HARRAP'S
MINI

English-French
DICTIONARY

DICTIONNAIRE
Français-Anglais

HARRAP'S MINI

English-French

DICTIONARY

DICTIONNAIRE

Français-Anglais

Editor
Rédacteur

Michael Janes

Consultant Editors
Avec la collaboration de
Fabrice Antoine
Isabelle Elkaim

HARRAP

This edition published in Great Britain 1999
by Chambers Harrap Publishers Ltd
7 Hopetoun Crescent, Edinburgh EH7 4AY

First published as
Harrap's Mini French Dictionary

ISBN 0 245 60625 4 (UK)
ISBN 0 245 50366 8 (France)

New edition 1994
Reprinted 1994, 1995 (twice), 1996, 1997, 1998, 1999

Dépôt légal pour cette édition : mai 1994

Typeset by Hewer Text Composition Services, Edinburgh
Printed and bound in Great Britain by
Caledonian International Book Manufacturing Ltd, Glasgow

Contents/Table des matières

Trademarks

Words considered to be trademarks have been designated in this dictionary by the symbol
®. However, no judgment is implied concerning the legal status of any trademark by virtue
of the presence or absence of such a symbol.

Marques Déposées

Les termes considérés comme des marques déposées sont signalés dans ce dictionnaire par
le symbole ®. Cependant, la présence ou l'absence de ce symbole ne constitue nullement
une indication quant à la valeur juridique de ces termes.

Preface

This is the second edition of Harrap's *Mini French-English Dictionary*. Many new words and phrases have been added, and entries have been presented in an even clearer and more attractive form. Our aim is for the dictionary to continue to be an up-to-date, practical and reliable work of reference, providing translations of the most useful words and expressions of French and English.

Entries in the dictionary consist of headwords followed by pronunciation and part of speech. When there is more than one translation, context words in brackets are supplied to help the user make the correct choice. Further guidance in the understanding of translations is provided by the use of labels to indicate the level of style (eg *Fam* for 'familiar' or colloquial) or to define a particular usage or field (eg *Am* for 'American' or *Mus* for 'music'). Context words and labels are also given when considered helpful for the understanding of single translations (eg **article** *n* (*object, in newspaper*) & *Gram* article *m*, or **putty** *n* mastic *m* (*pour vitres*)). The user is also helped by having context indicators and labels in French in the French section and in English in the English section of the dictionary.

Style and field labels follow bracketed indicators (eg **corner** *vt* (*market*) *Com* monopoliser, or **bidule** *nm* (*chose*) *Fam* whatsit). In the event of more than one translation within a grammatical category being qualified by the same style or field label, the label may then precede (see **trucker** where *Am* covers both senses given).

The user will find in the text important abbreviated words in English (eg BA, HIV) and in French (eg PCV, OVNI), useful geographical information such as names of countries, and a wide coverage of American words and usage (eg diaper, pinkie). The vocabulary includes French and English colloquialisms and slang, and important technical jargon. Comparatives and superlatives of English adjectives are also indicated.

In order to save space, some derived words are included within the entry of a headword. All such words are highlighted by means of the symbol ●. Derivatives may be written in full or abbreviated, as is usually the case for important derived forms (such as English **-ly** or French **-ment**).

An oblique stroke in bold is used to mark the stem of a headword at which point the derived ending is added. A bold dash stands for the headword or the portion of the headword to the left of the oblique stroke (eg **awkward** *a* . . . ●**-ly** *adv* . . . ; **boulevers/er** ... *vt* ... ●**-ement** *nm*)

An oblique stroke within an entry is a useful space-saving device to separate non-interchangeable parts of a phrase or expression matched exactly in French and English (eg **to be able to swim/drive** savoir nager/conduire is to be understood as: **to be able to swim** savoir nager and **to be able to drive** savoir conduire).

In common with other Harrap dictionaries, when a headword appears in an example in the same form, it is represented by its initial letter (eg **at h.** stands for **at home** in headword **home**). This applies whether the headword starts a new line or appears within an entry (eg **household** *a* . . . **h. name** . . .).

The pronunciation of both English and French is shown using the latest symbols of the International Phonetic Alphabet. Pronunciation is given for headwords at the start of an entry, and, as an additional help to the user, for those words within the entry where the correct pronunciation may be difficult to derive (eg ● **aristocratie** [-asi] not [-ati]; ● **rabid** [ˈræbɪd] not [ˈreɪbɪd]).

Preface

Stress in English is indicated for headwords and for derived words in which stress differs from that of a headword (eg **miracle** ['mɪrɪk(ə)l] and ● **mi'raculous**). American English pronunciation is listed wherever it is considered to show a marked difference from that of British English (eg **tomato** [tə'mɑːtəʊ], *Am* tə'meɪtəʊ). American spelling is also supplied if sufficiently different from British (eg **tire** and **tyre**, **plow** and **plough**).

An original feature of this dictionary is its semantic approach to the order and arrangement of entries: the meaning of words determines the structure of entries. Important semantic categories have been indicated by bold Arabic numerals within an entry (eg **1, 2, 3, 4**) (see **bolt**, **tail**, **général**) or have been entered as separate headwords (see **bug**[1] and **bug**[2], **draw**[1] and **draw**[2], **start**[1] and **start**[2]). The different grammatical divisions of separate headwords are easily identified by means of the symbol **‖**.

Words are usually entered under the headword from which they are considered to derive (eg ● **astronomer** follows **astronomy**, and ● **planétaire** follows **planète**). Present and past participles (used as adjectives) are, in most cases, entered, usually in abbreviated form, within an entry immediately after the infinitive, any other derived words there may be following in alphabetical order (eg **exagér/er** *vt* . . . ●**-é** *a* . . . ● **exagération** *nf*; **accommodat/e** *vt* . . . ●**-ing** *a* . . . ●**accommo'dation** *n*.

The author wishes to express his gratitude to Stuart Fortey and Hazel Curties for their substantial contributions to the first edition of this dictionary, and to his wife, Susan, for her help with Americanisms.

M. Jane
London 1994

Préface

Voici la seconde édition du Harrap's *Mini Dictionnaire Anglais-Français*. De nombreux mots et locutions y apparaissent pour la première fois et la présentation des articles y est encore plus claire et plus agréable. Ce dictionnaire veut être, comme dans sa première édition, un ouvrage de référence moderne, pratique et fiable, où l'on trouvera les traductions des mots et expressions les plus courants du français comme de l'anglais.

Chaque article de ce dictionnaire présente le mot d'entrée suivi de sa prononciation, puis de la catégorie grammaticale à laquelle il appartient. Lorsque plusieurs traductions sont apportées, des indications de contexte sont données entre parenthèses pour guider l'utilisateur vers la traduction adéquate. Le sens des différentes traductions est éclairé encore davantage par les indications de niveau de langue (par exemple: *Fam* pour 'familier') ou de domaines d'utilisation (par exemple: *Am* pour 'américain' ou *Mus* pour 'musique') données sous forme abrégée. Les mêmes indications, de contexte, de niveau de langue ou de domaine d'utilisation, accompagnent également une traduction unique d'un mot d'entrée lorsque celle-ci peut être ambiguë (par exemple: **article** *n* (*object, in newspaper*) & *Gram* article *m*, ou **putty** *n* mastic *m* (*pour vitres*)). L'accès à l'ouvrage est également facilité par l'utilisation d'indications en français dans la partie anglais-français et en anglais dans la partie français-anglais.

Les indications de niveau de langue et de domaine d'utilisation viennent à la suite de celles entre parenthèses (par exemple: **corner** *vt* (*market*) *Com* monopoliser, ou **bidule** *nm* (*chose*) *Fam* whatsit). Lorsque plusieurs traductions dans la même catégorie grammaticale sont définies par la même indication, celle-ci peut venir en tête (voir **trucker** où l'indication *Am* concerne les deux sens envisagés).

L'utilisateur trouvera dans cet ouvrage des abréviations courantes, tant anglaises (par exemple: BA, HIV) que françaises (par exemple: PCV, OVNI), de précieux éléments de géographie tels que des noms de pays, ainsi qu'une large sélection d'américanismes (par exemple: diaper, pinkie). Le lexique retenu comprend des mots et expressions familiers et argotiques, tant en français qu'en anglais, et des termes techniques courants. De plus, les comparatifs et superlatifs des adjectifs anglais sont indiqués.

Par souci de concision, certains mots dérivés sont donnés dans le corps des articles. Tous ces mots sont alors repérés par le symbole ●. Les dérivés sont donnés soit sous leur forme complète, soit en abrégé, ce qui est généralement le cas pour les formes dérivées courantes (telles que celles en -ly en anglais ou en -ment en français).

On utilise une barre oblique en gras pour isoler le radical d'un mot d'entrée à la suite duquel une terminaison sera ajoutée lors d'une dérivation. Un tiret en gras remplace le mot d'entrée ou la partie de ce mot qui précède la barre oblique (par exemple: **awkward** *a* ...●—**ly** *adv* ...; **boulevers/er** *vt* ... ●—**ant** *a* ... ●—**ement** *nm*).

Toujours par souci de concision, on utilise dans le corps d'un article une barre oblique pour mettre en parallèle des expressions sans répéter un élément qui ne varie pas (par exemple: **to be able to swim/drive** savoir nager/conduire se lira: **to be able to swim** savoir nager, **to be able to drive** savoir conduire).

Comme il est d'usage dans les autres dictionnaires Harrap, lorsqu'un mot d'entrée est repris sans modification dans un exemple, il est remplacé par sa première lettre. Cela est le cas aussi bien lorsque le mot figure au début d'un article (par exemple: **at h.** se lira **at home** dans l'article **home**) ou apparaît dans le corps d'un article (par exemple: ● **household** *a* ... **h. name** ...).

ix

Préface

La prononciation de l'anglais comme du français est fournie; elle utilise la notation la plus moderne de l'Alphabet Phonétique International. On donne la prononciation des mots d'entrée en début d'article, et, par souci de clarté, pour tout mot au sein de l'article dont il pourrait être difficile de déduire la prononciation (par exemple: ●aristocratie [-asi] et non [-ati]; ● rabid ['ræbɪd] et non ['reɪbɪd]).

L'accent tonique est indiqué pour les mots d'entrée anglais et pour les dérivés chaque fois que l'accentuation diffère de celle du mot principal (par exemple: **miracle** ['mɪrək(ə)l] et ● **mi'raculous**). Les prononciations américaines sont indiquées chaque fois qu'elles diffèrent nettement de celles de l'anglais britannique (par exemple: **tomato** [tə'mɑːtəʊ, *Am* tə'meɪtəʊ]). On a également fait figurer l'orthographe américaine lorsqu'elle est notablement différente de celles de l'anglais britannique (par exemple: **tire** et **tyre**, **plow** et **plough**).

Une des caractéristiques originales de ce dictionnaire est son approche sémantique du classement et de l'organisation des articles: c'est le sens des mots qui détermine l'organisation des articles. Les catégories sémantiques importantes sont indiquées par des chiffres arabes en gras (voir **bolt**, **tail**, **général**) ou donnent lieu à des articles séparés (voir **bug**[1] et **bug**[2], **draw**[1] et **draw**[2], **start**[1] et **start**[2]). Au sein d'un article, les différentes catégories grammaticales sont repérables aisément grâce au symbole ▮ qui le précède.

Les mots apparaissent en général sous les mots d'entrée dont ils sont dérivés (par exemple: ●**astronomer** suit **astronomy**, et ● **planétaire** suit **planète**). Les participes présents et passés (pris comme adjectifs), sont, dans la plupart des cas, placés, généralement en abrégé, à la suite de l'infinitif dont ils sont dérivés; tous les autres dérivés éventuels apparaissent ensuite par ordre alphabétique (par exemple: **exagér/er** *vt* … **-é** *a* … ●**exagération** *nf*; **accommodat/e** *vt* … ●**-ing** *a* … ●**accommo'dation** *n*.

L'auteur tient à exprimer sa gratitude envers Stuart Fortey et Hazel Curties pour leur importante contribution à la première édition du présent dictionnaire, et à son épouse, Susan, pour ses conseils et suggestions concernant les américanismes.

M. Janes
Londres 1994

x

Grammar Notes

n French, the feminine of an adjective is formed, when regular, by adding e to the masculine form (eg grand, grande; carré, carrée; fin, fine). If the masculine already ends in e, the feminine is the same as the masculine (eg utile). Irregular feminine forms of adjectives eg généreux, généreuse; léger, légère; doux, douce) are given on the French-English side of the dictionary. They are listed in the following way: généreux, -euse; léger, -ère; doux, douce. On the English-French side, French adjectives are shown in the masculine but highly irregular feminine forms (eg frais, fraîche; faux, fausse) have been included as an additional help to the user.

To form the plural of a French noun or adjective s is usually added to the singular (eg arbre, arbres; taxi, taxis; petit, petits). The plural form of a noun ending in s, x or z (eg pois, croix, nez) is the same as that of the singular. Plurals of nouns and adjectives which do not follow these general rules are listed in the French section, including the plurals of French compounds where the formation of the plural involves a change *other than* the addition of final s (eg chou-fleur, choux-fleurs; arc-en-ciel, arcs-en-ciel). The plurals of compounds which are formed simply by adding s (eg tire-bouchon) are not given.

The irregular plurals of French nouns and irregular masculine plurals of French adjectives) ending in al, eau, eu, au, ail and ou are listed on the French-English side (eg cerveau, -x; général, -aux). Included on the English-French side, as an additional help to the user, are the plurals of French nouns (and adjectives) ending in al, eu and au where s, and not the usual x, forms the plural (eg pneu, pneus; naval, navals) and of those nouns in ail and ou where the plural is formed with x, and not the usual s (eg vitrail, vitraux; chou, choux).

In English also, s is added to form the plural of a noun (eg cat, cats; taxi, taxis) but a noun ending in ch, s, sh, x or z forms its plural by the addition of es, pronounced [-ɪz] (eg glass, glasses; match, matches). (Note that when ch is pronounced [k], the plural is in s, eg monarch, monarchs.) When a noun ends in y preceded by a consonant, y is changed to es to form the plural (eg army, armies). English plurals not following these general rules are given on the English-French side, including the plurals of English compounds where the formation of the plural involves a change other than the addition of final s (eg brother-in-law, brothers-in-law). Common English irregular plurals involving a change of vowel (eg tooth, teeth) are given, for convenience, at both singular and plural headword positions.

Most French verbs have regular conjugations though some display spelling anomalies see French Verb Conjugations on p (i)). In the French section an asterisk is used to mark an irregular verb, and refers the user to the table of irregular verbs on p (iii).

Most English verbs form their past tense and past participle by adding ed to the infinitive eg look, looked) or d to an infinitive already ending in e (eg love, loved). When a verb ends n y preceded by a consonant, y becomes ied (eg satisfy, satisfied). To form the third person singular of a verb in the present tense s is added to the infinitive (eg know, knows) but an nfinitive in ch, s, sh, x or z forms its third person singular by the addition of es, pronounced -ɪz] (eg dash, dashes). When an infinitive ends in y preceded by a consonant, y is changed to ies to form the third person singular (eg satisfy, satisfies).

The English present participle is formed by the addition of ing to the infinitive (eg look, ooking) but final e is omitted when an infinitive ends in e (eg love, loving). When the nfinitive ends in a single consonant preceded by a vowel (eg tug), the final consonant is usually doubled in the past tense, past and present participles (eg tug, tugged, tugging). The doubling of consonants in English verbs is indicated in the text in the following way: **tug** .. *vt* (**-gg-**).

Irregular English verb conjugations are given in the English headword list, and a summary of the most important irregular verbs may also be found on p (xiii).

Notes sur la grammaire

En français, le féminin d'un adjectif se forme régulièrement en ajoutant e au masculin (par exemple: grand, grande; carré, carrée; fin, fine). Lorsque le masculin se termine déjà par e, le féminin est identique (par exemple: utile). Les féminins d'adjectifs qui ne se conforment pas à ces règles (par exemple: généreux, généreuse; léger, légère; doux, douce) sont donnés dans la partie français-anglais où ils sont notés comme suit: généreux, -euse; léger, -ère; doux, douce. Dans la partie anglais-français, on ne donne que le masculin des adjectifs, mais, par souci de fournir une information complémentaire utile, on indique les féminins irréguliers remarquables (par exemple: frais, fraîche; faux, fausse).

On forme en général le pluriel d'un nom ou d'un adjectif français en ajoutant s au singulier (par exemple: arbre, arbres; taxi, taxis; petit, petits). Le pluriel d'un nom se terminant par s, x ou z (par exemple: pois, croix, nez) est identique au singulier. Les pluriels des noms et adjectifs qui font exception à ces règles générales sont signalés dans la partie français-anglais, de même que les pluriels des mots composés français dont le passage au pluriel appelle une modification *autre que* le simple ajout d'un s final (par exemple: chou-fleur, choux-fleurs; arc-en-ciel, arcs-en-ciel). Les pluriels des mots composés ne sont pas donnés lorsqu'ils se forment par simple ajout d'un s (par exemple: tire-bouchon).

Les pluriels irréguliers des noms français, de même que ceux des adjectifs masculins, qui se terminent par al, eau, au, ail et ou sont indiqués dans la partie français-anglais (par exemple: cerveau, -x; général, -aux). Un complément d'information est fourni, dans la partie anglais-français, par la mention des pluriels des noms et adjectifs français qui se terminent par al, eu et au et forment leur pluriel en s au lieu de x (par exemple: pneu, pneus; naval, navals); il en va de même pour ceux qui se terminent par ail et ou et qui forment leur pluriel en x, au lieu de s (par exemple: vitrail, vitraux; chou, choux).

De la même façon, en anglais, on forme le pluriel des noms en ajoutant s (par exemple: cat, cats; taxi, taxis) mais on ajoutera es, prononcé [-ɪz], aux noms qui se terminent par ch, s, sh, x ou z (par exemple: glass, glasses; match, matches). (Noter cependant que lorsque ch se prononce [k], le pluriel est en s, comme dans monarch, monarchs.) Lorsqu'un nom se termine par un y précédé d'une consonne, ce y devient ies au pluriel (par exemple: army, armies). Les pluriels des noms anglais qui font exception à ces règles générales sont signalés dans la partie anglais-français, de même que les pluriels des mots composés anglais dont le passage au pluriel entraîne une modification autre que le simple ajout d'un s final (par exemple: brother-in-law, brothers-in-law). Pour faciliter la recherche, on a fait figurer comme mots d'entrée les pluriels irréguliers de mots anglais usuels qui se forment par modification de voyelle (par exemple: tooth, teeth).

La plupart des verbes français ont des conjugaisons régulières; cependant, certains subissent des variations orthographiques (voir: Conjugaisons des verbes français à la page (i)). Dans la partie français-anglais, un astérisque signale un verbe irrégulier et renvoie à la table des verbes irréguliers donnée en page (iii).

En anglais, le passé et le participe passé des verbes se forment dans la plupart des cas en ajoutant ed à l'infinitif (par exemple: look, looked) ou seulement d lorsque l'infinitif se termine par un e (par exemple: love, loved). Lorsqu'un verbe se termine par un y précédé d'une consonne, ce y devient ied (par exemple: satisfy, satisfied). La troisième personne du singulier d'un verbe au présent se forme en ajoutant s à l'infinitif (par exemple: know, knows), mais on ajoutera es, prononcé [-ɪz], aux infinitifs qui se terminent par ch, s, sh, x ou z (par exemple: dash, dashes). Enfin, lorsqu'un verbe se termine par un y précédé d'une

Notes sur la grammaire

consonne, ce y devient **ies** à la troisième personne du singulier (par exemple: satisfy, satisfies).

Le participe présent en anglais se forme en ajoutant la désinence **ing** à l'infinitif (par exemple: look, looking); lorsqu'un infinitif comporte un **e** final, celui-ci disparaît (par exemple: love, loving). Lorsque l'infinitif se termine par une seule consonne précédée d'une voyelle (par exemple: tug), la consonne finale est le plus souvent doublée au passé et aux participes passé et présent (par exemple: tug, tugged, tugging). Le doublement des consonnes dans les verbes anglais est signalé comme suit: **tug** ... *vt* (**-gg-**).

Les formes des verbes irréguliers anglais sont données dans la partie anglais-français et une liste récapitulative des verbes irréguliers usuels figure en page (xiii).

Abbreviations

Abréviations

adjective	*a*	adjectif
abbreviation	*abbr, abrév*	abréviation
adverb	*adv*	adverbe
agriculture	*Agr*	agriculture
American	*Am*	américain
anatomy	*Anat*	anatomie
architecture	*Archit*	architecture
slang	*Arg*	argot
article	*art*	article
cars, motoring	*Aut*	automobile
auxiliary	*aux*	auxiliaire
aviation, aircraft	*Av*	aviation
biology	*Biol*	biologie
botany	*Bot*	botanique
British	*Br*	britannique
Canadian	*Can*	canadien
carpentry	*Carp*	menuiserie
chemistry	*Ch*	chimie
cinema	*Cin*	cinéma
commerce	*Com*	commerce
computing	*Comptr*	informatique
conjunction	*conj*	conjonction
cookery	*Culin*	cuisine
definite	*def, déf*	défini
demonstrative	*dem, dém*	démonstratif
economics	*Econ, Écon*	économie
electricity	*El, Él*	électricité
et cetera	*etc*	et cetera
feminine	*f*	féminin
familiar	*Fam*	familier
football	*Fb*	football
figurative	*Fig*	figuré
finance	*Fin*	finance
feminine plural	*fpl*	féminin pluriel
French	*Fr*	français
geography	*Geog, Géog*	géographie
geology	*Geol, Géol*	géologie
geometry	*Geom, Géom*	géométrie
grammar	*Gram*	grammaire
history	*Hist*	histoire
humorous	*Hum*	humoristique
indefinite	*indef, indéf*	indéfini
indicative	*indic*	indicatif
infinitive	*inf*	infinitif
interjection	*int*	interjection

Abbreviations　　　　　　　Abréviations

invariable	*inv*	invariable
ironic	*Iron*	ironique
legal, law	*Jur*	juridique
linguistics	*Ling*	linguistique
literary	*Lit, Litt*	littéraire
literature	*Liter, Littér*	littérature
masculine	*m*	masculin
mathematics	*Math*	mathématiques
medicine	*Med, Méd*	médecine
carpentry	*Menuis*	menuiserie
meteorology	*Met, Mét*	météorologie
military	*Mil*	militaire
masculine plural	*mpl*	masculin pluriel
music	*Mus*	musique
noun	*n*	nom
nautical	*Nau*	nautique
noun feminine	*nf*	nom féminin
noun masculine	*nm*	nom masculin
noun masculine and feminine	*nmf*	nom masculin et féminin
computing	*Ordinat*	informatique
pejorative	*Pej, Péj*	péjoratif
philosophy	*Phil*	philosophie
photography	*Phot*	photographie
physics	*Phys*	physique
plural	*pl*	pluriel
politics	*Pol*	politique
possessive	*poss*	possessif
past participle	*pp*	participe passé
prefix	*pref, préf*	préfixe
preposition	*prep, prép*	préposition
present participle	*pres p, p prés*	participe présent
present tense	*pres t*	temps présent
pronoun	*pron*	pronom
psychology	*Psy*	psychologie
past tense	*pt*	prétérit
	qch	quelque chose
	qn	quelqu'un
registered trademark	®	marque déposée
radio	*Rad*	radio
railway, *Am* railroad	*Rail*	chemin de fer
relative	*rel*	relatif
religion	*Rel*	religion
school	*Sch, Scol*	école
singular	*sing*	singulier

slang	*Sl*	argot
someone	*s.o.*	
sport	*Sp*	sport
something	*sth*	
subjunctive	*sub*	subjonctif
suffix	*suff*	suffixe
technical	*Tech*	technique
telephone	*Tel, Tél*	téléphone
textiles	*Tex*	industrie textile
theatre	*Th*	théâtre
television	*TV*	télévision
typography, printing	*Typ*	typographie
university	*Univ*	université
United States	*US*	États-Unis
auxiliary verb	*v aux*	verbe auxiliaire
intransitive verb	*vi*	verbe intransitif
impersonal verb	*v imp*	verbe impersonnel
pronominal verb	*vpr*	verbe pronominal
transitive verb	*vt*	verbe transitif
transitive and	*vti*	verbe transitif et
intransitive verb		intransitif
vulgar	*Vulg*	vulgaire

Pronunciation of French

Table of Phonetic Symbols

Vowels

[i]	vite, cygne, sortie		[y]	cru, sûr, rue
[e]	été, donner		[ø]	feu, meule, nœud
[ɛ]	elle, mais, père		[œ]	œuf, jeune
[a]	chat, fameux		[ə]	le, refaire, entre
[ɑ]	pas, âgé		[ɛ̃]	vin, plein, faim, saint
[ɔ]	donne, fort, album		[ɑ̃]	enfant, temps, paon
[o]	dos, chaud, peau		[ɔ̃]	mon, nombre
[u]	tout, cour, roue		[œ̃]	lundi, humble

Consonants

[p]	pain, absolu, frapper		[n]	né, canne
[b]	beau, abbé		[ɲ]	campagne
[t]	table, nette		[ŋ]	jogging
[d]	donner, sud		[']	This symbol is placed before
[k]	camp, képi, qui			the phonetics of a word
[g]	garde, guerre, second			beginning with h to show that
[f]	feu, phrase			there is no elision or liaison:
[v]	voir, wagon			the preceding word must not
[s]	sou, cire, nation			be abbreviated (eg la hache
[z]	cousin, zéro			and not l'hache), and the final
[ʃ]	chose, schéma			consonant of the preceding
[ʒ]	gilet, jeter			word must not be pronounced
[l]	lait, facile, elle			(eg les haches: [leaʃ] and not
[r]	rare, rhume, barreau			[lezaʃ]).
[m]	mon, flamme			

Semi-consonants

[j]	piano, voyage, fille
[w]	ouest, noir, tramway
[ɥ]	muet, lui

Prononciation de l'anglais
Tableau des Signes Phonétiques
Voyelles et diphtongues

[i:]	bee, police	[ɒ]	lot, what
[ɪə]	beer, real	[ɔ:]	all, saw
[ɪ]	bit, added	[ɔɪ]	boil, toy
[e]	bet, said	[əʊ]	low, soap
[eɪ]	date, nail	[ʊ]	put, wool
[eə]	bear, air	[u:]	shoe, too
[æ]	bat, plan	[ʊə]	poor, sure
[aɪ]	fly, life	[ʌ]	cut, some
[ɑ:]	art, ask	[ɜ:]	burn, learn
[aʊ]	fowl, house	[ə]	china, annoy
		[(ə)]	relation

Consonnes

[p]	pat, top	[ð]	that, breathe
[b]	but, tab	[h]	hat, rehearse
[t]	tap, patter	[l]	lad, all
[d]	dab, ladder	[r]	red, sorry
[k]	cat, kite	[ʳ]	better, here (*représente un r*
[g]	go, rogue		*final qui se prononce en*
[f]	fat, phrase		*liaison devant une voyelle,*
[v]	veal, rave		*par exemple* 'here is' [hɪərɪz])
[s]	sat, ace	[m]	mat, hammer
[z]	zero, houses	[n]	no, banner
[ʃ]	dish, pressure	[ŋ]	singing, link
[ʒ]	pleasure	[j]	yet, onion
[tʃ]	charm, rich	[w]	wall, quite
[dʒ]	judge, rage	[']	*marque l'accent tonique;*
[θ]	thank, breath		*précède la syllabe accentuée*

A

A, a [eɪ] n A, a m; **5A** (number) 5 bis; **A1** (dinner etc) Fam super, superbe.

a [ə, stressed eɪ] (before vowel or mute h) **an** [ən, stressed æn] indef art **1** un, une; a man un homme; **an apple** une pomme.

2 (= def art in Fr) **sixty pence a kilo** soixante pence le kilo; **50 km an hour** 50 km à l'heure; **I have a broken arm** j'ai le bras cassé.

3 (art omitted in Fr) **he's a doctor** il est médecin; **Caen, a town in Normandy** Caen, ville de Normandie; **what a man!** quel homme!

4 (a certain) **a Mr Smith** un certain M. Smith.

5 (time) **twice a month** deux fois par mois.

6 (some) **to make a noise/a fuss** faire du bruit/des histoires.

aback [ə'bæk] adv **taken a.** déconcerté.

abandon [ə'bændən] **1** vt abandonner. **2** n (freedom of manner) laisser-aller m.

abashed [ə'bæʃt] a confus, gêné.

abate [ə'beɪt] vi (of storm, pain) se calmer.

abbey ['æbɪ] n abbaye f.

abbot ['æbət] n abbé m.

abbreviate [ə'briːvɪeɪt] vt abréger. ● **abbreviation** [-'eɪʃ(ə)n] n abréviation f.

abdicate ['æbdɪkeɪt] vti abdiquer.

abdomen ['æbdəmən] n abdomen m.

abduct [əb'dʌkt] vt (kidnap) enlever. ● **abduction** [əb'dʌkʃ(ə)n] n enlèvement m, rapt m.

abet [ə'bet] vt (-tt-) **to aid and a. s.o.** Jur être le complice de qn.

abide [ə'baɪd] **1** vi **to a. by** (promise etc) rester fidèle à. **2** vt supporter; **I can't a. him** je ne peux pas le supporter.

ability [ə'bɪlɪtɪ] n capacité f (to do pour faire), aptitude f (to do à faire); **to the best of my a.** de mon mieux.

abject ['æbdʒekt] a abject; **a. poverty** la misère.

ablaze [ə'bleɪz] a en feu; **a. with** (light) resplendissant de.

able ['eɪb(ə)l] a (-er, -est) capable, compétent; **to be a. to do** être capable de faire, pouvoir faire; **to be a. to swim/drive** savoir nager/conduire. ● **a.-'bodied** a robuste. ● **ably** adv habilement.

abnormal [æb'nɔːm(ə)l] a anormal. ● **abnor'mality** n anomalie f; (of body) difformité f. ● **abnormally** adv Fig exceptionnellement.

aboard [ə'bɔːd] adv Nau à bord; **all a.** Rail en voiture ▮ prep **a. the ship** à bord du navire; **a. the train** dans le train.

abolish [ə'bɒlɪʃ] vt supprimer, abolir. ● **abolition** [æbə'lɪʃ(ə)n] n suppression f, abolition f.

aboriginal [æbə'rɪdʒən(ə)l] n aborigène m.

abort [ə'bɔːt] vt (space flight, computer program) abandonner. ● **abortion** [-ʃ(ə)n] n Med avortement m; **to have an a.** se faire avorter. ● **abortive** a (plan etc) manqué, avorté.

abound [ə'baʊnd] vi abonder (in en).

about [ə'baʊt] adv **1** (approximately) à peu près, environ; (at) **a. two o'clock** vers deux heures.

2 (here and there) çà et là, ici et là; (ideas, flu) Fig ça et là; (rumour) qui circule; **to look a.** regarder autour de soi; **to follow a.** suivre partout; **to bustle a.** s'affairer; **there are lots a.** il en a beaucoup; **(out and) a.** (after illness) sur pied, guéri; **(up and) a.** (out of bed) levé, debout; **a turn, a face** Mil demi-tour m; Fig volte-face f inv.

▮ prep **1** (around) **a. the garden** autour du jardin; **a. the streets** par or dans les rues.

2 (*near to*) **a. here** par ici.
3 (*concerning*) au sujet de; **to talk a.** parler de; **a book a.** un livre sur; **what's it (all) a.?** de quoi s'agit-il?; **what** or **how a. me?** et moi alors?; **what** or **how a. a drink?** que dirais-tu de prendre un verre?
4 (+ *inf*) **a. to do** sur le point de faire.
above [ə'bʌv] *adv* au-dessus; (*in sky*) ci-dessus; **from a.** d'en haut; **floor a.** étage *m* supérieur or du dessus ‖ *prep* au-dessus de; **a. all** par-dessus tout, surtout; **he's a. me** (*in rank*) c'est mon supérieur; **a. lying** incapable de mentir; **a. asking** trop fier pour demander. ● **a.-'mentioned** a susmentionné. ● **aboveboard** a ouvert, honnête ‖ *adv* sans tricherie, cartes sur table.
abrasive [ə'breɪsɪv] a (*substance*) abrasif; (*rough*) *Fig* rude, dur; (*irritating*) agaçant.
abreast [ə'brest] *adv* côte à côte, de front; **four a.** par rangs de quatre; **to keep a. of** or **with** se tenir au courant de.
abridge [ə'brɪdʒ] *vt* (*book etc*) abréger.
abroad [ə'brɔːd] *adv* (*in* or *to a foreign country*) à l'étranger; **from a.** de l'étranger.
abrupt [ə'brʌpt] a (*sudden*) brusque; (*person*) brusque, abrupt; (*slope, style*) abrupt. ●—**ly** *adv* (*suddenly*) brusquement; (*rudely*) avec brusquerie.
abscess ['æbses] *n* abcès *m*.
abscond [əb'skɒnd] *vi* *Jur* s'enfuir.
absence ['æbsəns] *n* absence *f*; **in the a. of sth** à défaut de qch, faute de qch; **a. of mind** distraction *f*.
absent ['æbsənt] a absent (**from** de); (*look*) distrait; **a.-'minded** a distrait. ● **a.-'mindedness** *n* distraction *f*. ● **absen'tee** *n* absent, -ente *mf*.
absolute ['æbsəluːt] a (*power etc*) absolu; (*proof etc*) indiscutable; (*coward etc*) parfait, véritable. ●—**ly** *adv* absolument; (*forbidden*) formellement.
absolve [əb'zɒlv] *vt* *Rel Jur* absoudre; **to a. from** (*vow*) libérer de.
absorb [əb'zɔːb] *vt* (*liquid etc*) absorber;

(*shock*) amortir; **to become absorbed in** (*work*) s'absorber dans. ●—**ing** a (*work*) absorbant; (*book, film*) prenant. ● **absorbent** a absorbant; **a. cotton** *Am* coton *m* hydrophile *f*, ouate *f*. ● **absorber** *n* **shock a.** *Aut* amortisseur *m*.
abstain [əb'steɪn] *vi* s'abstenir (**from** de). ● **abstention** [-enʃ(ə)n] *n* abstention *f*.
abstract ['æbstrækt] **1** a & *n* abstrait (*m*). **2** *n* (*summary*) résumé *m*.
absurd [əb'sɜːd] a absurde, ridicule. ● **absurdity** *n* absurdité *f*.
abundant [ə'bʌndənt] a abondant. ● **abundance** *n* abondance *f*. ● **abundantly** *adv* **a. clear** tout à fait clair.
abuse [ə'bjuːs] *n* (*abusing*) abus *m* (**of** de); (*of child*) mauvais traitements *mpl*; (*curses*) injures *fpl* ‖ [ə'bjuːz] *vt* (*misuse*) abuser de; (*ill-treat*) maltraiter; (*speak ill of*) dire du mal de; (*insult*) injurier. ● **abusive** [ə'bjuːsɪv] a (*person*) grossier; (*words*) injurieux.
abysmal [ə'bɪzm(ə)l] a (*bad*) *Fam* désastreux, exécrable.
abyss [ə'bɪs] *n* abîme *m*.
academic [ækə'demɪk] a (*year etc*) universitaire; (*scholarly*) érudit, intellectuel; (*issue etc*) *Pej* théorique ‖ *n* (*teacher*) universitaire *mf*.
academy [ə'kædəmɪ] *n* (*society*) académie *f*; *Mil* école *f*; *Mus* conservatoire *m*.
accede [ək'siːd] *vi* **to a. to** (*request, throne, position*) accéder à.
accelerate [ək'seləreɪt] *vt* accélérer ‖ *vi* s'accélérer; *Aut* accélérer. ● **acceleration** [-'reɪʃ(ə)n] *n* accélération *f*. ● **accelerator** *n* *Aut* accélérateur *m*.
accent ['æksənt] *n* accent *m*. ● **accentuate** [æk'sentʃʊeɪt] *vt* accentuer.
accept [ək'sept] *vt* accepter. ●—**ed** a (*opinion*) reçu; (*fact*) reconnu. ● **acceptable** a (*worth accepting, tolerable*) acceptable. ● **acceptance** *n* acceptation *f*; (*approval, favour*) accueil *m* favorable.
access ['ækses] *n* accès *m* (**to sth** à qch, **to s.o.** auprès de qn). ● **ac'cessible** a

accessible.

accessories [ək'sesərɪz] *npl* (*objects*) accessoires *mpl*.

accident ['æksɪdənt] *n* accident *m*; **by a.** (*by chance*) par accident; (*unintentionally*) accidentellement, sans le vouloir. ● **a.-prone** *a* qui attire les accidents. ● **acci'dental** *a* accidentel, fortuit. ● **acci'dentally** *adv* accidentellement, par mégarde; (*by chance*) par accident.

acclaim [ə'kleɪm] *vt* (*cheer*) acclamer; (*praise*) faire l'éloge de ▮ *n* (*critical*) a. éloges *mpl* (de la critique).

acclimate ['æklɪmeɪt] *vti Am* = **acclimatize.** ● **ac'climatize** *vt* acclimater ▮ *vi* s'acclimater.

accommodat/e [ə'kɒmədeɪt] *vt* (*of house*) loger, recevoir; (*have room for*) avoir de la place pour (mettre); (*oblige*) rendre service à. ● **—ing** *a* accommodant, obligeant. ● **accommodation** [-'deɪʃ(ə)n] *n* (*lodging*) logement *m*; (*rented room or rooms*) chambre(s) *f(pl)*; *pl* (*in hotel Am*) chambre(s) *f(pl)*.

accompany [ə'kʌmpənɪ] *vt* accompagner. ● **accompaniment** *n* accompagnement *m*. ● **accompanist** *n Mus* accompagnateur, -trice *mf*.

accomplice [ə'kʌmplɪs] *n* complice *mf*.

accomplish [ə'kʌmplɪʃ] *vt* (*task, duty*) accomplir; (*aim*) atteindre. ● **—ed** *a* accompli. ● **—ment** *n* accomplissement *m*, (*thing achieved*) réalisation *f*; *pl* (*skills*) talents *mpl*.

accord [ə'kɔːd] **1** *n* accord *m*; **of my own a.** volontairement, de mon plein gré. **2** *vt* (*grant*) accorder. ● **accordance** *n* **in a. with** conformément à.

according [ə'kɔːdɪŋ] *prep* selon, d'après, suivant. ● **accordingly** *adv* en conséquence.

accordion [ə'kɔːdɪən] *n* accordéon *m*.

accost [ə'kɒst] *vt* accoster, aborder.

account [ə'kaʊnt] **1** *n Com* compte *m*; **accounts department** comptabilité *f*. **2** *n* (*report*) compte rendu *m*, récit *m*; (*explanation*) explication *f*; **by all accounts** au dire de tous; **to give a good a.**

of oneself s'en tirer à son avantage ▮ *vi* **to a. for** (*explain*) expliquer; (*give reckoning of*) rendre compte de; (*represent*) représenter. **3** (*expressions*) **on a. of** à cause de; **on no a.** en aucun cas; **of some a.** d'une certaine importance; **to take into a.** tenir compte de. ● **accountable** *a* responsable (**for** de, **to** devant).

accountant [ə'kaʊntənt] *n* comptable *mf*. ● **accountancy** *n* comptabilité *f*.

accumulate [ə'kjuːmjʊleɪt] *vt* accumuler, amasser ▮ *vi* s'accumuler. ● **accumulation** [-'leɪʃ(ə)n] *n* accumulation *f*; (*mass*) amas *m*.

accurate ['ækjʊrət] *a* exact, précis. ● **accuracy** *n* exactitude *f*, précision *f*. ● **accurately** *adv* avec précision.

accus/e [ə'kjuːz] *vt* accuser (**of** de). ● **—ed** *n* **the a.** *Jur* l'inculpé, -ée *mf*, l'accusé, -ée *mf*. ● **accusation** [ækjʊ'zeɪʃ(ə)n] *n* accusation *f*.

accustom [ə'kʌstəm] *vt* habituer, accoutumer. ● **—ed** *a* habitué (**to sth** à qch, **to doing** à faire); **to get a. to** s'habituer à, s'accoutumer à.

ace [eɪs] *n* (*card, person*) as *m*.

ache [eɪk] *n* douleur *f*, mal *m*; **to have an a. in one's arm** avoir mal au bras ▮ *vi* faire mal; **my head aches** la tête me fait mal; **I'm aching all over** j'ai mal partout; **to be aching to do** brûler de faire. ● **aching** *a* douloureux.

achieve [ə'tʃiːv] *vt* (*success, result*) obtenir; (*aim*) atteindre; (*ambition*) réaliser; (*victory*) remporter; **he can never a. anything** il n'arrive jamais à faire quoi que ce soit. ● **—ment** *n* (*success*) réussite *f*; (*of ambition*) réalisation *f*.

acid ['æsɪd] *a & n* acide (*m*).

acknowledge [ək'nɒlɪdʒ] *vt* reconnaître (**as** pour); (*greeting*) répondre à; **to a.** (**receipt of**) accuser réception de. ● **acknowledge(e)ment** *n* reconnaissance *f*; (*of letter*) accusé *m* de réception; (*receipt*) reçu *m*; (*confession*) aveu *m* (**of** de).

acne ['æknɪ] *n* acné *f*.

acorn ['eɪkɔːn] *n Bot* gland *m*.

acoustics [ə'kuːstɪks] *npl* acoustique *f*.

acquaint [ə'kweɪnt] *vt* to a. s.o. with sth informer qn de qch; **to be acquainted with** (*person*) connaître; (*fact*) savoir; **we are acquainted** on se connaît. ● **acquaintance** *n* connaissance *f*.

acquire [ə'kwaɪər] *vt* acquérir; (*taste*) prendre (**for** à); (*friends*) se faire; **acquired taste** goût *m* qui s'acquiert.

acquit [ə'kwɪt] *vt* (-**tt**-) **to a. s.o.** (**of a crime**) acquitter qn. ● **acquittal** *n* acquittement *m*.

acre ['eɪkər] *n* acre *f* (= 0,4 hectare).

acrimonious [ækrɪ'məʊnɪəs] *a* acerbe.

acrobat ['ækrəbæt] *n* acrobate *mf*. ● **acro'batic** *a* acrobatique. ● **acro'batics** *npl* acrobaties *fpl*.

across [ə'krɒs] *adv & prep* (*from side to side* (*of*)) d'un côté à l'autre (de); (*on the other side* (*of*)) de l'autre côté (de); (*crossways*) en travers (de); **to be a kilometre/***etc* **a.** (*wide*) avoir un kilomètre/*etc* de large; **to walk** *or* **go a.** (*street etc*) traverser.

acrylic [ə'krɪlɪk] *n* acrylique *m*; **a. socks/** *etc* chaussettes *fpl/etc* en acrylique.

act [ækt] **1** *n* (*deed*) acte *m*; **a. of parliament**) loi *f*; **caught in the a.** pris sur le fait; **a. of walking** action *f* de marcher.
2 *n* (*of play*) *Th* acte *m*; (*in circus, cabaret*) numéro *m*; **to put on an a.** *Fam* jouer la comédie ∥ *vt* (*part in play or film*) jouer ∥ *vi Th Cin* jouer; (*pretend*) jouer la comédie.
3 *vi* (*do sth, behave*) agir; **to a. as** (*secretary etc*) faire office de; (*of object*) servir de; **to a. (up)on** (*affect*) agir sur; (*advice*) suivre; **to a. on behalf of** représenter. ● **acting 1** *a* (*manager etc*) intérimaire. **2** *n* (*actor's art*) jeu *m*; (*career*) théâtre *m*.

action ['ækʃ(ə)n] *n* action *f*; *Mil* combat *m*; *Jur* procès *m*, action *f*; **to take a.** prendre des mesures; **to put into a.** (*plan*) exécuter; **out of a.** hors

d'usage, hors (de) service; (*person*) hors (de) combat.

active ['æktɪv] *a* actif; (*interest, dislike*) vif; (*volcano*) en activité ∥ *n Gram* actif *m*. ● **activate** *vt* (*mechanism*) actionner. ● **ac'tivity** *n* activité *f*; (*in street*) animation *f*.

actor ['æktər] *n* acteur *m*. ● **actress** *n* actrice *f*.

actual ['æktʃʊəl] *a* réel, véritable; (*example*) concret; **the a. book** le livre même. ● —**ly** *adv* (*truly*) réellement; (*in fact*) en réalité, en fait.

acupuncture ['ækjʊpʌŋktʃər] *n* acupuncture *f*.

acute [ə'kjuːt] *a* aigu (*f* -uë); (*emotion*) vif, profond; (*shortage*) grave. ● —**ly** *adv* (*to suffer, feel*) vivement, profondément. ● —**ness** *n* acuité *f*.

ad [æd] *n Fam* pub *f*; (*private, in newspaper*) annonce *f*; **small ad,** *Am* **want ad** petite annonce.

AD [eɪ'diː] *abbr* (*anno Domini*) après Jésus-Christ.

adamant ['ædəmənt] *a* inflexible; **to be a. that** maintenir cela.

adapt [ə'dæpt] *vt* adapter (**to** à); **to a.** (**oneself**) s'adapter. ● **adaptable** *a* (*person*) souple, capable de s'adapter. ● **adaptor** *n* (*plug*) prise *f* multiple.

add [æd] *vt* ajouter (**to** à, **that** que); **to a.** (**up** *or* **together**) additionner; **to a. in** inclure ∥ *vi* **to a. to** (*increase*) augmenter; **to a. up to** (*total*) s'élever à; (*mean*) signifier; (*represent*) constituer; **it all adds up** *Fam* ça s'explique. ● **adding machine** *n* machine *f* à calculer. ● **addition** [ə'dɪʃ(ə)n] *n* addition *f*; **in a.** de plus; **in a. to** en plus de. ● **a'dditional** *a* supplémentaire.

adder ['ædər] *n* vipère *f*.

addict ['ædɪkt] *n* (*drugs etc*) intoxiqué, -ée *mf*; *Fig* jazz/*etc* **a.** fana(tique) *mf* du jazz/*etc*; **drug a.** drogué, -ée *mf*. ● **a'ddicted** *a* **to be a. to** (*music, sport*) se passionner pour; (*have the habit of*) avoir la manie de; **a. to drink** alcoolique; **a. to cigarettes** accroché à la cigarette. ● **addiction** [ə'dɪkʃ(ə)n] *n* (*habit*) manie *f*; (*dependency*) dépendance *f*; **drug** a. toxicomanie *f*. ● a'**ddictive** *a* qui crée une dépendance.

additive ['ædɪtɪv] *n* additif *m*.

address [ə'dres, *Am* 'ædres] *n* (*on letter etc*) adresse *f*; (*speech*) allocution *f* ‖ [ə'dres] *vt* (*person*) s'adresser à; (*audience*) parler devant; (*words*) adresser (**to** à); (*letter*) mettre l'adresse sur.

adenoids ['ædɪnɔɪdz] *npl* végétations *fpl* (adénoïdes).

adept [ə'dept] *a* expert (**in, at** à).

adequate ['ædɪkwət] *a* (*quantity etc*) suffisant; (*acceptable*) convenable; (*person*) compétent; (*performance*) acceptable. ● **adequately** *adv* suffisamment; convenablement.

adhere [əd'hɪər] *vi* **to a.** to adhérer à; (*decision, rule*) s'en tenir à. ● **adhesive** *a* & *n* adhésif *m*.

adjective ['ædʒɪktɪv] *n* adjectif *m*.

adjoining [ə'dʒɔɪnɪŋ] *a* voisin.

adjourn [ə'dʒɜːn] *vt* (*postpone*) ajourner; (*session*) lever, suspendre ‖ *vi* lever la séance; **to a. to** (*go*) passer à.

adjust [ə'dʒʌst] *vt* (*machine*) régler, ajuster; (*prices, salaries*) ajuster; (*arrange*) arranger; **to a.** (**oneself**) **to** s'adapter à. ●—**able** *a* (*seat*) réglable. ●—**ment** *n Tech* réglage *m*; (*of person*) adaptation *f*.

ad-lib [æd'lɪb] *vi* (-**bb**-) improviser ‖ *a* (*joke etc*) improvisé.

administer [əd'mɪnɪstər] *vt* (*manage, dispense*) administrer (**to** à). ● **administration** [-'streɪʃ(ə)n] *n* administration *f*; (*government*) gouvernement *m*. ● **administrative** *a* administratif.

admiral ['ædmərəl] *n* amiral *m*.

admir/e [əd'maɪər] *vt* admirer (**for** pour, **for doing** de faire). ●—**ing** *a* admiratif. ●—**er** *n* admirateur, -trice *mf*. ● a'**dmirable** *a* admirable. ● **admiration** [ædmə'reɪʃ(ə)n] *n* admiration *f*.

admit [əd'mɪt] *vt* (-**tt**-) (*let in*) laisser entrer, admettre; (*acknowledge*) reconnaître, admettre (**that** que) ‖ *vi* **to a. to** sth (*confess*) avouer qch. ● **admission** *n* (*entry to theatre etc*) entrée *f* (**to** à, de); (*to club, school*) admission *f*; (*acknowledgment*) aveu *m*; **a.** (**charge**) (*prix m d'*)entrée *f*. ● **admittance** *n* entrée *f*; '**no a.**' 'entrée interdite'. ● **admittedly** [-ɪdlɪ] *adv* c'est vrai (que).

ado [ə'duː] *n* **without further a.** sans (faire) plus de façons.

adolescent [ædə'les(ə)nt] *n* adolescent, -ente *mf*. ● **adolescence** *n* adolescence *f*.

adopt [ə'dɒpt] *vt* (*child, method, attitude etc*) adopter. ●—**ed** *a* (*child*) adoptif; (*country*) d'adoption. ● **adoption** [-ʃ(ə)n] *n* adoption *f*.

adore [ə'dɔːr] *vt* adorer (**doing** faire); **he adores being flattered** il adore qu'on le flatte. ● **adorable** *a* adorable.

adorn [ə'dɔːn] *vt* (*room, book*) orner; (*person, dress*) parer.

Adriatic [eɪdrɪ'ætɪk] *n* **the A.** l'Adriatique *f*.

adrift [ə'drɪft] *a* & *adv Nau* à la dérive.

adult ['ædʌlt, ə'dʌlt] *n* adulte *mf* ‖ *a* (*animal etc*) adulte; **a. class/film/etc** classe *f*/film *m*/etc pour adultes. ● **adulthood** *n* âge *m* adulte.

adultery [ə'dʌltərɪ] *n* adultère *m*.

advance [əd'vɑːns] *n* (*movement, money*) avance *f*; (*of science*) progrès *mpl*; *pl* (*of love, friendship*) avances *fpl*; **in a.** à l'avance, d'avance; (*to arrive*) en avance; **in a. of s.o.** avant qn.

‖ *a* (*payment*) anticipé; **a. booking** réservation *f*.

‖ *vt* (*put forward, lend*) avancer; (*science, one's work*) faire avancer.

‖ *vi* (*go forward, progress*) avancer; **to a. towards s.o.** (s')avancer vers qn. ● **advanced** *a* avancé; (*studies*) supérieur; (*course*) de niveau supérieur.

advantage [əd'vɑːntɪdʒ] *n* avantage *m* (**over** sur); **to take a. of** (*situation*) profiter de; (*person*) tromper, exploiter.

advent ['ædvent] *n* arrivée *f*, avènement *m*; **A.** *Rel* l'Avent *m*.

adventure [əd'ventʃər] *n* aventure *f* ‖ *a*

(film etc) d'aventures. ● **adventurer** n aventurier, -ière mf.

adverb ['ædvɜːb] n adverbe m.

adverse ['ædvɜːs] a hostile, défavorable.

advert ['ædvɜːt] n Fam pub f; *(private, in newspaper)* annonce f.

advertis/e ['ædvətaɪz] vt *(commercially)* faire de la publicité pour; *(privately)* passer une annonce pour vendre; *(make known)* annoncer ▮ vi faire de la publicité; *(privately)* passer une annonce (**for** pour trouver). ●—**ing** n publicité f. ● **advertiser** n annonceur m.

advertisement [əd'vɜːtɪsmənt, Am ædvə'taɪzmənt] n publicité f; *(private, in newspaper)* annonce f; *(poster)* affiche f; **classified a**. petite annonce; **the advertisements** TV la publicité.

advice [əd'vaɪs] n conseil(s) m(pl); Com avis m; **a piece of a**. un conseil.

advis/e [əd'vaɪz] vt conseiller; *(recommend)* recommander; *(notify)* informer; **to a. s.o. to do** conseiller à qn de faire; **to a. against** déconseiller. ●—**able** a *(wise)* prudent (**to do** de faire); *(action)* à conseiller. ● **adviser** or **advisor** n conseiller, -ère mf.

advocate 1 ['ædvəkət] n *(of cause)* défenseur m, avocat, -ate mf. **2** ['ædvəkeɪt] vt préconiser, recommander.

aerial ['eərɪəl] n antenne f.

aerobics [eə'rəʊbɪks] npl aérobic f.

aerodrome ['eərədrəʊm] n aérodrome m.

aeroplane ['eərəpleɪn] n avion m.

aerosol ['eərəsɒl] n aérosol m.

afar [ə'faːr] adv **from a**. de loin.

affable ['æfəb(ə)l] a affable, aimable.

affair [ə'feər] n *(matter, concern)* affaire f; *(love)* a. liaison f; **state of affairs** situation f.

affect [ə'fekt] vt *(concern, move)* toucher, affecter; *(harm)* nuire à; *(influence)* influer sur. ●—**ed** a *(manner)* affecté; *(by disease)* atteint.

affection [ə'fekʃ(ə)n] n affection f *(for* pour). ● **affectionate** a affectueux.

affix [ə'fɪks] vt apposer.

afflict [ə'flɪkt] vt affliger (**with** de).

affluent ['æfluənt] a riche; **a. society** société f d'abondance. ● **affluence** n richesse f.

afford [ə'fɔːd] vt *(pay for)* avoir les moyens d'acheter, pouvoir se payer; **he can't a. the time (to read it)** il n'a pas le temps (de le lire); **I can a. to wait** je peux me permettre d'attendre. ●—**able** a *(price etc)* abordable.

Afghanistan [æf'gænɪstaːn] n Afghanistan m. ● **Afghan** a & n afghan, -ane (mf).

afield [ə'fiːld] adv **further a**. plus loin; **too far a**. trop loin.

afloat [ə'fləʊt] adv *(ship, swimmer, business)* à flot; **life a**. la vie sur l'eau.

afoot [ə'fʊt] adv **there's something a**. il se trame quelque chose; **there's a plan a. to . . .** on prépare un projet pour. . . .

afraid [ə'freɪd] a **to be a**. avoir peur (**of, to** de); **to make s.o. afraid** faire peur à qn; **he's a. (that) she may be ill** il a peur qu'elle (ne) soit malade; **I'm a. he's out** *(I regret to say)* je regrette, il est sorti.

afresh [ə'freʃ] adv de nouveau.

Africa ['æfrɪkə] n Afrique f. ● **African** a & n africain, -aine (mf).

after ['aːftər] adv après; **the month a**. le mois suivant, le mois d'après ▮ prep après; **a. all** après tout; **a. eating** après avoir mangé; **day a. day** jour après jour; **time a. time** bien des fois; **a. you!** je vous en prie!; **ten a. four** Am quatre heures dix; **to be a. sth/s.o.** *(seek)* chercher qch/qn ▮ conj après que; **a. she saw you** après qu'il t'a vu.

aftereffects ['aːftərɪfekts] npl suites fpl, séquelles fpl. ● **aftermath** [-maːθ] n suites fpl. ● **after'noon** n après-midi m or f inv; **in the a**. l'après-midi; **good a.!** *(hello)* bonjour!; *(goodbye)* au revoir! ● **after'noons** adv Am l'après-midi. ● **aftersales service** n service m après-vente. ● **aftershave (lotion)** n lotion f après-rasage. ● **afterthought** n réflexion f après coup; **as an a**. après coup.

● **afterward(s)** *adv* après, plus tard.

afters ['ɑ:ftəz] *npl Fam* dessert *m*.

again [ə'gen, ə'geɪn] *adv* de nouveau, encore une fois; **to go down/up a.** redescendre/remonter; **he won't do it a.** il ne le fera plus; **never a.** plus jamais; **a. and a.,** time and (time) a. bien des fois; **what's his name a.?** comment s'appelle-t-il déjà?

against [ə'genst, ə'geɪnst] *prep* contre; **to go** *or* **be a.** s'opposer à; **a. the law** illégal; **a law a. drinking** une loi qui interdit de boire; **a. the light** à contre-jour.

age [eɪdʒ] *n* âge *m*; **(old) a.** vieillesse *f*; **five years of a.** âgé de cinq ans; **to be of a.** être majeur; **under a.** trop jeune, mineur; **to wait (for) ages** *Fam* attendre une éternité; **a. group** tranche *f* d'âge; **a. limit** limite *f* d'âge ▮ *vti* (*pres p* **ag(e)ing**) vieillir. ● **aged** [eɪdʒd] *a.* **ten** âgé de dix ans; ['eɪdʒɪd] vieux, âgé; **the a.** les personnes *fpl* âgées.

agenda [ə'dʒendə] *n* ordre *m* du jour.

agent ['eɪdʒənt] *n* agent *m*; (*dealer for cars etc*) concessionnaire *mf*. ● **agency** *n* (*office*) agence *f*.

aggravate ['ægrəveɪt] *vt* (*make worse*) aggraver; **to a. s.o.** *Fam* exaspérer qn. ● **aggravation** [-'veɪʃ(ə)n] *n* (*bother*) *Fam* ennui(s) *m(pl)*.

aggression [ə'greʃ(ə)n] *n* agression *f*. ● **aggressive** *a* agressif. ● **aggressor** *n* agresseur *m*.

agile ['ædʒaɪl, *Am* 'ædʒ(ə)l] *a* agile.

agitate ['ædʒɪteɪt] *vt* (*worry*) agiter; **to be agitated** être agité.

ago [ə'gəʊ] *adv* **a year a.** il y a un an; **how long a.?** il y a combien de temps (de cela)?; **as long a. as 1800** (déjà) en 1800.

agog [ə'gɒg] *a* (*excited*) en émoi.

agony ['ægənɪ] *n* (*pain*) douleur *f* atroce; (*anguish*) angoisse *f*; **to be in a.** souffrir horriblement. ● **agonize** *vi* se faire beaucoup de souci.

agree [ə'gri:] *vi* (*come to an agreement*) se mettre d'accord; (*be in agreement*) être d'accord (**with** avec); (*of facts,*

dates etc) concorder; *Grammar* s'accorder; **to a. (up)on** (*decide*) convenir de; **to a. to sth/to doing** consentir à qch/à faire; **it doesn't a. with me** (*food, climate*) ça ne me réussit pas.

▮ *vt* **to a. to do** accepter de faire; **to a. that** (*admit*) admettre que. ● **agreed** *a* (*time, place*) convenu; **we are a.** nous sommes d'accord; **a.!** entendu!

agreeable [ə'gri:əb(ə)l] *a* **1** (*pleasant*) agréable. **2 to be a.** (*agree*) être d'accord. ● **agreement** *n* accord *m* (**with** avec); **in a. with/on** d'accord avec/sur.

agriculture ['ægrɪkʌltʃər] *n* agriculture *f*. ● **agri**cultural *a* agricole.

aground [ə'graʊnd] *adv* **to run a.** (*of ship*) (s')échouer.

ah! [ɑ:] *int* ah!

ahead [ə'hed] *adv* (*in space*) en avant; (*leading*) en tête; (*in the future*) dans l'avenir; **a.** (*of time*) en avance (**sur** l'horaire); **one hour/etc a.** une heure/ *etc* d'avance (**of** sur); **a. of** (*space*) devant; (*time, progress*) en avance sur; **to get a.** prendre de l'avance; **to think a.** penser à l'avenir; **straight a.** (*to walk*) tout droit; (*to look*) droit devant soi.

aid [eɪd] *n* (*help*) aide *f*; (*device*) accessoire *m*; (*visual*) moyen *m*, support *m*; **with the a. of** (*a stick etc*) à l'aide de; **in a. of** (*charity etc*) au profit de ▮ *vt* aider (s.o. to do qn à faire).

AIDS [eɪdz] *n Med* SIDA *m*; **A. virus** virus *m* du SIDA.

ailing ['eɪlɪŋ] *a* souffrant; (*company*) en difficulté. ● **ailment** *n* ennui *m* de santé.

aim [eɪm] *n* but *m*; **to take a.** viser; **with the a. of** dans le but de ▮ *vt* (*gun*) braquer, diriger (**at** sur); (*stone*) lancer (**at** à, vers); **aimed at children/etc** (*product*) destiné aux enfants/*etc* ▮ *vi* viser; **to a. at s.o.** viser qn; **to a. to do** *or* **at doing** avoir l'intention de faire. ● **—less** *a*, ● **—lessly** *adv* sans but.

air [eər] **1** *n* air *m*; **in the open a.** en plein air; **by a.** (*to travel*) en *or* par avion; (*letter, goods*) par avion; **to go on the a.**

(person) passer à l'antenne; (programme) être diffusé; **to throw (up) in(to) the a.** jeter en l'air ▮ a (raid, base etc) aérien; **a. fare** prix m du billet d'avion; **a. force/hostess** armée f/hôtesse f de l'air; **a. terminal** aérogare f ▮ vt (room) aérer; **airing cupboard** armoire f sèche-linge.

2 n (appearance, tune) air m.

airborne ['eəbɔːn] a en (cours de) vol; **to become a.** (of aircraft) décoller. ● **airconditioned** a climatisé. ● **air-conditioning** n climatisation f. ● **aircraft** n inv avion(s) m(pl); **a. carrier** porte-avions m inv. ● **airfield** n terrain m d'aviation. ● **airgun** n carabine f à air comprimé. ● **airletter** n aérogramme m. ● **airline** n ligne f aérienne; **a. ticket** billet m d'avion. ● **airliner** n avion m de ligne. ● **airmail** n poste f aérienne; **by a.** par avion. ● **airman** n (pl -men) aviateur m. ● **airplane** n Am avion m. ● **airpocket** n trou m d'air. ● **airport** n aéroport m. ● **airship** n dirigeable m. ● **airsickness** n mal m de l'air. ● **airstrip** n terrain m d'atterrissage. ● **airtight** a hermétique. ● **air traffic controller** n contrôleur m aérien, aiguilleur m du ciel.

airy ['eəri] a (-ier, -iest) (room) bien aéré.

aisle [aɪl] n (in plane, supermarket, cinema etc) allée f; (in church) allée f centrale.

ajar [ə'dʒɑːr] a & adv (door) entrouvert.

akin [ə'kɪn] a **a. (to)** apparenté (à).

à la mode [ælæ'məʊd] a Culin Am avec de la crème glacée.

alarm [ə'lɑːm] n (warning, fear, device in house or car) alarme f; (mechanism) sonnerie f (d'alarme); **false a.** fausse alerte f; **a. (clock)** réveil m ▮ vt (frighten) alarmer; (worry) inquiéter; **to be alarmed** s'inquiéter (**at** de).

alas! [ə'læs] int hélas!

album ['ælbəm] n (book, record) album m.

alcohol ['ælkəhɒl] n alcool m. ● **alco'holic** a (person) alcoolique ▮ n (person)

alcoolique mf. ● **alcoholism** n alcoolisme m.

alcove ['ælkəʊv] n alcôve f.

ale [eɪl] n bière f.

alert [ə'lɜːt] a (paying attention) vigilant; (mind, baby) éveillé ▮ n alerte f; **on the a.** sur le qui-vive ▮ vt alerter.

A level ['eɪlev(ə)l] n (exam) Br = épreuve f de bac.

algebra ['ældʒɪbrə] n algèbre f.

Algeria [æl'dʒɪərɪə] n Algérie f. ● **Algerian** a & n algérien, -ienne (mf).

alias ['eɪlɪəs] adv alias ▮ n nom m d'emprunt.

alibi ['ælɪbaɪ] n alibi m.

alien ['eɪlɪən] n étranger, -ère mf. ● **alienate** vt **to a. s.o.** (make unfriendly) se mettre qn à dos.

alight [ə'laɪt] **1** a (fire) allumé; (building) en feu; **to set a.** mettre le feu à. **2** vi descendre (**from** de).

align [ə'laɪn] vt **to a. oneself with** Pol s'aligner sur.

alike [ə'laɪk] **1** a (people, things) semblables, pareils; **to look** or **be a.** se ressembler. **2** adv de la même manière.

alimony ['ælɪmənɪ, Am 'ælɪməʊnɪ] n Jur pension f alimentaire.

alive [ə'laɪv] a vivant, en vie; **a. with** (insects etc) grouillant de; **to keep a.** (custom, memory) entretenir, perpétuer; **a. and kicking** Fam plein de vie.

all [ɔːl] a tout, toute, pl tous, toutes; **a. day** toute la journée; **a. (the) men** tous les hommes; **for a. his wealth** malgré toute sa fortune.

▮ pron tous mpl, toutes fpl; (everything) tout; **a. will die** tous mourront; **my sisters are a. here** toutes mes sœurs sont ici; **he ate it a., he ate a. of it** il a tout mangé; **take a. of it** prends (le) tout; **a. (that) he has** tout ce qu'il a; **a. of us** nous tous; **a. in a.** à tout prendre; **in a., a. told** en tout; **a. but impossible/etc** presque impossible/etc; **anything at a.** quoi que ce soit; **if he comes at a.** s'il vient effectivement; **if there's any wind at a.** s'il y a le moindre vent; **nothing at**

a. rien du tout; **not at a.** pas du tout; (after 'thank you') il n'y a pas de quoi. ∥ adv tout; **a. alone** tout seul; **a. bad** entièrement mauvais; **a. over** (everywhere) partout; (finished) fini; six-**a.** Fb six buts partout; **a. in** Fam épuisé. ●**a.-night** a (party) qui dure toute la nuit. ●**a.-out** a (effort) énergique. ●**a.-purpose** a (tool) universel. ●**a.-round** a (knowledge) approfondi; (athlete) complet. ●**a.-time** a (record) jamais atteint; **to reach an a.-time low/high** arriver au point le plus bas/le plus haut.

allegation [ælɪ'geɪʃ(ə)n] n accusation f.

alleg/e [ə'ledʒ] vt prétendre (**that** que). ●**—ed** a (author, culprit) présumé; **he is a. to be** on prétend qu'il est.

allegiance [ə'liːdʒəns] n fidélité f (**to** à).

allegory ['ælɪgərɪ, Am 'æləgɔːrɪ] n allégorie f.

allergy ['ælədʒɪ] n allergie f. ●**allergic** [ə'lɜːɪk] a allergique (**to** à).

alleviate [ə'liːvɪeɪt] vt (pain etc) soulager; (burden etc) alléger.

alley ['ælɪ] n ruelle f; **blind a.** impasse f. ●**alleyway** n ruelle f.

alliance [ə'laɪəns] n alliance f.

allied ['ælaɪd] a (country) allié.

alligator ['ælɪgeɪtər] n alligator m.

allocate ['æləkeɪt] vt (assign) attribuer, allouer (**to** à); (distribute) répartir.

allot [ə'lɒt] vt (-tt-) (assign) attribuer; (distribute) répartir ● **—ment** n (land) lopin m de terre (loué pour la culture).

allow [ə'laʊ] 1 vt permettre; (give) accorder (**s.o. sth** qch à qn); (a request) accéder à; **to a. a discount** accorder une réduction; **to s.o. to do** permettre à qn de faire; **to a. an hour/a metre** (estimated period or quantity) prévoir une heure/un mètre; **a. me!** permettez(-moi)!; **it's not allowed** c'est interdit; **you're not allowed to go** on vous interdit de partir. 2 vi **to a. for sth** tenir compte de qch.

allowance [ə'laʊəns] n allocation f; (for travel, housing, food) indemnité f; (for duty-free goods) tolérance f; **to make allowances for** (person) être indulgent envers; (thing) tenir compte de.

alloy ['ælɔɪ] n alliage m.

all right [ɔːl'raɪt] a (satisfactory) bien inv; (unharmed) sain et sauf; (undamaged) intact; (without worries) tranquille; **it's all r.** ça va; **I'm all r.** (healthy) je vais bien ∥ adv (well) bien; **all r.!** (agreement) d'accord!; **I received your letter all r.** (emphatic) j'ai bien reçu votre lettre.

ally ['ælaɪ] n allié, -ée mf.

almanac ['ɔːlmənæk] n almanach m.

almighty [ɔːl'maɪtɪ] a tout-puissant; (enormous) Fam terrible.

almond ['ɑːmənd] n amande f.

almost ['ɔːlməʊst] adv presque; **he a. fell**/etc il a failli tomber/etc.

alone [ə'ləʊn] a & adv seul; **an expert a. can . . .** seul un expert peut . . .; **to leave a.** (person) laisser tranquille; (thing) ne pas toucher à.

along [ə'lɒŋ] prep (all) **a.** (tout) le long de; **to go** or **walk a.** (street) passer par; **a. here** par ici; **a. with** avec ∥ adv **all a.** (all the time) dès le début; (all the way) d'un bout à l'autre; **to move a.** avancer; **he'll be** or **come a.** il viendra.

alongside [əlɒŋ'saɪd] prep & adv à côté (de); **a. the kerb** le long du trottoir.

aloof [ə'luːf] a distant ∥ adv à distance; **to keep a.** garder ses distances (**from** par rapport à).

aloud [ə'laʊd] adv à haute voix.

alphabet ['ælfəbet] n alphabet m. ●**alpha'betical** a alphabétique.

Alps [ælps] npl **the A.** les Alpes fpl. ●**alpine** a (club, range etc) alpin; (scenery) alpestre.

already [ɔːl'redɪ] adv déjà.

alright [ɔːl'raɪt] adv Fam = **all right**.

Alsatian [æl'seɪʃ(ə)n] n (dog) berger m allemand, chien-loup m.

also ['ɔːlsəʊ] adv aussi, également.

altar ['ɔːltər] n autel m.

alter ['ɔːltər] vt changer; (clothing) retoucher ∥ vi changer. ●**alteration** [-'reɪʃ(ə)n] n changement m; retouche *f*; *pl* (*to building*) travaux *mpl*.

alternate [ɔːlˈtɜːnət] *a* alterné; **on a. days** tous les deux jours ‖ [ˈɔːltəneɪt] *vi* alterner (**with** avec) ‖ *vt* faire alterner. ●—**ly** *adv* alternativement.

alternative [ɔːlˈtɜːnətɪv] *a* (*other*) **an a. way**/*etc* une autre façon/*etc*; **a. answers**/*etc* d'autres réponses/*etc* (différentes) ‖ *n* (*choice*) alternative *f*. ●—**ly** *adv* (**or**) **a.** (*or else*) ou alors, ou bien.

although [ɔːlˈðəʊ] *adv* bien que (+ *sub*).

altitude [ˈæltɪtjuːd] *n* altitude *f*.

altogether [ɔːltəˈɡeðər] *adv* (*completely*) tout à fait; (*on the whole*) somme toute; **how much a.?** combien en tout?

aluminium [æljʊˈmɪnjəm] (*Am* **aluminum** [əˈluːmɪnəm]) *n* aluminium *m*.

always [ˈɔːlweɪz] *adv* toujours.

am [æm, *unstressed* əm] *see* **be**.

a.m. [eɪˈem] *adv* du matin.

amalgamate [əˈmælɡəmeɪt] *vi* (*of organizations*) fusionner.

amass [əˈmæs] *vt* (*riches*) amasser.

amateur [ˈæmətər] *n* amateur *m*; **a. painter**/*etc* peintre/*etc* amateur ‖ *a* (*interest, sports*) d'amateur.

amaz/e [əˈmeɪz] *vt* stupéfier, étonner. ●—**ed** *a* stupéfait (**at sth** de qch), étonné (**at sth** par *or* de qch); (*filled with wonder*) émerveillé; **a. at seeing**/*etc* stupéfait *or* étonné de voir/*etc*. ●—**ing** *a* stupéfiant; (*incredible*) extraordinaire. ● **amazement** *n* stupéfaction *f*.

ambassador [æmˈbæsədər] *n* ambassadeur *m*; (*woman*) ambassadrice *f*.

amber [ˈæmbər] *n* ambre *m*; **a.** (**light**) (*of traffic signal*) *Aut* (feu *m*) orange *m*.

ambiguous [æmˈbɪɡjʊəs] *a* ambigu (*f* -uë).

ambition [æmˈbɪʃ(ə)n] *n* ambition *f*. ● **ambitious** *a* ambitieux.

amble [ˈæmb(ə)l] *vi* marcher d'un pas tranquille.

ambulance [ˈæmbjʊləns] *n* ambulance *f*; **a. driver** ambulancier, -ière *mf*.

ambush [ˈæmbʊʃ] *n* embuscade *f* ‖ *vt* prendre en embuscade; **to be ambushed** tomber dans une embuscade.

amend [əˈmend] *vt* (*text*) modifier; *Pol* (*law etc*) amender. ●—**ment** *n Pol* amendement *m*.

amends [əˈmendz] *npl* **to make a. for** réparer; **to make a.** réparer son erreur.

amenities [əˈmiːnɪtɪz, *Am* əˈmenɪtɪz] *npl* (*of sports club etc*) équipement *m*; (*of town*) aménagements *mpl*.

America [əˈmerɪkə] *n* Amérique *f*; **North/South A.** Amérique du Nord/du Sud. ● **American** *a* & *n* américain, -aine (*mf*).

amicab/le [ˈæmɪkəb(ə)l] *a* amical. ●—**ly** *adv* amicalement; *Jur* à l'amiable.

amid(st) [əˈmɪd(st)] *prep* au milieu de, parmi.

amiss [əˈmɪs] *adv* & *a* mal (à propos); **sth is a.** (*wrong*) qch ne va pas.

ammonia [əˈməʊnjə] *n* (*gas*) ammoniac *m*; (*liquid*) ammoniaque *f*.

ammunition [æmjʊˈnɪʃ(ə)n] *n* munitions *fpl*.

amnesty [ˈæmnəstɪ] *n* amnistie *f*.

amok [əˈmɒk] *adv* **to run a.** (*of crowd*) se déchaîner; (*of person*) devenir fou furieux.

among(st) [əˈmʌŋ(st)] *prep* (*amidst*) parmi; (*between*) entre; **a. the crowd/books** parmi la foule/les livres; **a. themselves/friends** entre eux/amis; **a. the French**/*etc* (*group*) chez les Français/*etc*.

amorous [ˈæmərəs] *a* (*look*) polisson; (*person*) d'humeur polissonne.

amount [əˈmaʊnt] **1** *n* quantité *f*; (*sum of money*) somme *f*; (*total of bill, Am check etc*) montant *m*; (*scope, size*) importance *f*. **2** *vi* **to a. to** s'élever à; (*mean*) *Fig* signifier; (*represent*) représenter.

amp [æmp] *n El* ampère *m*.

ample [ˈæmp(ə)l] *a* (*enough*) largement assez de; (*roomy*) ample; (*reasons, means*) solides; **you have a. time** tu as largement le temps; **that's a.** c'est largement suffisant. ● **amply** *adv* amplement.

amplify [ˈæmplɪfaɪ] *vt* (*sound etc*) amplifier. ● **amplifier** *n El* amplificateur *m*.

amputate ['æmpjʊteɪt] vt amputer. ● **amputation** [-'teɪʃ(ə)n] n amputation f.

amus/e [ə'mjuːz] vt amuser; **to keep s.o. amused** amuser qn. ● **—ing** a amusant. ● **—ement** n amusement m; (pastime) distraction f; pl (at fairground) attractions fpl; (gambling machines) machines fpl à sous; **a. arcade** salle f de jeux; **a. park** parc m d'attractions.

an [æn, unstressed ən] see **a**.

an(a)emic [ə'niːmɪk] a anémique.

an(a)esthetic [ænɪs'θetɪk] n anesthésie f; (substance) anesthésique m; **general/ local a.** anesthésie f générale/locale.

analogy [ə'nælədʒɪ] n analogie f.

analyse ['ænəlaɪz] vt analyser. ● **analysis**, pl **-yses** [ə'næləsɪs, -ɪsiːz] n analyse f. ● **analyst** n analyste mf. ● **ana'lytical** a analytique.

anarchy ['ænəkɪ] n anarchie f. ● **anarchist** n anarchiste mf.

anathema [ə'næθəmə] n **it is (an) a. to me** j'ai une sainte horreur de cela.

anatomy [ə'nætəmɪ] n anatomie f.

ancestor ['ænsestər] n ancêtre m.

anchor ['æŋkər] n ancre f; **to weigh a.** lever l'ancre ▮ vt (ship) mettre à l'ancre ▮ vi jeter l'ancre. ● **—ed** a ancré.

anchovy ['æntʃəvɪ, Am æn'tʃəʊvɪ] n anchois m.

ancient ['eɪnʃənt] a ancien; (pre-medieval) antique; (person) d'un grand âge.

and [ænd, unstressed ən(d)] conj et; **a knife a. fork** un couteau et une fourchette; **two hundred a. two** deux cent deux; **better a. better** de mieux en mieux; **go a. see** va voir.

anecdote ['ænɪkdəʊt] n anecdote f.

angel ['eɪndʒəl] n ange m. ● **an'gelic** a angélique.

anger ['æŋgər] n colère f; **in a., out of a.** sous le coup de la colère ▮ vt mettre en colère, fâcher.

angle ['æŋg(ə)l] n angle m; **at an a.** en biais.

angler ['æŋglər] n pêcheur, -euse mf à la ligne. ● **angling** n pêche f à la ligne.

Anglican ['æŋglɪkən] a & n anglican, -ane (mf).

Anglo- ['æŋgləʊ] pref anglo-. ● **Anglo-'Saxon** a & n anglo-saxon, -onne (mf).

angora [æŋ'gɔːrə] n (wool) angora m.

angry ['æŋgrɪ] a (-ier, -iest) (person) en colère, fâché; (look) fâché; (letter, words) indigné; **to get a.** se fâcher, se mettre en colère (with contre). ● **angrily** adv en colère; (to speak) avec colère.

anguish ['æŋgwɪʃ] n angoisse f.

angular ['æŋgjʊlər] a (face) anguleux.

animal ['ænɪməl] a (kingdom, fat etc) animal ▮ n animal m, bête f.

animate ['ænɪmət] a (alive) animé. ● **animated** a animé; **to become a.** s'animer. ● **animation** [-'meɪʃ(ə)n] n animation f.

aniseed ['ænɪsiːd] n Culin anis m.

ankle ['æŋk(ə)l] n cheville f; **a. sock** socquette f.

annex [ə'neks] vt annexer.

annex(e) ['æneks] n (building) annexe f.

annihilate [ə'naɪəleɪt] vt anéantir.

anniversary [ænɪ'vɜːsərɪ] n (of event) anniversaire m.

announc/e [ə'naʊns] vt annoncer; (birth, marriage) faire part de. ● **—ement** n (statement) annonce f; (of birth, marriage, death) avis m. ● **—er** n TV speaker m, speakerine f.

annoy [ə'nɔɪ] vt (inconvenience) ennuyer, gêner; (irritate) agacer, contrarier. ● **—ed** a fâché, contrarié; **to get a.** se fâcher (with contre). ● **—ing** a ennuyeux, contrariant. ● **annoyance** n ennui m, contrariété f.

annual ['ænjʊəl] a annuel ▮ n (children's book) album m.

anomaly [ə'nɒməlɪ] n anomalie f.

anon [ə'nɒn] adv Hum tout à l'heure.

anonymous [ə'nɒnɪməs] a anonyme; **to remain a.** garder l'anonymat.

anorak ['ænəræk] n anorak m.

anorexia [ænə'reksɪə] n anorexie f. ● **anorexic** a & n anorexique (mf).

another [ə'nʌðər] a & pron un(e) autre; **a. man** (different) un autre homme; **a. month** (additional) encore un mois, un autre mois; **a. ten** encore dix; **one a.** l'un(e) l'autre, *pl* les un(e)s les autres; **they love one a.** ils s'aiment (l'un l'autre).

answer ['ɑːnsər] *n* réponse *f*; (*to problem*) solution (**to** de); **in a.** to en réponse à.
 ▮ *vt* (*person, question, letter, phone*) répondre à; (*prayer, wish*) exaucer; **he answered 'yes'** il a répondu 'oui'; **to a. the bell** *or* **the door** ouvrir la porte.
 ▮ *vi* répondre; **to a. back** (*rudely*) répondre; **to a. for s.o./sth** répondre de qn/qch; **answering machine** répondeur *m*. ● **answerable** *a* responsable (**for sth** de qch, **to s.o.** devant qn).

ant [ænt] *n* fourmi *f*.

antagonize [æn'tægənaɪz] *vt* provoquer (l'hostilité de).

Antarctic [æn'tɑːktɪk] *n* the A. l'Antarctique *m*.

antelope ['æntɪləʊp] *n* antilope *f*.

antenatal [æntɪ'neɪt(ə)l] *a* prénatal (*mpl* -als) ▮ *n* examen *m* prénatal.

antenna[1], *pl* -ae [æn'tenə, -iː] *n* (*of insect etc*) antenne *f*.

antenna[2] [æn'tenə] *n* (*pl* -as) (*for TV, radio*) *Am* antenne *f*.

anthem ['ænθəm] *n* **national a.** hymne *m* national.

anthology [æn'θɒlədʒɪ] *n* recueil *m*.

anti- [ˈæntɪ, *Am* ˈæntaɪ] *pref* anti-. ● **anti'biotic** *n* antibiotique *m*. ● **antibody** ['æntɪbɒdɪ] *n* anticorps *m*. ● **anti'climax** *n* chute *f* dans l'ordinaire; (*letdown*) déception *f*. ● **anti'clockwise** *adv* dans le sens inverse des aiguilles d'une montre. ● **antifreeze** *n* *Aut* antigel *m*. ● **anti'histamine** *n* *Med* antihistaminique *m*. ● **anti-Se'mitic** *a* antisémite. ● **anti-'Semitism** *n* antisémitisme *m*. ● **anti'septic** *a* & *n* antiseptique (*m*). ● **anti'social** *a* (*misfit*) asocial; (*unsociable*) peu sociable.

anticipate [æn'tɪsɪpeɪt] *vt* (*foresee*) prévoir; (*expect*) s'attendre à. ● **anticipation** [-'peɪʃ(ə)n] *n* attente *f*; **in a. of** en prévision de, dans l'attente de.

antics ['æntɪks] *npl* singeries *fpl*.

antiquated ['æntɪkweɪtɪd] *a* (*phrase, custom*) vieilli; (*person*) vieux jeu *inv*; (*machine etc*) antédiluvien.

antique [æn'tiːk] *a* (*furniture etc*) ancien; (*of Greek or Roman period*) antique; **a. dealer** antiquaire *mf*; **a. shop** magasin *m* d'antiquités ▮ *n* antiquité *f*, objet *m* ancien.

antlers ['æntləz] *n* (*of deer*) *npl* bois *mpl*.

Antwerp ['æntwɜːp] *n* Anvers *m* or *f*.

anus ['eɪnəs] *n* anus *m*.

anvil ['ænvɪl] *n* enclume *f*.

anxiety [æŋ'zaɪətɪ] *n* (*worry*) inquiétude *f* (**about** au sujet de); (*fear*) anxiété *f*.

anxious ['æŋkʃəs] *a* (*worried*) inquiet (**about** de, pour); (*troubled*) anxieux; (*eager*) impatient (**to do** de faire); **I'm a. (that)** he should leave je tiens beaucoup à ce qu'il parte. ● **-ly** *adv* (*to wait*) impatiemment.

any ['enɪ] *a* 1 (*in questions*) du, de la, des; **have you a. milk/tickets?** avez-vous du lait/des billets?; **is there a. man (at all) who . . . ?** y a-t-il un homme (quelconque) qui . . . ?
 2 (*negative*) de; (*not the slightest*) aucun; **he hasn't got a. milk/tickets** il n'a pas de lait/de billets; **there isn't a. proof/doubt** il n'y a aucune preuve/ aucun doute.
 3 (*no matter which*) n'importe quel.
 4 (*every*) tout; **at a. moment** à tout moment; **in a. case, at a. rate** de toute façon.
 ▮ *pron* 1 (*no matter which one*) n'importe lequel; (*somebody*) quelqu'un; **if a. of you** si l'un d'entre vous.
 2 (*quantity*) en; **have you got a.?** en as-tu?; **I don't see a.** je n'en vois pas.
 ▮ *adv* **not a. further/happier/***etc* pas loin/plus heureux/*etc*; **I don't see him a. more** je ne le vois plus; **a. more tea?** encore du thé?, encore un peu de thé?; **a. better?** (un peu) mieux?

anybody ['enɪbɒdɪ] *pron* 1 (*somebody*) quelqu'un; **do you see a.?** vois-tu quelqu'un?; **more than a.** plus que tout autre. **2** (*negative*) personne; **he doesn't know a.** il ne connaît personne. **3** (*no matter who*) n'importe qui; **a. would think that** . . . on croirait que. . . .

nyhow ['enɪhaʊ] *adv* (*at any rate*) de toute façon; (*badly*) n'importe comment; (*in confusion*) sens dessus dessous.

nyone ['enɪwʌn] *pron* = **anybody.**

nyplace ['enɪpleɪs] *adv Am* = **anywhere.**

nything ['enɪθɪŋ] *pron* **1** (*something*) quelque chose; **can you see a.?** voyez-vous quelque chose? **2** (*negative*) rien; **he doesn't do a.** il ne fait rien; **without a.** sans rien. **3** (*everything*) tout; **a. you like** (*tout) ce que tu veux; **like a.** (*to work, run etc*) *Fam* comme un fou. **4** (*no matter what*) **a. (at all)** n'importe quoi.

nyway ['enɪweɪ] *adv* (*at any rate*) de toute façon.

nywhere ['enɪweər] *adv* **1** (*no matter where*) n'importe où. **2** (*everywhere*) partout; **a. you go** où que vous alliez, partout où vous allez; **a. you like** (là) où tu veux. **3** (*somewhere*) quelque part; **is he going a.?** va-t-il quelque part? **4** (*negative*) nulle part; **he doesn't go a.** il ne va nulle part; **without a. to put it** sans un endroit où le mettre

part [ə'pɑ:t] *adv* **1** (*separated*) **we kept them a.** nous les tenions séparés; **with legs (wide) a.** les jambes écartées; **they are a metre a.** ils se trouvent à un mètre l'un de l'autre; **to come a.** (*of two objects*) se séparer; (*of knot etc*) se défaire; **to tell two things/people a.** distinguer deux choses/personnes. **2** (*to pieces*) **to tear a.** mettre en pièces; (*of building etc*) **to take a.** démonter. **3 a. from** (*except for*) à part.

partment [ə'pɑ:tmənt] *n* (*flat*) *Am* appartement *m*; **a. house** *Am* immeuble *m* (*d'habitation*).

pathy ['æpəθɪ] *n* apathie *f*. ● **apa'thetic** *a* apathique.

pe [eɪp] *n* singe *m* ▮ *vt* (*imitate*) singer.

aperitif [ə'perəti:f] *n* apéritif *m*.

aperture ['æpətʃʊər] *n* ouverture *f*.

apiece [ə'pi:s] *adv* chacun; **a pound a.** une livre (la) pièce *or* chacun.

apologetic [əpɒlə'dʒetɪk] *a* (*letter*) plein d'excuses; **to be a. (about)** s'excuser (de). ● **apologetically** *adv* en s'excusant.

apology [ə'pɒlədʒɪ] *n* excuses *fpl*. ● **apologize** *vi* s'excuser (**for** de); **to a. to s.o.** faire ses excuses à qn (**for** pour).

apostle [ə'pɒs(ə)l] *n* apôtre *m*.

apostrophe [ə'pɒstrəfɪ] *n* apostrophe *f*.

appal [ə'pɔ:l] (*Am* **appall**) *vt* (**-ll-**) consterner; **to be appalled (at)** être horrifié (de). ● **appalling** *a* épouvantable.

apparatus [æpə'reɪtəs, *Am* -'rætəs] *n* (*equipment, organization*) appareil *m*; (*in gym*) agrès *mpl*.

apparent [ə'pærənt] *a* (*obvious, seeming*) apparent; **it's a. that** il est évident que. ● **—ly** *adv* apparemment.

appeal [ə'pi:l] *n* (*charm*) attrait *m*; (*interest*) intérêt *m*; (*call*) & *Jur* appel *m*.
▮ *vt* **to a. to** (*s.o., s.o.'s kindness*) faire appel à; **to a. to s.o.** (*attract*) plaire à qn; (*interest*) intéresser qn; **to a. to s.o. for sth** demander qch à qn; **to a. to s.o. to do** supplier qn de faire.
▮ *vi Jur* faire appel. ● **appealing** *a* (*attractive*) séduisant.

appear [ə'pɪər] *vi* (*become visible*) apparaître; (*present oneself*) se présenter; (*seem, be published*) paraître; (*on stage, in film*) jouer; (*in court*) comparaître; **it appears that** (*it seems*) il semble que (+ *sub or indic*); (*it is rumoured*) il paraîtrait que (+ *indic*). ● **appearance** *n* (*act*) apparition *f*; (*look*) apparence *f*; **to put in an a.** faire acte de présence.

appease [ə'pi:z] *vt* (*soothe*) apaiser.

appendix, *pl* **-ixes** *or* **-ices** [ə'pendɪks, -ɪksɪz, -ɪsi:z] *n* (*in book*) & *Anat* appendice *m*. ● **appendicitis** [əpendɪ'saɪtɪs] *n* appendicite *f*.

appetite ['æpɪtaɪt] *n* appétit *m*. ● **appetizer** *n* (*drink*) apéritif *m*; (*food*) amuse-gueule *m inv*. ● **appetizing** *a* appétissant.

applaud [ə'plɔːd] vt (clap) applaudir; (approve of) approuver ▮ vi applaudir. ● **applause** n applaudissements mpl.

apple ['æp(ə)l] n pomme f; **stewed apples,** Am **a. sauce** compote f de pommes; **cooking a.** pomme f à cuire; **a. pie** tarte f aux pommes; **a. tree** pommier m.

appliance [ə'plaɪəns] n appareil m.

applicant ['æplɪkənt] n candidat, -ate mf (for à). ● **application** [-'keɪʃ(ə)n] n (for job) candidature f; (for membership) demande f d'adhésion; (request) demande f (for de); **a. (form)** (job) formulaire m de candidature.

apply [ə'plaɪ] **1** vt (put on, carry out) appliquer; (brake) Aut appuyer sur; **to a. oneself to** s'appliquer à. **2** vi (be relevant) s'appliquer (to à); **to a. for** (job) poser sa candidature à; **to a. to s.o.** (ask) s'adresser à qn (for pour). ● **applied** a Math Ling etc appliqué.

appoint [ə'pɔɪnt] vt (person) nommer (**to sth** à qch); (director etc) nommer; (secretary etc) engager; (time, place) fixer; **at the appointed time** à l'heure dite. ● **—ment** n nomination f; (meeting) rendez-vous m inv; (post) situation f.

appraisal [ə'preɪz(ə)l] n évaluation f.

appreciate [ə'priːʃɪeɪt] **1** vt (enjoy, value) apprécier; (understand) comprendre; (be grateful for) être reconnaissant de. **2** vi prendre de la valeur. ● **appreci'ation** n **1** (gratitude) reconnaissance f; (judgment) appréciation f. **2** (rise in value) augmentation f (de la valeur). ● **appreciative** a (grateful) reconnaissant (of de); (favourable) élogieux.

apprehensive [æprɪ'hensɪv] a inquiet (**about** de, au sujet de).

apprentice [ə'prentɪs] n apprenti, -ie mf. ● **apprenticeship** n apprentissage m.

approach [ə'prəʊtʃ] vt (person, door etc) s'approcher de; (age, result, town) approcher de; (subject) aborder; (accost) aborder (qn) ▮ vi (of person, vehicle) s'approcher; (of date etc) approcher ▮ n (method) façon f de s'y

prendre; (path, route) (voie f d')acc... m; **at the a. of** à l'approche de.

appropriate [ə'prəʊprɪət] a (plac... clothes, remark, means etc) qui co... vient (to or for sth à qch). ● **—ly** a... convenablement.

approve [ə'pruːv] vt approuver; **to a. ... sth** approuver qch; **I don't a. of him** il ... me plaît pas; **I a. of his going** je trouv... bon qu'il y aille. ● **approval** n approba... tion f; **on a.** (goods) à l'essai.

approximate [ə'prɒksɪmət] a approx... matif. ● **—ly** adv à peu prè... approximativement. ● **approximatio...** [-'meɪʃ(ə)n] n approximation f.

apricot ['eɪprɪkɒt] n abricot m.

April ['eɪprəl] n avril m; **to make an ...** **fool of s.o.** faire un poisson d'avril à q...

apron ['eɪprən] n (garment) tablier m.

apt [æpt] a (remark, reply, time etc) qui convient; (word, name) bien chois... (student) doué; **it's a. to fall** (likel... (in general) ça a tendance à tomber; (o... particular occasion) ça pourrait bie... tomber. ● **aptitude** n aptitude f (for ... pour); (of student) don m (for pour).

aqualung ['ækwəlʌŋ] n scaphandre ... autonome.

aquarium [ə'kweərɪəm] n aquarium m...

Aquarius [ə'kweərɪəs] n (sign) le Ve... seau.

aquatic [ə'kwætɪk] a (plant etc) aqua... tique; (sport) nautique.

aqueduct ['ækwɪdʌkt] n aqueduc m.

Arab ['ærəb] a & n arabe (mf). ● **Arabi...** [ə'reɪbɪən] a arabe. ● **Arabic** a &... (language) arabe (m); **A. numeral...** chiffres mpl arabes.

arbiter ['ɑːbɪtər] n arbitre m. ● **arbitra...** vti arbitrer.

arbitrary ['ɑːbɪtrərɪ] a (decision et...) arbitraire.

arc [ɑːk] n (of circle) arc m.

arcade [ɑː'keɪd] n (for shops) (smal... passage m couvert; (large) galerie marchande.

arch [ɑːtʃ] n (of bridge) arche f; (of building) voûte f; (of foot) cambrure ...

◀ vt (one's back etc) arquer, courber.
● **archway** n passage m voûté, voûte f.

rch(a)eology [ɑːkɪˈɒlədʒɪ] n archéologie f. ● **arch(a)eologist** n archéologue mf.

rchaic [ɑːˈkeɪɪk] a archaïque.

rchbishop [ɑːtʃˈbɪʃəp] n archevêque m.

rch-enemy [ɑːtʃˈenəmɪ] n ennemi m numéro un.

rcher [ˈɑːtʃər] n archer m. ● **archery** n tir m à l'arc.

rchipelago [ɑːkɪˈpeləgəʊ] n (pl -oes or -os) archipel m.

rchitect [ˈɑːkɪtekt] n architecte mf. ● **architecture** n architecture f.

rchives [ˈɑːkaɪvz] npl archives fpl.
● **archivist** [ˈɑːkɪvɪst] n archiviste m.

rctic [ˈɑːktɪk] a arctique; (weather) polaire, glacial ▮ n the A. l'Arctique m.

rdent [ˈɑːdənt] a (supporter) ardent.

rduous [ˈɑːdjʊəs] a pénible, ardu.

re [ɑːr] see be.

rea [ˈeərɪə] n Geog région f; Geom superficie f; (of town) quartier m; Mil zone f; (domain) Fig domaine m, secteur m; **parking a.** aire f de stationnement; **dining/kitchen a.** coin-repas m/coin-cuisine m; **a. code** (phone number) Am indicatif m.

rena [əˈriːnə] n (for sports etc) & Fig arène f.

ren't [ɑːnt] = are not.

Argentina [ɑːdʒənˈtiːnə] n Argentine f.
● **Argentinian** a & n argentin, -ine (mf).

rguab/le [ˈɑːgʊəb(ə)l] a discutable.
● —**ly** adv on pourrait soutenir que.

rgue [ˈɑːgjuː] vi (quarrel) se disputer (with avec, about au sujet de); (reason) raisonner (with avec, about sur) ▮ vt (matter) discuter; **to a. that** (maintain) soutenir que.

rgument [ˈɑːgjəmənt] n (quarrel) dispute f; (reasoning) argument m; (debate) discussion f; **to have an a.** se disputer. ● **argu'mentative** a querelleur.

rid [ˈærɪd] a aride.

Aries [ˈeəriːz] n (sign) le Bélier.

rise [əˈraɪz] vi (pt arose, pp arisen) (of

problem opportunity etc) se présenter; (result) résulter (from de).

aristocracy [ærɪˈstɒkrəsɪ] n aristocratie f. ● **aristocrat** [ˈærɪstəkræt, Am əˈrɪstəkræt] n aristocrate mf. ● **aristo'cratic** a aristocratique.

arithmetic [əˈrɪθmətɪk] n arithmétique f.

ark [ɑːk] n Noah's a. l'arche f de Noé.

arm [ɑːm] 1 n bras m; **with open arms** à bras ouverts. 2 vt (with weapon) armer (with de). ● **armband** n brassard m; (for swimming) manchon m. ● **armchair** n fauteuil m. ● **armpit** n aisselle f. ● **armrest** n accoudoir m.

armistice [ˈɑːmɪstɪs] n armistice m.

armour [ˈɑːmər] n (of knight etc) armure f; (of tank etc) blindage m. ● **armoured** or **armour-plated** a (car etc) blindé.

arms [ɑːmz] npl (weapons) armes fpl.

army [ˈɑːmɪ] n armée f; **to join the a.** s'engager ▮ a (uniform etc) militaire.

aroma [əˈrəʊmə] n arôme m.

arose [əˈrəʊz] pt of arise.

around [əˈraʊnd] prep autour de; (approximately) environ, autour de ▮ adv autour; **all a.** tout autour; **to follow s.o. a.** suivre qn partout; **to rush a.** courir çà et là; **a. here** par ici; **he's still a.** il est encore là; **there's a lot of flu a.** il y a pas mal de grippe en ce moment; **up and a.** (after illness) Am sur pied.

arouse [əˈraʊz] vt (suspicion etc) éveiller, susciter; (sexually) exciter (qn).

arrange [əˈreɪndʒ] vt arranger; (time, meeting) fixer; **it was arranged that** il était convenu que; **to a. to do** s'arranger pour faire. ● —**ment** n (layout, agreement) arrangement m; pl (préparatifs mpl; (plans) projets mpl; **to make arrangements to** s'arranger pour.

array [əˈreɪ] n (display) étalage m.

arrears [əˈrɪəz] npl (payment) arriéré m; **to be in a.** avoir du retard dans ses paiements.

arrest [əˈrest] vt (criminal) arrêter ▮ n arrestation f; **under a.** en état d'arrestation.

arrive [əˈraɪv] vi arriver (at à). ● **arrival** n

arrivée f; **new a.** nouveau venu m, nouvelle venue f; (baby) nouveau-né, -ée mf.

arrogant ['ærəgənt] a arrogant. ● **arrogance** n arrogance f.

arrow ['ærəʊ] n flèche f.

arsenal ['ɑ:sən(ə)l] n arsenal m.

arson ['ɑ:s(ə)n] n incendie m volontaire. ● **arsonist** n incendiaire mf.

art [ɑ:t] n art m; **work of a.** œuvre f d'art; **faculty of arts** faculté f des lettres; **a. school** école f des beaux-arts.

artery ['ɑ:tərɪ] n Anat Aut artère f.

artful ['ɑ:tfəl] a rusé, astucieux.

arthritis [ɑ:'θraɪtɪs] n arthrite f.

artichoke ['ɑ:tɪtʃəʊk] n (globe) a. artichaut m; (Jerusalem) a. topinambour m.

article ['ɑ:tɪk(ə)l] n (object, in newspaper) & Gram article m; **a. of clothing** vêtement m; **articles of value** objets mpl de valeur.

articulate [ɑ:'tɪkjʊlət] a (person) qui s'exprime clairement ‖ [ɑ:'tɪkjʊleɪt] vti (speak) articuler; **articulated lorry** semi-remorque m.

artificial [ɑ:tɪ'fɪʃ(ə)l] a artificiel. ● **artificially** adv artificiellement.

artillery [ɑ:'tɪlərɪ] n artillerie f.

artist ['ɑ:tɪst] n (painter, actor etc) artiste mf. ● **artiste** [ɑ:'tiːst] n (singer, dancer) artiste m. ● **ar'tistic** a (pattern etc) artistique; (person) artiste.

artless ['ɑ:tləs] a naturel, naïf.

as [æz, unstressed əz] adv & conj **1** (manner etc) comme; **as you like** comme tu veux; **such as** comme, tel que; **dressed up as a clown** déguisé en clown; **as much** or **as hard as I can** (au)tant que je peux; **as it is** (to leave sth) comme ça, tel quel; **as if, as though** comme si.

2 (comparison) **as tall as you** aussi grand que vous; **is he as tall as you?** est-il aussi or si grand que vous?; **as white as a sheet** blanc comme un linge; **as much** or **as hard as you** autant que vous; **the same as** le même que; **twice as big as** deux fois plus grand que.

3 (though) **(as) clever as he is** si or aus[si] intelligent qu'il soit.

4 (capacity) **as a teacher** comme pr[o]fesseur, en tant que professeur; **to ac[t] as a father** agir en père.

5 (reason) puisque, comme; **as it's lat[e]** puisqu'il est tard, comme il est tard.

6 (time) **as I was leaving** comme j[e] partais; **as one grows older** à mesur[e] que l'on vieillit; **as he slept** pendan[t] qu'il dormait; **as from, as of** (time) partir de.

7 (concerning) **as for that, as to tha[t]** quant à cela.

8 (+ inf) **so as to** de manière à; **so stupi[d]** as **to** assez bête pour.

asap [eɪeseɪ'piː] abbr (as soon as poss[i]ble) le plus tôt possible.

asbestos [æs'bestəs] n amiante f.

ascend [ə'send] vt (throne) monter su[r] (mountain) faire l'ascension de. ● **as[cent]** n ascension f (of de); (slope) côte [f].

ascertain [æsə'teɪn] vt établir; (truth[)] découvrir; **to a. that** s'assurer que.

ash [æʃ] n **1** (of cigarette etc) cendre f; A[sh] **Wednesday** mercredi n des Cendres[.] **2** (tree) frêne m. ● **ashtray** n cendrier [n]

ashamed [ə'ʃeɪmd] a **to be** or **feel a** avoir honte (of s.o./sth de qn/qch); **t[o]** **be a. of oneself** avoir honte.

ashen ['æʃən] a (face) pâle.

ashore [ə'ʃɔːr] adv **to go a.** débarque[r] **to put s.o. a.** débarquer qn.

Asia ['eɪʃə, 'eɪʒə] n Asie f. ● **Asian** a asiatique ‖ n Asiatique mf.

aside [ə'saɪd] adv de côté; **to take o[ne]** draw s.o. **a.** prendre qn à part; **to step a[.]** s'écarter; **a. from** Am en dehors de.

ask [ɑ:sk] vt demander; (invite) invite[r] (to à); **to a. (s.o.) a question** poser un[e] question (à qn); **to a. s.o. (for) st[h]** demander qch à qn; **to a. s.o. to d[o]** demander à qn de faire; **to a. to d[o]** demander à faire.

‖ vi demander; **to a. for sth/s.o.** deman[der] der qch/qn; **to a. for sth back** redeman[der] der qch; **to a. about sth** se renseigner su[r] qch; **to a. after** or **about s.o.** demande[r]

des nouvelles de qn; **to a. s.o. about sth/
s.o.** interroger qn sur qch/qn; **asking
price** prix *m* demandé.

askance [ə'skɑːns] *adv* **to look a. at**
regarder avec méfiance.

askew [ə'skjuː] *adv* de biais, de travers.

asleep [ə'sliːp] *a* endormi; **to be a.**
dormir; **to fall a.** s'endormir.

asparagus [ə'spærəgəs] *n* (*shoots for
cooking*) asperges *fpl*.

aspect ['æspekt] *n* aspect *m*; (*of house*)
orientation *f*.

asphyxiate [əs'fɪksɪeɪt] *vt* asphyxier.

aspire [ə'spaɪər] *vi* **to a.** to aspirer à.
● **aspiration** [æspə'reɪʃ(ə)n] *n* aspiration
f.

aspirin ['æsprɪn] *n* aspirine *f*.

ass [æs] *n* (*animal*) âne *m*; (*person*) Fam
imbécile *mf*, âne *m*.

assailant [ə'seɪlənt] *n* agresseur *m*.

assassin [ə'sæsɪn] *n* Pol assassin *m*.
● **assassinate** *vt* assassiner. ● **assassi-
nation** [-'neɪʃ(ə)n] *n* assassinat *m*.

assault [ə'sɔːlt] *n* Mil assaut *m*; (*crime*)
agression *f* ‖ *vt* (*attack*) agresser;
(*woman*) violenter. ● **assault** *vt* violenter.

assemble [ə'semb(ə)l] *vt* (*objects, ideas*)
assembler; (*people*) rassembler; (*machine*) monter ‖ *vi* se rassembler. ● **assembly** *n* (*meeting*) assemblée *f*; Sch
rassemblement *m*; ‖ **a. line** (*in factory*)
chaîne *f* de montage.

assert [ə'sɜːt] *vt* affirmer (**that** que);
(*rights*) revendiquer. ● **assertion**
[-ʃ(ə)n] *n* (*statement*) affirmation *f*.

assess [ə'ses] *vt* (*estimate*) évaluer;
(*decide amount of*) fixer le montant
de. ● —**ment** *n* évaluation *f*.

asset ['æset] *n* (*advantage*) atout *m*; *pl*
(*of business*) biens *mpl*.

assign [ə'saɪn] *vt* (*give*) attribuer; (*day
etc*) fixer; (*appoint*) nommer. ● —**ment** *n*
(*task*) mission *f*; Sch devoir *m*.

assimilate [ə'sɪmɪleɪt] *vt* assimiler ‖ *vi*
s'assimiler.

assist [ə'sɪst] *vti* aider (**in doing, to do** à
faire). ● **assistance** *n* aide *f*; **to be of a. to
s.o.** aider qn. ● **assistant** *n* assistant,

-ante *mf*; (*in shop*) vendeur, -euse *mf*
‖ *a* adjoint.

associate [ə'səuʃɪeɪt] *vt* associer (**with**
sth à *or* avec qch, **with s.o.** à qn) ‖ *vi* to
a. with s.o. (*mix socially*) fréquenter qn;
(*in business venture*) s'associer à *or* avec
qn ‖ [ə'səuʃɪət] *n* & *a* associé, -ée (*mf*).
● **association** [-'eɪʃ(ə)n] *n* association *f*.

assorted [ə'sɔːtɪd] *a* (*different*) variés;
(*foods*) assortis. ● **assortment** *n* assortiment *m*.

assume [ə'sjuːm] *vt* **1** (*suppose*) supposer, présumer (**that** que). **2** (*take on*)
prendre; (*responsibility, role*) assumer;
(*attitude, name*) adopter; **assumed
name** nom *m* d'emprunt. ● **assumption**
[ə'sʌmpʃ(ə)n] *n* supposition *f*.

assure [ə'ʃuər] *vt* assurer (**s.o. that** à qn
que, **s.o. of** qn de). ● **assurance** *n*
assurance *f*.

asterisk ['æstərɪsk] *n* astérisque *m*.

asthma ['æsmə] *n* asthme *m*. ● **asth'matic**
a & *n* asthmatique (*mf*).

astonish [ə'stɒnɪʃ] *vt* étonner; **to be
astonished** s'étonner (**at sth** de qch).
● —**ing** *a* étonnant. ● **astonishment** *n*
étonnement *m*.

astound [ə'staund] *vt* stupéfier, étonner.
● —**ing** *a* stupéfiant.

astray [ə'streɪ] *adv* **to go a.** s'égarer; **to
lead a.** égarer.

astride [ə'straɪd] *adv* à califourchon
‖ *prep* à cheval sur.

astrology [ə'strɒlədʒɪ] *n* astrologie *f*.
● **astrologer** *n* astrologue *mf*.

astronaut ['æstrənɔːt] *n* astronaute *mf*.

astronomy [ə'strɒnəmɪ] *n* astronomie *f*.
● **astronomer** *n* astronome *mf*.

astute [ə'stjuːt] *a* (*crafty*) rusé; (*clever*)
astucieux.

asylum [ə'saɪləm] *n* asile *m*.

at [æt, *unstressed* ət] *prep* **1** à; **at the end** à
la fin; **at work** au travail; **at six (o'clock)**
à six heures; **at Easter** à Pâques.
2 chez; **at the doctor's** chez le médecin;
at home chez soi, à la maison.
3 en; **at sea** en mer; **at war** en guerre;
good at (*geography etc*) fort en.

4 contre; **angry at** fâché contre.

5 sur; **to shoot at** tirer sur; **at my request** sur ma demande.

6 de; **to laugh at** rire de; **surprised at** surpris de.

7 (au)près de; **at the window** (au)près de la fenêtre.

8 par; **to come in at the door** entrer par la porte; **six at a time** six par six.

9 (phrases) **at night** la nuit; **to look at** regarder; **to be (hard) at it** travailler dur; **he's always (on) at me** Fam il est toujours après moi.

ate [et, Am eıt] pt of eat.

atheist ['eıθııst] n athée mf.

Athens ['æθınz] n Athènes m or f.

athlete ['æθliːt] n athlète mf. ● **ath'letic** a athlétique; **a. meeting** réunion f sportive. ● **ath'letics** npl athlétisme m.

Atlantic [ət'læntık] a (coast) atlantique ‖ n the A. l'Atlantique m.

atlas ['ætləs] n atlas m.

atmosphere ['ætməsfıər] n atmosphère f.

atom ['ætəm] n atome m; **a. bomb** bombe f atomique. ● **a'tomic** a (bomb etc) atomique.

atone [ə'təʊn] vi **to a. for** expier.

atrocious [ə'trəʊʃəs] a atroce. ● **atrocity** n atrocité f.

attach [ə'tætʃ] vt attacher (**to** à); (document) joindre (**to** à); **attached to** (fond of) attaché à. ● **—ment** n (tool) accessoire m; (affection) attachement m (**to s.o.** à qn).

attaché case [ə'tæʃeıkeıs] n attaché-case m, mallette f.

attack [ə'tæk] n attaque f; (of illness) crise f; **heart a.** crise f cardiaque ‖ vti attaquer. ● **—er** n agresseur m.

attain [ə'teın] vt (aim, rank) parvenir à; (ambition) réaliser.

attempt [ə'tempt] n tentative f; **to make an a. to** do tenter de faire; **an a. on s.o.'s life** attentat m contre qn ‖ vt tenter; (task) entreprendre; **to a. to** do tenter de faire; **attempted murder** tentative f de meurtre.

attend [ə'tend] vt (meeting etc) assister à; (course) suivre; (school, church) aller à; (patient) soigner; **well-attended** (course) très suivi; (meeting) où il y a du monde ‖ vi assister; **to a. to** (take care of) s'occuper de (travail, client etc).

attendance [ə'tendəns] n présence f (**at** à); (school) a. scolarité f; **in a. de** service. ● **attendant** n employé, -ée mf; (in service station) pompiste mf; (in museum) gardien, -ienne mf.

attention [ə'tenʃ(ə)n] n attention f; **to pay a.** faire attention (**to** à); **a.!** Mil garde-à-vous!; **a. to detail** minutie f. ● **attentive** a (heedful) attentif (**to** à); (thoughtful) attentionné (**to** pour).

attic ['ætık] n grenier m.

attitude ['ætıtjuːd] n attitude f.

attorney [ə'tɜːnı] n (lawyer) Am avocat m; **district a.** Am = procureur m (de la République).

attract [ə'trækt] vt attirer. ● **attraction** [-ʃ(ə)n] n (charm, appeal) attrait m; (person, place etc) attraction f; (between people) attirance f.

attractive [ə'træktıv] a (house, car etc) beau (f belle); (price, offer etc) intéressant; **a. girl** belle fille f; **a. boy** beau garçon m.

attribute 1 ['ætrıbjuːt] n (quality) attribut m. **2** [ə'trıbjuːt] vt (ascribe) attribuer (**to** à).

aubergine ['əʊbəʒiːn] n aubergine f.

auburn ['ɔːbən] a (hair) châtain roux.

auction ['ɔːkʃən] n vente f (aux enchères) ‖ vt **to a. (off)** vendre (aux enchères). ● **auctio'neer** n commissaire-priseur m.

audacity [ɔː'dæsıtı] n audace f.

audible ['ɔːdıb(ə)l] a perceptible.

audience ['ɔːdıəns] n (of speaker, musician) auditoire m, public m; Th Cin spectateurs mpl, public m; Rad auditeurs mpl; (interview) audience f; **TV a.** téléspectateurs mpl.

audio ['ɔːdıəʊ] a (cassette etc) audio inv. ● **audiotypist** n dactylo f au magnétophone, audiotypiste mf. ● **audio-'visual**

a audio-visuel.

audit ['ɔ:dɪt] *vt* (*accounts*) vérifier.
● **auditor** *n* commissaire *m* aux comptes.

audition [ɔ:'dɪʃ(ə)n] *n* audition *f* ‖ *vti*
auditionner.

augur ['ɔ:gər] *vi* to a. well être de bon
augure.

August ['ɔ:gəst] *n* août *m*.

aunt [ɑ:nt] *n* tante *f*. ● **auntie** *or* **aunty** *n*
Fam tata *f*.

au pair [əʊ'peər] *adv* au pair ‖ *n* au p.
(girl) jeune fille *f* au pair.

aura ['ɔ:rə] *n* (*of place*) atmosphère *f*; (*of
person*) aura *f*.

austere [ɔ:'stɪər] *a* austère. ● **austerity** *n*
austérité *f*.

Australia [ɒ'streɪlɪə] *n* Australie *f*. ● **Australian** *a* & *n* australien, -ienne (*mf*).

Austria ['ɒstrɪə] *n* Autriche *f*. ● **Austrian**
a & *n* autrichien, -ienne (*mf*).

authentic [ɔ:'θentɪk] *a* authentique.
● **authenticate** *vt* authentifier.

author ['ɔ:θər] *n* auteur *m*.

authority [ɔ:'θɒrɪtɪ] *n* autorité *f*; (*permission*) autorisation *f* (to do de faire);
to be in a. (*in charge*) être responsable.
● **authori'tarian** *a* & *n* autoritaire (*mf*).
● **authoritative** *a* (*report, book*) qui fait
autorité; (*tone, person*) autoritaire.

authorize ['ɔ:θəraɪz] *vt* autoriser (to do à
faire). ● **authorization** [-'zeɪʃ(ə)n] *n*
autorisation *f* (to do de faire).

autistic [ɔ:'tɪstɪk] *a* autiste.

autobiography [ɔ:təʊbaɪ'ɒgrəfɪ] *n* auto-
biographie *f*.

autocratic [ɔ:tə'krætɪk] *a* autocratique.

autograph ['ɔ:təgrɑ:f] *n* autographe *m*
‖ *vt* dédicacer (for à).

automatic [ɔ:tə'mætɪk] *a* automatique.
● **automatically** *adv* automatiquement.

automation [ɔ:tə'meɪʃ(ə)n] *n* automatisation *f*.

automobile ['ɔ:təməbi:l] *n* *Am* auto-
(mobile) *f*.

autonomous [ɔ:'tɒnəməs] *a* autonome.
● **autonomy** *n* autonomie *f*.

autopsy ['ɔ:tɒpsɪ] *n* autopsie *f*.

autumn ['ɔ:təm] *n* automne *m*.

auxiliary [ɔ:g'zɪljərɪ] *a* & *n* auxiliaire
(*mf*); a. (verb) (verbe *m*) auxiliaire *m*.

avail [ə'veɪl] 1 *vt* to a. oneself of tirer
avantage de. 2 *n* to no a. en vain.

available [ə'veɪləb(ə)l] *a* (*thing, person*)
disponible; a. to all (*education etc*)
accessible à tous. ● **availa'bility** *n* dis-
ponibilité *f*.

avalanche ['ævəlɑ:nʃ] *n* avalanche *f*.

Ave *abbr* = avenue.

avenge [ə'vendʒ] *vt* venger; to a. oneself
se venger (on de).

avenue ['ævənju:] *n* avenue *f*; (*way to a
result*) Fig voie *f*.

average ['ævərɪdʒ] *n* moyenne *f*; on a. en
moyenne ‖ *a* moyen ‖ *vt* (*do*) faire en
moyenne; (*reach*) atteindre la moyenne
de.

averse [ə'vɜ:s] *a* to be a. to doing
répugner à faire.

avert [ə'vɜ:t] *vt* (*prevent*) éviter.

aviary ['eɪvɪərɪ] *n* volière *f*.

aviation [eɪvɪ'eɪʃ(ə)n] *n* aviation *f*.

avid ['ævɪd] *a* avide (for de).

avocado [ævə'kɑ:dəʊ] *n* (*pl* -os) a. (pear)
avocat *m*.

avoid [ə'vɔɪd] *vt* éviter; to a. doing éviter
de faire. ●—**able** *a* évitable.

await [ə'weɪt] *vt* attendre.

awake [ə'weɪk] *vi* (*pt* awoke, *pp* awoken)
se réveiller ‖ *vt* réveiller ‖ *a* (wide-)a.
éveillé; to keep s.o. a. empêcher qn de
dormir; he's (still) a. il ne dort pas
(encore). ● **awaken** 1 *vti* = awake. 2
vt to a. s.o. to sth faire prendre conscience de qch à qn. ● **awakening** *n*
réveil *m*.

award [ə'wɔ:d] *vt* (*money, prize*) attribuer; (*damages*) accorder ‖ *n* (*prize*)
prix *m*, récompense *f*; (*scholarship*)
bourse *f*.

aware [ə'weər] *a* a. of (*conscious*) conscient de; (*informed*) au courant de; to
become a. of se rendre compte de,
prendre conscience de; to be *or* become
a. that (*realize*) se rendre compte que.
●—**ness** *n* conscience *f*.

awash [ə'wɒʃ] *a* inondé (with de).

away [ə'weɪ] *adv* **1** (*distant*) loin; **far a. au loin**, très loin; **5 km a.** à 5 km (de distance).

2 (*in time*) **ten days a.** dans dix jours.

3 (*absent, gone*) parti, absent; **a. with you!** va-t-en!; **to drive a.** partir (en voiture); **to fade a.** disparaître complètement.

4 (*continuously*) **to work/talk**/*etc* **a.** travailler/parler/*etc* sans arrêt.

5 to play a. *Sp* jouer à l'extérieur.

awe [ɔː] *n* crainte *f* (*mêlée de respect*).

● **awesome** *a* (*impressive*) imposant; (*frightening*) effrayant; (*marvellous*) *Fam* super.

awful ['ɔːfəl] *a* affreux; (*terrifying*) épouvantable; (*ill*) malade; **an a. lot of** *Fam* un nombre incroyable de; **I feel a. (about it)** j'ai vraiment honte. ● **—ly** *adv* (*very*) (*good, pretty etc*) extrêmement; (*bad, late etc*) affreusement.

awhile [ə'waɪl] *adv* (*to stay, wait*) un peu.

awkward ['ɔːkwəd] *a* **1** (*clumsy*) maladroit. **2** (*difficult*) difficile; (*cumbersome*) gênant; (*tool*) peu commode; (*time*) mal choisi; (*silence*) gêné. ● **—ly** *adv* maladroitement; (*placed*) à un endroit peu pratique.

awning ['ɔːnɪŋ] *n* (*over shop, window*) store *m*; (*of hotel*) marquise *f*.

awoke, awoken [ə'wəʊk, ə'wəʊk(ə)n] *pt* & *pp of* **awake**.

axe [æks] (*Am* **ax**) *n* hache *f*; (*reduction*) *Fig* coupe *f* sombre ▮ *vt* réduire; (*job etc*) supprimer.

axis, *pl* **axes** ['æksɪs, 'æksiːz] *n* axe *m*.

axle ['æks(ə)l] *n* essieu *m*.

B

B, b [bi:] n B, b m; **2B** (number) 2 ter.

BA abbr = **Bachelor of Arts.**

babble ['bæb(ə)l] vi (mumble) bre-douiller ‖ n inv (of voices) rumeur f.

baboon [bə'bu:n] n babouin m.

baby ['beɪbɪ] n bébé m; b. boy petit garçon m; **b. girl** petite fille f; **b. tiger**/etc bébé-tigre/etc m; **b. clothes/ toys**/etc vêtements mpl/jouets mpl/etc de bébé; **b. carriage** Am voiture f d'enfant. ●**b.-minder** n gardien, -ienne mf d'enfants. ●**b.-sit** vi (pt & pp -sat, pres p -sitting) garder les enfants, faire du baby-sitting. ●**b.-sitter** n baby-sitter mf. ●**b.-walker** n trotteur m, youpala® m.

babyish ['beɪbɪʃ] a Pej de bébé; (puerile) enfantin.

bachelor ['bætʃələr] n 1 célibataire m. 2 **B. of Arts/of Science** licencié, -ée mf ès lettres/ès sciences.

back¹ [bæk] n (of person, animal) dos m; (of chair) dossier m; (of hand) revers m; (of house) arrière m, derrière m; (of vehicle, head) arrière m; (of room) fond m; (of page) verso m; (of fabric) envers m; Fb arrière m; **at the b. of** (book) à la fin de; **in the b. of** (vehicle) à l'arrière de; **b. to front** devant derrière, à l'envers; **to get s.o.'s b. up** Fam irriter qn; **in b. of** Am derrière.

back² [bæk] a (wheel, seat) arrière inv; **b. door** porte f de derrière; **b. room** pièce f du fond; **b. number** (of magazine etc) vieux numéro m; **b. pay** rappel m de salaire; **b. street** rue f écartée; **b. tooth** molaire f.

back³ [bæk] adv (behind) en arrière; **far b.,** a long way b. loin derrière; **a month b.** il y a un mois; **to stand b.** (of house) être en retrait (**from** par rapport à); **to go b. and forth** aller et venir; **to come b.** revenir; **he's b.** il est de retour, il est revenu; **the trip there and b.** le voyage aller et retour.

back⁴ [bæk] vt (with money) financer; (horse etc) parier sur, jouer; (vehicle) faire reculer; **to b. s.o (up)** (support) appuyer qn; **to b. up** Comptr sauvegarder.

‖ vi **to b. down** se dégonfler; **to b. out** (withdraw) se retirer; (of vehicle) sortir en marche arrière; **to b. up** (of vehicle) faire marche arrière.

backache ['bækeɪk] n mal m de dos. ●**back'bencher** n Pol membre m sans portefeuille. ●**backcloth** n toile f de fond. ●**back'date** vt (cheque, Am check) antidater. ●**back'handed** a (compliment) équivoque. ●**backhander** n (bribe) Fam pot-de-vin m. ●**backpack** n sac m à dos. ●**backrest** n dossier m. ●**backside** n (buttocks) Fam derrière m. ●**back'stage** adv dans les coulisses. ●**backstroke** n Sp dos m crawlé. ●**backup** n (support) appui m; (tail-back) Am embouteillage m; Comptr sauvegarde f; **b. lights** Aut Am feux mpl de recul. ●**backwater** n (place) trou m perdu. ●**back'yard** n arrière-cour f; Am jardin m (à l'arrière d'une maison).

backbone ['bækbəʊn] n colonne f vertébrale; (main support) pivot m.

backer ['bækər] n (supporter) partisan m; Sp parieur, -euse mf; Fin bailleur m de fonds.

backfire [bæk'faɪər] vi 1 Aut pétarader. 2 (of plot etc) échouer.

backgammon ['bækgæmən] n trictrac m.

background ['bækgraʊnd] n fond m; (events) Fig antécédents mpl; (education) formation f; (environment) milieu m; (social, political etc conditions) contexte m; **b. music** musique f de fond.

backing ['bækɪŋ] n (aid) soutien m; (material) support m, renfort m.

backlash ['bæklæʃ] n retour m de flamme.

backlog ['bæklɒg] n b. of work travail m en retard.

backward ['bækwəd] a (person, country etc) arriéré; (glance etc) en arrière ‖ adv = **backwards**. ●—ness n (of country etc) retard m. ●**backwards** adv en arrière; (to walk) à reculons; (to fall) à la renverse; **to go** or **move b.** reculer; **to go b. and forwards** aller et venir.

bacon ['beɪkən] n lard m; (in rashers) bacon m; **b. and eggs** œufs mpl au bacon.

bacteria [bæk'tɪərɪə] npl bactéries fpl.

bad [bæd] a (**worse, worst**) mauvais; (wicked) méchant; (accident, wound etc) grave; (tooth) carié; (arm, leg) malade; (pain) violent; **to feel b.** (ill) se sentir mal; **things are b.** ça va mal; **not b.!** pas mal!; **to go b.** (of fruit, meat) se gâter; (of milk) tourner; **too b.!** tant pis! ●**b.-'mannered** a mal élevé. ●**b.-'tempered** a grincheux.

badge [bædʒ] n (of plastic) badge m; (of metal, bearing logo) pin's m; (of postman, policeman) plaque f; (on school uniform) insigne m.

badger ['bædʒər] n (animal) blaireau m.

badly ['bædlɪ] adv mal; (hurt) grièvement; **b. affected** très touché; **to be b. mistaken** se tromper lourdement; **b. off** dans la gêne; **to want b.** avoir grande envie de.

badminton ['bædmɪntən] n badminton m.

baffle ['bæf(ə)l] vt (person) déconcerter.

bag [bæg] 1 n sac m; pl (luggage) valises fpl, bagages mpl; (under the eyes) poches fpl; **bags of** Fam (lots of) beaucoup de; **an old b.** une vieille taupe. 2 vt (-gg-) (take, steal) Fam piquer.

baggage ['bægɪdʒ] n bagages mpl; **b. car** Am fourgon m; **b. handler** bagagiste m; **b. room** Am consigne f.

baggy ['bægɪ] a (-ier, -iest) (trousers, Am pants) faisant des poches.

bagpipes ['bægpaɪps] npl cornemuse f.

Bahamas [bə'hɑːməz] npl the B. les Bahamas fpl.

bail [beɪl] 1 n Jur caution f; **on b.** en liberté provisoire ‖ vt **to b. (out)** fournir une caution pour; **to b. out** (person, company) venir en aide à. 2 vi **to b. out** Av sauter (en parachute).

bailiff ['beɪlɪf] n Jur huissier m.

bait [beɪt] 1 n amorce f, appât m. 2 vt (annoy) asticoter, tourmenter.

bak/e [beɪk] vt (faire) cuire (au four) ‖ vi (of cook) faire de la pâtisserie or du pain; (of cake etc) cuire (au four); **it's baking (hot)** Fam on cuit. ●—ed a (potatoes, apples) au four; **b. beans** haricots mpl blancs (à la tomate). ●—ing n cuisson f.

baker ['beɪkər] n boulanger, -ère mf. ●**bakery** n boulangerie f.

balaclava [bælə'klɑːvə] n b. (helmet) passe-montagne m.

balance ['bæləns] n équilibre m; (of account) solde m; (remainder) reste m; Econ Pol balance f; **to lose one's b.** perdre l'équilibre; **to strike a b.** trouver le juste milieu; **in the b.** incertain; **b. sheet** bilan m ‖ vt tenir en équilibre (on sur); (budget, account) équilibrer; (compensate for) compenser ‖ vi (of person) se tenir en équilibre, s'équilibrer; (of accounts) être en équilibre; **to b. out** (even out) s'équilibrer.

balcony ['bælkənɪ] n balcon m.

bald [bɔːld] a (-er, -est) chauve; (tyre, Am tire) lisse; **b. patch** tonsure f. ●**b.-'headed** a chauve. ●**baldness** n calvitie f.

bale [beɪl] 1 n (of cotton etc) balle f. 2 vi **to b. out** Av sauter (en parachute).

balk [bɔːk] vi reculer (**at** devant).

ball[1] [bɔːl] n balle f; (inflated) Fb Rugby etc ballon m; Billiards bille f; (of string, wool) pelote f; (sphere) boule f; (of meat or fish) boulette f; **on the b.** (alert) Fam éveillé; **he's on the b.** (efficient, know-

ledgeable) *Fam* il connaît son affaire, il est au point; **it's a whole new b. game** *Am* c'est une tout autre affaire.

ball² [bɔːl] *n* (*dance*) bal *m* (*pl* bals).

ballad ['bæləd] *n* (*poem*) ballade *f*.

ballast ['bæləst] *n* lest *m*.

ballet ['bæleɪ] *n* ballet *m*. ●**balle'rina** *n* ballerine *f*.

balloon [bə'luːn] *n* (*toy*) & *Av* ballon *m*.

ballot ['bælət] *n* (*voting*) scrutin *m*.

ballpoint ['bɔːlpɔɪnt] *n* **b. (pen)** stylo *m* à bille.

ballroom ['bɔːlruːm] *n* salle *f* de danse.

balmy ['bɑːmɪ] *a* (**-ier, -iest**) (*crazy*) *Fam* dingue, timbré.

Baltic ['bɔːltɪk] *n* **the B.** la Baltique.

bamboo [bæm'buː] *n* bambou *m*.

ban [bæn] *n* interdiction *f* ‖ *vt* (**-nn-**) interdire; **to ban s.o. from doing** interdire à qn de faire; **to b. from** (*club etc*) exclure de.

banal [bə'nɑːl, *Am* 'beɪn(ə)l] *a* banal (*mpl* **-als**).

banana [bə'nɑːnə] *n* banane *f*.

band [bænd] **1** *n* (*strip*) bande *f*; **rubber or elastic b.** élastique *m*. **2** *n* (*group of people*) bande *f*; *Mus* (*pop group*) groupe *m*; (*brass*) **b.** fanfare *f* ‖ *vi* **to b. together** se grouper.

bandage ['bændɪdʒ] *n* (*strip*) bande *f*; (*dressing*) bandage *m* ‖ *vt* **to b. (up)** (*arm, leg*) bander; (*wound*) mettre un bandage sur.

Band-Aid® ['bændeɪd] *n* pansement *m* adhésif.

bandit ['bændɪt] *n* bandit *m*.

bandwagon ['bændwægən] *n* **to jump on the b.** *Fig* suivre le mouvement.

bandy¹ ['bændɪ] *a* (**-ier, -iest**) (*person*) bancal (*mpl* **-als**); (*legs*) arqué. ●**b.-'legged** *a* bancal (*mpl* **-als**).

bandy² ['bændɪ] *vt* **to b. about** (*story etc*) faire circuler.

bang¹ [bæŋ] *n* (*noise*) coup *m* (violent); (*of gun*) détonation *f*; (*of door*) claquement *m* ‖ *vt* cogner, frapper; (*door*) (faire) claquer; **to b. one's head** se cogner la tête; **to b. down** (*lid*) rabattre

(violemment) ‖ *vi* cogner, frapper; (*of door*) claquer; **to b. into sth/s.o.** heurter qch/qn ‖ *int* vlan!, pan!; **to go (off) b.** éclater.

bang² [bæŋ] *adv* *Fam* (*exactly*) exactement; **b. in the middle** en plein milieu; **b. on six** à six heures tapantes.

banger ['bæŋər] *n* **1** *Culin Fam* saucisse *f*. **2 old b.** (*car*) *Fam* tacot *m*.

bangle ['bæŋg(ə)l] *n* bracelet *m* (rigide).

bangs [bæŋz] *npl* (*of hair*) *Am* frange *f*.

banish ['bænɪʃ] *vt* bannir.

banister ['bænɪstər] *n* **banister(s)** rampe *f* (d'escalier).

banjo ['bændʒəʊ] *n* (*pl* **-os** *or* **-oes**) banjo *m*.

bank [bæŋk] **1** *n* (*of river*) bord *m*; (*raised*) berge *f*; **the Left B.** (*in Paris*) la Rive gauche.
2 *n* *Com* banque *f*; **b. account** compte *m* en banque; **b. card** carte *f* d'identité bancaire; **b. holiday** jour *m* férié; **b. note** billet *m* de banque; **b. rate** taux *m* d'escompte ‖ *vt* (*money*) mettre en banque ‖ *vi* avoir un compte en banque (**with** à).
3 *vi* (*of aircraft*) virer.
4 *vi* **to b. on s.o./sth** (*rely on*) compter sur qn/qch. ●**-ing** *a* bancaire ‖ *n* (*activity*) la banque. ●**banker** *n* banquier *m*.

bankrupt ['bæŋkrʌpt] *a* **to go b.** faire faillite ‖ *vt* mettre en faillite. ●**bankruptcy** *n* faillite *f*.

banner ['bænər] *n* (*at rallies, on two poles*) banderole *f*; (*flag*) bannière *f*.

banns [bænz] *npl* bans *mpl*.

banquet ['bæŋkwɪt] *n* banquet *m*.

banter ['bæntər] *vti* plaisanter ‖ *n* plaisanterie *f*.

baptism ['bæptɪzəm] *n* baptême *m*. ●**bap'tize** *vt* baptiser.

bar [bɑːr] **1** *n* barre *f*; (*of gold*) lingot *m*; (*of chocolate*) tablette *f*; (*on window*) barreau *m*; **b. of soap** savonnette *f*; **behind bars** (*criminal*) sous les verrous; **the B.** *Jur* le barreau.
2 *n* (*pub, counter*) bar *m*.

3 n (*group of notes*) Mus mesure f.

4 vt (-rr-) **to b. s.o.'s way** bloquer le passage à qn.

5 vt (*prohibit*) interdire (**s.o. from doing** à qn de faire); (*exclude*) exclure (**from** à). ● **barmaid** n serveuse f de bar. ● **barman** or **bartender** n barman m.

Barbados [bɑːˈbeɪdɒs] n Barbade f.

barbarian [bɑːˈbeərɪən] n barbare mf. ● **barbaric** a barbare.

barbecue [ˈbɑːbɪkjuː] n barbecue m ‖ vt griller (au barbecue).

barbed wire [bɑːbdˈwaɪər] n fil m de fer barbelé; (*fence*) barbelés mpl.

barber [ˈbɑːbər] n coiffeur m (*pour hommes*).

bare [beər] a (-er, -est) nu; (*tree etc*) dénudé; (*cupboard, Am closet*) vide; the **b. necessities** le strict nécessaire; **with his b. hands** à mains nues. ● **barefoot** adv nu-pieds ‖ a aux pieds nus. ● **bare'headed** a & adv nu-tête inv.

barely [ˈbeəlɪ] adv (*scarcely*) à peine.

bargain [ˈbɑːgɪn] n (*deal*) marché m, affaire f; **a b.** (*cheap buy*) une occasion, une bonne affaire; **to make a b.** faire un marché (**with** avec); **into the b.** par-dessus le marché; **b. price** prix m exceptionnel; **b. counter** rayon m des soldes ‖ vi (*negotiate*) négocier; (*haggle*) marchander; **to b. for sth** (*expect*) s'attendre à qch.

barge [bɑːdʒ] **1** n chaland m, péniche f. **2** vi **to b. in** (*enter a room*) faire irruption; (*interrupt s.o.*) interrompre; **to b. into** (*hit*) se cogner contre.

bark [bɑːk] **1** n (*of tree*) écorce f. **2** vi (*of dog*) aboyer ‖ n aboiement m. ● —**ing** n aboiements mpl.

barley [ˈbɑːlɪ] n orge f.

barmy [ˈbɑːmɪ] a (-ier, -iest) (*crazy*) Fam dingue, timbré.

barn [bɑːn] n (*for crops etc*) grange f; ● **barnyard** n basse-cour f.

barometer [bəˈrɒmɪtər] n baromètre m.

baron [ˈbærən] n baron m; **press/oil b.** magnat m de la presse/du pétrole. ● **baroness** n baronne f.

barracks [ˈbærəks] npl caserne f.

barrage [ˈbærɑːʒ, Am bəˈrɑːʒ] n (*across river*) barrage m; **a b. of** (*questions etc*) un feu roulant de.

barrel [ˈbærəl] n **1** (*cask*) tonneau m; (*of oil*) baril m. **2** (*of gun*) canon m.

barren [ˈbærən] a stérile; (*style*) Fig aride.

barrette [bəˈret] n (*hair slide*) Am barrette f.

barricade [ˈbærɪkeɪd] n barricade f ‖ vt barricader; **to b. oneself (in)** se barricader.

barrier [ˈbærɪər] n barrière f; Fig obstacle m, barrière f; (**ticket**) **b.** Rail portillon m.

barring [ˈbɑːrɪŋ] prep sauf, excepté.

barrister [ˈbærɪstər] n avocat m.

barrow [ˈbærəʊ] n (*wheelbarrow*) brouette f; (*cart*) charrette f à bras.

barter [ˈbɑːtər] vt troquer, échanger (**for** contre) ‖ n troc m, échange m.

base [beɪs] **1** n (*bottom*) base f; (*of tree, lamp*) pied m. **2** n Mil base f. **3** vt baser, fonder (**on** sur); **based in London** basé à Londres. ● **baseboard** n Am plinthe f.

baseball [ˈbeɪsbɔːl] n base-ball m.

basement [ˈbeɪsmənt] n sous-sol m.

bash [bæʃ] n (*bang*) coup m; **to have a b.** (*try*) Fam essayer un coup ‖ vt (*hit*) cogner; (*ill-treat*) malmener; **to b. s.o. up** tabasser qn; **to b. down** (*door*) défoncer. ● —**ing** n (*thrashing*) Fam raclée f.

bashful [ˈbæʃfəl] a timide.

basic [ˈbeɪsɪk] a essentiel, de base; (*elementary*) élémentaire; (*pay, food*) de base; (*room, house*) tout simple ‖ n **the basics** Fam l'essentiel m. ● **basically** [-klɪ] adv au fond.

basil [ˈbæz(ə)l] n basilic m.

basin [ˈbeɪs(ə)n] n bassine f; (*for soup, food*) (grand) bol m; (*of river*) bassin m; (*sink*) lavabo m.

basis, pl **-ses** [ˈbeɪsɪs, -siːz] n (*of agreement etc*) bases fpl; **on the b. of** d'après; **on that b.** dans ces conditions; **on a weekly b.** chaque semaine.

bask [bɑːsk] vi se chauffer.

basket ['ba:skit] n panier m; (for bread, laundry, litter) corbeille f. ● **basketball** n basket(-ball) m.

Basque [bæsk] a & n basque (mf).

bass [beis] n Mus basse f.

bastard ['ba:stəd] 1 n & a (child) bâtard, -arde (mf). 2 n Pej Sl salaud m, salope f.

bat [bæt] 1 n (animal) chauve-souris f. 2 n Cricket Baseball batte f; Table Tennis raquette f; **off my own b.** de ma propre initiative ▮ vt (-tt-) (ball) frapper. 3 vt **she didn't b. an eyelid** elle n'a pas sourcillé.

batch [bætʃ] n (of people) groupe m; (of letters) paquet m; (of loaves) fournée f; (of papers) liasse f.

bated ['beitid] a **with b. breath** en retenant son souffle.

bath [ba:θ] n (pl -s [ba:ðz]) bain m; (tub) baignoire f; **to have** or **take a b.** prendre un bain; **b. towel** serviette f de bain; **swimming baths** piscine f ▮ vt baigner. ● **bathrobe** n peignoir m (de bain); Am robe f de chambre. ● **bathroom** n salle f de bain(s); (toilet) Am toilettes fpl. ● **bathtub** n baignoire f.

bath/e [beið] vt baigner; (wound) laver ▮ vi se baigner; Am prendre un bain ▮ n **to go for a b.** se baigner. ●**—ing** n ▮ baignade(r) f(nl); **b. costume** or **suit** maillot m de bain.

baton ['bætən, Am bə'tɒn] n (of conductor) baguette f; (of policeman) matraque f.

battalion [bə'tæljən] n bataillon m.

batter ['bætər] 1 n pâte f à frire. 2 vt (person) rouer de coups; (object) frapper (à coups redoublés); (baby) martyriser. ● **—ed** a (car) cabossé; **b. wife** femme f battue. ● **—ing** n **to take a b.** souffrir beaucoup.

battery ['bætəri] n Aut Mil batterie f; (in radio, appliance etc) pile f.

battle ['bæt(ə)l] n bataille f; (struggle) lutte f; **b. dress** tenue f de campagne ▮ vi se battre, lutter. ● **battlefield** n champ m de bataille. ● **battleship** n cuirassé m.

baulk [bɔ:k] vi reculer (**at** devant).

bawdy ['bɔ:di] a (-ier, -iest) grossier.

bawl [bɔ:l] vti **to b. (out)** beugler, brailler; **to b. s.o. out** Am Sl engueuler qn.

bay [bei] n 1 (of coastline) baie f. 2 (for loading etc) aire f. 3 (in room) renfoncement m; **b. window** bow-window m. 4 **to keep** or **hold at b.** (enemy, dog etc) tenir en respect.

bayonet ['beiənit] n baïonnette f.

bazaar [bə'za:r] n (market, shop) bazar m; (charity sale) vente f de charité.

BC [bi:'si:] abbr (before Christ) avant Jésus-Christ.

be [bi:] vi (pres t **am, are, is**; pt **was, were**; pp **been**; pres p **being**) 1 être; **it is green/small** c'est vert/petit; **he's a doctor** il est médecin; **he's an Englishman** c'est un Anglais; **it's him** c'est lui; **it's 3 (o'clock)** il est trois heures; **it's the sixth of May,** Am **it's May sixth** c'est or nous sommes le six mai.

2 avoir; **to be hot/right/lucky** avoir chaud/raison/de la chance; **my feet are cold** j'ai froid aux pieds; **he's 20** (age) il a 20 ans; **to be 2 metres high** avoir 2 mètres de haut; **to be 6 feet tall** mesurer 1,80 m.

3 (health) aller; **how are you?** comment vas-tu?; **I'm well** je vais bien.

4 (exist) être; **the best painter there is** le meilleur peintre qui soit; **leave me be** laissez-moi (tranquille); **that may be** cela se peut.

5 (go, come) **I've been to see her** je suis allé or j'ai été la voir; **he's (already) been** il est (déjà) venu.

6 (weather, calculations) faire; **it's fine** il fait beau; **it's foggy** il y a du brouillard; **2 and 2 are 4** 2 et 2 font 4.

7 (cost) coûter, faire; **it's 20 pence** ça coûte 20 pence; **how much is it?** ça fait combien?, c'est combien?

8 (auxiliary) **I am/was doing** je fais/faisais; **I'll be staying** je resterai, je vais rester; **I'm listening to the radio** (in the process of) je suis en train d'écouter la radio; **he was killed** il a été tué, on l'a tué; **I've been waiting (for) two hours**

j'attends depuis deux heures; **it is said**
on dit; **to be pitied** à plaindre.
9 (*in questions and answers*) **isn't it?,
aren't you?** *etc* n'est-ce pas?, non?; **I
am!, he is!** *etc* oui!
10 (+ *inf*) **he is to come at once** (*must*) il
doit venir tout de suite; **he's shortly to
go** (*intends to*) il va bientôt partir.
11 there is *or* **are** il y a; (*pointing*) voilà;
here is *or* **are** voici; **there she is** la voilà;
here they are les voici.
beach [biːtʃ] *n* plage *f*.
beacon ['biːkən] *n Nau Av* balise *f*;
(*lighthouse*) phare *m*.
bead [biːd] *n* perle *f*; (*of rosary*) grain *m*;
(*of sweat*) goutte *f*; **(string of) beads**
collier *m*.
beak [biːk] *n* bec *m*.
beaker ['biːkər] *n* gobelet *m*.
beam [biːm] *n* **1** (*of wood*) poutre *f*. **2** *n*
(*of sunlight*) rayon *m*; (*of headlight,
flashlight*) faisceau *m* ▮ *vi* (*of light*)
rayonner; (*of person*) rayonner (de
joie); (*smile*) sourire largement.
● **beaming** *a* (*radiant*) radieux.
bean [biːn] *n* haricot *m*; (*of coffee*) grain
m; **(broad) b.** fève *f*. ● **beanshoots** *or*
beansprouts *npl* germes *mpl* de soja.
bear[1] [beər] *n* (*animal*) ours *m*.
bear[2] [beər] *vt* (*pt* **bore**, *pp* **borne**) (*carry,
show*) porter; (*endure*) supporter; (*re-
semblance*) offrir; (*responsibility*) assumer; **to b. in mind** tenir compte de; **to b.
out** corroborer.
▮ *vi* **to b. left/right** (*turn*) tourner à
gauche/droite; **to b. north/***etc* (*go*) aller
en direction du nord/*etc*; **to b. (up)on**
(*relate to*) se rapporter à; **to b. with s.o.**
être patient avec qn; **to b. up** ne pas se
décourager; **b. up!** du courage!
bearable ['beərəb(ə)l] *a* supportable.
beard [biəd] *n* barbe *f*; **to have a b.**
porter la barbe. ● **bearded** *a* barbu.
bearing ['beəriŋ] *n* (*relevance*) relation *f*
(**on** avec); (*posture, conduct*) maintien
m; **to get one's bearings** s'orienter.
beast [biːst] *n* bête *f*, animal *m*; (*cruel
person*) brute *f*. ● **beastly** *a Fam* (*bad*)

vilain; (*spiteful*) méchant.
beat [biːt] *n* (*of heart, drum*) battement
m; (*of policeman*) ronde *f*; *Mus* mesure
f, rythme *m*.
▮ *vt* (*pt* **beat**, *pp* **beaten**) battre; (*defeat*)
vaincre, battre; **to b. a drum** battre du
tambour; **b. it!** *Fam* fichez le camp!; **to
b. back** *or* **off** repousser; **to b. in** *or* **down**
(*door*) défoncer; **to b. s.o. up** tabasser
qn.
▮ *vi* battre; (*at door*) frapper (**at** à); **to b.
about** *or* **around the bush** *Fam* tourner
autour du pot; **to b. down** (*of rain*)
tomber à verse; (*of sun*) taper. ● **beating** *n* (*blows, defeat*) raclée *f*; (*of heart,
drums*) battement *m*; **to take a b.**
souffrir beaucoup. ● **beater** *n* (*for
eggs*) batteur *m*.
beautiful ['bjuːtɪf(ə)l] *a* (très) beau (*f*
belle); (*superb*) merveilleux. ● **beauti-
fully** *adv* (*after verb*) à merveille; (*before adjective*) merveilleusement.
beauty ['bjuːtɪ] *n* (*quality, woman*)
beauté *f*; **it's a b.!** (*car etc*) c'est une
merveille!; **b. parlour** institut *m* de
beauté; **b. spot** (*on skin*) grain *m* de
beauté; (*in countryside*) endroit *m* pittoresque.
beaver ['biːvər] *n* castor *m* ▮ *vi* **to b.
away** travailler dur (**at sth** à qch).
because [bɪ'kɒz] *conj* parce que; **b. of** à
cause de.
beck [bek] *n* **at s.o.'s b. and call** aux
ordres de qn.
beckon ['bekən] *vti* **to b. (to) s.o.** faire
signe à qn (**to do** de faire).
become [bɪ'kʌm] *vi* (*pt* **became**, *pp*
become) devenir; **to b. a painter** devenir peintre; **to b. worried** commencer à
s'inquiéter; **what has b. of her?** qu'est-
elle devenue?
becoming [bɪ'kʌmɪŋ] *a* (*clothes*) seyant;
(*modesty*) bienséant.
bed [bed] *n* lit *m*; (*of sea*) fond *m*; (*flower
bed*) parterre *m*; **to go to b.** (aller) se
coucher; **in b.** couché; **to get out of b.** se
lever; **b. and breakfast** (*in hotel etc*)
chambre *f* avec petit déjeuner. **air b.**

matelas *m* pneumatique. ● **bedclothes**
npl couvertures *fpl* et draps *mpl*. ● **bedding** *n* literie *f*. ● **bedridden** *a* alité.
● **bedroom** *n* chambre *f* à coucher.
● **bedside** *n* chevet *m* ▮ *a* (*lamp, book,
table*) de chevet. ● **bed'sitter** *or* **bedsit** *n*
chambre *f* meublée. ● **bedspread** *n*
dessus-de-lit *m inv*. ● **bedtime** *n* heure
f du coucher.

bedlam ['bedləm] *n* (*noise*) *Fam* chahut
m.

bedraggled [bɪ'dræg(ə)ld] *a* (*clothes,
person*) débraillé.

bee [biː] *n* abeille *f*. ● **beehive** *n* ruche *f*.
● **beekeeping** *n* apiculture *f*.

beech [biːtʃ] *n* (*tree, wood*) hêtre *m*.

beef [biːf] *n* bœuf *m*. ● **beefburger** *n*
hamburger *m*. ● **beefy** *a* (**-ier, -iest**)
Fam musclé, costaud.

been [biːn] *pp* of **be**.

beer [bɪər] *n* bière *f*; **b. glass** chope *f*.

beet [biːt] *n* *Am* = **beetroot**. ● **beetroot** *n*
betterave *f* (*potagère*).

beetle ['biːt(ə)l] **1** *n* scarabée *m*; (*any
beetle-shaped insect*) bestiole *f*. **2** *vi* **to b.
off** *Fam* se sauver.

befit [bɪ'fɪt] *vt* (**-tt-**) convenir à.

before [bɪ'fɔːr] *adv* avant; (*already*)
déjà; (*in front*) devant; **the month b.** le
mois d'avant; **the day b.** la veille; **I've
never done it b.** je ne l'ai (encore) jamais
fait.
▮ *prep* (*time*) avant; (*place*) devant; **the
year b. last** il y a deux ans.
▮ *conj* avant que (+ ne + *sub*), avant
(+ *inf*); **b. he goes** avant qu'il (ne)
parte; **b. going** avant de partir. ● **beforehand** *adv* à l'avance.

befriend [bɪ'frend] *vt* offrir son amitié à,
aider.

beg [beg] *vt* (**-gg-**) **to b. (for)** solliciter,
demander; (*bread, money*) mendier; **to
b. s.o. to do** supplier qn de faire; **to b.
the question** esquiver la question ▮ *vi* (*in
street etc*) mendier; **to go begging** (*of
food, articles*) ne pas trouver d'ama-
teurs.

beggar ['begər] *n* mendiant, -ante *mf*;

lucky b. *Fam* veinard, -arde *mf*.

begin [bɪ'gɪn] *vt* (*pt* **began**, *pp* **begun**,
pres p **beginning**) commencer; (*campaign*) lancer; (*conversation*) engager;
to b. doing *or* **to do** commencer *or* se
mettre à faire ▮ *vi* commencer (**with** par,
by doing par faire); **to b. with** (*first*)
d'abord. ● **—ning** *n* commencement *m*,
début *m*. ● **beginner** *n* débutant,
-ante *mf*.

begrudge [bɪ'grʌdʒ] *vt* (*envy*) envier
(**s.o. sth** qch à qn); (*give unwillingly*)
donner à contrecœur; **to b. doing sth**
faire qch à contrecœur.

behalf [bɪ'hɑːf] *n* **on b. of** pour, au nom
de; (*in the interests of*) en faveur de.

behave [bɪ'heɪv] *vi* se conduire; (*of
machine*) fonctionner; **to b.** (**oneself**)
se tenir bien; (*of child*) être sage.
● **behaviour** (*Am* **behavior**) *n* conduite
f, comportement *m*.

behead [bɪ'hed] *vt* décapiter.

behind [bɪ'haɪnd] **1** *prep* derrière; (*in
progress*) en retard sur ▮ *adv* derrière;
(*late*) en retard (**with** *or* **in one's work/**
etc dans son travail/*etc*). **2** *n* (*buttocks*)
Fam derrière *m*.

beholden [bɪ'həʊldən] *a* redevable (**to** à,
for de).

beige [beɪʒ] *a* & *n* beige (*m*).

Beijing [beɪ'dʒɪŋ] *n* Beijing *m or* f.

being ['biːɪŋ] *n* (*person, soul*) être *m*; **to
come into b.** naître, être créé.

belated [bɪ'leɪtɪd] *a* tardif.

belch [beltʃ] **1** *vi* (*of person*) faire un
renvoi ▮ *n* renvoi *m*. **2** *vt* **to b.** (**out**)
(*smoke*) vomir.

Belgium ['beldʒəm] *n* Belgique *f*. ● **Belgian** ['beldʒən] *a* & *n* belge (*mf*).

belie [bɪ'laɪ] *vt* démentir.

belief [bɪ'liːf] *n* croyance *f* (**in s.o./sth** en
qn/qch); (*trust*) confiance *f*, foi *f*;
(*opinion*) opinion *f*.

believe [bɪ'liːv] *vti* croire (**in sth** à qch,
in God en Dieu); **b. so** je crois que oui;
to b. in doing croire qu'il faut faire; **he
doesn't b. in smoking** il désapprouve
que l'on fume. ● **—able** *a* croyable.

●**-er** n Rel croyant, -ante mf; **to be a b. in** = believe **in**.

belittle [bɪ'lɪt(ə)l] vt dénigrer.

bell [bel] n (of church etc) cloche f; (small) clochette f; (in phone, mechanism) sonnerie f; (on door, bicycle) sonnette f. ●**bellboy** n Am groom m.

belligerent [bɪ'lɪdʒərənt] a belligérant.

bellow ['beləʊ] vi beugler, mugir.

bellows ['beləʊz] npl soufflet m.

belly ['belɪ] n ventre m; **b. button** Fam nombril m. ●**bellyache** n Fam mal m au ventre. ●**bellyful** n **to have had a b.** Sl en avoir plein le dos.

belong [bɪ'lɒŋ] vi appartenir (**to** à); **to b. to** (club) être membre de; **the cup belongs here** la tasse se range ici. ●**-ings** npl affaires fpl.

beloved [bɪ'lʌvɪd] a & n bien-aimé, -ée (mf).

below [bɪ'ləʊ] prep au-dessous de ▮ adv en dessous; **see b.** (in book) voir ci-dessous.

belt [belt] **1** n ceinture f; (in machine) courroie f ▮ vi **to b. up** attacher sa ceinture. **2** vt (hit) Sl rosser. **3** vi **to b. (along)** (rush) Sl filer à toute allure; **b. up!** (shut up) Sl boucle-la!

bemused [bɪ'mjuːzd] a perplexe.

bench [bentʃ] n (seat) banc m; (work table) établi m; **the B.** Jur la magistrature (assise); (court) le tribunal.

bend [bend] n courbe f; (in river, pipe) coude m; (in road) virage m; (of arm, knee) pli m; **round the b.** (mad) Fam cinglé ▮ vt (pt & pp bent) courber; (leg, arm) plier; (head) baisser ▮ vi (of branch) plier; (of road) tourner; **to b. (down)** (stoop) se baisser; **to b. (over** or **forward)** se pencher.

beneath [bɪ'niːθ] prep au-dessous de, sous ▮ adv au-dessous.

benefactor ['benɪfæktər] n bienfaiteur m.

beneficial [benɪ'fɪʃəl] a bénéfique.

benefit ['benɪfɪt] n avantage m; (money) allocation f; pl (of education etc) bienfaits mpl; **child b.** allocations fpl familiales; **for your (own) b.** pour vous, pour votre bien; **to be of b.** faire du bien (**to** à); **to give s.o. the b. of the doubt** accorder à qn le bénéfice du doute. ▮ vt faire du bien à; (be useful to) profiter à. ▮ vi **you'll b. from it** ça vous fera du bien; **to b. from doing** gagner à faire.

benevolent [bɪ'nevələnt] a bienveillant.

benign [bɪ'naɪn] a (kind) bienveillant; **b. tumour** Med tumeur f bénigne.

bent [bent] **1** pt & pp of bend ▮ a (nail) tordu; (dishonest) Fam corrompu; **b. on doing** résolu à faire. **2** n (talent) aptitude f (**for** pour); (inclination) penchant m (**for** pour).

bequeath [bɪ'kwiːð] vt léguer (**to** à). ●**bequest** n legs m.

bereaved [bɪ'riːvd] a endeuillé ▮ n **the b.** la famille (or la femme etc) du défunt or de la défunte. ●**bereavement** n deuil m.

beret ['bereɪ, Am bə'reɪ] n béret m.

berk [bɜːk] n Sl imbécile mf.

Bermuda [bə'mjuːdə] n Bermudes fpl.

berry ['berɪ] n baie f.

berserk [bə'zɜːk] a **to go b.** devenir fou.

berth [bɜːθ] n **1** (in ship, train) couchette f. **2** (anchorage) mouillage m ▮ vi (of ship) mouiller.

beset [bɪ'set] vt (pt & pp beset, pres p besetting) assaillir (qn); **b. with obstacles/etc** semé or hérissé d'obstacles/etc.

beside [bɪ'saɪd] prep à côté de; **that's b. the point** ça n'a rien à voir.

besides [bɪ'saɪdz] prep (in addition to) en plus de; (except) excepté; **there are ten of us b.** Paul nous sommes dix sans compter Paul ▮ adv de plus; (moreover) d'ailleurs.

besiege [bɪ'siːdʒ] vt (of soldiers, crowd) assiéger.

bespectacled [bɪ'spektɪk(ə)ld] a à lunettes.

best [best] a meilleur (**in** de); **the b. part of** (most) la plus grande partie de; **the b. thing** le mieux; **b. man** (at wedding) témoin m.

▮ n **the b. (one)** le meilleur, la meilleure;

it's for the b. c'est pour le mieux; **at b.** au mieux; **to do one's b.** faire de son mieux; **to the b. of my knowledge** autant que je sache; **to make the b. of** s'accommoder de (*situation etc*); **in one's Sunday b.** endimanché; **all the b.!** portez-vous bien!; (*in letter*) amicalement.

‖ *adv* **(the) b.** (*to play etc*) le mieux; (*to like, love*) le plus; **the b. loved** le plus aimé. ● **b.-'seller** *n* (*book*) best-seller *m*.

bestow [bɪ'stəʊ] *vt* accorder (**on** à).

bet [bet] *n* pari *m* ‖ *vti* (*pt & pp* **bet** *or* **betted,** *pres p* **betting**) parier (**on** sur, **that** que); **you b.!** *Fam* (*of course*) tu parles! ● **betting** *n* pari(s) *m*(*pl*); **b. shop** *or* **office** bureau *m* du pari mutuel.

betray [bɪ'treɪ] *vt* trahir; **to b. to s.o.** (*give away to*) livrer à qn. ● **betrayal** *n* (*disloyalty*) trahison *f*.

better ['betər] *a* meilleur (**than** que); **she's (much) b.** (*in health*) elle va (bien) mieux; **he's b. than** (*at sports*) il joue mieux que; (*at French etc*) il est plus fort que; **that's b.** c'est mieux; **to get b.** (*recover*) se remettre; (*improve*) s'améliorer; **it's b. to go** il vaut mieux partir.

‖ *adv* mieux (**than** que); **I had b. go** il vaut mieux que je parte; **all the b.** tant mieux (**for** pour).

‖ *n* **to get the b. of s.o.** l'emporter sur qn; **change for the b.** amélioration *f*.

‖ *vt* (*improve*) améliorer; **to b. oneself** améliorer sa condition.

between [bɪ'twiːn] *prep* entre; **b. you and me** entre nous; **in b. sth and sth/two things** entre qch et qch/deux choses.

‖ *adv* **in b.** (*space*) au milieu; (*time*) dans l'intervalle.

beverage ['bevərɪdʒ] *n* boisson *f*.

beware [bɪ'weər] *vi* **to b. of** (*s.o., sth*) se méfier de; **b.!** méfiez-vous!; **'b. of the trains'** 'attention aux trains'.

bewilder [bɪ'wɪldər] *vt* dérouter.

beyond [bɪ'jɒnd] *prep* (*further than*) au-delà de; (*reach, doubt*) hors de; **b. belief** incroyable; **b. my means** au-dessus de

mes moyens; **it's b. me** ça me dépasse ‖ *adv* au-delà.

bias ['baɪəs] *n* penchant *m* (**towards** pour); (*prejudice*) préjugé *m*, parti pris *m*. ● **bias(s)ed** *a* partial; **to be b. against** avoir des préjugés contre.

bib [bɪb] *n* (*baby's*) bavoir *m*.

bible ['baɪb(ə)l] *n* bible *f*; **the B.** la Bible. ● **biblical** ['bɪblɪk(ə)l] *a* biblique.

bibliography [bɪblɪ'ɒgrəfɪ] *n* bibliographie *f*.

biceps ['baɪseps] *n Anat* biceps *m*.

bicker ['bɪkər] *vi* se chamailler.

bicycle ['baɪsɪk(ə)l] *n* bicyclette *f*.

bid¹ [bɪd] *vt* (*pt & pp* **bid,** *pres p* **bidding**) (*sum of money*) offrir, faire une offre de ‖ *vi* faire une offre (**for** pour) ‖ *n* (**at** *auction*) offre *f*, enchère *f*; (*for doing a job*) soumission *f*; (*attempt*) tentative *f*. ● **bidder** *n* **to the highest b.** au plus offrant.

bid² [bɪd] *vt* (*pt* **bade** [bæd], *pp* **bidden** *or* **bid,** *pres p* **bidding**) (*command*) commander (**s.o. to do** à qn de faire); (*say, wish*) dire, souhaiter.

bide [baɪd] *vt* **to b. one's time** attendre le bon moment.

big [bɪg] *a* (**bigger, biggest**) grand, gros (*f* **grosse**); (*in age, generous*) grand; (*in bulk, amount*) gros. **b. deal!** *Fam* (*bon*) et alors!; **b. toe** gros orteil *m* ‖ *adv* **to talk b.** *fanfaronner* ● **bighead** *n* *or* **big'headed** *a Fam* (*conceited*) prétentieux, -euse (*mf*); (*boasting*) vantard, -arde (*mf*). ● **bigshot** *or* **bigwig** *n Fam* gros bonnet *m*.

bigot ['bɪgət] *n* sectaire *mf*. ● **bigoted** *a* sectaire.

bike [baɪk] *n Fam* vélo *m*.

bikini [bɪ'kiːnɪ] *n* deux-pièces *m inv*; **b. briefs** mini-slip *m*.

bile [baɪl] *n* bile *f*.

bilingual [baɪ'lɪŋgwəl] *a* bilingue.

bill¹ [bɪl] **1** *n* (*invoice*) facture *f*, note *f*; (*in restaurant*) addition *f*; (*in hotel*) note *f*; (*banknote*) *Am* billet *m* ‖ *vt* **to b. s.o.** envoyer la facture à qn. **2** *n* (*proposed law*) projet *m* de loi; **b. of rights**

déclaration f des droits. **3** n (poster) Th affiche f ▮ vt Th mettre à l'affiche. ●**billboard** n Am panneau m d'affichage. ●**billfold** n Am portefeuille m.

bill² n (of bird) bec m.

billiard ['bɪljəd] a (table etc) de billard. ●**billiards** n (jeu m de) billard m.

billion ['bɪljən] n milliard m. ●**billio'naire** n milliardaire mf.

bin [bɪn] n boîte f; (for bread) huche f, boîte f; (for litter) poubelle f.

bind [baɪnd] **1** vt (pt & pp bound) (fasten) attacher, lier; (book) relier; (unite) lier; **to b. s.o. to do** obliger qn à faire. **2** n (bore) Fam plaie f. ●**—ing 1** n (of book) reliure f. **2** a (contract) irrévocable; **to be b. on s.o.** (legally) lier qn.

binge [bɪndʒ] n **to go on a b.** Fam faire la bringue.

bingo ['bɪŋgəʊ] n loto m.

binoculars [bɪ'nɒkjʊləz] npl jumelles fpl.

biochemistry [baɪəʊ'kemɪstrɪ] n biochimie f.

biodegradable [baɪəʊdɪ'greɪdəb(ə)l] a biodégradable.

biography [baɪ'ɒgrəfɪ] n biographie f.

biology [baɪ'ɒlədʒɪ] n biologie f. ●**bio'logical** a biologique.

birch [bɜːtʃ] n **(silver) b.** (tree) bouleau m.

bird [bɜːd] n oiseau m; (fowl) volaille f; **b.'s-eye view** vue f d'ensemble. ●**birdseed** n grains mpl de millet.

biro® ['baɪərəʊ] n (pl -os) stylo m à bille, bic® m.

birth [bɜːθ] n naissance f; **to give b. to** donner naissance à; **b. certificate** acte m de naissance; **b. control** limitation f des naissances. ●**birthday** n anniversaire m; **happy b.!** bon anniversaire!; **b. party** fête f d'anniversaire. ●**birthmark** n tache f de vin. ●**birthrate** n (taux m de) natalité f.

biscuit ['bɪskɪt] n biscuit m, gâteau m sec; Am petit pain m au lait.

bishop ['bɪʃəp] n évêque m; (in chess) fou m.

bit¹ [bɪt] n **1** morceau m; (of string, time)

bout m; **a b.** (a little) un peu; **a tiny b.** un tout petit peu; **quite a b.** (very) très; (a lot) beaucoup; **not a b.** pas du tout; **a b. of luck** une chance; **b. by b.** petit à petit; **in bits** en morceaux; **to come to bits** se démonter.

2 (coin) pièce f.

3 (of horse) mors m.

4 (computer information) bit m.

bit² [bɪt] pt of **bite.**

bitch [bɪtʃ] **1** n chienne f; (woman) Pej Fam garce f.

bite [baɪt] n (wound) morsure f; (from insect) piqûre f; (mouthful) bouchée f; **a b. to eat** un morceau à manger ▮ vti (pt bit, pp bitten) mordre; (of insect) piquer, mordre; **to b. one's nails** se ronger les ongles; **to sth off** arracher qch d'un coup de dent(s).

bitter ['bɪtər] **1** a (person, taste etc) amer; (cold, wind) glacial; (criticism) acerbe; (conflict) violent; **to feel b.** être plein d'amertume (about à cause de). **2** n bière f (pression). ●**—ly** adv (to cry, regret) amèrement; **it's b. cold** il fait un froid glacial. ●**—ness** n amertume f; violence f.

bizarre [bɪ'zɑːr] a bizarre.

blab [blæb] vi (-bb-) jaser. ●**blabber** vi jaser. ●**blabbermouth** n jaseur, -euse mf.

black [blæk] a (-er, -est) noir; **b. eye** œil m poché; **to give s.o. a b. eye** pocher l'œil à qn; **b. and blue** (bruised) couvert de bleus; **b. sheep** Fig brebis f galeuse; **b. ice** verglas m; **b. pudding** boudin m ▮ n (colour) noir m; (person) Noir, -e mf ▮ vi **to b. out** (faint) s'évanouir. ●**blacken** vt noircir. ●**blackish** a noirâtre.

blackberry ['blækbərɪ, Am -berɪ] n mûre f. ●**blackbird** n merle m. ●**blackboard** n tableau m (noir); **on the b.** au tableau. ●**black'currant** n cassis m. ●**blackleg** n (strike breaker) jaune m. ●**blacklist** n liste f noire ▮ vt mettre sur la liste noire. ●**blackmail** n chantage m ▮ vt faire chanter. ●**blackmailer** n maître chanteur m. ●**blackout** n panne f d'électricité; (*fainting fit*) syncope *f*; (*news*) b. black-out *m*. ●**blacksmith** *n* forgeron *m*.

blackguard ['blægɑːd, -gəd] *n* canaille *f*.

bladder ['blædər] *n* vessie *f*.

blade [bleɪd] *n* lame *f*; (*of grass*) brin *m*.

blame [bleɪm] *vt* accuser; **to b. s.o. for sth** rejeter la responsabilité de qch sur qn; (*reproach*) reprocher qch à qn; **you're to b.** c'est ta faute ∥ *n* faute *f*. ●—**less** *a* irréprochable.

bland [blænd] *a* (**-er, -est**) (*food*) (*mild*) sans saveur particulière; (*insipid*) fade.

blank [blæŋk] *a* (*paper, page*) blanc (*f* blanche), vierge; (*cheque, Am check*) en blanc; (*look*) vide; (*refusal*) absolu; **b. tape** cassette *f* vierge ∥ *a* & *n* **b. (space)** blanc *m*; **b. (cartridge)** cartouche *f* à blanc.

blanket ['blæŋkɪt] **1** *n* couverture *f*; (*of snow*) couche *f* ∥ *vt* (*cover*) Fig recouvrir. **2** *a* (*term etc*) général.

blare [bleər] *vi* **to b. (out)** (*of radio*) beugler; (*of music*) retentir.

blasphemy ['blæsfəmɪ] *n* blasphème *m*.

blast [blɑːst] **1** *n* explosion *f*; (*air from explosion*) souffle *m*; (*of wind*) rafale *f*; (**at**) **full b.** (*loud*) à plein volume ∥ *vt* (*blow up*) faire sauter; **to b. s.o.** Fam réprimander qn. **2** *int* Fam zut!, merde! ●—**ed** *a* Fam fichu, ●**blast-off** *n* (*of spacecraft*) mise *f* à feu.

blaz/e [bleɪz] **1** *n* (*flame*) flamme *f*; (*fire*) feu *m*; (*large*) incendie *m*; **b. of light** torrent *m* de lumière ∥ *vi* (*of fire*) flamber; (*of sun*) flamboyer. **2** *vt* **to b. a trail** marquer la voie. ●—**ing** *a* (*burning*) en feu; (*bloody*) brûlant.

blazer ['bleɪzər] *n* blazer *m*.

bleach [bliːtʃ] *n* (*household*) eau *f* de Javel; (*for hair*) décolorant *m* ∥ *vt* (*hair*) décolorer; (*linen*) blanchir.

bleak [bliːk] *a* (**-er, -est**) (*appearance*) morne; (*future, situation*) sombre; (*countryside*) désolé.

bleary ['blɪərɪ] *a* (*eyes*) troubles, voilés.

bleat [bliːt] *vi* bêler.

bleed [bliːd] *vti* (*pt & pp* **bled**) saigner;

to b. to death perdre tout son sang. ●—**ing** *a* (*wound*) saignant.

bleep [bliːp] *n* bip *m* ∥ *vt* appeler au bip-(bip). ●**bleeper** *n* bip(-bip) *m*.

blemish ['blemɪʃ] *n* (*fault*) défaut *m*; (*on fruit, reputation*) tache *f*.

blend [blend] *n* mélange *m* ∥ *vt* mélanger (**with** à); ∥ *vi* se mélanger; (*go together*) se marier (**with** avec). ●—**er** *n* (*for food*) mixer *m*.

bless [bles] *vt* bénir; **b. you!** (*sneezing*) à vos souhaits! ●—**ed** [-ɪd] *a* **1** saint, béni; **2** (*blasted*) Fam fichu, sacré. ●—**ing** *n* bénédiction *f*; (*benefit*) bienfait *m*; **what a b. that . . .** quelle chance que. . . .

blew [bluː] *pt of* **blow**[2].

blight [blaɪt] *n* (*scourge*) fléau *m*; **to be a b. on** avoir une influence néfaste sur; **urban b.** (*area*) quartier *m* délabré; (*condition*) délabrement *m* (de quartier).

blimey! ['blaɪmɪ] *int* Fam zut!, mince!

blind [blaɪnd] **1** *a* aveugle; **b. person** aveugle *mf*; **he's b. to** (*fault*) il ne voit pas; **b. alley** impasse *f* ∥ *n* **the b.** les aveugles *mpl* ∥ *vt* (*of light etc*) aveugler (*qn*). **2** *n* (*on window*) store *m*. ●—**ly** *adv* aveuglément. ●—**ness** *n* cécité *f*.

blinders ['blaɪndəz] *npl* (*of horse*) Am œillères *fpl*.

blindfold ['blaɪndfəʊld] *n* bandeau *m* ∥ *vt* bander les yeux à ∥ *adv* les yeux bandés.

blink [blɪŋk] *vi* (*of person*) cligner des yeux; (*of eyes*) cligner; (*of light*) clignoter ∥ *vt* **to b. one's eyes** cligner des yeux ∥ *n* clignement *m*. ●—**ing** *a* (*bloody*) Fam sacré.

blinkers ['blɪŋkəz] *npl* (*of horse*) œillères *fpl*; (*indicators*) Aut clignotants *mpl*.

bliss [blɪs] *n* félicité *f*. ●**blissful** *a* (*wonderful*) merveilleux. ●**blissfully** *adv* (*happy*) parfaitement.

blister ['blɪstər] *n* (*on skin*) ampoule *f*.

blitz [blɪts] *n* (*onslaught*) Fam offensive *f*.

blizzard ['blɪzəd] *n* tempête *f* de neige.

bloated ['bləʊtɪd] *a* gonflé.

blob [blɒb] *n* (*of water*) (grosse) goutte *f*;

(*of ink*) tache *f*.

block [blɒk] **1** *n* (*of stone etc*) bloc *m*; (*of buildings*) pâté *m* (de maisons); **b. of flats** immeuble *m*; **a b. away** *Am* une rue plus loin; **b. capitals** *or* **letters** majuscules *fpl*.

2 *vt* (*obstruct*) bloquer; (*pipe*) boucher; (*s.o.'s view*) boucher; **to b. off** (*road*) barrer; (*light*) intercepter; **to b. up** (*pipe, hole*) bloquer. ●**blo'ckade** *n* blocus *m* ▮ *vt* bloquer. ●**blockbuster** *n Cin* film *m* à grand spectacle. ●**blockhead** *n Fam* imbécile *mf*.

bloke [bləʊk] *n Fam* type *m*.

blond [blɒnd] *a* & *n* blond (*m*). ●**blonde** *a* & *n* blonde (*f*).

blood [blʌd] *n* sang *m* ▮ *a* (*group, cell*) sanguin; (*poisoning, bank*) du sang; **b. donor/bath** donneur, -euse *mf*/bain *m* de sang; **b. pressure** tension *f* (artérielle); **to have high b. pressure** avoir de la tension; **b. test** analyse *f* de sang. ●**bloodhound** *n* (*dog, detective*) limier *m*. ●**bloodshed** *n* effusion *f* de sang. ●**bloodshot** *a* (*eye*) injecté de sang. ●**bloodstained** *a* taché de sang. ●**bloodthirsty** *a* sanguinaire.

bloody ['blʌdɪ] **1** *a* (-ier, -iest) sanglant. **2** *a* (*weather, liar etc*) *Fam* sale ▮ *adv* (*very, completely*) *Fam* vachement. ●**b.-'minded** *a* hargneux.

bloom [bluːm] *n* fleur *f*; **in b.** en fleur(s) ▮ *vi* fleurir. ●**—ing** *a* **1** (*in bloom*) en fleur(s). **2** (*bloody*) *Fam* sacré, fichu.

blossom ['blɒsəm] *n* fleur(s) *f*(*pl*) ▮ *vi* fleurir; **to b. (out)** (*of person*) s'épanouir.

blot [blɒt] *n* tache *f* ▮ *vt* (-tt-) (*stain*) tacher; **to b. out** (*obliterate*) effacer. ●**blotting paper** *n* (papier *m*) buvard *m*.

blotch [blɒtʃ] *n* tache *f*. ●**blotchy** *a* (-ier, -iest) couvert de taches; (*face*) marbré.

blouse [blaʊz, *Am* blaʊs] *n* chemisier *m*.

blow[1] [bləʊ] *n* (*with fist etc*) coup *m*; **to come to blows** en venir aux mains.

blow[2] [bləʊ] *vt* (*pt* **blew**, *pp* **blown**) (*of wind*) pousser (*un navire etc*), chasser (*la pluie etc*); (*smoke*) souffler; (*bubbles*)

faire; (*trumpet*) souffler dans; **to b. a fuse** faire sauter un plomb; **to b. one's nose** se moucher; **to b. a whistle** siffler ▮ *vi* (*of wind, person*) souffler; (*of fuse*) sauter; (*of papers etc*) (*in wind*) s'éparpiller.

blow away *vt* (*of wind*) emporter (*qch*) ▮ *vi* (*of hat etc*) s'envoler ▮ **to blow down** *vt* (*chimney etc*) faire tomber ▮ *vi* tomber ▮ **to blow off** *vt* (*hat etc*) emporter ▮ *vi* s'envoler ▮ **to blow out** *vt* (*candle*) souffler ▮ *vi* (*of light*) s'éteindre. ●**blowout** *n* (*of tyre, Am tire*) éclatement *m*. ▮ **to blow over 1** *vti* = **blow down**. **2** *vi* (*of quarrel etc*) passer ▮ **to blow up** *vt* (*building etc*) faire sauter; (*pump up*) gonfler; (*photo*) agrandir ▮ *vi* (*explode*) exploser. ●**blow-up** *n* (*of photo*) agrandissement *m*.

blow-dry ['bləʊdraɪ] *n* brushing *m*.

blowlamp ['bləʊlæmp] *n* chalumeau *m*.

blowtorch ['bləʊtɔːʃ] *n Am* chalumeau *m*.

blowy ['bləʊɪ] *a* **it's b.** *Fam* il y a du vent.

bludgeon ['blʌdʒən] *n* gourdin *m* ▮ *vt* matraquer.

blue [bluː] *a* (**bluer, bluest**) bleu (*mpl* bleus); **b. film** *Fam* film *m* porno ▮ *n* bleu *m* (*pl* bleus); **the blues** (*depression*) *Fam* le cafard. ●**bluebell** *n* jacinthe *f* des bois. ●**blueberry** *n* airelle *f*. ●**blueprint** *n Fig* plan *m* (de travail).

bluff [blʌf] *vti* bluffer ▮ *n* bluff *m*.

blunder ['blʌndər] *n* (*mistake*) gaffe *f* ▮ *vi* faire une gaffe.

blunt [blʌnt] *a* (-er, -est) (*edge*) émoussé; (*pencil*) mal taillé; (*person, speech*) franc (*f* franche), brusque. ●**—ly** *adv* carrément.

blur [blɜːr] *n* tache *f* floue ▮ *vt* (-rr-) rendre flou. ●**blurred** *a* (*image*) flou.

blurb [blɜːb] *n Fam* résumé *m* publicitaire, laïus *m*.

blurt [blɜːt] *vt* **to b. (out)** (*secret*) laisser échapper; (*excuse*) bredouiller.

blush [blʌʃ] *vi* rougir (**with** de).

blustery ['blʌstərɪ] *a* (*weather*) de grand vent.

boar [bɔːr] n (wild) b. sanglier m.

board¹ [bɔːd] 1 n (piece of wood) planche f; (for notices) tableau m; (for games) plateau m; (cardboard) carton m; (committee) conseil m, commission f; (of examiners) Sch jury m (pl jurys); b. (of directors) conseil m d'administration; on b. (ship, aircraft) à bord (de). 2 vt (ship, aircraft) monter à bord de; (bus, train) monter dans; to b. up (door) boucher. ● **boarding** n (of passengers) embarquement m; b. pass carte f d'embarquement. ● **boardwalk** n Am promenade f.

board² [bɔːd] n (food) pension f; b. and lodging (chambre f avec) pension f ‖ vi (lodge) être en pension (with chez); boarding house pension f (de famille); boarding school pensionnat m. ● **boarder** n pensionnaire mf.

boast [bəʊst] vi se vanter (about, of de) ‖ vt se glorifier de; to b. that one can do sth se vanter de (pouvoir) faire qch ‖ n vantardise f. ● **-ing** n vantardise f. ● **boastful** a vantard.

boat [bəʊt] n bateau m; (small) barque f, canot m; (liner) paquebot m; in the same b. Fig logé à la même enseigne. ● **-ing** n canotage m.

bob [bɒb] vi (-bb-) to b. (up and down) (on water) danser sur l'eau.

bobby [bɒbɪ] n 1 (policeman) Fam flic m, agent m. 2 b. pin Am pince f à cheveux.

bode [bəʊd] vi to b. well/ill être de bon/mauvais augure.

body [bɒdɪ] n 1 corps m; (institution) organisme m; b. building culturisme m; b. warmer gilet m matelassé. ● **bodily** a (need) physique. ● **bodyguard** n garde m du corps, Fam gorille m. ● **bodywork** n carrosserie f.

bog [bɒg] n marécage m ‖ vt to get bogged down s'enliser. ● **boggy** a (-ier, -iest) marécageux.

boggle [bɒg(ə)l] vi the mind boggles cela confond l'imagination.

bogus [bəʊgəs] a faux (f fausse).

boil¹ [bɔɪl] n (pimple) furoncle m.

boil² [bɔɪl] vi bouillir; to b. down to Fig se ramener à; to b. over (of milk etc) déborder ‖ vt to b. (up) faire bouillir ‖ n to come to the b. bouillir; to bring to the b. amener à ébullition. ● **-ed** a (beef) bouilli; (potato) à l'anglaise; b. egg œuf m à la coque. ● **-ing** a to be at b. point (of liquid) bouillir; b. (hot) bouillant; it's b. (hot) (weather) il fait une chaleur infernale.

boiler [bɔɪlər] n chaudière f; b. suit bleus mpl (de travail).

boisterous [bɔɪstərəs] a (noisy) tapageur; (child) turbulent.

bold [bəʊld] a (-er, -est) hardi; in b. type en (caractères) gras. ● **-ness** n hardiesse f.

bollard [bɒləd, bɒlɑːd] n Aut borne f.

bolster [bəʊlstər] 1 n (pillow) traversin m, polochon m. 2 vt to b. (up) (support) soutenir.

bolt [bəʊlt] 1 n (on door etc) verrou m; (for nut) boulon m ‖ vt (door) fermer au verrou. 2 vi (dash) se précipiter; (run away) détaler; (of horse) s'emballer. 3 n b. (of lightning) éclair m. 4 vt (food) engloutir.

bomb [bɒm] n bombe f; letter b. lettre f piégée ‖ vt (from the air) bombarder; (of terrorist) faire sauter une bombe dans or à. ● **-ing** n bombardement m; (by terrorist) attentat m à la bombe. ● **bomber** n (aircraft) bombardier m; (terrorist) plastiqueur m. ● **bombshell** n to come as a b. tomber comme une bombe.

bombard [bɒmˈbɑːd] vt bombarder (with de). ● **-ment** n bombardement m.

bona fide [bəʊnəˈfaɪdɪ, Am -ˈfaɪd] a sérieux.

bond [bɒnd] n (link) lien m; (investment certificate) bon m, obligation f; (promise) engagement m; (adhesion) adhérence f.

bone [bəʊn] 1 n os m; (of fish) arête f; b. china porcelaine f tendre ‖ vt (meat) désosser. 2 vi to b. up on (subject) Am Fam bûcher.

bone-dry [bəʊn'draɪ] *a* tout à fait sec. ●**b.-idle** *a* paresseux comme une couleuvre.

bonfire ['bɒnfaɪər] *n* (*for celebration*) feu *m* de joie; (*for dead leaves*) feu *m* (de jardin).

bonkers ['bɒŋkəz] *a* (*crazy*) *Fam* dingue.

bonnet ['bɒnɪt] *n* (*hat*) bonnet *m*; (*of vehicle*) capot *m*.

bonus ['bəʊnəs] *n* prime *f*; **no claims b.** *Aut* bonus *m*.

bony ['bəʊnɪ] *a* (**-ier, -iest**) (*thin*) osseux; (*fish*) plein d'arêtes.

boo [bu:] *vti* siffler ▮ *npl* sifflets *mpl*.

boob [bu:b] *n* (*mistake*) *Fam* gaffe *f* ▮ *vi Sl* gaffer.

booby-trap ['bu:bɪtræp] *n* engin *m* piégé ▮ *vt* (**-pp-**) piéger.

book¹ [bʊk] *n* livre *m*; (*of tickets*) carnet *m*; (*record*) registre *m*; *pl* (*accounts*) comptes *mpl*; (*exercise*) **b.** cahier *m*; (**bank**) **b.** livret *m* (de banque).

book² [bʊk] *vt* **to b. (up)** (*seat etc*) réserver; **to b. s.o.** *Jur* donner un procès-verbal à qn; **to b. (down)** (*write down*) inscrire; (**fully**) **booked (up)** (*hotel, concert*) complet ▮ *vi* **to b. (up)** réserver des places; **to b. in** (*in hotel*) prendre une chambre; (*sign register*) signer le registre. ●**booking** *n* réservation *f*; **b. office** bureau *m* de location, guichet *m*.

bookcase ['bʊkkeɪs] *n* bibliothèque *f*. ●**bookends** *npl* serre-livres *m inv*. ●**bookkeeper** *n* comptable *mf*. ●**bookkeeping** *n* comptabilité *f*. ●**booklet** *n* brochure *f*. ●**bookmaker** *n* bookmaker *m*. ●**bookmark** *n* marque *f*, marque-page *m*. ●**bookseller** *n* libraire *mf*. ●**bookshelf** *n* rayon *m*. ●**bookshop** *or Am* **bookstore** *n* librairie *f*. ●**bookstall** *n* kiosque *m* (à journaux).

boom [bu:m] **1** *vi* (*of thunder, gun etc*) gronder ▮ *n* grondement *m*. **2** *n Econ* expansion *f*, boom *m*.

boon [bu:n] *n* avantage *m*.

boost [bu:st] *vt* (*increase*) augmenter; (*product*) faire de la réclame pour; (*economy*) stimuler; (*morale*) remonter ▮ *n* **to give a b. to** = to boost. ●**—er** *n* (*injection*) (piqûre *f* de) rappel *m*.

boot [bu:t] **1** *n* (*shoe*) botte *f*; (*ankle*) **b.** bottillon *m*; **to get the b.** *Fam* être mis à la porte; **b. polish** cirage *m* ▮ *vt* (*kick*) donner un coup *or* des coups de pied à; **to b. out** mettre à la porte. **2** *n Aut* coffre *m*. **3** *n* **to b.** en plus.

booth [bu:ð, bu:θ] *n* (*for phone*) cabine *f*; (*at fair*) baraque *f*; (*voting*) isoloir *m*.

booty ['bu:tɪ] *n* (*stolen goods*) butin *m*.

booz/e [bu:z] *n Fam* alcool *m*, boisson(s) *f*(*pl*) ▮ *vi Fam* boire (beaucoup). ●**—er** *n Fam* (*person*) buveur, -euse *mf*.

border ['bɔ:dər] *n* (*of country*) frontière *f*; (*edge*) bord *m*; (*of garden*) bordure *f* ▮ *vt* **to b. (on)** (*country*) toucher à; **to b. (up)on** (*verge on*) être voisin de. ●**borderline** *n* frontière *f*; **b. case** cas *m* limite.

bor/e¹ [bɔ:r] **1** *vt* (*weary*) ennuyer; **to be bored** s'ennuyer; **I'm bored with that** ça m'ennuie ▮ *n* (*person*) raseur, -euse *mf*; **it's a b.** c'est ennuyeux. **2** *vt* (*hole*) percer. **3** *n* (*of gun*) calibre *m*. ●**—ing** *a* ennuyeux. ●**boredom** *n* ennui *m*.

bore² [bɔ:r] *pt of* **bear²**.

born [bɔ:n] *a* né; **to be b.** naître; **he was b.** il est né.

borne [bɔ:n] *pp of* **bear²**.

borough ['bʌrə] *n* (*town*) municipalité *f*; (*part of town*) arrondissement *m*.

borrow ['bɒrəʊ] *vt* emprunter (**from** à). ●**—ing** *n* emprunt *m*.

Bosnia ['bɒznɪə] *n* Bosnie *f*.

bosom ['bʊzəm] *n* (*chest*) poitrine *f*, seins *mpl*; (*breast*) & *Fig* sein *m*; **b. friend** ami, -ie *mf* intime.

boss [bɒs] *n Fam* patron, -onne *mf*, chef *m* ▮ *vt* **to b. s.o. around** *or* **about** *Fam* commander qn. ●**bossy** *a* (**-ier, -iest**) *Fam* autoritaire.

boss-eyed [bɒs'aɪd] *a* **to be b.-eyed** loucher.

bosun ['bəʊs(ə)n] *n* maître *m* d'équipage.

botany ['bɒtənɪ] *n* botanique *f*. ●**bo'tanical** *a* botanique.

botch [bɒtʃ] vt to b. (up) (spoil) bâcler.

both [bəʊθ] a les deux ▌pron tous or toutes (les) deux; **b. (of) the boys** les deux garçons; **b. of us** nous deux ▌adv (at the same time) à la fois; **b. you and I** vous et moi.

bother ['bɒðər] vt (annoy, worry) ennuyer; (disturb) déranger; (pester) importuner; (hurt etc) (of foot etc) gêner; **to b. doing** or **to do** se donner la peine de faire; **I can't be bothered!** je n'en ai pas envie! ▌vi **to b. about** (worry about) se préoccuper de; (deal with) s'occuper de ▌n (trouble) ennui m; (effort) peine f; (inconvenience) dérangement m; **(oh) b.!** zut alors!

bottle ['bɒt(ə)l] n bouteille f; (small) flacon m; (for baby) biberon m; (hotwater) **b.** bouillotte f; **b. opener** ouvre-bouteilles m inv; **b. bank** conteneur m pour verre usagé ▌vt mettre en bouteilles; **to b. up** (feeling) contenir. ● **bottlefeed** vt (pt & pp -**fed**) nourrir au biberon. ● **bottleneck** n (in road) goulot m d'étranglement; (traffic hold-up) bouchon m.

bottom ['bɒtəm] n (of sea, box) fond m; (of page, hill) bas m; (buttocks) Fam derrière m; (of table) bout m; **to be at the b.** of the class être le dernier de la classe ▌a (shelf) inférieur; (of bus) b. **floor** rez-de-chaussée m; **b. part** partie f inférieure.

bought [bɔːt] pt & pp of **buy.**

boulder ['bəʊldər] n rocher m.

boulevard ['buːləvɑːd] n boulevard m.

bounce [baʊns] **1** vi (of ball) rebondir; (of person) faire des bonds ▌vt faire rebondir ▌n (re)bond m. **2** vi (of cheque, Am check) Fam être sans provision.

bound¹ [baʊnd] pt & pp of **bind. ▌a** to do (obliged) obligé de faire; (certain) sûr de faire; **it's b. to happen/snow/etc** ça arrivera/il neigera/etc sûrement; **b. for** (of person, ship) en route pour; (of train, plane) à destination de. **2** a b. up with (connected) lié à.

bound² [baʊnd] n (leap) bond m ▌vi

bondir.

boundary ['baʊnd(ə)ri] n limite f.

bounds [baʊndz] npl **out of b.** (place) interdit.

bouquet [bəʊˈkeɪ, buː-] n (of flowers, wine) bouquet m.

bout [baʊt] n (of fever, coughing etc) accès m; (of asthma etc) crise f; Boxing combat m; (session) séance f; **a b. of flu** une grippe.

boutique [buːˈtiːk] n boutique f (de mode).

bow¹ [bəʊ] n (weapon) arc m; Mus archet m; (knot) nœud m; **b. tie** nœud m papillon. ● **b.-'legged** a aux jambes arquées.

bow² [baʊ] **1** n (with knees bent) révérence f; (nod) salut m ▌vt (one's head) incliner ▌vi s'incliner (**to** devant); (nod) incliner la tête (**to** devant). **2** n Nau proue f.

bowels ['baʊəlz] npl intestins mpl.

bowl [bəʊl] n (for food) bol m; (basin) cuvette f; (for sugar) sucrier m; (for salad) saladier m; (for fruit) (of glass, plastic) coupe f. **2** vt Cricket lancer la balle. **3** vt **to b. s.o. over** (astound) bouleverser qn. ● —**ing** n (tenpin) b. bowling m; **b. alley** bowling m.

bowler ['bəʊlər] n **b. (hat)** (chapeau m) melon m.

bowls [bəʊlz] npl (game) boules fpl.

box [bɒks] **1** n boîte f; (large) caisse f; (of cardboard) carton m; Th loge f; TV Fam télé f; **b. office** bureau m de location; **b. room** (lumber room) débarras m; (bedroom) petite chambre f (carrée) ▌vt to b. **(up)** mettre en boîte; **to b. in** (enclose) enfermer.

2 vi Boxing boxer. ● —**ing** n **1** boxe f; **b. ring** ring m. **2 B. Day** le lendemain de Noël. ● **boxer** n boxeur m.

boy [bɔɪ] n garçon m; **English b.** jeune Anglais m; **old b.** Sch ancien élève m; **oh b.!** mon Dieu!

boycott ['bɔɪkɒt] vt boycotter ▌n boycottage m.

boyfriend ['bɔɪfrend] n (petit) ami m.

bra [brɑː] n soutien-gorge m.

brace [breɪs] **1** n (dental) appareil m; pl (trouser straps) bretelles fpl. **2** vt **to b. oneself for** (news, shock) se préparer à.

bracelet [breɪslɪt] n bracelet m.

bracket [brækɪt] n (for shelf etc) équerre f; (round sign) Typ parenthèse f; (square sign) Typ crochet m; Fig groupe m, tranche f ▮ vt mettre entre parenthèses or crochets.

brag [bræg] vi (-gg-) se vanter (about, of de). ●**bragging** n vantardise f.

braid [breɪd] vt (hair) Am tresser ▮ n Am tresse f.

Braille [breɪl] n braille m.

brain [breɪn] **1** n cerveau m; (of animal, bird) cervelle f; **to have brains** (sense) avoir de l'intelligence; **b. drain** fuite f des cerveaux. **2** vt (hit) Fam assommer. ●**brainstorm** n Am idée f géniale. ●**brainwash** vt faire un lavage de cerveau à. ●**brainwave** n idée f géniale.

brainy [breɪnɪ] a (-ier, -iest) Fam intelligent.

brak/e [breɪk] n frein m; **b. light** Aut stop m ▮ vi freiner. ●**—ing** n freinage m.

bramble [bræmb(ə)l] n (bush) ronce f.

bran [bræn] n (of wheat) son m.

branch [brɑːntʃ] n branche f; (of road) embranchement m; (of store, office) succursale f ▮ vi **to b. off** (of road) bifurquer; **to b. out** (of firm, person) étendre ses activités (into à).

brand [brænd] **1** n (trademark) marque f; (variety) type m. **2** vt **to be branded as** avoir une réputation de.

brandish [brændɪʃ] vt brandir.

brand-new [brænd'njuː] a tout neuf (f toute neuve), flambant neuf (f flambant neuve).

brandy [brændɪ] n cognac m; (made with pears etc) eau-de-vie f.

brash [bræʃ] a effronté.

brass [brɑːs] n cuivre m; **the top b.** (officers, executives) Fam les huiles fpl; **b. band** fanfare f.

brassiere [bræzɪər, Am brə'zɪər] n soutien-gorge m.

brat [bræt] n (badly behaved) sale gosse mf.

brave [breɪv] a (-er, -est) courageux, brave ▮ vt (danger etc) braver. ●**bravery** n courage m.

brawl [brɔːl] n (fight) bagarre f ▮ vi se bagarrer.

brawn [brɔːn] n muscles mpl. ●**brawny** a (-ier, -iest) musclé.

bray [breɪ] vi (of ass) braire.

brazen [breɪz(ə)n] a (shameless) effronté.

Brazil [brə'zɪl] n Brésil m. ●**Brazilian** a & n brésilien, -ienne (mf).

breach [briːtʃ] **1** n violation f; (of contract) rupture f ▮ vt (code) violer. **2** n (gap) brèche f ▮ vt (wall) ouvrir une brèche dans.

bread [bred] n inv pain m; **loaf of b.** pain m; (slice or piece of) b. and butter tartine f. ●**breadbin** or Am **breadbox** n boîte f à pain. ●**breadboard** n planche f à pain. ●**breadcrumb** n miette f (de pain); pl Culin chapelure f. ●**breadline** n **on the b.** indigent. ●**breadwinner** n soutien f de famille.

breadth [bretθ] n largeur f.

break [breɪk] vt (pt **broke**, pp **broken**) casser; (into pieces) briser; (silence, spell) rompre; (strike, heart, ice) briser; (record) Sp battre; (law) violer; (one's promise) manquer à; (journey) interrompre; (news) annoncer (to à); (habit) se débarrasser de; **to b. open** (safe) percer; **to b. new ground** innover. ▮ vi (se) casser; se briser; se rompre; (of voice) s'altérer; (of boy's voice) muer; (of weather) se gâter; (of news) éclater; (of day) se lever; (stop work) faire la pause; **to b. loose** s'échapper; **to b. with** s.o. rompre avec qn.

▮ n cassure f; (in bone) fracture f; (with person, group) rupture f; (in journey) interruption f; (rest) repos m; (in activity, for tea) pause f; Sch récréation f; (in weather) changement m; **a lucky b.** Fam une chance. ●**breaking point** n **at b. point** (person) sur le point de craquer.

breakable ['breɪkəb(ə)l] *a* fragile.

break away *vi* se détacher ▌ *vt* détacher ▌ **to break down** *vt* (*door*) enfoncer; (*analyse*) analyser ▌ *vi* (*of vehicle, machine*) tomber en panne; (*of talks*) échouer; (*collapse*) (*of person*) s'effondrer. ● **breakdown** *n* panne *f*; analyse *f*; (*in talks*) rupture *f*; (*nervous*) dépression *f*; **b. lorry** dépanneuse *f*. ▌ **to break in** *vi* (*of burglar*) entrer par effraction ▌ *vt* (*door*) enfoncer; (*horse*) dresser; (*vehicle*) *Am* roder. ● **break-in** *n* cambriolage *m*. ▌ **to break into** *vt* (*safe*) forcer ▌ **to break off** *vt* détacher; (*relations*) rompre ▌ *vi* se détacher; (*stop*) s'arrêter; **to break off with s.o.** rompre avec qn ▌ **to break out** *vi* (*of war, fire*) éclater; (*escape*) s'échapper ▌ **to break through** *vi* (*of sun*) percer ▌ *vt* (*defences*) percer. ● **breakthrough** *n* (*discovery*) percée *f*, découverte *f*. ▌ **to break up** *vt* mettre en morceaux; (*marriage*) briser; (*fight*) mettre fin à ▌ *vi* (*of group*) se disperser; (*of marriage*) se briser; (*from school*) partir en vacances. ● **breakup** *n* fin *f*; (*in marriage*) rupture *f*.

breakfast ['brekfəst] *n* petit déjeuner *m*.

breast [brest] *n* sein *m*; (*of chicken*) blanc *m*. ● **breastfeed** *vt* (*pt & pp* **-fed**) allaiter. ● **breaststroke** *n* brasse *f*.

breath [breθ] *n* haleine *f*, souffle *m*; **out of b.** (tout) essoufflé; **to get a b. of air** prendre l'air; **to take a deep b.** respirer profondément; **under one's b.** tout bas. ● **breathalyser®** *n* alcootest® *m*. ● **breathtaking** *a* sensationnel.

breath/e [briːð] *vti* respirer; **to b.** in aspirer; **to b. out** expirer; **to b. air into** sth souffler dans qch. ● **—ing** *n* respiration *f*; **b. space** moment *m* de repos. ● **breather** *n Fam* moment *m* de repos.

bred [bred] *pt & pp* de **breed 1** ▌ *a* **well-b.** bien élevé.

breeches ['brɪtʃɪz] *npl* culotte *f*.

breed [briːd] **1** *vt* (*pt & pp* **bred**) (*animals*) élever ▌ *vi* (*of animals*) se reproduire. **2** *n* race *f*, espèce *f*. ● **—ing** *n* élevage *m*;

reproduction *f*. ● **breeder** *n* éleveur, -euse *mf*.

breeze [briːz] *n* brise *f*. ● **breezy** *a* (**-ier, -iest**) (*weather, day*) frais (*f* fraîche).

brevity ['brevɪtɪ] *n* brièveté *f*.

brew [bruː] *vt* (*beer*) brasser; (*plot*) préparer; **to b. tea** préparer du thé; (*infuse*) (faire) infuser du thé ▌ *vi* (*of storm*) se préparer; (*of tea*) infuser; **something is brewing** il se prépare quelque chose ▌ *n* (*drink*) breuvage *m*; (*of tea*) infusion *f*. ● **brewery** *n* brasserie *f*.

bribe [braɪb] *n* pot-de-vin *m* ▌ *vt* acheter (*qn*). ● **bribery** *n* corruption *f*.

brick [brɪk] *n* brique *f*; (*child's*) cube *m* ▌ *vt* **to b. up** (*gap, door*) murer. ● **bricklayer** *n* maçon *m*. ● **brickwork** *n* (*bricks*) briques *fpl*.

bride [braɪd] *n* mariée *f*; **the b. and groom** les mariés *mpl*. ● **bridegroom** *n* marié *m*. ● **bridesmaid** *n* demoiselle *f* d'honneur.

bridge [brɪdʒ] **1** *n* pònt *m*; (*on ship*) passerelle *f* ▌ *vt* **to b. a gap** combler une lacune. **2** *n Cards* bridge *m*.

bridle ['braɪd(ə)l] *n* (*for horse*) bride *f*; **b. path** allée *f* cavalière.

brief[1] [briːf] *a* (**-er, -est**) bref (*f* brève); **in b.** en résumé. ● **—ly** *adv* (*quickly*) en vitesse.

brief[2] [briːf] (*instructions*) *Mil Pol etc* instructions *fpl* ▌ *vt* donner des instructions à; (*inform*) mettre au courant (*on* de). ● **—ing** *n Mil Pol* instructions *fpl*.

briefcase ['briːfkeɪs] *n* serviette *f*.

briefs [briːfs] *npl* (*underpants*) slip *m*.

brigade [brɪ'geɪd] *n* brigade *f*.

bright [braɪt] *a* (**-er, -est**) (*star, eyes, situation, future*) brillant; (*colour, light*) vif; (*weather, room*) clair; (*clever*) intelligent; (*happy*) joyeux; (*idea*) génial; **b. interval** *Met* éclaircie *f* ▌ *adv* **b. and early** de bonne heure. ● **—ly** *adv* avec éclat. ● **—ness** *n* éclat *m*.

brighten ['braɪt(ə)n] *vt* **to b. (up)** (*room*) égayer ▌ *vi* **to b. (up)** (*of weather*) s'éclaircir; (*of face*) s'éclairer.

brilliant ['brɪljənt] *a* (*light*) éclatant;

(*clever*) brillant; (*fantastic*) *Fam* super. ● **brilliance** *n* éclat *m*; (*of person*) grande intelligence *f*.

brim [brɪm] *n* bord *m* ▮ *vi* (**-mm-**) to b. over déborder (**with** de).

bring [brɪŋ] *vt* (*pt & pp* brought) (*person, vehicle*) amener; (*object*) apporter; (*to cause*) amener; to b. sth to (*perfection, a peak etc*) porter qch à; to b. to an end mettre fin à; to b. to mind rappeler.

bring about *vt* provoquer ▮ to bring along *vt* (*object*) apporter; (*person*) amener ▮ to bring back *vt* (*person*) ramener; (*object*) rapporter; (*memories*) rappeler ▮ to bring down *vt* (*object*) descendre; (*overthrow*) faire tomber; (*reduce*) réduire ▮ to bring forward *vt* (*in time or space*) avancer ▮ to bring in *vt* (*object*) rentrer; (*person*) faire entrer; (*introduce*) introduire; (*income*) rapporter ▮ to bring off *vt* (*task*) mener à bien; (*object*) sortir ▮ to bring out *vt* (*object*) sortir; (*person*) faire sortir; (*meaning*) faire ressortir; (*book*) publier; (*product*) lancer ▮ to bring round *vt Med* ranimer (*qn*); (*convert*) convertir (*qn*) (**to** à) ▮ to bring to *Med* *vt* ranimer (*qn*) ▮ to bring together *vt* (*friends etc*) réunir; (*reconcile*) réconcilier ▮ to bring up *vt* (*object*) monter; (*child etc*) élever; (*subject*) mentionner; (*food*) vomir.

brink [brɪŋk] *n* bord *m*.

brisk [brɪsk] *a* (**-er, -est**) vif; at a b. pace vite. ● **—ly** *adv* (*to walk*) vite.

bristle [ˈbrɪs(ə)l] *n* poil *m* ▮ *vi* se hérisser.

Britain [ˈbrɪt(ə)n] *n* Grande-Bretagne *f*. ● **British** *a* britannique; the B. Isles les îles *fpl* Britanniques ▮ *n* the B. les Britanniques *mpl*. ● **Briton** *n* Britannique *mf*.

Brittany [ˈbrɪtənɪ] *n* Bretagne *f*.

brittle [ˈbrɪt(ə)l] *a* fragile.

broach [brəʊtʃ] *vt* (*topic*) entamer.

broad [brɔːd] *a* (**-er, -est**) (*wide*) large; (*outline*) général; (*accent*) prononcé; in b. daylight en plein jour; b. bean fève *f*; b. jump *Sp Am* saut *m* en longueur. ● b.-

'minded *a* à l'esprit large. ● b.-'shouldered *a* large d'épaules. ● broaden *vt* élargir ▮ *vi* s'élargir. ● broadly *adv* b. (speaking) en gros.

broadcast [ˈbrɔːdkɑːst] *vt* (*pt & pp* broadcast) diffuser, retransmettre ▮ *vi* (*of station*) émettre; (*person*) parler à la radio or à la télévision ▮ *n* émission *f*.

broccoli [ˈbrɒkəlɪ] *n inv* brocolis *mpl*.

brochure [ˈbrəʊʃər] *n* brochure *f*, dépliant *m*.

broil [brɔɪl] *vti* griller.

broke [brəʊk] 1 *pt of* break. 2 *a* (*penniless*) fauché. ● **broken** *pp of* break ▮ *a* (*man, voice, line*) brisé; in b. English en mauvais anglais; b. home foyer *m* brisé. ● broken-'down *a* (*machine*) (tout) déglingué.

broker [ˈbrəʊkər] *n* courtier, -ière *mf*.

brolly [ˈbrɒlɪ] *n* (*umbrella*) *Fam* pépin *m*.

bronchitis [brɒŋˈkaɪtɪs] *n* bronchite *f*.

bronze [brɒnz] *n* bronze *m* ▮ *a* (*statue etc*) en bronze.

brooch [brəʊtʃ] *n* (*ornament*) broche *f*.

brood [bruːd] 1 *n* couvée *f*, nichée *f*. 2 *vi* méditer tristement (**over** sur); to b. over (*a plan*) ruminer. ● **broody** *a* (**-ier, -iest**) (*person*) maussade.

brook [brʊk] *n* ruisseau *m*.

broom [bruːm] *n* balai *m*. ● **broomstick** *n* manche *m* à balai.

Bros *abbr* (Brothers) Frères *mpl*.

broth [brɒθ] *n* bouillon *m*.

brothel [ˈbrɒθ(ə)l] *n* maison *f* close.

brother [ˈbrʌðər] *n* frère *m*. ● b.-in-law *n* (*pl* brothers-in-law) beau-frère *m*. ● **brotherly** *a* fraternel.

brought [brɔːt] *pt & pp of* bring.

brow [braʊ] *n* 1 (*forehead*) front *m*. 2 (*of hill*) sommet *m*.

brown [braʊn] *a* (**-er, -est**) brun; (*reddish*) marron; (*hair*) châtain; (*tanned*) bronzé ▮ *n* brun *m*; marron *m* ▮ *vt* (*of sun*) bronzer (*la peau*); (*Culin*) faire dorer; to be browned off *Fam* en avoir marre.

Brownie [ˈbraʊnɪ] *n* (*girl scout*) jeannette *f*.

browse [brauz] *vi* (*in bookshop*) feuilleter des livres; (*in shop*) regarder; **to b. through** (*book*) feuilleter.

bruis/e [bru:z] *vt* **to b. one's knee/etc** se faire un bleu au genou/etc ‖ *n* bleu *m*, contusion *f*. ●**—ed** *a* couvert de bleus.

brunch [brʌntʃ] *n* brunch *m*.

brunette [bru:'net] *n* brunette *f*.

brunt [brʌnt] *n* **to bear the b. of** (*attack etc*) subir le plus gros de.

brush [brʌʃ] *n* brosse *f*; (*for shaving*) blaireau *m*; (*for sweeping*) balayette *f*; (*action*) coup *m* de brosse ‖ *vt* (*teeth, hair*) brosser; (*clothes*) donner un coup de brosse à; **to b. aside** écarter; **to b. away** or **off** enlever; **to b. up (on)** (*language*) se remettre à ‖ *vi* **to b. against** effleurer. ●**brushwood** *n* broussailles *fpl*.

Brussels ['brʌs(ə)lz] *n* Bruxelles *m* or *f*; **B. sprouts** choux *mpl* de Bruxelles.

brutal ['bru:t(ə)l] *a* brutal. ●**bru'tality** *n* brutalité *f*.

brute [bru:t] *n* (*animal, person*) brute *f*.

BSc, *Am* **BS** *abbr* = **Bachelor of Science.**

bubble ['bʌb(ə)l] *n* (*of air, soap, in boiling liquid*) bulle *f*; **b. bath** bain *m* moussant; **b. gum** bubble-gum *m* ‖ *vi* bouillonner; **to b. over** déborder (**with** de).

buck [bʌk] **1** *n Am Fam* dollar *m*. **2** *n* (*animal*) mâle *m*. **3** *vt* **to b. up** remonter le moral à (*qn*) ‖ *vi* **to b. up** (*become livelier*) reprendre du poil de la bête; (*hurry*) se grouiller.

bucket ['bʌkɪt] *n* seau *m*.

buckle ['bʌk(ə)l] **1** *n* boucle *f* ‖ *vt* boucler. **2** *vti* (*warp*) voiler. **3** *vi* **to b. down to** (*task*) s'atteler à.

bud [bʌd] *n* (*of tree*) bourgeon *m*; (*of flower*) bouton *m* ‖ *vi* (*-dd-*) bourgeonner; pousser des boutons. ●**budding** *a* (*talent*) naissant; (*doctor etc*) en herbe.

Buddhist ['budɪst] *a* & *n* bouddhiste (*mf*).

buddy ['bʌdɪ] *n Am Fam* copain *m*, pote *m*.

budge [bʌdʒ] *vi* bouger ‖ *vt* faire bouger.

budgerigar ['bʌdʒərɪgɑːr] *n* perruche *f*.

budget ['bʌdʒɪt] *n* budget *m* ‖ *vi* **to b. for** inscrire au budget.

budgie ['bʌdʒɪ] *n Fam* perruche *f*.

buff [bʌf] **1** *a* **b.(-coloured)** chamois *inv*. **2** *n jazz/etc* **b.** *Fam* fana(tique) *mf* de jazz/etc.

buffalo ['bʌfələu] *n* (*pl* -oes *or* -o) buffle *m*; (**American**) bison *m*.

buffer ['bʌfər] *n* (*on train*) tampon *m*; (*at end of track*) butoir *m*.

buffet¹ ['bufeɪ] *n* (*table, meal, café*) buffet *m*; **cold b.** viandes *fpl* froides; **b. car** (*on train*) voiture-bar *f*.

buffet² ['bʌfɪt] *vt* (*of waves*) battre (*navire etc*).

bug¹ [bʌg] **1** *n* (*any insect*) bestiole *f*; (*germ*) *Fam* microbe *m*, virus *m*. **2** *n Fam* (*in machine*) défaut *m*; (*in computer program*) erreur *f*. **3** *n* (*listening device*) micro *m* (*clandestin*) ‖ *vt* (*-gg-*) (*room*) installer des micros dans.

bug² [bʌg] *vt* (*-gg-*) (*annoy*) *Fam* embêter.

buggy ['bʌgɪ] *n* (**baby**) **b.** poussette *f*; (*folding pushchair*) poussette-canne *f*; (*pram*) *Am* landau *m* (*pl* -aus).

bugle ['bju:g(ə)l] *n* clairon *m*.

build [bɪld] **1** *n* (*of person*) carrure *f*. **2** *vt* (*pt* & *pp* **built**) construire; (*house, town*) construire, bâtir ‖ *vi* bâtir, construire. **3** *vt* **to b. up** (*increase*) augmenter; (*collection*) constituer; (*business*) monter; (*speed*) prendre; (*reputation*) bâtir ‖ *vi* (*of tension, pressure*) augmenter, monter; (*of dust*) s'accumuler.

builder ['bɪldər] *n* (*of houses etc*) (*workman*) maçon *m*; (*contractor*) entrepreneur *m*.

building ['bɪldɪŋ] *n* bâtiment *m*; (*flats, offices*) immeuble *m*; (*action*) construction *f*; **b. society** = société *f* de crédit immobilier.

built-in [bɪlt'ɪn] *a* (*cupboard, Am closet*) encastré; (*part of machine*) incorporé.

built-up [bɪlt'ʌp] *a* urbanisé; **b.-up area** agglomération *f*.

bulb [bʌlb] n (of plant) oignon m; (of lamp) ampoule f.
Bulgaria [bʌl'geərɪə] n Bulgarie f. ● **Bulgarian** a & n bulgare (mf).
bulg/e [bʌldʒ] vi **to b. (out)** se renfler, bomber. ● **—ing** n renflement m. ● **—ing** a renflé, bombé; **to be b.** (of bag etc) être plein à craquer (**with** de).
bulk [bʌlk] n inv (of building etc) volume m; (of person) grosseur f; **the b. of** (most) la majeure partie de; **in b.** (to buy, sell) en gros. ● **bulky** a (**-ier, -iest**) gros (f grosse).
bull [bʊl] n taureau m.
bulldog ['bʊldɒg] n bouledogue m.
bulldozer ['bʊldəʊzər] n bulldozer m.
bullet ['bʊlɪt] n balle f (de revolver etc). ● **bulletproof** a (jacket, Am vest) pare-balles inv; (car) blindé.
bulletin ['bʊlətɪn] n bulletin m; **b. board** Am tableau m d'affichage.
bullfight ['bʊlfaɪt] n corrida f. ● **bullring** n arène f.
bull's-eye ['bʊlzaɪ] n (of target) centre m; **to hit the b.-eye** faire mouche.
bully ['bʊlɪ] n (grosse) brute f ● **vt** brutaliser; **to b. into doing** forcer à faire.
bum [bʌm] **1** n Fam (loafer) clochard, -arde mf; (good-for-nothing) propre mf à rien ● **vi** (-mm-) **to b. (around)** se balader. **2** n (buttocks) Fam derrière m; **b. bag** banane f.
bumblebee ['bʌmb(ə)lbiː] n bourdon m.
bump [bʌmp] vt (of car etc) heurter; **to b. one's head/knee** se cogner la tête/le genou; **to b. into** se cogner contre; (of car) rentrer dans; (meet) tomber sur ● **vi** **to b. along** (on rough road) (in car etc) cahoter.
● **n** (impact) choc m; (jerk) cahot m; (on road, body) bosse f. ● **bumper** n (of car etc) pare-chocs m inv ● a (crop etc) exceptionnel; **b. cars** autos fpl tamponneuses. ● **bumpy** a (**-ier, -iest**) (road, ride) cahoteux.
bun [bʌn] n (cake) petit pain m au lait.
bunch [bʌntʃ] n (of flowers) bouquet m; (of keys) trousseau m; (of bananas)

régime m; (of people) bande f; **b. of grapes** grappe f de raisin; **a b. of** (mass) Fam un tas de.
bundle ['bʌnd(ə)l] **1** n paquet m; (of papers) liasse f; (of firewood) fagot m. **2** vt (put) fourrer; (push) pousser (**into** dans). **3** vti **to b. (oneself) up** se couvrir (bien).
bung [bʌŋ] **1** vt **to b. up** (stop up) boucher. **2** vt (toss) Fam balancer.
bungalow ['bʌŋgələʊ] n bungalow m.
bungle ['bʌŋg(ə)l] vt gâcher.
bunion ['bʌnjən] n (on toe) oignon m.
bunk [bʌŋk] n Rail Nau couchette f; **b. beds** lits mpl superposés.
bunker ['bʌŋkər] n Mil Golf bunker m.
bunny ['bʌnɪ] n **b. (rabbit)** Fam Jeannot m lapin.
buoy [bɔɪ] n bouée f.
buoyant ['bɔɪənt] a (cheerful) gai, optimiste.
burden ['bɜːd(ə)n] n fardeau m; (of tax) poids m ● vt accabler (**with** de).
bureau, pl **-eaux** ['bjʊərəʊ, -əʊz] n (office) bureau m; (desk) secrétaire m; (chest of drawers) Am commode f.
bureaucracy [bjʊə'rɒkrəsɪ] n bureaucratie f. ● **bureaucrat** ['bjʊərəkræt] n bureaucrate mf.
burger ['bɜːgər] n Fam hamburger m.
burglar ['bɜːglər] n cambrioleur, -euse mf; **b. alarm** alarme f antivol. ● **burglarize** vt Am cambrioler. ● **burglary** n cambriolage m. ● **burgle** vt cambrioler.
burial ['berɪəl] n enterrement m.
burly ['bɜːlɪ] a (**-ier, -iest**) costaud.
Burma ['bɜːmə] n Birmanie f. ● **Bur'mese** a & n birman, -ane (mf).
burn [bɜːn] n brûlure f.
● **vt** (pt & pp **burned** or **burnt**) brûler; **burnt alive** brûlé vif; **to b. down** (house) détruire par le feu.
● **vi** brûler; **to b. down** (of house) brûler (complètement), être réduit en cendres; **to b. out** (of fire) s'éteindre; (of fuse) sauter. ● **—ing** a en feu; (fire, light) allumé; (topic etc) Fig brûlant ● **n smell of b.** odeur f de brûlé. ● **burner** n (of

stove) brûleur *m*.

burp [bɜːp] *n Fam* rot *m* ▮ *vi Fam* roter.

burrow [ˈbʌrəʊ] *n* (*hole*) terrier *m* ▮ *vti* creuser.

burst [bɜːst] *n* (*of laughter*) éclat *m*; (*of applause*) salve *f*; (*of thunder*) coup *m*; (*explosion*) éclatement *m*; (*surge*) élan *m*; (*fit*) accès *m*.
▮ *vi* (*pt & pp* burst) (*with force*) éclater; (*of bubble, balloon, boil, tyre, cloud*) crever; **to b. into** (*room*) faire irruption dans; **to b. into tears** fondre en larmes; **to b. into flames** prendre feu; **to b. out laughing** éclater de rire.
▮ *vt* (*bubble, balloon etc*) crever. ● **bursting** *a* (*full*) plein à craquer (**with** de).

bury [ˈberɪ] *vt* (*dead person*) enterrer; (*hide*) enfouir; (*plunge*) plonger; **buried in one's work**/*etc* plongé dans son travail/*etc*.

bus [bʌs] *n* (auto)bus *m*; (*long-distance*) (auto)car *m* ▮ *a* (*driver, ticket etc*) d'autobus; d'autocar; **b. shelter** Abribus® *m*; **b. station** gare *f* routière; **b. stop** arrêt *m* d'autobus.

bush [bʊʃ] *n* buisson *m*; **the b.** (*land*) la brousse. ● **bushy** *a* (**-ier, -iest**) (*hair, tail etc*) broussailleux.

bushed [bʊʃt] *a* (*tired*) *Fam* crevé.

business [ˈbɪznɪs] *n* affaires *fpl*, commerce *m*; (*shop*) commerce *m*; (*task, concern, matter*) affaire *f*; **big b.** les grosses entreprises *fpl* commerciales; **on b.** (*to travel*) pour affaires; **it's your b. to ...** c'est à vous de ...; **that's none of your b.!, mind you own b.!** ça ne vous regarde pas!
▮ *a* commercial; (*meeting, trip*) d'affaires; **b. hours** (*office*) heures *fpl* de travail; (*shop*) heures *fpl* d'ouverture; **b. card** carte *f* de visite. ● **businesslike** *a* sérieux, pratique. ● **businessman** *n* (*pl* -men) homme *m* d'affaires. ● **businesswoman** *n* (*pl* -women) femme *f* d'affaires.

busker [ˈbʌskər] *n* musicien, -ienne *mf* des rues.

bust [bʌst] **1** *n* (*sculpture*) buste *m*;

(*woman's breasts*) poitrine *f*. **2** *a* (*broken*) *Fam* fichu; **to go b.** (*bankrupt*) faire faillite.

bustl/e [ˈbʌs(ə)l] *vi* s'affairer ▮ *n* activité *f*. ● **-ing** *a* (*street*) bruyant.

busy [ˈbɪzɪ] *a* (**-ier, -iest**) occupé (**doing** à faire); (*active*) actif; (*day*) chargé; (*street*) animé; (*phone*) *Am* occupé; **to be b. doing** être en train de faire; **b. signal** *Am* sonnerie *f* 'occupé' ▮ *vt* **to b. oneself** s'occuper (**with sth** à qch, **doing** à faire). ● **busybody** *n* **to be a b.** faire la mouche du coche.

but [bʌt, *unstressed* bət] **1** *conj* mais. **2** *prep* (*except*) sauf; **b. for that** sans cela; **b. for him** sans lui; **no one b. you** personne d'autre que toi. **3** *adv* (*only*) ne ... que, seulement; **he's b. a boy** ce n'est qu'un garçon.

butane [ˈbjuːteɪn] *n* (*gas*) butane *m*.

butcher [ˈbʊtʃər] *n* boucher *m*; **b.'s shop** boucherie *f* ▮ *vt* (*people*) massacrer; (*animal*) abattre.

butler [ˈbʌtlər] *n* maître *m* d'hôtel.

butt [bʌt] **1** *n* (*of cigarette*) mégot *m*; (*of gun*) crosse *f*; (*buttocks*) *Am Fam* derrière *m*; **b. for ridicule** objet *m* de risée. **2** *vi* **to b. in** interrompre.

butter [ˈbʌtər] *n* beurre *m*; **b. dish** beurrier *m* ▮ *vt* beurrer. ● **buttercup** *n* bouton-d'or *m*. ● **buttermilk** *n* lait *m* de beurre

butterfly [ˈbʌtəflaɪ] *n* papillon *m*; **to have butterflies** *Fam* avoir le trac; **b. stroke** brasse *f* papillon.

buttock [ˈbʌtək] *n* fesse *f*.

button [ˈbʌtən] *n* bouton *m*; (*of phone*) touche *f*; (*badge*) *Am* badge *m* ▮ *vt* **to b. (up)** boutonner ▮ *vi* **to b. (up)** (*of garment*) se boutonner. ● **buttonhole** *n* boutonnière *f*; (*flower*) fleur *f*.

buy [baɪ] *vt* (*pt & pp* bought) acheter (**from s.o.** à qn, **for s.o.** à *or* pour qn); (*story etc*) *Am Fam* croire, avaler; **to b. back** racheter; **to b. up** acheter en bloc ▮ *n* **a good b.** une bonne affaire. ● **-er** *n* acheteur, -euse *mf*.

buzz [bʌz] **1** *vi* bourdonner; **to b. off** *Fam*

décamper ▌ n bourdonnement m. **2** n (phone call) **to give s.o. a b.** passer un coup de fil à qn. ●—**er** n interphone m; (of bell, clock) sonnerie f.

by [baɪ] prep **1** (agent) par; de; **hit/ chosen/etc by** frappé/choisi/etc par; **surrounded/followed/etc by** entouré/ suivi/etc de; **a book by . . .** un livre de . . . .

2 (manner, means) **by sea** par mer; **by mistake** par erreur; **by car** en voiture; **by bicycle** à bicyclette; **by doing** en faisant; **one by one** un à un; **day by day** de jour en jour; **by sight/day/far** de vue/jour/loin; **by the door** (through) par la porte; **(all) by oneself** tout seul.

3 (next to) à côté de; (near) près de; **by the lake/sea** au bord du lac/de la mer; **to go** or **pass by the bank** passer devant la banque.

4 (before in time) avant; **by Monday** avant lundi; **by now** à cette heure-ci; **by yesterday** (dès) hier.

5 (amount, measurement) à; **by the kilo** au kilo; **paid by the hour** payé à l'heure; **taller by a metre** plus grand d'un mètre.

6 (according to) à, d'après; **by my watch** à or d'après ma montre; **it's fine** or **all right by me** si vous voulez.

▌ adv **close by** tout près; **to go by, pass by** passer; **to put by** mettre de côté; **by and large** en gros. ●**by-election** n élection f partielle. ●**by-law** n arrêté (municipal) m. ●**by-product** n sousproduit m.

bye(-bye)! [baɪ('baɪ)] int Fam salut!, au revoir!

bypass ['baɪpɑːs] n déviation f (routière) ▌ vt (town) contourner; (ignore) Fig éviter de passer par.

bystander ['baɪstændər] n spectateur, -trice mf.

C

C, c [siː] *n* C, c *m*.

c *abbr* = **cent**.

cab [kæb] *n* taxi *m*; (*of train driver etc*) cabine *f*.

cabaret ['kæbəreɪ] *n* (*show*) spectacle *m*.

cabbage ['kæbɪdʒ] *n* chou *m* (*pl* choux).

cabin ['kæbɪn] *n* (*on ship, aircraft*) cabine *f*; (*hut*) cabane *f*; **c. crew** *Av* équipage *m*.

cabinet ['kæbɪnɪt] **1** *n* (*cupboard, Am closet*) armoire *f*; (*for display*) vitrine *f*; **(filing) c.** classeur *m* (de bureau). **2** *n* (*government ministers*) gouvernement *m*; **c. meeting** conseil *m* des ministres; **c. minister** ministre *m*. ● **c.-maker** *n* ébéniste *m*.

cable ['keɪb(ə)l] *n* câble *m*; **c. car** téléphérique *m*; (*on tracks*) funiculaire *m*; **c. television** la télévision par câble; **to have c.** *Fam* avoir le câble ‖ *vt* (*message etc*) câbler (**to** à).

caboose [kə'buːs] *n* *Rail* *Am* fourgon *m* (de queue).

cache [kæʃ] *n* **an arms' c.** une cache d'armes.

cackle ['kæk(ə)l] *vi* (*of hen*) caqueter ‖ *n* caquet *m*.

cactus, *pl* -**ti** *or* -**tuses** ['kæktəs, -taɪ, -təsɪz] *n* cactus *m*.

caddie ['kædɪ] *n* *Golf* caddie *m*.

cadet [kə'det] *n* *Mil* élève *m* officier.

cadge [kædʒ] *vt* (*meal*) se faire payer (**off s.o.** par qn); **to c. money off s.o.** taper qn.

Caesarean [sɪ'zeərɪən] *n* *Med* césarienne *f*.

café ['kæfeɪ] *n* café(-restaurant) *m*. ● **cafeteria** [kæfɪ'tɪərɪə] *n* cafétéria *f*.

caffeine ['kæfiːn] *n* caféine *f*.

cage [keɪdʒ] *n* cage *f*.

Cairo ['kaɪərəʊ] *n* Le Caire.

cajole [kə'dʒəʊl] *vt* amadouer, enjôler.

cake [keɪk] *n* gâteau *m*; (*small*) pâtisserie *f*; **c. shop** pâtisserie *f*.

caked [keɪkt] *a* **c. mud/blood** boue *f*/sang *m* séché(e).

calamine ['kæləmaɪn] *n* **c. (lotion)** lotion *f* apaisante (à la calamine).

calamity [kə'læmɪtɪ] *n* calamité *f*.

calcium ['kælsɪəm] *n* calcium *m*.

calculat/e ['kælkjʊleɪt] *vti* calculer; **to c. that** *Fam* supposer que; **calculated risk** risque *m* calculé. ● —**ing** *a* (*shrewd*) calculateur. ● **calculation** [-'leɪʃ(ə)n] *n* calcul *m*. ● **calculator** *n* **(pocket) c.** calculatrice *f* (de poche).

calculus ['kælkjʊləs] *n* *Math* calcul *m*.

calendar ['kælɪndər] *n* calendrier *m*; (*diary*) *Am* agenda *m*.

calf [kɑːf] *n* (*pl* **calves**) **1** (*animal*) veau *m*. **2** *Anat* mollet *m*.

calibre ['kælɪbər] (*Am* **caliber**) *n* calibre *m*.

call [kɔːl] *n* appel *m*; (*shout*) cri *m*; (*visit*) visite *f*; **(telephone) c.** communication *f*, appel *m* téléphonique; **to make a c.** *Tel* téléphoner (**to** à); **on c.** de garde; **c. box** *n* *Am* cabine *f* (téléphonique).

‖ *vt* appeler; (*shout*) crier; (*wake up*) réveiller; (*person to meeting*) convoquer (**to** à); (*attention*) attirer (**to** sur); (*truce*) demander; **he's called David** il s'appelle David; **to c. a meeting** convoquer une assemblée; **to c. s.o. a liar/** *etc* traiter qn de menteur/*etc*; **to c. into question** mettre en question.

‖ *vi* appeler; (*cry out*) crier; (*visit*) passer.

call back *vti* rappeler ‖ **to call by** *vi* (*visit*) passer ‖ **to call for** *vt* (*require*) demander; (*summon*) appeler; (*collect*) passer prendre ‖ **to call in** *vt* (*into room etc*) faire venir *or* entrer; (*police*) appeler ‖ *vi* **to c. in** (**on s.o.**) (*visit*) passer (chez qn); **c.-in programme** *Rad* émission *f* à ligne ouverte █ **to call off** *vt* (*cancel*) annuler; (*dog*) rappeler █ **to call on** *vt* (*visit*) passer voir, passer chez; **to call on s.o. to do** inviter qn à faire; (*urge*) sommer qn de faire █ **to call out** *vt* (*shout*) crier; (*doctor*) appeler █ *vi* (*shout*) crier; **to call out for** demander à haute voix █ **to call round** *vi* (*visit*) passer █ **to call up** *vt Tel* appeler; (*recruits*) *Mil* appeler, mobiliser. ● **call-up** *n Mil* appel *m*, mobilisation *f*.

caller ['kɔːlər] *n* visiteur, -euse *mf*; *Tel* correspondant, -ante *mf*.

calling ['kɔːlɪŋ] *n* vocation *f*; **c. card** *Am* carte *f* de visite.

callous ['kæləs] *a* cruel, insensible.

callus ['kæləs] *n* durillon *m*, cal *m*.

calm [kɑːm] *a* (-er, -est) calme, tranquille; **keep c.!** (*don't panic*) du calme! █ *n* calme *m* █ *vt* **to c. (down)** calmer █ *vi* **to c. down** se calmer. ● **-ly** *adv* calmement.

Calor gas ['kælɔːgæs] *n* butagaz® *m*.

calorie ['kælərɪ] *n* calorie *f*.

camcorder [kæm'kɔːdər] *n* caméscope *m*.

came [keɪm] *pt of* **come**.

camel ['kæməl] *n* chameau *m*.

camellia [kə'miːlɪə] *n Bot* camélia *m*.

camera ['kæmrə] *n* appareil (photo) *m*; (**TV** *or* **film**) *c.* caméra *f*. ● **cameraman** *n* (*pl* **-men**) cameraman *m*.

camouflage ['kæməflɑːʒ] *n* camouflage *m* █ *vt* camoufler.

camp¹ [kæmp] *n* camp *m*; **c. bed** lit *m* de camp █ *vi* **to c. (out)** camper. ● **-ing** *n Sp* camping *m*; **c. site** (terrain *m* de) camping *m*. ● **camper** *n* (*person*) campeur, -euse *mf*; (*vehicle*) camping-car *m*. ● **campfire** *n* feu *m* de camp. ● **campsite** *n* camping *m*.

camp² [kæmp] *a* (*affected*) affecté (et risible).

campaign [kæm'peɪn] *n Pol Mil etc* campagne *f* █ *vi* faire campagne. ● **-er** *n* militant, -ante *mf* (**for** pour).

campus ['kæmpəs] *n Univ* campus *m*.

can¹ [kæn, *unstressed* kən] *v aux* (*pres t* **can**; *pt* **could**) (*be able to*) pouvoir; (*know how to*) savoir; **he couldn't help me** il ne pouvait pas m'aider; **if I c.** si je peux; **she c. swim** elle sait nager; **if I could swim** si je savais nager; **he could do it tomorrow** il pourrait le faire demain; **he could have done it** il aurait pu le faire; **you could be wrong** (*possibility*) tu as peut-être tort; **he can't be dead** (*probability*) il ne peut pas être mort; **c. I come in?** puis-je entrer?; **I c. see** je vois.

can² [kæn] *n* (*for water etc*) bidon *m*; (*for food, beer*) boîte *f* █ *vt* (**-nn-**) mettre en boîte. ● **canned** *a* en boîte, en conserve; **c. food** conserves *fpl*. ● **can-opener** *n* ouvre-boîtes *m inv*.

Canada ['kænədə] *n* Canada *m*. ● **Canadian** [kə'neɪdɪən] *a* & *n* canadien, -ienne (*mf*).

canal [kə'næl] *n* canal *m*.

canary [kə'neərɪ] *n* canari *m*, serin *m*.

cancel ['kænsəl] *vt* (**-ll-**, *Am* **-l-**) (*flight, appointment etc*) annuler; (*goods, taxi etc*) décommander; (*train*) supprimer; (*stamp*) oblitérer; **to c. a ticket** (*punch*) (*with date*) composter un billet; (*with hole*) poinçonner un billet; **to c. each other out** s'annuler. ● **cancellation** [-'leɪʃ(ə)n] *n* annulation *f*; suppression *f*; oblitération *f*.

cancer ['kænsər] *n* cancer *m*; **C.** (*sign*) le Cancer; **c. patient** cancéreux, -euse *mf*. ● **cancerous** *a* cancéreux.

candid ['kændɪd] *a* franc (*f* franche). ● **candour** (*Am* **candor**) *n* franchise *f*.

candidate ['kændɪdeɪt] *n* candidat, -ate *mf*.

candle ['kænd(ə)l] *n* bougie *f*; (*in church*) cierge *m*. ● **candlelight** *n* by **c.** à la (lueur d'une) bougie; **to have dinner by c.** dîner aux chandelles. ● **candlestick** *n* bougeoir *m*; (*tall*) chandelier *m*.

candy ['kændɪ] *n Am* bonbon(s) *m(pl)*; **c. store** *Am* confiserie *f*. ● **candyfloss** *n* barbe *f* à papa.

cane [keɪn] *n* (*stick*) canne *f*; (*for punish-*

ing) rotin *m*; *Sch* baguette *f* ‖ *vt* (*punish*) fouetter.

canister ['kænɪstər] *n* boîte *f* (*en métal*).

cannabis ['kænəbɪs] *n* (*drug*) haschisch *m*.

cannibal ['kænɪbəl] *n* cannibale *mf*.

cannon ['kænən] *n* (*pl* -s *or inv*) canon *m*.

cannot ['kænɒt] = **can not**.

canny ['kænɪ] *a* (-**ier, -iest**) rusé, malin.

canoe [kə'nu:] *n* canoë *m*, kayak *m*;
●—**ing** *n* to go c. *Sp* faire du canoë-kayak. ●**canoeist** *n* canoéiste *mf*.

canopy ['kænəpɪ] *n* (*hood of pram or Am baby carriage*) capote *f*; (*small roof*) auvent *m*; (*over bed, altar etc*) dais *m*.

can't [kɑːnt] = **can not**.

cantaloup(e) ['kæntəlu:p, *Am* -ləʊp] *n* (*melon*) cantaloup *m*.

cantankerous [kæn'tæŋkərəs] *a* grincheux, acariâtre.

canteen [kæn'ti:n] *n* (*in school, factory etc*) cantine *f*; (*flask*) gourde *f*; **c. of cutlery** ménagère *f*.

canvas ['kænvəs] *n* (*grosse*) toile *f*; (*for embroidery*) canevas *m*.

canvass ['kænvəs] *vt* (*an area*) faire du démarchage dans; **to c. s.o.** *Pol* solliciter des voix de qn; *Com* solliciter des commandes de qn. ●—**ing** *n* *Com Pol* démarchage *m*. ●—**er** *n* *Pol* agent *m* électoral; *Com* démarcheur, -euse *mf*.

canyon ['kænjən] n cañon m, canyon m.

cap¹ [kæp] *n* **1** (*hat*) casquette *f*; (*for shower, of sailor*) bonnet *m*; (*of soldier*) képi *m*. **2** (*of bottle, tube*) bouchon *m*; (*of milk or beer bottle*) capsule *f*; (*of pen*) capuchon *m*. **3** (*of child's gun*) amorce *f*.

cap² [kæp] *vt* (-**pp**-) (*outdo*) surpasser; **to c. it all** pour comble; **capped with** (*crowned*) surmonté de.

capable ['keɪpəb(ə)l] *a* (*person*) capable (**of sth** de qch, **of doing** de faire); **c. of** (*situation etc*) susceptible de. ●**capa'bility** *n* capacité *f*.

capacity [kə'pæsɪtɪ] *n* (*of container*) capacité *f*; (*ability*) aptitude *f*, capacité *f* (**for sth** pour qch, **for doing** à faire); **in**

my c. as en ma qualité de; **in an advisory/***etc* **c.** à titre consultatif/*etc*; **filled to c.** absolument plein, comble.

cape [keɪp] *n* **1** (*cloak*) cape *f*; (*of cyclist*) pèlerine *f*. **2** *Geog* cap *m*; **C. Town** Le Cap.

caper ['keɪpər] **1** *n* (*activity*) *Sl* affaire *f*; (*prank*) *Fam* farce *f*. **2** *n* *Bot Culin* câpre *f*.

capital ['kæpɪtəl] **1** *a* (*punishment, importance*) capital ‖ *n* **c.** (*city*) capitale *f*; **c. (letter)** majuscule *f*, capitale *f*. **2** *n* (*money*) capital *m*. ●**capitalist** *a* & *n* capitaliste (*mf*).

capitalize ['kæpɪtəlaɪz] *vi* **to c. on** tirer parti de.

capricious [kə'prɪʃəs] *a* capricieux.

Capricorn ['kæprɪkɔ:n] *n* (*sign*) le Capricorne.

capsize [kæp'saɪz] *vi* (*of boat*) chavirer ‖ *vt* (faire) chavirer.

capsule ['kæpsəl, 'kæpsju:l] *n* (*medicine, of spaceship etc*) capsule *f*.

captain ['kæptɪn] *n* capitaine *m* ‖ *vt* (*team*) être le capitaine de.

caption ['kæpʃ(ə)n] *n* (*under illustration*) légende *f*.

captivating ['kæptɪveɪtɪŋ] *a* captivant.

captive ['kæptɪv] *n* prisonnier, -ière *mf*. ●**cap'tivity** *n* captivité *f*.

capture ['kæptʃər] *vt* (*person, animal*) prendre, capturer; (*town*) prendre; (*attention*) capter; (*represent on film etc*) rendre ‖ *n* capture *f*.

car [kɑ:r] *n* voiture *f*, auto *f*; *Rail* wagon *m*, voiture *f*; **c. boot sale** (*sorte de*) braderie *f*; **c. ferry** ferry-boat *m*; **c. hire** location *f* de voitures; **c. park** parking *m*; **c. phone** téléphone *m* de voiture; **c. radio** autoradio *m*; **c. rental** *Am* = **c. hire**; **c. wash** (*machine*) lave-auto *m*. ●**carfare** *n* *Am* frais *mpl* de voyage. ●**carport** *n* auvent *m* (*pour voiture*). ●**carsick** *a* **to be c.** être malade en voiture.

carafe [kə'ræf] *n* carafe *f*.

caramel ['kærəməl] *n* caramel *m*.

carat ['kærət] *n* carat *m*.

caravan ['kærəvæn] n Aut caravane f; (horse-drawn) roulotte f; **c. site** camping m pour caravanes.

carbohydrates [kɑːbəʊ'haɪdreɪts] npl (in diet) féculents mpl.

carbon ['kɑːbən] n carbone m; **c. copy** double m (au carbone); **c. paper** (papier m) carbone m.

carburettor [kɑːbjʊ'retər] (Am **carburetor** ['kɑːbəreɪtər]) n carburateur m.

carcinogenic [kɑːsɪnə'dʒenɪk] a cancérigène.

card [kɑːd] n carte f; (cardboard) carton m; (index) **c.** fiche f; **c. index** fichier m; **c. game** jeu m de cartes; (game of cards) partie f de cartes; **c. table** table f de jeu; **to play cards** jouer aux cartes; **on** or **Am in the cards** Fam très vraisemblable. ●**cardboard** n carton m. ●**cardphone** n téléphone m à carte.

cardiac ['kɑːdɪæk] a cardiaque.

cardigan ['kɑːdɪgən] n gilet m.

cardinal ['kɑːdɪn(ə)l] 1 a (number, point) cardinal. 2 n (priest) cardinal m.

care [keər] 1 vi **to c. about** (feel concern about) se soucier de, s'intéresser à; **I don't c.** ça m'est égal; **I couldn't c. less** Fam je m'en fiche; **who cares?** qu'est-ce que ça fait?

2 vi (like) aimer, vouloir; **would you c. to try?** voulez-vous essayer?, aimeriez-vous essayer?; **to c. for** (a drink, a change etc) avoir envie de; **to c. about** or **for s.o.** (be fond of) avoir de la sympathie pour qn; **to c. for s.o.** (look after) s'occuper de qn; (sick person) soigner qn.

3 n (attention) soin(s) m(pl); (protection) garde f, soin m; (anxiety) souci m; **to take c. not to do** faire attention à ne pas faire; **to take c. to do** veiller à faire; **to take c. of** s'occuper de (qch, qn); (sick person) prendre soin de; **to take c. of oneself** (manage) se débrouiller; (keep healthy) faire bien attention à soi.

career [kə'rɪər] n carrière f.

carefree ['keəfriː] a insouciant.

careful ['keəf(ə)l] a (exact, thorough)

soigneux (**about** de); (work) soigné; (cautious) prudent; **to be c. of** or **with** faire attention à; **to be c. not to do** faire attention à ne pas faire. ●**-ly** adv avec soin; prudemment.

careless ['keələs] a négligent; (absentminded) étourdi; (work) peu soigné; **c. about** peu soigneux de.

caress [kə'res] n caresse f ǁ vt (stroke) caresser; (kiss) embrasser.

caretaker ['keəteɪkər] n gardien, -ienne mf, concierge mf.

cargo ['kɑːgəʊ] n (pl -oes, Am -os) cargaison f; **c. boat** cargo m.

Caribbean [kærɪ'biːən, Am kə'rɪbɪən] a caraïbe ǁ n **the C. (Islands)** les Antilles fpl.

caricature ['kærɪkətʃʊər] n caricature f.

caring ['keərɪŋ] a (loving) aimant; (understanding) très humain.

carnation [kɑː'neɪʃən] n œillet m.

carnival ['kɑːnɪvəl] n carnaval m (pl -als).

carol ['kærəl] n chant m (de Noël).

carp [kɑːp] n (fish) carpe f.

carpenter ['kɑːpɪntər] n (for house building) charpentier m; (for light woodwork) menuisier m. ●**carpentry** n charpenterie f; menuiserie f.

carpet ['kɑːpɪt] n tapis m; (wall-to-wall) moquette f; **c. sweeper** balai m mécanique ǁ vt recouvrir d'un tapis or d'une moquette. ●**-ing** n (carpets) tapis mpl; (wall-to-wall) **c.** moquette f.

carriage ['kærɪdʒ] n (of train, horsedrawn) voiture f; Com transport m; **c. paid** port payé. ●**carriageway** n (of road) chaussée f.

carrier ['kærɪər] n Med porteur, -euse mf; Com entreprise f de transports; **c. (bag)** sac m (en plastique).

carrot ['kærət] n carotte f.

carry ['kærɪ] vt porter; (goods) transporter; (by wind) emporter; (sound) conduire; (motion) Pol faire passer, voter; (sell) stocker; (in calculation) Math retenir; **to c. sth too far** pousser qch trop loin ǁ vi (of sound) porter.

carry away *vt* emporter; **to be** *or* **get carried away** (*excited*) s'emballer ▌**to carry back** *vt* (*thing*) rapporter; (*person*) ramener ▌**to carry off** *vt* emporter; (*kidnap*) enlever; (*prize*) remporter; **to c. it off** réussir ▌**to carry on** *vt* continuer (*doing* à faire); (*conduct*) diriger, mener; (*sustain*) soutenir ▌*vi* continuer; (*behave*) *Pej* se conduire (mal); (*complain*) se plaindre; **to c. on with sth** continuer qch ▌**to carry out** *vt* (*plan, order, promise*) exécuter, réaliser; (*repair, reform*) effectuer; (*duty*) accomplir; (*meal*) *Am* emporter ▌**to carry through** *vt* (*plan etc*) mener à bonne fin.

carryall ['kærɪɔːl] *n* *Am* fourre-tout *m* *inv*. ● **carrycot** *n* (nacelle *f*) porte-bébé *m*.

cart [kɑːt] **1** *n* (*horse-drawn*) charrette *f*; (*in supermarket*) *Am* caddie® *m*; (*serving*) *Am* table *f* roulante. **2** *vt* (*goods, people*) transporter; **to c. (around)** *Fam* trimbal(l)er; **to c. away** emporter.

carton ['kɑːtən] *n* (*box*) carton *m*; (*of milk, fruit juice etc*) brique *f*; (*of cigarettes*) cartouche *f*; (*of cream*) pot *m*.

cartoon [kɑː'tuːn] *n* (*in newspaper*) dessin *m* (humoristique); (*film*) dessin *m* animé; (*strip*) c. bande *f* dessinée. ● **cartoonist** *n* dessinateur, -trice *mf* (humoristique).

cartridge ['kɑːtrɪdʒ] *n* (*of firearm, pen, camera, tape deck*) cartouche *f*; (*of record player*) cellule *f*.

carv/e [kɑːv] *vt* (*cut*) tailler (*out of* dans); (*initials etc*) graver; (*sculpt*) sculpter; **to c. (up)** (*meat*) découper; **to c. up** (*country*) dépecer, morceler. ● **—ing** *n* **wood c.** sculpture *f* sur bois.

cascade [kæs'keɪd] *vi* (*fall*) tomber; (*hang*) pendre.

case [keɪs] *n* **1** (*instance, in hospital*) cas *m*; *Jur* affaire *f*; *Phil* arguments *mpl*; **in any c.** en tout cas; **in c. it rains** pour le cas où il pleuvrait; **in c. of** en cas de; **(just) in c.** à tout hasard. **2** (*bag*) valise *f*; (*crate*) caisse *f*; (*for pen, glasses, camera, violin, cigarettes*) étui *m*; (*for* *jewels*) coffret *m*.

cash [kæʃ] *n* argent *m*; **to pay (in) c.** payer en espèces *or* en liquide; **to pay c. (down)** (*not on credit*) payer comptant; **c. price** prix *m* (au) comptant; **c. desk** caisse *f*; **c. machine** distributeur *m* de billets; **c. register** caisse *f* enregistreuse. ▌*vt* **to c. a cheque** *or* *Am* **check** (*of person*) encaisser un chèque; (*of bank*) payer un chèque; **to c. in on** *Fam* profiter de.

cashier ['kæʃɪər] *n* caissier, -ière *mf*.

cashew ['kæʃuː] *n* **c.** noix *f* de cajou *m*.

cashmere ['kæʃmɪər] *n* cachemire *m*.

casino [kə'siːnəʊ] *n* (*pl* **-os**) casino *m*.

casket ['kɑːskɪt] *n* (*box*) coffret *m*; (*coffin*) cercueil *m*.

casserole ['kæsərəʊl] *n* (*covered dish*) cocotte *f*; (*stew*) ragoût *m* en cocotte.

cassette [kə'set] *n* (*audio, video*) cassette *f*; *Phot* cartouche *f*; **c. player** lecteur *m* de cassettes; **c. recorder** magnétophone *m* à cassettes.

cast [kɑːst] **1** *n* (*actors*) acteurs *mpl*; (*list of actors*) distribution *f*; (*mould*) moulage *m*; (*for broken bone*) plâtre *m*. **2** *vt* (*pt & pp* **cast**) (*throw*) jeter; (*light, shadow*) projeter; (*glance*) jeter (**at** à); (*metal*) couler; (*role*) *Th* distribuer; **to c. doubt/a spell on** jeter le doute/un sort sur; **to c. one's mind back** se reporter en arrière; **to c. a vote** voter; **to c. aside** rejeter; **to c. off** (*chains etc*) se libérer de; **to c. off its skin** (*of animal*) muer. **3** *vi* **to c. off** (*of ship*) appareiller. **4** *n* **c. iron** fonte *f*. ● **c.-'iron** *a* (*pan etc*) en fonte; (*will*) *Fig* de fer; (*alibi*) *Fig* en béton.

castaway ['kɑːstəweɪ] *n* naufragé, -ée *mf*.

caster ['kɑːstər] *n* (*wheel*) roulette *f*; **c. sugar** sucre *m* en poudre.

castle ['kɑːs(ə)l] *n* château *m*; *Chess* tour *f*.

castoffs ['kɑːstɒfs] *npl* vieux vêtements *mpl*.

castor ['kɑːstər] *n* (*wheel*) roulette *f*; **c. oil** huile *f* de ricin; **c. sugar** sucre *m* en poudre.

castrate [kæ'streɪt] *vt* châtrer.

casual ['kæʒjʊəl] *a* (*remark*) fait en passant; (*stroll*) sans but; (*meeting*) fortuit; (*offhand*) désinvolte; (*worker*) temporaire; (*work*) irrégulier; **c. clothes** vêtements *mpl* sport; **a c. acquaintance** quelqu'un que l'on connaît un peu. ●**casually** *adv* (*informally*) avec désinvolture; (*to remark*) en passant.

casualty ['kæʒjʊəltɪ] *n* (*dead*) mort *m*, morte *f*; (*wounded*) blessé, -ée *mf*; (*accident victim*) accidenté, -ée *mf*; **casualties** morts et blessés *mpl*; **c. (department)** (*in hospital*) (service *m* des) urgences *fpl*.

cat [kæt] *n* chat *m*; (*female*) chatte *f*; **c. food** pâteé *n*.

catalogue ['kætəlɒg] (*Am* **catalog**) *n* catalogue *m* ǁ *vt* cataloguer.

catalyst ['kætəlɪst] *n Ch & Fig* catalyseur *m*.

catalytic [kætə'lɪtɪk] *a* **c. converter** *Aut* pot *m* catalytique.

catapult ['kætəpʌlt] *n* (*toy*) lance-pierres *m inv*.

cataract ['kætərækt] *n* (*eye condition*) cataracte *f*.

catarrh [kə'tɑːr] *n* gros rhume *m*.

catastrophe [kə'tæstrəfɪ] *n* catastrophe *f*. ●**cata'strophic** *a* catastrophique.

catch [kætʃ] *vt* (*pt & pp* **caught**) (*ball, thief, illness, train etc*) attraper; (*grab*) prendre, saisir; (*surprise*) (sur)prendre; (*understand*) saisir; (*attention*) attirer; (*on nail etc*) accrocher (**on** à); (*finger etc*) se prendre (**in** dans); **to c. sight of** apercevoir; **to c. fire** prendre feu; **to c. one's breath** (*rest*) reprendre haleine; **I didn't c. the train**/*etc* j'ai manqué le train/*etc*; **to c. s.o. doing** (sur)prendre qn à faire; **to c. s.o. out** prendre qn en défaut; **to c. s.o. up** rattraper qn.

ǁ *vi* (*of fire*) prendre; **her skirt (got) caught in the door** sa jupe s'est prise *or* coincée dans la porte; **to c. on** (*became popular*) prendre; (*understand*) saisir; **to c. up** se rattraper; **to**

c. up with s.o. rattraper qn.
ǁ *n* (*captured animal*) capture *f*, prise *f*; (*haul of fish*) pêche *f*; (*trick, snare*) piège *m*; (*on door*) loquet *m*. ●**catching** *a* contagieux.

catchy ['kætʃɪ] *a* (**-ier, -iest**) (*tune*) *Fam* facile à retenir.

category ['kætɪgərɪ] *n* catégorie *f*. ●**cate'gorical** *a* catégorique.

cater ['keɪtər] *vi* **to c. for** *or* **to** (*need, taste*) satisfaire; (*of book etc*) s'adresser à (*enfants, étudiants etc*). ●**—er** *n* traiteur *m*.

caterpillar ['kætəpɪlər] *n* chenille *f*.

cathedral [kə'θiːdrəl] *n* cathédrale *f*.

Catholic ['kæθlɪk] *a & n* catholique (*mf*). ●**Ca'tholicism** *n* catholicisme *m*.

cattle ['kæt(ə)l] *npl* bétail *m*, bestiaux *mpl*.

caucus ['kɔːkəs] *n Pol Am* comité *m* électoral.

caught [kɔːt] *pt & pp* of **catch**.

cauldron ['kɔːldrən] *n* chaudron *m*.

cauliflower ['kɒlɪflaʊər] *n* chou-fleur *m*.

cause [kɔːz] *n* (*origin, reason, ideal etc*) & *Jur* cause *f* ǁ *vt* causer; **to c. sth/s.o. to fall**/*etc* faire tomber/*etc* qch/qn.

caution ['kɔːʃ(ə)n] *n* (*care*) prudence *f*; (*warning*) avertissement *m* ǁ *vt* (*warn*) avertir; **to c. s.o. against sth** mettre qn en garde contre qch. ●**cautious** *a* prudent. ●**cautiously** *adv* prudemment.

cavalier [kævə'lɪər] *a* (*selfish*) cavalier.

cavalry ['kævəlrɪ] *n* cavalerie *f*.

cave [keɪv] **1** *n* caverne *f*, grotte *f*. **2** *vi* **to c. in** (*fall in*) s'effondrer. ●**caveman** *n* (*pl* **-men**) homme *m* des cavernes.

cavern ['kævən] *n* caverne *f*.

caviar(e) ['kævɪɑːr] *n* caviar *m*.

cavity ['kævɪtɪ] *n* cavité *f*.

CD [siː'diː] *n abbr* (*compact disc or Am disk*) CD *m*.

cease [siːs] *vti* cesser (**doing** de faire). ●**c.-fire** *n* cessez-le-feu *m inv*. ●**ceaseless** *a* incessant.

cedar ['siːdər] *n* (*tree, wood*) cèdre *m*.

ceiling ['si:lɪŋ] n (of room, Fig on wages etc) plafond m.

celebrat/e ['selɪbreɪt] vt (event) fêter; (mass) célébrer ‖ vi faire la fête; **we should c. (that)!** il faut fêter ça! il faut fêter ça! il faut fêter ça! a célèbre. ●**celebration** [-'breɪʃ(ə)n] n (event) fête f; **the celebrations** les festivités fpl.

celebrity [sə'lebrətɪ] n (person) célébrité f.

celery ['selərɪ] n céleri m.

cell [sel] n cellule f; El élément m.

cellar ['selər] n cave f.

cello ['tʃeləʊ] n (pl -os) violoncelle m. ●**cellist** n violoncelliste m.

cellophane® ['seləfeɪn] n cellophane® f.

cellular ['seljʊlər] a **c. blanket** couverture f en cellular; **c. phone** téléphone m cellulaire.

Celsius ['selsɪəs] a Celsius inv.

Celt [kelt] n Celte mf. ●**Celtic** a celtique, celte.

cement [sɪ'ment] n ciment m; **c. mixer** bétonnière f ‖ vt cimenter.

cemetery ['semətrɪ, Am 'semətərɪ] n cimetière m.

censor ['sensər] vt (film etc) censurer. ●**censorship** n censure f.

cent [sent] n (coin) cent m.

centenary [sen'ti:nərɪ, Am sen'tenərɪ] n centenaire m.

centigrade ['sentɪɡreɪd] a centigrade.

centimetre ['sentɪmi:tər] n centimètre m.

centipede ['sentɪpi:d] n mille-pattes m inv.

centre ['sentər] (Am **center**) n centre m; **c. forward** Fb avant-centre m ‖ vt centrer; Phot cadrer ‖ vi **to c. on** (of question) tourner autour de. ●**central** a central. ●**centralize** vt centraliser.

century ['sentʃərɪ] n siècle m.

ceramic [sə'ræmɪk] a (tile etc) de céramique.

cereal ['sɪərɪəl] n céréale f; (breakfast) **c.** céréales fpl (pour petit déjeuner).

ceremony ['serɪmənɪ] n (event) cérémonie f; **to stand on c.** faire des cérémonies or des façons.

certain ['sɜːtən] a (sure, particular) cer-

tain; **c. people** certaines personnes fpl; **she's c. to come** c'est certain qu'elle viendra; **I'm not c. what to do** je ne sais pas très bien ce qu'il faut faire; **to be c. of sth/that** être certain de qch/que; **for c. (to say, know)** avec certitude; **to make c. of (fact)** s'assurer de; (seat etc) s'assurer. ●**—ly** adv certainement; (yes) bien sûr; (without fail) sans faute. ●**certainty** n certitude f.

certificate [sə'tɪfɪkɪt] n certificat m; Univ diplôme m.

certify ['sɜːtɪfaɪ] vt (document etc) certifier; **certified public accountant** Am expert-comptable m.

chaffinch ['tʃæfɪntʃ] n (bird) pinson m.

chain [tʃeɪn] n (of rings, mountains) chaîne f; (of ideas, events) enchaînement m, suite f; (of lavatory) chasse f d'eau; **c. reaction** réaction f en chaîne; **to be a c.-smoker** fumer cigarette sur cigarette; **c. saw** tronçonneuse f; **c. store** magasin m à succursales multiples ‖ vt **to c. (down)** enchaîner; **to c. (up)** (dog) mettre à l'attache.

chair [tʃeər] n chaise f; (armchair) fauteuil m; Univ chaire f; **c. lift** télésiège m ‖ vt (meeting) présider. ●**chairman** n (pl -men) président, -ente mf. ●**chairmanship** n présidence f.

chalet ['ʃæleɪ] n chalet m.

chalk [tʃɔːk] n craie f ‖ vt écrire à la craie; **to c. up** (success) Fig remporter. ●**chalky** a (-ier, -iest) crayeux.

challeng/e ['tʃælɪndʒ] n défi m; (task) challenge m, gageure f ‖ vt défier (**s.o. to do** qn de faire); (dispute) contester; **to c. s.o. to a game** inviter qn à jouer. ●**—ing** a (job) exigeant; (book) stimulant. ●**challenger** n Sp challenger m.

chamber ['tʃeɪmbər] n (room, of gun etc) chambre f; **c. of commerce** chambre f de commerce ‖ a (music, orchestra) de chambre; **c. pot** pot m de chambre. ●**chambermaid** n femme f de chambre.

chamois ['ʃæmɪ] n **c. (leather)** peau f de chamois.

champagne [ʃæm'peɪn] n champagne m.

champion ['tʃæmpɪən] n champion, -onne mf; **c. skier** champion, -onne de ski ▮ vt (support) se faire le champion de. ●**championship** n championnat m.

chance [tʃɑːns] n (luck) hasard m; (possibility) chances fpl; (opportunity) occasion f; (risk) risque m; **by c.** par hasard; **by any c.** (possibly) par hasard; **to take a c.** tenter le coup.
▮ a (remark) fait au hasard; (meeting) fortuit; (occurrence) accidentel.
▮ vt **to c. doing** prendre le risque de faire; **to c. it** risquer le coup.

chancellor ['tʃɑːnsələr] n Pol etc chancelier m.

chandelier [ʃændəˈlɪər] n lustre m.

change [tʃeɪndʒ] n changement m; (money) monnaie f; **for a c.** pour changer; **it makes a c. from** ça change de; **a c. of clothes** des vêtements de rechange.
▮ vt (modify) changer; (exchange) échanger (for contre); (money, wheel) changer; (transform) transformer (qn, qch) (into en); **to c. trains/one's skirt/etc** changer de train/de jupe/etc; **to c. gear/the subject** changer de vitesse/de sujet.
▮ vi (alter) changer; (change clothes) se changer; **to c. into** se changer en; **to c. over** passer (from de, to à); **changing room** vestiaire m. ●**changeable** a (weather, mood etc) changeant. ●**change-over** n passage m (from de, to à).

channel ['tʃæn(ə)l] n TV chaîne f, canal m; (for irrigation) rigole f; (for boats) chenal m; (groove) rainure f; (of inquiry etc) voie f; **to go through the usual channels** passer par la voie normale; **the C.** Geog la Manche; **the C. Islands** les îles anglo-normandes ▮ vt (-ll-, Am -l-) (energies, crowd etc) canaliser (into vers).

chant [tʃɑːnt] vt (slogan) scander ▮ vi (of demonstrators) scander des slogans.

chaos ['keɪɒs] n chaos m. ●**cha'otic** a (room) sens dessus dessous; (situation) chaotique.

chap [tʃæp] 1 n (fellow) Fam type m; **old c.!** mon vieux! 2 n (on skin) gerçure f.

chapel [tʃæp(ə)l] n chapelle f.

chaperon(e) ['ʃæpərəʊn] n chaperon m.

chaplain ['tʃæplɪn] n aumônier m.

chapped [tʃæpt] a (hand, lip etc) gercé.

chapter ['tʃæptər] n chapitre m.

char [tʃɑːr] 1 vt (-rr-) carboniser; (scorch) brûler légèrement. 2 n (cleaning woman) Fam femme f de ménage.

character ['kærɪktər] n (of person, place etc) & Typ caractère m; (in book, film) personnage m; (strange person) numéro m. ●**characte'ristic** a & n caractéristique (f).

charade [ʃəˈrɑːd, Am ʃəˈreɪd] n (game) charade f (mimée); (travesty) parodie f, comédie f.

charcoal ['tʃɑːkəʊl] n charbon m (de bois); (crayon) fusain m, charbon m.

charge[1] [tʃɑːdʒ] n (cost) prix m; pl (expenses) frais mpl; **there's a c. (for it)** c'est payant; **to make a c. for sth** faire payer qch; **free of c.** gratuit; **extra c.** supplément m ▮ vt (amount) demander (for pour); **to c. s.o.** Com faire payer qn; **to c. sth to s.o.** mettre qch sur le compte de qn.

charge[2] [tʃɑːdʒ] n (in battle) charge f; Jur accusation f; (responsibility) charge f; (care) garde f; **to take c. of** prendre en charge; **to be in c. of** (child) avoir la garde de; (office) être responsable de; **the person in c.** le or la responsable; **who's in c. here?** qui commande ici? ▮ vt (battery, soldiers) charger; Jur accuser (with de) ▮ vi (rush) se précipiter; **c.!** Mil chargez! ●**charger** n (for battery) chargeur m.

chariot ['tʃærɪət] n (Roman etc) char m.

charity ['tʃærɪtɪ] n (kindness, alms) charité f; (society) œuvre f charitable; **to give to c.** faire la charité.

charm [tʃɑːm] n (attractiveness, spell) charme m; (trinket) breloque f ▮ vt charmer. ●**—ing** a charmant.

chart [tʃɑːt] n (map) carte f; (table)

tableau *m*; **(pop) charts** hit-parade *m* ▌ *vt* (*route*) porter sur la carte.

charter ['tʃɑːtər] *n* (*aircraft*) charter *m*; **c. flight** (vol *m*) charter *m* ▌ *vt* (*aircraft etc*) affréter. ●**chartered accountant** *n* expert-comptable *m*.

charwoman ['tʃɑːwumən] *n* (*pl* -**women**) femme *f* de ménage.

chase [tʃeɪs] *n* poursuite *f*, chasse *f* ▌ *vt* poursuivre; **to c. s.o. away** *or* **off** chasser qn ▌ *vi* **to c. after s.o./sth** courir après qn/qch.

chasm ['kæzəm] *n* abîme *m*, gouffre *m*.

chassis ['ʃæsɪ, *Am* 'tʃæsɪ] *n* Aut châssis *m*.

chaste [tʃeɪst] *a* chaste.

chat [tʃæt] *n* petite conversation *f*; **to have a c.** bavarder ▌ *vi* (-**tt**-) causer, bavarder (**with** avec) ▌ *vt* **to c. s.o. up** Fam baratiner qn.

chatty ['tʃætɪ] *a* (-**ier**, -**iest**) (*person*) bavard; (*style*) familier.

chatter ['tʃætər] *vi* bavarder; (*of birds*) jacasser; **his teeth are chattering** il claque des dents ▌ *n* bavardage *m*; jacassement *m*. ●**chatterbox** *n* bavard, -arde *mf*.

chauffeur ['ʃəufər] *n* chauffeur *m* (de maître).

chauvinist ['ʃəuvɪnɪst] *n* (male) **c.** Pej macho *m*, phallocrate *m*.

cheap [tʃiːp] *a* (-**er**, -**est**) bon marché *inv*, pas cher; (*rate*, *fare*) réduit; (*worthless*) sans valeur; (*mean*, *petty*) mesquin; **cheaper** moins cher, meilleur marché ▌ *adv* (*to buy*) (à) bon marché. ●**cheaply** *adv* (à) bon marché.

cheat [tʃiːt] *vt* (*deceive*) tromper; (*defraud*) frauder; **to c. s.o. out of sth** escroquer qch à qn ▌ *vi* (*at games etc*) tricher ▌ *n* tricheur, -euse *mf*; (*crook*) escroc *m*. ●—**ing** *n* (*at games etc*) tricherie *f*. ●**cheater** *n* Am = **cheat**.

check[1] [tʃek] *a* (*dress etc*) à carreaux ▌ *n* (*pattern*) carreaux *mpl*. ●**checked** *a* à carreaux.

check[2] [tʃek] *vt* (*examine*) vérifier; (*inspect*) contrôler; (*mark off*, *tick*) cocher;

pointer; (*stop*) arrêter, enrayer; (*restrain*) contenir, maîtriser; (*baggage*) Am mettre à la consigne.

▌ *vi* vérifier; **to c. on sth** vérifier qch.

▌ *n* vérification *f*; (*inspection*) contrôle *m*; (*halt*) arrêt *m*; Chess échec *m*; (*curb*) frein *m*; (*tick*) Am = croix *f*; (*receipt*) Am reçu *m*; (*bill in restaurant etc*) Am addition *f*; (*cheque*) Am chèque *m*; **to keep a c. on** contrôler; **to put a c. on** mettre un frein à. ●**checkbook** *n* Am carnet *m* de chèques. ●**checking account** *n* Am compte *m* courant. ●**checkmate** *n* Chess échec et mat *m*. ●**checkroom** *n* Am vestiaire *m*; (*left-luggage office*) Am consigne *f*.

checkered ['tʃekəd] *a* Am = **chequered**.

checkers ['tʃekəz] *npl* Am jeu *m* de dames. ●**checkerboard** *n* Am damier *m*.

check in *vi* (*luggage*) enregistrer ▌ *vi* (*at hotel*) signer le registre; (*arrive*) arriver; (*at airport*) se présenter (à l'enregistrement). ●**check-in** *n* (*at airport*) enregistrement *m* (des bagages) ▌**to check off** *vt* (*names on list etc*) cocher ▌**to check out** *vi* (*confirm*) confirmer ▌ *vi* (*at hotel*) régler sa note. ●**checkout** *n* (*in supermarket*) caisse *f*. ▌**to check up** *vi* vérifier. ●**checkup** *n* Med bilan *m* de santé.

cheddar ['tʃedər] *n* (*cheese*) cheddar *m*.

cheek [tʃiːk] *n* joue *f*; (*impudence*) Fig culot *m*. ●**cheeky** *a* (-**ier**, -**iest**) (*person*, *reply etc*) insolent.

cheep [tʃiːp] *vi* (*of bird*) piauler.

cheer [tʃɪər] *n* **cheers** (*shouts*) acclamations *fpl*; **cheers!** Fam à votre santé! ▌ *vt* (*applaud*) acclamer; **to c. up** donner du courage à; (*amuse*) égayer ▌ *vi* applaudir; **to c. up** prendre courage; s'égayer; **c. up!** (du) courage! ●—**ing** *n* (*shouts*) acclamations *fpl*.

cheerful ['tʃɪəfəl] *a* gai.

cheerio! [tʃɪərɪ'əu] *int* salut!, au revoir!

cheese [tʃiːz] *n* fromage *m*. ●**cheeseburger** *n* cheeseburger *m*. ●**cheesecake** *n* tarte *f* au fromage blanc.

cheetah ['tʃiːtə] *n* guépard *m*.

chef [ʃef] *n* (*cook*) chef *m*.

chemical ['kemɪkəl] a chimique ∥n produit m chimique.

chemist ['kemɪst] n (pharmacist) pharmacien, -ienne mf; (scientist) chimiste mf; **c.'s shop** pharmacie f. ● **chemistry** n chimie f.

cheque [tʃek] n chèque m. ● **chequebook** n carnet m de chèques.

chequered ['tʃekəd] a (pattern) à carreaux.

cherish ['tʃerɪʃ] vt (hope) nourrir; (person) chérir.

cherry ['tʃerɪ] n cerise f; **c. brandy** cherry m.

chess [tʃes] n échecs mpl. ● **chessboard** n échiquier m.

chest [tʃest] n **1** Anat poitrine f. **2** (box) coffre m; **c. of drawers** commode f.

chestnut ['tʃesnʌt] n châtaigne f ∥a (hair) châtain; **c. tree** châtaignier m.

chew [tʃuː] vt **to c. (up)** mâcher ∥vi mastiquer; **chewing gum** chewing-gum m.

chick [tʃɪk] n poussin m. ● **chicken 1** n poulet m. **2** a (cowardly) Fam froussard ∥vi **to c. out** Fam se dégonfler. ● **chickenpox** n varicelle f.

chickpea ['tʃɪkpiː] n pois m chiche.

chicory ['tʃɪkərɪ] n (for salad) endive f; (in coffee etc) chicorée f.

chide [tʃaɪd] vt gronder.

chief [tʃiːf] n chef m; **in c.** (commander, editor) en chef ∥a (main, highest in rank) principal. ● **—ly** adv principalement, surtout.

chilblain ['tʃɪlbleɪn] n engelure f.

child, pl **children** [tʃaɪld, 'tʃɪldrən] n enfant mf; **c. care** (for working parents) crèches fpl et garderies fpl; **c. minder** nourrice f, assistante f maternelle. ● **childbearing** n (act) accouchement m. ● **childbirth** n accouchement m. ● **childhood** n enfance f. ● **childish** a puéril, enfantin. ● **childlike** a naïf, innocent.

Chile ['tʃɪlɪ] n Chili m.

chill [tʃɪl] n froid m; (coldness in feelings) froideur f; (illness) refroidissement m;

to catch a c. prendre froid ∥vt (wine, melon) faire rafraîchir; (meat) réfrigérer; **to c. s.o.** (with cold etc) faire frissonner qn (with de); **to be chilled to the bone** être transi; **chilled wine** vin m frais. ● **chilly** a (-ier, -iest) froid; **it's c.** il fait (un peu) froid.

chilli ['tʃɪlɪ] n (pl -ies) piment m (de Cayenne).

chime [tʃaɪm] vi (of bell) carillonner; (of clock) sonner ∥n carillon m; sonnerie f.

chimney ['tʃɪmnɪ] n cheminée f. ● **chimneypot** n tuyau m de cheminée. ● **chimneysweep** n ramoneur m.

chimpanzee [tʃɪmpæn'ziː] n chimpanzé m.

chin [tʃɪn] n menton m.

china ['tʃaɪnə] n inv porcelaine f ∥a en porcelaine.

China ['tʃaɪnə] n Chine f. ● **Chi'nese** n chinois ∥n inv (person) Chinois, -oise mf; (language) chinois m; (meal) Fam repas m chinois.

chink [tʃɪŋk] n (slit) fente f.

chip [tʃɪp] vt (-pp-) (cup, blade) ébrécher; (paint) écailler ∥vi **to c. in** Fam contribuer ∥n (splinter) éclat m; (break) ébréchure f; (microchip) puce f; (counter) jeton m; pl (French fries) frites fpl; (crisps) Am chips fpl. ● **chipboard** n (bois m) aggloméré m.

chiropodist [kɪ'rɒpədɪst] n pédicure mf.

chirp [tʃɜːp] vi (of bird) pépier.

chirpy ['tʃɜːpɪ] a (-ier, -iest) gai, plein d'entrain.

chisel ['tʃɪz(ə)l] n ciseau m ∥vt (-ll-, Am -l-) ciseler.

chitchat ['tʃɪttʃæt] n bavardage m.

chivalrous ['ʃɪvəlrəs] a (man) galant.

chives [tʃaɪvz] npl ciboulette f.

chlorine ['klɔːriːn] n chlore m. ● **chlorinated** a **c. water** eau f chlorée.

choc-ice ['tʃɒkaɪs] n (ice cream) esquimau m.

chock-a-block [tʃɒkə'blɒk] or **chock'full** a Fam archiplein.

chocolate ['tʃɒklɪt] n chocolat m; **milk c.** chocolat au lait; **plain** or Am **bittersweet**

c. chocolat à croquer ▮*a* (*cake*) au chocolat; (*egg*) en chocolat; (*colour*) chocolat *inv*.

choice [tʃɔɪs] *n* choix *m*; **from c.** de son propre choix ▮*a* (*goods*) de choix.

choir ['kwaɪər] *n* chœur *m*. ●**choirboy** *n* jeune choriste *m*.

choke [tʃəʊk] **1** *vt* (*person*) étrangler, étouffer; (*clog*) boucher (*tuyau*); **to c. back** (*sobs etc*) étouffer ▮*vi* s'étrangler, étouffer; **to c. on** (*fish bone etc*) s'étrangler avec. **2** *n Aut* starter *m*.

cholera ['kɒlərə] *n* choléra *m*.

cholesterol [kə'lestərɒl] *n* cholestérol *m*.

choose [tʃuːz] *vt* (*pt* **chose**, *pp* **chosen**) choisir; **to c. to do** (*make a firm choice*) choisir de faire; (*decide*) juger bon de faire ▮*vi* choisir; **as I/you c.** comme il me/vous plaît. ●**choos(e)y** *a* (*-sier, -siest*) difficile (**about** sur).

chop [tʃɒp] **1** *n* (*of lamb, pork*) côtelette *f*; **to get the c.** *Sl* être flanqué à la porte. **2** *n* (*-pp-*) couper (à la hache); (*food*) hacher; **to c. down** (*tree*) abattre; **to c. off** (*branch, finger*) couper; **to c. up** couper en morceaux. ●**chopper** *n* hachoir *m*; (*helicopter*) *Sl* hélico *m*.

choppy ['tʃɒpɪ] *a* (*sea*) agité.

chopsticks ['tʃɒpstɪks] *npl Culin* baguettes *fpl* (*pour manger*).

chord [kɔːd] *n Mus* accord *m*.

chore [tʃɔːr] *n* travail *m* (*routinier*) (*unpleasant*) corvée *f*; *pl* (*household*) (travaux *mpl* du) ménage *m*.

choreographer [kɒrɪ'ɒɡrəfər] *n* chorégraphe *mf*.

chorus ['kɔːrəs] *n* (*of song*) refrain *m*; (*singers*) chœur *m*.

chose, chosen [tʃəʊz, 'tʃəʊz(ə)n] *pt* & *pp* of **choose**.

Christ [kraɪst] *n* Christ *m*. ●**Christian** ['krɪstʃən] *a* & *n* chrétien, -ienne (*mf*); **C. name** prénom *m*.

christen ['krɪs(ə)n] *vt* (*person, ship*) baptiser. ●**—ing** *n* baptême *m*.

Christmas ['krɪsməs] *n* Noël *m*; **at C. (time)** à (la) Noël; **Merry** *or* **Happy C.** Joyeux Noël; **Father C.** le père Noël ▮*a*

(*tree, card, day, party etc*) de Noël; **C. box** étrennes *fpl*; **C. Eve** la veille de Noël.

chrome [krəʊm] *or* **chromium** *n* chrome *m*.

chronic ['krɒnɪk] *a* (*disease, state etc*) chronique.

chronicle ['krɒnɪk(ə)l] *n* chronique *f*.

chronological [krɒnə'lɒdʒɪk(ə)l] *a* chronologique.

chrysanthemum [krɪ'sænθəməm] *n* chrysanthème *m*.

chubby ['tʃʌbɪ] *a* (*-ier, -iest*) (*person, hands*) potelé; (*cheeks*) rebondi.

chuck [tʃʌk] *vt* (*throw*) *Fam* jeter, lancer; **to c. away** (*old clothes etc*) *Fam* balancer; **to c. out** (*old clothes, person etc*) *Fam* balancer; **to c. in** *or* **up** (*job*) *Fam* laisser tomber.

chuckle ['tʃʌk(ə)l] *vi* glousser, rire ▮*n* gloussement *m*.

chug [tʃʌɡ] *vi* (*-gg-*) **to c. along** (*of vehicle*) avancer lentement (*en faisant teuf-teuf*).

chum [tʃʌm] *n Fam* copain *m*. ●**chummy** *a* (*-ier, -iest*) *Fam* amical; **c. with** copain avec.

chunk [tʃʌŋk] *n* (*gros*) morceau *m*.

church [tʃɜːtʃ] *n* église *f*; **in c.** à l'église. ●**churchgoer** *n* pratiquant, -ante *mf*. ●**churchyard** *n* cimetière *m*.

churlish ['tʃɜːlɪʃ] *a* (*rude*) grossier; (*bad-tempered*) hargneux.

chute [ʃuːt] *n* (*in pool, playground*) toboggan *m*; (*for rubbish, Am garbage*) vide-ordures *m inv*.

chutney ['tʃʌtnɪ] *n* condiment *m* épicé (à base de fruits).

CID [siːaɪ'diː] *abbr* (*Criminal Investigation Department*) *Br* = PJ *f*.

cider ['saɪdər] *n* cidre *m*.

cigar [sɪ'ɡɑːr] *n* cigare *m*.

cigarette [sɪɡə'ret] *n* cigarette *f*; **c. end** mégot *m*; **c. lighter** briquet *m*.

cinch [sɪntʃ] *n* **it's a c.** *Fam* (*easy*) c'est facile; (*sure*) c'est (sûr et) certain.

Cinderella [sɪndə'relə] *n* Cendrillon *f*.

cine-camera ['sɪnɪkæmrə] *n* caméra *f*.

cinema ['sɪnəmə] n cinéma m. ●**cine-magoer** n cinéphile mf.

cinnamon ['sɪnəmən] n Bot Culin cannelle f.

circle ['sɜːk(ə)l] n (shape, group, range etc) cercle m; (around eyes) cerne m; Th balcon m; pl (political etc) milieux mpl ▮ vt (move round) faire le tour de; (word) encadrer ▮ vi (of aircraft, bird) décrire des cercles.

circuit ['sɜːkɪt] n (electrical path, in sport etc) circuit m; **c. breaker** El disjoncteur m.

circular ['sɜːkjʊlər] a circulaire ▮ n (letter) circulaire f; (advertisement) prospectus m.

circulate ['sɜːkjʊleɪt] vi circuler ▮ vt faire circuler. ●**circulation** [-'leɪʃ(ə)n] n circulation f; (of newspaper etc) tirage m.

circumcised ['sɜːkəmsaɪzd] a circoncis.

circumference [sɜː'kʌmfərəns] n circonférence f.

circumstance ['sɜːkəmstæns] n circonstance f; pl Com situation f financière; **in** or **under no circumstances** en aucun cas.

circus ['sɜːkəs] n cirque m.

CIS abbr (Commonwealth of Independent States) CEI f.

cistern ['sɪstən] n (for lavatory) réservoir m (de la chasse d'eau).

citadel ['sɪtəd(ə)l] n citadelle f.

citizen ['sɪtɪz(ə)n] n citoyen, -enne mf; (of town) habitant, -ante mf; **Citizens' Band** (Radio) la CB. ●**citizenship** n citoyenneté f.

citrus ['sɪtrəs] a **c. fruit(s)** agrumes mpl.

city ['sɪtɪ] n (grande) ville f, cité f; **c. centre** centre-ville m; **c. hall** Am hôtel m de ville.

civic ['sɪvɪk] a (duty) civique; (centre) administratif; (authorities) municipal.

civil ['sɪv(ə)l] a **1** (rights, war, marriage etc) civil; **c. servant** fonctionnaire mf; **c. service** fonction f publique. **2** (polite) poli.

civilian [sɪ'vɪljən] a & n civil, -ile (mf).

civilize ['sɪvɪlaɪz] vt civiliser. ●**civiliza-tion** [-'zeɪʃ(ə)n] n civilisation f.

claim [kleɪm] vt (one's due etc) réclamer, revendiquer; (benefit, payment etc) demander à bénéficier de; **to c. that** (assert) prétendre que ▮ n (demand) revendication f; (statement) affirmation f; (complaint) réclamation f; (right) droit m (**to** à); (insurance) c. demande f d'indemnité. ●**claimant** n demandeur, -euse mf.

clam [klæm] n (shellfish) palourde f.

clamber ['klæmbər] vi grimper; **to c. up the stairs** grimper l'escalier.

clamour ['klæmər] (Am clamor) n clameur f ▮ vi **to c. for** demander à grands cris.

clamp [klæmp] n (clip-like) pince f; (large, iron) crampon m; (wheel) c. Aut sabot m (de Denver) ▮ vt serrer; (car) mettre un sabot à ▮ vi **to c. down** sévir (**on** contre). ●**clampdown** n coup m d'arrêt, restriction f (**on** à).

clan [klæn] n clan m.

clang [klæŋ] n son m métallique. ●**clanger** n Sl gaffe f; **to drop a c.** faire une gaffe.

clap [klæp] **1** vti (-pp-) (applaud) applaudir; **to c.** (one's hands) battre des mains. **2** vt (-pp-) (put) Fam fourrer. ●**clapped-'out** a (car, person) Fam HS. ●**clapping** n applaudissements mpl.

claret ['klærət] n (wine) bordeaux m rouge.

clarify ['klærɪfaɪ] vt clarifier. ●**clarifi-cation** [-'ɪkeɪʃ(ə)n] n clarification f.

clarinet [klærɪ'net] n clarinette f.

clarity ['klærətɪ] n (of expression etc) clarté f; (of sound) pureté f.

clash [klæʃ] vi (of plates, pans) s'entre-choquer; (of interests, armies) se heurter; (of colours) jurer (**with** avec); (of people) se bagarrer; (coincide) tomber en même temps (**with** que) ▮ n (noise) choc m, heurt m; (of interests) conflit m.

clasp [klɑːsp] vt (hold) serrer; **to c. one's hands** joindre les mains ▮ n (fastener) fermoir m; (of belt) boucle f.

class [klɑːs] *n* classe *f*; (*lesson*) cours *m*; (*university grade*) mention *f*; **the c. of 1993** *Am* la promotion de 1993 ∥ *vt* classer. ● **classmate** *n* camarade *mf* de classe. ● **classroom** *n* (salle *f* de) classe *f*.

classic [ˈklæsɪk] *a* classique ∥ *n* (*writer, work etc*) classique *m*; **to study classics** étudier les humanités *fpl*. ● **classical** *a* classique.

classify [ˈklæsɪfaɪ] *vt* classer, classifier. ● **classification** [-ˈkeɪʃ(ə)n] *n* classification *f*.

classy [ˈklɑːsɪ] *a* (**-ier, -iest**) *Fam* chic *inv*.

clatter [ˈklætər] *n* bruit *m*, fracas *m*.

clause [klɔːz] *n* (*in sentence*) proposition *f*; (*in document*) *Jur* clause *f*.

claw [klɔː] *n* (*of lobster*) pince *f*; (*of cat, sparrow etc*) griffe *f*; (*of eagle*) serre *f* ∥ *vt* (*scratch*) griffer.

clay [kleɪ] *n* argile *f*.

clean [kliːn] *a* (**-er, -est**) propre; (*clear-cut*) net (*f* nette); (*joke*) pour toutes les oreilles; **c. living** vie *f* saine.
∥ *adv* (*utterly*) complètement, carrément; (*to break, cut*) net.
∥ *n* **to give sth a c.** nettoyer qch.
∥ *vt* nettoyer; (*wash*) laver; (*wipe*) essuyer; **to c. one's teeth** se brosser *or* se laver les dents; **to c. out** (*room etc*) nettoyer; (*empty*) vider; **to c. up** (*room etc*) nettoyer; (*reform*) *Fig* épurer.
∥ *vi* **to c. (up)** faire le nettoyage.
● **cleaning** *n* nettoyage *m*; (*housework*) ménage *m*; **c. woman** femme *f* de ménage. ● **cleaner** *n* femme *f* de ménage; (**dry**) **c.** teinturier, -ière *mf*. ● **cleanly** *adv* (*to break, cut*) net.

clean-cut [kliːnˈkʌt] *a* net (*f* nette). ● **clean-'shaven** *a* (*with no beard etc*) glabre. ● **clean-up** *n* *Fig* purge *f*, coup *m* de balai.

cleanliness [ˈklenlɪnɪs] *n* propreté *f*.

cleans/e [klenz] *vt* nettoyer; *Fig* purifier; **cleansing cream** crème *f* démaquillante. ● **—er** *n* (*for skin*) démaquillant *m*.

clear [klɪər] *a* (**-er, -est**) (*sky, water,*

sound, thought etc) clair; (*glass*) transparent; (*outline, photo*) net (*f* nette), clair; (*profit, majority*) net (*f* nette); (*mind*) lucide; (*road*) libre, dégagé; (*obvious*) évident, clair (**that** que); (*certain*) certain; (*complete*) entier; **to be c. of** (*free of*) être libre de; (*out of*) être hors de; **to make oneself c.** se faire comprendre; **c. conscience** conscience *f* nette.
∥ *adv* **to keep** *or* **steer c. of** se tenir à l'écart de; **to get c. of** (*away from*) s'éloigner de.
∥ *vt* (*path, table*) débarrasser, dégager; (*land*) défricher; (*fence*) franchir; (*obstacle*) éviter; (*person*) *Jur* disculper; (*cheque, Am check*) faire passer (sur un compte); (*debts*) liquider; (*through customs*) dédouaner; (*for security*) autoriser; **to c. one's throat** s'éclaircir la gorge.
∥ *vi* **to c. (up)** (*of weather*) s'éclaircir; (*of fog*) se dissiper. ● **clearing** *n* (*in woods*) clairière *f*. ● **clearly** *adv* clairement; (*obviously*) évidemment.

clearance [ˈklɪərəns] *n* (*sale*) soldes *mpl*; (*space*) dégagement *m*; (*permission*) autorisation *f*.

clear away [klɪərəˈweɪ] *vt* (*remove*) enlever ∥ *vi* (*of fog*) se dissiper ∥ **to c. off** *vi* (*leave*) *Fam* filer ∥ *vt* (*table*) débarrasser ∥ **to c. out** *vt* (*empty*) vider; (*clean*) nettoyer; (*remove*) enlever ∥ **to c. up** *vi* (*mystery etc*) éclaircir ∥ *vti* (*tidy*) ranger.

clear-cut [klɪərˈkʌt] *a* net (*f* nette). ● **clear-'headed** *a* lucide.

clearway [ˈklɪəweɪ] *n* route *f* à stationnement interdit.

clement [ˈklemənt] *a* clément.

clementine [ˈkleməntaɪn] *n* clémentine *f*.

clench [klentʃ] *vt* (*fist, teeth*) serrer.

clergyman [ˈklɜːdʒɪmən] *n* (*pl* **-men**) ecclésiastique *m*.

clerical [ˈklerɪk(ə)l] *a* (*job*) d'employé; (*work*) de bureau; (*error*) d'écriture.

clerk [klɑːk, *Am* klɜːk] *n* employé, -ée *mf* (de bureau); (*in store*) *Am* vendeur, -euse *mf*; **solicitor's c.** *Br* clerc *m* de notaire.

clever ['klevər] a (-er, -est) intelligent; (smart, shrewd) astucieux; (skilful) habile (at sth à qch, at doing à faire); (ingenious) (machine, plan) ingénieux; (gifted) doué; c. at (English etc) fort en; c. with one's hands habile de ses mains.

cliché ['kli:ʃeɪ] n (idea) cliché m.

click [klɪk] n déclic m, bruit m sec ▮ vi (of machine etc) faire un déclic; it suddenly clicked (I realized) Fam j'ai compris tout à coup.

client ['klaɪənt] n client, -ente mf. • clientele [kli:ən'tel] n clientèle f.

cliff [klɪf] n falaise f.

climate ['klaɪmɪt] n Met & Fig climat m.

climax ['klaɪmæks] n point m culminant; (sexual) orgasme m.

climb [klaɪm] vt to c. (up) (steps) monter; (hill, mountain) gravir, faire l'ascension de; (tree, ladder) monter à; to c. (over) (wall) escalader; to c. down (from) (wall, tree, hill) descendre de.
▮ vi (of plant) grimper; to c. (up) (up steps etc) monter; (up hill etc) gravir; to c. down descendre.
▮ n montée f. •—ing n (mountain) c. alpinisme m. • climber n (mountaineer) alpiniste mf.

clinch [klɪntʃ] vt (deal) conclure.

cling [klɪŋ] vi (pt & pp clung) se cramponner (to à); (stick) adhérer (to à). • clingfilm n film m plastique.

clinic ['klɪnɪk] n (private) clinique f; (health centre) centre m médical.

clink [klɪŋk] vi tinter ▮ vt faire tinter ▮ n tintement m.

clip [klɪp] 1 vt (-pp-) (cut) couper; (hedge) tailler; (ticket) poinçonner. 2 n (for paper) trombone m; (fastener) attache f; (of brooch, of cyclist, for hair) pince f ▮ vt (-pp-) to c. (on) (attach) attacher. 3 n (of film) extrait m. • clipping n (from newspaper) Am: coupure f. • clippers npl (for hair) tondeuse f; (for finger nails) coupe-ongles m inv.

cloak [kləʊk] n (grande) cape f. • cloakroom n vestiaire m; (lavatory)

toilettes fpl.

clobber ['klɒbər] vt (hit) Sl tabasser.

clock [klɒk] n (large) horloge f; (small) pendule f; Aut compteur m; (alarm) c. réveil m; a race against the c. une course contre la montre; round the c. vingt-quatre heures sur vingt-quatre; c. tower clocher m.
▮ vt Sp chronométrer; to c. up (miles) (in car) Fam faire.
▮ vi to c. in or out (of worker) pointer. • clockwise adv dans le sens des aiguilles d'une montre. • clockwork a mécanique ▮ n to go like c. aller or marcher comme sur des roulettes.

clog [klɒg] 1 n (shoe) sabot m. 2 vt (-gg-) to c. (up) (obstruct) boucher.

cloister ['klɔɪstər] n cloître m.

close[1] [kləʊs] a (-er, -est) (place, relative etc) proche; (collaboration, resemblance, connection) étroit; (friend) intime; (contest) serré; (atmosphere) Met lourd; to have a c. shave or call l'échapper belle.
▮ adv c. (by), c. at hand (tout) près; c. to près de; c. behind juste derrière; c. on (almost) Fam pas loin de; we stood c. together nous étions debout serrés les uns contre les autres; to follow c. suivre de près. • c.-'cropped a (hair) (coupé) ras. • c.-'knit (group etc) a très uni. • c.-up n gros plan m.

close[2] [kləʊz] n (end) fin f; to bring sth to a c. mettre fin a qch; to draw to a c. tirer à sa fin.
▮ vt (door, shop etc) fermer; (discussion) clore; (opening) boucher; (road) barrer; (gap) réduire; (deal) conclure; to c. the meeting lever la séance.
▮ vi se fermer; (end) se terminer; (of shop) fermer. • closing n fermeture f; c. date date f limite; c. time heure f de fermeture.

close down vti (for good) fermer (définitivement) ▮ close in vt (enclose) enfermer ▮ vi (approach) approcher ▮ to close up vi (of shopkeeper) fermer; (of line of people) se resserrer.

closely ['kləʊslɪ] *adv* (*to follow, guard*) de près; (*to listen*) attentivement; **c. linked** étroitement lié (**to** à); **to hold s.o. c.** tenir qn contre soi.

closet ['klɒzɪt] *n Am* (*cupboard*) placard *m*; (*wardrobe*) penderie *f*.

closure ['kləʊʒər] *n* fermeture *f*.

clot [klɒt] **1** *n* (*of blood*) caillot *m* ‖ *vi* (*of blood*) se coaguler. **2** *n* (*person*) *Fam* imbécile *mf*.

cloth [klɒθ] *n* tissu *m*, étoffe *f*; (*for dishes*) torchon *m*; (*tablecloth*) nappe *f*.

cloth/e [kləʊð] *vt* habiller, vêtir (**in** de). ● **—ing** *n* (*clothes*) vêtements *mpl*; **an article of c.** un vêtement.

clothes [kləʊðz] *npl* vêtements *mpl*; **to put one's c. on** s'habiller; **c. shop** magasin *m* d'habillement; **c. brush** brosse *f* à habits; **c. peg**, *Am* **c. pin** pince *f* à linge; **c. line** corde *f* à linge.

cloud [klaʊd] *n* nuage *m* ‖ *vi* **to c. over** (*of sky*) se couvrir. ● **cloudburst** *n* averse *f*. ● **cloudy** *a* (**-ier, -iest**) (*weather, sky*) couvert, nuageux; **it's c.** le temps est couvert.

clout [klaʊt] **1** *n* (*blow*) *Fam* taloche *f* ‖ *vt* *Fam* flanquer une taloche à. **2** *n* *Pol Fam* influence *f*, pouvoir *m*.

clove [kləʊv] *n* clou *m* de girofle; **c. of garlic** gousse *f* d'ail.

clover ['kləʊvər] *n* trèfle *m*.

clown [klaʊn] *n* clown *m* ‖ *vi* **to c. (around)** faire le clown.

club [klʌb] **1** *n* (*weapon*) matraque *f*; (*golf*) **c.** (*stick*) club *m* ‖ *vt* (**-bb-**) matraquer. **2** *n* (*society*) club *m*. **3** *n* **club(s)** *Cards* trèfle *m*. ● **club soda** *n Am* eau *f* gazeuse.

cluck [klʌk] *vi* (*of hen*) glousser.

clue [kluː] *n* indice *m*; (*of crossword*) définition *f*; (*to mystery*) clef *f*; **I don't have a c.** *Fam* je n'en ai pas la moindre idée. ● **clueless** *a Fam* stupide, nul (*f* nulle).

clump [klʌmp] *n* (*of flowers, trees*) massif *m*.

clumsy ['klʌmzɪ] *a* (**-ier, -iest**) maladroit; (*shape*) lourd; (*tool*) peu commode.

clung [klʌŋ] *pt* & *pp* of **cling**.

cluster ['klʌstər] *n* groupe *m*; (*of flowers*) grappe *f* ‖ *vi* se grouper.

clutch [klʌtʃ] **1** *vt* (*hold tight*) serrer; (*cling to*) se cramponner à; (*grasp*) saisir ‖ *vi* **to c. at** essayer de saisir. **2** *n Aut* embrayage *m*; (*pedal*) pédale *f* d'embrayage.

clutter ['klʌtər] *n* (*objects*) fouillis *m* ‖ *vt* **to c. (up)** (*room etc*) encombrer (**with** de).

cm *abbr* (*centimetre*) cm.

co- [kəʊ] *pref* co-.

Co *abbr* (*company*) Cie.

coach [kəʊtʃ] **1** *n* (*of train*) voiture *f*, wagon *m*; (*bus*) autocar *m*; (*horse-drawn*) carrosse *m*. **2** *n* (*person*) *Sp* entraîneur, -euse *mf* ‖ *vt* (*pupil*) donner des leçons (particulières) à; (*sportsman etc*) entraîner; **to c. s.o. for** (*exam*) préparer qn à.

coal [kəʊl] *n* charbon *m* ‖ *a* (*merchant*) de charbon; (*cellar, bucket, shovel*) à charbon; **c. fire** feu *m* de cheminée. ● **coalfield** *n* bassin *m* houiller. ● **coalmine** *n* mine *f* de charbon.

coarse [kɔːs] *a* (**-er, -est**) (*person, manners*) grossier, vulgaire; (*surface*) rude; (*fabric*) grossier.

coast [kəʊst] *n* côte *f*. ● **coastal** *a* côtier. ● **coastguard** *n* (*person*) garde *m* maritime, garde-côte *m*. ● **coastline** *n* littoral *m*.

coaster ['kəʊstər] *n* (*for glass etc*) dessous *m* de verre.

coat [kəʊt] *n* manteau *m*; (*jacket*) veste *f*; (*of animal*) pelage *m*; (*of paint*) couche *f*; **c. of arms** armoiries *fpl* ‖ *vt* couvrir (**with** de); (*with chocolate*) enrober (**with** de); **coated tongue** langue *f* chargée. ● **—ing** *n* couche *f*.

coathanger ['kəʊthæŋər] *n* cintre *m*.

coax [kəʊks] *vt* amadouer; **to c. s.o. into doing** amadouer qn pour qu'il fasse.

cob [kɒb] *n* **corn on the c.** épi *m* de maïs.

cobbled ['kɒb(ə)ld] *a* pavé. ● **cobblestone** *n* pavé *m*.

cobbler ['kɒblər] n cordonnier m.

cobweb ['kɒbweb] n toile f d'araignée.

cocaine [kəʊ'keɪn] n cocaïne f.

cock [kɒk] 1 n (rooster) coq m; (male bird) (oiseau m) mâle m. 2 vt (gun) armer. ●c.-a-doodle-'doo n & int cocorico (m). ●c.-and-'bull story n histoire f à dormir debout.

cocker ['kɒkər] n c. (spaniel) cocker m.

cockerel ['kɒk(ə)rəl] n coquelet m.

cock-eyed ['kɒk'aɪd] a Fam 1 (cross-eyed) bigleux. 2 (crooked) de travers. 3 (crazy) absurde, stupide.

cockle ['kɒk(ə)l] n (shellfish) coque f.

cockney ['kɒknɪ] a & n cockney (mf) (natif des quartiers est de Londres).

cockpit ['kɒkpɪt] n Av poste m de pilotage.

cockroach ['kɒkrəʊtʃ] n cafard m.

cocktail ['kɒkteɪl] n (drink) cocktail m; (fruit) c. macédoine f (de fruits); c. party cocktail m; prawn c. crevettes fpl à la mayonnaise.

cocky ['kɒkɪ] a (-ier, -iest) Fam trop sûr de soi, arrogant.

cocoa ['kəʊkəʊ] n cacao m.

coconut ['kəʊkənʌt] n noix f de coco; c. palm cocotier m.

cocoon [kə'ku:n] n cocon m.

cod [kɒd] n morue f; (bought fresh) cabillaud m. ●c.-liver 'oil n huile f de foie de morue.

COD [si:əʊ'di:] abbr (cash on delivery) contre remboursement.

code [kəʊd] n code m ▍ vt coder.

co-educational [kəʊedjʊ'keɪʃən(ə)l] a (school, teaching) mixte.

coerce [kəʊ'ɜ:s] vt contraindre (s.o. into doing qn à faire). ●coercion [-ʃ(ə)n] n contrainte f.

coexist [kəʊɪg'zɪst] vi coexister. ●coexistence n coexistence f.

coffee ['kɒfɪ] n café m; white c., Am c. with milk café m au lait; (in restaurant etc) (café m) crème m; black c. café m noir; c. bar café m; c. break pause-café f; c. table table f basse. ●coffeepot n cafetière f.

coffers ['kɒfəz] npl (funds) coffres mpl.

coffin ['kɒfɪn] n cercueil m.

cog [kɒg] n (tooth of wheel) dent f; (person) Fig rouage m.

cognac ['kɒnjæk] n cognac m.

cohabit [kəʊ'hæbɪt] vi (of unmarried people) vivre en concubinage.

coherent [kəʊ'hɪərənt] a (idea etc) cohérent; (way of speaking) compréhensible.

coil [kɔɪl] n (of wire, rope etc) rouleau m; (of snake) anneau m; El bobine f; (contraceptive) stérilet m ▍ vt (rope) enrouler.

coin [kɔɪn] n pièce f (de monnaie); c. bank Am tirelire f ▍ vt (word) Fig forger; to c. a phrase pour ainsi dire. ●c.-operated a automatique.

coincide [kəʊɪn'saɪd] vi coïncider (with avec). ●co'incidence n coïncidence f.

coke [kəʊk] n 1 (fuel) coke m. 2 (Coca-Cola®) coca m.

colander ['kʌləndər, 'kɒl-] n (for vegetables etc) passoire f.

cold [kəʊld] n froid m; Med rhume m; to catch c. prendre froid; to get a c. s'enrhumer.
▍ a (-er, -est) froid; to be or feel c. (of person) avoir froid; my hands are c. j'ai froid aux mains; it's c. (of weather) il fait froid; to get c. (of weather) se refroidir; (of food) refroidir; in c. blood de sang-froid; c. cream crème f de beauté; c. meats, Am c. cuts assiette f anglaise. ●c.-'blooded a (person) cruel; (murder) de sang-froid. ●coldness n froideur f.

coleslaw ['kəʊlslɔ:] n salade f de chou cru.

colic ['kɒlɪk] n Med coliques fpl.

collaborate [kə'læbəreɪt] vi collaborer (on à). ●collaboration [-'reɪʃ(ə)n] n collaboration f.

collage ['kɒlɑːʒ] n (picture) collage m.

collapse [kə'læps] vi (of person, building) s'effondrer; (of government) tomber; (faint) se trouver mal ▍ n effondrement m; (of government) chute f.

collar ['kɒlər] n (on garment) col m; (of dog) collier m ▮ vt (seize) Fam saisir (qn) au collet; (buttonhole) retenir (qn). ● **collarbone** n clavicule f.

colleague ['kɒli:g] n collègue mf.

collect [kə'lekt] vt (pick up) ramasser; (gather) rassembler, recueillir; (taxes) percevoir; (rent) encaisser; (stamps etc as hobby) collectionner; (call for) (passer) prendre; **to c. money** (in street, church) quêter (for pour) ▮ vi (of dust) s'accumuler; (in street, church) quêter (for pour) ▮ adv **to call c.** Am téléphoner en PCV.

collection [kə'lekʃ(ə)n] n (of objects) collection f; (of poems etc) recueil m; (of money in church etc) quête f; (of mail) levée f; (of taxes) perception f.

collector [kə'lektər] n (of stamps etc) collectionneur, -euse mf.

college ['kɒlɪdʒ] n université f; (within university) collège m; Pol Rel collège m; Mus conservatoire m; **art c.** école f des beaux-arts.

collide [kə'laɪd] vi entrer en collision (with avec). ● **collision** n collision f.

colliery ['kɒlɪərɪ] n houillère f.

colloquial [kə'ləʊkwɪəl] a (word etc) familier.

collusion [kə'lu:ʒ(ə)n] n collusion f.

cologne [kə'ləʊn] n eau f de Cologne.

colon ['kəʊlən] n 1 (punctuation mark) deux-points m inv. 2 Anat côlon m.

colonel ['kɜ:n(ə)l] n colonel m.

colony ['kɒlənɪ] n colonie f.

colonial [kə'ləʊnɪəl] a colonial. ● **'colonize** vt coloniser.

colossal [kə'lɒs(ə)l] a colossal.

colour ['kʌlər] n (Am color) n couleur f. ▮ a (photo, TV set) en couleurs; (problem) racial; **c. supplement** (of newspaper) supplément m illustré; **off c.** (not well) mal fichu.
▮ vt colorer; **to c. (in)** (drawing) colorier. ● **—ed** a (person, pencil) de couleur; (glass, water) coloré. ● **—ing** n (in food) colorant m; (complexion) teint m; (with crayons) coloriage m; (shade,

effect) coloris m; **c. book** album m de coloriages. ● **colour-blind** a daltonien. ● **colourful** a (crowd) coloré; (person) pittoresque.

colt [kəʊlt] n (horse) poulain m.

column ['kɒləm] n colonne f; (newspaper feature) chronique f. ● **columnist** n chroniqueur m; **gossip c.** échotier, -ière mf.

coma ['kəʊmə] n coma m; **in a c.** dans le coma.

comb [kəʊm] n peigne m ▮ vt (hair) peigner; (search) Fig ratisser; **to c. one's hair** se peigner.

combat ['kɒmbæt] n combat m.

combine[1] [kəm'baɪn] vt (activities, qualities, elements) combiner; (efforts) joindre; **our combined efforts produced a result** en joignant nos efforts nous avons obtenu un résultat ▮ vi s'unir; (of elements) se combiner. ● **combination** [-'neɪʒ(ə)n] n combinaison f; (of qualities) réunion f; (of events) concours m.

combine[2] ['kɒmbaɪn] n 1 Com association f; (cartel) cartel m. 2 **c. harvester** Agr moissonneuse-batteuse f.

combustion [kəm'bʌstʃ(ə)n] n combustion f.

come [kʌm] vi (pt came, pp come) venir (from de, to à); **to c. first** (in race) arriver premier; (in exam) être le premier; **o. and see me** viens me voir; **I've just c. from** j'arrive de; **to c. home** rentrer; **coming!** j'arrive!; **to c. as a surprise (to)** surprendre; **to c. close to doing** faillir faire; **nothing came of it** ça n'a abouti à rien; **to c. true** se réaliser; **c. May**/etc Fam en mai/etc; **how c. that...?** Fam comment se fait-il que...?

come about vi (happen) se faire, arriver ▮ **to c. across** vi (of speech) faire de l'effet; (of feelings) se montrer ▮ vt (person, reference) tomber sur; (lost object) trouver (par hasard) ▮ **to come along** vi venir (with avec); (progress) of work etc) avancer; **c. along!** allons! ▮ **to come apart** vi (of two objects) se séparer ▮ **to c. away** vi (leave, come off) partir

to come back vi revenir; (return home) rentrer. ● **comeback** n (of actor, politician etc) retour m. **to come by** vt (obtain) obtenir; (find) trouver. **to come down** vi descendre; (of rain, price) tomber; (of building) être démoli. ▌vt (stairs, hill etc) descendre; **to c. down with** (illness) attraper. ● **comedown** n Fam humiliation f. **to come for** vt venir chercher (qch, qn). **to come forward** vi (volunteer) se présenter; **to c. forward with sth** offrir qch. **to come in** vi entrer; (of tide) monter; (of train) arriver; Pol arriver au pouvoir; (of money) rentrer; **to c. in for** (criticism) essuyer. **to come into** vt (room etc) entrer dans; (money) hériter de. **to come off** vi (of button etc) se détacher, partir; (succeed) réussir; (happen) avoir lieu. ▌vt (fall from) tomber de; (get down from) descendre de. **to come on** vi (progress) (of work etc) avancer; (start) commencer; (of play) être joué; **c. on!** allez! **to come out** vi sortir; (of sun, book) paraître; (of stain) partir; (of photo) réussir; **to c. out (on strike)** se mettre en grève. **to come over** vi (visit) venir, passer (**to** chez); **to c. over to** (approach) s'approcher de; **to c. over funny** se trouver mal. ▌vt (take hold of) (of feeling) saisir (qn). **to come round** vi (visit) venir, passer (**to** chez); (of date) revenir; (regain consciousness) revenir à soi. **to come through** vi (survive) s'en tirer. ▌vt (crisis etc) se tirer indemne de. **to come to** vi (regain consciousness) revenir à soi. ▌vt (amount to) Com revenir à; (a decision) parvenir à; **to c. to an end** toucher à sa fin; **to c. to understand/etc** en venir à comprendre/etc. **to come under** vt (heading) être classé sous; (s.o.'s influence) tomber sous. **to come up** vi (rise) monter; (of plant) sortir; (of question, job) se présenter. ▌vt (stairs etc) monter. **to come up against** vt (wall, problem) se heurter à. **to come up to** vt (reach) arriver jusqu'à; (approach) s'approcher de. **to come up with** vt (idea, money) trouver. **to come upon** vt (book, reference) tomber sur.

comedy ['kɒmɪdɪ] n comédie f. ● **co'median** n (acteur m) comique m, actrice f comique.

comet ['kɒmɪt] n comète f.

comeuppance [kʌm'ʌpəns] n **he got his c.** Pej Fam il n'a eu que ce qu'il mérite.

comfort ['kʌmfət] n confort m; (consolation) réconfort m, consolation f; **to like one's comforts** aimer ses aises fpl. ▌vt consoler; (cheer) réconforter. ● **—er** n (quilt) Am édredon m.

comfortable ['kʌmfətəb(ə)l] a (chair, house etc) confortable; (rich) aisé; **he's c.** (in chair etc) il est à l'aise, il est bien; **make yourself c.** mets-toi à l'aise. ● **comfortably** adv (to sit) confortablement; **to live c.** vivre à l'aise.

comic ['kɒmɪk] a comique. ▌n (actor) comique m; (actress) actrice f comique; (magazine) illustré m; **c. strip** bande f dessinée. ● **comical** a comique, drôle.

coming ['kʌmɪŋ] a (future) à venir. ▌n **comings and goings** allées fpl et venues

comma ['kɒmə] n Gram virgule f.

command [kə'mɑːnd] n (order) commander (**s.o.** to do à qn de faire); (control) commander (régiment, navire etc). ▌vi commander. ▌n (order) ordre m; (authority) commandement m; (mastery) maîtrise f (**of** de); Comptr commande f; **at one's c.** (disposal) à sa disposition; **to be in c. (of)** (ship, army etc) commander; (situation) être maître (de); **commanding officer** commandant m. ● **commander** n Mil commandant m.

commandment [kə'mɑːndmənt] n Rel commandement m.

commandeer [kɒmən'dɪər] vt réquisitionner.

commando [kə'mɑːndəʊ] n (pl **-os** or **-oes**) Mil commando m.

commemorate [kə'meməreɪt] vt commémorer.

commence [kə'mens] *vti* commencer (**doing** à faire).

commend [kə'mend] *vt* (*praise*) louer; (*recommend*) recommander. ●**—able** *a* louable.

comment ['kɒment] *n* commentaire *m*, remarque *f*; **'no c.!'** 'rien à dire' ‖ *vi* faire des commentaires *or* des remarques (**on** sur); **to c. on** (*text, event*) commenter ‖ *vt* **to c. that** remarquer que. ●**commentary** *n* commentaire *m*; (**live**) **c.** *TV Rad* reportage *m*. ●**commentator** *n TV Rad* commentateur, -trice *mf*.

commerce ['kɒmɜːs] *n* commerce *m*. ●**co'mmercial 1** *a* commercial; **c. traveller** voyageur *m* de commerce. **2** *n* (*advertisement*) *TV* publicité *f*; **the commercials** *TV* la publicité.

commiserate [kə'mɪzəreɪt] *vi* **to c. with** s.o. s'apitoyer sur (le sort de) qn.

commission [kə'mɪʃ(ə)n] *n* (*fee, group*) commission *f*; (*order for work*) commande *f* ‖ *vt* (*artist*) passer une commande à; (*book*) commander.

commissionaire [kəmɪʃə'neər] *n* (*in hotel etc*) commissionnaire *m*. ●**commissioner** *n* (*police*) **c.** préfet *m* (de police).

commit [kə'mɪt] *vt* (**-tt-**) (*crime*) commettre; (*bind*) engager (*qn*); (*devote*) consacrer (*efforts etc*) (**to** à); **to c. suicide** se suicider; **to c. to memory** apprendre par cœur; **to c. to prison** incarcérer; **to c. oneself** (*make a promise*) s'engager (**to** à). ●**—ment** *n* (*duty, responsibility*) obligation *f*; (*promise*) engagement *m*; (*devotion*) dévouement *m*.

committee [kə'mɪtɪ] *n* comité *m*.

commodity [kə'mɒdɪtɪ] *n* produit *m*.

common ['kɒmən] **1** *a* (**-er, -est**) (*shared, vulgar*) commun; (*frequent*) courant, commun; **in c.** (*shared*) en commun (**with** avec); **to have nothing in c.** n'avoir rien de commun (**with** avec); **in c. with** (*like*) comme; **C. Market** Marché *m* commun; **c. room** (*for students*) salle *f* commune; (*for teachers*)

salle *f* des professeurs; **c. or garden** ordinaire.

2 *n* (*land*) terrain *m* communal; **House of Commons** *Pol* Chambre *f* des Communes; **the Commons** les Communes *fpl*. ●**commonly** *adv* (*generally*) en général; (*vulgarly*) d'une façon commune.

commonplace [kɒmənpleɪs] *a* banal (*mpl* -als).

commonsense [kɒmən'sens] *n* sens *m* commun, bon sens *m*.

Commonwealth ['kɒmənwelθ] *n* **the C.** le Commonwealth.

commotion [kə'məʊʃ(ə)n] *n* agitation *f*.

communal [kə'mjuːn(ə)l] *a* (*shared*) (*bathroom etc*) commun; (*of the community*) communautaire.

commune 1 ['kɒmjuːn] *n* (*district*) commune *f*; (*group*) communauté *f*. **2** [kə'mjuːn] *vi* **to c. with nature/God** être en communion avec la nature/Dieu. ●**co'mmunion** *n* communion *f* (**with** avec).

communicate [kə'mjuːnɪkeɪt] *vt* communiquer; (*illness*) transmettre ‖ *vi* (*of person, rooms etc*) communiquer. ●**communication** [-'keɪʃ(ə)n] *n* communication *f*; **c. cord** *Rail* signal *m* d'alarme.

communiqué [kə'mjuːnɪkeɪ] *n Pol etc* communiqué *m*.

communism ['kɒmjʊnɪz(ə)m] *n* communisme *m*. ●**communist** *a* & *n* communiste (*mf*).

community [kə'mjuːnɪtɪ] *n* communauté *f*; **the student c.** les étudiants *mpl*; **c. centre** centre *m* socio-culturel; **c. worker** animateur, -trice *mf* socio-culturel(le).

commut/e [kə'mjuːt] *vi* (*travel*) faire la navette (**to work** pour se rendre à son travail). ●**—ing** *n* trajets *mpl* journaliers. ●**commuter** *n* banlieusard, -arde *mf*; **c. train** train *m* de banlieue.

compact[1] [kəm'pækt] *a* (*car, substance*) compact; **c. disc** *or Am* **disk** ['kɒmpækt] disque *m* compact.

compact[2] ['kɒmpækt] *n* (*for face powder*)

poudrier *m*.

companion [kəm'pænjən] *n* (*person*) compagnon *m*, compagne *f*. ● **companionship** *n* camaraderie *f*.

company ['kʌmpənɪ] *n* (*companionship, business*) compagnie *f*; (*guests*) invités, -ées *mfpl*; (*people present*) assemblée *f*; **to keep s.o. c.** tenir compagnie à qn; **to keep good c.** avoir de bonnes fréquentations; **he's good c.** c'est un bon compagnon; **c. car** voiture *f* de société.

compare [kəm'peər] *vt* comparer (**with,** **to** à); **compared to** *or* **with** en comparaison de ‖ *vi* être comparable, se comparer (**with** à). ● **comparable** ['kɒmpərəb(ə)l] *a* comparable (**with,** **to** à).

comparative [kəm'pærətɪv] *a* (*relative*) relatif; (*method etc*) comparatif; (*law etc*) comparé. ● **comparatively** *adv* relativement. ● **comparison** *n* comparaison *f* (**with** avec).

compartment [kəm'pɑːtmənt] *n* compartiment *m*.

compass ['kʌmpəs] *n* **1** (*for direction*) boussole *f*; (*on ship*) compas *m*. **2** (*for drawing etc*) *Am* compas *m*; (**pair of**) **compasses** compas *m*.

compassion [kəm'pæʃ(ə)n] *n* compassion *f*.

compatible [kəm'pætɪb(ə)l] *a* compatible.

compatriot [kəm'pætrɪət, kəm'peɪtrɪət] *n* compatriote *mf*.

compel [kəm'pel] *vt* (**-ll-**) forcer, contraindre (**to do** à faire); **compelled to do** forcé *or* contraint de faire. ● **compelling** *a* irrésistible.

compensate ['kɒmpənseɪt] *vt* **to c. s.o.** dédommager qn (**for** de) ‖ *vi* compenser; **to c. for sth** (*make up for*) compenser qch. ● **compensation** *n* [-'seɪʃ(ə)n] *n* (*financial*) dédommagement *m*; **in c. for** en compensation de.

compère ['kɒmpeər] *n* *TV* *Rad* animateur, -trice *mf* ‖ *vt* (*a show*) animer.

compete [kəm'piːt] *vi* (*in race etc*) concourir; **to c. (with s.o.)** rivaliser (avec

qn); *Com* faire concurrence (à qn); **to c.** **for sth** se disputer qch; **to c. in a race** courir dans une course.

competent ['kɒmpɪtənt] *a* compétent (**to** **do** pour faire); (*sufficient*) suffisant; (*knowledge etc*) suffisant. ● **—ly** *adv* avec compétence. ● **competence** *n* compétence *f*.

competition [kɒmpɪ'tɪʃ(ə)n] *n* (*rivalry*) compétition *f*, concurrence *f*; **a c.** (*contest*) un concours; *Sp* une compétition. ● **competitive** *a* (*price, market*) compétitif; (*person*) aimant la compétition; **c. examination** concours *m*. ● **competitor** *n* concurrent, -ente *mf*.

compile [kəm'paɪl] *vt* (*dictionary*) rédiger; (*list*) dresser.

complacent [kəm'pleɪsənt] *a* content de soi. ● **complacence** *or* **complacency** *n* autosatisfaction *f*.

complain [kəm'pleɪn] *vi* se plaindre (**to** à; **of,** **about** de; **that** que). ● **complaint** *n* plainte *f*; (*in shop etc*) réclamation *f*; *Med* maladie *f*; (**cause for**) **c.** sujet *m* de plainte.

complement ['kɒmplɪmənt] *n* complément *m* ‖ ['kɒmplɪment] *vt* compléter. ● **comple'mentary** *a* complémentaire.

complete [kəm'pliːt] *a* (*total*) complet; (*finished*) achevé; **a c. idiot** un parfait imbécile ‖ *vt* (*add sth missing to*) compléter; (*finish*) achever; (*a form*) remplir. ● **—ly** *adv* complètement. ● **completion** [-ʃ(ə)n] *n* achèvement *m*.

complex ['kɒmpleks] **1** *a* complexe. **2** *n* (*feeling, buildings*) complexe *m*; **housing** **c.** grand ensemble *m*. ● **com'plexity** *n* complexité *f*.

complexion [kəm'plekʃ(ə)n] *n* (*of the face*) teint *m*.

complicat/e ['kɒmplɪkeɪt] *vt* compliquer. ● **—ed** *a* compliqué. ● **complication** [-'keɪʃ(ə)n] *n* complication *f*.

complicity [kəm'plɪsɪtɪ] *n* complicité *f*.

compliment ['kɒmplɪmənt] *n* compliment *m*; **compliments of the season** meilleurs vœux pour Noël et la nouvelle année ‖ ['kɒmplɪment] *vt* complimenter. ● **compli'mentary** *a* **1** (*flattering*) flatteur. **2** (*free*) (offert) à titre gracieux; (*ticket*) de faveur.

comply [kəm'plaɪ] *vi* obéir (**with** à).

component [kəm'pəʊnənt] *n* (*of structure, self-assembly furniture etc*) élément *m*; (*of machine*) pièce *f*; (*chemical*) composant *m*.

compos/e [kəm'pəʊz] *vt* composer; **to c. oneself** se calmer. ●**—ed** *a* calme. ●**—er** *n Mus* compositeur, -trice *mf*. ●**composition** [kɒmpə'zɪʃ(ə)n] *n Mus Liter Ch* composition *f*; (*school essay*) rédaction *f*.

compost ['kɒmpɒst, *Am* 'kɒmpəʊst] *n* compost *m*.

composure [kəm'pəʊʒər] *n* calme *m*, sang-froid *m*.

compound ['kɒmpaʊnd] *n* (*substance, word*) composé *m*; (*area*) enclos *m* ▮ *a* (*substance, word*) composé; (*sentence, number*) complexe.

comprehend [kɒmprɪ'hend] *vt* comprendre. ●**comprehension** [-ʃ(ə)n] *n* compréhension *f*. ●**comprehensive** *a* complet; (*view, measure*) d'ensemble; (*insurance*) tous risques *inv* ▮ *a* & *n* **c. (school)** = collège *m* d'enseignement secondaire.

compress [kəm'pres] *vt* (*gas, air*) comprimer.

comprise [kəm'praɪz] *vt* (*consist of*) comprendre; (*make up*) constituer.

compromise ['kɒmprəmaɪz] *vt* compromettre ▮ *vi* accepter un compromis ▮ *n* compromis *m*.

compulsion [kəm'pʌlʃ(ə)n] *n* contrainte *f*. ●**compulsive** *a* (*smoker, gambler, liar*) invétéré.

compulsory [kəm'pʌlsərɪ] *a* obligatoire.

computer [kəm'pjuːtər] *n* ordinateur *m*; **c. game** jeu *m* électronique; **c. operator** opérateur, -trice *mf* sur ordinateur; **c. program** programme *m* informatique; **c. science** informatique *f*; **c. scientist** informaticien, -ienne *mf*. ●**computerized** *a* informatisé. ●**computing** *n* informatique *f*.

comrade ['kɒmreɪd] *n* camarade *mf*.

con [kɒn] *vt* (**-nn-**) (*deceive*) *Sl* rouler, escroquer ▮ *n Sl* escroquerie *f*; **c. man** escroc *m*.

concave ['kɒnkeɪv] *a* concave.

conceal [kən'siːl] *vt* (*hide*) dissimuler, cacher (*objet, sentiment*) (**from s.o.** à qn).

concede [kən'siːd] *vt* concéder (**to** à, **that** que) ▮ *vi* céder.

conceit [kən'siːt] *n* vanité *f*. ●**conceited** *a* vaniteux.

conceiv/e [kən'siːv] *vt* (*idea, child etc*) concevoir; (*believe*) voir ▮ *vi* (*of woman*) concevoir; **to c. of** concevoir. ●**—able** *a* concevable, envisageable (**that** que + *sub*).

concentrate ['kɒnsəntreɪt] *vt* concentrer ▮ *vi* (*mentally & converge*) se concentrer (**on** sur); **to c. on doing** s'appliquer à faire; **to c. on one's exams/etc** se consacrer particulièrement à ses examens/*etc*. ●**concentration** [-'treɪʃ(ə)n] *n* concentration *f*; **c. camp** camp *m* de concentration.

concept ['kɒnsept] *n* concept *m*. ●**conception** [kən'sepʃ(ə)n] *n* (*idea*) & *Med* conception *f*.

concern [kən'sɜːn] *vt* concerner; **to be concerned** (*anxious*) être inquiet; **to be concerned with/about** s'occuper de/s'inquiéter de; **the main person concerned** le principal intéressé ▮ *n* (*matter*) affaire *f*; (*anxiety*) inquiétude *f*; **his c. for** son souci de; (*business*) c. entreprise *f* ●**—ing** *prep* en ce qui concerne.

concert ['kɒnsət] *n* concert *m*; **c. hall** salle *f* de concert. ●**c.-goer** *n* habitué, -ée *mf* des concerts.

concerted [kən'sɜːtɪd] *a* (*effort*) concerté.

concertina [kɒnsə'tiːnə] *n* concertina *m*.

concession [kən'seʃ(ə)n] *n* concession *f* (**to** à).

conciliation [kənsɪlɪ'eɪʃ(ə)n] *n* conciliation *f*.

concise [kən'saɪs] *a* concis. ●**—ly** *adv* avec concision. ●**concision** [-ʒ(ə)n] *n* concision *f*.

conclude [kən'kluːd] *vt* (*end, settle*) conclure; **to c. that** (*infer*) conclure que ‖ *vi* (*of event*) se terminer (**with** par); (*of speaker*) conclure. ●**conclusion** [-ʒ(ə)n] *n* conclusion *f*; **in c.** pour conclure. ●**conclusive** *a* concluant.

concoct [kən'kɒkt] *vt* (*dish*) Pej concocter; (*scheme*) combiner. ●**concoction** [-ʃ(ə)n] *n* (*substance*) Pej mixture *f*.

concourse [ˈkɒŋkɔːs] *n* (*hall*) hall *m*.

concrete [ˈkɒŋkriːt] **1** *n* béton *m* ‖ *a* en béton. **2** *a* (*real, positive*) concret.

concurrently [kən'kʌrəntlɪ] *adv* simultanément.

concussion [kən'kʌʃ(ə)n] *n* Med commotion *f* (cérébrale).

condemn [kən'dem] *vt* condamner (*qn*) (**to** à); (*building*) déclarer inhabitable.

condense [kən'dens] *vt* condenser. ●**condensation** [kɒndən'seɪʃ(ə)n] *n* (*mist*) buée *f*.

condescend [kɒndɪ'send] *vi* condescendre (**to do** à faire).

condiment [ˈkɒndɪmənt] *n* condiment *m*.

condition [kən'dɪʃ(ə)n] **1** *n* (*stipulation, circumstance, state etc*) condition *f*; **on c. that one does** à condition de faire, à condition que l'on fasse; **in good c.** en bon état; **out of c.** en mauvaise forme. **2** *vt* (*action, person*) conditionner. ●**conditional** *a* conditionnel; **to be c. upon** dépendre de.

conditioner [kən'dɪʃənər] *n* (*hair*) c. après-shampooing *m*.

condo [ˈkɒndəʊ] *n abbr* (*pl* -os) Am = **condominium**.

condolences [kən'dəʊlənsɪz] *npl* condoléances *fpl*.

condom [ˈkɒndəm, -dɒm] *n* préservatif *m*, capote *f* (anglaise).

condominium [kɒndə'rɪɪnɪəm] *n* Am (*building*) copropriété *f*; (*apartment*) appartement *m* dans une copropriété.

condone [kən'dəʊn] *vt* (*overlook*) fermer les yeux sur; (*forgive*) excuser.

conducive [kən'djuːsɪv] *a* **c. to** favorable à.

conduct [ˈkɒndʌkt] *n* (*behaviour*) conduite *f* ‖ [kən'dʌkt] *vt* (*lead*) conduire, mener (*touristes, enquête etc*); (*orches-*

tra) diriger; (*electricity, heat*) conduire; **to c. oneself** se conduire. ●—**ed** *a* (*visit*) guidé; **c. tour** excursion *f* accompagnée; (*of building etc*) visite *f* guidée.

conductor [kən'dʌktər] *n* Mus chef *m* d'orchestre; (*on bus*) receveur *m*; (*on train*) Am chef *m* de train. ●**conductress** *n* (*on bus*) receveuse *f*.

cone [kəʊn] *n* cône *m*; (*of ice cream*) cornet *m*; **traffic c.** cône *m* de chantier.

confectioner [kən'fekʃənər] *n* (*of sweets, Am candies*) confiseur, -euse *mf*. ●**confectionery** *n* confiserie *f*.

confederation [kɒnfedə'reɪʃ(ə)n] *n* confédération *f*.

confer [kən'fɜːr] **1** *vt* (-rr-) (*grant*) conférer (**on** à); **to c. a degree on** remettre un diplôme à. **2** *vi* (-rr-) (*talk together*) se consulter; **to c. with s.o.** consulter qn.

conference [ˈkɒnfərəns] *n* conférence *f*; (*scientific etc*) congrès *m*.

confess [kən'fes] **1** *vt* avouer (**that** que, **to s.o.** à qn) ‖ *vi* (*crime etc*) avouer. **2** *vt* Rel confesser ‖ *vi* se confesser. ●**confession** [-ʃ(ə)n] *n* aveu(x) *m(pl)*; Rel confession *f*.

confetti [kən'fetɪ] *n* confettis *mpl*.

confide [kən'faɪd] *vt* confier (**to** à, **that** que) ‖ *vi* **to c. in** (*talk to*) se confier à.

confidence [ˈkɒnfɪdəns] *n* (*trust*) confiance *f*; (**self-**)**c.** confiance *f* en soi; **in c.** en confidence; **motion of no c.** Pol motion *f* de censure; **c. trick** escroquerie *f*. ●**confident** *a* sûr; (**self-**)**c.** sûr de soi. ●**confidently** *adv* avec confiance.

confidential [kɒnfɪ'denʃəl] *a* confidentiel. ●—**ly** *adv* en confidence.

confine [kən'faɪn] *vt* **1** (*limit*) limiter (**to** à); **to c. oneself to doing** se limiter à faire. **2** (*keep prisoner*) enfermer (*qn*) (**to, in** dans). ●—**ed** *a* (*space*) réduit; **to be confined to bed** cloué au lit.

confirm [kən'fɜːm] *vt* confirmer (**that** que); (*strengthen*) raffermir. ●—**ed** *a* (*bachelor*) endurci; (*smoker*) invétéré. ●**confirmation** [kɒnfə'meɪʃ(ə)n] *n* confirmation *f*.

confiscate [ˈkɒnfɪskeɪt] *vt* confisquer

(from s.o. à qn).

conflict ['kɒnflɪkt] n conflit m
‖ [kən'flɪkt] vi être en contradiction
(**with** avec); (of dates, events, TV programmes) tomber en même temps (**with**
que). ●**—ing** a (views etc) contradic-
toires; (dates) incompatibles.

conform [kən'fɔ:m] vi (of person) se
conformer (**to** à); (of ideas etc) être
en conformité. ●**conformist** a & n
conformiste mf.

confound [kən'faʊnd] vt (surprise, puzzle) confondre.

confront [kən'frʌnt] vt (danger, problems) faire face à; **to c. s.o.** (be face
to face with) se trouver en face de qn;
(oppose) s'opposer à qn. ●**confrontation**
[kɒnfrən'teɪʃ(ə)n] n confrontation f.

confus/e [kən'fju:z] vt (make unsure)
embrouiller (qn); **to c. with** (mistake
for) confondre avec. ●**—ed** a (situation, noises etc) confus; **to be c.** (of
person) s'y perdre; **to get c.** s'embrouiller. ●**—ing** a déroutant. ●**confusion**
[-ʒ(ə)n] n confusion f; **in c.** en désordre.

congealed [kən'dʒi:ld] a **c. blood** sang m
coagulé.

congenial [kən'dʒi:nɪəl] a sympathique.

congenital [kən'dʒenɪtəl] a congénital.

congested [kən'dʒestɪd] a (street) encombré (district) surpeuplé; (nose)
bouché; (lungs) congestionné. ●**congestion** [-tʃ(ə)n] n encombrement m;
(traffic) encombrement(s) m(pl); Med
congestion f.

Congo ['kɒŋgəʊ] n Congo m.

congratulate [kən'grætʃʊleɪt] vt féliciter (**s.o. on sth** qn de qch, **s.o. on
doing sth** qn d'avoir fait qch). ●**congratulations** [-'leɪʃ(ə)nz] npl félicitations fpl (**on** pour).

congregate ['kɒŋgrɪgeɪt] vi se rassembler. ●**congregation** [-'geɪʃ(ə)n] n
(worshippers) fidèles mfpl.

congress ['kɒŋgrəs] n congrès m; **C.**
Pol Am le Congrès. ●**Congressman** n
(pl **-men**) Am membre m du Congrès.
●**Con'gressional** a Am du Congrès.

conical ['kɒnɪk(ə)l] a conique.

conifer ['kɒnɪfər] n (tree) conifère m.

conjugal ['kɒndʒʊgəl] a conjugal.

conjugate ['kɒndʒʊgeɪt] vt (verb) conjuguer. ●**conjugation** [-'geɪʃ(ə)n] n conjugaison f.

conjunction [kən'dʒʌŋkʃ(ə)n] n Gram
conjonction f; **in c. with** conjointement
avec.

conjunctivitis [kəndʒʌŋktɪ'vaɪtɪs] n con-
jonctivite f.

conjur/e ['kʌndʒər] vt **to c. (up)** (by
magic) faire apparaître; **to c. up** (memories etc) Fig évoquer; **conjuring trick**
tour m de prestidigitation. ●**—er** n
prestidigitateur, -trice mf.

conk [kɒŋk] vi **to c. out** (break down)
Fam tomber en panne.

connect [kə'nekt] vt relier (**with, to** à);
(telephone, washing machine etc) brancher; **to c. with** Tel mettre (qn) en
communication avec; (in memory) associer (qch, qn) avec.
‖ vi (be connected) être relié; **to c. with**
(of train, bus) assurer la correspondance avec. ●**—ed** a (facts etc) liés;
to be c. with (have dealings with, relate
to) être lié à.

connection [kə'nekʃ(ə)n] n (link) rapport m, relation f (**with** avec); (train, bus
etc) correspondance f; (phone call)
communication f; pl (contacts) relations
fpl; **in c. with** à propos de.

connive [kə'naɪv] vi **to c. at** fermer les
yeux sur; **to c. together** agir en complicité.

connotation [kɒnə'teɪʃ(ə)n] n connotation f.

conquer ['kɒŋkər] vt (country, freedom
etc) conquérir; (enemy, habit) vaincre.
●**—ing** a victorieux. ●**conqueror** n
conquérant, -ante mf. ●**conquest** n
conquête f.

cons [kɒnz] npl **the pros and (the) c.** le
pour et le contre.

conscience ['kɒnʃəns] n conscience f.

conscientious [kɒnʃɪ'enʃəs] a consciencieux. ●**—ness** n application f, sérieux

m.

conscious ['kɒnʃəs] *a* (*awake*) conscient; (*intentional*) délibéré; **c. of sth** (*aware*) conscient de qch; **to be c. of doing** avoir conscience de faire. ●**—ly** *adv* (*knowingly*) consciemment. ●**—ness** *n* **to lose/regain c.** perdre/reprendre connaissance.

conscript ['kɒnskrɪpt] *n Mil* conscrit *m* ▮ [kən'skrɪpt] *vt* enrôler (par conscription). ●**conscription** [kən'skrɪpʃ(ə)n] *n* conscription *f.*

consecutive [kən'sekjʊtɪv] *a* consécutif. ●**—ly** *adv* consécutivement.

consensus [kən'sensəs] *n* consensus *m.*

consent [kən'sent] *vi* consentir (**to** à) ▮ *n* consentement *m*; **by common c.** de l'aveu de tous; **by mutual c.** d'un commun accord.

consequence ['kɒnsɪkwəns] *n* (*result*) conséquence *f*; (*importance*) importance *f.* ●**consequently** *adv* par conséquent.

conservative [kən'sɜːvətɪv] *a* **1** (*view*) traditionnel; (*estimate*) modeste. **2** *a & n* **C.** *Br Pol* conservateur, -trice (*mf*).

conservatory [kən'sɜːvətrɪ] *n* (*room*) véranda *f.*

conserve [kən'sɜːv] *vt* (*energy, water etc*) économiser, faire des économies de; (*preserve*) préserver (*privilèges, faune etc*); **to c. one's strength** économiser ses forces. ●**conservation** [kɒnsə'veɪʃ(ə)n] *n* (*energy-saving*) économies *fpl* d'énergie; (*of nature*) protection *f* de l'environnement; **c. area** zone *f* naturelle protégée.

consider [kən'sɪdər] *vt* considérer (**that** que); (*take into account*) tenir compte de; **I'll c. it** j'y réfléchirai; **to c. doing** envisager de faire; **all things considered** tout compte fait. ●**consideration** [-'reɪʃ(ə)n] *n* (*thought, thoughtfulness, reason*) considération *f*; **under c.** à l'étude; **to take into c.** prendre en considération.

considerable [kən'sɪdərəb(ə)l] *a* (*large*) considérable; (*much*) beaucoup de. ●**considerably** *adv* beaucoup, considé-

rablement.

considerate [kən'sɪdərət] *a* plein d'égards (**to** pour), attentionné (**to** à l'égard de).

considering [kən'sɪdərɪŋ] *prep* compte tenu de; **c. that** étant donné que.

consign [kən'saɪn] *vt* (*send*) expédier (*marchandises*) (**to** à). ●**—ment** *n* (*goods*) arrivage *m.*

consist [kən'sɪst] *vi* consister (**of** en, **in** dans, **in doing** à faire).

consistent [kən'sɪstənt] *a* (*unchanging*) constant; (*coherent*) (*ideas etc*) cohérent, logique; **to be c. with** concorder avec. ●**—ly** *adv* (*always*) constamment. ●**consistency** *n* **1** (*of liquid etc*) consistance *f.* **2** (*of ideas etc*) cohérence *f.*

console¹ [kən'səʊl] *vt* consoler. ●**consolation** [kɒnsə'leɪʃ(ə)n] *n* consolation *f*; **c. prize** lot *m* de consolation.

console² ['kɒnsəʊl] *n* (*control desk*), console *f.*

consolidate [kən'sɒlɪdeɪt] *vt* consolider.

consonant ['kɒnsənənt] *n* consonne *f.*

conspicuous [kən'spɪkjʊəs] *a* (*noticeable*) visible, en évidence; (*striking*) remarquable; (*showy*) voyant; **to make oneself c.** se faire remarquer.

conspire [kən'spaɪər] *vi* (*plot*) conspirer (**against** contre); **to c. to do** comploter de faire. ●**conspiracy** [-'spɪrəsɪ] *n* conspiration *f.*

constable ['kʌnstəb(ə)l] *n* (*police*) **c.** agent *m* (de police); **chief c.** = préfet *m* de police.

constant ['kɒnstənt] *a* (*frequent*) incessant; (*unchanging*) constant. ●**constantly** *adv* constamment, sans cesse.

constellation [kɒnstə'leɪʃ(ə)n] *n* constellation *f.*

constipated ['kɒnstɪpeɪtɪd] *a* constipé. ●**constipation** [-'peɪʃ(ə)n] *n* constipation *f.*

constituent [kən'stɪtjʊənt] *n Pol* électeur, -trice *mf.* ●**constituency** *n* circonscription *f* électorale; (*voters*) électeurs *mpl.*

constitute ['kɒnstɪtjuːt] *vt* constituer.

● **constitution** [-'tju:ʃ(ə)n] n (of person)
& Pol constitution f. ● **consti'tutional** a
Pol constitutionnel.
constraint [kən'streınt] n contrainte f.
constrict [kən'strıkt] vt (tighten, narrow)
resserrer; (movement) gêner.
construct [kən'strʌkt] vt construire.
● **construction** [-ʃ(ə)n] n construction
f; **under c.** en construction. ● **constructive** a constructif.
consul ['kɒnsəl] n consul m. ● **consular** a
consulaire. ● **consulate** n consulat m.
consult [kən'sʌlt] vt consulter ‖ vi **to c.
with** discuter avec; **consulting room** (of
doctor) cabinet m de consultation.
● **consultation** [kɒnsəl'teıʃ(ə)n] n consultation f.
consultancy [kən'sʌltənsı] n **c. (firm)**
cabinet m d'experts-conseils; **c. fee**
honoraires mpl de conseils. ● **consultant** n (doctor) spécialiste mf; (financial, legal) expert-conseil m.
consum/e [kən'sju:m] vt (food, supplies
etc) consommer; (of grief, hate etc)
dévorer (qn); **to be consumed by** (grief
etc) être dévoré de. ● **—er** n consommateur, -trice mf; **gas/electricity c.**
abonné, -ée mf au gaz/à l'électricité;
c. goods/society biens mpl/société f
de consommation. ● **consumption**
[-'sʌmpʃ(ə)n] n consommation f (of de).
contact ['kɒntækt] n contact m; (person)
contact m, relation f; **in c. with** en
contact avec; **c. lenses** lentilles fpl or
verres mpl de contact ‖ vt contacter, se
mettre en contact avec.
contagious [kən'teıdʒəs] a contagieux.
contain [kən'teın] vt (enclose, hold back)
contenir. ● **—er** n récipient m; (for
transporting goods) conteneur m.
contaminate [kən'tæmıneıt] vt contaminer.
contemplate ['kɒntəmpleıt] vt (look at)
contempler; (consider) envisager (**doing**
de faire).
contemporary [kən'tempərərı] a contemporain (**with** de); (pattern, style
etc) moderne ‖ n (person) contempo-

rain, -aine mf.
contempt [kən'tempt] n mépris m; **to hold
in c.** mépriser. ● **contemptible** a méprisable. ● **contemptuous** a dédaigneux (**of**
de).
contend [kən'tend] vi **to c. with** (problem
etc) faire face à; **to c. with s.o.** (deal
with) avoir affaire à qn; (compete)
rivaliser avec qn. ● **—er** n concurrent,
-ente mf.
content¹ [kən'tent] a satisfait (**with** de);
he's c. to do il ne demande pas mieux
que de faire. ● **—ed** a satisfait.
content² ['kɒntent] n (of text etc) (subject
matter) contenu m; pl (of container,
letter etc) (total within) contenu m;
(**table of) contents** (of book) table f
des matières; **alcoholic c.** teneur f en
alcool.
contentious [kən'tenʃəs] a (issue) liti-
gieux.
contest [kən'test] vt (dispute) contester;
(fight for) disputer ‖ ['kɒntest] n (competition) concours m; (fight) lutte f.
● **con'testant** n concurrent, -ente mf;
(in fight) adversaire mf.
context ['kɒntekst] n contexte m.
continent ['kɒntınənt] n continent m; **the
C.** l'Europe f (continentale). ● **con-
ti'nental** a européen; Geog continental; **c. breakfast** petit déjeuner m à la
française.
contingent [kən'tındʒənt] **1** a **to be c.
upon** dépendre de. **2** nm (group) contingent m. ● **contingency** n éventualité f;
c. plan plan m d'urgence.
continual [kən'tınjʊəl] a continuel.
● **continually** adv continuellement.
continue [kən'tınju:] vt continuer (**to do**
or **doing** à or de faire); **to c. (with)** (work
etc) poursuivre, continuer; (resume)
reprendre; **to be continued** (of story) à
suivre ‖ vi continuer; (resume) reprendre. ● **continuation** [-'eıʃ(ə)n] n
continuation f; (resumption) reprise f;
(new episode) suite f.
continuous [kən'tınjʊəs] a continu; **c.
film programme** cinéma m permanent.

●**continuously** *adv* sans interruption.

contort [kən'tɔːt] *vt* (*twist*) tordre; **to c. oneself** se contorsionner.

contour ['kɒntʊər] *n* contour *m*.

contraception [kɒntrə'sepʃ(ə)n] *n* contraception *f*. ●**contraceptive** *a* & *n* contraceptif (*m*).

contract[1] ['kɒntrækt] *n* contrat *m*; **c. work** travail *m* en sous-traitance. ●**con'tractor** *n* entrepreneur *m*.

contract[2] [kən'trækt] *vt* (*illness, debt, muscle etc*) contracter ▌*vi* (*of heart*) se contracter. ●**contraction** [-ʃ(ə)n] *n* (*of muscle, word*) contraction *f*.

contradict [kɒntrə'dɪkt] *vt* contredire. ●**contradiction** [-ʃ(ə)n] *n* contradiction *f*. ●**contradictory** *a* contradictoire.

contralto [kən'træltəʊ] *n* (*pl* -os) contralto *m*.

contraption [kən'træpʃ(ə)n] *n* *Fam* engin *m*, machin *m*.

contrary ['kɒntrərɪ] *a* contraire (**to** à) ▌*adv* **c. to** contrairement à ▌*n* contraire *m*; **on the c.** au contraire; **unless you, I** *etc* **hear to the c.** sauf avis contraire.

contrast **1** ['kɒntrɑːst] *n* contraste *m*; **in c.** to par opposition à. **2** [kən'trɑːst] *vi* contraster (**with** avec) ▌*vt* mettre en contraste. ●**—ing** *a* (*colours, opinions etc*) opposés.

contravene [kɒntrə'viːn] *vt* (*law*) enfreindre.

contribute [kən'trɪbjuːt] *vt* donner (**to** à); (*article*) écrire (**to** pour); **to c. money to** contribuer à ▌*vi* **to c.** contribuer à; (*publication*) collaborer à. ●**contribution** [kɒntrɪ'bjuːʃ(ə)n] *n* contribution *f*; (*to fund etc*) cotisation(s) *f(pl)*; (*newspaper article*) article *m*. ●**contributor** *n* (*to newspaper*) collaborateur, -trice *mf*; (*of money*) donateur, -trice *mf*.

contrive [kən'traɪv] *vt* **to c. to do** trouver moyen de faire.

contrived [kən'traɪvd] *a* artificiel.

control [kən'trəʊl] *vt* (**-ll-**) (*business, organization*) diriger; (*traffic*) régler; (*prices, quality, situation, emotion*) contrôler; (*child, animal*) tenir; **to c. oneself** se contrôler.

▌*n* (*authority*) autorité *f* (**over** sur); (*over prices, quality*) contrôle *m*; (*over one's emotions*) maîtrise *f*; **the controls** (*of train etc*) les commandes *fpl*; (*knobs*) *TV Rad* les boutons *mpl*; (**self-**)**c.** le contrôle de soi-même, la maîtrise (de soi); **to keep s.o. under c.** tenir qn; **to bring under c.** (*fire, inflation*) maîtriser; **everything is under c.** tout est en ordre; **in c. of** (*situation, vehicle*) maître de; **I'm in c.** (*of situation*) j'ai la situation en main; **to lose c. of** (*situation, vehicle*) perdre le contrôle de; **out of c.** (*situation, crowd*) difficilement maîtrisable; **c. tower** *Av* tour *f* de contrôle. ●**controller** *n* **air traffic c.** contrôleur *m* aérien, aiguilleur *m* du ciel.

controversy ['kɒntrəvɜːsɪ] *n* controverse *f*. ●**contro'versial** *a* (*book, author*) contesté, controversé; (*doubtful*) discutable.

convalesce [kɒnvə'les] *vi* (*rest*) être en convalescence. ●**convalescence** *n* convalescence *f*. ●**convalescent home** *n* maison *f* de convalescence.

convector [kən'vektər] *n* **c.** (**heater**) convecteur *m*.

convenience [kən'viːnɪəns] *n* commodité *f*; (*advantage*) avantage *m*; **at your c.** quand vous voudrez; (*public*) **conveniences** toilettes *fpl*; **c. food(s)** plats *mpl* tout préparés; **c. store** magasin *m* de proximité.

convenient [kən'viːnɪənt] *a* commode, pratique; (*well-situated*) bien situé (**for the shops**/*etc* par rapport aux magasins/*etc*); (*moment*) convenable, opportun; **to be c. (for)** (*suit*) convenir (à). ●**—ly** *adv* **c. situated** bien situé.

convent ['kɒnvənt] *n* couvent *m*.

convention [kən'venʃ(ə)n] *n* (*custom*) usage *m*, convention *f*; (*meeting*) assemblée *f*; (*agreement*) convention *f*. ●**conventional** *a* conventionnel.

converg/e [kən'vɜːdʒ] *vi* converger. ●**—ing** *a* convergent.

conversant [kən'vɜːsənt] *a* to be c. with (*custom, author etc*) connaître; (*fact*) savoir.

conversation [kɒnvə'seɪʃ(ə)n] *n* conversation *f*. ● **conversational** *a* (*tone*) de la conversation.

converse 1 [kən'vɜːs] *vi* s'entretenir (**with** avec). **2** ['kɒnvɜːs] *a & n* inverse (*m*). ● **conversely** *adv* inversement.

convert [kən'vɜːt] *vt* (*change*) convertir (**into** en); (*building*) aménager (**into** en); **to c. s.o.** *Rel* convertir qn (**to** à) ▮ ['kɒnvɜːt] *n* converti, -ie *mf*.

convertible [kən'vɜːtəb(ə)l] *n* (*car*) (voiture *f*) décapotable *f* ▮ *a* (*sofa*) convertible.

convex ['kɒnveks] *a* convexe.

convey [kən'veɪ] *vt* (*goods, people*) transporter; (*sound, message, order*) transmettre; (*idea*) communiquer (**to** à); (*evoke*) évoquer; (*water etc through pipes*) amener. ● **conveyor belt** *n* tapis *m* roulant.

convict ['kɒnvɪkt] *n* forçat *m* ▮ [kən'vɪkt] *vt* reconnaître *or* déclarer coupable (**of** de). ● **conviction** [-ʃ(ə)n] *n* *Jur* condamnation *f*; (*belief*) conviction *f*.

convinc/e [kən'vɪns] *vt* convaincre, persuader (**of** de). ●—**ing** *a* convaincant.

convoluted [kɒnvə'luːtɪd] *a* (*argument, style*) compliqué, tarabiscoté.

convoy ['kɒnvɔɪ] *n* (*ships, cars*) convoi *m*.

convulsion [kən'vʌlʃ(ə)n] *n* convulsion *f*.

coo [kuː] *vi* (*of dove*) roucouler.

cook [kʊk] *vt* (*food*) (faire) cuire; **to c. up** *Fam* inventer ▮ *vi* (*of food*) cuire; (*of person*) faire la cuisine; **what's cooking?** *Fam* qu'est-ce qui se passe? ▮ *n* (*person*) cuisinier, -ière *mf*. ●—**ing** *n* cuisine *f*; **c. apple** pomme *f* à cuire. ● **cooker** *n* (*stove*) cuisinière *f*.

cookbook ['kʊkbʊk] *n* livre *m* de cuisine. ● **cookery** *n* cuisine *f*; **c. book** livre *m* de cuisine.

cookie ['kʊkɪ] *n* *Am* biscuit *m*, gâteau *m* sec.

cool [kuːl] *a* (**-er, -est**) (*weather, place, drink etc*) frais (*f* fraîche); (*having cooled down*) (*tea etc*) qui n'est plus très chaud; (*calm*) (*manner, person*) calme; (*unfriendly*) (*reception etc*) froid; **I feel c.** (*cold*) j'ai (un peu) froid; (*no longer hot*) j'ai moins chaud; **to keep sth c.** tenir qch au frais. ▮ *n* (*of evening*) fraîcheur *f*; **to keep/lose one's c.** garder/perdre son sang-froid. ▮ *vt* **to c.** (**down**) refroidir, rafraîchir. ▮ *vi* **to c.** (**down** or **off**) (*of hot liquid*) refroidir; (*of enthusiasm*) se refroidir; (*of anger, angry person*) se calmer; **to c. off** (*refresh oneself by drinking, swimming etc*) se rafraîchir. ● **cooler** *n* (*for food*) glacière *f*. ● **coolly** *adv* calmement; (*to welcome*) froidement. ● **coolness** *n* fraîcheur *f*; (*unfriendliness*) froideur *f*.

cool-headed [kuːl'hedɪd] *a* calme.

coop [kuːp] **1** *n* (*for chickens*) poulailler *m*. **2** *vt* **to c. s.o. up** enfermer qn.

co-op ['kəʊɒp] *n* *Am* appartement *m* en copropriété.

co-operate [kəʊ'ɒpəreɪt] *vi* coopérer (**in** à, **with** avec). ● **co-operation** [-'reɪʃ(ə)n] *n* coopération *f*.

co-operative [kəʊ'ɒpərətɪv] *a* coopératif ▮ *n* coopérative *f*.

co-ordinate [kəʊ'ɔːdɪneɪt] *vt* coordonner.

▮▮▮ [ɒp] *n* (*policeman*) *Fam* flic *m*.

cope [kəʊp] *vi* **to c. with** s'occuper de; (*problem*) faire face à; **(to be able) to c.** (*savoir*) se débrouiller.

co-pilot ['kəʊpaɪlət] *n* copilote *m*.

copper ['kɒpər] *n* (*metal*) cuivre *m*; *pl* (*coins*) petite monnaie *f*.

copy ['kɒpɪ] *n* copie *f*; (*of book, magazine etc*) exemplaire *m* ▮ *vti* copier ▮ *vt* **to c. out** or **down** (*text, letter etc*) (re)copier. ● **copyright** *n* copyright *m*.

coral ['kɒrəl] *n* corail *m*; **c. reef** récif *m* de corail.

cord [kɔːd] **1** *n* (*heavy string*) corde *f*; (*of curtain etc*) cordon *m*; *El* cordon *m* électrique; **vocal cords** cordes *fpl* vocales. **2** *npl* (*trousers, Am pants*) *Fam* velours m.

cordial ['kɔːdɪəl] **1** a (friendly) cordial. **2** n (fruit) c. sirop m.

cordon ['kɔːdən] n cordon m ▮ vt **to c. off** (of police) interdire l'accès de (lieu).

corduroy ['kɔːdərɔɪ] n (fabric) velours m côtelé; pl (trousers, Am pants) pantalon m en velours (côtelé).

core [kɔːr] n (of apple etc) trognon m; (of problem) cœur m; (group of people) noyau m ▮ vt (apple) vider.

cork [kɔːk] n liège m; (for bottle) bouchon m ▮ vt **to c. (up)** (bottle) boucher. ● **corkscrew** n tire-bouchon m.

corn [kɔːn] n **1** (wheat) blé m; (maize) Am maïs m; **c. on the cob** épi m de maïs. **2** (hard skin on foot) cor m. ● **corned beef** n corned-beef m. ● **cornflakes** npl céréales fpl. ● **cornflour** (Am **cornstarch**) n farine f de maïs, maïzena® f.

corner ['kɔːnər] **1** n coin m; (bend in road) virage m; Fb corner m; **in a (tight) c.** dans une situation difficile; **around the c.** (shops etc) à deux pas. **2** vt (person in corridor etc) coincer; (animal) acculer; (market) Com monopoliser ▮ vi Aut prendre un virage.

cornet ['kɔːnɪt] n (of ice cream) cornet m.

Cornwall ['kɔːnwəl] n Cornouailles f. ● **Cornish** a de Cornouailles.

corny ['kɔːnɪ] a (-ier, -iest) (joke) rebattu.

coronary ['kɒrənərɪ] n Med infarctus m.

coronation [kɒrə'neɪʃ(ə)n] n couronnement m, sacre m.

coroner ['kɒrənər] n coroner m (officier de police judiciaire qui enquête en cas de mort suspecte).

corporal ['kɔːpərəl] **1** n Mil caporal(-chef) m. **2** a **c. punishment** châtiment m corporel.

corporation [kɔːpə'reɪʃ(ə)n] n (business) société f commerciale.

corporate ['kɔːpərət] a (decision etc) collectif.

corps [kɔːr, pl kɔːz] n Mil Pol corps m.

corpse [kɔːps] n cadavre m.

corpulent ['kɔːpjulənt] a corpulent.

correct [kə'rekt] a (right, accurate) (answer etc) exact, correct; (proper) correct; **he's c.** il a raison ▮ vt corriger. ● **-ly** adv correctement. ● **correction** [-ʃ(ə)n] n correction f.

correspond [kɒrɪ'spɒnd] vi **1** (agree, be similar) correspondre (**to, with** à). **2** (by letter) correspondre (**with** avec). ● **-ing** a (matching) correspondant. ● **correspondence** n correspondance f; **c. course** cours m par correspondance. ● **correspondent** n (journalist) envoyé, -ée mf.

corridor ['kɒrɪdɔːr] n couloir m.

corrode [kə'rəud] vt ronger, corroder ▮ vi se corroder; (rust) rouiller.

corrugated ['kɒrəgeɪtɪd] a **c. iron** tôle f ondulée; **c. cardboard** carton m.

corrupt [kə'rʌpt] vt corrompre ▮ a corrompu. ● **corruption** [-ʃ(ə)n] n corruption f.

corset ['kɔːsɪt] n (boned) corset m; (elasticated) gaine f.

Corsica ['kɔːsɪkə] n Corse f.

cos [kɒs] n **c. (lettuce)** (laitue f) romaine f.

cosh [kɒʃ] n matraque f ▮ vt matraquer.

cosmetic [kɒz'metɪk] n produit m de beauté ▮ a (surgery) esthétique; Fig superficiel.

cosmic ['kɒzmɪk] a cosmique. ● **cosmonaut** n cosmonaute mf.

cosset ['kɒsɪt] vt choyer.

cost [kɒst] vti (pt & pp cost) coûter; **how much does it c.?** ça coûte or ça vaut combien?; **to c. the earth** Fam coûter les yeux de la tête ▮ n prix m; **to my c.** à mes dépens; **at all costs** à tout prix; **the c. of living** le coût de la vie. ● **c.-effective** a rentable. ● **costly** a (-ier, -iest) (expensive) coûteux; (valuable) de valeur.

co-star ['kəustɑːr] n Cin Th partenaire mf.

costume ['kɒstjuːm] n costume m; (woman's suit) tailleur m; (swimming) **c.** maillot m (de bain); **c. jewellery** or Am **jewelry** bijoux mpl de fantaisie.

cosy ['kəuzɪ] **1** a (-ier, -iest) (house etc)

douillet (f -ette); **make yourself c.** mets-toi à l'aise; **we're c.** on est bien ici. **2** n (tea) c. couvre-théière m.

cot [kɒt] n (for baby) lit m d'enfant; (camp bed) Am lit m de camp.

cottage ['kɒtɪdʒ] n petite maison f de campagne; (thatched) **c.** chaumière f; **c. cheese** fromage m blanc (maigre).

cotton ['kɒtən] n coton m; (yarn) fil m (de coton); **c. wool,** Am **absorbent c.** coton m hydrophile, ouate f; **c. candy** Am barbe f à papa ▮ a (shirt etc) de ou en coton.

couch [kaʊtʃ] n canapé m.

couchette [ku:'ʃet] n (on train) couchette f.

cough [kɒf] **1** n toux f; **c. syrup** or **mixture** sirop m contre la toux ▮ vi tousser ▮ vt **to c. up** (blood) cracher. **2** vti **to c. up** (pay) Sl casquer.

could [kʊd, unstressed kəd] see **can**[1].

couldn't ['kʊd(ə)nt] = could not.

council ['kaʊns(ə)l] n conseil m; (town or city) **c.** conseil m municipal; **c. flat/ house** appartement m/maison f loué(e) à la municipalité, = HLM m or f. ● **councillor** n (town) **c.** conseiller m municipal.

counsel ['kaʊnsəl] n inv (advice) conseil m ▮ vt (-ll-, Am -l-) conseiller (s.o. to do à qn de faire). ● **counsellor** (Am **counselor**) n conseiller, -ère mf.

count[1] [kaʊnt] vt compter; **not counting Paul** sans compter Paul; **to c. in** (include) inclure; **to c. out** (exclude) exclure; (money) compter. ▮ vi (calculate, be important) compter; **to c. on s.o./sth** (rely on) compter sur qn/qch; **to c. on doing** compter faire. ▮ n **he's lost c. of** or **he can't keep c. of the books he has** il ne sait plus combien il a de livres. ● **countdown** n compte m à rebours.

count[2] [kaʊnt] n (title) comte m.

countenance ['kaʊntɪnəns] n (face) Lit mine f, expression f.

counter ['kaʊntər] **1** n (in shop, bar etc) comptoir m; (in bank etc) guichet m. **2** n (in games) jeton m. **3** adv **c. to** à l'encontre de. **4** vt (threat) répondre à; (decision) s'opposer à; (effect) neutraliser; (blow) parer ▮ vi riposter (with par).

counter- ['kaʊntər] pref contre-.

counteract [kaʊntə'rækt] vt (influence etc) neutraliser.

counterattack ['kaʊntərətæk] n contre-attaque f ▮ vti contre-attaquer.

counterclockwise [kaʊntə'klɒkwaɪz] a & adv Am dans le sens inverse des aiguilles d'une montre.

counterfeit ['kaʊntəfɪt] a faux (f fause) ▮ n contrefaçon f, faux m ▮ vt contre-faire.

counterfoil ['kaʊntəfɔɪl] n souche f.

counterpart ['kaʊntəpɑːt] n (thing) équivalent m; (person) homologue mf.

counterproductive [kaʊntəprə'dʌktɪv] a (action) inefficace, qui produit l'effet contraire.

countess ['kaʊntɪs] n comtesse f.

countless ['kaʊntləs] a innombrable.

country ['kʌntrɪ] n pays m; (regarded with affection) patrie f; (opposed to town) campagne f ▮ a (house etc) de campagne; **c. dancing** la danse folklo-rique. ● **countryside** n campagne f.

county ['kaʊntɪ] n comté m.

coup [ku:, pl ku:z] n Pol coup m d'État.

couple ['kʌp(ə)l] n (of people) couple m; **a c. of** deux ou trois; (a few) quelques.

coupon ['ku:pɒn] n (voucher for gift, meal etc) bon m.

courage ['kʌrɪdʒ] n courage m. ● **courageous** [kə'reɪdʒəs] a courageux.

courgette [kʊə'ʒet] n courgette f.

courier ['kʊrɪər] n (for tourists) guide m; (messenger) messager m; **c. service** service m de messagerie.

course [kɔːs] **1** n (duration, movement) cours m; (of ship) route f; (way) Fig route f, chemin m; **c. (of action)** ligne f de conduite; (option) parti m; **in the c. of** au cours de; **in due c.** en temps utile. **2** n (lessons) Sch Univ cours m; **c. of lectures** série f de conférences.

3 c. (of treatment) Med traitement m.
4 n (of meal) plat m; **first c.** entrée f.
5 n (racecourse) champ m de courses;
(golf) c. terrain m (de golf).
6 adv **of c.!** bien sûr!, mais oui!; **of c. not!**
bien sûr que non!

court [kɔːt] 1 n (of king etc) cour f; Jur
cour f, tribunal m; (tennis) c. court m
(de tennis); **high c.** cour f suprême; **to
take s.o to c.** poursuivre qn en justice;
c. **shoe** escarpin m.
2 vt (woman) faire la cour à; (danger)
aller au-devant de. ●**courthouse** n palais m de justice. ●**courtroom** n salle f du
tribunal. ●**courtyard** n cour f.

courteous ['kɜːtɪəs] a poli, courtois.
●**courtesy** n politesse f, courtoisie f.

courtier ['kɔːtɪər] n Hist courtisan m.

court-martial [kɔːt'mɑːʃəl] n conseil m
de guerre ‖ vt (-ll-, Am -l-) faire passer
en conseil de guerre.

cousin ['kʌz(ə)n] n cousin, -ine mf.

Coventry ['kɒvəntrɪ] n **to send s.o. to C.**
(punish) mettre qn en quarantaine.

cover ['kʌvər] n (lid) couvercle m; (of
book) couverture f; (for furniture, typewriter) housse f; **the covers** (on bed) les
couvertures fpl et les draps mpl; **to take
c.** se mettre à l'abri; c. **charge** (in
restaurant) couvert m; c. **note** certificat
m provisoire d'assurance.
‖ vt couvrir (with de); (protect) protéger, couvrir; (distance) parcourir, couvrir; (insure) assurer; **to c. over** (floor etc)
recouvrir; **to c. up** recouvrir; (truth,
tracks) dissimuler; (scandal) étouffer.
‖ vi **to c. (oneself) up** (wrap up) se
couvrir; **to c. up for s.o.** couvrir qn.
●**cover-up** n tentative f pour camoufler
une affaire.

coverage ['kʌvərɪdʒ] n TV etc reportage
m (of sur).

coveralls ['kʌvərɔːlz] npl Am bleu m de
travail.

covering ['kʌvərɪŋ] n (wrapping) enveloppe f; (layer) couche f; c. **letter** lettre f
jointe (à un document).

covet ['kʌvɪt] vt convoiter.

cow [kaʊ] 1 n vache f; (nasty woman)
Fam chameau m. 2 vt **to be cowed**
(afraid) être intimidé. ●**cowboy** n
cow-boy m. ●**cowshed** n étable f.

coward ['kaʊəd] n lâche mf. ●**cowardly** a
lâche. ●**cowardice** n lâcheté f.

cower ['kaʊər] vi (with fear) trembler.

coy [kɔɪ] a (-er, -est) qui fait son or sa
timide.

coyote [kaɪ'əʊtɪ] n (wolf) Am coyote m.

cozy ['kəʊzɪ] a Am = **cosy**.

crab [kræb] 1 n crabe m. 2 vi (-bb-)
(complain) Fam rouspéter. ●**crabby** a
(-ier, -iest) (person) grincheux.

crack¹ [kræk] n fente f; (in glass, china,
bone) fêlure f; (in skin) crevasse f;
(noise) craquement m; (of whip) claquement m; (joke) Fam plaisanterie f (at
aux dépens de); **at the c. of dawn** au
point du jour.
‖ vt (glass, ice) fêler; (nut) casser; (skin)
crevasser; (whip) faire claquer; (joke)
lancer; (code) déchiffrer; (safe) percer.
‖ vi se fêler; se crevasser; (of branch,
wood) craquer; **to get cracking** (get to
work) Fam s'y mettre; **to c. down on**
sévir contre; **to c. up** (mentally) Fam
craquer. ●**cracker** n 1 (biscuit) biscuit m
(salé). 2 (firework) pétard m; Christmas
c. diablotin m. ●**crackers** a (mad) Sl
cinglé. ●**crackpot** n Fam cinglé, -ée m.

crack² [kræk] a (first-rate) de premier
ordre; c. **shot** tireur m d'élite.

crackle ['kræk(ə)l] vi (of fire) crépiter;
(of sth frying) grésiller ‖ n crépitement
m; grésillement m.

cradle ['kreɪd(ə)l] n berceau m ‖ vt
bercer.

craft [krɑːft] 1 n (skill) art m; (job) métier
m (artisanal). 2 n inv (boat) bateau m.
●**craftsman** n (pl -men) artisan m.
●**craftsmanship** n (skill) art m

crafty ['krɑːftɪ] a (-ier, -iest) astucieux,
Pej rusé.

crag [kræg] n rocher m à pic.

cram [kræm] vt (-mm-) **to c. sth into**
(force) fourrer qch dans; **to c. with** (fill)
bourrer de ‖ vi **to c. into** (of people)

s'entasser dans; **to c. (for an exam)** bachoter.

cramp [kræmp] *n Med* crampe *f* (**in** à).

cramped [kræmpt] *a* (*in a room or one's clothes*) à l'étroit; **in c. conditions** à l'étroit.

cranberry ['krænbəri] *n* canneberge *f*.

crane [kreɪn] *n* (*machine, bird*) grue *f*.

crank [kræŋk] **1** *n* (*person*) *Fam* excentrique *mf*; (*fanatic*) fanatique *mf*. **2** *n* (*handle*) *Tech* manivelle *f*. ● **cranky** *a* (**-ier, -iest**) excentrique; (*bad-tempered*) *Am* grincheux.

crannies ['krænɪz] *npl* **nooks and c.** coins et recoins *mpl*.

crash [kræʃ] *n* accident *m*; (*of firm*) faillite *f*; (*noise*) fracas *m*; (*of thunder*) coup *m*; **c. course/diet** cours *m*/régime *m* intensif; **c. barrier** glissière *f* de sécurité; **c. helmet** casque *m* (anti-choc); **c. landing** atterrissage *m* en catastrophe.

‖ *int* (*of fallen object*) patatras!

‖ *vt* (*car*) avoir un accident avec; **to c. one's car into** faire rentrer sa voiture dans.

‖ *vi* (*of car, plane*) s'écraser; **to c. into** rentrer dans; **the cars crashed into each other** les voitures se sont percutées; **to (down)** (*fall*) tomber; (*break*) se casser. ● **crash-land** *vi* atterrir en catastrophe.

crate [kreɪt] *n* (*large*) caisse *f*; (*small*) cageot *m*; (*for bottles*) casier *m*.

crater ['kreɪtər] *n* cratère *m*.

cravat [krə'væt] *n* foulard *m* (*autour du cou*).

craving ['kreɪvɪŋ] *n* désir *m*, grand besoin *m* (**for** de).

crawl [krɔːl] *vi* ramper; (*of child*) marcher à quatre pattes; (*of vehicle*) avancer au pas; **to be crawling with** grouiller de **‖** *n Swimming* crawl *m*; **to move at a c.** *Aut* avancer au pas.

crayfish ['kreɪfɪʃ] *n inv* (*freshwater*) écrevisse *f*.

crayon ['kreɪən] *n* crayon *m* de couleur (*en cire*).

craze [kreɪz] *n* manie *f* (**for** de). ● **crazed**

a affolé.

crazy ['kreɪzɪ] *a* (**-ier, -iest**) fou (*f* folle); **c. about sth** fana de qch; **c. about s.o.** fou de qn.

creak [kriːk] *vi* (*of hinge*) grincer; (*floorboards*) craquer. ● **creaky** *a* grinçant; qui craque.

cream [kriːm] *n* crème *f*; **c. cake** gâteau *m* à la crème; **c.(-coloured)** crème *inv*; **c. cheese** fromage *m* blanc **‖** *vt* **to c. off** *Fig* écrémer. ● **creamy** *a* (**-ier, -iest**) crémeux.

crease [kriːs] *vt* froisser **‖** *vi* se froisser **‖** *n* pli *m*. ● **c.-resistant** *a* infroissable.

create [kriː'eɪt] *vt* créer; (*impression, noise*) faire. ● **creation** [-ʃ(ə)n] *n* création *f*. ● **creative** *a* (*person, activity*) créatif. ● **creator** *n* créateur, -trice *f*.

creature ['kriːtʃər] *n* animal *m*, bête *f*; (*person*) créature *f*.

crèche [kreʃ] *n* (*nursery*) crèche *f*.

credentials [krɪ'denʃəlz] *npl* références *fpl*; (*identity*) pièces *fpl* d'identité; (*of diplomat*) lettres *fpl* de créance.

credible ['kredɪb(ə)l] *a* croyable; (*politician, information*) crédible. ● **credi'bility** *n* crédibilité *f*.

credit ['kredɪt] *n* (*financial*) crédit *m*; (*merit*) mérite *m*; *Univ* unité *f* de valeur; *pl* (*of film*) générique *m*; **to give c. to** (*person*) *Fig* reconnaître le mérite de; (*statement*) ajouter foi à; **to be a c. to** faire honneur à; **on c.** à crédit; **in c.** (*account*) créditeur; **to one's c.** *Fig* à son actif; **c. balance** solde *m* créditeur; **c. card** carte *f* de crédit; **c. facilities** facilités *fpl* de paiement.

‖ *vt* (*of bank*) créditer (**s.o. with sth** qn de qch). ● **creditor** *n* créancier, -ière *mf*. ● **creditworthy** *a* solvable.

creed [kriːd] *n* credo *m*.

creek [kriːk] *n* (*stream*) *Am* ruisseau *m*; (*bay*) crique *f*.

creep [kriːp] **1** *vi* (*pt & pp* **crept**) ramper; (*silently*) se glisser (furtivement); (*slowly*) avancer lentement. **2** *n* (*person*) *Sl* salaud *m*; **it gives me the creeps**

Fam ça me fait froid dans le dos.
● **creepy** *a* (**-ier, -iest**) *Fam* terrifiant;
(*nasty*) vilain. ● **creepy-'crawly** or *Am*
creepy-'crawler *n Fam* bestiole *f.*

cremate [krɪ'meɪt] *vt* incinérer. ● **crema-**
tion [-ʃ(ə)n] *n* crémation *f.* ● **cre-**
ma'torium *n* crématorium *m.*
● **crematory** ['kri:mətə:rɪ] *n Am* crématorium *m.*

crêpe [kreɪp] *n* (*fabric, rubber*) crêpe *m*;
c. paper papier *m* crêpon.

crept [krept] *pt & pp of* **creep 1.**

crescent ['kres(ə)nt] *n* croissant *m*;
(*street*) rue *f* (en demi-lune).

cress [kres] *n* cresson *m.*

crest [krest] *n* (*of wave, mountain*) crête
f; (*of hill*) sommet *m.*

Crete [kri:t] *n* Crète *f.*

cretin ['kretɪn, *Am* 'kri:t(ə)n] *n* crétin,
-ine *mf*

crevice ['krevɪs] *n* (*crack*) crevasse *f*,
fente *f.*

crew [kru:] *n* (*of ship, plane*) équipage *m*;
(*gang*) équipe *f*; **c. cut** (coupe *f* en)
brosse *f.* ● **c.-neck(ed)** *a* à col ras.

crib [krɪb] *n* 1 (*cot*) *Am* lit *m* d'enfant;
(*cradle*) berceau *m*; *Rel* crèche *f.* 2 *n* (*list
of answers*) *Sch* pompe *f*, antisèche *f*
▮ *vti* (**-bb-**) copier.

crick [krɪk] *n* **c. in the neck** torticolis *m.*

cricket ['krɪkɪt] *n* 1 (*game*) cricket *m.* 2
(*insect*) grillon *m.*

crime [kraɪm] *n* crime *m*; (*not serious*)
délit *m*; (*criminal practice*) criminalité *f.*
● **criminal** *a & n* criminel, -elle (*mf*); **c.**
record casier *m* judiciaire.

crimson ['krɪmz(ə)n] *a & n* cramoisi (*m*).

cringe [krɪndʒ] *vi* reculer (**from** devant).

crinkle ['krɪŋk(ə)l] *vt* froisser ▮ *vi* se
froisser.

crippl/e ['krɪp(ə)l] *n* (*disabled*) infirme *mf*
▮ *vt* rendre infirme, estropier; (*nation
etc*) *Fig* paralyser. ● **—ed** *a* infirme; **c.**
with (*rheumatism, pains*) perclus de.

crisis, *pl* **-ses** ['kraɪsɪs, -si:z] *n* crise *f.*

crisp [krɪsp] 1 *a* (**-er, -est**) (*biscuit*)
croustillant; (*apple*) croquant; (*snow*)
craquant; (*air*) vif. 2 *npl* (**potato**) **crisps**

(**pommes** *fpl*) **chips** *fpl*; **packet of crisps**
sachet *m* de chips. ● **crispbread** *n* pain *m*
suédois.

criss-cross ['krɪskrɒs] *a* (*lines*) entre-
croisés ▮ *vi* s'entrecroiser ▮ *vt* sillonner
(en tous sens).

criterion, *pl* **-ia** [kraɪ'tɪərɪən, -ɪə] *n* critère
m.

critic ['krɪtɪk] *n* critique *m.* ● **critical** *a*
critique. ● **critically** *adv* (*to examine*) en
critique; **c. ill** gravement, malade.
● **criticism** *n* critique *f.* ● **criticize** *vti*
critiquer.

croak [krəʊk] *vi* (*of frog*) croasser ▮ *n*
croassement *m.*

Croatia [krəʊ'eɪʃə] *n* Croatie *f.*

crochet ['krəʊʃeɪ] *vt* faire au crochet ▮ *vi*
faire du crochet ▮ *n* (*travail m au*)
crochet *m.*

crockery ['krɒkərɪ] *n* (*cups etc*) vaisselle
f.

crocodile ['krɒkədaɪl] *n* crocodile *m.*

crocus ['krəʊkəs] *n* crocus *m.*

crony ['krəʊnɪ] *n Pej Fam* copain *m*,
copine *f.*

crook [krʊk] *n* 1 (*thief*) escroc *m.* 2
(*shepherd's stick*) houlette *f.*

crooked ['krʊkɪd] *a* (*stick*) courbé;
(*path*) tortueux; (*hat, picture*) de travers; (*deal, person*) malhonnête ▮ *adv* de
travers.

crop [krɒp] 1 *n* (*harvest*) récolte *f*;
(*produce*) culture *f.* 2 *vt* (**-pp-**) (*hair*)
couper (ras) ▮ *n* **c. of hair** chevelure *f.* 3
vi (**-pp-**) **to c. up** se présenter, survenir.
● **cropper** *n* **to come a c.** *Sl* (*fall*)
ramasser une pelle; (*fail*) échouer.

croquet ['krəʊkeɪ] *n* (*game*) croquet *m.*

cross[1] [krɒs] 1 *n* croix *f*; **a c. between**
(*animal*) un croisement entre *or* de; *Fig*
un compromis entre.
2 *vt* (*street, room etc*) traverser; (*barrier*) franchir; (*legs*) croiser; (*cheque,
Am check*) barrer; **to c. off** *or* **out** (*word,
name etc*) rayer; **to c. over** (*road etc*)
traverser; **it never crossed my mind
that...** il ne m'est pas venu à l'esprit
que... ▮ *vi* (*of paths*) se croiser; **to c.**

over traverser. ●**c.-country 'race** *n* cross(-country) *m*. ●**c.-examination** [-'neɪʃ(ə)n] *n* contre-interrogatoire *m*. ●**c.-e'xamine** *vt* interroger. ●**c.-'eyed** *a* qui louche. ●**c.-'reference** *n* renvoi *m*. ●**c.-section** -ʃ(ə)n] *n* coupe *f* transversale; (*sample*) échantillon *m*.

cross² [krɒs] *a* (*angry*) fâché (**with** contre).

crossfire ['krɒsfaɪər] *n* feux *mpl* croisés.

crossing ['krɒsɪŋ] *n* (*by ship*) traversée *f*; (**pedestrian**) c. passage *m* protégé.

crossroads ['krɒsrəʊdz] *n* carrefour *m*.

crosswalk ['krɒswɔːk] *n Am* passage *m* protégé.

crossword ['krɒswɜːd] *n* c. (**puzzle**) mots *mpl* croisés.

crotch [krɒtʃ] *n* (*of garment, person*) entrejambe *m*.

crotchety ['krɒtʃɪtɪ] *a* grincheux.

crouch [kraʊtʃ] *vi* to c. (**down**) s'accroupir. ●**—ing** *a* accroupi.

croupier ['kruːpɪər] *n* (*in casino*) croupier *m*.

crow [krəʊ] **1** *n* corbeau *m*; **as the c. flies** à vol d'oiseau. **2** *vi* (*of cock*) chanter. ●**crowbar** *n* levier *m*.

crowd [kraʊd] *n* foule *f*; (*particular group*) bande *f*; **quite a c.** beaucoup de monde.
vi to c. into (*of people*) s'entasser dans, to c. round s.o./sth se presser autour de qn/qch; **to c. together** se serrer.
vt (*fill*) remplir; **to c. sth into** (*press*) entasser qch dans. ●**crowded** *a* plein (**with** de); **it's very c.!** il y a beaucoup de monde!

crown [kraʊn] *n* (*of king etc*) couronne *f*; **C. jewels** joyaux *mpl* de la Couronne *vt* couronner.

crucial ['kruːʃəl] *a* crucial.

crucifix ['kruːsɪfɪks] *n* crucifix *m*.

crude [kruːd] *a* (**-er, -est**) (*manners, person, language*) grossier; (*painting, work*) rudimentaire; **c. oil** pétrole *m* brut.

cruel [krʊəl] *a* (**crueller, cruellest**) cruel.

● **cruelty** *n* cruauté *f*; **an act of c.** une cruauté.

cruet ['kruːɪt] *n* c. (**stand**) salière *f*, poivrière *f* et huilier *m*.

cruis/e [kruːz] *n* croisière *f* *vi* (*of ship*) croiser; (*of car*) rouler; (*of plane*) voler; (*of tourists*) faire une croisière; **cruising speed** *Nau Av* vitesse *f* de croisière. ●**—er** *n* (*ship*) croiseur *m*.

crumb [krʌm] *n* miette *f*.

crumble ['krʌmb(ə)l] *vt* (*bread*) émietter *vi* (*in small pieces*) s'effriter; (*of bread*) s'émietter; (*become ruined*) tomber en ruine. ●**crumbly** *a* (*pastry etc*) friable.

crummy ['krʌmɪ] *a* (**-ier, -iest**) *Fam* moche.

crumpet ['krʌmpɪt] *n* petite crêpe *f* grillée (*servie beurrée*).

crumple ['krʌmp(ə)l] *vt* froisser *vi* se froisser.

crunch [krʌntʃ] *vt* (*food*) croquer. ●**crunchy** *a* (**-ier, -iest**) (*apple etc*) croquant; (*bread, biscuit, Am cookie*) croustillant.

crusade [kruːˈseɪd] *n* croisade *f*.

crush [krʌʃ] **1** *n* (*crowd*) cohue *f*; (*rush*) bousculade *f*; **to have a c. on s.o.** *Fam* en pincer pour qn. **2** *vt* écraser; (*hope*) détruire; (*clothes*) froisser; (*cram*) entasser (**into** dans). ●**—ing** *a* (*defeat*) écrasant.

crust [krʌst] *n* croûte *f* ●**crusty** *a* (**-ier, -iest**) (*bread*) croustillant.

crutch [krʌtʃ] *n* **1** *Med* béquille *f*. **2** (*crotch*) entrejambe *m*.

crux [krʌks] *n* **the c. of the matter** le nœud de l'affaire.

cry [kraɪ] *n* (*shout*) cri *m*; **to have a c.** *Fam* pleurer.
vi (*weep*) pleurer; **to c. (out)** pousser un cri, crier; (*exclaim*) s'écrier; **to c. (out) for** *of person*) demander (à grands cris); **to be crying out for** (*of thing*) avoir grand besoin de; **to c. off** (*sth*) se désintéresser (de qch); **to c. over sth/s.o.** pleurer (sur) qch/qn.
vt to c. (**out**) (*shout*) crier. ●**crying** *n* cris *mpl*; (*weeping*) pleurs *mpl*.

crypt [krɪpt] *n* crypte *f*.

crystal ['krɪst(ə)l] *n* cristal *m*. • **c.-'clear** *a* (water, sound) cristallin; *Fig* clair comme le jour.

cub [kʌb] *n* **1** (of animal) petit *m*, petite *f*. **2** (scout) louveteau *m*.

Cuba ['kju:bə] *n* Cuba *m*. • **Cuban** *a* & *n* cubain, -aine (*mf*).

cubbyhole ['kʌbɪhəʊl] *n* cagibi *m*.

cube [kju:b] *n* cube *m*; (of meat etc) dé *m*. • **cubic** *a* (metre etc) cube; **c. capacity** volume *m*; *Aut* cylindrée *f*.

cubicle ['kju:bɪk(ə)l] *n* (for changing clothes) cabine *f*; (in hospital) box *m*.

cuckoo ['kʊku:, *Am* 'ku:ku:] *n* (bird) coucou *m*; **c. clock** coucou *m*.

cucumber ['kju:kʌmbər] *n* concombre *m*.

cuddle ['kʌd(ə)l] *vt* (hug) serrer (dans ses bras); (caress) câliner ‖ *vi* (of lovers) se serrer; **to (kiss and) c.** s'embrasser; **to c. up to s.o.** (huddle) se serrer contre qn ‖ *n* caresse *f*. • **cuddly** *a* (-ier, -iest) *a* câlin, caressant; (toy) doux (*f* douce).

cudgel ['kʌdʒəl] *n* trique *f*, gourdin *m*.

cue [kju:] *n* **1** *Th* réplique *f*; (signal) signal *m*. **2** (billiard) c. queue *f* (de billard).

cuff [kʌf] *n* (of shirt etc) poignet *m*; (of trousers) *Am* revers *m*; **off the c.** impromptu; **c. link** bouton *m* de manchette.

cul-de-sac ['kʌldəsæk] *n* impasse *f*.

culminate ['kʌlmɪneɪt] *vi* **to c. in** finir par.

culprit ['kʌlprɪt] *n* coupable *mf*.

cult [kʌlt] *n* culte *m*.

cultivat/e ['kʌltɪveɪt] *vt* (land, mind etc) cultiver. • **—ed** *a* cultivé. • **cultivation** [-'veɪʃ(ə)n] *n* culture *f*; **fields under c.** cultures *fpl*.

culture ['kʌltʃər] *n* culture *f*. • **cultural** *a* culturel. • **cultured** *a* cultivé.

cumbersome ['kʌmbəsəm] *a* encombrant.

cunning ['kʌnɪŋ] *a* astucieux; *Pej* rusé ‖ *n* astuce *f*; *Pej* ruse *f*.

cup [kʌp] *n* tasse *f*; (goblet, prize) coupe *f*; **c. final** *Fb* finale *f* de la coupe. • **cupful**

n tasse *f*.

cupboard ['kʌbəd] *n* armoire *f*; (built into wall) placard *m*.

cuppa ['kʌpə] *n* *Fam* tasse *f* de thé.

curable ['kjʊərəb(ə)l] *a* guérissable.

curate ['kjʊərɪt] *n* vicaire *m*.

curator [kjʊə'reɪtər] *n* (of museum) conservateur *m*.

curb [kɜ:b] **1** *n* (kerb) *Am* bord *m* du trottoir. **2** *vt* (feelings) refréner; (ambitions) modérer; (expenses) limiter ‖ *n* frein *m*; **to put a c. on** mettre un frein à.

curd cheese ['kɜ:dtʃi:z] *n* fromage *m* blanc (maigre).

curdle ['kɜ:d(ə)l] *vi* se cailler.

cure [kjʊər] *vt* (illness, person) guérir (of de) ‖ *n* remède *m* (for contre); (recovery) guérison *f*; **rest c.** cure *f* de repos.

curfew ['kɜ:fju:] *n* couvre-feu *m*.

curio ['kjʊərɪəʊ] *n* (pl -os) bibelot *m*.

curious ['kjʊərɪəs] *a* (odd) curieux; (inquisitive) curieux (about de); **c. to know** curieux de savoir. • **curi'osity** *n* curiosité *f*.

curl [kɜ:l] **1** *vti* (hair) boucler, friser ‖ *n* boucle *f*. **2** *vi* **to c. up** (shrivel) se racornir; **to c. (oneself) up** (into a ball) se pelotonner. • **—er** *n* bigoudi *m*. • **curly** *a* (-ier, -iest) bouclé; (with tight curls) frisé.

currant ['kʌrənt] *n* (dried grape) raisin *m* de Corinthe; (fruit) groseille *f*.

currency ['kʌrənsɪ] *n* (money) monnaie *f*; (foreign) **c.** devises *fpl* (étrangères).

current ['kʌrənt] **1** *a* (fashion etc) actuel; (opinion, use, phrase) courant; (year, month) en cours; **c. affairs** questions *fpl* d'actualité; **c. events** actualité *f*; **the c. issue** (of magazine etc) le dernier numéro. **2** *n* (of river) & *El* courant *m*. • **—ly** *adv* actuellement, à présent.

curriculum, *pl* **-la** [kə'rɪkjʊləm, -lə] *n* programme *m* (scolaire); **c. vitæ** curriculum vitae *m* inv.

curry ['kʌrɪ] *n* curry *m*, cari *m*.

curse [kɜ:s] *n* malédiction *f*; (swearword) juron *m*; (scourge) fléau *m* ‖ *vt* maudire ‖ *vi* (swear) jurer.

cursor ['kɜːsər] n (on computer screen) curseur m.

cursory ['kɜːsərɪ] a (trop) rapide, superficiel.

curt [kɜːt] a brusque. ●—**ly** adv d'un ton brusque.

curtail [kɜː'teɪl] vt (visit etc) écourter; (expenses) réduire.

curtain ['kɜːt(ə)n] n rideau m.

curts(e)y ['kɜːtsɪ] n révérence f ▮ vi faire une révérence.

curve [kɜːv] n courbe f; (in road) virage m ▮ vt courber ▮ vi se courber; (of road) tourner.

cushion ['kʊʃən] n coussin m ▮ vt (shock) amortir. ●**cushioned** a (seat) rembourré; ●**against** Fig protégé contre.

cushy ['kʊʃɪ] a (-ier, -iest) (job, life) Fam pépère, facile.

custard ['kʌstəd] n crème f anglaise; (when set) crème f renversée.

custody ['kʌstədɪ] n (care) garde f; to take s.o. into c. Jur mettre qn en détention préventive.

custom ['kʌstəm] n coutume f; (customers) clientèle f. ●**customary** a habituel; it is c. to il est d'usage de. ●**custom-built** or **customized** a (car etc) (fait) sur commande. ●**custom-made** a (shirt etc) (fait) sur mesure.

customer ['kʌstəmər] n client, -ente mf.

customs ['kʌstəmz] n(pl) (the) c. la douane; (duties) droits mpl de douane; c. officer douanier m.

cut [kʌt] n (mark) coupure f; (stroke) coup m; (of clothes, hair) coupe f; (in salary, prices etc) réduction f; (of meat) morceau m ▮ vt (pt & pp cut, pres p cutting) couper; (meat) découper; (glass, tree) tailler; (salary, price etc) réduire; (tooth) percer; to c. open ouvrir (au couteau etc); to c. short (visit) abréger ▮ vi (of person, scissors) couper.

cut away vt (remove) enlever ▮ **to cut back (on)** vti réduire. ●**cutback** n réduc-

tion f ▮ **to cut down** vt (tree) abattre, couper ▮ **to cut down (on)** vti réduire ▮ **to cut in** vi (interrupt) interrompre ▮ **to cut into** vi (cake etc) entamer ▮ **to cut off** vt couper; (isolate) isoler ▮ **to cut out** vi (of car engine) caler ▮ vt (article) découper; (garment) tailler; (remove) enlever; (eliminate) supprimer; to c. out drinking (stop) s'arrêter de boire; c. it out! Fam ça suffit!; c. out to be a doctor/etc fait pour être médecin/etc. ●**cutout** n (picture) découpage m; El coupe-circuit m inv. ▮ **to cut up** vt couper (en morceaux); c. up about démoralisé par.

cute [kjuːt] a (-er, -est) (pretty) Fam mignon (f mignonne).

cutlery ['kʌtlərɪ] n couverts mpl.

cutlet ['kʌtlɪt] n (of veal etc) côtelette f.

cut-price [kʌt'praɪs] a à prix réduit.

cutting ['kʌtɪŋ] n coupe f; (newspaper article) coupure f; (plant) bouture f; c. edge tranchant m.

CV [siː'viː] n abbr curriculum (vitae) m inv.

cwt abbr = hundredweight.

cyanide ['saɪənaɪd] n cyanure m.

cycle ['saɪk(ə)l] 1 n bicyclette f, vélo m; c. path or track piste f cyclable; c. race course f cycliste ▮ vi aller à bicyclette (to à); Sp faire de la bicyclette. 2 n (series, period) cycle m ▮ vi cycling n cyclisme m. ●**cyclist** n cycliste mf.

cyclone ['saɪkləʊn] n cyclone m.

cylinder ['sɪlɪndər] n cylindre m.

cymbal ['sɪmb(ə)l] n cymbale f.

cynic ['sɪnɪk] n cynique mf. ●**cynical** a cynique.

Cyprus ['saɪprəs] n Chypre f. ●**Cypriot** ['sɪprɪət] a & n cypriote (mf).

cyst [sɪst] n Med kyste m.

Czech [tʃek] a & n tchèque (mf). ●**Czecho'slovak** a & n tchécoslovaque (mf). ●**Czechoslo'vakia** n Tchécoslovaquie f. ●**Czechoslo'vakian** a & n tchécoslovaque (mf).

D

D, d [diː] *n* D, d *m*. ● **D.-day** *n* le jour J.

dab [dæb] *vt* (-bb-) (*wound etc*) tamponner; **to d. sth on sth** appliquer qch (à petits coups) sur qch.

dabble ['dæb(ə)l] *vi* **to d. in** s'occuper *or* se mêler un peu de.

Dacron® ['dækrɒn] *n Am* tergal® *m*.

dad [dæd] *n Fam* papa *m*. ● **daddy** *n Fam* papa *m*; **d. longlegs** (*cranefly*) tipule *f*; (*spider*) *Am* faucheur *m*.

daffodil ['dæfədɪl] *n* jonquille *f*.

daft [dɑːft] *a* (-er, -est) *Fam* idiot, bête.

dagger ['dægər] *n* poignard *m*.

dahlia ['deɪljə, *Am* 'dæljə] *n* dahlia *m*.

daily ['deɪlɪ] *a* quotidien, journalier ‖ *adv* chaque jour ‖ *n* **d.** (**paper**) quotidien *m*; **d.** (**help**) (*cleaning woman*) femme *f* de ménage.

dainty ['deɪntɪ] *a* (-ier, -iest) délicat; (*pretty*) mignon (*f* -onne).

dairy ['deərɪ] *n* (*on farm*) laiterie *f*; (*shop*) crémerie *f*; **d. product/produce** produit *m*/produits *mpl* laitier(s) ‖ *a* laitier.

daisy ['deɪzɪ] *n* pâquerette *f*.

dale [deɪl] *n Lit* vallée *f*.

dam [dæm] *n* (*wall*) barrage *m* ‖ *vt* (-mm-) (*river*) barrer.

damag/e ['dæmɪdʒ] *n* dégâts *mpl*; (*harm*) préjudice *m*; *pl Jur* dommages-intérêts *mpl* ‖ *vt* (*object*) endommager, abîmer; (*eyesight, health*) abîmer; (*plans, reputation etc*) *Fig* compromettre. ● **—ing** *a* (*harmful*) préjudiciable (**to** à).

damn [dæm] *vt* (*condemn*) condamner; *Rel* damner; **d. him!** *Fam* qu'il aille se faire voir! ‖ *int* **d.** (**it**)! *Fam* merde! ‖ *n* **he doesn't care a d.** *Fam* il s'en fiche pas mal ‖ *a* (*awful*) *Fam* fichu, sacré ‖ *adv* (*very*) *Fam* vachement. ● **—ed** *a Fam* = **damn** *a* & *adv*.

damp [dæmp] *a* (-er, -est) humide ‖ *n* humidité *f*. ● **damp(en)** *vt* humecter; **to**

d. (**down**) (*enthusiasm*) refroidir. ● **dampness** *n* humidité *f*.

danc/e [dɑːns] *n* danse *f*; (*social event*) bal *m* (*pl* bals); **d. hall** salle *f* de danse ‖ *vi* danser ‖ *vt* (*waltz etc*) danser. ● **—ing** *n* danse *f*. ● **dancer** *n* danseur, -euse *f*.

dandelion ['dændɪlaɪən] *n* pissenlit *m*.

dandruff ['dændrʌf] *n* pellicules *fpl*.

Dane [deɪn] *n* Danois, -oise *mf*.

danger ['deɪndʒər] *n* danger *m* (**to** pour); **in d.** en danger; **to be in d. of** (*threatened by*) menacé de; **to be in d. of falling/etc** risquer de tomber/*etc*; **d. zone** zone *f* dangereuse. ● **dangerous** *a* (*place, illness, person etc*) dangereux (**to** pour). ● **dangerously** *adv* **d. ill** gravement malade.

dangle ['dæŋg(ə)l] *vt* balancer ‖ *vi* (*hang*) pendre; (*swing*) se balancer.

Danish ['deɪnɪʃ] *a* danois ‖ *n* (*language*) danois *m*.

dar/e [deər] *vt* oser (**do** faire); **she d. not come** elle n'ose pas venir; **he doesn't d.** (**to**) **go** il n'ose pas y aller; **I d. say he tried** il a sans doute essayé; **to d. s.o. to do** défier qn de faire. ● **—ing** *a* audacieux. ● **daredevil** *n* casse-cou *m inv*.

dark [dɑːk] *a* (-er, -est) obscur, noir, sombre; (*colour*) foncé, sombre; (*skin, hair*) brun, foncé; (*eyes*) sombre; (*gloomy*) sombre; **it's d.** il fait nuit *or* noir; **d. glasses** lunettes *fpl* noires. ‖ *n* noir *m*, obscurité *f*; **after d.** après la tombée de la nuit. ● **d.-'haired** *a* aux cheveux bruns. ● **d.-'skinned** *a* brun. ● **darken** *vt* assombrir, obscurcir ‖ *vi* s'assombrir. ● **darkness** *n* obscurité *f*, noir *m*.

darkroom ['dɑːkruːm] *n Phot* chambre *f* noire.

darling ['dɑːlɪŋ] *n* (*favourite*) chouchou, -oute *mf*; (**my**) **d.** (mon) chéri, (ma) chérie; **he's a d.** c'est un amour; **be a d.!** sois un ange! à chéri.

darn [dɑːn] **1** *vt* (*socks*) repriser. **2** *int* **d. it!** bon sang!

dart [dɑːt] **1** *vi* (*dash*) se précipiter (**for** vers). **2** *n* *Sp* fléchette *f*; *pl* (*game*) fléchettes *fpl*. ●**dartboard** *n* cible *f*.

dash [dæʃ] **1** *n* (*run, rush*) ruée *f*; **to make a d.** se précipiter (**for** vers) ‖ *vi* se précipiter; **to d. off** *or* **away** partir *or* filer en vitesse ‖ *vt* jeter (avec force); (*hopes*) *Fig* briser; **to d. off** (*letter*) faire en vitesse. **2** *n* **a d. of** un (petit) peu de. **3** *n* (*handwritten stroke*) trait *m*; *Typ* tiret *m*.

dashboard ['dæʃbɔːd] *n Aut* tableau *m* de bord.

data ['deɪtə] *npl* données *fpl*; **d. base** base *f* de données; **d. processing** informatique *f*.

date[1] [deɪt] *n* (*time*) date *f*; (*meeting*) *Fam* rendez-vous *m inv*; (*person*) *Fam* copain, -ine *mf* (*avec qui on a un rendez-vous*); **up to d.** moderne; (*information*) à jour; (*well-informed*) au courant (**on** de); **out of d.** (*old-fashioned*) démodé; (*expired*) périmé; **d. stamp** (*tampon m*) dateur *m*; (*mark*) cachet *m*.
‖ *vt* (*letter etc*) dater; (*girl, boy*) *Fam* sortir avec.
‖ *vi* (*become out of date*) dater; **to d. back to** *or* **from** dater de.

date[2] [deɪt] *n* (*fruit*) datte *f*.

datebook ['deɪtbʊk] *n Am* agenda *m*.

daub [dɔːb] *vt* barbouiller (**with** de).

daughter ['dɔːtər] *n* fille *f*. ●**d.-in-law** (*pl* **daughters-in-law**) belle-fille *f*.

daunt [dɔːnt] *vt* décourager, rebuter. ●**—less** *a* intrépide.

dawdl/e ['dɔːd(ə)l] *vi* traîner. ●**—er** *n* traînard, -arde *mf*.

dawn [dɔːn] *n* aube *f*, aurore *f* ‖ *vi* (*of day*) se lever; (*of new era*) naître; **it dawned upon him that...** il lui est venu à l'esprit que....

day [deɪ] *n* jour *m*; (*whole day long*) journée *f*; *pl* (*period*) époque *f*, temps *mpl*; **all d.** (**long**) toute la journée; **the**

following *or* **next d.** le lendemain; **the d. before** la veille; **the d. before yesterday** or **before last** avant-hier; **the d. after tomorrow** après-demain; **d. boarder** demi-pensionnaire *mf*; (*person*) *Fam* crèche *f*; **d. return** *Rail* aller et retour *m* (*pour une journée*); **d. tripper** excursionniste *mf*. ●**d.-to-'day** *a* quotidien, journalier; **on a d.-to-day basis** (*every day*) journellement.

daybreak ['deɪbreɪk] *n* point *m* du jour. ●**daycare** *n* (*for children*) service *m* de garderie. ●**daydream** *n* rêverie *f* ‖ *vi* rêvasser. ●**daylight** (*lumière f du*) jour *m*; **it's d.** il fait jour. ●**daytime** *n* journée *f*, jour *m*.

daze [deɪz] *vt* (*by blow*) étourdir ‖ *n* **in a d.** étourdi; (*because of drugs*) hébété.

dazzle ['dæz(ə)l] *vt* éblouir.

dead [ded] *a* mort; (*numb*) (*arm etc*) engourdi; (*telephone*) sans tonalité; **in d. centre** au beau milieu; **to be a d. loss** (*of person*) *Fam* n'être bon à rien; **it's a d. loss** *Fam* ça ne vaut rien; **d. silence** un silence de mort; **a d. stop** un arrêt complet; **d. end** (*street*) impasse *f*; **a d.-end job** un travail sans avenir.
‖ *adv* (*completely*) absolument; (*very*) très; **d. beat** *Fam* éreinté; **d. drunk** *Fam* ivre mort; **to stop d.** s'arrêter net.
‖ *n* **the d.** les morts *mpl*. ●**deadline** *n* date *f* limite; (*hour*) heure *f* limite.

deaden ['ded(ə)n] *vt* (*shock*) amortir; (*pain*) calmer; (*feeling*) émousser.

deadly ['dedli] *a* (*-ier, -iest*) (*enemy, silence*) mortel; (*weapon*) meurtrier; **d. sins** péchés *mpl* capitaux.

deaf [def] *a* sourd; **d. and dumb** sourd-muet ‖ *n* **the d.** les sourds *mpl*. ●**deafen** *vt* assourdir. ●**deafness** *n* surdité *f*.

deal[1] [diːl] *n* **a good** *or* **great d.** (*a lot*) beaucoup (**of** de).

deal[2] [diːl] *n* **1** *Com* marché *m*, affaire *f*; **to give s.o. a fair d.** traiter qn équitablement; **it's a d.** d'accord; **big d.!** *Iron* la belle affaire!
2 *vt* (*pt & pp* **dealt** [delt]) (*blow*) porter (**to** à); **to d.** (**out**) (*cards*) donner.

3 vi (trade) traiter (**with s.o.** avec qn); **to d. in** faire le commerce de; **to d. with** (take care of) s'occuper de; (concern) (of book etc) traiter de. ● **dealings** npl relations fpl (**with** avec); Com transactions fpl.

dealer ['di:lər] n marchand, -ande mf (**in** de); (agent) dépositaire mf; (for cars) concessionnaire mf; (in drugs) revendeur, -euse mf (de drogues).

dean [di:n] n Rel Univ doyen m.

dear [diər] a (-er, -est) (loved, expensive) cher; (price) élevé; **D. Sir** (in letter) Monsieur; **D. Uncle** (mon) cher oncle; **oh d.!** oh là là!, oh mon Dieu! ∥ n (my) **d.** (darling) (mon) chéri, (ma) chérie; (friend) mon cher, ma chère; **she's a d.** c'est un amour; **be a d.!** sois un ange! ● **dearly** adv (to love) tendrement; (very much) beaucoup; **to pay d. for sth** payer qch cher.

dearth [dɜ:θ] n manque m, pénurie f.

death [deθ] n mort f; **to put to d.** mettre à mort; **to be bored to d.** s'ennuyer à mourir; **to be sick to d.** en avoir vraiment marre; **many deaths** (people killed) de nombreux morts mpl; **d. certificate** acte m de décès; **d. duty** or **duties**, Am **d. taxes** droits mpl de succession; **d. penalty** peine f de mort; **d. rate** mortalité f; **d. sentence** condamnation f à mort; **it's a d. trap** il y a danger de mort. ● **deathbed** n lit m de mort. ● **deathly** a (silence) de mort ∥ adv **d. pale** d'une pâleur mortelle.

debat/e [dɪ'beɪt] vti discuter; **to d. whether to leave/**etc se demander si on doit partir/etc ∥ n débat m, discussion f. ● **—able** a discutable; **its d. whether...** il est difficile de dire si....

debit ['debɪt] n débit m; **in d.** (account) débiteur; **d. balance** solde m débiteur ∥ vt débiter (**s.o. with sth** qn de qch).

debris ['debri:] n débris mpl.

debt [det] n dette f; **to be in d.** avoir des dettes; **to be 50 dollars in d.** devoir 50 dollars; **to run** or **get into d.** faire des dettes. ● **debtor** n débiteur, -trice mf.

debut ['debju:] n Th début m.

decade [dekeɪd] n décennie f.

decadent ['dekədənt] a décadent. ● **decadence** n décadence f.

decaffeinated [di:'kæfɪneɪtɪd] a décaféiné.

decal ['di:kæl] n Am décalcomanie f.

decant [dɪ'kænt] vt (wine) décanter. ● **—er** n carafe f.

decapitate [dɪ'kæpɪteɪt] vt décapiter.

decathlon [dɪ'kæθlən] n Sp décathlon m.

decay [dɪ'keɪ] vi (go bad) se gâter; (rot) pourrir; (of tooth) se carier; (of building) tomber en ruine ∥ n pourriture f; (of building) délabrement m; (of tooth) carie(s) f(pl). ● **—ing** a (meat, fruit etc) pourrissant.

deceased [dɪ'si:st] a décédé, défunt ∥ n **the d.** le défunt, la défunte; pl les défunt(e)s.

deceit [dɪ'si:t] n tromperie f. ● **deceitful** a trompeur.

deceive [dɪ'si:v] vti tromper; **to d. one-self** se faire des illusions.

December [dɪ'sembər] n décembre m.

decent ['di:sənt] a (respectable) convenable, décent; (good) bon (f bonne); (kind) gentil (f -ille). ● **decency** n décence f; (kindness) gentillesse f.

deception [dɪ'sepʃ(ə)n] n tromperie f. ● **deceptive** a trompeur.

decide [dɪ'saɪd] vt (question etc) décider, régler; (s.o.'s career, fate etc) décider de; **to d. to do** décider de faire; **to d. that** décider que; **to d. s.o. to** décider qn à faire.

∥ vi (make decisions) décider; (make up one's mind) se décider (**on doing** à faire); **to d. on sth** décider de qch; (choose) se décider pour qch; **the deciding factor** le facteur décisif. ● **decided** a (firm) décidé (clear) net (f nette).

decimal ['desɪməl] a décimal; **d. point** virgule f ∥ n décimale f.

decimate ['desɪmeɪt] vt décimer.

decipher [dɪ'saɪfər] vt déchiffrer.

decision [dɪ'sɪʒ(ə)n] n décision f.

decisive [dɪ'saɪsɪv] a (defeat, tone etc)

décisif; (victory) net (f nette).

deck [dek] 1 n Nau pont m; **top d.** (of bus) impériale f. 2 n **d. of cards** jeu m de cartes. 3 n (of record player) platine f. ● **deckchair** n chaise f longue.

declare [dɪ'kleər] vt déclarer (**that** que); (verdict, result) proclamer. ● **declaration** [deklə'reɪʃ(ə)n] n déclaration f; proclamation f.

decline [dɪ'klaɪn] 1 vi (become less) (of popularity etc) être en baisse; (deteriorate) (of health etc) décliner; **to d. in importance** perdre de l'importance ‖ n déclin m; (fall) baisse f. 2 vt (offer etc) refuser, décliner; **to d. to do** refuser de faire.

decod/e [diː'kəʊd] vt (message) décoder. ● **—er** n Comptr TV décodeur m.

decompose [diːkəm'pəʊz] vi (rot) se décomposer.

decor ['deɪkɔːr] n décor m.

decorate ['dekəreɪt] vt (cake, room, soldier) décorer (**with** de); (hat, skirt etc) orner (**with** de); (paint etc) peindre (et tapisser) (pièce, maison). ● **decoration** [-'reɪʃ(ə)n] n décoration f. ● **decorative** à décoratif. ● **decorator** n (house painter etc) peintre m décorateur; (interior) m. décorateur, -trice mf.

decreas/e [dɪ'kriːs] vti diminuer ‖ ['diːkriːs] n diminution f (**in** de). ● **—ing** a (number etc) décroissant.

decree [dɪ'kriː] n Pol Rel décret m; Jur jugement m; (municipal) arrêté m ‖ vt (pt & pp **decreed**) décréter (**that** que).

decrepit [dɪ'krepɪt] a (building) en ruine.

dedicat/e ['dedɪkeɪt] vt (devote) consacrer (**to** à); (book) dédier (**to** à). ● **—ed** a (teacher etc) consciencieux. ● **dedication** [-'keɪʃ(ə)n] n (in book) dédicace f; (devotion) dévouement m.

deduce [dɪ'djuːs] vt (conclude) déduire (**from** de, that que).

deduct [dɪ'dʌkt] vt (subtract) déduire (**from** de); (from wage, account) prélever (**from** sur). ● **deduction** [-ʃ(ə)n] n déduction f.

deed [diːd] n action f, acte m; (feat)

exploit m; Jur acte m (notarié).

deep [diːp] a (**-er, -est**) profond; (snow) épais (f épaisse); (voice) grave; (note) Mus bas (f basse); **to be six metres/etc d.** avoir six mètres/etc de profondeur; **d. in thought** absorbé dans ses pensées; **the d. end** (in swimming pool) le grand bain; **d. red** rouge foncé. ● **—ly** adv (grateful, to breathe, regret etc) profondément. ● **deep-'freeze** vt surgeler ‖ n congélateur m. ● **d.-'rooted** or **d.-'seated** a bien ancré, profond.

deepen ['diːpən] vt approfondir; (increase) augmenter ‖ vi devenir plus profond.

deer [dɪər] n inv cerf m.

deface [dɪ'feɪs] vt (damage) dégrader; (daub) barbouiller.

default [dɪ'fɔːlt] n **by d.** Comptr Jur par défaut; **to win by d.** gagner par forfait.

defeat [dɪ'fiːt] vt (opponent etc) battre, vaincre ‖ n défaite f.

defect[1] ['diːfekt] n défaut m. ● **de'fective** a défectueux.

defect[2] [dɪ'fekt] vi Pol déserter; **to d. to** (the enemy etc) passer à.

defence [dɪ'fens] (Am **defense**) n défense f; **the body's defences** la défense de l'organisme (**against** contre); **in his d.** Jur à sa décharge. ● **defenceless** a sans défense. ● **defensive** a défensif ‖ n **on the d.** sur la défensive.

defend [dɪ'fend] vt défendre. ● **defendant** n (accused) Jur prévenu, -ue mf. ● **defender** n (of title) Sp détenteur, -trice mf.

defense [dɪ'fens] n Am = **defence**.

defer [dɪ'fɜːr] vt (**-rr-**) (postpone) différer.

defiant [dɪ'faɪənt] a (tone, attitude etc) de défi; (person) rebelle. ● **defiance** n (resistance) défi m (**of** à); **in d. of** (contempt) au mépris de.

deficient [dɪ'fɪʃənt] a (not adequate) insuffisant; (faulty) défectueux; **to be d. in** manquer de. ● **deficiency** n manque m; (of vitamins etc) carence f; (flaw) défaut m.

deficit ['defɪsɪt] *n* déficit *m*.

define [dɪ'faɪn] *vt* définir.

definite ['defɪnɪt] *a* (*date, plan*) précis, déterminé; (*reply, improvement*) net (*f* nette); (*order, offer*) ferme; (*certain, sure*) certain; **d. article** *Gram* article *m* défini. ●**—ly** *adv* certainement; (*considerably*) nettement; (*to say*) catégoriquement.

definition [defɪ'nɪʃ(ə)n] *n* définition *f*.

deflect [dɪ'flekt] *vt* (*bullet etc*) faire dévier; **to d. s.o. from sth** détourner qn de qch.

deformed [dɪ'fɔ:md] *a* (*body*) difforme. ●**deformity** *n* difformité *f*.

defraud [dɪ'frɔ:d] *vt* (*customs etc*) frauder; **to d. s.o. of sth** escroquer qch à qn.

defrost [di:'frɒst] *vt* (*fridge*) dégivrer; (*food*) décongeler.

defuse [di:'fju:z] *vt* (*bomb, conflict*) désamorcer.

defy [dɪ'faɪ] *vt* (*person, death etc*) défier; (*efforts*) résister à; **to d. s.o. to do** défier qn de faire.

degenerate [dɪ'dʒenəreɪt] *vi* dégénérer (**into** en).

degrade [dɪ'greɪd] *vt* dégrader.

degree [dɪ'gri:] *n* 1 (*angle, temperature etc*) degré *m*; **it's 20 degrees** il fait 20 degrés; **not in the slightest d.** pas du tout; **to such a d.** à tel point (**that** que). 2 *Univ* diplôme *m*; (*Bachelor's*) licence *f*; (*Master's*) maîtrise *f*; (*PhD*) doctorat *m*.

dehydrated [di:haɪ'dreɪtɪd] *a* déshydraté; **to get d.** se déshydrater.

de-ice [di:'aɪs] *vt* (*car window etc*) dégivrer.

dejected [dɪ'dʒektɪd] *a* abattu, découragé. ●**dejection** *n* abattement *m*.

delay [dɪ'leɪ] *vt* retarder; (*payment*) différer ▮ *vi* (*be slow*) tarder (**doing, in doing** à faire); (*linger*) s'attarder ▮ *n* (*lateness*) retard *m*; (*waiting period*) délai *m*; **without d.** sans tarder.

delectable [dɪ'lektəb(ə)l] *a* délectable.

delegate 1 ['delɪgeɪt] *vt* déléguer (**to** à). 2 ['delɪgət] *n* délégué, -ée *mf*. ●**delegation**

[-'geɪʃ(ə)n] *n* délégation *f*.

delete [dɪ'li:t] *vt* rayer, supprimer. ●**deletion** [-ʃ(ə)n] *n* (*thing deleted*) rature *f*.

deliberate[1] [dɪ'lɪbərət] *a* (*intentional*) intentionnel, délibéré; (*slow*) mesuré. ●**—ly** *adv* (*intentionally*) exprès; (*to walk*) avec mesure.

deliberate[2] [dɪ'lɪbəreɪt] *vi* délibérer ▮ *vt* délibérer sur.

delicate ['delɪkət] *a* délicat. ●**delicacy** *n* délicatesse *f*; (*food*) mets *m* délicat.

delicatessen [delɪkə'tesən] *n* traiteur *m* et épicerie *f* fine.

delicious [dɪ'lɪʃəs] *a* délicieux.

delight [dɪ'laɪt] *n* (*pleasure*) délice *m*, (grand) plaisir *m*, joie *f*; (*delicious food etc*) délice *m*; *pl* (*pleasures, things*) délices *fpl*; **to take d. in sth/in doing** se délecter de qch/à faire ▮ *vt* réjouir ▮ *vi* **to d. in doing** se délecter à faire. ●**—ed** *a* ravi, enchanté (**with sth** de qch, **to do** de faire, **that** que).

delightful [dɪ'laɪtfəl] *a* charmant; (*meal, perfume*) délicieux.

delinquent [dɪ'lɪŋkwənt] *a & n* délinquant, -ante (*mf*).

delirious [dɪ'lɪərɪəs] *a* délirant; **to be d.** avoir le délire, délirer.

deliver [dɪ'lɪvər] *vt* 1 (*goods, milk etc*) livrer; (*letters*) distribuer; (*hand over*) remettre (**to** à). 2 (*rescue*) délivrer (**from** de). 3 (*give birth to*) mettre au monde. 4 (*speech*) prononcer; (*warning*) lancer; (*blow*) porter. ●**delivery** *n* 1 livraison *f*; (*of letters*) distribution *f*; (*handing over*) remise *f*. 2 (*birth*) accouchement *m*. ●**deliveryman** *n* (*pl* **-men**) livreur *m*.

delude [dɪ'lu:d] *vt* tromper; **to d. oneself** se faire des illusions. ●**delusion** [-ʒ(ə)n] *n* illusion *f*.

deluge ['delju:dʒ] *n* (*of water, questions etc*) déluge *m*.

de luxe [dɪ'lʌks] *a* de luxe.

delve [delv] *vi* **to d. into** (*question, past*) fouiller; (*books*) fouiller dans.

demand [dɪ'mɑ:nd] *vt* exiger (**sth from s.o.** qch de qn); (*rights, more pay*) revendiquer; **to d. that** exiger que; **to**

d. to know insister pour savoir ‖ n exigence f; (claim) revendication f; (for goods) demande f; **in great d.** très demandé; **to make demands on s.o.** exiger beaucoup de qn. ● **demanding** a exigeant.

demean [dɪ'miːn] vt **to d. oneself** s'abaisser. ● **—ing** a dégradant.

demeanour [dɪ'miːnər] (Am **demeanor**) n (behaviour) comportement m.

demerara [deməˈreərə] n **d. (sugar)** sucre m roux.

demister [diːˈmɪstər] n Aut dispositif m de désembuage.

demo ['deməʊ] n (pl **-os**) (demonstration) Fam manif f.

demobilize [diːˈməʊbɪlaɪz] vt démobiliser.

democracy [dɪˈmɒkrəsɪ] n démocratie f. ● **democrat** ['deməkræt] n démocrate mf. ● **demoˈcratic** a démocratique; (person) démocrate.

demolish [dɪˈmɒlɪʃ] vt démolir. ● **demolition** [deməˈlɪʃ(ə)n] n démolition f.

demon ['diːmən] n démon m.

demonstrate ['demənstreɪt] vt démontrer; (machine) faire une démonstration de; **to d. how to do** montrer comment faire ‖ vi (protest) manifester. ● **demonstration** [-ˈstreɪʃ(ə)n] n démonstration f; (protest) manifestation f. ● **demonstrator** n (protester) manifestant, -ante mf.

demonstrative [dɪˈmɒnstrətɪv] a & n Gram démonstratif (m).

demoralize [dɪˈmɒrəlaɪz] vt démoraliser.

demote [dɪˈməʊt] vt rétrograder.

den [den] n tanière f.

denial [dɪˈnaɪəl] n (of rumour) démenti m; (of truth etc) dénégation f; **to issue a d.** publier un démenti.

denim ['denɪm] n (toile f de) coton m; pl (jeans) (blue-)jean m.

Denmark ['denmɑːk] n Danemark m.

denomination [dɪnɒmɪˈneɪʃ(ə)n] n Rel confession f, religion f; (of coin, banknote) valeur f.

denote [dɪˈnəʊt] vt dénoter.

denounce [dɪˈnaʊns] vt (person, injustice etc) dénoncer (**to** à); **to d. s.o. as a spy/** etc accuser qn publiquement d'être un espion/etc.

dense [dens] a (**-er, -est**) dense; (stupid) Fam lourd, bête. ● **—ly** adv **d. populated/**etc très peuplé/etc. ● **density** n densité f.

dent [dent] n (in car, metal etc) bosse f; **full of dents** (car etc) cabossé ‖ vt cabosser.

dental ['dent(ə)l] a dentaire; **d. surgeon** chirurgien m dentiste. ● **dentist** n dentiste mf. ● **dentistry** n médecine f dentaire. ● **dentures** npl dentier m.

deny [dɪˈnaɪ] vt nier (**doing** avoir fait, **that** que); (rumour) démentir; (authority) rejeter; **to d. s.o. sth** refuser qch à qn.

deodorant [diːˈəʊdərənt] n déodorant m.

depart [dɪˈpɑːt] vi partir; (deviate) s'écarter (**from** de). ● **—ed** n **the d.** le défunt, la défunte.

department [dɪˈpɑːtmənt] n département m; (in office) service m; (in shop) rayon m; Univ section f, département m; **that's your d.** (sphere) c'est ton rayon; **d. store** grand magasin m.

departure [dɪˈpɑːtʃər] n départ m; **a d. from** (custom, rule) un écart par rapport à; **to be a new d. for** constituer une nouvelle voie pour; **d. lounge** (in airport) salle f de départ.

depend [dɪˈpend] vi dépendre (**on, upon** de); **to d. (up)on** (rely on) compter sur (**for sth** pour qch). ● **—able** a (person, information, machine etc) sûr. ● **dependant** n personne f à charge.

dependent [dɪˈpendənt] a dépendant (**on, upon** de); (relative) à charge; **to be d. (up)on** dépendre de.

depict [dɪˈpɪkt] vt (describe) dépeindre; (in pictures) représenter.

deplete [dɪˈpliːt] vt (use up) épuiser; (reduce) réduire.

deplor/e [dɪˈplɔːr] vt déplorer. ● **—able** a déplorable.

deploy [dɪˈplɔɪ] vt (troops etc) déployer.

deport [dɪ'pɔːt] vt (foreigner etc) expulser.

deposit [dɪ'pɒzɪt] 1 vt (object, money etc) déposer ▌n (in bank) dépôt m; (part payment) acompte m; (against damage) caution f; (on bottle) consigne f. **d. account** compte m d'épargne. 2 n (sediment) dépôt m; (of gold, oil etc) gisement m. ● **depositor** n déposant, -ante mf.

depot ['depəʊ, Am 'diːpəʊ] n dépôt m; (railroad station) Am gare f; (bus) **d.** Am gare f routière.

depraved [dɪ'preɪvd] a dépravé. ● **depravity** [dɪ'prævɪtɪ] n dépravation f.

depreclate [dɪ'priːʃɪeɪt] vi (in value) se déprécier. ● **depreciation** [-'eɪʃ(ə)n] n dépréciation f.

depress [dɪ'pres] vt (discourage) déprimer; (push down) appuyer sur. ● **—ed** a (person) déprimé; (industry) (in decline) en déclin; (in crisis) en crise; **to get d.** se décourager. ● **depression** [-ʃ(ə)n] n dépression f.

depriv/e [dɪ'praɪv] vt priver (**of** de). ● **—ed** a (child etc) déshérité.

depth [depθ] n profondeur f; **in the depths of** (forest, despair) au plus profond de; (winter) au cœur de; **in d.** en profondeur.

deputize ['depjʊtaɪz] vi assurer l'intérim (**for s.o.** de qn).

deputy ['depjʊtɪ] n (replacement) remplaçant, -ante mf; (assistant) adjoint, -ointe mf; **d. (sheriff)** Am shérif m adjoint; **d. chairman** vice-président, -ente mf.

derailed [dɪ'reɪld] a **to be d.** (of train) dérailler. ● **derailment** n déraillement m.

derby ['dɜːbɪ] n (hat) Am (chapeau m) melon m.

derelict ['derɪlɪkt] a (building etc) abandonné.

deride [dɪ'raɪd] vt tourner en dérision. ● **derisory** a (amount etc) dérisoire.

derive [dɪ'raɪv] vt **to d. from sth** (pleasure etc) tirer de qch; **to be derived from** (of word etc) dériver de. ● **derivation** [derɪ'veɪʃ(ə)n] n Ling dérivation f.

dermatologist [dɜːmə'tɒlədʒɪst] n dermatologue mf.

derogatory [dɪ'rɒgət(ə)rɪ] a (word) péjoratif; (remark) désobligeant (**to** pour).

derrick ['derɪk] n (over oil well) derrick m.

derv [dɜːv] n gazole m, gas-oil m.

descend [dɪ'send] vi descendre (**from** de); **to d. upon** (of tourists) envahir; (attack) faire une descente sur; **in descending order** en ordre décroissant ▌vt (stairs) descendre; **to be descended from** descendre de. ● **descendant** n descendant, -ante mf. ● **descent** n (of aircraft etc) descente f. 2 (ancestry) origine f.

describe [dɪ'skraɪb] vt décrire. ● **description** [-ʃ(ə)n] n description f; (on passport) signalement m; **of every d.** de toutes sortes. ● **descriptive** a descriptif.

desecrate ['desɪkreɪt] vt profaner.

desert[1] ['dezət] n désert m; **d. animal** animal m du désert; **d. island** île f déserte.

desert[2] [dɪ'zɜːt] vt abandonner, déserter; **to d. s.o.** (of luck etc) abandonner qn ▌vi Mil déserter. ● **—ed** a (place) désert. ● **—er** n Mil déserteur m.

deserv/e [dɪ'zɜːv] vt mériter (**to do** faire). ● **—ing** a (person) méritant; (cause) louable; **d. of** digne de.

desiccated ['desɪkeɪtɪd] a (des)séché.

design [dɪ'zaɪn] 1 vt (car, dress, furniture etc) dessiner; (devise) (project etc); **designed to do/for s.o.** conçu pour faire/pour qn; **well designed** bien conçu.
▌n (pattern) motif m, dessin m; (sketch) plan m, dessin m; (type of dress or car) modèle m; (planning) conception f, création f; **industrial d.** dessin m industriel; **to study d.** étudier le design.
2 n (aim) dessein m; **by d.** intentionnellement. ● **designer** n (artistic, industrial) dessinateur, -trice mf; (of clothes) styliste mf; (well-known) couturier m; **d. clothes** vêtements mpl griffés.

designate ['dezɪgneɪt] *vt* désigner.

desir/e [dɪ'zaɪər] *n* désir *m*; **I've got no d. to** je n'ai aucune envie de ∥ *vt* désirer (**to do** faire). ●—**able** *a* désirable.

desk [desk] *n* (*in school*) table *f*; (*in office*) bureau *m*; (*in shop*) caisse *f*; (**reception**) **d.** (*in hotel etc*) réception *f*; **d. clerk** (*in hotel*) *Am* réceptionniste *mf*.

desolate ['desələt] *a* (*deserted*) désolé; (*dreary, bleak*) triste; (*person*) affligé.

despair [dɪ'speər] *n* désespoir *m*; **to be in d.** être au désespoir ∥ *vi* désespérer (**of s.o.** de qn, **of doing** de faire).

despatch [dɪ'spætʃ] *vt & n* = **dispatch**.

desperate ['despərət] *a* désespéré; (*criminal*) capable de tout; **to be d. for** (*money, love etc*) avoir désespérément besoin de; (*a cigarette, baby etc*) mourir d'envie d'avoir. ●**desperation** [-'reɪʃ(ə)n] *n* désespoir *m*; **in d.** (*as a last resort*) en désespoir de cause.

despicable [dɪ'spɪkəb(ə)l] *a* méprisable.

despise [dɪ'spaɪz] *vt* mépriser.

despite [dɪ'spaɪt] *prep* malgré.

despondent [dɪ'spɒndənt] *a* découragé.

despot ['despɒt] *n* despote *m*.

dessert [dɪ'zɜːt] *n* dessert *m*. ●**dessert-spoon** *n* cuillère *f* à dessert.

destination [destɪ'neɪʃ(ə)n] *n* destination *f*.

destine ['destɪn] *vt* destiner (**for à, to do** à faire); **it was destined to happen** ça devait arriver.

destiny ['destɪnɪ] *n* destin *m*; (*fate of individual*) destinée *f*.

destitute ['destɪtjuːt] *a* (*poor*) indigent.

destroy [dɪ'strɔɪ] *vt* détruire; (*horse*) abattre; (*cat, dog*) faire piquer.

destruction [dɪ'strʌkʃ(ə)n] *n* destruction *f*. ●**destructive** *a* (*person, war*) destructeur; (*child*) qui casse tout.

detach [dɪ'tætʃ] *vt* détacher (**from** de). ●—**ed** *a* (*indifferent*) détaché; **d. house** maison *f* individuelle.

detachable [dɪ'tætʃəb(ə)l] *a* (*lining*) amovible.

detachment [dɪ'tætʃmənt] *n* (*attitude*) &

Mil détachement *m*.

detail ['diːteɪl, *Am* dɪ'teɪl] *n* détail *m*; **in d.** en détail ∥ *vt* raconter en détail. ●—**ed** *a* (*account etc*) détaillé.

detain [dɪ'teɪn] *vt* retenir; (*prisoner*) détenir; (*in hospital*) garder, hospitaliser. ●**detention** [dɪ'tenʃ(ə)n] *n* (*school punishment*) retenue *f*; (*in prison*) détention *f*.

detect [dɪ'tekt] *vt* (*find*) découvrir; (*see, hear*) distinguer; (*mine*) détecter; (*illness*) dépister.

detective [dɪ'tektɪv] *n* inspecteur *m* de police, policier *m* (en civil); (*private*) détective *m* (privé); **d. film/novel** film *m*/roman *m* policier.

detector [dɪ'tektər] *n* détecteur *m*; **smoke d.** détecteur *m* de fumée.

deter [dɪ'tɜːr] *vt* (-**rr**-) **to d. s.o.** dissuader *or* décourager qn (**from doing** de faire, **from sth** de qch).

detergent [dɪ'tɜːdʒənt] *n* détergent *m*.

deteriorate [dɪ'tɪərɪəreɪt] *vi* se détériorer. ●**deterioration** [-'reɪʃ(ə)n] *n* détérioration *f*.

determin/e [dɪ'tɜːmɪn] *vt* déterminer; (*price*) fixer; **to d. to do** se déterminer à faire. ●—**ed** *a* (*look, person*) déterminé; **to d. to do** décidé à faire; **I'm d. she'll succeed** je suis bien décidé à ce qu'elle réussisse.

deterrent [dɪ'terənt, *Am* dɪ'taɪrənt] *n Mil* force *f* de dissuasion; **to be a d.** *Fig* être dissuasif.

detest [dɪ'test] *vt* détester (**doing** faire). ●—**able** *a* détestable.

detonate ['detəneɪt] *vt* faire exploser. ●**detonator** *n* détonateur *m*.

detour ['diːtʊər] *n* détour *m*.

detract [dɪ'trækt] *vi* **to d. from** (*make less*) diminuer.

detriment ['detrɪmənt] *n* **to the d. of** au détriment de. ●**detri'mental** *a* préjudiciable (**to** à).

devalue [diːˈvæljuː] *vt* (*money*) & *Fig* dévaluer. ●**devaluation** [-'eɪʃ(ə)n] *n* dévaluation *f*.

devastat/e ['devəsteɪt] *vt* (*lay waste*)

dévaster; (*upset, shock*) Fig foudroyer
(*qn*). ●—**ing** *a* (*storm etc*) dévastateur;
(*overwhelming*) (*news etc*) accablant;
(*shock*) terrible.

develop [dɪ'veləp] *vt* développer; (*area,
land*) mettre en valeur; (*habit, illness*)
contracter; (*talent*) manifester; *Phot*
développer; **to d. a liking for** prendre
goût à.
▮ *vi* se développer; (*of event, crisis*) se
produire; (*of talent, illness*) se manifester; **to d. into** devenir; **developing country** pays *m* en voie de développement.
●—**er** *n* (*property*) **d.** promoteur *m* (de
construction). ●—**ment** *n* développement *m*; (**housing**) **d.** lotissement
m; (*large*) grand ensemble *m*; **a (new) d.**
(*in situation*) un fait nouveau.

deviate ['di:vɪeɪt] *vi* dévier (**from** de); **to
d. from the norm** s'écarter de la norme.

device [dɪ'vaɪs] *n* dispositif *m*; (*scheme*)
procédé *m*; **left to one's own devices**
livré à soi-même.

devil ['dev(ə)l] *n* diable *m*; **a or the d. of a
problem** *Fam* un problème épouvanta-
ble; **I had a or the d. of a job** *Fam* j'ai eu
un mal fou (**doing, to do** à faire); **what/
where/why the d.?** *Fam* que/où/pour-
quoi diable? ●**devilish** *a* diabolique.

devious ['di:vɪəs] *a* (*mind, behaviour*)
tortueux; **he's d.** il a l'esprit tortueux.

devise [dɪ'vaɪz] *vt* (*a plan*) combiner; (*a
plot*) tramer; (*invent*) inventer.

devoid [dɪ'vɔɪd] *a* **d.** of dénué de.

devolution [di:və'lu:ʃ(ə)n] *n Pol* décen-
tralisation *f*.

devot/e [dɪ'vəʊt] *vt* consacrer (**to** à).
●—**ed** *a* dévoué; (*admirer*) fervent.
●**devo'tee** *n Sp Mus* passionné, -ée
mf. ●**devotion** [-ʃ(ə)n] *n* dévouement
m (**to s.o.** à qn).

devour [dɪ'vaʊər] *vt* dévorer.

devout [dɪ'vaʊt] *a* dévot; (*supporter*)
fervent.

dew [dju:] *n* rosée *f*. ●**dewdrop** *n* goutte *f*
de rosée.

diabetes [daɪə'bi:ti:z] *n Med* diabète *m*.
●**diabetic** [-'betɪk] *n* diabétique *mf* ▮ *a*

diabétique; **d. jam**/*etc* confiture *f*/*etc*
pour diabétiques.

diabolical [daɪə'bɒlɪk(ə)l] *a* (*bad*) épouvantable.

diagnose ['daɪəgnəʊz, *Am* -'nəʊs] *vt*
diagnostiquer. ●**diagnosis**, *pl* -**oses**
[daɪəg'nəʊsɪs, -əʊsi:z] *n* diagnostic *m*.

diagonal [daɪ'æg(ə)l] *a* diagonal ▮ *n*
d. (*line*) diagonale *f*. ●—**ly** *adv* en
diagonale.

diagram ['daɪəgræm] *n* schéma *m*, diagramme *m*; *Geom* figure *f*.

dial ['daɪəl] *n* cadran *m* ▮ *vt* (-**ll-**, *Am* -**l-**)
(*phone number*) faire, composer; (*per-
son*) appeler; **d. tone** *Am* tonalité *f*.
●**dialling** *a* **d. code** indicatif *m*; **d. tone**
tonalité *f*.

dialect ['daɪəlekt] *n* (*regional*) dialecte *m*;
(*rural*) patois *m*.

dialogue ['daɪəlɒg] (*Am* **dialog**) *n* dialogue *m*.

dialysis, *pl* -**yses** [daɪ'ælɪsɪs, -ɪsi:z] *n*
Med dialyse *f*.

diameter [daɪ'æmɪtər] *n* diamètre *m*.
●**dia'metrically** *adv* (*opposed*) diamétra-
lement.

diamond ['daɪəmənd] **1** *n* (*stone*) diamant *m*; (*shape*) losange *m*; (**baseball**)
d. terrain *m* (de baseball); **d.
necklace**/*etc* rivière *f*/*etc* de diamants.
2 *n* & *npl Cards* carreau *m*.

diaper ['daɪəpər] *n* (*for baby*) *Am* couche
f.

diaphragm ['daɪəfræm] *n* diaphragme
m.

diarr(o)ea [daɪə'ri:ə] *n* diarrhée *f*.

diary ['daɪərɪ] *n* (*calendar*) agenda *m*;
(*private*) journal *m* (intime).

dice [daɪs] *n inv* dé *m* (à jouer) ▮ *vt* (*food*)
couper en dés.

dictaphone® ['dɪktəfəʊn] *n* dicta-
phone® *m*.

dictate [dɪk'teɪt] *vt* dicter (**to** à) ▮ *vi*
dicter; **to d. to s.o.** (*order around*) faire
la loi à qn. ●**dictation** [-ʃ(ə)n] *n* dictée *f*.

dictator [dɪk'teɪtər] *n* dictateur *m*. ●**dictatorship** *n* dictature *f*.

diction ['dɪkʃ(ə)n] *n* langage *m*; (*way of*

speaking) diction *f*.

dictionary ['dɪkʃənərɪ] *n* dictionnaire *m*; **English d.** dictionnaire *m* d'anglais.

did [dɪd] *pt of* **do**.

die [daɪ] **1** *vi* (*pt & pp* **died**, *pres p* **dying**) mourir (**of, from** de); **to be dying to do** mourir d'envie de faire; **to be dying for sth** avoir une envie folle de qch; **to d. away** (*of noise*) mourir; **to d. down** (*of fire*) mourir; (*of storm*) se calmer; **to d. off** mourir (les uns après les autres); **to d. out** (*of custom*) mourir.

2 *n* (*in engraving*) coin *m*; **the d. is cast** *Fig* les sorts sont jetés.

diehard ['daɪhɑːd] *n* réactionnaire *mf*.

diesel ['diːzəl] *a & n* **d. (engine)** (moteur *m*) diesel *m*; **d. (oil)** gazole *m*.

diet ['daɪət] *n* (*for losing weight*) régime *m*; (*usual food*) alimentation *f*; **to go on a d.** faire un régime ∥ *vi* suivre un régime. ●**dietary** *a* diététique; **d. fibre** fibre(s) *f(pl)* alimentaire(s). ●**die'tician** *n* diététicien, -ienne *mf*.

differ ['dɪfər] *vi* différer (**from** de); (*disagree*) ne pas être d'accord (**from** avec).

difference ['dɪf(ə)rəns] *n* différence *f* (**in** de); **d. (of opinion)** différend *m*; **it makes no d.** ça n'a pas d'importance; **it makes no d. to me** ça m'est égal. ●**different** *a* différent (**from, to** de); (*another*) autre; (*various*) divers, différents. ●**differently** *adv* autrement (**from, to** que).

differentiate [dɪfə'renʃɪət] *vti* différencier (**from** de) ∥ *vti* **to d. (between)** faire la différence entre.

difficult ['dɪfɪkəlt] *a* difficile (**to do** à faire); **it's d. for us to...** il nous est difficile de.... ●**difficulty** *n* difficulté *f*; **to have d. doing** avoir du mal à faire; **to be in d.** avoir des difficultés; **to have d. with** avoir des ennuis avec.

diffident ['dɪfɪdənt] *a* (*person*) qui manque d'assurance.

diffuse [dɪ'fjuːz] *vt* (*spread*) diffuser.

dig [dɪg] *vt* (*pt & pp* **dug**, *pres p* **digging**) (*ground, garden*) bêcher; (*hole, grave etc*) creuser; **to d. sth into** (*push*) planter

qch dans; **to d. out** (*from ground*) déterrer; (*accident victim*) dégager; (*find*) *Fam* dénicher; **to d. up** (*from ground*) déterrer; (*weed*) arracher; (*earth*) retourner; (*street*) piocher. ∥ *vi* (*dig a hole*) creuser; **to d. in** (*eat*) *Fam* manger; **to d. into** (*s.o.'s past*) fouiller dans; (*one's savings*) puiser dans; (*meal*) *Fam* attaquer.

∥ *n* (*with spade*) coup *m* de bêche; (*with elbow*) coup *m* de coude; (*remark*) *Fam* coup *m* de griffe.

digest [daɪ'dʒest] *vti* digérer ●**digestion** [-tʃ(ə)n] *n* digestion *f*. ●**digestive** *a* digestif.

digger ['dɪgər] *n* (*machine*) pelleteuse *f*.

digit ['dɪdʒɪt] *n* (*number*) chiffre *m*. ●**digital** *a* (*watch*) numérique.

dignified ['dɪgnɪfaɪd] *a* digne. ●**dignify** *vt* donner de la dignité à. ●**dignity** *n* dignité *f*.

digress [daɪ'gres] *vi* faire une digression; **to d. from** s'écarter de.

digs [dɪgz] *npl* *Fam* chambre *f* (meublée).

dilapidated [dɪ'læpɪdeɪtɪd] *a* (*house*) délabré.

dilemma [daɪ'lemə] *n* dilemme *m*.

diligent ['dɪlɪdʒənt] *a* assidu, appliqué; **to be d. in doing sth** faire qch avec zèle. ●**diligence** *n* zèle *m*, assiduité *f*.

dilute [daɪ'luːt] *vt* diluer ●**dilué**

dim [dɪm] *a* (**dimmer, dimmest**) (*light*) faible; (*colour*) terne; (*room*) sombre; (*memory, outline*) vague; (*person*) stupide ∥ *vt* (**-mm-**) (*light*) baisser; (*memory*) estomper; **to d. one's headlights** *Am* se mettre en code. ●**dimly** *adv* (*to shine*) faiblement; (*vaguely*) vaguement.

dime [daɪm] *n* *US Can* (pièce *f* de) dix cents *mpl*; **a d. store** = un Prisunic®, un Monoprix®.

dimension [daɪ'menʃ(ə)n] *n* dimension *f*; (*extent*) *Fig* étendue *f*. ●**dimensional** *a* **two-d.** à deux dimensions.

diminish [dɪ'mɪnɪʃ] *vti* diminuer.

diminutive [dɪ'mɪnjʊtɪv] **1** *a* (*tiny*) minuscule. **2** *a* & *n Gram* diminutif (*m*).

dimmers ['dɪməz] *npl* (*low beams*) *Am Aut* phares *mpl* code *inv*, codes *mpl*.

dimple ['dɪmp(ə)l] *n* fossette *f*.

dimwit ['dɪmwɪt] *n* idiot, -ote *mf*. ● **dim'witted** *a* idiot.

din [dɪn] **1** *n* (*noise*) vacarme *m*. **2** *vt* (**-nn-**) to d. into s.o. that rabâcher à qn que.

din/e [daɪn] *vi* dîner (**on** de); to d. out dîner en ville; **dining car** *Rail* wagon-restaurant *m*; **dining room** salle *f* à manger. ● **—er** *n* dîneur, -euse *mf*; *Rail* wagon-restaurant *m*; (*short-order restaurant*) *Am* petit restaurant *m*.

dinghy ['dɪŋgɪ] *n* petit canot *m*; (**rubber**) **d.** canot *m* pneumatique.

dingy ['dɪndʒɪ] *a* (**-ier**, **-iest**) (*room etc*) minable; (*colour*) terne.

dinner ['dɪnər] *n* (*evening meal*) dîner *m*; (*lunch*) déjeuner *m*; **to have d.** dîner; **to have s.o. to d.** avoir qn à dîner; **d. jacket** smoking *m*; **d. party** dîner *m* (à la maison); **d. plate** grande assiette *f*; **d. service**, **d. set** service *m* de table.

dinosaur ['daɪnəsɔːr] *n* dinosaure *m*.

dip [dɪp] *vt* (**-pp-**) plonger; **to d. one's headlights** se mettre en code ‖ *vi* (*of road*) plonger; **to d. into** (*pocket, savings*) puiser dans; (*book*) feuilleter ‖ *n* (*in road*) petit creux *m*; **to go for a d.** (*swim*) faire trempette.

diphtheria [dɪp'θɪərɪə] *n* diphtérie *f*.

diphthong ['dɪfθɒŋ] *n* diphtongue *f*.

diploma [dɪ'pləʊmə] *n* diplôme *m*.

diplomacy [dɪ'pləʊməsɪ] *n* (*tact*) & *Pol* diplomatie *f*. ● **'diplomat** *n* diplomate *mf*. ● **diplo'matic** *a* diplomatique; **to be d.** (*tactful*) être diplomate.

dipper ['dɪpər] *n* **the big d.** (*at fairground*) les montagnes *fpl* russes.

dire ['daɪər] *a* affreux; (*poverty, need*) extrême.

direct [daɪ'rekt] **1** *a* (*result, flight, person etc*) direct; (*danger*) immédiat ‖ *adv* directement.
2 *vt* (*work, one's attention*) diriger;

(*letter, remark*) adresser (**to** à); (*efforts*) orienter (**to**, **towards** vers); (*film*) réaliser; (*play*) mettre en scène; **to d. s.o. to** (*place*) indiquer à qn le chemin de; **to d. s.o. to do** charger qn de faire. ● **directly** *adv* (*without detour*) directement; (*at once*) tout de suite; (*to speak*) franchement; **d. behind**/*etc* juste derrière/*etc* ‖ *conj Fam* aussitôt que (+ *indic*).

direction [daɪ'rek∫(ə)n] *n* direction *f*, sens *m*; (*management*) direction *f*; *pl* (*orders*) indications *fpl*; **directions (for use)** mode *m* d'emploi; **in the opposite d.** en sens inverse.

director [daɪ'rektər] *n* directeur, -trice *mf*; (*of film*) réalisateur, -trice *mf*; (*of play*) metteur *m* en scène; (*board member in firm*) administrateur, -trice *mf*.

directory [daɪ'rektərɪ] *n* (*phone book*) annuaire *m* (du téléphone); (*of streets*) guide *m*; *Comptr* répertoire *m*; **d. inquiries** *Tel* renseignements *mpl*.

dirt [dɜːt] *n* saleté *f*; (*earth*) terre *f*; **d. cheap** *Fam* très bon marché; **d. road** chemin *m* de terre; **d. track** *Sp* cendrée *f*.

dirty ['dɜːtɪ] *a* (**-ier**, **-iest**) sale; (*job*) salissant; (*obscene, unpleasant*) sale; (*word*) grossier; **to get d.** se salir; **to get sth d.** salir qch; **a d. joke** une histoire cochonne; **a d. trick** un sale tour ‖ *vt* salir ‖ *vi* se salir.

dis- [dɪs] *pref* dé-, dés-.

disabled [dɪs'eɪb(ə)ld] *a* handicapé ‖ *n* **the d.** les handicapés *mpl*. ● **disa'bility** *n* infirmité *f*.

disadvantage [dɪsəd'vɑːntɪdʒ] *n* désavantage *m*.

disagree [dɪsə'griː] *vi* ne pas être d'accord (**with** avec); (*of figures*) ne pas concorder; **to d. with s.o.** (*of food etc*) ne pas réussir à qn. ● **—able** *a* désagréable. ● **—ment** *n* désaccord *m*; (*quarrel*) différend *m*.

disappear [dɪsə'pɪər] *vi* disparaître. ● **disappearance** *n* disparition *f*.

disappoint [dɪsəˈpɔɪnt] vt décevoir; **I'm disappointed with it** ça m'a déçu. ●**—ing** a décevant. ●**—ment** n déception f.

disapprov/e [dɪsəˈpruːv] vi to d. of s.o./sth désapprouver qn/qch; **I d.** je suis contre. ●**—ing** a (look etc) désapprobateur. ● disapproval n désapprobation f.

disarm [dɪsˈɑːm] vti désarmer. ● disarmament n désarmement m.

disarray [dɪsəˈreɪ] n in d. (army, party) en plein désarroi; (clothes) en désordre.

disaster [dɪˈzɑːstər] n désastre m; **d. area** région f sinistrée. ● disastrous a désastreux.

disband [dɪsˈbænd] vt disperser ∥ vi se disperser.

disbelief [dɪsbəˈliːf] n incrédulité f.

disc [dɪsk] (Am **disk**) n disque m; **identity d.** plaque f d'identité; **d. jockey** disc-jockey m.

discard [dɪsˈkɑːd] vt (get rid of) se débarrasser de; (plan, hope etc) Fig abandonner.

discern [dɪˈsɜːn] vt discerner. ●**—ing** a (person) averti, sagace. ●**—ment** n discernement m.

discharge [dɪsˈtʃɑːdʒ] vt (patient, employee) renvoyer; (soldier) libérer; (gun, accused person) décharger; (liquid) déverser ∥ vi (of wound) suppurer ∥ [ˈdɪstʃɑːdʒ] n (of gun, electrical) décharge f; (of liquid, pus) écoulement m; (dismissal) renvoi m; (freeing) libération f.

disciple [dɪˈsaɪp(ə)l] n disciple m.

discipline [ˈdɪsɪplɪn] n (behaviour, subject) discipline f ∥ vt (control) discipliner; (punish) punir. ● discipli'narian n to be a (strict) d. être très à cheval sur la discipline.

disclaim [dɪsˈkleɪm] vt (responsibility) (dé)nier.

disclose [dɪsˈkləʊz] vt révéler. ● disclosure n révélation f.

disco [ˈdɪskəʊ] n (pl -os) Fam discothèque f.

discolour [dɪsˈkʌlər] (Am **discolor**) vt décolorer; (teeth) jaunir.

discomfort [dɪsˈkʌmfət] n (physical) douleur f; (mental) malaise m; **I get d. from my wrist** mon poignet me gêne.

disconcert [dɪskənˈsɜːt] vt déconcerter.

disconnect [dɪskəˈnekt] vt (unfasten etc) détacher; (unplug) débrancher; (wires) déconnecter; (gas, telephone) couper.

discontent [dɪskənˈtent] n mécontentement m. ● discontented a mécontent.

discontinu/e [dɪskənˈtɪnjuː] vt cesser, interrompre. ●**—ed** a (article) Com qui ne se fait plus.

discord [ˈdɪskɔːd] n (disagreement) discorde f.

discotheque [ˈdɪskətek] n (club) discothèque f.

discount 1 [ˈdɪskaʊnt] n (on article) remise f, réduction f; **at a d.** (to buy, sell) à prix réduit; **d. store** solderie f. **2** [dɪsˈkaʊnt] vt (story etc) ne pas tenir compte de.

discourage [dɪsˈkʌrɪdʒ] vt décourager (s.o. from doing qn de faire); **to get discouraged** se décourager. ●**—ment** n découragement m.

discourteous [dɪsˈkɜːtɪəs] a discourtois.

discover [dɪsˈkʌvər] vt découvrir (that que). ● discovery n découverte f.

discredit [dɪsˈkredɪt] vt (cast slur on) discréditer ∥ n discrédit m.

discreet [dɪsˈkriːt] a (unassuming, reserved etc) discret. ● discretion [dɪsˈkreʃ(ə)n] n discrétion f; **I'll use my own d.** je ferai comme bon me semblera.

discrepancy [dɪsˈkrepənsɪ] n divergence f, contradiction f (between entre).

discriminat/e [dɪsˈkrɪmɪneɪt] vi to d. against faire de la discrimination contre. ●**—ing** a (person) averti, sagace; (ear) fin. ● discrimination [-ˈneɪʃ(ə)n] n (against s.o.) discrimination f; (judgment) discernement m; (distinction) distinction f.

discus [ˈdɪskəs] n Sp disque m.

discuss [dɪsˈkʌs] vt (talk about) discuter de (politique etc); (examine in detail) discuter (projet, question, prix). ● discussion [-ˈʃ(ə)n] n discussion f; under d.

(*matter etc*) en question.

disdain [dɪs'deɪn] *n* dédain *m*.

disease [dɪ'ziːz] *n* maladie *f*. ● **diseased** *a* malade.

disembark [dɪsɪm'bɑːk] *vti* débarquer.

disenchant [dɪsɪn'tʃɑːnt] *vt* désenchanter. ● **—ment** *n* désenchantement *m*.

disentangle [dɪsɪn'tæŋg(ə)l] *vt* (*string etc*) démêler; **to d. oneself from** se dégager de.

disfavour ['dɪsfeɪvər] (*Am* **disfavor**) *n* défaveur *f*.

disfigure [dɪs'fɪgər] *vt* défigurer.

disgrac/e [dɪs'greɪs] *n* (*shame*) honte *f* (**to** à); (*disfavour*) disgrâce *f* ‖ *vt* déshonorer. ● **—ed** *a* (*politician etc*) disgracié.

disgraceful [dɪs'greɪsfəl] *a* honteux (**of s.o.** de la part de qn). ● **disgracefully** *adv* honteusement.

disgruntled [dɪs'grʌnt(ə)ld] *a* mécontent.

disguise [dɪs'gaɪz] *vt* déguiser (**as** en) ‖ *n* déguisement *m*; **in d.** déguisé.

disgust [dɪs'gʌst] *n* dégoût *m* (**for, at, with** de); **in d.** dégoûté ‖ *vt* dégoûter. ● **—ed** *a* dégoûté (**at, by, with** de); **to be d. with s.o.** (*annoyed*) être fâché contre qn. ● **—ing** *a* dégoûtant.

dish [dɪʃ] **1** *n* (*container, food*) plat *m*; **the dishes** la vaisselle. **2** *vt* **to d. out** *Fam* distribuer; **to d. out** *or* **up** (*food*) servir.

dishcloth ['dɪʃklɒθ] *n* (*for washing*) lavette *f*; (*for drying*) torchon *m*.

dishearten [dɪs'hɑːt(ə)n] *vt* décourager.

dishevelled [dɪ'ʃevəld] (*Am* **disheveled**) *a* (*person, hair*) hirsute, ébouriffé.

dishonest [dɪs'ɒnɪst] *a* malhonnête. ● **dishonesty** *n* malhonnêteté *f*.

dishonour [dɪs'ɒnər] (*Am* **dishonor**) *n* déshonneur *m* ‖ *vt* déshonorer. ● **—able** *a* peu honorable.

dishtowel ['dɪʃtaʊəl] *n* torchon *m*.

dishwasher ['dɪʃwɒʃər] *n* lave-vaisselle *m inv*.

dishy ['dɪʃɪ] *a* (**-ier, -iest**) (*woman, man*) *Fam* sexy, qui a du chien.

disillusion [dɪsɪ'luːʒ(ə)n] *vt* décevoir; **to be disillusioned (with)** être déçu (de).

disincentive [dɪsɪn'sentɪv] *n* mesure *f* dissuasive; **to be a d. to s.o.** décourager qn.

disinclined [dɪsɪŋ'klaɪnd] *a* peu disposé (**to** à).

disinfect [dɪsɪn'fekt] *vt* désinfecter. ● **disinfectant** *a* & *n* désinfectant (*m*).

disintegrate [dɪs'ɪntɪgreɪt] *vi* se désintégrer.

disinterested [dɪs'ɪntrɪstɪd] *a* (*impartial*) désintéressé; (*uninterested*) *Fam* indifférent (**in** à).

disk [dɪsk] *n* **1** *Am* = **disc. 2** (*of computer*) disque *m*; **hard d.** disque *m* dur; **d. drive** lecteur *m* de disquettes *or* de disques. ● **diskette** [dɪs'ket] *n* disquette *f*.

dislike [dɪs'laɪk] *vt* ne pas aimer (**doing** faire); **he doesn't d. it** ça ne lui déplaît pas ‖ *n* aversion *f* (**for, of** pour); **to take a d. to s.o./sth** prendre qn/qch en grippe.

dislocate ['dɪsləkeɪt] *vt* (*limb*) disloquer; **to d. one's shoulder** se démettre l'épaule.

dislodge [dɪs'lɒdʒ] *vt* faire bouger, déplacer; (*enemy*) déloger.

disloyal [dɪs'lɔɪəl] *a* déloyal.

dismal ['dɪzməl] *a* morne, triste. ● **—ly** *adv* (*to fail, behave*) lamentablement.

dismantle [dɪs'mænt(ə)l] *vt* (*machine*) démonter.

dismay [dɪs'meɪ] *vt* consterner ‖ *n* consternation *f*.

dismiss [dɪs'mɪs] *vt* (*from job*) renvoyer (**from** de); (*official*) destituer; (*appeal*) *Jur* rejeter; (*thought, suggestion etc*) *Fig* écarter; **d.!** *Mil* rompez! ● **dismissal** *n* renvoi *m*; destitution *f*.

dismount [dɪs'maʊnt] *vi* descendre (**from** de).

disobey [dɪsə'beɪ] *vt* désobéir à ‖ *vi* désobéir. ● **disobedience** *n* désobéissance *f*. ● **disobedient** *a* désobéissant.

disorder [dɪs'ɔːdər] *n* (*confusion*) désordre *m*; (*illness*) troubles *mpl*; (*riots*) désordres *mpl*. ● **disorderly** *a* (*behaviour, room*) désordonné; (*meeting*) houleux.

disorganized [dɪs'ɔːgənaɪzd] *a* désorganisé.

disorientate [dɪsˈɔːrɪənteɪt] (*Am* **disorient** [dɪsˈɔːrɪənt]) *vt* désorienter.

disown [dɪsˈəʊn] *vt* désavouer, renier.

disparaging [dɪsˈpærɪdʒɪŋ] *a* peu flatteur, désobligeant.

disparity [dɪsˈpærətɪ] *n* écart *m*, disparité *f* (**between** entre).

dispatch [dɪsˈpætʃ] *vt* (*send*) expédier (*lettre etc*); (*troops, messenger*) envoyer; (*finish*) expédier (*travail etc*) ▌ *n* (*sending*) expédition *f* (**of** de); (*report*) dépêche *f*.

dispel [dɪsˈpel] *vt* (**-ll-**) dissiper.

dispensary [dɪsˈpensərɪ] *n* (*in hospital*) pharmacie *f*; (*in chemist's shop*) officine *f*.

dispense [dɪsˈpens] **1** *vt* (*give out*) distribuer; (*medicine*) préparer. **2** *vi* **to d. with** (*do without*) se passer de. ● **dispenser** *n* (*device*) distributeur *m*; **cash d.** distributeur *m* de billets.

disperse [dɪsˈpɜːs] *vt* disperser ▌ *vi* se disperser. ● **dispersal** *n* dispersion *f*.

dispirited [dɪsˈpɪrɪtɪd] *a* découragé.

displace [dɪsˈpleɪs] *vt* (*refugees, furniture*) déplacer; (*replace*) supplanter.

display [dɪsˈpleɪ] *vt* montrer; (*notice, electronic data*) afficher; (*painting, goods*) exposer; (*courage*) faire preuve de ▌ *n* (*in shop*) étalage *m*; (*of electronic data*) affichage *m*; (*of force*) déploiement *m*; (*of anger*) manifestation *f*; (*of paintings*) exposition *f*; **d.** (**unit**) (*of computer*) moniteur *m*; **on d.** exposé.

displeas/e [dɪsˈpliːz] *vt* déplaire à. ● **—ed** *a* mécontent (**with** de). ● **displeasure** *n* mécontentement *m*.

disposal [dɪsˈpəʊzəl] *n* (*sale*) vente *f*; (*of waste*) évacuation *f*; **at the d. of** à la disposition de.

dispos/e¹ [dɪsˈpəʊz] *vi* **to d. of** (*get rid of*) se débarrasser de; (*throw away*) jeter (*papier etc*); (*one's time, money*) disposer de; (*sell*) vendre. ● **—able** *a* (*plate etc*) à jeter, jetable; (*income*) disponible.

dispose² [dɪsˈpəʊz] *vt* **to d. s.o. to do** disposer qn à faire; **disposed to do** disposé à faire; **well-disposed towards** bien disposé envers.

disposition [dɪspəˈzɪʃ(ə)n] *n* (*character*) naturel *m*; (*readiness*) inclination *f*.

disproportionate [dɪsprəˈpɔːʃ(ə)nət] *a* disproportionné.

disprove [dɪsˈpruːv] *vt* réfuter.

dispute [dɪsˈpjuːt] *n* (*quarrel*) dispute *f*; *Pol* conflit *m*; *Jur* litige *m*; **beyond d.** incontestable; **in d.** (*matter*) débattu; (*facts, territory*) contesté; (*competence*) en question ▌ *vt* (*claim etc*) contester.

disqualify [dɪsˈkwɒlɪfaɪ] *vt* (*make unfit*) rendre inapte (**from** à); *Sp* disqualifier; **to d. s.o. from driving** retirer son permis à qn.

disregard [dɪsrɪˈgɑːd] *vt* ne tenir aucun compte de ▌ *n* indifférence *f* (**for** à); (*for the law*) désobéissance *f* (**for** à).

disrepair [dɪsrɪˈpeər] *n* **in (a state of) d.** en mauvais état.

disrepute [dɪsrɪˈpjuːt] *n* **to bring into d.** jeter le discrédit sur.

disrespect [dɪsrɪˈspekt] *n* manque *m* de respect. ● **disrespectful** *a* irrespectueux (**to** envers).

disrupt [dɪsˈrʌpt] *vt* (*traffic, class etc*) perturber; (*communications*) interrompre; (*plan, s.o.'s books etc*) déranger. ● **disruption** [-ʃ(ə)n] *n* perturbation *f*; (*of plan etc*) dérangement *m*. ● **disruptive** *a* (*child*) turbulent.

dissatisfied [dɪˈsætɪsfaɪd] *a* mécontent (**with** de). ● **dissatisfaction** [-ˈfækʃ(ə)n] *n* mécontentement *m* (**with** devant).

dissect [daɪˈsekt] *vt* disséquer.

dissent [dɪˈsent] *n* dissentiment *m*.

dissertation [dɪsəˈteɪʃ(ə)n] *n* *Univ* mémoire *m*.

dissident [ˈdɪsɪdənt] *a* & *n* dissident, -ente (*mf*).

dissimilar [dɪˈsɪmɪlər] *a* différent (**to** de).

dissipate [ˈdɪsɪpeɪt] *vt* (*clouds, fears etc*) dissiper; (*energy*) gaspiller.

dissociate [dɪˈsəʊʃɪeɪt] *vt* dissocier (**from** de).

dissolve [dɪ'zɒlv] vt dissoudre ‖ vi se dissoudre.

dissuade [dɪ'sweɪd] vt dissuader (**from doing** de faire); **to d. s.o. from sth** détourner qn de qch.

distance ['dɪstəns] n distance f; **in the d.** au loin; **from a d.** de loin; **at a d.** à quelque distance; **it's within walking d.** on peut y aller à pied; **to keep one's d.** garder ses distances.

distant ['dɪstənt] a éloigné, lointain; (relative) éloigné; (reserved) distant.

distaste [dɪs'teɪst] n aversion f (**for** pour). ●**distasteful** a désagréable.

distil [dɪs'tɪl] vt (-ll-) distiller; **distilled water** (for car, iron) eau f déminéralisée.

distinct [dɪs'tɪŋkt] a 1 (clear) (voice, light etc) distinct; (difference, improvement) net (f nette), marqué. 2 (different) distinct (**from** de).

distinction [dɪs'tɪŋkʃ(ə)n] n distinction f; Univ mention f très bien.

distinctive [dɪs'tɪŋktɪv] a distinctif. ●**—ly** adv distinctement; (to forbid) formellement; (definitely) sensiblement; **d. possible** tout à fait possible.

distinguish [dɪs'tɪŋgwɪʃ] vti distinguer (**from** de, **between** entre); **distinguishing mark** signe m particulier. ●**—ed** a distingué.

distort [dɪs'tɔːt] vt déformer. ●**—ed** a (false) faux (f fausse).

distract [dɪs'trækt] vt distraire (**from** de). ●**—ed** a (troubled) préoccupé; (with worry) éperdu. ●**—ing** a (noise) gênant.

distraction [dɪs'trækʃ(ə)n] n (lack of attention, amusement) distraction f.

distraught [dɪs'trɔːt] a éperdu, affolé.

distress [dɪs'tres] n (pain) douleur f; (anguish, misfortune) détresse f; **in d.** (ship) en détresse; (poverty) dans la détresse ‖ vt affliger. ●**—ing** a affligeant.

distribute [dɪs'trɪbjuːt] vt distribuer; (spread evenly) répartir. ●**distribution** [-'bjuːʃ(ə)n] n distribution f. ●**distributor** n Aut Cin etc distributeur m; (commercial dealer) concessionnaire

mf.

district ['dɪstrɪkt] n région f; (of town) quartier m; (administrative) district m; **postal d.** division f postale; **d. attorney** Am = procureur m (de la République); **d. nurse** infirmière f visiteuse.

distrust [dɪs'trʌst] vt se méfier de ‖ n méfiance f (**of** de). ●**distrustful** a méfiant; **to be d. of** se méfier de.

disturb [dɪs'tɜːb] vt (sleep, water) troubler; (papers, belongings) déranger; **to d. s.o.** (bother) déranger qn; (worry) troubler qn. ●**—ed** a (person) (mentally) perturbé. ●**—ing** a (worrying) inquiétant.

disturbance [dɪs'tɜːbəns] n (noise) tapage m; pl (riots) troubles mpl.

disuse [dɪs'juːs] n **to fall into d.** tomber en désuétude. ●**disused** [-'juːzd] a désaffecté.

ditch [dɪtʃ] **1** n fossé m. **2** vt (dump) Fam se débarrasser de.

dither ['dɪðər] vi Fam hésiter, tergiverser.

ditto ['dɪtəʊ] adv idem.

divan [dɪ'væn] n divan m.

div/e [daɪv] vi (pt dived, Am dove [dəʊv]) plonger; (rush) se précipiter, se jeter ‖ n (of swimmer, goalkeeper) plongeon m; (of submarine) plongée f; (of aircraft) piqué m. ●**—ing** n (underwater) plongée f sous-marine; **d. board** plongeoir m. ●**diver** n plongeur, -euse mf.

diverge [daɪ'vɜːdʒ] vi diverger (**from** de). ●**divergent** a divergent.

diverse [daɪ'vɜːs] a divers. ●**diversity** n diversité f.

divert [daɪ'vɜːt] vt (attention, person etc) détourner (**from** de); (traffic) dévier; (aircraft) dérouter; (amuse) divertir. ●**diversion** [-ʃ(ə)n, Am -ʒ(ə)n] n Aut déviation f; (distraction) & Mil diversion f.

divide [dɪ'vaɪd] vt diviser (**into** en); **to d. sth (off)** séparer qch (**from sth** de qch); **to d. sth up** (share out) partager qch; **to d. one's time between** partager son temps entre ‖ vi (of group, road) se diviser. ● **divided** a (*family etc*) divisé; (*opinions*) partagés.

dividend ['dɪvɪdend] n Fin dividende m.

divine [dɪ'vaɪn] a divin.

division [dɪ'vɪʒ(ə)n] n division f; (*dividing object*) séparation f. ● **divisible** a divisible. ● **divisive** [-'vaɪsɪv] a qui cause des dissensions.

divorc/e [dɪ'vɔːs] n divorce m ‖ vt (*husband, wife*) divorcer d'avec ‖ vi divorcer. ● **—ed** a divorcé (**from** d'avec); **to get d.** divorcer. ● **divorcee** [dɪvɔː'siː, Am dɪvɔː'seɪ] n divorcé, -ée mf.

divulge [dɪ'vʌldʒ] vt divulguer.

DIY [diːaɪ'waɪ] n abbr (*do-it-yourself*) bricolage m.

dizzy ['dɪzɪ] a (*-ier, -iest*) **to be** or **feel d.** avoir le vertige; **to make s.o. (feel) d.** donner le vertige à qn. ● **dizziness** n vertige m.

DJ [diː'dʒeɪ] n abbr = disc jockey.

do [duː] **1** v aux (*3rd person sing pres t* **does**; pt **did**; pp **done**; pres p **doing**) **do you know?** savez-vous?, est-ce que vous savez?; **I do not** or **don't see** je ne vois pas; **he did say so** (*emphasis*) il l'a bien dit; **do stay here now**; **you know him, don't you?** tu le connais, n'est-ce pas?; **neither do I** moi non plus; **so do I** moi aussi; **oh, does he?** (*surprise*) ah oui?; **don't!** non!

2 vt faire; **to do nothing but sleep** ne faire que dormir; **what does she do?** (*in general*), **what is she doing?** (*now*) qu'est-ce qu'elle fait?, que fait-elle?; **what have you done (with)...?** qu'as-tu fait (de)...?; **well done** (*congratulations*) bravo!; (*steak etc*) bien cuit; **that'll do me** (*suit*) ça fera mon affaire; **I've been done** (*cheated*) Fam je me suis fait avoir; **to do s.o. out of sth** escroquer qch à qn; **I'm done (in)** (*tired*) Sl je suis claqué; **he's done for** Fam il est fichu; **to do in** (*kill*) Sl supprimer; **to do out** (*clean*) nettoyer; **to do over** (*redecorate*) refaire; **to do up** (*coat, button*) boutonner; (*zip, Am zipper*) fermer; (*house*) refaire; (*goods*) embal-

ler; **do yourself up (well)!** (*wrap up*) couvre-toi (bien)!

3 vi (*get along*) aller, marcher; (*suit*) faire l'affaire, convenir; (*be enough*) suffire; (*finish*) finir; **how do you do?** (*introduction*) enchanté; (*greeting*) bonjour; **he did well** or **right to leave** il a bien fait de partir; **do as I do** fais comme moi; **to make do** se débrouiller; **to do away with sth/s.o.** supprimer qch/qn; **I could do with a coffee/etc** (*need, want*) j'aimerais bien (prendre) un café/etc; **to do without sth/s.o.** se passer de qch/qn; **to have to do with** (*relate to*) avoir à voir avec; (*concern*) concerner.

4 n (pl **dos** or **do's**) (*party*) Fam soirée f, fête f; **the do's and don'ts** ce qu'il faut faire ou ne pas faire.

docile ['dəʊsaɪl] a docile.

dock [dɒk] **1** n (*for ship*) dock m ‖ vi (*at quayside*) se mettre à quai; (*of spacecraft*) s'arrimer. **2** n Jur banc m des accusés. ● **—er** n docker m. ● **dockyard** n chantier m naval.

doctor ['dɒktər] **1** n Med médecin m, docteur m; Univ docteur m. **2** vt (*text, food*) altérer. ● **doctorate** ['dɒktərət] n doctorat m (**in** ès, en).

doctrine ['dɒktrɪn] n doctrine f.

document ['dɒkjʊmənt] n document m. ● **documentary** n (*film*) documentaire m.

dodge [dɒdʒ] vt (*question, acquaintance etc*) esquiver; (*pursuer*) échapper à; (*tax*) éviter de payer ‖ vi (*to one side*) faire un saut (de côté); **to d. through** (*crowd*) se faufiler dans ‖ n mouvement m de côté; (*trick*) Fig truc m.

dodgems ['dɒdʒəmz] npl autos fpl tamponneuses.

dodgy ['dɒdʒɪ] a (*-ier, -iest*) Fam (*tricky*) délicat; (*dubious*) douteux; (*unreliable*) peu sûr.

doe [dəʊ] n (*deer*) biche f.

does [dʌz] see **do**. ● **doesn't** ['dʌz(ə)nt] = **does not**.

dog[1] [dɒg] n chien m; (*female*) chienne f;

d. biscuit biscuit *m* pour chien; **d. food** pâtée *f*; **d. collar** *Fam* col *m* de pasteur. ● **d.-eared** *a* (*page etc*) écorné. ● **d.-'tired** *a Fam* claqué.

dog² [dɒg] *vt* (**-gg-**) (*follow*) poursuivre.

dogged ['dɒgɪd] *a* obstiné. ● **—ly** *adv* obstinément.

doggy ['dɒgɪ] *n Fam* toutou *m*; **d. bag** (*in restaurant*) petit sac *m* pour emporter les restes.

doghouse ['dɒghaʊs] *n Am* niche *f*.

dogmatic [dɒg'mætɪk] *a* dogmatique.

dogsbody ['dɒgzbɒdɪ] *n Pej* factotum *m*, sous-fifre *m*.

doing ['duːɪŋ] *n* that's your d. c'est toi qui as fait ça; **doings** *Fam* activités *fpl*.

do-it-yourself [duːɪtjə'self] *n* bricolage *m* ‖ *a* (*store, book*) de bricolage.

doldrums ['dɒldrəmz] *npl* to be in the d. (*of person*) avoir le cafard; (*of business*) être en plein marasme.

dole [dəʊl] **1** *n* **d.** (*money*) allocation *f* de chômage; to go on the d. s'inscrire au chômage. **2** *vt* to d. out distribuer au compte-gouttes.

doll [dɒl] *n* poupée *f*; **doll's house**, *Am* **dollhouse** maison *f* de poupée.

dollar ['dɒlər] *n* dollar *m*.

dollop ['dɒləp] *n* (*of food*) gros morceau *m*.

dolphin ['dɒlfɪn] *n* (*sea animal*) dauphin *m*.

domain [dəʊ'meɪn] *n* (*land, sphere*) domaine *m*.

dome [dəʊm] *n* dôme *m*, coupole *f*.

domestic [də'mestɪk] *a* familial, domestique; (*animal*) domestique; (*trade, flight*) intérieur; **d. science** arts *mpl* ménagers.

dominant ['dɒmɪnənt] *a* dominant; (*person*) dominateur.

dominate ['dɒmɪneɪt] *vti* dominer.

domineering [dɒmɪ'nɪərɪŋ] *a* dominateur.

dominion [də'mɪnjən] *n* domination *f*; (*land*) territoire *m*.

domino ['dɒmɪnəʊ] *n* (*pl* **-oes**) domino *m*; *pl* (*game*) dominos *mpl*.

don [dɒn] *n Univ* professeur *m*.

donate [dəʊ'neɪt] *vt* faire don de; (*blood*) donner ‖ *vi* donner. ● **donation** [-ʃ(ə)n] *n* don *m*.

done [dʌn] *pp* of **do**.

donkey ['dɒŋkɪ] *n* âne *m*; **for d.'s years** *Fam* depuis belle lurette.

donor ['dəʊnər] *n* (*of blood, organ*) donneur, -euse *mf*.

don't [dəʊnt] = **do not.**

doom [duːm] *n* ruine *f*; (*fate*) destin *m*; (*gloom*) *Fam* tristesse *f* ‖ *vt* condamner (**to** à); **to be doomed** (**to failure**) être voué à l'échec.

door [dɔːr] *n* porte *f*; (*of vehicle*) portière *f*, porte *f*; **out of doors** dehors; **d.-to-door salesman** démarcheur *m*. ● **doorbell** *n* sonnette *f*. ● **doorknob** *n* bouton *m* or poignée *f* de porte. ● **doorknocker** *n* marteau *m*. ● **doorman** *n* (*pl* **-men**) (*of hotel etc*) portier *m*, concierge *m*. ● **doormat** *n* paillasson *m*. ● **doorstep** *n* seuil *m*. ● **doorstop(per)** *n* butoir *m* (de porte). ● **doorway** *n* **in the d.** dans l'encadrement de la porte.

dope [dəʊp] **1** *n* (*drugs*) *Fam* drogue *f*; (*for horse, athlete*) dopant *m* ‖ *vt* doper. **2** *n* (*idiot*) *Fam* imbécile *mf*. ● **dopey** *a* (**-ier, -iest**) *Fam* (*stupid*) abruti; (*sleepy*) endormi.

dormant ['dɔːmənt] *a* (*volcano, matter*) en sommeil.

dormer ['dɔːmər] *n* **d.** (**window**) lucarne *f*.

dormitory ['dɔːmɪtrɪ, *Am* 'dɔːmɪtɔːrɪ] *n* dortoir *m*; *Am* résidence *f* (universitaire).

dormouse, *pl* **-mice** ['dɔːmaʊs, -maɪs] *n* loir *m*.

dose [dəʊs] *n* dose *f*; (*of hard work*) *Fig* période *f* ‖ *vt* **to d. oneself** (**up**) se bourrer de médicaments. ● **dosage** *n* (*amount*) dose *f*.

dosshouse ['dɒshaʊs] *n Sl* asile *m* (de nuit).

dossier ['dɒsɪeɪ] *n* (*papers*) dossier *m*.

dot [dɒt] *n* point *m*; **polka d.** pois *m*; **on the d.** *Fam* à l'heure pile ‖ *vt* (**-tt-**) (*an i*) mettre un point sur; **dotted with**

parsemé de; **dotted line** pointillé *m*.
● **dot matrix printer** *n Comptr* imprimante *f* matricielle.

dot/e [dəʊt] *vt* **to d. on** être gaga de.
●—**ing** *a* affectueux; **her d. husband** son mari qui lui passe tout.

dotty ['dɒtɪ] *a* (**-ier, -iest**) *Fam* cinglé.

double ['dʌb(ə)l] *a* double; **a d. bed** un grand lit; **a d. room** une chambre pour deux personnes; **d. 's'** deux 's'; **d. three four two** (*phone number*) trente-trois quarante-deux.
‖ *adv* (*twice*) deux fois, le double; (*to fold*) en deux; **he earns d. what I earn** il gagne le double de moi or deux fois plus que moi.
‖ *n* double *m*; (*person*) double *m*, sosie *m*; (*stand-in*) *Cin* doublure *f*; **on the d.** au pas de course.
‖ *vt* doubler; **to d. over** (*fold*) replier; **doubled over in pain** plié (en deux) de douleur.
‖ *vi* doubler; **to d. back** (*of person*) revenir en arrière; **to d. up** (*with pain, laughter*) être plié (en deux).

double-bass [dʌb(ə)l'beɪs] *n Mus* contrebasse *f*. ● **d.-'breasted** *a* (*jacket*) croisé. ● **d.-'cross** *vt* tromper.
● **d.-'decker** (*bus*) *n* autobus *m* à impériale. ● **d.-'glazing** *n* (*window*) double vitrage *m*. ● **d.-'parking** *n* stationnement *m* ̶i̶n̶ ̶d̶o̶u̶b̶l̶e̶ ̶f̶i̶l̶e̶. ● **d.-'quick** *adv* ̶i̶n̶ vitesse.

doubly ['dʌblɪ] *adv* doublement.

doubt [daʊt] *n* doute *m*; **to be in d. about** avoir des doutes sur; **no d.** (*probably*) sans doute; **in d.** (*result, career etc*) dans la balance ‖ **to doubt** *vt* douter de; **to d. whether** or **that** or **if** douter que (+ *sub*).

doubtful ['daʊtfəl] *a* (*person, future etc*) incertain; (*dubious*) douteux; **to be d.** (*about sth*) avoir des doutes (sur qch); **it's d. whether** or **that** or **if** ce n'est pas certain que (+ *sub*). ● **doubtless** *adv* sans doute.

dough [dəʊ] *n* pâte *f*; (*money*) *Fam* fric *m*, blé *m*.

doughnut ['dəʊnʌt] *n* beignet *m* (rond).

dove[1] [dʌv] *n* colombe *f*.
dove[2] [dəʊv] *Am pt of* **dive**.
Dover ['dəʊvər] *n* Douvres *m or f*.

dowdy ['daʊdɪ] *a* (**-ier, -iest**) peu élégant, sans chic.

down[1] [daʊn] *adv* en bas; (*to the ground*) par terre; (*from upstairs*) descendu; (*of sun*) couché; (*of curtain, temperature*) baissé; (*of tyre, Am tire*) dégonflé; **d. in writing** inscrit; (**lie**) **d.!** (*to dog*) couché!; **to come** or **go d.** descendre; **to come d. from** (*place*) arriver de; **to fall d.** tomber (par terre); **d. there** or **here** en bas; **d. with traitors/etc!** à bas les traîtres/*etc*!; **d. with (the) flu** grippé; **to feel d.** (*depressed*) *Fam* avoir le cafard; **d. to** (*in numbers, dates etc*) jusqu'à; **d. payment** acompte *m*; **d. under** aux antipodes, en Australie.
‖ *prep* (*at bottom of*) en bas de; (*from top to bottom of*) du haut en bas de; (*along*) le long de; **to go d.** (*hill, street, stairs*) descendre; **to live d. the street** habiter plus loin dans la rue.
‖ *vt* **to d. a drink** vider un verre.

down[2] [daʊn] *n* (*on bird, person etc*) duvet *m*.

down-and-out ['daʊnənaʊt] *a* sur le pavé ‖ *n* clochard, -arde *mf*. ● **downbeat** *a* (*gloomy*) *Fam* pessimiste. ● **downcast** *a* découragé. ● **downfall** *n* chute *f*. ● ̶d̶o̶w̶n̶'̶h̶e̶a̶r̶t̶e̶d̶ ̶*̶a̶*̶ ̶d̶é̶c̶o̶u̶r̶a̶g̶é̶ ̶d̶é̶p̶r̶i̶m̶é̶
● **down'hill** *adv* en pente; **to go d.** descendre; (*of sick person, business*) aller de pire en plus mal. ● **downmarket** *a Com* bas de gamme; (*neighbourhood etc*) populaire; (*person*) ordinaire. ● **downpour** *n* averse *f*, pluie *f* torrentielle. ● **downright** *a* (*rogue*) véritable; (*refusal*) catégorique ‖ *adv* (*rude etc*) franchement. ● **downscale** *a Am* = **downmarket**. ● **downstairs** [daʊnsteəz] *a* (*room, neighbours*) d'en bas ‖ [daʊn'steəz] *adv* (*to live etc*) en bas; **to come** or **go d.** descendre l'escalier. ● **down'stream** *adv* en aval.
● **down-to-'earth** *a* terre-à-terre *inv*.
● **down'town** *adv* en ville; **d. Chicago/**

etc le centre de Chicago/*etc*. ● **downward** *a* vers le bas; (*path*) qui descend. ● **downward(s)** *adv* vers le bas.

Down's [daʊnz] *a* D. syndrome mongolisme *m*.

dowry ['daʊərɪ] *n* dot *f*.

doze [dəʊz] *n* petit somme *m* ▮ *vi* sommeiller; **to d. off** s'assoupir. ● **dozy** *a* (-ier, -iest) somnolent; (*silly*) *Fam* gourde.

dozen ['dʌz(ə)n] *n* douzaine *f*; **a d.** (*eggs, books etc*) une douzaine de; **dozens of** *Fig* des dizaines de.

Dr *abbr* (*Doctor*) Docteur.

drab [dræb] *a* terne; (*weather*) gris.

draft [drɑːft] **1** *n* (*outline*) ébauche *f*; (*of letter*) brouillon *m* ▮ *vt* **to d.** (**out**) (*sketch out*) faire le brouillon de; (*write out*) rédiger. **2** *n* *Mil Am* conscription *f* ▮ *vt* (*conscript*) appeler (sous les drapeaux). **3** *n* *Am* = **draught**.

draftsman ['drɑːftsmən] *n* (*pl* -men) *Am* = **draughtsman**.

drafty ['drɑːftɪ] *a* *Am* = **draughty**.

drag [dræg] *vt* (-gg-) traîner; (*river*) draguer; **to d. s.o./sth along** (en)traîner qn/qch; **to d. s.o. away from** arracher qn à; **to d. s.o. into** entraîner qn dans ▮ *vi* traîner; **to d. on** *or* **out** (*last a long time*) se prolonger ▮ *n* *Fam* (*boring task*) corvée *f*; (*person*) raseur, -euse *mf*; **in d.** (*clothing*) en travesti.

dragon ['drægən] *n* dragon *m*. ● **dragonfly** *n* libellule *f*.

drain [dreɪn] *n* (*sewer*) égout *m*; (*outside house*) puisard *m*; (*in street*) bouche *f* d'égout; **it's down the d.** (*wasted*) *Fam* c'est fichu; **to be a d. on** (*resources, patience*) épuiser.
▮ *vt* (*tank, glass*) vider; (*vegetables*) égoutter; (*land*) drainer; (*resources*) épuiser; **to d.** (**off**) (*liquid*) faire écouler.
▮ *vi* **to d.** (**off**) (*of liquid*) s'écouler; **draining board** paillasse *f*. ● **drainage** *n* (*sewers*) système *m* d'égouts. ● **drainer** *n* (*board*) paillasse *f*; (*rack, basket*) égouttoir *m*.

drainboard ['dreɪnbɔːd] *n* *Am* paillasse *f*.

● **drainpipe** *n* tuyau *m* d'évacuation.

drake [dreɪk] *n* canard *m* (mâle).

drama ['drɑːmə] *n* (*event*) drame *m*; (*dramatic art*) théâtre *m*; **d. critic** critique *m* dramatique.

dramatic [drə'mætɪk] *a* dramatique; (*very great, striking*) spectaculaire. ● **dramatically** *adv* (*to change, drop etc*) de façon spectaculaire.

dramatist ['dræmətɪst] *n* dramaturge *m*. ● **dramatize** *vt* (*exaggerate*) dramatiser; (*novel etc*) adapter (pour la scène *or* l'écran).

drank [dræŋk] *pt* of **drink**.

drape [dreɪp] *vt* (*person, shoulder*) draper (**with** de) ▮ *n* **drapes** (*heavy curtains*) *Am* rideaux *mpl*.

drastic ['dræstɪk] *a* radical; **d. reductions** (*in shop*) soldes *mpl* monstres. ● **drastically** *adv* radicalement.

draught [drɑːft] (*Am* **draft**) **1** *n* (*wind*) courant *m* d'air; **d. excluder** bourrelet *m* (*de porte, de fenêtre*). **2** *npl* (*game*) dames *fpl*. ● **draught beer** *n* bière *f* pression. ● **draughtboard** *n* damier *m*.

draughtsman ['drɑːftsmən] *n* (*pl* -men) dessinateur, -trice *mf* (industriel(le) *or* technique).

draughty ['drɑːftɪ] *a* (-ier, -iest) (*room*) plein de courants d'air.

draw[1] [drɔː] *n* *Sp* match *m* nul; (*of lottery*) tirage *n* au sort; (*attraction*) attraction *f*.

▮ *vt* (*pt* **drew**, *pp* **drawn**) (*pull*) tirer; (*pass, move*) passer (**over** sur, **into** dans); (*prize*) gagner; (*money from bank*) retirer (**from** de); (*salary*) toucher; (*attract*) attirer; (*comfort*) puiser (**from** dans); **to d. sth to a close** mettre fin à qch; **to d. a match** *Sp* faire match nul; **to d. out** (*money*) retirer; **to d. up** (*chair*) approcher; (*contract, list, plan*) dresser; **to d. (up)on** (*savings*) puiser dans.

▮ *vi* *Sp* faire match nul; **to d. near (to)** s'approcher (de); (*of time*) approcher (de); **to d. to a close** tirer à sa fin; **to d. back** (*go backwards*) reculer; **to d. in** (*of** *days*) diminuer; (*of train*) arriver (en gare); **to d. up** (*of vehicle*) s'arrêter.

draw² [drɔ:] *vt* (*pt* **drew**, *pp* **drawn**) (*picture*) dessiner; (*circle*) tracer; (*distinction*) *Fig* faire (**between** entre) ∎ *vi* (*as artist*) dessiner.

drawback ['drɔ:bæk] *n* inconvénient *m*.

drawbridge ['drɔ:brɪdʒ] *n* pont-levis *m*.

drawer ['drɔ:r] *n* (*in furniture*) tiroir *m*.

drawing ['drɔ:ɪŋ] *n* dessin *m*; **d. board** planche *f* à dessin; **d. pin** punaise *f*; **d. room** salon *m*.

drawl [drɔ:l] *vi* parler d'une voix traînante ∎ *n* voix *f* traînante.

drawn [drɔ:n] *pp of* **draw**[1,2] ∎ *a* (*face*) tiré; **d. match** *or* **game** match *m* nul.

dread [dred] *vt* (*exam etc*) appréhender; **to d. doing** appréhender de faire ∎ *n* crainte *f*.

dreadful ['dredfəl] *a* épouvantable; (*child*) insupportable; (*ill*) malade; **I feel d. about it** j'ai vraiment honte. ●**—ly** *adv* terriblement; **to be d. sorry** regretter infiniment.

dream [dri:m] *vi* (*pt & pp* **dreamed** *or* **dreamt** [dremt]) rêver (**of**, **about** de, **or about doing** faire); **I wouldn't d. of it!** pas question! ∎ *vt* rêver (**that** que); **to d. sth up** imaginer qch ∎ *n* rêve *m*; **to have a d.** faire un rêve (**about** de); **to have dreams of** rêver de; **a d. house**/*etc* une maison/*etc* de rêve. ●**dreamer** *n* rêveur, -euse *mf*. ●**dreamy** *a* (**-ier**, **-iest**) rêveur.

dreary ['drɪərɪ] *a* (**-ier**, **-iest**) (*gloomy*) morne; (*monotonous*) monotone; (*boring*) ennuyeux.

dredge [dredʒ] *vt* (*river*) draguer.

dregs [dregz] *npl* **the d.** (*in liquid, of society*) la lie.

drench [drentʃ] *vt* tremper; **to get drenched** se faire tremper (jusqu'aux os).

dress [dres] **1** *n* (*woman's garment*) robe *f*; (*style of dressing*) tenue *f*; **d. circle** *Th* (premier) balcon *m*; **d. rehearsal** *Th* (répétition *f*) générale *f*.
2 *vt* (*person*) habiller; (*wound*) panser;

(*salad*) assaisonner; **to get dressed** s'habiller; **dressed for tennis** en tenue de tennis.
∎ *vi* s'habiller; **to d. up** (*smartly*) bien s'habiller; (*in disguise*) se déguiser (**as** en). ●**dressmaker** *n* couturière *f*. ●**dressmaking** *n* couture *f*.

dresser ['dresər] **1** (*furniture*) vaisselier *m*; *Am* coiffeuse *f*. **2 she's a good d.** elle s'habille toujours bien.

dressing ['dresɪŋ] *n Med* pansement *m*; (*seasoning*) assaisonnement *m*; **d. gown** robe *f* de chambre; **d. room** *Th* loge *f*; **d. table** coiffeuse *f*.

dressy ['dresɪ] *a* (**-ier**, **-iest**) (*smart*) chic *inv*; (*too*) **d.** trop habillé.

drew [dru:] *pt of* **draw**[1,2].

dribble ['drɪb(ə)l] **1** *vi* (*of baby*) baver; (*of liquid*) tomber goutte à goutte. ∎ **2** *vi Fb* dribbler ∎ *vt* (*ball*) dribbler.

dribs [drɪbz] *npl* **in d. and drabs** par petites quantités; (*to arrive*) par petits groupes.

dried [draɪd] *a* (*fruit*) sec *f* sèche; (*milk*) en poudre; (*flowers*) séché.

drier ['draɪər] *n* = **dryer**.

drift [drɪft] *vi* être emporté par le vent *or* le courant; (*of ship*) dériver; (*of snow*) s'amonceler; **to d. about** (*aimlessly*) se promener sans but; **to d. apart** (*of husband and wife*) devenir des étrangers l'un pour l'autre; **to d. into crime**/*etc* sombrer dans le crime/*etc*.
∎ *n* mouvement *m*; (*direction*) sens *m*; (*of snow*) congère *f*; (*meaning*) sens *m* général. ●**driftwood** *n* bois *m* flotté.

drill [drɪl] **1** *n* (*tool*) perceuse *f*; (*bit*) mèche *f*; (*pneumatic*) marteau *m* piqueur; (*dentist's*) roulette *f* ∎ *vt* percer; (*tooth*) fraiser; (*oil well*) forer ∎ *vi* **to d. for oil** faire de la recherche pétrolière. **2** *n* (*exercise*) *Mil Sch* exercice(s) *m(pl)* ∎ *vi* faire l'exercice.

drink [drɪŋk] *n* boisson *f*; (*alcoholic*) verre *m*; **to give s.o. a d.** donner (quelque chose) à boire à qn; **to have a d.** boire quelque chose; (*alcoholic drink*) prendre un verre.

❚ *vt* (*pt* **drank**, *pp* **drunk**) boire; **to d. sth down** *or* **up** boire qch.

❚ *vi* boire (**out of** dans); **to d. up** finir son verre; **to d. to s.o.** boire à la santé de qn; **drinking bout** beuverie *f*; **drinking chocolate** chocolat *m* en poudre; **drinking water** eau *f* potable. ● **drinkable** *a* (*fit for drinking*) potable; (*not unpleasant*) buvable. ● **drinker** *n* buveur, -euse *mf*.

drip [drɪp] *vi* (**-pp-**) dégouliner; (*of washing, vegetables*) s'égoutter; (*of tap, Am faucet*) goutter ❚ *vt* (*paint etc*) laisser couler ❚ *n* (*drop*) goutte *f*; (*sound*) bruit *m* de goutte; *Med* goutte-à-goutte *m inv*; (*fool*) *Fam* nouille *f*. ● **d.-dry** *a* (*shirt etc*) sans repassage. ● **dripping** *a* & *adv* **d.** (**wet**) dégoulinant.

drive [draɪv] *n* promenade *f* en voiture; (*energy*) énergie *f*; (*campaign*) campagne *f*; (*road to house*) allée *f*; **an hour's d.** une heure de voiture; **left-hand d.** (*vehicle or Am à*) conduite *f* à gauche; **disk d.** *Comptr* lecteur *m* de disquettes. ❚ *vt* (*pt* **drove**, *pp* **driven**) (*vehicle, train, passenger*) conduire (**to** à); (*machine*) actionner; (*chase away*) chasser; **to d. s.o. to do** pousser qn à faire; **to d. s.o. to despair** réduire qn au désespoir; **to d. s.o. mad** *or* **crazy** rendre qn fou; **to d. the rain against** (*of wind*) rabattre la pluie contre; **he drives a Ford** il a une Ford.

❚ *vi* (*drive a car*) conduire; (*go by car*) rouler; **to d. on the left** rouler à gauche; **to d. to Paris**/*etc* aller (en voiture) à Paris/*etc*; **what are you driving at?** *Fig* où veux-tu en venir?

drive along *vi* (*in car*) rouler ❚ **to drive away** *vt* (*chase*) chasser ❚ *vi* partir (en voiture) ❚ **to drive back** *vt* (*passenger*) ramener (en voiture); (*enemy*) repousser ❚ *vi* revenir (en voiture) ❚ **to drive in** *vt* (*nail etc*) enfoncer ❚ **to drive off** *vi* (*in car*) partir en voiture ❚ **to drive on** *vi* (*in car*) continuer ❚ **to drive out** *vt* (*chase away*) chasser (*qn, qch*) ❚ **to drive up** *vi* arriver (en voiture).

drive-in [draɪvɪn] *n* (*movie theater*) *Am* drive-in *m*.

drivel ['drɪv(ə)l] *n* (*nonsense*) idioties *fpl*.

driver ['draɪvər] *n* (*of car etc*) conducteur, -trice *mf*; (*train or engine*) **d.** mécanicien *m*; **she's a good d.** elle conduit bien; **driver's license** *Am* permis *m* de conduire.

driveway ['draɪvweɪ] *n* (*to house*) allée *f*.

driving ['draɪvɪŋ] **1** *n* *Aut* conduite *f*; **d. lesson** leçon *f* de conduite; **d. licence** permis *m* de conduire; **d. school** autoécole *f*. **2** *a* **d. force** force *f* agissante.

drizzle ['drɪz(ə)l] *n* bruine *f* ❚ *vi* bruiner. ● **drizzly** *a* **it's d.** il bruine.

dromedary ['drɒmədərɪ, *Am* 'drɒmɪderɪ] *n* dromadaire *m*.

drone [drəʊn] *n* (*hum*) bourdonnement *m*; (*purr*) ronronnement *m* ❚ *vi* (*of engine*) ronronner.

drool [druːl] *vi* (*slaver*) baver; **to d. over** *Fig* s'extasier devant.

droop [druːp] *vi* (*of flower*) se faner; (*of head*) pencher; (*of eyelid*) tomber.

drop [drɒp] **1** *n* (*of liquid*) goutte *f*. **2** *n* (*fall*) baisse *f*, chute *f* (**in** de); (*distance of fall*) hauteur *f* (de chute); (*jump*) *Av* saut *m*.

❚ *vt* (**-pp-**) laisser tomber; (*price, voice*) baisser; (*bomb*) larguer; (*passenger, goods from vehicle*) déposer; (*put*) mettre; (*leave out*) faire sauter; (*get rid of*) supprimer; (*team member*) écarter; **to d. s.o. off** (*from vehicle*) déposer qn; **to d. a line** écrire un petit mot (**to** à); **to d. a hint** faire une allusion; **to d. a hint that** laisser entendre que; **to d. a word in s.o.'s ear** glisser un mot à l'oreille de qn.

❚ *vi* (*fall*) tomber; (*of price*) baisser; **he's ready to d.** *Fam* il tombe de fatigue; **to d. back** *or* **behind** rester en arrière; **to d. by** *or* **in** (*visit s.o.*) passer (chez qn); **to d. off** (*fall asleep*) s'endormir; (*fall off*) tomber; (*of interest, sales*) diminuer; **to d. out** (*fall out*) tomber; (*withdraw*) se retirer; (*of student*) laisser tomber ses études. ● **drop-out** *n* (*student*) étudiant, -ante *mf* qui abandonne ses études.

• **dropper** n Med compte-gouttes m inv.
• **droppings** npl (of animal) crottes fpl;
(of bird) fiente f.

drought [draut] n sécheresse f.

drove [drəuv] pt of drive.

droves [drəuvz] npl in d. en foule.

drown [draun] vi se noyer ‖ vt noyer; to
d. oneself, be drowned se noyer. • **—ing**
a (man etc) qui se noie ‖ n (death)
noyade f.

drowse [drauz] vi sommoler. • **drowsy** a
(-ier, -iest) somnolent; to feel or be d.
avoir sommeil; to make s.o. d. assoupir
qn.

drudge [drʌdʒ] n homme m or femme f
de peine. • **drudgery** n corvée(s) f(pl).

drug [drʌg] n Med médicament m,
drogue f; (narcotic) stupéfiant m, drogue f; Fig drogue f; **drugs** (narcotics in
general) la drogue; to be on drugs, take
drugs se droguer; d. addict drogué, -ée
mf; d. taking usage m de la drogue ‖ vt
(-gg-) droguer (qn); (drink) mêler un
somnifère à. • **druggist** n Am pharmacien, -ienne mf. • **drugstore** n Am
drugstore m.

drum [drʌm] n Mus tambour m; (for oil)
bidon m; **the drums** (of orchestra etc)
la batterie ‖ vi (-mm-) Mus battre du
tambour ‖ vt I tried to d. it into him j'ai
essayé de le lui faire rentrer dans le
crâne, to d. up business attirer les
clients. • **drummer** n (joueur, -euse mf
de) tambour m; (in pop group) batteur
m. • **drumstick** n Mus baguette f (de
tambour); (of chicken) pilon m.

drunk [drʌŋk] pp of drink ‖ a ivre; to get
d. s'enivrer ‖ n ivrogne mf. • **drunkard** n
ivrogne mf. • **drunken** a (person) (regularly) ivrogne; (driver) ivre; d. driving
conduite f en état d'ivresse.

dry [drai] a (drier, driest) sec (f sèche);
(well, river) à sec; (day) sans pluie; (wit)
caustique; (subject, book) aride; to keep
sth d. tenir qch au sec; to wipe sth d.
essuyer qch; to run d. se tarir; to feel or
be d. (thirsty) avoir soif.
‖ vt sécher; (clothes in tumble drier) faire

sécher; (by wiping) essuyer; to d. sth off
or up sécher qch.
‖ vi sécher; to d. off sécher; to d. up
sécher; (dry the dishes) essuyer la
vaisselle; (run dry) (of stream) se tarir. • **drier** n (for hair, clothes) séchoir
m; (helmet-style for hair) casque m.
• **dryness** n sécheresse f.

dry-clean [drai'kli:n] vt nettoyer à sec.
• **—er** n teinturier, -ière mf; the d.-
cleaner's (shop) le pressing.

dual ['dju:əl] a double; d. carriageway
route f à deux voies (séparées).

dub [dʌb] vt (-bb-) (film) doubler.

dubious ['dju:brəs] a (offer, person etc)
douteux; I'm d. about going je me
demande si je dois y aller; to be d.
about sth douter de qch.

duchess ['dʌtʃis] n duchesse f.

duck [dʌk] 1 n canard m. 2 vi se baisser
(vivement) ‖ vt (head) baisser. • **duckling** n caneton m.

dud [dʌd] a Fam (coin) faux (f fausse);
(cheque, Am check) en bois; (watch etc)
qui ne marche pas.

due[1] [dju:] a (money, sum) dû (to à);
(rent, bill) à payer; (respect) qu'on doit
(to à); (proper) qui convient; to fall d.
échoir; she's d. for (salary increase etc)
elle doit or devrait recevoir; he's d. (to
arrive) (is awaited) il doit arriver; I'm d.
there he doit être là-bas; in d. course (at
proper time) en temps utile; (finally) à la
longue; d. to (caused by) dû à; (because
of) à cause de.
‖ n dû m; pl (of club) cotisation f;
(official charges) droits mpl.

due[2] [dju:] adv d. north/south/etc plein
nord/sud/etc.

duel ['dju:əl] n duel m.

duet [dju:'et] n duo m.

duffel, duffle ['dʌf(ə)l] a d. bag sac m de
marin; d. coat duffel-coat m.

dug [dʌg] pt & pp of dig.

duke [dju:k] n duc m.

dull [dʌl] a (-er, -est) (boring) ennuyeux;
(colour, character) terne; (weather)
maussade; (sound, ache) sourd; (mind)

lourd; (*edge*) émoussé ▮ *vt* (*sound, pain*) amortir; (*senses*) émousser; (*mind*) engourdir. ●**-ness** *n* (*of life, town*) monotonie *f*; (*of colour*) manque *m* d'éclat.

duly ['dju:lɪ] *adv* (*properly*) comme il convient; (*in fact*) en effet; (*in due time*) en temps utile.

dumb [dʌm] *a* (**-er, -est**) muet (*f* muette); (*stupid*) idiot, bête *f*.

dumbfound [dʌm'faʊnd] *vt* sidérer, ahurir.

dummy [dʌmɪ] **1** *n* (*of baby*) sucette *f*; (*for clothes*) mannequin *m*; (*of ventriloquist*) pantin *m*; (*fool*) *Fam* idiot, -ote *mf*. **2** *a* factice, faux (*f* fausse).

dump [dʌmp] *vt* (*rubbish, Am garbage*) déposer; **to d. (down)** (*put down*) déposer; **to d. s.o.** (*ditch*) *Fam* plaquer qn ▮ *n* (*for ammunition*) *Mil* dépôt *m*; (*dull town*) *Fam* trou *m*; (*house*) *Fam* baraque *f*; (*rubbish* or *Am garbage*) **d.** tas *m* d'ordures; (*place*) dépôt *m* d'ordures; (*untidy room*) dépotoir *m*; **to be (down) in the dumps** *Fam* avoir le cafard; **d. truck** camion *m* à benne basculante.

dumpling ['dʌmplɪŋ] *n Culin* boulette *f* (de pâte).

dumpy ['dʌmpɪ] *a* (**-ier, -iest**) (*person*) boulot, gros et court.

dunce [dʌns] *n* cancre *m*, âne *m*.

dune [dju:n] *n* (**sand**) **d.** dune *f*.

dung [dʌŋ] *n* (*of horse*) crotte *f*; (*of cattle*) bouse *f*; (*manure*) fumier *m*.

dungarees [dʌŋɡə'ri:z] *npl* (*of child, workman*) salopette *f*; (*jeans*) *Am* jean *m*.

dungeon ['dʌndʒən] *n* cachot *m*.

dunk [dʌŋk] *vt* (*bread etc*) tremper.

dupe [dju:p] *vt* duper.

duplex ['du:pleks] *n* (*apartment*) *Am* duplex *m*.

duplicate ['dju:plɪkeɪt] *vt* (*key etc*) faire un double de; (*on machine*) polycopier ▮ ['dju:plɪkət] *n* double *m*; **in d.** en deux exemplaires; **a d. copy** une copie en double; **a d. key** un double de la clef.

durable ['djʊərəb(ə)l] *a* (*material*) résistant; (*friendship*) durable.

duration [djʊə'reɪʃ(ə)n] *n* durée *f*.

duress [djʊ'res] *n* **under d.** sous la contrainte.

during ['djʊərɪŋ] *prep* pendant.

dusk [dʌsk] *n* (*twilight*) crépuscule *m*.

dust [dʌst] **1** *n* poussière *f*; **d. cloth** *Am* chiffon *m*; **d. cover** (*for furniture*) housse *f*; (*for book*) jaquette *f* ▮ *vt* (*furniture etc*) essuyer (la poussière de) ▮ *vi* faire la poussière. **2** *vt* (*sprinkle*) saupoudrer (**with** de). ●**dustbin** *n* poubelle *f*. ●**dustcart** *n* camion-benne *m*. ●**dustman** *n* (*pl* **-men**) éboueur *m*. ●**dustpan** *n* petite pelle *f* (à poussière).

duster ['dʌstər] *n* chiffon *m*.

dusty ['dʌstɪ] *a* (**-ier, -iest**) poussiéreux.

Dutch [dʌtʃ] *a* hollandais; néerlandais ▮ *n* (*language*) hollandais *m*; **the D.** (*people*) les Hollandais *mpl*. ●**Dutchman** *n* (*pl* **-men**) Hollandais *m*. ●**Dutchwoman** *n* (*pl* **-women**) Hollandaise *f*.

dutiful ['dju:tɪfəl] *a* (*son, child*) respectueux, obéissant.

duty ['dju:tɪ] *n* devoir *m*; (*tax*) impôt *m*; (*responsibilities*) fonctions *fpl*; **on d.** (*policeman, teacher*) de service; (*doctor*) de garde; **off d.** libre. ●**d.-'free** *a* (*goods, shop*) hors-taxe *inv*.

duvet [du:'veɪ] *n* couette *f*.

dwarf [dwɔ:f] *n* nain *m*, naine *f*.

dwell [dwel] *vi* (*pt & pp* **dwelt**) demeurer; **to d. on** penser sans cesse à; (*speak about*) parler sans cesse de. ●**-ing** *n* habitation *f*.

dwindl/e ['dwɪnd(ə)l] *vt* diminuer (peu à peu). ●**-ing** *a* (*interest etc*) décroissant.

dye [daɪ] *n* teinture *f* ▮ *vt* teindre; **to d. green/etc** teindre en vert/*etc*.

dying ['daɪɪŋ] *pres p of* **die 1** ▮ *a* (*person*) mourant; (*custom*) qui se perd; (*words*) dernier.

dyke [daɪk] *n* (*wall*) digue *f*.

dynamic [daɪ'næmɪk] *a* dynamique.

dynamite ['daɪnəmaɪt] *n* dynamite *f* ▮ *vt* dynamiter.

dynamo ['daɪnəməʊ] *n* (*pl* **-os**) dynamo *f*.

dysentery ['dɪsɪntrɪ] *n Med* dysenterie *f*.

dyslexic [dɪs'leksɪk] *a & n* dyslexique (*mf*).

E

E, e [iː] *n* E, e *m.*

each [iːtʃ] *a* à chaque **‖** *pron* e. (one) chacun, -une; **e. other** l'un(e) l'autre, *pl* les un(e)s les autres; **to see e. other** se voir (l'un(e) l'autre); **e. of us** chacun, -une d'entre nous.

eager ['iːgər] *a* impatient (**to do** de faire); (*enthusiastic*) plein d'enthousiasme; **to be e. for** désirer vivement; **to be e. to do** (*want*) tenir (beaucoup) à faire. ●**—ly** *adv* (**to work** *etc*) avec enthousiasme; (**to await**) avec impatience. ●**—ness** *n* impatience *f* (**to do** de faire); (*zeal*) enthousiasme *m* (**for sth** pour qch).

eagle ['iːg(ə)l] *n* aigle *m.*

ear¹ [ɪər] *n* oreille *f*; **all ears** *Fam* tout ouïe; **to play it by e.** *Fam* agir selon la situation. ●**earache** *n* mal *m* d'oreille. ●**eardrum** *n* tympan *m.*

ear² [ɪər] *n* (*of corn*) épi *m.*

earl [ɜːl] *n* comte *m.*

early ['ɜːlɪ] *a* (**-ier, -iest**) (*first*) premier; (*death*) prématuré; (*age*) jeune; (*painting, work*) de jeunesse; (*reply*) rapide; (*retirement*) anticipé; (*ancient*) ancien; **it's e.** (*on clock*) il est tôt; (*referring to meeting etc*) c'est tôt; **it's too e. to get up** il est trop tôt pour se lever; **to be e.** (*ahead of time*) être en avance; (*in getting up*) être matinal; **to have an e. meal/night** manger/se coucher de bonne heure; **in e. summer** au début de l'été.
‖ *adv* tôt, de bonne heure; (*ahead of time*) en avance; (**to book**) à l'avance; (**to die**) prématurément; **as e. as possible** le plus tôt possible; **earlier (on)** plus tôt; **at the earliest** au plus tôt.

earmark ['ɪərmɑːk] *vt* (*funds*) assigner (**for** à).

earmuffs ['ɪərmʌfs] *npl* protège-oreilles *m inv.*

earn [ɜːn] *vt* gagner; (*interest*) *Fin* rapporter. ●**—ings** *npl* (*wages*) rémunérations *fpl*; (*profits*) bénéfices *mpl.*

earnest ['ɜːnɪst] *a* sérieux; (*sincere*) sincère **‖** *n* **in e.** sérieusement; **it's raining in e.** il pleut pour de bon; **he's in e.** il est sérieux.

earphones ['ɪəfəʊnz] *npl* casque *m.* ●**earplug** *n* boule *f* Quiès®. ●**earring** *n* boucle *f* d'oreille. ●**earshot** *n* **within e.** à portée de voix.

earth [ɜːθ] *n* (*world, ground*) terre *f*; *El* terre *f*, masse *f*; **nothing/nobody on e.** rien/personne au monde; **where/what on e.?** où/que diable?

earthenware ['ɜːθənweər] *n* faïence *f* **‖** *a* en faïence.

earthly ['ɜːθlɪ] *a* (*possessions*) terrestre; **for no e. reason** *Fam* sans la moindre raison.

earthquake ['ɜːθkweɪk] *n* tremblement *m* de terre.

earwig ['ɪəwɪg] *n* (*insect*) perce-oreille *m.*

ease [iːz] **1** *n* (*facility*) facilité *f*; (*physical*) bien-être *m*; (*mental*) tranquillité *f*; **with e.** facilement; (*ill*) **at e.** (*mal*) à l'aise; **at e.** (*of mind*) tranquille.
2 *vt* (*pain*) soulager; (*mind*) calmer; (*tension*) diminuer; **to e. sth off/along** enlever/déplacer qch doucement; **to e. oneself through** se glisser par.
‖ *vi* **to e. (off** *or* **up)** (*become less*) (*of pressure*) diminuer; (*of demand*) baisser; (*of pain*) se calmer; (*not work so hard*) se relâcher.

easel ['iːz(ə)l] *n* chevalet *m.*

easily ['iːzɪlɪ] *adv* facilement; **e. the best/** *etc* de loin le meilleur/*etc.*

east [iːst] *n* est *m*; (**to the) e. of** à l'est de; **the E.** (*Eastern Europe*) l'Est *m*; (*Orient*) l'Orient *m.*

Easter *a* (*coast*) est *inv*; (*wind*) d'est; **E. Africa** Afrique *f* orientale.

▮ *adv* à l'est, vers l'est. • **eastbound** *a* (*traffic*) en direction de l'est. • **easterly** *a* (*point*) est *inv*; (*direction*) de l'est; (*wind*) d'est. • **eastern** *a* (*coast*) est *inv*; E. France l'Est *m* de la France; E. Europe Europe *f* de l'Est. • **eastward(s)** *a* & *adv* vers l'est.

Easter ['iːstər] *n* Pâques *m sing or fpl*; Happy E.! joyeuses Pâques!; E. egg œuf *m* de Pâques.

easy ['iːzɪ] *a* (**-ier, -iest**) facile; (*life*) tranquille; (*pace*) modéré; **it's e. to do** c'est facile à faire; **e. chair** fauteuil *m* (rembourré).

▮ *adv* doucement; **go e. on** (*sugar etc*) vas-y doucement avec; (*person*) ne sois pas trop dur avec; **take it e.** (*rest*) repose-toi; (*work less*) ne te fatigue pas; (*calm down*) calme-toi; (*go slow*) ne te presse pas. • **easygoing** *a* (*carefree*) insouciant; (*easy to get along with*) facile à vivre.

eat [iːt] *vt* (*pt* **ate** [et, *Am* eɪt], *pp* **eaten** ['iːt(ə)n]) manger; (*meal*) prendre; **to e. sth up** (*finish*) finir qch ▮ *vi* manger; **to e. into sth** (*of acid*) ronger qch; **to e. out** manger dehors; **eating place** restaurant *m*. • **eater** *n* **big e.** gros mangeur *m*, grosse mangeuse *f*.

eau de Cologne [əʊdəkə'ləʊn] *n* eau *f* de Cologne.

eaves [iːvz] *npl* avant-toit *m*. • **eavesdrop** *vti* (**-pp-**) **to e. (on)** écouter (de façon indiscrète).

ebb [eb] *n* reflux *m*; **e. and flow** le flux et le reflux; **at a low e.** (*patient, spirits*) *Fig* très bas ▮ *vi* refluer; **to e. (away)** (*of strength*) *Fig* décliner.

ebony ['ebənɪ] *n* (*wood*) ébène *f*.

EC [iː'siː] *n abbr* (*European Community*) CEE *f*.

eccentric [ɪk'sentrɪk] *a* & *n* excentrique (*mf*).

echo ['ekəʊ] *n* (*pl* **-oes**) écho *m* ▮ *vt* (*sound*) répercuter; (*repeat*) *Fig* répéter ▮ *vi* **the explosion/etc echoed** l'écho de l'explosion/*etc* se répercuta; **the room/etc echoes** la pièce/*etc* est sonore.

éclair [eɪ'kleər] *n* (*cake*) éclair *m*.

eclipse [ɪ'klɪps] *n* (*of sun etc*) éclipse *f*.

ecology [ɪ'kɒlədʒɪ] *n* écologie *f*.

economic [iːkə'nɒmɪk] *a* économique; (*profitable*) rentable. • **economical** *a* économique; (*thrifty*) économe. • **economics** *n* science *f* économique; (*of a business etc*) aspect *m* financier.

economy [ɪ'kɒnəmɪ] *n* économie *f*; **e. class** (*on aircraft*) classe *f* touriste. • **economist** *n* économiste *mf*. • **economize** *vti* économiser (**on** sur).

ecstasy ['ekstəsɪ] *n* extase *f*. • **ecstatic** *a* extasié; **to be e. about** s'extasier sur.

ECU [eɪ'kjuː] *n abbr* (*European Currency Unit*) ECU *m inv*.

eczema ['eksɪmə] *n Med* eczéma *m*.

edge [edʒ] *n* bord *m*; (*of forest*) lisière *f*; (*of town*) abords *mpl*; (*of page*) marge *f*; (*of knife*) tranchant *m*; **on e.** (*person*) énervé; (*nerves*) tendu ▮ *vt* (*clothing etc*) border (**with** de) ▮ *vti* **to e. (oneself) into** (*move*) se glisser dans; **to e. (oneself) forward** avancer doucement. • **edging** *n* (*border*) bordure *f*.

edgeways ['edʒweɪz] (*Am* **edgewise**) *adv* **to get a word in e.** *Fam* placer un mot.

edgy ['edʒɪ] *a* (**-ier, -iest**) énervé.

edible ['edɪb(ə)l] *a* (*mushroom etc*) comestible; (*not unpleasant*) mangeable.

edifice ['edɪfɪs] *n* (*building*) édifice *m*.

Edinburgh ['edɪnb(ə)rə] *n* Édimbourg *m or f*.

edit ['edɪt] *vt* (*newspaper*) diriger; (*article*) mettre au point; (*film*) monter; (*text*) éditer; (*compile*) rédiger (*dictionnaire etc*); (*cut out*) couper.

editor ['edɪtər] *n* (*of newspaper*) rédacteur, -trice *mf* en chef; (*of review*) directeur, -trice *mf*; (*compiler of dictionary, newspaper column*) rédacteur, -trice *mf*; (*of text*) éditeur, -trice *mf*; (*proofreader*) correcteur, -trice *mf*; *TV Rad* réalisateur, -trice *mf*; **the e. in chief** (*of newspaper*) le rédacteur *or* la rédactrice en chef. • **editorial** *a* de la rédaction; **e. staff** rédaction *f* ▌ *n* éditorial *m*.

edition [ɪ'dɪʃ(ə)n] *n* édition *f*.

educate ['edjukeɪt] *vt* (*family, children*) éduquer; (*in school*) instruire; (*pupil, mind*) former, éduquer; **to be educated at** faire ses études à; **(well-)educated** (*person*) instruit. ●**education** [-'keɪʃ(ə)n] *n* éducation *f*; (*teaching*) instruction *f*, enseignement *m*; (*training*) formation *f*. ●**edu'cational** *a* (*establishment*) d'enseignement; (*method, theory*) pédagogique; (*game, film*) éducatif; (*experience*) instructif.

EEC [iːiː'siː] *n abbr* (*European Economic Community*) CEE *f*.

eel [iːl] *n* anguille *f*.

eerie ['ɪərɪ] *a* (*-ier, -iest*) sinistre, étrange.

efface [ɪ'feɪs] *vt* effacer.

effect [ɪ'fekt] **1** *n* (*result, impression*) effet *m* (**on** sur); **in e.** en fait; **to put into e.** mettre en application; **to come into e.**, **take e.** (*of law*) entrer en vigueur; **to take e.** (*of drug*) agir; **to have an e.** (*of medicine*) faire de l'effet; **to have no e.** rester sans effet. **2** *vt* (*carry out*) effectuer.

effective [ɪ'fektɪv] *a* (*efficient*) efficace; (*striking*) frappant; (*actual*) effectif; **to become e.** (*of law*) prendre effet. ●—**ly** *adv* efficacement; (*in fact*) effectivement.

effeminate [ɪ'femɪnɪt] *a* efféminé.

efficient [ɪ'fɪʃ(ə)nt] *a* (*method, organization*) efficace; (*person*) compétent, efficace; (*machine*) performant. ●**efficiency** *n* efficacité *f*; (*of machine*) performances *fpl*. ●**efficiently** *adv* efficacement; **to work e.** (*of machine*) bien fonctionner.

effigy ['efɪdʒɪ] *n* effigie *f*.

effort ['efət] *n* effort *m*; **to make an e.** faire un effort (**to** pour); **it isn't worth the e.** ça ne *or* n'en vaut pas la peine. ●**effortlessly** *adv* facilement, sans effort.

effusive [ɪ'fjuːsɪv] *a* (*person*) expansif; (*thanks, excuses*) sans fin.

e.g. [iː'dʒiː] *abbr* (*exempli gratia*) par exemple.

egg[1] [eg] *n* œuf *m*; **e. timer** sablier *m*; ●**eggcup** *n* coquetier *m*. ●**eggplant** *n Am* aubergine *f*. ●**eggshell** *n* coquille *f* (d'œuf).

egg[2] [eg] *vt* **to e. on** (*encourage*) inciter (**to do** à faire).

ego ['iːgəʊ] *n* (*pl* **-os**) **the e.** l'ego *m*; **one's e.** (*self-image*) son image *f* de soi; (*self-esteem*) son amour-propre *m*. ●**egoist** ['egəʊɪst] *n* égoïste *mf*.

Egypt ['iːdʒɪpt] *n* Égypte *f*. ●**Egyptian** [ɪ'dʒɪpʃən] *a & n* égyptien, -ienne (*mf*).

eh? [eɪ] *int Fam* hein?

eiderdown ['aɪdədaʊn] *n* édredon *m*.

eight [eɪt] *a & n* huit (*m*). ●**eigh'teen** *a & n* dix-huit (*m*). ●**eighth** *a & n* huitième (*mf*). ●**eightieth** *a & n* quatre-vingtième (*mf*). ●**eighty** *a & n* quatre-vingts (*m*); **e.-one** quatre-vingt-un.

Eire ['eərə] *n* Eire *f*, République *f* d'Irlande.

either ['aɪðər] **1** *a & pron* (*one or other*) l'un(e) ou l'autre; (*with negative*) ni l'un(e) ni l'autre; (*each*) chaque; **on e. side** de chaque côté. **2** *adv* **she can't swim e.** elle ne sait pas nager non plus; **I don't e.** (ni) moi non plus. **3** *conj* **e.** ... **or** ou (bien) ... ou (bien), soit ... soit; (*with negative*) ni ... ni.

eject [ɪ'dʒekt] *vt* (*from hall etc*) expulser (*qn*) (**from** de) ▌ *vi* (*of pilot*) s'éjecter.

eke [iːk] *vt* **to e. out** (*income*) faire durer; **to e. out a living** gagner (difficilement) sa vie.

elaborate [ɪ'læbərət] *a* compliqué; (*preparation*) minutieux; (*meal*) raffiné ▌ [ɪ'læbəreɪt] *vt* (*theory*) élaborer ▌ *vi* entrer dans les détails (**on** de).

elapse [ɪ'læps] *vi* s'écouler.

elastic [ɪ'læstɪk] *a* élastique; **e. band** élastique *m* ▌ *n* (*fabric*) élastique *m*.

elated [ɪ'leɪtɪd] *a* transporté de joie.

elbow ['elbəʊ] *n* coude *m* ▌ *vt* **to e. one's way** se frayer un chemin (à coups de coude) (**through** à travers).

elder[1] ['eldər] a & n (of two people) aîné, -ée (mf).

elder[2] ['eldər] n (tree) sureau m.

elderly ['eldəlɪ] a assez âgé ‖ n the e. les personnes fpl âgées. ● **eldest** a & n aîné, -ée (mf); **his** or **her** e. **brother** l'aîné de ses frères.

elect [ɪ'lekt] vt (by voting) élire (qn) (to à); **to e. to do** choisir de faire ‖ a **the president e.** le président désigné. ● **election** [ɪ'lekʃ(ə)n] n élection f; **general e.** élections fpl législatives ‖ a (campaign) électoral; (day, results) du scrutin.

electoral [ɪ'lektər(ə)l] a électoral. ● **electorate** [ɪ'lektərət] n électorat m.

electric [ɪ'lektrɪk] a électrique; **e. blanket** couverture f chauffante; **e. shock** décharge f électrique. ● **electrical** a électrique. ● **electrician** [-'trɪʃən] n électricien m. ● **elec'tricity** n électricité f.

electrify [ɪ'lektrɪfaɪ] vt Rail électrifier; (excite) Fig électriser.

electrocute [ɪ'lektrəkjuːt] vt électrocuter.

electronic [ɪlektrɒnɪk] a électronique. ● **electronics** n électronique f.

elegant ['elɪgənt] a élégant. ● **elegance** n élégance f. ● **elegantly** adv avec élégance.

element ['elɪmənt] n (component, chemical etc) élément m; (of heater, kettle) résistance f; **an e. of truth** un grain de vérité; **the human e.** le facteur humain; **in one's e.** dans son élément.

elementary [elɪ'ment(ə)rɪ] a élémentaire; (school) Am primaire.

elephant ['elɪfənt] n éléphant m.

elevate ['elɪveɪt] vt élever (**to** à). ● **elevation** [-'veɪʃ(ə)n] n élévation f (**of** de); (height) altitude f.

elevator ['elɪveɪtər] n Am ascenseur m.

eleven [ɪ'lev(ə)n] a & n onze (m). ● **elevenses** [ɪ'lev(ə)nzɪz] n Fam pause-café f (vers onze heures du matin). ● **eleventh** a & n onzième (mf).

elf [elf] n (pl **elves**) lutin m.

elicit [ɪ'lɪsɪt] vt tirer, obtenir (**from** de).

elision [ɪ'lɪʒ(ə)n] n (of vowel) élision f.

eligible ['elɪdʒəb(ə)l] a (for post etc) admissible (**for** à); **to be e. for sth** (entitled to) avoir droit à qch; **an e. young man** (suitable as husband) un beau parti.

eliminate [ɪ'lɪmɪneɪt] vt supprimer (**from** de); (applicant, possibility) éliminer.

elite [eɪ'liːt] n élite f (**of** de).

elk [elk] n (animal) élan m.

elm [elm] n (tree, wood) orme m.

elocution [elə'kjuːʃ(ə)n] n élocution f.

elongated ['iːlɒŋgeɪtɪd] a allongé.

elope [ɪ'ləʊp] vi s'enfuir (**with** avec).

eloquent ['eləkwənt] a éloquent.

else [els] adv d'autre; **someone e.** quelqu'un d'autre; **everybody e.** tous les autres; **nobody/nothing e.** personne/rien d'autre; **something e.** autre chose; **anything e.?** (in shop etc) autre chose?; **anything e. to add?** encore quelque chose à ajouter?; **somewhere e.** ailleurs, autre part; **nowhere e.** nulle part ailleurs; **who e.?** qui d'autre?; **how e.?** de quelle autre façon?; **or e.** ou bien, sinon. ● **elsewhere** adv ailleurs.

elude [ɪ'luːd] vt (of word, name) échapper à (qn); (question) éluder; (blow) esquiver. ● **elusive** a (enemy, aims) insaisissable; (reply) évasif.

emaciated [ɪ'meɪsɪeɪtɪd] a émacié.

embankment [ɪm'bæŋkmənt] n (of path etc) talus m; (of river) berge f.

embargo [ɪm'bɑːgəʊ] n (pl **-oes**) embargo m.

embark [ɪm'bɑːk] vi (s')embarquer; **to e. on** (start) commencer; (launch into) se lancer dans. ● **embarkation** [embɑː'keɪʃ(ə)n] n embarquement m.

embarrass [ɪm'bærəs] vt embarrasser, gêner. ● **—ing** a (question etc) embarrassant. ● **—ment** n embarras m, gêne f.

embassy ['embəsɪ] n ambassade f.

embedded [ɪm'bedɪd] a (stick, bullet etc) enfoncé (**in** dans).

embellish [ɪm'belɪʃ] vt embellir.

embers ['embəz] npl braise(s) f(pl).

embezzl/e [ɪm'bez(ə)l] vt (money) détourner. ● **—er** n escroc m, voleur m.

embittered [ɪm'bɪtəd] a (person) aigri.

emblem ['embləm] n emblème m.

embody [ɪm'bɒdɪ] vt (express) exprimer; (represent) incarner; (include) réunir.

embossed [ɪm'bɒst] a (pattern, characters) en relief; (paper) gaufré.

embrace [ɪm'breɪs] vt prendre dans ses bras, étreindre; (include, adopt) embrasser ▮ vi s'étreindre, s'embrasser ▮ n étreinte f.

embroider [ɪm'brɔɪdər] vt (cloth) broder. ● **embroidery** n broderie f.

embryo ['embrɪəʊ] n (pl -os) embryon m.

emcee [em'siː] n Am présentateur, -trice mf.

emerald ['emərəld] n émeraude f.

emerge [ɪ'mɜːdʒ] vi apparaître (from de); (from hole) sortir; (of truth, from water) émerger; **it emerges that** il apparaît que.

emergency [ɪ'mɜːdʒənsɪ] n urgence f; **in an e.** en cas d'urgence ▮ a (measure etc) d'urgence; (exit, brake) de secours; **e. ward** or Am **room** salle f des urgences; **e. landing** atterrissage m forcé.

emery ['emərɪ] a **e. board** lime f à ongles en carton.

emigrant ['emɪgrənt] n émigrant, -ante mf. ● **emigrate** vi émigrer.

eminent ['emɪnənt] a éminent.

emission [ɪ'mɪʃ(ə)n] n (of pollutant) émission f.

emotion [ɪ'məʊʃ(ə)n] n (strength of feeling) émotion f; (joy, love etc) sentiment m. ● **emotional** a (person, reaction) émotif; (story, speech) émouvant; (moment) d'intense émotion. ● **emotive** a (word) affectif; **an e. issue** une question sensible.

emperor ['empərər] n empereur m.

emphasize ['emfəsaɪz] vt souligner (that que); (word, fact, syllable) appuyer sur.

emphasis ['emfəsɪs] n (in word or phrase) accent m; (insistence) insistance f; **to lay** or **put e. on** mettre l'accent sur.

emphatic [em'fætɪk] a (refusal etc) (clear) catégorique; (forceful) énergi-

que; **to be e. about** insister sur; **she was e.** elle a été catégorique. ● **emphatically** adv (to refuse etc) catégoriquement; énergiquement.

empire ['empaɪər] n empire m.

employ [ɪm'plɔɪ] vt (person, means) employer. ● **employee** [ɪm'plɔɪiː] n employé, -ée mf. ● **employer** n patron, -onne mf. ● **employment** n emploi m; **place of e.** lieu m de travail; **e. agency** bureau m de placement.

empress ['emprɪs] n impératrice f.

empty ['emptɪ] a (-ier, -iest) vide; (threat, promise etc) vain; **on an e. stomach** à jeun; **to return e.-handed** revenir les mains vides.

▮ n empties (bottles) bouteilles fpl vides.

▮ vt **to e. (out)** (box, liquid etc) vider; (vehicle) décharger; (objects in box etc) sortir (from de).

▮ vi (of building, tank etc) se vider. ● **emptiness** n vide m.

emulsion [ɪ'mʌlʃ(ə)n] n (paint) peinture f acrylique (mate).

enable [ɪ'neɪb(ə)l] vt **to e. s.o. to do** permettre à qn de faire.

enamel [ɪ'næm(ə)l] n émail m (pl émaux) ▮ a en émail.

enamoured [ɪn'æməd] a **e. of** (thing) séduit par; (person) amoureux de.

encase [ɪn'keɪs] vt (cover) recouvrir (in de).

enchanting [ɪn'tʃɑːntɪŋ] a enchanteur.

encircle [ɪn'sɜːk(ə)l] vt entourer; Mil encercler.

enclos/e [ɪn'kləʊz] vt (send with letter) joindre (in, with à); (fence off) clôturer; **to e. sth with** (a wall etc) entourer qch de. ● **—ed** a (space) clos; (receipt etc) ci-joint; (market) couvert.

enclosure [ɪn'kləʊʒər] n (in letter) pièce f jointe; (place) enceinte f.

encompass [ɪn'kʌmpəs] vt (include) inclure.

encore ['ɒŋkɔːr] int & n bis (m).

encounter [ɪn'kaʊntər] vt rencontrer ▮ n rencontre f.

encourage [ɪn'kʌrɪdʒ] vt encourager (to

do à faire). ●—ment n encouragement m.

encroach [ɪn'krəʊtʃ] vi empiéter (**on, upon** sur).

encyclop(a)edia [ɪnsaɪklə'piːdɪə] n encyclopédie f.

end [end] n (of street, box etc) bout m; (of meeting, month, book etc) fin f; (purpose) fin f, but m; **at an e.** (discussion etc) fini; (patience) à bout; **in the e.** à la fin; **to come to an e.** prendre fin; **to put an e. to, bring to an e.** mettre fin à; **there's no e. to it** ça n'en finit plus; **no e. of** Fam beaucoup de; **six days on e.** six jours d'affilée; **for days on e.** pendant des jours et des jours; **to stand a box on e.** mettre une boîte debout.
▮ a (row, house) dernier; **e. product** Com produit m fini; Fig résultat m.
▮ vt finir, terminer (**with** par); (rumour) mettre fin à.
▮ vi finir, se terminer; **to e. in failure** se solder par un échec; **to e. up doing finir** par faire; **to e. up in** (London etc) se retrouver à; **he ended up in prison/a doctor** il a fini en prison/médecin.

endanger [ɪn'deɪndʒər] vt mettre en danger; **endangered species** espèce f menacée.

endearing [ɪn'dɪərɪŋ] a (person) sympathique.

endeavour [ɪn'devər] (Am **endeavor**) vi s'efforcer (**to do** de faire) ▮ n effort m (**to do** pour faire).

ending ['endɪŋ] n fin f; (of word) terminaison f.

endive ['endɪv, Am 'endaɪv] n (curly) chicorée f; (smooth) endive f.

endless ['endləs] a (speech, series etc) interminable; (countless) innombrable.
●—ly adv interminablement.

endorse [ɪn'dɔːs] vt (cheque, Am check) endosser; (action, plan) approuver. ●—ment n (on driving licence) = point(s) enlevé(s) sur le permis de conduire.

endow [ɪn'daʊ] vt (institution) doter (**with** de); **endowed with** (person) Fig

doté de.

endure [ɪn'djʊər] 1 vt (bear) supporter (**doing** de faire). 2 vi (last) durer.
● **endurance** n endurance f, résistance f.

enemy ['enəmɪ] n ennemi, -ie mf; **the e.** Mil l'ennemi m ▮ a (tank etc) ennemi.

energy ['enədʒɪ] n énergie f ▮ a (crisis, resources etc) énergétique. ● **ener'getic** a énergique; **to feel e.** se sentir en pleine forme.

enforce [ɪn'fɔːs] vt (law) faire respecter; (discipline) imposer (**on** à).

engag/e [ɪn'geɪdʒ] vt (take on) engager, prendre ▮ vi **to e. in** (launch into) se lancer dans; (be involved in) être mêlé à.
● —**ed** a 1 (person, toilet, phone) occupé; **e. in doing** occupé à faire; **to be e. in business**/etc être dans les affaires/etc. 2 **e.** (**to be married**) fiancé; **to get e.** se fiancer.

engaging [ɪn'geɪdʒɪŋ] a (smile) engageant.

engagement [ɪn'geɪdʒmənt] n (to marry) fiançailles fpl; (meeting) rendez-vous m inv; (undertaking) engagement m; **e. ring** bague f de fiançailles.

engine ['endʒɪn] n Aut moteur m; Rail locomotive f; Nau machine f; **e. driver** mécanicien m.

engineer [endʒɪ'nɪər] n ingénieur m; (repairer) dépanneur, -euse mf; (train driver) Am mécanicien m; **civil e.** ingénieur m des travaux publics. ●—**ing** n ingénierie f; (**civil**) **e.** génie m civil; (**mechanical**) **e.** mécanique f.

England ['ɪŋglənd] n Angleterre f.

English ['ɪŋglɪʃ] a anglais; **the E. Channel** la Manche ▮ n (language) anglais m; **the E.** (people) les Anglais mpl.
● **Englishman** n (pl -**men**) Anglais m.
● **English-speaking** a anglophone.
● **Englishwoman** n (pl -**women**) Anglaise f.

engrav/e [ɪn'greɪv] vt graver. ●—**ing** n gravure f. ● **engraver** n graveur m.

engrossed [ɪn'grəʊst] a **e. in one's work/ book** absorbé par son travail/dans sa lecture.

engulf [ɪn'gʌlf] vt engloutir.

enhance [ɪn'hɑːns] vt (beauty etc) rehausser; (value) augmenter.

enigma [ɪ'nɪgmə] n énigme f.

enjoy [ɪn'dʒɔɪ] vt aimer (**doing** faire); (meal) apprécier; (good health etc) jouir de; **to e. the evening** passer une bonne soirée; **to e. oneself** s'amuser; **to e. being in London/etc** se plaire à Londres/etc. ●—**able** a agréable; (meal) excellent. ●—**ment** n plaisir m.

enlarge [ɪn'lɑːdʒ] vt agrandir ‖ vi s'agrandir. ●—**ment** n Phot agrandissement m.

enlighten [ɪn'laɪt(ə)n] vt éclairer (**s.o. on** or **about sth** qn sur qch). ●—**ing** a instructif.

enlist [ɪn'lɪst] vi (in the army etc) s'engager ‖ vt (recruit) engager; (supporter) recruter; (support) obtenir.

enliven [ɪn'laɪv(ə)n] vt (meeting etc) animer.

enormous [ɪ'nɔːməs] a énorme; (explosion, blow) terrible; (success, patience) immense. ●—**ly** adv (very much) énormément; (very) extrêmement.

enough [ɪ'nʌf] a & n assez (de); **e. time/cups/etc** assez de temps/de tasses/etc; **to have e. to live on** avoir de quoi vivre; **to have e. to drink** avoir assez à boire; **to have had e. of** en avoir assez de; **that's e.**, ça suffit, c'est assez ‖ adv (to work etc) assez; **big/good/etc e.** assez grand/bon/etc (**to** pour); **strangely e.**, he left chose curieuse, il est parti.

enquire [ɪn'kwaɪər] vi = **inquire**.

enquiry [ɪn'kwaɪərɪ] n = **inquiry**.

enrage [ɪn'reɪdʒ] vt mettre en rage.

enrich [ɪn'rɪtʃ] vt enrichir; (soil) fertiliser.

enrol [ɪn'rəʊl] (Am **enroll**) vi (-**ll**-) s'inscrire (**in**, **for** à) ‖ vt inscrire. ●—**ment** (Am **enrollment**) n inscription f.

ensemble [ɒn'sɒmb(ə)l] n (clothes) & Mus ensemble m.

ensu/e [ɪn'sjuː] vi s'ensuivre. ●—**ing** a (day, year etc) suivant; (event) qui s'ensuit.

ensure [ɪn'ʃʊər] vt assurer; **to e. that** (make sure) s'assurer que.

entail [ɪn'teɪl] vt (imply, involve) supposer.

entangle [ɪn'tæŋg(ə)l] vt emmêler, enchevêtrer; **to get entangled** s'empêtrer (**in** dans).

enter ['entər] vt (room, vehicle, army etc) entrer dans; (road) s'engager dans; (university) s'inscrire à; (write down) inscrire (**in** dans, **on** sur); (data) Comptr entrer, introduire (données etc); **to e. s.o. for** (exam) présenter qn à; **to e. a painting/etc in** (competition) présenter un tableau/etc à; **it didn't e. my head** or **mind** ça ne m'est pas venu à l'esprit (**that** que).

‖ vi entrer; **to e. for** (race, exam) s'inscrire pour; **to e. into** (conversation, relations) entrer en; (career) entrer dans; (negotiations, explanation) entamer; (agreement) conclure.

enterpris/e ['entəpraɪz] n (undertaking, firm) entreprise f; (spirit) initiative f. ●—**ing** a (person) plein d'initiative.

entertain [entə'teɪn] vt amuser, distraire; (guest) recevoir; (idea, possibility) envisager; (hope) nourrir ‖ vi (receive guests) recevoir. ●—**ing** a amusant. ● **entertainer** n artiste mf. ● **entertainment** n amusement m, distraction f; (show) spectacle m.

enthral(l) [ɪn'θrɔːl] vt (-**ll**-) (delight) captiver.

enthuse [ɪn'θjuːz] vi **to e. over** Fam s'emballer pour.

enthusiasm [ɪn'θjuːzɪæz(ə)m] n enthousiasme m. ● **enthusiast** n enthousiaste mf; **jazz/etc e.** passionné, -ée mf de jazz/etc.

enthusiastic [ɪnθuːzɪ'æstɪk] a enthousiaste; (golfer etc) passionné; **to be e. about** (hobby) être passionné de; (gift etc) être emballé par; **to get e.** s'emballer (**about** pour). ● **enthusiastically** adv avec enthousiasme.

entic/e [ɪn'taɪs] vt attirer (par la ruse) (**into** dans); **to e. s.o. to do** entraîner qn (par la ruse) à faire. ● **—ing** a séduisant.

entire [ɪn'taɪər] a entier. ● **—ly** adv tout à fait, entièrement. ● **entirety** [ɪn'taɪərətɪ] n in its e. en entier.

entitl/e [ɪn'taɪt(ə)l] vt to e. s.o. to do donner à qn le droit de faire; **to e. s.o. to sth** donner à qn (le) droit à qch. ● **—ed** a (book) intitulé; **to be e. to do** avoir le droit de faire; **to be e. to sth** avoir droit à qch.

entity ['entɪtɪ] n entité f.

entrance ['entrəns] n entrée f (to de); (to university) admission f (to à); **e. examination** examen m d'entrée.

entrant ['entrənt] n (in race) concurrent, -ente mf; (for exam) candidat, -ate mf.

entreat [ɪn'triːt] vt supplier (to do de faire).

entrée ['ɒntreɪ] n (main dish) Am plat m principal.

entrench [ɪn'trentʃ] vt to e. oneself Mil & Fig se retrancher.

entrust [ɪn'trʌst] vt confier (to à); **to e. s.o. with sth** confier qch à qn.

entry ['entrɪ] n (way in, action) entrée f; (bookkeeping item) écriture f; (term in dictionary or logbook) entrée f; (thing to be judged in competition) objet m (or œuvre f or projet m) soumis au jury; **e. form** feuille f d'inscription; **'no e.'** (on door etc) 'entrée interdite'; (road sign) 'sens interdit'.

enumerate [ɪ'njuːməreɪt] vt énumérer.

enunciate [ɪ'nʌnsɪeɪt] vt (word) articuler.

envelop [ɪn'veləp] vt envelopper (in mystery/etc de mystère/etc).

envelope ['envələʊp] n enveloppe f.

envious ['envɪəs] a envieux (of sth de qch); **e. of s.o.** jaloux de qn. ● **enviable** a enviable.

environment [ɪn'vaɪərənmənt] n milieu m; **the e.** (natural) l'environnement m; **e.-friendly** (product) qui ne nuit pas à l'environnement. ● **environ'mental** a du milieu; de l'environnement, écologique.

envisage [ɪn'vɪzɪdʒ] vt (imagine) envi-

sager (**doing** de faire); (foresee) prévoir.

envision [ɪn'vɪʒ(ə)n] vt Am = **envisage**.

envoy ['envɔɪ] n (messenger) envoyé, -ée mf.

envy ['envɪ] n envie f ‖ vt envier (s.o. sth qch à qn).

epic ['epɪk] a épique ‖ n épopée f; (screen) **e. film** m à grand spectacle.

epidemic [epɪ'demɪk] n épidémie f.

epidural [epɪ'djʊərəl] n Med (anesthésie f) péridurale f.

epilepsy ['epɪlepsɪ] n épilepsie f. ● **epi'leptic** a & n épileptique (mf).

episode ['epɪsəʊd] n épisode m.

epitaph ['epɪtɑːf] n épitaphe f.

epithet ['epɪθet] n épithète f.

epitome [ɪ'pɪtəmɪ] n **the e. of** l'exemple même de. ● **epitomize** vt incarner.

epoch ['iːpɒk] n époque f. ● **e.-making** a (event) qui fait date.

equal ['iːkwəl] a égal (to à); **with e. hostility** avec la même hostilité; **on an e. footing** sur un pied d'égalité (with avec); **to be e. to** (in quantity, number) égaler; **e. to** (task) Fig à la hauteur de. ‖ n (person) égal, -ale mf; **to treat s.o. as an e.** traiter qn en égal or d'égal à égal. ‖ vt (-ll-, Am -l-) égaler (in beauty/etc en beauté/etc); **equals sign** Math signe m d'égalité. ● **equal** adv (to an equal degree, also) également; (to divide) in parts égales; **he's e. stupid** (just as) il est tout aussi bête.

equality [ɪ'kwɒlɪtɪ] n égalité f.

equalize ['iːkwəlaɪz] vi (score) Sp égaliser.

equate [ɪ'kweɪt] vt mettre sur le même pied (with que), assimiler (with à).

equation [ɪ'kweɪʒ(ə)n] n Math équation f.

equator [ɪ'kweɪtər] n équateur m; **at** or **on the e.** sous l'équateur.

equilibrium [iːkwɪ'lɪbrɪəm] n équilibre m.

equinox ['iːkwɪnɒks] n équinoxe m.

equip [ɪ'kwɪp] vt (-pp-) équiper (with de); **(well-)equipped with** pourvu de; **(well-)equipped to do** compétent pour faire. ●—ment n équipement m, matériel m.

equities ['ekwɪtɪz] npl (shares) Com actions fpl (ordinaires).

equivalent [ɪ'kwɪvələnt] a & n équivalent (m). ●**equivalence** n équivalence f.

era ['ɪərə, Am 'erə] n époque f; (historical, geological) ère f.

eradicate [ɪ'rædɪkeɪt] vt supprimer; (evil, prejudice) extirper.

erase [ɪ'reɪz, Am ɪ'reɪs] vt effacer. ●**eraser** n (rubber for pencil marks) gomme f.

erect [ɪ'rekt] 1 a (upright) (bien) droit. 2 vt (build) construire; (statue, monument) ériger; (scaffolding, tent) monter.

erode [ɪ'rəʊd] vt éroder; (confidence etc) Fig miner, ronger.

erotic [ɪ'rɒtɪk] a érotique.

err [ɜːr] vi (be wrong) se tromper.

errand ['erənd] n commission f, course f.

erratic [ɪ'rætɪk] a (service, machine etc) capricieux, fantaisiste; (person, behaviour) lunatique; (results etc) irrégulier.

error ['erər] n (mistake) erreur f; to do sth in e. faire qch par erreur.

erupt [ɪ'rʌpt] vi (of volcano) entrer en éruption; (of war, violence) éclater. ●**eruption** [-ʃ(ə)n] n (of volcano) éruption f (of de); (of violence) flambée f.

escalate ['eskəleɪt] vi (of war, violence) s'intensifier; (of prices) monter en flèche.

escalator ['eskəleɪtər] n escalier m roulant.

escapade ['eskəpeɪd] n (prank) frasque f.

escape [ɪ'skeɪp] vi (of gas, animal, prisoner etc) s'échapper; to e. from (person) échapper à; (place) s'échapper de; escaped prisoner évadé, -ée mf. ▮ vt (death) échapper à; (punishment) éviter; that name escapes me ce nom m'échappe.
▮ n (of gas) fuite f; (of person) évasion f, fuite f; to have a lucky or narrow e. l'échapper belle.

escort ['eskɔːt] n Mil Nau escorte f; (of woman) cavalier m ▮ [ɪ'skɔːt] vt escorter.

Eskimo ['eskɪməʊ] n (pl -os) Esquimau, -aude mf ▮ a esquimau (inv or f -aude).

esoteric [esəʊ'terɪk] a obscur, ésotérique.

especially [ɪ'speʃəlɪ] adv (tout) spécialement; (particularly) particulièrement; e. as d'autant plus que.

espionage ['espɪənɑːʒ] n espionnage m.

esplanade ['espləneɪd] n esplanade f.

espresso [e'spresəʊ] n (pl -os) (café m) express m.

Esq [ɪ'skwaɪər] abbr (esquire) J. Smith Esq (on envelope) Monsieur J. Smith.

essay ['eseɪ] n Sch rédaction f; Univ dissertation f; (literary) essai m (on sur).

essence ['esəns] n essence f; Culin extrait m; (main point) essentiel m (of de); in e. essentiellement.

essential [ɪ'senʃ(ə)l] a (principal, necessary) essentiel; it's e. that il est indispensable que (+ sub) ▮ npl the essentials l'essentiel m (of de); (of grammar) les éléments mpl. ●—ly adv essentiellement.

establish [ɪ'stæblɪʃ] vt établir; (state, society) fonder; (well-)established (business company) solide; (fact) reconnu; she's (well-)established elle a une réputation établie. ●—ment n (institution, business company) établissement m; the E. les classes fpl dirigeantes.

estate [ɪ'steɪt] n (land) terre(s) f(pl), propriété f; (property after death) Jur succession f; housing e. lotissement m; (workers') cité f (ouvrière); industrial e. zone f industrielle; e. agency agence f immobilière; e. agent agent m immobilier; e. car break m.

esteem [ɪ'stiːm] vt estimer; highly esteemed très estimé ▮ n estime f.

esthetic [es'θetɪk] a Am esthétique.

estimate ['estɪmeɪt] vt (value, consider) estimer (that que) ▮ ['estɪmət] n (assessment, judgment) évaluation f; (price for work to be done) devis m; rough e.

chiffre *m* approximatif.

estuary ['estjuərı] *n* estuaire *m*.

etc [et'setərə] *adv* etc.

etch [etʃ] *vti* graver à l'eau forte. ●—**ing** *n* (*picture*) eau-forte *f*.

eternal [ı'tɜ:n(ə)l] *a* éternel. ●**eternity** *n* éternité *f*.

ethical ['eθık(ə)l] *a* moral, éthique.

Ethiopia [i:θı'əʊpıə] *n* Éthiopie *f*. ●**Ethiopian** *a* & *n* éthiopien, -ienne (*mf*).

ethnic ['eθnık] *a* (*minority etc*) ethnique; **e.** music/*etc* musique *f*/*etc* traditionnelle (*d'Afrique etc*).

etiquette ['etıket] *n* (*rules*) bienséances *fpl*; (*diplomatic*) *e.* protocole *m*.

etymology [etı'mɒlədʒı] *n* étymologie *f*.

eucalyptus [ju:kə'lıptəs] *n* (*tree*) eucalyptus *m*.

euphemism ['ju:fəmız(ə)m] *n* euphémisme *m*.

euphoria [ju:'fɔ:rıə] *n* euphorie *f*.

Euro- ['jʊərəʊ] *pref* euro-; **Euro-MP** membre *m* du parlement européen.

Europe ['jʊərəp] *n* Europe *f*. ●**European** [jʊərə'pi:ən] *a* & *n* européen, -éenne (*mf*).

evacuate [ı'vækjʊeıt] *vt* évacuer.

evade [ı'veıd] *vt* éviter; (*pursuer, tax*) échapper à; (*law, question*) éluder.

evaluate [ı'væljʊeıt] *vt* évaluer (**at** à).

evaporate [ı'væpəreıt] *vi* (*of liquid*) s'évaporer; **evaporated milk** lait *m* concentré.

evasion [ı'veıʒ(ə)n] *n* **e. of** (*pursuer*) fuite *f* devant; **tax e.** évasion *f* fiscale.

evasive [ı'veısıv] *a* évasif.

eve [i:v] *n* **on the e. of** à la veille de.

even ['i:v(ə)n] **1** *a* (*flat*) uni, égal; (*equal*) égal; (*regular*) régulier; (*number*) pair; **to get e. with s.o.** se venger de qn; **we're e.** (*quits*) nous sommes quittes; (*in score*) nous sommes à égalité; **to break e.** (*financially*) s'y retrouver ‖ *vt* **to e. sth** (**out** *or* **up**) égaliser qch.
2 *adv* même; **e. better/more** encore mieux/plus; **e. if** *or* **though** même si; **e. so** quand même. ●**evenly** *adv* de manière égale; (*regularly*) régulière-

ment.

evening ['i:vnıŋ] *n* soir *m*; (*whole evening, event*) soirée *f*; **in the e.** le soir; **at seven in the e.** à sept heures du soir; **every Tuesday e.** tous les mardis soir; **all e. (long)** toute la soirée ‖ *a* (*newspaper, meal etc*) du soir; **e. performance** *Th* soirée *f*; **e. dress** (*of man*) tenue *f* de soirée; (*of woman*) robe *f* du soir.

event [ı'vent] *n* événement *m*; *Sp* épreuve *f*; **in the e. of death** en cas de décès; **in any e.** en tout cas. ●**eventful** *a* (*journey etc*) mouvementé; (*occasion*) mémorable.

eventual [ı'ventʃʊəl] *a* final. ●**eventu'ality** *n* éventualité *f*. ●**eventually** *adv* finalement, à la fin; (*some day* or *other*) un jour ou l'autre.

ever ['evər] *adv* jamais; **has he. seen it?** l'a-t-il jamais vu?; **more than e.** plus que jamais; **nothing e.** jamais rien; **hardly e.** presque jamais; **the first e.** le tout premier; **e. since** (*that event etc*) depuis; **e. since then** depuis lors, dès lors; **for e.** (*for always*) pour toujours; (*continually*) sans cesse; **the best one e.** le meilleur fils du monde; **e. so sorry/happy/***etc* vraiment désolé/heureux/*etc*; **thank you e. so much** merci mille fois; **it's e. such a pity** c'est vraiment dommage; **why e. not?** mais pourquoi pas?

evergreen ['evəgri:n] *n* arbre *m* à feuilles persistantes. ●**ever'lasting** *a* éternel. ●**ever'more** *adv* **for e.** à (tout) jamais.

every ['evrı] *a* chaque; **e. child** chaque enfant, tous les enfants; **e. one** chacun; **e. single one** tous (sans exception); **e. second** *or* **other day** tous les deux jours; **her e. gesture** ses moindres gestes; **e. bit as big** tout aussi grand (**as** que); **e. so often, e. now and then** de temps en temps.

everybody ['evrıbɒdı] *pron* tout le monde; **e. in turn** chacun à son tour. ●**everyday** *a* (*happening*), de tous les jours; (*ordinary*) banal (*mpl* -als); **in e.**

use d'usage courant. ● **everyone** pron = **everybody**. ● **everyplace** adv Am = **everywhere**. ● **everything** pron tout; e. I have tout ce que j'ai. ● **everywhere** adv partout; e. she goes où qu'elle aille, partout où elle va.

evict [ɪ'vɪkt] vt expulser (**from** de). ● **eviction** [-ʃ(ə)n] n expulsion f.

evidence ['evɪdəns] n (proof) preuve(s) f(pl); (given by witness) témoignage m; **to give e.** témoigner (**against** contre); **e.** of (wear etc) des signes mpl de; **in e.** (noticeable) (bien) en vue.

evident ['evɪdənt] a évident (**that** que); **it is e. from...** il apparaît de... (**that** que). ● **—ly** adv (obviously) évidemment; (apparently) apparemment.

evil ['i:v(ə)l] a (influence, person etc) malfaisant; (deed, advice, system) mauvais ‖ n mal m; **to speak e.** dire du mal (**about, of** de).

evoke [ɪ'vəʊk] vt (recall, conjure up) évoquer. ● **evocative** [ɪ'vɒkətɪv] a évocateur.

evolution [i:və'lu:ʃ(ə)n] n évolution f.

evolve [ɪ'vɒlv] vi (of society, idea etc) évoluer ‖ vt (system etc) développer.

ewe [ju:] n brebis f.

ex- [eks] pref ex-; **ex-wife** ex-femme f.

exact [ɪg'zækt] **1** a (accurate, precise) exact; **to be e. about sth** préciser qch. ‖ vt (demand) exiger (**from** de); (money) extorquer (**from** à). ● **—ing** a exigeant. ● **—ly** adv exactement.

exaggerate [ɪg'zædʒəreɪt] vti exagérer. ● **exaggeration** [-'reɪʃ(ə)n] n exagération f.

exam [ɪg'zæm] n abbr (examination) examen m.

examine [ɪg'zæmɪn] vt examiner; (accounts, luggage) vérifier; (passport) contrôler; (question) interroger (élève, témoin). ● **examination** [-'neɪʃ(ə)n] n Sch Univ examen m; (inspection) examen m; (of passport) contrôle m; **class e.** devoir m surveillé or sur table. ● **examiner** n Sch examinateur, -trice mf.

example [ɪg'zɑːmp(ə)l] n exemple m; for

e. par exemple; **to set an e.** or **a good e.** donner l'exemple or le bon exemple (**to** à); **to set a bad e.** donner le mauvais exemple.

exasperate [ɪg'zɑːspəreɪt] vt exaspérer.

excavate ['ekskəveɪt] vt (dig) creuser; (for relics etc) fouiller; (uncover) déterrer.

exceed [ɪk'siːd] vt dépasser. ● **—ingly** adv extrêmement.

excel [ɪk'sel] vi (-ll-) **to e. in** or **at sth** être excellent en qch.

excellent ['eksələnt] a excellent. ● **excellence** n excellence f.

except [ɪk'sept] prep sauf, excepté; **e. for** à part; **e. that** sauf que; **e. if** sauf si; **to do nothing e. wait** ne rien faire sinon attendre ‖ vt excepter.

exception [ɪk'sepʃ(ə)n] n exception f; **with the e. of** à l'exception de; **to take e. to** (object to) désapprouver; (be hurt by) s'offenser de. ● **exceptional** a exceptionnel. ● **exceptionally** adv exceptionnellement.

excerpt ['eksɜːpt] n (from film etc) extrait m.

excess ['ekses] n excès m; (surplus) Com excédent m; **to e.** à l'excès; **e. calories/** etc des calories fpl/etc en trop; **e. fare** supplément m (de billet); **e. luggage** or **baggage** excédent m de bagages; **e. weight** kilos mpl en trop.

excessive [ɪk'sesɪv] a excessif. ● **excessively** adv (too, too much) excessivement; (very) extrêmement.

exchange [ɪks'tʃeɪndʒ] vt échanger (**for** contre) ‖ n échange m; (of foreign currencies) change m; (telephone) e. central m (téléphonique); **in e.** en échange (**for** de).

Exchequer [ɪks'tʃekər] n **Chancellor of the E.** = ministre m des Finances.

excitable [ɪk'saɪtəb(ə)l] a excitable.

excit/e [ɪk'saɪt] vt (enthuse) passionner; (agitate, provoke, stimulate) exciter. ● **—ed** a (happy) surexcité; (nervous) énervé; **to get e.** (nervous, enthusiastic) s'exciter; **to be e. about** (new car *etc*) se réjouir de. ●**—ing** *a* (*book, adventure etc*) passionnant. ●**excitement** *n* agitation *f*, excitation *f*; (*emotion*) vive émotion *f*.

exclaim [ɪk'skleɪm] *vti* s'exclamer (that que). ●**exclamation** [ekskləˈmeɪʃ(ə)n] *n* exclamation *f*; **e. mark** *or Am* **point** point *m* d'exclamation.

exclude [ɪks'kluːd] *vt* exclure (**from** de). ●**exclusion** [-ʒ(ə)n] *n* exclusion *f*.

exclusive [ɪk'skluːsɪv] *a* exclusif; (*club, group*) fermé; (*interview, news item*) en exclusivité; **e. of wine**/*etc* vin/*etc* non compris.

excruciating [ɪk'skruːʃɪeɪtɪŋ] *a* insupportable, atroce.

excursion [ɪk'skɜːʃ(ə)n] *n* excursion *f*.

excuse [ɪk'skjuːz] *vt* (*forgive*) excuser (**s.o. for doing** qn d'avoir fait, qn de faire); (*exempt*) dispenser (**from** de); **e. me for asking** permettez-moi de demander; **e. me!** excusez-moi!, pardon! ▮ [ɪk'skjuːs] *n* excuse *f*; **to make an e.** se trouver une excuse; **it was an e. for** cela a servi de prétexte à.

ex-directory [eksdaɪ'rektərɪ] *a* (*telephone number*) sur la liste rouge.

execute ['eksɪkjuːt] *vt* (*criminal, order etc*) exécuter. ●**execution** [-'kjuːʃ(ə)n] *n* exécution *f*. ●**exe'cutioner** *n* bourreau *m*.

executive [ɪg'zekjʊtɪv] *a* (*job*) de cadre; (*car, plane*) de direction; (*power*) exécutif ▮ *n* (*person*) cadre *m*; (*board, committee*) bureau *m*; **the e.** *Pol* l'exécutif *m*; (**senior**) **e.** cadre *m* supérieur; **junior e.** jeune cadre *m*; **sales e.** cadre *m* commercial.

exemplify [ɪg'zemplɪfaɪ] *vt* (*show*) illustrer; (*serve as example of*) servir d'exemple de.

exempt [ɪg'zempt] *a* dispensé (**from** de) ▮ *vt* dispenser (**from** de). ●**exemption** [-ʃ(ə)n] *n* dispense *f*.

exercise ['eksəsaɪz] *n Sch Sp Mil* exercice *m*; **e. book** cahier *m* ▮ *vt* (*muscles, rights etc*) exercer; (*dog, horse etc*) promener; (*tact, judgment etc*) faire preuve de ▮ *vi* (*take exercise*) faire de l'exercice.

exert [ɪg'zɜːt] *vt* exercer; (*force*) employer; **to e. oneself** (*physically*) dépenser; **don't e. yourself** ne te fatigue pas. ●**exertion** [-ʃ(ə)n] *n* effort *m*.

exhaust [ɪg'zɔːst] **1** *vt* (*use up, tire*) épuiser; **to become exhausted** s'épuiser. **2** *n* **e.** (*pipe*) *Aut* tuyau *m* d'échappement; **e.** (*fumes*) gaz *mpl* d'échappement. ●**—ing** *a* épuisant. ●**exhaustion** [[-st∫(ə)n] *n* épuisement *m*.

exhaustive [ɪg'zɔːstɪv] *a* (*study etc*) complet, exhaustif.

exhibit [ɪg'zɪbɪt] *vt* (*put on display*) exposer; (*courage etc*) montrer ▮ *n* objet *m* exposé; *Jur* pièce *f* à conviction.

exhibition [egzɪ'bɪʃ(ə)n] *n* exposition *f*; **an e. of** (*skill, arrogance etc*) une démonstration de. ●**exhibitionist** *n* exhibitionniste *mf*.

exhibitor [ɪg'zɪbɪtər] *n* exposant, -ante *mf*.

exhilarating [ɪg'zɪləreɪtɪŋ] *a* (*experience etc*) grisant; (*air*) vivifiant. ●**exhilaration** [-'reɪʃ(ə)n] *n* joie *f*.

exile ['egzaɪl] *vt* exiler ▮ *n* (*absence*) exil *m*; (*person*) exilé, -ée *mf*.

exist [ɪg'zɪst] *vi* exister; (*live*) vivre (**on** de). ●**—ing** *a* (*situation*) actuel; (*law*) existant. ●**existence** *n* existence *f*; **to come into e.** être créé; **to be in e.** exister.

exit ['eksɪt, 'egzɪt] *n* (*action, door, window*) sortie *f*.

exodus ['eksədəs] *n inv* exode *m*.

exonerate [ɪg'zɒnəreɪt] *vt* (*from blame*) disculper (**from** de).

exorbitant [ɪg'zɔːbɪtənt] *a* exorbitant.

exotic [ɪg'zɒtɪk] *a* exotique.

expand [ɪk'spænd] *vt* (*knowledge, influence etc*) étendre; (*trade, idea*) développer; (*production*) augmenter; (*gas, metal*) dilater ▮ *vi* (*trade*) se développer; augmenter; se dilater; **to e. on** développer ses idées sur; **expanding sector** *Com* secteur *m* en (pleine) expansion.

expanse [ɪk'spæns] *n* étendue *f*.

expansion [ɪk'spænʃ(ə)n] *n* (*of economy, gas, metal etc*) expansion *f*; (*of trade etc*) développement *m*.

expatriate [eks'pætrɪət, *Am* eks'peɪtrɪət] *a & n* expatrié, -ée (*mf*).

expect [ɪk'spekt] *vt* (*anticipate*) s'attendre à; (*think*) penser (that que); (*suppose*) supposer (that que); (*await*) attendre (*qn*); **to e. sth from s.o./sth** attendre qch de qn/qch; **to e. to do** compter faire; **to e. that** s'attendre à ce que (+ *sub*); **I e. you to come** (*want*) je compte que vous viendrez; **it was expected** c'était prévu (that que); **she's expecting (a baby)** elle attend un bébé.

expectancy [ɪk'spektənsɪ] *n* **life e.** espérance *f* de vie. ● **expectant** *a* **e. mother** future mère *f*.

expectation [ekspek'teɪʃ(ə)n] *n* attente *f*; **to come up to s.o.'s expectations** répondre à l'attente de qn.

expedient [ɪks'piːdɪənt] *a* avantageux; (*suitable*) opportun ▮ *n* expédient *m*.

expedition [ekspɪ'dɪʃ(ə)n] *n* expédition *f*.

expel [ɪk'spel] *vt* (**-ll-**) (*from school*) renvoyer; (*foreigner, demonstrator etc*) expulser (**from** de).

expenditure [ɪk'spendɪtʃər] *n* (*money*) dépenses *fpl*.

expense [ɪk'spens] *n* frais *mpl*; **business/ travelling expenses** frais *mnl* généraux/ de déplacement; **at the e. of s.o./sth** (*causing harm*) aux dépens de qn/qch; **one's e. account** sa note de frais (professionnels).

expensive [ɪk'spensɪv] *a* (*goods, hotel etc*) cher; (*tastes*) de luxe; **to be e.** coûter or être cher. ●**—ly** *adv* (*dressed etc*) luxueusement.

experience [ɪk'spɪərɪəns] *n* (*knowledge, event*) expérience *f*; **from** or **by e.** par expérience; **he has had e. of this work** il a déjà fait ce travail; **I've had e. of driving** j'ai déjà conduit; **practical e.** pratique *f* ▮ *vt* (*undergo*) connaître; (*difficulty*) éprouver. ●**—ed** *a* (*person*) expérimenté; (*eye, ear*) exercé; **to be e.**

in s'y connaître en.

experiment [ɪk'sperɪmənt] *n* expérience *f* ▮ [ɪk'sperɪment] *vi* faire une expérience *or* des expériences; **to e. with sth** (*in science*) expérimenter qch. ● **experi'mental** *a* expérimental.

expert ['ekspɜːt] *n* expert *m* (**on, in** en) ▮ *a* expert (**in sth** en qch, **in** *or* **at doing** à faire); **e. advice** le conseil d'un expert; **e. touch** grande habileté *f*. ● **expertise** [-'tiːz] *n* compétence *f* (**in** en).

expir/e [ɪk'spaɪər] *vi* expirer. ●**—ed** *a* (*ticket, passport etc*) périmé.

expiry [ɪk'spaɪərɪ] (*Am* **expiration** [ekspə'reɪʃ(ə)n]) *n* expiration *f*; **e. date** (*on ticket*) date *f* d'expiration; (*on product*) date *f* limite d'utilisation.

explain [ɪk'spleɪn] *vt* expliquer (**to** à, **that** que); (*reasons*) exposer; **to e. sth away** justifier qch. ● **explanation** [eksplə'neɪʃ(ə)n] *n* explication *f*.

explanatory [ɪk'splænət(ə)rɪ] *a* explicatif.

expletive [ɪk'spliːtɪv, *Am* 'eksplətɪv] *n* juron *m*.

explicit [ɪk'splɪsɪt] *a* explicite. ●**—ly** *adv* explicitement.

explode [ɪk'spləʊd] *vi* exploser ▮ *vt* faire exploser.

exploit 1 [ɪk'splɔɪt] *vt* (*person, land etc*) exploiter. **2** ['eksplɔɪt] *n* (*feat*) exploit *m*. ● **exploitation** [-'teɪʃ(ə)n] *n* exploitation *f*.

explore [ɪk'splɔːr] *vt* explorer; (*causes etc*) examiner. ● **exploration** [eksplə'reɪʃ(ə)n] *n* exploration *f*.

exploratory [ɪk'splɒrət(ə)rɪ] *a* (*talks etc*) préliminaire, exploratoire; **e. operation** *Med* sondage *m*.

explorer [ɪk'splɔːrər] *n* explorateur, -trice *mf*.

explosion [ɪk'spləʊʒ(ə)n] *n* explosion *f*.

explosive [ɪk'spləʊsɪv] *a* (*weapon, situation*) explosif; **e. device** engin *m* explosif ▮ *n* explosif *m*.

export ['ekspɔːt] *n* exportation *f* ▮ [ɪk'spɔːt] *vt* exporter (**to** vers, **from**

de). ● **ex'porter** n exportateur, -trice mf;
(country) pays m exportateur.

expose [ık'spəʊz] vt (leave uncovered) &
Phot exposer; (plot, scandal etc) révéler;
(crook etc) démasquer; **to e. s.o. to**
(subject to) exposer qn à.

exposure [ık'spəʊʒər] n exposition f (to
à); Phot pose f; **to die of e.** mourir de
froid.

express [ık'spres] **1** vt exprimer; **to e.**
oneself s'exprimer. **2** a (letter, delivery) exprès inv; (train) rapide, express
inv; (order) exprès; (intention) explicite; **with the e. purpose of** dans le
seul but de ▮ adv (to send) par exprès
▮ n (train) rapide m, express m inv.
● **expression** [-ʃ(ə)n] n (phrase, look)
expression f; **an e. of** (gratitude etc)
un témoignage de. ● **expressly** adv
expressément.

expressive [ık'spresıv] a expressif.

expressway [ık'spreswei] n Am autoroute f.

exquisite [ık'skwızıt] a exquis. ● **—ly** adv
d'une façon exquise.

ex-serviceman [eks'sɜːvɪsmən] n (pl -men)
ancien combattant m.

extend [ık'stend] vt (arm, business)
étendre; (line, visit, meeting) prolonger
(**by** de); (hand) tendre (**to s.o.** à qn);
(house) agrandir; (time limit) reculer;
(help, thanks) offrir (**to** à) ▮ vi (of wall,
plain etc) s'étendre (**to** jusqu'à); (in
time) se prolonger.

extension [ık'stenʃ(ə)n] n (in time) prolongation f; (of meaning) extension f;
(for table) rallonge f; (to building)
agrandissement(s) m(pl); (of phone)
appareil m supplémentaire; (of office
phone) poste m; **e. (cable** or **lead)**
rallonge f.

extensive [ık'stensıv] a étendu, vaste;
(repairs, damage) important. ● **exten-**
sively adv (very much) énormément,
considérablement; **to be e. damaged**
subir des dégâts importants.

extent [ık'stent] n (scope) étendue f;
(size) importance f; **to a large/certain**

e. dans une large/certaine mesure; **to**
such an e. that à tel point que.

extenuating [ık'stenjʊeɪtɪŋ] a **e. circum-**
stances circonstances fpl atténuantes.

exterior [ıks'tɪərɪər] a & n extérieur (m).

exterminate [ık'stɜːmɪneɪt] vt (people,
animals) exterminer.

external [ek'stɜːn(ə)l] a extérieur; **for e.**
use (medicine) à usage externe.

extinct [ık'stıŋkt] a (volcano) éteint;
(species, animal) disparu.

extinguish [ık'stıŋgwıʃ] vt éteindre. ● **—er**
n (fire) e. extincteur m.

extort [ık'stɔːt] vt (money) extorquer
(**from** à). ● **extortion** n Jur extorsion f
de fonds. ● **extortionate** a (price etc)
exorbitant.

extra ['ekstrə] a (additional) supplémentaire; **one e. glass** un verre de or en plus;
(any) e. bread? encore du pain?; **to be e.**
(spare) être en trop; (cost more) être en
supplément; **e. charge** or **portion** supplément m; **e. time** Fb prolongation f.
▮ adv to pay e. payer un supplément;
wine costs or **is 3 francs e.** il y a un
supplément de 3F pour le vin; **e. big**
plus grand que d'habitude.
▮ n (perk) à-côté m; Cin Th figurant,
-ante mf; pl (expenses) frais mpl
supplémentaires.

extra- ['ekstrə] pref extra-. ● **e.-'dry** a
(champagne) brut. ● **e.-'strong** a extra-
fort.

extract [ık'strækt] vt extraire (**from** de);
(tooth, promise) arracher; (money) sou-
tirer (**from** à) ▮ ['ekstrækt] n (of book
etc, food substance) extrait m.

extra-curricular [ekstrəkə'rıkjʊlər, Am
-erı] a (activities) extrascolaire.

extradite ['ekstrədaıt] vt extrader. ● **ex-**
tradition [-'dıʃ(ə)n] n extradition f.

extraordinary [ık'strɔːdən(ə)rı, Am -erı]
a extraordinaire.

extra-special [ekstrə'speʃəl] a (occasion)
très spécial; (care) tout particulier.

extravagant [ık'strævəgənt] a (behaviour, idea etc) extravagant; (wasteful
with money) dépensier. ● **extravagance**

n (wastefulness) prodigalité *f; (thing bought)* folle dépense *f; (wasteful expenses)* prodigalités *fpl.*

extreme [ɪk'stri:m] *a (exceptional, furthest)* extrême; *(danger, poverty, importance)* très grand ‖ *n (furthest degree)* extrême *m;* **to carry** *or* **take sth to extremes** pousser qch à l'extrême; **extremes of temperature** températures *fpl* extrêmes. ● **extremely** *adv* extrêmement.

extremist [ɪk'stri:mɪst] *a & n* extrémiste *(mf).*

extremity [ɪk'stremɪtɪ] *n* extrémité *f.*

extricate ['ekstrɪkeɪt] *vt (free)* dégager *(qn, qch)* **(from** de).

extrovert ['ekstrəvɜ:t] *n* extraverti, -ie *mf.*

exuberant [ɪg'z(j)u:bərənt] *a* exubérant.

eye¹ [aɪ] *n* œil *m (pl* yeux); **before my very eyes** sous mes yeux; **as far as the e. can see** à perte de vue; **to have one's e.**

on *(house, car)* avoir en vue; **to keep an e. on** surveiller; **to lay** *or* **set eyes on** voir; **to take one's eyes off** s.o./sth quitter qn/qch des yeux; **to catch s.o.'s e.** attirer l'attention de qn; **keep your eyes open!** ouvrez l'œil!; **we don't see e. to e.** nous ne voyons pas les choses du même œil; **to be an e.-opener for s.o.** *Fam* être une révélation pour qn.

eye² [aɪ] *vt* regarder; *(with envy)* dévorer des yeux; *(with lust)* reluquer.

eyeball ['aɪbɔ:l] *n* globe *m* oculaire. ● **eyebrow** *n* sourcil *m.* ● **eyeglasses** *npl (spectacles) Am* lunettes *fpl.* ● **eyelash** *n* cil *m.* ● **eyelid** *n* paupière *f.* ● **eyeliner** *n* eye-liner *m.* ● **eye shadow** *n* ombre *f* à paupières. ● **eyesight** *n* vue *f.* ● **eyesore** *n (building etc)* horreur *f.* ● **eyestrain** *n* **to have e.** avoir les yeux qui tirent. ● **eyewitness** *n* témoin *m* oculaire.

F

F, f [ef] n F, f m.

fable ['feɪb(ə)l] n fable f.

fabric ['fæbrɪk] n (cloth) tissu m, étoffe f.

fabricate ['fæbrɪkeɪt] vt (invent, make) fabriquer.

fabulous ['fæbjuləs] a (wonderful) Fam formidable; (incredible, legendary) fabuleux.

façade [fə'sɑːd] n (of building) & Fig façade f.

face [feɪs] n (of person) visage m, figure f; (of clock) cadran m; (of cube, mountain) face f; (of cliff) paroi f; **f. down** (person) face contre terre; (thing) tourné à l'envers; **f. to f.** face à face; **in the f. of** devant; (despite) en dépit de; **to save/lose f.** sauver/perdre la face; **to make** or **pull faces** faire des grimaces; **f. powder** poudre f; **f. value** (of stamp etc) valeur f.

▮ vt (danger, enemy, problem etc) faire face à; (accept) accepter; (look in the face) regarder (qn) en face; **to f., be facing** (be opposite) être en face de; (of window, room etc) donner sur (le jardin etc); **faced with** (problem) confronté à; (defeat) menacé par; (bill) contraint à payer; **he can't f. leaving** il n'a pas le courage de partir.

▮ vi (of house) être orienté (north/etc au nord/etc); (of person) se tourner; (be turned) être tourné (towards vers); **to f. up to** (danger, problem) faire face à; (fact) accepter; **about f.!** Am Mil demitour!

facecloth ['feɪsklɒθ] n gant m de toilette.

facelift ['feɪslɪft] n Med lifting m; (of building) ravalement m.

faceless ['feɪsləs] a anonyme.

facetious [fə'siːʃəs] a (person) facétieux; (remark) plaisant.

facial ['feɪʃ(ə)l] a du visage ▮ n soin m du visage.

facile ['fæsaɪl, Am 'fæs(ə)l] a facile, superficiel.

facilitate [fə'sɪlɪteɪt] vt faciliter.

facilities [fə'sɪlɪtɪz] npl (for sports, cooking etc) équipements mpl; (in harbour, airport) installations fpl; (possibilities) facilités fpl; (means) moyens mpl; **special f.** (conditions) conditions fpl spéciales (for pour); **credit f.** facilités fpl de paiement.

fact [fækt] n fait m; **as a matter of f., in f.** en fait; **the facts of life** les choses fpl de la vie.

faction ['fækʃ(ə)n] n (group) faction f.

factor ['fæktər] n (element) facteur m.

factory ['fækt(ə)rɪ] n usine f; **arms f.** manufacture f d'armes.

factual ['fæktʃʊəl] a objectif, basé sur les faits; (error) de fait.

faculty ['fæk(ə)ltɪ] n (aptitude) & Univ faculté f.

fad [fæd] n (fashion) folie f, mode f (for de).

fade [feɪd] vi (of flower) se faner; (of light) baisser; (of colour) passer; (of fabric) se décolorer; (of memory etc) s'effacer.

fag [fæg] n **1** (cigarette) Fam clope m or f; **f. end** mégot m. **2** (homosexual) Am Sl Pej pédé m.

fail [feɪl] vi (of person, plan etc) échouer; (of business) faire faillite; (of health, sight, light) baisser; (of memory, strength) défaillir; (of brakes) Aut lâcher; (of engine) tomber en panne; **to f. in an exam** échouer à un examen; **to f. in one's duty** manquer à son devoir.

▮ vt (exam) rater, échouer à; (candidate) refuser, recaler; **to f. s.o.** (let down) laisser tomber qn; (of words) manquer à qn; **to f. to do** (*forget*) manquer de faire; (*not be able*) ne pas arriver à faire ‖ *n* **without f.** à coup sûr. ●**failed** *a* (*attempt, poet*) manqué. ●**failing** *n* (*fault*) défaut *m* ‖ *prep* à défaut de; **f. that** à défaut.

failure ['feɪljər] *n* échec *m*; (*of business*) faillite *f*; (*of engine, machine*) panne *f*; (*person*) raté, -ée *mf*; **f. to do** incapacité *f* de faire; **her f. to leave** le fait qu'elle n'est pas partie; **to end in f.** se solder par un échec; **heart f.** arrêt *m* du cœur.

faint [feɪnt] **1** *a* (*-er, -est*) (*weak*); (*voice, trace, hope etc*) faible; (*colour*) pâle; **I haven't got the faintest idea** je n'en ai pas la moindre idée. **2** *a* **to feel f.** se trouver mal ‖ *vi* s'évanouir. ●**—ly** *adv* (*weakly*) faiblement; (*slightly*) légèrement.

fair[1] [feər] *n* foire *f*; (*for charity*) fête *f*; (*funfair*) fête *f* foraine. ●**fairground** *n* champ *m* de foire.

fair[2] [feər] **1** *a* (*-er, -est*) (*just*) juste; (*game, fight*) loyal; **she is/that is f. to him** elle est juste envers lui/c'est juste pour lui; **f. (and square)** honnête(ment); **f. play** fair-play *m inv*; **that's not f. play!** ce n'est pas du jeu!; **f. enough!** très bien! ‖ *adv* **to play, fight** loyalement.

2 *a* (*rather good*) passable, assez bon; (*price, warning*) raisonnable; **a f. amount (of)** pas mal (de); **f. copy** copie *f* au propre.

3 *a* (*wind*) favorable; (*weather*) beau. ●**fairly** *adv* **1** (*to treat*) équitablement; (*to play, fight, act*) loyalement. **2** (*rather*) assez, plutôt; **f. sure** presque sûr. ●**fairness** *n* justice *f*; (*of person*) impartialité *f*. ●**fair-'sized** *a* assez grand.

fair[3] [feər] *a* (*hair, person*) blond; (*complexion, skin*) clair. ●**fair-'haired** *a* blond. ●**fair-'skinned** *a* à la peau claire.

fairy ['feərɪ] *n* fée *f*; **f. tale** or **story** conte *m* de fées.

faith [feɪθ] *n* foi *f*; **to have f. in s.o.** avoir confiance en qn; **to put one's f. in**

(*justice etc*) se fier à; **in good f.** de bonne foi. ●**faithful** *a* fidèle (**to** à). ●**faithfully** *adv* fidèlement; **yours f.** (*in letter*) veuillez agréer l'expression de mes salutations distinguées.

fake [feɪk] *n* (*document etc*) faux *m*; (*person*) imposteur *m* ‖ *vt* (*document, signature etc*) falsifier; (*election*) truquer ‖ *vi* (*pretend*) faire semblant ‖ *a* faux (*f* fausse); (*elections*) truqué.

falcon ['fɔːlkən] *n* faucon *m*.

fall [fɔːl] *n* chute *f*; (*in price, demand etc*) baisse *f* (**in** de); **the f.** (*season*) *Am* l'automne *m*.

‖ *vi* (*pt* **fell**, *pp* **fallen**) tomber; **to f. into** (*hole, trap*) tomber dans; **to f. off** or **down sth, f. out of sth** tomber de qch; **to f. on a Monday**/*etc* (*of event*) tomber un lundi/*etc*; **to f. over sth** (*chair etc*) tomber en butant contre qch; (*balcony etc*) tomber de qch; **to f. victim** devenir victime (**to** de); **to f. asleep** s'endormir; **to f. ill** tomber malade; **to f. due** échoir.

fall apart *vi* (*of machine*) tomber en morceaux; (*of group*) se désagréger ‖ **to fall away** (*come off*) se détacher, tomber ‖ **to fall back on** *vt* (*as last resort*) se rabattre sur ‖ **to fall behind** *vi* rester en arrière; (*in work, payment*) prendre du retard ‖ **to fall down** *vi* tomber, (*of building*) s'effondrer ‖ **to fall for** *vt* (*person*) tomber amoureux de; (*trick*) se laisser prendre à ‖ **to fall in** *vi* (*collapse*) s'écrouler ‖ **to fall off** *vi* (*come off*) se détacher, tomber; (*of numbers*) diminuer ‖ **to fall out** *vi* (*quarrel*) se brouiller (**with** avec) ‖ **to fall over** *vi* tomber; (*of table, vase*) se renverser ‖ **to fall through** *vi* (*of plan*) tomber à l'eau.

fallacy ['fæləsɪ] *n* erreur *f*; *Phil* faux raisonnement *m*.

fallout ['fɔːlaʊt] *n* (*radioactive*) retombées *fpl*.

fallow ['fæləʊ] *a* (*land*) en jachère.

false [fɔːls] *a* faux (*f* fausse); **f. teeth** fausses dents *fpl* ●**falsehood** *n* mensonge *m*.

falsify ['fɔːlsɪfaɪ] *vt* falsifier.

falter ['fɔːltər] *vi* (*of step*) chanceler; (*of voice*) hésiter.

fame [feɪm] *n* renommée *f*.

familiar [fə'mɪljər] *a* (*task, person, atmosphere etc*) familier (**to** à); (*event*) habituel; **f. with** s.o. (*too friendly*) familier avec qn; **to be f. with** (*know*) connaître; **to make oneself f. with** se familiariser avec; **he looks f.** (**to me**) je l'ai déjà vu (quelque part). ● **famili'arity** *n* familiarité *f* (**with** avec); (*of event, sight etc*) caractère *m* familier.

familiarize [fə'mɪljəraɪz] *vt* **to f. oneself with** se familiariser avec.

family ['fæmɪlɪ] *n* famille *f* ‖ *a* (*name, doctor etc*) de famille; (*problems*) familial; **f. man** père *m* de famille.

famine ['fæmɪn] *n* famine *f*.

famished ['fæmɪʃt] *a* affamé.

famous ['feɪməs] *a* célèbre (**for** pour).

fan¹ [fæn] *n* (*held in hand*) éventail *m*; (*mechanical*) ventilateur *m*; **f. heater** radiateur *m* soufflant ‖ *vt* (**-nn-**) (*person etc*) éventer; (*fire*) attiser.

fan² [fæn] *n* (*of person*) fan *mf*; *Sp* supporter *m*; **to be a jazz/sports f.** être passionné de jazz/de sport.

fanatic [fə'nætɪk] *n* fanatique *mf*. ● **fanatical** *a* fanatique.

fanciful ['fænsɪfəl] *a* fantaisiste.

fancy ['fænsɪ] **1** *n* (*whim*) fantaisie *f*; (*liking*) goût *m*; **to take a f. to** s.o. se prendre d'affection pour qn; **I took a f. to it**, **it took my f.** j'en ai eu envie ‖ *a* (*hat, button etc*) fantaisie *inv*; (*car*) de luxe; (*house, restaurant*) chic; **f. dress** travesti *m*; **f.-dress ball** bal *m* masqué. **2** *vt* (*want*) avoir envie de; **to f. that** (*think*) croire que; **f. that!** (*donc*)!; **he fancies her** *Fam* elle lui plaît.

fanfare ['fænfeər] *n* *Mus* fanfare *f*.

fang [fæŋ] *n* (*of dog, wolf*) croc *m*; (*of snake*) crochet *m*.

fanny ['fænɪ] *n* (*buttocks*) *Am Fam* derrière *m*; **f. pack** banane *f*.

fantastic [fæn'tæstɪk] *a* fantastique.

fantasy ['fæntəsɪ] *n* (*imagination*) fantaisie *f*; (*dream*) rêve *m*; (*fanciful, sexual*) fantasme *m*. ● **fantasize** *vi* fantasmer (**about** sur).

far [fɑːr] *adv* (**farther** *or* **further**, **farthest** *or* **furthest**) (*distance*) loin; **f. bigger/more expensive/etc** beaucoup plus grand/plus cher/*etc* (**than** que); **f. advanced** très avancé; **how f. is it to...?** combien y a-t-il d'ici à...?; **is it f. to...?** sommes-nous, suis-je *etc* loin de...?; **how f. are you going?** jusqu'où vas-tu?; **how f. has he got with?** (*plans, work etc*) où en est-il de?; **so f.** (*time*) jusqu'ici; (*place*) jusque-là; **as f. as** (*place*) jusqu'à; **as f. as I know** autant que je sache; **as f. as I'm concerned** en ce qui me concerne; **f. from doing** loin de faire; **f. away** *or* **off** au loin; **to be f. away** être loin (**from** de); **by f.** de loin.

‖ *a* (*other*) (*side, end*) autre; **it's a f. cry from** on est loin de; **the F. East** l'Extrême-Orient *m*.

faraway [fɑːrə'weɪ] *a* (*country*) lointain; (*look*) distrait. ● **far-'fetched** *a* tiré par les cheveux. ● **far-'off** *a* lointain. ● **far-'reaching** *a* de grande portée.

farce [fɑːs] *n* farce *f*. ● **farcical** *a* grotesque.

fare [feər] **1** *n* (*price of journey*) (*in bus etc*) prix *m* du billet; (*in taxi*) prix *m* de la course. **2** *n* (*food*) nourriture *f*. **3** *vi* (*manage*) se débrouiller; **how did she f.?** comment ça s'est passé (pour elle)?

farewell [feə'wel] *n* & *int* adieu (*m*).

farm [fɑːm] *n* ferme *f*; **on a f.** dans une ferme ‖ *a* (*worker, produce*) agricole; **f. land** terres *fpl* cultivées ‖ *vt* cultiver. ● **—ing** *n* agriculture *f*; (*breeding*) élevage *m*; **dairy f.** industrie *f* laitière. ● **farmer** *n* fermier, -ière *mf*.

farmhand ['fɑːmhænd] *n* ouvrier, -ière *mf* agricole. ● **farmhouse** *n* ferme *f*. ● **farmyard** *n* basse-cour *f*.

farther ['fɑːðər] *adv* plus loin; **f. forward** plus avancé; **to get f. away** s'éloigner. ● **farthest** *a* le plus éloigné ‖ *adv* le plus loin.

fascinate ['fæsɪneɪt] *vt* fasciner. ●**fascination** [-'neɪʃ(ə)n] *n* fascination *f*.

fascist ['fæʃɪst] *a* & *n* fasciste (*mf*).

fashion ['fæʃ(ə)n] **1** *n* (*style in clothes etc*) mode *f*; **in f.** à la mode; **out of f.** démodé; **f. designer** (grand) couturier *m*; **f. show** présentation *f* de collections. **2** *n* (*manner*) façon *f*; (*custom*) habitude *f*. **3** *vt* (*make*) façonner. ●**fashionable** *a* à la mode; (*place*) chic *inv*; **it's f. to do that** il est de bon ton de faire cela.

fast [fɑ:st] **1** *a* (**-er, -est**) rapide; **to be f.** (*of clock*) avancer (**by** de); **f. colour** couleur *f* grand teint *inv*; **f. food** restauration *f* rapide; **f. food restaurant** fast-food *m* ‖ *adv* (*quickly*) vite; **how f.?** à quelle vitesse?; **f. asleep** profondément endormi. **2** *vi* (*go without food*) jeûner ‖ *n* jeûne *m*.

fasten ['fɑ:s(ə)n] *vt* attacher (**to** à); (*door, window*) fermer (bien); **to f. down** or **up** attacher qch ‖ *vi* (*of dress etc*) s'attacher; (*of door, window*) se fermer. ●**fastener** or **fastening** *n* (*clip*) attache *f*; (*of garment*) fermeture *f*; (*of bag*) fermoir *m*; (*hook*) agrafe *f*.

fastidious [fə'stɪdɪəs] *a* difficile (à contenter), exigeant.

fat [fæt] **1** *n* graisse *f*; (*on meat*) gras *m*; **vegetable f.** huile *f* végétale. **2** *a* (**fatter, fattest**) gras (*f* grasse); (*cheeks, salary*) gros (*f* grosse); **to get f.** grossir.

fatal ['feɪt(ə)l] *a* mortel; (*mistake, blow etc*) Fig fatal (*mpl* fatals). ●**—ly** *adv* (*wounded*) mortellement.

fatality [fə'tælɪt] *n* **1** (*person killed*) victime *f*. **2** (*of event*) fatalité *f*.

fate [feɪt] *n* destin *m*, sort *m*; (*of person*) sort *m*. ●**fated** *a* **our meeting/etc was f.** notre rencontre/*etc* devait arriver. ●**fateful** *a* (*important*) fatal; (*prophetic*) fatidique; (*disastrous*) néfaste.

father ['fɑ:ðər] *n* père *m*. ●**f.-in-law** *n* (*pl* **fathers-in-law**) beau-père *m*. ●**fatherhood** *n* paternité *f*. ●**fatherly** *a* paternel.

fathom ['fæðəm] **1** *n* Nau brasse *f* (= *1,8 m*). **2** *vt* **to f. (out)** (*understand*) comprendre.

fatigue [fə'ti:g] *n* fatigue *f*.

fatten ['fæt(ə)n] *vt* engraisser. ●**—ing** *a* (*food*) qui fait grossir.

fatty ['fætɪ] *a* (**-ier, -iest**) (*food*) gras (*f* grasse) ‖ *n* (*person*) Fam gros lard *m*.

faucet ['fɔ:sɪt] *n* (*tap*) Am robinet *m*.

fault [fɔ:lt] *n* (*blame*) faute *f*; (*defect*) défaut *m*; (*mistake*) erreur *f*; Geol faille *f*; **it's your f.** c'est ta faute; **to find f. (with)** critiquer ‖ *vt* **to f. s.o./sth** trouver des défauts chez qn/à qch. ●**faultless** *a* irréprochable. ●**faulty** *a* (**-ier, -iest**) défectueux.

favour ['feɪvər] (*Am* **favor**) *n* (*act of kindness*) service *m*; (*approval*) faveur *f*; **to do s.o. a f.** rendre service à qn; **in f.** (*fashion*) en vogue; **in f. of** (*for the sake of*) au profit de; **to be in f. of** (*support*) être pour; (*prefer*) préférer ‖ *vt* (*encourage*) favoriser; (*prefer*) préférer; (*support*) être partisan de. ●**favourable** *a* favorable (**to** à).

favourite ['feɪv(ə)rɪt] (*Am* **favorite**) *a* favori, préféré ‖ *n* favori, -ite *mf*. ●**favouritism** *n* favoritisme *m*.

fawn [fɔ:n] *n* (*deer*) faon *m* ‖ *a* & *n* (*colour*) fauve (*m*).

fax [fæks] *n* (*machine*) télécopieur *m*, fax *m*; (*message*) télécopie *f*, fax *m* ‖ *vt* (*message*) faxer; **to f. s.o.** envoyer une télécopie *or* un fax à qn.

fear [fɪər] *n* crainte *f*, peur *f*; **for f. of doing** de peur de faire; **for f. that** de peur que (+ *ne* + *sub*); **there are fears he might leave** on craint qu'il ne parte ‖ *vt* craindre; **I f. he might leave** je crains qu'il ne parte. ●**fearful** *a* (*timid*) peureux; (*awful*) (*noise etc*) affreux. ●**fearless** *a* intrépide. ●**fearsome** *a* redoutable.

feasible ['fi:zəb(ə)l] *a* (*practicable*) faisable; (*theory etc*) plausible.

feast [fi:st] *n* festin *m*; Rel fête *f* ‖ *vi* banqueter; **to f. on** (*cakes etc*) se régaler de.

feat [fi:t] *n* exploit *m*; **f. of skill** tour *m* d'adresse.

feather ['feðər] *n* plume *f*; **f. duster**

plumeau *m*.

feature ['fi:tʃər] **1** *n* (*of face, person*) trait *m*; (*of thing, place, machine*) caractéristique *f*; **f. (article)** article *m* de fond; **f. (film)** grand film *m*. **2** *vt* (*of newspaper, film etc*) (*present*) présenter; (*portray*) représenter; **a film featuring Chaplin** un film avec Charlot en vedette ‖ *vi* (*appear*) figurer (**in** dans).

February ['februərɪ, *Am* -erɪ] *n* février *m*.

fed [fed] *pt* & *pp* of **feed** ‖ **to be f. up** *Fam* en avoir marre *or* ras le bol (**with** de).

federal ['fedərəl] *a* fédéral. ●**federation** [-'reɪʃ(ə)n] *n* fédération *f*.

fee [fi:] *n* (*price*) prix *m*; **fee(s)** (*professional*) honoraires *mpl*; (*for registration, examination*) droits *mpl*; **to charge a f. (for a job)** se faire payer (pour un travail); **school** *or* **tuition fees** frais *mpl* de scolarité; **entrance f.** droit *m or* prix *m* d'entrée; **membership fee(s)** cotisation *f*.

feeble ['fi:b(ə)l] *a* (**-er, -est**) faible; (*excuse*) pauvre; (*joke, attempt*) pitoyable.

feed [fi:d] *n* (*for animal*) aliments *mpl*; (*baby's breast feed*) tétée *f*; (*baby's bottle feed*) biberon *m* ‖ *vt* (*pt* & *pp* **fed**) donner à manger à, nourrir; (*breastfeed*) allaiter (*un bébé*); (*bottlefeed*) donner le biberon à (*un bébé*); **to f. s.o. sth** faire manger qch à qn; **to f. sth into** (*machine*) introduire qch dans; (*computer*) entrer qch dans.
‖ *vi* (*eat*) manger; **to f. on** se nourrir de.

feedback ['fi:dbæk] *n* réaction(s) *f(pl)*.

feel [fi:l] *n* (*touch*) toucher *m*; (*feeling*) sensation *f*.
‖ *vt* (*pt* & *pp* **felt**) (*be aware of*) sentir; (*experience*) éprouver; (*touch*) tâter; **to f. that** avoir l'impression que; **to f. one's way** avancer à tâtons.
‖ *vi* (*tired, old etc*) se sentir; **to f. (about)** (*grope*) tâtonner; (*in pocket etc*) fouiller (**for sth** pour trouver qch); **it feels hard** c'est dur (au toucher); **I f. hot/sleepy/hungry/***etc* j'ai chaud/sommeil/faim/

etc; **she feels better** elle va mieux; **to f. like sth** (*want*) avoir envie de qch; **it feels like cotton** on dirait du coton; **to f. as if** avoir l'impression que; **what do you f. about...?** que pensez-vous de...?; **I f. bad about it** ça m'ennuie; **to f. up to doing** être (assez) en forme pour faire.

feeler ['fi:lər] *n* (*of snail*) antenne *f*; **to put out a f.** *Fig* lancer un ballon d'essai.

feeling ['fi:lɪŋ] *n* (*emotion, impression*) sentiment *m*; (*physical*) sensation *f*; **a f. for s.o.** de la sympathie pour qn.

feet [fi:t] *see* **foot¹**.

feline ['fi:laɪn] *a* félin.

fell [fel] **1** *pt of* **fall**. **2** *vt* (*tree*) abattre.

fellow ['feləʊ] *n* **1** (*man, boy*) type *m*; **an old f.** un vieux; **poor f.!** pauvre malheureux! **2** (*companion*) **f. being** semblable *m*; **f. countryman, f. countrywoman** compatriote *mf*; **f. passenger** compagnon *m* de voyage, compagne *f* de voyage. **3** (*of society*) membre *m*.

fellowship ['feləʊʃɪp] *n* camaraderie *f*; (*group*) association *f*; (*scholarship*) bourse *f* universitaire.

felony ['felənɪ] *n* crime *m*.

felt¹ [felt] *pt* & *pp* of **feel**.

felt² [felt] *n* feutre *m*; **f.-tip (pen)** crayon *m* feutre.

female ['fi:meɪl] *a* (*name, voice etc*) féminin; (*animal*) femelle; **f. student** étudiante *f* ‖ *n* (*woman*) femme *f*; (*girl*) fille *f*; (*animal*) femelle *f*.

feminine ['femɪnɪn] *a* féminin. ●**feminist** *a* & *n* féministe (*mf*).

fenc/e [fens] **1** *n* barrière *f*, clôture *f*; (*in race*) obstacle *m* ‖ *vt* **to f. (in)** (*land*) clôturer. **2** *vi* (*with sword*) faire de l'escrime. ●**—ing** *n Sp* escrime *f*.

fend [fend] **1** *vi* **to f. for oneself** se débrouiller. **2** *vt* **to f. off** (*blow*) parer.

fender ['fendər] *n* (*of car*) *Am* aile *f*.

ferment ['fɜːment] *n* ferment *m*; (*excitement*) *Fig* effervescence *f* ‖ [fə'ment] *vi* fermenter.

fern [fɜːn] *n* fougère *f*.

ferocious [fə'rəʊʃəs] *a* féroce. ●**ferocity** [fə'rɒsɪtɪ] *n* férocité *f*.

ferret ['ferɪt] n (animal) furet m ‖ vt to f. out dénicher.

Ferris wheel ['ferɪswiːl] n grande roue f.

ferry ['ferɪ] n ferry-boat m; (small, for river) bac m ‖ vt transporter.

fertile ['fɜːtaɪl, Am 'fɜːt(ə)l] a (land, imagination) fertile; (person, animal) fécond. ●**fertilize** vt (land) fertiliser; (egg) féconder. ●**fertilizer** n engrais m.

fervent ['fɜːv(ə)nt] a fervent.

fester ['festər] vi (of wound) suppurer.

festival ['festɪv(ə)l] n Mus Cin festival m (pl -als); Rel fête f.

festive ['festɪv] a (atmosphere etc) de fête; (mood) joyeux; **f. season** période f des fêtes. ●**festivities** npl festivités fpl.

fetch [fetʃ] vt 1 (bring) amener (qn); (object) apporter; **to (go and) f.** aller chercher; **to f. sth in** rentrer qch; **to f. sth out** sortir qch. 2 (be sold for) rapporter (ten pounds/etc dix livres/etc).

fête [feɪt] n fête f.

fetish ['fetɪʃ] n (obsession) manie f; **to make a f. of** être obsédé par.

fetus ['fiːtəs] n Am fœtus m.

feud [fjuːd] n querelle f, dissension f.

feudal ['fjuːd(ə)l] a féodal.

fever ['fiːvər] n fièvre f; **to have a f.** (temperature) avoir de la fièvre; **a high f.** une forte fièvre. ●**feverish** a (person, activity) fiévreux.

few [fjuː] a & pron peu (de); **f. towns/etc** peu de villes/etc; **a f. towns/etc** quelques villes/etc; **f. of them** peu d'entre eux; **a f.** quelques-un(e)s (of de); **a f. of us** quelques-uns d'entre nous; **one of the f. books** l'un des rares livres; **quite a f.** a good f. bon nombre (de); **a f. more books/etc** encore quelques livres/etc; **f. and far between** rares (et espacés); **f. came** peu sont venus; **every f. days** tous les trois ou quatre jours.

fewer ['fjuːər] a & pron moins (de) (than que); **f. houses (than)** moins de maisons (que); **no f. than** pas moins de. ●**fewest** ['fjuːɪst] a & pron le moins (de).

fiancé(e) [fɪ'ɒnseɪ] n fiancé, -ée mf.

fiasco [fɪ'æskəʊ] n (pl -os, Am -oes) fiasco m.

fib [fɪb] n Fam blague f, bobard m ‖ vi (-bb-) Fam raconter des blagues.

fibre ['faɪbər] (Am fiber) n fibre f; (in diet) fibre(s) f(pl). ●**fibreglass** n fibre f de verre.

fickle ['fɪk(ə)l] a inconstant.

fiction ['fɪkʃ(ə)n] n (imagination) fiction f; (works of) f. romans mpl; **that's pure f.** ce sont des histoires. ●**fictional** or **fictitious** [-'tɪʃəs] a fictif.

fiddle ['fɪd(ə)l] 1 n (violin) Fam violon m. 2 vi Fam **to f. about** (waste time) traînailler; **to f. (about) with** (watch, pen etc) tripoter; (cars) bricoler. 3 n (dishonest act) Fam combine f ‖ vt (accounts etc) Fam falsifier. ●**fiddler** n 1 Fam joueur, -euse mf de violon. 2 (swindler) Fam combinard, -arde m.

fiddly ['fɪdlɪ] a (-ier, -iest) (task) délicat.

fidget ['fɪdʒɪt] vi **to f. (about)** gigoter; **to f. (about) with** tripoter ‖ n personne f qui ne tient pas en place. ●**fidgety** a agité, remuant.

field [fiːld] n champ m; Sp terrain m; (sphere) domaine m; **f. glasses** jumelles fpl; **f. marshal** maréchal m.

fiend [fiːnd] n démon m; (sex) f. Fam satyre m. ●**fiendish** a (cruel) diabolique; (awful) abominable.

fierce [fɪəs] a (-er, -est) féroce; (attack, wind) furieux.

fiery ['faɪərɪ] a (-ier, -iest) (person, speech) fougueux.

fiesta [fɪ'estə] n fiesta f.

fifteen [fɪf'tiːn] a & n quinze (m). ●**fifteenth** a & n quinzième (mf).

fifth [fɪfθ] a & n cinquième (mf); **a f.** un cinquième.

fifty ['fɪftɪ] a & n cinquante (m); **a f.-fifty chance** une chance sur deux. ●**fiftieth** a & n cinquantième (mf).

fig [fɪg] n figue f; **f. tree** figuier m.

fight [faɪt] n bagarre f; Mil Boxing combat m; (struggle) lutte f; (quarrel) dispute f; **to put up a f.** bien se défendre. ‖ vi (pt & pp fought) se battre (against contre); (*struggle*) lutter (**for** pour, **against** contre); (*quarrel*) se disputer; **to f. back** se défendre; **to f. over sth** se disputer qch.

❚ *vt* se battre avec (*qn*); (*evil*) lutter contre; **to f. a battle** livrer bataille; **to f. an election** se présenter à une élection; **to f. back** (*tears*) refouler; **to f. off** (*attacker*) repousser; **to f. it out** se bagarrer. ●**fighting** *n Mil* combat(s) *m(pl)*; (*brawling*) bagarres *fpl*; **f. troops** troupes *fpl* de combat. ●**fighter** *n* (*determined person*) battant, -ante *mf*; (*in brawl*) combattant, -ante *mf*; *Boxing* boxeur *m*; (*aircraft*) chasseur *m*.

figment ['figmənt] *n* **a f. of one's imagination** une création de son esprit.

figurative ['figjʊrətiv] *a* (*meaning*) figuré. ●**-ly** *adv* au figuré.

figure¹ ['figər, *Am* 'figjər] *n* **1** (*numeral*) chiffre *m*; (*price*) prix *m*; *pl* (*arithmetic*) calcul *m*. **2** (*shape*) forme *f*; (*outline*) silhouette *f*; (*of woman*) ligne *f*; **she has a nice f.** elle est bien faite. **3** (*diagram* & *Liter*) figure *f*; **a f. of speech** (*figurative usage*) une façon de parler; **f. skating** patinage *m* artistique. **4** (*important person*) figure *f*.

figure² ['figər, *Am* 'figjər] *vt* **to f. that** (*guess*) penser que; **to f. out** arriver à comprendre; (*problem*) résoudre; (*answer*) trouver; (*price*) calculer ❚ *vi* (*make sense*) s'expliquer; **to f. on doing** compter faire.

figurehead ['figəhed] *n* (*of organization*) potiche *f*.

filch [filtʃ] *vt* (*steal*) voler (**from** à).

file¹ [fail] **1** *n* (*tool*) lime *f* ❚ *vt* **to f.** (**down**) limer.

2 *n* (*folder*, *information*) dossier *m*; (*loose-leaf*) classeur *m*; (*for card index*, *computer data*) fichier *m*; **to be on f.** figurer au dossier ❚ *vt* (*application*, *complaint*) déposer; **to f.** (**away**) (*document*) classer.

3 *n* **in single f.** en file ❚ *vi* **to f. in/out** entrer/sortir à la queue leu leu; **to f. past** (*general*, *coffin*) défiler devant.

●**filing cabinet** *n* classeur *m*.

fill [fil] *vt* remplir (**with** de); (*tooth*) plomber; (*need*) répondre à; **to f. in** (*form*, *hole*) remplir; **to f. s.o. in on sth** mettre qn au courant de qch; **to f. out** (*form*) remplir; **to f. up** (*container*, *form*) remplir.

❚ *vi* **to f.** (**up**) se remplir; **to f. out** (*get fatter*) grossir; **to f. up** *Aut* faire le plein.

❚ *n* **to eat one's f.** manger à sa faim; **to have had one's f. of s.o./sth** en avoir assez de qn/qch. ●**filling** *a* (*meal*) nourrissant ❚ *n* (*in tooth*) plombage *m*; *Culin* garniture *f*; **f. station** poste *m* d'essence.

fillet ['filit, *Am* fi'lei] *n Culin* filet *m* ❚ *vt* (*pt* & *pp Am* ['fi'leid]) (*fish*) découper en filets.

filly ['fili] *n* (*horse*) pouliche *f*.

film [film] *n* film *m*; (*layer*) pellicule *f* ❚ *a* (*festival*) du film; (*studio*, *critic*) de cinéma; **f. fan** or **buff** cinéphile *mf*; **f. maker** cinéaste *m*; **f. star** vedette *f* (de cinéma) ❚ *vt* filmer ❚ *vi* (*of film maker*, *actor*) tourner.

Filofax® ['failəʊfæks] *n* (agenda *m*) organiseur *m*.

filter ['filtər] *n* filtre *m*; **f. tip** (bout *m*) filtre *m*; **f.-tipped cigarette** cigarette *f* (à bout) filtre ❚ *vt* filtrer ❚ *vi* filtrer (**through sth** à travers qch).

filth [filθ] *n* saleté *f*; (*obscenities*) *Fig* saletés *fpl*. ●**filthy** *a* (**-ier, -iest**) (*hands*, *shoes etc*) sale; (*language*) obscène.

fin [fin] *n* (*of fish*, *seal*) nageoire *f*.

final ['fain(ə)l] *a* (*last*) dernier; (*decision*) définitif ❚ *n Sp* finale *f*; *pl Univ* examens *mpl* de dernière année. ●**finalist** *n Sp* finaliste *mf*. ●**finalize** *vt* (*plan*) mettre au point; (*date*) fixer. ●**finally** *adv* (*lastly*, *eventually*) enfin; (*once and for all*) définitivement.

finale [fi'nɑ:li] *n Mus* finale *m*.

finance ['fainæns] *n* finance *f*; *pl* (*of person*) finances *fpl*; (*of company*) situation *f* financière ❚ *vt* financer.

financial [fai'nænʃəl] *a* financier; **f. year** année *f* budgétaire. ●**-ly** *adv* financièrement.

find [faɪnd] n (discovery) trouvaille f ▮ vt
(pt & pp **found**) trouver; (sth or s.o. lost)
retrouver; **to f. difficulty doing** éprouver de la difficulté à faire; **I f. that** je
trouve que; **to f. s.o. guilty** Jur déclarer
qn coupable.

find out vt (secret etc) découvrir; (person) démasquer ▮ vi (inquire) se renseigner (**about** sur); **to f. out about sth**
(discover) découvrir qch.

findings ['faɪndɪŋz] npl conclusions fpl.

fine¹ [faɪn] n (money) amende f; (for
driving offence) contravention f ▮ vt **to
f. s.o.** (£10/etc) infliger une amende (de
dix livres/etc) à qn.

fine² [faɪn] **1** a (-er, -est) (thin, not
coarse) fin; (distinction) subtil ▮ adv
(to cut, write) menu. **2** a (-er, -est)
(very good) excellent; (weather, statue)
beau (f belle); **it's f.** (weather) il fait
beau; **he's f.** (healthy) il va bien ▮ adv
(well) très bien.

finery ['faɪnərɪ] n (clothes) parure f.

finger ['fɪŋgər] n doigt m; **little f.** petit
doigt m; **middle f.** majeur m; **f. mark**
trace f de doigt ▮ vt toucher (des
doigts). ●**fingernail** n ongle m.
●**fingerprint** n empreinte f (digitale).
●**fingertip** n bout m du doigt.

finicky ['fɪnɪkɪ] a (precise) méticuleux;
(difficult) difficile (about sur).

finish ['fɪnɪʃ] n (end) fin f; (of race)
arrivée f; (of article, car etc) finition
f; **paint with a matt f.** peinture f mate.
▮ vt **to f.** (off or up) finir, terminer; **to f.
doing** finir de faire; **to f. s.o. off** (kill)
achever qn.
▮ vi (of meeting etc) finir, se terminer;
(of person) finir, terminer; **to have
finished with** (object) ne plus avoir
besoin de; (situation, person) en avoir
fini avec; **to f. off** or **up** (of person) finir,
terminer; **to f. up in** (end up in) se
retrouver à; **to f. up doing** finir par
faire; **to put the finishing touch to sth**
mettre la dernière main à qch. ●**finished** a (ended, ruined etc) fini.

finite ['faɪnaɪt] a fini.

Finland ['fɪnlənd] n Finlande f. ●**Finn** n
Finlandais, -aise mf. ●**Finnish** a finlandais ▮ n (language) finnois m.

fir ['fɜːr] n (tree, wood) sapin m.

fire¹ ['faɪər] n feu m; (accidental) incendie m; (electric heater) radiateur m; **to
light** or **make a f.** faire du feu; **to set f. to**
mettre le feu à; **to catch f.** prendre feu;
on f. en feu; **(there's a) f.!** au feu!; **f.!** Mil
feu!; **f. alarm** alarme f d'incendie; **f.
brigade,** Am **f. department** pompiers
mpl; **f. engine** (vehicle) voiture f de
pompiers; **f. escape** escalier m de secours; **f. station** caserne f de pompiers.

fire² ['faɪər] vt (cannon) tirer; **to f. a gun**
tirer un coup de fusil or de pistolet; **to f.
questions at s.o.** bombarder qn de
questions; **to f. s.o.** (dismiss) renvoyer
qn ▮ vi tirer (**at** sur); **firing squad**
peloton m d'exécution.

firearm ['faɪərɑːm] n arme f à feu.
●**firecracker** n Am pétard m. ●**fire-
guard** n garde-feu m inv. ●**fireman** n
(pl -**men**) (sapeur-)pompier m. ●**fireplace** n cheminée f. ●**fireproof** a
(door) ignifugé. ●**fireside** n coin m du
feu. ●**firewood** n bois m de chauffage.
●**firework** n fusée f; (firecracker) pétard
m; **a f. display, fireworks** feu m d'artifice.

firm [fɜːm] **1** n Com entreprise f, maison
f. **2** a (-er, -est) (earth, decision etc)
ferme; **f. with s.o.** (strict) ferme avec qn
▮ adv **to stand f.** tenir bon. ●—**ly** adv
fermement; (to speak) d'une voix
ferme.

first [fɜːst] a premier; **f. cousin** cousin,
-ine mf germain(e).
▮ adv (firstly) d'abord, premièrement;
(for the first time) pour la première fois;
f. of all tout d'abord; **at f.** d'abord; **to
come f.** (in race) arriver premier; (in
exam) être premier.
▮ n premier, -ière mf; **from the f.** dès le
début; **f. aid** premiers secours mpl; **f.
(gear)** Aut première f.

first-class [fɜːst'klɑːs] a excellent; (tick-

et, seat) de première (classe); (*mail*) ordinaire ▮ *adv* (*to travel*) en première. ●**f.-'hand** *a* **to have (had) f.-hand experience of** avoir fait l'expérience personnelle de. ●**f.-'rate** *a* excellent.

firstly ['fɜːstlɪ] *adv* premièrement.

fish [fɪʃ] *n inv* poisson *m*; **f. market** marché *m* aux poissons; **f. bone** arête *f*; **f. fingers**, *Am* **f. sticks** *Culin* bâtonnets *mpl* de poisson; **f. shop** poissonnerie *f*; **f.-and-chip shop** boutique *f* de fritures.

▮ *vi* pêcher; **to f. for** (*salmon etc*) pêcher; ▮ *vt* **to f. out** (*from water*) repêcher; (*from pocket etc*) sortir. ●**—ing** *n* pêche *f*; **to go f.** aller à la pêche; **f. boat/**etc bateau *m/etc* de pêche; **f. net** (*of fisherman*) filet *m* (de pêche); (*of angler*) épuisette *f*; **f. rod** canne *f* à pêche. ●**fisherman** *n* (*pl* **-men**) pêcheur *m*. ●**fishmonger** *n* poissonnier, -ière *mf*.

fishy ['fɪʃɪ] *a* (**-ier, -iest**) (*story etc*) louche.

fist [fɪst] *n* poing *m*. ●**fistful** *n* poignée *f*.

fit¹ [fɪt] **1** *a* (**fitter, fittest**) (*healthy*) en bonne santé; (*in good shape*) en forme; (*suitable*) propre (**for à, to do** à faire); (*worthy*) digne (**for** de, **to do** de faire); (*able*) apte (**for** à, **to do** à faire); **f. to eat** bon à manger; **to see f. to do** juger à propos de faire; **to keep f.** se maintenir en forme.

2 *vt* (**-tt-**) (*of clothes*) aller (bien) à (*qn*); (*match*) répondre à, correspondre à; (*put in*) poser (*fenêtre, moquette etc*); **to f. sth** (**on**) **to sth** (*put*) poser qch sur qch; (*fix*) fixer qch à qch; **to f.** (**out** *or* **up**) **with sth** (*house, ship etc*) équiper de qch; **to f. in** (*insert*) faire entrer qch; **to f. s.o. in** (*find time to see*) prendre qn; **to f.** (**in**) **sth** (*go in*) aller dans qch; **to f.** (**on**) **sth** (*go on*) aller sur qch. ▮ *vi* (*of clothes*) aller (bien) (**à** *qn*); **this shirt fits** (*fits me*) cette chemise me va (bien); **to f. in** (*go in*) entrer, aller; (*of facts, plans*) s'accorder (**with** avec); **he doesn't f. in** il ne peut pas s'intégrer.

▮ *n* **a good f.** (*clothes*) à la bonne taille; **a**

close *or* **tight f.** ajusté. ●**fitted** *a* (*cupboard*) encastré; (*garment*) ajusté; **f. carpet** moquette *f*; **f. kitchen** cuisine aménagée. ●**fitting 1** *a* (*suitable*) convenable. **2** *n* (*of clothes*) essayage *m*; **f. room** (*booth*) cabine *f* d'essayage. **3** *npl* (*in house etc*) installations *fpl*.

fit² [fɪt] *n* (*attack*) *Med & Fig* accès *m*, crise *f*; **a f. of crying** une crise de larmes; **in fits and starts** par à-coups.

fitment ['fɪtmənt] *n* (*furniture*) meuble *m* encastré.

fitness ['fɪtnɪs] *n* (*health*) santé *f*; (*for job*) aptitudes *fpl* (**for** pour).

fitter ['fɪtər] *n* *Tech* monteur, -euse *mf*.

five [faɪv] *a & n* cinq (*m*). ●**fiver** *n* *Br Fam* billet *m* de cinq livres; *Am Fam* billet *m* de cinq dollars.

fix [fɪks] **1** *vt* (*make firm, decide*) fixer; (*tie with rope*) attacher; (*mend*) réparer; (*deal with*) arranger; (*prepare, cook*) préparer, faire; (*rig*) *Fam* truquer; (*bribe*) *Fam* acheter; (*put*) mettre (*ses espoirs etc*) (**on** en); **to f.** (**on**) (*lid etc*) mettre en place; **to f. up** (*trip etc*) arranger; **to f. s.o. up with a job/**etc procurer un travail/etc à qn.

2 *n in a f.* *Fam* dans le pétrin. ●**fixed** *a* (*idea, price etc*) fixe; **how's he f. for...?** *Fam* (*cash*) a-t-il assez de...?; (*tomorrow*) qu'est-ce qu'il fait pour...?

fixture ['fɪkstʃər] **1** *n* *Sp* rencontre *f* (*prévue*). **2** *npl* **fixtures** (*in house*) installations *fpl*.

fizz [fɪz] *vi* (*of champagne*) pétiller. ●**fizzy** *a* (**-ier, -iest**) pétillant.

fizzle ['fɪz(ə)l] *vi* **to f. out** (*of firework*) rater; (*of plan*) *Fig* tomber à l'eau.

flabbergasted ['flæbəgɑːstɪd] *a* *Fam* sidéré.

flabby ['flæbɪ] *a* (**-ier, -iest**) (*skin, person*) mou (*f* molle), flasque.

flag [flæg] **1** *n* drapeau *m*; *Nau* pavillon *m*; (*for charity*) insigne *m*; **f. stop** *Am* arrêt *m* facultatif ▮ *vt* (**-gg-**) **to f. down** (*taxi*) faire signe à. **2** *vi* (**-gg-**) (*of conversation*) languir; (*of worker*) fléchir. ●**flagpole** *n* mât *m*.

flagrant ['fleɪgrənt] a flagrant.

flair [fleər] n (intuition) flair m; **to have a f. for** (talent) avoir un don pour.

flake [fleɪk] n (of snow etc) flocon m; (of soap, metal) paillette f ▮ vi **to f. (off)** (of paint) s'écailler. ● **flaky** a **f. pastry** pâte f feuilletée.

flamboyant [flæm'bɔɪənt] a (person, manner) extravagant.

flame [fleɪm] n flamme f; **to burst into flame(s), go up in flames** prendre feu.

flaming ['fleɪmɪŋ] a (a damn) Fam fichu.

flamingo [flə'mɪŋgəʊ] n (pl -os or -oes) (bird) flamant m.

flammable ['flæməb(ə)l] a inflammable.

flan [flæn] n tarte f.

flank [flæŋk] n flanc m ▮ vt flanquer; **flanked by** flanqué de.

flannel ['flæn(ə)l] n (cloth) flanelle f; (face) f. gant m de toilette.

flap [flæp] 1 vi (-pp-) (of wings, sail etc) battre ▮ vt **to f. its wings** (of bird) battre des ailes. 2 n (of pocket, envelope) rabat m; (of table) abattant m.

flare [fleər] n Mil fusée f éclairante; (for runway) balise f ▮ vi (blaze) flamber; **to f. up** (of fire) prendre; (of violence, war) éclater; (get angry) s'emporter. ● **f.-up** n (of violence, fire) flambée f.

flared [fleəd] a (skirt) évasé; (trousers, Am pants) (à) pattes d'éléphant.

flash [flæʃ] n (of light) éclat m, (of genius) éclair m; Phot flash m; **f. of lightning** éclair m; **news f.** flash m; **in a f.** en un clin d'œil.
▮ vi (shine) briller; (on and off) clignoter.
▮ vt (a light) projeter; (aim) diriger (on, at sur); **to f. one's (head)lights** faire un appel de phares. ● **flashback** n retour m en arrière. ● **flashlight** n (torch) lampe f de poche; Phot flash m.

flashy ['flæʃɪ] a (-ier, -iest) a voyant, tape-à-l'œil inv.

flask [flɑːsk] n thermos® m or f inv; (for brandy, medicine etc) flacon m.

flat[1] [flæt] a (flatter, flattest) plat; (tyre or Am tire, battery) à plat; (nose) aplati;

(beer) éventé; (refusal) net (f nette); (rate, fare) fixe; **f. fee** prix m unique; **to put sth (down)** f. mettre qch à plat; **to be f.-footed** avoir les pieds plats.
▮ adv **to sing f.** chanter trop bas; **to fall f. on one's face** tomber à plat ventre; **in two minutes f.** en deux minutes pile; **f. out** (to work) d'arrache-pied; (to run) à toute vitesse.
▮ n (puncture) Aut crevaison f; (of hand) plat m; Mus bémol m. ● **flatly** adv (to deny, refuse etc) catégoriquement.

flat[2] [flæt] n (rooms) appartement m.

flatten ['flæt(ə)n] vt (crops) coucher; (town) raser; **to f. (out)** (metal etc) aplatir.

flatter ['flætər] vt flatter. ● **—ing** a (remark etc) flatteur; **it's a f. hat** ce chapeau vous avantage. ● **flattery** n flatterie f.

flaunt [flɔːnt] vt (show off) faire étalage de; (defy) Am narguer, défier.

flautist ['flɔːtɪst] n flûtiste mf.

flavour ['fleɪvər] (Am **flavor**) n (taste) goût m, saveur f; (of ice cream etc) parfum m ▮ vt (food) (with seasoning) assaisonner; (ice cream etc) parfumer (with à); **lemon-flavoured** (parfumé) au citron. ● **—ing** n assaisonnement m; (in cake, ice cream etc) parfum m.

flaw [flɔː] n défaut m. ● **flawless** a parfait.

flax [flæks] n lin m.

flea [fliː] n puce f; **f. market** marché m aux puces. ● **fleapit** n Fam cinéma m miteux.

fleck [flek] n (mark) petite tache f.

flee [fliː] vi (pt & pp fled) s'enfuir, fuir ▮ vt (place) s'enfuir de; (danger etc) fuir.

fleece [fliːs] n 1 (sheep's coat) toison f. 2 vt (rob) Fam voler (qn).

fleet [fliːt] n (of ships) flotte f; **a f. of buses**/etc (of company) un parc d'autobus/etc; (shuttle service) une noria d'autobus/etc.

fleeting ['fliːtɪŋ] a (visit, moment) bref (f brève).

Flemish ['flemɪʃ] a flamand ▮ n (lan-

guage) flamand *m*.

flesh [fleʃ] *n* chair *f*; **in the f.** en chair et en os; **he's your f. and blood** (*child*) c'est la chair de ta chair; (*brother etc*) il est de ton sang. ●**fleshy** *a* (**-ier, -iest**) charnu.

flew [fluː] *pt of* **fly**[2].

flex [fleks] **1** *vt* (*limb*) fléchir; (*muscle*) faire jouer. **2** *n* (*wire*) fil *m* (souple); (*for telephone*) cordon *m*.

flexible ['fleksɪb(ə)l] *a* (*person, wire etc*) souple.

flick [flɪk] *vt* donner un petit coup à; **to f. sth off** (*remove*) enlever qch (d'une chiquenaude); **to f. a switch** pousser un bouton **‖** *vi* **to f. through** (*pages*) feuilleter **‖** *n* (*with finger*) chiquenaude *f*; (*with whip etc*) petit coup *m*; **f. knife** couteau *m* à cran d'arrêt.

flicker ['flɪkər] *vi* (*of flame, light*) vaciller; (*of needle*) osciller.

flier ['flaɪər] *n* **1** (*leaflet*) *Am* prospectus *m*. **2** **high f.** (*ambitious person*) jeune loup *m*.

flies [flaɪz] *npl* (*on trousers, Am pants*) braguette *f*.

flight [flaɪt] *n* **1** (*of bird, aircraft etc*) vol *m*; **f. to/from** vol *m* à destination de/en provenance de; **to have a good f.** faire bon voyage; **f. attendant** steward *m or* hôtesse *f* de l'air; **f. deck** cabine *f* de pilotage. **2** (*floor, storey, Am story*) étage *m*; **f. of stairs** escalier *m*. **3** (*escape*) fuite *f* (**from** de); **to take f.** prendre la fuite.

flimsy ['flɪmzɪ] *a* (**-ier, -iest**) (*cloth etc*) (*light*) (trop) léger; (*thin*) (trop) mince; (*excuse*) mince.

flinch [flɪntʃ] *vi* (*with pain*) tressaillir; **to f. from** (*duty*) se dérober à; **without flinching** (*complaining*) sans broncher.

fling [flɪŋ] *vt* (*pt & pp* **flung**) lancer; **to f. open** (*door*) ouvrir brutalement.

flint [flɪnt] *n* silex *m*; (*for cigarette lighter*) pierre *f*.

flip [flɪp] *vt* (**-pp-**) (*with finger*) donner une chiquenaude à **‖** *vi* **to f. through** (*book*) feuilleter.

flip-flops ['flɪpflɒps] *npl* tongs *fpl*.

flippant ['flɪpənt] *a* irrévérencieux; (*offhand*) désinvolte.

flipper ['flɪpər] *n* (*of swimmer*) palme *f*; (*of seal*) nageoire *f*.

flirt [fləːt] *vi* flirter (**with** avec) **‖** *n* flirteur, -euse *mf*.

flit [flɪt] *vi* (**-tt-**) (*fly*) voltiger.

float [fləʊt] *n Fishing* flotteur *m*; (*in parade*) char *m* **‖** *vi* flotter (**on** sur); **to f. down the river** descendre la rivière. ●**—ing** *a* (*wood etc*) flottant; **f. voters** électeurs *mpl* indécis.

flock [flɒk] *n* (*of sheep*) troupeau *m*; (*of birds*) volée *f*; (*of tourists etc*) foule *f* **‖** *vi* venir en foule.

flog [flɒg] *vt* (**-gg-**) **1** (*beat*) flageller. **2** (*sell*) *Sl* vendre.

flood [flʌd] *n* inondation *f*; (*of letters, tears etc*) *Fig* flot *m*, déluge *m* **‖** *vt* (*field, house etc*) inonder (**with** de) **‖** *vi* (*of river*) déborder; (*of building*) être inondé; **to f. in** (*of money*) affluer; **to f. into** (*of tourists etc*) envahir (*un pays etc*). ●**—ing** *n* inondation *f*; (*floods*) inondations *fpl*.

floodlight ['flʌdlaɪt] *n* projecteur *m* **‖** *vt* (*pt & pp* **floodlit**) illuminer; **floodlit match** *Sp* (match *m* en) nocturne *f*.

floor [flɔːr] *n* **1** (*ground*) sol *m*; (*wooden etc in building*) plancher *m*; (*storey, Am story*) étage *m*; (*dance*) **f.** piste *f* (de danse); **on the f.** par terre; **on the first f.** au premier étage; (*ground floor*) *Am* au rez-de-chaussée; **f. show** spectacle *m* (de cabaret). **2** *vt* (*knock down*) terrasser; (*puzzle*) stupéfier. ●**floorboard** *n* planche *f*.

flop [flɒp] **1** *vi* (**-pp-**) **to f. down** (*collapse*) s'effondrer. **2** *vi* (**-pp-**) *Fam* (*fail*) échouer; (*of play, film etc*) faire un four **‖** *n Fam* échec *m*, four *m*. *Th Cin* four *m*.

floppy ['flɒpɪ] *a* (**-ier, -iest**) (*soft*) mou (*f* molle); (*clothes*) (trop) large; **f. disk** (*of computer*) disquette *f*.

floral ['flɔːrəl] *a* floral; (*material, pattern*) à fleurs.

florist ['flɒrɪst] *n* fleuriste *mf*.

floss [flɒs] n (dental) f. fil m (de soie) dentaire.

flotilla [flə'tɪlə] n Nau flottille f.

flounce [flaʊns] n (on dress etc) volant m.

flounder ['flaʊndər] 1 vi (in water, speech etc) patauger. 2 n (fish) carrelet m.

flour ['flaʊər] n farine f.

flourish ['flʌrɪʃ] 1 vi (of person, business, plant) prospérer; (of the arts) fleurir. 2 vt (wave) brandir (bâton etc). 3 n (decoration) fioriture f; Mus fanfare f. ●—ing a prospère.

flout [flaʊt] vt narguer, braver.

flow [fləʊ] vi couler; (of electric current) circuler; (of hair) flotter; (of traffic) s'écouler; **to f. in** (of people, money) affluer; **to f. into the sea** (of river) se jeter dans la mer ‖ n (of river) courant m; (of tide) flux m; (of current, information, blood) circulation f; (of traffic, liquid) écoulement m; (of visitors, insults) flot m; **f. chart** organigramme m. ●**flowing** a (movement) gracieux; (style) coulant.

flower ['flaʊər] n fleur f; **in f.** en fleurs; **f. bed** parterre m; **f. pot** pot m de fleurs; **f. shop** (boutique f de) fleuriste mf ‖ vi fleurir. ●—ed a (dress) à fleurs. ●—ing a (in bloom) en fleurs; (with flowers) (shrub etc) à fleurs. ●**flowery** a (material) à fleurs.

flown [fləʊn] pp of **fly**[2].

flu [fluː] n (influenza) Fam grippe f.

fluctuate ['flʌktʃʊeɪt] vi varier. ●**fluctuation(s)** [-'eɪʃ(ə)n(z)] n(pl) (in prices etc) fluctuations fpl (in de).

fluent ['fluːənt] a **he's f. in Russian, his Russian is f.** il parle couramment le russe; **to be f., be a f. speaker** s'exprimer avec facilité. ●—**ly** adv (to speak a language) couramment.

fluff [flʌf] n (of material) peluche(s) f(pl); (on floor) moutons mpl. ●**fluffy** a (-ier, -iest) (bird) duveteux; (material) pelucheux; (toy) en peluche; **light and f.** (cake) très léger.

fluid ['fluːɪd] a fluide; (plans) flexible ‖ n fluide m.

fluke [fluːk] n Fam coup m de chance; **by a f.** par raccroc.

flung [flʌŋ] pt & pp of **fling**.

flunk [flʌŋk] vi (in exam) Am Fam être collé ‖ vt Am Fam (exam) être collé à; (pupil) coller.

fluorescent [flʊə'res(ə)nt] a fluorescent.

fluoride ['flʊəraɪd] n fluor m; **f. toothpaste** dentifrice m au fluor.

flurry ['flʌrɪ] n 1 (of activity) poussée f. 2 (of snow) rafale f.

flush [flʌʃ] 1 n (blush) rougeur f; (of youth, beauty) éclat m ‖ vi (blush) rougir. 2 vt **to f. sth (out)** (clean) nettoyer qch à grande eau; **to f. the pan** or **toilet** tirer la chasse d'eau; **to s.o. out** (chase away) faire sortir qn (from de). 3 a (level) de niveau (with de). ●**flushed** a (cheeks etc) rouge; **f. with** (success) ivre de.

fluster ['flʌstər] vt énerver; **to get flustered** s'énerver.

flute [fluːt] n flûte f. ●**flutist** n Am flûtiste mf.

flutter ['flʌtər] vi (of bird) voltiger; (of wing) battre; (of flag) flotter (mollement) ‖ vt **to f. its wings** battre des ailes.

fly[1] [flaɪ] n (insect) mouche f.

fly[2] [flaɪ] vi (pt **flew**, pp **flown**) (of bird, aircraft etc) voler; (of passenger) aller en avion; (of time) passer vite; (of flag) flotter; **to f. away** or **off** s'envoler; **to f. out** (of passenger) partir en avion; (from room) sortir à toute vitesse; **I must f.!** il faut que je file!; **to f. at s.o.** (attack) sauter sur qn.

‖ vt (aircraft) piloter; (passengers) transporter (par avion); (airline) voyager par; (flag) arborer; (kite) faire voler; **to f. the French flag** battre pavillon français; **to f. across** or **over** (country etc) survoler. ●**flying** n (flight) vol m; (air travel) (as passenger) l'avion m; ‖ a (doctor, personnel) volant; **with f. colours** (to succeed) haut la main; **f. saucer** soucoupe f volante; **f. visit** visite f éclair inv; **f. time** (length) Av durée f du vol; **ten hours'/**etc f. **time** dix heures/ etc de vol.

fly³ [flaɪ] n (on trousers) braguette f.

flyby ['flaɪbaɪ] n Av Am défilé m aérien. ● **fly-by-night** a (firm) véreux. ● **flyover** n (bridge) toboggan m. ● **flypast** n Av défilé m aérien.

foal [fəʊl] n poulain m.

foam [fəʊm] n (on sea, in mouth) écume f; (on beer) mousse f; **f. rubber** caoutchouc m mousse; **f. mattress/**etc matelas m/etc mousse ▮ vi (of sea, mouth) écumer; (of beer, soap) mousser.

fob [fɒb] vt (-bb-) **to f. s.o. off with sth** se débarrasser de qn en lui donnant or lui racontant qch.

focus ['fəʊkəs] n (of attention, interest) centre m; Geom etc foyer m; **in f.** (photo etc) net (f nette); **out of f.** flou ▮ vt (image, camera) mettre au point; (efforts) concentrer (**on** sur) ▮ vti to f. (**one's attention**) **on** se tourner vers; **to f.** (**one's eyes**) **on** fixer les yeux sur.

fodder ['fɒdər] n fourrage m.

foe [fəʊ] n ennemi, -ie mf.

foetus ['fiːtəs] n fœtus m.

fog [fɒg] n brouillard m. ● **fogbound** a bloqué par le brouillard. ● **foglamp** or **foglight** n Aut (phare m) anti-brouillard m.

fogey ['fəʊgɪ] n **old f.** vieille baderne f.

foggy ['fɒgɪ] a (-ier, -iest); **it's f.** il y a du brouillard; **f. weather** brouillard m; **on a f. day** par un jour de brouillard; **she hasn't the foggiest idea** Fam elle n'en a pas la moindre idée.

foil [fɔɪl] **1** n (for cooking) papier m alu(minium). **2** n (contrasting person) repoussoir m. **3** vt (plans etc) déjouer.

fold¹ [fəʊld] n (in paper etc) pli m ▮ vt plier; (wrap) envelopper (**in** dans); **to f. away** or **down** or **up** (chair etc) plier; **to f. back** or **over** (blanket etc) replier; **to f. one's arms** (se) croiser les bras ▮ vi (of chair etc) se plier; **to f. away** or **down** or **up** (of chair etc) se plier; **to f. back** or **over** (of blanket etc) se replier. ● **—ing** a (chair etc) pliant. ● **folder** n (file holder)

chemise f; (pamphlet) dépliant m.

fold² [fəʊld] n (for sheep) parc m à moutons.

-fold [fəʊld] suff **tenfold** a par dix ▮ adv dix fois.

foliage ['fəʊlɪɪdʒ] n feuillage m.

folk [fəʊk] **1** npl (Am folk) gens mpl or fpl; **my folks** (parents) Fam mes parents mpl; **old f.** les vieux mpl. **2** a (dance etc) folklorique; **f. music** (contemporary) (musique f) folk m.

folklore ['fəʊklɔːr] n folklore m.

follow ['fɒləʊ] vt suivre; (career) poursuivre; **followed by** suivi de; **to f. s.o. around** suivre qn partout; **to f. through** (plan, idea etc) poursuivre jusqu'au bout; **to f. up** (idea, story) creuser; (clue, suggestion) suivre; (letter) donner suite à.

▮ vi (of person, event etc) suivre; **it follows that** il s'ensuit que; **to f. on** (come after) suivre. ● **following 1** a suivant ▮ prep à la suite de. **2** n (supporters) partisans mpl; **to have a large f.** (of TV programme, fashion) être très suivi.

follower ['fɒləʊər] n (supporter) partisan m.

folly ['fɒlɪ] n folie f; **an act of f.** une folie.

fond [fɒnd] a (**-er, -est**) (loving) tendre; (doting) indulgent; **to be (very) f. of** aimer beaucoup. ● **—ness** n prédilection f (**for sth** pour qch); (for people) affection f (**for** pour).

fondle ['fɒnd(ə)l] vt caresser.

food [fuːd] n nourriture f; (particular substance) aliment m; (cooking) cuisine f; (for cats, dogs etc) pâtée f; pl (foodstuffs) aliments mpl ▮ a (needs etc) alimentaire; **f. poisoning** intoxication f alimentaire. ● **foodstuffs** npl denrées fpl alimentaires.

fool [fuːl] n imbécile mf; (**you**) **silly f.!** espèce d'imbécile!; **to make a f. of s.o.** (ridicule) ridiculiser qn; **to play the f.** faire l'imbécile ▮ vt (trick) rouler ▮ vi **to f. (about** or **around)** faire l'imbécile; (waste time) perdre son temps.

foolhardy ['fuːlhɑːdɪ] a téméraire.

foolish ['fuːlɪʃ] a bête. ●—ly bêtement.
●—ness n bêtise f.

foolproof ['fuːlpruːf] a (scheme etc) infaillible.

foot[1], pl **feet** [fʊt, fiːt] n pied m; (of animal) patte f; (measure) pied m (= 30,48 cm); **at the f. of** (page, stairs) au bas de; (table) au bout de; **on f.** à pied; **on one's feet** (standing) debout; **f. brake** Aut frein m au plancher.

foot[2] [fʊt] vt (bill) payer.

football ['fʊtbɔːl] n (game) football m; (ball) ballon m. ●**footballer** n joueur, -euse mf de football. ●**footbridge** n passerelle f. ●**foothills** npl contreforts mpl. ●**foothold** n prise f (de pied); Fig position f; **to gain a f.** prendre pied. ●**footlights** npl Th rampe f. ●**footmark** n empreinte f (de pied). ●**footnote** n note f au bas de la page; Fig post-scriptum m. ●**footpath** n sentier m; (at roadside) chemin m (piétonnier). ●**footprint** n empreinte f (de pied or de pas). ●**footstep** n pas m; **to follow in s.o.'s footsteps** suivre les traces de qn. ●**footwear** n chaussures fpl.

footing ['fʊtɪŋ] n prise f (de pied); Fig position f; **on an equal f.** sur un pied d'égalité.

for [fɔːr, unstressed fər] **1** prep pour; (for a distance or period of) pendant; (in spite of) malgré; **f. you/me/etc** pour toi/moi/etc; **what's it f.?** ça sert à quoi?; **f. love** par amour; **to swim f.** (towards) nager vers; **a train f.** un train à destination de, un train pour; **the road f. London** la route (en direction) de Londres; **to come f. dinner** venir dîner; **it's time f. breakfast** c'est l'heure du petit déjeuner; **to sell sth f. seven dollars** vendre qch sept dollars; **what's the Russian f. 'book'?** comment dit-on 'livre' en russe?; **she walked f. a kilometre** elle a marché pendant un kilomètre; **he was away f. a month** (throughout) il a été absent pendant un mois; **he won't be back f. a month**

il ne sera pas de retour avant un mois; **he's been here f. a month** (he's still here) il est ici depuis un mois; **I haven't seen him f. ten years** voilà dix ans que je ne l'ai vu, je ne l'ai pas vu depuis dix ans; **it's easy/possible f. her to do it** il lui est facile/possible de le faire; **it's f. you to say** c'est à toi de dire; **f. that to be done** pour que ça soit fait.
2 conj (because) car.

forbid [fə'bɪd] vt (pt **forbad(e)**, pp **forbidden**, pres p **forbidding**) interdire, défendre (s.o. to do à qn de faire); **to f. s.o. sth** interdire or défendre qch à qn. ●**forbidden** a (fruit etc) défendu; **she is f. to leave** il lui est interdit de partir.

force [fɔːs] n force f; **the (armed) forces** Mil les forces armées; **by (sheer) f.** de force; **in f.** (rule) en vigueur; (in great numbers) en grand nombre.
∎ vt forcer (qn) (to do à faire); (impose) imposer (on à); (door, lock) forcer; (confession) arracher (from à); **to f. one's way into** entrer de force dans; **to f. back** (enemy) faire reculer; **to f. down** (aircraft) forcer à atterrir; **to f. sth into sth** faire entrer qch de force dans qch; **to f. sth out** faire sortir qch de force. ●**forced** a **f. to do** obligé or forcé de faire; **a f. smile** un sourire forcé.

forceful ['fɔːsfəl] a énergique.
●—ly adv énergiquement. ●—ness n force f.

forceps ['fɔːseps] n forceps m.

forcibly ['fɔːsəblɪ] adv (by force) de force.

ford [fɔːd] n gué m.

fore [fɔːr] n **to come to the f.** passer au premier plan.

forearm ['fɔːrɑːm] n avant-bras m inv.

foreboding [fɔː'bəʊdɪŋ] n (feeling) pressentiment m.

forecast ['fɔːkɑːst] vt (pt & pp **forecast**) prévoir ∎ n prévision f; (of weather) prévisions fpl; Sp pronostic m.

forecourt ['fɔːkɔːt] n (of hotel etc) avant-cour f; (of petrol or Am gas station) aire f (de service), devant m.

forefinger ['fɔːfɪŋgər] n index m.

forefront ['fɔːfrʌnt] n **in the f. of** au

premier rang de.

forego [fɔːˈgəʊ] vt (pp **foregone**) renoncer à.

foreground [ˈfɔːgraʊnd] n premier plan m.

forehead [ˈfɒrɪd, ˈfɔːhed] n (brow) front m.

foreign [ˈfɒrən] a étranger; (trade) extérieur; (travel, correspondent) à l'étranger; (produce) de l'étranger; **F. Minister**, Br **F. Secretary** ministre m des Affaires étrangères. ● **foreigner** n étranger, -ère mf.

foreman [ˈfɔːmən] n (pl -men) (worker) contremaître m.

foremost [ˈfɔːməʊst] 1 a principal. 2 adv **first and f.** tout d'abord.

forensic [fəˈrensɪk] a (laboratory, evidence) médico-légal; **f. medicine** médecine f légale.

forerunner [ˈfɔːrʌnər] n précurseur m.

foresee [fɔːˈsiː] vt (pt **foresaw**, pp **foreseen**) prévoir. ● **-able** a prévisible.

foreshadow [fɔːˈʃædəʊ] vt présager.

foresight [ˈfɔːsaɪt] n prévoyance f.

forest [ˈfɒrɪst] n forêt f.

forestall [fɔːˈstɔːl] vt devancer.

foretaste [ˈfɔːteɪst] n avant-goût m (of de).

foretell [fɔːˈtel] vt (pt & pp **foretold**) prédire.

forever [fəˈrevər] adv (for always) pour toujours; (continually) sans cesse.

forewarn [fɔːˈwɔːn] vt avertir.

foreword [ˈfɔːwɜːd] n avant-propos m inv.

forfeit [ˈfɔːfɪt] vt (lose) perdre ∥ n (penalty) peine f; (in game) gage m.

forg/e [fɔːdʒ] 1 (signature, money) contrefaire; (document) falsifier. 2 vi **to f. ahead** (progress) aller de l'avant. 3 vt (metal) forger ∥ n forge f. ● **-ed** a (passport etc) faux (f fausse); **f. money** fausse monnaie f. ● **-er** n (of documents etc) faussaire m.

forgery [ˈfɔːdʒərɪ] n faux m.

forget [fəˈget] vt (pt **forgot**, pp **forgotten**, pres p **forgetting**) oublier (**to do** de

faire); **f. it!** Fam (it doesn't matter) peu importe!; **to f. oneself** s'oublier ∥ vi oublier; **to f. about** oublier.

forgetful [fəˈgetfəl] a **he's f.** il n'a pas de mémoire.

forgiv/e [fəˈgɪv] vt (pt **forgave**, pp **forgiven**) pardonner (**s.o. sth** qch à qn). ● **-ing** a indulgent. ● **forgiveness** n pardon m.

forgo [fɔːˈgəʊ] vt (pp **forgone**) renoncer à.

fork [fɔːk] 1 n (for eating) fourchette f; (for garden) fourche f. 2 vi (of road) bifurquer; **to f. left** (in vehicle) prendre à gauche ∥ n (in road) bifurcation f. 3 vt **to f. out** (money) Fam allonger. ● **-ed** a fourchu. ● **forklift truck** n chariot m élévateur.

forlorn [fəˈlɔːn] a (forsaken) abandonné; (unhappy) triste.

form [fɔːm] n (shape, type, style) forme f; (document) formulaire m; Sch classe f; **in the f. of** en forme de; **on f., in good f.** en (pleine) forme ∥ vt (group, basis, character) former; (habit) contracter; (an opinion) se former; (constitute) constituer, former; **to f. part of** faire partie de ∥ vi (appear) se former. ● **formation** [-ˈmeɪʃ(ə)n] n formation f.

formal [ˈfɔːm(ə)l] a (person, tone etc) cérémonieux; (stuffy) compassé; (official) (announcement etc) officiel; (denial, structure, logic) formel; **f. dress** tenue f de cérémonie; **f. education** éducation f scolaire. ● **for'mality** n (requirement) formalité f. ● **formally** adv (to declare etc) officiellement; **f. dressed** en tenue de cérémonie.

format [ˈfɔːmæt] n (layout) présentation f; (size) format m ∥ vt Comptr formater.

formative [ˈfɔːmətɪv] a formateur.

former [ˈfɔːmər] 1 a (previous) (teacher, job, house etc) ancien; (situation, life) antérieur; **my f. colleague** mon ancien collègue; **in f. days** autrefois. 2 a (of two) premier ∥ pron **the f.** celui-là, celle-là, le premier, la première. ● **-ly** adv (in

the past) autrefois; (*before*) avant.
formidable ['fɔːmɪdəb(ə)l] *a* effroyable.
formula ['fɔːmjʊlə] *n* 1 (*pl* -as *or* -ae [-iː]) formule *f*. 2 (*pl* -as) (*baby food*) lait *m* maternisé (en poudre).
forsake [fə'seɪk] *vt* (*pt* forsook, *pp* forsaken) abandonner.
fort [fɔːt] *n* Mil fort *m*.
forte ['fɔːteɪ, *Am* fɔːt] *n* (*strong point*) fort *m*.
forth [fɔːθ] *adv* en avant; **and so f.** et ainsi de suite; **to go back and f.** aller et venir.
forthcoming [fɔːθ'kʌmɪŋ] *a* 1 (*event*) à venir; (*book, film*) qui va sortir; **my f. book** mon prochain livre. 2 (*available*) disponible. 3 (*open*) (*person*) communicatif.
forthright ['fɔːθraɪt] *a* direct, franc (*f* franche).
forthwith [fɔːθ'wɪð] *adv* sur-le-champ.
fortieth ['fɔːtɪəθ] *a* & *n* quarantième (*mf*).
fortify ['fɔːtɪfaɪ] *vt* (*strengthen*) fortifier; **to f. s.o.** (*of food, drink*) réconforter qn. ●**fortification** [-'keɪʃ(ə)n] *n* fortification *f*.
fortnight ['fɔːtnaɪt] *n* quinze jours *mpl*. ●—**ly** *a* bimensuel ▮ *adv* tous les quinze jours.
fortress ['fɔːtrɪs] *n* forteresse *f*.
fortunate ['fɔːtʃənɪt] *a* (*choice, event etc*) heureux; **to be f.** (*of person*) avoir de la chance; **it's f. that** c'est heureux que (+ *sub*). ●—**ly** *adv* heureusement.
fortune ['fɔːtʃuːn] *n* (*wealth*) fortune *f*; (*luck*) chance *f*; (*chance*) sort *m*; **to have the good f. to** do avoir la chance de faire; **to tell s.o.'s f.** dire la bonne aventure à qn; **to make one's f.** faire fortune. ●**f.-teller** *n* diseur, -euse *mf* de bonne aventure.
forty ['fɔːtɪ] *a* & *n* quarante (*m*).
forum ['fɔːrəm] *n* forum *m*.
forward ['fɔːwəd] *adv* **forward(s)** en avant; **to go f.** avancer; **from this time f.** désormais ▮ *a* (*movement*) en avant; (*child*) Fig précoce; (*impudent*) effronté

▮ *n* Fb avant *m* ▮ *vt* (*letter*) faire suivre; (*goods*) expédier.
fossil ['fɒs(ə)l] *n* fossile *m*.
foster ['fɒstər] 1 *vt* (*music, art etc*) encourager. 2 *vt* (*child*) élever en famille d'accueil ▮ *a* (*child, parents*) adoptif; **f. home** *or* **family** famille *f* d'accueil.
fought [fɔːt] *pt* & *pp* of **fight**.
foul [faʊl] 1 *a* (-er, -est) (*smell, taste, weather etc*) infect; (*language*) grossier; **to be f.-mouthed** avoir un langage grossier. 2 *n* Sp coup *m* irrégulier; Fb faute *f* ▮ *a* **f. play** Sp jeu *m* irrégulier; Jur acte *m* criminel. 3 *vt* **to f. (up)** salir; (*pipe, drain*) encrasser; **to f. up** (*plans*) Fam gâcher.
found[1] [faʊnd] *pt* & *pp* of **find**.
found[2] [faʊnd] *vt* (*town etc*) fonder; (*opinion etc*) fonder, baser (**on** sur). ●—**er**[1] *n* fondateur, -trice *mf*.
foundation [faʊn'deɪʃ(ə)n] *n* (*basis of agreement etc*) bases *fpl*; **the foundations** (*of building*) les fondations *fpl*; **without f.** sans fondement.
founder[2] ['faʊndər] *vi* (*of ship*) sombrer.
foundry ['faʊndrɪ] *n* fonderie *f*.
fountain ['faʊntɪn] *n* fontaine *f*; **f. pen** stylo(-plume) *m*.
four [fɔːr] *a* & *n* quatre (*m*); **on all fours** à quatre pattes; **f.-letter word** = mot *m* de cinq lettres. ●**fourfold** *a* quadruple ▮ *adv* au quadruple. ●**foursome** *n* (*two couples*) deux couples *mpl*. ●**fourteen** *a* & *n* quatorze (*m*). ●**fourth** *a* & *n* quatrième (*mf*).
fowl [faʊl] *n* (*hens etc*) la volaille; **a f.** une volaille.
fox [fɒks] *n* 1 renard *m*. 2 *vt* (*puzzle*) mystifier; (*trick*) tromper.
foxglove ['fɒksɡlʌv] *n* Bot digitale *f*.
foyer ['fɒɪeɪ, *Am* 'fɔɪər] *n* Th foyer *m*; (*in hotel*) hall *m*.
fraction ['frækʃ(ə)n] *n* fraction *f*.
fracture ['fræktʃər] *n* fracture *f* ▮ *vt* fracturer; **to f. one's leg**/*etc* se fracturer la jambe/*etc* ▮ *vi* se fracturer.
fragile ['frædʒaɪl, *Am* 'frædʒ(ə)l] *a* fragile.

fragment ['frægmənt] n fragment m.

fragrant ['freɪgrənt] a parfumé. ●**fragrance** n parfum m.

frail [freɪl] a (-er, -est) (person, health etc) fragile.

frame [freɪm] **1** n (of building, person) charpente f; (of picture, bicycle) cadre m; (of window) châssis m; (of spectacles) monture f; **f. of mind** humeur f. **|** vt (picture) encadrer; (proposals, ideas) Fig formuler. **2** vt **to f. s.o.** Fam monter un coup contre qn. ●**framework** n structure f; **in the f. of** (context) dans le cadre de.

franc [fræŋk] n franc m.

France [frɑːns] n France f.

franchise ['fræntʃaɪz] n **1** Pol droit m de vote. **2** (right to sell product) franchise f.

Franco- ['fræŋkəʊ] pref franco-.

frank [fræŋk] a **1** (-er, -est) (honest) franc (f franche). **2** vt (letter) affranchir. ●**-ly** adv franchement. ●**-ness** n franchise f.

frankfurter ['fræŋkfɜːtər] n saucisse f de Francfort.

frantic ['fræntɪk] a (activity, shouts) frénétique; (rush, efforts) effréné; (person) hors de soi; **f. with joy** fou de joie. ●**frantically** adv (to run etc) comme un fou.

fraternity [frə'tɜːnɪtɪ] n Univ Am association f de camarades de classe; **the publishing/etc f.** la grande famille de l'édition/etc. ●**fraternize** ['frætənaɪz] vi fraterniser (**with** avec).

fraud [frɔːd] n **1** (crime) fraude f. **2** (person) imposteur m. ●**fraudulent** a frauduleux.

fraught [frɔːt] a **f. with** plein de; **to be f.** (of situation, person) être tendu.

fray [freɪ] **1** vi (of garment) s'effilocher; (of rope) s'user. **2** n (fight) rixe f. ●**-ed** a **my nerves are f.** j'ai les nerfs à vif.

freak [friːk] n phénomène m, monstre m; **a jazz/etc f.** Fam une(e) fana de jazz/etc **|** a (result, weather etc) anormal.

freckle ['frek(ə)l] n tache f de rousseur.

●**freckled** a couvert de taches de rousseur.

free [friː] a (**freer, freest**) (at liberty, not occupied) libre; (without cost) gratuit; (lavish) généreux (**with** de); **to get f.** se libérer; **f. to do** libre de faire; **f. of charge** gratuit; **f. of** (pain, person etc) débarrassé de; (trapped person) dégager; **f. gift** prime f; **f. kick** Fb coup m franc; **f.-range egg** œuf m de ferme; **f. speech** liberté f d'expression; **f. trade** libre-échange m. **|** adv **f.** (of charge) gratuitement. **|** vt (pt & pp **freed**) (prisoner, country etc) libérer; (trapped person) dégager; (untie) détacher.

freedom ['friːdəm] n liberté f; **f. from** (worry, responsibility) absence f de.

Freefone® ['friːfəʊn] Tel = numéro m vert. ●**free-for-'all** n mêlée f générale. ●**freehold** n propriété f foncière libre. ●**freelance** a indépendant **|** n collaborateur, -trice mf indépendant(e). ●**freeloader** n (sponger) parasite m. ●**Freemason** n franc-maçon m. ●**freeway** n Am autoroute f.

freely ['friːlɪ] adv (to speak, circulate etc) librement; (to give) libéralement.

freez/e [friːz] vi (pt **froze**, pp **frozen**) geler; **to f. to death** mourir de froid; **f.!** Am ne bougez plus!; **to f. up** or **over** geler; (of window) se givrer. **|** vt (food) congeler; (credits, river) geler; (prices, wages) bloquer; **frozen food** surgelés mpl. **|** n (freezing weather) gel m; (of prices etc) blocage m. ●**-ing** a (weather) glacial; (hands, person) gelé; **it's f.** on gèle; **I'm f. cold** j'ai très froid **|** n **below f.** au-dessous de zéro. ●**freezer** n (deep-freeze) congélateur m; (in fridge) freezer m.

freight [freɪt] n (goods, price for transport) fret m; (transport) transport m; **f. train** Am train m de marchandises. ●**-er** n (ship) cargo m.

French [frentʃ] a français; (teacher) de français; (embassy) de France; **F. fries**

Am frites *fpl* ▌ *n* (*language*) français *m*;
the F. (*people*) les Français *mpl*.
● **Frenchman** *n* (*pl* **-men**) Français *m*.
● **French-speaking** *a* francophone.
● **Frenchwoman** *n* (*pl* **-women**) Française *f*.

frenzy ['frenzı] *n* frénésie *f*. ● **frenzied** *a*
(*shouts*) frénétique; (*attack*) violent.

frequent ['fri:kwənt] *a* fréquent; **f. visitor**
habitué, -ée *mf* (**to** de) ▌ [frı'kwent] *vt*
fréquenter. ● **frequency** *n* fréquence *f*.
● **frequently** *adv* fréquemment.

fresh [freʃ] *1 a* (**-er, -est**) frais (*f* fraîche);
(*new*) nouveau (*f* nouvelle); (*impudent*)
Fam culotté; **to get some f. air** prendre
l'air. *2 adv* **to be f. from** arriver tout
juste de; (*university*) sortir tout juste de.
● **—ly** *adv* (*arrived, picked etc*) fraîchement. ● **—ness** *n* fraîcheur *f*.

freshen ['freʃən] *vi* **to f. up** (*have a wash*)
faire un brin de toilette ▌ *vt* **to f. up**
(*house*) retaper; **to f. s.o. up** (*of bath*)
rafraîchir qn. ● **—er** *n* **air f.** désodorisant *m*.

fret [fret] *vi* (**-tt-**) (*worry*) se faire du
souci; (*of baby*) pleurer. ● **fretful** *a* (*baby
etc*) grognon (*f* -onne).

friction ['frɪkʃ(ə)n] *n* friction *f*.

Friday ['fraıdı, *Am* -deı] *n* vendredi *m*;
Good F. Vendredi Saint.

fridge [frɪdʒ] *n* frigo *m*.

fried [traɪd] *pt & pp of* **fry** ▌ *a* (*fish etc*)
frit; **f. egg** œuf *m* sur le plat.

friend [frend] *n* ami, -ie *mf*; (*from school,
work*) camarade *mf*; **to be friends with**
s.o. être ami avec qn; **to make friends** se
lier (**with** avec). ● **friendly** *a* (**-ier, -iest**)
aimable, gentil (**to** avec); (*child, animal*)
gentil; (*attitude, smile*) amical; **some f.
advice** un conseil d'ami; **to give s.o. some
advice**, **be on f. terms with s.o.** être en
bons termes avec qn. ● **friendship** *n*
amitié *f*.

frieze [fri:z] *n Archit* frise *f*.

frigate ['frɪgət] *n* (*ship*) frégate *f*.

fright [fraıt] *n* peur *f*; **to have a f.** avoir
peur; **to give s.o. a f.** faire peur à qn.
● **frighten** *vt* effrayer; **to f. away** *or* **off**

(*animal, person*) faire fuir. ● **frightened**
a effrayé; **to be f.** avoir peur (**of** de).
● **frightening** *a* effrayant.

frightful ['fraıtfəl] *a* affreux.

frigid ['frɪdʒɪd] *a* (*greeting etc*) froid;
(*woman*) frigide.

frill [frıl] *n* **1** (*on dress etc*) volant *m*.
2 frills (*useless embellishments*) fioritures *fpl*; **no frills** (*machine*, *Br* holiday, *Am* vacation) sans rien de
superflu.

fringe [frındʒ] **1** *n* (*of hair*, *on clothes etc*)
frange *f*. **2** *n* (*of forest*) lisière *f*; **on the f.
of society** en marge de la société ▌ *a*
(*group*) marginal; **f. benefits** avantages
mpl divers.

Frisbee® ['frızbi:] *n* Frisbee® *m*.

frisk [frısk] **1** *vt* (*search*) fouiller (au
corps). **2** *vi* **to f. (about)** gambader.

fritter ['frıtər] **1** *vt* **to f. away** (*waste*)
gaspiller. **2** *n Culin* beignet *m*.

frivolous ['frıvələs] *a* frivole.

frizzy ['frızı] *a* (*hair*) crépu.

fro [frəʊ] *adv* **to go to and f.** aller et venir.

frock [frɒk] *n* (*dress*) robe *f*; (*of monk*)
froc *m*.

frog [frɒg] *n* grenouille *f*. ● **frogman** *n* (*pl*
-men) homme-grenouille *m*.

frolic ['frɒlık] *vi* (*pt & pp* **frolicked**) **to f.
(about)** gambader.

from [frɒm, *unstressed* frəm] *prep* **1** de; **a
letter f. une lettre de**; **to suffer f.** souffrir
de; **where are you f.?** d'où êtes-vous?; **a
train f.** un train en provenance de; **to be
ten metres (away) f. the house** être à dix
mètres de la maison.

2 (*time onwards*) à partir de, dès,
depuis; **f. today (on)**, **as f. today** à
partir d'aujourd'hui, dès aujourd'hui;
f. her childhood dès *or* depuis son
enfance.

3 (*numbers, prices, onwards*) à partir de;
f. five francs à partir de cinq francs.

4 (*away from*) à; **to take/hide/borrow f.**
prendre/cacher/emprunter à.

5 (*out of*) dans; sur; **to take f.** (*box*)
prendre dans; (*table*) prendre sur; **to
drink f. a cup** boire dans une tasse; **to**

drink (straight) f. the bottle boire à la bouteille.

6 (*according to*) d'après; **f. what I saw** d'après ce que j'ai vu.

7 (*cause*) par; **f. habit**/*etc* par habitude/ etc.

8 (*on behalf of*) de la part de; **tell her f. me** dis-lui de ma part.

front [frʌnt] *n* (*of garment, building*) devant *m*; (*of boat, car*) avant *m*; (*of crowd*) premier rang *m*; (*of book*) début *m*; *Mil Pol Met* front *m*; (*beach*) front *m* de mer; **in f. (of)** devant; **in f.** (*ahead*) en avant; (*in race*) en tête; **in the f.** (*in vehicle*) à l'avant; (*of house*) devant.

▮ *a* (*tooth etc*) de devant; (*part, wheel, car seat*) avant *inv*; (*row, page*) premier; **f. door** porte *f* d'entrée; **f. line** *Mil* front *m*; **f. room** (*lounge*) salon *m*; **f. runner** *Fig* favori, -ite *mf*; **f.-wheel drive** (*on vehicle*) traction *f* avant.

frontier [ˈfrʌntɪər] *n* frontière *f*.

frost [frɒst] *n* gel *m*, gelée *f*; (*frozen drops on window, grass etc*) givre *m* ▮ *vi* **to f. up** (*of window etc*) se givrer. ●**frostbite** *n* gelure *f*. ●**frostbitten** *a* gelé.

frosted [ˈfrɒstɪd] *a* (*glass*) dépoli.

frosting [ˈfrɒstɪŋ] *n* (*icing*) *Am Culin* glaçage *m*.

frosty [ˈfrɒstɪ] *a* (**-ier, -iest**) (*air, night etc*) glacial; (*window*) givré; **it's f.** il gèle.

froth [frɒθ] *n* mousse *f* ▮ *vi* mousser.

frown [fraʊn] *n* froncement *m* de sourcils ▮ *vi* froncer les sourcils; **to f. (up)on** *Fig* désapprouver.

froze, frozen [frəʊz, ˈfrəʊz(ə)n] *pt & pp* of **freeze**.

frugal [ˈfruːg(ə)l] *a* (*meal, life, person*) frugal.

fruit [fruːt] *n* fruit *m*; (*some*) **f.** (*one item*) un fruit; (*more than one*) des fruits; **to like f.** aimer les fruits; **f. basket** corbeille *f* à fruits; **f. drink** boisson *f* aux fruits; **f. juice** jus *m* de fruit; **f. salad** salade *f* de fruits; **f. tree** arbre *m* fruitier; **f. machine** *Fig* machine *f* à

sous. ●**fruitcake** *n* cake *m*. ●**fruitful** *a* (*meeting*) fructueux. ●**fruitless** *a* stérile.

frustrat/e [frʌˈstreɪt] *vt* (*person*) frustrer; (*plans*) faire échouer; (*ambitions*) décevoir. ●**—ed** *a* (*mentally, sexually*) frustré. ●**—ing** *a* irritant. ●**frustration** [-ˈstreɪʃ(ə)n] *n* frustration *f*.

fry [fraɪ] **1** *vt* faire frire ▮ *vi* frire. **2** *n* **small f.** (*people*) menu fretin *m*. ●**—ing** *n* friture *f*; **f. pan** poêle *f* (à frire).

ft *abbr* (*measure*) = **foot, feet.**

fuddy-duddy [ˈfʌdɪdʌdɪ] *n* **he's an old f.-duddy** *Fam* c'est un vieux schnoque.

fudge [fʌdʒ] **1** *n* (*sweet, Am candy*) caramel *m* mou. **2** *vt* **to f. the issue** refuser d'aborder le problème.

fuel [fjʊəl] *n* combustible *m*; *Aut* carburant *m*; **f. (oil)** mazout *m*; **f. tank** *Aut* réservoir *m*.

fugitive [ˈfjuːdʒɪtɪv] *n* fugitif, -ive *mf*.

fulfil, *Am* **fulfill** [fʊlˈfɪl] *vt* (**-ll-**) (*ambition, dream*) réaliser; (*condition, duty, promise*) remplir; (*desire*) satisfaire; **to f. oneself** s'épanouir. ●**fulfilling** *a* satisfaisant. ●**fulfilment** or *Am* **fulfillment** *n* (*feeling*) satisfaction *f*.

full [fʊl] *a* (**-er, -est**) plein (**of** de); (*bus, theatre etc*) complet; (*life, day*) rempli; (*skirt*) ample; **the f. price** le prix fort; **to pay f. fare** payer plein tarif; **a f. member** un membre à part entière; **a f. hour** une heure entière; **to be f. (up)** (*of person*) n'avoir plus faim; (*of hotel*) être complet; **at f. speed** à toute vitesse; **f. name** (*on form*) nom et prénom; **f. stop** *Gram* point *m*.

▮ *adv* **to know f. well** savoir fort bien.

▮ *n* **in f.** (*to read sth, publish sth*) en entier; (*to write one's name*) en toutes lettres; **to pay in f.** tout payer; **to the f.** (*completely*) tout à fait.

full-back [ˈfʊlbæk] *n* *Fb* arrière *m*. ●**f.-'length** *a* (*film*) de long métrage; (*portrait*) en pied; (*dress*) long. ●**f.-'scale** *a* (*model etc*) grandeur nature *inv*; (*operation, attack etc*) de grande envergure. ●**f.-'sized** *a* (*model*) grandeur nature *inv*. ● f.-'time *a* & *adv* à plein temps.

fully ['fʊlɪ] *adv* entièrement; (*thoroughly*) à fond; (*at least*) au moins.

fully-fledged, *Am* **full-fledged** ['fʊl(ɪ)'fledʒd] *a* (*engineer etc*) diplômé; (*member*) à part entière.

fumble ['fʌmb(ə)l] *vi* **to f.** (**about**) (*grope*) tâtonner; (*search*) fouiller (**for** pour trouver); **to f.** (**about**) **with** tripoter.

fume [fjuːm] **1** *vi* (*of person*) rager. **2** *npl* **fumes** vapeurs *fpl*; (*from car exhaust*) gaz *mpl*.

fumigate ['fjuːmɪgeɪt] *vt* désinfecter (par fumigation).

fun [fʌn] *n* amusement *m*; **to be** (**good**) **f.** être très amusant; **to have** (**some**) **f.** s'amuser; **to make f. of, poke f. at** se moquer de; **for f.** pour le plaisir.

function ['fʌŋkʃ(ə)n] **1** *n* (*role, duty* & *Math* fonction *f*; (*party*) réception *f*; (*ceremony*) cérémonie *f* (publique). **2** *vi* (*work*) fonctionner. ● **functional** *a* fonctionnel.

fund [fʌnd] *n* (*for pension etc*) caisse *f*, fonds *m*; (*of knowledge*) Fig fond *m*; *pl* (*money resources*) fonds *mpl*; (*for special purpose*) crédits *mpl* ▮ *vt* (*with money*) fournir des fonds or des crédits à.

fundamental [fʌndə'ment(ə)l] *a* fondamental.

funeral ['fjuːnərəl] *n* enterrement *m* ▮ *a* (*service, march*) funèbre.

funfair ['fʌnfeər] *n* fête *f* foraine; (*larger*) parc *m* d'attractions.

fungus, *pl* **-gi** ['fʌŋgəs, -gaɪ] *n* Bot champignon *m*; (*mould*, *Am* mold) moisissure *f*.

funnel ['fʌn(ə)l] *n* **1** (*of ship*) cheminée *f*. **2** (*for pouring*) entonnoir *m*.

funny ['fʌnɪ] *a* (**-ier, -iest**) (*amusing*) drôle; (*strange*) bizarre; **a f. idea** une drôle d'idée; **to feel f.** ne pas se sentir très bien.

fur [fɜːr] *n* **1** (*of animal, for wearing*) fourrure *f*; (*of dog, cat*) pelage *m*, poil *m*. **2** *n* (*in kettle*) dépôt *m* (de tartre) ▮ *vi* (**-rr-**) **to f.** (**up**) s'entartrer.

furious ['fjʊərɪəs] *a* (*violent, angry*) furieux (**with, at** contre); (*efforts*) acharné.

furnace ['fɜːnɪs] *n* (*forge*) fourneau *m*.

furnish ['fɜːnɪʃ] *vt* **1** (*room*) meubler. **2** (*supply*) fournir (**s.o. with sth** qch à qn). ● **-ings** *npl* ameublement *m*.

furniture ['fɜːnɪtʃər] *n* meubles *mpl*; **a piece of f.** un meuble.

furrow ['fʌrəʊ] *n* (*on brow*) & Agr sillon *m*.

furry ['fɜːrɪ] *a* (*animal*) à poil; (*toy*) en peluche.

further ['fɜːðər] **1** *adv* & *a* = **farther. 2** *adv* (*more*) davantage, plus; (*besides*) en outre ▮ *a* (*additional*) supplémentaire; **f. details** de plus amples détails; **a f. case**/*etc* (*another*) un autre cas/*etc*; **without f. delay** sans plus attendre; **f. education** enseignement *m* post-scolaire. **3** *vt* (*cause, research*) promouvoir. ● **furthermore** *adv* en outre. ● **furthest** *a* & *adv* = **farthest.**

furtive ['fɜːtɪv] *a* (*smile etc*) furtif; (*person*) sournois.

fury ['fjʊərɪ] *n* (*violence, anger*) fureur *f*.

fuse [fjuːz] **1** *vt* **to f. the lights** faire sauter les plombs ▮ *vi* **the lights** *etc* **have fused** les plombs ont sauté ▮ *n* (*wire*) fusible *m*. **2** *n* (*of bomb*) amorce *f*. **3** *vt* (*metal*) fondre; (*join together*) réunir par fusion. ● **fused** *a* (*electric plug*) avec fusible incorporé.

fuselage ['fjuːzəlaːʒ] *n* Av fuselage *m*.

fusion ['fjuːʒ(ə)n] *n* Phys Biol fusion *f*.

fuss [fʌs] *n* chichis *mpl*, façons *fpl*; (*noise*) agitation *f*; **what a f.!** quelle histoire!; **to kick up** or **make a f.** faire des histoires; **to make a f. of** être aux petits soins pour.

▮ *vi* faire des chichis; (*worry*) se tracasser (**about** pour); (*rush about*) s'agiter; **to f. over s.o.** être aux petits soins pour qn. ● **fusspot** or *Am* **fussbudget** *n* Fam enquiquineur, -euse *mf*. ● **fussy** *a* (**-ier, -iest**) tatillon; (*difficult*) difficile (**about** sur).

futile ['fjuːtaɪl, *Am* 'fjuːt(ə)l] *a* futile, vain.

future ['fjuːtʃər] n avenir m; Gram futur m; **in f.** (from now on) à l'avenir; **in the f.** (one day) un jour (futur) ‖ a futur.
fuze [fjuːz] n, vt & vi Am = **fuse 1 & 2**.

fuzz [fʌz] n Am (of material) peluche(s) f(pl); (on floor) moutons mpl.
fuzzy ['fʌzɪ] a (-ier, -iest) (picture, idea) flou; **f. hair** cheveux mpl crépus.

G

G, g [dʒiː] *n* G, g *m*. ● **G.-string** *n* (*cloth*) cache-sexe *m inv*.

gabble ['gæb(ə)l] *vi* (*chatter*) jacasser; (*indistinctly*) bredouiller ‖ *n* baragouin *m*.

gad [gæd] *vi* (-dd-) **to g. about** vadrouiller.

gadget ['gædʒɪt] *n* gadget *m*.

Gaelic ['geɪlɪk, 'gælɪk] *a & n* gaélique (*m*).

gag [gæg] **1** *n* (*over mouth*) bâillon *m* ‖ *vt* (-gg-) (*victim etc*) bâillonner. **2** *n* (*joke*) plaisanterie *f*; *Cin Th* gag *m*. **3** *vi* (-gg-) (*choke*) s'étouffer (**on** avec).

gaiety ['geɪtɪ] *n* gaieté *f*. ● **gaily** *adv* gaiement.

gain [geɪn] *vt* (*obtain, win*) gagner; (*experience, reputation*) acquérir; **to g. speed/weight** prendre de la vitesse/du poids; **to g. popularity** gagner en popularité ‖ *vi* (*of watch*) avancer; **to g. in strength** gagner en force; **to g. on** (*catch up with*) rattraper ‖ *n* (*increase*) augmentation *f* (**in** de); (*profit*) bénéfice *m*.

gait [geɪt] *n* (*walk*) démarche *f*.

gala ['gɑːlə, *Am* 'geɪlə] *n* gala *m*; **swimming g.** concours *m* de natation.

galaxy ['gæləksɪ] *n* galaxie *f*.

gale [geɪl] *n* grand vent *m*, rafale *f* (de vent).

gall [gɔːl] *n* **1** (*impudence*) *Fam* effronterie *f*; **g. bladder** vésicule *f* biliaire. **2** *vt* (*vex*) blesser, froisser.

gallant ['gælənt] *a* (*chivalrous*) galant; (*brave*) courageux.

galleon ['gælɪən] *n* (*ship*) *Hist* galion *m*.

gallery ['gælərɪ] *n* (*room*) galerie *f*; (*for public, press*) tribune *f*; **art g.** (*private*) galerie *f* d'art; (*public*) musée *m* d'art.

Gallic ['gælɪk] *a* (*French*) français.

gallivant ['gælɪvænt] *vi* **to g. (about)** *Fam*

vadrouiller.

gallon ['gælən] *n* gallon *m* (*Br* = 4,5 *litres, Am* = 3,8 *litres*).

gallop ['gæləp] *n* galop *m* ‖ *vi* galoper; **galloping inflation** l'inflation *f* galopante.

gallows ['gæləuz] *npl* potence *f*.

gallstone ['gɔːlstəun] *n Med* calcul *m* biliaire.

galore [gə'lɔːr] *adv* à gogo, en abondance.

galoshes [gə'lɒʃɪz] *npl* (*shoes*) caoutchoucs *mpl*.

gambl/e ['gæmb(ə)l] *vi* jouer (**on** sur, **with** avec) ‖ *vt* (*bet*) parier, jouer (**ten dollars**/*etc* dix dollars/*etc*); **to g. (away)** (*lose*) perdre (au jeu) ‖ *n* (*risk*) coup *m* risqué. ●**—ing** *n* jeu *m*. ●**gambler** *n* joueur, -euse *mf*.

game [geɪm] **1** *n* jeu *m*; (*of football, cricket etc*) match *m*; (*of tennis, chess, cards*) partie *f*; **to have a g. of** jouer un match de; faire une partie de; **games** *Sch* le sport. **2** *n* (*animals, birds*) gibier *m*. **3** *a* (*brave*) courageux; **g. for sth** (*willing to do*) prêt à qch; **I'm g.** je suis partant. **4** *a* **to have a g. leg** être boiteux. ●**gamekeeper** *n* garde-chasse *m*.

gammon ['gæmən] *n* (*ham*) jambon *m* fumé.

gammy ['gæmɪ] *a Fam* = **game 4**.

gang [gæŋ] *n* (*of children, friends etc*) bande *f*; (*of workers*) équipe *f*; (*of criminals*) gang *m* ‖ *vi* **to g. up on** or **against** se mettre à plusieurs contre. ●**gangster** *n* gangster *m*.

gangrene ['gæŋgriːn] *n* gangrène *f*.

gangway ['gæŋweɪ] *n* passage *m*; (*in train*) couloir *m*; (*in bus, theatre etc*) allée *f*; (*footbridge*) *Av Nau* passerelle *f*.

gaol [dʒeɪl] *n & vt* = **jail**.

gap [gæp] *n* (*empty space*) trou *m*; (*in*

time) intervalle *m*; (*in knowledge*) lacune *f*; **the g. between** (*difference*) l'écart *m* entre.

gap/e [geɪp] *vi* (*stare*) rester bouche bée; **to g. at** regarder bouche bée. ● **—ing** *a* (*hole, wound*) béant.

garage ['gæra:(d)ʒ, *Am* gəˈra:ʒ] *n* garage *m* ‖ *vt* mettre au garage.

garbage ['ga:bɪdʒ] *n Am* ordures *fpl*; **g. can** poubelle *f*; **g. man** éboueur *m*; **g. truck** camion-benne *m*.

garden ['ga:d(ə)n] *n* jardin *m*; **the gardens** (*park*) le parc; **g. centre** (*store*) jardinerie *f*; **g. party** garden-party *f* ‖ *vi* jardiner. ● **—ing** *n* jardinage *m*. ● **gardener** *n* jardinier, -ière *mf*.

gargle ['ga:g(ə)l] *vi* se gargariser.

garish ['geərɪʃ, *Am* 'gærɪʃ] *a* (*clothes*) voyant, criard; (*light*) cru.

garland ['ga:lənd] *n* guirlande *f*.

garlic ['ga:lɪk] *n* ail *m*; **g. sausage** saucisson *m* à l'ail.

garment ['ga:mənt] *n* vêtement *m*.

garret ['gærət] *n* (*room*) mansarde *f*.

garrison ['gærɪsən] *n Mil* garnison *f*.

garter ['ga:tər] *n* (*round leg*) jarretière *f*; (*attached to belt*) *Am* jarretelle *f*.

gas [gæs] *n* gaz *m inv*; (*gasoline*) *Am* essence *f*; **g. cooker/mask/meter/etc** cuisinière *f*/masque *m*/compteur *m*/*etc* à gaz; **g. fire** *or* **heater** appareil *m* de chauffage à gaz; **g. heating** chauffage *m* au gaz; **g. pipe** tuyau *m* de gaz; **g. station** *Am* station-service *f*; **g. stove** cuisinière *f* à gaz; (*portable*) réchaud *m* à gaz ‖ *vt* (**-ss-**) (*poison*) asphyxier (*qn*).

gash [gæʃ] *n* entaille *f* ‖ *vt* (*skin*) entailler; **to g. one's knee** se faire une blessure profonde au genou.

gasket ['gæskɪt] *n Aut* joint *m* de culasse.

gasman ['gæsmæn] *n* (*pl* **-men**) employé *m* du gaz.

gasoline ['gæsəli:n] *n Am* essence *f*.

gasp [ga:sp] *vi* haleter (*for breath*) ‖ *n* halètement *m*. **2** *vi* **to g. in surprise**/ *etc* avoir le souffle coupé de surprise/ *etc*.

gassy ['gæsɪ] *a* (**-ier, -iest**) (*drink*) gazeux.

gastric ['gæstrɪk] *a* (*ulcer etc*) gastrique.

gasworks ['gæswɜ:ks] *n* usine *f* à gaz.

gate [geɪt] *n* (*at level crossing, field etc*) barrière *f*; (*metal, of garden*) grille *f*; (*of castle, in airport etc*) porte *f*; (*at stadium*) entrée *f*. ● **gateway** *n* **the g. to success** le chemin du succès.

gâteau, *pl* **-eaux** ['gætəʊ, -əʊz] *n* gros gâteau *m* à la crème.

gatecrash ['geɪtkræʃ] *vti* **to g. (a party)** s'inviter de force à (une réception).

gather ['gæðər] *vt* (*people, objects*) rassembler; (*pick up*) ramasser; (*flowers*) cueillir; (*information*) recueillir; (*fabric*) froncer; **I g. that...** je crois comprendre que...; **to g. speed** prendre de la vitesse; **to g. in** (*crops*) rentrer; (*exam papers*) ramasser; **to g. (up) one's strength** rassembler ses forces.
‖ *vi* (*of people*) se rassembler; (*of clouds*) se former; (*of dust*) s'accumuler; **to g. round** (*come closer*) s'approcher; **to g. round s.o.** entourer qn. ● **gathering** *n* (*group*) rassemblement *m*.

gaudy ['gɔːdɪ] *a* (**-ier, -iest**) voyant, criard.

gauge [geɪdʒ] *n* (*instrument*) jauge *f*, indicateur *m* ‖ *vt* (*estimate*) évaluer, jauger; (*measure*) mesurer.

gaunt [gɔːnt] *a* (*thin*) décharné.

gauze [gɔːz] *n* (*fabric*) gaze *f*.

gave [geɪv] *pt of* **give**.

gawk [gɔːk] *vi* **to g. (at)** regarder bouche bée.

gawp [gɔːp] *vi* = **gawk**.

gay [geɪ] *a* (**-er, -est**) **1** *a & n* homosexuel (*m*), homo (*m inv*). **2** (*cheerful*) gai; (*colour*) vif, gai.

gaze [geɪz] *n* regard *m* (fixe) ‖ *vi* regarder; **to g. at** regarder (fixement).

gazelle [gəˈzel] *n* (*animal*) gazelle *f*.

GB [dʒiːˈbiː] *abbr* (*Great Britain*) Grande-Bretagne *f*.

GCE [dʒiːsiːˈiː] *abbr Br* (*General Certificate of Education*) = épreuve *f* de bac.

GCSE [dʒiːsiːesˈiː] *abbr Br* (*General Certificate of Secondary Education*)

= épreuve *f* de brevet.

gear [gɪər] **1** *n* équipement *m*, matériel *m*; (*belongings*) affaires *fpl*; (*clothes*) *Fam* vêtements; (*speed*) *Aut* vitesse *f*; **in g.** *Aut* en prise; **not in g.** *Aut* au point mort; **g. lever,** *Am* **g. shift** levier *m* de (changement de) vitesse. **2** *vt* (*adapt*) adapter (**to** à); **geared up to do** prêt à faire; **to g. oneself up for** se préparer pour. ● **gearbox** *n* boîte *f* de vitesses.

geel [dʒi:] *int Am Fam* ça alors!

geese [gi:s] *see* goose.

Geiger counter [ˈgaɪgəkaʊntər] *n* compteur *m* Geiger.

gel [dʒel] *n* (*substance*) gel *m*.

gelignite [ˈdʒelɪgnaɪt] *n* dynamite *f* (au nitrate de soude).

gem [dʒem] *n* pierre *f* précieuse; (*person of value*) *Fig* perle *f*; (*thing of value*) bijou *m* (*pl* -oux).

Gemini [ˈdʒemɪnaɪ] *n* (*sign*) les Gémeaux *mpl*.

gen [dʒen] *n* (*information*) *Fam* tuyaux *mpl*.

gender [ˈdʒendər] *n* Gram genre *m*; (*of person*) sexe *m*.

gene [dʒi:n] *n* (*of cell*) gène *m*.

general [ˈdʒenərəl] **1** *a* général; **in g.** en général; **the g. public** le (grand) public; **for g. use** à l'usage du public; **g. delivery** *Am* poste *f* restante; **to be g.** (*widespread*) être très répandu. **2** *n* (*officer*) *Mil* général *m*.

generalize [ˈdʒen(ə)rəlaɪz] *vti* généraliser. ● **generalization** [-ˈzeɪʃ(ə)n] *n* généralisation *f*.

generally [ˈdʒen(ə)rəlɪ] *adv* généralement; **g. speaking** en général.

generate [ˈdʒenəreɪt] *vt* (*heat*) produire; (*fear, hope etc*) engendrer.

generation [dʒenəˈreɪʃ(ə)n] *n* génération *f*; **g. gap** conflit *m* des générations.

generator [ˈdʒenəreɪtər] *n* El groupe *m* électrogène.

generous [ˈdʒenərəs] *a* généreux (**with** de); (*helping, meal*) copieux. ● **gene'rosity** *n* générosité *f*. ● **generously** *adv* généreusement.

genetic [dʒɪˈnetɪk] *a* génétique; **g. engineering** génie *m* génétique. ● **genetics** *n* génétique *f*.

Geneva [dʒɪˈniːvə] *n* Genève *m* or *f*.

genial [ˈdʒiːnɪəl] *a* (*kind*) affable; (*cheerful*) jovial.

genie [ˈdʒiːnɪ] *n* (*goblin*) génie *m*.

genital [ˈdʒenɪt(ə)l] *a* génital ● *npl* **genitals** organes *mpl* génitaux.

genius [ˈdʒiːnɪəs] *n* (*ability, person*) génie *m*; **to have a g. for doing/sth** avoir le génie pour faire/de qch.

gent [dʒent] *n* **gents' shoes** *Com* chaussures *fpl* pour hommes; **the gents** les toilettes *fpl* pour hommes.

gentle [ˈdʒent(ə)l] *a* (**-er, -est**) (*person, sound, slope etc*) doux (*f* douce); (*hint, reminder*) discret; (*touch, breeze*) léger; (*exercise, speed*) modéré; **to be g. with** s.o. traiter qn avec douceur. ● **gentleman** *n* (*pl* **-men**) monsieur *m*; (*well-bred*) gentleman *m*. ● **gentleness** *n* douceur *f*. ● **gently** *adv* doucement; (*smoothly*) (*to land in aircraft etc*) en douceur.

genuine [ˈdʒenjuɪn] *a* (*leather etc*) véritable; (*signature etc*) authentique; (*sincere*) sincère. ●**—ly** *adv* (*surprised etc*) véritablement; (*to think etc*) sincèrement.

geography [dʒɪˈɒgrəfɪ] *n* géographie *f*. ● **geo'graphical** *a* géographique.

geology [dʒɪˈɒlədʒɪ] *n* géologie *f*. ● **geo'logical** *a* géologique.

geometry [dʒɪˈɒmɪtrɪ] *n* géométrie *f*. ● **geo'metric(al)** *a* géométrique.

geranium [dʒɪˈreɪnɪəm] *n* géranium *m*.

geriatric [dʒerɪˈætrɪk] *a* (*hospital*) gériatrique; **g. ward** service *m* de gériatrie.

germ [dʒɜːm] *n* Med microbe *m*; (*seed*) Biol & Fig germe *m*.

German [ˈdʒɜːmən] *a* allemand; **G. measles** *Med* rubéole *f*; **G. shepherd** (*dog*) *Am* berger *m* allemand ● *n* (*person*) Allemand, -ande *mf*; (*language*) allemand *m*.

Germany [ˈdʒɜːmənɪ] *n* Allemagne *f*.

gesticulate [dʒesˈtɪkjʊleɪt] *vi* gesticuler.

gesture [ˈdʒestʃər] *n* geste *m* ● *vi* **to g.**

s.o. to do faire signe à qn de faire.
get [get] **1** vt (pt & pp **got**, pp Am **gotten**, pres p **getting**) (obtain) obtenir, avoir; (find) trouver; (buy) acheter; (receive) recevoir, avoir; (catch) attraper; (bus, train) prendre; (seize) prendre, saisir; (fetch) aller chercher (qn, qch); (put) mettre; (derive) tirer (**from** de); (understand) comprendre, saisir; (prepare) préparer; (lead) mener; (hit with fist, stick etc) atteindre; (reputation) se faire; **I have got**, Am **I have gotten** j'ai; **to g. s.o. to do sth** faire faire qch à qn; **to g. sth built/etc** faire construire/ etc qch; **to g. things going** or **started** faire démarrer les choses; **to g. sth to s.o.** (send) faire parvenir qch à qn; **to g. s.o. to sth** (bring) amener qn à qch.
2 vi (go) aller (**to** à); (arrive) arriver (**to** à); (become) devenir; **to g. caught/run over/etc** se faire prendre/écraser/etc; **to g. dressed/washed** s'habiller/se laver; **to g. paid** être payé; **where have you got** or **Am gotten to?** où en es-tu?; **you've got to stay** (must) tu dois rester; **to g. to do** (succeed in doing) parvenir à faire; **I'm getting to understand** (starting) je commence à comprendre; **to g. working** (start) se mettre à travailler.
get about or **(a)round** vi se déplacer; (of news) circuler ▌ **to get across** vt (road) traverser; (message) communiquer; **to g. s.o. across** faire traverser qn ▌ vi traverser; **to g. across to s.o. that** faire comprendre à qn que ▌ **to get along** vi (manage) se débrouiller; (progress) avancer; (be on good terms) s'entendre (**with** avec) ▌ **to get at** vt (reach) parvenir à, atteindre; **what is he getting at?** où veut-il en venir? ▌ **to get away** vi (leave) partir, s'en aller; (escape) s'échapper; **to g. away with a crime** s'en tirer avec une amende. ● **getaway** n (escape) fuite f. ▌ **to get back** vt (recover) récupérer; (replace) remettre ▌ vi (return) revenir, retourner; (move back) reculer ▌ **to get by** vi (pass) passer; (manage) se débrouiller ▌ **to get down** vi (go down) descendre

(**from** de); **to g. down to** (task, work) se mettre à ▌ vt (bring down) descendre (**from** de); **to g. s.o. down** (depress) Fam déprimer qn ▌ **to get in** vt (bicycle, washing etc) rentrer; (buy) acheter; **to g. s.o. in** (call for) faire venir qn; **to g. in a car/etc** monter dans une voiture/etc ▌ vi (enter) entrer; (come home) rentrer; (enter vehicle or train) monter; (of plane, train) arriver; (of candidate) Pol être élu ▌ **to get into** vt entrer dans; (vehicle, train) monter dans; (habit) prendre; **to g. into bed/a rage** se mettre au lit/en colère ▌ **to get off** vi (leave) partir; (from vehicle or train) descendre (**from** de); (finish work) sortir; (be acquitted) Jur être acquitté ▌ vt (remove) enlever; (send) expédier; **to g. off a chair** se lever d'une chaise; **to g. off a bus** descendre d'un bus ▌ **to get on** vt (shoes, clothes) mettre; (bus, train) monter dans ▌ vi (progress) marcher, avancer; (manage) se débrouiller; (succeed) réussir; (enter bus or train) monter; (be on good terms) s'entendre (**with** avec); **how are you getting on?** comment ça va?; **to g. on to s.o.** (on phone) contacter qn; **to g. on with** (task) continuer ▌ **to get out** vi sortir; (from vehicle or train) descendre (**of** de); **to g. out of** (obligation) échapper à; (danger) se tirer de; (habit) perdre ▌ vt (remove) enlever; (bring out) sortir (qch), faire sortir (qn) ▌ **to get over** vt (road) traverser; (obstacle) surmonter; (fence) franchir; (illness) se remettre de; (surprise) revenir de; (ideas) communiquer ▌ vi (cross) traverser; (visit) passer ▌ **to get round** vt (obstacle) contourner ▌ vi (visit) passer; **to g. round to doing** en venir à faire ▌ **to get through** vi (pass) passer; (finish) finir; (pass exam) être reçu; **to g. through to s.o.** (on the phone) contacter qn ▌ vt (hole etc) passer par; (task, meal) venir à bout de; (exam) être reçu à ▌ **to get together** vi (of people) se rassembler. ● **get-together** n réunion f. ▌ **to get up** vi (rise) se lever (**from** de); **to**

g. up to (in book) en arriver à; **to g. up to something** or **to mischief** faire des bêtises ▮ vt (ladder, stairs etc) monter; **to g. sth up** (bring up) monter qch. ● **get-up** n (clothes) Fam accoutrement m.

geyser ['gi:zər] n 1 (water heater) chauffe-eau m inv (à gaz). 2 Geol geyser m.

Ghana ['gɑ:nə] n Ghana m.

ghastly ['gɑ:stlɪ] a (-ier, -iest) (horrible) affreux; (pale) blême, pâle.

gherkin ['gɜ:kɪn] n cornichon m.

ghetto ['getəʊ] n (pl -os) ghetto m; **g. blaster** Fam mini-stéréo f portable.

ghost [gəʊst] n fantôme m; **g. story** histoire f de fantômes; **g. town** ville f fantôme.

giant ['dʒaɪənt] n géant m ▮ a (tree, packet etc) géant, gigantesque; (steps) de géant.

gibberish ['dʒɪbərɪʃ] n baragouin m.

gibe [dʒaɪb] vi railler; **to g. at** railler ▮ n raillerie f.

giblets ['dʒɪblɪts] npl (of fowl) abats mpl.

giddy ['gɪdɪ] a (-ier, -iest) **to be** or **feel g.** (at height) avoir le vertige; (in room) avoir un or des vertige(s); **to make s.o. g.** donner le vertige à qn. ● **giddiness** n vertige m.

gift [gɪft] n cadeau m; (talent, donation) don m; **g. voucher** or **token** chèque-cadeau m. ● **gifted** a doué (with de, for pour). ● **giftwrapped** a en paquet-cadeau.

gig [gɪg] n Mus Fam engagement m.

gigantic [dʒaɪˈgæntɪk] a gigantesque.

giggle ['gɪg(ə)l] vi rire (bêtement) ▮ n petit rire m bête; **to have the giggles** avoir le fou rire.

gills [gɪlz] npl (of fish) ouïes fpl.

gimmick ['gɪmɪk] n (trick, object) truc m.

gin [dʒɪn] n (drink) gin m.

ginger ['dʒɪndʒər] 1 a (hair) roux (f rousse). 2 n Bot Culin gingembre m; **g. beer** boisson f gazeuse au gingembre. ● **gingerbread** n pain m d'épice.

gipsy ['dʒɪpsɪ] n bohémien, -ienne mf; (Central European) Tsigane mf.

giraffe [dʒɪˈræf, dʒɪˈrɑ:f] n girafe f.

girder ['gɜ:dər] n (metal beam) poutre f.

girdle ['gɜ:d(ə)l] n (belt) ceinture f; (corset) gaine f.

girl ['gɜ:l] n (petite) fille f, fillette f; (young woman) jeune fille f; (daughter) fille f; **English g.** jeune Anglaise f; **g. guide** éclaireuse f. ● **girlfriend** n amie f; (of boy) petite amie f.

giro ['dʒaɪrəʊ] n (welfare payment) chèque m de paiement d'indemnités (maladie or chômage); **bank g.** virement m bancaire; **g. account** compte m courant postal.

gist [dʒɪst] n **to get the g. of** comprendre l'essentiel de.

give [gɪv] vt (pt gave, pp given) donner (to à); (support) apporter; (a smile, gesture) faire; (a sigh) pousser; (a look) jeter; (a blow) porter; **g. me York 234** (phone number) passez-moi le 234 à York; **to g. way** (of branch, person etc) céder (to à); (collapse) (of roof etc) s'effondrer; Aut céder la priorité (to à) ▮ n (in fabric) élasticité f.

give away vt (free of charge) donner; (prize) distribuer; (secret) révéler; (betray) trahir (qn) ▮ **to give back** vt (return) rendre ▮ **to give in** vi (surrender) céder (to à) ▮ vt (hand in) remettre ▮ **to give off** vt (smell, heat) dégager ▮ **to give out** vt (hand out) distribuer; (news) announcer ▮ vi (of patience) s'épuiser ▮ **to give over** vt (devote) consacrer (to à) ▮ vi **g. over!** (stop) Fam arrête! ▮ **to give up** vi abandonner, renoncer ▮ vt abandonner, renoncer à; (seat) céder (to à); (prisoner) livrer (to à); **to g. up smoking** cesser de fumer.

given ['gɪv(ə)n] a (fixed) donné; **to be g. to doing** (prone to) avoir l'habitude de faire; **g. your age** (in view of) étant donné votre âge.

glacier ['glæsɪər, Am 'gleɪʃər] n glacier m.

glad [glæd] a (person) content (of, about de; that que + sub); **I'm g. to know that...** je suis content de savoir que....

●**gladly** adv (willingly) volontiers.

glamour ['glæmər] n (charm) enchantement m; (splendour) éclat m; (of éclat) prestige m. ●**glamorous** a (person, dress etc) séduisant; (job) prestigieux.

glance [glɑːns] n coup m d'œil ▮ vi jeter un coup d'œil (at à, sur).

gland [glænd] n glande f.

glar/e [gleər] **1** vi to g. at s.o. foudroyer qn (du regard) ▮ n regard m furieux. **2** vi (of sun) briller d'un éclat aveuglant ▮ n éclat m aveuglant. ●—**ing** a (light) éblouissant; (sun) aveuglant; (injustice) flagrant; a g. mistake une faute grossière.

glass [glɑːs] n verre m; (mirror) miroir m, glace f; a pane of g. une vitre, un carreau; g. door porte f vitrée. ●**glasses** npl (spectacles) lunettes fpl. ●**glassful** n (plein) verre m.

glaze [gleɪz] vt (door) vitrer; (pottery) vernisser ▮ n (on pottery) vernis m.

gleam [gliːm] n lueur f ▮ vi (re)luire.

glean [gliːn] vt (information) glaner.

glee [gliː] n joie f. ●**gleeful** a joyeux.

glen [glen] n vallon m.

glib [glɪb] a (person) qui a la parole facile; (speech) peu sincère.

glid/e [glaɪd] vi glisser; (of aircraft, bird) planer. ●—**ing** n Av Sp vol m à voile. ●**glider** n Av planeur m.

glimmer ['glɪmər] vi luire (faiblement) ▮ n (light, of hope etc) lueur f.

glimpse [glɪmps] n aperçu m; to catch or get a g. of entrevoir.

glisten ['glɪs(ə)n] vi (of wet surface) briller; (of water) miroiter.

glitter ['glɪtər] vi scintiller, briller.

gloat [gləʊt] vi jubiler (over à l'idée de).

globe [gləʊb] n globe m. ●**global** a (universal) mondial; (comprehensive) global.

gloom [gluːm] n (sadness) tristesse f; (darkness) obscurité f. ●**gloomy** a (-ier, -iest) (sad) triste; (pessimistic) pessimiste; (dark) sombre.

glorified ['glɔːrɪfaɪd] a it's a g. barn/etc ce n'est guère plus qu'une grange/etc.

glorious ['glɔːrɪəs] a (splendid) magnifique; (full of glory) glorieux.

glory ['glɔːrɪ] n gloire f; (great beauty) splendeur f.

gloss [glɒs] n (shine) brillant m; g. paint peinture f brillante; g. finish brillant m. ●**glossy** a (-ier, -iest) (photo) glacé; (magazine) de luxe.

glossary ['glɒsərɪ] n glossaire m.

glove [glʌv] n gant m; g. compartment Aut (shelf) vide-poches m inv; (enclosed) boîte f à gants.

glow [gləʊ] vi (of sky, fire) rougeoyer; (of lamp) luire; (of eyes, person) Fig rayonner (with de) ▮ n rougeoiement m; (of lamp) lueur f. ●—**ing** a (account, terms etc) très favorable.

glucose ['gluːkəʊs] n glucose m.

glue [gluː] n colle f ▮ vt coller (to, on à); with one's eyes glued to Fam les yeux fixés sur; glued to the television Fam cloué devant la télévision.

glum [glʌm] a (glummer, glummest) triste.

glut [glʌt] n (of goods, oil etc) surplus m (of de).

glutton ['glʌt(ə)n] n glouton, -onne mf; g. for work bourreau m de travail; g. for punishment masochiste mf. ●**gluttony** n gloutonnerie f.

GMT [dʒiːem'tiː] abbr (Greenwich Mean Time) GMT.

gnarled [nɑːld] a noueux.

gnash [næʃ] vt to g. one's teeth grincer des dents.

gnat [næt] n (petit) moustique m.

gnaw [nɔː] vti ronger.

go [gəʊ] **1** vi (3rd person sing pres t goes; pt went; pp gone; pres p going) aller (to à, from de); (depart) partir, s'en aller; (disappear) disparaître, partir; (be sold) se vendre; (function) marcher; (progress) aller, marcher; (become) devenir; (of time) passer; (of hearing, strength) baisser; (of fuse) sauter; (of bulb) griller; (of material) s'user; to go well/badly (of event) se passer bien/mal; she's going to do (is about to, intends to) elle va faire; **it's all gone** (finished) il n'y en a plus; **to go and get** (fetch) aller chercher; **to go and see** aller voir; **to go riding/on a trip/**etc faire du cheval/un voyage/etc; **to let go of** lâcher; **to go to a doctor/**etc aller voir un médecin/etc; **to get things going** faire démarrer les choses; **is there any beer going?** (available) y a-t-il de la bière?; **two hours/**etc **to go** (still left) encore deux heures/etc. **2** n (pl **goes**) (attempt) coup m; (energy) dynamisme m; **to have a go at** (doing) sth essayer (de faire) qch; **at one go** d'un seul coup; **on the go** actif; **to make a go of** sth (make a success of) réussir qch.

go about or **(a)round** vi se déplacer; (of news, rumour) circuler ▌ **to go about** vt (one's duties etc) s'occuper de; **to know how to go about it** savoir s'y prendre ▌ **to go across** vt traverser ▌ vi (cross) traverser; (go) aller (**to** à) ▌ **to go after** vt (chase) poursuivre; (seek) (re)chercher; (job) essayer d'obtenir ▌ **to go against** vi (of result) être défavorable à; (s.o.'s wishes) aller contre ▌ **to go ahead** vi avancer; (continue) continuer; (start) commencer; **go ahead!** allez-y!; **to go ahead with** (plan etc) poursuivre. ● **go-ahead** a dynamique ▌ n **to get the go-ahead** avoir le feu vert ▌ **to go along** vi aller; (move forward, progress) avancer; **to go along with** (agree) être d'accord avec ▌ **to go away** vi partir, s'en aller ▌ **to go back** vi retourner; (in time) remonter; (step back) reculer; **to go back on** (promise) revenir sur ▌ **to go by** vi passer ▌ vt (judge from) juger d'après; (instruction) suivre ▌ **to go down** vi descendre; (fall down) tomber; (of ship) couler; (of sun) se coucher; (of storm) s'apaiser; (of temperature, price) baisser; (of tyre, Am tire) se dégonfler; **to go down well** (of speech) être bien reçu; **to go down with** (illness) attraper ▌ vt **to go down the stairs/street** descendre l'escalier/la rue ▌ **to go for** vt (fetch) aller chercher; (attack) attaquer; (like) Fam aimer

beaucoup ▌ **to go forward(s)** vi avancer ▌ **to go in** vi (r)entrer; (of sun) se cacher; **to go in for** (exam) se présenter à; (hobby, sport) faire ▌ vt **to go in a room/**etc entrer dans une pièce/etc ▌ **to go into** vt (room etc) entrer dans; (question) examiner ▌ **to go off** vi (leave) partir; (go bad) se gâter; (of alarm) se déclencher; (of gun) partir; (of event) se passer ▌ vt (one's food) perdre le goût de ▌ **to go on** vi continuer (**doing** à faire); (travel) poursuivre sa route; (happen) se passer; (last) durer; (of time) passer; **to go on at** (nag) Fam s'en prendre à ▌ **to go out** vi sortir; (of light, fire) s'éteindre; (of newspaper, product) être distribué (**to** à); **to go out to work** travailler (au dehors) ▌ **to go over** vi (go) aller (**to** à); (cross over) traverser; (to enemy) passer (**to** à); **to go over to s.o.('s)** faire un saut chez qn ▌ vt examiner; (in one's mind) repasser; (speech) revoir; (touch up) retoucher ▌ **to go round** vi (turn) tourner; (make a detour) faire le tour; (be sufficient) suffire; **to go round to s.o.('s)** faire un saut chez qn; **enough to go round** assez pour tout le monde ▌ vt (corner) tourner; (world) faire le tour de ▌ **to go through** vi passer ▌ vt (suffer) subir; (examine) examiner; (search) fouiller; (spend) dépenser; (wear out) user; (perform) accomplir; **to go through with** (carry out) aller jusqu'au bout de ▌ **to go under** vi (of ship, person, firm) couler ▌ **to go up** vi monter; (explode) sauter ▌ vt **to go up the stairs/street** monter l'escalier/la rue ▌ **to go without** vi se passer de.

goad [gəʊd] vt **to g. s.o. (on)** aiguillonner qn.

go-ahead ['gəʊəhed] a dynamique ▌ n **to get the g.** avoir le feu vert.

goal [gəʊl] n but m. ● **goalkeeper** n Fb gardien m de but, goal m. ● **goalpost** n Fb poteau m de but.

goat [gəʊt] n chèvre f.

gobble ['gɒb(ə)l] vt **to g. (up)** engloutir

go-between ['gəʊbɪtwiːn] *n* intermédiaire *mf*.

goblin ['gɒblɪn] *n* (*evil spirit*) lutin *m*.

god [gɒd] *n* dieu *m*; G. Dieu *m*; **the gods** *Th Fam* le poulailler. ● **g.-forsaken** *a* (*place*) perdu.

godchild ['gɒdtʃaɪld] *n* (*pl* **-children**) filleul, -eule *mf*. ● **goddaughter** *n* filleule *f*. ● **godfather** *n* parrain *m*. ● **godmother** *n* marraine *f*. ● **godson** *n* filleul *m*.

goddam(n) ['gɒdæm] *a Am Fam* foutu.

goddess ['gɒdɪs] *n* déesse *f*.

godsend ['gɒdsend] *n* **to be a g.** (*of thing, person*) être un don du ciel.

goes [gəʊz] *see* go 1.

gofer ['gəʊfər] *n Am Sl* bonniche *f*.

goggles ['gɒg(ə)lz] *npl* (*spectacles*) lunettes *fpl* (*de protection, de plongée*).

going ['gəʊɪŋ] **1** *n* (*conditions*) conditions *fpl*; **it's hard** *or* **heavy g.** c'est difficile. **2** *a* **the g. price** le prix pratiqué (**for** pour); **the g. rate** le tarif en vigueur; **a g. concern** une entreprise qui marche bien. ● **goings-on** *npl Pej* activités *fpl*.

go-kart ['gəʊkɑːt] *n Sp* kart *m*.

gold [gəʊld] *n* or *m* ▮ *a* (*watch etc*) en or; (*coin, dust*) d'or; **g. medal** *Sp* médaille *f* d'or. ● **golden** *a* (*in colour*) doré; (*rule*) d'or; **a g. opportunity** une occasion en or. ● **goldmine** *n* mine *f* d'or. ● **gold-'plated** *a* plaqué or. ● **goldsmith** *n* orfèvre *m*.

goldfish ['gəʊldfɪʃ] *n* poisson *m* rouge.

golf [gɒlf] *n* golf *m*. ● **golfer** *n* golfeur, -euse *mf*.

gondola ['gɒndələ] *n* (*boat*) gondole *f*.

gone [gɒn] *pp* of go 1 ▮ *a* **it's g. two** *Fam* il est plus de deux heures.

gong [gɒŋ] *n* gong *m*.

goo [guː] *n Fam* truc *m* collant *or* visqueux.

good [gʊd] *a* (**better, best**) bon (*f* bonne); (*kind*) gentil; (*weather*) beau; (*well-behaved*) sage; **my g. friend** mon cher ami; **a g. fellow** *or* **guy** un brave type; **a g. (long) walk** une bonne promenade; **very g.!** (*all right*) très bien!; **that's g. of**

you c'est gentil de ta part; **to feel g.** se sentir bien; **that isn't g. enough** (*bad*) ça ne va pas; (*not sufficient*) ça ne suffit pas; **it's g. for us** ça nous fait du bien; **g. at French**/*etc* (*at school*) bon *m* (en français/*etc*); **to be g. with** (*children*) savoir s'y prendre avec; **it's a g. thing (that)...** heureusement que...; **a g. many, a g. deal (of)** beaucoup (**of** de); **as g. as** (*almost*) pratiquement; **g. afternoon, g. morning** bonjour; (*on leaving*) au revoir; **g. evening** bonsoir; **g. night** bonsoir; (*before going to bed*) bonne nuit.

▮ *n* (*advantage, virtue*) bien *m*; **for her own g.** pour son bien; **for the g. of** (*one's family etc*) pour; **it will do you g.** ça te fera du bien; **it's no g. crying/shouting/** *etc* ça ne sert à rien de pleurer/crier/*etc*; **that's no g.** (*worthless*) ça ne vaut rien; (*not all right, bad*) ça ne va pas; **what's the g. of crying/**etc? à quoi bon pleurer/*etc*?; **for g.** (*to leave etc*) pour de bon. ● **g.-for-nothing** *a & n* propre à rien (*mf*). ● **g.-'looking** *a* beau (*f* belle).

goodbye! [gʊd'baɪ] *int* au revoir!

goodness ['gʊdnɪs] *n* bonté *f*; **my g.!** mon Dieu!

goods [gʊdz] *npl* marchandises *fpl*; (*articles for sale*) articles *mpl*; **g. train** train *m* de marchandises.

goodwill [gʊd'wɪl] *n* bonne volonté *f*; (*zeal*) zèle *m*.

gooey ['guːɪ] *a Fam* gluant, poisseux.

goof [guːf] *vi* **to g. (up)** (*blunder*) *Am* faire une gaffe.

goose, *pl* **geese** [guːs, giːs] *n* oie *f*; **g. pimples** *or* **bumps** chair *f* de poule. ● **gooseflesh** *n* chair *f* de poule.

gooseberry ['gʊzbərɪ, *Am* 'guːsberɪ] *n* groseille *f* à maquereau.

gorge [gɔːdʒ] **1** *n* (*ravine*) gorge *f*. **2** *vt* **to g. oneself** se gaver (**on** de).

gorgeous ['gɔːdʒəs] *a* magnifique.

gorilla [gə'rɪlə] *n* gorille *m*.

gormless ['gɔːmləs] *a Fam* stupide.

gorse [gɔːs] *n inv* ajonc(s) *m(pl)*.

gory ['gɔːrɪ] *a* (**-ier, -iest**) (*bloody*) san-

glant; (details) Fig horrible.
gosh! [gɒʃ] int Fam mince (alors)!
go-slow [gəʊ'sləʊ] n (strike) grève f perlée.
gospel ['gɒspəl] n évangile m.
gossip ['gɒsɪp] n (talk) bavardage(s) m(pl); (malicious) cancan(s) m(pl); (person) commère f ‖ vi bavarder; (maliciously) cancaner.
got [gɒt] pt & Br pp of get.
Gothic ['gɒθɪk] a gothique.
gotten ['gɒt(ə)n] Am pp of get.
gourmet ['gʊəmeɪ] n gourmet m; g. restaurant restaurant m gastronomique.
gout [gaʊt] n Med goutte f.
govern ['gʌvən] vt (rule) gouverner; (city, province) administrer; (emotion) maîtriser; (influence) déterminer ‖ vi Pol gouverner; **governing body** conseil m d'administration. ● **governess** n gouvernante f.
government ['gʌvənmənt] n gouvernement m; (local) administration f.
governor ['gʌvənər] n gouverneur m; (of school) administrateur, -trice mf.
gown [gaʊn] n (of woman) robe f; (of judge, lecturer) toge f.
GP [dʒiː'piː] n abbr (general practitioner) (médecin m) généraliste m.
grab [græb] vt (-bb-) to g. (hold of) saisir; to g. sth from s.o. arracher qch à qn.
grace [greɪs] 1 n (charm, gracefulness) & Rel grâce f; (extension of time) délai m de grâce; **10 days' g.** 10 jours de grâce. 2 vt (adorn) orner; (honour) honorer (with de). ● **graceful** a gracieux. ● **gracefully** adv (to dance etc) avec grâce.
gracious ['greɪʃəs] a (kind) aimable (to envers).
grade [greɪd] n catégorie f; Mil grade m; (of product) qualité f; (level) niveau m; (in exam etc) note f; (class in school) Am classe f; **g. school** Am école f primaire; **g. crossing** Am passage m à niveau ‖ vt (classify) classer; (colours etc) graduer; (school paper) noter.
gradient ['greɪdɪənt] n (slope) inclinaison

f.
gradual ['grædʒʊəl] a progressif; (slope) doux (f douce). ●—**ly** adv progressivement, peu à peu.
graduate ['grædʒʊeɪt] vi Univ obtenir son diplôme; Am Sch obtenir son baccalauréat; to g. from sortir de ‖ ['grædʒʊət] n diplômé, -ée mf, licencié, -ée mf. ● **graduation** [-'eɪʃ(ə)n] n Univ remise f des diplômes.
graduated ['grædʒʊeɪtɪd] a (tube etc) gradué.
graffiti [grə'fiːtɪ] npl graffiti mpl.
graft [grɑːft] n Med Bot greffe f ‖ vt greffer (on to à).
grain [greɪn] n (seed) grain m; (cereals) céréales fpl; (in wood) fibre f; (in leather, paper) grain m.
gram(me) [græm] n gramme m.
grammar ['græmər] n grammaire f; g. school Br lycée m. ● **gra'mmatical** a grammatical.
grand [grænd] 1 a (-er, -est) (splendid) magnifique; (style) grandiose; (gesture) majestueux; g. piano piano m à queue; the g. tour (of town etc) la visite complète. 2 n inv Am Sl mille dollars mpl; Br Sl mille livres fpl.
grandchild ['græntʃaɪld] n (pl -children) petit(e)-enfant mf. ● **grand(d)ad** n Fam papi m. ● **granddaughter** n petite-fille f. ● **grandfather** n grand-père m. ● **grandma** [-mɑː] n Fam mamie f. ● **grandmother** n grand-mère f. ● **grandpa** [-pɑː] n Fam papi m. ● **grandparents** npl grands-parents mpl. ● **grandson** n petit-fils m.
grandstand ['grænstænd] n Sp tribune f.
granite ['grænɪt] n granit(e) m.
granny ['grænɪ] n Fam mamie f.
grant [grɑːnt] 1 vt accorder (to à); (request) accéder à; (prayer, wish) exaucer; (admit) admettre (that que); to take sth for granted considérer qch comme acquis; I take it for granted that... je présume que.... 2 n subvention f; (for study) Univ bourse f.

granulated ['grænjʊleɪtɪd] *a* g. **sugar** sucre *m* cristallisé.

grape [greɪp] *n* grain *m* de raisin; *pl* le raisin, les raisins *mpl*; **to eat (some) grapes** manger du raisin *or* des raisins.

grapefruit ['greɪpfruːt] *n* pamplemousse *m*.

graph [græf, grɑːf] *n* courbe *f*; **g. paper** papier *m* millimétré.

graphic ['græfɪk] *a* (*description*) explicite, vivant; (*art*) graphique; **g. design** arts *mpl* graphiques. ● **graphics** *npl* *Comptr* graphiques *mpl*.

grapple ['græp(ə)l] *vi* **to g. with** (*person, problem*) se colleter avec.

grasp [grɑːsp] *vt* (*seize, understand*) saisir ▮ *n* (*firm hold*) prise *f*; (*understanding*) compréhension *f*; (*knowledge*) connaissance *f*; **within s.o.'s g.** (*reach*) à la portée de qn.

grass [grɑːs] *n* herbe *f*; (*lawn*) gazon *m*; **the g. roots** *Pol* la base. ● **grasshopper** *n* sauterelle *f*. ● **grassland** *n* prairie *f*.

grat/e [greɪt] **1** *n* (*for fireplace*) grille *f* de foyer. **2** *vt* (*cheese etc*) râper. **3** *vi* (*of sound*) grincer (**on sth** sur qch); **to g. on the ears** écorcher les oreilles. ● **-ing 1** *a* (*sound*) grinçant. **2** *n* (*bars*) grille *f*. ● **grater** *n* *Culin* râpe *f*.

grateful ['greɪtfəl] *a* reconnaissant (**to** à, **for** de); (*words, letter*) de remerciement; (*attitude*) plein de reconnaissance; **I'm g. (to you) for your help** je vous suis reconnaissant de votre aide; **g. thanks** mes sincères remerciements.

gratified ['grætɪfaɪd] *a* (*pleased*) très content (**by sth** de qch, **to do** de faire). ● **gratifying** *a* très satisfaisant *or* agréable.

gratis ['grætɪs] *adv* gratis.

gratitude ['grætɪtjuːd] *n* reconnaissance *f*, gratitude *f* (**for** de).

gratuity [grə'tjuːɪtɪ] *n* (*tip*) pourboire *m*.

grave[1] [greɪv] *n* tombe *f*; **g. digger** fossoyeur *m*. ● **gravestone** *n* pierre *f* tombale. ● **graveyard** *n* cimetière *m*; **auto g.** *Am Fam* cimetière *m* de voitures.

grave[2] [greɪv] *a* (**-er, -est**) (*serious*) grave.

gravel ['græv(ə)l] *n* gravier *m*.

gravitate ['grævɪteɪt] *vi* **to g. towards** (*be drawn towards*) être attiré vers; (*move towards*) se diriger vers.

gravity ['grævɪtɪ] *n* **1** *Phys* pesanteur *f*. **2** (*seriousness*) gravité *f*.

gravy ['greɪvɪ] *n* jus *m* de viande.

gray [greɪ] *a* & *vi Am* = **grey**.

graze [greɪz] **1** *vt* (*scrape*) écorcher; (*touch lightly*) frôler ▮ *n* (*wound*) écorchure *f*. **2** *vi* (*of cattle*) paître.

grease [griːs] *n* graisse *f* ▮ *vt* graisser. ● **greaseproof** (**paper**) *a* & *n* papier *m* sulfurisé. ● **greasy** *a* (**-ier, -iest**) plein de graisse; (*hair*) gras.

great [greɪt] *a* (**-er, -est**) grand; (*excellent*) *Fam* magnifique; **a g. deal** *or* **number (of), a g. many** beaucoup (de); **a very g. age** un âge très avancé; **the greatest team**/*etc* (*best*) la meilleure équipe/*etc*; **Greater London** le grand Londres. ● **g.-'grandfather** *n* arrière-grand-père *m*. ● **g.-'grandmother** *n* arrière-grand-mère *f*.

Great Britain [greɪt'brɪt(ə)n] *n* Grande-Bretagne *f*.

greatly ['greɪtlɪ] *adv* (*much*) beaucoup; (*very*) très; **I g. prefer** je préfère de beaucoup.

Greece [griːs] *n* Grèce *f*.

greed [griːd] *n* avidité *f* (**for** de); (*for food*) gourmandise *f*. ● **greedy** *a* (**-ier, -iest**) avide (**for** de); (*for food*) glouton (*f* -onne), gourmand.

Greek [griːk] *a* grec (*f* grecque) ▮ *n* Grec *m*, Grecque *f*; (*language*) grec *m*.

green [griːn] *a* (**-er, -est**) vert; (*immature*) *Fig* inexpérimenté; *Pol* vert, écologiste; **to turn** *or* **go g.** devenir vert; (*of garden etc*) verdir; **to get the g. light** avoir le (feu) vert; **g. with envy** *Fig* vert de jalousie; **g. card** *US* permis *m* de travail.

▮ *n* (*colour*) vert *m*; (*lawn*) pelouse *f*; (*village square*) place *f* gazonnée; *pl* (*vegetables*) légumes *mpl* verts; **the**

Greens *Pol* les Verts. ● **greenery** *n* (*plants, leaves*) verdure *f*. ● **greengrocer** *n* marchand, -ande *mf* de légumes. ● **greenhouse** *n* serre *f*; **the g. effect** l'effet *m* de serre.

Greenland ['gri:nlənd] *n* Groenland *m*.

greet [gri:t] *vt* (*with a nod etc*) saluer (*qn*); (*welcome, receive*) accueillir; **to g. s.o.** (*of sight*) s'offrir aux regards de qn. ● **—ing** *n* salutation *f*; (*welcome*) accueil *m*; *pl* (*for birthday, festival*) vœux *mpl*; **greetings card** carte *f* de vœux.

grenade [grə'neɪd] *n* (*bomb*) grenade *f*.

grew [gru:] *pt of* grow.

grey [greɪ] *a* (*-er, -est*) gris; (*pale*) (*complexion*) blême; **to be going g.** grisonner ▮ *vi* **to be greying** être grisonnant. ● **g.-'haired** *a* aux cheveux gris. ● **greyhound** *n* lévrier *m*.

grid [grɪd] *n* (*grating, on map*) grille *f*.

griddle ['grɪd(ə)l] *n* (*on stove*) plaque *f* à griller.

grief [gri:f] *n* chagrin *m*, douleur *f*; **to come to g.** (*of driver, pilot etc*) avoir un accident; (*of plan*) échouer.

grieve [gri:v] *vi* s'affliger (*over sth de* qch); **to g. for s.o.** pleurer qn ▮ *vt* peiner, affliger. ● **grievance** *n* grief *m*; *pl* (*complaints*) doléances *fpl*; **to have a g. against s.o.** avoir à se plaindre de qn.

grill [grɪl] *n* (*utensil*) gril *m*; (*dish*) grillade *f* ▮ *vti* griller.

grille [grɪl] *n* (*metal bars*) grille *f*.

grim [grɪm] *a* (*grimmer, grimmest*) (*face, future*) sombre; (*horrifying*) sinistre; (*bad*) *Fam* affreux; **a g. determination** une volonté inflexible.

grimace ['grɪməs] *n* grimace *f* ▮ *vi* grimacer.

grime [graɪm] *n* crasse *f*. ● **grimy** *a* (*-ier, -iest*) crasseux.

grin [grɪn] *vi* (*-nn-*) avoir un large sourire ▮ *n* large sourire *m*.

grind [graɪnd] **1** *vt* (*pt & pp* ground) (*coffee, pepper etc*) moudre; (*meat*) *Am* hacher; (*blade, tool*) aiguiser; **to g. one's teeth** grincer des dents ▮ *vi* **to** **to a halt** s'arrêter (progressivement). **2** *n* (*work, routine*) *Fam* corvée *f*. ● **grinder** *n* **coffee g.** moulin *m* à café.

grip [grɪp] *vt* (*-pp-*) (*seize*) saisir; (*hold*) tenir serré; (*of story*) *Fig* empoigner (*qn*) ▮ *n* (*hold*) prise *f*; (*with hand*) poigne *f*; (*on situation*) contrôle *m*; (*handle*) poignée *f*; **to get to grips with** (*problem*) s'attaquer à; **in the g. of** (*despair etc*) en proie à. ● **gripping** *a* (*film etc*) passionnant.

grisly ['grɪzlɪ] *a* (*gruesome*) horrible.

gristle ['grɪs(ə)l] *n* *Culin* cartilage *m*.

grit [grɪt] **1** *n* (*sand*) sable *m*; (*gravel*) gravillon *m* ▮ *vt* (*-tt-*) (*road*) sabler. **2** *n* (*courage*) *Fam* cran *m*. **3** *vt* (*-tt-*) **to g.** **one's teeth** serrer les dents.

groan [grəʊn] *vi* (*with pain, as a complaint*) gémir ▮ *n* gémissement *m*.

grocer ['grəʊsər] *n* épicier, -ière *mf*; **g.'s shop** épicerie *f*. ● **grocery** *n* (*shop*) *Am* épicerie *f*; *pl* (*food*) provisions *fpl*.

groggy ['grɒgɪ] *a* (*-ier, -iest*) (*shaky*) pas solide sur les jambes; (*from a blow*) groggy.

groin [grɔɪn] *n* *Anat* aine *f*; (*genitals*) bas-ventre *m*.

groom [gru:m] **1** *n* (*bridegroom*) marié *m*. **2** *n* (*for horses*) lad *m* ▮ *vt* (*horse*) panser; **well groomed** (*person*) très soigné.

groove [gru:v] *n* (*slot for sliding door etc*) rainure *f*.

grope [grəʊp] *vi* **to g. (about)** tâtonner; **to g. for** chercher à tâtons.

gross [grəʊs] *a* **1** (*total*) (*weight, income*) brut; **g. national product** *Econ* produit *m* national brut. **2** (*-er, -est*) (*coarse*) grossier; (*injustice*) flagrant. ● **—ly** *adv* (*very*) extrêmement.

grotesque [grəʊ'tesk] *a* (*ludicrous*) grotesque; (*frightening*) monstrueux.

grotto ['grɒtəʊ] *n* (*pl* -oes *or* -os) grotte *f*.

grotty ['grɒtɪ] *a* (*-ier, -iest*) *Fam* (*ugly*) moche; (*of poor quality*) nul.

ground[1] [graʊnd] **1** *n* terre *f*, sol *m*; (*for camping, football etc*) terrain *m*; (*electrical wire*) *Am* terre *f*; *pl* (*reasons*) raisons *fpl*, motifs *mpl*; (*gardens*) parc *m*; **on the g.** (*lying, sitting*) par terre; **to lose g.** perdre du terrain; **g. crew** (*at airport*) personnel *m* au sol; **g. floor** rez-de-chaussée *m inv*; **g. frost** gelée *f* blanche.

2 *vt* (*aircraft*) bloquer *or* retenir au sol. ● **grounding** *n* connaissances *fpl* (de fond) (**in** en). ● **groundnut** *n* arachide *f*. ● **groundsheet** *n* tapis *m* de sol. ● **groundwork** *n* préparation *f*.

ground² [graʊnd] *pt & pp of* **grind** ‖ *a* (*coffee*) moulu; **g. meat** viande *f* hachée ‖ *npl* (*coffee*) **grounds** marc *m* (de café).

group [gruːp] *n* groupe *m* ‖ *vt* **to g. (together)** grouper ‖ *vi* se grouper. ● **—ing** *n* (*group*) groupe *m*.

grove [graʊv] *n* bocage *m*.

grovel [ˈgrɒv(ə)l] *vi* (**-ll-**, *Am* **-l-**) *Pej* ramper, s'aplatir (**to s.o.** devant qn).

grow [graʊ] *vi* (*pt* **grew**, *pp* **grown**) (*of person*) grandir; (*of plant, hair*) pousser; (*increase*) augmenter, grandir; (*of firm, town*) se développer; **to g. fat(ter)** grossir; **to g. to like** finir par aimer; **to g. into** devenir; **to g. out of** (*one's clothes*) devenir trop grand pour; (*a habit*) perdre; **to g. up** devenir adulte; **when I g. up** quand je serai grand.

‖ *vt* (*plant, crops*) cultiver; (*beard, hair*) laisser pousser. ● **growing** *a* (*child*) qui grandit; (*number, discontent*) grandissant. ● **grown** *a* (*man, woman*) adulte. ● **grown-up** *n* grande personne *f*, adulte *mf*.

growl [graʊl] *vi* grogner (**at** contre) ‖ *n* grognement *m*.

growth [graʊθ] *n* croissance *f*; (*increase*) augmentation *f* (**in** de); (*lump*) *Med* tumeur *f* (**on** à).

grub [grʌb] *n* (*food*) *Fam* bouffe *f*.

grubby [ˈgrʌbɪ] *a* (**-ier, -iest**) sale.

grudg/e [grʌdʒ] **1** *n* rancune *f*; **to have a g. against s.o.** garder rancune à qn. **2** *vt* (*give*) donner à contrecœur; (*reproach*) reprocher (**s.o. sth** qch à qn); **to g. doing sth** faire qch à contrecœur. ● **—ingly** *adv* (*to give etc*) à contrecœur.

gruelling, *Am* **grueling** [ˈgruəlɪŋ] *a* (*day, detail etc*) éprouvant, atroce.

gruesome [ˈgruːsəm] *a* horrible.

gruff [grʌf] *a* (**-er, -est**) (*voice, person*) bourru.

grumble [ˈgrʌmb(ə)l] *vi* (*complain*) râler, grogner (**about, at** contre).

grumpy [ˈgrʌmpɪ] *a* (**-ier, -iest**) grincheux.

grunt [grʌnt] *vti* grogner ‖ *n* grognement *m*.

guarantee [gærənˈtiː] *n* garantie *f* ‖ *vt* garantir (**against** contre); **to g. s.o. that** garantir à qn que. ● **guarantor** *n* garant, -ante *mf*.

guard [gɑːd] *n* (*vigilance, soldiers etc*) garde *f*; (*individual person*) garde *m*; *Rail* chef *m* de train; **to keep a g. on** surveiller; **under g.** sous surveillance; **on one's g.** sur ses gardes; **to catch s.o. off his g.** prendre qn au dépourvu; **on g. (duty)** de garde; **to stand g.** monter la garde.

‖ *vt* (*protect*) protéger (**against** contre); (*watch over*) surveiller, garder.

‖ *vi* **to g. against** (*protect oneself*) se prémunir contre; (*prevent*) empêcher. ● **guardian** *n* (*of child*) *Jur* tuteur, -trice *mf*; (*protector*) gardien, -ienne *mf*.

guerrilla [gəˈrɪlə] *n* (*person*) guérillero *m*; **g. warfare** guérilla *f*.

guess [ges] *n* conjecture *f*; (*intuition*) intuition *f*; (*estimate*) estimation *f*; **to make a g.** (essayer de) deviner; **at a g.** à vue de nez ‖ *vt* deviner (**that** que); (*length, number etc*) estimer; (*suppose*) *Am* supposer (**that** que); (*think*) *Am* croire (**that** que) ‖ *vi* deviner; **I g.** *Am* je suppose; je crois. ● **guesswork** *n* hypothèse *f*; **by g.** à vue de nez.

guest [gest] *n* invité, -ée *mf*; (*in hotel*) client, -ente *mf*; (*at meal*) convive *mf*; **our g. speaker/etc** le conférencier/etc qui est notre invité. ● **guesthouse** *n* pension *f* de famille. ● **guestroom** *n* chambre *f* d'ami.

guffaw [gəˈfɔː] *vi* rire bruyamment.

guidance ['gaɪdəns] n (*advice*) conseils mpl.

guid/e [gaɪd] n (*person*) guide m; (*indication*) indication f; g. (**book**) guide m; (*girl*) g. éclaireuse f; g. **dog** chien m d'aveugle ▮ vt (*lead*) guider. ●—**ed** a (*missile*) guidé; g. **tour** visite f guidée. ● **guidelines** npl indications fpl (à suivre).

guild [gɪld] n association f.

guillotine ['gɪləti:n] n (*for execution*) guillotine f.

guilt [gɪlt] n culpabilité f. ● **guilty** a (-**ier**, -**iest**) coupable; g. **person** coupable mf; **to find s.o. g./not g.** déclarer qn coupable/non coupable.

guinea pig ['gɪnɪpɪg] n (*animal*) & Fig cobaye m.

guise [gaɪz] n **under the g. of** sous l'apparence de.

guitar [gɪ'tɑːr] n guitare f. ● **guitarist** n guitariste mf.

gulf [gʌlf] n (*in sea*) golfe m; (*chasm*) gouffre m; **a g. between** Fig un abîme entre.

gull [gʌl] n (*bird*) mouette f.

gullible ['gʌlɪb(ə)l] a crédule.

gulp [gʌlp] **1** vt **to g.** (**down**) avaler (vite) ▮ n (*of drink*) gorgée f. **2** vi (*with emotion*) avoir la gorge serrée.

gum¹ [gʌm] n Anat gencive f.

gum² [gʌm] **1** n (*glue*) colle f ▮ vt (-**mm**-) coller. **2** n (*for chewing*) chewing-gum m.

gun [gʌn] n pistolet m, revolver m; (*rifle*)

fusil m; (*firing shells*) canon m ▮ vt (-**nn**-) **to g. down** abattre. ● **gunfight** n échange m de coups de feu. ● **gunfire** n coups mpl de feu; Mil tir m d'artillerie. ● **gunman** n (pl -**men**) bandit m armé. ● **gunpoint** n **at g.** sous la menace d'une arme. ● **gunpowder** n poudre f à canon. ● **gunshot** n coup m de feu; g. **wound** blessure f par balle.

gunge [gʌndʒ] n Fam magma m.

gurgle ['gɜːg(ə)l] vi (*of water*) glouglouter; (*of baby*) gazouiller.

gush [gʌʃ] vi **to g.** (**out**) jaillir (**of** de).

gust [gʌst] n g. (**of wind**) rafale f (de vent). ● **gusty** a (-**ier**, -**iest**) (*weather*) venteux; (*day*) de vent.

gusto ['gʌstəʊ] n **with g.** avec entrain.

gut [gʌt] **1** n Anat intestin m; pl Fam (*insides*) ventre m; (*courage*) cran m. **2** vt (-**tt**-) (*of fire*) ne laisser que les quatre murs de (*maison etc*).

gutter ['gʌtər] n (*on roof*) gouttière f; (*in street*) caniveau m.

guy [gaɪ] n (*fellow*) Fam type m.

guzzle ['gʌz(ə)l] vi (*eat*) bâfrer ▮ vt (*eat*) engloutir (*qch*); (*drink*) siffler (*qch*).

gym [dʒɪm] n gym(nastique) f; (*gymnasium*) gymnase m; g. **shoes** tennis fpl or mpl. ● **gymnasium** [-'neɪzɪəm] n gymnase m. ● **gymnast** n gymnaste mf. ● **gym'nastics** n gymnastique f.

gynaecologist, Am **gynecologist** [gaɪnɪ'kɒlədʒɪst] n gynécologue mf.

gypsy ['dʒɪpsɪ] n = **gipsy.**

H

H, h [eɪtʃ] *n* H, h *m*; **H bomb** bombe *f* H.

haberdasher ['hæbədæʃər] *n* mercier, -ière *mf*; (*men's outfitter*) *Am* chemisier *m*.

habit ['hæbɪt] *n* **1** habitude *f*; **to be in/get into the h.** of doing avoir/prendre l'habitude de faire. **2** (*addiction*) *Med* accoutumance *f*; **a h.-forming drug** une drogue qui crée une accoutumance. **3** (*of monk, nun*) habit *m*.

habitual [hə'bɪtʃʊəl] *a* habituel; (*smoker etc*) invétéré.

habitat ['hæbɪtæt] *n* (*of animal, plant*) habitat *m*.

hack [hæk] **1** *vt* (*cut*) tailler. **2** *n* **h.** (**writer**) *Pej* écrivaillon *m*.

hacker ['hækər] *n Comptr* pirate *m* (informatique).

hackneyed ['hæknɪd] *a* (*saying*) rebattu.

had [hæd] *pt & pp of* have.

haddock ['hædək] *n* (*fish*) aiglefin *m*; **smoked h.** haddock *m*.

haemorrhage ['hemərɪdʒ] *n Med* hémorragie *f*.

haemorrhoids ['hemərɔɪdz] *npl* hémorroïdes *fpl*.

hag [hæg] *n* (**old**) **h.** (vieille) sorcière *f*.

haggard ['hægəd] *a* (*person, face*) hâve, émacié.

haggl/e ['hæg(ə)l] *vi* marchander; **to h. over** (*article*) marchander; (*price*) discuter. ●**—ing** *n* marchandage *m*.

Hague (The) [ðə'heɪg] *n* La Haye.

ha-ha! [hɑː'hɑː] *int* (*laughter*) ha, ha!

hail¹ [heɪl] *n Met & Fig* grêle *f* ‖ *vi Met* grêler; **it's hailing** il grêle. ●**hailstone** *n* grêlon *m*.

hail² [heɪl] **1** *vt* (*greet*) saluer; (*taxi*) héler. **2** *vi* **to h. from** (*of person*) être originaire de.

hair [heər] *n* (*on head*) cheveux *mpl*; (*on body, of animal*) poils *mpl*; **a h.** (*on*

head) un cheveu; (*on body, of animal*) un poil; **h. cream** brillantine *f*; **h. dryer** sèche-cheveux *m inv*; **h. spray** (bombe *f* de) laque *f*.

hairbrush ['heəbrʌʃ] *n* brosse *f* à cheveux. ●**haircut** *n* coupe *f* de cheveux; **to have a h.** se faire couper les cheveux. ●**hairdo** *n* (*pl* **-dos**) *Fam* coiffure *f*. ●**hairdresser** *n* coiffeur, -euse *mf*. ●**hairnet** *n* résille *f*. ●**hairpin** *n* épingle *f* à cheveux; **h. bend** *Aut* virage *m* en épingle à cheveux. ●**hair-raising** *a* effrayant. ●**hairslide** *n* barrette *f*. ●**hairstyle** *n* coiffure *f*.

-haired [heəd] *suff* long-/red-/etc haired aux cheveux longs/roux/etc.

hairy ['heərɪ] *a* (**-ier, -iest**) (*person, animal, body*) poilu; (*frightening*) *Fam* effrayant.

hake [heɪk] *n* (*fish*) colin *m*.

half [hɑːf] *n* (*pl* **halves**) moitié *f*, demi, -ie *mf*; (*of match*) *Sp* mi-temps *f*; **h. (of) the apple/**etc la moitié de la pomme/etc; **ten and a h.** dix et demi; **ten and a h. weeks** dix semaines et demie; **to cut in h.** couper en deux.

‖ *a* demi; **a h. a day, a h.-day** une demi-journée; **h. a dozen, a h.-dozen** une demi-douzaine; **at h. price** à moitié prix; **h. man h. beast** mi-homme mi-bête ‖ *adv* (*dressed, full etc*) à moitié, à demi; (*almost*) presque; **h. asleep** à moitié endormi; **h. past one** une heure et demie; **he isn't h. lazy/**etc *Fam* il est drôlement paresseux/etc; **h. as much as** moitié moins que.

half-back ['hɑːfbæk] *n Fb* demi *m*. ●**h.-'baked** *a* (*idea*) *Fam* à la manque. ●**h.-caste** *n* métis, -isse *mf*. ●**h.-'dozen** *n* demi-douzaine *f*. ●**h.-'hearted** *a* (*person, manner*) peu enthousiaste. ●**h.-'hour** *n* demi-heure *f*. ●**h.-'mast**

at h.-mast (*flag*) en berne. ●h.-'open *a* entrouvert. ●h.-'price *a* & *adv* à demi-prix. ●h.-'term *n* (*in British school*) petites vacances *fpl*. ●h.-'time *n* Sp mi-temps *f*. ●half'way *adv* à mi-chemin (*between entre*); to fill/*etc* h. remplir/*etc* à moitié; h. through (*book*) à la moitié de. ●h.-'wit *n* imbécile *mf*.

halibut ['hælɪbət] *n* (*fish*) flétan *m*.

hall [hɔːl] *n* (*room*) salle *f*; (*house entrance*) entrée *f*; (*of hotel*) hall *m*; (*mansion*) manoir *m*; h. of residence *Univ* résidence *f* universitaire; halls of residence cité *f* universitaire; lecture h. *Univ* amphithéâtre *m*.

hallmark ['hɔːlmɑːk] *n* (*on silver or gold*) poinçon *m*.

hallo! [hə'ləʊ] *int* = hello.

Hallowe'en [hæləʊ'iːn] *n* la veille de la Toussaint.

hallstand ['hɔːlstænd] *n* portemanteau *m*.

hallucination [həluːsɪ'neɪʃ(ə)n] *n* hallucination *f*.

hallway ['hɔːlweɪ] *n* entrée *f*.

halo ['heɪləʊ] *n* (*pl* -oes *or* -os) auréole *f*.

halt [hɔːlt] *n* halte *f*; to call a h. to mettre fin à ▮ *vi* (*of soldiers etc*) faire halte; (*of production etc*) s'arrêter ▮ *vt* arrêter ▮ *int* Mil halte!

halve [hɑːv] *vt* (*time, expense*) réduire de moitié, (*number*) diviser en deux.

ham [hæm] *n* jambon *m*; h. and eggs œufs *mpl* au jambon.

hamburger ['hæmbɜːgər] *n* hamburger *m*.

hammer ['hæmər] *n* marteau *m* ▮ *vt* (*nail*) enfoncer (into dans); (*metal*) marteler; (*defeat*) Fam battre à plate(s) couture(s); to h. out (*agreement*) mettre au point ▮ *vi* frapper (au marteau). ●—ing *n* (*defeat*) Fam raclée *f*.

hammock ['hæmək] *n* hamac *m*.

hamper ['hæmpər] 1 *vt* gêner. 2 *n* (*basket*) panier *m* (*à provisions*); (*laundry basket*) Am panier *m* à linge.

hamster ['hæmstər] *n* hamster *m*.

hand¹ [hænd] 1 *n* main *f*; to hold in one's h. tenir à la main; by h. (*to make, sew etc*) à la main; at *or* to h. (*within reach*) sous la main; (close) at h. (*person*) tout près; (*day etc*) proche; in h. (*situation*) bien en main; the matter in h. l'affaire *f* en question; on h. (*ready for use*) disponible; on the one h.... d'une part...; on the other h.... d'autre part...; hands up! (*in attack*) haut les mains!; (*to schoolchildren*) levez la main!; hands off! pas touche!; to give s.o. a (helping) h. donner un coup de main à qn; out of h. (*child*) impossible; (*situation*) incontrôlable; h. in h. la main dans la main; h. in h. with (*together with*) Fig de pair avec; at first h. de première main; h. luggage bagages *mpl* à main.

2 *n* (*worker*) ouvrier, -ière *mf*; (*of clock*) aiguille *f*; Cards jeu *m*.

hand² [hænd] *vt* (*give*) donner (to à); to h. down (*bring down*) descendre; (*knowledge*) transmettre (to à); to h. in remettre; to h. out distribuer; to h. over remettre; (*power*) transmettre; to h. round (*cakes*) passer.

handbag ['hændbæg] *n* sac *m* à main. ●handbook *n* (*manual*) manuel *m*; (*guide*) guide *m*. ●handbrake *n* frein *m* à main. ●handbrush *n* balayette *f*. ●handcuff *vt* passer les menottes à; to be handcuffed avoir les menottes aux poignets. ●handcuffs *npl* menottes *fpl*. ●hand'made *a* fait à la main. ●hand'picked *a* (*team member etc*) trié sur le volet. ●handrail *n* (*on stairs*) rampe *f*. ●handshake *n* poignée *f* de main. ●hands-on *a* (*experience*) pratique. ●handwriting *n* écriture *f*. ●hand'written *a* écrit à la main.

handful ['hændfʊl] *n* (*bunch*) poignée *f*; she's (quite) a h. elle est difficile.

handicap ['hændɪkæp] *n* (*disadvantage*) & Sp handicap *m* ▮ *vt* (-pp-) handicaper; to be handicapped (*after accident*) rester handicapé. ●handicapped *a* (*disabled*) handicapé.

handicraft ['hændıkrɑːft] n artisanat m
d'art. ●**handiwork** n (action) ouvrage m.
handkerchief ['hæŋkətʃıf] n (pl -fs)
mouchoir m.
handle ['hænd(ə)l] 1 n (of door) poignée
f; (of knife) manche m; (of bucket) anse
f; (of saucepan) queue f; (of pump) bras
m. 2 vt (manipulate) manier; (touch)
toucher à; (vehicle, ship) manœuvrer;
(deal with) s'occuper de.
handlebars ['hænd(ə)lbɑːz] npl guidon
m.
handout ['hændaʊt] n (leaflet) prospectus m; (money) aumône f.
handsome ['hænsəm] a (person, building
etc) beau (f belle); (profit) considérable;
(gift) généreux.
handy ['hændı] a (-ier, -iest) (convenient,
practical) commode, pratique; (skilful)
habile (at doing à faire); (within reach)
sous la main; (place) accessible; to come
in h. se révéler utile. ●**handyman** n (pl
-men) (DIY enthusiast) bricoleur m;
(workman) homme m à tout faire.
hang[1] [hæŋ] 1 vt (pt & pp hung) suspendre (on, from à); (on hook) accrocher (on, from à), suspendre;
(wallpaper) poser; (let dangle) laisser
pendre (from, out of de) ▌ vi (dangle)
pendre; (of fog, smoke) flotter. 2 to get
the h. of sth Fam arriver à comprendre
qch; to get the h. of doing Fam trouver
le truc pour faire. ●—**ing**[1] a suspendu
(from à); h. on (wall) accroché à.
hang[2] [hæŋ] vt (pt & pp hanged) (criminal) pendre (for pour) ▌ vi (of criminal)
être pendu. ●—**ing**[2] n Jur pendaison f.
●**hangman** n (pl -men) bourreau m.
hang about vi (loiter) traîner; (wait) Fam
attendre ▌to hang down vi (dangle)
pendre; (of hair) tomber ▌to hang on
vi (hold out) résister; (wait) Fam attendre; to h. on to (cling to) ne pas
lâcher; (keep) garder ▌to hang out vi
(washing) étendre; (flag) arborer ▌vi (of
shirt, tongue) pendre ▌to hang up vt
(picture etc) accrocher ▌vi (on phone)
raccrocher.

hangar ['hæŋər] n Av hangar m.
hanger ['hæŋər] n (coat) h. cintre m.
●**hanger-'on** n (pl hangers-on) (person)
Pej parasite m.
hang-glider [hæŋ'glaıdər] n deltaplane Ⓡ n. ●**hang-gliding** n vol m
libre. ●**hangover** n Fam gueule f de
bois. ●**hangup** n Fam complexe m.
hanker ['hæŋkər] vi to h. after avoir
envie de. ●—**ing** n (forte) envie f.
hankie, hanky ['hæŋkı] n Fam mouchoir
m.
hanky-panky [hæŋkı'pæŋkı] n inv Fam
(sexual behaviour) galipettes fpl.
haphazard [hæp'hæzəd] a au hasard, au
petit bonheur.
happen ['hæpən] vi arriver, se passer; to
h. to s.o./sth arriver à qn/qch; I h. to
know il se trouve que je sais; do you h.
to have...? est-ce que par hasard vous
avez...?; whatever happens quoi qu'il
arrive. ●—**ing** n événement m.
happy ['hæpı] a (-ier, -iest) heureux (to
do de faire, about sth de qch); I'm not
(too or very) h. about it ça ne me plaît
pas beaucoup; H. New Year! bonne
année!; H. Christmas! Joyeux Noël!
●**h.-go-'lucky** a insouciant. ●**happily**
adv joyeusement; (contentedly) tranquillement; (fortunately) heureusement. ●**happiness** n bonheur m.
harass ['hærəs, Am hə'ræs] vt harceler.
harbour ['hɑːbər] (Am harbor) 1 n port
m. 2 vt (criminal) cacher; (fear, secret)
nourrir.
hard [hɑːd] a (-er, -est) (not soft, severe,
difficult) dur; (fact) brut; (water) calcaire; to be h. on or to s.o. être dur avec
qn; to find it h. to sleep avoir du mal à
dormir; no h. feelings! sans rancune!;
h. of hearing dur d'oreille; h. core
(group) noyau m dur; h. disk Comptr disque m dur; h. evidence preuves fpl
tangibles; a h. frost une forte gelée; h.
labour Jur travaux mpl forcés; h. worker gros travailleur m; h. up (broke) Fam
fauché; to be h. up for manquer de.
▌adv (-er, -est) (to work, hit, freeze) dur;

(*to pull*) fort; (*to rain*) à verse; (*badly*) mal; **to think h.** réfléchir bien; **h. at work** en plein travail; **h. done by** traité injustement.

hard-and-fast [ha:dən(d)'fa:st] *a* (*rule*) strict. ● **'hardboard** *n* Isorel® *m*. ● **hard-'boiled** *a* (*egg*) dur. ● **hard'headed** *a* réaliste. ● **hard'wearing** *a* résistant. ● **hard-'working** *a* travailleur.

harden ['ha:d(ə)n] *vti* durcir; **to become hardened to** s'endurcir à. ● **—ed** *a* (*criminal*) endurci.

hardly ['ha:dlɪ] *adv* à peine; **h. anyone/ ever** presque personne/jamais.

hardness ['ha:dnɪs] *n* dureté *f*.

hardship ['ha:dʃɪp] *n* (*ordeal*) épreuve(s) *f(pl)*; (*deprivation*) privation(s) *f(pl)*.

hardware ['ha:dweər] *n inv* quincaillerie *f*; (*of computer*) *& Mil* matériel *m*.

hardy ['ha:dɪ] *a* (**-ier, -iest**) (*person, plant*) résistant.

hare [heər] *n* lièvre *m*.

harm [ha:m] *n* (*hurt*) mal *m*; (*wrong*) tort *m*; **to come to no h.** il ne lui arrivera rien ▮ *vt* (*physically*) faire du mal à (*qn*); (*health, interests etc*) nuire à; (*object*) endommager. ● **harmful** *a* nuisible. ● **harmless** *a* (*person, treatment, fumes*) inoffensif; (*hobby, act*) innocent.

harmonica [ha:'mɒnɪkə] *n* harmonica *m*.

harmonious [ha:'məʊnɪəs] *a* harmonieux.

harmonize ['ha:mənaɪz] *vt* harmoniser ▮ *vi* s'harmoniser.

harmony ['ha:mənɪ] *n* harmonie *f*.

harness ['ha:nɪs] *n* (*for horse, baby*) harnais *m* ▮ *vt* (*horse*) harnacher; (*energy*) *Fig* exploiter.

harp [ha:p] **1** *n Mus* harpe *f*. **2** *vt* **to h. on about sth** *Fam* ne pas s'arrêter de parler de qch.

harpoon [ha:'pu:n] *n* harpon *m*.

harrowing ['hærəʊɪŋ] *a* (*story, memory*) poignant; (*experience*) très éprouvant; (*cry, sight*) déchirant.

harsh [ha:ʃ] *a* (**-er, -est**) (*severe*) dur, sévère; (*winter, climate*) rude; (*sound*) discordant; (*voice*) rauque; (*taste*) âpre; (*surface*) rugueux; **h. light** lumière *f* crue. ● **—ly** *adv* durement, sévèrement. ● **—ness** *n* (*severity*) dureté *f*.

harvest ['ha:vɪst] *n* moisson *f*; (*of fruit*) récolte *f* ▮ *vt* moissonner; (*fruit*) récolter.

has [hæz] *see* **have**. ● **has-been** *n Fam* personne *f* finie.

hash [hæʃ] **1** *n Culin* hachis *m*. **2** *n* (*mess*) *Fam* gâchis *m*. **3** *n* (*hashish*) *Fam* hasch *m*, H *m*.

hashish ['hæʃi:ʃ] *n* haschisch *m*.

hassle ['hæs(ə)l] *n Fam* (*trouble*) histoires *fpl*; (*bother*) mal *m*, peine *f*.

haste [heɪst] *n* hâte *f*; **in h.** à la hâte; **to make h.** se hâter. ● **hasten** ['heɪs(ə)n] *vi* se hâter (**to do de faire**) ▮ *vt* hâter.

hasty ['heɪstɪ] *a* (**-ier, -iest**) (*sudden*) précipité; (*visit*) rapide; (*decision*) hâtif. ● **hastily** *adv* (*quickly*) à la hâte.

hat [hæt] *n* chapeau *m*; (*of child*) bonnet *m*; (*cap*) casquette *f*; **that's old h.** *Fam* (*old-fashioned*) c'est vieux jeu; (*stale*) c'est vieux comme les rues.

hatch [hætʃ] **1** *vi* (*of chick, egg*) éclore ▮ *vt* faire éclore; (*plot*) *Fig* tramer. **2** *n* (*in kitchen wall*) passe-plats *m inv*.

hatchback ['hætʃbæk] *n* (*car*) trois-portes *f inv*, cinq-portes *f inv*.

hatchet ['hætʃɪt] *n* hachette *f*.

hate [heɪt] *vt* détester, haïr; **to h. doing** *or* **to do** détester faire ▮ *n* haine *f*; **pet h.** *Fam* bête *f* noire. ● **hateful** *a* haïssable. ● **hatred** *n* haine *f*.

hatstand ['hætstænd] *n* portemanteau *m*.

haughty ['hɔ:tɪ] *a* (**-ier, -iest**) hautain.

haul [hɔ:l] **1** *vt* (*pull*) tirer; (*goods*) camionner. **2** *n* (*fish caught*) prise *f*; (*of thief*) butin *m*; **a long h.** un long voyage. ● **haulier** *or Am* **hauler** *n* transporteur *m* routier.

haunt [hɔ:nt] **1** *vt* hanter. **2** *n* endroit *m* favori; (*of criminal*) repaire *m*.

have [hæv] *n* (*3rd person sing pres t* **has**; *pt & pp* **had**; *pres p* **having**) *vt* avoir; (*meal, shower etc*) prendre; **he has got, he has** il a; **to h. a walk/dream** faire une

promenade/un rêve; **to h. a drink** prendre un verre; **to h. a wash** se laver; **to h. a pleasant holiday** *or Am* **vacation** (*spend*) passer d'agréables vacances; **will you h. . . .?** (*a cake, some tea etc*) est-ce que tu veux. . .?; **to let s.o. h. sth** donner qch à qn; **I won't h. this** (*allow*) je ne tolérerai pas ça; **you've had it!** *Fam* tu es fichu!; **to h. on** (*clothes*) porter; **to have something on** (*be busy*) être pris; **to h. s.o. over** *or* **round** inviter qn chez soi. **2** *v aux* avoir; (*with* monter, sortir *etc &* *pronominal verbs*) être; **to h. decided** avoir décidé; **to h. gone** être allé; **to h. cut oneself** s'être coupé; **she has been punished** elle a été punie; **I've just done it** je viens de le faire; **to h. to do** (*must*) devoir faire; **I've got to go, I h. to go** je dois partir, je suis obligé de partir, il faut que je parte; **I don't h.** to go je ne suis pas obligé de partir; **to h. sth done** faire faire qch; **he's had his suitcase brought up** il a fait monter sa valise; **she's had her hair cut** elle s'est fait couper les cheveux; **I've had my car stolen** on m'a volé mon auto; **I've been doing it for months** je le fais depuis des mois; **haven't I?, hasn't she?** *etc* n'est-ce pas?; **no I haven't!** non!; **yes I h.!** si!; **after he had eaten,** he left après avoir mangé, il partit.
3 *npl* **the haves and have-nots** les riches *mpl* et les pauvres *mpl*.

haven ['heɪv(ə)n] *n* refuge *m*.

haven't ['hævənt] = **have not**.

haversack ['hævəsæk] *n* (*shoulder bag*) musette *f*.

havoc ['hævək] *n* ravages *mpl*.

hawk [hɔːk] *n* (*bird*) & *Pol* faucon *m*.

hawthorn ['hɔːθɔːn] *n* aubépine *f*.

hay [heɪ] *n* foin *m*; **h. fever** rhume *m* des foins. ● **haystack** *n* meule *f* de foin.

haywire ['heɪwaɪər] *a* **to go h.** (*of machine*) se détraquer; (*of plan*) mal tourner.

hazard ['hæzəd] *n* risque *m*; **health h.** risque *m* pour la santé; **h.** (**warning**) **light** *Aut* feux *mpl* de détresse ▮ *vt*

(*guess, remark*) hasarder. ● **hazardous** *a* hasardeux.

haze [heɪz] *n* brume *f*. ● **hazy** *a* (**-ier, -iest**) (*weather*) brumeux; (*sun*) voilé; (*photo, idea*) flou; **I'm h. about my plans** je ne suis pas sûr de mes projets.

hazel ['heɪz(ə)l] *n* (*bush*) noisetier *m* ▮ *a* (*eyes*) noisette *inv*. ● **hazelnut** *n* noisette *f*.

he [hiː] *pron* il; (*stressed*) lui; **he wants** il veut; **he's a happy man** c'est un homme heureux; **he and I** lui et moi ▮ *n Fam* mâle *m*; **it's a he** (*baby*) c'est un garçon.

head [hed] **1** *n* (*of person, hammer etc*) tête *f*; (*leader*) chef *m*; (*headmaster*) directeur *m*; (*headmistress*) directrice *f*; **h. of hair** chevelure *f*; **h. first** la tête la première; **it didn't enter my h.** ça ne m'est pas venu à l'esprit; **to take it into one's h. to do** se mettre en tête de faire; **to shout one's h. off** *Fam* crier à tue-tête; **at the h. of** (*in charge of*) à la tête de; **at the h. of the list** en tête de liste; **at the h. of the page** en haut de (la) page; **it's above my h.** ça me dépasse; **to keep one's h.** garder son sang-froid; **it's coming to a h.** (*of situation*) ça devient critique; **heads or tails?** pile ou face?; **per h., a h.** (*each*) par personne; **h. cold** rhume *m* de cerveau.
2 *a* principal; (*gardener*) en chef; **h. waiter** maître *m* d'hôtel; **a h. start** une grosse avance.
3 *vt* (*group, firm*) être à la tête de; (*list*) être en tête de; (*vehicle*) diriger (*towards* vers); **to h. the ball** *Fb* faire une tête; **to h. off** (*person*) détourner de son chemin; (*prevent*) empêcher; **to be headed for** *Am* = **to h. for.**
4 *vi* **to h. for, be heading for** (*place*) se diriger vers; (*ruin*) *Fig* aller à. ● **heading** *n* (*of chapter, page*) titre *m*; (*of subject*) rubrique *f*; (*on letter etc*) en-tête *m*.

headache ['hedeɪk] *n* mal *m* de tête; (*difficulty, person*) *Fig* problème *m*; **to have a h.** avoir mal à la tête. ● **headlamp** *or* **headlight** *n* *Aut* phare *m*. ● **headline** *n* (*of newspaper*) manchette *f*; *pl* (*gros-*

titres *mpl*; *Rad TV* (grands) titres *mpl*.
● **headlong** *adv* (*to fall*) la tête la première; (*to rush*) tête baissée.
● **head′master** *n* (*of school*) directeur *m*. ● **head′mistress** *n* (*of school*) directrice *f*. ● **head-′on** *adv & a* (*to collide, collision*) de plein fouet. ● **headphones** *npl* casque *m* (à écouteurs). ● **headquarters** *npl Com Pol* siège *m* (central); *Mil* quartier *m* général. ● **headrest** *n* appuie-tête *m inv*. ● **headscarf** *n* (*pl* **-scarves**) foulard *m*. ● **headstrong** *a* têtu. ● **headway** *n* progrès *mpl*.

heady ['hedɪ] *a* (**-ier, -iest**) (*wine*) capiteux; (*speech*) impétueux.

heal [hiːl] *vi* (*of wound*) se cicatriser; (*of bruise*) disparaître; (*of bone*) se ressouder ‖ *vt* (*wound*) cicatriser; (*bruise*) faire disparaître; (*bone*) ressouder; (*person*) guérir.

health [helθ] *n* santé *f*; **h. food** aliment *m* naturel; **h. food shop** *or Am* **store** magasin *m* de produits diététiques; **h. food restaurant** restaurant *m* diététique; **h. resort** station *f* climatique; **the (National) H. Service** = la Sécurité Sociale. ● **healthy** *a* (**-ier, -iest**) (*person*) en bonne santé, sain; (*food, attitude*) sain; (*appetite*) robuste.

heap [hiːp] *n* tas *m*; heaps of (*money, people*) *Fam* des tas de; **to have heaps of time** *Fam* avoir largement le temps ‖ *vt* entasser; **to h. on s.o.** (*praise*) couvrir qn de; (*insults*) accabler qn de.

hear [hɪər] *vt* (*pt & pp* **heard** [hɜːd]) entendre; (*listen to*) écouter; (*learn*) apprendre (**that** que); **I heard him come** *or* **coming** je l'ai entendu venir; **have you heard the news?** connais-tu la nouvelle?; **h., h.!** bravo!
‖ *vi* entendre; (*get news*) recevoir des nouvelles (**from** de); **I've heard of** *or* **about him** j'ai entendu parler de lui; **she wouldn't h. of it** elle ne veut pas en entendre parler; **I wouldn't h. of it!** pas question! ● **hearing 1** *n* (*sense*) ouïe *f*; **h. aid** appareil *m* auditif. **2** (*of committee*) séance *f*; **to get a (fair) h.** avoir la

possibilité de s'exprimer. ● **hearsay** *n* **by h.** par ouï-dire; **it's h.** ce ne sont que des bruits qui courent.

hearse [hɜːs] *n* corbillard *m*.

heart [hɑːt] *n* cœur *m*; **heart(s)** *Cards* cœur *m*; (**off**) **by h.** par cœur; **to lose h.** perdre courage; **at h.** au fond; **his h. is set on it** il le veut à tout prix, il y tient; **h. attack** crise *f* cardiaque; **h. disease** maladie *f* de cœur.
● **heartache** ['hɑːteɪk] *n* chagrin *m*.
● **heartbeat** *n* battement *m* de cœur. ● **heartbreaking** *a* navrant, déchirant. ● **heartbroken** *a* inconsolable. ● **heartburn** *n Med* brûlures *npl* d'estomac.

hearten ['hɑːt(ə)n] *vt* encourager. ● **—ing** *a* encourageant.

hearth [hɑːθ] *n* foyer *m*.

hearty ['hɑːtɪ] *a* (**-ier, -iest**) (*appetite, meal*) gros (*f* grosse).

heat [hiːt] **1** *n* chaleur *f*; (*heating*) chauffage *m*; **in the h. of the argument** dans le feu de la discussion; **at low h.** *Culin* à feu doux; **h. wave** vague *f* de chaleur ‖ *vti* **to h. (up)** chauffer.
2 *n* (*in race, competition*) éliminatoire *f*; **it was a dead h.** ils sont arrivés ex aequo. ● **—ed** *a* (*swimming pool*) chauffé; (*argument*) passionné. ● **—ing** *n* chauffage *m*; **central h.** chauffage *m* central. ● **heater** *n* appareil *m* de chauffage; **water h.** chauffe-eau *m inv*.

heath [hiːθ] *n* (*land*) lande *f*.

heather ['heðər] *n* (*plant*) bruyère *f*.

heave [hiːv] *vt* (*lift*) soulever; (*pull*) tirer; (*drag*) traîner; (*throw*) *Fam* lancer; (*a sigh*) pousser ‖ *vi* (*of stomach, chest*) se soulever; (*feel sick*) *Fam* avoir des haut-le-cœur.

heaven ['hev(ə)n] *n* ciel *m*, paradis *m*; **h. knows when** *Fam* Dieu sait quand; **good heavens!** *Fam* mon Dieu! ● **—ly** *a* céleste; (*pleasing*) *Fam* divin.

heavy ['hevɪ] *a* (**-ier, -iest**) lourd; (*work, cold*) gros (*f* grosse); (*blow*) violent; (*rain*) fort; (*traffic*) dense; (*smoker, drinker*) grand; **a h. day** (*busy*) une journée chargée; **h. casualties** de nombreuses victimes; **h. snow** d'abondantes chutes de neige; **it's h. going** c'est difficile. ●**heavily** adv (to walk, tax) lourdement; (to breathe) péniblement; (to smoke, drink, snow) beaucoup; **h. in debt** lourdement endetté; **to rain h.** pleuvoir à verse. ●**heavyweight** n Boxing poids m lourd.

Hebrew ['hi:bru:] n (language) hébreu m.

heck [hek] int Fam zut! ▌ n = **hell** in expressions.

heckl/e ['hek(ə)l] vt interpeller. ●—**ing** n interpellations fpl.

hectic ['hektik] a (activity) fiévreux; (period) très agité; (trip) mouvementé; **h. life** vie f trépidante.

he'd [hi:d] = **he had** & **he would**.

hedge [hedʒ] **1** n (bushes) haie f. **2** vi (answer evasively) ne pas se mouiller.

hedgehog ['hedʒhɒg] n (animal) hérisson m.

heed [hi:d] vt faire attention à.

heel [hi:l] n talon m; **down at h.,** Am **down at the heels** (shabby) miteux; **h. bar** cordonnerie f express; (on sign) 'talon minute'.

hefty ['hefti] a (-ier, -iest) (large, heavy) gros (f grosse).

height [hait] n hauteur f; (of person) taille f; (of mountain, aircraft) altitude f; **the h. of** (success, fame) le sommet de; (folly) le comble de; **at the h. of** (summer, storm) au cœur de. ●**heighten** vt (tension, interest) augmenter.

heir [eər] n héritier m. ●**heiress** n héritière f.

held [held] pt & pp of **hold**.

helicopter ['helikɒptər] n hélicoptère m. ●**heliport** n héliport m.

hell [hel] n enfer m; **a h. of a lot (of)** Fam énormément (de); **what the h. are you doing?** Fam qu'est-ce que tu fous?; **to h. with him** Fam qu'il aille se faire voir; **h.!** Fam zut!; **h.-bent on doing,** Am **h.-bent to do** Fam acharné à faire.

he'll [hi:l] = **he will**.

hello! [hə'ləu] int bonjour!; (answering phone) allô!; (surprise) tiens!

helm [helm] n Nau barre f.

helmet ['helmit] n casque m.

help [help] n aide f, secours m; (cleaning woman) femme f de ménage; (office or shop workers) employés, -ées mfpl; **with the h. of** (stick etc) à l'aide de; **h.!** au secours!

▌ vt aider (s.o. do or to do qn à faire); **to h. s.o. to soup/etc** (serve) servir du potage/etc à qn; **h. yourself** servez-vous (to de); **to h. s.o. out** aider qn; (of trouble) dépanner qn; **to h. s.o. up** aider qn à monter; **I can't h. laughing** je ne peux (pas) m'empêcher de rire; **he can't h. being blind** ce n'est pas sa faute s'il est aveugle.

▌ vi **to h. (out)** aider. ●**helping** n (serving) portion f. ●**helper** n assistant, -ante mf.

helpful ['helpfəl] a (useful) utile; (person) serviable.

helpless ['helpləs] a (powerless) impuissant; (disabled) impotent.

helter-skelter [heltə'skeltər] n (slide) toboggan m.

hem [hem] n ourlet m ▌ vt (-mm-) (garment) ourler; **to be hemmed in** (surrounded) être cerné (by de); (unable to move) être coincé.

hemorrhage ['hemaridʒ] n Med hémorragie f.

hemorrhoids ['hemaroidz] npl hémorroïdes fpl.

hen [hen] n poule f. ●**henpecked** a (husband) dominé par sa femme.

hence [hens] adv **1** (therefore) d'où. **2** (from now) **ten years h.** d'ici dix ans. ●**henceforth** adv désormais.

henchman ['hentʃmən] n (pl -**men**) Pej acolyte m.

hepatitis [hepə'taitis] n hépatite f.

her [hɜːr] **1** pron la, l'; (after prep, 'than', 'it is') elle; (to h.) lui; **I see h.** je la vois; **I saw h.** je l'ai vue; **I give (to) h.** je lui donne; **with h.** avec elle. **2** poss a son, sa, pl ses.

herald ['herəld] vt annoncer.

herb [hɜːb, Am ɜːb] n herbe f; pl Culin fines herbes fpl. ●**herbal** a **h. tea** infusion f (d'herbes).

herd [hɜːd] n troupeau m.

here [hɪər] 1 adv ici; **h. is, h. are** voici; **she is h.** la voici; **summer is h.** l'été est là; **h. and there** çà et là; **h. you are!** (take this) tenez! 2 **int h.!** (calling s.o.'s attention) holà!; (giving s.o. sth) tenez! ●**here-a'bouts** adv par ici. ●**here'by** adv (to declare etc) par le présent acte. ●**here'with** adv (with letter) Com ci-joint.

hereditary [hɪˈredɪtərɪ] a héréditaire.

heritage ['herɪtɪdʒ] n héritage m.

hermit ['hɜːmɪt] n solitaire mf, ermite m.

hernia ['hɜːnɪə] n hernie f.

hero ['hɪərəʊ] n (pl -oes) héros m. ●**he'roic** a héroïque. ●**heroine** ['herəʊɪn] n héroïne f. ●**heroism** ['herəʊɪz(ə)m] n héroïsme m.

heroin ['herəʊɪn] n (drug) héroïne f.

heron ['herən] n (bird) héron m.

herring ['herɪŋ] n hareng m.

hers [hɜːz] poss pron le sien, la sienne, pl les sien(ne)s; **this hat is h.** ce chapeau est à elle ou est le sien; **a friend of h.** une amie à elle.

herself [hɜːˈself] pron elle-même; (reflexive) se, s'; (after prep) elle; **she cut h.** elle s'est coupée; **she thinks of h.** elle pense à elle.

hesitant ['hezɪtənt] a hésitant.

hesitate ['hezɪteɪt] vi hésiter (over, about sur) ‖ vt **to h. to do** hésiter à faire. ●**hesitation** [-'teɪʃ(ə)n] n hésitation f.

het up [het'ʌp] a Fam énervé.

hew [hjuː] vt (pp hewn or hewed) tailler.

hexagon ['heksəgən] n hexagone m. ●**hex'agonal** a hexagonal.

hey! [heɪ] int (calling s.o.) hé!; (surprise, annoyance) ho!

heyday ['heɪdeɪ] n in its h. à son âge d'or; **in my h.** à l'apogée de ma vie or de ma carrière.

hi! [haɪ] int Fam salut!

hibernate ['haɪbəneɪt] vi hiberner.

hiccup ['hɪkʌp] n hoquet m; Fig (petit) problème m; **to have (the) hiccups** avoir le hoquet ‖ vi hoqueter.

hide¹ [haɪd] vt (pt hid, pp hidden) cacher (from à) ‖ vi se cacher (from de). ●**h.-and-seek** n cache-cache m inv. ●**hide-out** n cachette f. ●**hiding** n 1 **to go into h.** se cacher; **h. place** cachette f. 2 **a good h.** (thrashing) Fam une bonne raclée.

hide² [haɪd] n (skin) peau f.

hideous ['hɪdɪəs] a (person, sight, weather etc) horrible. ●**—ly** adv (badly, very) horriblement.

hi-fi ['haɪfaɪ] n (system) chaîne f hi-fi ‖ a hi-fi inv.

high [haɪ] a (-er, -est) haut; (speed) grand; (price, number) élevé; (on drugs) Fam défoncé; **to be five metres h.** avoir ou faire cinq mètres de haut; **it is h. time that** il est grand temps que (+ sub); **h. fever** forte ou grosse fièvre f; **h. jump** Sp saut m en hauteur; **h. noon** plein midi m; **h. school** = lycée m; **h. spirits** entrain m; **h. spot** (of visit) point m culminant; (of show) clou m; **h. street** grand-rue f; **h. table** table f d'honneur; **h. voice** voix f aiguë.
‖ adv **h. (up)** (to fly, throw etc) haut; **to aim h.** viser haut.
‖ n **a new h., an all-time h.** (peak) un nouveau record.

highbrow ['haɪbraʊ] a & n intellectuel, -elle (mf).

high-chair ['haɪtʃeər] n chaise f haute. ●**h.-'class** a (service) de premier ordre, (building) de luxe. ●**h.-'handed** a tyrannique. ●**h.-'pitched** a (sound) aigu (f -uë). ●**h.-'powered** a (person) très dynamique. ●**h.-rise** a **h.-rise flats** tour f. ●**h.-'speed** a ultra-rapide; **h.-speed train** train m à grande vitesse. ●**h.-'strung** a Am nerveux. ●**h.-'up** a (person) Fam haut placé.

higher ['haɪər] a (number, speed etc) supérieur (to à); **h. education** enseignement m supérieur ‖ adv (to fly etc) plus haut (than que).

highlands ['haɪləndz] npl régions fpl montagneuses.

highlight ['haɪlaɪt] n (of visit, day) point m culminant; (of show) clou m; (in hair) reflet *m* ‖ *vt* souligner; (*with marker*) surligner. ●**highlighter** *n* (*coloured marker*) surligneur *m*.

highly ['haɪlɪ] *adv* (*very*) (*interesting, amusing etc*) très; (*to recommend*) chaudement; **h. paid** très bien payé; **to speak h. of** dire beaucoup de bien de; **h. strung** nerveux.

Highness ['haɪnɪs] *n* (*title*) Altesse *f*.

highroad ['haɪrəʊd] *n* grand-route *f*.

highway ['haɪweɪ] *n Am* autoroute *f*; **public h.** voie *f* publique; **H. Code** code *m* de la route.

hijack ['haɪdʒæk] *vt* (*aircraft, vehicle*) détourner ‖ *n* détournement *m*. ●**—ing** *n* (*air piracy*) piraterie *f* aérienne; (*hijack*) détournement *m*. ●**hijacker** *n* pirate *m* de l'air.

hik/e [haɪk] **1** *n* excursion *f* à pied ‖ *vi* marcher à pied. **2** *n* (*increase*) *Fam* hausse *f*. ●**—er** *n* excursionniste *mf*.

hilarious [hɪ'leərɪəs] *a* (*funny*) désopilant.

hill [hɪl] *n* colline *f*; (*small*) coteau *m*; (*slope*) pente *f*. ●**hillside** *n* **on the h.** à flanc de colline *or* de coteau. ●**hilly** *a* (*-ier, -iest*) accidenté.

hilt [hɪlt] *n* (*of sword*) poignée *f*; **to the h.** *Fig* au maximum.

him [hɪm] *pron* le, l'; (*after prep, 'than', 'it is'*) lui; **(to) h.** lui; **I see h.** je le vois; **I saw h.** je l'ai vu; **I give (to) h.** je lui donne; **with h.** avec lui.

himself [hɪm'self] *pron* lui-même; (*reflexive*) se, s'; (*after prep*) lui; **he cut h.** il s'est coupé; **he thinks of h.** il pense à lui.

hind [haɪnd] *a* **h. legs** pattes *fpl* de derrière.

hinder ['hɪndər] *vt* (*obstruct*) gêner; (*prevent*) empêcher (**from doing** de faire). ●**hindrance** *n* gêne *f*.

hindsight ['haɪndsaɪt] *n* **with h.** rétrospectivement.

Hindu ['hɪnduː] *a & n* hindou, -oue (*mf*).

hinge [hɪndʒ] **1** *n* charnière *f*. **2** *vi* **to h. on** dépendre de.

hint [hɪnt] *n* (*insinuation*) allusion *f*; (*sign*) indication *f*; (*trace*) trace *f*; *pl* (*advice*) conseils *mpl* ‖ *vt* laisser entendre (**that** que) ‖ *vi* **to h. at** faire allusion à.

hip [hɪp] *n* hanche *f*.

hippie ['hɪpɪ] *n* hippie *mf*.

hippopotamus [hɪpə'pɒtəməs] *n* hippopotame *m*.

hire ['haɪər] *vt* (*vehicle etc*) louer; (*worker*) engager; **to h. out** donner en location, louer ‖ *n* location *f*; **for h.** à louer; **h. purchase** vente *f* or achat *m* à crédit; **on h. purchase** à crédit.

his [hɪz] **1** *poss a* son, sa, *pl* ses. **2** *poss pron* le sien, la sienne, *pl* les sien(ne)s; **this hat is h.** ce chapeau est à lui *or* est le sien; **a friend of h.** un ami à lui.

Hispanic [hɪs'pænɪk] *a & n Am* hispano-américain, -aine (*mf*).

hiss [hɪs] *vti* siffler ‖ *n* sifflement *m*.

history ['hɪstərɪ] *n* (*study, events*) histoire *f*; **your medical h.** vos antécédents médicaux. ●**historian** *n* historien, -ienne *mf*. ●**historic(al)** *a* historique.

hit [hɪt] *vt* (*pt & pp* **hit**, *pres p* **hitting**) (*beat etc*) frapper; (*bump into*) heurter; (*reach*) atteindre; (*affect*) toucher; (*find*) rencontrer (*problème*); **to h. it off** *Fam* s'entendre bien (**with s.o.** avec qn).

‖ *vi* frapper; **to h. back** rendre coup pour coup; (*answer criticism etc*) riposter; **to h. out (at)** *Fam* attaquer; **to h. (up)on** (*find*) tomber sur.

‖ *n* (*blow*) coup *m*; (*play, film, book*) succès *m*; **h.** (*song*) chanson *f* à succès; **to make a h. with** *Fam* avoir un succès avec. ●**hit-and-run driver** *n* chauffard *m* (*qui prend la fuite*). ●**hit-or-'miss** *a* (*chancy*) aléatoire.

hitch [hɪtʃ] **1** *n* (*snag*) problème *m*. **2** *vt* (*fasten*) accrocher (**to** à). **3** *vti* **to h. (a lift** *or* **a ride)** *Fam* faire du stop (**to** jusqu'à).

hitchhik/e ['hɪtʃhaɪk] *vi* faire de l'autostop (**to** jusqu'à). ●**—ing** *n* auto-stop *m*. ●**hitchhiker** *n* auto-stoppeur, -euse *mf*.

hi-tech [haɪ'tek] *a* (*industry*) de pointe.

HIV [eɪtʃaɪ'viː] *n* HIV **positive/negative**

Med séropositif/séronégatif.

hive [haɪv] *n* ruche *f*.

hoard [hɔːd] *n* réserve *f*; (*of money*) trésor *m* § *vt* amasser.

hoarding ['hɔːdɪŋ] *n* panneau *m* d'affichage.

hoarse [hɔːs] *a* (-er, -est) (*person, voice*) enroué.

hoax [həʊks] *n* canular *m* § *vt* faire un canular à.

hob [hɒb] *n* (*on stove*) plaque *f* chauffante.

hobble ['hɒb(ə)l] *vi* (*walk*) boitiller.

hobby ['hɒbɪ] *n* passe-temps *m inv*; **my h.** mon passe-temps favori. ● **hobbyhorse** *n* (*favourite subject*) dada *m*.

hobnob ['hɒbnɒb] *vi* (-bb-) **to h. with** frayer avec.

hobo ['həʊbəʊ] *n* (*pl* -oes *or* -os) *Am* vagabond, -onde *mf*.

hockey ['hɒkɪ] *n* hockey *m*; **ice h.** hockey sur glace.

hodgepodge ['hɒdʒpɒdʒ] *n* fatras *m*.

hoe [həʊ] *n* binette *f* § *vt* biner.

hog [hɒg] **1** *n* (*pig*) cochon *m*, porc *m*. **2** *n* **to go the whole h.** *Fam* aller jusqu'au bout. **3** *vt* (-gg-) *Fam* monopoliser.

hoist [hɔɪst] *vt* hisser § *n* (*machine*) palan *m*.

hold [həʊld] *n* (*grip*) prise *f*; (*of ship*) cale *f*; (*of aircraft*) soute *f*; **to get h. of** (*grab*) saisir; (*contact*) joindre; (*find*) trouver. § *vt* (*pt & pp* held) tenir; (*breath, interest, heat, attention*) retenir; (*a post*) occuper; (*a record*) détenir; (*weight*) supporter; (*party, bazaar etc*) organiser; (*ceremony, mass*) célébrer; (*possess*) posséder; (*contain*) contenir; (*keep*) garder; **to h. hands** se tenir par la main; **to h. one's own** se débrouiller; (*of sick person*) se maintenir; **h. the line!** *Tel* ne quittez pas!; **h. it!** (*stay still*) ne bouge pas!; **to be held** (*of event*) avoir lieu.

§ *vi* (*of nail, rope*) tenir; (*of weather*) se maintenir; **to h. good** (*of argument*) valoir (**for** pour). ● **holdall** *n* (*bag*) fourre-tout *m inv*.

hold back *vt* (*crowd, tears*) contenir; (*hide*) cacher (**from** à) § **to hold down** *vt* (*price*) maintenir bas; (*keep*) garder (*un emploi*); (*person on ground*) maintenir au sol § **to hold off** *vt* (*enemy*) tenir à distance § *vi* **if the rain holds off** s'il ne pleut pas § **to hold on** *vi* (*wait*) attendre; (*stand firm*) tenir bon; **h. on!** *Tel* ne quittez pas!; **h. on (tight)!** tenez bon! § **to hold onto** *vt* (*cling to*) tenir bien; (*keep*) garder § **to hold out** *vt* (*offer*) offrir; (*arm*) étendre § *vi* (*resist*) résister; (*last*) durer § **to hold over** *vt* (*postpone*) remettre § **to hold up** *vt* (*raise*) lever; (*support*) soutenir; (*delay*) retarder; (*bank*) attaquer (à main armée).

holder ['həʊldər] *n* (*of passport, post*) titulaire *mf*; (*of record*) détenteur, -trice *mf*; (*container*) support *m*.

holdings ['həʊldɪŋz] *npl* *Fin* possessions *fpl*.

holdup ['həʊldʌp] *n* (*attack*) hold-up *m inv*; (*traffic jam*) bouchon *m*; (*delay*) retard *m*.

hole [həʊl] *n* trou *m* § *vi* **to h. up** (*hide*) *Fam* se terrer.

holiday ['hɒlɪdeɪ] *n* **holiday(s)** (*from work, school etc*) vacances *fpl*; **a h.** (*day off*) un congé; *Rel* une fête; **a (public *or* bank) h.**, *Am* **a legal h.** un jour férié; **on h.** en vacances; **holidays** *with pay* congés *mpl* payés § *a* (*camp, clothes etc*) de vacances. ● **holidaymaker** *n* vacancier, -ière *mf*.

Holland ['hɒlənd] *n* Hollande *f*.

hollow ['hɒləʊ] *a* creux § *n* creux *m* § *vt* **to h. out** creuser.

holly ['hɒlɪ] *n* houx *m*.

holster ['həʊlstər] *n* étui *m* de revolver.

holy ['həʊlɪ] *a* (-ier, -iest) saint; (*bread, water*) bénit; (*ground*) sacré.

homage ['hɒmɪdʒ] *n* hommage *m*; **to pay h. to** rendre hommage à.

home [həʊm] *n* maison *f*; (*country*) pays *m* (natal); **(old people's) h.** maison *f* de retraite; **at h.** à la maison, chez soi; **to make oneself at h.** se mettre à l'aise; **to play at h.** *Fb* jouer à domicile; **a broken**

h. un foyer désuni; **a good h.** une bonne famille; **to make one's h. in** s'installer à or en.

∥ *adv* à la maison, chez soi; **to go** or **come (back) h.** rentrer; **to be h.** être rentré; **to drive h.** ramener (*qn*) (en voiture); (*nail*) enfoncer.

∥ *a* (*life, cooking etc*) de famille, familial; *Pol* national; (*visit, match*) à domicile; **h. computer** ordinateur *m* domestique; **h. help** aide *f* ménagère; **H. Office** = ministère *m* de l'Intérieur; **h. rule** *Pol* autonomie *f*; **H. Secretary** = ministre *m* de l'Intérieur; **h. town** (*birth place*) ville *f* natale.

homecoming ['həʊmkʌmɪŋ] *n* retour *m* au foyer. ●**homeland** *n* patrie *f*. ●**homeloving** *a* casanier. ●**home'made** *a* (fait à la) maison *inv*.

homeless ['həʊmləs] *a* sans abri ∥ **the h.** les sans-abri *m inv*.

homely ['həʊmlɪ] *a* (-ier, -iest) (*simple*) simple; (*ugly*) *Am* laid.

homesick ['həʊmsɪk] *a* **to be h.** avoir envie de rentrer chez soi.

homeward ['həʊmwəd] *a* (*trip*) de retour ∥ *adv* **h. bound** sur le chemin de retour.

homework ['həʊmwɜːk] *n Sch* devoir(s) *m(pl)*.

homey ['həʊmɪ] *a* (-ier, -iest) *Am Fam* accueillant.

homicide ['hɒmɪsaɪd] *n* (*murder*) homicide *m*; **two homicides** *Am* deux meurtres *mpl*.

homosexual [həʊmə'seksʊəl] *a* & *n* homosexuel, -elle (*mf*).

honest ['ɒnɪst] *a* honnête; (*frank*) franc (*f* franche) (**with** avec); **the h. truth** la pure vérité; **to be (quite) h....** pour être franc.... ●**honesty** *n* honnêteté *f*; franchise *f*.

honey ['hʌnɪ] *n* miel *m*; (*person*) *Fam* chéri, -ie *mf*. ●**honeycomb** *n* rayon *m* de miel. ●**honeymoon** *n* lune *f* de miel; **to be on one's h.** être en voyage de noces. ●**honeysuckle** *n Bot* chèvrefeuille *f*.

honk [hɒŋk] *vi Aut* klaxonner ∥ *n* coup *m*

de klaxon®.

honour ['ɒnər] (*Am* **honor**) *n* honneur *m*; **in h. of** en l'honneur de; **honours degree** *Univ* = licence *f* ∥ *vt* honorer (**with** de). ●**honorary** *a* (*member*) honoraire; (*title*) honorifique. ●**honourable** *a* honorable.

hood [hʊd] *n* capuchon *m*; (*mask of robber*) cagoule *f*; (*soft car roof, roof of pram* or *Am baby carriage*) capote *f*; (*car bonnet*) capot *m*; (*above stove*) hotte *f*. ●**hooded** *a* (*person*) encapuchonné; (*coat*) à capuchon.

hoodlum ['huːdləm] *n* (*gangster*) *Fam* gangster *m*.

hoof, *pl* **-fs** or **-ves** [huːf, -fs, -vz] [hʊf, -fs, huːvz]) *n* sabot *m*.

hook [hʊk] *n* crochet *m*; (*on clothes*) agrafe *f*; *Fishing* hameçon *m*; **off the h.** (*phone*) décroché; **to let** or **get s.o. off the h.** tirer qn d'affaire ∥ *vt* **to h.** (**on** or **up**) accrocher (**to** à). ●**-ed** *a* (*nose, end, object*) recourbé; **h. on chess/etc** *Fam* enragé d'échecs/*etc*, accro des échecs/ *etc*; **to be h. on drugs** *Fam* être accro. ●**hooker** *n Fam* prostituée *f*.

hook(e)y ['hʊkɪ] *n* **to play h.** *Am Fam* sécher (la classe).

hooligan ['huːlɪgən] *n* vandale *m*, voyou *m*.

hoop [huːp] *n* cerceau *m*.

hoot [huːt] *vi Aut* klaxonner; (*of train*) siffler; (*of owl*) hululer ∥ *n Aut* coup *m* de klaxon®. ●**—er** *n Aut* klaxon® *m*; (*of factory*) sirène *f*.

hoover ['huːvər] *n* aspirateur *m* ∥ *vt* (*room*) passer l'aspirateur dans; (*carpet*) passer l'aspirateur sur.

hop [hɒp] *vi* (**-pp-**) (*of person*) sauter (à cloche-pied); (*of kangaroo etc*) sauter; (*of bird*) sautiller; **h. in!** (*in car*) montez!; **to h. on a bus** monter dans un autobus ∥ *vt* **h. it!** *Fam* fiche le camp! ∥ *n* (*leap*) saut *m*.

hope [həʊp] *n* espoir *m* ∥ *vi* espérer; **to h. for** (*wish for*) espérer; (*expect*) attendre; **I h. so/not** j'espère que oui/non ∥ *vt* espérer (**to** faire, **that** que).

hopeful ['həʊpfəl] *a* (*person*) optimiste;

(*promising*) prometteur; **to be h. that** avoir bon espoir que. ●**—ly** *adv* avec optimisme; (*one hopes*) on espère (que).

hopeless ['həʊpləs] *a* désespéré, sans espoir; (*useless*, *bad*) nul. ●**—ly** *adv* (*extremely*) (*lost*) complètement; (*in love*) éperdument.

hops [hɒps] *npl* (*for beer*) houblon *m*.

hopscotch ['hɒpskɒtʃ] *n* (*game*) marelle *f*.

horde [hɔːd] *n* horde *f*, foule *f*.

horizon [hə'raɪz(ə)n] *n* horizon *m*; **on the h.** à l'horizon.

horizontal [hɒrɪ'zɒnt(ə)l] *a* horizontal.

hormone ['hɔːməʊn] *n* hormone *f*.

horn [hɔːn] **1** *n* (*of animal*) corne *f*; *Aut* klaxon® *m*; *Mus* cor *m*. **2** *vi* **to h. in** *Am Fam* mêler son grain de sel.

hornet ['hɔːnɪt] *n* (*insect*) frelon *m*.

horny ['hɔːnɪ] *a* (**-ier**, **-iest**) (*aroused*) *Fam* excité.

horoscope ['hɒrəskəʊp] *n* horoscope *m*.

horrendous [hə'rendəs] *a* horrible.

horrible ['hɒrɪb(ə)l] *a* horrible, affreux. ●**horribly** *adv* horriblement.

horrid ['hɒrɪd] *a* horrible; (*child*) épouvantable.

horrific [hə'rɪfɪk] *a* horrible, horrifiant.

horrify ['hɒrɪfaɪ] *vt* horrifier.

horror ['hɒrər] *n* horreur *f*; (*little*) **h.** (*child*) *Fam* petit monstre *m*; **h. film** film *f* d'épouvante.

hors-d'œuvre [ɔː'dɜːv] *n* hors-d'œuvre *m inv*.

horse [hɔːs] *n* **1** cheval *m*; **to go h. riding** faire du cheval. **2 h. chestnut** marron *m* (d'Inde).

horseback ['hɔːsbæk] *n* **on h.** à cheval; **to go h. riding** *Am* faire du cheval. ●**horseplay** *n* jeux *mpl* brutaux. ●**horsepower** *n* cheval *m* (vapeur). ●**horseracing** *n* courses *fpl*. ●**horseradish** *n* radis *m* noir, raifort *m*. ●**horseshoe** *n* fer *m* à cheval.

hose [həʊz] *n* (*tube*) tuyau *m*; **garden h.** tuyau *m* d'arrosage. ●**hosepipe** *n* = **hose**.

hospice ['hɒspɪs] *n* (*for dying people*)

hospice *m*.

hospitable [hɒ'spɪtəb(ə)l] *a* accueillant. ●**hospi'tality** *n* hospitalité *f*.

hospital ['hɒspɪt(ə)l] *n* hôpital *m*; **in h.**, *Am* **in the h.** à l'hôpital ▌ *a* (*bed*, *food*) d'hôpital; (*staff*) hospitalier. ●**hospitalize** *vt* hospitaliser.

host [həʊst] *n* **1** (*man who receives guests*) hôte *m*; *TV Rad* présentateur, -trice *mf*. **2** **a h. of** (*many*) une foule de. ●**hostess** *n* (*in house*, *aircraft*, *nightclub*) hôtesse *f*.

hostage ['hɒstɪdʒ] *n* otage *m*; **to take/hold s.o. h.** prendre/retenir qn en otage.

hostel ['hɒst(ə)l] *n* foyer *m*; **youth h.** auberge *f* de jeunesse.

hostile ['hɒstaɪl, *Am* 'hɒst(ə)l] *a* hostile (**to**, **towards** à). ●**ho'stility** *n* hostilité *f* (**to**, **towards** envers); *pl Mil* hostilités *fpl*.

hot¹ [hɒt] *a* (**hotter**, **hottest**) chaud; (*spice*) fort; **to be** *or* **feel h.** avoir chaud; **it's h.** il fait chaud; **not so h. at** (*good at*) *Fam* pas très calé en; **h. dog** (*sausage*) hot-dog *m*. ●**hotbed** *n Pej* foyer *m* (**of** de). ●**hothead** *n* tête *f* brûlée. ●**hot'headed** *a* impétueux. ●**hotplate** *n* chauffe-plats *m inv*; (*on stove*) plaque *f* chauffante. ●**hot-'tempered** *a* emporté. ●**hot-'water bottle** *n* bouillotte *f*.

hot² [hɒt] *vi* (**-tt-**) **to h. up** (*increase*) s'intensifier; (*become dangerous or excited*) chauffer.

hotchpotch ['hɒtʃpɒtʃ] *n* fatras *m*.

hotel [həʊ'tel] *n* hôtel *m*; **h. room/etc** chambre *f*/etc d'hôtel; **h. prices** le prix des hôtels.

hotly ['hɒtlɪ] *adv* passionnément.

hound [haʊnd] **1** *vt* (*pursue*) traquer; (*bother*) harceler. **2** *n* (*dog*) chien *m* courant.

hour ['aʊər] *n* heure *f*; **half an h., a half-h.** une demi-heure; **a quarter of an h.** un quart d'heure; **paid fifty francs an h.** payé cinquante francs (de) l'heure; **ten miles an h.** dix miles à l'heure; **h. hand** (*of watch*, *clock*) petite aiguille *f*. ●**—ly**

a (*pay*) horaire; **an h. bus/***etc* un bus/*etc*
toutes les heures ▮ *adv* toutes les heures;
h. paid payé à l'heure.

house[1], *pl* **-ses** [haus, -zız] *n* maison *f*;
(*audience*) *Th* salle *f*; (*performance*) *Th*
séance *f*; **the H.** *Pol* la Chambre; **at** or
to my H. chez moi; **on the h.** (*free of
charge*) aux frais de la maison; **h. prices**
prix *mpl* immobiliers.

house/e[2] [hauz] *vt* loger; (*of building*)
abriter; **it is housed in** (*kept*) on le garde
dans. ●**—ing** *n* logement *m*; (*houses*)
logements *mpl*.

housebound ['hausbaund] *a* confiné
chez soi. ●**housebreaking** *n* *Jur* cambriolage *m*. ●**housebroken** *a* (*dog etc*)
Am propre. ●**household** *n* famille *f*; **h.
duties** soins *mpl* du ménage; **a h. name**
un nom très connu. ●**householder** *n*
(*owner*) propriétaire *mf*. ●**housekeeper**
n (*employee*) gouvernante *f*. ●**house-
keeping** *n* ménage *m* (*entretien*).
●**houseproud** *a* qui s'occupe méticuleu-
sement de sa maison. ●**housetrained** *a*
(*dog etc*) propre. ●**house-warming** *n* &
a **to have a h.-warming (party)** pendre la
crémaillère. ●**housewife** *n* (*pl* **-wives**)
ménagère *f*. ●**housework** *n* (*travaux
mpl* de) ménage *m*.

hovel ['hɒv(ə)l] *n* (*slum*) taudis *m*.

hover ['hɒvər] *vi* (*of bird, aircraft, Fig
danger*) planer. ●**hovercraft** *n* aéroglisseur *m*.

how [hau] *adv* comment; **h. come?** *Fam*
comment ça?; **h. do you do?** bonjour; **h.
long/high is...?** quelle est la longueur/
hauteur de...?; **h. much?, h. many?**
combien?; **h. much time/***etc*? combien
de temps/*etc*?; **h. many apples/***etc*?
combien de pommes/*etc*?; **h. about
some coffee?** (si on prenait) du café?;
h. about me? et moi?

however [hau'evər] **1** *adv* **h. big he may
be** si or quelque grand qu'il soit; **h. she
may do it** de quelque manière qu'elle le
fasse; **h. that may be** quoi qu'il en soit. **2**
conj cependant.

howl [haul] *vi* hurler; (*of wind*) mugir ▮ *n*
hurlement *m*; mugissement *m*; (*of
laughter*) éclat *m*.

howler ['haulər] *n* (*mistake*) *Fam* gaffe *f*.

HP [eıt['pi:] *abbr* = **hire purchase.**

hp *abbr* (*horsepower*) CV.

HQ [eıt['kju:] *abbr* = **headquarters.**

hub [hʌb] *n* (*of wheel*) moyeu *m*; *Fig*
centre *m*. ●**hubcap** *n* *Aut* enjoliveur
m.

huddle ['hʌd(ə)l] *vi* **to h. (together)** se
blottir (les uns contre les autres).

hue [hju:] *n* teinte *f*, couleur *f*.

huff [hʌf] *n* **in a h.** (*offended*) *Fam* fâché.

hug [hʌg] *vt* (**-gg-**) (*person*) serrer (dans
ses bras); **to h. the kerb/coast** serrer le
trottoir/la côte ▮ *n* **to give s.o. a h.** serrer
qn (dans ses bras).

huge [hju:dʒ] *a* énorme.

hull [hʌl] *n* (*of ship*) coque *f*.

hullo! [hʌ'ləu] *int* = **hello.**

hum [hʌm] *vi* (**-mm-**) (*of insect*) bourdonner; (*of person*) fredonner; (*of top*)
ronfler; (*of engine*) vrombir ▮ *vt* (*tune*)
fredonner ▮ *n* (*of insect*) bourdonnement *m*.

human ['hju:mən] *a* humain; **h. being**
être *m* humain ▮ *npl* humains *mpl*.

humane [hju:'meın] *a* (*kind*) humain.

humanity [hju:'mænətı] *n* (*human beings,
kindness*) humanité *f*.

humble ['hʌmb(ə)l] *a* humble ▮ *vt* humilier.

humbug ['hʌmbʌg] *n* (*talk*) fumisterie *f*;
(*person*) fumiste *mf*.

humdrum ['hʌmdrʌm] *a* monotone.

humid ['hju:mɪd] *a* humide. ●**hu'midity** *n*
humidité *f*.

humiliate [hju:'mılıeıt] *vt* humilier.
●**humiliation** [-'eı['(ə)n] *n* humiliation
f.

humour ['hju:mər] (*Am* **humor**) **1** *n* (*fun*)
humour *m*; (*temper*) humeur *f*; **to have
a sense of h.** avoir le sens de l'humour. **2**
vt **to h. s.o.** faire plaisir à qn. ●**humorous** *a* (*book etc*) humoristique; (*person*)
plein d'humour.

hump [hʌmp] *n* **1** (*lump, mound*) bosse *f*.

2 to have the h. (*depression*) *Fam* avoir le cafard. ● **humpback bridge** *n Aut* pont *m* en dos d'âne.

hunch [hʌntʃ] **1** *n* (*idea*) *Fam* intuition *f*. **2** *vt* (*one's shoulders*) voûter. ● **hunchback** *n* bossu, -ue *mf*.

hundred ['hʌndrəd] *a & n* cent (*m*); **a h. pages** cent pages; **two h. pages** deux cents pages; **hundreds of** des centaines de. ● **hundredth** *a & n* centième (*mf*). ● **hundredweight** *n* 112 livres (= 50,8 kg); *Am* 100 livres (= 45,3 kg).

hung [hʌŋ] *pt & pp* of **hang**[1].

Hungary ['hʌŋgəri] *n* Hongrie *f*. ● **Hungarian** [hʌŋ'geəriən] *a & n* hongrois, -oise (*mf*) ▮ *n* (*language*) hongrois *m*.

hunger ['hʌŋgər] *n* faim *f*. ● **hungry** *a* (-ier, -iest) **to be** or **feel h.** avoir faim; **to go h.** souffrir de la faim; **to make s.o. h.** donner faim à qn.

hunk [hʌŋk] *n* (*gros*) morceau *m*.

hunt [hʌnt] *n* (*search*) recherche *f* (**for** de); (*for animals*) chasse *f* ▮ *vt* (*animals*) chasser; (*pursue*) poursuivre; (*seek*) chercher; **to h. down** (*fugitive etc*) traquer ▮ *vi* (*kill animals*) chasser; **to h. for sth** (re)chercher qch. ● **—ing** *n* chasse *f*. ● **hunter** *n* chasseur *m*.

hurdle ['hɜːd(ə)l] *n* (*fence*) *Sp* haie *f*; (*problem*) *Fig* obstacle *m*.

hurl [hɜːl] *vt* (*stone, abuse etc*) lancer (**at** à); **to h. oneself at s.o.** se ruer sur qn.

hurray! [hʊ'reɪ] *int* hourra!

hurricane ['hʌrɪkən, *Am* 'hʌrɪkeɪn] *n* ouragan *m*.

hurried ['hʌrɪd] *a* (*steps, decision*) précipité; (*work*) fait à la hâte; **to be h.** être pressé.

hurry ['hʌrɪ] *n* hâte *f*; **in a h.** à la hâte; **to be in a h.** être pressé; **to be in a h. to do** avoir hâte de faire; **there's no h.** rien ne presse ▮ *vi* se dépêcher (**to do** de faire); **to h. out** sortir à la hâte; **to h. towards** se précipiter vers; **to h. up** se dépêcher ▮ *vt* (*person*) bousculer; **to h. one's meal** manger à toute vitesse; **to h. one's work** se précipiter dans son travail; **to h. s.o. out** faire sortir

qn à la hâte.

hurt [hɜːt] *vt* (*pt & pp* hurt) (*physically*) faire du mal à; (*emotionally*) faire de la peine à; (*offend*) blesser; (*damage*) nuire à (*réputation etc*); **to h. s.o.'s feelings** blesser qn ▮ *vi* faire mal ▮ *n* mal *m*. ● **hurtful** *a* (*remark*) blessant.

hurtle ['hɜːt(ə)l] *vi* **to h. along** aller à toute vitesse; **to h. down** dégringoler.

husband ['hʌzbənd] *n* mari *m*.

hush [hʌʃ] *n* silence *m* ▮ *int* chut! ▮ *vt* **to h. up** (*scandal*) étouffer. ● **hush-hush** *a* *Fam* ultra-secret.

husk [hʌsk] *n* (*of rice, grain*) enveloppe *f*.

husky ['hʌskɪ] *a* (-ier, -iest) (*voice*) enroué.

hustle ['hʌs(ə)l] **1** *vt* (*shove*) bousculer (qn). **2** *n* **h. and bustle** tourbillon *m*.

hut [hʌt] *n* cabane *f*, hutte *f*.

hutch [hʌtʃ] *n* (*for rabbit*) clapier *m*.

hyacinth ['haɪəsɪnθ] *n* jacinthe *f*.

hybrid ['haɪbrɪd] *a & n* hybride (*m*).

hydrangea [haɪ'dreɪndʒə] *n* (*shrub*) hortensia *m*.

hydrant ['haɪdrənt] *n* (*fire*) **h.** bouche *f* d'incendie.

hydrofoil ['haɪdrəfɔɪl] *n* hydrofoil *m*.

hydrogen ['haɪdrədʒən] *n* hydrogène *m*.

hyena [haɪ'iːnə] *n* (*animal*) hyène *f*.

hygiene ['haɪdʒiːn] *n* hygiène *f*. ● **hygienic** *a* hygiénique.

hymn [hɪm] *n Rel* cantique *m*.

hype [haɪp] *n Fam* grand battage *m* publicitaire.

hyper- ['haɪpər] *pref* hyper-.

hypermarket ['haɪpəmɑːkɪt] *n* hypermarché *m*.

hyphen ['haɪf(ə)n] *n* trait *m* d'union. ● **hyphenated** *a* (*word*) à trait d'union.

hypnotism ['hɪpnətɪz(ə)m] *n* hypnotisme *m*. ● **hypnotize** *vt* hypnotiser.

hypoallergenic [haɪpəʊælə'dʒenɪk] *a* hypoallergénique.

hypocrisy [hɪ'pɒkrɪsɪ] *n* hypocrisie *f*. ● **hypocrite** ['hɪpəkrɪt] *n* hypocrite *mf*. ● **hypo'critical** *a* hypocrite.

hypothesis, *pl* -eses [haɪ'pɒθɪsɪs, -ɪsiːz] *n*

hypothèse *f*. ● **hypothetical** [-'θetɪk(ə)l]
a hypothétique
hysterical [hɪ'sterɪk(ə)l] *a* (*very upset*)
qui a une crise de nerfs; (*funny*) *Fam*
désopilant. ● **hysterically** *adv* (*to cry*)
sans pouvoir s'arrêter; **to laugh h.** rire
aux larmes. ● **hysterics** *npl* (*tears etc*)
crise *f* de nerfs; (*laughter*) crise *f* de rire.

I

I, i [aɪ] n I, i m.

I [aɪ] pron je, j'; (stressed) moi; **I want** je veux; **he and I** lui et moi.

ice¹ [aɪs] n glace f; (on road) verglas m; **i. cream** glace f; **i. cube** glaçon m ‖ vi **to i.** (over or up) (of lake) geler; (of window) se givrer.

ice² [aɪs] vt (cake) glacer. ● **icing** n (on cake etc) glaçage m.

iceberg ['aɪsbɜːg] n iceberg m. ● **icebox** n Am réfrigérateur m. ● **ice-'cold** a glacial; (drink) glacé. ● **ice-skating** n patinage m (sur glace).

Iceland ['aɪslənd] n Islande f. ● **Ice'landic** a islandais.

icicle ['aɪsɪk(ə)l] n glaçon m (naturel).

icy ['aɪsɪ] a (-ier, -iest) (water, hands, room) glacé; (weather) glacial; (road) verglacé.

ID [aɪdiː] n pièce f d'identité.

I'd [aɪd] = I had & I would.

idea [aɪ'dɪə] n idée f; **I have an i. that...** j'ai l'impression que...; **that's the i.!** Fam c'est ça!; **not the slightest or foggiest i.** pas la moindre idée.

ideal [aɪ'dɪəl] a idéal (mpl -aux or -als) ‖ n idéal m (pl -aux or -als). ● **idealist** n idéaliste mf. ● **ideally** adv idéalement; **i. we should stay** l'idéal, ce serait de rester or que nous restions.

identical [aɪ'dentɪk(ə)l] a identique (to, with à).

identify [aɪ'dentɪfaɪ] vt identifier; **to i. (oneself) with** s'identifier avec. ● **identi-fication** [-'keɪʃ(ə)n] n identification f; (document) pièce f d'identité.

identikit [aɪ'dentɪkɪt] n portrait-robot m.

identity [aɪ'dentɪtɪ] n identité f; **i. card** carte f d'identité.

idiom ['ɪdɪəm] n expression f idioma-tique. ● **idio'matic** a idiomatique.

idiosyncrasy [ɪdɪə'sɪŋkrəsɪ] n particu-

larité f.

idiot ['ɪdɪət] n idiot, -ote mf. ● **idi'otic** a idiot, bête.

idle ['aɪd(ə)l] a (unoccupied) inactif; (lazy) paresseux; (unemployed) au chômage; (machine) au repos; (pro-mise, pleasure) vain; (rumour) sans fondement; **an i. moment** un moment de loisir ‖ vi (of engine) tourner au ralenti ‖ vt **to i. away** (time) gaspiller. ● **idler** n paresseux, -euse mf.

idol ['aɪd(ə)l] n idole f. ● **idolize** vt (adore) traiter comme une idole.

i.e. [aɪ'iː] abbr (id est) c'est-à-dire.

if [ɪf] conj si; **if he comes** s'il vient; **even if** même si; **if so** dans ce cas; **if not** sinon; **if only I were rich** si seulement j'étais riche; **if only to look** ne serait-ce que pour regarder; **as if** comme si; **if necessary** s'il le faut.

igloo ['ɪgluː] n igloo m.

ignite [ɪg'naɪt] vt mettre le feu à ‖ vi prendre feu. ● **ignition** [ɪg'nɪʃ(ə)n] n Aut allumage m; **to switch on/off the i.** mettre/couper le contact.

ignorance ['ɪgnərəns] n ignorance f (of de). ● **ignorant** a ignorant (of de).

ignore [ɪg'nɔːr] vt ne prêter aucune attention à, ne tenir aucun compte de (qch); (pretend not to recognize) faire semblant de ne pas reconnaître (qn).

ill [ɪl] a (sick) malade; (bad) mauvais; **i. will** malveillance f ‖ npl ills (misfor-tunes) maux mpl ‖ adv mal; **to speak i. of** dire du mal de.

I'll [aɪl] = I will or I shall.

ill-advised [ɪləd'vaɪzd] a peu judicieux. ● **ill-'fated** a malheureux. ● **ill-in'formed** a mal renseigné. ● **ill-'mannered** a mal élevé. ● **ill-'natured** a (mean, unkind) désagréable. ● **ill-'timed** a inopportun. ● **ill-'treat** vt maltraiter.

illegal [ɪˈliːg(ə)l] a illégal.

illegible [ɪˈledʒəb(ə)l] a illisible.

illegitimate [ɪlɪˈdʒɪtɪmət] a illégitime.

illicit [ɪˈlɪsɪt] a illicite.

illiterate [ɪˈlɪtərət] a & n illettré, -ée (mf). ● **illiteracy** n analphabétisme m.

illness [ˈɪlnɪs] n maladie f.

illuminate [ɪˈluːmɪneɪt] vt (street etc) éclairer; (monument etc for special occasion) illuminer. ● **illuminations** [-ˈneɪʃ(ə)nz] npl (decorative lights) illuminations fpl.

illusion [ɪˈluːʒ(ə)n] n illusion f (about sur); **to be under the i. that** avoir l'illusion que.

illustrate [ˈɪləstreɪt] vt (with pictures, examples) illustrer (**with** de). ● **illustration** [-ˈstreɪʃ(ə)n] n illustration f.

image [ˈɪmɪdʒ] n image f; **(public) i.** (of company) image f de marque; **he's the i. of his brother** c'est tout le portrait de son frère.

imaginary [ɪˈmædʒɪn(ə)rɪ] a imaginaire.

imagination [ɪmædʒɪˈneɪʃ(ə)n] n imagination f.

imaginative [ɪˈmædʒɪnətɪv] a (plan, person etc) plein d'imagination.

imagin/e [ɪˈmædʒɪn] vt (picture to oneself) (s')imaginer (**that** que); (suppose) imaginer (**that** que); **you're imagining (things)!** tu te fais des illusions! ● **—able** a imaginable; **the worst thing i.** le pire que l'on puisse imaginer.

imbecile [ˈɪmbəsiːl, Am ˈɪmbəs(ə)l] a & n imbécile (mf).

imbued [ɪmˈbjuːd] a **i. with** (ideas) imprégné de.

imitate [ˈɪmɪteɪt] vt imiter. ● **imitation** [-ˈteɪʃ(ə)n] n imitation f; **i. jewellery** or Am **jewelry** bijoux mpl fantaisie; **i. leather** similicuir m.

immaculate [ɪˈmækjʊlət] a (person, shirt etc) impeccable.

immaterial [ɪməˈtɪərɪəl] a peu important.

immature [ɪməˈtjʊər] a (person) qui manque de maturité; (animal) jeune.

immediate [ɪˈmiːdɪət] a immédiat. ● **immediately** adv (at once) tout de suite, immédiatement; **i. above/below** juste au-dessus/en dessous ‖ conj (as soon as) dès que.

immense [ɪˈmens] a immense. ● **immensely** adv extraordinairement.

immerse [ɪˈmɜːs] vt (in liquid) plonger; **immersed in work** plongé dans le travail. ● **immersion** [-ʃ(ə)n] n **i. heater** chauffe-eau m inv électrique.

immigrate [ˈɪmɪgreɪt] vi immigrer. ● **immigrant** n immigré, -ée mf ‖ a immigré. ● **immigration** [-ˈgreɪʃ(ə)n] n immigration f.

imminent [ˈɪmɪnənt] a imminent.

immobile [ɪˈməʊbaɪl, Am ɪˈməʊb(ə)l] a immobile. ● **immobilize** vt immobiliser.

immoral [ɪˈmɒrəl] a immoral.

immortal [ɪˈmɔːt(ə)l] a immortel. ● **immortalize** vt immortaliser.

immune [ɪˈmjuːn] a (naturally) immunisé (**to** contre); (vaccinated) vacciné; **i. to** Fig à l'abri de. ● **immunize** vt vacciner (**against** contre).

imp [ɪmp] n diablotin, lutin m.

impact [ˈɪmpækt] n (shock) impact; (effect) effet m (**on** sur).

impair [ɪmˈpeər] vt détériorer; (hearing, health) abîmer.

impale [ɪmˈpeɪl] vt empaler.

impart [ɪmˈpɑːt] vt communiquer (**to** à).

impartial [ɪmˈpɑːʃ(ə)l] a impartial.

impassable [ɪmˈpɑːsəb(ə)l] a (road) impraticable; (river) infranchissable.

impassive [ɪmˈpæsɪv] a impassible.

impatient [ɪmˈpeɪʃ(ə)nt] a impatient (**to do** de faire); **i. with s.o.** intolérant à l'égard de qn. ● **impatience** n impatience f. ● **impatiently** adv avec impatience.

impeccable [ɪmˈpekəb(ə)l] a (manners, person) impeccable.

impecunious [ɪmpɪˈkjuːnɪəs] a sans le sou.

impede [ɪmˈpiːd] vt (hamper) gêner; **to i. s.o. from doing** (prevent) empêcher qn de faire.

impediment [ɪmˈpedɪmənt] n (speech) n défaut m d'élocution.

impending [ɪmˈpendɪŋ] a imminent.

imperative [ɪm'perətɪv] a (necessary) indispensable; **it is i. that** il est indispensable que (+ sub) **‖** n Gram impératif m.

imperfect [ɪm'pɜːfɪkt] **1** a imparfait; (goods) défectueux. **2** a & n i. (tense) Gram imparfait m. ● **imperfection** [ɪmpə'fekʃ(ə)n] n imperfection f.

imperial [ɪm'pɪərɪəl] a impérial; **i. measure** Br mesure f légale (anglo-saxonne).

impersonal [ɪm'pɜːsən(ə)l] a impersonnel.

impersonate [ɪm'pɜːsəneɪt] vt (pretend to be) se faire passer pour; (on TV etc) imiter. ● **impersonation** [-'neɪʃ(ə)n] n imitation f. ● **impersonator** n (on TV etc) imitateur, -trice mf.

impertinent [ɪm'pɜːtɪnənt] a impertinent (to envers). ● **impertinence** n impertinence f.

impervious [ɪm'pɜːvɪəs] a imperméable (to à).

impetuous [ɪm'petjʊəs] a impétueux.

impetus ['ɪmpɪtəs] n impulsion f.

impinge [ɪm'pɪndʒ] vi **to i. on** (affect) affecter; (encroach on) empiéter sur.

impish ['ɪmpɪʃ] a (naughty) espiègle.

implant [ɪm'plɑːnt] vt (surgically) implanter (**in** dans); (ideas) inculquer (**in** à).

implement[1] ['ɪmplɪmənt] n (tool) instrument m; (utensil) ustensile m.

implement[2] ['ɪmplɪment] vt (carry out) mettre en œuvre, exécuter.

implicate ['ɪmplɪkeɪt] vt impliquer (**in** dans). ● **implication** [-'keɪʃ(ə)n] n (consequence) conséquence f; (involvement) implication f; (impact) portée f; **by i.** implicitement.

implicit [ɪm'plɪsɪt] a (implied) implicite; (obedience etc) absolu. ●—**ly** adv implicitement.

implore [ɪm'plɔːr] vt implorer (**s.o. to do** qn de faire).

imply [ɪm'plaɪ] vt (suggest) laisser entendre (**that** que); (assume) impliquer (**that** que); (insinuate) insinuer (**that** que). ● **implied** a implicite.

impolite [ɪmpə'laɪt] a impoli.

import [ɪm'pɔːt] vt (goods etc) importer (**from** de) **‖** ['ɪmpɔːt] n (imported product) importation f. ● **im'porter** n importateur, -trice mf.

importance [ɪm'pɔːtəns] n importance f; **to be of i.** avoir de l'importance; **of no i.** sans importance.

important [ɪm'pɔːtənt] a important (**that** que (+ sub)).

impose [ɪm'pəʊz] vt imposer (**on** à); (fine, punishment) infliger (**on** à) **‖** vi (cause trouble) déranger; **to i. on s.o.** déranger qn. ● **imposition** [-pə'zɪʃ(ə)n] n (inconvenience) dérangement m.

imposing [ɪm'pəʊzɪŋ] a (building) impressionnant.

impossible [ɪm'pɒsəb(ə)l] a impossible (**to do** à faire); **it is i. (for us) to do it** (nous) est impossible de faire; **it is i. that** il est impossible que (+ sub) **‖** n **to do the i.** faire l'impossible. ● **impossi'bility** n impossibilité f.

impostor [ɪm'pɒstər] n imposteur m.

impotent ['ɪmpətənt] a Med impuissant.

impound [ɪm'paʊnd] vt (of police) saisir, confisquer.

impoverished [ɪm'pɒvərɪʃt] a appauvri.

impracticable [ɪm'præktɪkəb(ə)l] a impraticable.

impractical [ɪm'præktɪk(ə)l] a peu réaliste.

imprecise [ɪmprɪ'saɪs] a imprécis.

impregnable [ɪm'pregnəb(ə)l] a (fortress etc) imprenable.

impresario [ɪmprɪ'sɑːrɪəʊ] n (pl -os) impresario m.

impress [ɪm'pres] vt impressionner (qn); **to i. sth on s.o.** faire comprendre qch à qn.

impression [ɪm'preʃ(ə)n] n impression f; **to be under** or **have the i. that** avoir l'impression que. ● **impressionable** a (person) impressionnable.

impressionist [ɪm'preʃənɪst] n (entertainer) imitateur, -trice mf.

impressive [ɪm'presɪv] a impressionnant.

imprint [ɪm'prɪnt] *vt* imprimer ▮ ['ɪmprɪnt] *n* empreinte *f*.

imprison [ɪm'prɪz(ə)n] *vt* emprisonner. ●**—ment** *n* emprisonnement *m*; **life i.** la prison à vie.

improbable [ɪm'prɒbəb(ə)l] *a* peu probable; (*story, excuse*) invraisemblable. ● **improba'bility** *n* improbabilité *f*.

improper [ɪm'prɒpər] *a* (*indecent*) indécent; (*wrong*) (*use etc*) incorrect.

improve [ɪm'pruːv] *vt* améliorer; (*mind*) cultiver; **to i. oneself** se cultiver ▮ *vi* s'améliorer; (*of business*) reprendre; **to i. on** (*do better than*) faire mieux que. ●**—ment** *n* amélioration *f* (**in** de); (*progress*) progrès *m(pl)*; **to be an i. on sth** être supérieur à qch.

improvise ['ɪmprəvaɪz] *vti* improviser. ● **improvisation** [-'zeɪʃ(ə)n] *n* improvisation *f*.

impudent ['ɪmpjʊdənt] *a* impudent.

impulse ['ɪmpʌls] *n* impulsion *f*; **on i.** sur un coup de tête. ● **im'pulsive** *a* (*person, act*) impulsif, irréfléchi.

impunity [ɪm'pjuːnɪtɪ] *n* **with i.** impunément.

impurity [ɪm'pjʊərɪtɪ] *n* impureté *f*.

in [ɪn] *prep* **1** dans; **in the box/the school/ etc** dans la boîte/l'école/*etc*; **in an hour('s time)** dans une heure; **in luxury** dans le luxe; **in so far as** dans la mesure où.

2 à; **in school** à l'école; **in the sun** au soleil; **in Paris** à Paris; **in the USA** aux USA; **in Portugal** au Portugal; **in fashion** à la mode; **in ink** à l'encre; **in spring** au printemps.

3 en; **in summer/May/French** en été/mai/français; **in Spain** en Espagne; **in secret** en secret; **in an hour** (*during that period*) en une heure; **in doing** en faisant; **dressed in black** habillé en noir; **in all** en tout.

4 de; **in a soft voice** d'une voix douce; **the best in the class** le meilleur de la classe; **an increase in** une augmentation de; **at six in the evening** à six heures du soir.

5 chez; **in children/animals** chez les enfants/les animaux; **in Shakespeare** chez Shakespeare.

6 in the rain sous la pluie; **in the morning** le matin; **he hasn't done it in years** ça fait des années qu'il ne l'a pas fait; **in an hour** (*at the end of that period*) au bout d'une heure; **one in ten** un sur dix; **in tens** dix par dix; **in thousands** par milliers; **in here** ici; **in there** là-dedans.

▮ *adv* **to be in** (*home*) être là, être à la maison; (*of train*) être arrivé; (*in fashion*) être à la mode; (*in season*) être de saison; (*in power*) *Pol* être au pouvoir; **day in day out** jour après jour; **we're in for some rain/trouble** on va avoir de la pluie/des ennuis; **it's the in thing** *Fam* c'est dans le vent.

▮ *npl* **the ins and outs of** les moindres détails de.

in- [ɪn] *pref* in-.

inability [ɪnə'bɪlɪtɪ] *n* incapacité *f* (**to do** de faire).

inaccessible [ɪnək'sesəb(ə)l] *a* inaccessible.

inaccurate [ɪn'ækjʊrət] *a* inexact. ● **inaccuracy** *n* (*error*) inexactitude *f*.

inaction [ɪn'ækʃ(ə)n] *n* inaction *f*.

inactive [ɪn'æktɪv] *a* inactif; (*mind*) inerte.

inadequate [ɪn'ædɪkwət] *a* (*quantity*) insuffisant; (*person*) pas à la hauteur; (*work*) médiocre. ● **inadequacy** *n* insuffisance *f*.

inadvertently [ɪnəd'vɜːtəntlɪ] *adv* par inadvertance.

inadvisable [ɪnəd'vaɪzəb(ə)l] *a* (*action*) à déconseiller; **it is i. to ...** il est déconseillé de....

inanimate [ɪn'ænɪmət] *a* inanimé.

inappropriate [ɪnə'prəʊprɪət] *a* (*unsuitable*) (*place, remark etc*) qui ne convient pas.

inarticulate [ɪnɑː'tɪkjʊlət] *a* (*person*) incapable de s'exprimer; (*sound*) inarticulé.

inasmuch as [ɪnəz'mʌtʃəz] *adv* (*be-*

cause) vu que; (*to the extent that*) en ce sens que.

inattentive [ɪnə'tentɪv] *a* inattentif (**to** à).

inaugural [ɪ'nɔːgjʊrəl] *a* inaugural. ● **inaugurate** *vt* (*building*) inaugurer. ● **inauguration** [-'reɪʃ(ə)n] *n* inauguration *f*.

inborn [ɪn'bɔːn] *a* inné.

Inc *abbr* (*Incorporated*) *Am Com* SA, SARL.

incalculable [ɪn'kælkjʊləb(ə)l] *a* incalculable.

incapable [ɪn'keɪpəb(ə)l] *a* incapable (**of doing** de faire); **i. of** (*pity etc*) inaccessible à.

incapacitate [ɪnkə'pæsɪteɪt] *vt* (*for work*) rendre incapable (*de travailler*).

incendiary [ɪn'sendɪərɪ] *a* (*bomb*) incendiaire.

incense 1 [ɪn'sens] *vt* mettre en colère. **2** ['ɪnsens] *n* (*substance*) encens *m*.

incentive [ɪn'sentɪv] *n* encouragement *m*, motivation *f*; **to give s.o. an i. to work** encourager qn à travailler.

incessant [ɪn'ses(ə)nt] *a* incessant. ● **—ly** *adv* sans cesse.

incest ['ɪnsest] *n* inceste *m*.

inch [ɪntʃ] *n* pouce *m* (= *2,54 cm*); **within an i. of** (*success*) à deux doigts de; **i. by i.** petit à petit ‖ *vi* **to i. forward** avancer petit à petit.

incident ['ɪnsɪdənt] *n* incident *m*; (*in book, film etc*) épisode *m*.

incidental [ɪnsɪ'dent(ə)l] *a* (*additional*) accessoire, secondaire. ● **—ly** *adv* (*by the way*) à propos.

incinerator [ɪn'sɪnəreɪtər] *n* incinérateur *m*.

incision [ɪn'sɪʒ(ə)n] *n* incision *f*.

incite [ɪn'saɪt] *vt* inciter (**to do** à faire). ● **—ment** *n* incitation *f* (**to do** à faire).

incline 1 [ɪn'klaɪn] *vt* (*bend*) incliner; **to be inclined to do** (*feel a wish to*) avoir bien envie de faire; (*tend to*) avoir tendance à faire. **2** ['ɪnklaɪn] *n* (*slope*) inclinaison *f*. ● **inclination** [-'neɪʃ(ə)n] *n* (*tendency*) inclination *f*; (*desire*) envie *f* (**to do** de faire).

includ/e [ɪn'kluːd] *vt* (*contain*) com-

prendre; **my invitation includes you** mon invitation s'adresse aussi à vous; **to be included** être compris; (*on list*) être inclus. ● **—ing** *prep* y compris; **i. service** service *m* compris; **up to and including Monday** jusqu'à lundi inclus.

inclusion [ɪn'kluːʒ(ə)n] *n* inclusion *f*.

inclusive [ɪn'kluːsɪv] *a* inclus; **from the fourth to the tenth of May i.** du quatre jusqu'au dix mai inclus; **to be i. of** comprendre; **i. charge** prix *m* global.

incoherent [ɪnkəʊ'hɪərənt] *a* incohérent.

income ['ɪnkʌm] *n* revenu *m* (**from** de); **private i.** rentes *fpl*; **i. tax** impôt *m* sur le revenu.

incoming ['ɪnkʌmɪŋ] *a* (*president etc*) nouveau (*f* nouvelle); **i. tide** marée *f* montante; **i. calls** *Tel* appels *mpl* de l'extérieur.

incompatible [ɪnkəm'pætəb(ə)l] *a* incompatible (**with** avec).

incompetent [ɪn'kɒmpɪtənt] *a* incompétent.

incomplete [ɪnkəm'pliːt] *a* incomplet.

incomprehensible [ɪnkɒmprɪ'hensəb(ə)l] *a* incompréhensible.

inconceivable [ɪnkən'siːvəb(ə)l] *a* inconcevable.

inconclusive [ɪnkən'kluːsɪv] *a* peu concluant.

incongruous [ɪn'kɒŋgrʊəs] *a* (*building, colours*) qui jure(nt) (**with** avec); (*remark*) incongru; (*absurd*) absurde.

inconsiderate [ɪnkən'sɪdərət] *a* (*action, remark*) irréfléchi; (*person*) pas très gentil (**towards** avec).

inconsistent [ɪnkən'sɪstənt] *a* (*reports etc*) en contradiction (**with** avec); (*person*) inconséquent, incohérent. ● **inconsistency** *n* incohérence *f*.

inconspicuous [ɪnkən'spɪkjʊəs] *a* peu en évidence.

inconvenient [ɪnkən'viːnɪənt] *a* (*moment, situation etc*) gênant; (*house, school*) mal situé; **it's i. (for me) to...** ça me dérange de.... ● **inconvenience** *n* (*bother*) dérangement *m*; (*disadvantage*) inconvénient *m* ‖ *vt* déranger.

gêner.

incorporate [ɪnˈkɔːpəreɪt] vt (contain) contenir; (introduce) incorporer (**into** dans); **incorporated society** Am société f anonyme, société f à responsabilité limitée.

incorrect [ɪnkəˈrekt] a inexact; **you're i.** vous avez tort.

increas/e [ɪnˈkriːs] vi augmenter; (of effort, noise) s'intensifier; **to i. in weight** prendre du poids ▮ vt augmenter; intensifier ▮ [ˈɪnkriːs] n augmentation f (**in, of** de); intensification f (**in, of** de); **on the i.** en hausse. ●—**ing** a (amount etc) croissant. ●—**ingly** adv de plus en plus.

incredible [ɪnˈkredəb(ə)l] a incroyable. ● **incredibly** adv incroyablement.

incredulous [ɪnˈkredjʊləs] a incrédule.

increment [ˈɪŋkrəmənt] n augmentation f.

incriminat/e [ɪnˈkrɪmɪneɪt] vt incriminer. ●—**ing** a compromettant.

incubate [ˈɪŋkjʊbeɪt] vt (eggs) couver. ● **incubator** n (for baby, eggs) couveuse f.

incur [ɪnˈkɜːr] vt (-rr-) (expenses) faire; (loss) subir; (debt) contracter; (criticism) s'attirer.

incurable [ɪnˈkjʊərəb(ə)l] a incurable.

indebted [ɪnˈdetɪd] a **i. to s.o. for sth/for doing sth** redevable à qn de qch/d'avoir fait qch.

indecent [ɪnˈdiːs(ə)nt] a (obscene) indécent. ● **indecency** n (crime) outrage m à la pudeur.

indecisive [ɪndɪˈsaɪsɪv] a (person, answer) indécis.

indeed [ɪnˈdiːd] adv en effet; **very good/** etc **i.** vraiment très bon/etc; **yes i.!** bien sûr!; **thank you very much i.!** merci infiniment!

indefinite [ɪnˈdefɪnət] a (feeling, duration) indéfini; (plan) mal déterminé. ●—**ly** adv indéfiniment.

indelible [ɪnˈdeləb(ə)l] a (ink, memory) indélébile; **i. pen** stylo m à encre indélébile.

indemnify [ɪnˈdemnɪfaɪ] vt indemniser (**for** de). ● **indemnity** n (compensation) indemnité f.

indented [ɪnˈdentɪd] a (edge) dentelé.

independent [ɪndɪˈpendənt] a indépendant (**of** de); (reports) de sources différentes. ● **independence** n indépendance f. ● **independently** adv de façon indépendante; **i. of** indépendamment de.

indestructible [ɪndɪˈstrʌktəb(ə)l] a indestructible.

index [ˈɪndeks] n (in book) index m; (in library) catalogue m; (number, sign) indice m; **i. card** fiche f; **i. finger** index m ▮ vt (classify) classer. ● **i.-linked** a (wages etc) indexé (**to** sur).

India [ˈɪndɪə] n Inde f. ● **Indian** a & n indien, -ienne (mf).

indicate [ˈɪndɪkeɪt] vt indiquer (**that** que); **I was indicating right** Aut j'avais mis mon clignotant droit. ● **indication** [-ˈkeɪʃ(ə)n] n (sign) indice m, indication f; (idea) idée f.

indicative [ɪnˈdɪkətɪv] a **i. of** (symptomatic) symptomatique de ▮ n (mood) Gram indicatif m.

indicator [ˈɪndɪkeɪtər] n (instrument) indicateur m; (sign) indication f (**of** de); Aut clignotant m.

indict [ɪnˈdaɪt] vt inculper (**for** de).

Indies [ˈɪndɪz] npl **the West I.** les Antilles fpl.

indifferent [ɪnˈdɪf(ə)rənt] a indifférent (**to** à); (mediocre) médiocre. ● **indifference** n indifférence f (**to** à).

indigestion [ɪndɪˈdʒestʃ(ə)n] n problèmes mpl de digestion; (**an attack of**) **i.** une indigestion.

indignant [ɪnˈdɪgnənt] a indigné (**at** de); **to become i.** s'indigner. ●—**ly** adv avec indignation. ● **indignation** [-ˈneɪʃ(ə)n] n indignation f.

indigo [ˈɪndɪgəʊ] n & a (colour) indigo m & a inv.

indirect [ɪndaɪˈrekt] a indirect. ●—**ly** adv indirectement.

indiscreet [ɪndɪˈskriːt] a indiscret.

indiscriminate [ɪndɪˈskrɪmɪnət] a (ran-

dom) fait, donné *etc* au hasard; (*person*) qui manque de discernement. ● —**ly** *adv* (*at random*) au hasard.
indispensable [ɪndɪ'spensəb(ə)l] *a* indispensable (**to** à).
indisposed [ɪndɪ'spəʊzd] *a* (*unwell*) indisposé.
indisputable [ɪndɪ'spjuːtəb(ə)l] *a* incontestable.
indistinct [ɪndɪ'stɪŋkt] *a* indistinct.
indistinguishable [ɪndɪ'stɪŋgwɪʃəb(ə)l] *a* indifférenciable (**from** de).
individual [ɪndɪ'vɪdʒʊəl] *a* (*separate, personal*) individuel; (*specific*) particulier ‖ *n* (*person*) individu *m*. ● **individualist** *n* individualiste *mf*. ● **individually** *adv* (*separately*) individuellement; (*unusually*) de façon (très) personnelle.
indivisible [ɪndɪ'vɪzəb(ə)l] *a* indivisible.
Indo-China [ɪndəʊ'tʃaɪnə] *n* Indochine *f*.
indoctrinate [ɪn'dɒktrɪneɪt] *vt* endoctriner. ● **indoctrination** [-'neɪʃ(ə)n] *n* endoctrinement *m*.
Indonesia [ɪndəʊ'niːʒə] *n* Indonésie *f*.
indoor ['ɪndɔːr] *a* (*games, shoes etc*) d'intérieur; (*swimming pool etc*) couvert. ● **in'doors** *adv* à l'intérieur; **to go** *or* **come i.** rentrer.
induce [ɪn'djuːs] *vt* (*persuade*) persuader (*qn*) (**to do** de faire); (*cause*) provoquer. ● **inducement** *n* incitation *f*.
indulge [ɪn'dʌldʒ] *vt* (*s.o.'s wishes*) satisfaire; (*child etc*) gâter; **to i. oneself** se gâter ‖ *vi* **to i. in** (*ice cream etc*) se permettre; (*vice etc*) s'adonner à. ● **indulgence** *n* indulgence *f*. ● **indulgent** *a* indulgent (**to** envers).
industrial [ɪn'dʌstrɪəl] *a* industriel; (*conflict*) du travail; **to take i. action** se mettre en grève; **i. estate**, *Am* **i. park** zone *f* industrielle. ● **industrialist** *n* industriel *m*. ● **industrialized** *a* industrialisé.
industrious [ɪn'dʌstrɪəs] *a* travailleur.
industry ['ɪndəstrɪ] *n* industrie *f*; (*hard work*) application *f*.
inedible [ɪn'edəb(ə)l] *a* immangeable.
ineffective [ɪnɪ'fektɪv] *a* (*measure etc*) inefficace; (*person*) incapable.

ineffectual [ɪnɪ'fektʃʊəl] *a* = **ineffective**.
inefficient [ɪnɪ'fɪʃ(ə)nt] *a* (*person, measure etc*) inefficace; (*machine*) peu performant. ● **inefficiency** *n* inefficacité *f*.
inept [ɪ'nept] *a* (*unskilled*) peu habile (**at sth** à qch); (*incompetent*) incapable.
inequality [ɪnɪ'kwɒlɪtɪ] *n* inégalité *f*.
inert [ɪ'nɜːt] *a* inerte.
inescapable [ɪnɪ'skeɪpəb(ə)l] *a* inéluctable.
inevitable [ɪn'evɪtəb(ə)l] *a* inévitable. ● **inevitably** *adv* inévitablement.
inexcusable [ɪnɪk'skjuːzəb(ə)l] *a* inexcusable.
inexorable [ɪn'eksərəb(ə)l] *a* inexorable.
inexpensive [ɪnɪk'spensɪv] *a* bon marché *inv*.
inexperience [ɪnɪk'spɪərɪəns] *n* inexpérience *f*. ● **inexperienced** *a* inexpérimenté.
inexplicable [ɪnɪk'splɪkəb(ə)l] *a* inexplicable.
infallible [ɪn'fæləb(ə)l] *a* infaillible.
infamous ['ɪnfəməs] *a* (*evil*) infâme. ● **infamy** *n* infamie *f*.
infancy ['ɪnfənsɪ] *n* petite enfance *f*; **to be in its i.** (*of technique etc*) en être à ses premiers balbutiements.
infant ['ɪnfənt] *n* (*child*) petit(e) enfant *mf*; (*baby*) nourrisson *m*; **i. school** classes *fpl* préparatoires. ● **infantile** [-aɪl] *a* (*illness, reaction*) infantile.
infantry ['ɪnfəntrɪ] *n* infanterie *f*.
infatuated [ɪn'fætʃʊeɪtɪd] *a* amoureux (**with s.o.** de qn). ● **infatuation** [-'eɪʃ(ə)n] *n* engouement *m* (**for, with** pour).
infect [ɪn'fekt] *vt* infecter; **to become** *or* **get infected** s'infecter. ● **infection** [-ʃ(ə)n] *n* infection *f*. ● **infectious** [-ʃəs] *a* (*disease, person*) contagieux.
infer [ɪn'fɜːr] *vt* (**-rr-**) déduire (**from** de, **that** que).
inferior [ɪn'fɪərɪər] *a* inférieur (**to** à); (*goods, work*) de qualité inférieure ‖ *n* (*person*) inférieur, -eure *mf*. ● **infer'iority** *n* infériorité *f*.
infernal [ɪn'fɜːn(ə)l] *a* infernal.
inferno [ɪn'fɜːnəʊ] *n* (*pl* **-os**) (*blaze*)

brasier m; (hell) enfer m.

infertile [ɪnˈfɜːtaɪl, Am ɪnˈfɜːt(ə)l] a (person, land) stérile.

infest [ɪnˈfest] vt infester (**with** de).

infidelity [ɪnfɪˈdelɪtɪ] n infidélité f.

infighting [ˈɪnfaɪtɪŋ] n (within group) luttes fpl intestines.

infiltrate [ˈɪnfɪltreɪt] vi s'infiltrer (**into** dans) ▮ vt (group etc) s'infiltrer dans.

infinite [ˈɪnfɪnɪt] a & n infini (m). ●—**ly** adv infiniment. ● in'**finity** n Math Phot infini m.

infinitive [ɪnˈfɪnɪtɪv] n Gram infinitif m.

infirm [ɪnˈfɜːm] a infirme. ● **infirmary** n (hospital) hôpital m.

inflam/e [ɪnˈfleɪm] vt enflammer. ●—**ed** a (throat etc) enflammé. ● **inflammable** a inflammable. ● **inflammation** [ɪnfləˈmeɪʃ(ə)n] n Med inflammation f.

inflate [ɪnˈfleɪt] vt (balloon, prices etc) gonfler. ● **inflatable** a gonflable. ● **inflation** [-ʃ(ə)n] n Econ inflation f. ● **inflationary** a Econ inflationniste.

inflection [ɪnˈflek(ʃ)ən] n Gram flexion f.

inflexible [ɪnˈfleksəb(ə)l] a inflexible.

inflict [ɪnˈflɪkt] vt (wound) occasionner (**on** à); (punishment) infliger (**on** à); **to i. pain on s.o.** faire souffrir qn.

influence [ˈɪnfluəns] n influence f; **under the i. of** (drugs) sous l'effet de; **under the i. (of drink)** Jur en état d'ébriété ▮ vt influencer. ● **influential** [-ˈenʃəl] a **to be i.** avoir une grande influence.

influenza [ɪnfluˈenzə] n Med grippe f.

influx [ˈɪnflʌks] n afflux m (**of** de).

info [ˈɪnfəʊ] n Fam tuyaux mpl, renseignements mpl (**on** sur).

inform [ɪnˈfɔːm] vt informer (**of** de, **that** que); **to keep s.o. informed of** tenir qn au courant de ▮ vi **to i. on s.o.** dénoncer qn.

informal [ɪnˈfɔːm(ə)l] a (manner, person etc) simple, décontracté; (tone, expression) familier; (announcement) officieux; (meeting) non-officiel. ● **informally** adv sans cérémonie; (to dress) simplement; (to discuss) à titre non-officiel; (to meet) officieusement.

informant [ɪnˈfɔːmənt] n informateur, -trice mf.

information [ɪnfəˈmeɪʃ(ə)n] n (facts) renseignements mpl (**about, on** sur); (knowledge) & Comptr information f; **a piece of i.** un renseignement; **to get some i.** se renseigner.

informative [ɪnˈfɔːmətɪv] a instructif.

informer [ɪnˈfɔːmər] n (police) i. indicateur, -trice mf.

infrequent [ɪnˈfriːkwənt] a peu fréquent. ●—**ly** adv rarement.

infringe [ɪnˈfrɪndʒ] vt (rule) contrevenir à ▮ vi **to i. upon** (encroach on) empiéter sur.

infuriat/e [ɪnˈfjʊərɪeɪt] vt exaspérer. ●—**ing** a exaspérant.

ingenious [ɪnˈdʒiːnɪəs] a ingénieux. ● **ingenuity** [ɪndʒɪˈnjuːɪtɪ] n ingéniosité f.

ingrained [ɪnˈgreɪnd] a (prejudice) enraciné; **i. dirt** crasse f.

ingratiate [ɪnˈgreɪʃɪeɪt] vt **to i. oneself with** s'insinuer dans les bonnes grâces de.

ingredient [ɪnˈgriːdɪənt] n ingrédient m.

inhabit [ɪnˈhæbɪt] vt habiter. ●—**able** a habitable. ● **inhabitant** n habitant, -ante mf.

inhale [ɪnˈheɪl] vt (smell etc) aspirer; (fumes etc) respirer; **to i. the smoke** (of smoker) avaler la fumée.

inherent [ɪnˈhɪərənt] a inhérent (**in** à).

inherit [ɪnˈherɪt] vt hériter (de). ● **inheritance** n héritage m.

inhibit [ɪnˈhɪbɪt] vt (hinder) gêner; (prevent) empêcher (**from doing** de faire); **to be inhibited** avoir des inhibitions. ● **inhibition** [-ˈbɪʃ(ə)n] n inhibition f.

inhospitable [ɪnhɒˈspɪtəb(ə)l] a peu accueillant, inhospitalier.

inhuman [ɪnˈhjuːmən] a (not human, cruel) inhumain. ● **inhu'mane** a (not kind) inhumain.

initial [ɪˈnɪʃ(ə)l] a premier, initial ▮ npl **initials** (letters) initiales fpl; (signature) paraphe m ▮ vt (**-ll-**, Am **-l-**) parapher. ●—**ly** adv au début.

initiate [ɪˈnɪʃɪeɪt] vt (reform) amorcer;

(*attack, fashion*) lancer; (*policy*) inaugurer; **to i. s.o. into** initier qn à.

initiative [ɪ'nɪʃətɪv] n initiative f.

inject [ɪn'dʒekt] vt injecter (**into** sth dans qch); **to i. sth into s.o.** faire une piqûre de qch à qn. ● **injection** [-ʃ(ə)n] n injection f, piqûre f.

injur/e ['ɪndʒər] vt (*physically*) blesser, faire du mal à; **to i. one's foot**/*etc* se blesser au pied/*etc*. ●—**ed** a blessé ▌ **n the i.** les blessés *mpl*. ● **injury** n (*to flesh*) blessure f; (*fracture*) fracture f; (*sprain*) foulure f; (*bruise*) contusion f.

injustice [ɪn'dʒʌstɪs] n injustice f.

ink [ɪŋk] n encre f; **Indian i.** encre f de Chine. ● **inkwell** n encrier m.

inkling ['ɪŋklɪŋ] n (petite) idée f.

inlaid [ɪn'leɪd] a (*marble*) incrusté (**with** de); (*wood*) marqueté.

inland ['ɪnlənd] a intérieur; **the I. Revenue** Br le fisc ▌ [ɪn'lænd] adv à l'intérieur (*des terres*).

in-laws ['ɪnlɔːz] npl Fam belle-famille f.

inlet ['ɪnlet] n (*of sea*) crique f.

inmate ['ɪnmeɪt] n (*of prison*) détenu, -ue mf; (*of asylum*) interné, -ée mf.

inn [ɪn] n auberge f.

innards ['ɪnədz] npl Fam entrailles fpl.

innate [ɪ'neɪt] a inné.

inner ['ɪnər] a intérieur; (*feelings*) intime; **an i. circle** (*group of people*) un cercle restreint; **the i. city** les quartiers du centre-ville; **i. tube** (*of tyre, Am tire*) chambre f à air. ● **innermost** a le plus profond.

inning ['ɪnɪŋ] n Baseball tour m de batte. ● **innings** n inv Cricket tour m de batte.

innkeeper ['ɪnkiːpər] n aubergiste mf.

innocent ['ɪnəs(ə)nt] a innocent. ● **innocence** n innocence f.

innovate ['ɪnəveɪt] vi innover. ● **innovation** [-'veɪʃ(ə)n] n innovation f.

innuendo [ɪnjʊ'endəʊ] n (pl -oes or -os) insinuation f.

innumerable [ɪ'njuːmərəb(ə)l] a innombrable.

inoculate [ɪ'nɒkjʊlet] vt vacciner (**against** contre). ● **inoculation** [-'leɪʃ(ə)n] n vacci-

nation f.

inoffensive [ɪnə'fensɪv] a inoffensif.

inopportune [ɪn'ɒpətjuːn] a inopportun.

inordinate [ɪ'nɔːdɪnət] a excessif. ●—**ly** adv excessivement.

in-patient ['ɪnpeɪʃ(ə)nt] n malade mf hospitalisé(e).

input ['ɪnpʊt] n (*computer operation*) entrée f; (*data*) données fpl; (*resources*) ressources fpl.

inquest ['ɪnkwest] n enquête f.

inquire [ɪn'kwaɪər] vi se renseigner (**about** sur); **to i. after s.o.** demander des nouvelles de qn; **to i. into** faire une enquête sur ▌ vt demander; **to i. how to get to** demander le chemin de.

inquiry [ɪn'kwaɪərɪ] n demande f de renseignements; (*investigation*) enquête f; **to make inquiries** demander des renseignements; (*of police*) enquêter.

inquisitive [ɪn'kwɪzɪtɪv] a curieux. ● **inquisitively** adv avec curiosité.

inroads ['ɪnrəʊdz] npl (*attacks*) incursions fpl (**into** dans); **to make i. in** (*start on*) entamer.

insane [ɪn'seɪn] a fou (f folle). ● **insanity** n folie f.

insatiable [ɪn'seɪʃəb(ə)l] a insatiable.

inscribe [ɪn'skraɪb] vt inscrire; (*book*) dédicacer (**to** à). ● **inscription** [-skrɪpʃ(ə)n] n inscription f; dédicace f.

insect ['ɪnsekt] n insecte m; **i. repellent** crème f anti-insecte. ● **in'secticide** n insecticide m.

insecure [ɪnsɪ'kjʊər] a (*not securely fixed*) mal fixé; (*furniture, ladder*) branlant; (*uncertain*) incertain; (*person*) qui manque d'assurance.

insemination [ɪnsemɪ'neɪʃ(ə)n] n **artificial i.** Med insémination f artificielle.

insensitive [ɪn'sensɪtɪv] a insensible (**to** à). ● **insen'sitivity** n insensibilité f.

inseparable [ɪn'sep(ə)rəb(ə)l] a inséparable (**from** de).

insert [ɪn'sɜːt] vt insérer (**in, into** dans). ● **insertion** [-ʃ(ə)n] n insertion f.

inshore ['ɪnʃɔːr] a côtier ▌ adv près de la

côte.

inside [ɪn'saɪd] *adv* dedans, à l'intérieur; **come i.!** entrez! ∥ *prep* à l'intérieur de; *(time)* en moins de ∥ *n* dedans *m*, intérieur *m*; *pl (stomach) Fam* ventre *m*; **on the i.** à l'intérieur *(of de)*; **i. out** *(socks etc)* à l'envers; *(to know etc)* à fond.
∥ ['ɪnsaɪd] *a* intérieur; *(information)* obtenu à la source; **the i. lane** *Aut* la voie de gauche, *Am* la voie de droite.

insider [ɪn'saɪdər] *n* initié, -ée *mf*; **i. dealing** *(on Stock Exchange)* délit *m* d'initié.

insidious [ɪn'sɪdɪəs] *a* insidieux.

insight ['ɪnsaɪt] *n* perspicacité *f*; *(into question etc)* aperçu *m* **(into** de).

insignificant [ɪnsɪg'nɪfɪkənt] *a* insignifiant. ● **insignificance** *n* insignifiance *f*.

insincere [ɪnsɪn'sɪər] *a* peu sincère. ● **insincerity** *n* manque *m* de sincérité.

insinuate [ɪn'sɪnjʊeɪt] *vt Pej* insinuer **(that** que).

insipid [ɪn'sɪpɪd] *a* insipide.

insist [ɪn'sɪst] *vi* insister **(on doing** pour faire); **to i. on sth** *(demand)* exiger qch; *(assert)* affirmer qch ∥ *vt (order)* insister **(that** pour que + *sub*); *(declare)* affirmer **(that** que).

insistence [ɪn'sɪstəns] *n* insistance *f*; **her i. on seeing me** l'insistance qu'elle met à vouloir me voir. ● **insistent** *a* insistant; **to be i. (that)** insister (pour que + *sub*). ● **insistently** *adv* avec insistance.

insolent ['ɪnsələnt] *a* insolent. ● **insolence** *n* insolence *f*.

insoluble [ɪn'sɒljʊb(ə)l] *a* insoluble.

insolvent [ɪn'sɒlvənt] *a* insolvable.

insomnia [ɪn'sɒmnɪə] *n* insomnie *f*.

insomuch as [ɪnsəʊ'mʌtʃəz] *adv* = **inasmuch as.**

inspect [ɪn'spekt] *vt* inspecter; *(tickets)* contrôler. ● **inspection** [-ʃ(ə)n] *n* inspection *f*; *(of tickets)* contrôle *m*. ● **inspector** *n* inspecteur, -trice *mf*; *(on train)* contrôleur, -euse *mf*.

inspire [ɪn'spaɪər] *vt* inspirer **(s.o. with sth** qch à qn); **to be inspired to do** avoir l'inspiration de faire. ● **inspiration** [-spə'reɪʃ(ə)n] *n* inspiration *f*; *(person)* source *f* d'inspiration.

instability [ɪnstə'bɪlɪtɪ] *n* instabilité *f*.

install [ɪn'stɔːl] *(Am* **instal)** *vt* installer. ● **installation** [-stə'leɪʃ(ə)n] *n* installation *f*.

instalment [ɪn'stɔːlmənt] *(Am* **installment)** *n (of money)* acompte *m*; *(of serial, story)* épisode *m*; *(of publication)* fascicule *m*; **to buy on the i. plan** *Am* acheter à crédit.

instance ['ɪnstəns] *n (example)* exemple *m*; *(case)* cas *m*; **for i.** par exemple; **in the first i.** en premier lieu.

instant ['ɪnstənt] *a* immédiat; **i. coffee** café instantané *or* soluble; **of the 3rd i.** *(in letter)* Com du 3 courant ∥ *n (moment)* instant *m*; **this (very) i.** *(at once)* à l'instant. ● **instantly** *adv* immédiatement.

instead [ɪn'sted] *adv* plutôt, au lieu de cela; **i. of (doing) sth** au lieu de (faire) qch; **i. of s.o.** à la place de qn; **i. (of him or her)** à sa place.

instep ['ɪnstep] *n (of foot)* cou-de-pied *m*; *(of shoe)* cambrure *f*.

instigate ['ɪnstɪgeɪt] *vt* provoquer. ● **instigator** *n* instigateur, -trice *mf*.

instil [ɪn'stɪl] *vt* (**-ll-**) *(idea)* inculquer **(into** à); *(courage)* insuffler **(into** à).

instinct ['ɪnstɪŋkt] *n* instinct *m*; **by i.** d'instinct. ● **instinctive** *a* instinctif. ● **instinctively** *adv* instinctivement.

institute ['ɪnstɪtjuːt] **1** *n* institut *m*. **2** *vt (rule)* instituer; *(inquiry, proceedings)* Jur entamer.

institution [ɪnstɪ'tjuːʃ(ə)n] *n (organization, custom etc)* institution *f*; **educational/financial i.** établissement *m* scolaire/financier.

instruct [ɪn'strʌkt] *vt (teach)* enseigner **(s.o. in sth** qch à qn); **to i. s.o. about sth** *(inform)* instruire qn de qch; **to i. s.o. to do** *(order)* charger qn de faire. ● **instruction** [-ʃ(ə)n] *n (teaching)* instruction *f*; *pl (for use)* mode *m* d'emploi; *(orders)* instructions *fpl*. ● **instructive** *a* instructif. ● **instructor** n professeur m; (for skiing) moniteur, -trice mf; **driving i.** moniteur, -trice mf d'auto-école.

instrument ['ɪnstrəmənt] n instrument m. ● **instru'mental** a Mus instrumental; **to be i. in sth/in doing sth** contribuer à qch/à faire qch.

insubordinate [ɪnsə'bɔːdɪnət] a indiscipliné.

insufferable [ɪn'sʌfərəb(ə)l] a intolérable.

insufficient [ɪnsə'fɪʃənt] a insuffisant. ● **—ly** adv insuffisamment.

insular ['ɪnsjʊlər] a (climate) insulaire; (views) étroit.

insulate ['ɪnsjʊleɪt] vt (against cold and electrically) isoler; (against sound) insonoriser; **to i. s.o. from** protéger qn de; **insulating tape** chatterton m. ● **insulation** [-'leɪʃ(ə)n] n isolation f; insonorisation f; (material) isolant m.

insulin ['ɪnsjʊlɪn] n insuline f.

insult [ɪn'sʌlt] vt insulter ‖ ['ɪnsʌlt] n insulte f (to à).

insure [ɪn'ʃʊər] vt 1 (car, goods etc) assurer (against contre). 2 Am = **ensure**. ● **insurance** n assurance f; **i. company** compagnie f d'assurances; **i. policy** police f d'assurance.

insurmountable [ɪnsə'maʊntəb(ə)l] a insurmontable.

intact [ɪn'tækt] a intact.

intake ['ɪnteɪk] n (of food) consommation f; (of students, schoolchildren) admissions fpl.

intangible [ɪn'tændʒəb(ə)l] a intangible.

integral ['ɪntɪɡrəl] a intégral; **to be an i. part of** faire partie intégrante de.

integrate ['ɪntɪɡreɪt] vt intégrer (into dans); **integrated school** école f où se pratique la déségrégation raciale ‖ vi s'intégrer (into dans). ● **integration** [-'ɡreɪʃ(ə)n] n intégration f; (racial) déségrégation f raciale.

integrity [ɪn'teɡrɪtɪ] n intégrité f.

intellect ['ɪntɪlekt] n (cleverness, faculty) intelligence f. ● **inte'llectual** a & n intellectuel, -elle (mf).

intelligence [ɪn'telɪdʒəns] n intelligence f. ● **intelligent** a intelligent.

intelligible [ɪn'telɪdʒəb(ə)l] a compréhensible.

intend [ɪn'tend] 1 a (gift, remark etc) destiner (for à); **to be intended to do/ for s.o.** être destiné à faire/à qn; **to i. to do** avoir l'intention de faire. ● **—ed** a (deliberate) voulu.

intention [ɪn'tenʃ(ə)n] n intention f (of doing de faire).

intentional [ɪn'tenʃ(ə)n(ə)l] a voulu; **it wasn't i.** ce n'était pas fait exprès. ● **—ly** adv exprès.

intense [ɪn'tens] a intense; (interest) vif. ● **—ly** adv intensément; Fig extrêmement.

intensify [ɪn'tensɪfaɪ] vt intensifier ‖ vi s'intensifier.

intensity [ɪn'tensətɪ] n intensité f.

intensive [ɪn'tensɪv] a intensif; **in i. care** Med en réanimation.

intent [ɪn'tent] **1** a (look) attentif; **i. on doing** résolu à faire; **i. on** (task) absorbé par. **2** n intention f; **to all intents and purposes** en fait.

inter [ɪn'tɜːr] vt (-rr-) enterrer.

inter- [ɪntə(r)] pref inter-.

interact [ɪntə'rækt] vi (of people) agir conjointement; Ch interagir. ● **interaction** [-ʃ(ə)n] n interaction f. ● **interactive** a Comptr interactif.

intercept [ɪntə'sept] vt intercepter.

interchange ['ɪntətʃeɪndʒ] n (on road) échangeur m. ● **inter'changeable** a interchangeable.

inter-city [ɪntə'sɪtɪ] a **i.-city train** train m de grandes lignes.

intercom ['ɪntəkɒm] n interphone m.

interconnect/ed [ɪntəkə'nektɪd] a (facts etc) liés. ● **—ing** a **i. rooms** pièces fpl communicantes.

intercourse ['ɪntəkɔːs] n (sexual) rapports mpl.

interdependent [ɪntədɪ'pendənt] a interdépendant; (parts of machine) solidaire.

interest ['ɪnt(ə)rɪst] n intérêt m; (money) intérêts mpl; **his** or **her i. is** (hobby etc) ce qui l'intéresse c'est; **to take an i.** in sth/s.o. s'intéresser à qch/qn; **to lose i.** in se désintéresser de; **to be of i. to s.o.** intéresser qn.

‖ *vt* intéresser. ● **interested** *a* (*motive, person*) intéressé; **to be i. in sth/s.o.** s'intéresser à qch/qn; **I'm i. in doing** ça m'intéresse de faire; **are you i.?** ça vous intéresse? ● **interesting** *a* intéressant.

interface ['ɪntəfeɪs] *n* Comptr & Fig interface *f*.

interfer/e [ɪntə'fɪər] *vi* se mêler des affaires des autres; **to i. in** s'ingérer dans; **to i. with** (*upset*) déranger; (*touch*) toucher (à). ● **—ing** *a* (*person*) qui se mêle de tout. ● **interference** *n* ingérence *f*; Rad parasites *mpl*.

interim ['ɪntərɪm] *n* **in the i.** entre-temps ‖ *a* (*measure etc*) provisoire.

interior [ɪn'tɪərɪər] *a* intérieur ‖ *n* intérieur *m*; **Department of the I.** Am ministère *m* de l'Intérieur.

interjection [ɪntə'dʒekʃ(ə)n] *n* Gram interjection *f*.

interlock [ɪntə'lɒk] *vi* Tech s'emboîter.

interloper ['ɪntələʊpər] *n* intrus, -use *mf*.

interlude ['ɪntəluːd] *n* TV interlude *m*; Th entracte *m*.

intermediary [ɪntə'miːdɪərɪ] *a* & *n* intermédiaire (*mf*).

intermediate [ɪntə'miːdɪət] *a* intermédiaire; (*course*) de niveau moyen.

intermission [ɪntə'mɪʃ(ə)n] *n* Cin Th entracte *m*.

intermittent [ɪntə'mɪtənt] *a* intermittent. ● **—ly** *adv* par intermittence.

intern 1 [ɪn'tɜːn] *vt* Pol interner. **2** ['ɪntɜːn] *n* (*doctor*) Am interne *mf* (des hôpitaux).

internal [ɪn'tɜːn(ə)l] *a* interne; (*flight, policy*) intérieur; **the I. Revenue Service** Am le service des impôts, le fisc.

international [ɪntə'næʃ(ə)nəl] *a* international ‖ *n* (*match*) rencontre *f* internationale; (*player*) international *m*.

interplanetary [ɪntə'plænɪt(ə)rɪ] *a* interplanétaire.

interplay ['ɪntəpleɪ] *n* interaction *f*.

interpret [ɪn'tɜːprɪt] *vt* interpréter ‖ *vi* faire l'interprète. ● **interpreter** *n* interprète *mf*.

interrelated [ɪntərɪ'leɪtɪd] *a* en corrélation.

interrogate [ɪn'terəgeɪt] *vt* interroger. ● **interrogation** [-'geɪʃ(ə)n] *n* interrogation *f*; (*by police*) interrogatoire *m*.

interrogative [ɪntə'rɒgətɪv] *a* & *n* Gram interrogatif (*m*).

interrupt [ɪntə'rʌpt] *vt* interrompre. ● **interruption** [-ʃ(ə)n] *n* interruption *f*.

intersect [ɪntə'sekt] *vt* couper ‖ *vi* se couper, s'entrecouper. ● **intersection** [-ʃ(ə)n] *n* (*crossroads*) croisement *m*, intersection *f*; (*of lines*) intersection *f*.

interval ['ɪntəv(ə)l] *n* intervalle *m*; Th Cin entracte *m*; **at intervals** (*time*) de temps à autre; (*space*) par intervalles; **bright intervals** éclaircies *fpl*.

intervene [ɪntə'viːn] *vi* (*of person*) intervenir; (*of event*) survenir; **ten years intervened** dix années s'écoulèrent. ● **intervention** [-'venʃ(ə)n] *n* intervention *f*.

interview ['ɪntəvjuː] *n* entrevue *f*, entretien *m* (with avec); TV etc interview *f*; **to call s.o. for an i.** convoquer qn ‖ *vt* avoir une entrevue avec; TV etc interviewer. ● **—er** *n* TV etc interviewer *m*.

intestine [ɪn'testɪn] *n* intestin *m*.

intimate¹ ['ɪntɪmət] *a* intime; (*friendship*) profond; (*knowledge*) approfondi. ● **intimacy** *n* intimité *f*.

intimate² ['ɪntɪmeɪt] *vt* (*hint*) suggérer (that que).

intimidate [ɪn'tɪmɪdeɪt] *vt* intimider. ● **intimidation** [-'deɪʃ(ə)n] *n* intimidation *f*.

into ['ɪntuː, *unstressed* 'ɪntə] *prep* **1** dans; **to put i.** mettre dans; **to go i.** (*room, detail*) entrer dans. **2** en; **to translate i.** traduire en; **to change s.o. i.** transformer ou changer qn en; **to go i. town** aller en ville; **i. pieces** (*to break*) en morceaux. **3 to be i. yoga**/*etc* Fam être à fond dans le yoga/*etc*.

intolerable [ɪn'tɒlərəb(ə)l] *a* intolérable

(that que + *sub*).

intolerant [in'tɒlərənt] *a* intolérant (**of** de). ● **intolerance** *n* intolérance *f*.

intonation [intə'neiʃ(ə)n] *n Ling* intonation *f*.

intoxicate [in'tɒksikeit] *vt* enivrer. ● **intoxicated** *a* ivre.

intra- ['intrə] *pref* intra-.

intransigent [in'trænsidʒənt] *a* intransigeant.

intransitive [in'trænsitiv] *a Gram* intransitif.

intravenous [intrə'vi:nəs] *a Med* intraveineux.

intrepid [in'trepid] *a* intrépide.

intricate ['intrikət] *a* complexe, compliqué. ● **intricacy** *n* complexité *f*.

intrigue 1 [in'tri:g] *vt* (*interest*) intriguer; **I'm intrigued to know...** je suis curieux de savoir.... **2** ['intri:g] *n* (*plot*) intrigue *f*. ● **—ing** *a* (*news etc*) curieux.

intrinsic [in'trinsik] *a* intrinsèque.

introduce [intrə'dju:s] *vt* (*bring in, insert*) introduire (**into** dans); (*programme, subject*) présenter; **to i. s.o. to s.o.** présenter qn à qn; **to i. s.o. to Dickens/etc** faire découvrir Dickens/etc à qn.

introduction [intrə'dʌkʃ(ə)n] *n* introduction *f*; (*of person to person*) présentation *f*; **her i. to** (*life abroad etc*) son premier contact avec. ● **introductory** *a* (*words*) d'introduction; (*speech*) de présentation; (*course*) d'initiation.

introspective [intrə'spektiv] *a* introspectif.

introvert ['intrəvɜ:t] *n* introverti, -ie *mf*.

intrude [in'tru:d] *vi* (*of person*) déranger (**on s.o.** qn). ● **intruder** *n* intrus, -use *mf*. ● **intrusion** [-ʒ(ə)n] *n* (*bother*) dérangement *m*; (*interference*) intrusion *f* (**into** dans); **forgive my i.** pardonnez-moi de vous avoir dérangé.

intuition [intju:'iʃ(ə)n] *n* intuition *f*. ● **in'tuitive** *a* intuitif.

inundate ['inʌndeit] *vt* inonder (**with** de); **inundated with work/letters/etc** submergé de travail/lettres/etc.

invade [in'veid] *vt* envahir; **to i. s.o.'s privacy** violer la vie privée de qn. ● **—er** *n* envahisseur, -euse *mf*.

invalid[1] [in'vælid] *a & n* malade (*mf*); (*through injury*) infirme (*mf*); **i. car** voiture *f* d'infirme.

invalid[2] [in'vælid] *a* (*ticket etc*) non valable.

invaluable [in'væljuəb(ə)l] *a* (*help etc*) inestimable.

invariable [in'veəriəb(ə)l] *a* invariable. ● **invariably** *adv* (*always*) toujours.

invasion [in'veiʒ(ə)n] *n* invasion *f*; **i. of s.o.'s privacy** atteinte *f* à la vie privée de qn.

invent [in'vent] *vt* inventer. ● **invention** [-ʃ(ə)n] *n* invention *f*. ● **inventive** *a* inventif. ● **inventor** *n* inventeur, -trice *mf*.

inventory ['invənt(ə)ri] *n* inventaire *m*.

invert [in'vɜ:t] *vt* (*order etc*) intervertir; (*object*) retourner; **inverted commas** guillemets *mpl*.

invest [in'vest] *vt* (*money*) placer, investir (**in** dans); (*time, effort*) consacrer (**in** à) ● *vi* **to i. in** (*project*) placer son argent dans; (*company*) investir dans; (*new radio etc*) *Fig* se payer. ● **investment** *n* investissement *m*, placement *m*. ● **investor** *n* (*in shares*) actionnaire *mf*; (*saver*) épargnant, -ante *mf*.

investigate [in'vestigeit] *vt* examiner, étudier; (*crime*) enquêter sur. ● **investigation** [-'geiʃ(ə)n] *n* examen *m*, étude *f*; (*inquiry by journalist, police etc*) enquête *f* (**of, into** sur). ● **investigator** *n* (*detective*) enquêteur, -euse *mf*; (*private*) détective *m*.

invigilate [in'vidʒileit] *vi* être de surveillance (**à un examen**). ● **invigilator** *n* surveillant, -ante *mf*.

invigorating [in'vigəreitiŋ] *a* stimulant.

invincible [in'vinsəb(ə)l] *a* invincible.

invisible [in'vizəb(ə)l] *a* invisible; **i. ink** encre *f* sympathique.

invite [in'vait] *vt* inviter (**to do** à faire); (*ask for*) demander; (*give occasion for*) provoquer, appeler; **to i. s.o. out** inviter qn (à sortir); **to i. s.o. over** inviter qn (à venir) **‖** ['ɪnvaɪt] *n Fam* invitation *f*. ● **—ing** *a* engageant; (*food*) appétissant. ● **invitation** [-'teɪʃ(ə)n] *n* invitation *f*.

invoice ['ɪnvɔɪs] *n* facture *f* **‖** *vt* facturer.

invoke [ɪn'vəʊk] *vt* invoquer.

involuntary [ɪn'vɒləntərɪ] *a* involontaire.

involve [ɪn'vɒlv] *vt* (*include*) mêler (*qn*) (**in** à); (*associate*) associer (*qn*) (**in** à); (*entail*) entraîner; **to get involved** (*commit oneself*) s'engager (**in** dans); **the job involves going abroad** le poste nécessite des déplacements à l'étranger. ● **involved** *a* (*concerned*) concerné; (*committed*) engagé (**in** dans); (*complicated*) compliqué; **the factors/etc i.** (*at stake*) les facteurs/etc en jeu; **the person i.** la personne en question; **i. with s.o.** mêlé aux affaires de qn; (*emotionally*) amoureux de qn. ● **involvement** [ɪn'vɒlvmənt] *n* participation *f* (**in** à); (*commitment*) engagement *m* (**in** dans); (*emotional*) liaison *f*.

invulnerable [ɪn'vʌln(ə)rəb(ə)l] *a* invulnérable.

inward ['ɪnwəd] *a & adv* (*movement, to move*) vers l'intérieur **‖** *a* (*inner*) intérieur; (*thoughts*) intime. ● **inwardly** *adv* (*to laugh, curse etc*) intérieurement. ● **inwards** [-wədz] *adv* vers l'intérieur.

iodine ['aɪədiːn, *Am* -'aɪədaɪn] *n* (*antiseptic*) teinture *f* d'iode.

IOU [aɪəʊ'juː] *n abbr* (*I owe you*) reconnaissance *f* de dette.

IQ [aɪ'kjuː] *n abbr* (*intelligence quotient*) QI *m inv*.

Iran [ɪ'rɑːn, ɪ'ræn] *n* Iran *m*. ● **Iranian** [ɪ'reɪnɪən] *a & n* iranien, -ienne (*mf*).

Iraq [ɪ'rɑːk] *n* Irak *m*. ● **Iraqi** *a & n* irakien, -ienne (*mf*).

irascible [ɪ'ræsəb(ə)l] *a* irascible.

irate [aɪ'reɪt] *a* furieux.

Ireland ['aɪələnd] *n* Irlande *f*. ● **Irish** *a* irlandais **‖** *n* (*language*) irlandais *m*; **the I.** (*people*) les Irlandais *mpl*. ● **Irishman** *n* (*pl* -**men**) Irlandais *m*. ● **Irishwoman** *n* (*pl* -**women**) Irlandaise *f*.

iris ['aɪərɪs] *n Anat Bot* iris *m*.

irk [ɜːk] *vt* ennuyer. ● **irksome** [-səm] *a* ennuyeux.

iron ['aɪən] *n* fer *m*; (*for clothes*) fer *m* (à repasser); **old i., scrap i.** ferraille *f* **‖** *vt* (*clothes*) repasser; **to i. out** (*difficulties*) aplanir. ● **—ing** *n* repassage *m*; **i. board** planche *f* à repasser.

ironmonger ['aɪənmʌŋgər] *n* quincaillier, -ière *mf*.

irony ['aɪərənɪ] *n* ironie *f*. ● **i'ronic(al)** *a* ironique.

irradiate [ɪ'reɪdɪeɪt] *vt* irradier; **irradiated food** aliments *mpl* irradiés.

irrational [ɪ'ræʃən(ə)l] *a* (*person*) peu rationnel; (*act*) irrationnel; (*fear*) irraisonné.

irrefutable [ɪrɪ'fjuːtəb(ə)l] *a* irréfutable.

irregular [ɪ'regjʊlər] *a* irrégulier. ● **irregu'larity** *n* irrégularité *f*.

irrelevant [ɪ'reləvənt] *a* sans rapport (**to** avec); (*activity*) peu utile; **that's i.** ça n'a rien à voir. ● **irrelevance** *n* manque *m* de rapport.

irreparable [ɪ'rep(ə)rəb(ə)l] *a* (*harm, loss*) irréparable.

irreplaceable [ɪrɪ'pleɪsəb(ə)l] *a* irremplaçable.

irrepressible [ɪrɪ'presəb(ə)l] *a* (*laughter etc*) irrépressible.

irresistible [ɪrɪ'zɪstəb(ə)l] *a* (*person, charm etc*) irrésistible.

irrespective of [ɪrɪ'spektɪvəv] *prep* sans tenir compte de.

irresponsible [ɪrɪ'sponsəb(ə)l] *a* (*act*) irréfléchi; (*person*) irresponsable.

irretrievable [ɪrɪ'triːvəb(ə)l] *a* irréparable.

irreversible [ɪrɪ'vɜːsəb(ə)l] *a* (*process*) irréversible; (*decision*) irrévocable.

irrevocable [ɪ'revəkəb(ə)l] *a* irrévocable.

irrigate ['ɪrɪgeɪt] *vt* irriguer. ● **irrigation** [-'geɪʃ(ə)n] *n* irrigation *f*.

irritat/e ['ɪrɪteɪt] *vt* (*annoy, inflame*) irriter. ● **—ing** *a* irritant. ● **irritable** *a* (*easily annoyed*) irritable. ● **irritation** [-'teɪʃə)n] *n* (*anger, inflammation*) irritation *f*.

is [ɪz] *see* be.
islam ['ɪzlɑːm] *n* islam *m*. ●**islamic** [ɪz'læmɪk] *a* islamique.
island ['aɪlənd] *n* île *f*. ●**isle** [aɪl] *n* île *f*; **the British Isles** les îles Britanniques.
isn't ['ɪz(ə)nt] = **is not**.
isolate ['aɪsəleɪt] *vt* isoler (**from** de). ●**isolated** *a* (*remote, unique*) isolé. ●**isolation** [-'leɪʃ(ə)n] *n* isolement *m*; **in i.** isolément.
Israel ['ɪzreɪl] *n* Israël *m*. ●**Is'raeli** *a & n* israélien, -ienne (*mf*).
issue ['ɪʃuː] *vt* (*book etc*) publier; (*tickets*) distribuer; (*passport*) délivrer; (*an order*) donner; (*warning*) lancer; (*supply*) fournir (**with** de, **to** à) ▮ *vi* **to i. from** (*of smell*) se dégager de ▮ *n* (*of newspaper, magazine*) numéro *m*; (*matter*) question *f*; (*outcome*) résultat *m*; (*of stamps etc*) émission *f*; **at i.** (*at stake*) en cause; **to make an i. of** faire toute une affaire de.
isthmus ['ɪsməs] *n* Geog isthme *m*.
it [ɪt] *pron* **1** (*subject*) il, elle; (*object*) le, la, l'; (**to) it** (*indirect object*) lui; **it bites** il mord; **I've done it** je l'ai fait.
2 (*impersonal*) il; **it's snowing** il neige; **it's hot** il fait chaud.
3 (*non specific*) ce, cela, ça; **it's good c'est bon; who is it?** qui est-ce?; **that's it!** (*I agree*) c'est ça!, (*it's done*) ça y est!; **to consider it wise to do** juger prudent de

faire; **it was Paul who...** c'est Paul qui...; **to have it in for s.o.** Fam en vouloir à qn.
4 of it, from it, about it en; **in it, to it, at it** y; **on it** dessus; **under it** dessous.
italics [ɪ'tælɪks] *npl* italique *m*.
Italy ['ɪtəlɪ] *n* Italie *f*. ●**l'talian** *a & n* italien, -ienne (*mf*) ▮ *n* (*language*) italien *m*.
itch [ɪtʃ] *n* démangeaison(s) *f(pl)* ▮ *vi* démanger; (*of person*) avoir des démangeaisons; **his arm itches** son bras le démange; **I'm itching to do** Fig ça me démange de faire. ●—**ing** *n* démangeaison(s) *f(pl)*. ●**itchy** *a* **I have an i. hand** j'ai une main qui me démange; **I'm i.** j'ai des démangeaisons.
item ['aɪtəm] *n* (*object for sale in newspaper etc*) article *m*; (*matter*) question *f*; **news i.** information *f*. ●**itemize** *vt* (*invoice etc*) détailler.
itinerant [aɪ'tɪnərənt] *a* (*musician*) ambulant; (*judge*) itinérant.
itinerary [aɪ'tɪnərərɪ] *n* itinéraire *m*.
its [ɪts] *poss a* son, sa, *pl* ses.
itself [ɪt'self] *pron* lui-même, elle-même; (*reflexive*) se, s'; **goodness i.** la bonté même; **by i.** tout seul.
IUD [aɪjuː'diː] *n abbr* (*intrauterine device*) stérilet *m*.
ivory ['aɪvərɪ] *n* ivoire *m*.
ivy ['aɪvɪ] *n* lierre *m*.

J

J, j [dʒeɪ] n J, j m.

jab [dʒæb] vt (-bb-) (knife etc) enfoncer (into dans); (prick) piquer (qn) (with sth du bout de qch) ▮ n coup m (sec); (injection) Fam piqûre f.

jabber ['dʒæbər] vi bavarder.

jack [dʒæk] 1 n Aut cric m ▮ vt to j. up (vehicle) soulever (avec un cric); (price) Fig augmenter. 2 n Cards valet m. 3 n j. of all trades homme m à tout faire. ●j.-in-the-box n diable m (à ressort).

jackal ['dʒæk(ə)l] n (animal) chacal m.

jackass ['dʒækæs] n (fool) idiot, -ote mf.

jackdaw ['dʒækdɔː] n (bird) choucas m.

jacket ['dʒækɪt] n (short coat) veste f; (of man's suit) veston m; (bulletproof) gilet m; (dust) j. (of book) jaquette f; j. potato pomme f de terre en robe des champs.

jack-knife ['dʒæknaɪf] 1 n couteau m de poche. 2 vi (of lorry, truck) se mettre en travers de la route.

jackpot ['dʒækpɒt] n gros lot m.

jacuzzi [dʒəˈkuːzɪ] n (bath, pool) jacuzzi m.

jaded ['dʒeɪdɪd] a blasé.

jagged ['dʒægɪd] a déchiqueté.

jaguar ['dʒægjʊər, Am -waːr] n (animal) jaguar m.

jail [dʒeɪl] n prison f ▮ vt emprisonner (for theft/etc pour vol/etc); to j. s.o. for ten years condamner qn à dix ans de prison.

jam¹ [dʒæm] n (preserve) confiture f. ●jamjar n pot m à confiture.

jam² [dʒæm] 1 n (traffic) j. embouteillage m; in a j. (trouble) Fam dans le pétrin. 2 vt (-mm-) (squeeze, make stuck) coincer, bloquer; (street etc) encombrer; Rad brouiller; to j. sth into (cram) (en)tasser qch dans; to j. on (brakes) bloquer.

▮ vi (get stuck) se coincer, se bloquer; to j. into (of crowd) s'entasser dans. ●jammed a (machine etc) coincé, bloqué; (street etc) encombré. ●jam-'packed a (hall etc) bourré de monde.

Jamaica [dʒəˈmeɪkə] n Jamaïque f.

jangle ['dʒæŋg(ə)l] vi cliqueter.

janitor ['dʒænɪtər] n Am concierge m.

January ['dʒænjʊərɪ, Am -erɪ] n janvier m.

Japan [dʒəˈpæn] n Japon m. ●Japa'nese a & n inv (pl inv) japonais, -aise (mf) ▮ n (language) japonais m.

jar [dʒɑːr] 1 n (container) pot m; (large, glass) bocal m. 2 n (jolt) choc m ▮ vt (-rr-) (shake) ébranler. 3 vi (-rr-) (of noise) grincer; (of note) Mus détonner; (of colours) jurer (with avec). ●jarring a (noise) discordant.

jargon ['dʒɑːgən] n jargon m.

jaundice ['dʒɔːndɪs] n Med jaunisse f. ●jaundiced a (bitter) aigri; to take a j. view of voir d'un mauvais œil.

jaunt [dʒɔːnt] n (journey) balade f.

jaunty ['dʒɔːntɪ] a (-ier, -iest) (carefree) insouciant; (cheerful) allègre.

javelin ['dʒævlɪn] n javelot m.

jaw [dʒɔː] n mâchoire f.

jaywalker ['dʒeɪwɔːkər] n piéton m imprudent.

jazz [dʒæz] n jazz m ▮ vt to j. up Fam (enliven) animer; (room) égayer.

jealous ['dʒeləs] a jaloux (f -ouse) (of de). ●jealousy n jalousie f.

jeans [dʒiːnz] npl (pair of) j. jean m.

jeep® [dʒiːp] n jeep® f.

jeer [dʒɪər] vti to j. (at) (mock) railler; (boo) huer ▮ npl jeers (boos) huées fpl. ●—ing n (of crowd) huées fpl.

jell [dʒel] vi (of ideas etc) Fam prendre tournure.

jello® ['dʒeləʊ] n inv (dessert) Am gelée f. ●jelly n (preserve, dessert) gelée f.

● **jellyfish** n méduse f.

jeopardy ['dʒepədɪ] n danger m. ● **jeopardize** vt mettre en danger.

jerk [dʒɜːk] 1 vt donner une secousse à ‖ n secousse f. 2 n (person) (stupid) j. Fam crétin, -ine mf. ● **jerky** a (-ier, -iest) (movement etc) saccadé.

jersey ['dʒɜːzɪ] n (garment) tricot m (de laine); Fb maillot m; (cloth) jersey m.

Jersey ['dʒɜːzɪ] n Jersey f.

jest [dʒest] n plaisanterie f; **in j.** pour rire.

Jesus ['dʒiːzəs] n Jésus m.

jet [dʒet] 1 n (plane) avion m à réaction ‖ a (engine) à réaction; **j. lag** fatigue f (due au décalage horaire). 2 n (of steam etc) jet m. ● **jet-lagged** a Fam qui souffre du décalage horaire.

jet-black [dʒet'blæk] a (noir) de jais.

jettison ['dʒetɪs(ə)n] vt (cargo) Nau jeter à la mer; (fuel) Av larguer.

jetty ['dʒetɪ] n jetée f; (landing-place) embarcadère m.

Jew [dʒuː] n (man) Juif m; (woman) Juive f. ● **Jewish** a juif.

jewel ['dʒuːəl] n bijou m (pl -oux); (in watch) rubis m. ● **jeweller** or Am **jeweler** n bijoutier, -ière mf. ● **jewellery** or Am **jewelry** n bijoux mpl.

jibe [dʒaɪb] vi & n = gibe.

jiffy ['dʒɪfɪ] n Fam instant m.

Jiffy bag® ['dʒɪfɪbæg] n enveloppe f matelassée.

jigsaw ['dʒɪgsɔː] n **j. (puzzle)** puzzle m.

jilt [dʒɪlt] vt (lover) laisser tomber.

jingle ['dʒɪŋg(ə)l] vi (of keys, bell etc) tinter ‖ vt faire tinter ‖ n tintement m.

jinx [dʒɪŋks] n (person, object) portemalheur m inv.

jitters ['dʒɪtəz] npl **to have the j.** Fam avoir la frousse. ● **jittery** a **to be j.** Fam avoir la frousse.

job [dʒɒb] n (task, work) travail m; (post) poste m, emploi m, situation f; **to have a (hard) j. doing** or **to do** Fam avoir du mal à faire; **to have the j. of doing** (unpleasant task) être obligé de faire; (for a living etc) être chargé de faire; **it's**

a good j. (that) Fam heureusement que (+ indic); **out of a j.** au chômage. ● **jobcentre** n agence f nationale pour l'emploi. ● **jobless** a au chômage.

jockey ['dʒɒkɪ] n jockey m.

jocular ['dʒɒkjʊlər] a jovial, amusant.

jog [dʒɒg] 1 n (shake) secousse f; (nudge) coup m de coude ‖ vt (-gg-) (shake) secouer; (push) pousser; (memory) Fig rafraîchir. 2 vi (-gg-) **to j. along** (of vehicle) cahoter; (of work) aller tant bien que mal. 3 vi (-gg-) Sp faire du jogging. ● **jogging** n Sp jogging m.

john [dʒɒn] n **the j.** (lavatory) Am Fam le petit coin.

join [dʒɔɪn] 1 vt (put together) joindre; (wires, pipes) raccorder; (words, towns) relier; **to j. s.o.** (catch up with, meet) rejoindre qn; (go with) se joindre à qn (**in doing** pour faire); **to j. hands** se donner la main; **to j. together** or **up** (objects) joindre.
‖ vi (of roads, rivers etc) se rejoindre; **to j.** (together or up) (of objects) se joindre (**with** à); **to j. in** prendre part; **to j. in a game**/etc prendre part à un jeu/etc.
‖ n raccord m, joint m.
2 vt (become a member of) s'inscrire à (club, parti); (army, police, company) entrer dans; **to j. the queue** or Am **line** prendre la queue.
‖ vi (become a member) devenir membre; **to j. up** Mil s'engager.

joiner ['dʒɔɪnər] n menuisier m.

joint [dʒɔɪnt] 1 n Anat articulation f; Culin rôti m; Tech joint m. 2 n (nightclub) Fam boîte f. 3 n (cigarette) Fam joint m. 4 a (decision etc) commun; **j. account** compte m joint; **j. efforts** efforts mpl conjugués.

jok/e [dʒəʊk] n plaisanterie f; (trick) tour m ‖ vi plaisanter (**about** sur). ●**—er** n plaisantin m; Cards joker m. ●**—ingly** adv en plaisantant.

jolly ['dʒɒlɪ] 1 a (-ier, -iest) (happy) gai; (drunk) Fam éméché. 2 adv (very) Fam rudement; **j. good!** très bien!

jolt [dʒəʊlt] vt (shake) secouer; **to j. s.o.**

(of vehicle) cahoter qn; *(shock)* secouer qn ▮ *n* cahot *m*, secousse *f*; *(shock)* secousse *f*.

Jordan ['dʒɔːd(ə)n] *n* Jordanie *f*.

jostle ['dʒɒs(ə)l] *vti (push)* bousculer ▮ *vi (push each other)* se bousculer **(for sth** pour obtenir qch).

jot [dʒɒt] *vt* (-tt-) **to j. down** noter. ● **jotter** *n (notepad)* bloc-notes *m*.

journal ['dʒɜːn(ə)l] *n (periodical)* revue *f*. ● **journalism** *n* journalisme *m*. ● **journalist** *n* journaliste *mf*.

journey ['dʒɜːnɪ] *n (trip)* voyage *m*; *(distance)* trajet *m*; **to go on a j.** partir en voyage.

jovial ['dʒəʊvɪəl] *a* jovial.

joy [dʒɔɪ] *n* joie *f*; **the joys of** *(mother-hood etc)* les plaisirs *mpl* de. ● **joyful** *a* joyeux. ● **joyride** *n* équipée *f* en voiture volée, rodéo *m*.

joystick ['dʒɔɪstɪk] *n (of aircraft, computer)* manche *m* à balai.

JP [dʒeɪ'piː] *abbr* = **Justice of the Peace.**

jubilant ['dʒuːbɪlənt] *a* **to be j.** jubiler.

judder ['dʒʌdər] *vi (shake)* vibrer ▮ *n* vibration *f*.

judg/e [dʒʌdʒ] *n* juge *m* ▮ *vti* juger; **judging by** à en juger par. ● **—(e)ment** *n* jugement *m*.

judicial [dʒuː'dɪʃ(ə)l] *a* judiciaire. ● **judiciary** *n* magistrature *f*.

judo ['dʒuːdəʊ] *n* judo *m*.

jug [dʒʌɡ] *n* cruche *f*; *(for milk)* pot *m*.

juggernaut ['dʒʌɡənɔːt] *n (truck)* poids *m* lourd, mastodonte *m*.

juggl/e ['dʒʌɡ(ə)l] *vi* jongler ▮ *vt* jongler avec. ● **—er** *n* jongleur, -euse *mf*.

juice [dʒuːs] *n* jus *m*; *(in stomach)* suc *m*. ● **juicy** *a* (-ier, -iest) *(fruit)* juteux; *(story)* *Fig* savoureux.

jukebox ['dʒuːkbɒks] *n* juke-box *m*.

July [dʒuː'laɪ] *n* juillet *m*.

jumble ['dʒʌmb(ə)l] *vt* **to j. (up)** *(objects, facts etc)* mélanger ▮ *n (disorder)* fouillis *m*; **j. sale** vente *f* de charité; *(for school etc)* vente *f* (au profit de l'école etc).

jumbo ['dʒʌmbəʊ] *a* géant; **j. jet** gros-

porteur *m*.

jump [dʒʌmp] *n (leap)* saut *m*, bond *m*; *(start)* sursaut *m*; *(increase)* hausse *f*; **j. rope** *Am* corde *f* à sauter.

▮ *vi* sauter **(at** sur); *(start)* sursauter; **to j. to conclusions** tirer des conclusions hâtives; **to j. in** or **on** *(train, vehicle)* monter or sauter dans; **to j. off** or **out** sauter; *(from bus etc)* descendre; **to j. off sth, j. out of sth** sauter de qch; **to j. out of the window** sauter par la fenêtre; **to j. up** se lever d'un bond.

▮ *vt (ditch)* sauter; **to j. the lights** *Aut* griller un feu rouge; **to j. the rails** *(of train)* dérailler; **to j. the queue** passer avant son tour; **to j. rope** *Am* sauter à la corde.

jumper ['dʒʌmpər] *n* pull(-over) *m*; *(dress)* *Am* robe *f* chasuble.

jumpy ['dʒʌmpɪ] *a* (-ier, -iest) nerveux.

junction ['dʒʌŋkʃ(ə)n] *n (crossroads)* carrefour *m*; **j. 23** *(exit on motorway)* la sortie 23.

June [dʒuːn] *n* juin *m*.

jungle ['dʒʌŋɡ(ə)l] *n* jungle *f*.

junior ['dʒuːnɪər] *a (younger)* plus jeune; *(in rank etc)* subalterne; *(teacher, doctor)* jeune; **to be s.o.'s j.** être plus jeune que qn; *(in rank, status)* être au-dessous de qn; **Smith j.** Smith fils; **j. school** école *f* primaire; **j. high school** *Am* = collège *m* d'enseignement secondaire ▮ *n* cadet, -ette *mf*; *Sch* petit, -ite *mf*; *Sp* junior *mf*.

junk [dʒʌŋk] **1** *n (objects)* bric-à-brac *m inv*; *(metal)* ferraille *f*; *(inferior, goods)* camelote *f*; *(waste)* ordures *fpl*; **j. food** aliment *m* peu nutritif; **j. shop** (boutique *f* de) brocanteur *m*. **2** *vt (get rid of)* *Am Fam* balancer.

junkie ['dʒʌŋkɪ] *n* *Fam* drogué, -ée *mf*.

junta ['dʒʌntə, *Am* 'hʊntə] *n* *Pol* junte *f*.

jury ['dʒʊərɪ] *n (in competition)* & *Jur* jury *m*.

just [dʒʌst] **1** *adv (exactly, only)* juste; **she has/had j. left** elle vient/venait de partir; **I've j. come from** j'arrive de; **I'm j. coming!** j'arrive!; **he'll (only) j. catch the bus** il aura son bus de justesse; **he j.**

missed it il l'a manqué de peu; **j. as big/**
etc tout aussi grand/*etc* (as que); **j.**
listen! écoute donc!; **j. a moment!** un
instant!; **j. over ten** un peu plus de dix; **j.**
one un(e) seul(e) (**of** de); **j. about**
(*approximately*) à peu près; (*almost*)
presque; **j. about to do** sur le point de
faire. **2** *a* (*fair*) juste (**to** envers).

justice ['dʒʌstɪs] *n* justice *f*; **to do j. to**
(*meal*) faire honneur à; **J. of the Peace**
juge *m* de paix.

justify ['dʒʌstɪfaɪ] *vt* justifier; **to be**
justified in doing être fondé à faire.
● **justi'fiable** *a* justifiable. ● **justification**
[-'keɪʃ(ə)n] *n* justification *f*.

jut [dʒʌt] *vi* (-tt-) **to j. out** faire saillie; **to j.**
out over sth surplomber qch.

juvenile ['dʒuːvənaɪl] *n* adolescent, -ente
mf ‖ *a* (*court, book etc*) pour enfants;
(*delinquent*) jeune; (*behaviour*) puéril.

K

K, k [keɪ] *n* K, k *m*.

kaleidoscope [kəˈlaɪdəskəʊp] *n* kaléidoscope *m*.

kangaroo [kæŋgəˈruː] *n* (*pl* -oos) kangourou *m*.

karate [kəˈrɑːtɪ] *n Sp* karaté *m*.

kebab [kəˈbæb] *n* brochette *f*.

keel [kiːl] *n Nau* quille *f* ▮ *vi* to k. over (*of boat*) chavirer.

keen [kiːn] *a* (*eager*) plein d'enthousiasme; (*edge*) aiguisé; (*interest*) vif; (*mind*) pénétrant; (*wind*) coupant; **k. eyesight** vue *f* perçante; **a k. sportsman** un passionné de sport; **to be k. to do** *or* **on doing** (*want*) tenir (beaucoup) à faire; **to be k. on doing** (*like*) aimer (beaucoup) faire; **to be k. on** (*music, sport etc*) être passionné de; **he is k. on her/the idea** elle/l'idée lui plaît beaucoup.

keep¹ [kiːp] *vt* (*pt & pp* kept) garder; (*shop, car*) avoir; (*diary, promise*) tenir; (*family*) entretenir; (*rule*) respecter; (*feast day*) célébrer; (*delay*) retenir; **to k. doing** (*continue*) continuer à faire; **to k. sth clean** tenir *or* garder qch propre; **to be k. on** (*music,* *sport etc*) ; **to k. sth from s.o.** (*hide*) cacher qch à qn; **to k. s.o. from doing** (*prevent*) empêcher qn de faire; **to k. s.o. waiting/working** faire attendre/travailler qn; **to k. sth going** (*engine*) laisser qch en marche; **to k. an appointment** se rendre à un rendez-vous.

▮ *vi* (*remain*) rester; (*continue*) continuer; (*of food*) se garder; **how is he keeping?** comment va-t-il?; **to k. still** rester tranquille; **to k. left** tenir sa gauche; **to k. from doing** (*refrain*) s'abstenir de faire; **to k. going** (*continue*) continuer; **to k. at it** continuer à le faire.

▮ *n* (*food*) nourriture *f*, subsistance *f*; **to**

have one's k. être logé et nourri; **for keeps** *Fam* pour toujours.

keep² [kiːp] *n* (*tower*) *Hist* donjon *m*.

keep away *vt* (*person*) éloigner (**from** de) ▮ *vi* ne pas s'approcher (**from** de) ▮ **to keep back** *vt* (*crowd*) contenir; (*delay*) retenir; (*hide*) cacher (**from** à) ▮ *vi* ne pas s'approcher (**from** de) ▮ **to keep down** *vt* (*restrict*) limiter; (*price, costs*) maintenir bas ▮ **to keep in** *vt* empêcher (*qn*) de sortir; (*as punishment*) *Sch* consigner (*élève*) ▮ **to keep off** *vt* (*person*) éloigner; **'k. off the grass'** ne pas marcher sur les pelouses' ▮ *vi* (*not go near*) ne pas s'approcher; **if the rain keeps off** s'il ne pleut pas ▮ **to keep on** *vt* (*hat, employee*) garder; **to k. on doing** continuer à faire ▮ **to keep out** *vt* empêcher (*qn*) d'entrer ▮ *vi* rester en dehors (**of** de) ▮ **to keep to** *vt* (*subject, path*) ne pas s'écarter de; (*room*) garder; **to k. to the left** tenir la gauche ▮ **to keep up** *vt* (*continue*) continuer (**doing sth** à faire qch); (*road, building*) entretenir ▮ *vi* (*continue*) continuer; (*follow*) suivre; **to k. up with s.o** (*follow*) suivre qn.

keeper [ˈkiːpər] *n* (*in park, zoo*) gardien, -ienne *mf*.

keeping [ˈkiːpɪŋ] *n* **in k. with** en rapport avec.

keepsake [ˈkiːpseɪk] *n* souvenir *m*.

keg [keg] *n* tonnelet *m*.

kennel [ˈken(ə)l] *n* niche *f*; (*for boarding dogs*) chenil *m*.

Kenya [ˈkiːnjə, ˈkenjə] *n* Kenya *m*.

kept [kept] *pt & pp of* keep¹ ▮ *a* **a well k.** (*house etc*) bien tenu.

kerb [kɜːb] *n* bord *m* du trottoir.

kernel [ˈkɜːn(ə)l] *n* (*of nut*) amande *f*.

kerosene [ˈkerəsiːn] *n* (*paraffin*) *Am* pétrole *m* (lampant).

ketchup ['ketʃəp] n ketchup m.

kettle ['ket(ə)l] n bouilloire f; **the k. is boiling** l'eau bout.

key [ki:] n clef f, clé f; (of piano, typewriter, computer) touche f ▮ a (industry, post etc) clef (f inv), clé (f inv); **k. person** pivot m; **k. ring** porte-clefs m inv ▮ vt Comptr **to k. in** (data) saisir. ●**keyboard** n clavier m. ●**keyhole** n trou m de (la) serrure. ●**keynote** n (of speech) note f dominante.

keyed [ki:d] a **to be k. up** avoir les nerfs tendus.

khaki ['kɑ:kɪ] a kaki a inv.

kick [kɪk] n coup m de pied; (of horse) ruade f; **for kicks** Fam pour le plaisir ▮ vt donner un coup de pied à; (of horse) lancer une ruade à; **to k. down** or **in** (door etc) démolir à coups de pied; **to k. out** (throw out) Fam flanquer dehors ▮ vi donner des coups de pied; (of horse) ruer; **to k. off** Fb donner le coup d'envoi; (start) démarrer. ●**k.-off** n Fb coup m d'envoi.

kid [kɪd] **1** n (child) Fam gosse mf; **my k. brother** Am Fam mon petit frère. **2** n (goat) chevreau m. **3** vti (-dd-) (joke, tease) Fam blaguer.

kidnap ['kɪdnæp] vt (-pp-) kidnapper. ●**kidnapper** n ravisseur, -euse mf.

kidney ['kɪdnɪ] n Anat rein m; Culin rognon m; **k. machine** coeur m rein artificiel.

kill [kɪl] vt tuer; **my feet are killing me** Fam je ne sens plus mes pieds; **to k. off** détruire ▮ vi tuer ▮ n mise f à mort; (prey) animaux mpl tués. ●**-ing** n (of person) meurtre m; (of group) massacre m; (of animal) mise f à mort; **to make a k.** Fin réussir un beau coup. ●**killer** n tueur, -euse mf.

killjoy ['kɪldʒɔɪ] n rabat-joie m inv.

kiln [kɪln] n (for pottery) four m.

kilo ['ki:ləʊ] n (pl -os) kilo m. ●**kilogram(me)** ['kɪləʊgræm] n kilogramme m.

kilometre [kɪ'lɒmɪtər] n (Am **kilometer**) kilomètre m.

kilowatt ['kɪləʊwɒt] n kilowatt m.

kilt [kɪlt] n kilt m.

kin [kɪn] n **one's next of k.** son plus proche parent.

kind¹ [kaɪnd] n (sort) sorte f, genre m, espèce f (of de); **all kinds of** toutes sortes de; **what k. of drink/etc is it?** qu'est-ce que c'est comme boisson/etc?; **nothing of the k.!** absolument pas!; **k. of worried/sad/etc** plutôt inquiet/triste/etc; **it's the only one of its k.** c'est unique en son genre; **we are two of a k.** nous nous ressemblons.

kind² [kaɪnd] a (-er, -est) (helpful, pleasant) gentil (to avec, pour); **that's k. of you** c'est gentil or aimable à vous. ●**k.-'hearted** a qui a bon cœur.

kindergarten ['kɪndəgɑ:t(ə)n] n jardin m d'enfants.

kindle ['kɪnd(ə)l] vt allumer.

kindly ['kaɪndlɪ] adv avec bonté; **k. wait/etc** ayez la bonté d'attendre/etc ▮ a (person) bienveillant.

kindness ['kaɪndnɪs] n gentillesse f.

king [kɪŋ] n roi m. ●**k.-size(d)** a géant; (cigarette) long. ●**kingdom** n royaume m; **animal/plant k.** règne m animal/végétal.

kingfisher ['kɪŋfɪʃər] n martin-pêcheur m.

kinky ['kɪŋkɪ] a (-ier, -iest) (person) qui a des goûts bizarres; (clothes) bizarre.

kinship ['kɪnʃɪp] n parenté f.

kiosk ['ki:ɒsk] n kiosque m; (telephone) **k.** cabine f (téléphonique).

kipper ['kɪpər] n (herring) kipper m.

kiss [kɪs] n baiser m; **the k. of life** Med le bouche-à-bouche ▮ vt (person) embrasser; **to k. s.o.'s hand** baiser la main de qn ▮ vi s'embrasser.

kit [kɪt] n équipement m, matériel m; (of articles) trousse f; (belongings) affaires fpl; (do-it-yourself) **k.** kit m; **first-aid k.** trousse f de pharmacie; **tool k.** trousse f à outils; **k. bag** sac m (de soldat etc) ▮ vt (-tt-) **to k. s.o. out** équiper qn (with de).

kitchen ['kɪtʃɪn] n cuisine f; **k. cabinet**

buffet *m* de cuisine; **k. garden** jardin *m* potager; **k. sink** évier *m*; **k. units** éléments *mpl* de cuisine. ● **kitche'nette** *n* coin-cuisine *m*.

kite [kaɪt] *n* (*toy*) cerf-volant *m*.

kitten ['kɪt(ə)n] *n* chaton *m*.

kitty ['kɪtɪ] *n* (*fund*) cagnotte *f*.

kiwi ['ki:wi:] *n* (*bird, fruit*) kiwi *m*.

km *abbr* (*kilometre*) km.

knack [næk] *n* (*skill*) coup *m* (de main) (**of doing** pour faire); **to have a** *or* **the k. of doing** (*tendency*) avoir le don de faire.

knapsack ['næpsæk] *n* sac *m* à dos.

knead [ni:d] *vt* (*dough*) pétrir.

knee [ni:] *n* genou *m*; **to go down on one's knees** se mettre à genoux; **k. pad** *Sp* genouillère *f*. ● **kneecap** *n Anat* rotule *f*.

kneel [ni:l] *vi* (*pt & pp* **knelt** *or* **kneeled**) **to k. (down)** s'agenouiller; **to be kneeling (down)** être à genoux.

knew [nju:] *pt of* **know**.

knickers ['nɪkəz] *npl* (*woman's undergarment*) slip *m*; (*longer*) culotte *f*.

knife [naɪf] *n* (*pl* **knives**) couteau *m*; (*penknife*) canif *m* ▮ *vt* poignarder.

knight [naɪt] *n* chevalier *m*; *Chess* cavalier *m* ▮ *vt* **to be knighted** *Br* être fait chevalier. ● **knighthood** *n Br* titre *m* de chevalier.

knit [nɪt] *vt* (**-tt-**) tricoter; **to k. one's brow** froncer les sourcils ▮ *vi* tricoter; **to k. together** (*of bones*) se souder. ● **knitting** *n* (*activity, material*) tricot *m*; **k. needle** aiguille *f* à tricoter. ● **knitwear** *n* tricots *mpl*.

knob [nɒb] *n* (*on door etc*) bouton *m*; (*of butter*) noix *f*.

knock [nɒk] *vt* (*strike*) frapper; (*collide with*) heurter; (*criticize*) *Fam* critiquer; **to k. one's head on sth** se cogner la tête contre qch; **to k. to the ground** jeter à terre ▮ *vi* (*strike*) frapper; **to k. against** *or* **into** (*bump into*) heurter ▮ *n* (*blow*) coup *m*; (*collision*) heurt *m*; **there's a k. at the door** quelqu'un frappe; **I heard a k.** j'ai entendu frapper.

knock about *vt* (*ill-treat*) malmener ▮ **to**

knock back *vt* (*drink, glass etc*) *Fam* s'envoyer (derrière la cravate) ▮ **to knock down** *vt* (*vase, pedestrian etc*) renverser; (*house, wall etc*) abattre; (*price*) baisser ▮ **to knock in** *vt* (*nail*) enfoncer ▮ **to knock off** *vt* (*person, object*) faire tomber (**from** de); (*steal*) *Fam* piquer; **to knock £5 off the price** baisser le prix de cinq livres ▮ *vi* (*stop work*) *Fam* s'arrêter de travailler ▮ **to knock out** *vt* (*make unconscious*) assommer; *Boxing* mettre k.-o.; (*beat in competition*) éliminer; **to k. oneself out** (*tire*) *Fam* s'esquinter (**doing** à faire). ● **knock-out** *n Boxing* knock-out *m*. ▮ **to knock over** *vt* (*pedestrian, vase etc*) renverser ▮ **to knock up** *vt* (*meal*) *Fam* préparer à la hâte.

knocker ['nɒkər] *n* (*for door*) marteau *m*.

knot [nɒt] **1** *n* (*in rope etc*) nœud *m* ▮ *vt* (**-tt-**) nouer. **2** *n* (*unit of speed*) *Nau* nœud *m*.

know [nəʊ] *vt* (*pt* **knew**, *pp* **known**) (*facts, language etc*) savoir; (*person, place etc*) connaître; (*recognize*) reconnaître (**by** à); **to k. that** savoir que; **to k. how to do** savoir faire; **for all I k.** (autant) que je sache; **I'll let you k.** je vous le ferai savoir; **I'll have you k. that** ... sachez que ...; **to k. (a lot) about** (*person, event*) en savoir long sur; (*cars, sewing etc*) s'y connaître en; **to get to k. (about) sth** apprendre qch; **to get to k. s.o.** (*meet*) faire la connaissance de qn. ▮ *vi* savoir; **I k.** je (le) sais; **I wouldn't k.** je n'en sais rien; **I k. about that** je suis au courant; **do you k. of a good dentist/** *etc*? connais-tu un bon dentiste/*etc*?; **you should k. better than to do that** tu es trop intelligent pour faire ça; **you should have known better** tu aurais dû réfléchir.

▮ *n* **in the k.** *Fam* au courant. ● **knowingly** *adv* (*consciously*) sciemment. ● **known** *a* connu; **a k. expert** un expert reconnu; **well k.** (bien) connu (**that** que); **she is k. to be** ... on sait qu'elle est ... .

know-all ['nəʊɔːl] *or Am* **know-it-all** *n Pej*
je-sais-tout *mf inv*. ● **know-how** *n* (*skill*)
savoir-faire *m inv*.
knowledge ['nɒlɪdʒ] *n* connaissance *f* (**of**
de); (*learning*) connaissances *fpl*, savoir
m; **to** (**the best of**) **my k.** à ma connaissance; **general k.** culture *f* générale.
● **knowledgeable** *a* bien informé (**about**
sur).

knuckle ['nʌk(ə)l] **1** *n* articulation *f* (du
doigt). **2** *vi* **to k. down to** (*task*) *Fam*
s'atteler à.
Koran [kə'rɑːn] *n* **the K.** le Coran.
Korea [kə'rɪə] *n* Corée *f*.
kosher ['kəʊʃər] *a* (*food*) kascher *inv*.
Kuwait [kjuː'weɪt] *n* Koweït *m*.

L

L, l [el] L, l *m*.

lab [læb] *n Fam* labo *m*. ● **laboratory** [lə'bɒrət(ə)rɪ, *Am* 'læbrətɔrɪ] *n* laboratoire *m*; **language l.** laboratoire *m* de langues.

label ['leɪb(ə)l] *n* étiquette *f* ‖ *vt* (-ll-, *Am* -l-) (*with price*) étiqueter; (*for identification*) mettre une étiquette sur.

laborious [lə'bɔːrɪəs] *a* laborieux.

labour ['leɪbər] (*Am* **labor**) *n* (*work*) travail *m*; (*workers*) main-d'œuvre *f*; **L.** *Br Pol* les travaillistes *mpl*; **in l.** (*woman*) en train d'accoucher ‖ *a* (*market, situation*) du travail; **l. dispute** conflit *m* ouvrier; **l. force** main-d'œuvre *f*; **l. union** *Am* syndicat *m* ‖ *vi* (*toil*) peiner. ● **labourer** *n* (*on roads etc*) manœuvre *m*; (*on farm*) ouvrier *m* agricole.

labyrinth ['læbɪrɪnθ] *n* labyrinthe *m*.

lace [leɪs] **1** *n* (*cloth*) dentelle *f*. **2** *n* (*of shoe etc*) lacet *m* ‖ *vt* **to l. (up)** (*shoe etc*) lacer.

lack [læk] *n* manque *m*; **for l. of** à défaut de ‖ *vt* manquer de ‖ *vi* **to be lacking** manquer (**in** de).

lacquer ['lækər] *n* (*for wood, hair*) laque *f*.

lad [læd] *n* gamin *m*, garçon *m*.

ladder ['lædər] *n* échelle *f*; (*in stocking*) maille *f* filée ‖ *vti* (*stocking*) filer.

laden ['leɪd(ə)n] *a* chargé (**with** de).

ladle ['leɪd(ə)l] *n* louche *f*.

lady ['leɪdɪ] *n* dame *f*; **a young l.** une jeune fille; (*married*) une jeune femme; **Ladies and Gentlemen!** Mesdames, Mesdemoiselles, Messieurs!; **l. doctor** femme *f* médecin; **l. friend** amie *f*; **the ladies' room, the** les toilettes *fpl* pour dames. ● **ladybird** *or Am* **ladybug** *n* coccinelle *f*. ● **ladylike** *a* (*manner*) distingué; **she's (very) l.** elle est très grande dame.

lag [læg] **1** *vi* (-gg-) **to l. behind** (*in progress*) avoir du retard; (*dawdle*) traîner; **to l. behind s.o.** avoir du retard sur qn. **2** *vt* (-gg-) (*pipe*) calorifuger.

lager ['lɑːgər] *n* bière *f* blonde.

lagoon [lə'guːn] *n* lagune *f*; (*small, coral*) lagon *m*.

laid [leɪd] *pt* & *pp* of **lay²**. ● **l.-'back** *a Fam* relax.

lain [leɪn] *pp* of **lie¹**.

lair [leər] *n* tanière *f*.

lake [leɪk] *n* lac *m*.

lamb [læm] *n* agneau *m*. ● **lambswool** *n* laine *f* d'agneau, lambswool *m*.

lame [leɪm] *a* (-er, -est) (*person, argument*) boiteux; (*excuse*) piètre; **to be l.** boiter.

lament [lə'ment] *n* lamentation *f* ‖ *vt* **to l. (over)** se lamenter sur.

laminated ['læmɪneɪtɪd] *a* (*glass*) feuilleté.

lamp [læmp] *n* lampe *f*; (*on vehicle*) feu *m*. ● **lamppost** *n* lampadaire *m* (*de rue*). ● **lampshade** *n* abat-jour *m inv*.

lanai [lə'naɪ] *n Am* véranda *f*.

lance [lɑːns] **1** *n* (*weapon*) lance *f*. **2** *vt* inciser.

land¹ [lænd] *n* terre *f*; (*country*) pays *m*; (*plot of*) **l.** terrain *m* ‖ *a* (*transport etc*) terrestre; (*reform*) agraire; (*tax*) foncier.

land² [lænd] *vi* (*of aircraft*) atterrir, se poser; (*of ship*) mouiller; (*of passengers*) débarquer; (*of bomb*) tomber; **to l. up** (*end up*) se retrouver.
‖ *vt* (*aircraft*) poser; (*passengers, cargo*) débarquer; (*job, prize*) *Fam* décrocher; **to l. s.o. in trouble** *Fam* mettre qn dans le pétrin; **to be landed with** *Fam* (*person*) avoir sur les bras; (*fine*) ramasser.
● **landing** *n* **1** *Av* atterrissage *m*; *Nau* débarquement *m*; **forced l.** atterrissage

m forcé; **l. stage** débarcadère *m*. **2** *n* (*at top of stairs*) palier *m*.

landlady ['lændleɪdɪ] *n* propriétaire *f*; (*of pub*) patronne *f*. ●**landlord** *n* propriétaire *m*; (*of pub*) patron *m*. ●**landmark** *n* point *m* de repère. ●**landslide** *n* éboulement *m*; *Pol* raz-de-marée *m inv* électoral.

landscape ['lændskeɪp] *n* paysage *m*.

lane [leɪn] *n* (*in country*) chemin *m*; (*in town*) ruelle *f*; (*division of road*) voie *f*; (*line of traffic*) file *f*; *Av Nau Sp* couloir *m*.

language ['læŋgwɪdʒ] *n* (*English etc*) langue *f*; (*faculty, style*) langage *m*; **computer l.** langage *m* machine ▮ *a* (*laboratory*) de langues; (*teacher, studies*) de langue(s).

languish ['læŋgwɪʃ] *vi* languir (**for, after** après).

lanky ['læŋkɪ] *a* (**-ier, -iest**) dégingandé.

lantern ['læntən] *n* lanterne *f*.

lap [læp] **1** *n* (*of person*) genoux *mpl*; **in the l. of luxury** dans le plus grand luxe. **2** *n Sp* tour *m* (de piste). **3** *vt* (**-pp-**) **to l. up** (*drink*) laper. **4** *vi* (**-pp-**) **to l. over** (*overlap*) se chevaucher.

lapel [lə'pel] *n* (*of jacket etc*) revers *m*.

lapse [læps] **1** *n* (*fault*) faute *f*; (*weakness*) défaillance *f*; **a l. of memory** un trou de mémoire ▮ *vi* commettre une faute; **to l.** into retomber dans. **2** *n* (*interval*) intervalle *m*; **a l. of time** un intervalle (**between** entre). **3** *vi* (*expire*) (*of ticket etc*) se périmer; (*of subscription*) prendre fin; (*of insurance policy*) cesser d'être valable.

laptop ['læptɒp] *a* **l. computer** ordinateur *m* portable.

lard [lɑːd] *n* saindoux *m*.

larder ['lɑːdər] *n* (*cupboard*) garde-manger *m inv*.

large [lɑːdʒ] *a* (**-er, -est**) (*in size or extent*) grand; (*in volume, bulkiness*) gros (*f* grosse); **to grow** or **get l.** grossir, grandir; **at l.** (*of prisoner, animal*) en liberté; (*as a whole*) en général; **by and l.** dans l'ensemble.

●**l.-scale** *a* (*operation etc*) de grande envergure. ●**largely** *adv* (*to a great extent*) en grande mesure.

lark [lɑːk] **1** *n* (*bird*) alouette *f*. **2** *n* (*joke*) *Fam* rigolade *f*, blague *f* ▮ *vi* **to l. about** *Fam* s'amuser.

larva, *pl* **-vae** ['lɑːvə, -viː] *n* (*of insect*) larve *f*.

laryngitis [lærɪn'dʒaɪtɪs] *n* laryngite *f*.

lasagna [lə'zænjə] *n* lasagne *f*.

laser ['leɪzər] *n* laser *m*; **l. beam** rayon *m* laser.

lash[1] [læʃ] *n* (*with whip*) coup *m* de fouet ▮ *vt* (*strike*) fouetter; (*tie*) attacher (**to** à) ▮ *vi* **to l. out** (*spend wildly*) *Fam* claquer son argent; **to l. out at** envoyer des coups à; (*criticize*) *Fig* fustiger.

lash[2] [læʃ] *n* (*eyelash*) cil *m*.

lashings ['læʃɪŋz] *npl* **l. of** (*jam etc*) *Fam* une montagne de.

lass [læs] *n* jeune fille *f*.

lasso [læ'suː, *Am* 'læsəʊ] *n* (*pl* **-os**) lasso *m* ▮ *vt* attraper au lasso.

last[1] [lɑːst] *a* dernier; **the l. ten lines** les dix dernières lignes; **l. but one** avant-dernier; **l. night** (*evening*) hier soir; (*night*) la nuit dernière.

▮ *adv* (*lastly*) en dernier lieu, enfin; (*on the last occasion*) (pour) la dernière fois; **to leave l.** sortir en dernier.

▮ *n* (*person, object*) dernier, -ière *mf*; (*end*) fin *f*; **the l. of the beer**/*etc* le reste de la bière/*etc*; **at** (**long**) **l.** enfin. ●**l.-ditch** *a* (*attempt*) désespéré. ●**l.-minute** *a* de dernière minute. ●**lastly** *adv* en dernier lieu, enfin.

last[2] [lɑːst] *vi* durer; **to l.** (**out**) (*endure*) tenir; (*of money, supplies*) durer. ●**—ing** *a* durable.

latch [lætʃ] **1** *n* loquet *m*; **the door is on the l.** la porte n'est pas fermée à clef. **2** *vi* **to l. on to** (*idea etc*) *Fam* adopter.

late[1] [leɪt] *a* (**-er, -est**) (*not on time*) en retard (**for** à); (*meal, season, hour*) tardif; (*stage*) avancé; (*edition*) dernier; **he's an hour l.** il a une heure de retard; **to make s.o. l.** mettre qn en retard; **it's l.** il est tard; **Easter**/*etc* **is l.**

Pâques/*etc* est tard; **in l.** June/*etc* fin juin/*etc*; **a later edition**/*etc* une édition/ *etc* plus récente; **the latest edition**/*etc* la dernière édition/*etc*; **to take a later train** prendre un train plus tard; **at a later date** à une date ultérieure; **the latest date** la date limite; **at the latest** au plus tard; **of l.** dernièrement. ▮ *adv (in the day, season etc)* tard; (*not on time*) en retard; **it's getting l.** il se fait tard; **later (on)** plus tard; **no later than** pas plus tard que.

late² [leɪt] *a* the **l. Mr Smith**/*etc* (*deceased*) feu Monsieur Smith/*etc*.

latecomer ['leɪtkʌmər] *n* retardataire *mf*. ●**lately** *adv* dernièrement. ●**lateness** *n* (*of person, train etc*) retard *m*; **constant l.** des retards continuels.

latent ['leɪtənt] *a* latent.

lateral ['lætərəl] *a* latéral.

lathe [leɪð] *n Tech* tour *m*.

lather ['lɑːðər] *n* mousse *f* (de savon) ▮ *vt* savonner.

Latin ['lætɪn] *a* latin; **L. America** Amérique *f* latine ▮ *n* (*language*) latin *m*. ●**Latin American** *a* d'Amérique latine ▮ *n* Latino-Américain, -aine *mf*.

latitude ['lætɪtjuːd] *n Geog & Fig* latitude *f*.

latter ['lætər] *a* (*later, last-named*) dernier; (*second*) deuxième ▮ *n* dernier, -ière *mf*; second, -onde *mf*. ●**—ly** *adv* récemment, dernièrement.

laudable ['lɔːdəb(ə)l] *a* louable.

laugh [lɑːf] *n* rire *m*; **to have a l.** rire ▮ *vi* rire (**at, about de**) ▮ *vt* **to l. off** tourner en plaisanterie. ●**—ing** *a* riant; **it's no l. matter** il n'y a pas de quoi rire; **to be the l. stock** of être la risée de. ●**laughable** *a* ridicule. ●**laughter** *n* rire(s) *m(pl)*; **to roar with l.** rire aux éclats.

launch [lɔːntʃ] **1** *n* (*motor boat*) vedette *f* **2** *vt* (*rocket, boat, fashion etc*) lancer ▮ *vi* **to l. (out) into** (*begin*) se lancer dans ▮ *n* lancement *m*.

launder ['lɔːndər] *vt* (*clothes*) blanchir; (*money from drugs*) *Fig* blanchir.

launderette [lɔːndə'ret] *or Am* **Laundro-**

mat® *n* laverie *f* automatique.

laundry ['lɔːndrɪ] *n* (*place*) blanchisserie *f*; (*clothes*) linge *m*.

lava ['lɑːvə] *n Geol* lave *f*.

lavatory ['lævətrɪ] *n* cabinets *mpl*.

lavender ['lævəndər] *n* lavande *f*.

lavish ['lævɪʃ] *a* prodigue (**with** de); (*helping, meal*) généreux; (*house*) somptueux ▮ *vt* prodiguer (**on s.o.** à qn).

law [lɔː] *n* (*rule, rules*) loi *f*; (*study, profession*) droit *m*; **court of l.**, **l. court** cour *f* de justice; **l. and order** l'ordre public; **l. student** étudiant, -ante *mf* en droit. ●**lawful** *a* (*action, age etc*) légal. ●**lawless** *a* (*country*) anarchique.

lawn [lɔːn] *n* pelouse *f*, gazon *m*; **l. mower** tondeuse *f* (à gazon); **l. tennis** tennis *m* (sur gazon).

lawsuit ['lɔːsuːt] *n* procès *m*.

lawyer ['lɔːjər] *n* (*in court*) avocat *m*; (*for wills, sales*) notaire *m*; (*legal expert*) juriste *m*.

lax [læks] *a* (*person*) négligent; (*discipline*) relâché; **to be l. in doing sth** négliger de faire qch.

laxative ['læksətɪv] *n* laxatif *m*.

lay¹ [leɪ] *a* (*non-religious*) laïque; **l. person** profane *mf*. ●**layman** *n* (*pl* **-men**) (*non-specialist*) profane *mf*.

lay² [leɪ] (*pt & pp* **laid**) **1** *vt* (*put down*) poser; (*blanket*) étendre (**over** sur); (*trap*) tendre; (*money*) miser (**on** sur); (*accusation*) porter; **to l. the table** mettre la table; **to l. bare** mettre à nu; **to l. waste** ravager; **to l. s.o. open to** exposer qn à; **to l. one's hands on** mettre la main sur. **2** *vt* (*egg*) pondre.

lay³ [leɪ] *pt of* **lie¹**.

layabout ['leɪəbaʊt] *n Fam* fainéant, -ante *mf*. ●**lay-by** *n* (*pl* **-bys**) *Aut* aire *f* de stationnement *or* de repos. ●**layout** *n* disposition *f*; *Typ* mise *f* en pages.

lay down *vt* (*put down*) poser; (*arms*) déposer; (*condition*) (im)poser; **to l. down the law** faire la loi (**to** à) ▮ **to lay into** *vt Fam* attaquer ▮ **to lay off** *vt* (*worker*) licencier ▮ *vi* (*stop*) *Fam* arrêter; **l. off!** (*don't touch*) *Fam* pas touche! ∎**to lay on** *vt* (*install*) installer; (*supply*) fournir ∎**l. out** *vt* (*garden*) dessiner; (*house*) concevoir; (*prepare*) préparer; (*display*) disposer; (*money*) *Fam* mettre (on dans); **to be laid up** (*in bed*) être alité.

layer ['leɪər] *n* couche *f*.

layman ['leɪmən] *n see* lay[1].

laze [leɪz] *vi* **to l.** (**about** *or* **around**) paresser.

lazy ['leɪzɪ] *a* (**-ier, -iest**) (*person etc*) paresseux. ●**lazybones** *n Fam* paresseux, -euse *mf*.

lb *abbr* (*libra*) = **pound** (*weight*).

lead[1] [liːd] *vt* (*pt & pp* led) (*guide, take*) mener, conduire (to à); (*team, government etc*) diriger; (*life*) mener; **to l. s.o. in/out/etc** faire entrer/sortir/etc qn; **to l. s.o. to do** (*cause*) amener qn à faire; **to l. the way** montrer le chemin; **easily led** influençable; **to l. s.o. away** *or* **off** emmener (qn); **to l. s.o. back** ramener qn. ∎ *vi* (*of street, door etc*) mener, conduire (to à); (*in race*) être en tête; (*in match*) mener; (*go ahead*) aller devant; **to l. to** (*result in*) aboutir à; (*cause*) causer, amener; **to l. up to** (*of street etc*) conduire à, mener à; (*precede*) précéder.

∎ *n* (*distance or time ahead*) avance *f* (**over** sur); (*example*) exemple *m*; (*clue*) piste *f*; (*star part*) *Cin Th* rôle *m* principal; (*for dog*) laisse *f*; (*wire*) *El* fil *m*; **to take the l.** prendre la tête; **to be in the l.** (*in race*) être en tête; (*in match*) mener.

lead[2] [led] *n* (*metal*) plomb *m*; (*of pencil*) mine *f*; **l. pencil** crayon *m* à mine de plomb. ●**leaded** *a* (*petrol, Am* gas) au plomb. ●**lead-free** *a* (*petrol, Am* gas) sans plomb.

leader ['liːdər] *n* chef *m*; *Pol* dirigeant, -ante *mf*; (*of strike*) meneur, -euse *mf*; (*guide*) guide *m*. ●**leadership** *n* direction *f*; (*qualities*) qualités *fpl* de chef; (*leaders*) *Pol* dirigeants *mpl*.

leading ['liːdɪŋ] *a* (*main*) principal;

(*important*) important; (*front*) (*runner, car etc*) de tête; **a l. figure** un personnage marquant; **the l. lady** *Cin* la vedette féminine; **l. article** (*in newspaper*) éditorial *m*.

leaf [liːf] **1** *n* (*pl* leaves) *Bot* feuille *f*; (*of book*) feuillet *m*; (*of table*) rallonge *f*. **2** *vi* **to l.** (**through**) (*book*) feuilleter.

leaflet ['liːflɪt] *n* prospectus *m*; (*containing instructions*) notice *f*.

league [liːg] *n* (*alliance*) ligue *f*; *Sp* championnat *m*; **in l. with** *Pej* de connivence avec.

leak [liːk] *n* (*of gas etc*) fuite *f*; (*in boat*) voie *f* d'eau ∎ *vi* (*of liquid, pipe, tap etc*) fuir; (*of ship*) faire eau ∎ *vt* (*liquid*) répandre; (*information*) *Fig* divulguer. ●**—age** *n* fuite *f*; (*amount lost*) perte *f*.

lean[1] [liːn] *a* (**-er, -est**) (*thin*) maigre; (*year*) difficile.

lean[2] [liːn] *vi* (*pt & pp* leaned *or* leant [lent]) (*of object*) pencher; (*of person*) se pencher; **to l. against/on sth** (*of person*) s'appuyer contre/sur qch; **to l. back against** s'adosser à; **to l. forward** (*of person*) se pencher (en avant); **to l. over** (*of person*) se pencher; (*of object*) pencher ∎ *vt* appuyer (qch) (**against** contre); **to l. one's head on/out of sth** pencher la tête sur/par qch. ●**leaning 1** *a* penché; **l. against** appuyé contre. **2** *npl* tendances *fpl* (**towards** à). ●**lean-to** *n* (*pl* -tos) (*building*) appentis *m*.

leap [liːp] *n* (*jump*) bond *m*, saut *m*; (*increase*) *Fig* bond *m*; **l. year** année *f* bissextile ∎ *vi* (*pt & pp* leaped *or* leapt [lept]) bondir; (*of flames*) jaillir; (*of profits*) faire un bond. ●**leapfrog** *n* saute-mouton *m inv*.

learn [lɜːn] *vt* (*pt & pp* learned *or* learnt) apprendre (**that** que); **to l.** (**how**) **to do** apprendre à faire ∎ *vi* apprendre; **to l. about** (*study*) étudier; (*hear about*) apprendre. ●**—ed** [-ɪd] *a* savant. ●**—ing** *n* (*of language*) apprentissage *m* (**of** de); (*knowledge*) érudition *f*. ●**learner** *n* débutant, -ante *mf*.

lease [liːs] n bail m ‖ vt (house etc) louer à bail.

leash [liːʃ] n laisse f; **on a l.** en laisse.

least [liːst] a the l. (smallest amount of) le moins de; (slightest) le moindre; **he has the l. talent** il a le moins de talent (**of all** de tous); **the l. effort**/etc le moindre effort/etc.
‖ n the l. le moins; **at l.** du moins; (with quantity) au moins; **not in the l.** pas du tout.
‖ adv (to work, eat etc) le moins; (with adjective) le or la moins; **l. of all** surtout pas.

leather ['leðər] n cuir m; (wash) l. peau f de chamois.

leave [liːv] 1 n (holiday, Am vacation) congé m; (consent) & Mil permission f; **l. of absence** congé m exceptionnel.
2 vt (pt & pp left) (allow to remain, forget) laisser; (go away from) quitter; **to l. the table** sortir de table; **to l. s.o. in charge of s.o./sth** laisser à qn la garde de qn/qch; **to l. sth with s.o.** (entrust) laisser qch à qn; **to be left (over)** rester; **there's no bread/etc left** il ne reste plus de pain/etc; **I'll l. it to you** je m'en remets à toi; **to l. go (of)** (release) lâcher; **to l. behind** (not take) laisser; (in race, at school) distancer; **to l. off** (lid) ne pas mettre; **to l. on** (hat, gloves) garder; **to l. out** (forget to put) oublier (de mettre) (accent etc); (word, line) sauter; (exclude) exclure.
‖ vi (go away) partir (**from** de, **for** pour); **to l. off** (stop) Fam s'arrêter. ● **leavings** npl restes mpl.

Lebanon ['lebənən] n Liban m.
● **Leba'nese** a & n libanais, -aise (mf).

lecture ['lektʃər] 1 n (public speech) conférence f; (as part of series) Univ cours m (magistral) ‖ vi faire une conférence or un cours. 2 vt (scold) faire la morale à ‖ n (scolding) sermon m.
● **lecturer** n conférencier, -ière mf; Univ professeur m.

led [led] pt & pp of **lead**[1].

ledge [ledʒ] n (on wall, window) rebord m.

ledger ['ledʒər] n Com grand livre m.

leek [liːk] n poireau m.

leer [lɪər] vi **to l. (at)** lorgner ‖ n regard m sournois.

leeway ['liːweɪ] n (freedom) liberté f d'action; (safety margin) marge f de sécurité.

left[1] [left] pt & pp of **leave** 2 ‖ a **l. luggage office** consigne f. ● **leftovers** npl restes mpl.

left[2] [left] a (side, hand etc) gauche ‖ adv à gauche ‖ n gauche f; **on** or **to the l.** à gauche (**of** de). ● **l.-hand** a à or de gauche; **on the l.-hand side** à gauche (**of** de). ● **l.-'handed** a (person) gaucher. ● **l.-wing** a Pol de gauche.

leg [leg] n jambe f; (of dog, bird etc) patte f; (of table) pied m; (of journey) étape f; (of chicken) cuisse f de poulet; **l. of lamb** gigot m d'agneau; **to pull s.o.'s l.** (make fun of) mettre qn en boîte. ● **l.-room** n place f pour les jambes.

legacy ['legəsɪ] n Jur & Fig legs m.

legal ['liːg(ə)l] a (lawful) légal; (affairs, adviser) juridique; **l. aid** assistance f judiciaire; **l. expert** juriste m; **l. proceedings** procès m. ● **legalize** vt légaliser.
● **legally** adv légalement.

legend ['ledʒənd] n (story, inscription) légende f. ● **legendary** a légendaire.

leggings ['legɪŋz] npl jambières fpl.

legible ['ledʒəb(ə)l] a lisible. ● **legibly** adv lisiblement.

legion ['liːdʒən] n Mil & Fig légion f.

legislation [ledʒɪs'leɪʃ(ə)n] n (laws) législation f; (piece of) l. loi f. ● **legislative** ['ledʒɪslətɪv] a législatif.

legitimate [lɪ'dʒɪtɪmət] a (reason, child etc) légitime.

legless ['legləs] a (drunk) Fam (complètement) bourré.

leg-room n see **leg**.

leisure ['leʒər, Am 'liːʒər] n **l. (time)** loisirs mpl; **l. activities** loisirs mpl; **l. centre** centre m de loisirs; **at (one's) l.** à tête reposée. ● **—ly** a (walk, occupation) peu fatigant; (*meal, life*) calme; **at a l. pace** sans se presser.

lemon ['lemən] *n* citron *m*; **l. drink, l. squash** citronnade *f*; **l. tea** thé *m* au citron. ●**lemo'nade** *n* (*fizzy*) limonade *f*; (*still*) *Am* citronnade *f*.

lend [lend] *vt* (*pt & pp* **lent**) prêter (**to** à); (*charm, colour etc*) *Fig* donner (**to** à). ●**—er** *n* prêteur, -euse *mf*.

length [leŋθ] *n* longueur *f*; (*section of rope, pipe etc*) morceau *m*; (*of road*) tronçon *m*; (*of cloth*) métrage *m*; (*duration*) durée *f*; **l. of time** temps *m*; **at l.** (*at last*) enfin; (*in detail*) dans le détail. ●**lengthen** *vt* allonger; (*in time*) prolonger; ●**lengthy** *a* (*-ier, -iest*) long.

lenient ['liːnɪənt] *a* indulgent (**to** envers). ●**leniently** *adv* avec indulgence.

lens [lenz] *n* lentille *f*; (*in spectacles*) verre *m*; (*of camera*) objectif *m*.

Lent [lent] *n* *Rel* Carême *m*.

lentil ['lent(ə)l] *n* *Bot Culin* lentille *f*.

Leo ['liːəʊ] *n* (*sign*) le Lion.

leopard ['lepəd] *n* léopard *m*.

leotard ['liːətɑːd] *n* collant *m* (*de danse*).

leper ['lepər] *n* lépreux, -euse *mf*. ●**leprosy** *n* lèpre *f*.

lesbian ['lezbɪən] *n* lesbienne *f*.

less [les] *a & n* moins (**de**) (**than** que); **l. time/etc** moins de temps/etc; **she has l. (than you)** elle en a moins (que toi); **l. than a kilo/ten/etc** (*with quantity, number*) moins d'un kilo/de dix/etc ▮ *adv* (*to sleep, know etc*) moins (**than** que); **l. (often)** moins souvent; **l. and l.** de moins en moins; **one l.** un(e) de moins. ▮ *prep* moins; **l. six francs** moins six francs.

-less [ləs] *suff* sans; **childless** sans enfants.

lessen ['les(ə)n] *vti* diminuer.

lesser ['lesər] *a* moindre ▮ **n the l. of** le or la moindre de.

lesson ['les(ə)n] *n* leçon *f*; **an English l.** une leçon *or* un cours d'anglais.

lest [lest] *conj Lit* de peur que (+ ne + sub).

let[1] [let] **1** *vt* (*pt & pp* **let**, *pres p* **letting**) (*allow*) laisser (**s.o. do** qn faire); **to l. s.o. have sth** donner qch à qn. **2** *v aux* **l. us eat/go/etc, l.'s eat/go/etc** mangeons/partons/etc; **l.'s go for a stroll** allons nous promener; **l. him come** qu'il vienne.

let[2] [let] *vt* (*pt & pp* **let**, *pres p* **letting**) **to l. (out)** (*house, room etc*) louer.

let down *vt* (*lower*) baisser; (*hair*) dénouer; (*dress*) rallonger; (*tyre, Am tire*) dégonfler; **to l. s.o. down** décevoir qn; **the car l. me down** la voiture est tombée en panne. ▮**to let in** *vt* (*person, dog*) faire entrer; (*noise, light*) laisser entrer; **to l. s.o. in on sth** mettre qn au courant de qch; **to l. oneself in for trouble** s'attirer les ennuis ▮**to let off** *vt* (*firework, gun*) faire partir; **to l. s.o. off** laisser partir qn; (*not punish*) ne pas punir qn; (*clear of crime*) disculper qn; **to l. s.o. off doing** dispenser qn de faire ▮**to let on** *vi* **not to l. on** *Fam* ne rien dire; **to l. on that** *Fam* (*admit*) avouer que ▮**to let out** *vt* faire *or* laisser sortir; (*prisoner*) relâcher; (*cry, secret*) laisser échapper; (*skirt*) élargir; **to l. s.o. out (of the house)** ouvrir la porte à qn ▮**to let up** *vi* (*of rain etc*) s'arrêter.

letdown ['letdaʊn] *n* déception *f*.

lethal ['liːθ(ə)l] *a* (*blow etc*) mortel; (*weapon*) meurtrier.

lethargic [lə'θɑːdʒɪk] *a* léthargique.

letter ['letər] *n* (*message, part of word*) lettre *f*; **l. bomb** lettre *f* piégée; **l. writer** correspondant, -ante *mf*. ●**letterbox** *n* boîte *f* aux *or* à lettres. ●**lettering** *n* (*letters*) lettres *fpl*.

lettuce ['letɪs] *n* laitue *f*, salade *f*.

letup ['letʌp] *n* arrêt *m*, répit *m*.

leuk(a)emia [luː'kiːmɪə] *n* leucémie *f*.

level ['lev(ə)l] **1** *n* niveau *m*; (*rate*) taux *m* (*a surface*) plat; (*object on ground*) d'aplomb; (*equal in score*) à égalité (**with** avec); (*in height*) au même niveau (**with** que); **l. crossing** *Rail* passage *m* à niveau ▮ *vt* (**-ll-**, *Am* **-l-**) (*surface, differ-*

ences) aplanir, niveler; (*building*) raser; (*gun*) braquer (at sur); (*accusation*) lancer (at contre) ▮ *vi* to l. **off** *or* **out** (*stabilize*) se stabiliser.
2 *n* **on the l.** *Fam* (*honest*) honnête; (*frankly*) honnêtement ▮ *vi* (-ll-, *Am* -l-) to l. **with s.o.** *Fam* être franc avec qn. ● **level-headed** *a* équilibré.

lever ['li:vər, *Am* 'levər] *n* levier *m*.

levy ['levɪ] *vt* (*tax*) lever ▮ *n* (*tax*) impôt *m*.

lewd [lu:d] *a* (-er, -est) obscène.

liable ['laɪəb(ə)l] *a* l. to (*dizziness etc*) sujet à; (*fine, tax*) passible de; l. to do susceptible de faire; l. for responsable de. ● **lia'bility** *n* responsabilité *f* (for de); (*disadvantage*) handicap *m*; *pl* (*debts*) dettes *fpl*.

liaise [lɪ'eɪz] *vi* travailler en liaison (**with** avec). ● **liaison** *n* (*contact*) & *Mil* liaison *f*.

liar ['laɪər] *n* menteur, -euse *mf*.

libel ['laɪb(ə)l] *vt* (-ll-, *Am* -l-) diffamer (par écrit) ▮ *n* diffamation *f*.

liberal ['lɪbərəl] *a* (*open-minded*) & *Pol* libéral; (*generous*) généreux (**with** de) ▮ *n Pol* libéral, -ale *mf*.

liberate ['lɪbəreɪt] *vt* libérer. ● **liberation** [-'reɪʃ(ə)n] *n* libération *f*.

liberty ['lɪbətɪ] *n* liberté *f*; **at l.** to do libre de faire; **what a l.!** *Fam* quel culot!; **to take liberties with s.o.** se permettre des familiarités avec qn.

Libra ['li:brə] *n* (*sign*) la Balance.

library ['laɪbrərɪ] *n* bibliothèque *f*. ● **li'brarian** *n* bibliothécaire *mf*.

libretto [lɪ'bretəʊ] *n* (*pl* -os) *Mus* livret *m*.

Libya ['lɪbjə] *n* Libye *f*. ● **Libyan** *a* & *n* libyen, -enne (*mf*).

lice [laɪs] *see* **louse**.

licence, *Am* **license** ['laɪsəns] *n* (*document*) permis *m*, autorisation *f*; (*for driving*) permis *m*; *Com* licence *f*; **pilot's l.** brevet *m* de pilote; **l. fee** *Rad TV* redevance *f*; **l. plate/number** *Aut* plaque *f*/numéro *m* d'immatriculation.

license ['laɪsəns] *vt* accorder un permis *or* une licence à, autoriser; **licensed**

premises établissement *m* qui a une licence de débit de boissons.

lick [lɪk] *vt* lécher; (*defeat*) *Fam* écraser; **to be licked** (*by problem*) *Fam* être dépassé. ● **-ing** *n* (*defeat*) *Fam* déculottée *f*.

licorice ['lɪkərɪʃ, -rɪs] *n Am* réglisse *f*.

lid [lɪd] *n* **1** (*of box etc*) couvercle *m*. **2** (*of eye*) paupière *f*.

lie¹ [laɪ] *vi* (*pt* lay, *pp* lain, *pres p* lying) (*in flat position*) s'allonger, s'étendre; (*remain*) rester; (*be*) être; (*in grave*) reposer; **to be lying** (*on the grass etc*) être allongé *or* étendu; **he lay asleep** il dormait; **here lies** (*on tomb*) ci-gît; **the problem lies in** le problème réside dans.

lie² [laɪ] *vi* (*pt* & *pp* lied, *pres p* lying) (*tell lies*) mentir ▮ *n* mensonge *m*; **to give the l. to sth** (*show as untrue*) démentir qch.

lie about *or* **around** *vi* (*of objects, person*) traîner ▮ **to lie down** *vi* s'allonger, se coucher; **lying down** allongé, couché ▮ **to lie in** *vi Fam* faire la grasse matinée. ● **lie-down** *n* to have a **l.-down** = **lie down**. ● **lie-in** *n* to have a **l.-in** = **lie in**.

lieutenant [lef'tenənt, *Am* lu:'tenənt] *n* lieutenant *m*.

life [laɪf] *n* (*pl* **lives**) vie *f*; (*of battery*) durée *f* (de vie); **to come to l.** (*of party etc*) s'animer; **loss of l.** perte *f* en vies humaines; **l. insurance** assurance-vie *f*; **l. jacket** gilet *m* de sauvetage; **l. peer** pair *m* à vie; **l. preserver** *Am* ceinture *f* de sauvetage; **l. span** durée *f* de vie; **l. style** style *m* de vie.

lifebelt ['laɪfbelt] *n* ceinture *f* de sauvetage. ● **lifeboat** *n* canot *m* de sauvetage. ● **lifebuoy** *n* bouée *f* de sauvetage. ● **lifeguard** *n* maître nageur *m* (sauveteur). ● **lifeless** *a* sans vie. ● **lifelike** *a* qui semble vivant. ● **lifelong** *a* de toute sa vie; (*friend*) de toujours. ● **lifesize(d)** *a* grandeur nature *inv*. ● **lifetime** *n* vie *f*; *Fig* éternité *f*; **in my l.** de mon vivant; **a once-in-a-l. experience** l'expérience de votre vie.

lift [lɪft] *vt* lever; (*ban, siege*) *Fig* lever;

(idea etc) Fig voler **(from à)**; **to l. down or off** *(take down)* descendre **(from de)**; **to l. out** *(take out)* sortir; **to l. up** *(arm, object)* lever.

‖ *vi (of fog)* se lever; **to l. off** *(of space vehicle)* décoller. ● **lift-off** *n (of space vehicle)* décollage *m*.

ligament ['lɪgəmənt] *n* ligament *m*.

light¹ [laɪt] *n* lumière *f*; *(on vehicle)* feu *m*; *(vehicle headlight)* phare *m*; **by the l. of** à la lumière de; **in the l. of** *(considering)* à la lumière de; **against the l.** à contre-jour; **to bring to l.** mettre en lumière; **to throw l. on** *(matter)* éclaircir; **do you have a l.?** *(for cigarette)* est-ce que vous avez du feu?; **to set l. to** mettre le feu à; **l. bulb** ampoule *f* (électrique).

‖ *vt (pt & pp lit or lighted) (match, fire, gas)* allumer; **to l. (up)** *(room)* éclairer; *(cigarette)* allumer. ● **lighting** *n (lights)* éclairage *m*.

light² [laɪt] *a (bright, not dark)* clair; **a l. green jacket** une veste vert clair.

light³ [laɪt] *a (in weight, strength etc)* léger; **l. rain** pluie *f* fine; **to travel l.** voyager avec peu de bagages. ● **l.-'headed** *a (giddy, foolish)* étourdi. ● **l.-'hearted** *a* gai.

lighten ['laɪt(ə)n] *vt* **to l. a weight** *or* **a load** diminuer un poids.

lighter ['laɪtər] *n (for cigarettes etc)* briquet *m*; *(for cooker, Am stove)* allume-gaz *m inv*.

lighthouse ['laɪthaʊs] *n* phare *m*.

lightly ['laɪtlɪ] *adv* légèrement. ● **lightness** *n* légèreté *f*.

lightning ['laɪtnɪŋ] *n (flashes)* éclairs *mpl*; *(charge)* la foudre; *(flash of)* l. éclair *m*; **l. conductor** *or Am* **rod** paratonnerre *m*.

lightweight ['laɪtweɪt] *a (cloth, shoes etc)* léger.

like¹ [laɪk] *prep* comme; **l. this** comme ça; **what's he l.?** comment est-il?; **to be** *or* **look l.** ressembler à; **what was the book l.?** comment as-tu trouvé le livre?;

what does it smell l.? cela sent quoi?; **I have one l. it** j'en ai un pareil.

‖ *adv* **nothing l. as big**/*etc* loin d'être aussi grand/*etc*.

‖ *conj (as) Fam* comme; **do l. I do** fais comme moi.

‖ *n ... and the l. ...* et ainsi de suite; **the likes of you** des gens de ton acabit.

‖ *a (alike)* semblable, pareil.

like² [laɪk] *vt* aimer (bien) **(to do, doing** faire**)**; **I l. him** je l'aime bien, il me plaît; **she likes it here** elle se plaît ici; **to l. sth/ s.o. best** aimer mieux qch/qn, aimer qch/qn le plus; **I'd l. to come** je voudrais (bien) *or* j'aimerais (bien) venir; **I'd l. a kilo of apples** je voudrais un kilo de pommes; **would you l. an apple?** voulez-vous une pomme?; **if you l.** si vous voulez. ● **liking** *n* **a l. for** *(person)* de la sympathie pour; *(thing)* du goût pour; **to my l.** à mon goût.

likeable ['laɪkəb(ə)l] *a* sympathique.

likely ['laɪklɪ] *a (-ier, -iest) (result etc)* probable; *(excuse)* vraisemblable; **a l. excuse!** *Iron* belle excuse!; **it's l. (that) she'll come**, **she's l. to come** il est probable qu'elle viendra; **he's not l. to come** il ne risque pas de venir.

‖ *adv* **very l.** très probablement; **not l.!** pas question! ● **likelihood** *n* probabilité *f*; **there isn't much l. that** il y a peu de chances que (*+ sub*).

liken ['laɪkən] *vt* comparer **(to à)**.

likeness ['laɪknɪs] *n* ressemblance *f*; **a family l.** un air de famille.

likewise ['laɪkwaɪz] *adv (similarly)* même, pareillement.

lilac ['laɪlək] *n* lilas *m* ‖ *a (colour)* lilas *inv*.

Lilo® ['laɪləʊ] *n (pl -os)* matelas *m* pneumatique.

lily ['lɪlɪ] *n* lis *m*, lys *m*; **l. of the valley** muguet *m*.

limb [lɪm] *n (of body)* membre *m*.

limber ['lɪmbər] *vi* **to l. up** faire des exercices d'assouplissement.

lime [laɪm] *n* **1** *(fruit)* citron *m* vert. **2** *(tree)* tilleul *m*. **3** *(substance)* chaux *f*.

limelight ['laɪmlaɪt] *n* **in the l.** (*glare of publicity*) en vedette.

limit ['lɪmɪt] *n* limite *f*; **that's the l.!** *Fam* c'est le comble!; **within limits** dans une certaine limite ▌ *vt* limiter (**to** à); **to l. oneself to doing** se borner à faire. ● **—ed** *a* (*restricted*) limité; **l. company** *Com* société *f* à responsabilité limitée; **(public) l. company** (*with shareholders*) société *f* anonyme; **to a l. degree** jusqu'à un certain point. ● **limitation** [-'teɪʃ(ə)n] *n* limitation *f*.

limousine [lɪmə'ziːn] *n* (*airport etc shuttle*) *Am* voiture-navette *f*; (*car*) limousine *f*.

limp [lɪmp] **1** *vi* (*of person*) boiter ▌ *n* **to have a l.** boiter. **2** *a* (**-er, -est**) (*soft*) mou (*f* molle); (*flabby*) flasque.

linchpin ['lɪntʃpɪn] *n* (*person*) pivot *m*.

linctus ['lɪŋktəs] *n Med* sirop *m* (contre la toux).

line¹ [laɪn] *n* ligne *f*; (*of poem*) vers *m*; (*wrinkle*) ride *f*; (*track*) voie *f*; (*rope*) corde *f*; (*row*) rangée *f*, ligne *f*; (*of vehicles, people*) file *f*; (*business*) métier *m*; **one's lines** (*of actor*) son texte *m*; **on the l.** (*phone*) au bout du fil; (*at risk*) (*job etc*) menacé; **hold the l.!** *Tel* ne quittez pas!; **the hot l.** *Tel* le téléphone rouge; **to stand in l.** *Am* faire la queue; **to step** *or* **get out of l.** (*misbehave*) faire une incartade; **in l. with** conforme à; **he's in l. for** (*promotion etc*) il doit recevoir; **to drop a l.** (*send a letter*) *Fam* envoyer un mot (**to** à); **where do we draw the l.?** où fixer les limites? ▌ *vt* **to l. the street** (*of trees*) border la rue; (*of people*) faire la haie le long de la rue; **to l. up** (*children, objects*) aligner; (*arrange*) organiser; (*get ready*) préparer; **to have sth lined up** (*in mind*) avoir qch en vue; **lined face** visage *m* ridé; **lined paper** papier *m* réglé.
▌ *vi* **to l. up** s'aligner; (*queue up*) *Am* faire la queue. ● **line-up** *n* (*row*) file *f*; (*of TV programmes*) programme(s) *m(pl)*; (*of TV guests*) invités *mpl*.

line² [laɪn] *vt* (*clothes*) doubler; **to l. one's pockets** *Fig* se remplir les poches. ● **lining** *n* (*of clothes*) doublure *f*.

linen ['lɪnɪn] *n* (*sheets etc*) linge *m*; (*material*) (toile *f* de) lin *m*; **l. basket** panier *m* à linge.

liner ['laɪnər] *n* **1** (**ocean**) **l.** paquebot *m*. **2** (**dust**)**bin l.**, *Am* **garbage can l.** sac *m* poubelle.

linesman ['laɪnzmən] *n* (*pl* **-men**) *Fb etc* juge *m* de touche.

linger ['lɪŋgər] *vi* **to l. (on)** (*of person*) s'attarder; (*of smell, memory*) persister; (*of doubt*) subsister.

lingo ['lɪŋgəʊ] *n* (*pl* **-oes**) *Hum Fam* jargon *m*.

linguist ['lɪŋgwɪst] *n* linguiste *mf*; **to be a good l.** être doué pour les langues. ● **lin'guistic** *a* linguistique. ● **lin'guistics** *n* linguistique *f*.

link [lɪŋk] *vt* (*connect*) relier (**to** à); (*relate, associate*) lier (**to** à); **to l. up** relier ▌ *vi* **to l. up** (*of companies, countries etc*) s'associer; (*of computers*) se connecter; (*of roads*) se rejoindre ▌ *n* (*connection*) lien *m*; (*of chain*) maillon *m*; (*by road, rail*) liaison *f*.

lino ['laɪnəʊ] *n* (*pl* **-os**) lino *m*.

lint [lɪnt] *n Med* tissu *m* ouaté; (*fluff*) peluche(s) *f(pl)*.

lion ['laɪən] *n* lion *m*; **l. cub** lionceau *m*; **l. tamer** dompteur, -euse *mf* de lions. ● **lioness** *n* lionne *f*.

lip [lɪp] *n* lèvre *f*; (*rim*) bord *m*. ● **l.-read** *vi* (*pt & pp* **-read** [red]) lire sur les lèvres. ● **lipstick** *n* bâton *m* de rouge; (*substance*) rouge *m* à lèvres.

liqueur [lɪ'kjʊər, *Am* lɪ'kɜːr] *n* liqueur *f*.

liquid ['lɪkwɪd] *n & a* liquide (*m*).

liquidate ['lɪkwɪdeɪt] *vt* (*debt, Fam person*) liquider.

liquidizer ['lɪkwɪdaɪzər] *n* mixer *m*. ● **liquidize** *vt* passer au mixer.

liquor ['lɪkər] *n* alcool *m*; **l. store** magasin *m* de vins et de spiritueux.

liquorice ['lɪkərɪʃ, -rɪs] *n* réglisse *f*.

lira, *pl* **lire** ['lɪərə, 'lɪəreɪ] *n* (*currency*) lire *f*.

lisp [lɪsp] *vi* zézayer ▌ *n* **to have a l.**

zézayer.

list [lɪst] n liste f ● vt (one's possessions etc) faire la liste de; (names) mettre sur la liste; (name one by one) énumérer; **listed building** monument m classé. ●—**er** n (to radio) auditeur, -trice mf; **to be a good l.** savoir écouter.

listen ['lɪsən] vi écouter; **to l. to** écouter; **to l. (out) for** guetter (le bruit or les cris etc de). ●—**er** n (to radio) auditeur, -trice mf; **to be a good l.** savoir écouter.

listless ['lɪstləs] a apathique.

lit [lɪt] pt & pp of **light¹**.

litany ['lɪtənɪ] n Rel litanies fpl.

liter ['liːtər] n Am litre m.

literal ['lɪtərəl] a littéral; (not exaggerated) réel. ●—**ly** adv littéralement; (really) réellement; **he took it l.** il l'a pris au pied de la lettre.

literate ['lɪtərət] a qui sait lire et écrire. ● **literacy** n capacité f de lire et d'écrire; (of country) degré m d'alphabétisation.

literature ['lɪt(ə)rɪtʃər] n littérature f; (pamphlets etc) documentation f. ● **literary** a littéraire.

lithe [laɪð] a agile, souple.

litigation [lɪtɪ'geɪʃ(ə)n] n Jur litige m.

litre ['liːtər] n (Am **liter**) n litre m.

litter ['lɪtər] n **1** (rubbish, Am garbage) détritus m; (papers) papiers mpl; **l. basket** or **bin** boîte f à ordures ▮ vt **to l.** (with papers) (street etc) laisser traîner des papiers dans; **a street littered with** une rue jonchée de. **2** n (young animals) portée f.

little¹ ['lɪt(ə)l] **1** a (small) petit; **the l. ones** les petits; **a l.** un (petit) peu.

little² ['lɪt(ə)l] **1** a & n (not much) peu (de); **l. time/money/etc** peu de temps/d'argent/etc; **I've l. left** il m'en reste peu; **she eats l.** elle mange peu; **to have l. to say** avoir peu de chose à dire; **as l. as possible** le moins possible.

2 a & n a l. (some) un peu (de); **a l. money/time/etc** un peu d'argent/de temps/etc; **I have a l.** j'en ai un peu; **the l. that I have** le peu que j'ai.

3 adv (somewhat, rather) peu; **a l. heavy/etc** un peu lourd/etc; **to work/etc a l.** travailler/etc un peu; **l. by l.** peu à peu.

live¹ [lɪv] vi vivre; (reside) habiter, vivre; **where do you l.?** où habitez-vous? ▮ vt (life) mener, vivre; **to l. it up** Fam mener la grande vie.

live² [laɪv] **1** a (electric wire) sous tension; (switch) mal isolé; (plugged in) (appliance) branché; (alive) (animal etc) vivant; (ammunition) réel; **a real l. king** un roi en chair et en os. **2** a & adv Rad TV en direct; **a l. broadcast** une émission en direct; **a l. audience** le or un public.

live down vt faire oublier (avec le temps) ▮ **to live off** or **on** vt (eat) vivre de; (sponge on) vivre aux crochets de (qn) ▮ **to live on** vi (of memory etc) survivre ▮ **to live through** vt (experience) vivre; (survive) survivre à ▮ **to live up to** vt (s.o.'s expectations) se montrer à la hauteur de.

livelihood ['laɪvlɪhʊd] n **my l.** mon gagne-pain; **to earn one's l.** gagner sa vie.

lively ['laɪvlɪ] a (-ier, -iest) (person, style) vif, vivant; (street) vivant; (interest, mind) vif; (day) mouvementé; (discussion) animé.

liven ['laɪv(ə)n] vt **to l. up** (person) égayer; (party) animer ▮ vi **to l. up** (of person, party) s'animer.

liver ['lɪvər] n foie m.

livestock ['laɪvstɒk] n bétail m.

livid ['lɪvɪd] a (angry) furieux; (blue, grey) (complexion) livide.

living ['lɪvɪŋ] **1** a (alive) vivant; **not a l. soul** (nobody) personne; **within l. memory** de mémoire d'homme; **the l.** les vivants mpl. **2** n (livelihood) vie f; **to make** or **earn a** or **one's l.** gagner sa vie; **to work for a l.** travailler pour vivre; **the cost of l.** le coût de la vie; **l. conditions** conditions fpl de vie. ● **living room** n salle f de séjour.

lizard ['lɪzəd] n lézard m.

llama ['lɑːmə] n (animal) lama m.

load [ləʊd] n (object carried, burden) charge f; (strain, weight) poids m; **a l. of, loads of** (people, money etc) Fam un

tas de, énormément de.
▌ vt (*truck, gun etc*) charger (**with** de); **to l. s.o. down with** charger qn de de; **to l. up** (*car, ship etc*) charger (**with** de).
▌ vi **to l. (up)** charger la voiture, le navire *etc*. ●**loaded** *a* (*gun, vehicle etc*) chargé; (*rich*) *Fam* plein aux as; **l. (down) with** (*debts*) accablé de.

loaf [ləʊf] **1** *n* (*pl* **loaves**) pain *m*; *French* **l.** baguette *f*. **2** *vi* **to l. (about)** fainéanter. ●**—er** *n* fainéant, -ante *mf*.

loan [ləʊn] *n* (*money lent*) prêt *m*; (*money borrowed*) emprunt *m*; **on l.** **from** prêté par; (**out**) **on l.** (*book*) sorti ▌ vt (*lend*) prêter (**to** à).

loath [ləʊθ] *a* **l. to do** *Lit* peu disposé à faire.

loathe [ləʊð] *vt* détester (**doing** faire).

lobby ['lɒbɪ] **1** *n* (*of hotel*) vestibule *m*, hall *m*; *Th* foyer *m*. **2** *n Pol* groupe *m* de pression, lobby *m* ▌ vt faire pression sur.

lobe [ləʊb] *n* (*of ear*) lobe *m*.

lobster ['lɒbstər] *n* homard *m*; (*spiny*) langouste *f*.

local ['ləʊk(ə)l] *a* local; (*regional*) régional; (*of the neighbourhood*) du *or* de quartier; (*of the region*) de la région; **are you l.?** êtes-vous du coin *or* d'ici?; **a l. phone call** (*within town*) une communication urbaine ▌ *n* (*pub*) *Fam* bistrot *m* du coin, pub *m*; **she's a l.** elle est du coin; **the locals** les gens du coin.

locality [ləʊˈkælɪtɪ] *n* (*neighbourhood*) environs *mpl*; (*region*) région *f*; (*place*) lieu *m*.

locally ['ləʊkəlɪ] *adv* dans le coin; (*around here*) par ici.

locate [ləʊˈkeɪt] *vt* (*find*) trouver, repérer; (*pain, noise, leak*) localiser; **to be located** (*situated*) être situé. ●**location** [-ʃ(ə)n] *n* (*site*) emplacement *m*; **on l.** *Cin* en extérieur.

lock [lɒk] **1** *vt* (*door, car etc*) fermer à clef ▌ vi fermer à clef ▌ *n* (*on door etc*) serrure *f*; (**anti-theft**) **l.** *Aut* antivol *m*; **under l. and key** sous clef. **2** *n* (*on canal*) écluse *f*. **3** *n* (*of hair*) mèche *f*.

lock away *vt* (*prisoner, jewels etc*) enfermer ▌ **to lock in** *vt* (*person*) enfermer; **to lock s.o. in sth** enfermer qn dans qch ▌ **to l. out** *vt* (*person*) (*accidentally*) enfermer dehors ▌ **to lock up** *vt* (*house, car etc*) fermer à clef; (*prisoner, jewels etc*) enfermer ▌ vi fermer à clef.

locker ['lɒkər] *n* casier *m*; (*for luggage*) casier *m* de consigne automatique; (*for clothes*) vestiaire *m* (métallique); **l. room** *Sp Am* vestiaire *m*.

locket ['lɒkɪt] *n* (*jewel*) médaillon *m*.

locksmith ['lɒksmɪθ] *n* serrurier *m*.

loco ['ləʊkəʊ] *a Sl* cinglé, fou (*f* folle).

locomotion [ləʊkəˈməʊʃ(ə)n] *n* locomotion *f*. ●**locomotive** *n* locomotive *f*.

locum ['ləʊkəm] *n* (*doctor*) remplaçant, -ante *mf*.

locust ['ləʊkəst] *n* criquet *m*, sauterelle *f*.

lodge [lɒdʒ] **1** *vt* (*person*) loger; **to l. a complaint** porter plainte ▌ vi (*of bullet*) se loger (**in** dans); **to be lodging** (*accommodated*) être logé (**with** chez). **2** *n* (*house*) pavillon *m* de gardien; (*of porter*) loge *f*.

lodger ['lɒdʒər] *n* (*room and meals*) pensionnaire *mf*; (*room only*) locataire *mf*.

lodgings ['lɒdʒɪŋz] *npl* (*flat, Am apartment*) logement *m*; (*room*) chambre *f*; **in l.** en meublé.

loft [lɒft] *n* (*attic*) grenier *m*.

lofty ['lɒftɪ] *a* (**-ier, -iest**) (*high, noble*) élevé; (*proud, superior*) hautain.

log [lɒg] **1** *n* (*tree trunk*) tronc *m* d'arbre; (*for fire*) bûche *f*; **l. fire** feu *m* de bois. **2** *vt* (**-gg-**) (*facts*) noter. ●**logbook** *n Nau* journal *m* de bord; *Av* carnet *m* de vol.

loggerheads (at) [æt'lɒgəhedz] *adv* en désaccord (**with** avec).

logic ['lɒdʒɪk] *n* logique *f*. ●**logical** *a* logique. ●**logically** *adv* logiquement.

logistics [lə'dʒɪstɪks] *n* logistique *f*.

logo ['ləʊgəʊ] *n* (*pl* **-os**) logo *m*.

loin [lɔɪn] *n* (*meat*) filet *m*.

loiter ['lɔɪtər] *vi* traîner.

loll [lɒl] *vi* (*in armchair etc*) se prélasser.

lollipop ['lɒlɪpɒp] n (sweet, Am candy) sucette f; (ice) esquimau m. ●**lolly** n Fam sucette f; (ice) l. esquimau m.

London ['lʌndən] n Londres m or f ▮ a (taxi etc) londonien. ●**Londoner** n Londonien, -ienne mf.

lone [ləʊn] a solitaire. ●**loneliness** n solitude f. ●**lonely** a (-ier, -iest) (road, life etc) solitaire; (person) seul, solitaire. ●**loner** n solitaire mf.

long[1] [lɒŋ] a (-er, -est) long (f longue); to be ten metres l. avoir dix mètres de long; to be six weeks l. durer six semaines; how l. is...? quelle est la longueur de...?; (time) quelle est la durée de...?; a l. time longtemps; in the l. run à la longue; l. jump Sp saut m en longueur.

2 adv (a long time) longtemps; l. before longtemps avant; l. ago il y a longtemps qu'il est ici?; how l. ago? il y a combien de temps?; not l. ago il y a peu de temps; before l. sous peu; no longer ne plus; she no longer swims elle ne nage plus; a bit longer (to wait etc) encore un peu; I won't be l. je n'en ai pas pour longtemps; don't be l. dépêche-toi; all summer l. tout l'été; l. live the queen vive la reine; as l. as, so l. as (provided that) pourvu que (+ sub); as l. as I live tant que je [...]

long[2] [lɒŋ] vi to l. for sth avoir très envie de qch; to l. to do avoir très envie de faire. ●**—ing** n désir m, envie f.

long-distance [lɒŋ'dɪstəns] a (race) de fond; (phone call) interurbain; (flight) long-courrier. ●**long'haired** a aux cheveux longs. ●**long-life** a (battery) longue durée inv; (milk) longue conservation. ●**long-'playing** a l.-playing record 33 tours m inv. ●**long-range** a (forecast) à long terme. ●**long'sighted** a Med presbyte. ●**long-'term** a à long terme. ●**long'winded** a (speech, speaker) verbeux.

longways ['lɒŋweɪz] adv en longueur.

loo [luː] n the l. (toilet) Fam le petit coin.

look [lʊk] n regard m; (appearance) air m; (good) looks un beau physique; to have a l. (at) jeter un coup d'œil (à), regarder; to have a l. (for) chercher; to have a l. (a)round regarder; (walk) faire un tour; let me have a l. fais voir; I like the l. of him il me fait bonne impression.
▮ vti regarder; to l. s.o. in the face regarder qn dans les yeux; to l. tired/happy/etc sembler or avoir l'air fatigué/heureux/etc; to l. pretty/ugly être joli/laid; to l. one's age faire son âge; you l. like or as if you're tired on dirait que tu es fatigué; it looks like it! c'est probable; to l. like a child avoir l'air d'un enfant; to l. like an apple avoir l'air d'être une pomme; you l. like my brother tu ressembles à mon frère; it looks like rain (to me) il me semble qu'il va pleuvoir; what does he l. like? comment est-il?; to l. well or good (of person) avoir bonne mine; you l. good in that hat/etc ce chapeau/etc te va très bien; that looks bad (action etc) ça fait mauvais effet.

look after vt (deal with) s'occuper de (qch, qn); (sick person, hair) soigner; (keep safely) garder (for s.o. pour qn); to l. after oneself (in health) faire bien attention à soi; (manage) se débrouiller ▮ to look around vt visiter ▮ vi (have a look) regarder; (walk round) faire un tour ▮ to look at vt regarder; (consider) considérer ▮ to look away vi détourner les yeux ▮ to look back vi regarder derrière soi ▮ to look down vi baisser les yeux; (from a height) regarder en bas; to l. down on (scornfully) mépriser ▮ to look for vt chercher ▮ to look forward to vt (event) attendre avec impatience; to l. forward to doing avoir hâte de faire ▮ to look in vi regarder (à l'intérieur); to l. in on s.o. passer voir qn ▮ to look into vt examiner; (find out about) se renseigner sur ▮ to look on vi (watch) regarder ▮ vt (consider) considérer ▮ to look out vi (be careful) faire attention (for à); to l. out for (seek) chercher; to look (out) on to (of window, *house etc*) donner sur ▌**to look over** *vt* examiner, regarder de près; (*briefly*) parcourir; (*region, town*) parcourir, visiter ▌**to look round** *vt* visiter ▌*vi* regarder; (*walk round*) faire un tour; (*look back*) se retourner ▌**to look through** *vt* = look over ▌**to look up** *vi* (*of person*) lever les yeux; (*into the air*) regarder en l'air; (*improve*) s'améliorer; **to l. up to s.o.** *Fig* respecter qn ▌*vt* (*word*) chercher; **to l. s.o. up** (*visit*) passer voir qn.

-looking ['lʊkɪŋ] *suff* **pleasant-/tired-/etc l.** à l'air agréable/fatigué/*etc*.

lookout ['lʊkaʊt] *n* (*high place*) observatoire *m*; (*soldier*) guetteur *m*; **l.** (*post*) poste *m* de guet; (*on ship*) vigie *f*; **to be on the l.** faire le guet; **to be on the l. for** guetter.

loom [lu:m] **1** *vi* **to l.** (**up**) (*of mountain etc*) apparaître indistinctement; (*of event etc*) paraître imminent. **2** *n Tex* métier *m* à tisser.

loony ['lu:nɪ] *n & a Sl* imbécile (*mf*).

loop [lu:p] *n* (*in river etc*) & *Av* boucle *f*.

loophole ['lu:phəʊl] *n* (*in rules*) point *m* faible, lacune *f*; (*way out*) échappatoire *f*.

loose [lu:s] *a* (**-er, -est**) (*screw, belt, knot*) desserré; (*tooth*) branlant; (*page*) détaché; (*clothes*) flottant; (*hair*) dénoué; (*wording, translation*) approximatif; (*link*) vague; (*discipline*) relâché; (*articles*) *Com* en vrac; (*cheese, tea etc*) *Com* au poids; (*having escaped*) (*animal*) échappé; (*prisoner*) évadé; **l. change** petite monnaie *f*; **l. covers** housses *fpl*; **l. living** vie *f* dissolue; **to come** *or* **get l.** (*of knot, screw*) se desserrer; (*of page*) se détacher; **to get l.** (*of dog*) se détacher; **to set** *or* **turn l.** (*dog etc*) lâcher.

▌*n* **on the l.** (*prisoner*) évadé; (*animal*) échappé.

loosely ['lu:slɪ] *adv* (*to hang*) lâchement; (*to hold, tie*) sans serrer; (*to translate*) librement; (*to link*) vaguement.

loosen ['lu:s(ə)n] *vt* (*knot, belt, screw*)

desserrer; (*rope*) détendre; (*grip*) relâcher.

loot [lu:t] *n* butin *m*; (*money*) *Sl* fric *m* ▌*vt* piller. ●**—ing** *n* pillage *m*. ●**looter** *n* pillard, -arde *mf*.

lop [lɒp] *vt* (**-pp-**) **to l. (off)** couper.

lop-sided [lɒp'saɪdɪd] *a* (*crooked*) de travers; **to walk l.-sided** se déhancher.

lord [lɔ:d] *n* seigneur *m*; (*British title*) lord *m*; **the L.** (*God*) le Seigneur; **L. knows if...** Dieu sait si...; **oh L.!** *Fam* mince!; **the House of Lords** *Pol* la Chambre des Lords. ●**lordship** *n* **Your L.** (*to judge*) Monsieur le juge.

lorry ['lɒrɪ] *n* camion *m*; (*heavy*) poids *m* lourd; **l. driver** camionneur *m*; **long-distance l. driver** routier *m*.

lose [lu:z] *vt* (*pt & pp* **lost**) perdre; **to get lost** (*of person*) se perdre; **the ticket/etc got lost** on a perdu le billet/*etc*; **I've lost my bearings** je suis désorienté; **the clock loses six minutes a day** la pendule retarde de six minutes par jour; **to l. one's life** perdre la vie (*in dans*).

▌*vi* perdre; **to l. out** être perdant; **to l. to s.o.** *Sp* être battu par qn. ●**—ing** *a* (*number, team*) perdant; **a l. battle** une bataille perdue d'avance. ●**loser** *n* (*in contest etc*) perdant, -ante *mf*; (*failure in life*) *Fam* paumé, -ée *mf*.

loss [lɒs] *n* perte *f*; **to sell at a l.** vendre à perte; **at a l. to do sth** (*unable*) incapable de faire qch.

lost [lɒst] *pt & pp of* lose ▌*a* perdu; **l. property**, *Am* **l. and found** objets *mpl* trouvés.

lot¹ [lɒt] *n* (*destiny*) sort *m*; (*batch, plot of land*) lot *m*; **to draw lots** tirer au sort.

lot² [lɒt] **the l.** (*everything*) tout; **the l. of you** vous tous; **a l. of, lots of** beaucoup de; **a l. beaucoup**; **quite a l.** pas mal (*of* de); **such a l.** tellement (*of* de); **what a l. of flowers/water/etc!** regarde toutes ces fleurs/toute cette eau/*etc*!; **what a l.!** quelle quantité!; **what a l. of flowers/etc you have!** (ce) que vous avez (beaucoup de) fleurs/*etc*!

lotion ['ləʊʃ(ə)n] *n* lotion *f*.

lottery ['lɒtəri] n loterie f.

lotto ['lɒtəu] n (game) loto m.

loud [laud] a (-er, -est) (voice, music) fort; (noise, cry) grand; (gaudy) voyant ▮ adv (to shout etc) fort; **out l.** tout haut. ●—**ly** adv (to speak, shout etc) fort. ●**loud'hailer** n mégaphone m. ●**loud'speaker** n haut-parleur m; (for speaking to crowd) porte-voix m inv.

lounge [laundʒ] 1 n salon m; **departure l.** (in airport) salle f d'embarquement; **l. suit** complet m veston. 2 vi (in armchair etc) se prélasser; **to l. about** (idle) paresser; (stroll) flâner.

louse, pl **lice** [laus, lais] 1 n (insect) pou m. 2 n inv (person) Pej Sl salaud m.

lousy ['lauzi] a (-ier, -iest) (food, weather etc) Fam infect.

lout [laut] n rustre m.

lovable ['lʌvəb(ə)l] a adorable.

love [lʌv] n amour m; **in l.** amoureux (**with** de); **they're in l.** ils s'aiment; **yes, my l.** oui, mon amour.
▮ vt aimer; (like very much) aimer (beaucoup) (**to do, doing** faire); **give him** or **her my l.** (greeting) dis-lui bien des choses de ma part; **l. affair** liaison f (amoureuse); **15 l.** Tennis 15 à rien. ●**loving** a affectueux.

lovely ['lʌvli] a (-ier, -iest) (pleasing) agréable; (excellent) excellent, (pretty) joli; (charming) charmant; (kind) gentil; **l. to see you!** je suis ravi de te voir; **l. and warm**/etc bien chaud/etc.

lover ['lʌvər] n (man) amant m; (woman) maîtresse f; **a l. of** (music, art etc) un amateur de; **a nature l.** un amoureux de la nature.

low[1] [ləu] a (-er, -est) bas (f basse); (speed, income, intelligence) faible; (opinion, quality) mauvais; **she's l. on** (money etc) elle n'a plus beaucoup de; **to feel l.** être déprimé; **in a l. voice** à voix basse; **lower** inférieur.
▮ adv (-er, -est) bas; **to turn (down) l.** mettre plus bas; **to run l.** (of supplies) s'épuiser.
▮ n **to reach an all-time l.** (of prices etc)

atteindre leur niveau le plus bas.

low[2] [ləu] vi (of cattle) meugler.

low beams [ləu'bi:mz] npl Aut Am codes mpl. ●**low-'calorie** a (diet) (à) basses calories. ●**low-'cut** a décolleté. ●**lowdown** à Fam méprisable. ●**'lowdown** n (facts) Fam tuyaux mpl. ●**low-'fat** a (milk) écrémé; (cheese) allégé. ●**low-key** a (discreet) discret. ●**lowland(s)** n plaine f. ●**low-'salt** a (food) à faible teneur en sel.

lower ['ləuər] vt baisser; (by rope) descendre; **to l. oneself** Fig s'abaisser. ●—**ing** n (drop) baisse f.

lowly ['ləuli] a (-ier, -iest) humble.

lox [lɒks] n Am saumon m fumé.

loyal ['lɔiəl] a fidèle (**to** à), loyal (**to** envers). ●**loyalty** n fidélité f, loyauté f.

lozenge ['lɒzindʒ] n (tablet) pastille f; (shape) losange m.

LP [el'pi:] n abbr (long-playing record) 33 tours m inv.

L-plates ['elpleits] npl Aut plaques fpl d'apprenti conducteur.

Ltd abbr (Limited) Com SARL.

lubricate ['lu:brikeit] vt lubrifier; Aut graisser. ●**lubrication** [-'keiʃ(ə)n] n Aut graissage m.

lucid ['lu:sid] a lucide.

luck [lʌk] n (chance, good fortune) chance f; (fate) hasard m, fortune f; **bad l.** malchance f, malheur m; **hard l.!** pas de chance!; **to be in l.** avoir de la chance.

lucky ['lʌki] a (-ier, -iest) (person) chanceux, heureux; (guess, event) heureux; **to be l.** avoir de la chance (**to do** de faire); **it's l. that** c'est une chance que (+ sub); **I've had a l. day** j'ai eu de la chance aujourd'hui; **l. charm** porte-bonheur m inv; **l. number**/etc chiffre m/etc porte-bonheur. ●**luckily** adv heureusement.

lucrative ['lu:krətiv] a lucratif.

ludicrous ['lu:dikrəs] a ridicule.

ludo ['lu:dəu] n jeu m des petits chevaux.

lug [lʌg] vt (-gg-) (pull) traîner; **to l. sth around** trimbaler qch.

luggage ['lʌgɪdʒ] n bagages mpl; **a piece of l.** un bagage; **hand l.** bagages mpl à main; **l. compartment** compartiment m à bagages.

lukewarm ['lu:kwɔ:m] a tiède.

lull [lʌl] **1** n arrêt m; (in storm) accalmie f. **2** vt (-ll-) **to l. s.o. to sleep** endormir qn.

lullaby ['lʌləbaɪ] n berceuse f.

lumber[1] ['lʌmbər] n (timber) bois m de charpente; (junk) bric-à-brac m inv.
● **lumberjack** n Am Can bûcheron m.
● **lumberjacket** n blouson m.

lumber[2] ['lʌmbər] vt **to l. s.o. with sth/ s.o.** Fam coller qch/qn à qn; **he got lumbered with the chore** il s'est appuyé la corvée.

luminous ['lu:mɪnəs] a (colour, paper etc) fluo inv; (dial, clock) lumineux.

lump [lʌmp] n morceau m; (bump) bosse f; (swelling) grosseur f; **l. sum** somme f forfaitaire ∥ vt **to l. together** réunir; Fig Pej mettre dans le même sac. ● **lumpy** a (-ier, -iest) (soup) grumeleux; (surface) bosselé.

lunacy ['lu:nəsɪ] n folie f.

lunar ['lu:nər] a lunaire.

lunatic ['lu:nətɪk] n fou m, folle f.

lunch [lʌntʃ] n déjeuner m; **to have l.** déjeuner; **l. break, l. hour, l. time** heure f du déjeuner ∥ vi déjeuner (on, off de).
● **lunchbox** n boîte f à sandwichs.

luncheon ['lʌntʃ(ə)n] n déjeuner m; **l. meat** pâté m de viande, = mortadelle f; **l. voucher** chèque-déjeuner m.

lung [lʌŋ] n poumon m; **l. cancer** cancer m du poumon.

lunge [lʌndʒ] vi-**to l. at s.o.** se ruer sur qn.

lurch [lɜ:tʃ] **1** vi (of person) tituber. **2** n **to leave s.o. in the l.** Fam laisser qn en plan.

lure [lʊər] vt attirer (par la ruse) (into dans) ∥ n (attraction) attrait m.

lurid ['lʊərɪd] a (horrifying) horrible; (sensational) à sensation; (gaudy) voyant.

lurk [lɜ:k] vi (hide) se cacher (in dans); (prowl) rôder; (of suspicion etc) persister.

luscious ['lʌʃəs] a (food) appétissant.

lush [lʌʃ] a (vegetation) luxuriant; (surroundings etc) opulent.

lust [lʌst] n (for person, object) convoitise f (for de); (for power, knowledge) soif f (for de) ∥ vi **to l. after** convoiter; (power etc) avoir soif de.

lustre ['lʌstər] (Am **luster**) n (gloss) lustre m.

Luxembourg ['lʌksəmbɜ:g] n Luxembourg m.

luxury ['lʌkʃərɪ] n luxe m ∥ a (goods, car etc) de luxe. ● **luxurious** [lʌg'ʒʊərɪəs] a luxueux.

lying ['laɪɪŋ] pres p of **lie**[1] & [2] ∥ n le mensonge ∥ a (journalist etc) menteur.

lynch [lɪntʃ] vt lyncher.

lyric ['lɪrɪk] a lyrique ∥ npl **lyrics** (of song) paroles fpl. ● **lyrical** a (enthusiastic etc) lyrique.

M

M, m [em] *n* M, m *m*.

m *abbr* **1** (*metre*) mètre *m*. **2** (*mile*) mile *m*.

MA [em'eɪ] *abbr* = Master of Arts.

mac [mæk] *n* (*raincoat*) *Fam* imper *m*.

macaroni [mækə'rəʊnɪ] *n* macaroni(s) *m(pl)*; **m. cheese** macaroni(s) au gratin.

machine [mə'ʃiːn] *n* machine *f*; **change/ cash m.** distributeur *m* de monnaie/ billets. ● **machinegun** *n* (*heavy*) mitrailleuse *f*; (*portable*) mitraillette *f*. ● **machinery** *n* machines *fpl*; (*works*) mécanisme *m*; *Fig* rouages *mpl*. ● **machinist** *n* (*on sewing machine*) piqueur, -euse *mf*.

macho ['mætʃəʊ] *n* (*pl* **-os**) macho *m* ‖ *a* (*attitude etc*) macho (*f inv*).

mackerel ['mækrəl] *n inv* (*fish*) maquereau *m*.

mackintosh ['mækɪntɒʃ] *n* imperméable *m*.

mad [mæd] *a* (**madder, maddest**) fou (*f* folle); **m. dog** chien *m* enragé; **m. (at)** (*angry*) furieux (contre); **m. about** (*person*) fou de; (*films etc*) passionné de; **to drive s.o. m.** rendre qn fou; (*irritate*) énerver qn; **to run/etc like m.** courir/etc comme un fou *or* une folle.

Madagascar [mædə'gæskər] *n* Madagascar *f*.

madam ['mædəm] *n* (*married*) madame *f*; (*unmarried*) mademoiselle *f*.

maddening ['mæd(ə)nɪŋ] *a* exaspérant.

made [meɪd] *pt* & *pp* of **make**.

Madeira [mə'dɪərə] *n* (*island*) Madère *f*; (*wine*) madère *m*.

madhouse ['mædhaʊs] *n Fam* maison *f* de fous. ● **madly** *adv* (*in love etc*) follement; (*desperately*) désespérément. ● **madman** *n* (*pl* **-men**) fou *m*. ● **madness** *n* folie *f*.

Mafia ['mæfɪə] *n* maf(f)ia *f*.

magazine [mægə'ziːn] *n* (*periodical*) magazine *m*, revue *f*; (*broadcast*) *TV Rad* magazine *m*.

maggot ['mægət] *n* ver *m*, asticot *m*.

magic ['mædʒɪk] *n* magie *f* ‖ *a* (*wand etc*) magique. ● **magical** *a* magique. ● **magician** [mə'dʒɪʃən] *n* magicien, -ienne *mf*.

magistrate ['mædʒɪstreɪt] *n* magistrat *m*.

magnet ['mægnɪt] *n* aimant *m*. ● **magnetic** *a* magnétique. ● **magnetism** *n* magnétisme *m*.

magnificent [mæg'nɪfɪsənt] *a* magnifique.

magnify ['mægnɪfaɪ] *vt* (*image*) grossir; (*sound*) amplifier; **magnifying glass** loupe *f*.

magnolia [mæg'nəʊlɪə] *n* (*tree*) magnolia *m*.

magpie ['mægpaɪ] *n* (*bird*) pie *f*.

mahogany [mə'hɒgənɪ] *n* acajou *m*.

maid [meɪd] *n* (*servant*) bonne *f*; **old m.** *Pej* vieille fille *f*.

maiden ['meɪd(ə)n] *n Old-fashioned* jeune fille *f* ‖ *a* (*speech, flight*) inaugural, -ale, -aux, -ales; **m. name** nom *m* de jeune fille.

mail [meɪl] *n* (*system*) poste *f*; (*letters*) courrier *m* ‖ *a* (*bag etc*) postal; **m. order** vente *f* par correspondance; **m. van** (*vehicle*) camion *m* des postes ‖ *vt* (*letter*) poster; **mailing list** liste *f* d'adresses. ● **mailbox** *n Am* boîte *f* aux *or* à lettres. ● **mailman** *n* (*pl* **-men**) *Am* facteur *m*.

maim [meɪm] *vt* mutiler, estropier.

main [meɪn] **1** *a* principal; **the m. thing is to…** l'essentiel est de…; **m. line** *Rail* grande ligne *f*; **m. road** grand-route *f*. **2** *n* **water/gas m.** conduite *f* d'eau/de gaz; **the mains** *El* le secteur; **a mains radio** une radio secteur. ● **—ly** *adv* surtout.

mainland ['meɪnlænd] *n* continent *m*.

● **mainstay** n (of family etc) soutien m; (of policy) pilier m. ● **mainstream** n tendance f dominante.

maintain [meɪn'teɪn] vt (continue) maintenir (tradition etc); (vehicle, family etc) entretenir; **to m. law and order** faire respecter l'ordre public; **to m. that** affirmer or maintenir que. ● **maintenance** n (of vehicle, road etc) entretien m; (alimony) pension f alimentaire.

maisonette [meɪzə'net] n duplex m.

maître d' [meɪtrə'diː] n (in restaurant) Am maître m d'hôtel.

maize [meɪz] n (cereal) maïs m.

majesty ['mædʒəstɪ] n majesté f; **Your M.** Votre Majesté. ● **ma'jestic** a majestueux.

major ['meɪdʒər] **1** a (main, great) & Mus majeur; **a m. road** une grande route. **2** n Mil commandant m. **3** n (subject) Univ Am dominante f ▮ vi **to m. in** se spécialiser en.

Majorca [mə'jɔːkə] n Majorque f.

majorette [meɪdʒə'ret] n majorette f.

majority [mə'dʒɒrɪtɪ] n majorité f (of de); **in the m.** en majorité; **the m. of people** la plupart des gens ▮ a (vote etc) majoritaire.

make [meɪk] vt (pt & pp made) faire; (tool, vehicle etc) fabriquer; (decision) prendre; (friends, salary) se faire; (destination) arriver à; **to m. s.o. happy/tired/etc** rendre qn heureux/fatigué/ etc; **she made the train** (did not miss) elle a eu le train; **to m. s.o. do sth** faire faire qch à qn; **to m. oneself heard** se faire entendre; **to m. oneself at home** se mettre à l'aise; **to m. sth ready** préparer qch; **to m. do** (manage) se débrouiller (with avec); **to m. do with** (be satisfied with) se contenter de; **to m. it** arriver; (succeed) réussir; **I m. it five o'clock** j'ai cinq heures; **what do you m. of it?** qu'en penses-tu?; **you're made** (for life) ton avenir est assuré; **to m. believe** (pretend) faire semblant (that one is d'être); **to m. good** (loss) compenser; (damage) réparer; **to m. light of sth** prendre qch à la légère.

▮ n (brand) marque f; **of French/etc m.** de fabrication française/etc.

make-believe ['meɪkbəliːv] n **it's m.-believe** (story etc) c'est (de la) pure invention.

make for vi (go towards) aller vers ▮ **make off** vi (run away) se sauver ▮ **to make out** vt (see) distinguer; (understand) comprendre; (write) faire (chèque, liste); (claim) prétendre (that que) ▮ vi (manage) Fam se débrouiller ▮ **make up** vt (story) inventer; (put together) faire (collection, liste, lit etc); (prepare) préparer; (form) former; (loss) compenser; (quantity) compléter; (quarrel) régler; (one's face) maquiller ▮ vti **to m. (it) up** (of friends) se réconcilier; **to m. up for** (loss, damage) compenser; (lost time, mistake) rattraper. ● **make-up** n (for face) maquillage m; (of object etc) constitution f; **to wear m.-up** se maquiller.

maker ['meɪkər] n (of product) fabricant, -ante mf.

makeshift ['meɪkʃɪft] n expédient m ▮ a (arrangement etc) de fortune.

makings ['meɪkɪŋz] npl **the m. of** les éléments mpl (essentiels) de; **to have the m. of a pianist/etc** avoir l'étoffe d'un pianiste/etc.

malaise [mæ'leɪz] n malaise m.

malaria [mə'leərɪə] n malaria f.

Malaysia [mə'leɪzɪə] n Malaisie f.

male [meɪl] a Biol Bot etc mâle; (clothes, sex) masculin ▮ n mâle m.

malevolent [mə'levələnt] a malveillant.

malfunction [mæl'fʌŋkʃ(ə)n] n mauvais fonctionnement m ▮ vi fonctionner mal.

malice ['mælɪs] n méchanceté f; **to bear s.o. m.** vouloir du mal à qn. ● **malicious** [mə'lɪʃəs] a malveillant.

malignant [mə'lɪgnənt] a **m. tumour** Med tumeur f maligne.

mall [mɔːl] n (shopping) m. (covered) galerie f marchande; Am centre m commercial.

mallet ['mælɪt] n (tool) maillet m.

malnutrition [mælnjuːˈtrɪʃ(ə)n] n malnutrition f, sous-alimentation f.

malt [mɔːlt] n malt m.

Malta ['mɔːltə] n Malte f. ● **Mal'tese** a & n maltais, -aise (mf).

mammal ['mæm(ə)l] n mammifère m.

mammoth ['mæməθ] a (large) monstre ‖ n (extinct animal) mammouth m.

man [mæn] n (pl **men** [men]) homme m; (player) Sp joueur m; (chess piece) pièce f; **to be m. and wife** être mari et femme; **my old m.** Fam (father) mon père; (husband) mon homme; **yes old m.!** Fam oui mon vieux!
‖ vt (-nn-) (be on duty at) être de service à; (ship) pourvoir d'un équipage; (guns) servir; **manned spacecraft** engin m spatial habité. ● **manhood** n (period) âge m d'homme. ● **manhunt** n chasse f à l'homme. ● **man'kind** n le genre humain. ● **manly** a (-ier, -iest) viril. ● **man-'made** a artificiel; (fibre) synthétique.

manage ['mænɪdʒ] vt (run) diriger; (handle) manier; (take) Fam prendre; (eat) Fam manger; (contribute) Fam donner; **to m. to do** (succeed) réussir à faire; (by being smart) se débrouiller pour faire; **I'll m. it** j'y arriverai.
‖ vi (succeed) y arriver; (make do) se débrouiller (with avec); **to m. without sth** se passer de qch; **the managing director** le PDG. ● **manageable** a (parcel, person, car etc) maniable (feasible) (task etc) faisable. ● **management** n (running, managers) direction f; (of property) gestion f; (executive staff) cadres mpl.

manager ['mænɪdʒər] n directeur m; (of shop, café) gérant m; (business) m. (of boxer etc) manager m. ● **manage'ress** n directrice f; gérante f. ● **managerial** [mænə'dʒɪərɪəl] a **m. job** m poste de direction; **the m. staff** les cadres mpl.

mandarin ['mændərɪn] 1 a & n m. (orange) mandarine f. 2 n (high-ranking official) haut fonctionnaire m.

mandate ['mændeɪt] n Pol mandat m.

mandatory ['mændətərɪ] a obligatoire.

mane [meɪn] n crinière f.

maneuver [mə'nuːvər] n & vti Am = manoeuvre.

mangle ['mæŋ(ə)l] vt (damage) mutiler.

mango ['mæŋɡəʊ] n (pl **-oes** or **-os**) (fruit) mangue f.

manhandle [mæn'hænd(ə)l] vt maltraiter.

manhole ['mænhəʊl] n trou m d'homme; **m. cover** plaque f d'égout.

mania ['meɪnɪə] n manie f. ● **maniac** n fou m, folle f; **sex m.** obsédé m sexuel.

manicure ['mænɪkjʊər] n soin m des mains ‖ vt (person) manucurer; (s.o.'s nails) faire.

manifest ['mænɪfest] 1 a (plain) manifeste. 2 vt (show) manifester.

manifesto [mænɪ'festəʊ] n (pl **-os** or **-oes**) Pol manifeste m.

manifold ['mænɪfəʊld] a multiple.

manipulate [mə'nɪpjʊleɪt] vt manœuvrer; (facts, electors) Pej manipuler.

manner ['mænər] n (way) manière f; (behaviour) attitude f; pl (social habits) manières fpl; **to have no manners** être mal élevé; **in this m.** de cette manière; **all m. of** toutes sortes de. ● **mannered** a **well-/bad-m.** bien/mal élevé.

mannerism ['mænərɪz(ə)m] n Pej tic m.

manoeuvre [mə'nuːvər] (Am **maneuver**) n manœuvre f ‖ vti manœuvrer.

manor ['mænər] n **m.** (house) manoir m.

manpower ['mænpaʊər] n (labour) main-d'œuvre f; Mil effectifs mpl.

mansion ['mænʃ(ə)n] n hôtel m particulier; (in country) manoir m.

manslaughter ['mænslɔːtər] n Jur homicide m involontaire.

mantelpiece ['mænt(ə)lpiːs] n (shelf) cheminée f.

manual ['mænjʊəl] 1 a (work etc) manuel. 2 n (book) manuel m.

manufactur/e [mænjʊ'fæktʃər] vt fabriquer ‖ n fabrication f. ● **—er** n fabricant, -ante mf.

manure [mə'njʊər] n fumier m.

manuscript ['mænjʊskrɪpt] n manuscrit m.

many ['menɪ] a & n beaucoup (de); **m. things** beaucoup de choses; **m. came** beaucoup sont venus; **very m.,** a good or great **m.** un très grand nombre (de); **m. of** un grand nombre de; **m. of them** un grand nombre d'entre eux; **m. times** bien des fois; **m. kinds** toutes sortes (of de); **how m.?** combien (de)?; **too m.** trop (de); **one too m.** un de trop; **there are too m. of them** ils sont trop nombreux; so **m.** tant (de); **as m. books/etc** as autant de livres/etc que; **as m. as** (up to) jusqu'à.

map [mæp] n (of country, region) carte f; (of town, bus network etc) plan m ∥ vt (-pp-) **to m. out** (road) faire le tracé de; (one's day etc) Fig organiser.

maple ['meɪp(ə)l] n (tree, wood) érable m.

mar [maːr] vt (-rr-) gâter.

marathon ['mærəθən] n marathon m.

marble ['maːb(ə)l] n (substance) marbre m; (toy ball) bille f.

march [maːtʃ] n Mil marche f ∥ vi (of soldiers etc) défiler; (walk in step) marcher (au pas); **to m. in/out** Fig entrer/sortir d'un pas décidé; **to m. past** défiler ∥ **to. past s.o.** défiler devant qn. ●**m.-past** n défilé m.

March [maːtʃ] n mars m.

mare [meər] n jument f.

margarine [maːdʒəˈriːn] n margarine f.

marge [maːdʒ] n Fam margarine f.

margin ['maːdʒɪn] n (of page etc) marge f; ●**marginal** a (unimportant) négligeable; **m. seat** Pol siège m disputé. ●**marginally** adv très légèrement.

marigold ['mærɪgəʊld] n (flower) souci m.

marijuana [mærɪˈwaːnə] n marijuana f.

marina [məˈriːnə] n marina f.

marine [məˈriːn] 1 a (life etc) marin. 2 n (soldier) fusilier m marin, Am marine m.

marionette [mærɪəˈnet] n marionnette f.

marital ['mærɪt(ə)l] a matrimonial; (re-lations) conjugal; **m. status** situation f de famille.

maritime ['mærɪtaɪm] a (climate etc) maritime.

mark¹ [maːk] n (symbol) marque f; (stain, trace) trace f, tache f; (token, sign) signe m; (for school exercise etc) note f; (target) but m; (model of machine etc) série f; **up to the m.** (person, work) à la hauteur.

∥ vt marquer; (exam etc) corriger, noter; **to m. time** Mil marquer le pas; Fig piétiner; **to m. down** (price) baisser; **to m. off** séparer; (on list) cocher; (area) délimiter; **to m. up** (price) augmenter. ●**marked** a (noticeable) marqué. ●**marking(s)** n(pl) (on animal etc) marques fpl; (on road) signalisation f horizontale.

mark² [maːk] n (currency) mark m.

marker ['maːkər] n (pen) marqueur m; (bookmark) signet m.

market ['maːkɪt] n marché m; **on the black m.** au marché noir; **the Common M.** le Marché commun; **m. value** valeur f marchande; **m. price** prix m courant; **m. gardener** maraîcher, -ère mf ∥ vt (sell) vendre; (launch) commercialiser. ●**—ing** n marketing m.

marksman ['maːksmən] n (pl -men) tireur m d'élite.

marmalade ['maːməleɪd] n confiture f d'oranges.

maroon [məˈruːn] a (colour) bordeaux inv.

marooned [məˈruːnd] a abandonné; (in snowstorm etc) bloqué (by par).

marquee [maːˈkiː] n (for concerts etc) chapiteau m; (awning) Am marquise f.

marquis ['maːkwɪs] n marquis m.

marriage ['mærɪdʒ] n mariage m; **m. bureau** agence f matrimoniale; **m. certificate** extrait m d'acte de mariage.

marrow ['mærəʊ] n 1 (of bone) moelle f. 2 (vegetable) courge f.

marr/y ['mærɪ] vt épouser, se marier avec; (of priest etc) marier ∥ vi se marier. ●**—ied** a marié; (life) conjugal; **m. name** nom *m* de femme mariée; **to get m.** se marier.

marsh [maːʃ] *n* marais *m*, marécage *m*. ● **marshland** *n* marécages *mpl*. ● **marsh'mallow** *n* Culin (pâte *f* de) guimauve *f*.

marshal ['maːʃ(ə)l] 1 *n* (*in army*) maréchal *m*; (*in airforce*) général *m*; (*at public event*) membre *m* du service d'ordre; Jur Am shérif *m*. 2 *vt* (-ll-, Am -l-) (*gather*) rassembler.

martial ['maːʃ(ə)l] *a* martial; **m. law** loi *f* martiale.

Martian ['maːʃ(ə)n] *n & a* martien, -ienne (*mf*).

martyr ['maːtər] *n* martyr, -yre *mf*. ● **martyrdom** *n* martyre *m*.

marvel ['maːv(ə)l] *n* (*wonder*) merveille *f* ‖ *vi* (-ll-, Am -l-) s'émerveiller (**at** de).

marvellous ['maːv(ə)ləs] (Am **marvelous**) *a* merveilleux.

Marxist ['maːksɪst] *a & n* marxiste (*mf*).

marzipan ['maːzɪpæn] *n* pâte *f* d'amandes.

mascara [mæ'skaːrə] *n* mascara *m*.

mascot ['mæskɒt] *n* mascotte *f*.

masculine ['mæskjʊlɪn] *a* masculin.

mash [mæʃ] *n* (*potatoes*) purée *f* ‖ *vt* **to m. (up)** (*crush*) écraser (en purée); **mashed potatoes** purée *f* (de pommes de terre).

mask [maːsk] *n* masque *m* ‖ *vt* (*cover, hide*) masquer (**from** à).

masochist ['mæsəkɪst] *n* masochiste *mf*.

mason ['meɪs(ə)n] *n* maçon *m*. ● **masonry** *n* maçonnerie *f*.

masquerade [maːskə'reɪd] *vi* **to m. as** se faire passer pour.

mass[1] [mæs] 1 *n* (*quantity*) masse *f*; **a m. of** (*many*) une multitude de; (*pile*) un tas de, une masse de; **masses of** des masses de; **the masses** (*people*) les masses *fpl*. ‖ *a* (*education*) des masses; (*demonstration*) de masse; (*protests, departure*) en masse; (*unemployment*) massif; (*hysteria*) collectif; **m. media** mass media *mpl*; **m. production** produc-

tion *f* en série. 2 *vi* (*of troops*) se masser. ● **mass-pro'duce** *vt* fabriquer en série.

mass[2] [mæs] *n* Rel messe *f*.

massacre ['mæsəkər] *n* massacre *m* ‖ *vt* massacrer.

massage ['mæsaːʒ] *n* massage *m* ‖ *vt* masser. ● **ma'sseur** *n* masseur *m*. ● **ma'sseuse** *n* masseuse *f*.

massive ['mæsɪv] *a* (*huge*) énorme; (*solid*) (*building etc*) massif. ● **—ly** *adv* énormément.

mast [maːst] *n* Nau mât *m*; Rad TV pylône *m*.

master ['maːstər] *n* maître *m*; (*in secondary school*) professeur *m*; **a m.'s degree** une maîtrise (**in** de); **M. of Arts/Science** (*person*) Maître *m* ès lettres/sciences; **m. of ceremonies** (*presenter*) Am animateur, -trice *mf*; **m. key** passe-partout *m inv*; **m. plan** plan *m* or stratégie d'ensemble; **old m.** (*painting*) tableau *m* de maître.

‖ *vt* (*control*) maîtriser; (*subject, situation*) dominer; **she has mastered Latin** elle possède le latin. ● **masterly** *a* magistral. ● **mastery** *n* maîtrise *f* (**of** de).

mastermind ['maːstəmaɪnd] *n* (*person*) cerveau *m* (**behind** derrière) ‖ *vt* organiser.

masterpiece ['maːstəpiːs] *n* chef-d'œuvre *m*.

mastic ['mæstɪk] *n* mastic *m* (silicone).

masturbate ['mæstəbeɪt] *vi* se masturber.

mat[1] [mæt] *n* tapis *m*; (*of straw*) natte *f*; (*at door*) paillasson *m*; (*for table*) (*of fabric*) napperon *m*; (*hard*) dessous-de-plat *m inv*; (*place*) **m.** set *m* (de table).

mat[2] [mæt] *a* (*paint*) mat (*f* mate).

match[1] [mætʃ] *n* (*stick*) allumette *f*; **book of matches** pochette *f* d'allumettes. ● **matchbox** *n* boîte *f* d'allumettes. ● **matchstick** *n* allumette *f*.

match[2] [mætʃ] *n* (*game*) match *m*; (*equal*) égal, -ale *mf*; (*marriage*) mariage *m*; **to be a good m.** (*of colours, people etc*) être bien assortis.

vt (*of clothes, colour etc*) aller (bien) avec; **to m. (up)** (*plates etc*) assortir; **to m. (up to)** (*equal*) égaler; (*s.o.'s hopes or expectations*) répondre à; **to be well-matched** (*of colours, people etc*) être (bien) assortis.
● **vi** (*go with each other*) être assortis.
● **matching** *a* (*dress etc*) assorti.

mate [meɪt] **1** *n* (*friend*) camarade *mf*; (*of animal*) mâle *m*, femelle *f*; **builder's/electrician's/***etc* **m.** aide-maçon/-électricien/*etc* *m*. **2** *vi* (*of animals*) s'accoupler (**with** avec). **3** *n Chess* mat *m*.

material [mə'tɪərɪəl] **1** *a* (*need etc*) matériel; (*important*) important. **2** *n* (*substance*) matière *f*; (*cloth*) tissu *m*; **material(s)** (*equipment*) matériel *m*; **building materials** matériaux *mpl* de construction.

materialist [mə'tɪərɪəlɪst] *n* matérialiste *mf*. ● **materia'listic** *a* matérialiste.

materialize [mə'tɪərɪəlaɪz] *vi* se matérialiser.

maternal [mə'tɜːn(ə)l] *a* maternel. ● **maternity** *n* maternité *f* ● *a* (*clothes*) de grossesse; (*allowance, leave*) de maternité; **m. hospital** maternité *f*.

mathematical [mæθə'mætɪk(ə)l] *a* mathématique. ● **mathematician** [-mə'tɪʃ(ə)n] *n* mathématicien, -ienne *mf*. ● **mathematics** *n* mathématiques *fpl*. ● **maths** *or Am* **math** *n Fam* maths *fpl*.

matinée ['mætɪneɪ] *n Th Cin* matinée *f*.

matrimony ['mætrɪmənɪ] *n* mariage *m*. ● **matri'monial** *a* matrimonial.

matrix, *pl* **-ices** ['meɪtrɪks, -ɪsiːz] *n Math* matrice *f*.

matron ['meɪtrən] *n* (*nurse*) infirmière *f* (en) chef; *Lit* mère *f* de famille, dame *f* âgée. ● **matronly** *a* (*air*) de mère de famille; (*stout*) corpulent.

matt [mæt] *a* (*paint, paper*) mat (*f* mate).

matter¹ ['mætər] *n* matière *f*; (*subject, affair*) affaire *f*, question *f*; **no m.!** peu importe!; **no m. what she does** quoi qu'elle fasse; **no m. where you go** où que tu ailles; **no m. who you are** qui que

vous soyez; **what's the m.?** qu'est-ce qu'il y a?; **what's the m. with you?** qu'est-ce que tu as?; **there's something the m.** il y a quelque chose qui ne va pas; **there's something the m. with my leg** j'ai quelque chose à la jambe; **there's nothing the m. with him** il n'a rien.
● **vi** (*be important*) importer (**to** à); **it doesn't m. if/who/***etc* peu importe si/qui/*etc*; **it doesn't m.!** ça ne fait rien!, peu importe! ● **matter-of-'fact** *a* (*person, manner*) terre à terre.

matter² ['mætər] *n* (*pus*) *Med* pus *m*.

matting ['mætɪŋ] *n* **a piece of m., some m.** une natte.

mattress ['mætrəs] *n* matelas *m*.

mature [mə'tʃʊər] *a* mûr; (*cheese*) fait ● **vi** mûrir; (*of cheese*) se faire. ● **maturity** *n* maturité *f*.

maul [mɔːl] *vt* (*of animal*) mutiler.

mausoleum [mɔːsə'lɪəm] *n* mausolée *m*.

mauve [məʊv] *a* & *n* (*colour*) mauve (*m*).

maximum ['mæksɪməm] *n* (*pl* **-ima** [-ɪmə] *or* **-imums**) maximum *m* ● *a* maximum (*f inv*). ● **maximize** [-maɪz] *vt* porter au maximum.

may [meɪ] *v aux* (*pt* **might**) **1** (*possibility*) **he m. come** il peut arriver; **he might come** il pourrait arriver; **I m.** *or* **might be wrong** ce se peut que je me trompe; **you m.** *or* **might have** tu aurais pu; **I m.** *or* **might have forgotten it** je l'ai peut-être oublié; **we m.** *or* **might as well go** nous ferions aussi bien de partir; **she's afraid I m.** *or* **might get lost** elle a peur que je ne me perde.
2 (*permission*) **m. I stay?** puis-je rester?; **m. I?** vous permettez?; **you m.** go tu peux partir.
3 (*wish*) **m. you be happy** (que tu) sois heureux.

May [meɪ] *n* mai *m*.

maybe ['meɪbiː] *adv* peut-être.

mayonnaise [meɪə'neɪz] *n* mayonnaise *f*.

mayor [meər] *n* (*man, woman*) maire *m*.

maze [meɪz] *n* labyrinthe *m*.

MC [em'si:] *abbr* = master of ceremonies.

me [mi:] *pron* me, m'; *(after prep, 'than', 'it is' etc)* moi; **(to) me** me, m'; **she knows me** elle me connaît; **he helps me** il m'aide; **he gives (to) me** il me donne; **with me** avec moi.

meadow ['medəʊ] *n* pré *m*, prairie *f*.

meagre ['mi:gər] *(Am* **meager)** *a* maigre.

meal [mi:l] *n (food)* repas *m*.

mean¹ [mi:n] *vt (pt & pp meant* [ment])
(signify) vouloir dire, signifier; *(intend)* destiner **(for** à); *(result in)* entraîner; *(represent)* représenter; *(refer to)* faire allusion à; **to m. to do** *(intend)* avoir l'intention de faire; **I m. it** je suis sérieux; **to m. something to s.o.** *(matter)* avoir de l'importance pour qn; **I didn't m. to!** je ne l'ai pas fait exprès!; **you were meant to come** vous étiez censé venir.

mean² [mi:n] *a* **(-er, -est)** *(with money etc)* avare; *(petty)* mesquin; *(nasty)* méchant; *(inferior)* misérable. ●**-ness** *n (greed)* avarice *f*; *(nastiness)* méchanceté *f*.

mean³ [mi:n] *a (average) (distance etc)* moyen **l** *n (middle position)* milieu *m*; *(average) Math* moyenne *f*.

meander [mɪ'ændər] *vi (of river)* faire des méandres.

meaning ['mi:nɪŋ] *n* sens *m*, signification *f*. ●**meaningful** *a* significatif. ●**meaningless** *a* qui n'a pas de sens.

means [mi:nz] *n(pl) (method)* moyen(s) *m(pl)* **(to do, of doing** faire); *(wealth)* moyens *mpl*; **by m. of** *(stick etc)* au moyen de; *(work etc)* à force de; **by all m.!** très certainement!; **by no m.** nullement; **private m.** fortune *f* personnelle.

meant [ment] *pt & pp of* **mean¹**.

meantime ['mi:ntaɪm] *adv & n* **(in the) m.** entre-temps. ●**meanwhile** *adv* entre-temps.

measles ['mi:z(ə)lz] *n* rougeole *f*.

measly ['mi:zlɪ] *a (contemptible) Fam* minable.

measure ['meʒər] *n (action, amount)* mesure *f*; *(ruler)* règle *f*; **made to m.**

fait sur mesure **l** *vt* mesurer; *(adjust)* adapter **(to** à); **to m. up** *(plank etc)* mesurer **l** *vi* **to m. up to** *(task etc)* être à la hauteur de.

measurement ['meʒəmənt] *n (of chest, waist etc)* tour *m*; *pl (dimensions)* mesures *fpl*; **your hip/etc measurement(s)** votre tour de hanches/etc.

meat [mi:t] *n* viande *f*; *(of crab, lobster etc)* chair *f*; **m. diet** régime *m* carné. ●**meatball** *n* boulette *f* (de viande).

Mecca ['mekə] *n* la Mecque.

mechanic [mɪ'kænɪk] *n* mécanicien, -ienne *mf*. ●**mechanical** *a* mécanique. ●**mechanics** *n (science)* mécanique *f*; *pl (working parts)* mécanisme *m*.

mechanism ['mekənɪz(ə)m] *n* mécanisme *m*.

medal ['med(ə)l] *n* médaille *f*. ●**medallion** *n* médaillon *m*. ●**medallist** *(Am* **medalist)** *n* médaillé, -ée *mf*; **to be a gold/silver m.** *Sp* être médaille d'or/d'argent.

meddle ['med(ə)l] *vi (interfere)* se mêler **(in** de); *(tamper)* toucher **(with** à).

media ['mi:dɪə] *npl* **1** *(the mass)* **m.** les médias *mpl*. **2** *see* **medium 2.**

mediaeval [medɪ'i:v(ə)l] *a* médiéval.

median ['mi:dɪən] *a & n* **m. (strip)** *Aut Am* bande *f* médiane.

mediate ['mi:dɪeɪt] *vi* servir d'intermédiaire **(between** entre). ●**mediator** *n* médiateur, -trice *mf*.

Medicaid ['medɪkeɪd] *n Am* = assistance *f* médicale aux défavorisés.

medical ['medɪk(ə)l] *a* médical; *(school, studies)* de médecine; *(student)* en médecine; **m. insurance** assurance *f* maladie **l** *n (in school, army)* visite *f* médicale.

Medicare ['medɪkeər] *n Am* = assistance *f* médicale aux personnes âgées.

medication [medɪ'keɪʃ(ə)n] *n* médicaments *mpl*.

medicine ['medəsən] *n* médicament *m*; *(science)* médecine *f*; **m. cabinet, m. chest** (armoire *f* à) pharmacie *f*.

medieval [medɪ'i:v(ə)l] *a* médiéval.

mediocre [miːdɪˈəʊkər] a médiocre.

meditate ['medɪteɪt] vi méditer (on sur).

Mediterranean [medɪtəˈreɪnɪən] a méditerranéen ∎ n the M. la Méditerranée.

medium ['miːdɪəm] 1 a (average, middle) moyen. 2 n (pl media ['miːdɪə]) Phys véhicule m; Biol milieu m; (for conveying data) support m; through the m. of par l'intermédiaire de; happy m. juste milieu m. 3 n (person) médium m. ∎ m.-sized a moyen, de taille moyenne.

medley ['medlɪ] n mélange m; Mus potpourri m.

meek [miːk] a (-er, -est) doux (f douce).

meet [miːt] vt (pt & pp met) (person, team etc) rencontrer; (person by arrangement) retrouver; (pass in street, road etc) croiser; (fetch) (aller or venir) chercher; (wait for) attendre; (debt, danger) faire face à; (need) combler; (be introduced to) faire la connaissance de; to arrange to m. s.o. donner rendez-vous à qn.
∎ vi (of people, teams, rivers) se rencontrer; (of people by arrangement) se retrouver; (be introduced) se connaître; (of club etc) se réunir; (of trains, vehicles) se croiser.
∎ n to make a m. with s.o. Fam donner rendez-vous à qn.

meeting ['miːtɪŋ] n réunion f; (large) assemblée f; (between two people) (by chance) rencontre f; (arranged) rendez-vous m inv; in a m. en conférence.

meet up vi (of people) se rencontrer; (by arrangement) se retrouver; to m. up with s.o. rencontrer qn; retrouver qn ∎ to meet with vt (accident, problem) avoir; (refusal) essuyer; (difficulty) rencontrer; to m. with s.o. Am rencontrer qn; (by arrangement) retrouver qn.

mega- ['megə] pref méga-.

megaphone ['megəfəʊn] n porte-voix m inv.

melancholy ['melənkəlɪ] n mélancolie f.

mellow ['meləʊ] a (-er, -est) (fruit) mûr; (voice, wine) moelleux; (character) mûri par l'expérience ∎ vi (of person) s'adou-

cir.

melodrama ['melədrɑːmə] n mélodrame m.

melody ['melədɪ] n mélodie f.

melon ['melən] n melon m.

melt [melt] vi fondre; to m. into (merge) Fig se fondre dans ∎ vt (faire) fondre; to m. down (metal object) fondre; melting point point m de fusion; melting pot Fig creuset m.

member ['membər] n membre m; M. of Parliament député m. ∎ membership n adhésion f (of à); (members) membres mpl; m. (fee) cotisation f.

memento [məˈmentəʊ] n (pl -os or -oes) (object) souvenir m.

memo ['meməʊ] n (pl -os) note f.

memoirs ['memwɑːz] npl (essays) mémoires mpl.

memorable ['memərəb(ə)l] a mémorable.

memorial [məˈmɔːrɪəl] a (plaque) commémoratif ∎ n mémorial m.

memory ['memərɪ] n mémoire f; (recollection) souvenir m; in m. of à la mémoire de. ∎ memorize vt apprendre par cœur.

men [men] see man; the men's room les toilettes fpl pour hommes.

menace ['menɪs] n danger m; (threat) menace f; (nuisance) Fam plaie f ∎ vt menacer.

mend [mend] vt (repair) réparer; (clothes) raccommoder; to m. one's ways se corriger ∎ n to be on the m. (after illness) aller mieux.

menial ['miːnɪəl] a inférieur.

meningitis [menɪnˈdʒaɪtɪs] n Med méningite f.

menopause ['menəpɔːz] n ménopause f.

menstruation [menstrʊˈeɪʃ(ə)n] n menstruation f.

mental ['ment(ə)l] a mental; (hospital) psychiatrique; m. block blocage m; m. strain tension f nerveuse. ∎—ly adv he's m. handicapped c'est un handicapé mental; she's m. ill c'est une malade mentale.

mentality [men'tæləti] n mentalité f.

mention ['menʃ(ə)n] vt mentionner, faire mention de; **not to m....** sans parler de...; **don't m. it!** il n'y a pas de quoi! ‖ n mention f.

menu ['menju:] n (in restaurant) & Comptr menu m.

MEP [emi:'pi:] n abbr (Member of the European Parliament) membre m du Parlement européen.

mercenary ['mɜːsɪnəri] n mercenaire m.

merchandise ['mɜːtʃəndaiz] n (articles) marchandises fpl; (total stock) marchandise f.

merchant ['mɜːtʃ(ə)nt] n (trader) négociant, -ante mf; (shopkeeper, Am storekeeper) commerçant m, -ante mf; **m. bank** banque f de commerce; **m. navy** or Am **marine** marine f marchande.

mercury ['mɜːkjʊri] n mercure m.

mercy ['mɜːsi] n pitié f; Rel miséricorde f; **to beg for m.** demander grâce; **at the m. of** à la merci de. ● **merciful** a miséricordieux (**to** pour). ● **merciless** a impitoyable.

mere [mɪər] a simple; (only) ne... que; **she's a m. child** ce n'est qu'une enfant; **it's a m. kilometre** ça ne fait qu'un kilomètre; **by m. chance** par pur hasard. ●—**ly** adv (tout) simplement.

merg/e [mɜːdʒ] vi (blend) se mêler (**with** à); (of roads) se rejoindre; (of companies) fusionner ‖ vt (companies) & Comptr fusionner. ●—**er** n Com fusion f.

meringue [mə'ræŋ] n (cake) meringue f.

merit ['merit] n mérite m ‖ vt mériter.

mermaid ['mɜːmeid] n (woman) sirène f.

merry ['meri] a (-ier, -iest) gai; (drunk) éméché; **M. Christmas** Joyeux Noël. ● **m.-go-round** n (at funfair etc) manège m. ● **m.-making** n réjouissances fpl.

mesh [meʃ] n (of net) maille f; (fabric) tissu m à mailles; **wire m.** grillage m.

mesmerize ['mezməraiz] vt hypnotiser.

mess¹ [mes] **1** n (confusion) désordre m, pagaïe f; (muddle) gâchis m; (dirt) saleté f; **in a m.** sens dessus dessous; (trouble)

dans le pétrin; (sorry state) dans un triste état; **to make a m. of** gâcher.

2 vt **to m. s.o. about** (bother) Fam déranger qn; **to m. up** (spoil) gâcher; (dirty) salir; (room) mettre sens dessous.

‖ vi **to m. about** (have fun) s'amuser; (play the fool) faire l'idiot; **to m. about with sth** (fiddle with) s'amuser avec qch. ● **messy** a (-ier, -iest) (untidy) en désordre; (dirty) sale.

mess² [mes] n Mil mess m inv.

message ['mesidʒ] n message m.

messenger ['mesindʒər] n messager, -ère mf; (in office, hotel) coursier, -ière mf.

Messiah [mɪ'saiə] n Messie m.

Messrs ['mesəz] npl **M. Brown** Messieurs or MM Brown.

messy ['mesi] a see **mess¹**.

met [met] pt & pp of **meet**.

metal ['met(ə)l] n métal m; **m. ladder**/etc échelle f/etc métallique. ● **me'tallic** a (sound) métallique; (paint) métallisé. ● **metalwork** n (craft) travail m des métaux.

metaphor ['metəfər] n métaphore f. ● **meta'phorical** a métaphorique.

mete [mi:t] vt **to m. out** (punishment) infliger (**to** à).

meteor ['mi:tiər] n météore m.

meteorology [mi:tiə'rɒlədʒi] n météorologie f.

meter¹ ['mi:tər] n (device) compteur m; (parking) m. parcmètre m; **m. maid** Aut Fam & Am contractuelle f.

meter² ['mi:tər] n (measurement) Am mètre m.

method ['meθəd] n méthode f. ● **me'thodical** a méthodique.

Methodist ['meθədist] a & n Rel méthodiste (mf).

methylated ['meθɪleitid] a **m. spirit(s)** alcool m à brûler. ● **meths** n Fam = methylated spirits.

meticulous [mɪ'tikjʊləs] a méticuleux.

metre ['mi:tər] (Am **meter**) n mètre m. ● **metric** ['metrik] a métrique.

metropolitan [metrə'pɒlɪtən] *a* métropolitain.

mew [mjuː] *vi (of cat)* miauler.

mews [mjuːz] *n (street)* ruelle *f*; **m. flat** appartement *m* chic *(aménagé dans une ancienne écurie)*.

Mexico ['meksɪkəʊ] *n* Mexique *m*. ● **Mexican** *a & n* mexicain, -aine *(mf)*.

miaow [miːˈaʊ] *vi (of cat)* miauler ▮ *n* miaulement *m* ▮ *int* miaou.

mice [maɪs] *see* mouse.

mickey ['mɪkɪ] *n* **to take the m. out of s.o.** *Fam* charrier qn.

micro- ['maɪkrəʊ] *pref* micro-.

microbe ['maɪkrəʊb] *n* microbe *m*.

microchip ['maɪkrəʊtʃɪp] *n Comptr* puce *f*.

microfilm ['maɪkrəʊfɪlm] *n* microfilm *m*.

microlight ['maɪkrəʊlaɪt] *n Av* ULM *m*.

microphone ['maɪkrəfəʊn] *n* micro *m*.

microprocessor [maɪkrəʊ'prəʊsesər] *n* microprocesseur *m*.

microscope ['maɪkrəskəʊp] *n* microscope *m*.

microwave ['maɪkrəʊweɪv] *n* **m. (oven)** four *m* à micro-ondes.

mid [mɪd] *a* **(in) m.-June** (à) la mi-juin; **(in) m. morning** au milieu de la matinée; **in m. air** en plein ciel.

midday [mɪd'deɪ] *n* midi *m* ▮ *a (sun etc)* de midi.

middle ['mɪd(ə)l] *n* milieu *m*; *(waist)* *Fam* taille *f*; **(right) in the m. of** au (beau) milieu de; **in the m. of saying/working/etc** en train de dire/travailler/*etc.*
▮ *a (central)* du milieu; *(class, quality)* moyen; *(name)* deuxième; **the M. Ages** le moyen âge; **in m. age** vers la cinquantaine; **the M. East** le Moyen-Orient. ● **m.-'aged** *a* d'un certain âge. ● **m.-'class** *a* bourgeois.

middling ['mɪdlɪŋ] *a* moyen, passable.

midge [mɪdʒ] *n (fly)* moucheron *m*.

midget ['mɪdʒɪt] *n* nain *m*, naine *f*.

Midlands ['mɪdləndz] *npl* **the M.** les comtés *mpl* du centre de l'Angleterre.

midnight ['mɪdnaɪt] *n* minuit *f*.

midst [mɪdst] *n* **in the m. of** au milieu de; **in our/their m.** parmi nous/eux.

midsummer [mɪd'sʌmər] *n* milieu *m* de l'été.

midway [mɪd'weɪ] *a & adv* à mi-chemin.

midweek [mɪd'wiːk] *n* milieu *m* de la semaine.

midwife ['mɪdwaɪf] *n (pl* **-wives)** sage-femme *f*.

midwinter [mɪd'wɪntər] *n* milieu *m* de l'hiver.

miffed [mɪft] *a Fam* vexé **(by** de).

might [maɪt] **1** *see* may. **2** *n (strength)* force *f*. ● **mighty** *a* **(-ier, -iest)** puissant; *(very great) Fam* sacré ▮ *adv (very) Am Fam* rudement.

migraine ['miːgreɪn, 'maɪgreɪn] *n* migraine *f*.

migrate [maɪ'greɪt] *vi (of people)* émigrer; *(of birds)* migrer. ● **migrant** *a & n* **m. (worker)** migrant, -ante *(mf)*.

mike [maɪk] *n Fam* micro *m*.

mild [maɪld] *a* **(-er, -est)** *(weather, taste etc)* doux *(f* douce); *(beer, punishment)* léger; *(medicine, illness)* bénin *(f* bénigne); *(exercise)* modéré. ● **—ly** *adv* doucement; *(slightly)* légèrement; **to put it m.** pour ne pas dire plus. ● **—ness** *n (of weather)* douceur *f*.

mildew ['mɪldjuː] *n (on cheese etc)* moisissure *f*.

mile [maɪl] *n* mile *m (=* 1,6 *km)*; **to walk for miles** marcher pendant des kilomètres; **miles better** *Fam* bien mieux. ● **mileage** *n* = kilométrage *m*; *(per gallon)* = consommation *f* aux cent kilomètres. ● **mileometer** *n* = **milometer**. ● **milestone** *n* = borne *f* kilométrique; *Fig* jalon *m*.

militant ['mɪlɪtənt] *a & n* militant, -ante *(mf)*.

military ['mɪlɪt(ə)rɪ] *a* militaire.

militate ['mɪlɪteɪt] *vi (of arguments etc)* militer **(against** contre).

milk [mɪlk] *n* lait *m* ▮ *a (chocolate)* au lait; *(bottle)* à lait; *(diet)* lacté; *(produce)* laitier; **m. float** voiture *f* de laitier; **m. shake** milk-shake *m* ▮ *vt (cow)* traire;

(*exploit*) *Fig* exploiter. ● **milkman** n (*pl* -men) laitier m. ● **milky** a (-ier, -iest) (*diet*) lacté; (*coffee, tea*) au lait; **the M. Way** la Voie lactée.

mill [mɪl] **1** n moulin m; (*factory*) usine f; **cotton m.** filature f de coton; **paper m.** papeterie f. **2** vi **to m. around** (*of crowd*) grouiller. ● **miller** n meunier, -ière mf. ● **millstone** n (*burden*) boulet m (**round one's neck** qu'on traîne).

millet ['mɪlɪt] n *Bot* millet m.

milli- [mɪlɪ] *pref* milli-.

millimetre ['mɪlɪmi:tər] (*Am* **millimeter**) n millimètre m.

million ['mɪljən] n million m; **a m. men/** *etc* un million d'hommes/*etc*; **two m.** deux millions. ● **millio'naire** n millionnaire mf.

milometer [maɪ'lɒmətər] n = compteur m (kilométrique).

mime [maɪm] n (*actor*) mime mf; (*art*) mime m ‖ vti mimer.

mimic ['mɪmɪk] vt (-ck-) imiter ‖ n imitateur, -trice mf.

minaret [mɪnə'ret] n (*of mosque*) minaret m.

mince [mɪns] n (*meat*) viande f hachée, hachis m; (*fruit*) *Am* = **mincemeat** ‖ vt hacher. ● **mincemeat** n (*dried fruit*) mélange m de fruits secs; (*meat*) = **mince.** ● **mincer** n hachoir m.

mind¹ [maɪnd] n esprit m; (*sanity*) raison f; (*memory*) mémoire f; (*head*) tête f; **to change one's m.** changer d'avis; **to my m.** à mon avis; **in two minds** (*undecided*) irrésolu; **to make up one's m.** se décider; **to be on s.o.'s m.** préoccuper qn; **out of one's m.** (*mad*) fou; **to bring to m.** (*recall*) rappeler; **to bear in m.** (*remember*) se souvenir de; **to have in m.** (*person, plan*) songer à; **to have a good m. to do sth** avoir bien envie de faire qch.

mind² [maɪnd] vti (*pay attention to*) faire attention à; (*look after*) garder; (*noise, dirt etc*) être gêné par; **m. you don't fall** prends garde de ne pas tomber; **m. you do it** n'oublie pas de le faire; **do you m.**

if? (*I smoke etc*) ça vous gêne si?; (*I leave etc*) ça ne vous fait rien si?; **I don't m.** ça m'est égal; **I wouldn't m. a cup of tea** j'aimerais bien une tasse de thé; **I m. that...** ça me gêne que...; **never m.!** ça ne fait rien!; (*don't worry*) ne vous en faites pas!; **m. (out)!** (*watch out*) attention!; **m. you...** remarquez, ...; **m. your own business!** ça ne vous regarde pas!

mind-boggling ['maɪndbɒglɪŋ] a stupéfiant.

minder ['maɪndər] n (*for children*) nourrice f; (*bodyguard*) *Fam* gorille m; **child m.** nourrice f.

mindless ['maɪndləs] a stupide.

mine¹ [maɪn] *poss pron* le mien, la mienne, *pl* les mien(ne)s; **this hat is m.** ce chapeau est à moi or est le mien; **a friend of m.** un ami à moi.

min/e² [maɪn] **1** n (*for coal, gold etc*) & *Fig* mine f ‖ vt (*coal etc*) extraire. **2** n (*explosive*) mine f ‖ vt (*bridge etc*) miner. ● **—ing** n exploitation f minière. ● **miner** n mineur m.

mineral ['mɪnərəl] a & n minéral (m); **m. water** eau f minérale.

mingle ['mɪŋ(ə)l] vi se mêler (**with** à); **to m. with** (*socially*) fréquenter.

mingy ['mɪndʒɪ] a (-ier, -iest) (*mean*) *Fam* radin.

mini ['mɪnɪ] *pref* mini-.

miniature ['mɪnɪtʃər] a (*train etc*) miniature *inv* ‖ n miniature f; **in m.** en miniature.

minibus ['mɪnɪbʌs] n minibus m. ● **minicab** n (radio-)taxi m.

minim ['mɪnɪm] n *Mus* blanche f.

minimum ['mɪnɪməm] n (*pl* -ima [-ɪmə] or -imums) minimum m ‖ a minimum (f inv). ● **minimal** a minimal. ● **minimize** [-maɪz] vt minimiser.

mining ['maɪnɪŋ] n *see* **mine²**.

minister ['mɪnɪstər] n *Pol* ministre m; *Rel* pasteur m. ● **mini'sterial** a *Pol* ministériel. ● **ministry** n *Pol* ministère m.

mink [mɪŋk] n (*animal, fur*) vison m.

minor ['maɪnər] a (*detail, operation etc*)

petit; *Mus Rel etc* mineur ∥ *n Jur* mineur, -eure *mf*.

Minorca [mɪˈnɔːkə] *n* Minorque *f*.

minority [maɪˈnɒrɪti] *n* minorité *f*; **in the** *or* **a m.** en minorité ∥ *a* minoritaire.

mint [mɪnt] **1** *n* (*place*) Hôtel *m* de la Monnaie; **a m. (of money)** *Fig* une petite fortune ∥ *vt* (*money*) frapper ∥ *a* (*stamp*) neuf. **2** *n* (*herb*) menthe *f*; (*sweet, Am candy*) bonbon *m* à la menthe; **m. tea/etc** thé *m*/etc à la menthe.

minus [ˈmaɪnəs] *prep* moins; (*without*) *Fam* sans; **it's m. ten (degrees)** il fait moins dix (degrés) ∥ *n* **m. (sign)** (signe *m*) moins *m*.

minute¹ [ˈmɪnɪt] **1** *n* minute *f*; **any m. (now)** d'une minute à l'autre; **m. hand** (*of clock*) grande aiguille *f*. **2** *npl* **minutes** (*of meeting*) procès-verbal *m*.

minute² [maɪˈnjuːt] *a* (*tiny*) minuscule; (*careful*) minutieux.

miracle [ˈmɪrək(ə)l] *n* miracle *m*. ● **miˈraculous** *a* miraculeux.

mirage [ˈmɪrɑːʒ] *n* mirage *m*.

mirror [ˈmɪrər] *n* miroir *m*, glace *f*; *Aut* rétroviseur *m* ∥ *vt* refléter.

mirth [mɜːθ] *n* *Lit* gaieté *f*, hilarité *f*.

misapprehension [mɪsæprɪˈhenʃ(ə)n] *n* malentendu *m*.

misbehave [mɪsbɪˈheɪv] *vi* se conduire mal.

miscalculate [mɪsˈkælkjʊleɪt] *vt* mal calculer ∥ *vi* *Fig* se tromper. ● **misˈcalculation** [-ˈleɪʃ(ə)n] *n* erreur *f* de calcul.

miscarriage [mɪsˈkærɪdʒ] *n* **to have a m.** *Med* faire une fausse couche; **m. of justice** erreur *f* judiciaire. ● **misˈcarry** *vi* *Med* faire une fausse couche.

miscellaneous [mɪsɪˈleɪnɪəs] *a* divers.

mischief [ˈmɪstʃɪf] *n* espièglerie *f*; (*malice*) méchanceté *f*; **to get into m.** faire des bêtises; **to make m. for s.o.** créer des ennuis à qn; **to do s.o. a m.** faire mal à qn. ● **mischievous** *a* (*naughty*) espiègle; (*malicious*) méchant.

misconception [mɪskənˈsepʃ(ə)n] *n* idée

f fausse.

misconduct [mɪsˈkɒndʌkt] *n* mauvaise conduite *f*.

misdeed [mɪsˈdiːd] *n* méfait *m*.

misdemeanor [mɪsdɪˈmiːnər] *n* *Am Jur* délit *m*.

misdirect [mɪsdɪˈrekt] *vt* (*letter*) mal adresser; (*person*) mal renseigner.

miser [ˈmaɪzər] *n* avare *mf*. ● **-ly** *a* avare.

miserable [ˈmɪzərəb(ə)l] *a* (*wretched*) misérable; (*unhappy*) malheureux; (*awful*) affreux; (*salary*) dérisoire.

misery [ˈmɪzəri] *n* (*suffering*) souffrances *fpl*; (*sadness*) tristesse *f*; (*person*) *Fam* grincheux, -euse *mf*; *pl* (*misfortunes*) misères *fpl*.

misfire [mɪsˈfaɪər] *vi* (*of plan*) rater.

misfit [ˈmɪsfɪt] *n* *Pej* inadapté, -ée *mf*.

misfortune [mɪsˈfɔːtʃuːn] *n* malheur *m*.

misgivings [mɪsˈgɪvɪŋz] *npl* (*doubts*) doutes *mpl* (**about** sur); (*fears*) craintes *fpl*.

misguided [mɪsˈgaɪdɪd] *a* (*action etc*) imprudent; **to be m.** (*of person*) se tromper.

mishandle [mɪsˈhænd(ə)l] *vt* (*affair, situation*) traiter avec maladresse.

mishap [ˈmɪshæp] *n* (*hitch*) contretemps *m*; (*accident*) mésaventure *f*.

misinform [mɪsɪnˈfɔːm] *vt* mal renseigner.

misinterpret [mɪsɪnˈtɜːprɪt] *vt* mal interpréter.

mislay [mɪsˈleɪ] *vt* (*pt & pp* **mislaid**) égarer.

mislead [mɪsˈliːd] *vt* (*pt & pp* **misled**) tromper. ● **-ing** *a* trompeur.

mismanage [mɪsˈmænɪdʒ] *vt* mal administrer.

misnomer [mɪsˈnəʊmər] *n* nom *m* *or* terme *m* impropre.

misplace [mɪsˈpleɪs] *vt* (*lose*) égarer.

misprint [ˈmɪsprɪnt] *n* faute *f* d'impression.

mispronounce [mɪsprəˈnaʊns] *vt* mal prononcer.

misrepresent [mɪsreprɪˈzent] *vt* présenter sous un faux jour.

miss¹ [mɪs] vt (train, target, opportunity etc) manquer, rater; (not see) ne pas voir; (not understand) ne pas comprendre; (deceased person etc) regretter; (sth just lost) remarquer l'absence de; **he misses Paris/her** Paris/elle lui manque; **I m. you** tu me manques; **we'll be missed** on remarquera notre absence; **don't m. seeing this play** ne manque pas de voir cette pièce; **to m. sth out** (leave out) sauter qch.
‖ vi manquer, rater; **to m. out** (lose a chance) rater l'occasion; **to m. out on** (opportunity) rater.
‖ n coup m manqué; **we had a near m.** on l'a échappé belle; **I'll give it a m.** Fam (not go) je n'y irai pas. ●**missing** a absent; (in war, after disaster) disparu; (object) manquant; **there are two cups/students m.** il manque deux tasses/deux étudiants m; **to go m.** disparaître.

miss² [mɪs] n (woman) mademoiselle f; **Miss Brown** Mademoiselle or Mlle Brown.

misshapen [mɪsˈʃeɪp(ə)n] a difforme.

missile [ˈmɪsaɪl, Am ˈmɪs(ə)l] n (rocket) missile m; (object thrown) projectile m.

mission [ˈmɪʃ(ə)n] n mission f. ●**missionary** n missionnaire m.

missive [ˈmɪsɪv] n (letter) missive f.

misspell [mɪsˈspel] vt (pt & pp -ed or misspelt) mal écrire.

mist [mɪst] n (fog) brume f; (on glass) buée f ‖ vi **to m. over** or **up** s'embuer.

mistake [mɪˈsteɪk] n erreur f, faute f; **to make a m.** se tromper, faire (une) erreur; **by m.** par erreur.
‖ vt (pt mistook, pp mistaken) (meaning, intention etc) se tromper sur; **to m. the date/etc** se tromper de date/etc; **you can't m. it** (face, car etc) il est impossible de ne pas le reconnaître; **to m. s.o./sth for** prendre qn/qch pour. ●**mistaken** a (idea) erroné; **to be m.** (of person) se tromper. ●**mistakenly** adv par erreur.

mister [ˈmɪstər] n Fam monsieur m.

mistletoe [ˈmɪs(ə)ltəʊ] n Bot gui m.

mistreat [mɪsˈtriːt] vt maltraiter.

mistress [ˈmɪstrɪs] n maîtresse f; (in secondary school) professeur m; (in primary school) institutrice f.

mistrust [mɪsˈtrʌst] n méfiance f ‖ vt se méfier de.

misty [ˈmɪstɪ] a (-ier, -iest) (foggy) brumeux; (glass) embué.

misunderstand [mɪsʌndəˈstænd] vti (pt & pp -stood) mal comprendre. ●**misunderstanding** n malentendu m.

misuse [mɪsˈjuːz] vt (word, tool) mal employer; (power etc) abuser de ‖ [mɪsˈjuːs] n (of word) emploi m abusif; (of tool) usage m abusif; (of power etc) abus m.

mite [maɪt] n **1** (insect) mite f. **2** (poor) m. (child) (pauvre) petit, -ite mf.

mitigate [ˈmɪtɪgeɪt] vt atténuer.

mitt(en) [mɪt, ˈmɪt(ə)n] n (glove) moufle f.

mix [mɪks] vt mélanger, mêler; (cement, cake) préparer; (salad) remuer; **to m. up** (drinks, papers etc) mélanger; (make confused) embrouiller (qn); (mistake) confondre (with avec); **to be mixed up with s.o.** être mêlé aux affaires de qn.
‖ vi se mêler; (of colours) s'allier; **to m. with s.o.** (socially) fréquenter qn; **she doesn't m.** elle n'est pas sociable.
‖ n (mixture) mélange m. ●**mixed** a (school, marriage) mixte; (feelings) mitigés; (chocolates etc) assortis; **m. grill** assortiment m de grillades; **to be m. up** (of person) être désorienté; (of facts etc) être embrouillé. ●**mixer** n (electric, for food) mixe(u)r m; **to be a good m.** (of person) être sociable. ●**mixture** n mélange m; (for cough) sirop m. ●**mix-up** n confusion f.

mm abbr (millimetre) mm.

moan [məʊn] vi (groan) gémir; (complain) se plaindre (**to** à, **about** de, **that** que) ‖ n gémissement m; plainte f.

moat [məʊt] n douve(s) f(pl).

mob [mɒb] n (crowd) foule f, cohue f; (gang) bande f ‖ vt (-bb-) (person, store etc) assiéger.

mobile ['məʊbaɪl, Am 'məʊb(ə)l] a mobile; (having a car) Fam motorisé; **m. home** mobil-home m; **m. library** bibliobus m; **m. phone** téléphone m portatif ‖ n (Am [məʊbiːl]) (ornament) mobile m. ● **mo'bility** n mobilité f.

mobilize ['məʊbɪlaɪz] vti mobiliser.

moccasin ['mɒkəsɪn] n (shoe) mocassin m.

mocha ['məʊkə] n (coffee) moka m.

mock [mɒk] 1 vt se moquer de; (mimic) singer ‖ vi se moquer (at de). 2 a (false) simulé; **m. exam** examen m blanc. ●—**ing** a moqueur. ● **mockery** n (act) moquerie f; (parody) parodie f; **to make a m. of sth** tourner qch en ridicule.

mock-up ['mɒkʌp] n (model) maquette f.

mod cons [mɒd'kɒnz] npl abbr (modern conveniences) tout le confort moderne.

mode [məʊd] n (manner) & Comptr mode m.

model ['mɒd(ə)l] n (example, person posing for artist etc) modèle m; (fashion) m. mannequin m; (scale) m. modèle m (réduit).

‖ a (behaviour, student etc) modèle; (car, plane etc) modèle réduit inv; **m. railway** train n miniature.

‖ vt (clay etc) modeler (hats etc) présenter (les modèles de); **to m. sth/s.o. on** modeler qch/qn sur.

‖ vi (for fashion) être mannequin; (pose for artist) poser.

modem ['məʊdəm] n Comptr modem m.

moderate[1] ['mɒdərət] a modéré; (in speech) mesuré ‖ n Pol modéré, -ée mf. ●—**ly** adv modérément; (averagely) moyennement.

moderate[2] ['mɒdəreɪt] vt (tone down) modérer. ● **moderation** [-'reɪʃ(ə)n] n modération f; **in m.** avec modération.

modern ['mɒd(ə)n] a moderne; **m. languages** langues fpl vivantes.

modernize ['mɒdənaɪz] vt moderniser ‖ vi se moderniser.

modest ['mɒdɪst] a modeste. ● **modesty** n (quality) modestie f.

modify ['mɒdɪfaɪ] vt (alter) modifier;

(tone down) modérer. ● **modification** [-'keɪʃ(ə)n] n modification f.

mohair ['məʊheər] n mohair m.

moist [mɔɪst] a (-er, -est) humide; (sticky) moite. ● **moisten** ['mɔɪs(ə)n] vt humecter.

moisture ['mɔɪstʃər] n humidité f; (on glass) buée f. ● **moisturizer** n (for skin) crème f hydratante.

molar ['məʊlər] n (tooth) molaire f.

molasses [mə'læsɪz] n (treacle) Am mélasse f.

mold [məʊld] Am = **mould**.

mole [məʊl] n 1 (on skin) grain m de beauté. 2 (animal, spy) taupe f.

molecule ['mɒlɪkjuːl] n molécule f.

molest [mə'lest] vt (annoy) importuner; (child, woman) Jur attenter à la pudeur de.

molt [məʊlt] Am = **moult**.

molten ['məʊlt(ə)n] a (metal) en fusion.

mom [mɒm] n Am Fam maman f.

moment ['məʊmənt] n moment m; **this (very) m.** (now) à l'instant; **the m. she leaves** dès qu'elle partira; **any m.** (now) d'un moment à l'autre.

momentary ['məʊməntərɪ, Am -erɪ] a momentané. ● **momentarily** (Am [məʊmən'terɪlɪ]) adv (temporarily) momentanément; (soon) Am tout à l'heure.

momentum [məʊ'mentəm] n (speed) élan m; **to gather m.** (of ideas etc) gagner du terrain.

mommy ['mɒmɪ] n Am Fam maman f.

Monaco ['mɒnəkəʊ] n Monaco f.

monarch ['mɒnək] n monarque m. ● **monarchy** n monarchie f.

monastery ['mɒnəst(ə)rɪ] n monastère m.

Monday ['mʌndɪ, Am -deɪ] n lundi m.

monetary ['mʌnɪt(ə)rɪ] a monétaire.

money ['mʌnɪ] n argent m; **to get one's m.'s worth** en avoir pour son argent; **m. order** mandat m. ● **moneybox** n tirelire f. ● **moneychanger** n changeur m. ● **moneylender** n prêteur, -euse mf sur gages. ● **moneymaking** a lucratif.

● **money-spinner** n Fam mine f d'or.
mongrel ['mʌŋgrəl] n (dog) bâtard m.
monitor ['mɒnɪtər] 1 n (screen, device) Comptr TV etc moniteur m. 2 vt (radio broadcast) écouter; (check) contrôler.
monk [mʌŋk] n moine m, religieux m.
monkey ['mʌŋkɪ] n singe m; **m. wrench** clef f anglaise.
mono ['mɒnəʊ] a (record etc) mono inv. ▮ n **in m.** en monophonie.
mono- ['mɒnəʊ] pref mono-.
monologue ['mɒnəlɒg] n monologue m.
monopoly [mə'nɒpəlɪ] n monopole m. ● **monopolize** vt monopoliser.
monotony [mə'nɒtənɪ] n monotonie f. ● **monotonous** a monotone.
monsoon [mɒn'suːn] n (wind, rain) mousson f.
monster ['mɒnstər] n monstre m. ● **mon'strosity** n monstruosité f. ● **monstrous** a (terrible, enormous) monstrueux.
month [mʌnθ] n mois m. ● **monthly** a mensuel ▮ n (periodical) mensuel m ▮ adv (every month) mensuellement.
Montreal [mɒntrɪ'ɔːl] n Montréal m or f.
monument ['mɒnjʊmənt] n monument m.
moo [muː] vi meugler ▮ n meuglement m.
mooch [muːtʃ] vi **to m. around** Fam flâner.
mood [muːd] n (of person) humeur f; (of country) état m d'esprit; Gram mode m; **in a good/bad m.** de bonne/mauvaise humeur; **to be in the m. to do** être d'humeur à faire. ● **moody** a (-ier, -iest) (bad-tempered) de mauvaise humeur; (changeable) d'humeur changeante.
moon [muːn] n lune f; **full m.** pleine lune; **over the m.** (delighted) Fam ravi (about de). ● **moonlight** n clair m de lune; **by m.** au clair de lune.
moor [mʊər] 1 vt Nau amarrer ▮ vi mouiller. 2 n (open land) lande f.
moose [muːs] n inv (animal) élan m.
mop [mɒp] n balai m (à laver); **dish m.** lavette f; **m. of hair** tignasse f ▮ vt (-pp-)

to m. (up) (floor etc) essuyer; **to m. up** (liquid) éponger.
mope [məʊp] vi **to m. about** errer comme une âme en peine.
moped ['məʊped] n mobylette® f.
moral ['mɒrəl] a moral ▮ n (of story) morale f; pl (standards) moralité f. ● **morale** [mə'rɑːl, Am mə'ræl] n moral m. ● **mo'rality** n (morals) moralité f.
morbid ['mɔːbɪd] a morbide.
more [mɔːr] a & n plus (de) (than que); (other) d'autres; **m. cars/etc** plus de voitures/etc; **he has m. (than you)** il en a plus (que toi); **a few m. months** encore quelques mois; **(some) m. tea/ etc** encore du thé/etc; **(some) m. details** d'autres détails; **m. than a kilo/ten** (with quantity, number) plus d'un kilo/de dix. ▮ adv (tired, rapidly etc) plus (than que); **m. and m.** de plus en plus; **m. or less** plus ou moins; **the m. he shouts the m. hoarse he gets** plus il crie plus il s'enroue; **she doesn't have any m.** n'en a plus.
moreover [mɔːr'əʊvər] adv de plus.
morgue [mɔːg] n (mortuary) morgue f.
morning ['mɔːnɪŋ] n matin m; (duration of morning) matinée f; **in the m.** le matin; (tomorrow) demain matin; **at seven in the m.** à sept heures du matin; **every Tuesday m.** tous les mardis matin ▮ a du matin. ● **mornings** adv Am le matin.
Morocco [mə'rɒkəʊ] n Maroc m. ● **Moroccan** a & n marocain, -aine (mf).
moron ['mɔːrɒn] n crétin, -ine mf.
morphine ['mɔːfiːn] n morphine f.
Morse [mɔːs] n & a **M. (code)** morse m.
mortal ['mɔːt(ə)l] a & n mortel, -elle (mf).
mortar ['mɔːtər] n mortier m.
mortgage ['mɔːgɪdʒ] n prêt-logement m.
mortician [mɔː'tɪʃ(ə)n] n Am entrepreneur m de pompes funèbres.
mortuary ['mɔːtʃʊərɪ] n morgue f.
mosaic [məʊ'zeɪɪk] n mosaïque f.
Moscow ['mɒskəʊ, Am 'mɒskaʊ] n Moscou m or f.

Moses ['məʊzɪz] a M. basket couffin m.
Moslem ['mɒzlɪm] a & n musulman,
-ane (mf).
mosque [mɒsk] n mosquée f.
mosquito [mɒ'ski:təʊ] n (pl -oes) moustique m; **m. net** moustiquaire f.
moss [mɒs] n mousse f (plante).
most [məʊst] a & n the m. (greatest in
amount etc) le plus (de); **I have (the) m.
books** j'ai le plus de livres; **I have (the)
m.** j'en ai le plus; **m. (of the) books/etc**
la plupart des livres/etc; **m. (of the) cake/
etc** la plus grande partie du gâteau/etc;
m. of them la plupart d'entre eux; **m. of
it** la plus grande partie; **at (the very) m.**
tout au plus; **to make the m. of sth**
profiter (au maximum) de qch. ▪ adv
(le) plus; (very) très; the **m.
beautiful** le plus beau, la plus belle
(in, de); **to talk (the) m.** parler le
plus; **m. of all** surtout. ● **mostly** adv
surtout.
MOT [eməʊ'ti:] n abbr (Ministry of
Transport) = contrôle m obligatoire
des véhicules de plus de trois ans.
motel [məʊ'tel] n motel m.
moth [mɒθ] n papillon m de nuit; (in
clothes) mite f. ● **m.-eaten** a mité.
● **mothball** n boule f de naphtaline.
mother ['mʌðər] n mère f; **M.'s Day** la
fête des Mères; **m. tongue** langue f
maternelle. ● **motherhood** n maternité
f. ● **motherly** a maternel.
mother-in-law ['mʌðərɪnlɔ:] n (pl
mothers-in-law) belle-mère f. ● **m.-of-
pearl** n (substance) nacre f. ● **m.-to-'be**
n (pl mothers-to-be) future mère f.
motion ['məʊʃ(ə)n] n (of arm etc) mouvement m; Pol motion f; **to set in m.**
mettre en mouvement; **m. picture** film
m ▪ vti to m. (to) s.o. to do faire signe à
qn de faire. ● **-less** a immobile.
motive ['məʊtɪv] n motif m (for de).
motivate ['məʊtɪveɪt] vt (person, decision) motiver. ● **motivation** [-'veɪʃ(ə)n]
n motivation f; (incentive) encouragement m.
motley ['mɒtlɪ] a (collection) hétéroclite.

motor ['məʊtər] n (engine) moteur m;
(car) Fam auto f ▪ a (industry etc)
automobile; (accident) d'auto; **m. boat**
canot m automobile ▪ vi (drive) rouler
en auto. ● **-ing** n Sp automobilisme m;
school of m. auto-école f.
motorbike ['məʊtəbaɪk] n Fam moto f.
● **motorcar** n automobile f. ● **motorcycle**
n moto f. ● **motorcyclist** n motocycliste
mf. ● **motorist** n automobiliste mf.
● **motorway** n autoroute f.
motto ['mɒtəʊ] n (pl -oes or -os) devise f.
mould [məʊld] (Am mold) 1 n (shape)
moule m ▪ vt (clay etc) mouler; (character) modeler. 2 n (growth) moisissure
f. ● **mouldy** (Am moldy) a (-ier, -iest)
moisi; **to go m.** moisir.
moult [məʊlt] (Am molt) vi muer. ● **-ing**
n mue f.
mound [maʊnd] n (of earth) tertre m;
(untidy pile) Fig monceau m.
mount [maʊnt] 1 n (frame for photo or
slide) cadre m; (horse) monture f ▪ vt
(horse, jewel, photo etc) monter; (ladder
etc) monter sur ▪ vi to m. (up) (on horse)
se mettre en selle. 2 vi (increase, rise)
monter; **to m. up** (add up) chiffrer (to à);
(accumulate) s'accumuler.
Mount [maʊnt] n (in place names) mont
m.
mountain ['maʊntɪn] n montagne f; **m.
bike** VTT m inv. ● **mountai'neer** n
alpiniste mf. ● **mountai'neering** n alpinisme m. ● **mountainous** a montagneux.
mourn [mɔ:n] vti to m. (for) s.o., **m.** the
loss of s.o. pleurer (la perte de) qn; **she's
mourning** elle est en deuil. ● **-ing** n
deuil m; **in m.** en deuil. ● **mourner** n
parent, -ente mf or ami, -ie mf du
défunt or de la défunte.
mouse, pl **mice** [maʊs, maɪs] n (animal)
& Comptr souris f. ● **mousetrap** n
souricière f.
mousse [mu:s] n mousse f (dessert).
moustache [mə'stɑ:ʃ, Am 'mʌstæʃ] n
moustache f.
mouth [maʊθ] n (pl -s [maʊðz]) bouche f;
(of dog, lion etc) gueule f; (of river)

embouchure *f*; (*of cave*) entrée *f*.
●**mouthful** *n* (*of food*) bouchée *f*;
●**mouthorgan** *n* harmonica *m*.
●**mouthpiece** *n* *Mus* embouchure *f*; (*spokesperson*) porte-parole *m* *inv*.
●**mouthwash** *n* bain *m* de bouche.
●**mouth-watering** *a* appétissant.

movable ['mu:vəb(ə)l] *a* mobile.

move [mu:v] *n* mouvement *m*; (*change of house*) déménagement *m*; (*change of job*) changement *m* d'emploi; (*in game*) coup *m*, (*one's turn*) tour *m*; (*act*) démarche *f*; (*attempt*) tentative *f*; **to make a m.** (*leave*) se préparer à partir; (*act*) passer à l'action; **to get a m. on** *Fam* se dépêcher; **on the m.** en marche.

▮ *vt* déplacer, remuer, bouger; (*arm, leg*) remuer; (*put*) mettre; (*transport*) transporter; (*piece in game*) jouer; **to m. s.o.** (*emotionally*) émouvoir qn; (*transfer in job*) muter qn; **to m. house** déménager.

▮ *vi* bouger, remuer; (*go*) aller (**to** à); (*pass*) passer (**to** à); (*change seats*) changer de place; (*progress*) avancer; (*act*) agir; (*play*) jouer; (*out of house*) déménager; **to m. to a new house**/*etc* aller habiter une nouvelle maison/*etc*; **to m. into a house** emménager dans une maison.

▮ **move about** *or* **around** *vi* déplacer, (*fidget*) remuer ▮ **to move along** *vi* avancer ▮ **to move away** *vi* (*go away*) s'éloigner; (*move house*) déménager ▮ **to move back** *vt* (*chair etc*) reculer; (*to its position*) remettre ▮ *vi* reculer; (*return*) retourner ▮ **to move down** *vt* descendre (*qch*) ▮ **to move forward** *vti* avancer ▮ **to move in** *vi* (*into house*) emménager ▮ **to move off** *vi* (*go away*) s'éloigner; (*of vehicle*) démarrer ▮ **to move on** *vi* avancer; **m. on!** circulez! ▮ **to move out** *vi* (*out of house*) déménager ▮ **to move over** *vt* pousser ▮ *vi* (*make room*) se pousser ▮ **to move up** *vi* (*on seats etc*) se pousser.

moveable ['mu:vəb(ə)l] *a* mobile.

movement ['mu:vmənt] *n* (*action, group etc*) & *Mus* mouvement *m*.

movie ['mu:vɪ] *n* *Fam* film *m*; **the movies** (*cinema*) le cinéma; **m. camera** caméra *f*; **m. theater** *Am* cinéma *m*.

moving ['mu:vɪŋ] *a* en mouvement; (*touching*) émouvant; **m. stairs** escalier *m* mécanique.

mow [məʊ] *vt* (*pp* **mown** *or* **mowed**) (*field*) faucher; **to m. the lawn** tondre le gazon; **to m. down** (*kill*) *Fig* faucher.
●—**er** *n* (*lawn*) **m.** tondeuse *f* (à gazon).

MP [em'pi:] *n* *abbr* (*Member of Parliament*) député *m*.

Mr ['mɪstər] *n* **Mr Brown** Monsieur *or* M. Brown.

Mrs ['mɪsɪz] *n* (*married woman*) **Mrs Brown** Madame *or* Mme Brown.

Ms [mɪz] *n* (*married or unmarried woman*) **Ms Brown** Madame *or* Mme Brown.

MSc [emes'si:], *Am* **MS** *abbr* = **Master of Science**.

much [mʌtʃ] *a* & *n* beaucoup (de); **not m. time/money**/*etc* pas beaucoup de temps/d'argent/*etc*; **not m.** pas beaucoup; **m. of sth** (*a good deal of*) une bonne partie de qch; **as m. as** autant que; **as m. wine**/*etc* as autant de vin/*etc* que; **as m. as you like** autant que tu veux, **twice/three as m.** deux fois plus (de); **how m.?** combien (de)?; **too m.** trop (de); **so m.** tant (de); **I know this m.** je sais ceci (du moins); **it's not m. of a garden** ce n'est pas merveilleux comme jardin.

▮ *adv* **very m.** beaucoup; **not (very) m.** pas beaucoup.

muck [mʌk] **1** *n* (*manure*) fumier *m*; (*filth*) *Fig* saleté *f*.
2 *vi* **to m. about** *Fam* (*have fun*) s'amuser; (*play the fool*) faire l'idiot; **to m. about with sth** (*fiddle with*) *Fam* s'amuser avec qch; (*interfere in*) *Fam* participer, contribuer.

▮ *vt* **to m. s.o. about** *Fam* embêter qn; **to m. sth up** *Fam* gâcher qch ●**m.-up** *n* *Fam* gâchis *m*. ● **mucky** *a* (**-ier, -iest**) sale.

mud [mʌd] *n* boue *f*. ● **muddy** *a* (**-ier, -iest**) (*water, road*) boueux; (*hands etc*) couvert de boue. ● **mudguard** *n* garde-boue *m inv*.

muddle ['mʌd(ə)l] *n* (*mix-up*) confusion *f*; (*mess*) désordre *m*; **in a m.** (*person*) désorienté; (*mind, ideas*) embrouillé ‖ *vt* (*person, facts etc*) embrouiller; (*papers*) mélanger ‖ *vi* **to m. through** *Fam* se débrouiller.

muesli ['mjuːzlɪ] *n* muesli *m*.

muffin ['mʌfɪn] *n* (*cake*) sorte de petite brioche.

muffl/e ['mʌf(ə)l] *vt* (*noise*) assourdir. ● **—ed** *a* (*noise*) sourd. ● **—er** *n Aut Am* silencieux *m*.

mug [mʌg] **1** *n* grande tasse *f*; (*beer*) m. chope *f*. **2** *n* (*face*) *Fam* gueule *f*. **3** *n* (*fool*) *Fam* niais, -aise *mf*. **4** *vt* (**-gg-**) (*in street*) agresser, attaquer. ● **mugger** *n* agresseur *m*. ● **mugging** *n* agression *f*.

muggy ['mʌgɪ] *a* (**-ier, -iest**) (*weather*) lourd.

mule [mjuːl] *n* (*male*) mulet *m*; (*female*) mule *f*.

multi- ['mʌltɪ] *pref* multi-.

multicoloured ['mʌltɪkʌləd] (*Am* **multicolored**) *a* multicolore.

multimillionaire [mʌltɪmɪljə'neər] *n* milliardaire *mf*.

multiple ['mʌltɪp(ə)l] *a* multiple ‖ *n Math* multiple *m*.

multiply ['mʌltɪplaɪ] *vt* multiplier ‖ *vi* (*of animals, insects*) se multiplier. ● **multiplication** [-'keɪʃ(ə)n] *n* multiplication *f*.

multistorey [mʌltɪ'stɔːrɪ] (*Am* **multistoried**) *a* à étages.

multitude ['mʌltɪtjuːd] *n* multitude *f*.

mum [mʌm] *n Fam* maman *f*.

mumble ['mʌmb(ə)l] *vti* marmotter.

mummy ['mʌmɪ] *n* **1** (*mother*) *Fam* maman *f*. **2** (*body*) momie *f*.

mumps [mʌmps] *n* oreillons *mpl*.

munch [mʌntʃ] *vti* (*chew*) mastiquer; (*eat*) *Fam* manger à belles dents.

mundane [mʌn'deɪn] *a* banal (*mpl* -als).

municipal [mjuː'nɪsɪp(ə)l] *a* municipal.

mural ['mjʊərəl] *n* fresque *f*, peinture *f* murale.

murder ['mɜːdər] *n* meurtre *m*, assassinat *m*; **it's m.** (*dreadful*) *Fam* c'est affreux ‖ *vt* (*kill*) assassiner. ● **—er** *n* meurtrier, -ière *mf*, assassin *m*.

murky ['mɜːkɪ] *a* (**-ier, -iest**) obscur; (*water, business, past*) trouble.

murmur ['mɜːmər] *n* murmure *m* ‖ *vti* murmurer.

muscle ['mʌs(ə)l] *n* muscle *m*. ● **muscular** *a* (*arm etc*) musclé.

museum [mjuː'zɪəm] *n* musée *m*.

mush [mʌʃ] *n* (*soft mass*) bouillie *f*. ● **mushy** *a* (**-ier, -iest**) (*food etc*) en bouillie.

mushroom ['mʌʃrʊm] *n* champignon *m*.

music ['mjuːzɪk] *n* musique *f*; **m. centre** chaîne *f* stéréo compacte; **m. hall** music-hall *m*; **m. lover** mélomane *mf*; **canned** *or* **piped m.** musique *f* (de fond) enregistrée. ● **musical** *a* musical; (*instrument*) de musique; **to be m.** être musicien ‖ *n* (*film, play*) comédie *f* musicale. ● **musician** [-'zɪʃ(ə)n] *n* musicien, -ienne *mf*.

Muslim ['mʊzlɪm] *a & n* musulman, -ane (*mf*).

muslin ['mʌzlɪn] *n* (*cotton*) mousseline *f*.

mussel ['mʌs(ə)l] *n* (*shellfish*) moule *f*.

must [mʌst] *v aux* **1** (*necessity*) **you m. obey** tu dois obéir, il faut que tu obéisses. **2** (*certainty*) **she m. be clever** elle doit être intelligente; **I m. have seen it** j'ai dû le voir ‖ *n* **this is a m.** ceci est indispensable.

mustache ['mʌstæʃ] *n Am* moustache *f*.

mustard ['mʌstəd] *n* moutarde *f*.

muster ['mʌstər] *vt* (*gather*) rassembler (*troupes, courage etc*).

mustn't ['mʌs(ə)nt] = **must not**.

musty ['mʌstɪ] *a* (**-ier, -iest**) (*smell*) de moisi; **it smells m.**, **it's m.** ça sent le moisi.

mute [mjuːt] *a* (*silent*) & *Ling* muet (*f* muette).

muted ['mjuːtɪd] *a* (*criticism*) voilé.

mutilate ['mjuːtɪleɪt] *vt* mutiler.

mutiny ['mju:tɪnɪ] *n* mutinerie *f* ‖ *vi* se mutiner.

mutter ['mʌtər] *vti* marmonner.

mutton ['mʌt(ə)n] *n* (*meat*) mouton *m*.

mutual ['mju:tʃʊəl] *a* (*help etc*) mutuel; (*friend etc*) commun; **m. fund** *Fin Am* fonds *m* commun de placement. ●—**ly** *adv* mutuellement.

muzzle ['mʌz(ə)l] *n* (*for animal*) muselière *f*; (*snout*) museau *m* ‖ *vt* museler.

my [maɪ] *poss a* mon, ma, *pl* mes.

myself [maɪ'self] *pron* moi-même; (*reflexive*) me, m'; (*after prep*) moi; **I wash m.** je me lave; **I think of m.** je pense à moi.

mystery ['mɪstərɪ] *n* mystère *m*. ●**my'sterious** *a* mystérieux.

mystical ['mɪstɪk(ə)l] *a* mystique.

mystify ['mɪstɪfaɪ] *vt* (*bewilder*) laisser perplexe; (*fool*) mystifier.

myth [mɪθ] *n* mythe *m*. ●**my'thology** *n* mythologie *f*.

N

N, n [en] *n* N, n *m*.

nab [næb] *vt* (-bb-) (*catch*) *Fam* épingler.

naff [næf] *a* *Fam* (*stupid*) bête; (*unfashionable*) ringard.

nag [næg] *vt* (-gg-) **to n. s.o.** (*pester*) embêter qn (**to do** pour qu'il fasse); (*find fault with*) critiquer qn. ● **nagging** *a* (*doubt, headache*) qui subsiste.

nail [neɪl] **1** *n* (*of finger, toe*) ongle *m*; **n. file/polish** lime *f*/vernis *m* à ongles. **2** *n* (*metal*) clou *m* ‖ *vt* **to n. (down)** (*lid etc*) clouer.

naïve [naɪ'i:v] *a* naïf.

naked ['neɪkɪd] *a* (*person*) (tout) nu; (*flame*) nu; **to see with the n. eye** voir à l'œil nu.

name [neɪm] *n* nom *m*; (*reputation*) réputation *f*; **my n. is...** je m'appelle...; **in the n. of** au nom de; **to put one's n. down for** (*school, course*) s'inscrire à; **to call s.o. names** injurier qn; **first n.** prénom *m*; **last n.** nom *m* de famille; **n. plate** plaque *f*.
‖ *vt* nommer; (*ship, street*) baptiser; (*date, price*) fixer; **he was named after** *or Am* **for...** il a reçu le nom de....

namely ['neɪmlɪ] *adv* (*that is*) à savoir.

namesake ['neɪmseɪk] *n* (*person*) homonyme *m*.

nanny ['nænɪ] *n* nurse *f*; (*grandmother*) *Fam* mamie *f*.

nap [næp] *n* (*sleep*) petit somme *m*; **to have** *or* **take a n.** faire un petit somme; (*after lunch*) faire la sieste ‖ *vi* (-pp-) sommeiller.

nape [neɪp] *n* **n. (of the neck)** nuque *f*.

napkin ['næpkɪn] *n* (*at table*) serviette *f*. ● **nappy** *n* (*for baby*) couche *f*. ● **nappy-liner** *n* protège-couche *m*.

narcotic [nɑː'kɒtɪk] *a* & *n* narcotique (*m*).

narrate [nə'reɪt] *vt* raconter. ● **narrative** ['nærətɪv] *n* (*story*) récit *m*. ● **narrator** narrateur, -trice *mf*.

narrow ['nærəʊ] *a* (-er, -est) étroit ‖ *vi* (*of path*) se rétrécir ‖ *vt* **to n. (down)** (*choice, meaning etc*) limiter. ● **—ly** *adv* (*to miss etc*) de justesse; **he n. escaped** *or* **missed being killed**/*etc* il a failli être tué/*etc*. ● **narrow-minded** [nærəʊ'maɪndɪd] *a* borné.

nasty ['nɑːstɪ] *a* (-ier, -iest) (*bad*) mauvais, vilain; (*spiteful*) méchant (**to, towards** avec). ● **nastily** *adv* (*to behave*) méchamment; (*to rain*) horriblement.

nation ['neɪʃ(ə)n] *n* nation *f*. ● **national** ['næʃən(ə)l] *a* national; **n. anthem** hymne *m* national; **N. Health Service** = Sécurité *f* Sociale; **n. insurance** = assurances *fpl* sociales ‖ *n* (*citizen*) ressortissant, -ante *mf*. ● **nationalist** *n* nationaliste *mf*. ● **natio'nality** *n* nationalité *f*. ● **nationalize** *vt* nationaliser. ● **nationally** *adv* (*to travel etc*) dans le pays (tout) entier.

nationwide ['neɪʃənwaɪd] *a* & *adv* dans le pays (tout) entier.

native ['neɪtɪv] *a* (*country*) natal (*mpl* -als); (*habits, costume*) du pays; (*tribe*) indigène; **n. language** langue *f* maternelle; **to be an English n. speaker** parler l'anglais comme langue maternelle ‖ *n* (*formerly, non-European in colony*) indigène *mf*; **to be a n. of** être originaire de.

NATO ['neɪtəʊ] *n* *abbr* (*North Atlantic Treaty Organization*) OTAN *f*.

natter ['nætər] *vi* *Fam* bavarder.

natural ['nætʃ(ə)rəl] *a* naturel; (*actor, gardener etc*) né. ● **naturally** *adv* (*as normal, of course*) naturellement; (*by nature*) de nature; (*to behave etc*) avec naturel.

naturalized ['nætʃ(ə)rəlaızd] *a* to become n. se faire naturaliser.

nature ['neɪtʃər] *n* (*natural world, character*) nature *f*; **by n.** de nature; **n. study** sciences *fpl* naturelles.

naught ['nɔːt] *n* Math zéro *m*.

naught/y ['nɔːtɪ] *a* (-ier, -iest) (*child*) vilain, malicieux; (*joke, story*) osé. ●—**iness** *n* mauvaise conduite *f*.

nausea ['nɔːzɪə] *n* nausée *f*. ●**nauseate** *vt* écœurer. ●**nauseous** ['nɔːʃəs] *a* to feel n. (*sick*) Am avoir envie de vomir.

nautical ['nɔːtɪk(ə)l] *a* nautique.

naval ['neɪv(ə)l] *a* naval (*mpl* -als); (*hospital*) maritime; (*officer*) de marine.

nave [neɪv] *n* (*of church*) nef *f*.

navel ['neɪv(ə)l] *n* nombril *m*.

navigate ['nævɪgeɪt] *vi* naviguer ∥ *vt* (*boat*) diriger; (*river*) naviguer sur. ●**navigation** [-'geɪʃ(ə)n] *n* navigation *f*. ●**navigator** *n* Av Nau navigateur *m*.

navy ['neɪvɪ] *n* marine *f* ∥ *a* **n. (blue)** bleu marine *inv*.

Nazi ['nɑːtsɪ] *a* & *n* Pol Hist nazi, -ie (*mf*).

near [nɪər] *adv* (-er, -est) près; **quite n.** tout près; **to draw n.** (s')approcher (**to** de); (*of date*) approcher; **n. to** près de; **to come n. to being killed/***etc* faillir être tué/*etc*; **n. enough** (*more or less*) plus ou moins.

∥ *prep* (-er, -est) **n. (to)** près de; **n. the bed** près du lit; **n. (to) the end** vers la fin; **to come n. s.o.** s'approcher de qn.

∥ *a* (-er, -est) proche; **the nearest hospital** l'hôpital le plus proche; **the nearest way** la route la plus directe; **in the n. future** dans un avenir proche; **to the nearest franc** (*to calculate*) à un franc près; **n. side** *Aut* côté *m* gauche, *Am* côté *m* droit.

∥ *vt* (*approach*) approcher de; **nearing completion** près d'être achevé. ●**near'by** *adv* tout près ∥ ['nɪəbaɪ] *a* proche.

nearly ['nɪəlɪ] *adv* presque; **she (very) n. fell** elle a failli tomber; **not n. as clever/** *etc* **as** loin d'être aussi intelligent/*etc*

que.

neat [niːt] *a* (-er, -est) (*clothes, work*) soigné, propre; (*room*) bien rangé; (*style*) élégant; (*pleasant*) Fam agréable; (*good*) Fam super; **to drink one's whisky n.** prendre son whisky sec. ●—**ly** *adv* avec soin; (*skilfully*) habilement.

necessary ['nesɪs(ə)rɪ] *a* nécessaire; **it's n. to do** il est nécessaire de faire; **to make it n. for s.o. to do** mettre qn dans la nécessité de faire; **to do what's n.** faire le nécessaire (**for** pour). ●**nece'ssarily** *adv* **not n.** pas forcément.

necessity [nɪ'sesɪtɪ] *n* (*obligation, need*) nécessité *f*; **there's no n. for you to do that** tu n'es pas obligé de faire cela; **to be a n.** être indispensable; **the (bare) necessities** le (strict) nécessaire. ●**necessitate** *vt* nécessiter.

neck[1] [nek] *n* cou *m*; (*of dress, horse*) encolure *f*; (*of bottle*) col *m*; **low n.** (*of dress*) décolleté *m*; **n. and n.** Sp à égalité. ●**necklace** *n* collier *m*. ●**neckline** *n* encolure *f*. ●**necktie** *n* cravate *f*.

neck[2] [nek] *vi* (*kiss etc*) Fam se peloter.

nectarine ['nektəriːn] *n* (*fruit*) nectarine *f*.

need [niːd] **1** *n* (*necessity, want, poverty*) besoin *m*; **in n.** dans le besoin; **to be in n. of** avoir besoin de; **there's no n. (for you) to do that** tu n'as pas besoin de faire cela, il n'est pas besoin de

∥ *vt* avoir besoin de; **you n. it** tu en as besoin; **it needs an army** *or* **an army is needed to do that** il faut une armée pour faire cela; **this sport needs patience** ce sport demande de la patience; **her hair needs cutting** il faut qu'elle se fasse couper les cheveux.

2 *v aux* **n. he wait?** est-il obligé d'attendre?; **I needn't have rushed** ce n'était pas la peine de me presser. ●**needlessly** *adv* inutilement. ●**needy** *a* (-ier, -iest) *a* nécessiteux.

needle ['niːd(ə)l] **1** *n* aiguille *f*; (*of record player*) saphir *m*. **2** *vt* (*irritate*) Fam agacer. ●**needlework** *n* couture *f*; (*object*) ouvrage *m*.

negative ['negətɪv] a négatif ▮ n Phot négatif m; (word) Gram négation f; (form) Gram forme f négative; **to answer in the n.** répondre par la négative.

neglect [nɪ'glekt] vt (person, health, work, duty etc) négliger; (garden, car) ne pas s'occuper de; **to n. to do** négliger de faire ▮ n (of person) manque m de soins (of envers); (carelessness) négligence f; **in a state of n.** (garden, house) mal tenu. ● **neglected** a (appearance) négligé; (garden, house) mal tenu; **to feel n.** sentir qu'on vous néglige.

negligent ['neglɪdʒənt] a négligent. ● **negligence** n négligence f.

negligible ['neglɪdʒəb(ə)l] a négligeable.

negotiate [nɪ'gəʊʃɪeɪt] **1** vti (discuss) négocier. **2** vt (fence, obstacle) franchir; (bend) Aut négocier. ● **negotiation** [-'eɪʃ(ə)n] n négociation f; **in n.** with en pourparlers avec.

Negro ['niːgrəʊ] n (pl **-oes**) often Pej (man) Noir m; (woman) Noire f.

neigh [neɪ] vi (of horse) hennir.

neighbour ['neɪbər] (Am **neighbor**) n voisin, -ine mf. ● **neighbourhood** n (district) quartier m; (neighbours) voisinage m; **in the n. of ten pounds** dans les dix livres. ● **neighbouring** a voisin. ● **neighbourly** a (feeling etc) amical; **they're n. (people)** ils sont bons voisins.

neither ['naɪðər, Am 'niːðər] adv ni...nor ni... ni; **you n. me** ni toi ni moi; **he n. sings nor dances** il ne chante ni ne danse.

▮ conj (not either) (ne)...non plus; **n. will I go** je n'y irai pas non plus; **n. do I, n. can I** etc (ni) moi non plus.

▮ a (not) n. boy (came) aucun des deux garçons (n'est venu); **on n. side** ni d'un côté ni de l'autre.

▮ pron **n. (of them)** ni l'un(e) ni l'autre, aucun(e) (des deux).

neon ['niːɒn] a (lighting etc) au néon; **n. sign** enseigne f au néon.

nephew ['nevjuː, 'nefjuː] n neveu m.

nerve [nɜːv] n nerf m; (courage) courage m (**to do** de faire); (confidence) assurance f; (calm) sang-froid m; (impudence) Fam culot m (**to do** de faire); **you get on my nerves** Fam tu me tapes sur les nerfs; **to have an attack of nerves** (anxiety) avoir le trac; **a bundle of nerves** (person) Fam un paquet de nerfs; **to have bad nerves** être nerveux; **n. centre** centre m nerveux. ● **n.-racking** a éprouvant pour les nerfs.

nervous ['nɜːvəs] a (tense) nerveux; (worried) inquiet (**about** de); (uneasy) mal à l'aise; **to be or feel n.** (before exam etc) avoir le trac. ● **—ly** adv nerveusement; (worriedly) avec inquiétude.

nest [nest] n nid m; **n. egg** (money saved) pécule m ▮ vi (of bird) se nicher.

nestle ['nes(ə)l] vi se pelotonner (**up to** contre).

net [net] **1** n filet m; **n. curtain** voilage m. **2** a (profit, weight etc) net (f nette) ▮ vt (-tt-) (of person etc) gagner net; **this venture netted them....** cette entreprise leur a rapporté.... ● **netting** n (nets) filets mpl; (mesh) mailles fpl; (wire) n. grillage m.

Netherlands (the) [ðə'neðələndz] npl les Pays-Bas mpl.

nettle ['net(ə)l] n ortie f.

network ['netwɜːk] n réseau m.

neurotic [njʊ'rɒtɪk] a & n névrosé, -ée (mf).

neuter ['njuːtər] **1** a & n Gram neutre (m). **2** vt (cat) châtrer.

neutral ['njuːtrəl] a neutre; (policy) de neutralité ▮ n **in n.** (gear) Aut au point mort. ● **neutralize** vt neutraliser.

never ['nevər] adv **1** (not ever) (ne...) jamais; **she n. lies** elle ne ment jamais; **n. in my life** jamais de ma vie; **n. again** plus jamais. **2** (not) Fam **I n. did it** je ne l'ai pas fait. ● **n.-ending** a interminable.

nevertheless [nevəðə'les] adv néanmoins.

new [njuː] a (**-er, -est**) nouveau (f nouvelle); (brand-new) neuf (f neuve); **a n. glass/pen/etc** (different) un autre verre/stylo/etc; **a n. boy** (in school) un nouveau; **what's n.?** Fam quoi de neuf?

n. look (*of person*) nouveau look *m*; a n.-born baby un nouveau-né, une nouveau-née. ●**newcomer** *n* nouveau-venu *m*, nouvelle-venue *f*. ●**new'fangled** *a* (trop) moderne. ●**newly** *adv* (*recently*) nouvellement; **the n.-weds** les nouveaux mariés.

news [nju:z] *n* nouvelle(s) *f(pl)*; (*in the media*) informations *fpl*, actualités *fpl*; **sports/etc n.** (*newspaper column*) chronique *f* sportive/etc; **a piece of n., some n.** une nouvelle; (*in the media*) une information; **n. flash** flash *m*.

newsagent ['nju:zeɪdʒənt] *n* marchand, -ande *mf* de journaux. ●**newscaster** *n* présentateur, -trice *mf*. ●**newsdealer** *n* *Am* = newsagent. ●**newsletter** *n* (*of club etc*) bulletin *m*. ●**newspaper** *n* journal *m*. ●**newsprint** *n* papier *m* (de) journal. ●**newsreader** *n* présentateur, -trice *mf* *Fam* plein de nouvelles.

newt [nju:t] *n* (*animal*) triton *m*.

New Zealand [nju:'zi:lənd] *n* Nouvelle-Zélande *f* ▮ *a* néo-zélandais. ●**New Zealander** *n* Néo-Zélandais, -aise *mf*.

next [nekst] *a* prochain; (*room, house*) d'à-côté; (*following*) suivant; **n. month** (*in the future*) le mois prochain; **he returned the n. month** (*in the past*) il revint le mois suivant; **the n. day** le lendemain; **the n. morning** le lendemain matin; **within the n. ten days** d'ici (à) dix jours; (**by) this time n. week** d'ici (à) la semaine prochaine; **from one year to the n.** d'une année à l'autre; **you're n.** c'est ton tour; **n. (please)!** (au) suivant!; **the n. size** la taille au-dessus; **to live/etc n. door** habiter/etc à côté (**to** de); **n.-door neighbour** voisin *m* d'à-côté.

▮ *n* (*in series etc*) suivant, -ante *mf*.

▮ *adv* (*afterwards*) ensuite, après; (*now*) maintenant; **when you come n.** la prochaine fois que tu viendras.

▮ *prep* **n. to** (*beside*) à côté de; **n. to nothing** presque rien.

NHS [eneɪtʃ'es] *n* *abbr* (*National Health Service*) = Sécurité *f* Sociale.

nib [nɪb] *n* (*of pen*) plume *f*, bec *m*.

nibble ['nɪb(ə)l] *vti* (*eat*) grignoter; (*bite*) mordiller.

nice [naɪs] *a* (**-er, -est**) (*pleasant*) agréable; (*charming*) charmant; (*good*) bon (*f* bonne); (*fine*) beau (*f* belle); (*pretty*) joli; (*kind*) gentil (**to** avec); (*respectable*) bien *inv*; **it's n. here** c'est bien ici; **n. and easy/etc** (*very*) bien facile/etc. ●**n.-'looking** *a* beau (*f* belle). ●**nicely** *adv* agréablement; (*kindly*) gentiment; (*well*) bien.

niceties ['naɪsɪtɪz] *npl* (*subtleties*) subtilités *fpl*.

niche [ni:ʃ, nɪtʃ] *n* **1** (*recess*) niche *f*. **2** (*job*) **to make a n. for oneself** faire son trou.

nick [nɪk] **1** *n* (*on wood*) entaille *f*; (*in blade*) brèche *f*. **2** *n* (*prison*) *Sl* taule *f* ▮ *vt* (*steal, arrest*) *Sl* piquer. **3** *n* **in the n. of time** juste à temps.

nickel ['nɪk(ə)l] *n* (*metal*) nickel *m*; (*coin*) *Am* pièce *f* de cinq cents.

nickname ['nɪkneɪm] *n* surnom *m*; (*short form*) diminutif *m* ▮ *vt* surnommer.

nicotine ['nɪkəti:n] *n* nicotine *f*.

niece [ni:s] *n* nièce *f*.

Nigeria [naɪ'dʒɪərɪə] *n* Nigéria *m*. ●**Nigerian** *a* & *n* nigérian, -ane (*mf*).

niggling ['nɪglɪŋ] *a* (*trifling*) insignifiant; (*doubt*) persistant.

night [naɪt] *n* nuit *f*; (*evening*) soir *m*; **at n.** la nuit; **last n.** (*evening*) hier soir; (*night*) cette nuit, la nuit dernière; **to have an early/late n.** se coucher tôt/tard; **to have a good night('s sleep)** bien dormir; **first n.** *Th* première *f* ▮ *a* (*work etc*) de nuit; (*life*) nocturne; **n. school** cours *mpl* du soir; **n. watchman** veilleur *m* de nuit.

nightcap ['naɪtkæp] *n* boisson *f* (*prise avant de se coucher*). ●**nightclub** *n* boîte *f* de nuit. ●**nightdress** or **nightgown** or *Fam* **nightie** *n* (*woman's*) chemise *f* de nuit. ●**nightfall** *n* **at n.** à la tombée de la nuit. ●**nightlight** *n* veilleuse *f*. ●**nightmare** *n* cauchemar *m*. ●**nighttime** *n* nuit *f*.

nightingale ['naɪtɪŋgeɪl] n rossignol m.

nightly ['naɪtlɪ] adv chaque nuit or soir ▎a de chaque nuit or soir.

nil [nɪl] n (nothing) & Sp zéro m; **the risk is n.** le risque est nul.

Nile [naɪl] n the N. le Nil.

nimble ['nɪmb(ə)l] a (-er, -est) agile.

nine [naɪn] a & n neuf (m). ●**nine'teen** a & n dix-neuf (m). ●**ninetieth** a & n quatre-vingt-dixième (mf). ●**ninety** a & n quatre-vingt-dix (m). ●**ninth** a & n neuvième (mf); **a n.** un neuvième.

nip [nɪp] **1** vt (-pp-) (pinch, bite) pincer ▎n pinçon m; **there's a n. in the air** ça pince. **2** vi (-pp-) **to n. round to s.o.** Fam faire un saut chez qn; **to n. in/out** (dash) Fam entrer/sortir un instant.

nipple ['nɪp(ə)l] n bout m de sein; (on baby's bottle) Am tétine f.

nippy ['nɪpɪ] a (-ier, -iest) **it's n.** (weather) Fam ça pince.

nitwit ['nɪtwɪt] n (fool) Fam idiot, -ote mf.

nitrogen ['naɪtrədʒən] n azote m.

no [nəʊ] adv & n non (m inv); **no!** non!; **no more than ten/a kilo/etc** pas plus de dix/d'un kilo/etc; **no less than ten/etc** pas moins de dix/etc; **no more time/etc** plus de temps/etc; **no more/less than you** pas plus/moins que vous.
▎a aucun(e); pas de; **I have no idea** je n'ai aucune idée; **no child came** aucun enfant n'est venu; **I have no money/ time/etc** je n'ai pas d'argent/de temps/ etc; **of no importance/etc** sans importance/etc; **with no gloves/etc** on sans gants/etc; **'no smoking'** 'défense de fumer'; **no way!** Fam pas question!; **no one = nobody.**

noble ['nəʊb(ə)l] a (-er, -est) noble. ●**no'bility** n noblesse f. ●**nobleman** n (pl -men) noble m.

nobody ['nəʊbɒdɪ] pron (ne...) personne; **n. came** personne n'est venu; **he knows n.** il ne connaît personne; **n.!** personne!

nod [nɒd] **1** vti (-dd-) **to n.** (one's head) faire un signe de tête ▎n signe m de tête.

2 vi (-dd-) **to n. off** (go to sleep) s'assoupir.

noise [nɔɪz] n bruit m; (of bell, drum) son m; **to make a n.** faire du bruit.

noisy ['nɔɪzɪ] a (-ier, -iest) bruyant. ●**noisily** adv bruyamment.

nominal ['nɒmɪn(ə)l] a (value) nominal; (rent, salary) symbolique.

nominate ['nɒmɪneɪt] vt (appoint) nommer; (as candidate) proposer (**for** comme candidat à). ●**nomi'nation** [-'neɪʒ(ə)n] n nomination f; (as candidate) proposition f de candidat.

non- [nɒn] pref non-.

non-committal [nɒnkə'mɪt(ə)l] a (answer, person) évasif.

nondescript ['nɒndɪskrɪpt] a quelconque, très ordinaire.

none [nʌn] pron aucun(e) mf; (in filling out a form) néant; **n. of them** aucun d'eux; **she has n. (at all)** elle n'en a pas (du tout); **n. (at all) came** pas un(e) seul(e) n'est venu(e); **n. of the cake/etc** pas une seule partie du gâteau/etc; **n. of the trees/etc** aucun des arbres/etc; **n. of it** or **this** rien (de ceci).
▎adv **n. too hot/etc** pas tellement chaud/ etc; **he's n. the wiser/etc** il n'est pas plus sage/etc. ●**none the'less** adv néanmoins.

nonentity [nɒ'nentɪtɪ] n (person) nullité f.

non-existent [nɒnɪg'zɪstənt] a inexistant.

non-fiction [nɒn'fɪkʃ(ə)n] n littérature f non-romanesque; (in library) ouvrages mpl généraux.

nonplus [nɒn'plʌs] vt (-ss-) dérouter.

nonsense ['nɒnsəns] n absurdités fpl; **that's n.** c'est absurde.

non-smoker [nɒn'sməʊkər] n (person) non-fumeur, -euse mf; (train compartment) compartiment m non-fumeurs.

non-stick [nɒn'stɪk] a (pan) anti-adhésif.

non-stop [nɒn'stɒp] a sans arrêt; (train, flight) direct ▎adv (to work) sans arrêt; (to fly) sans escale.

noodles ['nuːd(ə)lz] npl nouilles fpl; (in soup) vermicelle(s) m(pl).

nook [nʊk] n coin m; **in every n. and cranny** dans tous les coins (et recoins).

noon [nu:n] *n* midi *m*; **at n.** à midi ▮ *a* (*sun etc*) de midi.

no-one ['nəʊwʌn] *pron* = **nobody.**

noose [nu:s] *n* (*loop*) nœud *m* coulant; (*of hangman*) corde *f*.

nor [nɔ:r] *conj* ni; **neither you n.** me ni toi ni moi; **she neither drinks n. smokes** elle ne fume ni ne boit; **n. do I, n. can I** *etc* (ni) moi non plus; **n. will I (go)** je n'y irai pas non plus.

norm [nɔ:m] *n* norme *f*.

normal ['nɔ:m(ə)l] *a* normal ▮ *n* **above/below n.** au-dessus/au-dessous de la normale. ●**normally** *adv* normalement.

Normandy ['nɔ:məndɪ] *n* Normandie *f*.

north [nɔ:θ] *n* nord *m*; **(to the) n. of** au nord de.

▮ *a* (*coast*) nord *inv*; (*wind*) du nord; **N. America/Africa** Amérique *f*/Afrique *f* du Nord; **N. American** (*a & n*) nord-américain, -aine (*mf*).

▮ *adv* au nord, vers le nord. ●**northbound** *a* (*traffic*) en direction du nord. ●**north-'east** *n & a* nord-est *m & a inv.* ●**northerly** ['nɔ:ðəlɪ] *a* (*point*) nord *inv*; (*direction, wind*) du nord. ●**northern** ['nɔ:ðən] *a* (*coast*) nord *inv*; (*town*) du nord; **N. France** le Nord de la France; **N. Europe** Europe *f* du Nord; **N. Ireland** Irlande *f* du Nord. ●**northerner** *n* habitant, -ante *mf* du Nord. ●**northward(s)** *a & adv* vers le nord. ●**north-'west** *n & a* nord-ouest *m & a inv.*

Norway ['nɔ:weɪ] *n* Norvège *f*. ●**Nor'wegian** [-'wi:dʒən] *a & n* norvégien, -ienne (*mf*) ▮ *n* (*language*) norvégien *m*.

nose [nəʊz] *n* nez *m*; **her n. is bleeding** elle saigne du nez; **to turn one's n. up** *Fig* faire le dégoûté (**at** devant). ●**nosebleed** *n* saignement *m* de nez. ●**nosedive** *n Av* piqué *m*.

nosey ['nəʊzɪ] *a* (*-ier, -iest*) indiscret; **n. parker** fouineur, -euse *mf*.

nosh [nɒʃ] *n Fam* (*light meal*) (petit) en-cas *m*; (*food*) bouffe *f*.

nostalgic [nɒ'stældʒɪk] *a* nostalgique.

nostril ['nɒstr(ə)l] *n* (*of person*) narine *f*;

(*of horse*) naseau *m*.

nosy ['nəʊzɪ] *a* = **nosey.**

not [nɒt] *adv* **1** (ne...) pas; **he's n. there, he isn't there** il n'est pas là; **n. yet** pas encore; **why n.?** pourquoi pas?; **n. one reply/etc** pas une seule réponse/*etc*; **n. at all** pas du tout; (*after 'thank you'*) je vous en prie. **2** non; **I think/hope n.** je pense/j'espère que non; **isn't she?, don't you?** *etc* non?

notable ['nəʊtəb(ə)l] *a* (*remarkable*) notable. ●**notably** *adv* (*noticeably*) notablement; (*particularly*) notamment.

notch [nɒtʃ] **1** *n* (*in wood*) encoche *f*, entaille *f*; (*in belt, wheel*) cran *m*. **2** *vt* **to n. up** (*a score*) marquer.

note [nəʊt] *n* (*comment, tone etc*) *& Mus* note *f*; (*banknote*) billet *m*; (*piano key*) touche *f*; (*message, letter*) petit mot *m*; **to take n. of, make a n. of** prendre note de.

▮ *vt* (*take note of, notice*) noter; **to n. down** (*word etc*) noter. ●**notebook** *n* carnet *m*; *Sch* cahier *m*. ●**notepad** *n* bloc-notes *m*. ●**notepaper** *n* papier *m* à lettres.

noted ['nəʊtɪd] *a* **to be n. for** être connu pour.

nothing ['nʌθɪŋ] *pron* (ne...) rien; **he knows n.** il ne sait rien; **n. to do/eat/** *etc* rien à faire/manger/*etc*; **n. big/** *etc* rien de grand/*etc*; **n. much** pas grand-chose; **n. but** (*problems etc*) rien que; **I've got n. to do with it** je n'y suis pour rien; **I can do n. (about it)** je n'y peux rien; **to come to n.** (*of efforts etc*) ne rien donner; **for n.** (*in vain, free of charge*) pour rien; **to have n. on** être tout nu.

▮ *adv* **n. like as large/***etc* loin d'être aussi grand/*etc*.

notice ['nəʊtɪs] *n* (*notification*) avis *m*; (*in newspaper*) annonce *f*; (*sign*) pancarte *f*; (*poster*) affiche *f*; (*review of film etc*) critique *f*; (*attention*) attention *f*; **n. (of dismissal)** congé *m*; **to give (in) one's n.** (*resignation*) donner sa démission; **to give s.o. (advance) n.** (*inform*) avertir qn (**of** de); **to take n.** faire attention (**of** de);

to bring sth to s.o.'s n. porter qch à la connaissance de qn; **until further n.** jusqu'à nouvel ordre; **at short n.** au dernier moment; **n. board** tableau *m* d'affichage.

▮ *vt* (*person, fact, danger etc*) remarquer; **I n. that** je m'aperçois que, je remarque que. ●**noticeable** *a* visible; **that's n.** ça se voit; **she's n.** elle se fait remarquer.

notify ['nəʊtɪfaɪ] *vt* (*inform*) avertir (**s.o. of sth** qn de qch); (*announce*) notifier (**to** à). ●**notification** [-'keɪʃ(ə)n] *n* avis *m*.

notion ['nəʊʃ(ə)n] *n* (*thought*) idée *f*; (*awareness*) notion *f*; **some n. of** (*knowledge*) quelques notions de.

notorious [nəʊ'tɔːrɪəs] *a* (*event, person*) tristement célèbre; (*stupidity, criminal*) notoire.

notwithstanding [nɒtwɪθ'stændɪŋ] *prep* malgré ▮ *adv* tout de même.

nougat ['nuːgɑː, 'nʌgət] *n* nougat *m*.

nought [nɔːt] *n* *Math* zéro *m*.

noun [naʊn] *n* *Gram* nom *m*.

nourish ['nʌrɪʃ] *vt* nourrir. ●**—ing** *a* nourrissant. ●**—ment** *n* nourriture *f*.

novel ['nɒv(ə)l] **1** *n* roman *m*. **2** *a* (*new*) nouveau (*f* nouvelle). ●**novelist** *n* romancier, -ière *mf*. ●**novelty** *n* (*object, idea*) nouveauté *f*.

November [nəʊ'vembər] *n* novembre *m*.

novice ['nɒvɪs] *n* novice *mf* (**at** en).

now [naʊ] *adv* maintenant; **just n., right n.** en ce moment; **I saw her just n.** je l'ai vue à l'instant; **for n.** pour le moment; **from n. on** désormais; **before n.** avant; **n. and then** de temps à autre; **n. hot, n. cold** tantôt chaud, tantôt froid; **n. (then)!** bon!; (*telling s.o. off*) allons!; **n. it happened that...** or il advint que... ▮ *conj* **n. (that)** maintenant que. ●**nowadays** *adv* aujourd'hui, de nos jours.

noway ['nəʊweɪ] *adv* *Am* nullement.

nowhere ['nəʊweər] *adv* nulle part; **n. else** nulle part ailleurs; **n. near the house** loin de la maison; **n. near enough** loin d'être assez.

nozzle ['nɒz(ə)l] *n* (*of hose*) jet *m*; (*of*

tube) embout *m*.

nuance ['njuːɑːns] *n* nuance *f*.

nuclear ['njuːklɪər] *a* nucléaire; **n. scientist** spécialiste *mf* du nucléaire.

nucleus, *pl* **-clei** ['njuːklɪəs, -klɪaɪ] *n* noyau *m*.

nude [njuːd] *a* nu ▮ *n* (*figure*) nu *m*; **in the n.** (tout) nu. ●**nudist** *n* nudiste *mf* ▮ *a* (*camp*) de nudistes.

nudge [nʌdʒ] *vt* pousser du coude ▮ *n* coup *m* de coude.

nuisance ['njuːs(ə)ns] *n* embêtement *m*; (*person*) peste *f*; **that's a n.** c'est embêtant; **he's being a n.** il nous embête, il m'embête *etc*.

null [nʌl] *a* **n. (and void)** nul (et non avenu).

numb [nʌm] *a* (*hand etc*) engourdi; **n. with cold** engourdi par le froid ▮ *vt* engourdir.

number ['nʌmbər] *n* nombre *m*; (*of page, house, telephone etc*) numéro *m*; **a dance n.** un numéro de danse; **a n. of** un certain nombre de; **n. plate** (*of vehicle*) plaque *f* d'immatriculation ▮ *vt* (*page etc*) numéroter; (*include, count, amount to*) compter.

numeral ['njuːm(ə)rəl] *n* chiffre *m*.

numerical [njuː'merɪk(ə)l] *a* numérique.

numerous ['njuːmərəs] *a* nombreux.

nun [nʌn] *n* religieuse *f*.

nurse [nɜːs] **1** *n* infirmière *f*; (*male*) **n.** infirmier *m*. **2** *vt* (*look after*) soigner; (*suckle*) nourrir, allaiter; (*a grudge*) *Fig* nourrir. ●**—ing** *a* (*mother*) qui allaite; **the n. staff** le personnel infirmier ▮ *n* (*care*) soins *mpl*; (*job*) profession *f* d'infirmière *or* d'infirmier; **n. home** clinique *f*.

nursery ['nɜːsərɪ] *n* chambre *f* d'enfants; (*for plants, trees*) pépinière *f*; (*day*) **n.** (*school*) crèche *f*; **n. rhyme** chanson *f* enfantine; **n. school** école *f* maternelle.

nut[1] [nʌt] *n* fruit *m* à coque; (*walnut*) noix *f*; (*hazelnut*) noisette *f*; (*peanut*) cacah(o)uète *f*; **Brazil/cashew n.** noix *f* du Brésil/de cajou. ●**nutcracker(s)** *n(pl)* casse-noix *m inv*. ●**nutshell** **in a n.** *Fig*

en un mot.
nut² [nʌt] *n* **1** (*for bolt*) écrou *m*. **2** (*person*) *Sl* cinglé, -ée *mf*. ● **nutcase** *n* *Sl* cinglé, -ée *mf*. ● **nuts** *a* *Sl* cinglé (**about** de).

nutmeg ['nʌtmeg] *n* muscade *f*.
nutritious [njuː'trɪʃəs] *a* nutritif. ● **nutrition** [-ʃ(ə)n] *n* nutrition *f*.
nylon ['naɪlɒn] *n* nylon *m*; *pl* (*stockings*) bas *mpl* nylon ‖ *a* (*shirt etc*) en nylon.

O

O, o [əʊ] n O, o m.

oaf [əʊf] n balourd, -ourde mf.

oak [əʊk] n chêne m.

OAP [əʊeɪ'piː] n abbr (old age pensioner) retraité, -ée mf.

oar [ɔːr] n aviron m, rame f.

oasis, pl **oases** [əʊ'eɪsɪs, əʊ'eɪsiːz] n oasis f.

oath [əʊθ] n (pl -s [əʊðz]) (promise) serment m; (profanity) juron m; **to take an o.** to do faire le serment de faire.

oats [əʊts] npl avoine f; (porridge) o. flocons mpl d'avoine.

obedient [ə'biːdɪənt] a obéissant. ● **obedience** n obéissance f (**to** à).

obese [əʊ'biːs] a obèse.

obey [ə'beɪ] vt (person, order etc) obéir à; **to be obeyed** être obéi ∥ vi obéir.

obituary [ə'bɪtʃʊərɪ] n nécrologie f.

object[1] ['ɒbdʒɪkt] n (thing) objet m; (aim) but m, objet m; Gram complément m (d'objet); **that's no o.** (no problem) ça ne pose pas de problème.

object[2] [əb'dʒekt] vi to o. to sth/s.o. désapprouver qch/qn; **I o. to you(r) doing that** ça me gêne que tu fasses ça; **I o.!** je proteste!

objection [əb'dʒekʃ(ə)n] n objection f; **I've got no o.** ça ne me gêne pas, je n'y vois pas d'objection. ● **objectionable** a très désagréable.

objective [əb'dʒektɪv] 1 n (aim, target) objectif m. 2 a (opinion etc) objectif. ● **objectively** adv objectivement.

obligation [ɒblɪ'geɪʃ(ə)n] n obligation f; **under an o. to do** dans l'obligation de faire.

obligatory [ə'blɪgət(ə)rɪ] a (compulsory) obligatoire; (imposed by custom) de rigueur.

oblig/e [ə'blaɪdʒ] vt 1 (compel) contraindre (**s.o. to do** qn à faire); **obliged to do**

contraint à faire. 2 (help) rendre service à (qn); **obliged to s.o.** reconnaissant à qn (**for** de); **much obliged!** merci infiniment! ● **-ing** a (kind) serviable.

oblique [ə'bliːk] a (line etc) oblique; (reference) indirect.

obliterate [ə'blɪtəreɪt] vt effacer.

oblivion [ə'blɪvɪən] n oubli m. ● **oblivious** a inconscient (**to, of** de).

oblong ['ɒblɒŋ] a (elongated) oblong (f oblongue); (rectangular) rectangulaire ∥ n rectangle m.

obnoxious [əb'nɒkʃəs] a odieux.

oboe ['əʊbəʊ] n Mus hautbois m.

obscene [əb'siːn] a obscène. ● **obscenity** n obscénité f.

obscure [əb'skjʊər] a (word, actor etc) obscur ∥ vt (hide) cacher; (confuse) embrouiller.

observatory [əb'zɜːvət(ə)rɪ] n observatoire m.

observe [əb'zɜːv] vt (notice, respect) observer; (say) (faire) remarquer (**that** que); **to o. the speed limit** respecter la limitation de vitesse. ● **observant** a observateur. ● **observation** [ɒbzə'veɪʃ(ə)n] n (observing, remark) observation f; (by police) surveillance f; **under o.** (hospital patient) en observation. ● **observer** n observateur, -trice mf.

obsess [əb'ses] vt obséder. ● **obsession** [-ʃ(ə)n] n obsession f; **to have an o. with** or **about sth** avoir l'obsession de qch. ● **obsessive** a (memory, idea) obsédant; (fear) obsessif; (neurotic) obsessionnel; **to be o. about sth** avoir l'obsession de qch.

obsolete ['ɒbsəliːt] a (out of date) dépassé; (ticket) périmé; (machinery) archaïque.

obstacle ['ɒbstək(ə)l] n obstacle m.

obstinate ['ɒbstɪnət] a (person, resistance

etc) obstiné, opiniâtre; (*pain*) rebelle.
obstruct [əb'strʌkt] *vt* (*block*) boucher; (*hinder*) gêner. ● **obstruction** [-ʃ(ə)n] *n* (*act, state*) & *Med Pol Sp* obstruction *f*; (*obstacle*) obstacle *m*; (*in pipe*) bouchon *m*. ● **obstructive** *a* to be o. faire de l'obstruction.
obtain [əb'teɪn] *vt* obtenir. ● **—able** *a* (*available*) disponible.
obvious ['ɒbvɪəs] *a* évident (that que); **he's the o. man to see** c'est évidemment l'homme qu'il faut voir. ● **—ly** *adv* (*evidently, of course*) évidemment.
occasion [ə'keɪʒ(ə)n] *n* (*time, opportunity*) occasion *f*; (*event, ceremony*) événement *m*; **on the o. of** à l'occasion de; **on** o. à l'occasion.
occasional [ə'keɪʒənəl] *a* (*infrequent*) qu'on fait, voit *etc* de temps en temps; (*rain, showers*) intermittent; **she drinks the o.** whisky elle boit un whisky de temps en temps. ● **occasionally** *adv* de temps en temps.
occupy ['ɒkjʊpaɪ] *vt* (*house, time, space, post etc*) occuper; **to keep oneself occupied** s'occuper (**doing** à faire). ● **occupant** *n* (*inhabitant*) occupant, -ante *mf*. ● **occupation** [-'peɪʃ(ə)n] *n* (*activity*) occupation *f*; (*job*) emploi *m*; (*trade*) métier *m*; (*profession*) profession *f*; **the o. of** (*country etc*) l'occupation *f* de. ● **occu'pational** *a* **o. hazard** risque *m* du métier. ● **occupier** *n* (*of house*) occupant, -ante *mf*; *Mil* occupant *m*.
occur [ə'kɜːr] *vi* (**-rr-**) (*happen*) avoir lieu; (*be found*) se rencontrer; (*arise*) se présenter; **it occurs to me that...** il me vient à l'esprit que.... ● **occurrence** [ə'kʌrəns] *n* (*event*) événement *m*; (*existence*) existence *f*.
ocean ['əʊʃ(ə)n] *n* océan *m*.
o'clock [ə'klɒk] *adv* (**it's**) **three** o'c./*etc* (il est) trois heures/*etc*.
octagon ['ɒktəgən] *n* octogone *m*.
October [ɒk'təʊbər] *n* octobre *m*.
octopus ['ɒktəpəs] *n* pieuvre *f*.
OD [əʊ'diː] *vi* **to OD on heroin**/*etc* prendre une overdose d'héroïne/*etc*.

odd [ɒd] *a* **1** (*strange*) bizarre, curieux; **an o. size** une taille peu courante.
2 (*number*) impair.
3 (*left over*) **I have an o. penny** il me reste un penny; **a few o. stamps** quelques timbres (qui restent); **the odd man out** l'exception *f*; **sixty o.** soixante et quelques; **an o. glove**/*etc* un gant/*etc* dépareillé.
4 (*occasional*) qu'on fait, voit *etc* de temps en temps; **to find the o. mistake** trouver de temps en temps une erreur; **o. jobs** (*around house*) menus travaux *mpl*; **o. job man** homme *m* à tout faire. ● **oddity** *n* (*person*) personne *f* bizarre; (*object*) curiosité *f*. ● **oddly** *adv* bizarrement; **o. enough, he was...** chose curieuse, il était.... ● **oddment** *n Com* fin *f* de série.
odds [ɒdz] *npl* **1** (*in betting*) cote *f*; (*chances*) chances *fpl*. **2** **it makes no o.** (*no difference*) *Fam* ça ne fait rien. **3** **at o.** (*in disagreement*) en désaccord (**with** avec). **4** **o. and ends** petites choses.
odious ['əʊdɪəs] *a* détestable, odieux.
odometer [əʊ'dɒmɪtər] *n Am* compteur *m* (kilométrique).
odour ['əʊdər] (*Am* **odor**) *n* odeur *f*.
of [əv, *stressed* ɒv] *prep* de, d' (**le** = **du, de** + **les** = **des**); **of the table** de la table; **of the boy** du garçon; **of the boys** des garçons; **of a book** d'un livre; **of wood**/*etc* de or en bois/*etc*; **of it, of them** en; **she has a lot of it** *or* **of them** elle en a beaucoup; **a friend of his** un ami à lui, un de ses amis; **there are ten of us** nous sommes dix; **that's nice of you** c'est gentil de ta part; **of no value**/*etc* sans valeur/*etc*; **a man of fifty** un homme de cinquante ans; **the fifth of June** le cinq juin.
off [ɒf] **1** *adv* (*gone away*) parti; (*light, gas, radio etc*) éteint, fermé; (*tap, Am faucet*) fermé; (*switched off at mains*) coupé; (*detached*) détaché; (*removed*) enlevé; (*cancelled*) annulé; (*not fit to eat or drink*) mauvais; (*milk, meat*) tourné; **2 km o.** à 2 km (d'ici or de

là); **to be** *ou* **go o.** (*leave*) partir; **where are you o. to?** où vas-tu?; **he has his hat o.** il a enlevé son chapeau; **with his,** *my etc* **gloves o.** sans gants; **a day o.** un jour de congé; **time o.** du temps libre; **I'm o. today** j'ai congé aujourd'hui; **5% o.** une réduction de 5%; **hands o.!** pas touche!; **on and o.** (*sometimes*) de temps à autre; **to be better o.** (*wealthier, in a better position*) être mieux.
2 *prep* (*from*) de; (*distant*) éloigné de; **to get o. the bus/***etc* descendre du bus/*etc*; **to take sth o. the table/***etc* prendre qch sur la table/*etc*; **to eat o. a plate** manger dans une assiette; **to keep o. the grass** ne pas marcher sur les pelouses; **she's o. her food** elle ne mange plus rien; **o. Dover/***etc Nau* au large de Douvres/*etc*; **o. limits** interdit; **the o. side** *Aut* le côté droit, *Am* le côté gauche.

offal ['ɒf(ə)l] *n Culin* abats *mpl*.

off-colour ['ɒfkʌlər] *a* (*ill*) patraque; (*indecent*) scabreux. ● **off'hand** *a* (*abrupt*) brusque, impoli ‖ *adv* (*to say, know etc*) comme ça. ● **off-licence** *n* magasin *m* de vins et de spiritueux. ● **off-line** *a* (*computer*) autonome. ● **off'load** *vt* **to o.-load sth onto s.o.** (*task etc*) se décharger de qch sur qn. ● **off-'peak** *a* (*traffic*) aux heures creuses; (*rate, price*) heures creuses *inv*. ● **off-putting** *a Fam* rebutant. ● **off'side** *a* **to be o.** *Fb* être hors jeu. ● **off'stage** *a & adv* dans les coulisses. ● **off-the-peg** (*Am* **off-the-rack**) *a* (*clothes*) de confection. ● **off-the-'wall** *a* (*crazy*) *Am* dément.

offence [ə'fens] (*Am* **offense**) *n* (*crime*) délit *m*; (*to take o.* s'offenser (**at** de); **to give o.** (*to s.o.*) offenser (qn).

offend [ə'fend] *vt* froisser, offenser (*qn*); **to be offended** (**at**) se froisser (de), s'offenser (de). ● **offender** *n* (*criminal*) délinquant, -ante *mf*; (*habitual*) récidiviste *mf*.

offensive [ə'fensɪv] **1** *a* (*unpleasant*) choquant; (*words etc*) insultant (**to s.o.** pour qn); (*weapon*) offensif; **o. to s.o.** (*of person*) insultant avec qn. **2** *n*

Mil & Fig offensive *f*.

offer ['ɒfər] *n* offre *f*; **on** (*special*) **o.** *Com* en promotion ‖ *vt* offrir; (*opinion, remark*) proposer; **to o. to do** offrir *or* proposer de faire. ● —**ing** *n* (*gift*) offrande *f*.

office ['ɒfɪs] *n* **1** (*room*) bureau *m*; (*of doctor*) *Am* cabinet *m*; **head o.** siège *m* central; **o. block** *or* **building** immeuble *m* de bureaux. **2** (*post*) fonction *f*; (*duty*) fonctions *fpl*; **to be in o.** (*of political party*) être au pouvoir.

officer ['ɒfɪsər] *n* (*in the army, navy etc*) officier *m*; (*in company*) responsable *mf*, directeur, -trice *mf*; (*police*) **o.** agent *m* (de police).

official [ə'fɪʃ(ə)l] **1** *a* officiel. **2** *n* (*person of authority*) responsable *mf*, officiel *m*; (*civil servant*) fonctionnaire *mf*; (*employee*) employé, -ée *mf*. ● **officially** *adv* officiellement.

officiate [ə'fɪʃɪeɪt] *vi* (*preside*) présider; *Rel* officier.

offing ['ɒfɪŋ] *n* **in the o.** en perspective.

offset ['ɒfset, ɒf'set] *vt* (*pt & pp* **offset**, *pres p* **offsetting**) (*compensate for*) compenser; (*s.o.'s beauty etc by contrast*) faire ressortir.

offshoot ['ɒfʃuːt] *n* (*of organization, group etc*) ramification *f*.

offspring ['ɒfsprɪŋ] *n* progéniture *f*.

often ['ɒf(t)ən] *adv* souvent; **how o.?** combien de fois?; **how o. do they run?** (*trains, buses etc*) il y en a tous les combien?; **once too o.** une fois de trop; **every so o.** de temps en temps.

ogre ['əʊgər] *n* ogre *m*.

oh! [əʊ] *int* oh!, ah!; (*pain*) aïe!; **oh yes!** mais oui!; **oh yes?** ah oui?, ah bon?

oil [ɔɪl] *n* huile *f*; (*extracted from ground*) pétrole *m*; (*fuel*) mazout *m* ‖ *a* (*industry, product*) pétrolier; (*painting, paints*) à l'huile; **o. lamp** lampe *f* à pétrole; **o. change** *Aut* vidange *f* ‖ *vt* (*machine*) graisser, huiler.

oilcan ['ɔɪlkæn] *n* burette *f*. ● **oilfield** *n* gisement *m* de pétrole. ● **oilskin(s)** *n*(*pl*) (*garment*) ciré *m*. ● **oily** *a* (**-ier, -iest**) (*substance, skin*) huileux; (*hands*) graisseux; (*food*) gras (*f* grasse).

ointment ['ɔɪntmənt] *n* pommade *f*.

OK, okay [əʊ'keɪ] *a* & *adv see* **all right ▌** *vt* (*pt* & *pp* OKed, okayed, *pres p* OKing, okaying) approuver.

old [əʊld] *a* (**-er, -est**) vieux (*f* vieille); (*former*) ancien; *how o. is he?* quel âge a-t-il?; *he's ten years o.* il a dix ans, il est âgé de dix ans; *he's older than me* il est plus âgé que moi; **an older son** un fils aîné; **the oldest son** le fils aîné; *o.* **enough to do** assez grand pour faire; *o.* **enough to marry** en âge de se marier; *o.* **age** vieillesse *f*; *o.* **man** vieillard *m*; *o.* **woman** vieille femme *f*; **to get** *or* **grow old(er)** vieillir (*f people*) les vieux *mpl*.

olden ['əʊld(ə)n] *a* **in o. days** jadis.

old-fashioned [əʊld'fæʃənd] *a* (*out-of-date*) démodé; (*person*) rétro *inv*.

olive ['ɒlɪv] *n* olive *f* **▌** *a* **o. (green)** (vert) olive *inv*; *o.* **oil** huile *f* d'olive.

Olympic [ə'lɪmpɪk] *a* (*games etc*) olympique.

ombudsman ['ɒmbʊdzmən] *n* (*pl* **-men**) médiateur *m*.

omelet(te) ['ɒmlɪt] *n* omelette *f*; *cheese/ etc* **o.** omelette au fromage/*etc*.

omen ['əʊmən] *n* augure *m*. **● ominous** *a* de mauvais augure; (*tone*) menaçant.

omit [əʊ'mɪt] *vt* (**-tt-**) omettre (**to do** de faire). **● omission** *n* [-ʃ(ə)n] *n* omission *f*.

on [ɒn] *prep* **1** (*position*) sur; **on the chair** sur la chaise; **to put on (to)** mettre sur. **2** (*concerning, about*) sur; **an article on** un article sur; **to speak on Dickens**/*etc* parler sur Dickens/*etc*. **3** (*manner, means*) **on foot** à pied; **on the blackboard** au tableau; **on the radio** à la radio; **on the train**/*etc* dans le train/ *etc*; **on holiday**, *Am* **on vacation** en vacances; **to be on** (*course*) suivre; (*project*) travailler à; (*salary*) toucher; (*team, committee*) être membre de; **to keep** *or* **stay on** (*path etc*) suivre; **it's on me!** (*I'll pay*) *Fam* c'est moi qui paie! **4** (*time*) **on Monday** lundi; **on Mondays**

le lundi; **on May 3rd** le 3 mai; **on the evening of May 3rd** le 3 mai au soir; **on my arrival** à mon arrivée. **5** (+ *present participle*) en; **on seeing this** en voyant ceci.

▌ *adv* (*ahead*) en avant; (*in progress*) en cours; (*lid, brake*) mis; (*light, radio*) allumé; (*gas, tap, Am faucet*) ouvert; (*machine*) en marche; **to (and on)** sans cesse; **to play**/*etc* **on** continuer à jouer/ *etc*; **she has her hat on** elle a mis *or* elle porte son chapeau; **he has something/ nothing on** il est habillé/tout nu; **the strike is on** la grève aura lieu; **what's on?** *TV* qu'y a-t-il à la télé?; *Cin Th* qu'est-ce qu'on joue?; **there's a film on** on passe un film; **I've been on to him** (*on phone*) je l'ai eu au bout du fil; **from then on** à partir de là. **● on-coming** *a* (*vehicle*) qui vient en sens inverse. **● on-going** *a* (*project*) en cours. **● on-line** *a* (*computer*) en ligne.

once [wʌns] *adv* (*on one occasion*) une fois; (*formerly*) autrefois; *o.* **a month**/ *etc* une fois par mois/*etc*; *o.* **again**, *o.* **more** encore une fois; **at o.** tout de suite; **all at o.** (*suddenly*) tout à coup; (*at the same time*) à la fois; *o.* **and for all** une fois pour toutes **▌** *conj* une fois que.

one [wʌn] *a* **1** un, une; *o.* **man** un homme, *or* **woman** une femme; **page** *o.* la page un; **twenty-o.** vingt-et-un **2** (*only*) seul; **my o. (and only) aim** mon seul et unique but. **3** (*same*) même; **in the o. bus** dans le même bus.

▌ *pron* **1** un, une; **do you want o.?** en veux-tu (un)?; **he's o. of us** il est des nôtres; **o. of them** l'un d'eux, l'une d'elles; **a big/small**/*etc* o. un grand/ petit/*etc*; **she's o.** (*a teacher, gardener etc*) elle l'est; **this o.** celui-ci, celle-ci; **that o.** celui-là, celle-là; **the o. who** *or* **which** celui *or* celle qui; **Paul's o.** *Fam* c'est celui de Paul; **it's my o.** *Fam* c'est à moi; **another o.** un(e) autre. **2** (*impersonal*) on; *o.* **knows** on sait; **it**

helps o. ça nous or vous aide; **one's family** sa famille.

one-'armed [wʌn'a:md] a (person) manchot. ● **one-'eyed** a borgne. ● **one-legged** [-legɪd] a a o.-legged man or woman unijambiste mf. ● **one-'off** or Am **one-of-a-'kind** a Fam unique, exceptionnel. ● **one-parent family** n famille f monoparentale. ● **one-'sided** a (judgment etc) partial; (contest) inégal; (decision) unilatéral. ● **one-time** a (former) ancien. ● **one-'way** a (street) à sens unique; (traffic) en sens unique; (ticket) simple.

oneself [wʌn'self] pron soi-même; (reflexive) se, s'; **to cut o.** se couper.

onion ['ʌnjən] n oignon m.

onlooker ['ɒnlʊkər] n spectateur, -trice mf.

only ['əʊnlɪ] a seul; **the o. house**/etc la seule maison/etc; **the o. one** le seul, la seule; **an o. son** un fils unique.
‖ adv seulement, ne... que; **I o. have ten** je n'en ai que dix, j'en ai dix seulement; **if o.** si seulement; **not o.** non seulement; **I have o. just seen it** je viens tout juste de le voir; **he knows** lui seul le sait.
‖ conj (but) Fam seulement; **o. I can't** seulement je ne peux pas.

onset ['ɒnset] n (of disease etc) début m; (of old age) approche m.

onslaught ['ɒnslɔ:t] n attaque f.

onto ['ɒntu:, unstressed 'ɒntə] prep = **on to**.

onus ['əʊnəs] n inv **the o. is on you** c'est votre responsabilité (**to do** de faire).

onward(s) ['ɒnwəd(z)] adv en avant; **from that time o.** à partir de là.

ooze [u:z] vi **to o. (out)** suinter.

opaque [əʊ'peɪk] a opaque.

open ['əʊpən] a ouvert; (view, road) dégagé; (car) décapoté; (meeting) public (f -ique); (post, job) vacant; (attempt, envy) manifeste; (airline ticket) open inv; **wide o.** grand ouvert; **in the o. air** en plein air; **the o. spaces** les grands espaces; **it's o. to doubt** c'est douteux; **o. to** (criticism, attack) exposé à; (ideas, suggestions) ouvert à; **I've got an o. mind on it** je n'ai pas d'opinion arrêtée là-dessus; **to leave o.** (date) ne pas préciser.
‖ n (out) **in the o.** (outside) en plein air; **to sleep (out) in the o.** dormir à la belle étoile; **to bring (out) into the o.** (reveal) divulguer.
‖ vt ouvrir; (legs) écarter; **to o. out** or **up** ouvrir.
‖ vi (of flower, door, eyes etc) s'ouvrir; (of shop, office, person) ouvrir; (of play) débuter; (of film) sortir; **the door opens** (is opened by s.o.) la porte s'ouvre; (can open) la porte ouvre; **to o. on to** (of window) donner sur; **to o. out** or **up** s'ouvrir; **to o. out** (widen) s'élargir; **to o. up** (open a or the door) ouvrir.

open-air ['əʊpən'eər] a (pool, market etc) en plein air. ● **o.-'necked** a (shirt) sans cravate. ● **o.-'plan** a (office etc) sans cloisons.

opening ['əʊpənɪŋ] n ouverture f; (career prospect, trade outlet) débouché m; **late o.** nocturne f ‖ a (time, speech) d'ouverture; **o. night** Th première f.

openly ['əʊpənlɪ] adv (not secretly, frankly) ouvertement; (publicly) publiquement. ● **openness** n (frankness) franchise f.

opera ['ɒprə] n opéra m; **o. glasses** jumelles fpl de théâtre. ● **ope'ratic** a d'opéra.

operat/e ['ɒpəreɪt] **1** vi (of surgeon) opérer (**on s.o.** qn, **for** de). **2** vi (of machine etc) fonctionner; (proceed) opérer ‖ vt faire fonctionner; (business) gérer. ● **—ing** a o. theatre, Am o. room salle f d'opération; **o. wing** Med bloc m opératoire. ● **operation** [-'reɪʃ(ə)n] n Med Mil Math etc opération f; (working) fonctionnement m; **in o.** (machine) en service; **to have an o.** se faire opérer. ● **operative** ['ɒpərətɪv] a (scheme, measure etc) en vigueur.

operator ['ɒpəreɪtər] n (on phone) standardiste mf; (on machine) opérateur, -trice mf; **tour o.** organisateur, -trice mf de voyages.

opinion [ə'pɪnjən] n opinion f, avis m; in

my o. à mon avis.

opium ['əʊpɪəm] n opium m.

opponent [ə'pəʊnənt] n adversaire mf.

opportune ['ɒpətjuːn] a opportun.

opportunity [ɒpə'tjuːnɪtɪ] n occasion f (**to do**, of doing de faire); pl (**prospects**) perspectives fpl; **equal opportunities** des chances fpl égales.

oppos/e [ə'pəʊz] vt (person, measure etc) s'opposer à; (motion) Pol faire opposition à. ●**—ed** a opposé (**to** à); **as o. to** par opposition à. ●**—ing** a (team, interests) opposé. ●**opposition** [ɒpə'zɪʃ(ə)n] n opposition f (**to** à); the o. (rival camp) l'adversaire m; (in business) la concurrence; **he put up no o.** il n'a opposé aucune résistance.

opposite ['ɒpəzɪt] a (side etc) opposé; (house) d'en face; **one's o. number** son homologue mf ‖ adv (to sit etc) en face ‖ prep o. (**to**) en face de ‖ n the o. le contraire.

oppress [ə'pres] vt (treat cruelly) opprimer; (of heat, anguish) oppresser. ●**oppression** [-ʃ(ə)n] n oppression f. ●**oppressive** a (heat, weather) étouffant; (régime) oppressif; (ruler) tyrannique.

opt [ɒpt] vi to o. **for sth** décider pour qch; to o. **to do** choisir de faire; to o. **out** refuser de participer (**of** à) ‖ **option** [-ʃ(ə)n] n (choice) choix m; Sch matière f à option; **she has no o.** elle n'a pas le choix. ●**optional** a facultatif; **o. extra** (on car) accessoire m en option.

optical ['ɒptɪk(ə)l] a (instrument etc) d'optique; (lens, fibre etc) optique.

optician [ɒp'tɪʃ(ə)n] n opticien, -ienne mf.

optimism ['ɒptɪmɪz(ə)m] n optimisme m. ●**optimist** n optimiste mf. ●**opti'mistic** a optimiste.

optimum ['ɒptɪməm] a optimum; the o. **temperature** la température optimum.

opulent ['ɒpjʊlənt] a opulent.

or [ɔːr] conj ou; **one or two** un ou deux; **he doesn't drink or smoke** il ne boit ni ne

fume; **ten or so** environ dix.

oral ['ɔːrəl] a oral ‖ n (exam) oral m.

orange ['ɒrɪndʒ] 1 n (fruit) orange f; o. **juice** jus m d'orange. 2 a & n (colour) orange a & m inv. ●**orangeade** n orangeade f.

orator ['ɒrətər] n orateur m.

orbit ['ɔːbɪt] n (of planet etc) orbite f ‖ vt (sun etc) graviter autour de.

orchard ['ɔːtʃəd] n verger m.

orchestra ['ɔːkɪstrə] n orchestre m; **the o.** (seats in theater) Am l'orchestre m.

orchid ['ɔːkɪd] n orchidée f.

ordain [ɔː'deɪn] vt (priest) ordonner.

ordeal [ɔː'diːl] n épreuve f.

order ['ɔːdər] n (command) ordre m; (purchase) commande f; **in o.** (passport etc) en règle; (drawer etc) en ordre; **in (numerical) o.** dans l'ordre numérique; **in working o.** en état de marche; **in o. to do** pour faire; **in o. that** pour que (+ sub); **it's in o. to smoke**/etc (allowed) il est permis de fumer/etc; **out of o.** (machine) en panne; (telephone) en dérangement; **to make an o.** (purchase) passer une commande.
‖ vt (command) ordonner (**s.o. to do** à qn de faire); (meal, goods etc) commander; (taxi) appeler; **to o. s.o. around** commander qn.
‖ vi (in café etc) commander.

orderly ['ɔːdəlɪ] 1 a (tidy) ordonné; (mind) méthodique; (crowd) discipliné. 2 n Mil planton m; (in hospital) garçon m de salle.

ordinal ['ɔːdɪnəl] a (number) ordinal.

ordinary ['ɔːd(ə)nrɪ] a (usual, commonplace) ordinaire; (average) moyen; **an o. individual** un simple particulier; **in o. use** d'usage courant; **in the o. way** normalement; **it's out of the o.** ça sort de l'ordinaire.

ore [ɔːr] n minerai m.

organ ['ɔːgən] n 1 Anat & Fig organe m. 2 Mus orgue m, orgues fpl; **barrel o.** orgue m de Barbarie.

organic [ɔː'gænɪk] a organique; (vegetables etc) biologique.

organization [ɔːɡənaɪˈzeɪʃ(ə)n] *n* (*arrangement, association*) organisation *f.*

organize/e [ˈɔːɡənaɪz] *vt* organiser. ● —**er** *n* organisateur, -trice *mf*; (*personal*) o. (agenda *m*) organiseur *m.*

orgasm [ˈɔːɡæz(ə)m] *n* orgasme *m.*

orgy [ˈɔːdʒɪ] *n* orgie *f.*

orient [ˈɔːrɪənt] *vt Am* = **orientate.** ● **orientate** *vt* orienter.

Orient [ˈɔːrɪənt] *n* the O. l'Orient *m.* ● **ori'ental** *a* oriental.

orifice [ˈɒrɪfɪs] *n* orifice *m.*

origin [ˈɒrɪdʒɪn] *n* origine *f.*

original [əˈrɪdʒɪn(ə)l] *a* (*idea, artist etc*) original; (*first*) premier; (*copy, version*) original ‖ *n* (*document etc*) original *m.* ● **origi'nality** *n* originalité *f.* ● **originally** *adv* (*at first*) au départ; **she comes o. from** elle est originaire de.

originate [əˈrɪdʒɪneɪt] *vi* (*begin*) prendre naissance (**in** dans); **to o. from** (*of idea etc*) émaner de ‖ *vt* être l'auteur de.

ornament [ˈɔːnəmənt] *n* (*on dress etc*) ornement *m*; (*vase etc*) bibelot *m.* ● **orna'mental** *a* décoratif, ornemental.

orphan [ˈɔːf(ə)n] *n* orphelin, -ine *mf.* ● **orphaned** *a* orphelin; **he was o. by the accident** l'accident l'a rendu orphelin. ● **orphanage** *n* orphelinat *m.*

orthodox [ˈɔːθədɒks] *a* orthodoxe.

orthop(a)edic [ɔːθəˈpiːdɪk] *a* orthopédique *f.*

Oscar [ˈɒskər] *n Cin* oscar *m.*

ostensibly [ɒˈstensɪblɪ] *adv* apparemment.

ostentatious [ɒstenˈteɪʃ(ə)s] *a* prétentieux.

ostrich [ˈɒstrɪtʃ] *n* autruche *f.*

other [ˈʌðər] *a* autre; **o. doctors** d'autres médecins; **o. people** d'autres; **the o. one** l'autre *mf*; **I have no o. gloves than these** je n'ai pas d'autres gants que ceux-ci. ‖ *pron* the o. l'autre *mf*; (*some*) **others** d'autres; **some do, others don't** les uns le font, les autres ne le font pas; **none o. than** nul autre que. ‖ *adv* o. than autrement que. ● **otherwise** *adv & conj* autrement ‖ *a* (*different*)

(tout) autre.

OTT [əʊtiːˈtiː] *a abbr* (*over the top*) *Fam* outrancier.

otter [ˈɒtər] *n* loutre *f.*

ouch! [aʊtʃ] *int* aïe!, ouille!

ought [ɔːt] *v aux* 1 (*obligation, desirability*) **you o. to leave** tu devrais partir; **I o. to have done it** j'aurais dû le faire; **he said he o. to stay** il a dit qu'il devait rester. 2 (*probability*) **it o. to be ready** ça devrait être prêt.

ounce [aʊns] *n* once *f* (= 28,35 g).

our [aʊər] *poss a* notre, *pl* nos. ● **ours** *pron* le nôtre, la nôtre, *pl* les nôtres; **this book is o.** ce livre est à nous or est le nôtre; **a friend of o.** un ami à nous. ● **our'selves** *pron* nous-mêmes, (*reflexive & after prep*) nous; **we wash o.** nous nous lavons.

oust [aʊst] *vt* évincer (**from** de).

out [aʊt] *adv* (*outside*) dehors; (*not at home etc*) sorti; (*light, fire*) éteint; (*news, secret*) connu; (*flower*) ouvert; (*book*) publié; (*eliminated from game*) éliminé; **to be** or **go o. a lot** sortir beaucoup; **he's o. in Italy** il est (parti) en Italie; **to have a day o.** sortir pour la journée; **5 km o.** *Nau* à 5 km du rivage; **the sun's o.** il fait (du) soleil; **the tide's o.** la marée est basse; **the trip** or **journey o.** l'aller *m*; **o. there** là-bas.

‖ *prep* o. of (*outside*) en dehors de; (*danger, reach, water*) hors de; (*without*) sans; **o. of the window** par la fenêtre; **o. of pity/love/etc** par pitié/amour/etc; **to drink/take/copy o. of sth** boire/prendre/copier dans qch; **made o. of** (*wood etc*) fait en; **to make sth o. of a box/etc** faire qch avec une boîte/etc; **she's o. of town** elle n'est pas en ville; **four o. of five** quatre sur cinq; **o. of the blue** de manière inattendue; **to feel o. of place** ne pas se sentir intégré.

out-and-out [ˈaʊtənaʊt] *a* (*cheat, liar etc*) achevé. ● **o.-of-'date** *a* (*expired*) périmé; (*old-fashioned*) démodé. ● **o.-of-'doors** *adv* dehors. ● **o.-of-the-'way** *a* (*place*) écarté.

outbid [aʊt'bɪd] vt (pt & pp **outbid**, pres p **outbidding**) to o. s.o. (sur)enchérir sur qn.

outboard ['aʊtbɔːd] a o. motor (of boat) moteur m hors-bord inv.

outbreak ['aʊtbreɪk] n (of war, epidemic) début m; (of violence) éruption f; (of fever) accès m; (of hostilities) ouverture f.

outburst ['aʊtbɜːst] n (of anger, joy) explosion f; (of violence) flambée f.

outcast ['aʊtkɑːst] n (social) o. paria m.

outcome ['aʊtkʌm] n résultat m, issue f.

outcry ['aʊtkraɪ] n tollé m.

outdated [aʊt'deɪtɪd] a démodé.

outdo [aʊt'duː] vt (pt outdid, pp outdone) surpasser (in en).

outdoor ['aʊtdɔːr] a (pool, market, life) en plein air; (game) de plein air; o. clothes tenue f pour sortir. ● out'doors adv dehors.

outer ['aʊtər] a extérieur; o. space l'espace m (cosmique).

outfit ['aʊtfɪt] n (clothes) costume m; (for woman) toilette f; (toy) panoplie f (de cow-boy etc); (kit) trousse f; (group, gang) Fam bande f; sports/ski o. tenue f de sport/de ski.

outgoing ['aʊtɡəʊɪŋ] 1 a (minister etc) sortant; (mail) en partance; o. calls Tel appels mpl vers l'extérieur. 2 a (sociable) liant. 3 npl outgoings (expenses) dépenses fpl.

outgrow [aʊt'ɡrəʊ] vt (pt outgrew, pp outgrown) (clothes) devenir trop grand pour; (habit) perdre (en grandissant).

outhouse ['aʊthaʊs] n (of mansion, farm) dépendance f; (lavatory) Am cabinets mpl extérieurs.

outing ['aʊtɪŋ] n sortie f, excursion f.

outlandish [aʊt'lændɪʃ] a (weird) bizarre.

outlast [aʊt'lɑːst] vt durer plus longtemps que; (survive) survivre à.

outlaw ['aʊtlɔː] n hors-la-loi m inv ‖ vt (ban) proscrire.

outlay ['aʊtleɪ] n (expense) dépense(s) f(pl).

outlet ['aʊtlet] n (market for goods) débouché m; (for liquid) sortie f; El prise f de courant; (for feelings, energy) exutoire m; retail o. point m de vente; factory o. magasin m d'usine.

outline ['aʊtlaɪn] n (shape) contour m; (rough) o. (of article, plan etc) esquisse f; the broad or general outline(s) les grandes lignes ‖ vt (plan, situation) esquisser; (book, speech) résumer; to be outlined against (of tree etc) se profiler sur.

outlive [aʊt'lɪv] vt survivre à.

outlook ['aʊtlʊk] n inv (for future) perspective(s) f(pl); (point of view) perspective f (on sur); (weather forecast) prévisions fpl.

outlying ['aʊtlaɪɪŋ] a (remote) isolé.

outmoded [aʊt'məʊdɪd] a démodé.

outnumber [aʊt'nʌmbər] vt être plus nombreux que.

outpatient ['aʊtpeɪʃ(ə)nt] n malade mf en consultation externe.

outpost ['aʊtpəʊst] n avant-poste m.

output ['aʊtpʊt] n rendement m, production f; (computer data) données fpl de sortie; (computer process) sortie f.

outrage ['aʊtreɪdʒ] n (scandal) scandale m; (anger) indignation f; (crime) atrocité f; bomb o. attentat m à la bombe ‖ vt (morals) outrager; outraged by sth indigné de qch.

outrageous [aʊt'reɪdʒəs] a (shocking) scandaleux; (hat etc) grotesque; (atrocious) atroce.

outright [aʊt'raɪt] adv (to say, tell) franchement; (completely) complètement; (to be killed) sur le coup ‖ ['aʊtraɪt] a (complete) complet; (lie) pur; (refusal) catégorique; (winner) incontesté.

outset ['aʊtset] n at the o. au début; from the o. dès le départ.

outside [aʊt'saɪd] adv (au) dehors, à l'extérieur; to go o. sortir.
‖ prep à l'extérieur de, en dehors de; (beyond) Fig en dehors de; o. my room à la porte de ma chambre.
‖ n extérieur m, dehors m.

▌['aʊtsaɪd] a extérieur; **the o. lane** Aut la voie de droite or Am de gauche; **an o. chance** une faible chance. ● **out'sider** n (stranger) étranger, -ère mf; Sp outsider m.

outsize ['aʊtsaɪz] a (clothes) grande taille inv.

outskirts ['aʊtskɜːts] npl banlieue f.

outsmart [aʊt'smɑːt] vt être plus malin que.

outspoken [aʊt'spəʊk(ə)n] a (frank) franc (f franche).

outstanding [aʊt'stændɪŋ] a remarquable; (problem, business) non réglé; (debt) impayé; work o. travail m à faire.

outstay [aʊt'steɪ] vt **to o. one's welcome** abuser de l'hospitalité de son hôte.

outstretched [aʊt'stretʃt] a (arm) tendu.

outstrip [aʊt'strɪp] vt (-pp-) devancer.

outward ['aʊtwəd] a (sign, appearance) extérieur; (movement) vers l'extérieur; **o. journey** or **trip** aller m. ● **outward(s)** adv vers l'extérieur.

outweigh [aʊt'weɪ] vt (be more important than) l'emporter sur.

outwit [aʊt'wɪt] vt (-tt-) être plus malin que.

oval ['əʊv(ə)l] a & n ovale (m).

ovary ['əʊvərɪ] n Anat ovaire m.

oven ['ʌv(ə)n] n four m; **o. glove** gant m isolant.

over ['əʊvər] prep (on) sur; (above) au-dessus de; (on the other side of) de l'autre côté de; **bridge o. the river** pont m sur le fleuve; **to jump/look**/etc **o. sth** sauter/regarder/etc par-dessus qch; **to fall o. the balcony** tomber du balcon; **she fell o. it** elle en est tombée; **o. it** (on) dessus; (above) au-dessus; (to jump etc) par-dessus; **to criticize**/etc **o. sth** (about) critiquer/etc à propos de qch; **o. the phone** au téléphone; **o. the holidays** pendant les vacances; **o. ten days** (more than) plus de dix jours; **men o. sixty** les hommes de plus de soixante ans; **o. and above** en plus de; **he's o. his flu** il est remis de sa grippe; **all o. Spain** dans toute l'Espagne; **all o. the carpet** partout sur le tapis.

▌adv (above) (par-)dessus; (finished) fini; (danger) passé; (again) encore; (too) trop; **jump o.!** sautez par-dessus!; **o. here** ici; **o. there** là-bas; **to come** or **go o.** (visit) passer; **to ask s.o. o.** inviter qn (à venir); **he's o. in Italy** il est (parti) en Italie; **she's o. from Paris** elle est venue de Paris; **all o.** (everywhere) partout; **it's all o.!** (finished) c'est fini!; **kilo or o.** un kilo ou plus; **I have ten o.** il m'en reste dix; **there's some bread o.** il reste du pain; **o. and o. (again)** à plusieurs reprises; **to start all o. (again)** recommencer à zéro; **o. pleased**/etc trop content/etc.

over-abundant [əʊvərə'bʌndənt] a surabondant. ● **o.-de'veloped** a trop développé. ● **o.-fa'miliar** a trop familier. ● **o.-in'dulge** vt (one's desires) céder trop facilement à; (person) trop gâter.

overall 1 [əʊvər'ɔːl] a (length etc) total; (result etc) global ▌adv globalement. **2** ['əʊvərɔːl] n blouse f (de travail); pl (of workman) bleu m de travail.

overbearing [əʊvə'beərɪŋ] a autoritaire.

overboard ['əʊvəbɔːd] adv à la mer.

overbook [əʊvə'bʊk] vt (flight, hotel) surréserver.

overcast [əʊvə'kɑːst] a (sky) couvert.

overcharge [əʊvə'tʃɑːdʒ] vt **to o. s.o. for sth** faire payer qch trop cher à qn.

overcoat ['əʊvəkəʊt] n pardessus m.

overcome [əʊvə'kʌm] vt (pt overcame, pp overcome) (problem) surmonter; (shyness etc) vaincre; **to be o. by** (fatigue, grief) être accablé par; (fumes, temptation) succomber à.

overcook [əʊvə'kʊk] vt faire cuire trop.

overcrowded [əʊvə'kraʊdɪd] a (house, country) surpeuplé; (bus, train) bondé.

overdo [əʊvə'duː] vt (pt overdid, pp overdone) exagérer; Culin faire cuire trop; **to o. it** ne pas y aller doucement; **don't o. it!** vas-y doucement!

overdose ['əʊvədəʊs] n overdose f.

overdraft ['əʊvədrɑːft] n Fin découvert m. ● **over'drawn** a (account) à découvert.

overdue [əuvə'dju:] a (train etc) en retard; (debt) arriéré.

overeat [əuvər'i:t] vi manger trop.

overestimate [əuvər'estimeit] vt surestimer.

overexcited [əuvərik'saitid] a surexcité.

overflow 1 [əuvə'fləu] vi (of river, bath etc) déborder; **to be overflowing with** (of town, house etc) regorger de (visiteurs etc). **2** ['əuvəfləu] n (outlet) trop-plein m.

overgrown [əuvə'grəun] a envahi par la végétation; **o. with** (weeds etc) envahi par.

overhaul 1 [əuvə'hɔ:l] vt (vehicle, schedule etc) réviser **2** ['əuvəhɔ:l] n révision f.

overhead [əuvə'hed] adv au-dessus; ['əuvəhed] **1** a (cable etc) aérien. **2** npl (expenses) frais mpl généraux.

overhear [əuvə'hiər] vt (pt & pp overheard) surprendre, entendre.

overheat [əuvə'hi:t] vt surchauffer vi (of engine) chauffer.

overjoyed [əuvə'dʒɔid] a fou (f folle) de joie.

overland ['əuvəlænd] a & adv par voie de terre.

overlap [əuvə'læp] vi (-pp-) se chevaucher vt chevaucher

overleaf [əuvə'li:f] adv au verso.

overload [əuvə'ləud] vt surcharger.

overlook [əuvə'luk] vt **1** (not notice) ne pas remarquer; (forget) oublier; (ignore) passer sur. **2** (of window etc) donner sur; (of tower, fort) dominer.

overly ['əuvəli] adv excessivement.

overnight [əuvə'nait] adv (pendant) la nuit; (suddenly) Fig du jour au lendemain; **to stay o.** passer la nuit ['əuvənait] a (train, flight) de nuit; (stay) d'une nuit; **o. stop** arrêt m pour la nuit.

overpass ['əuvəpæs] n (bridge) Am toboggan m.

overpopulated [əuvə'pɒpuleitid] a surpeuplé.

overpower [əuvə'pauər] vt (physically) maîtriser; (defeat) vaincre; Fig accabler. ●—**ing** a (heat etc) accablant.

overpriced [əuvə'praist] a trop cher.

overrated [əuvə'reitid] a surfait.

overreact [əuvəri'ækt] vi réagir excessivement.

overrid/e [əuvə'raid] vt (pt overrode, pp overridden) (invalidate) annuler; (take no notice of) passer outre à; (be more important than) l'emporter sur. ●—**ing** a (importance) primordial; **my o. consideration** ma priorité.

overrule [əuvə'ru:l] vt (decision) annuler; (objection) repousser.

overrun [əuvə'rʌn] vt (pt overran, pp overrun, pres p overrunning) **1** (invade) envahir. **2** (go beyond) aller au-delà de.

overseas [əuvə'si:z] adv (Africa etc) outre-mer; (abroad) à l'étranger ['əuvəsi:z] a (visitor etc) d'outremer; étranger; (trade) extérieur.

oversee [əuvə'si:] vt (pt oversaw, pp overseen) (work) superviser.

overshadow [əuvə'ʃædəu] vt (make less important) éclipser; (make gloomy) assombrir.

oversight ['əuvəsait] n oubli m, omission f; (mistake) erreur f.

oversimplify [əuvə'simplifai] vti trop simplifier.

oversleep [əuvə'sli:p] vi (pt & pp overslept) dormir trop longtemps.

overspend [əuvə'spend] vi dépenser trop.

overstaffed [əuvə'stɑ:ft] a au personnel pléthorique.

overstay [əuvə'stei] vt **to o. one's welcome** abuser de l'hospitalité de son hôte.

overstep [əuvə'step] vt (-pp-) (limit) dépasser; **to o. the mark** dépasser les bornes.

overt ['əuvɜ:t] a manifeste.

overtake [əuvə'teik] vt (pt overtook, pp overtaken) dépasser; (vehicle) doubler, dépasser vi (in vehicle) doubler, dépasser.

overthrow [əuvə'θrəu] vt (pt overthrew,

pp overthrown) (*dictator etc*) renverser.
overtime ['əʊvətaɪm] *n* heures *fpl* sup-plémentaires ▌*adv* to work o. faire des heures supplémentaires.
overtones ['əʊvətəʊnz] *npl* (*traces*) note *f*, nuance *f* (**of** de).
overture ['əʊvətjʊər] *n Mus & Fig* ouverture *f*.
overturn [əʊvə'tɜːn] *vi* (*of car, boat*) se retourner ▌*vt* (*chair etc*) renverser; (*car, boat*) retourner.
overweight [əʊvə'weɪt] *a* to be o. (*of person*) avoir des kilos en trop.
overwhelm [əʊvə'welm] *vt* (*of feelings, heat etc*) accabler; (*defeat*) écraser; (*amaze*) bouleverser. ●**—ed** *a* (*over-joyed*) ravi (**by, with** de); o. with (*work, offers*) submergé de; o. by (*gift etc*) vivement touché par. ●**—ing** *a* (*heat etc*) accablant; (*majority, defeat*) écrasant; (*desire*) irrésistible; (*impres-sion*) dominant. ●**—ingly** *adv* (*to vote*) en masse.
overwork [əʊvə'wɜːk] *n* surmenage *m* ▌*vi* se surmener.
overwrought [əʊvə'rɔːt] *a* (*tense*) tendu.
owe [əʊ] *vt* (*money, respect etc*) devoir

(**to** à); **to o. it to oneself to do** se devoir de faire. ●**owing 1** *a* (*money*) dû. **2** *prep* **o. to** à cause de.
owl [aʊl] *n* hibou *m* (*pl* hiboux).
own [əʊn] **1** *a* propre; **my o. house** ma propre maison ▌*pron* **it's my (very) o.** c'est à moi (tout seul); **a house of his o.** sa propre maison; (**all**) **on one's o.** (*alone*) tout seul; **to get one's o. back** se venger (**on s.o.** de qn, **for sth** de qch); **to come into one's o.** (*fulfil oneself*) s'épanouir.
2 *vt* (*possess*) posséder; **who owns this ball/etc?** à qui appartient cette balle/etc?
3 *vi* **to o. up** (*confess*) avouer (**to sth** qch). ●**owner** *n* propriétaire *mf*. ●**own-ership** *n* possession *f*; **home o.** accession *f* à la propriété.
ox, *pl* **oxen** [ɒks, 'ɒks(ə)n] *n* bœuf *m*.
oxygen ['ɒksɪdʒ(ə)n] *n* oxygène *m* ▌*a* (*mask, tent*) à oxygène.
oyster ['ɔɪstər] *n* huître *f*.
oz *abbr* (*ounce*) once *f*.
ozone ['əʊzəʊn] *n* ozone *m*; **o. layer** couche *f* d'ozone. ●**o.-friendly** *a* (*pro-duct*) qui préserve la couche d'ozone.

P

P, p [piː] *n* P, p *m*.

p [piː] *abbr* = **penny, pence**.

pa [pɑː] *n Fam* papa *m*.

pace [peɪs] *n* (*speed, step*) pas *m*; **to keep p. with** (*follow*) suivre; (*in work, progress*) se maintenir à la hauteur de ‖ *vi* **to p. up and down** faire les cent pas. ● **pacemaker** *n* (*for heart*) stimulateur *m* cardiaque.

Pacific [pəˈsɪfɪk] *a* (*coast etc*) pacifique ‖ *n* **the P.** le Pacifique.

pacify [ˈpæsɪfaɪ] *vt* (*country*) pacifier; (*crowd, angry person*) calmer; (*nervous person*) apaiser. ● **pacifier** *n* (*of baby*) *Am* sucette *f*. ● **pacifist** *n* pacifiste *mf*.

pack¹ [pæk] *n* (*bundle, packet*) paquet *m*; (*rucksack*) sac *m* (à dos); (*of animal*) charge *f*; (*of hounds, wolves*) meute *f*; (*of runners*) *Sp* peloton *m*; (*of cards*) jeu *m*; (*of lies*) tissu *m*.

pack² [pæk] *vt* (*fill*) remplir (**with** de); (*suitcase*) faire; (*object into box etc*) emballer; (*object into suitcase*) mettre dans sa valise; (*crush*) tasser ‖ *vi* (*fill one's bags*) faire ses valises. ● **packed** *a* (*bus, room etc*) bourré; **p. lunch** panier-repas *m*. ● **packing** *n* (*material, action*) emballage *m*; **p. case** caisse *f* d'emballage.

pack away *vt* (*tidy away*) ranger ‖ **to pack down** *vt* (*crush*) tasser ‖ **to pack in** *vt* (*give up*) laisser tomber; (*stop*) arrêter; **p. it in!** laisse tomber! ‖ **to pack into** *vt* (*cram*) entasser dans; (*put*) mettre dans ‖ *vi* (*crowd into*) s'entasser dans ‖ **to pack up** *vt* (*put into box*) emballer; (*give up*) *Fam* laisser tomber ‖ *vi Fam* (*stop*) s'arrêter; (*of machine, vehicle*) tomber en rade.

package [ˈpækɪdʒ] *n* paquet *m*; (*computer programs*) progiciel *m*; **p. tour** voyage *m* organisé ‖ *vt* emballer. ●**-ing** *n* (*material*) emballage *m*.

packet [ˈpækɪt] *n* paquet *m*; **to make/cost a p.** *Fam* faire/coûter beaucoup d'argent.

pact [pækt] *n* pacte *m*.

pad [pæd] *n* (*of cloth etc*) tampon *m*; (*for writing*) bloc *m*; (*on knee*) *Sp* genouillère *f*; (*room*) *Sl* piaule *f*; **launch(ing) p.** aire *f* de lancement ‖ *vt* (**-dd-**) (*armchair etc*) rembourrer; (*jacket etc*) matelasser; **to p. out** (*text*) délayer. ● **padding** *n* rembourrage *m*.

paddle [ˈpæd(ə)l] **1** *vi* (*dip one's feet*) se mouiller les pieds; **paddling pool** (*inflatable*) piscine *f* gonflable; (*purpose-built*) pataugeoire *f* ‖ **n to have a (little) p.** se mouiller les pieds. **2** *n* (*pole*) pagaie *f*; **p. boat** bateau *m* à roues ‖ *vt* **to p. a canoe** pagayer.

paddock [ˈpædək] *n* enclos *m*; (*at racecourse*) paddock *m*.

padlock [ˈpædlɒk] *n* (*on door etc*) cadenas *m*; (*on bicycle, moped*) antivol *m* ‖ *vt* (*door etc*) cadenasser.

p(a)ediatrician [piːdɪəˈtrɪʃ(ə)n] *n* (*doctor*) pédiatre *mf*.

pagan [ˈpeɪgən] *a & n* païen, -enne (*mf*).

page [peɪdʒ] **1** *n* (*of book etc*) page *f*. **2** *n* **p. (boy)** (*in hotel etc*) groom *m*; (*at court*) *Hist* page *m*; (*at wedding*) garçon *m* d'honneur ‖ *vt* **to p. s.o.** faire appeler qn. ● **pager** *n* récepteur *m* d'appel.

pageant [ˈpædʒənt] *n* grand spectacle *m* historique.

pagoda [pəˈgəʊdə] *n* pagode *f*.

paid [peɪd] *pt & pp of* **pay** ‖ *a* (*assassin etc*) à gages; **to put p. to** (*hopes, plans*) anéantir.

pail [peɪl] *n* seau *m*.

pain [peɪn] *n* (*physical*) douleur *f*; (*grief*)

peine *f*; *pl* (*efforts*) efforts *mpl*; **to have a p. in one's arm** avoir mal *or* une douleur au bras; **to be in p.** souffrir; **to take (great) pains to do** se donner du mal à faire; **to take (great) pains not to do** prendre bien soin de ne pas faire; **to be a p. (in the neck)** (*of person*) *Fam* être casse-pieds. ● **painkiller** *n* calmant *m*; **on painkillers** sous calmants.

painful ['peɪnfəl] *a* (*illness, arm, sight etc*) douloureux; (*difficult*) pénible. ● **painless** *a* sans douleur; (*operation*) indolore; (*easy*) *Fam* facile.

painstaking ['peɪnzteɪkɪŋ] *a* (*person*) soigneux; (*work*) soigné.

paint [peɪnt] *n* peinture *f*; *pl* (*in box, tube*) couleurs *fpl*; **p. stripper** décapant ▮ *vti* peindre; **to p. sth blue**/*etc* peindre qch en bleu/*etc*. ●—**ing** *n* (*activity*) peinture *f*; (*picture*) tableau *m*, peinture *f*. ● **painter** *n* peintre *m*.

paintbrush ['peɪntbrʌʃ] *n* pinceau *m*.

pair [peər] *n* (*two*) paire *f*; (*man and woman*) couple *m*; **a p. of shorts** un short.

pajamas [pə'dʒɑːməz] *npl Am* = **pyjamas.**

Pakistan [pɑːkɪ'stɑːn] *n* Pakistan *m*. ● **Pakistani** *a* & *n* pakistanais, -aise (*mf*).

pal [pæl] *n Fam* copain *m*, copine *f* ▮ *vi* (-ll-) **to p. up** devenir copains; **to p. up with s.o.** devenir copain avec qn.

palace ['pælɪs] *n* palais *m*. ● **palatial** [pə'leɪʃ(ə)l] *a* comme un palais.

palatable ['pælətəb(ə)l] *a* (*food*) agréable; (*idea etc*) acceptable.

palate ['pælɪt] *n Anat* palais *m*.

pale [peɪl] *a* (-**er, -est**) (*face, colour etc*) pâle; **p. ale** bière *f* blonde ▮ *vi* pâlir.

Palestine ['pæləstaɪn] *n* Palestine *f*. ● **Pale'stinian** *a* & *n* palestinien, -ienne (*mf*).

palette ['pælɪt] *n* (*of artist*) palette *f*.

pall [pɔːl] **1** *vi* devenir insipide *or* ennuyeux (**on** pour). **2** *n* (*of smoke*) voile *m*.

pallid ['pælɪd] *a* pâle. ● **pallor** *n* pâleur *f*.

pally ['pælɪ] *a* (-**ier, -iest**) *Fam* copain

am, copine *af* (**with** avec).

palm [pɑːm] **1** *n* (*of hand*) paume *f*. **2** *n* **p. (tree)** palmier *m*; **p. leaf** palme *f*; **P. Sunday** les Rameaux *mpl*. **3** *vt Fam* **to p. sth off** refiler qch (**on s.o.** à qn); **to p. s.o. off on s.o.** coller qn à qn.

palmist ['pɑːmɪst] *n* chiromancien, -ienne *mf*.

palpitation [pælpɪ'teɪʃ(ə)n] *n* palpitation *f*.

paltry ['pɔːltrɪ] *a* (-**ier, -iest**) (*sum etc*) dérisoire; **a p. excuse** une piètre excuse.

pamper ['pæmpər] *vt* dorloter.

pamphlet ['pæmflɪt] *n* brochure *f*.

pan [pæn] **1** *n* casserole *f*; (*for frying*) poêle *f* (à frire); (*of lavatory*) cuvette *f*. **2** *vi* (-**nn-**) **to p. out** (*succeed*) aboutir.

pancake ['pænkeɪk] *n* crêpe *f*.

panda ['pændə] *n* (*animal*) panda *m*; **P. car** = voiture *f* pie *inv* (de la police).

pandemonium [pændɪ'məʊnɪəm] *n* (*chaos*) chaos *m*; (*uproar*) tumulte *m*.

pander ['pændər] *vi* **to p. to** (*tastes, fashion etc*) sacrifier à; **to p. to s.o.** se plier aux désirs de qn.

pane [peɪn] *n* vitre *f*, carreau *m*.

panel ['pæn(ə)l] *n* **1** (*of door etc*) panneau *m*; (**control**) **p.** *Tech El* console *f*; (**instrument**) **p.** *Av Aut* tableau *m* de bord. **2** (*of judges*) jury *m*; (*of experts*) groupe *m*; **a p. of guests** des invités; **a p. game** *TV Rad* un jeu par équipes. ● **panelled** (*Am* **paneled**) *a* (*room etc*) lambrissé. ● **panelling** (*Am* **paneling**) *n* lambris *m*.

pangs [pæŋz] *npl* **p. of conscience** remords *mpl* (de conscience); **p. of hunger** tiraillements *mpl* d'estomac.

panic ['pænɪk] *n* panique *f*; **to get into a p.** paniquer ▮ *vi* (-**ck-**) s'affoler, paniquer. ● **p.-stricken** *a* affolé. ● **panicky** (*person*) *a Fam* qui s'affole facilement.

panorama [pænə'rɑːmə] *n* panorama *m*.

pansy ['pænzɪ] *n Bot* pensée *f*.

pant [pænt] *vi* (*gasp*) haleter.

panther ['pænθər] *n* panthère *f*.

panties ['pæntɪz] *npl* (*female underwear*) slip *m*; (*longer*) culotte *f*.

pantomime ['pæntəmaɪm] n spectacle m de Noël.

pantry ['pæntrɪ] n (larder) garde-manger m inv.

pants [pænts] npl (male underwear) slip m; (long) caleçon m; (trousers) Am pantalon m.

pantyhose ['pæntɪhəʊz] n (tights) Am collant(s) m(pl).

paper ['peɪpər] n papier m; (newspaper) journal m; (wallpaper) papier m peint; (exam) épreuve f (écrite); (student's exercise) copie f; (learned article) exposé m, communication f; **brown p.** papier m d'emballage; **to put sth down on p.** mettre qch par écrit.
▮a (bag etc) en papier; (cup, plate) en carton; **p. clip** trombone m; **p. knife** coupe-papier m inv; **p. shop** marchand m de journaux.
▮vt (room, wall) tapisser.

paperback ['peɪpəbæk] n (book) livre m de poche. ●**paperboy** n livreur m de journaux. ●**paperweight** n presse-papiers m inv. ●**paperwork** n Com écritures fpl; (red tape) paperasserie f.

paprika ['pæprɪkə] n paprika m.

par [pɑːr] n **on a p.** au même niveau (with que); **below p.** (unwell) Fam pas en forme.

parable ['pærəb(ə)l] n (story) parabole f.

paracetamol [pærə'siːtəmɒl] n paracétamol m; (tablet) comprimé m de paracétamol.

parachute ['pærəʃuːt] n parachute m; **to drop by p.** (men, supplies) parachuter.

parade [pə'reɪd] **1** n (procession) défilé m; (ceremony) Mil parade f; **fashion p.** défilé m de mode ▮vi Mil etc défiler; **to p. about** (walk about) se balader ▮vt faire étalage de. **2** n (street) avenue f.

paradise ['pærədaɪs] n paradis m.

paradox ['pærədɒks] n paradoxe m. ●**para'doxically** adv paradoxalement.

paraffin ['pærəfɪn] n pétrole m (lampant); (wax) Am paraffine f; **p. lamp** lampe f à pétrole.

paragraph ['pærəgrɑːf] n paragraphe m;

'new p.' 'à la ligne'.

parakeet ['pærəkiːt] n perruche f.

parallel ['pærəlel] a (comparable) & Math parallèle (with, to à); **to run p. to** or with être parallèle à ▮n (comparison) & Geog parallèle m; (line) Math parallèle f.

paralysis [pə'ræləsɪs] n paralysie f.

paralyse ['pærəlaɪz] (Am -lyze) vt paralyser.

paramount ['pærəmaʊnt] a **of p. importance** de la plus haute importance.

paranoia [pærə'nɔɪə] n paranoïa f. ●**'paranoid** a paranoïaque.

parapet ['pærəpɪt] n parapet m.

paraphernalia [pærəfə'neɪlɪə] n attirail m.

paraphrase ['pærəfreɪz] n paraphrase f ▮vt paraphraser.

parasite ['pærəsaɪt] n (person, animal) parasite m.

parasol ['pærəsɒl] n (over table, on beach) parasol m; (lady's) ombrelle f.

paratroops ['pærətruːps] npl Mil parachutistes mpl.

parcel ['pɑːs(ə)l] **1** n colis m, paquet m; **to be part and p. of** faire partie intégrante de. **2** vt (-ll-, Am -l-) **to p. sth up** faire un paquet de qch.

parched [pɑːtʃt] a **to be parched** (thirsty) être assoiffé.

parchment ['pɑːtʃmənt] n parchemin m.

pardon ['pɑːd(ə)n] n (by king, president etc) grâce f; (forgiveness) pardon m; Jur grâce f; **general p.** amnistie f; **I beg your p.** (apologize) je vous prie de m'excuser; (not hearing) vous dites?; **p.?** (not hearing) comment?; **p. (me)!** (sorry) pardon! ▮vt pardonner (s.o. for sth qch à qn); **to p. s.o.** (of king etc) gracier qn.

parent ['peərənt] n père m, mère f; one's **parents** ses parents mpl; **p. company** maison f mère. ●**parental** [pə'rent(ə)l] a (responsibility etc) des parents.

Paris ['pærɪs] n Paris m or f. ●**Parisian** [pə'rɪzɪən, Am pə'riː∫ən] a & n parisien, -ienne (mf).

parish ['pærɪʃ] n Rel paroisse f; (civil)

commune f ▌ a (church, register) paroissial; **p. council** conseil m municipal.

park [pɑːk] **1** n (garden) parc m. **2** vt (vehicle) garer ▌ vi Aut se garer; (remain parked) stationner. ● **parking** n stationnement m; **'no p.'** 'défense de stationner'; **p. light** veilleuse f; **p. lot** Am parking m; **p. meter** parcmètre m; **p. place** or **space** place f de parking; **p. ticket** contravention f.

parkway ['pɑːkweɪ] n Am avenue f.

parliament ['pɑːləmənt] n parlement m. ● **parliamentary** a parlementaire.

parlour ['pɑːlər] (Am **parlor**) n (in mansion) (petit) salon m; **ice-cream p.** Am salon m de glaces.

parochial [pəˈrəʊkɪəl] a (mentality) Pej de clocher; (person) Pej provincial; **p. school** Am école f catholique.

parody ['pærədɪ] n parodie f ▌ vt parodier.

parole [pəˈrəʊl] n **on p.** Jur en liberté conditionnelle.

parquet ['pɑːkeɪ] n **p. (floor)** parquet m.

parrot ['pærət] n perroquet m.

parry ['pærɪ] vt (blow) parer; (question) éluder.

parsimonious [pɑːsɪˈməʊnɪəs] a parcimonieux.

parsley ['pɑːslɪ] n persil m.

parsnip ['pɑːsnɪp] n panais m.

parson ['pɑːs(ə)n] n (Protestant priest) pasteur m.

part¹ [pɑːt] n partie f; (of machine) pièce f; (of periodical) fascicule m; (of serial) épisode m; (role in play etc) rôle m; (in hair) Am raie f; **to take p.** participer (in à); **to take s.o.'s p.** prendre parti pour qn; **in p.** en partie; **for the most p.** dans l'ensemble; **to be a p. of** faire partie de; **on the p. of** (on behalf of) de la part de; **for my p.** pour ma part; **in these parts** dans ces parages; **p. exchange** reprise f; **to take in p. exchange** reprendre; **p. payment** paiement m partiel.

▌ adv (partly) en partie.

part² [pɑːt] vt (separate) séparer; **to p. company with s.o.** quitter qn ▌ vi (of

friends etc) se quitter; (of married couple) se séparer; **to p. with sth** (get rid of) se séparer de qch.

partake [pɑːˈteɪk] vi (pt **partook**, pp **partaken**) **to p. in** participer à.

partial ['pɑːʃəl] a (not total) partiel; (biased) partial (**towards** envers); **to be p. to sth** (fond of) Fam avoir un faible pour qch.

participate [pɑːˈtɪsɪpeɪt] vi participer (in à). ● **participant** n participant, -ante mf. ● **participation** n participation f.

participle [pɑːˈtɪsɪp(ə)l] n Gram participe m.

particle ['pɑːtɪk(ə)l] n (of atom, dust) particule f; (of truth) grain m.

particular [pəˈtɪkjʊlər] **1** a (specific, special) particulier; (fussy) difficile (**about** sur); (showing care) méticuleux; **this p. book** ce livre-ci en particulier; **in p.** en particulier. **2** npl **particulars** détails mpl, renseignements mpl; (address etc) coordonnées fpl. ● **—ly** adv particulièrement.

parting ['pɑːtɪŋ] **1** n (in hair) raie f. **2** n (separation) séparation f ▌ a (gift, words) d'adieu.

partition [pɑːˈtɪʃ(ə)n] **1** n (in room) cloison f ▌ vt **to p. off** cloisonner. **2** n (of country) partition f ▌ vt (country) partager.

partly ['pɑːtlɪ] adv en partie; **p. English p. French** moitié anglais moitié français.

partner ['pɑːtnər] n (in business) associé, -ée mf; (lover, spouse) & Sp Pol partenaire mf; (dancing) n cavalier, -ière mf. ● **partnership** n association f; **in p. with** en association avec.

partridge ['pɑːtrɪdʒ] n perdrix f.

part-time [pɑːtˈtaɪm] a & adv à temps partiel.

party ['pɑːtɪ] n **1** (gathering) (formal) réception f; (with friends) soirée f; (for birthday) fête f. **2** (group) groupe m; Pol parti m; (in contract, lawsuit) partie f; **rescue p.** équipe f de secours; **innocent p.** innocent, -ente mf; **p. line** Tel ligne f partagée; Pol ligne f du parti;

p. **ticket** billet *m* collectif.

pass[1] [paːs] *n* (*entry permit*) laissez-passer *m inv*; (*free ticket*) *Th etc* billet *m* de faveur; (*over mountains*) col *m*; *Fb etc* passe *f*; to **get a p.** (*in exam*) être reçu (**in French**/*etc* en français/*etc*); to **make a p. at s.o.** faire des avances à qn; **p. mark** (*in exam*) moyenne *f*.

pass[2] [paːs] *vi* (*go, come, disappear*) passer (**to** à, **through** par); (*overtake in vehicle*) dépasser; (*in exam*) être reçu (**in French**/*etc* en français/*etc*); **he can p. for thirty** on lui donnerait trente ans.

▮ *vt* (*move, spend, give etc*) passer (**to** à); (*go past*) passer devant (*immeuble etc*); (*vehicle*) dépasser; (*exam*) être reçu à; (*candidate*) recevoir; (*opinion*) prononcer (**on** sur); (*remark*) faire; (*allow*) autoriser; (*bill, law*) (*of parliament*) voter; **to p. s.o.** (*in street*) croiser qn.

passable ['paːsəb(ə)l] *a* (*not bad*) passable; (*road*) praticable; (*river*) franchissable.

passage ['pæsɪdʒ] *n* (*of text, act of passing etc*) passage *m*; (*of time*) écoulement *m*; (*corridor*) couloir *m*; (*by boat*) traversée *f*. ● **passageway** *n* (*corridor*) couloir *m*; (*alleyway*) passage *m*.

pass along *vi* passer ▮ **to pass away** *vi* (*die*) mourir ▮ **to pass by** *vi* passer (à côté) ▮ *vt* (*building etc*) passer devant; **to p. by s.o.** (*in street*) croiser qn ▮ **to pass off** *vi* (*happen*) se passer ▮ *vt* to p. oneself off as se faire passer pour; **to p. sth off on s.o.** refiler qch à qn ▮ **to pass on** *vt* (*message, illness etc*) transmettre (**to** à) ▮ **to pass out** *vi* (*faint*) s'évanouir ▮ *vt* (*hand out*) distribuer ▮ **to pass over** *vt* (*ignore*) passer sur (*qch*) ▮ **to pass round** *vt* (*cakes, document etc*) faire passer; (*hand out*) distribuer (*tracts etc*) ▮ **to pass through** *vi* passer ▮ **to pass up** *vt* (*chance etc*) laisser passer.

passbook ['paːsbʊk] *n* livret *m* de caisse d'épargne.

passenger ['pæsɪndʒər] *n* passager, -ère

mf; *Rail* voyageur, -euse *mf*.

passer-by [paːsə'baɪ] *n* (*pl* **passers-by**) passant, -ante *f*.

passing ['paːsɪŋ] *a* (*vehicle etc*) qui passe; (*beauty*) passager ▮ *n* (*of vehicle etc*) passage *m*; (*of time*) écoulement *m*; **in p.** en passant.

passion ['pæʃ(ə)n] *n* passion *f*; to **have a p. for** (*cars etc*) avoir la passion de. ● **passionate** *a* passionné.

passive ['pæsɪv] *a* (*not active*) & *Gram* passif ▮ *n Gram* passif *m*; **in the p.** au passif.

Passover ['paːsəʊvər] *n Rel* Pâque *f*.

passport ['paːspɔːt] *n* passeport *m*; **p. control** le contrôle des passeports.

password ['paːswɜːd] *n* mot *m* de passe.

past [paːst] 1 *n* (*time, history*) passé *m*; **in the p.** (*formerly*) dans le temps.

▮ *a* (*gone by*) passé; (*former*) ancien; **these p. months** ces derniers mois; **in the p. tense** *Gram* au passé.

2 *prep* (*in front of*) devant; (*after*) après; (*further than*) plus loin que; (*too old for*) trop vieux pour; **p. four o'clock** quatre heures passées; **to be p. fifty** avoir cinquante ans passés.

▮ *adv* devant; **to go p.** passer (devant); **to run p.** passer en courant.

pasta ['pæstə] *n Culin* pâtes *fpl*.

paste [peɪst] 1 *n* (*mixture*) pâte *f*; (*of meat*) pâté *m*; (*of fish*) beurre *m*. 2 *n* (*glue*) colle *f* (blanche) ▮ *vt* coller; **to p. up** (*notice etc*) coller.

pastel ['pæstəl, *Am* pæ'stel] *n* pastel *m*.

pasteurized ['pæstəraɪzd] *a* (*milk*) pasteurisé.

pastille ['pæstɪl, *Am* pæ'stiːl] *n* pastille *f*.

pastime ['paːstaɪm] *n* passe-temps *m inv*.

pastor ['paːstər] *n Rel* pasteur *m*.

pastry ['peɪstrɪ] *n* (*dough*) pâte *f*; (*cake*) pâtisserie *f*.

pasture ['paːstʃər] *n* pâturage *m*.

pasty ['pæstɪ] *n Culin* petit pâté *m* (en croûte).

pat [pæt] *vt* (**-tt-**) (*cheek etc*) tapoter; (*animal*) caresser ▮ *n* petite tape; caresse *f*.

patch [pætʃ] n (for clothes) pièce f; (over eye) bandeau m; (of colour) tache f; (of fog) nappe f; (of ice) plaque f; **a cabbage p.** un carré de choux; **bad p.** Fig mauvaise période f ‖ vt **to p. (up)** (clothing) rapiécer; **to p. up** (quarrel) régler. ● **patchwork** n patchwork m. ● **patchy** a (-ier, -iest) inégal.

patent ['peɪtənt] 1 a a patent. 2 n brevet m (d'invention) ‖ vt (faire) breveter. ● —**ly** adv manifestement; **p. obvious** absolument évident.

paternal [pə'tɜ:n(ə)l] a paternel.

path [pɑ:θ] n (pl -s [pɑ:ðz]) sentier m, chemin m; (in park) allée f; (of river) cours m; (of bullet) trajectoire f. ● **pathway** n sentier m, chemin m.

pathetic [pə'θetik] a (results etc) lamentable.

pathology [pə'θɒlədʒɪ] n pathologie f.

patient ['peɪʃ(ə)nt] 1 a patient. 2 n (in hospital) malade mf, patient, -ente mf; (on doctor's or dentist's list) patient, -ente mf. ● **patience** n patience f; **to have p.** prendre patience; **to lose p.** perdre patience (**with s.o.** avec qn); **to play p.** (card game) faire des réussites. ● **patiently** adv patiemment.

patio ['pætɪəʊ] n (pl -os) terrasse f; **p. doors** porte-fenêtre f.

patriot ['peɪtrɪət] n patriote mf. ● **patriotic** a patriotique; (person) patriote. ● **patriotism** n patriotisme m.

patrol [pə'trəʊl] n patrouille f; **police p. car** voiture f de police ‖ vi (-ll-) patrouiller ‖ vt patrouiller dans. ● **patrolman** n (pl -men) Am agent m de police.

patron ['peɪtrən] n (of artist) protecteur, -trice mf; (customer) client, -ente mf; (of theatre etc) habitué, -ée mf. ● **patronize/** ['pætrənaɪz, Am 'peɪtrənaɪz] vt Pej traiter (qn) avec condescendance. ● —**ing** a condescendant.

patter ['pætər] 1 n (of footsteps) petit bruit m; (of rain) crépitement m ‖ vi (of rain) crépiter. 2 n (talk) baratin m.

pattern ['pæt(ə)n] n dessin m, motif m;

(paper model for garment) patron m; Fig modèle m; (plan) plan m; (tendency) tendance f; (of a crime) scénario m. ● **patterned** a (dress, cloth) à motifs.

paunch [pɔ:ntʃ] n panse f, bedon m.

pauper ['pɔ:pər] n pauvre mf.

pause [pɔ:z] n pause f; (in conversation) silence m ‖ vi (stop) faire une pause; (hesitate) hésiter.

pav/e [peɪv] vt paver; **to p. the way for** Fig ouvrir la voie à. ● —**ing** n (surface) pavage m; **p. stone** pavé m.

pavement ['peɪvmənt] n trottoir m; (roadway) Am chaussée f.

pavilion [pə'vɪljən] n (building) pavillon m.

paw [pɔ:] n patte f ‖ vt (of animal) donner des coups de patte à.

pawn [pɔ:n] 1 n Chess pion m. 2 vt mettre en gage. ● **pawnbroker** n prêteur, -euse mf sur gages. ● **pawnshop** n bureau m de prêteur sur gages.

pay [peɪ] n salaire m; (of workman) paie f; (of soldier) solde f; **p. day** jour m de paie; **p. slip** or Am **stub** bulletin m de paie.

‖ vt (pt & pp paid) (person, sum) payer; (deposit) verser; (of investment) rapporter; (compliment, visit) faire (**to** à); **to p. s.o.** **to do** or **for doing** payer qn pour faire; **to p. s.o. for sth** payer qch à qn; **to p. money into one's account** or **the bank** verser de l'argent sur son compte; **to p. homage** or **tribute** rendre hommage à.

‖ vi payer; **to p. a lot** payer cher; **it pays to be cautious** on a intérêt à être prudent. ● **paying** a (guest) payant; (profitable) (scheme etc) rentable.

payable ['peɪəb(ə)l] a (due) payable; **a cheque** or Am **check p. to** un chèque à l'ordre de.

pay back vt (person, loan) rembourser; **I'll p. you back for this!** je te revaudrai ça! ‖ **to pay for** vt (qch) ‖ **to pay in** vt (cheque, Am check) verser (**to one's account** sur son compte) ‖ **to pay off** vt (debt, person) rembourser; (in instalments) rembourser par acomptes; **to p. off** an old score *Fig* régler un vieux compte ▮ *vi* (*be successful*) être payant ▮ **to pay out** *vt* (*spend*) dépenser ▮ **to pay up** *vti* payer.

paycheck ['peɪtʃek] *n Am* chèque *m* de règlement de salaire. ●**payoff** *n Fam* (*reward*) récompense *f*. ●**payphone** *n* téléphone *m* public. ●**payroll** *n* **to be on the p. of** (*factory etc*) être employé par.

payment ['peɪmənt] *n* paiement *m*; (*of deposit*) versement *m*; **on p. of 20 francs** moyennant 20 francs.

PC [pi:'si:] *n abbr* = **personal computer**.

PE [pi:'i:] *n abbr* (*physical education*) EPS *f*.

pea [pi:] *n* pois *m*; **garden** *or* **green peas** petits pois *mpl*; **p. soup** soupe *f* aux pois.

peace [pi:s] *n* paix *f*; **p. of mind** tranquillité *f* d'esprit; **in p.** en paix; **at p.** en paix (**with** avec); **to have (some) p. and quiet** avoir la paix; **to disturb the p.** troubler l'ordre public. ●**p.-loving** *a* pacifique.

peaceful ['pi:sfəl] *a* paisible, calme; (*demonstration, coexistence*) pacifique.

peach [pi:tʃ] *n* (*fruit*) pêche *f* ▮ *a* (*colour*) pêche *inv*.

peacock ['pi:kɒk] *n* paon *m*.

peak [pi:k] *n* (*mountain top*) sommet *m* (*mountain*) pic *m*; (*of cap*) visière *f*; (*of fame etc*) *Fig* sommet *m*; **the traffic is at its p.** la circulation est à son maximum ▮ *a* (*hours, period*) de pointe; (*production*) maximum. ●**peaked cap** *n* casquette *f*.

peaky ['pi:kɪ] *a* (**-ier**, **-iest**) *Fam* (*ill*) patraque; (*pale*) pâlot.

peal [pi:l] *n* (*of laughter*) éclat *m*; (*of thunder*) roulement *m*; **p. of bells** carillon *m* ▮ *vi* (*of bells*) carillonner.

peanut ['pi:nʌt] *n* cacah(o)uète *f*; **p. butter** beurre *m* de cacah(o)uètes.

pear [peər] *n* poire *f*; **p. tree** poirier *m*.

pearl [pɜ:l] *n* perle *f*; **p. necklace** collier *m* de perles.

peasant ['pezənt] *n* paysan, -anne *mf*.

peashooter ['pi:ʃu:tər] *n* sarbacane *f*.

peat [pi:t] *n* tourbe *f*.

pebble ['peb(ə)l] *n* (*stone*) caillou *m* (*pl* -oux) (*on beach*) galet *m*. ●**pebbly** *a* (*beach*) (couvert) de galets.

pecan ['pi:kæn] *n* (*nut*) *Am* noix *f* de pécan.

peck [pek] *vti* **to p. (at)** (*of bird*) picorer (*du pain etc*); donner un coup de bec à (*qn*) ▮ *n* coup *m* de bec; (*kiss*) *Fam* bécot *m*.

peckish ['pekɪʃ] *a* **to be p.** (*hungry*) *Fam* avoir un petit creux.

peculiar [pɪ'kju:lɪər] *a* (*strange*) bizarre; (*special*) particulier (**to** à). ●**peculiarity** *n* (*feature*) particularité *f*.

pedal ['ped(ə)l] *n* pédale *f*; **p. boat** pédalo *m* ▮ *vi* (**-ll-**, *Am* **-l-**) pédaler ▮ *vt* **to p. a bicycle** faire marcher un vélo; (*ride*) rouler en vélo. ●**pedalbin** *n* poubelle *f* à pédale.

pedantic [pə'dæntɪk] *a* pédant.

peddl/e ['ped(ə)l] *vt* colporter; (*drugs*) faire le trafic de. ●**—er** *n* (*door-to-door*) colporteur, -euse *mf*; (*in street*) camelot *m*; **drug p.** revendeur, -euse *mf* de drogues.

pedestal ['pedɪst(ə)l] *n Archit & Fig* piédestal *m*.

pedestrian [pə'destrɪən] *n* piéton *m*; **p. crossing** passage *m* pour piétons. ●**pedestrianized** *a* **p. street** rue *f* piétonne *ou* piétonnière.

pediatrician [pi:dɪə'trɪʃ(ə)n] *n* (*doctor*) pédiatre *m*.

pedigree ['pedɪgri:] *n* (*of dog etc*) pedigree *m*; (*of person*) ascendance *f* ▮ *a* (*dog etc*) de race.

pedlar ['pedlər] *n* (*door-to-door*) colporteur, -euse *mf*; (*in street*) camelot *m*.

pee [pi:] *n* **to go for a p.** *Fam* faire pipi.

peek [pi:k] *n* **to have a p.** = **to peek** ▮ *vi* jeter un petit coup d'œil (**at** à).

peel [pi:l] *n* (*of vegetable, fruit*) épluchure(s) *f(pl)*; **a piece of p., some p.** une épluchure ▮ *vt* (*apple, potato etc*) éplucher; **to p. off** (*label etc*) décoller ▮ *vi* (*of* *sunburnt skin*) peler; (*of paint*) s'écailler. ●**—ings** *npl* éplucherure *fpl*. ●**peeler** *n* (*potato*) **p.** éplucheur *m*.

peep [piːp] 1 *n* to have a **p.** = to peep ‖ *vi* jeter un petit coup *m* d'œil; to **p.** out se montrer; **peeping Tom** voyeur, -euse *mf*. 2 *vi* (*of bird*) pépier. ●**peephole** *n* judas *m*.

peer [pɪər] 1 *n* (*equal*) pair *m*, égal, -ale *mf*; (*noble*) pair *m*. 2 *vi* to **p.** (at) regarder attentivement (*comme pour mieux voir*). ●**peerage** *n* (*rank*) pairie *f*.

peeved [piːvd] *a* Fam irrité.

peevish ['piːvɪʃ] *a* grincheux, irritable.

peg [peg] *n* (*for coat, hat*) patère *f*; (*for clothes*) pince *f* (à linge); (*for tent*) piquet *m*; (*wooden*) cheville *f*; to buy sth off the **p.** acheter qch en prêt-à-porter.

pejorative [pɪ'dʒɒrətɪv] *a* péjoratif.

Peking [piː'kɪŋ] *n* Pékin *m* or *f*.

pelican ['pelɪk(ə)n] *n* (*bird*) pélican *m*; **p. crossing** passage *m* pour piétons (*avec feux à déclenchement manuel*).

pellet ['pelɪt] *n* (*of paper*) boulette *f*; (*for gun*) grain *m* de plomb *m*.

pelt [pelt] 1 *vi* it's pelting (down) (*raining*) il pleut à verse. 2 *vt* to **p.** s.o. with (*stones etc*) bombarder qn de. 3 *n* (*skin*) peau *f*.

pelvis ['pelvɪs] *n* Anat bassin *m*.

pen [pen] 1 *n* (*fountain pen*) stylo *m* (à plume); (*ballpoint*) stylo *m* (à bille); (*dipped in ink*) porte-plume *m inv*; **p. friend, p. pal** correspondant, -ante *mf*; **p. name** pseudonyme *m*; **p. nib** (bec *m* de) plume *f* ‖ *vt* (**-nn-**) (*write*) écrire. 2 *n* (*enclosure for baby, sheep or cattle*) parc *m*.

penal ['piːn(ə)l] *a* (*code etc*) pénal; (*colony*) pénitentiaire. ●**penalize** *vt* (*punish*) Sp pénaliser (**for** pour); (*handicap*) désavantager.

penalty ['pen(ə)ltɪ] *n* (*prison sentence*) peine *f*; (*fine*) amende *f*; Sp pénalisation *f*; Fb penalty *m*; Rugby pénalité *f*.

pence [pens] *npl see* **penny.**

pencil ['pens(ə)l] *n* crayon *m*; in **p.** au

crayon; **p. case** trousse *f*; **p. sharpener** taille-crayon(s) *m inv* ‖ *vt* (**-ll-**, Am **-l-**) to **p. in** (*note down*) noter provisoirement.

pendant ['pendənt] *n* (*around neck*) pendentif *m*.

pending ['pendɪŋ] 1 *a* (*matter*) en suspens. 2 *prep* (*until*) en attendant.

pendulum ['pendjʊləm] *n* (*of clock*) balancier *m*.

penetrat/e ['penɪtreɪt] *vt* (*substance*) pénétrer; (*secret*) découvrir; (*forest, group*) pénétrer dans. ●**—ing** *a* (*mind etc*) pénétrant.

penguin ['peŋgwɪn] *n* manchot *m*.

penicillin [penɪ'sɪlɪn] *n* pénicilline *f*.

peninsula [pə'nɪnsjʊlə] *n* presqu'île *f*, péninsule *f*.

penis ['piːnɪs] *n* pénis *m*.

penitent ['penɪtənt] *a* repentant.

penitentiary [penɪ'tenʃərɪ] *n* Am prison *f* (centrale).

penknife ['pennaɪf] *n* (*pl* **-knives**) canif *m*.

pennant ['penənt] *n* (*flag*) fanion *m*.

penny ['penɪ] *n* 1 (*pl* **pennies**) (*coin*) penny *m*; Am Can cent *m*; I don't have a **p.** Fig je n'ai pas le or un sou. 2 (*pl* **pence** [pens]) (*value, currency*) penny *m*. ●**penniless** *a* sans le sou.

pension ['penʃ(ə)n] *n* pension *f*; (*retirement*) **p.** retraite *f*; to retire on a **p.** toucher une retraite; **p. scheme** régime *m* de retraite ‖ *vt* to **p.** s.o. off mettre qn à la retraite. ●**—er** *n* pensionné, -ée *mf*; (*on retirement pension*) retraité, -ée *mf*; old age **p.** retraité, -ée *mf*.

Pentagon ['pentəgən] *n* the P. Am Pol le Pentagone.

Pentecost ['pentɪkɒst] *n* (*Whitsun*) Am Pentecôte *f*.

penthouse ['penthaʊs] *n* appartement *m* de luxe (*construit sur le toit d'un immeuble*).

pent-up ['pent'ʌp] *a* (*feelings*) refoulé.

penultimate [pɪ'nʌltɪmət] *a* avant-dernier.

people ['piːp(ə)l] *npl* (*in general*) gens *mpl or fpl*; (*specific persons*) personnes *fpl*; **the p.** (*citizens*) le peuple; **old p.** les personnes *fpl* âgées; **old people's home** hospice *m* de vieillards; (*private*) maison *f* de retraite; **two p.** deux personnes; **English p.** les Anglais *mpl*; **p. think that…** on pense que… ∥ *n* (*nation*) peuple *m*.

pep [pep] *n Fam* dynamisme; **p. talk** petit laïus d'encouragement ∥ *vt* (**-pp-**) **to p. s.o. up** (*perk up*) ragaillardir qn.

pepper ['pepər] *n* poivre *m*; (*vegetable*) poivron *m* ∥ *vt* poivrer. ● **pepperpot** *n* poivrière *f*.

peppermint ['pepəmint] *n* (*flavour*) menthe *f*; (*sweet, Am candy*) bonbon *m* à la menthe.

per [pɜːr] *prep* par; **p. annum** par an; **p. head, p. person** par personne; **p. cent** pour cent; **50 pence p. kilo** 50 pence le kilo; **40 km p. hour** 40 km à l'heure. ● **per'centage** *n* pourcentage *m*.

perceive [pə'siːv] *vt* (*see, hear*) percevoir; (*notice*) remarquer (**that** que). ● **perception** [-ʃ(ə)n] *n* perception *f* (of de); (*intuition*) intuition *f*. ● **perceptive** *a* (*person*) perspicace; (*study, remark*) pénétrant.

perch [pɜːtʃ] **1** *n* (*for bird*) perchoir *m* ∥ *vi* (*of bird*) se percher (**on** sur); (*of person*) *Fig* se percher ∥ *vt* (*put*) percher. **2** *n* (*fish*) perche *f*.

percolator ['pɜːkəleɪtər] *n* cafetière *f*; (*in café or restaurant*) percolateur *m*.

perennial [pə'renɪəl] **1** *a* (*complaint etc*) perpétuel. **2** *a* (*plant*) vivace ∥ *n* plante *f* vivace.

perfect ['pɜːfɪkt] *a* parfait ∥ *a & n* **p.** (**tense**) *Gram* parfait *m* ∥ [pə'fekt] *vt* (*piece of work*) parachever; (*technique*) mettre au point; (*one's French etc*) parfaire ses connaissances en. ● **'perfectly** *adv* parfaitement.

perfection [pə'fekʃ(ə)n] *n* perfection *f*; **to p.** à la perfection. ● **perfectionist** *n* perfectionniste *m*.

perforate ['pɜːfəreɪt] *vt* perforer. ● **perforation** [-'reɪʃ(ə)n] *n* perforation *f*.

perform [pə'fɔːm] *vt* (*task, miracle*)

accomplir; (*one's duty, a function*) remplir; (*surgical operation*) pratiquer (**on** sur); (*a play, piece of music*) jouer ∥ *vi* (*act, play*) jouer; (*sing*) chanter; (*dance*) danser; (*of circus animal*) faire un numéro; (*of machine, vehicle*) fonctionner; (*in one's job*) réussir.

performance [pə'fɔːməns] *n* **1** (*show*) (*in theatre*) représentation *f*, séance *f*; (*in concert hall, cinema, Am movie theater*) séance *f*. **2** (*of actor, musician etc*) interprétation *f*; (*of athlete, machine etc*) performance *f*; (*in job, of company*) performances *fpl*; (*fuss*) *Fam* histoire(s) *f(pl)*.

performer [pə'fɔːmər] *n* (*entertainer*) artiste *mf*.

perfume ['pɜːfjuːm] *n* parfum *m*.

perhaps [pə'hæps] *adv* peut-être; **p. not** peut-être que non.

peril ['perɪl] *n* péril *m*; **at your p.** à vos risques et péril. ● **perilous** *a* périlleux.

period ['pɪərɪəd] **1** *n* période *f*; (*historical*) époque *f*; (*time limit*) délai *m*; (*lesson*) *Sch* leçon *f*; (*full stop*) *Am Gram* point *m*; **in the p. of a month** l'espace d'un mois; **I refuse, p.!** *Am* je refuse, un point c'est tout! ∥ *a* (*furniture*) d'époque; (*costume*) de l'époque. **2** *n* (*monthly*) **period(s)** (*of woman*) règles *fpl*.

periodic [pɪərɪ'ɒdɪk] *a* périodique. ● **periodical** *n* (*magazine*) périodique *m*.

peripheral [pə'rɪfər(ə)l] *a* (*question*) sans rapport direct (**to** avec); (*region etc*) & *Comptr* périphérique ∥ *npl* **peripherals** *Comptr* périphériques *mpl*.

periscope ['perɪskəʊp] *n* périscope *m*.

perish ['perɪʃ] *vi* (*die*) périr; (*of food, substance*) se détériorer. ●**—ing** (*cold, weather*) *Fam* glacial. ● **perishable** *a* (*food*) périssable ∥ *npl* **perishables** denrées *fpl* périssables.

perjury ['pɜːdʒərɪ] *n* parjure *m*; **to commit p.** se parjurer.

perk [pɜːk] **1** *vi* **to p. up** (*become livelier*) reprendre du poil de la bête ∥ *vt* **to p. s.o. up** remonter qn. **2** *n* (*in job*) avantage *m* en nature. ● **perky** *a* (**-ier,** **-iest**) (*cheerful*) guilleret.

perm [pɜːm] *n* (*of hair*) permanente *f* ▮ *vt* **to have one's hair permed** se faire faire une permanente.

permanent ['pɜːmənənt] *a* permanent; (*address*) fixe. ●**—ly** *adv* à titre permanent.

permeate ['pɜːmɪeɪt] *vt* **to p. (through)** **sth** (*of liquid etc*) pénétrer qch.

permissible [pə'mɪsəb(ə)l] *a* permis.

permission [pə'mɪʃ(ə)n] *n* permission *f* (**to do** de faire); **to ask/give p.** demander/donner la permission.

permissive [pə'mɪsɪv] *a* (trop) tolérant, laxiste.

permit [pə'mɪt] *vt* (**-tt-**) permettre (**s.o. to** **do** à qn de faire); **weather permitting** si le temps le permet ▮ ['pɜːmɪt] *n* permis *m*; (*entrance pass*) laissez-passer *m* inv.

perpendicular [pɜːpən'dɪkjʊlər] *a* & *n* perpendiculaire (*f*).

perpetrate ['pɜːpɪtreɪt] *vt* (*crime*) commettre, perpétrer. ● **perpetrator** *n* auteur *m*.

perpetual [pə'petʃʊəl] *a* perpétuel. ● **perpetuate** *vt* perpétuer.

perplex [pə'pleks] *vt* rendre perplexe, dérouter. ●**—ed** *a* perplexe. ●**—ing** *a* déroutant.

persecute ['pɜːsɪkjuːt] *vt* persécuter. ● **persecution** [-'kjuːʃ(ə)n] *n* persécution *f*.

persever/e [pɜːsɪ'vɪər] *vi* persévérer (**in** dans). ●**—ing** *a* (*persistent*) persévérant. ● **perseverance** *n* persévérance *f*.

Persian ['pɜːʃ(ə)n, 'pɜːʒ(ə)n] *a* (*language, cat etc*) persan; **the P. Gulf** le golfe Persique ▮ *n* (*language*) persan *m*.

persist [pə'sɪst] *vi* persister (**in doing** à faire, **in sth** dans qch). ● **persistence** *n* persistance *f*. ● **persistent** *a* (*person*) obstiné; (*fever etc*) persistant; (*noise etc*) continuel.

person ['pɜːs(ə)n] *n* personne *f*; **in p.** en personne.

personal ['pɜːsən(ə)l] *a* personnel; (*application*) en personne; (*friend, hygiene*)

intime; (*life*) privé; (*indiscreet*) indiscret; **p. assistant** secrétaire *m* particulier, secrétaire *f* particulière; **p.** **computer** ordinateur *m* personnel; **p.** **stereo** baladeur *m*. ●**—ly** *adv* personnellement; (*in person*) en personne.

personality [pɜːsə'nælətɪ] *n* (*character, famous person*) personnalité *f*; **a tele-** **vision p.** une vedette de la télévision.

personify [pə'sɒnɪfaɪ] *vt* personnifier.

personnel [pɜːsə'nel] *n* (*staff*) personnel *m*.

perspective [pə'spektɪv] *n* (*artistic &* *viewpoint*) perspective *f*; **in p.** *Fig* sous son vrai jour.

Perspex ['pɜːspeks] *n* Plexiglas® *m*.

perspire [pə'spaɪər] *vi* transpirer. ● **per-** **spiration** [pɜːspə'reɪʃ(ə)n] *n* transpiration *f*.

persuade [pə'sweɪd] *vt* persuader (**s.o.** **to do** qn de faire). ● **persuasion** [-ʒ(ə)n] *n* persuasion *f*; (*creed*) religion *f*. ● **per-** **suasive** *a* (*person, argument etc*) persuasif.

pert [pɜːt] *a* (*impertinent*) impertinent; (*lively*) plein d'entrain.

pertain [pə'teɪn] *vi* **to p. to** (*relate*) se rapporter à; (*belong*) appartenir à.

pertinent ['pɜːtɪnənt] *a* pertinent.

perturb [pə'tɜːb] *vt* troubler, perturber.

Peru [pə'ruː] *n* Pérou *m*. ● **Peruvian** *a* & *n* péruvien, -ienne (*mf*).

peruse [pə'ruːz] *vt* lire (attentivement); (*skim through*) parcourir.

pervade [pə'veɪd] *vt* se répandre dans. ● **pervasive** *a* qui se répand partout.

perverse [pə'vɜːs] *a* (*awkward*) contrariant; (*obstinate*) entêté; (*wicked*) pervers. ● **perversion** *n* [-ʃ(ə)n, *Am* -ʒ(ə)n] perversion *f*.

pervert [pə'vɜːt] *vt* pervertir; (*mind*) corrompre; (*truth*) travestir ▮ ['pɜːvɜːt] *n* (**sexual**) **p.** détraqué, -ée *mf*, pervers, -erse *mf*.

pesky ['peskɪ] *a* (**-ier, -est**) *Am Fam* embêtant.

pessimism ['pesɪmɪz(ə)m] *n* pessimisme *m*. ● **pessimist** *n* pessimiste *mf*. ● **pes-**

si'mistic a pessimiste.

pest [pest] n animal m or insecte m nuisible; (person) casse-pieds mf inv, peste f.

pester ['pestər] vt harceler (**with questions de** questions); **to p. s.o. to do sth/ for sth** harceler qn pour qu'il fasse qch/ jusqu'à ce qu'il donne qch.

pesticide ['pestisaid] n pesticide m.

pet [pet] **1** n animal m (domestique); (favourite person) chouchou, -oute mf; **yes p.** Fam oui mon chou; **to have** or **keep a p.** avoir un animal chez soi ∎ a (dog, cat etc) domestique; (favourite) favori; **the p. shop** magasin m d'animaux; **p. hate** bête f noire.

2 vt (-tt-) (fondle) caresser; (sexually) Fam peloter ∎ vi Fam se peloter.

petal ['pet(ə)l] n pétale m.

peter ['piːtər] vi **to p. out** (dry up) tarir; (die out) mourir; (disappear) disparaître.

petite [pə'tiːt] a (woman) menue.

petition [pə'tɪʃ(ə)n] n (signatures) pétition f; (request) Jur requête f.

petrified ['petrifaid] a (frightened) pétrifié de terreur.

petrol ['petrəl] n essence f; **p. can** bidon m à essence; **p. station** station-service f; **p. tank** réservoir m (d'essence).

petroleum [pə'trəuliəm] n pétrole m.

petticoat ['petikəut] n jupon m.

petty ['peti] a (-ier, -iest) (minor) petit; (trivial) insignifiant; (mean) mesquin; **p. cash** Com petite caisse f, menue monnaie f.

petulant ['petjulənt] a irritable.

pew [pjuː] n banc m d'église; **take a p.!** Hum assieds-toi!

pewter ['pjuːtər] n étain m.

phallic ['fælik] a phallique.

phantom ['fæntəm] n fantôme m.

pharmacy ['fɑːməsi] n pharmacie f. ●**pharmacist** n pharmacien, -ienne mf.

pharyngitis [færin'dʒaitəs] n Med pharyngite f.

phase [feiz] n (stage) phase f ∎ vt **to p. sth in/out** introduire/supprimer qch

progressivement.

PhD [piːeitʃ'diː] n abbr (Doctor of Philosophy) (university degree) doctorat m.

pheasant ['fezənt] n (bird) faisan m.

phenomenon, pl -ena [fi'nɒminən, -inə] n phénomène m. ●**phenomenal** a phénoménal.

philanthropist [fi'lænθrəpist] n philanthrope mf.

philately [fi'lætəli] n. philatélie. ●**philatelist** n philatéliste mf.

Philippines ['filipiːnz] npl **the P.** les Philippines fpl.

philistine ['filistain] n béotien, -ienne mf.

philosophy [fi'lɒsəfi] n philosophie f. ●**philosopher** n philosophe mf. ●**philo'sophical** a philosophique; (resigned) Fig philosophe.

phlegm [flem] n (in throat) glaires fpl.

phobia ['fəubiə] n phobie f.

phone [fəun] n téléphone m; **on the p.** (speaking here) au téléphone; (at other end) au bout du fil; **to be on the p.** (as subscriber) avoir le téléphone; **p. call** coup m de fil or de téléphone; **to make a p. call** téléphoner (**to** à); **p. book** annuaire m; **p. booth**, **p. box** cabine f téléphonique; **p. number** numéro m de téléphone.

∎ vt **to p. s.o. (up)** téléphoner à qn; **to p. s.o. back** rappeler qn.

∎ vi **to p. (up)** téléphoner; **to p. back** rappeler.

phonetic [fə'netik] a phonétique.

phoney ['fəuni] a (-ier, -iest) Fam (jewels, writer etc) faux (f fausse); (company, excuse) bidon inv ∎ n Fam (impostor) imposteur m; (insincere person) faux-jeton m.

phonograph ['fəunəgræf] n Am électrophone m.

photo ['fəutəu] n (pl -os) photo f; **to take a p. of** prendre une photo de; **to have one's p. taken** se faire prendre en photo.

photocopy ['fəutəukɒpi] n photocopie f ∎ vt photocopier. ●**photocopier** n (machine) photocopieuse f.

photogenic [fəʊtəʊ'dʒenɪk] a photogénique.

photograph ['fəʊtəʊgræf] n photographie f ▮ vt photographier. ● **photographer** [fə'tɒgrəfər] n photographe mf. ● **photo'graphic** a photographique. ● **photography** [fə'tɒgrəfɪ] n (activity) photographie f.

photostat® ['fəʊtəʊstæt] n = **photocopy**.

phrase [freɪz] n (saying) expression f; (idiom) & Gram locution f ▮ vt (express) exprimer. ● **phrasebook** n (for tourists) manuel m de conversation.

Phys Ed [fɪz'ed] n abbr (physical education) Am EPS f.

physical ['fɪzɪk(ə)l] a physique; (object, world) matériel; **p. examination** examen m médical; **p. education** éducation f physique; ● **physically** adv physiquement; **p. impossible** matériellement impossible.

physician [fɪ'zɪʃ(ə)n] n médecin m.

physics ['fɪzɪks] n (science) physique f. ● **physicist** n physicien, -ienne mf.

physiology [fɪzɪ'ɒlədʒɪ] n physiologie f.

physiotherapy [fɪzɪəʊ'θerəpɪ] n kinésithérapie f. ● **physiotherapist** n kinésithérapeute mf.

physique [fɪ'ziːk] n (appearance) physique m; (constitution) constitution f.

piano [pɪ'ænəʊ] n (pl -os) piano m. ● **pianist** ['pɪənɪst] n pianiste mf.

pick [pɪk] n (choice) choix m; **to take one's p.** faire son choix, choisir; **the p. of** (best) le meilleur de.
▮ vt (choose) choisir; (flower, fruit etc) cueillir; (hole) faire (**in** dans); (pimple etc) gratter; (lock) crocheter; **to p. one's nose** se mettre les doigts dans le nez; **to p. a fight** chercher la bagarre (**with** avec); **to p. holes in** Fig relever les défauts de.
pick at vt **to p. at one's food** picorer ▮ **pick off** vt (remove) enlever; (shoot) abattre un à un ▮ **to pick on** vt (nag, blame) s'en prendre à (qn) ▮ **to pick out** vt (choose) choisir; (identify) reconnaître ▮ **to pick up** vt (sth dropped) ramasser;

(fallen person or chair) relever; (person into air, weight) soulever; (a cold) attraper; (habit, accent, speed) prendre; (fetch, collect) (passer) prendre; (find) trouver; (programme) Rad capter; (survivor) recueillir; (arrest) arrêter; (learn) apprendre ▮ vi (improve) s'améliorer; (of business, trade) reprendre; (of patient) aller mieux; (resume) continuer.

pick(axe) (Am **-ax**) ['pɪk(æks)] n (tool) pioche f; **ice pick** pic m à glace.

picket ['pɪkɪt] n (striker) gréviste mf; **p. (line)** piquet m (de grève) ▮ vt (factory) installer des piquets de grève aux portes de.

pickle ['pɪk(ə)l] **1** npl **pickles** (vegetables) pickles mpl; Am concombres mpl, cornichons mpl ▮ vt mariner; **pickled onion/etc** oignon m/etc au vinaigre. **2** n **in a p.** (trouble) Fam dans le pétrin.

pick-me-up ['pɪkmiːʌp] n (drink) Fam remontant m.

pickpocket ['pɪkpɒkɪt] n pickpocket m.

pick-up ['pɪkʌp] n **1 p.-up (truck)** pick-up m. **2 p.-up point** (for bus passengers) point m de ramassage.

picky ['pɪkɪ] a (-ier, -iest) (choosey) Am difficile.

picnic ['pɪknɪk] n pique-nique m; **p. basket** or **hamper** panier m à pique-nique ▮ vi (-ck-) pique-niquer.

picture ['pɪktʃər] **1** n image f; (painting) tableau m, peinture f; (drawing) dessin m; (photo) photo f; (film) film m; **the pictures** Fam le cinéma; **to put s.o. in the p.** Fig mettre qn au courant; **p. frame** cadre m. **2** vt (imagine) s'imaginer (**that** que).

picturesque [pɪktʃə'resk] a pittoresque.

pie [paɪ] n (open) tarte f; (with pastry on top) tourte f; **meat p.** pâté m en croûte; **cottage p.** hachis m Parmentier.

piece [piːs] n morceau m; (of fabric, machine, in game) pièce f; (coin) pièce f; **bits and pieces** des petites choses; **in pieces** en morceaux; **to smash to pieces** briser en morceaux; **to take to pieces**

(*machine*) démonter; **to come to pieces** se démonter; **a p. of news/advice/***etc* une nouvelle/un conseil/*etc*; **in one p.** (*object*) intact; (*person*) indemne.
‖ *vt* **to p. together** (*facts*) reconstituer. ● **piecemeal** *adv* petit à petit ‖ *a* (*unsystematic*) peu méthodique.

pier [pɪər] *n* (*for walking, with entertainments*) jetée *f*.

pierc/e [pɪəs] *vt* percer (*qch*); (*of cold, bullet*) transpercer (*qn*). ● **-ing** *a* (*voice etc*) perçant; (*wind etc*) glacial.

pig [pɪg] *n* cochon *m*, porc *m*; (*glutton*) goinfre *m*. ● **piggy** *a* (*greedy*) *Fam* goinfre.

pigeon [ˈpɪdʒɪn] *n* pigeon *m*. ● **pigeon-hole** *n* casier *m* ‖ *vt* classer.

piggyback [ˈpɪgɪbæk] *n* **to give s.o. a p.** porter qn sur le dos.

piggybank [ˈpɪgɪbæŋk] *n* tirelire *f* (*en forme de cochon*).

pigheaded [pɪgˈhedɪd] *a* obstiné.

pigment [ˈpɪgmənt] *n* pigment *m*.

pigsty [ˈpɪgstaɪ] *n* porcherie *f*.

pigtail [ˈpɪgteɪl] *n* (*hair*) natte *f*.

pike [paɪk] *n* (*fish*) brochet *m*.

pilchard [ˈpɪltʃəd] *n* pilchard *m* (*grosse sardine*).

pile¹ [paɪl] *n* tas *m*; (*neatly arranged*) pile *f*; (*fortune*) *Fam* fortune *f*; **piles of** *Fam* beaucoup de ‖ *vt* **to p. (up)** entasser; (*neatly*) empiler ‖ *vi* **to p. into** (*crowd into*) s'entasser dans; **to p. up** (*accumulate*) s'accumuler. ● **p.-up** *n* *Aut* carambolage *m*.

pile² [paɪl] *n* (*of carpet*) poils *mpl*.

piles [paɪlz] *npl* *Med* hémorroïdes *fpl*.

pilfer [ˈpɪlfər] *vt* (*steal*) chaparder (**from** s.o. à qn). ● **-ing** *n* chapardage *n*.

pilgrim [ˈpɪlgrɪm] *n* pèlerin *m*. ● **pilgrimage** *n* pèlerinage *n*.

pill [pɪl] *n* pilule *f*; **to be on the p.** prendre la pilule; **to go on/off the p.** se mettre à/ arrêter la pilule.

pillage [ˈpɪlɪdʒ] *vti* piller ‖ *n* pillage *m*.

pillar [ˈpɪlər] *n* pilier *m*. ● **p.-box** *n* boîte *f* aux *or* à lettres (*située sur le trottoir*).

pillion [ˈpɪljən] *adv* **to ride p.** (*on motorbike*) monter derrière.

pillow [ˈpɪləʊ] *n* oreiller *m*. ● **pillowcase** *n* taie *f* d'oreiller.

pilot [ˈpaɪlət] **1** *n* (*of aircraft*) pilote *m* ‖ *vt* piloter ‖ *a* **p. light** (*on appliance*) voyant *m*. **2** *a* (*experimental*) (-)pilote; **p. scheme** projet(-)pilote *m*.

pimento [pɪˈmentəʊ] *n* (*pl -os*) piment *m*.

pimple [ˈpɪmp(ə)l] *n* bouton *m*.

pin [pɪn] *n* épingle *f*; (*drawing pin*) punaise *f*; *Tech* goupille *f*; **to have pins and needles** *Fam* avoir des fourmis (**in** dans); **p. money** argent *m* de poche.
‖ *vt* (**-nn-**) **to p. (on)** (*attach*) épingler (**to** sur, à); (*to wall*) punaiser (**to, on** à); **to p. one's hopes on** mettre tous ses espoirs dans; **to p. on** (**to**) s.o. (*crime*) accuser qn de; **to p. sth down** immobiliser qch; (*fix*) fixer qch; **to p. s.o. down** *Fig* forcer qn à préciser ses idées; **to p. up** (*notice*) punaiser, afficher.

PIN [pɪn] *n abbr* (*personal identification number*) **PIN number** code *m* confidentiel.

pinafore [ˈpɪnəfɔːr] *n* (*apron*) tablier *m*; (*dress*) robe *f* chasuble.

pinball [ˈpɪnbɔːl] *n* flipper *m*; **p. machine** flipper *m*.

pincers [ˈpɪnsəz] *npl* (*tool*) tenailles *fpl*.

pinch [pɪntʃ] **1** *n* (*mark*) pinçon *m*; (*of salt*) pincée *f*; **to give s.o. a p.** pincer qn; **at a p.,** *Am* **in a p.** (*if necessary*) au besoin ‖ *vt* pincer. **2** *vt* (*steal*) *Fam* piquer (**from** à); (*arrest*) pincer.

pincushion [ˈpɪnkʊʃ(ə)n] *n* pelote *f* (à épingles).

pine [paɪn] **1** *n* (*tree, wood*) pin *m*; **p. forest** pinède *f*. **2** *vi* **to p. for** désirer vivement (retrouver).

pineapple [ˈpaɪnæp(ə)l] *n* ananas *m*.

ping-pong [ˈpɪŋpɒŋ] *n* ping-pong *m*.

pink [pɪŋk] *a* & *n* (*colour*) rose (*m*).

pinkie [ˈpɪŋkɪ] *n* *Am* petit doigt *m*.

pinnacle [ˈpɪnək(ə)l] *n* *Fig* apogée *n*.

pinpoint [ˈpɪnpɔɪnt] *vt* (*locate*) repérer; (*define*) définir.

pinstripe [ˈpɪnstraɪp] *a* (*suit*) rayé.

pint [paɪnt] n pinte f (Br = 0,57 litre, Am = 0,47 litre); **a p. of beer** = un demi.

pinup ['pɪnʌp] n (girl) pin-up f inv.

pioneer [paɪə'nɪər] n pionnier, -ière mf.

pious ['paɪəs] a (person, deed) pieux.

pip [pɪp] **1** n (of fruit) pépin m. **2** npl the **pips** (sound) Rad etc le top.

pipe [paɪp] **1** n tuyau m; (of smoker) pipe f; Mus pipeau m; **the pipes** (bagpipes) la cornemuse; **to smoke a p.** fumer la pipe; **p. cleaner** cure-pipe m; **p. dream** chimère f. **2** vi **to p. down** (shut up) Fam la boucler. ● **piping** n (pipes) tuyaux mpl; **length of p.** tuyau m ▌ adv **it's p. hot** (soup etc) c'est très chaud.

pipeline ['paɪplaɪn] n pipeline m; **it's in the p.** Fig c'est en route.

pirate ['paɪərət] n pirate m ▌ a (radio, ship) pirate. ● **piracy** n piraterie f. ● **pirated** a (book, CD etc) pirate.

Pisces ['paɪsiːz] npl (sign) les Poissons mpl.

pistachio [pɪ'stæʃɪəʊ] n (pl -os) (fruit, flavour) pistache f.

pistol ['pɪstəl] n pistolet m.

piston ['pɪst(ə)n] n Aut piston m.

pit [pɪt] **1** n (hole) trou m; (coalmine) mine f; (quarry) carrière f; (of stomach) creux m; Th orchestre. **2** vt (-tt-) **to p. one's wits against** se mesurer à. **3** n (stone of fruit) Am noyau m; (smaller) pépin m.

pitch¹ [pɪtʃ] **1** n Fb etc terrain m. **2** n (degree) degré m; (of voice) hauteur f; Mus ton m. **3** vt (tent) dresser; (camp) établir; (ball) lancer; **a pitched battle** Mil une bataille rangée; Fig une belle bagarre. **4** vi (of ship) tanguer. **5** vi **to p. in** (cooperate) Fam se mettre de la partie.

pitch² [pɪtʃ] n (tar) poix f. ● **p.-'black** or **p.-'dark** a noir comme dans un four.

pitcher ['pɪtʃər] n cruche f.

pitchfork ['pɪtʃfɔːk] n fourche f (à foin).

pitfall ['pɪtfɔːl] n (trap) piège m.

pith [pɪθ] n (of orange) peau f blanche.

pitiful ['pɪtɪfəl] a pitoyable. ● **pitiless** a impitoyable.

pitta ['piːtə] adj **p.** bread pitta m.

pittance ['pɪtəns] n (income) revenu m or salaire m misérable.

pitted ['pɪtɪd] a (face) grêlé.

pitter-patter ['pɪtəpætər] n = **patter 1.**

pity ['pɪtɪ] n pitié f; **(what) a p.!** (quel) dommage!; **it's a p.** c'est or il est dommage (that que (+ sub), **to do de** faire); **to take p. on s.o.** avoir pitié de qn ▌ vt plaindre.

pivot ['pɪvət] n pivot m ▌ vi pivoter.

pizza ['piːtsə] n pizza f.

placard ['plækɑːd] n (notice) affiche f.

placate [plə'keɪt, Am 'pleɪkeɪt] vt calmer.

place [pleɪs] n endroit m, lieu m; (house) maison f; (seat, position, rank) place f; **in the first p.** en premier lieu; **to take p.** avoir lieu; **p. of work** lieu m de travail; **market p.** place f du marché; Fin marché m; **at my p., to my p.** (house) chez moi; **some p.** (somewhere) Am quelque part; **no p.** (nowhere) Am nulle part; **all over the p.** partout; **to lose one's p.** perdre sa place; (in book) perdre sa page; **p. setting** couvert m; **to set** or **lay three places** mettre trois couverts; **to take the p. of** remplacer; **in p. of** à la place de; **out of p.** (remark) déplacé; (object) pas à sa place; **p. mat** set m (de table).

▌ vt (put, invest) & Sp placer; (an order) passer (with s.o. à qn); **to p. s.o.** (identify) remettre qn.

placid ['plæsɪd] a placide.

plague [pleɪg] **1** n (disease) peste f; (nuisance) Fam plaie f. **2** vt (pester) harceler (with de).

plaice [pleɪs] n (fish) carrelet m.

plaid [plæd] n (fabric) tissu m écossais.

plain¹ [pleɪn] a (-er, -est) (clear, obvious) clair; (simple) simple; (madness) pur; (without a pattern) uni; (woman, man) sans beauté; (sheer) pur; **in p. clothes** en civil; **to make it p. to s.o. that** faire comprendre à qn que ▌ adv (tired etc) tout bonnement. ● **—ly** adv clairement; (frankly) franchement.

plain² [pleɪn] n Geog plaine f.

plaintiff ['pleɪntɪf] n Jur plaignant, -ante mf.

plait [plæt] n tresse f ‖ vt tresser.

plan [plæn] n projet m; (elaborate) plan m; (economic, of house, book etc) plan m; **the best p. would be to...** le mieux serait de...; **according to p.** comme prévu; **to have no plans** (be free) n'avoir rien de prévu; **master p.** stratégie f or plan m d'ensemble.
‖ vt (-nn-) (foresee) prévoir, projeter; (organize) organiser; (prepare) préparer; (design) concevoir; **to p. to do** or **on doing** avoir l'intention de faire; **as planned** comme prévu.
‖ vi faire des projets; **to p. for** (rain, disaster) prévoir.

plane [pleɪn] 1 n (aircraft) avion m. 2 n (tool) rabot m ‖ vt raboter. 3 n **p. (tree)** platane m. 4 n (level) & Fig plan m.

planet ['plænɪt] n planète f. ● **planetary** a planétaire.

plank [plæŋk] n planche f.

planner ['plænər] n **(town) p.** urbaniste mf.

planning ['plænɪŋ] n (economic, industrial, commercial) planification f; **family p.** planning m familial.

plant [plɑ:nt] 1 n plante f; **house p.** plante f verte ‖ vt (flower, field) planter (with en, de); (bomb) Fig poser; **to p. sth on s.o.** cacher qch sur qn. 2 n (factory) usine f; (machinery) matériel m. ● **plantation** [-'teɪʃ(ə)n] n (trees etc) plantation f.

plaque [plæk] n (commemorative plate) plaque f.

plaster ['plɑ:stər] n plâtre m; (sticking) **p.** sparadrap m; **p. of Paris** plâtre m à mouler; **in p.** (arm etc) dans le plâtre; **p. cast** Med plâtre m ‖ vt plâtrer; **to p. down** (hair) plaquer; **to p. with** (cover) couvrir de. ●—**ed** a (drunk) Fam bourré.

plastic ['plæstɪk] a (object) en plastique; (substance) plastique; **p. surgery** chirurgie f esthétique ‖ n plastique m.

plasticine® ['plæstɪsi:n] n pâte f à modeler.

plate [pleɪt] n (dish) assiette f; (metal sheet on door etc) plaque f; (book illustration) gravure f; **to have a lot on one's p.** (work) avoir du pain sur la planche; **p. glass** verre m à vitre. ● **plateful** n assiettée f.

plateau ['plætəʊ] n (pl -s or -x) Geog plateau m.

platform ['plætfɔ:m] n (at train station) quai m; (on bus etc) plate-forme f; (for speaker etc) estrade f.

platinum ['plætɪnəm] n (metal) platine m ‖ a **p.** or **p.-blond(e) hair** cheveux mpl platinés.

platonic [plə'tɒnɪk] a (love etc) platonique.

platoon [plə'tu:n] n Mil section f.

plausible ['plɔ:zəb(ə)l] a (argument etc) plausible.

play [pleɪ] n Th pièce f (de théâtre); (amusement, looseness) jeu m; **a p. on words** un jeu de mots; **to come into p.** entrer en jeu.
‖ vt (part, tune etc) jouer; (game) jouer à; (instrument) jouer de; (match) disputer (with avec); (team, opponent) jouer contre; (record, compact disc) passer; (radio) faire marcher; **to p. the fool** faire l'idiot; **to p. a part in** sth contribuer à faire/à qch; **to p. it cool** Fam garder son sang-froid.
‖ vi jouer (with avec, at à); (of tape recorder etc) marcher; **what are you playing at?** Fam qu'est-ce que tu fais?
● **play about** or **around** vi jouer, s'amuser ‖ **to play back** vt (tape) réécouter ‖ **to play down** vt (reduce importance of) minimiser ‖ **to play out** vt (scene etc) jouer; **to be played out** (of idea etc) Fam être périmé ‖ **to play up** vi (of child, machine etc) Fam faire des siennes ‖ vt Fam (of child etc) faire enrager (qn); (of bad back etc) tracasser (qn).

play-act ['pleɪækt] vi jouer la comédie.
● **playboy** n playboy m. ● **playground** n Sch cour f de récréation; (with swings etc) terrain m de jeux. ● **playgroup** n =

playschool. ● **playmate** n camarade mf.
● **playpen** n parc m (pour enfants).
● **playroom** n (in house) salle f de jeux.
● **playschool** n garderie f (d'enfants).
● **playtime** n Sch récréation f. ● **playwright** n dramaturge mf.

player ['pleɪər] n (in game, of instrument) joueur, -euse mf; Th acteur m, actrice f; **clarinet/etc** p. joueur, -euse mf de clarinette/etc; **cassette/CD** p. lecteur m de cassettes/de CD.

playful ['pleɪfəl] a enjoué; (child) joueur.

playing ['pleɪɪŋ] n jeu m; p. **card** carte f à jouer; p. **field** terrain m de jeu.

plc [pi:el'si:] abbr (public limited company) SA.

plea [pli:] n (request) appel m; to make a p. of guilty plaider coupable. ● **plead** vi Jur plaider; to p. with s.o. to do implorer qn de faire; to p. for (help etc) implorer ‖ vt Jur plaider; (as excuse) alléguer.

pleasant ['plezənt] a agréable (to avec).
● —**ly** adv agréablement.

pleasantries ['plezəntriz] npl (polite remarks) civilités fpl.

please [pli:z] adv s'il vous plaît, s'il te plaît; p. **do!** bien sûr!, je vous en prie!; '**no smoking p.**' 'prière de ne pas fumer'.
‖ vt to p. s.o. plaire à qn; (satisfy) contenter qn; **hard to p.** difficile (à contenter), exigeant; p. **yourself!** comme tu veux!
‖ vi plaire; **do as you p.** fais comme tu veux; **as much** or **as many as you p.** autant qu'il vous plaira; **as you p.** autant qu'il vous plaira. ● **pleased** a content (**with** de, **that** que (+ sub), to do de faire); p. **to meet you!** enchanté!
● **pleasing** a agréable.

pleasure ['pleʒər] n plaisir m; p. **boat** bateau m de plaisance. ● **pleasurable** a très agréable.

pleat [pli:t] n (in skirt) pli m. ● **pleated** a plissé.

pledge [pledʒ] n (promise) promesse f (to do de faire) ‖ vt promettre (to do de faire).

plenty ['plentɪ] n abondance f; **in** p. en

abondance; p. **of** beaucoup de; **that's** p. c'est assez. ● **plentiful** a abondant.

pliable ['plaɪəb(ə)l] a souple.

pliers ['plaɪəz] npl (tool) pince(s) f(pl).

plight [plaɪt] n situation f critique; (sorry) p. triste situation f.

plimsoll ['plɪmsəʊl] n (chaussure f de) tennis m.

plinth [plɪnθ] n socle m.

plod [plɒd] vi (**-dd-**) to p. (**along**) avancer or travailler laborieusement; to p. **through** (book) lire laborieusement. ● **plodding** a (slow) lent; (step) pesant.

plonk [plɒŋk] 1 vt to p. sth (**down**) (drop) Fam poser qch (bruyamment). 2 n (wine) Sl pinard m.

plot [plɒt] 1 n complot m (**against** contre); (story) intrigue f ‖ vti (**-tt-**) comploter (to do de faire). 2 n p. (**of land**) terrain m; (patch in garden) carré m de terre; **building** p. terrain m à bâtir. 3 vt (**-tt-**) to p. (**out**) (route) déterminer; (diagram) tracer.

plough [plaʊ] (Am **plow**) n charrue f ‖ vt (field) labourer; to p. **money into** mettre beaucoup d'argent dans ‖ vi labourer; to p. **into** (crash into) percuter; to p. **through** (snow) avancer péniblement dans; (fence, wall) défoncer. ● **ploughman** n (pl -**men**) p.'s **lunch** Culin assiette f composée (de crudités et fromage).

plow [plaʊ] Am = **plough**.

ploy [plɔɪ] n stratagème m.

pluck [plʌk] 1 vt (fowl) plumer; (flower) cueillir; (eyebrows) épiler; (string) Mus pincer. 2 n courage m ‖ vt to p. **up** courage s'armer de courage.

plug [plʌg] 1 n (of cotton wool, Am absorbent cotton etc) tampon m; (for sink, bath) bonde f; (wall) p. (for screw) cheville f ‖ vt (**-gg-**) to p. (**up**) (stop up) boucher. 2 n El fiche f, prise f (mâle); (socket) prise f de courant ‖ vt (**-gg-**) to p. **in** brancher. 3 n Aut bougie f. 4 vt (**-gg-**) (book etc) Fam faire du battage publicitaire pour. ● **plughole** n trou m (du lavabo etc).

plum [plʌm] n prune f; **a** p. **job** Fam un

travail en or.

plumb [plʌm] 1 *vt* to p. in (*washing machine*) raccorder. 2 *adv* (*crazy etc*) *Am Fam* complètement.

plumber ['plʌmər] *n* plombier *m*. ● **plumbing** *n* plomberie *f*.

plume [plu:m] *n* (*feather*) plume *f*; (*on hat etc*) plumet *m*.

plummet ['plʌmɪt] *vi* (*of prices*) dégringoler; (*of aircraft etc*) plonger.

plump [plʌmp] 1 *a* (-er, -est) (*person, arm etc*) potelé; (*cheek*) rebondi. 2 *vi* to p. for (*choose*) se décider pour, choisir.

plunder ['plʌndər] *vt* piller ∥*n* (*act*) pillage *m*; (*goods*) butin *m*.

plung/e [plʌndʒ] *vt* plonger (qch) (**into** dans) ∥*vi* (*dive*) plonger (**into** dans); (*fall*) tomber (**from** de); (*rush*) se lancer; **plunging neckline** décolleté *m* plongeant ∥*n* (*dive*) plongeon *m*; (*fall*) chute *f*; **to take the p.** Fig sauter le pas. ● **-er** *n* ventouse *f* (*pour déboucher un tuyau*).

plural ['pluərəl] *a* (*form*) pluriel; (*noun*) au pluriel ∥*n* pluriel *m*; **in the p.** au pluriel.

plus [plʌs] *prep* plus; (*as well as*) en plus de; **two p. two** deux plus deux ∥*a* (*factor*) & *El* positif; **twenty p.** vingt et quelques ∥*n* (*sign*) *Math* (signe *m*) plus *m*; **that's a p.** c'est un plus.

plush [plʌʃ] *a* (-er, -est) somptueux.

ply [plaɪ] 1 *vt* (*a trade*) exercer. 2 *vi* to p. **between** (*travel*) faire la navette entre. 3 *vt* to p. s.o. **with** (*whisky etc*) faire boire continuellement à qn; (*questions*) bombarder qn de.

plywood ['plaɪwʊd] *n* contre-plaqué *m*.

p.m. [pi:'em] *adv* (*afternoon*) de l'après-midi; (*evening*) du soir.

PM [pi:'em] *n abbr* (*Prime Minister*) Premier ministre *m*.

pneumatic [nju:'mætɪk] *a* **p. drill** marteau piqueur *m*.

pneumonia [nju:'məʊnɪə] *n* pneumonie *f*.

poach [pəʊtʃ] 1 *vt* (*egg*) pocher. 2 *vi* (*hunt, steal*) braconner ∥*vt* (*employee*

from rival company) débaucher. ● **—ing** *n* braconnage *m*. ● **poacher** *n* 1 (*person*) braconnier *m*. 2 (*egg*) p. pocheuse *f*.

PO Box [pi:əʊ'bɒks] *abbr* (*Post Office Box*) boîte *f* postale, BP *f*.

pocket ['pɒkɪt] *n* poche *f*; (*small area*) *Fig* petite zone *f*; (*of resistance*) poche *f*; **I'm 50 francs out of p.** j'ai perdu 50 francs ∥*a* (*money, handkerchief etc*) de poche ∥*vt* (*gain*) empocher. ● **pocketbook** *n* (*notebook*) carnet *m*; (*handbag*) *Am* sac *m* à main. ● **pocketful** *n* a p. of une pleine poche de.

pockmarked ['pɒkmɑ:kt] *a* (*face*) grêlé.

pod [pɒd] *n* cosse *f*.

podgy ['pɒdʒɪ] *a* (-ier, -iest) (*person*) rondelet (*f* -ette); (*arm etc*) dodu.

podiatrist [pə'daɪətrɪst] *n Am* pédicure *mf*.

podium ['pəʊdɪəm] *n* podium *m*.

poem ['pəʊɪm] *n* poème *m*. ● **poet** *n* poète *m*. ● **po'etic** *a* poétique. ● **poetry** *n* poésie *f*.

point [pɔɪnt] 1 *n* (*of knife etc*) pointe *f*; *pl Rail* aiguillage *m*; (*power*) p. *El* prise *f* (de courant).

2 *n* (*dot, position, score, degree etc*) point *m*; (*decimal*) virgule *f*; (*meaning*) sens *m*; (*importance*) intérêt *m*; (*remark*) remarque *f*; **p. of view** point *m* de vue; **at this p.** (*in time*) en ce moment, on the pr of doing sur le point de faire; **what's the p.?** à quoi bon? (of waiting/*etc* attendre/*etc*); **there's no p.** (**in**) **staying**/*etc* ça ne sert à rien de rester/*etc*; **that's not the p.** il ne s'agit pas de ça; **that's beside the p.** c'est à côté de la question; **to the p.** pertinent; **his good points** ses qualités *fpl*; **his bad points** ses défauts *mpl*.

3 *vt* (*aim*) pointer (**at** sur); (*vehicle*) tourner (**towards** vers); **to p. the way** indiquer le chemin (**to** à); **to p. one's finger at** montrer du doigt; **to p. out** (*show*) indiquer; (*mention*) signaler (**to** à, **that** que).

∥*vi* montrer du doigt; **to p. at** *or* **to s.o./ sth** (*with finger*) montrer qn/qch; **to p.**

to (*indicate*) indiquer; **to p. east** indiquer l'est; **to be pointing at** (*of gun*) être braqué sur.

point-blank [pɔɪnt'blæŋk] *adv* & *a* (*to shoot, a shot*) à bout portant; (*to refuse, a refusal*) Fig (tout) net.

pointed ['pɔɪntɪd] *a* pointu; (*remark, criticism*) Fig pertinent; (*incisive*) mordant.

pointer ['pɔɪntər] *n* (*on dial etc*) index *m*; (*advice*) conseil *m*; (*clue*) indice *m*.

pointless ['pɔɪntləs] *a* inutile. ●—**ly** *adv* inutilement.

poise [pɔɪz] *n* (*confidence*) assurance *f*; (*composure*) calme *m*; (*grace*) grâce *f*. ● **poised** *a* (*composed*) calme; (*hanging*) suspendu; **p. to attack**/*etc* prêt à attaquer/*etc*.

poison ['pɔɪz(ə)n] *n* poison *m*; (*of snake*) venin *m* ▮ *vt* empoisonner; **to p. s.o.'s mind** corrompre qn. ● **poisoning** *n* empoisonnement *m*. ● **poisonous** *a* (*substance*) toxique; (*snake*) venimeux; (*plant*) vénéneux.

poke [pəʊk] *vt* pousser (*du doigt, avec un bâton etc*); (*fire*) tisonner; **to p. sth into** sth fourrer *or* enfoncer qch dans qch; **to p. one's finger at s.o.** pointer son doigt vers qn; **to p. one's nose into** fourrer le nez dans; **to p. one's head out of the window** passer la tête par la fenêtre; **to p. out s.o.'s eye** crever un œil à qn. ▮ *vi* pousser; **to p. about** *or* **around in** (*drawer etc*) fouiner dans. ▮ *n* (*jab*) (petit) coup *m*; (*shove*) poussée *f*. ● **poker n 1** (*for fire*) tisonnier *m*. **2** *Cards* poker *m*.

poky ['pəʊkɪ] *a* (**-ier, -iest**) (*small*) exigu (*f* -guë) *et* misérable; (*slow*) *Am* lent.

Poland ['pəʊlənd] *n* Pologne *f*. ● **Pole** *n* Polonais, -aise *mf*.

pole [pəʊl] *n* **1** (*rod*) perche *f*; (*fixed*) poteau *m*; (*for flag*) mât *m*. **2** *Geog* pôle *m*; **North/South P.** pôle Nord/Sud. ● **polar** *a* polaire; **p. bear** ours *m* blanc.

police [pə'liːs] *n* police *f*; **extra p.** des renforts *mpl* de police ▮ *a* (*inquiry, dog, State etc*) policier; **p. car** voiture *f* de police; **p. force** police *f*; **p. station** commissariat *m* de police.

▮ *vt* (*city etc*) maintenir l'ordre dans; (*frontier*) contrôler. ● **policeman** *n* (*pl* -**men**) agent *m* de police. ● **policewoman** *n* (*pl* -**women**) femme-agent *f*.

policy ['pɒlɪsɪ] *n* **1** *Pol Econ etc* politique *f*; (*individual course of action*) règle *f*. **2** (**insurance**) **p.** police *f* (d'assurance); **p. holder** assuré, -ée *mf*.

polio ['pəʊlɪəʊ] *n* polio *f*; **p. victim** polio *mf*.

polish ['pɒlɪʃ] *vt* (*floor, shoes etc*) cirer; (*metal*) astiquer; (*rough surface, Fig style*) polir; **to p. off** (*food, work etc*) *Fam* liquider; **to p. up** (*one's French etc*) travailler ▮ *n* (*for shoes*) cirage *m*; (*for floor, furniture*) cire *f*; (*shine*) vernis *m*; **to give sth a p.** faire briller qch. ● **polished** *a* (*manners*) raffiné.

Polish ['pəʊlɪʃ] *a* polonais ▮ *n* (*language*) polonais *m*.

polite [pə'laɪt] *a* (**-er, -est**) poli (**to, with** avec). ●—**ly** *adv* poliment. ●—**ness** *n* politesse *f*.

political [pə'lɪtɪk(ə)l] *a* politique. ● **politician** [pɒlɪ'tɪʃ(ə)n] *n* homme *m or* femme *f* politique. ● **politics** ['pɒlɪtɪks] *n* politique *f*.

polka ['pɒlkə, *Am* 'pəʊlkə] *n* (*dance*) polka *f*; **p. dot** pois *m*.

poll [pəʊl] *n* (*voting*) scrutin *m*, élection *f*; (*vote*) vote *m*; **to go to the polls** aller aux urnes; (**opinion**) **p.** sondage *m* (d'opinion) ▮ *vt* (*votes*) obtenir. ●—**ing** *n* élections *fpl*; **p. booth** isoloir *m*; **p. station**, *Am* **p. place** bureau *m* de vote.

pollen ['pɒlən] *n* pollen *m*.

pollute [pə'luːt] *vt* polluer. ● **pollutant** *n* polluant *m*. ● **pollution** [-ʃ(ə)n] *n* pollution *f*.

polo ['pəʊləʊ] *n* *Sp* polo *m*; **p. neck** (*sweater*) col *m* roulé.

polyester [pɒlɪ'estər] *n* polyester *m* ▮ *a* (*shirt etc*) en polyester.

polytechnic [pɒlɪ'teknɪk] *n* institut *m* universitaire de technologie, IUT *m*.

polythene ['pɒlɪθiːn] *n* polyéthylène *m*

p. bag sac *m* en plastique.

pomegranate ['pɒmɪgrænɪt] *n* (*fruit*) grenade *f*.

pomp [pɒmp] *n* pompe *f*.

pompous ['pɒmpəs] *a* pompeux.

pond [pɒnd] *n* étang *m*; (*artificial*) bassin *m*.

ponder ['pɒndər] *vt* **to p. (over)** sth réfléchir à qch ▮ *vi* réfléchir.

pong [pɒŋ] *n Sl* mauvaise odeur *f*.

pony ['pəʊnɪ] *n* poney *m*. ● **ponytail** *n* (*hair*) queue *f* de cheval.

poodle ['pu:d(ə)l] *n* caniche *m*.

poohl [pu:] *int* bah!; (*bad smell*) ça pue!

pool [pu:l] **1** *n* (*puddle*) flaque *f*; (*of blood*) mare *f*; (*for swimming*) piscine *f*. **2** *n* (*of experience, talent*) réservoir *m*; (*of advisers*) réserve *f*; (*of typists*) pool *m*; (**football**) **pools** pronostics *mpl* (*sur les matchs de football*) ▮ *vt* (*share*) mettre en commun; (*combine*) unir. **3** *n* (*billiards*) billard *m* américain.

pooped [pu:pt] *a* (*exhausted*) *Am Fam* vanné, crevé.

poor [pʊər] *a* (**-er, -est**) (*not rich, deserving pity*) pauvre; (*bad*) mauvais; (*weak*) faible; **p. thing!** le *or* la pauvre! ▮ **the p.** les pauvres *mpl*. ● **-ly 1** *adv* (*badly*) mal; (*clothed*) pauvrement. **2** *a* (*ill*) malade.

pop [pɒp] ▮ *n* (*noise*) bruit *m* sec; **to go p.** faire pan; (*of champagne bottle*) faire pop ▮ *vt* (**-pp-**) (*balloon etc*) crever ▮ *vi* (*burst*) crever; (*of ears*) se déboucher. **2** *vt* (*put*) *Fam* mettre ▮ *vi Fam* (*go*) **to p. in** entrer (un instant); **to p. off** (*leave*) partir; **to p. out** sortir (un instant); **to p. over** *or* **round** faire un saut (**to** chez); **to p. up** (*of person, question etc*) surgir.

pop² [pɒp] **1** *n* (*music*) pop *m* ▮ *a* (*concert, singer etc*) pop *inv*. **2** *n* (*father*) *Am Fam* papa *m*. **3** *n* (**soda**) **p.** (*drink*) soda *m*.

popcorn ['pɒpkɔ:n] *n* pop-corn *m*.

pope [pəʊp] *n* pape *m*.

poplar ['pɒplər] *n* (*tree*) peuplier *m*.

popper ['pɒpər] *n* (*on clothes etc*) pression *f*.

poppy ['pɒpɪ] *n* (*wild*) coquelicot *m*; (*cultivated*) pavot *m*.

popsicle® ['pɒpsɪk(ə)l] *n* (*ice lolly*) *Am* = esquimau *m*.

popular ['pɒpjʊlər] *a* (*person, song etc*) populaire; (*fashionable*) à la mode; **to be p. with** plaire beaucoup à. ● **popu'larity** *n* popularité *f* (**with** auprès de).

populated ['pɒpjʊleɪtɪd] *a* **highly/sparsely/etc p.** très/peu/*etc* peuplé; **p. by** peuplé de.

population [pɒpjʊ'leɪʃ(ə)n] *n* population *f*.

porcelain ['pɔ:səlɪn] *n* porcelaine *f*.

porch [pɔ:tʃ] *n* porche *m*; (*veranda*) *Am* véranda *f*.

porcupine ['pɔ:kjʊpaɪn] *n* porc-épic *m*.

pore [pɔ:r] **1** *n* (*of skin*) pore *m*. **2** *vi* **to p. over** (*book etc*) étudier de près.

pork [pɔ:k] *n* (*meat*) porc *m*; **p. pie** pâté *m* (de porc) en croûte.

pornography [pɔ:'nɒgrəfɪ] *n* (*Fam* **porn**) pornographie *f*. ● **porno'graphic** *a* pornographique.

porpoise ['pɔ:pəs] *n* (*sea animal*) marsouin *m*.

porridge ['pɒrɪdʒ] *n* porridge *m* (*bouillie de flocons d'avoine*).

port [pɔ:t] **1** *n* (*harbour*) port *m*; **p. of call** escale *f* ▮ *a* (*authorities etc*) portuaire. **2** *n* **p. (side)** (*left*) Nau Av bâbord *m*. **3** *n* (*wine*) porto *m*.

portable ['pɔ:təb(ə)l] *a* portable, portatif.

porter ['pɔ:tər] *n* (*for luggage*) porteur *m*; (*doorman at hotel*) portier *m*.

portfolio [pɔ:t'fəʊlɪəʊ] *n* (*pl* **-os**) (*for documents*) serviette *f*; *Pol Fin* portefeuille *m*.

porthole ['pɔ:thəʊl] *n* Nau Av hublot *m*.

portion ['pɔ:ʃ(ə)n] *n* (*share, helping*) portion *f*; (*of train, book etc*) partie *f*.

portly ['pɔ:tlɪ] *a* (**-ier, -iest**) corpulent.

portrait ['pɔ:trɪt] *n* portrait *m*.

portray [pɔ:'treɪ] *vt* (*describe*) représenter. ● **portrayal** *n* représentation *f*.

Portugal ['pɔ:tjʊg(ə)l] *n* Portugal.

● **Portu'guese** a & n inv portugais, -aise (mf) ▮ n (language) portugais m.

pose [pəʊz] 1 n (of model etc) pose f ▮ vi (of model etc) poser (for pour); **to p. as a lawyer**/etc se faire passer pour un avocat/etc. 2 vt (question) poser.

posh [pɒʃ] a Fam (smart) chic inv; (snobbish) snob (f inv).

position [pə'zɪʃ(ə)n] n (place, opinion etc) position f; (job, circumstances) situation f; (customer window in bank etc) guichet m; **in a p. to do** en mesure de faire; **in a good p. to do** bien placé pour faire; **in p.** en place, en position ▮ vt (camera etc) mettre en position; (put) placer.

positive ['pɒzɪtɪv] a positif; (progress, change) réel; (sure) certain (of de, that que); **p. reply** (yes) réponse f affirmative; **a p. genius** Fam un vrai génie. ●—**ly** adv (for certain) positivement; (completely) complètement; (categorically) catégoriquement; (to reply) par l'affirmative.

possess [pə'zes] vt posséder. ●**possession** [-ʃ(ə)n] n possession f; pl (belongings) biens mpl; **in p. of** en possession de. ●**possessive** a (person, adjective etc) possessif ▮ n Gram possessif m.

possible ['pɒsəb(ə)l] a possible; **it is p.** (**for us**) **to do it** il (nous) est possible de le faire; **it is p. that** il est possible que (+ sub); **as far as p.** autant que possible; **if p.** si possible; **as much or as many as p.** le plus possible.

possibility [pɒsɪ'bɪlɪtɪ] n possibilité f; **there's some p. that** il est (tout juste) possible que (+ sub); **she has possibilities** elle promet; **it's a distinct p.** c'est bien possible.

possibly adv 1 (perhaps) peut-être. 2 (with can, could etc) **if you p.** can si cela t'est possible; **to do all one p. can** faire tout son possible; **he cannot p. stay** il ne peut absolument pas rester.

post¹ [pəʊst] n (system) poste f; (letters) courrier m; **by p.** par la poste; **to catch/**

miss the p. avoir/manquer la levée; **p. office** (bureau m de) poste f; **the P. Office** (administration) les postes fpl ▮ vt (put in postbox) poster, mettre à la poste; (send) envoyer; **to keep s.o. posted** Fig tenir qn au courant.

post² [pəʊst] n (job, place) & Mil poste m ▮ vt (sentry, guard) poster; (employee) affecter (to à). ●—**ing** n (appointment) affectation f.

post³ [pəʊst] n (pole) poteau m; (of door) montant m; **winning p.** Sp poteau m d'arrivée ▮ vt **to p. (up)** (notice etc) afficher, coller.

post- [pəʊst] pref post-; **p.-1800** après 1800.

postage ['pəʊstɪdʒ] n tarif m (postal), tarifs mpl (postaux) (**to** pour); **p. stamp** timbre-poste m.

postal ['pəʊstəl] a (services, district etc) postal; **p. order** mandat m postal.

postbag ['pəʊstbæg] n sac m postal. ● **postbox** n boîte f aux or à lettres. ● **postcard** n carte f postale. ● **postcode** n code m postal. ● **post-'free** adv franco.

postdate [pəʊst'deɪt] vt postdater.

poster ['pəʊstər] n affiche f; (for decoration) poster m.

postgraduate [pəʊst'grædʒʊət] n étudiant, -ante mf de troisième cycle.

postman ['pəʊstmən] n (pl -men) facteur m. ● **postmark** n cachet m de la poste. ● **postmaster** n receveur m (des postes).

post-mortem [pəʊst'mɔːtəm] n **p.-mortem** (**examination**) autopsie f (**on** de).

postpone [pəʊ'spəʊn] vt remettre (for de, until à). ●—**ment** n remise f.

posture ['pɒstʃər] n (of body) posture f; Fig attitude f.

postwar ['pəʊstwɔːr] a d'après-guerre.

posy ['pəʊzɪ] n petit bouquet m (de fleurs).

pot [pɒt] 1 n pot m; (for cooking) marmite f; **pots and pans** casseroles fpl; **jam p.** pot m à confiture; **to take p. luck** (with food) manger à la fortune du pot; **to go to p.** Fam aller à la ruine; **gone to p.** (person, plans etc) Fam fichu.

2 n (drug) Fam hasch m.

potato [pə'teɪtəʊ] n (pl -oes) pomme f de terre; **p. crisps**, Am **p. chips** pommes fpl chips.

potbelly ['pɒtbelɪ] n bedaine f. ● **potbellied** a ventru.

potent ['pəʊtənt] a (drug, remedy etc) puissant; (drink) fort.

potential [pə'tenʃ(ə)l] a (client, sales) éventuel; (danger, resources) potentiel; (leader etc) en puissance ‖ n potentiel m; Fig (perspectives fpl d')avenir m; **to have p.** (of person, company etc) avoir de l'avenir. ● **-ly** adv potentiellement.

pothole ['pɒthəʊl] n (in road) nid m de poules; (cave) caverne f. ● **potholing** n spéléologie f.

potion ['pəʊʃ(ə)n] n breuvage m magique; Med potion f.

potshot ['pɒtʃɒt] n **to take a p.** faire un carton (at sur).

potted ['pɒtɪd] a **1** (plant) en pot. **2** (version etc) abrégé, condensé.

potter ['pɒtər] **1** n (person) potier m. **2** vi **to p. (about)** bricoler. ● **pottery** n (art) poterie f; (objects) poteries fpl; **a piece of p.** une poterie.

potty ['pɒtɪ] **1** n pot m (de bébé). **2** a (-ier, -iest) (mad) Fam toqué.

pouch [paʊtʃ] n petit sac m; (of kangaroo) poche f; (for tobacco) blague f.

pouf(fe) [pu:f] n (seat) pouf m.

poultry ['pəʊltrɪ] n volaille f.

pounce [paʊns] vi (leap) sauter, bondir (on sur) ‖ n bond m.

pound [paʊnd] **1** n (weight) livre f (= 453,6 grammes); (money) livre f (sterling). **2** n (for cars, dogs) fourrière f. **3** vt (spices etc) piler; (meat) attendrir; (bombard) Mil pilonner; (ville); (thump) tambouriner sur, marteler (table etc); (of sea) battre (bateau etc) ‖ vi (of heart) battre à tout rompre.

pour [pɔ:r] vt (liquid) verser; **to p. money into sth** investir beaucoup d'argent dans qch ‖ vi **it's pouring (down)** il pleut à verse; **pouring rain** pluie f torrentielle.

pour away vt (liquid) vider ‖ **to pour in** vt (liquid) verser ‖ vi (of water, rain, sunshine) entrer à flots; (of people, money) affluer ‖ **to pour off** vt (liquid) vider ‖ **to pour out** vt (liquid) verser; (cup etc) vider ‖ vi (of liquid) couler à flots; (of people) sortir en masse; (of smoke) s'échapper (from de).

pout [paʊt] vti **to p. (one's lips)** faire la moue ‖ n moue f.

poverty ['pɒvətɪ] n pauvreté f; **(extreme) p.** la misère f. ● **p.-stricken** a (person) indigent.

powder ['paʊdər] n poudre f; **p. puff** houppette f; **p. room** toilettes fpl (pour dames) ‖ vt (body, skin) poudrer; **to p. one's face** or **nose** se poudrer. ● **-ed** a (milk, eggs) en poudre.

power ['paʊər] n (ability, authority) pouvoir m; (strength, nation) & Math Tech puissance f; (energy) énergie f; (current) El courant m; **in p.** Pol au pouvoir; **in one's p.** en son pouvoir; **p. cut** coupure f de courant; **p. station**, Am **p. plant** centrale f (électrique) ‖ vt **to be powered by** être actionné par; (gas, oil etc) fonctionner à. ● **powerful** a puissant. ● **powerless** a impuissant (**to do** à faire).

PR [pi:'ɑ:r] n abbr = public relations.

practical ['præktɪk(ə)l] a (tool, knowledge, person etc) pratique; **p. joke** farce f. ● **practi'calities** npl (of scheme, situation etc) aspect m pratique.

practically ['præktɪk(ə)lɪ] adv (almost) pratiquement.

practice ['præktɪs] n (exercise, way of proceeding) pratique f; (habit) habitude f; (training) entraînement m; (rehearsal) répétition f; (clients) clientèle f; **to be out of p.** manquer d'entraînement; **to put into p.** mettre en pratique; **to be in p.** (of doctor, lawyer) exercer.

practise ['præktɪs] (Am **practice**) vt (sport, art etc) pratiquer; (medicine, law etc) exercer; (flute, piano etc) s'exercer à; (language) (s'exercer à) parler (on avec); (work at) travailler (ses maths etc) ∎ vi Mus Sp s'exercer; (of doctor, lawyer) exercer. ●—ed a (experienced) chevronné; (ear, eye) exercé. ●—ing a (Catholic etc) pratiquant.

practitioner [præk'tɪʃ(ə)nər] n general p. (médecin m) généraliste m.

pragmatic [præg'mætɪk] a pragmatique.

prairie(s) ['preərɪ(z)] n(pl) (in North America) Prairies fpl.

praise [preɪz] vt louer (qn) (for sth de qch); **to p. s.o. for doing** louer qn d'avoir fait ∎ n louange(s) f(pl), éloge(s) m(pl); **in p. of** à la louange de. ● **praiseworthy** a digne d'éloges.

pram [præm] n landau m (pl -aus).

prance [prɑːns] vi **to p. about** (of dancer) caracoler; (strut) se pavaner; (go about) Fam se balader.

prank [præŋk] n (trick) farce f.

prawn [prɔːn] n crevette f (rose).

pray [preɪ] vi prier; **to p. for good weather/a miracle** prier pour avoir du beau temps/pour un miracle ∎ vt **to p. that** prier pour que (+ sub).

prayer [preər] n prière f.

pre- [priː] pref **p.-1800** avant 1800.

preach [priːtʃ] vti prêcher; **to p. to s.o.** Rel & Fig prêcher qn; **to p. a sermon** faire un sermon.

prearrange [priːə'reɪndʒ] vt arranger à l'avance.

precarious [prɪ'keərɪəs] a précaire.

precaution [prɪ'kɔːʃ(ə)n] n précaution f (of doing de faire); **as a p.** par précaution.

preced/e [prɪ'siːd] vti précéder; **to p. sth by sth** faire précéder qch de qch. ●—**ing** a précédent.

precedence ['presɪdəns] n **to take p. over** (priority) avoir la priorité sur. ● **precedent** n précédent m.

precinct ['priːsɪŋkt] n (of convent etc) enceinte f; (electoral district) Am circonscription f; (police district) Am secteur m; (for shopping) zone f piétonnière or piétonne.

precious ['preʃəs] **1** a précieux. **2** adv **p.**

few, p. little Fam très peu (de).

precipice ['presɪpɪs] n (sheer face) Geog à-pic m inv; (chasm) Fig précipice m.

precipitate [prɪ'sɪpɪteɪt] vt (hasten, throw) & Ch précipiter; (reaction etc) provoquer.

precise [prɪ'saɪs] a précis; (person) minutieux. ●—**ly** adv (accurately, exactly) précisément; **at 3 o'clock p.** à 3 heures précises. ● **precision** [-ʒ(ə)n] n précision f.

preclude [prɪ'kluːd] vt (prevent) empêcher (**from doing** de faire); (possibility) exclure.

precocious [prɪ'kəʊʃəs] a (child) précoce.

preconception [priːkən'sep(ʃ)(ə)n] n préconception f.

precondition [priːkən'dɪʃ(ə)n] n préalable m.

predate [priː'deɪt] vt (precede) précéder; (document) antidater.

predator ['predətər] n (animal) prédateur m.

predecessor ['priːdɪsesər] n prédécesseur m.

predicament [prɪ'dɪkəmənt] n situation f fâcheuse.

predict [prɪ'dɪkt] vt prédire. ● **predictable** a prévisible. ● **prediction** [-ʃ(ə)n] n prédiction f.

predispose [priːdɪ'spəʊz] vt prédisposer (**to do** à faire).

predominant [prɪ'dɒmɪnənt] a prédominant. ●—**ly** adv (almost all) pour la plupart. ● **predominate** vi prédominer (**over** sur).

pre-empt [priː'empt] vt (decision etc) devancer.

preen [priːn] vt (feathers) lisser; **she's preening herself** Fig elle se bichonne.

prefab ['priːfæb] n Fam maison f préfabriquée. ● **prefabricated** [-'fæbrɪkeɪtɪd] a préfabriqué.

preface ['prefɪs] n préface f.

prefect ['priːfekt] n Sch élève mf chargé(e) de la discipline; (French official) préfet m.

prefer [prɪ'fɜːr] vt (-rr-) préférer (**to** à).

aimer mieux (to que); **to p.** to do préférer faire, aimer mieux faire.

preferable ['prefərəb(ə)l] *a* préférable (to à). • **preferably** *adv* de préférence.

preference ['prefərəns] *n* préférence *f* (for pour); **in p.** to de préférence à. • **prefe'rential** *a* (*treatment*) de faveur; (*terms etc*) préférentiel.

prefix ['pri:fiks] *n* préfixe *m*.

pregnant ['pregnənt] *a* (*woman*) enceinte; (*animal*) pleine; **five months p.** enceinte de cinq mois. • **pregnancy** *n* (*of woman*) grossesse *f*.

prehistoric [pri:hi'stɒrik] *a* préhistorique.

prejudic/e ['predʒədis] *n* préjugé *m*; (*people's attitude*) préjugés *mpl*; *Jur* préjudice *m*; **to be full of p.** être plein de préjugés ‖ *vt* (*person*) prévenir (**against** contre); (*success etc*) porter préjudice à. • **—ed** *a* (*idea*) partial; **she's p.** elle a des préjugés *or* un préjugé (**against** contre).

preliminary [pri'liminəri] *a* (*speech, inquiry, exam etc*) préliminaire ‖ *npl* pre-lininaries préliminaires *mpl*.

prelude ['prelju:d] *n* prélude *m* (to à).

premarital [pri:'mærit(ə)l] *a* avant le mariage.

premature ['premətʃʊər, *Am* pri:mə-'tʊər] *a* prématuré.

premeditate [pri:'mediteit] *vt* préméditer.

premier ['premiər, *Am* pri'miər] *n* Premier ministre *m*.

première ['premiər, *Am* pri'mjeər] *n* Th Cin première *f*.

premises ['premisiz] *npl* locaux *mpl*; **on the p.** sur les lieux; **off the p.** hors des lieux.

premium ['pri:miəm] *n* Fin prime *f*; (*insurance*) p. prime *f* (d'assurance); **p. bond** bon *m* à lots.

premonition [premə'niʃ(ə)n, *Am* pri:mə'niʃ(ə)n] *n* pressentiment *m*.

prenatal [pri:'neit(ə)l] *a Am* prénatal (*mpl* -als).

preoccupy [pri:'ɒkjʊpai] *vt* (*worry*) préoccuper; **to be preoccupied** être préoccupé (**with** de).

prepaid [pri:'peid] *a* (*reply*) payé.

prepar/e [pri'peər] *vt* préparer (sth for qch pour, s.o. for qn à); **to p.** to do se préparer à faire ‖ *vi* **to p. for** (*journey, occasion*) faire des préparatifs pour; (*exam*) préparer. • **—ed** *a* (*ready*) prêt, disposé (**to do** à faire); **to be p. for sth** (*expect*) s'attendre à qch. • **preparation** [prepə'reiʃ(ə)n] *n* préparation *f*; *pl* préparatifs *mpl* (**for** de).

preparatory [prə'pærət(ə)ri] *a* préparatoire; **p. school** = prep school.

preposition [prepə'ziʃ(ə)n] *n Gram* préposition *f*.

preposterous [pri'pɒstərəs] *a* absurde.

prep school ['prepsku:l] *n* école *f* primaire privée; *Am* école *f* secondaire privée.

prerecorded [pri:ri'kɔ:did] *a* (*message etc*) enregistré à l'avance; **p. broadcast** *Rad TV* émission *f* en différé.

prerequisite [pri:'rekwizit] *n* (condition *f*) préalable *m*.

prerogative [pri'rogətiv] *n* prérogative *f*.

preschool ['pri:sku:l] *a* (*age etc*) préscolaire.

prescrib/e [pri'skraib] *vt* (*of doctor*) prescrire. • **—ed** *a* (*textbook*) (inscrit) au programme. • **prescription** [-ʃ(ə)n] *n* (*for medicine*) ordonnance *f*; **on p.** sur ordonnance.

presence ['prezəns] *n* présence *f*; **in the p. of** en présence de; **p. of mind** présence *f* d'esprit.

present¹ ['prezənt] **1** *a* (*not absent*) présent (**at** à, **in** dans). **2** *a* (*year, state etc*) actuel, présent; (*job, house etc*) actuel; **the p. tense** le présent ‖ *n* **the p.** (*time, tense*) le présent *m*; **for the p.** pour le moment; **at p.** à présent. **3** *n* (*gift*) cadeau *m*. • **—ly** *adv* (*soon*) tout à l'heure; (*now*) à présent.

present² [pri'zent] *vt* (*show, introduce etc*) présenter (**to** à); (*concert etc*) donner; **to p. s.o. with** (*gift*) offrir à qn; (*prize*) remettre à qn. • **—able** *a* présen-

table. ●—**er** n présentateur, -trice mf.
●**presentation** [prezən'teɪʃ(ə)n] n présentation f; (of prize) remise f.
preserve [prɪ'zɜ:v] **1** vt (keep) conserver; (fruit etc) mettre en conserve. **2** n **preserve(s)** (jam) confiture f. **3** n (sphere) domaine m. ●**preservation** [prezə'veɪʃ(ə)n] n conservation f. ●**preservative** n (in food) agent m de conservation. ●**preserver** n life p. Am gilet m de sauvetage.
preside [prɪ'zaɪd] vi présider; **to p. over a meeting** présider une réunion.
president ['prezɪdənt] n président, -ente mf. ●**presidency** n présidence f. ●**presidential** a présidentiel.
press[1] [pres] **1** n (newspapers) presse f; (printing) p. presse f ‖ a (conference etc) de presse. **2** n (machine for pressing trousers etc) presse f; (for making wine) pressoir m.
press[2] [pres] vt (button, doorbell etc) appuyer sur; (tube, lemon) presser; (hand) serrer; (clothes) repasser; (insist on) insister sur; **to p. s.o. to do** (urge) presser qn de faire; **to p. charges** Jur engager des poursuites (against contre) ‖ vi (with finger) appuyer (on sur); (of weight) faire pression (on sur); ‖ n **to give sth a p.** (trousers, Am pants etc) repasser qch.
press down vt (button etc) appuyer sur ‖ **to press for** vt (demand) insister pour obtenir (qch) ‖ **to press on** vi (carry on) continuer (with sth qch).
pressed [prest] a (hard) p. (busy) débordé; **to be hard p.** (in difficulties) être en difficultés; **to be p. for** (time, money) être à court de.
pressing ['presɪŋ] a (urgent) pressant.
press-stud ['presstʌd] n bouton-pression m.
press-up ['presʌp] n (exercise) pompe f.
pressure ['preʃər] n pression f; **the p. of work** le surmenage; **p. cooker** cocotte-minute f; **p. group** groupe m de pression; **under p.** (worker, to work) sous pression ‖ vt **to p. s.o.** faire pression sur

qn (**into doing** pour qu'il fasse). ●**pressurize** vt Av pressuriser; **to p. s.o.** faire pression sur qn (**into doing** pour qu'il fasse).
prestige [pre'sti:ʒ] n prestige m.
presume [prɪ'zju:m] vt (suppose) présumer (**that** que). ●**presumably** adv (you'll come etc) je présume que. ●**presumption** [-'zʌmpʃ(ə)n] n (supposition) présomption f.
pretence [prɪ'tens] (Am **pretense**) n (sham) feinte f; (claim, affectation) prétention f; **to make a p. of doing sth** feindre de faire qch; **under false pretences** sous des prétextes fallacieux.
pretend [prɪ'tend] vt (make believe) faire semblant (**to do** de faire, **that** que); (maintain) prétendre (**to do** de faire, **that** que) ‖ vi faire semblant.
pretentious [prɪ'tenʃəs] a prétentieux.
pretext ['pri:tekst] n prétexte m; **on the p. of/that** sous prétexte de/que.
pretty ['prɪtɪ] **1** a (-ier, -iest) joli. **2** adv Fam (rather, quite) assez; **p. well, p. much** (almost) pratiquement.
prevail [prɪ'veɪl] vi (be prevalent) prédominer; (win) prévaloir (**against** contre); **to p. (up)on s.o.** persuader qn (**to do** de faire). ●—**ing** a (most common) courant; (situation) actuel; (wind) dominant.
prevalent ['prevalənt] a courant, répandu. ●**prevalence** n fréquence f; (predominance) prédominance f.
prevent [prɪ'vent] vt empêcher (**from doing** de faire). ●**preventable** a évitable. ●**prevention** [-ʃ(ə)n] n prévention f.
preview ['pri:vju:] n (of film, painting) avant-première f.
previous ['pri:vɪəs] a précédent; (experience) préalable; **she's had a p. job** elle a déjà eu un emploi ‖ adv **p. to** avant. ●—**ly** adv avant.
prewar ['pri:wɔ:r] a d'avant-guerre.
prey [preɪ] n proie f; **to be (a) p. to** être en proie à; **bird of p.** rapace m ‖ vi **to p. on** (of animal) faire sa proie de; (of person) abuser de; **to p. on s.o.'s mind**

tracasser qn.

price [praɪs] n (of object, success etc) prix m; **to pay a high p. for sth** payer cher qch; Fig payer chèrement qch ∥ a (control, war, rise etc) des prix; **p. list** tarif m ∥ vt **it's priced at £5** ça coûte cinq livres. ● **priceless** a (jewel etc) inestimable. ● **pricey** a (-ier, -iest) Fam cher.

prick [prɪk] vt (jab) piquer (with avec); (burst) crever; **to p. up one's ears** dresser l'oreille ∥ n piqûre f.

prickle ['prɪk(ə)l] n (of animal, plant) piquant m. ● **prickly** a (-ier, -iest) (plant, beard) piquant; (animal) hérissé.

pride [praɪd] n (satisfaction) fierté f; (exaggerated) orgueil m; (self-respect) amour-propre m; **to take p. in** (person, work etc) être fier de; (look after) prendre soin de; **to take p. in doing sth** mettre (toute) sa fierté à faire qch ∥ vt **to p. oneself on sth/on doing** s'enorgueillir de qch/de faire.

priest [priːst] n prêtre m.

priggish ['prɪgɪʃ] a suffisant.

prim [prɪm] a (primmer, primmest) **p. (and proper)** (affected) bégueule; (neat) impeccable.

primary ['praɪmərɪ] a (main, basic) principal; Sch Pol Geol etc primaire; **of p. importance** de première importance; **p. school** école f primaire ∥ n (election) Am primaire f. ● **primarily** [Am praɪ'merɪlɪ] adv essentiellement.

prime [praɪm] 1 a (reason etc) principal; (quality) premier; (example, condition) excellent, parfait; **of p. importance** de première importance; **P. Minister** Premier ministre m; **p. number** nombre m premier. 2 n **in the p. of life** dans la force de l'âge. 3 vt (gun) amorcer; (surface) apprêter. ● **primer** n 1 (book) premier livre m. 2 (paint) apprêt m.

primitive ['prɪmɪtɪv] a (society, conditions etc) primitif.

primrose ['prɪmrəʊz] n Bot primevère f (jaune).

prince [prɪns] n prince m. ● **prin'cess** n

princesse f.

principal ['prɪnsɪp(ə)l] **1** a (main) principal. **2** n (of school) directeur, -trice mf; (of university) président, -ente mf. ● **—ly** adv principalement.

principality [prɪnsɪ'pælətɪ] n principauté f.

principle ['prɪnsɪp(ə)l] n principe m; **in p.** en principe; **on p.** par principe.

print [prɪnt] n (of finger, foot etc) empreinte f; (letters) caractères mpl; (engraving) gravure f; (fabric, textile design) imprimé m; (photo) épreuve f; **in p.** (book) disponible; **out of p.** (book) épuisé.
∥ vt (book etc) imprimer; (photo) tirer; (write) écrire en caractères d'imprimerie; **to p. out** (of computer) imprimer. ● **printed** a imprimé; **p. matter** imprimés mpl. ● **printing** n (action) Typ impression f; (technique, art) imprimerie f; **p. press** Typ presse f.

printer ['prɪntər] n (of computer) imprimante f; (person) imprimeur m. ● **printout** n (of computer) sortie f sur imprimante.

prior ['praɪər] a précédent, antérieur; (experience) préalable ∥ adv **p. to sth/to doing** avant qch/de faire.

priority [praɪ'ɒrɪtɪ] n priorité f (over sur).

prise [praɪz] vt **to p. open/off** (box, lid) ouvrir/enlever (en faisant levier).

prison ['prɪz(ə)n] n prison f; **in p.** en prison ∥ a (life etc) pénitenciaire; (camp) de prisonniers; **p. officer** gardien, -ienne mf de prison. ● **prisoner** n prisonnier, -ière mf; **to take s.o. p.** faire qn prisonnier.

pristine ['prɪstiːn] a (condition) parfait; (primitive) primitif.

privacy ['praɪvəsɪ] n intimité f; (quiet place) coin m retiré; **to give s.o. some p.** laisser qn seul.

private ['praɪvɪt] **1** a privé; (lesson, car etc) particulier; (report, letter) confidentiel; (personal) personnel; (dinner etc) intime; **a p. citizen** un simple particulier; **p. detective, p. investiga-**

tor, *Fam* p. eye détective *m* privé; **p. parts** parties *fpl* génitales; **p. place** coin *m* retiré; **p. secretary** secrétaire *m* particulier, secrétaire *f* particulière; **p. tutor** professeur *m* particulier.

‖ *n* **in p.** en privé; (*to have dinner etc*) dans l'intimité.

2 *n Mil* (simple) soldat *m*. ● **privately** *adv* en privé; (*personally*) à titre personnel; (*to have dinner etc*) dans l'intimité; **p. owned** appartenant à un particulier.

privatize ['praɪvətaɪz] *vt* privatiser.

privet ['prɪvɪt] *n* (*bush*) troène *m*.

privilege ['prɪvɪlɪdʒ] *n* privilège *m*. ● **privileged** *a* privilégié; **to be p. to do sth** avoir le privilège de faire qch.

prize¹ [praɪz] *n* prix *m*; (*in lottery*) lot *m*; **the first p.** (*in lottery*) le gros lot ‖ *a* (*essay etc*) primé; **a p. fool**/*etc Hum* un parfait idiot/*etc*. ● **p.-giving** *n* distribution *f* des prix. ● **p.-winner** *n* lauréat, -ate *mf*; (*in lottery*) gagnant, -ante *mf*.

prize² [praɪz] *vt* = **prise**.

pro [prəʊ] *n* (*professional*) *Fam* pro *mf*.

pro- [prəʊ] *pref* pro-.

probable ['prɒbəb(ə)l] *a* probable (**that** que); (*convincing*) vraisemblable. ● **proba'bility** *n* probabilité *f*; **in all p.** selon toute probabilité. ● **probably** *adv* probablement.

probation [prə'beɪʃ(ə)n] *n* **on p.** *Jur* en liberté surveillée; **p. officer** responsable *mf* des délinquants mis en liberté surveillée.

probe [prəʊb] *n* (*inquiry*) enquête *f* (**into** dans) ‖ *vt* (*investigate*) & *Med* sonder; (*examine*) examiner (*situation etc*) ‖ *vi* (*investigate*) faire des recherches; **to p. into** (*origins etc*) sonder.

problem ['prɒbləm] *n* problème *m*; **he's got a drug/a drink p.** c'est un drogué/un alcoolique; **no p.!** *Fam* pas de problème!; **to have a p. doing** avoir du mal à faire. ● **proble'matic** *a* problématique; **it's p. whether** il est douteux que (+ *sub*).

procedure [prə'siːdʒər] *n* procédure *f*.

proceed [prə'siːd] *vi* (*go*) avancer, aller; (*act*) procéder; (*continue*) continuer; **to p. to** (*next question etc*) passer à; **to p. with** (*task etc*) continuer; **to p. to do sth** se mettre à faire qch.

proceedings [prə'siːdɪŋz] *npl* (*events*) événements *mpl*; (*meeting*) séance *f*; (*discussions*) débats *mpl*; **to take** (**legal**) **proceedings** intenter un procès (**against** contre).

proceeds ['prəʊsiːdz] *npl* (*profits from sale etc*) produit *m*.

process ['prəʊses] **1** *n* (*method*) procédé *m* (**for doing** pour faire); (*chemical, economic etc*) processus *m*; **in the p. of doing** en train de faire. **2** *vt* (*food, data etc*) traiter; (*examine*) examiner; (*photo*) développer; **processed cheese** fromage *m* fondu. ● **processor** *n* **food p.** robot *m* (ménager); **word p.** machine *f* à *or* de traitement de texte.

procession [prə'seʃ(ə)n] *n* cortège *m*, défilé *m*.

proclaim [prə'kleɪm] *vt* proclamer (**that** que); **to p. s.o. king** proclamer qn roi.

procrastinate [prə'kræstɪneɪt] *vi* tergiverser.

procure [prə'kjʊər] *vt* obtenir; **to p. sth for s.o.** procurer qch à qn.

prod [prɒd] *vti* (**-dd-**) **to p. (at)** pousser (*du coude etc*); **to p. s.o. into doing** *Fig* pousser qn à faire ‖ *n* (petit) coup *m*.

prodigal ['prɒdɪg(ə)l] *a* (*son etc*) prodigue.

prodigy ['prɒdɪdʒɪ] *n* prodige *m*; **child p.** enfant *mf* prodige.

produce¹ [prə'djuːs] *vt* (*manufacture, yield etc*) produire; (*bring out*) sortir (*pistolet, mouchoir etc*); (*passport, proof*) présenter; (*profit*) rapporter; (*cause*) provoquer, produire; (*publish*) publier; (*film*) produire; **oil-producing country** pays *m* producteur de pétrole. ● **pro'ducer** *n* (*of goods, film*) producteur, -trice *mf*.

produce² ['prɒdjuːs] *n* (*agricultural etc*) produits *mpl*.

product ['prɒdʌkt] n Com Math etc &
Fig produit m.

production [prə'dʌkʃ(ə)n] n production
f; (of play) mise f en scène; **to work on
the p. line** travailler à la chaîne.
● **productive** [prə'dʌktɪv] a (land, meeting
etc) productif. ● **produc'tivity** n productivité f.

profane [prə'feɪn] a (sacrilegious) sacrilège. ● **profanities** npl (swear words)
grossièretés fpl.

profess [prə'fes] vt professer; **to p. to be**
prétendre être.

profession [prə'feʃ(ə)n] n profession f.
● **professional** a professionnel; (man,
woman) qui exerce une profession
libérale; (army) de métier; (diplomat) de
carrière; (piece of work) de professionnel ∥ n professionnel, -elle mf; (doctor,
lawyer etc) membre m des professions
libérales. ● **professionally** adv professionnellement; (to meet s.o.) dans le
cadre de son travail.

professor [prə'fesər] n professeur m
(d'université); Am enseignant, -ante
mf d'université.

proficient [prə'fɪʃ(ə)nt] a compétent (**in**
en). ● **proficiency** n compétence f.

profile ['prəʊfaɪl] n profil m; **in p.** de
profil.

profit ['prɒfɪt] n profit m, bénéfice m; **to
sell at a p.** vendre à profit; **p. motive**
recherche f du profit ∥ vi **to p. by** or
from sth tirer profit de qch. ● **p.-making**
a à but lucratif; **non p.-making** sans but
lucratif.

profitable ['prɒfɪtəb(ə)l] a Com & Fig
rentable. ● **profitably** adv avec profit.

profound [prə'faʊnd] a (silence, remark
etc) profond. ● **-ly** adv profondément.

profusely [prə'fjuːslɪ] adv (to bleed)
abondamment; (to thank) avec effusion; **to apologize p.** se répandre en
excuses.

program¹ ['prəʊɡræm] n (of computer)
programme m; **computer p.** programme
m informatique ∥ vt (-mm-) (computer)
programmer. ● **programmer** n (compu-

ter) p. programmeur, -euse mf.

programme, Am **program²** ['prəʊɡræm]
n programme m; (broadcast) émission f
∥ vt (machine, VCR etc) programmer.

progress ['prəʊɡres] n progrès m(pl); **to
make p.** faire des progrès; (when driving
etc) bien avancer; **in p.** en cours
∥ [prə'ɡres] vi progresser; (of story,
meeting) se dérouler. ● **progression**
[prə'ɡreʃ(ə)n] n progression f.

progressive [prə'ɡresɪv] a (gradual)
progressif; (company, ideas) progressiste.

prohibit [prə'hɪbɪt] vt interdire (**s.o. from
doing** à qn de faire); **we're prohibited
from leaving**/etc il nous est interdit de
partir/etc. ● **prohibitive** a (price etc)
prohibitif.

project 1 ['prɒdʒekt] n (plan) projet m
(**for sth** pour qch, **to do** pour faire);
(undertaking) entreprise f; (at school)
étude f; (housing) p. Am cité f (ouvrière). **2** [prə'dʒekt] vt (throw, show etc)
projeter ∥ vi (jut out) faire saillie.
● **projection** [prə'dʒekʃ(ə)n] n projection f; (projecting object) saillie f.
● **pro'jector** n (for films or slides) projecteur m.

proliferate [prə'lɪfəreɪt] vi proliférer.

prolific [prə'lɪfɪk] a prolifique.

prolong [prə'lɒŋ] vt prolonger.

promenade [prɒmə'nɑːd] n (at seaside)
promenade f.

prominent ['prɒmɪnənt] a (person) important; (nose) proéminent; (chin,
tooth) saillant; (striking) frappant;
(conspicuous) (bien) en vue. ● **-ly** adv
(displayed) bien en vue.

promiscuous [prə'mɪskjʊəs] a (person)
qui mène une vie très libre; (behaviour)
immoral.

promis/e ['prɒmɪs] n promesse f; **to show
p.**, **be full of p.** être prometteur ∥ vt
promettre (**s.o. sth**, **sth to s.o.** qch à qn;
to do faire; **that que**) ∥ vi **I p.!** je te le
promets!; **p.?** promis? ● **-ing** a (situation) prometteur (f -euse); (person) qui
promet.

promote [prə'məʊt] *vt* (*product, research*) promouvoir; (*good health, awareness*) favoriser; **to p. s.o.** (*in job*) donner de l'avancement à qn; **promoted (to) manager/***etc* promu directeur/*etc.* ● **promotion** [-ʃ(ə)n] *n* (*of person*) avancement *m*, promotion *f*; (*of research etc*) promotion *f*.

prompt [prɒmpt] **1** *a* (*speedy*) rapide; (*punctual*) à l'heure; **p. to act** prompt à agir ▌*adv* **at 8 o'clock p.** à 8 heures pile. **2** *vt* (*urge*) inciter (*qn*) (**to do** à faire); (*cause*) provoquer. **3** *vt* (*actor*) souffler (son rôle) à. ● —**ness** *n* rapidité *f.*

prone [prəʊn] *a* **1 p. to sth** (*illnesses, accidents etc*) prédisposé à; **to be p. to do sth** avoir tendance à faire qch. **2** (*lying flat*) sur le ventre.

prong [prɒŋ] *n* (*of fork*) dent *f.*

pronoun ['prəʊnaʊn] *n Gram* pronom *m.*

pronounce [prə'naʊns] *vt* (*say, declare*) prononcer ▌*vi* (*articulate*) prononcer. ● **pronunciation** [prənʌnsɪ'eɪʃ(ə)n] *n* prononciation *f.*

proof [pru:f] **1** *n* (*evidence*) preuve(s) *fpl*; (*of book, photo*) épreuve *f.* **2** *a* **p. against** (*material*) à l'épreuve de (*feu, acide etc*). ● **proofreader** *n Typ* correcteur, -trice *mf.*

prop [prɒp] **1** *n* (*for wall etc*) étai *m* ▌*vt* (**-pp-**) **to p. up** (*ladder etc*) appuyer (**against** contre); (*one's head*) caler; (*wall*) étayer. **2** *n* **prop(s)** *Th* accessoire(s) *m(pl).*

propaganda [prɒpə'gændə] *n* propagande *f.*

propel [prə'pel] *vt* (**-ll-**) (*drive, hurl*) propulser. ● **propeller** *n Av Nau* hélice *f.*

proper ['prɒpər] *a* (*suitable, respectable*) convenable; (*right*) bon (*f* bonne); (*downright*) véritable; (*noun, meaning*) propre; **the p. address/method/***etc* (*right*) la bonne adresse/méthode/*etc*; **the village/***etc* **p.** le village/*etc* proprement dit. ● —**ly** *adv* comme il faut, convenablement; **very p.** (*quite rightly*) à juste titre.

property ['prɒpətɪ] **1** *n* (*building*) propriété *f*; (*possessions*) biens *mpl*, propriété *f* ▌*a* (*market, company etc*) immobilier; (*tax*) foncier; **p. owner** propriétaire *m* foncier. **2** *n* (*of substance etc*) propriété *f.*

prophecy ['prɒfɪsɪ] *n* prophétie *f.* ● **prophesy** [-ɪsaɪ] *vti* prophétiser; **to p. that** prédire que.

prophet ['prɒfɪt] *n* prophète *m.* ● **pro'phetic** *a* prophétique.

proportion [prə'pɔːʃ(ə)n] *n* (*ratio*) proportion *f*; (*portion*) partie *f*; *pl* (*size*) dimensions *fpl*, proportions *fpl*; **in p.** en proportion (**to** de); **out of p.** hors de proportion (**to** avec) ▌*vt* **well proportioned** bien proportionné. ● **proportional** *or* **proportionate** *a* proportionnel (**to** à).

propose [prə'pəʊz] *vt* (*suggest*) proposer (**to** à, **that** que + *sub*)); **to p. to do, p. doing** se proposer de faire ▌*vi* faire une demande (en mariage) (**to** à). ● **proposal** *n* proposition *f*; (*of marriage*) demande *f* (en mariage). ● **proposition** [prɒpə'zɪʃ(ə)n] *n* proposition *f*; (*matter*) *Fig* affaire *f.*

proprietor [prə'praɪətər] *n* propriétaire *mf.*

pros [prəʊz] *npl* **the p. and cons** le pour et le contre.

prosaic [prəʊ'zeɪɪk] *a* prosaïque.

prose [prəʊz] *n* prose *f*; (*translation*) thème *m.*

prosecute ['prɒsɪkjuːt] *vt* poursuivre (en justice) (**for stealing/***etc* pour vol/*etc*). ● **prosecution** [-'kjuːʃ(ə)n] *n Jur* poursuites *fpl*; **the p.** (*lawyers*) = le ministère public.

prospect¹ ['prɒspekt] *n* (*outlook, possibility*) perspective *f* (**of doing** de faire, **of sth** de qch); (*future*) **prospects** perspectives *fpl* d'avenir; **it has prospects** c'est prometteur; **she has prospects** elle a de l'avenir. ● **pro'spective** *a* (*possible*) éventuel; (*future*) futur.

prospect² [prə'spekt] *vi* **to p. for** (*gold etc*) chercher. ● **prospector** *n* prospecteur, -trice *mf*.

prospectus [prə'spektəs] *n* (*leaflet*) prospectus *m*; *Univ* guide *m* (de l'étudiant).

prosper ['prɒspər] *vi* prospérer.
● **pro'sperity** *n* prospérité *f*. ● **prosperous** *a* (*wealthy*) riche, prospère; (*thriving*) prospère.

prostitute ['prɒstɪtjuːt] *n* prostituée *f*.
● **prostitution** [-'tjuːʃ(ə)n] *n* prostitution *f*.

prostrate ['prɒstreɪt] *a* (*prone*) sur le ventre; (*worshipper, servant*) prosterné ‖ [prɒ'streɪt] *vt* **to p. oneself** se prosterner (**before** devant).

protagonist [prəʊ'tægənɪst] *n* protagoniste *mf*.

protect [prə'tekt] *vt* protéger (**from** de, **against** contre); (*interests*) sauvegarder.
● **protection** [-ʃ(ə)n] *n* protection *f*.
● **protective** *a* (*clothes, screen etc*) de protection; (*person, attitude etc*) protecteur (*f* -trice).

protein ['prəʊtiːn] *n* protéine *f*.

protest ['prəʊtest] *n* protestation *f* (**against** contre); **in p.** en signe de protestation ‖ [prə'test] *vt* protester (**that** que); (*one's innocence*) protester de ‖ *vi* protester (**against** contre); (*of students etc*) contester. ● —**er** *n* (*student etc*) contestataire *m*.

Protestant ['prɒtɪstənt] *a & n* protestant, -ante (*mf*).

protocol ['prəʊtəkɒl] *n* protocole *m*.

protracted [prə'træktɪd] *a* prolongé.

protractor [prə'træktər] *n* (*for measuring*) rapporteur *m*.

protrude [prə'truːd] *vi* dépasser; (*of tooth*) avancer. ● —**ing** *a* (*tooth*) qui avance.

proud [praʊd] *a* (-er, -est) fier (**of** de, **to do** de faire); (*superior to others*) orgueilleux. ● —**ly** *adv* fièrement; orgueilleusement.

prove [pruːv] *vt* prouver (**that** que); **to p. oneself** faire ses preuves ‖ *vi* **to p. difficult**/*etc* s'avérer difficile/*etc*.

proverb ['prɒvɜːb] *n* proverbe *m*.
● **pro'verbial** *a* proverbial.

provide [prə'vaɪd] *vt* (*supply*) fournir (**s.o. with sth** qch à qn); **to p. s.o. with sth** (*equip*) pourvoir qn de qch ‖ *vi* **to p. for s.o.** pourvoir aux besoins de qn; (*s.o.'s future*) assurer l'avenir de qn; **to p. for sth** (*make allowance for*) prévoir qch. ● **provided** *or* **providing** *conj* **p.** (**that**) pourvu que (+ *sub*).

province ['prɒvɪns] *n* province *f*; (*field of knowledge*) *Fig* domaine *m*; **the provinces** la province; **in the provinces** en province. ● **pro'vincial** *a & n* provincial, -ale (*mf*).

provision [prə'vɪʒ(ə)n] *n* (*supply*) provision *f*; (*clause*) disposition *f*; **to make p. for** = **to provide for.**

provisional [prə'vɪʒən(ə)l] *a* provisoire.
● —**ly** *adv* provisoirement.

provocation [prɒvə'keɪʃ(ə)n] *n* provocation *f*.

provocative [prə'vɒkətɪv] *a* (*person, remark etc*) provocant.

provoke [prə'vəʊk] *vt* (*annoy*) agacer; (*rouse*) provoquer (*qn*) (**to do, into doing** à faire); (*cause*) provoquer (*réaction etc*).

prow [praʊ] *n Nau* proue *f*.

prowess ['praʊes] *n* (*bravery*) courage *m*; (*skill*) talent *m*.

prowl [praʊl] *vi* **to p. (around)** rôder ‖ *n* **to be on the p,** rôder. ● —**er** *n* rôdeur, -euse *mf*.

proxy ['prɒksɪ] *n* **by p.** par procuration.

prude [pruːd] *n* prude *f*. ● **prudish** *a* prude.

prudent ['pruːdənt] *a* prudent. ● —**ly** *adv* prudemment.

prune [pruːn] **1** *n* (*dried plum*) pruneau *m*. **2** *vt* (*tree, bush*) tailler, élaguer.

pry [praɪ] **1** *vi* être indiscret; **to p. into** se mêler de; (*s.o.'s reasons etc*) chercher à découvrir. **2** *vt* **to p. open** *Am* forcer (en faisant levier). ● —**ing** *a* indiscret.

PS [piː'es] *abbr* (*postscript*) P.-S.

psalm [sɑːm] *n* psaume *m*.

pseudo- ['sjuːdəʊ] *pref* pseudo-.

pseudonym ['sjuːdənɪm] *n* pseudonyme *m*.

psychiatry [saɪ'kaɪətrɪ] *n* psychiatrie *f*.
● **psychi'atric** *a* psychiatrique. ● **psychiatrist** *n* psychiatre *mf*.

psychic ['saɪkɪk] *a* (méta)psychique; **I'm not p.** *Fam* je ne suis pas devin.

psycho- ['saɪkəʊ] *pref* psycho-. ● **psycho'analyst** *n* psychanalyste *mf*.

psychology [saɪ'kɒlədʒɪ] *n* psychologie *f*. ● **psycho'logical** *a* psychologique. ● **psychologist** *n* psychologue *mf*.

psychopath ['saɪkəʊpæθ] *n* psychopathe *mf*.

PTO *abbr* (please turn over) TSVP.

pub [pʌb] *n* pub *m*.

puberty ['pjuːbətɪ] *n* puberté *f*.

public ['pʌblɪk] *a* public (*f* -ique); (*library, swimming pool*) municipal; **in the p. eye** très en vue; **p. company** société *f* par actions; **p. figure** personnalité *f* connue; **p. house** pub *m*; **p. life** la vie publique; **p. relations** relations *fpl* publiques.
I *n* public *m*; **in p.** en public; **a member of the p.** un simple particulier. ● **—ly** *adv* publiquement; **p. owned company** entreprise *f* nationalisée.

publican ['pʌblɪk(ə)n] *n* patron, -onne *mf* d'un pub.

publication [pʌblɪ'keɪʃ(ə)n] *n* (book etc) publication *f*.

publicity [pʌb'lɪsɪtɪ] *n* publicité *f*. ● **'publicize** *vt* rendre public; (advertise) faire de la publicité pour.

public-spirited [pʌblɪk'spɪrɪtɪd] *a* to be **p.-spirited** avoir le sens civique.

publish ['pʌblɪʃ] *vt* publier; (book, author) éditer, publier; **'published weekly'** 'paraît toutes les semaines'. ● **—ing** *n* (profession) édition *f*. ● **publisher** *n* éditeur, -trice *mf*.

pucker ['pʌkər] *vt* **to p. (up)** (brow, lips) plisser **I** *vi* **to p. (up)** se plisser.

pudding ['pʊdɪŋ] *n* pudding *m*; Christmas **p.** pudding *m*; **rice p.** riz *m* au lait.

puddle ['pʌd(ə)l] *n* flaque *f* (d'eau).

pudgy ['pʌdʒɪ] *a* (-ier, -iest) = **podgy**.

puerile ['pjʊəraɪl] *a* puérile.

puff [pʌf] *n* (of smoke, wind, air) bouffée

f **I** *vi* (blow, pant) souffler; **to p. at** (cigar) tirer sur **I** *vt* (smoke) souffler (into dans); **to p. out** (cheeks) gonfler. ● **puffy** *a* (-ier, -iest) (swollen) gonflé.

puke [pjuːk] *vi* (vomit) Sl dégueuler.

pull [pʊl] *n* (attraction) attraction *f*; **to give sth a p.** tirer qch **I** *vt* (draw, tug) tirer; (tooth) arracher; (trigger) appuyer sur; (muscle) se claquer; **to p. sth apart** or **to bits** mettre qch en pièces; **to p. a face** faire la moue **I** *vi* (tug) tirer (at, on sur); (go, move) aller; **to p. at** or **on** tirer (sur).

pull along *vt* (drag) traîner (to jusqu'à) **I** **to pull away** *vt* (move) éloigner; (snatch) arracher (from à) **I** *vi* Aut démarrer; **to p. away from** s'éloigner de **I** **to pull back** *vi* (withdraw) Mil etc se retirer **I** *vt* retirer; (curtains) ouvrir **I** **to pull down** *vt* (lower) baisser; (knock down) faire tomber; (demolish) démolir **I** **to pull in** *vt* (drag into room etc) faire entrer (de force); (stomach) rentrer; (crowd) attirer **I** *vi* (arrive) arriver; (stop) Aut se garer; **to p. into the station** (of train) entrer en gare **I** **to pull off** *vt* enlever; (plan, deal) Fig mener à bien **I** **to pull on** *vt* (boots etc) mettre **I** **to pull out** *vt* (tooth, hair) arracher; (cork, pin) enlever (from de); (from pocket etc) tirer, sortir (from de); (troops) retirer **I** *vi* (to overtake) Aut déboîter; (leave) partir; (withdraw) se retirer **I** **to pull over** *vt* (drag) traîner (to jusqu'à); (knock down) faire tomber **I** *vi* Aut se ranger (sur le côté) **I** **to pull through** *vi* s'en tirer **I** **to pull oneself together** *vt* se ressaisir **I** **to pull up** *vt* (socks, blind, Am shade etc) remonter; (plant, tree) arracher **I** *vi* Aut s'arrêter.

pulley ['pʊlɪ] *n* poulie *f*.

pullout ['pʊlaʊt] *n* (in newspaper etc) supplément *m* détachable.

pullover ['pʊləʊvər] *n* pull(-over) *m*.

pulp [pʌlp] *n* (of fruit) pulpe *f*; **in a p.** Fig en bouillie.

pulpit ['pʊlpɪt] *n* (in church) chaire *f*.

pulse [pʌls] n 1 Med pouls m. 2 pulses (plant seeds) graines fpl de légumineuse.

pulverize ['pʌlvəraɪz] vt (grind, defeat) pulvériser.

pumice ['pʌmɪs] n p. (stone) pierre f ponce.

pump [pʌmp] 1 n pompe f; petrol p., Am gas p. pompe f à essence; (petrol) p. attendant pompiste mf ∎ vt pomper; (blood, round body) faire circuler; (money) Fig injecter (into dans); to p. s.o. (for information) tirer les vers du nez à qn; to p. air into, to p. up (mattress etc) gonfler. 2 n (shoe) (for sports) tennis m; (for dancing) escarpin m.

pumpkin ['pʌmpkɪn] n potiron m.

pun [pʌn] n calembour m.

punch[1] [pʌntʃ] n (blow) coup m de poing; (force) Fig punch m; p. line (of joke) astuce f finale ∎ vt (person) donner un coup de poing à (on the chin au menton). ●p.-up n Fam bagarre f.

punch[2] [pʌntʃ] 1 n (for paper) perforeuse f; (for tickets) poinçonneuse f ∎ vt (ticket) poinçonner, (with date) composter; (paper) perforer; to p. a hole in sth faire un trou dans qch. 2 n (drink) punch m.

punctual ['pʌŋktʃʊəl] a (on time) à l'heure; (regularly) ponctuel. ●—ly adv à l'heure; (regularly) ponctuellement.

punctuate ['pʌŋktʃʊeɪt] vt ponctuer (with de). ●punctuation [-'eɪʃ(ə)n] n ponctuation f; p. mark signe m de ponctuation.

puncture ['pʌŋktʃər] n (in tyre, Am tire) crevaison f; to have a p. crever ∎ vti (burst) crever.

pungent ['pʌndʒənt] a âcre, piquant.

punish ['pʌnɪʃ] vt punir (for sth de qch, for doing pour avoir fait). ●—ing a (tiring) éreintant. ●—ment n punition f, châtiment m; capital p. peine f capitale; to take a lot of p. (damage) Fig en encaisser.

punitive ['pjuːnɪtɪv] a (measure etc)

punitif.

punk [pʌŋk] n p. (rock) (music) le punk (rock); p. (rocker) (fan) punk mf ∎ a punk inv.

punnet ['pʌnɪt] n (of strawberries) barquette f.

punt [pʌnt] n barque f (à fond plat). ●—ing n canotage m. ●punter n 1 (gambler) parieur, -euse mf. 2 (customer) Fam client, -ente mf.

puny ['pjuːnɪ] a (-ier, -iest) (sickly) chétif; (small) (effort) faible.

pup ['pʌp] n (dog) chiot m.

pupil ['pjuːp(ə)l] n 1 (in school) élève mf. 2 (of eye) pupille f.

puppet ['pʌpɪt] n marionnette f; p. show spectacle m de marionnettes.

puppy ['pʌpɪ] n (dog) chiot m.

purchas/e ['pɜːtʃɪs] n (article, buying) achat m ∎ vt acheter (from s.o. à qn, for s.o. à or pour qn). ●—er n acheteur, -euse mf.

pure [pjʊər] a (-er, -est) pur.

purée ['pjʊəreɪ] n purée f.

purely ['pjʊəlɪ] adv (only) strictement.

purge [pɜːdʒ] n Pol purge f ∎ vt (rid) purger (of de); (group) Pol épurer.

purify ['pjʊərɪfaɪ] vt purifier.

puritanical [pjʊərɪ'tænɪk(ə)l] a puritain.

purple ['pɜːp(ə)l] a violet (f -ette); to go p. (with anger) devenir pourpre ∎ n violet m.

purpose ['pɜːpəs] n 1 (aim) but m; for this p. dans ce but; on p. exprès; to serve no p. ne servir à rien; for the purposes of pour les besoins de. 2 (determination) résolution f; to have a sense of p. être résolu. ●p.-'built a construit spécialement. ●—posely adv exprès.

purr [pɜːr] vi ronronner ∎ n ronron(nement) m.

purse [pɜːs] n 1 (for coins) porte-monnaie m inv; (handbag) Am sac m à main. 2 vt to p. one's lips pincer les lèvres.

purser ['pɜːsər] n Nau commissaire m du bord.

pursue [pə'sjuː] vt (chase, seek, continue) poursuivre; (fame, pleasure) recher-

cher; (*course of action*) suivre. ● **pursuit**
n poursuite *f*; (*activity, pastime*) occupation *f*.

pus [pʌs] *n* pus *m*.

push [puʃ] *n* (*shove*) poussée *f*; **to give
s.o./sth a p.** pousser qn/qch; **to give s.o.
the p.** *Fam* flanquer qn à la porte.
▮ *vt* pousser (**to, as far as** jusqu'à);
(*button*) appuyer sur; (*lever*) abaisser;
(*drugs*) *Fam* revendre; **to p. sth into/
between** enfoncer *or* fourrer qch dans/
entre; **to p. sth off the table** faire tomber
qch de la table (en le poussant); **to p.
s.o. off a cliff** pousser qn du haut d'une
falaise; **to be pushing forty/***etc Fam*
friser la quarantaine/*etc*.
▮ *vi* pousser; (*on button etc*) appuyer (**on**
sur).

push about *or* **around** *vt* (*bully*) *Fam*
marcher sur les pieds à (**qn**) ▮ **to push
aside** *vt* (*person, objection*) écarter ▮ **to
push away** *or* **back** *vt* repousser ▮ **to
push down** *vt* (*button*) appuyer sur;
(*lever*) abaisser ▮ **to push for** *vt* faire
pression pour obtenir (**qch**) ▮ **to push in**
vi (*in queue, Am line*) *Fam* resquiller ▮ **to
push off** *vi* (*leave*) *Fam* filer; **p. off!** *Fam*
fiche le camp! ▮ **to push on** *vi* continuer
(**with sth** qch); (*in journey*) poursuivre
sa route ▮ **to push over** *vt* renverser ▮ **to
push through** *vt* (*law*) faire adopter ▮ *vti*
to push (*one's way*) **through** se frayer un
chemin (**a crowd** à travers une foule)
▮ **to push up** *vt* (*lever, sleeve, collar*)
relever; (*increase*) augmenter.

pushbike ['puʃbaɪk] *n Fam* vélo *m*.
● **push-button** *n* bouton *m*; (*of phone*)
touche *f*; **p.-button phone** téléphone *m* à
touches. ● **pushchair** *n* poussette *f*.
● **pushover** *n* **to be a p.** *Fam* être
facile. ● **push-up** *n* (*exercise*) *Am*
pompe *f*.

pushed [puʃt] *a* **to be p. (for time)** être
très bousculé.

pusher ['puʃər] *n* (*of drugs*) revendeur,
-euse *mf* (de drogue).

pushy ['puʃɪ] *a* (**-ier, -iest**) *Pej* arrogant;

(*in job*) arriviste.

puss(y) ['pus(ɪ)] *n* (*cat*) minou *m*.

put [put] *vt* (*pt & pp put, pres p putting*)
mettre; (*money, savings*) placer (**into**
dans); (*problem, argument*) présenter
(**to** à); (*question*) poser (**to** à); (*say*)
dire; (*estimate*) évaluer (**at** à); **to p.
pressure on sth/s.o.** faire pression sur
qch/qn; **to p. it bluntly** pour parler
franc.

put across *vt* (*message etc*) communiquer (**to** à) ▮ **to put aside** *vt* (*money,
object*) mettre de côté ▮ **to put away** *vt*
(*in its place*) ranger (*livre, voiture etc*);
(*criminal*) mettre en prison; (*insane
person*) enfermer ▮ **to put back** *vt* (*replace, postpone*) remettre; (*receiver*) *Tel*
raccrocher; (*progress, clock*) retarder
▮ **to put by** *vt* (*money*) mettre de côté
▮ **to put down** *vt* (*on floor etc*) poser;
(*passenger*) déposer; (*a deposit*) *Fin*
verser; (*write down*) inscrire; (*attribute*) attribuer (**to** à); (*kill*) faire piquer
(*chien etc*) ▮ **to put forward** *vt* (*clock,
meeting, argument*) avancer; (*opinion*)
exprimer; (*candidate*) proposer (**for** à)
▮ **to put in** *vt* (*sth into box etc*) mettre
dedans; (*insert*) introduire; (*add*) ajouter; (*install*) installer; (*application, request*) faire; (*enrol*) inscrire (**qn**) (**for** à);
(*spend*) passer (*une heure etc*) (*doing* à
faire) ▮ **to put off** *vt* (*postpone*) renvoyer
(à plus tard); (*passenger*) déposer; (*gas,
radio*) fermer; (*dismay*) déconcerter; **to
p. s.o. off** dissuader qn (*doing* de faire);
(*disgust*) dégoûter qn (**sth de** qch); **to
p. s.o. off doing** (*disgust*) ôter à qn l'envie
de faire ▮ **to put on** *vt* (*clothes etc*)
mettre; (*weight*) prendre; (*film, play*)
jouer; (*gas, radio*) mettre, allumer;
(*record, cassette*) passer; (*clock*) avancer; **to p. s.o. on** (*tease*) *Am* faire
marcher qn; **she p. me on to you** elle
m'a donné votre adresse ▮ **to put out** *vt*
(*take outside*) sortir; (*arm, leg*) étendre;
(*hand*) tendre; (*tongue*) tirer; (*gas, light*)
éteindre, fermer; (*inconvenience*) déranger; (*upset*) déconcerter ▮ **to p.**

through *vt Tel* passer (*qn*) (**to** à) **▌to put together** *vt* mettre ensemble; (*assemble*) assembler; (*compose*) composer; (*prepare*) préparer **▌to put up** *vi* (*stay*) descendre (**at a hotel** à un hôtel) **▌** *vt* (*lift*) lever; (*window*) remonter; (*tent, statue, ladder*) dresser; (*flag*) hisser; (*building*) construire; (*umbrella*) ouvrir; (*picture, poster*) mettre; (*price, numbers*) augmenter; (*resistance*) offrir; (*candidate*) proposer (**for** à); (*guest*) loger **▌to put up with** *vt* (*tolerate*) supporter (*qch, qn*).

putt [pʌt] *n Golf* putt *m*. ● **putting** *n Golf* putting *m*; **p. green** green *m*.

putter ['pʌtər] *vi* **to p. around** *Am* bri-coler.

putty ['pʌtɪ] *n* mastic *m* (*pour vitres*).

put-you-up ['pʊtjuːʌp] *n* canapé-lit *m*.

puzzl/e ['pʌz(ə)l] *n* mystère *m*; (*jigsaw*) puzzle *m* **▌** *vt* laisser perplexe **▌** *vi* **to p. over** (*problem etc*) se creuser la tête sur. ● **—ed** *a* perplexe. ● **—ing** *a* curieux.

PVC [piːviːˈsiː] *n* (*plastic*) PVC *m*.

pyjama [pɪˈdʒɑːmə] *a* (*jacket etc*) de pyjama. ● **pyjamas** *npl* pyjama *m*; **a pair of p.** un pyjama; **to be in p.** être en pyjama.

pylon ['paɪlən] *n* pylône *m*.

pyramid ['pɪrəmɪd] *n* pyramide *f*.

Pyrenees [pɪrəˈniːz] *npl* **the P.** les Pyrénées *fpl*.

Q

Q, q [kju:] *n* Q, q *m*.

quack [kwæk] *n* **1** (*of duck*) coin-coin *m inv*. **2** (*doctor*) charlatan *m*.

quad(rangle) ['kwɒd(ræŋg(ə)l)] *n* (*of college, school*) cour *f*.

quadruple [kwɒ'dru:p(ə)l] *vti* quadrupler.

quadruplets [kwɒ'dru:plɪts] (*Fam* **quads** [kwɒdz]) *npl* quadruplés, -ées *mfpl*.

quail [kweɪl] *n* (*bird*) caille *f*.

quaint [kweɪnt] *a* (**-er, -est**) pittoresque; (*old-fashioned*) vieillot (*f* -otte); (*odd*) bizarre.

quake [kweɪk] *n Fam* tremblement *m* de terre.

Quaker ['kweɪkər] *n* quaker, -eresse *mf*.

qualification [kwɒlɪfɪ'keɪʃ(ə)n] *n* **1** (*diploma*) diplôme *m*; (*competence*) compétence *f*; *pl* (*skills*) qualités *fpl* nécessaires (**for** pour, **to do** pour faire). **2** (*reservation*) réserve *f*.

qualify ['kwɒlɪfaɪ] **1** *vt* (*make competent*) & *Sp* qualifier (**qn**) (**for sth** pour qch, **to do** pour faire) ● *vi* obtenir son diplôme (**as a doctor**/*etc* de médecin/*etc*); *Sp* se qualifier (**for** pour); **to q. for** (*post*) remplir les conditions requises pour. **2** *vt* (*opinion, statement*) nuancer; *Gram* qualifier. ● **qualified** *a* (*able*) qualifié (**to do** pour faire); (*teacher etc*) diplômé; (*success*) limité; (*opinion*) nuancé; (*support*) conditionnel.

quality ['kwɒlɪtɪ] *n* qualité *f*.

qualms [kwɑ:mz] *npl* (*scruples*) scrupules *mpl*.

quandary ['kwɒndrɪ] *n* **in a q.** bien embarrassé.

quantity ['kwɒntɪtɪ] *n* quantité *f*; **in q.** (*to purchase etc*) en grande(s) quantité(s). ● **quantify** *vt* quantifier.

quarantine ['kwɒrəntiːn] *n Med* quarantaine *f* ▌ *vt* mettre en quarantaine.

quarrel ['kwɒrəl] *n* dispute *f*; **to pick a q.** chercher des histoires (**with s.o.** à qn). ▌ *vi* (**-ll-, *Am* -l-**) se disputer (**with s.o.** avec qn). ● **quarrelling** *or Am* **quarreling** *n* (*quarrels*) disputes *fpl*. ● **quarrelsome** *a* querelleur.

quarry ['kwɒrɪ] *n* (*to extract stone etc*) carrière *f*.

quart [kwɔːt] *n* litre *m* (*mesure approximative*) (*Br* = 1,14 *litres, Am* = 0,95 *litre*).

quarter ['kwɔːtər] **1** *n* quart *m*; (*money*) *Am Can* quart *m* de dollar; (*of fruit, moon*) quartier *m*; **to divide sth into quarters** diviser qch en quatre; **q. (of a) pound** quart *m* de livre; **a q. past nine**, *Am* **a q. after nine** neuf heures et un quart; **a q. to nine** neuf heures moins le quart; **from all quarters** de toutes parts. **2** *n* (*district*) quartier *m*; (*living*) **quarters** logement(s) *m(pl)*; (*of soldier*) quartier(s) *m(pl)*.

quarterly ['kwɔːtəlɪ] *a* (*magazine etc*) trimestriel ▌ *adv* trimestriellement ▌ *n* publication *f* trimestrielle.

quartet(te) [kwɔː'tet] *n Mus* quatuor *m*; (*jazz*) **q.** quartette *m*.

quartz [kwɔːts] *n* quartz *m* ▌ *a* (*watch etc*) à quartz.

quash [kwɒʃ] *vt* (*rebellion*) réprimer; (*verdict*) *Jur* casser.

quaver ['kweɪvər] **1** *n Mus* croche *f*. **2** *vi* chevroter.

quay [ki:] *n Nau* quai *m*. ● **quayside** *n* on the q. sur les quais.

queasy ['kwi:zɪ] *a* (**-ier, -iest**) **to feel** *or* **be q.** avoir mal au cœur.

Quebec [kwɪ'bek] *n* le Québec.

queen [kwi:n] *n* reine *f*; *Chess Cards* dame *f*; **the q. mother** la reine mère.

queer ['kwɪər] *a* (**-er, -est**) (*odd*) bizarre; (*ill*) *Fam* patraque.

quell [kwel] *vt* (*revolt etc*) réprimer.

quench [kwentʃ] *vt* **to q. one's thirst** se désaltérer.

query ['kwɪərɪ] *n* question *f* ∥ *vt* poser des questions sur.

quest [kwest] *n* quête *f* (**for** de); **in q. of** en quête de.

question ['kwestʃ(ə)n] *n* question *f*; **there's no q. of it, it's out of the q.** c'est hors de question; **without q.** incontestable(ment); **in q.** en question; **q. mark** point *m* d'interrogation.

∥ *vt* interroger (*qn*) (**about** sur); (*doubt*) mettre (*qch*) en question; **to q. whether** douter que (+ *sub*). ● **questionable** *a* douteux. ● **questio'nnaire** *n* questionnaire *m*.

queue [kjuː] *n* (*of people*) queue *f*; (*of cars*) file *f*; **to form a q.** faire la queue ∥ *vi* **to q. (up)** faire la queue (**for** pour).

quibble ['kwɪb(ə)l] *vi* ergoter, discuter (**over** sur).

quiche [kiːʃ] *n* (*tart*) quiche *f*.

quick [kwɪk] **1** *a* (**-er, -est**) rapide; **q. to react** prompt à réagir; **be q.!** fais vite!; **to have a q. shower/meal/etc** se doucher/manger/*etc* en vitesse ∥ *adv* (**-er, -est**) vite. **2** *n* **to cut s.o. to the q.** blesser qn au vif. ● **q.-'tempered** *a* irascible. ● **q.-'witted** *a* à l'esprit vif.

quicken ['kwɪk(ə)n] *vt* accélérer ∥ *vi* s'accélérer.

quickly ['kwɪklɪ] *adv* vite.

quicksands ['kwɪksændz] *npl* sables *mpl* mouvants.

quid [kwɪd] *n inv Fam* livre *f* (sterling).

quiet [kwaɪət] *a* (**-er, -est**) (*silent, peaceful*) tranquille, calme; (*machine, vehicle*) silencieux; (*voice, sound*) doux (*f* douce); (*private*) intime; **to be** or **keep q.** (*shut up*) se taire; (*make no noise*) ne pas faire de bruit; **q.!** silence!; **to keep q.**

about sth ne pas parler de qch; **on the q.** (*secretly*) *Fam* en cachette.

quieten ['kwaɪət(ə)n] *vti* **to q. (down)** (se) calmer.

quietly ['kwaɪətlɪ] *adv* tranquillement; (*not loudly*) doucement; (*silently*) silencieusement; (*secretly*) en cachette.

quilt [kwɪlt] *n* édredon *m*; (*continental*) q. (*duvet*) couette *f* ∥ *vt* (*pad*) matelasser; **quilted jacket** veste *f* matelassée.

quintet(te) [kwɪn'tet] *n* quintette *m*.

quintuplets [kwɪn'tjuːplɪts, *Am* -'tʌplɪts] (*Fam* **quins** [kwɪnz], *Am* **quints** [kwɪnts]) *npl* quintuplés, -ées *mfpl*.

quip [kwɪp] *n* (*remark*) boutade *f*.

quirk [kwɜːk] *n* bizarrerie *f*; (*of fate*) caprice *m*.

quit [kwɪt] *vt* (*pt & pp* **quit** *or* **quitted**, *pres p* **quitting**) (*leave*) quitter; **to q. doing** arrêter de faire ∥ *vi* (*give up*) abandonner; (*resign*) démissionner.

quite [kwaɪt] *adv* (*entirely*) tout à fait; (*really*) vraiment; (*rather*) assez; **q. a genius** un véritable génie; **q. (so)** exactement!; **q. a lot** pas mal (**of** de); **q. a (long) time ago** il y a pas mal de temps.

quits [kwɪts] *a* quitte (**with** envers); **to call it q.** en rester là.

quiver ['kwɪvər] *vi* (*of person*) frémir (**with** de); (*of voice*) trembler.

quiz [kwɪz] *n* (*pl* **quizzes**) (*test*) test *m*; **q. (programme)** *TV Rad* jeu(-concours) *m* ∥ *vt* (**-zz-**) questionner.

quota ['kwəʊtə] *n* quota *m*.

quote [kwəʊt] *vt* citer; (*reference number*) *Com* rappeler; (*price*) indiquer ∥ *vi* **to q. from** (*book*) citer ∥ *n* = **quotation**; **in quotes** entre guillemets. ● **quotation** [-'teɪʃ(ə)n] *n* citation *f*; (*estimate*) *Com* devis *m*; **q. marks** guillemets *mpl*; **in q. marks** entre guillemets.

R

R, r [ɑːr] n R, r m.

rabbi ['ræbaɪ] n rabbin m.

rabbit ['ræbɪt] n lapin m.

rabble ['ræb(ə)l] n **the r.** Pej la populace.

rabies ['reɪbiːz] n Med rage f. ●**rabid** ['ræbɪd] a (dog) enragé.

raccoon [rə'kuːn] n (animal) raton m laveur.

rac/e¹ [reɪs] n (contest) course f ‖ vt (horse) faire courir; (engine) emballer; **to r.** (against or with) **s.o.** faire une course avec qn ‖ vi (run) courir; (of engine) s'emballer. ●**—ing** n courses fpl; **r. car** voiture f de course; **r. driver** coureur m automobile. ●**racecourse** n champ m de courses. ●**racehorse** n cheval m de course. ●**racetrack** n (for horses) Am champ m de courses; (for cars etc) piste f.

race² [reɪs] n (group) race f; **r. relations** rapports mpl entre les races.

racial ['reɪʃəl] a racial. ●**racialism** n racisme m. ●**racism** ['reɪsɪz(ə)m] n racisme m. ●**racist** a & n raciste (mf).

rack [ræk] **1** n (for bottles, letters etc) casier m; (for drying dishes) égouttoir m; (luggage) (on bus, train) filet m à bagages; (on bicycle) porte-bagages m inv; (roof) **r.** (of car) galerie f. **2** vt **to r. one's brains** se creuser la cervelle. **3** n **to go to r. and ruin** (of building) tomber en ruine.

racket ['rækɪt] n **1** (for tennis) raquette f. **2** (din) vacarme m. **3** (crime) racket m; (scheme) combine f; **the drugs r.** le trafic de (la) drogue.

racoon [rə'kuːn] n (animal) raton m laveur.

racy ['reɪsɪ] a (-ier, -iest) (description etc) piquant; (suggestive) osé.

radar ['reɪdɑːr] n radar m ‖ a (control, trap etc) radar inv.

radiant ['reɪdɪənt] a (person) rayonnant (with de), radieux.

radiate ['reɪdɪeɪt] vt (heat) dégager; (joy) Fig rayonner de ‖ vi (of heat, lines) rayonner (from de). ●**radiation** [-'eɪʃ(ə)n] n (of heat) rayonnement m (of de); (radioactivity) radiation f.

radiator ['reɪdɪeɪtər] n (of central heating, vehicle) radiateur m.

radical ['rædɪk(ə)l] a radical ‖ n (person) Pol radical, -ale mf.

radio ['reɪdɪəʊ] n (pl -os) radio f; **on** or **over the r.** à la radio; **car r.** autoradio m; **r. set** poste m de radio; **r. operator** radio m ‖ vt **to r. s.o.** appeler qn par radio. ●**r.-con'trolled** a radioguidé.

radioactive [reɪdɪəʊ'æktɪv] a radioactif. ●**radioac'tivity** n radioactivité f.

radiographer [reɪdɪ'ɒɡrəfər] n (technician) radiologue m. ●**radiologist** n (doctor) radiologue mf.

radish ['rædɪʃ] n radis m.

radius, pl **-dii** ['reɪdɪəs, -dɪaɪ] n (of circle) rayon m; **within a r. of 10 km** dans un rayon de 10 km.

RAF [ɑːreɪ'ef] n abbr (Royal Air Force) armée f de l'air (britannique).

raffle ['ræf(ə)l] n tombola f.

raft [rɑːft] n (boat) radeau m.

rag [ræɡ] n **1** (old clothing) haillon m; (for dusting etc) chiffon m; **in rags** (clothes) en loques; (person) en haillons. **2** (newspaper) torchon m. **3** (procession) carnaval m d'étudiants (au profit d'œuvres de charité).

ragamuffin ['ræɡəmʌfɪn] n va-nu-pieds m inv.

rag/e [reɪdʒ] n (anger) rage f; **to fly into a r.** se mettre en rage; **to be all the r.** (of fashion) faire fureur ‖ vi (be angry) rager; (of storm, battle) faire rage. ●**—ing** a (storm, fever) violent.

ragged ['rægɪd] *a* (*clothes*) en loques; (*person*) en haillons.

raid [reɪd] *n* Mil raid *m*; (*by police*) descente *f*; (*by thieves*) hold-up *m inv*; **air r.** raid *m* aérien ▮ *vt* faire un raid *or* une descente *or* un hold-up dans; *Av* attaquer; (*fridge etc*) *Fam* dévaliser. ● **raider** *n* (*criminal*) malfaiteur *m*.

rail [reɪl] **1** *n* (*for train*) rail *m*; **by r.** (*to travel*) par le train; (*to send*) par chemin de fer; **to go off the rails** (*of train*) dérailler ▮ *a* (*ticket*) de chemin de fer; (*strike*) des cheminots. **2** *n* (*rod on balcony*) balustrade *f*; (*on stairs*) rampe *f*; (*curtain rod*) tringle *f*; (*towel*) r. porte-serviettes *m inv*. ● **railing** *n* (*of balcony*) balustrade *f*; *pl* (*fence*) grille *f*.

railcard ['reɪlkɑːd] *n* carte *f* de chemin de fer. ● **railroad** *n Am* = **railway**; **r. track** voie *f* ferrée. ● **railway** *n* (*system*) chemin *m* de fer; (*track*) voie *f* ferrée ▮ *a* (*ticket*) de chemin de fer; (*timetable*) des chemins de fer; **r. line** (*route*) ligne *f* de chemin de fer; (*track*) voie *f* ferrée; **r. station** gare *f*.

rain [reɪn] *n* pluie *f*; **in the r.** sous la pluie; **I'll give you a r. check** *Am Fam* j'accepterai volontiers à une date ultérieure ▮ *vi* pleuvoir; **to r. (down)** (*of blows, bullets*) pleuvoir; **it's raining** il pleut. ● **rainbow** *n* arc-en-ciel *m*. ● **raincoat** *n* imper(méable) *m*. ● **raindrop** *n* goutte *f* de pluie. ● **rainfall** *n* (*amount*) précipitations *fpl*. ● **rainforest** *n* forêt *f* tropicale (humide). ● **rainwater** *n* eau *f* de pluie. ● **rainy** *a* (**-ier, -iest**) pluvieux; **the r. season** la saison des pluies.

raise [reɪz] *vt* (*lift*) lever; (*child, family, animal, voice*) élever; (*crops*) cultiver; (*salary, price*) augmenter; (*temperature*) faire monter; (*question*) soulever; (*taxes*) lever; **to r. s.o.'s hopes** faire naître les espérances de qn; **to r. money** réunir des fonds ▮ *n* (*pay rise*) *Am* augmentation *f* (de salaire).

raisin ['reɪz(ə)n] *n* raisin *m* sec.

rake [reɪk] *n* râteau *m* ▮ *vt* (*garden*) ratisser; **to r. (up)** (*leaves*) ratisser; **to**

r. in (*money*) *Fam* ramasser à la pelle.

rally ['rælɪ] *vt* (*unite, win over*) rallier (**to** à); **to r. support** rallier des partisans (**for** autour de) ▮ *vi* se rallier (**to** à); (*recover*) reprendre ses forces; **to r. round** (s.o.) (*help*) venir en aide (à qn) ▮ *n* Pol rassemblement *m*; *Aut* rallye *m*.

ram [ræm] **1** *n* (*animal*) bélier *m*. **2** *vt* (**-mm-**) (*vehicle*) emboutir; **to r. sth into sth** enfoncer qch dans qch.

RAM [ræm] *n abbr* = **random access memory**.

rambl/e ['ræmb(ə)l] **1** *n* (*hike*) randonnée *f* ▮ *vi* faire une randonnée *or* des randonnées. **2** *vi* (*in talk*) *Pej* discourir. ● **—er** *n* promeneur, -euse *mf*.

rambling ['ræmblɪŋ] **1** *a* (*house*) construit sans plan; (*spread out*) vaste. **2** *a* (*speech*) décousu.

ramp [ræmp] *n* (*slope for wheelchair etc*) rampe *f* (d'accès); (*in garage*) pont *m* (de graissage); '**r.**' *Aut* 'dénivellation'.

rampage ['ræmpeɪdʒ] *n* **to go on the r.** (*of crowd*) se déchaîner; (*loot*) se livrer au pillage.

rampant ['ræmpənt] *a* **to be r.** (*of crime, disease*) sévir.

rampart ['ræmpɑːt] *n* rempart *m*.

ramshackle ['ræmʃæk(ə)l] *a* délabré.

ran [ræn] *pt of* **run**.

ranch [rɑːntʃ] *n Am* ranch *m*; **r. house** maison *f* genre bungalow (sur sous-sol).

rancid ['rænsɪd] *a* rance.

random ['rændəm] *n* **at r.** au hasard ▮ *a* (*choice*) (fait) au hasard; (*sample*) prélevé au hasard; **r. check** (*by police*) contrôle-surprise *m*; **r. access memory** *Comptr* mémoire *f* vive.

randy ['rændɪ] *a* (**-ier, -iest**) *Fam* excité.

rang [ræŋ] *pt of* **ring**[2].

range [reɪndʒ] **1** *n* (*of gun, voice etc*) portée *f*; (*of singer's voice*) étendue *f*; (*of aircraft, ship*) rayon *m* d'action; (*of colours, prices, products*) gamme *f*; (*of sizes*) choix *m*; (*of temperature*) variations *fpl* ▮ *vi* (*vary*) varier (**from** de, **to** à); (*extend*) s'étendre. **2** *n* (*of moun-*

tains) chaîne *f*; (*grassland*) *Am* prairie *f*. **3** *n* (*stove*) *Am* cuisinière *f*. **4** *n* (*shooting or rifle*) r. (*at funfair*) stand *m* de tir; (*outdoors*) champ *m* de tir.

ranger ['reɪndʒər] *n* garde *m* forestier.

rank [ræŋk] **1** *n* (*position, class*) rang *m*; (*grade*) *Mil* grade *m*; **the r. and file** (*workers etc*) la base; **taxi r.** station *f* de taxi ▮ *vti* **to r. among** compter parmi. **2** *a* (**-er, -est**) (*smell*) fétide.

ransack ['rænsæk] *vt* (*search*) fouiller; (*plunder*) saccager.

ransom ['ræns(ə)m] *n* (*money*) rançon *f*; **to hold s.o. to r.** rançonner qn.

rant [rænt] *vi* **to r. (and rave)** tempêter (**at** contre).

rap [ræp] **1** *n* petit coup *m* sec ▮ *vi* (**-pp-**) frapper (**at** à). **2** *n* (*music*) rap *m*.

rape [reɪp] *vt* violer ▮ *n* viol *m*. ● **rapist** *n* violeur *m*.

rapid ['ræpɪd] **1** *a* rapide. **2** *npl* **rapids** (*of river*) rapides *mpl*. ● **rapidly** *adv* rapidement.

rapture ['ræptʃər] *n* **to go into raptures** s'extasier (**about** sur). ● **rapturous** *a* (*welcome, applause*) enthousiaste.

rare [reər] *a* (**-er, -est**) rare; (*meat*) bleu; (*medium*) r. (*meat*) saignant; **it's r. for her to do it** il est rare qu'elle le fasse. ● **—ly** *adv* rarement. ● **rarity** *n* (*quality, object*) rareté *f*.

rarefied ['reərɪfaɪd] *a* raréfié.

raring ['reərɪŋ] *a* **r. to start**/*etc* impatient de commencer/*etc*.

rascal ['rɑːsk(ə)l] *n* coquin, -ine *mf*.

rash [ræʃ] **1** *n* (*on skin*) (*patches*) rougeurs *fpl*; (*spots*) (éruption *f* de) boutons *mpl*. **2** *a* (**-er, -est**) irréfléchi. ● **—ly** *adv* sans réfléchir.

rasher ['ræʃər] *n* tranche *f* de lard.

raspberry ['rɑːzbərɪ, *Am* -berɪ] *n* (*fruit*) framboise *f*.

rasping ['rɑːspɪŋ] *a* (*voice*) âpre.

rat [ræt] **1** *n* rat *m*; **the r. race** *Fig* la course au bifteck, the jungle. **2** *vi* (**-tt-**) **to r. on** *Fam* (*denounce*) cafarder sur; (*promise*) manquer à.

rate [reɪt] *n* (*level, percentage*) taux *m*;

(*speed*) vitesse *f*; (*price*) tarif *m*; **exchange/interest r.** taux *m* de change/d'intérêt; **insurance rates** primes *fpl* d'assurance; **postage r.** tarif *m* postal; **r. of flow** débit *m*; **at a r.** d'une vitesse de; (*amount*) à raison de; **at this r.** (*slow speed*) à ce train-là; **at any r.** en tout cas; **the success r.** (*chances*) les chances *fpl* de succès.

2 *vt* (*evaluate*) évaluer; (*regard*) considérer (**as** comme); (*deserve*) mériter; **to be highly rated** être très apprécié.

rather ['rɑːðər] *adv* (*preferably, quite*) plutôt; **I'd r. stay** j'aimerais mieux *or* je préférerais rester (**than** que); **I'd r. you came** j'aimerais mieux *or* je préférerais que vous veniez; **r. than leave**/*etc* plutôt que de partir/*etc*; **r. more tired**/*etc* un peu plus fatigué/*etc* (**than** que).

ratify ['rætɪfaɪ] *vt* ratifier.

rating ['reɪtɪŋ] *n* classement *m*; (*wage level*) indice *m*; **credit r.** *Fin* degré *m* de solvabilité; **the ratings** *TV* l'indice *m* d'écoute.

ratio ['reɪʃɪəʊ] *n* (*pl* **-os**) proportion *f*.

ration ['ræʃ(ə)n, *Am* 'reɪʃ(ə)n] *n* ration *f*; *pl* (*food*) vivres *mpl* ▮ *vt* rationner. ● **—ing** *n* rationnement *m*.

rational ['ræʃən(ə)l] *a* (*a thought etc*) rationnel; (*person*) raisonnable. ● **rationalize** *vt* (*organize*) rationaliser; (*explain*) justifier. ● **rationally** *adv* raisonnablement.

rattle ['ræt(ə)l] **1** *n* (*baby's toy*) hochet *m*; (*of sports fan*) crécelle *f* ▮ *vi* faire du bruit; (*of window*) trembler ▮ *vt* (*shake*) secouer; (*window*) faire trembler; (*keys*) faire cliqueter. **3** *vt* **to r. s.o.** (*make nervous*) *Fam* ébranler qn; **to r. off** (*poem etc*) *Fam* débiter (à toute vitesse). ● **rattlesnake** *n* serpent *m* à sonnette.

ratty ['rætɪ] *a* (**-ier, -iest**) **1** (*shabby*) *Am Fam* minable. **2 to get r.** (*annoyed*) *Fam* prendre la mouche.

raucous ['rɔːkəs] *a* (*noisy*) bruyant.

ravage ['rævɪdʒ] *vt* ravager.

rav/e [reɪv] *vi* (*talk nonsense*) divaguer;

(*rage*) tempêter (**at** contre); **to r. about** (*enthuse*) ne pas tarir d'éloges sur. ●—**ing** *a* **to be r. mad** être fou furieux.

raven ['reɪv(ə)n] *n* corbeau *m*.

ravenous ['rævənəs] *a* (*appetite*) vorace; **I'm r.** j'ai une faim de loup.

ravine [rə'viːn] *n* ravin *m*.

ravioli [rævɪ'əʊlɪ] *n* ravioli *mpl*.

ravishing ['rævɪʃɪŋ] *a* (*beautiful*) ravissant.

raw [rɔː] *a* (**-er, -est**) (*vegetable etc*) cru; (*sugar, data*) brut; (*skin*) écorché; (*immature*) inexpérimenté; (*weather*) rigoureux; **r. material** matière *f* première.

Rawlplug® ['rɔːlplʌg] *n* cheville *f*.

ray [reɪ] *n* (*of light, sun etc*) rayon *m*; (*of hope*) *Fig* lueur *f*.

rayon ['reɪɒn] *n* rayonne *f* **‖** *a* en rayonne.

razor ['reɪzər] *n* rasoir *m*; **r. blade** lame *f* de rasoir.

Rd *abbr* = **road**.

re- [riː, rɪ] *pref* ré-, re-, r-.

reach [riːtʃ] *vt* (*place, distant object, aim*) atteindre; (*gain access to*) accéder à; (*of letter*) parvenir à (*qn*); (*contact*) joindre (*qn*); (*conclusion*) arriver à; **to r. s.o.** (*over*) **sth** (*hand over*) passer qch à qn. **‖** *vi* (*extend*) s'étendre (**to** à); **to r. (out)** (*with arm*) (é)tendre le bras (**for** pour prendre).

‖ *n* portée *f*; **within r. of** à portée de; (*near*) à proximité de; **within (easy) r.** (*object*) à portée de main; (*shops*) facilement accessible.

react [rɪ'ækt] *vi* réagir (**against** contre, **to** à). ●**reaction** *n* -ʃ(ə)n *n* réaction *f*. ●**reactionary** *a* & *n* réactionnaire (*mf*).

reactor [rɪ'æktər] *n* réacteur *m* (*nucléaire*).

read [riːd] *vt* (*pt & pp* **read** [red]) lire; (*meter*) relever; *qc* (*of instrument*) indiquer; **to r. French/etc** *Br Univ* faire des études de français/*etc* **‖** *vi* lire; **to r. to s.o.** faire la lecture à qn **‖** *n* **to have a r.** *Fam* faire un peu de lecture. ●—**able**

a lisible. ●—**er** *n* lecteur, -trice *mf*; (*book*) livre *m* de lecture.

read about *vt* lire quelque chose sur (*qn, qch*) **‖ to read back** *vt* relire **‖ to read out** *vt* lire (*qch*) (à haute voix) **‖ to read over** *vt* relire **‖ to read through** *vt* (*skim*) parcourir **‖ to read up (on)** *vt* (*study*) étudier.

readdress [riːə'dres] *vt* (*letter*) faire suivre.

readily ['redɪlɪ] *adv* (*willingly*) volontiers; (*easily*) facilement. ●**readiness** *n* **in r. for** prêt pour.

reading ['riːdɪŋ] *n* lecture *f*; (*of meter*) relevé *m*; (*by instrument*) indication *f*; (*variant*) variante *f* **‖** *a* (*room, book*) de lecture; **r. matter** choses *fpl* à lire; **r. lamp** (*desk*) lampe *f* de bureau; (*bedside*) lampe *f* de chevet.

readjust [riːə'dʒʌst] *vt* (*instrument*) régler; (*salary*) réajuster **‖** *vi* se réadapter (**to** à).

read-only [riːd'əʊnlɪ] *a* **r.-only memory** *Comptr* mémoire *f* morte.

ready ['redɪ] *a* (**-ier, -iest**) prêt (**to do** à faire, **for sth** à *or* pour qch); (*quick*) *Fig* prompt (**to do** à faire); **to get sth/s.o. r.** préparer qch/qn; **to get r.** se préparer (**for sth** à *or* pour qch, **to do** à faire); **r. cash** argent *m* liquide. ●**r.-'cooked** *a* tout cuit. ●**r.-'made** *a* tout fait; **r.-made clothes** le prêt-à-porter *m*.

real [rɪəl] *a* vrai, véritable (*world, fact etc*) réel; **in r. life** dans la réalité; **r. estate** *Am* immobilier *m* **‖** *adv* *Fam* vraiment; **r. stupid** vraiment bête.

realist ['rɪəlɪst] *n* réaliste *mf*. ●**rea'listic** *a* réaliste.

reality [rɪ'ælətɪ] *n* réalité *f*; **in r.** en réalité.

realize ['rɪəlaɪz] *vt* **1** (*know*) se rendre compte de; (*understand*) comprendre (**that** que); **to r. that** (*know*) se rendre compte que. **2** (*carry out*) réaliser. ●**realization** *n* -'zeɪʃ(ə)n *n* (*awareness*) (prise *f* de) conscience *f*.

really ['rɪəlɪ] *adv* vraiment; **is it r. true?** est-ce bien vrai?

realm [relm] n (*kingdom*) royaume m; (*of science etc*) Fig domaine m.

realtor ['rɪəltər] n Am agent m immobilier.

ream [ri:m] n (*of paper*) rame f.

reap [ri:p] vt (*field, crop*) moissonner.

reappear [ri:ə'pɪər] vi réapparaître.

rear [rɪər] **1** n (*back part*) arrière m; **in** or **at the r.** à l'arrière (**of** de); **from the r.** par derrière ∎ a arrière inv, de derrière; **r.-view mirror** Aut rétroviseur m. **2** vt (*family, animals*) élever; (*one's head*) relever. **3** vi **to r. (up)** (*of horse*) se cabrer.

rearrange [ri:ə'reɪndʒ] vt (*hair, room*) réarranger; (*plans*) changer.

reason ['ri:z(ə)n] n (*cause, sense*) raison f; **the r. for/why...** la raison de/pour laquelle...; **for no r.** sans raison; **that stands to r.** c'est logique; **within r.** avec modération; **to have every r. to believe/** etc avoir tout lieu de croire/etc. ∎ vi raisonner; **to r. with s.o.** raisonner qn. ● **reasoning** n raisonnement m.

reasonable ['ri:zənəb(ə)l] a raisonnable. ● **reasonably** adv raisonnablement; (*fairly, rather*) assez.

reassur/e [ri:ə'ʃʊər] vt rassurer. ● **-ing** a rassurant. ● **reassurance** n réconfort m.

rebate ['ri:beɪt] n (*discount on purchase*) ristourne f; (*refund*) remboursement m (partiel).

rebel ['reb(ə)l] n rebelle mf; (*against parents etc*) révolté, -ée mf ∎ [rɪ'bel] vi (**-ll-**) se révolter (**against** contre). ● **re'bellion** n révolte f. ● **re'bellious** a (*child etc*) rebelle.

rebound [rɪ'baʊnd] vi (*of ball*) rebondir; (*of stone*) ricocher; (*of lies etc*) Fig retomber (**on** sur) ∎ ['ri:baʊnd] n rebond m; ricochet m.

rebuff [rɪ'bʌf] vt repousser ∎ n rebuffade f.

rebuild [ri:'bɪld] vt (pt & pp **rebuilt**) reconstruire.

rebuke [rɪ'bju:k] vt réprimander ∎ n réprimande f.

recall [rɪ'kɔ:l] vt (*remember*) se rappeler (**that** que, **doing** avoir fait); (*call back*) rappeler; **to r. sth to s.o.** rappeler qch à qn ∎ n rappel m.

recap [ri:'kæp] vti (**-pp-**) récapituler ∎ n récapitulation f. ● **reca'pitulate** vti récapituler.

recapture [ri:'kæptʃər] vt (*prisoner etc*) reprendre; (*rediscover*) retrouver; (*recreate*) recréer.

reced/e [rɪ'si:d] vi s'éloigner; (*of floods*) baisser. ● **-ing** a (*forehead*) fuyant; **his hair(line) is r.** son front se dégarnit.

receipt [rɪ'si:t] n (*for payment, object left etc*) reçu m (**for** de); (*for letter, parcel*) accusé m de réception; pl (*money taken*) recettes fpl; **to acknowledge r.** accuser réception (**of** de); **on r. of** dès réception de.

receiv/e [rɪ'si:v] vt recevoir; (*stolen goods*) receler. ● **-er** n (*of phone*) combiné m; Rad récepteur m; (*of stolen goods*) receleur, -euse mf; (*in bankruptcy*) administrateur m judiciaire; **to pick up the r.** (*of phone*) décrocher.

recent ['ri:sənt] a récent; **in r. months** ces mois-ci. ● **-ly** adv récemment.

receptacle [rɪ'septək(ə)l] n récipient m.

reception [rɪ'sep(ə)n] n (*party, welcome etc*) & Rad réception f; **r. (desk)** réception f. ● **receptionist** n secrétaire mf, réceptionniste mf.

receptive [rɪ'septɪv] a réceptif (**to an idea/**etc à une idée/etc).

recess [rɪ'ses, Am 'ri:ses] n **1** (*holiday, Am vacation*) vacances fpl; Sch Am récréation f. **2** (*alcove*) renfoncement m; (*nook*) & Fig recoin m.

recession [rɪ'se(ə)n] n Econ récession f.

recharge [ri:'tʃɑ:dʒ] vt (*battery*) recharger. ● **-able** a (*battery*) rechargeable.

recipe ['resɪpɪ] n Culin & Fig recette f (**for** de, **for doing** pour faire).

recipient [rɪ'sɪpɪənt] n (*of award, honour*) récipiendaire m.

reciprocal [rɪ'sɪprək(ə)l] a réciproque. ● **reciprocate** vt (*compliment*) retourner ∎ vi (*do the same*) en faire autant.

recital [rɪ'saɪt(ə)l] n Mus récital m.

recite [rɪ'saɪt] vt (poem etc) réciter; (list) énumérer.

reckless ['rekləs] a (rash) imprudent. ●—ly adv imprudemment.

reckon ['rek(ə)n] vt (calculate) calculer; (count) compter; (think) penser (that que) ▮ vi to r. with s.o./sth (take into account) compter avec qch/qn; to r. on sth/s.o. (rely on) compter sur qch/qn; to r. on doing compter faire. ●—ing n calcul(s) m(pl).

reclaim [rɪ'kleɪm] vt 1 (ask for back) réclamer; (luggage at airport) récupérer. 2 (land) mettre en valeur.

recline [rɪ'klaɪn] vi (of person) être allongé; reclining seat siège m à dossier inclinable.

recluse [rɪ'kluːs] n reclus, -use mf.

recognize ['rekəgnaɪz] vt reconnaître (by à, that que). ●recognition [-'nɪʃ(ə)n] n reconnaissance f; to change beyond r. devenir méconnaissable; to gain r. être reconnu.

recoil [rɪ'kɔɪl] vi reculer (from doing à l'idée de faire, from sth à la vue de qch).

recollect [rekə'lekt] vt se souvenir de; to r. that se souvenir que. ●recollection [-'lekʃ(ə)n] n souvenir m.

recommend [rekə'mend] vt recommander (to à, for pour); to r. s.o. to do recommander à qn de faire. ●recommendation [-'deɪʃ(ə)n] n recommandation f.

reconcile ['rekənsaɪl] vt (person) réconcilier (with, to avec); (opinions etc) concilier; to r. oneself to sth se résigner à qch.

reconditioned [riːkən'dɪʃ(ə)nd] a (engine etc) refait (à neuf).

reconsider [riːkən'sɪdər] vt reconsidérer ▮ vi revenir sur sa décision.

record 1 ['rekɔːd] n (disc) disque m; r. library discothèque f; r. player électrophone m.

2 n (best performance) Sp etc record m ▮ a (number etc) record inv; in r. time en un temps record.

3 n (report) rapport m; (register) registre m; (mention) mention f; (note) note f; (background) antécédents mpl; (case history) dossier m; (police) r. casier m judiciaire; (public) records archives fpl; to keep a r. of noter; off the r. à titre confidentiel; their safety r. leurs résultats mpl en matière de sécurité.

4 [rɪ'kɔːd] vt (on tape etc, in register etc) enregistrer; (in diary) noter ▮ vi (on tape etc) enregistrer. ●recorded a enregistré; (prerecorded) (TV programme) en différé; (fact) attesté; letter sent (by) r. delivery = lettre f avec avis de réception. ●recording n enregistrement m.

recorder [rɪkɔːdər] n Mus flûte f à bec; (tape) r. magnétophone m.

recount [rɪ'kaʊnt] vt (relate) raconter.

recoup [rɪ'kuːp] vt (loss) récupérer.

recourse ['riːkɔːs] n to have r. to avoir recours à.

recover [rɪ'kʌvər] 1 vt (get back) retrouver. 2 vi (from illness, shock etc) se remettre (from de); (of economy) se redresser. ●recovery n 1 (from illness) guérison f; Econ redressement m. 2 the r. of sth la récupération de qch.

recreate [riːkri'eɪt] vt recréer.

recreation [rekri'eɪʃ(ə)n] n récréation f. ●recreational a (activity etc) de loisir.

recruit [rɪ'kruːt] n recrue f ▮ vt recruter; to r. s.o. to do (persuade) embaucher qn pour faire.

rectangle ['rektæŋɡ(ə)l] n rectangle m. ●rec'tangular a rectangulaire.

rectify ['rektɪfaɪ] vt rectifier.

rector ['rektər] n (priest) pasteur m (anglican).

recuperate [rɪ'kuːpəreɪt] vi récupérer (ses forces).

recur [rɪ'kɜːr] vi (-rr-) (of event) se reproduire; (of illness) réapparaître; (of theme) revenir. ●recurrence [rɪ'kʌrəns] n (of illness) réapparition f. ●recurrent [rɪ'kʌrənt] a fréquent.

recycle [riː'saɪk(ə)l] vt (material) recycler.

red [red] a (redder, reddest) rouge; (hair) roux (f rousse); to turn or go r. rougir;

R. Cross Croix-Rouge *f*; **R. Indian** Peau-Rouge *mf*; **r. light** *(traffic light)* feu *m* rouge; **the r.-light district** le quartier des prostituées; **r. tape** *Fig* paperasserie *f* (administrative). ▮*n (colour)* rouge *m*; **in the r.** *(company, account, person)* dans le rouge. ●**r.-'handed** *adv* **caught r.-handed** pris en flagrant délit. ●**r.-'hot** *a* brûlant.

redecorate [riː'dekəreɪt] *vt (room etc)* refaire ▮ *vi* refaire la peinture et les papiers.

redeem [rɪ'diːm] *vt (restore to favour, buy back)* racheter; *(debt)* rembourser; *(convert into cash)* réaliser; **redeeming feature** bon point *m*.

redhead ['redhed] *n* roux *m*, rousse *f*.

redirect [riːdaɪ'rekt] *vt (mail)* faire suivre.

redo [riː'duː] *vt (pt* **redid***, pp* **redone***) (exercise, house etc)* refaire.

reduce [rɪ'djuːs] *vt* réduire **(to** à, **by** de); *(temperature)* faire baisser; **at a reduced price** *(ticket, goods)* à prix réduit. ●**reduction** [rɪ'dʌkʃ(ə)n] *n* réduction *f* (in de); *(of temperature)* baisse *f*.

redundant [rɪ'dʌndənt] *a (not needed)* de trop; **to make r.** *(worker)* mettre au chômage, licencier. ●**redundancy** *n (of worker)* licenciement *m*; **r. pay** indemnité *f* de licenciement.

reed [riːd] *n* **1** *Bot* roseau *m*. **2** *Mus* anche *f*.

reef [riːf] *n* récif *m*, écueil *m*.

reek [riːk] *vi (a)* puer; **to r. of sth** *(smell)* & *Fig* puer qch.

reel [riːl] **1** *n (of thread, film)* bobine *f*; *(film itself)* bande *f*; *(for fishing line)* moulinet *m*. **2** *vi (stagger)* chanceler; *(of mind)* chavirer. **3** *vt* **to r. off** *(from memory)* débiter (à toute vitesse).

re-entry [riː'entrɪ] *n (of spacecraft)* rentrée *f*.

re-establish [riːɪ'stæblɪʃ] *vt* rétablir.

ref [ref] *n abbr (referee) Sp Fam* arbitre *m*.

refectory [rɪ'fektərɪ] *n* réfectoire *m*.

refer [rɪ'fɜːr] *vi (-rr-)* **to r. to** *(mention)* faire allusion à; *(speak of)* parler de; *(apply to)* s'appliquer à; *(consult)* se reporter à ▮ *vt* **to r. sth to s.o.** soumettre qch à qn; **to r. s.o. to** *(article etc)* renvoyer qn à.

referee [refə'riː] *n Fb Boxing etc* arbitre *m*; *(for job)* répondant, -ante *mf* ▮ *vt* arbitrer.

reference ['refərəns] *n (in book, for job etc)* référence *f*; *(indirect)* allusion *f* (to à); *(mention)* mention *f* (to de); **with r. to** concernant; *Com* suite à; **r. book** ouvrage *m* de référence.

referendum [refə'rendəm] *n* référendum *m*.

refill [riː'fɪl] *vt* remplir (à nouveau); *(lighter, pen etc)* recharger ▮ ['riːfɪl] *n* recharge *f*; **a r.** *(drink)* un autre verre.

refine [rɪ'faɪn] *vt (oil, sugar, manners)* raffiner; *(metal)* affiner; *(technique, machine)* perfectionner. ●**refinement** *n (of person)* raffinement *m*; *pl (improvements)* améliorations *fpl*. ●**refinery** *n* raffinerie *f*.

reflect [rɪ'flekt] **1** *vt (light, image etc)* refléter, réfléchir; *Fig* refléter; **to be reflected** *(of light etc)* se refléter ▮ *vi* **to r. on s.o.** *(of prestige etc)* rejaillir sur qn; **to r. badly on s.o.** nuire à l'image de qn. **2** *vi (think)* réfléchir (on à). ●**reflection** [-ʃ(ə)n] *n* **1** *(image)* & *Fig* reflet *m*; *(reflecting)* réflexion *f* (of de). **2** *(thought)* réflexion (on sur); **on r.** tout bien réfléchi.

reflector [rɪ'flektər] *n* réflecteur *m*.

reflex ['riːfleks] *n* & *a* réflexe *(m)*; **r. action** réflexe *m*.

reflexive [rɪ'fleksɪv] *a (verb)* réfléchi.

reform [rɪ'fɔːm] *n* réforme *f* ▮ *vt* réformer; *(person, conduct)* corriger ▮ *vi (of person)* se réformer.

refrain [rɪ'freɪn] **1** *vi* s'abstenir *(from doing* de faire). **2** *n Mus* refrain *m*.

refresh [rɪ'freʃ] *vt (of bath, drink)* rafraîchir; *(of sleep, rest)* délasser; **to r. one's memory** se rafraîchir la mémoire. ●**—ing** *a (drink etc)* rafraîchissant; *(sleep)* réparateur; *(pleasant)* agréable.

● **refresher course** n cours m de recyclage. ● **refreshments** npl (drinks) rafraîchissements mpl; (snacks) petites choses fpl à grignoter.

refrigerate [rɪ'frɪdʒəreɪt] vt (food) conserver au frais. ● **refrigerator** n réfrigérateur m.

refuel [riː'fjuːəl] vi (-ll-, Am -l-) Av se ravitailler ‖ vt Av ravitailler.

refuge ['refjuːdʒ] n refuge m; **to take r.** se réfugier.

refugee [refjuːˈdʒiː] n réfugié, -ée mf.

refund [rɪ'fʌnd] vt rembourser (s.o. sth qn de qch) ‖ ['riːfʌnd] n remboursement m.

refuse¹ [rɪ'fjuːz] vt refuser (s.o. sth qch à qn, to do de faire) ‖ vi refuser. ● **refusal** n refus m.

refuse² ['refjuːs] n (rubbish) ordures fpl; **r. collector** éboueur m; **r. dump** dépôt m d'ordures.

refute [rɪ'fjuːt] vt réfuter.

regain [rɪ'geɪn] vt (lost ground, favour) regagner; (health, sight) retrouver; **to r. one's strength** retrouver ses forces; **to r. consciousness** reprendre connaissance.

regard [rɪ'gɑːd] vt (consider) considérer, regarder; (concern) regarder, concerner; **as regards** en ce qui concerne ‖ n considération f (for pour); **to have (a) high r. for s.o.** estimer qn; **with r. to** en ce qui concerne; **to give one's regards to s.o.** transmettre son meilleur souvenir à qn. ● **—ing** prep en ce qui concerne.

regardless [rɪ'gɑːdləs] a **r. of** sans tenir compte de ‖ adv (all the same) quand même.

regatta [rɪ'gætə] n régates fpl.

reggae ['regeɪ] n (music) reggae m.

régime [reɪ'ʒiːm] n Pol régime m.

regiment ['redʒɪmənt] n régiment m.

region ['riːdʒ(ə)n] n région f; **in the r. of £50/etc** (about) dans les 50 livres/etc, environ 50 livres/etc. ● **regional** a régional.

register ['redʒɪstər] n registre m; Sch cahier m d'appel; (electoral) liste f électorale; **to take the r.** Sch faire l'appel.

‖ vt (birth, death) déclarer; (record, note) enregistrer; (express) exprimer; (indicate) indiquer.

‖ vi (enrol) s'inscrire (for a course à un cours); (in hotel) signer le registre; **it hasn't registered (with me)** Fam je n'ai pas encore réalisé ça. ● **registered** a (member) inscrit; (letter, package) recommandé; **to send by r. post** envoyer en recommandé.

registration [redʒɪ'streɪʃ(ə)n] n (enrolment) inscription f; **r. (number)** Aut numéro m d'immatriculation; **r. document** Aut = carte f grise.

registry ['redʒɪstrɪ] a **r. office** bureau m de l'état civil.

regret [rɪ'gret] vt (-tt-) regretter (doing, to do de faire; that que (+ sub)); **I r. to hear that...** je suis désolé d'apprendre que... ‖ n regret m. ● **regretfully** adv **r., I...** à mon grand regret, je.... ● **regrettable** a regrettable (that que (+ sub)).

regroup [riː'gruːp] vi se regrouper.

regular ['regjʊlər] a (steady, even) régulier; (surface) uni; (usual) habituel; (price, size) normal; (listener) fidèle; (staff) permanent; **a r. guy** Am Fam un chic type ‖ n (in bar etc) habitué, -ée mf. ● **regularly** adv régulièrement.

regulate ['regjʊleɪt] vt régler.

regulation [regjʊˈleɪʃ(ə)n] n **regulations** (rules) règlement m ‖ a (uniform etc) réglementaire.

rehabilitate [riːhəˈbɪlɪteɪt] vt (in public esteem) réhabiliter; (drug addict) désintoxiquer; (wounded soldier) réadapter.

rehearse [rɪ'hɜːs] vt (a play, piece of music etc) répéter; (prepare) Fig préparer ‖ vi répéter. ● **rehearsal** n Th etc répétition f.

reign [reɪn] n règne m; **in the r. of** sous le règne de ‖ vi régner (over sur).

reimburse [riːɪm'bɜːs] vt rembourser (for de).

rein [reɪn] n see **reins**.

reindeer ['reɪndɪər] n inv renne m.

reinforce [riːɪn'fɔːs] vt renforcer (with

de); **reinforced concrete** béton *m* armé. •**—ments** *npl* (*troops*) renforts *mpl*.

reins [reɪnz] *npl* (*for horse*) rênes *fpl*; (*for baby*) bretelles *fpl* de sécurité (avec laisse).

reinstate [riːɪnˈsteɪt] *vt* réintégrer.

reiterate [riːˈɪtəreɪt] *vt* (*say again*) réitérer.

reject [rɪˈdʒekt] *vt* rejeter, refuser ‖ [ˈriːdʒekt] *n* Com article *m* de rebut ‖ *a* (*article*) de deuxième choix; **r. shop** solderie *f*. •**rejection** [rɪˈdʒekʃ(ə)n] *n* rejet *m*; (*of candidate etc*) refus *m*.

rejoic/e [rɪˈdʒɔɪs] *vi* (*celebrate*) faire la fête; (*be delighted*) se réjouir (**over** or **at sth** de qch). •**—ing(s)** *n(pl)* réjouissance(s) *f(pl)*.

rejoin [rɪˈdʒɔɪn] *vt* (*join up with*) rejoindre.

rejuvenate [rɪˈdʒuːvəneɪt] *vt* rajeunir.

relapse [rɪˈlæps] *n* Med rechute *f* ‖ *vi* Med rechuter.

relat/e [rɪˈleɪt] **1** *vt* (*narrate*) raconter (**that** que). **2** *vt* (*connect*) établir un rapport entre (*faits etc*); **to r. sth to** (*link*) rattacher qch à ‖ *vi* **to r. to** (*apply to*) se rapporter à; (*get along with*) s'entendre avec. •**—ed** *a* (*linked*) lié (**to** à); (*languages*) apparentés; **to be r. to s.o.** (*by family*) être parent de qn.

relation [rɪˈleɪʃ(ə)n] *n* (*relative*) parent, -ente *mf*; (*relationship*) rapport *m*, relation *f* (**between** entre); **what r. are you to him?** quel est ton lien de parenté avec lui?; **international relations** relations *fpl* internationales. •**relationship** *n* (*in family*) lien(s) *m(pl)* de parenté; (*relations*) relations *fpl*; (*connection*) rapport *m*.

relative [ˈrelətɪv] **1** *n* (*person*) parent, -ente *mf*. **2** *a* relatif (**to** à); (*qualities etc of two or more people*) respectif; **r. to** (*compared to*) relativement à. •**—ly** *adv* relativement.

relax [rɪˈlæks] **1** *vt* (*person, mind*) détendre ‖ *vi* se détendre; **r.!** (*calm down*) du calme! **2** *vt* (*grip, pressure etc*) relâcher; (*restrictions, control*) assouplir.

•**—ed** *a* (*person, atmosphere*) décontracté. •**—ing** *a* (*bath etc*) délassant.

•**relaxation** [riːlækˈseɪʃ(ə)n] *n* (*rest*) détente *f*.

relay [ˈriːleɪ] *n* relais *m*; **r. race** course *f* de relais ‖ *vt* (*message etc*) Rad retransmettre, Fig transmettre (**to** à).

release [rɪˈliːs] *vt* (*free*) libérer (**from** de); (*bomb, s.o.'s hand*) lâcher; (*spring*) déclencher; (*brake*) desserrer; (*film, record*) sortir; (*news*) publier; (*trapped person*) dégager; (*tension*) éliminer. ‖ *n* (*of prisoner etc*) libération *f*; (*of film etc*) sortie *f* (**of** de); (*film*) nouveau film *m*; **a happy r.** (*s.o.'s death*) une délivrance; **press r.** communiqué *m* de presse; **to be on general r.** (*of film*) passer dans toutes les salles.

relent [rɪˈlent] *vi* (*change one's mind*) revenir sur sa décision. •**—less** *a* implacable.

relevant [ˈreləvənt] *a* pertinent (**to** à); (*useful*) utile; **that's not r.** ça n'a rien à voir. •**relevance** *n* pertinence *f* (**to** à); (*connection*) rapport *m* (**to** avec).

reliable [rɪˈlaɪəb(ə)l] *a* (*person, information etc*) fiable, sérieux; (*machine*) fiable. •**relia'bility** *n* fiabilité *f*; (*of person*) sérieux *m*, fiabilité *f*.

reliance [rɪˈlaɪəns] *n* (*dependence*) dépendance *f* (**on** de); (*trust*) confiance *f* (**on** en).

relic [ˈrelɪk] *n* relique *f*; *pl* (*of the past*) vestiges *mpl*.

relief [rɪˈliːf] *n* (*from pain etc*) soulagement *m* (**from** à); (*help, supplies*) secours *m*; (*in art*) & Geog relief *m*; **tax r.** dégrèvement *m*; **to be on r.** Am recevoir l'aide sociale ‖ *a* (*train, bus*) supplémentaire; **r. road** route *f* de délestage.

relieve [rɪˈliːv] *vt* (*pain etc*) soulager; (*boredom*) dissiper; (*take over from*) relayer (qn); (*help*) secourir; **to r. s.o. of sth** (*rid*) débarrasser qn de qch; **to r. congestion in** (*street*) décongestionner.

religion [rɪˈlɪdʒ(ə)n] *n* religion *f*. •**religious** *a* religieux.

relinquish [rɪˈlɪŋkwɪʃ] *vt* (*give up*) abandonner; (*let go*) lâcher.

relish ['relɪʃ] *n* (*seasoning*) assaisonnement *m*; (*liking*) goût *m* (**for** pour); **to eat with r.** manger de bon appétit ▮ *vt* (*food etc*) savourer; (*like*) aimer (**doing** faire).

reload [riː'ləʊd] *vt* (*gun, camera*) recharger.

relocate [riːləʊ'keɪt, *Am* riː'ləʊkeɪt] *vi* (*to new place*) déménager; **to r. in** *or* **to** s'installer à.

reluctant [rɪ'lʌktənt] *a* peu enthousiaste (**to do** pour faire); **a r. teacher/***etc* un professeur/*etc* malgré lui. ●**reluctance** *n* manque *m* d'enthousiasme (**to do** à faire). ●**reluctantly** *adv* sans enthousiasme.

rely [rɪ'laɪ] *vi* **to r. (up)on** (*count on*) compter sur; (*be dependent on*) dépendre de.

remain [rɪ'meɪn] **1** *vi* rester. **2** *npl* **remains** restes *mpl*. ●**—ing** *a* qui reste(nt). ●**remainder** *n* reste *m*; **the r.** (*remaining people*) les autres *mfpl*.

remand [rɪ'mɑːnd] *vt* **to r. (in custody)** *Jur* placer en détention préventive.

remark [rɪ'mɑːk] *n* remarque *f* ▮ *vt* (*say*) (faire) remarquer (**that** que) ▮ *vi* **to r. on sth** faire des remarques sur qch. ●**—able** *a* remarquable (**for** par). ●**—ably** *adv* remarquablement.

remarry [riː'mærɪ] *vi* se remarier.

remedial [rɪ'miːdɪəl] *a* **r. class** cours *m* de rattrapage; **r. exercises** gymnastique *f* corrective.

remedy ['remɪdɪ] *vt* remédier à ▮ *n* remède *m* (**for** contre, à).

remember [rɪ'membər] *vt* se souvenir de, se rappeler; **to r. that/doing** se rappeler que/d'avoir fait; **to r. to do** (*not forget to do*) penser à faire; **r. me to him** *or* **her!** rappelle-moi à son bon souvenir! ▮ *vi* se souvenir, se rappeler. ●**remembrance** *n* **in r. of** en souvenir de.

remind [rɪ'maɪnd] *vt* rappeler (**s.o. of sth** qch à qn, **s.o. that** à qn que); **to r. s.o. to do** faire penser à qn à faire. ●**—er** *n* (*of event & letter*) rappel *m*; (*note to do sth*) pense-bête *m*; **to give s.o. a r. to do sth** faire penser à qn à faire qch.

reminisce [remɪ'nɪs] *vi* raconter *or* se rappeler ses souvenirs (**about** de). ●**reminiscent** *a* **r. of** qui rappelle.

remiss [rɪ'mɪs] *a* négligent.

remittance [rɪ'mɪtəns] *n* (*sum*) paiement *m*.

remnant ['remnənt] *n* (*remaining part*) reste *m*; (*of fabric*) coupon *m*; (*oddment*) fin *f* de série.

remodel [riː'mɒd(ə)l] *vt* (**-ll-**, *Am* **-l-**) remodeler.

remorse [rɪ'mɔːs] *n* remords *m*(*pl*) (**for** pour). ●**—less** *a* implacable.

remote [rɪ'məʊt] *a* (**-er**, **-est**) **1** (*far-off*) lointain, éloigné; (*isolated*) isolé; (*aloof*) distant; **r. from** loin de; **r. control** télécommande *f*. **2** (*slight*) petit; **not the remotest idea** pas la moindre idée. ●**—ly** *adv* (*slightly*) un peu; **not r. aware/***etc* nullement conscient/*etc*.

remould ['riːməʊld] *n* pneu *m* rechapé.

remove [rɪ'muːv] *vt* (*clothes, stain etc*) enlever (**from s.o.** à qn, **from sth** de qch); (*withdraw*) retirer; (*lead away*) emmener (**to** à); (*obstacle, threat, word*) supprimer; (*fear, doubt*) dissiper. ●**removable** *a* (*lining etc*) amovible. ●**removal** *n* enlèvement *m*; suppression *f*; **r. man** déménageur *m*; **r. van** camion *m* de déménagement. ●**remover** *n* (*for make-up*) démaquillant *m*; (*for nail polish*) dissolvant *m*; (*for stains*) détachant *m*.

remunerate [rɪ'mjuːnəreɪt] *vt* rémunérer.

rename [riː'neɪm] *vt* (*street*) rebaptiser; **to r. a file** *Comptr* renommer un fichier.

render ['rendər] *vt* (*give, make*) rendre; *Mus* interpréter. ●**—ing** *n* *Mus* interprétation *f*; (*translation*) traduction *f*.

rendez-vous ['rɒndɪvuː, *pl* -vuːz] *n inv* rendez-vous *m inv*.

reneg(u)e [rɪ'niːg, rɪ'neɪg] *vi* **to r. on** (*promise*) revenir sur.

renew [rɪ'njuː] *vt* renouveler; (*resume*)

reprendre; (*library book*) renouveler le prêt de. ●—ed *a* (*efforts*) renouvelés; (*attempt*) nouveau (*f* nouvelle). ●renewal *n* renouvellement *m*; (*resumption*) reprise *f*.

renounce [rɪˈnaʊns] *vt* (*give up*) renoncer à; (*disown*) renier.

renovate [ˈrenəveɪt] *vt* (*house*) rénover; (*painting*) restaurer.

renown [rɪˈnaʊn] *n* renommée *f*. ●renowned *a* renommé (*for* pour).

rent [rent] *n* (*for house etc*) loyer *m*; **r. collector** encaisseur *m* de loyers ▌ *vt* louer; **to r. out** louer; **rented car** voiture *f* de location. ●**rent-'free** *adv* sans payer de loyer ▌ *a* gratuit. ●**rental** *n* (*of television, car*) (prix *m* de) location *f*; (*of telephone*) abonnement *m*.

reopen [riːˈəʊpən] *vti* rouvrir.

reorganize [riːˈɔːɡənaɪz] *vt* (*company etc*) réorganiser.

rep [rep] *n Fam* représentant, -ante *mf* de commerce.

repair [rɪˈpeər] *vt* réparer ▌ *n* réparation *f*; **beyond r.** irréparable; **in good/bad r.** en bon/mauvais état; 'road under r.' *Aut* 'travaux'; **r. man** réparateur *m*.

repatriate [riːˈpætrɪeɪt] *vt* rapatrier.

repay [riːˈpeɪ] *vt* (*pt & pp* **repaid**) (*pay back*) rembourser; (*kindness*) payer de retour; (*reward*) récompenser (*for* de). ●—ment *n* remboursement *m*; récompense *f*.

repeal [rɪˈpiːl] *vt* (*law*) abroger ▌ *n* abrogation *f*.

repeat [rɪˈpiːt] *vt* répéter (*that* que); (*promise, threat*) réitérer; (*class*) *Sch* redoubler; **to r. oneself** se répéter ▌ *vi* répéter; **to r. on s.o.** (*of food*) *Fam* revenir à qn ▌ *n TV Rad* rediffusion *f*. ●—ed *a* (*attempts etc*) répétés; (*efforts*) renouvelés. ●—edly *adv* de nombreuses fois.

repel [rɪˈpel] *vt* (**-ll-**) repousser. ●repellent *a* repoussant.

repent [rɪˈpent] *vi* se repentir (*of* de). ●repentance *n* repentir *m*. ●repentant *a* repentant.

repercussions [riːpəˈkʌʃ(ə)nz] *npl* répercussions *fpl*.

repertory [ˈrepət(ə)rɪ] *n Th & Fig* répertoire *m*; **r. (theatre)** théâtre *m* de répertoire.

repetition [repɪˈtɪʃ(ə)n] *n* répétition *f*. ●repetitious *or* re'petitive *a* répétitif.

replace [rɪˈpleɪs] *vt* (*take the place of*) remplacer (*by, with* par); (*put back*) remettre; **to r. the receiver** *Tel* raccrocher. ●—ment *n* remplacement *m* (*of* de); (*person*) remplaçant, -ante *mf*; (*machine part*) pièce *f* de rechange.

replay [ˈriːpleɪ] *n Sp* match *m* rejoué; (*instant*) **r.** *TV* répétition *f* immédiate (au ralenti) ▌ [riːˈpleɪ] *vt* (*on tape recorder etc*). repasser.

replica [ˈreplɪkə] *n* copie *f* exacte.

reply [rɪˈplaɪ] *vti* répondre (*to* à, *that* que) ▌ *n* réponse *f*; **in r.** en réponse (*to* à).

report [rɪˈpɔːt] *n* (*account*) rapport *m*; (*of meeting*) compte rendu *m*; (*in media*) reportage *m*; *Sch* bulletin *m*; (*rumour*) rumeur *f*; **r. card** *Am* bulletin *m* (scolaire).

▌ *vt* (*give account of*) rapporter, rendre compte de; (*announce*) annoncer (*that* que); (*notify*) signaler (*to* à); (*inform on*) dénoncer (*to* à); (*in newspaper*) faire un reportage sur.

▌ *vi* faire un rapport; (*of journalist*) faire un reportage (*on* sur); (*go*) se présenter (*to* à, **to s.o.** chez qn). ●reported *a* (*speech*) *Gram* indirect; **it is r. that** on dit que; **r. missing** porté disparu. ●reporter *n* reporter *m*.

repossess [riːpəˈzes] *vt Jur* reprendre possession de.

represent [reprɪˈzent] *vt* représenter. ●representation [-'teɪʃ(ə)n] *n* représentation *f*. ●representative *a* représentatif (*of* de) ▌ *n* représentant, -ante *mf*; *Pol Am* député *m*.

repress [rɪˈpres] *vt* (*feeling, tears*) réprimer, refouler; (*uprising*) réprimer. ●—ed *a Psy* refoulé.

reprieve [rɪˈpriːv] *n Jur* commutation *f*;

(*temporary*) sursis m ▮ *vt* accorder une commutation *or* un sursis à.

reprimand ['reprimɑ:nd] *n* réprimande *f* ▮ *vt* réprimander.

reprisal [rɪ'praɪz(ə)l] *n* **reprisals** représailles *fpl*; **as a r. for** en représailles de.

reproach [rɪ'prəʊtʃ] *n* (*blame*) reproche *m*; **beyond r.** sans reproche ▮ *vt* reprocher (**s.o. for sth** qch à qn). ●**reproachfully** *adv* d'un ton *or* d'un air réprobateur.

reproduce [ri:prə'dju:s] *vt* reproduire ▮ *vi* *Biol Bot* se reproduire. ●**reproduction** [-'dʌkʃ(ə)n] *n* (*of sound etc*) & *Biol Bot* reproduction *f*.

reptile ['reptaɪl] *n* reptile *m*.

republic [rɪ'pʌblɪk] *n* république *f*. ●**republican** *a* & *n* républicain, -aine (*mf*).

repudiate [rɪ'pju:dɪeɪt] *vt* (*behaviour, violence etc*) condamner; (*accusation*) rejeter; (*idea*) répudier.

repugnant [rɪ'pʌgnənt] *a* répugnant; **he's r. to me** il me répugne.

repulse [rɪ'pʌls] *vt* repousser. ●**repulsive** *a* repoussant.

reputable ['repjʊtəb(ə)l] *a* de bonne réputation. ●**repute** [rɪ'pju:t] *n* r. de bonne réputation. ●**re'puted** *a* réputé (**to be** pour être).

reputation [repjʊ'teɪʃ(ə)n] *n* réputation *f*; **to have a r. for being** avoir la réputation d'être.

request [rɪ'kwest] *n* demande *f* (**for** de); **on r. sur demande**; **at s.o.'s r.** à la demande de qn; **r. stop** (*for bus*) arrêt *m* facultatif ▮ *vt* demander (**sth from s.o.** qch à qn; **s.o. to do** à qn de faire).

require [rɪ'kwaɪər] *vt* (*of thing*) (*necessitate*) demander; (*demand*) exiger; (*of person*) avoir besoin de (*qch, qn*); (*staff*) rechercher; **to r. s.o. to do** (*order*) exiger de qn qu'il fasse; **if required** s'il le faut; **the required qualities**/*etc* les qualités/*etc* qu'il faut; **required condition** *f* requise. ●**—ment** *n* (*need*) exigence *f*; (*condition*) condition *f* (requise).

requisite ['rekwɪzɪt] *n* (*for travel etc*) article *m*; **toilet requisites** articles *mpl*

de toilette.

requisition [rekwɪ'zɪʃ(ə)n] *vt* réquisitionner ▮ *n* réquisition *f*.

reroute [ri:'ru:t] *vt* (*aircraft etc*) dérouter.

rerun ['ri:rʌn] *n* *Cin* reprise *f*; *TV* rediffusion *f*.

reschedule [ri:'ʃedju:l, *Am* ri:'skedju:l] *vt* (*meeting*) déplacer.

rescu/e ['reskju:] *vt* (*save*) sauver; (*set free*) délivrer (**from** de) ▮ *n* (*action*) sauvetage *m* (**of** de); (*help, troops*) secours *mpl*; **to go to s.o.'s r.** aller au secours de qn; **to the r.** à la rescousse ▮ *a* (*team, operation*) de sauvetage. ●**—er** *n* sauveteur *m*.

research [rɪ'sɜ:tʃ] *n* recherches *fpl* (**on, into** sur); **some r.** des recherches, de la recherche; **a piece of r.** un travail de recherche ▮ *vi* faire des recherches. ●**—er** *n* chercheur, -euse *mf*.

resemble [rɪ'zemb(ə)l] *vt* ressembler à. ●**resemblance** *n* ressemblance *f* (**to** avec).

resent [rɪ'zent] *vt* (*be angry about*) s'indigner de; (*be bitter about*) éprouver de l'amertume à l'égard de; **I r. that** ça m'indigne. ●**resentful** *a* **to be r.** éprouver de l'amertume. ●**resentment** *n* amertume *f*.

reservation [rezə'veɪʃ(ə)n] *n* **1** (*booking*) réservation *f*; (*doubt*) réserve *f*; **to make a r.** réserver. **2** (*land*) **Am** réserve *f*; **central r.** (*on road*) terre-plein *m*.

reserve [rɪ'zɜ:v] **1** *vt* (*room, decision etc*) réserver; (*right*) se réserver ▮ *n* (*reticence*) réserve *f*.

2 *n* (*land, stock*) réserve *f*; **r.** (*player*) remplaçant, -ante *mf*; **the reserves** (*troops*) les réserves *fpl*; **nature r.** réserve *f* naturelle; **in r.** en réserve; **r. tank** *Av Aut* réservoir *m* de secours. ●**reserved** *a* (*person, room*) réservé.

reservoir ['rezəvwɑ:r] *n* (*of water etc*) & *Fig* réservoir *m*.

reshape [ri:'ʃeɪp] *vt* (*industry etc*) réorganiser.

reshuffle [ri:'ʃʌf(ə)l] *n* (*cabinet*) **r.** remaniement *m* (ministériel).

reside [rɪˈzaɪd] *vi* résider.

residence [ˈrezɪdəns] *n* (*home*) résidence *f*; (*of students*) foyer *m*; **in r.** (*doctor*) sur place; **r. permit** permis *m* de séjour. ● **'resident** *n* habitant, -ante *mf*; (*of hotel*) pensionnaire *mf*; (*foreigner*) résident, -ente *mf* ▮ *a* **to be r. in London** résider à Londres. ● **resi'dential** *a* (*neighbourhood etc*) résidentiel.

resign [rɪˈzaɪn] *vt* (*one's post*) démissionner de; **to r. oneself to sth/to doing** se résigner à qch/à faire ▮ *vi* démissionner (**from** de); **to r. from one's job** démissionner. ● **—ed** *a* résigné. ● **resignation** [rezɪgˈneɪʃ(ə)n] *n* (*from job*) démission *f*; (*attitude*) résignation *f*.

resilient [rɪˈzɪlɪənt] *a* élastique; (*person*) *Fig* résistant.

resin [ˈrezɪn] *n* résine *f*.

resist [rɪˈzɪst] *vt* (*attack etc*) résister à; **to r. doing sth** se retenir de faire qch; **she can't r. cakes** elle ne peut pas résister devant des gâteaux; **he can't r. her** (*indulgence*) il ne peut rien lui refuser; (*charm*) il ne peut pas résister à son charme ▮ *vi* résister. ● **resistance** *n* résistance *f* (**to** à). ● **resistant** *a* résistant (**to** à).

resit [riːˈsɪt] *vt* (*pt & pp* **resat**, *pres p* **resitting**) (*exam*) repasser.

resolute [ˈrezəluːt] *a* résolu. ● **resolution** [-ˈluːʃ(ə)n] *n* résolution *f*.

resolv/e [rɪˈzɒlv] *vt* résoudre (**to do** faire, **that que**) ▮ *n* résolution *f*. ● **—ed** *a* résolu (**to do** à faire).

resort [rɪˈzɔːt] **1** *vi* **to r. to sth** (*turn to*) avoir recours à qch; **to r. to doing** en venir à faire ▮ *n* **as a last r.** en dernier ressort. **2** *n* (*holiday or Am* **vacation**) **r. station** *f* de vacances; **seaside** *or Am* **beach r.** station *f* balnéaire; **ski r.** station de ski.

resounding [rɪˈzaʊndɪŋ] *a* (*success*) retentissant.

resources [rɪˈsɔːsɪz, rɪˈzɔːsɪz] *npl* (*wealth, means*) ressources *fpl* ● **resourceful** *a* (*person, scheme*) ingénieux.

respect [rɪˈspekt] *n* respect *m* (**for** pour, de); (*aspect*) égard *m*; **with r. to** en ce qui concerne; **with all due r.** sans vouloir vous vexer ▮ *vt* respecter.

respectable [rɪˈspektəb(ə)l] *a* (*honourable, quite good*) respectable; (*satisfying*) (*results, score etc*) honnête; (*clothes, behaviour*) convenable.

respectful [rɪˈspektfəl] *a* respectueux (**to** envers, **of** de).

respective [rɪˈspektɪv] *a* respectif. ● **—ly** *adv* respectivement.

respond [rɪˈspɒnd] *vi* répondre (**to** à); **to r. to treatment** bien réagir au traitement. ● **response** *n* réponse *f*; **in r. to** en réponse à.

responsible [rɪˈspɒnsəb(ə)l] *a* responsable (**for** de, **to s.o.** devant qn); (*job*) à responsabilités. ● **responsi'bility** *n* responsabilité *f*. ● **responsibly** *adv* de façon responsable.

responsive [rɪˈspɒnsɪv] *a* (*reacting*) qui réagit bien; (*alert*) éveillé; (*attentive*) qui fait attention; **r. to** (*kindness*) sensible à; (*suggestion*) réceptif à.

rest[1] [rest] *n* (*relaxation*) repos *m*; (*support*) support *m*; **to have** *or* **take a r.** se reposer; **to put s.o.'s mind at r.** tranquilliser qn; **r. home** maison *f* de repos; **r. room** *Am* toilettes *fpl*.

▮ *vi* (*relax*) se reposer; **to r. on** (*of argument*) reposer sur; **I won't r. till** je n'aurai de repos que (+ *sub*); **to be resting on sth** (*of hand etc*) être posé sur qch; **a resting place** un lieu de repos.

▮ *vt* (*lean*) appuyer (**on** sur); (*base*) fonder; (*eyes etc*) reposer; (*horse etc*) laisser reposer.

rest[2] [rest] *n* (*remainder*) reste *m* (**of** de); **the r.** (*others*) les autres *mfpl*; **the r. of the men/etc** les autres hommes/etc ▮ *vi* (*remain*) **r. assured** soyez assuré (**that** que).

restaurant [ˈrestərɒnt] *n* restaurant *m*; **r. car** *Rail* wagon-restaurant *m*.

restful [ˈrestfəl] *a* reposant.

restless [ˈrestləs] *a* agité. ● **—ness** *n* agitation *f*.

restore [rɪ'stɔːr] vt (give back) rendre (**to** à); (order, peace) rétablir; (building, painting) restaurer.

restrain [rɪ'streɪn] vt (person) retenir; maîtriser; (crowd, anger, inflation) contenir; **to r. s.o. from doing** retenir qn de faire; **to r. oneself** se retenir, se maîtriser. ● **restraint** n (moderation) retenue f; (restriction) contrainte f.

restrict [rɪ'strɪkt] vt restreindre (**to** à). ● **—ed** a (space, use) restreint. ● **restriction** [-ʃ(ə)n] n restriction f.

result [rɪ'zʌlt] n résultat m; **as a r.** en conséquence; **as a r. of** par suite de ∎ vi résulter (**from** de); **to r. in** aboutir à.

resume [rɪ'zjuːm] vti (begin or take again) reprendre; **to r. doing** se remettre à faire. ● **resumption** [rɪ'zʌmpʃ(ə)n] n reprise f.

résumé ['rezjʊmeɪ] n Am curriculum vitae m inv.

resurface [riː'sɜːfɪs] vt (road) refaire le revêtement de.

resurgence [rɪ'sɜːdʒəns] n réapparition f.

resurrect [rezə'rekt] vt (custom etc) ressusciter.

retail ['riːteɪl] n (vente f au) détail m ∎ a (price, shop) de détail ∎ vi se vendre (au détail) (**at** à) ∎ adv (to sell) au détail. ● **—er** n détaillant, -ante mf.

retain [rɪ'teɪn] vt (freshness, heat etc) conserver; (hold back, remember) retenir. ● **retainer** n (fee) acompte m. ● **retention** [rɪ'tenʃ(ə)n] n (memory) mémoire f.

retaliate [rɪ'tælɪeɪt] vi riposter (**against s.o.** contre qn, **against an attack** à une attaque). ●

retarded [rɪ'tɑːdɪd] a (mentally) **r.** arriéré.

retch [retʃ] vi avoir un or des haut-le-cœur.

rethink [riː'θɪŋk] vt (pt & pp rethought) repenser.

reticent ['retɪsənt] a réticent.

retir/e [rɪ'taɪər] **1** vi (from work) prendre sa retraite; **retiring age** l'âge m de la retraite. **2** vi (withdraw) se retirer (**from** de, **to** à); (go to bed) aller se coucher. ● **—ed** a (no longer working) retraité. ● **retirement** n retraite f; **on my r.** dès mon départ à la retraite; **r. age** l'âge m de la retraite.

retort [rɪ'tɔːt] vt rétorquer.

retrace [riː'treɪs] vt (past event) se remémorer; **to r. one's steps** revenir sur ses pas.

retract [rɪ'trækt] vt (statement etc) rétracter ∎ vi (of person) se rétracter.

retrain [riː'treɪn] vi se recycler ∎ vt recycler.

retread ['riːtred] n pneu m rechapé.

retreat [rɪ'triːt] n (withdrawal) retraite f; (place) refuge m ∎ vi se retirer (**from** de); (of troops) battre en retraite.

retrieve [rɪ'triːv] vt (recover) récupérer; (rescue) sauver (**from** de); (loss, error) réparer; (data) Comptr récupérer. ● **retrieval** n **information r.** recherche f documentaire; Comptr recherche f de données.

retroactive [retrəʊ'æktɪv] a (pay increase etc) avec effet rétroactif.

retrospect ['retrəspekt] n **in r.** rétrospectivement. ● **retro'spective 1** a (law, effect) rétroactif. **2** n (of film director etc) rétrospective f.

return [rɪ'tɜːn] vi (come back) revenir; (go back) retourner; (go back home) rentrer; **to r. to** (subject) revenir à. ∎ vt (give back) rendre; (put back) remettre; (bring back) rapporter; (send back) renvoyer; (candidate) Pol élire.

∎ n retour m; (on investment) rendement m; pl (profits) bénéfices mpl; **r. (ticket)** (billet m d')aller et retour m; **tax r.** déclaration f de revenus; **many happy returns (of the day)!** bon anniversaire!; **in r.** en échange (**for** de).

∎ a (trip, flight etc) (de) retour; **r. match** or **game** match m retour. ● **returnable** a (bottle) consigné.

reunion [riː'juːnɪən] n réunion f.

● **reu'nite** *vt* réunir; **to be reunited with s.o.** retrouver qn.

rev [rev] *n Aut Fam* tour *m* ▮ *vt* (-vv-) **to r. (up)** (*engine*) *Fam* faire ronfler.

revamp [riːˈvæmp] *vt* (*method etc*) *Fam* remanier.

reveal [rɪˈviːl] *vt* (*make known*) révéler (*that* que); (*make visible*) laisser voir. ● —**ing** *a* (*sign etc*) révélateur.

revel [ˈrev(ə)l] *vi* (-ll-, *Am* -l-) faire la fête; **to r. in sth** se délecter de qch. ● **reveller** (*Am* **reveler**) *n* noceur, -euse *mf*.

revelation [revəˈleɪʃ(ə)n] *n* révélation *f*.

revenge [rɪˈvendʒ] *n* vengeance *f*; **to get** *or* **have one's r.** se venger (**on s.o.** de qn, **on s.o. for sth** de qch sur qn); **in r.** pour se venger.

revenue [ˈrevənjuː] *n* revenu *m*.

reverence [ˈrevərəns] *n* révérence *f*.

reverend [ˈrev(ə)rənd] *n* **R. Smith** (*Anglican*) le révérend Smith; (*Catholic*) l'abbé *m* Smith; (*Jewish*) le rabbin Smith.

reversal [rɪˈvɜːsəl] *n* (*of situation*) renversement *m*; (*of policy, opinion*) revirement *m*; (*of fortune*) revers *m*.

reverse [rɪˈvɜːs] *a* (*order, image etc*) inverse; **r. side** (*of coin etc*) revers *m*; (*of paper*) verso *m*.
▮ *n* contraire *m*; (*of coin, fabric etc*) revers *m*; (*of paper*) verso *m*; **in r.** (**gear**) *Aut* en marche arrière.
▮ *vt* (*situation*) renverser; (*order, policy*) inverser; (*decision*) annuler; **to r. the charges** *Tel* téléphoner en PCV.
▮ *vti* **to r. (the car)** faire marche arrière; **to r. in/out** rentrer/sortir en marche arrière; **reversing lights** feux *mpl* de recul.

revert [rɪˈvɜːt] *vi* **to r. to** revenir à.

review [rɪˈvjuː] **1** *vt* (*book etc*) faire la critique de; (*troops*) passer en revue; (*situation*) réexaminer; (*salary*) réviser ▮ *n* (*of book etc*) critique *f*. **2** *n* (*magazine*) revue *f*. ● —**er** *n* critique *m*.

revise [rɪˈvaɪz] *vt* (*opinion, notes, text*) réviser ▮ *vi* (*for exam*) réviser (**for**

pour). ● **revision** [rɪˈvɪʒ(ə)n] *n* révision *f*.

revitalize [riːˈvaɪt(ə)laɪz] *vt* revitaliser.

revival [rɪˈvaɪvəl] *n* (*of custom, business, play*) reprise *f*; (*of faith, fashion*) renouveau *m*.

revive [rɪˈvaɪv] *vt* (*unconscious person, memory*) ranimer; (*dying person*) réanimer; (*custom, fashion*) ressusciter; (*hope, interest*) faire renaître ▮ *vi* (*of unconscious person*) reprendre connaissance; (*of hope, interest*) renaître.

revoke [rɪˈvəʊk] *vt* (*decision*) annuler; (*contract*) révoquer.

revolt [rɪˈvəʊlt] **1** *n* révolte *f* ▮ *vi* (*rebel*) se révolter (**against** contre). **2** *vt* (*disgust*) révolter. ● —**ing** *a* dégoûtant.

revolution [revəˈluːʃ(ə)n] *n* révolution *f*. ● **revolutionary** *a* & *n* révolutionnaire (*mf*).

revolve [rɪˈvɒlv] *vi* tourner (**around** autour de); **revolving door(s)** (porte *f* à) tambour *m*.

revolver [rɪˈvɒlvər] *n* revolver *m*.

revulsion [rɪˈvʌlʃ(ə)n] *n* (*disgust*) dégoût *m*.

reward [rɪˈwɔːd] *n* récompense *f* (**for** de) ▮ *vt* récompenser (**s.o. for sth** qn de *or* pour qch). ● —**ing** *a* qui vaut la peine; (*satisfying*) satisfaisant; (*financially*) rémunérateur.

rewind [riːˈwaɪnd] *vt* (*pt* & *pp* **rewound**) (*tape*) rembobiner ▮ *vi* se rembobiner.

rewire [riːˈwaɪər] *vt* (*house*) refaire l'installation électrique de.

rewrite [riːˈraɪt] *vt* (*pt* **rewrote**, *pp* **rewritten**) récrire; (*edit*) réécrire.

rhetoric [ˈretərɪk] *n* rhétorique *f*.

rheumatism [ˈruːmətɪz(ə)m] *n Med* rhumatisme *m*; **to have r.** avoir des rhumatismes.

rhinoceros [raɪˈnɒsərəs] *n* rhinocéros *m*.

rhubarb [ˈruːbɑːb] *n* rhubarbe *f*.

rhyme [raɪm] *n* rime *f*; (*poem*) vers *mpl* ▮ *vi* rimer (**with** avec).

rhythm [ˈrɪð(ə)m] *n* rythme *m*. ● **rhythmic(al)** *a* rythmique.

rib [rɪb] *n Anat* côte *f*.

ribbon ['rɪbən] n ruban m; **to tear to ribbons** mettre en lambeaux.

rice [raɪs] n riz m. ●**ricefield** n rizière f.

rich [rɪtʃ] a (-er, -est) (person, food etc) riche; **r. in** riche en ∎ **n the r.** les riches mpl. ●**riches** npl richesses fpl. ●**richly** adv (illustrated etc) richement.

rick [rɪk] vt **to r. one's back** se tordre le dos.

rickety ['rɪkɪtɪ] a (furniture) branlant.

rid [rɪd] vt (pt & pp rid, pres p ridding) débarrasser (of de); **to get r. of, r. oneself of** se débarrasser de. ●**riddance** n **good r.!** Fam bon débarras!

ridden ['rɪd(ə)n] pp of **ride**.

-ridden ['rɪd(ə)n] suff **debt-r.** criblé de dettes; **disease-r.** en proie à la maladie.

riddle ['rɪd(ə)l] **1** n (puzzle) énigme f. **2** vt **riddled with** (bullets, holes, mistakes) criblé de; (corruption) en proie à.

ride [raɪd] n (on bicycle, by car etc) promenade f; (distance) trajet m; (in taxi) course f; **to go for a (car) r.** faire une promenade (en voiture); **to give s.o. a r.** (in car) emmener qn en voiture; **to take s.o. for a r.** (deceive) Fam mener qn en bateau.

∎ vi (pt **rode**, pp **ridden**) aller (à bicyclette, à moto, à cheval etc) (**to** à); **to r., go riding** (on horse) monter (à cheval); **to be riding in a car** être en voiture.

∎ vt (a particular horse) monter; (distance) faire (à cheval etc); **to r. a horse or horses** monter à cheval; **I was riding (on) a bicycle/donkey** j'étais à bicyclette/à dos d'âne; **to know how to r. a bicycle** savoir faire de la bicyclette; **to r. a bicycle** aller à bicyclette à.

rider ['raɪdər] n (on horse) cavalier, -ière mf; (cyclist) cycliste mf.

ridge [rɪdʒ] n (of roof, mountain) arête f, crête f.

ridicule ['rɪdɪkjuːl] n ridicule m; **to hold up to r.** tourner en ridicule; **object of r.** objet m de risée ∎ vt tourner en ridicule, ridiculiser. ●**ri'diculous** a ridicule.

riding ['raɪdɪŋ] n (horse) r. équitation f; **r. boots** bottes fpl de cheval.

rife [raɪf] a (widespread) répandu.

riffraff ['rɪfræf] n racaille f.

rifle ['raɪf(ə)l] n fusil m.

rift [rɪft] n (in political party) scission f; (disagreement) désaccord m; (crack) fissure f.

rig [rɪg] **1** n (oil) r. derrick m; (at sea) plate-forme f pétrolière. **2** vt (-gg-) (result, election) Pej truquer; (equipment) installer. **3** vt (-gg-) **to r. out** (dress) Fam habiller.

right¹ [raɪt] **1** a (correct) bon (f bonne), exact; (fair) juste; (angle) Math droit; **to be r.** (of person) avoir raison (**to do** de faire); **it's the r. road** c'est la bonne route; **the r. choice/time** le bon choix/moment; **it's the r. time** (accurate) c'est l'heure exacte; **the clock is r.** la pendule est à l'heure; **he's the r. man** c'est l'homme qu'il faut; **the r. thing to do** la meilleure chose à faire; **it's not r. to steal** ce n'est pas bien de voler; **it doesn't look r.** il y a quelque chose qui ne va pas; **to put r.** (error) corriger; (fix) arranger; **to put s.o. r.** (inform) éclairer qn; **r.!** bien!; **that's r.** c'est ça, c'est exact.

∎ adv (straight) (tout) droit; (completely) tout à fait; (correctly) juste; (well) bien; **she did r.** elle a bien fait; **r. round** tout autour (**sth** de qch); **r. behind** juste derrière; **r. here** ici même; **r. away, r. now** tout de suite.

∎ n **to be in the r.** avoir raison; **r. and wrong** le bien et le mal.

2 all r. see all right.

right² [raɪt] a (not left) (hand, side etc) droit ∎ adv à droite ∎ n droite f; **on or to the r.** à droite (of de). ●**r.-hand** a à or de droite; **on the r.-hand side** à droite (of de); **r.-hand man** bras m droit. ●**r.-'handed** a (person) droitier. ●**r.-wing** a Pol de droite.

right³ [raɪt] n (entitlement) droit m (**to do** de faire); **to have a r. to sth** avoir droit à qch; **r. of way** Aut priorité f; **human rights** les droits de l'homme.

righteous ['raɪtʃəs] a (person) vertueux;

(*cause, indignation*) juste.
rightful ['raɪtfəl] *a* légitime. ●—**ly** *adv* légitimement.
rightly ['raɪtlɪ] *adv* bien, correctement; (*justifiably*) à juste titre; **r. or wrongly** à tort ou à raison.
rigid ['rɪdʒɪd] *a* rigide. *f*.
rigmarole ['rɪgmərəʊl] *n* (*process*) procédure *f* compliquée.
rigour ['rɪgər] (*Am* **rigor**) *n* rigueur *f*. ●**rigorous** *a* rigoureux.
rim [rɪm] *n* (*of cup etc*) bord *m*; (*of wheel*) jante *f*.
rind [raɪnd] *n* (*of cheese*) croûte *f*; (*of bacon*) couenne *f*.
ring[1] [rɪŋ] *n* (*for finger, curtain etc*) anneau *m*; (*for finger with jewel*) bague *f*; (*of people, chairs*) cercle *m*; (*of smoke*) rond *m*; (*gang*) bande *f*; (*at circus*) piste *f*; *Boxing* ring *m*; (*burner on stove*) brûleur *m*; **diamond r.** bague *f* de diamants; **to have rings under one's eyes** avoir les yeux cernés; **r. road** route *f* de ceinture; (*motorway*) périphérique *m*.
▮ *vt* **to r. (round)** entourer (**with** de); (*item on list etc*) encadrer. ●**ringleader** *n* *Pej* (*of gang*) chef *m* de bande; (*of rebellion*) meneur, -euse *mf*.
ring[2] [rɪŋ] *n* (*sound*) sonnerie *f*; **there's a r.** on sonne; **to give s.o. a r.** (*phone call*) passer un coup de fil à qn.
▮ *vi* (*pt* **rang**, *pp* **rung**) (*of bell, phone, person etc*) sonner; (*of sound, words*) retentir; (*of ears*) bourdonner; (*on phone*) téléphoner.
▮ *vt* sonner; **to r. s.o.** (*on phone*) téléphoner à qn; **to r. the (door)bell** sonner (à la porte); **that rings a bell** *Fam* ça me rappelle quelque chose. ●**ringing tone** *n* (*on phone*) sonnerie *f*.
ring back *vi* (*phone*) rappeler ▮ *vt* **to r. s.o. back** rappeler qn ▮ **to ring off** *vi* (*after phoning*) raccrocher ▮ **to ring out** *vi* (*of bell*) sonner; (*of sound*) retentir ▮ **to ring up** *vi* (*phone*) téléphoner ▮ *vt* **to r. s.o. up** téléphoner à qn.
rink [rɪŋk] *n* (*ice-skating*) patinoire *f*.

rinse [rɪns] *vt* rincer; **to r. one's hands** (*remove soap*) se rincer les mains; **to r. out** rincer ▮ *n* (*hair colouring*) shampooing *m* colorant; **to give sth a r.** rincer qch.
riot ['raɪət] *n* (*uprising*) émeute *f*; (*fighting*) bagarres *fpl*; **a r. of colour** *Fig* une orgie de couleurs; **to run r.** (*of crowd*) se déchaîner; **the r. police** = les CRS *mpl* ▮ *vi* (*rise up*) faire une émeute; (*fight*) se bagarrer. ●—**er** *n* émeutier, -ière *mf*; (*vandal*) casseur *m*. ●**riotous** *a* (*crowd etc*) tapageur.
rip [rɪp] *vt* (**-pp-**) déchirer; **to r. off** (*button etc*) arracher; **to r. s.o. off** (*deceive*) *Fam* rouler qn; **to r. out** (*telephone etc*) arracher (**from** de); **to r. sth up** déchirer qch ▮ *vi* (*of cloth*) se déchirer ▮ *n* déchirure *f*; **it's a r.-off** *Fam* c'est du vol organisé.
ripe [raɪp] *a* (**-er, -est**) mûr; (*cheese*) fait. ●**ripen** *vti* mûrir.
ripple ['rɪp(ə)l] *n* (*on water*) ride *f*; (*of laughter*) *Fig* cascade *f* ▮ *vi* (*of water*) se rider.
rise [raɪz] *vi* (*pt* **rose**, *pp* **risen**) (*of temperature, balloon, price etc*) monter, s'élever; (*of hope*) grandir; (*of sun, curtain*) se lever; (*of dough*) lever; (*get up from chair or bed*) se lever; **to r. in price** augmenter de prix; **to r. to the surface** remonter à la surface; **to r. (up)** (*rebel*) se soulever (**against** contre); **to r. to power** accéder au pouvoir.
▮ *n* (*in price etc*) hausse *f* (**in** de); (*in river*) crue *f*; (*of leader*) *Fig* ascension *f*; (*of technology*) essor *m*; (*to power*) accession *f*; (*slope in ground*) montée *f*; (**pay**) **r.** augmentation *f* (de salaire); **to give r. to sth** donner lieu à qch. ●**rising** *n* (*of curtain*) lever *m*; (*revolt*) soulèvement *m* ▮ *a* (*sun*) levant; (*number*) croissant; **r. prices** la hausse des prix.
riser ['raɪzər] *n* **early r.** lève-tôt *mf inv*; **late r.** lève-tard *mf inv*.
risk [rɪsk] *n* risque *m* (**of doing** de faire, **in doing** à faire); **at r.** (*person*) en danger;

(*job*) menacé; **at your own r.** à tes risques et périls ‖ *vt* (*one's life etc*) risquer; **she won't r. leaving** elle ne se risquera pas à partir; **let's r. it** risquons le coup. ● **risky** *a* (**-ier, -iest**) (*full of risks*) risqué.

rite [raɪt] *n* rite *m*; **the last rites** *Rel* les derniers sacrements *mpl.* ● **ritual** *a & n* rituel (*m*).

rival ['raɪv(ə)l] *a* (*company etc*) rival; (*forces, claim*) opposé ‖ *n* rival, -ale *mf* ‖ *vt* (**-ll-**, *Am* **-l-**) (*compete with*) rivaliser avec (**in** de); (*equal*) égaler (**in** en). ● **rivalry** *n* rivalité *f* (**between** entre).

river ['rɪvər] *n* (*small*) rivière *f*; (*flowing into sea*) fleuve *m*; **the R. Thames** la Tamise ‖ *a* (*port etc*) fluvial; **r. bank** rive *f*. ● **riverside** *a & n* (**by the**) **r.** au bord de l'eau.

riveting ['rɪvɪtɪŋ] *a* (*story etc*) fascinant.

Riviera [rɪvɪ'eərə] *n* **the (French) R.** la Côte d'Azur.

roach [rəʊtʃ] *n* (*cockroach*) *Am* cafard *m*.

road [rəʊd] *n* route *f* (**to** qui va à); (*small*) chemin *m*; (*in town*) rue *f*; (*roadway*) chaussée *f*; (*path*) *Fig* voie *f*, chemin *m*, route *f* (**to** de); **the Paris r.** la route de Paris; **across** *or* **over the r.** (*building etc*) en face; **by r.** par la route. ‖ *a* (*map, safety*) routier; (*accident*) de la route; **r. hog** *Fam* chauffard *m*; **to have r. sense** (*of child*) avoir conscience des dangers de la rue; **r. sign** panneau *m* (routier); **r. works** travaux *mpl.* ● **road-block** *n* barrage *m* routier. ● **roadside** *n & n* (**by the**) **r.** au bord de la route. ● **roadway** *n* chaussée *f.* ● **roadworthy** *a* (*vehicle*) en état de marche.

roam [rəʊm] *vt* parcourir ‖ *vi* errer; **to r. (about) the streets** (*of child, dog*) traîner dans les rues.

roar [rɔːr] *vi* (*of lion, wind, engine*) rugir; (*of person*) hurler; (*of thunder*) gronder; **to r. with laughter** éclater de rire ‖ *vt* **to r. (out)** (*threat etc*) hurler ‖ *n* rugissement *m*; hurlement *m*; grondement *m*.

● **—ing** *a* **a r. fire** une belle flambée; **to do a r. trade** vendre beaucoup (**in** de).

roast [rəʊst] *vt* rôtir; (*coffee*) griller ‖ *vi* (*of meat*) rôtir ‖ *n* (*meat*) rôti *m* ‖ *a* (*chicken etc*) rôti; **r. beef** rosbif *m*.

rob [rɒb] *vt* (**-bb-**) (*person*) voler; (*bank*) attaquer; (*shop, house etc*) (*by breaking in*) cambrioler; **to r. s.o. of sth** voler qch à qn; (*deprive*) priver qn de qch. ● **robber** *n* voleur, -euse *mf.* ● **robbery** *n* vol *m*; **it's daylight r.!** c'est du vol organisé; **armed r.** vol m à main armée.

robe [rəʊb] *n* (*dressing gown*) robe *f* de chambre; (*of priest, judge*) robe *f.*

robin ['rɒbɪn] *n* (*bird*) rouge-gorge *m*.

robot ['rəʊbɒt] *n* robot *m*.

robust [rəʊ'bʌst] *a* robuste.

rock¹ [rɒk] **1** *vt* (*baby, boat*) bercer, balancer; (*branch*) balancer; (*violently*) secouer ‖ *vi* (*sway*) se balancer; (*of building*) trembler. **2** *n Mus* rock *m*. ● **—ing** *a* **r. chair/horse** fauteuil *m/* cheval *m* à bascule.

rock² [rɒk] *n* (*substance*) roche *f*; (*boulder, rock face*) rocher *m*; (*stone*) *Am* pierre *f*; **a stick of r.** (*sweet*) un bâton de sucre d'orge; **r. face** paroi *f* rocheuse; **on the rocks** (*whisky*) avec des glaçons; (*marriage*) en pleine débâcle. ● **r.-'bottom** *n* (*prices*) les plus bas ● **r.-climbing** *n* varappe *f.*

rockery ['rɒkərɪ] *n* (*in garden*) rocaille *f.*

rocket ['rɒkɪt] *n* fusée *f* ‖ *vi* (*of prices*) *Fig* monter en flèche.

rocky ['rɒkɪ] *a* (**-ier, -iest**) (*road*) rocailleux.

rod [rɒd] *n* (*wooden*) baguette *f*; (*metal*) tige *f*; (*of curtain*) tringle *f*; (*for fishing*) canne *f* (à pêche).

rode [rəʊd] *pt of* **ride**.

rodent ['rəʊdənt] *n* (*animal*) rongeur *m*.

rodeo ['rəʊdɪəʊ, *Am* rəʊ'deɪəʊ] *n* (*pl* **-os**) *Am* rodéo *m*.

roe [rəʊ] *n* (*eggs*) œufs *mpl* de poisson.

rogue [rəʊg] *n* (*dishonest*) crapule *f*; (*mischievous*) coquin, -ine *mf.*

role [rəʊl] *n* rôle *m*.

roll [rəʊl] *n* (*of paper etc*) rouleau *m*;

(*small bread loaf*) petit pain *m*; (*of fat*) bourrelet *m*; (*of drum, thunder*) roulement *m*; (*list*) liste *f*; **to have a r. call** faire l'appel.

▮ *vi* (*of ball etc*) rouler; (*of person, animal*) se rouler; **to r. into a ball** (*of animal*) se rouler en boule; **r. on tonight!** *Fam* vivement ce soir!. ▮ *vt* rouler (*qch, qn*).

roll down *vt* (*car window etc*) baisser; (*slope*) descendre (en roulant) ▮ **to roll in** *vi* (*flow in*) *Fam* affluer ▮ **to roll out** *vt* (*dough*) étaler ▮ **to roll over** *vi* (*many times*) se rouler; (*once*) se retourner ▮ *vt* retourner ▮ **to roll up** *vt* (*map, cloth*) rouler; (*sleeve, trousers, Am pants*) retrousser ▮ *vi* (*arrive*) *Fam* s'amener.

roller ['rəʊlər] *n* (*for hair, painting etc*) rouleau *m*; **r. coaster** (*at funfair*) montagnes *fpl* russes. ● **roller-skate** *n* patin *m* à roulettes ▮ *vi* faire du patin à roulettes.

rolling-pin ['rəʊlɪŋpɪn] *n* rouleau *m* à pâtisserie.

ROM [rɒm] *n abbr* = **read-only memory.**

Roman ['rəʊmən] **1** *a* & *n* romain, -aine (*mf*). **2 R. Catholic** *a* & *n* catholique (*mf*).

romance [rəʊ'mæns] *n* (*love*) amour *m*; (*affair*) aventure *f* amoureuse; (*story*) histoire *f* d'amour; (*charm*) poésie *f*. ● **romantic** *a* (*of love, tenderness etc*) romantique ▮ *n* (*person*) romantique *mf*.

Romania [rəʊ'meɪnɪə] *n* Roumanie *f*. ● **Romanian** *a* & *n* roumain, -aine *mf* ▮ *n* (*language*) roumain *m*.

romp [rɒmp] *vi* s'ébattre (bruyamment); **to r. through an exam** avoir un examen les doigts dans le nez.

rompers ['rɒmpəz] *npl* (*for baby*) barboteuse *f*.

roof [ruːf] *n* toit *m*; (*of tunnel, cave*) plafond *m*; **r. of the mouth** voûte *f* du palais; **r. rack** (*of car*) galerie *f*. ● **rooftop** *n* toit *m*.

rook [rʊk] *n* **1** (*bird*) corneille *f*. **2** *Chess* tour *f*.

room [ruːm, rʊm] *n* **1** (*in house etc*) pièce *f*; (*bedroom*) chambre *f*; (*large, public*) salle *f*; **men's r., ladies' r.** *Am* toilettes *fpl*. **2** (*space*) place *f* (**for** pour); (*some*) **r.** de la place. ● **roommate** *n* camarade *mf* de chambre. ● **roomy** *a* (**-ier, -iest**) spacieux; (*clothes*) ample.

roost [ruːst] *vi* (*of bird*) se percher.

rooster ['ruːstər] *n* coq *m*.

root [ruːt] **1** *n* (*of plant etc*) & *Math* racine *f*; (*origin*) *Fig* origine *f*; **to take r.** (*of plant, person*) prendre racine; **to put down (new) roots** *Fig* s'enraciner; **r. cause** cause *f* première ▮ *vt* **r. out** (*destroy*) extirper. **2** *vi* **to r. for** (*cheer, support*) *Fam* encourager. ● **rooted** *a* **deeply r.** bien enraciné (**in** dans).

rope [rəʊp] *n* corde *f*; *Nau* cordage *m*; **to know the ropes** *Fam* être au courant ▮ *vt* **to r. s.o. in** *Fam* embrigader qn (**to do** pour faire); **to r. off** (*of police etc*) interdire l'accès de.

rop(e)y ['rəʊpɪ] *a* (**-ier, -iest**) *Fam* (*thing*) minable; (*person*) patraque.

rosary ['rəʊzərɪ] *n Rel* chapelet *m*.

rose¹ [rəʊz] *n* (*flower*) rose *f*; (*colour*) rose *m*; **r. bush** rosier *m*.

rose² [rəʊz] *pt of* **rise.**

rosé ['rəʊzeɪ] *n* (*wine*) rosé *m*.

rosemary ['rəʊzmərɪ] *n Bot Culin* romarin *m*.

roster ['rɒstər] *n* (**duty**) **r.** liste *f* (de service).

rostrum ['rɒstrəm] *n* tribune *f*; *Sp* podium *m*.

rosy ['rəʊzɪ] *a* (**-ier, -iest**) (*pink*) rose; (*future*) *Fig* tout en rose.

rot [rɒt] *n* pourriture *f*; (*nonsense*) *Fam* inepties *fpl* ▮ *vti* (**-tt-**) **to r. (away)** pourrir.

rota ['rəʊtə] *n* liste *f* (de service).

rotary ['rəʊtərɪ] *a* rotatif ▮ *n* (*for traffic*) *Am* sens *m* giratoire.

rotate [rəʊ'teɪt] *vi* tourner ▮ *vt* faire tourner.

rote [rəʊt] *n* **by r.** machinalement.

rotten ['rɒt(ə)n] *a* (*fruit, weather etc*) pourri; (*bad*) *Fam* moche; (*corrupt*)

pourri; **to feel r.** (*ill*) être mal fichu.
● **rotting** *a* (*meat, fruit etc*) qui pourrit.
rough¹ [rʌf] *a* (**-er, -est**) (*surface*) rugueux, rude; (*plank, bark*) rugueux; (*ground*) inégal, (*manners, voice, task*) rude; (*coarse*) grossier; (*brutal*) brutal; (*neighbourhood*) mauvais; (*sea*) agité; **a r. child** (*unruly*) un enfant turbulent; **to feel r.** (*ill*) *Fam* être mal fichu; **r. and ready** (*conditions etc*) grossier (mais adéquat).
▍*adv* (*to sleep, live*) à la dure; (*to play*) brutalement.
▍*vi* **to r. up** (*hair*) ébouriffer; (*person*) *Fam* malmener. ● **roughen** *vt* rendre rude. ● **roughly¹** *adv* (*not gently*) rudement; (*coarsely*) grossièrement; (*brutally*) brutalement.
rough² [rʌf] *a* (**-er, -est**) (*calculation, figure etc*) approximatif; **r. guess,** approximation *f*; **r. book** cahier *m* de brouillon; **r. copy, r. draft** brouillon *m*; **r. paper** du papier brouillon ▍*vt* **r. out** (*plan*) ébaucher. ● **-ly²** *adv* (*approximately*) à peu de (choses) près.
roughage ['rʌfidʒ] *n* (*in food*) fibres *fpl* (alimentaires).
roulette [ru:'let] *n* roulette *f*.
round [raʊnd] **1** *adv* autour; **all r., right r.** tout autour; **to go r. to s.o.'s** passer chez qn; **to ask r.** inviter chez soi; **r. here** par ici; **the long way r.** le chemin le plus long.
▍*prep* autour de; **r. about** (*approximately*) environ; **r.** (*about*) **midday** vers midi; **to go r. a corner** tourner un coin. **2** *a* (**-er, -est**) rond; **r. trip** *Am* aller (et) retour *m*.
3 *n* (*slice*) tranche *f*; (*sandwich*) sandwich *m*; *Sp Pol* manche *f*; (*of golf*) partie *f*; *Boxing* round *m*; (*of talks*) série *f*; (*of drinks*) tournée *f*; **to be on one's round(s)** (*of milkman*) faire sa tournée; (*of doctor*) faire ses visites; (*of policeman*) faire sa ronde; **delivery r.** livraisons *fpl*, tournée *f*; **r. of applause** salve *f* d'applaudissements.
▍*vt* **to r. off** (*meal, speech etc*) terminer

(*with* par); **to r. up** (*gather*) rassembler; (*price*) arrondir au chiffre supérieur.
● **r.-'shouldered** *a* voûté. ● **rounded** *a* arrondi.
roundabout ['raʊndəbaʊt] **1** *a* indirect, détourné. **2** *n* (*at funfair*) manège *m*; (*road junction*) rond-point *m* (à sens giratoire).
rounders ['raʊndəz] *npl Sp* sorte de baseball.
roundup ['raʊndʌp] *n* (*of criminals*) rafle *f*.
rous/e [raʊz] *vt* éveiller; **roused** (**to** anger) en colère; **to r. to action** inciter à agir. ● **-ing** *a* (*welcome*) enthousiaste.
rout [raʊt] *n* (*defeat*) déroute *f* ▍*vt* mettre en déroute.
route 1 [ru:t] *n* itinéraire *m*; (*of ship, aircraft*) route *f*; **bus r.** ligne *f* d'autobus. **2** [raʊt] *n* (*delivery round*) *Am* tournée *f*.
routine [ru:'ti:n] **1** *n* routine *f*; **one's daily r.** (*in office*) son travail journalier; **the daily r.** (*monotony*) le train-train quotidien ▍*a* (*inquiry, work etc*) de routine. **2** *n* (*on stage*) numéro *m*.
rove [rəʊv] *vi* errer ▍*vt* parcourir.
row¹ [rəʊ] **1** *n* (*line*) rang *m*, rangée *f*; (*one behind another*) file *f*; **two days in a r.** deux jours de suite. **2** *vi* (*in boat*) ramer ▍*vt* (*boat*) faire aller à la rame; **r. boat** *Am* bateau *m* à rames. ● **-ing** *n* canotage *m*; *Sp* aviron *m*; **r. boat** bateau *m* à rames.
row² [raʊ] *n Fam* (*noise*) vacarme *m*; (*quarrel*) dispute *f* ▍*vi Fam* se disputer (**with** avec).
rowdy ['raʊdi] *a* (**-ier, -iest**) chahuteur (et brutal).
royal ['rɔɪəl] *a* royal; **Royal Air Force** armée *f* de l'air (britannique) ▍*npl* **the royals** *Fam* la famille royale. ● **royalty 1** *n* (*persons*) personnages *mpl* royaux. **2** *npl* (*from book*) droits *mpl* d'auteur; (*from invention*) royalties *fpl*.
rpm [ɑ:pi:'em] *abbr* (*revolutions per minute*) *Aut* tours/minute *mpl*.

rub [rʌb] *vt* (-bb-) frotter; (*person*) frictionner; **to r. shoulders with** Fig côtoyer ▮ *vi* frotter ▮ *n* (*massage*) friction *f*; **to give sth a r.** frotter qch. ●**rubbing alcohol** *n* Am alcool *m* à 90°.

rub away *vt* (*mark*) effacer ▮ **to rub down** *vt* (*person*) frictionner; (*with sandpaper*) poncer (*qch*) ▮ **to rub in** *vt* (*cream*) faire pénétrer (en massant); **to r. it in** Pej Fam retourner le couteau dans la plaie ▮ **to rub off** *vt* (*mask*) effacer ▮ *vi* (*of mark*) partir; (*of manners*) Fig déteindre (**on s.o.** sur qn) ▮ **to rub out** *vt* (*mark*) effacer.

rubber [rʌbər] *n* caoutchouc *m*; (*eraser*) gomme *f*; (*for blackboard*) brosse *f*; (*contraceptive*) Am Sl capote *f*. **r. stamp** tampon *m*.

rubbish ['rʌbɪʃ] 1 *n* (*waste*) ordures *fpl*; (*junk*) saletés *fpl*; (*nonsense*) Fig idioties *fpl*; **that's r.** (*absurd*) c'est absurde; (*worthless*) ça ne vaut rien; **r. bin** poubelle *f*; **r. dump** décharge *f* (*publique*); (*untidy place*) dépotoir *m*. 2 *vt* **to r. s.o./sth** (*criticize*) Fam dénigrer qn/qch. ●**rubbishy** *a* (*book, film etc*) nul; (*goods*) de mauvaise qualité.

rubble ['rʌb(ə)l] *n* décombres *mpl*.

ruby ['ru:bɪ] *n* (*gem*) rubis *m*.

rucksack ['rʌksæk] *n* sac *m* à dos.

rudder ['rʌdər] *n* gouvernail *m*.

ruddy ['rʌdɪ] *a* (-ier, -iest) 1 (*complexion*) coloré. 2 (*bloody*) Sl fichu.

rude [ru:d] *a* (-er, -est) (*impolite*) impoli (**to** envers); (*coarse, insolent*) grossier (**to** envers); (*indecent*) obscène. ●**—ness** *n* impolitesse *f*; grossièreté *f*.

rudiments ['ru:dɪmənts] *npl* rudiments *mpl*.

ruffian ['rʌfɪən] *n* voyou *m*.

ruffle ['rʌf(ə)l] *vt* (*hair*) ébouriffer; **to r. s.o.** (*offend*) froisser qn.

rug [rʌg] *n* carpette *f*; (*over knees*) plaid *m*; (*bedside*) r. descente *f* de lit.

rugby ['rʌgbɪ] *n* **r.** (*football*) rugby *m*.

rugged ['rʌgɪd] *a* (*surface*) rugueux, rude; (*terrain*) accidenté; (*person, features*) rude.

ruin ['ru:ɪn] *n* (*destruction, building etc*) ruine *f*; **in ruins** (*building*) en ruine ▮ *vt* (*health, country, person*) ruiner; (*clothes*) abîmer; (*effect, meal, party*) gâter. ●**ruinous** *a* ruineux.

rule [ru:l] 1 *n* (*principle*) règle *f*; (*regulation*) règlement *m*; (*custom*) coutume *f*; (*authority*) autorité *f*; Pol gouvernement *m*; **against the rules** or Am **rule** contraire au règlement; **as a r.** en règle générale.

▮ *vt* (*country*) gouverner; (*decide*) Jur Sp décider (**that** que); **to r. s.o.** (*dominate*) mener qn; **to r. out** (*exclude*) exclure.

▮ *vi* (*of king etc*) régner (**over** sur); (*of judge*) statuer (**on** sur).

2 *n* (*for measuring*) règle *f*. ●**ruling** *a* (*class*) dirigeant; (*party*) Pol au pouvoir ▮ *n* Jur Sp décision *f*.

ruler ['ru:lər] *n* 1 (*for measuring*) règle *f*. 2 (*king, queen etc*) souverain, -aine *mf*; Pol dirigeant, -ante *m*.

rum [rʌm] *n* rhum *m*.

Rumania [ru:'meɪnɪə] *see* **Romania**.

rumble ['rʌmb(ə)l] *vi* (*of train, thunder*) gronder; (*of stomach*) gargouiller.

rummage ['rʌmɪdʒ] *vi* **to r.** (**about**) farfouiller; **r. sale** (*used clothes etc*) Am vente *f* de charité.

rumour ['ru:mər] (*Am* **rumor**) *n* bruit *m*, rumeur *f*. ●**rumoured** *a* **it is r. that** on dit que.

rump [rʌmp] *n* (*of horse*) croupe *f*; **r. steak** rumsteck *m*.

rumple ['rʌmp(ə)l] *vt* (*clothes*) chiffonner.

run [rʌn] *n* (*series*) série *f*; (*period*) période *f*; (*running*) course *f*; (*outing*) tour *m*; (*journey*) parcours *m*; (*rush*) ruée *f* (**on** sur); (*for skiing*) piste *f*; (*in cricket, baseball*) point *m*; (*in stocking*) maille *f* filée; **to go for a r.** (aller) faire une course à pied; (*in vehicle*) (aller) faire un tour; **on the r.** (*prisoner*) en fuite; **to have the r. of** (*house etc*) avoir à sa disposition; **in the long r.** à la longue.

▮ *vi* (*pt* **ran**, *pp* **run**, *pres p* **running**) courir; (*of river, nose, pen, tap or Am* faucet) couler; (of colour in washing) déteindre; (of ink) baver; (of play, film) se jouer; (of contract) être valide; (last) durer; (pass) passer; (function) marcher; (idle) Aut tourner; (of stocking) filer; **to r. down/in/etc** descendre/entrer/etc en courant; **to r. for president** être candidat à la présidence; **to r. between** (of bus) faire le service entre; **to go running** Sp faire du jogging; **it runs into a hundred pounds** ça va chercher dans les cent livres; **it runs in the family** ça tient de famille.

▮vt (risk) courir; (marathon etc) courir, prendre part à; (temperature, errand) faire; (machine) faire fonctionner; (engine) Aut faire tourner; (drive) Aut conduire; (goods) transporter (to à); (business, country) diriger; (courses, events) organiser; (house) tenir; (computer program) exécuter; (article) publier (on sur); (bath) faire couler; **to r. one's hand over** passer la main sur; **to r. its course** (of illness etc) suivre son cours; **to r. 5 km** Sp faire 5 km de course à pied; **to r. a car** avoir une voiture.

run about or **around** vi courir çà et là ▮**to run across** vt (meet) tomber sur (qn) ▮**to run along** vi r. along! filez! ▮**to run away** vi s'enfuir, se sauver (from de) ▮**to run down** vt (pedestrian) renverser; (belittle) Fig dénigrer; (restrict) limiter peu à peu. ● **run-'down** a (weak, tired) à plat; (district) délabré ▮**to run in** vt (vehicle) roder ▮**to run into** vt (meet) tomber sur; (crash into) Aut percuter; **to r. into debt** s'endetter ▮**to run off** vi (flee) s'enfuir (with avec) ▮**to run out** vi (of stocks) s'épuiser; (of lease) expirer; (of time) manquer; **to r. out of** (time, money) manquer de; **we've r. out of coffee** on n'a plus de café ▮vt **to r. s.o. out of** chasser qn de ▮**to run over** vi (of liquid) déborder ▮vt (kill pedestrian) écraser; (knock down pedestrian) renverser; (notes, text) revoir ▮**to run round** vt (surround) entourer ▮**to run**

through vt (recap) revoir ▮**to run up** vt (debts, bill) laisser s'accumuler.

runaway ['rʌnəweɪ] n fugitif, -ive mf ▮a (car, horse) emballé; (lorry, Am truck) fou (f folle) (inflation) galopant.

rung[1] [rʌŋ] n (of ladder) barreau m.

rung[2] [rʌŋ] pp of **ring**[2].

runner ['rʌnər] n Sp etc coureur m; **r. bean** haricot m (grimpant). ● **runner-'up** n Sp second, -onde mf.

running ['rʌnɪŋ] n (on foot) course f; (of machine) fonctionnement m; (of business, country) direction f; **to be out of the r.** ne plus être dans la course ▮a (commentary) simultané; **six days/etc r.** six jours/etc de suite.

runny ['rʌnɪ] a (-ier, -iest) (cream etc) liquide; (nose) qui coule.

run-of-the-mill [rʌnəvðə'mɪl] a ordinaire.

runway ['rʌnweɪ] n Av piste f (d'envol).

rupture ['rʌptʃər] n Med hernie f ▮vt rompre.

rural ['rʊərəl] a rural.

rush[1] [rʌʃ] vi (move fast) se précipiter, se ruer (at sur, towards vers); (of blood) affluer (to à); (hurry) se dépêcher (to do de faire); **to r. out** partir en vitesse.

▮vt **to r. s.o.** (hurry) bousculer qn; **to r. s.o. to hospital** or Am **to the hospital** transporter qn d'urgence à l'hôpital; **to r.** (through) sth (job, meal etc) faire, manger etc qch en vitesse; **to be rushed into** (decision, answer etc) être forcé à prendre, donner etc.

▮n ruée f (for vers); (confusion) bousculade f; (hurry) hâte f; (of orders) avalanche f; **in a r.** pressé (**to do** de faire); **to leave in a r.** partir en vitesse; **the r. hour** l'heure f d'affluence; **a r. job** un travail d'urgence.

rushes[2] ['rʌʃɪz] npl (plants) joncs mpl.

rusk [rʌsk] n biscotte f.

russet ['rʌsɪt] a brun roux inv.

Russia ['rʌʃə] n Russie f. ● **Russian** a & n russe (mf) ▮n (language) russe m.

rust [rʌst] n rouille f ▮vi (se) rouiller.

● **rustproof** a inoxydable. ● **rusty** a (-ier,
-iest) (metal, Fig memory etc) rouillé.
rustic ['rʌstɪk] a rustique.
rustle ['rʌs(ə)l] 1 vi (of leaves) bruire. 2 vt
to r. up Fam (prepare) préparer (repas
etc).
rut [rʌt] n ornière f; to be in a r. Fig être

encroûté.
ruthless ['ruːθləs] a (attack, person etc)
impitoyable; (in taking decisions) très
ferme. ● —ly adv (mercilessly) impi-
toyablement.
rye [raɪ] n seigle m; r. bread pain m de
seigle.

S

S, s [es] n S, s m.

Sabbath ['sæbəθ] n (Jewish) sabbat m; (Christian) dimanche m.

sabotage ['sæbətɑːʒ] n sabotage m ‖ vt saboter. ● **saboteur** [-'tɜːr] n saboteur, -euse mf.

saccharin ['sækərɪn] n saccharine f.

sachet ['sæʃeɪ] n (of lavender etc) sachet m; (of shampoo) dosette f.

sack [sæk] 1 n (bag) sac m. 2 vt (dismiss) Fam virer ‖ n Fam to get the s. se faire virer; to give s.o. the s. virer qn. 3 vt (town etc) mettre à sac. ● —**ing** n 1 (cloth) toile f à sac. 2 (dismissal) Fam renvoi m.

sacrament ['sækrəmənt] n Rel sacrement m.

sacred ['seɪkrɪd] a (holy) sacré.

sacrifice ['sækrɪfaɪs] n sacrifice m ‖ vt sacrifier (to à, pour).

sad [sæd] a (sadder, saddest) triste. ● **sadden** vt attrister. ● **sadly** adv tristement; (unfortunately) malheureusement; (very) (inadequate etc) très. ● **sadness** n tristesse f.

saddle ['sæd(ə)l] n selle f ‖ vt (horse) seller; **to s. s.o. with sth/s.o.** (debt, relative etc) Fam coller qch/qn à qn. ● **saddlebag** n sacoche f.

sadistic [sə'dɪstɪk] a sadique.

sae [eseɪ'iː] abbr = stamped addressed envelope.

safari [sə'fɑːrɪ] n safari m; **to be or go on s.** faire un safari.

safe[1] [seɪf] a (-er, -est) (person) en sécurité; (equipment, toy, animal) sans danger; (place, investment, method) sûr; (bridge, ladder) solide; (prudent) prudent; **s. (and sound)** sain et sauf; **it's s. to go out** on peut sortir sans danger; **the safest thing is...** le plus sûr est de...; **s. from** à l'abri de; **to be on the s. side** pour plus de sûreté; **in s. hands** en mains sûres; **s. journey!** bon voyage! ● **safe'keeping** n **for s.** à garder en sécurité. ● **safely** adv (without accident) sans accident; (without risk) sans risque; (in a safe place) en lieu sûr.

safe[2] [seɪf] n (for money etc) coffre-fort m.

safeguard ['seɪfgɑːd] n sauvegarde f (against contre) ‖ vt sauvegarder.

safety ['seɪftɪ] n sécurité f; (solidity) solidité f ‖ a (belt, device, screen, margin) de sécurité; (pin, razor, chain, valve) de sûreté; **s. precaution** mesure f de sécurité.

sag [sæg] vi (-gg-) (of roof, ground) s'affaisser; (of breasts) tomber; (of cheeks) pendre. ● **sagging** a (roof, ground) affaissé; (breasts) tombant.

saga ['sɑːgə] n Liter saga f; (bad sequence of events) Fig feuilleton m.

sage [seɪdʒ] n 1 Bot Culin sauge f. 2 (wise man) sage m.

Sagittarius [sædʒɪ'teərɪəs] n (sign) le Sagittaire.

Sahara [sə'hɑːrə] n the S. (desert) le Sahara.

said [sed] pt & pp of say.

sail [seɪl] vi (navigate) naviguer; (leave) partir; Sp faire de la voile; **to s. into port** entrer au port; **to s. round the world/an island** faire le tour du monde/d'une île en bateau; **to s. through** (exam) Fig passer haut la main.
‖ vt (boat) piloter; (seas) parcourir.
‖ n voile f; **to set s.** (of boat) partir (for à destination de). ● —**ing** n navigation f; Sp voile f; (departure) départ m; (crossing) traversée f; **s. boat** voilier m. ● **sailboard** n planche f (à voile). ● **sailboat** n Am voilier m.

sailor ['seɪlər] n marin m, matelot m.

saint [seɪnt] n saint m, sainte f.

sake [seɪk] n for my/your/his/etc s. pour moi/toi/lui/etc; **(just) for the s. of eating/etc** simplement pour manger/etc; **for heaven's** or **God's s.** pour l'amour de Dieu.

salad ['sæləd] n (vegetables, fruit etc) salade f; **s. bowl** saladier m; **s. cream** mayonnaise f; **s. dressing** sauce f de salade.

salami [sə'lɑːmɪ] n salami m.

salary ['sælərɪ] n (professional) traitement m; (wage) salaire m.

sale [seɪl] n vente f; **sale(s)** (at reduced prices) Com soldes mpl; **in a** or **the s.**, Am **on s.** (cheaply) en solde; **on s.** (available) en vente; **(up) for s.** à vendre; **to put up for s.** mettre en vente; **s. price** Com prix m de solde; • **salesclerk** n Am vendeur, -euse mf. • **salesman** n (pl -men) (in shop) vendeur m; (travelling) s., Am (traveling) s., représentant m (de commerce). • **saleswoman** n (pl -women) vendeuse f; (who travels) représentante f (de commerce).

saliva [sə'laɪvə] n salive f.

sallow ['sæləʊ] a (-er, -est) jaunâtre.

salmon ['sæmən] n saumon m.

salmonella [sælmə'nelə] n (poisoning) salmonellose f.

salon ['sælɒn] n beauty/hairdressing s. salon m de beauté/de coiffure.

saloon [sə'luːn] n (car) berline f; (on ship) salon m; (bar) Am bar m; **s. bar** (of pub) salle f chic.

salt [sɔːlt] n sel m; **bath salts** sels mpl de bain; **s. free** sans sel; **s. water** eau f salée ▌ vt saler. • **saltcellar** or Am **saltshaker** n salière f. • **salty** a (-ier, -iest) a salé.

salute [sə'luːt] n Mil salut m; (of guns) salve f ▌ vt (greet) Mil saluer ▌ vi Mil faire un salut.

salvage ['sælvɪdʒ] vt (save) sauver (**from** de); (iron etc to be used again) récupérer ▌ n (saved goods) objets mpl sauvés (d'un naufrage etc); **s. operation/etc** opération f/etc de sauvetage.

salvation [sæl'veɪʃ(ə)n] n salut m; **the S. Army** l'armée f du Salut.

same [seɪm] a même; **the (very) s. house as** (exactement) la même maison que ▌ pron **the s.** le même, la même, pl les mêmes; **it's all the s. to me** ça m'est égal; **all** or **just the s.** tout de même; **to do the s.** en faire autant.

sample ['sɑːmp(ə)l] n échantillon m; (of blood) prélèvement m ▌ vt (wine, cheese etc) goûter; (product) essayer; (army life etc) goûter de.

sanctify ['sæŋktɪfaɪ] vt sanctifier.

sanctimonious [sæŋktɪ'məʊnɪəs] a (person, manner) tartufe.

sanction ['sæŋkʃ(ə)n] n (approval, punishment) sanction f ▌ vt (approve) sanctionner.

sanctuary ['sæŋktʃʊərɪ, Am -erɪ] n Rel sanctuaire m; (refuge) & Pol asile m; (for animals) réserve f.

sand [sænd] n sable m ▌ vt (road) sabler; **to s. (down)** (wood etc) poncer. • **sandbag** n sac m de sable. • **sandcastle** n château m de sable. • **sandpaper** n papier m de verre ▌ vt (wood) poncer. • **sandstone** n (rock) grès m.

sandal ['sænd(ə)l] n sandale f.

sandwich ['sænwɪdʒ] **1** n sandwich m; **cheese/etc s.** sandwich au fromage/etc; **hero** or **submarine s.** Am gros sandwich m coupé dans une baguette; **s. bar** snack-bar m (qui ne vend que des sandwichs). **2** vt **to s. (in)** (fit in) intercaler; **sandwiched in between** (caught) coincé entre.

sandy ['sændɪ] a **1** (-ier, -iest) (beach) de sable; (road, ground) sablonneux. **2** (hair) blond roux inv.

sane [seɪn] a (-er, -est) (person) sain (d'esprit); (idea, attitude) raisonnable.

sang [sæŋ] pt of **sing**.

sanitary ['sænɪtərɪ, Am -erɪ] a (fittings) sanitaire; (clean) hygiénique; **s. towel** or Am **napkin** serviette f hygiénique. • **sanitation** [-'teɪʃ(ə)n] n hygiène f (publique); (plumbing) installations fpl sanitaires.

sanity ['sænɪtɪ] n (of person) santé f mentale; (reason) raison f.

sank [sæŋk] pt of **sink²**.

Santa Claus ['sæntəklɔːz] n le père Noël.

sap [sæp] **1** n Bot sève f. **2** vt (-pp-) (weaken) miner (énergie etc).

sapphire ['sæfaɪər] n (jewel) saphir m.

sarcastic [sɑːˈkæstɪk] a sarcastique.

sardine [sɑːˈdiːn] n sardine f.

Sardinia [sɑːˈdɪnɪə] n Sardaigne f.

sash [sæʃ] n (on dress) ceinture f; (of mayor etc) écharpe f.

sat [sæt] pt & pp of **sit**.

Satan ['seɪt(ə)n] n Satan m.

satchel ['sætʃ(ə)l] n cartable m.

satellite ['sætəlaɪt] n satellite m; **s. (country)** pays m satellite; **s. dish** antenne f parabolique or satellite; **s. TV** télévision f par satellite.

satin ['sætɪn] n satin m.

satire ['sætaɪər] n satire f (on contre). ● **sa'tirical** a satirique. ● **satirize** vt faire la satire de.

satisfaction [sætɪsˈfækʃ(ə)n] n satisfaction f. ● **satisfactory** a satisfaisant.

satisfy ['sætɪsfaɪ] vt satisfaire (qn); (convince) persuader (qn) (that que); (demand, condition) satisfaire à; **to s. oneself that** s'assurer que; **satisfied (with)** satisfait (de). ● **—ing** a satisfaisant; (meal) substantiel.

satsuma [sæt'suːmə] n (fruit) satsuma f.

saturate ['sætʃəreɪt] vt (soak) tremper; (fill) saturer (**with** de).

Saturday ['sætədɪ, -deɪ] n samedi m.

sauce [sɔːs] n **1** sauce f; **tomato s.** sauce tomate. **2** (impudence) Fam toupet m. ● **saucy** a (-ier, -iest) (impudent) impertinent.

saucepan ['sɔːspən] n casserole f.

saucer ['sɔːsər] n soucoupe f.

Saudi Arabia [saʊdɪəˈreɪbɪə, Am sɔːdɪəˈreɪbɪə] n Arabie f Séoudite.

sauna ['sɔːnə] n sauna m.

sausage ['sɒsɪdʒ] n (cooked, for cooking) saucisse f; (dried, for slicing) saucisson m.

savage ['sævɪdʒ] a (fierce) féroce; (bru-

tal, cruel) brutal, sauvage ‖n (brute) sauvage mf ‖vt (of animal, critic etc) attaquer (férocement).

save¹ [seɪv] vt (rescue) sauver (**from** de); (keep) garder; (money, time) économiser; Comptr sauvegarder; (stamps) collectionner; (problems) éviter; **to s. s.o. from doing** (prevent) empêcher qn de faire; **that will s. him or her (the bother of) going** ça lui évitera d'y aller; **to s. up (money)** économiser.
‖vi to save (up) faire des économies (**for** sth, **to buy** sth pour acheter qch).
‖n Fb arrêt m. ● **saving** n (of time, money) économie f (of de); (thrifty habit) l'épargne f; pl (money) économies fpl; **savings account** compte m d'épargne; **savings bank** caisse f d'épargne.

save² [seɪv] prep (except) sauf.

saveloy ['sævəlɔɪ] n cervelas m.

saviour ['seɪvjər] (Am **savior**) n sauveur m.

savour ['seɪvər] (Am **savor**) vt savourer. ● **savoury** (Am **savory**) a (not sweet) Culin salé.

saw¹ [sɔː] n scie f ‖vt (pt **sawed**, pp **sawn** or **sawed**) scier; **to s. off** scier; **a sawn-off** or Am **sawed-off shotgun** un fusil à canon scié. ● **sawdust** n sciure f.

saw² [sɔː] pt of **see**.

saxophone ['sæksəfəʊn] n saxophone m.

say [seɪ] vt (pt & pp **said** [sed]) dire (**to** à, **that** que); (of dial etc) marquer; **to s. again** répéter; **what do you s. to a walk?** que dirais-tu d'une promenade?; **(let's) s. tomorrow** disons demain; **to s. nothing of** ... sans parler de...; **that's to s.** c'est-à-dire.
‖vi dire; **you don't s.!** Fam sans blague!; **s.!** Am Fam dis donc!; **that goes without saying** ça va sans dire.
‖n to have one's s. dire ce que l'on a à dire; **to have no s.** ne pas avoir voix au chapitre (**in** pour). ● **saying** n dicton m, proverbe m.

scab [skæb] n (of wound) croûte f.

scaffold ['skæfəld] n échafaudage m; (gallows) échafaud m. ●—ing n échafaudage m.

scald [skɔːld] vt (burn, cleanse) ébouillanter ▮ n brûlure f.

scale [skeɪl] 1 n (of map, wages etc) échelle f; (of numbers) série f; Mus gamme f; on a small/large s. sur une petite/grande échelle; s. model modèle m réduit ▮ vt to s. down réduire (proportionnellement). 2 n (on fish) écaille f ▮ vt (teeth) détartrer. 3 vt (wall) escalader.

scales [skeɪlz] npl (for weighing) balance f; (bathroom) s. pèse-personne m; (baby) s. pèse-bébé m.

scallion ['skæljən] n Am oignon m vert.

scallop ['skɒləp] n coquille f Saint-Jacques.

scalp [skælp] n Med cuir m chevelu.

scalpel ['skælp(ə)l] n scalpel m.

scam [skæm] n (swindle) Am Fam escroquerie f.

scamper ['skæmpər] vi to s. off détaler.

scampi ['skæmpɪ] npl scampi mpl.

scan [skæn] 1 vt (-nn-) (look at briefly) parcourir (des yeux); (scrutinize) scruter; (of radar) balayer. 2 n to have a s. (of pregnant woman) passer une échographie.

scandal ['skænd(ə)l] n (disgrace) scandale m; (gossip) médisances fpl; to cause a s. (of book etc) causer un scandale; (of conduct etc) faire scandale. ●**scandalize** vt scandaliser. ●**scandalous** a scandaleux.

Scandinavia [skændɪ'neɪvɪə] n Scandinavie f. ●**Scandinavian** a & n scandinave (mf).

scanner ['skænər] n Med Comptr scanner m.

scant [skænt] a (meal, amount) insuffisant; s. attention/regard peu d'attention/de cas. ●**scanty** a (-ier, -iest) insuffisant; (bikini etc) minuscule.

scapegoat ['skeɪpgəʊt] n bouc m émissaire.

scar [skɑːr] n cicatrice f ▮ vt (-rr-)

marquer d'une cicatrice; Fig marquer.

scarce [skeəs] a (-er, -est) (food, book etc) rare; ●**scarcely** adv à peine. ●**scarcity** n (shortage) pénurie f.

scare [skeər] n to give s.o. a s. faire peur à qn; bomb s. alerte f à la bombe ▮ vt faire peur à; to s. off (person) faire fuir; (animal) effaroucher. ●**scared** a (look, people) effrayé; to be s. (stiff) avoir (très) peur. ●**scarecrow** n épouvantail m.

scarf [skɑːf] n (pl scarves) (long) écharpe f; (square, for women) foulard m.

scarlet ['skɑːlət] a écarlate; s. fever scarlatine f.

scary ['skeərɪ] a (-ier, -iest) it's s. Fam ça fait peur.

scathing ['skeɪðɪŋ] a (remark) acerbe; to be s. about critiquer de façon acerbe.

scatter ['skætər] vt (disperse) disperser (foule, nuages etc); (throw or cast about) éparpiller (papiers etc); (spread) répandre ▮ vi (of crowd) se disperser. ●—**ing** n a s. of houses/etc quelques maisons/etc dispersées. ●**scatterbrain** n écervelé, -ée mf.

scaveng/e ['skævɪndʒ] vi fouiller dans les ordures (for pour trouver). ●—**er** n clochard, -arde mf (qui fait les poubelles).

scenario [sɪ'nɑːrɪəʊ] n (pl -os) Cin & Fig scénario m.

scene [siːn] n (setting, fuss) & Th scène f; (of crime, accident) lieu m; (incident) incident m; (view) vue f; behind the scenes Th dans les coulisses; on the s. sur les lieux; to make a s. faire une scène (à qn). ●**scenery** n paysage m; Th décor(s) m(pl). ●**scenic** a (beauty) pittoresque; (route) touristique.

scent [sent] n (fragrance, perfume) parfum m; (animal's track) piste f ▮ vt parfumer (with de); (smell) flairer.

sceptical ['skeptɪk(ə)l] a (Am skeptical) sceptique.

schedule ['ʃedjuːl, Am 'skedʒʊl] n (of work etc) programme m; (timetable) horaire m; (list) liste f; on s. (on time) scheme 303 scotch

à l'heure; (up to date) à jour; **ahead of s.** en avance; **to be behind s.** avoir du retard; **according to s.** comme prévu. ▮ vt (to plan) prévoir; (event) fixer le programme de. ● **scheduled** a (planned) prévu; (service, flight, train etc) régulier; **she's s. to leave at 8** elle doit partir à 8 h.

schem/e [ski:m] n (plan) plan m (**to do** pour faire); (dishonest trick) combine f; (arrangement) arrangement m. ●**—ing** a intrigant ▮n Pej machinations fpl. ● **schemer** n intrigant, -ante mf.

scholar ['skɒlər] n érudit, -ite mf; (specialist) spécialiste mf; (grant holder) boursier, -ière mf. ● **scholarly** a érudit. ● **scholarship** n érudition f; (grant) bourse f (d'études).

school [sku:l] n école f; (teaching, lessons) classe f; (college) Am Fam université f; (within university) institut m, département m; **in** or **at s.** à l'école; **secondary s.,** Am **high s.** collège m, lycée m; **public s.** école f privée; Am école publique; **s. of motoring** auto-école f; **summer s.** cours mpl d'été or de vacances. ▮ a (year, book, equipment etc) scolaire; (hours) de classe; **s. fees** frais mpl de scolarité; **s. yard** Am cour f (de récréation). ● **schooling** n (learning) instruction f; (attendance) scolarité f.

schoolboy ['sku:lbɔɪ] n écolier m. ● **schoolchildren** npl écoliers mpl. ● **schoolgirl** n écolière f. ● **school-'leaver** n jeune mf qui a terminé ses études secondaires. ● **schoolmaster** n (primary) instituteur m; (secondary) professeur m. ● **schoolmate** n camarade mf de classe. ● **schoolmistress** n institutrice f; professeur m. ● **schoolteacher** n (primary) instituteur, -trice mf; (secondary) professeur m.

science ['saɪəns] n science f; **to study s.** étudier les sciences ▮ a (subject) scientifique; (teacher) de sciences; **s. fiction** science-fiction f. ● **scien'tific** a scientifique. ● **scientist** n scientifique mf.

scissors ['sɪzəz] npl ciseaux mpl; **a pair of s.** une paire de ciseaux.

sclerosis [sklɪ'rəʊsɪs] n **multiple s.** sclérose f en plaques.

scoff [skɒf] **1** vi to **s. at** (scorn) se moquer de. **2** vti (eat) Fam bouffer.

scold [skəʊld] vt gronder (**for doing** pour avoir fait).

scone [skəʊn, skɒn] n petit pain m au lait.

scoop [sku:p] n (shovel) pelle f (à main); Culin cuillère f; (in newspaper) exclusivité f ▮ vt (prizes) rafler; **to s. out** (hollow out) évider; **to s. up** ramasser (avec une pelle or une cuillère).

scoot [sku:t] vi (rush, leave) Fam filer.

scooter ['sku:tər] n (child's) trottinette f; (motorcycle) scooter m.

scope [skəʊp] n (range) étendue f; (competence) compétence(s) f(pl); (limits) limites fpl; **s. for sth/for doing** (opportunity) des possibilités fpl de qch/de faire.

scorch [skɔ:tʃ] vt (linen, grass etc) roussir ▮n s. (**mark**) brûlure f légère. ●**—ing** a (day) torride; (sun, sand) brûlant.

score[1] [skɔ:r] n Sp score m; Cards marque f; Mus partition f; (of film) musique f; **a s. to settle** Fig un compte à régler; **on that s.** à cet égard ▮ vt (point, goal) marquer; (exam mark) avoir; (success) remporter ▮ vi marquer un point or un but; (count points) marquer les points. ● **scoreboard** n Sp tableau or f d'affichage.

score[2] [skɔ:r] n a **s. (of)** (twenty) une vingtaine (de); **scores of** Fig un grand nombre de.

scorn [skɔ:n] vt mépriser ▮n mépris m. ● **scornful** a méprisant; **to be s. of** mépriser. ● **scornfully** adv avec mépris.

Scorpio ['skɔ:pɪəʊ] n (sign) le Scorpion.

scorpion ['skɔ:pɪən] n scorpion m.

Scot [skɒt] n Écossais, -aise mf. ● **Scotland** n Écosse f. ● **Scotsman** n (pl -men) Écossais m. ● **Scotswoman** n (pl -women) Écossaise f. ● **Scottish** a écossais.

scotch [skɒtʃ] **1** a **s. tape**® Am scotch®

m. **2** *vt* (*rumour*) étouffer; (*attempt*) faire échouer.

Scotch [skɒtʃ] *n* (*whisky*) scotch *m*.

scot-free [skɒt'friː] *adv* sans être puni.

scoundrel ['skaʊndr(ə)l] *n* vaurien *m*.

scour ['skaʊər] *vt* (*pan*) récurer; (*streets*) *Fig* parcourir (**for** à la recherche de). ●—**er** *n* tampon *m* à récurer.

scourge [skɜːdʒ] *n* fléau *m*.

scout [skaʊt] **1** *n* (*soldier*) éclaireur *m*; (**boy**) **s.** scout *m*; **girl s.** *Am* éclaireuse *f*; **s. camp** camp *m* scout. **2** *vi* **to s. round for** chercher.

scowl [skaʊl] *vi* se renfrogner; **to s. at s.o.** regarder qn d'un air mauvais.

scraggy ['skrægɪ] *a* (**-ier**, **-iest**) (*bony*) maigrichon.

scram [skræm] *vi* (**-mm-**) *Fam* filer.

scramble ['skræmb(ə)l] **1** *vi* **to s. for** se ruer vers; **to s. up** (*climb*) grimper; **to s. through** traverser avec difficulté. **2** *vt* (*egg*) brouiller.

scrap [skræp] **1** *n* (*piece*) petit morceau *m* (of de); (*of information, news*) fragment *m*; *pl* (*food*) restes *mpl*; **s. paper** (*papier m*) brouillon *m*.

2 *n* (*metal*) ferraille *f*; **to sell for s.** vendre à la casse ‖ *a* (*yard, heap*) de ferraille; **s. dealer** marchand *m* de ferraille; **s. metal** ferraille *f*; **on the s. heap** *Fig* au rebut ‖ *vt* (**-pp-**) se débarrasser de; (*vehicle*) mettre à la ferraille; (*plan, idea*) *Fig* abandonner.

3 *n* (*fight*) *Fam* bagarre *f*. ● **scrapbook** *n* album *m* (*pour collages etc*).

scrap/e [skreɪp] **1** *vt* racler, gratter; (*skin, knee etc*) érafler ‖ *vi* **to s. against** frotter contre ‖ *n* (*on skin*) éraflure *f*. **2** *n* **to get into a s.** *Fam* s'attirer des ennuis. ●—**er** *n* racloir *m*.

scrape away *or* **off** *vt* (*mud etc*) racler ‖ **to scrape through** *vi* (*in exam*) réussir de justesse ‖ **to scrape together** *vt* (*money, people*) réunir (difficilement).

scratch [skrætʃ] **1** *n* (*mark, injury*) éraflure *f*; (*on glass*) rayure *f*; **to start from s.** (re)partir de zéro; **it isn't up to s.** ce n'est pas au niveau.

‖ *vt* (*arm etc that itches*) gratter; (*skin, furniture etc*) érafler; (*glass*) rayer; (*with claw*) griffer; (*one's name*) graver (**on** sur).

‖ *vi* (*relieve an itch*) se gratter; (*of cat etc*) griffer; (*for cancer etc*) gratter.

scrawl [skrɔːl] *vt* gribouiller ‖ *n* gribouillis *m*.

scrawny ['skrɔːnɪ] *a* (**-ier**, **-iest**) (*bony*) maigrichon.

scream [skriːm] *vti* crier, hurler; **to s. at s.o.** crier après qn; **to s. with pain** hurler de douleur ‖ *n* cri *m* (*perçant*).

screech [skriːtʃ] *vi* crier, hurler; (*of tyres, Am tires*) crisser; (*of brakes*) hurler.

screen [skriːn] **1** *n* écran *m*; (**folding**) **s.** paravent *m* ‖ *vt* (*hide*) cacher (**from s.o.** à qn); (*protect*) protéger (**from** de); (*a film*) projeter; (*visitors, documents*) filtrer; (*for cancer etc*) faire subir un test de dépistage à (*qn*) (**for** pour). ●—**ing** *n* (*of film*) projection *f*; (*selection*) tri *m*; *Med* (*test m de*) dépistage *m*. ● **screenplay** *n* *Cin* scénario *m*.

screw [skruː] *n* vis *f* ‖ *vt* visser (**to** à); **to s. down** *or* **on** visser; **to s. off** dévisser; **to s. up** (*paper*) chiffonner; (*eyes*) plisser; (*mess up*) *Sl* gâcher. ● **screwdriver** *n* tournevis *m*. ● **screwy** *a* (**-ier**, **-iest**) (*idea, person*) farfelu.

scribble ['skrɪb(ə)l] *vti* griffonner ‖ *n* griffonnage *m*.

scrimmage ['skrɪmɪdʒ] *n* *Fb Am* mêlée *f*.

script [skrɪpt] *n* (*of film*) scénario *m*; (*of play*) texte *m*; (*in exam*) copie *f*; (*system of writing*) écriture *f*; (*handwriting*) script *m*.

Scripture(s) ['skrɪptʃə(z)] *n(pl)* *Rel* Écriture *f* (sainte), (Saintes) Écritures *fpl*.

scroll [skrəʊl] *n* rouleau *m* (de parchemin).

scroung/e [skraʊndʒ] *vt* (*meal*) se faire payer (**off s.o.** par qn); (*system of writing*) *Fig* écriture *f*; **to s. money off** *or* **from s.o.** taper qn ‖ *vi* vivre en parasite; **to s. around for** *Pej* chercher. ●—**er** *n* parasite *m*.

scrub [skrʌb] **1** vt (**-bb-**) (surface) nettoyer (à la brosse); (pan) récurer; (washing) frotter; **scrubbing brush** brosse f dure ‖ n to give sth a s. = to scrub sth; **s. brush** Am brosse f dure. **2** n (land) broussailles fpl.

scruff [skrʌf] n **by the s. of the neck** par la peau du cou.

scruffy ['skrʌfɪ] a (**-ier, -iest**) (untidy) négligé; (dirty) malpropre.

scrum [skrʌm] n Rugby mêlée f.

scruple ['skru:p(ə)l] n scrupule m. ● **scrupulous** a scrupuleux. ● **scrupulously** adv (completely) (clean, honest) absolument.

scrutinize ['skru:tɪnaɪz] vt scruter. ● **scrutiny** n examen m minutieux.

scuba diving ['sku:bədaɪvɪŋ] n la plongée sous-marine.

scuff [skʌf] vt **to s. (up)** (scrape) érafler.

scuffle ['skʌf(ə)l] n bagarre f.

sculpt [skʌlpt] vti sculpter. ● **sculptor** n sculpteur m. ● **sculpture** n (art, object) sculpture f ‖ vti sculpter.

scum [skʌm] n **1** (on liquid) écume f. **2** Pej (people) racaille f; **the s. of** (society) la lie de.

scurry ['skʌrɪ] vi (rush) se précipiter; **to s. off** décamper.

scuttle ['skʌt(ə)l] **1** vt (ship) saborder. **2** vi **to s. off** filer.

scythe [saɪð] n faux f.

sea [si:] n mer f; **(out) at s.** en mer; **by s.** par mer; **by** or **beside the s.** au bord de la mer; **to be all at s.** Fig nager complètement ‖ a (level, breeze) de la mer; (water, fish) de mer; (air, salt) marin; (battle, power) naval; (route) maritime; **s. bed** fond m de la mer; **s. lion** otarie f. ● **seaboard** ['si:bɔ:d] n littoral m. ● **seafood** n fruits mpl de mer. ● **seafront** n front m de mer. ● **seagull** n mouette f. ● **seaman** n (pl **-men**) marin m. ● **seaplane** n hydravion m. ● **seaport** n port m de mer. ● **seashell** n coquillage m. ● **seashore** n bord m de la mer. ● **seasick** a **to be s.** avoir le mal de mer. ● **seasickness** n mal m de mer. ● **seaside** n bord m de la mer. ● **seaweed** n algue(s) f(pl). ● **seaworthy** a (ship) en état de naviguer.

seal [si:l] **1** n (animal) phoque m. **2** n (mark, design) sceau m; (of wax on document etc) cachet m (de cire) ‖ vt (document, container) sceller; (stick down) cacheter (enveloppe etc); (with putty) boucher; **to s. off** (of police, troops) interdire l'accès de (quartier, lieu).

seam [si:m] n (in cloth) couture f; (of coal etc) veine f.

search [sɜ:tʃ] n recherche f (**for** de); (of person, place) fouille f; **in s. of** à la recherche de; **to do a s. for sth** Comptr rechercher qch; **s.** party équipe f de secours ‖ vt (person, place) fouiller (**for** pour trouver); **to s. (through) one's papers/etc for sth** chercher qch dans ses papiers/etc ‖ vi chercher; **to s. for sth** chercher qch. ● **searchlight** ['sɜ:tʃlaɪt] n projecteur m.

season ['si:z(ə)n] n **1** n saison f; **the festive s.** la période des fêtes; **in (the) high s.** en pleine saison; **in the low s.** en basse saison; **a Truffaut s.** Cin un cycle Truffaut; **s. ticket** carte f d'abonnement. **2** vt (food) assaisonner; **highly seasoned** (dish) relevé. ●**—ing** n Culin assaisonnement m.

seasonal ['si:zən(ə)l] a saisonnier.

seasoned ['si:zənd] a (worker etc) expérimenté.

seat [si:t] n (for sitting, centre) & Pol siège m; (on train, bus) banquette f; Cin Th fauteuil m; (place) place f; (of trousers, Am pants) fond m; **to take** or **have a s.** s'asseoir; **s. belt** ceinture f de sécurité. ‖ vt (at table) placer (qn); (on one's lap) asseoir (qn); **the room seats 50** la salle a 50 places (assises); **be seated!** asseyez-vous! ● **seated** a (sitting) assis. ● **seating** n (seats) places fpl assises; **s. capacity** nombre m de places assises.

secluded [sɪ'klu:dɪd] a (remote) isolé.

● **seclusion** [-ʒ(ə)n] *n* solitude *f*.

second[1] ['sekənd] *a* deuxième, second; **every s. week** une semaine sur deux; **in s. (gear)** *Aut* en seconde; **to be s. in command** commander en second.

❚ *adv* **to come s.** *Sp* se classer deuxième; **the s. biggest** le deuxième en ordre de grandeur; **the s. richest country** le deuxième pays le plus riche.

❚ *n* (*person, object*) deuxième *mf*, second, -onde *mf*; *pl* (*goods*) articles *mpl* de second choix; **Louis the S.** Louis Deux.

❚ *vt* (*motion*) appuyer. ● **s.-'class** *a* (*ticket on train etc*) de seconde (*classe*); (*mail*) non urgent. ● **s.-'rate** *a* médiocre.

second[2] ['sekənd] *n* (*part of minute*) seconde *f*; **s. hand** (*of clock, watch*) trotteuse *f*.

second[3] [sɪ'kɒnd] *vt* (*employee*) détacher (**to** à).

secondary ['sekəndərɪ] *a* secondaire.

secondhand [sekənd'hænd] **1** *a* & *adv* (*not new*) d'occasion. **2** *a* (*report, news*) de seconde main.

secondly ['sekəndlɪ] *adv* deuxièmement.

secret ['siːkrɪt] *a* secret ❚ *n* secret *m*; **in s.** en secret. ● **secrecy** *n* (*discretion, silence*) secret *m*; **in s.** en secret.

secretary ['sekrət(ə)rɪ] *n* secrétaire *mf*; **Foreign S.**, *Am* **S. of State** = ministre *m* des Affaires étrangères. ● **secre'tarial** *a* (*work, post*) de secrétaire; (*school*) de secrétariat.

secretive ['siːkrətɪv] *a* (*person*) cachottier; (*organization*) qui a le goût du secret; **to be s. about** être très discret sur.

sect [sekt] *n* secte *f*.

section ['sekʃ(ə)n] *n* (*of town, country, book etc*) partie *f*; (*of road, wood etc*) section *f*; (*of machine, furniture*) élément *m*; (*department*) section *f*; (*in store*) rayon *m*; **the sports/etc s.** (*of newspaper*) la page des sports/*etc* ❚ *vt* **to s. off** (*separate*) séparer.

sector ['sektər] *n* secteur *m*.

secular ['sekjʊlər] *a* (*teaching etc*) laïque; (*music, art*) profane.

secure [sɪ'kjʊər] **1** *a* (*person, valuables*) en sûreté, en sécurité; (*place*) sûr; (*solid, firm*) solide; (*door, window*) bien fermé; (*certain*) assuré; **s. from** à l'abri de; (*emotionally*) se sécurise ❚ *vt* (*fasten*) attacher; (*window etc*) bien fermer; (*success etc*) *Fig* assurer.

2 *vt* (*obtain*) procurer (**sth for s.o.** qch à qn); **to s. sth** (**for oneself**) se procurer qch. ● **securely** *adv* (*firmly*) solidement; (*safely*) en sûreté.

security [sɪ'kjʊərətɪ] *n* sécurité *f*; (*for loan, bail*) caution *f*; **s. guard** agent *m* de sécurité; (*transferring money*) convoyeur *m* de fonds.

sedan [sɪ'dæn] *n* (*saloon*) *Aut Am* berline *f*.

sedate [sɪ'deɪt] **1** *a* calme. **2** *vt* mettre sous calmants. ● **sedation** [-ʃ(ə)n] *n* **under s.** sous calmants.

sedative ['sedətɪv] *n* calmant *m*.

sedentary ['sedəntərɪ] *a* sédentaire.

sediment ['sedɪmənt] *n* sédiment *m*.

sedition [sə'dɪʃ(ə)n] *n* sédition *f*.

seduce [sɪ'djuːs] *vt* séduire. ● **seduction** [sɪ'dʌkʃ(ə)n] *n* séduction *f*. ● **seductive** *a* (*person, offer*) séduisant.

see[1] [siː] *vti* (*pt* **saw**, *pp* **seen**) voir; **we'll on verra** (**bien**); **I s.!** je vois!; **I saw him run(ning)** je l'ai vu courir; **to s. reason** entendre raison; **s. who it is** va voir qui c'est; **s. you (later)!** à tout à l'heure!; **s. you (soon)!** à bientôt!; **to s. that** (*take care that*) = **to s. to it that.**

see about *vt* (*deal with*) s'occuper de; (*consider*) songer à ❚ **to see off** *vt* accompagner (*qn*) (*à la gare etc*) ❚ **to see out** *vt* raccompagner (*qn*) ❚ **to see through** *vt* (*task*) mener à bonne fin; **to s. s.o. through** (*be enough for*) suffire à qn ❚ **to see to** *vt* (*deal with*) s'occuper de (*qch, qn*); (*mend*) réparer (*qch*); **to s. to it that** veiller à ce que (+ *sub*); (*check*) s'assurer que; **to s. s.o. to** (*accompany*) raccompagner qn à.

seed [siːd] *n* graine *f*; (*in grape*) pépin *m*;

(source) Fig germe; **to go to s.** (of lettuce etc) monter en graine. ● **seedling** n (plant) semis m.

seedy ['si:dɪ] a (-ier, -iest) miteux.

seeing ['si:ɪŋ] conj **s. (that)** vu que.

seek [si:k] vt (pt & pp sought) chercher (**to do** à faire); (ask for) demander (**from** à); **to s. (after)** rechercher; **to s. out** aller trouver.

seem [si:m] vi sembler (**to do** faire); **it seems that...** (impression) il semble que... (+ sub or indic); (rumour) il paraît que...; **it seems to me that...** il me semble que...; **we s. to know each other** il me semble qu'on se connaît; **I can't s. to do it** je n'arrive pas à le faire. ● **—ingly** adv apparemment.

seemly ['si:mlɪ] a convenable.

seen [si:n] pp of **see**.

seep [si:p] vi (ooze) suinter; **to s. into** s'infiltrer dans.

seesaw ['si:sɔ:] n (jeu m de) bascule f.

seethe [si:ð] vi **to s. with anger** bouillir de colère; **to s. with people** (swarm) grouiller de monde.

see-through ['si:θru:] a (dress etc) transparent.

segment ['segmənt] n segment m; (of orange) quartier m.

segregate ['segrɪgeɪt] vt séparer; **(racially) segregated** (school) où se pratique la ségrégation raciale. ● **segregation** [-'geɪʃ(ə)n] n ségrégation f.

seize [si:z] **1** vt saisir; (power, land) s'emparer de **|** vi **to s. (up)on** (offer etc) saisir. **2** vi **to s. up** (of engine) (se) gripper.

seizure ['si:ʒər] n Med crise f; **s. of power** prise f de pouvoir.

seldom ['seldəm] adv rarement.

select [sɪ'lekt] vt choisir (**from** parmi); (candidates, players etc) sélectionner **|** a (chosen) choisi; (exclusive) sélect, chic inv. ● **selection** [-ʃ(ə)n] n sélection f. ● **selective** a (memory etc) sélectif; **to be s.** (of person) opérer un choix; (choosey) être difficile (**about sth** sur

qch).

self [self] n (pl **selves**) **he's back to his old s.** Fam il est redevenu lui-même. ● **s.-a'ssurance** n assurance f. ● **s.-a'ssured** a sûr de soi. ● **s.-'catering** a où l'on fait la cuisine soi-même. ● **s.-con'fessed** a (liar etc) de son propre aveu. ● **s.-'confidence** n assurance f. ● **s.-'confident** a sûr de soi. ● **s.-'conscious** a gêné. ● **s.-con'tained** a (flat, Am apartment) indépendant. ● **s.-con'trol** n maîtrise f de soi. ● **s.-de'fence** (Am **-defense**) n Jur légitime défense f. ● **s.-'discipline** n autodiscipline f. ● **s.-em'ployed** a qui travaille à son compte. ● **s.-es'teem** n amour-propre m. ● **s.-'evident** a évident, qui va de soi. ● **s.-ex'planatory** a qui tombe sous le sens. ● **s.-'governing** a autonome. ● **s.-im'portant** a suffisant. ● **s.-in'dulgent** a qui ne se refuse rien. ● **s.-'interest** n intérêt m (personnel). ● **s.-'pity** n to feel **s.-pity** s'apitoyer sur son propre sort. ● **s.-'portrait** n autoportrait m. ● **s.-re'liant** a indépendant. ● **s.-re'spect** n amour-propre m. ● **s.-'righteous** a trop content de soi. ● **s.-'sacrifice** n abnégation f. ● **s.-'satisfied** a content de soi. ● **s.-'service** n & a libre-service (m inv). ● **s.-su'fficient** a indépendant. ● **s.-su'pporting** a financièrement indépendant.

selfish ['selfɪʃ] a égoïste; (motive) intéressé. ● **selfishness** n égoïsme m.

sell [sel] vt (pt & pp **sold**) vendre; (idea etc) Fig faire accepter; **she sold it to me for twenty pounds** elle me l'a vendu vingt livres; **to s. back** revendre; **to s. off** liquider; **to have** or **be sold out of sth** n'avoir plus de qch; **this book is sold out** ce livre est épuisé.

| vi (of product) se vendre; (of idea etc) Fig être accepté; **to s. up** vendre sa maison; Com **vendre son affaire**; **selling price** prix m de vente. ● **sell-by date** n (on product) date f limité de vente. ● **seller** n vendeur, -euse mf. ● **sellout** n

it was a s. *Th Cin* tous les billets ont été vendus.

sellotape® ['seləteɪp] *n* scotch® *m* ▮ *vt* scotcher.

semblance ['sembləns] *n* semblant *m*.

semen ['si:mən] *n* sperme *m*.

semester [sɪ'mestər] *n Univ* semestre *m*.

semi- ['semɪ] *pref* semi-, demi-. ● **semibreve** [-briːv] *n Mus* ronde *f*. ● **semicircle** *n* demi-cercle *m*. ● **semi'circular** *a* semi-circulaire. ● **semi'colon** *n* point-virgule *m*. ● **semide'tached** *a* **s. house** maison *f* jumelle. ● **semi'final** *n Sp* demi-finale *f*. ● **semi(trailer)** *n Am* semi-remorque *m*.

seminar ['semɪnɑːr] *n Univ* séminaire *m*.

semolina [semə'liːnə] *n* semoule *f*.

senate ['senɪt] *n Pol* sénat *m*. ● **senator** *n Pol* sénateur *m*.

send [send] *vt* (*pt & pp* **sent**) envoyer (**to** à); **to s. s.o. for sth/s.o.** envoyer qn chercher qch/qn; **to s. s.o. mad** rendre qn fou; **to s. s.o. packing** *Fam* envoyer promener qn. ● **—er** *n* expéditeur, -trice *mf*; **'return to s.'** 'retour à l'expéditeur'.

send away *vt* envoyer (**to** à); (*dismiss*) renvoyer ▮ *vi* **to s. away for sth** commander qch (par courrier) ▮ **to send back** *vt* renvoyer ▮ **to send for** *vt* (*doctor etc*) faire venir; (*by mail*) commander (par courrier) ▮ **to send in** *vt* (*form*) envoyer; (*person*) faire entrer ▮ **to send off** *vt* (*letter etc*) envoyer (**to** à) ▮ *vi* **= send away** ▮ **to send on** *vt* (*letter, luggage*) faire suivre ▮ **to send out** *vt* (*invitation etc*) envoyer ▮ *vi* (*from room etc*) faire sortir (*qn*); **to s. out for** (*meal etc*) envoyer chercher ▮ **to send up** *vt* (*luggage etc*) faire monter; (*rocket, balloon*) lancer.

send-off ['sendɒf] *n* **to give s.o. a s.-off** *Fam* faire des adieux chaleureux à qn.

send-up ['sendʌp] *n Fam* parodie *f*.

senile ['siːnaɪl] *a* gâteux, sénile.

senior ['siːnɪər] *a* (*older*) plus âgé; (*position, rank, executive*) supérieur; (*teacher, partner*) principal; **to be s.o.'s s.** être plus âgé que qn; (*in rank, status*) être au-dessus de qn; **Brown s.** Brown père; **s. citizen** personne *f* âgée; **s. year** *Sch Univ Am* dernière année *f*.

▮ *n* aîné, -ée *mf*; *Sch* grand, grande *mf*; *Sch Univ Am* étudiant, -ante *mf* de dernière année; *Sp* senior *mf*. ● **seni'ority** *n* (*in service*) ancienneté *f*; (*in rank*) supériorité *f*.

sensation [sen'seɪʃ(ə)n] *n* sensation *f*. ● **sensational** *a* (*event*) qui fait sensation; (*terrific*) *Fam* sensationnel.

sense [sens] *n* (*faculty, awareness, meaning*) sens *m*; **s. of smell** odorat *m*; **a s. of** (*shame etc*) un sentiment de; **a s. of warmth/pleasure** une sensation de chaleur/plaisir; **a s. of direction** le sens de l'orientation; **to have a s. of humour** avoir de l'humour; **to have (good) s.** avoir du bon sens; **to have the s. to do** avoir l'intelligence de faire; **to make s.** (*of story etc*) avoir un sens, tenir debout; **to make s. of** comprendre. ▮ *vt* sentir (intuitively) (**that** que).

senseless ['sensləs] *a* (*stupid, meaningless*) insensé.

sensibility [sensɪ'bɪlɪtɪ] *n* sensibilité *f*; *pl* (*touchiness*) susceptibilité *f*.

sensible ['sensəb(ə)l] *a* (*wise*) raisonnable; (*clothes, shoes*) pratique.

sensitive ['sensɪtɪv] *a* (*responsive, painful*) sensible; (*delicate*) (*skin, question*) délicat; (*touchy*) susceptible (**about** à propos de); **s. to** (*the cold etc*) sensible à. ● **sensi'tivity** *n* sensibilité *f*; (*touchiness*) susceptibilité *f*.

sensual ['senʃʊəl] *a* (*bodily, sexual*) sensuel. ● **sensuous** *a* (*pleasing, refined*) sensuel.

sent [sent] *pt & pp* of **send**.

sentence ['sentəns] **1** *n Gram* phrase *f*. **2** *n* (*punishment, in prison*) peine *f*; (*conviction*) condamnation *f*; **to pass s.** prononcer une condamnation (**on s.o.** contre qn) ▮ *vt* **to s. s.o. to 3 years** condamner qn à 3 ans de prison.

sentiment ['sentɪmənt] *n* sentiment *m*. ● **senti'mental** *a* sentimental.

sentry ['sentrɪ] n sentinelle f.

separate ['sepərət] a (distinct) séparé; (independent) indépendant; (different) différent ▮ ['sepəreɪt] vt séparer (from de). ▮ vi se séparer (from de). ●**separately** adv séparément. ●**separation** [sepə'reɪʃ(ə)n] n séparation f.

September [sep'tembər] n septembre m.

septic ['septɪk] a (wound) infecté; **to turn s.** s'infecter.

sequel ['si:kw(ə)l] n suite f.

sequence ['si:kwəns] n (order) ordre m; (series) succession f; Mus Cards séquence f; **film s.** séquence de film; **in s.** dans l'ordre.

sequin ['si:kwɪn] n paillette f.

Serbia ['sɜ:bɪə] n Serbie f.

serene [sə'ri:n] a serein.

sergeant ['sɑ:dʒənt] n Mil sergent m; (in police force) brigadier m.

serial ['sɪərɪəl] n (story, film) feuilleton m; **s. number** (on appliance etc) numéro de série.

series ['sɪərɪz] n inv série f; (book collection) collection f.

serious ['sɪərɪəs] a sérieux; (illness, mistake, tone) grave, sérieux; (damage) important. ●**—ly** adv sérieusement; (ill) gravement; **to take s.** prendre au sérieux. ●**—ness** n sérieux m; (of illness, situation etc) gravité f.

sermon ['sɜ:mən] n sermon m.

serpent ['sɜ:pənt] n serpent m.

serrated [sə'reɪtɪd] a (knife) à dents (de scie).

servant ['sɜ:vənt] n (in house etc) domestique mf; (person who serves) Fig serviteur m; **public s.** fonctionnaire mf.

serve [sɜ:v] vt (meal, cause etc) servir; (at table, in shop etc) servir (**to s.o.** à qn, **s.o. with sth** qch à qn); (of train, bus etc) desservir (un village, quartier etc); (supply with electricity etc) alimenter; (apprenticeship) faire; **to s. a sentence** (in prison) purger une peine; **it serves its purpose** ça fait l'affaire; (**it) serves you right!** Fam ça t'apprendra!; **to s. up or out** (meal etc) servir.

▮ vi servir (**as de**); **to s. on** (committee) être membre de; **to s. to show/etc** servir à montrer/etc.

▮ Tennis service m.

service ['sɜ:vɪs] n (serving, help, dishes etc) & Mil Rel Tennis service m; (machine or vehicle repair) révision f; **to be of s.** to être utile à; **the (armed) services** les forces fpl armées; **s. (charge)** (in restaurant) service m; **s. area** (on motorway) aire f de service; **s. station** station-service f.

▮ vt (machine, vehicle) réviser. ●**servicing** n Aut révision f.

serviceable ['sɜ:vɪsəb(ə)l] a (usable) utilisable; (useful) commode.

serviceman ['sɜ:vɪsmən] n (pl -men) n militaire m.

serviette [sɜ:vɪ'et] n serviette f (de table).

serving ['sɜ:vɪŋ] n (of food) portion f.

session ['seʃ(ə)n] n séance f; Univ Am semestre m universitaire.

set [set] **1** n (of keys, needles, tools etc) jeu m; (of stamps, numbers) série f; (of people) groupe m; Math ensemble m; (of books) collection f; (of dishes) service m; (scenery) Th Cin décor m; (stage) Th Cin plateau m; (hairstyle) mise f en plis; Tennis set m; **television** or **TV s.** téléviseur m; **chess s.** (box) jeu d'échecs; **the skiing s.** le monde du ski.

2 a (time, price etc) fixe; (lunch) à prix fixe; (school book etc) au programme; (speech) préparé à l'avance; (in one's habits) régulier; (situated) situé; **s. phrase** expression f consacrée; **the s. menu** le plat du jour; **dead s. against** absolument opposé à; **s. on doing** résolu à faire; **to be s. on sth** vouloir qch à tout prix; **all s.** (ready) prêt (**to do** pour faire).

3 vt (pt & pp set, pres p. setting) (put) mettre, poser; (date, limit etc) fixer; (record) Sp établir; (mechanism, clock) régler; (alarm clock) mettre (**for** pour); (arm etc in plaster) plâtrer; (task) donner (**for s.o.** à qn);

(*trap*) tendre; (*problem*) poser; (*diamond*) monter; (*precedent*) créer; **to have one's hair s.** se faire faire une mise en plis; **to s. loose** (*dog*) lâcher (on contre).

▮ *vi* (*of sun*) se coucher; (*of jelly, Am jello*®) prendre; (*of bone*) se ressouder.

set about *vt* (*begin*) se mettre à (qch); **to s. about doing sth** se mettre à faire qch ▮ **to set back** *vt* (*in time*) retarder (qn); (*cost*) *Fam* coûter (à qn) ▮ **to set down** *vt* (*object*) déposer ▮ **to set in** *vi* (*start*) commencer ▮ **to set off** *vt* (*bomb*) faire exploser; (*mechanism*) déclencher; (*beauty*) *Fig* rehausser; **to s. s.o. off crying**/*etc* faire pleurer/*etc* qn ▮ *vi* (*leave*) partir ▮ **to set out** *vt* (*display, explain*) exposer (**to** à); (*arrange*) disposer ▮ *vi* (*leave*) partir; **to s. out to do** entreprendre de faire ▮ **to set up** *vt* (*tent, statue*) dresser; (*table*) installer; (*business*) créer, monter; (*meeting*) organiser; (*government*) établir; (*inquiry*) ouvrir ▮ *vi* **to s. up in business** monter une affaire.

setback ['setbæk] *n* (*hitch*) revers *m*; *Med* rechute *f*.

setsquare ['setskweər] *n Math* équerre *f*.

settee [se'ti:] *n* canapé *m*.

setting ['setɪŋ] *n* (*surroundings*) cadre *m*; (*of sun*) coucher *m*.

settle ['set(ə)l] *vt* (*decide, arrange, pay*) régler; (*date*) fixer; (*place in position*) placer; (*person*) installer (*dans son lit etc*); (*nerves*) calmer; (*land*) coloniser; **let's s. things** arrangeons les choses; **that's (all) settled** c'est décidé *or* réglé.

▮ *vi* (*live*) s'installer; (*of dust*) se déposer; (*of bird*) se poser; (*of snow*) tenir; **to s. (down) into** (*armchair*) s'installer dans; (*job*) s'habituer à; **to s. (up) with s.o.** (*pay*) régler qn; **to s. down** (*in chair or house*) s'installer; (*calm down*) se calmer; (*in one's lifestyle*) se ranger; **to s. down to** (*get used to*) s'habituer à; (*work*) se mettre à; **to s. for** accepter; **to s. in** s'installer. ● **settled** *a* (*weather*) stable. ● **settlement** *n* (*agreement*) ac-

cord *m*; (*payment*) règlement *m*; (*colony*) colonie *f*. ● **settler** *n* colon *m*.

setup ['setʌp] *n Fam* situation *f*.

seven ['sev(ə)n] *a & n* sept (*m*). ● **seven'teen** *a & n* dix-sept (*m*). ● **seventh** *a & n* septième (*mf*). ● **seventieth** *a & n* soixante-dixième (*mf*). ● **seventy** *a & n* soixante-dix (*m*); **s.-one** soixante et onze.

sever ['sevər] *vt* sectionner, couper; (*relations*) *Fig* rompre.

several ['sev(ə)rəl] *a & pron* plusieurs (of d'entre).

severe [sə'vɪər] *a* (*tone, judge etc*) sévère; (*winter*) rigoureux; (*test*) dur; (*injury*) grave; (*blow, pain*) violent; (*cold, frost*) intense; **a s. cold** *Med* un gros rhume; **s. with s.o.** sévère envers qn. ● **severely** *adv* (*to punish*) sévèrement; (*damaged*) gravement; **to be s. handicapped** souffrir d'un handicap sévère.

sew [səʊ] *vti* (*pt* **sewed**, *pp* **sewn** [səʊn] *or* **sewed**) coudre; **to s. on** (*button*) (re)coudre; **to s. up** (*tear*) (re)coudre. ● **—ing** *n* couture *f*; **s. machine** machine *f* à coudre.

sewage ['su:ɪdʒ] *n* eaux *fpl* d'égout. ● **sewer** ['su:ər] *n* égout *m*.

sewn [səʊn] *pp* of **sew**.

sex [seks] *n* (*gender*) sexe *m*; (*activity*) relations *fpl* sexuelles; **the opposite s.** l'autre sexe; **to have s. with** coucher avec ▮ *a* (*education, life etc*) sexuel; **s. maniac** obsédé, -ée *mf* sexuel(le). ● **sexist** *a & n* sexiste (*mf*). ● **sexual** *a* sexuel. ● **sexy** *a* (**-ier, -iest**) (*book, clothes, person*) sexy *inv*; (*aroused*) qui a envie (de faire l'amour).

sextet [sek'stet] *n* sextuor *m*.

sh! [ʃ] *int* chut! [ʃyt].

shabby ['ʃæbɪ] *a* (**-ier, -iest**) (*room etc*) minable; (*person*) pauvrement vêtu; (*mean*) *Fig* mesquin.

shack [ʃæk] *n* cabane *f*.

shackles ['ʃæk(ə)lz] *npl* chaînes *fpl*.

shade [ʃeɪd] *n* ombre *f*; (*of colour*) ton *m*; (*of opinion, meaning*) nuance *f*; (*of* *lamp*) abat-jour *m inv*; (*window*) s. *Am* store *m*; **in the s.** à l'ombre; **a s. taller/** *etc* (*slightly*) un rien plus grand/*etc* ▮ *vt* (*of tree*) ombrager; **to s. in** (*drawing*) ombrer. ●**shady** *a* (**-ier, -iest**) (*place*) ombragé; (*person etc*) *Fig* louche.

shadow ['ʃædəʊ] **1** *n* ombre *f*. **2** *a* **s. cabinet** *Br Pol* cabinet *m* fantôme. **3** *vt* **to s. s.o.** (*follow*) filer qn. ●**shadowy** *a* (**-ier, -iest**) (*form etc*) obscur, vague.

shaft [ʃɑːft] *n* **1** (*of tool*) manche *m*; (*in machine*) arbre *m*; **s. of light** trait *m* de lumière. **2** (*of mine*) puits *m*; (*of lift, Am elevator*) cage *f*.

shaggy ['ʃægɪ] *a* (**-ier, -iest**) (*hair, beard*) broussailleux; (*dog*) à longs poils.

shake [ʃeɪk] *vt* (*pt* **shook**, *pp* **shaken**) secouer; (*bottle, fist*) agiter; (*belief etc*) *Fig* ébranler; (*upset*) bouleverser; **to s. the windows** (*of shock*) ébranler les vitres; **to s. one's head** (*say no*) secouer la tête; **to s. hands with** serrer la main à; **we shook hands** nous nous sommes serré la main; **to s. off** (*dust etc*) secouer; (*cough, pursuer*) *Fig* se débarrasser de; **to s. up** (*organization*) réorganiser; **to s. s.o. up** (*disturb, rouse to action*) secouer qn; **s. yourself out of it!** secoue-toi! ▮ *vi* trembler (**with** de).

▮ *n* secousse *f*; **to give sth a s.** secouer qch. ●**shake-up** *n Fig* (grande) réorganisation *f*.

shaky ['ʃeɪkɪ] *a* (**-ier, -iest**) tremblant; (*ladder*) branlant; (*memory, health*) chancelant; (*on one's legs, in a language*) mal assuré.

shall [ʃæl, *unstressed* ʃəl] *v aux* **1** (*future*) **I s. come, I'll come** je viendrai; **we s. not come, we shan't come** nous ne viendrons pas. **2** (*question*) **s. I leave?** veux-tu que je parte?; **s. we leave?** on part? **3** (*order*) **he s. do it if I order it** il devra le faire si je l'ordonne.

shallow ['ʃæləʊ] *a* (**-er, -est**) (*water, river etc*) peu profond; (*fig Pej*) superficiel.

sham [ʃæm] *n* (*pretence*) comédie *f*; (*person*) imposteur *m*; **it's a s.** c'est du bidon! ▮ *a* (*false*) faux (*f* fausse);

(*emotion*) feint ▮ *vt* (**-mm-**) feindre.

shambles ['ʃæmb(ə)lz] *n* désordre *m*, pagaille *f*; **to be a s.** être en pagaille; **to make a s. of** (*room etc*) mettre en pagaille.

shame [ʃeɪm] *n* (*feeling, disgrace*) honte *f*; **it's a s.** c'est dommage (**to do** de faire); **it's a s. (that)** c'est dommage que (+ *sub*); **what a s.!** (quel) dommage!; **to put s.o. to s.** faire honte à qn ▮ *vt* (*disgrace*) faire honte à. ●**shameful** *a* honteux. ●**shameless** *a* (*brazen*) effronté; (*indecent*) impudique.

shammy ['ʃæmɪ] *n Fam* peau *f* de chamois.

shampoo [ʃæm'puː] *n* shampooing *m* ▮ *vt* (*carpet*) shampooiner; **to s. s.o.'s hair** faire un shampooing à qn.

shandy ['ʃændɪ] *n* (*beer*) panaché *m*.

shan't [ʃɑːnt] = **shall not**.

shanty[1] ['ʃæntɪ] *n* (*hut*) baraque *f*. ●**shantytown** *n* bidonville *f*.

shanty[2] ['ʃæntɪ] *n* **sea s.** chanson *f* de marins.

shape [ʃeɪp] *n* forme *f*; **in (good) s.** (*fit*) en (pleine) forme; **to be in good/bad s.** (*of vehicle, house etc*) être en bon/mauvais état; (*of business*) marcher bien/mal; **to take s.** (*of plan, book etc*) prendre forme; (*progress well*) avancer; **in the s. of** en forme de.

▮ *vt* (*fashion*) façonner (**into** en); (*one's life*) *Fig* déterminer.

▮ *vi* **to s. up** (*of plans*) prendre (bonne) tournure; (*of pupil, wrongdoer*) s'y mettre. ●**-shaped** *suff* **pear-s.**/*etc* en forme de poire/*etc*. ●**shapeless** *a* informe. ●**shapely** *a* (**-ier, -iest**) (*woman, legs*) bien tourné.

share [ʃeər] *n* part *f* (**of, in** de); (*in company*) *Fin* action *f*; **to do one's (fair) s.** fournir sa part d'efforts; **stocks and shares** *Fin* valeurs *fpl* (boursières) ▮ *vt* (*meal, opinion etc*) partager (**with** avec); (*characteristic*) avoir en commun; **to s. sth out** partager *or* répartir qch (**among** entre) ▮ *vi* **to s. in sth** avoir sa part de qch. ●**shareholder** *n Fin* actionnaire *mf*.

shark [ʃɑːk] *n* (*fish*) requin *m*.

sharp [ʃɑːp] **1** *a* (**-er, -est**) (*knife, blade etc*) tranchant; (*pointed*) pointu; (*point, pain, voice*) aigu (*f* -uë); (*mind*) vif; (*bend*) brusque; (*words, wind, tone*) âpre; (*eyesight*) perçant; (*outline*) net (*f* nette); (*lawyer etc*) *Pej* peu scrupuleux; **s. practice** *Pej* procédé(s) *m(pl)* malhonnête(s).
▌*adv* (*to stop*) net; **five o'clock**/*etc* **s.** cinq heures/*etc* pile; **s. right/left** tout de suite à droite/à gauche.
2 *n Mus* dièse *m*.

sharpen ['ʃɑːpən] *vt* (*knife*) aiguiser; (*pencil*) tailler. ●**-er** *n* (*for pencils*) taille-crayon(s) *m inv*.

sharply ['ʃɑːplɪ] *adv* (*suddenly*) brusquement; (*harshly*) vivement; (*clearly*) nettement.

shatter ['ʃætər] *vt* (*door, arm etc*) fracasser; (*glass*) faire voler en éclats; (*career, health*) briser; (*person, hopes*) anéantir ▌*vi* (*smash*) se fracasser; (*of glass*) voler en éclats. ●**-ed** *a* (*exhausted*) anéanti. ●**-ing** *a* (*defeat*) accablant; (*experience*) bouleversant.

shav/e [ʃeɪv] *vt* (*person, head*) raser; **to s. off one's beard** se raser la barbe ▌*vi* se raser ▌*n* **to have a s.** se raser; **to have a close s.** *Fig* l'échapper belle. ●**-ing** *n* (*strip of wood*) copeau *m*; **s. brush** blaireau *m*; **s. cream, s. foam** crème *f* à raser. ●**shaver** *n* rasoir *m* électrique.

shawl [ʃɔːl] *n* châle *m*.

she [ʃiː] *pron* elle *f*; **s. wants** elle veut; **she's a happy woman** c'est une femme heureuse ▌*n Fam* femelle *f*; **it's a s.** (*baby*) c'est une fille.

sheaf [ʃiːf] *n* (*pl* **sheaves**) (*of corn*) gerbe *f*.

shear [ʃɪər] *vt* tondre ▌*npl* **shears** cisaille(s) *f(pl)*; **pruning shears** sécateur *m*.

sheath [ʃiːθ] *n* (*pl* **-s** [shiːðz]) (*container*) fourreau *m*; (*contraceptive*) préservatif *m*.

shed [ʃed] **1** *n* (*in garden*) abri *m* (de jardin); (*for goods or machines*) hangar

m. **2** *vt* (*pt & pp* **shed**, *pres p* **shedding**) (*lose*) perdre; (*tears, warmth*) répandre; (*get rid of*) se défaire de; **to s. light on** *Fig* éclairer.

she'd [ʃiːd] = **she had** & **she would**.

sheep [ʃiːp] *n inv* mouton *m*. ●**sheepdog** *n* chien *m* de berger. ●**sheepskin** *n* peau *f* de mouton.

sheepish ['ʃiːpɪʃ] *a* penaud. ●**—ly** *adv* d'un air penaud.

sheer [ʃɪər] **1** *a* (*luck, madness*) pur; (*impossibility*) absolu; **it's s. hard work** ça demande du travail; **by s. hard work** à force de travail. **2** *a* (*cliff*) à pic ▌*adv* (*to rise*) à pic. **3** *a* (*fabric*) très fin.

sheet [ʃiːt] *n* (*on bed*) drap *m*; (*of paper etc*) feuille *f*; (*of glass, ice*) plaque *f*; (*dust cover*) housse *f*; (*canvas*) bâche *f*; **s. metal** tôle *f*.

sheikh [ʃeɪk] *n* scheik *m*, cheik *m*.

shelf [ʃelf] *n* (*pl* **shelves**) étagère *f*; (*in shop*) rayon *m*.

shell [ʃel] **1** *n* (*of egg etc*) coquille *f*; (*of tortoise*) carapace *f*; (*seashell*) coquillage *m*; (*of building*) carcasse *f* ▌*vt* (*peas*) écosser; (*nut, shrimp*) décortiquer. **2** *n* (*explosive*) obus *m* ▌*vt* (*town etc*) *Mil* bombarder. ●**shellfish** *npl* (*oysters etc*) fruits *mpl* de mer. ●**shell suit** *n* survêtement *m*.

she'll [ʃiːl] = **she will**.

shelter ['ʃeltər] *n* (*place, protection*) abri *m*; **to take s.** se mettre à l'abri (**from** de) ▌*vt* abriter (**from** de); (*criminal*) protéger ▌*vi* s'abriter. ●**-ed** *a* (*place*) abrité; (*life*) très protégé.

shelve [ʃelv] *vt* (*postpone*) laisser en suspens.

shelving ['ʃelvɪŋ] *n* (*shelves*) rayonnage(s) *m(pl)*; **s. unit** (*set of shelves*) étagère *f*.

shepherd ['ʃepəd] **1** *n* berger *m*; **s.'s pie** hachis *m* Parmentier. **2** *vt* **to s. s.o. around** piloter qn. ●**shepherdess** *n* bergère *f*.

sherbet ['ʃɜːbət] *n* (*powder*) poudre *f* acidulée; (*water ice*) *Am* sorbet *m*.

sheriff ['ʃerɪf] *n Am* shérif *m*.

sherry ['ʃerɪ] n sherry m.

shield [ʃiːld] n bouclier m; (on coat of arms) écu m; (screen) Tech écran m ‖ vt protéger (**from** de).

shift [ʃɪft] n (change) changement m (**of, in** de); (period of work) poste m; (workers) équipe f; **gear** s. Aut Am levier m de vitesse; **s. work** travail m en équipe.
‖ vt (move) bouger; (employee) muter (**to** à); (blame) rejeter (**on to** sur); **to s. places** changer de place; **to s. gear(s)** Aut Am changer de vitesse.
‖ vi bouger; (of views) changer; (pass) passer (**to** à); (go) aller (**to** à); **to s. over** or **up** se pousser.

shiftless ['ʃɪftləs] a (apathetic) mou (f molle); (lazy) paresseux.

shifty ['ʃɪftɪ] a (-ier, -iest) (sly) sournois; (dubious) louche.

shimmer ['ʃɪmər] vi chatoyer, miroiter.

shin [ʃɪn] n tibia m; **s. pad** n Sp jambière f.

shin/e [ʃaɪn] vi (pt & pp **shone** [ʃɒn, Am ʃəʊn]) briller ‖ vt (polish) faire briller; **to s. a light** or **a torch on sth** éclairer qch ‖ n (on shoes, cloth) brillant m; (on metal etc) éclat m. **●—ing** a (bright, polished) brillant.

shingle ['ʃɪŋg(ə)l] n (on beach) galets mpl.

shingles ['ʃɪŋg(ə)lz] n Med zona m.

shiny ['ʃaɪnɪ] a (-ier, -iest) (bright, polished) brillant; (clothes, through wear) lustré.

ship [ʃɪp] n navire m, bateau m; **by** s. en bateau ‖ vt (-pp-) (send) expédier (par mer); (transport) transporter (par mer). **● shipping** n (traffic) navigation f; (ships) navires mpl; **s. line** compagnie f de navigation.

shipbuilding ['ʃɪpbɪldɪŋ] n construction f navale. **● shipment** n (goods) cargaison f. **● shipowner** n armateur m. **● shipshape** a & adv en ordre. **● shipwreck** n naufrage m. **● shipwrecked** a naufragé; **to be** s. faire naufrage. **● shipyard** n chantier m naval.

shirk [ʃɜːk] vt (duty) se dérober à; (work) éviter de faire ‖ vi tirer au flanc.

shirt [ʃɜːt] n chemise f; (of woman) chemisier m; (of sportsman) maillot m. **● shirtsleeves** npl **in** (one's) s. en bras de chemise.

shiver ['ʃɪvər] vi frissonner (**with** de) ‖ n frisson m.

shoal [ʃəʊl] n (of fish) banc m.

shock [ʃɒk] n (emotional, physical) choc m; (impact) & Med choc m; (of explosion) secousse f; (electric) s. décharge f (électrique) (**from sth** en touchant qch); **suffering from** s. en état de choc; **to come as a** s. **to s.o.** stupéfier qn.
‖ a (tactics, wave) de choc; (effect, image) -choc inv; **s. absorber** Aut amortisseur m.
‖ vt (offend) choquer; (surprise) stupéfier. **● shocking** a affreux; (outrageous) scandaleux; (indecent) choquant. **● shockproof** a résistant au choc.

shoddy ['ʃɒdɪ] a (-ier, -iest) (goods) de mauvaise qualité.

shoe [ʃuː] n chaussure f, soulier m; (for horse) fer m; (brake) s. Aut sabot m (de frein); **in your shoes** Fig à ta place; **s. polish** cirage m ‖ vt (pt & pp **shod**) (horse) ferrer. **● shoehorn** n chausse-pied m. **● shoelace** n lacet m. **● shoeshop** n magasin m de chaussures. **● shoestring** n **on a** s. Fig avec peu d'argent (en poche).

shone [ʃɒn, Am ʃəʊn] pt & pp of **shine**.

shoo [ʃuː] vt **to s.** (away) chasser ‖ int ouste!

shook [ʃʊk] pt of **shake**.

shoot[1] [ʃuːt] vt (pt & pp **shot**) (kill) tuer (d'un coup de feu), abattre; (wound) blesser (d'un coup de feu); (execute) fusiller; (hunt) chasser; (gun) tirer un coup de; (missile, Fig glance) lancer (**to** à); (film) tourner; **to s. down** (aircraft) abattre.
‖ vi (with gun etc) tirer (**at** sur); Fb etc shooter; **to s. ahead/off** (rush) avancer/ partir à toute vitesse; **to s. up** (of price) monter en flèche; (grow) pousser vite;

(spurt) jaillir. ● **shooting** *n (shots)* coups *mpl* de feu; *(murder)* meurtre *m; (execution)* fusillade *f; (hunting)* chasse *f*. ● **shoot-out** *n Fam* fusillade *f*.

shoot² [ʃuːt] *n (on plant)* pousse *f*.

shop [ʃɒp] *n* magasin *m; (small)* boutique *f; (workshop)* atelier *m;* **at the baker's s.** à la boulangerie, chez le boulanger; **s. assistant** vendeur, -euse *mf;* **s. front** devanture *f;* **s. steward** délégué, -ée *mf* syndical(e); **s. window** vitrine *f*.

▮ *vi* (-pp-) faire ses courses *(at chez);* **to s. around** comparer les prix. ● **shopping** *n (goods)* achats *mpl;* **to go s.** faire des courses; **to do one's s.** faire ses courses; **s. bag** sac *m* à provisions; **s. centre** centre *m* commercial. ● **shopper** *n (customer)* client, -ente *mf;* **lots of shoppers** beaucoup de gens qui font leurs courses.

shopkeeper [ʃɒpkiːpər] *n* commerçant, -ante *mf*. ● **shoplifter** *n* voleur, -euse *mf* à l'étalage. ● **shoplifting** *n* vol *m* à l'étalage. ● **shopsoiled** *or Am* **shopworn** *a* abîmé.

shore [ʃɔːr] *n* 1 *(of sea, lake)* rivage *m; (coast)* côte *f*, bord *m* de (la) mer; *(beach)* plage *f;* **on s.** *(passenger)* à terre. 2 *vt* **to s. up** *(prop up)* étayer.

short [ʃɔːt] *a* (-er, -est) court; *(person, distance)* petit; *(syllable)* bref; *(impatient)* brusque; **a s. time** *or* **while ago** (il y a) peu de temps; **to be s. of money/time** être à court d'argent/de temps; **we're s. of ten men** il nous manque dix hommes; **money/time is s.** l'argent/le temps manque; **s. of** *(except)* sauf; *(before)* avant; **not far s. of** pas loin de; **s. of a miracle** à moins d'un miracle; **to be s. for** *(of name)* être l'abréviation de; **in s.** bref; **s. circuit** *El* court-circuit *m;* **s. cut** raccourci *m;* **s. list** liste *f* de candidats retenus.

▮ *adv* **to cut s.** *(hair)* couper court; *(visit etc)* raccourcir; *(person)* couper la parole à; **to get** *or* **run s.** manquer *(of de);* **to stop s.** s'arrêter net.

shortage [ʃɔːtɪdʒ] *n* manque *m*.

shortbread [ʃɔːtbred] *n* sablé *m*. ● **short-'change** *vt (buyer)* ne pas rendre juste à. ● **short-'circuit** *vt El & Fig* court-circuiter. ● **shortcoming** *n* défaut *m*. ● **shorthand** *n* sténo *f;* **s. typist** sténodactylo *f*. ● **short-'lived** *a* de courte durée. ● **short'sighted** *a Med & Fig* myope. ● **short-'sleeved** *a* à manches courtes. ● **short-'staffed** *a* à court de personnel. ● **short-'term** *a* à court terme.

shorten [ʃɔːt(ə)n] *vt (dress, text etc)* raccourcir.

shortening [ʃɔːt(ə)nɪŋ] *n Culin* matière *f* grasse.

shortly [ʃɔːtlɪ] *adv (soon)* bientôt; **s. after** peu après.

shorts [ʃɔːts] *npl* **(a pair of) s.** un short; *(boxer)* s. caleçon *m*.

shot [ʃɒt] *pt of* **shoot¹** *n (from gun)* coup *m; (bullet)* balle *f; Cin Phot* prise *f* de vues; *(injection) Med* piqûre *f;* **a good s.** *(person)* bon tireur; **to have a s. at (doing) sth** essayer de faire qch; **like a s.** *(at once)* tout de suite; **to be s. of** *Fam* être débarrassé de. ● **shotgun** *n* fusil *m* (de chasse).

should [ʃʊd, *unstressed* ʃəd] *v aux* **1** (= *ought to*) **you s. do it** vous devriez le faire; **I s. have stayed** j'aurais dû rester; **that s. be Paul** ça doit être Paul. **2** (= *would*) **I s. like to** j'aimerais bien; **it's strange she s. say no** il est étrange qu'elle dise non. **3** *(possibility)* **if he s. come** s'il vient; **I s. be free** si je suis libre.

shoulder [ʃəʊldər] *n* 1 épaule *f;* **(hard) s.** *(of motorway)* bas-côté *m;* **s. bag** sac *m* à bandoulière; **s. blade** omoplate *f;* **s. pad** *(of jacket)* épaulette *f*. **2** *vt (responsibility)* endosser.

shout [ʃaʊt] *n* cri *m;* **to give s.o. a s.** appeler qn ▮ *vi* **to s. (out)** crier; **to s. to s.o. to do** crier à qn de faire; **to s. at s.o.** *(scold)* crier après qn ▮ *vt* **to s. (out)** *(insult etc)* crier. ● **—ing** *n (shouts)* cris *mpl*.

shove [ʃʌv] *n* poussée *f;* **to give a s. (to)**

pousser ▌ *vt* pousser; (*put*) *Fam* fourrer (**into** dans) ▌ *vi* pousser; **to s. off** (*leave*) *Fam* ficher le camp; **to s. over** (*move over*) *Fam* se pousser.

shovel ['ʃʌv(ə)l] *n* pelle *f* ▌ *vt* (**-ll-**, *Am* **-l-**) **to s. (up)** (*snow*) enlever à la pelle; (*leaves etc*) ramasser à la pelle; **to s. sth into** *Fam* fourrer qch dans.

show [ʃəʊ] *n* Th TV spectacle *m*; Cin séance *f*; (*exhibition*) exposition *f*; (*of force*) démonstration *f* (**of** de); (*semblance*) semblant *m* (**of** de); (*ostentation*) parade *f*; **the Motor S.** le Salon de l'Automobile; (**just**) **for s.** pour l'effet; **on s.** (*painting etc*) exposé; **s. business** le monde du spectacle.

▌ *vt* (*pt* **showed**, *pp* **shown**) montrer (**to** à, **that** que); (*in exhibition*) exposer; (*film*) passer; (*indicate*) indiquer, montrer; **to s. s.o. to the door** reconduire qn; **I'll s. him!** *Fam* je vais lui apprendre!

▌ *vi* (*be visible*) se voir; (*of film*) passer.

show around *vt* faire visiter; **she was shown around the house** on lui a fait visiter la maison ▌ **to show in** *vt* (*visitor*) faire entrer ▌ **to show off** *vt* (*display*) *Pej* étaler; (*highlight*) faire valoir ▌ *vi* *Pej* crâner. ● **show-off** *n* *Pej* crâneur, -euse *mf*. ▌ **to show out** *vt* (*visitor*) reconduire ▌ **to show round** *vt* = **show around** ▌ **to show up** *vt* (*embarrass*) mettre (*qn*) dans l'embarras; (*fault*) faire ressortir ▌ *vi* ressortir (**against** sur); (*of person*) *Fam* arriver.

showcase ['ʃəʊkeɪs] *n* vitrine *f*. ● **showdown** *n* confrontation *f*. ● **showjumping** *n* Sp jumping *m*. ● **showpiece** *n* modèle *m* du genre. ● **showroom** *n* (*for cars*) salle *f* d'exposition.

shower ['ʃaʊər] *n* (*bath*) douche *f*; (*of rain*) averse *f*; (*of blows*) déluge *m*; **to have** *or* **take a s.** prendre une douche ▌ *vt* **to s. s.o. with** (*gifts, abuse*) couvrir qn de. ● **showery** *a* pluvieux.

showing ['ʃəʊɪŋ] *n* (*performance*) Cin séance *f*; (*of film*) projection *f* (**of** de); (*of team, player*) performance *f*.

shown [ʃəʊn] *pp of* **show**.

showy ['ʃəʊɪ] *a* (**-ier, -iest**) (*colour, hat*) voyant; (*person*) prétentieux.

shrank [ʃræŋk] *pt of* **shrink 1**.

shrapnel ['ʃræpn(ə)l] *n* éclats *mpl* d'obus.

shred [ʃred] *n* lambeau *m*; **not a s. of evidence** pas la moindre preuve ▌ *vt* (**-dd-**) mettre en lambeaux; (*cabbage, carrots*) râper. ● **shredder** *n* Culin râpe *f*; (*in office*) destructeur *m* de documents.

shrew [ʃru:] *n* (*woman*) *Pej* mégère *f*.

shrewd [ʃru:d] *a* (**-er, -est**) (*person, plan*) astucieux.

shriek [ʃri:k] *n* cri *m* (aigu) ▌ *vi* crier; **to s. with laughter** hurler de rire.

shrill [ʃrɪl] *a* (**-er, -est**) aigu (*f* -uë), strident.

shrimp [ʃrɪmp] *n* crevette *f* (grise).

shrine [ʃraɪn] *n* lieu *m* saint; (*tomb*) chasse *f*.

shrink [ʃrɪŋk] 1 *vi* (*pt* **shrank**, *pp* **shrunk** *or* **shrunken**) (*of clothes*) rétrécir; (*of audience, amount etc*) diminuer; **to s. from** reculer devant (**doing** l'idée de faire) ▌ *vt* rétrécir. 2 *n* (*person*) *Am* *Hum* psy(chiatre) *m*. ● **s.-wrapped** *a* emballé sous pellicule plastique.

shrivel ['ʃrɪv(ə)l] *vi* (**-ll-**, *Am* **-l-**) **to s. (up)** se ratatiner ▌ *vt* **to s. (up)** ratatiner.

shroud [ʃraʊd] *n* linceul *m* ▌ *vt* **shrouded in mist** enseveli sous la brume; **shrouded in mystery** enveloppé de mystère.

Shrove Tuesday [ʃrəʊv'tju:zdɪ] *n* Mardi *m* gras.

shrub [ʃrʌb] *n* arbuste *m*.

shrug [ʃrʌg] *vt* (**-gg-**) **to s. one's shoulders** hausser les épaules; **to s. off** (*dismiss*) écarter (dédaigneusement).

shrunk(en) ['ʃrʌŋk(ən)] *pp of* **shrink 1**.

shudder ['ʃʌdər] *vi* frémir (**with** de); (*of machine*) vibrer.

shuffle ['ʃʌf(ə)l] 1 *vt* (*cards*) battre. 2 *vti* **to s. (one's feet)** traîner les pieds.

shun [ʃʌn] *vt* (**-nn-**) fuir, éviter.

shunt [ʃʌnt] *vt* (*train*) aiguiller (**on to** sur); **we were shunted (to and fro)** *Fam* on nous a baladés (**from office to office/** *etc* de bureau en bureau/*etc*).

shush! [ʃʊʃ] *int* chut! [ʃyt].

shut [ʃʌt] *vt* (*pt & pp* shut, *pp* shutting) fermer; **to s.** one's finger in (*door etc*) se prendre le doigt dans ∥ *vi* (*of door etc*) se fermer; (*of shop, museum etc*) fermer; **the door doesn't s.** la porte ne ferme pas.

shut away *vt* (*lock away*) enfermer ∥ **to shut down** *vt* fermer ∥ *vi* (*of shop etc*) fermer (définitivement) ∥ **to shut in** *vt* (*lock in*) enfermer ∥ **to shut off** *vt* (*gas etc*) fermer; (*engine*) arrêter; (*isolate*) isoler ∥ **to shut out** *vt* (*light*) empêcher d'entrer; (*view*) boucher; **to s. s.o. out** (*accidentally*) enfermer qn dehors ∥ **to shut up** *vt* (*house etc*) fermer; (*lock up*) enfermer (*personne, objet précieux*); (*silence*) *Fam* faire taire (*qn*) ∥ *vi* (*be quiet*) *Fam* se taire.

shutter [ʃʌtər] *n* (*on window*) volet *m*; (*of shop*) rideau *m* (métallique); (*of camera*) obturateur *m*.

shuttle [ʃʌt(ə)l] *n* **s.** (*service*) navette *f*; **space s.** navette spatiale ∥ *vi* faire la navette.

shy [ʃaɪ] *a* (-er, -est) timide ∥ *vi* **to s. away** reculer (**from** s.o. devant qn, **from** doing à l'idée de faire). ●—**ness** *n* timidité *f*.

sibling [sɪblɪŋ] *n* frère *m*, sœur *f*.

Sicily [sɪsɪlɪ] *n* Sicile *f*.

sick [sɪk] *a* (-er, -est) (*ill*) malade; (*mind*) malsain; (*humour*) noir; **to be s.** (*vomit*) vomir; **off s., on s. leave** en congé de maladie; **to feel s.** avoir mal au cœur; **to be s. (and tired) of sth/s.o.** *Fam* en avoir marre de qch/qn; **he makes me s.** *Fam* il m'écœure ∥ **the s.** les malades *mpl* ∥ *vt* **to s. up** (*vomit*) *Fam* vomir. ●**sickbay** *n* infirmerie *f*. ●**sickbed** *n* lit *m* de malade.

sicken [sɪkən] **1** *vt* écœurer. **2** *vi* **to be sickening for** (*illness*) couver. ●—**ing** *a* écœurant.

sickly [sɪklɪ] *a* (-ier, -iest) maladif; (*pale*) pâle; (*taste*) écœurant.

sickness [sɪknɪs] *n* (*illness*) maladie *f*.

side [saɪd] *n* côté *m*; (*of hill, animal*)

flanc *m*; (*of road, river*) bord *m*; (*of question, character*) aspect *m*; *Sp* équipe *f*; **the right s.** (*of fabric*) l'endroit *m*; **the wrong s.** (*of fabric*) l'envers *m*; **at** *or* **by the s. of** (*nearby*) à côté de; **at** *or* **by my s.** à côté de moi, à mes côtés; **by s.** l'un à côté de l'autre; **to move to one s.** s'écarter; **on this s.** de ce côté; **on the other s.** de l'autre côté; **to take sides with s.o.** se ranger du côté de qn; **on our s.** de notre côté.

∥ *a* (*lateral*) latéral; (*view*) de côté; (*street*) transversal.

∥ *vi* **to s. with s.o.** se ranger du côté de qn. ●-**sided** *suff* **ten-s.** à dix côtés.

sideboard [saɪdbɔːd] *n* **1** buffet *m*. **2 sideboards** (*hair*) pattes *fpl*. ●**sideburns** *npl* (*hair*) *Am* pattes *fpl*. ●**sidelight** *n* *Aut* veilleuse *f*. ●**sideline** *n* (*activity*) activité *f* secondaire. ●**sidesaddle** *vt* (*to ride*) en amazone. ●**sidestep** *vt* (-pp-) éviter. ●**sidetrack** *vt* **to get sidetracked** s'écarter du sujet. ●**sidewalk** *n* *Am* trottoir *m*. ●**sideways** *adv & a* de côté.

siding [saɪdɪŋ] *n* *Rail* voie *f* de garage.

siege [siːdʒ] *n* *Mil* siège *m*.

siesta [sɪestə] *n* sieste *f*; **to take a s.** faire la sieste.

sieve [sɪv] *n* tamis *m*; (*for liquids*) passoire *f*. ●**sift** *vt* (*flour etc*) tamiser ∥ *vi* **to s. through** (*papers*) examiner (à la loupe).

sigh [saɪ] *n* soupir *m* ∥ *vti* soupirer.

sight [saɪt] *n* vue *f*; (*thing seen*) spectacle *m*; (*on gun*) mire *f*; **to lose s. of** perdre de vue; **to catch s. of** apercevoir; **to come into s.** apparaître; **at first s.** à première vue; **by s.** de vue; **in s.** (*target, end etc*) en vue; **out of s.** (*hidden*) caché; (*no longer visible*) disparu; **the (tourist) sights** les attractions *fpl* touristiques; **to set one's sights on** (*job etc*) viser. ●**sightseer** *n* touriste *mf*. ●**sightseeing** *n* **to go s.** faire du tourisme.

sign [saɪn] **1** *n* signe *m*; (*notice*) panneau *m*; (*over shop, inn*) enseigne *f*; **no s. of** aucune trace de; **to use s. language**

parler par signes.

2 vt (put signature to) signer; **to s. sth over** céder qch (to à) ‖ vi signer; **to s. for** (letter) signer le reçu de; **to s. in** (in hotel etc) signer le registre; **to s. on** (on the dole) s'inscrire au chômage; **to s. on** or **up** (of soldier, worker) s'engager; (for course) s'inscrire.

signal ['sɪɡnəl] n signal m; **busy s.** Tel Am sonnerie f 'occupé'; **traffic signals** feux mpl de circulation; **s. box**, Am **s. tower** Rail poste m d'aiguillage ‖ vt (-ll-, Am -l-) (be a sign of) indiquer; (arrival etc) signaler (to à) ‖ vi faire des signaux; (with indicator) Aut mettre son clignotant; **to s. (to) s.o. to do** faire signe à qn de faire. ● **signalman** n (pl **-men**) Rail aiguilleur m.

signature ['sɪɡnətʃər] n signature f; **s. tune** indicatif m (musical).

signet ring ['sɪɡnɪtrɪŋ] n chevalière f.

significant [sɪɡ'nɪfɪkənt] a (important, large) important. ● **significance** n (meaning) signification f; (importance) importance f. ● **significantly** adv (appreciably) sensiblement.

signify ['sɪɡnɪfaɪ] vt (mean, make known) signifier (that que).

signpost ['saɪnpəʊst] n poteau m indicateur ‖ vt flécher.

silence ['saɪləns] n silence m; **in s.** en silence ‖ vt faire taire. ● **silencer** n (on gun) silencieux m. ● **silent** a silencieux; (film, anger) muet (f muette); **to keep s.** garder le silence (about sur). ● **silently** adv silencieusement.

silhouette [sɪlu:'et] n silhouette f.

silicon ['sɪlɪkən] n silicium m; **s. chip** puce f de silicium.

silk [sɪlk] n soie f. ● **silky** a (-ier, -iest) soyeux.

sill [sɪl] n (of window) rebord m.

silly ['sɪlɪ] a (-ier, -iest) bête; **to do something s.** faire une bêtise.

silver ['sɪlvər] n argent m; (plates etc) argenterie f ‖ a (spoon etc) en argent, (hair, colour) argenté; **s. paper** papier m d'argent. ● **s.-'plated** a plaqué argent.

● **silversmith** n orfèvre m. ● **silverware** n argenterie f. ● **silvery** a (colour) argenté.

similar ['sɪmɪlər] a semblable (to à). ● **simi'larity** n ressemblance f (to avec). ● **similarly** adv de la même façon; (likewise) de même.

simile ['sɪmɪlɪ] n Liter comparaison f.

simmer ['sɪmər] vi Culin mijoter; (of water) frémir; (of revolt etc) couver; **to s. down** (calm down) Fam se calmer.

simple ['sɪmp(ə)l] a (-er, -est) (basic, easy etc) simple. ● **s.-'minded** a simple d'esprit. ● **simpleton** n nigaud, -aude mf. ● **sim'plicity** n simplicité f. ● **simplification** [-'keɪʃ(ə)n] n simplification f. ● **simplify** vt simplifier. ● **simply** adv (plainly, merely) simplement; (absolutely) absolument.

simultaneous [sɪməl'teɪnɪəs, Am saɪməl'teɪnɪəs] a simultané. ● **—ly** adv simultanément.

sin [sɪn] n péché m ‖ vi (-nn-) pécher.

since [sɪns] **1** prep (in time) depuis ‖ conj depuis que; **s. she's been here** depuis qu'elle est ici; **it's a year s.** I saw him ça fait un an que je ne l'ai pas vu ‖ adv (ever) s. depuis. **2** conj (because) puisque.

sincere [sɪn'sɪər] a sincère. ● **sincerely** adv sincèrement; **yours s.** (in letter) veuillez croire à mes sentiments dévoués. ● **sin'cerity** n sincérité f.

sinew ['sɪnju:] n Anat tendon m.

sinful ['sɪnfəl] a (act etc) coupable; **he's s.** c'est un pécheur; **that's s.** c'est un péché.

sing [sɪŋ] vti (pt sang, pp sung) chanter. ● **—ing** n (of bird & musical technique) chant m ‖ a (lesson etc) de chant. ● **singer** n chanteur, -euse mf.

singe [sɪndʒ] vt (cloth) roussir; (hair) brûler.

single ['sɪŋɡ(ə)l] a seul; (room, bed) pour une personne; (unmarried) célibataire; **not a s. book/**etc pas un seul livre/etc; **every s. day** tous les jours sans exception; **s. ticket** billet m; simple; **s. parent** père m or mère f célibataire; **s.-parent**

family famille *f* monoparentale; **s. European market** marché *m* unique européen.
❚ *n* (*ticket*) aller *m* (simple); (*record*) 45 tours *m inv*; *pl* **Tennis** simples *mpl*; **singles bar** bar *m* pour célibataires.
❚ *vt* **to s. out** (*choose*) choisir.
● **s.-'breasted** *a* (*jacket*) droit.
● **s.-'decker** *n* (*bus*) autobus *m* sans impériale. ● **s.-'handed** *a* sans aide.
● **s.-'minded** *a* (*person*) résolu.

singly ['sɪŋglɪ] *adv* (*one by on*) un à un.

singsong ['sɪŋsɒŋ] *n* **to get together for a s.** se réunir pour chanter.

singular ['sɪŋgjʊlər] *a Gram* (*form*) singulier; (*noun*) au singulier ❚ *n Gram* singulier *m*; **in the s.** au singulier.

sinister ['sɪnɪstər] *a* sinistre.

sink[1] [sɪŋk] *n* (*in kitchen*) évier *m*; (*washbasin*) lavabo *m*.

sink[2] [sɪŋk] *vi* (*pt* **sank**, *pp* **sunk**) (*of ship, person etc*) couler; (*of water level*) baisser; (*collapse, subside*) s'affaisser; **to s. (down) into** (*mud*) s'enfoncer dans; (*armchair*) s'affaler dans; **to s. in** (*of fact etc*) *Fam* rentrer (dans le crâne)?; **has that sunk in?** *Fam* as-tu compris ça?
❚ *vt* (*ship*) couler; **to s. into** (*knife etc*) enfoncer dans; (*money*) investir dans.

sinner ['sɪnər] *n* pécheur *m*, pécheresse *f*.

sinus ['saɪnəs] *n Anat* sinus *m inv*.
● **sinu'sitis** *n* sinusite *f*.

sip [sɪp] *vt* (**-pp-**) boire à petites gorgées ❚ *n* (*mouthful*) petite gorgée *f*; (*drop*) goutte *f*.

siphon ['saɪfən] *n* siphon *m* ❚ *vt* **to s. off** (*money*) détourner.

sir [sɜːr] *n* monsieur *m*; **S.** (*title*) sir.

siren ['saɪərən] *n* (*of factory etc*) sirène *f*.

sirloin ['sɜːlɔɪn] *n* aloyau *m*.

sissy ['sɪsɪ] *n* (*boy, man*) *Fam* femme-lette *f*.

sister ['sɪstər] *n* sœur *f*; (*nurse*) infirmière *f* en chef. ● **s.-in-law** *n* (*pl* **sisters-in-law**) belle-sœur *f*.

sit [sɪt] *vi* (*pp & pp* **sat**, *pres p* **sitting**) s'asseoir; (*for artist*) poser (**for** pour);

(*of assembly etc*) siéger; **to be sitting** être assis; **she was sitting reading** elle était assise à lire ❚ *vt* (*child on chair etc*) asseoir; (*exam*) se présenter à.

sit around *vi* traîner; (*do nothing*) ne rien faire ❚ **to sit back** *vi* (*in chair*) se caler; (*rest*) se reposer; (*do nothing*) ne rien faire ❚ **to sit down** *vi* s'asseoir; **to be sitting down** être assis ❚ *vt* asseoir (*qn*) ❚ **to sit for** *vt* (*exam*) se présenter à ❚ **to sit in on** *vt* (*lecture*) assister à ❚ **to sit on** (*jury*) être membre de ❚ **to sit through** *vt* (*film*) rester jusqu'au bout de ❚ **to sit up** *vi* **to s. up (straight)** s'asseoir (bien droit); **to s. up waiting for s.o.** ne pas se coucher en attendant qn.

site [saɪt] *n* (*position*) emplacement *m*; (*building*) chantier *m*; **launching s.** aire *f* de lancement.

sit-in ['sɪtɪn] *n Pol* sit-in *m inv*.

sitting ['sɪtɪŋ] *n* séance *f*; (*for one's portrait*) séance *f* de pose; (*in restaurant*) service *m*. ● **sitting room** *n* salon *m*.

situate ['sɪtʃʊeɪt] *vt* situer; **to be situated** être situé, se situer. ● **situation** [-'eɪʃ(ə)n] *n* situation *f*.

six [sɪks] *a & n* six (*m*). ● **six'teen** *a & n* seize (*m*). ● **sixth** *a & n* sixième (*mf*); **(lower) s. form** *Sch* = classe *f* de première; **(upper) s. form** *Sch* = classe *f* terminale. ● **sixtieth** *a & n* soixantième (*mf*). ● **sixty** *a & n* soixante (*m*).

size [saɪz] 1 *n* (*of person, clothes, packet etc*) taille *f*; (*measurements*) dimensions *fpl*; (*of town, sum, damage*) importance *f*; (*of shoes, gloves*) pointure *f*; (*of shirt*) encolure *f*; **hip/chest s.** tour *m* de hanches/de poitrine. **2** *vt* **to s. up** (*person*) jauger; (*situation*) évaluer. ● **sizeable** *a* assez grand or gros.

sizzle ['sɪz(ə)l] *vi* grésiller.

skate[1] [skeɪt] *n* patin *m* ❚ *vi* patiner.
● **—ing** *n* patinage *m*; **to go s.** faire du patinage; **s. rink** (*ice-skating*) patinoire *f*. ● **skateboard** *n* planche *f* à roulettes.
● **skater** *n* patineur, -euse *mf*.

skate[2] [skeɪt] *n* (*fish*) raie *f*.

skeleton ['skelɪt(ə)n] *n* squelette *m* ❚ *a*

(crew, staff) (réduit au) minimum.

skeptical ['skeptɪk(ə)l] *Am* = **sceptical**.

sketch [sketʃ] *n (drawing)* croquis *m; (comic play)* sketch *m;* **a rough s. of** *(plan)* une esquisse de ‖ *vt* **to s. (out)** *(idea etc)* esquisser ‖ *vi* faire un *or* des croquis. ● **sketchy** *a* (**-ier, -iest**) incomplet.

skewer ['skjuər] *n (for meat etc)* broche *f; (for kebab)* brochette *f.*

ski [skiː] *n (pl* **skis)** ski *m;* **s. lift** remonte-pente *m;* **s. mask** *Am* cagoule *f,* passe-montagne *m;* **s. pants** fuseau *m;* **s. run** piste *f* de ski ‖ *vi (pt* **skied** [skiːd], *pres p* **skiing)** faire du ski. ● **—ing** *n Sp* ski *m* ‖ *a (school, clothes etc)* de ski. ● **skier** *n* skieur, -euse *mf.*

skid [skɪd] *vi* (**-dd-**) *Aut* déraper; **to s. into sth** déraper et heurter qch ‖ *n* dérapage *m.*

skill [skɪl] *n* habileté *f,* adresse *f* (**at** à); *(technique)* technique *f;* **one's skills** *(aptitudes)* ses compétences *fpl.* ● **skilful** *or Am* **skillful** *a* habile (**at doing** à faire, **at sth** en qch). ● **skilled** *a* habile; *(worker)* qualifié; *(work)* de spécialiste.

skim [skɪm] **1** *vt* (**-mm-**) *(milk)* écrémer; *(soup)* écumer; **skimmed milk** lait *m* écrémé. **2** *vt* (**-mm-**) **to s. (over)** *(surface)* effleurer; **to s. through** *(book)* parcourir.

skimp [skɪmp] *vi (on food etc)* lésiner (**on** sur). ● **skimpy** *a* (**-ier, -iest**) *(clothes)* étriqué; *(meal)* insuffisant.

skin [skɪn] *n* peau *f;* **s. diving** plongée *f* sous-marine; **s. test** cuti-(réaction) *f* ‖ *vt* (**-nn-**) *(fruit)* peler. ● **s.-'deep** *a* superficiel. ● **s.-'tight** *a* moulant.

skinhead ['skɪnhed] *n* skinhead *m.*

skinny ['skɪnɪ] *a* (**-ier, -iest**) maigre.

skint [skɪnt] *a (penniless) Fam* fauché.

skip¹ [skɪp] **1** *vi* (**-pp-**) *(hop about)* sautiller; *(with rope)* sauter à la corde; **skipping rope** corde *f* à sauter. **2** *vt* (**-pp-**) *(miss)* sauter *(repas, classe etc);* **to s. classes** *(miss school)* sécher les cours.

skip² [skɪp] *n (container for rubbish)*

benne *f.*

skipper ['skɪpər] *n Nau Sp* capitaine *m.*

skirmish ['skɜːmɪʃ] *n* accrochage *m.*

skirt [skɜːt] **1** *n* jupe *f.* **2** *vt* **to s. round** contourner; **skirting board** *(on wall)* plinthe *f.*

skittle ['skɪt(ə)l] *n* quille *f;* **to play skittles** jouer aux quilles.

skive [skaɪv] *vi (shirk) Fam* tirer au flanc; **to s. off** *Fam* se défiler. ● **—er** *n Fam* tire-au-flanc *m inv.*

skulk [skʌlk] *vi* rôder (furtivement).

skull [skʌl] *n* crâne *m.*

skunk [skʌŋk] *n (animal)* mouffette *f.*

sky [skaɪ] *n* ciel *m.* ● **skydiving** *n* parachutisme *m* (en chute libre). ● **skylight** *n* lucarne *f.* ● **skyline** *n (outline of buildings)* ligne *f* d'horizon. ● **skyscraper** *n* gratte-ciel *m inv.*

slab [slæb] *n (of concrete etc)* bloc *m; (thin, flat)* plaque *f; (of chocolate)* tablette *f; (of meat)* tranche *f* épaisse; *(paving stone)* dalle *f.*

slack [slæk] *a* (**-er, -est**) *(knot, spring)* lâche; *(discipline, security)* relâché; *(trade)* faible; *(lax, careless)* négligent; *(worker, student)* peu sérieux; **s. periods** périodes *fpl* creuses; *(hours)* heures *fpl* creuses; **to be s.** *(of rope)* avoir du mou; *(in office etc)* être calme. ● **slacken** *vi* **to s. (off)** *(in effort)* se relâcher; *(of production, speed)* diminuer ‖ *vt* **to s. (off)** *(rope)* relâcher; *(pace, effort)* ralentir. ● **slackness** *n (of person)* négligence *f; (of rope)* mou *m.*

slacks [slæks] *npl* pantalon *m.*

slalom ['slɑːləm] *n (ski race)* slalom *m.*

slam [slæm] **1** *vt* (**-mm-**) *(door, lid)* claquer; *(hit)* frapper violemment; *(put down)* poser violemment; **to s. on the brakes** écraser le frein ‖ *vi (of door)* claquer ‖ *n* claquement *m.* **2** *vt* (**-mm-**) *(criticize) Fam* critiquer (avec virulence).

slander ['slɑːndər] *n* diffamation *f,* calomnie *f* ‖ *vt* diffamer.

slang [slæŋ] *n* argot *m* ‖ *a (word etc)* d'argot, argotique. ● **slanging match** *n*

Fam engueulade *f*.

slant [slɑ:nt] *n* inclinaison *f*; (*point of view*) Fig angle *m* (**on** sur) ▮ *vi* (*of roof*) être en pente; (*of writing*) pencher. ●—**ed** *or* ●—**ing** *a* penché; (*roof*) en pente.

slap [slæp] **1** *n* tape *f*; (*on face*) gifle *f* ▮ *vt* (-**pp**-) (*person*) donner une tape à; **to s. s.o.'s face** gifler qn; **to s. s.o.'s bottom** donner une fessée à qn.

2 *vt* (-**pp**-) (*put*) mettre; **to s. on** (*apply*) appliquer à la va-vite.

3 *adv* **s. in the middle** *Fam* en plein milieu. ●**slapdash** *a* (*person*) négligent; (*task*) fait à la va-vite ▮ *adv* à la va-vite. ●**slaphappy** *a Fam* je-m'en-fichiste. ●**slap-up** '**meal** *n Fam* gueuleton *m*.

slash [slæʃ] **1** *vt* (*with blade etc*) taillader; (*sever*) trancher ▮ *n* entaille *f*. **2** *vt* (*reduce*) réduire radicalement; (*prices*) écraser.

slat [slæt] *n* (*in blind, Am shade*) lame *f*.

slate [sleɪt] *n* ardoise *f*.

slaughter ['slɔ:tər] *vt* (*people*) massacrer; (*animal*) abattre ▮ *n* massacre *m*; abattage *m*. ●**slaughterhouse** *n* abattoir *m*.

slave [sleɪv] *n* esclave *mf* ▮ *vi* **to s.** (**away**) se crever (au travail). ●**slavery** *n* esclavage *m*. ●**slavish** *a* servile.

slay [sleɪ] *vt* (*pt* **slew**, *pp* **slain**) *Lit* tuer.

sleazy ['sli:zɪ] *a* (-**ier**, -**iest**) *Fam* sordide.

sledge [sledʒ] (*Am* **sled** [sled]) *n* luge *f*; (*horse-drawn*) traîneau *m*.

sledgehammer ['sledʒhæmər] *n* masse *f*.

sleek [sli:k] *a* (-**er**, -**est**) (*smooth*) lisse; (*manner*) *Pej* onctueux.

sleep [sli:p] *n* sommeil *m*; **to have a s., get some s.** dormir ▮ *vi* (*pt & pp* **slept**) dormir; (*spend the night*) coucher; **to go** *or* **get to s.** s'endormir; **to send s.o. to s.** endormir qn ▮ *vt* **to s. it off** *Fam*, **s. off a hangover** cuver son vin. ●—**ing** *a* (*asleep*) endormi; **s. bag** sac *m* de couchage; **s. car** wagon-lit *m*; **s. pill** somnifère *m*; **s. quarters** chambre(s) *f*(*pl*). ●**sleeper** *n* **1 to be a light s.** avoir le sommeil léger. **2** (*bed in train*) cou-

chette *f*; (*train*) train *m* couchettes. ●**sleepless** *a* (*night*) d'insomnie. ●**sleepwalker** *n* somnambule *mf*. ●**sleepy** *a* (-**ier**, -**iest**) (*town*) endormi; **to be s.** (*of person*) avoir sommeil.

sleet [sli:t] *n* neige *f* fondue ▮ *vi* **it's sleeting** il tombe de la neige fondue.

sleeve [sli:v] *n* (*of shirt etc*) manche *f*; (*of record*) pochette *f*; **long**-/**short**-**sleeved** à manches longues/courtes.

sleigh [sleɪ] *n* traîneau *m*.

slender ['slendər] *a* (*person*) mince; (*neck, hand*) fin; (*small*) *Fig* faible.

slept [slept] *pt & pp of* **sleep.**

slice [slaɪs] *n* tranche *f*; (*portion*) *Fig* partie *f* ▮ *vt* **to s.** (**up**) couper (en tranches); **to s. off** (*cut off*) couper.

slick [slɪk] **1** *a* (-**er**, -**est**) (*glib*) qui a la parole facile; (*manner*) mielleux; (*film, book*) bien fait mais superficiel. **2** *n* **oil s.** nappe *f* de pétrole; (*large*) marée *f* noire.

slid/e [slaɪd] *n* (*in playground*) toboggan *m*; (*on ice*) glissoire *f*; (*for hair*) barrette *f*; *Phot* diapositive *f*; (*in value etc*) (légère) baisse *f* ▮ *vi* (*pt & pp* **slid**) glisser ▮ *vt* (*letter etc*) glisser (**into** dans); (*table, chair etc*) faire glisser. ●—**ing** *a* (*door, panel*) coulissant; **s. roof** toit *m* ouvrant; **s. scale** *Com* échelle *f* mobile

slight [slaɪt] **1** *a* (-**er**, -**est**) (*noise, mistake etc*) léger, petit; (*chance*) faible; (*person, figure*) (*slim*) mince; (*frail*) frêle; **the slightest thing** la moindre chose; **not in the slightest** pas le moins du monde. **2** *vt* (*offend*) offenser; (*ignore*) bouder. ●—**ly** *adv* légèrement.

slim [slɪm] *a* (**slimmer, slimmest**) mince ▮ *vi* (-**mm**-) maigrir. ●**slimming** *a* (*diet*) amaigrissant.

slime [slaɪm] *n* boue *f* (visqueuse); (*of snail*) bave *f*. ●**slimy** *a* (-**ier**, -**iest**) boueux; (*sticky, Fig smarmy*) visqueux.

sling [slɪŋ] **1** *n* (*weapon*) fronde *f*; (*toy*) lance-pierres *m inv*; (*for arm*) écharpe *f*; **in a s.** en écharpe. **2** *vt* (*pt & pp* **slung**) (*throw*) jeter; **to s. out** *Fam* balancer. ●**slingshot** *n Am* lance-pierres *m inv*.

slip [slɪp] **1** *n* (*mistake*) erreur *f*; (*woman's undergarment*) combinaison *f*; **a s. of paper** (*bit*) un bout de papier; (*for filing*) une fiche de papier; **a s. of the tongue** un lapsus; **to give s.o. the s.** fausser compagnie à qn; **s. road** *Aut* bretelle *f* (d'accès *or* de sortie).
2 *vi* (**-pp-**) glisser ▮ *vt* (*slide*) glisser (*qch*) (**to à, into** dans); **it slipped his mind** ça lui est sorti de l'esprit.
slip away *vi* (*escape*) s'esquiver ▮ **to slip in** *vi* (*enter*) entrer furtivement ▮ **to slip into** *vt* (*room etc*) se glisser dans; (*bathrobe etc*) mettre, passer ▮ **to slip off** *vt* (*coat etc*) enlever ▮ **to slip on** *vt* (*coat etc*) mettre ▮ **to slip out** *vi* sortir furtivement; (*for a moment*) sortir (un instant); (*of secret*) s'éventer ▮ **to slip past** *vt* (*guard*) passer sans être vu de ▮ **to slip up** *vi* (*make a mistake*) gaffer.
slipcover ['slɪpkʌvər] *n Am* housse *f*.
slipper ['slɪpər] *n* pantoufle *f*.
slippery ['slɪpəri] *a* glissant.
slipshod ['slɪpʃɒd] *a* (*negligent*) négligent; (*slovenly*) négligé.
slip-up ['slɪpʌp] *n Fam* gaffe *f*.
slit [slɪt] *n* (*opening*) fente *f*; (*cut*) coupure *f* ▮ *vt* (*pt & pp* slit, *pres p* slitting) (*cut*) couper; **to s. open** (*sack*) éventrer.
slither ['slɪðər] *vi* glisser; (*of snake*) se couler.
sliver ['slɪvər] *n* (*of wood*) éclat *m*; (*of cheese etc*) fine tranche *f*.
slobber ['slɒbər] *vi* (*of dog etc*) baver (**over** sur).
slog [slɒg] *n* **a** (**hard**) **s.** (*effort*) un gros effort; (*work*) un travail dur ▮ *vi* (**-gg-**) **to s.** (**away**) bosser.
slogan ['sləʊgən] *n* slogan *m*.
slop [slɒp] *vi* (**-pp-**) **to s.** (**over**) (*spill*) se répandre ▮ *vt* répandre.
slop/e [sləʊp] *n* pente *f*; (*of mountain*) versant *m*; (*for skiing*) piste *f* ▮ *vi* (*of ground, roof etc*) être en pente. ●**—ing** *a* en pente; (*handwriting*) penché.
sloppy ['slɒpi] *a* (**-ier, -iest**) (*work, appearance*) négligé; (*person*) négligent; (*sentimental*) sentimental.

slot [slɒt] *n* (*slit*) fente *f*; (*groove*) rainure *f*; (*in programme*) *Rad TV* créneau *m*; **s. machine** distributeur *m* automatique; (*for gambling*) machine *f* à sous ▮ *vt* (**-tt-**) (*insert*) insérer (**into** dans) ▮ *vi* s'insérer (**into** dans).
slouch [slaʊtʃ] *vi* ne pas se tenir droit; (*have stoop*) avoir le dos voûté; (*in chair*) se vautrer (**in** dans); **slouching over** (*desk*) penché sur ▮ *n* mauvaise tenue *f*.
slovenly ['slʌvənli] *a* négligé.
slow [sləʊ] *a* (**-er, -est**) lent; (*business*) calme; **at a s. speed** à vitesse réduite; **to be a s. walker** marcher lentement; **to be s.** (*of clock, watch*) retarder; **to be five minutes s.** retarder de cinq minutes; **in s. motion** au ralenti ▮ *adv* lentement ▮ *vti* **to s. down** *or* **up** ralentir. ●**—ly** *adv* lentement; (*bit by bit*) peu à peu.
slowcoach ['sləʊkəʊtʃ] *n Fam* tortue *f*.
●**slow-down** (**strike**) *n Am* grève *f* perlée. ●**slowpoke** *n Am Fam* tortue *f*.
sludge [slʌdʒ] *n* gadoue *f*.
slug [slʌg] **1** *n* (*mollusc*) limace *f*. **2** *n* (*bullet*) *Am Sl* pruneau *m*. **3** *vt* (**-gg-**) (*hit*) *Am Fam* frapper.
sluggish ['slʌgɪʃ] *a* (*person*) amorphe; (*machine*) peu nerveux; (*business*) peu actif.
slum [slʌm] *n* (*house*) taudis *m*; **the slums** les quartiers *mpl* pauvres ▮ *a* (*district*) pauvre ▮ *vt* (**-mm-**) **to s. it** *Fam* (*have lean times*) manger de la vache enragée; (*mix with bad company*) s'encanailler.
slumber ['slʌmbər] *n Lit* sommeil *m*.
slump [slʌmp] **1** *n* baisse *f* soudaine (**in** de); (*in prices*) effondrement *m*; *Econ* crise *f* ▮ *vi* baisser; (*of prices*) s'effondrer. **2** *vi* **to s. into** (*armchair*) s'affaisser dans.
slung [slʌŋ] *pt & pp of* sling 2.
slur [slɜːr] **1** *vt* (**-rr-**) prononcer indistinctement. **2** *n* **to cast a s. on** (*reputation*) porter atteinte à. ●**slurred** *a* (*speech*) indistinct.
slush [slʌʃ] *n* (*snow*) neige *f* fondue.
slut [slʌt] *n Pej* (*immoral*) salope *f*;

(untidy) souillon *f*.

sly [slaɪ] *a* (**-er, -est**) *(cunning)* rusé ▮ *n* **on the s.** en cachette.

smack [smæk] **1** *n* claque *f*; gifle *f*; fessée *f* ▮ *vt (person)* donner une claque à; **to s. s.o.'s face** gifler qn; **to s. s.o.('s bottom)** donner une fessée à qn. **2** *adv* **s. in the middle** *Fam* en plein milieu. **3** *vi* **to s. of** avoir des relents de.

small [smɔːl] *a* (**-er, -est**) petit; **s. change** petite monnaie *f*; **s. talk** menus propos *mpl* ▮ *adv* (*to cut, chop*) menu ▮ *n* **the s. of the back** le creux *m* des reins. ● **smallholding** *n* petite ferme *f*. ● **small-scale** *a* *Fig* peu important.

smallpox ['smɔːlpɒks] *n* petite vérole *f*.

smarmy ['smɑːmɪ] *a* (**-ier, -iest**) *Pej Fam* visqueux.

smart[1] [smɑːt] *a* (**-er, -est**) *(in appearance)* élégant; *(clever)* intelligent; *(astute)* astucieux; *(quick)* rapide; **s. aleck** *Fam* je-sais-tout *mf inv*; **s. card** carte *f* à puce *or* à mémoire. ● **smarten** *vt* **to s. up** *(room etc)* embellir ▮ *vti* **to s. (oneself) up** se faire beau. ● **smartly** *adv* *(dressed)* avec élégance.

smart[2] [smɑːt] *vi* *(sting)* brûler, faire mal.

smash [smæʃ] *vt (break)* briser; *(shatter)* fracasser; *(record)* pulvériser; **to s. s.o.'s face** *Fam* casser la gueule à qn ▮ *vi* se briser ▮ *n (accident)* collision *f*; **s. hit** *Fam* succès *m* fou. ● **s.-up** *n* collision *f*.

smash down *or* **in** *vt (door)* enfoncer ▮ **smash into** *vt (of vehicle)* (r)entrer dans *(lampadaire etc)* ▮ **to smash up** *vt (vehicle)* esquinter; *(room)* démolir.

smashing ['smæʃɪŋ] *a Fam* formidable.

smattering ['smætərɪŋ] *n* **a s. of** *(French etc)* quelques notions *fpl*.

smear [smɪər] *vt (coat)* enduire *(with* de); *(stain)* tacher *(with* de); *(smudge)* laisser une trace sur ▮ *n (mark)* trace *f*; **s. campaign** campagne *f* de diffamation.

smell [smel] *n* odeur *f*; *(sense of)* s. odorat *m* ▮ *vt (pt & pp* **smelled** *or* **smelt**) sentir; *(of animal)* flairer ▮ *vi (stink)* sentir (mauvais); *(have a smell)*

avoir une odeur; **to s. of smoke**/*etc* sentir la fumée/*etc*. ● **smelly** *a* (**-ier, -iest**) **to be s.** sentir (mauvais).

smelt[1] [smelt] *pt & pp of* **smell**.

smelt[2] [smelt] *vt (ore)* fondre; **smelting works** fonderie *f*.

smile [smaɪl] *n* sourire *m* ▮ *vi* sourire (**at** s.o. à qn). ● **-ing** *a* souriant.

smirk [smɜːk] *n (smug)* sourire *m* suffisant; *(scornful)* sourire *m* goguenard.

smock [smɒk] *n* blouse *f*.

smog [smɒg] *n* brouillard *m* épais.

smoke [sməʊk] *n* fumée *f*; **to have a s.** fumer une cigarette *etc*; **s. detector** *or* **alarm** détecteur *m* de fumée.

▮ *vt (cigarette etc)* fumer; **smoked salmon**/*etc* saumon *m*/*etc* fumé.

▮ *vi* fumer; **'no smoking'** 'défense de fumer'; **smoking compartment** *Rail* compartiment *m* fumeurs. ● **smoker** *n* fumeur, -euse *mf*; *Rail* compartiment *m* fumeurs. ● **smokestack** *n* cheminée *f* (d'usine). ● **smoky** *a* (**-ier, -iest**) *(air)* enfumé; **it's s. here** il y a de la fumée ici.

smooth [smuːð] *a* (**-er, -est**) *(surface, skin etc)* lisse; *(movement)* régulier; *(flight)* agréable; *(cream)* onctueux; *(sea)* calme; *(person, manners)* *Pej* douceureux; **the s. running** la bonne marche *(of* de) ▮ *vt* **to s. down** *or* **out** *(dress, hair etc)* lisser; **to s. over** *(problems)* *Fig* aplanir. ● **-ly** *adv* (*dress*) en douceur.

smother ['smʌðər] *vt (stifle)* étouffer; **to s. with** *(kisses etc)* *Fig* couvrir de.

smoulder ['sməʊldər] *(Am* **smolder**) *vi (of fire, Fig passion etc)* couver.

smudge [smʌdʒ] *n* tache *f*, bavure *f* ▮ *vt (paper etc)* faire des taches sur.

smug [smʌg] *a (smile etc)* béat; *(person)* content de soi. ● **-ly** *adv* avec suffisance.

smuggle ['smʌg(ə)l] *vt* passer (en fraude); **smuggled goods** contrebande *f*. ● **-ing** *n* contrebande *f*. ● **smuggler** *n* contrebandier, -ière *mf*.

smut [smʌt] *n inv (obscenity)* cochonneries *fpl*.

snack [snæk] *n (meal)* casse-croûte *m*

inv; pl (things to eat) petites choses fpl à grignoter; (sweets, Am candies) friandises fpl; **to eat a s.** or **snacks** grignoter; **s. bar** snack(-bar) m.

snag [snæg] n (hitch) inconvénient m, problème m.

snail [sneɪl] n escargot m.

snake [sneɪk] n serpent m.

snap [snæp] **1** vt (-pp-) (break) casser (avec un bruit sec); (fingers) faire claquer; **to s. up a bargain** sauter sur une occasion ∥ vi se casser net; (of person) Fig parler sèchement (at à); **to s. off** (break off) se casser; **s. out of it!** Fam secoue-toi! ∥ n bruit m sec; Phot photo f; **s. (fastener)** pression f; **cold s.** Met coup m de froid.

2 a to make a s. decision décider sans réfléchir. ● **snapshot** n photo f.

snappy ['snæpɪ] a **make it s.!** Fam dépêche-toi!

snare [sneər] n piège m.

snarl [snɑːl] vi gronder (en montrant les dents). ● **s.-up** n Aut Fam embouteillage m.

snatch [snætʃ] vt saisir (d'un geste vif); (some rest etc) Fig (réussir à) prendre; **to s. sth from s.o.** arracher qch à qn.

sneak [sniːk] **1** vi (pt & pp Am sneaked or snuck) **to s. in/out** entrer/sortir furtivement; **to s. off** s'esquiver. **2** n (telltale) Fam rapporteur, -euse mf ∥ vi **to s. on s.o.** (of child) Fam rapporter sur qn. ● **sneaky** a (-ier, -iest) (sly) Fam sournois.

sneaker ['sniːkər] n (chaussure f de) tennis m.

sneer [snɪər] vi ricaner; **to s. at** se moquer de ∥ n ricanement m.

sneeze [sniːz] n éternuement m ∥ vi éternuer.

snicker ['snɪkər] vi Am = snigger.

snide [snaɪd] a (remark etc) sarcastique.

sniff [snɪf] vt renifler; **to s. glue** sniffer de la colle; **to s. out** (bargain) Fig renifler ∥ vi **to s. (at)** renifler. ● **sniffle** n **a s., the sniffles** Fam un petit rhume.

snigger ['snɪgər] vi ricaner.

snip [snɪp] n (bargain) Fam bonne affaire f; **to make a s.** couper ∥ vt (-pp-) **to s. (off)** couper.

sniper ['snaɪpər] n Mil tireur m embusqué.

snivel ['snɪv(ə)l] vi (-ll-, Am -l-) pleurnicher.

snob [snɒb] n snob mf. ● **snobbery** n snobisme m. ● **snobbish** a snob inv.

snooker ['snuːkər] n snooker m (sorte de jeu de billard).

snoop [snuːp] vi fourrer son nez partout; **to s. on s.o.** espionner qn.

snooze [snuːz] n petit somme m.

snor/e [snɔːr] vi ronfler. ● **—ing** n ronflements mpl.

snorkel ['snɔːk(ə)l] n Sp Nau tuba m.

snort [snɔːt] vi (grunt) grogner; (sniff) renifler; (of horse) renâcler.

snotty ['snɒtɪ] a (-ier, -iest) Fam (nose) qui coule; (handkerchief) plein de morve.

snout [snaʊt] n museau m.

snow [snəʊ] n neige f ∥ vi neiger; **it is snowing** il neige ∥ vt **to be snowed in** être bloqué par la neige; **to be s. under** (work) être submergé de. ● **snowball** n boule f de neige. ● **snowbound** a bloqué par la neige. ● **snowdrift** n congère f. ● **snowfall** n chute f de neige. ● **snowflake** n flocon m de neige. ● **snowman** n (pl -men) bonhomme m de neige. ● **snowplough** or Am **snowplow** n chasseneige m inv. ● **snowstorm** n tempête f de neige. ● **snowy** a (-ier, -iest) (weather etc) neigeux.

snub [snʌb] n rebuffade f ∥ vt (-bb-) (offer etc) rejeter; **to s. s.o.** snober qn.

snuff [snʌf] vt **to s. (out)** (candle) moucher.

snug [snʌg] a (house etc) douillet; (garment) bien ajusté; **we're s.** (in chair etc) on est bien; **s. in bed** bien au chaud dans son lit.

snuggle ['snʌg(ə)l] vi **to s. up to s.o.** se pelotonner contre qn.

so [səʊ] **1** adv (to such a degree) si, tellement (that que); (thus) ainsi; **so**

that (*purpose*) pour que (+ *sub*); (*result*) si bien que; **so as to do** pour faire; **I think so** je le pense; **do so!** faites-le!; **if so** si oui; **is that so?** c'est vrai?; **so am I,** so do **I** *etc* moi aussi; **so much** (*to work etc*) tant, tellement (**that** que); **so much courage**/*etc* tant or tellement de courage/*etc* (**that** que); **so many** tant, tellement; **so many books**/*etc* tant or tellement de livres/*etc* (**that** que); **ten or so** environ dix; **and so on** et ainsi de suite; **so long!** *Fam* au revoir! **2** *conj* (*therefore*) donc; (*in that case*) alors; **so what?** et alors? ● **So-and-so** *n* **Mr So-and-so** Monsieur Un tel. ● **so-'called** *a* prétendu, soi-disant *inv*. ● **so-so** *a Fam* comme ci comme ça.

soak [səʊk] *vt* (*drench*) tremper (*qn*); (*washing, food*) faire tremper; **soaked through** trempé jusqu'aux os; **to s. up** absorber ‖ *vi* (*of washing etc*) tremper; **to s. in** (*of liquid*) s'infiltrer. ● —**ing** *a* & *adv* **s.** (**wet**) trempé.

soap [səʊp] *n* savon *m*; **s. opera** feuilleton *m* (télé) à l'eau de rose; **s. powder** lessive *f*. ● **soapflakes** *npl* savon *m* en paillettes. ● **soapsuds** *npl* mousse *f* de savon. ● **soapy** *a* (-ier, -iest) *a* savonneux.

soar [sɔːr] *vi* (*of bird etc*) s'élever; (*of price*) monter (en flèche).

sob [sɒb] *n* sanglot *m* ‖ *vi* (-bb-) sangloter.

sober ['səʊbər] **1** *a* **he's s.** (*not drunk*) il n'est pas ivre ‖ *vti* **to s. up** dessoûler. **2** *a* (*serious*) sérieux; (*style*) sobre.

soccer ['sɒkər] *n* football *m*.

sociable ['səʊʃəb(ə)l] *a* (*person*) sociable.

social ['səʊʃəl] *a* social; **s. club** club *m*; **s. evening** soirée *f*; **to have a good s. life** sortir beaucoup; **s. security** (*aid*) aide *f* sociale; (*pension*) *Am* pension *f* de retraite; **s. services, S. Security =** Sécurité *f* sociale; **s. worker** assistant, -ante *mf* social(e). ● **socialize** *vi* (*mix*) se mêler aux autres. ● **socially** *adv* (*to meet s.o.*) en société.

socialist ['səʊʃəlɪst] *a* & *n* socialiste (*mf*).

society [sə'saɪətɪ] *n* (*community, club etc*) société *f*.

sociology [səʊsɪ'ɒlədʒɪ] *n* sociologie *f*.

sock [sɒk] *n* chaussette *f*.

socket ['sɒkɪt] *n* (*for electric plug*) prise *f* de courant; (*of lamp*) douille *f*; (*of eye*) orbite *f*.

sod [sɒd] *n* (*turf*) *Am* gazon *m*.

soda ['səʊdə] *n* **1** *Ch* soude *f*. **2 s.** (**water**) eau *f* gazeuse; **s.** (**pop**) *Am* soda *m*.

sofa ['səʊfə] *n* canapé *m*; **s. bed** canapé-lit *m*.

soft [sɒft] *a* (-er, -est) (*gentle, not stiff*) doux (*f* douce); (*butter, ground, paste*) mou (*f* molle); (*colour*) tendre; (*indulgent*) indulgent; (*cowardly*) *Fam* poltron; **it's too s.** (*radio etc*) ce n'est pas assez fort; **s. drink** boisson *f* non alcoolisée; **s. drugs** drogues *fpl* douces. ● **s.-'boiled** *a* (*egg*) à la coque. ● **soften** ['sɒf(ə)n] *vt* (*object*) ramollir; (*colour, light*) adoucir ‖ *vi* **to s. up** se ramollir. ● **softly** *adv* doucement. ● **softness** *n* douceur *f*.

software ['sɒftweər] *n inv* (*of computer*) logiciel *m*; **s. package** progiciel *m*.

soggy ['sɒgɪ] *a* (-ier, -iest) (*ground*) détrempé; (*biscuit, bread*) ramolli.

soil [sɔɪl] **1** *n* (*earth*) sol *m*, terre *f*. **2** *vt* (*dirty*) salir.

solar ['səʊlər] *a* solaire; **s. power** énergie *f* solaire.

sold [səʊld] *pt* & *pp* of **sell**.

solder ['sɒldər, *Am* 'sɒdər] *vt* souder ‖ *n* soudure *f*.

soldier ['səʊldʒər] **1** *n* soldat *m*, militaire *m*. **2** *vi* **to s. on** persévérer.

sole [səʊl] **1** *n* (*of shoe*) semelle *f*; (*of foot*) plante *f*. **2** *a* (*only*) seul, unique; (*rights*) *Com* exclusif. **3** *n* (*fish*) sole *f*. ● —**ly** *adv* uniquement.

solemn ['sɒləm] *a* (*formal*) solennel; (*serious*) grave.

solicit [sə'lɪsɪt] *vt* (*seek*) solliciter ‖ *vi* (*of prostitute*) racoler. ● **solicitor** *n* (*for wills etc*) notaire *m*.

solid ['sɒlɪd] a (car, meal, state etc) solide; (wall, ball) plein; (gold, rock) massif; (crowd, mass) compact; **s. line** ligne f continue; **frozen s.** entièrement gelé ▮ n Ch solide m; pl (foods) aliments mpl solides. ● **solidly** adv (built etc) solidement.

solidarity [sɒlɪ'dærɪtɪ] n solidarité f (with avec).

solitary ['sɒlɪtərɪ] a (lonely, alone) solitaire; (only) seul; **s. confinement** Jur isolement m (cellulaire). ● **solitude** n solitude f.

solo ['səʊləʊ] n (pl -os) Mus solo m ▮ a solo inv ▮ adv Mus en solo; (to fly) en solitaire. ● **soloist** n Mus soliste mf.

soluble ['sɒljʊb(ə)l] a soluble.

solution [sə'luːʃ(ə)n] n (to problem etc) & Ch solution f (to de).

solve [sɒlv] vt (problem etc) résoudre.

solvent ['sɒlvənt] **1** a (financially) solvable. **2** n Ch (dis)solvant m; **s. abuse** usage m de solvants hallucinogènes.

sombre ['sɒmbər] a sombre, triste.

some [sʌm] a **1** (amount, number) du, de la, des; **s. wine** du vin; **s. water** de l'eau; **s. dogs** des chiens; **s. pretty flowers** de jolies fleurs.

2 (unspecified) un, une; **s. man (or other)** un homme (quelconque); **s. charm** (a certain amount of) un certain charme; **s. other way** un autre moyen.

3 (a few) quelques, certains; (a little) un peu de.

▮ pron **1** (number) quelques-un(e)s, certain(e)s (of de).

2 (a certain quantity) en; **I want s.** j'en veux; **do you have s.?** en as-tu?; **s. of it is over** il en reste un peu.

▮ adv (about) quelque; **s. ten years** quelque dix ans.

somebody ['sʌmbɒdɪ] pron = someone. ● **someday** adv un jour. ● **somehow** adv (in some way) d'une manière ou d'une autre; (for some reason) on ne sait pourquoi. ● **someone** pron quelqu'un; **at s.'s house** chez qn; **s. small/etc** quelqu'un de petit/etc. ● **someplace**

adv Am quelque part. ● **something** pron quelque chose; **s. awful/etc** quelque chose d'affreux/etc; **s. of a liar/etc** un peu menteur/etc ▮ adv **she plays s. like...** elle joue un peu comme.... ● **sometime** adv un jour; **s. before his departure** avant son départ. ● **sometimes** adv quelquefois, parfois. ● **somewhat** adv quelque peu. ● **somewhere** adv quelque part; **s. about fifteen** environ quinze.

somersault ['sʌməsɔːlt] n (on ground) culbute f ▮ vi faire la culbute.

son [sʌn] n fils m. ● **s.-in-law** n (pl sons-in-law) gendre m.

song [sɒŋ] n chanson f. ● **songbook** n recueil m de chansons.

sonic ['sɒnɪk] a **s. boom** bang m (supersonique).

soon [suːn] adv (-er, -est) (in a short time) bientôt; (quickly) vite; (early) tôt; **s. after** peu après; **as s. as she leaves** aussitôt qu'elle partira; **no sooner had he spoken than** à peine avait-il parlé que; **I'd sooner leave** je préférerais partir; **I'd just as s. leave** j'aimerais autant partir; **sooner or later** tôt ou tard.

soot [sʊt] n suie f.

soothe [suːð] vt (pain, nerves) calmer.

sophisticated [sə'fɪstɪkeɪtɪd] a (person, taste) raffiné; (machine, method) sophistiqué.

sophomore ['sɒfəmɔːr] n Am étudiant, -ante mf de seconde année.

sopping ['sɒpɪŋ] a & adv **s. (wet)** trempé.

soppy ['sɒpɪ] a (-ier, -iest) Fam (silly) idiot, bête; (sentimental) sentimental.

soprano [sə'prɑːnəʊ] n (pl -os) Mus (singer) soprano mf.

sorbet ['sɔːbeɪ] n (water ice) sorbet m.

sorcerer ['sɔːsərər] n sorcier m.

sordid ['sɔːdɪd] a (act, street etc) sordide.

sore [sɔːr] a (-er, -est) (painful) douloureux; (angry) Am fâché (at contre); **she has a s. throat** elle a mal à la gorge; **he's still s.** Med il a encore mal ▮ n Med plaie

f. ●—**ness** n (pain) douleur f.

sorrow ['sɒrəʊ] n chagrin m, peine f.

sorry ['sɒrɪ] a (-ier, -iest) (sight etc) triste; **to be s.** (regret) être désolé, regretter (**to do** de faire); **I'm s. she can't come** je regrette qu'elle ne puisse pas venir; **I'm s. about the delay** excusez-moi de ce retard; **s.!** pardon!; **to say s.** demander pardon (**to** à); **to feel** or **be s. for s.o.** plaindre qn.

sort[1] [sɔːt] n espèce f, sorte f (**of** de); **all sorts of** toutes sortes de; **what s. of drink**/etc **is it?** qu'est-ce que c'est comme boisson/etc?; **s. of sad**/etc plutôt triste/etc.

sort[2] [sɔːt] vt (papers etc) trier; **to s. out** (classify, select) trier; (separate) séparer (**from** de); (arrange) arranger; (tidy) ranger; (problem) régler ▌vi **to s. through** (letters etc) trier; **sorting office** centre m de tri.

SOS [esəʊ'es] n SOS m.

sought [sɔːt] pt & pp de **seek.**

soul [səʊl] n âme f; **not a living s.** (nobody) personne, pas âme qui vive.

sound[1] [saʊnd] n son m; (noise) bruit m; **I don't like the s. of it** ça ne me plaît pas du tout; **s. barrier** mur m du son; **s. effects** bruitage m.

▌vt (bell, alarm etc) sonner; (bugle, horn) sonner de; (letter) Gram prononcer; **to s. one's horn** Aut klaxonner.

▌vi (of bell etc) sonner; (seem) sembler; **to s. like** sembler être; (resemble) ressembler à; **it sounds like** or **as if** il semble que (+ sub or indic). ● **soundproof** a insonorisé ▌vt insonoriser.

● **soundtrack** n (of film) bande f sonore.

sound[2] [saʊnd] a (-er, -est) (healthy) sain; (good, reliable) solide ▌adv **s. asleep** profondément endormi. ●—**ly** adv (asleep, to sleep) profondément.

sound[3] [saʊnd] vt (test, measure) sonder; **to s. s.o. out** sonder qn (**about** sur).

soup [suːp] n soupe f, potage m; **s. dish** or **plate** assiette f creuse.

sour ['saʊər] a (-er, -est) aigre; (milk) tourné; **to turn s.** (of wine) s'aigrir; (of

milk) tourner; (of friendship) se détériorer.

source [sɔːs] n (origin) source f.

south [saʊθ] n sud m; **(to the) s. of** au sud de.

▌a (coast) sud inv; (wind) du sud; **S. America**/**Africa** Amérique f/Afrique f du Sud; **S. American** (a & n) sud-américain, -aine (mf); **S. African** (a & n) sud-africain, -aine (mf).

▌adv au sud, vers le sud. ● **southbound** a (traffic) en direction du sud. ● **south-'east** n & a sud-est m & a inv. ● **southerly** ['sʌðəlɪ] a (point) sud inv; (direction, wind) du sud. ● **southern** ['sʌðən] a (town) du sud; (coast) sud inv; **S. Italy** le Sud de l'Italie; **S. Africa** Afrique f australe. ● **southerner** ['sʌðənər] n habitant, -ante mf du Sud. ● **southward(s)** a & adv vers le sud. ● **south-'west** n & a sud-ouest m & a inv.

souvenir [suːvə'nɪər] n (object) souvenir m.

sovereign ['sɒvrɪn] n souverain, -aine mf ▌a (State, authority) souverain.

sow[1] [səʊ] vt (pt sowed, pp sowed or sown) (seeds, doubt etc) semer.

sow[2] [saʊ] n (pig) truie f.

soya ['sɔɪə] n **s. (bean)** graine f de soja. ● **soybean** n Am graine f de soja.

spa [spɑː] n (town) station f thermale; (spring) source f minérale.

space [speɪs] n (gap, emptiness, atmosphere) espace m; (period) période f; (for parking) place f; **blank s.** espace m, blanc m; **to take up s.** (room) prendre de la place; **in the s. of** dans l'espace de a (voyage etc) spatial ▌vt **to s. out** espacer. ● **spacing** n **in double**/**single spacing** (to type) à double/simple interligne. ● **spaceman** n (pl -**men**) astronaute m. ● **spaceship** n engin m spatial. ● **spacesuit** n combinaison f spatiale. ● **spacewoman** n (pl -**women**) astronaute f.

spacious ['speɪʃəs] a spacieux, grand.

spade [speɪd] n **1** (for garden) bêche f; (of child) pelle f. **2 spade(s)** Cards pique m.

spaghetti [spə'getɪ] n spaghetti(s) mpl.
Spain [speɪn] n Espagne f.
span [spæn] n (of arch) portée f; (of wings) envergure f; (of life) Fig durée f ∎ vt (-nn-) (of bridge etc) enjamber (rivière etc); Fig couvrir.
Spaniard ['spænjəd] n Espagnol, -ole mf. ● **Spanish** a espagnol ∎ n (language) espagnol m. ● **Spanish-A'merican** a hispano-américain.
spaniel ['spænjəl] n épagneul m.
spank [spæŋk] vt donner une fessée à. ● **—ing** n fessée f.
spanner ['spænər] n (tool) clef f (à écrous); **adjustable s.** clef f à molette.
spare¹ [speər] 1 a (extra) de or en trop; (clothes, tyre, Am tire) de rechange; (wheel) de secours; (available) disponible; (bed, room) d'ami; **s. time** loisirs mpl ∎ n **s. (part)** Tech Aut pièce f détachée.
2 vt (do without) se passer de (qn, qch); (efforts) ménager; **to s. s.o.** (not kill) épargner qn; (details etc) épargner à qn; (time) accorder à qn; (money) donner à qn; **I can't s. the time** je n'ai pas le temps. ● **sparing** a to be s. with (butter etc) ménager. ● **sparingly** adv avec modération.
spare² [speər] a (lean) maigre.
spark [spɑːk] 1 n étincelle f. 2 vt to s. off (cause) provoquer. ● **spark(ing) plug** n Aut bougie f.
sparkl/e ['spɑːk(ə)l] vi (of diamond, star) étinceler ∎ n éclat m. ● **—ing** a (wine, water) pétillant.
sparrow ['spærəʊ] n moineau m.
sparse [spɑːs] a clairsemé.
spartan ['spɑːtən] a spartiate, austère.
spasm ['spæzəm] n (of muscle) spasme m; (of coughing etc) Fig accès m.
spastic ['spæstɪk] n handicapé, -ée mf moteur.
spat [spæt] pt & pp of **spit 1.**
spate [speɪt] n a s. of (orders etc) une avalanche de.
spatter ['spætər] vt (clothes, person etc) éclabousser (with de).

spawn [spɔːn] n (of fish etc) frai m ∎ vi frayer ∎ vt Fig engendrer.
speak [spiːk] vi (pt spoke, pp spoken) parler (about, of de); (in assembly) prendre la parole; **so to s.** pour ainsi dire; **to s. well of s.o./sth** dire du bien de qn/qch; **Bob speaking!** Tel Bob à l'appareil!; **that's spoken for** c'est pris; **to s. up** (more loudly) parler plus fort; (boldly) parler (franchement).
∎ vt (language) parler; (say) dire; **to s. one's mind** dire ce que l'on pense. ● **speaking** a to be on s. terms with s.o. parler à qn; **English-/French-speaking** qui parle anglais/français.
speaker ['spiːkər] n (public) orateur m; (in dialogue) interlocuteur, -trice mf; (loudspeaker) El haut-parleur m; (of stereo system) enceinte f; **to be a Spanish/etc s.** parler espagnol/etc.
spear [spɪər] n lance f.
spearmint ['spɪəmɪnt] a (sweet, Am candy) à la menthe; (flavour) de menthe; (chewing-gum) mentholé.
special ['speʃ(ə)l] a spécial; (care, attention) (tout) particulier; (favourite) préféré ∎ n **today's s.** (in restaurant) le plat du jour. ● **specialist** n spécialiste mf (in de). ● **speci'ality** n spécialité f. ● **specialize** vi se spécialiser (in dans). ● **specialized** a spécialisé. ● **specially** adv spécialement; (particularly) particulièrement. ● **specialty** n Am spécialité f.
species ['spiːʃiːz] n inv espèce f.
specific [spə'sɪfɪk] a précis, explicite. ● **specifically** adv (purposely) expressément; (exactly) précisément; (particularly) spécifiquement.
specify ['spesɪfaɪ] vt spécifier (that que). ● **specification** [-'keɪʃ(ə)n] n spécification f; pl (of machine etc) caractéristiques fpl.
specimen ['spesɪmɪn] n (example, person) spécimen m; (of blood) prélèvement m; (of urine) échantillon m.
speck [spek] n (stain) petite tache f; (of dust) grain m; (dot) point m.
speckled ['spek(ə)ld] a tacheté.

specs [speks] *npl Fam* lunettes *fpl*.
spectacle ['spektək(ə)l] *n* **1** (*sight*) spectacle *m*. **2 spectacles** (*glasses*) lunettes *fpl*. ● **spec'tacular** *a* spectaculaire. ● **spec'tator** *n Sp etc* spectateur, -trice *mf*.
spectrum, *pl* **-tra** ['spektrəm, -trə] *n Phys* spectre *m*; (*range*) *Fig* gamme *f*.
speculate ['spekjυleıt] *vi Fin Phil* spéculer; **to s. about** (*s.o.'s motives etc*) s'interroger sur ‖ *vt* **to s. that** conjecturer que. ● **speculation** *n Fin Phil* spéculation *f*; (*guessing*) conjectures *fpl* (**about** sur).
sped [sped] *pt & pp of* **speed 1**.
speech [spiːtʃ] *n* (*talk, lecture*) discours *m* (**on, about** sur); (*power of language*) parole *f*; (*diction*) élocution *f*; (*spoken language*) langage *m*; **freedom of s.** liberté *f* d'expression; **part of s.** catégorie *f* grammaticale. ● **—less** *a* muet (*f* muette) (**with** de).
speed [spiːd] **1** *n* (*rate*) vitesse *f*; (*swiftness*) rapidité *f*; **s. limit** *Aut* limitation *f* de vitesse ‖ *vt* (*pt & pp* **sped**) **to s. up** accélérer ‖ *vi* **to s. up** (*of person*) aller plus vite; (*of pace*) s'accélérer; **to s. past** passer à toute vitesse (**sth** devant qch). **2** *vi* (*pt & pp* **speeded**) (*drive too fast*) aller trop vite. ● **speeding** *n Aut* excès *m* de vitesse.
speedboat ['spiːdbəυt] *n* vedette *f*. ● **spee'dometer** *n Aut* compteur *m* (de vitesse). ● **speedway** *n Sp* piste *f* de vitesse pour motos; *Sp Aut Am* autodrome *m*.
speedy ['spiːdı] *a* (**-ier, -iest**) rapide. ● **speedily** *adv* rapidement.
spell[1] [spel] *n* (*magic*) charme *m* (*curse*) sort *m*; **under a s.** envoûté. ● **spellbound** *a* (*audience etc*) captivé.
spell[2] [spel] *n* (*period*) (courte) période *f*; (*while*) moment *m*; **cold s.** vague *f* de froid.
spell[3] [spel] *vt* (*pt & pp* **spelled** *or* **spelt**) (*write*) écrire; (*say aloud*) épeler; (*of letters*) former (*mot*); (*mean*) *Fig* signifier; **to be able to s.** savoir l'ortho-

graphe; **how is it spelt?** comment cela s'écrit-il?; **to s. out** *Fig* expliquer clairement. ● **—ing** *n* orthographe *f*; **s. mistake** faute *f* d'orthographe.
spelunking [spə'lʌŋkıŋ] *n* spéléologie *f*.
spend [spend] **1** *vt* (*pt & pp* **spent**) (*money*) dépenser (**on** pour) ‖ *vi* dépenser. **2** *vt* (*pt & pp* **spent**) (*time etc*) passer (**on sth** sur qch, **doing** à faire); (*energy*) consacrer (**on sth** à qch). ● **—ing** *n* **s. money** argent *m*. ● **spendthrift** *n* **to be a s.** être dépensier.
spent [spent] *pt & pp of* **spend**.
sperm [spɜːm] *n* (*pl* **sperm** *or* **sperms**) sperme *m*.
spew [spjuː] *vt* vomir.
sphere [sfıər] *n* (*of influence etc*) & *Geom Pol* sphère *f*; (*of music etc*) domaine *m*.
sphinx [sfıŋks] *n* sphinx *m*.
spice [spaıs] *n* épice *f*; (*interest etc*) *Fig* piment *m* ‖ *vt* épicer. ● **spicy** *a* (**-ier, -iest**) (*food*) épicé; (*story*) *Fig* pimenté.
spick-and-span [spıkən'spæn] *a* (*clean*) impeccable.
spider ['spaıdər] *n* araignée *f*; **s.'s web** toile *f* d'araignée.
spike [spaık] *n* (*of metal*) pointe *f*.
spill [spıl] *vt* (*pt & pp* **spilled** *or* **spilt**) (*liquid*) répandre, renverser (**on, over** sur) ‖ *vi* se répandre, se renverser.
spill out *vt* (*empty*) vider (*café, verre etc*) ‖ *vi* (*of coffee etc*) se renverser (**on, over** sur) ‖ **to spill over** *vi* (*of liquid*) déborder.
spin [spın] *n* (*motion*) tour *m*; (*car ride*) petit tour *m*; (*on washing machine*) essorage *m* ‖ *vt* (*pt & pp* **spun**, *pres p* **spinning**) (*wheel, top*) faire tourner; (*web, wool etc*) filer; (*washing*) essorer; **to s. out** (*speech*) faire durer. ‖ *vi* (*of spinner, spider*) filer; **to s.** (**round**) (*of dancer, wheel etc*) tourner; (*of head*) *Fig* tourner; (*of vehicle*) faire un tête-à-queue. ● **spinning** *a* **s. top** toupie *f*; **s. wheel** rouet *m*.
spinach ['spınıdʒ, *Am* -ıtʃ] *n* (*food*) épinards *mpl*.

spin-dry ['spɪndraɪ] vt essorer. ● **spin dryer** n essoreuse f.

spine [spaɪn] n Anat colonne f vertébrale; (spike of animal or plant) épine f. ● **spinal** a (injury) à la colonne vertébrale.

spinster ['spɪnstər] n célibataire f; Pej vieille fille f.

spiral ['spaɪərəl] 1 n spirale f ‖ a en spirale; (staircase) en colimaçon. 2 vi (-ll-, Am -l-) (of prices) monter en flèche.

spire ['spaɪər] n (of church) flèche f.

spirit ['spɪrɪt] n (soul etc) esprit m; (courage) Fig courage m; pl (drink) alcool m, spiritueux mpl; **spirit(s)** (morale) moral m; Ch alcool m; **in good spirits** de bonne humeur ‖ a (lamp) à alcool. ● **spirited** a (campaign, attack etc) vigoureux.

spiritual ['spɪrɪtʃʊəl] a (life etc) & Rel spirituel.

spit [spɪt] 1 n crachat m; (in mouth) salive f ‖ vi (pt & pp spat or spit, pres p spitting) cracher ‖ vt cracher; **to s. out** (re)cracher; **the spitting image of s.o.** le portrait (tout craché) de qn. 2 n (for meat) broche f.

spite [spaɪt] 1 n **in s. of** malgré; **in s. of the fact that** bien que (+ sub). 2 n (dislike) rancune f ‖ vt (annoy) contrarier. ● **spiteful** a méchant.

spittle ['spɪt(ə)l] n crachat m; (in mouth) salive f.

splash [splæʃ] vt éclabousser (with de, over sur); (spill) répandre ‖ vi (of mud etc) faire des éclaboussures; (of waves) clapoter; **to s. over sth/s.o.** éclabousser qch/qn; **to s.** (about) (in river, mud) patauger; (in bath) barboter ‖ n (mark) éclaboussure f; (of colour) Fig tache f; s.! plouf!

splendid ['splendɪd] a (wonderful, rich etc) splendide.

splint [splɪnt] n Med attelle f.

splinter ['splɪntər] n (of wood etc) éclat m; (in finger) écharde f.

split [splɪt] n fente f; (tear) déchirure f;

Pol scission f; **one's s.** (share) Fam sa part.

‖ vt (pt & pp **split**, pres p **splitting**) (break apart) fendre; (tear) déchirer; **to s.** (up) (group) diviser; (money, work) partager (between entre); **to s. one's sides (laughing)** se tordre (de rire).

‖ vi se fendre; (tear) se déchirer; **to s.** (up) (of group) se diviser; **to s.** up (of couple, friends etc) se séparer; (of lovers) rompre; (of crowd) se disperser. ● **split-up** n (of couple) séparation f, rupture f.

‖ a **a s. second** une fraction de seconde; **s.-level apartment** duplex m.

splutter ['splʌtər] vi (spit) (of person) crachoter; (of sparks, fat) crépiter.

spoil [spɔɪl] vt (pt & pp spoilt or spoiled) (make unpleasant) gâter; (damage, ruin) abîmer; (child, dog etc) gâter. ● **spoilsport** n rabat-joie m inv.

spoils [spɔɪlz] npl (rewards) butin m.

spoke[1] [spəʊk] n (of wheel) rayon m.

spoke[2] [spəʊk] pt of **speak**. ● **spoken** pp of **speak** ‖ a (language etc) parlé. ● **spokesman** n (pl -men) or **spokeswoman** n (pl -women) porte-parole m inv (for, of de).

sponge [spʌndʒ] 1 n éponge f; **s. bag** trousse f de toilette; **s. cake** gâteau m de Savoie ‖ vt **to s. down/off** laver/enlever à l'éponge. 2 vi **to s. off** or **on s.o.** Fam vivre aux crochets de qn. ● **sponger** n Fam parasite m.

sponsor ['spɒnsər] n (of appeal, advertiser etc) personne f assurant le patronage (of de); (for membership) parrain m, marraine f; Jur garant, -ante mf; Sp sponsor m ‖ vt (appeal etc) patronner; (member, company) parrainer; Sp sponsoriser. ● **sponsorship** n patronage m; parrainage m; sponsoring m.

spontaneous [spɒn'teɪnɪəs] a spontané. ● **—ly** adv spontanément.

spooky ['spuːkɪ] a (-ier, -iest) Fam qui donne le frisson.

spool [spuːl] n bobine f.

spoon [spuːn] n cuillère f. ● **spoonfeed** vt

(*pt* & *pp* **spoonfed**) (*help*) *Fig* mâcher le travail à. ● **spoonful** *n* cuillerée *f*.

sporadic [spə'rædɪk] *a* sporadique; **s. fighting** échauffourées *fpl*.

sport [spɔːt] **1** *n* sport *m*; **to play s.** *or Am* **sports** faire du sport; **sports club** club *m* sportif; **sports car/jacket/ground** voiture *f*/veste *f*/terrain *m* de sport; **sports results** résultats *mpl* sportifs. **2** *vt* (*wear*) arborer. ● **—ing** *a* (*attitude, person etc*) sportif; **that's s. of you** *Fig* c'est chic de ta part.

sportsman ['spɔːtsmən] *n* (*pl* **-men**) sportif *m*. ● **sportswear** *n* vêtements *mpl* de sport. ● **sportswoman** *n* (*pl* **-women**) sportive *f*. ● **sporty** *a* (**-ier, -iest**) sportif.

spot[1] [spɒt] *n* (*stain, mark*) tache *f*; (*dot*) point *m*; (*pimple*) bouton *m*; (*place*) endroit *m*, (*act*) *Th* numéro *m*; (*drop*) goutte *f*; **a s. of** *Fam* un peu de; **a soft s.** **for** un faible pour; **on the s.** sur place; (*accident*) **black s.** *Aut* point *m* noir; **s. check** contrôle *m* au hasard. ● **spotless** *a* (*clean*) impeccable. ● **spotlight** *n* *Th* projecteur *m*; (*for photography*) spot *m*. ● **spotted** *a* (*fur*) tacheté; (*dress*) à pois. ● **spotty** *a* (**-ier, -iest**) **1** (*face etc*) boutonneux. **2** (*patchy*) *Am* inégal.

spot[2] [spɒt] *vt* (**-tt-**) (*notice*) apercevoir.

spouse [spaʊs, spaʊz] *n* époux *m*, épouse *f*.

spout [spaʊt] **1** *n* (*of teapot etc*) bec *m*. **2** *vi* **to s.** (**out**) jaillir.

sprain [spreɪn] *n* foulure *f*; **to s. one's ankle/wrist** se fouler la cheville/le poignet.

sprang [spræŋ] *pt of* **spring**[1].

sprawl [sprɔːl] *vi* (*of town, person*) s'étaler; **to be sprawling** être étalé. ● *n* **the urban s.** les banlieues *fpl* tentaculaires.

spray [spreɪ] **1** *n* (*can*) bombe *f*; (*water drops*) gouttelettes *fpl*; (*from sea*) embruns *mpl*; **hair s.** laque *f* à cheveux ● *vt* (*liquid, surface*) vaporiser; (*plant, crops*) arroser, traiter; (*car*) peindre à la bombe. **2** *n* (*of flowers*) petit bouquet *m*.

spread [spred] *vt* (*pt* & *pp* **spread**) (*stretch, open out*) étendre; (*legs, fingers*) écarter; (*distribute*) répandre (**over** sur); (*paint, payment, visits*) étaler; (*news, germs*) propager; **to s. out** étendre; écarter; étaler. ● *vi* (*of fire, town, fog*) s'étendre; (*of news, epidemic*) se propager; **to s. out** (*of people*) se disperser. ● *n* (*of fire, germs, ideas*) propagation *f*; (*paste*) *Culin* pâte *f* (à tartiner); (*meal*) festin *m*; **cheese s.** fromage *m* à tartiner. ● **s.-'eagled** *a* bras et jambes écartés. ● **spreadsheet** *n* *Comptr* tableur *m*.

spree [spriː] *n* **to go on a spending s.** faire des achats extravagants.

sprightly ['spraɪtlɪ] *a* (**-ier, -iest**) alerte.

spring[1] [sprɪŋ] *n* (*metal device*) ressort *m*; (*leap*) bond *m* ● *vi* (*pt* **sprang**, *pp* **sprung**) (*leap*) bondir; **to s. to mind** venir à l'esprit; **to s. from** provenir de; **to s. up** surgir ● *vt* (*news*) annoncer brusquement (**on** à); **to s. a leak** (*of boat*) commencer à faire eau. ● **springboard** *n* tremplin *m*.

spring[2] [sprɪŋ] *n* (*season*) printemps *m*; **in** (**the**) **s.** au printemps; **s. onion** oignon *m* vert. ● **s.-'cleaning** *n* nettoyage *m* de printemps. ● **springlike** *a* printanier. ● **springtime** *n* printemps *m*.

spring[3] [sprɪŋ] *n* (*of water*) source *f*; **s. water** eau *f* de source.

sprinkl/e ['sprɪŋk(ə)l] *vt* (*sand etc*) répandre (**on, over** sur); **to s. with water, s. water on** asperger d'eau; **to s. with** (*sugar, salt, flour*) saupoudrer de. ● **—er** *n* (*in garden*) arroseur *m*.

sprint [sprɪnt] *n* *Sp* sprint *m* ● *vi* sprinter. ● **—er** *n* sprinter *m*, sprinteuse *f*.

sprout [spraʊt] **1** *vi* (*of seed etc*) germer, pousser; **to s. up** pousser vite; (*appear*) surgir ● *vt* (*leaves*) pousser. **2** *n* (**Brussels**) **s.** chou *m* de Bruxelles.

spruce [spruːs] *a* (**-er, -est**) (*neat*) pimpant ● *vt* **to s. oneself up** se faire beau.

sprung [sprʌŋ] *pp of* **spring**[1].

spry [spraɪ] *a* (**spryer, spryest**) (*old person*) alerte.

spud [spʌd] n (potato) Fam patate f.

spun [spʌn] pt & pp of **spin**.

spur [spɜːr] n (of horse rider) éperon m; (stimulus) Fig aiguillon m; **on the s. of the moment** sur un coup de tête ▮ vt (-rr-) **to s. s.o. on** (urge on) aiguillonner qn.

spurn [spɜːn] vt rejeter (avec mépris).

spurt [spɜːt] vi **to s. (out)** (of liquid) jaillir ▮ n (of energy) sursaut m; **to put on a s.** (rush) foncer.

spy [spaɪ] n espion, -onne mf; **s. hole** judas m; **s. ring** réseau m d'espionnage ▮ vi **s. on s.o.** espionner qn. ●**—ing** n espionnage m.

squabble ['skwɒb(ə)l] vi se chamailler (**over** à propos de) ▮ n chamaillerie f.

squad [skwɒd] n (group) & Mil escouade f; (team) Sp équipe f.

squadron ['skwɒdrən] n Mil escadron m; Nau Av escadrille f.

squalid ['skwɒlɪd] a sordide. ● **squalor** n conditions fpl sordides.

squall [skwɔːl] n (of wind) rafale f.

squander ['skwɒndər] vt (money, time) gaspiller (**on** en).

square ['skweər] n carré m; (on chessboard, graph paper) case f; (in town) place f ▮ a carré; (in order, settled) Fig en ordre; (meal) solide; (all) **s.** (quits) quitte (**with** envers) ▮ vt (settle) mettre en ordre, régler; (arrange) arranger; Math mettre au carré ▮ vi (tally) cadrer (**with** avec). ● **squarely** adv (honestly) honnêtement.

quash [skwɒʃ] 1 vt (crush) écraser; (squeeze) serrer ▮ n lemon/orange **s.** sirop m de citron/d'orange; (diluted) citronnade f/orangeade f. 2 n (game) squash m. 3 n (vegetable) Am courge f.

squat [skwɒt] 1 vi (-tt-) **to s. (down)** s'accroupir; **squatting (down)** accroupi. ● **squatter** n squatter m. 2 a (short and thick) trapu.

squeak [skwiːk] vi (of door) grincer; (of shoe) craquer; (of mouse) faire couic.

squeal [skwiːl] 1 vi pousser des cris aigus ▮ n cri m aigu. 2 vi **to s. on s.o.** (inform on) Fam balancer qn.

squeamish ['skwiːmɪʃ] a facilement dégoûté.

squeeze [skwiːz] vt (press) presser; (hand, arm) serrer; **to s. sth into sth** faire rentrer qch dans qch; **to s. (out)** (juice etc) faire sortir (**from** de). ▮ vi **to s. through/into/etc** (force oneself) se glisser par/dans/etc; **to s. in** trouver un peu de place; **to s. up** se serrer (**against** contre). ● **squeezer** n lemon **s.** presse-citron m.

squelch [skweltʃ] vi patauger (en faisant floc-floc).

squid [skwɪd] n (mollusc) calmar m.

squiggle ['skwɪg(ə)l] n gribouillis m; (line) ligne f onduleuse.

squint [skwɪnt] n **to have a s.** loucher ▮ vi loucher; (in the sunlight etc) plisser les yeux.

squirm [skwɜːm] vi (wriggle) se tortiller.

squirrel ['skwɪrəl, Am 'skwɜːrəl] n écureuil m.

squirt [skwɜːt] vt (liquid) faire gicler ▮ vi gicler ▮ n giclée f, jet m.

stab [stæb] vt (-bb-) (with knife etc) poignarder ▮ n **s. (wound)** coup m (de couteau).

stable[1] ['steɪb(ə)l] a (-er, -est) stable; **mentally s.** bien équilibré. ● **sta'bility** n stabilité f. ● **stabilize** vt stabiliser ▮ vi se stabiliser.

stable[2] ['steɪb(ə)l] n écurie f.

stack [stæk] n (heap) tas m; **stacks of** Fam un or des tas de ▮ vt **to s. (up)** entasser.

stadium ['steɪdɪəm] n Sp stade m.

staff [stɑːf] n personnel m; (of school) professeurs mpl; (of army) état-major m; **a member of s.** (in office) un(e) employé, -ée; **s. meeting** Sch conseil m des professeurs; **s. room** Sch salle f des professeurs.

stag [stæg] n cerf m.

stage[1] [steɪdʒ] n (platform) Th scène f; **the s.** (profession) le théâtre; **s. door** entrée f des artistes ▮ vt (play) monter;

Fig organiser. ● **s.-hand** *n* machiniste *m*.
● **s.-manager** *n* régisseur *m*.

stage² [steɪdʒ] *n* (*phase*) stade *m*, étape *f*;
(*of journey*) étape *f*; **in (easy) stages** par
étapes; **at an early s.** au début.

stagecoach ['steɪdʒkəʊtʃ] *n Hist* diligence *f*.

stagger ['stægər] **1** *vi* chanceler. **2** *vt*
(*holidays, Am vacation etc*) étaler. **3** *vt*
to s. s.o. stupéfier qn. ●**—ing** *a* stupéfiant.

stagnant ['stægnənt] *a* stagnant.
● **stag'nate** *vi* stagner.

staid [steɪd] *a* posé, sérieux.

stain [steɪn] **1** *vt* (*to mark*) tacher (**with**
de) ‖ *n* tache *f*; **s. remover** détachant *m*.
2 *vt* (*colour*) teinter (*du bois*); **stained
glass window** vitrail *m* (*pl* vitraux).
● **stainless steel** *n* inox *m*; **s.-steel
knife/etc** couteau *m*/*etc* en inox.

stair [steər] *n* **s.** (*step*) une marche; **the
stairs** (*staircase*) l'escalier *m*. ● **staircase** *or* **stairway** *n* escalier *m*.

stake [steɪk] **1** *n* (*post*) pieu *m*; (*for plant*)
tuteur *m* ‖ *vt* **to s. one's claim to**
revendiquer. **2** *n* (*betting*) enjeu *m*;
(*investment*) investissement *m*; **at s.** en
jeu ‖ *vt* (*bet*) jouer (**on** sur).

stale [steɪl] *a* (**-er, -est**) (*bread*) rassis (*f*
rassie); (*food*) pas frais (*f* fraîche); (*air*)
vicié; (*smell*) de renfermé; (*news*) *Fig*
vieux (*f* vieille).

stalemate ['steɪlmeɪt] *n Chess* pat *m*; *Fig*
impasse *f*.

stalk [stɔːk] **1** *n* (*of plant*) tige *f*; (*of fruit*)
queue *f*. **2** *vt* (*animal*) traquer.

stall [stɔːl] **1** *n* (*in market*) étal *m*; (*for
newspapers, flowers*) kiosque *m*; (*in
stable*) stalle *f*; **the stalls** *Cin* l'orchestre
m. **2** *vti Aut* caler. **3** *vi* **to s. (for time)**
chercher à gagner du temps.

stallion ['stæljən] *n* (*horse*) étalon *m*.

stamina ['stæmɪnə] *n* vigueur *f*, résistance *f*.

stammer ['stæmər] *vi* bégayer ‖ *n* bégaiement *m*; **to have a s.** être bègue.

stamp [stæmp] **1** *n* (*for postage, instrument*) timbre *m*; (*mark*) cachet *m*; **the s.**

of *Fig* la marque de; **s. collecting**
philatélie *f* ‖ *vt* (*document*) tamponner; (*letter*) timbrer; (*metal*) estamper;
to s. out (*rebellion*) écraser; (*disease*)
supprimer; **stamped addressed envelope,**
Am **stamped self-addressed envelope**
enveloppe *f* timbrée à votre adresse.
2 *vti* **to s. (one's feet)** taper des pieds.

stampede [stæm'piːd] *n* fuite *f* précipitée; (*rush*) ruée *f*.

stance [stɑːns] *n* position *f*.

stand [stænd] *n* (*position*) position *f*;
(*support*) support *m*; (*at exhibition*)
stand *m*; (*for spectators*) *Sp* tribune *f*;
(*witness*) *Am* barre *f*; **news/flower s.**
kiosque *m* à journaux/à fleurs.

‖ *vt* (*pt & pp* **stood**) (*pain, person etc*)
supporter; (*put straight*) mettre (debout); **to s. a chance** avoir une chance.

‖ *vi* être *or* se tenir (debout); (*get up*) se
lever; (*remain*) rester (debout); (*be
situated*) se trouver.

stand about *or* **around** *vi* (*in street etc*)
traîner ‖ **to stand aside** *vi* s'écarter ‖ **to
stand back** *vi* reculer ‖ **to stand by** *vi* (*do
nothing*) rester là (sans rien faire); (*be
ready*) être prêt (à intervenir *etc*) ‖ *vt*
(*friend*) rester fidèle à ‖ **to stand down** *vi*
(*withdraw*) se désister ‖ **to stand for** *vt*
(*mean*) signifier, représenter; *Pol* être
candidat à; (*put up with*) supporter ‖ **to
stand in for** *vt* (*replace*) remplacer ‖ **to
stand out** *vi* (*be conspicuous*) ressortir
(**against** sur) ‖ **to stand over** *vt* (*watch*)
surveiller (*qn*) ‖ **to stand up** *vt* mettre
debout ‖ *vi* (*get up*) se lever ‖ **to stand up
for** *vt* défendre ‖ **to stand up to** *vt* (*resist*)
résister à; (*defend onself*) tenir tête à
(*qn*).

standard ['stændəd] **1** *n* (*norm*) norme *f*;
(*level*) niveau *m*; (*of weight, gold*) étalon
m; **standards (of behaviour)** principes
mpl; **s. of living, living standards** niveau
m de vie; **up to s.** (*work etc*) au niveau;
(*person*) à la hauteur ‖ *a* (*average*)
ordinaire; (*model, size*) standard *inv*;
(*dictionary*) classique; **s. lamp** lampadaire *m*. **2** *n* (*flag*) étendard *m*. ● **stan-**

dardize *vt* standardiser.
standby ['stændbaɪ] *n* (*pl* **-bys**) **on s.** prêt à partir *or* à intervenir ▪ *a* (*battery etc*) de réserve; (*ticket*) *Av* sans garantie.
stand-in ['stændɪn] *n* *Th* doublure *f* (**for** de).
standing ['stændɪŋ] *a* debout *inv*; (*committee, offer*) permanent; **s. order** (*in bank*) virement *m* automatique ▪ *n* réputation *f*; (*social, professional*) rang *m*; (*financial*) situation *f*.
stand-offish [stænd'ɒfɪʃ] *a* (*person*) distant, froid.
standpoint ['stændpɔɪnt] *n* point *m* de vue.
standstill ['stændstɪl] *n* **to bring to a s.** immobiliser; **to come to a s.** s'immobiliser; **at a s.** immobile; (*negotiations*) paralysé.
stank [stæŋk] *pt of* **stink**.
stapl/e ['steɪp(ə)l] **1** *a* **s.** food *or* diet nourriture *f* de base. **2** *n* (*for paper etc*) agrafe *f* ▪ *vt* agrafer. ●**—er** *n* agrafeuse *f*.
star [stɑːr] *n* étoile *f*; (*person*) vedette *f*; **shooting s.** étoile *f* filante; **s. part** rôle *m* principal; **the Stars and Stripes, the S.-Spangled Banner** *Am* la bannière étoilée; **four-s.** (*petrol*) du super *f* (**-rr-**) (*of actor*) être la vedette (**in** de) ▪ *vt* (*of film*) avoir pour vedette. ●**stardom** *n* célébrité *f*. ●**starfish** *n* étoile *f* de mer.
starboard ['stɑːbəd] *n* *Nau* *Av* tribord *m*.
starch [stɑːtʃ] *n* (*for stiffening*) amidon *m*; (*in food*) fécule *f*. ●**starchy** *a* (**-ier, -iest**) **s. food**(**s**) féculents *mpl*.
stare [steər] *n* regard *m* (fixe) ▪ *vi* **to s. at s.o.** fixer qn/qch (du regard).
stark [stɑːk] *a* (**-er, -est**) (*place*) désolé; (*austere*) austère; (*fact, reality*) brutal; **to be in s. contrast** to contraster nettement avec ▪ *adv* **s. naked** complètement nu.
starling ['stɑːlɪŋ] *n* étourneau *m*.
start[1] [stɑːt] *n* commencement *m*, début *m*; (*of race*) départ *m*; (*lead*) *Sp* & *Fig* avance *f* (**on** sur); **to make a s.** commencer; **for a s.** pour commencer; **from**

the s. dès le début.
▪ *vt* commencer; (*fashion*) lancer; (*engine, vehicle*) mettre en marche; (*business*) fonder; **to s. a war/fire** (*cause*) provoquer une guerre/un incendie; **to s. doing** *or* **to do** commencer à faire.
▪ *vi* commencer (**with sth** par qch, **by doing** par faire); (*of vehicle*) démarrer; (*leave*) partir (**for** pour); **to s. with** (*firstly*) pour commencer; **s. post** *Sp* ligne *f* de départ; **s. from** à partir de. ●**starting** *a* (*point, line*) de départ; **s. post** *Sp* ligne *f* de départ; **s. from** à partir de. ●**starter** *n* (*in vehicle*) démarreur *m*; (*course of meal*) hors-d'œuvre *m inv*, entrée *f*; (*soup*) potage *m*; (*runner*) partant *m*.
start[2] [stɑːt] *vi* (*be startled, jump*) sursauter ▪ *n* sursaut *m*.
start back *vi* (*return*) repartir ▪ **to start off** *vi* (*leave*) partir (**for** pour) ▪ **to start on** *vt* commencer (qch); **to s. s.o. on** (*career*) lancer qn dans ▪ **to start out** *vi* = **start off** ▪ **to start up** *vt* (*engine, vehicle*) mettre en marche; (*business*) fonder ▪ *vi* (*of engine, vehicle*) démarrer.
startle ['stɑːt(ə)l] *vt* (*make jump*) faire sursauter; (*alarm*) *Fig* alarmer.
starve [stɑːv] *vi* souffrir de la faim; (*die*) mourir de faim; **I'm starving!** (*hungry*) je meurs de faim! ▪ *vt* (*make suffer*) faire souffrir de la faim; (*deprive*) *Fig* priver (**of** de). ●**starvation** [-'veɪʃ(ə)n] *n* faim *f*; **on a s. diet** à la diète.
stash [stæʃ] *vt* **to s. away** (*hide*) *Fam* cacher.
state[1] [steɪt] **1** *n* (*condition*) état *m*; **in no (fit) s.** to hors d'état de; **in a s.** (*bad shape*) dans un drôle d'état.
2 *n* **S.** (*nation etc*) État *m*; **the States** *Fam* les États-Unis *mpl* ▪ *a* (*secret*) d'État; (*control*) de l'État; (*school, education*) public; **s. visit** voyage *m* officiel. ●**s.-of-the-art** *a* (*technology etc*) de pointe; (*up-to-date*) dernier cri. ●**state-'owned** *a* étatisé. ●**statesman** *n* (*pl* **-men**) homme *m* d'État.
state[2] [steɪt] *vt* déclarer (**that** que); (*problem*) exposer; (*time, date*) fixer.

● **statement** n déclaration f; Jur déposition f; (bank) s. relevé m de compte.
stately ['steɪtlɪ] a (-ier, -iest) majestueux; **s. home** château m.
static ['stætɪk] a statique.
station ['steɪʃ(ə)n] n (for trains) gare f; (underground) station f; (social) rang m; (police) s. commissariat m (de police); **bus** or **coach s.** gare f routière; **radio/space s.** station f de radio/spatiale; **service** or **petrol** or Am **gas s.** station-service f; **s. wagon** Aut Am break m ‖ vt (troops) poster. ● **stationmaster** n Rail chef m de gare.
stationary ['steɪʃən(ə)rɪ] a (vehicle) à l'arrêt.
stationer ['steɪʃ(ə)nər] n papetier, -ière mf; **s.'s (shop)** papeterie f. ● **stationery** n articles mpl de bureau.
statistic [stə'tɪstɪk] n (fact) statistique f; **statistics** (science) la statistique.
statue ['stætʃuː] n statue f.
stature ['stætʃər] n stature f.
status ['steɪtəs] n (position) situation f; (legal, official) statut m; (prestige) standing m; **s. symbol** marque f de standing.
statute ['stætʃuːt] n (law) loi f, pl (of institution) statuts mpl.
staunch [stɔːntʃ] a (-er, -est) loyal, fidèle.
stave [steɪv] vt **to s. off** (disaster) conjurer; (hunger) tromper.
stay [steɪ] n (visit) séjour m ‖ vi (remain) rester; (reside) loger; (visit) séjourner; **to s. put** ne pas bouger. ● **s.-at-home** n Pej casanier, -ière mf.
stay away vi ne pas s'approcher (from de); **to s. away from** (school) ne pas aller à ‖ **to stay in** vi (at home) rester à la maison; (of nail, screw etc) tenir ‖ **to stay out** vi (outside) rester dehors; (not come home) ne pas rentrer; **to s. out of sth** (not interfere in) ne pas se mêler de qch; (avoid) éviter qch ‖ **to stay up** vi (at night) ne pas se coucher; (of fence etc) tenir; **to s. up late** se coucher tard.
stead [sted] n **to stand s.o. in good s.** être bien utile à qn; **in s.o.'s s.** à la place de

qn.
steadfast ['stedfɑːst] a (intention etc) ferme.
steady ['stedɪ] a (-ier, -iest) stable; (hand) sûr; (progress, speed, demand) régulier; (nerves) solide; **a s. boyfriend** un petit ami; **s. (on one's feet)** solide sur ses jambes ‖ vt (chair etc) maintenir (en place); (nerves) calmer. ● **steadily** adv (to walk) d'un pas assuré; (gradually) progressivement; (regularly) régulièrement; (continuously) sans arrêt.
steak [steɪk] n steak m, bifteck m. ● **steakhouse** n grill(-room) m.
steal[1] [stiːl] vti (pt stole, pp stolen) voler (from s.o. à qn).
steal[2] [stiːl] vi (pt stole, pp stolen) **to s. in/out** entrer/sortir furtivement. ● **stealthy** ['stelθɪ] a (-ier, -iest) furtif.
steam [stiːm] n vapeur f; (on glass) buée f; **to let off s.** Fam décompresser; **s. engine** locomotive f à vapeur ‖ vt (food) cuire à la vapeur; **to get steamed up** (of glass) se couvrir de buée ‖ vi (of kettle) fumer. ● **steamer** or **steamship** n (bateau m à) vapeur m; (liner) paquebot m. ● **steamroller** n rouleau m compresseur. ● **steamy** a (-ier, -iest) humide; (window) embué.
steel [stiːl] **1** n acier m; **s. industry** sidérurgie f. **2** vt **to s. oneself** s'armer de courage.
steep [stiːp] **1** a (-er, -est) (stairs, slope etc) raide; (hill, path) escarpé; (price) Fig excessif. **2** vt (soak) tremper (in dans). ● **—ly** adv (to rise) en pente raide, (of prices) Fig excessivement.
steeple ['stiːp(ə)l] n clocher m.
steer [stɪər] vt (vehicle, ship, person) diriger (towards vers) ‖ vi Nau tenir le gouvernail; **to s. towards** faire route vers; **to s. clear of** éviter. ● **—ing** n Aut direction f; **s. wheel** volant m.
stem [stem] **1** n (of plant) tige f. **2** vt (-mm-) **to s. (the flow of)** (stop) arrêter. **3** vi (-mm-) **to s. from** provenir de.
stench [stentʃ] n puanteur f.
stencil ['stens(ə)l] n (metal, plastic) po-

choir m; (paper, for typing) stencil m.
stenographer [stə'nɒgrəfər] n Am sténodactylo f.
step [step] n pas m; (of stairs) marche f; (on train, bus) marchepied m; (doorstep) pas m de la porte; (action) Fig mesure f; **(flight of) steps** escalier m; (outdoors) perron m; (ladder) escabeau m; **s. by s.** pas à pas; **in s. with** Fig en accord avec ▮ vi (-pp-) (walk) marcher (on sur). ● **stepladder** n escabeau m. ● **stepping-stone** n Fig tremplin m (to pour arriver à).
step aside vi s'écarter ▮ **to step back** vi reculer ▮ **to step down** vi descendre (from de); (withdraw) Fig se retirer ▮ **to step forward** vi faire un pas en avant ▮ **to step in** vi (intervene) intervenir ▮ **to step into** vt (car etc) monter dans ▮ **to step out** vi (of car etc) descendre (of de) ▮ **to step over** vt (obstacle) enjamber ▮ **to step up** vt (increase) augmenter; (speed up) activer.
stepbrother ['stepbrʌðər] n demi-frère m. ● **stepdaughter** n belle-fille f. ● **stepfather** n beau-père m. ● **stepmother** n belle-mère f. ● **stepsister** n demi-sœur f. ● **stepson** n beau-fils m.
stereo ['steriəʊ] n (pl -os) (record player etc) chaîne f (stéréo inv); **in s.** en stéréo; **(personal) s.** baladeur m ▮ a (record etc) stéréo inv; (broadcast) en stéréo. ● **stereotype** ['steriətaip] n stéréotype m.
sterile ['sterail, Am 'sterəl] a stérile. ● **sterilize** vt stériliser.
sterling ['stɜːlɪŋ] n (currency) livre(s) f(pl) sterling inv; **the pound s.** la livre sterling inv.
steroid ['stɪərɔɪd] n stéroïde m.
stern [stɜːn] **1** a (-er, -est) sévère. **2** n (of ship) arrière m.
stethoscope ['steθəskəʊp] n stéthoscope m.
stew [stjuː] n ragoût m; **s. pot** cocotte f ▮ vt (meat) faire en ragoût; (fruit) faire cuire; **stewed fruit** compote f ▮ vi cuire.
steward ['stjuːəd] n (on plane, ship) steward m; **shop s.** délégué, -ée mf

syndical(e). ● **stewar'dess** n (on plane) hôtesse f.
stick¹ [stik] n (of wood, chalk etc) bâton m; (for walking) canne f; **in the sticks** Pej Fam à la cambrousse.
stick² [stik] vt (pt & pp stuck) (glue) coller; (put) Fam mettre, fourrer; (tolerate) Fam supporter; **to s. sth into sth** fourrer qch dans qch ▮ vi coller (to à); (of food in pan) attacher (to dans); (of drawer etc) se coincer, être coincé; (remain) Fam rester; **sticking plaster** sparadrap m.
stick around vi Fam rester dans les parages ▮ **to stick by** vt rester fidèle à (qn) ▮ **to stick down** vt (envelope) coller; (put down) Fam poser ▮ **to stick on** vt (stamp) coller; (hat etc) mettre ▮ **to stick out** vt (tongue) tirer; (head) sortir; **to s. it out** Fam tenir le coup ▮ vi (of petticoat, balcony etc) dépasser ▮ **to stick up** vt (notice) coller, afficher; (hand) Fam lever ▮ **to stick up for** vt défendre.
sticker ['stikər] n (label) autocollant m.
stick-up ['stikʌp] n Fam hold-up m inv.
sticky ['stiki] a (-ier, -iest) collant; (label) adhésif; (problem) Fig difficile.
stiff [stif] a (-er, -est) raide; (leg etc) ankylosé; (brush) dur; (person) Fig guindé; (price) élevé; **to have a s. neck** avoir le torticolis; **to feel s.** être courbatu(ré); **to be bored s.** Fam s'ennuyer à mourir, frozen s. Fam complètement gelé. ● **stiffen** vt raidir ▮ vi se raidir. ● **stiffness** n raideur f.
stifle ['staif(ə)l] vt étouffer ▮ vi **it's stifling** on étouffe.
stigma ['stigmə] n (moral stain) flétrissure f; **there's no s. attached to...** il n'y a aucune honte à....
stiletto [sti'letəʊ] a **s. heel** talon m aiguille.
still¹ [stil] adv encore, toujours; (even) encore; (nevertheless) tout de même.
still² [stil] a (-er, -est) (not moving) immobile; (calm) calme, tranquille; (drink) non gazeux; **to keep** or **stand s.** rester tranquille; **s. life** nature f

morte. ● **stillborn** a mort-né.
stilt [stɪlt] n (pole) échasse f.
stilted ['stɪltɪd] a (speech, person) guindé.
stimulate ['stɪmjʊleɪt] vt stimuler. ● **stimulus**, pl **-li** [-laɪ] n (encouragement) stimulant m.
sting [stɪŋ] vti (pt & pp **stung**) (of insect, ointment etc) piquer ▌n piqûre f; (insect's organ) dard m.
stingy ['stɪndʒɪ] a (-ier, -iest) avare, mesquin; **s. with** (money, praise) avare de; (food) mesquin sur.
stink [stɪŋk] n puanteur f ▌vi (pt **stank** or **stunk**, pp **stunk**) puer; (of book, film etc) Fam être infect; **to s. of smoke/etc** empester la fumée/etc ▌vt **to s. out** (room) empester. ● **—ing** a Fam infect.
stint [stɪnt] 1 n (period) période f de travail; (share) part f de travail. 2 vi **to s. on** lésiner sur.
stipulate ['stɪpjʊleɪt] vt stipuler (that que).
stir [stɜ:r] n **to give sth a s.** remuer qch; **to cause** or **create a s.** Fig faire du bruit ▌vt (-rr-) (coffee, leaves etc) remuer; (excite) Fig exciter; (incite) inciter (**to do** à faire); **to s. up** (trouble) provoquer ▌vi remuer. ● **stirring** a (speech) émouvant.
stirrup ['stɪrəp] n étrier m.
stitch [stɪtʃ] n point m; (in knitting) maille f; (in wound) point m de suture; **a s.** (pain) un point de côté; **to be in stitches** Fam se tordre (de rire) ▌vt **to s. (up)** (sew up) coudre; (repair) recoudre; Med suturer.
stock [stɒk] n (supply) provision f, stock m; (of knowledge, jokes) fonds m, mine f; (family) souche f; (soup) bouillon m; **stocks and shares** Fin valeurs fpl (boursières); **in s.** (goods) en magasin, en stock; **out of s.** épuisé; **to take s.** Fig faire le point (**of** de); **s. phrase** expression f toute faite; **the S. Exchange** or **Market** la Bourse.
▌vt (sell) vendre; (keep in store) stocker; (shop, larder) approvisionner; **well-stocked** bien approvisionné.

▌vi **to s. up** s'approvisionner (**with** de, en).
stockbroker ['stɒkbrəʊkər] n agent m de change. ● **stockist** n dépositaire mf. ● **stockpile** vt stocker, amasser. ● **stocktaking** n Com inventaire m.
stocking ['stɒkɪŋ] n (garment) bas m.
stocky ['stɒkɪ] a (-ier, -iest) trapu.
stodgy ['stɒdʒɪ] a (-ier, -iest) (food) Fam lourd, indigeste.
stoke [stəʊk] vt (fire) entretenir; (furnace) alimenter.
stole[1] [stəʊl] n (shawl) étole f.
stole[2], **stolen** [stəʊl, 'stəʊl(ə)n] pt & pp of **steal**[1,2].
stomach ['stʌmək] 1 n (for digestion) estomac m; (front of body) ventre m. 2 vt (put up with) supporter. ● **stomach-ache** n mal m de ventre; **to have a s.-ache** avoir mal au ventre.
stone [stəʊn] n pierre f; (pebble) caillou m (pl -oux); (in fruit) noyau m; (in kidney) calcul m; (weight) = 6,348 kg; **a stone's throw away** Fig à deux pas d'ici ▌vt lancer des pierres sur.
stone- [stəʊn] pref complètement. ● **s.-'broke** a Am Sl fauché. ● **s.-'deaf** a sourd comme un pot.
stoned [stəʊnd] a (on drugs) Fam camé.
stony ['stəʊnɪ] a 1 (-ier, -iest) (path etc) caillouteux. 2 **s. broke** Sl fauché.
stood [stʊd] pt & pp of **stand**.
stool [stu:l] n tabouret m.
stoop [stu:p] 1 n **to have a s.** être voûté ▌vi se baisser; **to s. to doing** Fig s'abaisser à faire. 2 n (in front of house) Am perron m.
stop [stɒp] n (place, halt) arrêt m, halte f; (for plane, ship) escale f; Gram point m; **bus s.** arrêt m d'autobus; **to put a s. to sth** mettre fin à qch; **to come to a s.** s'arrêter; **s. light** (on vehicle) stop m; **s. sign** (on road) stop m.
▌vt (-pp-) arrêter; (end) mettre fin à; (prevent) empêcher (**from doing** de faire).
▌vi s'arrêter; (of pain, conversation etc) cesser; (stay) rester; **to s. eating/etc**

s'arrêter de manger/*etc*; **to s. snowing/** *etc* cesser de neiger/*etc.*

stop by *vi* passer (s.o.'s chez qn) ∥ **to stop off** *or* **over** *vi* (on journey) s'arrêter ∥ **to stop up** *vt* (sink, pipe etc) boucher.

stopgap ['stɒpgæp] *n* bouche-trou *m.*

stoppage ['stɒpɪdʒ] *n* (in work) arrêt *m* de travail; (strike) débrayage *m*; (in pay) retenue *f.*

stopper ['stɒpər] *n* bouchon *m.* ● **stopoff** *or* **stopover** *n* halte *f.* ● **stopwatch** *n* chronomètre *m.*

store [stɔːr] *n* (supply) provision *f*; (of information etc) mine *f*; (warehouse) entrepôt *m*; (shop) *Am* magasin *m*; (computer memory) mémoire *f*; (department) *Am* grand magasin *m*; **to have sth in s. for s.o.** (surprise) réserver qch à qn.

∥ *vt* (in warehouse etc) stocker; *Comptr* mettre en mémoire; **to s. (up)** (for future use) mettre en réserve; **to s. (away)** (furniture) entreposer. ● **storage** *n* **s. space** *or* **room** espace *m* de rangement; **s. capacity** *Comptr* capacité *f* de mémoire. ● **storekeeper** *n* (shopkeeper) *Am* commerçant, -ante *mf.* ● **storeroom** *n* (in house) débarras *m*; (in office, shop) réserve *f.*

storey ['stɔːrɪ] *n* étage *m.*

stork [stɔːk] *n* cigogne *f.*

storm [stɔːm] **1** *n* tempête *f*; (thunderstorm) orage *m.* **2** *vt* (attack) *Mil* prendre d'assaut. **3** *vi* **to s. out** (angrily) sortir comme une furie. ● **stormy** *a* (-ier, -iest) (weather, Fig meeting) orageux.

story ['stɔːrɪ] *n* **1** histoire *f*; (newspaper article) article *m*; **s. (line)** (plot) intrigue *f*; **short s.** *Liter* nouvelle *f*; **fairy s.** conte *m* de fées. **2** (of building) *Am* étage *m.* ● **storybook** *n* livre *m* d'histoires. ● **storyteller** *n* conteur, -euse *mf.*

stout [staut] **1** *a* (-er, -est) (person) corpulent; (volume) épais (*f* épaisse). **2** *n* (beer) bière *f* brune.

stove [stəuv] *n* (for cooking) cuisinière *f*; (solid fuel) fourneau *m*; (portable) ré-

chaud *m*; (for heating) poêle *m.*

stow [stəu] **1** *vt* **to s. away** (put away) ranger. **2** *vi* **to s. away** *Nau* voyager clandestinement. ● **stowaway** *n* *Nau* passager, -ère *mf* clandestin(e).

straddle ['stræd(ə)l] *vt* (chair, fence) se mettre *or* être à califourchon sur; (line in road) chevaucher.

straggl/e ['stræg(ə)l] *vi* (trail) traîner (en désordre). ● **—er** *n* traînard, -arde *mf.*

straight [streɪt] *a* (-er, -est) droit; (hair) raide; (route) direct; (tidy) en ordre; (frank) franc (*f* franche); (refusal) net (*f* nette); **let's get this s.** comprenons-nous bien; **to keep a s. face** garder son sérieux; **to put s.** (tidy) ranger.

∥ *adv* (to walk etc) droit; (directly) tout droit; (to drink whisky etc) sec; **s. away** tout de suite; **s. opposite** juste en face; **s. ahead** *or* **on** tout droit; **to look s. ahead** regarder droit devant soi. ● **straighten** *vt* **to s. (up)** (tie, hair, room) arranger; **to s. things out** arranger les choses. ● **straightforward** *a* (easy, clear) simple.

strain [streɪn] **1** *n* tension *f*; (tiredness) fatigue *f*; (mental) tension *f* nerveuse; (effort) effort *m* ∥ *vt* (muscle) se froisser; (ankle, wrist) se fouler; (eyes) fatiguer; (voice) forcer; *Fig* mettre à l'épreuve; **to s. one's ears** tendre l'oreille; **to s. ones back** se faire mal au dos ∥ *vi* fournir un effort (**to do** pour faire).

2 *vt* (soup etc) passer; (vegetables) égoutter.

3 *n* (breed) lignée *f*; (of virus) souche *f.* ● **strained** *a* (relations) tendu; (muscle) froissé; (ankle, wrist) foulé. ● **strainer** *n* passoire *f.*

strait [streɪt] *n* **1** strait(s) *Geog* détroit *m.* **2 in financial straits** dans l'embarras. ● **straitjacket** *n* camisole *f* de force.

strand [strænd] *n* (of wool) brin *m*; (of hair) mèche *f*; (of story) *Fig* fil *m.*

stranded ['strændɪd] *a* en rade.

strange [streɪndʒ] *a* (-er, -est) (odd) étrange; (unknown) inconnu. ● **strangely** *adv* étrangement; **s. (enough) she...** chose étrange elle.... ● **stranger**

n (*unknown*) inconnu, -ue *mf*; (*outsider*) étranger, -ère *mf*; **he's a s. here** il n'est pas d'ici.

strangle ['stræŋg(ə)l] *vt* étrangler. ● **strangler** *n* étrangleur, -euse *mf*.

strap [stræp] *n* sangle *f*, courroie *f*; (*on dress*) bretelle *f*; (*on watch*) bracelet *m*; (*on sandal*) lanière *f* ‖ *vt* (**-pp-**) **to s.** (**down** *or* **in**) attacher (avec une sangle).

strapping ['stræpɪŋ] *a* (*well-built*) robuste.

strategy ['strætədʒɪ] *n* stratégie *f*. ● **strategic** [strə'tiːdʒɪk] *a* stratégique.

straw [strɔː] *n* paille *f*; (*drinking*) paille *f*; **that's the last s.!** c'est le comble!

strawberry ['strɔːbərɪ, *Am* -berɪ] *n* fraise *f* ‖ *a* (*flavour, ice cream*) à la fraise; (*jam*) de fraises; (*tart*) aux fraises.

stray [streɪ] *a* (*animal*) perdu; **a few s. cars/etc** quelques rares voitures/*etc* ‖ *n* animal *m* perdu ‖ *vi* s'égarer; **to s. from** (*subject, path*) s'écarter de; **don't s. too far** ne t'éloigne pas.

streak [striːk] *n* (*line*) raie *f*; (*of light*) filet *m*; (*of colour*) strie *f*; (*of paint*) traînée *f*; (*trace*) *Fig* trace *f*; **grey/etc streaks** (*in hair*) mèches *fpl* grises/*etc*. ● **streaked** *a* strié, zébré; (*stained*) taché (**with** de).

stream [striːm] *n* (*brook*) ruisseau *m*; (*flow*) flot *m*; *Sch* classe *f* (de niveau) ‖ *vi* ruisseler (**with** de); **to s. in** (*of sunlight, people*) entrer à flots.

streamer ['striːmər] *n* (*paper*) serpentin *m*; (*banner*) banderole *f*.

streamlin/e ['striːmlaɪn] *vt* (*work etc*) rationaliser. ● **—ed** *a* (*shape*) aérodynamique.

street [striːt] *n* rue *f*; **s. door** porte *f* d'entrée; **s. lamp, s. light** lampadaire *m*; **s. map, s. plan** plan *m* des rues; ● **streetcar** *n* (*tram*) *Am* tramway *m*.

strength [streŋθ] *n* force *f*; (*health, energy*) forces *fpl*; (*of wood etc*) solidité *f*; **on the s. of** *Fig* en vertu de. ● **strengthen** *vt* (*building, position*) renforcer; (*body, limb*) fortifier.

strenuous ['strenjʊəs] *a* (*effort etc*) vigoureux, énergique; (*work*) ardu.

strep [strep] *a* **s. throat** *Am* forte angine *f*.

stress [stres] *n* (*pressure*) pression *f*; (*mental*) stress *m*; (*emphasis*) & *Gram* accent *m*; *Tech* tension *f*; **under s.** stressé ‖ *vt* insister sur; (*word*) accentuer; **to s. that** souligner que. ● **stressful** *a* stressant.

stretch [stretʃ] *vt* (*rope, neck*) tendre; (*shoe, rubber*) étirer; **to s. (out)** (*arm, leg*) étendre, allonger; **to s. (out) one's arm** (*reach out*) tendre le bras (**to take** pour prendre); **to s. one's legs** se dégourdir les jambes; **to s. out** (*visit*) prolonger

‖ *vi* (*of person, elastic*) s'étirer; (*of influence*) s'étendre; **to s. (out)** (*of plain etc*) s'étendre

‖ *n* (*area, duration*) étendue *f*; (*of road*) tronçon *m*; (*route, trip*) trajet *m*; **ten/etc hours at a s.** dix/*etc* heures d'affilée.

stretcher ['stretʃər] *n* brancard *m*.

strew [struː] *vt* (*pt* **strewed**, *pp* **strewed** *or* **strewn**) répandre; **strewn with** jonché de.

stricken ['strɪk(ə)n] *a* (*town, region etc*) sinistré; **s. with** (*illness*) atteint de.

strict [strɪkt] *a* (**-er, -est**) (*severe, absolute*) strict. ● **—ly** *adv* strictement; **s. forbidden** formellement interdit. ● **—ness** *n* sévérité *f*.

stride [straɪd] *n* (grand) pas *m*, enjambée *f*; **to make great strides** *Fig* faire de grands progrès ‖ *vi* (*pt* **strode**) **to s. across** *or* **over** enjamber; **to s. along/ out/etc** avancer/sortir/*etc* à grands pas.

strife [straɪf] *n inv* conflit(s) *m(pl)*.

strike [straɪk] **1** *n* (*attack*) *Mil* raid *m* (aérien).

‖ *vt* (*pt* & *pp* **struck**) (*hit, impress*) frapper; (*collide with*) heurter; (*a blow*) donner; (*a match*) frotter; (*gold*) trouver; (*of clock*) sonner (*l'heure*); **to s. a bargain** conclure un accord; **it strikes me that** il me semble que (+ *indic*); **how did it s. you?** quelle impression ça t'a fait?; **to s. s.o. down** (*of illness etc*) terrasser qn; **to s. s.o. off** (*from list*) rayer qn (**from** de); **to s. up a friendship** lier amitié (**with** avec).

‖ *vi* (*attack*) attaquer; **to s. back** (*retaliate*) riposter.

2 *n* (*of workers*) grève *f*; **to go (out) on s.** se mettre en grève (**for** pour obtenir. **against** pour protester contre); (*pt & pp* **struck**) (*of workers*) faire grève. ●**striking** *a* (*impressive*) frappant. ●**striker** *n* (*worker*) gréviste *mf*; Fb buteur *m*.

string [strɪŋ] *n* ficelle *f*; (*of anorak, apron*) cordon *m*; (*of violin, racket etc*) corde *f*; (*of pearls*) collier *m*; (*of insults*) chapelet *m*; (*of vehicles*) file *f*; (*of questions*) série *f*; **to pull strings** Fig faire jouer ses relations; **to pull strings for s.o.** pistonner qn. ‖ *a* (*instrument*) Mus à cordes; **s. bean** haricot *m* vert.

‖ *vt* (*pt & pp* **strung**) **to s. up** (*hang up*) suspendre. ●**stringed** *a* (*instrument*) Mus à cordes.

stringent ['strɪndʒ(ə)nt] *a* rigoureux.

strip [strɪp] **1** *n* (*piece*) bande *f*; (**thin**) **s.** (*of metal etc*) lamelle *f*; (*landing*) **s.** piste *f* d'atterrissage; **s.** cartoon, comic **s.** bande *f* dessinée.

2 *vt* (**-pp-**) (*undress*) déshabiller; (*bed*) défaire; (*machine*) démonter; **to s. off** (*remove*) enlever ‖ *vi* **to s. (off)** (*undress*) se déshabiller. ●**stripper** *n* (*woman*) strip-teaseuse *f*; (**paint**) **s.** décapant *m*.

stripe [straɪp] *n* rayure *f*; Mil galon *m*. ●**striped** *a* rayé (**with** de).

strive [straɪv] *vi* (*pt* **strove**, *pp* **striven**) s'efforcer (**to do** de faire, **for** d'obtenir).

strode [strəʊd] *pt of* **stride**.

stroke [strəʊk] **1** *n* (*movement*) coup *m*; (*of pen, genius*) trait *m*; (*of brush*) touche *f*; (*caress*) caresse *f*; Med coup *m* de sang, attaque *f*; (*swimming*) s. nage *f*; **at a s.** d'un coup; **a s. of luck** un coup de chance ‖ *vt* (*beard, cat etc*) caresser.

stroll [strəʊl] *n* promenade *f* ‖ *vi* se promener, flâner; **to s. in/etc** entrer/ etc sans se presser.

stroller ['strəʊlər] *n* (*for baby*) Am poussette *f*.

strong [strɒŋ] *a* (**-er, -est**) fort; (*shoes, chair, nerves etc*) solide; (*interest*) vif; (*measures*) énergique; **sixty s.** au nombre de soixante ‖ *adv* **to be going s.** aller toujours bien. ●**—ly** *adv* (*to protest, defend*) énergiquement; (*to advise*) fortement; (*to feel*) profondément. ●**strongbox** *n* coffre-fort *m*. ●**stronghold** *n* bastion *m*.

strove [strəʊv] *pt of* **strive**.

struck [strʌk] *pt & pp of* **strike 1 & 2**.

structure ['strʌktʃər] *n* structure *f*; (*building*) construction *f*. ●**structural** *a* structural; (*building defect*) de construction; **s. damage** (*to building*) dommage *m* au gros œuvre.

struggle ['strʌg(ə)l] *n* (*fight*) lutte *f* (**to do** pour faire); (*effort*) effort *m*; **to put up a s.** résister; **to have a s. doing** *or* **to do** avoir du mal à faire ‖ *vi* (*fight*) lutter, se battre (**with** avec); (*move about wildly*) se débattre; **to be struggling** (*financially*) avoir du mal; **to s. to do** s'efforcer de faire.

strum [strʌm] *vt* (**-mm-**) (*guitar*) gratter de.

strung [strʌŋ] *pt & pp of* **string** ‖ *a* **s. out** (*things*) espacés; (*washing*) étendu.

strut [strʌt] **1** *vi* (**-tt-**) **to s.** (**about** *or* **around**) se pavaner. **2** *n* (*support*) Tech étai *m*.

stub [stʌb] **1** *n* (*of pencil, cigarette etc*) bout *m*; (*of ticket, cheque, Am check*) talon *m* ‖ *vt* (**-bb-**) **to s. out** (*cigarette*) écraser. **2** *vt* (**-bb-**) **to s. one's toe** *or* **toe** cogner le doigt de pied (**on** contre).

stubble ['stʌb(ə)l] *n* barbe *f* de plusieurs jours.

stubborn ['stʌbən] *a* (*person*) entêté; (*cough, manner etc*) opiniâtre. ●**—ness** *n* entêtement *m*.

stuck [stʌk] *pt & pp of* **stick²** ‖ *a* (*caught, jammed*) coincé; **s. indoors** cloué chez soi; **I'm s.** (*unable to carry on*) je ne sais par quoi faire *or* dire *etc*; **to be s. with sth/s.o.** se farcir qch/qn. ● **s.-'up** *a Fam* prétentieux.

stud [stʌd] *n* **1** (*on football boot*) crampon *m*; (*earring*) clou *m* d'oreille; (*collar*) **s.** bouton *m* de col. **2** (*farm*) haras *m*; (*horses*) écurie *f*; (*stallion*) étalon *m*. ● **studded** *a* **s. with** (*covered*) constellé de.

student ['stjuːdənt] *n* *Univ* étudiant, -ante *mf*; *Sch* élève *mf*; **music**/*etc* **s.** étudiant, -ante en musique/*etc* ‖ *a* (*life*, *protest*) étudiant; (*restaurant*, *residence*, *grant*) universitaire.

studio ['stjuːdɪəʊ] *n* (*pl* **-os**) (*of painter etc*) & *Cin TV* studio *m*; **s. flat** *or Am* **apartment** studio *m*.

studious ['stjuːdɪəs] *a* (*person*) studieux.

study ['stʌdɪ] *n* étude *f*; (*office*) bureau *m* ‖ *vt* (*learn*, *observe*) étudier ‖ *vi* étudier; **to be a doctor**/*etc* faire des études pour devenir médecin/*etc*; **to s. for** (*exam*) préparer.

stuff [stʌf] **1** *n* (*thing*) truc *m*; (*substance*) substance *f*; (*things*) trucs *mpl*; (*possessions*) affaires *fpl*; **it's good s.** c'est bon (ça). **2** *vt* (*fill*) bourrer (**with** de); (*cushion*, *armchair etc*) rembourrer (**with** avec); (*animal*) empailler; (*put*) fourrer (**into** dans); (*chicken etc*) farcir; **my nose is stuffed (up)** j'ai le nez bouché. ● **—ing** *n* (*padding*) bourre *f*; *Culin* farce *f*.

stuffy ['stʌfɪ] *a* (**-ier, -iest**) (*room etc*) mal aéré; (*old-fashioned*) vieux jeu *inv*; **it smells s.** ça sent le renfermé.

stumble ['stʌmb(ə)l] *vi* trébucher (**over** sur); **to s. across** *or on* (*find*) tomber sur; **stumbling block** pierre *f* d'achoppement.

stump [stʌmp] *n* (*of tree*) souche *f*; (*of limb*) moignon *m*.

stun [stʌn] *vt* (**-nn-**) (*with punch etc*) étourdir; (*amaze*) *Fig* stupéfier. ● **stunned** *a* (*amazed*) stupéfait (**by** par). ● **stunning** *a* (*news*) stupéfiant; (*terrific*) *Fam* sensationnel.

stung [stʌŋ] *pt* & *pp* of **sting**.

stunk [stʌŋk] *pt* & *pp* of **stink**.

stunt [stʌnt] **1** *n* tour *m* (de force); *Cin* cascade *f*; (*trick*) truc *m*; **publicity s.** coup *m* de pub; **s. man** *Cin* cascadeur *m*; **s. woman** cascadeuse *f*. **2** *vt* (*growth*) retarder. ● **—ed** *a* (*person*) rabougri.

stupendous [stjuː'pendəs] *a* prodigieux.

stupid ['stjuːpɪd] *a* stupide, bête; **a s. thing** une stupidité; **s. fool** idiot, -ote *mf*. ● **stu'pidity** *n* stupidité *f*.

sturdy ['stɜːdɪ] *a* (**-ier, -iest**) robuste.

stutter ['stʌtər] *vi* bégayer ‖ *n* bégaiement *m*; **to have a s.** être bègue.

sty [staɪ] *n.* (*for pigs*) porcherie *f*.

sty(e) [staɪ] *n* (*on eye*) orgelet *m*.

style [staɪl] *n* style *m*; (*fashion*) mode *f*; (*design of dress etc*) modèle *m*; (*of hair*) coiffure *f*; **to have s.** avoir de la classe; **in s.** (*to live*, *travel*) dans le luxe ‖ *vt* (*design*) créer; **to s. s.o.'s hair** coiffer qn. ● **stylish** *a* chic *inv*, élégant. ● **stylist** *n* (*hair*) **s.** coiffeur, -euse *mf*.

sub- [sʌb] *pref* sous-, sub-.

subconscious [sʌb'kɒnʃəs] *a* & *n* subconscient (*m*).

subcontract [sʌbkən'trækt] *vt* sous-traiter. ● **subcontractor** *n* sous-traitant *m*.

subdivide [sʌbdɪ'vaɪd] *vt* subdiviser.

subdue [səb'djuː] *vt* (*country*) asservir; (*feelings*) maîtriser. ● **—ed** *a* (*light*) atténué; (*voice*, *tone*) bas (*f* basse); (*person*) qui manque d'entrain.

subject¹ ['sʌbdʒɪkt] *n* **1** (*matter*) & *Gram* sujet *m*; *Sch Univ* matière *f*; **s. matter** (*topic*) sujet *m*; (*content*) contenu *m*. **2** (*citizen*) ressortissant, -ante *mf*; (*of monarch*) sujet, -ette *mf*; (*in experiment*) sujet *m*.

subject² ['sʌbdʒekt] *a* **s. to** (*prone to*) sujet à (*maladie etc*); (*ruled by*) soumis à (*loi etc*); (*conditional upon*) sous réserve de; **prices are s. to change** les prix peuvent être modifiés ‖ [səb'dʒekt] *vt* soumettre (**to** à); (*expose*) exposer (**to** à).

subjective [səb'dʒektɪv] *a* subjectif. ● **—ly** *adv* subjectivement.

subjunctive [səb'dʒʌŋktɪv] *n* *Gram* subjonctif *m*.

sublet [sʌb'let] *vt* (*pt* & *pp* **sublet**, *pres p* **subletting**) sous-louer.

sublime [sə'blaɪm] *a* sublime; (*indifference*) suprême.

submarine ['sʌbməriːn] *n* sous-marin *m*.

submerge [səb'mɜːdʒ] *vt* (*flood*, *overwhelm*) submerger; (*immerse*) immerger (**in** dans).

submit [səb'mɪt] *vt* (-tt-) soumettre (**to** à) ▮ *vi* se soumettre (**to** à). ● **submission** [-ʃ(ə)n] *n* soumission *f*.

subordinate [sə'bɔːdɪnət] *a* subalterne; *Gram* subordonné ▮ *n* subordonné, -ée *mf* ▮ [sə'bɔːdɪneɪt] *vt* subordonner (**to** à).

subpoena [səb'piːnə] *vt* Jur citer ▮ *n* Jur citation *f*.

subscribe [səb'skraɪb] *vi* (*pay money*) cotiser (**to** à); **to s. to** (*take out subscription*) s'abonner à (*journal etc*); (*be a subscriber*) être abonné à (*journal etc*); (*fund*, *idea*) souscrire à. ● **subscriber** *n* (*to newspaper etc*) & *Tel* abonné, -ée *mf*. ● **subscription** [-'skrɪpʃ(ə)n] *n* abonnement *m*; (*to fund etc*) souscription *f*; (*to club*) cotisation *f*.

subsequent ['sʌbsɪkwənt] *a* postérieur (**to** à); **our s. problems** les problèmes que nous avons eus par la suite. ● **-ly** *adv* par la suite.

subside [səb'saɪd] *vi* (*of ground*, *building*) s'affaisser; (*of wind*) baisser. ● **subsidence** *n* affaissement *m*.

subsidiary [səb'sɪdɪərɪ, *Am* -erɪ] *a* accessoire ▮ *n* (*company*) filiale *f*.

subsidize ['sʌbsɪdaɪz] *vt* subventionner. ● **subsidy** *n* subvention *f*.

substance ['sʌbstəns] *n* substance *f*; (*firmness*) solidité *f*. ● **substantial** [səb'stænʃ(ə)l] *a* important; (*meal*) copieux. ● **sub'stantially** *adv* considérablement; **s. true/etc** en grande partie vrai/ *etc*; **s. different** très différent.

substandard [sʌb'stændəd] *a* de qualité inférieure.

substitute ['sʌbstɪtjuːt] *n* produit *m* de remplacement; (*person*) remplaçant, -ante

mf (**for** de); **there's no s. for...** rien ne peut remplacer... ▮ *vt* **to s. sth/s.o. for** substituer qch/qn à, remplacer qch/qn par ▮ *vi* **to s. for s.o.** remplacer qn.

subtitle ['sʌbtaɪt(ə)l] *n* sous-titre *m* ▮ *vt* sous-titrer.

subtle ['sʌt(ə)l] *a* (-er, -est) subtil.

subtotal [sʌb'təʊt(ə)l] *n* sous-total *m*.

subtract [səb'trækt] *vt* soustraire (**from** de). ● **subtraction** [-ʃ(ə)n] *n* soustraction *f*.

suburb ['sʌbɜːb] *n* banlieue *f*; **the suburbs** la banlieue; **in the suburbs** en banlieue. ● **su'burban** *a* (*train etc*) de banlieue. ● **su'burbia** *n* la banlieue.

subversive [səb'vɜːsɪv] *a* subversif.

subway ['sʌbweɪ] *n* passage *m* souterrain; *Rail Am* métro *m*.

succeed [sək'siːd] 1 *vi* réussir (**in doing** à faire, **in sth** dans qch). 2 *vt* **to s. s.o.** (*follow*) succéder à qn. ● **-ing** *a* (**in** *past*) suivant; (*in future*) futur; (*consecutive*) consécutif.

success [sək'ses] *n* succès *m*, réussite *f*; **to make a s. of sth** réussir qch; **he was a s.** il a eu du succès; **it was a s.** c'était réussi; **her s. in the exam** sa réussite à l'examen. ● **successful** *a* (*effort etc*) couronné de succès, réussi; (*outcome*) heureux; (*company*) prospère; (*candidate in exam*) admis, reçu; (*writer*, *film etc*) à succès; **to be s.** réussir (**in** dans, **in an exam** à un examen, **in doing** à faire). ● **successfully** *adv* avec succès.

succession [sək'seʃ(ə)n] *n* succession *f*, **ten days in s.** dix jours consécutifs; **in rapid s.** coup sur coup. ● **successive** *a* (*governments etc*) successif; **ten s. days** dix jours consécutifs. ● **successor** *n* successeur *m* (**of**, **to** de).

succulent ['sʌkjʊlənt] *a* succulent.

succumb [sə'kʌm] *vi* succomber (**to** à).

such [sʌtʃ] *a* (*of this or that kind*) tel, telle; **s. a car/etc** une telle voiture/*etc*; **s. happiness/s. noise/etc** (*so much*) tant ou tellement de bonheur/de bruit/*etc*; **s. as** comme, tel que; **s. and s.** tel ou tel. ▮ *adv* (*so very*) si; (*in comparisons*) aussi; **s. long trips** de si longs voyages; **s. a**

large helping une si grosse portion; **s. a kind woman as you** une femme aussi gentille que vous.
| pron **happiness/etc as s.** le bonheur/etc en tant que tel.

suck [sʌk] vt sucer; (of baby) téter (lait, biberon etc); **to s. (up)** (with straw, pump) aspirer | vi (of baby) téter. ●**—er** n (rubber pad) ventouse f.

suckle ['sʌk(ə)l] vt (of woman) allaiter | vi (of baby) téter.

suction ['sʌkʃ(ə)n] n succion f; **s. pad** ventouse f.

Sudan [suː'dɑːn] n Soudan m.

sudden ['sʌd(ə)n] a soudain; **all of a s.** tout à coup. ●**—ly** adv subitement.

suds [sʌdz] npl mousse f de savon.

sue [suː] vt poursuivre (en justice) | vi engager des poursuites (judiciaires).

suede [sweɪd] n daim m | a de daim.

suffer ['sʌfər] vi souffrir (from de); **to s. from pimples** avoir des boutons; **your work/etc will s.** ton travail/etc s'en ressentira | vt (loss etc) subir; (pain) ressentir. ●**—ing** n souffrance(s) f(pl). ●**sufferer** n (from misfortune) victime f; AIDS s. malade mf du SIDA; asthma s. asthmatique mf.

suffice [sə'faɪs] vi suffire.

sufficient [sə'fɪʃ(ə)nt] a (quantity) suffisant; **s. money/etc** suffisamment d'argent/etc. ●**—ly** adv suffisamment.

suffix ['sʌfɪks] n Gram suffixe m.

suffocate ['sʌfəkeɪt] vti suffoquer.

sugar ['ʃʊgər] n sucre m; **lump s.** sucre en morceaux; **brown s.** sucre m brun; **s. bowl** sucrier m; **s. cane/tongs** canne f/ pince f à sucre | vt sucrer. ●**sugary** a (taste) sucré.

suggest [sə'dʒest] vt (propose) suggérer, proposer (**to** à, **doing** de faire, **that** que (+ sub)); (evoke, imply) suggérer. ●**suggestion** [-tʃ(ə)n] n suggestion. ●**suggestive** a suggestif; **to be s. of** suggérer.

suicide ['suːɪsaɪd] n suicide m. ●**sui'cidal** a suicidaire.

suit[1] [suːt] **1** n (man's) costume m; (woman's) tailleur m; **flying/diving/ski**

s. combinaison f de vol/plongée/ski. **2** n (lawsuit) procès m. **3** n Cards couleur f.

suit[2] [suːt] vt (please, be acceptable to) convenir à; (of dress, colour etc) aller (bien) à; (adapt) adapter (**to** à); **it suits me to stay** ça m'arrange de rester; **suited to** (job, activity) fait pour; **well suited** (couple etc) bien assorti.

suitable ['suːtəb(ə)l] a qui convient (**for** à), convenable (**for** pour); (dress, colour) qui va (bien). ●**suitably** adv convenablement; **s. impressed** très impressionné.

suitcase ['suːtkeɪs] n valise f.

suite [swiːt] n (rooms) suite f; (furniture) mobilier m; **bedroom s.** (furniture) chambre f à coucher.

sulfur ['sʌlfər] n Am soufre m.

sulk [sʌlk] vi bouder. ●**sulky** a (-ier, -iest) boudeur.

sullen ['sʌlən] a maussade. ●**—ly** adv d'un air maussade.

sulphur ['sʌlfər] n soufre m.

sultan ['sʌltən] n sultan m.

sultana [sʌl'tɑːnə] n raisin m (de Smyrne).

sultry ['sʌltrɪ] a (-ier, -iest) (heat) étouffant.

sum [sʌm] **1** n (amount of money, total) somme f; (calculation) calcul m; pl (arithmetic) le calcul. **2** vt (-mm-) **to s. up** (facts etc) récapituler, résumer; (situation) évaluer; (person) jauger | vi **to s. up** récapituler.

summarize ['sʌməraɪz] vt résumer | vi récapituler. ●**summary** n résumé m.

summer ['sʌmər] n été m; **in (the) s.** en été | a d'été; **s. camp** Am colonie f de vacances; **s. holidays** or Am **vacation** grandes vacances fpl. ●**summertime** n été m; **in (the) s.** en été.

summit ['sʌmɪt] n (of mountain, power etc) sommet m; **s. (conference)** Pol conférence f au sommet.

summon ['sʌmən] vt appeler; (meeting, s.o. to meeting) convoquer (**to** à); **to s. s.o. to do** sommer qn de faire; **to s. up** (courage) rassembler.

summons ['sʌmənz] n Jur assignation f ▮ vt Jur assigner.

sumptuous ['sʌmptʃʊəs] a somptueux.

sun [sʌn] n soleil m; **in the s.** au soleil; **the sun is shining** il fait (du) soleil; **s. lotion/** etc crème f/etc solaire ▮ vt (-nn-) **to s. oneself** se chauffer au soleil.

sunbathe ['sʌnbeɪð] vi prendre un bain de soleil. ● **sunbed** n lit m à ultraviolets. ● **sunblock** n écran m total. ● **sunburn** n Med coup m de soleil; (tan) bronzage m. ● **sunburnt** a (tanned) bronzé; Med brûlé par le soleil. ● **sundial** n cadran m solaire. ● **sundown** n coucher m du soleil. ● **sunflower** n tournesol m. ● **sunglasses** npl lunettes fpl de soleil. ● **sunlamp** n lampe f à bronzer. ● **sunlight** n (lumière f du) soleil m. ● **sun lounge** n (in house) véranda f. ● **sunrise** n lever m du soleil. ● **sunroof** n Aut toit m ouvrant. ● **sunset** n coucher m du soleil. ● **sunshade** n (on table) parasol m. ● **sunshine** n soleil m. ● **sunstroke** n insolation f. ● **suntan** n bronzage m; **s. lotion/oil** crème f/huile f solaire. ● **suntanned** a bronzé.

sundae ['sʌndeɪ] n glace f aux fruits.

Sunday ['sʌndɪ, -deɪ] n dimanche m; **S. school** Rel = catéchisme m.

sundry ['sʌndrɪ] a divers ▮ n **all and s.** tout le monde.

sung [sʌŋ] pp of **sing**.

sunk [sʌŋk] pp of **sink**[2]. ● **sunken** a (treasure etc) submergé; (eyes) cave.

sunny ['sʌnɪ] a (-ier, -iest) (day etc) ensoleillé; **it's s.** il fait (du) soleil; **s. periods** or **intervals** éclaircies fpl.

super ['su:pər] a Fam super, sensationnel.

super- ['su:pər] pref super-.

superb [su:'pɜ:b] a superbe.

superficial [su:pə'fɪʃ(ə)l] a superficiel.

superfluous [su:'pɜ:flʊəs] a superflu.

superglue ['su:pəglu:] n colle f extraforte.

superhuman [su:pə'hju:mən] a surhumain.

superintendent [su:pərɪn'tendənt] n (po-

lice) s. commissaire m (de police).

superior [su:'pɪərɪər] a supérieur (**to** à); (goods) de qualité supérieure ▮ n (person) supérieur, -eure mf. ● **superi'ority** n supériorité f.

superlative [su:'pɜ:lətɪv] a sans pareil ▮ a & n Gram superlatif (m).

supermarket ['su:pəmɑ:kɪt] n supermarché m.

supernatural [su:pə'nætʃ(ə)rəl] a & n surnaturel (m).

superpower ['su:pəpaʊər] n Pol superpuissance f.

supersede [su:pə'si:d] vt supplanter.

supersonic [su:pə'sɒnɪk] a supersonique.

superstar ['su:pəstɑ:r] n Cin superstar f.

superstition [su:pə'stɪʃ(ə)n] n superstition f. ● **superstitious** a superstitieux.

supertanker ['su:pətæŋkər] n pétrolier m géant.

supervise ['su:pəvaɪz] vt (person, work) surveiller; (office, research) diriger. ● **supervision** [-'vɪʒ(ə)n] n surveillance f; direction f. ● **supervisor** n surveillant, -ante mf; (in office) chef m de service; (in store) chef m de rayon.

supper ['sʌpər] n dîner m, souper m; (late-night) souper m; **to have s.** dîner, souper.

supple ['sʌp(ə)l] a souple.

supplement ['sʌplɪmənt] n supplément m (**to** à) ▮ ['sʌplɪment] vt compléter. ● **supple'mentary** a supplémentaire.

supply [sə'plaɪ] vt (provide) fournir; (with electricity, gas, water) alimenter (**with** en); (equip) équiper (**with** de); **to s. s.o. with sth, s. sth to s.o.** fournir qch à qn.

▮ n (stock) réserve f; pl (equipment) matériel m; (food) **supplies** vivres mpl; (office) **supplies** fournitures fpl de bureau); **s. and demand** l'offre f et la demande; **to be in short s.** manquer; **s. ship/**etc navire m/etc ravitailleur. ● **supplier** n Com fournisseur m.

support [sə'pɔ:t] vt (bear weight of) supporter; (help, encourage) soutenir,

appuyer; (*be in favour of*) être en faveur de; (*family etc*) subvenir aux besoins de; (*endure*) supporter.
‖ *n* (*help*) soutien *m*, appui *m*; (*object*) support *m*; **means of s.** moyens *mpl* de subsistance; **income** *n Br* allocation *f* d'aide sociale; **in s. of s.o.** en faveur de qn. ● **supporter** *n* partisan *m*. ● **supporter** *m*. ● **supportive** *a* to be s. of s.o. soutenir qn.

suppos/e [sə'pəʊz] *vti* supposer (**that** que); **I'm supposed to work** *or* **be working** (*ought*) je suis censé travailler; **he's s. to be rich** on le dit riche; **I s.** (**so**) je pense; **you're tired, I s.** vous êtes fatigué, je suppose; **s.** *or* **supposing we go** (*suggestion*) si nous partions; **s.** *or* **supposing you're right** supposons que tu aies raison.

suppress [sə'pres] *vt* (*abuse etc*) supprimer; (*feelings*) réprimer; (*scandal, yawn, revolt, information*) étouffer.

supreme [suː'priːm] *a* suprême.

surcharge ['sɜːtʃɑːdʒ] *n* (*extra charge*) supplément *m*.

sure [ʃʊər] *a* (**-er, -est**) sûr (**of** de, **that** que); **she's s. to accept** c'est sûr qu'elle acceptera; **it's s. to snow** il va sûrement neiger; **to make s. of sth** s'assurer de qch; **for s.** à coup sûr, pour sûr; **s.!** bien sûr!; **be s. to do it!** ne manquez pas de le faire! ● **surely** *adv* sûrement; **he didn't refuse?** (*I hope*) il n'a tout de même pas refusé?

surf [sɜːf] *n* (*foam*) ressac *m*. ● **surfboard** *n* planche *f* (de surf). ● **surfing** *n Sp* surf *m*; **to go s.** faire du surf.

surface ['sɜːfɪs] *n* surface *f*; **s. area** superficie *f*; **s. mail** courrier *m* par voie(s) de surface **‖** *vi* (*of swimmer etc*) remonter à la surface; (*of person, thing*) *Fam* réapparaître.

surge ['sɜːdʒ] *n* (*of enthusiasm etc*) vague *f*; (*in prices etc*) montée *f* **‖** *vi* (*of crowd, hatred*) déferler; (*of prices etc*) monter (soudainement); **to s. forward** se lancer en avant.

surgeon ['sɜːdʒ(ə)n] *n* chirurgien *m*.

● **surgery** *n* (*doctor's office*) cabinet *m*; (*period*) consultation *f*; (*science*) chirurgie *f*; **to have s.** avoir une opération (**for** pour). ● **surgical** *a* chirurgical; (*appliance*) orthopédique; **s. spirit** alcool *m* à 90°.

surly ['sɜːlɪ] *a* (**-ier, -iest**) bourru.

surname ['sɜːneɪm] *n* nom *m* de famille.

surpass [sə'pɑːs] *vt* surpasser (**in** en).

surplus ['sɜːpləs] *n* surplus *m* **‖** *a* (*goods*) en surplus; **some s. material/***etc* un surplus de tissu/*etc*.

surpris/e [sə'praɪz] *n* surprise *f*; **to give s.o. a s.** faire une surprise à qn; **to take s.o. by s.** prendre qn au dépourvu **‖** *a* (*visit etc*) inattendu **‖** *vt* (*astonish*) étonner, surprendre; (*come upon*) surprendre. ● **—ed** *a* surpris (**that** que (+ *sub*), **at sth** de qch); **I'm s. at his stupidity** sa bêtise m'étonne; **I'm s. to see you** je suis surpris de te voir. ● **—ing** *a* surprenant. ● **—ingly** *adv* étonnamment.

surrender [sə'rendər] **1** *vi* se rendre (**to** à) **‖** *n Mil* capitulation *f*. **2** *vt* (*hand over*) remettre (**to** à); (*right, claim*) renoncer à.

surrogate ['sʌrəgət] *n* substitut *m*; **s. mother** mère *f* porteuse.

surround [sə'raʊnd] *vt* entourer (**with** de); (*of army, police*) encercler; **surrounded by** entouré de. ● **—ing** *a* environnant. ● **—ings** *npl* environs *mpl*; (*setting*) cadre *m*.

surveillance [sɜː'veɪləns] *n* (*of prisoner etc*) surveillance *f*.

survey [sə'veɪ] *vt* (*look at*) regarder; (*house*) inspecter; (*land*) arpenter **‖** ['sɜːveɪ] *n* enquête *f*; (*of opinion*) sondage *m*; (*of house*) inspection *f*. ● **sur'veyor** *n* (*of land*) géomètre *m*; (*of house*) expert *m*.

survive [sə'vaɪv] *vi* survivre **‖** *vt* survivre à (*qn, qch*). ● **survival** *n* (*act*) survie *f*; (*relic*) vestige *m*. ● **survivor** *n* survivant, -ante *mf*.

susceptible [sə'septəb(ə)l] *a* sensible (**to** à); **s. to colds/***etc* prédisposé aux rhumes/etc.

suspect ['sʌspekt] n & a suspect, -ecte (mf) ▌ [sə'spekt] vt soupçonner (**of** de qch, **of doing** d'avoir fait, **that** que); (question, doubt) suspecter (l'honnêteté de qn etc).

suspend [sə'spend] vt 1 (stop, postpone, dismiss) suspendre; (pupil) renvoyer; (passport) retirer; **suspended sentence** Jur condamnation f avec sursis. 2 (hang) suspendre (**from** à). ●**suspender** n (for stocking) jarretelle f; pl (for trousers, Am pants) Am bretelles fpl. ●**suspension** [-ʃ(ə)n] n (of vehicle) suspension f; **s. bridge** pont m suspendu.

suspense [sə'spens] n attente f (angoissée); (in film, book etc) suspense m.

suspicion [sə'spɪʃ(ə)n] n soupçon m; **to arouse s.** éveiller les soupçons; **with s.** avec méfiance; **under s.** considéré comme suspect. ●**suspicious** a (person) soupçonneux, méfiant; (behaviour) suspect; **s.(-looking)** suspect; **to be s. of** or **about** se méfier de.

sustain [sə'stein] vt (effort, theory) soutenir; (weight) supporter; (with food) nourrir; (damage, loss) subir; (injury) recevoir. ●**—able** a (growth rate etc) qui peut être maintenu. ●**sustenance** n (food) nourriture f; (quality) valeur f nutritive.

swab [swɒb] n Med (pad) tampon m; (specimen) prélèvement m.

swagger ['swægər] vi (walk) parader.

swallow ['swɒləʊ] 1 vt avaler; **to s. down** avaler; **to s. up** (savings etc) Fig engloutir ▌ vi avaler. 2 n (bird) hirondelle f.

swam [swæm] pt of **swim**.

swamp [swɒmp] n marécage m, marais m ▌ vt (flood, Fig overwhelm) submerger (**with** de). ●**swampy** a (-ier, -iest) marécageux.

swan [swɒn] n cygne m.

swap [swɒp] n échange m; pl (stamps etc) doubles mpl ▌ vt (-pp-) échanger (**for** contre); **to s. seats** changer de place ▌ vi échanger.

swarm [swɔ:m] n (of bees etc) essaim m

▌ vi (of streets, insects, people etc) fourmiller (**with** de).

swat [swɒt] vt (-tt-) (fly etc) écraser.

sway [swei] vi se balancer ▌ vt balancer; Fig influencer.

swear ['sweər] vt (pt **swore**, pp **sworn**) (promise) jurer (**to do** de faire, **that** que); **to s. an oath** prêter serment; **to s. s.o. to secrecy** faire jurer le silence à qn ▌ vi (curse) jurer, pester (**at** contre); **she swears by this lotion** elle ne jure que par cette lotion. ●**swearword** n gros mot m, juron m.

sweat [swet] n sueur f; **s. shirt** sweatshirt m ▌ vi (of person) transpirer, suer; **I'm sweating** je suis en sueur ▌ vt **to s. out** (a cold) se débarrasser de (en transpirant). ●**sweater** n (garment) pull m. ●**sweaty** a (-ier, -iest) (shirt etc) plein de sueur; (hand) moite; (person) (tout) en sueur.

Swede [swi:d] n Suédois, -oise mf. ●**Sweden** n Suède f. ●**Swedish** a suédois ▌ n (language) suédois m.

sweep [swi:p] n (with broom) coup m de balai ▌ vt (pt & pp **swept**) (with broom) balayer; (chimney) ramoner; (river) draguer ▌ vi balayer. ●**—ing** a (gesture) large; (change) radical; (statement) trop général.

sweep aside vt (dismiss) écarter ▌ **to sweep away** vt (leaves) balayer; (carry off) emporter ▌ **to sweep out** vt (room etc) balayer ▌ **to sweep through** vt (of fear) saisir (groupe); (of disease) ravager (pays) ▌ **to sweep up** vt (dust, floor etc) balayer.

sweet [swi:t] a (-er, -est) (not sour) doux (f douce); (tea, coffee, cake) sucré; (child, house, cat) mignon (f mignonne); (sound, smile) doux; (pleasant) agréable; (kind) aimable; **to have a s. tooth** aimer les sucreries; **s. potato** patate f douce; **s. shop** confiserie f. ▌ n (candy) bonbon m; (dessert) dessert m. ●**sweeten** vt (tea etc) sucrer; Fig adoucir. ●**sweetener** n (for tea etc) édulcorant m. ●**sweetly** adv (kindly) aimablement; (*agreeably*) agréablement. ●**sweetness** *n* douceur *f*; (*taste*) goût *m* sucré.

sweetheart ['swi:tha:t] *n* petit ami *m*, petite amie *f*.

swell[1] [swel] *vi* (*pt* **swelled**, *pp* **swollen** *or* **swelled**) (*of hand, leg etc*) enfler; (*of wood, dough*) gonfler; (*of river, numbers*) grossir; **to s. up** (*of hand etc*) enfler ‖ *vt* (*river, numbers*) grossir. ●—**ing** *n* *Med* enflure *f*.

swell[2] [swel] 1 *n* (*of sea*) houle *f*. 2 *a* (*very good*) *Am Fam* formidable.

swelter ['sweltər] *vi* étouffer. ●—**ing** *a* étouffant; **it's s.** on étouffe.

swept [swept] *pp* of **sweep**.

swerve [swa:v] *vi* (*of vehicle*) faire une embardée; (*while running*) faire un écart.

swift [swift] 1 *a* (**-er, -est**) rapide. 2 *n* (*bird*) martinet *m*. ●—**ly** *adv* rapidement.

swill [swil] *vt* (*beer etc*) *Fam* boire, siffler; **to s. sth (out)** laver qch (à grande eau).

swim [swim] *n* **to go for a s.** se baigner. ‖ *vi* (*pt* **swam**, *pp* **swum**, *pres p* **swimming**) nager; *Sp* faire de la natation; **to go swimming** aller nager; **to s. away** se sauver (à la nage). ‖ *vt* (*river*) traverser à la nage; (*length, crawl etc*) nager. ●**swimming** *n* natation *f*; **s. costume** maillot *m* de bain; **s. pool** piscine *f*; **s. trunks** slip *m* de bain. ●**swimmer** *n* nageur, -euse *mf*. ●**swimsuit** *n* maillot *m* de bain.

swindl/e ['swind(ə)l] *n* escroquerie *f* ‖ *vt* escroquer. ●—**er** *n* escroc *m*.

swine [swain] *n inv* (*person*) *Pej* salaud *m*.

swing [swiŋ] *n* (*in playground etc*) balançoire *f*; (*of pendulum*) oscillation *f*; (*in opinion*) revirement *m*; (*rhythm*) rythme *m*; **to be in full s.** battre son plein; **s. door** porte *f* de saloon. ‖ *vi* (*pt* & *pp* **swung**) (*sway*) se balancer; (*of pendulum*) osciller; (*turn*) virer; **to s. round** (*suddenly*) virer, tourner; (*of person*) se retourner (vivement); **to s.**

into action passer à l'action. ‖ *vt* (*arms etc*) balancer; (*axe*) brandir. ●—**ing** *a Fam* (*trendy*) dans le vent; (*lively*) plein de vie; (*music*) entraînant.

swipe [swaip] *vti* **to s. (at)** (*hit*) (essayer de) frapper (*qn, qch*). 2 *vt* **to s. sth** (*steal*) *Fam* piquer qch (**from s.o.** à qn).

swirl [swa:l] *vi* tourbillonner.

swish [swiʃ] 1 *a* (*posh*) *Fam* rupin, chic. 2 *vi* (*of whip etc*) siffler; (*of fabric*) froufrouter.

Swiss [swis] *a* suisse ‖ *n inv* Suisse *m*, Suissesse *f*; **the S.** les Suisses *mpl*.

switch [switʃ] *n El* bouton *m* (électrique), interrupteur *m*; (*change*) changement *m*; (*reversal*) revirement *m* (**in** de). ‖ *vt* (*money, employee*) transférer (**to** à); (*support*) reporter (**to** sur, **from** de); (*exchange*) échanger (**for** contre); **to s. places** *or* **seats** changer de place. ‖ *vi* **to s. to** (*change*) passer à. ●**switch-blade** *n Am* couteau *m* à cran d'arrêt. ●**switchboard** *n Tel* standard *m*; **s. operator** standardiste *mf*.

switch off *vt* (*lamp, gas, radio etc*) éteindre; (*engine*) arrêter; (*electricity*) couper ‖ **to switch on** *vt* (*lamp, gas, radio etc*) mettre, allumer; (*engine*) mettre en marche ‖ **to switch over** *vi* (*change TV channels*) changer de chaîne.

Switzerland ['switsələnd] *n* Suisse *f*.

swivel ['swiv(ə)l] *vi* (**-ll-,** *Am* **-l-**) **to s. (round)** (*of chair*) pivoter ‖ *a* **s. chair** fauteuil *m* pivotant.

swollen ['swəʊl(ə)n] *pp* of **swell**[1] ‖ *a* (*leg etc*) enflé; (*stomach*) gonflé.

swoon [swu:n] *vi Lit* se pâmer.

swoop [swu:p] 1 *vi* **to s. (down) on** (*of bird*) fondre sur. 2 *n* (*of police*) descente *f* ‖ *vi* faire une descente (**on** dans).

swop [swɒp] *n*, *vt* & *vi* = **swap**.

sword [sɔ:d] *n* épée *f*. ●**swordfish** *n* espadon *m*.

swore, sworn [swɔ:r, swɔ:n] *pt* & *pp* of **swear**.

swot [swɒt] *vti* (**-tt-**) **to s. (up)** (*study*)

Fam potasser; **to s. (up) for** (*exam*) *Fam* potasser.

swum [swʌm] *pp of* swim.

swung [swʌŋ] *pt & pp of* swing.

sycamore ['sɪkəmɔːr] *n* (*maple tree*) sycomore *m*; (*plane tree*) *Am* platane *m*.

syllable ['sɪləb(ə)l] *n* syllabe *f*.

syllabus ['sɪləbəs] *n* programme *m* (scolaire).

symbol ['sɪmb(ə)l] *n* symbole *m*. ● **sym'bolic** *a* symbolique. ● **symbolize** *vt* symboliser.

sympathy ['sɪmpəθɪ] *n* (*pity*) compassion *f*; (*understanding*) compréhension *f*; (*when s.o. dies*) condoléances *fpl*; (*solidarity*) solidarité *f* (**for** avec); (**political**) **sympathies** tendances *fpl* (politiques); **he's in s. with,** he has **sympathies with** (*workers in dispute*) il est du côté de. ● **sympa'thetic** *a* (*showing pity*) compatissant; (*understanding*) compréhensif; **s. to** bien disposé à l'égard de. ● **sympathize** *vi* **I s. (with you)** (*pity*) je suis désolé (pour vous); (*understanding*) je vous comprends. ● **sympathizer** *n Pol* sympathisant, -ante *mf*.

symphony ['sɪmfənɪ] *n* symphonie *f* ▮ *a* (*orchestra, concert*) symphonique.

symptom ['sɪmptəm] *n* symptôme *m*.

synagogue ['sɪnəgɒg] *n* synagogue *f*.

synchronize ['sɪŋkrənaɪz] *vt* synchroniser.

syndicate ['sɪndɪkət] *n* (*of businessmen*) syndicat *m*.

syndrome ['sɪndrəʊm] *n Med & Fig* syndrome *m*.

synonym ['sɪnənɪm] *n* synonyme *m*. ● **sy'nonymous** *a* synonyme (**with** de).

synopsis, *pl* **-opses** [sɪ'nɒpsɪs, -ɒpsi:z] *n* résumé *m*.

synthetic [sɪn'θetɪk] *a* synthétique.

Syria ['sɪrɪə] *n* Syrie *f*. ● **Syrian** *a & n* syrien, -ienne (*mf*).

syringe [sɪ'rɪndʒ] *n* seringue *f*.

syrup ['sɪrəp] *n* sirop *m*; (**golden**) **s.** (*treacle*) mélasse *f* (raffinée).

system ['sɪstəm] *n* (*structure etc*) & *Anat Comptr etc* système *m*; (*human body*) organisme *m*; (*order*) méthode *f*; **the immune s.** le système immunitaire; **operating s.** *Comptr* système *m* d'exploitation; **systems analyst** analyste-programmeur, -euse *mf*. ● **syste'matic** *a* systématique.

T

T, t [ti:] *n* T, t *m*. ● **T-shirt** *n* tee-shirt *m*.

ta! [tɑ:] *int Sl* merci!

tab [tæb] *n* (*cloth etc flap*) patte *f*; (*label*) étiquette *f*; (*on can of drink*) languette *f*; (*bill*) *Am* addition *f*; **to keep tabs on** *Fam* surveiller (de près).

table[1] ['teɪb(ə)l] *n* **1** (*furniture*) table *f*; **bedside/card/operating t.** table de nuit/ de jeu/d'opération; **to lay** *or* **set/clear the t.** mettre/débarrasser la table; (**sitting**) **at the t.** à table; **t. wine** vin *m* de table. **2** (*list*) table *f*; **t. of contents** table des matières. ● **tablecloth** *n* nappe *f*. ● **tablemat** *n* (*of cloth*) napperon *m*; (*hard*) dessous-de-plat *m inv*. ● **tablespoon** *n* = cuillère *f* à soupe. ● **tablespoonful** *n* (**to a t.**) = cuillère *f* à soupe.

table[2] ['teɪb(ə)l] *vt* (*motion*) *Pol* présenter; (*postpone*) *Am* ajourner.

tablet ['tæblɪt] *n* **1** (*pill*) comprimé *m*. **2** (*inscribed stone*) plaque *f*.

tabloid ['tæblɔɪd] *n* (*newspaper*) quotidien *m* populaire.

taboo [tə'bu:] *a* & *n* tabou (*m*).

tacit ['tæsɪt] *a* tacite.

tack [tæk] **1** *n* (*nail*) petit clou *m*; (*thumbtack*) *Am* punaise *f* ‖ *vt* **to t. (down)** clouer. **2** *n* (*stitch*) point *m* de bâti ‖ *vt* **to t. (down)** bâtir; **to t. on** (*add*) *Fig* ajouter. **3** *n* (*course of action*) *Fig* voie *f*.

tackle ['tæk(ə)l] **1** *n* (*gear*) matériel *m*. **2** *vt* (*problem etc*) s'attaquer à; (*thief*) saisir (à bras-le-corps); *Rugby* plaquer; *Fb* tacler.

tacky ['tækɪ] *a* (**-ier, -iest**) **1** (*wet*) pas sec (*f* sèche). **2** *Fam* (*in appearance*) moche; (*remark etc*) de mauvais goût.

tact [tækt] *n* tact *m*. ● **tactful** *a* (*remark etc*) plein de tact; **to be t.** (*of person*) avoir du tact. ● **tactfully** *adv* avec tact. ● **tactless** *a* qui manque de tact.

tactic ['tæktɪk] *n* **a t.** une tactique; **tactics** la tactique. ● **tactical** *a* tactique.

tadpole ['tædpəʊl] *n* têtard *m*.

taffy ['tæfɪ] *n* (*toffee*) *Am* caramel *m* (*dur*).

tag [tæg] **1** *n* (*label*) étiquette *f*. **2** *vi* (**-gg-**) **to t. along** (*follow*) suivre.

Tahiti [tɑ:'hi:tɪ] *n* Tahiti *m*.

tail [teɪl] **1** *n* (*of animal etc*) queue *f*; (*of shirt*) pan *m*; *pl* (*outfit*) queue-de-pie *f*; **t. end** fin *f*, bout *m*; **heads or tails?** pile ou face? **2** *vt* (*follow*) suivre, filer. **3** *vi* **to t. off** (*lessen*) diminuer. ● **tailback** *n* (*of traffic*) bouchon *m*. ● **tailgate** *n Aut* hayon *m*. ● **taillight** *n Aut Am* feu *m* arrière *inv*.

tailor ['teɪlər] *n* (*person*) tailleur ‖ *vt* (*adjust*) *Fig* adapter (**to**, **to suit** à). ● **t.-made** *a* fait sur mesure; **t.-made for** (*specially designed*) conçu pour.

tainted ['teɪntɪd] *a* (*air*) pollué; (*food*) gâté.

take [teɪk] *vt* (*pt* **took**, *pp* **taken**) prendre; (*prize*) remporter; (*exam*) passer; (*choice*) faire; (*contain*) contenir; *Math* soustraire (**from** de); (*tolerate*) supporter; (*bring*) amener (*qn* **to** à); (*by car*) conduire (*qn* **to** à); (*escort*) accompagner (*qn* **to** à); (*lead away*) emmener (*qn* **to** à); (*of road*) mener (*qn* **to** à); **to t. s.o. to** (*theatre etc*) emmener qn à; **to t. sth to s.o.** (ap)porter qch à qn; **to t. sth with one** emporter qch; **to t. s.o. home** (*on foot, by car*) ramener qn; **it takes an army/courage/***etc* il faut une armée/du courage/*etc* (**to do** pour faire); **I took an hour to do it** j'ai mis une heure à le faire.

take after *vt* **to t. after s.o.** ressembler à qn ‖ **take along** *vt* (*object*) emporter; (*person*) emmener ‖ **take apart** *vt* (*machine*) démonter ‖ **take away** *vt* (*thing*) emporter; (*person*) emmener; (*remove*) enlever (**from** à); *Math* soustraire (**from** de) ▮ **to take back** *vt* reprendre; (*return*) rapporter; (*accompany*) ramener (*qn*) (**to** à) ▮ **to take down** *vt* (*object*) descendre; (*notes*) prendre ▮ **to take in** *vt* (*chair, car etc*) rentrer; (*orphan*) recueillir; (*skirt*) reprendre; (*include*) comprendre; (*understand*) comprendre; (*deceive*) *Fam* rouler ▮ **to take off** *vt* (*remove*) enlever; (*lead away*) emmener; (*mimic*) imiter; *Math* déduire (**from** de) ▮ *vi* (*of aircraft*) décoller ▮ **to take on** *vt* (*work, staff, passenger, shape*) prendre ▮ **to take out** *vt* (*from pocket etc*) sortir; (*stain*) enlever; (*tooth*) arracher; (*insurance*) prendre; **to t. s.o. out to** (*theatre etc*) emmener qn à ▮ **to take over** *vt* (*company etc*) prendre la direction de; (*overrun*) envahir; (*buy out*) racheter (*compagnie*); **to t. over s.o.'s job** remplacer qn ▮ *vi* prendre la relève (**from** de); (*permanently*) prendre la succession (**from** de) ▮ **to take round** *vt* (*bring*) apporter (*qch*) (**to** à); amener (*qn*) (**to** à); (*distribute*) distribuer; (*visitor*) faire visiter ▮ **to take to** *vt* **to t. to doing** se mettre à faire; **I didn't t. to him/it** il/ça ne m'a pas plu ▮ **to take up** *vt* (*carry up*) monter; (*continue*) reprendre; (*space, time*) prendre; (*offer*) accepter; (*hobby*) se mettre à.

take-away ['teɪkəweɪ] *a* (*meal*) à emporter ▮ *n* (*shop*) restaurant *m* qui fait des plats à emporter; (*meal*) plat *m* à emporter. ● **takeoff** *n* (*of aircraft*) décollage *m*. ● **take-out** *a* & *n Am* = **take-away.** ● **take-over** *Com* rachat *m*.

taken ['teɪk(ə)n] *a* (*seat*) pris; **to be t. ill** tomber malade.

takings ['teɪkɪŋz] *npl* (*money*) recette *f*.

talcum ['tælkəm] *a* **t. powder** talc *m*.

tale [teɪl] *n* (*story*) conte *m*; (*account*) récit *m*; (*lie*) histoire *f*; **to tell tales** rapporter (**on** sur).

talent ['tælənt] *n* talent *m*; (*talented people*) talents *mpl*; **to have a t. for** avoir du talent pour. ● **talented** *a* doué.

talk [tɔːk] *n* (*words*) propos *mpl*; (*gossip*) bavardage(s) *m(pl)*; (*conversation*) conversation *f*; (*lecture*) exposé *m* (**on** sur); (*informal*) causerie *f* (**on** sur); (*interview*) entretien *m*; *pl* (*negotiations*) pourparlers *mpl*; **to have a t. with s.o.** parler avec qn; **there's t. of** on parle de. ▮ *vi* parler (**to** à; **with** avec; **about, of** de); (*chat*) bavarder; ▮ *vt* (*nonsense*) dire; **to t. politics** parler politique; **to t. s.o. into doing/out of doing** persuader qn de faire/de ne pas faire; **to t. sth over** discuter (de) qch. ● **talking-to** *n* **to give s.o. a t.-to** *Fam* passer un savon à qn.

talkative ['tɔːkətɪv] *a* bavard.

tall [tɔːl] *a* (**-er, -est**) (*person*) grand; (*tree, house, wall etc*) haut; **how t. are you?** combien mesures-tu?; **a t. story** *Fig* une histoire invraisemblable.

tally ['tælɪ] *vi* correspondre (**with** à).

tambourine [tæmbə'riːn] *n* tambourin *m*.

tame [teɪm] *a* (**-er, -est**) (*animal*) apprivoisé; (*person*) *Fig* docile; (*book*) fade ▮ *vt* apprivoiser; (*lion*) dompter.

tamper ['tæmpər] *vi* **to t. with** (*lock, car etc*) essayer de forcer; (*machine etc*) toucher à; (*text*) altérer. ● **t.-proof** *a* (*seal*) de sécurité; (*lock*) inviolable; (*jar*) à fermeture de sécurité.

tampon ['tæmpɒn] *n* tampon *m* (périodique).

tan [tæn] **1** *n* (*suntan*) bronzage *m* ▮ *vti* (**-nn-**) bronzer. **2** *a* (*colour*) marron clair *inv*.

tandem ['tændəm] *n* **1** (*bicycle*) tandem *m*. **2** **in t.** (*to work*) en tandem.

tang [tæŋ] *n* (*taste*) saveur *f* piquante; (*smell*) odeur *f* piquante. ● **tangy** *a* (**-ier, -iest**) piquant.

tangerine [tændʒə'riːn] *n* mandarine *f*.

tangle ['tæŋg(ə)l] *n* **to get into a t.** (*of rope*) s'enchevêtrer; (*of hair*) s'emmêler. ● **tangled** *a* enchevêtré; (*hair*) emmêlé; **to get t.** = **to get into a tangle.**

tank [tæŋk] *n* **1** (*for storing liquid or gas*) réservoir *m*; (*vat*) cuve *f*; (*fish*) **t.** aquarium *m*. **2** (*vehicle*) *Mil* char *m*. **3** *vi* **to t.**

up on (snacks etc) Fam se remplir le ventre de.

tanker ['tæŋkər] n (truck) Aut camion-citerne m; (oil) t. (ship) pétrolier m.

Tannoy® ['tænɔɪ] n over the T. au(x) haut-parleur(s).

tantalizing ['tæntəlaɪzɪŋ] a (irrésistible-ment) tentant.

tantamount ['tæntəmaʊnt] a it's t. to cela équivaut à.

tantrum ['tæntrəm] n colère f; to have a t. (of child) faire une colère.

tap [tæp] 1 n (for water) robinet m; on t. Fig disponible. 2 vti (-pp-) (hit) frapper légèrement, tapoter ▮ n petit coup m; t. dancing claquettes fpl. 3 vt (-pp-) (phone) placer sur table d'écoute. 4 vt (-pp-) (resources) exploiter.

tape [teɪp] 1 n ruban m; (sticky or adhesive) t. ruban adhésif; t. measure mètre m (à) ruban ▮ vt (stick) coller (avec du ruban adhésif). 2 n (for sound or video recording) bande f (magnétique or vidéo); t. recorder magnétophone m; t. deck platine f cassette ▮ vt (a film, music, voice etc) enregistrer; (event) faire une cassette de ▮ vi enregistrer.

taper ['teɪpər] 1 vi (of fingers etc) s'effiler; to t. off Fig diminuer. 2 n (candle) Rel cierge m. ●—ed a (trousers, Am pants) à bas étroits. ●—ing a (fingers) fuselé.

tapestry ['tæpɪstrɪ] n tapisserie f.

tar [tɑːr] n goudron m ▮ vt (-rr-) gou-dronner.

target ['tɑːgɪt] n cible f; (objective) objectif m; vt (campaign, product etc) destiner (at à); (age group etc) viser.

tariff ['tærɪf] n (tax) tarif m douanier; (price list) tarif m.

tarmac ['tɑːmæk] n macadam m (gou-dronné); (runway) piste f.

tarnish ['tɑːnɪʃ] vt ternir.

tarpaulin [tɑːˈpɔːlɪn] n bâche f (gou-dronnée).

tart [tɑːt] 1 n (pie) (open) tarte f; (with pastry on top) tourte f. 2 a (-er, -est) (taste) aigre.

tartan ['tɑːt(ə)n] n tartan m ▮ a (skirt etc)

écossais.

tartar ['tɑːtər] a t. sauce sauce f tartare.

task [tɑːsk] n travail m, tâche f; t. force Mil détachement m spécial; Pol com-mission f spéciale.

tassel ['tas(ə)l] n (on clothes etc) gland m.

taste [teɪst] n goût m; (general idea) Fig idée f, aperçu m; in good/bad t. de bon/mauvais goût; to have a t. of goûter; (try) goûter à ▮ vt (eat, drink) goûter; (try) goûter à; (make out the taste of) sentir (le goût de) ▮ vi to t. of or like avoir un goût de; to t. delicious/etc avoir un goût délicieux/etc. ●tasteful ['teɪstfəl] a de bon goût. ●taste-fully adv avec goût. ●tasteless a (food etc) sans goût; (joke etc) Fig de mauvais goût. ●tasty a (-ier, -iest) savoureux.

tattered ['tætəd] a (clothes) en lambeaux. ●tatters npl in t. en lambeaux.

tattoo [tæˈtuː] 1 n (pl -oos) (on body) tatouage m ▮ vt tatouer. 2 n (pl -oos) Mil spectacle m militaire.

tatty ['tætɪ] a (-ier, -iest) (clothes etc) Fam miteux.

taught [tɔːt] pt & pp of teach.

taunt [tɔːnt] vt railler ▮ n raillerie f.

Taurus ['tɔːrəs] n (sign) le Taureau.

taut [tɔːt] a (rope etc) tendu.

tavern ['tævən] n taverne f.

tax[1] [tæks] n (on goods) taxe f, impôt m; (on income) impôts mpl ▮ a fiscal; t. collector percepteur m; t. relief dégrè-vement m (d'impôt); (road) t. disc vignette f (automobile) ▮ vt (person) imposer; (goods) taxer. ●taxable a imposable. ●taxation [-ˈeɪʃ(ə)n] n (taxes) impôts mpl; the burden of t. le poids de l'impôt. ●tax-free a exempt d'impôts. ●taxman n (pl -men) Fam percepteur m. ●taxpayer n contri-buable mf.

tax[2] [tæks] vt (patience) mettre à l'épreuve; (tire) fatiguer.

taxi ['tæksɪ] 1 n taxi m; t. cab taxi m; t. rank, Am t. stand station f de taxis. 2 vi (of aircraft) rouler au sol.

TB [ti:'bi:] n tuberculose f.

tea [ti:] n thé m; (snack) goûter m; **high t.** goûter m (dînatoire); **to have t.** prendre le thé; (afternoon snack) goûter; **t. break** pause-thé f; **t. cloth** (for drying dishes) torchon m; **t. party** thé m; **t. set** service m à thé; **t. towel** torchon m. ● **teabag** n sachet m de thé. ● **teacup** n tasse f à thé. ● **teapot** n théière f. ● **tearoom** n salon m de thé. ● **teaspoon** n petite cuillère f. ● **teaspoonful** n cuillerée f à café. ● **teatime** n l'heure f du thé.

teach [ti:tʃ] vt (pt & pp taught) apprendre (s.o. sth qch à qn, that que); (in school etc) enseigner (s.o. sth qch à qn); **to t. s.o. (how) to do** apprendre à qn à faire ● ─ vi enseigner. ● ─**ing** n enseignement m ▮ a (method, material) pédagogique; **the t. profession** l'enseignement m; (teachers) le corps enseignant; **t. staff** personnel m enseignant.

teacher ['ti:tʃər] n professeur m; (in primary school) instituteur, -trice mf.

team [ti:m] n Sp équipe f; (of horses) attelage m; **t. mate** coéquipier, -ière mf ▮ vi **to t. up** faire équipe (with avec). ● **teamster** n Am routier m. ● **teamwork** n collaboration f.

tear[1] [teər] 1 n déchirure f ▮ vt (pt tore, pp torn) (rip) déchirer; (snatch) arracher (from s.o. à qn); **torn between** Fig tiraillé entre; **to t. down** (house) démolir; **to t. off** or **out** (remove with force) arracher; (receipt, stamp etc) détacher; **to t. up** déchirer ▮ vi (of cloth etc) se déchirer. 2 vi (pt tore, pp torn) **to t. along/off** (rush) aller/partir à toute vitesse.

tear[2] [tiər] n larme f; **in tears** en larmes; **close to tears** au bord des larmes. ● **tearful** a (eyes, voice) larmoyant; (person) en larmes. ● **teargas** n gaz m lacrymogène.

tearaway ['teərəwei] n Fam casse-cou m.

tease [ti:z] vt taquiner; (harshly) tourmenter.

teat [ti:t] n (of bottle, animal) tétine f.

technical ['teknik(ə)l] a technique. ● **techni'cality** n (detail) détail m technique. ● **technically** adv techniquement; Fig théoriquement. ● **tech'nician** n technicien, -ienne mf. ● **tech'nique** n technique f. ● **technocrat** n technocrate m. ● **techno'logical** a technologique. ● **tech'nology** n technologie f.

teddy ['tedi] n **t. (bear)** ours m (en peluche).

tedious ['ti:diəs] a fastidieux.

teem [ti:m] vi 1 (swarm) grouiller (**with** de). 2 **to t. (with rain)** pleuvoir à torrents.

teenage ['ti:neidʒ] a (boy, girl) adolescent; (fashion) pour adolescents. ● **teenager** n adolescent, -ente mf. ● **teens** npl **in one's t.** adolescent.

teeny (**weeny**) ['ti:ni('wi:ni)] a Fam minuscule.

tee-shirt ['ti:ʃɜ:t] n tee-shirt m.

teeth [ti:θ] see **tooth**.

teeth/e [ti:ð] vi faire ses dents. ● ─**ing** n dentition f; **t. ring** anneau m de dentition; **t. troubles** Fig difficultés fpl de mise en route.

teetotaller [ti:'təut(ə)lər] n personne f qui ne boit pas d'alcool.

tele- ['teli] pref télé-.

telecommunications [telikəmju:ni'keiʃ(ə)nz] npl télécommunications fpl.

telegram ['teligræm] n télégramme m.

telegraph ['teligra:f] a **t. pole/wire** poteau m/fil m télégraphique.

Telemessage® ['telimesidʒ] n (in UK) = télégramme m.

telephone ['telifəun] n téléphone m; **on the t.** (speaking) au téléphone ▮ a (call, line, message) téléphonique; **t. booth, t. box** cabine f téléphonique; **t. directory** annuaire m du téléphone; **t. number** numéro m de téléphone ▮ vi téléphoner ▮ vt (message) téléphoner (**to** à); **to t. s.o.** téléphoner à qn. ● **te'lephonist** n standardiste mf.

telephoto ['telifəutəu] a **t. lens** téléobjectif m.

teleprinter ['telɪprɪntər] n téléscripteur m.

telescope ['telɪskəup] n télescope m. ●**tele'scopic** a (umbrella etc) télescopique.

teletypewriter [telɪ'taɪpraɪtər] n Am téléscripteur m.

televise ['telɪvaɪz] vt retransmettre à la télévision. ●**tele'vision** n télévision f; on (the) t. à la télévision; t. set téléviseur m ▮ a (programme, screen etc) de télévision; (interview etc) télévisé.

telex ['teleks] n (service, message) télex m ▮ vt envoyer par télex.

tell [tel] vt (pt & pp told) dire (s.o. sth qch à qn, that que); (story) raconter; (distinguish) distinguer (from de); (know) savoir; to t. s.o. to do dire à qn de faire; to know how to t. the time savoir lire l'heure; to t. the difference voir la différence; to t. s.o. off Fam disputer qn.
▮ vi dire; (have an effect) avoir un effet; (know) savoir; to t. of or about sth/s.o. parler de qch/qn; to t. on s.o. Fam rapporter sur qn. ●**telltale** n Fam rapporteur, -euse mf.

teller ['telər] n (bank) t. guichetier, -ière mf (de banque).

telly ['telɪ] n Fam télé f.

temp [temp] n (secretary) Fam intérimaire mf.

temper ['tempər] 1 n (mood, nature) humeur f; to lose one's t. se mettre en colère; in a bad t. de mauvaise humeur; to have a (bad) t. avoir un caractère de cochon. 2 vt (moderate) tempérer.

temperament ['temp(ə)rəmənt] n tempérament m. ●**tempera'mental** a (person, machine) capricieux.

temperate ['tempərət] a (climate) tempéré.

temperature ['temp(ə)rətʃər] n température f; to have a t. Med avoir de la température or de la fièvre.

template ['templət] n (of plastic, metal etc) patron m.

temple ['temp(ə)l] n 1 (building) Rel temple m. 2 Anat tempe f.

tempo ['tempəu] n (pl -os) (of life etc) rythme m.

temporary ['temp(ə)rərɪ, Am -erɪ] a provisoire; (job) temporaire; (secretary) intérimaire.

tempt [tempt] vt tenter; tempted to do tenté de faire; to t. s.o. to do persuader qn de faire. ●**tempta-tion** [-'teɪʃ(ə)n] n tentation f.

ten [ten] a & n dix (m). ●**tenfold** a t. increase augmentation f par dix ▮ adv to increase t. (se) multiplier par dix.

tenacious [tə'neɪʃəs] a tenace.

tenant ['tenənt] n locataire nmf. ●**te-nancy** n (lease) location f; (period) occupation f.

tend [tend] 1 vi to t. to do avoir tendance à faire; to t. towards incliner vers. 2 vt (look after) s'occuper de. ●**tendency** n tendance f (to do à faire).

tender¹ ['tendər] a (soft, loving) tendre; (painful) sensible. ●**—ness** n tendresse f; (pain) (petite) douleur f.

tender² ['tendər] 1 vt (offer) offrir; to t. one's resignation donner sa démission. 2 n to be legal t. (of money) avoir cours. 3 n (for services etc) soumission f (for pour).

tenement ['tenəmənt] n immeuble m (de rapport).

tenner ['tenər] n Fam billet m de dix livres.

tennis ['tenɪs] n tennis m; table t. tennis de table; t. court court m (de tennis).

tenor ['tenər] n Mus ténor m.

tenpin ['tenpɪn] a t. bowling bowling m. ●**tenpins** n Am bowling m.

tense [tens] 1 a (-er, -est) (person, muscle, situation) tendu ▮ vt tendre, crisper. 2 n Gram temps m.

tension ['tenʃ(ə)n] n tension f.

tent [tent] n tente f; t. peg piquet m de tente.

tentacle ['tentək(ə)l] n tentacule m.

tentative ['tentətɪv] a (not definite) provisoire; (hesitant) timide. ●**—ly** adv provisoirement.

tenterhooks ['tentəhʊks] *npl* on t. (*anxious*) sur des charbons ardents.

tenth [tenθ] *a & n* dixième (*mf*); **a t.** un dixième.

tenuous ['tenjʊəs] *a* (*link*) ténu.

tepid ['tepɪd] *a* (*liquid*) & *Fig* tiède.

term [tɜːm] *n* (*word*) terme *m*; (*period*) période *f*; (*of school year*) trimestre *m*; (*semester*) *Am* semestre *m*; *pl* (*conditions*) conditions *fpl*; (*prices*) prix *mpl*; **t. (of office)** *Pol* mandat *m*; **easy terms** *Fin* facilités *fpl* de paiement; **on good/ bad terms** en bons/mauvais termes (**with** s.o. avec qn); **on close terms** intime (**with** avec); **in terms of** (*speaking of*) sur le plan de; **to come to terms with** (*situation*) faire face à; **in the long/ short t.** à long/court terme ‖ *vt* (*name, call*) appeler.

terminal ['tɜːmɪn(ə)l] **1** *n* (*air*) t. aérogare *f*; (*computer*) t. terminal *m* (d'ordinateur); (*oil*) t. terminal *m* (pétrolier). **2** *a* (*patient, illness*) incurable; **in its t. stage** (*illness*) en phase terminale. ● **—ly** *adv* **t. ill** (*patient*) incurable.

terminate ['tɜːmɪneɪt] *vt* mettre fin à; (*contract*) résilier; (*pregnancy*) interrompre.

terminus ['tɜːmɪnəs] *n* terminus *m*.

termite ['tɜːmaɪt] *n* (*insect*) termite *m*.

terrace ['terɪs] *n* terrasse *f*; (*houses*) maisons *fpl* en bande; **the terraces** *Sp* les gradins *mpl*. ● **terraced house** *n* maison *f* attenante aux maisons voisines.

terrain [tə'reɪn] *n* *Mil Geol* terrain *m*.

terrible ['terəb(ə)l] *a* affreux, terrible. ● **terribly** *adv* (*badly, very*) affreusement.

terrier ['terɪər] *n* (*dog*) terrier *m*.

terrific [tə'rɪfɪk] *a* (*excellent, very great*) *Fam* formidable, terrible. ● **terrifically** *adv* *Fam* (*extremely*) terriblement; (*extremely well*) terriblement bien.

terrify ['terɪfaɪ] *vt* terrifier; **to be terrified of** avoir très peur de. ● **—ing** *a* terrifiant.

territory ['terɪtərɪ] *n* territoire *m*.

terror ['terər] *n* terreur *f*; (*child*) *Fam* polisson, -onne *mf*. ● **terrorism** *n* terrorisme *m*. ● **terrorist** *n & a* terroriste (*mf*). ● **terrorize** *vt* terroriser.

terry(cloth) ['terɪ(klɒθ)] *n* tissu-éponge *m*.

terse [tɜːs] *a* laconique.

Terylene® ['terəliːn] *n* tergal® *m*.

test [test] *vt* (*try*) essayer; (*product, machine*) tester; (*pupil*) interroger; (*of doctor*) examiner (*les yeux etc*); (*analyse*) analyser (*le sang etc*); (*courage*) *Fig* éprouver.

‖ *n* (*trial*) essai *m*; (*of product*) test *m*; *Sch* interrogation *f*, test *m*; (*by doctor*) examen *m*; (*of blood etc*) analyse *f*; **driving t.** (examen *m* du) permis *m* de conduire; **eye t.** examen *m* de la vue.

‖ *a* (*pilot, flight*) d'essai; **t. match** *Sp* match *m* international; **t. tube** éprouvette *f*; **t. tube baby** bébé *m* éprouvette.

testament ['testəmənt] *n* testament *m*; **Old/New T.** *Rel* Ancien/Nouveau Testament.

testicle ['testɪk(ə)l] *n* *Anat* testicule *m*.

testify ['testɪfaɪ] *vi* *Jur* témoigner (**against** contre); **to t. to sth** témoigner de qch ‖ *vt* **to t. that** *Jur* témoigner que. ● **testi'monial** *n* références *fpl*.

tetanus ['tetənəs] *n* *Med* tétanos *m*.

tether ['teðər] *n* **at the end of one's t.** à bout (de nerfs).

text [tekst] *n* texte *m*. ● **textbook** *n* manuel *m* (scolaire).

textile ['tekstaɪl] *a & n* textile (*m*).

texture ['tekstʃər] *n* (*of fabric etc*) texture *f*; (*of paper, wood*) grain *m*.

Thames [temz] *n* **the T.** la Tamise.

than [ðən, *stressed* ðæn] *conj* **1** que; **happier t.** plus heureux que; **he has more t. you** il en a plus que toi; **fewer oranges t. plums** moins d'oranges que de prunes. **2** (*with numbers*) de; **more t. six** plus de six.

thank [θæŋk] *vt* remercier (**for sth** de qch, **for doing** d'avoir fait); **t. you** merci (**for sth** pour *or* de qch, **for doing** d'avoir fait); **no, t. you** (non) merci; **t.**

God, t. **heavens** Dieu merci.
▮**n**pl remerciements *mpl*; **(many)**
thanks! merci (beaucoup)!; **thanks to**
(*because of*) grâce à. ● **thankful** *a* reconnaissant (for de); t. that bien heureux
que (+ *sub*). ● **thankless** *a* ingrat.
●**Thanks'giving (day)** *n Am* jour *m*
d'action de grâce(s).

that [ðət, *stressed* ðæt] **1** *conj* que; **to say**
t. dire que.

2 *rel pron* (*subject*) qui; (*object*) que;
(*with prep*) lequel, laquelle, *pl* les-
quel(le)s; **the boy t. left** le garçon qui
est parti; **the book t.** I read le livre que
j'ai lu; **the carpet t.** I put it on le tapis sur
lequel je l'ai mis; **the house t. she told me
about** la maison dont elle m'a parlé; **the
day/morning t. she arrived** le jour/matin
où elle est arrivée.

3 *dem a* (*pl see* those) ce, cet (*before
vowel or mute h*), cette; (*opposed to
'this'*) ... + -là; **t. day** ce jour; ce
jour-là; **t. girl** cette fille; cette fille-là.

4 *dem pron* (*pl see* those) ça, cela; ce; **t.
(one)** celui-là *m*, celle-là *f*; **give me t.**
donne-moi ça *or* cela; **I prefer t. (one)** je
préfère celui-là; **before t.** avant ça *or*
cela; **t.'s right** c'est juste; **who's t.?** qui
est-ce?; **t.'s the house** c'est la maison;
(*pointing*) voilà la maison; **t. is (to
say)**... c'est-à-dire....

5 *adv* (*so*) *Fam* si; **not t. good** pas si bon;
t. high (*pointing*) haut comme ça; **t.
much** (*to cost etc*) (au)tant que ça.

thatched [θætʃt] *a* (*roof*) de chaume; **t.
cottage** chaumière *f*.

thaw [θɔ:] *n* dégel *m* ▮ *vi* dégeler; (*of
snow, ice*) fondre; (*of food*) décongeler;
it's thawing ça dégèle ▮ *vt* (*snow etc*)
faire fondre; **to t. (out)** (*food*) (faire)
décongeler.

the [ðə, *before vowel* ði, *stressed* ði:] *def
art* le, l', la, *pl* les; **t. roof** le toit; **t. man**
l'homme; **t. moon** la lune; **t. orange**
l'orange; **t. boxes** les boîtes; **the smallest** le plus petit; **of t., from t.** du, de l',
de la, *pl* des; **to t., at t.** au, à l', à la, *pl*
aux; **Elizabeth t. Second** Élisabeth

Deux.

theatre ['θɪətər] *n* (*place, art*) théâtre *m*.
●**theatregoer** *n* amateur *m* de théâtre.
●**the'atrical** *a* théâtral; **t. company**
troupe *f* de théâtre.

theft [θeft] *n* vol *m*.

their [ðeər] *poss a* leur, *pl* leurs; **t. house**
leur maison *f*. ● **theirs** [ðeəz] *poss pron*
le leur, la leur, *pl* les leurs; **this book is t.**
ce livre est à eux *or* est le leur; **a friend
of t.** un ami à eux.

them [ðəm, *stressed* ðem] *pron* les; (*after
prep, 'than', 'it is'*) eux *mpl*, elles *fpl*; **(to)
t.** leur; **I see t.** je les vois; **I give (to) t.** je
leur donne; **with t.** avec eux, avec elles;
ten of t. dix d'entre eux *or* elles; **all of t.
came** tous sont venus, toutes sont
venues; **I like all of t.** je les aime tous
or toutes.

theme [θi:m] *n* thème *m*; **t. music** musique *f* (de film); **t. song** chanson *f* (de
film); **t. park** parc *m* (de loisirs) à
thème.

themselves [ðem'selvz] *pron* eux-
mêmes *mpl*, elles-mêmes *fpl*; (*reflexive*) se, s'; (*after prep etc*) eux *mpl*,
elles *fpl*; **they wash t.** ils *or* elles se
lavent; **they think of t.** ils pensent à
eux, elles pensent à elles.

then [ðen] **1** *adv* (*at that time*) à cette
époque-là; (*just a moment ago*) à ce
moment-là; (*next*) ensuite, puis; **from t.
on** dès lors; **before t.** avant cela; **until t.**
jusque-là ▮ *a* **the t. mayor/**etc le maire/
etc de l'époque. **2** *conj* (*therefore*) donc,
alors.

theology [θɪ'ɒlədʒɪ] *n* théologie *f*.

theory ['θɪərɪ] *n* théorie *f*; **in t.** en
théorie. ● **theo'retical** *a* théorique.

therapy ['θerəpɪ] *n* thérapeutique *f*.
● **thera'peutic** *a* thérapeutique.

there [ðeər] *adv* là; (*down or over*) t. là-
bas; **on t.** là-dessus; **t. is, t. are** il y a;
(*pointing*) voilà; **t. he is** le voilà; **t. they
are** les voilà; **that man t.** cet homme-là;
t. (you are)! (*take this*) tenez!; **t., don't
cry!** allons, ne pleure pas! ● **there-
a'bout(s)** *adv* par là; (*in amount*) à

peu près. ●**there'after** adv après cela.
●**thereby** adv de ce fait. ●**therefore** adv
donc. ●**thereu'pon** adv sur ce.

thermal ['θɜːm(ə)l] a (underwear) en
thermolactyl®; t. **springs** eaux fpl thermales.

thermometer [θə'mɒmɪtər] n thermomètre m.

Thermos® ['θɜːməs] n (pl **-es**) T. (flask
or Am bottle) thermos® m or f inv.

thermostat ['θɜːməstæt] n thermostat m.

thesaurus [θɪ'sɔːrəs] n dictionnaire m de
synonymes.

these [ðiːz] 1 dem a (sing see **this**) ces;
(opposed to 'those') . . . + -ci; t. **men** ces
hommes; ces hommes-ci. 2 dem pron
(sing see **this**) t. (**ones**) ceux-ci mpl,
celles-ci fpl; t. **are my friends** ce sont
mes amis.

thesis, pl **theses** ['θiːsɪs, 'θiːsiːz] n thèse
f.

they [ðeɪ] pron 1 ils mpl, elles fpl;
(stressed) eux mpl, elles fpl; t. **go** ils
vont, elles vont; t. **are doctors** ce sont
des médecins. 2 (people in general) on; t.
say on dit. ●**they'd** = **they had** & **they
would**. ●**they'll** = **they will**.

thick [θɪk] a (**-er, -est**) épais (f épaisse);
(stupid) Fam lourd (à spread) en
couche épaisse; (to grow) dru ∎ n in the
t. **of** (battle etc) au cœur de ●**—ly** adv
(to spread) en couche épaisse; (to grow)
dru; (populated) très. ●**—ness** n épaisseur f.

thicken ['θɪk(ə)n] vt épaissir ∎ vi (of fog
etc) s'épaissir; (of cream etc) épaissir.

thickset [θɪk'set] a (person) trapu.
●**thick-skinned** a (person) peu sensible.

thief [θiːf] n (pl **thieves**) voleur, -euse mf.
●**thieving** a voleur ∎ n vol m.

thigh [θaɪ] n cuisse f.

thimble ['θɪmb(ə)l] n dé m (à coudre).

thin [θɪn] a (**thinner, thinnest**) (slice,
paper etc) mince; (person, leg) maigre,
mince; (soup) peu épais (f épaisse);
(crowd) clairsemé; (powder) fin ∎ adv
(to spread) en couche mince; (to cut)
en tranches minces ∎ vt (**-nn-**) to t.

(**down**) (paint etc) diluer. ●**—ly** adv en
couche mince; en tranches minces;
(disguised) à peine.

thing [θɪŋ] n chose f; one's **things**
(belongings) ses affaires fpl; **poor little
t.!** pauvre petit!; **how are things?** comment ça va?; **I'll think things over** j'y
réfléchirai; **for one t. . . . , and for another
t.** d'abord . . . et ensuite. ●**thingummy** n
Fam truc m, machin m.

think [θɪŋk] vi (pt & pp **thought**) penser
(about, of à); **to t.** (carefully) réfléchir
(about, of à); **to t. of doing** penser à
faire; **to t. a lot of** penser beaucoup de
bien de; **she doesn't t. much of it** ça ne
lui dit pas grand-chose; **I can't t. of it** je
n'arrive pas à m'en souvenir.
∎ vt penser (that que); **I . . . so** je pense or
crois que oui; **what do you t. of him?** que
penses-tu de lui?; **I thought it difficult** je
l'ai trouvé difficile; **to t. sth over** réfléchir à qch; **to t. sth up** inventer qch.
●**thinker** n penseur, -euse mf.

third [θɜːd] a troisième; t. **person** or **party**
tiers m; **t.-party insurance** assurance f
au tiers; T. **World** Tiers-Monde m ∎ n
troisième mf; **a t.** (fraction) un tiers
∎ adv **to come t.** se classer troisième.
●**—ly** adv troisièmement.

third-class [θɜːd'klɑːs] a de troisième
classe. ●**t.-rate** a (très) inférieur.

thirst [θɜːst] n soif f (for de). ●**thirsty**
a (**-ier, -iest**) **to be** or **feel t.** avoir soif; **to
make s.o. t.** donner soif à qn.

thirteen [θɜː'tiːn] a & n treize (m).
●**thirteenth** a & n treizième (mf).
●**'thirtieth** a & n trentième (mf).
●**'thirty** a & n trente (m).

this [ðɪs] 1 dem a (pl see **these**) ce, cet
(before vowel or mute h), cette; (opposed
to 'that') . . . + -ci; t. **book** ce livre; ce
livre-ci; t. **photo** cette photo; cette
photo-ci. 2 dem pron (pl see **these**)
ceci; ce; t. (**one**) celui-ci m, celle-ci f;
give me t. donne-moi ceci; **I prefer t.
(one)** je préfère celui-ci; **before t.** avant
ceci; **who's t.?** qui est-ce?; t. **is Paul** c'est
Paul; (pointing) voici Paul. 3 adv (so) t.

high (*pointing*) haut comme ceci; **t. far** (*until now*) jusqu'ici.

thistle ['θɪs(ə)l] *n* chardon *m*.

thorn [θɔːn] *n* épine *f*. ● **thorny** *a* (*-ier, -iest*) (*bush etc*) épineux.

thorough ['θʌrə] *a* (*careful*) minutieux; (*knowledge, examination*) approfondi; (*liar*) parfait; (*disaster*) complet; **to give sth a t. washing**/*etc* laver/*etc* qch à fond. ●**—ly** *adv* (*completely*) tout à fait; (*carefully*) avec minutie; (*to know, clean etc*) à fond.

thoroughbred ['θʌrəbred] *n* (*horse*) pur-sang *m inv*.

thoroughfare ['θʌrəfeər] *n* artère *f*, rue *f*; 'no t.' 'passage interdit'.

those [ðəʊz] **1** *dem a* (*sing see* that) ces; (*opposed to 'these'*) ... + -là; **t. men** mes hommes; ces hommes-là. **2** *dem pron* (*sing see* that) **t.** (*ones*) ceux-là *mpl*, celles-là *fpl*; **t. are my friends** ce sont mes amis.

though [ðəʊ] **1** *conj* (*even*) **t.** bien que .(*+ sub*); **as t.** comme si. **2** *adv* (*however*) pourtant.

thought [θɔːt] *pt & pp of* think ▮ *n* pensée *f*; (*careful*) réflexion *f*; **to have second thoughts** changer d'avis.

thoughtful ['θɔːtfəl] *a* (*considerate*) gentil, attentionné; (*pensive*) pensif. ● **thoughtfully** *adv* (*considerately*) gentiment. ● **thoughtless** *a* (*towards others*) pas très gentil; (*absent-minded*) étourdi. ● **thoughtlessly** *adv* (*inconsiderately*) pas très gentiment.

thousand ['θaʊzənd] *a & n* mille *a & m inv*; **a t. pages** mille pages; **two t. pages** deux mille pages; **thousands of** des milliers de.

thrash [θræʃ] **1** *vt* **to t. s.o.** donner une correction à qn; (*defeat*) écraser qn; **to t. out** (*plan*) élaborer (à force de discussions). **2** *vi* **to t. around** (*struggle*) se débattre. ●**—ing** *n* (*beating*) correction *f*.

thread [θred] *n* (*yarn*) & Fig fil *m*; (*of screw*) pas *m* ▮ *vt* (*needle, beads*) enfiler; **to t. one's way** se faufiler. ● **threadbare** *a*

élimé, râpé.

threat [θret] *n* menace *f*. ● **threaten** *vi* menacer ▮ *vt* menacer (**to do** de faire, **with sth** de qch). ● **threatening** *a* menaçant.

three [θriː] *a & n* trois (*m*); **t.-piece suite** canapé *m* et deux fauteuils. ● **threefold** *a* triple ▮ *adv* **to increase t.** tripler.

thresh [θreʃ] *vt Agr* battre.

threshold ['θreʃhəʊld] *n* seuil *m*.

threw [θruː] *pt of* throw.

thrifty ['θrɪftɪ] *a* (*-ier, -iest*) économe.

thrill [θrɪl] *n* frisson *m*; **to get a t. out of doing** prendre plaisir à faire ▮ *vt* (*delight*) réjouir; (*excite*) faire frissonner. ●**—ed** *a* ravi (**with sth** de qch, **to do** de faire). ●**—ing** *a* passionnant. ● **thriller** *n* film *m or* roman *m* à suspense.

thriv/e [θraɪv] *vi* (*of business, plant etc*) prospérer; **she thrives on hard work** le travail lui profite. ●**—ing** *a* prospère.

throat [θrəʊt] *n* gorge *f*.

throb [θrɒb] *vi* (*-bb-*) (*of heart*) palpiter; (*of engine*) vrombir; (*vibrate*) vibrer; **my finger is throbbing** mon doigt me fait des élancements.

throes [θrəʊz] *npl* **in the t. of** au milieu de; (*illness, crisis*) en proie à; **in the t. of doing** en train de faire.

throne [θrəʊn] *n* trône *m*.

throng [θrɒŋ] *Lit n* foule *f* ▮ *vi* (*rush*) affluer ▮ *vt* (*station etc*) se presser dans.

throttle ['θrɒt(ə)l] **1** *n Aut* accélérateur *m*. **2** *vt* (*strangle*) étrangler.

through [θruː] *prep* (*place*) à travers; (*window, door*) par; (*time*) pendant; (*means*) par; (*thanks to*) grâce à; **to go or get t.** (*forest etc*) traverser; (*hole etc*) passer par; (*wall etc*) passer à travers; **Tuesday t. Saturday** *Am* de mardi à samedi.

▮ *adv* à travers; **to go t.** (*cross*) traverser; (*pass*) passer; **to let t.** laisser passer; **to be t.** (*finished*) *Am* avoir fini; **we're t.** *Am* c'est fini entre nous; **I'm t. with the book** *Am* je n'ai plus besoin du livre; **all or right t.** (*to the end*) jusqu'au bout; **t. to or till** jusqu'à; **I'll put you t.** (*to him*)

Tel je vous le passe.
▮ *a* (*train, traffic*) direct; '**no t. road**' 'voie sans issue'.

throughout [θruːˈaʊt] *prep* **t. the neighbourhood**/*etc* dans tout le quartier/*etc*; **t. the day**/*etc* pendant toute la journée/*etc* ▮ *adv* (*everywhere*) partout; (*all the time*) tout le temps.

throughway [ˈθruːweɪ] *n Am* autoroute *f*.

throw [θrəʊ] *n* (*of stone etc*) jet *m*; *Sp* lancer *m*; (*of dice*) coup *m* ▮ *vt* (*pt* **threw**, *pp* **thrown**) jeter (**to, at** à); (*stone, ball*) lancer, jeter; (*hurl*) projeter; (*of horse*) désarçonner (*qn*); (*party*) donner.

throw away *vt* (*unwanted object*) jeter; (*waste*) *Fig* gâcher ▮ **to throw back** *vt* (*ball*) renvoyer (**to** à) ▮ **to throw in** *vt* (*as extra*) *Fam* donner en prime ▮ **to throw out** *vt* (*unwanted object*) jeter; (*suggestion*) repousser; (*expel*) mettre (*qn*) à la porte ▮ **to throw up** *vt Fam* (*job*) laisser tomber; (*food*) rendre ▮ *vi* (*vomit*) *Fam* rendre.

throwaway [ˈθrəʊəweɪ] *a* (*disposable*) jetable.

thrush [θrʌʃ] *n* (*bird*) grive *f*.

thrust [θrʌst] *n* (*push, lunge etc*) coup *m* ▮ *vt* (*pt* & *pp* **thrust**) (*push*) pousser; (*put*) mettre; **to t. sth into sth** (*stick, knife etc*) enfoncer qch dans qch.

thud [θʌd] *n* bruit *m* sourd.

thug [θʌg] *n* voyou *m*.

thumb [θʌm] *n* pouce *m* ▮ *vt* **to t.** (**through**) (*book*) feuilleter; **to t. a lift** *or* **a ride** *Fam* faire du stop. ● **thumbtack** *n Am* punaise *f*.

thump [θʌmp] *vt* (*person*) frapper, cogner sur; (*table*) taper sur; **to t. one's head** se cogner la tête (**on** contre) ▮ *vi* frapper, cogner (**on** sur); (*of heart*) battre à grands coups ▮ *n* (grand) coup *m*; (*noise*) bruit *m* sourd.

thunder [ˈθʌndər] *n* tonnerre *m* ▮ *vi* (*of guns etc*) tonner; **it's thundering** il tonne; **to t. past** passer dans un bruit de tonnerre. ● **thunderbolt** *n* coup *m* de foudre; (*event*) *Fig* coup *m* de

● **thunderclap** *n* coup *m* de tonnerre.
● **thunderstorm** *n* orage *m*.

Thursday [ˈθɜːzdɪ, -deɪ] *n* jeudi *m*.

thus [ðʌs] *adv* ainsi.

thwart [θwɔːt] *vt* (*plan, person*) contrecarrer.

thyme [taɪm] *n Bot Culin* thym *m*.

tiara [tɪˈɑːrə] *n* (*of woman*) diadème *m*.

tick [tɪk] **1** *n* (*of clock*) tic-tac *m* ▮ *vi* faire tic-tac; **to t. over** (*of engine, business*) tourner au ralenti. **2** *n* (*mark*) = croix *f* ▮ *vt* **to t.** (**off**) (*on list etc*) cocher; **to s.o. off** *Fam* passer un savon à qn. **3** *n* (*insect*) tique *f*. ● **—ing** *n* (*of clock*) tic-tac *m*; **to give s.o. a t.-off** *Fam* passer un savon à qn.

ticket [ˈtɪkɪt] *n* billet *m*; (*for bus, underground, cloakroom*) ticket *m*; (*for library*) carte *f*; (*fine*) *Aut Fam* contravention *f*; *Pol Am* liste *f*; (**price**) étiquette *f*; **t. collector** contrôleur, -euse *mf*; **t. office** guichet *m*.

tickle [ˈtɪk(ə)l] *vt* chatouiller ▮ *n* chatouillement *m*. ● **ticklish** *a* (*person*) chatouilleux; (*garment*) qui chatouille.

tidbit [ˈtɪdbɪt] *n* (*food*) *Am* bon morceau *m*.

tide [taɪd] **1** *n* marée *f*; **against the t.** *Nau* & *Fig* à contre-courant. **2** *vt* **to t. s.o. over** (*help out*) dépanner qn. ● **tidal** *a* (*river*) qui a une marée; **t. wave** raz-de-marée *m inv*; (*in public opinion etc*) *Fig* vague *f* de fond.

tidings [ˈtaɪdɪŋz] *npl Lit* nouvelles *fpl*.

tidy [ˈtaɪdɪ] *a* (**-ier, -iest**) (*place, toys etc*) bien rangé; (*clothes, hair*) soigné; (*person*) (*methodical*) ordonné; (*in appearance*) soigné; (*sum*) *Fam* joli; **to make t.** ranger ▮ *vt* **to t. sth** (**up** *or* **away**) ranger qch; **to t. out** (*drawer etc*) vider; **to t. oneself up** s'arranger ▮ *vi* **to t. up** ranger. ● **tidily** *adv* (*to put away etc*) soigneusement.

tie [taɪ] *n* (*around neck*) cravate *f*; (*string, strap etc*) & *Fig* lien *m*, attache *f*; *Sp* égalité *f* de points; (*drawn match*) match *m* nul ▮ *vt* (*fasten*) attacher, lier (**to** à); (*a knot*) faire (**in** à); (*shoe*) lacer;

(*link*) lier (**to** à) **‖** *vi Sp* finir à égalité de points; *Fb* faire match nul; (*in race*) être ex aequo.

tie down *vt* attacher; **to t. s.o. down to** (*date etc*) obliger qn à accepter **‖ to tie in** *vi* (*be linked*) être lié; **to t. in with** se rapporter à **‖ to tie up** *vt* attacher (*qn*) (**to** à); (*person*) ligoter; **tied up** (*linked*) lié (**with** avec); (*busy*) *Fam* occupé.

tier [tɪər] *n* (*seats*) gradin *m*; (*of cake*) étage *m*.

tiff [tɪf] *n* petite querelle *f*.

tiger ['taɪɡər] *n* tigre *m*.

tight [taɪt] *a* (**-er, -est**) (*clothes fitting too closely*) (trop) étroit, (trop) serré; (*skintight*) ajusté, collant; (*drawer, lid*) dur; (*knot, screw*) serré; (*rope, wire*) raide; (*control*) strict; (*schedule*) serré; **a t. spot** *Fam* une situation difficile; **it's a t. squeeze** il y a juste la place **‖** *adv* (*to hold, shut*) bien; (*to squeeze*) fort.
● **tighten** *vt* **to t. (up)** (*bolt etc*) (res)serrer; (*rope*) tendre; (*security*) *Fig* renforcer **‖** *vi* **to t. up on** se montrer plus strict à l'égard de. ● **tightly** *adv* (*to hold*) bien; (*to squeeze*) fort.

tight-fitting [taɪt'fɪtɪŋ] *a* (*garment*) ajusté.
● **tightfisted** *a* avare. ● **'tightrope** *n* corde *f* raide. ● **'tightwad** *n* *Am Fam* grippe-sou *m*.

tights [taɪts] *npl* collant(s) *m(pl)*.

tile [taɪl] *n* (*on roof*) tuile *f*; (*on wall or floor*) carreau *m* **‖** *vt* (*wall, floor*) carreler. ● **—ed** *a* (*roof*) de tuiles; (*wall, floor*) carrelé.

till [tɪl] **1** *prep & conj* = **until. 2** *n* (*for money*) caisse *f* (enregistreuse). **3** *vt* (*land*) cultiver.

tilt [tɪlt] *vti* pencher **‖** *n* inclinaison *f*.

timber ['tɪmbər] *n* bois *m* (de construction); (*trees*) arbres *mpl*.

time [taɪm] *n* temps *m*; (*point in time*) moment *m*; (*period in history*) époque *f*; (*on clock*) heure *f*; (*occasion*) fois *f*; *Mus* mesure *f*; **in (the course of) t.** avec le temps; **it's t. (to do)** il est temps (de faire); **some/most of the t.** une partie/la plupart du temps; **all of the t.** tout le

temps; **in a year's t.** dans un an; **a long t.** longtemps; **a short t.** peu de temps; **to have a good t.** s'amuser (bien); **to have a hard t. doing** avoir du mal à faire; **t. off** du temps libre; **in no t. (at all)** en rien de temps; **(just) in t.** (*to arrive*) à temps (**for** sth pour qch, **to do** pour faire); **from t. to t.** de temps en temps; **what is it?** quelle heure est-il?; **the right t.** l'heure *f* exacte; **on t.** à l'heure; **at the same t.** en même temps (**as** que); (*simultaneously*) à la fois; **for the t. being** pour le moment; **at the present t.** à l'heure actuelle; **at times** parfois; **(the) next t. you come** la prochaine fois que tu viendras; **one at a t.** un à un; **ten times** ten dix fois dix; **t. bomb** bombe *f* à retardement; **t. lag** décalage *m*; **t. limit** délai *m*; **t switch** = **timer; t. zone** fuseau *m* horaire.
● **time-consuming** *a* qui prend du temps.

timeless ['taɪmləs] *a* éternel.

timely ['taɪmlɪ] *a* à propos.

timer ['taɪmər] *n* (*device*) minuteur *m*, compte-minutes *m* *inv*; (*built into appliance*) programmateur *m*; (*plugged into socket*) prise *f* programmable.

timetable ['taɪmteɪb(ə)l] *n* horaire *m*; (*in school*) emploi *m* du temps.

timid ['tɪmɪd] *a* (*afraid*) craintif; (*shy*) timide.

timing ['taɪmɪŋ] *n* (*judgment of artist etc*) rythme *m*; **the t. of** (*time*) le moment choisi pour; **what good t.!** quelle synchronisation!

tin [tɪn] *n* (*metal*) étain *m*; (*coated steel or iron*) fer-blanc *m*; (*can*) boîte *f*; **cake t.** moule *m* à gâteaux; **t. opener** ouvre-boîtes *m* *inv*. ● **tinfoil** *n* papier *m* (d')aluminium. ● **tinned** *a* en boîte.

tinge [tɪndʒ] *n* teinte *f*. ● **tinged** *a* **t. with** (*pink etc*) teinté de; (*jealousy etc*) *Fig* empreint de.

tingle ['tɪŋɡ(ə)l] *vi* picoter; **it's tingling** ça

me picote.

tinker ['tɪŋkər] *vi* **to t. (about) with** bricoler.

tinkle ['tɪŋk(ə)l] *vi* tinter.

tinsel ['tɪns(ə)l] *n* guirlandes *fpl* de Noël.

tint [tɪnt] *n* teinte *f*; (*for hair*) shampooing *m* colorant. ●**tinted** *a* (*paper, glass*) teinté; **t. glasses** verres *mpl* teintés.

tiny ['taɪnɪ] *a* (**-ier, -iest**) tout petit.

tip¹ [tɪp] **1** *n* (*end*) bout *m*; (*pointed*) pointe *f*. **2** *n* (*money*) pourboire *m* ‖ *vt* (**-pp-**) (*waiter etc*) donner un pourboire à. **3** *n* (*advice*) conseil *m*; (*information*) & *Sp* tuyau *m*; **to get a t.-off** se faire tuyauter ‖ *vt* **to t. off** (*police*) prévenir. **4** *n* (*for rubbish, Am* garbage) décharge *f*.

tip² [tɪp] *vt* (**-pp-**) **to t.** (**up or over**) (*tilt*) pencher; (*overturn*) faire basculer; **to t.** (**out**) (*liquid, load*) déverser (**into** dans) ‖ *vi* **to t.** (**up or over**) (*tilt*) pencher; (*overturn*) basculer.

tipped [tɪpt] *a* **t. cigarette** cigarette *f* (à bout) filtre.

tipsy ['tɪpsɪ] *a* (**-ier, -iest**) (*drunk*) éméché.

tiptoe ['tɪptəʊ] *n* **on t.** sur la pointe des pieds ‖ *vi* marcher sur la pointe des pieds.

tiptop ['tɪptɒp] *a Fam* excellent.

tir/e¹ ['taɪər] *vt* fatiguer; **to t. s.o. out** épuiser qn ‖ *vi* se fatiguer. ●**-ed** *a* fatigué; **to be t.** of sth/s.o./doing en avoir assez de qch/qn/de faire; **to get t. of doing** se lasser de faire. ●**-ing** *a* fatigant. ●**tiredness** *n* fatigue *f*. ●**tireless** *a* infatigable. ●**tiresome** *a* ennuyeux.

tire² ['taɪər] *n Am* pneu *m* (*pl* pneus).

tissue ['tɪʃuː] *n* (*handkerchief*) mouchoir *m* en papier; *Biol* tissu *m*; **t. paper** papier *m* de soie.

tit [tɪt] *n* **to give t. for tat** rendre coup pour coup.

titbit ['tɪtbɪt] *n* (*food*) bon morceau *m*.

titillate ['tɪtɪleɪt] *vt* exciter.

title ['taɪt(ə)l] *n* (*name, claim*) & *Sp* titre *m*; **t. deed** titre *m* de propriété; **t. role** *Th Cin* rôle *m* principal.

to [tə, *stressed* tuː] *prep* **1** à; (*towards*) vers; (*of attitude, feelings*) envers; (*right up to*) jusqu'à; **give it to him** *or* **her** donne-le-lui; **to France** en France; **to Portugal** au Portugal; **to the butcher('s)**/etc chez le boucher/etc; **the road to London** la route de Londres; **the train to Paris** le train pour Paris; **kind/cruel/** etc **to s.o.** gentil/cruel/etc pour *or* envers qn; **it's ten (minutes) to one** il est une heure moins dix; **ten to one** (*proportion*) dix contre un; **one person to a room** une personne par chambre. **2** (*with infinitive*) **to say/do/**etc dire/ faire/etc; (*in order*) **to** pour; **she tried to** elle a essayé.

3 (*with adjective*) de; à; **happy/**etc **to do** heureux/etc de faire; **it's easy/difficult/** etc **to do** c'est facile/difficile/etc à faire. ‖ *adv* **to push to** (*door*) fermer.

toad [təʊd] *n* crapaud *m*.

toadstool ['təʊdstuːl] *n* champignon *m* (vénéneux).

toast [təʊst] **1** *n* pain *m* grillé; **piece** *or* **slice of t.** tranche *f* de pain grillé, toast *m* ‖ *vt* (*bread*) (faire) griller. **2** *n* (*drink*) toast *m* ‖ *vt* (*person*) porter un toast à; (*success, event*) arroser. ●**toaster** *n* grille-pain *m inv*.

tobacco [tə'bækəʊ] *n* (*pl* -os) tabac *m*; **t. store** *Am* (bureau *m* de) tabac *m*. ●**tobacconist** *n* buraliste *mf*; **t.'s (shop)** (bureau *m* de) tabac *m*.

toboggan [tə'bɒgən] *n* luge *f*.

today [tə'deɪ] *adv* & *n* aujourd'hui *m*.

toddler ['tɒdlər] *n* petit(e) enfant *mf* en bas âge.

to-do [tə'duː] *n* (*fuss*) *Fam* histoire *f*.

toe [təʊ] **1** *n* orteil *m*; **on one's toes** *Fig* vigilant. **2** *vt* **to t. the line** (*respect the rules*) se soumettre. ●**toenail** *n* ongle *m* du pied.

toffee ['tɒfɪ] *n* caramel *m* (dur); **t. apple** pomme *f* d'amour.

together [tə'geðər] *adv* ensemble; (*at the same time*) en même temps; **t. with** avec.

toil [tɔɪl] *n* labeur *m* ‖ *vi* travailler dur.

toilet ['tɔɪlɪt] *n* (*room*) toilettes *fpl*; (*bowl,*

seat) cuvette *f or* siège *m* des toilettes; **to go to the t.** aller aux toilettes ▌*a* (*articles*) de toilette; **t. flush** chasse *f* d'eau; **t. paper** papier *m* hygiénique; **t. roll** rouleau *m* de papier hygiénique; **t. water** (*perfume*) eau *f* de toilette. ● **toiletries** *npl* articles *mpl* de toilette.

token ['təʊkən] *n* (*disc, Am disk*) jeton *m*; (*voucher*) bon *m*; (*sign*) témoignage *m*; **gift t.** chèque-cadeau *m*; **book t.** chèque-livre *m*; **record t.** chèque-disque *m*.

told [təʊld] *pt & pp of* **tell** ▌*adv* **all t.** en tout.

tolerable ['tɒlərəb(ə)l] *a* (*bearable*) tolérable; (*fairly good*) passable.

tolerant ['tɒlərənt] *a* tolérant (**of** *à* l'égard de). ● **tolerance** *n* tolérance *f*.

tolerate ['tɒləreɪt] *vt* tolérer.

toll [təʊl] **1** *n* (*fee*) péage *m* ▌*a* (*road, bridge*) à péage. **2** *n* **the death t.** le nombre de morts. **3** *vi* (*of bell*) sonner. ● **tollfree number** *n Tel Am* = numéro *m* vert.

tomato [tə'mɑːtəʊ, *Am* tə'meɪtəʊ] *n* (*pl -oes*) tomate *f*.

tomb [tuːm] *n* tombeau *m*. ● **tombstone** *n* pierre *f* tombale.

tomboy ['tɒmbɔɪ] *n* (*girl*) garçon *m* manqué.

tomcat ['tɒmkæt] *n* matou *m*.

tomorrow [tə'mɒrəʊ] *adv & n* demain (*m*); **t. morning/evening** demain matin/soir; **the day after t.** après-demain.

ton [tʌn] *n* tonne *f* (*Br = 1016 kg, Am = 907 kg*); **metric t.** tonne *f* (= *1000 kg*); **tons of** (*lots of*) *Fam* des tonnes de.

tone [təʊn] *n* ton *m*; (*of telephone, radio*) tonalité *f*; **engaged t.** *Tel* sonnerie *f* 'occupé'; **in that t.** sur ce ton; **she's t.-deaf** elle n'a pas d'oreille ▌*vt* **to t. down** atténuer; **to t. up** (*muscles*) tonifier.

tongs [tɒŋz] *npl* **sugar t.** pince *f* à sucre.

tongue [tʌŋ] *n* langue *f*; **t. in cheek** ironique(ment).

tonic ['tɒnɪk] *n Med* fortifiant *m*; **t. (water)** eau *f* gazeuse (tonique); **gin and t.** gin-tonic *m*.

tonight [tə'naɪt] *adv & n* (*this evening*) ce soir (*m*); (*during the night*) cette nuit (*f*).

tonne [tʌn] *n* (*metric*) tonne *f*.

tonsil ['tɒns(ə)l] *n* amygdale *f*. ● **tonsillitis** [tɒnsə'laɪtəs] *n* **to have t.** avoir une angine.

too [tuː] *adv* **1** trop; **t. tired to play** trop fatigué pour jouer; **t. hard to solve** trop difficile à résoudre; **t. much, t. many** trop; **t. much salt/etc** trop de sel/etc; **t. many people/etc** trop de gens/etc; **one t. many** un de trop. **2** (*also*) aussi; (*moreover*) en plus.

took [tʊk] *pt of* **take**.

tool [tuːl] *n* outil *m*; **t. bag, t. kit** trousse *f* à outils.

tooth [tuːθ] *pl* **teeth** [tuːθ, tiːθ] *n* dent *f*; **milk/wisdom t.** dent de lait/de sagesse; **t. decay** carie *f* dentaire; **to have a sweet t.** aimer les sucreries. ● **toothache** ['tuːθeɪk] *n* mal *m* de dents; **to have a t.** avoir mal aux dents. ● **toothbrush** *n* brosse *f* à dents. ● **toothpaste** *n* dentifrice *m*. ● **toothpick** *n* cure-dent *m*.

top[1] [tɒp] *n* (*of mountain, tower, tree*) sommet *m*; (*of wall, ladder, page*) haut *m*; (*of table, surface*) dessus *m*; (*of list*) tête *f*; (*of car*) toit *m*; (*of bottle, tube*) bouchon *m*; (*bottle cap*) capsule *f*; (*of saucepan*) couvercle *m*; (*of pen*) capuchon *m*; **pyjama t.** haut *m or* veste *f* de pyjama; (**at the**) **t. of the class** le premier de la classe; **on t.** sur; (*in addition to*) *Fig* en plus de; **on t.** (*in bus etc*) en haut; **from t. to bottom** de fond en comble; **the big t.** (*circus*) le chapiteau.

▌*a* (*drawer, shelf*) du haut; (*step, layer*) dernier; (*upper*) supérieur; (*in rank, exam*) premier; (*chief*) principal; (*best*) meilleur; (*distinguished*) éminent; (*maximum*) maximum; **on the t. floor** au dernier étage; **in t. gear** *Aut* en quatrième vitesse; **at t. speed** à toute vitesse; **t. copy** original *m*; **t. hat** (*chapeau m*) haut-de-forme *m*. ● **top-level** *a* (*talks*) au sommet. ● **t.-'notch** *a Fam* excellent. ● **t.-'ranking** *a* (*official*) haut placé. ● **t.-'secret** *a* ultra-secret.

top² [tɒp] *vt* (**-pp-**) (*exceed*) dépasser; **to t. up** (*glass*) remplir (de nouveau); (*coffee, tea*) remettre; **topped with** *Culin* nappé de.

top³ [tɒp] *n* (*spinning*) t. toupie *f*.

topic ['tɒpɪk] *n* sujet *m*. ● **topical** *a* d'actualité.

topless ['tɒpləs] *a* (*woman*) aux seins nus.

topple ['tɒp(ə)l] *vi* **to t. (over)** tomber ▮ *vt* **to t. (over)** faire tomber.

topsy-turvy [tɒpsɪ'tɜːvɪ] *a & adv* sens dessus dessous [sɑ̃dsydsu].

torch [tɔːtʃ] *n* (*electric*) lampe *f* électrique; (*flame*) torche *f*.

tore [tɔːr] *pt of* tear¹.

torment [tɔː'ment] *vt* (*annoy*) agacer; (*make suffer*) tourmenter ▮ ['tɔːment] *n* tourment *m*.

tornado [tɔː'neɪdəʊ] *n* (*pl* **-oes**) tornade *f*.

torpedo [tɔː'piːdəʊ] *n* (*pl* **-oes**) torpille *f*.

torrent ['tɒrənt] *n* torrent *m*. ● **torrential** [tə'ren∫(ə)l] *a* torrentiel.

tortoise ['tɔːtəs] *n* tortue *f*. ● **tortoiseshell** *a* (*comb etc*) en écaille; (*spectacles*) à monture d'écaille.

torture ['tɔːtʃər] *n* torture *f* ▮ *vt* torturer.

Tory ['tɔːrɪ] *Pol n* tory *m* ▮ *a* tory *inv*.

toss [tɒs] *vt* (*throw*) jeter, lancer (**to** à); **to t. s.o.** (*about*) (*of boat, vehicle*) ballotter qn; **to t. a coin** jouer à pile ou face ▮ *vi* **to t.** (*about*), **t. and turn** (*in one's sleep*) se tourner et se retourner; **let's t. up, let's t. (up) for it** jouons-le à pile ou face.

tot [tɒt] *n* (*tiny*) **t.** petit(e) enfant *mf*.

total ['təʊt(ə)l] *a* total; **the t. sales** le total des ventes ▮ *n* total *m* ▮ *vt* (**-ll-**, *Am* **-l-**) (*of debt, invoice*) s'élever à; **to t. (up)** (*find the total of*) totaliser; **that totals $9** ça fait neuf dollars en tout. ● **—ly** *adv* totalement.

totter ['tɒtər] *vi* chanceler.

touch [tʌtʃ] *n* (*contact*) contact *m*; (*sense*) toucher *m*; (*of painter*) *Fb Rugby* touche *f*; **a t. of** (*small amount*) un petit peu de; **to put the finishing touches to** mettre la dernière touche à; **in t. with s.o.** en contact avec qn; **to be**

out of t. with ne plus être en contact avec; (*situation*) ne plus être au courant de; **to get in t.** se mettre en contact (**with** avec); **we lost t.** on s'est perdu de vue. ▮ *vt* toucher; (*interfere with, eat*) toucher à; (*move emotionally*) toucher; (*equal*) *Fig* égaler. ▮ *vi* (*of lines, hands etc*) se toucher; **don't t.!** n'y or ne touche pas! ● **touching** (*story etc*) touchant.

touch down *vi* (*of aircraft*) atterrir ▮ **to touch on** *vt* (*subject*) aborder ▮ **to touch up** *vt* (*photo etc*) retoucher.

touchdown ['tʌtʃdaʊn] *n* *Av* atterrissage *m*; *Rugby Am Fb* essai *m*. ● **touchline** *n* *Fb Rugby* (ligne *f* de) touche *f*.

touchy ['tʌtʃɪ] *a* (**-ier, -iest**) susceptible (**about** à propos de).

tough [tʌf] *a* (**-er, -est**) (*hard*) (*meat etc*) dur; (*sturdy*) solide; (*strong*) fort; (*difficult, harsh*) dur; (*businessman*) dur en affaires; **t. guy** dur *m*. ● **toughen** *vt* (*body, person*) endurcir; (*reinforce*) renforcer.

toupee ['tuːpeɪ] *n* postiche *m*.

tour [tʊər] *n* (*journey*) voyage *m*; (*visit*) visite *f*; (*by artist, team etc*) tournée *f*; (**package**) **t.** voyage *m* organisé; **on t.** en voyage; en tournée ▮ *vt* visiter; (*of artist etc*) être en tournée en *or* dans. ● **—ing** *n* tourisme *m*; **to go t.** faire du tourisme.

tourism ['tʊərɪz(ə)m] *n* tourisme *m*. ● **tourist** *n* touriste *mf* ▮ *a* (*region etc*) touristique; **t. office** syndicat *m* d'initiative.

tournament ['tʊənəmənt] *n* *Sp & Hist* tournoi *m*.

tout [taʊt] *vi* **to t. for** (*customers*) racoler ▮ *n* racoleur, -euse *mf*; **ticket t.** revendeur, -euse *mf* (en fraude) de billets.

tow [təʊ] *vt* (*car, boat*) remorquer; (*caravan, trailer*) tracter; **to t. away** (*vehicle*) emmener à la fourrière ▮ *n* '**on t.'**, *Am* '**in t.**' 'en remorque'; **t. truck** *Am* dépanneuse *f*. ● **towrope** *n* (*câble m* de) remorque *f*.

toward(s) [tə'wɔːd(z), *Am* tɔːd(z)] *prep* vers; (*of feelings*) envers; **cruel/etc t. s.o.**

cruel/*etc* envers qn; **money t.** de l'argent pour (acheter).

towel ['tauəl] *n* serviette *f* (de toilette); (*for dishes*) torchon *m*; **t. rail,** *Am* **t. rack** porte-serviettes *m inv.* ● **towelling** *or Am* **toweling** *n* tissu-éponge *m*; **(kitchen) t.** *Am* essuie-tout *m inv.*

tower ['tauər] *n* tour *f*; **block** tour *f*, immeuble *m* ∎ *vi* **to t. above** *or* **over** dominer. ● **-ing** *a* très haut.

town [taun] *n* ville *f*; **in t., (in)to t.** en ville; **out of t.** en province; **t. centre** centre-ville *m*; **t. council** conseil *m* municipal; **t. hall** mairie *f*; **t. planning** urbanisme *m*. ● **township** *n* (*in South Africa*) commune *f* (noire).

toxic ['tɒksɪk] *a* toxique.

toy [tɔɪ] *n* jouet *m*; **soft t.** (jouet *m* en) peluche *f* ∎ *a* (*gun*) d'enfant; (*house, car*) miniature *inv* ∎ *vi* **to t. with** (*idea etc*) caresses. ● **toyshop** *n* magasin *m* de jouets.

trace [treɪs] *n* trace *f* (**of** de); **to vanish without t.** disparaître sans laisser de traces ∎ *vt* (*draw*) tracer; (*with tracing paper*) (dé)calquer; (*find*) retrouver (la trace de); (*follow*) suivre (la piste de) (**to** à). ● **tracing** *n* (*drawing*) calque *m*; **t. paper** papier-calque *m inv.*

track [træk] *n* (*of animal, suspect, sports stadium etc*) piste *f*; *Rail* voie *f*; (*path*) chemin *m*; (*of rocket*) trajectoire *f*; (*racetrack*) *Am* champ *m* de courses; **the tracks** (*of wheels*) les traces *fpl*; **to keep t.** of suivre; **to lose t. of** (*friend*) perdre de vue; **on the right t.** sur la bonne voie; **t. event** *Sp* épreuve *f* sur piste; **t. record** *Fig* antécédents *mpl.* ∎ *vt* **to t. (down)** (*locate*) retrouver; (*pursue*) traquer. ● **track shoes** *npl Am* baskets *mpl*, tennis *mpl.* ● **tracksuit** *n Sp* survêtement *m.*

tract [trækt] *n* (*land*) étendue *f.*

tractor ['træktər] *n* tracteur *m.*

trade [treɪd] *n* commerce *m*; (*job*) métier *m*; (*exchange*) échange *m* ∎ *a* (*fair, secret*) commercial; (*barrier*) douanier; **t. union** syndicat *m*; **t. unionist**

syndicaliste *mf* ∎ *vi* faire du commerce (**with** avec); **to t. in** faire le commerce de ∎ *vt* échanger (**for** contre); **to t. sth in** (*old article*) faire reprendre qch. ● **trade-in** *n Com* reprise *f.*

trademark ['treɪdmɑːk] *n* marque *f* de fabrique; **(registered) t.** marque déposée.

trader ['treɪdər] *n* (*shopkeeper*) commerçant, -ante *mf.* ● **tradesman** *n* (*pl* -**men**) commerçant *m.*

trading ['treɪdɪŋ] *n* commerce *m* ∎ *a* (*port, debts etc*) commercial; (*nation*) commerçant.

tradition [trə'dɪʃ(ə)n] *n* tradition *f.* ● **tra'ditional** *a* traditionnel.

traffic ['træfɪk] **1** *n* (*on road*) circulation *f*; *Av Nau Rail* trafic *m*; **heavy t.** beaucoup de circulation; **t. circle** *Am* rond-point *m*; **t. cone** cône *m* de chantier; **t. island** refuge *m* (*pour piétons*); **t. jam** embouteillage *m*; **t. lights** feux *mpl* (de signalisation); (*when red*) feu *m* rouge; **t. sign** panneau *m* de signalisation. **2** *n* (*trade*) *Pej* trafic *m* (**in** de) ∎ *vi* (**-ck-**) trafiquer (**in** de). ● **trafficker** *n Pej* trafiquant, -ante *mf.*

tragedy ['trædʒədɪ] *n* tragédie *f.* ● **tragic** *a* tragique.

trail [treɪl] *n* (*of smoke, blood etc*) traînée *f*; (*track*) piste *f*, trace *f*; (*path*) sentier *m*; **in its t.** (*wake*) dans son sillage ∎ *vt* (*drag*) traîner; (*follow*) suivre (la piste de) ∎ *vi* (*on the ground etc*) traîner; **to t. (behind)** (*lag behind*) traîner. ● **-er** *n* **1** (*for car*) remorque *f*; *Am* caravane *f*; (*camper*) *Am* camping-car *m*; **t. truck** *Am* semi-remorque *m.* **2** *Cin* bande *f* annonce.

train [treɪn] **1** *n* train *m*; (*underground*) rame *f*; **to go** *or* **come by t.** prendre le train; **t. set** (*toy*) petit train *m.*

2 *n* (*procession*) file *f*; (*of events*) suite *f*; **my t. of thought** le fil de ma pensée.

3 *vt* (*teach*) former (**to do** à faire); *Sp* entraîner; (*animal, child*) dresser (**to do** à faire); (*ear*) exercer ∎ *vi* recevoir une formation (**as a doctor**/etc de médecin/etc); Sp s'entraîner. ● **trained** a (skilled) qualifié; (nurse, engineer etc) diplômé; (ear) exercé. ● **training** n formation f; Sp entraînement m; **to be in t.** Sp s'entraîner; (**teachers') t. college** école f normale.

trainee [treɪ'niː] n & a stagiaire (mf).

trainer ['treɪnər] n (of athlete, racehorse) entraîneur m; (of dog etc) dresseur m; **trainers** (shoes) baskets mpl, tennis mpl.

traipse [treɪps] vi **to t. around** (tiredly) traîner les pieds; (wander) se balader.

traitor ['treɪtər] n traître m.

tram [træm] n tramway m.

tramp [træmp] **1** n (vagrant) clochard, -arde mf; (woman) Pej traînée f. **2** vi (walk) marcher d'un pas lourd.

trample ['træmp(ə)l] vti **to t. sth** (underfoot), **t. on sth** piétiner qch.

trampoline [træmpə'liːn] n trampoline m.

trance [trɑːns] n **in a t.** en transe.

tranquil ['træŋkwɪl] a tranquille. ● **tranquillizer** n Med tranquillisant m.

trans- [træns, trænz] pref trans-.

transaction [trænz'ækʃ(ə)n] n (in bank) opération f; (on Stock Market) transaction f.

transatlantic [trænzət'læntɪk] a transatlantique.

transfer [træns'fɜːr] vt (-rr-) (person, goods etc) transférer (**to** à); (power) Pol faire passer (**to** à); **to t. the charges** téléphoner en PCV ▮['trænsfɜːr] n transfert m (**to** à); (of power) Pol passation f; (image) décalcomanie f; **bank** or **credit t.** virement m (bancaire).

transform [træns'fɔːm] vt transformer (**into** en). ● **transformation** [-fə'meɪʃ(ə)n] n transformation f. ● **transformer** n El transformateur m.

transfusion [træns'fjuːʒ(ə)n] n (**blood**) **t.** transfusion f (sanguine).

transistor [træn'zɪstər] n **t.** (**radio**) transistor m.

transit ['trænzɪt] n **in t.** en transit; **t.**

lounge Av salle f de transit.

transition [træn'zɪʒ(ə)n] n transition f. ● **transitional** a (government etc) de transition.

transitive ['trænsɪtɪv] a Gram transitif.

translate [træns'leɪt] vt traduire (**from** de, **into** en). ● **translation** n traduction f. ● **translator** n traducteur, -trice mf.

transmit [trænz'mɪt] vt (-tt-) (send, pass) transmettre ▮vti (broadcast) émettre. ● **transmission** [-ʃ(ə)n] n transmission f; (broadcast) émission f. ● **transmitter** n Rad TV émetteur m.

transparent [træns'pærənt] a transparent. ● **transparency** n transparence f; (slide) Phot diapositive f.

transpire [træn'spaɪər] vi (happen) Fam arriver; **it transpired that...** il s'est avéré que....

transplant [træns'plɑːnt] vt (plant) transplanter; (organ) Med greffer ▮['trænsplɑːnt] n Med greffe f.

transport [træn'spɔːt] vt transporter ▮['trænspɔːt] n transport m (**of** de); (**means of**) **t.** moyen m de transport; **public t.** les transports en commun; **t. café** routier m. ● **transportation** [-'teɪʃ(ə)n] n transport m; (means) moyen m de transport.

transvestite [trænz'vestaɪt] n travesti m.

trap [træp] n piège m; **t. door** trappe f ▮vt (-pp-) (animal) prendre (au piège); (jam) coincer, (cut off by snow etc) bloquer (**by** par).

trapeze [trə'piːz] n (in circus) trapèze m; **t. artist** trapéziste mf.

trappings ['træpɪŋz] npl signes mpl extérieurs.

trash [træʃ] n (nonsense) sottises fpl; (junk) bric-à-brac m inv; (waste) Am ordures fpl; (riffraff) Am racaille f. ● **trashcan** n Am poubelle f. ● **trashy** a (-ier, -iest) (book etc) qui ne vaut rien; (goods) de camelote.

trauma ['trɔːmə, 'traʊmə] n (shock) traumatisme m. ● **trau'matic** a traumatisant.

travel ['træv(ə)l] vi (-ll-, Am -l-) (on journey) voyager; (move, go) aller, se

déplacer ▌ vt (country, distance) parcourir ▌ n travel(s) voyages mpl; on one's travels en voyage ▌ a (agency, book) de voyages; t. brochure dépliant m touristique. ● travelled a to be well t. avoir beaucoup voyagé. ● travelling n voyages mpl ▌ a (bag etc) de voyage; (expenses) de déplacement; (musician) ambulant.

traveller ['trævələr] (Am traveler) n voyageur, -euse mf; traveller's cheque, Am traveler's check chèque m de voyage.

travelsickness ['trævəlsıknıs] n (in car) mal m de la route; (in aircraft) mal m de l'air.

travesty ['trævəstı] n parodie f.

trawler ['trɔːlər] n (ship) chalutier m.

tray [treı] n plateau m; (for office correspondence) corbeille f.

treacherous ['tretʃ(ə)rəs] a (road, conditions) très dangereux; (person, action) traître. ● treachery n traîtrise f.

treacle ['triːk(ə)l] n mélasse f.

tread [tred] vi (pt trod, pp trodden) (walk) marcher (on sur); (proceed) Fig avancer ▌ vt to t. sth into a carpet étaler qch (avec les pieds) sur un tapis ▌ n (step of stairs) marche f; (of tyre, Am tire) bande f de roulement.

treason ['triːz(ə)n] n trahison f.

treasure ['treʒər] n trésor m; t. hunt chasse f au trésor ▌ vt (value) tenir à; (keep) conserver (précieusement). ● treasurer n trésorier, -ière mf. ● Treasury n the T. Pol = le ministère des Finances.

treat [triːt] 1 vt (person, product etc) & Med traiter; (consider) considérer (as comme); to t. s.o. to sth offrir qch à qn. 2 n (special) t. petit extra m, gâterie f; (meal) régal m; to give s.o. a (special) t. donner une surprise à qn; it was a t. (for me) to do it ça m'a fait plaisir de le faire.

treatment ['triːtmənt] n (behaviour) & Med traitement m; rough t. mauvais traitements mpl.

treaty ['triːtı] n Pol traité m.

treble ['treb(ə)l] a triple ▌ vti tripler ▌ n le

triple; **it's t. the price** c'est le triple du prix.

tree [triː] n arbre m; **Christmas t.** arbre m or sapin m de Noël; **family t.** arbre m généalogique. ● t.-lined a bordé d'arbres. ● t.-top n cime f (d'un arbre). ● t.-trunk n tronc m d'arbre.

trek [trek] vi (-kk-) cheminer (péniblement) ▌ n voyage m (pénible); (distance) Fam tirée f.

tremble ['tremb(ə)l] vi trembler (with de). ● tremor n tremblement m; (earth) t. secousse f (sismique).

tremendous [trə'mendəs] a (huge) énorme; (dreadful) terrible; (wonderful) formidable.

trench [trentʃ] n tranchée f.

trend [trend] n tendance f (towards à); (fashion) mode f. ● trendy a (-ier, -iest) (person, clothes etc) Fam à la mode.

trepidation [trepı'deıʃ(ə)n] n inquiétude f.

trespass ['trespəs] vi s'introduire sans autorisation (on, upon dans); 'no trespassing' 'entrée interdite'.

trestle ['tres(ə)l] n tréteau m.

trial ['traıəl] n Jur procès m; (test) essai m; (ordeal) épreuve f; to go or be on t., être jugé, passer en jugement; to put s.o. on t. juger qn; by t. and error par tâtonnements ▌ a (period, flight) d'essai.

triangle ['traıæŋg(ə)l] n triangle m; (setsquare) Am équerre f. ● tri'angular a triangulaire.

tribe [traıb] n tribu f. ● tribal a tribal.

tribunal [traı'bjuːn(ə)l] n commission f; Mil tribunal m.

tributary ['trıbjʊtərı] n affluent m.

tribute ['trıbjuːt] n hommage m; to pay t. to rendre hommage à.

trick [trık] n (joke, of conjurer etc) tour m; (clever method) astuce f; to play a t. on s.o. jouer un tour à qn; card t. tour m de cartes; that will do the t. Fam ça fera l'affaire ▌ vt (deceive) tromper, attraper; to t. s.o. into doing sth amener qn à faire qch par la ruse. ● trickery n ruse f.

trickle ['trɪk(ə)l] n (of liquid) filet m; **a t. of** (letters) Fig un petit nombre de ∥ vi (flow) couler (lentement); **to t. in** (of letters etc) Fig arriver en petit nombre.

tricky ['trɪkɪ] a (-ier, -iest) (problem etc) difficile.

tricycle ['traɪsɪk(ə)l] n tricycle m.

trifl/e ['traɪf(ə)l] n (insignificant thing, money) bagatelle f; (dessert) diplomate m ∥ adv **a t. small**/etc un tantinet petit/etc ∥ vi **to t. with** (s.o.'s feelings) jouer avec. ●—**ing** a insignifiant.

trigger ['trɪɡər] n (of gun) gâchette f ∥ vt **to t. (off)** (start) déclencher.

trim [trɪm] **1** a (trimmer, trimmest) (neat) soigné; (slim) svelte. **2** n (cut) légère coupe f; **to have a t.** (haircut) se faire rafraîchir les cheveux ∥ vt (-mm-) couper (un peu); (finger nail, edge) rogner; (hair) rafraîchir. **3** n (on garment) garniture f; (on car) garnitures fpl ∥ vt (-mm-) **to t. with** orner de. ●**trimmings** npl garniture(s) f(pl); (extras) Fig accessoires mpl.

trinket ['trɪŋkɪt] n colifichet m.

trio ['triːəʊ] n (pl -os) (group) & Mus trio m.

trip [trɪp] **1** n (journey) voyage m; (outing) excursion f; **to take a t. to** (shops etc) aller à. **2** vi (-pp-) **to t. (over or up)** (stumble) trébucher; **to t. over sth** trébucher contre qch ∥ vt **to t. s.o. up** faire trébucher qn.

tripe [traɪp] n Culin tripes fpl; (nonsense) Fam bêtises fpl.

triple ['trɪp(ə)l] a triple ∥ vti tripler. ●**triplets** npl (children) triplés, -ées mfpl.

triplicate ['trɪplɪkət] n **in t.** en trois exemplaires.

tripod ['traɪpɒd] n trépied m.

tripper ['trɪpər] n **day t.** excursionniste mf.

trite [traɪt] a banal (mpl -als).

triumph ['traɪʌmf] n triomphe m (over sur) ∥ vi triompher (**over** de). ●**tri'umphant** a (team, army) triomphant; (success, welcome, return) triomphal.

trivial ['trɪvɪəl] a (unimportant) insignifiant; (trite) banal (mpl -als).

trod, trodden [trɒd, 'trɒd(ə)n] pt & pp of tread.

trolley ['trɒlɪ] n (for luggage) chariot m; (in supermarket) caddie® m; (for shopping) poussette f (de marché); **(tea) t.** table f roulante; **t. (car)** Am tramway m. ●**trolleybus** n trolley(bus) m.

trombone [trɒm'bəʊn] n Mus trombone m.

troop [truːp] n bande f; Mil troupe f; **the troops** (soldiers) les troupes fpl ∥ vi **to t. in/out/past** entrer/sortir/etc en masse. ●—**er** n (state) **t.** Am membre m de la police montée.

trophy ['trəʊfɪ] n coupe f, trophée m.

tropics ['trɒpɪks] npl **the t.** les tropiques mpl. ●**tropical** a tropical.

trot [trɒt] n (of horse) trot m; **on the t.** Fam de suite ∥ vi (-tt-) trotter; **to t. off** Hum Fam se sauver ∥ vt **to t. out** (say) Fam débiter.

trouble ['trʌb(ə)l] n (difficulty) ennui(s) m(pl); (effort) peine f (inconvenience) dérangement m; **trouble(s)** (social unrest, illness) troubles mpl; **to be in t.** avoir des ennuis; **to get into t.** s'attirer des ennuis (with avec); **to go to the t. of doing, take the t. to do** se donner la peine de faire; **I didn't put her to any t.** je ne l'ai pas dérangée; **to find the t.** trouver le problème, ∥ vt (inconvenience) déranger; (worry, annoy) ennuyer; (grieve) peiner; ●**troubled** a (worried) inquiet; (period) agité. ●**trouble-free** a (machine) qui ne tombe jamais en panne. ●**troublemaker** n Scol élément m perturbateur; Pol fauteur m de troubles.

troublesome ['trʌb(ə)ls(ə)m] a ennuyeux; (leg etc) qui fait mal.

trough [trɒf] n (for drinking) abreuvoir m; (for feeding) auge f; **t. of low pressure** Met dépression f.

trousers ['traʊzəz] npl pantalon m; **a pair of t., some t.** un pantalon; **(short) t.** culottes fpl courtes.

trout [traʊt] n truite f.

truant ['truːənt] n (pupil) absentéiste mf; **to play t.** sécher (la classe), faire l'école buissonnière.

truce [truːs] n Mil trêve f.

truck [trʌk] n 1 (lorry) camion m; Rail wagon m plat; **t. driver** camionneur m; (long-distance) routier m; **t. stop** (restaurant) Am routier m. 2 **t. farmer** Am maraîcher, -ère mf. ● **trucker** n Am (for goods) transporteur m routier; (driver) camionneur m, routier m.

trudge [trʌdʒ] vi marcher d'un pas pesant.

true [truː] a (-er, -est) vrai; (accurate) exact; **t. to** (promise etc) fidèle à; **to come t.** se réaliser; **to hold t.** (of argument) valoir (for pour). ● **truly** adv vraiment; (faithfully) fidèlement; **well and t.** bel et bien.

truffle ['trʌf(ə)l] n (mushroom) truffe f.

trump [trʌmp] n Cards atout m; **t. card** (advantage) Fig atout m.

trumpet ['trʌmpɪt] n trompette f.

truncheon ['trʌntʃ(ə)n] n (weapon) matraque f.

trundle ['trʌnd(ə)l] vti **to t. along** rouler bruyamment.

trunk [trʌŋk] n (of tree, body) tronc m; (of elephant) trompe f; (case) malle f; (of vehicle) Am coffre m; pl (for swimming) slip m de bain; (shorts) caleçon m de bain; **t. road** route f nationale.

truss [trʌs] vt **to t. (up)** (prisoner) ligoter.

trust [trʌst] n (faith) confiance f (in en); (group) Fin trust m; Jur fidéicommis m ▮ vt (person, judgment) avoir confiance en, se fier à; (instinct) se fier à; **to t. s.o. with sth, t. sth to s.o.** confier qch à qn; **I t. that** j'espère que ▮ vi **to t. in s.o.** avoir confiance en qn, se fier à qn. ● **trusted** a (friend, method etc) éprouvé. ● **trusting** a confiant. ● **trustworthy** a digne de confiance.

truth [truːθ] n (pl -s [truːðz]) vérité f; **there's some t. in...** il y a du vrai dans.... ● **truthful** a (statement) véridique; (person) sincère.

try [traɪ] 1 vt (attempt, sample, use) essayer; (s.o.'s patience) mettre à l'épreuve; **to t. doing** or **to do** essayer de faire; **to t. one's hand at** s'essayer à; **to t. one's luck** tenter sa chance ▮ vi essayer (for sth d'obtenir qch); **to t. hard** faire un gros effort; **t. and come!** essaie de venir! ▮ n (attempt) & Rugby essai m; **to have a t.** essayer; **at first's** au premier coup.

2 vt (person) Jur juger (for theft/etc pour vol/etc). ● **trying** a éprouvant.

try on vt (clothes, shoes) essayer ▮ **to try out** vt (car, method etc) essayer; (person) mettre à l'essai.

T-shirt ['tiːʃɜːt] n tee-shirt m.

tub [tʌb] n (basin) baquet m; (bath) baignoire f; (for ice cream) pot m.

tuba ['tjuːbə] n Mus tuba m.

tubby ['tʌbɪ] a (-ier, -iest) Fam dodu.

tube [tjuːb] n tube m; (underground railway) Fam métro m; (of tyre, Am tire) chambre f à air.

tuberculosis [tjuːbɜːkjuˈləʊsɪs] n tuberculose f.

TUC [tiːjuːˈsiː] n abbr (Trades Union Congress) = confédération f des syndicats britanniques.

tuck [tʌk] 1 vt (put) mettre; **to t. away** ranger; (hide) cacher; **to t. in** (shirt, blanket) rentrer; (person in bed) border; **to t. up** (sleeves) remonter. 2 vi **to t. in** (eat) Fam manger; **to t. into** (meal) Fam attaquer ▮ **t. shop** Sch boutique f à provisions.

Tuesday ['tjuːzdɪ, -deɪ] n mardi m.

tuft [tʌft] n (of hair, grass) touffe f.

tug [tʌɡ] 1 vt (-gg-) (pull) tirer ▮ vi tirer (at sur) ▮ n **to give sth a t.** tirer (sur) qch. 2 n tug(boat) remorqueur m.

tuition [tjuːˈɪʃ(ə)n] n enseignement m; (lessons) leçons fpl; (fee) frais mpl de scolarité.

tulip ['tjuːlɪp] n tulipe f.

tumble ['tʌmb(ə)l] vi **to t. (down** or **over)** (fall) dégringoler ▮ n dégringolade f; **t. dryer** or **drier** sèche-linge m inv.

tumbledown ['tʌmb(ə)ldaʊn] a délabré.

tumbler ['tʌmblər] n (glass) gobelet m.

tummy ['tʌmɪ] n Fam ventre m.

tumour ['tjuːmər] (Am tumor) n tumeur f.

tuna ['tjuːnə] n (fish) thon m.

tune [tjuːn] n (melody) air m; **in t.** (instrument) accordé; **out of t.** désaccordé; **to sing in t./out of t.** chanter juste/faux; **in t. with** Fig en accord avec ▮ vt **to t. (up)** (instrument) accorder; (engine) régler ▮ vi **to t.** (in (to) Rad TV se mettre à l'écoute (de). ● **tuning** n Aut réglage m; **t. fork** Mus diapason m.

tunic ['tjuːnɪk] n tunique f.

Tunisia [tjuːˈnɪzɪə] n Tunisie f.

tunnel ['tʌn(ə)l] n tunnel m; **the Channel T.** le tunnel sous la Manche ▮ vi (-ll-, Am -l-) percer un tunnel (**into** dans).

turban ['tɜːbən] n turban m.

turbine ['tɜːbaɪn, Am 'tɜːbɪn] n turbine f.

turbulence ['tɜːbjʊləns] n Av etc turbulences fpl.

turf [tɜːf] **1** n (grass) gazon m; **piece of t.** motte f de gazon. **2** vt **to t. s.o. out** Fam jeter qn dehors.

turkey ['tɜːkɪ] n dindon m, dinde f; (as food) dinde f.

Turkey ['tɜːkɪ] n Turquie f. ● **Turk** n Turc m, Turque f. ● **Turkish** a turc (f turque); **T. delight** loukoum m ▮ n (language) turc m.

turmoil ['tɜːmɔɪl] n confusion f; **in t.** en ébullition.

turn [tɜːn] n (movement, in game etc) tour m; (in road) tournant m; (of events) tournure f; Med crise f; **t. of phrase** tour m or tournure f (de phrase); **to take turns** se relayer; **in t.** à tour de rôle; **it's your t. (to play)** c'est à toi or (à) ton tour (de jouer); **to do s.o. a good t.** rendre service à qn; **the t. of the century** le début or la fin du siècle.

▮ vt tourner; (mattress, pancake) retourner; **to turn s.o./sth into** (change) changer or transformer qn/qch en; **to t. sth red/etc** rougir/etc qch; **she has turned twenty** elle a vingt ans passés; **it turns**

my stomach cela me soulève le cœur.

▮ vi (of wheel, driver etc) tourner; (turn head or body) se (re)tourner; (towards vers); (become) devenir; **to t. red/etc** rougir/etc; **to t. to** (question, adviser) se tourner vers; **to t. into** (change) se changer or se transformer en.

turn against vt se retourner contre (qn) ▮ **to turn around** vi (of person) se retourner ▮ **to turn away** vt (eyes) détourner (**from** de); (person) renvoyer ▮ vi se détourner ▮ **to turn back** vt (bed sheet etc) replier; (person) renvoyer; (clock) reculer (**to** jusqu'à) ▮ vi retourner (sur ses pas) ▮ **to turn down** vt (gas, radio etc) baisser; (fold down) rabattre; (refuse) refuser (qn, offre etc) ▮ **to turn in** vt (prisoner) Fam livrer (à la police) ▮ vi (go to bed) Fam se coucher ▮ **to turn off** vt (light, radio etc) éteindre; (tap, Am faucet) fermer; (machine) arrêter ▮ **to turn on** vt (light, radio etc) mettre, allumer; (tap, Am faucet) ouvrir; (machine) mettre en marche; **to t. s.o. on** (sexually) Fam exciter qn ▮ **to turn out** vt (light) éteindre; (contents of box) vider (**from** de); (produce) produire ▮ vi (of crowds) venir; (happen) se passer; **she turned out to be...** elle s'est révélée être... ▮ **to turn over** vt (page) tourner ▮ vi (of vehicle, person) se retourner ▮ **to turn round** vt (head, object) tourner; (vehicle) faire faire demi-tour à ▮ vi (of person) se retourner ▮ **to turn up** vt (radio, light etc) mettre plus fort; (collar) remonter ▮ vi (arrive) arriver; (be found) être retrouvé.

turning ['tɜːnɪŋ] n (street) petite rue f; (bend in road) tournant m; **t. point** (in time) tournant m.

turnip ['tɜːnɪp] n navet m.

turn-off ['tɜːnɒf] n (in road) embranchement m. ● **turnout** n (people) assistance f; (at polls) participation f. ● **turnover** n (sales) Com chiffre m d'affaires; (of stock, staff) rotation f; **apple t.** chausson m (aux pommes). ● **turnup** n (on trousers) revers m.

turnpike ['tɜːnpaɪk] n Am autoroute f à péage.

turnstile ['tɜːnstaɪl] n (gate) tourniquet m.

turntable ['tɜːnteɪb(ə)l] n (of record player) platine f.

turpentine ['tɜːpəntaɪn] (Fam **turps** [tɜːps]) n térébenthine f.

turquoise ['tɜːkwɔɪz] a turquoise inv.

turret ['tʌrɪt] n tourelle f.

turtle ['tɜːt(ə)l] n tortue f de mer; Am tortue f. ●**turtleneck** a (sweater) à col roulé ▮ n col m roulé.

tusk [tʌsk] n (of elephant) défense f.

tussle ['tʌs(ə)l] n bagarre f.

tutor ['tjuːtər] n professeur m particulier; (in British university) directeur, -trice mf d'études ▮ vt donner des cours particuliers à. ●**tu'torial** n Univ = travaux mpl dirigés.

tuxedo [tʌk'siːdəʊ] n (pl -os) Am smoking m.

TV [tiː'viː] n télé f.

twang [twæŋ] n (nasal) t. nasillement m.

tweed [twiːd] n tweed m; **t. jacket**/etc veste f/etc en tweed.

tweezers ['twiːzəz] npl pince f à épiler.

twelve [twelv] a & n douze (m). ●**twelfth** a & n douzième (mf).

twenty ['twentɪ] a & n vingt (m). ●**twen-tieth** a & n vingtième (mf).

twice [twaɪs] adv deux fois; **t. as heavy**/etc deux fois plus lourd/etc.

twiddle ['twɪd(ə)l] vti to t. (with) sth (knob etc) tripoter qch; to t. one's thumbs se tourner les pouces.

twig [twɪg] n (of branch) brindille f.

twilight ['twaɪlaɪt] n crépuscule m.

twin [twɪn] n jumeau m, jumelle f; **identical t.** vrai jumeau, vraie jumelle; **t. brother** frère m jumeau; **t. sister** sœur f jumelle; **t. beds** lits mpl jumeaux ▮ vt (-nn-) (town) jumeler. ●**twinning** n jumelage m.

twine [twaɪn] n (string) ficelle f.

twinge [twɪndʒ] n a **t. (of pain)** un élancement; a **t. of remorse** un pincement de remords.

twinkle ['twɪŋk(ə)l] vi (of star) scintiller;

(of eye) pétiller.

twirl [twɜːl] vi tournoyer ▮ vt faire tournoyer.

twist [twɪst] vt (wire, arm etc) tordre; (roll) enrouler (**round** autour de); (knob) tourner; **to t. one's ankle** se tordre la cheville; **to t. off** (lid) dévisser ▮ vi (wind) s'entortiller (**round** sth autour de qch); (of road, river) serpenter ▮ n (turn) tour m; (in road) zigzag m; (in rope) entortillement m; (in story) coup m de théâtre. ●**twisted** a (ankle, wire, mind) tordu. ●**twister** n tongue t. mot m ou expression f imprononçable.

twit [twɪt] n Fam idiot, -ote mf.

twitch [twɪtʃ] 1 n (nervous) tic m ▮ vi (of person) avoir un tic. 2 n (jerk) secousse f.

twitter ['twɪtər] vi (of bird) pépier.

two [tuː] a & n deux (m). ●**t.-'faced** a Fig hypocrite. ●**t.-piece** n (woman's suit) tailleur m; (swimsuit) deux-pièces m inv. ●**t.-'seater** n Aut voiture f à deux places. ●**t.-way** a **t.-way traffic** circulation f dans les deux sens; **t.-way radio** émetteur-récepteur m.

twofold ['tuːfəʊld] a double ▮ adv to **increase t.** doubler.

twosome ['tuːsəm] n couple m.

tycoon [taɪ'kuːn] n magnat m.

type¹ [taɪp] n 1 (sort) genre m, type m; (example) type m; **blood t.** groupe m sanguin. 2 (print) caractères mpl; **in large t.** en gros caractères.

typ/e² [taɪp] vti (write) taper (à la machine). ●**—ing** n dactylo f; **a page of t.** une page dactylographiée; **t. error** faute f de frappe. ●**typewriter** n machine f à écrire. ●**typewritten** a dactylographié. ●**typist** n dactylo f.

typhoid ['taɪfɔɪd] n Med typhoïde f.

typhoon [taɪ'fuːn] n Met typhon m.

typical ['tɪpɪk(ə)l] a typique (**of** de); (customary) habituel; **that's t. (of him)!** c'est bien lui!

tyranny ['tɪrənɪ] n tyrannie f. ●**tyrant** ['taɪərənt] n tyran m.

tyre ['taɪər] n pneu m (pl pneus).

U

U, u [juː] *n* U, u *m*. ● **U-turn** *n Aut* demitour *m*; *Fig* volte-face *f inv*.

udder ['ʌdər] *n* (*of cow etc*) pis *m*.

UFO [juːef'əʊ] *n abbr* (*unidentified flying object*) OVNI *m*.

ugh! [ɜː(h)] *int* pouah!

ugly ['ʌglɪ] *a* (**-ier, -iest**) laid. ● **ugliness** *n* laideur *f*.

UK [juːˈkeɪ] *abbr* = **United Kingdom**.

Ukraine [juːˈkreɪn] *n* the U. l'Ukraine *f*.

ulcer ['ʌlsər] *n* ulcère *m*.

ulterior [ʌlˈtɪərɪər] *a* u. motive arrière-pensée *f*.

ultimate ['ʌltɪmət] *a* (*final, last*) ultime; (*basic*) fondamental; (*authority*) suprême. ●**—ly** *adv* (*finally*) à la fin; (*fundamentally*) en fin de compte.

ultimatum [ʌltɪˈmeɪtəm] *n* ultimatum *m*.

ultramodern [ʌltrəˈmɒdən] *a* ultramoderne.

ultrasound ['ʌltrəsaʊnd] *n* (*scan, technique*) échographie *f*.

ultraviolet [ʌltrəˈvaɪələt] *a* ultraviolet.

umbrella [ʌmˈbrelə] *n* parapluie *m*; (*for sun*) parasol *m*.

umpire ['ʌmpaɪər] *n Sp* arbitre *m*.

umpteen [ʌmpˈtiːn] *a* u. times/*etc Fam* je ne sais combien de fois/*etc*. ● **umpteenth** *a Fam* énième.

un- [ʌn] *pref* in-, peu, non, sans.

UN [juːˈen] *abbr* = **United Nations**.

unabated [ʌnəˈbeɪtɪd] *adv* to continue u. se poursuivre avec la même intensité.

unable [ʌnˈeɪb(ə)l] *a* to be u. to do être incapable de faire; **he's u.** to swim il ne sait pas nager.

unabridged [ʌnəˈbrɪdʒd] *a* intégral.

unacceptable [ʌnəkˈseptəb(ə)l] *a* inacceptable.

unaccompanied [ʌnəˈkʌmpənɪd] *a* (*person*) non accompagné.

unaccountable [ʌnəˈkaʊntəb(ə)l] *a* inexplicable.

unaccounted [ʌnəˈkaʊntɪd] *a* to be (still) u. for rester introuvable.

unaccustomed [ʌnəˈkʌstəmd] *a* inaccoutumé; **to be u. to sth/to doing** ne pas être habitué à qch/à faire.

unaided [ʌnˈeɪdɪd] *adv* sans aide.

unanimous [juːˈnænɪməs] *a* unanime. ●**—ly** *adv* à l'unanimité.

unappetizing [ʌnˈæpɪtaɪzɪŋ] *a* peu appétissant.

unarmed [ʌnˈɑːmd] *a* non armé; **u. combat** combat *m* à mains nues.

unashamedly [ʌnəˈʃeɪmɪdlɪ] *adv* sans aucune honte.

unassailable [ʌnəˈseɪləb(ə)l] *a* inattaquable.

unassuming [ʌnəˈsjuːmɪŋ] *a* modeste.

unattached [ʌnəˈtætʃt] *a* (*independent, not married*) libre.

unattainable [ʌnəˈteɪnəb(ə)l] *a* (*aim*) inaccessible.

unattractive [ʌnəˈtræktɪv] *a* (*idea, appearance etc*) peu attrayant; (*ugly*) laid.

unauthorized [ʌnˈɔːθəraɪzd] *a* non autorisé.

unavailable [ʌnəˈveɪləb(ə)l] *a* (*person*) qui n'est pas disponible; (*article*) épuisé.

unavoidab/le [ʌnəˈvɔɪdəb(ə)l] *a* inévitable. ●**—ly** *adv* inévitablement; (*delayed*) pour une raison indépendante de sa volonté.

unaware [ʌnəˈweər] *a* to be u. of sth ignorer qch; **to be u. that** ignorer que. ● **unawares** *adv* to catch s.o. u. prendre qn au dépourvu.

unbalanced [ʌnˈbælənst] *a* (*mind, person*) déséquilibré.

unbearable [ʌnˈbeərəb(ə)l] *a* insupportable.

unbeatable [ʌnˈbiːtəb(ə)l] *a* imbattable.

● **unbeaten** a (player) invaincu; (record) non battu.

unbeknown(st) [ʌnbɪ'nəʊn(st)] a **u. to s.o.** à l'insu de qn.

unbelievable [ʌnbɪ'liːvəb(ə)l] a incroyable.

unbias(s)ed [ʌn'baɪəst] a impartial.

unblock [ʌn'blɒk] vt (sink etc) déboucher.

unborn [ʌn'bɔːn] a (child) à naître.

unbreakable [ʌn'breɪkəb(ə)l] a incassable. ● **unbroken** a intact; (continuous) continu; (record) non battu.

unbutton [ʌn'bʌt(ə)n] vt déboutonner.

uncalled-for [ʌn'kɔːldfɔːr] a déplacé.

uncanny [ʌn'kænɪ] a (-ier, -iest) étrange, mystérieux.

unceasing [ʌn'siːsɪŋ] a incessant.

unceremoniously [ʌnserɪ'məʊnɪəslɪ] adv (to treat) sans ménagement.

uncertain [ʌn'sɜːt(ə)n] a incertain (about, of de); **it's u. whether** or **that** il n'est pas certain que (+ sub); **I'm u. whether to stay** je ne sais pas très bien si je dois rester. ● **uncertainty** n incertitude f.

unchanged [ʌn'tʃeɪndʒd] a inchangé. ● **unchanging** a immuable.

unchecked [ʌn'tʃekt] adv (to spread etc) sans que rien ne soit fait.

uncivilized [ʌn'sɪvɪlaɪzd] a barbare.

uncle [ʌŋk(ə)l] n oncle m.

unclear [ʌn'klɪər] a (meaning) qui n'est pas clair; (result) incertain; **it's u. whether...** on ne sait pas très bien si...

uncomfortable [ʌn'kʌmftəb(ə)l] a (chair etc) inconfortable; (heat) désagréable; **she feels u.** (uneasy) elle est mal à l'aise.

uncommon [ʌn'kɒmən] a rare.

uncomplicated [ʌn'kɒmplɪkeɪtɪd] a simple.

uncompromising [ʌn'kɒmprəmaɪzɪŋ] a intransigeant.

unconcerned [ʌnkən'sɜːnd] a (indifferent) indifférent (by, with à).

unconditional [ʌnkən'dɪʃ(ə)nəl] a (offer) inconditionnel; (surrender) sans condition.

unconfirmed [ʌnkən'fɜːmd] a non confirmé.

unconnected [ʌnkə'nektɪd] a (facts, events etc) sans rapport (with avec).

unconscious [ʌn'kɒnʃəs] a (person) sans connaissance; (desire) inconscient; **u. of** inconscient de [ʌ n Psy inconscient m. ● **-ly** adv inconsciemment.

uncontrollable [ʌnkən'trəʊləb(ə)l] a (emotion, laughter) irrépressible.

unconventional [ʌnkən'venʃ(ə)nəl] a peu conventionnel; (person) anticonformiste.

unconvinced [ʌnkən'vɪnst] a **to be** or **remain u.** ne pas être convaincu (of de). ● **unconvincing** a peu convaincant.

uncooked [ʌn'kʊkt] a cru.

uncooperative [ʌnkəʊ'ɒp(ə)rətɪv] a peu coopératif.

uncork [ʌn'kɔːk] vt (bottle) déboucher.

uncouth [ʌn'kuːθ] a grossier.

uncover [ʌn'kʌvər] vt (conspiracy etc) découvrir.

undamaged [ʌn'dæmɪdʒd] a (goods) en bon état.

undaunted [ʌn'dɔːntɪd] a nullement découragé.

undecided [ʌndɪ'saɪdɪd] a (person) indécis (about sur); **I'm u. whether to do it** or **not** je n'ai pas décidé si je le ferai ou non.

undeniable [ʌndɪ'naɪəb(ə)l] a incontestable.

under ['ʌndər] prep sous; (less than) moins de; (according to) selon; **children u. nine** les enfants de moins de neuf ans; **u. the circumstances** dans les circonstances; **u. there** là-dessous; **u. it** dessous; **u. (the command of) s.o.** sous les ordres de qn; **u. repair** en réparation; **u. way** (in progress) en cours; (on the way) en route; **to get u. way** (of campaign etc) démarrer ‖ adv au-dessous.

under- ['ʌndər] pref sous-.

undercarriage ['ʌndəkærɪdʒ] n (of aircraft) train m d'atterrissage.

undercharge [ʌndə'tʃɑːdʒ] vt **I undercharged him (for it)** je ne (le) lui ai pas fait payer assez.

underclothes ['ʌndəkləʊðz] *npl* sous-vêtements *mpl*.

undercoat ['ʌndəkəʊt] *n* (*of paint*) couche *f* de fond.

undercooked [ʌndə'kʊkt] *a* pas assez cuit.

undercover [ʌndə'kʌvər] *a* (*agent, operation*) secret.

undercut [ʌndə'kʌt] *vt* (*pt & pp* undercut, *pres p* undercutting) *Com* vendre moins cher que.

underdeveloped [ʌndədɪ'veləpt] *a* (*country*) sous-développé.

underdog ['ʌndədɒg] *n* (*politically, socially*) opprimé, -ée *mf*.

underdone [ʌndə'dʌn] *a* pas assez cuit; (*steak*) saignant.

underestimate [ʌndər'estɪmeɪt] *vt* sous-estimer.

underfed [ʌndə'fed] *a* sous-alimenté.

underfoot [ʌndə'fʊt] *adv* sous les pieds.

undergo [ʌndə'gəʊ] *vt* (*pt* underwent, *pp* undergone) subir.

undergraduate [ʌndə'grædʒʊət] *n* étudiant, -ante *mf* (de licence).

underground ['ʌndəgraʊnd] *a* souterrain; (*secret*) *Fig* clandestin ▌*n Rail* métro *m*; (*organization*) *Pol* résistance *f* ▌[ʌndə'graʊnd] *adv* sous terre.

undergrowth ['ʌndəgrəʊθ] *n* sous-bois *m inv*.

underhand [ʌndə'hænd] *a* (*dishonest*) sournois.

underlying [ʌndə'laɪɪŋ] *a* (*basic*) fondamental; (*hidden*) profond.

underline [ʌndə'laɪn] *vt* (*word etc*) souligner.

undermine [ʌndə'maɪn] *vt* (*society, building, strength*) miner, saper.

underneath [ʌndə'niːθ] *prep* sous ▌*adv* (en) dessous; **the book u.** le livre d'en dessous ▌*n* dessous *m*.

underpaid [ʌndə'peɪd] *a* sous-payé.

underpants ['ʌndəpænts] *npl* slip *m*; (*loose, long*) caleçon *m*.

underpass ['ʌndəpɑːs] *n* (*for pedestrians*) passage *m* souterrain; (*for vehi-* cles) passage *m* inférieur.

underpriced [ʌndə'praɪst] *a* **it's u.** le prix est trop bas, c'est bradé.

underprivileged [ʌndə'prɪvɪlɪdʒd] *a* défavorisé.

underrate [ʌndə'reɪt] *vt* sous-estimer.

undershirt ['ʌndəʃɜːt] *n Am* tricot *m* de corps.

underside ['ʌndəsaɪd] *n* dessous *m*.

undersized [ʌndə'saɪzd] *a* trop petit.

underskirt ['ʌndəskɜːt] *n* jupon *m*.

understaffed [ʌndə'stɑːft] *a* à court de personnel.

understand [ʌndə'stænd] *vti* (*pt & pp* understood) comprendre; **I've been given to u. that** on m'a fait comprendre que. ●**—ing** *n* compréhension *f*; (*agreement*) accord *m*; (*sympathy*) entente *f*; **on the u. that** à condition que (+ *sub*) ▌*a* (*person*) compréhensif. ●**understood** *a* (*agreed*) entendu; (*implied*) sous-entendu.

understandab/le [ʌndə'stændəb(ə)l] *a* compréhensible. ●**—ly** *adv* naturellement.

understatement ['ʌndəsteɪtmənt] *n* euphémisme *m*.

understudy ['ʌndəstʌdɪ] *n Th* doublure *f*.

undertak/e [ʌndə'teɪk] *vt* (*pt* undertook, *pp* undertaken) (*task etc*) entreprendre; (*responsibility*) assumer; **to u. to do** entreprendre de faire. ●**—ing** *n* (*task*) entreprise *f*; (*promise*) promesse *f*; **to give an u.** promettre (**that** que).

undertaker ['ʌndəteɪkər] *n* entrepreneur *m* de pompes funèbres.

undertone ['ʌndətəʊn] *n* **in an u.** à mi-voix.

underwater [ʌndə'wɔːtər] *a* sous-marin ▌*adv* sous l'eau.

underwear ['ʌndəweər] *n* sous-vêtements *mpl*.

underweight [ʌndə'weɪt] *a* (*person*) qui ne pèse pas assez.

underworld ['ʌndəwɜːld] *n* **the u.** (*criminals*) le milieu, la pègre.

undesirable [ʌndɪ'zaɪərəb(ə)l] *a* peu

souhaitable (**that** que (+ *sub*)); (*person*) indésirable.

undetected [ʌndɪˈtektɪd] *a* **to go u.** passer inaperçu.

undies [ˈʌndɪz] *npl* (*female underwear*) *Fam* dessous *mpl.*

undignified [ʌnˈdɪɡnɪfaɪd] *a* qui manque de dignité.

undisciplined [ʌnˈdɪsɪplɪnd] *a* indiscipliné.

undisputed [ʌndɪˈspjuːtɪd] *a* incontesté.

undistinguished [ʌndɪˈstɪŋɡwɪʃt] *a* médiocre.

undivided [ʌndɪˈvaɪdɪd] *a* **my u. attention** toute mon attention.

undo [ʌnˈduː] *vt* (*pt* **undid**, *pp* **undone**) défaire; (*bound person, hands*) détacher. ●**—ing** *n* (*downfall*) perte *f.* ● **undone** *a* **to come u.** (*of knot etc*) se défaire.

undoubtedly [ʌnˈdaʊtɪdlɪ] *adv* sans aucun doute.

undreamt-of [ʌnˈdremtɒv] *a* insoupçonné.

undress [ʌnˈdres] *vi* se déshabiller ‖ *vt* déshabiller; **to get undressed** se déshabiller.

undrinkable [ʌnˈdrɪŋkəb(ə)l] *a* imbuvable.

undue [ʌnˈdjuː] *a* excessif. ● **unduly** *adv* excessivement.

unearned [ʌnˈɜːnd] *a* **u. income** rentes *fpl.*

unearth [ʌnˈɜːθ] *vt* (*from ground*) déterrer; (*discover*) *Fig* dénicher, déterrer.

unearthly [ʌnˈɜːθlɪ] *a* **at an u. hour** *Fam* à une heure impossible.

uneasy [ʌnˈiːzɪ] *a* (*ill at ease*) mal à l'aise; (*worried*) inquiet, inquiet; (*peace*). précaire; (*silence*) gêné.

uneconomic(al) [ʌniːkəˈnɒmɪk((ə)l)] *a* peu économique.

uneducated [ʌnˈedʒʊkeɪtɪd] *a* (*person*) inculte; (*accent*) populaire.

unemployed [ʌnɪmˈplɔɪd] *a* au chômage ‖ *n* **the u.** les chômeurs *mpl.* ● **unemployment** *n* chômage *m*; **u. benefit** allocation *f* de chômage.

unending [ʌnˈendɪŋ] *a* interminable.

unenthusiastic [ʌnɪnθjuːzɪˈæstɪk] *a* peu enthousiaste.

unenviable [ʌnˈenvɪəb(ə)l] *a* peu enviable.

unequal [ʌnˈiːkwəl] *a* inégal.

unequivocal [ʌnɪˈkwɪvək(ə)l] *a* sans équivoque.

uneven [ʌnˈiːv(ə)n] *a* inégal.

uneventful [ʌnɪˈventfəl] *a* (*trip, life etc*) sans histoires.

unexpected [ʌnɪkˈspektɪd] *a* inattendu. ●**—ly** *adv* à l'improviste; (*suddenly*) subitement; (*unusually*) exceptionnellement.

unexplained [ʌnɪkˈspleɪnd] *a* inexpliqué.

unfailing [ʌnˈfeɪlɪŋ] *a* (*optimism etc*) inébranlable.

unfair [ʌnˈfeər] *a* injuste (**to s.o.** envers qn); (*competition*) déloyal. ●**—ly** *adv* injustement. ●**—ness** *n* injustice *f.*

unfaithful [ʌnˈfeɪθfəl] *a* infidèle (**to** à).

unfamiliar [ʌnfəˈmɪlɪər] *a* inconnu; **to be u. with sth** ne pas connaître qch.

unfashionable [ʌnˈfæʃ(ə)nəb(ə)l] *a* (*subject etc*) démodé; (*restaurant etc*) peu chic *inv*, ringard; **it's u. to do it** n'est pas de bon ton de faire.

unfasten [ʌnˈfɑːs(ə)n] *vt* défaire.

unfavourable [ʌnˈfeɪv(ə)rəb(ə)l] (*Am* **unfavorable**) *a* défavorable.

unfeeling [ʌnˈfiːlɪŋ] *a* insensible.

unfinished [ʌnˈfɪnɪʃt] *a* inachevé.

unfit [ʌnˈfɪt] *a* en mauvaise santé; (*in bad shape*) pas en forme; (*unsuitable*) impropre (**for sth** à qch, **to do** à faire); (*unworthy*) indigne (**for sth** de qch, **to do** de faire); (*incapable*) inapte (**for sth** à qch, **to do** à faire).

unflinching [ʌnˈflɪntʃɪŋ] *a* (*fearless*) intrépide.

unfold [ʌnˈfəʊld] *vt* déplier; (*wings*) déployer ‖ *vi* (*of story*) se dérouler.

unforeseeable [ʌnfɔːˈsiːəb(ə)l] *a* imprévisible. ● **unforeseen** *a* imprévu.

unforgettable [ʌnfəˈɡetəb(ə)l] *a* inoubliable.

unforgivable [ʌnfəˈɡɪvəb(ə)l] *a* impardonnable.

unfortunate [ʌn'fɔːtʃ(ə)nət] a malheureux; (event) fâcheux; **you were u.** tu n'as pas eu de chance. ●—**ly** adv malheureusement.

unfounded [ʌn'faʊndɪd] a (rumour) sans fondement.

unfriendly [ʌn'frendlɪ] a froid, peu aimable (**to** avec).

unfulfilled [ʌnfʊl'fɪld] a (desire) insatisfait.

unfurnished [ʌn'fɜːnɪʃt] a non meublé.

ungainly [ʌn'geɪnlɪ] a (clumsy) gauche.

ungodly [ʌn'gɒdlɪ] a **at an u. hour** Fam à une heure impossible.

ungrateful [ʌn'greɪtfəl] a ingrat.

unhappy [ʌn'hæpɪ] a (-ier, -iest) (sad) malheureux; **u. with** or **about sth** (not pleased) mécontent de qch; **he's u. about doing it** ça le dérange de le faire. ●**unhappiness** n tristesse f.

unharmed [ʌn'hɑːmd] a (person) indemne.

unhealthy [ʌn'helθɪ] a (-ier, -iest) (climate etc) malsain; (person) en mauvaise santé; (lungs) malade.

unheard-of [ʌn'hɜːdɒv] a (unprecedented) inouï.

unheeded [ʌn'hiːdɪd] a **it went u.** on n'en a pas tenu compte.

unhelpful [ʌn'helpfəl] a (person) peu serviable; (advice) peu utile.

unhook [ʌn'hʊk] vt (picture, curtain) décrocher; (dress) dégrafer.

unhurt [ʌn'hɜːt] a indemne.

unhygienic [ʌnhaɪ'dʒiːnɪk] a pas très hygiénique.

uniform ['juːnɪfɔːm] **1** n uniforme m. **2** a (regular) uniforme; (temperature) constant.

unify ['juːnɪfaɪ] vt unifier.

unimaginable [ʌnɪ'mædʒɪnəb(ə)l] a inimaginable. ●**unimaginative** a (person, plan etc) qui manque d'imagination.

unimpaired [ʌnɪm'peəd] a intact.

unimportant [ʌnɪm'pɔːtənt] a peu important.

uninhabitable [ʌnɪn'hæbɪtəb(ə)l] a inhabitable. ●**uninhabited** a inhabité.

uninhibited [ʌnɪn'hɪbɪtɪd] a (person) sans complexes.

uninjured [ʌn'ɪndʒəd] a indemne.

uninspiring [ʌnɪn'spaɪərɪŋ] a (subject etc) pas très inspirant.

unintelligible [ʌnɪn'telɪdʒəb(ə)l] a inintelligible.

unintentional [ʌnɪn'tenʃ(ə)nəl] a involontaire.

uninterested [ʌn'ɪntrɪstɪd] a indifférent (**in** à). ●**uninteresting** a (book etc) peu intéressant; (person) fastidieux.

uninterrupted [ʌnɪntə'rʌptɪd] a ininterrompu.

uninvited [ʌnɪn'vaɪtɪd] adv (to arrive) sans invitation. ●**uninviting** a peu attrayant.

union ['juːnɪən] n union f; (trade or Am labor union) syndicat m ‖ a syndical; **u. member** syndiqué, -ée mf; **the U. Jack** le drapeau britannique.

unique [juː'niːk] a unique. ●—**ly** adv exceptionnellement.

unisex ['juːnɪseks] a (clothes etc) unisexe.

unison ['juːnɪs(ə)n] n **in u.** à l'unisson (**with** de).

unit ['juːnɪt] n unité f; (of furniture etc) élément m; (group, team) groupe m; **psychiatric u.** service m de psychiatrie; **research u.** centre m de recherche; **u. trust** Fin fonds m commun de placement.

unite [juː'naɪt] vt unir; (country, party) unifier; **United Kingdom** Royaume-Uni m; **United Nations** (Organisation f des) Nations unies fpl; **United States (of America)** États-Unis mpl (d'Amérique) ‖ vi (of students etc) s'unir.

unity ['juːnətɪ] n unité f.

universal [juːnɪ'vɜːs(ə)l] a universel.

universe ['juːnɪvɜːs] n univers m.

university [juːnɪ'vɜːsɪtɪ] n université f; **at u.** à l'université ‖ a (teaching, town etc) universitaire; (student, teacher) d'université.

unjust [ʌn'dʒʌst] a injuste.

unjustified [ʌn'dʒʌstɪfaɪd] a injustifié.

unkempt [ʌn'kempt] a (appearance) négligé; (hair) mal peigné.

unkind [ʌn'kaɪnd] a peu gentil (to s.o. avec qn); (nasty) méchant (to s.o. avec qn).

unknowingly [ʌn'nəʊɪŋlɪ] adv inconsciemment.

unknown [ʌn'nəʊn] a inconnu ∥ n (person) inconnu, -ue mf; the u. Phil l'inconnu m; **u. (quantity)** Math & Fig inconnue f.

unlawful [ʌn'lɔ:fəl] a illégal.

unleaded [ʌn'ledɪd] a (petrol, Am gasoline) sans plomb.

unleash [ʌn'li:ʃ] vt (force etc) déchaîner.

unless [ʌn'les] conj à moins que (+ sub); **u. she comes** à moins qu'elle ne vienne; **u. you work harder, you'll fail** à moins de travailler plus dur, vous échouerez.

unlike [ʌn'laɪk] a différent ∥ prep **u. me, she...** à la différence de moi, elle...; **he's u. his father** il n'est pas comme son père; **that's u. him** ça ne lui ressemble pas.

unlikely [ʌn'laɪklɪ] a peu probable; (unbelievable) incroyable; **she's u. to win** il est peu probable qu'elle gagne.

unlimited [ʌn'lɪmɪtɪd] a illimité.

unlisted [ʌn'lɪstɪd] a (phone number) Am sur la liste rouge.

unload [ʌn'ləʊd] vt décharger.

unlock [ʌn'lɒk] vt ouvrir (avec une clef).

unlucky [ʌn'lʌkɪ] a (-ier, -iest) (person) malchanceux; (number etc) qui porte malheur; **you're u.** tu n'as pas de chance. ● **unluckily** adv malheureusement.

unmade [ʌn'meɪd] a (bed) défait.

unmanageable [ʌn'mænɪdʒəb(ə)l] a (child) difficile; (hair) difficile à coiffer.

unmanned [ʌn'mænd] a (spacecraft) inhabité.

unmarried [ʌn'mærɪd] a célibataire.

unmask [ʌn'mɑːsk] vt démasquer.

unmentionable [ʌn'menʃ(ə)nəb(ə)l] a dont il ne faut pas parler.

unmistakable [ʌnmɪ'steɪkəb(ə)l] a (obvious) indubitable; (face, voice) facilement reconnaissable.

unmitigated [ʌn'mɪtɪgeɪtɪd] a (disaster) absolu; (folly) pur.

unmoved [ʌn'mu:vd] a impassible (by devant); (unconcerned) indifférent (by à).

unnatural [ʌn'nætʃ(ə)rəl] a (not normal) pas naturel; (affected) qui manque de naturel.

unnecessary [ʌn'nesəs(ə)rɪ] a inutile.

unnerve [ʌn'nɜːv] vt déconcerter.

unnoticed [ʌn'nəʊtɪst] a **to go u.** passer inaperçu.

unobstructed [ʌnəb'strʌktɪd] a (view) dégagé.

unobtainable [ʌnəb'teɪnəb(ə)l] a impossible à obtenir.

unobtrusive [ʌnəb'tru:sɪv] a discret.

unoccupied [ʌn'ɒkjʊpaɪd] a (house) inoccupé; (seat) libre.

unofficial [ʌnə'fɪʃ(ə)l] a officieux; (visit) privé; (strike) sauvage.

unorthodox [ʌn'ɔ:θədɒks] a peu orthodoxe.

unpack [ʌn'pæk] vt (suitcase) défaire; (goods, belongings) déballer; **to u. a comb/etc from** sortir un peigne/etc de ∥ vi défaire sa valise; (take out goods) déballer.

unpaid [ʌn'peɪd] a (bill, sum) impayé; (work, worker) bénévole; (leave) non payé.

unpalatable [ʌn'pælətəb(ə)l] a désagréable.

unparalleled [ʌn'pærəleld] a sans égal.

unplanned [ʌn'plænd] a (visit, baby) imprévu.

unpleasant [ʌn'plezənt] a désagréable (to s.o. avec qn).

unplug [ʌn'plʌg] vt (-gg-) (appliance) débrancher.

unpopular [ʌn'pɒpjʊlər] a peu populaire; **to be u. with s.o.** ne pas plaire à qn.

unprecedented [ʌn'presɪdentɪd] a sans précédent.

unpredictable [ʌnprɪ'dɪktəb(ə)l] a imprévisible; (*weather*) indécis.

unprepared [ʌnprɪ'peəd] *a* **to be u. for sth** (*not expect*) ne pas s'attendre à qch.

unpretentious [ʌnprɪ'tenʃəs] *a* sans prétention.

unprofessional [ʌnprə'feʃ(ə)nəl] *a* (*person, behaviour*) pas très professionnel.

unpublished [ʌn'pʌblɪʃt] *a* inédit.

unpunished [ʌn'pʌnɪʃt] *a* **to go u.** rester impuni.

unqualified [ʌn'kwɒlɪfaɪd] *a* **1** (*teacher etc*) non diplômé; **he's u. to do** il n'est pas qualifié pour faire. **2** (*support*) sans réserve; (*success*) parfait.

unquestionable [ʌn'kwestʃ(ə)nəb(ə)l] *a* incontestable.

unravel [ʌn'ræv(ə)l] *vt* (**-ll-**, *Am* **-l-**) (*threads etc*) démêler; (*mystery*) *Fig* éclaircir.

unreal [ʌn'rɪəl] *a* irréel. ● **unrea'listic** *a* peu réaliste.

unreasonable [ʌn'riːz(ə)nəb(ə)l] *a* qui n'est pas raisonnable; (*price*) excessif.

unrecognizable [ʌnrekəg'naɪzəb(ə)l] *a* méconnaissable.

unrelated [ʌnrɪ'leɪtɪd] *a* (*facts etc*) sans rapport (**to** avec).

unrelenting [ʌnrɪ'lentɪŋ] *a* (*person*) implacable; (*effort*) acharné.

unreliable [ʌnrɪ'laɪəb(ə)l] *a* (*person*) peu sûr; (*machine*) peu fiable.

unrepentant [ʌnrɪ'pentənt] *a* impénitent.

unreservedly [ʌnrɪ'zɜːvɪdlɪ] *adv* sans réserve.

unrest [ʌn'rest] *n* agitation *f*.

unrestricted [ʌnrɪ'strɪktɪd] *a* illimité; (*access*) libre.

unripe [ʌn'raɪp] *a* (*fruit*) vert, pas mûr.

unroll [ʌn'rəʊl] *vt* dérouler ∥ *vi* se dérouler.

unruffled [ʌn'rʌf(ə)ld] *a* (*person*) calme.

unruly [ʌn'ruːlɪ] *a* (**-ier, -iest**) indiscipliné.

unsafe [ʌn'seɪf] *a* (*place, machine etc*) dangereux; (*person*) en danger.

unsaid [ʌn'sed] *a* **to leave sth u.** passer qch sous silence.

unsatisfactory [ʌnsætɪs'fækt(ə)rɪ] *a* peu satisfaisant. ● **un'satisfied** *a* insatisfait; **u. with** peu satisfait de.

unsavoury [ʌn'seɪv(ə)rɪ] (*Am* **unsavory**) *a* (*person, place*) répugnant.

unscathed [ʌn'skeɪðd] *a* indemne.

unscrew [ʌn'skruː] *vt* dévisser.

unscrupulous [ʌn'skruːpjʊləs] *a* peu scrupuleux.

unseemly [ʌn'siːmlɪ] *a* inconvenant.

unseen [ʌn'siːn] *n* (*translation*) version *f*.

unselfish [ʌn'selfɪʃ] *a* désintéressé.

unsettled [ʌn'set(ə)ld] *a* (*weather*) instable.

unshakeable [ʌn'ʃeɪkəb(ə)l] *a* inébranlable.

unshaven [ʌn'ʃeɪv(ə)n] *a* pas rasé.

unsightly [ʌn'saɪtlɪ] *a* laid, disgracieux.

unskilled [ʌn'skɪld] *a* **u. worker** ouvrier, -ière *mf* non qualifié(e).

unsociable [ʌn'səʊʃəb(ə)l] *a* peu sociable.

unsolved [ʌn'sɒlvd] *a* (*problem*) non résolu; (*mystery*) inexpliqué; (*crime*) dont l'auteur n'est pas connu.

unsound [ʌn'saʊnd] *a* (*construction*) peu solide; (*method*) peu sûr; (*decision*) peu judicieux.

unspeakable [ʌn'spiːkəb(ə)l] *a* (*horrible*) innommable.

unspecified [ʌn'spesɪfaɪd] *a* indéterminé.

unstable [ʌn'steɪb(ə)l] *a* instable.

unsteady [ʌn'stedɪ] *a* (*hand, voice, step etc*) mal assuré; (*table, ladder etc*) instable. ● **unsteadily** *adv* (*to walk*) d'un pas mal assuré.

unstuck [ʌn'stʌk] *a* **to come u.** (*of stamp etc*) se décoller; (*fail*) (*of person*) *Fam* se planter.

unsuccessful [ʌnsək'sesfəl] *a* (*attempt etc*) vain, infructueux; (*outcome, candidate*) malheureux; (*application*) non retenu; **to be u.** ne pas réussir (**in doing** à faire); (*of book, artist*) ne pas avoir de succès. ● **-ly** *adv* en vain.

unsuitable [ʌn'suːtəb(ə)l] *a* qui ne con-

vient pas (**for** à); (*manners, clothes*) peu
convenable. ●**unsuited** *a* **u. to** (*job,
activity*) peu fait pour; **they're u.** ils
ne sont pas compatibles.

unsupervised [ʌn'suːpəvaɪzd] *adv* (*to
play etc*) sans surveillance.

unsure [ʌn'ʃʊər] *a* incertain (**of, about**
de).

unsuspecting [ʌnsə'spektɪŋ] *a* qui ne se
doute de rien.

unsympathetic [ʌnsɪmpə'θetɪk] *a* incom-
préhensif; **u. to** indifférent à.

untangle [ʌn'tæŋg(ə)l] *vt* (*rope, hair etc*)
démêler.

untenable [ʌn'tenəb(ə)l] *a* (*position*) intenable.

unthinkable [ʌn'θɪŋkəb(ə)l] *a* impensable.

untidy [ʌn'taɪdɪ] *a* (**-ier, -iest**) (*clothes,
hair*) peu soigné; (*room*) en désordre;
(*person*) désordonné; (*in appearance*)
peu soigné.

untie [ʌn'taɪ] *vt* (*person, hands*) détacher;
(*knot, parcel*) défaire.

until [ʌn'tɪl] *prep* jusqu'à; **u. then** jusque-
là; **I didn't come u. yesterday** je ne suis
venu qu'hier; **not u. tomorrow** pas
avant demain ‖ *conj* jusqu'à ce que
(+ *sub*); **u. she comes** jusqu'à ce qu'elle
vienne; **do nothing u. I come** ne fais rien
avant que j'arrive.

untimely [ʌn'taɪmlɪ] *a* inopportun;
(*death*) prématuré.

untiring [ʌn'taɪərɪŋ] *a* infatigable.

untold [ʌn'təʊld] *a* (*wealth*) incalculable.

untoward [ʌntə'wɔːd] *a* fâcheux.

untranslatable [ʌntræns'leɪtəb(ə)l] *a* intraduisible.

untrue [ʌn'truː] *a* faux (*f* fausse).

unusable [ʌn'juːzəb(ə)l] *a* inutilisable.

unused 1 [ʌn'juːzd] *a* (*a new*) neuf (*f*
neuve); (*not in use*) inutilisé. **2**
[ʌn'juːst] *a* **u. to sth/to doing** peu
habitué à qch/à faire.

unusual [ʌn'juːʒʊəl] *a* exceptionnel;
(*strange*) étrange. ●—**ly** *adv* exceptionnellement.

unveil [ʌn'veɪl] *vt* dévoiler.

unwanted [ʌn'wɒntɪd] *a* (*useless*) dont
on n'a pas besoin; (*child*) non désiré.

unwelcome [ʌn'welkəm] *a* (*news, fact*)
fâcheux; (*gift, visit*) inopportun; (*person*) importun.

unwell [ʌn'wel] *a* indisposé.

unwieldy [ʌn'wiːldɪ] *a* (*package etc*)
encombrant.

unwilling [ʌn'wɪlɪŋ] *a* **he's u. to do** il ne
veut pas faire. ●—**ly** *adv* à contrecœur.

unwind [ʌn'waɪnd] **1** *vt* (*thread etc*)
dérouler ‖ *vi* se dérouler. **2** *vi* (*relax*)
Fam décompresser.

unwise [ʌn'waɪz] *a* imprudent.

unwittingly [ʌn'wɪtɪŋlɪ] *adv* involontairement.

unworkable [ʌn'wɜːkəb(ə)l] *a* (*idea etc*)
impraticable.

unworthy [ʌn'wɜːðɪ] *a* indigne (**of** de).

unwrap [ʌn'ræp] *vt* (**-pp-**) ouvrir, défaire.

unwritten [ʌn'rɪt(ə)n] *a* (*agreement*) tacite.

unzip [ʌn'zɪp] *vt* (**-pp-**) ouvrir (la fermeture éclair® de).

up [ʌp] *adv* en haut; (*in the air*) en l'air;
(*of sun*) levé; (*out of bed*) levé, debout;
(*finished*) fini; **to come** *or* **go up** monter;
prices are up les prix ont augmenté; **up
there** là-haut; **up above** au-dessus; **up on
the roof** sur le toit; **further** *or* **higher up**
plus haut; **up to** (*as far as*) jusqu'à;
(*task*) *Fig* à la hauteur de; **to be up to
doing** (*capable*) être de taille à faire; **it's
up to you to do it** c'est à toi de le faire;
that's up to you ça dépend de toi; **where
are you up to?** (*in book etc*) où en es-tu?;
what are you up to? que fais-tu?; **what's
up?** (*what's the matter?*) *Fam* qu'est-ce
qu'il y a?; **time's up** c'est l'heure; **to
walk up and down** marcher de long en
large; **to be up against** (*confront*) être
confronté à.

‖ *prep* (*a hill*) en haut de; (*a tree*) dans;
(*a ladder*) sur; **to go up** (*hill, stairs*)
monter.

‖ *npl* **to have ups and downs** avoir des
hauts et des bas.

up-and-coming [ʌpənd'kʌmiŋ] *a* plein d'avenir. ● **upbeat** *a* (*cheerful*) *Am Fam* optimiste. ● **upbringing** *n* éducation *f*. ● **upcoming** *a Am* imminent. ● **up'date** *vt* mettre à jour. ● **up'grade** *vt* (*job*) revaloriser; (*person*) promouvoir. ● **up'hill 1** *adv* to go u. monter. **2** [ˈʌphil] *a* (*struggle, task*) pénible. ● **up'hold** *vt* (*pt & pp* upheld) maintenir. ● **upkeep** *n* entretien *m*. ● **upmarket** *a Com* haut de gamme. ● **upright 1** *a & adv* (*straight*) droit. **2** *a* (*honest*) droit. ● **uprising** *n* insurrection *f*. ● **up'root** *vt* (*plant, person*) déraciner. ● **upside 'down** *adv* à l'envers; **to turn u. down** (*plans etc*) *Fig* chambouler. ● **up'stairs** *adv* en haut; to go u. monter (l'escalier); ‖ [ˈʌpsteəz] *a* (*room*) du dessus. ● **up'stream** *adv* en amont. ● **up'tight** *a Fam* (*tense*) crispé; (*angry*) en colère. ● **up-to-'date** *a* moderne; (*information*) à jour; (*well-informed*) au courant (**on** de). ● **upturn** *n* (*improvement*) amélioration *f* (**in** de). ● **upward** *a* (*movement*) ascendant; (*path*) qui monte; (*trend*) à la hausse. ● **upwards** *adv* vers le haut; **from five francs u.** à partir de cinq francs.

upheaval [ʌpˈhiːv(ə)l] *n* bouleversement *m*.

upholster [ʌpˈhəulstər] *vt* (*pad*) rembourrer; (*cover*) recouvrir. ● **upholstery** *n* (*padding*) rembourrage *m*; (*covering*) revêtement *m*; (*in car*) garniture *f*.

upon [əˈpɒn] *prep* sur.

upper [ˈʌpər] **1** *a* supérieur; **u. class** aristocratie *f*; **to have the u. hand** avoir le dessus. **2** *n* (*of shoe*) dessus *m*. ● **u.-'class** *a* aristocratique. ● **uppermost** *a* le plus haut; (*on top*) en dessus; (*in importance*) de la plus haute importance.

uproar [ˈʌprɔːr] *n* vacarme *m*, tapage *m*.

upset [ʌpˈset] *vt* (*pt & pp* upset, *pres p* upsetting) (*knock over, spill*) renverser; (*plans, stomach, routine etc*) déranger; **to u. s.o.** (*make sad*) faire de la peine à

qn; (*offend*) vexer qn; (*aggravate*) exaspérer qn ‖ *a* peiné; vexé; exaspéré; (*stomach*) dérangé ‖ [ˈʌpset] *n* (*in plans etc*) dérangement *m* (**in** de); (*grief*) peine *f*; **to have a stomach u.** avoir l'estomac dérangé.

upshot [ˈʌpʃɒt] *n* résultat *m*.

urban [ˈɜːbən] *a* urbain.

urchin [ˈɜːtʃin] *n* polisson, -onne *mf*.

urge [ɜːdʒ] *vt* **to u. s.o. to do** conseiller vivement à qn de faire; **to u. on** (*person, team*) encourager ‖ *n* forte envie *f*.

urgency [ˈɜːdʒənsɪ] *n* urgence *f*; (*of tone, request*) insistance *f*. ● **urgent** *a* urgent; (*tone*) insistant. ● **urgently** *adv* d'urgence.

urinal [juˈraɪn(ə)l] *n* urinoir *m*.

urine [ˈjuː(ə)rɪn] *n* urine *f*. ● **urinate** *vi* uriner.

urn [ɜːn] *n* urne *f*; (*for coffee or tea*) fontaine *f*.

us [əs, *stressed* ʌs] *pron* nous; (**to**) **us** nous; **she sees us** elle nous voit; **he gives** (**to**) **us** il nous donne; **with us** avec nous; **all of us** nous tous; **let's** *or* **let us eat!** mangeons!

US [juːˈes] *abbr* = United States.

USA [juːesˈeɪ] *abbr* = United States of America.

usage [ˈjuːsɪdʒ] *n* (*custom*) & *Ling* usage *m*.

use [juːs] *n* emploi *m*, usage *m*; (*usefulness*) utilité *f*; **to have the u. of** avoir l'usage de; **to make u. of** se servir de; **not in u.** hors d'usage; **ready for u.** prêt à l'emploi; **to be of u.** être utile; **it's no u. crying/etc** ça ne sert à rien de pleurer/ *etc*; **what's the u. of worrying/etc?** à quoi bon s'inquiéter/*etc*?, à quoi ça sert de s'inquiéter/*etc*?; **he's no u.** il est nul. ‖ [juːz] *vt* se servir de, utiliser, employer (**as** comme; **to do, for doing** pour faire); **it's used to do** *or* **for doing** ça sert à faire; **it's used as** ça sert de; **to u.** (**up**) (*fuel*) consommer; (*supplies*) épuiser; (*money*) dépenser.

used [juːzd] **1** *a* (*second-hand*) d'occasion. **2** [juːst] *v aux* **I u. to sing/***etc* avant, je chantais/*etc* ▌*a* **u. to sth/to doing** habitué à qch/à faire; **to get u. to** s'habituer à.

useful ['juːsfəl] *a* utile (**to** à); **to come in u.** être utile; **to make oneself u.** se rendre utile. ● **usefulness** *n* utilité *f*. ● **useless** *a* inutile; (*person*) nul.

user ['juːzər] *n* (*of road etc*) usager *m*; (*of machine, computer, dictionary*) utilisateur, -trice *mf*. ● **u.-friendly** *a Comptr* convivial.

usher ['ʌʃər] *n* (*in church or theatre*) placeur *m* ▌*vt* **to u. in** faire entrer (*qn*); (*period etc*) *Fig* inaugurer. ● **ushe'rette** *n Cin* ouvreuse *f*.

usual ['juːʒʊəl] *a* habituel, normal; **as u.** comme d'habitude ▌**in the u.** (*food, excuse etc*) *Fam* la même chose que d'habitude. ● **—ly** *adv* d'habitude.

usurp [juːˈzɜːp] *vt* usurper.

utensil [juːˈtens(ə)l] *n* ustensile *m*.

utility [juːˈtɪlətɪ] *n* (**public**) **u.** service *m* public.

utilize ['juːtɪlaɪz] *vt* utiliser.

utmost ['ʌtməʊst] *a* **the u. ease**/*etc* la plus grande facilité/*etc*; **the u. danger/limit**/*etc* un danger/une limite/*etc* extrême ▌*n* **to do one's u.** faire tout son possible (**to do** pour faire).

utter ['ʌtər] **1** *a* complet, total; (*folly*) pur; (*idiot*) parfait; **it's u. nonsense** c'est complètement absurde. **2** *vt* (*a cry, sigh*) pousser; (*a word*) dire; (*a threat*) proférer. ● **utterly** *adv* complètement.

U-turn ['juːtɜːn] *n Aut* demi-tour *m*; *Fig* volte-face *f inv*.

V

V, v [viː] n V, v m. ● **V.-neck** n (sweater etc) col m en V.

vacant ['veɪkənt] a (room, seat) libre; (post) vacant; (look) vague. ● **vacancy** n (post) poste m vacant; (room) chambre f libre; **'no vacancies'** (in hotel) 'complet'.

vacate [vəˈkeɪt, Am 'veɪkeɪt] vt quitter.

vacation [verˈkeɪʃ(ə)n] n Am vacances fpl; **on v.** en vacances. ●—**er** n Am vacancier, -ière mf.

vaccinate ['væksɪneɪt] vt vacciner. ● **vaccination** [-'neɪʃ(ə)n] n vaccination f. ● **vaccine** [-iːn] n vaccin m.

vacuum ['vækjʊ(ə)m] n vide m; **v. cleaner** aspirateur m; **v. flask** thermos® m or f inv vt (room) passer l'aspirateur dans; (carpet) passer l'aspirateur sur. ● **v.-packed** a emballé sous vide.

vagabond ['vægəbɒnd] n vagabond, -onde mf.

vagina [vəˈdʒaɪnə] n vagin m.

vagrant ['veɪɡrənt] n Jur vagabond, -onde mf.

vague [veɪɡ] a (-er, -est) vague; (outline, memory) flou; **he was v. (about it)** il est resté vague. ●—**ly** adv vaguement.

vain [veɪn] a (-er, -est) **1** (attempt, hope) vain; **in v.** en vain; **her efforts were in v.** ses efforts ont été inutiles. **2** (conceited) vaniteux. ●—**ly** adv (in vain) vainement.

valentine ['væləntaɪn] n (card) carte f de la Saint-Valentin.

valiant ['væljənt] a courageux. ● **valour** (Am **valor**) n bravoure f.

valid ['vælɪd] a (ticket, excuse etc) valable. ● **validate** vt valider. ● **va'lidity** n validité f.

valley ['vælɪ] n vallée f.

valuable ['væljʊəb(ə)l] a (object) de (grande) valeur; (help, time etc) précieux ▮npl **valuables** objets mpl de valeur.

value ['væljuː] n valeur f; **it's good v. (for money)** ça a un bon rapport qualité/prix; **v. added tax** taxe f à la valeur ajoutée ▮ vt (appreciate) attacher de la valeur à; (assess) évaluer. ● **valuation** [-'eɪʃ(ə)n] n (by expert) expertise f.

valve [vælv] n (of machine) soupape f; (in radio) lampe f; (of tyre, Am tire) valve f; (of heart) valvule f.

vampire ['væmpaɪər] n vampire m.

van [væn] n (small) camionnette f, fourgonnette f; (large) camion m; Rail fourgon m.

vandal ['vænd(ə)l] n vandale mf. ● **vandalism** n vandalisme m. ● **vandalize** vt saccager.

vanguard ['vænɡɑːd] n **in the v. of** (progress etc) à l'avant-garde de.

vanilla [vəˈnɪlə] n vanille f ▮ a (ice cream) à la vanille.

vanish ['vænɪʃ] vi disparaître.

vanity ['vænɪtɪ] n vanité f.

vantage point ['vɑːntɪdʒpɔɪnt] n (place, point of view) (bon) point m de vue.

vapour ['veɪpər] (Am **vapor**) n vapeur f; (on glass) buée f.

variable ['veərɪəb(ə)l] a variable. ● **variation** [-'eɪʃ(ə)n] n variation f.

varicose ['værɪkəʊs] a **v. veins** varices fpl.

variety [vəˈraɪətɪ] n **1** (diversity) variété f; **a v. of reasons**/etc (many) diverses raisons/etc; **a v. of (articles)** Com toute une gamme de. **2 v. show** Th spectacle m de variétés.

various ['veərɪəs] a divers. ●—**ly** adv diversement.

varnish ['vɑːnɪʃ] vt vernir ▮ n vernis m.

vary ['veərɪ] vti varier (**from** de). ● **varied** a varié.

vase [vɑːz, Am veɪs] n vase m.

Vaseline® ['væsəliːn] n vaseline f.

vast [vɑ:st] *a* vaste. ●**—ly** *adv* (*very*) infiniment.

vat [væt] *n* cuve *f*.

VAT [vi:eɪ'ti:, væt] *n abbr* (*value added tax*) TVA *f*.

Vatican [ˈvætɪkən] *n* the V. le Vatican.

vault [vɔ:lt] **1** *n* (*in bank*) salle *f* des coffres; (*tomb*) caveau *m*; (*roof*) voûte *f*. **2** *vti* (*jump*) sauter.

VCR [vi:si:'ɑ:r] *n abbr* (*video cassette recorder*) magnétoscope *m*.

VD [vi:'di:] *n abbr* (*venereal disease*) MST *f*.

VDU [vi:di:'ju:] *n abbr* (*visual display unit*) moniteur *m*.

veal [vi:l] *n* (*meat*) veau *m*.

veer [vɪər] *vi* (*of car*) virer; (*of wind*) tourner; **to v. off the road** quitter la route.

vegetable [ˈvedʒtəb(ə)l] *n* légume *m*; **v. garden** (jardin *m*) potager *m*; **v. oil** huile *f* végétale. ●**vege'tarian** *a* & *n* végétarien, -ienne (*mf*). ●**vegetation** [-'teɪʃ(ə)n] *n* végétation *f*.

vehicle [ˈvi:ɪk(ə)l] *n* véhicule *m*; **heavy goods v.** poids *m* lourd; **off-road v.** véhicule *m* tout terrain.

veil [veɪl] *n* (*covering*) & *Fig* voile *m*. ●**veiled** *a* (*criticism, woman etc*) voilé.

vein [veɪn] *n* (*in body or rock*) veine *f*; (*in leaf*) nervure *f*; (*mood*) *Fig* esprit *m*.

Velcro® [ˈvelkrəʊ] *n* Velcro® *m*.

velvet [ˈvelvɪt] *n* velours *m* ▮*a* de velours.

vending machine [ˈvendɪŋməʃi:n] *n* distributeur *m* automatique.

vendor [ˈvendər] *n* vendeur, -euse *mf*.

veneer [vəˈnɪər] *n* (*wood*) placage *m*; (*appearance*) *Fig* vernis *m*.

venerable [ˈven(ə)rəb(ə)l] *a* vénérable.

venetian [vəˈni:ʃ(ə)n] *a* **v. blind** store *m* vénitien.

vengeance [ˈvendʒəns] *n* vengeance *f*; **with a v.** (*to work, study etc*) furieusement; (*to rain, catch up etc*) pour de bon.

venison [ˈvenɪs(ə)n] *n* venaison *f*.

venom [ˈvenəm] *n* (*poison*) venin *m*.

vent [vent] **1** *n* (*hole*) orifice *m*; (*for air*) bouche *f* d'aération. **2** *n* **to give v. to** (*feeling*) donner libre cours à ▮*vt* (*one's anger*) décharger (**on** sur).

ventilate [ˈventɪleɪt] *vt* ventiler. ●**ventilation** [-'leɪʃ(ə)n] *n* (*in room*) aération *f*. ●**ventilator** *n* (*in wall etc*) ventilateur *m*.

ventriloquist [venˈtrɪləkwɪst] *n* ventriloque *mf*.

venture [ˈventʃər] *n* entreprise *f* (risquée); **my v. into** mon incursion *f* dans ▮*vt* (*opinion*) hasarder; **to v. to do** oser faire ▮*vi* s'aventurer, se risquer (**into** dans).

venue [ˈvenju:] *n* lieu *m* de rencontre.

veranda(h) [vəˈrændə] *n* véranda *f*.

verb [vɜ:b] *n* verbe *m*. ●**verbal** *a* (*skill etc*) verbal.

verdict [ˈvɜ:dɪkt] *n* verdict *m*.

verge [vɜ:dʒ] *n* (*of road*) accotement *m*; **on the v. of** *Fig* (*ruin, tears*) au bord de; **on the v. of doing** sur le point de faire ▮*vi* **to v. on** friser; (*of colour*) tirer sur.

verify [ˈverɪfaɪ] *vt* vérifier; (*passport etc*) contrôler.

vermin [ˈvɜ:mɪn] *n* (*animals*) animaux *mpl* nuisibles; (*insects, people*) vermine *f*.

versatile [ˈvɜ:sətaɪl, *Am* ˈvɜ:sət(ə)l] *a* (*mind*) souple; (*tool, computer*) polyvalent; **he's v.** il est polyvalent.

verse [vɜ:s] *n* (*part of song*) couplet *m*; (*poetry*) poésie *f*; (*of Bible*) verset *m*; **in v.** en vers.

versed [vɜ:st] *a* (**well**) **v. in** versé dans.

version [ˈvɜ:ʃ(ə)n, *Am* ˈvɜ:ʒ(ə)n] *n* version *f*.

versus [ˈvɜ:səs] *prep* contre.

vertical [ˈvɜ:tɪk(ə)l] *a* vertical.

very [ˈverɪ] **1** *adv* très; **I'm v. hot** j'ai très chaud; **v. much** beaucoup; **the v. first** le tout premier; **at the v. least** tout au moins; **at the v. latest** au plus tard. **2** *a* (*actual*) même; **his v. brother** son frère même; **to the v. end** jusqu'au bout.

vessel [ˈves(ə)l] *n Nau Anat Bot* vaisseau *m*; (*receptacle*) récipient *m*.

vest [vest] *n* tricot *m* de corps; (*woman's*)

chemise f (américaine); (*waistcoat*) *Am* gilet m.

vested ['vestɪd] a v. interests *Pol etc* intérêt(s) m(pl); she's got a v. interest in *Fig* elle est directement intéressée dans.

vestige ['vestɪdʒ] n vestige m; not a v. of truth pas un grain de vérité.

vet [vet] 1 n vétérinaire mf. 2 vt (-tt-) (*document*) examiner de près; (*candidate*) se renseigner à fond sur. ● **veteri'narian** n *Am* vétérinaire mf. ● **veterinary** a v. surgeon vétérinaire mf.

veteran ['vet(ə)rən] n vétéran m; (war) v. ancien combattant m.

veto ['viːtəʊ] n (pl -oes) (*refusal*) veto m inv; (*power*) droit m de veto ▮ vt mettre son veto à.

vex [veks] vt contrarier; vexed question question f controversée.

VHF [viːeɪtʃ'ef] n abbr (*very high frequency*) on VHF sur modulation de fréquence.

via ['vaɪə, *Am* 'vɪə] prep par, via.

viable ['vaɪəb(ə)l] a (*plan etc*) viable.

viaduct ['vaɪədʌkt] n viaduc m.

vibrate [vaɪ'breɪt] vi vibrer. ● **vibration** [-'breɪʃ(ə)n] n vibration f.

vicar ['vɪkər] n (*in Church of England*) pasteur m. ● **vicarage** n presbytère m.

vicarious [vɪ'keərɪəs] a (*emotion*) ressenti indirectement.

vice [vaɪs] n 1 (*depravity, fault*) vice m; v. squad brigade f des mœurs. 2 (*tool*) étau m.

vice- [vaɪs] pref vice-.

vice versa [vaɪs(ɪ)'vɜːsə] adv vice versa.

vicinity [və'sɪnɪtɪ] n environs mpl; in the v. of (*place, amount*) aux environs de.

vicious ['vɪʃəs] a (*spiteful*) méchant; (*violent*) brutal; v. circle cercle m vicieux. ● **—ly** adv méchamment; brutalement.

victim ['vɪktɪm] n victime f; to be the v. of être victime de. ● **victimize** vt persécuter.

Victorian [vɪk'tɔːrɪən] a victorien.

victory ['vɪktərɪ] n victoire f. ● **victor** n

vainqueur m. ● **vic'torious** a victorieux.

video ['vɪdɪəʊ] n (*cassette*) cassette f; v. cassette vidéocassette f; v. (recorder) magnétoscope m; on v. sur cassette; to make a v. of faire une cassette de ▮ a (*game, camera etc*) vidéo inv ▮ vt (*event*) faire une (vidéo)cassette de. ● **videotape** n bande f vidéo.

vie [vaɪ] vi (*pres p* vying) rivaliser (with avec).

Vienna [vɪ'enə] n Vienne m or f.

Vietnam [vjet'næm, *Am* -'nɑːm] n Viêt Nam m. ● **Vietna'mese** a & n vietnamien, -ienne (mf).

view [vjuː] n vue f; (*opinion*) opinion f, avis m; to come into v. apparaître; in my v. à mon avis; on v. (*exhibit*) exposé; in v. of (*fact*) compte tenu de; with a v. to doing afin de faire ▮ vt (*regard*) considérer; (*house*) visiter. ● **—er** n 1 TV téléspectateur, -trice mf. 2 (*for slides*) visionneuse f. ● **viewpoint** n point m de vue.

vigilant ['vɪdʒɪlənt] a vigilant. ● **vigilance** n vigilance f.

vigour ['vɪɡər] (*Am* vigor) n vigueur f. ● **vigorous** a (*person, speech etc*) vigoureux.

vile [vaɪl] a (-er, -est) (*base*) infâme; (*unpleasant*) abominable.

villa ['vɪlə] n grande maison f; (*holiday or Am vacation home*) maison f de vacances.

village ['vɪlɪdʒ] n village m. ● **villager** n villageois, -oise mf.

villain ['vɪlən] n canaille f; (*in story or play*) méchant m.

vindicate ['vɪndɪkeɪt] vt justifier.

vindictive [vɪn'dɪktɪv] a vindicatif, rancunier.

vine [vaɪn] n (*grapevine*) vigne f; v. grower viticulteur m. ● **vineyard** ['vɪnjəd] n vignoble m.

vinegar ['vɪnɪɡər] n vinaigre m.

vintage ['vɪntɪdʒ] 1 n (*year*) année f. 2 a (*wine*) de grand cru; (*car*) d'époque; (*film*) classique; (*good*) *Fig* bon.

vinyl ['vaɪn(ə)l] n vinyle m.

violate ['vaɪəleɪt] *vt* violer.

violence ['vaɪələns] *n* violence *f*. ● **violent** *a* violent; **a v. dislike** une aversion vive (**of** pour). ● **violently** *adv* violemment.

violet ['vaɪələt] **1** *a* & *n* (*colour*) violet (*m*). **2** *n* (*plant*) violette *f*.

violin [ˌvaɪə'lɪn] *n* violon *m*. ● **violinist** *n* violoniste *mf*.

VIP [ˌviːaɪ'piː] *n abbr* (*very important person*) personnage *m* de marque.

viper ['vaɪpər] *n* vipère *f*.

virgin ['vɜːdʒɪn] *n* vierge *f*; **to be a v.** (*of woman, man*) être vierge.

Virgo ['vɜːgəʊ] *n* (*sign*) la Vierge.

virile ['vɪraɪl, *Am* 'vɪrəl] *a* viril.

virtual ['vɜːtʃʊəl] *a* **1 it was a v. failure/** *etc* ce fut en fait un échec/*etc*. **2** *Phys Comptr* virtuel. ● **—ly** *adv* (*in fact*) en fait; (*almost*) pratiquement.

virtue ['vɜːtʃuː] *n* **1** (*goodness*) vertu *f*; (*advantage*) mérite *m*. **2 by v. of** en raison de. ● **virtuous** *a* vertueux.

virtuoso, *pl* **-si** [ˌvɜːtʃʊ'əʊsəʊ, -siː] *n* virtuose *mf*.

virulent ['vɪrʊlənt] *a* virulent.

virus ['vaɪərəs] *n* *Med Comptr* virus *m*.

visa ['viːzə] *n* visa *m*.

Visa® ['viːzə] *n* **V. (card)** carte *f* Visa®.

viscount ['vaɪkaʊnt] *n* vicomte *m*. ● **viscountess** *n* vicomtesse *f*.

vise [vaɪs] *n* (*tool*) *Am* étau *m*.

visible ['vɪzəb(ə)l] *a* visible. ● **visi'bility** *n* visibilité *f*.

vision ['vɪʒ(ə)n] *n* (*eyesight, foresight etc*) vision *f*; **a woman of v.** *Fig* une femme qui voit loin.

visit ['vɪzɪt] *n* visite *f*; (*stay*) séjour *m* ‖ *vt* (*place*) visiter; **to visit s.o.** rendre visite à qn; (*stay with*) faire un séjour chez qn ‖ *vi* être en visite (*Am* **with** chez). ● **—ing** *a* (*card, hours*) de visite. ● **visitor** *n* visiteur, -euse *mf*; (*guest*) invité, -ée *mf*; (*in hotel*) client, -ente *mf*.

visor ['vaɪzər] *n* (*of helmet*) visière *f*.

vista ['vɪstə] *n* (*view of place*) vue *f*.

visual ['vɪʒʊəl] *a* visuel; **v. aid** (*in teaching*) support *m* visuel. ● **visualize**

vt (*imagine*) se représenter.

vital ['vaɪt(ə)l] *a* essentiel; **it's v. that** il est essentiel que (+ *sub*); **of v. importance** d'importance capitale; **v. statistics** (*of woman*) mensurations *fpl*. ● **—ly** *adv* (*important*) extrêmement.

vitality [vaɪ'tælɪtɪ] *n* vitalité *f*.

vitamin ['vɪtəmɪn, *Am* 'vaɪtəmɪn] *n* vitamine *f*.

vivacious [vɪ'veɪʃəs] *a* plein d'entrain.

vivid ['vɪvɪd] *a* (*imagination*) vif; (*description*) vivant. ● **—ly** *adv* (*to describe*) de façon vivante; **to remember sth v.** avoir un vif souvenir de qch.

V-neck [viː'nek] *n* (*sweater etc*) col *m* en V.

vocabulary [və'kæbjʊlərɪ, *Am* -erɪ] *n* vocabulaire *m*.

vocal ['vəʊk(ə)l] *a* (*cords, music*) vocal; (*outspoken, noisy*) qui se fait entendre.

vocation [vəʊ'keɪʃ(ə)n] *n* vocation *f*. ● **vocational** *a* professionnel.

vociferous [və'sɪf(ə)rəs] *a* bruyant.

vodka ['vɒdkə] *n* vodka *f*.

vogue [vəʊg] *n* vogue *f*; **in v.** en vogue.

voice [vɔɪs] *n* voix *f*; **at the top of one's v.** à tue-tête ‖ *vt* (*opinion etc*) formuler.

void [vɔɪd] **1** *n* vide *m*. **2** *a* (*not valid*) *Jur* nul.

volatile ['vɒlətaɪl, *Am* 'vɒlət(ə)l] *a* (*person*) versatile; (*situation*) explosif.

volcano [vɒl'keɪnəʊ] *n* (*pl* **-oes**) volcan *m*.

volition [və'lɪʃ(ə)n] *n* **of one's own v.** de son propre gré.

volley ['vɒlɪ] *n* (*gunfire*) salve *f*; (*of insults*) bordée *f*; *Tennis* volée *f*. ● **volleyball** *n* *Sp* volley(-ball) *m*.

volt [vəʊlt] *n* *El* volt *m*. ● **voltage** *n* voltage *m*.

volume ['vɒljuːm] *n* (*book, capacity, loudness*) volume *m*.

voluntary ['vɒlənt(ə)rɪ, *Am* -terɪ] *a* volontaire; (*unpaid*) bénévole. ● **voluntarily** *adv* volontairement; bénévolement.

volunteer [vɒlən'tɪər] *n* volontaire *mf* ‖ *vi* se proposer (**for sth** pour qch, **to**

do pour faire) ▌*vt* (*information*) offrir (spontanément).

vomit ['vɒmɪt] *vti* vomir ▌*n* (*matter*) vomi *m*.

voracious [və'reɪʃəs] *a* (*appetite, reader etc*) vorace.

vot/e [vəʊt] *n* vote *m*; (*right to vote*) droit *m* de vote; **to win votes** gagner des voix; **v. of no confidence** *Pol* motion *f* de censure; **v. of thanks** discours *m* de remerciement ▌*vt* (*funds etc*) voter; **to be voted president** (*elected*) être élu président ▌*vi* voter; **to v. Labour** voter travailliste. ●—**ing** *n*

(*polling*) scrutin *m*. ● **voter** *n Pol* électeur, -trice *mf*.

vouch [vaʊtʃ] *vi* **to v. for** répondre de.

voucher ['vaʊtʃər] *n* (*for meals, gift etc*) chèque *m*; (*for price reduction*) bon *m* de réduction.

vow [vaʊ] *n* vœu *m* ▌*vt* (*obedience etc*) jurer (**to à**); **to v. to do** jurer de faire.

vowel ['vaʊəl] *n* voyelle *f*.

voyage ['vɔɪɪdʒ] *n* voyage *m* (par mer).

vulgar ['vʌlgər] *a* vulgaire.

vulnerable ['vʌln(ə)rəb(ə)l] *a* vulnérable.

vulture ['vʌltʃər] *n* vautour *m*.

W

W, w [ˈdʌb(ə)lju:] *n* W, w *m*.

wacky [ˈwækɪ] *a* (**-ier, -iest**) *Am Fam* farfelu.

wad [wɒd] *n* (*of banknotes, papers*) liasse *f*; (*of cotton wool, Am absorbent cotton*) tampon *m*.

waddle [ˈwɒd(ə)l] *vi* se dandiner.

wade [weɪd] *vi* to w. through (*mud, water etc*) patauger dans; (*book etc*) *Fig* avancer péniblement dans; **wading pool** *Am* (*inflatable*) piscine *f* gonflable; (*purpose-built*) pataugeoire *f*.

wafer [ˈweɪfər] *n* (*biscuit*) gaufrette *f*.

waffle [ˈwɒf(ə)l] **1** *n* (*talk*) *Fam* blabla *m* ‖ *vi* *Fam* parler pour ne rien dire, blablater. **2** *n* (*cake*) gaufre *f*.

wag [wæg] *vt* (**-gg-**) (*tail, finger*) remuer ‖ *vi* (*of tail*) remuer.

wage [weɪdʒ] **1** *n* **wage(s)** salaire *m*, paie *f*; **w. claim** revendication *f* salariale; **w. earner** salarié, -ée *mf*; (*breadwinner*) soutien *m* de famille; **w. freeze** blocage *m* des salaires; **w. increase** augmentation *f* de salaire. **2** *vt* (*campaign*) mener; **to w. war** faire la guerre (**on** à).

wager [ˈweɪdʒər] *n* pari *m*.

waggle [ˈwæg(ə)l] *vti* remuer.

wag(g)on [ˈwægən] *n* *Rail* wagon *m* (de marchandises); (*horse-drawn*) chariot *m*.

wail [weɪl] *vi* (*cry out, complain*) gémir; (*of siren*) hurler.

waist [weɪst] *n* taille *f*; **stripped to the w.** torse nu. ● **waistcoat** [ˈweɪskəʊt] *n* gilet *m*. ● **waistline** *n* taille *f*.

wait [weɪt] **1** *n* attente *f*; **to lie in w. (for)** guetter ‖ *vi* attendre; **to w. for s.o./sth** attendre qn/qch; **w. until I've gone, w. for me to go** attends que je sois parti; **to keep s.o. waiting** faire attendre qn; **I can't w. to do it** j'ai hâte de le faire. **2** *vi* (*serve*) **to w. at table** servir à table;

to w. on s.o. servir qn. ● **waiting** *n* attente *f*; ‘**no w.**’ (*street sign*) ‘arrêt interdit’ ‖ *a* **w. list/room** liste *f*/salle *f* d’attente.

wait around *vi* attendre ‖ **to wait behind** *vi* rester ‖ **to wait up** *vi* veiller; **to w. up for s.o.** attendre le retour de qn avant de se coucher.

waiter [ˈweɪtər] *n* garçon *m* (de café), serveur *m*; **w.!** garçon! ● **waitress** *n* serveuse *f*; **w.!** mademoiselle!

waive [weɪv] *vt* renoncer à; **to w. a requirement (for s.o.)** dispenser qn d’une condition requise.

wake[1] [weɪk] *vi* (*pt* **woke**, *pp* **woken**) **to w. (up)** se réveiller; **to w. up to** (*fact etc*) prendre conscience de ‖ *vt* **to w. (up)** réveiller. ● **waken** *vt* *Lit* éveiller ‖ *vi* *Lit* s’éveiller.

wake[2] [weɪk] *n* (*of ship*) & *Fig* sillage *m*; **in the w. of** *Fig* dans le sillage de.

Wales [weɪlz] *n* pays *m* de Galles; **the Prince of W.** le prince de Galles.

walk [wɔːk] *n* promenade *f*; (*shorter*) (*petit*) tour *m*; (*way of walking*) démarche *f*; (*path*) allée *f*, chemin *m*; **to go for a w., take a w.** faire une promenade; (*shorter*) faire un (petit) tour; **to take for a w.** (*child*) emmener se promener; (*baby, dog*) promener; **five minutes’ w. (away)** à cinq minutes à pied; **from all walks of life** *Fig* de toutes conditions sociales.

‖ *vi* marcher; (*stroll*) se promener; (*go on foot*) aller à pied; **w.!** (*don’t run*) ne cours pas!

‖ *vt* (*distance*) faire à pied; (*streets*) (par)courir; (*take for a walk*) promener (*bébé, chien*); **to w. s.o. to** (*station etc*) accompagner qn à.

walk away *vi* s’éloigner (**from** de); **to w. away with** (*steal*) *Fam* faucher ‖ **to walk**

in *vi* entrer; **to w. into** (*tree etc*) rentrer dans ▮ **to walk off** *vi* = **walk away** ▮ **to walk out** *vi* (*leave*) partir; **to w. out on s.o.** abandonner qn ▮ **to walk over** *vi* **to w. over to** (*go up to*) s'approcher de.

walker ['wɔːkər] *n* marcheur, -euse *mf*; (*for pleasure*) promeneur, -euse *mf*. ● **walking stick** *n* canne *f*. ● **walkout** *n* (*strike*) grève *f* surprise. ● **walkover** *n* (*in contest etc*) victoire *f* facile. ● **walkway** *n* **moving w.** trottoir *m* roulant.

walkie-talkie [wɔːkɪ'tɔːkɪ] *n* talkie-walkie *m*.

Walkman® ['wɔːkmən] *n* (*pl* **Walkmans**) baladeur *m*.

wall [wɔːl] *n* mur *m*; (*of cabin, tunnel, stomach*) paroi *f* ▮ *a* (*map etc*) mural. ● **walled** *a* **w. city** ville *f* fortifiée. ● **wallflower** *n Bot* giroflée *f*. ● **wallpaper** *n* papier *m* peint ▮ *vt* tapisser. ● **wall-to-wall 'carpet(ing)** *n* moquette *f*.

wallet ['wɒlɪt] *n* portefeuille *m*.

wallop ['wɒləp] *vt* (*hit*) *Fam* taper sur ▮ *n Fam* grand coup *m*.

wallow ['wɒləʊ] *vi* **to w. in** (*mud, vice etc*) se vautrer dans.

wally ['wɒlɪ] *n* (*idiot*) *Fam* andouille *f*.

walnut ['wɔːlnʌt] *n* (*nut*) noix *f*; (*tree, wood*) noyer *m*.

walrus ['wɔːlrəs] *n* (*animal*) morse *m*.

waltz [wɔːls, *Am* wɒlts] *n* valse *f* ▮ *vi* valser.

wand [wɒnd] *n* baguette *f* (magique).

wander ['wɒndər] *vi* (*of thoughts*) vagabonder; **to w. (about or around)** (*roam*) errer; (*stroll*) flâner; **to w. from** (*path, subject*) s'écarter de; **to w. off** s'éloigner ▮ *vt* **to w. the streets** errer dans les rues. ● —**ing** *a* (*life, tribe*) vagabond, nomade.

wane [weɪn] *vi* (*of moon, fame etc*) décroître ▮ *n* **to be on the w.** décroître.

wangle ['wæŋg(ə)l] *vt* (*obtain*) *Fam* se débrouiller pour obtenir.

want [wɒnt] *vt* vouloir (**to do** faire); (*ask for*) demander (qn); (*need*) avoir besoin de; **I w. him to go** je veux qu'il parte; **you're wanted** on vous demande ▮ *vi* **not**

to w. for (*not lack*) ne pas manquer de ▮ *n* (*lack*) manque *m* (**of** de); **for w. of** par manque de; **for w. of money/time** faute d'argent/de temps; **for w. of anything better** faute de mieux. ● **wanted** *a* (*criminal*) recherché par la police. ● **wanting** *a* (*inadequate*) insuffisant.

wanton ['wɒntən] *a* (*gratuitous*) gratuit; (*immoral*) *Old-fashioned* impudique.

war [wɔːr] *n* guerre *f*; **at w.** en guerre (**with** avec); **to declare w.** déclarer la guerre (**on** à); **w. memorial** monument *m* aux morts.

ward[1] [wɔːd] *n* **1** (*in hospital*) salle *f*. **2** (*child*) *Jur* pupille *mf*. **3** (*electoral division*) circonscription *f* électorale.

ward[2] [wɔːd] *vt* **to w. off** (*blow, anger*) détourner; (*danger*) éviter.

warden ['wɔːd(ə)n] *n* (*of institution, Am of prison*) directeur, -trice *mf*; (**traffic**) **w.** contractuel, -elle *mf*.

warder ['wɔːdər] *n* gardien *m* (de prison).

wardrobe ['wɔːdrəʊb] *n* (*cupboard, Am closet*) penderie *f*; (*clothes*) garde-robe *f*.

warehouse, *pl* -ses ['weəhaʊs, -zɪz] *n* entrepôt *m*.

wares [weəz] *npl* marchandises *fpl*.

warfare ['wɔːfeər] *n* guerre *f*. ● **warhead** *n* (*of missile*) ogive *f*.

warily ['weərɪlɪ] *adv* avec précaution.

warm [wɔːm] *a* (**-er, -est**) chaud; (*welcome, thanks etc*) *Fig* chaleureux; **to be** or **feel w.** avoir chaud; **it's (nice and) w.** (*of weather*) il fait (agréablement) chaud; **to get w.** (*of person, room*) se réchauffer ▮ *vt* **to w. (up)** (*person, food etc*) réchauffer ▮ *vi* **to w. up** (*of person, room, engine*) se réchauffer; (*of food, water*) chauffer. ● **warmly** *adv* (*to wrap up etc*) chaudement; (*to welcome etc*) *Fig* chaleureusement. ● **warmth** *n* chaleur *f*.

warn [wɔːn] *vt* avertir, prévenir (**that** que); **to w. s.o. against sth** mettre qn en garde contre qch; **to w. s.o. against doing** conseiller à qn de ne pas faire.

●**—ing** n avertissement m; (*advance notice*) (pré)avis m; Met avis m; (*device*) alarme f; **without w.** sans prévenir; **a note** or **word of w.** une mise en garde; **w. light** (*on appliance*) voyant m lumineux; **(hazard) w. lights** Aut feux mpl de détresse.

warp [wɔːp] vt (*wood etc*) voiler; (*judgment*) Fig pervertir; **a warped mind** un esprit tordu ∥ vi se voiler.

warpath ['wɔːpɑːθ] n **to be on the w.** (*angry*) Fam être d'humeur massacrante.

warrant ['wɒrənt] n Jur mandat m; **a w. for your arrest** un mandat d'arrêt contre vous; **search w.** mandat m de perquisition. ●**warranty** n Com garantie f.

warren ['wɒrən] n (*rabbit*) **w.** garenne f.

warring ['wɔːrɪŋ] a (*countries etc*) en guerre.

warrior ['wɒrɪər] n guerrier, -ière mf.

warship ['wɔːʃɪp] n navire m de guerre.

wart [wɔːt] n verrue f.

wartime ['wɔːtaɪm] n **in w.** en temps de guerre.

wary ['weərɪ] a (-ier, -iest) prudent; **to be w. of s.o./sth** se méfier de qn/qch; **to be w. of doing** hésiter beaucoup à faire.

was [wəz, *stressed* wɒz] *see* **be**.

wash [wɒʃ] n (*clothes*) lessive f; **to have a w.** se laver; **to give sth a w.** laver qch; **to do the w.** faire la lessive ∥ vt laver; **to w. one's hands** se laver les mains (Fig of sth de qch) ∥ vi (*have a wash*) se laver. ●**washable** a lavable. ●**washbasin** n lavabo m. ●**washcloth** n Am gant m de toilette. ●**washout** n (*event*) Fam fiasco m. ●**washroom** n Am toilettes fpl.

wash away vt (*stain*) faire partir (en lavant) ∥ vi (*of stain*) partir (au lavage) ∥ **to wash down** vt (*vehicle, deck*) laver à grande eau; (*food*) arroser (**with** de) ∥ **to wash off** vti = **wash away** ∥ **to wash out** vt (*bowl*) laver ∥ vti = **wash away** ∥ **to wash up** vt (*dishes*) laver ∥ vi (*do the dishes*) faire la vaisselle; (*have a wash*) Am se laver.

washer ['wɒʃər] n (*ring*) rondelle f, joint m.

washing ['wɒʃɪŋ] n (*act*) lavage m; (*clothes*) lessive f, linge m; **to do the w.** faire la lessive; **w. line** corde f à linge; **w. machine** machine f à laver; **w. powder** lessive f. ●**w.-'up** n vaisselle f; **to do the w.-up** faire la vaisselle; **w.-up liquid** produit m pour la vaisselle.

wasp [wɒsp] n guêpe f.

wastage ['weɪstɪdʒ] n gaspillage m; (*losses*) pertes fpl; **some w.** (*of goods*) du déchet.

waste [weɪst] n gaspillage m; (*of time*) perte f; (*rubbish, Am garbage*) déchets mpl; **w. disposal unit** broyeur m d'ordures; **w. products** déchets mpl; **w. ground** (*in town*) terrain m vague; **w. land** terres fpl incultes; **w. paper** vieux papiers mpl; **w. pipe** tuyau m d'évacuation ∥ vt (*money, food etc*) gaspiller; (*time, opportunity*) perdre; **to w. one's life** gâcher sa vie ∥ vi **to w. away** dépérir. ●**wasted** a (*effort*) inutile.

wastebin ['weɪstbɪn] n (*in kitchen*) poubelle f. ●**wastepaper basket** n corbeille f (à papier).

wasteful ['weɪstfəl] a (*person*) gaspilleur; (*process*) peu économique.

watch [wɒtʃ] **1** n (*small clock*) montre f. **2** n (*over suspect, baby etc*) surveillance f; **to keep (a) w. over** surveiller; **to keep w.** faire le guet ∥ vt regarder; (*observe*) observer; (*suspect, baby etc*) surveiller; (*be careful of*) faire attention à ∥ vi regarder; **to w. (out) for sth/s.o.** (*wait for*) guetter qch/qn; **to w. out** (*take care*) faire attention (**for** à); **w. out!** attention!; **to w. over** surveiller.

watchdog ['wɒtʃdɒg] n chien m de garde. ●**watchmaker** n horloger, -ère mf. ●**watchman** n (pl -men) **night w.** veilleur m de nuit. ●**watchstrap** n bracelet m de montre.

watchful ['wɒtʃfəl] a vigilant.

water ['wɔːtər] n eau f; **under w.** (*road etc*) inondé; (*to swim*) sous l'eau; **in hot**

w. *Fig* dans le pétrin; w. **cannon** lance *f* à eau; w. **ice** sorbet *m*; w. **lily** nénuphar *m*; w. **pistol** pistolet *m* à eau; w. **polo** *Sp* water-polo *m*; w. **skiing** ski *m* nautique; w. **tank** réservoir *m* d'eau. ▮ *vt* (*plant etc*) arroser; to w. **down** (*wine etc*) couper (d'eau); (*text*) édulcorer. ▮ *vi* (*of eyes*) larmoyer; **it makes my mouth** w. ça lui fait venir l'eau à la bouche. ● **watering can** *n* arrosoir *m*.

watercolour (*Am* **-color**) *n* (*picture*) aquarelle *f*; (*paint*) couleur *f* pour aquarelle. ● **watercress** *n* cresson *m* (de fontaine). ● **waterfall** *n* chute *f* d'eau. ● **waterlogged** *a* délavé. ● **watermark** *n* (*in paper*) filigrane *m*. ● **watermelon** *n* pastèque *f*. ● **waterproof** *a* (*material*) imperméable. ● **watershed** *n* (*turning point*) tournant *m* (décisif). ● **watertight** *a* (*container*) étanche. ● **waterway** *n* voie *f* navigable. ● **waterworks** *n* station *f* hydraulique.

watery ['wɔːtərɪ] *a* (*soup*) trop liquide; w. **tea** or **coffee** de la lavasse.

watt [wɒt] *n El* watt *m*.

wave [weɪv] *n* (*of sea*) & *Fig* vague *f*; (*in hair*) ondulation *f*; (*sign*) signe *m* (de la main); **medium/short** w. *Rad* ondes *fpl* moyennes/courtes; **long** w. *Rad* grandes ondes, ondes longues ▮ *vi* (*with hand*) faire signe (de la main); (*of flag*) flotter; **to** w. **to s.o.** (*greet*) saluer qn de la main ▮ *vt* (*arm, flag etc*) agiter; **to** w. **s.o. on** faire signe à qn d'avancer. ● **waveband** *n Rad* bande *f* de fréquence. ● **wavelength** *n Rad* & *Fig* longueur *f* d'ondes.

waver ['weɪvər] *vi* (*of person etc*) vaciller.

wavy ['weɪvɪ] *a* (**-ier, -iest**) (*line*) onduleux; (*hair*) ondulé.

wax [wæks] **1** *n* cire *f*; (*for ski*) fart *m* ▮ *vt* cirer; (*ski*) farter; (*car*) lustrer ▮ *a* (*candle etc*) de cire. **w. paper** *Culin Am* papier *m* paraffiné. **2** *vi* (*of moon*) croître. ● **waxworks** *npl* musée *m* de cire; (*dummies*) moulages *mpl* de cire.

way¹ [weɪ] *n* (*path, road*) chemin *m* (**to** de); (*direction*) sens *m*, direction *f*;

(*distance*) distance *f*; **all the** w., **the whole** w. (*to talk etc*) pendant tout le chemin; **this** w. par ici; **that** w. par là; **which** w.? par où?; **to lose one's** w. se perdre; **I'm on my** w. j'arrive; (*going*) je pars; **to make one's** w. **towards** se diriger vers; **the** w. **there** l'aller *m*; **the** w. **back** le retour; **the** w. **in** l'entrée *f*; **the** w. **out** la sortie; **a** w. **out of** (*problem*) *Fig* une solution à; **the** w. **is clear** *Fig* la voie est libre; **on the** w. **en route** (**to** pour); **by** w. **of** (*via*) par; **out of the** w. (*isolated*) isolé; **by the** w.... *Fig* à propos...; **to be** or **stand in s.o.'s** w. être sur le chemin de qn; **to get out of the** w. s'écarter; **a long** w. (**away** or **off**) très loin; **do it the other** w. **round** fais le contraire ▮ *adv* (*behind etc*) très loin; w. **ahead** très en avance (**of** sur).

way² [weɪ] *n* (*manner*) façon *f*; (*means*) moyen *m*; (*habit*) habitude *f*; (*particular*) égard *m*; **one's ways** (*behaviour*) ses manières *fpl*; **to get one's own** w. obtenir ce qu'on veut; (**in**) **this** w. de cette façon; **in a** w. dans un certain sens; w. **of life** mode *m* de vie; **no** w.! *Fam* pas question!

wayside ['weɪsaɪd] *n* **by the** w. au bord le la route.

wayward ['weɪwəd] *a* rebelle, capricieux.

WC [dʌb(ə)lju:'siː] *n* w-c *mpl*.

we [wiː] *pron* nous; **we** go nous allons; **we teachers** nous autres professeurs; **we never know** (*indefinite*) on ne sait jamais.

weak [wiːk] *a* (**-er, -est**) faible; (*tea, coffee*) léger; (*health, stomach*) fragile. ● w.-'**willed** *a* faible. ● **weaken** *vt* affaiblir ▮ *vi* faiblir. ● **weakling** *n* (*in body*) mauviette *f*; (*in character*) faible *mf*. ● **weakness** *n* faiblesse *f*; (*fault*) point *m* faible; **a** w. **for** (*liking*) un faible pour.

wealth [welθ] *n* richesse(s) *f(pl)*; **a** w. **of** (*abundance*) une profusion de. ● **wealthy** *a* (**-ier, -iest**) riche ▮ *n* **the** w. les riches *mpl*.

wean [wiːn] *vt* (*baby*) sevrer.

weapon ['wepən] *n* arme *f*.

wear [weər] **1** *vt* (*pt* **wore**, *pp* **worn**) (*have on body*) porter; (*put on*) mettre; **to have nothing to w.** n'avoir rien à se mettre ∎ *n* **men's/sports w.** vêtements *mpl* pour hommes/de sport; **evening w.** tenue *f* de soirée.

2 *vt* (*pt* **wore**, *pp* **worn**) (*material, patience etc*) user ∎ *vi* (*last*) faire de l'usage; (*become worn*) s'user ∎ *n* **w. (and tear)** usure *f*. ● **wearing** *a* (*tiring*) épuisant.

wear away *vt* (*clothes etc*) user; (*person*) épuiser ∎ *vi* s'user; (*of colours, ink*) s'effacer ∎ **to wear down** = **wear out** ∎ **to wear off** *vi* (*of colour, pain etc*) disparaître ∎ **to wear out** *vt* (*clothes etc*) user; (*person*) épuiser ∎ *vi* (*of clothes etc*) s'user.

weary ['wɪərɪ] *a* (**-ier**, **-iest**) (*tired*) fatigué (**of doing** de faire); (*tiring*) fatigant; (*look*) las (*f* **lasse**) ∎ *vi* **to w. of** se lasser de.

weasel ['wiːz(ə)l] *n* belette *f*.

weather ['weðər] *n* temps *m*; **what's the w. like?** quel temps fait-il?; **under the w.** (*ill*) patraque ∎ *vt* (*storm*) essuyer; (*crisis*) Fig surmonter. ● **weather-beaten** *a* (*face, person*) tanné. ● **weathercock** *n* girouette *f*. ● **weatherman** *n* (*pl* **-men**) *TV Rad Fam* présentateur *m* météo.

weav/e [wiːv] *vt* (*pt* **wove**, *pp* **woven**) (*cloth, Fig plot*) tisser; (*basket*) tresser ∎ *vi* **to w. in and out of** (*crowd, cars etc*) se faufiler entre. ● **—er** *n* tisserand, -ande *mf*.

web [web] *n* (*of spider*) toile *f*; (*of lies*) Fig tissu *m*.

wed [wed] *vt* (**-dd-**) (*marry*) épouser ∎ *vi* se marier.

we'd [wiːd] = **we had** & **we would**.

wedding ['wedɪŋ] *n* (*ceremony*) mariage *m*; **golden/silver w.** noces *fpl* d'or/d'argent ∎ *a* (*cake*) de noces; (*anniversary, present*) de mariage; (*dress*) de mariée; **w. ring**, *Am* **w. band** alliance *f*.

wedge [wedʒ] *n* (*under wheel etc*) cale *f* ∎ *vt* (*wheel, table etc*) caler; (*push*) enfoncer (**into** dans); **wedged (in)** between (*caught*) coincé entre.

Wednesday ['wenzdɪ, -deɪ] *n* mercredi *m*.

wee [wiː] *a* (*tiny*) Fam tout petit.

weed [wiːd] *n* mauvaise herbe *f*; **w. killer** désherbant *m* ∎ *vti* désherber ∎ *vt* **to w. out** Fig éliminer (**from** de). ● **weedy** *a* (**-ier**, **-iest**) (*person*) Fam maigre et chétif.

week [wiːk] *n* semaine *f*; **tomorrow w.**, **a w. tomorrow** demain en huit. ● **weekday** *n* jour *m* de semaine, jour *m* ouvrable. ● **week'end** *n* week-end *m*; **at** *or* **on** *or* **over the w.** ce week-end. ● **weekly** *a* hebdomadaire ∎ *adv* toutes les semaines ∎ *n* (*magazine*) hebdomadaire *m*.

weep [wiːp] *vi* (*pt* & *pp* **wept**) pleurer; (*of wound*) suinter ∎ **to w. for s.o.** pleurer qn; **weeping willow** saule *m* pleureur.

weigh [weɪ] *vt* peser; **to w. sth/s.o. down** (*with load*) surcharger qch/qn (**with** de); **to be weighed down by** (*of branch etc*) plier sous le poids de; **weighed down with** (*worry etc*) Fig accablé de; **to w. up** (*goods, chances*) peser ∎ *vi* peser. ● **weighing-machine** *n* balance *f*.

weight [weɪt] *n* poids *m*; **by w.** au poids; **to put on w.** grossir; **to lose w.** maigrir; **to pull one's w.** Fig faire sa part du travail; **w. lifter** haltérophile *mf*; **w. lifting** haltérophilie *f* ∎ *vt* **to w. sth (down)** faire tenir qch avec un poids; **to w. sth/s.o. down with** (*overload*) surcharger qch/qn de. ● **weighty** *a* (**-ier**, **-iest**) (*argument, subject*) Fig de poids.

weighting ['weɪtɪŋ] *n* (*on salary*) indemnité *f* de résidence.

weir [wɪər] *n* (*across river*) barrage *m*.

weird [wɪəd] *a* (**-ier**, **-iest**) (*odd*) bizarre; (*eerie*) mystérieux.

welcome ['welkəm] *a* (*pleasant*) agréable; (*timely*) opportun; **to be w.** (*warmly received, of person*) être bien reçu; **w.!** bienvenue!; **w. back!** bienvenue!; **to make s.o. (feel) w.** faire bon accueil à qn; **you're w.!** (*after 'thank you'*) il n'y a pas de quoi!; **a coffee/a break would be w.** un café/une pause ne ferait pas de mal; **w. to do** (*free*) libre de faire; **you're w. to my bike** mon vélo est à ta disposition. ∎ *n* accueil *m*; **to extend a w. to** (*greet*) souhaiter la bienvenue à. ∎ *vt* accueillir; (*warmly*) faire accueil à; **I w. you!** (*say welcome to you*) je vous souhaite la bienvenue! ● **welcoming** *a* (*smile*) accueillant; (*speech*) de bienvenue.

weld [weld] *vt* **to w. (together)** souder; (*groups*) *Fig* unir. ●**—ing** *n* soudure *f*. ● **welder** *n* soudeur *m*.

welfare ['welfeər] *n* (*material*) bien-être *m*; (*public aid*) aide *f* sociale; **to be on w.** *Am* percevoir des allocations; **the w. state** (*in Great Britain*) l'État-providence *m*; **w. work** assistance *f* sociale.

well[1] [wel] **1** *n* (*for water*) puits *m*; (*oil*) **w.** puits de pétrole. **2** *vi* **to w. up** (*rise*) monter.

well[2] [wel] *adv* (*better, best*) bien; **to do w.** (*succeed*) réussir; **you'd do w. to refuse** tu ferais bien de refuser; **w. done!** bravo!; **I, you, she** *etc* **might (just) as w. have left** il valait mieux partir; **as w.** (*also*) aussi; **as w. as** aussi bien que; **as w. as two cats, he has...** en plus de deux chats, il a.... ∎ *a* **she's w.** (*healthy*) elle va bien; **to get w.** se remettre; **all's w.** tout va bien. ∎ *int* eh bien!; **w., w.!** (*surprise*) tiens, tiens!; **huge, w., quite big** énorme, enfin, assez grand.

we'll [wi:l] = **we will** *or* **we shall.**

well-behaved [welbɪ'heɪvd] *a* sage. ● **w.-'being** *n* bien-être *m*. ● **w.-'built** *a* (*person, car*) solide. ● **w.-'heeled** *a* (*rich*) *Fam* nanti. ● **w.-in'formed** *a* bien informé. ● **w.-'known** *a* (*bien*) connu. ● **w.-'mannered** *a* bien élevé. ● **w.-'meaning** *a* bien intentionné. ● **w.-'off** *a* riche. ● **w.-'read** *a* instruit. ● **w.-'thought-of** *a* hautement considéré.

● **w.-thought-'out** *a* bien conçu. ● **w.-'timed** *a* opportun. ● **w.-to-'do** *a* riche. ● **w.-'tried** *a* (*method*) éprouvé. ● **w.-wishers** *npl* admirateurs, -trices *mfpl*.

wellington ['welɪŋtən] *n* **w. (boot)** botte *f* de caoutchouc.

Welsh [welʃ] *a* gallois; **W. rabbit** *or* **rarebit** *Culin* toast *m* au fromage ∎ *n* (*language*) gallois *m*; **the W.** (*people*) les Gallois *mpl*. ● **Welshman** *n* (*pl* -men) Gallois *m*. ● **Welshwoman** *n* (*pl* -women) Galloise *f*.

wend [wend] *vt* **to w. one's way** s'acheminer (**to** vers).

went [went] *pt of* **go 1.**

wept [wept] *pt of* **weep.**

were [wər, *stressed* wɜːr] *see* **be.**

west [west] *n* ouest *m*; **(to the) w. of** à l'ouest de; **the W.** *Pol* l'Occident *m*. ∎ *a* (*coast*) ouest *inv*; (*wind*) d'ouest; **W. Africa** Afrique *f* occidentale; **W. Indian** (*a & n*) antillais, -aise (*mf*); **the W. Indies** les Antilles *fpl.* ∎ *adv* à l'ouest, vers l'ouest. ● **westbound** *a* (*traffic*) en direction de l'ouest. ● **westerly** *a* (*point*) ouest *inv*; (*direction*) de l'ouest; (*wind*) d'ouest. ● **western** *a* (*coast*) ouest *inv*; (*culture etc*) *Pol* occidental; **W. Europe** Europe *f* de l'Ouest ∎ *n* (*film*) western *m.* ● **westward(s)** *a & adv* vers l'ouest.

wet [wet] *a* (**wetter, wettest**) mouillé; (*damp, rainy*) humide; (*day, month*) de pluie; **'w. paint'** 'peinture fraîche'; **to get w.** se mouiller; **to make w.** mouiller; **it's w.** (*raining*) il pleut; **w. suit** combinaison *f* de plongée ∎ *n* **the w.** (*rain*) la pluie; (*damp*) l'humidité *f* ∎ *vt* (**-tt-**) mouiller.

we've [wi:v] = **we have.**

whack [wæk] *n* (*blow*) grand coup *m* ∎ *vt* donner un grand coup à. ●**—ed** *a* (*tired*) *Fam* claqué. ●**—ing** *a* (*big*) *Fam* énorme.

whale [weɪl] *n* baleine *f*.

wham! [wæm] *int* vlan!

wharf [wɔːf] *n* (*pl* **wharfs** *or* **wharves**) (*for* *ships*) quai *m*.

what [wɒt] **1** *a* quel, quelle, *pl* quel(le)s; **w. book?** quel livre?; **w. a fool/**etc**!** quel idiot/*etc*!; **w. little she has** le peu qu'elle a.

2 *pron* (*in questions*) (*subject*) qu'est-ce qui; (*object*) (qu'est-ce) que; (*after prep*) quoi; **w.'s happening?** qu'est-ce qui se passe?; **w. does he do?** qu'est-ce qu'il fait?, que fait-il?; **w. is it?** qu'est-ce que c'est?; **w.'s that book?** c'est quoi, ce livre?; **w.!** (*surprise*) quoi!, comment!; **w.'s it called?** comment ça s'appelle?; **w. for?** pourquoi?; **w. about me/**etc**?** et moi/*etc*?; **w. about leaving/**etc**?** si on partait/*etc*?

3 *pron* (*indirect, relative*) (*subject*) ce qui; (*object*) ce que; **I know w. will happen/w. she'll do** je sais ce qui arrivera/ce qu'elle fera; **w. happens is. . .** ce qui arrive c'est que. . .; **w. I need** ce dont j'ai besoin.

whatever [wɒt'evər] *a* **w. (the) mistake/**etc quelle que soit l'erreur/*etc*; **of w. size** de n'importe quelle taille; **no chance w.** pas la moindre chance; **nothing w.** rien du tout ‖ *pron* (*no matter what*) quoi que (+ *sub*); **w. you do** quoi que tu fasses; **w. happens** quoi qu'il arrive; **w. is important** fais tout ce qui est important; **do w. you want** fais tout ce que tu veux.

what's-it ['wɒtsɪt] *n* (*thing*) *Fam* machin *m*.

whatsoever [wɒtsəʊ'evər] *a* & *pron* = **whatever**.

wheat [wiːt] *n* blé *m*, froment *m*. ● **wheatgerm** *n* germes *mpl* de blé.

wheedle ['wiːd(ə)l] *vt* **to w. s.o.** enjôler qn (**into doing** pour qu'il fasse); **to w. sth out of s.o.** obtenir qch de qn par la flatterie.

wheel [wiːl] *n* roue *f*; **at the w.** *Aut* au volant; *Nau* au gouvernail ‖ *vt* (*bicycle etc*) pousser. ● **wheelbarrow** *n* brouette *f*. ● **wheelchair** *n* fauteuil *m* roulant.

wheeze [wiːz] *vi* respirer bruyamment. ● **wheezy** *a* (**-ier, -iest**) poussif.

when [wen] *adv* quand ‖ *conj* quand, lorsque; **w. I finish, w. I've finished** quand j'aurai fini; **w. I saw him** *or* **w. I'd seen him, I left** après l'avoir vu, je suis parti; **the day/moment w.** le jour/moment où.

whenever [wen'evər] *conj* (*at whatever time*) quand; (*each time that*) chaque fois que.

where [weər] *adv* où; **w. are you from?** d'où êtes-vous? ‖ *conj* (là) où; **I found it w. she'd left it** je l'ai trouvé là où elle l'avait laissé; **the place/house w.** l'endroit/la maison où; **that's w. you'll find it** c'est là que tu le trouveras. ● **whereabouts** *adv* où (donc) ‖ *n* **in his w.** l'endroit m où il est. ● **whereas** *conj* alors que. ● **where'by** *adv* par quoi. ● **where'upon** *adv* sur quoi. ● **wher'ever** *conj* **w. you go** (*everywhere*) partout où tu iras, où que tu ailles; **I'll go w. you like** (*anywhere*) j'irai (là) où vous voudrez.

whet [wet] *vt* (**-tt-**) (*appetite*) aiguiser.

whether ['weðər] *conj* si; **I don't know w. to leave** je ne sais pas si je dois partir; **w. she does it or not** qu'elle le fasse ou non; **it's doubtful w.** il est douteux que (+ *sub*).

which [wɪtʃ] **1** *a* (*in questions etc*) quel, quelle, *pl* quel(le)s; **w. hat?** quel chapeau?; **in w. case** auquel cas.

2 *rel pron* (*subject*) qui; (*object*) que; (*after prep*) lequel, laquelle, *pl* lesquel(le)s; (*after clause*) ce qui; (*object*) ce que; **the house w.** is old la maison qui est vieille; **the book w. I like** le livre que j'aime; **the table w. I put it on** la table sur laquelle je l'ai mis; **the film of w. . . .** le film dont *or* duquel. . .; **she's ill, w. is sad** elle est malade, ce qui est triste; **he lies, w. I don't like** il ment, ce que je n'aime pas; **after w.** (*whereupon*) après quoi.

3 *pron* **w. (one)** (*in questions*) lequel, laquelle, *pl* lesquel(le)s; **w. (one) of us?** lequel *or* laquelle d'entre nous *or* de nous?; **w. (ones) are the best of these books?** quels sont les meilleurs de ces livres?

4 *pron* w. (one) (*the one that*) (*subject*) celui qui, celle qui, *pl* ceux qui, celles qui; (*object*) celui *etc* que; **show me w. (one) is red** montrez-moi celui *or* celle qui est rouge; **I know w. (ones) you want** je sais ceux *or* celles que vous désirez.

whichever [wɪtʃ'evər] *a & pron* w. book/ *etc or* w. of the books/*etc* you buy quel que soit le livre/*etc* que tu achètes; **take w. books** *or* **w. of the books interest you** prenez les livres qui vous intéressent; **take w. (one) you like** prends celui *or* celle que tu veux; **w. (ones) remain** ceux *or* celles qui restent.

whiff [wɪf] *n* (*puff*) bouffée *f*; (*smell*) odeur *f*.

while [waɪl] *conj* (*when*) pendant que; (*although*) bien que (+ *sub*); (*as long as*) tant que; (*whereas*) tandis que; **w. eating/***etc* en mangeant/*etc* **I** w. un moment; **all the w.** tout le temps **I** *vt* to w. away (*time*) passer. ● **whilst** [waɪlst] *conj* = **while.**

whim [wɪm] *n* caprice *m*.

whimper ['wɪmpər] *vi* (*of dog, person*) gémir faiblement; (*snivel*) pleurnicher.

whimsical ['wɪmzɪk(ə)l] *a* (*look, idea*) bizarre; (*person*) fantasque, capricieux.

whine [waɪn] *vi* gémir; (*complain*) Fig se plaindre.

whip [wɪp] *n* fouet *m* **I** *vt* (-pp-) fouetter; **whipped cream** crème *f* fouettée **I** *vi* (*rush*) aller à toute vitesse. ● **w.-round** *n* Fam collecte *f*.

whip off *vt* (*take off*) Fam enlever brusquement **I** **to whip out** *vt* (*from pocket etc*) Fam sortir brusquement (**from** de) **I** **to whip round** *vi* Fam faire un saut (**to s.o.'s** chez qn) **I** **to whip up** *vt* (*interest*) susciter; (*meal*) Fam préparer rapidement.

whirl [wɜːl] *vi* to w. (round) tourbillonner, tournoyer; (*of spinning top*) tourner **I** *vt* to w. (round) faire tourbillonner; faire tourner. ● **whirlpool** *n* tourbillon *m*; **w. bath** *Am* bain *m* à remous. ● **whirlwind** *n* tourbillon *m* (de vent).

whirr [wɜːr] *vi* (*of engine*) vrombir; (*of spinning top*) ronronner.

whisk [wɪsk] **1** *n* Culin fouet *m* **I** *vt* fouetter. **2** *vt* to w. away *or* off enlever rapidement; (*person*) emmener rapidement.

whiskers ['wɪskəz] *npl* (*of cat*) moustaches *fpl*; (*side*) w. favoris *mpl*.

whisky, *Am* **whiskey** ['wɪskɪ] *n* whisky *m*.

whisper ['wɪspər] *vti* chuchoter; **to w. sth to s.o.** chuchoter qch à l'oreille de qn **I** *n* chuchotement *m*.

whistle ['wɪs(ə)l] *n* sifflement *m*; (*object*) sifflet *m*; **to blow the** *or* **one's w.** siffler **I** *vti* siffler.

white [waɪt] *a* (-er, -est) blanc (*f* blanche); **to go** *or* **turn w.** blanchir. ● **w. coffee** café *m* au lait; **w. lie** pieux mensonge *m*; **w. man** blanc *m*; **w. woman** blanche *f* **I** *n* (*colour, of egg*) blanc *m*. ● **white-collar 'worker** *n* employé, -ée *mf* de bureau. ● **whiteness** *n* blancheur *f*. ● **whitewash** *vt* (*wall*) badigeonner; (*person*) Fig blanchir.

whiting ['waɪtɪŋ] *n inv* (*fish*) merlan *m*.

Whitsun ['wɪts(ə)n] *n* la Pentecôte.

whizz [wɪz] **1** *vi* to w. past *or* by (*rush*) passer à toute vitesse. **2** *a* w. kid *Fam* petit prodige *m*.

who [huː] *pron* qui; **w. did it?** qui (est-ce qui) a fait ça?; **the woman w.** la femme qui.

whoever [huː'evər] *pron* (*no matter who*) qui que ce soit qui; (*object*) qui que ce soit que; **w. has travelled** (*anyone who*) quiconque a voyagé; **w. you are** qui que vous soyez; **this man, w. he is** cet homme, quel qu'il soit; **w. did that?** qui donc a fait ça?

whodunit [huː'dʌnɪt] *n* (*detective story*) Fam polar *m*.

whole [həʊl] *a* entier; (*intact*) intact; **the w. time** tout le temps; **the w. apple** toute la pomme, la pomme (tout) entière; **the w. world** le monde entier; **the w. lot** le tout; **w. food** aliment *m* complet **I** *n* (*unit*) tout *m*; (*total*) totalité *f*; **the w. of**

the village le village (tout) entier, tout le village; **on the w.** dans l'ensemble. ●**whole-'hearted** *a or* **whole-'heartedly** *adv* sans réserve. ●**wholemeal** *or Am* **wholewheat** *a* (*bread*) complet.

wholesale ['həulseɪl] *n* **to deal in w.** *Com* faire de la vente en gros **‖** *a* (*price etc*) de gros; (*destruction etc*) *Fig* en masse **‖** *adv* (*to sell, buy*) au prix de gros; (*in bulk*) en gros; (*to destroy etc*) *Fig* en masse. ●**wholesaler** *n* grossiste *mf*.

wholesome ['həulsəm] *a* (*food, climate etc*) sain.

wholly ['həulɪ] *adv* entièrement.

whom [hu:m] *pron* (*object*) que; (*in questions and after prep*) qui; **w. did she see?** qui a-t-elle vu?; **the man you know** l'homme que tu connais; **with w.** avec qui.

whooping cough ['hu:pɪŋkɒf] *n* coqueluche *f*.

whopping ['wɒpɪŋ] *a* (*big*) *Fam* énorme.

whore [hɔ:r] *n* (*prostitute*) putain *f*.

whose [hu:z] *poss pron & a* à qui, de qui; **w. book is this?** à qui est ce livre?; **w. daughter are you?** de qui es-tu la fille?; **the woman w. book I have** la femme dont *or* de qui j'ai le livre; **the man w. mother I spoke to** l'homme à la mère de qui j'ai parlé.

why [waɪ] **1** *adv* pourquoi; **w. not?** pourquoi pas? **‖** *conj* **the reason w. they...** la raison pour laquelle ils.... **2** *int* (*surprise*) eh bien!, tiens!

wick [wɪk] *n* (*of candle, lighter*) mèche *f*.

wicked ['wɪkɪd] *a* (*evil*) méchant; (*mischievous*) malicieux. ●**—ness** *n* méchanceté *f*.

wicker ['wɪkər] *n* osier *m*; **w. basket** panier *m* d'osier.

wicket ['wɪkɪt] *n* (*cricket stumps*) guichet *m*.

wide [waɪd] *a* (**-er, -est**) (*ocean*) vaste; (*choice, variety*) grand; **to be three metres w.** avoir trois mètres de large **‖** *adv* (*to open*) tout grand; (*to fall*) loin du but. ●**wide-'awake** *a* éveillé.

●**widely** *adv* (*to travel*) beaucoup; (*to broadcast*) largement; **w. different** très différent; **it's w. believed that...** on pense généralement que.... ●**widen** *vt* élargir **‖** *vi* s'élargir.

widespread ['waɪdspred] *a* (très) répandu.

widow ['wɪdəu] *n* veuve *f*. ●**widowed** *a* **to be w.** (*of man*) devenir veuf; (*of woman*) devenir veuve. ●**widower** *n* veuf *m*.

width [wɪdθ] *n* largeur *f*.

wield [wi:ld] *vt* (*brandish*) brandir; (*power*) *Fig* exercer.

wife [waɪf] *n* (*pl* **wives**) femme *f*, épouse *f*.

wig [wɪg] *n* perruque *f*.

wiggle ['wɪg(ə)l] *vt* agiter; **to w. one's hips** tortiller des hanches **‖** *vi* (*of worm etc*) se tortiller; (*of tail*) remuer.

wild [waɪld] *a* (**-er, -est**) (*animal, flower etc*) sauvage; (*idea, life*) fou (*f* folle); (*look*) farouche; (*angry*) furieux (**with** contre); **w. with** (*joy etc*) fou de; **I'm not w. about it** *Fam* ça ne m'emballe pas; **to grow w.** (*of plant*) pousser à l'état sauvage; **to run w.** (*of animals*) courir en liberté; (*of crowd*) se déchaîner; **the W. West** *Am* le Far West **‖** *npl* **the wilds** les régions *fpl* sauvages. ●**wild-'goose chase** *n* fausse piste *f*. ●**wildlife** *n* faune *f*.

wilderness ['wɪldənəs] *n* désert *m*.

wildly ['waɪldlɪ] *adv* (*madly*) follement; (*violently*) violemment.

wile [waɪl] *n* ruse *f*, artifice *m*.

wilful ['wɪlfəl] *a* (*Am* **willful**) *a* (*intentional, obstinate*) volontaire.

will[1] *v aux* **he will come, he'll come** (*future tense*) il viendra (**won't he?** n'est-ce pas?); **you will not come, you won't come tu ne viendras pas** (**will you?** n'est-ce pas?); **w. you have a tea?** veux-tu prendre un thé?; **w. you be quiet!** veux-tu te taire!; **I w.!** (*yes*) oui!; **it won't open** ça ne veut pas s'ouvrir.

will[2] [wɪl] **1** *vt* (*intend*) *Old-fashioned* vouloir (**that** que (+ *sub*)); **to w. oneself to do** faire un effort de volonté pour faire ▌*n* volonté *f*; **ill** w. mauvaise volonté; **free w.** libre arbitre *m*; **of one's own free w.** de son plein gré; **against one's w.** à contrecœur; **at w.** (*to leave etc*) quand on veut. **2** *n* (*legal document*) testament *m*.

willing ['wɪlɪŋ] *a* (*helper, worker*) de bonne volonté; **to be w. to do** être disposé *or* prêt à faire, vouloir bien faire ▌*n* **to show w.** faire preuve de bonne volonté. ● —**ly** *adv* (*with pleasure*) volontiers; (*voluntarily*) volontairement. ● —**ness** *n* bonne volonté *f*; **her w. to do** son empressement *m* à faire.

willow ['wɪləʊ] *n* (*tree, wood*) saule *m*.

willpower ['wɪlpaʊər] *n* volonté *f*.

willy-nilly [wɪlɪ'nɪlɪ] *adv* bon gré mal gré.

wilt [wɪlt] *vi* (*of plant*) dépérir.

wily [waɪlɪ] *a* (**-ier, -iest**) rusé.

wimp [wɪmp] *n* *Fam* femmelette *f*, mauviette *f*.

win [wɪn] *n* (*victory*) victoire *f* ▌*vi* (*pt & pp* **won**, *pres p* **winning**) gagner ▌*vt* (*money, race etc*) gagner; (*victory, prize*) remporter; (*friends*) se faire; **to w. s.o. over** gagner qn (**to** à). ● **winning** *a* (*number, horse etc*) gagnant; (*team*) victorieux ▌*npl* **winnings** gains *mpl*.

wince [wɪns] *vi* faire une grimace (de douleur, dégoût *etc*).

winch [wɪntʃ] *n* treuil *m*.

wind¹ [wɪnd] *n* vent *m*; (*breath*) souffle *m*; **to have w.** (*in stomach*) avoir des gaz; **to get w. of sth** entendre parler de qch; **w. instrument** *Mus* instrument *m* à vent ▌*vt* **to w. s.o.** (*of blow*) couper le souffle à qn. ● **windcheater** *or* *Am* **windbreaker** *n* blouson *m*, coupe-vent *m inv*. ● **windfall** *n* (*unexpected money*) aubaine *f*. ● **windmill** *n* moulin *m* à vent. ● **windpipe** *n* *Anat* trachée *f*. ● **windscreen** *or* *Am* **windshield** *n* *Aut* pare-brise *m inv*; **w. wiper** essuie-glace *m inv*. ● **windsurfer** *n* (*person*) véliplanchiste *mf*. ● **windsurfing** *n* **to go w.** faire de la planche à voile. ● **windswept** *a* (*street etc*) balayé par les vents. ● **windy** *a* (**-ier, -iest**) **it's w.** (*of weather*) il y a du vent; **w. day** jour *m* de grand vent.

wind² [waɪnd] *vt* (*pt & pp* **wound**) (*roll*) enrouler (**round** autour de); (*clock*) remonter ▌*vi* (*of river, road*) serpenter. ● —**ing** *a* (*road etc*) sinueux; (*staircase*) tournant.

wind down *vt* (*car window*) baisser ▌**to wind up** *vt* (*clock*) remonter; (*meeting, speech*) terminer ▌*vi* (*end up*) finir (**doing** par faire); **to w. up with sth** se retrouver avec qch.

window ['wɪndəʊ] *n* fenêtre *f*; (*pane*) vitre *f*, carreau *m*; (*in vehicle or train*) vitre *f*; (*in shop*) vitrine *f*; (*counter*) guichet *m*; **French w.** porte-fenêtre *f*; **w. box** jardinière *f*; **w. cleaner** *or* *Am* **washer** laveur, -euse *mf* de carreaux; **w. ledge** = **windowsill**; **to go w. shopping** faire du lèche-vitrines. ● **windowpane** *n* vitre *f*, carreau *m*. ● **windowsill** *n* (*inside*) appui *m* de (la) fenêtre; (*outside*) rebord *m* de (la) fenêtre.

windy ['wɪndɪ] *a* *see* **wind¹**.

wine [waɪn] *n* vin *m*; **w. bar/bottle** bar *m*/bouteille *f* à vin; **w. cellar** cave *f* (à vin); **w. list** carte *f* des vins; **w. waiter** sommelier *m*. ● **wineglass** *n* verre *m* à vin. ● **wine-growing** *a* viticole.

wing [wɪŋ] *n* aile *f*; **the wings** *Th* les coulisses *fpl*. ● **winger** *n* *Fb* ailier *m*.

wink [wɪŋk] *vi* faire un clin d'œil (**at, to** à) ▌*n* clin *m* d'œil.

winner ['wɪnər] *n* gagnant, -ante *mf*; (*of argument, fight*) vainqueur *m*. ● **winning** *a & n see* **win**.

winter ['wɪntər] *n* hiver *m* ▌**in (the) w.** en hiver ▌*a* d'hiver. ● **wintertime** *n* hiver *m*. ● **wintry** *a* hivernal; **w. day** jour *m* d'hiver.

wipe [waɪp] *vt* essuyer; **to w. one's feet/hands** s'essuyer les pieds/les mains; **to w. away** *or* **off** *or* **up** (*liquid*) essuyer; **to w. out** (*clean*) essuyer; (*destroy*) anéantir; (*erase*) effacer ▌*vi* **to w. up** (*dry the dishes*) essuyer la vaisselle ▌*n* **to give sth a w.** donner un coup de torchon *or* d'éponge à qch. ●wiper n Aut essuie-glace m inv.

wir/e ['waɪər] n fil m; w. mesh or netting grillage m ‖ vt to w. sth (up) to sth (connect) El relier qch à qch; to w. a hall for sound sonoriser une salle. ●—ing n El installation f électrique.

wisdom ['wɪzdəm] n sagesse f.

wise [waɪz] a (-er, -est) (in knowledge) sage; (advisable) prudent. ●wisecrack n Fam (joke) astuce f; (sarcastic remark) sarcasme m. ●wisely adv prudemment.

-wise [waɪz] suff (with regard to) money/etc-wise question argent/etc.

wish [wɪʃ] vt souhaiter, vouloir (to do faire); I w. (that) you could help me/could have helped me je voudrais que/j'aurais voulu que vous m'aidiez; I w. I hadn't done that je regrette d'avoir fait ça; if you w. si tu veux; I w. you a happy birthday je vous souhaite (un) bon anniversaire; I w. I could si seulement je pouvais.
‖ vi w. for sth souhaiter qch.
‖ n (specific) souhait m, vœu m; (general) désir m; the w. for sth/to do le désir de qch/de faire; best wishes (on greeting card) meilleurs vœux mpl; (in letter) amitiés fpl; send him my best wishes fais-lui mes amitiés. ●wishful a it's w. thinking (on your part) tu rêves, tu prends tes désirs pour la réalité.

wisteria [wɪ'stɪərɪə] n Bot glycine f.

wistful ['wɪstfəl] a mélancolique et rêveur.

wit [wɪt] n 1 (humour) esprit m; (person) homme m or femme f d'esprit. 2 wit(s) (intelligence) intelligence f (to do of faire).

witch/e [wɪtʃ] n sorcière f. ●witchcraft n sorcellerie f.

with [wɪð] prep 1 avec; come w. me viens avec moi; w. no hat/etc sans chapeau/etc; I'll be right w. you je suis à vous dans une seconde; I'm w. you (I understand) Fam je te suis; w. it (up-to-date) Fam dans le vent.

2 (at the house etc of) chez; she's staying w. me elle loge chez moi.

3 (cause) de; to jump w. joy sauter de joie.

4 (instrument, means) avec, de; to write w. a pen écrire avec un stylo; to fill w. remplir de; satisfied w. satisfait de.

5 (description) à; w. blue eyes aux yeux bleus.

withdraw [wɪð'drɔ:] vt (pt withdrew, pp withdrawn) retirer (from de) ‖ vi se retirer. ●withdrawn a (person) renfermé. ●withdrawal n retrait m.

wither ['wɪðər] vi (of plant etc) se flétrir.

withhold [wɪð'həʊld] vt (pt & pp withheld) (permission etc) refuser (from à); (decision) différer; (money) retenir (from de); (information) cacher (from à).

within [wɪ'ðɪn] adv à l'intérieur ‖ prep (place, box etc) à l'intérieur de; w. 10 km (of) (less than) à moins de 10 km (de); (inside an area of) dans un rayon de 10 km (de); w. a month (to return etc) avant un mois; (to finish sth) en moins d'un mois; w. my means dans mes moyens; w. sight en vue.

without [wɪ'ðaʊt] prep sans; w. a tie/etc sans cravate/etc; w. doing sans faire.

withstand [wɪð'stænd] vt (pt & pp withstood) résister à.

witness ['wɪtnɪs] n (person) témoin m; to bear w. to témoigner de ‖ vt (accident etc) être le témoin de; (document) signer (pour attester l'authenticité de).

witty ['wɪtɪ] a (-ier, -iest) spirituel.

wives [waɪvz] see wife.

wizard ['wɪzəd] n magicien m; (genius) Fig génie m.

wobble ['wɒb(ə)l] vi (of chair etc) branler; (of cyclist, pile) osciller; (of jelly, Am jello®) trembler. ●wobbly a (table, tooth) branlant.

woe [wəʊ] n malheur m.

woke, woken [wəʊk, 'wəʊkən] pt & pp of wake[1].

wolf [wʊlf] 1 n (pl wolves) loup m. 2 vt to w. (down) (food) engloutir.

woman, pl **women** ['wumən, 'wimin] n femme f; **w. doctor** femme f médecin; **women drivers** les femmes fpl au volant; **w. friend** amie f; **w. teacher** professeur m femme; **women's** (clothes, attitudes etc) féminin. ●**womanhood** n to reach w. devenir (une) femme. ●**womanly** a féminin.

womb [wu:m] n utérus m.

women ['wimin] see **woman.**

won [wʌn] pt & pp of **win.**

wonder ['wʌndər] 1 n (marvel) merveille f, miracle m; (feeling) émerveillement m; **in w.** (to watch etc) émerveillé; **(it's) no w.** ce n'est pas étonnant (**that** que (+ sub)) ‖ vi (marvel) s'étonner (**at** de). 2 vt (ask oneself) se demander (**if** si, **why** pourquoi) ‖ vi (ask oneself questions) s'interroger (**about** au sujet de, sur); **I was just wondering** je réfléchissais.

wonderful ['wʌndəfəl] a (excellent, astonishing) merveilleux.

wonky ['wɒŋkɪ] a (-ier, -iest) Fam (table etc) bancal; (picture) de travers.

won't [wəunt] = **will not.**

woo [wu:] vt (voters etc) Fig chercher à plaire à.

wood [wud] n (material, forest) bois m. ●**wooded** a (valley etc) boisé. ●**wooden** a de or en bois; (manner, dancer etc) Fig raide. ●**woodland** n région f boisée. ●**woodpecker** n (bird) pic m. ●**woodwork** n (school subject) menuiserie f. ●**woodworm** n vers mpl (du bois); **it has w.** c'est vermoulu.

wool [wul] n laine f. ●**woollen** (Am **woolen**) a en laine ‖ npl **woollens**, Am **woolens** lainages mpl. ●**woolly** a (-ier, -iest) laineux; (unclear) Fig nébuleux ‖ n (garment) Fam lainage m.

word [wɜ:d] n mot m; (spoken) parole f, mot m; (promise) parole f; (command) ordre m; (news) nouvelles fpl; pl (of song etc) paroles fpl; **to have a w. with** s.o. parler à qn; (advise, criticize) avoir un mot avec qn; **in other words** autrement dit; **w. processing** traitement m de texte; **w. processor** machine f à or de traitement de texte ‖ vt (express) formuler. ●**wording** n termes mpl. ●**wordy** a (-ier, -iest) verbeux.

wore [wɔ:r] pt of **wear.**

work [wɜ:k] n travail m; (product, book etc) œuvre f, ouvrage m; (building or repair work) travaux mpl; **to be at w.** travailler; **farm w.** travaux mpl agricoles; **out of w.** au chômage; **a day off** un jour de congé; **he's off w.** il n'est pas allé travailler; **the works** (of clock etc) le mécanisme; **gas works** usine f à gaz; **w. force** main-d'œuvre f; **w. permit** permis m de travail; **w. station** poste m de travail.

‖ vi travailler; (of machine etc) marcher, fonctionner; (of drug) agir; **to w. loose** (of knot, screw) se desserrer; **to w. towards** (result, aim) travailler à.

‖ vt (person) faire travailler; (machine) faire marcher; (miracle) faire; (metal, wood etc) travailler.

workable ['wɜ:kəb(ə)l] a (plan) praticable.

workaholic [wɜ:kə'hɒlɪk] n Fam bourreau m de travail. ●'**workbench** n établi m. ●'**workman** n (pl **-men**) ouvrier m. ●'**workmate** n camarade mf de travail. ●'**workout** n Sp séance f d'entraînement m. ●'**workroom** n salle f de travail. ●'**workshop** n atelier m. ●**work-to-'rule** n grève f du zèle.

work at vt (improve) travailler (qch) ‖ **to work off** vt (debt) payer en travaillant; (excess fat) se débarrasser de (par l'exercice) ‖ **to work on** vt (book, problem) travailler à; (improve) travailler (son français etc) ‖ **to work out** vi (succeed) marcher; (do exercises) s'entraîner; **it works out at 50 francs** ça fait 50 francs ‖ vt (calculate) calculer; (problem) résoudre; (scheme) préparer; (understand) comprendre ‖ **to work up** vt **to w. up an appetite** s'ouvrir l'appétit; **to get worked up** s'énerver ‖ vi **it works up to** (climax) ça tend vers; **to w. up to** sth en venir à qch.

worker ['wɜːkər] n travailleur, -euse mf; (manual) ouvrier, -ière mf; (office) w. employé, -ée mf (de bureau).

working ['wɜːkɪŋ] a (day, clothes) de travail; (population) actif; w. class classe f ouvrière; in w. order en état de marche. ● working-'class a ouvrier.

world [wɜːld] n monde m; all over the w. dans le monde entier; the richest/etc in the world le or la plus riche/etc du monde ∎ a (war etc) mondial; (champion, cup, record) du monde. ● world-'famous a de renommée mondiale. ● worldly a (pleasures) de ce monde; (person) qui a l'expérience du monde. ● world'wide a universel.

worm [wɜːm] 1 n ver m. 2 vt to w. one's way into s'insinuer dans.

worn [wɔːn] pt of wear ∎ a (clothes etc) usé. ● worn-'out a (object) complètement usé; (person) épuisé.

worry ['wʌrɪ] n souci m ∎ vi s'inquiéter (about sth de qch, about s.o. pour qn) ∎ vt inquiéter; to be worried être inquiet (about au sujet de). ●—ing a inquiétant. ● worrier n anxieux, -euse mf.

worse [wɜːs] a pire, plus mauvais (than que); to get w. se détériorer; he's getting w. (in health) il va de plus en plus mal. ∎ adv plus mal (than que); I could do w. je pourrais faire pire; from bad to w. de mal en pis; to be w. off aller moins bien financièrement.

∎ n there's w. (to come) il y a pire encore; a change for the w. une détérioration. ● worsen vti empirer.

worship ['wɜːʃɪp] n culte m; his W. the Mayor Monsieur le Maire ∎ vt (-pp-) (person, god) adorer; (money) Pej avoir le culte de.

worst [wɜːst] a pire, plus mauvais ∎ adv (the) w. le plus mal ∎ n the w. (one) le or la pire, le or la plus mauvais(e); the w. (thing) is that... le pire c'est que...; at w. au pire; to be at its w. (of crisis) avoir atteint son paroxysme; to get the w. of it (in struggle etc) avoir le dessous.

worth [wɜːθ] n valeur f; to buy 50 pence

w. of chocolates acheter pour cinquante pence de chocolats ∎ a to be w. sth valoir qch; how much or what is it w.? ça vaut combien?; the film's w. seeing le film vaut la peine or Fam le coup d'être vu; it's w. (one's) while ça (en) vaut la peine or Fam le coup; it's w. (while) waiting ça vaut la peine d'attendre. ● worthless a qui ne vaut rien.

worthwhile [wɜːθ'waɪl] a (book, film etc) qui vaut la peine d'être lu, vu etc; (activity) qui (en) vaut la peine; (plan) valable; (satisfying) qui donne des satisfactions.

worthy ['wɜːðɪ] a (-ier, -iest) (person) digne; (cause, act) louable; w. of sth/ s.o. digne de qch/qn.

would [wʊd, unstressed wəd] v aux I w. stay, I'd stay (conditional tense) je resterais; he w. have done it il l'aurait fait; w. you help me, please? voulez-vous m'aider, s'il vous plaît?; w. you like some tea? voudriez-vous (prendre) du thé?; the wound wouldn't heal la blessure ne voulait pas cicatriser; I w. see her every day (used to) je la voyais chaque jour.

wound[1] [wuːnd] vt (hurt) blesser; the wounded les blessés mpl ∎ n blessure f.

wound[2] [waʊnd] pt & pp of wind[2].

wove, woven [wəʊv, 'wəʊv(ə)n] pt & pp of weave.

wow! [waʊ] int Fam oh là là!

wrap [ræp] vt (-pp-) to w. (up) envelopper; (parcel) emballer ∎ vti to w. (oneself) up (dress warmly) se couvrir ∎ n (shawl) châle m; plastic w. Am film m plastique. ● wrapping n (action, material) emballage m; w. paper papier m d'emballage. ● wrapper n (of sweet, Am candy) papier m.

wrath [rɒθ] n Lit courroux m.

wreak [riːk] vt to w. vengeance on se venger de; to w. havoc on ravager.

wreath [riːθ] n (pl -s [riːðz]) (of flowers) couronne f.

wreck [rek] n (ship) épave f; (sinking) naufrage m; (train etc) train m etc

accidenté; (*person*) épave *f* (humaine);
to be a nervous w. être à bout de
nerfs ▌*vt* (*object, Fig hopes etc*) détruire. ●**—age** *n* (*of plane etc*) débris
mpl. ●**—er** *n* (*truck*) *Am* dépanneuse *f*.

wren [ren] *n* (*bird*) roitelet *m*.

wrench [rentʃ] **1** *n* (*tool*) clef *f* (à écrous),
Am clef *f* à molette *f*. **2** *vt* (*tug at*) tirer
sur; (*twist*) tordre; **to w. sth from s.o.**
arracher qch à qn.

wrestl/e [ˈres(ə)l] *vi* lutter (**with s.o.**
avec qn); **to w. with** (*problem etc*)
Fig se débattre avec. ●**—ing** *n Sp* lutte
f; (**all-in**) w. catch *m*. ●**wrestler** *n*
lutteur, -euse *mf*; catcheur, -euse *mf*.

wretch [retʃ] *n* malheureux, -euse *mf*;
(*rascal*) misérable *mf*. ●**wretched** [-ɪd] *a*
(*poor, pitiful*) misérable; (*dreadful*) affreux; (*annoying*) maudit.

wriggle [ˈrɪg(ə)l] *vi* **to w.** (**about**) se
tortiller; (*of fish*) frétiller.

wring [rɪŋ] *vt* (*pt & pp* **wrung**) **to w.** (**out**)
(*clothes by hand*) tordre.

wrinkle [ˈrɪŋk(ə)l] *n* (*on skin*) ride *f*; (*in
cloth or paper*) pli *m* ▌*vt* (*skin*) rider;
(*cloth, paper*) plisser ▌*vi* se rider; faire
des plis.

wrist [rɪst] *n* poignet *m*. ●**wristwatch** *n*
montre *f*.

writ [rɪt] *n* acte *m* judiciaire; **to issue a w.
against s.o.** assigner qn (en justice).

write [raɪt] *vti* (*pt* **wrote**, *pp* **written**)
écrire. ●**w.-off** *n* a (**complete**) **w.-off**
(*car*) une véritable épave. ●**w.-up** *n*
(*report*) compte rendu *m*.

write away for *vt* (*details etc*) écrire pour
demander ▌**to write back** *vi* répondre
▌**to write down** *vt* noter ▌**to write off**
vt (*debt*) passer aux profits et pertes; **to
w. off for** = **write away for** ▌**to write out**
vt écrire; (*copy*) recopier ▌**to write up** *vt*
(*notes*) mettre à jour; **to w. up for** =

write away for.

writer [ˈraɪtər] *n* auteur *m* (**of** de);
(*literary*) écrivain *m*.

writhe [raɪð] *vi* (*in pain etc*) se tordre.

writing [ˈraɪtɪŋ] *n* (*handwriting*) écriture
f; *pl* (*of author*) écrits *mpl*; **to put sth
(down) in w.** mettre qch par écrit; **some
w.** (*on page*) quelque chose d'écrit; **w.
desk** secrétaire *m*; **w. pad** bloc *m* de
papier à lettres; (*for notes*) bloc-notes
m; **w. paper** papier *m* à lettres.

written [ˈrɪt(ə)n] *pp* of **write**.

wrong [rɒŋ] *a* (*sum, idea etc*) faux (*f*
fausse); (*direction, road etc*) mauvais;
(*unfair*) injuste; **to be w.** (*of person*)
avoir tort (**to do** de faire); (*mistaken*)
se tromper; **it's w. to swear**/*etc* c'est mal
de jurer/*etc*; **the clock's w.** la pendule
n'est pas à l'heure; **something's w.**
quelque chose ne va pas; **something's
w. with the phone** le téléphone ne
marche pas bien; **something's w. with
her arm** elle a quelque chose au bras;
nothing's w. tout va bien; **what's w. with
you?** qu'est-ce que tu as?; **the w. way
round** *or* **up** à l'envers.
▌*adv* mal; **to go w.** (*of plan*) mal
tourner; (*of machine*) tomber en
panne; (*of person*) se tromper.
▌*n* (*injustice*) injustice *f*; **to be in the w.**
être dans son tort; **right and w.** le bien et
le mal.
▌*vt* faire (du) tort à (qn). ●**wrongful** *a*
(*arrest*) arbitraire. ●**wrongly** *adv* (*to
inform, translate etc*) mal; (*to suspect
etc*) à tort.

wrote [rəʊt] *pt* of **write**.

wrought [rɔːt] *a* **w. iron** fer *m* forgé.
●**w.-'iron** *a* en fer forgé.

wrung [rʌŋ] *pt & pp* of **wring**.

wry [raɪ] *a* (**wryer, wryest**) (*comment*)
ironique; (*smile*) forcé.

X

X, x [eks] *n* X, x *m.*

xenophobia [zenə'fəʊbɪə, *Am* ziːnəʊ-] *n* xénophobie *f.*

Xerox® ['zɪərɒks] *n* photocopie *f* ‖ *vt* photocopier.

Xmas ['krɪsməs] *n Fam* Noël *m.*

X-ray ['eksreɪ] *n* (*photo*) radio(graphie) *f*; (*beam*) rayon *m* X; **to have an X-ray** passer une radio ‖ *vt* radiographier.

xylophone ['zaɪləfəʊn] *n* xylophone *m.*

Y

Y, y [waɪ] *n* Y, y *m.*

yacht [jɒt] *n* yacht *m.* ●**-ing** *n* yachting *m.*

Yank [jæŋk] *n Fam* Ricain, -aine *mf.*

yap [jæp] *vi* (**-pp-**) (*of dog*) japper.

yard [jɑːd] *n* **1** (*of farm, school etc*) cour *f*; (*for storage*) dépôt *m*, chantier *m*; (*garden*) *Am* jardin *m* (*à l'arrière de la maison*). **2** (*measure*) yard *m* (= 91,44 cm). ●**yardstick** *n* (*criterion*) critère *m.*

yarn [jɑːn] *n* **1** (*thread*) fil *m.* **2** (*tale*) *Fam* longue histoire *f.*

yawn [jɔːn] *vi* bâiller ‖ *n* bâillement *m.*

year [jɪər] *n* an *m*, année *f*; **school/tax y.** année *f* scolaire/fiscale; **this y.** cette année; **in the y. 1994** en (l'an) 1994; **he's ten years old** il a dix ans; **New Y. Nouvel An; New Year's Day** le jour de l'An; **New Year's Eve** la Saint-Sylvestre. ●**yearly** *a* annuel ‖ *adv* annuellement.

yearn [jɜːn] *vi* **to y. for s.o.** languir après qn; **to y. for sth** avoir très envie de qch; **to y. to do** avoir très envie de faire.

yeast [jiːst] *n* levure *f.*

yell [jel] *vti* **to y. (out)** hurler; **to y. at s.o.** (*scold*) crier après qn ‖ *n* hurlement *m.*

yellow ['jeləʊ] *a & n* (*colour*) jaune (*m*).

yes [jes] *adv* oui; (*contradicting negative*

question) si ‖ *n* oui *m inv.*

yesterday ['jestədɪ] *adv & n* hier (*m*); **y. morning/evening** hier matin/soir; **the day before y.** avant-hier.

yet [jet] **1** *adv* encore; (*already*) déjà; **she hasn't come (as) y.** elle n'est pas encore venue; **has he come y.?** est-il déjà arrivé?; **the best y.** le meilleur jusqu'ici. **2** *conj* (*nevertheless*) pourtant.

yew [juː] *n* (*tree, wood*) if *m.*

yield [jiːld] *n* (*of farm etc*) rendement *m*; (*profit*) rapport *m* ‖ *vt* (*produce*) produire; (*profit*) rapporter; (*give up*) céder (**to** à) ‖ *vi* (*surrender, give way*) céder (**to** à); (*of tree etc*) rendre; **'y.'** (*road sign*) *Am* 'cédez le passage'.

yoga ['jəʊgə] *n* yoga *m.*

yog(h)urt ['jɒgət, *Am* 'jəʊgɜːt] *n* yaourt *m.*

yoke [jəʊk] *n* (*for oxen*) & *Fig* joug *m.*

yolk [jəʊk] *n* jaune *m* (d'œuf).

you [juː] *pron* **1** (*polite form singular*) vous; (*familiar form singular*) tu; (*polite and familar form plural*) vous; (*object*) vous; te, t'; *pl* vous; (*after prep, 'than', 'it is'*) vous; toi; *pl* vous; **(to) y.** vous; te, t'; *pl* vous; **y. are** vous êtes; tu es; **I see y.** je vous vois; je te vois; **I give it to y.** je vous le donne; je te le donne; **with y.**

avec vous; avec toi; **y. teachers** vous autres professeurs; **y. idiot!** espèce d'imbécile!
2 (*indefinite*) on; (*object*) vous; te, t'; *pl* vous; **y. never know** on ne sait jamais. ● **you'd = you had & you would.** ● **you'll = you will.**

young [jʌŋ] *a* (**-er, -est**) jeune; **my young(er) brother** mon (frère) cadet; **her youngest brother** le cadet de ses frères; **the youngest son** le cadet ▌ *n* (*of animals*) petits *mpl*; **the y.** (*people*) les jeunes *mpl*. ● **youngster** *n* jeune *mf*.

your [jɔːr] *poss a* (*polite form singular, polite and familiar form plural*) votre, *pl* vos; (*familiar form singular*) ton, ta, *pl* tes; (*one's*) son, sa, *pl* ses.

yours [jɔːz] *poss pron* le vôtre, la vôtre, *pl* les vôtres; (*familiar form singular*) le tien, la tienne, *pl* les tien(ne)s; **this book is y.** ce livre est à vous *or* est le vôtre; ce livre est à toi *or* est le tien; **a friend of y.** un ami à vous; un ami à toi.

yourself [jɔːˈself] *pron* (*polite form*) vous-même; (*familiar form*) toi-même; (*reflexive*) vous; te, t'; (*after prep*) vous; toi; **you wash y.** vous vous lavez; tu te laves. ● **your'selves** *pron pl* vous-mêmes; (*reflexive & after prep*) vous.

youth [juːθ] *n* (*pl* **-s** [juːðz]) (*age, young people*) jeunesse *f*; (*young man*) jeune *m*; **y. club** maison *f* des jeunes. ● **youthful** *a* jeune.

yoyo [ˈjəʊjəʊ] *n* (*pl* **-os**) yo-yo *m inv.*

yucky [ˈjʌkɪ] *a Fam* dégueulasse.

yummy [ˈjʌmɪ] *a* (**-ier, -iest**) *Sl* délicieux.

yuppie [ˈyʌpɪ] *n* jeune cadre *m* dynamique.

Z

Z, z [zed, *Am* ziː] *n* Z, z *m.*

zany [ˈzeɪnɪ] *a* (**-ier, -iest**) farfelu.

zap [zæp] *vi Compu* effacer. ● **zapper** *n* (*for TV channels*) télécommande *f.*

zeal [ziːl] *n* zèle *m.* ● **zealous** [ˈzeləs] *a* zélé.

zebra [ˈziːbrə, ˈzebrə] *n* zèbre *m*; **z. crossing** passage *m* pour piétons.

zero [ˈzɪərəʊ] *n* (*pl* **-os**) zéro *m.*

zest [zest] *n* **1** (*enthusiasm*) entrain *m*; **z. for living** appétit *m* de vivre. **2** (*of lemon, orange*) zeste *m.*

zigzag [ˈzɪgzæg] *n* zigzag *m* ▌ *a & adv* en zigzag.

zinc [zɪŋk] *n* (*metal*) zinc *m.*

zip [zɪp] *n* **1** **z.** (**fastener**) fermeture *f* éclair®▌ *vt* (**-pp-**) **to z.** (**up**) fermer (avec une fermeture éclair®). **2** *vi* (**-pp-**) (*go quickly*) aller comme l'éclair. **3** *a* **z. code** *Am* code *m* postal. ● **zipper** *n Am* fermeture *f* éclair®.

zit [zɪt] *n* (*pimple*) *Am Fam* bouton *m.*

zodiac [ˈzəʊdɪæk] *n* zodiaque *m.*

zone [zəʊn] *n* zone *f*; (*division of city*) secteur *m.*

zoo [zuː] *n* (*pl* **zoos**) zoo *m*; **z. keeper** gardien, -ienne *mf* de zoo.

zoom [zuːm] **1** *vi* (*rush*) se précipiter; **to z. past** passer comme un éclair. **2** *n* **z. lens** zoom *m.*

zucchini [zuːˈkiːnɪ] *n* (*pl* **-ni** *or* **-nis**) *Am* courgette *f.*

FRENCH VERB CONJUGATIONS

Regular Verbs

	-ER Verbs	-IR Verbs	-RE Verbs
Infinitive	*donn/er*	*fin/ir*	*vend/re*
1 Present	je donne	je finis	je vends
	tu donnes	tu finis	tu vends
	il donne	il finit	il vend
	nous donnons	nous finissons	nous vendons
	vous donnez	vous finissez	vous vendez
	ils donnent	ils finissent	ils vendent
2 Imperfect	je donnais	je finissais	je vendais
	tu donnais	tu finissais	tu vendais
	il donnait	il finissait	il vendait
	nous donnions	nous finissions	nous vendions
	vous donniez	vous finissiez	vous vendiez
	ils donnaient	ils finissaient	ils vendaient
3 Past historic	je donnai	je finis	je vendis
	tu donnas	tu finis	tu vendis
	il donna	il finit	il vendit
	nous donnâmes	nous finîmes	nous vendîmes
	vous donnâtes	vous finîtes	vous vendîtes
	ils donnèrent	ils finirent	ils vendirent
4 Future	je donnerai	je finirai	je vendrai
	tu donneras	tu finiras	tu vendras
	il donnera	il finira	il vendra
	nous donnerons	nous finirons	nous vendrons
	vous donnerez	vous finirez	vous vendrez
	ils donneront	ils finiront	ils vendront
5 Subjunctive	je donne	je finisse	je vende
	tu donnes	tu finisses	tu vendes
	il donne	il finisse	il vende
	nous donnions	nous finissions	nous vendions
	vous donniez	vous finissiez	vous vendiez
	ils donnent	ils finissent	ils vendent
6 Imperative	donne	finis	vends
	donnons	finissons	vendons
	donnez	finissez	vendez
7 Present participle	donnant	finissant	vendant
8 Past participle	donné	fini	vendu

Note The conditional is formed by adding the following endings to the infinitive: -ais, -ais, -ait, -ions, -iez, -aient. Final 'e' is dropped in infinitives ending '-re'.

SPELLING ANOMALIES OF -ER VERBS

Verbs in **-ger** (eg **manger**) take an extra e before endings beginning with o or a: *Present* je mange, nous mangeons; *Imperfect* je mangeais, nous mangions; *Past historic* je mangeai, nous mangeâmes; *Present participle* mangeant. Verbs in **-cer** (eg **commencer**) change c to ç before endings beginning with o or a: *Present* je commence, nous commençons; *Imperfect* je commençais, nous commencions; *Past historic* je commençai, nous commençâmes; *Present participle* commençant. Verbs containing mute e in their penultimate syllable fall into two groups. In the first (eg **mener, peser, lever**), e becomes è before an unpronounced syllable in the present and subjunctive, and in the future and conditional tenses (eg je mène, ils mèneront). The second group contains most verbs ending in **-eler** and **-eter** (eg **appeler, jeter**). These verbs change l to **ll** and t to **tt** before an unpronounced syllable (eg j'appelle, ils appelleront; je jette, ils jetteront). However, the following verbs in **-eler** and **-eter** fall into the first group in which e changes to è before mute e (eg je modèle, ils modèleront; j'achète, ils achèteront): **déceler, démanteler, geler, marteler, modeler, peler, receler; acheter, fureter, haleter**. Derived verbs (eg **dégeler, racheter**) are conjugated in the same way. Verbs containing e acute in their penultimate syllable change é to è before the unpronounced endings of the present and subjunctive only (eg je cède but je céderai). Verbs in **-yer** (eg **essuyer**) change y to i before an unpronounced syllable in the present and subjunctive, and in the future and conditional tenses (eg j'essuie, ils essuieront). In verbs in **-ayer** (eg **balayer**), y may be retained before mute e (eg je balaie or balaye, ils balaieront or balayeront).

IRREGULAR VERBS

Listed below are those verbs considered to be the most useful. Forms and tenses not given are fully derivable, such as the third person singular of the present tense which is normally formed by substituting 't' for the final 's' of the first person singular, eg 'crois' becomes 'croit', 'dis' becomes 'dit'. Note that the endings of the past historic fall into three categories, the 'a' and 'i' categories shown at *donner*, and at *finir* and *vendre*, and the 'u' category which has the following endings: -us, -ut, -ûmes, -ûtes, -urent. Most of the verbs listed below form their past historic with 'u'. The imperfect may usually be formed by adding -ais, -ait, -ions, -iez, -aient to the stem of the first person plural of the present tense, eg 'je buvais' etc may be derived from 'nous buvons' (stem 'buv-' and ending '-ons'); similarly, the present participle may generally be formed by substituting -ant for -ons (eg buvant). The future may usually be formed by adding -ai, -as, -a, -ons, -ez, -ont to the infinitive or to an infinitive without final 'e' where the ending is -re (eg conduire). The imperative usually has the same forms as the second persons singular and plural and first person plural of the present tense.

1 = Present   2 = Imperfect   3 = Past historic   4= Future
5 = Subjunctive   6 = Imperative   7 = Present participle
8 = Past participle   n = nous   v = vous   † verbs conjugated with **être** only.

Irregular French Verbs

abattre	*like* **battre**
†s'abstenir	*like* **tenir**
accourir	*like* **courir**
accroître	*like* **croître** *except* 8 accru
accueillir	*like* **cueillir**
acquérir	1 j'acquiers, n acquérons 2 j'acquérais 3 j'acquis
	4 j'acquerrai 5 j'acquière 7 acquérant 8 acquis
adjoindre	*like* **atteindre**
admettre	*like* **mettre**
†aller	1 je vais, tu vas, il va, n allons, v allez, ils vont 4 j'irai
	5 j'aille, n allions, ils aillent 6 va, allons, allez (*but note* vas-y)
apercevoir	*like* **recevoir**
apparaître	*like* **connaître**
appartenir	*like* **tenir**
apprendre	*like* **prendre**
asseoir	1 j'assieds, il assied, n asseyons, ils asseyent 2 j'asseyais
	3 j'assis 4 j'assiérai 5 j'asseye 7 asseyant 8 assis
atteindre	1 j'atteins, n atteignons, ils atteignent 2 j'atteignais 3 j'atteignis
	4 j'atteindrai 5 j'atteigne 7 atteignant 8 atteint
avoir	1 j'ai, tu as, il a, n avons, v avez, ils ont 2 j'avais 3 j'eus
	4 j'aurai 5 j'aie, il ait, n ayons, ils aient 6 aie, ayons, ayez
	7 ayant 8 eu
battre	1 je bats, il bat, n battons 5 je batte
boire	1 je bois, n buvons, ils boivent 2 je buvais 3 je bus
	5 je boive, n buvions 7 buvant 8 bu
bouillir	1 je bous, n bouillons, ils bouillent 2 je bouillais
	3 *not used* 5 je bouille 7 bouillant
combattre	*like* **battre**
commettre	*like* **mettre**
comparaître	*like* **connaître**
comprendre	*like* **prendre**
compromettre	*like* **mettre**
concevoir	*like* **recevoir**
conclure	1 je conclus, n concluons, ils concluent 5 je conclue
concourir	*like* **courir**
conduire	1 je conduis, n conduisons 3 je conduisis 5 je conduise 8 conduit
connaître	1 je connais, il connaît, n connaissons 3 je connus
	5 je connaisse 7 connaissant 8 connu
conquérir	*like* **acquérir**
consentir	*like* **mentir**
construire	*like* **conduire**
contenir	*like* **tenir**
contraindre	*like* **atteindre**
contredire	*like* **dire** *except* 1 v contredisez
convaincre	*like* **vaincre**
convenir	*like* **tenir**

Irregular French Verbs

corrompre	*like* **rompre**
coudre	1 je couds, il coud, n cousons, ils cousent 3 je cousis 5 je couse 7 cousant 8 cousu
courir	1 je cours, n courons 3 je courus 4 je courrai 5 je coure 8 couru
couvrir	1 je couvre, n couvrons 2 je couvrais 5 je couvre 8 couvert
craindre	*like* **atteindre**
croire	1 je crois, n croyons, ils croient 2 je croyais 3 je crus 5 je croie, n croyions 7 croyant 8 cru
croître	1 je crois, il croît, n croissons 2 je croissais 3 je crûs 5 je croisse 7 croissant 8 crû, crue
cueillir	1 je cueille, n cueillons 2 je cueillais 4 je cueillerai 5 je cueille 7 cueillant
cuire	1 je cuis, n cuisons 2 je cuisais 3 je cuisis 5 je cuise 7 cuisant 8 cuit
débattre	*like* **battre**
décevoir	*like* **recevoir**
découvrir	*like* **couvrir**
décrire	*like* **écrire**
décroître	*like* **croître** *except* 8 décru
dédire (se)	*like* **dire**
déduire	*like* **conduire**
défaillir	1 je défaille, n défaillons 2 je défaillais 3 je défaillis 5 je défaille 7 défaillant 8 défailli
défaire	*like* **faire**
démentir	*like* **mentir**
démettre	*like* **mettre**
dépeindre	*like* **atteindre**
déplaire	*like* **plaire**
déteindre	*like* **atteindre**
détenir	*like* **tenir**
détruire	*like* **conduire**
†devenir	*like* **tenir**
dévêtir (se)	*like* **vêtir**
devoir	1 je dois, n devons, ils doivent 2 je devais 3 je dus 4 je devrai 5 je doive, n devions 6 *not used* 7 devant 8 dû, due, *pl* dus, dues
dire	1 je dis, n disons, v dites 2 je disais 3 je dis 5 je dise 7 disant 8 dit
disparaître	*like* **connaître**
dissoudre	1 je dissous, n dissolvons 2 je dissolvais 5 je dissolve 7 dissolvant 8 dissous, dissoute
distraire	1 je distrais, n distrayons 2 je distrayais 3 *none* 5 je distraie 7 distrayant 8 distrait
dormir	*like* **mentir**
éclore	1 il éclôt, ils éclosent 8 éclos

Irregular French Verbs

écrire	1 j'écris, n écrivons 2 j'écrivais 3 j'écrivis 5 j'écrive 7 écrivant 8 écrit
élire	*like* **lire**
émettre	*like* **mettre**
émouvoir	*like* **mouvoir** *except* 8 ému
endormir	*like* **mentir**
enduire	*like* **conduire**
†s'enfuir	*like* **fuir**
entreprendre	*like* **prendre**
entretenir	*like* **tenir**
entrevoir	*like* **voir**
entrouvrir	*like* **couvrir**
envoyer	4 j'enverrai
†s'éprendre	*like* **prendre**
éteindre	*like* **atteindre**
être	1 je suis, tu es, il est, n sommes, v êtes, ils sont 2 j'étais 3 je fus 4 je serai 5 je sois, n soyons, ils soient 6 sois, soyons, soyez 7 étant 8 été
exclure	*like* **conclure**
extraire	*like* **distraire**
faillir	(*defective*) 3 je faillis 4 je faillirai 8 failli
faire	1 je fais, n faisons, v faites, ils font 2 je faisais 3 je fis 4 je ferai 5 je fasse 7 faisant 8 fait
falloir	(*impersonal*) 1 il faut 2 il fallait 3 il fallut 4 il faudra 5 il faille 6 *none* 7 *none* 8 fallu
feindre	*like* **atteindre**
foutre	1 je fous, n foutons 2 je foutais 3 *none* 5 je foute 7 foutant 8 foutu
frire	(*defective*) 1 je fris, tu fris, il frit 4 je frirai (*rare*) 6 fris (*rare*) 8 frit (*for other persons and tenses use* faire frire)
fuir	1 je fuis, n fuyons, ils fuient 2 je fuyais 3 je fuis 5 je fuie 7 fuyant 8 fui
haïr	1 je hais, il hait, n haïssons
inclure	*like* **conclure**
induire	*like* **conduire**
inscrire	*like* **écrire**
instruire	*like* **conduire**
interdire	*like* **dire** *except* 1 v interdisez
interrompre	*like* **rompre**
intervenir	*like* **tenir**
introduire	*like* **conduire**
joindre	*like* **atteindre**
lire	1 je lis, n lisons 2 je lisais 3 je lus 5 je lise 7 lisant 8 lu
luire	*like* **nuire**
maintenir	*like* **tenir**

Irregular French Verbs

maudire	1 je maudis, n maudissons 2 je maudissais 3 je maudis 4 je maudirai 5 je maudisse 7 maudissant 8 maudit
médire	*like* **dire** *except* 1 v médisez
mentir	1 je mens, n mentons 2 je mentais 5 je mente 7 mentant
mettre	1 je mets, n mettons 2 je mettais 3 je mis 5 je mette 7 mettant 8 mis
moudre	1 je mouds, il moud, n moulons 2 je moulais 3 je moulus 5 je moule 7 moulant 8 moulu
†mourir	1 je meurs, n mourons, ils meurent 2 je mourais 3 je mourus 4 je mourrai 5 je meure, n mourions 7 mourant 8 mort
†naître	1 je nais, il naît, n naissons 2 je naissais 3 je naquis 4 je naîtrai 5 je naisse 7 naissant 8 né
nuire	1 je nuis, n nuisons 2 je nuisais 3 je nuisis 5 je nuise 7 nuisant 8 nui
obtenir	*like* **tenir**
offrir	*like* **couvrir**
omettre	*like* **mettre**
ouvrir	*like* **couvrir**
paître	(*defective*) 1 il paît 2 il paissait 3 *none* 4 il paîtra 5 il paisse 7 paissant 8 *none*
paraître	*like* **connaître**
parcourir	*like* **courir**
†partir	*like* **mentir**
†parvenir	*like* **tenir**
peindre	*like* **atteindre**
percevoir	*like* **recevoir**
permettre	*like* **mettre**
plaindre	*like* **atteindre**
plaire	1 je plais, il plaît, n plaisons 2 je plaisais 3 je plus 5 je plaise 7 plaisant 8 plu
pleuvoir	(*impersonal*) 1 il pleut 2 il pleuvait 3 il plut 4 il pleuvra 5 il pleuve 6 *none* 7 pleuvant 8 plu
poursuivre	*like* **suivre**
pourvoir	*like* **voir** *except* 4 je pourvoirai
pouvoir	1 je peux *or* je puis, tu peux, il peut, n pouvons, ils peuvent 2 je pouvais 3 je pus 4 je pourrai 5 je puisse 6 *not used* 7 pouvant 8 pu
prédire	*like* **dire** *except* 1 v prédisez
prendre	1 je prends, il prend, n prenons, ils prennent 2 je prenais 3 je pris 5 je prenne 7 prenant 8 pris
prescrire	*like* **écrire**
pressentir	*like* **mentir**
prévenir	*like* **tenir**
prévoir	*like* **voir** *except* 4 je prévoirai
produire	*like* **conduire**

Irregular French Verbs

promettre	*like* **mettre**
promouvoir	*like* **mouvoir** *except* 8 promu
proscrire	*like* **écrire**
†provenir	*like* **tenir**
rabattre	*like* **battre**
rasseoir	*like* **asseoir**
recevoir	1 je reçois, n recevons, ils reçoivent 2 je recevais 3 je reçus 4 je recevrai 5 je reçoive, n recevions, ils reçoivent 7 recevant 8 reçu
reconduire	*like* **conduire**
reconnaître	*like* **connaître**
reconstruire	*like* **conduire**
recoudre	*like* **coudre**
recourir	*like* **courir**
recouvrir	*like* **couvrir**
recueillir	*like* **cueillir**
redire	*like* **dire**
réduire	*like* **conduire**
refaire	*like* **faire**
rejoindre	*like* **atteindre**
relire	*like* **lire**
reluire	*like* **nuire**
remettre	*like* **mettre**
†renaître	*like* **naître**
rendormir	*like* **mentir**
renvoyer	*like* **envoyer**
†repartir	*like* **mentir**
repentir	*like* **mentir**
reprendre	*like* **prendre**
reproduire	*like* **conduire**
résoudre	1 je résous, n résolvons 2 je résolvais 3 je résolus 5 je résolve 7 résolvant 8 résolu
ressentir	*like* **mentir**
resservir	*like* **mentir**
ressortir	*like* **mentir**
restreindre	*like* **atteindre**
retenir	*like* **tenir**
†revenir	*like* **tenir**
revêtir	*like* **vêtir**
revivre	*like* **vivre**
revoir	*like* **voir**
rire	1 je ris, n rions 2 je riais 3 je ris 5 je rie, n riions 7 riant 8 ri
rompre	*regular except* 1 il rompt
rouvrir	*like* **couvrir**
satisfaire	*like* **faire**

Irregular French Verbs

savoir	1 je sais, n savons, il savent 2 je savais 3 je sus 4 je saurai 5 je sache 6 sache, sachons, sachez 7 sachant 8 su
séduire	*like* **conduire**
sentir	*like* **mentir**
servir	*like* **mentir**
sortir	*like* **mentir**
souffrir	*like* **couvrir**
soumettre	*like* **mettre**
sourire	*like* **rire**
souscrire	*like* **écrire**
soustraire	*like* **distraire**
soutenir	*like* **tenir**
†se souvenir	*like* **tenir**
subvenir	*like* **tenir**
suffire	1 je suffis, n suffisons 2 je suffisais 3 je suffis 5 je suffise 7 suffisant 8 suffi
suivre	1 je suis, n suivons 2 je suivais 3 je suivis 5 je suive 7 suivant 8 suivi
surprendre	*like* **prendre**
†survenir	*like* **tenir**
survivre	*like* **vivre**
taire	1 je tais, n taisons 2 je taisais 3 je tus 5 je taise 7 taisant 8 tu
teindre	*like* **atteindre**
tenir	1 je tiens, n tenons, ils tiennent 2 je tenais 3 je tins, tu tins, il tint, n tînmes, v tîntes, ils tinrent 4 je tiendrai 5 je tienne 7 tenant 8 tenu
traduire	*like* **conduire**
traire	*like* **distraire**
transmettre	*like* **mettre**
tressaillir	*like* **défaillir**
vaincre	1 je vaincs, il vainc, n vainquons 2 je vainquais 3 je vainquis 5 je vainque 7 vainquant 8 vaincu
valoir	1 je vaux, il vaut, n valons 2 je valais 3 je valus 4 je vaudrai 5 je vaille 6 *not used* 7 valant 8 valu
†venir	*like* **tenir**
vêtir	1 je vêts, n vêtons 2 je vêtais 5 je vête 7 vêtant 8 vêtu
vivre	1 je vis, n vivons 2 je vivais 3 je vécus 5 je vive 7 vivant 8 vécu
voir	1 je vois, n voyons 2 je voyais 3 je vis 4 je verrai 5 je voie, n voyions 7 voyant 8 vu
vouloir	1 je veux, il veut, n voulons, ils veulent 2 je voulais 3 je voulus 4 je voudrai 5 je veuille 6 veuille, veuillons, veuillez 7 voulant 8 voulu.

VERBES ANGLAIS IRRÉGULIERS

Infinitif	Prétérit	Participe passé
arise	arose	arisen
awake	awoke	awoken
be	was, were	been
bear	bore	borne
beat	beat	beaten
become	became	become
begin	began	begun
bend	bent	bent
bet	bet, betted	bet, betted
bid	bade, bid	bidden, bid
bind	bound	bound
bite	bit	bitten
bleed	bled	bled
blow	blew	blown
break	broke	broken
breed	bred	bred
bring	brought [brɔːt]	brought
broadcast	broadcast	broadcast
build	built	built
burn	burnt, burned	burnt, burned
burst	burst	burst
buy	bought [bɔːt]	bought
cast	cast	cast
catch	caught [kɔːt]	caught
choose	chose	chosen
cling	clung	clung
come	came	come
cost	cost	cost
creep	crept	crept
cut	cut	cut
deal	dealt [delt]	dealt
dig	dug	dug
dive	dived, *Am* dove [dəʊv]	dived
do	did	done
draw	drew	drawn
dream	dreamed, dreamt [dremt]	dreamed, dreamt
drink	drank	drunk
drive	drove	driven
dwell	dwelt	dwelt
eat	ate [et, *Am* eɪt]	eaten
fall	fell	fallen
feed	fed	fed
feel	felt	felt
fight	fought [fɔːt]	fought
find	found	found

Verbes anglais irréguliers

Infinitif	Prétérit	Participe passé
flee	fled	fled
fling	flung	flung
fly	flew	flown
forbid	forbad(e)	forbidden
forecast	forecast	forecast
foresee	foresaw	foreseen
forget	forgot	forgotten
forgive	forgave	forgiven
forsake	forsook (*rare*)	forsaken
freeze	froze	frozen
get	got	got, *Am* gotten
give	gave	given
go	went	gone
grind	ground	ground
grow	grew	grown
hang	hung, hanged	hung, hanged
have	had	had
hear	heard [hɜːd]	heard
hide	hid	hidden
hit	hit	hit
hold	held	held
hurt	hurt	hurt
keep	kept	kept
kneel	knelt, kneeled	knelt, kneeled
know	knew	known
lay	laid	laid
lead	led	led
lean	leant [lent], leaned	leant, leaned
leap	leapt [lept], leaped	leapt, leaped
learn	learnt, learned	learnt, learned
leave	left	left
lend	lent	lent
let	let	let
lie	lay	lain
light	lit, lighted	lit, lighted
lose	lost	lost
make	made	made
mean	meant [ment]	meant
meet	met	met
mislay	mislaid	mislaid
mislead	misled	misled
mistake	mistook	mistaken
misunderstand	misunderstood	misunderstood
mow	mowed	mown, mowed

Verbes anglais irréguliers

Infinitif	Prétérit	Participe passé
outdo	outdid	outdone
overcome	overcame	overcome
overdo	overdid	overdone
overtake	overtook	overtaken
pay	paid	paid
put	put	put
quit	quit, quitted	quit, quitted
read	read [red]	read
redo	redid	redone
rewind	rewound	rewound
rid	rid	rid
ride	rode	ridden
ring	rang	rung
rise	rose	risen
run	ran	run
saw	sawed	sawn, sawed
say	said [sed]	said
see	saw	seen
seek	sought [sɔːt]	sought
sell	sold	sold
send	sent	sent
set	set	set
sew	sewed	sewn, sewed
shake	shook [ʃʊk]	shaken
shed	shed	shed
shine	shone ([ʃɒn, *Am* ʃəʊn])	shone
shoot	shot	shot
show	showed	shown, showed
shrink	shrank	shrunk, shrunken
shut	shut	shut
sing	sang	sung
sink	sank	sunk
sit	sat	sat
sleep	slept	slept
slide	slid	slid
sling	slung	slung
slit	slit	slit
smell	smelt, smelled	smelt, smelled
sow	sowed	sown, sowed
speak	spoke	spoken
speed	sped, speeded	sped, speeded
spell	spelt, spelled	spelt, spelled
spend	spent	spent
spill	spilt, spilled	spilt, spilled

Verbes anglais irréguliers

Infinitif	Prétérit	Participe passé
spin	spun	spun
spit	spat, spit	spat, spit
split	split	split
spoil	spoilt, spoiled	spoilt, spoiled
spread	spread	spread
spring	sprang	sprung
stand	stood [stʊd]	stood
steal	stole	stolen
stick	stuck	stuck
sting	stung	stung
stink	stank, stunk	stunk
stride	strode	stridden (*rare*)
strike	struck	struck
string	strung	strung
strive	strove	striven
swear	swore	sworn
sweep	swept	swept
swell	swelled	swollen, swelled
swim	swam	swum
swing	swung	swung
take	took [tʊk]	taken
teach	taught [tɔːt]	taught
tear	tore	torn
tell	told	told
think	thought [θɔːt]	thought
throw	threw	thrown
thrust	thrust	thrust
tread	trod	trodden
undergo	underwent	undergone
understand	understood	understood
undertake	undertook	undertaken
upset	upset	upset
wake	woke	woken
wear	wore	worn
weave	wove	woven
weep	wept	wept
win	won [wʌn]	won
wind	wound [waʊnd]	wound
withdraw	withdrew	withdrawn
withhold	withheld	withheld
withstand	withstood	withstood
wring	wrung	wrung
write	wrote	written

NUMERALS

Cardinal numbers

LES NOMBRES

Les nombres cardinaux

nought	0	zéro
one	1	un
two	2	deux
three	3	trois
four	4	quatre
five	5	cinq
six	6	six
seven	7	sept
eight	8	huit
nine	9	neuf
ten	10	dix
eleven	11	onze
twelve	12	douze
thirteen	13	treize
fourteen	14	quatorze
fifteen	15	quinze
sixteen	16	seize
seventeen	17	dix-sept
eighteen	18	dix-huit
nineteen	19	dix-neuf
twenty	20	vingt
twenty-one	21	vingt et un
twenty-two	22	vingt-deux
thirty	30	trente
forty	40	quarante
fifty	50	cinquante
sixty	60	soixante
seventy	70	soixante-dix
eighty	80	quatre-vingts
eighty-one	81	quatre-vingt-un
ninety	90	quatre-vingt-dix
ninety-one	91	quatre-vingt-onze
a *or* one hundred	100	cent
a hundred and one	101	cent un
a hundred and two	102	cent deux
a hundred and fifty	150	cent cinquante
two hundred	200	deux cents
two hundred and one	201	deux cent un
two hundred and two	202	deux cent deux
a *or* one thousand	1 000 (1,000)	mille
a thousand and one	1 001 (1,001)	mille un
a thousand and two	1 002 (1,002)	mille deux
two thousand	2 000 (2,000)	deux mille
a *or* one million	1 000 000 (1,000,000)	un million

Ordinal numbers

first	1st	1er	premier
second	2nd	2e	deuxième
third	3rd	3e	troisième
fourth	4th	4e	quatrième
fifth	5th	5e	cinquième
sixth	6th	6e	sixième
seventh	7th	7e	septième
eighth	8th	8e	huitième
ninth	9th	9e	neuvième
tenth	10th	10e	dixième
eleventh	11th	11e	onzième
twelfth	12th	12e	douzième
thirteenth	13th	13e	treizième
fourteenth	14th	14e	quatorzième
fifteenth	15th	15e	quinzième
twentieth	20th	20e	vingtième
twenty-first	21st	21e	vingt et unième
twenty-second	22nd	22e	vingt deuxième
thirtieth	30th	30e	trentième

Les nombres ordinaux

Examples of usage

Exemples d'emplois

three (times) out of ten	*trois (fois) sur dix*
ten at a time, in *or* by tens, ten by ten	*dix par dix, dix à dix*
the ten of us/you, we ten/you ten	*nous dix/vous dix*
all ten of them *or* us *or* you	*tous les dix, toutes les dix*
there are ten of us/them	*nous sommes dix/elles sont dix*
(between) the ten of them	*à eux dix, à elles dix*
ten of them came/were living together	*ils sont venus/ils vivaient à dix*
page ten	*page dix*
Charles the Tenth	*Charles Dix*
to live at number ten	*habiter au (numéro) dix*
to be the tenth to arrive/to leave	*arriver/partir le dixième*
to come tenth, be tenth (*in a race*)	*arriver dixième, être dixième*
it's the tenth (today)	*nous sommes le dix (aujourd'hui)*
the tenth of May, May the tenth, *Am* May tenth	*le dix mai*
to arrive/be paid/*etc* on the tenth	*arriver/être payé/etc le dix*
to arrive/be paid/*etc* on the tenth of May *or* on May the tenth *or Am* on May tenth	*arriver/être payé/etc le dix mai*
by the tenth, before the tenth	*avant le dix, pour le dix*
it's ten (o'clock)	*il est dix heures*
it's half past ten	*il est dix heures et demie*
ten past ten, *Am* ten after ten	*dix heures dix*
ten to ten	*dix heures moins dix*
by ten (o'clock), before ten (o'clock)	*pour dix heures, avant dix heures*
to be ten (years old)	*avoir dix ans*
a child of ten, a ten-year-old (child)	*un enfant de dix ans*

DAYS and MONTHS

LES JOURS et LES MOIS

Monday *lundi*; Tuesday *mardi*; Wednesday *mercredi*; Thursday *jeudi*; Friday *vendredi*; Saturday *samedi*; Sunday *dimanche*

January *janvier*; February *février*; March *mars*; April *avril*; May *mai*; June *juin*; July *juillet*; August *août*; September *septembre*; October *octobre*; November *novembre*; December *décembre*

Examples of usage

Exemples d'emplois

on Monday (*eg* he arrives on Monday)	*lundi (par exemple il arrive lundi)*
(on) Mondays	*le lundi*
see you on Monday!	*à lundi!*
by Monday, before Monday	*avant lundi, pour lundi*
Monday morning/evening	*lundi matin/soir*
a week/two weeks on Monday, *Am* a week/two weeks from Monday	*lundi en huit/en quinze*
it's Monday (today)	*nous sommes (aujourd'hui) lundi*
Monday the tenth of May, Monday May the tenth, *Am* Monday May tenth	*(le) lundi dix mai*
on Monday the tenth of May, on Monday May the tenth *or Am* May tenth	*le lundi dix mai*
tomorrow is Tuesday	*demain c'est mardi*
in May	*en mai, au mois de mai*
every May, each May	*tous les ans en mai, chaque année en mai*
by May, before May	*avant mai, pour mai*

A

A, a [ɑ] *nm* A, a.

a [a] *voir* **avoir**.

à [a] *prép* (à + **le** = **au** [o], à + **les** = **aux** [o]) **1** (*direction: lieu*) to; (*temps*) till, to; **aller à Paris** to go to Paris; **de 3 à 4 h** from 3 till ou to 4 (o'clock). **2** (*position: lieu*) at, in; (*surface*) on; (*temps*) at; **être au bureau/à la ferme/au jardin/à Paris** to be at ou in the office/ on ou at the farm/in the garden/in Paris; **à la maison** at home; **à l'horizon** on the horizon; **à 8 h** at 8 (o'clock); **à mon arrivée** on (my) arrival; **à lundi!** see you (on) Monday! **3** (*description*) **l'homme à la barbe** the man with the beard; **verre à liqueur** liqueur glass. **4** (*attribution*) **donner qch à qn** to give sth to s.o., give s.o. sth. **5** (*devant inf*) **apprendre à lire** to learn to read; **travail à faire** work to do; **maison à vendre** house for sale; **prêt à partir** ready to leave. **6** (*appartenance*) **c'est** (son livre) **à lui** it's his (book); **c'est à vous de** (*décider, protester etc*) it's up to you to; (*lire, jouer etc*) it's your turn to. **7** (*prix*) for; **pain à 2F** loaf for 2F. **8** (*poids*) by; **vendre au kilo** to sell by the kilo. **9** (*vitesse*) **100 km à l'heure** 100km ou per hour. **10** (*moyen, manière*) **à bicyclette** by bicycle; **à la main** by hand; **à pied** on foot; **au crayon** with a pencil, in pencil; **au galop** at a gallop; **à la française** in the French style ou way; **deux à deux** two by two.

abaisser [abese] *vt* to lower ‖ **s'a.** *vpr* (*barrière*) to lower; (*température*) to drop; **s'a. à faire** to stoop to doing.

abandon [abɑ̃dɔ̃] *nm* abandonment;

desertion; *Sp* withdrawal; (*naturel*) abandon; **à l'a.** in a neglected state. ● **abandonner** *vt* (*travail, tentative*) to give up, abandon; (*endroit, animal*) to desert, abandon ‖ *vi* to give up; *Sp* to withdraw.

abasourdir [abazurdir] *vt* to stun, astound.

abat-jour [abaʒur] *nm inv* lampshade.

abats [aba] *nmpl* offal; (*de volaille*) giblets.

abattoir [abatwar] *nm* slaughterhouse.

abattre* [abatr] *vt* (*mur*) to knock down; (*arbre*) to cut down; (*personne, gros gibier*) to shoot; (*vache etc*) to slaughter; (*avion*) to shoot down; (*déprimer*) *Fig* to demoralize ‖ **s'a.** *vpr* (*tomber*) to collapse; (*oiseau*) to swoop down (**sur** on); **s'a. sur** (*pluie*) to come down on; (*tempête*) to hit.

abattu [abaty] *a* (*triste*) demoralized.

abbaye [abei] *nf* abbey.

abbé [abe] *nm* (*chef d'abbaye*) abbot; (*prêtre*) priest.

abcès [apsɛ] *nm* abscess.

abdomen [abdɔmɛn] *nm* stomach, abdomen. ● **abdominal, -aux** *a* abdominal.

abeille [abej] *nf* bee.

aberrant [aberɑ̃] *a* (*idée etc*) ludicrous, absurd.

abîme [abim] *nm* abyss, chasm, gulf.

abîmer [abime] *vt* to spoil, damage ‖ **s'a.** *vpr* to get spoilt.

abject [abʒɛkt] *a* abject, despicable.

aboiement [abwamɑ̃] *nm voir* **aboyer**.

abois (aux) [ozabwa] *adv* at bay.

abolir [abɔlir] *vt* to abolish. ● **abolition** *nf* abolition.

abominable [abɔminabl] *a* terrible.

abondant [abɔ̃dɑ̃] *a* plentiful, abundant. ● **abondamment** *adv* abundantly. ● **abondance** *nf* abundance (**de** of);

une a. de plenty of, an abundance of; **en a.** in abundance. ● **abonder** vi to abound (**en** in).

abonné, -ée [abɔne] nmf (à un journal, au téléphone) subscriber; Rail Sp Th season ticket holder; (du gaz etc) consumer. ● **abonnement** nm subscription; (**carte d'**)**a.** Rail Th season ticket. ● **s'abonner** vpr to subscribe, take out a subscription (**à** to); to buy a season ticket.

abord [abɔr] 1 nm (vue) **au premier a.** at first sight. 2 nmpl (environs) surroundings; **aux abords de** around, nearby.

abordable [abɔrdabl] a (prix, marchandises) affordable; (personne) approachable.

abord (d') [dabɔr] adv first.

abord/er [abɔrde] vi to land ‖ vt (personne, lieu) to approach; (problème) to tackle, approach. ● **—age** nm (assaut) Nau boarding.

about/ir [abutir] vi to succeed; **a. à** to end at, lead to, end up in; **n'a. à rien** to come to nothing. ● **—issement** nm (résultat) outcome.

aboyer [abwaje] vi to bark. ● **aboiement** nm bark; pl barking.

abréger [abreʒe] vt (récit) to shorten; (mot) to abbreviate. ● **abrégé** nm **en a.** (phrase) in shortened form; (mot) in abbreviated form.

abreuvoir [abrœvwar] nm (lieu) watering place; (récipient) drinking trough.

abréviation [abrevjasjɔ̃] nf abbreviation.

abri [abri] nm shelter; **a. (de jardin)** (garden) shed; **à l'a. de** (vent) sheltered from; (besoin) safe from; **sans a.** homeless. ● **Abribus**® nm bus shelter. ● **abriter** vt (protéger) to shelter; (loger) to house ‖ **s'a.** vpr to (take) shelter.

abricot [abriko] nm apricot. ● **abricotier** nm apricot tree.

abrupt [abrypt] a (pente etc) steep, sheer, abrupt; (personne) abrupt.

abrut/ir [abrytir] vt **a. qn** (travail, télévision) to turn s.o. into a vegetable. ● **—i,**

-ie nmf idiot ‖ a idiotic.

absence [apsɑ̃s] nf absence. ● **absent, -ente** a (personne) absent, away; (chose) missing ‖ nmf absentee. ● **s'absenter** vpr to go away.

absolu [apsɔly] a absolute. ● **—ment** adv absolutely.

absorb/er [apsɔrbe] vt to absorb; (manger) to eat. ● **—ant** a (papier) absorbent; (travail, lecture) absorbing. ● **absorption** nf absorption.

abstenir* (**s'**) [sapstənir] vpr Pol to abstain; **s'a. de qch/de faire** to refrain from sth/doing. ● **abstention** nf Pol abstention.

abstrait [apstrε] a abstract. ● **abstraction** nf abstraction; **faire a. de** to disregard, leave aside.

absurde [apsyrd] a & nm absurd. ● **absurdité** nf absurdity; **dire des absurdités** to talk nonsense.

abus [aby] nm abuse, misuse (**de** of); over-indulgence (**de** in); (injustice) abuse; **a. d'alcool** alcohol abuse. ● **abuser** vi to go too far; **a. de** (situation, personne) to take unfair advantage of; (autorité) to abuse, misuse; (friandises) to over-indulge in.

abusif, -ive [abyzif, -iv] a excessive; **emploi a.** Ling improper use, misuse.

acabit [akabi] nm **de cet a.** Péj of that ilk.

acacia [akasja] nm (arbre) acacia.

académie [akademi] nf academy; Univ = (regional) education authority. ● **académique** a academic.

acajou [akaʒu] nm mahogany; **cheveux a.** auburn hair.

acariâtre [akarjɑtr] a cantankerous.

accabl/er [akɑble] vt to overwhelm (**de** with); **a. d'injures** to heap insults upon; **accablé de dettes** (over)burdened with debt; **accablé de chaleur** overcome by heat; **chaleur accablante** oppressive heat. ● **—ement** nm dejection.

accalmie [akalmi] nf lull.

accaparer [akapare] vt to monopolize; (personne) to take up all the time of.

accéder [aksede] vi **a. à** (lieu) to reach;

(*pouvoir, trône, demande*) to accede to.

accélérer [akselere] *vi Aut* to accelerate ▌ *vt* (*travaux etc*) to speed up; (*allure, pas*) to quicken, speed up ▌ **s'a.** *vpr* to speed up. ● **accélérateur** *nm Aut* accelerator. ● **accélération** *nf* acceleration; speeding up.

accent [aksɑ̃] *nm* accent; (*sur une syllabe*) stress; **mettre l'a. sur** to stress. ● **accentuer** *vt* to emphasize, accentuate, stress ▌ **s'a.** *vpr* to become more pronounced.

accepter [aksepte] *vt* to accept; **a. de faire** to agree to do. ● **acceptable** *a* acceptable. ● **acceptation** *nf* acceptance.

accès [aksɛ] *nm* **1** access (**à** to); **'a. interdit** 'no entry'; **les a. de** (*routes*) the approaches to. **2** (*de folie, colère, toux*) fit; (*de fièvre*) bout. ● **accessible** *a* accessible; (*personne*) approachable.

accessoire [akseswar] *a* secondary ▌ *nmpl Th* props; (*de voiture etc*) accessories; **accessoires de toilette** toilet requisites.

accident [aksidɑ̃] *nm* accident; **a. d'avion/de train** plane/train crash; **par a.** by accident, by chance. ● **accidenté, -ée** *a* (*terrain*) uneven; (*région*) hilly; (*voiture*) damaged (in an accident). ● **accidentel, -elle** *a* accidental. ● **accidentellement** *adv* accidentally, unintentionally.

acclamer [aklame] *vt* to cheer, acclaim. ● **acclamations** *nfpl* cheers.

acclimater [aklimate] *vt*, **s'a.** *vpr* to acclimatize, *Am* acclimate.

accolade [akɔlad] *nf* (*embrassade*) embrace; *Typ* brace, bracket.

accoler [akɔle] *vt* to place (side by side) (**à** against).

accommod/er [akɔmɔde] *vt* to adapt; *Culin* to prepare; **s'a. à** to adapt (oneself) to. ● **—ant** *a* accommodating, easy to please.

accompagner [akɔ̃paɲe] *vt* (*personne*) to go *ou* come with, accompany, escort; (*chose*) & *Mus* to accompany. ● **accompagnateur, -trice** *nmf* (*de touristes*)

guide; (*musical*) accompanist. ● **accompagnement** *nm* (*musical*) accompaniment.

accompl/ir [akɔ̃plir] *vt* to carry out, fulfil, accomplish. ● **—i** *a* accomplished.

accord [akɔr] *nm* agreement; (*harmonie*) harmony; *Mus* chord; **être d'a.** to agree, be in agreement (**avec** with); **d'a.!** all right! ● **accorder** *vt* (*donner*) to grant; *Mus* to tune; *Gram* to make agree ▌ **s'a.** *vpr* to agree; (*s'entendre*) to get along.

accordéon [akɔrdeɔ̃] *nm* accordion.

accoster [akɔste] *vt* to accost; *Nau* to come alongside ▌ *vi Nau* to berth.

accotement [akɔtmɑ̃] *nm* roadside, shoulder, verge.

accouch/er [akuʃe] *vi* to give birth (**de** to) ▌ *vt* (*enfant*) to deliver. ● **—ement** *nm* delivery.

accouder (s') [sakude] *vpr* **s'a. à** *ou* **sur** to lean on (*with one's elbows*). ● **accoudoir** *nm* armrest.

accoupler (s') [sakuple] *vpr* (*animaux*) to mate (**à** with).

accourir* [akurir] *vi* to come running, run over.

accoutumer [akutyme] *vt* to accustom ▌ **s'a.** *vpr* to get accustomed (**à** to); **comme à l'accoutumée** as usual. ● **accoutumance** *nf* familiarization (**à** with); *Med* addiction.

accroc [akro] *nm* (*déchirure*) tear; (*difficulté*) hitch, snag.

accrocher [akrɔʃe] *vt* (*déchirer*) to catch; (*fixer*) to hook; (*suspendre*) to hang up (*on a hook*); (*heurter*) to hit, knock ▌ **s'a.** *vpr* (*ne pas céder*) to persevere; (*se disputer*) *Fam* to clash; **s'a. à** (*se cramponner etc*) to cling to; (*s'écorcher*) to catch oneself on. ● **accrochage** *nm Aut* minor collision, knock; (*friction*) *Fam* clash.

accroître* [akrwatr] *vt*, **s'a.** *vpr* to increase. ● **accroissement** *nm* increase.

accroupir (s') [sakrupir] *vpr* to squat *ou* crouch (down). ● **accroupi** *a* squatting, crouching.

accueil [akœj] *nm* welcome, reception. ●**accueillir*** *vt* to receive, welcome, greet. ●**accueillant** *a* welcoming.

acculer [akyle] *vt* **a. qn à qch** to drive s.o. to *ou* against sth.

accumuler [akymyle] *vt*, **s'a.** *vpr* to pile up, accumulate. ●**accumulation** *nf* accumulation.

accus/er [akyze] *vt* (*dénoncer*) to accuse; (*rendre responsable*) to blame (**de** for); (*révéler*) to show; (*faire ressortir*) to bring out; **a. réception** to acknowledge receipt (**de** of). ●**—é, -ée 1** *nmf* accused; (*cour d'assises*) defendant. **2** *a* prominent. ●**accusateur, -trice** *a* (*look*) accusing. ●**accusation** *nf* accusation; *Jur* charge.

acéré [asere] *a* sharp.

achalandé [aʃalɑ̃de] *a* **bien a.** (*magasin*) well-stocked.

acharner (s') [saʃarne] *vpr* **s'a. sur** (*attaquer*) to set upon, lay into; **s'a. contre** (*poursuivre*) to pursue (relentlessly); **s'a. à faire** to struggle to do, try desperately to do. ●**acharné** *a* (*travail, effort*) relentless. ●**acharnement** *nm* (*au travail*) (stubborn) determination.

achat [aʃa] *nm* purchase; *pl* shopping.

achet/er [aʃte] *vti* to buy, purchase; **a. à qn** (*vendeur*) to buy from s.o.; (*pour qn*) to buy for s.o. ●**—eur, -euse** *nmf* buyer, purchaser; (*dans un magasin*) shopper.

achever [aʃve] *vt* to finish (off); **a. de faire qch** (*personne*) to finish doing sth; **a. qn** (*tuer*) to finish s.o. off ▮**s'a.** *vpr* to end, finish.

acide [asid] *a* acid, sour ▮*nm* acid.

acier [asje] *nm* steel. ●**aciérie** *nf* steelworks.

acné [akne] *nf* acne.

acompte [akɔ̃t] *nm* part payment, deposit.

acoustique [akustik] *nf* acoustics.

acquérir* [akerir] *vt* (*obtenir*) to acquire, gain; (*acheter*) to purchase. ●**acquéreur** *nm* purchaser. ●**acquisition** *nf* purchase; acquisition.

acquiescer [akjese] *vi* to acquiesce (**à** to).

acquit [aki] *nm* receipt; **par a. de conscience** to ease one's conscience. ●**acquitter** *vt* (*accusé*) to acquit; (*dette*) to clear, pay; **s'a. de** (*devoir, promesse*) to discharge; **s'a. envers qn** to repay s.o. ●**acquittement** *nm* (*d'un accusé*) acquittal.

âcre [ɑkr] *a* bitter, acrid, pungent.

acrobate [akrɔbat] *nmf* acrobat. ●**acrobaties** *nfpl* acrobatics. ●**acrobatique** *a* acrobatic.

acrylique [akrilik] *a* & *nm* acrylic.

acte [akt] *nm* act, deed, action; *Th* act; **un a. de** an act of; **a. de naissance** birth certificate.

acteur, -trice [aktœr, -tris] *nmf* actor, actress.

actif, -ive [aktif, -iv] *a* active ▮*nm Gram* active.

action [aksjɔ̃] *nf* action; (*en Bourse*) share. ●**actionnaire** *nmf* shareholder. ●**actionner** *vt* to set in motion, activate, actuate.

activer [aktive] *vt* (*accélérer*) to speed up ▮**s'a.** *vpr* (*se dépêcher*) *Fam* to get a move on.

activité [aktivite] *nf* activity; **en a.** (*personne*) fully active; (*volcan*) active.

actualité [aktɥalite] *nf* (*événements*) current events; *pl TV* news; **d'a.** topical.

actuel, -elle [aktɥɛl] *a* (*présent*) present; (*contemporain*) topical. ●**actuellement** *adv* at present, at the present time.

acupuncture [akypɔ̃ktyr] *nf* acupuncture. ●**acupuncteur, -trice** *nmf* acupuncturist.

adapter [adapte] *vt* to adapt; (*ajuster*) to fit (**à** to); **s'a. à** (*s'habituer*) to adapt to, adjust to; (*tuyau etc*) to fit. ●**adaptateur, -trice** *nmf* adapter. ●**adaptation** *nf* adjustment; (*de roman*) adaptation.

additif [aditif] *nm* additive.

addition [adisjɔ̃] *nf* addition; (*au restaurant*) bill, *Am* check. ●**additionner** *vt* to add (**à** to); (*nombres*) to add up.

adhérer [adere] *vi* **a. à** (*coller*) to stick to; (*s'inscrire*) to join; (*pneu*) to grip.

● **adhérence** nf (de pneu) grip. ● **adhérent, -ente** nmf member.

adhésif, -ive [adezif, -iv] a & nm adhesive.

adieu, -x [adjø] int & nm farewell, goodbye.

adjectif [adʒɛktif] nm adjective.

adjoint, -ointe [adʒwɛ̃, -wɛ̃t] nmf assistant; **a. au maire** deputy mayor.

adjuger [adʒyʒe] vt (accorder) to award (prize).

admettre* [admɛtr] vt (laisser entrer, accueillir, reconnaître) to admit; (autoriser, tolérer) to allow; (candidat) to pass; **être admis à** (examen) to have passed.

administrer [administre] vt (gérer, donner) to administer. ● **administrateur, -trice** nmf administrator. ● **administratif, -ive** a administrative. ● **administration** nf administration; **l'A.** (service public) government service, the Civil Service.

admirer [admire] vt to admire. ● **admirable** a admirable. ● **admirateur, -trice** nmf admirer. ● **admiratif, -ive** a admiring. ● **admiration** nf admiration.

admissible [admisibl] a (comportement etc) acceptable. ● **admission** nf admission.

adolescent, -ente [adɔlesɑ̃, -ɑ̃t] nmf adolescent, teenager ● **adolescence** nf adolescence, Fam teens.

adopter [adɔpte] vt to adopt. ● **adoptif, -ive** a (fils, patrie) adopted. ● **adoption** nf adoption.

adorer [adɔre] vt Rel to worship; (chose, personne) to love, adore; **a. faire** to love ou adore doing. ● **adorable** a adorable. ● **adoration** nf worship; **être en a. devant** to love, adore.

adosser [adose] vt **a. qch à** to lean sth back against; **s'a. à** to lean back against.

adoucir [adusir] vt (voix, traits etc) to tone down ▮ **s'a.** vpr (temps) to turn milder; (caractère) to mellow. ● **adoucissement** nm **a. de la température** milder weather.

adresse [adrɛs] nf **1** (domicile) address. **2** (habileté) skill. ● **adresser** vt (lettre) to send; (remarque etc) to address; **a. la parole à** to speak to; **s'a. à** to speak to; (aller trouver) to go and see; (bureau) to inquire at; (être destiné à) to be aimed at.

Adriatique [adriatik] nf **l'A.** the Adriatic.

adroit [adrwa] a skilful, clever.

adulte [adylt] a adult ▮ nmf adult, grown-up; **être a.** to be an adult or a grown-up.

adverbe [adverb] nm adverb.

adversaire [adverser] nmf opponent. ● **adverse** a opposing.

aérer [aere] vt (chambre, lit) to air (out) ▮ **s'a.** vpr Fam to get some air. ● **aéré** a airy. ● **aération** nf ventilation. ● **aérien, -ienne** a (attaque, transport etc) air; (photo) aerial; (câble) overhead; **ligne aérienne** airline.

aérobic [aerɔbik] nf aerobics.

aéro-club [aerɔklœb] nm flying club. ● **aérodrome** nm aerodrome. ● **aérogare** nf air terminal. ● **aéroglisseur** nm hovercraft. ● **aéromodélisme** nm model aircraft building and flying. ● **aéronautique** nf aeronautics. ● **aéroport** nm airport. ● **aéroporté** a airborne. ● **aérosol** nm aerosol.

affaiblir [afeblir] vt, **s'a.** vpr to weaken.

affaire [afɛr] nf (question) matter; (scandale) affair; (procès) case; pl Com business; (d'intérêt public, personnel) affairs; (effets) belongings, things; **avoir a. à** to have to deal with; **c'est mon a.** that's my business ou affair ou concern; **faire une bonne a.** to get a good deal, get a bargain; **ça fera l'a.** that will do nicely; **toute une a.** (histoire) quite a business.

affairer (s') [safere] vpr bustle about. ● **affairé** a busy.

affaisser (s') [afese] vpr (personne) to collapse; (plancher) to give way; (sol) to subside. ● **affaissement** nm (du sol) subsidence.

affaler (s') [safale] vpr to flop down.

affamé [afame] *a* starving.

affecter [afɛkte] *vt* (*nommer à un poste*) to post.

affection [afɛksjɔ̃] *nf* (*attachement*) affection; (*maladie*) ailment. ● **affectionner** *vt* to be fond of. ● **affectueux, -euse** *a* affectionate, loving.

affermir [afɛrmir] *vt* (*autorité*) to strengthen.

affiche [afiʃ] *nf* notice; (*publicitaire*) poster; *Th* bill. ● **afficher** *vt* (*avis, affiche*) to put up, stick up; (*concert etc*) to put up a notice about; *Ordinat* to display. ● **affichage** *nm* (bill-)posting; *Ordinat* display; **panneau d'a.** hoarding, *Am* billboard.

affilée (d') [dafile] *adv* (*à la suite*) in a row, at a stretch.

affirmatif, -ive [afirmatif, -iv] *a* (*ton*) assertive, positive; (*proposition*) affirmative; **il a été a.** he was quite positive.

affirmer [afirme] *vt* to assert. ● **affirmation** *nf* assertion.

affliger [afliʒe] *vt* to distress.

affluence [aflyɑ̃s] *nf* crowd; **heure(s) d'a.** rush hour(s).

affluent [aflyɑ̃] *nm* tributary.

affoler [afɔle] *vt* to drive crazy; (*effrayer*) to terrify ▮ **s'a.** *vpr* to panic. ● **affolant** *a* terrifying. ● **affolement** *nm* panic.

affranchir [afrɑ̃ʃir] *vt* (*timbrer*) to stamp (*letter*).

affreux, -euse [afrø, -øz] *a* horrible, dreadful, awful. ● **affreusement** *adv* dreadfully, awfully.

affront [afrɔ̃] *nm* insult, affront; **faire un a. à** to insult.

affront/er [afrɔ̃te] *vt* to confront, face; (*mauvais temps, difficultés etc*) to brave. ● **—ement** *nm* confrontation.

affût [afy] *nm* **à l'a. de** *Fig* on the lookout for.

affûter [afyte] *vt* (*outil*) to sharpen.

Afghanistan [afganistɑ̃] *nm* Afghanistan.

afin [afɛ̃] *prép* **a. de** (+ *inf*) in order to ▮ *conj* **a. que** (+ *sub*) so that.

Afrique [afrik] *nf* Africa. ● **africain, -aine** *a* & *nmf* African.

agac/er [agase] *vt* (*personne*) to irritate, annoy. ● **—ement** *nm* irritation.

âge [aʒ] *nm* age; **quel â. as-tu?** how old are you?; **avant l'â.** before one's time; **d'un certain â.** middle-aged; **l'â. adulte** adulthood; **le moyen â.** the Middle Ages. ● **âgé** *a* elderly; **â. de six ans six** years old; **un enfant â. de six ans** a six-year-old child; **plus â. que** older than.

agence [aʒɑ̃s] *nf* agency; (*succursale*) branch office; **a. immobilière** estate agent's office, *Am* real estate office.

agenda [aʒɛ̃da] *nm* diary, *Am* datebook.

agenouiller (s') [saʒnuje] *vpr* to kneel (down); **être agenouillé** to be kneeling (down).

agent [aʒɑ̃] *nm* agent; **a. (de police)** policeman; **a. de change** stockbroker; **a. immobilier** estate agent, *Am* real estate agent.

agglomération [aglɔmerasjɔ̃] *nf* (*habitations*) built-up area; (*ville*) town.

aggloméré [aglɔmere] *nm* (*bois*) chipboard, fibreboard.

aggraver [agrave] *vt*, **s'a.** *vpr* to worsen. ● **aggravation** *nf* worsening.

agile [aʒil] *a* agile. ● **agilité** *nf* agility.

agir [aʒir] **1** *vi* to act. **2 s'agir** *v imp* **il s'agit d'argent/etc** it's a question *ou* matter of money/etc, it concerns money/etc; **de quoi s'agit-il?** what is it?, what's it about?

agiter [aʒite] *vt* (*remuer*) to stir; (*secouer*) to shake; (*brandir*) to wave ▮ **s'a.** *vpr* (*enfant*) to fidget. ● **agité** *a* (*mer*) rough; (*personne*) restless, agitated; (*enfant*) fidgety, restless. ● **agitation** *nf* (*de la mer*) roughness; (*d'une personne*) restlessness; (*nervosité*) agitation; (*de la rue*) bustle; *Pol* unrest.

agneau, -x [aɲo] *nm* lamb.

agonie [agɔni] *nf* death throes. ● **agoniser** *vi* to be dying.

agrafe [agraf] *nf* hook; (*pour papiers*) staple. ● **agrafer** *vt* (*robe etc*) to fasten, do up; (*papiers*) to staple. ● **agrafeuse**

nf stapler.

agrandir [agrɑ̃dir] *vt* to enlarge; (*grossir*) to magnify ▮ **s'a.** *vpr* to expand, grow. ● **agrandissement** *nm* (*de ville*) expansion; (*de maison*) extension; (*de photo*) enlargement.

agréable [agreabl] *a* pleasant, agreeable, nice. ● **—ment** [-əmɑ̃] *adv* pleasantly.

agréer [agree] *vt* to accept; **veuillez a. mes salutations distinguées** (*dans une lettre*) yours faithfully, *Am* sincerely yours.

agrès [agrɛ] *nmpl Nau* tackle, rigging; (*de gymnastique*) apparatus, *Am* equipment.

agresser [agrese] *vt* to attack; (*dans la rue, pour voler*) to mug. ● **agresseur** *nm* (*dans la rue*) mugger. ● **agression** *nf* attack; (*dans la rue*) mugging.

agressif, -ive [agresif, -iv] *a* aggressive. ● **agressivité** *nf* aggressiveness.

agricole [agrikɔl] *a* (*ouvrier, machine*) farm; **travaux agricoles** farm work.

agriculteur [agrikyltœr] *nm* farmer. ● **agriculture** *nf* farming, agriculture.

agripper [agripe] *vt* to clutch, grip; **s'a. à** to cling to, clutch, grip.

agrumes [agrym] *nmpl* citrus fruit(s).

aguets (aux) [ozagɛ] *adv* on the lookout.

ah! [ɑ] *int* ah!, oh!

ahuri [ayri] *a* astounded, bewildered.

ai [e] *voir* **avoir**.

aide [ed] *nf* help, assistance, aid; **à l'a. de** with the help *ou* aid of ▮ *nmf* (*personne*) assistant. ● **a.-mémoire** *nm inv Scol* handbook (*of facts etc*).

aider [ede] *vt* to help, assist, aid (**à faire** to do); **s'a. de** to make use of.

aïe! [aj] *int* ouch!, ow!

aie(s), aient [e] *voir* **avoir**.

aigle [egl] *nm* eagle.

aigre [egr] *a* (*acide*) sour; (*voix, vent*) sharp, cutting. ● **aigreur** *nf* sourness; (*de ton*) sharpness.

aigri [egri] *a* embittered, bitter.

aigu, -uë [egy] *a* (*douleur, crise etc*) acute; (*dents*) sharp, pointed; (*voix*) shrill.

aiguille [egɥij] *nf* (*à coudre, de pin*) needle; (*de montre*) hand; (*de balance*) pointer; **a.** (**rocheuse**) peak.

aiguill/er [egɥije] *vt* (*train*) to shunt, *Am* switch; (*personne*) to steer, direct. ● **—age** *nm* (*appareil*) *Rail* points, *Am* switches. ● **—eur** *nm Rail* signalman; **a. du ciel** air traffic controller.

aiguiser [eg(ɥ)ize] *vt* (*affiler*) to sharpen; (*appétit*) to whet.

ail [aj] *nm* garlic.

aile [ɛl] *nf* wing; (*de moulin*) sail; *Aut* wing, *Am* fender. ● **aileron** *nm* (*de requin*) fin. ● **ailier** [elje] *nm Fb* wing(er).

aille(s), aillent *voir* **aller**[1].

ailleurs [ajœr] *adv* somewhere else, elsewhere; **partout a.** everywhere else; **d'a.** (*du reste*) besides, anyway.

aimable [ɛmabl] *a* (*gentil*) kind; (*sympathique*) likeable, amiable; (*agréable*) pleasant. ● **—ment** [-əmɑ̃] *adv* kindly.

aimant [ɛmɑ̃] *nm* magnet. ● **aimanter** *vt* to magnetize.

aimer [eme] *vt* to love; **a.** (**bien**) (*apprécier*) to like, be fond of; **a. faire** to like doing *ou* to do; **j'aimerais qu'il vienne** I would like him to come; **a. mieux** to prefer; **ils s'aiment** they're in love.

aine [ɛn] *nf* groin.

aîné, -ée [ene] *a* (*de deux frères etc*) elder, older; (*de plus de deux*) eldest, oldest ▮ *nmf* (*enfant*) elder *ou* older (child); eldest *ou* oldest (child); **c'est mon a.** he's my senior.

ainsi [ɛ̃si] *adv* (*comme ça*) (in) this *ou* that way; (*alors*) so; **a. que** as well as; **et a. de suite** and so on; **pour a. dire** so to speak.

air [ɛr] *nm* **1** air; **en plein a.** in the open (air); outdoors; **en l'a.** (*up*) in the air; (*paroles, menaces*) empty; **ficher** *ou* **flanquer en l'a.** *Fam* (*jeter*) to chuck away; (*gâcher*) to mess up; (*dans l'a.* (*grippe, idées*) about, around. **2** (*expression*) look, appearance; **avoir l'a.** to look, seem; **avoir l'a. de** to look like. **2**

(*mélodie*) tune.

aire [ɛr] *nf* (*de stationnement etc*) & *Géom* area.

aisance [ɛzɑ̃s] *nf* (*facilité*) ease; (*prospérité*) affluence.

aise [ɛz] *nf* **à l'a.** (*dans un vêtement etc*) comfortable; (*dans une situation*) at ease; (*fortuné*) comfortably off; **aimer ses aises** to like one's comforts; **mal à l'a.** uncomfortable, ill at ease. ● **aisé** [eze] *a* (*fortuné*) comfortably off; (*facile*) easy. ● **aisément** *adv* easily.

aisselle [ɛsɛl] *nf* armpit.

ait [ɛ] *voir* avoir.

ajouré [aʒure] *a* (*dentelle etc*) openwork.

ajourner [aʒurne] *vt* to postpone, adjourn.

ajout [aʒu] *nm* addition. ● **ajouter** *vti* to add (à to); **s'a. à** to add to.

ajust/er [aʒyste] *vt* (*pièce, salaires*) to adjust; **a. à** (*adapter*) to fit to. ●—**é** *a* (*serré*) close-fitting.

alaise [alɛz] *nf* (waterproof) undersheet.

alambiqué [alɑ̃bike] *a* convoluted.

alarme [alarm] *nf* (*signal, inquiétude*) alarm; **jeter l'a.** to cause alarm; **a. antivol/d'incendie** burglar/fire alarm. ● **alarmer** *vt* to alarm; **s'a. de** to become alarmed at.

album [albɔm] *nm* (*de timbres etc*) album; (*de dessins*) sketchbook.

alcool [alkɔl] *nm* alcohol; (*spiritueux*) spirits; **a. à 90%** surgical spirit, *Am* rubbing alcohol; **a. à brûler** methylated spirit(s). ● **alcoolique** *a* & *nmf* alcoholic. ● **alcoolisée** *a* **boisson a.** alcoholic drink. ● **alcoolisme** *nm* alcoholism. ● **alcootest**® *nm* breath test; (*appareil*) breathalyzer.

aléas [alea] *nmpl* hazards, risks.

alentours [alɑ̃tur] *nmpl* surroundings, vicinity; **aux alentours de** in the vicinity of.

alerte [alɛrt] **1** *a* (*leste*) spry; (*éveillé*) alert. **2** *nf* alarm; **en état d'a.** on the alert; **a. aérienne** air-raid warning. ● **alerter** *vt* to warn, alert.

algèbre [alʒɛbr] *nf* algebra.

Alger [alʒe] *nm ou f* Algiers.

Algérie [alʒeri] *nf* Algeria. ● **algérien, -ienne** *a* & *nmf* Algerian.

algue(s) [alg] *nf(pl)* seaweed.

alibi [alibi] *nm* alibi.

aliéné, -ée [aljene] *nmf* insane person; *Péj* lunatic.

aligner [aliɲe] *vt* to line up, align ‖ **s'a.** *vpr* (*personnes*) to fall into line, line up; *Pol* to align oneself (**sur** with). ● **alignement** *nm* alignment.

aliment [alimɑ̃] *nm* food. ● **alimentaire** *a* (*ration, industrie etc*) food; **produits alimentaires** foods. ● **alimentation** *nf* (*action*) feeding; supply(ing); (*régime*) diet, nutrition; (*nourriture*) food; **magasin d'a.** grocer's, grocery store. ● **alimenter** *vt* (*nourrir*) to feed; (*fournir*) to supply (**en** with).

alité [alite] *a* bedridden.

allaiter [alete] *vti* to breastfeed (*baby*); (*animal*) to suckle.

allécher [aleʃe] *vt* to tempt.

allée [ale] *nf* (*de parc etc*) path, walk; (*de cinéma, supermarché etc*) aisle; (*devant une maison*) drive(way); **allées et venues** comings and goings.

allég/er [aleʒe] *vt* to make lighter. ●—**é** *a* (*fromage etc*) low-fat.

allégresse [alegrɛs] *nf* gladness, rejoicing.

Allemagne [almaɲ] *nf* Germany. ● **allemand, -ande** *a* & *nmf* German ‖ *nm* (*langue*) German.

aller[1] [ale] **1** *vi* (*aux* être) to go; (*montre etc*) to work, go; **a. à** (*convenir à*) to suit; **a. avec** (*vêtement*) to go with, match; **a. bien/mieux** (*personne*) to be well/better; **il va savoir/venir/etc** he'll know/come/etc, he's going to know/come/etc; **il va partir** he's about to leave, he's going to leave; **va voir!** go and see!; **comment vas-tu?, (comment) ça va?** how are you?; **ça va!** all right!, fine!; **ça va (comme ça)!** that's enough!; **allez-y** go on, go ahead; **allez! au lit!** come on *ou* go on, (to) bed!; **ça va de soi** that's obvious.

2 s'en aller *vpr* to go away; (*tache*) to

come out; **je m'en vais** I'm off.

aller² *nm* outward journey; **a. (simple)** single (ticket), *Am* one-way (ticket); **a. (et) retour** return (ticket), *Am* round-trip (ticket).

allergie [alɛrʒi] *nf* allergy. ● **allergique** *a* allergic (**à** to).

alliage [aljaʒ] *nm* alloy.

alliance [aljɑ̃s] *nf* (*anneau*) wedding ring; *Pol* alliance.

allier [alje] *vt* (*associer*) to combine (**à** with); ▌**s'a.** *vpr* (*pays*) to become allied (**à** with, to). ● **allié, -ée** *nmf* ally.

allô [alo] *int Tél* hello!

allocation [alɔkasjɔ̃] *nf* allowance, benefit; **a. (de) chômage** unemployment benefit; **allocations familiales** child benefit.

allocution [alɔkysjɔ̃] *nf* (short) speech.

allonger [alɔ̃ʒe] *vt* (*bras*) to stretch out; (*jupe*) to lengthen; ▌*vi* (*jours*) to get longer ▌**s'a.** *vpr* to stretch out. ● **allongé** *a* (*étiré*) elongated.

allumer [alyme] *vt* (*feu, pipe etc*) to light; (*électricité, radio*) to turn *ou* switch on ▌**s'a.** *vpr* (*lumière*) to come on; (*feu, guerre*) to flare up. ● **allumage** *nm* lighting; *Aut* ignition. ● **allume-gaz** *nm inv* gas lighter.

allumette [alymɛt] *nf* match.

allure [alyr] *nf* (*vitesse*) pace; (*de véhicule*) speed; (*démarche*) walk; (*air*) look.

allusion [alyzjɔ̃] *nf* allusion; (*voilée*) hint; **faire a. à** to refer *ou* allude to; to hint at.

alors [alɔr] *adv* (*en ce cas-là*) so, then; (*en ce temps-là*) then; **a. que** (*tandis que*) whereas; (*lorsque*) when; **et a.?** so what?

alouette [alwɛt] *nf* (sky)lark.

alourdir [alurdir] *vt* to weigh down ▌**s'a.** *vpr* to become heavy *ou* heavier. ● **alourdi** *a* heavy.

alpage [alpaʒ] *nm* mountain pasture. ● **Alpes** *nfpl* **les A.** the Alps. ● **alpin** *a* alpine. ● **alpinisme** *nm* mountaineering. ● **alpiniste** *nmf* mountaineer.

alphabet [alfabɛ] *nm* alphabet. ● **al-**

phabétique *a* alphabetical.

altérer [altere] **1** *vt* (*denrée, santé*) to spoil. **2** (*donner soif à*) to make thirsty. **3** **s'altérer** *vpr* (*santé, relations*) to deteriorate.

alternative [alternativ] *nf* alternative.

alterner [alterne] *vti* to alternate. ● **alternance** *nf* alternation.

altesse [altɛs] *nf* (*titre*) Highness.

altitude [altityd] *nf* height, altitude.

aluminium [alyminjɔm] *nm* aluminium, *Am* aluminum; **papier (d')a.,** *Fam* **papier (d')alu** tinfoil.

alunir [alynir] *vi* to land on the moon.

alvéole [alveɔl] *nf* (*de ruche*) cell; (*dentaire*) socket.

amabilité [amabilite] *nf* kindness; **faire des amabilités à** to show kindness to.

amadouer [amadwe] *vt* to coax.

amaigr/ir [amegrir] *vt* to make thin(ner); **régime amaigrissant** *Br* slimming diet, *Am* weight reduction diet. ● **—i** *a* thin(ner). ● **—issement** *nm* (*volontaire*) *Br* slimming, *Am* dieting.

amande [amɑ̃d] *nf* almond.

amarre [amar] *nf* (*mooring*) rope; *pl* moorings. ● **amarrer** (*bateau*) *vt* to moor.

amas [amɑ] *nm* heap, pile. ● **amasser** *vt* to pile up; (*fortune, preuves*) to amass ▌**s'a.** *vpr* to pile up.

amateur [amatœr] *nm* (*d'art etc*) lover; *Sp* amateur; (*travail*) *Péj* amateurish; **une équipe a.** an amateur team.

ambassade [ɑ̃basad] *nf* embassy. ● **ambassadeur, -drice** *nmf* ambassador.

ambiance [ɑ̃bjɑ̃s] *nf* atmosphere. ● **ambiant** *a* surrounding.

ambigu, -guë [ɑ̃bigy] *a* ambiguous. ● **ambiguïté** [-gɥite] *nf* ambiguity.

ambitieux, -euse [ɑ̃bisjø, -øz] *a* ambitious. ● **ambition** *nf* ambition.

ambulance [ɑ̃bylɑ̃s] *nf* ambulance. ● **ambulancier, -ière** *nmf* ambulance driver.

ambulant [ɑ̃bylɑ̃] *a* travelling, itinerant.

âme [ɑm] *nf* soul; **â. qui vive** a living soul.

améliorer [ameljɔre] *vt*, **s'a.** *vpr* to

improve. ● **amélioration** *nf* improvement.

amen [amɛn] *adv* amen.

aménag/er [amenaʒe] *vt* (*arranger, installer*) to fit out (en as); (*transformer*) to convert (en into); (*construire*) to set up. ●**—ement** *nm* fitting out; conversion; setting up.

amende [amɑ̃d] *nf* fine; **infliger une a. à** to impose a fine on.

amener [amne] *vt* to bring; (*causer*) to bring about.

amer, -ère [amɛr] *a* bitter. ● **amèrement** *adv* bitterly.

Amérique [amerik] *nf* America; **A. du Nord/du Sud** North/South America. ● **américain, -aine** *a* & *nmf* American.

amertume [amɛrtym] *nf* bitterness.

ameublement [amœbləmɑ̃] *nm* furniture.

ameuter [amøte] *vt* (*voisins*) to bring out.

ami, -e [ami] *nmf* friend; (*de la nature, des livres etc*) lover (**de** of); **petit a.** boyfriend; **petite amie** girlfriend.

amiable (à l') [alamjabl] *a* amicable ‖ *adv* amicably.

amiante [amjɑ̃t] *nm* asbestos.

amical, -aux [amikal, -o] *a* friendly. ●**—ement** *adv* in a friendly manner.

amiral, -aux [amiral, -o] *nm* admiral.

amitié [amitje] *nf* friendship; (*amabilité*) kindness; *pl* kind regards; **prendre qn en a.** to take a liking to s.o.

ammoniac [amɔnjak] *nm* (*gaz*) ammonia. ● **ammoniaque** *nf* (*liquide*) ammonia.

amnésie [amnezi] *nf* amnesia.

amnistie [amnisti] *nf* amnesty.

amoindrir [amwɛ̃drir] *vt*, **s'a.** *vpr* to decrease, diminish.

amonceler (s') [samɔ̃sle] *vpr* to pile up.

amont (en) [ɑ̃namɔ̃] *adv* upstream.

amorce [amɔrs] *nf* (*début*) start; (*de pêcheur*) bait; (*de pistolet d'enfant*) cap. ● **amorcer** *vt*, **s'a.** *vpr* to start.

amort/ir [amɔrtir] *vt* (*coup*) to cushion,

(*bruit*) to deaden. ●**—isseur** *nm* shock absorber.

amour [amur] *nm* love; **pour l'a. de** for the sake of; **mon a.** my darling, my love. ● **a.-propre** *nm* self-respect, self-esteem. ● **amoureux, -euse** *nmf* lover ‖ *a* **a. (de qn)** in love (with s.o.).

amovible [amɔvibl] *a* removable, detachable.

amphithéâtre [ɑ̃fiteatr] *nm* (*romain*) amphitheatre; *Univ* lecture hall.

ample [ɑ̃pl] *a* (*vêtement*) full, ample, roomy; (*provision*) full. ● **amplement** *adv* amply, fully; **a. suffisant** ample. ● **ampleur** *nf* (*de robe*) fullness; (*importance, étendue*) scale, extent; **prendre de l'a.** to grow.

amplifier [ɑ̃plifje] *vt* (*son, courant*) to amplify; (*exagérer*) to magnify ‖ **s'a.** *vpr* to increase. ● **amplificateur** *nm* *Él* amplifier.

ampoule [ɑ̃pul] *nf* (*électrique*) (light) bulb; (*aux pieds etc*) blister; (*de médicament*) phial.

amputer [ɑ̃pyte] *vt* (*membre*) to amputate; **a. qn de la jambe** to amputate s.o.'s leg. ● **amputation** *nf* amputation.

amuser [amyze] *vt* (*divertir*) to amuse, entertain ‖ **s'a.** *vpr* to enjoy oneself, have fun; **s'a. avec** to play with; **s'a. à faire** to amuse oneself doing. ● **amusant** *a* amusing. ● **amusement** *nm* amusement; (*jeu*) game.

amygdales [amidal] *nfpl* tonsils.

an [ɑ̃] *nm* year; **il a dix ans** he's ten (years old); **par a.** (*dix fois etc*) a ou per year; **Nouvel A.** New Year.

analogue [analɔg] *a* similar.

analyse [analiz] *nf* analysis; *Méd* test; **a. grammaticale** parsing. ● **analyser** *vt* to analyse; (*phrase*) to parse.

ananas [anana(s)] *nm* pineapple.

anarchie [anarʃi] *nf* anarchy. ● **anarchiste** *nmf* anarchist.

anatomie [anatɔmi] *nf* anatomy.

ancêtre [ɑ̃sɛtr] *nm* ancestor.

anche [ɑ̃ʃ] *nf* *Mus* reed.

anchois [ɑ̃ʃwa] *nm* anchovy.

ancien, -ienne [ɑ̃sjɛ̃, -jɛn] *a (vieux)* old; *(meuble)* antique; *(qui n'est plus)* former, ex-, old; *(antique)* ancient; *(dans une fonction)* senior; **a. élève** old boy, *Am* alumnus; **a. combattant** ex-serviceman, *Am* veteran.

▮ *nmf (par l'âge)* elder; *(dans une fonction)* senior; **les anciens** *(auteurs, peuples)* the ancients. ● **anciennement** *adv* formerly. ● **ancienneté** *nf* age; *(dans une fonction)* seniority.

ancre [ɑ̃kr] *nf* anchor; **jeter l'a.** to (cast) anchor; **lever l'a.** to weigh anchor. ● **ancrer** *vt (navire)* to anchor; *(idée) Fig* to root, fix.

andouille [ɑ̃duj] *nf (idiot) Fam* nitwit; **espèce d'a.!** *Fam* (you) nitwit!

âne [ɑn] *nm (animal)* donkey, ass; *(personne) Péj* ass.

anéant/ir [aneɑ̃tir] *vt* to annihilate, wipe out. ● **—issement** *nm* annihilation.

anecdote [anɛkdɔt] *nf* anecdote.

anémie [anemi] *nf* an(a)emia. ● **anémique** *a* an(a)emic. ● **s'anémier** *vpr* to become an(a)emic.

anémone [anemɔn] *nf* anemone.

ânerie [ɑnri] *nf* stupidity; *(action etc)* stupid thing. ● **ânesse** *nf* she-ass.

anesthésie [anɛstezi] *nf* an(a)esthesia; **a. générale/locale** general/local an(a)esthetic. ● **anesthésier** *vt* to an(a)esthetize.

ange [ɑ̃ʒ] *nm* angel; **être aux anges** to be in seventh heaven. ● **angélique** *a* angelic.

angine [ɑ̃ʒin] *nf* sore throat.

anglais, -aise [ɑ̃glɛ, -ɛz] *a* English ▮ *nmf* Englishman, Englishwoman; **les A.** the English ▮ *nm (langue)* English ▮ *af* **filer à l'anglaise** to take French leave.

angle [ɑ̃gl] *nm (point de vue)* & *Géom* angle; *(de rue)* corner.

Angleterre [ɑ̃glətɛr] *nf* England.

anglican, -ane [ɑ̃glikɑ̃, -an] *a* & *nmf* Anglican.

anglo- [ɑ̃glɔ] *préf* Anglo-. ● **anglophone** *a* English-speaking ▮ *nmf* English

speaker. ● **anglo-saxon, -onne** *a* & *nmf* Anglo-Saxon.

angoisse [ɑ̃gwas] *nf* (great) anxiety, anguish. ● **angoissant** *a* distressing. ● **angoissé** *a (personne)* in (a state of) anguish; *(geste, cri)* anguished.

angora [ɑ̃gɔra] *nm (laine)* angora.

anguille [ɑ̃gij] *nf* eel.

animal, -aux [animal, -o] *nm* animal ▮ *a (règne, graisse etc)* animal.

anim/er [anime] *vt (débat, groupe)* to lead; *(soirée)* to liven up; *(mécanisme)* to drive; **la joie qui animait son regard** the joy which made his face light up; **animé de** *(sentiment)* prompted by.

▮ **s'animer** *vpr (rue etc)* to come to life; *(yeux)* to light up. ● **animé** *a (rue conversation)* lively; *(doué de vie)* animate. ● **animateur, -trice** *nmf TV* compere, *Am* master of ceremonies, emcee; *(de club)* leader, organizer. ● **animation** *nf (des rues)* activity; *(de réunion)* liveliness; *(de visage)* brightness.

anis [ani(s)] *nm (boisson, parfum)* aniseed.

ankyloser (s') [sɑ̃kiloze] *vpr* to stiffen up. ● **ankylosé** *a* stiff.

anneau, -x [ano] *nm* ring; *(de chaîne)* link.

année [ane] *nf* year; **bonne a.!** Happy New Year!

annexe [anɛks] *nf (bâtiment)* annex(e). ● **annexer** *vt (pays)* to annex. ● **annexion** *nf* annexation.

anniversaire [aniversɛr] *nm (d'événement)* anniversary; *(de naissance)* birthday.

annonce [anɔ̃s] *nf (avis)* announcement; *(publicitaire)* advertisement; **petites annonces** classified advertisements, small ads. ● **annoncer** *vt (signaler)* to announce, report; *(vente)* to advertise; **a. le printemps** to herald spring; **s'a. pluvieux/difficile/etc** to look (like being) rainy/difficult/*etc*.

annuaire [anɥɛr] *nm (téléphonique)* phone book, directory.

annuel, -elle [anɥɛl] *a* annual, yearly.

annulaire [anylɛr] *nm* ring *ou* third finger.

annuler [anyle] *vt* (*visite etc*) to cancel; (*jugement*) to quash ∎ **s'a.** *vpr* to cancel each other out. ● **annulation** *nf* cancellation; quashing.

anodin [anɔdɛ̃] *a* harmless.

anomalie [anɔmali] *nf* (*bizarrerie*) anomaly.

ânon [anɔ̃] *nm* baby donkey.

ânonner [anɔne] *vt* to stumble through (*poem etc*).

anonymat [anɔnima] *nm* anonymity; **garder l'a.** to remain anonymous. ● **anonyme** *a* & *nmf* anonymous (person).

anorak [anɔrak] *nm* anorak.

anorexie [anɔreksi] *nf* anorexia. ● **anorexique** *a* & *nmf* anorexic.

anormal, -aux [anɔrmal, -o] *a* abnormal; (*enfant*) educationally subnormal.

anse [ɑ̃s] *nf* (*de tasse etc*) handle; (*baie*) cove.

Antarctique [ɑ̃tarktik] *a* antarctic ∎ *nm* **l'A.** the Antarctic, Antarctica.

antécédent [ɑ̃tesedɑ̃] *nm Gram* antecedent.

antenne [ɑ̃tɛn] *nf TV Rad* aerial, *Am* antenna; (*d'insecte*) antenna, feeler; **sur** *ou* **à l'a.** on the air.

antérieur [ɑ̃terjœr] *a* (*précédent*) former, previous, earlier; (*placé devant*) front; **membre a.** forelimb; **a. à** prior to.

anthropophage [ɑ̃trɔpɔfaʒ] *nm* cannibal.

antiatomique [ɑ̃tiatɔmik] *a* **abri a.** fallout shelter.

antibiotique [ɑ̃tibjɔtik] *nm* antibiotic.

antibrouillard [ɑ̃tibrujar] *a* & *nm* (**phare**) **a.** fog lamp.

antichoc [ɑ̃tiʃɔk] *a inv* shockproof.

anticip/er [ɑ̃tisipe] *vti* **a.** (**sur**) to anticipate. ● **-é** *a* (*retraite etc*) early; **avec mes remerciements anticipés** thanking you in advance.

anticonstitutionnel, -elle [ɑ̃tikɔ̃stitysjɔnɛl] *a* unconstitutional.

anticorps [ɑ̃tikɔr] *nm* antibody.

anticyclone [ɑ̃tisiklon] *nm* anticyclone.

antidémocratique [ɑ̃tidemɔkratik] *a* undemocratic.

antidérapant [ɑ̃tiderapɑ̃] *a* non-skid.

antidote [ɑ̃tidɔt] *nm* antidote.

antigel [ɑ̃tiʒɛl] *nm* antifreeze.

Antilles [ɑ̃tij] *nfpl* **les A.** the West Indies. ● **antillais, -aise** *a* & *nmf* West Indian.

antilope [ɑ̃tilɔp] *nf* antelope.

antimite [ɑ̃timit] *nm* **de l'a.** moth balls.

antipathique [ɑ̃tipatik] *a* disagreeable.

antipodes [ɑ̃tipɔd] *nmpl* **aux a.** (*partir*) to the antipodes; **aux a. de** (*la vérité etc*) poles apart from.

antique [ɑ̃tik] *a* ancient. ● **antiquaire** *nmf* antique dealer. ● **antiquité** *nf* (*temps, ancienneté*) antiquity; (*objet ancien*) antique.

antisémite [ɑ̃tisemit] *a* anti-Semitic. ● **antisémitisme** *nm* anti-Semitism.

antiseptique [ɑ̃tisɛptik] *a* & *nm* antiseptic.

antivol [ɑ̃tivɔl] *nm* anti-theft lock *ou* device.

antre [ɑ̃tr] *nm* (*de lion etc*) den.

anus [anys] *nm* anus.

Anvers [ɑ̃vɛr(s)] *nm ou f* Antwerp.

anxiété [ɑ̃ksjete] *nf* anxiety. ● **anxieux, -euse** *a* anxious.

août [u(t)] *nm* August. ● **aoûtien, -ienne** [ausjɛ̃, -jɛn] *nmf* August holidaymaker *ou Am* vacationer.

apaiser [apeze] *vt* (*personne*) to calm, pacify; (*faim*) to appease; (*douleur*) to soothe; (*craintes*) to calm ∎ **s'a.** *vpr* (*personne*) to calm down; (*tempête, douleur*) to die down. ● **apaisant** *a* soothing.

aparté [aparte] *nm* **en a.** in private.

apercevoir* [apersəvwar] *vt* to see; (*brièvement*) to catch a glimpse of; **s'a.** *de* to realize, notice; **s'a. que** to realize *ou* notice that. ● **aperçu** *nm* overall view.

apéritif [aperitif] *nm* aperitif.

apeuré [apœre] *a* frightened, scared.

aphone [afɔn] *a* voiceless, completely hoarse.

aphte [aft] *nm* mouth ulcer.

apiculture [apikyltyr] *nf* beekeeping.

apitoyer [apitwaje] *vt* to move (to pity); **s'a. sur** to pity.

aplanir [aplanir] *vt* (*terrain*) to level; (*difficulté*) to iron out, smooth out.

aplatir [aplatir] *vt* to flatten (out) **‖ s'a.** *vpr* (*s'étendre*) to lie flat; (*s'humilier*) to grovel; **s'a. contre** to flatten oneself against. ● **aplati** *a* flat.

aplomb [aplɔ̃] *nm* **d'a.** (*meuble etc*) level, straight; (*personnne*) (*sur ses jambes*) steady; (*bien portant*) in good shape.

apocalypse [apokalips] *nf* apocalypse; **d'a.** (*vision etc*) apocalyptic.

apogée [apoʒe] *nm* (*de carrière etc*) peak.

apostrophe [apostrɔf] *nf* **1** (*signe*) apostrophe. **2** (*interpellation*) sharp *ou* rude remark. ● **apostropher** *vt* to shout at.

apothéose [apoteoz] *nf* final triumph.

apôtre [apotr] *nm* apostle.

apparaître* [aparɛtr] *vi* (*se montrer*, *sembler*) to appear.

appareil [aparɛj] *nm* (*instrument*, *machine*) apparatus; (*électrique*) appliance; *Tél* telephone; (*avion*) aircraft; *Anat* system; **a.** (**photo**) camera; **a.** (**auditif**) hearing aid; **a.** (**dentaire**) brace; **qui est à l'a.?** *Tél* who's speaking?

appareiller [apareje] *vi Nau* to get under way.

apparence [aparɑ̃s] *nf* appearance; **en a.** outwardly; **sauver les apparences** to keep up appearances. ● **apparemment** [-amã] *adv* apparently. ● **apparent** *a* apparent; (*très visible*) conspicuous.

apparenté [aparɑ̃te] *a* (*semblable*) similar.

apparition [aparisjɔ̃] *nf* appearance; (*fantôme*) apparition.

appartement [apartəmɑ̃] *nm* flat, *Am* apartment.

appartenir* [apartənir] *vi* to belong (à to); **il vous appartient de** it's your responsibility to. ● **appartenance** *nf* membership (à of).

appât [apɑ] *nm* (*amorce*) bait. ● **appâter** *vt* (*attirer*) to lure.

appauvrir [apovrir] *vt* to make poorer **‖ s'a.** *vpr* to become poorer.

appel [apel] *nm* (*cri*, *attrait etc*) call; (*demande pressante*) & *Jur* appeal; *Mil* call-up; **faire l'a.** *Scol* to take the register; *Mil* to have a roll call; **faire a. à** to appeal to, call upon.

appeler [aple] *vt* (*personne*, *nom etc*) to call; (*en criant*) to call out to; *Mil* to call up; (*nécessiter*) to call for; **a. à l'aide** to call for help; **en a. à** to appeal to; **il est appelé à** (*de hautes fonctions*) he is marked out for; (*témoigner etc*) he is called upon to. **‖ s'appeler** *vpr* to be called; **il s'appelle Paul** his name is Paul. ● **appelé** *nm Mil* conscript. ● **appellation** *nf* (*nom*) term.

appendice [apɛ̃dis] *nm* (*du corps*, *de livre*) appendix. ● **appendicite** *nf* appendicitis.

appesantir (s') [sapəzɑ̃tir] *vpr* **s'a. sur** (*sujet*) to dwell upon.

appétit [apeti] *nm* appetite (**de** for); **mettre qn en a.** to whet s.o.'s appetite; **bon a.!** enjoy your meal! ● **appétissant** *a* appetizing.

applaud/ir [aplodir] *vti* to applaud, clap. ● **—issements** *nmpl* applause.

applique [aplik] *nf* wall lamp.

appliqu/er [aplike] *vt* to apply (à to); (*loi*, *décision*) to put into effect; **s'a. à** (*un travail*) to apply oneself to; (*concerner*) to apply to; **s'a. à faire** to take pains to do. ● **—é a** (*travailleur*) painstaking. ● **application** *nf* application.

appoint [apwɛ̃] *nm* **faire l'a.** to give the correct money *ou* change.

appontement [apɔ̃tmɑ̃] *nm* landing stage.

apport [apor] *nm* contribution.

apporter [aporte] *vt* to bring.

apposition [apozisjɔ̃] *nf Gram* apposition.

apprécier [apresje] *vt* (*aimer*, *percevoir*) to appreciate; (*évaluer*) to assess. ● **appréciable** *a* appreciable. ● **appréciation** *nf* (*de professeur*) comment (**sur** on); (*de distance etc*) assessment.

appréhender [apreɑ̃de] vt (craindre) to dread (**de faire** doing); (arrêter) to arrest, apprehend. ● **appréhension** nf anxiety, apprehension.

apprendre* [aprɑ̃dr] vti (étudier) to learn; (événement, fait) to hear of, learn of; (nouvelle) to hear; **a. à faire** to learn to do; **a. qch à qn** (enseigner) to teach s.o. sth; (informer) to tell s.o. sth; **a. à qn à faire** to teach s.o. to do; **a. que** to learn that; (être informé) to hear that.

apprenti, -ie [aprɑ̃ti] nmf apprentice; (débutant) novice. ● **apprentissage** nm apprenticeship; (d'une langue) learning (de of).

apprêter (s') [saprete] vpr to get ready (à faire to do).

apprivoiser [aprivwaze] vt to tame ▌ **s'a.** vpr to become tame. ● **apprivoisé** a tame.

approbation [aprɔbasjɔ̃] nf approval.

approche [aprɔʃ] nf approach.

approcher [aprɔʃe] vt (chaise etc) to draw up (de to); (personne) to come ou get close to, approach ▌ vi to draw near(er) (de to), approach ▌ **s'a.** vpr to come ou get near(er) (de to); **il s'est approché de moi** he came up to me.

approfond/ir [aprɔfɔ̃dir] vt (trou etc) to dig deeper; (question) to go into thoroughly. ● **—i** a thorough.

approprié [aprɔprije] a appropriate.

approprier (s') [saprɔprije] vpr **s'a. qch** to take sth, help oneself to sth.

approuver [apruve] vt (autoriser) to approve; (apprécier) to approve of.

approvisionner [aprɔvizjɔne] vt (ville etc) to supply (with provisions); (magasin) to stock ▌ **s'a.** vpr to get one's supplies (**de, en** of).

approximatif, -ive [aprɔksimatif, -iv] a approximate. ● **approximativement** adv approximately.

appui [apɥi] nm support; (pour coude etc) rest; (de fenêtre) sill. ● **appui-tête** nm ou **appuie-tête** nm inv headrest.

appuyer [apɥije] vt (soutenir) to sup-

port; **a. qch sur/contre** (poser) to rest ou lean sth on/against; **s'a.** sur to lean on, rest on; (compter) to rely on ▌ vi **a. sur** (bouton etc) to press; (être posé sur) to rest on.

après [aprɛ] **1** prép (temps) after; (espace) beyond; **a. un an** after a year; **a. le pont** beyond the bridge; **a. coup** after the event; **a. avoir mangé** after eating; **a. qu'il t'a vu** after he saw you ▌ adv after(wards); **l'année d'a.** the following year; **et a.?** and then what? **2** prép **d'a.** (selon) according to.

après-demain [apredmɛ̃] adv the day after tomorrow. ● **a.-midi** nm ou f inv afternoon. ● **a.-shampooing** nm (hair) conditioner. ● **a.-ski** nm ankle boot, snow boot.

apte [apt] a suited (à to), capable (à of). ● **aptitude** nf aptitude (à, pour for); **avoir des aptitudes pour qch** to have an aptitude for sth.

aquarelle [akwarɛl] nf watercolour.

aquarium [akwarjɔm] nm aquarium.

aquatique [akwatik] a aquatic.

arabe [arab] a & nmf Arab ▌ a & nm (langue) Arabic; **chiffres arabes** Arabic numerals. ● **Arabie** nf A. Séoudite Saudi Arabia.

arachide [araʃid] nf peanut.

araignée [areɲe] nf spider.

arbitraire [arbitrer] a arbitrary.

arbitre [arbitr] nm Fb Boxe referee; Tennis umpire; **libre a.** free will. ● **arbitrer** vt to referee; to umpire. ● **arbitrage** nm refereeing; umpiring.

arborer [arbɔre] vt (insigne, vêtement) to sport.

arbre [arbr] nm tree; Aut shaft, axle.

arbuste [arbyst] nm (small) shrub, bush.

arc [ark] nm (arme) bow; (voûte) arch; (de cercle) arc; **tir à l'a.** archery. ● **arcade** nf arch(way); pl arcade, arches.

arc-en-ciel [arkɑ̃sjɛl] nm (pl arcs-en-ciel) rainbow.

archaïque [arkaik] a archaic.

arche [arʃ] nf (voûte) arch; **l'a. de Noé**

Noah's ark.

archéologie [arkeolɔʒi] *nf* arch(a)eology. ● **archéologue** *nmf* arch(a)eologist.

archer [arʃe] *nm* archer.

archet [arʃɛ] *nm Mus* bow.

archevêque [arʃəvɛk] *nm* archbishop.

archipel [arʃipɛl] *nm* archipelago.

archiplein [arʃiplɛ̃] *a* chock-a-block.

architecte [arʃitɛkt] *nm* architect. ● **architecture** *nf* architecture.

archives [arʃiv] *nfpl* archives, records.

Arctique [arktik] *nm* **l'A.** the Arctic.

ardent [ardɑ̃] *a* (*passionné*) ardent, fervent; (*empressé*) eager; (*soleil*) scorching. ● **ardemment** [-amɑ̃] *adv* eagerly, fervently. ● **ardeur** *nf* (*énergie*) enthusiasm, fervour.

ardoise [ardwaz] *nf* slate.

are [ar] *nm* = 100 square metres.

arène [arɛn] *nf* (*pour taureaux*) bullring; *pl* bullring; *Hist* amphitheatre.

arête [arɛt] *nf* (*de poisson*) bone; (*de cube etc*) edge, ridge; (*de montagne*) ridge.

argent [arʒɑ̃] *nm* (*métal*) silver; (*monnaie*) money; **a. comptant** *ou* **liquide** cash. ● **argenterie** *nf* silverware.

Argentine [arʒɑ̃tin] *nf* Argentina. ● **argentin, -ine** *a* & *nmf* Argentinian.

argile [arʒil] *nf* clay.

argot [argo] *nm* slang.

argument [argymɑ̃] *nm* argument. ● **argumentation** *nf* arguments.

aride [arid] *a* arid, barren.

aristocrate [aristokrat] *nmf* aristocrat. ● **aristocratie** [-asi] *nf* aristocracy. ● **aristocratique** *a* aristocratic.

arithmétique [aritmetik] *nf* arithmetic.

armateur [armatœr] *nm* shipowner.

armature [armatyr] *nf* (*charpente*) framework; (*de lunettes, tente*) frame.

arme [arm] *nf* weapon; *pl* weapons, arms; **a. à feu** firearm. ● **armer** *vt* (*personne etc*) to arm (**de** with); (*fusil*) to cock; (*appareil photo*) to wind on ‖ **s'a.** *vpr* to arm oneself (**de** with). ● **armement(s)** *nm(pl)* arms.

armée [arme] *nf* army; **a. de l'air** air force.

armistice [armistis] *nm* armistice.

armoire [armwar] *nf* (*penderie*) wardrobe, *Am* closet; **a. à pharmacie** medicine chest *ou* cabinet.

armure [armyr] *nf* armour.

armurier [armyrje] *nm* gunsmith.

arôme [arom] *nm* (*goût*) flavour; (*odeur*) (pleasant) smell.

arpent/er [arpɑ̃te] *vt* (*terrain*) to survey; (*trottoir etc*) to pace up and down. ● **—eur** *nm* (land) surveyor.

arqué [arke] *a* arched, curved; (*jambes*) bandy.

arrache-pied (d') [daraʃpje] *adv* relentlessly.

arrach/er [araʃe] *vt* (*clou, dent, cheveux, page etc*) to pull out; (*plante*) to pull up; **a. qch à qn** to snatch sth from s.o.; (*aveu, argent*) to force sth out of s.o.; **a. qn de son lit** to drag s.o. out of bed. ● **—age** *nm* (*de plante*) pulling up.

arranger [arɑ̃ʒe] *vt* (*chambre, visite etc*) to fix up, arrange; (*voiture, texte etc*) to put right; (*différend*) to settle; **ça m'arrange** that suits me ‖ **s'a.** *vpr* (*se mettre d'accord*) to come to an agreement *ou* arrangement; (*finir bien*) to turn out fine; **s'a. pour faire** to arrange to do, manage to do. ● **arrangeant** *a* accommodating.

arrestation [arɛstasjɔ̃] *nf* arrest.

arrêt [arɛ] *nm* (*halte, endroit*) stop; (*action*) stopping; **temps d'a. pause;** à l'a. stationary; **a. de travail** (*grève*) stoppage; (*congé*) sick leave; **sans a.** constantly, non-stop.

arrêté [arete] *nm* order, decision.

arrêter [arete] *vt* to stop; (*appréhender*) to arrest; (*regard, date*) to fix ‖ *vi* to stop; **il n'arrête pas de critiquer/etc** he's always criticizing/etc, he doesn't stop criticizing/etc ‖ **s'a.** *vpr* to stop; **s'a. de faire** to stop doing.

arrière [arjɛr] *adv* **en a.** (*marcher etc*) backwards; (*rester*) behind; (*regarder*) back, behind; **en a. de qn/qch** behind s.o./sth ‖ *nm* & *a inv* back, rear; **à l'a.** in *ou* at the back; **faire marche a.** to reverse, back ‖ *nm Fb* (full) back.

arrière-boutique [arjerbutik] *nm* back room (*of a shop*). ● **a.-goût** *nm* aftertaste. ● **a.-grand-mère** *nf* great-grandmother. ● **a.-grand-père** *nm* (*pl* **arrière-grands-pères**) great-grand-father. ● **a.-pensée** *nf* ulterior motive. ● **a.-plan** *nm* background.

arrimer [arime] *vt* (*fixer*) to secure.

arriv/er [arive] *vi* (*aux être*) (*venir*) to arrive, come; (*survenir*) to happen; (*réussir*) to succeed; **a. à** (*atteindre*) to reach; **a. à faire** to manage to do, succeed in doing; **a. à qn** to happen to s.o. ‖ *v imp* **il m'arrive d'oublier**/*etc* I (sometimes) forget/*etc*. ● **—ée** *nf* arrival; *Sp* (*winning*) post. ● **arrivage** *nm* consignment.

arrogant [arɔgɑ̃] *a* arrogant.

arrond/ir [arɔ̃dir] *vt* (*chiffre, angle, jupe*) to round off; (*rendre rond*) to make round (*pebble etc*). ● **—i** *a* rounded.

arrondissement [arɔ̃dismɑ̃] *nm* (*d'une ville*) district.

arros/er [aroze] *vt* (*terre*) to water; (*succès*) to drink to. ● **—age** *nm* watering. ● **arrosoir** *nm* watering can.

art [ar] *nm* art; **film/critique d'a.** art film/critic; **arts ménagers** domestic science.

artère [arter] *nf Anat* artery; *Aut* main road.

artichaut [artiʃo] *nm* artichoke.

article [artikl] *nm* (*de presse, de commerce*) & *Gram* article; (*dans un contrat, catalogue*) item; **articles de toilette** toiletries.

articuler [artikyle] *vt* (*mot etc*) to articulate. ● **articulation** *nf Ling* articulation; *Anat* joint; **a. (du doigt)** knuckle.

artifice [artifis] *nm* **feu d'a.** (*spectacle*) firework display, fireworks.

artificiel, -elle [artifisjɛl] *a* artificial. ● **artificiellement** *adv* artificially.

artillerie [artijri] *nf* artillery. ● **artilleur** *nm* gunner.

artisan [artizɑ̃] *nm* craftsman, artisan. ● **artisanal, -aux** *a* **métier a.** craftsman's trade; **objet a.** object made by crafts-

men. ● **artisanat** *nm* (*métier*) craftsman's trade.

artiste [artist] *nmf* artist; *Th Mus Cin* performer, artist. ● **artistique** *a* artistic.

as [ɑs] *nm* (*carte, champion*) ace; **a. du volant** brilliant *ou* crack driver.

ascenseur [asɑ̃sœr] *nm* lift, *Am* elevator.

ascension [asɑ̃sjɔ̃] *nf* ascent; **l'A.** Ascension Day.

Asie [azi] *nf* Asia. ● **asiatique** *a* & *nmf* Asian, Asiatic.

asile [azil] *nm* (*abri*) shelter; *Pol* asylum; **a. (d'aliénés)** *Péj* (lunatic) asylum.

aspect [aspe] *nm* (*air*) appearance; (*perspective*) & *Gram* aspect.

asperges [asperʒ] *nfpl* asparagus.

asperger [asperʒe] *vt* (*par jeu ou accident*) to splash (**de** with); (*pour humecter*) to spray, sprinkle (**de** with).

aspérité [asperite] *nf* bump.

asphalte [asfalt] *nm* asphalt.

asphyxie [asfiksi] *nf* suffocation. ● **asphyxier** *vt* to suffocate, asphyxiate.

aspirateur [aspiratœr] *nm* vacuum cleaner, hoover® **passer (à) l'a.** to vacuum, hoover.

aspir/er [aspire] **1** *vt* (*liquide*) to suck up; (*respirer*) to breathe in, inhale. **2** *vi* **a. à** **qch** to aspire to sth. ● **—é** *a Ling* aspirate(d).

aspirine [aspirin] *nf* aspirin.

assagir (s') [sasaʒir] *vpr* to settle down.

assaill/ir [asajir] *vt* to attack; **a. de** (*questions etc*) to assail with. ● **—ant** *nm* attacker, assailant.

assaisonn/er [asɛzɔne] *vt* to season. ● **—ement** *nm* seasoning.

assassin [asasɛ̃] *nm* murderer. ● **assassinat** *nm* murder. ● **assassiner** *vt* to murder.

assaut [aso] *nm* onslaught, assault; **prendre d'a.** to (take by) storm.

assemblée [asɑ̃ble] *nf* (*personnes réunies*) gathering; (*parlement*) assembly; (*de fidèles*) congregation.

assembler [asɑ̃ble] *vt* to put together, assemble ‖ **s'a.** *vpr* to gather. ● **assem-**

blage nm (montage) assembly; (réunion d'objets) collection.

asseoir* [aswar] vt a. qn to sit s.o. (down), seat s.o. (sur on) **s'a.** vpr to sit (down).

assez [ase] adv enough; a. de pain/de gens enough bread/people; j'en ai a. I've had enough; a. grand/intelligent/ etc (suffisamment) big/clever/etc enough (pour faire to do); a. fatigué/etc (plutôt) fairly ou rather ou quite tired/ etc.

assidu [asidy] a (toujours présent) regular; (appliqué) diligent; a. auprès de qn attentive to s.o.

assléger [asjeʒe] vt (ville) to besiege; (magasin, vedette) to mob, crowd round; (importuner) to pester.

assiette [asjɛt] nf (récipient) plate; a. anglaise Culin (assorted) cold meats, Am cold cuts; ne pas être dans son a. Fig to be feeling out of sorts. ● **assiettée** nf plateful.

assimiler [asimile] vt to assimilate.

assis [asi] (pp de asseoir) a sitting (down); rester a. to remain seated; place assise seat (on bus etc).

assises [asiz] nfpl (cour d')a. court of assizes.

assistance [asistɑ̃s] nf 1 (assemblée) audience; (nombre de personnes présentes) attendance, turnout. 2 (aide) assistance; l'A. (publique) the child care service; enfant de l'A. child in care.

assister [asiste] 1 vt (aider) to help, assist. 2 vi a. à (réunion, cours etc) to attend, be present at; (accident) to witness. ● **assistant, -ante** nmf assistant; les assistants (spectateurs) the members of the audience; (témoins) the onlookers; assistant(e) social(e) social worker; assistante maternelle child minder, Am baby-sitter.

association [asɔsjasjɔ̃] nf association.

associer [asɔsje] vt to associate (à with); a. qn à (ses travaux) to involve s.o. in; (profits) to give s.o. a share in **s'a.** vpr to join forces; s'a. à (collaborer) to associate with, join forces with. ● **associé, -ée** nmf partner, associate.

assoiffé [aswafe] a thirsty (de for).

assombrir [asɔ̃bʀir] vt (obscurcir) to darken **s'a.** vpr (ciel) to cloud over.

assommer [asɔme] vt (personne) to knock unconscious; (animal) to stun, brain; (ennuyer) to bore stiff. ● **—ant** a (ennuyeux) tiresome, boring.

assortir [asɔrtir] vt, **s'a.** vpr to match. ● **assortis** apl (objets semblables) matching; (fromages etc variés) assorted. ● **assortiment** nm assortment.

assoupir (s') [sasupir] vpr to doze off. ● **assoupi** a (personne) drowsy.

assouplir [asuplir] vt (étoffe, muscles) to make supple; (corps) to limber up; (règles) to ease, relax. ● **—issement** nm exercices d'a. limbering-up exercises.

assourdir [asurdir] vt (personne) to deafen; (son) to muffle. ● **—issant** a deafening.

assujettir [asyʒetir] vt (soumettre) to subject (à to); (peuple) to subjugate.

assumer [asyme] vt (tâche, rôle) to assume, take on; (emploi) to take up, assume.

assurance [asyrɑ̃s] nf (aplomb) (self-) assurance; (promesse) assurance; (contrat) insurance; a. au tiers/tous risques third-party/comprehensive insurance; assurances sociales = national insurance, Am = social security.

assurer [asyre] vt (par un contrat) to insure; (travail etc) to carry out; a. à qn que to assure s.o. that; a. qn de qch, a. qch à qn to assure s.o. of sth. ● **s'assurer** vpr (par un contrat) to insure oneself, get insured (contre against); s'a. que/de to make sure that/of. ● **assuré, -ée** a (succès) assured, certain; (pas) firm, secure; (air) (self-)confident **|** nmf policyholder, insured person. ● **assureur** nm insurer.

astérisque [asterisk] nm asterisk.

asthme [asm] nm asthma. ● **asthmatique** a & nmf asthmatic.

asticot [astiko] nm maggot, Am worm.

astiquer [astike] vt to polish.

astre [astr] nm star.

astrologie [astrɔlɔʒi] nf astrology.

astronaute [astrɔnot] nmf astronaut.
● **astronautique** nf space travel.

astronomie [astrɔnɔmi] nf astronomy.
● **astronome** nmf astronomer. ● **astronomique** a astronomical.

astuce [astys] nf (pour faire qch) knack, trick; (invention) gadget; (plaisanterie) clever joke, (finesse) astuteness. ● **astucieux, -euse** a clever, astute.

atelier [atəlje] nm (d'ouvrier etc) workshop; (de peintre) studio.

athée [ate] nmf atheist.

Athènes [aten] nm ou f Athens.

athlète [atlɛt] nmf athlete. ● **athlétique** a athletic. ● **athlétisme** nm athletics.

atlantique [atlɑ̃tik] a Atlantic ▮ nm l'A. the Atlantic.

atlas [atlɑs] nm atlas.

atmosphère [atmɔsfɛr] nf atmosphere.
● **atmosphérique** a atmospheric.

atome [atom] nm atom. ● **atomique** [atɔmik] a (bombe, énergie etc) atomic.

atomiseur [atɔmizœr] nm spray.

atout [atu] nm trump (card); (avantage) Fig asset.

âtre [ɑtr] nm (foyer) hearth.

atroce [atrɔs] a atrocious; (crime) heinous, atrocious. ● **atrocités** nfpl (horreurs) atrocities.

attabler (s') [satable] vpr to sit down at the table. ● **attablé** a (seated) at the table.

attache [ataʃ] nf (objet) fastening; pl (liens) links.

attaché-case [ataʃekez] nm attaché case.

attach/er [ataʃe] vt (lier) to tie (up), attach (à to); (boucler, fixer) to fasten; **a. de l'importance à qch** to attach great importance to sth; **s'a. à** (se lier) to become attached to (s.o.); (se consacrer) to apply oneself to (task etc) ▮ vi (en cuisant) to stick. ● **—ant** a (enfant etc) likeable. ● **—ement** nm (affection) attachment (à to).

attaque [atak] nf attack; **a. aérienne** air raid. ● **attaquer** vt, **s'a. à** to attack; (difficulté, sujet) to tackle ▮ vi to attack. ● **attaquant, -ante** nmf attacker.

attarder (s') [satarde] vpr (en chemin) to dawdle, loiter; **s'a. sur** ou **à** (détails etc) to linger over.

atteindre* [atɛ̃dr] vt (parvenir à) to reach; (cible) to hit; (idéal) to achieve; (blesser) to hit, wound; **être atteint de** (maladie) to be suffering from.

atteinte [atɛ̃t] nf **hors d'a.** (objet, personne) out of reach.

attel/er [atle] vt (bêtes) to harness, hitch up; (remorque) to hook up. ● **—age** nm (crochet) hook (for towing); (bêtes) team.

attendre [atɑ̃dr] vt to wait for; (escompter) to expect (de of, from); **elle attend un bébé** she's expecting a baby; **a. que qn vienne** to wait for s.o. to come, wait until s.o. comes; **a. d'être informé** to wait to be informed.

▮ vi to wait; **faire a. qn** to keep s.o. waiting; **se faire a.** (réponse, personne etc) to be a long time coming; **attends voir!** Fam let me see!; **en attendant** meanwhile; **en attendant que** (+ sub) until.

▮ **s'attendre** vpr **s'a. à qch/à faire** to expect sth/to do; **s'a. à ce que qn fasse qch** to expect s.o. to do sth. ● **attendu** a (avec joie) eagerly-awaited; (prévu) expected.

attendrir [atɑ̃drir] vt (émouvoir) to move (to compassion) ▮ **s'a.** vpr to be moved (sur by). ● **attendrissant** a moving.

attentat [atɑ̃ta] nm attempt on s.o.'s life, murder attempt; **a. (à la bombe)** (bomb) attack.

attente [atɑ̃t] nf (temps) wait(ing); (espérance) expectation(s); **salle d'a.** waiting room.

attentif, -ive [atɑ̃tif, -iv] a (personne) attentive; (travail, examen) careful. ● **attentivement** adv attentively.

attention [atɑ̃sjɔ̃] nf attention; pl

(*égards*) consideration; **faire a. à** (*écouter, remarquer*) to pay attention to; (*prendre garde*) to be careful of; **faire a. (à ce) que** (+ *sub*) to be careful that; **a.! watch out!; a. là-voiture!** watch out for the car! ● **attentionné** *a* considerate.

atténuer [atenɥe] *vt* to mitigate, attenuate ▮**s'a.** *vpr* to subside.

atterré [atere] *a* être a. to be dismayed.

atterr/ir [aterir] *vi Av* to land. ● **—issage** *nm Av* landing; **a. forcé** crash landing.

attirail [atiraj] *nm* (*équipement*) *Fam* gear, equipment.

attirer [atire] *vt* (*faire venir, plaire à*) to attract; (*attention*) to attract, catch; **a. l'a. de qn sur** to draw s.o.'s attention to; **a. qch à qn** (*ennuis etc*) to bring s.o. sth; **a. dans** (*coin, piège*) to lure into ▮**s'a.** *vpr* (*ennuis etc*) to bring upon oneself. ● **attirant** *a* attractive.

attitude [atityd] *nf* attitude; (*maintien*) bearing.

attraction [atraksjɔ̃] *nf* attraction.

attrait [atre] *nm* attraction.

attrape [atrap] *nf* (*objet*) trick. ● **a.-nigaud** (*ruse*) *nm* trick.

attraper [atrape] *vt* (*ballon, maladie, voleur, train etc*) to catch; (*accent, contravention etc*) to pick up; **se laisser a.** (*duper*) to get taken in *ou* tricked; **se faire a.** (*gronder*) *Fam* to get a telling-off.

attrayant [atrejɑ̃] *a* attractive.

attribuer [atribɥe] *vt* (*donner*) to assign (à to); (*décerner*) to award (*prize*) (à to). ● **attribution** *nf* assignment; (*de prix*) awarding.

attribut [atriby] *nm Gram* predicate adjective; (*caractéristique*) attribute.

attrister [atriste] *vt* to sadden.

attrouper [atrupe] *vt*, **s'a.** *vpr* to gather. ● **attroupement** *nm* (*disorderly*) crowd.

au [o] *voir* à.

aubaine [oben] *nf* (**bonne**) **a.** stroke of good luck, godsend.

aube [ob] *nf* dawn; **dès l'a.** at the crack of dawn.

aubépine [obepin] *nf* hawthorn.

auberge [oberʒ] *nf* inn; **a. de jeunesse** youth hostel.

aubergine [oberʒin] *nf* aubergine, *Am* eggplant.

aucun, -une [okœ̃, -yn] *a* no, not any; **il n'a a. talent** he has no talent, he doesn't have any talent; **a. professeur n'est venu** no teacher has come ▮*pron* none, not any; **il n'en a a.** he has none (at all), he doesn't have any (at all); **a. d'entre nous** none of us; **a. des deux** neither of the two.

audace [odas] *nf* (*courage*) daring, boldness; (*impudence*) audacity. ● **audacieux, -euse** *a* daring, bold.

au-dessous [odsu] *prép* **au-d. de** (*arbre etc*) below, under, beneath; (*âge, prix*) under; (*température*) below.

au-dessus [odsy] *adv* above; over; on top; (à *l'étage supérieur*) upstairs ▮*prép* **au-d. de** above; (*âge, température, prix*) over; (*posé sur*) on top of.

au-devant de [odvɑ̃də] *prép* **aller au-d. de qn** to go to meet s.o.

audience [odjɑ̃s] *nf* (*entretien*) audience; *Jur* hearing.

audio [odjo] *a inv* (*cassette etc*) audio. ● **audio-visuel, -elle** *a* audio-visual.

auditeur, -trice [oditœr, -tris] *nmf Rad* listener; **les auditeurs** the audience. ● **audition** *nf* (*ouïe*) hearing; (*séance musicale*) recital. ● **auditoire** *nm* audience. ● **auditorium** *nm* concert hall; *Rad* recording studio (*for recitals*).

auge [oʒ] *nf* (*feeding*) trough.

augmenter [ogmɑ̃te] *vt* to increase (de by); (*prix, impôt*) to raise, increase; **a. qn** to give s.o. a rise *ou Am* raise ▮*vi* to increase (de by); (*prix*) to rise, go up, increase. ● **augmentation** *nf* increase (de in, of); **a. de salaire** (pay) rise, *Am* raise; **a. de prix** price rise *ou* increase.

augure [ogyr] *nm* être de bon/mauvais **a.** to be a good/bad omen.

aujourd'hui [oʒurdɥi] *adv* today; (*actuellement*) nowadays, today; **a. en**

quinze two weeks from today.

aumône [omon] *nf* alms.

aumônier [omonje] *nm* chaplain.

auparavant [oparavɑ̃] *adv* (*avant*) before(hand); (*d'abord*) first.

auprès de [opredə] *prép* (*assis, situé etc*) by, close to, next to; (*en comparaison de*) compared to.

auquel [okel] *voir* **lequel**.

aura, aurait [ora, ore] *voir* **avoir**.

auréole [oreɔl] *nf* (*de saint etc*) halo; (*sur tissu etc*) ring.

auriculaire [ɔrikyler] *nm* **l'a.** the little finger.

aurore [ɔrɔr] *nf* dawn, daybreak.

ausculter [ɔskylte] *vt* (*malade*) to examine (*with a stethoscope*); (*cœur*) to listen to.

aussi [osi] *adv* **1** (*comparaison*) as; **a. lourd que** as heavy as. **2** (*également*) too, also, as well; **moi a.** so do, can, am *etc* I; **a. bien que** as well as. **3** (*tellement*) so; **un repas a. délicieux** such a delicious meal, so delicious a meal. **4** *conj* (*donc*) therefore.

aussitôt [osito] *adv* immediately, at once; **a. que** as soon as; **a. levé, il partit** as soon as he was up, he left; **a. dit, a. fait** no sooner said than done.

austral, *mpl* -als [ostral] *a* southern.

Australie [ostrali] *nf* Australia. ●**australien, -ienne** *a & nmf* Australian.

autant [otɑ̃] *adv* **1 a. de ... que** (*quantité*) as much ... as; (*nombre*) as many ... as; **il a a. d'argent/de pommes que vous** he has as much money/as many apples as you. **2 a. de** (*tant de*) so much; (*nombre*) so many; **je n'ai jamais vu a. d'argent/de pommes** I've never seen so much money/so many apples; **pourquoi manges-tu a.?** why are you eating so much? **3 a. que** (*lire etc*) as much as; **il lit a. que vous/que possible** he reads as much as you/as possible; **il n'a jamais souffert a.** he's never suffered as *ou* so much; **a. que je sache** as far as I know; **d'a. (plus) que** all the more (so) since; **a. avouer/etc** we, you *etc* might as well confess/*etc*;

en faire/dire a. to do/say the same; **j'aimerais a. aller au musée** I'd just as soon go to the museum.

autel [otel] *nm* altar.

auteur [otœr] *nm* (*de livre*) author, writer; (*de chanson*) composer; (*de crime*) perpetrator; **droit d'a.** copyright; **droits d'a.** royalties.

authentique [otɑ̃tik] *a* genuine, authentic.

auto [oto] *nf* car; **autos tamponneuses** bumper cars, dodgems.

auto- [oto] *préf* self-.

autobus [otobys] *nm* bus.

autocar [otokar] *nm* bus, coach.

autocollant [otokɔlɑ̃] *nm* sticker ▮ *a* (*enveloppe etc*) self-seal.

autocuiseur [otokɥizœr] *nm* pressure cooker.

autodéfense [otodefɑ̃s] *nf* self-defence.

auto-école [otoekɔl] *nf* driving school, school of motoring.

autographe [otograf] *nm* autograph.

automate [otomat] *nm* automaton. ●**automatisation** *nf* automation. ●**automatiser** *vt* to automate.

automatique [otomatik] *a* automatic. ●**—ment** *adv* automatically.

automne [otɔn] *nm* autumn, *Am* fall.

automobile [otomɔbil] *nf* car, *Am* automobile. ●**automobiliste** *nmf* motorist, driver.

autonome [otonɔm] *a* (*région etc*) autonomous, self-governing; (*personne*) *Fig* independent; (*ordinateur*) off-line. ●**autonomie** *nf* autonomy.

autopsie [otɔpsi] *nf* autopsy, post-mortem.

autoradio [otoradjo] *nm* car radio.

autorail [otoraj] *nm* railcar.

autoriser [otɔrize] *vt* (*permettre*) to permit (**à faire** to do). ●**autorisation** *nf* permission, authorization.

autorité [otɔrite] *nf* authority. ●**autoritaire** *a* authoritarian.

autoroute [otorut] *nf* motorway, *Am* highway, freeway.

auto-stop [otostɔp] *nm* hitchhiking; **faire**

de l'a. to hitchhike. ● **auto-stoppeur, -euse** *nmf* hitchhiker.

autour [otur] *adv* around; **tout a.** all around ● *prép* **a. de** around.

autre [otr] *a & pron* other; **un a. livre** another book; **un a.** another (one); **d'autres** others; **d'autres médecins** other doctors; **as-tu d'autres questions?** have you any other *ou* further questions?; **qn/personne/rien d'a.** s.o./ no one/nothing else; **a. chose/part** something/somewhere else; **qui/quoi d'a.?** who/what else?; **l'un l'a., les uns les autres** each other; **l'un et l'a.** both (of them); **l'un ou l'a.** either (of them); **ni l'un ni l'a.** neither (of them); **les uns . . . les autres** some . . . others; **nous/vous autres Anglais** we/you English; **d'un moment à l'a.** any moment (now).

● **autrement** [otrəmã] *adv* (*différemment*) differently; (*sinon*) otherwise.

autrefois [otrəfwa] *adv* in the past, long ago.

Autriche [otriʃ] *nf* Austria. ● **autrichien, -ienne** *a & nmf* Austrian.

autruche [otryʃ] *nf* ostrich.

autrui [otrɥi] *pron* others, other people.

auvent [ovã] *nm* (*de tente, magasin*) awning.

aux [o] *voir* **à**.

auxiliaire [ɔksiljɛr] *a & nm* Gram (**verbe**) **a.** auxiliary (verb) ● *nmf* (*aide*) helper.

auxquels, -elles [okɛl] *voir* **lequel**.

av. *abrév* **avenue**.

avachir (s') [savaʃir] *vpr* (*soulier, personne*) to become flabby *ou* limp.

avait [avɛ] *voir* **avoir**.

aval (en) [ãnaval] *adv* downstream (**de** from).

avalanche [avalãʃ] *nf* avalanche.

avaler [avale] *vt* to swallow; **a. ses mots** to mumble ● *vi* to swallow.

avance [avãs] *nf* (*marche, acompte*) advance; (*de coureur, chercheur etc*) lead; *pl* (*diplomatiques*) overtures; **à l'a., d'a., par a.** in advance; **en a.** (*arriver, partir*) early; (*avant l'horaire prévu*) (ahead) of time; (*dans son déve-*

loppement) ahead, in advance; (*montre etc*) fast; **en a. sur** (*qn, son époque etc*) ahead of; **avoir une heure d'a.** (*train etc*) to be an hour early.

avancé [avãse] *a* (*âge, enfant etc*) advanced; (*season*) well advanced.

avancement [avãsmã] *nm* (*de personne*) promotion; (*de travail*) progress.

avancer [avãse] *vt* (*date, réunion*) to bring forward; (*main, chaise, pion*) to move forward; (*travail*) to speed up; (*argent*) to advance; (*montre*) to put forward.

▌*vi* (*personne, véhicule etc*) to move forward, advance; (*travail*) to progress, advance; (*faire saillie*) to jut out (**sur** over); **a. de cinq minutes** (*montre*) to be five minutes fast; **alors, ça avance?** are things progressing?

▌**s'avancer** *vpr* to move forward, advance.

avant [avã] *prép* before; **a. de voir** before seeing; **a. qu'il (ne) parte** before he leaves; **a. huit jours** within a week; **a. tout** above all; **a. toute chose** first and foremost; **a. peu** before long ● *adv* before; **en a.** (*mouvement*) forward; (*en tête*) ahead; **la nuit d'a.** the night before ▌*nm & a inv* front ▌*nm* (*joueur*) Fb forward.

avantage [avãtaʒ] *nm* advantage; (*bénéfice*) Fin benefit; **tirer a. de** to benefit from. ● **avantager** *vt* (*favoriser*) to favour. ● **avantageux, -euse** *a* (*prix etc*) worthwhile, attractive; **a. pour qn** advantageous to s.o.

avant-bras [avãbra] *nm inv* forearm. ● **a.-centre** *nm* Fb centre-forward. ● **a.-dernier, -ière** *a & nmf* last but one. ● **a.-garde** *nf* Mil advance guard; **d'a.-garde** (*idée, film etc*) avant-garde. ● **a.-goût** *nm* foretaste. ● **a.-guerre** *nm ou f* prewar period; **d'a.-guerre** pre-war. ● **a.-hier** [avãtjɛr] *adv* the day before yesterday. ● **a.-première** *nf* preview. ● **a.-propos** *nm inv* foreword. ● **a.-veille** *nf* **l'a.-veille (de)** two days before.

avare [avar] *a* miserly; **a. de** (*compliments etc*) sparing of ‖ *nmf* miser. ● **avarice** *nf* avarice.

avarie(s) [avari] *nf(pl)* damage. ● **avarié** *a* (*aliment*) rotting, rotten.

avec [avɛk] *prép* with; (*envers*) to(wards); **et a. ça?** (*dans un magasin*) *Fam* anything else? ‖ *adv* **il est venu a.** (*son chapeau etc*) *Fam* he came with it.

avenant [avnɑ̃] *a* pleasing, attractive.

avènement [avɛnmɑ̃] *nm* **l'a. de** the coming *ou* advent of; (*roi*) the accession of.

avenir [avnir] *nm* future; **à l'a.** (*désormais*) in future; **d'a.** (*personne, métier*) with future prospects.

aventure [avɑ̃tyr] *nf* adventure; (*en amour*) affair; **à l'a.** (*marcher etc*) aimlessly. ● **aventurer (s')** *vpr* to venture (**sur** on to, **dans** into, **à faire** to do). ● **aventureux, -euse** *a* (*personne, vie*) adventurous; (*risqué*) risky. ● **aventurier, -ière** *nmf* adventurer.

avenue [avny] *nf* avenue.

avérer (s') [savere] *vpr* (*juste etc*) to prove (to be); **il s'avère que** it turns out that.

averse [avers] *nf* shower, downpour.

aversion [aversjɔ̃] *nf* aversion (**pour** to).

avert/ir [avertir] *vt* (*mettre en garde, menacer*) to warn; (*informer*) to notify, inform. ● **—i** *a* informed. ● **—issement** *nm* warning. ● **—isseur** *nm* *Aut* horn; **a. d'incendie** fire alarm.

aveu, -x [avø] *nm* confession; **de l'a. de** by the admission of.

aveugle [avœgl] *a* blind ‖ *nmf* blind man, blind woman; **les aveugles** the blind. ● **aveuglément** [-emɑ̃] *adv* blindly. ● **aveugler** *vt* to blind.

aveuglette (à l') [alavœglɛt] *adv* blindly; **chercher qch à l'a.** to grope for sth.

aviateur, -trice [avjatœr, -tris] *nmf* airman, airwoman. ● **aviation** *nf* (*industrie, science*) aviation; (*armée de l'air*) air force; (*avions*) aircraft *inv*; **l'a.** *Sp* flying.

avide [avid] *a* (*d'argent*) greedy (**de** for); **a. d'apprendre**/*etc* eager to learn/*etc*. ● **—ment** [-əmɑ̃] *adv* greedily. ● **avidité** *nf* greed.

avilir [avilir] *vt* to degrade, debase.

avion [avjɔ̃] *nm* aircraft *inv*, (aero)plane, *Am* airplane; **a. à réaction** jet; **a. de ligne** airliner; **par a.** (*lettre*) airmail; **en a., par a.** (*voyager*) by plane, by air.

aviron [avirɔ̃] *nm* oar; **l'a.** *Sp* rowing; **faire de l'a.** to row, practise rowing.

avis [avi] *nm* opinion; *Pol Jur* judgment; (*communiqué*) notice; (*conseil*) & *Fin* advice; **à mon a.** in my opinion; **changer d'a.** to change one's mind.

avis/er [avize] *vt* to advise, inform; **s'a. de qch** to realize sth suddenly; **s'a. de faire** to venture to do. ● **—é a** prudent, wise; **bien/mal a.** well-/ill-advised.

avocat, -ate [avɔka, -at] **1** *nmf* barrister, *Am* attorney, counselor; (*d'une cause*) *Fig* advocate. **2** *nm* (*fruit*) avocado (pear).

avoine [avwan] *nf* oats; **farine d'a.** oatmeal.

avoir* [avwar] **1** *v aux* to have; **je l'ai/ l'avais vu** I've/I'd seen him.

2 *vt* (*posséder*) to have; (*obtenir*) to get; (*tromper*) *Fam* to take for a ride; **il a** he has, he's got; **qu'est-ce que tu as?** what's the matter with you?, what's wrong with you?; **j'ai à lui parler** I have to speak to her; **il n'a qu'à essayer** he only has to try; **a. faim/chaud**/*etc* to be *ou* feel hungry/hot/*etc*; **a. cinq ans**/*etc* to be five (years old)/*etc*; **en a. pour longtemps** to be busy for quite a while; **j'en ai pour dix minutes** this will take me ten minutes; (*ne bougez pas*) I'll be with you in ten minutes; **en a. pour son argent** to get *ou* have one's money's worth.

3 *v imp* **il y a** there is, *pl* there are; **il y a six ans** six years ago; **il n'y a pas de quoi!** don't mention it!; **qu'est-ce qu'il y a?** what's the matter?, what's wrong?

4 *nm* assets, property.

avoisinant

avoisinant [avwazinã] a neighbouring, nearby.

avort/er [avɔrte] vi (projet etc) Fig to miscarry, fail; (se faire) a. (femme) to have ou get an abortion. ●—ement nm abortion; Fig failure.

avou/er [avwe] vt to confess, admit (que that); (crime) to confess to, admit to; s'a. vaincu to admit defeat ‖ vi (coupable) to confess. ●—é a (ennemi, but) declared.

avril [avril] nm April; un poisson d'a. (farce) an April fool joke; faire un poisson d'a. à to make an April fool of.

axe [aks] nm Math Astron axis; (essieu) axle; (d'une politique) broad direction; grands axes (routes) main roads.

ayant [ejã] voir avoir.

azimuts [azimyt] nmpl dans tous les a. Fam here and everywhere; tous a. (guerre, publicité etc) all-out.

azote [azot] nm nitrogen.

azur [azyr] nm azure, (sky) blue; la Côte d'A. the (French) Riviera.

B

B, b [be] *nm* B, b.

babill/er [babije] *vi* to babble. ●**—age** *nm* babble.

babines [babin] *nfpl* (*lèvres*) chops.

babiole [babjɔl] *nf* (*objet*) knick-knack.

bâbord [babɔr] *nm Nau Av* port (side).

babouin [babwɛ̃] *nm* baboon.

baby-foot [babifut] *nm inv* table *ou* miniature football.

bac [bak] *nm* **1** (*bateau*) ferry(boat). **2** (*cuve*) tank; **b. à glace** ice tray; **b. à légumes** vegetable compartment. **3** *abrév* = **baccalauréat**.

baccalauréat [bakalɔrea] *nm* school leaving certificate.

bâche [baʃ] *nf* (*de toile*) tarpaulin; (*de plastique*) plastic sheet. ●**bâcher** *vt* to cover over (*with a tarpaulin ou plastic sheet*).

bachelier, -ière [baʃəlje, -jer] *nmf* holder of the *baccalauréat*.

bacille [basil] *nm* germ.

bâcler [bakle] *vt* (*travail*) to dash off carelessly, botch (up).

bactéries [bakteri] *nfpl* bacteria.

badaud, -aude [bado, -od] *nmf* (*inquisitive*) onlooker, bystander.

badge [badʒ] *nm* badge, *Am* button.

badigeon [badiʒɔ̃] *nm* whitewash. ●**badigeonner** *vt* (*mur*) to whitewash; (*écorchure*) to paint (*with antiseptic*).

badiner [badine] *vi* to jest, joke; **b. avec** (*prendre à la légère*) to trifle with.

bafouer [bafwe] *vt* to mock *ou* scoff at.

bafouiller [bafuje] *vti* to stammer.

bagage [bagaʒ] *nm* (*valise etc*) piece of luggage *ou* baggage; (*connaissances*) *Fig* (fund of) knowledge; *pl* (*ensemble des valises*) luggage, baggage. ●**bagagiste** *nm* baggage handler.

bagarre [bagar] *nf* fight, brawl; **aimer la b.** to like a fight *ou* a brawl. ●**bagarrer**

(se) *vpr* to fight, brawl; (*se disputer*) to fight, quarrel.

bagatelle [bagatel] *nf* trifle.

bagne [baɲ] *nm* convict prison; **c'est le b. ici** *Fig* this place is a real sweatshop *ou* workhouse. ●**bagnard** *nm* convict.

bagnole [baɲɔl] *nf Fam* car.

bagou(t) [bagu] *nm Fam* glibness; **avoir du b.** to have the gift of the gab.

bague [bag] *nf* (*anneau*) ring; (*de cigare*) band.

baguette [baget] *nf* (*canne*) stick; (*de chef d'orchestre*) baton; (*pain*) (long thin) loaf, baguette; *pl* (*de tambour*) drumsticks; (*pour manger*) chopsticks; **b. (magique)** (magic) wand; **mener qn à la b.** to rule s.o. with an iron hand.

bahut [bay] *nm* (*meuble*) chest, cabinet; (*lycée*) *Fam* school.

baie [be] *nf* **1** (*de côte*) bay. **2** *Bot* berry. **3** (*fenêtre*) picture window.

baignade [beɲad] *nf* swim, bathe; (*activité*) swimming, bathing; (*endroit*) bathing place.

baigner [beɲe] *vt* to bathe; (*enfant*) to bath, *Am* bathe; **baigné de** (*sueur, lumière*) bathed in; (*sang*) soaked in.

▮ *vi* **b. dans** (*tremper*) to be steeped in (*sauce etc*).

▮ **se baigner** *vpr* to go swimming *ou* bathing; (*dans une baignoire*) to have *ou* take a bath. ●**baigneur, -euse** **1** *nmf* bather. **2** *nm* (*poupée*) baby doll.

baignoire [beɲwar] *nf* bath (tub).

bail, *pl* **baux** [baj, bo] *nm* lease.

bâill/er [baje] *vi* to yawn. ●**—ement** *nm* yawn.

bâillon [bajɔ̃] *nm* gag. ●**bâillonner** *vt* (*victime, presse etc*) to gag.

bain [bɛ̃] *nm* bath; (*de mer*) swim, bathe; **prendre un b. de soleil** to sunbathe; **salle**

de bain(s) bathroom; **être dans le b.**
Fam to have got *ou Am* gotten into the
swing of things; **petit/grand b.** *(piscine)*
shallow/deep end; **b. de bouche**
mouthwash. ● **b.-marie** *nm* (pl **bains-
marie**) *Culin* double boiler.

baïonnette [bajɔnɛt] *nf* bayonet.

baiser [beze] *vt* **b. au front/sur la joue** to
kiss on the forehead/cheek ‖ *nm* kiss;
bons baisers *(dans une lettre)* (with)
love.

baisse [bɛs] *nf* fall, drop **(de** in); **en b.**
(température) falling; *(popularité)* de-
clining.

baisser [bese] *vt* *(voix, prix etc)* to
lower, drop; *(tête)* to bend; *(radio,
chauffage)* to turn down ‖ *vi* *(prix,
niveau etc)* to go down, drop; *(soleil)*
to go down; *(marée)* to go out; *(santé,
popularité)* *Fig* to decline ‖ **se b.** *vpr* to
bend down, stoop.

bajoues [baʒu] *nfpl* *(d'animal, de personne)* chops.

bal, *pl* **bals** [bal] *nm* ball; *(populaire)*
dance.

balade [balad] *nf* *Fam* walk; *(en auto)*
drive; *(excursion)* tour. ● **balader (se)**
vpr Fam *(à pied)* to (go for a) walk;
(excursionner) to tour (around); **se b.
(en voiture)** to go for a drive. ● **baladeur**
nm Walkman®, (personal) stereo

balafre [balafr] *nf* *(cicatrice)* scar; *(blessure)* gash, slash. ● **balafré** *a* scarred.

balai [balɛ] *nm* broom; **manche à b.**
broomstick; *Av Ordinat* joystick; **donner un coup de b.** to sweep up. ● **b.-
brosse** *nm* (pl **balais-brosses**) garden
brush *(for scrubbing paving stones)*.

balance [balɑ̃s] *nf* *(instrument)* (pair of)
scales; **la B.** *(signe)* Libra.

balancer [balɑ̃se] *vt* *(hanches, tête,
branches)* to sway; *(bras)* to swing;
(lancer) *Fam* to chuck; *(se débarrasser
de)* *Fam* to chuck out.

‖ **se balancer** *vpr* *(personne)* to swing
(from side to side); *(arbre, bateau etc)*
to sway; **je m'en balance!** I couldn't care
less! ● **balancier** *nm* *(d'horloge)* pendu-

lum; *(de montre)* balance wheel. ● **balançoire** *nf* *(suspendue)* swing; *(bascule)*
seesaw.

balayer [baleje] *vt* *(chambre)* to sweep
(out); *(rue, feuilles)* to sweep (up);
(enlever, chasser) to sweep away. ● **balayette** *nf* (hand) brush; *(balai)* short-
handled broom. ● **balayeur, -euse** *nmf*
(personne) roadsweeper ‖ *nf* *(véhicule)*
roadsweeper.

balbutier [balbysje] *vti* to stammer.

balcon [balkɔ̃] *nm* balcony; *Th* dress
circle.

baldaquin [baldakɛ̃] *nm* *(de lit etc)*
canopy.

baleine [balɛn] *nf* *(animal)* whale; *(de
parapluie)* rib.

balise [baliz] *nf* *Nau* beacon; *Av*
(ground) light; *Aut* road sign. ● **bali-
ser** *vt* to mark with beacons *ou* lights;
(route) to signpost. ● **balisage** *nm* *Nau*
beacons; *Av* lighting; *Aut* signposting.

ballade [balad] *nf* *(légende, poème long)*
ballad; *(poème court)* & *Mus* ballade.

ballant [balɑ̃] *a* *(bras, jambes)* dangling.

ballast [balast] *nm* ballast.

balle [bal] *nf* *(de tennis, golf etc)* ball;
(projectile) bullet; *(paquet)* bale; *pl
(francs)* *Fam* francs; **se renvoyer la b.**
to pass the buck (to each other).

ballet [balɛ] *nm* ballet. ● **ballerine** *nf*
ballerina.

ballon [balɔ̃] *nm* *(jouet d'enfant, dirigeable)* balloon; *(de sport)* ball; **b. de
football** football, *Am* soccer ball.

ballonné [balɔne] *am* *(ventre)* bloated.

ballot [balo] *nm* *(paquet)* bundle.

ballottage [balɔtaʒ] *nm* second ballot *(no
candidate having achieved the required
number of votes)*.

ballotter [balɔte] *vti* to shake (about).

balnéaire [balneer] *a* **station b.** seaside
resort, *Am* beach resort.

balourd, -ourde [balur, -urd] *nmf*
(clumsy) oaf.

Baltique [baltik] *nf* **la B.** the Baltic.

balustrade [balystrad] *nf* (hand)rail,
railing(s).

bambin [bãbɛ̃] *nm* tiny tot, toddler.

bambou [bãbu] *nm* bamboo.

ban [bã] *nm* (*applaudissements*) round of applause; *pl* (*de mariage*) banns; **mettre qn au b. de** to outlaw s.o. from; **un (triple) b. pour...** three cheers for..., a big hand for....

banal, *mpl* -**als** [banal] *a* (*fait, accident*) commonplace, banal; (*idée, propos*) banal, trite. ●**banalité** *nf* banality; *pl* (*propos*) banalities.

banane [banan] *nf* banana. ●**bananier** *nm* banana tree.

banc [bã] *nm* (*siège*) bench; (*de poissons*) shoal; **b. des accusés** *Jur* dock; **b. d'église** pew; **b. de sable** sandbank; **b. d'essai** *Fig* testing ground.

bancaire [bãkɛr] *a* **compte/etc b.** bank account/etc; **opération b.** banking operation.

bancal, *mpl* -**als** [bãkal] *a* (*personne*) bandy, bow-legged; (*meuble*) wobbly; (*idée*) shaky.

bandage [bãdaʒ] *nm* (*pansement*) bandage.

bande [bãd] *nf* **1** (*de terrain, papier etc*) strip; (*de film*) reel; (*de journal*) wrapper; (*rayure*) stripe; (*pansement*) bandage; (*sur la chaussée*) line; (*de fréquences*) *Rad* band; **b. (magnétique)** tape; **b. vidéo** videotape; **b. sonore** sound track; **une b. dessinée** a comic strip, a strip cartoon; **aimer la b. dessinée** to like comic strips *ou* comics. **2** (*groupe*) gang, band; **b. d'idiots!** you load of idiots!

bandeau, -**x** [bãdo] *nm* (*sur les yeux*) blindfold; (*pour la tête*) headband; (*pansement*) head bandage.

bander [bãde] *vt* (*blessure etc*) to bandage; (*yeux*) to blindfold; (*muscle*) to tense.

banderole [bãdrɔl] *nf* (*de manifestants*) banner.

bandit [bãdi] *nm* robber, gangster. ●**banditisme** *nm* crime.

bandoulière [bãduljɛr] *nf* shoulder strap; **en b.** slung across the shoulder.

banjo [bãdʒo] *nm Mus* banjo.

banlieue [bãljø] *nf* **la b.** the suburbs, the outskirts; **une b.** a suburb; **la grande b.** the outer suburbs; **de b.** (*maison etc*) suburban; **train de b.** commuter train. ●**banlieusard**, -**arde** *nmf* (*habitant*) suburbanite; (*voyageur*) commuter.

bannir [banir] *vt* (*exiler, supprimer*) to banish (**de** from).

banque [bãk] *nf* bank; (*activité*) banking.

banqueroute [bãkrut] *nf* (*fraudulent*) bankruptcy.

banquet [bãkɛ] *nm* banquet.

banquette [bãkɛt] *nf* (*de véhicule, train*) seat.

banquier [bãkje] *nm* banker.

banquise [bãkiz] *nf* ice floe *ou* field.

baptême [batɛm] *nm* christening, baptism; (*de navire*) christening; **b. de l'air** first flight. ●**baptiser** [batize] *vt* (*enfant*) to christen, baptize; (*appeler*) *Fig* to christen (*ship*).

baquet [bakɛ] *nm* (*pansement*) tub, basin.

bar [bar] *nm* (*lieu, comptoir*) bar.

baragouiner [baragwine] *vt* (*langue*) to gabble a few words of.

baraque [barak] *nf* hut, shack; (*maison*) *Fam* hovel; (*de forain*) stall. ●—**ment** *nm* (makeshift) huts.

baratin [baratɛ̃] *nm Fam* sweet talk; *Com* sales talk, patter. ●**baratiner** *vt* (*fille*) to chat up, *Am* sweet-talk.

barbare [barbar] *a* (*manières, crime*) barbaric; (*peuple, invasions*) barbarian ‖ *nmf* barbarian. ●**barbarie** *nf* (*cruauté*) barbarity.

barbe [barb] *nf* beard; **une b. de trois jours** three days' growth of beard; **se faire la b.** to shave; **la b.!** enough!; **quelle b.!** what a drag!; **b. à papa** candyfloss, *Am* cotton candy.

barbecue [barbəkju] *nm* barbecue.

barbelé [barbəle] *a* **fil de fer b.** barbed wire ‖ *nmpl* **barbelés** barbed wire.

barbiche [barbiʃ] *nf* goatee (beard).

barbot/er [barbɔte] *vi* (*s'agiter*) to splash about, paddle. ●—**euse** *nf* (*de bébé*) playsuit, rompers.

barbouill/er [barbuje] *vt* (*salir*) to smear; (*gribouiller*) to scribble; (*peindre*) to daub; **avoir l'estomac barbouillé** *Fam* to feel queasy. ●**—age** *nm* smear; scribble; daub.

barbu [barby] *a* bearded.

bardé [barde] *a* **b. de** (*décorations etc*) covered with.

barder [barde] *v imp* **ça va b.!** *Fam* there'll be fireworks!

barème [barɛm] *nm* (*des tarifs*) table; (*des salaires*) scale.

baril [bari(l)] *nm* barrel; **b. de poudre** powder keg; **b. de lessive** box of laundry detergent.

bariolé [barjole] *a* brightly-coloured.

barman, *pl* **-men** *ou* **-mans** [barman, -mɛn] *nm* barman, *Am* bartender.

baromètre [barɔmɛtr] *nm* barometer.

baron, -onne [barɔ̃, -ɔn] *nm* baron ‖ *nf* baroness.

baroque [barɔk] *a & nm Archit Mus etc* baroque.

barque [bark] *nf* (small) boat.

barre [bar] *nf* bar; *Nau* helm; (*trait*) line, stroke; **b. de soustraction** minus sign; **b. fixe** *Sp* horizontal bar. ●**barreau, -x** *nm* (*de fenêtre etc*) & *Jur* bar; (*d'échelle*) rung.

barr/er [bare] *vt* (*route etc*) to close (off); (*obstruer*) to block (off); (*porte*) to bar; (*chèque*) to cross; (*phrase*) to cross out; (*bateau*) to steer; **b. la route à qn, b. qn** to bar s.o.'s way; **'rue barrée'** 'road closed'. ●**barrage** *nm* (*sur une route*) roadblock; (*sur un fleuve*) dam.

barrette [barɛt] *nf* (*pince*) (hair)slide, *Am* barrette.

barricade [barikad] *nf* barricade. ●**barricader** *vt* to barricade ‖ **se b.** *vpr* to barricade oneself (**dans** in).

barrière [barjɛr] *nf* (*porte*) gate; (*clôture*) fence; (*obstacle, mur*) barrier.

barrique [barik] *nf* (large) barrel.

bas[1], basse [bɑ, bas] *a* (*table, prix etc*) low; (*action*) vile, base, mean; (*partie de ville*) lower; **au b. mot** at the very least;

enfant en b. âge young child; **avoir la vue basse** to be short-sighted.

‖ *adv* low; (*parler*) in a whisper, softly; **mettre b.** (*animal*) to give birth; **à b. les dictateurs**/*etc*! down with dictators/*etc*!

‖ *nm* (*de côte, page, mur etc*) bottom, foot; **tiroir**/*etc* **du b.** bottom drawer/*etc*; **en b.** down (below); (*par l'escalier*) downstairs; **en** *ou* **au b. de** at the foot *ou* bottom of; **de haut en b.** from top to bottom.

bas[2] [bɑ] *nm* (*chaussette*) stocking.

basané [bazane] *a* (*visage etc*) tanned.

bas-côté [bakote] *nm* (*de route*) roadside, shoulder, verge.

bascule [baskyl] *nf* (*balançoire*) seesaw; (**balance à**) **b.** weighing machine; **cheval/fauteuil à b.** rocking horse/chair. ●**basculer** *vti* (*personne*) to topple over; (*benne*) to tip up.

base [bɑz] *nf Ch Math Mil Av etc*; **bases** (*d'un argument, accord etc*) basis; **de b.** (*salaire etc*) basic; **produit à b. de lait** milk-based product. ●**baser** *vt* to base (**sur** on).

bas-fond [bafɔ̃] *nm* (*eau*) shallows.

basilic [bazilik] *nm Bot Culin* basil.

basilique [bazilik] *nf* basilica.

basket(-ball) [basket(bol)] *nm* basketball.

baskets [basket] *nfpl* (*chaussures*) trainers, *Am* track shoes.

basque [bask] *a & nmf* Basque.

basse [bas] 1 *voir* **bas[1]**. 2 *nf Mus* bass.

basse-cour [baskur] *nf* (*pl* **basses-cours**) farmyard.

bassement [basmɑ̃] *adv* basely, meanly. ●**bassesse** *nf* baseness, meanness; (*action*) vile *ou* base *ou* mean act.

bassin [basɛ̃] *nm* (*pièce d'eau*) pond; (*de port*) dock; (*de piscine*) pool; (*cuvette*) bowl, basin; *Anat* pelvis; *Géog* basin; **b. houiller** coalfield. ●**bassine** *nf* bowl.

basson [basɔ̃] *nm* (*instrument*) bassoon.

bastingage [bastɛ̃gaʒ] *nm* (ship's) rail.

bastion [bastjɔ̃] *nm Fig* bastion, stronghold.

bas-ventre [bavɑ̃tr] *nm* lower abdomen;

(*sexe*) *Fam* genitals.

bat [ba] *voir* **battre**.

bât [bɑ] *nm* packsaddle.

bataclan [bataklɑ̃] *nm Fam* paraphernalia; **et tout le b.** *Fam* and the whole caboodle.

bataille [bataj] *nf* battle; *Cartes* beggar-my-neighbour. ● **batailler** *vi* to fight, battle. ● **batailleur, -euse** *nmf* fighter ▮ *a* fond of fighting. ● **bataillon** *nm* batallion.

bâtard, -arde [bɑtar, -ard] *a* & *nmf* bastard; **chien b.** mongrel.

bateau, -x [bato] *nm* boat; (*grand*) ship.

batifoler [batifɔle] *vi Hum* to fool about.

bâtiment [bɑtimɑ̃] *nm* (*édifice*) building; (*navire*) vessel; **le b., l'industrie du b.** the building trade; **ouvrier du b.** building worker. ● **bâtir** *vt* (*construire*) to build; (*coudre*) to baste, tack; **terrain à b.** building site. ● **bâti** *a* **bien b.** well-built. ● **bâtisse** *nf Péj* building.

bâton [bɑtɔ̃] *nm* (*canne*) stick; (*d'agent*) baton; **b. de rouge** lipstick; **donner des coups de b. à qn** to beat s.o. (with a stick); **parler à bâtons rompus** to ramble from one subject to another; **mettre des bâtons dans les roues à qn** to put obstacles in s.o.'s way.

battage [bataʒ] *nm* (*du blé*) threshing; (*publicité*) *Fam* publicity, hype.

battant [batɑ̃] *nm* (*de porte etc*) flap; **porte à deux battants** double door.

battante [batɑ̃t] *af* **pluie b.** driving rain.

battement [batmɑ̃] *nm* **1** (*de tambour*) beat(ing); (*de paupières*) blink(ing); **b. de cœur** heartbeat. **2** (*délai*) interval.

batterie [batri] *nf Mil Aut* battery; **la b.** *Mus* the drums; **b. de cuisine** set of kitchen utensils.

batteur [batœr] *nm* **1** (*musicien*) drummer. **2 b. à œufs** egg beater.

battre* [batr] **1** *vt* (*frapper, vaincre*) to beat; (*blé*) to thresh; (*cartes*) to shuffle (*œufs*) to beat; (*à coups redoublés*) to batter; **b. la mesure** to beat time; **b. à mort** to batter *ou* beat to death.

▮ *vi* to beat; (*porte*) to bang; **b. des mains**

to clap (one's hands); **b. des paupières** to blink; **b. des ailes** (*oiseau*) to flap its wings.

2 se battre *vpr* to fight (**avec** with, **pour** for).

baume [bom] *nm* (*résine, consolation*) balm.

baux [bo] *voir* **bail**.

bavard, -arde [bavar, -ard] *a* (*élève etc*) talkative ▮ *nmf* chatterbox. ● **bavarder** *vi* to chat, chatter; (*divulguer des secrets*) to blab. ● **bavardage** *nm* chatting, chatter(ing).

bave [bav] *nf* dribble, slobber; foam; (*de limace*) slime. ● **baver** *vi* to dribble, slobber; (*chien enragé*) to foam; (*stylo*) to smudge; (*bouche*) slobbery; (*omelette*) runny. ● **baveux, -euse** *a* (*bouche*) slobbery; (*omelette*) runny. ● **bavoir** *nm* bib. ● **bavure** *nf* (*tache*) smudge; (*erreur*) blunder; **sans b.** flawless(ly).

bazar [bazar] *nm* (*magasin, marché*) bazaar; (*désordre*) mess, clutter; (*attirail*) *Fam* stuff, gear.

BCBG [besebeʒe] *a inv abrév* (*bon chic bon genre*) stylish, classy.

bd *abrév* boulevard.

BD [bede] *nf abrév* bande dessinée.

béant [beɑ̃] *a* (*plaie*) gaping; (*gouffre*) yawning.

beau (*or* **bel** *before vowel or mute h*), **belle**, *pl* **beaux, belles** [bo, bɛl] *a* (*femme, fleur, histoire etc*) beautiful; (*homme*) handsome, good-looking; (*voyage, temps*) fine, lovely; (*occasion, talent*) fine; **au b. milieu** right in the middle; **j'ai b. crier**/*etc* it's no use (my) shouting/*etc*; **un b. morceau** a good bit; **de plus belle** (*recommencer etc*) worse than ever.

▮ *nm* **le b.** the beautiful; **faire le b.** (*chien*) to sit up and beg.

▮ *nf Cartes etc* deciding game.

beaucoup [boku] *adv* (*lire etc*) a lot, a great deal; **aimer b.** to like very much *ou* a lot; **s'intéresser b. à** to be very interested in; **b. de** (*livres etc*) many, a lot *ou* a great deal of; (*courage etc*) a lot *ou* a great deal of, much; **pas b. d'argent**/*etc* not much money/*etc*; **j'en ai b.** (*quantité*) I have a lot; (*nombre*) I have lots; **b. plus** much more, a lot more; many more, a lot more (**que** than); **b. trop** much too much; much too many; **b. trop petit**/*etc* much too small/*etc*; **b. sont...** many are....

beau-fils [bofis] *nm* (*pl* **beaux-fils**) (*d'un précédent mariage*) stepson; (*gendre*) son-in-law. ● **b.-frère** *nm* (*pl* **beaux-frères**) brother-in-law. ● **b.-père** *nm* (*pl* **beaux-pères**) father-in-law; (*second mari de la mère*) stepfather.

beauté [bote] *nf* beauty; **institut** *ou* **salon de b.** beauty salon.

beaux-arts [bozar] *nmpl* fine arts. ● **b.-parents** *nmpl* parents-in-law.

bébé [bebe] *nm* baby; **b.-lion**/*etc* (*pl* **bébés-lions**/*etc*) baby lion/*etc*.

bec [bek] *nm* (*d'oiseau*) beak, bill; (*de cruche*) spout; (*bouche*) *Fam* mouth; *Mus* mouthpiece; **coup de b.** peck; **clouer le b. à qn** *Fam* to shut s.o. up.

bécasse [bekas] *nf* (*oiseau*) woodcock; (*personne*) *Fam* simpleton.

bêche [bɛʃ] *nf* spade. ● **bêcher** *vt* (*cultiver*) to dig.

becquée [beke] *nf* beakful; **donner la b. à** (*oiseau*) to feed. ● **becqueter** *vt* (*picorer*) to peck (at)

bedaine [bədɛn] *nf* *Fam* paunch, pot-belly. ● **bedonnant** *a* potbellied, paunchy.

bée [be] *af* **bouche b.** open-mouthed.

beffroi [befrwa] *nm* belfry.

bégayer [begeje] *vi* to stutter. ● **bègue** [beg] *nmf* stutterer ‖ *a* **être b.** to stutter.

beige [bɛʒ] *a* & *nm* beige.

beignet [bɛɲɛ] *nm* (*pâtisserie*) fritter.

Beijing [bɛidʒiŋ] *nm* *ou* f Beijing.

bel [bɛl] *voir* beau.

bêler [bele] *vi* to bleat.

belette [bəlɛt] *nf* weasel.

Belgique [bɛlʒik] *nf* Belgium. ● **belge** *a* & *nmf* Belgian.

bélier [belje] *nm* (*animal, machine*) ram; **le B.** (*signe*) Aries.

belle [bɛl] *voir* beau.

belle-fille [bɛlfij] *nf* (*pl* **belles-filles**) (*d'un précédent mariage*) stepdaughter; (*épouse d'un fils*) daughter-in-law. ● **b.-mère** *nf* (*pl* **belles-mères**) mother-in-law; (*deuxième femme du père*) stepmother. ● **b.-sœur** *nf* (*pl* **belles-sœurs**) sister-in-law.

belliqueux, -euse [belikø, -øz] *a* (*action, ton*) warlike; (*personne*) aggressive.

belvédère [belveder] *nm* (*sur une route*) viewpoint.

bémol [bemɔl] *nm* *Mus* flat.

bénédiction [benediksjɔ̃] *nf* blessing.

bénéfice [benefis] *nm* (*financier*) profit; (*avantage*) benefit. ● **bénéficier** *vi* **b. de** to benefit from. ● **bénéfique** *a* beneficial.

Bénélux [benelyks] *nm* Benelux.

bénévole [benevɔl] *a* & *nmf* voluntary (worker).

bénin, -igne [benɛ̃, -iɲ] *a* (*tumeur*) benign; (*accident*) minor.

bénir [benir] *vt* to bless; (*remercier*) to give thanks to. ● **bénit** *a* (*pain*) consecrated; **eau bénite** holy water. ● **bénitier** [-itje] *nm* (holy-water) stoup.

benjamin, -ine [bɛ̃ʒamɛ̃, -in] *nmf* youngest child; *Sp* young junior.

benne [bɛn] *nf* (*de camion*) (movable) container; (*de grue*) scoop; **camion à b. basculante** dump truck; **b. à ordures** skip, *Am* Dumpster®.

béquille [bekij] *nf* (*canne*) crutch; (*de moto*) stand.

berceau, -x [bɛrso] *nm* cradle.

bercer [bɛrse] *vt* (*balancer*) to rock; (*apaiser*) to soothe, lull. ● **—euse** *nf* lullaby.

béret [berɛ] *nm* beret.

berge [bɛrʒ] *nf* (*rive*) (raised) bank.

berger, -ère [bɛrʒe, -er] 1 *nm* shepherd; **chien (de) b.** sheepdog ‖ *nf* shepherdess. 2 *nm* **b. allemand** Alsatian (dog), *Am* German shepherd. ● **bergerie** *nf* sheepfold.

berlingot [bɛrlɛ̃go] *nm* (*bonbon*) boiled sweet, *Am* hard candy; (*à la menthe*) mint; (*emballage*) (milk) carton.

berne (en) [ɑbɛrn] *adv* at half-mast.

besogne [bəzɔɲ] *nf* job, task, work *inv*.

besoin [bəzwɛ̃] *nm* need; **avoir b. de** to need; **au b.** if necessary, if need be; **dans le b.** in need, needy.

bestial, -aux [bɛstjal, -o] *a* bestial, brutish. ● **bestiaux** *nmpl* livestock; (*bovins*) cattle. ● **bestiole** *nf* (*insecte*) bug.

bétail [betaj] *nm* livestock; (*bovins*) cattle.

bête¹ [bɛt] *nf* animal; (*insecte*) bug, creature; **b. noire** pet hate, pet peeve; **chercher la petite b.** (*critiquer*) to pick holes.

bête² [bɛt] *a* stupid, silly. ● **bêtement** *adv* stupidly; **tout b.** quite simply. ● **bêtise** *nf* stupidity; (*action, parole*) stupid *ou* silly thing.

béton [betɔ̃] *nm* concrete; **mur/etc en b.** concrete wall/*etc*; **b. armé** reinforced concrete. ● **bétonnière** *nf* cement *ou* concrete mixer.

betterave [bɛtrav] *nf* beetroot, *Am* beet; **b. sucrière** *ou* **à sucre** sugar beet.

beugler [bøgle] *vi* (*taureau*) to bellow; (*vache*) to moo; (*radio*) *Fig* to blare (out).

beur [bœr] *nm* = North African born in France of immigrant parents.

beurre [bœr] *nm* butter. ● **beurrer** *vt* to butter. ● **beurrier** *nm* butter dish.

beuverie [bøvri] *nf* drinking session.

bévue [bevy] *nf* blunder, mistake.

biais [bjɛ] *nm* (*moyen détourné*) device, expedient; **regarder de b.** to look at sidelong; **traverser en b.** to cross at an angle.

bibelot [biblo] *nm* (small) ornament, trinket.

biberon [bibrɔ̃] *nm* (feeding) bottle; **nourrir au b.** to bottlefeed.

bible [bibl] *nf* bible; **la B.** the Bible. ● **biblique** *a* biblical.

bibliobus [biblijobys] *nm* mobile library.

bibliographie [biblijografi] *nf* bibliography.

bibliothèque [biblijotɛk] *nf* library; (*meuble*) bookcase. ● **bibliothécaire** *nmf* librarian.

bic® [bik] *nm* ballpoint, biro®.

biceps [bisɛps] *nm* (*muscle*) biceps.

biche [biʃ] *nf* doe, hind; **ma b.** *Fig* my pet.

bicolore [bikɔlɔr] *a* two-coloured.

bicoque [bikɔk] *nf* *Péj* shack, hovel.

bicyclette [bisiklɛt] *nf* bicycle; **la b.** *Sp* cycling; **aller à b.** to cycle.

bidet [bidɛ] *nm* (*cuvette*) bidet.

bidon [bidɔ̃] **1** *nm* (*d'essence*) can; (*pour boissons*) canteen. **2** *nm* du **b.** *Fam* bull, baloney ‖ *a inv* (*simulé*) *Fam* phoney, fake.

bidonville [bidɔ̃vil] *nf* shantytown.

bidule [bidyl] *nm* (*chose*) *Fam* whatsit.

bien [bjɛ̃] *adv* well; **il joue b.** he plays well; **je vais b.** I'm fine *ou* well; **b. fatigué/souvent/etc** (*très*) very tired/often/*etc*; **merci b.!** thanks very much!; **b.! fine!, right!; b. des fois/des gens/etc** lots of *ou* many times/people/*etc*; **je l'ai b. dit** (*intensif*) I *did* say so; **c'est b. compris?** is that quite understood?; **tu as b. fait** you did right; **c'est b. fait (pour lui)** it serves him right.

‖ *a inv* (*convenable, à l'aise*) all right, fine; (*agréable*) nice, fine; (*compétent, bon*) good, fine; (*beau*) attractive; (*en forme*) well; **une fille b.** (*moralement*) a nice *ou* respectable girl; **ce n'est pas b. de...** it's not nice *ou* right to....

‖ *nm* (*avantage*) good; (*chose*) possession; **ça te fera du b.** it will do you good; **pour ton b.** for your own good; **le b. et le mal** good and evil; **biens de consommation** consumer goods. ● **bien-être** *nm* well-being.

bienfaisance [bjɛ̃fəzɑ̃s] *nf* œuvre de **b.** charity. ● **bienfaisant** *a* beneficial.

bienfait [bjɛ̃fɛ] *nm* (*générosité*) favour; (*d'un remède etc*) beneficial effect. ● **bienfaiteur, -trice** *nmf* benefactor, benefactress.

bienheureux, -euse [bjɛ̃nœrø, -øz] *a* blessed, blissful.

bien que [bjɛ̃k(ə)] *conj* (+*sub*) although.

bienséant [bjɛ̃seã] *a* proper.

bientôt [bjɛ̃to] *adv* soon; **à b.!** see you soon!; **il est b. dix heures/***etc* it's nearly ten o'clock/*etc*.

bienveillant [bjɛ̃vɛjã] *a* kindly.

bienvenu, -ue [bjɛ̃vny] *a* welcome ▮*nmf* **soyez le b.!** welcome! ▮*nf* **souhaiter la bienvenue à qn** to welcome s.o.

bière [bjɛr] *nf* (*boisson*) beer; **b. pression** draught beer.

bifteck [biftɛk] *nm* steak.

bifurquer [bifyrke] *vi* (*route etc*) to fork, branch off; (*véhicule*) to turn off, fork. ●**bifurcation** *nf* fork, junction.

bigarré [bigare] *a* (*étoffe etc*) mottled; (*foule, société*) motley.

bigler [bigle] *vi* (*loucher*) *Fam* to squint.

bigorneau, -x [bigɔrno] *nm* (*coquillage*) winkle.

bigot, -ote [bigo, -ɔt] *nmf Péj* churchy person ▮*a Péj* churchy, over-devout.

bigoudi [bigudi] *nm* (hair) curler *ou* roller.

bigrement [bigrəmã] *adv Fam* awfully.

bijou, -x [biʒu] *nm* jewel; (*ouvrage élégant*) *Fig* gem. ●**bijouterie** *nf* (*commerce*) jeweller's shop, *Am* jewelry shop; (*bijoux*) jewellery, *Am* jewelry. ●**bijoutier, -ière** *nmf* jeweller, *Am* jeweler.

bikini [bikini] *nm* bikini.

bilan [bilã] *nm Fin* balance sheet; (*résultat*) outcome; (*d'un accident*) (casualty) toll; **b. de santé** checkup.

bile [bil] *nf* bile; **se faire de la b.** *Fam* to worry.

bilingue [bilɛ̃g] *a* bilingual.

billard [bijar] *nm* (*jeu*) billiards; (*table*) billiard table.

bille [bij] *nf* (*d'enfant*) marble; (*de billard*) billiard ball; **stylo à b.** ballpoint (pen).

billet [bijɛ] *nm* ticket; **b. (de banque)** (bank)note, *Am* bill; **b. aller, b. simple** single ticket, *Am* one-way ticket; **b. (d')aller et retour** return ticket, *Am*

round trip ticket.

billot [bijo] *nm* (*de bois*) block.

bimensuel, -elle [bimãsɥɛl] *a* bimonthly.

biner [bine] *vt* to hoe. ●**binette** *nf* hoe.

biochimie [bjoʃimi] *nf* biochemistry.

biodégradable [bjodegradabl] *a* biodegradable.

biographie [bjografi] *nf* biography. ●**biographique** *a* biographical.

biologie [bjɔlɔʒi] *nf* biology. ●**biologique** *a* biological; (*légumes etc*) organic.

bip [bip] *nm* bleeper.

bique [bik] *nf Fam* nanny-goat.

bis [bis] *adv* (*cri*) *Th* encore; *Mus* repeat; **4 bis** (*numéro*) 4A ▮*nm Th* encore.

biscornu [biskɔrny] *a* distorted, misshapen; (*idée*) cranky.

biscotte [biskɔt] *nf* (*pain*) Melba toast.

biscuit [biskɥi] *nm* (*sucré*) biscuit, *Am* cookie; (*salé*) biscuit, *Am* cracker; **b. de Savoie** sponge (cake).

bise [biz] *nf* **1** (*vent*) north wind. **2** (*baiser*) *Fam* kiss.

bison [bizɔ̃] *nm* (American) buffalo, bison.

bisou [bizu] *nm Fam* kiss.

bissextile [bisɛkstil] *af* **année b.** leap year.

bistouri [bisturi] *nm* scalpel, lancet.

bistro(t) [bistro] *nm* bar, café.

bitume [bitym] *nm* (*revêtement*) asphalt.

bivouac [bivwak] *nm* (*campement*) bivouac.

bizarre [bizar] *a* peculiar, odd. ●**—ment** *adv* oddly. ●**bizarrerie** *nf* peculiarity.

blabla(bla) [blabla(bla)] *nm* claptrap.

blafard [blafar] *a* pale, pallid.

blague [blag] *nf* **1** (*plaisanterie, farce*) *Fam* joke; *pl* (*absurdités*) *Fam* nonsense; **sans b.!** you're joking! **2** (*à tabac*) pouch. ●**blaguer** *vi* to be joking ▮*vt* to tease (*s.o.*). ●**blagueur, -euse** *nmf* joker.

blaireau, -x [blero] *nm* **1** (*animal*) badger. **2** (*brosse*) shaving brush.

blâme [blɑm] *nm* (*critique*) criticism,

blame; (*réprimande*) rebuke. ● **blâmable** *a* blameworthy. ● **blâmer** *vt* to criticize, blame; (*réprimander*) to rebuke.

blanc, blanche [blɑ̃, blɑ̃ʃ] **1** *a* white; (*page etc*) blank; **nuit blanche** sleepless night ▮ *nmf* (*personne*) white man *ou* woman ▮ *nm* (*couleur*) white; (*de poulet*) breast; (*espace, interligne*) blank; **b. (d'œuf)** (egg) white; **laisser en b.** to leave blank; **chèque en b.** blank cheque *ou* Am check; **cartouche à b.** blank (cartridge).

2 *nf* Mus minim, *Am* half-note. ● **blanchâtre** *a* whitish. ● **blancheur** *nf* whiteness.

blanchir [blɑ̃ʃir] *vt* (*mur*) to whitewash; (*drap*) to launder; **b. qn** (*disculper*) to clear s.o. ▮ *vi* to turn white. ● **blanchissage** *nm* laundering. ● **blanchisserie** *nf* (*lieu*) laundry. ● **blanchisseur, -euse** *nmf* laundryman, laundrywoman.

blasé [blaze] *a* blasé.

blason [blazɔ̃] *nm* (*écu*) coat of arms.

blasphème [blasfɛm] *nf* blasphemy. ● **blasphématoire** *a* (*propos*) blasphemous. ● **blasphémer** *vti* to blaspheme.

blazer [blazœr] *nm* blazer.

blé [ble] *nm* wheat.

bled [blɛd] *nm* (*village etc*) Péj Fam dump of a place.

blême [blɛm] *a* sickly pale; **b. de colère** livid with anger.

bless/er [blese] *vt* to injure, hurt; (*avec un couteau, d'une balle etc*) to wound; (*offenser*) to hurt, offend; **se b. le** *ou* **au bras/etc** to hurt one's arm/*etc*. ● **—ant** *a* (*parole, personne*) hurtful. ● **—é, -ée** *nmf* casualty, injured *ou* wounded person. ● **blessure** *nf* injury; wound.

bleu [blø] *a* (*mpl* **bleus**) blue; **b. de colère** blue in the face ▮ *nm* (*pl* **-s**) (*couleur*) blue; (*contusion*) bruise; (*vêtement*) overalls; **bleus de travail** overalls; **se faire un b. au genou/etc** to bruise one's knee/*etc*. ● **bleuet** *nm* cornflower. ● **bleuir** *vti* to turn blue.

blindé [blɛ̃de] *a* (*voiture etc*) armoured; **porte blindée** reinforced steel door; **une**

vitre blindée bulletproof glass ▮ *nm* armoured vehicle.

bloc [blɔk] *nm* (*de pierre etc*) block; (*de papier*) pad; (*masse compacte*) unit; **en b.** all together; **à b.** (*visser etc*) tight, hard. ● **b.-notes** *nm* (*pl* **blocs-notes**) writing pad.

blocage [blɔkaʒ] *nm* (*des roues*) locking; **b. des prix** price freeze.

blond, -onde [blɔ̃, -ɔ̃d] *a* fair(-haired), blond ▮ *nm* fair-haired man; (*couleur*) blond ▮ *nf* fair-haired woman, blonde; (*bière*) **blonde** lager, pale *ou* light ale.

bloquer [blɔke] *vt* (*obstruer*) to block; (*coincer*) to jam; (*roue*) to lock; (*freins*) to slam on; (*salaires, prix*) to freeze; **bloqué par la neige** snowbound ▮ **se b.** *vpr* to jam, stick; (*roue*) to lock.

blottir (se) [səblɔtir] *vpr* (*dans un coin etc*) to crouch; (*dans son lit*) to snuggle down; **se b. contre** to snuggle up to.

blouse [bluz] *nf* (*tablier*) smock, overall; (*corsage*) blouse. ● **blouson** *nm* windcheater, *Am* windbreaker.

blue-jean(s) [bludʒin(z)] *nm* jeans, denims.

bluff [blœf] *nm* bluff. ● **bluffer** *vti* to bluff.

boa [bɔa] *nm* (*serpent, tour de cou*) boa.

bobine [bɔbin] *nf* (*de fil, film etc*) reel, spool; (*pour machine à coudre*) bobbin, spool; *El* coil.

bobo [bɔbo] *nm* (*langage enfantin*) hurt; **j'ai b.**, **ça fait b.** it hurts.

bocal, -aux [bɔkal, -o] *nm* glass jar; (*à poissons*) bowl.

bœuf, *pl* **-fs** [bœf, bø] *nm* (*animal*) ox (*pl* oxen), bullock; (*viande*) beef.

bof! [bɔf] *int* (*indifférence*) *Fam* don't know and don't care!, big deal!

bohémien, -ienne [bɔemjɛ̃, -jɛn] *a* et *nmf* gipsy.

boire* [bwar] *vt* to drink; (*absorber*) to soak up; (*paroles*) *Fig* to take in; **b. un coup** to have a drink; **offrir à b. à qn** to offer s.o. a drink; **b. à petits coups** to sip ▮ *vi* to drink.

bois¹ [bwa] *voir* **boire**.

bois² [bwa] *nm* (*matière, forêt*) wood.

(de construction) timber; pl (de cerf) antlers; **en** ou **de b.** wooden; **b. de chauffage** firewood; ● **boisé** a wooded. ● **boiserie(s)** nf(pl) panelling.

boisson [bwasɔ̃] nf drink.

boit [bwa] voir **boire.**

boîte [bwat] nf box; (de conserve) tin, Am can; (de bière) can; **b. de nuit** nightclub; **mettre qn en b.** Fam to pull s.o.'s leg. ● **boîtier** nm (de montre etc) case.

boiter [bwate] vi (personne) to limp. ● **boiteux, -euse** a lame; (projet etc) Fig shaky.

bol [bɔl] nm (récipient) bowl; **prendre un b. d'air** to get a breath of fresh air.

bolide [bɔlid] nm (véhicule) racing car.

bombard/er [bɔ̃barde] vt (ville etc) to bomb; (avec des obus) to shell; **b.** de (questions) to bombard with; (objets) to pelt with. ● —**ement** nm bombing; shelling. ● **bombardier** nm (avion) bomber.

bombe [bɔ̃b] nf (projectile) bomb; (de laque etc) spray; **faire l'effet d'une b.** Fig to be a bombshell, be quite unexpected.

bomb/er [bɔ̃be] vt **b. la poitrine** to throw out one's chest. ● —**é** a (vitre etc) rounded; (route) cambered.

bon¹, bonne [bɔ̃, bɔn] a 1 (satisfaisant etc) good.

2 (agréable) nice, good; **il fait b. se reposer** it's nice ou good to rest; **b. anniversaire!** happy birthday!

3 (charitable) kind, good (avec qn to s.o.).

4 (qui convient) right; **le b. choix/moment** the right choice/moment.

5 (approprié, apte) fit; **b. à manger** fit to eat; **ce n'est b. à rien** it's useless; **comme b. te semble** as you think fit; **c'est à savoir** it's worth knowing.

6 (prudent) wise, good; **croire b. de...** to think it wise ou good to....

7 (compétent) good; **b. en français** good at French.

8 (valable) good; **ce billet est encore b.** this ticket is still good.

9 (intensif) **un b. moment** a good while.

10 (locutions) **à quoi b.?** what's the use

ou point ou good?; **pour de b.** really (and truly); **ah b.?** is that so? ‖ adv **sentir b.** to smell good; **il fait b.** it's nice (and warm).

bon² [bɔ̃] nm (billet) coupon, voucher.

bonbon [bɔ̃bɔ̃] nm sweet, Am candy. ● **bonbonnière** nf sweet box, Am candy box.

bonbonne [bɔ̃bɔn] nf (bouteille) demijohn.

bond [bɔ̃] nm leap, bound; **faire un b.** to leap (into the air); (prix) to shoot up.

bonde [bɔ̃d] nf (bouchon) plug.

bondé [bɔ̃de] a packed, crammed.

bondir [bɔ̃dir] vi to leap.

bonheur [bɔnœr] nm happiness; (chance) good luck, good fortune; **par b.** luckily.

bonhomme, pl **bonshommes** [bɔnɔm, bɔ̃zɔm] nm fellow, guy; **b. de neige** snowman.

boniment(s) [bɔnimɑ̃] nm(pl) (baratin) patter.

bonjour [bɔ̃ʒur] nm & int good morning; (après-midi) good afternoon; **donner le b. à, dire b. à** to say hello to.

bonne¹ [bɔn] voir **bon¹.**

bonne² nf (domestique) maid.

bonnement [bɔnmɑ̃] adv **tout b.** simply.

bonnet [bɔnɛ] nm (de ski etc) cap; (de femme, d'enfant) hat, bonnet; (de soutien-gorge) cup; **b. d'âne** dunce's cap.

bonsoir [bɔ̃swar] nm & int (en rencontrant qn) good evening; (en quittant qn) goodbye; (au coucher) good night.

bonté [bɔ̃te] nf kindness, goodness.

boom [bum] nm Écon boom.

bord [bɔr] nm (rebord) edge; (rive) bank; (de chapeau) brim; (de verre) rim, brim, edge; **au b. de la mer/route** at ou by the seaside/roadside; **b. du trottoir** kerb, Am curb; **au b. de** (précipice) on the brink of; **au b. des larmes** on the verge of tears; **à bord (de)** Nau Av on board; **jeter par-dessus b.** to throw overboard.

bordeaux [bɔrdo] a inv maroon.

border [bɔrde] vt (lit, personne) to tuck in; **b. la rue/etc** (maisons, arbres etc) to line the street/etc.

bordure [bɔrdyr] *nf* border; **en b. de** bordering on.

borgne [bɔrɲ] *a* (*personne*) one-eyed, blind in one eye.

borne [bɔrn] *nf* (*pierre*) boundary mark; *pl* (*limites*) *Fig* bounds; **b. kilométrique** = milestone; **dépasser les bornes** to go too far.

born/er [bɔrne] *vt* (*limiter*) to confine; **se b. à** to confine oneself to. ●**—é** *a* (*personne*) narrow-minded.

Bosnie [bɔsni] *nf* Bosnia.

bosquet [bɔskɛ] *nm* grove, thicket.

bosse [bɔs] *nf* (*dans le dos*) hump; (*enflure*) bump, lump; (*de terrain*) bump; **avoir la b. de** *Fam* to have a flair for.

bosseler [bɔsle] *vt* (*déformer*) to dent.

bossu, -ue [bɔsy] *a* hunchbacked ‖ *nmf* (*personne*) hunchback.

botanique [bɔtanik] *nf* botany.

botte [bɔt] *nf* **1** (*chaussure*) boot. **2** (*de radis etc*) bunch; (*de paille*) bundle. ●**botter** *vt* (*ballon etc*) *Fam* to boot. ●**bottillon** *nm* *ou* **bottine** *nf* (ankle) boot.

Bottin® [bɔtɛ̃] *nm* phone book.

bouc [buk] *nm* billy goat; (*barbe*) goatee.

boucan [bukɑ̃] *nm* *Fam* din, racket.

bouche [buʃ] *nf* mouth; **faire la fine b.** *Péj* to turn up one's nose; **b. de métro** métro entrance; **b. d'égout** drain opening, manhole; **le b.-à-b.** the kiss of life. ●**bouchée** *nf* mouthful.

bouch/er[1] [buʃe] *vt* (*évier, nez etc*) to stop up, block (up); (*bouteille*) to cork; (*vue, rue etc*) to block; **se b. le nez** to hold one's nose.

boucher[2] [buʃe] *nm* butcher. ●**boucherie** *nf* butcher's (shop); (*carnage*) butchery.

bouchon [buʃɔ̃] *nm* stopper, top; (*de liège*) cork; (*de tube, bidon*) cap, top; *Pêche* float; (*embouteillage*) *Fig* traffic jam.

boucle [bukl] *nf* **1** (*de ceinture*) buckle; (*de fleuve etc*) & *Av* loop; (*de ruban*) bow; **b. d'oreille** earring. **2 b. (de cheveux)** curl.

boucler [bukle] **1** *vt* (*attacher*) to fasten,

buckle; (*travail etc*) to finish off; (*fermer*) *Fam* to lock up; (*encercler*) to surround, cordon off; **boucle-la!** *Fam* shut up! **2** *vt* (*cheveux*) to curl ‖ *vi* to be curly. ●**bouclé** *a* (*cheveux*) curly.

bouclier [buklije] *nm* shield.

bouddhiste [budist] *a* & *nmf* Buddhist.

bouder [bude] *vi* to sulk. ●**bouderie** *nf* sulkiness. ●**boudeur, -euse** *a* sulky.

boudin [budɛ̃] *nm* black pudding, *Am* blood sausage.

boue [bu] *nf* mud. ●**boueux, -euse** [bwø, -øz] *a* muddy.

bouée [bwe] *nf* buoy; **b. de sauvetage** lifebuoy; **b. (gonflable)** rubber ring.

bouffe [buf] *nf* *Fam* food, grub. ●**bouffer** *vti* (*manger*) to eat.

bouffée [bufe] *nf* (*de fumée*) puff; (*de parfum*) whiff.

bouffi [bufi] *a* puffy, bloated.

bouffon, -onne [bufɔ̃, -ɔn] *nm* buffoon.

bougeoir [buʒwar] *nm* candlestick.

bougeotte [buʒɔt] *nf* **avoir la b.** *Fam* to have the fidgets.

bouger [buʒe] *vi* to move; (*agir*) to stir ‖ *vt* to move.

bougie [buʒi] *nf* candle; *Aut* spark(ing) plug.

bougon, -onne [bugɔ̃, -ɔn] *a* *Fam* grumpy. ●**bougonner** *vi* *Fam* to grumble.

bouillabaisse [bujabɛs] *nf* fish soup.

bouillie [buji] *nf* porridge; (*pour bébé*) cereal; **en b.** in a mush, mushy.

bouill/ir*** [bujir] *vi* to boil; **b. à gros bouillons** to bubble, boil hard; **faire b. qch** to boil sth; **b. de colère** to be seething with anger. ●**—ant** *a* boiling. ●**bouilloire** *nf* kettle. ●**bouillon** *nm* (*aliment*) broth, stock; (*bulles*) bubbles. ●**bouillonner** *vi* to bubble. ●**bouillotte** *nf* hot water bottle.

boulanger, -ère [bulɑ̃ʒe, -ɛr] *nmf* baker. ●**boulangerie** *nf* baker's (shop).

boule [bul] *nf* (*sphère*) ball; *pl* (*jeu*) bowls; **b. de neige** snowball; **se mettre en b.** (*chat etc*) to curl up into a ball; (*en colère*) *Fam* to fly off the handle; **boules Quiès®** earplugs.

bouleau, -x [bulo] *nm* (silver) birch.

bouledogue [buldɔg] *nm* bulldog.

boulet [bule] *nm* (de forçat) ball and chain; **b. de canon** cannonball.

boulette [bulet] *nf* (de papier) ball; (de viande) meatball.

boulevard [bulvar] *nm* boulevard.

boulevers/er [bulverse] *vt* (déranger) to turn upside down; (émouvoir) to upset (greatly), distress; (vie de qn, pays) to disrupt. ●—**ant** *a* upsetting, distressing. ●—**ement** *nm* upheaval.

boulon [bulɔ̃] *nm* bolt.

boulot [bulo] *nm* (travail) *Fam* work; (emploi) *Fam* job.

boum [bum] **1** *int* & *nm* bang. **2** *nf* (surprise-partie) *Fam* party.

bouquet [buke] *nm* (de fleurs) bunch, bouquet; (d'arbres) clump; (de vin) bouquet; **c'est le b.!** that's the last straw!

bouquin [bukɛ̃] *nm* *Fam* book. ●**bouquiniste** *nmf* second-hand bookseller.

bourbeux, -euse [burbø, -øz] *a* muddy. ●**bourbier** *nm* (lieu, situation) quagmire.

bourdon [burdɔ̃] *nm* (insecte) bumble-bee. ●**bourdonner** *vi* to buzz, hum. ●**bourdonnement** *nm* buzzing, humming.

bourg [bur] *nm* (small) market town. ●**bourgade** *nf* (large) village.

bourgeois, -oise [burʒwa, -waz] *a* & *nmf* middle-class (person). ●**bourgeoisie** *nf* middle class.

bourgeon [burʒɔ̃] *nm* bud. ●**bourgeonner** *vi* to bud.

bourgmestre [burgmestr] *nm* (en Belgique, Suisse) burgomaster.

bourgogne [burgɔɲ] *nm* (vin) Burgundy.

bourrade [burad] *nf* (du coude etc) shove.

bourrage [buraʒ] *nm* **b. de crâne** brainwashing.

bourrasque [burask] *nf* squall, gust of wind.

bourratif, -ive [buratif, -iv] *a* (aliment) *Fam* filling, stodgy.

bourreau, -x [buro] *nm* executioner; **b. d'enfants** child batterer; **b. de travail** workaholic.

bourrelet [burlɛ] *nm* weather strip; **b. de graisse** roll of fat.

bourrer [bure] *vt* to stuff, cram (**de** with); (pipe, coussin) to fill; **b. de coups** to thrash; **b. le crâne à qn** to brainwash s.o.

bourrique [burik] *nf* ass.

bourru [bury] *a* surly, rough.

bourse [burs] *nf* (sac) purse; (d'études) grant, scholarship; **la B.** the Stock Exchange. ●**boursier, -ière** *nmf* *Scol Univ* grant holder, scholar.

boursouflé [bursufle] *a* (visage etc) puffy.

bousculer [buskyle] *vt* (heurter, pousser) to jostle; (presser) to rush, push. ●**bousculade** *nf* jostling, rush.

bouse [buz] *nf* **une b. (de vache)** a cowpat; **de la b. (de vache)** cow dung.

bousiller [buzije] *vt* *Fam* to mess up, wreck.

boussole [busɔl] *nf* compass.

bout [bu] *nm* end; (de langue, canne, doigt) tip; (de papier, pain, ficelle) bit; **un b. de temps/chemin** a little while/ way; **au b. d'un moment** after a while; **jusqu'au b.** (lire etc) (right) to the end; **à b. (de forces)** exhausted; **à b. de souffle** out of breath; **à b. de bras** at arm's length; **venir à b. de** (travail) to get through; (adversaire) to get the better of; **à b. portant** point-blank.

boutade [butad] *nf* (plaisanterie) quip, witticism.

boute-en-train [butɑ̃trɛ̃] *nm inv* (personne) live wire.

bouteille [butɛj] *nf* bottle; (de gaz) cylinder.

boutique [butik] *nf* shop.

bouton [butɔ̃] *nm* (bourgeon) bud; (au visage etc) pimple, spot; (de vêtement) button; (poussoir) (push-)button; (de porte, télévision) knob; **b. de manchette** cuff link. ●**b.-d'or** *nm* (pl **boutons-d'or**) buttercup. ●**boutonner** *vt*, **se b.** *vpr* to button (up). ● **boutonneux, -euse** *a* pimply, spotty. ● **boutonnière** *nf* buttonhole.

bouture [butyr] *nf* (*plante*) cutting.

bovins [bɔvɛ̃] *nmpl* cattle.

bowling [bolin] *nm* (tenpin) bowling; (*lieu*) bowling alley.

box, *pl* **boxes** [bɔks] *nm* (*garage*) lockup *ou* individual garage; (*d'écurie*) (loose) box; (*des accusés*) dock.

boxe [bɔks] *nf* boxing. ● **boxer** *vi* Sp to box ‖ *vt* Fam to whack, punch. ● **boxeur** *nm* boxer.

boyau, -x [bwajo] *nm* Anat gut; (*corde*) catgut; (*de bicyclette*) (racing) tyre *ou* Am tire.

boycotter [bɔjkɔte] *vt* to boycott.

BP [bepe] *nf abrév* (*boîte postale*) PO Box.

bracelet [brasle] *nm* bracelet, bangle; (*de montre*) strap, Am band.

braconner [brakɔne] *vi* to poach. ● **braconnier** *nm* poacher.

brader [brade] *vt* to sell off cheaply.

braguette [braget] *nf* (*de pantalon*) fly, flies.

braille [braj] *nm* Braille.

brailler [braje] *vti* to bawl.

braire* [brer] *vi* (*âne*) to bray.

braise(s) [brez] *nf(pl)* embers, live coals.

brancard [brãkar] *nm* (*civière*) stretcher; (*de charrette*) shaft. ● **brancardier** *nm* stretcher-bearer.

branche [brãʃ] *nf* (*d'arbre, d'une science etc*) branch; (*de compas*) leg, arm; (*de lunettes*) side (piece). ● **branchages** *nmpl* (cut *ou* fallen) branches.

branché [brãʃe] *a* (*informé*) Fam with it.

branch/er [brãʃe] *vt* (*lampe etc*) to plug in; (*installer*) to connect. ● **—ement** *nm* El connection.

brandir [brãdir] *vt* to brandish, flourish.

branle [brãl] *nm* **mettre en b.** to set in motion. ● **b.-bas** *nm inv* turmoil. ● **branlant** *a* (*table etc*) wobbly, shaky.

braquer [brake] **1** *vt* (*arme etc*) to point, aim (**sur** at); (*yeux*) to fix. **2** *vi* Aut to turn the steering wheel, steer.

bras [bra] *nm* arm; **en b. de chemise** in one's shirtsleeves; **b. dessus b. dessous** arm in arm; **à b. ouverts** with open arms; **son b. droit** Fig his right-hand man; **à tour de b.** with all one's might; **à b.-le-corps** round the waist. ● **brassard** *nm* armband. ● **brassée** *nf* armful.

brasier [brazje] *nm* blaze, inferno.

brasse [bras] *nf* (*nage*) breaststroke; (*mesure*) fathom; **b. papillon** butterfly stroke.

brasserie [brasri] *nf* (*usine*) brewery; (*café*) brasserie.

brassière [brasjer] *nf* (*de bébé*) vest, Am undershirt.

bravade [bravad] *nf* **par b.** out of bravado.

brave [brav] *a & nm* (*hardi*) brave (man); (*honnête*) good (man). ● **bravement** *adv* bravely. ● **braver** *vt* to defy.

bravo [bravo] *int* well done ‖ *nm* cheer.

bravoure [bravur] *nf* bravery.

break [brek] *nm* estate car, Am station wagon.

brebis [brəbi] *nf* ewe; **b. galeuse** (*indésirable*) black sheep.

brèche [brɛʃ] *nf* gap, breach.

bredouille [brəduj] *a* **rentrer b.** to come back empty-handed.

bredouiller [brəduje] *vti* to mumble.

bref, brève [bref, brev] *a* brief, short ‖ *adv* (*enfin*) **b.** in a word.

Brésil [brezil] *nm* Brazil. ● **brésilien, -ienne** *a & nmf* Brazilian.

Bretagne [brətaɲ] *nf* Brittany. ● **breton, -onne** *a & nmf* Breton.

bretelle [brətel] *nf* strap; (*route d'accès*) access road; *pl* (*pour pantalon*) braces, Am suspenders.

brève [brev] *voir* **bref**.

brevet [brəve] *nm* diploma; **b. (des collèges)** = GCSE (*examination for 16-year-olds*); **b. (d'invention)** patent. ● **breveter** *vt* to patent.

bribes [brib] *nfpl* scraps, bits.

bric-à-brac [brikabrak] *nm inv* bric-à-brac, jumble, junk.

bricole [brikɔl] *nf* (*objet, futilité*) trifle.

bricol/er [brikɔle] *vi* to do odd jobs ▮ *vt* (*réparer*) to patch up; (*fabriquer*) to put together. ●**—age** *nm* (*passe-temps*) do-it-yourself; (*petits travaux*) odd jobs; **salon/rayon du b.** do-it-yourself exhibition/department. ●**—eur, -euse** *nmf* handyman, handywoman.

bravoure [bravur] *nf* bravery.

bride [brid] *nf* (*de cheval*) bridle. ●**brider** *vt* (*cheval*) to bridle; **avoir les yeux bridés** to have slanting eyes.

bridge [bridʒ] *nm* (*jeu*) bridge.

brièvement [brijɛvmɑ̃] *adv* briefly. ●**brièveté** *nf* shortness, brevity.

brigade [brigad] *nf* (*de gendarmerie*) squad; *Mil* brigade. ●**brigadier** *nm* police sergeant; *Mil* corporal.

brigand [brigɑ̃] *nm* robber; (*enfant*) rascal.

brillant [brijɑ̃] *a* (*luisant*) shining; (*astiqué*) shiny; (*couleur*) bright; (*doué, remarquable*) *Fig* brilliant ▮ *nm* shine; (*diamant*) diamond. ●**brillamment** *adv* brilliantly.

briller [brije] *vi* to shine; **faire b.** (*meuble*) to polish (up).

brin [brɛ̃] *nm* (*d'herbe*) blade; (*de corde, fil*) strand; (*de muguet*) spray; **un b. de** *Fig* a bit of.

brindille [brɛ̃dij] *nf* twig.

bringuebaler [brɛ̃gbale] *vi* to shake about; (*véhicule*) to rattle along.

brio [brijo] *nm* (*virtuosité*) brilliance.

brioche [brijɔʃ] *nf* (*pâtisserie*) brioche (*light sweet bun*).

brique [brik] *nf* brick; (*de lait, jus de fruit*) carton.

briquer [brike] *vt* to polish (up).

briquet [brikɛ] *nm* (*cigarette*) lighter.

brise [briz] *nf* breeze.

briser [brize] *vt* to break; (*en morceaux*) to smash, break; (*espoir, carrière*) to wreck, shatter ▮ **se b.** *vpr* to break. ●**brisants** *nmpl* reefs.

britannique [britanik] *a* British ▮ *nmpl* **les Britanniques** the British.

broc [bro] *nm* pitcher, jug.

brocanteur, -euse [brɔkɑ̃tœr, -øz] *nmf* secondhand dealer (*in furniture etc*).

broche [broʃ] *nf* *Culin* spit; (*bijou*) brooch; *Méd* pin. ●**brochette** *nf* (*tige*) skewer; (*plat*) kebab.

brochet [broʃɛ] *nm* (*poisson*) pike.

brochure [broʃyr] *nf* brochure, booklet.

brocolis [brɔkɔli] *nmpl* broccoli.

broder [brode] *vt* to embroider (**de** with). ●**broderie** *nf* embroidery.

broncher [brɔ̃ʃe] *vi* (*bouger*) to budge; (*reculer*) to flinch; (*protester*) to balk.

bronches [brɔ̃ʃ] *nfpl* bronchial tubes. ●**bronchite** *nf* bronchitis.

bronze [brɔ̃z] *nm* bronze.

bronz/er [brɔ̃ze] *vt* to tan; **se (faire) b.** to sunbathe, get a (sun)tan ▮ *vi* to get (sun)tanned. ●**—age** *nm* (sun)tan, sunburn.

brosse [brɔs] *nf* brush; **b. à dents** toothbrush; **cheveux en b.** crew cut. ●**brosser** *vt* to brush; **se b. les dents/cheveux** to brush one's teeth/hair.

brouette [bruɛt] *nf* wheelbarrow.

brouhaha [bruaa] *nm* hubbub.

brouillard [brujar] *nm* fog; **il y a du b.** it's foggy.

brouille [bruj] *nf* disagreement, quarrel.

brouiller [bruje] **1** *vt* (*idées etc*) to mix up; (*vue*) to blur; (*œufs*) to scramble ▮ **se b.** *vpr* (*idées*) to be *ou* get confused; (*temps*) to cloud over; (*vue*) to get blurred. **2** *vt* (*amis*) to cause a split between ▮ **se b.** *vpr* to fall out (**avec** with).

brouillon [brujɔ̃] *nm* rough draft.

broussailles [brusaj] *nfpl* bushes.

brousse [brus] *nf* **la b.** the bush.

brouter [brute] *vti* to graze.

broyer [brwaje] *vt* to grind; (*doigt, bras*) to crush.

bru [bry] *nf* daughter-in-law.

brugnon [bryɲɔ̃] *nm* (*fruit*) nectarine.

bruine [brɥin] *nf* drizzle. ●**bruiner** *v imp* to drizzle.

bruissement [brɥismɑ̃] *nm* (*de feuilles*) rustle, rustling.

bruit [brɥi] *nm* noise, sound; (*nouvelle*) rumour; **faire du b.** to make a noise.

● **bruitage** nm Cin sound effects.

brûlant [brylɑ̃] a (objet, soleil) burning (hot); (sujet) Fig red-hot.

brûlé [bryle] nm **odeur de b.** smell of burning.

brûle-pourpoint (à) [abrylpurpwɛ̃] adv point-blank.

brûler [bryle] vt to burn; (consommer) to use up, burn; **b. un feu (rouge)** to go through ou jump the lights ▮ vi to burn; **b. (d'envie) de faire** to be dying to do ▮ **se b.** vpr to burn oneself.

brûlure [brylyr] nf burn; **brûlures d'estomac** heartburn.

brume [brym] nf mist, haze. ● **brumeux, -euse** a misty, hazy; (obscur) Fig hazy.

brun, brune [brœ̃, bryn] a brown; (cheveux) dark, brown; (personne) dark-haired ▮ nm (couleur) brown ▮ nmf dark-haired person. ● **brunir** vt (peau) to tan ▮ vi to turn brown; (cheveux) to go darker.

brushing [brœʃiŋ] nm blow-dry.

brusque [brysk] a (manière, personne etc) abrupt, blunt; (subit) sudden, abrupt. ● **brusquement** adv suddenly, abruptly. ● **brusquer** vt to rush. ● **brusquerie** nf abruptness.

brut [bryt] a (pétrole) crude; (sucre) unrefined; (soie) raw; (poids, revenu) gross.

brutal, -aux [brytal, -o] a (violent) savage, brutal; (enfant) rough; (franchise, réponse) crude, blunt. ● **brutaliser** vt to ill-treat. ● **brutalité** nf (violence, acte) brutality. ● **brute** nf brute.

Bruxelles [brysɛl] nm ou f Brussels.

bruyant [brɥijɑ̃] a noisy. ● **bruyamment** adv noisily.

bruyère [brɥijɛr] nf (plante) heather.

bu [by] pp de **boire**.

buanderie [bɥɑ̃dri] nf (lieu) laundry.

bûche [byʃ] nf log. ● **bûcher** nm (local) woodshed; (supplice) stake. ● **bûcheron** nm lumberjack, woodcutter.

budget [bydʒɛ] nm budget. ● **budgétaire** a budgetary; (année) financial.

buée [bɥe] nf mist, condensation.

buffet [byfɛ] nm (armoire) sideboard; (table, repas) buffet.

buffle [byfl] nm buffalo.

buis [bɥi] nm (arbre) box; (bois) boxwood.

buisson [bɥisɔ̃] nm bush.

buissonnière [bɥisɔnjɛr] af **faire l'école b.** to play truant ou Am hookey.

bulbe [bylb] nm bulb.

Bulgarie [bylgari] nf Bulgaria. ● **bulgare** a & nmf Bulgarian.

bulldozer [byldozœr] nm bulldozer.

bulle [byl] nf bubble; (de bande dessinée) balloon.

bulletin [byltɛ̃] nm (météo) report; (scolaire) report, Am report card; (communiqué, revue) bulletin; **b. de paie** pay slip ou Am stub; **b. de vote** ballot paper.

buraliste [byralist] nmf (au tabac) tobacconist.

bureau, -x [byro] nm **1** (table) desk. **2** (lieu) office; **b. de change** foreign exchange office, bureau de change; **b. de location** Th Cin box office; **b. de tabac** tobacconist's (shop), Am tobacco store. ● **bureautique** nf office automation.

burette [byrɛt] nf oilcan; Culin cruet.

burlesque [byrlɛsk] a (idée etc) ludicrous.

bus¹ [bys] nm bus.

bus² [by] pt de **boire**.

buste [byst] nm (torse, sculpture) bust.

but¹ [by(t)] nm (objectif) aim, goal; (cible) target; Fb goal; **aller droit au b.** to go straight to the point; **j'ai pour b. de...** my aim is to....

but² [by] pt de **boire**.

butane [bytan] nm (gaz) butane.

buter [byte] **1** vi **b. contre** to stumble over; (difficulté) Fig to come up against. **2 se buter** vpr (s'entêter) to become ou to obstinate. ● **buté** a obstinate.

butin [bytɛ̃] nm loot, haul, booty.

butiner [bytine] vi (abeille) to gather pollen and nectar.

butoir [bytwar] nm (pour train) buffer;

(*de porte*) stop(per).
butte [byt] **1** *nf* mound, hillock. **2 en b. à**
(*calomnie etc*) exposed to.
buvable [byvabl] *a* drinkable. ●**buveur,**

-euse *nmf* drinker.
buvard [byvar] *a* & *nm* (**papier**) **b.**
blotting paper.
buvette [byvet] *nf* refreshment bar.

C

C, c [se] *nm* C, c

c *abrév* centime.

c' [s] *voir* ce¹.

ça [sa] *pron dém* (*abrév de* cela) (*pour désigner*) that; (*plus près*) this; (*sujet indéfini*) it, that; **ça m'amuse que...** it amuses me that...; **où/quand/comment/ etc ça?** where?/when?/how?/*etc*; **ça va (bien)?** how's it going?; **ça va!** fine!, OK!; **ça alors!** (*surprise, indignation*) how about that!; **c'est ça** that's right; **et avec ça?** (*dans un magasin*) anything else?

ça [sa] *adv* **çà et là** here and there.

caban [kabɑ̃] *nm* (*veste*) reefer.

cabane [kaban] *nf* hut, cabin; (*à outils*) shed; (*à lapins*) hutch.

cabas [kaba] *nm* shopping bag.

cabillaud [kabijo] *nm* (fresh) cod.

cabine [kabin] *nf* (*de bateau*) cabin; *Tél* phone booth, phone box; (*de camion*) cab; (*d'ascenseur*) car; (*à la piscine*) cubicle; **c.** (*de pilotage*) cockpit; (*d'un grand avion*) flight deck; **c. d'essayage** fitting room.

cabinet [kabinɛ] *nm* (*de médecin*) surgery, *Am* office; (*d'avocat*) office; (*clientèle de médecin ou d'avocat*) practice; (*de ministre*) department; *pl* (*toilettes*) toilet, lavatory; **c. de toilette** (small) bathroom, toilet; **c. de travail** study.

câble [kɑbl] *nm* cable; (*cordage*) rope; **la télévision par c.** cable television; **le c.** *TV* cable. ● **câbler** *vt* **être câblé** *TV* to have cable.

cabosser [kabɔse] *vt* to dent.

cabrer (se) [səkabre] *vpr* (*cheval*) to rear (up).

cabri [kabri] *nm* (*chevreau*) kid.

cabrioles [kabriɔl] *nfpl* **faire des c.** (*sauts*) to cavort, caper (about).

cabriolet [kabriɔlɛ] *nm Aut* convertible.

cacah(o)uète [kakawɛt] *nf* peanut.

cacao [kakao] *nm* (*boisson*) cocoa.

cachalot [kaʃalo] *nm* sperm whale.

cache-cache [kaʃkaʃ] *nm inv* hide-and-seek. ● **c.-nez** *nm inv* scarf, muffler.

cachemire [kaʃmir] *nm* (*tissu*) cashmere.

cacher [kaʃe] *vt* to hide, conceal (à from); **je ne cache pas que...** I don't hide the fact that... **▌se c.** *vpr* to hide.

cachet [kaʃɛ] *nm* (*de la poste*) postmark; (*comprimé*) tablet; *Fig* distinctive character. ● **cacheter** *vt* to seal.

cachette [kaʃɛt] *nf* hiding place; **en c.** in secret; **en c. de qn** without s.o. knowing.

cachot [kaʃo] *nm* dungeon.

cachotteries [kaʃɔtri] *nfpl* secretiveness; (*petits secrets*) little mysteries. ● **cachottier, -ière** *a & nmf* secretive (person).

cacophonie [kakɔfɔni] *nf* cacophony.

cactus [kaktys] *nm* cactus.

cadavre [kadɑvr] *nm* corpse. ● **cadavérique** *a* (*teint etc*) cadaverous; **rigidité c.** rigor mortis.

caddie® [kadi] *nm* (supermarket) trolley *ou Am* cart.

cadeau, -x [kado] *nm* present, gift.

cadenas [kadnɑ] *nm* padlock. ● **cadenasser** *vt* to padlock.

cadence [kadɑ̃s] *nf* rhythm; *Mus* cadence; (*taux, vitesse*) rate; **en c.** in time.

cadet, -ette [kadɛ, -ɛt] *a* (*de deux frères etc*) younger; (*de plus de deux*) youngest **▌** *nmf* (*enfant*) younger (child); youngest (child); *Sp* junior; **c'est mon c.** he's my junior.

cadran [kadrɑ̃] *nm* (*de téléphone etc*) dial; (*de montre*) face; **c. solaire** sundial.

cadre [kadr] *nm* **1** (*de photo, vélo etc*) frame; (*décor*) setting; (*sur un imprimé*) box. **2** (*chef*) *Com* executive, manager; *pl* (*personnel*) *Com* management, managers.

cadrer [kadre] *vi* to tally (**avec** with).

cafard, -arde [kafar, -ard] *nm* **1** (*insecte*) cockroach. **2 avoir le c.** to be in the dumps; **ça me donne le c.** it depresses me. ●**cafardeux, -euse** *a* (*personne*) in the dumps.

café [kafe] *nm* coffee; (*bar*) café; **c. au lait, c. crème** white coffee, coffee with milk; **c. noir, c. nature** black coffee; **c. soluble** *ou* **instantané** instant coffee; **tasse de c.** cup of black coffee. ●**cafétéria** *nf* cafeteria. ●**cafetière** *nf* coffee-pot; (*électrique*) percolator.

cage [kaʒ] *nf* cage; **c. (d'escalier)** (stair)well; **c. des buts** *Fb* goal (area).

cageot [kaʒo] *nm* crate, box.

cagibi [kaʒibi] *nm* (storage) room.

cagnotte [kaɲɔt] *nf* (*tirelire*) kitty.

cagoule [kagul] *nf* (*de bandit, moine*) hood; (*d'enfant*) balaclava, *Am* ski mask.

cahier [kaje] *nm Scol* exercise book; (*carnet*) (note)book; **c. de brouillon** rough book, *Am* = scratch pad; **c. d'appel** register (in school).

cahin-caha [kaɛ̃kaa] *adv* **aller c.-caha** to jog along (with ups and downs).

cahot [kao] *nm* jolt, bump. ●**cahoter** *vi* (*véhicule*) to jolt along. ●**cahoteux, -euse** *a* bumpy.

caille [kaj] *nf* (*oiseau*) quail.

cailler [kaje] *vti*, **se c.** *vpr* (*sang*) to clot, congeal; (*lait*) to curdle; **faire c.** (*lait*) to curdle. ●**caillot** *nm* (*blood*) clot.

caillou, -x [kaju] *nm* stone; (*galet*) pebble. ●**caillouteux, -euse** *a* stony.

Caire [kɛr] *nm* **le C.** Cairo.

caisse [kɛs] *nf* (*boîte*) case, box; (*cageot*) crate; (*guichet*) cash desk, pay desk; (*de supermarché*) checkout; (*tambour*) drum; **c. (enregistreuse)** till, cash register; **c. d'épargne** savings bank.

caissier, -ière [kesje, -jɛr] *nmf* cashier; (*de supermarché*) checkout assistant.

cajoler [kaʒɔle] *vt* (*câliner*) to pamper, make a fuss of.

cajou [kaʒu] *nm* **noix de c.** cashew nut.

cake [kɛk] *nm* fruit cake.

calamité [kalamite] *nf* calamity.

calandre [kalɑ̃dr] *nf Aut* radiator grille.

calcaire [kalker] *a* (*eau*) hard ▮ *nm Géol* limestone.

calciné [kalsine] *a* charred, burnt to a cinder.

calcium [kalsjɔm] *nm* calcium.

calcul [kalkyl] *nm* calculation; (*discipline*) arithmetic.

calcul/er [kalkyle] *vt* to calculate. ●**—é** *a* (*risque etc*) calculated. ●**calculatrice** *nf* (*ordinateur*) calculator. ●**calculette** *nf* pocket calculator.

cale [kal] *nf* **1** (*pour maintenir*) wedge. **2** (*de bateau*) hold.

calé [kale] *a Fam* (*instruit*) clever (**en qch** at sth).

caleçon [kalsɔ̃] *nm* underpants, boxer shorts; **c. de bain** bathing trunks.

calendrier [kalɑ̃drije] *nm* (*mois et jours*) calendar; (*programme*) timetable.

cale-pied [kalpje] *nm* (*de bicyclette*) toe-clip.

calepin [kalpɛ̃] *nm* (pocket) notebook.

caler [kale] **1** *vt* (*meuble etc*) to wedge; (*appuyer*) to prop (up). **2** *vt* (*moteur*) to stall ▮ *vi* to stall.

calfeutrer [kalføtre] *vt* (*avec du bourrelet*) to draughtproof; **se c.** (**chez soi**) to shut oneself away *ou* up.

calibre [kalibr] *nm* (*diamètre*) calibre.

calice [kalis] *nm* (*vase*) *Rel* chalice.

californien, -ienne (kalifurɲɛ̃, (à) [akalifurʃɔ̃] *adv* astride; **se mettre à c. sur** to straddle.

câlin [kalɛ̃] *a* affectionate ▮ *nm* cuddle. ●**câliner** *vt* (*caresser*) to cuddle.

calleux, -euse [kalø, -øz] *a* covered in calluses, callous.

calme [kalm] *a* calm; (*journée etc*) quiet, calm ▮ *nm* calm(ness); **du c.!** keep quiet!; (*pas de panique*) keep calm!; **dans le c.** (*travailler, étudier*) in peace and quiet. ●**—ment** [-əmɑ̃] *adv* calmly.

calmer [kalme] *vt* (*douleur*) to soothe; (*inquiétude*) to calm; **c. qn** to calm s.o. (down) ▮ **se c.** *vpr* to calm down. ●**calmant** *nm* (*pour la nervosité*) sedative; (*la douleur*) painkiller; **sous calmants** under sedation; on painkillers.

calomnie [kalɔmni] *nf* slander; (*par écrit*) libel. ● **calomnier** *vt* to slander; to libel. ● **calomnieux, -euse** *a* slanderous; libellous.

calorie [kalɔri] *nf* calorie.

calot [kalo] *nm Mil* forage cap.

calotte [kalɔt] *nf Rel* skull cap; **c. glaciaire** icecap.

calque [kalk] *nm* (*dessin*) tracing; **(papier-)c.** tracing paper. ● **calquer** *vt* to trace; (*imiter*) *Fig* to copy.

calvaire [kalver] *nm Rel* calvary; *Fig* agony.

calvitie [kalvisi] *nf* baldness.

camarade [kamarad] *nmf* friend; **c. de jeu** playmate; **c. d'atelier** workmate, *Am* work colleague. ● **camaraderie** *nf* friendship, companionship.

cambouis [kãbwi] *nm* (dirty) oil.

cambrer [kãbre] *vt* to arch; **c. les reins** ou **le buste** to throw out one's chest.

cambriol/er [kãbrijɔle] *vt* to burgle, *Am* burglarize. ● **—age** *nm* burglary. ● **—eur, -euse** *nmf* burglar.

camélia [kamelja] *nm Bot* camellia.

camelot [kamlo] *nm* street hawker. ● **camelote** *nf* cheap goods, junk.

camembert [kamãber] *nm* Camembert (cheese).

caméra [kamera] *nf* (*TV ou* film) camera. ● **cameraman** *nm* (*pl* **-mans** *ou* **-men**) cameraman.

caméscope [kameskɔp] *nm* camcorder.

camion [kamjɔ̃] *nm* lorry, *Am* truck; **c. de déménagement** removal van, *Am* moving van. ● **c.-benne** *nm* (*pl* **camions-bennes**) dustcart, *Am* garbage truck. ● **c.-citerne** *nm* (*pl* **camions-citernes**) tanker, *Am* tank truck. ● **camionnette** *nf* van. ● **camionneur** *nm* (*conducteur*) lorry *ou Am* truck driver.

camisole [kamizɔl] *nf* **c. de force** straitjacket.

camomille [kamɔmij] *nf Bot* camomile; (*tisane*) camomile tea.

camoufl/er [kamufle] *vt* to camouflage. ● **—age** *nm* camouflage.

camp [kã] *nm* camp; **feu de c.** campfire; **lit de c.** camp bed; **c. de concentration** concentration camp; **dans mon c.** (*jeu*) on my side.

campagne [kãpaɲ] *nf* **1** country(side); **à la c.** in the country. **2** (*électorale, militaire etc*) campaign. ● **campagnard, -arde** *a* style/*etc* **c.** country style/*etc* ‖ *nm* countryman ‖ *nf* countrywoman.

camp/er [kãpe] *vi* to camp. ● **—ement** *nm* encampment, camp. ● **—eur, -euse** *nmf* camper.

camping [kãpiŋ] *nm* camping; (*terrain*) camp(ing) site. ● **c.-car** *nm* camper.

campus [kãpys] *nm Univ* campus.

Canada [kanada] *nm* Canada. ● **canadien, -ienne** *a* & *nmf* Canadian ‖ *nf* fur-lined jacket.

canaille [kanɑj] *nf* rogue, scoundrel.

canal, -aux [kanal, -o] *nm* (*artificiel*) canal; *TV* channel. ● **canalisation** *nf* (*de gaz etc*) mains, main pipe. ● **canaliser** *vt* (*rivière etc*) to canalize; (*diriger*) *Fig* to channel.

canapé [kanape] *nm* (*siège*) sofa, couch, settee.

canard [kanar] *nm* **1** duck; (*mâle*) drake. **2** (*journal*) *Péj* rag.

canari [kanari] *nm* canary.

cancans [kãkã] *nmpl* (malicious) gossip.

cancer [kãser] *nm* cancer; **le C.** (*signe*) Cancer. ● **cancéreux, -euse** *a* cancerous ‖ *nmf* cancer patient. ● **cancérigène** *a* carcinogenic.

cancre [kãkr] *nm* (*élève*) *Péj* dunce.

cancrelat [kãkrəla] *nm* cockroach.

candidat, -ate [kãdida, -at] *nmf* candidate; (*à un poste*) applicant, candidate; **être** *ou* **se porter c. à** to apply for. ● **candidature** *nf* application; *Pol* candidacy; **poser sa c.** to apply (**à** for).

cane [kan] *nf* (female) duck. ● **caneton** *nm* duckling.

canette [kanet] *nf* **1** (*de bière*) (small) bottle. **2** (*bobine*) spool.

canevas [kanva] *nm* (*toile*) canvas; (*ébauche*) framework, outline.

caniche [kaniʃ] *nm* poodle.

canicule [kanikyl] *nf* scorching heat; **la c.** (*période*) the dog days.

canif [kanif] *nm* penknife.

canin, -ine [kanin] *a* (*espèce, race*) canine; **exposition c.** dog show. **2** *nf* (*dent*) canine (tooth).

caniveau, -x [kanivo] *nm* gutter (*in street*).

canne [kan] *nf* (walking) stick; (*à sucre, de bambou*) cane; **c. à pêche** fishing rod.

cannelle [kanɛl] *nf Bot Culin* cinnamon.

cannette [kanɛt] *nf* = **canette**.

cannibale [kanibal] *nmf* & *a* cannibal.

canoë [kanɔe] *nm* canoe; *Sp* canoeing.

canon [kanɔ̃] *nm* (big) gun; *Hist* cannon; (*de fusil etc*) barrel.

cañon [kaɲɔ̃] *nm* canyon.

canot [kano] *nm* boat; **c. de sauvetage** lifeboat; **c. pneumatique** rubber dinghy.
● **canoter** *vi* to go boating.

cantatrice [kɑ̃tatris] *nf* opera singer.

cantine [kɑ̃tin] *nf* **1** (*réfectoire*) canteen; **manger à la c.** (*écolier*) to have school dinners *ou Am* school lunch. **2** (*coffre*) tin trunk.

cantique [kɑ̃tik] *nm* hymn.

canton [kɑ̃tɔ̃] *nm* (*en France*) district (*division of arrondissement*); (*en Suisse*) canton.

cantonade (à la) [alakɑ̃tɔnad] *adv* (*parler*) to all and sundry, to everyone in general.

cantonnier [kɑ̃tɔnje] *nm* road mender.

canyon [kaɲɔ̃] *nm* canyon.

caoutchouc [kautʃu] *nm* rubber; (*élastique*) rubber band; *pl* (*chaussures*) galoshes, (rubber) overshoes; **balle/etc en c.** rubber ball/etc; **c. mousse**® foam.
● **caoutchouteux, -euse** *a* rubbery.

CAP [seape] *nm abrév* (*certificat d'aptitude professionnelle*) technical and vocational diploma.

cap [kap] *nm Géog* cape, headland; (*direction*) *Nau* course; **mettre le c. sur** to steer a course for; **franchir le c. de** (*difficulté*) to get over the worst of; **franchir le c. de la trentaine/etc** to turn

thirty/etc.

capable [kapabl] *a* capable, able; **c. de faire** able to do, capable of doing.
● **capacité** *nf* ability, capacity; (*contenance*) capacity.

cape [kap] *nf* cape; (*grande*) cloak.

capillaire [kapiler] *a* **lotion/etc c.** hair lotion/etc.

capitaine [kapiten] *nm* captain.

capital, -ale, -aux [kapital, -o] **1** *a* major, fundamental; (*peine*) capital; (*péché*) deadly. **2** *a* **lettre capitale** capital letter ▮ *nf* (*lettre, ville*) capital. **3** *nm* & *nmpl* (*argent*) capital. ● **capitaliste** *a* & *nmf* capitalist.

capituler [kapityle] *vi* to surrender.
● **capitulation** *nf* surrender.

caporal, -aux [kapɔral, -o] *nm* corporal.

capot [kapo] *nm Aut* bonnet, *Am* hood.

capote [kapɔt] *nf Aut* hood, *Am* (convertible) top; *Mil* greatcoat; **c. (anglaise)** (*préservatif*) *Fam* condom.
● **capoter** *vi Aut Av* to overturn.

câpre [kɑpr] *nf Bot Culin* caper.

caprice [kapris] *nm* (passing) whim.
● **capricieux, -euse** *a* temperamental.

Capricorne [kaprikɔrn] *nm* **le C.** (*signe*) Capricorn.

capsule [kapsyl] *nf* (*spatiale*) & *Méd etc* capsule; (*de bouteille, pistolet d'enfant*) cap.

capter [kapte] *vt* (*signal, radio*) to pick up; (*attention*) to capture, win; (*eau*) to draw off.

captif, -ive [kaptif, -iv] *a* & *nmf* captive.
● **captiver** *vt* to fascinate, captivate.
● **captivité** *nf* captivity.

capture [kaptyr] *nf* catch, capture.
● **capturer** *vt* (*animal etc*) to capture.

capuche [kapyʃ] *nf* hood. ● **capuchon** *nm* hood; (*de stylo*) cap, top.

capucine [kapysin] *nf* (*plante*) nasturtium.

caqueter [kakte] *vi* (*poule, personne*) to cackle.

car [kar] **1** *conj* because, for. **2** *nm* bus, coach; **c. de police** police van.

carabine [karabin] *nf* rifle; **c. à air**

comprimé airgun.

caracoler [karakɔle] *vi* to prance, caper.

caractère[1] [karakter] *nm* (*lettre*) Typ character; **petits caractères** small letters; **caractères d'imprimerie** (block) capitals; **caractères gras** bold type *ou* characters.

caractère[2] [karakter] *nm* (*tempérament, nature*) character, nature; **avoir bon c.** to be good-natured. ● **caractériel, -ielle** *a* & *nmf* disturbed (child).

caractériser [karakterize] *vt* to characterize; **se c. par** to be characterized by.

caractéristique [karakteristik] *a* & *nf* characteristic.

carafe [karaf] *nf* decanter, carafe.

carambolage [karɑ̃bɔlaʒ] *nm* pileup (*of vehicles*).

caramel [karamɛl] *nm* caramel; (*bonbon dur*) toffee, *Am* taffy.

carapace [karapas] *nf* (*de tortue etc*) & *Fig* shell.

carat [kara] *nm* carat.

caravane [karavan] *nf* (*pour camper*) caravan, *Am* trailer; (*dans le désert*) caravan; **c. publicitaire** publicity convoy. ● **caravaning** *n* caravanning.

carbone [karbɔn] *nm* (**papier**) **c.** carbon (paper).

carboniser [karbɔnize] *vt* to burn (to ashes), char; **mourir carbonisé** to be burned to death.

carburant [karbyrɑ̃] *nm* Aut fuel. ● **carburateur** *nm* carburettor, *Am* carburetor.

carcasse [karkas] *nf* Anat carcass; (*d'immeuble etc*) frame, shell.

cardiaque [kardjak] *a* **être c.** to have a weak heart; **crise/problème c.** heart attack/trouble; **arrêt c.** cardiac arrest. ● **cardiologue** *nmf* heart specialist.

cardinal, -aux [kardinal, -o] 1 *a* (*nombre, point*) cardinal. 2 *nm* Rel cardinal.

Carême [karɛm] *nm* Lent.

carence [karɑ̃s] *nf* Méd deficiency.

caresse [karɛs] *nf* caress. ● **caresser** [karese] *vt* (*animal, enfant etc*) to stroke, pat; (*femme, homme*) to car-

ess; (*espoir*) to cherish.

cargaison [kargɛzɔ̃] *nf* cargo, freight. ● **cargo** *nm* cargo boat.

caricature [karikatyr] *nf* caricature. ● **caricaturer** *vt* to caricature.

carie [kari] *nf* **la c. (dentaire)** tooth decay; **une c.** a cavity. ● **cariée** *af* **dent c.** decayed *ou* bad tooth.

carillon [karijɔ̃] *nm* (*cloches*) chimes; (*horloge*) chiming clock. ● **carillonner** *vi* to chime.

carlingue [karlɛ̃g] *nf* (*fuselage*) Av cabin.

carnage [karnaʒ] *nm* carnage.

carnassier, -ière [karnasje, -jɛr] *a* carnivorous ❚ *nm* carnivore.

carnaval, *pl* **-als** [karnaval] *nm* carnival.

carnet [karnɛ] *nm* notebook; (*de timbres, chèques, adresses*) book; **c. de notes** school report, *Am* report card.

carnivore [karnivɔr] *a* carnivorous ❚ *nm* carnivore.

carotte [karɔt] *nf* carrot.

carpe [karp] *nf* carp.

carpette [karpɛt] *nf* rug.

carré [kare] *a* square; **mètre c.** square metre ❚ *nm* square; (*de jardin*) patch; **c. de soie** (square) silk scarf.

carreau, -x [karo] *nm* (*vitre*) (window) pane; (*pavé*) tile; (*sol*) tiled floor; (*couleur*) Cartes diamonds; **à carreaux** (*nappe etc*) check(ed).

carrel/er [karle] *vt* to tile. ● **—age** *nm* (*sol*) tiled floor.

carrefour [karfur] *nm* crossroads.

carrément [karemɑ̃] *adv* (*dire etc*) bluntly; (*complètement*) downright.

carrer (se) [səkare] *vpr* to settle down firmly.

carrière [karjɛr] *nf* 1 (*terrain*) quarry. 2 (*métier*) career.

carrosse [karɔs] *nm* Hist (horse-drawn) carriage. ● **carrossable** *a* suitable for vehicles. ● **carrosserie** *nf* Aut body(work).

carrure [karyr] *nf* build, breadth of shoulders.

cartable [kartabl] *nm* (*d'écolier*) satchel.

carte [kart] *nf* card; (*de lecteur*) ticket; *Géog* map; *Naut* chart; (*menu*) menu; **c. (postale)** (post)card; **c. (à jouer)** (playing) card; **jouer aux cartes** to play cards; **c. de crédit** credit card; **c. d'identité bancaire** bank card; **c. de visite** visiting card; (*professionnelle*) business card; **c. des vins** wine list; **c. grise** vehicle registration document; **avoir c. blanche** *Fig* to have a free hand.

cartilage [kartila3] *nm* cartilage.

carton [kart3] *nm* cardboard; (*boîte*) cardboard box, carton; **c. à dessin** portfolio. ● **cartonner** *vt* (*livre*) to case; **livre cartonné** hardback. ● **cartonnage** *nm* (*emballage*) cardboard package.

cartouche [kartuʃ] *nf* cartridge; (*de cigarettes*) carton; *Phot* cassette. ● **cartouchière** *nf* cartridge belt.

cas [kɑ] *nm* case; **en tout c.** in any case *ou* event; **en aucun c.** on no account; **en c. de besoin** if need be; **en c. d'accident** in the event of an accident; **en c. d'urgence** in an emergency; **au c. où elle tomberait** if she should fall; **pour le c. où il pleuvrait** in case it rains.

casaque [kazak] *nf* (*de jockey*) shirt.

cascade [kaskad] *nf* **1** waterfall; (*série*) *Fig* spate; **en c.** in succession. **2** *Cin* stunt. ● **cascadeur, -euse** *nmf Cin* stunt man, stunt woman.

case [kaz] *nf* **1** pigeonhole; (*de tiroir*) compartment; (*d'échiquier etc*) square; (*de formulaire*) box. **2** (*hutte*) hut, cabin.

caser [kaze] *vt Fam* (*ranger*) to place, stash.

caserne [kazern] *nf Mil* barracks; **c. de pompiers** fire station.

casier [kazje] *nm* pigeonhole; (*meuble à tiroirs*) filing cabinet; (*fermant à clef*) locker; **c. à bouteilles/à disques** bottle/record rack; **c. judiciaire** criminal record.

casino [kazino] *nm* casino.

casque [kask] *nm* helmet; (*de coiffeur*) (hair) dryer; **c. (à écouteurs)** head-

phones; **les Casques bleus** the UN peace-keeping force. ● **casqué** *a* helmeted.

casquette [kasket] *nf* (*coiffure*) cap.

casse [kɑs] *nf* (*action*) breakage; (*objets*) breakages; **mettre à la c.** to scrap. ● **casse-cou** [kɑsku] *nmf inv* (*personne*) *Fam* daredevil. ● **c.-croûte** *nm inv* snack. ● **c.-noisettes** *nm inv ou* **c.-noix** *nm inv* nutcracker(s). ● **c.-pieds** *nmf inv* (*personne*) *Fam* pain in the neck. ● **c.-tête** *nm inv* (*problème*) headache; (*jeu*) puzzle, brain teaser.

casser [kɑse] *vt* to break; (*noix*) to crack; (*annuler*) *Jur* to annul; **elle me casse les pieds** *Fam* she's getting on my nerves; **c. la figure à qn** *Fam* to smash s.o.'s face in ‖ *vi*, **se c.** *vpr* to break; **se c. la tête** *Fam* to rack one's brains; **se c. la figure** (*tomber*) *Fam* to come a cropper, *Am* take a spill. ● **cassant** *a* (*fragile*) brittle; (*brusque*) curt.

casserole [kasrɔl] *nf* (*sauce*)pan.

cassette [kaset] *nf* (*audio*) cassette; (*vidéo*) video, cassette; **sur c.** (*film*) on video; **faire une c. de** to make a video of.

cassis 1 [kasis] *nm* (*fruit*) blackcurrant; (*boisson*) blackcurrant liqueur. **2** [kasi] *nm* (*obstacle*) dip (*across road*).

cassoulet [kasulɛ] *nm* stew (*of meat and beans*).

caste [kast] *nf* caste.

castor [kastɔr] *nm* beaver.

castrer [kastre] *vt* to castrate.

cataclysme [kataklism] *nm* cataclysm.

catacombes [katak3b] *nfpl* catacombs.

catalogue [katalog] *nm*, *Am* catalog. ● **cataloguer** *vt* (*livres etc*) to catalogue, *Am* catalog.

catalyseur [katalizœr] *nm Ch & Fig* catalyst.

catalytique [katalitik] *a* **pot c.** *Aut* catalytic converter.

cataplasme [kataplasm] *nm Méd* poultice.

catapulte [katapylt] *nf Hist Av* catapult.

cataracte [katarakt] *nf* **1** *Méd* cataract. **2**

(*cascade*) falls.

catastrophe [katastrɔf] *nf* disaster, catastrophe; **atterrir en c.** to make an emergency landing. ● **catastrophique** *a* disastrous, catastrophic.

catch [katʃ] *nm* (all-in) wrestling. ● **catcheur, -euse** *nmf* wrestler.

catéchisme [kateʃism] *nm* catechism.

catégorie [kategɔri] *nf* category. ● **catégorique** *a* categorical.

cathédrale [katedral] *nf* cathedral.

catholicisme [katɔlisism] *nm* Catholicism. ● **catholique** *a & nmf* (Roman) Catholic; **pas (très) c.** (*affaire, personne*) *Fig* shady, dubious.

catimini (en) [ɑ̃katimini] *adv* on the sly.

cauchemar [koʃmar] *nm* nightmare.

cause [koz] *nf* cause; *Jur* case; **à c. de** because of, on account of; **pour c. de** on account of; **en connaissance de c.** in full knowledge of the facts; **mettre en c.** (*la bonne foi de qn etc*) to (call into) question; (*personne*) to implicate.

causer [koze] **1** *vt* (*provoquer*) to cause. **2** *vi* (*bavarder*) to chat (**de** about); (*discourir*) to talk. ● **causerie** *nf* talk. ● **causette** *nf* **faire la c.** *Fam* to have a little chat.

caustique [kostik] *a* (*substance, esprit*) caustic.

caution [kosjɔ̃] *nf* surety; (*pour libérer qn*) *Jur* bail.

cavalcade [kavalkad] *nf* *Fam* stampede.

cavaler [kavale] *vi* *Fam* to run, rush.

cavalerie [kavalri] *nf* *Mil* cavalry. ● **cavalier, -ière 1** *nmf* rider ‖ *nm* *Mil* trooper; *Échecs* knight. **2** *nm* (*pour danser*) partner. **3** *a* (*insolent*) offhand.

cave [kav] *nf* cellar. ● **caveau, -x** *nm* (*burial*) vault.

caverne [kavern] *nf* cave; **homme des cavernes** caveman.

caverneux, -euse [kavernø, -øz] *a* (*voix, rire*) hollow, deep-sounding.

caviar [kavjar] *nm* caviar(e).

cavité [kavite] *nf* hollow.

CCP [sesepe] *nm* abrév (*compte chèque postal*) PO Giro account, *Am* Post

Office checking account.

ce¹ [s(ə)] (*c' before e and é*) *pron dém* **1** it, that; **c'est toi/bon/etc** it's *ou* that's you/good/*etc*; **c'est un médecin** he's a doctor; **ce sont eux qui…** they are the people *ou* the ones who…; **c'est à elle de jouer** it's her turn to play; **est-ce que tu viens?** are you coming?; **sur ce** at this point, thereupon.

2 ce que, ce qui what; **je sais ce qui est bon/ce que tu veux** I know what is good/what you want; **ce que c'est beau!** it's so beautiful!, how beautiful it is!

ce², **cette**, *pl* **ces** [s(ə), sɛt, se] (*ce becomes cet before a vowel or mute h*) *a dém* this, that, *pl* these, those; (+ *-ci*) this, *pl* these; (+ *-là*) that, *pl* those; **cet homme** this *ou* that man; **cet homme-ci** this man; **cet homme-là** that man.

ceci [səsi] *pron dém* this; **écoutez bien c.** listen to this.

céder [sede] *vt* to give up (**à** to) ‖ *vi* (*personne*) to give in, give way (**à** to); (*branche, chaise etc*) to give way.

cédille [sedij] *nf* *Gram* cedilla.

cèdre [sɛdr] *nm* (*arbre, bois*) cedar.

CEE [seəə] *abrév* (*Communauté Économique Européenne*) EEC.

CEI [seəi] *nf abrév* (*Communauté des États Indépendants*) CIS.

ceinture [sɛ̃tyr] *nf* belt; (*de robe de chambre*) cord; (*taille*) *Anat* waist; **c. de sécurité** *Aut Av* seatbelt; **c. de sauvetage** lifebelt. ● **ceinturer** *vt* to seize round the waist.

cela [s(ə)la] *pron dém* (*pour désigner*) that; (*sujet indéfini*) it, that; **c. m'attriste que…** it saddens me that…; **quand/comment/etc c.?** when?/how?/*etc*; **c'est c.** that is so.

célèbre [selɛbr] *a* famous. ● **célébrité** *nf* fame; (*personne*) celebrity.

célébrer [selebre] *vt* to celebrate. ● **célébration** *nf* celebration (**de** of).

céleri [sɛlri] *nm* (*en branches*) celery.

célibataire [selibater] *a* (*non marié*) single, unmarried ‖ *nm* bachelor ‖ *nf* unmarried woman.

celle *voir* **celui.**

cellier [selje] *nm* storeroom (*for wine etc*).

cellophane® [selɔfan] *nf* cellophane®.

cellule [selyl] *nf* cell.

celui, celle, *pl* **ceux, celles** [səlɥi, sel, sø, sel] *pron dém* **1** the one, *pl* those, the ones; **c. de Jean** John's (one); **ceux de Jean** John's (ones), those of John. **2** (+ *-ci*) this one, *pl* these (ones); (*dont on vient de parler*) the latter; (+ *-là*) that one, *pl* those (ones); the former; **ceux-ci sont gros** these (ones) are big.

cendre [sɑ̃dr] *nf* ash.

cendrier [sɑ̃drije] *nm* ashtray.

Cendrillon [sɑ̃drijɔ̃] *nm* Cinderella.

censé [sɑ̃se] *a* supposed; **il n'est pas c. le savoir** he's not supposed to know.

censeur [sɑ̃sœr] *nm* censor; *Scol* assistant headmaster, *Am* assistant principal. ● **censure** *nf* **la c.** (*examen*) censorship; (*comité, service*) the censor. ● **censurer** *vt* (*film etc*) to censor.

cent [sɑ̃] ([sɑ̃t] *pl* [sɑ̃z] *before vowel and mute h except* **un** *and* **onze**) *a* & *nm* hundred; **c. pages** a *ou* one hundred pages; **deux cents pages** two hundred pages; **deux c. trois pages** two hundred and three pages; **cinq pour c.** five per cent. ● **centaine** *nf* **une c. (de)** about a hundred; **des centaines de** hundreds of. ● **centenaire** *a* & *nmf* centenarian ‖ *nm* (*anniversaire*) centenary. ● **centième** *a* & *nm* hundredth; **un c.** a hundredth. ● **centigrade** *a* centigrade. ● **centime** *nm* centime. ● **centimètre** *nm* centimetre; (*ruban*) tape measure.

central, -aux [sɑ̃tral, -o] **1** *a* central. **2** *nm* **c. (téléphonique)** (telephone) exchange. ● **centrale** *nf* (*usine*) power station, *Am* power plant. ● **centraliser** *vt* to centralize.

centre [sɑ̃tr] *nm* centre; **c. commercial** shopping centre *ou* mall. ● **c.-ville** *nm* (*pl* **centres-villes**) city *ou* town centre, *Am* downtown area. ● **centrer** *vt* to centre.

centuple [sɑ̃typl] *nm* hundredfold; **au c.** a hundredfold.

cep [sep] *nm* vine stock.

cependant [səpɑ̃dɑ̃] *conj* however, yet.

céramique [seramik] *nf* (*matière*) ceramic; (*art*) pottery, ceramics; **de** *ou* **en c.** ceramic.

cerceau, -x [serso] *nm* hoop.

cercle [serkl] *nm* (*forme, groupe*) circle.

cercueil [serkœj] *nm* coffin.

céréale [sereal] *nf* cereal.

cérébral, -aux [serebral, -o] *a* cerebral.

cérémonie [seremɔni] *nf* ceremony; **de c.** (*tenue etc*) ceremonial. ● **cérémonieux, -euse** *a* ceremonious.

cerf [ser] *nm* deer *inv*; (*mâle*) stag. ● **cerf-volant** *nm* (*pl* **cerfs-volants**) (*jouet*) kite.

cerise [s(ə)riz] *nf* cherry. ● **cerisier** *nm* cherry tree.

cerne [sern] *nm* (*cercle, marque*) ring. ● **cerner** *vt* to surround; **avoir les yeux cernés** to have rings under one's eyes.

certain [sertɛ̃] **1** *a* (*sûr*) certain, sure; **il est** *ou* **c'est c. que tu réussiras** you're certain *ou* sure to succeed; **je suis c. de réussir** I'm certain *ou* sure I'll succeed; **être c. de qch** to be certain *ou* sure of sth.

2 *a* (*imprécis, difficile à fixer*) certain; *pl* certain, some; **un c. temps** a certain (amount of) time ‖ *pron pl* some (people), certain people. ● **certainement** *adv* certainly. ● **certes** *adv* indeed, most certainly.

certificat [sertifika] *nm* certificate.

certifier [sertifje] *vt* to certify; **je vous certifie que** I assure you that.

certitude [sertityd] *nf* certainty; **avoir la c. que** to be certain that.

cerveau, -x [servo] *nm* (*organe*) brain; (*intelligence*) mind, brain(s); **rhume de c.** head cold.

cervelas [servəla] *nm* saveloy.

cervelle [servel] *nf* (*substance*) brain; *Culin* brains.

ces *voir* **ce²**.

CES [seøs] *nm abrév* (*collège d'enseignement secondaire*) comprehensive school, *Am* high school.

césarienne [sezarjɛn] *nf Méd* Caesarean.

cesse [sɛs] *nf* **sans c.** constantly.

cesser [sese] *vti* to stop; **faire c.** to put a stop to; **il ne cesse de parler** he doesn't stop talking. ●**cessez-le-feu** *nm inv* ceasefire.

c'est-à-dire [setadir] *conj* that is (to say), in other words.

cet, cette *voir* **ce²**.

ceux *voir* **celui**.

chacun, -une [ʃakœ̃, -yn] *pron* each (one), every one; (*tout le monde*) everyone.

chagrin [ʃagrɛ̃] *nm* grief, sorrow; **avoir du c.** to be very upset. ●**chagriner** *vt* to upset, distress.

chahut [ʃay] *nm* (*bruit*) racket. ●**chahuter** *vi* to create a racket ▮ *vt* (*professeur*) to be rowdy with, play up. ●**chahuteur, -euse** *nmf* rowdy.

chaîne [ʃɛn] *nf* chain; *TV* channel, network; (*de montagnes*) chain, range; **c. de montage** assembly line; **travail à la c.** production-line work; **c. hi-fi** hi-fi (system); **collision en c.** *Aut* multiple collision. ●**chaînette** *nf* (small) chain. ●**chaînon** *nm* (*anneau*) link.

chair [ʃɛr] *nf* flesh; (*couleur*) **c.** flesh-coloured; **en c. et en os** in the flesh; **la c. de poule** goose pimples *ou* bumps; **bien en c.** plump; **c. à saucisses** sausage meat.

chaise [ʃɛz] *nf* chair; **c. longue** deck-chair; **c. d'enfant, c. haute** high-chair.

châle [ʃal] *nm* shawl.

chalet [ʃalɛ] *nm* chalet.

chaleur [ʃalœr] *nf* heat; (*douce*) warmth; (*d'un accueil etc*) warmth. ●**chaleureux, -euse** *a* warm.

challenge [ʃalɑ̃ʒ] *nm Sp* challenge match.

chaloupe [ʃalup] *nf* (*bateau*) launch.

chalumeau, -x [ʃalymo] *nm* blowlamp, *Am* blowtorch.

chalut [ʃaly] *nm* trawl net. ●**chalutier** *nm* (*bateau*) trawler.

chamailler (se) [səʃamaje] *vpr* to squabble.

chamarré [ʃamare] *a* (*robe etc*) richly coloured.

chambouler [ʃɑ̃bule] *vt Fam* to make topsy-turvy, turn upside down.

chambre [ʃɑ̃br] *nf* (bed)room; *Pol Jur Tech Anat* chamber; **c. à coucher** bedroom; (*mobilier*) bedroom suite; **c. à air** (*de pneu*) inner tube; **C. des Communes** *Br Pol* House of Commons; **c. d'ami** guest *ou* spare room; **garder la c.** to stay indoors.

chameau, -x [ʃamo] *nm* camel.

chamois [ʃamwa] *nm* (*animal*) chamois; **peau de c.** wash leather, chamois, shammy.

champ [ʃɑ̃] *nm* field; (*domaine*) *Fig* field, scope; **c. de bataille** battlefield; **c. de courses** racecourse, *Am* racetrack; **c. de foire** fairground. ●**champêtre** *a* rural.

champagne [ʃɑ̃paɲ] *nm* champagne; **c. brut** extra-dry champagne.

champignon [ʃɑ̃piɲɔ̃] *nm Bot* mushroom; **c. vénéneux** toadstool, poisonous mushroom.

champion, -onne [ʃɑ̃pjɔ̃, -jɔn] *nmf* champion. ●**championnat** *nm* championship.

chance [ʃɑ̃s] *nf* luck; (*probabilité de réussir, occasion*) chance; **avoir de la c.** to be lucky; **tenter sa c.** to try one's luck; **c'est une c. que...** it's lucky that.... ●**chanceux, -euse** *a* lucky.

chancel/er [ʃɑ̃sle] *vi* to stagger. ●**—ant** *a* (*pas, santé*) faltering, shaky.

chancelier [ʃɑ̃səlje] *nm* chancellor.

chandail [ʃɑ̃daj] *nm* (thick) sweater.

chandelier [ʃɑ̃dəlje] *nm* candlestick.

chandelle [ʃɑ̃dɛl] *nf* candle; **voir trente-six chandelles** *Fig* to see stars; **en c.** (*tir*) straight into the air.

change [ʃɑ̃ʒ] *nm Fin* exchange; **le contrôle des changes** exchange control.

changer [ʃɑ̃ʒe] *vt* (*modifier, remplacer, échanger*) to change; **c. qn en** to change s.o. into; **ça la changera de ne pas travailler** it'll be a change for her not to be working.

▌*vi* to change; **c. de voiture/d'adresse/**
etc to change one's car/address/*etc*; **c.
de train/de place** to change trains/
places; **c. de vitesse/de sujet** to change
gear/the subject.

▌**se changer** *vpr* to change (one's
clothes). ●**changement** *nm* change; **aimer le c.** to like change.

chanson [ʃɑ̃sɔ̃] *nf* song. ●**chant** *nm*
singing; (*chanson*) song; (*hymne*)
chant; **c. de Noël** Christmas carol.

chant/er [ʃɑ̃te] *vi* to sing; (*coq*) to crow;
si ça te chante *Fam* if you feel like it;
faire c. qn to blackmail s.o. ▌*vt* to sing.
●**—ant** *a* (*air, voix*) melodious. ●**chantage** *nm* blackmail. ●**chanteur, -euse**
nmf singer.

chantier [ʃɑ̃tje] *nm* (building) site; (*sur
route*) roadworks; **c. naval** shipyard,
dockyard.

chantonner [ʃɑ̃tɔne] *vti* to hum.

chanvre [ʃɑ̃vr] *nm* hemp.

chaos [kao] *nm* chaos. ●**chaotique** *a*
chaotic.

chaparder [ʃaparde] *vt Fam* to pinch (à
from).

chapeau, -x [ʃapo] *nm* hat; (*de champignon, roue*) cap; **c.!** well done!

chapelet [ʃaplɛ] *nm* rosary; **un c. de**
(*saucisses, injures*) a string of

chapelle [ʃapɛl] *nf* chapel; **c. ardente**
chapel of rest.

chapelure [ʃaplyr] *nf* breadcrumbs.

chapiteau, -x [ʃapito] *nm* (*de cirque*) big
top; (*pour expositions etc*) marquee,
tent.

chapitre [ʃapitr] *nm* chapter; **sur le c. de**
on the subject of.

chaque [ʃak] *a* each, every.

char [ʃar] *nm* (*romain*) chariot; (*de
carnaval*) float; *Can Fam* car; **c. (d'assaut)** *Mil* tank.

charabia [ʃarabja] *nm Fam* gibberish.

charade [ʃarad] *nf* (*énigme*) riddle.

charbon [ʃarbɔ̃] *nm* coal; **c. de bois**
charcoal; **sur des charbons ardents** on
tenterhooks.

charcuterie [ʃarkytri] *nf* pork butcher's
shop; (*aliments*) cooked (pork) meats.
●**charcutier, -ière** *nmf* pork butcher.

chardon [ʃardɔ̃] *nm Bot* thistle.

charge [ʃarʒ] *nf* (*poids*) load; (*fardeau*)
burden; *Jur El Mil* charge; (*fonction*)
office; *pl* (*dépenses*) expenses; (*de locataire*) (maintenance) charges; **charges
sociales** national insurance contributions, *Am* Social Security contributions; **à c.** (*enfant, parent*) dependent;
à la c. de qn (*personne*) dependent on
s.o.; (*frais*) payable by s.o.; **prendre en
c.** to take charge of, take responsibility
for.

charg/er [ʃarʒe] *vt* to load; (*soldats,
batterie*) to charge; **se c. de** (*enfant,
tâche etc*) to take charge of; **c. qn de**
(*tâche etc*) to entrust s.o. with; (*paquets
etc*) to load s.o. with; **c. qn de faire** to
instruct s.o. to do. ●**—é, -ée** *a* (*personne, véhicule, arme etc*) loaded;
(*journée etc*) busy. ●**—ement** *nm* (*action*) loading; (*objet*) load.

chariot [ʃarjo] *nm* (*à bagages etc*) trolley, *Am* cart; (*de ferme*) waggon; (*de
machine à écrire*) carriage.

charité [ʃarite] *nf* (*secours, vertu*) charity; **faire la c.** to give to charity; **faire la
c. à** (*mendiant*) to give (money) to.
●**charitable** *a* charitable (**pour, envers**
towards).

charivari [ʃarivari] *nm Fam* din, hubbub.

charlatan [ʃarlatɑ̃] *nm* charlatan, quack.

charme [ʃarm] *nm* charm; (*magie*) spell.
●**charm/er** [ʃarme] *vt* to charm; **je suis
charmé de vous voir** I'm delighted to see
you. ●**—ant** *a* charming. ●**—eur, -euse**
a engaging.

charnière [ʃarnjɛr] *nf* hinge.

charogne [ʃarɔɲ] *nf* carrion.

charpente [ʃarpɑ̃t] *nf* frame(work); (*de
personne*) build. ●**charpentier** *nm* carpenter.

charple [ʃarpi] *nf* **mettre en c.** (*déchirer*)
to tear to shreds.

charrette [ʃarɛt] *nf* cart. ●**charrier** *vt*

(*transporter*) to cart; (*rivière*) to carry along (*sand etc*).

charrue [ʃary] *nf* plough, *Am* plow.

charter [ʃarter] *nm* (*vol*) charter (flight).

chas [ʃa] *nm* eye (*of a needle*).

chasse¹ [ʃas] *nf* hunting, hunt; (*poursuite*) chase; **c. sous-marine** underwater (harpoon) fishing; **c. à courre** hunting; **avion/pilote de c.** fighter plane/pilot; **faire la c. à** to hunt for; **c. à l'homme** manhunt.

chasse² [ʃas] *nf* **c. d'eau** toilet *ou* lavatory flush; **tirer la c.** to flush the toilet *ou* lavatory.

chass/er [ʃase] *vt* (*animal*) to hunt; (*papillon*) to chase; (*faire partir*) to chase (*s.o.*) away, drive (*s.o.*) out; (*mouche*) to brush away; (*odeur*) to get rid of ▮ *vi* to hunt. ●**—eur, -euse** *nmf* hunter ▮ *nm* (*d'hôtel*) pageboy, bellboy. ●**chasse-neige** *nm inv* snow-plough, *Am* snowplow.

châssis [ʃasi] *nm* frame; *Aut* chassis.

chaste [ʃast] *a* chaste. ●**chasteté** *nf* chastity.

chat [ʃa] *nm* cat; **un c. dans la gorge** a frog in one's throat; **d'autres chats à fouetter** other fish to fry; **c. perché** (*jeu*) tag.

châtaigne [ʃatɛɲ] *nf* chestnut. ●**châtaignier** *nm* chestnut tree. ●**châtain** *a inv* (chestnut) brown.

château, -x [ʃato] *nm* (*forteresse*) castle; (*palais*) palace, stately home; **c. fort** fortified castle; **c. d'eau** water tower; **c. de cartes** house of cards. ●**châtelain, -aine** *nmf* lord *ou* lady of the manor.

châtier [ʃatje] *vt* (*punir*) *Litt* to chastise.

châtiment [ʃatimɑ̃] *nm* punishment.

chaton [ʃatɔ̃] *nm* (*chat*) kitten.

chatouiller [ʃatuje] *vt* to tickle. ●**chatouillis** *nm* tickle; (*action*) tickling. ●**chatouilleux, -euse** *a* ticklish; (*irritable*) touchy.

chatte [ʃat] *nf* (she-)cat; **ma petite c.** *Fam* my darling.

chatterton [ʃatɛrtɔn] *nm* (adhesive) insulating tape.

chaud [ʃo] *a* hot; (*doux*) warm; **pleurer à chaudes larmes** to cry bitterly ▮ *nm* heat, warmth; **avoir c.** to be hot; to be warm; **il fait c.** it's hot; it's warm; **être au c.** to be in the warm. ●**chaudement** *adv* warmly.

chaudière [ʃodjer] *nf* boiler.

chauffage [ʃofaʒ] *nm* heating.

chauffard [ʃofar] *nm* road hog, reckless driver.

chauff/er [ʃofe] *vt* to heat up, warm up; (*métal*) to heat ▮ *vi* to heat up, warm up; (*moteur*) to overheat ▮ **se c.** *vpr* to warm oneself up. ●**—ant** *a* (*couverture*) electric; **plaque chauffante** hot plate. ●**—é** *a* (*piscine etc*) heated. ●**chauffe-bain** *nm ou* **chauffe-eau** *nm inv* water heater.

chauffeur [ʃofœr] *nm* *Aut* driver; (*employé*) chauffeur.

chaume [ʃom] *nm* (*pour toiture*) thatch; **toit de c.** thatched roof. ●**chaumière** *nf* thatched cottage.

chaussée [ʃose] *nf* road(way).

chausser [ʃose] *vt* (*chaussures*) to put on; **c. qn** to put shoes on (to) s.o.; **se c.** to put on one's shoes; **c. du 40** to take a size 40 shoe. ●**chausse-pied** *nm* shoe-horn.

chausson [ʃosɔ̃] *nm* slipper; (*de danse*) shoe; **c. (aux pommes)** apple turnover.

chaussure [ʃosyr] *nf* shoe.

chaussette [ʃoset] *nf* sock.

chauve [ʃov] *a* & *nmf* bald (person).

chauve-souris [ʃovsuri] *nf* (*pl* **chauves-souris**) (*animal*) bat.

chauvin, -ine [ʃovɛ̃, -in] *a* chauvinistic ▮ *nmf* chauvinist.

chaux [ʃo] *nf* lime; **blanc de c.** white-wash.

chavirer [ʃavire] *vti* *Nau* to capsize.

chef [ʃɛf] *nm* leader, head; (*de tribu*) chief; *Culin* chef; **en c.** (*commandant, rédacteur*) in chief; **c. d'atelier** (*shop*) foreman; **c. d'entreprise** company head; **c. d'équipe** foreman; **c. d'État** head of state; **c. de famille** head of the family; **c. de gare** stationmaster; **c. d'orchestre**

conductor. ● **chef-lieu** nm (pl **chefs-lieux**) chief town (of a département).

chef-d'œuvre [ʃɛdœvr] nm (pl **chefs-d'œuvre**) masterpiece.

chemin [ʃ(ə)mɛ̃] nm **1** road, path; (trajet, direction) way; **beaucoup de c. à faire** a long way to go; **dix minutes de c.** ten minutes' walk; **se mettre en c.** to set out, start out; **à mi-c.** half-way. **2 c. de fer** railway, Am railroad.

cheminot [ʃ(ə)mino] nm railway ou Am railroad employee.

cheminée [ʃ(ə)mine] nf fireplace; (encadrement) mantelpiece; (sur le toit) chimney; (de navire) funnel.

chemise [ʃ(ə)miz] nf shirt; (couverture cartonnée) folder; **c. de nuit** nightdress. ● **chemisette** nf short-sleeved shirt. ● **chemisier** nm (vêtement) blouse.

chenapan [ʃ(ə)napɑ̃] nm Hum rogue.

chêne [ʃɛn] nm (arbre, bois) oak.

chenet [ʃ(ə)nɛ] nm andiron.

chenil [ʃ(ə)ni(l)] nm kennels, Am kennel.

chenille [ʃ(ə)nij] nf caterpillar; (de char) Mil caterpillar track.

chèque [ʃɛk] nm cheque, Am check; **c. de voyage** traveller's cheque, Am traveler's check. ● **c.-repas** nm (pl **chèques-repas**) luncheon voucher, Am meal ticket. ● **chéquier** nm cheque book, Am checkbook.

cher, chère [ʃɛr] **1** a (aimé) dear (à to). **2** a (coûteux) expensive, dear; (quartier, hôtel etc) expensive; **payer c.** (objet) to pay a lot for; (erreur etc) Fig to pay dearly for.

cherch/er [ʃɛrʃe] vt to look for, search for; (du secours, la paix etc) to seek; (dans un dictionnaire) to look up; **c. ses mots** to fumble for one's words; **aller c.** to (go and) get ou fetch; **c. à faire** to attempt to do. ● **-eur, -euse** nmf research worker; **c. d'or** gold-digger.

chér/ir [ʃerir] vt to cherish. ● **-i, -ie** a dearly loved, beloved ‖ nmf darling.

chétif, -ive [ʃetif, -iv] a puny; (dérisoire) wretched.

cheval, -aux [ʃ(ə)val, -o] nm horse; (vapeur) Aut horsepower; **à c.** on horseback; **faire du c.** to go horse riding ou Am horseback riding; **à c. sur** straddling; **c. à bascule** rocking horse; **chevaux de bois** (manège) merry-go-round.

chevaleresque [ʃ(ə)valrɛsk] a chivalrous.

chevalet [ʃ(ə)valɛ] nm easel; (de menuisier) trestle.

chevalier [ʃ(ə)valje] nm knight.

chevalière [ʃ(ə)valjɛr] nf signet ring.

chevaline [ʃ(ə)valin] af **boucherie c.** horse butcher's (shop).

chevauchée [ʃ(ə)voʃe] nf (horse) ride.

chevaucher [ʃ(ə)voʃe] vt to straddle ‖ vi, **se c.** vpr to overlap.

chevelu [ʃ(ə)vly] a hairy. ● **chevelure** nf (head of) hair.

chevet [ʃ(ə)vɛ] nm bedhead; **table/livre de c.** bedside table/book; **au c. de** at the bedside of.

cheveu, -x [ʃ(ə)vø] nm **un c.** a hair; **cheveux** hair; **avoir les cheveux noirs** to have black hair; **couper les cheveux en quatre** Fig to split hairs.

cheville [ʃ(ə)vij] nf **1** Anat ankle. **2** (pour vis) (wall) plug; (pour joindre) peg, pin.

chèvre [ʃɛvr] nf goat; (femelle) nanny-goat. ● **chevreau, -x** nm (petit de la chèvre) kid.

chèvrefeuille [ʃɛvrəfœj] nm honeysuckle.

chevreuil [ʃəvrœj] nm roe deer; Culin venison.

chevron [ʃəvrɔ̃] nm (poutre) rafter; **à chevrons** (tissu, veste etc) herringbone.

chevronné [ʃəvrɔne] a seasoned, experienced.

chez [ʃe] prép **c. qn** at s.o.'s house, flat etc; **il est c. Jean/c. l'épicier** he's at John's (place)/at the grocer's; **il va c. Jean/c. l'épicier** he's going to John's (place)/to the grocer's; **c. moi, c. nous** at home; **je vais c. moi** I'm going home; **une habitude c. elle** a habit with her; **c. Mme Dupont** (adresse) care of ou c/o Mme Dupont; **c. Camus** in (the work of) Camus.

chic [ʃik] *a inv* smart, stylish; (*gentil*) *Fam* nice, decent ‖ *int* **c. (alors)!** great! ‖ *nm* style, elegance.

chicanes [ʃikan] *nfpl* (*obstacles*) zigzag barriers.

chiche [ʃiʃ] **1** *a* mean, niggardly; **c. de** sparing of. **2** *int* (*défi*) *Fam* I bet you I do, can *etc*; **c. que je parte sans lui** I bet I leave without him.

chicorée [ʃikɔre] *nf* (*à café*) chicory; (*pour salade*) endive.

chien [ʃjɛ̃] *nm* dog; **un mal de c.** *Fam* an awful lot of trouble; **temps de c.** *Fam* rotten weather. ● **c.-loup** *nm* (*pl chiens-loups*) wolfhound. ● **chienne** *nf* dog, bitch.

chiendent [ʃjɛ̃dɑ̃] *nm Bot* couch grass.

chiffon [ʃifɔ̃] *nm* rag; **c. (à poussière)** duster, *Am* dustcloth. ● **chiffonner** *vt* to crumple. ● **chiffonnier** *nm* ragman.

chiffre [ʃifr] *nm* figure, number; (*romain, arabe*) numeral; **c. d'affaires** (sales) turnover. ● **chiffrer** *vt* (*montant*) to assess, work out ‖ **se c.** *vpr* to amount to, work out at.

chignon [ʃiɲɔ̃] *nm* bun, chignon.

Chili [ʃili] *nm* Chile. ● **chilien, -ienne** *a & nmf* Chilean.

chimie [ʃimi] *nf* chemistry. ● **chimique** *a* chemical. ● **chimiste** *nmf* (research) chemist.

chimpanzé [ʃɛ̃pɑ̃ze] *nm* chimpanzee.

Chine [ʃin] *nf* China. ● **chinois, -oise** *a & nmf* Chinese ‖ *nmf* Chinese man *ou* woman, Chinese *inv*; **les C.** the Chinese ‖ *nm* (*langue*) Chinese.

chiot [ʃjo] *nm* pup(py).

chiper [ʃipe] *vt Fam* to pinch (**à** from).

chipie [ʃipi] *nf* **vieille c.** (*femme*) *Péj* old crab.

chipoter [ʃipɔte] *vi* (*discuter*) to quibble.

chips [ʃips] *nfpl* (potato) crisps, *Am* chips.

chiquenaude [ʃiknod] *nf* flick (of the finger).

chirurgie [ʃiryrʒi] *nf* surgery. ● **chirurgical, -aux** *a* surgical. ● **chirurgien** *nm* surgeon.

chlore [klɔr] *nm* chlorine.

choc [ʃɔk] *nm* (*d'objets*) impact, shock; (*émotion*) & *Méd* shock.

chocolat [ʃɔkɔla] *nm* chocolate; **c. à croquer** plain *ou Am* bittersweet chocolate; **c. au lait** milk chocolate; **c. glacé** choc-ice, *Am* chocolate ice-cream bar. ● **chocolaté** *a* chocolate-flavoured.

chœur [kœr] *nm* (*chanteurs, nef*) *Rel* choir; **en c.** (all) together, in chorus.

choir [ʃwar] *vi* **laisser c. qn** *Fam* to turn one's back on s.o.

chois/ir [ʃwazir] *vt* to choose, pick, select. ● **—i** *a* (*œuvres*) selected; (*terme*) well-chosen; (*public*) select. ● **choix** *nm* choice; (*assortiment*) selection; **morceau de c.** choice piece.

choléra [kɔlera] *nm* cholera.

cholestérol [kɔlesterɔl] *nm* cholesterol.

chôm/er [ʃome] *vi* (*ouvrier etc*) to be unemployed. ● **—age** *nm* unemployment; **au** *ou* **en c.** unemployed; **mettre en c. technique** to lay off. ● **—eur, -euse** *nmf* unemployed person; **les chômeurs** the unemployed.

chope [ʃɔp] *nf* beer mug; (*contenu*) pint.

choqu/er [ʃɔke] *vt* (*scandaliser*) to shock; (*commotionner*) to shake up. ● **—ant** *a* shocking.

chorale [kɔral] *nf* choral society. ● **choriste** *nmf* chorister.

chorégraphe [kɔregraf] *nmf* choreographer.

chose [ʃoz] *nf* thing; **état de choses** state of affairs; **dis-lui bien des choses de ma part** remember me to him *ou* her; **monsieur C.** Mr What's-his-name.

chou, -x [ʃu] *nm* cabbage; **choux de Bruxelles** Brussels sprouts; **mon c.!** my pet!; **c. à la crème** cream puff. ● **c.-fleur** *nm* (*pl choux-fleurs*) cauliflower.

chouchou, -oute [ʃuʃu, -ut] *nmf* (*favori*) *Fam* pet, darling. ● **chouchouter** *vt* to pamper.

choucroute [ʃukrut] *nf* sauerkraut.

chouette [ʃwet] **1** *nf* (*oiseau*) owl. **2** *a* (*chic*) *Fam* super, great.

choyer [ʃwaye] *vt* to pamper.

chrétien, -ienne [kretjɛ̃, -jɛn] *a* & *nmf* Christian. ●**Christ** [krist] *nm* Christ. ●**christianisme** *nm* Christianity.

chrome [krom] *nm* chrome, chromium. ●**chromé** *a* chrome- *ou* chromium-plated.

chronique [krɔnik] **1** *a* (*malade, chômage etc*) chronic. **2** *nf* (*à la radio*) report; (*dans le journal*) column. ●**chroniqueur** *nm Journ* reporter, columnist.

chronologie [krɔnɔlɔʒi] *nf* chronology. ●**chronologique** *a* chronological.

chronomètre [krɔnɔmetr] *nm* stopwatch. ●**chronométrer** *vt Sp* to time.

chrysanthème [krizɑ̃tem] *nm* chrysanthemum.

chuchot/er [ʃyʃɔte] *vti* to whisper. ●**—ement** *nm* whisper(ing).

chut! [ʃyt] *int* sh!, shush!

chute [ʃyt] *nf* fall; (*défaite*) (down)fall; **c. d'eau** waterfall; **c. de neige** snowfall; **c. de pluie** rainfall; **c. des cheveux** hair loss.

Chypre [ʃipr] *nf* Cyprus. ●**chypriote** *a* & *nmf* Cypriot.

ci [si] **1** *adv* **par-ci par-là** here and there. **2** *pron dém* **comme ci comme ça** so so. **3** *voir ce*², **celui**.

ci-après [siapre] *adv* below, hereafter. ●**ci-dessous** *adv* below. ●**ci-dessus** *adv* above. ●**ci-gît** *adv* here lies (*on gravestones*). ●**ci-joint** *a* (*inv before n*) (*dans une lettre*) enclosed (herewith).

cible [sibl] *nf* target.

cicatrice [sikatris] *nf* scar.

cicatriser [sikatrize] *vt*, **se c.** *vpr* to heal (up) (*leaving a scar*). ●**cicatrisation** *nf* healing (up).

cidre [sidr] *nm* cider.

Cie *abrév* (*compagnie*) Co.

ciel [sjel] *nm* **1** (*pl* **cieux**) sky; **à c. ouvert** (*piscine etc*) open-air. **2** (*pl* **cieux** [sjø]) *Rel* heaven; **juste c.!** good heavens!

cierge [sjerʒ] *nm Rel* candle.

cigale [sigal] *nf* (*insecte*) cicada.

cigare [sigar] *nm* cigar. ●**cigarette** *nf* cigarette.

cigogne [sigɔɲ] *nf* stork.

cil [sil] *nm* (eye)lash.

cime [sim] *nf* (*d'un arbre*) top; (*d'une montagne*) & *Fig* peak.

ciment [simɑ̃] *nm* cement. ●**cimenter** *vt* to cement.

cimetière [simtjer] *nm* cemetery, graveyard.

ciné [sine] *nm Fam* cinema. ●**c.-club** *nm* film society. ●**cinéaste** *nm* film maker. ●**cinéphile** *nmf* film buff.

cinéma [sinema] *nm* (*art*) cinema; (*salle*) cinema, *Am* movie theater; **aller au c.** to go to the movies *ou* the cinema; **acteur de c.** movie *ou* film actor. ●**cinématographique** *a* **industrie/etc c.** film industry/etc.

cinglé [sɛ̃gle] *a Fam* crazy.

cinq [sɛ̃k] *nm* five ‖ *a* ([sɛ̃] *before consonant*) five. ●**cinquième** *a* & *nmf* fifth; **un c.** a fifth.

cinquante [sɛ̃kɑ̃t] *a* & *nm* fifty. ●**cinquantaine** *nf* **une c. (de)** about fifty. ●**cinquantième** *a* & *nmf* fiftieth.

cintre [sɛ̃tr] *nm* coathanger.

cirage [siraʒ] *nm* (shoe) polish.

circoncis [sirkɔ̃si] *a* circumcised.

circonférence [sirkɔ̃ferɑ̃s] *nf* circumference.

circonflexe [sirkɔ̃fleks] *a Gram* circumflex.

circonscrire [sirkɔ̃skrir] *vt* to circumscribe. ●**circonscription** *nf* division; **c. (électorale)** constituency, *Am* district.

circonspect, -ecte [sirkɔ̃spe(kt), -ekt] *a* cautious.

circonstance [sirkɔ̃stɑ̃s] *nf* circumstance; **pour/en la c.** for/on this occasion; **de c.** (*habit, parole etc*) appropriate. ●**circonstancié** *a* detailed. ●**circonstanciel, -ielle** *a Gram* adverbial.

circuit [sirkɥi] *nm Sp Él Fin* circuit; (*voyage*) tour, trip.

circulaire [sirkyler] *a* circular ‖ *nf* (*lettre*) circular.

circulation [sirkylasjɔ̃] *nf* circulation; *Aut* traffic. ●**circuler** *vi* to circulate;

(*véhicule, train*) to travel, go, move; (*passant*) to walk about; (*rumeur*) to go round, circulate; **faire c.** to circulate; (*piétons*) to move on; **circulez!** keep moving!

cire [sir] *nf* wax; (*pour meubles*) polish, wax. ●**cirer** *vt* to polish.

ciré [sire] *nm* (*vêtement*) oilskin(s).

cirque [sirk] *nm* circus.

cisaille(s) [sizaj] *nf(pl)* shears. ●**ciseau, -x** *nm* chisel; (**une paire de**) **ciseaux** (a pair of) scissors.

citadelle [sitadel] *nf* citadel.

cité [site] *nf* city; **c.** (**ouvrière**) housing estate (*for workers*), *Am* housing project; **c. universitaire** (students') halls of residence, *Am* university dormitory complex. ●**citadin, -ine** *nmf* city dweller ▮ *a* urban.

citer [site] *vt* to quote; *Jur* to summon. ●**citation** *nf* quotation; *Jur* summons.

citerne [sitern] *nf* (*réservoir*) tank.

citoyen, -enne [sitwajɛ̃, -en] *nmf* citizen.

citron [sitrɔ̃] *nm* lemon; **c. pressé** (fresh) lemon juice. ●**citronnade** *nf* lemon drink, (still) lemonade.

citrouille [sitruj] *nf* pumpkin.

civet [sivɛ] *nm* stew; **c. de lièvre** jugged hare.

civière [sivjɛr] *nf* stretcher.

civil [sivil] **1** *a* (*guerre, mariage etc*) civil; (*non militaire*) civilian; **année civile** calendar year. **2** *nm* civilian; **dans le c.** in civilian life; **en c.** (*policier*) in plain clothes; (*soldat*) in civilian clothes.

civilisation [sivilizasjɔ̃] *nf* civilization. ●**civiliser** *vt* to civilize ▮ **se c.** *vpr* to become civilized. ●**civilisé** *a* civilized.

civique [sivik] *a* civic; **instruction c.** *Scol* civics.

clair [kler] *a* (*distinct, limpide, évident*) clear; (*éclairé*) light; (*pâle*) light(-coloured); **bleu/vert c.** light blue/green; **il fait c.** it's light ou bright ▮ *adv* (*voir*) clearly ▮ *nm* **c. de lune** moonlight; **tirer au c.** (*question etc*) to clear up. ●**—ement** *adv* clearly.

clairière [klerjɛr] *nf* clearing.

clairon [klerɔ̃] *nm* bugle. ●**claironner** *vt* (*annoncer*) to trumpet forth.

clairsemé [klersəme] *a* sparse.

clairvoyant [klervwajɑ̃] *a* (*perspicace*) clear-sighted.

clam/er [klame] *vt* to cry out. ●**—eur** *nf* clamour, outcry.

clan [klɑ̃] *nm* clan, clique, set.

clandestin [klɑ̃destɛ̃] *a* secret, clandestine; (*journal, mouvement*) underground; **passager c.** stowaway.

clapier [klapje] *nm* (rabbit) hutch.

claque [klak] *nf* smack, slap. ●**claquer** *vt* (*porte*) to slam, bang; (*fouet*) to crack; **se c. un muscle** to pull a muscle; **faire c.** (*doigts*) to snap; (*langue*) to click; (*fouet*) to crack.

▮ *vi* (*porte*) to slam, bang; (*drapeau*) to flap; (*coup de feu*) to ring out; **elle claque des dents** her teeth are chattering. ●**claquage** *nm* pulled muscle; **faire un c.** to pull a muscle. ●**claquement** *nm* (*de porte*) slam(ming).

claquettes [klaket] *nfpl* tap dancing.

clarifier [klarifje] *vt* to clarify.

clarinette [klarinet] *nf* clarinet.

clarté [klarte] *nf* light, brightness; (*précision*) clarity.

classe [klɑs] *nf* class; **aller en c.** to go to school; **c. ouvrière/moyenne** working/middle class; **avoir de la c.** to have class.

class/er [klɑse] *vt* to classify; (*papiers*) to file; (*candidats*) to grade; (*affaire*) to close; **se c. premier** to come first. ●**—ement** *nm* classification; filing; grading; (*rang*) place; *Sp* placing. ●**—eur** *nm* (*meuble*) filing cabinet; (*portefeuille*) (loose leaf) file ou binder.

classique [klasik] *a* classical; (*typique*) classic. ●**classicisme** *nm* classicism.

clause [kloz] *nf* clause.

clavecin [klavsɛ̃] *nm Mus* harpsichord.

clavicule [klavikyl] *nf* collarbone.

clavier [klavje] *nm* keyboard.

clé, clef [kle] *nf* key; (*outil*) spanner, wrench; *Mus* clef; **fermer à c.** to lock; **sous c.** under lock and key; **c. de contact** ignition key; **poste/industrie c.** key

post/industry; **prix clés en main** (*voiture*) on-the-road price.
clément [klemã] *a* clement.
clémentine [klemãtin] *nf* clementine.
clerc [klɛr] *nm* (*de notaire*) clerk. ●**clergé** *nm* clergy.
cliché [kliʃe] *nm Phot* negative; (*idée*) cliché.
client, -ente [klijã, -ãt] *nmf* (*de magasin etc*) customer; (*d'un avocat etc*) client; (*d'un médecin*) patient; (*d'hôtel*) guest. ●**clientèle** *nf* customers; (*d'un avocat*) practice; (*d'un médecin*) practice, patients.
cligner [kliɲe] *vi* **c. des yeux** (*ouvrir et fermer*) to blink; (*fermer à demi*) to screw up one's eyes; **c. de l'œil** to wink.
clignot/er [kliɲote] *vi* to blink; (*lumière*) to flicker; (*étoile*) to twinkle. ●**—ant** *nm Aut* indicator, *Am* directional signal.
climat [klima] *nm Mét* & *Fig* climate. ●**climatique** *a* climatic.
climatisation [klimatizasjɔ̃] *nf* air-conditioning. ●**climatiser** *vt* to air-condition.
clin d'œil [klɛ̃dœj] *nm* wink; **en un c. d'œil** in no time (at all).
clinique [klinik] *nf* (private) clinic.
clip [klip] *nm* (*film*) video (clip).
cliqueter [klikte] *vi* to clink. ●**cliquetis** *nm* clink(ing).
clochard, -arde [klɔʃar, -ard] *nmf* down-and-out, tramp.
cloche [klɔʃ] *nf* **1** bell; **c. à fromage** cheese cover. **2** (*personne*) *Fam* idiot, oaf. ●**clocher** *nm* bell tower; (*en pointe*) steeple. ●**clochette** *nf* (small) bell.
cloche-pied (à) [aklɔʃpje] *adv* **sauter à c.-pied** to hop on one foot.
cloison [klwazɔ̃] *nf* partition. ●**cloisonner** *vt* to partition.
cloître [klwatr] *nm* cloister.
clope [klɔp] *nm ou f* (*cigarette*) *Fam* fag, smoke, *Am* butt.
clopin-clopant [klɔpɛ̃klɔpã] *adv* **aller c.-clopant** to hobble.
cloque [klɔk] *nf* blister.
clore [klɔr] *vt* (*débat, lettre*) to close.

●**clos, close** *a* (*incident*) closed; (*espace*) enclosed.
clôture [klotyr] *nf* (*barrière*) fence; (*fermeture*) closing. ●**clôturer** *vt* to enclose; (*compte, séance etc*) to close.
clou [klu] *nm* (*furoncle*) boil; **le c. (du spectacle)** *Fam* the star attraction; **les clous** (*passage*) pedestrian crossing. ●**clouer** *vt* to nail; **cloué au lit** confined to bed. ●**clouté** *a* (*pneus*) studded; **passage c.** pedestrian crossing, *Am* crosswalk.
clown [klun] *nm* clown.
club [klœb] *nm* (*association*) club.
cm *abrév* (*centimètre*) cm.
co- [kɔ] *préf* co-.
coaguler [kɔagyle] *vti*, **se c.** *vpr* (*sang*) to clot.
coaliser (se) [səkɔalize] *vpr* to form a coalition, join forces. ●**coalition** *nf* coalition.
coasser [kɔase] *vi* (*grenouille*) to croak.
cobaye [kɔbaj] *nm* (*animal*) & *Fig* guinea pig.
cobra [kɔbra] *nm* (*serpent*) cobra.
coca [kɔka] *nm* (*Coca-Cola®*) coke.
cocaïne [kɔkain] *nf* cocain.
cocarde [kɔkard] *nf* rosette; *Av* roundel.
cocasse [kɔkas] *a* droll, comical.
coccinelle [kɔksinɛl] *nf* ladybird, *Am* ladybug.
cocher[1] [kɔʃe] *vt* to tick (off), *Am* check (off).
cocher[2] [kɔʃe] *nm* coachman.
cochon, -onne [kɔʃɔ̃, -ɔn] **1** *nm* pig; (*mâle*) hog; **c. d'Inde** guinea pig. **2** *nmf* (*personne sale*) (dirty) pig ▮ *a* (*histoire, film*) dirty. ●**cochonnerie(s)** *nf(pl)* (*obscénité(s)*) filth; (*pacotille*) *Fam* trash, rubbish.
cocktail [kɔktɛl] *nm* (*boisson*) cocktail; (*réunion*) cocktail party.
coco [kɔko] *nm* **noix de c.** coconut. ●**cocotier** *nm* coconut palm.
cocon [kɔkɔ̃] *nm* cocoon.
cocorico [kɔkɔriko] *int* & *nm* cock-a-doodle-doo.
cocotte [kɔkɔt] *nf* (*marmite*) casserole; **c.**

minute® pressure cooker.

code [kɔd] *nm* code; **codes, phares c.** *Aut* dipped headlights, *Am* low beams; **C. de la route** Highway Code, *Am* traffic regulations. ● **coder** *vt* to code.

coéquipier, -ière [kɔekipje, -jɛr] *nmf* team mate.

cœur [kœr] *nm* heart; (*couleur*) *Cartes* hearts; **au c. de** (*ville, hiver etc*) in the heart of; **par c.** (off) by heart; **ça me (sou)lève le c.** that turns my stomach; **à c. ouvert** (*opération*) open-heart; **avoir mal au c.** to feel sick; **avoir le c. gros** to have a heavy heart; **ça me tient à c.** that's important to me; **avoir bon c.** to be kind-hearted; **de bon c.** (*offrir*) willingly; (*rire*) heartily; **si le c. vous en dit** if you so desire.

coffre [kɔfr] *nm* chest; (*de banque*) safe; (*de voiture*) boot, *Am* trunk. ● **c.-fort** *nm* (*pl* **coffres-forts**) safe. ● **coffret** *nm* (*à bijoux etc*) box.

cognac [kɔɲak] *nm* cognac.

cogner [kɔɲe] *vti* to knock, bang; **se c. la tête/etc** to knock *ou* bang one's head/ *etc*; **se c. à qch** to knock *ou* bang into sth.

cohérent [kɔerɑ̃] *a* coherent.

cohue [kɔy] *nf* crowd, mob.

coiff/er [kwafe] *vt* **c. qn** to do s.o.'s hair; **se c.** to do one's hair; **c. qn d'un chapeau** to put a hat on s.o.; **se c. d'un chapeau** to put on a hat. ● **—eur, -euse**[1] *nmf* (*pour hommes*) barber, hairdresser; (*pour dames*) hairdresser. ● **—euse**[2] *nf* dressing table. ● **coiffure** *nf* hat, headgear; (*arrangement*) hairstyle; (*métier*) hairdressing.

coin [kwɛ̃] *nm* (*angle*) corner; (*endroit*) spot; (*de terre, de ciel*) patch; **du c.** (*magasin, gens etc*) local; **dans le c.** in the (local) area; **au c. du feu** by the fireside.

coincer [kwɛ̃se] *vt* (*mécanisme, tiroir*) to jam ‖ **se c.** *vpr* (*mécanisme etc*) to get stuck *ou* jammed; **se c. le doigt** to get one's finger stuck. ● **coincé** *a* (*tiroir etc*) stuck, jammed.

coïncider [kɔɛ̃side] *vi* to coincide. ● **coïncidence** *nf* coincidence.

coing [kwɛ̃] *nm* (*fruit*) quince.

col [kɔl] *nm* (*de chemise*) collar; (*de bouteille*) & *Anat* neck; (*de montagne*) pass; **c. roulé** polo neck, *Am* turtleneck.

colère [kɔlɛr] *nf* anger; **une c.** (*accès*) a fit of anger; **en c.** angry (**contre** with); **se mettre en c.** to lose one's temper. ● **coléreux, -euse** *a* quick-tempered.

colimaçon (en) [ɑ̃kɔlimasɔ̃] *adv* **escalier en c.** spiral staircase.

colique [kɔlik] *nf* diarrh(o)ea.

colis [kɔli] *nm* parcel, package.

collaborer [kɔlabɔre] *vi* to collaborate (**avec** with, **à** on); **c. à** (*journal*) to contribute to. ● **collaborateur, -trice** *nmf* collaborator; contributor. ● **collaboration** *nf* collaboration; contribution.

collage [kɔlaʒ] *nm* (*œuvre*) collage.

collant [kɔlɑ̃] **1** *a* (*papier*) sticky; (*vêtement*) skin-tight. **2** *nm* (pair of) tights; (*de danse*) leotard.

colle [kɔl] *nf* (*transparente*) glue; (*blanche*) paste; (*question*) *Fam* poser, teaser; (*punition*) *Scol Arg* detention.

collecte [kɔlɛkt] *nf* (*quête*) collection. ● **collecter** *vt* to collect.

collectif, -ive [kɔlɛktif, -iv] *a* collective; (*hystérie, démission*) mass; **billet c.** group ticket. ● **collectivement** *adv* collectively. ● **collectivité** *nf* community.

collection [kɔlɛksjɔ̃] *nf* collection. ● **collectionner** *vt* (*timbres etc*) to collect. ● **collectionneur, -euse** *nmf* collector.

collège [kɔlɛʒ] *nm* (secondary) school, *Am* (high) school; (*électoral*) college. ● **collégien** *nm* schoolboy. ● **collégienne** *nf* schoolgirl.

collègue [kɔlɛg] *nmf* colleague.

coller [kɔle] *vt* (*timbre etc*) to stick; (*à la colle transparente*) to glue; (*à la colle blanche*) to paste; (*affiche*) to stick up; (*papier peint*) to hang; (*mettre*) *Fam* to stick, shove; **c. contre** (*nez, oreille etc*) to press against; **c. qn** (*consigner*) *Scol* to keep s.o. in; **être collé à** (*examen*) *Fam* to fail, flunk ▮ *vi* to stick, cling. ● **colleur, -euse** *nmf* c. **d'affiches** billsticker.

collet [kɔlɛ] *nm* (*piège*) snare; **prendre qn au c.** to grab s.o. by the scruff of the neck.

collier [kɔlje] *nm* (*bijou*) necklace; (*de chien, cheval*) & *Tech* collar.

colline [kɔlin] *nf* hill.

collision [kɔlizjɔ̃] *nf* (*de véhicules*) collision; **entrer en c. avec** to collide with.

colloque [kɔlɔk] *nm* symposium.

colmater [kɔlmate] *vt* (*fuite, fente*) to seal.

colombe [kɔlɔ̃b] *nf* dove.

colon [kɔlɔ̃] *nm* settler, colonist. ● **colonial, -aux** *a* colonial. ● **colonie** *nf* colony; **c. de vacances** (children's) holiday camp *ou Am* vacation camp, *Am* = summer camp.

coloniser [kɔlɔnize] *vt* (*région*) to colonize.

colonel [kɔlɔnɛl] *nm* colonel.

colonne [kɔlɔn] *nf* column; **c. vertébrale** spine.

color/er [kɔlɔre] *vt* to colour; **c. en vert** to colour green. ● **—ant** *a & nm* colouring. ● **—é** *a* (*verre etc*) coloured; (*foule*) colourful.

coloriage [kɔlɔrjaʒ] *nm* colouring; (*dessin*) coloured drawing. ● **colorier** *vt* (*dessin etc*) to colour (in). ● **coloris** *nm* (*effet*) colouring; (*nuance*) shade.

colosse [kɔlɔs] *nm* giant. ● **colossal, -aux** *a* colossal.

colporter [kɔlpɔrte] *vt* to peddle, hawk.

coma [kɔma] *nm* coma; **dans le c.** in a coma.

combat [kɔ̃ba] *nm* fight. ● **combatif, -ive** *a* (*personne*) eager to fight; (*esprit*) fighting.

combatt/re* [kɔ̃batr] *vti* to fight. ● **—ant** *nm* (*bagarreur*) *Fam* fighter, brawler.

combien [kɔ̃bjɛ̃] **1** *adv* (*quantité*) how much; (*nombre*) how many; **c. de** (*temps, argent etc*) how much; (*gens, livres etc*) how many.

2 *adv* (*à quel point*) how; **tu verras c. il est bête** you'll see how silly he is. **3** *adv* (*distance*) **c. y a-t-il d'ici à...?** how far is it to...? **4** *nm inv* **le c. sommes-nous?** *Fam* what date is it?; **tous les c.?** *Fam* how often?

combin/er [kɔ̃bine] *vt* (*assembler*) to combine. ● **—é** *nm* (*de téléphone*) receiver. ● **combinaison** *nf* **1** combination; (*manœuvre*) scheme. **2** (*vêtement de femme*) slip; (*de mécanicien*) boiler suit, *Am* overalls; **c. de vol/plongée/ski** flying/diving/ski suit; **c. spatiale** spacesuit.

comble [kɔ̃bl] **1** *nm* **le c. de** (*la joie etc*) the height of; **c'est un ou le c.!** that's the limit! **2** *nmpl* **sous les combles** beneath the roof, in the loft *ou* attic. **3** *a* (*bondé*) packed.

combler [kɔ̃ble] *vt* (*trou etc*) to fill; (*vœu*) to fulfil; **c. son retard** to make up lost time; **c. qn de** (*joie*) to fill s.o. with; **je suis comblé** I'm completely satisfied.

combustible [kɔ̃bystibl] *nm* fuel ▮ *a* combustible.

comédie [kɔmedi] *nf* comedy; **c. musicale** musical; **jouer la c.** *Fig* to put on an act, pretend; **c'est de la c.** (*faux*) it's a sham. ● **comédien** *nm* actor. ● **comédienne** *nf* actress.

comestible [kɔmɛstibl] *a* edible.

comète [kɔmɛt] *nf* comet.

comique [kɔmik] *a* (*amusant*) *Fig* funny, comical; (*acteur etc*) comic.

comité [kɔmite] *nm* committee.

commande [kɔmɑ̃d] **1** *nf* (*achat*) order; **sur c.** to order. **2** *nfpl* **les commandes** (*d'un avion etc*) the controls.

command/er [kɔmɑ̃de] **1** *vt* (*diriger, exiger, dominer*) to command; (*faire fonctionner*) to control ▮ *vi* **c. à qn de faire** to command s.o. to do. **2** *vt* (*acheter*) to order. ● **—ant** *nm Nau* captain; **c. de bord** *Av* captain. ● **—ement** *nm* (*autorité*) command; *Rel* commandment. ● **commando** *nm Mil* commando.

comme [kɔm] *adv & conj* **1** like; **un peu c.**

a bit like; **c. moi** like me; **c. cela** like that.

2 as; **il parle c. il écrit** he speaks as he writes; **blanc c. neige** (as) white as snow; **c. si as if; c. pour faire** as if to do; **c. par hasard** as if by chance; **c. ami** (*en tant que*) as a friend; **qu'as-tu c. diplômes?** what do you have in the way of certificates?; **joli c. tout** *Fam* ever so pretty.

❚ *adv* (*exclamatif*) **regarde c. il pleut!** look how it's raining!; **c. c'est petit!** isn't it small!

❚ *conj* (*temps*) as; (*cause*) as, since; **c. elle entrait** (just) as she was coming in; **c. tu es mon ami** as *ou* since you're my friend.

commémoration [kɔmemɔrasjɔ̃] *nf* commemoration.

commenc/er [kɔmɑ̃se] *vti* to begin, start (**à faire** to do, doing; **par** with; **par faire** by doing); **pour c.** to begin with. ●**—ement** *nm* beginning, start.

comment [kɔmɑ̃] *adv* how; **c. le sais-tu?** how do you know?; **et c.!** and how!; **c.?** (*répétition*) pardon?, what?; (*surprise*) what?; **c.!** (*indignation*) what!; **c. est-il?** what is he like?; **c. faire?** what's to be done?; **c. t'appelles-tu?** what's your name?; **c. allez-vous?** how are you?

commentaire [kɔmɑ̃tɛr] *nm* (*explications*) commentary; (*remarque*) comment. ●**commenter** *vt* to comment (up)on.

commerçant, -ante [kɔmɛrsɑ̃, -ɑ̃t] *nmf* shopkeeper ❚ *a* **quartier/etc c.** shopping district/etc.

commerce [kɔmɛrs] *nm* trade, commerce; (*magasin*) shop, business; **de c.** (*voyageur, maison, tribunal*) commercial; **chambre de c.** chamber of commerce; **faire du c.** to trade (**avec** with); **dans le c.** (*objet*) (on sale) in the shops *ou Am* stores. ●**commercial, -aux** *a* commercial.

commettre* [kɔmɛtr] *vt* (*délit etc*) to commit; (*erreur*) to make.

commissaire [kɔmisɛr] *nm* **c. (de police)**

police superintendent *ou Am* chief. ●**c.-priseur** *nm* (*pl* **commissaires-priseurs**) auctioneer. ●**commissariat** *nm* **c. (de police)** (central) police station.

commission [kɔmisjɔ̃] *nf* (*course*) errand; (*message*) message; (*pourcentage*) commission (**sur** on); **faire les commissions** to do the shopping.

commode [kɔmɔd] **1** *a* (*pratique*) handy; (*simple*) easy; **il n'est pas c.** (*pas aimable*) he's unpleasant. **2** *nf* chest of drawers, *Am* dresser.

commun [kɔmœ̃] *a* (*collectif, habituel*) common; (*frais, cuisine etc*) shared; (*action, démarche etc*) joint; **ami c.** mutual friend; **peu c.** uncommon; **en c.** in common; **transports en c.** public transport; **avoir** *ou* **mettre en c.** to share. ●**—ément** [kɔmynemɑ̃] *adv* commonly.

communauté [kɔmynote] *nf* community.

commune [kɔmyn] *nf* (*municipalité française*) commune; **les Communes** *Br Pol* the Commons. ●**communal, -aux** *a* local, municipal.

communication [kɔmynikasjɔ̃] *nf* communication; **c. (téléphonique)** (telephone) call; **mauvaise c.** *Tél* bad line.

communi/er [kɔmynje] *vi* to receive Holy Communion. ●**—ant, -ante** *nmf Rel* communicant. ●**communion** *nf* communion; *Rel* (Holy) Communion.

communiqu/er [kɔmynike] *vt* to communicate, pass on; **se c. à** (*feu, rire*) to spread to ❚ *vi* (*personne, pièces etc*) to communicate. ●**—é** *nm* (*avis*) (official) statement; **c. de presse** press release.

communisme [kɔmynism] *nm* communism. ●**communiste** *a & nmf* communist.

commutateur [kɔmytatœr] *nm* (*bouton*) *Él* switch.

compact [kɔ̃pakt] *a* (*foule, matière*) dense; (*appareil, véhicule*) compact.

compagne [kɔ̃paɲ] *nf* (*camarade*) friend; (*épouse*) companion.

compagnie [kɔ̃paɲi] *nf* (*présence, société*) company; **tenir c. à qn** to keep s.o. company.

compagnon [kɔ̃paɲɔ̃] *nm* companion; (*ouvrier*) workman; **c. de route** travelling companion, fellow traveller; **c. de jeu** playmate; **c. de travail** fellow worker, workmate.

comparaître* [kɔ̃paretr] *vi* Jur to appear (in court) (**devant** before).

comparer [kɔ̃pare] *vt* to compare (**à** to, **with**) ∥ **se c.** *vpr* to be compared (**à** to, **with**). ● **comparable** *a* comparable. ● **comparaison** *nf* comparison (**avec** with); *Littér* simile. ● **comparatif** *nm* Gram comparative.

compartiment [kɔ̃partimɑ̃] *nm* compartment.

compas [kɔ̃pa] *nm* **1** (*pour mesurer etc*) (pair of) compasses, Am compass. **2** (*boussole*) Nau compass.

compassion [kɔ̃pasjɔ̃] *nf* compassion.

compatible [kɔ̃patibl] *a* compatible (**avec** with).

compatir [kɔ̃patir] *vi* to sympathize; **c. à** (*la douleur etc de qn*) to share in.

compatriote [kɔ̃patrijɔt] *nmf* compatriot.

compenser [kɔ̃pɑ̃se] *vt* to make up for, compensate for ∥ *vi* to compensate. ● **compensation** *nf* compensation; **en c. de** in compensation for.

compétent [kɔ̃petɑ̃] *a* competent. ● **pétence** *nf* competence.

compétition [kɔ̃petisjɔ̃] *nf* competition; (*épreuve*) Sp event; **de c.** (*esprit, sport*) competitive. ● **compétitif, -ive** *a* competitive.

complaisant [kɔ̃plezɑ̃] *a* kind, obliging. ● **complaisance** *nf* kindness.

complément [kɔ̃plemɑ̃] *nm* complement; **le c.** (*le reste*) the rest. ● **complémentaire** *a* complementary; (*détails*) additional.

complet, -ète [kɔ̃plɛ, -ɛt] **1** *a* complete; (*train, hôtel etc*) full; (*aliment*) whole. **2** *nm* (*costume*) suit. ● **complètement** *adv* completely.

compléter [kɔ̃plete] *vt* to complete; (*ajouter à*) to complement; (*somme*) to make up ∥ **se c.** *vpr* (*caractères*) to complement each other.

complexe [kɔ̃plɛks] **1** *a* complex. **2** *nm* (*sentiment, construction*) complex; **avoir des complexes** to be hung up, have hang-ups.

complication [kɔ̃plikasjɔ̃] *nf* complication.

complice [kɔ̃plis] *nm* accomplice ∥ *a* (*regard*) knowing; (*attitude*) conniving. ● **complicité** *nf* complicity.

compliment [kɔ̃plimɑ̃] *nm* compliment; *pl* (*éloges*) compliments; (*félicitations*) congratulations.

compliquer [kɔ̃plike] *vt* to complicate ∥ **se c.** *vpr* (*situation*) to get complicated. ● **compliqué** *a* (*mécanisme, histoire etc*) complicated.

complot [kɔ̃plo] *nm* plot (**contre** against). ● **comploter** [kɔ̃plɔte] *vti* to plot (**de faire** to do).

comporter [kɔ̃pɔrte] **1** *vt* to contain. **2 se comporter** *vpr* to behave; (*joueur, voiture*) to perform. ● **comportement** *nm* behaviour; (*de joueur etc*) performance.

compos/er [kɔ̃poze] *vt* (*former, constituer*) to make up, compose; (*musique*) to compose; (*numéro*) Tél to dial; **se c. de**, **être composé de** to be composed of. ● **—ant** *nm* (*chimique, électronique*) component. ● **—é** *a* (*mot etc*) & *Ch* compound; **temps c.** compound tense; **passé c.** perfect (tense) ∥ *nm* compound.

compositeur, -trice [kɔ̃pozitœr, -tris] *nmf* Mus composer.

composition [kɔ̃pozisjɔ̃] *nf* Mus Littér Ch composition; Scol test, class exam; **c. française** Scol French essay.

composter [kɔ̃pɔste] *vt* (*billet*) to punch.

compote [kɔ̃pɔt] *nf* stewed fruit, Am sauce; **c. de pommes** stewed apples, Am applesauce.

compréhensible [kɔ̃preɑ̃sibl] *a* understandable, comprehensible. ● **compréhensif, -ive** *a* (*personne*) understanding. ● **compréhension** *nf* understanding.

comprendre* [kɔ̃prɑ̃dr] *vt* to understand; (*comporter*) to include, comprise; **je n'y comprends rien** I don't understand anything about it; **ça se comprend** that's understandable. ● **compris** *a* (*inclus*) included (**dans** in); **tout c.** (all) inclusive; **y c.** including.

compresse [kɔ̃prɛs] *nf Méd* compress.

comprim/er [kɔ̃prime] *vt* to compress. ● **—é** *nm Méd* tablet.

compromettre* [kɔ̃prɔmɛtr] *vt* to compromise. ● **compromis** *nm* compromise.

comptable [kɔ̃tabl] *a nmf* bookkeeper; (*expert*) accountant. ● **comptabilité** *nf* (*comptes*) accounts; (*service*) accounts department.

comptant [kɔ̃tɑ̃] *a* **argent c.** (hard) cash ‖ *adv* **payer c.** to pay (in) cash; **(au) c.** (*acheter, vendre*) for cash.

compte [kɔ̃t] *nm* (*comptabilité*) account; (*calcul*) count; (*nombre*) (right) number; **avoir un c. en banque** to have a bank account; **c. chèque** cheque account, *Am* checking account; **tenir c. de** to take into account; **c. tenu de** considering; **se rendre c. de** to realize; **rendre c. de** (*exposer*) to report on; (*justifier*) to account for; **à son c.** (*travailler*) for oneself; (*s'installer*) on one's own; **pour le c. de** on behalf of; **en fin de c.** all things considered; **avoir un c. à régler avec qn** to have a score to settle with s.o.; **c. à rebours** countdown. ● **compte-gouttes** *nm inv Méd* dropper; **au c.-gouttes** very sparingly.

compter [kɔ̃te] *vt* (*calculer*) to count; (*prévoir*) to allow, reckon; **c. faire** to expect to do; (*avoir l'intention de*) to intend to do; **c. qch à qn** (*facturer*) to charge s.o. for sth. ‖ *vi* (*calculer, avoir de l'importance*) to count; **c. sur** to rely on; **c. avec** to reckon with; **c. parmi** to be (numbered) among. ● **compteur** *nm El* meter; **c. (de vitesse)** *Aut* speedometer; **c. (kilométrique)** milometer, clock, *Am* odometer.

compte rendu [kɔ̃trɑ̃dy] *nm* report; (*de livre, film*) review.

comptoir [kɔ̃twar] *nm* (*de magasin*)

counter; (*de café*) bar; (*de bureau*) (reception) desk.

comte [kɔ̃t] *nm* (*noble*) count; *Br* earl. ● **comtesse** *nf* countess.

con, conne [kɔ̃, kɔn] *a* (*idiot*) *Fam* (damn) stupid ‖ *nmf Fam* (damn) stupid fool.

concave [kɔ̃kav] *a* concave.

concentrer [kɔ̃sɑ̃tre] *vt* to concentrate; (*attention etc*) to focus, concentrate ‖ **se c.** *vpr* (*réfléchir*) to concentrate. ● **concentré** *a* (*lait*) condensed; (*attentif*) concentrating (hard) ‖ *nm* **c. de tomates** tomato purée. ● **concentration** *nf* concentration.

concentrique [kɔ̃sɑ̃trik] *a* concentric.

concerner [kɔ̃sɛrne] *vt* to concern; **en ce qui me concerne** as far as I'm concerned.

concert [kɔ̃sɛr] *nm Mus* concert; (*de louanges*) chorus; **de c.** (*agir*) together.

concerter (se) [səkɔ̃sɛrte] *vpr* to consult (together).

concession [kɔ̃sesjɔ̃] *nf* concession (**à** to). ● **concessionnaire** *nmf Com* (authorized) dealer, agent.

concev/oir* [kɔ̃səvwar] *vt* (*imaginer, éprouver, engendrer*) to conceive; (*comprendre*) to understand. ● **—able** *a* conceivable.

concierge [kɔ̃sjɛrʒ] *nmf* caretaker, *Am* janitor.

concili/er [kɔ̃silje] *vt* (*choses*) to reconcile. ● **—ant** *a* conciliatory.

concis [kɔ̃si] *a* concise, terse.

concitoyen, -enne [kɔ̃sitwajɛ̃, -ɛn] *nmf* fellow citizen.

conclu/re* [kɔ̃klyr] *vt* (*terminer, régler*) to conclude; **c. que** (*déduire*) to conclude that; **c. un marché** to make a deal ‖ *vi* (*orateur etc*) to conclude. ● **—ant** *a* conclusive. ● **conclusion** *nf* conclusion.

concombre [kɔ̃kɔ̃br] *nm* cucumber.

concorde [kɔ̃kɔrd] *nf* concord, harmony.

concord/er [kɔ̃kɔrde] *vi* (*faits etc*) to agree; **c. avec** to match. ● **—ant** *a* in agreement.

concourir* [kɔ̃kurir] *vi* (*candidat*) to compete (**pour** for); **c. à** (*un but*) to contribute to.

concours [kɔ̃kur] *nm* Scol Univ competitive examination; (*jeu*) competition; (*aide*) assistance; (*de circonstances*) combination; **c. hippique** horse show, show-jumping event.

concret, -ète [kɔ̃krɛ, -ɛt] *a* concrete. ● **concrétiser** *vt* to give concrete form to ▮ **se c.** *vpr* to materialize.

conçu [kɔ̃sy] *pp de* **concevoir** ▮ *a* **c. pour faire/pour qn** designed to do/for s.o.; **bien c.** (*maison etc*) well designed.

concurrent, -ente [kɔ̃kyrɑ̃, -ɑ̃t] *nmf* competitor. ● **concurrence** *nf* competition; **faire c. à** to compete with. ● **concurrencer** *vt* to compete with.

condamn/er [kɔ̃dane] *vt* to condemn; (*accusé*) to sentence (**à** to); (*porte*) to block up; (*pièce*) to keep locked; **c. qn à une amende** to fine s.o. ● **-é, -ée** *nmf* Jur condemned man *ou* woman; **être c.** (*malade*) to be a hopeless case, be terminally ill. ● **condamnation** *nf* Jur sentence; (*censure*) condemnation.

condenser [kɔ̃dɑ̃se] *vt*, **se c.** *vpr* to condense.

condescendant [kɔ̃desɑ̃dɑ̃] *a* condescending.

condiment [kɔ̃dimɑ̃] *nm* condiment.

condition [kɔ̃disjɔ̃] *nf* (*état, stipulation, rang*) condition; *pl* (*clauses, tarifs*) Com terms; **à c. de faire, à c. que l'on fasse** providing *ou* provided (that) one does. ● **conditionnel** *nm* Gram conditional.

conditionn/er [kɔ̃disjɔne] *vt* (*influencer*) to condition. ● **-é à** (*réflexe*) conditioned; **à air c.** (*pièce etc*) air-conditioned.

condoléances [kɔ̃dɔleɑ̃s] *nfpl* sympathy, condolences.

conducteur, -trice [kɔ̃dyktœr, -tris] *nmf* Aut Rail driver.

conduire* [kɔ̃dɥir] **1** *vt* to lead; Aut to drive; (*eau*) to carry; (*affaire etc*) & Él to conduct; **c. qn à** (*accompagner*) to take s.o. to. **2 se conduire** *vpr* to behave.

conduite [kɔ̃dɥit] *nf* conduct, behaviour; Aut driving (**de** of); (*d'eau, de gaz*) main; (*d'entreprise etc*) conduct; **c. à gauche** (*volant*) left-hand drive.

cône [kon] *nm* cone.

confection [kɔ̃fɛksjɔ̃] *nf* making (**de** of); **vêtements de c.** ready-to-wear clothes; **magasin de c.** clothes shop, Am clothing store. ● **confectionner** *vt* (*gâteau, robe*) to make.

confédération [kɔ̃federasjɔ̃] *nf* confederation.

conférence [kɔ̃ferɑ̃s] *nf* conference; (*exposé*) lecture; **en c.** in a meeting. ● **conférencier, -ière** *nmf* lecturer.

confesser [kɔ̃fese] *vt* to confess ▮ **se c.** *vpr* Rel to confess (**à** to). ● **confession** *nf* confession. ● **confessionnal, -aux** *nm* Rel confessional.

confettis [kɔ̃feti] *nmpl* confetti.

confiance [kɔ̃fjɑ̃s] *nf* trust, confidence; **faire c. à qn, avoir c. en qn** to trust s.o.; **c. en soi** (self-)confidence; **poste/abus de c.** position/breach of trust; **homme de c.** reliable man; **en toute c.** (*acheter*) quite confidently. ● **confiant** *a* trusting; (*sûr de soi*) confident; **être c. en** *ou* **dans** to have confidence in.

confidence [kɔ̃fidɑ̃s] *nf* (*secret*) confidence; **en c.** in confidence; **faire une c. à qn** to confide in s.o. ● **confident** *nm* confidant. ● **confidente** *nf* confidante. ● **confidentiel, -ielle** *a* confidential.

confier [kɔ̃fje] *vt* **c. à qn** (*enfant, objet*) to give s.o. to look after, entrust s.o. with; **c. un secret/etc à qn** to confide a secret/ etc to s.o.; **se c. à qn** to confide in s.o.

confirmer [kɔ̃firme] *vt* to confirm (**que** that). ● **confirmation** *nf* confirmation.

confiserie [kɔ̃fizri] *nf* (*magasin*) sweet shop, Am candy store; *pl* (*produits*) confectionery, sweets, Am candy. ● **confiseur, -euse** *nmf* confectioner.

confisquer [kɔ̃fiske] *vt* to confiscate (**à qn** from s.o.).

confit [kɔ̃fi] *a* **fruits confits** crystallized *ou* candied fruit. ● **confiture** *nf* jam.

preserves.

conflit [kɔ̃fli] *nm* conflict.

confondre [kɔ̃fɔ̃dr] *vt* (*choses, personnes*) to mix up, confuse; (*consterner, étonner*) to confound; **c. qch/qn avec** to mistake sth/s.o. for **‖ se c.** *vpr* (*s'unir*) to merge; **se c. en excuses** to be very apologetic.

conforme [kɔ̃fɔrm] *a* **c. à** in accordance with, in keeping with; (*modèle*) true to; **copie c. à l'original** true copy, copy true to the original. **● conformément** *adv* **c. à** in accordance with.

conformer (se) [səkɔ̃fɔrme] *vpr* to conform (**à** to).

conformiste [kɔ̃fɔrmist] *a* & *nmf* conformist. **● conformité** *nf* conformity.

confort [kɔ̃fɔr] *nm* comfort. **● confortable** *a* comfortable.

confrère [kɔ̃frɛr] *nm* colleague.

confronter [kɔ̃frɔ̃te] *vt Jur etc* to confront (**avec** with); **confronté à** confronted with. **● confrontation** *nf* confrontation.

confus [kɔ̃fy] *a* (*esprit, situation, idée, bruit etc*) confused; (*gêné*) embarrassed; **je suis c.!** (*désolé*) I'm terribly sorry! **● confusément** *adv* indistinctly, vaguely. **● confusion** *nf* confusion; (*gêne, honte*) embarrassment.

congé [kɔ̃ʒe] *nm* leave (of absence); (*vacances*) holiday, *Am* vacation; (*avis pour locataire*) notice (to quit); (*pour salarié*) notice (of dismissal); **c. de maladie** sick leave; **congés payés** paid holidays *ou Am* vacation; **donner son c. à** (*employé, locataire*) to give notice to; **prendre c. de** to take leave of.

congédier [kɔ̃ʒedje] *vt* (*domestique etc*) to dismiss.

congeler [kɔ̃ʒle] *vt* to freeze. **● congélateur** *nm* freezer, deep-freeze. **● congélation** *nf* freezing.

congère [kɔ̃ʒɛr] *nf* snowdrift.

congestion [kɔ̃ʒɛstjɔ̃] *nf* **c. cérébrale** *Méd* stroke.

Congo [kɔ̃go] *nm* Congo. **● congolais, -aise** *a* & *nmf* Congolese.

congratuler [kɔ̃gratyle] *vt Iron* to congratulate.

congrès [kɔ̃grɛ] *nm* congress.

conifère [kɔnifɛr] *nm* conifer.

conique [kɔnik] *a* conic(al), cone-shaped.

conjecture [kɔ̃ʒɛktyr] *nf* conjecture.

conjoint [kɔ̃ʒwɛ̃] *nm* spouse; *pl* husband and wife.

conjonction [kɔ̃ʒɔ̃ksjɔ̃] *nf Gram* conjunction.

conjoncture [kɔ̃ʒɔ̃ktyr] *nf* circumstances; *Écon* economic situation.

conjugal, -aux [kɔ̃ʒygal, -o] *a* conjugal.

conjuguer [kɔ̃ʒyge] *vt* (*verbe*) to conjugate; (*efforts*) to combine **‖ se c.** *vpr* (*verbe*) to be conjugated. **● conjugaison** *nf Gram* conjugation.

conjur/er [kɔ̃ʒyre] *vt* (*danger*) to avert; (*mauvais sort*) to ward off; **c. qn** to beg s.o., implore s.o. (**de faire** to do).

connaissance [kɔnesɑ̃s] *nf* knowledge; (*personne*) acquaintance; *pl* (*science*) knowledge (**en** of); **faire la c. de qn, faire c. avec qn** (*inconnu*) to meet s.o., make s.o.'s acquaintance; (*ami, époux etc*) to get to know s.o.; **à ma c.** as far as I know; **avoir c. de** to be aware of; **perdre c.** to lose consciousness, faint; **sans c.** unconscious. **● connaisseur** *nm* connoisseur.

connaître* [kɔnɛtr] *vt* to know; (*rencontrer*) to meet; (*un succès*) to have; (*un malheur*) to experience; **faire c.** to make known **‖ se c.** *vpr* (*amis etc*) to get to know each other; **nous nous connaissons déjà** we've met before; **s'y c. à** *ou* **en qch** to know (all) about sth.

connerie [kɔnri] *nf Fam* (*bêtise*) (damn) stupidity; (*action*) (damn) stupid thing; *pl* (*paroles*) (damn) stupid nonsense.

connivence [kɔnivɑ̃s] *nf* connivance.

connu *pp de* **connaître ‖** *a* (*célèbre*) well-known.

conquér/ir* [kɔ̃kerir] *vt* (*pays, marché etc*) to conquer. **●—ant, -ante** *nmf* conqueror. **● conquête** *nf* conquest; **faire la c. de** (*pays, marché etc*) to conquer.

consacrer [kɔ̃sakre] vt (temps, vie etc) to devote (à to); **se c. à** to devote oneself to.

consciemment [kɔ̃sjamɑ̃] adv consciously.

conscience [kɔ̃sjɑ̃s] nf 1 (psychologique) consciousness; **la c. de qch** the awareness of sth; **avoir/prendre c. de** to be/ become aware ou conscious of. 2 (morale) conscience; **avoir mauvaise c.** to have a guilty conscience; **c. professionnelle** conscientiousness. ● **consciencieux, -euse** a conscientious. ● **conscient** a conscious; **c. de** aware ou conscious of.

conscrit [kɔ̃skri] nm Mil conscript.

consécutif, -ive [kɔ̃sekytif, -iv] a consecutive; **c. à** following upon.

conseil[1] [kɔ̃sɛj] nm un c. a piece of advice, some advice; **des conseils** advice.

conseil[2] [kɔ̃sɛj] nm (assemblée) council, committee; **c. d'administration** board of directors; **c. des ministres** (réunion) Pol cabinet meeting.

conseiller[1] [kɔ̃seje] vt (guider, recommander) to advise; **c. qch à qn** to recommend sth to s.o.; **c. à qn de faire** to advise s.o. to do. ● **conseiller**[2], **-ère** nmf (expert) consultant, adviser; (d'un conseil) councillor, Am councillor; **c. municipal** town councillor, Am councilman.

consentir* [kɔ̃sɑ̃tir] vi **c. à** to consent to. ● **—ement** nm consent.

conséquence [kɔ̃sekɑ̃s] nf consequence; (conclusion) conclusion; **en c.** accordingly; **sans c.** (importance) of no importance.

conséquent (par) [parkɔ̃sekɑ̃] adv consequently.

conservateur, -trice [kɔ̃sɛrvatœr, -tris] 1 a & nmf Pol Conservative. 2 nm (de musée) curator.

conservatoire [kɔ̃sɛrvatwar] nm school (of music, drama).

conserve [kɔ̃sɛrv] nf conserves canned

ou tinned food; **de** ou **en c.** canned, tinned; **mettre en c.** to can, tin.

conserver [kɔ̃sɛrve] vt (ne pas perdre) to keep, retain; (fruits, tradition etc) to preserve; **se c.** vpr (aliment) to keep. ● **conservation** nf preservation.

considérable [kɔ̃siderabl] a considerable.

considérer [kɔ̃sidere] vt to consider (que that, comme to be); **tout bien considéré** all things considered. ● **considération** nf (respect) regard, esteem; **prendre en c.** to take into consideration.

consigne [kɔ̃siɲ] nf (instruction) orders; (de gare) left-luggage office, Am baggage checkroom; Scol detention; (somme) deposit; **c. automatique** (de gare) luggage lockers, Am baggage lockers. ● **consigner** vt (bouteille etc) to charge a deposit on; (élève) Scol to keep in.

consistant [kɔ̃sistɑ̃] a (sauce, bouillie) thick; (repas) solid. ● **consistance** nf (de liquide) consistency.

consister [kɔ̃siste] vi **c. en/dans** to consist of/in; **c. à faire** to consist in doing.

console [kɔ̃sɔl] nf Tech Él console.

consoler [kɔ̃sɔle] vt to comfort, console; **se c. de** (la mort de qn etc) to get over. ● **consolation** nf comfort, consolation.

consolider [kɔ̃sɔlide] vt to strengthen.

consommer [kɔ̃sɔme] vt (aliment, carburant etc) to consume vi (au café) to drink; **c. beaucoup/peu** (véhicule) to be heavy/light on petrol ou Am gas. ● **consommateur, -trice** nmf Com consumer; (au café) customer. ● **consommation** nf consumption; (boisson) drink; **biens/société de c.** consumer goods/society.

consonne [kɔ̃sɔn] nf consonant.

conspirer [kɔ̃spire] vi to plot, conspire (contre against). ● **conspirateur, -trice** nmf plotter. ● **conspiration** nf plot, conspiracy.

constant [kɔ̃stɑ̃] a constant. ● **constamment** adv constantly. ● **constance** nf constancy.

constat [kɔsta] *nm* (official) report; **dresser un c. d'échec** to acknowledge one's failure.

constater [kɔstate] *vt* to note, observe (**que** that); (*vérifier*) to establish; (*enregistrer*) to record; **je ne fais que c.** I'm merely stating a fact. ● **constatation** *nf* (*remarque*) observation.

constellation [kɔstelasjɔ] *nf* constellation. ● **constellé** *a* **c. de** (*étoiles, joyaux*) studded with.

consterner [kɔstɛrne] *vt* to distress, dismay. ● **consternation** *nf* distress, dismay.

constipé [kɔstipe] *a* constipated. ● **constipation** *nf* constipation.

constituer [kɔstitɥe] *vt* (*composer*) to make up; (*représenter*) to represent; (*organiser*) to form; **constitué de** made up of; **se c. prisonnier** to give oneself up. ● **constitution** *nf* (*santé*) & *Pol* constitution; (*composition*) composition. ● **constitutionnel, -elle** *a* constitutional.

constructeur [kɔstryktœr] *nm* builder; (*fabricant*) maker (**de** of). ● **constructif, -ive** *a* constructive. ● **construction** *nf* (*de pont etc*) building, construction (**de** of); (*édifice*) building; (*de théorie etc*) & *Gram* construction; **matériaux/jeu de c.** building materials/set.

construire* [kɔstrɥir] *vt* (*maison, route etc*) to build, construct; (*phrase, théorie etc*) to construct.

consul [kɔsyl] *nm* consul. ● **consulat** *nm* consulate.

consulter [kɔsylte] **1** *vt* to consult ‖ **se c.** *vpr* to consult (each other), confer. **2** *vi* (*médecin*) to hold surgery, *Am* hold office hours. ● **consultation** *nf* consultation; **cabinet de c.** *Méd* surgery, *Am* (doctor's) office; **heures de c.** *Méd* surgery hours, *Am* office hours.

consumer [kɔsyme] *vt* (*détruire, miner*) to consume.

contact [kɔtakt] *nm* contact; (*toucher*) touch; *Aut* ignition; **être en c. avec** to be in touch *ou* contact with; **prendre c.** to get in touch (**avec** with); **entrer en c.**

avec to come into contact with; **prise de c.** first meeting; **mettre/couper le c.** *Aut* to switch on/off the ignition; **lentilles** *ou* **verres de c.** contact lenses. ● **contacter** *vt* to contact.

contagieux, -euse [kɔtaʒjø, -øz] *a* (*maladie, rire*) contagious, infectious; **c'est c.** it's catching *ou* contagious. ● **contagion** *nf* *Méd* infection.

contaminer [kɔtamine] *vt* to contaminate.

conte [kɔt] *nm* tale; **c. de fée** fairy tale.

contempler [kɔtɑple] *vt* to gaze at. ● **contemplation** *nf* contemplation.

contemporain, -aine [kɔtɑporɛ, -ɛn] *a* & *nmf* contemporary.

contenance [kɔtnɑs] *nf* **1** (*d'un récipient*) capacity. **2** **perdre c.** (*allure*) to lose one's composure.

contenir* [kɔtnir] *vt* (*renfermer*) to contain; (*avoir comme capacité*) to hold; (*contrôler*) to hold back, contain ‖ **se c.** *vpr* to contain oneself. ● **conteneur** *nm* (freight) container.

content [kɔtɑ] *a* pleased, happy, glad (**de faire** to do); **c. de qn/qch** pleased *ou* happy with s.o./sth; **c. de soi** self-satisfied; **non c. d'avoir fait** not content with having done.

content/er [kɔtɑte] *vt* to satisfy, please; **se c. de** to be content *ou* happy with. ● **—ement** *nm* contentment, satisfaction.

contenu [kɔtny] *nm* (*de récipient*) contents; (*de texte, film etc*) content.

cont/er [kɔte] *vt* (*histoire etc*) to tell (**à** to). ● **—eur, -euse** *nmf* storyteller.

contestable [kɔtestabl] *a* debatable.

contestataire [kɔtestater] *a* **étudiant/ ouvrier c.** student/worker protester ‖ *nmf* protester. ● **contestation** *nf* (*discussion*) dispute; **faire de la c.** to protest (against the Establishment).

conteste (sans) [sɑkɔtest] *adv* unquestionably.

contester [kɔteste] **1** *vi* (*étudiants etc*) to protest ‖ *vt* to protest against. **2** *vt* (*fait etc*) to dispute, contest.

contexte [kɔ̃tɛkst] *nm* context.

contigu, -uë [kɔ̃tigy] *a* **c. (à)** (*maisons etc*) adjoining.

continent [kɔ̃tinɑ̃] *nm* continent; (*opposé à une île*) mainland. ● **continental, -aux** *a* continental.

continu [kɔ̃tiny] *a* continuous. ● **continuel, -elle** *a* continual. ● **continuellement** *adv* continually.

continuer [kɔ̃tinɥe] *vt* to continue, carry on (**à** *ou* **de faire** doing); (*prolonger*) to continue ‖ *vi* to continue, go on.

contorsion [kɔ̃tɔrsjɔ̃] *nf* contortion. ● **se contorsionner** *vpr* to contort oneself.

contour [kɔ̃tur] *nm* outline, contour; *pl* (*de route, rivière*) twists, bends.

contourner [kɔ̃turne] *vt* (*colline etc*) to go round, skirt; (*difficulté, loi*) to get round.

contraception [kɔ̃trasɛpsjɔ̃] *nf* contraception. ● **contraceptif, -ive** *a & nm* contraceptive.

contracter [kɔ̃trakte] *vt* (*muscle, habitude, dette etc*) to contract ‖ **se c.** *vpr* (*cœur etc*) to contract.

contractuel, -elle [kɔ̃traktɥɛl] *nmf* traffic warden, *Am* meter man *ou* maid.

contradiction [kɔ̃tradiksjɔ̃] *nf* contradiction. ● **contradictoire** *a* (*propos etc*) contradictory; (*rapports, théories*) conflicting.

contraindre* [kɔ̃trɛ̃dr] *vt* to compel, force (**à faire** to do). ● **contraignant** *a* constraining, restricting. ● **contrainte** *nf* constraint.

contraire [kɔ̃trɛr] *a* opposite; (*défavorable*) contrary; **c. à** contrary to ‖ *nm* opposite; (**bien**) **au c.** on the contrary. ● **—ment** *adv* **c. à** contrary to.

contrari/er [kɔ̃trarje] *vt* (*projet, action*) to spoil, thwart; (*personne*) to annoy. ● **—ant** *a* (*action etc*) annoying; (*personne*) difficult, perverse. ● **contrariété** *nf* annoyance.

contraste [kɔ̃trast] *nm* contrast. ● **contraster** *vi* to contrast (**avec** with).

contrat [kɔ̃tra] *nm* contract.

contravention [kɔ̃travɑ̃sjɔ̃] *nf* (*pour stationnement interdit*) (parking) ticket; (*amende*) *Aut* fine.

contre [kɔ̃tr] *prép & adv* against; (*en échange de*) (in exchange) for; **échanger c.** to exchange for; **fâché c.** angry with; **six voix c. deux** six votes to two; **Nîmes c. Arras** (*match*) Nîmes versus *ou* against Arras; **un médicament c.** (*toux etc*) a medicine for; **par c.** on the other hand; **tout c. qch/qn** close to sth/s.o.

contre- *préf* counter-.

contre-attaque [kɔ̃tratak] *nf* counterattack. ● **contre-attaquer** *vt* to counterattack.

contrebalancer [kɔ̃trəbalɑ̃se] *vt* to counterbalance; (*compenser*) *Fig* to offset.

contrebande [kɔ̃trəbɑ̃d] *nf* (*fraude*) smuggling; (*marchandises*) smuggled goods; **de c.** (*tabac etc*) smuggled; **faire de la c.** to smuggle; **passer qch en c.** to smuggle sth. ● **contrebandier, -ière** *nmf* smuggler.

contrebas (en) [ɑ̃kɔ̃trəba] *adv & prép* **en c. (de)** down below.

contrebasse [kɔ̃trəbas] *nf* *Mus* double-bass.

contrecarrer [kɔ̃trəkare] *vt* to thwart, frustrate.

contrecœur (à) [akɔ̃trəkœr] *adv* reluctantly.

contrecoup [kɔ̃trəku] *nm* (indirect) effect *ou* consequence.

contredire* [kɔ̃trədir] *vt* to contradict ‖ **se c.** *vpr* to contradict oneself.

contrée [kɔ̃tre] *nf* region, land.

contrefaçon [kɔ̃trəfasɔ̃] *nf* counterfeiting, forgery; (*objet imité*) counterfeit, forgery.

contre-indiqué [kɔ̃trɛ̃dike] *a* (*médicament*) dangerous, not recommended.

contre-jour (à) [akɔ̃trəʒur] *adv* against the (sun)light.

contremaître [kɔ̃trəmɛtr] *nm* foreman.

contrepartie [kɔ̃trəparti] *nf* **en c.** in exchange.

contre-pied [kɔ̃trəpje] *nm* **le c.-pied d'une opinion/attitude** the (exact) opposite view/attitude.

contre-plaqué [kɔ̃trəplake] *nm* plywood.

contrepoids [kɔ̃trəpwa] *nm* **faire c. (à)** to counterbalance.

contresens [kɔ̃trəsɑ̃s] *nm* misinterpretation; (*en traduisant*) mistranslation; **à c.** the wrong way.

contretemps [kɔ̃trətɑ̃] *nm* hitch, mishap; **à c.** (*arriver etc*) at the wrong moment.

contribu/er [kɔ̃tribɥe] *vi* to contribute (**à** to). ●**—able** *nmf* taxpayer. ●**contribution** *nf* contribution; (*impôt*) tax; **mettre qn à c.** to use s.o.'s services.

contrit [kɔ̃tri] *a* (*air etc*) contrite.

contrôle [kɔ̃trol] *nm* inspection, check(ing) (**de** of); (*des prix, de la qualité*) control; (*maîtrise*) control; **un c.** (*examen*) a check (**sur** on); **le c. de soi(-même)** self-control; **le c. des naissances** birth control; **un c. d'identité** an identity check. ●**contrôler** *vt* (*examiner*) to inspect, check; (*maîtriser, surveiller*) to control ▮ **se c.** *vpr* (*se maîtriser*) to control oneself. ●**contrôleur, -euse** *nmf* (*de train*) (ticket) inspector; (*au quai*) ticket collector; (*de bus*) conductor, conductress; **c. de la navigation aérienne** air-traffic controller.

contrordre [kɔ̃trɔrdr] *nm* change of orders.

controverse [kɔ̃trɔvɛrs] *nf* controversy.

contumace (par) [parkɔ̃tymas] *adv* Jur in one's absence.

contusion [kɔ̃tyzjɔ̃] *nf* bruise.

convainc/re [kɔ̃vɛ̃kr] *vt* to convince (**de** of); **c. qn de faire** to persuade s.o. to do. ●**—ant** *a* convincing. ●**—u** *a* (*certain*) convinced (**de** of).

convalescent, -ente [kɔ̃valesɑ̃, -ɑ̃t] *nmf* convalescent ▮ *a* **être c.** to convalesce. ●**convalescence** *nf* convalescence; **être en c.** to convalesce.

convenable [kɔ̃vnabl] *a* (*acceptable*) (*réponse etc*) suitable; (*correct*) (*tenue etc*) decent. ●**—ment** [-əmɑ̃] *adv* suitably; decently.

convenance [kɔ̃vnɑ̃s] *nf* **convenances** (*usages*) convention(s), proprieties; **à**

sa **c.** to one's satisfaction *ou* taste.

conven/ir* [kɔ̃vnir] *vi* **1 c. à** (*être fait pour*) to be suitable for; (*plaire à, aller à*) to suit; **ça convient** (*date etc*) that's suitable; **il convient de faire** it's advisable to do. **2 c. de** (*lieu etc*) to agree upon; (*erreur*) to admit. ●**—u** *a* (*prix etc*) agreed.

convention [kɔ̃vɑ̃sjɔ̃] *nf* (*accord*) agreement, convention. ●**conventionné** *a* **médecin c.** = National Health Service doctor (*bound by agreement with the State*).

conversation [kɔ̃vɛrsasjɔ̃] *nf* conversation.

conversion [kɔ̃vɛrsjɔ̃] *nf* conversion. ●**convertir** *vt* to convert (**à** to, **en** into) ▮ **se c.** *vpr* to be converted, convert. ●**convertible** *nm* (**canapé**) **c.** bed settee.

convexe [kɔ̃vɛks] *a* convex.

conviction [kɔ̃viksjɔ̃] *nf* (*certitude, croyance*) conviction; **pièce à c.** Jur exhibit.

convier [kɔ̃vje] *vt* to invite (**à une soirée/** *etc* to a party/*etc*).

convive [kɔ̃viv] *nmf* guest (*at table*).

convoi [kɔ̃vwa] *nm* (*véhicules, personnes etc*) convoy; Rail train; **c. (funèbre)** funeral procession.

convoyeur [kɔ̃vwajœr] *nm* **c. de fonds** security guard (*transferring money*).

convoquer [kɔ̃vɔke] *vt* (*candidats, membres etc*) to summon *ou* invite (to attend); (*assemblée*) to convene, summon; **c. qn à** to summon *ou* invite s.o. to. ●**convocation** *nf* (*lettre*) (written) notice to attend.

convulsion [kɔ̃vylsjɔ̃] *nf* convulsion.

coopérer [kɔɔpere] *vi* to co-operate (**à** in, **avec** with). ●**coopération** *nf* co-operation.

coordonnées *nfpl* [kɔɔrdɔne] (*adresse, téléphone*) Fam contact address and phone number, particulars.

copain [kɔpɛ̃] *nm* Fam (*camarade*) pal; (*petit ami*) boyfriend; **être c. avec** to be pals with.

copeau, -x [kɔpo] *nm* (*de bois*) shaving.

copie [kɔpi] *nf* copy; (*devoir, examen*) paper. ●**copier** *vti* to copy; *Scol* to copy, crib (*sur* from). ●**copieur, -euse** *nmf* (*élève etc*) copycat.

copieux, -euse [kɔpjø, -øz] *a* plentiful, copious.

copine [kɔpin] *nf Fam* (*camarade*) pal; (*petite amie*) girlfriend; **être c. avec** to be pals with.

copropriété [kɔprɔprijete] *nf* joint ownership; (**immeuble en**) **c.** block of flats in joint ownership, *Am* condominium.

coq [kɔk] *nm* rooster, cock; **passer du c. à l'âne** to jump from one subject to another.

coque [kɔk] *nf* **1** (*de noix*) shell; (*fruit de mer*) cockle; **œuf à la c.** boiled egg. **2** (*de navire*) hull.

coquelicot [kɔkliko] *nm* poppy.

coqueluche [kɔklyʃ] *nf Méd* whooping cough.

coquet, -ette [kɔke, -et] *a* (*chic*) smart; (*joli*) pretty; (*somme*) *Fam* tidy. ●**coquetterie** *nf* smartness; (*goût de la toilette*) dress sense.

coquetier [kɔktje] *nm* egg cup.

coquille [kɔkij] *nf* shell; **c. Saint-Jacques** scallop. ●**coquillage** *nm* shellfish *inv*; (*coquille*) shell.

coquin, -ine [kɔkɛ̃, -in] *nmf* rascal ‖ *a* mischievous; (*histoire*) naughty.

cor [kɔr] *nm Mus* horn; **c. (au pied)** corn; **réclamer** *ou* **demander à c. et à cri** to clamour for.

corail, -aux [kɔraj, -o] *nm* coral.

Coran [kɔrã] *nm* **le C.** the Koran.

corbeau, -x [kɔrbo] *nm* crow; (**grand**) **c.** raven.

corbeille [kɔrbɛj] *nf* basket; **c. à papier** waste paper basket.

corbillard [kɔrbijar] *nm* hearse.

cordage [kɔrdaʒ] *nm Nau* rope.

corde [kɔrd] *nf* rope; (*plus mince*) cord; (*de raquette, violon etc*) string; **instrument à cordes** *Mus* string instrument; **c. à linge** (washing- *ou* clothes-)line; **c. à sauter** skipping rope, *Am* jump rope; **usé jusqu'à la c.** threadbare;

cordes vocales vocal cords; **pas dans mes cordes** *Fam* not my line. ●**cordée** *nf* roped (climbing) party. ●**cordelette** *nf* (fine) cord.

cordial, -aux [kɔrdjal, -o] *a* warm. ●**cordialité** *nf* warmth.

cordon [kɔrdɔ̃] *nm* (*de tablier, sac etc*) string; (*de rideau*) cord, rope; (*de soulier*) lace; (*d'agents de police*) cordon; (*ombilical*) cord. ●**c.-bleu** *nm* (*pl* **cordons-bleus**) first-class cook.

cordonnier [kɔrdɔnje] *nm* shoe repairer. ●**cordonnerie** *nf* shoe repair *ou* repairer's shop.

Corée [kɔre] *nf* Korea. ●**coréen, -enne** *a* & *nmf* Korean.

coriace [kɔrjas] *a* (*aliment, personne*) tough.

corne [kɔrn] *nf* (*de chèvre etc*) horn; (*de cerf*) antler; (*matière, instrument*) horn; (*angle, pli*) corner.

cornée [kɔrne] *nf Anat* cornea.

corneille [kɔrnɛj] *nf* crow.

cornemuse [kɔrnəmyz] *nf* bagpipes.

corner [kɔrne] **1** *vt* (*page*) to turn down the corner of, dog-ear. **2** [kɔrner] *nm Fb* corner.

cornet [kɔrne] *nm* (*de glace*) cornet, cone; **c. (de papier)** (paper) cone.

corniche [kɔrniʃ] *nf* (*route*) cliff road; *Archit* cornice.

cornichon [kɔrniʃɔ̃] *nm* **1** (*concombre*) gherkin. **2** (*niais*) *Fam* clot, twit.

corps [kɔr] *nm* body; *Mil Pol* corps; **c. électoral** electorate; **c. enseignant** teaching profession; **garde du c.** bodyguard; **un c. de bâtiment** a main building; **c. et âme** body and soul; **lutter c. à c.** to fight hand-to-hand; **à son c. défendant** under protest; **prendre c.** (*projet*) to take shape; **faire c. avec** to form a part of, belong with. ●**corporel, -elle** *a* bodily; (*châtiment*) corporal.

corpulent [kɔrpylã] *a* stout, corpulent. ●**corpulence** *nf* stoutness, corpulence.

correct [kɔrekt] *a* (*exact*) correct; (*bienséant, honnête*) proper, correct; (*passable*) adequate. ●**—ement** [-əmã] *adv*

correctly; properly; adequately. ● **correcteur, -trice 1** *a* **verres correcteurs** corrective lenses. **2** *nmf Scol* examiner.
correction [kɔrɛksjɔ̃] *nf* correction; (*punition*) thrashing; (*exactitude, bienséance*) correctness; **la c. de** (*devoirs, examen*) the marking of. ● **correctionnel** *am* **tribunal c.** magistrates' court, *Am* police court.
correspondance [kɔrɛspɔ̃dɑ̃s] *nf* correspondence; (*de train, d'autocar*) connection, *Am* transfer.
correspond/re [kɔrɛspɔ̃dr] **1** *vi* (*s'accorder*) to correspond (**à** to, with). **2** *vi* (*écrire*) to correspond (**avec** with). ● **—ant, -ante** *a* corresponding ‖ *nmf* correspondent; (*d'un élève etc*) pen friend, *Am* pen pal; *Tél* caller.
corrida [kɔrida] *nf* bullfight.
corridor [kɔridɔr] *nm* corridor.
corrig/er [kɔriʒe] *vt* (*texte, injustice etc*) to correct; (*devoir*) to mark, correct; (*châtier*) to beat, punish; **c. qn de** (*défaut*) to cure s.o. of; **se c. de** to cure oneself of. ● **—é** *nm Scol* model (answer), correct version.
corromp/re* [kɔrɔ̃pr] *vt* to corrupt; (*soudoyer*) to bribe. ● **—u** *a* corrupt. ● **corruption** *nf* (*de juge etc*) bribery; (*vice*) corruption.
corsage [kɔrsaʒ] *nm* (*chemisier*) blouse; (*de robe*) bodice.
Corse [kɔrs] *nf* Corsica. ● **corse** *a* & *nmf* Corsican.
corser (se) [səkɔrse] *vpr* **l'affaire se corse** things are hotting up. ● **corsé** *a* (*café*) strong; (*sauce, histoire*) spicy.
cortège [kɔrtɛʒ] *nm* (*défilé*) procession; (*suite*) retinue; **c. officiel** (*automobiles*) motorcade.
corvée [kɔrve] *nf* chore, drudgery.
cosmos [kɔsmɔs] *nm* (*univers*) cosmos; (*espace*) outer space. ● **cosmonaute** *nmf* cosmonaut.
cosse [kɔs] *nf* (*de pois etc*) pod.
cossu [kɔsy] *a* (*maison etc*) opulent.
costaud [kɔsto] *a Fam* brawny ‖ *nm Fam* strong man.

costume [kɔstym] *nm* (*déguisement*) costume; (*complet*) suit. ● **se costumer** *vpr* **se c. en** to dress up as; **bal costumé** fancy-dress ball, costume ball.
cote [kɔt] *nf* (*évaluation, popularité*) rating; (*des valeurs boursières*) quotation; **c. d'alerte** danger level.
côte [kot] *nf* **1** *Anat* rib; (*de mouton*) chop; (*de veau*) cutlet; **c. à c.** side by side. **2** (*montée*) hill; (*versant*) hillside. **3** (*littoral*) coast.
côté [kote] *nm* side; (*direction*) way; **de l'autre c.** on the other side (**de** of); (*direction*) the other way; **de ce c.** (*passer*) this way; **du c. de** (*vers, près de*) towards; **de c.** (*se jeter, regarder, mettre de l'argent etc*) to one side; **à c.** nearby; (*pièce*) in the other room; (*maison*) next door; **la maison (d')à c.** the house next door; **à c. de** next to, beside; (*comparaison*) compared to; **venir de tous côtés** to come from all directions; **d'un c.** on the one hand; **de mon c.** for my part; **à mes côtés** by my side; **laisser de c.** (*travail*) to neglect; **le bon c.** (*d'une affaire*) the bright side (**de** of).
coteau, -x [kɔto] *nm* (small) hill; (*versant*) hillside.
côtelé [kotle] *am* **velours c.** cord(uroy).
côtelette [kotlɛt] *nf* (*d'agneau, de porc*) chop; (*de veau*) cutlet.
côtier, -ière [kotje, -jɛr] *a* coastal.
cotiser [kɔtize] *vi* to contribute (**à** to, **pour** towards); **c. (à)** (*club*) to subscribe (to) ‖ **se c.** *vpr* to club together (**pour acheter** to buy). ● **cotisation** *nf* (*de club*) dues, subscription; (*de retraite etc*) contribution(s).
coton [kɔtɔ̃] *nm* cotton; **c. (hydrophile)** cotton wool, *Am* (absorbent) cotton.
côtoyer [kotwaje] *vt* **c. qn** (*fréquenter*) to rub shoulders with s.o.
cou [ku] *nm* neck; **sauter au c. de qn** to throw one's arms around s.o.; **jusqu'au c.** *Fig* up to one's eyes *ou* ears.
couchage [kuʃaʒ] *nm* **sac de c.** sleeping bag.

couche [kuʃ] *nf* **1** (*épaisseur*) layer; (*de peinture*) coat; **couches sociales** social strata. **2** (*pour bébé*) nappy, *Am* diaper. **3 faire une fausse c.** *Méd* to have a miscarriage.

coucher [kuʃe] *vt* to put to bed; (*héberger*) to put up; (*allonger*) to lay (down *ou* out) ▮ *vi* to sleep (**avec** with) ▮ **se c.** *vpr* to go to bed; (*s'allonger*) to lie flat *ou* down; (*soleil*) to go down ▮ *nm* **c. de soleil** sunset. ● **couchant** *a* (*soleil*) setting. ● **couché** *a* **être c.** to be in bed; (*étendu*) to be lying (down).

couchette [kuʃet] *nf* (*de train*) sleeper, sleeping berth; (*de bateau*) bunk.

coucou [kuku] *nm* (*oiseau*) cuckoo; (*pendule*) cuckoo clock; (*fleur*) cowslip.

coude [kud] *nm* elbow; (*de chemin, rivière*) bend; **se serrer les coudes** to help one another, stick together; **c. à c.** side by side; **coup de c.** nudge; **pousser du c.** to nudge.

coudre² [kudr] *vti* to sew.

couenne [kwan] *nf* (pork) crackling.

couette [kwet] *nf* (*édredon*) duvet, continental quilt.

couffin [kufɛ̃] *nm* (*de bébé*) Moses basket, *Am* bassinet.

couler¹ [kule] *vi* (*eau etc*) to flow; (*robinet, nez, sueur*) to run; (*fuir*) to leak. ● **—ée** *nf* **c. de lave** lava flow.

couler² [kule] *vi* (*bateau, nageur*) to sink; **c. à pic** to sink to the bottom ▮ *vt* to sink.

couleur [kulœr] *nf* colour; (*colorant, paint*); *Cartes* suit; *pl* (*teint*) colour; **c. chair** flesh-coloured; **de c.** (*homme, habit etc*) coloured; **photo/etc en couleurs** colour photo/etc; **téléviseur c.** colour TV set.

couleuvre [kulœvr] *nf* (grass) snake.

coulisses [kulis] *nfpl* **dans les c.** *Th* in the wings, backstage.

coulissant [kulisɑ̃] *a* (*porte etc*) sliding.

couloir [kulwar] *nm* corridor; (*de circulation, d'une piste*) lane; (*dans un bus*) gangway.

coup [ku] *nm* blow, knock; (*léger*) tap, touch; (*choc moral*) blow; (*de fusil etc*) shot; (*d'horloge*) & *Sp* stroke; (*aux échecs etc*) move; (*fois*) *Fam* time; **donner des coups à** to hit; **c. de brosse** brush(-up); **c. de chiffon** wipe (with a rag); **c. de sonnette** ring (on a bell); **c. de dents** bite; **c. de chance** stroke of luck; **c. d'État** coup; *Fam* nasty blow; **mauvais c.** piece of mischief; **c. franc** *Fb* free kick; **tenter le c.** *Fam* to have a go; **réussir son c.** to bring it off; **faire les quatre cents coups** to get into all kinds of mischief; **tenir le c.** to hold out; **avoir/attraper le c.** to have/get the knack; **sous le c. de** (*émotion etc*) under the influence of; **il est dans le c.** *Fam* he's in the know; **après c.** afterwards, after the event; **sur le c. de midi** on the stroke of twelve; **tué sur le c.** killed outright; **à c. sûr** for sure; **c. sur c.** (*à la suite*) one after the other; **tout à c., tout d'un c.** suddenly; **d'un seul c.** in one go; **du premier c.** *Fam* (at the) first go; **du c.** (*de ce fait*) as a result; **pour le c.** this time.

coupable [kupabl] *a* guilty (**de** of); **déclarer c.** *Jur* to convict, find guilty ▮ *nmf* guilty person, culprit.

coupe [kup] *nf* **1** (*trophée*) cup; (*à fruits*) dish; (*à boire*) goblet, glass. **2** (*de vêtement etc*) cut; **c. de cheveux** haircut.

coupe-ongles [kupɔ̃gl] *nm inv* (nail) clippers. ● **c.-papier** *nm inv* paper knife. ● **c.-vent** *nm* windcheater, *Am* windbreaker.

couper [kupe] *vt* to cut; (*arbre*) to cut down; (*téléphone, vivres etc*) to cut off; (*courant*) to switch off; (*faim, souffle etc*) to take away; (*vin*) to water down; (*morceler*) to cut up; (*croiser*) to cut across; **c. la parole à qn** to cut s.o. short. ▮ *vi* to cut; **ne coupez pas!** *Tél* hold the line!

▮ **se couper** *vpr* (*routes*) to intersect; **se c. au doigt** to cut one's finger. ● **coupant** *a* sharp.

couple [kupl] *nm* couple.

couplet [kuplɛ] *nm* verse.

coupole [kupɔl] *nf* dome.

coupon [kupɔ̃] *nm* (*tissu*) remnant, oddment; (*ticket, titre*) coupon; **c. réponse** reply coupon.

coupure [kupyr] *nf* cut; (*de journal*) cutting, *Am* clipping; (*billet*) banknote, *Am* bill; **c. d'électricité** blackout, power cut.

cour [kur] *nf* 1 court(yard); **c. (de récréation)** *Scol* playground, *Am* school yard. 2 (*de roi*) & *Jur* court. 3 (*de femme, d'homme*) courtship; **faire la c. à qn** to court s.o.

courage [kuraʒ] *nm* courage; **perdre c.** to lose heart *ou* courage; **s'armer de c.** to pluck up courage; **bon c.!** good luck! ● **courageux, -euse** *a* courageous.

couramment [kuramɑ̃] *adv* (*parler*) fluently; (*souvent*) frequently.

courant [kurɑ̃] 1 *a* (*fréquent*) common; (*modèle, taille*) standard; (*compte, langage*) current; (*affaires*) routine; **eau courante** running water. 2 *nm* (*de l'eau, électrique*) current; **c. d'air** draught, *Am* draft; **dans le c. de** (*mois etc*) during the course of; **être/mettre au c.** to know/tell (**de** about).

courbature [kurbatyr] *nf* (*muscular*) ache. ● **courbaturé** *a* aching (all over).

courbe [kurb] *a* curved ∥ *nf* curve. ● **courber** *vti* to bend ∥ **se c.** *vpr* to bend (over).

courgette [kurʒɛt] *nf* courgette, *Am* zucchini.

courir* [kurir] *vi* to run; (*se hâter*) to rush; (*à bicyclette, en auto*) to race; **en courant** (*vite*) in a rush; **le bruit court que...** there's a rumour going around that...; **faire c.** (*nouvelle*) to spread. ∥ *vt* (*risque*) to run; (*épreuve sportive*) to run (in); (*danger*) to face; (*magasins, cafés*) to go round; (*filles*) to run after. ● **coureur** *nm Sp etc* runner; (*cycliste*) cyclist; (*automobile*) racing driver.

couronne [kurɔn] *nf* (*de roi, dent*) crown; (*pour enterrement*) wreath. ● **couronner** (*roi etc*) *vt* to crown. ● **couronnement** *nm* (*de roi etc*) coronation.

courrier [kurje] *nm* post, mail; **par retour du c.** by return of post, *Am* by return mail.

courroie [kurwa] *nf* (*attache*) strap; (*de transmission*) *Tech* belt.

cours [kur] *nm* 1 (*de maladie, rivière, astre, pensées etc*) course; (*d'une monnaie etc*) rate; **c. d'eau** river, stream; **suivre son c.** (*déroulement*) to follow its course; **en c.** (*travail*) in progress; (*année*) current; (*affaires*) outstanding; **en c. de route** on the way; **au c. de** during.

2 (*leçon*) class; (*série de leçons*) course; (*conférence*) lecture; **c. magistral** lecture; **faire c.** (*professeur*) to teach.

course[1] [kurs] *nf* (*action*) run(ning); (*épreuve de vitesse*) & *Fig* race; *pl* (*de chevaux*) races; **cheval de c.** racehorse; **voiture de c.** racing car.

course[2] [kurs] *nf* (*commission*) errand, *pl* (*achats*) shopping; **faire une c.** to run an errand; **faire les courses** to do the shopping.

coursier, -ière [kursje, -jɛr] *nmf* messenger.

court [kur] 1 *a* short ∥ *adv* (*couper, s'arrêter*) short; **tout c.** quite simply; **à c. de** (*argent etc*) short of; **pris de c.** caught unawares. 2 *nm Tennis* court. ● **c.-circuit** *nm* (*pl* **courts-circuits**) *Él* short circuit. ● **c.-circuiter** *vt* to short-circuit.

courtois [kurtwa] *a* courteous. ● **courtoisie** *nf* courtesy.

couru [kury] *a* **c'est c.** (*d'avance*) *Fam* it's a sure thing.

couscous [kuskus] *nm Culin* couscous.

cousin, -ine [kuzɛ̃, -in] *nmf* cousin.

coussin [kusɛ̃] *nm* cushion.

cousu [kuzy] *a* sewn; **c. main** handsewn.

coût [ku] *nm* cost. ● **coûter** *vti* to cost; **ça coûte combien?** how much is it?, how much does it cost?; **coûte que coûte** at all costs; **c. les yeux de la tête** to cost the earth. ● **coûtant** *am* **prix c.** cost price.

coûteux, -euse [kutø, -øz] *a* costly,

expensive.

coûteau, -x [kuto] *nm* knife; **coup de c.** stab; **retourner le c. dans la plaie** *Fig* to rub it in.

coutume [kutym] *nf* custom; **avoir c. de faire** to be accustomed to doing; **comme de c.** as usual.

couture [kutyr] *nf* sewing, needlework; (*métier*) dressmaking; (*raccord*) seam; **maison de c.** fashion house. ● **couturier** *nm* fashion designer. ● **couturière** *nf* dressmaker.

couvent [kuvã] *nm* (*pour religieuses*) convent; (*pour moines*) monastery.

couv/er [kuve] *vt* (*œufs*) to sit on, hatch; (*rhume etc*) to be getting; **c. des yeux** to look at enviously ‖ *vi* (*poule*) to brood; (*feu*) to smoulder; (*mal, complot*) to be brewing. ● **—ée** *nf* (*oiseaux*) brood. ● **couveuse** *nf* (*pour nouveaux-nés, œufs*) incubator.

couvercle [kuverkl] *nm* lid, cover.

couvert [kuver] **1** *nm* (*cuillère, fourchette, couteau*) (set of) cutlery; **mettre le c.** to set *ou* lay the table; **table de cinq couverts** table set *ou* laid for five. **2** *nm* **se mettre à c.** to take cover. **3** *a* covered (**de** with, in); (*ciel*) overcast.

couverture [kuvertyr] *nf* (*de lit*) blanket; (*de livre etc*) cover; **c. chauffante** electric blanket.

couvre-feu [kuvrəfø] *nm* (*pl* **-x**) curfew. ● **c.-lit** *nm* bedspread. ● **c.-pied** *nm* quilt.

couvrir* [kuvrir] *vt* to cover (**de** with); (*voix*) to drown ‖ **se c.** *vpr* (*s'habiller*) to wrap up, cover up; (*se coiffer*) to cover one's head; (*ciel*) to cloud over. ● **couvreur** *nm* roofer.

cow-boy [kɔbɔj] *nm* cowboy.

crabe [krab] *nm* crab.

cracher [kraʃe] *vi* to spit ‖ *vt* to spit (out). ● **crachat** *nm* spit, spittle.

crack [krak] *nm* *Fam* ace, wizard, real champ.

craie [kre] *nf* chalk.

craindre* [krɛ̃dr] *vt* (*personne, mort, douleur etc*) to be afraid of, fear; (*chaleur, froid etc*) to be sensitive to;

c. de faire to be afraid of doing; **je crains qu'elle ne vienne** I'm afraid *ou* I fear (that) she might come; **c. pour qch** to fear for sth; **ne craignez rien** don't be afraid, have no fear.

crainte [krɛ̃t] *nf* fear; **de c. de faire** for fear of doing; **de c. que** (+ *sub*) for fear that. ● **craintif, -ive** *a* timid.

cramoisi [kramwazi] *a* crimson.

crampe [krãp] *nf* *Méd* cramp.

cramponner (se) [səkrãpɔne] *vpr* **se c. à** to hold on to, cling to.

crampons [krãpɔ̃] *nmpl* (*de chaussures*) studs.

cran [krã] *nm* **1** (*entaille*) notch; (*de ceinture*) hole; **c. d'arrêt** catch; **couteau à c. d'arrêt** flick-knife, *Am* switchblade; **c. de sûreté** safety catch. **2** (*audace*) *Fam* pluck, guts.

crâne [kran] *nm* skull; (*tête*) *Fam* head. ● **crânienne** *af* **boîte c.** skull, cranium.

crapaud [krapo] *nm* toad.

crapule [krapyl] *nf* villain, scoundrel.

craqueler [krakle] *vt*, **se c.** *vpr* to crack.

craqu/er [krake] *vi* (*branche*) to snap; (*bois sec*) to crack; (*sous la dent*) to crunch; (*se déchirer*) to split, rip; (*personne*) to break down, reach breaking point. ● **—ement** *nm* snapping *ou* cracking (sound).

crasse [kras] *nf* filth ● **crasseux, -euse** *a* filthy.

cratère [krater] *nm* crater.

cravache [kravaʃ] *nf* horsewhip, riding crop.

cravate [kravat] *nf* (*autour du cou*) tie.

crawl [krol] *nm* (*nage*) crawl.

crayon [krɛjɔ̃] *nm* (*en bois*) pencil; **c. de couleur** coloured pencil; (*en cire*) crayon; **c. à bille** ballpoint (pen). ● **crayonner** *vt* to pencil.

créateur, -trice [kreatœr, -tris] *nmf* creator. ● **créatif, -ive** *a* creative. ● **création** *nf* creation. ● **créativité** *nf* creativity.

créature [kreatyr] *nf* (*être*) creature.

crèche [krɛʃ] *nf* (*de Noël*) manger, crib; (*pour bébé*) (day) nursery, crèche.

crédit [kredi] *nm* (*influence*) & *Fin* credit;

pl (*sommes*) funds; **à c.** (*acheter*) on credit, on hire purchase; **faire c.** (*prêter*) to give credit (à to). ●**créditeur, -euse** *a* **compte c.** account in credit; **solde c.** credit balance.

créer [kree] *vt* to create.

crémaillère [kremajer] *nf* **pendre la c.** to have a house-warming (party).

crématorium [krematɔrjɔm] *nm* crematorium, *Am* crematory.

crème [krɛm] *nf* cream; (*dessert*) cream dessert; **café c.** white coffee, coffee with cream *ou* milk; **c. Chantilly** whipped cream; **c. glacée** ice cream; **c. à raser** shaving cream; **c. anglaise** custard *a inv* cream(-coloured). ●**crémerie** *nf* (*magasin*) dairy (shop). ●**crémeux, -euse** *a* creamy. ●**crémier, -ière** *nmf* dairyman, dairywoman.

créneau, -x [kreno] *nm Hist* crenellation; *Com* gap; *TV Rad* slot; **faire un c.** *Aut* to park between two vehicles.

créole [kreɔl] *nmf* Creole **‖** *nm Ling* Creole.

crêpe [krɛp] **1** *nf Culin* pancake. **2** *nm* (*tissu*) crepe; (*caoutchouc*) crepe (rubber). ●**crêperie** *nf* pancake bar.

crépiter [krepite] *vi* to crackle.

crépu [krepy] *a* (*cheveux, personne*) frizzy.

crépuscule [krepyskyl] *nm* twilight, dusk.

cresson [krɛsɔ̃] *nm* (water)cress.

crête [krɛt] *nf* (*de montagne, d'oiseau*) crest; **c. de coq** cockscomb.

Crète [krɛt] *nf* Crete.

crétin, -ine [kretɛ̃, -in] *nmf* cretin, idiot.

creuser [krøze] **1** *vt* (*terre, sol*) to dig (a hole *ou* holes in); (*trou, puits*) to dig; (*évider*) to hollow out); **c. l'estomac** to whet the appetite. **2 se creuser** *vpr* (*joues etc*) to become hollow; **se c. la tête** *ou* **la cervelle** to rack one's brains.

creux, -euse [krø, -øz] *a* (*tube, joues, paroles etc*) hollow; (*estomac*) empty; (*sans activité*) slack; **assiette creuse** soup plate **‖** *nm* hollow; (*de l'estomac*) pit; (*moment*) slack period.

crevaison [krəvezɔ̃] *nf* (*de pneu*) puncture, flat.

crevasse [krəvas] *nf* (*trou*) crevice, crack; (*de glacier*) crevasse.

crever [krəve] *vi* (*bulle, pneu etc*) to burst; (*mourir*) *Fam* to die; **c. de faim** *Fam* to be starving **‖** *vt* to burst; (*œil*) to put *ou* knock out; **c. qn** *Fam* to wear s.o. out; **ça (vous) crève les yeux** *Fam* it's staring you in the face. ●**crevant** *a* (*fatigant*) *Fam* exhausting. ●**crevé** *a* (*fatigué*) *Fam* worn out; (*mort*) *Fam* dead.

crevette [krəvet] *nf* (*grise*) shrimp; (*rose*) prawn.

cri [kri] *nm* (*de joie, surprise*) cry, shout; (*de peur*) scream; (*de douleur, d'alarme*) cry; (*appel*) call, cry.

criard [krijar] *a* (*son*) screeching; (*couleur*) gaudy, showy.

criblé [krible] *a* **c. de** (*balles, dettes etc*) riddled with.

cric [krik] *nm Aut* jack.

crier [krije] *vi* to shout (out), cry (out); (*de peur*) to scream; (*oiseau*) to chirp; **c. après qn** *Fam* to shout at s.o. **‖** *vt* (*injure, ordre*) to shout (out); (*son innocence etc*) to proclaim.

crime [krim] *nm* crime; (*assassinat*) murder. ●**criminalité** *nf* crime (in general). ●**criminel, -elle** *a* criminal **‖** *nmf* criminal; (*assassin*) murderer.

crinière [krinjer] *nf* mane.

crique [krik] *nf* creek, cove.

criquet [krike] *nm* locust.

crise [kriz] *nf* crisis; (*accès*) attack; (*de colère etc*) fit; (*pénurie*) shortage; **c. de conscience** (moral) dilemma.

crisp/er [krispe] *vt* (*visage*) to make tense; (*poing*) to clench; (*muscle*) to tense; **c. qn** *Fam* to aggravate s.o. ●**—ant** *a* aggravating. ●**—é** *a* (*personne*) tense.

crisser [krise] *vi* (*pneu, roue*) to screech; (*neige*) to crunch.

cristal, -aux [kristal, -o] *nm* crystal; (*objets*) crystal(ware).

critère [kriter] *nm* criterion.

critiquable [kritikabl] *a* open to criticism.

critique [kritik] *a* critical ‖ *nf* (*reproche*) criticism; (*analyse de film, livre etc*) review; (*de texte*) critique; **faire la c. de** (*film etc*) to review ‖ *nm* critic. ● **critiquer** *vt* to criticize.

croasser [krɔase] *vi* (*corbeau*) to caw.

Croatie [krɔasi] *nf* Croatia.

croc [kro] *nm* (*dent*) fang.

croc-en-jambe [krɔkɑ̃ʒɑ̃b] *nm* (*pl crocs-en-jambe*) = **croche-pied**.

croche-pied [krɔʃpje] *nm* **faire un c.-pied à qn** to trip s.o. up.

crochet [krɔʃe] *nm* (*pour accrocher*) & *Boxe* hook; (*aiguille*) crochet hook; (*travail*) crochet; *Typ* (square) bracket; **faire qch au c.** to crochet sth; **faire un c.** (*personne*) to make a detour *ou* side trip.

crochu [krɔʃy] *a* (*nez*) hooked.

crocodile [krɔkɔdil] *nm* crocodile.

crocus [krɔkys] *nm Bot* crocus.

croire* [krwar] *vt* to believe; (*estimer*) to think, believe (**que** that); **j'ai cru la voir** I thought I saw her; **je crois que oui** I think *ou* believe so; **je n'en crois pas mes yeux** I can't believe my eyes; **il se croit malin/quelque chose** he thinks he's smart/quite something ‖ *vi* to believe (**à, en** in).

croiser [krwaze] *vt* (*jambes, ligne etc*) to cross; (*bras*) to fold, cross; **c. qn** to pass *ou* meet s.o.

‖ **se croiser** *vpr* (*voitures etc*) to pass *ou* meet (each other); (*routes*) to cross, intersect; (*lettres*) to cross in the post *ou* mail. ● **croisé** *a* (*bras*) folded, crossed; (*veston*) double-breasted; **mots croisés** crossword. ● **croisement** *nm* (*de routes*) crossroads, intersection; (*action*) crossing; (*de véhicules*) passing.

croisière [krwazjer] *nf* cruise.

croître* [krwatr] *vi* (*plante etc*) to grow; (*augmenter*) to grow, increase. ● **croissant 1** *nm* crescent; (*pâtisserie*) croissant. **2** *a* (*nombre etc*) growing. ● **croissance** *nf* growth.

croix [krwa] *nf* cross.

croque-monsieur [krɔkmɔsjø] *nm inv* toasted cheese and ham sandwich. ● **c.-mort** *nm Fam* undertaker's assistant.

croqu/er [krɔke] *vt* (*manger*) to crunch ‖ *vi* (*fruit etc*) to be crunchy. ● **—ant** *a* (*biscuit etc*) crunchy. ● **croquette** *nf Culin* croquette.

croquis [krɔki] *nm* sketch.

crosse [krɔs] *nf* (*de fusil*) butt; (*de hockey*) stick; (*d'évêque*) crook.

crotte [krɔt] *nf* (*de lapin etc*) droppings, mess. ● **crottin** *nm* (*horse*) dung.

crouler [krule] *vi* **c. sous une charge** (*porteur*) to totter beneath a burden.

croupe [krup] *nf* (*de cheval*) rump. ● **croupion** *nm* (*de poulet*) parson's nose, *Am* pope's nose.

croupier [krupje] *nm* (*au casino*) croupier.

croupir [krupir] *vi* (*eau*) to stagnate, become foul.

croustill/er [krustije] *vi* to be crusty; to be crunchy. ● **—ant** *a* (*pain*) crusty; (*biscuit*) crunchy.

croûte [krut] *nf* (*de pain etc*) crust; (*de fromage*) rind; (*de plaie*) scab; **casser la c.** *Fam* to have a snack. ● **croûton** *nm* crust (*at end of loaf*); *pl* (*avec soupe*) croûtons.

croyable [krwajabl] *a* credible, believable. ● **croyance** *nf* belief (**à, en** in). ● **croyant, -ante** *a* **être c.** to be a believer ‖ *nmf* believer.

CRS [seers] *nmpl abrév* (*Compagnies républicaines de sécurité*) riot police, State security police.

cru¹ [kry] *pp de* **croire**.

cru² [kry] **1** *a* (*aliment etc*) raw; (*propos*) crude. **2** *nm* (*vignoble*) vineyard; **un grand c.** (*vin*) a vintage wine.

cruauté [kryote] *nf* cruelty (**envers** to).

cruche [kryʃ] *nf* pitcher, jug.

crucial, -aux [krysjal, -o] *a* crucial.

crucifier [krysifje] *vt* to crucify. ● **crucifix** [krysifi] *nm* crucifix. ● **crucifixion** *nf* crucifixion.

crudités [krydite] *nfpl Culin* assorted

raw vegetables.

crue [kry] *nf* (*de cours d'eau*) swelling, flood; **en c.** in spate.

cruel, -elle [kryɛl] *a* cruel (**envers, avec** to).

crustacés [krystase] *nmpl* shellfish.

crypte [kript] *nf* crypt.

Cuba [kyba] *nm* Cuba. ● **cubain, -aine** *a* & *nmf* Cuban.

cube [kyb] *nm* cube; *pl* (*jeu*) building blocks ‖ *a* (*mètre etc*) cubic.

cueillir* [kœjir] *vt* to pick, gather. ● **cueillette** *nf* picking, gathering; (*fruits cueillis*) harvest.

cuiller, cuillère [kɥijɛr] *nf* spoon; **petite c., c. à café** teaspoon; **c. à soupe** soup spoon, table spoon. ● **cuillerée** *nf* spoonful; **c. à café** teaspoonful; **c. à soupe** tablespoonful.

cuir [kɥir] *nm* leather; (*peau épaisse d'un animal vivant*) hide; **c. chevelu** scalp.

cuire* [kɥir] *vt* to cook; (*à l'eau*) to boil; **c. (au four)** to bake; (*viande*) to roast ‖ *vi* to cook; to boil; to bake; to roast; **faire c.** to cook.

cuisant [kɥizɑ̃] *a* (*affront, blessure etc*) stinging.

cuisine [kɥizin] *nf* (*pièce*) kitchen; (*art*) cookery, cooking; (*aliments, préparation*) cooking; **faire la c.** to cook, do the cooking; **livre de c.** cook(ery) book; **haute c.** high-class cooking. ● **cuisiner** *vti* to cook. ● **cuisinier, -ière** *nmf* cook. ● **cuisinière** (*appareil*) cooker, stove, *Am* range.

cuisse [kɥis] *nf* thigh; (*de poulet, mouton*) leg.

cuisson [kɥisɔ̃] *nm* cooking.

cuit [kɥi] *pp de* **cuire** ‖ *a* cooked; **bien c.** well done *ou* cooked.

cuivre [kɥivr] *nm* (*rouge*) copper; (*jaune*) brass.

cul [ky] *nm* (*derrière*) *Fam* backside; (*de bouteille etc*) bottom. ● **c.-de-sac** *nm* (*pl* **culs-de-sac**) dead end, cul-de-sac.

culbute [kylbyt] *nf* (*saut*) sommersault; (*chute*) (backward) tumble; **faire une c.** to sommersault; to tumble. ● **culbuter**

vt (*personne, chaise*) to knock over.

culminant [kylminɑ̃] **a point c.** (*de réussite, montagne etc*) peak.

culot [kylo] *nm* (*aplomb*) *Fam* nerve, cheek. ● **culotté** a **être c.** *Fam* to have plenty of nerve *ou* cheek.

culotte [kylɔt] *nf Sp* (pair of) shorts; (*de femme*) (pair of) knickers *ou Am* panties; **culottes (courtes)** (*de jeune garçon*) short trousers *ou Am* pants; **c. de cheval** riding breeches.

culpabilité [kylpabilite] *nf* guilt.

culte [kylt] *nm* (*de dieu*) worship; (*religion*) form of worship, religion; (*service protestant*) service; (*admiration*) *Fig* cult.

cultiver [kyltive] *vt* (*terre*) to farm, cultivate; (*plantes*) to grow ‖ **se c.** *vpr* to improve one's mind. ● **cultivé** *a* (*esprit, personne*) cultured, cultivated. ● **cultivateur, -trice** *nmf* farmer.

culture [kyltyr] *nf* **1** (*action, agriculture*) farming; (*de légumes*) growing; *pl* (*terres*) fields (under cultivation); (*plantes*) crops. **2** (*éducation, civilisation*) culture; **c. générale** general knowledge. ● **culturel, -elle** *a* cultural.

cumuler [kymyle] *vt* **c. deux fonctions** to hold two offices (at the same time).

cupide [kypid] *a* avaricious. ● **cupidité** *nf* avarice.

curable [kyrabl] *a* curable.

cure [kyr] *nf* **1** (course of) treatment, cure. **2** (*résidence*) presbytery. ● **curé** *nm* (parish) priest.

curer [kyre] *vt* to clean out; **se c. le nez/ les dents** to pick one's nose/teeth. ● **cure-dent** *nm* toothpick. ● **cure-ongles** *nm inv* nail cleaner. ● **cure-pipe** *nm* pipe cleaner.

curieux, -euse [kyrjø, -øz] *a* (*bizarre*) curious; (*indiscret*) inquisitive, curious (**de** about); **c. de savoir** curious to know ‖ *nmf* inquisitive person; (*badaud*) onlooker. ● **curiosité** *nf* (*de personne, forme etc*) curiosity; (*chose*) curiosity; (*spectacle*) unusual sight.

curriculum (vitæ) [kyrikylɔm(vite)] *nm*

inv curriculum (vitae), *Am* résumé.
curseur [kyrsœr] *nm* (*d'un ordinateur*) cursor.
cuve [kyv] *nf* vat; (*réservoir*) & *Phot* tank. ●**cuvée** *nf* (*récolte de vin*) vintage. ●**cuvette** *nf* (*récipient*) & *Géog* basin, bowl; (*des toilettes*) bowl, pan.
CV [seve] *nm abrév* (*curriculum vitae*) CV, *Am* résumé.
cyanure [sjanyr] *nm* cyanide.
cycle [sikl] *nm* **1** (*série, révolution*) cycle. **2** (*bicyclette*) cycle. ●**cyclable** *a* piste c. cycle path *ou* track. ●**cyclique** *a* cyclic(al).

cyclisme [siklism] *nm Sp* cycling. ●**cycliste** *nmf* cyclist ‖ *a* course c. cycle *ou* bicycle race; **champion c.** cycling champion; **coureur c.** racing cyclist.
cyclomoteur [siklɔmɔtœr] *nm* moped.
cyclone [siklon] *nm* cyclone.
cygne [siɲ] *nm* swan.
cylindre [silɛ̃dr] *nm* cylinder. ●**cylindrée** *nf Aut* (engine) capacity. ●**cylindrique** *a* cylindrical.
cymbale [sɛ̃bal] *nf* cymbal.
cynique [sinik] *a* cynical. ●**cynisme** *nm* cynicism.
cyprès [siprɛ] *nm* (*arbre*) cypress.

D

D, d [de] *nm* D, d.

d' [d] *voir* de[1,2].

d'abord [dabɔr] *adv* (*en premier lieu, au début*) first.

dactylo [daktilo] *nf* (*personne*) typist; (*action*) typing. ● **dactylographie** *nf* typing. ● **dactylographier** *vt* to type.

dada [dada] *nm* (*manie*) hobby horse, pet subject.

dahlia [dalja] *nm* dahlia.

daigner [dɛɲe] *vt* **d. faire** to condescend to do.

daim [dɛ̃] *nm* fallow deer; (*mâle*) buck; (*cuir*) suede.

dalle [dal] *nf* paving stone; (*funèbre*) (flat) gravestone. ● **dallé** *a* (*pièce, cour etc*) paved.

daltonien, -ienne [daltɔnjɛ̃, -jɛn] *a & n* colour-blind (person).

dame [dam] *nf* **1** lady; (*mariée*) married lady. **2** *Échecs Cartes* queen; (*au jeu de dames*) king; (**jeu de**) **dames** draughts, *Am* checkers. ● **damier** *nm* draughtboard, *Am* checkerboard.

damner [dane] *vt* to damn; **faire d.** *Fam* to torment, drive mad.

dandiner (se) [sədɑ̃dine] *vpr* to waddle.

Danemark [danmark] *nm* Denmark. ● **danois, -oise** *a* Danish ▮ *nmf* **Dane** ▮ *nm* (*langue*) Danish.

danger [dɑ̃ʒe] *nm* danger; **en d.** in danger; **mettre en d.** to endanger; **en cas de d.** in an emergency; **en d. de mort** in mortal danger; **'d. de mort'** (*panneau*) 'danger'; **être sans d.** to be safe; **pas de d.!** *Fam* no way! ● **dangereux, -euse** *a* dangerous (**pour** to). ● **dangereusement** *adv* dangerously.

dans [dɑ̃] *prép* **1** in; (*changement de lieu*) into; (*à l'intérieur de*) inside; **d. le jardin** in the garden; **d. la boîte** *ou* inside the box; **mettre d.** to put in(to); **entrer d.** to go in(to); **d. Paris** in Paris (itself); **d. un rayon de** within (a radius of); **marcher d. les rues** to walk through *ou* about the streets.

2 (*provenance*) from, out of; **boire/prendre/etc d.** to drink/take/*etc* from *ou* out of.

3 (*temps futur*) in; **d. deux jours/etc** in two days/*etc*, in two days'/*etc* time.

4 (*quantité approximative*) about; **d. les dix francs/etc** (*quantité*) about ten francs/*etc*.

danse [dɑ̃s] *nf* dance; (*art*) dancing. ● **danser** *vti* to dance. ● **danseur, -euse** *nmf* dancer.

dard [dar] *nm* (*d'insecte*) sting.

date [dat] *nf* date; **de longue d.** (*amitié etc*) of long-standing; **en d. du...** dated the...; **d. d'expiration** expiry *or Am* expiration date; **d. limite** deadline; **d. limite de vente** sell-by date; **d. de naissance** date of birth.

dater [date] *vt* (*lettre etc*) to date ▮ *vi* (*être dépassé*) to date, be dated; **d. de** to date back to, date from; **à d. de** as from.

datte [dat] *nf* (*fruit*) date. ● **dattier** *nm* date palm.

dauphin [dofɛ̃] *nm* dolphin.

davantage [davɑ̃taʒ] *adv* (*quantité*) more; (*temps*) longer; **d. de temps/etc** more time/*etc*; **d. que** more than; longer than.

de[1] [d(ə)] (**d'** before a vowel or mute h; **de** + **le** = **du**, **de** + **les** = **des**) *prép* **1** (*complément d'un nom*) of; **les rayons du soleil** the rays of the sun, the sun's rays; **le livre de Paul** Paul's book; **la ville de Paris** the city of Paris; **un pont de fer** an iron bridge; **une augmentation/diminution de salaire/etc** an increase/decrease in salary/*etc*.

2 (*complément d'un adjectif*) **digne de**

worthy of; **heureux de partir** happy to leave; **content de qch/qn** pleased with sth/s.o.

3 (*complément d'un verbe*) **parler de** to speak of *ou* about; **se souvenir de** to remember; **décider de faire** to decide to do; **traiter qn de lâche** to call s.o. a coward.

4 (*provenance: lieu & temps*) from; **venir/dater de** to come/date from; **mes amis du village** my friends from the village, my village friends.

5 (*agent*) **accompagné de** accompanied by.

6 (*moyen*) **armé de** armed with; **se nourrir de** to live on.

7 (*manière*) **d'une voix douce** in *ou* with a gentle voice.

8 (*cause*) **mourir de faim** to die of hunger; **sauter de joie** to jump for joy.

9 (*temps*) **travailler de nuit** to work by night; **six heures du matin** six o'clock in the morning.

10 (*mesure*) **avoir** *ou* **faire six mètres de haut, être haut de six mètres** to be six metres high; **homme de trente ans** thirty-year-old man; **gagner cent francs de l'heure** to earn a hundred francs an hour.

de² [d(ə)] *art partitif* some; **elle boit du vin** she drinks (some) wine, **il ne boit pas de vin** (*négation*) he doesn't drink (any) wine; **il y a six de tués** (*avec un nombre*) there are six killed.

de³ [d(ə)] *art indéf pl* **de, des** some; **des fleurs** (some) flowers; **de jolies fleurs** (some) pretty flowers; **d'agréables soirées** (some) pleasant evenings.

dé [de] *nm* (*à jouer*) dice; (*à coudre*) thimble; **jouer aux dés** to play dice.

déambuler [deãbyle] *vi* to stroll.

débâcle [debakl] *nf Mil* rout; (*ruine*) downfall.

déball/er [debale] *vt* to unpack; (*étaler*) to display. ●—**age** *nm* unpacking; display.

débandade [debãdad] *nf* (*mad*) rush, stampede.

débarbouiller (se) [sədebarbuje] to wash one's face.

débarcadère [debarkader] *nm* quay, wharf.

débardeur [debardœr] *nm* (*vêtement*) slipover, *Am* (sweater) vest.

débarqu/er [debarke] *vt* (*passagers*) to land; (*marchandises*) to unload ‖ *vi* (*passagers*) to land, disembark; (*être naïf*) *Fam* not to be quite with it; **d. chez qn** *Fam* to turn up suddenly at s.o.'s place. ●—**ement** *nm* landing; (*de marchandises*) unloading; *Mil* landing.

débarras [debara] *nm* lumber room, *Am* storeroom; **bon d.!** *Fam* good riddance! ●**débarrasser** *vt* (*chambre, table etc*) to clear (**de** of); **d. qn de** (*ennemi, soucis etc*) to rid s.o. of; (*manteau etc*) to relieve s.o. of; **se d. de** to get rid of.

débat [deba] *nm* discussion, debate. ●**débattre*** **1** *vt* to discuss; **d. (d')une question** to discuss *ou* debate a question; **prix à d.** price by arrangement. **2 se débattre** *vpr* to struggle *ou* fight (to get free).

débauche [deboʃ] *nf* debauchery. ●**débauché** *a* (*libertin*) debauched.

débaucher [deboʃe] *vt* **d. qn** (*licencier*) to lay s.o. off; (*détourner*) *Fam* to entice s.o. away from his work.

débile [debil] *a* (*esprit, enfant etc*) weak, feeble; *Péj Fam* idiotic.

débit [debi] *nm* **1** (*vente*) turnover, sales; (*de fleuve*) (rate of) flow; (*d'un orateur*) delivery; **d. de boissons** bar, café; **d. de tabac** tobacconist's shop, *Am* tobacco store. **2** (*compte*) debit.

débiter [debite] *vt* **1** (*découper*) to cut up, slice up (**en** into); (*dire*) *Péj* to utter, spout. **2** (*compte*) to debit. ●**débiteur, -trice** *nmf* debtor ‖ **a solde d.** debit balance; **son compte est d.** his account is in debit.

déblayer [debleje] *vt* (*terrain, décombres*) to clear.

débloquer [debloke] **1** *vt* (*mécanisme*) to unjam; (*freins*) to release; (*compte, prix, crédits*) to unfreeze. **2** *vi* (*diva-*

guer) *Fam* to talk nonsense.

déboires [debwar] *nmpl* disappointments.

déboiser [debwaze] *vt* (*terrain*) to clear (of trees).

déboît/er [debwate] **1** *vt* **se d. l'épaule**/*etc* to dislocate one's shoulder/*etc*. **2** *vi Aut* to pull out, change lanes. ● **—ement** *nm Méd* dislocation.

débonnaire [deboner] *a* good-natured.

déborder [deborde] *vi* (*fleuve, liquide*) to overflow; (*en bouillant*) to boil over; **l'eau déborde du vase** the water is running over the top of the vase *ou* is overflowing the vase; **d. de** (*vie, joie etc*) *Fig* to be bubbling over with.

▮ *vt* (*dépasser*) to go *ou* extend beyond; **débordé de travail**/*visites* snowed under with work/visits. ● **débordement** *nm* overflowing; (*de joie, activité*) outburst.

débouché [debuʃe] *nm* (*carrière*) (career) opening *ou* prospect; (*marché pour produit*) outlet.

déboucher [debuʃe] **1** *vt* (*bouteille*) to open, uncork; (*lavabo, tuyau*) to clear, unblock. **2** *vi* (*surgir*) to emerge, come out (**de** from); **d. sur** (*rue*) to lead out onto, lead into.

débourser [deburse] *vt* to pay out.

debout [d(ə)bu] *adv* standing (up); **mettre d.** (*planche etc*) to stand up, put upright; **se mettre d.** to stand *ou* get up; **se tenir** *ou* **rester d.** (*personne*) to stand (up), remain standing (up); **être d.** (*levé*) to be up (and about); **d.!** get up!; **ça ne tient pas d.** (*théorie etc*) that doesn't hold water.

déboutonner [debutɔne] *vt* to unbutton, undo.

débraillé [debraje] *a* (*tenue etc*) slovenly.

débrancher [debrɑ̃ʃe] *vt Él* to unplug, disconnect ▮ *vi* (*se détendre*) *Fam* to unwind, take a break.

débrayer [debreje] *vi* **1** *Aut* to press the clutch. **2** (*se mettre en grève*) to stop work.

débris [debri] *nmpl* fragments, scraps;

(*restes*) remains; (*détritus*) rubbish, *Am* garbage.

débrouiller [debruje] **1** *vt* (*écheveau etc*) to unravel; (*affaire*) to sort out. **2 se débrouiller** *vpr Fam* to manage, get by; **se d. pour faire** to manage to do. ● **débrouillard** *a* smart, resourceful.

débroussailler [debrusaje] *vt* (*chemin*) to clear (of brushwood).

débusquer [debyske] *vt* (*gibier, personne*) to drive out, dislodge.

début [deby] *nm* beginning, start; **au d.** at the beginning; **faire ses débuts** (*sur la scène etc*) to make one's debut. ● **débuter** *vi* to start, begin; (*dans une carrière*) to start out in life; (*sur la scène etc*) to make one's debut. ● **débutant, -ante** *nmf* beginner.

déca [deka] *nm Fam* decaffeinated coffee.

décacheter [dekaʃte] *vt* (*lettre etc*) to open, unseal.

décadence [dekadɑ̃s] *nf* decadence, decay.

décaféiné [dekafeine] *a* decaffeinated.

décalcomanie [dekalkɔmani] *nf* (*image*) transfer, *Am* decal.

décal/er [dekale] *vt* **1** (*dans le temps*) to change the time of (*departure etc*); (*dans l'espace*) to shift *ou* move (slightly) (*chair etc*). **2** (*ôter les cales de*) to unwedge. ● **—age** *nm* (*écart*) gap, discrepancy; **d. horaire** time difference; **souffrir du d. horaire** to suffer from jet lag.

décalquer [dekalke] *vt* (*dessin*) to trace.

décamper [dekɑ̃pe] *vi* to clear off.

décap/er [dekape] *vt* (*métal*) to clean, scrape down; (*surface peinte*) to strip. ● **—ant** *nm* cleaning agent; (*pour enlever la peinture*) paint remover *ou* stripper.

décapiter [dekapite] *vt* to behead, decapitate.

décapotable [dekapɔtabl] *a & nf* (*voiture*) convertible.

décapsul/er [dekapsyle] *vt* **d. une bouteille** to take the top *ou* cap off a bottle. ● **—eur** *nm* bottle-opener.

décarcasser (se) [sədekarkase] *vpr Fam* to flog oneself to death (**pour faire** doing).

décéd/er [desede] *vi* to die. ●**—é** *a* deceased.

déceler [desle] *vt* (*trouver*) to detect.

décembre [desɑ̃br] *nm* December.

décennie [deseni] *nf* decade.

décent [desɑ̃] *a* (*bienséant, acceptable*) decent. ●**décemment** [-amɑ̃] *adv* decently. ●**décence** *nf* decency.

déception [desɛpsjɔ̃] *nf* disappointment. ●**décevoir*** *vt* to disappoint. ●**décevant** *a* disappointing.

décerner [deserne] *vt* (*prix etc*) to award.

décès [desɛ] *nm* death.

déchaîner [deʃene] *vt* (*colère, violence*) to unleash; **d. l'enthousiasme** to set off wild enthusiasm. **‖ se déchaîner** *vpr* (*tempête, rires*) to break out; (*foule*) to run riot; (*personne*) to fly into a rage. ●**déchaîné** *a* (*foule, flots*) wild, raging. ●**déchaînement** [-ɛnmɑ̃] *nm* (*de rires, de haine etc*) outburst; (*de violence*) outbreak; **le d. de la tempête** the raging of the storm.

déchanter [deʃɑ̃te] *vi Fam* to become disillusioned.

décharge [deʃarʒ] *nf* **d. (publique)** (rubbish) dump *ou* tip, *Am* (garbage) dump; **d. (électrique)** (electric) shock; **recevoir une d. (électrique)** to get a shock.

décharger [deʃarʒe] *vt* to unload; (*batterie*) El to discharge; **d. qn de** (*travail etc*) to relieve s.o. of **‖ se d.** *vpr* (*batterie*) to go flat. ●**déchargement** *nm* unloading.

déchausser (se) [sədeʃose] *vpr* to take one's shoes off; (*dent*) to get loose.

dèche [dɛʃ] *nf* **être dans la d.** *Fam* to be flat broke.

déchéance [deʃeɑ̃s] *nf* (*déclin*) decay, decline.

déchet [deʃɛ] *nm* **déchets** (*restes*) (*de viande etc*) scraps; (*industriels etc*) waste (products); (*ordures*) rubbish, *Am* garbage; **il y a du d.** there's some waste.

déchiffrer [deʃifre] *vt* (*message, mauvaise écriture*) to decipher.

déchiqueter [deʃikte] *vt* to tear to shreds.

déchirer [deʃire] *vt* (*page etc*) to tear (up), rip (up); (*vêtement*) to tear, rip; (*ouvrir*) to tear *ou* rip open; (*air*) (*bruit*) to pierce the air; **ce bruit me déchire les oreilles** this noise is ear-splitting. **‖ se déchirer** *vpr* (*robe etc*) to tear, rip; **se d. un muscle** to tear a muscle. ●**déchirant** *a* (*douloureux*) heart-breaking. ●**déchirement** *nm* (*souffrance*) heartbreak. ●**déchirure** *nf* tear, rip; **d. musculaire** torn muscle.

décider [deside] *vt* (*envoi, opération*) to decide on; **d. que** to decide that; **d. de faire** to decide to do; **d. qn (à faire)** to persuade s.o. (to do) **‖** *vi* **d. de** (*destin de qn*) to decide; (*voyage etc*) to decide on **‖ se d.** *vpr* to be decided; **se d. (à faire)** to make up one's mind (to do); **se d. pour qch** to decide on sth *ou* in favour of sth. ●**décidé** *a* (*air, ton*) determined, decided; **c'est d.** it's settled; **être d. à faire** to be determined to do. ●**décidément** *adv* undoubtedly.

décilitre [desilitr] *nm* decilitre.

décimal, -aux [desimal, -o] *a* decimal. ●**décimale** *nf* decimal.

décimètre [desimɛtr] *nm* decimetre; **double d.** ruler.

décisif, -ive [desizif, -iv] *a* decisive. ●**décision** *nf* decision (**de faire** to do); (*fermeté*) determination; **prendre une d.** to make a decision; **avec d.** decisively.

déclarer [deklare] *vt* to declare (**que** that); (*vol, décès etc*) to notify; **d. qn coupable** to convict s.o., find s.o. guilty; **d. la guerre** to declare war (**à** on) **‖ se d.** *vpr* (*incendie, maladie*) to break out; (*s'expliquer*) to declare one's views; **se d. contre** to come out against. ●**déclaration** *nf* declaration; (*de vol etc*) notification; (*commentaire*) statement, comment; **d. d'impôts** tax return.

déclasser [deklase] *vt* (*livres etc*) to put out of order; (*hôtel etc*) to downgrade; **d. qn** *Sp* to relegate s.o. (in the placing).

déclencher [deklɑ̃ʃe] *vt* (*mécanisme*) to set *ou* trigger off, start (off); (*attaque*) to launch; (*provoquer*) *Fig* to trigger off (*crisis, reaction*) **se d.** *vpr* (*alarme etc*) to go off; (*attaque, grève*) to start. ●**déclenchement** *nm* (*d'un appareil*) release.

déclic [deklik] *nm* (*bruit*) click; (*mécanisme*) catch, trigger.

déclin [deklɛ̃] *nm* decline. ●**décliner 1** *vi* (*forces etc*) to decline, wane; (*jour*) to draw to a close. **2** *vt* (*refuser*) to decline.

décod/er [dekode] *vt* (*message*) to decode. ●**—eur** *nm* decoder.

décoiffer [dekwafe] *vt* **d. qn** to mess up s.o.'s hair; **se d.** to mess up one's hair.

décoincer [dekwɛse] *vt* to unjam.

décoller [dekɔle] **1** *vi* (*avion etc*) to take off. **2** *vt* (*timbre etc*) to unstick ‖ **se d.** *vpr* to come unstuck. ●**décollage** *nm* (*d'avion*) takeoff.

décolleté [dekɔlte] *a* (*robe*) low-cut ‖ *nm* (*de robe*) low neckline.

décolorer [dekɔlɔre] *vt* (*tissu*) to fade, discolour; (*cheveux*) to bleach ‖ **se d.** *vpr* (*tissu*) to fade. ●**décoloration** *nf* discolo(u)ration; bleaching.

décombres [dekɔ̃br] *nmpl* rubble, ruins.

décommander [dekɔmɑ̃de] *vt* (*marchandises, invitation*) to cancel; (*invités*) to put off ‖ **se d.** *vpr* to cancel (one's appointment).

décomposer [dekɔ̃poze] *vt* to decompose ‖ **se d.** *vpr* (*pourrir*) to decompose; (*visage*) to become distorted.

décompresser [dekɔ̃prese] *vi* *Psy Fam* to unwind.

décompte [dekɔ̃t] *nm* deduction; (*détail*) breakdown. ●**décompter** *vt* to deduct.

déconcerter [dekɔ̃sɛrte] *vt* to disconcert.

déconfit [dekɔ̃fi] *a* downcast. ●**déconfiture** *nf* (state of) collapse *ou* defeat.

décongeler [dekɔ̃ʒle] *vt* (*faire*) **d.** (*aliment*) to thaw, defrost ‖ *vi* **mettre qch à**

d. to thaw *ou* defrost sth.

déconnecter [dekɔnɛkte] *vt* *Él* & *Fig* to disconnect.

déconner [dekɔne] *vi* (*divaguer*) *Arg* to talk a lot of nonsense.

déconseiller [dekɔ̃seje] *vt* **d. qch à qn** to advise s.o. against sth; **d. à qn de faire** to advise s.o. against doing; **c'est déconseillé** it is not advisable.

déconsidérer [dekɔ̃sidere] *vt* to discredit.

décontenancer [dekɔ̃tnɑ̃se] *vt* to disconcert ‖ **se d.** *vpr* to lose one's composure.

décontracter [dekɔ̃trakte] *vt* (*muscle*) to relax ‖ **se d.** *vpr* to relax.

décor [dekɔr] *nm* *Th Cin etc* scenery, decor; (*paysage*) scenery; (*d'intérieur*) decoration; (*cadre, ambiance*) setting; **les décors** *Th etc* the scenery; **un d.** *Th etc* a set.

décorer [dekɔre] *vt* (*maison, soldat etc*) to decorate (**de** with). ●**décorateur, -trice** *nmf* (interior) decorator; *Th* stage designer. ●**décoratif, -ive** *a* decorative. ●**décoration** *nf* decoration.

décortiquer [dekɔrtike] *vt* (*graine*) to husk; (*homard etc*) to shell.

découdre [dekudr] *vt* to unstitch ‖ *vi* **en d.** (**avec qn**) *Fam* to fight it out (with s.o.) ‖ **se d.** *vpr* to come unstitched.

découp/er [dekupe] *vt* (*viande*) to carve; (*article de journal etc*) to cut out; **se d. sur** to stand out against. ●**—é** *a* (*côte*) jagged. ●**découpage** *nm* carving; cutting out; (*image*) cutout.

décourager [dekuraʒe] *vt* (*dissuader, démoraliser*) to discourage (**de faire** from doing) ‖ **se d.** *vpr* to get discouraged. ●**découragement** *nm* discouragement.

décousu [dekuzy] *a* unstitched; (*propos, idées*) *Fig* disconnected.

découverte [dekuvɛrt] *nf* discovery; **partir à la d.** to explore; **partir** *ou* **aller à la d. de qch** to go in search of sth.

découvrir* [dekuvrir] *vt* (*trésor, terre etc*) to discover; (*secret, vérité etc*) to find out, discover; (*casserole etc*) to take the lid off; (*dénuder*) to uncover, expose; (*voir*) to perceive; **d. que** to discover *ou* find out that ▮ **se d.** *vpr* (*dans son lit*) to push the bedclothes off; (*enlever son chapeau*) to take one's hat off; (*ciel*) to clear (up). ●**découvert 1** *a* (*terrain*) open; (*tête etc*) bare; **à d.** exposed, unprotected; **agir à d.** to act openly. **2** *nm* (*d'un compte*) overdraft.

décrasser [dekrase] *vt* (*nettoyer*) to clean.

décrépit [dekrepi] *a* (*vieillard*) decrepit.

décret [dekrɛ] *nm* decree.

décrier [dekrije] *vt* to run down, disparage.

décrire* [dekrir] *vt* to describe.

décrocher[1] [dekrɔʃe] *vt* (*détacher*) to unhook; (*tableau*) to take down; (*obtenir*) *Fam* to get, land; (*le téléphone*) to pick up the phone ▮ **se d.** *vpr* (*tableau*) to fall down. ●**décroché** *a* (*téléphone*) off the hook.

décrocher[2] [dekrɔʃe] *vi* *Fam* (*abandonner*) to give up; (*perdre le fil*) to be unable to follow, lose track.

décroître* [dekrwatr] *vi* to decrease, decline; (*eaux*) to subside; (*jours*) to draw in.

décrypter [dekripte] *vt* to decipher, decode.

déçu [desy] *pp de* **décevoir** ▮ *a* disappointed.

décupler [dekyple] *vti* to increase tenfold.

dédaigner [dedeɲe] *vt* (*personne, richesse etc*) to scorn, despise; (*repas*) to turn up one's nose at; (*ne pas tenir compte de*) to disregard. ●**dédaigneux, -euse** *a* scornful (**de** of).

dédain [dedɛ̃] *nm* scorn, disdain (**pour, de** for).

dédale [dedal] *nm* maze, labyrinth.

dedans [d(ə)dɑ̃] *adv* inside; **de d.** from (the) inside; **en d.** on the inside; **au-d. (de), au d. (de)** inside; **tomber d.** (*trou*) to fall in (it); **mettre d.** (*tromper*) *Fam* to take in; **je me suis fait rentrer d.**

(*accident de voiture*) *Fam* someone went into me ▮ *nm* **le d.** the inside.

dédicace [dedikas] *nf* dedication, inscription. ●**dédicacer** *vt* (*livre etc*) to inscribe, dedicate (**à** to).

dédier [dedje] *vt* to dedicate.

dédire (se) [sədedir] *vpr* to go back on one's word.

dédommag/er [dedɔmaʒe] *vt* to compensate (**de** for). ●**—ement** *nm* compensation.

dédouaner [dedwane] *vt* (*marchandises*) to clear through customs.

dédoubler [deduble] *vt* (*classe etc*) to split into two; **d. un train** to run an extra train ▮ **se d.** *vpr* to be in two places at once.

déduire* [dedɥir] *vt* (*retirer*) to deduct (**de** from); (*conclure*) to deduce (**de** from). ●**déductible** *a* (*frais*) deductible. ●**déduction** *nf* (*raisonnement*) & *Com* deduction.

déesse [dees] *nf* goddess.

défaillir* [defajir] *vi* (*s'évanouir*) to faint; (*forces, mémoire*) to fail; **sans d.** without flinching. ●**défaillance** *nf* (*évanouissement*) fainting fit; (*faiblesse*) weakness; (*panne*) fault; **une d. cardiaque** heart failure.

défaire* [defɛr] *vt* (*nœud etc*) to undo, untie; (*valises*) to unpack; (*installation*) to take down; (*coiffure*) to mess up ▮ **se d.** *vpr* (*nœud etc*) to come undone *ou* untied; **se d. de** to get rid of. ●**défait** *a* (*lit*) unmade; (*cheveux*) dishevelled, untidy; (*visage*) drawn.

défaite [defɛt] *nf* defeat.

défaut [defo] *nm* (*faiblesse de caractère*) fault, shortcoming; (*de fabrication*) defect; (*de diamant*) flaw; (*désavantage*) drawback; **le d. de la cuirasse** the chink in the armour; **faire d.** to be lacking; **le temps me fait d.** I lack time; **à d. de** for want of; **prendre qn en d.** to catch s.o. out; **ou, à d....** or, failing that....

défavorable [defavɔrabl] *a* unfavourable (**à** to). ●**défavoriser** *vt* to put at a disadvantage, be unfair to.

défection [defɛksjɔ̃] *nf* defection, desertion; **faire d.** to desert; (*ne pas venir*) to fail to turn up.

défectueux, -euse [defɛktɥø, -øz] *a* faulty, defective.

défendre [defɑ̃dr] **1** *vt* (*protéger*) to defend (**contre** against) **I se d.** *vpr* to defend oneself; **se d. de** (*pluie etc*) to protect oneself from; **se d. de faire** (*s'empêcher de*) to refrain from doing; **je me défends (bien) en anglais**/*etc Fam* I can hold my own in English/*etc*.
2 *vt* **d. à qn de faire qch** (*interdire*) to forbid s.o. to do sth, not allow s.o. to do sth; **d. qch à qn** to forbid s.o. sth.

défense [defɑ̃s] *nf* **1** (*protection*) defence, *Am* defense; **sans d.** defenceless. **2** (*interdiction*) **'d. de fumer'** 'no smoking'; **'d. (absolue) d'entrer'** '(strictly) no entry'. **3** (*d'éléphant*) tusk. **● défenseur** *nm* defender; (*des faibles*) protector, defender. **● défensif, -ive** *a* defensive **I nf sur la défensive** on the defensive.

déferler [defɛrle] *vi* (*vagues*) to break; **d. dans** *ou* **sur** (*foule*) to surge *ou* sweep into.

défi [defi] *nm* challenge; **lancer un d. à qn** to challenge s.o.; **mettre qn au d. de faire qch** to challenge *ou* defy s.o. to do sth; **relever un d.** to take up *ou* accept a challenge.

déficience [defisjɑ̃s] *nf Méd* deficiency.

déficit [defisit] *nm* deficit. **● déficitaire** *a* (*budget etc*) in deficit.

défier¹ [defje] *vt* (*provoquer*) to challenge (**à** to); **d. qn de faire** to challenge *ou* defy s.o. to do.

défier² (**se**) [sədefje] *vpr* **se d. de** *Litt* to distrust. **● défiance** *nf* distrust (**de** of).

défigurer [defigyre] *vt* to disfigure. **●—é** *a* disfigured.

défilé [defile] *nm* **1** (*cortège*) procession; (*de manifestants*) march; *Mil* parade; (*de visiteurs*) stream. **2** *Géog* pass, gorge.

défiler [defile] *vi* (*manifestants, mili-*taires) to march (**devant** past); (*paysage, jours*) to pass by; (*visiteurs*) to keep coming and going; (*images*) to flash by (on the screen); *Ordinat* to scroll **I se d.** *vpr Fam* (*s'éloigner*) to sneak off; (*éviter d'agir*) to cop out.

défin/ir [definir] *vt* to define. **●—i** *a* definite; **article d.** *Gram* definite article. **● définition** *nf* definition; (*de mots croisés*) clue.

définitif, -ive [definitif, -iv] *a* final, definitive **I nf en définitive** in the final analysis, finally. **● définitivement** *adv* (*partir, exclure*) permanently, for good.

déflagration [deflagrasjɔ̃] *nf* explosion.

défoncer [defɔ̃se] **1** *vt* (*porte, mur etc*) to smash in ou down; (*trottoir, route etc*) to dig up. **2 se défoncer** *vpr* (*drogué*) *Fam* to get high (**à** on). **● défoncé** *a* **1** (*route*) full of potholes, bumpy. **2** (*drogué*) *Fam* high.

déformation [defɔrmasjɔ̃] *nf* distortion; (*de membre*) deformity; **c'est de la d. professionnelle** it's a case of being conditioned by one's job.

déformer [defɔrme] *vt* (*objet*) to put ou knock out of shape; (*doigt, main*) to deform **I se d.** *vpr* to lose its shape. **● déformé** *a* (*objet*) misshapen; (*corps*) deformed; **chaussée déformée** uneven road surface, bumpy road.

défouler (**se**) [sədefule] *vpr Fam* to let off steam.

défrayer [defreje] *vt* **d. la chronique** to be the talk of the town.

défricher [defriʃe] *vt* (*terrain*) to clear (for cultivation).

défriser [defrize] *vt* (*cheveux*) to straighten.

défroisser [defrwase] *vt* (*papier*) to smooth out.

défroqué [defrɔke] *a* (*prêtre*) defrocked.

défunt, -unte [defœ̃, -œ̃t] *a* (*mort*) departed; **son d. mari** her late husband **I nmf le d., la défunte** the deceased, the departed.

dégager [degaʒe] *vt* (*passage, voie*) to clear (**de** of); (*odeur*) to give off; (*idée,*

conclusion) to bring out; **d. qn de** *(décombres)* to free s.o. from.
❚ *vi Fb* to clear the ball (down the pitch); **d.!** *Fam* clear the way!

❚ **se dégager** *vpr (rue, ciel)* to clear; **se d. (de)** *(personne)* to free oneself (from); **se d. de** *(odeur)* to come out of *(kitchen etc).* ● **dégagé** *a (ciel)* clear; *(allure)* easy-going; *(vue)* open. ● **dégagement** *nm (action)* clearing; *Fb* clearance, kick; **itinéraire de d.** *Aut* relief road.

dégainer [degene] *vti (arme)* to draw.

dégarnir [degarnir] *vt* to clear, empty; *(compte)* to strip; *(arbre de Noël)* to take down the decorations from ❚ **se d.** *vpr (crâne)* to go bald; *(salle)* to clear, empty. ● **dégarni** *a (salle)* nearly bare; *(tête)* balding; **front d.** receding hairline.

dégâts [dega] *nmpl* damage; **limiter les d.** *Fig* to prevent matters getting worse, limit the damage.

dégel [deʒɛl] *nm* thaw. ● **dégeler** *vt* to thaw (out); *(crédits)* to unfreeze ❚ *vi* to thaw (out) ❚ *v imp* to thaw ❚ **se d.** *vpr (personne, situation)* to thaw (out).

dégénér/er [deʒenere] *vi* to degenerate (**en** into). ● **—é, -ée** *a* & *nmf* degenerate.

dégingandé [deʒɛ̃gɑ̃de] *a* gangling, lanky.

dégivrer [deʒivre] *vt (réfrigérateur)* to defrost; *Aut Av* to de-ice.

déglinguer (se) [sədeglɛ̃ge] *vpr Fam* to fall to bits. ● **déglingué** *a* falling to bits.

dégonfler [degɔ̃fle] *vt (pneu etc)* to let the air out of, let down ❚ **se d.** *vpr (pneu etc)* to go down; *(se montrer lâche) Fam* to chicken out, get cold feet. ● **dégonflé, -ée** *a (pneu)* flat; *(lâche) Fam* chicken, yellow ❚ *nmf Fam* yellow belly.

dégouliner [deguline] *vi* to trickle, drip.

dégourdi [degurdi] *a (malin)* smart, sharp.

dégourdir (se) [sədegurdir] *vpr* **se d. les jambes** to stretch one's legs.

dégoût [degu] *nm* disgust; **le d. de** *(la vie, les gens etc)* disgust for; **avoir du d. pour qch** to have a (strong) dislike ou

distaste for sth. ● **dégoûter** *vt* to disgust; **d. qn de qch** to put s.o. off sth, *Am* (be enough) to make s.o. sick of sth; **se d. de** to take a (strong) dislike to. ● **dégoûtant** *a* disgusting. ● **dégoûté** *a* disgusted; **d. de** sick of, disgusted with *ou* by; **elle est partie dégoûtée** she left in disgust; **il n'est pas d.** *(difficile)* he's not too fussy.

dégradation [degradɑsjɔ̃] *nf* degradation; *(de situation, état etc)* deterioration; *pl (dégâts)* damage.

dégrader [degrade] **1** *vt (avilir)* to degrade; *(mur etc)* to deface, damage ❚ **se d.** *vpr (édifice, situation)* to deteriorate. **2** *vt (couleur)* to shade off. ● **dégradant** *a* degrading.

dégrafer [degrafe] *vt (vêtement)* to unfasten, undo.

dégraisser [degrese] *vt* **1** *(bœuf)* to take the fat off; *(bouillon)* to skim. **2** *(entreprise) Fam* to slim down *(by laying off workers).*

degré [dəgre] *nm (angle, température etc)* degree; **enseignement du premier/ second d.** primary/secondary education; **au plus haut d.** *(avare etc)* extremely.

dégriffé [degrife] *a* **vêtement d.** unlabelled designer garment *(sold in seconds store).*

dégringoler [degrɛ̃gole] *vi* to tumble (down); **faire d. qch** to topple sth over ❚ *vt (escalier)* to rush down. ● **dégringolade** *nf* tumble.

dégrossir [degrosir] *vt (travail)* to rough out.

déguerpir [degerpir] *vi* to clear off *ou* out, make tracks.

dégueulasse [degœlas] *a Fam* disgusting, lousy.

déguiser [degize] *vt (pour tromper)* to disguise; **d. qn en** *(costumer)* to dress s.o. up as ❚ **se d.** *vpr* to dress oneself up *(en* as); *(pour tromper)* to disguise oneself *(en* as). ● **déguisement** *nm* disguise; *(de bal costumé etc)* fancy dress, costume.

déguster [degyste] vt (goûter) to taste, sample; (apprécier) to relish. ● **dégustation** nf tasting, sampling.

dehors [dəɔr] adv outside, out; (hors de chez soi) out; **en d.** on the outside; **en d. de la maison/etc** outside the house/etc; **en d. de la ville/fenêtre** out of town/the window; **en d. de** (excepté) Fig apart from; **au-d. (de), au d. (de)** outside; **déjeuner/jeter/etc d.** to lunch/throw/etc out ▮nm (extérieur) outside.

déjà [deʒa] adv already; **est-il d. parti?** has he left yet ou already?; **elle l'a d. vu** she's seen it before, she's already seen it; **c'est d. pas mal** Fam that's not bad at all; **quand partez-vous, d.?** Fam when did you say you are leaving?

déjeuner [deʒœne] vi (à midi) to (have) lunch; (le matin) to (have) breakfast ▮nm lunch; **petit d.** breakfast.

déjouer [deʒwe] vt (intrigue, plan) to thwart, foil.

delà [d(ə)la] adv **au-d. (de), au d. (de)** beyond; **au-d. du pont/etc** beyond ou past the bridge/etc.

délabrer (se) [sədelabre] vpr (édifice) to become dilapidated; (santé) to give out, fail. ● **délabré** a dilapidated.

délacer [delase] vt (chaussures) to undo.

délai [dele] nm time limit; (répit, sursis) extra time, extension; **dans un d. de dix jours** within ten days; **sans d.** without delay; **dans les plus brefs délais** as soon as possible; **dernier d.** final date.

délaisser [delese] vt to neglect.

délasser (se) [sədelase] vpr to relax. ● **délassement** nm relaxation, diversion.

délavé [delave] a (tissu, jean) faded.

délayer [deleje] vt (mélanger) to mix (with liquid).

delco [dɛlko] nm Aut distributor.

délégu/er [delege] vt to delegate (à to). ● **—é, -ée** nmf delegate. ● **délégation** nf delegation.

délestage [delɛstaʒ] nm **itinéraire de d.** alternative route (to relieve congestion).

délibéré [delibere] a (résolu) deter-

mined; (intentionnel) deliberate; **de propos d.** deliberately. ● **—ment** adv (à dessein) deliberately.

délibérer [delibere] vi (se consulter) to deliberate (**de** about).

délicat [delika] a (santé, travail etc) delicate; (question) tricky, delicate; (geste) tactful; (exigeant) particular. ● **délicatement** adv delicately; tactfully.

délice [delis] nm delight. ● **délicieux, -euse** a (mets, fruit etc) delicious; (endroit, parfum etc) delightful.

délier [delje] vt to untie, undo; (langue) Fig to loosen; **d. qn de** to release s.o. from.

délimiter [delimite] vt (terrain) to mark off; (sujet) to define.

délinquant, -ante [delɛ̃kɑ̃, -ɑ̃t] a & nmf delinquent. ● **délinquance** nf delinquency.

délire [delir] nm Méd delirium; (exaltation) frenzy. ● **délirer** vi Méd to be delirious; (dire n'importe quoi) to rave. ● **délirant** a (malade) delirious; (joie) frenzied, wild; (déraisonnable) utterly absurd.

délit [deli] nm offence, Am offense; **d. d'initié** (à la Bourse) insider trading.

délivrer [delivre] vt **1** (prisonnier, otage) to release, (set) free; **d. qn de** (souci, obligation etc) to rid s.o. of. **2** (passeport, billet etc) to issue.

déloger [deloʒe] vt to force ou drive out; Mil to dislodge.

déloyal, -aux [delwajal, -o] a disloyal; (concurrence) unfair.

delta [dɛlta] nm (d'un fleuve) delta.

deltaplane® [dɛltaplan] nm (engin) hang-glider.

déluge [delyʒ] nm flood; (de pluie) downpour.

déluré [delyre] a (fille, air) Péj brazen.

démagogie [demagɔʒi] nf demagogy.

demain [d(ə)mɛ̃] adv tomorrow; **à d.!** see you tomorrow!

demande [d(ə)mɑ̃d] nf request (**de qch** for sth); (d'emploi) application; (de renseignements) inquiry; Écon demand; **demandes d'emploi** (*dans le journal*) situations ou jobs wanted.

demander [d(ə)mɑ̃de] *vt* to ask for; (*emploi*) to apply for; (*nécessiter*) to require; **d. le chemin/l'heure** to ask the way/the time; **d. qch à qn** to ask s.o. for sth; **d. à qn de faire** to ask s.o. to do; **d. si/où** to ask *ou* inquire whether/where; **on te demande!** you're wanted!; **ça demande du temps** it takes time; **être très demandé** to be in great demand. ‖ **se demander** *vpr* to wonder, ask oneself (**pourquoi** why, **si** if).

démanger [demɑ̃ʒe] *vti* to itch; **son bras le démange** his arm itches. ●**démangeaison** *nf* itch; **avoir des démangeaisons** to be itching.

démanteler [demɑ̃tle] *vt* (*organisation etc*) to break up.

démaquiller (se) [sədemakije] *vpr* to take off one's make-up. ●**démaquillant** *nm* make-up remover.

démarche [demarʃ] *nf* walk; gait; **d. intellectuelle** thought process; **faire des démarches** to go through the process (**pour faire** of doing); **faire des démarches auprès de qn** to approach s.o.

démarcheur, -euse [demarʃœr, -øz] *nmf* *Com* door-to-door salesman *ou* saleswoman.

démarquer [demarke] *vt* (*prix*) to mark down.

démarr/er [demare] *vi* (*moteur de voiture etc*) to start (up); (*partir en voiture*) to move *ou* drive off ‖ *vt* (*commencer*) *Fam* to start. ●**-age** *nm* *Aut* start; **d. en côte** hill start. ●**-eur** *nm* *Aut* starter.

démasquer [demaske] *vt* to expose.

démêler [demele] *vt* (*cheveux etc*) to disentangle.

démêlés [demele] *nmpl* **avoir des d. avec la justice** to have a brush with *or* unpleasant dealings with the law.

déménag/er [demenaʒe] *vi* to move (out), move house ‖ *vt* (*meubles*) to remove, *Am* move. ●**-ement** *nm* move, moving (house); **camion de d.**

removal van, *Am* moving van. ●**—eur** *nm* removal man, *Am* (furniture) mover.

démener (se) [sədemne] *vpr* to fling oneself about; **se d. pour faire** to spare no effort to do.

dément [demɑ̃] *a* insane; (*génial*) *Fam* fantastic.

démentir [demɑ̃tir] *vt* (*nouvelle, faits etc*) to deny.

démerder (se) [sədemerde] *vpr* (*se débrouiller*) *Fam* to manage (by oneself).

démesuré [demezyre] *a* excessive.

démettre [demetr] *vt* **1 se d. l'épaule**/*etc* to dislocate one's shoulder/*etc*. **2 d. qn de ses fonctions** to dismiss s.o. from his post.

demeurant (au) [odəmœrɑ̃] *adv* for all that, nonetheless.

demeure [dəmœr] *nf* **1** (*belle maison*) mansion. **2 mettre qn en d. de faire** to summon *ou* instruct s.o. to do.

demeurer [dəmœre] *vi* **1** (*aux être*) (*rester*) to remain. **2** (*aux avoir*) (*habiter*) to live, reside.

demi, -ie [d(ə)mi] *a* half; **d.-journée** half-day; **une heure et demie** an hour and a half; (*horloge*) half past one ‖ *adv* (à) **d. plein** half-full; **ouvrir à d.** to open halfway ‖ *nmf* (*moitié*) half ‖ *nm* (*verre*) (half-pint) glass of beer; *Fb* half-back ‖ *nf* (à l'horloge) half-hour.

demi-cercle [d(ə)miserkl] *nm* semicircle. ●**d.-douzaine** *nf* **une d.-douzaine (de)** a half-dozen, half a dozen. ●**d.-finale** *nf* *Sp* semifinal. ●**d.-frère** *nm* stepbrother, half brother. ●**d.-heure** *nf* **une d.-heure** a half-hour, half an hour. ●**d.-mot** *nm* **tu comprendras à d.-mot** you'll understand without my having to spell it out. ●**d.-pension** *nf* half-board, *Am* breakfast and one meal. ●**d.-pensionnaire** *nmf* day boarder, *Am* day student. ●**d.-sel** *a inv* (*beurre*) slightly salted. ●**d.-sœur** *nf* stepsister, half sister. ●**d.-tarif** *nm & a inv* (*billet*) (à) **d.-tarif** half-price. ●**d.-tour** *nm* about turn, *Am* about face; *Aut* U-turn; **faire d.-tour**

(*à pied*) to turn back; (*en voiture*) to make a U-turn.

démission [demisjɔ̃] *nf* resignation; **donner sa d.** to hand in one's resignation.
● **démissionner** *vi* to resign.

démocratie [demɔkrasi] *nf* democracy.
● **démocratique** *a* democratic.

démoder (se) [sədemɔde] *vpr* to go out of fashion. ● **démodé** *a* old-fashioned.

démographie [demɔgrafi] *nf* demography.

demoiselle [d(ə)mwazɛl] *nf* (*jeune fille*) young lady; (*célibataire*) single woman; **d. d'honneur** (*à un mariage*) bridesmaid.

démolir [demɔlir] *vt* (*maison*) to knock *ou* pull down, demolish; (*jouet*) to demolish. ● **démolition** *nf* demolition; **en d.** being demolished.

démon [demɔ̃] *nm* **petit d.** (*enfant*) little devil.

démonstratif, -ive [demɔ̃stratif, -iv] *a* (*caractère*) demonstrative; **adjectif d.** *Gram* demonstrative adjective ∥ *nm* demonstrative.

démonstration [demɔ̃strasjɔ̃] *nf* demonstration; **faire une d.** to give a demonstration; **faire la d. d'un appareil** to demonstrate an appliance.

démonter [demɔ̃te] *vt* (*mécanisme*) to take apart, dismantle; (*installation*) to take down; **une mer démontée** a stormy sea ∥ **se d.** *vpr* to come apart; (*installation*) to come down; (*personne*) *Fig* to be put out *ou* disconcerted.

démontrer [demɔ̃tre] *vt* to show, demonstrate.

démoraliser [demɔralize] *vt* to demoralize ∥ **se d.** *vpr* to become demoralized.

démordre [demɔrdr] *vi* **il ne démordra pas de** (*son opinion etc*) he won't budge from.

démouler [demule] *vt* (*gâteau*) to turn out (*from its mould*).

démunir [demynir] *vt* **d. qn de** to deprive s.o. of; **se d.** to part with.

dénaturer [denatyre] *vt* (*propos, faits etc*) to misrepresent, distort; (*goût*) to alter.

déneiger [deneʒe] *vt* to clear of snow.

dénicher [deniʃe] *vt* (*trouver*) to dig up; (*ennemi, fugitif*) to hunt out, flush out.

dénier [denje] *vt* (*responsabilité, droit*) to deny; **d. qch à qn** to deny s.o. sth.

dénigrer [denigre] *vt* to denigrate.

dénivellation [denivelasjɔ̃] *nf* unevenness; (*pente*) gradient; *pl* (*relief*) bumps.

dénombrer [denɔ̃bre] *vt* to count, number.

dénomm/er [denɔme] *vt* to name. ● **—é, -ée** *nmf* **un d. Dupont** a man named Dupont.

dénoncer [denɔ̃se] *vt* (*injustice etc*) to denounce (**à** to); **d. qn** (*au professeur*) to tell on s.o. (**à** to) ∥ **se d.** *vpr* (*à la police*) to give oneself up (**à** to); (*au professeur*) to own up (**à** to). ● **dénonciateur, -trice** *nmf* *Scol* telltale.

dénouement [denumɑ̃] *nm* outcome, ending; *Th* dénouement.

dénouer [denwe] *vt* (*nœud, corde*) to undo, untie; (*cheveux*) to let down ∥ **se d.** *vpr* (*nœud*) to come undone *ou* untied; (*cheveux*) to come down.

dénoyauter [denwajɔte] *vt* (*prune etc*) to stone, *Am* to pit.

denrée [dɑ̃re] *nf* food(stuff); **denrées alimentaires** foods.

dense [dɑ̃s] *a* dense. ● **densité** *nf* density.

dent [dɑ̃] *nf* tooth (*pl* teeth); (*de fourchette*) prong; **d. de lait/sagesse** milk/wisdom tooth; **faire ses dents** (*enfant*) to be teething; **coup de d.** bite; **rien à se mettre sous la d.** nothing to eat.
● **dentaire** *a* dental.

dentelé [dɑ̃tle] *a* (*côte*) jagged; (*feuille*) serrated.

dentelle [dɑ̃tɛl] *nf* lace.

dénud/er [denyde] *vt* to (lay) bare. ● **—é** *a* bare.

dénué [denɥe] *a* **d. de sens**/*etc* devoid of sense/*etc*.

dénuement [denymɑ̃] *nm* destitution;

dans le d. poverty-stricken.
déodorant [deɔdɔrɑ̃] *nm* deodorant.
dépanner [depane] *vt* (*voiture etc*) to repair; **d. qn** *Fam* to help s.o. out. ● **dépannage** *nm* (emergency) repair; **voiture/service de d.** breakdown vehicle/service. ● **dépanneur** *nm* (*de télévision*) repairman; (*de voiture*) breakdown mechanic, emergency car mechanic. ● **dépanneuse** *nf* (*voiture*) breakdown lorry, *Am* wrecker, tow truck.

dépareillé [depareje] *a* (*chaussure etc*) odd, not matching; (*collection*) incomplete.

départ [depar] *nm* departure; (*d'une course*) start; **point/ligne de d.** starting point/post; **au d.** at the outset, at the start; **au d. de Paris/etc** (*excursion etc*) leaving from Paris/*etc*.

départager [departaʒe] *vt* (*concurrents*) to decide between.

département [departəmɑ̃] *nm* department. ● **départemental, -aux** *a* departmental; **route départementale** secondary road.

départir (se) [sədepartir] *vpr* **se d. de** (*attitude*) to depart from, abandon.

dépass/er [depase] *vt* (*véhicule, bicyclette etc*) to overtake; (*endroit*) to go past; (*date limite, durée*) to go beyond; **d. qn** (*en hauteur*) to be taller than s.o.; (*surclasser*) to be ahead of s.o.; **ça me dépasse** *Fig* that's (quite) beyond me ▌*vi* (*jupon, clou etc*) to stick out, show. ● **-é** *a* (*démodé*) outdated; (*incapable*) unable to cope. ● **-ement** *nm* *Aut* overtaking, passing.

dépayser [depeize] *vt* to disorientate, *Am* disorient.

dépecer [depəse] *vt* (*animal*) to cut up.

dépêche [depɛʃ] *nf* telegram; (*diplomatique*) dispatch. ● **dépêcher** *vt* to dispatch ▌**se d.** *vpr* to hurry (up).

dépeigné [depeɲe] *a* **être d.** to have untidy hair.

dépeindre* [depɛ̃dr] *vt* to depict, describe.

dépendre [depɑ̃dr] **1** *vi* to depend (**de** on,

upon); **d. de** (*appartenir à*) to belong to; (*être soumis à*) to be dependent on; **ça dépend de toi** that depends on you. **2** *vt* (*décrocher*) to take down. ● **dépendance** **1** *nf* dependence; **sous la d. de qn** under s.o.'s domination. **2** *nfpl* (*bâtiments*) outbuildings.

dépens [depɑ̃] *nmpl* **aux d. de** at the expense of.

dépense [depɑ̃s] *nf* (*frais*) expense, expenditure; (*d'électricité etc*) consumption. ● **dépenser** *vt* (*argent*) to spend; (*électricité etc*) to use; (*forces*) to exert; (*énergie*) to expend ▌**se d.** *vpr* to exert oneself.

dépensier, -ière [depɑ̃sje, -jɛr] *a* wasteful.

déperdition [deperdisjɔ̃] *nf* (*de chaleur etc*) loss.

dépérir [deperir] *vi* (*personne*) to waste away; (*plante*) to wither.

dépêtrer (se) [sədepetre] *vpr* *Fam* to extricate oneself (**de** from).

dépeupler [depœple] *vt* to depopulate.

dépilatoire [depilatwar] *nm* hair remover.

dépister [depiste] *vt* (*criminel etc*) to track down; (*maladie*) to detect.

dépit [depi] *nm* resentment, pique; **en d. de** in spite of; **en d. du bon sens** (*mal*) atrociously. ● **dépité** *a* vexed.

déplacer [deplase] *vt* (*objet, meuble etc*) to shift, move ▌**se d.** *vpr* (*aiguille d'une montre, personne etc*) to move; (*voyager*) to travel (about). ● **déplacé** *a* (*propos*) out of place; **personne déplacée** (*réfugié*) displaced person. ● **déplacement** *nm* (*voyage*) (business) trip; **frais de d.** travelling *ou Am* traveling expenses.

déplaire* [depler] *vi* **d. à qn** to displease s.o.; **ça me déplaît** I don't like it; **cet aliment lui déplaît** he *ou* she dislikes this food; **il se déplaît à Paris** he doesn't like it in Paris. ● **déplaisant** *a* unpleasant.

déplier [deplije] *vt* to open out, unfold. ● **-ant** *nm* (*prospectus*) leaflet.

déplor/er [deplɔre] *vt* (*regretter*) to

deplore; **d. que** (+ *sub*) to deplore the fact that, regret that. ● **—able** *a* regrettable, deplorable.

déployer [deplwaje] *vt* (*ailes*) to spread; (*journal, carte etc*) to unfold, open (out); (*courage etc*) to display ‖ **se d.** *vpr* (*drapeau*) to unfurl.

déport/er [deporte] *vt* **1** (*dévier*) to carry *ou* veer (off course). **2** (*dans un camp de concentration*) *Hist* to send to a concentration camp, deport. ● **—é, -ée** *nmf* (concentration camp) inmate. ● **déportation** *nf* internment (in a concentration camp).

déposer [depoze] *vt* (*poser*) to put down; (*laisser*) to leave; (*argent*) to deposit; (*plainte*) to lodge; (*ordures*) to dump; (*marque de fabrique*) to register; **d. qn** (*en voiture*) to drop s.o. (off); **d. une lettre à la poste** to drop a letter in the post, mail *ou* post a letter; **d. son bilan** (*entreprise*) to go into liquidation, file for bankruptcy.
‖ *vi Jur* to testify; (*liquide*) to leave a deposit.
‖ **se déposer** *vpr* (*poussière, lie*) to settle.

dépositaire [depoziter] *nmf* (*vendeur*) agent.

dépôt [depo] *nm* (*de vin etc*) deposit, sediment; (*à la banque*) deposit; (*d'autobus, de trains*) depot; (*entrepôt*) warehouse; **d. d'ordures** rubbish *ou* Am garbage dump; **laisser qch à qn en d.** to give s.o. sth for safekeeping.

dépotoir [depotwar] *nm* rubbish dump, Am garbage dump.

dépouille [depuj] *nf* (*d'un animal*) hide, skin; **d.** (**mortelle**) (*d'un défunt*) mortal remains.

dépouillé [depuje] *a* (*arbre*) bare; (*style*) austere.

dépouiller [depuje] *vt* **d. qn de** (*déposséder*) to deprive s.o. of; **d. un scrutin** to count votes.

dépourvu [depurvy] *a* **d. de** devoid of; **prendre qn au d.** to catch s.o. unawares.

dépravé [deprave] *a* depraved.

déprécier [depresje] *vt* (*monnaie, im-* *meuble etc*) to depreciate; (*dénigrer*) to disparage ‖ **se d.** *vpr* (*baisser*) to depreciate, lose (its) value.

dépression [depresjɔ̃] *nf* (*sur le sol*) & *Psy* depression; **zone de d.** trough of low pressure; **d.** (**nerveuse**) (nervous) breakdown; **d. économique** slump. ● **dépressif, -ive** *a* depressive.

déprime [deprim] *nf* **la d.** (*dépression*) *Fam* the blues.

déprim/er [deprime] *vt* to depress. ● **—é** *a* depressed.

depuis [dəpɥi] *prép* since; **d. lundi/1990** since Monday/1990; **d. qu'elle est partie** since she left; **j'habite ici d. un mois** I've been living here for a month; **d. quand êtes-vous là?** how long have you been here?; **d. peu/longtemps** for a short/long time; **je le connais d. toujours** I've known him all my life; **d. des siècles** *Fam* for ages; **d. Paris jusqu'à Londres** from Paris to London ‖ *adv* since (then).

député [depyte] *nm* (*à l'Assemblée nationale*) deputy, = Br MP, = Am congressman, congresswoman.

déraciner [derasine] *vt* (*arbre, personne etc*) to uproot; (*préjugés*) to eradicate, root out.

déraill/er [deraje] *vi* **1** (*train*) to jump the rails, be derailed; **faire d.** to derail. **2** (*divaguer*) *Fam* to talk drivel. ● **—ement** *nm* (*de train*) derailment. ● **—eur** *nm* (*de bicyclette*) derailleur (gear change).

déraisonnable [derezonabl] *a* unreasonable.

déranger [derɑ̃ʒe] *vt* (*affaires*) to disturb, upset; (*projets*) to mess up, upset; (*vêtements*) to mess up; **d. qn** to disturb *ou* bother s.o.; **je viendrai si ça ne te dérange pas** I'll come if that's not imposing; **ça vous dérange si je fume?** do you mind if I smoke?; **avoir l'estomac dérangé** to have an upset stomach.
‖ **se déranger** *vpr* to put oneself to a lot of trouble (**pour faire** to do), (*se déplacer*) to move; **ne te dérange pas!** don't bother! ● **dérangement** *nm* (*gêne*) both-

er, inconvenience; **excusez-moi pour le d.** I'm sorry to disturb *ou* bother you; **en d.** (*téléphone etc*) out of order.

dérap/er [derape] *vi* to skid. ●—**age** *nm* skid.

dérégler [deregle] *vt* (*télévision etc*) to put out of order; (*estomac, habitudes*) to upset ‖ **se d.** *vpr* (*montre, appareil*) to go wrong. ● **déréglé** *a* (*appareil*) out of order; (*vie, mœurs*) dissolute, wild.

dérider [deride] *vt*, **se d.** *vpr* to cheer up.

dérision [derizjɔ̃] *nf* derision, mockery; **tourner en d.** to mock; **par d.** derisively. ● **dérisoire** *a* ridiculous, derisory.

dérivatif [derivatif] *nm* distraction (à from).

dérive [deriv] *nf* **partir à la d.** (*navire*) to drift out to sea. ● **dériver** *vi* (*bateau*) to drift ‖ *vt* (*cours d'eau*) to divert; *Ling* to derive (**de** from).

dermatologie [dermatolɔʒi] *nf* dermatology.

dernier -ière [dɛrnje, -jɛr] *a* last; (*nouvelles, mode*) latest; (*étage*) top; (*degré*) highest; **le d. rang** the back *ou* last row; **ces derniers mois** these past few months; **en d.** last.

‖ *nmf* last (person *ou* one); **ce d.** (*de deux*) the latter; (*de plusieurs*) the last-mentioned; **être le d. de la classe** to be (at the) bottom of the class; **le d. des derniers** the lowest of the low; **le d. de mes soucis** the least of my worries. ● **d.-né, dernière-née** *nmf* youngest (child). ● **dernièrement** *adv* recently.

dérober [derɔbe] *vt* (*voler*) to steal (à from) ‖ **se d.** *vpr* to get out of one's obligations; (*s'esquiver*) to slip away; (*éviter de répondre*) to dodge the issue; **ses jambes se sont dérobées sous lui** his legs gave way beneath him. ● **dérobé** *a* (*porte etc*) hidden, secret.

dérogation [derɔgasjɔ̃] *nf* exemption, (special) dispensation.

dérouiller [deruje] *vt* **d. qn** (*battre*) *Fam* to thrash s.o.; **se d. les jambes** *Fam* to stretch one's legs.

dérouler [derule] *vt* (*tapis etc*) to unroll;

(*fil*) to unwind ‖ **se d.** *vpr* (*événement*) to take place, pass off.

dérouter [derute] *vt* (*avion, navire*) to divert, reroute; (*candidat etc*) to baffle.

derrick [derik] *nm* oil rig.

derrière [dɛrjɛr] *prép & adv* behind; **d. moi** behind me, *Am* in back of me; **assis d.** (*dans une voiture*) sitting in the back; **par d.** (*attaquer*) from behind, from the rear ‖ *nm* (*de maison etc*) back, rear; (*fesses*) behind, bottom; **patte de d.** hind leg; **roue de d.** back *ou* rear wheel.

des [de] *voir* **de**[1,2,3], **le**.

dès [dɛ] *prép* from; **d. le début** (right) from the start; **d. cette époque** (as) from that time, from that time on; **d. le sixième siècle** as early as the sixth century; **d. qu'elle viendra** as soon as she comes.

désabusé [dezabyze] *a* disillusioned.

désaccord [dezakɔr] *nm* disagreement; **être en d. avec qn** to be at odds with s.o. ● **désaccordé** *a* (*violon etc*) out of tune.

désaffecté [dezafɛkte] *a* (*gare etc*) disused.

désagréable [dezagreabl] *a* unpleasant, disagreeable.

désagréger (se) [sədezagreʒe] *vpr* to disintegrate, break up.

désagrément [dezagremɑ̃] *nm* annoyance, trouble.

désaltérer [dezaltere] *vt* **d. qn** to quench s.o.'s thirst; **se d.** to quench one's thirst.

désamorcer [dezamɔrse] *vt* (*obus, conflit*) to defuse.

désapprouver [dezapruve] *vt* to disapprove of ‖ *vi* to disapprove. ● **désapprobateur, -trice** *a* disapproving.

désarçonner [dezarsɔne] *vt* (*jockey*) to throw, unseat; (*déconcerter*) *Fig* to nonpluss.

désarm/er [dezarme] *vt* (*émouvoir*) & *Mil* to disarm. ●—**ant** *a* (*charme etc*) disarming.

désarroi [dezarwa] *nm* (*angoisse*) distress.

désarticulé [dezartikyle] *a* (*pantin, clown*) double-jointed.

désastre [dezastr] *nm* disaster. ● **désastreux, -euse** *a* disastrous.

désavantage [dezavɑ̃taʒ] *nm* (*inconvénient*) drawback, disadvantage; (*gêne*) handicap, disadvantage. ● **désavantager** *vt* to put at a disadvantage, handicap.

désavouer [dezavwe] *vt* (*livre, personne etc*) to disown.

désaxé, -ée [dezakse] *a & nmf* unbalanced (person).

desceller (se) [sədesele] *vpr* to come loose.

descendant, -ante [desɑ̃dɑ̃, -ɑ̃t] **1** *a* (*marée*) outgoing. **2** *nmf* (*personne*) descendant.

descendre [desɑ̃dr] *vi* (*aux être*) to come *ou* go down (**de** from); (*d'un train etc*) to get off (**de** from); (*d'un arbre*) to climb down (**de** from); (*nuit, thermomètre*) to fall; (*marée*) to go out; **d. à l'hôtel** to put up at a hotel; **d. chez un ami** to stay with a friend; **d. de** (*être issu de*) to be descended from; **d. en courant/flânant**/*etc* to run/stroll/*etc* down. ‖ *vt* (*aux avoir*) (*escalier*) to come *ou* go down; (*objet*) to bring *ou* take down; **d. qn** (*tuer*) *Fam* to bump s.o. off.

descente [desɑ̃t] *nf* (*d'avion etc*) descent; (*pente*) slope; (*de police*) raid (**dans** upon); **il fut accueilli à sa d. d'avion** he was met as he got off the plane; **d. à skis** downhill run; **d. de lit** (*tapis*) bedside rug.

descriptif, -ive [dɛskriptif, -iv] *a* descriptive. ● **description** *nf* description.

désemparé [dezɑ̃pare] *a* at a total loss, distraught.

désemplir [dezɑ̃plir] *vi* **ce magasin**/*etc* **ne désemplit pas** this shop/*etc* is always crowded.

désenfler [dezɑ̃fle] *vi* (*enflure*) to go down.

déséquilibre [dezekilibr] *nm* (*inégalité*) imbalance; (*mental*) unbalance; **en d.** (*meuble etc*) unsteady. ● **déséquilibrer** *vt* to throw off balance; (*esprit, personne*) *Fig* to unbalance.

désert [dezɛr] *a* deserted; **île déserte** desert island ‖ *nm* desert. ● **désertique** *a* **région**/*etc* **d.** desert region/*etc*.

déserter [dezɛrte] *vti* to desert. ● **déserteur** *nm* (*soldat*) deserter.

désespérer [dezɛspere] *vi* to despair (**de** of) ‖ *vt* to drive to despair ‖ **se d.** *vpr* (be in) despair. ● **désespérant** *a* (*enfant etc*) that drives one to despair, hopeless. ● **désespéré** *a* (*personne*) in despair, despairing; (*cas, situation*) desperate, hopeless; (*efforts, cris*) desperate.

désespoir [dezɛspwar] *nm* despair; **en d. de cause** in desperation.

déshabiller [dezabije] *vt* to undress, strip ‖ **se d.** *vpr* to get undressed, undress.

désherb/er [dezɛrbe] *vti* to weed. ● **—ant** *nm* weed killer.

déshérit/er [dezerite] *vt* to disinherit. ● **—é** *a* (*pauvre*) underprivileged.

déshonor/er [dezɔnɔre] *vt* to disgrace, dishonour. ● **—ant** *a* dishonourable.

déshydrater [dezidrate] *vt* to dehydrate ‖ **se d.** *vpr* to become dehydrated.

désigner [deziɲe] *vt* (*montrer*) to point to, point out; (*choisir*) to appoint, designate; (*signifier*) to indicate.

désinence [dezinɑ̃s] *nf Gram* ending.

désinfect/er [dezɛ̃fɛkte] *vt* to disinfect. ● **—ant** *nm & a* disinfectant. ● **désinfection** *nf* disinfection.

désinformation [dezɛ̃fɔrmasjɔ̃] *nf* (*dans la presse*) disinformation.

désintégrer (se) [sədezɛ̃tegre] *vpr* to disintegrate.

désintéresser (se) [sədezɛ̃terese] *vpr* **se d. de** to lose interest in. ● **désintéressé** *a* (*altruiste*) disinterested.

désintoxiquer [dezɛ̃tɔksike] *vt* (*alcoolique, drogué*) to treat for alcoholism *ou* drug abuse.

désinvolte [dezɛ̃vɔlt] *a* (*dégagé*) easygoing, casual; (*insolent*) offhand. ● **désinvolture** *nf* casualness; offhandedness.

désir [dezir] *nm* desire, wish. ● **désirer** *vt* to want, desire; (*convoiter*) to desire;

je **désire** venir I would like to come, I wish ou want to come; je **désire** que tu viennes I want you to come; ça laisse à d. it leaves something ou a lot to be desired.

désister (se) [sedeziste] vpr (candidat etc) to withdraw.

désobé/ir [dezɔbeir] vi to disobey; d. à qn to disobey s.o. ●—**issant** a disobedient. ●**désobéissance** nf disobedience (à to).

désobligeant [dezɔbliʒɑ̃] a disagreeable.

désodorisant [dezɔdɔrizɑ̃] nm air freshener.

désœuvré [dezœvre] a idle, unoccupied.

désoler [dezɔle] vt to distress, upset (very much) ▮ se d. vpr to be distressed ou upset (de at). ●**désolé** a (région) desolate; (affligé) distressed; être d. (navré) to be sorry (que (+ sub) that, de faire to do).

désolidariser (se) [sedesɔlidarize] vpr to dissociate oneself (de from).

désopilant [dezɔpilɑ̃] a hilarious.

désordonné [dezɔrdɔne] a (personne, chambre) untidy, messy.

désordre [dezɔrdr] nm (de papiers, affaires, idées) mess, muddle, disorder; (dans une classe) disturbance; (de cheveux, pièce) untidiness; pl (émeutes) disorder, unrest; en d. untidy, messy.

désorganiser [dezɔrganize] vt to disorganize.

désorienté [dezɔrjɑ̃te] a disorientated, Am disoriented.

désormais [dezɔrmɛ] adv from now on, in future.

désosser [dezɔse] vt (viande) to bone.

despote [dɛspɔt] nm tyrant, despot.

desquels, desquelles [dekɛl] voir lequel.

dessaisir (se) [sadesezir] vpr se d. de qch to part with sth.

dessaler [desale] vt (poisson etc) to remove the salt from (by smoking).

dessécher [deseʃe] vt (végétation) to dry up, wither; (bouche, gorge) to parch, dry; (fruits) to desiccate, dry ▮ se d. vpr

(plante) to wither, dry up; (peau) to dry (up).

dessein [desɛ̃] nm dans le d. de faire with the aim of doing; à d. intentionally.

desserrer [desere] vt (ceinture etc) to loosen; (poing) to open; (frein) to release; il n'a pas desserré les dents he didn't open his mouth ▮ se d. vpr to come loose.

dessert [desɛr] nm dessert, sweet.

desserte [desɛrt] nf assurer la d. de (village etc) to provide a (bus ou train) service to.

desservir [desɛrvir] vt 1 (table) to clear (away). 2 d. qn to harm s.o., do s.o. a disservice. 3 le car/etc dessert ce village the bus/etc provides a service to ou stops at this village.

dessin [desɛ̃] nm drawing; (motif) design, pattern; d. animé (film) cartoon; d. (humoristique) (dans un journal) cartoon; école de d. art school. ●**dessinateur, -trice** nmf drawer; d. humoristique cartoonist; d. de modes dress designer; d. industriel draughtsman, Am draftsman.

dessiner [desine] vt to draw; (meuble, robe etc) to design ▮ se d. vpr (colline etc) to stand out, be outlined; (projet) to take shape.

dessous [d(ə)su] adv under(neath), beneath, below; en d. (sous) under(neath) ▮ nm underneath; drap de d. bottom sheet; pl (vêtements) underclothes; les gens du d. the people downstairs; avoir le d. to get the worst of it. ●d.-de-plat nm inv table mat.

dessus [d(ə)sy] adv (marcher, écrire) on it; (monter) on top (of it), on it; (lancer, passer) over it; par-d. (sauter etc) over (it); par-d. tout above all ▮ nm top; drap de d. top sheet; avoir le d. to have the upper hand, get the best of it; les gens du d. the people upstairs. ●d.-de-lit nm inv bedspread.

destin [destɛ̃] nm fate, destiny.

destinataire [destinatɛr] nmf addressee.

destination [destinɑsjɔ̃] nf (lieu) destination; **à d. de** (*train etc*) (going) to, (bound) for.

destiner [destine] *vt* **d. qch à qn** to intend *ou* mean sth for s.o.; **d. qn à** (*carrière, fonction*) to intend s.o. for; **se d. à** (*carrière etc*) to intend to take up.

destituer [destitɥe] *vt* (*fonctionnaire etc*) to dismiss (from office).

destruction [destryksjɔ̃] *nf* destruction.

désuet, -ète [desɥe, -et] *a* obsolete.

détachement [detaʃmɑ̃] *nm* **1** (*indifférence*) detachment. **2** (*de fonctionnaire*) (temporary) transfer; (*de troupes*) detachment.

détacher[1] [detaʃe] *vt* (*ceinture, vêtement*) to undo; (*mains*) to untie; (*ôter*) to take off, detach; **d. qn** (*libérer*) to untie s.o.; (*affecter*) to transfer s.o. (on assignment) (**à** to) **‖ se d.** *vpr* (*chien, prisonnier*) to break loose; (*se dénouer*) to come undone; **se d. (de qch)** (*fragment*) to come off (sth); **se d. de** (*amis*) to break away from; **se d. (sur)** (*ressortir*) to stand out (against).

détach/er[2] [detaʃe] *vt* (*linge etc*) to remove the spots *ou* stains from. **●—ant** *nm* stain remover.

détail [detaj] *nm* **1** detail; **en d.** in detail; **le d. de** (*dépenses etc*) a breakdown of. **2 de d.** (*magasin, prix*) retail; **vendre au d.** to sell retail; (*par petites quantités*) to sell separately.

détaillant, -ante [detajɑ̃, -ɑ̃t] *nmf* retailer.

détaill/er [detaje] *vt* (*énumérer*) to detail. **●—é** *a* (*récit, facture etc*) detailed.

détaler [detale] *vi* Fam to run off.

détartrer [detartre] *vt* (*chaudière, dents etc*) to scale.

détaxer [detakse] *vt* (*denrée etc*) to reduce the tax on, on; (*supprimer*) to take the tax off; **produit détaxé** duty-free article.

détecter [detekte] *vt* to detect.

détective [detektiv] *nm* **d. (privé)** (private) detective.

déteindre* [detɛ̃dr] *vi* (*couleur ou étoffe au lavage*) to run; (*au soleil*) to fade; **ton**

tablier bleu a déteint sur ma chemise the blue of your apron has come off on(to) my shirt.

dételer [detle] *vt* (*chevaux*) to unhitch.

détendre [detɑ̃dr] *vt* (*arc etc*) to slacken, relax; (*atmosphère*) to ease; **d. qn** to relax s.o. **‖ se d.** *vpr* (*arc etc*) to slacken, get slack; (*atmosphère*) to ease; (*se reposer*) to relax; (*rapports*) to become less strained.

déten/ir* [detnir] *vt* (*record, pouvoir, titre*) to hold; (*secret, objet volé*) to be in possession of; (*prisonnier*) to hold, detain. **●—u, -ue** *nmf* prisoner. **● détention** *nf* (*d'armes*) possession; (*captivité*) detention; **placer en d. préventive** (*en prison*) to remand in custody.

détente [detɑ̃t] *nf* **1** (*repos*) relaxation. **2** (*gâchette*) trigger.

détergent [detɛrʒɑ̃] *nm* detergent.

détériorer [deterjɔre] *vt* (*abîmer*) to damage **‖ se d.** *vpr* (*empirer*) to deteriorate. **● détérioration** *nf* (*d'une situation etc*) deterioration (**de** in).

détermin/er [detɛrmine] *vt* (*préciser*) to determine; (*causer*) to bring about; **d. qn à faire** to induce s.o. to do, make s.o. do; **se d. à faire** to resolve *ou* determine to do. **●—ant** *a* (*motif*) deciding; (*rôle*) decisive. **●—é** *a* (*précis*) specific; (*résolu*) determined.

déterrer [detere] *vt* to dig up, unearth.

détest/er [deteste] *vt* to hate, detest; **d. faire** to hate doing *ou* to do, detest doing. **●—able** *a* awful, terrible.

détonation [detɔnasjɔ̃] *nf* explosion, blast.

détonner [detɔne] *vi* (*contraster*) to jar, be out of place.

détour [detur] *nm* (*crochet*) detour; (*de route etc*) bend, curve; **sans d.** (*parler*) without beating around the bush.

détourner [deturne] *vt* (*dévier*) to divert; (*tête*) to turn (away); (*avion*) to hijack; (*conversation, sens*) to change; (*fonds*) to embezzle; **d. qn de** (*son devoir, ses amis*) to take s.o. away from; (*sa* to lead s.o. away from; **d. les yeux** to look away.

‖ **se détourner** *vpr* to turn aside *ou* away. ● **détourné, -ée** *a* (*chemin, moyen*) roundabout, indirect. ● **détournement** *nm* **d. (d'avion)** hijack(ing); **d. (de fonds)** embezzlement.

détraquer [detrake] *vt* (*mécanisme*) to break, put out of order ‖ **se d.** *vpr* (*machine*) to go wrong; **se d. l'estomac** to upset one's stomach. ● **détraqué, -ée** *a* out of order; (*cerveau*) deranged ‖ *nmf* crazy *ou* deranged person.

détresse [detres] *nf* distress; **en d.** (*navire, âme*) in distress; **dans la d.** (*misère*) in (great) distress.

détriment de (au) [odetrimådə] *prép* to the detriment of.

détritus [detritys] *nmpl* rubbish, *Am* garbage.

détroit [detrwa] *nm* *Géog* strait(s), sound.

détromper (se) [sədetrõpe] *vpr* **détrompez-vous!** don't you believe it!

détrousser [detruse] *vt* (*voyageur etc*) to rob.

détruire* [detrɥir] *vt* (*ravager, tuer*) to destroy; (*santé*) to ruin, destroy.

dette [dɛt] *nf* debt; **avoir des dettes** to be in debt.

DEUG [dœg] *nm abrév* (*diplôme d'études universitaires générales*) degree taken after two years' study.

deuil [dœj] *nm* (*affliction, vêtements*) mourning; (*mort de qn*) bereavement; **être en d.** to be in mourning.

deux [dø] *a & nm* two; **d. fois** twice, two times; **mes d. sœurs** both my sisters, my two sisters; **tous (les) d.** both. ● **d.-pièces** *nm inv* (*maillot de bain*) bikini; (*appartement*) two-roomed flat *ou Am* apartment. ● **d.-points** *nm inv Gram* colon. ● **d.-roues** *nm inv* two-wheeled vehicle.

deuxième [døzjem] *a & nmf* second. ● **—ment** *adv* secondly.

dévaler [devale] *vt* (*escalier*) to race down ‖ *vi* (*tomber*) to tumble down.

dévaliser [devalize] *vt* (*personne, banque etc*) rob.

dévaloriser [devalɔrize] *vt* (*diplôme, marchandises*) to reduce in value, devalue ‖ **se d.** *vpr* to become devalued.

dévaluer [devalɥe] *vt* (*monnaie*) to devalue. ● **dévaluation** *nf* devaluation.

devancer [d(ə)våse] *vt* to get *ou* be ahead of; (*question etc*) to anticipate, forestall.

devant [d(ə)vå] *prép & adv* in front (of); **d. (l'hôtel/etc)** in front (of the hotel/ etc); **passer d. (l'église/etc)** to go past (the church/etc); **assis d.** (*dans une voiture*) sitting in the front; **par d.** from *ou* at the front; **loin d.** a long way ahead *ou* in front; **d. le danger** in the face of danger.

‖ *nm* front; **roue/porte de d.** front wheel/ door; **patte de d.** foreleg; **prendre les devants** (*action*) to take the initiative.

devanture [d(ə)våtyr] *nf* (*vitrine*) shop window; (*façade*) shop front.

dévaster [devaste] *vt* to ruin, devastate.

développer [devlɔpe] *vt* (*muscles, photos*) to develop ‖ **se d.** *vpr* to develop. ● **développement** *nm* development; *Phot* developing, processing; **les pays en voie de d.** the developing countries.

devenir* [dəvnir] *vi* (*aux* être) to become; (*vieux etc*) to get, become; (*rouge etc*) to turn, go, become; **d. un papillon/ un homme/etc** to grow into a butterfly/ a man/etc; **d. médecin** to become a doctor; **qu'est-il devenu?** what's become of him *ou* it?

dévergonder (se) [sədevergõde] *vpr* to fall into dissolute ways.

déverser [deverse] *vt* (*liquide, rancune*) to pour out; (*bombes, ordures*) to dump ‖ **se d.** *vpr* (*liquide*) to empty, pour out (**dans** into).

dévêtir (se) [sədevetir] *vpr Litt* to undress.

dévier [devje] *vt* (*circulation etc*) to divert; (*coup etc*) to deflect ‖ *vi* (*de ses principes etc*) to deviate (**de** from); (*de sa route*) to veer (off course). ● **dévia-**

tion nf (chemin) bypass; (itinéraire provisoire) diversion, Am detour.

deviner [d(ə)vine] vt to guess (que that); (avenir) to predict; **d. (le jeu de) qn** to see through s.o. ● **devinette** nf riddle.

devis [d(ə)vi] nm estimate (of cost of work to be done).

dévisager [devizaʒe] vt **d. qn** to stare at s.o.

devise [d(ə)viz] nf (légende) motto; (monnaie) (foreign) currency.

dévisser [devise] vt to unscrew, undo ‖ **se d.** vpr (bouchon) to unscrew; (se desserrer) to come loose.

dévoiler [devwale] vt (secret) to disclose.

devoir*[1] [d(ə)vwar] v aux **1** (nécessité) **je dois refuser** I must refuse, I have (got) to refuse; **j'ai dû refuser** I had to refuse. **2** (forte probabilité) **il doit être tard** it must be late; **elle a dû oublier** she must have forgotten; **il ne doit pas être bête** he can't be stupid.
3 (obligation) **tu dois apprendre tes leçons** you must learn your lessons; **il aurait dû venir** he should have come, he ought to have come; **vous devriez rester** you should stay, you ought to stay.
4 (événement prévu) **elle doit venir** she's supposed to be coming, she's due to come; **le train devait arriver à midi** the train was due (to arrive) at noon.

devoir*[2] [d(ə)vwar] **1** vt to owe; **d. de l'argent à qn** to owe s.o. money, owe money to s.o. **2** nm (obligation) duty; **devoir(s)** (exercice(s)) à faire à la maison) homework; **faire ses devoirs** to do one's homework; **d. sur table** class exam(ination).

dévolu [devɔly] nm **jeter son d. sur** to set one's heart on.

dévorer [devɔre] vt (manger) to eat up.

dévot, -ote [devo, -ɔt] a & nmf devout ou pious (person).

dévouer (se) [sədevwe] vpr (à une tâche) to dedicate oneself, devote oneself (à to); **se d. (pour qn)** (se sacrifier) to sacrifice oneself (for s.o.). ● **dévoué** a (ami, femme etc) devoted (à qn to s.o.);

(soldat etc) dedicated. ● **dévouement** [-umã] nm devotion, dedication.

diabète [djabɛt] nm (maladie) diabetes. ● **diabétique** a & nmf diabetic.

diable [djɑbl] nm devil; **le d.** the Devil; **habiter au d.** to live miles from anywhere.

diabolo [djabɔlo] nm (boisson) lemonade ou Am lemon soda flavoured with syrup.

diacre [djakr] nm Rel deacon.

diadème [djadɛm] nm (bijou féminin) tiara.

diagnostic [djagnɔstik] nm diagnosis.

diagonale [djagɔnal] nf diagonal (line); **en d.** diagonally.

diagramme [djagram] nm (schéma) diagram; (courbe) graph.

dialecte [djalɛkt] nm dialect.

dialogue [djalɔg] nm conversation; Pol Cin Th Littér dialogue.

dialyse [djaliz] nf Méd dialysis.

diamant [djamã] nm diamond.

diamètre [djamɛtr] nm diameter.

diapason [djapazɔ̃] nm Mus tuning fork.

diaphragme [djafragm] nm diaphragm.

diapositive, Fam **diapo** [djapozitiv, djapo] nf (colour) slide, transparency.

diarrhée [djare] nf diarrh(o)ea.

dictateur [diktatœr] nm dictator. ● **dictature** nf dictatorship.

dict/er [dikte] vt to dictate (à to). ● **—ée** nf dictation.

dictionnaire [diksjɔner] nm dictionary.

dicton [diktɔ̃] nm saying, adage.

dièse [djez] a & nm Mus sharp.

diesel [djezɛl] a & nm (moteur) **d.** diesel (engine).

diète [djet] nf (jeûne) starvation diet; (régime) strict) diet; **mettre qn à la d.** to put s.o. on a starvation diet ou a (strict) diet.

diététique [djetetik] nf dietetics ‖ a **aliment** ou **produit d.** health food; **magasin d.** health-food shop.

dieu, -x [djø] nm god; **D.** God; **D. merci!** thank God!, thank goodness!

diffamation [difamasjɔ̃] nf defamation;

(*en paroles*) slander; (*par écrit*) libel; **campagne de d.** smear campaign.

différé [difere] *nm* **en d.** (*émission*) (pre)recorded.

différence [diferãs] *nf* difference (**de** in); **à la d. de** unlike; **faire la d. entre** to make a distinction between.

différend [diferã] *nm* difference (of opinion).

différent [diferã] *a* different (**de** from, to); *pl* (*divers*) different, various. ● **différemment** [-amã] *adv* differently (**de** from, to).

différer [difere] **1** *vi* to differ (**de** from). **2** *vt* (*remettre*) to postpone, defer.

difficile [difisil] *a* difficult; (*exigeant*) fussy, hard to please; **c'est d. à faire** it's hard *ou* difficult to do; **il (nous) est d. de faire ça** it's hard *ou* difficult (for us) to do that.

difficulté [difikylte] *nf* difficulty (**à faire** in doing); **en d.** in a difficult situation.

difforme [diform] *a* deformed, misshapen.

diffus [dify] *a* (*lumière, style*) diffuse.

diffuser [difyze] *vt* (*émission, nouvelle etc*) to broadcast; (*lumière, chaleur*) to diffuse; (*livre*) to distribute.

digérer [diʒere] *vt* to digest; (*endurer*) *Fam* to stomach; **avoir du mal à d.** to have trouble digesting.

digestif, -ive [diʒestif, -iv] *a* (*tube, sucs etc*) digestive ∥ *nm* after-dinner liqueur. ● **digestion** *nf* digestion.

digitale [diʒital] *af* **empreinte d.** fingerprint.

digne [diɲ] *a* (*méritant*) worthy; (*air, attitude etc*) dignified; **d. de qn** worthy of s.o.; **d. d'admiration/etc** worthy of *ou* deserving of admiration/etc. ● **dignité** *nf* dignity; **manquer de d.** to have no self-respect.

digression [digresjɔ̃] *nf* digression.

digue [dig] *nf* dike; (*en bord de mer*) sea wall.

dilapider [dilapide] *vt* to squander, waste.

dilater [dilate] *vt*, **se d.** *vpr* to expand.

dilemme [dilem] *nm* dilemma.

diligence [diliʒãs] *nf* **1** (*rapidité*) speedy efficiency. **2** (*véhicule*) *Hist* stagecoach.

diluer [dilɥe] *vt* to dilute (**in** dans).

diluvienne [dilyvjen] *af* **pluie d.** torrential rain.

dimanche [dimãʃ] *nm* Sunday.

dimension [dimãsjɔ̃] *nf* (*mesure*) dimension; (*taille*) size; **à deux dimensions** two-dimensional.

diminuer [diminɥe] *vt* to reduce, decrease; (*frais*) to cut down, reduce; (*forces physiques*) to diminish, lessen, reduce ∥ *vi* (*réserves, nombre*) to decrease, diminish; (*jours*) to get shorter; (*prix*) to decrease. ● **diminution** *nf* reduction, decrease (**de** in).

diminutif, -ive [diminytif, -iv] *a* & *nm Gram* diminutive ∥ *nm* (*prénom*) nickname.

dinde [dɛ̃d] *nf* turkey. ● **dindon** *nm* turkey (cock).

dîner [dine] *vi* to have dinner; (*au Canada, en Belgique etc*) to (have) lunch ∥ *nm* dinner; lunch; (*soirée*) dinner party.

dînette [dinet] *nf* (*jouet*) doll's dinner service *ou* set.

dingue [dɛ̃g] *a Fam* crazy, nuts ∥ *nmf Fam* nutcase.

dinosaure [dinozor] *nm* dinosaur.

diphtongue [diftɔ̃g] *nf Ling* diphthong.

diplomate [diplɔmat] *nmf Pol* diplomat; (*négociateur habile*) diplomatist ∥ *a* (*habile, plein de tact*) diplomatic. ● **diplomatie** [-asi] *nf* (*tact*) & *Pol* diplomacy; (*carrière*) diplomatic service.

diplôme [diplom] *nm* certificate, diploma; *Univ* degree. ● **diplômé, -ée** *a* & *nmf* qualified (person); **être d. (de)** *Univ* to be a graduate (of).

dire* [dir] *vt* (*mot, avis etc*) to say; (*vérité, secret, heure etc*) to tell; **d. des bêtises** to talk nonsense; **d. qch à qn** to tell s.o. sth, say sth to s.o.; **d. à qn que** to tell s.o. that, say to s.o. that; **d. à qn de faire** to tell s.o. to do; **d. du mal/du bien de** to speak ill/well of; **on dirait un**

château it looks like a castle; **on dirait du Mozart** it sounds like Mozart; **on dirait du cabillaud** it tastes like cod; **ça ne me dit rien** (*envie*) I don't feel like that; (*souvenir*) it doesn't ring a bell; **dites donc!** look (here)!; **autrement dit** in other words; **à vrai d.** to tell the truth; **ça ne se dit pas** that's not said.
∥*nm* **au d.** according to.

direct [dirɛkt] *a* direct; **train d.** fast train ∥*nm* **en d.** (*émission*) live. ●—**ement** [-əmɑ̃] *adv* directly; (*immédiatement*) straight (away), directly.

directeur, -trice [dirɛktœr, -tris] *nmf* director; (*d'école*) headmaster, headmistress, *Am* principal ∥*a* (*principe*) guiding; **idées** *ou* **lignes directrices** guidelines.

direction [dirɛksjɔ̃] *nf* **1** (*sens*) direction; **en d. de** (*train*) (going) to, for. **2** (*de société, club*) running, management; (*d'études*) supervision; **avoir la d. de** to be in charge of; **sous la d. de** (*orchestre*) conducted by; **la d.** (*équipe dirigeante*) the management.

dirigeable [diriʒabl] *a* & *nm* (**ballon) d.** airship, dirigible.

dirigeant [diriʒɑ̃] *a* (*classe*) ruling ∥*nm* (*de pays*) leader; (*d'entreprise, club*) manager.

diriger [diriʒe] *vt* (*société, club*) to run, manage; (*parti, groupe, débat*) to lead; (*véhicule*) to steer; (*orchestre*) to conduct; (*études*) to supervise; (*orienter*) to turn (*vers* towards); (*arme, lumière*) to point (*vers* towards); **se d. vers** (*lieu, objet*) to make one's way towards, head for; (*dans une carrière*) to turn towards.

dirigisme [diriʒism] *nm* Écon state control.

dis, disant [di, dizɑ̃] *voir* **dire**.

discerner [disɛrne] *vt* (*voir*) to make out, discern; (*différencier*) to distinguish.

disciple [disipl] *nm* disciple, follower.

discipline [disiplin] *nf* (*règle, matière*) discipline.

discipliner (se) [sədisipline] *vpr* to dis-

cipline oneself. ●**discipliné** *a* well-disciplined.

discontinu [diskɔ̃tiny] *a* (*ligne*) discontinuous; (*bruit etc*) intermittent. ●**discontinuer** *vi* **sans d.** without stopping.

disconvenir [diskɔ̃vnir] *vi* **je n'en disconviens pas** I don't deny it.

discordant [diskɔrdɑ̃] *a* (*son*) discordant; (*témoignages*) conflicting; (*couleurs*) clashing.

discothèque [diskɔtɛk] *nf* record library; (*club*) discotheque, disco.

discours [diskur] *nm* speech. ●**discourir** *vi Péj* to speechify, hold forth.

discréditer [diskredite] *vt* to discredit, bring into disrepute ∥ **se d.** *vpr* (*personne*) to become discredited.

discret, -ète [diskrɛ, -ɛt] *a* (*personne, manière etc*) discreet; (*vêtement*) simple. ●**discrètement** *adv* discreetly; (*s'habiller*) simply. ●**discrétion** *nf* discretion; **vin**/*etc* **à d.** as much wine/*etc* as one wants.

discrimination [diskriminasjɔ̃] *nf* (*ségrégation*) discrimination.

disculper [diskylpe] *vt* to exonerate (*de* from).

discussion [diskysjɔ̃] *nf* discussion; (*conversation*) talk; (*querelle*) argument; **pas de d.!** no argument!

discuter [diskyte] *vt* to discuss; (*familièrement*) to talk over; (*contester*) to question; **ça peut se d.** that's arguable ∥ *vi* (*parler*) to talk (**de** about, **avec** with); (*répliquer*) to argue; **de** *ou* **sur qch** to discuss sth. ●**discuté** *a* (*auteur*) much discussed; (*théorie, question*) disputed, controversial.

dise, disent [diz] *voir* **dire**.

diseuse [dizœz] *nf* **d. de bonne aventure** fortune-teller.

disgracieux, -euse [disgrasjø, -øz] *a* ungainly.

disjoindre [disʒwɛ̃dr] *vt* (*questions*) to treat separately. ●**disjoint** *a* (*questions*) unconnected.

disjoncteur [disʒɔ̃ktœr] *nm* Él circuit breaker.

disloquer (se) [sədisloke] *vpr* (*meuble etc*) to fall apart; (*cortège*) to break up; **se d. le bras** to dislocate one's arm.
disons [dizɔ̃] *voir* **dire**.
dispar/aître* [disparetr] *vi* to disappear; (*être porté manquant*) to go missing; **d. en mer** to be lost at sea; **faire d.** to remove, get rid of. ●**—u** *a* (*soldat etc*) missing; **être porté d.** to be reported missing. ●**disparition** *nf* disappearance; (*mort*) death.
dispensaire [dispãser] *nm* community health centre.
dispense [dispãs] *nf* exemption. ●**dispenser** *vt* (*soins, bienfaits etc*) to dispense; **d. qn de** (*obligation*) to exempt s.o. from; **se d. de faire** to spare oneself the bother of doing.
disperser [disperse] *vt* to disperse, scatter; (*efforts*) to dissipate **‖ se d.** *vpr* (*foule*) to disperse; **elle se disperse trop** she tries to do too many things at once.
disponible [disponibl] *a* (*article, place etc*) available; (*esprit*) alert.
dispos [dispo] *am* **frais et d.** refreshed.
disposé [dispoze] *a* **bien/mal d.** in a good/bad mood; **bien d. envers** well-disposed towards; **d. à faire** prepared *ou* disposed to do.
disposer [dispoze] *vt* (*objets*) to arrange; **se d. à faire** to prepare to do **‖ vi d. de qch** to have sth at one's disposal; (*utiliser*) to make use of sth; **d. de qn** *Péj* to take advantage of s.o.
dispositif [dispozitif] *nm* (*mécanisme*) device; **d. policier** police presence.
disposition [dispozisjɔ̃] *nf* arrangement; (*de maison, page*) layout; (*humeur*) frame of mind; *pl* (*aptitudes*) ability, aptitude (**pour** for); **à la d. de qn** at s.o.'s disposal; **prendre ses** *ou* **des dispositions** (*préparatifs*) to make arrangements; (*pour l'avenir*) to make provision; **dans de bonnes dispositions à l'égard de** well-disposed towards.
disproportionné [disprɔpɔrsjɔne] *a* disproportionate.
dispute [dispyt] *nf* quarrel. ●**disputer** *vt*

(*match*) to play; (*rallye*) to compete in; **d. qch à qn** (*prix, première place etc*) to fight with s.o. for *ou* over sth; **d. qn** (*gronder*) *Fam* to tell s.o. off **‖ se d.** *vpr* to quarrel (**avec** with); (*match*) to take place; **se d. qch** to fight over sth.
disqualifier [diskalifje] *vt* (*équipe etc*) to disqualify.
disque [disk] *nm* (*de musique*) record; (*cercle*) disc, *Am* disk; (*d'ordinateur*) disk; **d. compact** compact disc *ou Am* disk. ●**disquette** *nf* (*d'ordinateur*) floppy (disk), diskette.
disséminer [disemine] *vt* (*graines, mines etc*) to scatter; (*idées*) *Fig* to disseminate.
disséquer [diseke] *vt* to dissect.
dissertation [disertasjɔ̃] *nf Scol* essay.
dissimuler [disimyle] *vt* (*cacher*) to hide, conceal (**à** from) **‖ se d.** *vpr* to hide (oneself), conceal oneself.
dissipé [disipe] *a* (*élève*) unruly; (*vie*) dissipated.
dissiper [disipe] *vt* (*brouillard, craintes*) to dispel; (*fortune*) to squander, dissipate; **d. qn** to distract s.o. **‖ se d.** *vpr* (*brume*) to clear, lift; (*craintes*) to disappear; (*élève*) to misbehave.
dissolu [disɔly] *a* (*vie etc*) dissolute.
dissolvant [disɔlvã] *a & nm* solvent; (*pour vernis à ongles*) nail polish remover.
dissoudre* [disudr] *vt, se d.* *vpr* to dissolve.
dissuader [disɥade] *vt* to dissuade, deter (**de qch** from sth, **de faire** from doing). ●**dissuasion** *nf* dissuasion; **force de d.** *Mil* deterrent.
distance [distãs] *nf* distance; **à deux mètres de d.** two metres apart; **à d.** at *ou* from a distance. ●**distancer** *vt* to leave behind.
distant [distã] *a* distant; **d. de dix kilomètres** (*éloigné*) ten kilometres away; (*à intervalles*) ten kilometres apart.
distendre [distãdr] *vt, se d.* *vpr* to distend.
distiller [distile] *vt* to distil. ●**distillerie** *nf*

(*lieu*) distillery.

distinct, -incte [distɛ̃, -ɛ̃kt] *a* (*différent*) distinct, separate (**de** from); (*net*) clear, distinct. ● **distinctement** *adv* distinctly, clearly.

distinguer [distɛ̃ge] *vt* (*différencier*) to distinguish; (*voir*) to make out; **d. le bien du mal** to tell good from evil ‖ **se d.** *vpr* (*s'illustrer*) to distinguish oneself; **se d. de** (*différer*) to be distinguishable from. ● **distingué** *a* (*bien élevé, éminent*) distinguished; **sentiments distingués** (*formule épistolaire de politesse*) yours faithfully, *Am* sincerely.

distraction [distraksjɔ̃] *nf* amusement, distraction; (*étourderie*) (fit of) absent-mindedness. ● **distraire*** *vt* (*divertir*) to entertain, amuse ‖ **se d.** *vpr* to amuse oneself. ● **distrait** *a* absent-minded. ● **distrayant** *a* entertaining.

distribuer [distribɥe] *vt* (*donner*) to hand *ou* give out, distribute; (*courrier*) to deliver; (*cartes*) to deal.

distributeur [distribytœr] *nm* *Aut Cin Com* distributor; **d. (automatique)** vending machine; **d. de billets** *Rail* ticket machine; (*de billets de banque*) cash dispenser *ou* machine.

distribution [distribysjɔ̃] *nf* distribution; (*du courrier*) delivery.

dit [di] *voir* **dire** ‖ *a* (*convenu*) agreed; (*surnommé*) called.

dites [dit] *voir* **dire**.

divaguer [divage] *vi* (*dérailler*) to rave, talk drivel.

divan [divɑ̃] *nm* divan, couch.

divers, -erses [diver, -ers] *a* (*varié*) varied, diverse; *pl* (*distincts*) various; **d. groupes** (*plusieurs*) various groups.

divertir [divertir] *vt* to entertain ‖ **se d.** *vpr* to enjoy oneself. ● **divertissement** *nm* entertainment.

dividende [dividɑ̃d] *nm* *Math Fin* dividend.

divin [divɛ̃] *a* divine. ● **divinité** *nf* divinity.

diviser [divize] *vt*, **se d.** *vpr* to divide (**en** into). ● **division** *nf* division.

divorce [divɔrs] *nm* divorce. ● **divorcer** *vi* to get *ou* be divorced, divorce; **d. d'avec qn** to divorce s.o. ● **divorcé, -ée** *a* divorced (**d'avec** from) ‖ *nmf* divorcee.

divulguer [divylge] *vt* to divulge.

dix [dis] (**dix** *before consonant*, [diz] *before vowel* & *nm* ten. ● **dixième** [dizjɛm] *a* & *nmf* tenth; **un d.** a tenth. ● **dix-huit** [dizɥit] *a* & *nm* eighteen. ● **dix-neuf** [diznœf] *a* & *nm* nineteen. ● **dix-sept** [disset] *a* & *nm* seventeen.

dizaine [dizen] *nf* **une d. (de)** about ten.

docile [dɔsil] *a* submissive, docile.

dock [dɔk] *nm* *Nau* dock. ● **docker** [dɔker] *nm* docker.

docteur [dɔktœr] *nm* *Méd Univ* doctor (**ès, en** of). ● **doctorat** *nm* doctorate, = PhD (**ès, en** in).

doctrine [dɔktrin] *nf* doctrine.

document [dɔkymɑ̃] *nm* document. ● **documentaire** *a* documentary ‖ *nm* (*film*) documentary. ● **documentaliste** *nmf* information officer; (*à l'école*) (school) librarian.

documenter (se) [sədɔkymɑ̃te] *vpr* to collect information. ● **documenté** *a* (**bien** *ou* **très**) **d.** (*personne*) well-informed. ● **documentation** *nf* (*documents*) documentation.

dodeliner [dɔdline] *vi* **d. de la tête** to nod (one's head).

dodo [dodo] *nm* (*langage enfantin*) **faire d.** to sleep; **aller au d.** to go to bye-byes.

dodu [dɔdy] *a* a chubby, plump.

dogue [dɔg] *nm* (*chien*) mastiff.

doigt [dwa] *nm* finger; **d. de pied** toe; **petit d.** little finger, *Am* pinkie; **un d. de vin/etc** a drop of wine/etc; **à deux doigts de** within an ace of; **savoir qch sur le bout du d.** to have sth at one's finger tips.

doigté [dwate] *nm* *Mus* fingering, touch; (*savoir-faire*) tact.

dois, doit [dwa] *voir* **devoir**[1,2].

doléances [dɔleɑ̃s] *nfpl* (*plaintes*) grievances.

dollar [dɔlar] *nm* dollar.

domaine [dɔmen] *nm* (*terres*) estate.

domain; (*sphère*) province, domain.

dôme [dom] *nm* dome.

domestique [dɔmɛstik] *a* (*vie, usage, marché etc*) domestic; **travaux domestiques** housework; **animal d.** domestic animal, pet ▮ *nmf* servant.

domicile [dɔmisil] *nm* home; **travailler à d.** to work at home; **livrer à d.** (*pain etc*) to deliver (to the house).

dominer [dɔmine] *vt* to dominate; (*situation, sentiment*) to master, dominate; (*être supérieur à*) to surpass; (*tour, rocher*) to tower above, dominate; (*valley, building etc*) to dominate; (*être le plus fort*) to dominate; (*être le plus important*) to predominate ▮ **se d.** *vpr* to control oneself. ● **dominateur, -trice** *a* domineering. ● **domination** *nf* domination.

domino [dɔmino] *nm* domino; *pl* (*jeu*) dominoes.

dommage [dɔmaʒ] **1** *nm* (**c'est**) **d.!** it's a pity *ou* a shame! (**quel**) **d.!** what a pity *ou* a shame! **2** *nmpl* (*dégâts*) damage; **dommages-intérêts** *Jur* damages.

dompt/er [dõte] *vt* (*animal*) to tame. ● **—eur, -euse** *nmf* (*de lions*) lion tamer.

DOM-TOM [dɔmtɔm] *nmpl abrév* (*départements et territoires d'outre-mer*) (French) overseas departments and territories.

don [dõ] *nm* (*cadeau, aptitude*) gift; (*charité*) donation.

donc [dõ(k)] *conj* so, then; (*par conséquent*) so, therefore; **asseyez-vous d.!** (*intensif*) will you sit down!; **allons d.!** come on!

donjon [dõʒõ] *nm* (*de château*) keep.

données [dɔne] *nfpl* (*information*) data; (*de problème*) (known) facts.

donner [dɔne] *vt* to give; (*récolte, résultat*) to produce; (*sa place*) to give up; (*cartes*) to deal; **pourriez-vous me d. l'heure?** could you tell me the time?; **d. un coup à** to hit; **d. à réparer** to take (in) to be repaired; **d. raison à qn** to say s.o. is right; **ça donne soif/faim** it makes

you thirsty/hungry; **c'est donné** *Fam* it's dirt cheap; **étant donné** (*la situation etc*) considering, in view of; **étant donné que** considering (that).

▮ *vi* **d. sur** (*fenêtre*) to overlook, look out onto; (*porte*) to open onto; **d. dans** (*piège*) to fall into.

▮ **se donner** *vpr* (*se consacrer*) to devote oneself (à to); **se d. du mal** to go to a lot of trouble (**pour faire** to do); **s'en d. à cœur joie** to have a whale of a time. ● **donneur, -euse** *nmf* giver; (*de sang, d'organe*) donor; *Cartes* dealer.

dont [dõ] *pron rel* (= *de qui, duquel, de quoi etc*) (*personne*) of whom; (*chose*) of which; (*appartenance: personne*) whose; (*appartenance: chose*) of which, whose; **une mère d. le fils est malade** a mother whose son is ill; **la fille d. il est fier** the daughter he is proud of *ou* of whom he is proud; **les outils d. j'ai besoin** the tools I need; **la façon d. elle joue** the way (in which) she plays; **cinq enfants d. deux filles** five children two of whom are daughters.

doper (se) [sǝdɔpe] *vpr* to take dope.

dorénavant [dɔrenavã] *adv* henceforth.

dor/er [dɔre] *vt* (*objet*) to gild; **se (faire) d. au soleil** to sunbathe. ● **—é** *a* (*objet*) gilt, gold; (*couleur*) golden.

dorloter [dɔrlɔte] *vt* to pamper, coddle.

dormir* [dɔrmir] *vi* to sleep; (*être endormi*) to be asleep.

dortoir [dɔrtwar] *nm* dormitory.

dos [do] *nm* (*de personne, d'animal*) back; (*de livre*) spine; **à d. d'âne** (*riding*) on a donkey; **'voir au d.'** (*verso*) 'see over'.

dose [doz] *nf* dose; (*quantité administrée*) dosage. ● **doser** *vt* (*remède*) to measure out the dose of; (*équilibrer*) to strike the correct balance between. ● **dosage** *nm* measuring out (*of dose*); équilibre balance.

dossard [dɔsar] *nm* Sp number (*fixed on back*).

dossier [dɔsje] *nm* **1** (*de siège*) back. **2** (*papiers*) file, dossier; (*classeur*) folder, file.

dot [dɔt] *nf* dowry.

doter [dɔte] *vt* (*hôpital etc*) to endow; **d. de** (*matériel*) to equip with.

douane [dwan] *nf* customs. ● **douanier, -ière** *nm* customs officer.

doublage [dublaʒ] *nm* (*de film*) dubbing.

double [dubl] *a & adv* double ‖ *nm* (*copie*) copy, duplicate; **le d. (de)** (*quantité*) twice as much (as).

doubler [duble] **1** *vt* (*augmenter*) to double; (*vêtement*) to line; (*film*) to dub; (*acteur*) to stand in for; (*classe à l'école*) to repeat. **2** *vti* (*en voiture*) to overtake, pass.

doublure [dublyr] *nf* (*étoffe*) lining; *Th* understudy; *Cin* stand-in, double.

douce [dus] *voir* **doux.** ● **doucement** *adv* (*délicatement*) gently; (*à voix basse*) softly; (*lentement*) slowly; (*sans bruit*) quietly. ● **douceur** *nf* (*de miel etc*) sweetness; (*de peau etc*) softness; (*de temps*) mildness; (*de personne*) gentleness; *pl* (*sucreries*) sweets, *Am* candies.

douche [duʃ] *nf* shower. ● **doucher** *vt* **d. qn** to give s.o. a shower ‖ **se d.** *vpr* to take *ou* have a shower.

doué [dwe] *a* gifted, talented (**en** at); (*intelligent*) clever; **il est d. pour** he has a gift *ou* talent for.

douille [duj] *nf* (*d'ampoule*) *Él* socket; (*de cartouche*) case.

douillet, -ette [dujɛ, -ɛt] *a* (*lit etc*) soft, cosy, *Am* cozy; **tu es d.** (*délicat*) you're such a baby.

douleur [dulœr] *nf* (*mal*) pain; (*chagrin*) sorrow, grief. ● **douloureux, -euse** *a* (*maladie, membre, décision etc*) painful.

doute [dut] *nm* doubt; **sans d.** no doubt, probably; **sans aucun d.** without (any *ou* a) doubt. ● **douter** *vi* to doubt; **d. de qch/qn** to doubt sth/s.o.; **se d. de qch** to suspect sth; **je m'en doute** I would think so, I suspect so. ● **douteux, -euse** *a* doubtful; (*louche, médiocre*) dubious.

Douvres [duvr] *nm ou f* Dover.

doux, douce [du, dus] *a* (*miel etc*) sweet; (*peau, lumière etc*) soft; (*temps*) mild;

(*personne, pente etc*) gentle.

douze [duz] *a & nm* twelve. ● **douzaine** *nf* (*douze*) dozen; (*environ*) about twelve; **une d. d'œufs**/*etc* a dozen eggs/*etc*. ● **douzième** *a & nmf* twelfth.

doyen, -enne [dwajɛ̃, -ɛn] *nmf Rel Univ* dean; **d. (d'âge)** oldest person.

dragée [draʒe] *nf* sugared almond.

dragon [dragɔ̃] *nm* (*animal*) dragon.

draguer [drage] *vt* **1** (*rivière etc*) to dredge. **2** *Arg* (*faire du baratin à*) to chat (*s.o.*) up, *Am* smooth-talk (*s.o.*).

drame [dram] *nm* drama; (*catastrophe*) tragedy. ● **dramatique** *a* dramatic; **auteur d.** playwright, dramatist; **film d.** drama.

drap [dra] *nm* (*de lit*) sheet; **d. housse** fitted sheet; **d. de bain** bath towel.

drapeau, -x [drapo] *nm* flag; **être sous les drapeaux** to be doing one's military service.

dresser [drese] **1** *vt* (*échelle, statue*) to put up, erect; (*oreille*) to prick up; (*liste*) to draw up, make out ‖ **se d.** *vpr* (*personne*) to stand up; (*statue, montagne*) to rise up, stand; **se d. contre** (*abus*) to stand up against. **2** *vt* (*animal*) to train. ● **dressage** *nm* training. ● **dresseur, -euse** *nmf* trainer.

dribbler [drible] *vti Fb* to dribble.

drogue [drɔg] *nf* (*médicament*) *Péj* drug; **une d.** (*stupéfiant*) a drug; **la d.** drugs, dope. ● **droguer** *vt* (*victime*) to drug; (*malade*) to dose up ‖ **se d.** *vpr* to take drugs, be on drugs; (*malade*) to dose oneself up. ● **drogué, -ée** *nmf* drug addict.

droguerie [drɔgri] *nf* hardware shop *ou* *Am* store. ● **droguiste** *nmf* owner of a *droguerie*.

droit¹ [drwa] *nm* (*privilège*) right; (*d'inscription etc*) fee(s), dues; *pl* (*de douane*) duty; **le d.** (*science juridique*) law; **avoir d. à** to be entitled to; **avoir le d. de faire** to be entitled to do, have the right to do.

droit² [drwa] *a* (*route, ligne etc*) straight; (*vertical*) (*mur etc*) upright, straight;

(angle) right; *(honnête) Fig* upright
▌ *adv* straight; **tout d.** straight *ou* right
ahead. ● **droite¹** *nf (ligne)* straight line.
droit³ [drwa] *a (côté, bras etc)* right ▌*nm*
(coup) Boxe right. ● **droite²** *nf* **la d.**
(côté) the right (side); *Pol* the right
(wing); **à d.** *(tourner)* (to the) right;
(rouler etc) on the right; **de d.** *(fenêtre
etc)* right-hand; *(politique, candidat)*
right-wing; **à d. de** on *ou* to the right
of; **à d. et à gauche** *(voyager etc)* here,
there and everywhere.
droitier, -ière [drwatje, -jɛr] *a & nmf*
right-handed (person).
droiture [drwatyr] *nf* uprightness.
drôle [drol] *a* funny; **d. d'air/de type**
funny look/fellow. ●**—ment** *adv* fun-
nily; *(extrêmement) Fam* terribly,
dreadfully.
dromadaire [drɔmadɛr] *nm* dromedary.
dru [dry] *a (herbe etc)* thick, dense ▌*adv*
tomber d. *(pluie)* to pour down heavily;
pousser d. to grow thick(ly).
du [dy] **= de + le** *(voir* **de¹,²,³** *& le).*
dû, due [dy] *a* **d. à** *(accident etc)* due to
▌*nm* due; *(argent)* dues.
duc [dyk] *nm* duke. ● **duchesse** *nf* duchess.
duel [dɥɛl] *nm* duel.
dûment [dymɑ̃] *adv* duly.
dune [dyn] *nf (sand)* dune.
duo [dɥo] *nm Mus* duet.

dupe [dyp] *nf* dupe, fool ▌*a* **d. de** duped
by, fooled by.
duplex [dypleks] *nm* split-level flat, *Am*
duplex.
duplicata [dyplikata] *nm inv* duplicate.
duquel *voir* **lequel.**
dur [dyr] *a (substance)* hard; *(difficile)*
hard, tough; *(hiver, personne, ton)*
harsh; *(œuf)* hard-boiled; **d. d'oreille**
hard of hearing; **d. à cuire** *Fam* hard-
bitten, tough ▌*adv (travailler)* hard
▌*nm Fam* tough guy.
durable [dyrabl] *a* durable.
durant [dyrɑ̃] *prép* during.
durcir [dyrsir] *vti,* **se d.** *vpr* to harden.
durée [dyre] *nf (de film etc)* length;
(période) duration; **disque de longue d.**
long-playing record. ● **durer** *vi* to last;
ça dure depuis... it's been going on
for....
dureté [dyrte] *nf* hardness; *(de ton etc)*
harshness.
duvet [dyvɛ] *nm* **1** *(d'oiseau, de visage)*
down. **2** *(sac)* sleeping bag.
dynamique [dinamik] *a* dynamic ▌*nf*
(force) dynamic force. ● **dynamisme**
nm dynamism.
dynamite [dinamit] *nf* dynamite.
dynamo [dinamo] *nf* dynamo.
dynastie [dinasti] *nf* dynasty.
dysenterie [disɑ̃tri] *nf Méd* dysentery.
dyslexique [disleksik] *a & nmf* dyslexic.

E

E, e [ə, ø] *nm* E, e.

EAO [øao] *nm abrév (enseignement assisté par ordinateur)* computer-aided learning.

eau, -x [o] *nf* water; **e. douce** *(non salée)* fresh water; *(du robinet)* soft water; **e. salée** salt water; **e. de Cologne** eau de Cologne; **grandes eaux** *(d'un parc)* ornamental fountains; **tomber à l'e.** *(projet)* to fall through; **ça lui fait venir l'e. à la bouche** it makes his *ou* her mouth water. ● **e.-de-vie** *nf (pl* eaux-de-vie*)* brandy. ● **e.-forte** *nf (pl* eaux-fortes*) (gravure)* etching.

ébahir [ebair] *vt* to astound, dumbfound.

ébattre (s') [sebatr] *vpr* to run about, play about.

ébauche [eboʃ] *nf (esquisse)* (rough) outline, (rough) sketch.

ébène [eben] *nf (bois)* ebony.

ébéniste [ebenist] *nm* cabinet-maker.

éberlué [eberlɥe] *a Fam* dumbfounded.

éblouir [ebluir] *vt* to dazzle.

éboueur [ebwœr] *nm* dustman, *Am* garbage collector.

ébouillanter (s') [sebujɑ̃te] *vpr* to scald oneself.

ébouler (s') [sebule] *vpr (falaise etc)* to crumble; *(roches)* to fall. ● **éboulement** *nm* landslide. ● **éboulis** *nm (mass of)* fallen debris.

ébouriffé [eburife] *a* dishevelled.

ébranler [ebrɑ̃le] *vt (mur, confiance etc)* to shake; *(santé)* to weaken; *(personne)* to shake, shatter ‖ **s'é.** *vpr (train etc)* to move off.

ébrécher [ebreʃe] *vt (assiette)* to chip.

ébriété [ebrijete] *nf* **en état d'é.** under the influence of drink.

ébrouer (s') [sebrue] *vpr (se secouer)* to shake oneself (about).

ébruiter [ebrɥite] *vt (nouvelle etc)* to make known, divulge.

ébullition [ebylisjɔ̃] *nf* boiling; **être en é.** *(eau)* to be boiling.

écaille [ekaj] *nf (de poisson)* scale; *(de tortue, d'huître)* shell; *(pour lunettes)* tortoise-shell. ● **écailler 1** *vt (poisson)* to scale; *(huître)* to shell. **2 s'écailler** *vpr (peinture)* to flake (off), peel.

écarlate [ekarlat] *a & nf* scarlet.

écarquiller [ekarkije] *vt* **é. les yeux** to open one's eyes wide.

écart [ekar] *nm (intervalle)* gap; *(embardée)* swerve; *(différence)* difference (de in, entre between); **écarts de** *(conduite etc)* lapses in; **le grand é.** *(de gymnaste)* the splits; **à l'é.** out of the way; **à l'é. de** away from.

écarter [ekarte] *vt (objets)* to move apart; *(jambes, rideaux)* to open; **é. qch de qch** to move sth away from sth; **é. qn de** *(exclure)* to keep s.o. out of; *(éloigner)* to keep *ou* take s.o. away from ‖ **s'é.** *vpr (s'éloigner)* to move away (de from); *(se séparer)* to move aside (de from). ● **écarté** *a (endroit)* remote; **les jambes écartées** with legs (wide) apart. ● **écartement** *nm (espace)* gap, distance (de between).

ecclésiastique [eklezjastik] *nm* clergyman.

écervelé [eservəle] *a* scatterbrained.

échafaud [eʃafo] *nm (pour exécution)* scaffold.

échafaudage [eʃafodaʒ] *nm (de peintre etc)* scaffold(ing).

échalote [eʃalɔt] *nf* shallot, scallion.

échancré [eʃɑ̃kre] *a (encolure)* V-shaped, scooped.

échange [eʃɑ̃ʒ] *nm* exchange; **en é.** in exchange (de for). ● **échanger** *vt* to exchange (contre for).

échangeur [eʃãʒœr] *nm* (*intersection*) Aut interchange.

échantillon [eʃãtijõ] *nm* sample. ● **échantillonnage** *nm* (*collection*) range (of samples).

échapper [eʃape] *vi* é. à qn to escape from s.o.; é. à la mort to escape death; son nom m'échappe his *ou* her name escapes me; ça lui a échappé (des mains) it slipped out of his *ou* her hands; **l'é. belle** to have a close shave **∥s'é.** *vpr* (*s'enfuir*) to escape (de from); (*gaz, eau*) to escape, come out; (*cycliste*) to pull *ou* break away. ● **échappée** *nf* (*de cycliste*) breakaway. ● **échappement** *nm* **tuyau d'é.** Aut exhaust pipe; **pot d'é.** Aut silencer, Am muffler.

écharde [eʃard] *nf* (*de bois*) splinter.

écharpe [eʃarp] *nf* scarf; (*de maire*) sash; **en é.** (*bras*) in a sling.

échasse [eʃas] *nf* (*bâton*) stilt.

échauffer [eʃofe] *vt* (*moteur*) to overheat; (*esprits*) to excite **∥s'é.** *vpr* (*discussion, sportif*) to warm up.

échéance [eʃeãs] *nf* (*date limite*) date (due), expiry *ou* Am expiration date; (*paiement*) payment (due); **à brève/longue é.** (*projet, emprunt*) short-/long-term.

échéant (le cas) [ləkazeʃeã] *adv* if the occasion should arise, possibly.

échec [eʃɛk] *nm* 1 (*insuccès*) failure. 2 **les échecs** (*jeu*) chess; **en é.** in check; **é.!** check!; **é. et mat!** checkmate!

échelle [eʃɛl] *nf* 1 (*marches*) ladder; **faire la courte é. à qn** to give s.o. a leg up *ou* Am a boost. 2 (*dimension*) scale.

échelon [eʃlõ] *nm* (*d'échelle*) rung; (*de fonctionnaire*) grade.

échelonner [eʃlɔne] *vt* (*paiements*) to spread out, space out **∥ s'é.** *vpr* to be spread out.

échevelé [eʃəvle] *a* (*ébouriffé*) dishevelled; (*course, danse etc*) wild.

échine [eʃin] *nf* Anat backbone, spine.

échiquier [eʃikje] *nm* (*plateau*) chessboard.

écho [eko] *nm* (*d'un son*) echo; *pl* (*dans la presse*) gossip (items), local news; **avoir des échos de** to hear some news about; **se faire l'é. de** (*opinions etc*) to echo.

échographie [ekografi] *nf* (ultrasound) scan; **passer une é.** (*femme enceinte*) to have a scan.

échouer [eʃwe] 1 *vi* to fail; **é. à** (*examen*) to fail. 2 *vi*, **s'échouer** *vpr* (*navire*) to run aground.

éclabousser [eklabuse] *vt* to splash, spatter (de with). ● **éclaboussure** *nf* splash.

éclair [eklɛr] 1 *nm* (*lumière*) flash; (*d'orage*) flash of lightning. 2 *nm* (*gâteau*) éclair.

éclairage [eklɛraʒ] *nm* (*de pièce etc*) lighting.

éclaircir [eklɛrsir] *vt* (*couleur etc*) to make lighter; (*mystère*) to clear up **∥s'é.** *vpr* (*ciel*) to clear (up); (*situation*) to become clear; **s'é. la voix** to clear one's throat. ● **éclaircie** *nf* (*durée*) sunny spell. ● **éclaircissement** *nm* (*explication*) clarification.

éclairer [eklere] *vt* (*pièce etc*) to light (up); (*avec une lampe etc*) to give s.o. some light **∥** *vi* (*lampe*) to give light **∥ s'é.** *vpr* (*visage*) to light up, brighten up; **s'é. à la bougie** to use candlelight; **s'é. à l'électricité** to have electric lighting. ● **éclairé** *a* (*averti*) enlightened; **bien/mal é.** (*illuminé*) well/badly lit.

éclaireur, -euse [eklerœr, -øz] *nmf* (boy) scout, (girl) guide.

éclat [ekla] *nm* 1 (*de la lumière*) brightness; (*de phare*) Aut glare; (*splendeur*) brilliance; (*de la jeunesse*) bloom. 2 (*de verre ou de bois*) splinter; (*de rire, colère*) (out)burst; **éclats de voix** noisy outbursts, shouts.

éclat/er [eklate] *vi* (*pneu etc*) to burst; (*bombe*) to go off, explode; (*verre*) to shatter; (*guerre, incendie*) to break out; (*orage, scandale*) to break; **é. de rire** to burst out laughing; **é. en sanglots** to burst into tears. ● **—ant** *a* (*lumière, couleur, succès*) brilliant. ● **—ement** *nm* (*de pneu etc*) bursting; (*de bombe*) explosion.

éclipse [eklips] *nf* (*du soleil, d'une célébrité etc*) eclipse. ● **éclipser** *vt* to eclipse ▮ **s'é.** *vpr* (*soleil*) to be eclipsed; (*partir*) *Fam* to slip away.

éclopé, -ée [eklope] *a* & *nmf* lame (person).

éclore [eklɔr] *vi* (*œuf*) to hatch; (*fleur*) to open (out), blossom. ● **éclosion** *nf* hatching; opening, blossoming.

écluse [eklyz] *nf* (*de canal*) lock.

écœur/er [ekœre] *vt* (*aliment etc*) to make (*s.o.*) feel sick. ● **—ant** *a* disgusting, sickening.

école [ekɔl] *nf* school; **à l'é.** in *ou* at school; **aller à l'é.** to go to school; **é. de danse/dessin** dancing/art school; **é. normale** teachers' training college; **é. publique** state school, *Am* public school. ● **écolier, -ière** *nmf* schoolboy, schoolgirl.

écologie [ekɔlɔʒi] *nf* ecology. ● **écologique** *a* ecological. ● **écologiste** *a* (*programme etc*) environmentalist ▮ *nmf* environmentalist.

économe [ekɔnɔm] *a* thrifty, economical.

économie [ekɔnɔmi] *nf* (*activité économique, vertu*) economy; *pl* (*argent*) savings; **une é. de** (*gain*) a saving of; **faire des économies** to save (up); **é. dirigée** planned economy. ● **économique** *a* **1** (*doctrine etc*) economic; **science é.** economics. **2** (*bon marché*) economical.

économiser [ekɔnɔmize] *vt* (*forces, argent, énergie etc*) to save ▮ *vi* to economize (**sur** on).

économiste [ekɔnɔmist] *nmf* economist.

écoper [ekɔpe] **1** *vt* (*bateau*) to bail out, bale out. **2** *vi Fam* to cop it; **é. (de)** (*punition*) to cop, get.

écorce [ekɔrs] *nf* (*d'arbre*) bark; (*de fruit*) peel, skin.

écorcher [ekɔrʃe] *vt* (*érafler*) to graze; **é. les oreilles** to grate on one's ears ▮ **s'é.** *vpr* to graze oneself. ● **écorchure** *nf* graze.

Écosse [ekɔs] *nf* Scotland. ● **écossais, -aise** *a* Scottish; (*tissu*) tartan; (*whisky*) Scotch ▮ *nmf* Scot.

écosser [ekɔse] *vt* (*pois*) to shell.

écouler [ekule] **1** *vt* (*se débarrasser de*) to dispose of; (*marchandises*) to sell (off), clear. **2 s'écouler** *vpr* (*eau*) to flow out; (*temps*) to pass, elapse. ● **écoulé** *a* (*années*) past. ● **écoulement** *nm* **1** (*de liquide, véhicules*) flow; (*de temps*) passage. **2** (*de marchandises*) sale, selling.

écourter [ekurte] *vt* (*séjour, discours etc*) to cut short; (*texte, tige etc*) to shorten.

écoute [ekut] *nf* listening; **à l'é.** *Rad* tuned in, listening in (**de** to). ● **écouter** *vt* to listen to ▮ *vi* to listen; (*aux portes etc*) to eavesdrop. ● **écouteur** *nm* (*de téléphone*) earpiece; *pl* (*casque*) earphones, headphones.

écran [ekrɑ̃] *nm* screen; **le petit é.** television.

écraser [ekraze] *vt* (*broyer*) to crush; (*cigarette*) to put out; (*piéton*) to run over; (*vaincre*) to beat (hollow), crush; **écrasé de** (*travail, douleur*) overwhelmed with; **se faire é.** *Aut* to get run over ▮ **s'é.** *vpr* (*avion, voiture*) to crash (**contre** into); **s'é. dans** (*foule*) to crush *ou* squash into. ● **écrasant** *a* (*victoire, chaleur*) overwhelming.

écrémer [ekreme] *vt* (*lait*) to skim; **lait écrémé** skimmed milk.

écrevisse [ekrəvis] *nf* (*crustacé*) crayfish *inv*.

écrier (s') [ekrije] *vpr* to exclaim (**que** that).

écrin [ekrɛ̃] *nm* (*jewel*) case.

écrire* [ekrir] *vt* to write; (*noter*) to write (down); (*en toutes lettres*) to spell; **é. à la machine** to type ▮ *vi* to write ▮ **s'é.** *vpr* (*mot*) to be spelled *ou* spelt. ● **écrit** *nm* written document, paper; (*examen*) written paper; **par é.** in writing.

écriteau, -x [ekrito] *nm* notice, sign.

écriture [ekrityr] *nf* (*système*) writing; (*personnelle*) (hand)writing; *pl Com* accounts; **les Écritures** *Rel* the Scripture(s).

écrivain

écrivain [ekrivɛ̃] *nm* author, writer.
écrou [ekru] *nm* (*de boulon*) nut.
écrouer [ekrue] *vt* to imprison.
écrouler (s') [sekrule] *vpr* (*édifice, blessé etc*) to collapse.
écrue [ekry] *af* **toile é.** unbleached linen; **soie é.** raw silk.
ÉCU [eky] *nm abrév* (*European Currency Unit*) ECU.
écueil [ekœj] *nm* (*rocher*) reef; (*obstacle*) *Fig* pitfall.
écuelle [ekɥɛl] *nf* (*bol*) bowl.
éculé [ekyle] *a* (*chaussure*) worn out at the heel; (*plaisanterie*) *Fig* hackneyed.
écume [ekym] *nf* (*de mer, bave d'animal etc*) foam. ● **écumer** *vt Culin* to skim; (*piller*) to plunder ‖ *vi* to foam (**de rage** with anger).
écureuil [ekyrœj] *nm* squirrel.
écurie [ekyri] *nf* stable.
écusson [ekysɔ̃] *nm* (*en étoffe*) badge.
écuyer, -ère [ekɥije, -er] *nmf* (*cavalier*) (horse) rider, equestrian.
eczéma [egzema] *nm Méd* eczema.
édenté [edɑ̃te] *a* toothless.
édifice [edifis] *nm* building. ● **édifier** *vt* (*bâtiment*) to erect.
Édimbourg [edɛ̃bur] *nm ou f* Edinburgh.
éditer [edite] *vt* (*publier*) to publish. ● **éditeur, -trice** *nmf* publisher. ● **édition** *nf* (*livre, journal*) edition; (*métier*) publishing.
édredon [edrədɔ̃] *nm* eiderdown.
éducateur, -trice [edykatœr, -tris] *nmf* educator.
éducatif, -ive [edykatif, -iv] *a* educational.
éducation [edykasjɔ̃] *nf* (*enseignement*) education; (*façon d'élever*) upbringing; **avoir de l'é.** to have good manners; **é. physique** physical education. ● **éduquer** *vt* (*à l'école*) to educate (*s.o.*); (*à la maison*) to bring (*s.o.*) up; (*esprit*) to educate, train.
effacer [efase] *vt* (*gommer*) to rub out, erase; (*en lavant*) to wash out; (*avec un chiffon*) to wipe away ‖ **s'e.** *vpr* (*souvenir, couleur etc*) to fade; (*se placer en

retrait) to step *ou* draw aside. ● **effacé** *a* (*modeste*) self-effacing.
effarant [efarɑ̃] *a Fam* incredible.
effaroucher [efaruʃe] *vt* to scare away.
effectif, -ive [efektif, -iv] **1** *a* (*réel*) effective, real. **2** *nm* (*de classe etc*) total number, size; *pl* (*employés*) & *Mil* manpower. ● **effectivement** *adv* (*en effet*) actually, effectively.
effectuer [efektɥe] *vt* (*expérience etc*) to carry out; (*paiement, trajet etc*) to make.
efféminé [efemine] *a* effeminate.
effervescent [efervesɑ̃] *a* (*mélange, jeunesse*) effervescent.
effet [efɛ] *nm* **1** (*résultat*) effect; (*impression*) impression, effect (**sur** on); **faire de l'e.** (*remède etc*) to be effective; **rester sans e.** to have no effect; **en e.** indeed, in fact; **sous l'e. de la colère** (*agir*) in anger; **e. de serre** greenhouse effect. **2 e. de commerce** bill, draft.
effets [efɛ] *nmpl* (*vêtements*) clothes, things.
efficace [efikas] *a* (*mesure etc*) effective; (*personne*) efficient. ● **efficacité** *nf* effectiveness; efficiency.
effilocher (s') [sefiloʃe] *vpr* to fray.
effleurer [eflœre] *vt* (*frôler*) to skim, touch (lightly); (*question*) *Fig* to touch on; **e. qn** (*pensée etc*) to cross s.o.'s mind.
effondrer (s') [sefɔ̃dre] *vpr* (*projet, édifice, personne*) to collapse. ● **effondrement** *nm* collapse; (*abattement*) dejection.
efforcer (s') [seforse] *vpr* **s'e. de faire** to try (hard) *ou* endeavour to do.
effort [efɔr] *nm* effort; **sans e.** (*réussir etc*) effortlessly; **faire des efforts** to try (hard), make an effort.
effraction [efraksjɔ̃] *nf* **pénétrer par e.** (*cambrioleur*) to break in; **vol avec e.** housebreaking.
effrayer [efreje] *vt* to frighten, scare ‖ **s'e.** *vpr* to be frightened *ou* scared. ● **effrayant** *a* frightening, scary.
effriter (s') [sefrite] *vpr* to crumble

(away).

effroi [efrwa] *nm* (*frayeur*) dread. ● **effroyable** *a* dreadful, appalling.

effronté [efrɔ̃te] *a* (*enfant etc*) insolent, cheeky. ● **effronterie** *nf* insolence.

effusion [efyzjɔ̃] *nf* **1** e. de sang bloodshed. **2** (*manifestation de tendresse*) emotional outburst; **avec e.** effusively.

égal, -ale, -aux [egal, -o] *a* equal (à to); (*uniforme, régulier*) even; **ça m'est é.** I don't care ∥ *nmf* (*personne*) equal; **traiter qn d'é. à é. ou en é.** to treat s.o. as an equal; **sans é.** without match. ● **-ement** *adv* (*aussi*) also, as well; (*au même degré*) equally. ● **égaler** *vt* to equal, match (en in); **3 plus 4 égale(nt) 7** 3 plus 4 equals 7.

égaliser [egalize] *vt* to equalize; (*terrain*) to level ∥ *vi Sp* to equalize.

égalité [egalite] *nf* equality; (*régularité*) evenness; **à é. (de score)** *Sp* even, equal (in points); **signe d'é.** *Math* equals sign.

égard [egar] *nm* **à l'é. de** (*envers*) towards; (*concernant*) with respect *ou* regard to; **avoir des égards pour qn** to have respect *ou* consideration for s.o.; **à cet é.** in this respect.

égarer [egare] *vt* (*objet*) to mislay ∥ **s'é.** *vpr* to lose one's way, get lost; (*objet*) to get mislaid, go astray.

égayer [egeje] *vt* (*pièce*) to brighten up; **é. qn** (*réconforter, amuser*) to cheer s.o. up.

églantier [eglɑ̃tje] *nm* (*arbre*) wild rose. ● **églantine** *nf* (*fleur*) wild rose.

église [egliz] *nf* church.

égoïsme [egɔism] *nm* selfishness. ● **égoïste** *a* & *nmf* selfish (person).

égorger [egɔrʒe] *vt* to cut the throat of.

égosiller (s') [segɔzije] *vpr* to scream one's head off, bawl out.

égout [egu] *nm* sewer; **eaux d'é.** sewage.

égoutter [egute] *vt* (*vaisselle*) to drain; (*légumes*) to strain, drain ∥ **s'é.** *vpr* to drain; to strain; (*linge*) to drip. ● **égouttoir** *nm* (*panier*) (dish) drainer.

égratigner (s') [segratiɲe] *vpr* (*en tom-*

bant etc) to scratch oneself. ● **égratignure** *nf* scratch.

égrener [egrəne] *vt* (*raisins*) to pick off; (*épis*) to shell.

Égypte [eʒipt] *nf* Egypt. ● **égyptien, -ienne** [-sjɛ̃, -sjɛn] *a* & *nmf* Egyptian.

eh! [e] *int* hey!; **eh bien!** well!

éhonté [eɔ̃te] *a* shameless; **mensonge é.** barefaced lie.

éjecter [eʒɛkte] *vt* to eject.

élaborer [elabɔre] *vt* (*système etc*) to elaborate. ● **élaboration** *nf* elaboration.

élaguer [elage] *vt* (*arbre, texte etc*) to prune.

élan [elɑ̃] *nm* (*vitesse*) momentum, impetus; (*impulsion*) impulse; (*fougue*) fervour, spirit; **prendre son é.** *Sp* to take a run (up).

élancé [elɑ̃se] *a* (*personne, taille etc*) slender.

élancer (s') [selɑ̃se] *vpr* (*bondir*) to leap *ou* rush (forward); **s'é. vers le ciel** (*tour*) to soar up (high) into the sky.

élargir [elarʒir] *vt* (*chemin*) to widen; (*vêtement*) to let out; (*esprit, débat*) to broaden ∥ **s'é.** *vpr* (*sentier etc*) to widen out; (*vêtement*) to stretch.

élastique [elastik] *a* (*objet*) elastic; (*règlement, notion*) flexible, supple ∥ *nm* (*lien*) elastic *ou* rubber band; (*tissu*) elastic.

élection [elɛksjɔ̃] *nf* election; **é. partielle** by-election. ● **électeur, -trice** *nmf* voter, elector. ● **électoral, -aux** *a* **campagne électorale** election campaign; **liste électorale** register of electors; **collège é.** electoral college.

électricien [elɛktrisjɛ̃] *nm* electrician. ● **électricité** *nf* electricity; **coupure d'é.** power cut. ● **électrique** *a* (*pendule, décharge*) electric; (*courant, fil*) electric(al); (*effet*) *Fig* electric.

électrocuter [elɛktrɔkyte] *vt* to electrocute.

électrogène [elɛktrɔʒɛn] *a* **groupe é.** *Él* generator.

électroménager [elɛktrɔmenaʒe] *am* **appareil é.** household electrical appliance.

électron [elektrɔ̃] *nm* electron. ●**électronicien, -ienne** *nmf* electronics engineer. ●**électronique** *a* electronic; **microscope é.** electron microscope ▮ *nf* electronics.

électrophone [elektrɔfɔn] *nm* record player.

élégant [elegɑ̃] *a* (*style, solution etc*) elegant; (*bien habillé*) smart, elegant. ●**élégamment** *adv* elegantly; smartly. ●**élégance** *nf* elegance; **avec é.** elegantly; (*s'habiller*) smartly, elegantly.

élément [elemɑ̃] *nm* (*composante, personne*) & *Ch* element; (*de meuble*) unit; (*d'ensemble*) *Math* member; *pl* (*notions*) rudiments, elements; **dans son é.** (*milieu*) in one's element.

élémentaire [elemɑ̃tɛr] *a* basic; (*cours, école etc*) elementary.

éléphant [elefɑ̃] *nm* elephant. ●**éléphantesque** *a* (*énorme*) *Fam* elephantine.

élevage [ɛlvaʒ] *nm* breeding, rearing; **é. de bovins** cattle rearing; **faire l'é. de** to breed, rear.

élévation [elevasjɔ̃] *nf* raising; *Géom* elevation; **é. de** (*hausse*) rise in.

élève [elɛv] *nmf Scol* pupil.

élevé [ɛlve] *a* (*haut*) high; (*noble*) noble; **bien/mal é.** well-/bad-mannered.

élever [ɛlve] *vt* (*prix, voix etc*) to raise; (*enfant*) to bring up, raise; (*animal*) to breed, rear ▮**s'é.** *vpr* (*prix, ton etc*) to rise; (*cerf-volant*) to rise (up) into the sky; **s'é. à** (*prix etc*) to amount to; **s'é. contre** to rise up against.

éleveur, -euse [ɛlvœr, -øz] *nmf* breeder.

éligible [eliʒibl] *a Pol* eligible (à for).

élimé [elime] *a* (*tissu*) threadbare.

éliminer [elimine] *vt* to eliminate. ●**élimination** *nf* elimination. ●**éliminatoire** *a* épreuve *Sp* qualifying round, heat; *Scol* qualifying exam; **note é.** *Scol* disqualifying mark ▮*nfpl* **éliminatoires** *Sp* qualifying rounds.

élire* [elir] *vt Pol* to elect (à to).

élite [elit] *nf* elite (de of); **les élites** the elite; **troupes/***etc* **d'e.** crack *ou* elite

troops/*etc.*

elle [el] *pron f* **1** (*sujet*) she; (*chose, animal*) it; *pl* they; **e. est** she is; it is; **elles sont** they are. **2** (*complément*) her; (*chose, animal*) it; *pl* them; **pour e.** for her; **pour elles** for them; **plus grande qu'e./qu'elles** taller than her/them. ●**e.-même** *pron f* herself; (*chose, animal*) itself; *pl* themselves.

élocution [elɔkysjɔ̃] *nf* diction; **défaut d'é.** speech defect.

éloge [elɔʒ] *nm* (*compliment*) praise; (*panégyrique*) eulogy. ●**élogieux, -euse** *a* laudatory.

éloigné [elwaɲe] *a* (*lieu*) far away, remote; (*date, parent*) distant; **é. de** (*village, maison etc*) far (away) from; (*très différent*) far removed from.

éloignement [elwaɲ(ə)mɑ̃] *nm* remoteness, distance; (*absence*) separation (de from).

éloigner [elwaɲe] *vt* (*chose, personne*) to move *ou* take away (de from); (*malade, moustiques*) to keep away; (*crainte, idée*) to get rid of, banish; (*échéance*) to put off; **é. qn de** (*sujet, but*) to get s.o. away from ▮**s'é.** *vpr* (*partir*) to move *ou* go away (de from); (*dans le passé*) to become (more) remote; **s'é. de** (*sujet, but*) to get away from.

élongation [elɔ̃gasjɔ̃] *nf Méd* pulled muscle.

éloquent [elɔkɑ̃] *a* eloquent. ●**éloquence** *nf* eloquence.

élu, -ue [ely] *pp de* **élire** ▮ *nmf Pol* elected member *ou* representative.

émail, -aux [emaj, -o] *nm* enamel; **casserole/***etc* **en é.** enamel saucepan/*etc.*

émanciper [emɑ̃sipe] *vt* (*femmes*) to emancipate ▮**s'é.** *vpr* to become emancipated.

émaner [emane] *vt* **e. de** to come *ou* emanate from. ●**émanations** *nfpl* (*odeurs*) smells; (*vapeurs*) fumes; **é. toxiques** toxic fumes.

emballer [ɑ̃bale] **1** *vt* (*dans une caisse etc*) to pack; (*dans du papier*) to wrap (up). **2** *vt* **e. qn** (*passionner*) *Fam* to thrill s.o. ‖**s'e.** *vpr* (*personne*) *Fam* to get carried away; (*cheval*) to bolt; (*moteur*) to race. ●**emballé** *a Fam* enthusiastic. ●**emballage** *nm* (*action*) packing; wrapping; (*caisse*) packaging; **papier d'e.** wrapping (paper).

embarcadère [ābarkader] *nm* quay, wharf.

embarcation [ābarkasjō] *nf* (small) boat.

embardée [ābarde] *nf Aut* (sudden) swerve; **faire une e.** to swerve.

embargo [ābargo] *nm* embargo.

embarquer [ābarke] *vt* (*passagers*) to take on board; (*marchandises*) to load (up); **e. qn dans** (*affaire*) *Fam* to involve s.o. in ‖ *vi*, **s'e.** *vpr* to (go on) board, embark; **s'e. dans** (*aventure etc*) *Fam* to embark on. ●**embarquement** *nm* (*de passagers*) boarding.

embarras [ābara] *nm* (*gêne*) embarrassment; (*difficulté*) difficulty, trouble; (*obstacle*) obstacle; **dans l'e.** in difficulty, in an awkward situation; (*financièrement*) in difficulties.

embarrasser [ābarase] *vt* (*obstruer*) to clutter; **e. qn** to be in s.o.'s way; (*déconcerter*) to embarrass s.o.; **s'e. de** to burden oneself with; (*se soucier*) to bother oneself about. ●**embarrassant** *a* (*paquet*) cumbersome; (*question*) embarrassing.

embauche [ābof] *nf* (*action*) hiring; (*travail*) work. ●**embaucher** *vt* (*ouvrier*) to hire, take on.

embaumer [ābome] *vt* (*parfumer*) to give a sweet smell to ‖ *vi* to smell sweet.

embellir [ābelir] *vt* (*personne*) to make more attractive; (*texte, vérité*) to embellish ‖ *vi* (*jeune fille etc*) to blossom out.

embêter [ābete] *vt Fam* (*agacer*) to annoy, bother; (*ennuyer*) to bore ‖**s'e.** *vpr Fam* to get bored. ●**embêtant** *a Fam* annoying; boring. ●**embêtement** [-etmā] *nm Fam* **un e.** (some) trouble *ou* bother; **des embêtements** trouble, bother.

emblée (d') [dāble] *adv* right away.

emblème [āblem] *nm* emblem.

emboîter [ābwate] *vt*, **s'e.** *vpr* (*tuyau(x)*) to fit together; **e. le pas à qn** to follow close on s.o.'s heels; (*imiter*) *Fig* to follow in s.o.'s footsteps.

embouchure [ābuʃyr] *nf* (*de fleuve*) mouth; *Mus* mouthpiece.

embourber (s') [sāburbe] *vpr* (*véhicule*) & *Fig* to get bogged down.

embouteillage [ābuteja3] *nm* traffic jam.

embouteillé [ābuteje] *a* (*rue etc*) congested.

emboutir [ābutir] *vt* (*voiture*) to knock *ou* crash into.

embranchement [ābrāʃmā] *nm* (*de voie*) junction; (*division du règne animal*) branch.

embraser [ābraze] *vt* to set ablaze ‖**s'e.** *vpr* (*prendre feu*) to flare up.

embrasser [ābrase] *vt* **e. qn** (*donner un baiser à*) to kiss s.o.; (*serrer contre soi*) to embrace *ou* hug s.o.; (*une croyance etc*) to embrace a belief/*etc* ‖**s'e.** *vpr* to kiss (each other). ●**embrassade** *nf* embrace, hug.

embrasure [ābrazyr] *nf* (*de fenêtre, porte*) opening.

embrayer [ābreje] *vi* to let in *ou* engage the clutch. ●—**age** [-eja3] *nm* (*mécanisme, pédale*) *Aut* clutch.

embrigader [ābrigade] *vt Péj* to recruit.

embrocher [ābroʃe] *vt* (*volaille etc*) to put on a spit, skewer.

embrouiller [ābruje] *vt* (*fils*) to tangle (up); (*papiers etc*) to mix up; **e. qn** to confuse s.o. ‖**s'e.** *vpr* to get confused *ou* muddled (**dans** in, with).

embroussaillé [ābrusaje] *a* (*barbe, chemin*) bushy.

embruns [ābrœ̄] *nmpl* (sea) spray.

embryon [ābrijō] *nm* embryo.

embûches [ābyʃ] *nfpl* (*difficultés*) traps, pitfalls.

embusquer (s') [sābyske] *vpr* to lie in ambush. ●**embuscade** *nf* ambush.

éméché [emeʃe] *a* (*ivre*) *Fam* tipsy.

émeraude [ɛmrod] *nf* & *a inv* emerald.

émerger [emerʒe] *vi* to emerge (de
from).

émerveiller [emerveje] *vt* to amaze, fill
with wonder ∎ **s'é.** *vpr* to marvel (de at).
● **émerveillement** *nm* wonder, amazement.

émett/re* [emetr] *vt* (*lumière, son etc*) to
give out; (*message radio*) to broadcast;
(*timbre, monnaie*) to issue; (*opinion,
vœu*) to express. ●**—eur** *nm* (*poste*) é.
Rad transmitter.

émeute [emøt] *nf* riot. ● **émeutier, -ière**
nmf rioter.

émietter [emjete] *vt*, **s'é.** *vpr* (*pain etc*) to
crumble.

émigr/er [emigre] *vi* (*personne*) to emigrate. ●**—ant, -ante** *nmf* emigrant. ●**—é,
-ée** *nmf* exile, émigré. ● **émigration** *nf*
emigration.

éminent [eminɑ̃] *a* eminent.

émissaire [emiser] *nm* emissary.

émission [emisjɔ̃] *nf* (*de radio etc*)
programme, broadcast; (*diffusion*)
transmission; (*de timbre, monnaie*)
issue.

emmagasiner [ɑ̃magazine] *vt* to store
(up).

emmanchure [ɑ̃mɑ̃ʃyr] *nf* (*de vêtement*)
arm hole.

emmêler [ɑ̃mele] *vt* (*fil, cheveux*) to
tangle (up) ∎ **s'e.** *vpr* to get tangled.

emménager [ɑ̃menaʒe] *vi* (*dans un logement*) to move in; **e. dans** to move into.

emmener [ɑ̃mne] *vt* to take (à to); **e. qn
faire une promenade** to take s.o. for a
walk; **e. qn en voiture** to give s.o. a lift
ou Am a ride, drive s.o. (à to).

emmerder [ɑ̃merde] *vt Arg* to annoy,
bug; (*ennuyer*) to bore stiff ∎ **s'e.** *vpr
Arg* to get bored stiff. ● **emmerdement**
nm Arg bother, trouble. ● **emmerdeur,
-euse** *nmf* (*personne*) *Arg* pain in the
neck.

emmitoufler (s') [sɑ̃mitufle] *vpr* to wrap
(oneself) up (dans in).

émoi [emwa] *nm* excitement; **en é.** agog.

émotion [emosjɔ̃] *nf* (*sentiment*) emotion; (*trouble*) excitement; **donner des**
émotions à qn give s.o. a scare. ● **émotif, -ive** *a* emotional.

émoussé [emuse] *a* (*pointe*) blunt;
(*sentiment*) dulled.

émouvoir* [emuvwar] *vt* (*affecter*) to
move, touch ∎ **s'é.** *vpr* to be moved
ou touched. ● **émouvant** *a* moving,
touching.

empailler [ɑ̃paje] *vt* (*animal*) to stuff.

empaqueter [ɑ̃pakte] *vt* to pack(age).

emparer (s') [sɑ̃pare] *vpr* **s'e. de** to take,
grab.

empâter (s') [sɑ̃pate] *vpr* to fill out, get
fat(ter).

empêch/er [ɑ̃peʃe] *vt* to prevent, stop; **e.
qn de faire** to prevent *ou* stop s.o.
(from) doing; **n'empêche qu'elle a raison** *Fam* all the same she's right; **elle ne
peut pas s'e. de rire** she can't help
laughing. ●**—ement** [-εʃmɑ̃] *nm* difficulty, hitch; **avoir un e.** to have something come up at the last minute (*to
prevent or delay an action*).

empereur [ɑ̃prœr] *nm* emperor.

empester [ɑ̃peste] *vt* (*tabac etc*) to stink
of; (*pièce*) to make stink, stink out; **e.
qn** to stink s.o. out ∎ *vi* to stink.

empêtrer (s') [sɑ̃petre] *vpr* to get entangled (dans in).

emphase [ɑ̃faz] *nf* pomposity. ● **emphatique** *a* pompous.

empiéter [ɑ̃pjete] *vi* **e. sur** to encroach
upon.

empiffrer (s') [sɑ̃pifre] *vpr Fam* to gorge
oneself (de with).

empiler [ɑ̃pile] *vt*, **s'e.** *vpr* to pile up (sur
on); **s'e. dans** (*personnes*) to pile into
(*building, car etc*).

empire [ɑ̃pir] *nm* (*territoires*) empire;
(*autorité*) hold, influence; **sous l'e. de**
(*peur etc*) in the grip of.

empirer [ɑ̃pire] *vi* to worsen, get worse.

emplacement [ɑ̃plasmɑ̃] *nm* (*de stationnement*) place; (*d'une construction*) site,
location.

emplette [ɑ̃plet] *nf* purchase; **faire des
emplettes** to do some shopping.

emplir [ɑ̃plir] *vt*, **s'e.** *vpr* to fill (de

with).

emploi [ɑ̃plwa] *nm* **1** (*usage*) use; **e. du temps** timetable; **mode d'e.** directions (for use). **2** (*travail*) job, employment; **l'e.** (*travail*) *Écon Pol* employment; **sans e.** unemployed.

employer [ɑ̃plwaje] *vt* (*utiliser*) to use; **e. qn** to employ s.o. ∥**s'e.** *vpr* (*expression etc*) to be used; **s'e. à faire** to devote oneself to doing. ●**employé, -ée** *nmf* employee; (*de bureau, banque*) clerk, employee. ●**employeur, -euse** *nmf* employer.

empocher [ɑ̃pɔʃe] *vt* (*argent*) to pocket.

empoigner [ɑ̃pwaɲe] *vt* (*saisir*) to grab.

empoisonner [ɑ̃pwazɔne] *vt* (*personne, aliment etc*) to poison; (*empester*) to stink out; (*gâter*) to bedevil; **e. qn** (*embêter*) *Fam* to get on s.o.'s nerves ∥**s'e.** *vpr* (*par accident*) to be poisoned; (*volontairement*) to poison oneself. ●**empoisonnant** *a* (*embêtant*) *Fam* irritating. ●**empoisonnement** *nm* poisoning; (*ennui*) *Fam* trouble.

emporter [ɑ̃pɔrte] *vt* (*prendre*) to take (away) (**avec soi** with one); (*enlever*) to take away; (*entraîner*) to carry away; (*par le vent*) to blow off *ou* away; (*par les vagues*) to sweep away; (*par la maladie*) to carry off; **l'e. sur qn** to get the upper hand over s.o.; **il l'a emporté** he won.

∥**s'emporter** *vpr* to lose one's temper (**contre** with). ●**emporté** *a* (*caractère*) hot-tempered.

empoté [ɑ̃pɔte] *a Fam* clumsy.

empreint [ɑ̃prɛ̃] *a* **e. de** *Litt* stamped with, heavy with.

empreinte [ɑ̃prɛ̃t] *nf* (*marque*) & *Fig* mark, stamp; **e. (digitale)** fingerprint; **e. (de pas)** footprint.

empresser (s') [sɑ̃prese] *vpr* **s'e. de faire** to hasten to do. ●**empressé** *a* eager, attentive. ●**empressement** [-ɛsmɑ̃] *nm* (*hâte*) eagerness; (*auprès de qn*) attentiveness.

emprise [ɑ̃priz] *nf* hold (**sur** over).

emprisonn/er [ɑ̃prizɔne] *vt* to jail,

imprison; (*enfermer*) *Fig* to confine. ●**-ement** *nm* imprisonment.

emprunt [ɑ̃prœ̃] *nm* (*argent etc*) loan; (*mot*) *Ling* borrowed word; **nom d'e.** assumed name. ●**emprunter** *vt* (*argent etc*) to borrow (**à qn** from s.o.); (*route etc*) to use; **e. à** (*tirer de*) to derive *ou* borrow from.

ému [emy] *pp de* **émouvoir** ∥ *a* (*attendri*) moved; (*attristé*) upset; (*apeuré*) nervous; **une voix émue** a voice charged with emotion.

émulation [emylasjɔ̃] *nf* emulation.

en¹ [ɑ̃] *prép* **1** (*lieu*) in; (*direction*) to; **être en ville/en France** to be in town/in France; **aller en ville/en France** to go (in)to town/to France.

2 (*temps*) in; **en février** in February; **en été** in summer; **d'heure en heure** from hour to hour.

3 (*moyen, état etc*) by; in; on; at; **en avion** by plane; **en groupe** in a group; **en fleur** in flower; **en vain** in vain; **en congé** on leave; **en mer** at sea; **en guerre** at war.

4 (*matière*) in; **en bois** in wood, wooden; **chemise en nylon** nylon shirt; **c'est en or** it's (made of) gold.

5 (*domaine*) **étudiant en lettres** arts *ou* humanities student; **docteur en médecine** doctor of medicine.

6 (*comme*) **en cadeau** as a present; **en ami** as a friend.

7 (+ *participe présent*) **en mangeant/etc** while eating/etc; **en apprenant que. . .** on hearing that. . .; **en souriant** smiling, with a smile; **en ne disant rien** by saying nothing; **sortir en courant** to run out.

8 (*transformation*) into; **traduire en français/etc** to translate into French/ etc.

en² [ɑ̃] *pron* & *adv* **1** (= *de là*) from there; **j'en viens** I've just come from there. **2** (= *de ça, lui, eux etc*) **il en est content** he's pleased with it *ou* him *ou* them; **en parler** to talk about it; **en mourir** to die of *ou* from it; **elle m'en frappa** she struck me with it. **3** (*partitif*) some; **j'en ai** I have some; **en veux-tu?** do you want some *ou* àny?; **donne-lui-en** give some to him *ou* her; **je t'en supplie** I beg you (to).

ENA [ena] *abrév (École Nationale d'Administration)* school training top civil servants. ●**énarque** *nmf* student *ou* former student of ENA.

encadr/er [ɑ̃kadre] *vt (tableau)* to frame; *(entourer d'un trait)* to circle *(word)*; *(étudiants)* to supervise, train; *(prisonnier)* to flank; **je ne peux pas l'e.** *Fam* I can't stand him *ou* her. ●**—ement** *nm (de porte, photo)* frame; **personnel d'e.** training and supervisory staff.

encaisser [ɑ̃kese] *vt (argent, loyer etc)* to collect; *(chèque)* to cash; *(coup) Fam* to take; **je ne peux pas l'e.** *Fam* I can't stand him *ou* her.

encart [ɑ̃kar] *nm (feuille)* insert; **e. publicitaire** publicity insert.

en-cas [ɑ̃kɑ] *nm inv (repas)* snack.

encastrer [ɑ̃kastre] *vt* to build in *(dans* to), embed *(dans* into).

enceinte [ɑ̃sɛ̃t] **1** *af (femme)* pregnant; **e. de six mois**/*etc* six months/*etc* pregnant. **2** *nf (muraille)* (surrounding) wall; *(espace)* enclosure; **e. (acoustique)** (loud)speakers.

encens [ɑ̃sɑ̃] *nm* incense.

encercler [ɑ̃serkle] *vt* to surround.

enchaîner [ɑ̃ʃene] *vt (animal)* to chain (up); *(prisonnier)* to put in chains, chain (up); *(idées etc)* to link (up) ‖ *vi (continuer à parler)* to continue ‖ **s'e.** *vpr (idées etc)* to be linked (up).

enchant/er [ɑ̃ʃɑ̃te] *vt (ravir)* to delight; *(ensorceler)* to bewitch, enchant. ●**—é** *a (ravi)* delighted (**de** with, **que** (+ *sub*) that); *(magique)* enchanted; **e. de faire votre connaissance!** pleased to meet you! ●**—ement** *nm* delight; **comme par e.** as if by magic. ●**—eur** *nm (sorcier)* magician.

enchère [ɑ̃ʃer] *nf (offre)* bid; **vente aux enchères** auction; **mettre aux enchères** to (put up for) auction.

enchevêtrer [ɑ̃ʃvetre] *vt* to (en)tangle

‖ **s'e.** *vpr* to get entangled *(dans* in).

enclave [ɑ̃klav] *nf* enclave.

enclencher [ɑ̃klɑ̃ʃe] *vt Tech* to engage.

enclin [ɑ̃klɛ̃] *a* **e. à** inclined *ou* prone to.

enclos [ɑ̃klo] *nm (terrain, clôture)* enclosure.

enclume [ɑ̃klym] *nf* anvil.

encoche [ɑ̃kɔʃ] *nf* nick, notch *(à* in).

encoignure [ɑ̃kwaɲyr] *nf* corner.

encolure [ɑ̃kɔlyr] *nf (de cheval, vêtement)* neck; *(tour du cou)* collar (size).

encombre (sans) [sɑ̃zɑ̃kɔ̃br] *adv* without a hitch.

encombr/er [ɑ̃kɔ̃bre] *vt (pièce etc)* to clutter up (**de** with); *(rue)* to congest (**de** with); **e. qn** to hamper s.o.; **s'e. de** to burden oneself with. ●**—ant** *a (paquet)* bulky; *(présence)* awkward. ●**—é** *a (lignes téléphoniques)* jammed. ●**—ement** *nm (d'objets)* clutter; *(de rue)* traffic jam.

encontre de (à l') [alɑ̃kɔ̃trədə] *adv* against; *(contrairement à)* contrary to.

encore [ɑ̃kɔr] *adv* **1** *(toujours)* still; **tu es e. là?** are you still here?

2 *(avec négation)* yet; **pas e.** not yet; **je ne suis pas e.** prêt I'm not ready yet.

3 *(de nouveau)* again; **essaie e.** try again.

4 *(de plus, en plus)* **e. un café** another coffee, one more coffee; **e. une fois** (once) again, once more; **e. un another** (one), one more; **e. du pain** (some) more bread; **e. quelque chose** something else; **qui/quoi e.?** who/what else?.

5 *(avec comparatif)* even, still; **e. mieux** even better, better still.

6 *(aussi)* **mais e.** but also.

7 si e. *(si seulement)* if only; **et e.!** *(à peine)* if that!, only just!

8 e. que (+ *sub*) although.

encourag/er [ɑ̃kuraʒe] *vt* to encourage (**à faire** to do). ●**—eant** *a* encouraging. ●**—ement** *nm* encouragement.

encrasser [ɑ̃krase] *vt* to clog up (with dirt).

encre [ɑ̃kr] *nf* ink; **e. de Chine** Indian *ou* *Am* India ink. ●**encrier** *nm* inkpot.

encroûter (s') [sɑ̃krute] *vpr Péj* to get

into a rut, get set in one's ways; **s'e. dans** (*habitude*) to get stuck in.

encyclopédie [ãsiklɔpedi] *nf* encyclop(a)edia.

endetter [ãdete] *vt* **e. qn** to get s.o. into debt **‖ s'e.** *vpr* to get into debt. ● **endettement** *nm* (*dettes*) debts.

endiguer [ãdige] *vt* (*fleuve*) to dam (up); (*réprimer*) *Fig* to stem.

endimanché [ãdimãʃe] *a* in one's Sunday best.

endive [ãdiv] *nf* chicory, endive.

endoctriner [ãdɔktrine] *vt* to indoctrinate.

endolori [ãdɔlɔri] *a* painful, aching.

endommager [ãdɔmaʒe] *vt* to damage.

endormir* [ãdɔrmir] *vt* (*enfant etc*) to put to sleep; (*ennuyer*) to send to sleep **‖ s'e.** *vpr* to fall asleep, go to sleep. ● **endormi** *a* asleep, sleeping; (*indolent*) *Fam* sluggish.

endosser [ãdose] *vt* (*vêtement*) to put on; (*responsabilité*) to assume; (*chèque*) to endorse.

endroit [ãdrwa] *nm* **1** place, spot; **à cet e. du récit** at this point in the story; **par endroits** in places. **2** (*de tissu*) right side; **à l'e.** (*vêtement*) right side out.

enduire* [ãdɥir] *vt* to smear, coat (**de** with). ● **enduit** *nm* coating; (*de mur*) plaster.

endurant [ãdyrã] *a* tough. ● **endurance** *nf* endurance.

endurc/ir [ãdyrsir] *vt* **e. qn à** (*douleur etc*) to harden s.o. to; **s'e.** to become hardened (**à** to). ●—**i** *a* (*insensible*) hardened; (*célibataire*) confirmed.

endurer [ãdyre] *vt* to endure, bear.

énergie [enerʒi] *nf* energy; **avec é.** (*protester etc*) forcefully. ● **énergétique** *a* **ressources énergétiques** energy resources; **aliment é.** energy food. ● **énergique** *a* (*dynamique*) energetic; (*remède*) powerful; (*mesure, ton*) forceful. ● **énergiquement** *adv* energetically.

énergumène [energymɛn] *nmf* *Péj* rowdy character.

énerver [enerve] *vt* **é. qn** (*irriter*) to get

on s.o.'s nerves; (*rendre nerveux*) to make s.o. nervous **‖ s'é.** *vpr* to get worked up. ● **énervé** *a* on edge.

enfance [ãfãs] *nf* childhood; **c'est l'e. de l'art** it's child's play.

enfant [ãfã] *nmf* child (*pl* children); **e. en bas âge** infant; **e. de chœur** *Rel* altar boy; **e. prodige** child prodigy; **bon e.** (*caractère*) good natured; **c'est un jeu d'e.** it's child's play. ● **enfanter** *vt* to give birth to. ● **enfantillage** *nm* childishness. ● **enfantin** *a* (*voix, joie*) childlike; (*simple*) easy; (*puéril*) childish.

enfer [ãfer] *nm* hell; **d'e.** (*bruit, vision*) infernal; **à un train d'e.** at breakneck speed.

enfermer [ãferme] *vt* to lock up; **s'e. dans** (*chambre etc*) to lock oneself up in; (*attitude etc*) *Fig* to maintain stubbornly.

enfiler [ãfile] *vt* (*aiguille*) to thread; (*perles etc*) to string; (*vêtement*) *Fam* to pull on.

enfin [ãfɛ̃] *adv* (*à la fin*) finally, at last; (*en dernier lieu*) lastly; (*en somme*) in a word; (*conclusion résignée*) well; **e. bref** (*en somme*) *Fam* in a word; **mais e.** but; (*mais*) **e.!** for heaven's sake!

enflammer [ãflame] *vt* to set fire to; (*allumette*) to light; (*irriter*) to inflame (*throat etc*); (*imagination, colère*) to excite **‖ s'e.** *vpr* to catch fire; **s'e. de colère** to flare up. ● **enflammé** *a* (*discours*) fiery.

enfler [ãfle] *vt* to swell **‖** *vi* *Méd* to swell (up). ● **enflure** *nf* swelling.

enfoncer [ãfɔse] *vt* (*clou etc*) to knock in, bang in; (*porte, voiture*) to smash in; **e. dans qch** (*couteau, mains etc*) to plunge into sth **‖ s'e.** *vpr* (*s'enliser*) to sink (**dans** into); **s'e. dans** (*pénétrer*) to plunge into, disappear (deep) into.

enfouir [ãfwir] *vt* to bury.

enfourcher [ãfurʃe] *vt* (*cheval etc*) to mount, bestride.

enfourner [ãfurne] *vt* to put in the oven.

enfuir* (**s'**) [sãfɥir] *vpr* to run away *ou* off (**de** from).

enfumer [ɑ̃fyme] vt (pièce) to fill with smoke; (personne) to smoke out.

engager [ɑ̃gaʒe] vt (discussion, combat) to start; (bijou etc) to pawn; (parole) to pledge; (capitaux) to tie up, invest; **e. qn** (embaucher) to hire s.o.; (lier) to bind s.o., commit s.o. ▮**s'e.** vpr (dans l'armée) to enlist; (sportif) to enter (pour for); (action, jeu) to start; (au service d'une cause) to commit oneself; **s'e. à faire** to undertake to do; **s'e. dans** (voie) to enter; (affaire etc) to get involved in. ● **engageant** a engaging, inviting. ● **engagé** a (écrivain etc) committed. ● **engagement** nm (promesse) commitment; (dans une compétition sportive) entry; (combat) Mil engagement; **prendre l'e. de faire** to undertake to do.

engelure [ɑ̃ʒlyr] nf chilblain.

engendrer [ɑ̃ʒɑ̃dre] vt (causer) to generate.

engin [ɑ̃ʒɛ̃] nm machine, device; **e. spatial** spaceship; **e. explosif** explosive device.

englober [ɑ̃glɔbe] vt to include, embrace.

engloutir [ɑ̃glutir] vt (nourriture) to wolf (down); (faire disparaître) to swallow up.

engouement [ɑ̃gumɑ̃] nm craze.

engouffrer [ɑ̃gufre] **1** vt (avaler) to wolf (down); (fortune) to consume. **2 s'engouffrer** vpr **s'e. dans** to sweep ou rush into.

engourdir [ɑ̃gurdir] vt (membre) to numb; (esprit) to dull ▮**s'e.** vpr to go numb.

engrais [ɑ̃grɛ] nm (naturel) manure; (chimique) fertilizer.

engraisser [ɑ̃grese] vt (animal) to fatten (up) ▮ vi, **s'e.** vpr to get fat.

engrenage [ɑ̃grənaʒ] nm Tech gears; Fig mesh, chain, web.

engueuler [ɑ̃gœle] vt **e. qn** Fam to give s.o. hell, bawl s.o. out. ● **engueulade** nf Fam (réprimande) bawling out, dressing-down; (dispute) slanging match, row.

enhardir [ɑ̃ardir] vt to make bolder; **s'e. à faire** to make bold to do.

énième [enjɛm] a Fam umpteenth.

énigme [enigm] nf riddle, enigma.

enivrer (s') [sɑ̃nivre] vpr to get drunk (de on).

enjamber [ɑ̃ʒɑ̃be] vt to step over; (pont etc) to span (river etc). ● **enjambée** nf stride.

enjeu, -x [ɑ̃ʒø] nm (mise) stake(s).

enjoliver [ɑ̃ʒɔlive] vt to embellish. ● **enjoliveur** [ɑ̃ʒɔlivœr] nm Aut hubcap.

enjoué [ɑ̃ʒwe] a playful, cheerful.

enlacer [ɑ̃lase] vt (serrer dans ses bras) to clasp.

enlaidir [ɑ̃ledir] vt to make ugly ▮ vi to grow ugly.

enlevé [ɑ̃lve] a (scène, danse etc) well-rendered.

enlever [ɑ̃lve] vt to take away, remove (à qn from s.o.); (vêtement) to take off, remove; (tache) to take out, remove; (enfant etc) to kidnap; (ordures) to collect ▮**s'e.** vpr (tache) to come out; (vernis) to come off. ● **enlèvement** nm (d'enfant) kidnapping.

enliser (s') [sɑ̃lize] vpr (véhicule) & Fig to get bogged down (dans in).

enneigé [ɑ̃neʒe] a snow-covered. ● **enneigement** nm snow coverage; **bulletin d'e.** snow report.

ennemi, -ie [ɛnmi] nmf enemy ▮ a (personne) hostile (de to); **pays/soldat e.** enemy country/soldier.

ennui [ɑ̃nɥi] nm boredom; (mélancolie) weariness; **un e.** (tracas) (some) trouble; **des ennuis** trouble; **l'e., c'est que...** the annoying thing is that....

ennuyer [ɑ̃nɥije] vt (agacer) to bother, annoy; (préoccuper) to bother; (fatiguer) to bore ▮**s'e.** vpr to get bored. ● **ennuyé** a (air) bored; **je suis très e.** (confus) I feel bad (about it). ● **ennuyeux, -euse** a (fastidieux) boring; (contrariant) annoying.

énoncé [enɔ̃se] nm (de texte) wording, terms.

énoncer [enɔ̃se] vt to state, express.

enorgueillir (s') [sānɔrgœjir] *vpr* **s'e. de** to pride oneself on.

énorme [enɔrm] *a* enormous, huge. ●**énormément** *adv* enormously; **e. de** an enormous amount of. ●**énormité** *nf* (*dimension*) enormity; (*faute*) (enormous) blunder.

enquérir (s') [sākerir] *vpr* **s'e. de** to inquire about.

enquête [āket] *nf* (*de police etc*) investigation; (*judiciaire*) inquiry; (*sondage*) survey. ●**enquêter** *vi* (*police etc*) to investigate; **e. sur** (*crime*) to investigate. ●**enquêteur, -euse** *nmf* (*policier etc*) investigator; (*sondeur*) researcher.

enraciner (s') [sārasine] *vpr* to take root; **enraciné dans** (*souvenir*) rooted in; **bien enraciné** (*préjugé etc*) deep-rooted.

enrag/er [āraʒe] *vi* to be furious (**de faire** about doing); **faire e. qn** to get on s.o.'s nerves. ●**-é** *a* (*chien*) rabid; **devenir e.** (*furieux*) to become furious; **rendre qn e.** to make s.o. furious.

enrayer [āreje] *vt* (*maladie etc*) to check ▮**s'e.** *vpr* (*fusil*) to jam.

enregistr/er [ārʒistre] *vt* 1 (*par écrit, sur bande*) to record; (*sur registre*) to register; (*constater*) to note, register; (**faire**) **e.** (*bagages*) to register, *Am* check. 2 (*musique, émission etc*) to record; **ça enregistre** it's recording. ●**-ement** *nm* (*des bagages*) registration, *Am* checking; (*d'un acte*) registration; (*sur bande etc*) recording.

enrhumer [āryme] *vpr* to catch a cold; **être enrhumé** to have a cold.

enrichir [āriʃir] *vt* to enrich (**de** with) ▮**s'e.** *vpr* (*personne*) to get rich.

enrober [ārɔbe] *vt* to coat (**de** in); **enrobé de chocolat** chocolate-coated.

enrôler [ārole] *vt*, **s'e.** *vpr* to enlist.

enrouer (s') [sārwe] *vpr* to get hoarse. ●**enroué** *a* hoarse.

enrouler [ārule] *vt* (*fil etc*) to wind; (*tapis etc*) to roll up; **s'e. dans** (*couvertures*) to wrap oneself up in; **s'e. sur ou autour de qch** to wind round sth.

ensanglanté [āsāglāte] *a* bloodstained.

enseigne [āsɛɲ] *nf* (*de magasin etc*) sign; **e. lumineuse** neon sign; **logés à la même e.** *Fig* in the same boat.

enseign/er [āsɛɲe] *vt* to teach; **e. qch à qn** to teach s.o. sth; **il enseigne** he teaches. ●**-ant, -ante** [-ɛɲā, -āt] *nmf* teacher. ●**-ement** [-ɛɲmā] *nm* education; (*action, métier*) teaching; **être dans l'e.** to be a teacher.

ensemble [āsābl] 1 *adv* together. 2 *nm* (*d'objets*) group, set; *Math* set; (*vêtement féminin*) outfit; *Mus* ensemble; **l'e. du personnel** (*totalité*) the whole (of the) staff; **l'e. des enseignants** all (of) the teachers; **dans l'e.** on the whole; **vue/etc d'e.** general view/*etc*.

ensevelir [āsəvlir] *vt* to bury.

ensoleillé [āsɔleje] *a* (*endroit, journée*) sunny.

ensommeillé [āsɔmeje] *a* sleepy.

ensorceler [āsɔrsəle] *vt* (*envoûter, séduire*) to bewitch.

ensuite [āsчit] *adv* (*puis*) next, then; (*plus tard*) afterwards.

entaille [ātaj] *nf* (*fente*) notch; (*blessure*) gash. ●**entailler** *vt* to notch; to gash.

entamer [ātame] *vt* (*pain, peau etc*) to cut (into); (*bouteille, boîte etc*) to start (on); (*négociations etc*) to enter into, start; (*capital*) to eat into; (*métal, plastique*) to damage.

entasser [ātase] *vt*, **s'e.** *vpr* (*objets*) to pile up; (**s')e. dans** (*passagers etc*) to crowd ou pile into; **ils s'entassaient sur la plage** they were crowded (together) on the beach.

entendre [ātādr] *vt* to hear; **e. parler de** to hear of; **e. dire que** to hear (it said) that; **e. raison** to listen to reason; **laisser e. à qn** to give s.o. to understand that ▮**s'entendre** *vpr* **s'e. (sur)** (*être d'accord*) to agree (on); **s'e. (avec qn)** (*s'accorder*) to get along ou on (with s.o.); **on ne s'entend plus!** (*à cause du bruit etc*) we can't hear ourselves speak!

entendu [ātādy] *a* (*convenu*) agreed; (*compris*) understood; (*sourire, air*) knowing; **e.!** all right!; **bien e.** of course.

entente [ɑ̃tɑ̃t] *nf* (*accord*) agreement, understanding; (**bonne**) **e.** (*amitié*) good relationship.

entériner [ɑ̃terine] *vt* to ratify.

enterrer [ɑ̃tere] *vt* (*défunt etc*) to bury; (*projet*) *Fig* to scrap. ● **enterrement** *nm* burial; (*funérailles*) funeral.

en-tête [ɑ̃tɛt] *nm* (*de papier*) heading; **papier à en-tête** headed paper.

entêter (s') [sɑ̃tete] *vpr* to persist (**à faire** in doing). ● **entêté** *a* (*têtu*) stubborn. ● **entêtement** [ɑ̃tɛtmɑ̃] *nm* stubbornness; (**à faire qch**) persistence.

enthousiasme [ɑ̃tuzjasm] *nm* enthusiasm. ● **enthousiasmer** *vt* to fill with enthusiasm; **s'e. pour** to be ou get enthusiastic about ou over. ● **enthousiaste** *a* enthusiastic.

enticher (s') [sɑ̃tiʃe] *vpr* **s'e. de** to become infatuated with.

entier, -ière [ɑ̃tje, -jɛr] 1 *a* (*total*) whole, entire; (*intact*) intact; (*absolu*) absolute, complete; **le pays tout e.** the whole ou entire country; **nombre e.** *Math* whole number ‖ *nm* (*unité*) whole; **en e.** completely. 2 *a* (*caractère*) unyielding. ● **entièrement** *adv* entirely.

entonner [ɑ̃tɔne] *vt* (*air*) to start singing.

entonnoir [ɑ̃tɔnwar] *nm* (*ustensile*) funnel.

entorse [ɑ̃tɔrs] *nf* *Méd* sprain; **e. à** (*règlement*) infringement of.

entortiller [ɑ̃tɔrtije] *vt* **e. qch autour de qch** (*dans du papier etc*) to wrap sth around sth; **e. qn** *Fam* to dupe s.o., get round s.o. ‖ **s'e.** *vpr* (*lierre etc*) to wind, twist.

entourage [ɑ̃turaʒ] *nm* (*proches*) circle of family and friends.

entourer [ɑ̃ture] *vt* to surround (**de** with); (*envelopper*) to wrap (**de** in); **entouré de** surrounded by; **e. qn de** **ses bras** to put one's arms round s.o.

entracte [ɑ̃trakt] *nm* *Th* interval, *Am* intermission.

entraide [ɑ̃trɛd] *nf* mutual aid. ● **s'entraider** [sɑ̃trede] *vpr* to help each other.

entrain [ɑ̃trɛ̃] *nm* spirit, liveliness; **plein d'e.** lively.

entraînant [ɑ̃trenɑ̃] *a* (*musique*) lively.

entraîner [ɑ̃trene] 1 *vt* to carry away; (*causer*) to bring about; (*impliquer*) to entail, involve; **e. qn** (*emmener*) to lead s.o. (away); (*de force*) to drag s.o. (away); **e. qn à faire** (*amener*) to lead s.o. to do. 2 *vt* (*athlète, cheval etc*) to train (**à** for) ‖ **s'e.** *vpr* *Sp* to train. ● **entraîneur** [-nœr] *nm* (*d'athlète*) coach; (*de cheval*) trainer.

entrave [ɑ̃trav] *nf* (*obstacle*) *Fig* hindrance (**à** to). ● **entraver** *vt* to hinder, hamper.

entre [ɑ̃tr(ə)] *prép* between; (*parmi*) among(st); **l'un d'e. vous** one of you; (**soit dit**) **e. nous** between you and me; **e. deux âges** middle-aged; **e. autres** among other things.

entrebâill/er [ɑ̃trəbaje] *vt* (*porte*) to open slightly. ● **—é** *a* slightly open, ajar.

entrechoquer (s') [sɑ̃trəʃɔke] *vpr* (*bouteilles etc*) to chink.

entrecôte [ɑ̃trəkot] *nf* (*boned ou Am* filleted) rib steak.

entre-deux-guerres [ɑ̃trədøgɛr] *nm inv* inter-war period.

entrée [ɑ̃tre] *nf* (*action*) entry, entrance; (*porte*) entrance; (*accès*) admission, entry (**de** to); (*vestibule*) entrance hall; (*billet*) ticket (for admission); (*plat*) first course; *Ordinat* input; (*mot dans un dictionnaire etc*) entry; **à son e.** as he ou she came in; **'e. interdite'** 'no entry'; **'e. libre'** 'admission free'; **e. de service** tradesmen's entrance; **e. en matière** (*d'un discours*) opening.

entrefaites (sur ces) [syrsezɑ̃trəfɛt] *adv* at that moment.

entrefilet [ɑ̃trəfilɛ] *nm* (*dans un journal*) (news) item.

entrejambe [ɑ̃trəʒɑ̃b] *nm* crutch, crotch.

entrelacer [ɑ̃trəlase] *vt*, **s'e.** *vpr* to intertwine.

entremêler [ɑ̃trəmele] *vt*, **s'e.** *vpr* to intermingle.

entremets [ātrəmɛ] nm (plat) dessert, sweet.

entremise [ātrəmiz] nf par l'e. de qn through s.o.

entreposer [ātrəpoze] vt to store. ● **entrepôt** nm warehouse.

entreprendre* [ātrəprādr] vt (travail, voyage etc) to undertake; **e. de faire** to do.

entrepreneur [ātrəprənœr] nm (en bâtiment) (building) contractor.

entreprise [ātrəpriz] nf 1 (firme) company, firm. 2 (opération) undertaking.

entrer [ātre] vi (aux être) (aller) to go in, enter; (venir) to come in, enter; **e. dans** to go into; (pièce) to come ou go into, enter; (arbre etc) Aut to crash into; (club) to join; **e. à l'universite**/etc to go to ou start university/etc; **entrez!** come in!; **faire/laisser e. qn** to show/ let s.o. in ▮ vt Ordinat to enter, key in.

entresol [ātrəsɔl] nm mezzanine (floor).

entre-temps [ātrətā] adv meanwhile.

entretenir* [ātrətnir] vt 1 (voiture, maison etc) to maintain; (relations, souvenir) to keep up; (famille) to keep, maintain; **e. sa forme/sa santé** to keep fit/healthy. 2 **e. qn de** to talk to s.o. about; **s'e. de** to talk about (avec with).

entretien [ātrətjɛ̃] nm 1 (de route, maison etc) maintenance. 2 (dialogue) conversation; (entrevue) interview.

entrevoir* [ātrəvwar] vt (rapidement) to catch a glimpse of; (pressentir) to (fore)see.

entrevue [ātrəvy] nf interview.

entrouvrir* [ātruvrir] vt, **s'e.** vpr to half-open. ● **entrouvert** a (porte, fenêtre) half-open, ajar.

énumérer [enymere] vt to list, enumerate. ● **énumération** nf list(ing).

envah/ir [āvair] vt to invade; (herbe etc) to overrun (garden); **e. qn** (doute, peur etc) to overcome s.o. ● **—issant** a (voisin etc) intrusive. ● **—isseur** nm invader.

enveloppe [āvlɔp] nf (pour lettre) envelope; **mettre sous e.** to put into an envelope; **e. timbrée à votre adresse** stamped addressed envelope, Am stamped self-addressed envelope.

envelopper [āvlɔpe] vt to wrap (up) (dans in) ▮ **s'e.** vpr to wrap oneself (up) (dans in).

envenimer (s') [sāvnime] vpr to turn septic; Fig to become acrimonious.

envergure [āvɛrgyr] nf (de personne) calibre; (ampleur) scope, importance; **de grande e.** (réforme etc) wide-ranging.

envers [āvɛr] prép towards, Am toward(s), to. 2 nm (de tissu) wrong side; (de médaille) reverse side; **à l'e.** (chaussette) inside out; (pantalon) back to front; (la tête en bas) upside down; (à contresens) the wrong way.

envie [āvi] nf 1 (jalousie) envy; (désir) longing, desire; **avoir e. de qch** to want sth; **j'ai e. de faire** I feel like doing; **elle meurt d'e. de faire** she's dying to do; **ça me fait e.** I really like that. ● **envier** vt to envy (qch à qn s.o. sth). ● **envieux, -euse** a & nmf envious (person); **faire des envieux** to cause envy.

environ [āvirɔ̃] adv (à peu près) about ▮ nmpl surroundings, outskirts; **aux environs de** (Paris, Noël, dix francs etc) around.

environner [āvirɔne] vt to surround. ● **environnant** a surrounding. ● **environnement** nm environment.

envisager [āvizaʒe] vt to consider; (imaginer comme possible) to envisage, Am envision; **e. de faire** to consider doing.

envol [āvɔl] nm (d'oiseau) taking flight; (d'avion) takeoff; **piste d'e.** Av runway. ● **s'envoler** vpr (oiseau) to fly away; (avion) to take off; (chapeau etc) to blow away.

envoûter [āvute] vt to bewitch.

envoyer* [āvwaje] vt to send; (lancer) to throw; (gifle) to give; **e. chercher qn** to send for s.o. ▮ **s'e.** vpr Fam (repas etc) to put ou stash away. ● **envoyé, -ée** nmf envoy; (reporter) correspondent. ● **en-**

voyeur *nm* sender; **'retour à l'e.'** 'return to sender'.

épagneul, -eule [epaɲœl] *nmf* spaniel.

épais, -aisse [epɛ, -ɛs] *a* thick. ● **épaisseur** *nf* thickness; *(dimension)* depth. ● **épaissir** *vti*, **s'é.** *vpr* to thicken.

épancher (s') [sepɑ̃ʃe] *vpr* *(parler)* to pour out one's heart.

épanouir (s') [sepanwir] *vpr* *(fleur)* to blossom, open out; *(personne)* *Fig* to blossom (out); *(visage)* to beam. ● **épanoui** *a* *(fleur, personne)* in full bloom; *(visage)* beaming. ● **épanouissement** *nm* *(éclat)* full bloom; *(de la personnalité)* fulfilment.

épargne [eparɲ] *nf* *(qualité, vertu)* thrift; *(sommes d'argent)* savings. ● **épargner** *vt* *(argent)* to save; *(ennemi etc)* to spare; **e. qch à qn** *(ennuis, chagrin etc)* to spare s.o. sth. ● **épargnant, -ante** *nmf* saver.

éparpiller [eparpije] *vt*, **s'é.** *vpr* to scatter. ● **épars** *a* scattered.

épatant [epatɑ̃] *a* *Fam* marvellous.

épater [epate] *vt* *Fam* to stun, astound.

épaule [epol] *nf* shoulder. ● **épauler** *vt* *(fusil)* to raise (to one's shoulder); **é. qn** *(aider)* to back s.o. up. ● **épaulette** *nf* *(d'une veste)* shoulder pad.

épave [epav] *nf* *(bateau, personne)* wreck.

épée [epe] *nf* sword.

épeler [eple] *vt* *(mot)* to spell.

éperdu [eperdy] *a* wild (**de** with); *(besoin)* desperate; *(regard)* distraught. ● **—ment** *adv* *(aimer)* madly; **elle s'en moque e.** she couldn't care less.

éperon [eprɔ̃] *nm* *(de cavalier, coq)* spur.

épervier [epervje] *nm* sparrowhawk.

éphémère [efemɛr] *a* short-lived.

épi [epi] *nm* *(de blé etc)* ear; *(mèche de cheveux)* tuft of hair.

épice [epis] *nf* *Culin* spice. ● **épicer** *vt* to spice. ● **épicé** *a* *(plat, récit etc)* spicy.

épicier, -ière [episje, -jɛr] *nmf* grocer. ● **épicerie** *nf* *(magasin)* grocer's (shop), *Am* grocery (store); **é. fine** delicatessen.

épidémie [epidemi] *nf* epidemic.

épiderme [epidɛrm] *nm* *Anat* skin.

épier [epje] *vt* *(observer)* to watch closely; **é. qn** to spy on s.o.

épilepsie [epilɛpsi] *nf* epilepsy. ● **épileptique** *a* & *nmf* epileptic.

épiler [epile] *vt* *(jambe)* to remove unwanted hair from; *(sourcil)* to pluck.

épilogue [epilog] *nm* epilogue.

épinards [epinar] *nmpl* spinach.

épine [epin] *nf* **1** *(de plante)* thorn; *(d'animal)* spine, prickle. **2 é. dorsale** *Anat* spine. ● **épineux, -euse** *a* *(tige, question)* thorny.

épingle [epɛ̃gl] *nf* pin; **é. de ou à nourrice, é. de sûreté** safety pin; **é. à linge** clothes peg, *Am* clothes pin; **é. à cheveux** hairpin; **tiré à quatre épingles** very spruce.

épique [epik] *a* epic.

épisode [epizɔd] *nm* episode. ● **épisodique** *a* occasional.

épithète [epitɛt] *nf* *(adjectif)* attribute.

éploré [eplɔre] *a* *(veuve, air)* tearful.

éplucher [eplyʃe] *vt* *(carotte, pomme etc)* to peel; *(salade)* to clean. ● **épluchure** *nf* peeling.

éponge [epɔ̃ʒ] *nf* sponge. ● **éponger** *vt* *(liquide)* to sponge up, mop up; *(carrelage)* to sponge (down), mop; **s'é. le front** to mop one's brow.

épopée [epɔpe] *nf* epic.

époque [epɔk] *nf* *(date)* time, period; *(historique)* age; **meubles d'é.** period furniture; **à l'é.** at the *ou* that time.

épouse [epuz] *nf* wife.

épouser [epuze] *vt* **1 é. qn** to marry s.o. **2** *(opinion etc)* to espouse; *(forme)* to assume.

épousseter [epuste] *vt* to dust.

épouvantable [epuvɑ̃tabl] *a* terrifying; *(très mauvais)* appalling.

épouvantail [epuvɑ̃taj] *nm* scarecrow.

épouvante [epuvɑ̃t] *nf* *(peur)* terror; *(appréhension)* dread; **film d'é.** horror film. ● **épouvanter** *vt* to terrify.

époux [epu] *nm* husband, *pl* husband and wife.

éprendre* (s') [seprɑ̃dr] *vpr* **s'é. de qn** to

fall in love with s.o.

épreuve [eprœv] *nf* (*examen*) test; (*sportive*) event; (*malheur*) hardship, ordeal; *Phot* print; *Typ* proof; **mettre à l'é.** to put to the test; **à toute é.** (*patience*) unfailing; (*nerfs*) rock-solid.

éprouver [epruve] *vt* to test; (*sentiment etc*) to feel; **é. qn** (*mettre à l'épreuve*) to put s.o. to the test; (*faire souffrir*) to distress s.o. ●**éprouvant** *a* (*pénible*) trying. ●**éprouvé** *a* (*sûr*) well-tried.

éprouvette [epruvɛt] *nf* test tube; **bébé é.** test tube baby.

épuiser [epɥize] *vt* (*personne, provisions, sujet*) to exhaust ‖**s'é.** *vpr* (*réserves, patience*) to run out; **s'é. à faire** to exhaust oneself doing. ●**épuisant** *a* exhausting. ●**épuisé** *a* exhausted; (*marchandise*) out of stock; (*édition*) out of print; **é. de fatigue** exhausted.

épuisette [epɥizɛt] *nf* fishing net (*on pole*).

épuration [epyrasjɔ̃] *nf* purification; **station d'é.** purification works.

équateur [ekwatœr] *nm* equator; **sous l'é.** at *ou* on the equator. ●**équatorial, -aux** *a* equatorial.

équation [ekwɑsjɔ̃] *nf* *Math* equation.

équerre [ekɛr] *nf* **é.** (**à dessiner**) set square, *Am* triangle; **d'é.** straight, square.

équilibre [ekilibr] *nm* balance; **tenir** *ou* **mettre en é.** to balance (**sur** on); **se tenir en é.** to keep one's balance; **perdre l'é.** to lose one's balance. ●**équilibrer** *vt* (*budget*) to balance ‖**s'é.** *vpr* (*comptes*) to balance.

équipage [ekipaʒ] *nm* *Nau Av* crew.

équipe [ekip] *nf* team; (*d'ouvriers*) gang; **é. de secours** search party; **é. de nuit** night shift; **faire é. avec** to team up with. ●**équipier, -ière** *nmf* team member.

équiper [ekipe] *vt* to equip (**de** with) ‖**s'é.** *vpr* to equip oneself. ●**équipement** *nm* equipment; (*de camping, ski etc*) gear.

équitable [ekitabl] *a* fair.

équitation [ekitasjɔ̃] *nf* (horse) riding, *Am* (horseback) riding.

équivalent [ekivalɑ̃] *a* & *nm* equivalent.

équivoque [ekivɔk] *a* (*ambigu*) equivocal; (*douteux*) dubious ‖*nf* ambiguity.

érable [erabl] *nm* (*arbre, bois*) maple.

érafler [erafle] *vt* to graze. ●**éraflure** *nf* graze.

éraillée [erɑje] *af* **voix é.** rasping voice.

ère [ɛr] *nf* era; **avant notre è.** BC.

érection [erɛksjɔ̃] *nf* (*de monument etc*) erection.

éreinter [erɛ̃te] *vt* (*fatiguer*) to exhaust.

ériger [eriʒe] *vt* to erect; **s'é. en** to set oneself up as.

ermite [ermit] *nm* hermit.

érosion [erozjɔ̃] *nf* erosion.

érotique [erotik] *a* erotic.

err/er [ere] *vi* to wander. ●**—ant** *a* wandering; **chien e.** stray dog.

erreur [erœr] *nf* mistake, error; **par e.** by mistake, in error; **dans l'e.** mistaken; **faire erreur** (*au téléphone*) to dial the wrong number. ●**erroné** *a* erroneous.

es *voir* **être**.

ès [ɛs] *prép* of; **licencié/docteur ès lettres** = BA/PhD.

escabeau, -x [ɛskabo] *nm* stepladder.

escadrille [ɛskadrij] *nf* (*groupe d'avions*) flight. ●**escadron** *nm* squadron.

escalade [ɛskalad] *nf* climbing; (*des prix, de la violence etc*) escalation. ●**escalader** *vt* to climb.

escale [ɛskal] *nf* *Av* stop(over); *Nau* port of call; **faire e. à** *Av* to stop (over) at; *Nau* to put in at; **vol sans e.** non-stop flight.

escalier [ɛskalje] *nm* stairs; **l'e., les escaliers** the stairs; **e. mécanique** *ou* **roulant** escalator; **e. de secours** fire escape; **e. de service** service stairs.

escalope [ɛskalɔp] *nf* *Culin* escalope.

escamoter [ɛskamɔte] *vt* (*faire disparaître*) to make vanish.

escapade [eskapad] *nf* (*excursion*) jaunt; **faire une e.** to run off.

escargot [eskargo] *nm* snail.

escarmouche [eskarmuʃ] *nf* skirmish.

escarpé [eskarpe] *a* steep. ● **escarpement** [*nm*] (*côte*) steep slope.

escarpin [eskarpɛ̃] *nm* (*soulier*) pump.

escient [esjɑ̃] *nm* **à bon e.** judiciously.

esclaffer (s') [sesklafe] *vpr* to roar with laughter.

esclandre [esklɑ̃dr] *nm* (*noisy*) scene.

esclave [esklav] *nmf* slave. ● **esclavage** *nm* slavery.

escompter [eskɔ̃te] *vt* **1** (*espérer*) to anticipate (**faire doing**), expect (**faire to do**). **2** *Com* to discount.

escorte [eskɔrt] *nf* *Mil Nau etc* escort.

escrime [eskrim] *nf* *Sp* fencing; **faire de l'e.** to fence.

escrimer (s') [seskrime] *vpr* to slave away (**à faire** at doing).

escroc [eskro] *nm* crook, swindler. ● **escroquer** *vt* **e. qn** to swindle s.o.; **e. qch à qn** to swindle s.o. out of sth. ● **escroquerie** *nf* swindling; **une e.** a swindle; **c'est de l'e.** *Fam* it's a rip-off.

espace [espas] *nm* space; **e. vert** garden, park. ● **espacer** *vt* to space out ‖ **s'e.** (*maisons, visites etc*) to become less frequent.

espadrille [espadrij] *nf* rope-soled sandal.

Espagne [espaɲ] *nf* Spain. ● **espagnol, -ole** *a* Spanish ‖ *nmf* Spaniard ‖ *nm* (*langue*) Spanish.

espèce [espes] **1** *nf* (*race*) species; (*genre*) kind, sort; **e. d'idiot!** (you) silly fool! **2** *nfpl* (*argent*) **en espèces** in cash.

espérance [esperɑ̃s] *nf* hope; **e. de vie** life expectancy.

espérer [espere] *vt* to hope for; **e. que** to hope that; **e. faire** to hope to do ‖ *vi* to hope; **j'espère (bien)!** I hope so!; **e. en qch** to trust in sth.

espiègle [espjɛgl] *a* mischievous.

espion, -onne [espjɔ̃, -ɔn] *nmf* spy. ● **espionnage** *nm* spying, espionage. ● **espionner** *vt* to spy on.

esplanade [esplanad] *nf* esplanade.

espoir [espwar] *nm* hope; **sans e.** (*cas etc*) hopeless.

esprit [espri] *nm* (*attitude, fantôme*) spirit; (*intellect*) mind; (*humour*) wit; **venir à l'e. de qn** to cross s.o.'s mind; **avoir de l'e.** to be witty; **perdre l'e.** to go out of one's mind.

esquimau, -aude, -os [eskimo, -od, -o] **1** *a* & *nmf* Eskimo. **2** *nm* (*glace*) choc-ice (*on a stick*), *Am* chocolate ice-cream bar.

esquinter [eskɛ̃te] *vt Fam* (*voiture etc*) to damage, bash; **s'e. à faire** (*se fatiguer*) to wear oneself out doing.

esquisse [eskis] *nf* (*croquis, plan*) sketch. ● **esquisser** *vt* to sketch; **e. un geste** to make a (slight) gesture.

esquiver [eskive] *vt* (*coup, problème*) to dodge ‖ **s'e.** *vpr* to slip away.

essai [ese] *nm* (*preuve*) test; (*tentative*) try, attempt; *Rugby* try; *Littér* essay; **à l'e.** (*objet*) *Com* on approval; **pilote d'e.** test pilot; **période d'e.** trial period; **coup d'e.** first attempt.

essaim [esɛ̃] *nm* swarm (*of bees etc*).

essayer [eseje] *vt* to try (**de faire** to do); (*vêtement*) to try on; (*méthode*) to try (**out**). ● **essayage** *nm* (*de costume*) fitting; **salon d'e.** fitting room.

essence [esɑ̃s] *nf* **1** *Aut* petrol, *Am* gas; (*extrait*) essence; **poste d'e.** filling station. ▯ *Phil* essence.

essentiel, -ielle [esɑ̃sjɛl] *a* essential (**à, pour** for) ‖ *nm* **l'e.** the main thing ou point; (*quantité*) the main part (**de** of). ● **essentiellement** *adv* essentially.

essieu, -x [esjø] *nm* axle.

essor [esɔr] *nm* (*de pays, d'entreprise etc*) development, expansion; **en plein e.** (*industrie etc*) booming.

essor/er [esɔre] *vt* (*linge*) to wring; (*dans une essoreuse*) to spin-dry; (*dans une machine à laver*) to spin. ● **—euse** *nf* (*électrique*) spin dryer.

essouffler [esufle] *vt* to make (s.o.) out of breath ‖ **s'e.** *vpr* to get out of breath.

essuyer [esɥije] **1** *vt* to wipe ‖ **s'e.** *vpr* to wipe oneself. **2** *vt* (*subir*) to suffer. ● **essuie-glace** *nm inv* windscreen wiper, *Am* windshield wiper. ● **essuie-mains** *nm inv* (hand) towel.

est[1] [ε] *voir* être.

est[2] [est] *nm* east; **à l'e.** in the east; (*direction*) (to the) east (**de** of); **d'e.** (*vent*) east(erly); **de l'e.** eastern ‖ *a inv* (*côte*) east(ern).

estampe [εstɑ̃p] *nf* (*gravure*) print.

esthéticienne [εstetisjεn] *nf* beautician.

esthétique [εstetik] *a* aesthetic, *Am* esthetic.

estime [εstim] *nf* regard.

estimer [εstime] *vt* (*tableau etc*) to value (à at); (*calculer*) to estimate; (*juger*) to consider (*que* that); **e. dangereux**/*etc* **de faire qch** to consider it dangerous/*etc* to do sth; **e. qn** to have high regard for s.o.; **s'e. heureux**/*etc* to consider oneself happy/*etc*. ● **estimation** *nf* (*de mobilier etc*) valuation; (*calcul*) estimation.

estival, -aux [εstival, -o] *a* travail/température/*etc* **estival(e)** summer work/temperature/*etc*.

estomac [εstɔma] *nm* stomach.

estomper [εstɔ̃pe] *vt* (*rendre flou*) to blur ‖ **s'e.** *vpr* to become blurred.

estrade [εstrad] *nf* (*tribune*) platform.

estropi/er [εstrɔpje] *vt* to cripple. ● **—é, -ée** *nmf* cripple.

estuaire [εstɥεr] *nm* estuary.

et [e] *conj* and; **vingt et un**/*etc* twenty-one/*etc*; **et moi?** what about me?

étable [etabl] *nf* cowshed.

établi [etabli] *nm* (work)bench.

établir [etablir] *vt* to establish; (*installer*) to set up; (*plan, liste*) to draw up ‖ **s'é.** *vpr* (*habiter*) to settle; (*épicier etc*) to set up shop as. ● **établissement** *nm* (*action, bâtiment, institution*) establishment; *Com* company, establishment; **é. scolaire** school.

étage [etaʒ] *nm* (*d'immeuble*) floor, storey, *Am* story; (*de fusée etc*) stage; **à l'é.** upstairs; **au premier é.** on the first *ou Am* second floor; **maison à deux étages** two-storeyed *ou Am* -storied house.

étagère [etaʒεr] *nf* shelf.

étain [etε̃] *nm* (*métal*) tin; (*de gobelet etc*) pewter.

étais, était [etε] *voir* être.

étal, pl étals [etal] *nm* (*au marché*) stall.

étalage [etalaʒ] *nm* (*vitrine*) display window; **faire é. de** to show off, make a show *ou* display of.

étaler [etale] *vt* (*disposer*) to lay out; (*en vitrine*) to display; (*beurre etc*) to spread; (*vacances*) to stagger; (*érudition etc*) to show off ‖ **s'é.** *vpr* (*s'affaler*) to sprawl; (*tomber*) *Fam* to fall flat; **s'é. sur** (*congés, paiements etc*) to be spread over.

étalon [etalɔ̃] *nm* **1** (*cheval*) stallion. **2** (*modèle*) standard; **é.-or** gold standard.

étanche [etɑ̃ʃ] *a* watertight; (*montre*) waterproof.

étancher [etɑ̃ʃe] *vt* (*soif*) to quench, slake.

étang [etɑ̃] *nm* pond.

étant [etɑ̃] *voir* être.

étape [etap] *nf* (*de voyage etc*) stage; (*lieu*) stop(over); **faire é.** à to stop off *ou* over at; **par petites étapes** in easy stages.

état [eta] *nm* **1** (*condition*) state; (*registre, liste*) statement, list; **en bon é.** in good condition; **en (bon) é.** de marche in (good) working order; **en é.** de faire in a position to do; **hors d'é.** de faire not in a position to do; **é. d'esprit** state of mind; **é. d'âme** mood; **é. civil** civil status (*birth, marriage, death etc*); **faire é.** de (*mention*) to mention; (**ne pas**) **être dans son é. normal** (not) to be one's usual self. **2** É. (*nation*) State; **homme d'É.** statesman. ● **étatisé** *a* state-controlled.

état-major [etamaʒɔr] *nm* (*pl* **états-majors**) (*d'un parti etc*) senior staff.

États-Unis [etazyni] *nmpl* É.-Unis (**d'Amérique**) United States (of America).

étau, -x [eto] *nm Tech* vice, *Am* vise.

été[1] [ete] *nm* summer.

été[2] [ete] *pp de* être.

éteindre* [etε̃dr] *vt* (*feu etc*) to put out; (*lampe etc*) to turn *ou* switch off ‖ *vi* to switch off ▌**s'é.** *vpr* (*feu*) to go out; (*personne*) to pass away; (*race*) to die out; (*amour*) to die. ●**éteint** *a* (*feu, bougie*) out; (*lampe, lumière*) off; (*volcan*) extinct; (*voix*) faint.

étendre [etɑ̃dr] *vt* (*linge*) to hang out; (*nappe*) to spread (out); (*beurre*) to spread; (*agrandir*) to extend; le **bras**/*etc* to stretch out one's arm/*etc*; **é. qn** to stretch s.o. out ▌**s'é.** *vpr* (*personne*) to stretch (oneself) out; (*plaine etc*) to stretch; (*feu*) to spread; **s'é. sur** (*sujet*) to dwell on. ●**étendu** *a* (*forêt, vocabulaire etc*) extensive; (*personne*) stretched out. ●**étendue** *nf* (*importance*) extent; (*surface*) area; (*d'eau*) expanse, stretch.

éternel, -elle *a* eternal. ●**s'éterniser** *vpr* (*débat etc*) to drag on endlessly; (*visiteur etc*) to stay for ever. ●**éternité** *nf* eternity.

éternu/er [eternɥe] *vi* to sneeze. ●**—ement** [-ymɑ̃] *nm* sneeze.

êtes [et] *voir* **être**.

Éthiopie [etjɔpi] *nf* Ethiopia. ●**éthiopien, -ienne** *a & nmf* Ethiopian.

éthique [etik] *a* ethical ▌*nf Phil* ethics.

ethnie [etni] *nf* ethnic group. ●**ethnique** *a* ethnic.

étinceler [etɛ̃sle] *vi* to sparkle. ●**étincelle** *nf* spark.

étiqueter [etikte] *vt* to label. ●**étiquette** *nf* **1** (*marque*) label. **2** (*protocole*) etiquette.

étirer (s') [setire] *vpr* to stretch (oneself).

étoffe [etɔf] *nf* material.

étoile [etwal] *nf* **1** star; **à la belle é.** in the open. **2 é. de mer** starfish. ●**étoilé** *a* (*ciel*) starry; **la bannière étoilée** *Am* the Star-Spangled Banner.

étonner [etɔne] *vt* to surprise ▌**s'é.** *vpr* to be surprised (**de qch** at sth, **que** (+ *sub*) that). ●**étonnant** *a* (*ahurissant*) surprising; (*remarquable*) amazing. ●**étonnement** *nm* surprise.

étouffer [etufe] *vt* (*tuer*) to suffocate, smother; (*bruit*) to muffle; (*feu*) to smother; (*révolte, sentiment*) to stifle;

(*scandale*) to hush up ▌**on étouffe!** it's stifling!; **é. de colère** to choke with anger ▌**s'é.** *vpr* (*en mangeant*) to choke (**sur, avec** on); (*mourir*) to suffocate. ●**étouffant** *a* (*air*) stifling.

étourdi, -ie [eturdi] *a* thoughtless ▌*nmf* scatterbrain. ●**étourderie** *nf* thoughtlessness; **une (faute d')é.** a thoughtless blunder.

étourd/ir [eturdir] *vt* to stun; (*vin, vitesse*) to make dizzy; (*abrutir*) to deafen. ●**—issant** *a* (*bruit*) deafening; (*remarquable*) stunning. ●**—issement** *nm* (*malaise*) dizzy spell.

étrange [etrɑ̃ʒ] *a* strange, odd.

étranger, -ère [etrɑ̃ʒe, -er] *a* (*d'un autre pays*) foreign; (*non familier*) strange (**à** to) ▌*nmf* foreigner; (*inconnu*) stranger; **à l'é.** abroad; **de l'é.** from abroad.

étrangler [etrɑ̃gle] *vt* **é. qn** (*tuer*) to strangle s.o.; (*col*) to choke s.o. ▌**s'é.** *vpr* (*de colère, en mangeant etc*) to choke.

être* [etr] **1** *vi* to be; **il est tailleur** he's a tailor; **est-ce qu'elle vient?** is she coming?; **il vient, n'est-ce pas?** he's coming, isn't he?; **est-ce qu'il aime le thé?** does he like tea?; **nous sommes dix** there are ten of us; **nous sommes le dix** today is the tenth (of the month); **où en es-tu?** how far have you got?; **il a été à Paris** (*est allé*) he has been to Paris; **elle est de Paris** she's from Paris; **elle est de la famille** she's one of the family; **il est cinq heures** it's five (o'clock); **il était une fois** once upon the time, there was; **c'est à lire** (*obligation*) this has to be read; **c'est à voir** (*exposition etc*) it's well worth seeing; **c'est à lui** it's his; **cela étant** that being so.

2 *v aux* (*avec venir, partir etc*) to have; **elle est arrivée** she has arrived.

3 *nm* **ê. humain** human being.

étreindre [etrɛ̃dr] *vt* to grip; (*avec amour*) to embrace.

étrennes [etren] *nfpl* New Year gift; (*gratification*) = Christmas box *ou* tip.

étrier [etrije] *nm* stirrup.

étroit [etrwa] *a* narrow; (*vêtement*) tight; (*lien, collaboration etc*) close; **être à l'é.** to be cramped. ● **étroitement** *adv* (*surveiller etc*) closely. ● **étroitesse** *nf* narrowness; (*de lien etc*) closeness; **é. d'esprit** narrow-mindedness.

étude [etyd] *nf* 1 (*action, ouvrage*) study; (*salle d'*)**é.** *Scol* study room; **à l'é.** (*projet*) under consideration; **faire des études de** (*médecine etc*) to study. 2 (*de notaire etc*) office.

étudiant, -ante [etydjã, -ãt] *nmf & a* student.

étudier [etydje] *vti* to study.

étui [etɥi] *nm* (*à lunettes etc*) case.

eu, eue [y] *pp de* avoir.

euh! [ø] *int* hem!, er!, well!

eurent [yr] *voir* avoir.

euro- [øro] *préf* Euro-.

eurocrate [ørɔkrat] *nmf* Eurocrat.

eurodollar [ørɔdɔlar] *nm* Eurodollar.

Europe [ørɔp] *nf* Europe; **l'E. (des douze)** the Twelve (countries of the Common Market). ● **européen, -enne** *a & nmf* European.

eut [y] *voir* avoir.

euthanasie [øtanazi] *nf* euthanasia.

eux [ø] *pron* (*sujet*) they; (*complément*) them; (*réfléchi, emphase*) themselves. ● **eux-mêmes** *pron* themselves.

évacuer [evakɥe] *vt* to evacuate; (*liquide*) to drain off.

évader (s') [sevade] *vpr* to escape (*de* from). ● **évadé, -ée** *nmf* escaped prisoner.

évaluer [evalɥe] *vt* (*fortune etc*) to estimate; (*meuble etc*) to value.

évangile [evãʒil] *nf* gospel; **É.** Gospel.

évanouir (s') [sevanwir] *vpr Méd* to faint, pass *ou* black out; (*espoir, crainte etc*) to vanish. ● **évanoui** *a Méd* unconscious. ● **évanouissement** *nm* (*syncope*) blackout.

évaporer (s') [sevapɔre] *vpr* to evaporate; (*disparaître*) *Fam* to vanish into thin air.

évasion [evazjɔ̃] *nf* escape (**d'un lieu** from a place); (*hors de la réalité*)

escapism; **é. fiscale** tax evasion.

éveil [evɛj] *nm* awakening; **en é.** on the alert.

éveiller [eveje] *vt* (*susciter*) to arouse ∥ **s'é.** *vpr* to awake(n) (**à** to); (*sentiment, idée*) to be aroused.

événement [evenmã] *nm* event.

éventail [evãtaj] *nm* 1 (*instrument portatif*) fan. 2 (*choix*) range.

éventer [evãte] *vt* **1 é. qn** to fan s.o. ∥ **s'éventer** *vpr* (*bière, parfum*) to turn stale.

éventrer [evãtre] *vt* (*oreiller etc*) to rip open; (*animal*) to open up.

éventuel, -elle [evãtɥɛl] *a* possible. ● **éventuellement** *adv* possibly.

évêque [evɛk] *nm* bishop.

évertuer (s') [severtɥe] *vpr* **s'é. à faire** to do one's utmost to do, struggle to do.

évident [evidã] *a* obvious (**que** that); (*facile*) *Fam* easy. ● **évidemment** [-amã] *adv* obviously. ● **évidence** *nf* obviousness; **une é.** an obvious fact; **nier l'é.** to deny the obvious; **être en é.** to be conspicuous; **mettre en é.** (*fait*) to underline; **se rendre à l'é.** to face the facts.

évier [evje] *nm* (kitchen) sink.

évincer [evɛ̃se] *vt* (*concurrent, président etc*) to oust (**de** from).

éviter [evite] *vt* to avoid (**de faire** doing); **é. qch à qn** to spare s.o. sth.

évolu/er [evɔlɥe] *vi* **1** (*changer*) to develop, change; (*société, idée, situation*) to evolve; (*maladie*) to develop. **2** (*se déplacer*) to move. ● **—é** *a* (*pays*) advanced; (*personne*) enlightened. ● **évolution** *nf* **1** (*changement*) development; evolution. **2** (*d'un danseur etc*) movement.

évoquer [evɔke] *vt* to evoke, call to mind.

ex [ɛks] *nmf* (*mari, femme*) *Fam* ex.

ex- [ɛks] *préf* ex-; **ex-mari** ex-husband.

exact [ɛgzakt] *a* (*précis*) exact, accurate; (*juste, vrai*) correct, right; (*ponctuel*) punctual. ● **exactement** *adv* exactly. ● **exactitude** *nf* accuracy; correctness;

punctuality.

ex aequo [ɛgzeko] *adv* être classés ex ae. Sp to tie, be equally placed.

exagér/er [ɛgzaʒere] *vt* to exaggerate ‖ *vi* (*parler*) to exaggerate; (*agir*) to overdo it, go too far. ●—é *a* excessive. ●exagération *nf* exaggeration; (*excès*) excessiveness.

exalter [ɛgzalte] *vt* (*glorifier*) to exalt; (*passionner*) to fire, stir.

examen [ɛgzamɛ̃] *nm* examination; (*bac etc*) exam(ination); e. blanc mock exam(ination). ●examinateur, -trice *nmf Scol* examiner. ●examiner *vt* to examine.

exaspérer [ɛgzaspere] *vt* (*énerver*) to aggravate, exasperate.

exaucer [ɛgzose] *vt* (*désir*) to grant.

excéder [ɛksede] *vt* 1 (*dépasser*) to exceed. 2 e. qn (*énerver*) to exasperate s.o. ●excédent *nm* surplus, excess; e. de bagages excess luggage *ou Am* baggage.

excellent [ɛksɛlɑ̃] *a* excellent.

excentrique [ɛksɑ̃trik] *a* & *nmf* eccentric.

excepté [ɛksɛpte] *prép* except.

exception [ɛksɛpsjɔ̃] *nf* exception; à l'e. de except (for); faire e. to be an exception. ●exceptionnel, -elle *a* exceptional. ●exceptionnellement *adv* exceptionally.

excès [ɛksɛ] *nm* excess; *pl* (*de table*) over-eating. e. de vitesse *Aut* speeding. ●excessif, -ive *a* excessive.

excitation [ɛksitasjɔ̃] *nf* (*agitation*) excitement.

exciter [ɛksite] *vt* (*faire naître*) to excite, rouse, stir; e. qn (*énerver*) to provoke s.o.; (*enthousiasmer*) to thrill s.o., excite s.o. ‖ s'e. *vpr* (*devenir nerveux*) to get excited. ●excitant *a Fam* exciting ‖ *nm* stimulant. ●excité *a* excited.

exclamer (s') [ɛksklame] *vpr* to exclaim. ●exclamation *nf* exclamation.

excl/ure* [ɛksklyr] *vt* (*écarter*) to exclude (de from); (*chasser*) to expel (de from); e. qch (*rendre impossible*) to preclude sth. ●—u *a* (*solution etc*) out

of the question; (*avec une date*) exclusive.

exclusif, -ive [ɛksklyzif, -iv] *a* (*droit, modèle, préoccupation*) exclusive. ●exclusivité *nf Com* exclusive rights; (*dans la presse*) scoop; en e. (*film*) having an exclusive showing (à at).

exclusion [ɛksklyzjɔ̃] *nf* exclusion; à l'e. de with the exception of.

excursion [ɛkskyrsjɔ̃] *nf* trip, outing; (à *pied*) hike.

excuse [ɛkskyz] *nf* (*prétexte*) excuse; *pl* (*regrets*) apology; faire des excuses to apologize (à to). ●excuser *vt* to excuse (qn d'avoir fait, qn de faire s.o. for doing) ‖ s'e. *vpr* to apologize (de for, auprès de to); excusez-moi!, je m'excuse! excuse me!

exécrable [ɛgzekrabl] *a* atrocious.

exécuter [ɛgzekyte] *vt* 1 (*travail*) to carry out; (*jouer*) *Mus* to perform; (*broderie etc*) to produce; (*programme informatique*) to run. 2 e. qn (*tuer*) to execute s.o. 3 s'exécuter *vpr* to comply. ●exécution *nf* 1 carrying out; performance; production. 2 (*mise à mort*) execution.

exécutif [ɛgzekytif] *am* pouvoir e. executive power ‖ *nm* l'e. Pol the executive.

exemplaire [ɛgzɑ̃pler] 1 *a* exemplary. 2 *nm* (*livre etc*) copy; photocopier un document en double e. to make two photocopies of a document.

exemple [ɛgzɑ̃pl] *nm* example; par e. for example, for instance; donner l'e. to set an example (à to); prendre e. sur qn to follow s.o.'s example; c'est un e. de vertu/*etc* he's a model of virtue/*etc*; (ça) par e.! *Fam* good heavens!.

exempt [ɛgzɑ̃] *a* e. de (*dispensé de*) exempt from. ●exempter *vt* to exempt (de from).

exercer [ɛgzerse] *vt* (*voix, droits*) to exercise; (*autorité, influence*) to exert (sur over); (*profession*) to practise; e. qn à (*couture etc*) to train s.o. in; e. qn à faire to train s.o. to do ‖ *vi* (*médecin etc*) to practise ‖ s'e. *vpr* (*influence etc*) to be exerted; **s'e. (à qch)** (*sportif etc*) to practise (sth); **s'e. à faire** to practise doing.

exercice [ɛgzɛrsis] *nm* (*physique etc*) & *Scol* exercise; **faire de l'e., prendre de l'e.** to (take) exercise; **l'e. de** (*pouvoir etc*) the exercise of; **en e.** (*fonctionnaire*) in office; (*médecin etc*) in practice.

exhaustif, -ive [ɛgzostif, -iv] *a* exhaustive.

exhiber [ɛgzibe] *vt* to exhibit, show.

exiger [ɛgziʒe] *vt* to demand, require (**de** from, **que** (+ *sub*) that). ● **exigeant** *a* demanding. ● **exigence** *nf* demand, requirement; **d'une grande e.** very demanding.

exigu, -uë [ɛgzigy] *a* (*appartement etc*) cramped, tiny.

exil [ɛgzil] *nm* exile. ● **exiler** *vt* to exile ‖**s'e.** *vpr* to go into exile. ● **exilé, -ée** *nmf* (*personne*) exile.

existence [ɛgzistɑ̃s] *nf* existence. ● **exister** *vi* to exist ‖**v il existe...** (*sing*) there is...; (*pl*) there are....

exode [ɛgzɔd] *nm* exodus.

exonérer [ɛgzɔnere] *vt* to exempt (**de** from).

exorbitant [ɛgzɔrbitɑ̃] *a* exorbitant.

exorciser [ɛgzɔrsize] *vt* to exorcize.

exotique [ɛgzɔtik] *a* exotic.

expansif, -ive [ɛkspɑ̃sif, -iv] *a* expansive, effusive.

expansion [ɛkspɑ̃sjɔ̃] *nf* (*d'un commerce, pays, gaz*) expansion; **en (pleine) e.** (fast) expanding.

expatrier (s') [sɛkspatrije] *vpr* to leave one's country.

expectative [ɛkspɛktativ] *nf* **être dans l'e.** to be waiting to see what happens.

expédier [ɛkspedje] *vt* **1** (*envoyer*) to send off. **2** (*affaires, client*) to dispose of quickly, dispatch. ● **expéditeur, -trice** *nmf* sender. ● **expédition** *nf* **1** (*envoi*) dispatch. **2** (*voyage*) expedition.

expérience [ɛksperjɑ̃s] *nf* (*connaissance*) experience; (*scientifique*) experiment; **faire l'e. de qch** to experience sth; **être sans e.** to have no experience.

expériment/er [ɛksperimɑ̃te] *vt* *Phys Ch* to try out, experiment with. ● **—é** *a* experienced.

expert [ɛkspɛr] *a* expert, skilled (**en** in) ‖*nm* expert (en on, in); (*d'assurances*) valuer. ● **e.-comptable** *nm* (*pl* **experts-comptables**) = chartered accountant, = *Am* certified public accountant. ● **expertise** *nf* (*évaluation*) (expert) appraisal.

expirer [ɛkspire] **1** *vti* to breathe out. **2** *vi* (*mourir*) to pass away; (*finir, cesser*) to expire. ● **expiration** *nf* (*échéance*) expiry, *Am* expiration; **arriver à e.** to expire.

explication [ɛksplikasjɔ̃] *nf* explanation; (*mise au point*) discussion.

explicite [ɛksplisit] *a* explicit.

expliquer [ɛksplike] *vt* to explain (**à** to, **que** that) ‖**s'e.** *vpr* (*discuter*) to talk things over (**avec** with); **s'e. qch** (*comprendre*) to understand sth; **ça s'explique** that is understandable.

exploit [ɛksplwa] *nm* feat, exploit.

exploit/er [ɛksplwate] *vt* (*champs*) to farm; (*ferme, entreprise*) to run; (*mine*) to work; (*profiter de*) *Fig* to exploit. ● **—ant, -ante** *nmf* farmer. ● **exploitation** *nf* **1** farming; running; working; (*entreprise*) concern; **e.** (**agricole**) farm. **2** *Péj* exploitation.

explorer [ɛksplɔre] *vt* to explore. ● **explorateur, -trice** *nmf* explorer. ● **exploration** *nf* exploration.

exploser [ɛksploze] *vi* (*gaz etc*) to explode; (*bombe*) to blow up, explode; **e.** (**de colère**) *Fam* to explode; **faire e.** (*bombe*) to explode. ● **explosif, -ive** *a* & *nm* explosive. ● **explosion** *nf* explosion; (*de colère, joie*) outburst.

exporter [ɛkspɔrte] *vt* to export (**vers** to, **de** from). ● **exportateur, -trice** *nmf* exporter ‖*a* exporting. ● **exportation** *nf* (*produit*) export; (*action*) export(ation).

expos/er [ɛkspoze] *vt* (*présenter, soumettre*) & *Phot* to expose (**à** to); (*tableau etc*) to exhibit; (*marchan-*

dises) to display; (*idée, théorie*) to set out; (*vie*) to risk; **s'e. à** to expose oneself to. ●**–é 1** *a* **bien e.**₊(*édifice*) having a good exposure; **e. au sud**/*etc* facing south/*etc*. **2** *nm* (*compte rendu*) account (**de** of); (*présentation*) talk.

exposition [ɛkspozisjɔ̃] *nf* (*salon*) exhibition; (*de marchandises etc*) display.

exprès[1] [ɛksprɛ] *adv* on purpose, intentionally; (*spécialement*) specially.

exprès[2], **-esse** [ɛksprɛs] **1** *a* (*ordre, condition*) express. **2** *a inv* **lettre**/**colis e.** express letter/parcel.

express [ɛksprɛs] *a & nm inv* (*train*) express; (*café*) espresso.

expressif, -ive [ɛkspresif, -iv] *a* expressive. ●**expression** *nf* (*phrase, mine etc*) expression. ●**exprimer** *vt* to express ▌**s'e.** *vpr* to express oneself.

exproprier [ɛksprɔprije] *vt* to seize the property of by compulsory purchase.

expulser [ɛkspylse] *vt* to expel (**de** from); (*joueur*) *Sp* to send off; (*locataire*) to evict. ●**expulsion** *nf* expulsion; sending off; eviction.

exquis [ɛkski] *a* (*nourriture*) delicious.

extasier (s') [sɛkstazje] *vpr* to be in raptures (**sur** over).

extensible [ɛkstɑ̃sibl] *a* expandable. ●**extension** *nf* extension; (*essor*) expansion.

exténué [ɛkstenɥe] *a* exhausted.

extérieur [ɛksterjœr] *a* outside; (*surface*) outer, external; (*signe*) outward; (*politique*) foreign; **e. à** external to ▌*nm* outside; **à l'e. (de)** outside; **à l'e.** (*match*) away; **en e.** *Cin* on location. ●**—ement**

adv externally; (*en apparence*) outwardly. ●**extérioriser** *vt* to express.

exterminer [ɛkstɛrmine] *vt* to exterminate, wipe out.

externat [ɛkstɛrna] *nm* (*école*) day school.

externe [ɛkstɛrn] **1** *a* external. **2** *nmf* (*élève*) day pupil; *Méd* non-resident hospital doctor, *Am* extern.

extincteur [ɛkstɛ̃ktœr] *nm* fire extinguisher.

extorquer [ɛkstɔrke] *vt* to extort (**à** from). ●**extorsion** *nf* extortion; **e. de fonds** (*crime*) extortion.

extra [ɛkstra] **1** *a inv* (*très bon*) *Fam* top-quality. **2** *nm inv* *Culin* (extra-special) treat; (*serviteur*) extra hand *ou* help.

extra- [ɛkstra] *préf* extra-. ●**e.-fin** *a* extra-fine. ●**e.-fort** *a* extra-strong.

extradition [ɛkstradisjɔ̃] *nf* extradition. ●**extrader** *vt* to extradite.

extraire* [ɛkstrɛr] *vt* to extract (**de** from); (*charbon*) to mine. ●**extrait** *nm* extract; **e. de naissance** (copy of one's) birth certificate.

extraordinaire [ɛkstraɔrdinɛr] *a* extraordinary.

extraterrestre [ɛkstraterɛstr] *a & nmf* extraterrestrial.

extravagant [ɛkstravagɑ̃] *a* extravagant.

extraverti, -ie [ɛkstraverti] *nmf* extrovert.

extrême [ɛkstrɛm] *a & nm* extreme; **pousser à l'e.** to take *ou* carry to extremes. ●**E.-Orient** *nm* Far East. ●**extrêmement** *adv* extremely. ●**extrémiste** *a & nmf* extremist. ●**extrémité** *nf* (*bout*) end; *pl* (*excès*) extremes.

F

F, f [εf] *nm* F, f.
F *abrév* **franc(s).**
fa [fa] *nm* (*note de musique*) F.
fable [fɑbl] *nf* fable.
fabricant, -ante [fabrikɑ̃, -ɑ̃t] *nmf* manufacturer. ● **fabrication** *nf* manufacture; **f. artisanale** small-scale manufacture.
fabrique [fabrik] *nf* factory; **marque de f.** trade mark.
fabriquer [fabrike] *vt* to make; (*en usine*) to manufacture; **qu'est-ce qu'il fabrique?** *Fam* what's he up to?
fabuleux, -euse [fabylø, -øz] *a* (*légendaire, incroyable*) fabulous.
fac [fak] *nf abrév* (*faculté*) *Fam* university; **à la f.** at university, *Am* at school.
façade [fasad] *nf* (*de bâtiment*) front; (*apparence*) *Fig* pretence, façade.
face [fas] *nf* face; (*de cube etc*) side; (*de monnaie*) head; **en f.** opposite; **en f. de** opposite, facing; (*en présence de*) in front of, face to face with; **f. à** (*vis-à-vis*) facing; **f. à f.** face to face; **f. à un problème** faced with a problem; **faire f. à** (*situation*) to face, face up to; **regarder qn en f.** to look s.o. in the face; **de f.** (*photo*) full-face.
facette [faset] *nf* (*de diamant, problème etc*) facet.
fâcher [fɑʃe] *vt* to anger ‖ **se f.** *vpr* to get angry (**contre** with); **se f. avec qn** (*se brouiller*) to fall out with s.o. ● **fâché** *a* (*air*) angry; (*amis*) on bad terms; **f. de qch** sorry about sth.
facho [faʃo] *a & nmf Fam* fascist.
facile [fasil] *a* easy; (*caractère, humeur*) easygoing; **c'est f. à faire** it's easy to do; **il nous est f. de faire ça** it's easy for us to do that; **f. à vivre** easy to get along with, easygoing. ● **—ment** *adv* easily. ● **facilité** *nf* (*simplicité*) easiness; (*à faire qch*) ease; **facilités de paiement** *Com* easy

terms; **avoir des facilités pour qch** to have an aptitude for sth. ● **faciliter** *vt* to make easier, facilitate.
façon [fasɔ̃] *nf* 1 way; **la f. dont elle parle** the way (in which) she talks; **f. (d'agir)** behaviour; **façons** (*manières*) manners; **une f. de parler** a manner of speaking; **de toute f.** anyway; **de f. à** so as to; **de f. générale** generally speaking; **d'une f. ou d'une autre** one way or another; **à ma f.** my way, (in) my own way; **faire des façons** to make a fuss. 2 (*coupe de vêtement*) cut, style.
façonner [fasɔne] *vt* (*travailler, former*) to fashion, shape; (*fabriquer*) to manufacture.
facteur [faktœr] *nm* 1 postman, *Am* mailman. 2 (*élément*) factor. ● **factrice** *nf* postwoman, *Am* mail woman.
facture [faktyr] *nf Com* bill, invoice. ● **facturer** *vt* to bill, invoice.
facultatif, -ive [fakyltatif, -iv] *a* optional; **arrêt f.** request stop.
faculté [fakylte] *nf* 1 (*aptitude*) faculty; (*possibilité*) freedom (**de faire** to do); **une f. de travail** a capacity for work. 2 (*d'université*) faculty; **à la f.** at university, *Am* at school.
fade [fad] *a* insipid; (*nourriture*) bland.
fagot [fago] *nm* bundle (of firewood).
faible [fɛbl] *a* weak; (*bruit*) faint; (*vent*) slight; (*revenus*) small; **f. en anglais/***etc* poor at English/*etc* ‖ *nm* (*personne*) weakling; **avoir un f. pour** to have a weakness *ou* a soft spot for. ● **faiblement** *adv* weakly; (*légèrement*) slightly; (*éclairer*) faintly. ● **faiblesse** *nf* weakness; faintness; slightness; (*défaut, syncope*) weakness.
faiblir [feblir] *vi* (*forces*) to weaken; (*courage, vue*) to fail; (*vent*) to slacken.
faïence [fajɑ̃s] *nf* (*matière*) earthenware.

pl (objets) crockery, earthenware.
faille[1] [faj] *nf Géol* fault; *Fig* flaw.
faille[2] [faj] *voir* **falloir**.
faillible [fajibl] *a* fallible.
faillir* [fajir] *vi* **1 il a failli tomber** he almost *ou* nearly fell. **2 f. à** *(devoir)* to fail in.
faillite [fajit] *nf Com* bankruptcy; **faire f.** to go bankrupt.
faim [fɛ̃] *nf* hunger; **avoir f.** to be hungry; **donner f. à qn** to make s.o. hungry; **manger à sa f.** to eat one's fill; **mourir de f.** to die of starvation; *(avoir très faim) Fig* to be starving.
fainéant, -ante [feneɑ̃, -ɑ̃t] *a* idle ▮ *nmf* idler. ● **fainéantise** *nf* idleness.
faire* [fɛr] **1** *vt (bruit, faute, gâteau, voyage etc)* to make; *(devoir, ménage etc)* to do; *(rêve, chute)* to have; *(sourire)* to give; *(promenade, sieste)* to have, take; *(guerre)* to wage, make; **ça fait dix mètres de large** *(mesure)* it's *ou* that's ten metres wide; **ça fait dix francs** *(prix)* it's *ou* that's ten francs; **2 et 2 font 4** 2 and 2 are 4; **qu'a-t-il fait (de)?** what's he done (with)?; **que f.?** what's to be done? **f. du tennis/du piano**/*etc* to play tennis/the piano/*etc*; **f. du droit**/*etc* to study law/*etc*; **f. l'idiot** to play the fool; **ça ne fait rien** that doesn't matter; **comment as-tu fait pour...?** how did you manage to...?
2 *vi (agir)* to do; *(paraître)* to look; **il fait vieux** he looks old; **elle ferait bien de partir** she'd do well to leave.
3 *v imp* **il fait beau/froid**/*etc* it's fine/cold/*etc*; **quel temps fait-il?** what's the weather like?; **ça fait deux ans que je ne l'ai pas vu** I haven't seen him for two years; **ça fait un an que je suis là** I've been here for a year.
4 *v aux (+ inf)*: **f. construire une maison** to have *ou* get a house built (**pour** s.o., **par qn** by s.o.); **f. souffrir**/*etc* **qn** to make s.o. suffer/*etc*; **se f. couper les cheveux** to have one's hair cut; **se f. obéir**/*etc* to make oneself obeyed/*etc*;

se f. tuer/*etc* to get *ou* be killed/*etc*.
5 se faire *vpr (fabrication)* to be made; *(activité)* to be done; **se f. des illusions** to have illusions; **se f. des amis** to make friends; **se f. vieux**/*etc* to get old/*etc*; **il se fait tard** it's getting late; **comment se fait-il que?** how is it that?; **ça se fait beaucoup** people do that a lot; **se f. à** to get used to; **ne t'en fais pas!** don't worry!
faire-part [fɛrpar] *nm inv (de mariage etc)* announcement.
fais, fait [fɛ] *voir* **faire**.
faisable [fəzabl] *a* feasible.
faisan [fəzɑ̃] *nm (oiseau)* pheasant.
faisceau, -x [feso] *nm (lumineux)* beam.
fait [fɛ] **1** *pp de* **faire** ▮ *a (fromage)* ripe; *(yeux)* made up; *(ongles)* polished; *(homme)* grown; **tout f.** ready made; **bien f.** *(jambes, corps etc)* shapely; **c'est bien f.!** it serves you right!
2 *nm* event; *(donnée, réalité)* fact; **prendre qn sur le f.** to catch s.o. red-handed *ou* in the act; **du f. de** on account of; **f. divers** *(rubrique de journal)* (miscellaneous) news item; **au f.** *(à propos)* by the way; **aller au f.** to get to the point; **en f.** in fact; **en f. de** in the matter of.
faîte [fɛt] *nm (haut)* top; *(apogée) Fig* height.
faites [fɛt] *voir* **faire**.
falaise [falɛz] *nf* cliff.
falloir* [falwar] **1** *v imp* **il faut qch/qn** I, you, we *etc* need sth/s.o.; **il lui faut un stylo** he *ou* she needs a pen; **il faut partir**/*etc* I, you, we *etc* have to go/*etc*; **il faut que je parte** I have to go; **il faudrait qu'elle reste** she ought to stay; **il faut un jour** it takes a day **(pour faire** to do); **comme il faut** proper(ly); **s'il le faut** if need be.
2 s'en falloir *v imp* **il s'en est fallu de peu qu'il ne pleure** he almost cried; **tant s'en faut** far from it.
falsifier [falsifje] *vt (texte etc)* to falsify.
famé (mal) [malfame] *a* of ill repute.
fameux, -euse [famø, -øz] *a (célèbre)* famous; *(excellent) Fam* first-class; **pas**

f. *Fam* not much good.

familial, -aux [familjal, -o] *a* family; **ennuis/etc familiaux** family problems/ *etc.*

familier, -ière [familje, -jɛr] *a* (*bien connu*) familiar (**à** to); (*amical*) friendly, informal; (*locution*) colloquial, familiar; **f. avec qn** (over)familiar with s.o.; **animal f.** pet. ● **se familiariser** *vpr* to familiarize oneself (**avec** with). ● **familiarité** *nf* familiarity (**avec** with). ● **familièrement** *adv* (*parler*) informally.

famille [famij] *nf* family; **en f.** (*dîner etc*) with one's family; **un père de f.** a family man.

famine [famin] *nf* famine.

fan [fɑ̃] *nm* (*admirateur*) *Fam* fan.

fana [fana] *nmf Fam* fan; **être f. de** to be crazy about.

fanatique [fanatik] *a* fanatical ‖ *nmf* fanatic. ● **fanatisme** *nm* fanaticism.

faner (se) [səfane] *vpr* (*fleur, beauté*) to fade. ● **fané** *a* faded.

fanfare [fɑ̃far] *nf* (*orchestre*) brass band.

fanfaron, -onne [fɑ̃farɔ̃, -ɔn] *a* boastful ‖ *nmf* braggart.

fanion [fanjɔ̃] *nm* (*drapeau*) pennant.

fantaisie [fɑ̃tezi] *nf* (*caprice*) whim, fancy; (*imagination*) imagination; (**de**) **f.** (*bouton etc*) novelty, fancy. ● **fantaisiste** *a* (*pas sérieux*) fanciful; (*excentrique*) unorthodox.

fantasme [fɑ̃tasm] *nm Psy* fantasy.

fantasque [fɑ̃task] *a* whimsical.

fantassin [fɑ̃tasɛ̃] *nm Mil* infantryman.

fantastique [fɑ̃tastik] *a* (*imaginaire, excellent*) fantastic.

fantôme [fɑ̃tom] *nm* ghost ‖ *a* **ville f.** ghost town.

faon [fɑ̃] *nm* (*animal*) fawn.

farce[1] [fars] *nf* practical joke, prank; *Th* farce; **magasin de farces et attrapes** joke shop. ● **farceur, -euse** *nmf* (*blagueur*) practical joker.

farce[2] [fars] *nf* (*viande*) stuffing. ● **farcir** *vt Culin* to stuff.

fard [far] *nm* make-up. ● **se farder** *vpr* (*se maquiller*) to make up.

fardeau, -x [fardo] *nm* burden, load.

farfelu [farfəly] *a Fam* crazy, bizarre.

farine [farin] *nf* (*de blé*) flour.

farouche [faruʃ] *a* **1** (*timide*) shy, unsociable; (*animal*) easily scared. **2** (*violent*) fierce.

fart [far(t)] *nm* (ski) wax. ● **farter** *vt* (*skis*) to wax.

fascicule [fasikyl] *nm* volume.

fasciner [fasine] *vt* to fascinate. ● **fascination** *nf* fascination.

fasciste [faʃist] *a* & *nmf* fascist.

fasse(s), fassent [fas] *voir* **faire.**

faste [fast] *nm* ostentation, display.

fastidieux, -euse [fastidjø, -øz] *a* tedious.

fatal, *mpl* -als [fatal] *a* (*mortel*) fatal; (*inévitable*) inevitable; (*moment*) fateful; **c'était f.!** it was bound to happen! ● **—ement** *adv* inevitably. ● **fatalité** *nf* (*destin*) fate.

fatigant [fatigɑ̃] *a* (*épuisant*) tiring; (*ennuyeux*) tiresome.

fatigue [fatig] *nf* tiredness, fatigue.

fatiguer [fatige] *vt* to tire; (*yeux*) to strain; (*importuner*) to annoy; (*raser*) to bore ‖ *vi* (*moteur*) to strain ‖ **se f.** *vpr* (*se lasser*) to get tired, tire (**de** of); (*travailler*) to tire oneself out (**à faire** doing). ● **fatigué** *a* tired, weary (**de** of).

faubourg [fobur] *nm* suburb.

fauché [foʃe] *a* (*sans argent*) *Fam* (flat) broke.

faucher [foʃe] *vt* **1** (*herbe*) to mow; (*blé*) to reap; **f. qn** (*renverser*) *Fig* to knock s.o. down, mow s.o. down. **2** (*voler*) *Fam* to snatch, pinch.

faucille [fosij] *nf* (*instrument*) sickle.

faucon [fokɔ̃] *nm* (*oiseau*) hawk, falcon.

faudra, faudrait [fodra, fodrɛ] *voir* **falloir.**

faufiler (se) [səfofile] *vpr* to edge one's way (**dans** through, into; **entre** between).

faune [fon] *nf* wildlife, fauna.

faussaire [fosɛr] *nm* forger.

fausse [fos] *voir* **faux**[1]. ● **faussement** *adv*

falsely.

fausser [fose] vt (réalité etc) to distort; **f. compagnie à qn** to give s.o. the slip.

fausseté [foste] nf (d'un raisonnement etc) falseness; (hypocrisie) duplicity.

faut [fo] voir **falloir**.

faute [fot] nf (erreur) mistake; (responsabilité) fault; (péché) sin; Fb foul; **c'est ta f.** it's your fault; **f. de temps**/etc for lack of time/etc; **f. de mieux** for want of anything better; **sans f.** without fail; **f. d'impression** printing error.

fauteuil [fotœj] nm armchair; **f. roulant** wheelchair; **f. d'orchestre** Th seat in the stalls.

fauteur [fotœr] nm **f. de troubles** troublemaker.

fautif, -ive [fotif, -iv] a (personne) at fault; (erroné) faulty.

fauve [fov] nm wild animal, big cat.

faux¹, fausse [fo, fos] a (pas vrai) false, untrue; (pas exact) wrong; (monnaie) forged, counterfeit; (voix) out of tune; **f. diamant**/etc imitation ou fake diamond/etc ▮ adv (chanter) out of tune ▮ nm (contrefaçon) forgery. ●**f.-filet** nm Culin sirloin. ●**f.-monnayeur** nm counterfeiter.

faux² [fo] nf (instrument) scythe.

faveur [favœr] nf favour; **en f. de** (au profit de) in aid ou favour of; **de f.** (billet) complimentary; (traitement) preferential. ●**favorable** a favourable (à to). ●**favori, -ite** a & nmf favourite. ●**favoriser** vt to favour. ●**favoritisme** nm favouritism.

favoris [favori] nmpl sideburns, sideboards.

fax [faks] nm (appareil, message) fax. **faxer** [fakse] vt (message) to fax.

fébrile [febril] a feverish.

fécond [fekɔ̃] a (femme, idée etc) fertile. ●**fécondité** nf fertility.

fécule [fekyl] nf starch. ●**féculents** nmpl (aliments) carbohydrates.

fédéral, -aux [federal, -o] a federal. ●**fédération** nf federation.

fée [fe] nf fairy. ●**féerique** a fairy(-like),

magical.

feindre* [fɛdr] vt to feign, affect, sham; **f. de faire** to pretend to do. ●**feinte** nf sham, pretence; Boxe Mil feint.

fêler [fele] vt, **se f.** vpr (tasse etc) to crack. ●**fêlure** nf crack.

féliciter [felisite] vt to congratulate (qn **de** ou **sur** s.o. on); **se f. de** to congratulate oneself on. ●**félicitations** nfpl congratulations (pour on).

félin [felɛ̃] a & nm feline.

femelle [fǝmel] a & nf (animal) female.

féminin [feminɛ̃] a (prénom etc) female; (trait, intuition etc) & Gram feminine; (mode, revue etc) women's. ●**féministe** a & nmf feminist.

femme [fam] nf woman (pl women); (épouse) wife; **f. médecin** woman doctor; **f. de ménage** cleaning woman; **f. de chambre** (chamber)maid; **f. d'affaires** businesswoman; **f. au foyer** housewife; **bonne f.** Fam woman.

fémur [femyr] nm thighbone.

fendiller (se) [sǝfɑ̃dije] vpr to crack.

fendre [fɑ̃dr] vt (bois etc) to split; (foule) to force one's way through; (air) to cleave; (cœur) Fig to break ▮ **se f.** vpr (se fissurer) to crack.

fenêtre [f(ǝ)netr] nf window.

fenouil [fǝnuj] nm Bot Culin fennel.

fente [fɑ̃t] nf (palissade, jupe etc) slit; (de rocher) split, crack.

féodal, -aux [feɔdal, -o] a feudal.

fer [fer] nm iron; (partie métallique de qch) metal (part); **barre de f.** iron bar; **fil de f.** wire; **boîte en f.** tin, Am can; **f. à cheval** horseshoe; **f. (à repasser)** iron (for clothes); **f. forgé** wrought iron; **santé de f.** Fig cast-iron health. ●**fer-blanc** nm (pl **fers-blancs**) tin (-plate).

fera, ferai(t) etc [fǝra, fǝre] voir **faire**.

férié [ferje] a **jour f.** (public) holiday.

ferme¹ [ferm] nf farm; (maison) farm(house).

ferme² [ferm] a (beurre, décision etc) firm; (pas, voix) steady; (autoritaire) firm (**avec** with) ▮ adv (discuter) keen-

ly; **s'ennuyer f.** to be bored stiff.
● **—ment** [-əmɑ̃] *adv* firmly.
fermentation [fɛrmɑ̃tasjɔ̃] *nf* fermentation. ● **fermenter** *vi* to ferment.
fermer [fɛrme] *vt* to close, shut; *(gaz etc)* to turn *ou* switch off; *(vêtement)* to do up; *(passage)* to block; **f. (à clef)** to lock; **f. un magasin**/*etc (définitivement)* to close *ou* shut (down) a shop/*etc* ‖ *vi*, **se f.** *vpr* to close, shut. ● **fermé** *a (porte, magasin etc)* closed, shut; *(route etc)* closed; *(gaz etc)* off.
fermeté [fɛrməte] *nf* firmness; *(de voix)* steadiness.
fermeture [fɛrmətyr] *nf* closing, closure; *(heure)* closing time; **f. éclair**® zip (fastener), *Am* zipper.
fermier, -ière [fɛrmje, -jɛr] *nmf* farmer.
fermoir [fɛrmwar] *nm* clasp, (snap) fastener.
féroce [feros] *a* fierce, savage. ● **férocité** *nf* ferocity.
feront [fərɔ̃] *voir* **faire**.
ferraille [fɛrɑj] *nf* scrap metal, old iron; **mettre à la f.** to scrap.
ferré [fɛre] *a* **voie ferrée** railway, *Am* railroad; *(rails)* track.
ferrer [fɛre] *vt (cheval)* to shoe.
ferronnerie [fɛrɔnri] *nf* ironwork.
ferroviaire [fɛrɔvjɛr] *a* **compagnie f.** railway company, *Am* railroad company.
fertile [fɛrtil] *a (terre, imagination)* fertile; **f. en incidents** eventful. ● **fertilité** *nf* fertility.
fervent [fɛrvɑ̃] *a* fervent. ● **ferveur** *nf* fervour.
fesse [fɛs] *nf* buttock; **les fesses** one's behind. ● **fessée** *nf* spanking.
festin [fɛstɛ̃] *nm (banquet)* feast.
festival, *pl* **-als** [fɛstival] *nm Mus Cin etc* festival.
festivités [fɛstivite] *nfpl* festivities.
fête [fɛt] *nf (civile)* holiday; *Rel* festival; *(entre amis)* party; **f. de famille** family celebration; **c'est sa f.** it's his *ou* her saint's day; **f. des Mères** Mother's Day; **f. du travail** Labour Day; **jour de f.** (public) holiday; **faire la f.** to have a

good time; **les fêtes** *(de Noël)* the Christmas holidays. ● **fêter** *vt (événement)* to celebrate.
feu¹, -x [fø] *nm* fire; *(de réchaud)* burner; *(lumière)* *Aut Nau Av* light; *(de dispute)* *Fig* heat; **feux (tricolores)** traffic lights; **feux de détresse** (hazard) warning lights; **feux de position** *Aut* parking lights; **feux de croisement** *Aut* dipped headlights, *Am* low beams; **tous feux éteints** *Aut* without lights; **f. rouge** *Aut (lumière)* red light; *(objet)* traffic lights; **mettre le f. à** to set fire to; **en f.** on fire, ablaze; **faire du f.** to light *ou* make a fire; **prendre f.** to catch fire; **avez-vous du f.?** have you got a light?; **donner le f. vert** to give the go-ahead (à to); **à f. doux** *Culin* on a low light *ou* heat; **au f.!** fire!; **f.!** *Mil* fire!; **coup de f.** *(bruit)* gunshot.
feu² [fø] *a inv* late; **f. ma tante** my late aunt.
feuille [fœj] *nf* leaf; *(de papier etc)* sheet; **f. d'impôt** tax form *ou* return; **f. de paye** pay slip *ou Am* stub; **f. de présence** attendance sheet. ● **feuillage** *nm* leaves.
feuillet [fœjɛ] *nm (de livre)* leaf. ● **feuilleter** *vt (livre)* to flip through; **pâte feuilletée** puff pastry *ou Am* paste.
feuilleton [fœjtɔ̃] *nm* serial; **f. télévisé** television serial.
feutre [føtr] *nm* felt; *(chapeau)* felt hat; **crayon f.** felt-tip (pen). ● **feutré** *a (bruit)* muffled; **à pas feutrés** silently.
février [fevrije] *nm* February.
fiable [fjabl] *a* reliable. ● **fiabilité** *nf* reliability.
fiacre [fjakr] *nm Hist* hackney carriage.
fiancer (se) [səfjɑ̃se] *vpr* to become engaged (avec to). ● **fiancé** *nm* fiancé; *pl* **engaged couple.** ● **fiancée** *nf* fiancée. ● **fiançailles** *nfpl* engagement.
fibre [fibr] *nf* fibre; **f. (alimentaire)** roughage, fibre; **f. de verre** fibreglass.
ficelle [fisɛl] *nf* **1** string. **2** *(pain)* long thin loaf. ● **ficeler** *vt* to tie up.
fiche [fiʃ] *nf* **1** *(carte)* index card; *(papier)* form, slip. **2** *El (prise)* plug.

● **fichier** *nm* card index, file; *Ordinat* file.

fiche(r) [fiʃ(e)] *vt* (*pp* **fichu**) *Fam* (*faire*) to do; (*donner*) to give; (*jeter*) to throw; (*mettre*) to put; **f. le camp** to shove off; **fiche-moi la paix!** leave me alone!; **se f. de qn** to make fun of s.o.; **je m'en fiche!** I don't give a damn!

ficher [fiʃe] *vt* **1** (*enfoncer*) to drive in. **2** (*renseignement sur une personne*) to put on file.

fichu [fiʃy] *a Fam* (*mauvais*) lousy, rotten; (*capable*) able (**de faire** to do); **c'est f.** (*abîmé*) *Fam* it's had it; **mal f.** (*malade*) not well.

fictif, -ive [fiktif, -iv] *a* fictitious. ● **fiction** *nf* fiction.

fidèle [fidɛl] *a* faithful (**à** to) ∥ *nmf* (*client*) regular (customer); **les fidèles** (*croyants*) the faithful; (*à l'église*) the congregation. ● **fidélité** *nf* fidelity.

fier (se) [səfje] *vpr* **se f. à** to trust.

fier, fière [fjɛr] *a* proud (**de** of). ● **fièrement** *adv* proudly. ● **fierté** *nf* pride.

fièvre [fjɛvr] *nf* fever; (*agitation*) frenzy; **avoir de la f.** to have a temperature *ou* a fever. ● **fiévreux, -euse** *a* feverish.

figer [fiʒe] *vt* to congeal; **f. qn** (*paralyser*) *Fig* to freeze s.o. ∥ **se f.** *vpr* (*liquide*) to congeal; (*sourire, personne*) *Fig* to freeze. ● **figé** *a* (*locution*) set, fixed; (*regard*) frozen, (*société*) fossilized.

fignoler [fiɲɔle] *vt Fam* to round off meticulously, refine.

figue [fig] *nf* fig; **mi-f., mi-raisin** (*accueil etc*) neither good nor bad, mixed. ● **figuier** *nm* fig tree.

figurant, -ante [figyrɑ̃, -ɑ̃t] *nmf Cin Th* extra.

figure [figyr] *nf* **1** (*visage*) face. **2** (*personnage*) & *Géom* figure; **faire f. de favori** to be considered the favourite. ● **figurer** *vi* to appear ∥ **se f.** *vpr* to imagine; **figurez-vous que...?** would you believe that...? ● **figuré** *a* (*sens*) figurative ∥ *nm* **au f.** figuratively.

fil [fil] *nm* **1** (*de coton, pensée etc*) thread; **f. dentaire** dental floss; **de f. en aiguille** bit by bit. **2** (*métallique*) wire; **f. de fer**

wire; **passer un coup de f. à qn** *Tél* to give s.o. a ring, call s.o. up; **au bout du f.** *Tél* on the line. **3** (*de couteau*) edge. **4 au f. de l'eau/des jours** with the current/the passing of time.

filante [filɑ̃t] *af* **étoile f.** shooting star.

filature [filatyr] *nf* **1** (*usine*) textile mill. **2** (*de policiers etc*) shadowing; **prendre en f.** to shadow.

file [fil] *nf* line; (*couloir*) *Aut* lane; **f. d'attente** queue, *Am* line; **en f. (indienne)** in single file; **chef de f.** leader.

filer [file] **1** *vt* (*coton etc*) to spin. **2** *vt* **f. qn** (*suivre*) to shadow s.o. **3** *vt Fam* **f. qch à qn** (*objet*) to slip s.o. sth; **f. un coup de pied/etc à qn** to give s.o. a kick/ *etc*. **4** *vi* (*partir*) to rush off; (*bas, collant*) to ladder, run; **filez!** hop it!; **f. entre les doigts de qn** to slip through s.o.'s fingers.

filet [file] *nm* **1** (*à bagages*) *Rail* (luggage) rack; (*de pêche*) & *Sp* net; **f. (à provisions)** net bag (*for shopping*). **2** (*d'eau*) trickle. **3** (*de poisson, viande*) fillet.

filiale [filjal] *nf* subsidiary (company).

filière [filjɛr] *nf* (*de drogue*) network; **suivre la f. (normale)** (*pour obtenir qch*) to go through the official channels; (*employé*) to work one's way up.

filigrane [filigran] *nm* (*sur papier*) watermark.

fille [fij] *nf* **1** girl; **petite f.** (little *ou* young) girl; **jeune f.** girl, young lady; **vieille f.** *Péj* old maid. **2** (*parenté*) daughter. ● **f.-mère** *nf* (*pl* **filles-mères**) *Péj* unmarried mother. ● **fillette** *nf* little girl.

filleul [fijœl] *nm* godson. ● **filleule** *nf* goddaughter.

film [film] *nm* **1** film, movie; (*pour photo*) film; **f. muet/parlant** silent/talking film *ou* movie; **f. policier** thriller. **2 f. plastique** (*pour aliments*) cling film, *Am* plastic wrap. ● **filmer** *vt* (*personne, scène*) to film.

filon [filɔ̃] *nm Géol* seam; **trouver le (bon) f.** to strike it lucky.

fils [fis] *nm* son; **Dupont f.** Dupont

junior.

filtre [filtr] *nm* filter; **(à bout) f.** (*cigarette*) (filter-)tipped; **(bout) f.** filter tip.
● **filtrer** *vt* to filter; (*personne, nouvelles*) to scrutinize ▮ *vi* to filter (through).

fin [fɛ̃] **1** *nf* end; (*but*) end, aim; **mettre f. à** to put an end to; **prendre f.** to come to an end; **tirer à sa f.** to draw to an end *ou* a close; **sans f.** endless; **à la f.** in the end; **arrêtez, à la f.!** stop, for heaven's sake!; **f. de semaine** weekend; **f. mai** at the end of May.
2 *a* (*pointe, tissu etc*) fine; (*peu épais*) thin; (*esprit, oreille*) sharp; (*plat*) delicate, choice; (*intelligent*) clever; **au f. fond de** in the depths of ▮ *adv* (*couper, moudre*) finely.

final, -aux *ou* **-als** [final, -o] *a* final ▮ *nm Mus* finale. ● **finale** *nf Sp* final. ● **finalement** *adv* finally; (*en somme*) after all.

finance [finɑ̃s] *nf* finance. ● **financer** *vt* to finance. ● **financement** *nm* financing.

financier, -ière [finɑ̃sje, -jɛr] *a* financial ▮ *nm* financier.

finesse [fines] *nf* (*de pointe etc*) fineness; (*de taille etc*) thinness; (*de plat*) delicacy; (*d'esprit, de goût*) finesse.

finir [finir] *vti* to finish; **f. bien/mal** (*histoire etc*) to have a happy/unhappy ending; **f. de faire** (*achever*) to finish doing; (*cesser*) to stop doing; **f. par faire** to end up *ou* finish up doing; **en f. avec** to put an end to, finish with; **elle n'en finit pas de pleurer** there's nothing that can make her stop crying. ● **fini** *a* (*produit*) finished; (*univers etc*) & *Math* finite; **c'est f.** it's over; **il est f.** (*fichu*) he's done for *ou* finished. ● **finition** *nf* (*action*) *Tech* finishing; (*résultat*) finish.

Finlande [fɛ̃lɑ̃d] *nf* Finland. ● **finlandais, -aise** *a* Finnish ▮ *nmf* Finn.

firme [firm] *nf* (*entreprise*) firm, company.

fisc [fisk] *nm* tax authorities, = Inland Revenue, = *Am* Internal Revenue. ● **fiscal, -aux** *a* fiscal, tax. ● **fiscalité** *nf* tax system; (*charges*) taxation.

fissure [fisyr] *nf* crack. ● **se fissurer** *vpr* to crack.

fixation [fiksasjɔ̃] *nf* (*action*) fixing; (*dispositif*) fastening; *Psy* fixation.

fixe [fiks] *a* fixed; (*prix, heure*) set, fixed; **idée f.** obsession; **regard f.** stare; **être au beau f.** *Mét* to be set fair ▮ *nm* (*paie*) fixed salary. ● **—ment** [-əmɑ̃] *adv* **regarder f.** to stare at.

fixer [fikse] *vt* (*attacher*) to fix (à to); (*date etc*) to fix; **f. (du regard)** to stare at; **être fixé** (*décidé*) to be decided; **comme ça on est fixé!** (*renseigné*) we've got the picture! ▮ **se f.** *vpr* (*regard*) to become fixed; (*s'établir*) to settle.

flacon [flakɔ̃] *nm* (small) bottle.

flageoler [flaʒɔle] *vi* to shake, tremble.

flageolet [flaʒɔlɛ] *nm Bot Culin* (dwarf) kidney bean.

flagrant [flagrɑ̃] *a* (*injustice etc*) flagrant, glaring; **pris en f. délit** caught in the act.

flair [flɛr] *nm* **1** (*d'un chien etc*) (sense of) smell, scent. **2** (*clairvoyance*) intuition, flair. ● **flairer** *vt* to smell.

flamand, -ande [flamɑ̃, -ɑ̃d] *a* Flemish ▮ *nmf* Fleming ▮ *nm* (*langue*) Flemish.

flamant [flamɑ̃] *nm* **f. (rose)** (*oiseau*) flamingo.

flambant [flɑ̃bɑ̃] *adv* **f. neuf** brand new.

flambeau, -x [flɑ̃bo] *nm* torch.

flambée [flɑ̃be] *nf* blaze; (*de colère, des prix etc*) *Fig* surge; (*de violence*) flare-up.

flamber [flɑ̃be] *vi* to burn, blaze ▮ *vt* (*aiguille*) *Méd* to sterilize; (*poulet*) to singe.

flamboyer [flɑ̃bwaje] *vi* to blaze.

flamme [flam] *nf* flame; **en flammes** on fire.

flan [flɑ̃] *nm* (*dessert*) custard tart, baked custard.

flanc [flɑ̃] *nm* side; (*d'une armée, d'un animal*) flank; **tirer au f.** *Arg* to shirk.

flancher [flɑ̃ʃe] *vi Fam* to give in, weaken.

Flandre(s) [flɑ̃dr] *nf(pl)* Flanders.

flanelle [flanɛl] *nf* (*tissu*) flannel.

flâner [flɑne] *vi* to stroll. ● **flânerie** *nf* (*action*) strolling; (*promenade*) stroll.

flanquer [flãke] vt 1 to flank (de with). 2 Fam (jeter) to chuck; (donner) to give; f. qn à la porte to throw s.o. out.

flaque [flak] nf puddle.

flash, pl **flashes** [flaʃ] nm 1 Phot (éclair) flashlight; (dispositif) flash(gun). 2 TV Rad (news) flash.

flatt/er [flate] vt to flatter. ●—é a flattered (de qch by sth, de faire to do, que that). ●**flatterie** nf flattery. ●**flatteur, -euse** nmf flatterer ▮ a flattering.

fléau, -x [fleo] nm 1 (catastrophe) scourge; (personne) plague. 2 Agr flail.

flèche [flɛʃ] nf arrow; (d'église) spire; **monter en f.** (prix) to shoot up, (sky)rocket. ●**flécher** [fleʃe] vt to sign-post (with arrows). ●**fléchette** nf dart; pl (jeu) darts.

fléchir [fleʃir] vt (membre) to flex, bend; **f. qn** Fig to move s.o., persuade s.o. ▮ vi (membre) to bend; (poutre) to sag; (faiblir) to give way; (baisser) to fall off.

flegme [flɛgm] nm composure. ●**flegmatique** a phlegmatic, stolid.

flemme [flɛm] nf Fam laziness; **il a la f.** he can't be bothered.

flétrir [fletrir] vt, **se f.** vpr to wither.

fleur [flœr] nf flower; (d'arbre) blossom; **en fleur(s)** in flower; in blossom; **à fleurs** (tissu) flowered, flowery; **à ou dans la f. de l'âge** in the prime of life.

fleur/ir [flœrir] vi to flower, to blossom; (arbre) to blossom; (art, commerce etc) Fig to flourish ▮ vt (table etc) to decorate with flowers. ●—a (jardin) in bloom; (tissu) flowered, flowery; (style) flowery, florid. ●**fleuriste** nmf florist.

fleuve [flœv] nm river.

flexible [flɛksibl] a pliable, flexible. ●**flexibilité** nf flexibility.

flexion [flɛksjɔ̃] nf 1 Anat flexion, flexing. 2 Gram inflexion.

flic [flik] nm (agent de police) Fam cop.

flipper [flipœr] nm (jeu) pinball; (appareil) pinball machine.

flirt [flœrt] nm (rapports) flirtation; (personne) flirt. ●**flirter** vi to flirt (avec with).

flocon [flɔkɔ̃] nm (de neige) flake; **flocons de maïs** cornflakes.

floraison [flɔrɛzɔ̃] nf flowering; **en pleine f.** in full bloom. ●**floral, -aux** a floral.

flore [flɔr] nf flora.

florissant [flɔrisã] a flourishing.

flot [flo] nm (de souvenirs etc) flood; pl (de mer) waves; (de lac) waters; **à f.** (bateau, personne) afloat; **mettre à f.** (bateau, firme) to launch; **remettre qn à f.** to restore s.o.'s fortunes; **couler à flots** (argent, vin etc) to flow freely.

flotte [flɔt] nf 1 Nau Av fleet. 2 Fam (pluie) rain; (eau) water.

flottement [flɔtmã] nm (hésitation) indecision.

flott/er [flɔte] vi to float; (drapeau) to fly; (pleuvoir) Fam to rain. ●—**eur** nm Pêche etc float.

flou [flu] a (photo) fuzzy, blurred; (idée) hazy, fuzzy.

fluctuant [flyktyã] a (prix, opinions) fluctuating. ●**fluctuations** nfpl fluctuation(s) (de in).

fluet, -ette [flyɛ, -ɛt] a thin, slender.

fluide [flɥid] a (liquide) & Fig fluid ▮ nm (liquide) fluid.

fluo [flyo] a inv (couleur etc) luminous, fluorescent.

fluorescent [flyoresã] a fluorescent.

flûte [flyt] 1 nf Mus flute. 2 nf (verre) champagne glass. 3 int heck!. ●**flûtiste** nmf flautist, Am flutist.

fluvial, -aux [flyvjal, -o] a navigation/etc **fluviale** river navigation/etc.

flux [fly] nm (abondance) flow; **f. et reflux** ebb and flow.

focal, -aux [fɔkal, -o] a focal. ●**focaliser** vt (intérêt etc) to focus.

fœtus [fetys] nm foetus, Am fetus.

foi [fwa] nf faith; **être de bonne/mauvaise f.** to be/not to be (completely) sincere; **avoir la f.** (être croyant) to have faith; **ma f., oui!** yes, indeed!

foie [fwa] nm liver.

foin [fwɛ̃] nm hay.

foire [fwar] *nf* fair; **faire la f.** *Fam* to have a ball.

fois [fwa] *nf* time; **une f.** once; **deux f.** twice, two times; **trois f.** three times; **deux f. trois** two times three; **chaque f. que** whenever; **une f. qu'il sera arrivé** once he has arrived; **à la f.** at the same time; **à la f. riche et heureux** both rich and happy; **une autre f.** (*elle fera attention etc*) next time; **des f.** *Fam* sometimes; **une f. pour toutes** once and for all.

foison [fwazɔ̃] *nf* **à f.** in plenty. ● **foisonner** *vi* to abound (**de, en** in).

fol [fɔl] *voir* **fou.**

folichon, -onne [fɔliʃɔ̃, -ɔn] *a* **pas f.** not much fun.

folie [fɔli] *nf* madness; **faire une f.** to do a foolish thing; (*dépense*) to be very extravagant; **aimer qn à la f.** to be madly in love with s.o..

folklore [fɔlklɔr] *nm* folklore. ● **folklorique** *a* **musique/etc f.** folk music/*etc.*

folle [fɔl] *voir* **fou.** ● **follement** *adv* madly.

foncé [fɔ̃se] *a* (*couleur*) dark.

foncer [fɔ̃se] **1** *vi* (*aller vite*) to tear along; **f. sur qn** to charge into *ou* at s.o. **2** *vti* (*couleur*) to darken.

foncier, -ière [fɔ̃sje, -jɛr] *a* **1** fundamental, basic. **2** (*propriété*) landed. ● **foncièrement** *adv* fundamentally.

fonction [fɔ̃ksjɔ̃] *nf* (*rôle*) & *Math* function; (*emploi*) office, post, duty; **f. publique** the public *ou* civil service; **faire f. de** (*personne*) to act as; (*objet*) to serve *ou* act as; **en f. de** according to; **prendre ses fonctions** to take up one's post *ou* duties. ● **fonctionnaire** *nmf* civil servant.

fonctionn/er [fɔ̃ksjɔne] *vi* (*machine etc*) to work; (*organisation*) to function; **faire f. de.** to operate, work. ● **—ement** *nm* working.

fond [fɔ̃] *nm* (*de boîte, jardin etc*) bottom; (*de salle etc*) back; (*arrière-plan*) background; (*de problème etc*) essence; **au f. de** at the bottom of; at the back of; **au f.** basically; **à f.** (*connaître etc*)

thoroughly; **de f. en comble** from top to bottom; **de f.** (*course*) long-distance; **bruit de f.** background noise; **f. de teint** foundation cream; **f. sonore** background music.

fondamental, -aux [fɔ̃damɑ̃tal, -o] *a* fundamental, basic.

fond/er [fɔ̃de] *vt* (*ville etc*) to found; (*famille*) to start; (**se**) **f. sur** to base (oneself) on; **bien fondé** well-founded. ● **—ement** *nm* foundation. ● **fondateur, -trice** *nmf* founder. ● **fondation** *nf* (*création, œuvre*) foundation (**de** of).

fonderie [fɔ̃dri] *nf* (*usine*) smelting works.

fondre [fɔ̃dr] *vt* to melt; (*métal*) to melt down; **faire f.** (*sucre etc*) to dissolve ▮ *vi* to melt; (*se dissoudre*) to dissolve; **f. en larmes** to burst into tears ▮ **se f.** *vpr* to merge; **se f. en eau** (*glaçon etc*) to melt (away); **se f. dans** (*la brume etc*) to disappear *ou* merge into.

fonds [fɔ̃] **1** *nmpl* (*argent*) funds. **2** *nm* **un f.** (*de commerce*) a business. **3** *nm* (*culturel etc*) *Fig* fund.

fondue [fɔ̃dy] *nf Culin* fondue.

font [fɔ̃] *voir* **faire.**

fontaine [fɔ̃tɛn] *nf* (*construction*) fountain; (*source*) spring.

fonte [fɔ̃t] *nf* **1** (*des neiges*) melting. **2** (*fer*) cast iron; **en f.** (*poêle etc*) cast-iron.

football [futbol] *nm* football, soccer. ● **footballeur, -euse** *nmf* footballer.

footing [futiŋ] *nm Sp* jogging.

forage [fɔraʒ] *nm* drilling, boring.

forain [fɔrɛ̃] *a* (*marchand*) itinerant; **fête foraine** (fun)fair.

force [fɔrs] *nf* force; (*physique, morale*) strength; (*nucléaire*) power; **de toutes ses forces** with all one's strength; **de f.** by force; **en f.** (*attaquer*) in force; **à f. de lire**/*etc* through reading/*etc*, after much reading/*etc*; **cas de f. majeure** circumstances beyond one's control; **dans la f. de l'âge** in the prime of life.

forcer [fɔrse] *vt* (*porte, attention etc*) to force; (*voix*) to strain; **f. qn à faire** to

force *ou* compel s.o. to do.
‖ *vi* (*y aller trop fort*) to overdo it.
‖ **se forcer** *vpr* to force oneself (**à faire** to do). ● **forcé** *a* forced (**de faire** to do); **un sourire f.** a forced smile; **c'est f.** *Fam* it's inevitable. ● **forcément** *adv* obviously; **pas f.** not necessarily.

forcené, -ée [fɔrsəne] *nmf* madman, madwoman.

forer [fɔre] *vt* to drill, bore.

forêt [fɔrɛ] *nf* forest. ● **forestier** *nm* (**garde**) **f.** forester, *Am* (forest) ranger.

forfait [fɔrfɛ] *nm* **1** (*prix*) all-inclusive price. **2 déclarer f.** *Sp* to withdraw from the game. ● **forfaitaire à prix f.** all-inclusive price.

forge [fɔrʒ] *nf* forge. ● **forger** *vt* (*métal, liens etc*) to forge. ● **forgeron** *nm* (black)smith.

formaliser (se) [səfɔrmalize] *vpr* to take offence *ou* *Am* offense (**de** at).

formalité [fɔrmalite] *nf* formality.

format [fɔrma] *nm* size.

formater [fɔrmate] *vt* (*disquette*) to format.

formation [fɔrmasjɔ̃] *nf* education, training; **f. permanente** continuing education.

forme [fɔrm] *nf* (*contour*) shape, form; (*manière, genre*) form; *pl* (*de femme*) figure; **en f. de poire/etc** pear-/etc shaped; **en (pleine) f.** in good shape *ou* form; **en bonne et due f.** in due form; **prendre f.** to take shape.

formel, -elle [fɔrmɛl] *a* (*structure, logique etc*) formal; (*démenti*) categorical, formal; (*preuve*) positive. ● **formellement** *adv* (*interdire*) strictly.

former [fɔrme] *vt* (*groupe, caractère etc*) to form; (*apprenti*) to train ‖ **se f.** *vpr* (*apparaître*) to form.

formidable [fɔrmidabl] *a* terrific, tremendous.

formulaire [fɔrmyler] *nm* (*feuille*) form.

formule [fɔrmyl] *nf* formula; (*phrase*) (set) expression; **f. de politesse** polite form of address. ● **formuler** *vt* to formulate.

fort¹ [fɔr] *a* strong; (*pluie, mer, chute de neige*) heavy; (*voix, radio*) loud; (*fièvre*) high; (*élève*) bright; (*pente*) steep; (*chances*) good; **f. en** (*maths etc*) good at; **c'est plus f. qu'elle** she can't help it; **c'est un peu f.** *Fam* that's a bit much; **à plus forte raison** all the more reason.
‖ *adv* (*frapper, pleuvoir*) hard; (*parler*) loud(ly); (*serrer*) tight; **sentir f.** to have a strong smell.
‖ *nm* **c'est son f.** that's his *ou* her strong point; **au plus f. de** in the thick of.

fort² [fɔr] *nm* *Hist Mil* fort. ● **forteresse** *nf* fortress.

fortifier [fɔrtifje] *vt* to strengthen, fortify ‖ **se f.** *vpr* (*malade*) to fortify oneself. ● **fortifiant** *nm* *Méd* tonic. ● **fortification** *nf* fortification.

fortuit [fɔrtɥi] *a* **rencontre/etc fortuite** chance meeting/etc.

fortune [fɔrtyn] *nf* (*argent, hasard*) fortune; **faire f.** to make one's fortune; **de f.** (*moyens etc*) makeshift. ● **fortuné** *a* (*riche*) well-to-do.

fosse [fos] *nf* (*trou*) pit; (*tombe*) grave.

fossé [fose] *nm* ditch; (*douve*) moat; (*désaccord*) *Fig* gulf, gap.

fossette [fosɛt] *nf* dimple.

fossile [fɔsil] *nm* & *a* fossil.

fou (or fol before vowel or mute h), **folle** [fu, fɔl] *a* (*personne, projet etc*) mad, insane, crazy; (*ardeur, temps*) tremendous; (*envie*) wild, mad; (*espoir*) foolish; **f. de** (*musique etc*) mad about; **f. de joie** wildly happy ‖ *nmf* madman, madwoman ‖ *nm* (*bouffon*) jester; *Échecs* bishop; **faire le f.** to play the fool.

foudre [fudr] *nf* **la f.** lightning; **coup de f.** *Fig* love at first sight. ● **foudroyer** *vt* to strike by lightning; *Él* to electrocute. ● **foudroyant** *a* (*succès etc*) staggering.

fouet [fwɛ] *nm* whip; *Culin* (egg) whisk. ● **fouetter** *vt* to whip; (*œufs*) to whisk; **crème fouettée** whipped cream.

fougère [fuʒer] *nf* fern.

fougue [fug] *nf* fire, ardour.

fouille [fuj] **1** *nf* (*de personne, bagages etc*) search. **2** *nfpl* **fouilles** (archéologiques) excavation, dig. ●**fouiller 1** vti (creuser) to dig. **2** vt (personne, maison etc) to search ▮ vi **f. dans** (tiroir etc) to search through.

fouillis [fuji] nm jumble, mess.

fouiner [fwine] vi Fam to nose about (**dans** in).

foulard [fular] nm (head) scarf.

foule [ful] nf crowd; **une f. de** (objets etc) a mass of; **un bain de f.** a walkabout.

foulée [fule] nf Sp stride; **dans la f.** Fam at one and the same time. ●**foulure** nf sprain.

fouler (se) [safule] vpr **se f. la cheville/** etc to sprain one's ankle/etc; **il ne se foule pas (la rate)** Fam he doesn't exactly exert himself. ●**foulure** nf sprain.

four [fur] nm **1** oven. **2 petit f.** (gâteau) (small) fancy cake.

fourbe [furb] a deceitful.

fourbu [furby] a (fatigué) dead beat.

fourche [furʃ] nf fork. ●**fourchette** nf **1** Culin fork. **2** (de salaires etc) bracket.

fourgon [furgɔ̃] nm (camion) van; (mortuaire) hearse. ●**fourgonnette** nf (small) van.

fourmi [furmi] nf **1** (insecte) ant. **2 avoir des fourmis** (dans les jambes etc) to have pins and needles. ●**fourmilière** nf anthill. ●**fourmiller** vi to teem, swarm (**de** with).

fournaise [furnez] nf (chambre etc) Fig furnace.

fourneau, -x [furno] nm (poêle) stove; (four) furnace; **haut f.** blast furnace.

fournée [furne] nf (de pain, gens) batch.

fournir [furnir] vt to supply, provide; (effort) to make; **f. qch à qn** to supply s.o. with sth ▮ **se f.** vpr to get one's supplies (**chez** from), shop (**chez** at). ●**fourni** a (barbe) bushy; **bien f.** (boutique) well-stocked. ●**fournisseur** nm (commerçant) supplier. ●**fourniture** nf (action) supply(ing) (**de** of); pl (objets) supplies.

fourré [fure] **1** a (gant etc) fur-lined; (gâteau) jam- ou cream-filled; **coup f.** (traîtrise) stab in the back. **2** nm Bot thicket.

fourreau, -x [furo] nm (gaine) sheath.

fourrer [fure] vt Fam (mettre) to stick; (flanquer) to chuck; **f. qch dans la tête de qn** to knock sth into s.o.'s head; **f. son nez dans** to poke one's nose into ▮ **se f.** vpr to put ou stick oneself (**dans** in).

fourrure [furyr] nf (pour vêtement etc, de chat etc) fur.

fourre-tout [furtu] nm inv (sac) holdall, Am carryall.

fourrière [furjer] nf (lieu) pound.

foutre* [futr] vt Arg = **fiche(r)**. ●**foutu** a Arg = **fichu**. ●**foutaise** nf Arg rubbish, bull.

foyer [fwaje] nm (maison, famille) home; (d'étudiants etc) hostel; (âtre) hearth; (lieu de réunion) club; **fonder un f.** to start a family.

fracas [fraka] nm din. ●**fracasser** vt, **se f.** vpr to smash.

fraction [fraksjɔ̃] nf fraction.

fracture [fraktyr] nf fracture; **se faire une f. au bras/**etc to fracture one's arm/etc. ●**fracturer** vt (porte etc) to break (open); **se f. la jambe/**etc to fracture one's leg/etc.

fragile [fraʒil] a (verre, santé etc) fragile; (enfant etc) frail. ●**fragilité** nf fragility; (d'un enfant etc) frailty.

fragment [fragmɑ̃] nm fragment.

frais¹, fraîche [frɛ, frɛʃ] a (poisson, souvenir etc) fresh; (temps) cool, (plutôt désagréable) chilly; (boisson) cold, cool; (œuf) new-laid, fresh; (peinture) wet; **servir f.** (vin etc) to serve chilled; **boire f.** to drink something cold ou cool; **il fait f.** it's cool; (froid) it's chilly ▮ nm **prendre le f.** to get some fresh air; **mettre au f.** to put in a cool place; (au réfrigérateur) to refrigerate. ●**fraîcheur** nf freshness; coolness. ●**fraîchir** vi (temps) to get cooler ou chillier.

frais² [frɛ] nmpl expenses; **à mes f.** at my (own) expense; **faire des f.** to go to some expense; **faire les f.** to bear the cost (de of); **f. de scolarité** school fees; **faux f.** incidental expenses; **f. généraux** running expenses, overheads.

fraise [frez] *nf* 1 (*fruit*) strawberry. 2 (*de dentiste*) drill. ●**fraisier** *nm* (*plante*) strawberry plant.

framboise [frɑ̃bwaz] *nf* raspberry. ●**framboisier** *nm* raspberry cane.

franc¹, franche [frɑ̃, frɑ̃ʃ] *a* 1 (*personne, réponse etc*) frank; (*visage, gaieté*) open. 2 (*zone*) free; **coup f.** *Fb* free kick; **f. de port** carriage paid. ●**franchement** *adv* (*honnêtement*) frankly; (*vraiment*) really; (*sans ambiguïté*) clearly.

franc² [frɑ̃] *nm* (*monnaie*) franc.

France [frɑ̃s] *nf* France. ●**français, -aise** *a* French ▮*nmf* Frenchman, Frenchwoman; **les F.** the French ▮*nm* (*langue*) French.

franchir [frɑ̃ʃir] *vt* (*fossé*) to jump (over), clear; (*frontière etc*) to cross; (*porte*) to go through; (*distance*) to cover; (*limites*) to exceed.

franchise [frɑ̃ʃiz] *nf* 1 frankness; **en toute f.** quite frankly. 2 (*exemption*) *Com* exemption; **'f. postale'** 'official paid'.

franc-maçon [frɑ̃masɔ̃] *nm* (*pl* **francs-maçons**) Freemason.

franco- [frɑ̃ko] *préf* Franco-.

francophone [frɑ̃kofɔn] *a* French-speaking ▮*nmf* French speaker.

frange [frɑ̃ʒ] *nf* (*de cheveux*) fringe, *Am* bangs.

frappe [frap] *nf* 1 (*dactylographie*) typing; (*de dactylo etc*) touch; **faute de f.** typing error. 2 **force de f.** *Mil* strike force.

frapper [frape] *vt* (*battre*) to hit, strike; **f. qn** (*surprendre*) to strike s.o. ▮*vi* (*à la porte etc*) to knock (à at); **f. du pied** to stamp (one's foot) ▮**se f.** *vpr* (*se tracasser*) *Fam* to worry. ●**frappant** *a* striking. ●**frappé** *a* (*vin*) chilled.

fraternel, -elle [fraternel] *a* fraternal, brotherly. ●**fraternité** *nf* fraternity, brotherhood.

fraude [frod] *nf* (*crime*) fraud; (*à un examen*) cheating; (**faire**) **passer qch en f.** to smuggle sth; **prendre qn en f.** to catch s.o. cheating; **f. fiscale** tax evasion. ●**frauder** *vi Jur* to commit fraud; (*à un examen*) to cheat (à in).

frayer (se) [səfreje] *vpr* **se f. un passage** to clear a way (à travers, dans through).

frayeur [frejœr] *nf* fright.

fredonner [frədɔne] *vt* to hum.

freezer [frizœr] *nm* (*de réfrigérateur*) freezer.

frégate [fregat] *nf* (*navire*) frigate.

frein [frɛ̃] *nm* brake; **donner un coup de f.** to brake (hard); **mettre un f. à** *Fig* to put a curb on. ●**freiner** *vi Aut* to brake ▮*vt* (*gêner*) *Fig* to check, curb. ●**freinage** *nm Aut* braking.

frêle [frel] *a* frail, fragile.

frelon [frəlɔ̃] *nm* (*guêpe*) hornet.

frémir [fremir] *vi* (*trembler*) to shudder (de with); (*feuille*) to quiver; (*eau chaude*) to simmer.

frêne [fren] *nm* (*arbre, bois*) ash.

frénésie [frenezi] *nf* frenzy. ●**frénétique** *a* frenzied, frantic.

fréquent [frekɑ̃] *a* frequent. ●**fréquemment** [-amɑ̃] *adv* frequently. ●**fréquence** *nf* frequency.

fréquenter [frekɑ̃te] *vt* (*école, église*) to attend; **f. qn** to see s.o. ▮**se f.** *vpr* (*fille et garçon*) to see each other; (*voisins*) to see each other socially. ●**fréquenté** *a* **très f.** (*lieu*) very busy; **mal f.** of ill repute.

frère [frer] *nm* brother.

fresque [fresk] *nf* (*œuvre peinte*) fresco.

fret [fre] *nm* freight.

frétiller [fretije] *vi* (*poisson*) to wriggle; **f. de** (*impatience*) to quiver with.

friable [frijabl] *a* crumbly.

friand [frijɑ̃] *a* **f. de** fond of, partial to. ●**friandises** *nfpl* sweets, *Am* candies.

fric [frik] *nm* (*argent*) *Fam* cash, dough.

friche (en) [ɑ̃friʃ] *adv* fallow.

friction [friksjɔ̃] *nf* 1 massage, rub(-down). 2 (*désaccord*) friction. ●**frictionner** *vt* to rub (down).

frigidaire® [frizider] nm fridge. ●**frigo** nm Fam fridge. ●**frigorifié** a (personne) Fam very cold. ●**frigorifique** a (vitrine) refrigerated.

frigide [frizid] a frigid.

frileux, -euse [frilø, -øz] a être f. to feel the cold.

frime [frim] nf Fam sham, show.

fringale [frɛ̃gal] nf Fam raging appetite.

fringant [frɛ̃gɑ̃] a (allure etc) dashing.

fringues [frɛ̃g] nfpl (vêtements) Fam togs, clothes.

friper [fripe] vt to crumple ‖ **se f.** vpr to get crumpled. ●**fripé** a (visage) crumpled.

fripouille [fripuj] nf rogue, scoundrel.

frire* [frir] vti to fry; **faire f.** to fry.

frise [friz] nf Archit frieze.

fris/er [frize] 1 vti (cheveux) to curl; **f. les cheveux à qn** to curl s.o.'s hair. **2** vt **f. la trentaine** to be close to thirty; **f. le ridicule** to be almost ridiculous. ●—**é** a curly.

frisquet [friskɛ] am chilly, coldish.

frisson [frisɔ̃] nm shiver; (de peur etc) shudder; **avoir des frissons** to be shivering; **donner le f. à qn** to give s.o. the creeps ou shivers. ●**frissonner** vi (de froid) to shiver; (de peur etc) to shudder (de with).

frit [fri] pp de **frire** ‖ a (poisson etc) fried. ●**frites** nfpl chips, Am French fries. ●**friteuse** nf (deep) fryer. ●**friture** nf (matière) (frying) oil ou fat; (aliment) fried fish; (bruit) Rad Tél crackling.

frivole [frivɔl] a frivolous.

froid [frwa] a cold; **garder la tête froide** to keep a cool head ‖ nm cold; **avoir/ prendre f.** to be/catch cold; **avoir f. aux mains** to have cold hands; **il fait f.** it's cold; **jeter un f.** to cast a chill (dans over); **être en f.** to be on bad terms (avec with). ●**froideur** nf (insensibilité) coldness.

froiss/er [frwase] 1 vt, **se f.** vpr (tissu etc) to crumple; **se f. un muscle** to strain a muscle. **2** vt **f. qn** to offend s.o.; **se f.** to take offence ou Am offense (de at).

frôler [frole] vt (toucher) to brush against; (raser) to skim; (la mort etc) to come within an ace of.

fromage [frɔmaʒ] nm cheese; **f. blanc** soft white cheese. ●**fromager, -ère** nm (fabricant) cheesemaker. ●**fromagerie** nf (magasin) cheese shop.

froment [frɔmɑ̃] nm wheat.

fronce [frɔ̃s] nf (pli dans un tissu) gather, fold. ●**froncer** vt 1 (étoffe) to gather. **2 f. les sourcils** to frown.

fronde [frɔ̃d] nf (arme) sling.

front [frɔ̃] nm forehead, brow; Mil Pol front; **de f.** (heurter) head-on; (côte à côte) abreast; (à la fois) (all) at once.

frontière [frɔ̃tjɛr] nf border, frontier ‖ a inv ville/etc f. border town/etc. ●**frontalier, -ière** a ville/etc **frontalière** border town/etc.

frotter [frɔte] vt to rub; (pour nettoyer) to scrub; (allumette) to strike; **se f. le dos** to scrub one's back ‖ vi to rub; (nettoyer, laver) to scrub.

frousse [frus] nf Fam fear; **avoir la f.** to be scared. ●**froussard, -arde** nmf Fam coward.

fructifier [fryktifje] vi (arbre, capital) to bear fruit. ●**fructueux, -euse** a (profitable) fruitful.

frugal, -aux [frygal, -o] a frugal.

fruit [frɥi] nm fruit; **des fruits, les fruits** fruit; **fruits de mer** seafood; **porter ses fruits** (placement etc) to bear fruit. ●**fruité** a fruity. ●**fruitier, -ière** a arbre **f.** fruit tree ‖ nmf fruiterer.

frustr/er [frystre] vt **f. qn** to frustrate s.o.; **f. qn de** to deprive s.o. of. ●—**é** a frustrated.

fuel [fjul] nm (fuel) oil, heating oil.

fugitif, -ive [fyʒitif, -iv] 1 nmf runaway, fugitive. **2** a (passager) fleeting.

fugue [fyg] nf 1 Mus fugue. **2** (absence) flight; **faire une f.** to run away.

fuir* [fɥir] vi to run away, flee; (gaz, robinet, stylo etc) to leak ‖ vt (éviter) to shun, avoid. ●**fuite** nf (évasion) flight (de from); (de gaz, documents etc) leak; **en f.** on the run; **prendre la f.** to take away *ou* off, take flight; **délit de f.** *Aut* hit-and-run offence *or Am* offense.

fulgurant [fylgyrɑ̃] *a* **progrès fulgurants** spectacular progress; **vitesse fulgurante** lightning speed.

fumée [fyme] *nf* smoke; (*vapeur*) steam, fumes.

fum/er [fyme] *vi* to smoke; (*liquide brûlant*) to steam ‖ *vt* to smoke. ●—**é** *a* (*poisson, verre etc*) smoked. ●—**eur, -euse** *nmf* smoker; **compartiment fumeurs** *Rail* smoking compartment.

fumet [fyme] *nm* aroma, smell.

fumeux, -euse [fymø, -øz] *a* (*idée etc*) hazy.

fumier [fymje] *nm* manure, dung; (*tas*) dunghill.

fumiste [fymist] *nmf* (*étudiant etc*) timewaster, good-for-nothing.

funambule [fynɑ̃byl] *nmf* tightrope walker.

funèbre [fynɛbr] *a* (*service, marche etc*) funeral; (*lugubre*) gloomy. ●**funérailles** *nfpl* funeral.

funeste [fynɛst] *a* (*désastreux*) catastrophic.

funiculaire [fynikyler] *nm* funicular.

fur et à mesure (au) [ofyreamzyr] *adv* as one goes along; **au f. et à m. que** as.

furent [fyr] *voir* **être**.

fureter [fyr(ə)te] *vi Péj* to pry *ou* ferret about.

fureur [fyrœr] *nf* (*violence*) fury; (*colère*) rage, fury; **faire f.** (*mode etc*) to be all the rage. ●**furie** *nf* (*colère, mégère*) fury. ●**furieux, -euse** *a* (*violent, en colère*) furious (**contre** with, at); (*vent*) raging; **avoir une furieuse envie de faire qch** to have a tremendous urge to do sth.

furoncle [fyrɔ̃kl] *nm Méd* boil.

fusain [fyzɛ̃] *nm* (*crayon, dessin*) charcoal.

fuseau, -x [fyzo] *nm* **1** (*pantalon*) ski pants. **2 f. horaire** time zone.

fusée [fyze] *nf* rocket.

fuselage [fyzlaʒ] *nm Av* fuselage.

fusible [fyzibl] *nm El* fuse.

fusil [fyzi] *nm* rifle, gun; (*de chasse*) shotgun; **coup de f.** gunshot. ●**fusillade** *nf* (*tirs*) gunfire. ●**fusiller** *vt* (*exécuter*) to shoot; **f. qn du regard** *Fam* to glare at s.o.

fusion [fyzjɔ̃] *nf* **1** melting; *Phys Biol* fusion; **en f.** (*métal*) molten. **2** *Com* merger; (*union*) fusion. ●**fusionner** *vti Com* to merge.

fut [fy] *voir* **être**.

fût [fy] *nm* (*tonneau*) barrel, cask.

futé [fyte] *a* cunning, smart.

futile [fytil] *a* (*propos, prétexte etc*) frivolous, futile; (*personne*) frivolous.

futur [fytyr] *a* future; **future mère** mother-to-be ‖ *nm* future; *Gram* future (tense).

fuyant [fɥijɑ̃] *voir* **fuir** ‖ *a* (*front*) receding; (*personne*) evasive. ●**fuyard** *nm* runaway, deserter.

G

G, g [ʒe] *nm* G, g.

gabardine [gabardin] *nf* (*tissu, imperméable*) gabardine.

gabarit [gabari] *nm* size, dimension.

gâcher [gɑʃe] *vt* (*gâter*) to spoil; (*occasion, argent*) to waste; (*vie, travail*) to mess up. ● **gâchis** *nm* (*gaspillage*) waste; (*désordre*) mess.

gâchette [gɑʃɛt] *nf* (*d'arme à feu*) trigger.

gadget [gadʒɛt] *nm* gadget.

gadoue [gadu] *nf* (*boue*) dirt, sludge; (*neige*) slush.

gaffe [gaf] *nf* (*bévue*) *Fam* blunder, gaffe. ● **gaffer** *vi* to blunder.

gag [gag] *nm* *Cin Th etc* gag.

gaga [gaga] *a Fam* senile, gaga.

gage [gaʒ] 1 *nm* (*garantie*) security; **mettre en g.** to pawn; **en g. de** (*fidélité etc*) as a token of. 2 *nmpl* (*salaire*) pay; **tueur à gages** hired killer, hitman. 3 *nm* (*au jeu*) forfeit.

gagnant, -ante [gaɲɑ̃, -ɑ̃t] *a* (*billet, cheval*) winning ▮ *nmf* winner.

gagner [gaɲe] 1 *vt* (*par le travail*) to earn; **g. sa vie** to earn one's living. 2 *vt* (*par le jeu*) to win; **g. une heure/etc** (*économiser*) to save an hour/etc; **g. du temps** (*temporiser*) to gain time; **g. du terrain/du poids** to gain ground/weight ▮ *vi* (*être vainqueur*) to win. 3 *vt* (*atteindre*) to reach ▮ *vi* (*incendie etc*) to spread.

gai [ge] *a* (*personne, air etc*) cheerful; (*ivre*) merry, tipsy. ● **gaiement** *adv* cheerfully. ● **gaieté** *nf* (*de personne etc*) cheerfulness.

gaillard [gajar] *a* vigorous; (*grivois*) coarse ▮ *nm* (*robuste*) strapping fellow.

gain [gɛ̃] *nm* (*profit*) gain, profit; *pl* (*salaire*) earnings; (*au jeu*) winnings.

un g. de temps a saving of time; **obtenir g. de cause** to win one's case.

gaine [gɛn] *nf* 1 (*sous-vêtement*) girdle. 2 (*étui*) sheath.

gala [gala] *nm* gala, official reception.

galant [galɑ̃] *a* (*homme*) gallant; (*ton, propos*) *Hum* amorous. ● **galanterie** *nf* (*courtoisie*) gallantry.

galaxie [galaksi] *nf* galaxy.

galbe [galb] *nm* curve, contour.

galère [galɛr] *nf* (*navire*) *Hist* galley.

galerie [galri] *nf* 1 (*passage, salle, magasin etc*) gallery; *Th* balcony; **g. (d'art)** (*art*) gallery. 2 (*porte-bagage*) *Aut* roof rack.

galet [galɛ] *nm* pebble.

galette [galɛt] *nf* round, flat, flaky cake; (*crêpe*) pancake.

Galles [gal] *nfpl* **pays de G.** Wales. ● **gallois, -oise** *a* (*navire*) Welsh ▮ *nm* (*langue*) Welsh ▮ *nmf* Welshman, Welshwoman.

gallicisme [galisism] *nm* (*mot etc*) gallicism.

galon [galɔ̃] *nm* (*ruban*) braid; (*de soldat*) stripe; **prendre du g.** *Mil & Fig* to get promoted.

galop [galo] *nm* gallop; **aller au g.** to gallop; **g. d'essai** *Fig* trial run. ● **galoper** *vi* (*cheval*) to gallop; **inflation galopante** galloping inflation.

galopin [galopɛ̃] *nm* urchin, rascal.

gambader [gɑ̃bade] *vi* to leap about.

gambas [gɑ̃bas] *nfpl* scampi.

gamelle [gamɛl] *nf* *Fam* pan; (*de chien*) bowl; (*d'ouvrier*) lunch tin ou box.

gamin, -ine [gamɛ̃, -in] *nmf* (*enfant*) *Fam* kid ▮ *a* playful, naughty.

gamme [gam] *nf* *Mus* scale; (*série*) range.

gang [gɑ̃g] *nm* (*de malfaiteurs*) gang. ● **gangster** *nm* gangster.

gangrène [gɑ̃grɛn] *nf* gangrene.

gant [gɑ̃] nm glove; **g. de toilette** facecloth; **boîte à gants** glove compartment;
jeter/relever le g. Fig to throw down/
take up the gauntlet. ● **ganté** a (main)
gloved; (personne) wearing gloves.

garage [garaʒ] nm Aut garage; **voie de g.**
Rail siding; Fig dead end. ● **garagiste**
nmf garage mechanic.

garant, -ante [garɑ̃, -ɑ̃t] nmf (personne)
Jur guarantor; **se porter g. de** to guarantee, vouch for ‖ nm (garantie) guarantee.

garantie [garɑ̃ti] nf guarantee; **garan-
tie(s)** (de police d'assurance) cover.
● **garantir** vt to guarantee (**contre**
against); **g. à qn que** to assure ou
guarantee s.o. that; **g. de** (protéger)
to protect from.

garce [gars] nf Péj Fam bitch.

garçon [garsɔ̃] nm boy; (jeune homme)
young man; **g. (de café)** waiter; **g.
manqué** tomboy.

garde [gard] **1** nm (gardien) guard;
(soldat) guardsman; **g. du corps** bodyguard; **G. des Sceaux** Justice Minister.
2 nf (d'enfants, de bagages etc) care,
custody (de of); **avoir la g. de** to be in
charge of; **prendre g.** to pay attention (**à
qch** to sth), be careful (**à qch** of sth);
prendre g. de ne pas faire to be careful
not to do; **mettre qn en g.** to warn s.o.
(**contre** against); **mise en g.** warning; **de
g.** on duty; **monter la g.** to stand guard;
sur ses gardes on one's guard; **chien de
g.** watchdog; **à la g. à vue** (police) custody.
3 nf (escorte, soldats) guard.

garde-à-vous [gardavu] nm inv Mil
(position of) attention. ● **g.-chasse** nm
(pl **gardes-chasses**) gamekeeper. ● **g.-
côte** nm (personne) coastguard. ● **g.-
manger** nm inv (armoire) food safe. ●
g.-robe nf (habits) wardrobe.

garder [garde] vt to keep; (vêtement) to
keep on; (surveiller) to watch (over);
(défendre) to guard; **g. la chambre** to
stay in one's room; **g. le lit** to stay in
bed ‖ **se g.** vpr (aliment) to keep; **se g. de
qch** (éviter) to beware of sth; **se g. de**

faire to take care not to do.

garderie [gardəri] nf crèche, nursery.

gardien, -ienne [gardjɛ̃, -jɛn] nmf
(d'immeuble etc) caretaker, Am janitor; (de prison) (prison) guard; (de
zoo, parc) keeper; (de musée) attendant, Am guard; **g. de but** Fb goalkeeper; **gardienne d'enfants** child
minder; **g. de nuit** night watchman; **g.
de la paix** policeman ‖ am **ange g.**
guardian angel.

gare [gar] **1** nf Rail station; **g. routière**
bus ou coach station. **2** int **g. à** watch ou
look out for; **sans crier g.** without
warning.

garer [gare] vt (voiture etc) to park ‖ **se
g.** vpr Aut to park.

gargariser (se) [səgargarize] vpr to
gargle.

gargouiller [garguje] vi (fontaine, eau) to
gurgle; (ventre) to rumble.

garnement [garnəmɑ̃] nm rascal, urchin.

garn/ir [garnir] vt (équiper) to fit out,
furnish (**de** with); (remplir) to fill;
(magasin) to stock (**de** with); (orner)
to decorate; (enjoliver) to trim (**de**
with); Culin to garnish. ● **—i** a
(plat) served with vegetables; **bien g.**
(portefeuille) Fig well-lined. ● **garniture**
nf Culin garnish, trimmings; pl Aut
fittings, upholstery; **g. de lit** bed linen.

garnison [garnizɔ̃] nf Mil garrison.

gars [gɑ] nm Fam fellow, guy.

gas-oil [gazwal] nm diesel (oil).

gaspill/er [gaspije] vt to waste. ● **—age**
nm waste.

gastrique [gastrik] a gastric.

gastronome [gastronɔm] nmf gourmet.
● **gastronomie** nf gastronomy.

gâteau, -x [gɑto] nm cake; **g. de riz** rice
pudding; **g. sec** (sweet) biscuit, Am
cookie; **c'était du g.** (facile) Fam it
was a piece of cake.

gâter [gɑte] vt to spoil ‖ **se g.** vpr
(aliment, dent) to go bad; (temps,
situation) to get worse; (relations) to
turn sour. ● **gâté** a (dent, fruit etc) bad.

gâteux, -euse [gɑtø, -øz] a senile, soft in

the head.

gauche[1] [goʃ] *a* (*côté, main etc*) left ▌ *nf*
la g. (*côté*) the left (side); *Pol* the left
(wing); **à g.** (*tourner etc*) (to the) left;
(*marcher etc*) on the left(-hand) side; **de
g.** (*fenêtre etc*) left-hand; (*parti, politique etc*) left-wing; **à g. de** on *ou* to the
left of. ● **gaucher, -ère** *a* & *nmf* left-
handed (person). ● **gauchiste** *a* & *nmf*
Pol (extreme) leftist.

gauche[2] [goʃ] *a* (*maladroit*) awkward.

gaufre [gofr] *nf Culin* waffle. ● **gaufrette**
nf wafer (biscuit).

gaule [gol] *nf* long pole; *Pêche* fishing
rod.

Gaule [gol] *nf* (*pays*) *Hist* Gaul. ● **gau-
lois** *a* Gallic; (*propos etc*) *Fig* earthy,
bawdy ▌ *nmpl* **les G.** *Hist* the Gauls.

gaver (se) [səgave] *vpr* to stuff oneself
(de with).

gaz [gaz] *nm inv* gas; **réchaud/masque/**
etc **à g.** gas stove/mask/*etc.*

gaze [gɑz] *nf* (*tissu*) gauze.

gazelle [gazɛl] *nf* (*animal*) gazelle.

gazer [gaze] *vi* **ça gaze!** everything's just
fine!

gazette [gazɛt] *nf* (*journal*) *Vieilli* newspaper.

gazeux, -euse [gazø, -øz] *a* (*boisson,
eau*) fizzy, carbonated.

gazinière [gazinjɛr] *nf* gas cooker *ou Am*
stove.

gazole [gazɔl] *nm* diesel (oil).

gazon [gazɔ̃] *nm* grass, lawn.

gazouiller [gazuje] *vi* (*oiseau*) to chirp;
(*bébé, ruisseau*) to babble.

geai [ʒɛ] *nm* (*oiseau*) jay.

géant, -ante [ʒeɑ̃, -ɑ̃t] *nmf* giant ▌ *a*
giant; **c'est g.!** *Fam* it's terrific *ou*
brilliant!

Geiger [ʒeʒɛr] *nm* **compteur G.** Geiger
counter.

gel [ʒɛl] *nm* **1** (*temps, glace*) frost; (*de
crédits*) *Écon* freezing. **2** (*pour cheveux
etc*) gel. ● **geler** *vti* to freeze; **on gèle ici**
it's freezing here ▌ *v imp* **il gèle** it's
freezing. ● **gelé** *a* frozen. ● **gelée** *nf*
frost; *Culin* jelly, *Am* jello®.

gélule [ʒelyl] *nf* (*médicament*) capsule.

Gémeaux [ʒemo] *nmpl* **les G.** (*signe*)
Gemini.

gém/ir [ʒemir] *vi* to groan. ● **—issement**
nm groan.

gencive [ʒɑ̃siv] *nf Anat* gum.

gendarme [ʒɑ̃darm] *nm* gendarme (*soldier performing police duties*). ● **gendarmerie** *nf* police force; (*local*) police
headquarters.

gendre [ʒɑ̃dr] *nm* son-in-law.

gène [ʒɛn] *nm Biol* gene.

gêne [ʒɛn] *nf* (*trouble physique*) discomfort; (*confusion*) embarrassment; (*dérangement*) bother, trouble; **dans la g.**
in financial difficulties.

gêner [ʒene] *vt* (*déranger, irriter*) to
bother; (*troubler*) to embarrass; (*mouvement*) to hamper; (*circulation*) *Aut* to
hold up, block; **g. qn** (*par sa présence*)
to be in s.o.'s way; **ça ne me gêne pas** I
don't mind (**si** if).
▌ **se gêner** *vpr* (*se déranger*) to put
oneself out; **ne te gêne pas pour moi!**
don't mind me! ● **gênant** *a* (*objet*)
cumbersome; (*présence, situation*) awkward; (*bruit*) annoying. ● **gêné** *a* (*intimidé*) embarrassed; (*mal à l'aise*)
awkward, uneasy; (*silence, sourire*)
awkward.

généalogique [ʒenealɔʒik] *a* genealogi-
cal; **arbre g.** family tree.

général, -aux [ʒeneral, -o] **1** *a* general; **en
g.** in general. **2** *nm* (*officier*) *Mil* general.
● **générale** *nf Th* dress rehearsal. ● **généralement** *adv* generally. ● **généralité** *nf*
generality.

généralisation [ʒeneralizasjɔ̃] *nf* generalization. ● **généraliser** *vti* to generalize
▌ **se g.** *vpr* to become general *ou* widespread.

généraliste [ʒeneralist] *nmf Méd* general
practitioner, GP.

générateur [ʒeneratœr] *nm Él* generator.

génération [ʒenerasjɔ̃] *nf* generation.

généreux, -euse [ʒenerø, -øz] *a* generous (de with). ● **généreusement** *adv*
generously. ● **générosité** *nf* generosity.

générique [ʒenerik] nm (de film) credits.

genèse [ʒənɛz] nf genesis.

genêt [ʒəne] nm (plante) broom.

génétique [ʒenetik] nf genetics ▮ a genetic.

Genève [ʒənɛv] nm ou f Geneva.

génial, -aux [ʒenjal -o] a (personne, invention) brilliant; (formidable) Fam fantastic.

génie [ʒeni] nm 1 (aptitude, personne) genius; **avoir le g. pour faire/de qch** to have a genius for doing/for sth. 2 **g. civil** civil engineering; **g. génétique** genetic engineering; **g. informatique** computer engineering.

génisse [ʒenis] nf (vache) heifer.

genou, -x [ʒ(ə)nu] nm knee; **être à genoux** to be kneeling (down); **se mettre à genoux** to kneel (down); **prendre qn sur ses genoux** to take s.o. on one's lap ou knee.

genre [ʒɑ̃r] nm 1 (espèce) kind, sort; (attitude) manner, way; **le g. humain** mankind. 2 Littér Cin genre; Gram gender; Biol genus.

gens [ʒɑ̃] nmpl people; (hommes) people; **jeunes g.** young people; (hommes) young men.

gentil, -ille [ʒɑ̃ti, -ij] a nice; **g. avec qn** nice ou kind to s.o.; **sois g.** (sage) be good. ● **gentillesse** nf kindness; **avoir la g. de faire** to be kind enough to do. ● **gentiment** adv (aimablement) kindly; (sagement) nicely.

géographie [ʒeografi] nf geography. ● **géographique** a geographical.

géologie [ʒeɔlɔʒi] nf geology. ● **géologue** nmf geologist.

géomètre [ʒeɔmɛtr] nm surveyor.

géométrie [ʒeɔmetri] nf geometry. ● **géométrique** a geometric(al).

géranium [ʒeranjɔm] nm Bot geranium.

gérant, -ante [ʒerɑ̃, -ɑ̃t] nmf manager, manageress; **g. d'immeubles** landlord's agent.

gerbe [ʒɛrb] nf (de blé) sheaf; (de fleurs) bunch; (d'étincelles) shower.

gercer [ʒɛrse] vi, **se g.** vpr (peau, lèvres) to become chapped. ● **gerçure** nf chap;

avoir des gerçures aux mains/lèvres to have chapped hands/lips.

gérer [ʒere] vt (commerce etc) to manage.

germain [ʒɛrmɛ̃] a **cousin g.** first cousin.

germanique [ʒɛrmanik] a Germanic.

germe [ʒɛrm] nm (microbe) germ; (de plante) shoot; (d'une idée) Fig seed, germ. ● **germer** vi (graine) to start to grow; (pomme de terre) to sprout; (idée) to germinate.

geste [ʒɛst] nm gesture; **ne pas faire un g.** (ne pas bouger) not to make a move; **faire un g. de la main** to wave one's hand. ● **gesticuler** vi to gesticulate.

gestion [ʒɛstjɔ̃] nf (action) management. ● **gestionnaire** nmf administrator.

ghetto [geto] nm ghetto.

gibecière [ʒibsjɛr] nf shoulder bag.

gibier [ʒibje] nm (animaux etc) game.

giboulée [ʒibule] nf shower, downpour.

gicl/er [ʒikle] vi (liquide) to spurt, squirt; (boue) to splash; **faire g.** to spurt, squirt. ● **—ée** nf jet, spurt. ● **—eur** nm (de carburateur) Aut jet.

gifle [ʒifl] nf slap (in the face). ● **gifler** vt **g. qn** to slap s.o., slap s.o.'s face.

gigantesque [ʒigɑ̃tɛsk] a gigantic.

gigot [ʒigo] nm leg of mutton ou lamb.

gigoter [ʒigɔte] vi Fam to wriggle, fidget.

gilet [ʒile] nm (cardigan) cardigan; (de costume) waistcoat, Am vest; **g. de sauvetage** life jacket; **g. pare-balles** bulletproof jacket ou Am vest.

gingembre [ʒɛ̃ʒɑ̃br] nm Bot Culin ginger.

girafe [ʒiraf] nf giraffe.

giratoire [ʒiratwar] a **sens g.** Aut roundabout, Am traffic circle.

girofle [ʒirɔfl] nm **clou de g.** Bot clove.

girouette [ʒirwɛt] nf weathercock, Am weather vane.

gisement [ʒizmɑ̃] nm (de minerai, pétrole) deposit.

gitan, -ane [ʒitɑ̃, -an] nmf (Spanish) gipsy.

gîte [ʒit] nm (abri) resting place.

givre [ʒivr] nm frost. ● **givré** a frost-covered.

glabre [glabr] *a* (*visage*) smooth.

glace [glas] *nf* **1** (*eau gelée*) ice; (*crème glacée*) ice cream. **2** (*vitre*) window; (*miroir*) mirror; **il est resté de g.** he showed no emotion.

glacer [glase] **1** *vt* to chill; **g. qn** (*paralyser*) to chill s.o. **2** *vt* (*gâteau*) to ice, (*au jus*) to glaze. ● **glacé** *a* **1** (*eau, main, pièce, vent*) icy; (*accueil*) *Fig* icy, chilly. **2** (*thé, café*) iced; (*marron*) candied.

glacial, -aux [glasjal, -o] *a* icy.

glacier [glasje] *nm* **1** *Géol* glacier. **2** (*vendeur*) ice-cream man.

glacière [glasjɛr] *nf* (*boîte, endroit*) ice-box.

glaçon [glasɔ̃] *nm* *Culin* ice cube.

glaïeul [glajœl] *nm* *Bot* gladiolus.

glaise [glɛz] *nf* clay.

gland [glɑ̃] *nm* *Bot* acorn.

glande [glɑ̃d] *nf* gland.

glander [glɑ̃de] *vi* *Fam* to fritter away one's time.

glaner [glane] *vt* (*blé, renseignement etc*) to glean.

glas [glɑ] *nm* (*de cloche*) knell.

glauque [glok] *a* sea-green.

gliss/er [glise] *vi* (*involontairement*) to slip; (*volontairement*) (*sur glace etc*) to slide; (*tiroir etc*) to slide; **faire g. un tiroir/etc** to slide a drawer/etc; **ça glisse** it's slippery ∥ *vt* (*introduire*) to slip (*sth*) (**dans** into); (*murmurer*) to whisper; **se g. dans/sous** to slip into/under. ● **—ant** *a* slippery. ● **glissade** *nf* (*involontaire*) slip; (*volontaire*) slide. ● **glissement** *nm* **g. à gauche** *Pol* swing ou shift to the left; **g. de terrain** *Géol* landslide.

glissière [glisjɛr] *nf* **porte à g.** sliding door.

global, -aux [glɔbal, -o] *a* total, global; **somme globale** lump sum. ● **—ement** *adv* collectively, as a whole.

globe [glɔb] *nm* globe; **g. de l'œil** eyeball.

globule [glɔbyl] *nm* (*du sang*) corpuscle.

gloire [glwar] *nf* glory; (*personne célèbre*) celebrity; **à la g. de** in praise of.

● **glorieux, -euse** *a* glorious. ● **glorifier** *vt* to glorify; **se g. de** to glory in.

glouglou [gluglu] *nm* (*de liquide*) gurgle.

glouss/er [gluse] *vi* (*poule*) to cluck. ● **—ement** *nm* cluck(ing).

glouton, -onne [glutɔ̃, -ɔn] *a* greedy ∥ *nmf* glutton.

gluant [glyɑ̃] *a* sticky.

glucose [glykoz] *nm* glucose.

glycine [glisin] *nf* *Bot* wisteria.

gnon [ɲɔ̃] *nm* *Fam* blow, punch.

goal [gol] *nm* *Fb* goalkeeper.

gobelet [gɔblɛ] *nm* (*de plastique, papier*) cup.

gober [gɔbe] *vt* (*œuf, mouche etc*) to swallow (whole); (*propos*) *Fam* to swallow.

godasse [gɔdas] *nf* *Fam* shoe.

godet [gɔdɛ] *nm* (*récipient*) pot.

goéland [gɔelɑ̃] *nm* (sea)gull.

gogo (à) [agogo] *adv* *Fam* galore.

goguenard [gɔgnar] *a* mocking.

goinfre [gwɛ̃fr] *nm* (*glouton*) *Fam* pig, guzzler. ● **se goinfrer** *vpr* *Fam* to stuff oneself (**de** with).

golf [gɔlf] *nm* golf; (*terrain*) golf course. ● **golfeur, -euse** *nmf* golfer.

golfe [gɔlf] *nm* gulf, bay.

gomme [gɔm] *nf* (*à effacer*) rubber, *Am* eraser. ● **gommer** *vt* (*effacer*) to rub out, erase.

gomme (à la) [alagɔm] *adv* *Fam* useless.

gond [gɔ̃] *nm* (*de porte etc*) hinge.

gondole [gɔ̃dɔl] *nf* (*bateau*) gondola. ● **gondolier** *nm* gondolier.

gondoler [gɔ̃dɔle] **1** *vi*, **se g.** *vpr* (*planche*) to warp. **2 se gondoler** *vpr* (*rire*) *Fam* to split one's sides.

gonflable [gɔ̃flabl] *a* inflatable.

gonfler [gɔ̃fle] *vt* (*pneu*) to pump up; (*en soufflant*) to blow up; (*poitrine*) to swell out ∥ *vi*, **se g.** *vpr* to swell; **se g. de** (*orgueil, émotion*) to swell with. ● **gonflé** *a* swollen; **être g.** *Fam* (*courageux*) to have plenty of pluck; (*insolent*) to have plenty of nerve. ● **gonfleur** *nm* (*air*) pump.

gorge [gɔrʒ] *nf* **1** throat. **2** *Géog* gorge.

gorgé [gɔrʒe] *a* g. de (*saturé*) gorged with.

gorgée [gɔrʒe] *nf* mouthful (*of wine etc*); **petite g.** sip; **d'une seule g.** in one gulp.

gorille [gɔrij] *nm* (*animal*) gorilla.

gosier [gozje] *nm* throat.

gosse [gɔs] *nmf* (*enfant*) *Fam* kid.

gouache [gwaʃ] *nf* (*peinture*) gouache.

goudron [gudrɔ̃] *nm* tar. ● **goudronner** *vt* to tar.

gouffre [gufr] *nm* gulf, chasm.

goulot [gulo] *nm* (*de bouteille*) neck; **boire au g.** to drink from the bottle.

goulu [guly] *a* greedy.

gourde [gurd] *nf* **1** water bottle. **2** (*personne*) *Péj Fam* chump, oaf.

gourdin [gurdɛ̃] *nm* club, cudgel.

gourer (se) [səgure] *vpr Fam* to make a mistake.

gourmand, -ande [gurmã, -ãd] *a* (over)fond of food; **g. de** fond of ▮ *nmf* hearty eater. ● **gourmandise** *nf* (over)fondness for food; *pl* (*mets*) delicacies.

gourmet [gurmε] *nm* gourmet.

gourmette [gurmεt] *nf* identity bracelet.

gousse [gus] *nf* **g. d'ail** clove of garlic.

goût [gu] *nm* taste; **de bon g.** in good taste; **sans g.** tasteless; **par g.** from *ou* by choice; **prendre g. à qch** to take a liking to sth, **avoir du g. (*personne*) to have good taste; **avoir un g. de noisette/*etc*** to taste of hazelnut/*etc*.

goûter [gute] *vt* (*aliment*) to taste; **g. à qch** to taste (a little of) sth ▮ *vi* to have an afternoon snack ▮ *nm* afternoon snack, tea.

goutte [gut] *nf* drop; **couler g. à g.** to drip. ● **g.-à-goutte** *nm inv Méd* drip. ● **gouttelette** *nf* droplet. ● **goutter** *vi* (*eau, robinet, nez*) to drip (**de** from).

gouttière [gutjεr] *nf* (*d'un toit*) gutter.

gouvernail [guvεrnaj] *nm* (*pale*) rudder; (*barre*) helm.

gouvernante [guvεrnãt] *nf* governess.

gouvernement [guvεrnəmã] *nm* government. ● **gouvernemental, -aux** *a* politique/*etc* **gouvernementale** government

policy/*etc*; **l'équipe gouvernementale** the government.

gouvern/er [guvεrne] *vti Pol & Fig* to govern, rule. ● **-ants** *nmpl* rulers. ● **-eur** *nm* governor.

grâce [grɑs] **1** *nf* (*charme*) & *Rel* grace; **de bonne/mauvaise g.** with good/bad grace; **donner le coup de g. à** to finish off; **faire g. de qch à qn** to spare s.o. sth; **être dans les bonnes grâces de qn** to be in favour with s.o. **2** *prép* **g. à** thanks to.

gracier [grasje] *vt* (*condamné*) to pardon.

gracieux, -euse [grasjø, -øz] *a* **1** (*élégant*) graceful; (*aimable*) gracious. **2** (*gratuit*) gratuitous; **à titre g.** free (of charge). ● **gracieusement** *adv* gracefully; graciously; free (of charge).

grade [grad] *nm Mil* rank; **monter en g.** to be promoted. ● **gradé** *nm Mil* non-commissioned officer.

gradin [gradɛ̃] *nm Th etc* tier (of seats).

graduer [gradɥe] *vt* (*règle*) to graduate; (*exercices*) to grade (*for difficulty*).

graffiti [grafiti] *nmpl* graffiti.

grain [grɛ̃] *nm* (*de blé etc*) & *Fig* grain; (*de café*) bean; (*de poussière*) speck; *pl* (*céréales*) grain; **g. de beauté** mole; (*sur le visage*) beauty spot; **g. de raisin** grape.

graine [grεn] *nf* seed; **mauvaise g.** (*enfant*) *Péj* rotten egg.

graisse [grεs] *nf* fat; (*lubrifiant*) grease. ● **graissage** *nm Aut* lubrication. ● **graisser** *vt* to grease. ● **graisseux, -euse** *a* (*vêtement etc*) greasy, oily; **tissu g.** fatty tissue.

grammaire [gramεr] *nf* grammar; **livre de g.** grammar (book). ● **grammatical, -aux** *a* grammatical.

gramme [gram] *nm* gram(me).

grand, grande [grã, grãd] *a* big, large; (*en hauteur*) tall; (*chaleur, découverte, âge etc*) great; (*bruit*) loud; (*différence*) big, great; (*maître*) great; (*âme*) noble; **g. frère/*etc*** (*plus âgé*) big brother/*etc*; **g. air** the open air; **il est g. temps** it's high time (**que** that).

‖*adv* g. ouvert (*yeux, fenêtre*) wide-open; **ouvrir g.** to open wide; **en g.** on a grand *ou* large scale.

‖*nmf Scol* senior; (*adulte*) grown-up.

grand-chose [grɑ̃ʃoz] *pron* **pas g.-chose** not much. ● **g.-mère** *nf* (*pl* **grands-mères**) grandmother. ● **g.-père** *nm* (*pl* **grands-pères**) grandfather. ● **g.-route** *nf* main road. ● **grands-parents** *nmpl* grandparents.

Grande-Bretagne [grɑ̃dbrətaɲ] *nf* Great Britain.

grandeur [grɑ̃dœr] *nf* (*importance, gloire*) greatness; (*dimension*) size; (*splendeur*) grandeur; **g. nature** life-size.

grandiose [grɑ̃djoz] *a* grandiose, grand.

grandir [grɑ̃dir] *vi* to grow; **g. de 2 cm** to grow 2 cm ‖ *vt* **g. qn** (*faire paraître plus grand*) to make s.o. seem taller.

grange [grɑ̃ʒ] *nf* barn.

granit(e) [granit] *nm* granite.

graphique [grafik] *a* (*signe, art*) graphic ‖ *nm* graph; *pl Ordinat* graphics.

grappe [grap] *nf* (*de fruits etc*) cluster; **g. de raisin** bunch of grapes.

gras, grasse [grɑ, grɑs] *a* (*personne etc*) fat; (*aliment*) fatty; (*graisseux*) greasy; (*plante, contour*) thick; **matières grasses** fat; **foie g.** *Culin* foie gras, fatted goose liver; **caractères g.** bold type ‖ *nm* (*de viande*) fat.

gratifier [gratifje] *vt* **g. qn de** to present *ou* favour s.o. with.

gratin [gratɛ̃] *nm* **macaronis/chou-fleur au g.** macaroni/cauliflower cheese.

gratis [gratis] *adv Fam* free (of charge).

gratitude [gratityd] *nf* gratitude.

gratte-ciel [gratsjɛl] *nm inv* skyscraper.

gratter [grate] *vt* (*avec un outil etc*) to scrape; (*avec les ongles etc*) to scratch; (*boue*) to scrape off; **ça me gratte** *Fam* it itches ‖ *vi* (*à la porte etc*) to scratch; (*tissu*) to be scratchy ‖ **se g.** *vpr* to scratch oneself.

gratuit [gratɥi] *a* (*billet etc*) free; (*hypothèse, acte*) gratuitous. ● **gratuité** *nf* **la g. de l'enseignement/etc** free education/etc. ● **gratuitement** *adv* free (of charge);

(*sans motif*) gratuitously.

gravats [grava] *nmpl* rubble, debris.

grave [grav] *a* serious; (*voix*) deep, low; (*visage*) grave, solemn; **ce n'est pas g.!** it's not important!; **accent g.** grave [grɑːv] accent. ● **—ment** *adv* (*malade, menacé*) seriously; (*dignement*) gravely.

grav/er [grave] *vt* (*sur métal etc*) to engrave; (*sur bois*) to carve; (*dans sa mémoire*) to imprint. ● **—eur** *nm* engraver.

gravier [gravje] *nm* gravel. ● **gravillons** *nmpl* gravel, (loose) chippings.

gravir [gravir] *vt* to climb (with effort).

gravité [gravite] *nf* **1** (*de situation etc*) seriousness; (*solennité*) gravity. **2** *Phys* gravity.

graviter [gravite] *vi* to revolve (**autour** around).

gravure [gravyr] *nf* (*image*) print; (*action, art*) engraving; **g. sur bois** (*objet*) woodcut.

gré [gre] *nm* **à son g.** (*goût*) to his *ou* her taste; (*désir*) as he *ou* she pleases; **de son plein g.** of one's own free will; **contre le g. de qn** against s.o.'s will; **bon g. mal g.** willy-nilly; **savoir g. à qn de qch** to be grateful to s.o. for sth.

Grèce [grɛs] *nf* Greece. ● **grec, grecque** *a* & *nmf* Greek ‖ *nm* (*langue*) Greek.

greffe [grɛf] **1** *nf* (*de peau, d'arbre etc*) graft; (*d'organe*) transplant. **2** *nm Jur* record office. ● **greffer** *vt* (*peau etc*) & *Bot* to graft (**à** on to); (*organe*) to transplant. ● **greffier** *nm* clerk (of the court).

grêle [grɛl] **1** *nf* hail. **2** *a* (*fin*) spindly, (very) thin. ● **grêler** *v imp* to hail. ● **grêlon** *nm* hailstone.

grelot [grəlo] *nm* (small round) bell (*that jingles*).

grelotter [grəlɔte] *vi* to shiver (**de** with).

grenade [grənad] *nf* **1** *Bot* pomegranate. **2** (*projectile*) *Mil* grenade. ● **grenadine** *nf* pomegranate syrup.

grenier [grənje] *nm* attic; *Agr* granary.

grenouille [grənuj] *nf* frog.

grès [grɛ] *nm* (*roche*) sandstone; (*po-*

terie) stoneware.

grésiller [grezije] *vi Culin* to sizzle; *Rad* to crackle.

grève [grɛv] *nf* **1** strike; **g. de la faim** hunger strike; **g. du zèle** work-to-rule, *Am* rule-book slow-down; **g. tournante** strike by rota; **se mettre en g.** to go (out) on strike. **2** (*de mer*) shore. ● **gréviste** *nmf* striker.

gribouiller [gribuje] *vti* to scribble. ● **gribouillis** *nm* scribble.

grief [grijɛf] *nm* (*plainte*) grievance.

grièvement [grijɛvmɑ̃] *adv* **g. blessé** seriously injured.

griffe [grif] *nf* **1** (*ongle*) claw; **sous la g. de qn** (*pouvoir*) in s.o.'s clutches. **2** (*de couturier*) (designer) label; (*tampon*) printed signature. ● **griffer** *vt* to scratch, claw.

griffonner [grifɔne] *vt* to scribble.

grignoter [griɲɔte] *vti* to nibble.

gril [gril] *nm* (*ustensile de cuisine*) grill. ● **grillade** [grijad] *nf* (*viande*) grill. ● **grille-pain** *nm inv* toaster. ● **griller** *vt* (*viande*) to grill, broil; (*pain*) to toast; (*café*) to roast; (*ampoule*) *El* to blow; **g. un feu rouge** *Aut Fam* to drive through *ou* jump a red light ‖ *vi* **mettre à g.** to put on the grill.

grille [grij] *nf* (*clôture*) railings; (*porte*) (iron) gate, (*de radiateur*) *Aut* grid, grille; (*des salaires*) *Fig* scale; (*de fenêtre*) bars, grating. ● **grillage** *nm* wire mesh *ou* netting.

grillon [grijɔ̃] *nm* (*insecte*) cricket.

grimace [grimas] *nf* (*pour faire rire*) (funny) face; (*de dégoût, douleur*) grimace; **faire des grimaces/la g.** to make faces/a face. ● **grimacer** *vi* to make faces *ou* a face; (*de dégoût etc*) to grimace (**de** with).

grimp/er [grɛ̃pe] *vi* to climb (**à qch** up sth) ‖ *vt* to climb. ● —**ant** *a* (*plante*) climbing.

grinc/er [grɛ̃se] *vi* to creak, grate; **g. des dents** to grind one's teeth. ● —**ement** *nm* creaking; grinding.

grincheux, -euse [grɛ̃ʃø, -øz] *a* grumpy.

grippe [grip] *nf* **1** (*maladie*) flu. **2 prendre qch/qn en g.** to take a strong dislike to sth/s.o. ● **grippé** *a* **être g.** to have (the) flu.

gris [gri] *a* grey, *Am* gray; (*temps*) dull, grey ‖ *nm* grey, *Am* gray. ● **grisaille** *nf* greyness, *Am* grayness. ● **grisâtre** *a* greyish, *Am* grayish.

griser [grize] *vt* (*vin etc*) to make (*s.o.*) tipsy; (*air vif, succès*) to exhilarate (*s.o.*).

grisonner [grizɔne] *vi* (*cheveux, personne*) to go grey *ou Am* gray.

grive [griv] *nf* (*oiseau*) thrush.

grivois [grivwa] *a* bawdy.

Groenland [grɔɛnlɑ̃d] *nm* Greenland.

grogn/er [grɔɲe] *vi* (*personne*) to grumble, growl (**contre** at); (*cochon*) to grunt. ● —**ement** *nm* grumble, growl; grunt. ● **grognon** *a* grumpy.

grommeler [grɔmle] *vti* to grumble, mutter.

gronder [grɔ̃de] *vi* (*chien*) to growl; (*tonnerre, camion*) to rumble ‖ *vt* (*réprimander*) to scold, tell off. ● **gronde-ment** *nm* growl; rumble.

groom [grum] *nm* page (boy), *Am* bell-boy.

gros, grosse [gro, gros] *a* big; (*gras*) fat; (*épais*) thick; (*effort, progrès*) great; (*somme, fortune*) large; (*averse, rhume*) heavy; (*faute*) serious, gross, (*bruit*) loud; **g. mot** swear word. ‖ *adv* **risquer g.** to take a big risk; **en g.** (*globalement*) roughly; (*écrire*) in big letters; (*vendre*) wholesale, in bulk. ‖ *nmf* (*personne*) fat man, fat woman. ‖ *nm* **le g. de** the bulk of; **de g.** (*prix, marché*) wholesale; **commerce/maison de g.** wholesale trade/company.

groseille [grozɛj] *nf* (*white ou red*) currant; **g. à maquereau** gooseberry.

grossesse [grosɛs] *nf* pregnancy.

grosseur [grosœr] *nf* **1** (*volume*) size; (*obésité*) weight. **2** (*tumeur*) *Méd* lump.

grossier, -ière [grosje, -jɛr] *a* (*tissu, traits*) rough, coarse; (*personne, manières*) rude, coarse; (*erreur*) gross;

être g. envers (*insolent*) to be rude to.
• **grossièrement** *adv* (*calculer*) roughly;
(*répondre*) rudely, coarsely; (*se tromper*) grossly. • **grossièreté** *nf* roughness;
coarseness; (*insolence*) rudeness; (*mot*)
rude word.

grossir [grosir] *vi* (*personne*) to put on
weight; (*bosse, foule etc*) to swell, get
bigger ‖ *vt* to swell; (*exagérer*) *Fig* to
magnify ‖ *vti* (*verre, loupe etc*) to magnify; **verre grossissant** magnifying glass.

grossiste [grosist] *nmf Com* wholesaler.

grotesque [grɔtɛsk] *a* (*risible*) ludicrous.

grotte [grɔt] *nf* cave, grotto.

grouiller [gruje] *vi* (*rue, fourmis etc*) to
be swarming (**de** with).

groupe [grup] *nm* group; **g. sanguin**
blood group; **g. scolaire** (*bâtiments*)
school block. • **grouper** *vt*, **se g.** *vpr*
to group (together).

grue [gry] *nf* (*machine, oiseau*) crane.

grumeau, -x [grymo] *nm* (*dans une sauce
etc*) lump.

gruyère [gryjɛr] *nm* gruyère (cheese).

gué [ge] *nm* ford; **passer à g.** to ford.

guenilles [gənij] *nfpl* rags (and tatters).

guenon [gənɔ̃] *nf* female monkey.

guépard [gepar] *nm* cheetah.

guêpe [gɛp] *nf* wasp.

guère [gɛr] *adv* (**ne**)... **g.** hardly; **il ne
sort g.** he hardly goes out.

guéridon [geridɔ̃] *nm* pedestal table.

guérilla [gerija] *nf* guerrilla warfare.

guérir [gerir] *vt* (*personne, maladie*) to
cure (**de** of); (*blessure*) to heal ‖ *vi* to get
better, recover; (*blessure*) to heal;
(*rhume*) to get better; **g. de** (*fièvre etc*)
to get over, recover from ‖ **se g.** *vpr* to
get better. • **guéri** *a* cured, better.
• **guérison** *nf* (*de personne*) recovery;
(*de maladie*) cure; (*de blessure*) healing. • **guérisseur, -euse** *nmf* faith
healer.

guerre [gɛr] *nf* war; (*chimique*) warfare;
en g. at war (**avec** with); **faire la g.** to
wage *ou* make war (**à** on, against);

crime/cri/*etc* **de g.** war crime/cry/*etc*.
• **guerrier, -ière** *a* (*nation*) war-like;
danse guerrière war dance; **chant g.**
battle song ‖ *nmf* warrior.

guet [gɛ] *nm* **faire le g.** to be on the
lookout. • **guetter** *vt* to be on the
lookout for.

guet-apens [getapɑ̃] *nm inv* ambush.

gueule [gœl] *nf* (*d'animal, de canon*)
mouth; (*figure*) *Fam* face; **avoir la g.
de bois** *Fam* to have a hangover; **faire la
g.** *Fam* to sulk. • **gueuler** *vti Fam* to
bawl (out).

gui [gi] *nm Bot* mistletoe.

guichet [giʃɛ] *nm* (*de gare, cinéma etc*)
ticket office; (*de banque etc*) window;
Th box office; **à guichets fermés** *Th Sp*
with all tickets sold in advance. • **guichetier, -ière** *nmf* (*de banque etc*) counter clerk, *Am* teller; (*à la gare*) ticket
office clerk.

guide [gid] **1** *nm* (*personne, livre etc*)
guide. **2** *nfpl* (*rênes*) reins. • **guider** *vt* to
guide; **se g. sur un manuel**/*etc* to use a
handbook/*etc* as a guide.

guidon [gidɔ̃] *nm* (*de bicyclette etc*)
handlebar(s).

guignol [giɲɔl] *nm* (*spectacle*) = Punch
and Judy show.

guillemets [gijmɛ] *nmpl Typ* inverted
commas; **entre g.** in inverted commas.

guillotine [gijɔtin] *nf* guillotine.

guimauve [gimov] *nf Bot Culin* marshmallow.

guindé [gɛ̃de] *a* (*peu naturel*) stiff;
(*affecté*) (*style*) stilted.

guirlande [girlɑ̃d] *nf* garland, wreath.

guise [giz] *nf* **n'en faire qu'à sa g.** to do
as one pleases; **en g. de** by way of.

guitare [gitar] *nf* guitar. • **guitariste** *nmf*
guitarist.

gymnase [ʒimnɑz] *nm* gymnasium.
• **gymnastique** *nf* gymnastics.

gynécologie [ʒinekɔlɔʒi] *nf* gynaecology, *Am* gynecology. • **gynécologue**
nmf gynaecologist, *Am* gynecologist.

H

H, h [aʃ] *nm* H, h; **l'heure H** zero hour; **bombe H** H-bomb.

ha! ['ɑ] *int* ah!, oh!; **ha, ha!** (*rire*) ha-ha!

habile [abil] *a* skilful (**à qch** at sth, **à faire** at doing); **h. de ses doigts** dextrous, clever with one's fingers. ●**habileté** *nf* skill.

habiller [abije] *vt* to dress (**de** in); (*fournir en vêtements*) to clothe; **h. qn en soldat/etc** (*déguiser*) to dress s.o. up as a soldier/*etc* ‖ **s'h.** *vpr* to dress, get dressed; (*avec élégance*) to dress up. ●**habillé** *a* dressed (**de** in, **en** as a); (*costume, robe*) smart.

habit [abi] *nm* costume, outfit; *pl* (*vêtements*) clothes.

habitable [abitabl] *a* (*maison*) fit to live in.

habitation [abitasjɔ̃] *nf* house, dwelling; (*action de résider*) living.

habiter [abite] *vi* to live (**à, en, dans** in) ‖ *vt* (*maison, région*) to live in. ●**—ant, -ante** *nmf* (*de pays etc*) inhabitant; (*de maison*) occupant. ●**—é** *a* (*région*) inhabited; (*maison*) occupied.

habitude [abityd] *nf* habit; **avoir l'h. de qch** to be used to sth; **avoir l'h. de faire** to be used to doing; **prendre l'h. de faire** to get into the habit of doing; **d'h.** usually; **comme d'h.** as usual.

habituel, -elle [abityɛl] *a* usual. ●**habituellement** *adv* usually.

habituer [abitɥe] *vt* **h. qn à** to accustom s.o. to; **être habitué à** to be used *ou* accustomed to ‖ **s'h.** *vpr* to get accustomed (**à** to). ●**habitué, -ée** *nmf* regular (customer *ou* visitor).

hache [aʃ] *nf* axe, *Am* ax.

hach/er [aʃe] *vt* (*au couteau*) to chop (up); (*avec un appareil*) to mince, *Am* grind. ●**—é** *a* **1** (*viande*) minced, *Am* ground; (*légumes*) chopped. **2** (*style*) jerky, broken. ●**hachis** *nm* (*viande*) mince, minced *ou Am* ground meat. ●**hachoir** *nm* (*couteau*) chopper; (*appareil*) mincer, *Am* grinder.

haie ['ɛ] *nf* (*clôture*) hedge; (*rangée*) row; **course de haies** (*coureurs*) hurdle race; (*chevaux*) steeplechase.

haillons ['ɑjɔ̃] *nmpl* rags (and tatters).

haine ['ɛn] *nf* hatred.

haïr* ['air] *vt* to hate.

halage [alaʒ] *nm* towing; **chemin de h.** towpath.

hâle ['ɑl] *nm* suntan. ●**hâlé** *a* suntanned.

haleine [alɛn] *nf* breath; **hors d'h.** out of breath; **perdre h.** to get out of breath; **de longue h.** (*travail*) long-term; **tenir en h.** to hold in suspense.

halet/er ['alte] *vi* to pant. ●**—ant** *a* panting.

hall ['ol] *nm* (*de gare*) main hall, concourse; (*de maison*) hall(way); (*d'hôtel*) lobby.

halle ['al] *nf* (*covered*) market; **les halles** the central food market.

hallucination [alysinasjɔ̃] *nf* hallucination. ●**hallucinant** *a* extraordinary.

halte ['alt] *nf* (*arrêt*) stop; **faire h.** to stop ‖ *int* stop!, *Mil* halt!

haltères [alter] *nmpl* weights. ●**haltérophilie** *nf* weight lifting.

hamac ['amak] *nm* hammock.

hameau, -x ['amo] *nm* hamlet.

hameçon [amsɔ̃] *nm* (*fish*) hook; **mordre à l'h.** *Pêche & Fig* to swallow the bait.

hanche ['ɑ̃ʃ] *nf* *Anat* hip.

hand(-)ball ['ɑ̃dbal] *nm* *Sp* handball.

handicapé, -ée ['ɑ̃dikape] *a & nmf* handicapped (person); **h. moteur** spastic.

hangar ['ɑ̃gar] *nm* (*entrepôt*) shed; (*pour avions*) hangar.

hanneton ['antɔ̃] *nm* cockchafer.

hanté ['ɑ̃te] *a* haunted.

hantise ['ɑ̃tiz] *nf* **la h. de** an obsession with.

happer ['ape] *vt* (*saisir*) to catch, snatch; (*par la gueule*) to snap up.

haras ['ara] *nm* stud farm.

harassé ['arase] *a* (*fatigué*) exhausted.

harceler ['arsəle] *vt* to harass, torment (**de** with).

hardi ['ardi] *a* bold, daring. ● **hardiesse** *nf* boldness, daring.

hareng ['arɑ̃] *nm* herring.

hargneux, -euse ['arɲø, -øz] *a* bad-tempered.

haricot ['ariko] *nm* (*blanc*) (haricot) bean; (*vert*) green bean, French bean.

harmonica [armɔnika] *nm* harmonica, mouthorgan.

harmonie [armɔni] *nf* harmony. ● **harmonieux, -euse** *a* harmonious. ● **harmoniser** *vt, s'h. vpr* to harmonize.

harnacher ['arnaʃe] *vt* (*cheval etc*) to harness. ● **harnais** *nm* (*de cheval, bébé*) harness.

harpe ['arp] *nf* harp.

harpon ['arpɔ̃] *nm* harpoon. ● **harponner** *vt* (*baleine*) to harpoon.

hasard ['azar] *nm* **le h.** chance; **un h.** a coincidence; **par h.** by chance; **si par h.** if by any chance; **au h.** at random; **à tout h.** just in case. ● **hasarder** *vt* (*remarque*) to venture, hazard; **se h. dans** to venture into; **se h. à faire** to risk doing, venture to do. ● **hasardeux, -euse** *a* risky, hazardous.

haschisch ['aʃiʃ] *nm* hashish.

hâte ['ɑt] *nf* haste, speed; (*impatience*) eagerness; **à la h.**, **en h.** in a hurry, hurriedly; **avoir h. de faire** (*désireux*) to be eager to do. ● **hâter** *vt* (*pas, départ etc*) to hasten **|| se h. vpr** to hurry (**de faire** to do).

hausse ['os] *nf* rise (**de** in); **en h.** rising. ● **hausser** *vt* (*prix, voix etc*) to raise; (*épaules*) to shrug; **se h. sur la pointe des pieds** to stand on tip-toe.

haut ['o] *a* (*montagne etc*) high; (*de taille*) tall; (*note de musique, tempéra-* *ture, rang etc*) high; **à haute voix** aloud; **h. de 5 mètres** 5 metres high *ou* tall; **la haute couture** high fashion; **en haute mer** out at sea.

|| adv (*voler, viser etc*) high (up); (*parler*) loud, loudly; (*lire, penser*) aloud, out loud; **h. placé** (*personne*) in a high position; **plus h.** (*dans un texte*) above, further back.

|| nm (*partie haute*) top; **en h. de** at the top of; **en h.** (*loger*) upstairs; (*regarder*) up; (*mettre*) on (the) top; **d'en h.** from high up, from up above; **avoir 5 mètres de h.** to be 5 metres high *ou* tall; **des hauts et des bas** *Fig* ups and downs.

hautain ['otɛ̃] *a* haughty.

hautbois ['obwa] *nm Mus* oboe.

haut-de-forme ['odfɔrm] *nm* (*pl* **hauts-de-forme**) top hat.

hautement ['otmɑ̃] *adv* (*tout à fait, très*) highly. ● **hauteur** *nf* height; *Géog* hill; (*orgueil*) *Péj* haughtiness; **à la h.** de (*objet*) level with; (*rue*) opposite; **il n'est pas à la h.** he isn't up to it; **saut en h.** *Sp* high jump.

haut-parleur ['oparlœr] *nm* loudspeaker.

Haye (La) [la'ɛ] *nf* The Hague.

hayon ['ɛjɔ̃,'ajɔ̃] *nm* (*porte*) *Aut* hatchback.

hé! [e] *int* **hé** (**là**) (*appel*) hey!

hebdomadaire [ebdɔmadɛr] *a* weekly **|| nm** (*publication*) weekly.

héberg/er [ebɛrʒe] *vt* to put up, accommodate. ● **—ement** *nm* accommodation.

hébété [ebete] *a* dazed, stupefied.

hébreu, -x [ebrø] *am* Hebrew **|| nm** (*langue*) Hebrew.

hécatombe [ekatɔ̃b] *nf* (great) slaughter.

hectare [ɛktar] *nm* hectare (= *2.47 acres*).

hégémonie [eʒemɔni] *nf* supremacy.

hein! [ɛ̃] *int Fam* (*surprise etc*) eh!

hélas! [elas] *int* unfortunately.

héler [ele] *vt* (*taxi etc*) to hail.

hélice [elis] *nf Av Nau* propeller.

hélicoptère [elikɔptɛr] *nm* helicopter. ● **héliport** *nm* heliport.

helvétique [elvetik] *a* Swiss.

hémicycle [emisikl] *nm* semicircle; *Pol Fig* French National Assembly.

hémisphère [emisfɛr] *nm* hemisphere.

hémorragie [emɔraʒi] *nf Méd* h(a)emorrhage; **h. cérébrale** stroke.

hémorroïdes [emɔrɔid] *nfpl* piles, h(a)emorrhoids.

henn/ir [enir] *vi* to neigh. ●**—issement** *nm* neigh.

hépatite [epatit] *nf* hepatitis.

herbe [ɛrb] *nf* grass; (*pour soigner*) herb; **mauvaise h.** weed; **fines herbes** *Culin* herbs; **en h.** (*blés*) green; (*poète etc*) *Fig* budding. ●**herbage** *nm* grassland. ●**herbicide** *nm* weed killer. ●**herbivore** *a* grass-eating, herbivorous.

hercule [ɛrkyl] *nm* Hercules, strong man.

hérédité [eredite] *nf* heredity. ●**héréditaire** *a* hereditary.

hérétique [eretik] *a* heretical ‖ *nmf* heretic.

hériss/er ['erise] *vt* (*poils*) to bristle (up); **h. qn** (*irriter*) to ruffle s.o.'s feathers ‖ **se h.** *vpr* (*poils*) to bristle (up); (*personne*) to get ruffled. ●**hérisson** ['erisɔ̃] *nm* (*animal*) hedgehog.

hérit/er [erite] *vti* to inherit (**qch de qn** sth from s.o.); **h. de qch** to inherit sth. ●**—age** *nm* (*biens*) inheritance; (*culturel, politique etc*) *Fig* heritage. ●**héritier** *nm* heir. ●**héritière** *nf* heiress.

hermétique [ɛrmetik] *a* airtight; (*obscur*) *Fig* impenetrable.

hermine [ɛrmin] *nf* (*animal, fourrure*) ermine.

hernie ['ɛrni] *nf Méd* hernia.

héron ['erɔ̃] *nm* (*oiseau*) heron.

héros ['ero] *nm* hero. ●**héroïne** [erɔin] *nf* **1** (*femme*) heroine. **2** (*drogue*) heroin. ●**héroïque** [erɔik] *a* heroic.

hésit/er [ezite] *vi* to hesitate (**sur** over, about; **entre** between; **à faire** to do); (*en parlant*) to falter, hesitate. ●**—ant** *a* (*personne*) hesitant; (*pas, voix*) unsteady, faltering. ●**hésitation** *nf* hesitation; **avec h.** hesitantly.

hétérogène [eterɔʒɛn] *a* diverse, heterogeneous.

hêtre ['ɛtr] *nm* (*arbre, bois*) beech.

heu! ['ø] *int* (*hésitation*) er!

heure [œr] *nf* (*mesure*) hour; (*moment*) time; **quelle h. est-il?** what time is it?; **il est six heures** it's six (o'clock); **six heures moins cinq** five to six; **six heures cinq** five past *ou Am* after six; **à l'h.** (*arriver*) on time; (*être payé*) by the hour; **dix kilomètres à l'h.** ten kilometres an hour; **de bonne h.** early; **de dernière h.** (*nouvelle*) latest; **tout à l'h.** (*futur*) later; (*passé*) a moment ago; **à toute h.** (*continuellement*) at all hours; **24 heures sur 24** 24 hours a day; **faire des heures supplémentaires** to work overtime; **heures creuses** off-peak *ou* slack periods; **l'h. d'affluence, l'h. de pointe** (*circulation etc*) rush hour; (*dans les magasins*) peak period.

heureux, -euse [œrø, -øz] *a* happy; (*chanceux*) lucky, fortunate; **h. de qch/de voir qn** (*satisfait*) happy *ou* glad about sth/to see s.o. ‖ *adv* (*vivre, mourir*) happily. ●**heureusement** *adv* (*par chance*) fortunately, luckily (**pour** for).

heurter ['œrte] *vt* (*cogner*) to knock, bump, hit (**contre** against); (*mur, piéton*) to bump into, hit; **h. qn** (*choquer*) to offend s.o., upset s.o.; ‖ **se h. à to** bump into, hit; (*difficultés*) *Fig* to come up against.

hexagone [ɛgzagɔn] *nm* hexagon; **l'H.** *Fig* France.

hiberner [ibɛrne] *vi* to hibernate.

hibou, -x ['ibu] *nm* owl.

hic ['ik] *nm* **voilà le h.** *Fam* that's the snag.

hideux, -euse ['idø, -øz] *a* hideous.

hier [(i)jɛr] *adv* & *nm* yesterday; **h. soir** last *ou* yesterday night, yesterday evening.

hiérarchie ['jerarʃi] *nf* hierarchy. ●**hiérarchique** *a* (*ordre*) hierarchical; **par la voie h.** through (the) official channels.

hi-fi ['ifi] *a inv* & *nf inv* hi-fi.

hilarant [ilarɑ̃] *a* hilarious.

hindou, -oue [ɛ̃du] *a* & *nmf* Hindu.

hippique [ipik] *a* **concours h.** horse show, show-jumping event. ● **hippodrome** *nm* racecourse, racetrack (*for horses*).

hippopotame [ipɔpɔtam] *nm* hippopotamus.

hirondelle [irɔ̃dɛl] *nf* (*oiseau*) swallow.

hisser ['ise] *vt* (*voile, fardeau etc*) to hoist, raise ‖ **se h.** *vpr* to raise oneself (up).

histoire [istwar] *nf* (*science, événements*) history; (*récit, mensonge*) story; (*affaire*) *Fam* business, matter; **des histoires** (*ennuis*) trouble; (*façons, chichis*) fuss; **toute une h.** (*problème*) quite a lot of trouble; (*chichis*) quite a lot of fuss; **sans histoires** (*voyage etc*) uneventful. ● **historien, -ienne** *nmf* historian. ● **historique** *a* historical; (*lieu, événement*) historic.

hiver [iver] *nm* winter. ● **hivernal, -aux** *a* froid/*etc* **h.** winter *ou* wintery cold/*etc*.

HLM ['aʃɛlɛm] *nm ou f abrév* (*habitation à loyer modéré*) = council flats, *Am* = low-rent apartment building (*sponsored by government*).

hocher ['ɔʃe] *vt* **h. la tête** (*pour dire oui*) to nod one's head; (*pour dire non*) to shake one's head.

hochet ['ɔʃe] *nm* (*jouet*) rattle.

hockey ['ɔkɛ] *nm* hockey; **h. sur glace** ice hockey.

holà! ['ɔla] *int* (*arrêtez*) hold on!, stop!; (*pour appeler*) hello!

hold-up ['ɔldœp] *nm inv* (*attaque*) hold-up.

Hollande ['ɔlɑ̃d] *nf* Holland. ● **hollandais, -aise** *a* Dutch ‖ *nmf* Dutchman, Dutchwoman; **les H.** the Dutch ‖ *nm* (*langue*) Dutch.

homard ['ɔmar] *nm* lobster.

homéopathie [ɔmeɔpati] *nf* hom(o)eopathy.

homicide [ɔmisid] *nm* murder, homicide; **h. involontaire** manslaughter.

hommage [ɔmaʒ] *nm* tribute, homage (à to); **rendre h.** à to pay tribute *ou*

homage to.

homme [ɔm] *nm* man (*pl* men); **l'h.** (*espèce*) man(kind); **des vêtements d'h.** men's clothes; **d'h.** à **h.** man to man; **l'h. de la rue** *Fig* the man in the street; **h. d'affaires** businessman. ● **h.-grenouille** *nm* (*pl* **hommes-grenouilles**) frogman.

homogène [ɔmɔʒɛn] *a* homogeneous.

homologue [ɔmɔlɔg] *nmf* counterpart, opposite number.

homologuer [ɔmɔlɔge] *vt* to approve *ou* recognize officially.

homonyme [ɔmɔnim] *nm* (*mot*) homonym; (*personne*) namesake.

homosexuel, -elle [ɔmɔsɛksɥɛl] *a* & *nmf* homosexual.

Hongrie ['ɔ̃gri] *nf* Hungary. ● **hongrois, -oise** *a* & *nmf* Hungarian ‖ *nm* (*langue*) Hungarian.

honnête [ɔnɛt] *a* honest; (*satisfaisant*) decent, fair. ● **honnêtement** *adv* honestly; decently. ● **honnêteté** *nf* honesty.

honneur [ɔnœr] *nm* (*dignité, faveur*) honour; (*mérite*) credit; **en l'h. de** in honour of; **faire h. à** (*sa famille etc*) to be a credit to; (*par sa présence*) to do honour to; (*repas*) *Fam* to do justice to; **invité d'h.** guest of honour; **avoir la place d'h.** to have the place of honour. ● **honorable** *a* honourable; (*résultat, salaire etc*) *Fig* respectable. ● **honoraire 1** *a* (*membre*) honorary. **2** *nmpl* (*d'avocat etc*) fees. ● **honorer** *vt* to honour (**de** with); **h. qn** (*conduite etc*) to do credit to s.o. ● **honorifique** *a* (*titre*) honorary.

honte ['ɔ̃t] *nf* shame; **avoir h.** to be *ou* feel ashamed (**de qch/de faire** of sth/to do, of doing); **faire h. à qn** to put s.o. to shame. ● **honteux, -euse** *a* (*confus*) ashamed; (*scandaleux*) shameful; **être h. de** to be ashamed of.

hop! ['ɔp] *int* **allez, h.!** jump!; (*pars*) off you go!

hôpital, -aux [ɔpital, -o] *nm* hospital; **à l'h.** in hospital, *Am* in the hospital.

hoquet ['ɔkɛ] *nm* hiccup; **avoir le h.** to have (the) hiccups.

horaire [ɔrɛr] a (salaire etc) hourly; (vitesse) per hour ▮ nm timetable.

horizon [ɔrizɔ̃] nm horizon; (vue, paysage) view; **à l'h.** on the horizon.

horizontal, -aux [ɔrizɔ̃tal, -o] a horizontal.

horloge [ɔrlɔ̃ʒ] nf clock. ● **horloger, -ère** nmf watchmaker. ● **horlogerie** nf watchmaker's (shop); (industrie) watchmaking.

hormis ['ɔrmi] prép Litt save, except (for).

hormone [ɔrmɔn] nf hormone.

horodateur [ɔrɔdatœr] nm pay and display ticket machine.

horoscope [ɔrɔskɔp] nm horoscope.

horreur [ɔrœr] nf horror; pl (propos) horrible things; **faire h. à** to disgust; **avoir h. de** to hate. ● **horrible** a horrible, awful. ● **horriblement** adv horribly. ● **horrifiant** a horrifying. ● **horrifié** a horrified.

hors ['ɔr] prép **h. de** (maison, boîte etc) out of, outside; (danger, haleine) Fig out of; **h. de soi** (furieux) beside oneself; **être h. jeu** Fb to be offside. ● **h.-bord** nm inv speedboat. ● **h.-concours** a inv noncompeting. ● **h.-d'œuvre** nm inv Culin hors-d'œuvre, starter. ● **h.-jeu** nm inv Fb offside. ● **h.-la-loi** nm inv outlaw. ● **h.-taxe** a inv (magasin, objet) duty free.

hortensia [ɔrtɑ̃sja] nm (arbrisseau) hydrangea.

horticulteur, -trice [ɔrtikyltœr, -tris] nmf horticulturalist. ● **horticulture** nf horticulture.

hospice [ɔspis] nm (pour vieillards) geriatric hospital; (pour malades incurables) hospice.

hospitalier, -ière [ɔspitalje, -jɛr] a **1** (accueillant) hospitable. **2** Méd personnel/etc **hospitalier** hospital staff/etc; **centre h.** hospital (complex). ● **hospitaliser** vt to hospitalize. ● **hospitalité** nf hospitality.

hostile [ɔstil] a hostile (à to, towards). ● **hostilité** nf hostility (envers to, towards); pl Mil hostilities.

hôte [ot] **1** nm (qui reçoit) host. **2** nmf (invité) guest. ● **hôtesse** nf hostess; **h. (de l'air)** (air) hostess.

hôtel [otɛl] nm hotel; **h. particulier** mansion, town house; **h. de ville** town hall, Am city hall. ● **hôtelier, -ière** nmf hotel-keeper, hotelier ▮ a **industrie/etc hôtelière** hotel industry/etc. ● **hôtellerie** nf **1** (auberge) inn, hostelry. **2** (métier) hotel trade.

hotte ['ɔt] nf **1** (panier) basket (carried on back). **2** (de cheminée etc) hood.

houblon ['ubl̃ɔ] nm **le h.** Bot hops.

houille ['uj] nf coal; **h. blanche** hydroelectric power. ● **houiller, -ère** a **bassin h.** coalfield; **industrie houillère** coal industry.

houle ['ul] nf (de mer) swell, surge. ● **houleux, -euse** a (mer) rough; (réunion etc) Fig stormy.

houppette ['upet] nf powder puff.

hourra ['ura] nm & int hurray.

housse ['us] nf (protective) cover.

houx ['u] nm holly.

hublot ['yblo] nm Nau Av porthole.

huer ['ɥe] vt to boo. ● **huées** nfpl boos.

huile [ɥil] nf oil; **peinture à l'h.** oil painting. ● **huileux, -euse** a oily.

huis [ɥi] nm **à h. clos** Jur in camera.

huissier [ɥisje] nm (introducteur) usher; (officier) Jur bailiff.

huit ['ɥit] a (['ɥi] before consonant) eight; **h. jours** a week ▮ nm eight. ● **huitaine** nf (semaine) week; **une h. (de)** about eight. ● **huitième** a & nmf eighth; **un h.** an eighth.

huître [ɥitr] nf oyster.

humain [ymɛ̃] a a human; (compatissant) humane ▮ nmpl humans. ● **humanitaire** a humanitarian. ● **humanité** nf (genre humain, sentiment) humanity.

humble [œ̃bl] a humble. ● **humblement** adv humbly.

humecter [ymɛkte] vt to moisten.

humer ['yme] vt (sentir) to smell.

humeur [ymœr] nf (caprice) mood; (caractère) temperament; (irritation) bad temper; **de bonne/mauvaise h.** in

a good/bad mood.
humide [ymid] *a* damp, wet; (*route*) wet;
(*main, yeux*) moist; **climat/temps h.**
(*chaud*) humid climate/weather;
(*froid, pluvieux*) damp *ou* wet climate/
weather. ● **humidité** *nf* humidity; (*plutôt
froide*) damp(ness).
humili/er [ymilje] *vt* to humiliate.
● **—ant** *a* humiliating. ● **humiliation** *nf*
humiliation. ● **humilité** *nf* humility.
humour [ymur] *nm* humour; **avoir de l'h.**
ou **le sens de l'h.** to have a sense of
humour. ● **humoristique** *a* (*ton etc*)
humorous.
hurl/er ['yrle] *vi* (*loup, vent*) to howl;
(*personne*) to scream, yell (out) ▮ *vt*
(*slogans, injures etc*) to scream, yell
out. ● **—ement** *nm* howl; scream, yell.
hutte ['yt] *nf* hut.
hydrater [idrate] *vt* (*peau*) to moisturize;
crème hydratante moisturizing cream.
hydraulique [idrolik] *a* hydraulic.
hydravion [idravjɔ̃] *nm* seaplane.
hydrogène [idrɔʒɛn] *nm Ch* hydrogen.
hydrophile [idrɔfil] *a* **coton h.** cotton
wool, *Am* (absorbent) cotton.
hyène [jɛn] *nf* (*animal*) hyena.

hygiaphone [iʒjafɔn] *nm* (hygienic) grill
(*for speaking through in ticket office etc*).
hygiène [iʒjɛn] *nf* hygiene. ● **hygiénique**
a hygienic; (*conditions*) sanitary; **papier
h.** toilet paper.
hymne [imn] *nm* **h. national** national
anthem.
hyper- [iper] *préf* hyper-.
hypermarché [ipermarʃe] *nm* hypermarket.
hypertension [ipertɑ̃sjɔ̃] *nf* high blood
pressure.
hypoallergénique [ipɔalerʒenik] *a* hypoallergenic.
hypnose [ipnoz] *nf* hypnosis. ● **hypnotiser** *vt* to hypnotize. ● **hypnotisme** *nm*
hypnotism.
hypocrisie [ipɔkrizi] *nf* hypocrisy. ● **hypocrite** *a* hypocritical ▮ *nmf* hypocrite.
hypothèque [ipɔtɛk] *nf* mortgage. ● **hy-
pothéquer** *vt* (*maison, avenir*) to mortgage.
hypothèse [ipɔtɛz] *nf* (*supposition*) assumption; (*en sciences*) hypothesis;
dans l'h. où... supposing (that)....
hystérie [isteri] *nf* hysteria. ● **hystérique**
a hysterical.

I

I, i [i] nm I, i.

iceberg [isberg] nm iceberg.

ici [isi] adv here; **par i.** (passer) this way; (habiter) around here; **jusqu'i.** (temps) up to now; (lieu) as far as this ou here; **d'i. peu** before long; **i. Dupont!** Tél this is Dupont!, Dupont speaking!; **je ne suis pas d'i.** I'm a stranger around here; **les gens d'i.** the people around here, the locals.

idéal, -aux ou **-als** [ideal, -o] a & nm ideal; **c'est l'i.** Fam that's the ideal thing. ● **idéaliser** vt to idealize. ● **idéaliste** a idealistic ‖ nmf idealist.

idée [ide] nf idea; **il m'est venu à l'i. que** it occurred to me that; **se faire une i. de** to imagine, get an idea of; **se faire des idées** Fam to imagine things; **avoir dans l'i. de faire** to have it in mind to do; **i. fixe** obsession.

identifier [idɑ̃tifje] vt to identify (à, avec with); **s'i.** à ou avec to identify (oneself) with. ● **identique** a identical (à to, with). ● **identité** nf identity; **carte d'i.** identity card.

idéologie [ideɔlɔʒi] nf ideology. ● **idéologique** a ideological.

idiome [idjom] nm (langue) idiom. ● **idiomatique** a idiomatic.

idiot, -ote [idjo, -ɔt] a silly, idiotic ‖ nmf idiot. ● **idiotie** [-ɔsi] nf (état) idiocy; **une i.** a silly ou an idiotic thing.

idole [idɔl] nm idol.

idylle [idil] nf (amourette) romance.

if [if] nm yew (tree).

igloo [iglu] nm igloo.

ignare [iɲar] a Péj ignorant.

ignifugé [iɲifyʒe] a fireproof(ed).

ignoble [iɲɔbl] a vile, revolting.

ignorant [iɲɔrɑ̃] a ignorant (de of). ● **ignorance** nf ignorance.

ignorer [iɲɔre] vt not to know; **j'ignore**

si I don't know if; **je n'ignore pas les difficultés** I'm not unaware of the difficulties; **i. qn** to ignore s.o.

il [il] pron m (personne) he; (chose, animal) it; **il est** he is; it is; **il pleut** it's raining; **il est vrai que** it's true that; **il y a** there is; pl there are; **il y a six ans** (temps écoulé) six years ago; **il y a une heure qu'il travaille** (durée) he has been working for an hour; **qu'est-ce qu'il y a?** what's the matter?; **il n'y a pas de quoi!** don't mention it!; **il doit/peut y avoir** there must/may be.

île [il] nf island; **les îles Britanniques** the British Isles.

illégal, -aux [ilegal, -o] a illegal.

illégitime [ileʒitim] a (enfant, revendication) illegitimate; (non fondé) unfounded.

illettré, -ée [iletre] a & nmf illiterate.

illicite [ilisit] a unlawful, illicit.

illimité [ilimite] a unlimited.

illisible [ilizibl] a (écriture) illegible; (livre) unreadable.

illuminer [ilymine] vt to light up ‖ **s'i.** vpr (visage, ciel) to light up. ● **illuminé** a (monument) floodlit. ● **illumination** nf (action, lumière) illumination.

illusion [ilyzjɔ̃] nf illusion (sur about); **se faire des illusions** to delude oneself (sur about). ● **illusionniste** nmf conjurer.

illustre [ilystr] a famous, illustrious.

illustrer [ilystre] vt (d'images, par des exemples) to illustrate (de with) ‖ **s'i.** vpr to become famous. ● **illustré** a (livre, magazine) illustrated ‖ nm (périodique) comic. ● **illustration** nf illustration.

îlot [ilo] nm **1** (île) small island. **2** (maisons) block.

ils [il] pron mpl they; **ils sont** they are.

image [imaʒ] nf picture; (ressemblance,

symbole) image; *(dans une glace)* reflection; **i. de marque** *(de firme etc)* (public) image.

imagination [imaʒinɑsjɔ̃] *nf* imagination.

imaginer [imaʒine] *vt (envisager, supposer)* to imagine; *(inventer)* to devise ▮ **s'i.** *vpr (se figurer)* to imagine (**que** that); *(se voir)* to picture oneself. ● **imaginaire** *a* imaginary.

imbattable [ɛ̃batabl] *a* unbeatable.

imbécile [ɛ̃besil] *a* idiotic ▮ *nmf* idiot. ● **imbécillité** *nf* **une i.** *(action, parole)* an idiotic thing.

imbiber [ɛ̃bibe] *vt* to soak (**de** with, in).

imbriquer (s') [ɛ̃brike] *vpr (questions etc)* to overlap, be interconnected.

imbuvable [ɛ̃byvabl] *a* undrinkable; *(personne) Fam* insufferable.

imiter [imite] *vt* to imitate; *(contrefaire)* to forge; **i. qn** *(pour rire)* to mimic s.o.; *(faire comme)* to do the same as s.o. ● **imitateur, -trice** *nmf (artiste) Th* impersonator, mimic. ● **imitation** *nf* imitation.

immaculé [imakyle] *a (sans tache, sans péché)* immaculate.

immangeable [ɛ̃mɑ̃ʒabl] *a* inedible.

immatriculer [imatrikyle] *vt* to register; **se faire i.** to register. ● **immatriculation** *nf* registration.

immédiat [imedja] *a* immediate ▮ *nm* **dans l'i.** for the time being. ● **immédiatement** *adv* immediately.

immense [imɑ̃s] *a* immense, vast. ● **immensité** *nf* immensity, vastness.

immerger [imɛrʒe] *vt* to immerse, put under water.

immeuble [imœbl] *nm* building; *(d'habitation)* block of flats, *Am* apartment building; *(de bureaux)* office building *ou* block.

immigr/er [imigre] *vi* to immigrate. ● **—é, -ée** *a & nmf* immigrant. ● **immigration** *nf* immigration.

imminent [iminɑ̃] *a* imminent.

immiscer (s') [simise] *vpr* to interfere (**dans** in).

immobile [imɔbil] *a* still, motionless. ● **immobiliser** *vt* to bring to a stop ▮ **s'i.** *vpr* to come to a stop.

immobilier, -ière [imɔbilje, -jer] *a* **vente immobilière** sale of property; **agent i.** estate agent, *Am* real estate agent.

immodéré [imɔdere] *a* immoderate.

immonde [imɔ̃d] *a* filthy.

immoral, -aux [imɔral, -o] *a* immoral.

immortel, -elle [imɔrtɛl] *a* immortal.

immuable [imɥabl] *a* unchanging.

immuniser [imynize] *vt* to immunize (**contre** against); **immunisé contre** *(à l'abri de) Méd & Fig* immune to *ou* from. ● **immunitaire** *a (déficience, système etc) Méd* immune. ● **immunité** *nf* immunity; **i. parlementaire** parliamentary immunity.

impact [ɛ̃pakt] *nm* impact (**sur** on).

impair [ɛ̃per] *a (nombre)* odd, uneven.

imparable [ɛ̃parabl] *a (coup etc)* unavoidable.

impardonnable [ɛ̃pardɔnabl] *a* unforgivable.

imparfait [ɛ̃parfɛ] **1** *a (connaissance etc)* imperfect. **2** *nm (temps) Gram* imperfect.

impartial, -aux [ɛ̃parsjal, -o] *a* fair, unbiased.

impasse [ɛ̃pas] *nf (rue)* dead end, blind alley; *(situation) Fig* stalemate, impasse; **dans l'i.** *(négociations)* in deadlock.

impassible [ɛ̃pasibl] *a* impassive, unmoved.

impatient [ɛ̃pasjɑ̃] *a* impatient; **i. de faire** eager *ou* impatient to do. ● **impatience** *nf* impatience. ● **impatienter** *vt* to annoy ▮ **s'i.** *vpr* to get impatient.

impayé [ɛ̃peje] *a* unpaid.

impeccable [ɛ̃pekabl] *a (propre)* immaculate, impeccable.

impénétrable [ɛ̃penetrabl] *a (forêt, mystère etc)* impenetrable.

impensable [ɛ̃pɑ̃sabl] *a* unthinkable.

imper [ɛ̃per] *nm Fam* raincoat, mac.

impératif, -ive [ɛ̃peratif, -iv] *a (consigne, ton)* imperative ▮ *nm Gram* imperative.

impératrice [ɛperatris] *nf* empress.

imperceptible [ɛpersɛptibl] *a* imperceptible (à to).

impérial, -aux [ɛperjal, -o] *a* imperial.

impérieux, -euse [ɛperjø, -øz] *a* (*autoritaire*) imperious; (*besoin*) pressing.

imperméable [ɛpermeabl] **1** *a* (*tissu, manteau*) waterproof. **2** *nm* raincoat, mackintosh.

impersonnel, -elle [ɛpersɔnɛl] *a* impersonal.

impertinent [ɛpertinɑ̃] *a* impertinent (envers to). ● **impertinence** *nf* impertinence.

imperturbable [ɛpertyrbabl] *a* (*personne*) unruffled.

impétueux, -euse [ɛpetɥø, -øz] *a* impetuous.

impitoyable [ɛpitwajabl] *a* ruthless, pitiless.

implacable [ɛplakabl] *a* implacable, relentless.

implanter [ɛplɑ̃te] *vt* (*industrie, mode etc*) to establish ▮ **s'i.** *vpr* to become established.

implicite [ɛplisit] *a* implicit.

impliquer [ɛplike] *vt* (*entraîner*) to imply; **i. que** (*supposer*) to imply that; **i. qn** (*engager*) to implicate s.o. (**dans** in).

implorer [ɛplɔre] *vt* to implore (**qn de faire** s.o. to do).

impoli [ɛpɔli] *a* rude, impolite. ● **impolitesse** *nf* rudeness; **une i.** an act of rudeness.

impopulaire [ɛpɔpylɛr] *a* unpopular.

important [ɛpɔrtɑ̃] *a* (*personnage, événement etc*) important; (*quantité, somme etc*) large, considerable; (*dégâts, retard*) considerable, great ▮ *nm* **l'i., c'est de...** the important thing is to.... ● **importance** *nf* importance, significance; (*taille*) size; (*de dégâts*) extent; **ça n'a pas d'i.** it doesn't matter.

importer [ɛpɔrte] **1** *v imp* to matter, be important (à to); **il importe de faire** it's important to do; **peu importe, n'importe** it doesn't matter; **n'importe qui/quoi/où/quand/comment** anyone/anything/ anywhere/any time/anyhow.

2 *vt* (*marchandises etc*) to import (**de** from). ● **importateur, -trice** *nmf* importer. ● **importation** *nf* (*objet*) import; (*action*) import(ing); **d'i.** (*article*) imported.

importuner [ɛpɔrtyne] *vt* to inconvenience, trouble.

imposer [ɛpoze] **1** *vt* **i. qch à qn** to impose sth on s.o. ▮ *vi* **en i. à qn** to impress s.o., command respect from s.o. ▮ **s'i.** *vpr* (*chez qn*) Péj to impose; (*s'affirmer*) to assert oneself; (*aller de soi*) to stand out; (*être nécessaire*) to be essential.

2 *vt* Fin to tax. ● **imposable** *a* Fin taxable.

impossible [ɛpɔsibl] *a* impossible (**à faire** to do); **il (nous) est i. de faire** it is impossible for us to do; **il est i. que** (+ *sub*) it is impossible that ▮ *nm* **faire l'i.** to do the impossible. ● **impossibilité** *nf* impossibility.

imposteur [ɛpɔstœr] *nm* impostor.

impôt [ɛpo] *nm* tax; *pl* (*contributions*) (income) tax, taxes; **i. sur le revenu** income tax; (**service des**) **impôts** tax authorities.

impotent [ɛpɔtɑ̃] *a* crippled, disabled.

impraticable [ɛpratikabl] *a* (*chemin etc*) impassable.

imprécis [ɛpresi] *a* imprecise.

imprégner [ɛpreɲe] *vt* to permeate, saturate (**de** with) ▮ **s'i.** *vpr* to become permeated *ou* saturated (**de** with); **imprégné de** (*idées*) imbued *ou* infused with.

imprenable [ɛprənabl] *a* Mil impregnable.

impresario [ɛpresarjo] *nm* (*business*) manager.

impression [ɛpresjɔ̃] *nf* **1** impression; **avoir l'i.** to have the feeling *ou* impression that; **faire bonne i. à qn** to make a good impression on s.o. **2** Typ printing.

impressionn/er [ɛpresjɔne] *vt* (*émou-*

voir) to make a strong impression on; (*influencer*) to impress. ●**—ant** *a* impressive. ●**impressionnable** *a* impressionable.

imprévisible [ɛ̃previzibl] *a* unforeseeable. ●**imprévu** *a* unexpected ‖ *nm* **en cas d'i.** in case of anything unexpected.

imprim/er [ɛ̃prime] *vt* (*livre etc*) to print; (*trace*) to impress (**dans** in). ●**—ante** *nf* (*d'ordinateur*) printer. ●**—é** *nm* (*formulaire*) printed form; **'imprimés'** (*par la poste*) 'printed matter'. ●**imprimerie** *nf* (*technique*) printing; (*lieu*) printing works, *Am* print shop. ●**imprimeur** *nm* printer.

improbable [ɛ̃prɔbabl] *a* improbable, unlikely.

impromptu [ɛ̃prɔ̃pty] *a & adv* impromptu.

impropre [ɛ̃prɔpr] *a* inappropriate; **i. à qch** unfit for sth.

improviser [ɛ̃prɔvize] *vti* to improvise.

improviste (à l') [alɛ̃prɔvist] *adv* unexpectedly; **prendre qn à l'i.** to catch s.o. unawares.

imprudent [ɛ̃prydɑ̃] *a* (*personne, action*) careless, foolish; **il est i. de** it is unwise *ou* foolish to. ●**imprudence** *nf* carelessness, foolishness; **commettre une i.** to do something foolish.

impudent [ɛ̃pydɑ̃] *a* impudent.

impudique [ɛ̃pydik] *a* lewd.

impuissant [ɛ̃pɥisɑ̃] *a* helpless; *Méd* impotent.

impulsif, -ive [ɛ̃pylsif, -iv] *a* impulsive. ●**impulsion** *nf* impulse; **donner une i. à** (*élan*) *Fig* to give an impetus *ou* impulse to.

impunément [ɛ̃pynemɑ̃] *adv* with impunity. ●**impuni** *a* unpunished.

impur [ɛ̃pyr] *a* impure. ●**impureté** *nf* impurity.

imputer [ɛ̃pyte] *vt* to attribute (**à** to).

inabordable [inabɔrdabl] *a* (*prix*) prohibitive; (*lieu*) inaccessible.

inacceptable [inaksɛptabl] *a* unacceptable.

inaccessible [inaksesibl] *a* inaccessible.

inachevé [inaʃve] *a* unfinished.

inactif, -ive [inaktif, -iv] *a* inactive. ●**inaction** *nf* inactivity, inaction.

inadapté, -ée [inadapte] *a & nmf* maladjusted (person).

inadmissible [inadmisibl] *a* unacceptable.

inadvertance (par) [parinadvertɑ̃s] *adv* inadvertently.

inaltérable [inalterabl] *a* (*matière*) that does not deteriorate; (*sentiment*) unchanging.

inanimé [inanime] *a* (*mort*) lifeless; (*évanoui*) unconscious; (*matière*) inanimate.

inanition [inanisjɔ̃] *nf* **mourir d'i.** to die of starvation.

inaperçu [inapɛrsy] *a* **passer i.** to go unnoticed.

inapplicable [inaplikabl] *a* inapplicable.

inappréciable [inapresjabl] *a* invaluable.

inapte [inapt] *a* unsuited (**à qch** to sth), inept (**à qch** at sth); *Mil* unfit ●**inaptitude** *nf* ineptitude, incapacity.

inattaquable [inatakabl] *a* unassailable.

inattendu [inatɑ̃dy] *a* unexpected.

inattentif, -ive [inatɑ̃tif, -iv] *a* inattentive, careless; **i. à** (*soucis, danger etc*) heedless of. ●**inattention** *nf* lack of attention; **dans un moment d'i.** in a moment of distraction.

inaudible [inodibl] *a* inaudible.

inaugurer [inogyre] *vt* (*politique, édifice*) to inaugurate; (*école*) to open; (*statue*) to unveil. ●**inauguration** *nf* inauguration; opening; unveiling.

inavouable [inavwabl] *a* shameful.

incalculable [ɛ̃kalkylabl] *a* incalculable.

incandescent [ɛ̃kɑ̃desɑ̃] *a* white-hot.

incapable [ɛ̃kapabl] *a* **i. de faire** unable to do, incapable of doing ‖ *nmf* (*personne*) incompetent. ●**incapacité** *nf* incapacity, inability (**de faire** to do); *Méd* disability, incapacity.

incarcérer [ɛ̃karsere] *vt* to incarcerate.

incarner [ɛ̃karne] *vt* to embody. ●**incarnation** *nf* embodiment.

incassable [ɛ̃kɑsabl] *a* unbreakable.

incendie [ɛ̃sɑ̃di] *nm* fire; **i. criminel** arson; **i. de forêt** forest fire. ● **incendiaire** *nmf* arsonist ‖ *a (bombe)* incendiary; *(paroles)* inflammatory. ● **incendier** *vt* to set fire to.

incertain [ɛ̃sɛrtɛ̃] *a* uncertain; *(temps)* unsettled; *(entreprise)* chancy; *(contour)* indistinct. ● **incertitude** *nf* uncertainty.

incessamment [ɛ̃sesamɑ̃] *adv* without delay.

incessant [ɛ̃sesɑ̃] *a* continual.

inceste [ɛ̃sɛst] *nm* incest.

inchangé [ɛ̃ʃɑ̃ʒe] *a* unchanged.

incidence [ɛ̃sidɑ̃s] *nf (influence)* effect.

incident [ɛ̃sidɑ̃] *nm* incident; *(accroc)* hitch.

incinérer [ɛ̃sinere] *vt (ordures)* to incinerate; *(cadavre)* to cremate.

inciser [ɛ̃size] *vt* to make an incision in.

incisif, -ive¹ [ɛ̃sizif, -iv] *a* incisive, sharp.

incisive² [ɛ̃siziv] *nf (dent)* incisor (tooth).

inciter [ɛ̃site] *vt* to urge *(s.o.)* **(à faire** to do).

incliner [ɛ̃kline] *vt (courber)* to bend; *(pencher)* to tilt, incline; **i. la tête** *(approuver)* to nod one's head; *(révérence)* to bow (one's head). ‖ **s'incliner** *vpr (se courber)* to bow (down); *(s'avouer vaincu)* to admit defeat; *(chemin)* to slope down; *(bateau)* to heel over. ● **inclinaison** *nf* incline, slope. ● **inclination** *nf (de tête)* nod; *(révérence)* bow; *(goût)* inclination.

incl/ure* [ɛ̃klyr] *vt* to include; *(enfermer)* to enclose. ● **—us** *a* inclusive; **du quatre jusqu'au dix mai i.** from the fourth to the tenth of May inclusive; **jusqu'à lundi i.** up to and including Monday.

incohérent [ɛ̃kɔerɑ̃] *a* incoherent.

incollable [ɛ̃kɔlabl] *a Fam* infallible, unbeatable.

incolore [ɛ̃kɔlɔr] *a* colourless; *(vernis)* clear.

incomber [ɛ̃kɔ̃be] *vi* **i. à qn** *(devoir)* to fall to s.o.

incommoder [ɛ̃kɔmɔde] *vt* to bother.

incomparable [ɛ̃kɔ̃parabl] *a* incomparable.

incompatible [ɛ̃kɔ̃patibl] *a* incompatible, inconsistent **(avec** with).

incompétent [ɛ̃kɔ̃petɑ̃] *a* incompetent.

incomplet, -ète [ɛ̃kɔ̃plɛ, -ɛt] *a* incomplete; *(fragmentaire)* scrappy, sketchy.

incompréhensible [ɛ̃kɔ̃preɑ̃sibl] *a* incomprehensible.

incompréhension [ɛ̃kɔ̃preɑ̃sjɔ̃] *nf* lack of understanding. ● **incompris, -ise** *a* misunderstood ‖ *nmf* greatly misunderstood person.

inconcevable [ɛ̃kɔ̃svabl] *a* inconceivable.

inconciliable [ɛ̃kɔ̃siljabl] *a* irreconcilable.

inconditionnel, -elle [ɛ̃kɔ̃disjɔnɛl] *a* unconditional.

inconfortable [ɛ̃kɔ̃fɔrtabl] *a* uncomfortable.

incongru [ɛ̃kɔ̃gry] *a* unseemly, incongruous.

inconnu, -ue [ɛ̃kɔny] *a* unknown **(à** to) ‖ *nmf (étranger)* stranger; *(auteur)* unknown ‖ *nf Math* unknown (quantity).

inconscient [ɛ̃kɔ̃sjɑ̃] *a* unconscious; *(imprudent)* thoughtless; **i. de qch** unaware of sth ‖ *nm* **l'i.** *Psy* the unconscious. ● **inconsciemment** [-amɑ̃] *adv* unconsciously. ● **inconscience** *nf (physique)* unconsciousness; *(irréflexion)* thoughtlessness.

inconsidéré [ɛ̃kɔ̃sidere] *a* thoughtless.

inconsolable [ɛ̃kɔ̃sɔlabl] *a* heartbroken, cut up.

inconstant [ɛ̃kɔ̃stɑ̃] *a* fickle.

incontestable [ɛ̃kɔ̃tɛstabl] *a* undeniable. ● **incontesté** *a* undisputed.

incontrôlé [ɛ̃kɔ̃trole] *a* unchecked. ● **incontrôlable** *a* unverifiable.

inconvenant [ɛ̃kɔ̃vnɑ̃] *a* improper.

inconvénient [ɛ̃kɔ̃venjɑ̃] *nm (désavantage)* drawback; *(risque)* risk; **si vous n'y voyez pas d'i.** if you have no objection(s).

incorporer [ɛ̃kɔrpɔre] *vt (introduire*

admettre) to incorporate (**dans** into); (*ingrédient*) to blend (**à** with); *Mil* to enrol, *Am* enroll.

Incorrect [ɛkɔrɛkt] *a* (*inexact*) incorrect; (*grossier*) impolite. ● **incorrection** *nf* (*faute*) impropriety, error; **une i.** (*grossièreté*) an impolite word *ou* act.

incorrigible [ɛkɔriʒibl] *a* incorrigible.

incorruptible [ɛkɔryptibl] *a* incorruptible.

incrédule [ɛkredyl] *a* incredulous. ● **incrédulité** *nf* disbelief.

incriminer [ɛkrimine] *vt* to incriminate.

incroyable [ɛkrwajabl] *a* incredible, unbelievable.

incrusté [ɛkryste] *a* **i. de** (*orné*) inlaid with.

incruster (s') [sɛkryste] *vpr* (*chez qn*) *Fam* to be difficult to get rid of, outstay one's welcome.

incubation [ɛkybasjɔ̃] *nf* incubation.

inculp/er [ɛkylpe] *vt* *Jur* to charge (**de** with). ● **—é, -ée** *nmf* **l'i.** the accused. ● **inculpation** *nf* charge.

inculquer [ɛkylke] *vt* to instil (**à** into).

inculte [ɛkylt] *a* (*terre*) uncultivated; (*personne*) uneducated.

incurable [ɛkyrabl] *a* incurable.

incursion [ɛkyrsjɔ̃] *nf* incursion.

incurver [ɛkyrve] *vt* to curve.

Inde [ɛd] *nf* India.

indécent [ɛdesɑ̃] *a* indecent.

indéchiffrable [ɛdeʃifrabl] *a* undecipherable.

indécis [ɛdesi] *a* (*hésitant*) undecided; (*de tempérament*) indecisive; (*résultat, victoire*) undecided.

indéfendable [ɛdefɑ̃dabl] *a* undefensible.

indéfini [ɛdefini] *a* (*indéterminé*) indefinite; (*imprécis*) undefined; **article i.** *Gram* indefinite article. ● **indéfiniment** *adv* indefinitely. ● **indéfinissable** *a* indefinable.

indéformable [ɛdeformabl] *a* (*vêtement*) which keeps its shape.

indélébile [ɛdelebil] *a* (*encre, souvenir*) indelible.

indélicat [ɛdelika] *a* (*grossier*) indelicate; (*malhonnête*) unscrupulous.

indemne [ɛdɛmn] *a* unhurt.

indemniser [ɛdɛmnize] *vt* to indemnify, compensate (**de** for). ● **indemnité** *nf* (*dédommagement*) compensation; (*allocation*) allowance.

indéniable [ɛdenjabl] *a* undeniable.

indépendant [ɛdepɑ̃dɑ̃] *a* independent (**de** of); (*chambre*) self-contained; (*journaliste*) freelance. ● **indépendance** *nf* independence.

indescriptible [ɛdeskriptibl] *a* indescribable.

indésirable [ɛdezirabl] *a* & *nmf* undesirable.

indestructible [ɛdestryktibl] *a* indestructible.

indéterminé [ɛdetermine] *a* indeterminate. ● **indétermination** *nf* (*doute*) indecision.

index [ɛdeks] *nm* (*doigt*) index finger, forefinger; (*liste*) index.

indexer [ɛdekse] *vt* *Écon* to index-link (**sur** to).

indicateur, -trice [ɛdikatœr, -tris] **1** *nm* *Rail* guide, timetable; *Tech* indicator, gauge. **2** *a* **poteau i.** signpost; **panneau i.** road sign.

indicatif, -ive [ɛdikatif -iv] **1** *a* indicative (**de** of) ▮ *nm* (*à la radio*) signature tune; (*téléphonique*) dialling code, *Am* area code. **2** *nm* *Gram* indicative.

indication [ɛdikasjɔ̃] *nf* (*renseignement*) (piece of) information; **indications** (*pour aller quelque part*) directions.

indice [ɛdis] *nm* (*dans une enquête*) clue; (*des prix*) index; (*de salaire*) grade; **i. d'écoute** *TV Rad* rating.

indien, -ienne [ɛdjɛ̃, -jɛn] *a* & *nmf* Indian.

indifférent [ɛdiferɑ̃] *a* indifferent (**à** to). ● **indifférence** *nf* indifference (**à** to).

indigène [ɛdiʒɛn] *a* & *nmf* native.

indigent [ɛdiʒɑ̃] *a* (very) poor.

indigeste [ɛdiʒɛst] *a* indigestible. ● **indigestion** *nf* (attack of) indigestion.

indigne [ɛdiɲ] *a* (*personne*) unworthy; **i.**

de qn/qch unworthy of s.o./sth.

indigner [ɛ̃diɲe] vt i. qn to make s.o. indignant **‖ s'i.** vpr to be ou become indignant (**de** at). ● **indignation** nf indignation.

indiqu/er [ɛ̃dike] vt (montrer) to show, indicate; (dire) to tell, point out; **i. du doigt** to point to ou at. ●—**é** a (heure) appointed; (conseillé) recommended; (adéquat) appropriate.

indirect [ɛ̃dirɛkt] a indirect. ●—**ement** [-əmã] adv indirectly.

indiscipliné [ɛ̃disipline] a unruly.

indiscret, -ète [ɛ̃diskrɛ, -ɛt] a (curieux) Péj inquisitive, prying; (indélicat) indiscreet, tactless. ● **indiscrétion** nf indiscretion.

indiscutable [ɛ̃diskytabl] a indisputable.

indispensable [ɛ̃dispɑ̃sabl] a essential.

indisposé [ɛ̃dispoze] a (malade) unwell, indisposed. ● **indisposition** nf indisposition.

indissoluble [ɛ̃disɔlybl] a (liens etc) solid.

indistinct, -incte [ɛ̃distɛ̃(kt), -ɛ̃kt] a unclear, indistinct.

individu [ɛ̃dividy] nm individual. ● **individualiste** a individualistic **‖** nmf individualist. ● **individuel, -elle** a individual.

Indochine [ɛ̃dɔʃin] nf Indo-China.

indolent [ɛ̃dɔlɑ̃] a indolent.

indolore [ɛ̃dɔlɔr] a painless.

indomptable [ɛ̃dɔ̃tabl] a (volonté) indomitable.

Indonésie [ɛ̃dɔnezi] nf Indonesia.

indue [ɛ̃dy] af **à une heure i.** at an ungodly hour.

induire* [ɛ̃dɥir] vt **i. qn en erreur** to lead s.o. astray.

indulgent [ɛ̃dylʒɑ̃] a indulgent (**envers** to, **avec** with). ● **indulgence** nf indulgence.

industrie [ɛ̃dystri] nf industry. ● **industrialisé** a industrialized. ● **industriel, -elle** a industrial **‖** nm industrialist.

inébranlable [inebrɑ̃labl] a (certitude, personne) unshakeable, unwavering.

inédit [inedi] a (texte) unpublished;

(nouveau) Fig original.

inefficace [inefikas] a (mesure etc) ineffective, ineffectual; (personne) inefficient.

inégal, -aux [inegal, -o] a unequal; (sol, humeur) uneven. ● **inégalable** a incomparable. ● **inégalité** nf (injustice) inequality; (physique) difference; (irrégularité) unevenness.

inéluctable [inelyktabl] a inescapable.

inepte [inɛpt] a absurd, inept.

inépuisable [inepɥizabl] a inexhaustible.

inerte [inɛrt] a inert; (corps) lifeless.

inespéré [inespere] a unhoped-for.

inestimable [inestimabl] a priceless.

inévitable [inevitabl] a inevitable, unavoidable.

inexact [inɛgzakt] a (erroné) inaccurate, inexact; **c'est i.!** it's incorrect! ● **inexactitude** nf inaccuracy; (manque de ponctualité) lack of punctuality.

inexcusable [inɛkskyzabl] a inexcusable.

inexistant [inɛgzistɑ̃] a non-existent.

inexorable [inɛgzɔrabl] a inexorable.

inexpérience [inɛksperjɑ̃s] nf inexperience. ● **inexpérimenté** a (personne) inexperienced.

inexplicable [inɛksplikabl] a inexplicable. ● **inexpliqué** a unexplained.

inexprimable [inɛksprimabl] a beyond words, inexpressible.

inextricable [inɛkstrikabl] a inextricable.

infaillible [ɛ̃fajibl] a infallible.

infaisable [ɛ̃fəzabl] a (travail etc) that cannot be done.

infamant [ɛ̃famɑ̃] a ignominious.

infâme [ɛ̃fɑm] a (odieux) vile, infamous; (taudis) squalid.

infanterie [ɛ̃fɑ̃tri] nf infantry.

infantile [ɛ̃fɑ̃til] a infantile.

infarctus [ɛ̃farktys] nm **un i.** Méd a coronary.

infatigable [ɛ̃fatigabl] a tireless.

infect [ɛ̃fɛkt] a (odeur) foul; (café etc) vile.

infecter [ɛ̃fɛkte] **1** vt (air) to contaminate. **2** vt Méd to infect ▮ **s'i.** vpr to get infected. ● **infectieux, -euse** a infectious. ● **infection** nf **1** Méd infection. **2** (odeur) stench.

inférieur, -eure [ɛ̃ferjœr] a (partie) lower; (qualité etc) inferior; **à l'étage i.** on the floor below; **i. à** inferior to; (plus petit que) smaller than. ● **infériorité** nf inferiority.

infernal, -aux [ɛ̃fernal, -o] a infernal.

infesté [ɛ̃feste] a (de requins/fourmis/ etc) shark/ant/etc -infested.

infidèle [ɛ̃fidɛl] a unfaithful (à to). ● **infidélité** nf unfaithfulness; **une i.** (acte) an infidelity.

infiltrer (s') [sɛ̃filtre] vpr (liquide) to seep (through) (**dans** into); (lumière) to filter (through) (**dans** into); **s'i. dans** (groupe, esprit) Fig to infiltrate.

infime [ɛ̃fim] a (très petit) tiny.

infini [ɛ̃fini] a infinite ▮ nm Math Phot infinity; Phil infinite; **à l'i.** (beaucoup) endlessly; Math to infinity. ● **infiniment** adv infinitely; (regretter, remercier) very much. ● **infinité** nf **une i. de** an infinite amount of.

infinitif [ɛ̃finitif] nm Gram infinitive.

infirme [ɛ̃firm] a & nmf disabled (person). ● **infirmité** nf disability.

infirmer [ɛ̃firme] vt to invalidate.

infirmerie [ɛ̃firməri] nf sick room, sickbay. ● **infirmier** nm male nurse. ● **infirmière** nf nurse.

inflammable [ɛ̃flamabl] a (in)flammable.

inflammation [ɛ̃flamasjɔ̃] nf Méd inflammation.

inflation [ɛ̃flasjɔ̃] nf Écon inflation.

infléchir [ɛ̃fleʃir] vt (courber) to inflect, bend; (modifier) to shift.

inflexible [ɛ̃fleksibl] a inflexible.

infliger [ɛ̃fliʒe] vt to inflict (à on); (amende) to impose (à on).

influence [ɛ̃flyɑ̃s] nf influence. ● **influencer** vt to influence. ● **influençable** a easily influenced. ● **influent** a influential.

information [ɛ̃fɔrmasjɔ̃] nf information; (nouvelle) piece of news; **les informa-** tions the news.

informatique [ɛ̃fɔrmatik] nf (science) computer science; (technique) data processing. ● **informaticien, -ienne** nmf computer scientist. ● **informatiser** vt to computerize.

informe [ɛ̃fɔrm] a shapeless.

informer [ɛ̃fɔrme] vt to inform (**de** of, about; **que** that) ▮ **s'i.** vpr to inquire (**de** about; **si** if, whether).

infortuné [ɛ̃fɔrtyne] a ill-fated, hapless.

infraction [ɛ̃fraksjɔ̃] nf (délit) offence, Am offense; **i. à** breach of.

infranchissable [ɛ̃frɑ̃ʃisabl] a (mur, fleuve) impassable.

infructueux, -euse [ɛ̃fryktɥø, -øz] a fruitless.

infusion [ɛ̃fyzjɔ̃] nf (tisane) herb ou herbal tea.

ingénier (s') [sɛ̃ʒenje] vpr to exercise one's wits (**à faire** in order to do).

ingénieur [ɛ̃ʒenjœr] nm engineer; **femme i.** woman engineer. ● **ingénierie** [-iri] nf engineering; **i. mécanique** mechanical engineering.

ingénieux, -euse [ɛ̃ʒenjø, -øz] a ingenious. ● **ingéniosité** nf ingenuity.

ingénu [ɛ̃ʒeny] a artless, naïve.

ingérer (s') [sɛ̃ʒere] vpr to interfere (**dans** in). ● **ingérence** nf interference.

ingrat [ɛ̃gra] a (personne) ungrateful (envers to); (tâche) thankless; (âge) awkward. ● **ingratitude** nf ingratitude.

ingrédient [ɛ̃gredjɑ̃] nm ingredient.

inhabitable [inabitabl] a uninhabitable. ● **inhabité** a uninhabited.

inhabituel, -elle [inabitɥɛl] a unusual.

inhalation [inalasjɔ̃] nf inhalation; **faire des inhalations** to inhale.

inhérent [inerɑ̃] a inherent (à in).

inhibé [inibe] a inhibited.

inhospitalier, -ière [inɔspitalje, -jɛr] a inhospitable.

inhumain [inymɛ̃] a (cruel) inhuman.

inhumer [inyme] vt to bury. ● **inhumation** nf burial.

inimaginable [inimaʒinabl] a unimaginable.

inimitable [inimitabl] *a* inimitable.

inimitié [inimitje] *nf* enmity.

ininflammable [inɛ̃flamabl] *a* (*tissu etc*) non-flammable.

inintelligible [inɛ̃teliʒibl] *a* unintelligible.

inintéressant [inɛ̃teresɑ̃] *a* uninteresting.

ininterrompu [inɛ̃terɔ̃py] *a* continuous.

initial, -aux [inisjal, -o] *a* initial. ● **initiale** *nf* (*lettre*) initial.

initiative [inisjativ] *nf* 1 initiative. 2 **syndicat d'i.** tourist office.

initier [inisje] *vt* to initiate (à into); **s'i. à** (*art, science*) to become acquainted with *ou* initiated into. ● **Initiation** *nf* initiation.

injecter [ɛ̃ʒekte] *vt* to inject; **injecté de sang** bloodshot. ● **injection** *nf* injection.

injure [ɛ̃ʒyr] *nf* insult; *pl* abuse, insults. ● **injurier** *vt* to insult, abuse. ● **injurieux, -euse** *a* abusive, insulting (**pour** to).

injuste [ɛ̃ʒyst] *a* (*contraire à la justice*) unjust; (*non équitable*) unfair. ● **injustice** *nf* injustice.

injustifiable [ɛ̃ʒystifjabl] *a* unjustifiable. ● **injustifié** *a* unjustified.

inlassable [ɛ̃lasabl] *a* untiring.

inné [ine] *a* innate, inborn.

innocent, -ente [inɔsɑ̃, -ɑ̃t] *a* innocent (**de** of) ● *nmf* *Jur* innocent person. ● **innocence** *nf* innocence. ● **innocenter** *vt* **i. qn** to clear s.o. (**de** of).

innombrable [inɔ̃brabl] *a* countless.

innommable [inɔmabl] *a* unspeakable, foul.

innover [inɔve] *vi* to innovate. ● **innovation** *nf* innovation.

inoccupé [inɔkype] *a* unoccupied.

inoculer [inɔkyle] *vt* **i. qch à qn** to infect *ou* inoculate s.o. with sth.

inodore [inɔdɔr] *a* odourless.

inoffensif, -ive [inɔfɑ̃sif, -iv] *a* harmless, inoffensive.

inonder [inɔ̃de] *vt* to flood; (*mouiller*) to soak; **inondé de soleil** bathed in sunlight. ● **inondation** *nf* flood; (*action*) flooding (**de** of).

inopiné [inɔpine] *a* unexpected.

inopportun [inɔpɔrtœ̃] *a* inopportune.

inoubliable [inublijabl] *a* unforgettable.

inouï [inwi] *a* incredible, extraordinary.

inox [inɔks] *nm* stainless steel; **couteau**/ *etc* **en i.** stainless-steel knife/*etc*. ● **inoxydable** *a* **acier i.** stainless steel.

inqualifiable [ɛ̃kalifjabl] *a* (*indigne*) unspeakable.

inquiet, -iète [ɛ̃kjɛ, -jɛt] *a* worried, anxious (**de** about).

inquiéter [ɛ̃kjete] *vt* (*préoccuper*) to worry; (*police*) to bother, harass (*suspect etc*) ● **s'i.** *vpr* to worry (**de** about). ● **inquiétant** *a* worrying.

inquiétude [ɛ̃kjetyd] *nf* worry, anxiety; **donner de l'i. à qn** to give s.o. cause for concern.

insaisissable [ɛ̃sezisabl] *a* elusive.

insalubre [ɛ̃salybr] *a* unhealthy.

insanités [ɛ̃sanite] *nfpl* (*idioties*) absurdities.

insatiable [ɛ̃sasjabl] *a* insatiable.

insatisfait [ɛ̃satisfɛ] *a* unsatisfied, dissatisfied.

inscrire* [ɛ̃skrir] *vt* to write *ou* put down; (*sur un registre*) to register; (*graver*) to inscribe; **i. qn** to enrol s.o., *Am* enroll s.o. ● **s'i.** *vpr* to put one's name down; **s'i. à** (*club, parti*) to join; (*examen*) to enrol *ou Am* enroll for, register for. ● **inscription** *nf* enrolment, *Am* enrollment, registration; (*sur écriteau etc*) inscription; **frais d'i.** *Univ* tuition fees.

insecte [ɛ̃sekt] *nm* insect. ● **insecticide** *nm* & *a* insecticide.

insécurité [ɛ̃sekyrite] *nf* insecurity.

insémination [ɛ̃seminasjɔ̃] *nf* **i. artificielle** *Méd* artificial insemination.

insensé [ɛ̃sɑ̃se] *a* senseless, absurd.

insensible [ɛ̃sɑ̃sibl] *a* (*indifférent*) insensitive (à to); (*graduel*) imperceptible, very slight. ● **insensibilité** *nf* insensitivity.

inséparable [ɛ̃separabl] *a* inseparable (**de** from).

insérer [ɛ̃sere] *vt* to insert (**dans** into,

in); **s'i. dans** (*société, groupe*) to become accepted by.

insidieux, -euse [ɛsidjø, -øz] *a* insidious.

insigne [ɛsiɲ] *nm* badge, emblem; *pl* (*de maire etc*) insignia.

insignifiant [ɛsiɲifjɑ̃] *a* insignificant.

insinuer [ɛsinɥe] *vt Péj* to insinuate (**que** that). ● **insinuation** *nf* insinuation.

insipide [ɛsipid] *a* insipid.

insister [ɛsiste] *vi* to insist (**pour faire** on doing); (*persévérer*) *Fam* to persevere; **i. sur** (*détail, syllabe etc*) to stress; **i. pour que** (+ *sub*) to insist that. ● **insistance** *nf* insistence, persistence.

insolation [ɛsɔlasjɔ̃] *nf Méd* sunstroke.

insolent [ɛsɔlɑ̃] *a* (*impoli*) insolent; (*luxe*) indecent. ● **insolence** *nf* insolence.

insolite [ɛsɔlit] *a* unusual, strange.

insoluble [ɛsɔlybl] *a* insoluble.

insolvable [ɛsɔlvabl] *a Fin* insolvent.

insomnie [ɛsɔmni] *nf* insomnia; *pl* (periods of) insomnia; **nuit d'i.** sleepless night.

insondable [ɛsɔ̃dabl] *a* unfathomable.

insonoriser [ɛsɔnɔrize] *vt* to sound-proof.

insouciant [ɛsusjɑ̃] *a* carefree.

insoumis [ɛsumi] *a* rebellious.

insoupçonnable [ɛsupsɔnabl] *a* beyond suspicion. ● **insoupçonné** *a* unsuspected.

insoutenable [ɛsutnabl] *a* unbearable; (*théorie*) untenable.

inspecter [ɛspɛkte] *vt* to inspect. ● **inspecteur, -trice** *nmf* inspector. ● **inspection** *nf* inspection.

inspirer [ɛspire] **1** *vt* to inspire; **i. qch à qn** to inspire s.o. with sth; **s'i. de** to take one's inspiration from. **2** *vi Méd* to breathe in. ● **inspiration** *nf* **1** inspiration. **2** *Méd* breathing in.

instable [ɛstabl] *a* (*meuble*) shaky, unsteady; (*temps*) unsettled; (*caractère, situation*) unstable.

installer [ɛstale] *vt* (*appareil, meuble etc*) to install, put in; (*étagère*) to put up;

(*équiper*) to fit out, fix up; **i. qn** (*dans une fonction, un logement*) to install s.o. **▮ s'installer** *vpr* (*s'asseoir, s'établir*) to settle (down); (*médecin etc*) to set oneself up; **s'i. dans** (*maison*) to move into. ● **installation** *nf* putting in; fitting out; moving in; *pl* (*appareils*) fittings, installations; (*bâtiments*) facilities.

instance [ɛstɑ̃s] *nf* **tribunal de première i.** = magistrates' court; **en i. de divorce** waiting for a divorce; **en i. de départ** about to depart.

instant [ɛstɑ̃] *nm* moment, instant; **à l'i.** a moment ago; **pour l'i.** for the moment. ● **instantané** *a* instantaneous; **café i.** instant coffee **▮** *nm* snapshot.

instaurer [ɛstɔre] *vt* to found, set up.

instigateur, -trice [ɛstigatœr, -tris] *nmf* instigator.

instinct [ɛstɛ̃] *nm* instinct; **d'i.** instinctively. ● **instinctif, -ive** *a* instinctive.

instituer [ɛstitɥe] *vt* (*règle, régime*) to establish.

institut [ɛstity] *nm* institute; **i. de beauté** beauty salon; **i. universitaire de technologie** polytechnic, technical college.

instituteur, -trice [ɛstitytœr, -tris] *nmf* primary *ou Am* elementary school teacher.

institution [ɛstitysjɔ̃] *nf* (*organisation etc*) institution; *Scol* private school.

instructif, -ive [ɛstryktif, -iv] *a* instructive.

instruction [ɛstryksjɔ̃] *nf* education, schooling; *Mil* training; *Jur* investigation; *pl* (*ordres*) instructions.

instruire* [ɛstrɥir] *vt* to teach, educate; *Mil* to train; *Jur* to investigate **▮ s'i.** *vpr* to educate oneself. ● **instruit** *a* educated.

instrument [ɛstrymɑ̃] *nm* instrument; (*outil*) implement.

insu de (à l') [alɛsyd(ə)] *prép* without the knowledge of.

insuffisant [ɛsyfizɑ̃] *a* (*en qualité*) inadequate; (*en quantité*) inadequate, insufficient. ● **insuffisance** *nf* inadequacy.

insulaire [ɛsyler] *a* insular **▮** *nmf* islander.

insuline [ɛ̃sylin] nf Méd insulin.

insulte [ɛ̃sylt] nf insult (à to). ● **insulter** vt to insult.

insupportable [ɛ̃sypɔrtabl] a unbearable.

insurger (s') [sɛ̃syrʒe] vpr to rise (up), rebel (**contre** against). ● **insurrection** nf uprising.

insurmontable [ɛ̃syrmɔ̃tabl] a insurmountable, insuperable.

intact [ɛ̃takt] a intact.

intangible [ɛ̃tãʒibl] a intangible.

intarissable [ɛ̃tarisabl] a inexhaustible.

intégral, -aux [ɛ̃tegral, -o] a full, complete; (édition) unabridged. ● **intégralement** adv in full, fully. ● **intégralité** nf whole (the of); **dans son i.** in full.

intègre [ɛ̃tɛgr] a upright, honest. ● **intégrité** nf integrity.

intégrer [ɛ̃tegre] vt to integrate (**dans** in) ‖ **s'i.** vpr to become integrated, adapt. ● **intégrante** af **faire partie i. de** to be part and parcel of.

intellectuel, -elle [ɛ̃telektɥel] a & nmf intellectual.

intelligent [ɛ̃teliʒã] a intelligent, clever. ● **intelligemment** [-amã] adv intelligently. ● **intelligence** nf intelligence.

intelligible [ɛ̃teliʒibl] a intelligible.

intempéries [ɛ̃tãperi] nfpl **les i.** bad weather.

intempestif, -ive [ɛ̃tãpestif, -iv] a untimely.

intenable [ɛ̃t(ə)nabl] a (position) untenable; (enfant) unruly, uncontrollable.

intendant, -ante [ɛ̃tãdã, -ãt] nmf Scol bursar. ● **intendance** nf Scol bursar's office.

intense [ɛ̃tãs] a intense; (trafic) heavy. ● **intensif, -ive** a intensive.

intensifier [ɛ̃tãsifje] vt, **s'i.** vpr to intensify.

intensité [ɛ̃tãsite] nf intensity.

intenter [ɛ̃tãte] vt **i. un procès à qn** Jur to institute proceedings against s.o.

intention [ɛ̃tãsjɔ̃] nf intention; **avoir l'i. de faire** to intend to do; **à l'i. de qn** for s.o. ● **intentionné a bien i.** well-intentioned.

inter- [ɛ̃ter] préf inter-.

interactif, -ive [ɛ̃teraktif, -iv] a Ordinat interactive.

intercalaire [ɛ̃terkaler] a & nm (**feuille) i.** (dans un classeur) divider.

intercaler [ɛ̃terkale] vt to insert.

intercepter [ɛ̃tersepte] vt to intercept.

interchangeable [ɛ̃terʃãʒabl] a interchangeable.

interclasse [ɛ̃terklas] nm Scol break (between classes).

intercontinental, -aux [ɛ̃terkɔ̃tinãtal, -o] a intercontinental.

interd/ire* [ɛ̃terdir] vt to forbid, not to allow (**qch à qn** s.o. sth); (film etc) to ban; **i. à qn de faire** (médecin, père etc) not to allow s.o. to do, forbid s.o. to do; (santé etc) to prevent s.o. from doing. ● —**It** a forbidden, not allowed; **il est i. de** it is forbidden to; **'stationnement i.'** 'no parking'. ● **interdiction** nf ban (**de** on); **'i. de fumer'** 'no smoking'.

intéress/er [ɛ̃terese] vt to interest; **s'i.** à to take an interest in, be interested in. ● —**ant** a (captivant) interesting; (prix etc) attractive. ● —**é, -ée** a (avide) self-interested; (concerné) concerned.

intérêt [ɛ̃terɛ] nm interest; Péj self-interest; pl Fin interest; **tu as i. à faire** you'd do well to do.

interface [ɛ̃terfas] nf Ordinat interface.

intérieur [ɛ̃terjœr] a (cour, paroi) inner, interior; (poche) inside; (politique, vol) internal, domestic; (vie, sentiment) inner, inward; (mer) inland.
‖ nm (de boîte etc) inside (**de** of); (de maison) interior, inside; (de pays) interior; **à l'i. (de)** inside; **ministère de l'I.** Home Office, Am Department of the Interior. ● **intérieurement** adv (dans le cœur) inwardly.

intérim [ɛ̃terim] nm **assurer l'i.** to deputize (**de** for); **président/etc par i.** acting president/etc. ● **intérimaire** a temporary.

interligne [ɛ̃terliɲ] nm Typ space (between the lines), spacing.

interlocuteur, -trice [ɛterlɔkytœr, -tris] *nmf Pol* negotiator; **mon i.** the person I am, was *etc* speaking to.

interloqué [ɛterlɔke] *a* dumbfounded.

interlude [ɛterlyd] *nm Mus TV* interlude.

intermède [ɛtermed] *nm* (*interruption*) & *Th* interlude.

intermédiaire [ɛtermedjer] *a* intermediate ▌*nmf* intermediary; **par l'i. de** through (the medium of).

interminable [ɛterminabl] *a* endless.

intermittence [ɛtermitãs] *nf* **par i.** intermittently.

international, -aux [ɛternasjɔnal, -o] *a* international ▌*nm* (*joueur*) *Sp* international.

interne [ɛtern] **1** *a* (*douleur etc*) internal; (*oreille*) inner. **2** *nmf* (*élève*) boarder; **i. (des hôpitaux)** houseman, *Am* intern. ● **internat** *nm* (*école*) boarding school.

interner [ɛterne] *vt* (*prisonnier*) to intern; (*aliéné*) to confine.

interpeller [ɛterpele] *vt* (*appeler*) to shout at *ou* to; (*dans une réunion*) to question; (*police*) *Jur* to take in for questioning.

interphone [ɛterfɔn] *nm* intercom.

interplanétaire [ɛterplaneter] *a* interplanetary.

interposer (s') [sɛterpoze] *vpr* (*dans une dispute etc*) to intervene (**dans** in).

interprète [ɛterpret] *nmf Ling* interpreter; (*chanteur*) singer; *Th Mus* performer. ● **interpréter** *vt* (*expliquer*) to interpret; (*chanter*) to sing; (*jouer*) *Th* to play, perform; (*exécuter*) *Mus* to perform.

interroger [ɛterɔʒe] *vt* to question. ● **interrogatif, -ive** *a* & *nm Gram* interrogative. ● **interrogation** *nf* question; (*action*) questioning; (*épreuve*) *Scol* test. ● **interrogatoire** *nm Jur* interrogation.

interrompre* [ɛterɔ̃pr] *vt* to interrupt, break off; **i. qn** to interrupt s.o. ▌**s'i.** *vpr* (*personne*) to break off, stop. ● **inter-**

rupteur *nm* (*électrique*) switch. ● **interruption** *nf* interruption; (*des hostilités, du courant*) break (**de** in).

intersection [ɛterseksjɔ̃] *nf* intersection.

interstice [ɛterstis] *nm* crack, chink.

interurbain [ɛteryrbɛ̃] *a* & *nm* (**téléphone**) **i.** long-distance telephone service.

intervalle [ɛterval] *nm* (*écart*) gap, space; (*temps*) interval; **dans l'i.** (*entretemps*) in the meantime.

intervenir* [ɛtervənir] *vi* (*s'interposer, agir*) to intervene; (*survenir*) to occur; **être intervenu** (*accord*) to be reached. ● **intervention** *nf* intervention; **i. (chirurgicale)** operation.

intervertir [ɛtervertir] *vt* to invert.

interview [ɛtervju] *nf* (*d'un journaliste etc*) interview. ● **interviewer** [-vjuve] *vt* to interview.

intestin [ɛtestɛ̃] *nm* bowel. ● **intestinal, -aux** *a* intestinal; **grippe intestinale** gastric flu.

intime [ɛtim] *a* intimate; (*ami*) close; (*vie, journal, mariage*) private ▌*nmf* close friend. ● **intimité** *nf* intimacy; privacy; **dans l'i.** (*mariage etc*) in private.

intimider [ɛtimide] *vt* to intimidate, frighten.

intituler [ɛtityle] *vt* to entitle ▌**s'i.** *vpr* to be entitled.

intolérable [ɛtɔlerabl] *a* intolerable (**que** (+ *sub*) that). ● **intolérance** *nf* intolerance.

intonation [ɛtɔnasjɔ̃] *nf Ling* intonation; (*ton*) tone.

intoxiquer [ɛtɔksike] *vt* (*empoisonner*) to poison; *Psy Pol* to brainwash ▌**s'i.** *vpr* to be *ou* become poisoned. ● **intoxication** *nf* poisoning; *Psy Pol* brainwashing; **i. alimentaire** food poisoning.

intraduisible [ɛtradɥizibl] *a* difficult to translate.

intraitable [ɛtretabl] *a* uncompromising.

intransigeant [ɛtrãziʒã] *a* intransigent.

intransitif, -ive [ɛtrãzitif, -iv] *a* & *nm Gram* intransitive.

intraveineux, -euse [ɛ̃travenø, -øz] *a* *Méd* intravenous.

intrépide [ɛ̃trepid] *a* (*courageux*) fearless, intrepid.

intrigue [ɛ̃trig] *nf* intrigue; (*de film, roman etc*) plot. ● **intriguer 1** *vi* to scheme, intrigue. **2** *vt* **i. qn** (*intéresser*) to intrigue s.o.

intrinsèque [ɛ̃trɛ̃sɛk] *a* intrinsic.

introduire* [ɛ̃trɔdɥir] *vt* (*présenter*) to introduce, bring in; (*insérer*) to put in (**dans** to), insert (**dans** into); (*faire entrer*) to show (*s.o.*) in; **s'i. dans** to get into. ● **introduction** *nf* (*texte, action*) introduction.

introuvable [ɛ̃truvabl] *a* nowhere to be found.

introverti, -ie [ɛ̃trɔvɛrti] *nmf* introvert.

intrus, -use [ɛ̃try, -yz] *nmf* intruder. ● **intrusion** *nf* intrusion (**dans** into).

intuition [ɛ̃tɥisjɔ̃] *nf* intuition.

inusable [inyzabl] *a* *Fam* hard-wearing, durable.

inusité [inyzite] *a* *Gram* unused.

inutile [inytil] *a* useless, unnecessary. ● **—ment** *adv* (*vainement*) needlessly.

inutilisable [inytilizabl] *a* unusable.

invaincu [ɛ̃vɛ̃ky] *a* *Sp* unbeaten.

invalide [ɛ̃valid] *a* & *nmf* disabled (person); **i. de guerre** disabled ex-soldier.

invalider [ɛ̃valide] *vt* to invalidate.

invariable [ɛ̃varjabl] *a* invariable.

invasion [ɛ̃vazjɔ̃] *nf* invasion.

invective [ɛ̃vɛktiv] *nf* invective.

invendable [ɛ̃vɑ̃dabl] *a* unsaleable. ● **invendu** *a* unsold.

inventaire [ɛ̃vɑ̃tɛr] *nm* (*liste*) *Com* inventory; **faire l'i.** *Com* to do the stock-taking.

inventer [ɛ̃vɑ̃te] *vt* (*créer*) to invent; (*imaginer*) to make up. ● **inventeur, -trice** *nmf* inventor. ● **inventif, -ive** *a* inventive. ● **invention** *nf* invention.

inverse [ɛ̃vɛrs] *a* (*sens*) opposite; (*ordre*) reverse; *Math* inverse ▌ *nm* **l'i.** the reverse, the opposite. ● **inversement** *adv* conversely. ● **inverser** *vt* (*ordre*)

to reverse. ● **inversion** *nf* *Gram etc* inversion.

investigation [ɛ̃vɛstigasjɔ̃] *nf* investigation.

invest/ir [ɛ̃vɛstir] **1** *vti* *Com* to invest (**dans** in). **2** *vt* **i. qn de** (*fonction etc*) to invest s.o. with. ● **—issement** *nm* *Com* investment. ● **investiture** *nf* *Pol* nomination.

invétéré [ɛ̃vetere] *a* inveterate.

invincible [ɛ̃vɛ̃sibl] *a* invincible.

invisible [ɛ̃vizibl] *a* invisible.

invit/er [ɛ̃vite] *vt* to invite; **i. qn à faire** to invite *ou* ask s.o. to do; (*inciter*) to tempt s.o. to do; **s'i.** (*chez qn*) to gatecrash. ● **—é, -ée** *nmf* guest. ● **invitation** *nf* invitation.

invivable [ɛ̃vivabl] *a* unbearable.

involontaire [ɛ̃vɔlɔ̃tɛr] *a* (*geste etc*) unintentional.

invoquer [ɛ̃vɔke] *vt* (*argument etc*) to put forward; (*appeler*) to call upon.

invraisemblable [ɛ̃vrɛsɑ̃blabl] *a* incredible; (*improbable*) improbable.

invulnérable [ɛ̃vylnerabl] *a* invulnerable.

iode [jɔd] *nm* **teinture d'i.** (*antiseptique*) iodine.

ira, irai(t) [ira, irɛ] *voir* aller[1].

Irak [irak] *nm* Iraq. ● **irakien, -ienne** *a* & *nmf* Iraqi.

Iran [irɑ̃] *nm* Iran. ● **iranien, -ienne** *a* & *nmf* Iranian.

iris [iris] *nm* *Anat Bot* iris.

Irlande [irlɑ̃d] *nf* Ireland. ● **irlandais, -aise** *a* Irish ▌ *nmf* Irishman, Irishwoman; **les I.** the Irish ▌ *nm* (*langue*) Irish.

ironie [irɔni] *nf* irony. ● **ironique** *a* ironic(al).

iront [irɔ̃] *voir* aller[1].

irradier [iradje] *vt* to irradiate.

irraisonné [irɛzɔne] *a* irrational.

irréconciliable [irekɔ̃siljabl] *a* irreconcilable.

irréel, -elle [ireɛl] *a* unreal.

irréfléchi [irefleʃi] *a* thoughtless.

irréfutable [irefytabl] *a* irrefutable.

irrégulier, -lère [iregylje, -jer] *a* irregular.

irrémédiable [iremedjabl] *a* irreparable.

irremplaçable [irɑ̃plasabl] *a* irreplaceable.

irréparable [ireparabl] *a* (*véhicule etc*) beyond repair; (*tort, perte*) irreparable.

irrépressible [irepresibl] *a* (*rires etc*) irrepressible.

irréprochable [ireprɔʃabl] *a* beyond reproach, irreproachable.

irrésistible [irezistibl] *a* (*personne, charme etc*) irresistible.

irrespirable [irespirabl] *a* unbreathable.

irresponsable [irespɔ̃sabl] *a* (*personne*) irresponsible.

irréversible [ireversibl] *a* irreversible.

irrévocable [irevɔkabl] *a* irrevocable.

irriguer [irige] *vt* to irrigate. ● **irrigation** *nf* irrigation.

irrit/er [irite] *vt* to irritate. ● **—ant** *a* irritating. ● **irritable** *a* irritable. ● **irritation** *nf* (*colère*) & *Méd* irritation.

irruption [irypsjɔ̃] *nf* **faire i. dans** to burst into.

islam [islam] *nm* Islam. ● **islamique** *a* Islamic.

Islande [islɑ̃d] *nf* Iceland. ● **islandais, -aise** *a* Icelandic.

isoler [izole] *vt* to isolate (**de** from); (*du froid etc*) & *Él* to insulate ‖ **s'i.** *vpr* to

cut oneself off, isolate oneself. ● **isolant** *nm* insulation (material). ● **isolé** *a* isolated; **i. de** cut off *ou* isolated from. ● **isolation** *nf* insulation. ● **isolement** *nm* isolation.

isoloir [izɔlwar] *nm* polling booth.

Israël [israel] *nm* Israel. ● **israélien, -ienne** *a* & *nmf* Israeli. ● **israélite** *a* Jewish.

issu [isy] *a* **être i. de** to come from.

issue [isy] *nf* (*sortie*) way out, exit; (*solution*) way out; (*résultat*) outcome; **rue** *etc* **sans i.** dead end; **situation** *etc* **sans i.** *Fig* dead end; **à l'i. de** at the close of.

isthme [ism] *nm Géog* isthmus.

Italie [itali] *nf* Italy. ● **italien, -ienne** *a* & *nmf* Italian ‖ *nm* (*langue*) Italian.

italique [italik] *a Typ* italic ‖ *nm* italics.

itinéraire [itinerer] *nm* route, itinerary.

IUT [iyte] *nm abrév* **institut universitaire de technologie.**

IVG [iveʒe] *nf abrév* (*interruption volontaire de grossesse*) (voluntary) abortion.

ivoire [ivwar] *nm* ivory; **statuette/etc en i.** *ou* **d'i.** ivory statuette/etc.

ivre [ivr] *a* drunk (**de** with). ● **ivresse** *nf* drunkenness; **en état d'i.** under the influence of drink. ● **ivrogne** *nmf* drunk(ard).

J

J, j [ʒi] *nm* J, j; **le jour J.** D-day.

j' [ʒ] *voir* **je.**

jachère (en) [ɑ̃ʒaʃɛr] *adv* (*champ*) fallow; **être en j.** to lie fallow.

jacinthe [ʒasɛ̃t] *nf* hyacinth.

jacuzzi [ʒakuzi] *nm* (*baignoire*) jacuzzi.

jadis [ʒadis] *adv* long ago, once.

jaguar [ʒagwar] *nm* (*animal*) jaguar.

jaillir [ʒajir] *vi* (*liquide*) to spurt (out), gush (out); (*lumière*) to beam out, shine (forth); (*cri*) to burst out.

jais [ʒɛ] *nm* (*noir*) **de j.** jet-black.

jalon [ʒalɔ̃] *nm* (*piquet*) marker. ●**jalonner** *vt* to mark (out); (*border*) to line.

jaloux, -ouse [ʒalu, -uz] *a* jealous (**de** of). ●**jalousie** *nf* jealousy.

Jamaïque [ʒamaik] *nf* Jamaica.

jamais [ʒamɛ] *adv* **1** (*négatif*) never; **sans j. sortir** without ever going out; **elle ne sort j.** she never goes out; **j. de la vie** (*absolutely*) never! **2** (*positif*) ever; **à (tout) j.** for ever; **si j.** if ever.

jambe [ʒɑ̃b] *nf* leg; **prendre ses jambes à son cou** to take to one's heels.

jambon [ʒɑ̃bɔ̃] *nm Culin* ham.

jante [ʒɑ̃t] *nf* (*de roue*) rim.

janvier [ʒɑ̃vje] *nm* January.

Japon [ʒapɔ̃] *nm* Japan. ●**japonais, -aise** *a* Japanese ▮*nmf* Japanese man *ou* woman, Japanese *inv*; **les J.** the Japanese ▮*nm* (*langue*) Japanese.

japper [ʒape] *vi* (*chien etc*) to yap, yelp.

jaquette [ʒakɛt] *nf* (*d'homme*) tailcoat, morning coat; (*de femme, livre*) jacket.

jardin [ʒardɛ̃] *nm* garden; **j. d'enfants** kindergarten, playschool; **j. public** park; (*plus petit*) gardens. ●**jardinage** *nm* gardening. ●**jardiner** *vi Fam* to garden ▮*vt* garden centre. ●**jardinier** *nm* gardener. ●**jardinière** *nf* (*personne*) gardener; (*caisse à fleurs*) window box; **j. (de légumes)** mixed vegetable dish; **j. d'enfants** kindergarten teacher.

jargon [ʒargɔ̃] *nm* jargon.

jarretelle [ʒartɛl] *nf* (*de gaine*) suspender, *Am* garter. ●**jarretière** *nf* (*autour de la jambe*) garter.

jaser [ʒaze] *vi* (*bavarder*) to jabber.

jatte [ʒat] *nf* (*bol*) bowl.

jaune [ʒon] *a* yellow ▮*nm* (*couleur*) yellow; **j. d'œuf** (egg) yolk. ●**jaunâtre** *a* yellowish. ●**jaunir** *vti* to turn yellow. ●**jaunisse** *nf Méd* jaundice.

Javel (eau de) [odʒavɛl] *nf* bleach.

javelot [ʒavlo] *nm* javelin.

jazz [dʒaz] *nm* jazz.

je [ʒ(ə)] *pron* (**j'** before vowel or mute h) I; **je suis** I am.

jean [dʒin] *nm* (*pair of*) jeans.

jeep® [dʒip] *nf* jeep®.

jerrycan [(d)ʒerikan] *nm* petrol *ou Am* gasoline can; (*pour l'eau*) water can.

jersey [ʒɛrze] *nm* (*tissu*) jersey.

Jersey [ʒɛrzɛ] *nf* Jersey.

Jésus [ʒezy] *nm* Jesus.

jet [ʒɛ] *nm* throw; (*de vapeur*) burst; (*de lumière*) flash; (*de tuyau d'arrosage*) nozzle; **j. d'eau** fountain; **premier j.** (*ébauche*) first draft.

jetable [ʒ(ə)tabl] *a* (*rasoir etc*) disposable.

jetée [ʒ(ə)te] *nf* pier, jetty.

jeter [ʒ(ə)te] *vt* to throw (**à** to, **dans** into); (*à la poubelle*) to throw away; (*ancre, sort*) to cast; (*cri*) to let out; (*éclat*) to throw out; **j. un coup d'œil sur** *ou* **à** to have *ou* take a look at; (*rapidement*) to glance at.

▮**se jeter** *vpr* to throw oneself; **se j. sur** to pounce on; **se j. contre** (*véhicule*) to crash into; **se j. dans** (*fleuve*) to flow into.

jeton [ʒ(ə)tɔ̃] *nm* (*pièce*) token; (*au jeu*) chip.

jeu, -x [ʒø] *nm* **1** game; (*amusement*) play; (*d'argent*) gambling; *Th* acting; *Mus* playing; **j. de mots** play on words; **jeux de société** parlour *ou* indoor games; **j. télévisé** television quiz; **en j.** (*en cause*) at stake; (*forces*) at work; **entrer en j.** to come into play.

2 (*série complète*) set; (*de cartes*) pack, deck, *Am* deck; (*cartes en main*) hand; **j. d'échecs** (*boîte, pièces*) chess set.

jeudi [ʒødi] *nm* Thursday.

jeun (à) [aʒœ̃] *adv* on an empty stomach; **être à j.** to have eaten no food.

jeune [ʒœn] *a* young; (*inexpérimenté*) inexperienced; **jeunes gens** young people ▮*nmf* young person; **les jeunes** young people. ●**jeunesse** *nf* youth; (*apparence*) youthfulness; **la j.** (*jeunes*) the young.

jeûne [ʒøn] *nm* fast; (*action*) fasting. ●**jeûner** *vi* to fast.

joaillier, -ère [ʒɔaje, -jɛr] *nmf* jeweller, *Am* jeweler. ●**joaillerie** *nf* (*magasin*) jewellery *ou Am* jewelry shop.

jockey [ʒɔke] *nm* jockey.

jogging [dʒɔgiŋ] *nm Sp* jogging; (*vêtement*) jogging suit; **faire du j.** to jog.

joie [ʒwa] *nf* joy, delight; **feu de j.** bonfire.

joindre* [ʒwɛ̃dr] *vt* (*mettre ensemble, relier*) to join; (*efforts*) to combine; (*insérer dans une enveloppe*) to enclose (**à** with); **j. qn** (*contacter*) to get in touch with s.o.; **j. les deux bouts** *Fam* to make ends meet; **se j. à** (*un groupe etc*) to join. ●**joint** *a* (*efforts*) joint; **à pieds joints** with feet together ▮*nm Tech* joint; (*de robinet*) washer.

joker [ʒɔkɛr] *nm Cartes* joker.

joli [ʒɔli] *a* nice, lovely; (*femme, enfant*) pretty.

jonc [ʒɔ̃] *nm Bot* rush.

joncher [ʒɔ̃ʃe] *vt* **jonché de** strewn *ou* littered with.

jonction [ʒɔ̃ksjɔ̃] *nf* (*de routes etc*) junction.

jongler [ʒɔ̃gle] *vi* to juggle (**avec** with). ●**—eur, -euse** *nmf* juggler.

jonquille [ʒɔ̃kij] *nf* daffodil.

Jordanie [ʒɔrdani] *nf* Jordan.

joue [ʒu] *nf Anat* cheek.

jouer [ʒwe] *vi* to play; (*acteur*) to act; (*au tiercé etc*) to gamble, bet; (*être important*) to count; **j. au tennis/aux cartes/etc** to play tennis/cards/etc; **j. du piano/etc** to play the piano/etc; **j. aux courses** to bet on the horses; **j. des coudes** to use one's elbows; **à toi de j.!** it's your turn (to play).

▮*vt* (*musique, tour, jeu, rôle*) to play; (*pièce, film*) to put on; (*risquer*) to bet, gamble (**sur** on); **se j. de** (*se moquer*) to scoff at; (*difficultés*) to make light of.

jouet [ʒwe] *nm* toy.

joueur, -euse [ʒwœr, -øz] *nmf* player; (*au tiercé etc*) gambler; **beau j.** good loser.

joufflu [ʒufly] *a* (*visage*) chubby; (*enfant*) chubby-cheeked.

joug [ʒu] *nm Agr & Fig* yoke.

jouir [ʒwir] *vi* **j. de** (*savourer, avoir*) to enjoy. ●**jouissance** *nf* enjoyment; (*usage*) *Jur* use.

joujou, -x [ʒuʒu] *nm Fam* toy.

jour [ʒur] *nm* day; (*lumière*) (day)light; (*ouverture*) gap, opening; (*aspect*) *Fig* light; **il fait j.** it's light; **en plein j.** in broad daylight; **de nos jours** nowadays; **du j. au lendemain** overnight; **au j. le j.** from day to day; **le j. de l'An** New Year's Day; **les beaux jours** (*l'été*) summer; **mettre à j.** to bring up to date; **donner le j. à** to give birth to; **quel j. sommes-nous?** what day is it?

journal, -aux [ʒurnal, -o] *nm* (news)paper; (*spécialisé*) journal; (*intime*) diary; **j. (parlé)** *Rad* news bulletin. ●**journalisme** *nm* journalism. ●**journaliste** *nmf* journalist.

journalier, -ère [ʒurnalje, -jɛr] *a* daily.

journée [ʒurne] *nf* day; **pendant la j.** during the day(time); **toute la j.** all day (long).

jovial, -aux [ʒɔvjal, -o] *a* jovial, jolly. ●**jovialité** *nf* jollity.

joyau, -aux [ʒwajo] *nm* jewel.

joyeux, -euse [ʒwajø, -øz] *a* merry, happy; **j. anniversaire!** happy birthday!; **j. Noël!** merry *ou* happy Christmas!

jubiler [ʒybile] *vi* to be jubilant.

jucher (se) [səʒyʃe] *vpr* to perch (**sur** on).

judas [ʒyda] *nm* (*de porte*) peephole.

judiciaire [ʒydisjɛr] *a* judicial, legal.

judicieux, -euse [ʒydisjø, -øz] *a* sensible, judicious.

judo [ʒydo] *nm* judo.

juge [ʒyʒ] *nm* judge; **j. d'instruction** examining magistrate; **j. de touche** *Fb* linesman.

jugé (au) [oʒyʒe] *adv* by guesswork.

jugement [ʒyʒmɑ̃] *nm* judg(e)ment; (*verdict*) *Jur* sentence; **passer en j.** *Jur* to stand trial.

juger [ʒyʒe] *vt* to judge; (*au tribunal*) to try (*s.o.*); (*estimer*) to consider (**que** that); **j. utile/etc de faire** to consider it useful/*etc* to do.

juguler [ʒygyle] *vt* to check, suppress.

juif, juive [ʒqif, ʒqiv] *a* Jewish ‖ *nmf* Jew.

juillet [ʒqijɛ] *nm* July.

juin [ʒɥɛ̃] *nm* June.

jumeau, -elle, *pl* **-eaux, -elles** [ʒymo, -ɛl] *a* twin; **frère j.** twin brother; **sœur jumelle** twin sister; **lits jumeaux** twin beds ‖ *nmf* twin. ● **jumeler** *vt* (*villes*) to twin. ● **jumelage** *nm* twinning.

jumelles [ʒymɛl] *nfpl* (*pour regarder*) binoculars; **j. de théâtre** opera glasses.

jument [ʒymɑ̃] *nf* mare.

jungle [ʒœ̃gl] *nf* jungle.

junior [ʒynjɔr] *nm & a inv Sp* junior.

junte [ʒœ̃t] *nf Pol* junta.

jupe [ʒyp] *nf* skirt. ● **jupon** *nm* petticoat.

jurer [ʒyre] **1** *vi* (*dire un gros mot*) to swear (**contre** at). **2** *vt* (*promettre*) to swear (**que** that, **de faire** to do); **j. de qch** to swear to sth. **3** *vi* (*contraster*) to clash (**avec** with). ● **juré** *a* (*ennemi*) sworn ‖ *nm Jur* juror.

juridiction [ʒyridiksjɔ̃] *nf* jurisdiction.

juridique [ʒyridik] *a* legal. ● **juriste** *nmf* legal expert.

juron [ʒyrɔ̃] *nm* swearword.

jury [ʒyri] *nm Jur* jury; (*examinateurs*) board of (examiners).

jus [ʒy] *nm* juice; (*de viande*) gravy; **j. d'orange** orange juice.

jusque [ʒysk] *prép* **jusqu'à** (*espace*) as far as, (right) up to; (*temps*) until, (up) till, to; (*même*) even; **jusqu'à dix francs/etc** (*limite*) up to ten francs/*etc*; **jusqu'en mai/etc** until May/*etc*; **jusqu'où?** how far?; **jusqu'ici** as far as this; (*temps*) up till now; **jusqu'à présent** up till now; **j. dans/sous/etc** right into/under/*etc*; **j. chez moi** as far as my place; **en avoir j.-là** *Fam* to be fed up.
‖ *conj* **jusqu'à ce qu'il vienne** until he comes.

juste [ʒyst] *a* (*équitable*) fair, just; (*légitime*) just; (*exact*) right, correct; (*étroit*) tight; (*remarque*) sound; **un peu j.** (*quantité, qualité*) barely enough; **très j.!** quite right!
‖ *adv* (*deviner, compter*) correctly, right, accurately; (*chanter*) in tune; (*seulement, exactement*) just; **au j.** exactly; **tout j.** (*à peine, seulement*) only just; **un peu j.** (*mesurer, compter*) a bit on the short side; **à 3 heures j.** on the stroke of 3. ● **justement** *adv* exactly, precisely, just; (*avec justesse ou justice*) justly.

justesse [ʒystɛs] *nf* (*exactitude*) accuracy; **de j.** (*éviter, gagner etc*) just.

justice [ʒystis] *nf* justice; (*autorités*) law; **en toute j.** in all fairness; **rendre j. à qn** to do justice to s.o.

justifier [ʒystifje] *vt* to justify; **j. de qch** to prove sth ‖ **se j.** *vpr Jur* to clear oneself (**de** of); (*attitude etc*) to be justified. ● **justificatif, -ive** *a* **document j.** supporting document, proof. ● **justification** *nf* justification; (*preuve*) proof.

juteux, -euse [ʒytø, -øz] *a* juicy.

juvénile [ʒyvenil] *a* youthful.

juxtaposer [ʒykstapoze] *vt* to juxtapose.

K

K, k [ka] *nm* K, k.

kaki [kaki] *a inv* khaki.

kaléidoscope [kaleidoskop] *nm* kaleidoscope.

kangourou [kãguru] *nm* **1** (*animal*) kangaroo. **2**® (*porte-bébé*) baby sling.

karaté [karate] *nm Sp* karate.

kascher [kaʃɛr] *a inv Rel* kosher.

kayak [kajak] *nm* (*bateau*) *Sp* canoe.

képi [kepi] *nm* (*coiffure*) *Mil* cap, kepi.

kermesse [kɛrmɛs] *nf* charity fête; (*en Belgique etc*) village fair.

kidnapper [kidnape] *vt* to kidnap.

kilo [kilo] *nm* kilo. ●**kilogramme** *nm* kilo(gram).

kilomètre [kilɔmɛtr] *nm* kilometre. ●**kilométrage** *nm Aut* = mileage.

●**kilométrique** *a* **borne k.** = milestone.

kilowatt [kilɔwat] *nm* kilowatt.

kinésithérapie [kineziterapi] *nf* physiotherapy. ●**kinésithérapeute** *nmf* physiotherapist.

kiosque [kjɔsk] *nm* (*à journaux*) kiosk, stall; **k. à musique** bandstand.

kit [kit] *nm* (self-assembly) kit; **meuble en k.** self-assembly (furniture) unit.

klaxon® [klaksɔn] *nm Aut* horn, hooter. ●**klaxonner** *vi* to hoot, *Am* honk.

km *abrév* (*kilomètre*) km.

k.-o. [kao] *a inv* **mettre k.-o.** to knock out.

Koweït [kɔwɛjt] *nm* Kuwait.

kyste [kist] *nm Méd* cyst.

L

L, l [ɛl] *nm* L, l.

l', la [l, la] *voir* le.

la [la] *nm* (note de musique) A.

là [la] **1** *adv* (lieu) there; (chez soi) in, home; **je reste là** I'll stay here; **c'est là que** that's where; **là où il est** where he is; **à cinq mètres de là** five metres away; **de là son échec** (cause) hence his *ou* her failure; **jusque-là** (lieu) as far as that; **passe par là** go that way.
2 *adv* (temps) then; **jusque-là** up till then.
3 *int* **oh là là!** oh dear!; **alors là!** well!
4 *voir* ce², celui.

là-bas [lɑba] *adv* over there.

label [label] *nm Com* label, mark (of quality, origin etc).

labo [labo] *nm Fam* lab. ● **laboratoire** *nm* laboratory; **l. de langues** language laboratory.

laborieux, -euse [labɔrjø, -øz] *a* (pénible) laborious; (personne) industrious; **les classes laborieuses** the working classes.

labour [labur] *nm* ploughing, *Am* plowing. ● **labourer** *vt* (avec charrue) to plough, *Am* plow; (visage etc) *Fig* to furrow.

labyrinthe [labirɛ̃t] *nm* maze, labyrinth.

lac [lak] *nm* lake.

lacer [lase] *vt* to lace (up). ● **lacet** *nm* **1** (shoe- *ou* boot-)lace. **2** (de route) twist, zigzag; **route en l.** winding *ou* zigzag road.

lâche [lɑʃ] **1** *a* cowardly ‖ *nmf* coward. **2** *a* (détendu) loose, slack. ● **lâcheté** *nf* cowardice; **une l.** (action) a cowardly act.

lâcher [lɑʃe] *vt* (main etc) to let go of; (bombe) to drop; (place, études) to give up; (juron) to utter; **l. qn** (laisser tranquille) *Fam* to leave s.o. (alone);

(abandonner) *Fam* to drop s.o.; **l. prise** to let go ‖ *vi* (corde) to give way.

lacrymogène [lakrimɔʒɛn] *a* **gaz l.** tear gas.

lacté [lakte] *a* **régime l.** milk diet; **la Voie lactée** the Milky Way.

lacune [lakyn] *nf* gap, deficiency.

là-dedans [lad(ə)dɑ̃] *adv* (lieu) in there, inside. ● **là-dessous** *adv* underneath. ● **là-dessus** *adv* on there; (monter) on top; (alors) thereupon. ● **là-haut** *adv* up there; (à l'étage) upstairs.

lagon [lagɔ̃] *nm* (small) lagoon. ● **lagune** *nf* lagoon.

laid [lɛ] *a* ugly; (ignoble) wretched. ● **laideur** *nf* ugliness.

laine [lɛn] *nf* wool; **de l., en l.** woollen, *Am* woolen. ● **lainage** *nm* (vêtement) woolly, woollen garment; (étoffe) woollen material; *pl* (vêtements) woollens.

laïque [laik] *a* (école) non-denominational; (vie) secular; (tribunal) lay.

laisse [lɛs] *nf* lead, leash; **en l.** on a lead *ou* leash.

laisser [lese] *vt* to leave; **l. qn partir/entrer/etc** (permettre) to let s.o. go/come in/etc; **l. qch à qn** to let s.o. have sth, leave sth with s.o.; **laissez-moi le temps de faire** give me *ou* leave me time to do it; **l. qn seul** to leave s.o. (all) alone; **je vous laisse** I'm leaving now; **se l. aller/faire** to let oneself go/be pushed around; **se l. surprendre par l'orage** to get caught out by the storm. ● **laisser-aller** *nm inv* carelessness. ● **laissez-passer** *nm inv* (sauf-conduit) pass.

lait [lɛ] *nm* milk; **dent de l.** milk tooth. ● **laitage** *nm* milk product. ● **laiterie** *nf* dairy. ● **laitier, -ière** *a* **produit l.** dairy product ‖ *nm* (livreur) milkman; (vendeur) dairyman ‖ *nf* dairywoman.

laiton [letɔ̃] *nm* brass.

laitue [lety] *nf* lettuce.

lama [lama] *nm* (*animal*) llama.

lambeau, -x [lɑ̃bo] *nm* shred, bit; **mettre en lambeaux** to tear to shreds; **tomber en lambeaux** to fall to bits.

lambiner [lɑ̃bine] *vi Fam* to dawdle.

lambris [lɑ̃bri] *nm* panelling.

lame [lam] *nf* **1** (*de couteau etc*) blade; (*de métal*) strip; **l. de parquet** floorboard. **2** (*vague*) wave; **l. de fond** ground swell.

lamelle [lamel] *nf* thin strip.

lamenter (se) [səlamɑ̃te] *vpr* to moan, lament; **se l. sur** to lament (over). ● **lamentable** *a* (*mauvais*) terrible; (*voix, cri*) mournful.

lampadaire [lɑ̃pader] *nm* standard lamp; (*de rue*) street lamp.

lampe [lɑ̃p] *nf* lamp; (*au néon*) light; **l. de poche** torch, *Am* flashlight.

lampion [lɑ̃pjɔ̃] *nm* Chinese lantern.

lance [lɑ̃s] *nf* spear; (*de tournoi*) *Hist* lance; (*extrémité de tuyau*) nozzle; **l. d'incendie** fire hose.

lance-pierres [lɑ̃spjer] *nm inv* catapult.

lancer [lɑ̃se] *vt* (*jeter*) to throw (**à** to); (*avec force*) to hurl; (*fusée, produit, mode, navire etc*) to launch; (*appel, ultimatum etc*) to issue; (*cri*) to utter; (*bombe*) to drop; (*regard*) to cast (**à** at) ▮ **se l.** *vpr* (*se précipiter*) to rush; **se l. dans** (*aventure, discussion*) to launch into ▮ *nm* **un l.** a throw; **le l. de** the throwing of. ● **lancement** *nm* (*de fusée, navire etc*) launch(ing).

lancinant [lɑ̃sinɑ̃] *a* (*douleur*) shooting; (*obsédant*) haunting.

landau [lɑ̃do] *nm* (*pl* **-s**) pram, *Am* baby carriage.

lande [lɑ̃d] *nf* moor, heath.

langage [lɑ̃gaʒ] *nm* (*système, faculté d'expression*) language; **l. machine** computer language.

lange [lɑ̃ʒ] *nm* (baby) blanket. ● **langer** *vt* (*bébé*) to change.

langouste [lɑ̃gust] *nf* (spiny) lobster. ● **langoustine** *nf* (Dublin Bay) prawn.

langue [lɑ̃g] *nf* tongue; *Ling* language; **l. maternelle** mother tongue; **langues vivantes** modern languages; **de l. anglaise/française** English-/French-speaking; **mauvaise l.** (*personne*) gossip. ● **languette** *nf* (*patte*) tongue.

lanière [lanjer] *nf* (*de cuir*) strap.

lanterne [lɑ̃tern] *nf* lantern; (*électrique*) lamp; *pl Aut* sidelights, parking lights.

lapalissade [lapalisad] *nf* statement of the obvious, truism.

laper [lape] *vt* (*boire*) to lap up ▮ *vi* to lap.

lapin [lapɛ̃] *nm* rabbit; **mon (petit) l.!** my dear!; **poser un l. à qn** *Fam* to stand s.o. up.

laps [laps] *nm* **un l. de temps** a lapse of time.

lapsus [lapsys] *nm* slip (of the tongue).

laque [lak] *nf* lacquer; **l. à cheveux** (hair) lacquer.

laquelle [lakel] *voir* **lequel**.

larbin [larbɛ̃] *nm Fam & Péj* flunkey.

lard [lar] *nm* (*fumé*) bacon; (*gras*) (pig's) fat. ● **lardon** *nm Culin* strip of bacon *ou* fat.

large [larʒ] *a* wide, broad; (*vêtement*) loose; (*idées, esprit*) broad; (*grand*) large; **de six mètres** six metres wide; **l. d'esprit** broad-minded. ▮ *adv* (*calculer*) liberally.

▮ *nm* breadth, width; **avoir six mètres de l.** to be six metres wide; **le l.** (*mer*) the open sea; **au l. de Cherbourg** *Nau* off Cherbourg; **être au l. dans** (*vêtement*) to have lots of room in. ● **largement** *adv* widely; (*ouvrir*) wide; (*au moins*) easily; (*servir, payer*) liberally; **avoir l. le temps** to have plenty of time. ● **largeur** *nf* width, breadth; (*d'esprit*) breadth.

larguer [large] (*large*) *vt* (*bombe etc*) to drop; **l. les amarres** *Nau* to cast off.

larme [larm] *nf* tear; (*goutte*) *Fam* drop; **en larmes** in tears; **rire aux larmes** to laugh till one cries.

larve [larv] *nf* (*d'insecte*) larva, grub.

larvé [larve] *a* latent, underlying.

laryngite [larɛ̃ʒit] *nf Méd* laryngitis.

las, lasse [lɑ, lɑs] *a* tired, weary (**de** of).
● **lasser** *vt* to tire, weary; **se l. de** to tire of.

laser [lazer] *nm* laser; **rayon l.** laser beam.

lasso [laso] *nm* lasso; **prendre au l.** to lasso.

latent [latɑ̃] *a* latent.

latéral, -aux [lateral, -o] *a* lateral; **rue latérale** side street.

latin, -ine [latɛ̃, -in] *a* & *nmf* Latin ‖ *nm* (*langue*) Latin.

latitude [latityd] *nf* *Géog* & *Fig* latitude.

latte [lat] *nf* slat, lath; (*de plancher*) board.

lauréat, -ate [lɔrea, -at] *nmf* (*prize*)winner.

laurier [lɔrje] *nm* *Bot* laurel, bay; **du l.** *Culin* bay leaves.

lavabo [lavabo] *nm* washbasin, sink; *pl* (*cabinet*) toilet(s), *Am* washroom.

lavande [lavɑ̃d] *nf* lavender.

lave [lav] *nf* *Géol* lava.

lave-auto [lavoto] *nm* *Can* car wash.
● **l.-linge** *nm inv* washing machine.
● **l.-vaisselle** *nm inv* dishwasher.

laver [lave] *vt* to wash; **l. qn de** (*soupçon etc*) *Fig* to clear s.o. of ‖ **se l.** *vpr* to wash, *Am* wash up; **se l. les mains** to wash one's hands. ● **lavable** *a* washable. ● **lavage** *nm* washing; **l. de cerveau** *Psy* brainwashing. ● **laverie** *nf* (*automatique*) launderette, *Am* Laundromat®. ● **lavette** *nf* dish cloth. ● **laveur** *nm* **l. de carreaux** window cleaner *ou Am* washer.

laxatif, -ive [laksatif, -iv] *nm* & *a* laxative.

laxiste [laksist] *a* permissive, lax.

layette [lejet] *nf* baby clothes.

le, la, *pl* **les** [l(ə), la, le] (**le** & **la** become **l'** before a vowel or mute h) **1** *art déf* (à + **le** = **au**, à + **les** = **aux**; de + **le** = **du**, de + **les** = **des**) the; **le garçon** the boy; **la fille** the girl; **les petits/rouges/etc** the little ones/red ones/*etc*; **mon ami le plus intime** my closest friend.

2 (*généralisation*) **la beauté** beauty; **la**

France France; **les Français** the French; **les hommes** men; **aimer le café** to like coffee.

3 (*possession*) **il ouvrit la bouche** he opened his mouth; **se blesser au pied** to hurt one's foot; **avoir les cheveux blonds** to have blond hair.

4 (*mesure*) **dix francs le kilo** ten francs a kilo.

5 (*temps*) **elle vient le lundi/le matin** she comes on Mondays/in the morning(s); **l'an prochain** next year.

‖ *pron* (*homme*) him; (*femme*) her; (*chose, animal*) it; *pl* them; **je la vois** I see her; I see it; **je le vois** I see him; I see it; **je les vois** I see them; **es-tu fatigué? — je le suis;** are you tired? — I am; **je le crois** I think so.

lécher [leʃe] *vt* to lick; **se l. les doigts** to lick one's fingers. ● **lèche-vitrines** *nm* **faire du l.-vitrines** *Fam* to go window-shopping.

leçon [ləsɔ̃] *nf* lesson; **servir de l. à qn** to teach s.o. a lesson.

lecteur, -trice [lektœr, -tris] *nmf* reader; *Univ* (foreign language) assistant; **l. de cassettes/de CD** cassette/CD player.
● **lecture** *nf* reading; *pl* (*livres*) books.

légal, -aux [legal, -o] *a* legal; (*médecine*) forensic. ● **légaliser** *vt* to legalize. ● **légalité** *nf* legality (**de** of)

légende [leʒɑ̃d] *nf* **1** (*histoire*) legend. **2** (*de plan*) key; (*de photo*) caption.
● **légendaire** *a* legendary.

léger, -ère [leʒe, -er] *a* light; (*bruit, fièvre etc*) slight; (*café, thé*) weak; (*bière, tabac*) mild; (*frivole*) frivolous; (*irréfléchi*) careless; **à la légère** (*agir*) rashly. ● **légèrement** *adv* lightly; (*un peu*) slightly; (*à la légère*) rashly.
● **légèreté** *nf* lightness; frivolity.

légion [leʒjɔ̃] *nf* *Mil* & *Fig* legion; **L. d'honneur** Legion of Honour.

législatif, -ive [leʒislatif, -iv] *a* legislative; (*élections*) parliamentary. ● **législation** *nf* legislation. ● **législature** *nf* (*période*) *Pol* term of office.

légitime [leʒitim] *a* (*action, enfant etc*)

legitimate; **être en état de l. défense** to be acting in self-defence. ● **légitimité** *nf* legitimacy.

legs [leg] *nm* Jur legacy, bequest; *(héritage)* Fig legacy. ● **léguer** *vt* to bequeath (**à** to).

légume [legym] *nm* vegetable.

lendemain [lɑ̃dmɛ̃] *nm* **le l.** the next day; **le l. de** the day after; **le l. matin** the next morning.

lent [lɑ̃] *a* slow. ● **lentement** *adv* slowly. ● **lenteur** *nf* slowness.

lentille [lɑ̃tij] *nf* **1** Bot Culin lentil. **2** *(verre)* lens.

léopard [leɔpar] *nm* leopard.

lèpre [lɛpr] *nf* leprosy.

lequel, laquelle, *pl* **lesquels, lesquelles** [ləkɛl, lakɛl, lekɛl] (+ **à** = **auquel, à laquelle, auxquel(le)s**; + **de** = **duquel, de laquelle, desquel(le)s**) **1** *pron rel (choose, animal)* which; *(personne)* who, *(indirect)* whom; **dans l.** in which; **parmi lesquels** *(choses, animaux)* among which; *(personnes)* among whom. **2** *pron interrogatif* which (one); **l. veux-tu?** which (one) do you prefer?

les [le] *voir* **le.**

léser [leze] *vt (personne)* Jur to wrong.

lésiner [lezine] *vi* to be stingy (**sur** with).

lessive [lesiv] *nf (produit)* washing powder, (laundry) detergent; *(linge)* washing; **faire la l.** to do the wash(ing). ● **lessiver** *vt* to scrub, wash.

lessivé [lesive] *a (fatigué)* Fam shattered.

lester [leste] *vt* to ballast, weight down.

leste [lest] *a (agile)* nimble.

léthargique [letarʒik] *a* lethargic.

lettre [lɛtr] *nf (missive, caractère)* letter; **en toutes lettres** *(mot)* in full; *(nombre)* in words; **les lettres** *(discipline)* letters. ● **lettré, -ée** *a* well-read ■ *nmf* scholar.

leucémie [løsemi] *nf* leuk(a)emia.

leur [lœr] **1** *a poss* their; **l. chat** their cat; **leurs voitures** their cars ■ *pron poss* **le l., la l., les leurs** theirs. **2** *pron inv (indirect)* (to) them; **il l. est facile de...** it's easy for them to....

leurre [lœr] *nm* illusion; *(tromperie)* trickery.

lever [l(ə)ve] *vt* to lift (up); raise; *(blocus, interdiction)* to lift; *(séance)* to close; *(camp)* to strike; **l. les yeux** to look up.

■ *vi (pâte)* to rise.

■ **se lever** *vpr* to get up; *(soleil, rideau)* to rise; *(jour)* to break; *(brume)* to clear, lift.

■ *nm* **le l. du soleil** sunrise; **le l. du rideau** Th the curtain (up). ● **levant** *a (soleil)* rising. ● **levé** *a* **être l.** *(debout)* to be up. ● **levée** *nf (d'interdiction)* lifting; *(du courrier etc)* collection.

levier [ləvje] *nm* lever; *(pour soulever)* crowbar.

lèvre [lɛvr] *nf* lip; **du bout des lèvres** half-heartedly.

lévrier [levrije] *nm* greyhound.

levure [ləvyr] *nf* yeast.

lexique [lɛksik] *nm* vocabulary, glossary.

lézard [lezar] *nm* lizard.

lézarde [lezard] *nf* crack. ● **se lézarder** *vpr* to crack.

liaison [ljɛzɔ̃] *nf (rapport)* connection; *(routière etc)* link; *(entre mots)* liaison; **l.** *(amoureuse)* love affair.

liane [ljan] *nf* Bot jungle vine, liana.

liasse [ljas] *nf* bundle.

Liban [libɑ̃] *nm* Lebanon. ● **libanais, -aise** *a* & *nmf* Lebanese.

libeller [libele] *vt (contrat etc)* to word, draw up; *(chèque)* to make out.

libellule [libelyl] *nf* dragonfly.

libéral, -ale, -aux [liberal, -o] *a* & *nmf* liberal.

libérer [libere] *vt (prisonnier etc)* to (set) free, release; *(pays, esprit)* to liberate (de from); **l. qn de** to free s.o. of ou from

■ **se l.** *vpr* to free oneself (**de** from). ● **libération** *nf* freeing; release; liberation.

liberté [liberte] *nf* freedom; **en l. provisoire** Jur on bail; **mettre en l.** to free, release; **mise en l.** release.

libraire [librɛr] *nmf* bookseller. ● **li-**

brairie *nf* bookshop.

libre [libr] *a* free (**de** qch from sth, **de faire** to do); (*voie*) clear; (*place*) vacant, free; (*école*) private (and religious). ●**l.-échange** *nm Écon* free trade. ●**l.-service** *nm* (*pl* **libres-services**) (*magasin etc*) self-service. ●**librement** [-əmã] *adv* freely.

Libye [libi] *nf* Libya. ●**libyen, -enne** *a* & *nmf* Libyan.

licence [lisãs] *nf Sp* permit; *Com* licence, *Am* license; *Univ* (Bachelor's) degree; **l. ès lettres/sciences** arts/ science degree, = BA/BSc, = *Am* BA/BS. ●**licencié, -ée** *a* & *nmf* graduate; **l. ès lettres/sciences** Bachelor of Arts/Science, = BA/BSc, = *Am* BA/ BS.

licencier [lisãsje] *vt* (*employé*) to lay off. ●**licenciement** *nm* dismissal.

lie [li] *nf* (*du vin*) dregs.

liège [ljɛʒ] *nm* (*matériau*) cork.

lien [ljɛ̃] *nm* (*rapport*) link, connection; (*ficelle*) tie; **l. de parenté** family tie.

lier [lje] *vt* (*attacher*) to tie (up); (*relier*) to link (up), connect; **l. qn** (*unir, engager*) to bind s.o.; **amis très liés** very close friends ▮ **se l.** *vpr* (*idées etc*) to tie in, link together; **se l. avec qn** to make friends with s.o.

lierre [ljɛr] *nm* ivy.

lieu, -x [ljø] *nm* place; (*d'un accident*) scene; **les lieux** (*locaux*) the premises; **sur les lieux** on the spot; **avoir l.** to take place; **donner l. à qch** to give rise to sth; **au l. de** instead of; **en premier l.** in the first place; **en dernier l.** lastly; **l. commun** commonplace. ●**l.-dit** *nm* (*pl* **lieux-dits**) *Géog* locality.

lieutenant [ljøtnã] *nm* lieutenant.

lièvre [ljɛvr] *nm* hare.

ligament [ligamã] *nm* ligament.

ligne [liɲ] *nf* (*trait, contour, transport*) line; (*belle silhouette*) figure; (*rangée*) row, line; (**se**) **mettre en l.** to line up; **en l.** *Tél* connected, through; (*ordinateur*) on-line; **les grandes lignes** (*de train*) the main line (services); *Fig* the broad

outline; **à la l.** *Gram* new paragraph; **entrer en l. de compte** to be taken into account; **pilote de l.** airline pilot.

lignée [liɲe] *nf* line, ancestry.

ligoter [ligɔte] *vt* to tie up.

liguer (se) [səlige] *vpr* to join together, conspire (**contre** against).

lilas [lila] *nm* lilac ▮ *a inv* (*couleur*) lilac.

limace [limas] *nf* slug.

limande [limãd] *nf* (*poisson*) lemon sole.

lime [lim] *nf* (*outil*) file. ●**limer** *vt* to file.

limite [limit] *nf* limit (**à** to); (*de propriété etc*) boundary; *pl Fb* boundary lines; **dépasser les limites** to go beyond the bounds. ▮ *a* (*cas*) extreme; (*vitesse, âge etc*) maximum; **date l.** latest date, deadline; **date l. de vente** *Com* sell-by date. ●**limitation** *nf* limitation; (*de vitesse, poids*) limit. ●**limiter** *vt* to limit, restrict (**à** to); (*délimiter*) to border; **se l. à faire** to limit *ou* restrict oneself to doing.

limoger [limɔʒe] *vt* (*destituer*) to dismiss.

limonade [limɔnad] *nf* (fizzy) lemonade.

limpide [lɛ̃pid] *a* (crystal) clear.

lin [lɛ̃] *nm Bot* flax; (*tissu*) linen.

linceul [lɛ̃sœl] *nm* shroud.

linge [lɛ̃ʒ] *nm* (*pièces de tissu*) linen; (*à laver*) washing, linen; **l. (de corps)** underwear. ●**lingerie** *nf* (*de femmes*) underwear, lingerie.

lingot [lɛ̃go] *nm* **l. d'or** gold bar.

linguiste [lɛ̃gɥist] *nmf* linguist. ●**linguistique** *a* linguistic ▮ *nf* linguistics.

lino [lino] *nm Fam* lino. ●**linoléum** *nm* linoleum.

linotte [linɔt] *nf* **tête de l.** *Fig* scatterbrain.

lion [ljɔ̃] *nm* lion; **le L.** (*signe*) Leo. ●**lionceau, -x** *nm* lion cub. ●**lionne** *nf* lioness.

liqueur [likœr] *nf* liqueur.

liquide [likid] *a* liquid; **argent l.** ready cash ▮ *nm* liquid; **du l.** (*argent*) ready cash; **payer en l.** to pay cash.

liquider [likide] *vt* (*dette, stock etc*) to liquidate; (*affaire, travail*) *Fam* to wind up, finish off ● **liquidation** nf liquidation; (vente) (clearance) sale.

lire¹ᵃ [lir] vti to read.

lire² [lir] nf (monnaie) lira.

lis¹ [lis] nm (plante, fleur) lily.

lis², lisant, lise(nt) etc [li, lizɑ̃, liz] voir **lire¹**.

lisible [lizibl] a (écriture) legible.

lisière [lizjer] nf edge, border.

lisse [lis] a smooth. ● **lisser** vt to smooth; (plumes) to preen.

liste [list] nf list; **l. électorale** register of electors, Am voting register; **sur la l. rouge** (numéro) Tél ex-directory, Am unlisted.

lit¹ [li] nm bed; **l. d'enfant** cot, Am crib; **lits superposés** bunk beds. ● **literie** nf bedding, bed clothes.

lit² [li] voir **lire¹**.

litanie [litani] nf (énumération) Fig long list (de of).

litière [litjer] nf (couche de paille) litter.

litige [litiʒ] nm dispute; Jur litigation.

litre [litr] nm litre, Am liter.

littéraire [literer] a literary. ● **littérature** nf literature.

littéral, -aux [literal, -o] a literal.

littoral [litɔral] nm coast(line).

livide [livid] a (pâle) (ghastly) pale.

livre [livr] **1** nm book; **l. de poche** paperback (book); **l. de bord** Nau logbook. **2** nf (monnaie, poids) pound. ● **livret** nm (registre) book; Mus libretto; **l. scolaire** school report book; **l. de famille** family registration book; **l. de caisse d'épargne** bankbook.

livrer [livre] vt (marchandises) to deliver (à to); (secret) to give away; **l. qn à** (la police etc) to give s.o. over ou up to; **l. bataille** to do battle.

‖ **se livrer** vpr (se rendre) to give oneself up (à to); (se confier) to confide (à in); **se l. à** (habitude, excès etc) to indulge in; (activité) to devote oneself to. ● **livraison** nf delivery. ● **livreur, -euse** nmf delivery man, delivery woman.

lobe [lɔb] nm Anat lobe.

local, -aux [lɔkal, -o] **1** a local. **2** nm (pièce) room; pl (bâtiment) premises.

localité [lɔkalite] nf locality.

locataire [lɔkater] nmf tenant; (chez le propriétaire) lodger.

location [lɔkasjɔ̃] nf (de maison etc) renting; (de voiture) hiring; (par propriétaire) renting (out), letting; hiring (out); (réservation) booking; (loyer) rental; (bail) lease; **en l.** on hire; **voiture de l.** hired ou rented car.

locomotion [lɔkɔmosjɔ̃] nf moyen de transport.

locomotive [lɔkɔmotiv] nf (de train) engine.

locution [lɔkysjɔ̃] nf phrase.

loge [lɔʒ] nf (de concierge) lodge; (d'acteur) dressing-room; (de spectateur) Th box.

loger [lɔʒe] vt (recevoir, mettre) to accommodate, house; (héberger) to put up; **l. qch dans** to fit sth in; **être logé et nourri** to have board and lodging.

‖ vi (à l'hôtel etc) to put up; (habiter) to live; (trouver à) **se l.** to find somewhere to live; **se l. dans** (balle) to lodge (itself) in. ● **logement** nm accommodation, lodging; (appartement) flat, Am apartment; (maison) house; **le l.** housing. ● **logeur, -euse** nmf landlord, landlady.

logiciel [lɔʒisjel] nm (d'ordinateur) software inv.

logique [lɔʒik] a logical ‖ nf logic. ●**—ment** adv logically.

logistique [lɔʒistik] nf logistics.

logo [lɔgo] nm logo.

loi [lwa] nf law; (du Parlement) act; **projet de l.** Pol bill; **faire la l.** to lay down the law (à to).

loin [lwɛ̃] adv far (away ou off); **Boston est l. (de Paris)** Boston is a long way away (from Paris); **plus l.** further, farther; (ci-après) further on; **au l.** in the distance; **de l.** from a distance; (de beaucoup) by far; **c'est l., tout ça** (passé) that was a long time ago; **l. de là** Fig far from it. ● **lointain** a distant, far-off ‖ nm **dans le l.** in the distance.

loisirs [lwazir] *nmpl* (*temps libre*) spare time, leisure (time); (*distractions*) leisure activities.

Londres [lɔ̃dr] *nm ou f* London. ●**londonien, -ienne** *a* London, of London ▮ *nmf* Londoner.

long, longue [lɔ̃, lɔ̃g] *a* long; **être l. (à faire) to be a long time** *ou* slow (in doing); **l. de deux mètres** two metres long.

▮ *nm* **avoir deux mètres de l.** to be two metres long; **(tout) le l. de** (*espace*) (all) along; **de l. en large** (*marcher etc*) up and down; **en l. et en large** thoroughly; **à la longue** in the long run; **tomber de tout son l.** to fall flat. ●**l.-courrier** *nm Av* long-distance airliner. ●**longue-vue** *nf* (*pl* **longues-vues**) telescope.

longer [lɔ̃ʒe] *vt* to go along; (*forêt, mer*) to skirt; (*mur*) to hug.

longitude [lɔ̃ʒityd] *nf* longitude.

longtemps [lɔ̃tɑ̃] *adv* (for) a long time; **trop/avant l.** too/before long; **aussi l. que** as long as.

longue [lɔ̃g] *voir* **long.** ●**longuement** *adv* at length. ●**longueur** *nf* length; **saut en l.** *Sp* long jump; **à l. de journée** all day long; **l. d'onde** *Rad & Fig* wavelength.

lopin [lɔpɛ̃] *nm* **l. de terre** plot of land.

loque [lɔk] *nf* **l. (humaine)** (*personne*) human wreck.

loques [lɔk] *nfpl* rags.

loquet [lɔkɛ] *nm* latch.

lorgner [lɔrɲe] *vt* (*convoiter*) to eye.

lors [lɔr] *adv* **l. de** at the time of; **depuis l., dès l.** from then on.

lorsque [lɔrsk(ə)] *conj* when.

losange [lozɑ̃ʒ] *nm* (*forme*) diamond.

lot [lo] *nm* **1** (*de loterie*) prize; **gros l.** top prize. **2** (*de marchandises etc*) batch. ●**loterie** *nf* lottery, raffle. ●**lotissement** *nm* (*terrain*) building plot; (*habitations*) housing estate *ou* Am development.

lotion [losjɔ̃] *nf* lotion.

loto [loto] *nm* (*jeu*) lotto.

louable [lwabl] *a* praiseworthy.

louange [lwɑ̃ʒ] *nf* praise.

louche [luʃ] **1** *nf* Culin ladle. **2** *a* (*suspect*)

shady, fishy.

loucher [luʃe] *vi* to squint; **l. sur** Fam to eye.

louer [lwe] *vt* **1** (*prendre en location*) to rent (*house etc*); (*voiture*) to hire, rent; (*donner en location*) to rent (out), let; (*réserver*) to book; **l. à bail** to lease; **maison/chambre à l.** house/room to let. **2** (*exalter*) to praise (**de** for); **se l. de** to be highly satisfied with.

loufoque [lufɔk] *a* (*fou*) Fam nutty.

loukoum [lukum] *nm* Turkish delight.

loup [lu] *nm* wolf; **avoir une faim de l.** to be ravenous.

loupe [lup] *nf* magnifying glass.

louper [lupe] *vt* Fam (*train etc*) to miss; (*examen*) to fail; (*travail*) to mess up.

lourd [lur] *a* heavy (Fig **de** with); (*temps, chaleur*) close, sultry; (*faute*) gross; (*tâche*) arduous ▮ *adv* **peser l.** (*malle etc*) to be heavy. ●**lourdement** *adv* heavily.

loutre [lutr] *nf* otter.

louveteau, -x [luvto] *nm* (*scout*) cub (scout).

louvoyer [luvwaje] *vi* (*tergiverser*) to hedge, be evasive.

loyal, -aux [lwajal, -o] *a* (*honnête*) fair (**envers** to); (*dévoué*) loyal (**envers** to). ●**loyauté** *nf* fairness; loyalty.

loyer [lwaje] *nm* rent.

lu [ly] *pp de* **lire¹**.

lubie [lybi] *nf* whim.

lubrifi/er [lybrifje] *vt* to lubricate. ●**—ant** *nm* lubricant.

lucarne [lykarn] *nf* (*fenêtre*) skylight.

lucide [lysid] *a* lucid. ●**lucidité** *nf* lucidity.

lucratif, -ive [lykratif, -iv] *a* lucrative.

lueur [lɥœr] *nf* (*lumière*) & Fig glimmer.

luge [lyʒ] *nf* sledge, Am sled.

lugubre [lygybr] *a* gloomy.

lui [lɥi] *pron mf* (*complément indirect*) (to) him; (*femme*) (to) her; (*chose, animal*) (to) it; **je le lui ai montré** I showed it to him *ou* her; **il lui est facile de . . .** it's easy for him *ou* for her to . . . .

▮ *pron m* **1** (*après une préposition*) him;

pour/avec/*etc* **lui** for/with/*etc* him; **il ne pense qu'à lui** he only thinks of himself. **2** (*complément direct*) him; (*animal*) it; **elle n'aime que lui** she only loves him. **3** (*sujet*) **elle est plus grande que lui** she's taller than he is *ou* than him; **lui, il ne viendra pas** (*emphatique*) he won't come; **c'est lui qui...** he is the one who.... ● **lui-même** *pron* himself; (*chose, animal*) itself.

luire* [lɥir] *vi* to shine, gleam. ● **luisant** *a* (*métal etc*) shiny.

lumière [lymjɛr] *nf* light; **à la l. de** by the light of; (*grâce à*) *Fig* in the light of; **faire toute la l. sur** *Fig* to clear up. ● **luminaire** *nm* (*appareil*) lighting appliance. ● **lumineux, -euse** *a* (*idée, ciel etc*) bright, brilliant; (*cadran etc*) luminous; **faisceau l.** beam of light.

lunaire [lyner] *a* lunar.

lunatique [lynatik] *a* temperamental.

lundi [lœdi] *nm* Monday.

lune [lyn] *nf* moon; **l. de miel** honeymoon.

lunette [lynet] *nf* **1 lunettes** glasses, spectacles; (*de protection, plongée*) goggles; **lunettes de soleil** sunglasses. **2** (*astronomique*) telescope; **l. arrière** *Aut* rear window.

lurette [lyret] *nf* **il y a belle l.** a long time ago.

lustre [lystr] *nm* (*éclairage*) chandelier. ● **lustré** *a* (*par l'usure*) shiny.

lutin [lytɛ̃] *nm* elf, imp, goblin.

lutte [lyt] *nf* fight, struggle; *Sp* wrestling; **l. des classes** class warfare. ● **lutter** *vi* to fight, struggle; *Sp* to wrestle. ● **lutteur, -euse** *nmf* fighter; *Sp* wrestler.

luxe [lyks] *nm* luxury; **article de l.** luxury article; **modèle de l.** de luxe model. ● **luxueux, -euse** *a* luxurious.

Luxembourg [lyksãbur] *nm* Luxembourg.

luxure [lyksyr] *nf* lewdness, lust.

luzerne [lyzɛrn] *nf Bot* lucerne, *Am* alfalfa.

lycée [lise] *nm* (secondary) school, *Am* high school. ● **lycéen, -enne** *nmf* pupil *ou* student (*at a lycée*).

lyncher [lɛ̃ʃe] *vt* to lynch.

lyophiliser [ljɔfilize] *vt* (*café etc*) to freeze-dry.

lyrique [lirik] *a* (*poème etc*) lyric; (*passionné*) *Fig* lyrical; **artiste l.** opera singer.

lys [lis] *nm* = **lis**[1].

M

M, m [ɛm] *nm* M, m.

m *abrév* (*mètre*) metre.

M [məsjø] *abrév* = **Monsieur**.

m' [m] *voir* me.

ma [ma] *voir* mon.

macadam [makadam] *nm* (*goudron*) tarmac.

macaron [makarɔ̃] *nm* (*gâteau*) macaroon.

macaroni(s) [makarɔni] *nm(pl)* macaroni.

macédoine [masedwan] *nf* **m.** (**de légumes**) mixed vegetables; **m.** (**de fruits**) fruit salad.

macérer [masere] *vti* Culin to soak.

mâcher [maʃe] *vt* to chew; **il ne mâche pas ses mots** he doesn't mince matters.

machin [maʃɛ̃] *nm* Fam (*chose*) what's-it; (*personne*) what's-his-name.

machinal, -aux [maʃinal, -o] *a* instinctive. **●—ement** *adv* instinctively.

machine [maʃin] *nf* machine; (*locomotive, moteur*) engine; **m. à coudre** sewing machine; **m. à écrire** typewriter; **m. à laver** washing machine. **●machiniste** *nm* (*conducteur*) driver; Th stage-hand.

macho [matʃo] *nm* macho.

mâchoire [maʃwar] *nf* jaw.

mâchonner [maʃone] *vt* to chew, munch.

maçon [masɔ̃] *nm* builder; bricklayer; mason. **●maçonnerie** *nf* (*travaux*) building work; (*ouvrage de briques*) brickwork; (*de pierres*) masonry.

maculer [makyle] *vt* Litt to stain (**de** with).

Madagascar [madagaskar] *nf* Madagascar.

madame, *pl* **mesdames** [madam, medam] *nf* madam; **bonjour mesdames** good morning (ladies); **Madame** *ou* **Mme Legras** Mrs *ou* Ms Legras; **Madame**

(*dans une lettre*) Dear Madam.

madeleine [madlɛn] *nf* (small) sponge cake.

mademoiselle, *pl* **mesdemoiselles** [madmwazɛl, medmwazɛl] *nf* miss; **bonjour mesdemoiselles** good morning (ladies); **Mademoiselle** *ou* **Mlle Legras** Miss Legras; **Mademoiselle** (*dans une lettre*) Dear Madam.

madère [mader] *nm* (*vin*) Madeira.

Madère [mader] *nf* (*île*) Madeira.

maf(f)ia [mafja] *nf* Mafia.

magasin [magazɛ̃] *nm* shop, Am store; (*entrepôt*) warehouse; **grand m.** department store; **en m.** in stock. **●magasinier** *nm* warehouseman.

magazine [magazin] *nm* (*revue*) magazine.

magie [maʒi] *nf* magic. **●magicien, -ienne** *nmf* magician. **●magique** *a* (*baguette etc*) magic; (*mystérieux, enchanteur*) magical.

magistral, -aux [maʒistral, -o] *a* masterly, magnificent.

magistrat [maʒistra] *nm* magistrate.

magnat [magna] *nm* tycoon, magnate.

magner (se) [səmaɲe] *vpr* Fam to hurry up.

magnétique [maɲetik] *a* magnetic.

magnétophone [maɲetofɔn] (*Fam* **magnéto**) *nm* tape recorder; **m. à cassettes** cassette recorder. **●magnétoscope** *nm* video (recorder), VCR.

magnifique [maɲifik] *a* magnificent.

magnolia [maɲɔlja] *nm* (*arbre*) magnolia.

magot [mago] *nm* (*économies*) Fam nest egg.

magouille(s) [maguj] *nf(pl)* Fam fiddling.

mai [mɛ] *nm* May.

maigre [mɛgr] *a* thin; (*viande*) lean;

(*fromage, yaourt*) low-fat; (*repas, salaire, espoir*) meagre. ● **maigreur** *nf* thinness. ● **maigrir** *vi* to get thin(ner).

maille [maj] *nf* (*de tricot*) stitch; (*de filet*) mesh. ● **maillon** *nm* (*de chaîne*) link.

maillet [maje] *nm* (*outil*) mallet.

maillot [majo] *nm* (*de sportif*) jersey, shirt; **m. (de corps)** vest, *Am* undershirt; **m. (de bain)** (*de femme*) swimsuit; (*d'homme*) (swimming) trunks.

main [mɛ̃] *nf* hand; **tenir à la m.** to hold in one's hand; **à la m.** (*faire, écrire etc*) by hand; **haut les mains!** hands up!; **donner un coup de m. à qn** *Fig* to lend s.o. a (helping) hand; **sous la m.** handy; **la m. dans la m.** hand in hand; **avoir la m. heureuse** to be lucky; **en m. propre** (*remettre qch*) in person; **attaque à m. armée** armed raid *ou* attack; **prêter m.-forte à** to lend assistance to. ● **main-d'œuvre** *nf* (*travail*) manpower, labour; (*salariés*) work force.

maint [mɛ̃] *a Litt* many a; **maintes fois, à maintes reprises** many a time.

maintenant [mɛ̃tnɑ̃] *adv* now; (*de nos jours*) nowadays; **m. que** now that; **dès m.** from now on.

maintenir [mɛ̃tnir] *vt* (*conserver*) to keep; (*retenir*) to hold, keep; (*affirmer*) to maintain (que that) **‖ se m.** *vpr* (*durer*) to be maintained; (*rester*) to keep. ● **maintien** *nm* maintenance (de of); (*allure*) bearing.

maire [mɛr] *nm* mayor. ● **mairie** *nf* town hall, *Am* city hall; (*administration*) town council, *Am* city hall.

mais [mɛ] *conj* but; **m. oui, m. si** yes of course; **m. non** definitely not.

maïs [mais] *nm* (*céréale*) maize, *Am* corn.

maison [mɛzɔ̃] *nf* (*bâtiment*) house; (*chez-soi, asile*) home; (*entreprise*) company, firm; (*famille*) household; **à la m.** at home; **aller à la m.** to go home; **m. individuelle** detached house; **m. de la culture** arts centre; **m. des jeunes** youth club; **m. de retraite** old people's home **‖** *a inv* (*tarte etc*) homemade.

maître [mɛtr] *nm* master; **se rendre m. de** (*incendie*) to bring under control; **être m. de** (*situation*) to be in control of; **m. de soi** in control of oneself; **m. (d'école)** teacher; **m. d'hôtel** (*restaurant*) head waiter; **m. nageur** (*sauveteur*) swimming instructor (and lifeguard); **m. chanteur** blackmailer.

maîtresse [mɛtrɛs] *nf* mistress; **m. (d'école)** teacher; **m. de maison** hostess **‖** *af* (*idée, poutre*) main; (*carte*) master.

maîtrise [mɛtriz] *nf* (*habileté, contrôle*) mastery (**de** of); (*diplôme*) Master's degree (**de** in); **m. (de soi)** self-control. ● **maîtriser** *vt* (*incendie*) to (bring under) control; (*émotion*) to master, control; (*sujet*) to master; **m. qn** to overpower s.o. **‖ se m.** *vpr* to control oneself.

majesté [maʒɛste] *nf* majesty; **Votre M.** (*titre*) Your Majesty. ● **majestueux, -euse** *a* majestic.

majeur [maʒœr] **1** *a* (*important*) & *Mus* major; **être m.** *Jur* to be of age; **la majeure partie de** most of. **2** *nm* (*doigt*) middle finger.

majorer [maʒɔre] *vt* to raise, increase.

majorette [maʒɔrɛt] *nf* (drum) majorette.

majorité [maʒɔrite] *nf* majority (**de** of); (*âge*) *Jur* coming of age, majority; (*gouvernement*) government. ● **majoritaire** *a* **scrutin m.** first-past-the-post voting system; **être m. aux élections** to win the elections.

Majorque [maʒɔrk] *nf* Majorca.

majuscule [maʒyskyl] *a* capital **‖** *nf* capital letter.

mal, maux [mal, mo] **1** *nm* (*douleur*) pain; (*dommage*) harm; (*maladie*) illness; **dire du m. de qn** to say bad things about s.o.; **m. de dents** toothache; **m. de gorge** sore throat; **m. de tête** headache; **m. de ventre** stomach-ache; **avoir le m. de mer** to be seasick; **avoir le m. du pays/etc** to be homesick/etc; **avoir m. à la tête/gorge/etc** to have a headache/ sore throat/etc; **ça (me) fait m., j'ai m.** it hurts (me); **faire du m. à** to hurt; **avoir**

du m. à faire to have trouble doing; se
donner du m. pour faire to go to a lot of
trouble to do; le bien et le m. good and
evil.
2 *adv* (*travailler etc*) badly; (*entendre,
comprendre*) not too well; aller m.
(*projet*) to be going badly; (*personne*)
Méd to be bad *ou* ill; être m. (à l'aise)
uncomfortable; se trouver m. to (feel)
faint; (ce n'est) pas m.! (that's) not bad!;
pas m. (*beaucoup*) *Fam* quite a lot (de
of); c'est m. de mentir it's wrong to lie.
malade [malad] a ill, sick; (*arbre, dent*)
diseased; (*estomac, jambe*) bad; être m.
du cœur to have a bad heart ∥ *nmf* sick
person; (*d'un médecin*) patient. ● maladie *nf* illness, disease. ● maladif, -ive a
(*personne*) sickly; (*morbide*) morbid.
maladroit [maladrwa] a clumsy, awkward; (*indélicat*) tactless.
malaise [malɛz] *nm* (*angoisse*) uneasi-
ness, malaise; (*indisposition*) feeling of
faintness *ou* discomfort; avoir un m. to
feel faint *ou* dizzy.
malaisé [maleze] a difficult.
Malaisie [malɛzi] *nf* Malaysia.
malaria [malarja] *nf* malaria.
malaxer [malakse] *vt* (*pétrir*) to knead.
malchance [malʃɑ̃s] *nf* bad luck; une m.
a mishap. ● malchanceux, -euse a unlucky.
mâle [mɑl] a male; (*viril*) manly ∥ *nm*
male.
malédiction [malediksjɔ̃] *nf* curse.
maléfique [malefik] a evil.
malencontreux, -euse [malɑ̃kɔ̃trø, -øz]
a unfortunate.
malentendant, -ante [malɑ̃tɑ̃dɑ̃, -ɑ̃t] *nmf*
person who is hard of hearing.
malentendu [malɑ̃tɑ̃dy] *nm* misunderstanding.
malfaçon [malfasɔ̃] *nf* defect.
malfaisant [malfəzɑ̃] a evil, harmful.
malfaiteur [malfɛtœr] *nm* criminal.
malgré [malgre] *prép* in spite of; m. tout
after all; m. moi in spite of myself,
reluctantly.
malhabile [malabil] a clumsy.

malheur [malœr] *nm* (*événement, malchance*) misfortune; (*accident*) mishap;
par m. unfortunately. ● malheureux,
-euse a (*triste*) unhappy, miserable;
(*fâcheux*) unfortunate; (*malchanceux*)
unlucky ∥ *nmf* (*infortuné*) poor man
ou woman, (poor) wretch. ● malheureusement *adv* unfortunately.
malhonnête [malɔnɛt] a dishonest.
● malhonnêteté *nf* dishonesty; une m.
(*action*) a dishonest act.
malice [malis] *nf* mischievousness.
● malicieux, -euse a mischievous.
malin, -igne [malɛ̃, -iɲ] a (*astucieux*)
clever, smart; (*tumeur*) *Méd* malignant; un m. plaisir a malicious pleasure.
malintentionné [malɛ̃tɑ̃sjɔne] a ill-inten-
tioned (à l'égard de towards).
malle [mal] *nf* (*coffre*) trunk; (*de véhicule*) boot, *Am* trunk. ● mallette *nf*
small suitcase; (*pour documents*) attaché case.
malmener [malməne] *vt* to manhandle.
malodorant [malɔdɔrɑ̃] a smelly.
malpoli [malpɔli] a rude.
malpropre [malprɔpr] a (*sale*) dirty.
malsain [malsɛ̃] a unhealthy.
Malte [malt] *nf* Malta. ● maltais, -aise a
& *nmf* Maltese.
maltraiter [maltrete] *vt* to ill-treat.
malveillant [malvɛjɑ̃] a malevolent.
● malveillance *nf* malevolence, ill will.
malvenu [malvəny] a uncalled-for.
maman [mamɑ̃] *nf* mum(my), *Am*
mom(my).
mamelle [mamɛl] *nf* (*d'animal*) teat; (*de
vache*) udder.
mamie [mami] *nf* grandma, granny.
mammifère [mamifɛr] *nm* mammal.
manche [mɑ̃ʃ] 1 *nf* (*de vêtement*) sleeve;
Sp Cartes round; la M. *Géog* the
Channel. 2 *nm* (*d'outil etc*) handle; m.
à balai broomstick; (*d'avion, d'ordinateur*) joystick. ● manchette *nf* 1 (*de
chemise etc*) cuff. 2 (*de journal*) headline.
manchot, -ote [mɑ̃ʃo, -ɔt] 1 a & *nmf* one-
armed *ou* one-handed (person). 2 *nm*

(oiseau) penguin.

mandarine [mɑ̃darin] *nf (fruit)* tangerine.

mandat [mɑ̃da] *nm* **1** *(postal)* money order. **2** *Pol* mandate; **m. d'arrêt** warrant **(contre qn** for s.o.'s arrest). ● **mandataire** *nmf (délégué)* representative, proxy.

manège [manɛʒ] *nm* **1** *(à la foire)* merry-go-round, roundabout; *(lieu)* riding-school; *(piste)* ring. **2** *(intrigue)* ploy, trickery *(no pl)*.

manette [manɛt] *nf* lever, handle.

mangeoire [mɑ̃ʒwar] *nf (feeding)* trough.

manger [mɑ̃ʒe] *vt* to eat; *(corroder)* to eat into; *(fortune)* to eat up; **donner à m. à** to feed ‖ *vi* to eat; **on mange bien ici** the food is good here; **m. à sa faim** to have enough to eat ‖ *nm* food. ● **mangeable** *a* eatable.

mangue [mɑ̃g] *nf (fruit)* mango.

manie [mani] *nf* mania, craze **(de** for). ● **maniaque** *a* fussy ‖ *nmf* fusspot, *Am* fussbudet.

manier [manje] *vt* to handle. ● **maniable** *a* easy to handle. ● **maniement** *nm* handling.

manière [manjɛr] *nf* way, manner; *pl (politesse)* manners; **de toute m.** anyway, anyhow; **de cette m.** (in) this way; **de m. à faire** so as to do; **à ma m.** (in) my own way; **la m. dont elle parle** the way (in which) she talks; **d'une m. générale** generally speaking; **faire des manières** to make a fuss.

manif [manif] *nf Fam* demo.

manifeste [manifɛst] **1** *a (évident)* manifest, obvious. **2** *nm Pol* manifesto.

manifester [manifɛste] **1** *vt (sa colère etc)* to show, manifest ‖ **se m.** *vpr (maladie etc)* to show itself; *(apparaître)* to appear. **2** *vi (dans la rue)* to demonstrate. ● **manifestant, -ante** *nmf* demonstrator. ● **manifestation** *nf* **1** *(défilé)* demonstration; *(réunion, fête)* event. **2** *(expression)* expression, manifestation.

manigancer [manigɑ̃se] *vt* to plot.

manipuler [manipyle] *vt (manier)* to handle; *(faits, électeurs) Péj* to manipulate.

manivelle [manivɛl] *nf Aut* crank.

mannequin [mankɛ̃] *nm (personne)* (fashion) model; *(statue)* dummy.

manœuvre [manœvr] **1** *nm (ouvrier)* labourer. **2** *nf (opération) & Mil* manoeuvre, *Am* maneuver; *(action)* manoeuvring; *(intrigue)* scheme. ● **manœuvrer** *vti (véhicule etc)* to manoeuvre, *Am* maneuver.

manoir [manwar] *nm* manor house.

manque [mɑ̃k] *nm* lack **(de** of); *(lacune)* gap; *pl (défauts)* shortcomings; **m. à gagner** loss of profit.

manquer [mɑ̃ke] *vt (cible, train etc)* to miss; *(ne pas réussir)* to make a mess of, ruin.

‖ *vi (faire défaut)* to be short *ou* lacking; *(être absent)* to be absent **(à** from); *(être en moins)* to be missing *ou* short; **m. de** *(pain, argent etc)* to be short of; *(attention etc)* to lack; **m. à** *(son devoir)* to fail in; *(sa parole)* to break; **ça manque de sel/**etc there isn't enough salt/etc; **elle/cela lui manque** he misses her/that; **ça n'a pas manqué** that was bound to happen; **je ne manquerai pas de venir** I won't fail to come; **elle a manqué (de) tomber** she nearly fell.

‖ *v imp* **il manque/il nous manque dix tasses** there are/we are ten cups short. ● **manquant** *a* missing. ● **manqué** *a (médecin, pilote etc)* failed.

mansarde [mɑ̃sard] *nf* attic.

manteau, -x [mɑ̃to] *nm* coat.

manucure [manykyr] *nmf* manicurist.

manuel, -elle [manɥɛl] **1** *a (travail etc)* manual. **2** *nm* handbook, manual; *(scolaire)* textbook.

manuscrit [manyskri] *nm* manuscript; *(tapé à la machine)* typescript.

mappemonde [mapmɔ̃d] *nf* map of the world; *(sphère)* globe.

maquereau, -x [makro] *nm (poisson)* mackerel.

maquette [maket] *nf* (scale) model.

maquiller [makije] *vt* (*visage*) to make up; (*vérité etc*) *Péj* to fake ‖ **se m.** to make (oneself) up. ●**maquillage** *nm* (*fard*) make-up.

maquis [maki] *nm Bot* scrub, bush.

maraîcher, -ère [mareʃe, -ɛʃer] *nmf* market gardener, *Am* truck farmer.

marais [marɛ] *nm* marsh; **m. salant** saltern.

marasme [marasm] *nm Écon* stagnation.

marathon [maratɔ̃] *nm* marathon.

marbre [marbr] *nm* marble.

marc [mar] *nm* (*eau-de-vie*) marc, brandy; **m. (de café)** coffee grounds.

marchand, -ande [marʃɑ̃, -ɑ̃d] *nmf* shopkeeper, trader; (*de voitures, meubles*) dealer; **m. de journaux** (*dans la rue*) newsvendor; (*dans un magasin*) newsagent, *Am* news dealer; **m. de légumes** greengrocer; **m. de poissons** fishmonger; **m. de couleurs** hardware merchant *ou* dealer ‖ *a* (*valeur*) market; **prix m.** trade price.

marchander [marʃɑ̃de] *vi* to haggle ‖ *vt* (*objet, prix*) to haggle over.

marchandise(s) [marʃɑ̃diz] *nf(pl)* goods, merchandise.

marche [marʃ] *nf* 1 (*d'escalier*) step, stair. 2 (*trajet*) walk; *Mil Mus* march; (*de train, véhicule*) movement; **la m.** *Sp* walking; **faire m. arrière** *Aut* to reverse; **un train en m.** a moving train; **mettre qch en m.** to start sth (up); **la bonne m. de** (*opération, machine*) the smooth running of.

marcher [marʃe] *vi* (*à pied*) to walk; (*poser le pied*) to tread, step (**dans** in); (*fonctionner*) to work, go; (*prospérer*) to go well; *Mil* to march; **faire m.** (*machine*) to work; (*entreprise*) to run; **ça marche?** *Fam* how's it going?

marché [marʃe] *nm* (*lieu*) market; (*contrat*) deal; **faire son** *ou* **le m.** to do one's shopping (*in the market*); **être bon m.** to be cheap; **vendre (à) bon m.** to sell cheap(ly); **c'est meilleur m.** it's cheaper; **par-dessus le m.** into the bargain; **au m. noir** on the black market; **le M. commun** the Common Market.

marchepied [marʃəpje] *nm* (*de train, bus*) step(s).

mardi [mardi] *nm* Tuesday; **M. gras** Shrove Tuesday.

mare [mar] *nf* (*étang*) pond; (*flaque*) pool.

marécage [marekaʒ] *nm* swamp, marsh. ●**marécageux, -euse** *a* swampy, marshy.

maréchal, -aux [mareʃal, -o] *nm Fr Mil* marshal.

marée [mare] *nf* tide; **m. haute/basse** high/low tide; **m. noire** oil slick.

marelle [marel] *nf* (*jeu*) hopscotch.

margarine [margarin] *nf* margarine.

marge [marʒ] *nf* (*de cahier etc*) margin; **en m. de** (*en dehors de*) on the fringe(s) of.

marguerite [margərit] *nf* (*fleur*) daisy.

mari [mari] *nm* husband.

mariage [marjaʒ] *nm* marriage; (*cérémonie*) wedding; **demande en m.** proposal (of marriage).

marier [marje] *vt* (*couleurs*) to blend; **m. qn** (*prêtre, maire etc*) to marry s.o. ‖ **se m.** *vpr* to get married; marry; **se m. avec qn** to get married to s.o., marry s.o. ●**marié** *a* married ‖ *nm* (bride)groom; **les mariés** the bride and (bride)groom. ●**mariée** *nf* bride.

marin [marɛ̃] *a* (*flore*) marine; (*mille*) nautical; **air/sel m.** sea air/salt ‖ *nm* sailor. ●**marine** *nf* **m. (de guerre)** navy; **m. marchande** merchant navy ‖ *a & nm inv* (*bleu*) **m.** (*couleur*) navy (blue).

marina [marina] *nf* marina.

mariner [marine] *vti Culin* to marinate.

marionnette [marjɔnɛt] *nf* puppet.

maritime [maritim] *a* (*droit, climat etc*) maritime; **port m.** seaport; **gare m.** harbour station.

mark [mark] *nm* (*monnaie*) mark.

marmelade [marməlad] *nf* **m. (de fruits)** stewed fruit.

marmite [marmit] *nf* (cooking) pot.

marmonner [marmɔne] *vti* to mutter.

Maroc [marɔk] *nm* Morocco. ●**marocain, -aine** *a* & *nmf* Moroccan.

maroquinerie [marɔkinri] *nf* leather goods shop. ●**maroquinier** *nm* leather goods dealer.

marque [mark] *nf* (*trace, signe*) mark; (*de produit*) make, brand; (*points*) Sp score; **m. de fabrique** trademark; **m. déposée** (registered) trademark; **la m. de** (*preuve*) the stamp of; **de m.** (*hôte, visiteur*) distinguished; (*produit*) of quality.

marquer [marke] *vt* (*par une marque*) to mark; (*écrire*) to note down; (*indiquer*) to show, mark; (*point, but*) Sp to score; **m. les points** Sp to keep (the) score ▌ *vi* (*laisser une trace*) to leave a mark; (*date, événement*) to stand out; Sp to score. ●**marquant** *a* outstanding. ●**marqueur** *nm* (*crayon*) marker.

marquis [marki] *nm* marquis. ●**marquise** *nf* marchioness.

marraine [marɛn] *nf* godmother.

marre [mar] *nf* **en avoir m.** *Fam* to be fed up (**de** with).

marrer (se) [səmare] *vpr Fam* to have a good laugh. ●**marrant** *a Fam* funny.

marron [marɔ̃] *nm* chestnut; (*couleur*) (chestnut) brown ▌ *a inv* (*couleur*) (chestnut) brown. ●**marronnier** *nm* (horse) chestnut tree.

mars [mars] *nm* March.

marteau, -x [marto] *nm* hammer; (*de porte*) (door)knocker; **m. piqueur** pneumatic drill. ●**marteler** *vt* to hammer.

martial, -aux [marsjal, -o] *a* martial; **cour martiale** court-martial.

martien, -ienne [marsjɛ̃, -jɛn] *nmf* & *a* Martian.

martinet [martinɛ] *nm* (*fouet*) (small) whip.

martin-pêcheur [martɛ̃peʃœr] *nm* (*pl* **martins-pêcheurs**) (*oiseau*) kingfisher.

martyr, -yre [martir] *nmf* (*personne*) martyr; **enfant m.** battered child. ●**martyriser** *vt* to torture; (*enfant*) to batter.

marxiste [marksist] *a* & *nmf* Marxist.

mascara [maskara] *nm* mascara.

mascarade [maskarad] *nf* masquerade.

mascotte [maskɔt] *nf* mascot.

masculin [maskylɛ̃] *a* male; (*viril*) masculine, manly; *Gram* masculine; (*vêtement, équipe*) men's ▌ *nm Gram* masculine.

masochiste [mazɔʃist] *nmf* masochist ▌ *a* masochistic.

masque [mask] *nm* mask. ●**masquer** *vt* (*dissimuler*) to mask (**à** from); (*cacher à la vue*) to block off.

massacre [masakr] *nm* slaughter, massacre. ●**massacrer** *vt* to slaughter, massacre; (*abîmer*) *Fam* to ruin.

massage [masaʒ] *nm* massage.

masse [mas] *nf* **1** (*volume*) mass; (*gros morceau, majorité*) bulk (**de** of); **en m.** in large numbers; **manifestation de m.** mass demonstration; **une m. de** (*tas*) a mass of; **des masses de** *Fam* masses of. **2** (*outil*) sledgehammer. **3** *Él* earth, *Am* ground.

masser [mase] **1** *vt* (*pétrir*) to massage. **2 se masser** *vpr* (*foule*) to form, mass. ●**masseur** *nm* masseur. ●**masseuse** *nf* masseuse.

massif, -ive [masif, -iv] **1** *a* massive; (*or, chêne etc*) solid; **départs massifs** mass departure(s). **2** *nm* (*d'arbres, de fleurs*) clump; *Géog* massif.

massue [masy] *nf* (*bâton*) club.

mastic [mastik] *nm* (*pour vitres*) putty; (*pour bois*) filler; **m. (silicone)** mastic. ●**mastiquer** *vt* **1** (*vitre*) to putty; (*bois*) to fill. **2** (*mâcher*) to chew.

masturber (se) [səmastyrbe] *vpr* to masturbate.

masure [mazyr] *nf* tumbledown house.

mat, mate [mat] *a* (*papier, couleur*) mat(t); (*bruit*) dull. **2** *am inv* & *nm Échecs* (check)mate; **faire m.** to (check)mate.

mât [ma] *nm* (*de navire*) mast; (*poteau*) pole.

match [matʃ] *nm Sp* match, *Am* game; **m. nul** tie, draw.

matelas [matla] *nm* mattress; **m. pneumatique** air bed. ●**matelassé** *a* (*tissu*)

quilted, padded.
matelot [matlo] *nm* sailor, seaman.
mater [mate] *vt* (*enfant etc*) to subdue.
matérialiser [materjalize] *vt*, **se m.** *vpr* to materialize.
matérialiste [materjalist] *a* materialistic ▮ *nmf* materialist.
matériaux [materjo] *nmpl* (building) materials.
matériel, -ielle [materjɛl] **1** *a* (*dégâts etc*) material. **2** *nm* (*de camping*) equipment, material(s); (*d'ordinateur*) hardware *inv*.
maternel, -elle [maternɛl] *a* (*amour, femme etc*) maternal, motherly; (*parenté*) maternal ▮ *nf* (**école**) **maternelle** nursery school. ● **maternité** *nf* (*état*) motherhood; (*hôpital*) maternity hospital; **congé de m.** maternity leave.
mathématique [matematik] *a* mathematical ▮ *nfpl* mathematics. ● **mathématicien, -ienne** *nmf* mathematician. ● **maths** [mat] *nfpl Fam* maths, *Am* math.
matière [matjer] *nf* (*à l'école*) subject; (*de livre*) subject matter; (*substance*) material; **la m.** *Phys* matter; **m. première** raw material; **en m. d'art/***etc* as regards art/*etc*, in art/*etc*.
matin [matɛ̃] *nm* morning; **le m.** (*chaque matin*) in the morning(s); **à sept heures du m.** at seven in the morning; **tous les mardis m.** every Tuesday morning; **de bon m., au petit m.** very early (in the morning). ● **matinal, -aux** *a* (*personne*) early; **soleil m.** morning sun; **être m.** to be an early riser. ● **matinée** *nf* morning; *Th* matinée; **faire la grasse m.** to sleep late.
matraque [matrak] *nf* (*de policier*) truncheon, *Am* billy (club); (*de malfaiteur*) cosh. ● **matraquer** *vt* (*frapper*) to club; (*publicité etc*) to plug.
matrice [matris] *nf Math* matrix. ● **matricielle** *af* **imprimante m.** *Ordinat* dot-matrix printer.
matricule [matrikyl] *nm* (registration) number.

matrimonial, -aux [matrimɔnjal, -o] *a* matrimonial.
maturité [matyrite] *nf* maturity.
maudire* [modir] *vt* to curse. ● **maudit** *a* (*sacré*) cursed, damned.
maugréer [mogree] *vi* to grumble (**contre** at).
mausolée [mozole] *nm* mausoleum.
maussade [mosad] *a* (*personne etc*) bad-tempered, moody; (*temps*) gloomy.
mauvais [movɛ] *a* bad; (*méchant*) wicked, evil; (*mal choisi*) wrong; (*mer*) rough; **plus m.** worse; **le plus m.** the worst; **il fait m.** the weather's bad; **être m. en** (*anglais etc*) to be bad at; **être en mauvaise santé** to be in bad health ▮ *adv* **ça sent m.** it smells bad ▮ *nm* **le bon et le m.** the good and the bad.
mauve [mov] *a* & *nm* (*couleur*) mauve.
maux [mo] *voir* **mal**.
maximum [maksimɔm] *nm* maximum; **le m. de** (*force etc*) the maximum (amount of); **au m.** as much as possible; (*tout au plus*) at most ▮ *a* maximum. ● **maximal, -aux** *a* maximum.
mayonnaise [majonɛz] *nf* mayonnaise.
mazout [mazut] *nm* (fuel) oil.
me [m(ə)] (**m'** before vowel or mute h) *pron* **1** (*complément direct*) me; **il me voit** he sees me. **2** (*indirect*) (**to**) me; **elle me parle** she speaks to me; **tu me l'as dit** you told me. **3** (*réfléchi*) myself; **je me lave** I wash myself.
mec [mek] *nm* (*individu*) *Arg* guy, bloke.
mécanicien [mekanisjɛ̃] *nm* mechanic; *Rail* train driver, *Am* engineer.
mécanique [mekanik] *a* mechanical; **jouet m.** wind-up toy ▮ *nf* (*science*) mechanics; (*mécanisme*) mechanism. ● **mécanisme** *nm* mechanism.
mécène [mesen] *nm* patron (of the arts).
méchant [meʃɑ̃] *a* (*cruel*) wicked, malicious; (*enfant*) naughty; (*chien*) vicious; **ce n'est pas m.** (*grave*) *Fam* it's nothing much. ● **méchamment** *adv* maliciously; (*très*) *Fam* terribly. ● **méchanceté** *nf* malice, wickedness; **une m.** a malicious word *ou* act.

mèche [mɛʃ] nf 1 (de cheveux) lock; pl (reflets) highlights. 2 (de bougie) wick; (de pétard) fuse; (de perceuse) drill, bit. 3 de m. avec qn (complicité) Fam in collusion with s.o.

méconnaissable [mekɔnɛsabl] a unrecognizable. ● **méconnu** a unrecognized.

mécontent [mekɔ̃tɑ̃] a dissatisfied (de with). ● **mécontenter** vt to displease, dissatisfy. ● **mécontentement** nm dissatisfaction, discontent.

médaille [medaj] nf (décoration) medal; (bijou) medallion; (pour chien) name tag; être m. d'or/d'argent Sp to be a gold/silver medallist ● **médaillon** nm (bijou) locket, medallion.

médecin [medsɛ̃] nm doctor, physician. ● **médecine** nf medicine; étudiant en m. medical student. ● **médical, -aux** a medical. ● **médicament** nm medicine.

médias [medja] nmpl (mass) media. ● **médiatique** a campagne/etc m. media campaign/etc.

médiéval, -aux [medjeval, -o] a medi(a)eval.

médiocre [medjɔkr] a second-rate, mediocre. ● **médiocrité** nf mediocrity.

médire* [medir] vi m. de qn to speak ill of s.o. ● **médisance(s)** nf(pl) malicious gossip; une m. a piece of malicious gossip.

méditer [medite] vt (conseil etc) to meditate on; m. de faire to consider doing ‖ vi to meditate (sur on).

Méditerranée [mediterane] nf la M. the Mediterranean. ● **méditerranéen, -enne** a Mediterranean.

médium [medjɔm] nm (spirite) medium.

méduse [medyz] nf jellyfish.

meeting [mitiŋ] nm Pol Sp meeting, rally.

méfait [mefɛ] nm Jur misdeed; pl (dégâts) ravages.

méfier (se) [s(ə)mefje] vpr se m. de to distrust, mistrust; (faire attention à) to watch out for; **méfie-toi!** watch out!; je me méfie I'm suspicious ou distrustful. ● **méfiant** a suspicious, distrustful. ● **mé-**

fiance nf distrust, mistrust.

mégarde (par) [parmegard] adv inadvertently, by mistake.

mégot [mego] nm Fam cigarette butt ou end.

meilleur, -eure [mɛjœr] a better (que than); le m. résultat/etc the best result/ etc ‖ nmf le m., la meilleure the best (one).

mélancolie [melɑ̃kɔli] nf melancholy, gloom. ● **mélancolique** a melancholy, gloomy.

mélange [melɑ̃ʒ] nm mixture, blend; (opération) mixing. ● **mélanger** vt (mêler) to mix; (brouiller) to mix (up), muddle ‖ se m. vpr to mix.

mélasse [melas] nf treacle, Am molasses.

mêler [mele] vt to mix, mingle (à with); (odeurs, thèmes) to combine; m. qn à (impliquer) to involve s.o. in ‖ se m. vpr to mix, mingle (à with); se m. à (la foule etc) to join; mêle-toi de ce qui te regarde! mind your own business! ● **mêlée** nf Rugby scrum.

mélodie [melɔdi] nf melody. ● **mélodieux, -euse** a melodious.

mélodrame [melɔdram] nm melodrama.

melon [m(ə)lɔ̃] nm 1 (fruit) melon. 2 (chapeau) m. bowler (hat), Am derby.

membre [mɑ̃br] nm 1 Anat limb. 2 (d'un groupe) member.

même [mɛm] 1 a same; en m. temps at the same time (que as); il est la bonté m. he is kindness itself; lui-m./vous-m./etc himself/yourself/etc ‖ pron le m., la m. the same (one); les mêmes the same (ones).

2 adv (y compris, aussi) even; m. si even if; ici m. in this very place; tout de m., quand m. all the same; de m. likewise; de m. que just as.

mémento [memɛ̃to] nm (aide-mémoire) handbook.

mémoire [memwar] 1 nf memory; à la m. de in memory of; m. morte/vive Ordinat read-only/random access memory. 2 nm Univ dissertation; pl Littér mémoirs. ● **mémorable** *a* memorable.

menace [mənas] *nf* threat, menace.
● **menacer** *vt* to threaten (**de faire** to
do). ● **menaçant** *a* threatening.

ménage [menaʒ] *nm* (*entretien*) house-
keeping; (*couple*) couple; **faire le m.** to
do the housework; **faire bon m. avec** to
get on happily with. ● **ménager¹, -ère** *a*
appareil m. domestic *ou* household
appliance; **travaux ménagers** housework
▌*nf* (*femme*) housewife.

ménag/er² [menaʒe] *vt* (*arranger*) to
prepare *ou* arrange (carefully);
(*épargner*) to use sparingly; **m. qn** to
treat *ou* handle s.o. carefully. ● **-ement**
nm (*soin*) care; **sans m.** (*brutalement*)
brutally.

mendier [mɑ̃dje] *vi* to beg ▌*vt* to beg for.
● **mendiant, -ante** *nmf* beggar.

men/er [məne] *vt* (*personne, vie etc*) to
lead; (*enquête*) to carry out; (*affaires*) to
run; **m. qn à** (*accompagner*) to take s.o.
to; **m. qch à bien** *Fig* to carry sth through
▌*vi Sp* to lead; **m. à** (*rue etc*) to lead to.
● **-eur, -euse** *nmf* (*de révolte*)
(ring)leader.

méningite [menɛ̃ʒit] *nf Méd* meningitis.

ménopause [menopoz] *nf* menopause.

menottes [mənɔt] *nfpl* handcuffs.

mensonge [mɑ̃sɔ̃ʒ] *nm* lie; (*action*) lying.

mensuel, -elle [mɑ̃sɥɛl] *a* monthly ▌*nm*
(*revue*) monthly. ● **mensualité** *nf*
monthly payment.

mensurations [mɑ̃syrasjɔ̃] *nfpl* measurements.

mental, -aux [mɑ̃tal, -o] *a* mental.
● **mentalité** *nf* mentality.

menthe [mɑ̃t] *nf* mint.

mention [mɑ̃sjɔ̃] *nf* mention, reference;
(*à un examen*) distinction; **faire m. de** to
mention. ● **mentionner** *vt* to mention.

ment/ir* [mɑ̃tir] *vi* to lie, tell lies (**à** to).
● **-eur, -euse** *nmf* liar.

menton [mɑ̃tɔ̃] *nm* chin.

menu [məny] **1** *nm* (*liste de plats*) &
Ordinat menu. **2** *a* (*mince*) slender, fine;
(*peu important*) minor, petty ▌*adv*

(*hacher*) small ▌*nm* **par le m.** in detail.

menuisier [mənɥizje] *nm* carpenter,
joiner. ● **menuiserie** *nf* carpentry, join-
ery; (*ouvrage*) woodwork.

méprendre (se) [səmeprɑ̃dr] *vpr* **se m.
sur** to be mistaken about.

mépris [mepri] *nm* contempt (**pour** for);
au m. de without regard to. ● **mépriser**
vt to despise, scorn. ● **méprisant** *a*
contemptuous, scornful.

méprisable [meprizabl] *a* despicable.

mer [mɛr] *nf* sea; (*marée*) tide; **en m.** at
sea; **par m.** by sea; **aller à la m.** to go to
the seaside.

mercenaire [mɛrsənɛr] *nm* mercenary.

mercerie [mɛrsəri] *nf* (*magasin*) haberdasher's, *Am* notions store.

merci [mɛrsi] **1** *int & nm* thank you,
thanks (**de, pour** for); (*non*) **m.!** no,
thank you! **2** *nf* **à la m. de** at the mercy
of.

mercredi [mɛrkrədi] *nm* Wednesday.

mercure [mɛrkyr] *nm* mercury.

merde! [mɛrd] *int Fam* (bloody) hell!

mère [mɛr] *nf* mother; **m. de famille**
mother (of a family); **maison m.** *Com*
parent company.

méridional, -ale, -aux [meridjɔnal, -o] *a*
southern ▌*nmf* southerner.

meringue [mərɛ̃g] *nf* (*gâteau*) meringue.

mérite [merit] *nm* merit. ● **mériter** *vt* (*être
digne de*) to deserve; (*valoir*) to be
worth; **m. de réussir**/*etc* to deserve to
succeed/*etc.*

merlan [mɛrlɑ̃] *nm* (*poisson*) whiting.

merle [mɛrl] *nm* blackbird.

merveille [mɛrvɛj] *nf* wonder, marvel;
à m. wonderfully (well). ● **merveilleux,
-euse** *a* wonderful, marvellous, *Am*
marvelous ▌*nm* **le m.** the supernatural.

mes [me] *voir* **mon.**

mésange [mezɑ̃ʒ] *nf* (*oiseau*) tit.

mésaventure [mezavɑ̃tyr] *nf* slight mishap.

mesdames [medam] *voir* **madame.**

mesdemoiselles [medmwazɛl] *voir* **mademoiselle.**

mésentente [mezãtãt] nf disagreement.

mesquin [meskɛ̃] a mean, petty.

message [mesaʒ] nm message. ● **messager, -ère** nmf messenger.

messageries [mesaʒri] nfpl Com courier service.

messe [mes] nf mass (church service).

Messie [mesi] nm Messiah.

messieurs [mesjø] voir **monsieur**.

mesure [mazyr] nf (dimension) measurement; (action) measure; (retenue) moderation; (cadence) Mus time, beat; **fait sur m.** made to measure; **à m. que** as, as soon ou as fast as; **dans la m. où** in so far as; **dans une certaine m.** to a certain extent; **en m. de** able to.

mesurer [mazyre] vt to measure; (juger, estimer) to calculate, assess; (argent, temps) to ration (out); **m. 1 mètre 83** (personne) to be six feet tall; (objet) to measure six feet.

met(s) [mɛ] voir **mettre**.

métal, -aux [metal, -o] nm metal. ● **métallique** a (éclat) metallic; **pont**/etc **m.** metal bridge/etc. ● **métallisé** a **bleu**/etc **m.** metallic blue/etc.

métallurgie [metalyrʒi] nf (industrie) steel industry; (science) metallurgy.

métaphore [metafɔr] nf metaphor. ● **métaphorique** a metaphorical.

météo [meteo] nf (bulletin) weather forecast.

météore [meteɔr] nm meteor.

météorologie [meteɔrɔlɔʒi] nf (science) meteorology; (service) weather bureau. ● **météorologique** a meteorological; **bulletin**/etc **m.** weather report/etc.

méthode [metɔd] nf (manière, soin) method; (livre) course. ● **méthodique** a methodical.

méticuleux, -euse [metikylø, -øz] a meticulous.

métier [metje] nm 1 (travail) job; (manuel) trade; (intellectuel) profession; **homme de m.** specialist. **2 m.** (à tisser) loom.

métis, -isse [metis] a & nmf half-caste.

métrage [metraʒ] nm (tissu) length; (de

film) footage; **long m.** (film) full-length film; **court m.** (film) short (film).

mètre [metr] nm (mesure) metre, Am meter; (règle) (metre) rule; **m. carré** square metre; **m. (à ruban)** tape measure. ● **métrique** a metric.

métro [metro] nm underground, Am subway.

métropolitain [metrɔpɔlitɛ̃] a metropolitan.

mets [mɛ] nm (aliment) dish.

mette(s), mettent [mɛt] voir **mettre**.

metteur en scène [metœrãsɛn] nm Th producer; Cin director.

mettre* [metr] vt to put; (table) to set, lay; (vêtement, lunettes) to put on, wear; (chauffage, radio etc) to put on, switch on; (réveil) to set (à for); **j'ai mis une heure** it took me an hour; **m. en colère** to make angry; **m. à l'aise** (rassurer) to put ou set at ease; **m. en liberté** to free; **m. en bouteille(s)** to bottle; **mettons que** (+ sub) let's suppose that.

❚ **se mettre** vpr to put oneself; (debout) to stand; (assis) to sit; (objet) to go, be put; **se m. en short**/etc to get into one's shorts/etc; **se m. à table** to sit (down) at the table; **se m. à l'aise** to make oneself comfortable; **se m. au travail** to start work; **se m. à faire** to start doing; **se m. au beau/froid/chaud** (temps) to turn fine/cold/warm.

meuble [mœbl] nm piece of furniture; pl furniture. ● **meubler** vt to furnish. ● **meublé** nm furnished flat ou Am apartment.

meugler [møgle] vi (vache) to moo.

meule [møl] nf 1 (de foin) haystack. 2 (pour moudre) millstone.

meunier, -ière [mønje, -jɛr] nmf miller.

meurt [mœr] voir **mourir**.

meurtre [mœrtr] nm murder. ● **meurtrier, -ière** nmf murderer ❚ a deadly, murderous.

meurtrir [mœrtrir] vt to bruise.

meute [møt] nf (de chiens etc) pack.

Mexique [meksik] nm Mexico. ● **mexi-**

cain, -aine a & nmf Mexican.

mi [mi] nm (note de musique) E.

mi- [mi] préf **la mi-mars**/etc mid March/ etc; **à mi-distance** midway.

miaul/er [mjole] vi (chat) to miaow, mew. ●**—ement(s)** nm(pl) miaowing, mewing.

mi-bas [miba] nm inv (dans les dates) a sock.

miche [miʃ] nf round loaf.

mi-chemin (à) [amiʃmɛ̃] adv halfway.

mi-clos [miklo] a half-closed.

mi-côte (à) [amikot] adv halfway up ou down (the hill).

micro [mikro] nm **1** microphone, mike. **2** (ordinateur) Fam micro(-computer).

micro- [mikro] préf micro-.

microbe [mikrɔb] nm germ.

microfilm [mikrɔfilm] nm microfilm.

micro-onde [mikrɔɔ̃d] nf microwave; **four à micro-ondes** microwave oven.

microscope [mikrɔskɔp] nm microscope.

midi [midi] nm **1** (heure) twelve o'clock, noon, midday; (heure du déjeuner) lunchtime. **2** **le M.** the south of France.

mie [mi] nf **la m.** the soft part of the bread; **pain de m.** sandwich loaf.

miel [mjel] nm honey.

mien, mienne [mjɛ̃, mjɛn] pron poss **le m., la mienne, les miens, les miennes** mine; **les deux miens** my two ‖nmpl **les miens** (ma famille) my (own) people.

miette [mjet] nf (de pain etc) crumb; **réduire en miettes** to smash to pieces.

mieux [mjø] adv & a inv better (que than); (plus à l'aise) more comfortable; (plus beau) better-looking; **le m., la m., les m.** the best; (de deux) the better; **tu ferais m. de partir** you had better leave; **de m. en m.** better and better; **je ne demande pas m.** there's nothing I'd like better (que de faire than to do). ‖nm (amélioration) improvement; **faire de son m.** to do one's best; **faire qch au m.** to do sth in the best possible way.

mignon, -onne [miɲɔ̃, -ɔn] a (charmant) cute; (gentil) nice.

migraine [migren] nf headache; Méd migraine.

migration [migrasjɔ̃] nf migration.

mijoter [miʒɔte] vt Culin to cook (lovingly); (lentement) to simmer ‖vi to simmer.

mil [mil] nm inv (dans les dates) a thousand; **l'an deux m.** the year two thousand.

milieu, -x [miljø] nm (centre) middle; (cadre, groupe social) environment; (entre extrêmes) middle course; (espace) Phys medium; **au m. de** in the middle of; **le juste m.** the happy medium; **le m.** (de malfaiteurs) the underworld.

militaire [militer] a military; **service m.** military service ‖nm serviceman; (dans l'armée de terre) soldier.

milit/er [milite] vi (personne) to be a militant; (arguments etc) to militate (pour in favour of, contre against). ●**—ant, -ante** nmf militant.

mille [mil] **1** a & nm inv thousand; **m. hommes**/etc a ou one thousand men/ etc; **deux m.** two thousand; **mettre dans le m.** to hit the bull's-eye. **2** nm (mesure) mile. ●**m.-pattes** nm inv (insecte) centipede. ●**millième** a & nmf thousandth. ●**millier** nm thousand; **un m. (de)** a thousand or so.

millefeuille [milfœj] nm (gâteau) cream slice.

millénaire [milener] nm millennium.

millésime [milezim] nm date (on wine etc).

millet [mije] nm Bot millet.

milli- [mili] préf milli-.

milliard [miljar] nm billion, thousand million. ●**milliardaire** nmf multimillionaire.

millimètre [milimetr] nm millimetre.

million [miljɔ̃] nm million; **un m. de livres**/etc a million pounds/etc; **deux millions** two million. ●**millionnaire** nmf millionaire.

mime [mim] nmf (acteur) mime; **le m.** (art) mime. ●**mimer** vti to mime. ●**mimique** nf (mine) funny face.

mimosa [mimoza] *nm Bot* mimosa.

minable [minabl] *a (lieu, personne)* shabby; *(médiocre)* pathetic.

minaret [minarɛ] *nm (de mosquée)* minaret.

minauder [minode] *vi* to simper.

mince [mɛ̃s] **1** *a* thin; *(élancé)* slim; *(insignifiant)* slim, paltry. **2** *int* **m. (alors)!** oh heck! ● **mincir** *vi* to get slim(mer).

mine [min] *nf* **1** appearance; *(physionomie)* look; **avoir bonne/mauvaise m.** to look well/ill; **faire m. de faire** to appear to do, make as if to do. **2** *(gisement)* & *Fig* mine; **m. de charbon** coalmine. **3** *(de crayon)* lead. **4** *(engin explosif)* mine. ● **miner** *vt* **1** *(saper)* to undermine. **2** *(terrain)* to mine.

minéral [mineral] *nm* ore.

minéral, -aux [mineral, -o] *a* & *nm* mineral.

minéralogique [mineralɔʒik] *a* **plaque m.** *Aut* number *ou Am* license plate.

mineur, -eure [minœr] **1** *nm (ouvrier)* miner. **2** *a (jeune, secondaire)* & *Mus* minor ▮ *nmf Jur* minor. ● **minier, -lère** *a* **industrie/***etc* **minière** mining industry/ *etc.*

mini- [mini] *préf* mini-.

miniature [minjatyr] *nf* miniature ▮ *a inv* **train/***etc* **m.** miniature train/*etc.*

minibus [minibys] *nm* minibus.

minime [minim] *a* trifling, minimal.

minimum [minimɔm] *nm* minimum; **le m. de** *(force etc)* the minimum *(amount of)*; **au m.** at the very least ▮ *a* minimum. ● **minimal, -aux** *a* minimum, minimal.

ministre [ministr] *nm Pol Rel* minister; **m. de l'Intérieur** = Home Secretary, *Am* Secretary of the Interior. ● **ministère** *nm* ministry; *(gouvernement)* cabinet; **m. de Intérieur** = Home Office, *Am* Department of the Interior. ● **ministériel, -lelle** *a* ministerial; **remaniement m.** cabinet reshuffle.

Minitel® [minitɛl] *nm* = telephone-connected terminal for data bank consul-

tation.

minorité [minɔrite] *nf* minority; **en m.** in the *ou* a minority. ● **minoritaire** *a* **parti/** *etc* **m.** minority party/*etc*; **être m.** to be in the *ou* a minority.

Minorque [minɔrk] *nf* Minorca.

minuit [minɥi] *nm* midnight, twelve o'clock.

minuscule [minyskyl] **1** *a (petit)* tiny, minute. **2** *a* & *nf* **(lettre) m.** small letter.

minute [minyt] *nf* minute; **à la m.** *(tout de suite)* this *(very)* minute; **d'une m. à l'autre** any minute *(now)* ▮ *a inv* **aliments** *ou* **plats m.** convenience food(s). ● **minuter** *vt* to time. ● **minuterie** *nf* time switch *(for lighting in a stairway etc)*. ● **minuteur** *nm* timer.

minutieux, -euse [minysjø, øz] *a* meticulous.

mioche [mjoʃ] *nmf (enfant) Fam* kid.

mirabelle [mirabɛl] *nf* mirabelle plum.

miracle [mirakl] *nm* miracle; **par m.** miraculously. ● **miraculeux, -euse** *a* miraculous.

mirage [miraʒ] *nm* mirage.

miroir [mirwar] *nm* mirror. ● **miroiter** *vi* to gleam, shimmer.

mis [mi] *pp de* **mettre** ▮ *a* **bien m.** well dressed.

mise [miz] *nf* **1** *(action)* putting; **m. en marche** starting up; **m. en service** putting into service; **m. en scène** *Th* production; *Cin* direction; **m. à feu** *(de fusée)* blast-off. **2** *(argent)* stake. **3** *(tenue)* attire.

miser [mize] *vt (argent)* to stake *(sur on)* ▮ *vi* **m. sur** *(cheval)* to back; *(compter sur) Fam* to bank on.

misère [mizer] *nf (grinding)* poverty; *(malheur)* misery. ● **misérable** *a* miserable, wretched; *(très pauvre)* destitute; *(logement, quartier)* seedy.

miséricorde [mizerikɔrd] *nf* mercy.

missile [misil] *nm (fusée)* missile.

mission [misjɔ̃] *nf* mission; *(tâche)* task. ● **missionnaire** *nm* missionary.

missive [misiv] *nf (lettre) Litt* missive.

mistral [mistral] *nm inv (vent)* mistral.

mite [mit] *nf* (clothes) moth.

mi-temps [mitɑ̃] *nf* (*pause*) *Sp* half-time; (*période*) *Sp* half; **travailler à mi-t.** to work part-time.

miteux, -euse [mitø, -øz] *a* shabby.

mitigé [mitiʒe] *a* moderate, lukewarm.

mitrailler [mitraje] *vt* to machinegun; (*photographier*) *Fam* to click *ou* snap away at. ●**mitraillette** *nf* machinegun (*portable*). ●**mitrailleur** *a* **fusil m.** machinegun (*portable*). ●**mitrailleuse** *nf* machinegun (*heavy*).

mi-voix (à) [amivwa] *adv* in an undertone.

mixe(u)r [miksœr] *nm* (*pour mélanger*) mixer; (*pour rendre liquide*) liquidizer.

mixte [mikst] *a* mixed; (*école*) co-educational, mixed.

mixture [mikstyr] *nf Péj* mixture.

Mlle [madmwazɛl] *abrév* = **Mademoiselle.**

MM [mesjø] *abrév* = **Messieurs.**

mm *abrév* (**millimètre**) mm.

Mme [madam] *abrév* = **Madame.**

mobile [mɔbil] **1** *a* (*pièce*) moving; (*panneau*) mov(e)able; (*personne*) mobile; (*feuillets*) detachable, loose ▮*nm* (*œuvre d'art*) mobile. **2** *nm* (*motif*) motive (**de** for). ●**mobilité** *nf* mobility.

mobilier [mɔbilje] *nm* furniture.

mobiliser [mɔbilize] *vti* to mobilize.

mobylette® [mɔbilɛt] *nf* moped.

mocassin [mɔkasɛ̃] *nm* moccasin.

moche [mɔʃ] *a Fam* (*laid*) ugly; **c'est m.** (*mal*) it's lousy *ou* rotten.

modalités [mɔdalite] *nfpl* methods (**de** of).

mode [mɔd] **1** *nf* fashion; (*industrie*) fashion trade; **à la m.** fashionable, in fashion. **2** *nm* mode, method; **m. d'emploi** directions (for use); **m. de vie** way of life. **3** *nm Gram* mood.

modèle [mɔdɛl] *nm* (*schéma, exemple, personne*) model; **m.** (*réduit*) (scale) model. ●**modeler** *vt* to model (**sur** on).

modem [mɔdɛm] *nm Ordinat* modem.

modéré [mɔdere] *a* moderate.

modérer [mɔdere] *vt* to moderate; (*vitesse, température etc*) to reduce ▮**se m.** *vpr* to restrain oneself. ●**modération** *nf* moderation; reduction; **avec m.** in moderation.

moderne [mɔdɛrn] *a* modern ▮*nm* **le m.** (*mobilier*) modern furniture. ●**moderniser** *vt*, **se m.** *vpr* to modernize.

modeste [mɔdɛst] *a* modest. ●**modestie** *nf* modesty.

modifier [mɔdifje] *vt* to alter, modify. ●**modification** *nf* alteration, modification.

modique [mɔdik] *a* (*prix etc*) modest.

modulation [mɔdylasjɔ̃] *nf* **m. de fréquence** FM (*frequency modulation*).

moelle [mwal] *nf Anat* marrow; **m. épinière** spinal cord.

moelleux, -euse [mwalø, -øz] *a* (*lit, tissu*) soft.

mœurs [mœr(s)] *nfpl* (*morale*) morals; (*habitudes*) habits, customs.

mohair [mɔɛr] *nm* mohair.

moi [mwa] *pron* **1** (*après une préposition*) me; **pour/avec/***etc* **moi** for/with/*etc* me. **2** (*complément direct*) me; **laissez-moi** leave me. **3** (*complément indirect*) (to) me; **montrez-le-moi** shows it to me. **4** (*sujet*) I; **c'est moi qui vous le dis!** *I'm* telling you; **il est plus grand que moi** he's taller than I am *ou* than me; **moi, je veux bien** (*emphatique*) that's OK by me. **5** *nm inv Psy* self. ●**moi-même** *pron* myself.

moindre [mwɛ̃dr] *a* **la m. erreur/***etc* the slightest mistake/*etc*; **le m.** (**de mes problèmes** *etc*) the least (**de** of); (**de deux problèmes** *etc*) the lesser (**de** of).

moine [mwan] *nm* monk.

moineau, -x [mwano] *nm* sparrow.

moins [mwɛ̃] **1** *adv* ([mwɛz] *before vowel*) less (**que** than); **m. de** (*temps, travail etc*) less (**que** than), not so much (**que** as); (*gens, livres etc*) fewer (**que** than), not so many (**que** as); (*cent francs etc*) less than; **m. grand/***etc* not as big/*etc* (**que** as); **le m., la m., les m.**

(*travailler etc*) the least; **le m. grand, la m. grande, les m. grand(e)s** the smallest; **de m. en m.** [dəmwɛzãmwɛ] less and less; **au m., du m.** at least; **de m., en m.** (*qui manque*) missing; **dix ans/***etc* **de m.** ten years/*etc* less; **en m.** (*personne, objet*) less; (*personnes, objets*) fewer; **les m. de vingt ans** those under twenty; **à m. que** (+ *sub*) unless.
2 *prép Math* minus; **deux heures m. cinq** five to two; **il fait m. dix (degrés)** it's minus ten (degrees).

mois [mwa] *nm* month; **au m. de juin/***etc* in (the month of) June/*etc*.

mois/ir [mwazir] *vi* to go mouldy; (*attendre*) *Fam* to hang about. ●—**i** *a* mouldy, *Am* moldy ▮*nm* mould, *Am* mold; **sentir le m.** to smell musty. ● **moisissure** *nf* mould, mildew.

moisson [mwasɔ̃] *nf* harvest.

moite [mwat] *a* sticky, moist.

moitié [mwatje] *nf* half; **la m. de la pomme/***etc* half (of) the apple/*etc*; **à m.** (*remplir etc*) halfway; **à m. fermé/** *etc* half closed/*etc*; **à m. prix** (at *ou* for) half-price; **de m.** by half; **partager m. -moitié** *Fam* to split fifty-fifty.

moka [mɔka] *nm* (*café*) mocha.

mol [mɔl] *voir* **mou.**

molaire [mɔlɛr] *nf* (*dent*) back tooth, molar.

molester [mɔlɛste] *vt* to manhandle.

molette [mɔlɛt] *nf* **clé à m.** adjustable wrench *ou* spanner.

molle [mɔl] *voir* **mou.** ● **mollir** *vi* to go soft; (*courage*) to flag.

mollet [mɔlɛ] **1** *nm* (*de jambe*) calf. **2** *a* **œuf m.** soft-boiled egg.

môme [mom] *nm/f* (*enfant*) *Fam* kid.

moment [mɔmã] *nm* (*instant*) moment; (*période*) time; **en ce m.** at the moment; **par moments** at times; **au m. de partir** when just about to leave; **au m. où** just as, when; **du m. que** (*puisque*) seeing that. ● **momentané** *a* momentary.

momie [mɔmi] *nf* (*cadavre*) mummy.

mon, ma, *pl* **mes** [mɔ̃, ma, me] (**ma** *becomes* **mon** [mɔ̃n] *before a vowel or*

mute h) *a poss* my; **mon père** my father; **ma mère** my mother; **mon ami(e)** my friend; **mes parents** my parents.

Monaco [mɔnako] *nf* Monaco.

monarque [mɔnark] *nm* monarch. ● **monarchie** *nf* monarchy.

monastère [mɔnaster] *nm* monastery.

monceau, -x [mɔ̃so] *nm* heap, pile.

mondain, -aine [mɔ̃dɛ̃, -ɛn] *a* **réunion/ etc mondaine** society gathering/*etc*.

monde [mɔ̃d] *nm* world; (*milieu social*) set; **du m.** (*gens*) people; (*beaucoup de gens*) a lot of people; **un m. fou** a tremendous crowd; **le m. entier** the whole world; **tout le m.** everybody; **mettre au m.** to give birth to; **venir au m.** to come into the world; **pas le moins du m.!** not in the least! ● **mondial, -aux** *a* (*crise, renommée etc*) worldwide; **guerre mondiale** world war.

monégasque [mɔnegask] *a & nmf* Monegasque.

monétaire [mɔneter] *a* monetary.

moniteur, -trice [mɔniter, -tris] *nmf* **1** instructor; (*de colonie de vacances*) assistant, *Am* camp counselor. **2** (*écran*) *Ordinat etc* monitor.

monnaie [mɔnɛ] *nf* (*devise*) currency, money; (*pièces*) change; **pièce de m.** coin; (*petite*) **m.** (small) change; **faire de la m.** to get change; **faire de la m. à qn** to give s.o. change (**sur un billet** for a note *ou Am* bill); **c'est m. courante** *Fig* it's very frequent.

mono- [mɔno] *préf* mono-.

monologue [mɔnɔlɔg] *nm* monologue.

monoparentale [mɔnɔparãtal] *af* **famille m.** one-parent family.

monophonie [mɔnɔfɔni] *nf* **en m.** in mono.

monoplace [mɔnɔplas] *a & nmf* (*avion, voiture*) single-seater.

monopole [mɔnɔpɔl] *nm* monopoly.

monotone [mɔnɔtɔn] *a* monotonous.

monseigneur [mɔ̃sɛɲœr] *nm* (*évêque*) His *ou* Your Grace; (*prince*) His *ou* Your Highness.

monsieur, *pl* **messieurs** [məsjø, mesjø]

nm man, gentleman; **oui m.** yes sir; **oui messieurs** yes gentlemen; **M. Legras** Mr Legras; **Messieurs** *ou* **MM Legras** Messrs Legras; **Monsieur** (*dans une lettre*) Dear Sir.

monstre [mɔ̃str] *nm* monster ▮ *a* (*énorme*) *Fam* colossal. ● **monstrueux, -euse** *a* (*abominable, énorme*) monstrous.

mont [mɔ̃] *nm* (*montagne*) mount.

montage [mɔ̃taʒ] *nm* *Tech* assembling, assembly; *Cin* editing.

montagne [mɔ̃taɲ] *nf* mountain; **la m.** (*zone*) the mountains; **montagnes russes** roller coaster. ● **montagnard, -arde** *nmf* mountain dweller. ● **montagneux, -euse** *a* mountainous.

montant [mɔ̃tɑ̃] **1** *nm* (*somme*) amount. **2** *nm* (*de barrière*) post; (*d'échelle*) upright. **3** *a* (*marée*) rising; (*col*) stand-up; **chaussure montante** boot.

monte-charge [mɔ̃tʃarʒ] *nm inv* service lift *ou* *Am* elevator.

montée [mɔ̃te] *nf* (*ascension*) climb; (*chemin*) slope; (*des prix, des eaux*) rise.

monter [mɔ̃te] *vi* (*aux* **être**) (*personne*) to go up *ou* come up; (*s'élever*) (*ballon etc*) to go up; (*grimper*) to climb (up) (**sur** onto); (*prix*) to go up, rise; (*marée*) to come in; (*avion*) to climb; **m. dans un véhicule** to get in(to) a vehicle; **m. dans un train** to get on(to) a train; **m. sur** *ou* **à** (*échelle*) to climb (up); **m. sur le trône** to become king *ou* queen; **m. en courant/** *etc* to run/*etc* up; **m. (à cheval)** *Sp* to ride (a horse).

▮ *vt* (*aux* **avoir**) (*côte etc*) to climb (up); (*objet*) to bring *ou* take up; (*cheval*) to ride; (*tente, affaire*) to set up; (*machine*) to assemble; (*bijou*) to set, mount; (*pièce*) *Th* to stage; **m. l'escalier** to go *ou* come upstairs *ou* up the stairs; **faire m. qn** to show s.o. up.

▮ **se monter** *vpr* **se m. à** (*frais*) to amount to.

montre [mɔ̃tr] *nf* **1** (wrist)watch; **course contre la m.** race against time. **2 faire m. de** *Litt* to show.

Montréal [mɔ̃real] *nm ou f* Montreal.

montrer [mɔ̃tre] *vt* to show (**à** to); **m. qn/ qch du doigt** to point at s.o./sth; **m. à qn comment faire qch** to show s.o. how to do sth ▮ **se m.** *vpr* to show oneself; **se m. courageux/***etc* to be courageous/*etc*, show courage/*etc*.

monture [mɔ̃tyr] *nf* **1** (*de lunettes*) frame; (*de bijou*) setting **2** (*cheval*) mount.

monument [mɔnymɑ̃] *nm* monument; **m. aux morts** war memorial. ● **monumental, -aux** *a* (*imposant, énorme etc*) monumental.

moquer (se) [səmɔke] *vpr* **se m. de** to make fun of; **je m'en moque!** *Fam* I couldn't care less! ● **moquerie** *nf* mockery.

moquette [mɔkɛt] *nf* fitted carpet(s), *Am* wall-to-wall carpeting.

moral, -aux [mɔral, -o] *a* moral ▮ *nm* **le m.** spirits, morale. ● **morale** *nf* (*d'histoire*) moral; (*principes*) morals; (*code*) moral code; **faire la m. à qn** to lecture s.o. ● **moralité** *nf* (*mœurs*) morality; (*de fable, récit etc*) moral.

morbide [mɔrbid] *a* morbid.

morceau, -x [mɔrso] *nm* piece, bit; (*de sucre*) lump; (*de viande*) *Culin* cut; (*d'une œuvre littéraire*) extract. ● **morceler** *vt* (*terrain*) to divide up.

mordiller [mɔrdije] *vt* to nibble.

mordre [mɔrdr] *vti* to bite; **ça mord** *Pêche* I have a bite.

mordu, -ue [mɔrdy] *pp de* **mordre** ▮ *nmf* **un m. du jazz/***etc* *Fam* a jazz/*etc* fan.

morfondre (se) [səmɔrfɔ̃dr] *vpr* to get bored (waiting), mope (about).

morgue [mɔrg] *nf* (*lieu*) mortuary, morgue.

morne [mɔrn] *a* dismal, gloomy, dull.

morose [mɔroz] *a* morose, sullen.

morphine [mɔrfin] *nf* morphine.

mors [mɔr] *nm* (*de harnais*) bit.

morse [mɔrs] *nm* **1** Morse (code). **2** (*animal*) walrus.

morsure [mɔrsyr] *nf* bite.

mort[1] [mɔr] *nf* death; **un silence de m.** a deathly silence. ● **mortalité** *nf* death rate. ● **mortel, -elle** *a* (*hommes, ennemi* *etc*) mortal; (*accident*) fatal; (*ennuyeux*) *Fam* deadly (dull) ▮ *nmf* mortal.

mort², morte [mɔr, mɔrt] *a* (*personne, plante etc*) dead; **m. de fatigue** dead tired; **m. de froid** numb with cold; **m. de peur** frightened to death.
▮ *nmf* dead man, dead woman; **les morts** the dead; **de nombreux morts** (*victimes*) many casualties *ou* deaths; **le jour** *ou* **la fête des Morts** All Souls' Day. ●**morte-saison** *nf* off season. ●**mort-né** *a* (*enfant*) & *Fig* stillborn.

mortuaire [mɔrtɥɛr] *a* **couronne**/*etc* **m.** funeral wreath/*etc*.

morue [mɔry] *nf* cod.

mosaïque [mɔzaik] *nf* mosaic.

Moscou [mɔsku] *nm ou f* Moscow.

mosquée [mɔske] *nf* mosque.

mot [mo] *nm* word; **envoyer un m. à qn** to drop a line to s.o.; **bon m.** witticism; **mots croisés** crossword (puzzle); **m. de passe** password; **m. d'ordre** *Pol* resolution, order.

motard [mɔtar] *nm Fam* motorcyclist.

moteur¹ [mɔtœr] *nm* (*de véhicule etc*) engine, motor; *Él* motor.

moteur², -trice [mɔtœr, -tris] *a* (*nerf, muscle*) motor; **force motrice** driving force.

motif [mɔtif] *nm* **1** (*raison*) reason (de for). **2** (*dessin*) pattern.

motion [mɔsjɔ̃] *nf Pol* motion; **on a voté une m. de censure** a vote of no confidence was passed.

motivé [mɔtive] *a* motivated.

moto [mɔto] *nf* motorcycle, motorbike. ●**motocycliste** *nmf* motorcyclist.

motte [mɔt] *nf* (*de terre*) lump, clod; (*de beurre*) block.

mou (*or* **mol** *before vowel or mute h*), **molle** [mu, mɔl] *a* soft; (*sans énergie*) feeble ▮ *nm* **avoir du m.** (*cordage*) to be slack.

mouchard, -arde [muʃar, -ard] *nmf Péj* informer.

mouche [muʃ] *nf* (*insecte*) fly; **faire m.** to hit the bull's-eye. ●**moucheron** *nm* (*insecte*) gnat, midge.

moucher [muʃe] *vt* **m. qn** to wipe s.o.'s nose; **se m.** to blow one's nose.

mouchoir [muʃwar] *nm* handkerchief; (*en papier*) tissue.

moudre* [mudr] *vt* (*café, blé*) to grind.

moue [mu] *nf* long face, pout; **faire la m.** to pull a (long) face, to pout.

mouette [mwɛt] *nf* (sea)gull.

moufle [mufl] *nf* (*gant*) mitten.

mouiller [muje] **1** *vt* to wet, make wet ▮ **se m.** *vpr* to get (oneself) wet; (*se compromettre*) *Fam* to get involved (*by taking risks*). **2** *vi Nau* to anchor. ●**mouillé** *a* wet (de with).

moule¹ [mul] *nm* mould, *Am* mold; **m. à gâteaux** cake tin. ●**mouler** *vt* to mould, *Am* mold; (*vêtement*) to fit s.o. tightly. ●**moulant** *a* (*vêtement*) tight-fitting.

moule² [mul] *nf* (*animal*) mussel.

moulin [mulɛ̃] *nm* mill; **m. à vent** windmill; **m. à café** coffee-grinder.

moulinet [mulinɛ] *nm* (*de canne à pêche*) reel.

moulu [muly] *pp de* **moudre** ▮ *a* (*café*) ground.

mour/ir* [murir] *vi* (*aux être*) to die (de of, from); **m. de froid** to die of exposure; **m. de fatigue** *Fig* to be dead tired; **m. de peur** *Fig* to be frightened to death; **s'ennuyer à m.** to be bored to death; **je meurs de faim** I'm starving! ●**—ant, -ante** *a* dying; (*voix*) faint.

mousse [mus] **1** *nf Bot* moss. **2** *nf* (*écume*) foam, froth; (*de bière*) froth; (*de savon*) lather; **m. à raser** shaving foam. **3** *nf Culin* mousse. ●**mousser** *vi* (*bière etc*) to froth; (*savon*) to lather; (*eau savonneuse*) to foam. ●**mousseux** *nm* sparkling wine.

mousseline [muslin] *nf* (*coton*) muslin.

mousson [musɔ̃] *nf* (*vent*) monsoon.

moustache [mustaʃ] *nf* moustache, *Am* mustache; *pl* (*de chat etc*) whiskers. ●**moustachu** *a* wearing a moustache.

moustique [mustik] *nm* mosquito. ●**moustiquaire** *nf* mosquito net; (*en métal*) screen.

moutarde [mutard] *nf* mustard.

mouton [mutɔ̃] *nm* sheep *inv*; (*viande*) mutton; *pl* (*sur la mer*) white horses, *Am* whitecaps; **peau de m.** sheepskin.

mouvement [muvmã] *nm* (*geste, groupe etc*) & *Mus* movement; (*de colère*) outburst; (*impulsion*) impulse; **en m.** in motion. ● **mouvementé** *a* (*vie, voyage etc*) eventful.

mouvoir* [muvwar] *vi*, **se m.** *vpr* to move; **mû par** (*mécanisme*) driven by. ● **mouvant** *a* **sables mouvants** quicksands.

moyen¹, -enne [mwajɛ̃, -ɛn] *a* average; (*format etc*) medium(-sized); **classe moyenne** middle class ‖ *nf* average; (*à un examen*) pass mark; (*à un devoir*) half marks; **en moyenne** on average; **la moyenne d'âge** the average age.

moyen² [mwajɛ̃] *nm* (*procédé, façon*) means, way (**de faire** of doing, to do); *pl* (*capacités*) ability, powers; (*argent*) means; **au m. de** by means of; **il n'y a pas m. de faire** it's not possible to do; **je n'ai pas les moyens** (*argent*) I can't afford it.

MST [emeste] *nf abrév* (*maladie sexuellement transmissible*) sexually transmitted disease, STD.

muer [mɥe] *vi* (*animal*) to moult, *Am* molt; (*voix*) to break; **se m. en** *Litt* to become transformed into.

muet, -ette [mɥe, -ɛt] *a* (*infirme*) dumb; (*de surprise etc*) speechless; (*film etc*) silent; (*voyelle etc*) *Gram* silent, mute.

mufle [myfl] *nm* **1** (*d'animal*) muzzle, nose. **2** (*individu*) *Péj* lout.

mug/ir [myʒir] *vi* (*bœuf*) to bellow; (*vache*) to moo; (*vent*) *Fig* to roar. ● **—issement(s)** *nm(pl)* bellow(ing); moo(ing); roar(ing).

muguet [myɡe] *nm* lily of the valley.

mule [myl] *nf* **1** (*pantoufle*) mule. **2** (*animal*) (she-)mule. ● **mulet¹** *nm* (he-)mule.

mulet² [mylɛ] *nm* (*poisson*) mullet.

multi- [mylti] *préf* multi-.

multicolore [myltikɔlɔr] *a* multico-

loured.

multinationale [myltinasjɔnal] *nf* multinational.

multiple [myltipl] *a* (*nombreux*) numerous; (*varié*) multiple ‖ *nm Math* multiple. ● **multiplication** *nf* multiplication; (*augmentation*) increase. ● **multiplier** *vt* to multiply ‖ **se m.** *vpr* to increase; (*se reproduire*) to multiply.

multitude [myltityd] *nf* multitude.

municipal, -aux [mynisipal, -o] *a* municipal; **conseil m.** town *ou Am* city council. ● **municipalité** *nf* (*corps*) town *ou Am* city council; (*commune*) municipality.

munir [mynir] *vt* **m. de** to provide *ou* equip with.

munitions [mynisjɔ̃] *nfpl* ammunition.

mur [myr] *nm* wall; **m. du son** sound barrier. ● **muraille** *nf* (high) wall.

mûr [myr] *a* (*fruit etc*) ripe; (*personne*) mature; **d'âge m.** of mature years, middle-aged. ● **mûrement** *adv* (*réfléchir*) carefully. ● **mûrir** *vti* (*fruit*) to ripen; (*personne*) to mature.

mûre [myr] *nf* (*baie*) blackberry.

muret [myrɛ] *nm* low wall.

murmure [myrmyr] *nm* murmur. ● **murmurer** *vti* to murmur.

muscade [myskad] *nf* nutmeg.

muscle [myskl] *nm* muscle. ● **musclé** *a* (*bras*) muscular, brawny. ● **musculaire** *a* (*force, douleur etc*) muscular. ● **musculature** *nf* muscles.

museau, -x [myzo] *nm* (*de chien, chat*) nose, muzzle. ● **museler** *vt* (*animal, presse*) to muzzle. ● **muselière** *nf* (*appareil*) muzzle.

musée [myze] *nm* museum; **m. de peinture** (public) art gallery. ● **muséum** *nm* (natural history) museum.

music-hall [myzikol] *nm* variety theatre.

musique [myzik] *nf* music. ● **musical, -aux** *a* musical. ● **musicien, -ienne** *nmf* musician ‖ *a* **être très/assez m.** to be very/quite musical.

musulman, -ane [myzylmã, -an] *a* & *nmf* Muslim, Moslem.

mutation [mytɑsjɔ̃] *nf* (*d'employé*) transfer; **en pleine m.** *Fig* undergoing profound change.

mutilé, -ée [mytile] *nmf* **m. de guerre** disabled ex-serviceman *ou Am* veteran.

mutin [mytɛ̃] **1** *a* (*espiègle*) full of fun, saucy. **2** *nm* (*rebelle*) mutineer.

mutuel, -elle[1] [mytɥɛl] *a* (*réciproque*) mutual.

mutuelle[2] [mytɥɛl] *nf* friendly society, *Am* benefit society.

myope [mjɔp] *a & nmf Méd & Fig* shortsighted (person). ● **myopie** *nf* shortsightedness.

myosotis [mjozɔtis] *nm Bot* forget-me-not.

myrtille [mirtij] *nf* (*baie*) bilberry.

mystère [mister] *nm* mystery. ● **mystérieux, -euse** *a* mysterious.

mystifier [mistifje] *vt* to fool, deceive, hoax.

mystique [mistik] *a* mystical.

mythe [mit] *nm* myth. ● **mythologie** *nf* mythology.

N

N, n [ɛn] *nm* N, n.

n' [n] *voir* ne.

nacelle [nasɛl] *nf (de ballon)* basket, car, gondola.

nacre [nakr] *nf* mother-of-pearl. ● **nacré** *a* pearly.

nage [naʒ] *nf (swimming)* stroke; **n. libre** freestyle; **traverser à la n.** to swim across; **en n.** *Fig* sweating.

nageoire [naʒwar] *nf (de poisson)* fin.

nag/er [naʒe] *vi* to swim; **je nage complètement** *(je suis perdu)* *Fam* I'm all at sea █ *vt (crawl etc)* to swim. ● **-eur, -euse** *nmf* swimmer.

naguère [nagɛr] *adv Litt* not long ago.

naïf, -ïve [naif, -iv] *a* naïve, simple.

nain, naine [nɛ̃, nɛn] *nmf* dwarf.

naissance [nɛsɑ̃s] *nf (de personne, d'animal)* birth; *(de cou)* base; **donner n. à** *Fig* to give rise to; **de n.** from birth.

naître* [nɛtr] *vi* to be born; *(sentiment)* to arise *(de* from); **faire n.** *(soupçon etc)* to give rise to.

naïveté [naivte] *nf* simplicity, naïveté.

nanti [nɑ̃ti] *a (riche)* well-off █ *n* **les nantis** *Péj* the well-off.

naphtaline [naftalin] *nf* mothballs.

nappe [nap] *nf* **1** table cloth. **2** *(d'eau)* sheet; *(de gaz, pétrole)* layer; *(de brouillard)* blanket. ● **napperon** *nm (pour vase etc)* (cloth) mat.

narcotique [narkɔtik] *a & nm* narcotic.

narguer [narge] *vt* to flout, mock.

narine [narin] *nf* nostril.

narquois [narkwa] *a* sneering.

narration [narasjɔ̃] *nf (récit)* narration. ● **narrateur, -trice** *nmf* narrator.

nasal, -aux [nazal, -o] *a* nasal.

naseau, -x [nazo] *nm (de cheval)* nostril.

natal, mpl -als [natal] *a (pays etc)* native. ● **natalité** *nf* birthrate.

natation [natasjɔ̃] *nf* swimming.

natif, -ive [natif, -iv] *a & nmf* native; **être n. de** to be a native of.

nation [nasjɔ̃] *nf* nation; **les Nations Unies** the United Nations. ● **national, -aux** *a* national; **fête nationale** national holiday. ● **nationale** *nf (route)* trunk road, *Am* highway. ● **nationaliste** *a* *Péj* nationalistic █ *nmf* nationalist. ● **nationalité** *nf* nationality.

natte [nat] *nf* **1** *(de cheveux)* plait, *Am* braid. **2** *(tapis)* mat, (piece of) matting. ● **natter** *vt* to plait, *Am* braid.

naturaliser [natyralize] *vt (personne)* *Pol* to naturalize.

nature [natyr] *nf (monde naturel, caractère)* nature; **être de n. à** to be likely to; **payer en n.** *Fin* to pay in kind; **n. morte** *(tableau)* still life; **plus grand que n.** larger than life █ *a inv (omelette, yaourt etc)* plain; *(thé)* without milk.

naturel, -elle [natyrɛl] *a* natural; **mort naturelle** death from natural causes █ *nm (caractère)* nature; *(simplicité)* naturalness. ● **naturellement** *adv* naturally.

naufrage [nofraʒ] *nm* (ship)wreck; **faire n.** to be (ship)wrecked. ● **naufragé, -ée** *a & nmf* shipwrecked (person).

nausée [noze] *nf* nausea, sickness. ● **nauséabond** *a* nauseating, sickening.

nautique [notik] *a* nautical; **ski/etc n.** water skiing/etc.

naval, mpl -als [naval] *a* naval.

navet [navɛ] *nm* **1** *Bot Culin* turnip. **2** *(film etc)* *Péj* flop, dud.

navette [navɛt] *nf (transport)* shuttle (service); **faire la n.** to shuttle back and forth *(entre* between); **n. spatiale** space shuttle.

navigable [navigabl] *a (fleuve)* navigable.

navigateur [navigatœr] *nm* *Av Nau* navigator. ● **navigation** *nf* (*trafic de bateaux*) shipping.

naviguer [navige] *vi* (*bateau*) to sail.

navire [navir] *nm* ship.

navré [navre] *a* (*air*) grieved; **je suis n.** I'm (terribly) sorry (**de faire** to do).

nazi, -ie [nazi] *a & nmf* Pol Hist Nazi.

ne [n(ə)] (**n'** before vowel or mute h; used to form negative verb with **pas, jamais, personne, rien** etc) *adv* **1** (+ *pas*) not; **il ne boit pas** he does not *ou* doesn't drink; **il n'ose (pas)** he doesn't dare. **2** (with **craindre, avoir peur** etc) **je crains qu'il ne parte** I'm afraid he'll leave.

né [ne] *pp de* **naître** *a* **elle est née** she was born; **née Dupont** née Dupont.

néanmoins [neɑ̃mwɛ̃] *adv* nevertheless.

néant [neɑ̃] *nm* nothingness, void; (*sur un formulaire*) = none.

nécessaire [neseser] *a* necessary; (*inéluctable*) inevitable ▮ *nm* **le n.** (*biens*) the necessities; **le strict n.** the bare necessities; **n. de toilette** sponge bag; **faire le n.** to do what's necessary. ● **nécessité** *nf* necessity. ● **nécessiter** *vt* to require, necessitate. ● **nécessiteux, -euse** *a* needy.

nécrologie [nekrɔlɔʒi] *nf* obituary.

nectarine [nektarin] *nf* (*fruit*) nectarine.

néerlandais, -aise [neerlɑ̃dɛ, -ɛz] *a* Dutch ▮ *nmf* Dutchman, Dutchwoman ▮ *nm* (*langue*) Dutch.

nef [nɛf] *nf* (*d'église*) nave.

néfaste [nefast] *a* (*influence* etc) harmful (**à** to).

négatif, -ive [negatif, -iv] *a* negative ▮ *nm* Phot negative.

négation [negasjɔ̃] *nf* denial (**de** of); Gram negation; (*mot*) negative.

négligeable [negliʒabl] *a* negligible.

négligent [negliʒɑ̃] *a* careless, negligent. ● **négligence** *nf* (*défaut*) carelessness, negligence; (*faute*) (careless) error.

négliger [negliʒe] *vt* (*personne, travail, conseil* etc) to neglect; **n. de faire** to neglect to do ▮ **se n.** *vpr* (*négliger sa tenue ou sa santé*) to neglect oneself. ● **négligé** *a* (*tenue*) untidy, neglected;

(*travail*) careless.

négoci/er [negɔsje] *vti* to negotiate. ● **-ant, -ante** *nmf* merchant, trader. ● **négociateur, -trice** *nmf* negotiator. ● **négociation** *nf* negotiation.

neige [nɛʒ] *nf* snow; **n. fondue** sleet; **n. carbonique** dry ice. ● **neiger** *v imp* to snow; **il neige** it's snowing.

nénuphar [nenyfar] *nm* water lily.

néo [neo] *préf* neo-.

néon [neɔ̃] *nm* (*gaz*) neon; **éclairage au n.** neon lighting.

néo-zélandais, -aise [neozelɑ̃dɛ, -ɛz] *a* of *ou* from New Zealand ▮ *nmf* New Zealander.

nerf [nɛr] *nm* Anat nerve; **crise de nerfs** (fit of) hysterics; **un peu de n.!** Fam buck up!; **ça me tape sur les nerfs** Fam it gets on my nerves; **être sur les nerfs** Fig to be keyed up *ou* het up. ● **nerveux, -euse** *a* (*agité*) nervous; **cellule/**etc **nerveuse** nerve cell/etc. ● **nervosité** *nf* nervousness.

nescafé® [neskafe] *nm* instant coffee.

n'est-ce pas? [nɛspa] *adv* isn't he?, don't you? won't they? etc; **il fait beau, n'est-ce pas?** the weather's fine, isn't it?

net, nette [nɛt] **1** *a* (*image, refus*) clean; (*coupure, linge*) clean; (*soigné*) neat; (*copie*) fair ▮ *adv* (*s'arrêter*) dead; (*casser, couper*) clean; (*tuer*) outright; (*refuser*) flat(ly). **2** *a* (*poids, prix* etc) net. ● **nettement** *adv* clearly; (*bien plus*) definitely; (*bien plus*) definitely; **netteté** *nf* clearness; (*de travail*) neatness.

nettoyer [netwaje] *vt* to clean (up). ● **nettoyage** *nm* cleaning; **n. à sec** dry cleaning.

neuf¹, neuve [nœf, nœv] *a* new; **quoi de n.?** what's new(s)?; ▮ *nm* **remettre à n.** to make as good as new; **il y a du n.** there's been something new.

neuf² [nœf] *a & nm* ([nœv] before **heures** & **ans**) nine. ● **neuvième** *a & nmf* ninth.

neutre [nøtr] **1** *a* (*pays, personne* etc) neutral. **2** *a & nm* Gram neuter. ● **neutraliser** *vt* to neutralize.

neveu, -x [nəvø] nm nephew.

névrose [nevroz] nf neurosis. ● **névrosé, -ée** a & nmf neurotic.

nez [ne] nm nose; **n. à n.** face to face (avec with); **au n. de qn** (rire etc) in s.o.'s face.

ni [ni] conj **ni...ni** (+ ne) neither...nor; **ni Pierre ni Paul ne sont venus** neither Peter nor Paul came; **il n'a ni faim ni soif** he's neither hungry nor thirsty; **sans manger ni boire** without eating or drinking; **ni l'un(e) ni l'autre** neither (of them).

niais, -aise [njɛ, -ɛz] a silly, simple.

niche [niʃ] nf (de chien) kennel, Am doghouse; (cavité) niche, recess.

nicher [niʃe] vi (oiseau) to nest ▮ **se n.** vpr (oiseau) to nest; (se cacher) to hide oneself. ● **nichée** nf (chiens) litter; (oiseaux, enfants) brood.

nickel [nikɛl] nm (métal) nickel.

nicotine [nikotin] nf nicotine.

nid [ni] nm nest; **n. de poules** pothole (in road).

nièce [njɛs] nf niece.

nier [nje] vt to deny (que that) ▮ vi Jur to deny the charge.

nigaud, -aude [nigo, -od] nmf silly fool.

Nigéria [niʒerja] nm Nigeria.

n'importe [nɛ̃port] voir **importer 1.**

niveau, -x [nivo] nm (hauteur) level; (degré, compétence) standard, level; **n. de vie** standard of living; **au n. de qn** (élève etc) up to s.o.'s standard. ● **niveler** vt (surface) to level; (fortunes etc) to even (up).

noble [nɔbl] a noble ▮ nmf nobleman, noblewoman. ● **noblesse** nf (caractère, classe) nobility.

noce(s) [nɔs] nf(pl) wedding; **noces d'argent/d'or** silver/golden wedding; **faire la noce** Fam to have a good time.

nocif, -ive [nɔsif, -iv] a harmful.

nocturne [nɔktyrn] a nocturnal; **tapage nocturne** Jur disturbance (at night) ▮ nf (de magasins etc) late night opening; **(match en) n.** Sp floodlit match, Am night game.

Noël [nɔɛl] nm Christmas; **le père N.** Father Christmas, Santa Claus.

nœud [nø] nm **1** knot; (ruban) bow; **n. coulant** slipknot, noose; **n. papillon** bow tie; **le n. du problème** the crux of the problem. **2** (mesure) Nau knot.

noir, noire [nwar] a black; (nuit, lunettes etc) dark; (idées) gloomy; (âme) vile; (misère) dire; **roman n.** thriller; **il fait n.** it's dark ▮ nm (couleur) black; (obscurité) dark; **N.** (homme) black; **vendre au n.** to sell on the black market ▮ nf Mus crotchet, Am quarter note; **Noire** (femme) black.

noircir [nwarsir] vt to make black ▮ vi, **se n.** vpr to turn black.

noisette [nwazɛt] nf hazelnut.

noix [nwa] nf (du noyer) walnut; **n. de coco** coconut; **n. de beurre** knob of butter; **à la n.** Fam trashy.

nom [nɔ̃] nm name; Gram noun; **n. de famille** surname; **n. de jeune fille** maiden name; **n. propre** Gram proper noun; **au n. de qn** on s.o.'s behalf.

nomade [nɔmad] nmf nomad.

nombre [nɔ̃br] nm number; **ils sont au n. de dix** there are ten of them; **le plus grand n. de** the majority of. ● **nombreux, -euse** a (amis, livres etc) numerous, many; (famille) large; **peu n.** few; **venir n.** to come in large numbers.

nombril [nɔ̃bri(l)] nm navel.

nomination [nɔminasjɔ̃] nf appointment, nomination.

nommer [nɔme] vt (appeler) to name; **n. qn** (désigner) to appoint s.o. (à un poste/etc to a post/etc); **n. qn président** to nominate ou appoint s.o. chairman ▮ **se n.** vpr (s'appeler) to be called.

non [nɔ̃] adv & nm inv no; **tu viens ou n.?** are you coming or not?; **n. seulement** not only; **n. (pas) que** (+ sub)... not that...; **je crois que n.** I don't think so; **(ni) moi n. plus** neither do I, nor can etc I; **c'est bien, n.?** Fam it's all right, isn't it?

non- [nɔ̃] préf non-.

nonante [nɔnɑ̃t] a (en Belgique, en

Suisse) ninety.

non-fumeur, -euse [nɔ̃fymœr, -øz] *nmf* non-smoker.

nord [nɔr] *nm* north; **au n.** in the north; (*direction*) (to the) north (**de** of); **du n.** (*vent, direction*) northerly; (*ville*) northern; (*gens*) from *ou* in the north; **Amérique/Afrique du N.** North America/Africa; **l'Europe du N.** Northern Europe.

▮ *a inv* (*côte*) north(ern). ● **n.-africain, -aine** *a* & *nmf* North African. ● **n.-américain, -aine** *a* & *nmf* North American. ● **n.-est** *nm* & *a inv* north-east. ● **n.-ouest** *nm* & *a inv* north-west.

nordique [nɔrdik] *a* & *nmf* Scandinavian.

normal, -aux [nɔrmal, -o] *a* normal. ● **normale** *nf* norm, normality; **au-dessus/au-dessous de la n.** above/below normal. ● **normalement** *adv* normally.

normand, -ande [nɔrmɑ̃, -ɑ̃d] *a* & *nmf* Norman. ● **Normandie** *nf* Normandy.

norme [nɔrm] *nf* norm.

Norvège [nɔrvɛʒ] *nf* Norway. ● **norvégien, -ienne** *a* & *nmf* Norwegian ▮ *nm* (*langue*) Norwegian.

nos [no] *voir* **notre**.

nostalgie [nɔstalʒi] *nf* nostalgia.

notable [nɔtabl] *a* (*fait*) notable ▮ *nm* (*personne*) notable.

notaire [nɔter] *nm* solicitor, lawyer.

notamment [nɔtamɑ̃] *adv* particularly.

note [nɔt] *nf* (*remarque etc*) & *Mus* note; (*chiffrée*) *Scol* mark, *Am* grade; (*facture*) bill, *Am* check; **prendre n. de** to make a note of.

noter [nɔte] *vt* (*remarquer*) to note, notice; (*écrire*) to note down; (*devoir etc*) *Scol* to mark, *Am* grade.

notice [nɔtis] *nf* (*mode d'emploi*) instructions.

notifier [nɔtifje] *vt* **n. qch à qn** to notify s.o. of sth.

notion [nɔsjɔ̃] *nf* notion, idea; *pl* (*éléments*) rudiments.

notoire [nɔtwar] *a* (*criminel*) notorious; (*fait*) well-known.

notre, *pl* **nos** [nɔtr, no] *a poss* our. ● **nôtre** *pron poss* **le** *ou* **la n.**, **les nôtres** ours; ▮ *nmpl* **les nôtres** (*parents etc*) our (own) people.

nouer [nwe] *vt* (*lacets etc*) to tie, knot; (*amitié, conversation*) to strike up.

nougat [nuga] *nm* nougat.

nouilles [nuj] *nfpl* noodles.

nounours [nunurs] *nm* teddy bear.

nourrice [nuris] *nf* (*assistante maternelle*) child minder, nurse.

nourrir [nurir] *vt* (*alimenter*) to feed ▮ **se n.** *vpr* to eat; **se n. de** to feed on ▮ *vi* (*aliment*) to be nourishing. ● **nourrissant** *a* nourishing.

nourrisson [nurisɔ̃] *nm* infant.

nourriture [nurityr] *nf* food.

nous [nu] *pron* **1** (*sujet*) we; **n. sommes** we are. **2** (*complément direct*) us; **il n. connaît** he knows us. **3** (*indirect*) to us; **il n. l'a donné** he gave it to us. **4** (*réfléchi*) ourselves; **n. n. lavons** we wash ourselves. **5** (*réciproque*) each other; **n. n. détestons** we hate each other. ● **nous-mêmes** *pron* ourselves.

nouveau (*or* **nouvel** *before vowel or mute* h), **nouvelle**[1], *pl* **nouveaux, nouvelles** [nuvo, nuvɛl] *a* new ▮ *nmf Scol* new boy, new girl ▮ *nm* **du n.** something new; **de n., à n.** again. ● **n.-né, -ée** *a* & *nmf* new-born (baby). ● **nouveauté** *nf* novelty; *pl* (*livres*) new books; (*disques*) new releases.

nouvelle[2] [nuvɛl] *nf* **1 nouvelle(s)** (*information*) news; **une n.** a piece of news. **2** (*récit*) short story.

Nouvelle-Zélande [nuvɛlzelɑ̃d] *nf* New Zealand.

novembre [nɔvɑ̃br] *nm* November.

novice [nɔvis] *a* inexperienced.

noyade [nwajad] *nf* drowning.

noyau, -x [nwajo] *nm* (*de fruit*) stone, *Am* pit; (*d'atome, de cellule*) nucleus.

noyer[1] [nwaje] *vt* to drown; (*terres*) to flood ▮ **se n.** *vpr* to drown; (*se suicider*) to drown oneself. ● **noyé, -ée** *nmf* (*mort*) drowned man *ou* woman ▮ *a* **être n.** (*perdu*) *Fig* to be out of one's depth.

noyer² [nwaje] *nm* (*arbre*) walnut tree.

nu [ny] *a* (*personne*) naked; (*mains, chambre*) bare; **tout nu** (stark) naked, (in the) nude; **tête nue** bare-headed; **voir à l'œil nu** to see with the naked eye.

nuage [nɥaʒ] *nm* cloud. ● **nuageux, -euse** *a* cloudy.

nuance [nɥɑ̃s] *nf* (*de couleurs*) shade; (*de sens*) nuance. ● **nuancer** *vt* (*teintes*) to blend, shade; (*pensée*) to qualify.

nucléaire [nykleer] *a* nuclear.

nudiste [nydist] *nmf* nudist; **camp de nudistes** nudist camp.

nuée [nɥe] *nf Litt* **une n. de** (*foule*) a host of; (*groupe compact*) a cloud of.

nues [ny] *nfpl* **tomber des n.** to be astounded.

nuire* [nɥir] *vi* **n. à** (*personne, intérêts etc*) to harm. ● **nuisible** *a* harmful.

nuit [nɥi] *nf* night; (*obscurité*) dark(ness); **il fait n.** it's dark; **la n.** (*se promener etc*) at night; **cette n.** (*aujourd'hui*) tonight; (*hier*) last night; **bonne n.** good night; **voyager/travailler**

de n. to travel/work by night.

nul, nulle [nyl] **1** *a* (*médiocre*) hopeless, useless; (*risque etc*) non-existent, nil; (*non valable*) *Jur* null (and void); **faire match n.** *Sp* to tie, draw. **2** *a* (*aucun*) no; **nulle part** nowhere; **sans n. doute** without any doubt ‖ *pron m* (*aucun*) no one. ● **nullement** *adv* not at all.

numérique [nymerik] *a* numerical; (*affichage etc*) digital.

numéro [nymero] *nm* number; (*de journal*) issue; (*au cirque*) act; **un n. de danse** a dance number; **n. vert** *Tél* = 0800 number, = *Am* tollfree number; **quel n.!** (*personne*) *Fam* what a character! ● **numéroter** *vt* (*pages etc*) to number.

nu-pieds [nypje] *a inv* barefoot ‖ *nmpl* open sandals.

nuque [nyk] *nf* back *ou* nape of the neck.

nurse [nœrs] *nf* nanny, (children's) nurse.

nu-tête [nytɛt] *a inv* bare-headed.

nutritif, -ive [nytritif, -iv] *a* nutritious.

nylon [nilɔ̃] *nm* (*fibre*) nylon; **chemise**/*etc* **en n.** nylon shirt/*etc*.

O

O, o [o] *nm* O, o.

oasis [ɔazis] *nf* oasis.

obé/ir [ɔbeir] *vi* to obey; **o. à qn/qch** to obey s.o./sth. ●**—issant** *a* obedient. ●**obéissance** *nf* obedience (à to).

obèse [ɔbɛz] *a* & *nmf* obese (person).

objecter [ɔbʒɛkte] *vt* (*prétexte*) to put forward; **o. que** to object that; **on lui objecta son jeune âge** they objected that he *ou* she was too young. ●**objection** *nf* objection.

objectif, -ive [ɔbʒɛktif, -iv] **1** *nm* (*but*) objective; *Phot* lens. **2** *a* (*opinion etc*) objective. ●**objectivité** *nf* objectivity.

objet [ɔbʒɛ] *nm* (*chose, sujet*) object; (*de toilette*) article; **faire l'o. de** (*étude, critiques etc*) to be the subject of; (*soins, surveillance*) to be given, receive; **objets trouvés** (*bureau*) lost property, *Am* lost and found.

obligation [ɔbligasjɔ̃] *nf* (*devoir, nécessité*) obligation; *Fin* bond. ●**obligatoire** *a* compulsory, obligatory; (*inévitable*) *Fam* inevitable.

oblig/er [ɔbliʒe] *vt* **1** to force, compel, oblige (à faire to do); (*engager*) to bind; **être obligé de faire** to have to do, be compelled to do. **2** (*rendre service à*) to oblige; **être obligé à qn de qch** to be obliged to s.o. for sth. ●**—é** *a* (*obligatoire*) necessary; (*fatal*) *Fam* inevitable. ●**obligeance** *nf* kindness.

oblique [ɔblik] *a* oblique; **regard o.** sidelong glance; **en o.** at an (oblique) angle.

oblitérer [ɔblitere] *vt* (*timbre*) to cancel; **timbre oblitéré** (*non neuf*) used stamp.

obscène [ɔpsɛn] *a* obscene. ●**obscénité** *nf* obscenity.

obscur [ɔpskyr] *a* (*noir*) dark; (*peu clair, inconnu, humble*) obscure. ●**obscurcir** *vt* (*chambre etc*) to make dark(er) ‖ **s'o.**

vpr (*ciel*) to get dark(er). ●**obscurité** *nf* dark(ness).

obséd/er [ɔpsede] *vt* to obsess, haunt. ●**—ant** *a* haunting, obsessive. ●**—é, -ée** *nmf* maniac (de for); **o. sexuel** sex maniac.

obsèques [ɔpsɛk] *nfpl* funeral.

observer [ɔpsɛrve] *vt* (*regarder*) to watch, observe; (*remarquer, respecter*) to observe; **faire o. qch à qn** to point sth out to s.o. ●**observateur, -trice** *a* observant ‖ *nmf* observer. ●**observation** *nf* (*étude, remarque*) observation; (*reproche*) rebuke; (*de règle etc*) observance; **en o.** (*malade*) under observation. ●**observatoire** *nm* observatory; (*endroit élevé*) lookout (post).

obsession [ɔpsesjɔ̃] *nf* obsession.

obstacle [ɔpstakl] *nm* obstacle; **faire o.** to stand in the way of.

obstiner (s') [sɔpstine] *vpr* to be persistent; **s'o. à faire** to persist in doing. ●**obstiné** *a* stubborn, persistent, obstinate.

obstruction [ɔpstryksjɔ̃] *nf* *Méd Pol Sp* obstruction; **faire de l'o.** *Pol Sp* to be obstructive. ●**obstruer** *vt* to obstruct.

obtempérer [ɔptɑ̃pere] *vi* to obey (an order); **o. à** to obey.

obtenir* [ɔptənir] *vt* to get, obtain, secure.

obtus [ɔpty] *a* (*angle, esprit*) obtuse.

obus [ɔby] *nm* *Mil* shell.

occasion [ɔkazjɔ̃] *nf* **1** (*chance*) chance, opportunity (de faire to do); (*circonstance*) occasion; **à l'o.** on occasion; **à l'o. de** on the occasion of. **2** *Com* (*prix avantageux*) bargain; (*objet non neuf*) second-hand buy; **d'o.** second-hand, used. ●**occasionner** [ɔkazjɔne] *vt* to cause; **o. qch à qn** to cause s.o. sth.

occident [ɔksidɑ̃] nm l'O. Pol the West. ● **occidental, -aux** a Géog Pol western ∎ nmpl les occidentaux Pol Westerners.

occupant, -ante [ɔkypɑ̃, -ɑ̃t] nmf (habitant) occupant ∎ nm Mil forces of occupation.

occupation [ɔkypasjɔ̃] nf (activité etc) occupation.

occupé [ɔkype] a busy (à faire doing); (place, maison etc) occupied; (ligne) Tél engaged, Am busy; (taxi) hired.

occuper [ɔkype] vt (maison, pays etc) to occupy; (place, temps) to take up, occupy; (poste) to hold, occupy; **o. qn** (travail, jeu) to keep s.o. busy, occupy s.o.

∎ **s'occuper** vpr to keep (oneself) busy (à faire doing); **s'o. de** (affaire, problème etc) to deal with; (politique) to be engaged in; **s'o. de qn** (malade etc) to take care of s.o.; (client) to see to s.o., deal with s.o.; **occupe-toi de tes affaires!** mind your own business!

occurrence [ɔkyrɑ̃s] nf en l'o. in this case, as it happens.

océan [ɔseɑ̃] nm ocean.

ocre [ɔkr] nm & a inv (couleur) ochre.

octobre [ɔktɔbr] nm October.

octogone [ɔktɔgɔn] nm octagon.

octroyer [ɔktrwaje] vt Litt to grant (à to).

oculaire [ɔkyler] a témoin o. eyewitness; globe o. eyeball. ● **oculiste** nmf eye specialist.

odeur [ɔdœr] nf smell, odour; (de fleur) scent. ● **odorat** nm sense of smell.

odieux, -euse [ɔdjø, -øz] a horrible, odious.

œil, pl **yeux** [œj, jø] nm eye; **lever/baisser les yeux** to look up/down; **fermer l'o.** (dormir) to shut one's eyes; **fermer les yeux sur** to turn a blind eye to; **coup d'o.** (regard) look, glance; **jeter un coup d'o. sur** to (have a) look ou glance at; **à vue d'o.** visibly; **à l'o.** (gratuitement) Fam free; **o. poché** ou **au beurre noir** Fig black eye; **mon o.!** Fam (incrédulité) my foot!; (refus) no way!

œillères [œjer] nfpl (de cheval) & Fig blinkers, Am blinders.

œillet [œje] nm 1 Bot carnation. 2 (trou de ceinture) eyelet.

œuf, pl **œufs** [œf, ø] nm egg; pl (de poisson) (hard) roe; **o. sur le plat** fried egg; **o. dur** hard-boiled egg; **œufs brouillés** scrambled eggs.

œuvre [œvr] nf (travail, livre etc) work; **o. (de charité)** (organisation) charity; **o. d'art** work of art; **mettre tout en o.** to do everything possible (**pour faire** to do).

offense [ɔfɑ̃s] nf insult. ● **offenser** vt to offend; **s'o. de** to take offence at.

offensif, -ive [ɔfɑ̃sif, -iv] a offensive ∎ nf (attaque) offensive; (du froid) onslaught.

offert [ɔfer] pp de **offrir**.

office [ɔfis] nm 1 Rel service. 2 (pièce près de la cuisine) pantry. 3 (établissement) office, bureau; **d'o.** automatically; **faire o. de** to serve as; **ses bons offices** one's good offices.

officiel, -ielle [ɔfisjel] a (acte etc) official ∎ nm (personnage) official. ● **officiellement** adv officially. ● **officieux, -euse** a unofficial.

officier [ɔfisje] nm (dans l'armée etc) officer.

offre [ɔfr] nf offer; (aux enchères) bid; **l'o. et la demande** Écon supply and demand; **offres d'emploi** (dans un journal) job vacancies, situations vacant.

offrir* [ɔfrir] vt **o. qch (à qn)** (donner en cadeau) to give (s.o.) sth, give sth (to s.o.); (proposer) to offer (s.o.) sth, offer sth (to s.o.); **je lui ai offert de le loger** I offered to put him up ∎ **s'o.** vpr (cadeau etc) to treat oneself to; (se proposer) to offer oneself (**comme** as); **s'o. aux regards** (spectacle etc) to greet one's eyes. ● **offrant** nm **au plus o.** to the highest bidder.

offusquer [ɔfyske] vt to offend, shock.

ogive [ɔʒiv] nf (de fusée) nose cone; **o. nucléaire** nuclear warhead.

ogre [ɔgr] nm ogre.

oh! [o] int oh!

ohé! [ɔe] *int* hey (there)!

oie [wa] *nf* goose (*pl* geese).

oignon [ɔɲɔ̃] *nm* (*légume*) onion; (*de fleur*) bulb.

oiseau, -x [wazo] *nm* bird; **à vol d'o.** as the crow flies; **o. rare** (*être irremplaçable*) *Hum* rare bird.

oiseux, -euse [wazø, -øz] *a* (*inutile*) idle, vain.

oisif, -ive [wazif, -iv] *a* (*inactif*) idle. ● **oisiveté** *nf* idleness

oléoduc [ɔleɔdyk] *nm* oil pipeline.

olive [ɔliv] *nf* (*fruit*) olive; **huile d'o.** olive oil ▮ *a inv* (*couleur*) (**vert**) **o.** olive (green). ● **olivier** *nm* olive tree.

olympique [ɔlɛ̃pik] *a* (*jeux, record etc*) Olympic.

ombrage [ɔ̃braʒ] *nm* (*ombre*) shade. ● **ombragé** *a* shady.

ombre [ɔ̃br] *nf* (*d'arbre etc*) shade; (*de personne, objet*) shadow; **à l'o.** in the shade; **dans l'o.** (*comploter etc*) *Fig* in secret.

ombrelle [ɔ̃brɛl] *nf* sunshade, parasol.

omelette [ɔmlɛt] *nf* omelet(te); **o. au fromage**/*etc* cheese/*etc* omelet(te).

omettre* [ɔmɛtr] *vt* to omit (**de faire** to do).

omnibus [ɔmnibys] *a* & *nm* (**train**) **o.** slow *ou* stopping train.

omoplate [ɔmɔplat] *nf* shoulder blade.

on [ɔ̃] (*sometimes* **l'on** [lɔ̃]) *pron* (*les gens*) they, people; (*nous*) we, one; (*vous*) you, one; **on frappe** someone's knocking; **on dit** they say, people say, it is said; **on m'a dit que** I was told that.

oncle [ɔ̃kl] *nm* uncle.

onctueux, -euse [ɔ̃ktɥø, -øz] *a* (*liquide, crème*) creamy.

onde [ɔ̃d] *nf* *Rad Phys* wave; **grandes ondes** long wave; **ondes courtes/ moyennes** short/medium wave.

ondée [ɔ̃de] *nf* (*pluie*) (sudden) shower.

on-dit [ɔ̃di] *nm inv* rumour, hearsay.

ondulation [ɔ̃dylasjɔ̃] *nf* undulation; (*de cheveux*) wave. ● **onduler** *vi* to undulate; (*cheveux*) to be wavy.

onéreux, -euse [ɔnerø, -øz] *a* costly.

ongle [ɔ̃gl] *nm* (finger) nail.

ont [ɔ̃] *voir* **avoir.**

ONU [ɔny] *nf abrév* (*Organisation des nations unies*) UN.

onze [ɔ̃z] *a* & *nm* eleven. ● **onzième** *a* & *nmf* eleventh.

opaque [ɔpak] *a* opaque.

opéra [ɔpera] *nm* (*musique*) opera; (*édifice*) opera house. ● **opérette** *nf* operetta.

opérateur, -trice [ɔperatœr, -tris] *nmf* (*de prise de vues*) cameraman; (*sur machine*) operator.

opérer [ɔpere] **1** *vt* (*en chirurgie*) to operate on (*s.o.*) (**de** for); (*tumeur*) to remove; **se faire o.** to have an operation ▮ *vi* (*chirurgien*) to operate.

2 *vt* (*exécuter*) to carry out; (*choix*) to make ▮ *vi* (*agir*) to work, act; (*procéder*) to proceed ▮ **s'o.** (*se produire*) to take place. ● **opération** *nf* *Méd Mil Math etc* operation; *Fin* deal. ● **opératoire** *a* choc **o.** post-operative shock; **bloc o.** operating *ou* surgical wing.

opiner [ɔpine] *vi* **o.** (**de la tête** *ou* **du chef**) to nod assent.

opiniâtre [ɔpinjɑtr] *a* stubborn, obstinate.

opinion [ɔpinjɔ̃] *nf* opinion (**sur** about, on).

opium [ɔpjɔm] *nm* opium.

opportun, -une [ɔpɔrtœ̃, -yn] *a* opportune, timely. ● **opportunité** *nf* timeliness.

opposé [ɔpoze] *a* (*direction, opinion etc*) opposite; (*équipe, intérêts*) opposing; **être o. à** to be opposed to ▮ *nm* **l'o.** the opposite (**de** of); **à l'o.** (*côté*) on the opposite side (**de** from, to); **à l'o. de** (*contrairement à*) contrary to.

opposer [ɔpoze] *vt* (*résistance, argument*) to put up (**à** against); (*équipes*) to bring together; (*couleurs etc*) to contrast; **o. qn à qn** to set s.o. against s.o.; **o. qch à qch** (*objet*) to place sth opposite sth; **match qui oppose...** match between....

▮ **s'opposer** *vpr* (*équipes*) to play against each other; **s'o. à** (*mesure, personne etc*) to be opposed to, oppose; **je m'y oppose** I'm opposed to it, I oppose. ● **opposition** *nf* opposition (à to); **faire o. à** to oppose; (*chèque*) to stop.

oppress/er [ɔprese] *vt* (*gêner*) to oppress. ●**—ant** *a* oppressive. ● **oppression** *nf* oppression. ● **opprimer** *vt* (*tyranniser*) to oppress.

opter [ɔpte] *vi* **o. pour** to opt for.

opticien, -ienne [ɔptisjɛ̃, -jɛn] *nmf* optician.

optimisme [ɔptimism] *nm* optimism. ● **optimiste** *a* optimistic ‖ *nmf* optimist.

optimum [ɔptimɔm] *a* **la température o.** the optimum temperature.

option [ɔpsjɔ̃] *nf* (*choix*) option; (*chose*) optional extra.

optique [ɔptik] *a* (*verre, fibres*) optical ‖ *nf* optics; (*aspect*) *Fig* perspective; **d'o.** (*illusion, instrument*) optical.

opulent [ɔpylɑ̃] *a* opulent.

or [ɔr] **1** *nm* gold; **montre/etc en or** gold watch/etc; **d'or** (*règle, âge*) golden; (*cœur*) of gold; **mine d'or** goldmine; **affaire en or** (*achat*) bargain; (*commerce*) *Fig* goldmine; **or noir** (*pétrole*) *Fig* black gold. **2** *conj* (*cependant*) now, well.

orage [ɔraʒ] *nm* (*thunder*)storm. ● **orageux, -euse** *a* stormy.

oral, aux [ɔral, -o] *a* oral ‖ *nm* (*examen*) *Scol* oral.

orange [ɔrɑ̃ʒ] *nf* (*fruit*) orange; **o. pressée** (fresh) orange juice ‖ *a & nm inv* (*couleur*) orange. ● **orangeade** *nf* orangeade. ● **oranger** *nm* orange tree.

orateur [ɔratœr] *nm* speaker, orator.

orbite [ɔrbit] *nf* (*d'astre etc*) orbit; (*d'œil*) socket; **mettre sur o.** to put into orbit.

orchestre [ɔrkɛstr] *nm* (*classique*) orchestra; (*jazz, pop*) band; (*places*) *Th Cin* stalls, *Am* orchestra.

orchidée [ɔrkide] *nf* orchid.

ordinaire [ɔrdinɛr] *a* (*habituel, normal*) ordinary, *Am* regular; (*médiocre*) ordinary, average; **d'o., à l'o.** usually; **de l'essence o.** two-star (petrol), *Am* regular.

ordinal, -aux [ɔrdinal, -o] *a* (*nombre*) ordinal.

ordinateur [ɔrdinatœr] *nm* computer.

ordonnance [ɔrdɔnɑ̃s] *nf* **1** (*de médecin*) prescription. **2** (*décret*) *Jur* order, ruling. **3** (*soldat*) orderly.

ordonn/er [ɔrdɔne] *vt* **1** (*enjoindre*) to order (**que** + *sub*) that); **o. à qn de faire** to order s.o. to do. **2** (*prêtre*) to ordain. ● **—é** *a* (*personne etc*) tidy, orderly.

ordre [ɔrdr] *nm* (*commandement, classement etc*) order; (*absence de désordre*) tidiness (*of room, person etc*); **en o.** (*chambre etc*) tidy; **mettre en o., mettre de l'o. dans** to tidy (up); **jusqu'à nouvel o.** until further notice; **de l'o. de** (*environ*) of the order of; **de premier o.** first-rate; **à l'o. du jour** on the agenda; **les forces de l'o.** the police.

ordures [ɔrdyr] *nfpl* (*déchets*) rubbish, *Am* garbage.

oreille [ɔrɛj] *nf* ear; **faire la sourde o.** to take no notice, refuse to listen; **être tout oreilles** to be all ears; **casser les oreilles à qn** to deafen s.o.

oreiller [ɔreje] *nm* pillow.

oreillons [ɔrejɔ̃] *nmpl Méd* mumps.

ores (d') [ɔr] *adv* **d'ores et déjà** [ɔrzedeʒa] henceforth.

orfèvre [ɔrfɛvr] *nm* goldsmith, silversmith. ● **orfèvrerie** *nf* (*magasin*) gold smith's ou silversmith's shop; (*objets*) gold ou silver plate.

organe [ɔrgan] *nm Anat & Fig* organ. ● **organisme** *nm* **1** (*corps*) body; *Anat Biol* organism. **2** (*bureaux etc*) organization.

organisation [ɔrganizasjɔ̃] *nf* (*arrangement, association*) organization.

organiser [ɔrganize] *vt* to organize ‖ **s'o.** *vpr* to get organized. ● **organiseur** *nm* (**agenda**) **o.** Filofax®. ● **organisateur, -trice** *nmf* organiser.

orgasme [ɔrgasm] *nm* orgasm.

orge [ɔrʒ] *nf* barley.

orgie [ɔrʒi] *nf* orgy.

orgue [ɔrg] *nm Mus* organ ‖ *nfpl* organ; **grandes orgues** great organ.

orgueil [ɔrgœj] nm pride. ● **orgueilleux, -euse** a proud.

orient [ɔrjɑ̃] nm **l'O.** the Orient, the East; **Moyen-O., Proche-O.** Middle East; **Extrême-O.** Far East. ● **oriental, -ale, -aux** a (côte, pays etc) eastern; (du Japon, de la Chine) far-eastern, oriental.

orientation [ɔrjɑ̃tasjɔ̃] nf direction; (action) positioning; (de maison) aspect, orientation; (tendance) Pol Littér trend; **o. professionnelle** careers' advice; **sens de l'o.** sense of direction.

orienter [ɔrjɑ̃te] vt (lampe etc) to position, direct; (voyageur, élève etc) to direct; (maison) to orientate, Am orient **‖ s'o.** vpr to find one's bearings ou direction; **s'o. vers** (carrière etc) to move towards. ● **orienté** a (film etc) slanted; **o. à l'ouest** (appartement etc) facing west.

orifice [ɔris] nm opening, orifice.

originaire [ɔriʒinɛr] a **être o. de** (natif) to be a native of.

original, -ale, -aux [ɔriʒinal, -o] 1 a (idée, artiste etc) original **‖** nm (texte) original. 2 a & nmf (bizarre) eccentric. ● **originalité** nf originality; eccentricity.

origine [ɔriʒin] nf origin; **à l'o.** originally; **d'o.** (pneu etc) original; **pays d'o.** country of origin.

orme [ɔrm] nm (arbre, bois) elm.

ornement [ɔrnəmɑ̃] nm ornament. ● **orner** vt to decorate, adorn (de with).

ornière [ɔrnjɛr] nf (sillon) rut.

orphelin, -ine [ɔrfəlɛ̃, -in] nmf orphan. ● **orphelinat** nm orphanage.

orteil [ɔrtɛj] nm toe; **gros o.** big toe.

orthodoxe [ɔrtɔdɔks] a orthodox.

orthographe [ɔrtɔgraf] nf spelling. ● **orthographier** vt to spell.

orthopédie [ɔrtɔpedi] nf orthop(a)edics.

ortie [ɔrti] nf nettle.

os [ɔs, pl o] nm bone; **trempé jusqu'aux os** soaked to the skin.

OS [ɔɛs] abrév = **ouvrier spécialisé.**

oscar [ɔskar] nm Cin Oscar.

osciller [ɔsile] vi Tech to oscillate; (se balancer) to swing, sway; (varier) to fluctuate (entre between).

oseille [ozɛj] nf Bot Culin sorrel.

oser [oze] vti to dare; **o. faire** to dare (to) do. ● **osé** a bold, daring.

osier [ozje] nm wicker; **panier d'o.** wicker basket.

ossature [ɔsatyr] nf (du corps) frame; (de bâtiment) & Fig framework. ● **osseux, -euse** a (maigre) bony; **tissu/etc o.** bone/etc tissue.

ostensible [ɔstɑ̃sibl] a conspicuous.

otage [ɔtaʒ] nm hostage; **prendre qn en o.** to take s.o. hostage.

OTAN [ɔtɑ̃] nf abrév (Organisation du traité de l'Atlantique Nord) NATO.

otarie [ɔtari] nf (animal) sea lion.

ôter [ote] vt to take away, remove (à qn from s.o.); (vêtement) to take off, remove; (déduire) to take (away).

otite [ɔtit] nf ear infection.

oto-rhino [ɔtɔrino] nmf Méd Fam ear, nose and throat specialist.

ou [u] conj or; **ou bien** or else; **ou elle ou moi** either her or me.

où [u] adv & pron where; **le jour où** the day when; **la table où** the table on which; **l'état où** the condition in which; **par où?** which way? **d'où?** where from?; **d'où ma surprise/etc** hence my surprise/etc; **le pays d'où** the country from which; **où qu'il soit** wherever he may be.

ouate [wat] nf Méd cotton wool, Am absorbent cotton.

oubli [ubli] nm (défaut) forgetfulness; **l'o. de qch** forgetting sth; **un o.** a lapse of memory; (dans une liste etc) an oversight; **tomber dans l'o.** to fall into oblivion.

oublier [ublije] vt to forget (de faire to do); (faute) to overlook.

oubliettes [ublijɛt] nfpl dungeon.

ouest [wɛst] nm west; **à l'o.** in the west; (direction) (to the) west (de of); **d'o.** (vent) west(erly); **de l'o.** western; **l'Europe de l'O.** Western Europe **‖** a inv (côte) west(ern).

ouf! [uf] *int* (*soulagement*) what a relief!

oui [wi] *adv* & *nm inv* yes; **tu viens, o. ou non?** are you coming or aren't you?; **je crois que o.** I think so.

ouï-dire [widir] *nm inv* **par o.-dire** by hearsay.

ouïe[1] [wi] *nf* hearing; **être tout o.** *Hum* to be all ears.

ouïe[2]! [uj] *int* ouch!

ouïes [wi] *nfpl* (*de poisson*) gills.

ouille! [uj] *int* ouch!

ouragan [uragɑ̃] *nm* hurricane.

ourler [urle] *vt* to hem. ● **ourlet** *nm* hem.

ours [urs] *nm* bear; **o. blanc** polar bear.

oursin [ursɛ̃] *nm* (*animal*) sea urchin.

ouste! [ust] *int Fam* scram!

outil [uti] *nm* tool. ● **outiller** *vt* to equip. ● **outillage** *nm* tools.

outrage [utraʒ] *nm* insult (à to).

outrance [utrɑ̃s] *nf* (*excès*) excess. ; **à o.** (*travailler etc*) to excess.

outre [utr] *prép* besides ‖ *adv* **en o.** besides; **o. mesure** inordinately; **passer o.** to take no notice (à of). ● **o.-Manche** *adv* across the Channel. ● **o.-mer** *adv* overseas; **d'o.-mer** (*territoire*) overseas.

outrepasser [utrəpase] *vt* (*limite etc*) to go beyond, exceed.

outré [utre] *a* (*révolté*) outraged; (*excessif*) exaggerated.

ouvert [uver] *pp de* **ouvrir** ‖ *a* open; (*robinet, gaz etc*) on; **à bras ouverts** with open arms. ● **ouvertement** *adv* openly. ● **ouverture** *nf* opening; (*trou*) hole; (*avance*) & *Mus* overture; **o. d'esprit** open-mindedness.

ouvrable [uvrabl] *a* **jour o.** working day.

ouvrage [uvraʒ] *nm* (*travail, livre*) work; (*couture*) (needle)work; **un o.** (*travail*) a piece of work.

ouvreuse [uvrøz] *nf Cin* usherette.

ouvrier, -ière [uvrije, -jer] *nmf* worker; **o. qualifié/spécialisé** skilled/unskilled worker ‖ *a* (*quartier etc*) working-class; **classe ouvrière** working class.

ouvrir* [uvrir] *vt* to open (up); (*gaz, radio etc*) to turn on, switch on; (*inaugurer*) to open; (*hostilités*) to begin; (*appétit*) to whet ‖ *vi* to open; (*ouvrir la porte*) to open (up); ‖ **s'ouvrir** *vpr* (*porte, boîte etc*) to open (up); **s'o. la jambe** to cut one's leg open. ● **ouvre-boîtes** *nm inv* tin opener, *Am* can-opener. ● **ouvre-bouteilles** *nm inv* bottle opener.

ovaire [ɔver] *nm Anat* ovary.

ovale [ɔval] *a* & *nm* oval.

OVNI [ɔvni] *nm abrév* (*objet volant non identifié*) UFO.

oxygène [ɔksiʒen] *nm* oxygen; **masque/ etc à o.** oxygen mask/*etc*. ● **oxygénée** *af* **eau o.** (hydrogen) peroxide.

ozone [ozon] *nm* ozone; **couche d'o.** ozone layer.

P

P, p [pe] nm P, p.

pacifier [pasifje] vt to pacify. ●**pacifiste** nmf pacifist.

pacifique [pasifik] 1 a (manifestation etc) peaceful; (personne, peuple) peace-loving. 2 a (côte etc) Pacific; **Océan P.** Pacific Ocean ▮ nm **le P.** the Pacific.

pack [pak] nm (de lait etc) carton.

pacotille [pakɔtij] nf (camelote) trash.

pacte [pakt] nm pact.

pagaie [page] nf paddle. ●**pagayer** vi (ramer) to paddle.

pagaïe, pagaille [pagaj] nf (désordre) Fam mess, shambles.

page [paʒ] 1 nf (de livre etc) page; **à la p.** (personne) Fig up-to-date. 2 nm (à la cour) Hist page (boy).

pagode [pagɔd] nf pagoda.

paie [pɛ] nf pay, wages. ●**paiement** nm payment.

païen, -enne [pajɛ̃, -ɛn] a & nmf pagan, heathen.

paillasson [pajasɔ̃] nm (door)mat.

paille [paj] nf straw; (pour boire) (drinking) straw; **tirer à la courte p.** to draw lots; **sur la p.** Fig penniless.

paillette [pajɛt] nf (d'habit) sequin; pl (de savon) flakes; (d'or) gold dust.

pain [pɛ̃] nm bread; **un p.** a loaf (of bread); **p. grillé** toast; **p. complet** wholemeal bread; **p. d'épice** gingerbread; **p. de seigle** rye bread; **petit p.** roll; **avoir du p. sur la planche** (travail) Fig to have a lot on one's plate.

pair [pɛr] 1 a (numéro) even. 2 nm (personne) peer; **hors (de) p.** unrivalled; **au p.** (étudiante etc) au pair; **travailler au p.** to work as an au pair.

paire [pɛr] nf pair (de of).

paisible [pezibl] a (vie, endroit etc) peaceful; (caractère) quiet, placid.

paître* [pɛtr] vi to graze.

paix [pɛ] nf peace; (traité) peace treaty; **en p.** in peace (avec with); **avoir la p.** to have (some) peace and quiet.

Pakistan [pakistɑ̃] nm Pakistan. ●**pakistanais, -aise** a & nmf Pakistani.

palace [palas] nm luxury hotel.

palais [palɛ] nm 1 (château) palace; **P. de justice** law courts; **p. des sports** sports stadium. 2 Anat palate.

pâle [pɑl] a pale.

Palestine [palestin] nf Palestine. ●**Palestinien, -ienne** a & nmf Palestinian.

palette [palɛt] nf (de peintre) palette.

pâleur [pɑlœr] nf paleness, pallor. ●**pâlir** vi to turn ou go pale (de with).

palier [palje] nm 1 (d'escalier) landing; **être voisins de p.** to live on the same floor. 2 (niveau) level; (phase de stabilité) plateau; **par paliers** (étapes) in stages.

palissade [palisad] nf fence (of stakes).

pallier [palje] vt (difficultés etc) to alleviate.

palmarès [palmares] nm prize list; (des chansons) hit-parade.

palme [palm] nf 1 palm (leaf). 2 (de nageur) flipper. ●**palmier** nm palm (tree).

pâlot, -otte [pɑlo, -ɔt] a Fam pale.

palourde [palurd] nf (mollusque) clam.

palper [palpe] vt to feel, finger.

palpit/er [palpite] vi (cœur) to throb, palpitate; (frémir) to quiver. ●**—ant** a (film etc) thrilling.

pamplemousse [pɑ̃pləmus] nm grapefruit.

pan [pɑ̃] 1 nm (de chemise) tail; (de ciel) patch; **p. de mur** section of wall. 2 int bang!

panache [panaʃ] nm (plumes) plume; **avoir du p.** (fière allure) to have panache.

panaché [panaʃe] **1** a (mélangé) motley. **2** a & nm (**demi**) p. shandy (beer and lemonade).

pancarte [pɑ̃kart] nf sign, notice; (de manifestant) placard.

panda [pɑ̃da] nm (animal) panda.

pané [pane] a Culin breaded.

panier [panje] nm basket; **p. à linge** linen basket, Am (clothes) hamper; **p. à salade** (ustensile) salad basket; (voiture) Fam prison van.

panique [panik] nf panic; **pris de p.** panic-stricken ‖ a **peur p.** panic fear. ●**paniquer** vi to panic. ●**paniqué** a panic-stricken.

panne [pan] nf breakdown; **tomber en p.** to break down; **être en p.** to have broken down; **p. d'électricité** blackout, power cut; **tomber en p. sèche** to run out of petrol ou Am gas.

panneau, -x [pano] nm **1** (écriteau) sign, notice, board; **p. de signalisation** road ou traffic sign; **p. d'affichage** (publicité) hoarding, Am billboard. **2** (de porte etc) panel.

panoplie [panɔpli] nf **1** (jouet) outfit. **2** (gamme) (wide) range.

panorama [panɔrama] nm view, panorama.

pans/er [pɑ̃se] vt (main, plaie etc) to dress, bandage; (personne) to dress the wound(s) of, bandage (up). ●—**ement** nm (bande) dressing, bandage; **p. adhésif** sticking plaster, Am Band-Aid®.

pantalon [pɑ̃talɔ̃] nm (pair of) trousers ou Am pants; **en p.** in trousers, Am in pants.

panthère [pɑ̃tɛr] nf (animal) panther.

pantin [pɑ̃tɛ̃] nm (jouet) puppet, jumping jack; (personne) Péj puppet.

pantoufle [pɑ̃tufl] nf slipper.

paon [pɑ̃] nm peacock.

papa [papa] nm dad(dy); **fils à p.** Péj rich man's son, daddy's boy.

pape [pap] nm pope.

paperasse(s) [papras] nf(pl) Péj papers. ●**paperasserie** nf Péj (official) papers; (procédure) red tape.

papeterie [papetri] nf (magasin) stationer's shop; (articles) stationery.

papi [papi] nm grand(d)ad.

papier [papje] nm (matière) paper; **un p.** (feuille) a sheet ou piece of paper; (formulaire) a form; **sac/etc en p.** paper bag/etc; **papiers (d'identité)** (identity) papers; **p. hygiénique** toilet paper; **p. à lettres** writing paper; **du p. journal** (some) newspaper; **p. peint** wallpaper; **p. de verre** sandpaper.

papillon [papijɔ̃] nm **1** (insecte) butterfly; **p. (de nuit)** moth. **2** (contravention) Fam (parking) ticket.

paprika [paprika] nm Culin paprika.

Pâque [pɑk] nf **la P.** Rel Passover.

paquebot [pakbo] nm Nau (ocean) liner.

pâquerette [pɑkrɛt] nf daisy.

Pâques [pɑk] nm sing & nfpl Easter.

paquet [pakɛ] nm (de bonbons etc) packet; (colis) package; (de cigarettes) pack(et); (de cartes) pack, deck.

par [par] prép **1** (agent, manière, moyen) by; **choisi/etc p.** chosen/etc by; **p. le train** by train; **p. erreur** by mistake; **p. le travail/etc** by ou through work/etc; **apprendre p. un ami** to learn from ou through a friend; **commencer p. qch** (récit etc) to begin with sth.
2 (lieu) through; **p. la porte/etc** through ou by the door/etc; **jeter p. la fenêtre** to throw out (of) the window; **p. ici/là** (aller) this/that way; (habiter) around here/there.
3 (motif) out of, from; **p. pitié/etc** out of ou from pity/etc.
4 (temps) on; **p. un jour d'hiver/etc** on a winter's day/etc; **p. ce froid** in this cold; **p. le passé** in the past.
5 (distributif) **dix fois p. an/etc** ten times a ou per year/etc; **cent francs p. personne** a hundred francs a ou per person; **deux p. deux** two by two; **p. deux fois** twice.
6 (trop) **p. trop aimable/etc** far too kind/etc.

parabole [parabɔl] nf (récit) parable.

parabolique [parabɔlik] a **antenne p.**

satellite dish.

parachever [paraʃve] *vt* to perfect.

parachute [paraʃyt] *nm* parachute.
●**parachutisme** *nm* parachute jumping. ●**parachutiste** *nmf* parachutist;
Mil paratrooper.

parade [parad] *nf* **1** (*spectacle*) & *Mil*
parade. **2** *Boxe Escrime etc* parry;
(*riposte*) *Fig* parry.

paradis [paradi] *nm* heaven, paradise.

paradoxe [paradɔks] *nm* paradox.

paraffine [parafin] *nf* paraffin (wax).

parages [paraʒ] *nmpl* region, area (**de**
of); **dans ces p.** in these parts.

paragraphe [paragraf] *nm* paragraph.

paraître* [parɛtr] **1** *vi* (*sembler*) to seem,
look, appear; (*apparaître*) to appear **‖** *v
imp* **il paraît qu'il va partir** it appears *ou*
seems (that) he's leaving. **2** *vi* (*livre*) to
come out, be published; **faire p.** to
bring out.

parallèle [paralɛl] **1** *a* (*comparable*) &
Math parallel (**à** with, to); (*marché*)
Com unofficial. **2** *nm* (*comparaison*) &
Géog parallel.

paralyser [paralize] *vt* to paralyse; *Am*
paralyze. ●**paralysie** *nf* paralysis.

paramètre [parametr] *nm* parameter.

paranoïa [paranɔja] *nf* paranoia.
●**paranoïaque** *a* & *nmf* paranoid.

parapet [parapɛ] *nm* parapet.

paraphe [paraf] *nm* initials, signature.

paraphrase [parafraz] *nf* paraphrase.

parapluie [paraplɥi] *nm* umbrella.

parasite [parazit] *nm* (*personne, organisme*) parasite; *pl* (*à la radio*) interference.

parasol [parasɔl] *nm* sunshade, parasol.

paratonnerre [paratɔnɛr] *nm* lightning
conductor *ou Am* rod.

paravent [paravɑ̃] *nm* (folding) screen.

parc [park] *nm* **1** park; (*de château*)
grounds; **p. d'attractions** amusement
park. **2** (*de bébé*) (play) pen; **p. (de
stationnement**) car park, *Am* parking
lot.

parcelle [parsɛl] *nf* fragment, particle;
(*terrain*) plot; (*de vérité*) *Fig* grain.

parce que [parsk(ə)] *conj* because.

parchemin [parʃəmɛ̃] *nm* parchment.

parcimonieux, -euse [parsimɔnjø, -øz] *a*
parsimonious.

par-ci, par-là [parsiparla] *adv* here, there
and everywhere.

parcmètre [parkmɛtr] *nm* parking meter.

parcourir* [parkurir] *vt* (*région*) to travel
all over; (*distance*) to cover; (*texte*) to
glance through. ●**parcours** *nm* (*itinéraire*) route; (*distance*) distance;
(*voyage*) trip, journey; **p. de golf** (*terrain*) golf course.

par-derrière [parderjɛr] *voir* **derrière**.

par-dessous [pardəsu] *prép* & *adv* under(neath).

pardessus [pardəsy] *nm* overcoat.

par-dessus [pardəsy] *prép* & *adv* over
(the top of); **p.-dessus tout** above all.

par-devant [pardəvɑ̃] *voir* **devant**.

pardon [pardɔ̃] *nm* forgiveness, pardon;
p.! (*excusez-moi*) sorry!; **p.?** (*pour demander*) excuse me?, *Am* pardon me?;
demander p. to apologize (**à** to). ●**pardonner** *vt* to forgive; **p. qch à qn/à qn
d'avoir fait qch** to forgive s.o. for sth/
for doing sth.

pare-balles [parbal] *a inv* **gilet p.-balles**
bulletproof jacket *ou Am* vest.

pare-brise [parbriz] *nm inv Aut* windscreen, *Am* windshield.

pare-chocs [parʃɔk] *nm inv Aut* bumper.

pareil, -eille [parɛj] *a* similar; **p. à** the
same as, similar to; **être pareils** to be
the same, be similar *ou* alike; **un p.
désordre/etc** such a mess/*etc*; **en p. cas**
in such a case **‖** *adv Fam* the same **‖** *nmf*
sans p. unparalleled.

parent, -ente [parɑ̃, -ɑ̃t] *nmf* relative,
relation **‖** *nmpl* (*père et mère*) parents
‖ *a* related (**de** to). ●**parenté** *nf* (*lien*)
relationship.

parenthèse [parɑ̃tɛz] *nf* (*signe*) bracket,
Am parenthesis; (*digression*) digression; **entre parenthèses** in brackets,
Am in parentheses.

parer [pare] **1** *vt* (*coup*) to parry, ward
off **‖** *vi* **p. à** (*éventualité*) to be prepared

for. **2** vt (orner) to adorn (**de** with).
paresse [parɛs] nf laziness. ●**paresseux,
-euse** a lazy, idle ‖nmf lazy person.
parfaire [parfɛr] vt to perfect. ●**parfait** a
perfect; **p.!** excellent!. ●**parfaitement**
adv perfectly; (certainement) certainly.
parfois [parfwa] adv sometimes.
parfum [parfœ̃] nm (odeur) fragrance,
scent; (goût) flavour; (liquide) perfume, scent.
parfumer [parfyme] vt to perfume,
scent; (glace, crème etc) to flavour (**à**
with) ‖**se p.** vpr to put on perfume;
(habituellement) to wear perfume.
●**parfumé** a (savon, fleur) scented; **p.
au café/etc** coffee-/etc flavoured. ●**par-
fumerie** nf (magasin) perfume shop.
pari [pari] nm bet; pl Sp betting, bets; **p.
mutuel urbain** = the tote, Am pari-
mutuel. ●**parier** vti to bet (**sur** on, **que**
that).
Paris [pari] m ou f Paris. ●**parisien,
-ienne** a Parisian; **la banlieue parisien-
ne** the Paris suburbs ‖nmf Parisian.
parking [parkiŋ] nm (lieu) car park, Am
parking lot.
parlement [parləmɑ̃] nm parliament.
●**parlementaire** a parliamentary ‖nmf
member of parliament.
parlementer [parləmɑ̃te] vi to negotiate.
parler [parle] vi to talk, speak (**de** about,
of; **à** to); **tu parles!** Fam you must be
joking!; **sans p. de...** not to mention...
‖ vt (langue) to speak ‖**se p.** vpr (langue)
to be spoken. ●**parlé** a (langue) spoken.
parloir [parlwar] nm (de couvent, prison)
visiting room.
parmi [parmi] prép among(st).
parodie [parɔdi] nf parody.
paroi [parwa] nf wall; (de maison) (inside) wall; (de rocher) (rock) face.
paroisse [parwas] nf parish.
parole [parɔl] nf (mot, promesse) word;
(faculté, langage) speech; pl (d'une
chanson) words, lyrics; **adresser la p.
à** to speak to; **prendre la p.** to speak;
demander la p. to ask to speak.
parquer [parke] vt (bœufs) to pen; (gens)

to herd together, confine; (véhicule) to
park.
parquet [parkɛ] nm **1** (parquet)
floor(ing). **2** Jur Public Prosecutor's
office.
parrain [parɛ̃] nm Rel godfather. ●**parrainer** vt (course etc) to sponsor. ●**parrainage** nm sponsorship.
pars, part[1] [par] voir partir.
parsemé [parsəme] a **p. de** (sol) scattered
ou strewn with.
part[2] [par] nf (portion) share, part; (de
gâteau) portion; **prendre p. à** (activité)
to take part in; (la joie etc de qn) to
share; **de toutes parts** from ou on all
sides; **de p. et d'autre** on both sides;
d'une p...., d'autre p. on the one
hand..., on the other hand; **d'autre p.**
(d'ailleurs) moreover; **de la p. de** (provenance) from; **c'est de la p. de qui?** Tél
who's speaking?; **quelque p.** somewhere; **nulle p.** nowhere; **autre p.** somewhere else; **à p.** (mettre, prendre) aside;
(excepté) apart from; (personne) different; **un cas/etc à p.** a separate ou special
case/etc; **membre à p. entière** full member; **faire p. de qch à qn** to inform s.o. of
sth.
partage [partaʒ] nm (de gâteau, trésor
etc) sharing; (distribution) sharing out.
●**partager** vt (repas, joie etc) to share
(**avec** with); (distribuer) to share out
‖**se p.** vpr (bénéfices etc) to share
(between themselves etc); **se p. entre**
to divide one's time between.
partance (en) [ɑ̃partɑ̃s] adv (train etc)
about to depart (**pour** for).
partant [partɑ̃] nm Sp starter.
partenaire [partənɛr] nmf (coéquipier
etc) & Pol partner.
parterre [partɛr] nm **1** (de jardin etc)
flower bed. **2** Th stalls, Am orchestra.
parti [parti] nm Pol party; **prendre un p.**
to make a decision; **prendre p. pour** to
side with; **tirer p. de qch** to turn sth to
(good) account; **p. pris** (préjugé) prejudice.
partial, -aux [parsjal, -o] a biased.

participe [partisip] *nm* Gram participle.

particip/er [partisipe] *vi* **p. à** (*jeu etc*) to take part in, participate in; (*frais, joie etc*) to share (in). ●**—ant, -ante** *nmf* participant. ●**participation** *nf* participation; sharing; (*d'un acteur*) (personal) appearance; **p. (aux frais)** contribution (*towards expenses*).

particule [partikyl] *nf* particle.

particulier, -ière [partikylje, -jer] *a* (*spécial*) particular; (*privé*) private; (*bizarre*) peculiar; **p. à** peculiar to; **en p.** (*surtout*) in particular; (*à part*) in private ‖ *nm* private individual. ●**particularité** *nf* peculiarity. ●**particulièrement** *adv* particularly; **tout p.** especially.

partie [parti] *nf* part; (*de cartes, tennis etc*) game; (*de chasse*) & Jur party; **en p.** partly, in part; **en grande p.** mainly; **faire p. de** to be a part of; (*club etc*) to belong to; (*comité*) to be on. ●**partiel, -ielle** *a* partial ‖ *nm* (**examen**) **p.** Univ term exam.

partir* [partir] *vi* (*aux* **être**) (*aller*) to go; (*s'en aller*) to go, leave; (*se mettre en route*) to set off; (*s'éloigner*) to go (away); (*coup de feu*) to go off; (*tache*) to come out; **p. de** (*commencer par*) to start (off) with; **à p. de** (*date, prix*) from. ●**parti** *a* **bien p.** off to a good start.

partisan [partizã] *nm* supporter, follower ‖ *a* **être p. de qch/de faire** to be in favour of sth/of doing.

partition [partisjɔ̃] *nf* Mus score.

partout [partu] *adv* everywhere; **p. où tu vas** *ou* **iras** everywhere *ou* wherever you go.

paru [pary] *pp de* **paraître**.

parvenir* [parvənir] *vi* (*aux* **être**) **à** (*lieu*) to reach; (*objectif*) to achieve; **p. à faire** to manage to do.

parvis [parvi] *nm* square (*in front of church etc*).

pas¹ [pɑ] *adv* (*négatif*) not; (**ne**)**... p.** not; **je ne sais p.** I do not *ou* don't know; **je n'ai p. compris** I didn't under-

stand; **je voudrais ne pas sortir** I would like not to go out; **p. de pain/etc** no bread/*etc*; **p. encore** not yet; **p. du tout** not at all.

pas² [pɑ] *nm* **1** step; (*allure*) pace; (*bruit*) footstep; (*trace*) footprint; **à deux p. (de)** close by; **au p.** at a walking pace; **rouler au p.** (*véhicule*) to go dead slow(ly); **au p.** (*cadencé*) in step; **faire les cent p.** to walk up and down; **revenir sur ses p.** to go back on one's tracks; **marcher à p. de loup** to creep (silently); **faux p.** (*en marchant*) stumble; (*faute*) Fig blunder; **le p. de la porte** the doorstep.

2 (*de vis*) thread.

3 Géog straits; **le p. de Calais** the Straits of Dover.

passable [pɑsabl] *a* (*travail, résultat*) (just) average; **mention p.** Scol Univ pass.

passage [pɑsaʒ] *nm* (*action*) passing, passage; (*traversée*) Nau crossing; (*extrait, couloir*) passage; (*chemin*) path; **p. clouté** *ou* **pour piétons** (pedestrian) crossing, *Am* crosswalk; **p. souterrain** subway, *Am* underpass; **p. à niveau** level crossing, *Am* grade crossing; **'p. interdit'** 'no through traffic'; **'cédez le p.'** (*au carrefour*) 'give way', *Am* 'yield'; **être de p.** to be passing through (**à Paris**/*etc* Paris/*etc*).

passager, -ère [pɑsaʒe, -ɛr] **1** *nmf* passenger; **p. clandestin** stowaway. **2** *a* (*de courte durée*) passing, temporary.

passant, -ante [pɑsɑ̃, -ɑ̃t] **1** *a* (*rue*) busy ‖ *nmf* passer-by. **2** *nm* (*de ceinture etc*) loop.

passe [pɑs] *nf* Sp pass; **mot de p.** password; **une mauvaise p.** Fig a bad patch.

passé [pɑse] **1** *a* (*temps etc*) past; (*couleur*) faded; **la semaine passée** last week; **dix heures passées** after *ou* gone ten (o'clock); **être passé** (*personne*) to have been (and gone); (*orage*) to be over; **avoir vingt ans passés** to be over twenty ‖ *nm* (*temps, vie passée*) past; Gram past (tense). **2** *prép* after; **p. huit**

heures after eight (o'clock).
passe-montagne [pɑsmɔ̃taɲ] *nm* balaclava, *Am* ski mask.
passe-partout [pɑspartu] *nm inv* master
key.
passe-passe [pɑspɑs] *nm inv* **tour de
p.-passe** conjuring trick.
passeport [pɑspɔr] *nm* passport.
passer [pɑse] *vi (aux être ou avoir)*
(aller) to go, pass *(de* from, *à* to);
(traverser) to go through *ou* over;
(facteur) to come; *(temps)* to pass
(by), go by; *(film)* to be shown, be
on; *(douleur, mode)* to pass; *(couleur)*
to fade; *(courant)* to flow; **p. devant**
(maison etc) to go past *ou* by, pass (by);
p. à *ou* **par Paris** to pass through Paris;
p. à la boulangerie *ou* **chez le boulanger**
to go round to the baker's; **p. à la caisse**
to go over to the cash desk; **laisser p.**
(personne, lumière) to let through *ou* in;
(occasion) to let slip; **p. prendre** to fetch,
pick up; **p. voir qn** to drop in on s.o.; **p.
pour** *(riche etc)* to be taken for; **faire p.
qn pour** to pass s.o. off as; **p. sur** *(détail
etc)* to overlook, pass over; **p. en**
(seconde etc) Scol to pass up into; *Aut* to change up to.
∎ *vt (aux avoir) (frontière etc)* to cross,
pass; *(maison etc)* to pass, go past;
(donner) to pass, hand (**à** to); *(temps)*
to spend, pass (**à faire** doing); *(disque,
film, chemise)* to put on; *(loi)* to pass;
(examen) to take, sit (for); *(thé)* to
strain; *(café)* to filter; *(commande)* to
place; *(limites)* to go beyond; *(visite
médicale)* to have; **p. (son tour)** to
pass; **p. qch à qn** *(caprice etc)* to grant
s.o. sth; *(pardonner)* to excuse s.o. sth;
p. un coup d'éponge/etc à qch to go over
sth with a sponge/etc; **je vous passe...**
Tél I'm putting you through to....
∎ **se passer** *vpr (se produire)* to take
place, happen; *(douleur)* to go (away),
pass; **se p. de** to do *ou* go without; **se p.
de commentaires** to need no comment; **ça
s'est bien passé** it went off well.
passerelle [pasrɛl] *nf (pont)* footbridge;

(voie d'accès) Nau Av gangway.
passe-temps [pɑstɑ̃] *nm inv* pastime.
passible [pasibl] *a* **p. de** *(peine) Jur* liable
to.
passif, -ive [pasif, -iv] **1** *a* passive ∎ *nm
Gram* passive. **2** *nm Com* liabilities.
passion [pɑsjɔ̃] *nf* passion; **avoir la p.
des voitures/d'écrire/etc** to have a passion for cars/writing/etc. ● **passionner**
vt to thrill, fascinate; **se p. pour** to have
a passion for. ● **passionnant** *a* thrilling.
● **passionné, -ée** *a* passionate; **p. de qch**
passionately fond of sth ∎ *nmf* fan **(de**
of).
passoire [pɑswar] *nf (pour liquides)*
sieve; *(à thé)* strainer; *(à légumes)*
colander.
pastel [pastɛl] *nm* pastel; **dessin au p.**
pastel drawing ∎ *a inv* **ton p.** pastel
shade *ou* tone.
pastèque [pastɛk] *nf* watermelon.
pasteur [pastœr] *nm Rel* pastor.
pasteurisé [pastœrize] *a* pasteurized.
pastille [pastij] *nf* pastille, lozenge.
patate [patat] *nf Fam* spud, potato.
patauger [patoʒe] *vi (marcher)* to wade
(in the mud etc); *(barboter)* to splash
about.
pâte [pɑt] *nf (substance)* paste; *(à pain)*
dough; *(à tarte)* pastry; *(à frire)* batter;
pâtes (alimentaires) pasta; **p. à modeler**
plasticine®, modelling clay; **p. dentifrice** toothpaste.
pâté [pɑte] *nm* **1** *(charcuterie)* pâté; **p. (en
croûte)** meat pie. **2** *(de sable)* sand
castle; **p. de maisons** block of houses.
pâtée [pɑte] *nf (pour chien)* dog food;
(pour chat) cat food.
paternel, -elle [patɛrnɛl] *a (amour etc)*
paternal, fatherly; *(parenté)* paternal.
pâteux, -euse [pɑtø, -øz] *a (substance)*
doughy, pasty.
pathétique [patetik] *a* moving.
pathologie [patɔlɔʒi] *nf* pathology.
patience [pasjɑ̃s] *nf* patience; **perdre p.**
to lose patience.
patient, -ente [pasjɑ̃, -ɑ̃t] **1** *a* patient. **2**

nmf Méd patient. ● **patiemment** [-amã]
adv patiently. ● **patienter** *vi* to wait
(patiently).

patin [patɛ̃] *nm* skate; (*pour le parquet*)
cloth pad (*used for walking*); **p. à glace**
ice skate; **p. à roulettes** roller-skate.

patin/er [patine] *vi Sp* to skate; (*roue*) to
spin around; (*véhicule*) to slip (and
slide). ● **—age** *nm Sp* skating; **p. artistique** figure skating. ● **patinoire** *nf* skating rink, ice rink.

pâtir [patir] *vi* **p. de** to suffer from.

pâtisserie [patisri] *nf* pastry, cake;
(*magasin*) cake shop; (*art*) cake *ou*
pastry making. ● **pâtissier, -ière** *nmf*
pastrycook and cake shop owner.

patois [patwa] *nm Ling* patois.

patrie [patri] *nf* (native) country.

patrimoine [patrimwan] *nm* (*biens*) & *Fig*
heritage.

patriote [patrijɔt] *nmf* patriot ‖ *a* (*personne*) patriotic. ● **patriotique** *a* (*chant
etc*) patriotic.

patron, -onne [patrɔ̃, -ɔn] **1** *nmf* (*chef*)
boss, employer; (*propriétaire*) owner
(**de** of); (*gérant*) manager, manageress; (*de bar*) landlord, landlady. **2** *nm*
(*modèle de papier*) *Tex* pattern.
● **patronat** [patrɔna] *nm* employers.

patrouille [patruj] *nf* patrol. ● **patrouiller**
vi to patrol.

patte [pat] *nf* **1** (*membre*) leg; (*de chat,
chien*) paw; **marcher à quatre pattes** to
crawl. **2** (*languette*) tongue.

pattes [pat] *nfpl* (*favoris*) sideboards,
Am sideburns.

pâturage [patyraʒ] *nm* pasture.

paume [pom] *nf* (*de main*) palm.

paum/er [pome] *vt Fam* to lose. ● **—é,
-ée** *nmf* (*malheureux*) *Fam* down-and-
out, loser ‖ *a* **un coin** *ou* **trou p.** *Fam* a
dump.

paupière [popjɛr] *nf* eyelid.

pause [poz] *nf* (*arrêt*) break; (*dans le
discours etc*) pause.

pauvre [povr] *a* (*personne, terre etc*) poor
‖ *nmf* poor man, poor woman; **les
pauvres** the poor. ● **pauvreté** *nf* (*be-*

soin) poverty.

pavaner (se) [səpavane] *vpr* to strut
(about).

pav/er [pave] *vt* to pave. ● **—é** *nm* **un p.** a
paving stone; (*de vieille chaussée*) a
cobblestone; **sur le p.** *Fig* on the streets.

pavillon [pavijɔ̃] *nm* **1** (*maison*) (detached) house; (*d'hôpital*) ward; (*d'exposition*) pavilion. **2** (*drapeau*) flag.

pavoiser [pavwaze] *vi* (*exulter*) *Fig* to
rejoice.

pavot [pavo] *nm* (*cultivé*) poppy.

paye [pɛj] *nf* pay, wages. ● **payement** *nm*
payment.

payer [peje] *vt* (*personne, somme*) to
pay; (*service, objet, faute*) to pay for;
p. qn pour faire qch to pay s.o. to do *ou*
for doing sth; **p. qch à qn** (*offrir en
cadeau*) *Fam* to treat s.o. to sth ‖ *vi*
(*personne, métier, crime*) to pay.
● **payant** *a* (*hôte, spectateur*) paying;
(*place, entrée*) that one has to pay
for; (*rentable*) worthwhile.

pays [pei] *nm* country; (*région*) region;
du p. (*vin, gens etc*) local.

paysage [peizaʒ] *nm* landscape, scenery.

paysan, -anne [peizã, -an] *nmf* (small)
farmer.

Pays-Bas [peiba] *nmpl* **les P.-Bas** the
Netherlands.

PCV [peseve] *abrév* (*paiement contre
vérification*) **téléphoner en PCV** to reverse the charges, *Am* call collect.

PDG [pedeʒe] *abrév* = **président directeur général.**

péage [peaʒ] *nm* (*droit*) toll; (*lieu*) toll-
booth; **pont/etc à p.** toll bridge/*etc.*

peau, -x [po] *nf* skin; (*de fruit*) peel, skin;
(*cuir*) hide; (*fourrure*) fur, pelt; **faire p.
neuve** *Fig* to turn over a new leaf. ● **P.-
Rouge** *nmf* (*pl* **Peaux-Rouges**) (Red)
Indian.

pêche[1] [pɛʃ] *nf* (*activité*) fishing; (*poissons*) catch; **p. (à la ligne)** angling; **aller
à la p.** to go fishing. ● **pêcher**[1] *vi* to fish
‖ *vt* (*attraper*) to catch; (*chercher à
prendre*) to fish for. ● **pêcheur** *nm* fisherman; (*à la ligne*) angler.

pêche² [pɛʃ] nf (fruit) peach. ● **pêcher²** nm (arbre) peach tree.

péché [peʃe] nm sin.

pédagogie [pedagɔʒi] nf (science) education, teaching methods. ● **pédagogique** a educational. ● **pédagogue** nmf teacher.

pédale [pedal] nf pedal; **p. de frein** foot brake (pedal). ● **pédaler** vi to pedal.

pédalo [pedalo] nm pedal boat.

pédant [pedɑ̃] a pedantic.

pédé [pede] nm (homosexuel) Péj Fam queer.

pédiatre [pedjatr] nmf Méd children's doctor, p(a)ediatrician.

pédicure [pedikyr] nmf chiropodist, Am podiatrist.

peigne [pɛɲ] nm comb; **se donner un coup de p.** to give one's hair a comb. ● **peigner** vt (cheveux) to comb; **p. qn** to comb s.o.'s hair ▮ **se p.** vpr to comb one's hair.

peignoir [pɛɲwar] nm dressing gown, Am bathrobe; **p. (de bain)** bathrobe.

peinard [penar] a Fam quiet (and easy).

peindre* [pɛ̃dr] vt to paint; **p. en bleu**/etc to paint blue/etc ▮ vi to paint.

peine [pen] nf **1** (châtiment) punishment; **la p. de mort** the death penalty; **p. de prison** prison sentence; **'défense d'entrer sous p. d'amende'** 'trespassers will be prosecuted ou fined'.
2 (chagrin) sorrow, grief; **avoir de la p.** to be upset ou sad; **faire de la p. à qn** to upset s.o.
3 (effort, difficulté) trouble; **se donner de la p.** to go to a lot of trouble (**pour faire** to do); **avec p.** with difficulty; **ça vaut la p. d'attendre**/etc it's worth (while) waiting/etc; **ce n'est pas** ou **ça ne vaut pas la p.** it's not worth it ou worth bothering.
● **peiner 1** vt to upset, sadden. **2** vi to labour, struggle.

peine (à) [apen] adv hardly, scarcely.

peintre [pɛ̃tr] nm (artiste) painter; **p. (en bâtiment)** (house) painter, (painter and) decorator. ● **peinture** nf (tableau, activité) painting; (matière) paint; '**p.**

fraîche' 'wet paint'.

péjoratif, -ive [peʒɔratif, -iv] a pejorative, derogatory.

Pékin [pekɛ̃] nm ou f Peking.

pelage [pəlaʒ] nm (d'animal) coat, fur.

pêle-mêle [pɛlmɛl] adv in disorder.

peler [pəle] vt (fruit) to peel ▮ vi (peau) to peel.

pèlerin [pɛlrɛ̃] nm pilgrim. ● **pèlerinage** nm pilgrimage.

pélican [pelikɑ̃] nm (oiseau) pelican.

pelle [pɛl] nf shovel; (d'enfant) spade; **p. à tarte** cake server; **à la p.** (argent etc) Fam galore. ● **pelleteuse** nf Tech mechanical digger ou shovel.

pellicule [pelikyl] nf Phot film; (couche) layer, film; pl Méd dandruff.

pelote [p(ə)lɔt] nf (de laine) ball; (à épingles) pincushion; **p. (basque)** Sp pelota.

peloton [p(ə)lɔtɔ̃] nm **1** (cyclistes) Sp pack. **2** Mil squad; **p. d'exécution** firing squad.

pelotonner (se) [səp(ə)lɔtɔne] vpr to curl up (into a ball).

pelouse [p(ə)luz] nf lawn; Sp enclosure.

peluche [p(ə)lyʃ] nf (jouet en) **p.** soft toy; **chien**/etc **en p.** furry dog/etc; **ours en p.** teddy bear. **2** nfpl (flocons) fluff, lint. ● **pelucher** vi to get fluffy ou linty.

pelure [p(ə)lyr] nf (épluchure) peeling.

pénal, -aux [penal, -o] a (code etc) penal. ● **pénaliser** vt Sp Jur to penalize (**pour** for). ● **pénalité** nf Jur Rugby penalty.

penalty, pl **-ties** [penalti, -iz] nm Fb penalty.

penaud [pəno] a sheepish.

penchant [pɑ̃ʃɑ̃] nm (goût) liking (**pour** for); (tendance) inclination (**à qch** towards sth).

pencher [pɑ̃ʃe] vt (objet) to tilt; (tête) to lean ▮ vi (arbre etc) to lean (over) ▮ **se p.** vpr to lean (over ou forward); **se p. par** (fenêtre) to lean out of; **se p. sur** (problème etc) to examine. ● **penché** a leaning.

pendaison [pɑ̃dɛzɔ̃] nf hanging.

pendant [pɑ̃dɑ̃] prép (au cours de) during; **p. la nuit** during the night; **p. deux mois** (pour une période de) for two months; **p. que** while.

pendentif [pɑ̃dɑ̃tif] nm (collier) pendant.

penderie [pɑ̃dri] nf wardrobe, Am closet.

pendre [pɑ̃dr] vti to hang (à from); **p. qn** to hang s.o. ‖ **se p.** vpr (se suicider) to hang oneself; (se suspendre) to hang (à from). ● **pendu, -ue** a (objet) hanging (à from) ‖ nmf hanged man ou woman.

pendule [pɑ̃dyl] nf clock.

pénétrer [penetre] vi **p. dans** to enter; (profondément) to penetrate (into) ‖ vt (pluie etc) to penetrate (sth). ● **pénétration** nf penetration.

pénible [penibl] a difficult; (douloureux) painful; (ennuyeux) tiresome. ● **-ment** [-əmɑ̃] adv with difficulty; (avec douleur) painfully.

péniche [peniʃ] nf barge.

pénicilline [penisilin] nf penicillin.

péninsule [penɛ̃syl] nf peninsula.

pénis [penis] nm penis.

pénitence [penitɑ̃s] nf (punition) punishment; (peine) Rel penance.

pénitencier [penitɑ̃sje] nm prison.

pénombre [penɔ̃br] nf half-light, (semi-)darkness.

pensée [pɑ̃se] nf **1** thought. **2** (fleur) pansy.

penser [pɑ̃se] vi to think (à of, about); **p. à qch/à faire qch** (ne pas oublier) to remember sth/to do sth; **j'y pense** I'm thinking about it; **penses-tu!** you must be joking!

‖ vt to think (que that); (concevoir) to think out; **je pensais rester** (intention) I was thinking of staying; **je pense réussir** (espoir) I hope to succeed; **que pensez-vous de…?** what do you think of ou about…?; **je pense du bien de qn/qch** to think highly of s.o./sth. ● **pensant** a **bien p.** Péj orthodox. ● **pensif, -ive** a thoughtful.

pension [pɑ̃sjɔ̃] nf **1** boarding school; (somme à payer) board; **être en p.** to board, be a boarder (**chez** with); **p.**

complète full board, Am American plan. **2** (de retraite etc) pension; **p. alimentaire** maintenance allowance. ● **pensionnaire** nmf (élève) boarder; (d'hôtel) resident; (de famille) lodger. ● **pensionnat** nm boarding school; (élèves) boarders.

pentagone [pɛ̃tagɔn] nm **le P.** Am Pol the Pentagon.

pente [pɑ̃t] nf slope; **en p.** sloping.

Pentecôte [pɑ̃tkot] nf Whitsun, Am Pentecost.

pénurie [penyri] nf scarcity (de of).

pépin [pepɛ̃] nm **1** (de fruit) pip, Am seed, pit. **2** (ennui) Fam hitch, bother.

pépinière [pepinjɛr] nf Bot nursery.

pépite [pepit] nf (gold) nugget.

perçant [pɛrsɑ̃] a (cri, froid) piercing; (yeux) sharp, keen.

percée [pɛrse] nf (dans une forêt etc) opening; (avance technologique, attaque militaire) breakthrough.

percepteur [pɛrsɛptœr] nm tax collector. ● **perceptible** a perceptible (à to). ● **perception** nf **1** (bureau) tax office; (d'impôt) collection. **2** (sensation) perception.

perc/er [pɛrse] vt (trouer) to pierce; (avec une perceuse) to drill (a hole in); (trou, ouverture) to make, drill; (mystère) to uncover ‖ vi (soleil) to break through; (abcès) to burst. ● **—euse** nf (outil) drill.

percevoir* [pɛrsəvwar] vt **1** (sensation) to perceive; (son) to hear. **2** (impôt) to collect.

perche [pɛrʃ] nf (bâton) pole.

percher [pɛrʃe] vi (oiseau) to perch; (volailles) to roost ‖ **se p.** vpr (oiseau, personne) to perch. ● **perchoir** nm perch; (de volailles) roost.

percolateur [pɛrkɔlatœr] nm (de restaurant) percolator.

percuter [pɛrkyte] vt (véhicule) to crash into.

perdre [pɛrdr] vt to lose; (gaspiller) to waste; (habitude) to get out of; **p. de vue** to lose sight of.

▌*vi* to lose; **j'y perds** I lose out.
▌**se perdre** *vpr* (*s'égarer*) to get lost; **se p. dans les détails** to be *ou* get bogged down in details; **je m'y perds** I'm lost *ou* confused. ●**perdant, -ante** *nmf* loser. ●**perdu** *a* lost; (*gaspillé*) wasted; (*malade*) finished; (*lieu*) isolated; **une balle perdue** a stray bullet; **c'est du temps p.** it's a waste of time.

perdrix [pɛrdri] *nf* partridge.

père [pɛr] *nm* father.

péremptoire [perɑ̃ptwar] *a* peremptory.

perfection [pɛrfɛksjɔ̃] *nf* perfection; **à la p.** perfectly.

perfectionner (se) [səpɛrfɛksjɔne] *vpr* **se p. en anglais/etc** to improve one's English/etc. ●**perfectionné** *a* (*machine etc*) advanced. ●**perfectionnement** *nm* improvement; **cours de p.** refresher course. ●**perfectionniste** *nmf* perfectionist.

perforer [pɛrfɔre] *vt* (*pneu, intestin etc*) to perforate; (*billet, carte*) to punch; **carte perforée** punch card. ●**perforation** *nf* perforation; (*trou*) punched hole. ●**perforeuse** *nf* (paper) punch.

performance [pɛrfɔrmɑ̃s] *nf* (*d'athlète etc*) performance. ●**performant** *a* (highly) efficient.

péridurale [peridyral] *a & nf* (**anesthésie**) **p.** *Méd* epidural.

péril [peril] *nm* danger, peril; **à tes risques et périls** at your own risk. ●**périlleux, -euse** *a* dangerous, perilous; **saut p.** somersault (*in mid air*).

périmer (se) [səperime] *vpr* **laisser qch (se) p.** to allow sth to expire. ●**périmé** *a* (*billet etc*) expired.

période [perjɔd] *nf* period. ●**périodique** *a* periodic ▌*nm* (*revue*) periodical.

péripétie [peripesi] *nf* (unexpected) event.

périphérique [periferik] *a* (*quartier etc*) outlying, peripheral; **radio p.** = radio station broadcasting from outside France ▌*nm* & **a** (**boulevard**) **p.** (motorway) ring road, *Am* beltway ▌*nmpl Ordinat* peripherals.

périple [peripl] *nm* trip, tour.

pér/ir [perir] *vi* to perish, die. ●**—issable** *a* (*denrée*) perishable.

périscope [periskɔp] *nm* periscope.

perle [pɛrl] *nf* (*bijou*) pearl; (*de bois, verre etc*) bead.

permanent, -ente [pɛrmanɑ̃, -ɑ̃t] **1** *a* permanent; (*spectacle*) *Cin* continuous. **2** *nf* (*coiffure*) perm. ●**permanence** *nf* permanence; (*salle d'étude*) study room; (*service, bureau*) duty office; **être de p.** to be on duty; **en p.** permanently.

permettre* [pɛrmɛtr] *vt* to allow, permit; **p. à qn de faire qch** (*permission, possibilité*) to allow *ou* permit s.o. to do sth; **vous permettez?** may I?; **se p. de faire** to allow oneself to do, take the liberty to do; **je ne peux pas me p. de l'acheter** I can't afford to buy it.

permis [pɛrmi] *a* allowed, permitted ▌*nm* (*autorisation*) licence, *Am* license, permit; **p. de conduire** (*carte*) driving licence, *Am* driver's license; **p. de travail** work permit; **passer son p. de conduire** to take one's driving *ou* road test.

permission [pɛrmisjɔ̃] *nf* permission; (*congé*) *Mil* leave; **demander la p.** to ask permission (**de faire** to do).

permuter [pɛrmyte] *vt* to change round *ou* over, permutate.

Pérou [peru] *nm* Peru.

perpendiculaire [pɛrpɑ̃dikyler] *a & nf* perpendicular (**à** to).

perpétrer [pɛrpetre] *vt* (*crime*) to perpetrate.

perpétuel, -elle [pɛrpetɥɛl] *a* perpetual; (*incessant*) continual; (*rente*) for life. ●**perpétuer** *vt* to perpetuate. ●**perpétuité (à)** *adv* (*condamnation*) for life.

perplexe [pɛrplɛks] *a* perplexed, puzzled.

perquisition [pɛrkizisjɔ̃] *nf* (house) search (*by police*).

perron [pɛrɔ̃] *nm* (front) steps.

perroquet [perɔke] *nm* parrot.

perruche [peryʃ] *nf* budgerigar, *Am*

parakeet.
perruque [peryk] *nf* wig.
persan [persã] *a* (*tapis, chat etc*) Persian
∎ *nm* (*langue*) Persian.
persécuter [persekyte] *vt* (*tourmenter*)
to persecute; (*importuner*) to harass.
● **persécution** *nf* persecution.
persévér/er [persevere] *vi* to persevere
(**dans** in). ● **—ant** *a* persevering. ● **persévérance** *nf* perseverance.
persienne [persjen] *nf* (outside) shutter.
persil [persi] *nm* parsley.
persist/er [persiste] *vi* to persist (**à faire**
in doing, **dans qch** in sth). ● **—ant** *a*
persistent; **à feuilles persistantes** (*arbre
etc*) evergreen.
personnage [persɔnaʒ] *nm* (*célébrité*)
(important) person; *Th Littér* character.
personnalité [persɔnalite] *nf* (*indivi-
dualité, personnage*) personality.
personne [persɔn] **1** *nf* person; *pl* people;
grande p. grown-up, adult; **en p.** in
person. **2** *pron* (*négatif*) nobody, no
one; (**ne**)... **p.** nobody, no one; **je ne
vois p.** I don't see anybody *ou* anyone;
p. ne saura nobody *ou* no one will
know; **mieux que p.** better than anybody *ou* anyone.
personnel, -elle [persɔnɛl] **1** *a* personal;
(*joueur*) individualistic. **2** *nm* staff,
personnel. ● **personnellement** *adv* personally.
personnifier [persɔnifje] *vt* to personify.
perspective [perspektiv] *nf* (*art*) perspective; (*idée, possibilité*) prospect
(**de** of); **en p.** *Fig* in view.
perspicace [perspikas] *a* shrewd.
persuader [persɥade] *vt* to persuade (**qn
de faire** s.o. to do); **être persuadé que** to
be convinced that. ● **persuasif, -ive** *a*
persuasive. ● **persuasion** *nf* persuasion.
perte [pert] *nf* loss; (*gaspillage*) waste (**de
temps/ d'argent** of time/money); **à p. de
vue** as far as the eye can see; **vendre à p.**
to sell at a loss.
pertinent [pertinã] *a* relevant.
perturber [pertyrbe] *vt* (*trafic, cérémonie*

etc) to disrupt; (*ordre public, personne*)
to disturb. ● **perturbation** *nf* disruption.
● **p. atmosphérique** atmospheric disturbance.
pervers [perver] *a* wicked, perverse;
(*dépravé*) perverted. ● **perversion** *nf*
perversion. ● **pervertir** *vt* to pervert.
pesant [pəzã] *a* heavy ∎ *nm* **valoir son p.
d'or** to be worth one's *ou* its weight in
gold. ● **pesanteur** *nf* (*force*) gravity.
peser [pəze] *vt* to weigh ∎ *vi* to weigh; **p.
lourd** to be heavy; (*argument etc*) *Fig* to
carry weight; **p. sur** (*appuyer*) to bear
down upon; (*influer*) to bear upon; **p.
sur l'estomac** to lie (heavily) on the
stomach. ● **pèse-personne** *nm* (bathroom) scales.
pessimisme [pesimism] *nm* pessimism.
● **pessimiste** *a* pessimistic ∎ *nmf* pessimist.
peste [pest] *nf* (*maladie*) plague; (*personne*) *Fig* pest.
pester [peste] *vi* to curse; **p. contre qch/
qn** to curse sth/ s.o.
pétale [petal] *nm* petal.
pétanque [petãk] *nf* (*jeu*) bowls.
pétarader [petarade] *vi* to backfire.
pétard [petar] *nm* (*explosif*) firecracker.
péter [pete] *vi Fam* (*éclater*) to go bang
ou pop; (*se rompre*) to snap.
pétill/er [petije] *vi* (*champagne etc*) to
sparkle, fizz; (*yeux*) to sparkle. ● **—ant** *a*
(*eau, vin, yeux*) sparkling.
petit, -ite [p(ə)ti, -it] *a* small, little; (*de
taille*) short; (*bruit, coup*) slight; (*jeune*)
little; **tout p.** tiny; **un p. Français** a
(little) French boy ∎ *nmf* (little) boy,
(little) girl; (*personne*) small person;
Scol junior; *pl* (*d'animal*) young; (*de
chien*) pups; (*de chat*) kittens ∎ *adv* **p. à
p.** little by little. ● **p.-suisse** *nm* soft
cheese (*for dessert*).
petit-fils [p(ə)tifis] *nm* (*pl* petits-fils)
grandson. ● **petite-fille** *nf* (*pl* petites-
filles) granddaughter. ● **petits-enfants**
nmpl grandchildren.
pétition [petisjɔ̃] *nf* petition.
pétrifier [petrifje] *vt* (*de peur etc*) to

petrify.

pétrin [petrɛ̃] *nm* **être dans le p.** *Fam* to be in a fix.

pétrir [petrir] *vt* to knead.

pétrole [petrɔl] *nm* oil, petroleum; **p. (lampant)** paraffin, *Am* kerosene; **nappe de p.** (*sur la mer*) oil slick. ● **pétrolier, -ière** *a* **industrie pétrolière** oil industry ‖ *nm* (*navire*) oil tanker.

peu [pø] *adv* (*manger etc*) not much, little; **elle mange p.** she doesn't eat much, she eats little; **un p.** a little, a bit; **p. de sel/temps**/*etc* not much salt/time/*etc*, little salt/time/*etc*; **un p. de fromage**/*etc* a little cheese/*etc*, a bit of cheese/*etc*; **p. de gens**/*etc* few people/*etc*, not many people/*etc*; **p. sont...** few are...; **un (tout) petit p.** a (tiny) little bit; **p. intéressant**/*etc* not very interesting/*etc*; **p. de chose** not much; **p. à p.** little by little, gradually; **à p. près** more or less; **p. après/avant** shortly after/before.

peuple [pœpl] *nm* (*nation*) people; **les gens du p.** the common people. ● **peuplé** *a* (*region etc*) populated (**de** by); **très/peu**/*etc* **p.** highly/sparsely/*etc* populated.

peuplier [pøplije] *nm* (*arbre, bois*) poplar.

peur [pœr] *nf* fear; **avoir p.** to be afraid *ou* frightened *ou* scared (**de qch/qn** of sth/s.o.; **de faire** to do, of doing); **faire p. à qn** to frighten *ou* scare s.o.; **de p. que** (+ *sub*) for fear that; **de p. de faire** for fear of doing. ● **peureux, -euse** *a* easily frightened.

peut [pø] *voir* **pouvoir 1**.

peut-être [pøtɛtr] *adv* perhaps, maybe; **p.-être qu'il viendra** perhaps *ou* maybe he'll come.

peuvent, peux [pœv, pø] *voir* **pouvoir 1**.

phallique [falik] *a* phallic.

phare [far] *nm* *Nau* lighthouse; *Aut* headlight, headlamp; **faire un appel de phares** *Aut* to flash one's lights.

pharmacie [farmasi] *nf* chemist's shop, *Am* drugstore; (*science*) pharmacy; (*armoire*) medicine cabinet. ● **pharma-** **cien, -ienne** *nmf* chemist, pharmacist, *Am* druggist.

phase [faz] *nf* phase.

phénomène [fenɔmɛn] *nm* phenomenon; (*personne*) *Fam* eccentric.

philanthrope [filɑ̃trɔp] *nmf* philanthropist.

philatélie [filateli] *nf* stamp collecting, philately. ● **philatéliste** *nmf* stamp collector, philatelist.

Philippines [filipin] *nfpl* **les P.** the Philippines.

philosophe [filozɔf] *nmf* philosopher ‖ *a* (*résigné, sage*) philosophical. ● **philosophie** *nf* philosophy. ● **philosophique** *a* philosophical.

phobie [fɔbi] *nf* phobia.

phonétique [fɔnetik] *a* phonetic ‖ *nf* phonetics.

phoque [fɔk] *nm* (*animal*) seal.

photo [fɔto] *nf* photo; (*art*) photography; **p. d'identité** ID photo; **prendre une p. de, prendre en p.** to take a photo of; **se faire prendre en p.** to have one's photo taken ‖ *a inv* **appareil p.** camera. ● **photogénique** *a* photogenic.

● **photographe** *nmf* photographer. ● **photographie** *nf* (*art*) photography; (*image*) photograph. ● **photographier** *vt* to photograph. ● **photographique** *a* photographic.

photocopie [fɔtɔkɔpi] *nf* photocopy. ● **photocopier** *vt* to photocopy. ● **photocopieuse** *nf* (*machine*) photocopier.

photomaton® [fɔtɔmatɔ̃] *nm* photo booth.

phrase [fraz] *nf* (*mots*) sentence.

physicien, -ienne [fizisjɛ̃, -jɛn] *nmf* physicist.

physiologie [fizjɔlɔʒi] *nf* physiology.

physionomie [fizjɔnɔmi] *nf* face.

physique [fizik] **1** *a* physical ‖ *nm* (*corps*) physique. **2** *nf* (*science*) physics. ● **—ment** *adv* physically.

piaffer [pjafe] *vi* (*cheval*) to stamp; **p. d'impatience** *Fig* to fidget impatiently.

piano [pjano] *nm* piano; **p. droit/à queue**

upright/grand piano. ●**pianiste** nmf pianist.

piaule [pjol] nf (chambre) Fam room.

pic [pik] nm **1** (cime) peak. **2** (outil) pick(axe); **p. à glace** ice pick.

pic (à) [apik] adv (verticalement) sheer; **couler à p.** to sink to the bottom; **arriver à p.** Fig to arrive in the nick of time.

pichet [piʃɛ] nm jug, pitcher.

pickpocket [pikpɔkɛt] nm pickpocket.

picorer [pikɔre] vti to peck.

picoter [pikɔte] vt (yeux) to make smart; **les yeux me picotent** my eyes are smarting.

pie [pi] nf (oiseau) magpie.

pièce [pjɛs] nf **1** (de maison etc) room. **2** (de pantalon) patch; (écrit) Jur document; **p. (de monnaie)** coin; **p. (de théâtre)** play; **p. d'identité** identity card, proof of identity; **pièces détachées ou de rechange** (de véhicule etc) spare parts; **p. montée** = tiered wedding cake; **cinq dollars/etc (la) p.** five dollars/etc each.

pied [pje] nm foot (pl feet); (de meuble) leg; (de verre, lampe) base; (de lit, d'arbre, de colline) foot; Phot stand; **à p.** on foot; **aller à p.** to walk, go on foot; **au p. de** at the foot ou bottom of; **au p. de la lettre** Fig literally; **coup de p.** kick; **donner un coup de p.** to kick (à qn s.o.); **avoir p.** (nageur) to have a footing, touch the bottom; **sur p.** (debout, levé) up and about; **comme un p.** (mal) Fam dreadfully. ●**p.-noir** nmf (pl **pieds-noirs**) Algerian-born Frenchman ou Frenchwoman.

piédestal, -aux [pjedɛstal, -o] nm pedestal.

piège [pjɛʒ] nm (pour animal) & Fig trap. ●**piéger** vt (animal) to trap; (voiture etc) to booby-trap; **colis/voiture piégé(e)** parcel/car bomb.

pierre [pjɛr] nf stone; (précieuse) gem, stone; **p. (à briquet)** flint. ●**pierreries** nfpl gems, precious stones.

piétiner [pjetine] vt to trample (on) ∎ vi to stamp (one's feet); (marcher sur place) to mark time; (ne pas avancer) Fig to make no headway.

piéton [pjetɔ̃] nm pedestrian. ●**piétonne** a **rue p.** pedestrian(ized) street.

pieu, -x [pjø] nm (piquet) post, stake.

pieuvre [pjœvr] nf octopus.

pieux, -euse [pjø, -øz] a pious.

pif [pif] nm (nez) Fam nose.

pigeon [piʒɔ̃] nm pigeon; (personne) Fam dupe.

piger [piʒe] vti Fam to understand.

pigment [pigmɑ̃] nm pigment.

pile [pil] nf **1** n**p. (électrique)** battery; **radio à piles** battery radio. **2** nf (tas) pile; **en p.** in a pile. **3** nf **p.** (de **p. ou face)?** heads (or tails)?; **jouer à p. ou face** to toss up. **4** adv **s'arrêter p.** Fam to stop short ou dead; **à deux heures p.** Fam on the dot of two.

piler [pile] vt (amandes etc) to grind.

pilier [pilje] nm pillar.

pilon [pilɔ̃] nm (de poulet) drumstick.

piller [pije] vti to loot, pillage. ●**pillage** nm looting, pillage. ●**pillard, -arde** nmf looter.

pilote [pilɔt] nm Av Nau pilot; (de voiture, char) driver ∎ a **usine/etc (-)p.** pilot factory/etc. ●**piloter** vt (avion) to fly, pilot; (bateau) to pilot; (voiture) to drive; **p. qn** Fig to show s.o. around. ●**pilotage** nm piloting; **poste de p.** cockpit; **école de p.** flying school.

pilule [pilyl] nf pill; **prendre la p.** (femme) to be on the pill; **arrêter la p.** to go off the pill.

piment [pimɑ̃] nm pepper, pimento. ●**pimenté** a Culin spicy.

pin [pɛ̃] nm (arbre, bois) pine; **pomme de p.** pine cone.

pinailler [pinaje] vi Fam to quibble.

pince [pɛ̃s] nf (outil) pliers; (de cycliste) clip; (de crabe) pincer; **p. à linge** (clothes) peg ou Am pin; **p. à épiler** tweezers; **p. à sucre** sugar tongs; **p. (à cheveux)** hairgrip, Am bobby pin.

pincer [pɛ̃se] vt to pinch; (corde) Mus to pluck; **p. qn** (arrêter) Fam to nab s.o.; **se p. le doigt** to get one's finger caught (dans in). ● —é a (air) stiff. ● —ée nf (de sel etc) pinch (de of).

pinceau, -x [pɛ̃so] nm (paint)brush.

pinède [pined] nf pine forest.

pingouin [pɛ̃gwɛ̃] nm penguin, auk.

ping-pong [piŋpɔ̃g] nm table tennis, ping-pong.

pin's [pinz] nm inv badge, lapel pin.

pinson [pɛ̃sɔ̃] nm (oiseau) chaffinch.

pintade [pɛ̃tad] nf guinea fowl.

pioche [pjɔʃ] nf pick(axe). ● **piocher** vti (creuser) to dig (with a pick).

pion [pjɔ̃] nm 1 (au jeu de dames) piece; Échecs & Fig pawn. 2 Scol Fam master (in charge of discipline).

pionnier [pjɔnje] nm pioneer.

pipe [pip] nf (de fumeur) pipe; **fumer la p.** to smoke a pipe.

pipeau, -x [pipo] nm (flûte) pipe.

pipi [pipi] nm **faire p.** Fam to go for a pee.

pique [pik] 1 nm (couleur) Cartes spades. 2 nf (allusion) cutting remark.

pique-assiette [pikasjɛt] nmf inv scrounger.

pique-nique [piknik] nm picnic. ● **pique-niquer** vi to picnic.

piquer [pike] vt (percer) to prick; (langue, yeux) to sting; (coudre) to (machine-)stitch; **p. qn** (abeille) to sting s.o.; **p. qch dans** (enfoncer) to stick sth into; **p. qch** (voler) Fam to pinch sth; **p. une colère** Fam to fly into a rage; **p. une crise (de nerfs)** Fam to throw a fit; **p. une tête** to plunge headlong. ▮ vi (avion) to dive; (moutarde etc) to be hot.

▮ **se piquer** vpr to prick oneself; **se p. au doigt** to prick one's finger. ● **piquant** a (plante, barbe) prickly; (sauce, goût) pungent; (détail) spicy ▮ nm Bot prickle, thorn; (d'animal) spine, prickle.

piquet [pikɛ] nm 1 (pieu) stake, picket; (de tente) peg. 2 **p. (de grève)** picket (line), strike picket. 3 **au p.** Scol in the corner.

piqûre [pikyr] nf (d'abeille) sting; Méd injection; (d'épingle) prick; (point) stitch.

pirate [pirat] nm pirate; **p. de l'air** hijacker; **p. (informatique)** hacker ▮ a radio p. pirate radio.

pire [pir] a worse (que than); **le p. moment**/etc the worst moment/etc ▮ nmf **le ou la p.** the worst (one); **au p.** at (the very) worst; **s'attendre au p.** to expect the (very) worst.

pis [pi] 1 nm (de vache) udder. 2 a inv & adv Litt worse; **de mal en p.** from bad to worse.

pis-aller [pizale] nm inv (solution) stopgap.

piscine [pisin] nf swimming pool.

pissenlit [pisɑ̃li] nm dandelion.

pistache [pistaʃ] nf (graine, parfum) pistachio.

piste [pist] nf (traces) track, trail; Sp (race)track; (de cirque) ring; (de patinage) rink; (de magnétophone) track; **p. (d'envol)** runway; **p. cyclable** cycle track, Am bicycle path; **p. de danse** dance floor; **p. de ski** ski run ou slope; **tour de p.** Sp lap.

pistolet [pistɔlɛ] nm gun, pistol; (de peintre) spray gun; **p. à eau** water pistol.

piston [pistɔ̃] nm 1 Aut piston. 2 **avoir du p.** (appui) Fam to have connections.

pita [pita] nm pitta bread.

pitié [pitje] nf pity; **j'ai p. de lui, il me fait p.** I feel sorry for him, I pity him. ● **pitoyable** a pitiful.

piton [pitɔ̃] nm 1 (à crochet) hook. 2 Géog peak.

pitre [pitr] nm clown.

pittoresque [pitɔrɛsk] a picturesque.

pivert [pivɛr] nm (green) woodpecker.

pivot [pivo] nm pivot. ● **pivoter** vi (personne) to swing round; (fauteuil) to swivel; (porte) to revolve.

pizza [pidza] nf pizza. ● **pizzeria** nf pizzeria.

PJ [peʒi] nf abrév (police judiciaire) = CID, Am = FBI.

placard [plakar] nm 1 (armoire) cupboard, *Am* closet. **2 p. publicitaire** advertising poster. ● **placarder** *vt* (*affiche*) to stick up.

place [plas] *nf* (*endroit*, *rang*) & *Sp* place; (*espace*) room; (*lieu public*) square; (*siège*) seat, place; (*emploi*) job, position; **p. (de parking)** parking place *ou* space; **p. (financière)** (money) market; **à la p.** (*échange*) instead (**de** of); **à votre p.** in your place; **sur p.** on the spot; **en p.** in place; **mettre qch en p.** (*installer*) to set sth up; (*ranger*) to put sth in its place; **changer de p.** to change places; **changer qch de p.** to move sth; **faire de la place (à qn)** to make room (for s.o.).

placer [plase] *vt* (*mettre*) to place, put; (*invité*, *spectateur*) to seat; (*argent*) to invest (**dans** in); **p. un mot** to get a word in edgeways *ou Am* edgewise.

❚ se placer *vpr* (*debout*) to (go and) stand; (*s'asseoir*) to (go and) sit; (*objet*) to be put *ou* placed; (*cheval*, *coureur*) to be placed; **se p. troisième/** *etc Sp* to come third/*etc*. ● **placé** *a* (*objet*) & *Sp* placed; **bien/mal p. pour faire** in a good/bad position to do; **les gens haut placés** people in high places. ● **placement** *nm* (*d'argent*) investment.

placide [plasid] *a* placid.

plafond [plafɔ̃] *nm* ceiling.

plage [plaʒ] *nf* **1** beach; (*ville*) (seaside) resort. **2 p. arrière** *Aut* (back) window shelf.

plaider [plede] *vti Jur* to plead. ● **plaidoirie** *nf Jur* speech (for the defence *ou Am* defense). ● **plaidoyer** *nm* plea.

plaie [plɛ] *nf* (*blessure*) wound; (*coupure*) cut; (*corvée*, *personne*) *Fig* nuisance.

plaignant, -ante [plɛɲɑ̃, -ɑ̃t] *nmf Jur* plaintiff.

plaindre* [plɛ̃dr] **1** *vt* to feel sorry for, pity. **2 se plaindre** *vpr* (*protester*) to complain (**about**, **que** that); **se p. de** (*maux de tête etc*) to complain of *ou* about. ● **plainte** *nf* complaint; (*cri*) moan, groan.

plaine [plɛn] *nf Géog* plain.

plaire* [plɛr] *vi* **p. à qn** to please s.o.; **elle lui plaît** he likes her; **ça me plaît** I like it **❚** *v imp* **s'il vous** *ou* **te plaît** please **❚ se p.** *vpr* (*à Paris etc*) to like *ou* enjoy it; (*l'un l'autre*) to like each other.

plaisance [plɛzɑ̃s] *nf* **bateau de p.** pleasure boat; **navigation de p.** yachting.

plaisant [plɛzɑ̃] *a* (*drôle*) amusing; (*agréable*) pleasing. ● **plaisanter** *vi* to joke (**sur** about); **p. avec qch** to trifle with sth. ● **plaisanterie** *nf* joke; **par p.** for a joke.

plaisir [plɛzir] *nm* pleasure; **faire p. à qn** to please s.o.; **pour le p.** for fun, for the fun of it; **faites-moi le p. de...** would you be good enough to....

plan [plɑ̃] *nm* (*projet*, *dessin*) plan; (*de ville*) map, plan; (*Géom* plane; **au premier p.** in the foreground; **gros p.** *Phot Cin* close-up; **sur le p. politique/***etc* from the political/*etc* viewpoint, politically/*etc*; **de premier p.** of importance, major.

planche [plɑ̃ʃ] *nf* board, plank; **p. à repasser/à dessin** ironing/drawing board; **p. (à roulettes)** skateboard; **p. (à voile)** sailboard; **faire de la p. (à voile)** to go windsurfing; **faire la p.** to float on one's back.

plancher [plɑ̃ʃe] *nm* floor.

plan/er [plane] *vi* (*oiseau*, *avion*) to glide; **p. sur** (*mystère*) *Fig* to hang over; **vol plané** glide, gliding. ● **—eur** (*avion*) glider.

planète [planɛt] *nf* planet. ● **planétaire** *a* planetary.

planifier [planifje] *vt Écon* to plan. ● **planification** *nf Écon* planning. ● **planning** *nm* (*emploi du temps*) schedule; **p. familial** family planning.

planque [plɑ̃k] *nf* **1** (*travail*) *Fam* cushy job. **2** (*lieu*) *Fam* hide-out.

plant [plɑ̃] *nm* (*de légumes etc*) bed.

plante [plɑ̃t] *nf* **1** *Bot* plant; **p. verte** house plant; **jardin des plantes** botanical gardens. **2 p. des pieds** sole (of the foot).

planter [plɑ̃te] *vt* (*fleur etc*) to plant; (*clou, couteau*) to drive in; (*tente, drapeau*) to put up; **p. là** qn to leave s.o. standing ¶ **se p.** *vpr* **1 se p. devant** to come ou go and stand in front of. **2** (*tomber*) *Fam* to fall over; (*échouer*) *Fam* to fail.

plantation [plɑ̃tasjɔ̃] *nf* (*terrain*) bed; (*de café, d'arbres etc*) plantation.

plaque [plak] *nf* plate; (*de verre, métal, verglas*) sheet; (*de chocolat*) bar; (*commémorative*) plaque; (*tache*) *Méd* blotch; **p. chauffante** *Culin* hotplate; **p. tournante** (*carrefour*) *Fig* centre, hub; **p. minéralogique, p. d'immatriculation** *Aut* number *ou* *Am* license plate; **p. dentaire** (*dental*) plaque.

plaqu/er [plake] *vt* *Rugby* to tackle; (*aplatir*) to flatten (**contre** against); (*abandonner*) *Fam* to give (*sth*) up; **p. qn** *Fam* to ditch s.o. ¶ **—é** *a* (*bijou*) plated; **p. or** gold-plated ¶ *nm* **p. or** gold plate.

plastic [plastik] *nm* plastic explosive. ● **plastiquer** *vt* to blow up.

plastique [plastik] *a* (*art, substance*) plastic; **matière p.** plastic ¶ *nm* (*matière*) plastic; **en p.** (*bouteille etc*) plastic.

plat [pla] **1** *a* flat; (*mer*) calm; (*fade*) flat, dull; **à p. ventre** flat on one's face; **à p.** (*pneu, batterie*) flat; (*épuisé*) *Fam* exhausted; **poser à p.** to put *ou* lay (down) flat; **assiette plate** dinner plate; **eau plate** still water; **calme p.** dead calm ¶ *nm* (*de la main*) flat. **2** *nm* (*récipient, nourriture*) dish; (*partie du repas*) course; **p. du jour'** (*au restaurant*) 'today's special'.

platane [platan] *nm* plane tree.

plateau, -x [plato] *nm* (*pour servir*) tray; (*plate-forme*) *Cin TV* set; *Th* stage; *Géog* plateau; **p. à fromages** cheeseboard.

plate-bande [platbɑ̃d] *nf* (*pl* plates-bandes) flower bed.

plate-forme [platfɔrm] *nf* (*pl* plates-formes) platform; **p.-forme pétrolière** oil rig.

platine [platin] **1** *nm* (*métal*) platinum. **2** *nf* (*d'électrophone, de magnétophone*) deck.

plâtre [plɑtr] *nm* (*matière*) plaster; **un p.** *Méd* a plaster cast; **dans le p.** *Méd* in plaster; **les plâtres** (*d'une maison etc*) the plasterwork. ● **plâtrer** *vt* (*membre*) to put in plaster.

plausible [plozibl] *a* plausible.

plein [plɛ̃] *a* (*rempli, complet*) full; (*paroi*) solid; **p. de** full of; **en pleine mer** out at sea; **en pleine figure** right in the face; **en p. jour** in broad daylight. ¶ *prép et adv* **des billes p. les poches** pockets full of marbles; **du chocolat p. la figure** chocolate all over one's face; **p. de lettres/d'argent**/*etc* *Fam* lots of letters/money/*etc*.

¶ *nm* **faire le p. (d'essence)** *Aut* to fill up (the tank); **battre son p.** (*fête*) to be in full swing.

pleurer [plœre] *vi* to cry (**sur** over) ¶ *vt* (*regretter*) to mourn (for). ● **pleureur** *a* **saule p.** weeping willow. ● **pleurnicher** *vi* to snivel. ● **pleurs (en)** *adv* in tears.

pleuvoir* [pløvwar] *v imp* to rain; **il pleut** it's raining ¶ *vi* (*coups etc*) to rain down (**sur** on).

Plexiglas® [pleksiglas] *nm* Perspex®, *Am* Lucite®.

pli [pli] *nm* **1** (*de papier etc*) fold; (*de jupe, robe*) pleat; (*de pantalon, de bouche*) crease; (*faux*) **p.** crease; **mise en plis** (*coiffure*) set. **2** (*enveloppe*) *Com* envelope, letter. **3** *Cartes* trick.

pliable [plijabl] *a* (*facile à plier*) pliable.

plier [plije] *vt* to fold; (*courber*) to bend ¶ *vi* (*branche*) to bend ¶ **se p.** *vpr* (*lit, chaise etc*) to fold (up); **se p. à** to submit to, give in to. ● **pliant** *a* (*chaise etc*) folding; (*parapluie*) telescopic.

pliss/er [plise] *vt* (*front*) to wrinkle, crease; (*yeux*) to screw up; (*froisser*) to crease. ● **—é** *a* (*tissu, jupe*) pleated.

plomb [plɔ̃] *nm* (*métal*) lead; (*fusible*) *Él* fuse; *pl* (*de chasse*) lead shot; **essence sans p.** unleaded petrol *ou* *Am* gasoline.

de p. (*sommeil*) *Fig* heavy; (*soleil*) blazing.

plomb/er [plɔ̃be] *vt* (*dent*) *vt* to fill. ●—**é** *a* (*teint*) leaden. ●—**age** *nm* (*de dent*) filling.

plombier [plɔ̃bje] *nm* plumber. ● **plomberie** *nf* (*métier, installations*) plumbing.

plong/er [plɔ̃ʒe] *vi* (*personne, avion etc*) to dive; (*route, regard*) *Fig* to plunge ▮ *vt* (*mettre, enfoncer*) to plunge (dans into); **se p. dans** (*lecture etc*) to immerse oneself in. ●—**ée** *nf Sp* diving; (*de sous-marin*) submersion. ● **plongeoir** *nm* diving board. ● **plongeon** *nm* dive. ● **plongeur, -euse** *nmf* diver; (*employé de restaurant*) dishwasher.

plouf [pluf] *nm* & *int* splash.

plu [ply] *pp de* **plaire, pleuvoir.**

pluie [plɥi] *nf* rain; **sous la p.** in the rain.

plume [plym] *nf* 1 (*d'oiseau*) feather. 2 (*pour écrire*) *Hist* quill (pen); (*de stylo*) (pen) nib; **stylo à p.** (fountain) pen. ● **plumage** *nm* plumage. ● **plumer** *vt* (*volaille*) to pluck; **p. qn** (*voler*) *Fig* to fleece s.o. ● **plumier** *nm* pencil box.

plupart (la) [laplypar] *nf* most; **la p. des cas/**etc most cases/etc; **la p. du temps** most of the time; **la p. d'entre eux** most of them; **pour la p.** mostly.

pluriel, -ielle [plyrjɛl] *a* & *nm Gram* plural; **au p.** (*nom*) in the plural, plural.

plus¹ [ply] ([plyz] *before vowel*, [plys] *in end position*) 1 *adv comparatif* (*travailler etc*) more (que than); **p. d'un kilo/de dix/**etc (*quantité, nombre*) more than a kilo/ten/etc; **p. de thé/**etc (*davantage*) more tea/etc; **p. beau/rapidement/**etc more beautiful/rapidly/etc (que than); **p. tard** later; **p. petit** smaller; **de p. en p.** more and more; **de p. en p. vite** quicker and quicker; **p. ou moins** more or less; **en p.** in addition (de to); **de p.** more (que than); (*en outre*) moreover; **les enfants (âgés) de p. de dix ans** children over ten; **j'ai dix ans de p. qu'elle** I'm ten years older than she is; **il est p. de cinq heures** it's after five (o'clock); **p. il crie p. il**

s'enroue the more he shouts the more hoarse he gets.

2 *adv superlatif* **le p.** (*travailler etc*) most; **le p. beau/**etc the most beautiful/etc (de tous of all); (*de deux*) the more beautiful/etc; **le p. grand/**etc the biggest/etc; (*de deux*) the bigger/etc; **j'ai le p. de livres** I have (the) most books; **j'en ai le p.** I have (the) most.

plus² [ply] *adv de négation* (ne)... **p.** no more; **il n'a p. de pain** he has no more bread, he doesn't have any more bread; **tu n'es p. jeune** you're not young any more, you're no longer young; **elle ne le fait p.** she no longer does it, she doesn't do it any more *ou* any longer; **je ne la reverrai p.** I won't see her again; **je ne voyagerai p. jamais** I'll never travel again *ou* any more.

plus³ [plys] *prép* plus; **deux p. deux font quatre** two plus two are four; **il fait p. deux (degrés)** it's two degrees above freezing ▮ *nm* **le signe p.** the plus sign.

plusieurs [plyzjœr] *a* & *pron* several.

plus-que-parfait [plyskəparfɛ] *nm Gram* pluperfect.

plus-value [plyvaly] *nf* (*bénéfice*) profit.

plutôt [plyto] *adv* rather (que than).

pluvieux, -euse [plyvjø, -øz] *a* rainy, wet.

PMU [peɛmy] *abrév* = **pari mutuel urbain.**

pneu [pnø] *nm* (*pl* -**s**) (*de roue*) tyre, *Am* tire. ● **pneumatique** *a* **matelas p.** air bed; **canot p.** rubber dinghy.

pneumonie [pnømɔni] *nf* pneumonia.

poche [pɔʃ] *nf* pocket; (*de kangourou etc*) pouch; (*sac en papier etc*) bag; *pl* (*sous les yeux*) bags; **j'ai un franc en p.** I have one franc on me. ● **pochette** *nf* (*sac*) bag, envelope; (*d'allumettes*) hook; (*de disque*) sleeve, (*sac à main*) (clutch) bag; (*mouchoir*) pocket handkerchief.

pocher [pɔʃe] *vt* (*œufs*) to poach. **2 p. l'œil à qn** to give s.o. a black eye.

podium [pɔdjɔm] *nm Sp* podium, rostrum.

poêle [pwal] **1** nm stove. **2** nf **p.** (à frire) frying pan.

poème [pɔɛm] nm poem. ●**poésie** nf (art) poetry; **une p.** (poème) a poem. ●**poète** nm poet. ●**poétique** a poetic.

poids [pwa] nm weight; **au p.** by weight; **p. lourd** (heavy) lorry ou Am truck; **lancer le p.** Sp to put the shot.

poignard [pwaɲar] nm dagger; **coup de p.** stab. ●**poignarder** vt to stab.

poigne [pwaɲ] nf (étreinte) grip.

poignée [pwaɲe] nf (quantité) handful (**de** of); (de porte, casserole etc) handle; **p. de main** handshake; **donner une p. de main à** to shake hands with.

poignet [pwaɲɛ] nm wrist; (de chemise) cuff.

poil [pwal] nm hair; (pelage) coat, fur; pl (de brosse) bristles; (de tapis) pile; **de bon/mauvais p.** Fam in a good/bad mood; **à p.** (nu) Fam (stark) naked; **au p.** (parfait) Fam top-rate. ●**poilu** a hairy.

poinçon [pwɛ̃sɔ̃] nm (outil) awl; (marque) hallmark. ●**poinçonner** vt (billet) to punch; (bijou) to hallmark.

poing [pwɛ̃] nm fist; **coup de p.** punch.

point [pwɛ̃] nm (lieu, score, question etc) point; (sur i, à l'horizon etc) dot; (tache) spot; (note) Scol mark; (de couture) stitch; **sur le p. de faire** about to do, on the point of doing; **p.** (final) full stop, Am period; **p. d'exclamation** exclamation mark ou Am point; **p. d'interrogation** question mark; **points de suspension** suspension points; **p. de vue** (opinion) point of view, viewpoint; (endroit) viewing point; **à p.** (steak) medium rare; **à p. (nommé)** (arriver etc) at the right moment; **au p. mort** Aut in neutral; **p. de côté** (douleur) stitch (in one's side); **mal en p.** in bad shape; **mettre au p.** Phot to focus; Aut to tune; (technique etc) to elaborate; (éclaircir) Fig to clarify; **faire le p.** Fig to take stock, sum up. ●**point-virgule** nm (pl **points-virgules**) semicolon.

pointe [pwɛ̃t] nf (extrémité) tip, point; (clou) nail; (maximum) Fig peak; **sur la p. des pieds** on tiptoe; **en p.** pointed; **de p.** (technologie, industrie etc) state-of-the-art; **à la p. de** (progrès etc) Fig in the forefront of.

pointer [pwɛ̃te] **1** vt (cocher) to tick (off), Am check (off). **2** vt (braquer) to point (**sur**, **vers** at). **3** vi (employé) to clock in; (à la sortie) to clock out ▮ **se p.** vpr (arriver) Fam to show up.

pointillé [pwɛ̃tije] nm dotted line.

pointilleux, -euse [pwɛ̃tijø, -øz] a fussy.

pointu [pwɛ̃ty] a (en pointe) pointed.

pointure [pwɛ̃tyr] nf (de chaussure, gant) size.

poire [pwar] nf (fruit) pear. ●**poirier** nm pear tree.

poireau, -x [pwaro] nm leek.

pois [pwa] nm (légume) pea; (dessin) (polka) dot; **petits p.** (garden) peas, Am peas; **p. chiche** chickpea; **à p.** (vêtement) spotted.

poison [pwazɔ̃] nm poison.

poisseux, -euse [pwasø, -øz] a sticky.

poisson [pwasɔ̃] nm fish; **p. rouge** goldfish; **les Poissons** (signe) Pisces. ●**poissonnerie** nf fish shop. ●**poissonnier, -ière** nmf fishmonger.

poitrine [pwatrin] nf Anat chest; (de femme) bust; (de veau, mouton) Culin breast.

poivre [pwavr] nm pepper. ●**poivrer** vt to pepper. ●**poivré** a Culin (piquant) peppery. ●**poivrier** nm (ustensile) pepperpot.

poivron [pwavrɔ̃] nm (légume) pepper.

polar [pɔlar] nm (roman) Fam whodunit.

pôle [pol] nm Géog pole; **p. Nord/Sud** North/South Pole. ●**polaire** a polar.

polémique [pɔlemik] a controversial ▮ nf controversy.

poli [pɔli] **1** a (courtois) polite (**avec** to, with). **2** a (lisse) polished. ●**—ment** adv politely.

police [pɔlis] nf **1** police; **p. secours** emergency services; **faire** ou **assurer la p.** to maintain order (**dans** in). **2** p.

(d'assurance) (insurance) policy. ● **policier** a **enquête**/etc **policière** police inquiry/etc; **chien p.** police dog; **roman p.** detective novel ▮ nm policeman, detective.

polio [pɔljo] nf (maladie) polio.

polir [pɔlir] vt to polish.

polisson, -onne [pɔlisɔ̃, -ɔn] a naughty.

politesse [pɔlites] nf politeness.

politique [pɔlitik] a political; **homme p.** politician ▮ nf (activité, science) politics; (mesures, manières de gouverner) Pol policies; **une p.** (tactique) a policy.

pollen [pɔlɛn] nm pollen.

polluer [pɔlɥe] vt to pollute. ● **polluant** nm pollutant. ● **pollution** nf pollution.

polo [pɔlo] nm 1 (chemise) sweat shirt. 2 Sp polo.

polochon [pɔlɔʃɔ̃] nm Fam bolster.

Pologne [pɔlɔɲ] nf Poland. ● **polonais, -aise** a Polish ▮ nmf Pole ▮ nm (langue) Polish.

poltron, -onne [pɔltrɔ̃, -ɔn] a cowardly.

polycopié [pɔlikɔpje] nm Univ duplicated course notes.

polyester [pɔliɛstɛr] nm polyester; **chemise**/etc **en p.** polyester shirt/etc.

polyvalent [pɔlivalɑ̃] 1 a (rôle) multipurpose; (personne) all-round. 2 a & nf (école) **polyvalente** Can = secondary school, Am = high school.

pommade [pɔmad] nf ointment.

pomme [pɔm] nf 1 apple; **p. d'Adam** Anat Adam's apple. 2 **p. de terre** potato; **pommes frites** Am French fries; **pommes chips** potato crisps ou Am chips; **pommes vapeur** steamed potatoes. ● **pommier** nm apple tree.

pommette [pɔmɛt] nf cheekbone.

pompe [pɔ̃p] 1 nf pump; **p. à essence** petrol ou Am gas station; **p. à incendie** fire engine; **coup de p.** Fam tired feeling. 2 nf (chaussure) Fam shoe. 3 nf (en gymnastique) press-up, Am push-up. 4 nfpl **pompes funèbres** undertaker's; **entrepreneur de pompes funèbres** undertaker. ● **pomper** vt (eau) to pump out

(de of); (absorber) to soak up ▮ vi to pump.

pompeux, -euse [pɔ̃pø, -øz] a pompous.

pompier [pɔ̃pje] nm fireman; **voiture des pompiers** fire engine. ● **pompiste** nmf Aut petrol ou Am gas station attendant.

pomponner [pɔ̃pɔne] vt to doll up.

ponce [pɔ̃s] nf (**pierre**) **p.** pumice (stone). ● **poncer** vt to rub down, sand.

ponctuation [pɔ̃ktɥasjɔ̃] nf punctuation. ● **ponctuer** vt to punctuate (**de** with).

ponctuel, -elle [pɔ̃ktɥɛl] a (à l'heure) punctual; (unique) Fig one-off, Am one-of-a-kind.

pondéré [pɔ̃dere] a level-headed.

pondre [pɔ̃dr] vt (œuf) to lay ▮ vi (poule) to lay (eggs ou an egg).

poney [pɔne] nm pony.

pont [pɔ̃] nm bridge; (de bateau) deck; **faire le p.** Fig to take the intervening day(s) off (between two holidays); **p. aérien** airlift. ● **p.-levis** nm (pl **ponts-levis**) drawbridge.

pontife [pɔ̃tif] nm (**souverain**) **p.** pope.

pop [pɔp] nm & a inv Mus pop.

populaire [pɔpylɛr] a (qui plaît) popular; (quartier, milieu) working-class; (expression) colloquial. ● **popularité** nf popularity (**auprès de** with).

population [pɔpylasjɔ̃] nf population.

porc [pɔr] nm pig; (viande) pork.

porcelaine [pɔrsəlɛn] nf china, porcelain.

porc-épic [pɔrkepik] nm (pl **porcs-épics**) (animal) porcupine.

porche [pɔrʃ] nm porch.

porcherie [pɔrʃəri] nf (pig)sty.

pore [pɔr] nm pore.

pornographie [pɔrnɔgrafi] nf pornography. ● **pornographique** a pornographic.

port [pɔr] nm 1 port, harbour; **arriver à bon p.** to arrive safely. 2 (d'armes) carrying; (de barbe) wearing; (prix) carriage, postage.

portable [pɔrtabl] a (portatif) portable.

portail [pɔrtaj] nm (de jardin) gate.

portant [pɔrtɑ̃] a **bien p.** in good health.

portatif, -ive [pɔrtatif, -iv] *a* portable.

porte [pɔrt] *nf* door; (*de jardin*) gate; (*de ville*) entrance, *Hist* gate; (*d'embarquement*) *Av* (departure) gate; **p. d'entrée** front door; **p. coulissante** sliding door; **mettre à la p.** to throw out; (*renvoyer*) to fire, sack. ● **porte-fenêtre** *nf* (*pl* **portes-fenêtres**) French window, *Am* French door.

porte-avions [pɔrtavjɔ̃] *nm inv* aircraft carrier. ● **p.-bagages** *nm inv* luggage rack. ● **p.-bonheur** *nm inv* (*fétiche*) (lucky) charm. ● **p.-cartes** *nm inv* card holder. ● **p.-clefs** *nm inv* key ring. ● **p.-documents** *nm inv* briefcase. ● **p.-monnaie** *nm inv* purse. ● **p.-plume** *nm inv* pen (*for dipping in ink*). ● **p.-savon** *nm* soapdish. ● **p.-serviettes** *nm inv* towel rail *ou Am* rack. ● **p.-voix** *nm inv* loudspeaker, megaphone.

portée [pɔrte] *nf* **1** (*de fusil etc*) range; **à la p. de qn** within reach of s.o.; (*richesse, plaisir etc*) *Fig* within s.o.'s grasp; **à p. de la main** within (easy) reach; **à p. de voix** within earshot; **hors de p.** out of reach. **2** (*animaux*) litter. **3** (*importance, effet*) significance. **4** *Mus* stave.

portefeuille [pɔrtəfœj] *nm* wallet; *Pol Com* portfolio.

portemanteau, -x [pɔrtmɑ̃to] *nm* (*sur pied*) hatstand, hallstand; (*crochet*) coat *ou* hat peg.

porte-parole [pɔrtparɔl] *nm inv* (*homme*) spokesman; (*femme*) spokeswoman (**de** for).

porter [pɔrte] *vt* to carry; (*vêtement, lunettes, barbe etc*) to wear; (*trace, responsabilité, fruits etc*) to bear; (*regard*) to cast; (*attaque*) to make (**contre** against); (*inscrire*) to enter; **p. qch à** (*apporter*) to take *ou* bring sth to; **p. bonheur/malheur** to bring good/bad luck.

▮ *vi* (*voix*) to carry; (*canon*) to fire; (*vue*) to extend; (*coup*) to hit the mark; (*reproche*) to hit home; **p. sur** (*reposer sur*) to rest on; (*concerner*) to bear on;

(*accent*) to fall on.

▮ **se porter** *vpr* (*vêtement*) to be worn; **se bien/mal** to be well/ill; **comment te portes-tu?** how are you?; **se p. candidat** to stand as a candidate. ● **porteur, -euse** *nm Rail* porter ▮ *nmf Méd* carrier; (*de nouvelles, chèque*) bearer; **mère porteuse** surrogate mother.

portier [pɔrtje] *nm* doorkeeper. ● **portière** *nf* (*de véhicule, train*) door. ● **portillon** *nm* gate.

portion [pɔrsjɔ̃] *nf* (*partie*) portion; (*de nourriture*) helping, portion.

portique [pɔrtik] *nm* **1** *Archit* portico. **2** (*de balançoire etc*) crossbar.

porto [pɔrto] *nm* (*vin*) port.

portrait [pɔrtrɛ] *nm* portrait; **être le p. de** (*son père etc*) to be the image of; **faire un p.** to paint *ou* draw a portrait (**de** of). ● **p.-robot** *nm* (*pl* **portraits-robots**) identikit (picture), photofit.

portuaire [pɔrtɥer] *a* **installations portuaires** port facilities.

Portugal [pɔrtygal] *nm* Portugal. ● **portugais, -aise** *a* Portuguese ▮ *nmf* Portuguese man *ou* woman, Portuguese *inv*; **les P.** the Portuguese ▮ *nm* (*langue*) Portuguese.

pose [poz] *nf* **1** (*installation*) putting up; putting in; laying. **2** (*attitude*) pose; (*temps*) *Phot* exposure.

poser [poze] *vt* to put (down); (*papier peint, rideaux*) to put up; (*sonnette, chauffage*) to put in; (*moquette, fondations*) to lay; (*question*) to ask (**à qn** s.o.); (*conditions*) to lay down; **p. sa candidature** to apply (**à** for).

▮ *vi* (*modèle etc*) to pose (**pour** for).

▮ **se poser** *vpr* (*oiseau, avion*) to land; (*problème, question*) to arise; **se p. sur** (*yeux*) to fix on.

positif, -ive [pozitif, -iv] *a* positive.

position [pozisjɔ̃] *nf* (*emplacement, opinion etc*) position; **prendre p.** *Fig* to take a stand (**contre** against).

posologie [pozɔlɔʒi] *nf* (*de médicament*) dosage, directions.

posséder [pɔsede] *vt* to possess; (*mai-*

son, bien etc) to own, possess; (*bien connaître*) to master. ● **possessif, -ive** *a* (*personne, adjectif etc*) possessive ∎*nm Gram* possessive. ● **possession** *nf* possession; **en p. de** in possession of.

possible [pɔsibl] *a* possible (**à faire** to do); **il (nous) est p. de le faire** it is possible (for us) to do it; **il est p. que** (+ *sub*) it is possible that; **si p.** if possible; **le plus tôt/etc p.** as soon/etc as possible; **autant que p.** as far as possible; **le plus p.** as much *ou* as many as possible ∎*nm* **faire son p.** to do one's utmost (**pour faire** to do); **dans la mesure du p.** as far as possible. ● **possibilité** *nf* possibility.

post- [pɔst] *préf* post-.

postal, -aux [pɔstal, -o] *a* postal; **boîte postale** PO Box; **code p.** postcode, *Am* zip code.

postdater [pɔstdate] *vt* to postdate.

poste [pɔst] **1** *nf* (*service*) post, mail; **(bureau de) p.** post office; **Postes (et Télécommunications)** (*administration*) Post Office; **par la p.** by post, by mail; **p. aérienne** airmail; **mettre à la p.** to post, mail.
2 *nm* (*lieu, emploi*) post; **p. de secours** first aid post; **p. de police** police station; **p. d'essence** petrol *ou Am* gas station; **p. d'incendie** fire point (*containing fire-fighting equipment*).
3 *nm* (*appareil*) *Rad TV* set; *Tél* extension (number). ● **poster 1** *vt* (*lettre*) to post, mail. **2** *vt* **p. qn** (*placer*) *Mil* to post s.o. **3** [pɔstɛr] *nm* poster.

postérieur [pɔsterjœr] *a* (*document etc*) later; **p. à** after. ● **postérieurement** *adv* subsequently. ● **postérité** *nf* posterity.

postier, -ière [pɔstje, -jɛr] *nmf* postal worker.

postillonner [pɔstijɔne] *vi* to sputter.

postuler [pɔstyle] *vi* **p. (à un emploi)** to apply for a job.

posture [pɔstyr] *nf* posture.

pot [po] *nm* **1** (*récipient*) jar; (*à confiture*) jar; (*à lait*) jug; (*à bière*) mug; (*de crème, yaourt*) carton; (*de bébé*) potty; **p. de fleurs** flower pot; **prendre un p.** (*verre*) *Fam* to have a drink. **2** (*chance*) *Fam*

luck; **avoir du p.** to be lucky.

potable [pɔtabl] *a* drinkable; **'eau p.'** 'drinking water'.

potage [pɔtaʒ] *nm* soup.

potager [pɔtaʒe] *am & nm* (**jardin**) **p.** vegetable garden.

potasser [pɔtase] *vt* (*examen*) *Fam* to cram for.

pot-au-feu [pɔtofø] *nm inv* beef stew.

pot-de-vin [pɔdvɛ̃] *nm* (*pl* **pots-de-vin**) bribe.

poteau, -x [pɔto] *nm* post; **p. indicateur** signpost; **p. d'arrivée** *Sp* winning post; **p. télégraphique** telegraph pole.

potelé [pɔtle] *a* plump, chubby.

potence [pɔtɑ̃s] *nf* (*gibet*) gallows.

potentiel, -ielle [pɔtɑ̃sjɛl] *a & nm* potential.

poterie [pɔtri] *nf* (*art*) pottery; **une p.** a piece of pottery; **des poteries** (*objets*) pottery. ● **potier** *nm* potter.

potins [pɔtɛ̃] *nmpl* (*cancans*) gossip.

potion [pɔsjɔ̃] *nf* potion.

potiron [pɔtirɔ̃] *nm* pumpkin.

pou, -x [pu] *nm* louse; **poux** lice.

poubelle [pubɛl] *nf* dustbin, *Am* garbage can.

pouce [pus] *nm* **1** thumb; **un coup de p.** *Fam* a helping hand. **2** (*mesure*) *Hist & Fig* inch.

poudre [pudr] *nf* powder; **p. (à canon)** (*explosif*) gunpowder; **en p.** (*lait*) powdered; (*chocolat*) drinking; **sucre en p.** castor *ou* caster sugar. ● **se poudrer** *vpr* (*femme*) to powder one's face. ● **poudreux, -euse** *a* powdery ∎*nf* (*neige*) powder snow. ● **poudrier** *nm* (*powder*) compact.

pouf [puf] *nm* (*siège*) pouf(fe).

pouffer [pufe] *vi* **p. (de rire)** to burst out laughing.

poulain [pulɛ̃] *nm* (*cheval*) foal.

poule [pul] *nf* **1** hen; *Culin* fowl; **être une p. mouillée** (*lâche*) to be chicken. ● **poulailler** *nm* **1** henhouse. **2 le p.** *Th Fam* the gods, the gallery. ● **poulet** *nm* (*poule, coq*) chicken.

pouliche [puliʃ] *nf* (*jument*) filly.

poulie [puli] *nf* pulley.

poulpe [pulp] *nm* octopus.

pouls [pu] *nm* Méd pulse.

poumon [pumɔ̃] *nm* lung; **à pleins poumons** (*respirer*) deeply; (*crier*) loudly.

poupe [pup] *nf* Nau stern.

poupée [pupe] *nf* doll.

poupon [pupɔ̃] *nm* (*bébé*) baby; (*poupée*) doll.

pour [pur] **1** *prép* for; **p. toi**/*etc* for you/ *etc*; **partir p.** (*Paris, cinq ans etc*) to leave for; **elle est p.** she's in favour; **p. faire qch** (in order) to do sth, so as to do sth; **p. que tu saches** so (that) you may know; **p. quoi faire?** what for?; **trop petit**/*etc* **p. faire qch** too small/*etc* to do sth; **assez grand**/*etc* **p. faire qch** big/*etc* enough to do sth; **p. cela** for that reason; **p. ma part** (*quant à moi*) as for me; **jour p. jour** to the day; **dix p. cent** ten per cent; **acheter p. cinq francs de bonbons** to buy five francs' worth of sweets *ou* Am candies.

2 *nm* **le p. et le contre** the pros and cons.

pourboire [purbwar] *nm* tip (*money*).

pourcentage [pursɑ̃taʒ] *nm* percentage.

pourparlers [purparle] *nmpl* negotiations, talks.

pourpre [purpr] *a & nm* purple.

pourquoi [purkwa] *adv & conj* why; **p. pas?** why not? ‖ *nm inv* reason (**de** for); **le p. et le comment** the whys and wherefores.

pourra, pourrait *etc* [pura, purɛ] *voir* **pouvoir 1**.

pourrir [purir] *vi* to rot ‖ *vt* to rot; **p. qn** to corrupt s.o. ●**pourri** *a* (*fruit, temps, personne etc*) rotten.

poursuite [pursɥit] **1** *nf* chase; (*du bonheur, de créancier*) pursuit (**de** of); **se mettre à la p. de** to go after, chase (after). **2** *nfpl* Jur legal proceedings (**contre** against).

poursuivre* [pursɥivr] **1** *vt* to chase, go after; (*harceler*) to hound, pursue; (*but, idéal etc*) to pursue. **2** *vt* **p. qn** (*en justice*) (*au criminel*) to prosecute s.o.; (*au civil*) to sue s.o. **3** *vt* (*lecture, voyage* *etc*) to carry on (with), continue (with), pursue ‖ *vi*, **se p.** *vpr* to continue, go on. ●**poursuivant, -ante** *nmf* pursuer.

pourtant [purtɑ̃] *adv* yet, nevertheless.

pourvoir* [purvwar] *vi* **p. à** (*besoins etc*) to provide for.

pourvu que [purvyk(ə)] *conj* (*condition*) provided *ou* providing (that); (*souhait*) **p. qu'elle soit là!** I only hope (that) she's there!

pousse [pus] *nf* **1** (*bourgeon*) shoot. **2** (*croissance*) growth.

pousser [puse] **1** *vt* to push; (*cri*) to utter; (*soupir*) to heave; **p. qn à faire qch** to urge s.o. to do sth; **p. qn à bout** to push s.o. to his *ou* her limits ‖ *vi* to push ‖ **se p.** *vpr* (*se déplacer*) to move up or over.

2 *vi* (*croître*) to grow; **faire p.** (*plante, barbe etc*) to grow. ●**poussé** *a* (*travail, études*) advanced. ●**poussée** *nf* (*pression*) pressure; (*de fièvre etc*) outbreak.

poussette [puset] *nf* pushchair, Am stroller.

poussière [pusjer] *nf* dust; **dix francs et des poussières** Fam a bit over ten francs. ●**poussiéreux, -euse** *a* dusty.

poussin [pusɛ̃] *nm* (*poulet*) chick.

poutre [putr] *nf* (*en bois*) beam; (*en acier*) girder. ●**poutrelle** *nf* girder.

pouvoir* [puvwar] **1** *v aux* (*capacité*) can, be able to; (*permission, éventualité*) may, can; **je peux deviner** I can guess, I'm able to guess; **tu peux entrer** you may *ou* can come in; **il peut sortir** he may *ou* might be out; **elle pourrait/ pouvait venir** she might/could come; **j'ai pu l'obtenir** I managed to get it; **j'aurais pu l'obtenir** I could have got it *ou* Am gotten it; **je n'en peux plus** I'm utterly exhausted ‖ *v imp* **il peut neiger** it may snow ‖ **se pouvoir** *vpr* **il se peut qu'elle parte** (it's possible that) she might leave.

2 *nm* (*capacité, autorité*) power; **les pouvoirs publics** the authorities; **au p.** Pol in power; **en son p.** in one's power (**de faire** to do); **p. d'achat** purchasing power.

poux [pu] *voir* **pou.**

pragmatique [pragmatik] *a* pragmatic.

prairie [preri] *nf* meadow.

praline [pralin] *nf* sugared almond. ● **praliné** (*glace*) praline-flavoured.

praticable [pratikabl] *a* (*chemin, projet*) practicable.

pratique [pratik] **1** *a* (*connaissance, personne, outil etc*) practical. **2** *nf* (*exercice, procédé*) practice; (*expérience*) practical experience; **la p. de la natation/ du golf**/*etc* swimming/golfing/*etc*; **mettre en p.** to put into practice; **en p.** (*en réalité*) in practice.

pratiquement [pratikmɑ̃] *adv* (*presque*) practically; (*en réalité*) in practice.

pratiqu/er [pratike] *vt* (*sport, art etc*) to practise, *Am* practice; (*trou, route*) to make; (*opération*) to carry out; **p. la natation** to go swimming. ● **—ant, -ante** *a Rel* practising ∥ *nmf* churchgoer.

pré [pre] *nm* meadow.

pré- [pre] *préf* pre-.

préalable [prealabl] *a* prior, preliminary; **p. à** prior to ∥ *nm* precondition; **au p.** beforehand.

préau, -x [preo] *nm Scol* covered playground *ou Am* school yard.

préavis [preavi] *nm* (advance) notice (**de** of).

précaire [preker] *a* precarious.

précaution [prekosjɔ̃] *nf* (*mesure*) precaution; (*prudence*) caution; **par p.** as a precaution; **prendre la p. de faire** to take the precaution of doing.

précédent, -ente [presedɑ̃, -ɑ̃t] **1** *a* previous, preceding ∥ *nmf* previous one. **2** *nm* **un p.** (*exemple*) a precedent; **sans p.** unprecedented. ● **précéder** *vti* to precede; **faire p. qch de qch** to precede sth by sth.

prêcher [preʃe] *vti* to preach.

précieux, -euse [presjø, -øz] *a* precious.

précipice [presipis] *nm* chasm, precipice.

précipiter [presipite] *vt* (*hâter*) to hasten, rush; (*jeter*) to throw, hurl; (*plonger*) to plunge (**dans** into) ∥ **se p.** *vpr* (*se jeter*)

to throw *ou* hurl oneself; (*foncer*) to rush (**à, sur** on to); (*s'accélérer*) to speed up. ● **précipitamment** [-amɑ̃] *adv* hastily. ● **précipitation 1** *nf* haste. **2** *nfpl* (*pluie*) precipitation.

précis [presi] *a* precise; (*idée, mécanisme*) accurate, precise; **à deux heures précises** at two o'clock sharp. ● **préciser** *vt* to specify (**que** that) ∥ **se p.** *vpr* to become clear(er). ● **précision** *nf* precision; accuracy; (*détail*) detail; (*explication*) explanation.

précoce [prekɔs] *a* (*fruit etc*) early; (*enfant*) precocious.

préconiser [prekɔnize] *vt* to advocate (**que** that).

précurseur [prekyrsœr] *nm* forerunner.

prédécesseur [predesesœr] *nm* predecessor.

prédilection [predilɛksjɔ̃] *nf* (special) liking; **de p.** favourite.

prédire* [predir] *vt* to predict (**que** that). ● **prédiction** *nf* prediction.

prédisposer [predispoze] *vt* to predispose (**à qch** to sth, **à faire** to do).

prédomin/er [predomine] *vi* to predominate. ● **—ant** *a* predominant.

préfabriqué [prefabrike] *a* prefabricated.

préface [prefas] *nf* preface.

préférable [preferabl] *a* preferable (**à** to).

préférence [preferɑ̃s] *nf* preference (**pour** for); **de p.** preferably; **de p. à** in preference to. ● **préférentiel, -ielle** *a* preferential.

préfér/er [prefere] *vt* to prefer (**à** to); **p. faire** to prefer to do; **je préférerais rester** I would rather stay, I would prefer to stay. ● **—é, -ée** *a* & *nmf* favourite.

préfet [prefɛ] *nm* prefect (*chief administrator in a department*); **p. de police** prefect of police (*Paris chief of police*). ● **préfecture** *nf* prefecture; **p. de police** Paris police headquarters.

préfixe [prefiks] *nm* prefix.

préhistoire [preistwar] *nf* prehistory.

●**préhistorique** a prehistoric.
préjudice [preʒydis] nm Jur prejudice, harm; **porter p. à** to prejudice, harm.
préjugé [preʒyʒe] nm prejudice; **avoir des préjugés** to be prejudiced (**contre** against); **être plein de préjugés** to be full of prejudice.
prélasser (se) [səprelase] vpr to lounge (about).
prélever [prel(ə)ve] vt (échantillon) to take (**sur** from); (somme) to deduct (**sur** from). ●**prélèvement** nm taking; deduction; **p. automatique** Fin standing order, Am automatic deduction.
préliminaire [preliminɛr] a preliminary ‖ nmpl preliminaries.
prélude [prelyd] nm prelude (à to).
prématuré [prematyre] a premature ‖ nm (bébé) premature baby.
préméditer [premedite] vt to premeditate.
premier, -ière [prəmje, -jɛr] a first; (enfance) early; (page de journal) front, first; (qualité, nécessité, importance) prime; **nombre p.** Math prime number; **le p. rang** the front ou first row; **à la première occasion** at the earliest opportunity; **P. ministre** Prime Minister.
‖ nmf first (one); **arriver le p, ou en p.** to arrive first; **être le p. de la classe** to be (at the) top of the class.
‖ nm (date) first; (étage) first ou Am second floor; **le p. de l'an** New Year's Day.
‖ nf première (wagon, billet) first class; Scol = sixth form, Am = twelfth grade; Aut first (gear); Th première. ●**premier-né** nm, **première-née** nf firstborn (child). ●**premièrement** adv firstly.
prémonition [premɔnisjɔ̃] nf premonition.
prénatal, mpl -als [prenatal] a antenatal, Am prenatal.
prendre* [prɑ̃dr] vt to take (**à qn** from s.o.); (attraper) to catch, get; (voyager par) to take, travel by (train etc); (douche, bain) to take, have; (repas)

to have; (photo) to take; (temps) to take (up); (ton, air) to put on; **p. qn pour** (un autre) to mistake s.o. for; (considérer) to take s.o. for; **p. feu** to catch fire; **p. de la place** to take up room; **p. du poids/de la vitesse** to put on weight/speed; **passer p. qn** to come and get s.o.; **à tout p.** on the whole; **qu'est-ce qui te prend?** what's got ou Am gotten into you?
‖ vi (feu) to catch; (ciment, gelée) to set; (greffe, vaccin) to take; (mode) to catch on.
‖ **se prendre** vpr (médicament) to be taken; (s'accrocher) to get caught; **se p. pour un génie/etc** to think one is a genius/etc; **s'y p. pour faire qch** to go ou set about doing sth; **s'en p. à** (critiquer, attaquer) to attack; (accuser) to blame.
prénom [prenɔ̃] nm first name.
préoccup/er [preɔkype] vt (inquiéter) to worry; (absorber) to preoccupy; **se p. de** to be worried about; to be preoccupied about. ●**—é** a worried. ●**préoccupation** nf worry.
préparer [prepare] vt to prepare (**qch pour** sth for); (repas etc) to get ready, prepare; (examen) to prepare (for), study for; **p. qch à qn** to prepare sth for s.o.; **p. qn à** (examen) to prepare ou coach s.o. for.
‖ **se préparer** vpr to get (oneself) ready (**à** ou **pour qch** for sth); **se p. à faire** to prepare to do. ●**préparatifs** nmpl preparations (**de** for). ●**préparation** nf preparation. ●**préparatoire** a preparatory.
préposé, -ée [prepoze] nmf employee; (facteur) postman, postwoman.
préposition [prepozisjɔ̃] nf Gram preposition.
préretraite [prerətrɛt] nf early retirement.
prérogative [prerɔgativ] nf prerogative.
près [prɛ] adv **p. de** (qn, qch) near (to), close to; **p. de deux ans/etc** (presque) nearly two years/etc; **p. de partir/etc**

about to leave/etc; **tout p.** nearby (**de qn/qch** s.o./sth), close by (**de qn/qch** s.o./sth); **de p.** (lire, suivre) closely; **à peu de chose p.** almost; **calculer au franc p.** to calculate to the nearest franc.

présage [prezaʒ] nm omen.

presbyte [prɛsbit] a & nmf long-sighted (person).

prescrire* [prɛskrir] vt (médicament) to prescribe. ● **prescription** nf (instruction) & Jur prescription.

présence [prezɑ̃s] nf presence; (à l'école etc) attendance (à at); **feuille de p.** attendance sheet; **en p. de** in the presence of.

présent¹ [prezɑ̃] **1** a (non absent) present (à at, dans in); **les personnes présentes** those present. **2** a (actuel) present ∎ nm (temps) present; Gram present (tense); **à p.** at present, now; **dès à p.** as from now.

présent² [prezɑ̃] nm (cadeau) present.

présenter [prezɑ̃te] vt (offrir, montrer, animer etc) to present; **p. qn à qn** to introduce ou present s.o. to s.o.

∎ **se présenter** vpr to introduce ou present oneself (à to); (chez qn) to show up; (occasion etc) to arise; **se p. à** (examen) to take; (élections) to run in; **ça se présente bien** it looks promising. ● **présentable** a presentable. ● **présentateur, -trice** nmf TV announcer, presenter. ● **présentation** nf presentation; introduction.

préserver [prezɛrve] vt to protect, preserve (**de, contre** from). ● **préservatif** nm condom, sheath.

présidence [prezidɑ̃s] nf (de nation) presidency; (de firme etc) chairmanship. ● **président, -ente** nmf (de nation) president; (de réunion, firme) chairman, chairwoman; **p. directeur général** (chairman and) managing director, Am chief executive officer. ● **présidentiel, -ielle** a presidential.

présider [prezide] vt (réunion) to chair, preside over ∎ vi to preside.

présomption [prezɔ̃psjɔ̃] nf (supposition, suffisance) presumption.

presque [prɛsk(ə)] adv almost, nearly; **p. jamais/rien** hardly ou scarcely ever/anything.

presqu'île [prɛskil] nf peninsula.

presse [prɛs] nf (journaux, appareil) press; Typ (printing) press; **conférence/agence de p.** press conference/agency.

presse-citron [prɛssitrɔ̃] nm lemon squeezer. ● **p.-papiers** nm inv paperweight.

pressentir* [presɑ̃tir] vt (deviner) to sense (**que** that). ● **pressentiment** nm foreboding.

presser [prese] vt (serrer) to squeeze, press; (bouton) to press; (fruit) to squeeze; **p. le pas** to speed up.

∎ vi (temps) to press; (affaire) to be urgent; **rien ne presse** there's no hurry.

∎ **se presser** vpr (se serrer) to squeeze (together); (se hâter) to hurry (**de faire** to do); (se grouper) to crowd, swarm. ● **pressant** a urgent. ● **pressé** a (personne) in a hurry; (travail) urgent; (air) hurried.

pressing [presiŋ] nm (magasin) dry cleaner's.

pression [presjɔ̃] nf **1** pressure; **faire p. sur qn** to put pressure on s.o., pressurize s.o. **2** (bouton) snap (fastener), press-stud.

pressuriser [presyrize] vt Av to pressurize.

prestation [prɛstasjɔ̃] nf **1** (allocation) allowance, benefit. **2** (performance) performance.

prestidigitateur, -trice [prɛstidiʒitatœr, -tris] nmf conjurer. ● **prestidigitation** nf **tour de p.** conjuring trick.

prestige [prɛstiʒ] nm prestige.

présumer [prezyme] vt to presume (**que** that).

prêt¹ [prɛ] a (préparé) ready (**à faire** to do, **à qch** for sth). ● **p.-à-porter** [prɛtaporte] nm (pl **prêts-à-porter**) ready-to-wear clothes.

prêt² [prɛ] *nm* (*emprunt*) loan.

prétend/re [pretɑ̃dr] *vt* to claim (**que** that); (*vouloir*) to intend (**faire** to do); **p. être/savoir** to claim to be/to know; **elle se prétend riche** she claims to be rich ‖ *vi* **p. à** (*titre etc*) to lay claim to. ●—**ant** *nm* (*amoureux*) suitor. ●—**u** *a* so-called.

prétentieux, -euse [pretɑ̃sjø, -øz] *a* & *nmf* conceited (person). ● **prétention** *nf* (*vanité*) pretension; (*revendication, ambition*) claim.

prêter [prete] *vt* (*argent, objet*) to lend (**à** to); (*attribuer*) to attribute (**à** to); **p. attention** to pay attention (**à** to); **p. serment** to take an oath; **se p. à** (*consentir à*) to agree to; (*sujet etc*) to lend itself to.

prétérit [preterit] *nm* *Gram* preterite (tense).

prétexte [pretekst] *nm* excuse, pretext; **sous p. de/que** on the pretext of/that.

prêtre [prɛtr] *nm* priest; **grand p.** high priest.

preuve [prœv] *nf* **preuve(s)** proof, evidence; **faire p. de** to show; **faire ses preuves** (*personne*) to prove oneself; (*méthode*) to prove itself.

prévon/ir [prevɔnir] *vt* 1 (*avertir*) to warn (**que** that); (*aviser*) to inform, tell (**que** that). 2 (*désir, question*) to anticipate; (*malheur*) to avert. ●—**u, -ue** *nmf* *Jur* defendant, accused. ● **prévention** *nf* prevention; **p. routière** road safety.

prévision [previzjɔ̃] *nf* (*opinion*) & *Mét* forecast; **en p. de** in expectation of.

prévoir [prevwar] *vt* (*anticiper*) to foresee (**que** that); (*prédire*) to forecast (**que** that); (*temps*) *Mét* to forecast; (*organiser*) to plan (for); (*préparer*) to provide, make provision for; **un repas est prévu** a meal is provided; **au moment prévu** at the appointed time; **comme prévu** as expected, as planned; **prévu pour** (*véhicule, appareil etc*) designed for.

prévoyant [prevwajɑ̃] *a* **être p.** to have foresight.

prier [prije] 1 *vi* *Rel* to pray (**pour** for) ‖ *vt* **p. Dieu pour qu'il nous accorde qch** to pray (to God) for sth. 2 *vt* **p. qn de faire** to ask *ou* request s.o. to do; (*implorer*) to beg s.o. to do; **je vous en prie** (*faites donc, allez-y*) please; (*en réponse à 'merci'*) don't mention it; **se faire p.** to wait to be asked.

prière [prijer] *nf* prayer; **p. de répondre/** *etc* please answer/*etc*.

primaire [primer] *a* primary.

prime [prim] 1 *nf* (*d'employé*) bonus; (*d'État*) subsidy; **en p.** (*cadeau*) as a free gift; **p. (d'assurance)** (insurance) premium. 2 *a* **de p. abord** at the very first glance.

primeurs [primœr] *nfpl* early fruit and vegetables.

primevère [primver] *nf* primrose.

primitif, -ive [primitif, -iv] *a* (*société, art etc*) primitive; (*état, sens*) original.

primordial, -aux [primɔrdjal, -o] *a* vital.

prince [prɛ̃s] *nm* prince. ● **princesse** *nf* princess. ● **principauté** *nf* principality.

principal, -aux [prɛ̃sipal, -o] *a* main, chief, principal ‖ *nm* (*de collège*) principal, headmaster; **le p.** (*essentiel*) the main *ou* chief thing.

principe [prɛ̃sip] *nm* principle; **en p.** theoretically; (*normalement*) as a rule; **par p.** on principle.

printemps [prɛ̃tɑ̃] *nm* (*saison*) spring.

priorité [priorite] *nf* priority (**sur** over); **la p.** *Aut* the right of way; **la p. à droite** the right of way to traffic coming from the right; **'cédez la p.'** *Aut* 'give way', *Am* 'yield'; **en p.** as a matter of priority. ● **prioritaire** *a* **être p.** to have priority; *Aut* to have the right of way.

pris [pri] *pp de* **prendre** ‖ *a* (*place*) taken; (*crème, ciment*) set; (*nez*) congested; (*gorge*) infected; **être (très) p.** (*occupé*) to be (very) busy; **p. de** (*peur, panique*) stricken with.

prise [priz] *nf* taking; (*objet saisi*) catch; (*manière d'empoigner*) grip, hold; (*de judo etc*) hold; (*de ville*) capture; **p. (de courant)** *Él* (*mâle*) plug; (*femelle*) socket; **p. multiple** *Él* adaptor; **p. de sang** blood test; **p. de contact** first meeting; **p. de position** *Fig* stand; **être aux prises avec qn/qch** to be struggling with s.o./sth.

prison [prizɔ̃] *nf* prison, jail; (*réclusion*) imprisonment; **être en p.** to be in prison *ou* in jail; **mettre qn en p.** to send s.o. to prison, jail s.o. ●**prisonnier, -ière** *nmf* prisoner; **faire qn p.** to take s.o. prisoner.

privatiser [privatize] *vt* to privatize.

privé [prive] *a* private; **en p.** (*seul à seul*) in private ▌*nm* **dans le p.** *Com Fam* in the private sector.

priver [prive] *vt* to deprive (**de** of); **se p. de** to do without, deprive oneself of.

privilège [privilɛʒ] *nm* privilege. ●**privilégié, -ée** *a & nmf* privileged (person).

prix [pri] *nm* **1** (*d'un objet etc*) price; **à tout p.** at all costs; **à aucun p.** on no account; **hors (de) p.** exorbitant. **2** (*récompense*) prize.

pro- [pro] *préf* pro-.

probable [prɔbabl] *a* likely, probable (**que** that); **peu p.** unlikely. ●**probabilité** *nf* probability, likelihood; **selon toute p.** in all probability. ●**probablement** [-əmɑ̃] *adv* probably.

probant [prɔbɑ̃] *a* conclusive.

problème [prɔblɛm] *nm* problem.

procédé [prosede] *nm* process.

procéder [prosede] *vi* (*agir*) to proceed; **p. à** (*enquête etc*) to carry out. ●**procédure** *nf* procedure; *Jur* proceedings.

procès [prosɛ] *nm* (*criminel*) trial; (*civil*) lawsuit; **faire un p. à qn** to take s.o. to court.

processeur [prosɛsœr] *nm* (*d'ordinateur*) processor.

procession [prosesjɔ̃] *nf* procession.

processus [prosesys] *nm* process.

procès-verbal, -aux [prosɛverbal, -o] *nm* (*contravention*) (traffic) fine, ticket; (*de réunion*) minutes; (*constat*) *Jur* report.

prochain, -aine [prɔʃɛ, -ɛn] **1** *a* next; (*mort, arrivée*) impending; **un jour p.** one day soon ▌*nf* **à la prochaine!** *Fam*

see you soon!; **à la prochaine (station)** at the next stop. **2** *nm* (*semblable*) fellow (man). ●**prochainement** *adv* shortly, soon.

proche [prɔʃ] *a* (*espace*) near, close; (*temps*) close (at hand); (*parent, ami*) close; (*avenir*) near; **p. de** near (to), close to; **le P.-Orient** the Middle East ▌*nmpl* close relations.

proclamer [prɔklame] *vt* to proclaim, declare (**que** that).

procuration [prɔkyrasjɔ̃] *nf* **par p.** (*voter etc*) by proxy.

procurer [prɔkyre] *vt* **p. qch à qn** (*personne*) to obtain sth for s.o.; **se p. qch** to obtain sth.

procureur [prɔkyrœr] *nm* = *Br* public prosecutor, = *Am* district attorney.

prodige [prɔdiʒ] *nm* (*miracle*) wonder; (*personne*) prodigy. ●**prodigieux, -euse** *a* extraordinary.

prodiguer [prɔdige] *vt* **p. qch à qn** to lavish sth on s.o.

production [prɔdyksjɔ̃] *nf* production. ●**producteur, -trice** *nmf Com Cin* producer ▌*a* producing; **pays p. de pétrole** oil-producing country. ●**productif, -ive** *a* (*terre, réunion etc*) productive. ●**productivité** *nf* productivity.

produire* [prɔdɥir] **1** *vt* (*fabriquer*) to produce; (*causer*) to produce, bring about. **2 se produire** *vpr* (*événement etc*) to happen. ●**produit** *nm* (*article etc*) product; (*pour la vaisselle*) liquid; (*d'une vente, d'une collecte*) proceeds; *pl* (*de la terre*) produce; **p. (chimique)** chemical; **p. de beauté** cosmetic; **p. national brut** *Écon* gross national product.

proéminent [prɔeminɑ̃] *a* prominent.

prof [prɔf] *nm Fam* = **professeur.**

profane [prɔfan] *nmf* lay person.

proférer [prɔfere] *vt* to utter.

professeur [prɔfesœr] *nm* teacher; *Univ* lecturer, *Am* professor; (*titulaire d'une chaire*) *Univ* professor.

profession [prɔfesjɔ̃] *nf* occupation, vocation; (*manuelle*) trade; **p. libérale**

profession; **sans p.** not gainfully employed. ● **professionnel, -elle** *a* professional; (*école*) vocational ‖*nmf* professional.

profil [prɔfil] *nm* (*de personne, objet*) profile; **de p.** (viewed) from the side, in profile.

profit [prɔfi] *nm* profit; (*avantage*) advantage, profit; **tirer p. de** to benefit from *ou* by, profit by; **au p. de** for the benefit of. ● **profitable** *a* (*utile*) beneficial (à to). ● **profiter** *vi* p. de to take advantage of; **p. à qn** to profit s.o.

profond [prɔfɔ̃] *a* deep; (*esprit, joie etc*) profound, great; (*cause*) underlying; **p. de deux mètres** two metres deep ‖*adv* (*pénétrer etc*) deep ‖ **nm au plus p. de** in the depths of. ● **profondément** *adv* deeply; (*dormir*) soundly; (*triste, souhaiter*) profoundly. ● **profondeur** *nf* depth; *pl* depths (**de** of); **à six mètres de p.** at a depth of six metres; **en p.** (*étudier etc*) in depth.

progéniture [prɔʒenityr] *nf* (*enfants*) *Hum* offspring.

progiciel [prɔʒisjɛl] *nm* (*pour ordinateur*) (software) package.

programmateur [prɔgramatœr] *nm* (*de four etc*) timer.

programme [prɔgram] *nm* programme, *Am* program; (*d'une matière*) *Scol* syllabus; (*d'ordinateur*) program; **p. (d'études)** (*d'une école*) curriculum. ● **programmer** *vt* (*ordinateur*) to program. ● **programmeur, -euse** *nmf* (computer) programmer.

progrès [prɔgrɛ] *nm & nmpl* progress; **faire des p.** to make progress. ● **progresser** *vi* to progress. ● **progressif, -ive** *a* gradual, progressive. ● **progression** *nf* progression. ● **progressivement** *adv* gradually, progressively.

proie [prwa] *nf* prey; **être en p. à** to be (a) prey to, be tortured by.

projecteur [prɔʒɛktœr] *nm* (*de monument*) floodlight; (*de prison*) & *Mil* searchlight; *Th* spot(light); *Cin* projector.

projectile [prɔʒɛktil] *nm* missile.

projection [prɔʒɛksjɔ̃] *nf* hurling, projection; (*de film*) projection; (*séance*) showing.

projet [prɔʒɛ] *nm* plan; (*entreprise, étude*) project; **faire des projets d'avenir** to make plans for the future; **p. de loi** Pol bill.

projeter [prɔʒte] *vt* **1** (*lancer*) to hurl, project. **2** (*film, ombre*) to project; (*lumière*) to flash. **3** (*voyage, fête etc*) to plan; **p. de faire** to plan to do.

proliférer [prɔlifere] *vi* to proliferate.

prolifique [prɔlifik] *a* prolific.

prolonger [prɔlɔ̃ʒe] *vt* to extend, prolong ‖ **se p.** *vpr* (*séance, rue, effet*) to continue. ● **prolongation** *nf* (*dans le temps*) extension; *pl Fb* extra time. ● **prolongement** *nm* (*dans l'espace*) extension.

promenade [prɔmnad] *nf* (*à pied*) walk; (*en voiture*) drive, ride; (*en vélo, à cheval*) ride; (*action*) *Sp* walking; (*lieu*) walk, promenade; **faire une p. = se promener.** ● **promener** *vt* to take for a walk *ou* ride; **envoyer qn p.** *Fam* to send s.o. packing ‖ **se p.** *vpr* (*à pied*) to (go for a) walk; (*en voiture*) to (go for a) drive *ou* ride. ● **promeneur, -euse** *nmf* stroller, walker.

promesse [prɔmɛs] *nf* promise.

promettre* [prɔmɛtr] *vt* to promise (**qch à qn** s.o. sth, **que** that); **p. de faire qch** to promise to do sth; **r'est promis** it's a promise ‖ *vi* **p. (beaucoup)** *Fig* to be promising ‖ **se p.** *vpr* **se p. de faire qch** to resolve to do sth. ● **prometteur, -euse** *a* promising.

promontoire [prɔmɔ̃twar] *nm Géog* headland.

promoteur [prɔmɔtœr] *nm* **p. (immobilier)** property developer.

promotion [prɔmosjɔ̃] *nf* promotion; **en p.** (*produit*) on (special) offer. ● **promouvoir*** *vt* (*personne, produit etc*) to promote; **être promu** (*employé*) to be promoted (à to).

prompt [prɔ̃] *a* swift, prompt.

pronom [prɔnɔ̃] *nm Gram* pronoun.
● **pronominal, -aux** *a Gram* pronominal.

prononcer [prɔnɔ̃se] *vt* (*articuler*) to pronounce; (*dire*) to utter; (*discours*) to deliver; (*jugement*) *Jur* to pronounce, pass ‖ **se p.** *vpr* (*mot*) to be pronounced; (*personne*) to reach a decision (**sur** about, on); **se p. pour/contre qch** to come out in favour of/against sth. ● **prononciation** *nf* pronunciation.

pronostic [prɔnɔstik] *nm* (*prévision*) & *Sp* forecast.

propagande [prɔpagɑ̃d] *nf* propaganda.

propager [prɔpaʒe] *vt*, **se p.** *vpr* to spread.

prophète [prɔfɛt] *nm* prophet. ● **prophétie** [-fesi] *nf* prophecy. ● **prophétique** *a* prophetic.

propice [prɔpis] *a* favourable (**à** to).

proportion [prɔpɔrsjɔ̃] *nf* proportion; *Math* ratio; *pl* (*dimensions*) proportions. ● **proportionné** *a* proportionate (**à** to); **bien p.** well-proportioned. ● **proportionnel, -elle** *a* proportional (**à** to).

propos [prɔpo] **1** *nmpl* (*paroles*) remarks. **2** *nm* (*sujet*) subject; **à p. de** about; **à tout p.** for no reason, at every turn. **3** *adv* **à p.** (*arriver etc*) at the right time; **à p.** by the way.

proposer [prɔpoze] *vt* (*suggérer*) to suggest, propose (**qch à qn** sth to s.o., **que** (+ *sub*) that); (*offrir*) to offer (**qch à qn** s.o. sth, **de faire** to do); **je te propose de rester** I suggest (that) you stay; **se p. pour faire qch** to offer to do sth; **se p. de faire qch** to propose *ou* mean to do sth. ● **proposition** *nf* suggestion, proposal; (*de paix*) proposal; *Gram* clause.

propre[1] [prɔpr] *a* clean; (*soigné*) neat ‖ *nm* **mettre qch au p.** to make a fair copy of sth. ● **proprement**[1] *adv* cleanly; (*avec netteté*) neatly. ● **propreté** *nf* cleanliness; (*netteté*) neatness.

propre[2] [prɔpr] **1** *a* (*à soi*) own; **mon p. argent** my own money. **2** *a* **p. à** (*attribut, coutume etc*) peculiar to;

(*approprié*) well-suited to; **sens p.** literal meaning; **nom p.** proper noun ‖ *nm* **le p. de** (*qualité*) the distinctive quality of. ● **proprement**[2] *adv* **à p. parler** strictly speaking; **le village/etc p. dit** the village/ *etc* proper *ou* itself.

propriétaire [prɔprijetɛr] *nmf* owner; (*qui loue*) landlord, landlady; **p. foncier** landowner.

propriété [prɔprijete] *nf* **1** (*bien, maison*) property; (*droit*) ownership, property. **2** (*qualité*) property.

propulser [prɔpylse] *vt* (*faire avancer, projeter*) to propel.

prosaïque [prɔzaik] *a* prosaic, pedestrian.

proscrire* [prɔskrir] *vt* (*exiler*) to banish; (*interdire*) to ban. ● **proscrit, -ite** *nmf* (*personne*) exile.

prose [proz] *nf* prose.

prospecter [prɔspɛkte] *vt* (*sol*) to prospect; (*pétrole*) to prospect for; (*région*) *Com* to canvass. ● **prospection** *nf* prospecting; *Com* canvassing.

prospectus [prɔspɛktys] *nm* leaflet.

prospère [prɔspɛr] *a* (*florissant*) thriving; (*riche*) prosperous. ● **prospérer** *vi* to thrive, flourish, prosper. ● **prospérité** *nf* prosperity.

prosterner (se) [səprɔstɛrne] *vpr* to prostrate oneself (**devant** before).

prostituer (se) [səprɔstitɥe] *vpr* to prostitute oneself. ● **prostituée** *nf* prostitute. ● **prostitution** *nf* prostitution.

protagoniste [prɔtagɔnist] *nmf* protagonist.

protecteur, -trice [prɔtɛktœr, -tris] *nmf* protector ‖ *a* (*geste etc*) & *Écon* protective; (*ton, air*) *Péj* patronizing. ● **protection** *nf* protection; **de p.** (*écran etc*) protective.

protéger [prɔteʒe] *vt* to protect (**de** from, **contre** against) ‖ **se p.** *vpr* to protect oneself. ● **protège-cahier** *nm* exercise book cover.

proteine [prɔtein] *nf* protein.

protestant, -ante [prɔtɛstɑ̃, -ɑ̃t] *a* & *nmf* Protestant.

protester [prɔteste] *vi* to protest (**contre** against); **p. de** (*son innocence etc*) to protest. ● **protestation** *nf* protest (**contre** against); *pl* (*d'amitié*) declarations (**de** of).

prothèse [prɔtez] *nf* (**appareil de**) **p.** (*membre*) artificial limb; **p. (dentaire)** false teeth.

protocole [prɔtɔkɔl] *nm* protocol.

proue [pru] *nf Nau* bow(s), prow.

prouesse [prues] *nf* feat, exploit.

prouver [pruve] *vt* to prove (**que** that).

Provence [prɔvɑ̃s] *nf* Provence.

provenir* [prɔvnir] *vi* **p. de** to come from. ● **provenance** *nf* origin; **en p. de** from.

proverbe [prɔverb] *nm* proverb.

province [prɔvɛ̃s] *nf* province; **la p.** the provinces; **en p.** in the provinces; **de p.** (*ville etc*) provincial. ● **provincial, -ale, -aux** *a et nmf* provincial.

proviseur [prɔvizœr] *nm* (*de lycée*) headmaster, headmistress, *Am* principal.

provision [prɔvizjɔ̃] *nf* **1** (*réserve*) supply, stock; *pl* (*achats*) shopping; (*nourriture*) food: **panier/sac à provisions** shopping basket/bag. **2** (*somme*) funds; (*acompte*) advance payment; **chèque sans p.** dud cheque, *Am* bad check.

provisoire [prɔvizwar] *a* temporary, provisional. ●**—ment** *adv* temporarily, provisionally.

provoquer [prɔvɔke] *vt* **1** (*causer*) to bring about, provoke; (*désir*) to arouse. **2** (*défier*) to provoke (*s.o.*). ● **provocant** *a* provocative. ● **provocation** *nf* provocation.

proximité [prɔksimite] *nf* closeness; **à p.** close by; **à p. de** close to.

prude [pryd] *a* prudish.

prudent [prydɑ̃] *a* (*circonspect*) cautious, careful. ● **prudemment** [-amɑ̃] *adv* cautiously, carefully. ● **prudence** *nf* caution, care; **par p.** as a precaution.

prune [pryn] *nf* (*fruit*) plum. ● **pruneau, -x** *nm* prune. ● **prunier** *nm* plum tree.

prunelle [prynɛl] *nf* (*de l'œil*) pupil.

P.-S. [pees] *abrév* (*post-scriptum*) PS.

psaume [psom] *nm* psalm.

pseudo- [psødo] *préf* pseudo-.

pseudonyme [psødɔnim] *nm* pseudonym.

psychanalyste [psikanalist] *nmf* psychoanalyst.

psychiatre [psikjatr] *nmf* psychiatrist. ● **psychiatrie** *nf* psychiatry. ● **psychiatrique** *a* psychiatric.

psycho [psiko] *préf* psycho-.

psychologie [psikɔlɔʒi] *nf* psychology. ● **psychologique** *a* psychological. ● **psychologue** *nmf* psychologist.

PTT [petete] *nfpl abrév* (*Postes, Télégraphes, Téléphones*) Post Office.

pu [py] *pp de* **pouvoir 1.**

puanteur [pɥɑ̃tœr] *nf* stink, stench.

pub [pyb] *nf Fam* (*réclame*) advertising; (*annonce*) ad.

puberté [pyberte] *nf* puberty.

public, -ique [pyblik] *a* public ‖ *nm* public; (*de spectacle*) audience; **le grand p.** the general public; **en p.** in public.

publication [pyblikasjɔ̃] *nf* (*action, livre etc*) publication. ● **publier** *vt* to publish.

publicité [pyblisite] *nf* (*réclame*) advertising, publicity; (*annonce*) advertisement; *Rad TV* commercial; *Fig* publicity (**autour de** surrounding). ● **publicitaire** *a* **agence/etc p.** advertising agency/etc; **film p.** promotional film.

puce [pys] *nf* **1** flea; **le marché aux puces, les puces** the flea market. **2** (*d'un ordinateur*) (micro)chip.

puceron [pysrɔ̃] *nm* greenfly.

pudeur [pydœr] *nf* (*sense of*) modesty. ● **pudique** *a* modest.

puer [pɥe] *vi* to stink ‖ *vt* to stink of.

puériculture [pɥerikyltyr] *nf* infant care, child care. ● **puéricultrice** *nf* children's nurse.

puéril [pɥeril] *a* puerile.

puis [pɥi] *adv* then; **et p. quoi?** and so what?

puiser [pɥize] *vt* to draw, take (**dans**

from).

puisque [pɥisk(ə)] *conj* since, as.

puissant [pɥisɑ̃] *a* powerful. ● **puissance** *nf* (*force, nation*) & *Math Tech* power; **en p.** (*talent, danger etc*) potential.

puisse(s), puissent *etc* [pɥis] *voir* **pouvoir 1**.

puits [pɥi] *nm* well; (*de mine*) shaft.

pull(-over) [pyl(ɔver)] *nm* sweater, pullover.

pulpe [pylp] *nf* (*de fruits*) pulp.

pulvériser [pylverize] *vt* (*liquide*) to spray; (*broyer*) & *Fig* to pulverize. ● **pulvérisateur** *nm* spray.

punaise [pynez] *nf* **1** (*insecte*) bug. **2** (*clou*) drawing pin, *Am* thumbtack.

punch [pɔ̃ʃ] *nm* **1** (*boisson*) punch. **2** [pœnʃ] (*énergie*) punch.

punir [pynir] *vt* to punish (**de qch** for sth, **pour avoir fait qch** for doing sth). ● **punition** *nf* punishment.

pupille [pypij] **1** *nf* (*de l'œil*) pupil. **2** *nmf* (*enfant sous tutelle*) ward; **p. de la Nation** war orphan.

pupitre [pypitr] *nm* (*d'écolier*) desk; (*d'orateur*) lectern; *Ordinat* console.

pur [pyr] *a* pure; (*alcool*) neat, straight. ● **pureté** *nf* purity.

purée [pyre] *nf* purée; **p. (de pommes de terre)** mashed potatoes.

purge [pyrʒ] *nf* *Pol Méd* purge.

purger [pyrʒe] *vt* **1** (*conduite*) *Tech* to drain, clear. **2** (*peine*) *Jur* to serve.

purifier [pyrifje] *vt* to purify.

pur-sang [pyrsɑ̃] *nm inv* (*cheval*) thoroughbred.

pus[1] [py] *nm* (*liquide*) pus, matter.

pus[2]**, put** [py] *voir* **pouvoir 1**.

putain [pytɛ̃] *nf* *Péj Vulg* whore.

puzzle [pœzl] *nm* (*jigsaw*) puzzle, jigsaw.

p.-v. [peve] *nm inv* (*procès-verbal*) (traffic) fine.

pyjama [piʒama] *nm* pyjamas, *Am* pajamas; **un p.** a pair of pyjamas *ou Am* pajamas; **pantalon de p.** pyjama trousers, *Am* pajama bottoms; **être en p.** to be in pyjamas *ou Am* pajamas.

pylône [pilon] *nm* pylon.

pyramide [piramid] *nf* pyramid.

Pyrénées [pirene] *nfpl* **les P.** the Pyrenees.

pyromane [piroman] *nmf* arsonist.

Q

Q, q [ky] *nm* Q, q.

QI [kyi] *nm inv abrév* (*quotient intellectuel*) IQ.

qu' [k] *voir* que.

quadrill/er [kadrije] *vt* (*police etc*) to be positioned throughout, comb (*town etc*). ●—**é** *a* (*papier*) squared. ●**quadrillage** *nm* (*lignes*) squares.

quadruple [k(w)adrypl] *a* **q. de** fourfold ▮ *nm* **le q. de** four times as much as. ●**quadrupler** *vti* to quadruple. ●**quadruplés, -ées** *nmfpl* (*enfants*) quadruplets, quads.

quai [ke] *nm Nau* (*pour passagers*) quay; (*pour marchandises*) wharf; (*de fleuve*) embankment; *Rail* platform.

qualification [kalifikɑsjɔ̃] *nf* (*action*) *Sp* qualifying. ●**se qualifier** *vpr Sp* to qualify (**pour** for). ●**qualifié** *a* (*équipe etc*) that has qualified; (*ouvrier, main-d'œuvre*) skilled; **q. pour faire** qualified to do.

qualité [kalite] *nf* quality; **produit/etc de q.** high-quality product/*etc*; **en sa q. de** in one's capacity as.

quand [kɑ̃] *conj & adv* when; **q. je viendrai** when I come; **c'est pour q.?** (*réunion, mariage*) when is it?; **q. même** *Fam* all the same.

quant (à) [kɑ̃ta] *prép* as for.

quantité [kɑ̃tite] *nf* quantity; **une q., des quantités** (*beaucoup*) a lot (**de** of); **en q.** (*abondamment*) in abundance. ●**quantifier** *vt* to quantify.

quarante [karɑ̃t] *a & nm* forty. ●**quarantaine** *nf* **1 une q. (de)** (*nombre*) (about) forty. **2** *Méd* quarantine; **mettre en q.** *Méd* to quarantine. ●**quarantième** *a & nmf* fortieth.

quart [kar] *nm* **1** quarter; **q. (de litre)** quarter litre, quarter of a litre; **q. d'heure** quarter of an hour; **une heure** et q. an hour and a quarter; **il est une heure et q.** it's a quarter past *ou* Am after one; **une heure moins le q.** quarter to one. **2** *Nau* watch.

quartier [kartje] **1** *nm* neighbourhood, district; (*chinois etc*) quarter; **de q.** (*cinéma etc*) local. **2** *nm* (*de pomme, lune*) quarter; (*d'orange*) segment. **3** *nm(pl)* **quartier(s)** *Mil* quarters; **q. général** headquarters.

quartz [kwarts] *nm* quartz; **montre/etc à q.** quartz watch/*etc*.

quasi [kazi] *adv* almost.

quatorze [katɔrz] *a & nm* fourteen. ●**quatorzième** *a & nmf* fourteenth.

quatre [katr] *a & nm* four; **son q. heures** (*goûter*) *Fam* one's afternoon snack; **se mettre en q.** to go out of one's way (**pour faire** to do). ●**quatrième** *a & nmf* fourth.

quatre-vingt(s) [katrəvɛ̃] *a & nm* eighty; **q.-vingts ans** eighty years; **q.-vingt-un** eighty-one; **page q.-vingt** page eighty. ●**q.-vingt-dix** *a & nm* ninety.

quatuor [kwatɥɔr] *nm Mus* quartet(te).

que [k(ə)] (**qu'** before a vowel or mute h)
1 *conj* that; **je pense qu'elle restera** I think (that) she'll stay; **qu'elle vienne ou non** whether she comes or not; **qu'il s'en aille!** let him leave!; **ça fait un an q. je suis là** I've been here for a year.

2 (**ne**). . .**q.** only; **tu n'as qu'un franc** you only have one franc.

3 (*comparaison*) than; (*avec aussi, même, tel, autant*) as; **plus/moins âgé q. lui** older/younger than him; **aussi sage/etc q.** as wise/*etc* as; **le même q.** the same as.

4 *adv* (**ce**) **qu'il est bête!** (*comme*) how silly he is!; **q. de gens!** (*combien*) what a lot of people!

5 *pron rel* (*chose*) that, which; (*per-*

sonne) that, whom; **le livre q. j'ai** the book (that ou which) I have; **l'ami q. j'ai** the friend (that ou whom) I have. **6** pron interrogatif what; **q. fait-il?, qu'est-ce qu'il fait?** what is he doing?; **qu'est-ce qui est dans ta poche?** what's in your pocket?.

Québec [kebɛk] nm le Q. Quebec.

quel, quelle [kɛl] **1** a interrogatif what, which; (qui) who; **q. livre/acteur préférez-vous?** which ou what book/actor do you prefer?; **je sais q. est ton but** I know what your aim is ∥ pron interrogatif which (one); **q. est le meilleur?** which (one) is the best?
2 a exclamatif **q. idiot!** what a fool!
3 a rel **q. qu'il soit** (chose) whatever it may be; (personne) whoever it ou he may be.

quelconque [kɛlkɔ̃k] a **1** any (whatever), some (or other); **une raison q.** any reason (whatever), some reason (or other). **2** (banal) ordinary.

quelque [kɛlk(ə)] **1** a some; **quelques femmes/livres/etc** some ou a few women/books/etc; **les quelques amies qu'elle a** the few friends she has.
2 adv (environ) about, some; **q. peu** somewhat; **cent francs et q.** Fam a hundred francs and a bit.
3 pron **q. chose** something; (interrogation) anything, something; **il a q. chose** (un problème) Fig there's something the matter with him; **q. chose d'autre** something else; **q. chose de grand/etc** something big/etc.
4 adv **q. part** somewhere; (interrogation) anywhere, somewhere.

quelquefois [kɛlkəfwa] adv sometimes.
quelques-uns, -unes [kɛlkəzœ̃, -yn] pron pl some.

quelqu'un [kɛlkœ̃] pron someone, somebody; (interrogation) anyone, anybody, someone, somebody; **q. d'intelligent/etc** someone clever/etc.

querelle [kərɛl] nf quarrel, dispute. ● **se quereller** vpr to quarrel.

question [kɛstjɔ̃] nf question; (problème)

matter, question; **il est q. de faire qch** there's some talk about doing sth; **il a été q. de vous** we ou they talked about you; **il n'en est pas q.** it's out of the question; **en q.** in question; **hors de q.** out of the question; **(re)mettre en q.** to (call in) question. ● **questionnaire** nm questionnaire. ● **questionner** vt to question (**sur** about).

quête [kɛt] nf **1** (collecte) collection; **faire la q.** to collect money. **2** (recherche) quest (**de** for); **en q. de** in search of.

queue [kø] nf **1** (d'animal) tail; (de fleur) stem, stalk; (de fruit) stalk; (de poêle) handle; (de train) rear; **q. de cheval** (coiffure) ponytail; **à la q. leu leu** (marcher) in single file; **faire une q. de poisson** Aut to cut in (**à qn** in front of s.o.).
2 (file) queue, Am line; **faire la q.** to queue up, Am line up.

qui [ki] **1** pron interrogatif (personne) who; (en complément) whom; **q. (est-ce qui) est là?** who's there?; **q. désirez-vous voir?, q. est-ce que vous désirez voir?** who(m) do you want to see?; **à q. est ce livre?** whose book is this?; **je demande q. a téléphoné** I'm asking who phoned.
2 pron rel (sujet) (personne) who, that; (chose) which, that; **l'homme q. est là** the man who's here ou that's here; **la maison q. se trouve en face** the house which is ou that's opposite; **q. que vous soyez** (sans antécédent) whoever you are, whoever you may be.
3 pron rel (après prép) **la femme de q. je parle** the woman I'm talking about ou about whom I'm talking; **l'ami sur l'aide de q. je compte** the friend on whose help I rely.

quiche [kiʃ] nf quiche.

quiconque [kikɔ̃k] pron (celui qui) whoever; (n'importe qui) anyone.

quille [kij] nf **1** (de navire) keel. **2** (de jeu) (bowling) pin, skittle; **jouer aux quilles** to bowl, play skittles.

quincaillier, -ière [kɛ̃kaje, -jɛr] nmf

hardware dealer, ironmonger. ● **quin-caillerie** *nf* (*magasin*) hardware shop, ironmonger's.

quinte [kɛ̃t] *nf* q. (de toux) coughing fit.

quintette [kɛ̃tɛt] *nm Mus* quintet(te).

quintuple [kɛ̃typl] *a* q. de fivefold ‖ *nm* le q. de five times as much as. ● **quintuplés, -ées** *nmfpl* (*enfants*) quintuplets, quins.

quinze [kɛ̃z] *a & nm* fifteen; q. jours two weeks, a fortnight. ● **quinzaine** *nf* une q. (de) (*nombre*) (about) fifteen; q. (de jours) two weeks, a fortnight. ● **quinzième** *a & nmf* fifteenth.

quittance [kitɑ̃s] *nf* receipt.

quitte [kit] *a* even, quits (**envers** with); q. à faire even if it means doing.

quitter [kite] *vt* to leave; (*ôter*) to take off; q. qn des yeux to take one's eyes off s.o. ‖ *vi* ne quittez pas! *Tél* hold on!,

hold the line! ‖ **se q.** *vpr* (*se séparer*) to part, say goodbye.

quoi [kwa] *pron* what; (*après prép*) which; à q. penses-tu? what are you thinking about?; **après q.** after which; ce à q. je m'attendais what I was expecting; de q. manger/*etc* something to eat/*etc*; (*assez*) enough to eat/*etc*; de q. écrire something to write with; **q. que je dise** whatever I say; **il n'y a pas de q.!** (*en réponse à 'merci'*) don't mention it!; **c'est un idiot, q.!** (*non traduit*) *Fam* he's a fool!

quoique [kwak(ə)] *conj* (+ *sub*) (al)though.

quota [k(w)ɔta] *nm* quota.

quotidien, -ienne [kɔtidjɛ̃, -jɛn] *a* daily ‖ *nm* daily (paper). ● **quotidiennement** *adv* daily.

R

R, r [ɛr] *nm* R, r.

rabâcher [rɑbɑʃe] *vt* to repeat endlessly.

rabais [rɑbɛ] *nm* (price) reduction, discount.

rabaisser [rɑbese] *vt* (*dénigrer*) to belittle; **r. à** (*ravaler*) to reduce to.

rabattre* [rɑbatr] *vt* (*baisser*) to pull *ou* put down; (*refermer*) to close (down) **║se r.** *vpr* (*se refermer*) to close; (*barrière*) to come down; (*après avoir doublé un véhicule*) to cut in (**devant** in front of); **se r. sur** *Fig* to fall back on.

rabbin [rɑbɛ̃] *nm* rabbi; **grand r.** chief rabbi.

rabot [rɑbo] *nm* (*outil*) plane. ● **raboter** *vt* to plane.

rabougri [rɑbugri] *a* (*personne, plante*) stunted.

racaille [rɑkɑj] *nf* rabble, riffraff.

raccommoder [rɑkɔmɔde] **1** *vt* (*linge*) to mend; (*chaussette*) to darn. **2** *vt* (*réconcilier*) *Fam* to reconcile **║se r.** *vpr* *Fam* to make it up (**avec** with). ● **raccommodage** *nm* mending; darning.

raccompagner [rɑkɔ̃paɲe] *vt* to see *ou* take back (home); **r. qn à la porte** to see s.o. to the door, see s.o. out.

raccord [rɑkɔr] *nm* (*dispositif*) connection, connector; (*de papier peint*) join; **r. (de peinture)** touch-up. ● **raccorder** *vt*, **se r.** *vpr* to connect (up), join (up) (**à** with, to).

raccourc/ir [rɑkursir] *vt* to shorten **║** *vi* to get shorter; (*au lavage*) to shrink. ● **—i** *nm* (*chemin*) short cut.

raccrocher [rɑkrɔʃe] *vt* (*objet tombé*) to hang back up; (*téléphone*) to put down; **se r. à** to hold on to, cling to **║** *vi* *Tél* to hang up, ring off.

race [rɑs] *nf* (*groupe ethnique*) race; (*animale*) breed; **chien de r.** pedigree dog. ● **racial, -aux** *a* racial. ● **racisme** *nm* racism, racialism. ● **raciste** *a* & *nmf* racist, racialist.

rachat [rɑʃa] *nm* *Com* repurchase; (*de firme*) take-over. ● **racheter** *vt* to buy back; (*firme*) to take over, buy out; **r. un manteau/une voiture**/*etc* to buy another coat/car/*etc*; **r. des chaussettes/du pain**/*etc* to buy some more socks/bread/*etc* **║se r.** *vpr* to make amends.

racine [rɑsin] *nf* (*de plante, personne etc*) & *Math* root; **prendre r.** (*plante*) & *Fig* to take root.

racket [rɑkɛt] *nm* (*activité*) racketeering.

raclée [rɑkle] *nf* *Fam* thrashing, hiding.

racler [rɑkle] *vt* to scrape; (*enlever*) to scrape off; **se r. la gorge** to clear one's throat. ● **racloir** *nm* scraper.

racoler [rɑkɔle] *vt* (*prostituée, vendeur etc*) to accost (*s.o.*).

raconter [rɑkɔ̃te] *vt* (*histoire*) to tell, relate; **r. qch à qn** (*vacances etc*) to tell s.o. about sth; **r. à qn que** to tell s.o. that.

racornir (se) [sərɑkɔrnir] *vpr* to get hard.

radar [rɑdar] *nm* radar; **contrôle r.** (*pour véhicules etc*) radar control.

rade [rɑd] *nf* **1** *Nau* (natural) harbour. **2** **laisser qn en r.** *Fam* to leave s.o. stranded, abandon s.o.; **rester en r.** *Fam* to be left behind.

radeau, -x [rɑdo] *nm* raft.

radiateur [rɑdjatœr] *nm* (*électrique, à gaz*) heater; (*de chauffage central, voiture*) radiator.

radiation [rɑdjɑsjɔ̃] *nf* **1** *Phys* radiation. **2** (*suppression*) removal (**de** from).

radical, -ale, -aux [rɑdikal, -o] *a* radical **║** *nm* *Ling* stem **║** *nmf* *Pol* radical.

radier [rɑdje] *vt* to strike *ou* cross off (**de** from).

radieux, -euse [rɑdjø, -øz] *a* (*personne*,

visage) beaming, radiant; *(soleil)* brilliant; *(temps)* glorious.

radin, -ine [radɛ̃, -in] *a Fam* stingy.

radio [radjo] **1** *nf* radio; *(poste)* radio (set); **à la r.** on the radio. **2** *nf (photo) Méd* X-ray; **passer** *ou* **faire une r.** to have an X-ray, be X-rayed. **3** *nm (opérateur)* radio operator. ●**radioactif, -ive** *a* radioactive. ●**radioactivité** *nf* radioactivity. ●**radiodiffuser** *vt* to broadcast (on the radio). ●**radiographier** *vt* to X-ray. ●**radiologue** *nmf (technicien)* radiographer; *(médecin)* radiologist. ●**radio-réveil** *nm (pl* **radios-réveils)** radio alarm clock.

radis [radi] *nm* radish; **r. noir** horse-radish.

radoter [radɔte] *vi* to ramble (on), drivel (on).

radoucir (se) [səradusir] *vpr* to calm down; *(temps)* to become milder. ●**radoucissement** *nm* **r. (du temps)** milder weather.

rafale [rafal] *nf (vent)* gust, squall; *(de mitrailleuse)* burst.

raffermir [rafɛrmir] *vt* to strengthen; *(muscles etc)* to tone up ▮ **se r.** *vpr* to become stronger.

raffinement [rafinmɑ̃] *nm (de personne)* refinement.

raffiner [rafine] *vt (pétrole, sucre)* to refine. ●**raffinerie** *nf* refinery.

raffoler [rafɔle] *vi* **r. de** *(aimer)* to be mad *ou* wild about.

rafistoler [rafistɔle] *vt Fam* to patch up.

rafle [rafl] *nf (police)* raid.

rafler [rafle] *vt (enlever) Fam* to swipe, make off with.

rafraîchir [rafreʃir] *vt* to cool (down); *(remettre à neuf)* to brighten up; *(mémoire)* to refresh ▮ **se r.** *vpr (boire)* to refresh oneself; *(se laver)* to freshen (oneself) up; *(temps)* to get cooler. ●**rafraîchissant** *a* refreshing. ●**rafraîchissement** *nm* **1** *(de température)* cooling. **2** *(boisson)* cold drink; *pl (glaces etc)* refreshments.

rage [raʒ] *nf* **1** *(colère)* rage; **r. de dents**

violent toothache; **faire r.** *(incendie, tempête)* to rage. **2** *(maladie)* rabies. ●**rageant** *a Fam* infuriating.

ragots [rago] *nmpl Fam* gossip.

ragoût [ragu] *nm Culin* stew.

raid [rɛd] *nm Mil Av* raid.

raide [rɛd] *a (rigide, guindé)* stiff; *(côte)* steep; *(cheveux)* straight; *(corde)* tight ▮ *adv (grimper)* steeply; **tomber r. mort** to drop dead. ●**raidir** *vt,* **se r.** *vpr* to stiffen; *(corde)* to tighten.

raie [rɛ] *nf* **1** *(trait)* line; *(de tissu, zèbre)* stripe; *(de cheveux)* parting, *Am* part. **2** *(poisson)* skate, ray.

rail [raj] *nm (barre)* rail (for train); **le r.** *(transport)* rail.

railler [raje] *vt* to mock, make fun of. ●**raillerie** *nf* gibe.

rainure [renyr] *nf* groove.

raisin [rezɛ̃] *nm* **raisin(s)** grapes; **grain de r.** grape; **manger du r.** *ou* **des raisins** to eat grapes; **r. sec** raisin.

raison [rezɔ̃] *nf* **1** *(faculté, motif)* reason; **la r. de/pour laquelle...** the reason for/ why...; **pour raisons de famille**/*etc* for family/*etc* reasons; **en r. de** *(cause)* on account of; **à r. de** *(proportion)* at the rate of; **à plus forte r.** all the more so; **r. de plus** all the more reason **(pour faire** to do, for doing); **entendre r.** to listen to reason.

2 avoir r. to be right **(de faire** to do, in doing); **donner r. à qn** to agree with s.o.; *(événement etc)* to prove s.o. right; **avec r.** rightly. ●**raisonnable** *a* reasonable.

raisonn/er [rezɔne] *vi (penser)* to reason; *(discuter)* to argue ▮ **r. qn** to reason with s.o. ●—**ement** *nm (faculté, activité)* reasoning; *(propositions)* argument.

rajeunir [raʒœnir] *vt* to make *(s.o.)* (feel *ou* look) younger; *(personne âgée) Méd* to rejuvenate ▮ *vi* to get *ou* feel *ou* look younger.

rajouter [raʒute] *vt* to add (**à** to); **en r.** *Fig* to overdo it.

rajuster [raʒyste] *vt (mécanisme)* to readjust; *(vêtements)* to straighten, adjust; (*cheveux*) to rearrange.

ralentir [ralɑ̃tir] *vti*, **se r.** *vpr* to slow down. ● **ralenti** *nm Cin TV* slow motion; **au r.** (*filmer, travailler*) in slow motion; **tourner au r.** (*moteur, usine*) to tick over, *Am* turn over.

râler [rale] *vi* (*blessé*) to groan; (*mourant*) to give the death rattle; (*protester*) *Fam* to grouse, moan.

rallier [ralje] *vt* (*rassembler*) to rally; **r. qn à** (*convertir*) to win s.o. over to ● **se r.** *vpr* **se r. à** (*point de vue*) to come over *ou* round to.

rallonge [ralɔ̃ʒ] *nf* (*de table*) extension; (*fil électrique*) extension (lead). ● **rallonger** *vti* to lengthen.

rallumer [ralyme] *vt* (*feu, pipe*) to light again; (*lampe*) to switch on again; (*conflit, haine*) to rekindle.

rallye [rali] *nm Sp Aut* rally.

ramasser [ramase] **1** *vt* (*prendre par terre, réunir*) to pick up; (*ordures, copies*) to collect, pick up; (*fruits, coquillages*) to gather. **2 se ramasser** *vpr* (*se pelotonner*) to curl up. ● **ramassage** *nm* picking up; collection; gathering; **r. scolaire** school bus service.

ramassis [ramasi] *nm* **r. de** (*voyous etc*) *Péj* bunch of.

rambarde [rɑ̃bard] *nf* guardrail.

rame [ram] *nf* **1** (*aviron*) oar. **2** (*de métro*) train. **3** (*de papier*) ream. ● **ramer** *vi* to row.

rameau, -x [ramo] *nm* branch; **les Rameaux** *Rel* Palm Sunday.

ramener [ramne] *vt* to bring *ou* take (*s.o.*) back; (*paix, ordre etc*) to restore, bring back; (*remettre en place*) to put back; **r. à** (*réduire à*) to reduce to; **r. à la vie** to bring back to life.

ramollir [ramɔlir] *vt*, **se r.** *vpr* to soften.

ramon/er [ramɔne] *vt* (*cheminée*) to sweep. ● **—eur** *nm* (chimney)sweep.

rampe [rɑ̃p] *nf* **1** (*d'escalier*) banister(s). **2** (*pente*) ramp, slope; **r. (d'accès)** ramp; **r. de lancement** (*de fusées etc*) launch(ing) pad. **3** (*projecteurs*) *Th* footlights.

ramper [rɑ̃pe] *vi* to crawl.

rancard [rɑ̃kar] *nm* (*rendez-vous*) *Fam* date; (*renseignement*) *Arg* tip.

rancart [rɑ̃kar] *nm* **mettre au r.** *Fam* to throw out, scrap.

rance [rɑ̃s] *a* rancid.

ranch [rɑ̃tʃ] *nm* ranch.

rancœur [rɑ̃kœr] *nf* rancour, resentment.

rançon [rɑ̃sɔ̃] *nf* ransom; **la r. de** (*inconvénient*) the price of (*success, fame etc*).

rancune [rɑ̃kyn] *nf* grudge; **garder r. à qn** to bear s.o. a grudge; **sans r.!** no hard feelings! ● **rancunier, -ière** *a* spiteful, vindictive.

randonnée [rɑ̃dɔne] *nf* (*à pied*) hike, walk; (*en vélo*) ride.

rang [rɑ̃] *nm* (*rangée*) row, line; (*classement, grade*) rank; **les rangs** (*hommes*) *Mil* the ranks (**de** of); **se mettre en rang(s)** to line up (**par trois**/*etc* in threes/*etc*). ● **rangée** *nf* row, line.

ranger [rɑ̃ʒe] *vt* (*papiers etc*) to put away; (*chambre etc*) to tidy (up); (*chiffres, mots*) to arrange; (*voiture*) to park; **r. parmi** (*auteur etc*) to rank among ▮ **se r.** *vpr* (*élèves etc*) to line up; (*s'écarter*) to stand aside; (*voiture*) to pull over; (*s'assagir*) to settle down; **se r. à l'avis de qn** to fall in with s.o.'s opinion. ● **rangé** *a* (*chambre etc*) tidy; (*personne*) steady; (*bataille*) pitched. ● **rangements** *nmpl* (*placards*) storage space.

ranimer [ranime] *vt* (*réanimer, revigorer*) to revive; (*feu*) to poke, stir.

rapace [rapas] *nm* (*oiseau*) bird of prey.

rapatrier [rapatrije] *vt* to repatriate.

râpe [rɑp] *nf Culin* grater. ● **râper** *vt* (*fromage, carottes*) to grate. ● **râpé 1** *a* (*fromage etc*) grated ▮ *nm* grated cheese. **2** *a* (*vêtement*) threadbare.

rapetisser [raptise] *vi* to get smaller; (*au lavage*) to shrink.

rapide [rapid] *a* fast, quick, rapid ▮ *nm* (*train*) express (train); (*de fleuve*) rapid. ● **—ment** *adv* fast, quickly, rapidly.

● **rapidité** *nf* speed.
rapiécer [rapjese] *vt* to patch (up).
rappel [rapel] *nm* (*de diplomate*) recall; (*évocation*) reminder; (*paiement*) back pay; *pl Th* curtain calls; (**vaccination de**) **r.** *Méd* booster; **r. à l'ordre** call to order.
rappeler [raple] *vt* (*pour faire revenir*) & *Tél* to call back; (*souvenir, diplomate*) to recall; **r. qch à qn** (*redire*) to remind s.o. of sth *vi Tél* to call back ‖ **se r.** *vpr* (*histoire, personne etc*) to remember, recall (**que** that).
rapport [rapɔr] *nm* **1** (*lien*) connection, link; *pl* (*entre personnes*) relations; **rapports** (**sexuels**) (sexual) intercourse; **par r. à** compared to *ou* with; **se mettre en r. avec qn** to get in touch with s.o.; **ça n'a aucun r.!** it has nothing to do with it! **2** (*récit*) report. **3** (*revenu*) *Com* return, yield.
rapporter [rapɔrte] **1** *vt* to bring *ou* take back ‖ *vi* (*chien*) to retrieve. **2** *vt* (*récit*) to report ‖ *vi* (*moucharder*) *Fam* to tell tales. **3** *vt* (*profit*) *Com* to bring in, yield ‖ *vi* (*investissement*) *Com* to bring in a good return. ● **rapporteur, -euse 1** *nmf* (*mouchard*) telltale. **2** *nm* *Géom* protractor. **3** *nm* *Jur* reporter.
rapprocher [raprɔʃe] *vt* to bring closer (**de** to); (*chaise*) to pull up (**de** to); (*réconcilier*) to bring together ‖ **se r.** *vpr* to come *ou* get closer (**de** to). ● **rapprochement** *nm* reconciliation; (*rapport*) connection; (*comparaison*) comparison.
rapt [rapt] *nm* (*d'enfant*) abduction.
raquette [raket] *nf* (*de tennis*) racket; (*de ping-pong*) bat.
rare [rar] *a* rare; (*argent, main-d'œuvre etc*) scarce; (*barbe, herbe*) sparse; **il est r. que** (+ *sub*) it's seldom *ou* rare that. ● **se raréfier** *vpr* (*denrées etc*) to get scarce. ● **rarement** *adv* rarely, seldom.
ras [ra] *a* (*cheveux*) close-cropped; (*herbe, poil*) short; **en rase campagne** in the open country; **à r. bord** (*remplir*) to the brim; **au r. du sol** (*avion*) close to

the ground; **en avoir r. le bol** *Fam* to be fed up (**de** with); **pull** (**au**) **r. du cou** crew-neck(ed) pullover ‖ *adv* short.
raser [raze] **1** *vt* (*menton, personne*) to shave; (*barbe, moustache*) to shave off ‖ **se r.** *vpr* to (have a) shave. **2** *vt* (*démolir*) to knock down. **3** *vt* (*frôler*) to skim, brush. **4** *vt* (*ennuyer*) *Fam* to bore. ● **rasé** *a* **être bien r.** to have shaved, be clean-shaven; **mal r.** unshaven. ● **rasoir 1** *nm* razor; (*électrique*) shaver. **2** *a inv* *Fam* boring.
rassasier [rasazje] *vti* to satisfy; **être rassasié** to have had enough (**de** of).
rassembler [rasɑ̃ble] *vt* (*gens, objets*) to gather (together), assemble; (*courage*) to summon up ‖ **se r.** *vpr* to gather, assemble. ● **rassemblement** *nm* gathering.
rasseoir* (**se**) [səraswar] *vpr* to sit down again.
rassis, *f* **rassie** [rasi] *a* (*pain, brioche etc*) stale. ● **rassir** *vi* to turn stale.
rassur/er [rasyre] *vt* to reassure; **rassure-toi** don't worry, set your mind at rest. ● **—ant** *a* (*nouvelle*) reassuring, comforting.
rat [ra] *nm* rat.
ratatiner (**se**) [səratatine] *vpr* to shrivel (up); (*vieillard*) to become wizened.
râteau, -x [rato] *nm* (*outil*) rake.
rat/er [rate] *vt* (*bus, cible, occasion etc*) to miss; (*travail, gâteau etc*) to ruin; (*examen*) to fail ‖ *vi* (*projet etc*) to fail. ● **—é, -ée 1** *nmf* (*personne*) failure. **2** *nmpl* **avoir des ratés** *Aut* to backfire.
ratifier [ratifje] *vt* to ratify.
ration [rasjɔ̃] *nf* ration. ● **rationner** *vt* (*vivres, personne*) to ration. ● **rationnement** *nm* rationing.
rationaliser [rasjɔnalize] *vt* to rationalize.
rationnel, -elle [rasjɔnɛl] *a* (*pensée, méthode*) rational.
ratisser [ratise] *vt* **1** (*allée etc*) to rake; (*feuilles etc*) to rake up. **2** (*fouiller*) to comb.

raton [ratɔ̃] *nm* **r.** laveur rac(c)oon.
RATP [ɛratepe] *nf abrév* (*Régie autonome des transports parisiens*) = Paris municipal transport authority.
rattacher [ratɑʃe] *vt* (*lacets etc*) to tie up again; (*incorporer*) to join (à to); (*idée, question*) to link (à to); **r. qn à** (*son pays etc*) to bind s.o. to; **se r. à** to be linked to.
rattraper [ratrape] *vt* to catch; (*prisonnier etc*) to recapture; (*temps perdu*) to make up for; **r. qn** (*rejoindre*) to catch up with s.o. ∎ **se r.** *vpr* (*après une erreur*) to make up for it; **se r. à** (*branche etc*) to catch hold of. ● **rattrapage** *nm* **cours de r.** *Scol* remedial class.
rature [ratyr] *nf* crossing out, deletion. ● **raturer** *vt* to cross out, delete.
rauque [rok] *a* (*voix*) hoarse.
ravages [ravaʒ] *nmpl* havoc, devastation; (*du temps*) ravages; **faire des r.** to cause havoc *ou* widespread damage. ● **ravager** *vt* to devastate, ravage.
ravaler [ravale] *vt* **1** (*façade etc*) to clean (and restore). **2** (*sanglots*) to swallow.
ravi [ravi] *a* delighted (**de** with, **de faire** to do, **que** that).
ravin [ravɛ̃] *nm* ravine, gully.
ravioli [ravjɔli] *nmpl* ravioli.
rav/ir [ravir] *vt* **1** (*plaire à*) to delight; **à r.** (*chanter etc*) delightfully. **2** (*emporter*) to snatch (à from). ● **—issant** *a* beautiful, lovely. ● **ravisseur, -euse** *nmf* kidnapper.
raviser (se) [səravize] *vpr* to change one's mind.
ravitailler [ravitaje] *vt* to provide with supplies (**en** of), supply (**en** with); (*avion*) to refuel ∎ **se r.** *vpr* to stock up (with supplies). ● **ravitaillement** *nm* supplying; refuelling; (*denrées*) supplies.
ray/er [reje] *vt* (*érafler*) to scratch; (*mot etc*) to cross out; **r. qn de** (*liste*) to cross *ou* strike s.o. off. ● **—é** *a* scratched; (*tissu*) striped. ● **rayure** *nf* scratch; (*bande*) stripe; **à rayures** striped.
rayon [rejɔ̃] *nm* **1** (*de lumière, soleil etc*)

Phys ray; (*de cercle*) radius; (*de roue*) spoke; **r. d'action** range; **dans un r. de** within a radius of. **2** (*planche*) shelf; (*de magasin*) department. **3** (*de ruche*) honeycomb.
rayonn/er [rejone] *vi* to radiate; (*dans une région*) to travel around (*from a central base*); **r. de joie** to beam with joy. ● **—ant** *a* (*visage etc*) beaming, radiant (**de** with).
raz-de-marée [rɑdmare] *nm inv* tidal wave; (*bouleversement*) *Fig* upheaval; **r.-de-marée électoral** landslide.
re-, ré- [r(ə), re] *préf* re-.
ré [re] *nm* (*note de musique*) D.
réacteur [reaktœr] *nm* (*d'avion*) jet engine; (*nucléaire*) reactor.
réaction [reaksjɔ̃] *nf* reaction; **r. en chaîne** chain reaction; **avion à r.** jet (aircraft). ● **réactionnaire** *a* & *nmf* reactionary.
réadapter [readapte] *vt*, **se r.** *vpr* to readjust (à to). ● **réadaptation** *nf* readjustment.
réaffirmer [reafirme] *vt* to reaffirm.
réagir [reaʒir] *vi* to react (**contre** against, **à** to); (*se secouer*) *Fig* to shake oneself out of it.
réaliser [realize] *vt* (*projet etc*) to carry out, realize; (*rêve*) to fulfil; (*bénéfices, économies*) to make; (*film*) to direct; (*se rendre compte*) to realize (**que** that) ∎ **se r.** *vpr* (*vœu*) to come true; (*projet*) to materialize; (*personne*) to fulfil oneself. ● **réalisable** *a* (*plan*) workable; (*rêve*) attainable. ● **réalisateur, -trice** *nmf Cin TV* director.
réalisme [realism] *nm* realism. ● **réaliste** *a* realistic ∎ *nmf* realist.
réalité [realite] *nf* reality; **en r.** in fact, in reality.
réanimation [reanimasjɔ̃] *nf* resuscitation; (**service de) r.** intensive care unit. ● **réanimer** *vt Méd* to revive.
réarmer [rearme] *vt* (*fusil etc*) to reload ∎ *vi*, **se r.** *vpr* (*pays*) to rearm. ● **réarmement** *nm* rearmament.
rébarbatif, -ive [rebarbatif, -iv] *a* forbid-

ding, off-putting.

rebelle [rəbɛl] *a* rebellious; **troupes rebelles** rebel troops ‖ *nmf* rebel. ● **se rebeller** *vpr* to rebel (**contre** against). ● **rébellion** *nf* rebellion.

rebond [r(ə)bɔ̃] *nm* bounce; (*par ricochet*) rebound. ● **rebondir** *vi* to bounce; to rebound. ● **rebondissement** *nm* new development (**de** in).

rebord [r(ə)bɔr] *nm* edge; (*de plat*) rim; **r. de (la) fenêtre** windowsill, window ledge.

reboucher [r(ə)buʃe] *vt* (*flacon*) to put the top back on; (*trou*) to block in again.

rebours (à) [ar(ə)bur] *adv* the wrong way.

rebrousse-poil (à) [ar(ə)bruspwal] *adv* **prendre qn à r.-poil** *Fig* to rub s.o. up the wrong way.

rebrousser [r(ə)bruse] *vt* **r. chemin** to turn back.

rébus [rebys] *nm inv* rebus (*word guessing game*).

rebut [rəby] *nm* **mettre qch au r.** to throw sth out, scrap sth; **le r. de la société** *Péj* the dregs of society.

rebuter [r(ə)byte] *vt* (*décourager*) to put off; (*choquer*) to repel.

recaler [r(ə)kale] *vt* **r. qn** *Scol Fam* to fail s.o., flunk s.o.; **être recalé, se faire r.** *Scol Fam* to fail, flunk.

récapituler [rekapityle] *vti* to recapitulate.

recel [rəsɛl] *nm* receiving stolen goods. ● **receler** *vt* (*mystère, secret etc*) to contain; (*objet volé*) to receive.

recens/er [r(ə)sɑ̃se] *vt* (*population*) to take a census of; (*inventorier*) to make an inventory of. ● **—ement** *nm* census; inventory.

récent [resɑ̃] *a* recent. ● **récemment** [-amɑ̃] *adv* recently.

récépissé [resepise] *nm* (*reçu*) receipt.

récepteur [resɛptœr] *nm* *Tél Rad* receiver. ● **réception** *nf* (*accueil, soirée*) & *Rad* reception; (*de lettre etc*) *Com* receipt; (*d'hôtel etc*) reception (desk); **dès r. de** on receipt of. ● **réceptionniste**

nmf receptionist.

récession [resesjɔ̃] *nf* *Écon* recession.

recette [r(ə)sɛt] *nf* **1** *Culin & Fig* recipe (**de** for). **2** (*argent, bénéfice*) takings; **recettes** (*rentrées*) *Com* receipts.

recev/oir* [r(ə)səvwar] *vt* to receive; (*accueillir*) to welcome; **être reçu (à)** (*examen*) to pass; **être reçu premier** to come first ‖ *vi* to have guests *ou* receive visitors; (*médecin*) to see patients. ● **—eur, -euse** *nmf* (*d'autobus*) (bus) conductor, (bus) conductress; (*des postes*) postmaster, postmistress.

rechange (de) [r(ə)ʃɑ̃ʒ] *a* (*outil, pièce, etc*) spare; (*solution etc*) alternative; **vêtements de r.** a change of clothes.

réchapper [reʃape] *vi* **r. à** (*accident etc*) to come through; **en r.** to escape with one's life.

recharge [r(ə)ʃarʒ] *nf* (*de stylo etc*) refill. ● **recharger** *vt* (*fusil, appareil photo*) to reload; (*briquet, stylo etc*) to refill; (*batterie*) to recharge.

réchaud [reʃo] *nm* (portable) stove.

réchauffer [reʃofe] *vt* (*personne, aliment etc*) to warm up ‖ **se r.** *vpr* to warm oneself up; (*temps*) to get warmer. ● **réchauffement** *nm* (*de température*) rise (**de** in).

rêche [rɛʃ] *a* rough, harsh.

recherche [r(ə)ʃɛrʃ] *nf* **1** search, quest (**de** for); **à la r. de** in search of. **2 la r., des recherches** (*scientifique etc*) research (**sur** on, into); **faire des recherches** to (do) research; (*enquêter*) to make investigations. **3** (*raffinement*) studied elegance.

recherch/er [r(ə)ʃɛrʃe] *vt* (*personne, objet*) to search *ou* hunt for; (*cause, faveur*) to seek. ● **—é** *a* **1** (*très demandé*) in great demand; **r. pour meurtre** wanted for murder. **2** (*élégant*) elegant.

rechute [r(ə)ʃyt] *nf* *Méd* relapse.

récidive [residiv] *nf* *Jur* further offence *ou* *Am* offense. ● **récidiver** *vi* *Jur* to commit a further offence *ou* *Am* offense.

récif [resif] *nm* reef.

récipient [resipjɑ̃] *nm* container, receptacle.

réciproque [resiprɔk] *a* mutual, reciprocal. ●**—ment** *adv* (*l'un l'autre*) each other; **et r.** and vice versa.

récit [resi] *nm* (*histoire*) story; (*compte rendu*) account.

récital, *pl* -**als** [resital] *nm Mus* recital.

réciter [resite] *vt* to recite. ●**récitation** *nf* (*poème*) poem (*learnt by heart and recited aloud*).

réclame [reklam] *nf* advertising; (*annonce*) advertisement; **en r.** *Com* on (special) offer.

réclamer [reklame] *vt* (*demander*) to ask for (*sth*) back; (*revendiquer*) to claim ▮ *vi* to complain. ●**réclamation** *nf* complaint; (**bureau des**) **réclamations** complaints department.

reclasser [r(ə)klɑse] *vt* (*fiches etc*) to reclassify.

reclus, -use [rəkly, -yz] *a* (*vie*) cloistered.

réclusion [reklyzjɔ̃] *nf* imprisonment; **r. à perpétuité** life imprisonment.

recoin [rəkwɛ̃] *nm* nook, recess.

recoller [r(ə)kɔle] *vt* (*objet cassé*) to stick back together; (*enveloppe*) to stick back down.

récolte [rekɔlt] *nf* (*action*) harvest; (*produits*) crop, harvest. ●**récolter** *vt* to harvest, gather (in).

recommand/er [r(ə)kɔmɑ̃de] *vt* (*appuyer, conseiller*) to recommend (**à** to, **pour** for); **r. à qn de faire** to recommend s.o. to do; **lettre recommandée** registered letter. ●**—é** *nm* **envoyer en r.** to send by registered post ou mail. ●**recommandable** *a* **peu r.** not very commendable. ●**recommandation** *nf* (*appui, conseil*) recommendation.

recommencer [r(ə)kɔmɑ̃se] *vti* to start ou begin again.

récompense [rekɔ̃pɑ̃s] *nf* reward (**pour** for); (*prix*) award; **en r. de** in return for. ●**récompenser** *vt* to reward (**de, pour** for).

réconcilier (se) [sərekɔ̃silje] *vpr* to settle one's differences, make it up (**avec** with). ●**réconciliation** *nf* reconciliation.

reconduire* [r(ə)kɔ̃dɥir] *vt* **r. qn** to see ou take s.o. back; (**à la porte**) to show s.o. out.

réconfort [rekɔ̃fɔr] *nm* comfort. ●**réconforter** *vt* to comfort; (*revigorer*) to fortify. ●**réconfortant** *a* comforting; (*boisson etc*) fortifying.

reconnaissant [r(ə)kɔnɛsɑ̃] *a* grateful (**à qn de qch** to s.o. for sth). ●**reconnaissance¹** *nf* (*gratitude*) gratitude.

reconnaître* [r(ə)kɔnɛtr] *vt* to recognize (**à qch** by sth); (*admettre*) to admit, acknowledge (**que** that); (*terrain*) *Mil* to reconnoitre; **être reconnu coupable** to be found guilty ▮ **se r.** *vpr* (*s'orienter*) to find one's bearings. ●**reconnu** *a* (*chef, fait*) acknowledged, recognized. ●**reconnaissance²** *nf* recognition; (*aveu*) acknowledgment; *Mil* reconnaissance; **r. de dette** IOU.

reconstituant [r(ə)kɔ̃stitɥɑ̃] *adj* (*aliment, régime*) which restores one's strength.

reconstituer [r(ə)kɔ̃stitɥe] *vt* (*armée, parti*) to reconstitute; (*crime, quartier*) to reconstruct; (*faits*) to piece together.

reconstruire* [r(ə)kɔ̃strɥir] *vt* (*ville, fortune*) to rebuild.

reconvertir [r(ə)kɔ̃vertir] **1** *vt* (*bâtiment etc*) to reconvert. **2 se reconvertir** *vpr* to take up a new form of employment.

recopier [r(ə)kɔpje] *vt* to copy out.

record [r(ə)kɔr] *nm & a inv Sp* record.

recoudre* [r(ə)kudr] *vt* (*bouton*) to sew (back) on; (*vêtement*) to stitch (up).

recouper [r(ə)kupe] *vt* (*témoignage etc*) to tally with, confirm ▮ **se r.** *vpr* to tally, match ou tie up.

recourbé [r(ə)kurbe] *a* (*clou etc*) bent; (*nez*) hooked.

recours [r(ə)kur] *nm* recourse (**à** to); **avoir r. à** to resort to; (*personne*) to turn to; **notre dernier r.** our last resort. ●**recourir*** *vi* **r. à** to resort to; (*personne*) to turn to.

recouvrer [r(ə)kuvre] *vt* (*santé*) to recover.

recouvrir* [r(ə)kuvrir] vt (livre, meuble, sol etc) to cover; (de nouveau) to re-cover.

récréation [rekreasjɔ̃] nf recreation; (temps) Scol break, playtime.

recroquevillé [rəkrɔkvije] a (personne, papier etc) curled up.

recrudescence [rəkrydesɑ̃s] nf new out-break (de of).

recrue [rəkry] nf recruit. ● **recruter** vt to recruit. ● **recrutement** nm recruitment.

rectangle [rektɑ̃gl] nm rectangle. ● **rectangulaire** a rectangular.

rectifier [rektifje] vt (erreur etc) to correct, rectify; (ajuster) to adjust. ● **rectification** nf correction, rectifica-tion.

recto [rekto] nm front (of the page); r. verso (on) both sides (of the page).

reçu [r(ə)sy] pp de **recevoir** ▮ a (idée) conventional, received; (candidat) successful ▮ nm (écrit) Com receipt.

recueil [r(ə)kœj] nm (ouvrage) antho-logy, collection (de of).

recueillir* [r(ə)kœjir] **1** vt to collect, gather; (suffrages) to win, get; (pren-dre chez soi) to take (s.o.) in. **2 se recueillir** vpr to meditate; (devant un monument) to stand in silence.

recul [r(ə)kyl] nm (d'armée, de négocia-teur) retreat; (éloignement) distance; **avoir un mouvement de r.** (personne) to recoil.

reculer [r(ə)kyle] vi to move ou step back; Aut to reverse; (armée) to re-treat; **r. devant** Fig to shrink from ▮ vt to push ou move back; (différer) to postpone.

reculons (à) [ar(ə)kylɔ̃] adv backwards.

récupérer [rekypere] vt (objet prêté) to get back, recover; (ferraille etc) to salvage ▮ vi to get one's strength back, recover.

récurer [rekyre] vt (casserole etc) to scrub, scour; **poudre à r.** scouring powder.

recycler [r(ə)sikle] vt (matériaux) to recycle ▮ **se r.** vpr to retrain. ● **recyc-**

-lage nm recycling, retraining.

rédacteur, -trice [redaktœr, -tris] nmf writer; (de journal) editor; **r. en chef** editor (in chief). ● **rédaction** nf (action) writing; (de contrat) drawing up; (de-voir de français) essay, composition; (journalistes) editorial staff.

redemander [rədmɑ̃de] vt (pain etc) to ask for more; **r. qch à qn** to ask s.o. for sth back.

redescendre [r(ə)desɑ̃dr] vi (aux être) to come ou go back down ▮ vt (aux avoir) (objet) to bring ou take back down.

redevable [r(ə)dəvabl] a **être r. de qch à qn** (argent) to owe s.o. sth; Fig to be indebted to s.o. for sth.

redevance [r(ə)dəvɑ̃s] nf (taxe) TV licence fee; Tél rental charge.

rediffusion [rədifyzjɔ̃] nf (de film etc) repeat.

rédiger [rediʒe] vt to write; (contrat) to draw up.

redire* [r(ə)dir] **1** vt to repeat. **2** vi **avoir ou trouver à r. à qch** to find fault with sth.

redonner [r(ə)dɔne] vt to give back; (donner plus) to give more (bread etc); **r. un franc/etc** to give another franc/etc.

redoubler [r(ə)duble] vti **1** to increase; **r. de patience/etc** to be much more pa-tient/etc. **2** vt (une classe) to repeat a year ou Am a grade. ● **—ant, -ante** nmf pupil repeating a year ou Am a grade. ● **—ement** nm repeating a year ou Am a grade.

redouter [r(ə)dute] vt to dread (de faire doing). ● **—able** a formidable.

redresser [r(ə)drese] vt (objet tordu etc) to straighten (out); (économie, situa-tion) to put right ▮ **se r.** vpr (se mettre assis) to sit up; (debout) to stand up; (pays, situation etc) to put itself right, right itself.

réduction [redyksjɔ̃] nf reduction (de in); (prix réduit) discount; **en r.** (copie, modèle etc) small-scale.

réduire* [redɥir] vt to reduce (à to, de

by); **r. en cendres** to reduce to ashes; **se r. à** (*se ramener à*) to come down to, amount to ▌*vi* (**faire**) **r.** (*sauce*) to reduce, boil down. ●**réduit 1** *a* (*prix, vitesse*) reduced; (*modèle*) small-scale. **2** *nm* (*pièce*) *Péj* tiny room, cubbyhole.

réécrire [reekrir] *vt* (*texte*) to rewrite.

rééduquer [reedyke] *vt* (*membre*) *Méd* to re-educate; **r. qn** to rehabilitate s.o. ●**rééducation** *nf* re-education; rehabilitation.

réel, -elle [reɛl] *a* real ▌*nm* **le r.** reality. ●**réellement** *adv* really.

réexpédier [reɛkspedje] *vt* (*faire suivre*) to forward (*letter*); (*à l'envoyeur*) to return.

refaire* [r(ə)fɛr] *vt* (*exercice, travail*) to do again, redo; (*chambre*) to do up, redo; (*erreur, voyage*) to make again.

réfectoire [refɛktwar] *nm* refectory.

référendum [referᾶdɔm] *nm* referendum.

référer [refere] *vi* en **r. à** to refer the matter to ▌**se r.** *vpr* **se r. à** to refer to s.o. ●**référence** *nf* reference.

refermer [r(ə)fɛrme] *vt*, **se r.** *vpr* to close (again).

refiler [r(ə)file] *vt* (*donner*) *Fam* to palm off (à on).

réfléchir [refleʃir] **1** *vt* (*image*) to reflect ▌**se r.** *vpr* to be reflected. **2** *vi* (*penser*) to think (à about). ●**réfléchi** *a* (*personne*) thoughtful; (*décision*) carefully thought-out; (*verbe*) *Gram* reflexive.

reflet [r(ə)flɛ] *nm* (*image*) & *Fig* reflection; (*lumière*) glint; (*couleur*) tint. ●**refléter** *vt* (*image, sentiment etc*) to reflect ▌**se r.** *vpr* to be reflected.

réflexe [reflɛks] *nm* & *a* reflex.

réflexion [reflɛksjɔ̃] *nf* **1** (*de lumière etc*) reflection. **2** (*méditation*) thought, reflection; (*remarque*) remark; **r. faite** on second thoughts *ou* Am thought.

reflux [rəfly] *nm* (*de la mer*) ebb; (*de la foule*) backward surge.

réforme *nf* (*changement*) reform. ●**réformer 1** *vt* to reform ▌**se r.** *vpr* to mend one's ways. **2** *vt* (*soldat*) to discharge as unfit.

refouler [r(ə)fule] *vt* to force *ou* drive back; (*sentiment*) to repress; (*larmes*) to hold back.

réfractaire [refrakter] *a* **r. à** resistant to.

refrain [r(ə)frɛ̃] *nm* (*de chanson*) chorus, refrain.

réfrigérer [refriʒere] *vt* to refrigerate. ●**réfrigérateur** *nm* refrigerator.

refroidir [r(ə)frwadir] *vt* to cool (down); (*décourager*) *Fig* to put off; (*ardeur*) to cool, damp(en) ▌*vi* to get cold, cool down ▌**se r.** *vpr* (*prendre froid*) *Fam* to catch cold; (*temps*) to get cold. ●**refroidissement** *nm* cooling; (*rhume*) chill; **r. de la température** fall in the temperature.

refuge [r(ə)fyʒ] *nm* refuge; (*pour piétons*) (traffic) island; (*de montagne*) (mountain) hut. ●**se réfugier** *vpr* to take refuge. ●**réfugié, -ée** *nmf* refugee.

refus [r(ə)fy] *nm* refusal; **ce n'est pas de r.** *Fam* I won't say no. ●**refuser** *vt* to refuse (*qch à qn* s.o. sth, *de faire* to do); (*offre, invitation*) to turn down, refuse; (*candidat*) to fail ▌**se r.** *vpr* (*plaisir etc*) to deny oneself; **se r. à croire**/etc to refuse to believe/*etc.*

regagner [r(ə)gaɲe] *vt* (*récupérer*) to regain, get back; (*revenir à*) to get back to. ●**regain** *nm* **avec un r. d'énergie**/etc with renewed energy/*etc.*

régaler (se) [səregale] *vpr* to have a feast.

regard [rəgar] *nm* **1** (*coup d'œil, expression*) look; (*fixe*) stare; **jeter un r. sur** to glance at; **chercher du r.** to look (a)round for. **2 au r. de** in regard to.

regarder [rəgarde] **1** *vt* to look at; (*fixement*) to stare at; (*observer*) to watch; (*considérer*) to consider, regard (**comme** as); **r. qn faire qch** to watch s.o. do sth ▌*vi* to look; to stare; to watch; **r. à** (*dépense, qualité etc*) to pay attention to ▌**se r.** *vpr* (*personnes*) to look at each other.

2 *vt* (*concerner*) to concern; **ça ne te regarde pas!** it's none of your business!

régates [regat] *nfpl* regatta.
régie [reʒi] *nf* (*entreprise*) state-owned company; *Th* stage management; *Cin* TV production department.
régime [reʒim] *nm* 1 (*politique*) (form of) government; *Péj* régime. 2 *Méd* diet; **se mettre au r.** to go on a diet; **suivre un r.** to be on a diet. 3 (*de moteur*) speed; **à ce r.** *Fig* at this rate. 4 (*de bananes, dattes*) bunch.
régiment [reʒimã] *nm Mil* regiment.
région [reʒjɔ̃] *nf* region, area. ● **régional, -aux** *a* regional.
régisseur [reʒisœr] *nm* (*de propriété*) steward; *Th* stage manager; *Cin* assistant director.
registre [rəʒistr] *nm* register.
règle [regl] 1 *nf* (*principe*) rule; **en r.** (*papiers d'identité etc*) in order; **être en r.** avec qn to be right with s.o.; **r. générale** as a (general) rule. 2 *nf* (*instrument*) ruler. 3 *nfpl* (*de femme*) (monthly) period.
règlement [regləmã] *nm* 1 (*règles*) regulations; **contraire au r.** against the rules *ou Am* the rule. 2 (*de conflit, problème etc*) settling; (*paiement*) payment; **r. de comptes** *Fig* (violent) settling of scores. ● **réglementer** *vt* to regulate.
régler [regle] 1 *vt* (*problème etc*) to settle; (*mécanisme*) to adjust, regulate; (*moteur*) to tune. 2 *vti* (*payer*) to pay; **r. qn** to settle up with s.o.; **r. son compte à qn** *Fig* to settle old scores with s.o.
réglable [reglabl] *a* (*siège etc*) adjustable. ● **réglage** *nm* adjustment; (*de moteur*) tuning.
réglisse [reglis] *nf* liquorice, *Am* licorice.
règne [rɛɲ] *nm* (*de roi etc*) reign; (*animal, minéral, végétal*) kingdom. ● **régner** *vi* (*roi, silence*) to reign (**sur** over); (*prédominer*) to prevail; **faire r. l'ordre** to maintain (law and) order.
régresser [regrese] *vi* to regress.
regret [r(ə)grɛ] *nm* regret; **à r.** with regret; **être au r. de faire** to be sorry to do. ● **regretter** *vt* to regret; **r. qn** to

miss s.o.; **r. que** (+ *sub*) to be sorry that, regret that; **je (le) regrette** I'm sorry. ● **regrettable** *a* unfortunate, regrettable.
regrouper [r(ə)grupe] *vt*, **se r.** *vpr* to gather together.
régulariser [regylarize] *vt* (*situation*) to regularize.
régulier, -ière [regylje, -jɛr] *a* regular; (*progrès, vitesse*) steady; (*légal*) legal. ● **régularité** *nf* regularity; steadiness; legality. ● **régulièrement** *adv* regularly; (*normalement*) normally.
réhabiliter [reabilite] *vt* (*dans l'estime publique*) to rehabilitate.
réimpression [reɛ̃presjɔ̃] *nf* (*livre*) reprint.
rein [rɛ̃] *nm* kidney; *pl* (*dos*) (small of the) back; **r. artificiel** *Méd* kidney machine.
reine [rɛn] *nf* queen.
reine-claude [rɛnklod] *nf* greengage.
réintégrer [reɛ̃tegre] *vt* 1 (*fonctionnaire etc*) to reinstate. 2 (*lieu*) to return to.
réitérer [reitere] *vt* to repeat.
rejaillir [r(ə)ʒajir] *vi* to spurt (up *ou* out); **r. sur** *Fig* to rebound on.
rejet [r(ə)ʒɛ] *nm* (*refus*) & *Méd* rejection. ● **rejeter** *vt* to throw back; (*refuser*) & *Méd* to reject; **r. une erreur/etc sur qn** to put the blame for a mistake/etc on s.o.
rejoindre* [r(ə)ʒwɛ̃dr] *vt* (*famille, lieu etc*) to get *ou* go back to; (*route, rue*) to join; **r. qn** (*se joindre à*) to join *ou* meet s.o.; (*rattraper*) to catch up with s.o. ‖ **se r.** *vpr* (*personnes, routes*) to meet.
réjouir (se) [səreʒwir] *vpr* to be delighted (**de** at, about; **de faire** to do). ● **réjouissance** *nf* rejoicing; *pl* festivities.
relâche [r(ə)laʃ] *nf Th Cin* (temporary) closure; **faire r.** (*théâtre, cinéma*) to close; **sans r.** without a break.
relâcher [r(ə)laʃe] 1 *vt* (*corde etc*) to slacken; (*discipline, étreinte*) to relax; **r. qn** to release s.o. ‖ **se r.** *vpr* to slacken; (*discipline*) to get lax. 2 *vi* (*bateau*) to put in.

relais [r(ə)lɛ] *nm* *Él Rad TV* relay; **(course de) r.** *Sp* relay (race); **prendre le r.** to take over (**de** from).

relancer [r(ə)lɑ̃se] *vt* to throw back; (*moteur*) to restart; (*industrie etc*) to put back on its feet; **r. qn** (*solliciter*) to pester s.o.

relatif, -ive [r(ə)latif, -iv] *a* relative (**à** to). ● **relativement** *adv* (*assez*) relatively.

relation [r(ə)lɑsjɔ̃] *nf* (*rapport*) relation(ship); (*ami*) acquaintance; **entrer en relations avec** to come into contact with; **avoir des relations** (*amis influents*) to have connections.

relax(e) [rəlaks] *a* *Fam* relaxed, informal.

relaxer (se) [sər(ə)lakse] *vpr* to relax.

relayer [r(ə)leje] *vt* to take over from (*s.o.*), relieve (*s.o.*); (*émission*) to relay ▮ **se r.** *vpr* to take (it in) turns (**pour faire** to do).

relève [r(ə)lɛv] *nf* (*remplacement*) relief; **prendre la r.** to take over (**de** from).

relever [rəlve] *vt* to raise; (*personne tombée*) to help up; (*col*) to turn up; (*manches*) to roll up; (*compteur*) to read; (*cahiers, copies*) to collect; (*copier*) to note down; (*faute*) to pick *ou* point out; (*traces*) to find; (*défi*) to accept; (*sauce*) to season. ▮ *vi* **r. de** (*dépendre de*) to come under; (*maladie*) to get over. ▮ **se relever** *vpr* (*personne tombée*) to get up. ● **relevé** *nm* list; (*de compteur*) reading; **r. de compte** (*bank*) statement.

relief [rəljɛf] *nm* (*forme*) relief; **en r.** (*cinéma*) three-D; (*livre*) pop-up; **mettre en r.** *Fig* to highlight.

relier [rəlje] *vt* to connect, link (**à** to); (*livre*) to bind.

religion [r(ə)liʒjɔ̃] *nf* religion; (*foi*) faith. ● **religieux, -euse** *a* religious; **mariage r.** church wedding ▮ *nm* monk. ● **religieuse** *nf* 1 nun. 2 *Culin* cream bun.

relique [rəlik] *nf* relic.

relire* [r(ə)lir] *vt* to read again, reread.

reliure [rəljyr] *nf* (*de livre*) binding; (*art*) bookbinding.

reluire* [r(ə)lɥir] *vi* to shine, gleam. ● **reluisant** *a* shiny; **peu r.** *Fig* far from brilliant.

remanier [r(ə)manje] *vt* (*texte*) to revise; (*ministère*) to reshuffle.

remarier (se) [sər(ə)marje] *vpr* to remarry.

remarquable [rəmarkabl] *a* remarkable (**par** for). ● **—ment** [-əmã] *adv* remarkably.

remarque [r(ə)mark] *nf* remark; (*écrite*) note; **je lui en ai fait la r.** I remarked on it to him *ou* her.

remarquer [rəmarke] *vt* 1 (*apercevoir*) to notice (**que** that); **faire r.** to point out (**à** to, **que** that); **se faire r.** to attract attention; **remarque!** mind you!, you know! 2 (*dire*) to remark (**que** that).

remblayer [rɑ̃bleje] *vt* (*route*) to bank up; (*trou*) to fill in.

rembobiner [rɑ̃bɔbine] *vt*, **se r.** *vpr* (*bande*) to rewind.

rembourré [rɑ̃bure] *a* (*fauteuil etc*) padded.

rembourser [rɑ̃burse] *vt* to pay back, repay; (*billet*) to refund. ● **remboursement** *nm* repayment; refund; **envoi contre r.** cash on delivery.

remède [r(ə)mɛd] *nm* cure, remedy; (*médicament*) medicine. ● **remédier** *vi* **r. à** to remedy.

remémorer (se) [sər(ə)memɔre] *vpr* (*histoire etc*) to recollect, recall.

remercier [r(ə)mɛrsje] *vt* 1 to thank (**de** *qch*, **pour** *qch* for sth); **je vous remercie d'être venu** thank you for coming; **je vous remercie** (*non merci*) no thank you. 2 (*congédier*) to dismiss. ● **remerciements** *nmpl* thanks.

remettre* [r(ə)mɛtr] *vt* to put back, replace; (*vêtement*) to put back on; (*donner*) to hand over (**à** to); (*restituer*) to give back (**à** to); (*démission, devoir*) to hand in; (*différer*) to postpone (**à** until); (*ajouter*) to add more *ou* another; **r. en question** *ou* **cause** to call into question; **r. en état** to repair; **r. ça** *Fam* to start again; **se r. à** (*activité*) to go back to; **se r. à faire** to start to do again; **se r. de** (*chagrin, maladie*) to get over, recover from; **s'en r. à** to rely on.

remise [r(ə)miz] *nf* 1 (*rabais*) discount. 2 **r. de peine** *Jur* remission. 3 (*local*) shed; *Aut* garage.

remmener [rãmne] *vt* to take back.

remonte-pente [r(ə)mɔ̃tpãt] *nm* ski lift.

remonter [r(ə)mɔ̃te] *vi* (*aux* **être**) to come *ou* go back up; (*niveau, prix*) to rise again; (*dans le temps*) to go back (**à** to); **r. dans** (*voiture*) to get *ou* go back in(to); (*bus, train*) to get *ou* go back on(to); **r. sur** (*cheval, vélo*) to get back on(to); **r. à dix ans**/*etc* to go back ten years/*etc*.

▌ *vt* (*aux* **avoir**) (*escalier, pente*) to come *ou* go back up; (*porter*) to bring *ou* take back up; (*montre*) to wind up; (*relever*) to raise; (*col*) to turn up; (*objet démonté*) to put back together; **r. le moral à qn** to cheer s.o. up. ●**remontée** *nf* 1 (*de pente etc*) ascent; (*d'eau, de prix*) rise. 2 **r. mécanique** ski lift. ●**remontoir** *nm* (*de mécanisme, montre*) winder.

remontrance [r(ə)mɔ̃trãs] *nf* reprimand; **faire des remontrances à** to reprimand.

remords [r(ə)mɔr] *nm & nmpl* remorse; **avoir des r.** to feel remorse.

remorque [r(ə)mɔrk] *nf Aut* trailer; **prendre en r.** to tow; **en r.** on tow, *Am* in tow. ●**remorquer** *vt* (*voiture, bateau*) to tow. ●**remorqueur** *nm* tug(boat).

remous [r(ə)mu] *nm* eddy; (*de foule*) bustle.

rempart [rãpar] *nm* rampart.

remplacer [rãplase] *vt* to replace (**par** with, **by**); (*succéder à*) to take over from; (*temporairement*) to stand in for. ●**remplaçant, -ante** *nmf* (*personne*) replacement; (*enseignant*) substitute teacher; *Sp* reserve. ●**remplacement** *nm* replacement; **assurer le r. de qn** to stand in for s.o.; **en r. de** in place of.

remplir [rãplir] *vt* to fill (up) (**de** with); (*fiche etc*) to fill in *ou* out; (*condition, devoir*) to fulfil; (*fonctions*) to perform

▌ se r. *vpr* to fill (up). ●**rempli** *a* full (**de** of). ●**remplissage** *nm* filling; (*verbiage*) *Péj* padding.

remporter [rãpɔrte] *vt* 1 (*objet*) to take back. 2 (*prix, victoire*) to win; (*succès*) to achieve.

remuer [r(ə)mɥe] *vt* to move; (*café etc*) to stir; (*salade*) to toss; (*terre*) to turn over **▌** *vi* to move; (*gigoter*) to fidget **▌ se r.** *vpr* to move; (*se démener*) *Fig* to go to a lot of trouble. ●**remuant** *a* (*enfant*) restless, fidgety. ●**remue-ménage** *nm inv* commotion.

rémunérer [remynere] *vt* (*personne*) to pay; (*travail*) to pay for. ●**rémunération** *nf* payment (**de** for).

renaître* [r(ə)netr] *vi* (*fleur*) to grow again; (*espoir, industrie*) to revive.

renard [r(ə)nar] *nm* fox.

renchérir [rãʃerir] *vi* **r. sur ce que qn dit**/*etc* to go further than s.o. in what one says/*etc*.

rencontre [rãkɔ̃tr] *nf* meeting; (*inattendue*) encounter; *Sp* match, *Am* game; **aller à la r. de qn** to go to meet s.o. ●**rencontrer** *vt* to meet; (*difficulté, obstacle*) to come up against, encounter; (*équipe*) *Sp* to play **▌ se r.** *vpr* to meet.

rendement [rãdmã] *nm Agr* yield; *Fin* return, yield (*de personne, machine*) output.

rendez-vous [rãdevu] *nm inv* appointment; (*d'amoureux*) date; (*lieu*) meeting place; **donner r.-vous à qn, prendre r.-vous avec qn** to make an appointment with s.o.

rendormir* (**se**) [sərãdɔrmir] *vpr* to go back to sleep.

rendre [rãdr] *vt* (*restituer*) to give back, return; (*monnaie*) to give; (*hommage*) to pay; (*justice*) to dispense; (*armes*) to surrender; **r. célèbre/plus grand**/*etc* to make famous/bigger/*etc* **▌** *vti* (*vomir*) to throw up **▌ se r.** *vpr* (*capituler*) to surrender (**à** to); (*aller*) to go (**à** to); **se r. à** (*évidence, ordres*) to submit to; **se r. utile**/*etc* to make oneself useful/*etc*.

rênes [ren] *nfpl* reins.

renfermer [rɑ̃fɛrme] *vt* to contain ▮ **se r.** *vpr* **se r. (en soi-même)** to withdraw into oneself. ● **renfermé 1** *a* (*personne*) withdrawn. **2** *nm* **sentir le r.** (*chambre etc*) to smell stuffy.

renflement [rɑ̃fləmɑ̃] *nm* bulge.

renflouer [rɑ̃flue] *vt* (*navire*) & *Com* to refloat.

renfoncement [rɑ̃fɔ̃smɑ̃] *nm* recess; **dans le r. d'une porte** in a doorway.

renforcer [rɑ̃fɔrse] *vt* to strengthen, reinforce. ● **renfort** *nm* **des renforts** (*troupes*) reinforcements; **de r.** (*personnel*) back-up; **à grand r. de** *Fig* with (the help of) a great deal of.

renfrogner (se) [sərɑ̃frɔɲe] *vpr* to scowl.

renier [rənje] *vt* (*ami*, *pays etc*) to disown; (*foi*, *opinion*) to renounce.

renifler [r(ə)nifle] *vti* to sniff.

renne [rɛn] *nm* reindeer.

renom [rənɔ̃] *nm* (*popularité*) renown; (*réputation*) reputation (**de for**). ● **renommé** *a* famous, renowned (**pour for**). ● **renommée** *nf* fame.

renoncer [r(ə)nɔ̃se] *vi* **r. à qch** to give sth up, abandon sth; **r. à faire** to give up (the idea of) doing.

renouer [rənwe] **1** *vt* (*lacet etc*) to retie. **2** *vt* (*reprendre*) to renew ▮ *vi* **r. avec qch** (*tradition etc*) to revive sth; **r. avec qn** to take up with s.o. again.

renouveau, -x [r(ə)nuvo] *nm* revival.

renouveler [r(ə)nuvle] *vt* to renew; (*erreur*, *question*) to repeat ▮ **se r.** *vpr* (*incident*) to happen again; (*cellules*, *sang*) to be renewed. ● **renouvelable** *a* renewable. ● **renouvellement** *nm* renewal.

rénover [renɔve] *vt* (*édifice*, *meuble etc*) to renovate.

renseigner [rɑ̃sɛɲe] *vt* to inform, give some information to (**sur** about) ▮ **se r.** *vpr* to find out, inquire (**sur** about). ● **renseignement** *nm* (piece of) information; *pl* information; **les renseignements** (*au téléphone*) directory inquiries, *Am* information; **prendre** *ou* **demander des renseignements** to make inquiries.

rentable [rɑ̃tabl] *a* profitable. ● **rentabilité** *nf* profitability.

rente [rɑ̃t] *nf* (*private*) income; (*pension*) pension; **avoir des rentes** to have private means.

rentrée [rɑ̃tre] *nf* **1** (*retour*) return; (*d'acteur*) comeback; **r. (des classes)** beginning of term *ou* of the school year. **2 rentrées** (*argent*) receipts.

rentrer [rɑ̃tre] *vi* (*aux être*) to go *ou* come back, return; (*chez soi*) to go *ou* come (back) home; (*entrer*) to go *ou* come in; (*entrer de nouveau*) to go *ou* come back in; **r. dans** (*entrer dans*) to go *ou* come into; (*entrer de nouveau dans*) to go *ou* come back into; (*pays*) to return to; (*heurter*) to crash into; (*s'emboîter dans*) to fit into; (*catégorie*) to come under; **r. (en classe)** to go back to school.

▮ *vt* (*aux* **avoir**) to bring *ou* take in; (*voiture*) to put away; (*chemise*) to tuck in; (*griffes*) to draw in.

renverse (à la) [alarɑ̃vɛrs] *adv* (*tomber*) backwards.

renverser [rɑ̃vɛrse] *vt* (*mettre à l'envers*) to turn upside down; (*faire tomber*) to knock over *ou* down; (*piéton*) to knock down; (*liquide*) to spill, knock over; (*gouvernement*) to overthrow; (*tête*) to tip back ▮ **se r.** *vpr* (*bouteille*, *vase etc*) to fall over; (*liquide*) to spill. ● **renversement** *nm* (*de situation*) reversal.

renvoi [rɑ̃vwa] *nm* dismissal; expulsion; postponement; (*dans un livre*) (cross) reference. ● **renvoyer*** *vt* to send back, return; (*employé*) to dismiss; (*élève*) to expel; (*balle etc*) to throw back; (*ajourner*) to postpone (**à** until); (*lumière*, *image etc*) to reflect; **r. qn à** (*adresser à*) to refer s.o. to.

réorganiser [reɔrganize] *vt* to reorganize.

réouverture [reuvɛrtyr] *nf* reopening.

repaire [r(ə)pɛr] *nm* den.

répandre [repɑ̃dr] *vt* (*liquide*) to spill; (*nouvelle*) to spread; (*odeur*) to give off; (*lumière*, *larmes*, *chargement*) to shed;

(*gravillons etc*) to scatter ▮ **se r.** *vpr* (*nouvelle etc*) to spread; (*liquide*) to spill; **se r. dans** (*fumée, odeur*) to spread through. ● **répandu** *a* (*opinion, usage*) widespread; (*épars*) scattered.

reparaître [r(ə)parɛtr] *vi* to reappear.

réparer [repare] *vt* to repair, mend; (*erreur*) to put right; (*forces*) to restore; (*faute*) to make amends for. ● **réparateur, -trice** *nmf* repairer. ● **réparation** *nf* repair; **en r.** under repair.

repartir* [r(ə)partir] *vi* (*aux être*) to set off again; (*s'en retourner*) to go back; (*reprendre*) to start again; **r. à** *ou* **de zéro** to go back to square one.

répartir [repartir] *vt* to distribute; (*partager*) to share (out); (*classer*) to divide (up); (*étaler dans le temps*) to spread (out) (**sur** over). ● **répartition** *nf* distribution; sharing, division.

repas [r(ə)pɑ] *nm* meal; **prendre un r.** to have *ou* eat a meal.

repass/er [r(ə)pɑse] **1** *vi* to come *ou* go back ▮ *vt* (*traverser*) to go back over; (*examen*) to take again; (*leçon*) to go over; (*film*) to show again; (*bande magnétique*) to play back. **2** *vt* (*linge*) to iron. ● **—age** *nm* ironing.

repêcher [r(ə)peʃe] *vt* (*objet*) to fish out; (*candidat*) Fam to allow to pass.

repentir* (**se**) [sər(ə)pɑtir] *vpr* to be sorry (**de** for).

répercuter [reperkyte] *vt* (*son*) to echo ▮ **se r.** *vpr* to echo, reverberate.

repère [r(ə)pɛr] *nm* (*guide*) mark; (*jalon*) marker; **point de r.** (*espace, temps*) landmark. ● **repérer** *vt* (*remarquer*) Fam to spot ▮ **se r.** *vpr* to get one's bearings.

répertoire [repɛrtwar] *nm* **1** index; (*carnet*) (indexed) notebook; (*de fichiers*) Ordinat directory; **r. d'adresses** address book. **2** Th repertoire.

répéter [repete] *vti* to repeat; Th to rehearse ▮ **se r.** *vpr* (*radoter*) to repeat oneself; (*événement*) to happen again. ● **répétitif, -ive** *a* repetitive. ● **répétition** *nf* repetition; Th rehearsal; **r. générale**

Th (final) dress rehearsal.

repiquer [r(ə)pike] *vt* (*disque*) to tape, record (on tape).

répit [repi] *nm* rest; **sans r.** ceaselessly.

replacer [r(ə)plase] *vt* to replace, put back.

repli [r(ə)pli] *nm* fold; Mil withdrawal.

replier [r(ə)plije] **1** *vt* to fold (up); (*couverture*) to fold back; (*ailes, jambes*) to tuck in ▮ **se r.** *vpr* (*siège*) to fold up; (*couverture*) to fold back. **2 se replier** *vpr* Mil to withdraw; **se r. sur soi-même** Fig to withdraw into oneself.

réplique [replik] *nf* **1** (*réponse*) (sharp) reply; Th lines; **sans r.** (*argument*) irrefutable. **2** (*copie*) replica. ● **répliquer** *vt* to reply (sharply) (**que** that) ▮ *vi* (*être impertinent*) to answer back.

répondre [repɔdr] *vi* to answer, reply; (*être impertinent*) to answer back; **r. à qn** to answer s.o., reply to s.o.; (*avec impertinence*) to answer s.o. back; (*à lettre, question*) to answer, reply to; (*besoin*) to meet, answer; **r. de** (*garantir*) to answer for (*s.o., sth*). ▮ *vt* (*remarque etc*) to answer *ou* reply with; **r. que** to answer *ou* reply that. ● **répondeur** *nm* Tél answering machine.

réponse [repɔs] *nf* answer, reply; **en r. à** in answer *ou* reply to

reporter[1] [r(ə)pɔrte] *vt* to take back; (*différer*) to put off, postpone (**à** until); (*transcrire*) to transfer (**sur** to); **se r. à** (*texte etc*) to refer to. ● **reportage** *nm* (*news*) report, article; (*en direct*) commentary; (*métier*) reporting.

reporter[2] [r(ə)pɔrter] *nm* reporter.

repos [r(ə)po] *nm* rest; (*tranquillité*) peace (and quiet); (*de l'esprit*) peace of mind; **r.!** Mil at ease!; **jour de r.** day off; **de tout r.** (*situation etc*) safe.

reposer [r(ə)poze] **1** *vt* (*objet*) to put back down; (*problème, question*) to raise again. **2** *vt* (*délasser*) to rest, relax; **r. sa tête sur** (*appuyer*) to rest one's head on ▮ *vi* (*être enterré*) to rest, lie; **r. sur** (*bâtiment*) to be built on;

(*théorie etc*) to be based on, rest on ‖ **se r.** *vpr* to rest; **se r. sur qn** to rely on s.o. ●**reposant** *a* restful, relaxing.

repousser [r(ə)puse] **1** *vt* to push back; (*écarter*) to push away; (*attaque*) to beat off; (*différer*) to put off, postpone. **2** *vi* (*cheveux, feuilles*) to grow again.

reprendre* [r(ə)prɑ̃dr] *vt* (*objet*) to take back; (*évadé, ville*) to recapture; (*souffle*) to get back; (*activité*) to take up again, resume; (*refrain*) to take up; (*vêtement*) to alter; (*corriger*) to correct; (*pièce*) Th to put on again; **r. de la viande/un œuf/etc** to take some more meat/another egg/*etc*; **r. des forces** to get one's strength back; **r. ses esprits** to come round.

‖ *vi* (*plante*) to take root again; (*recommencer*) to start (up) again, resume; (*affaires*) to pick up; (*parler*) to go on.

‖ **se reprendre** *vpr* (*se ressaisir*) to get a grip on oneself; (*se corriger*) to correct oneself; **s'y r. à deux fois** to have another go (at it).

représenter [r(ə)prezɑ̃te] *vt* to represent; (*pièce de théâtre*) to perform ‖ **se r.** *vpr* (*s'imaginer*) to imagine. ●**représentant, -ante** *nmf* representative; **r. de commerce** (travelling) salesman *ou* saleswoman, sales representative. ●**représentation** *nf* representation; Th performance.

répression [represjɔ̃] *nf* suppression, repression; (*mesures de contrôle*) Pol repression. ●**réprimer** *vt* (*sentiment, révolte etc*) to suppress, repress.

repris [r(ə)pri] *nm* **r. de justice** hardened criminal.

reprise [r(ə)priz] *nf* (*recommencement*) resumption; Rad TV repeat; (*de pièce de théâtre*) revival; (*raccommodage*) mend; Boxe round; (*économique*) recovery, revival; (*d'un locataire*) money for fittings; (*de marchandise*) taking back; (*pour nouvel achat*) part exchange, trade-in; *pl* Aut acceleration;

à plusieurs reprises on several occasions. ●**repriser** *vt* (*chaussette etc*) to mend, darn.

réprobation [reprɔbasjɔ̃] *nf* disapproval.

reproche [r(ə)prɔʃ] *nm* criticism, reproach; **faire des reproches à qn** to criticize s.o.; **sans r.** beyond reproach. ●**reprocher** *vt* **r. qch à qn** to criticize *ou* blame *ou* reproach s.o. for sth.

reproduire* [r(ə)prɔdɥir] **1** *vt* (*modèle etc*) to copy, reproduce ‖ **se r.** *vpr* (*animaux*) to breed, reproduce. **2** **se reproduire** *vpr* (*incident etc*) to happen again. ●**reproduction** *nf* breeding, reproduction; (*copie*) copy.

reptile [rɛptil] *nm* reptile.

repu [rəpy] *a* (*rassasié*) satiated.

république [repyblik] *nf* republic. ●**républicain, -aine** *a* & *nmf* republican.

répugnant [repyɲɑ̃] *a* repulsive, disgusting. ●**répugnance** *nf* disgust, repugnance (**pour** for); (*manque d'enthousiasme*) reluctance. ●**répugner** *vi* **r. à qn** to be repulsive to s.o.; **r. à faire** to be loath to do.

réputation [repytasjɔ̃] *nf* reputation; **avoir la r. d'être franc** to have a reputation for being frank *ou* for frankness. ●**réputé** *a* (*célèbre*) renowned (**pour** for); **r. pour être** reputed to be.

requête [rəkɛt] *nf* request; Jur petition. ●**requis** *a* required.

requin [r(ə)kɛ̃] *nm* (*poisson*) & Fig shark.

réquisitoire [rekizitwar] *nm* (*critique*) indictment (**contre** of).

RER [ɛrøɛr] *nm abrév* (*Réseau express régional*) = express rail network serving Paris and its suburbs.

rescapé, -ée [rɛskape] *nmf* survivor.

rescousse (à la) [alarɛskus] *adv* to the rescue.

réseau, -x [rezo] *nm* network.

réserve [rezɛrv] *nf* **1** (*provision*) stock, reserve; (*entrepôt*) storeroom; **en r.** in reserve. **2** (*de chasse, pêche*) preserve; (*indienne*) reservation; **r. naturelle** nature reserve. **3** (*discrétion*) reserve;

(*restriction*) reservation; **sans r.** (*admiration etc*) unqualified; **sous r. de** subject to; **sous toutes réserves** without guarantee.

réserv/er [rezerve] *vt* (*garder*) to save, reserve (**à** for); (*place, table*) to book, reserve; (*surprise etc*) to hold in store (**à** for); **se r. pour** to save oneself for. ●**-é** *a* (*personne, place*) reserved. ●**réservation** *nf* reservation, booking.

réservoir [rezervwar] *nm* (*citerne*) tank; **r. d'essence** *Aut* petrol *ou Am* gas tank.

résidence [rezidɑ̃s] *nf* residence; **r. secondaire** second home; **r. universitaire** hall of residence, *Am* dormitory. ●**résidentiel, -ielle** (*quartier*) residential. ●**résider** *vi* to be resident, reside (**à, en, dans** in).

résidu [rezidy] *nm* residue, waste.

résigner (se) [səreziɲe] *vpr* to resign oneself (**à qch** to sth, **à faire** to doing).

résilier [rezilje] *vt* (*contrat*) to terminate.

résine [rezin] *nf* resin.

résistance [rezistɑ̃s] *nf* resistance (**à** to); (*conducteur*) *Él* (heating) element; **plat de r.** main dish.

résist/er [reziste] *vi* **r. à** to resist (*chaleur, fatigue*) to withstand; (*se défendre contre*) to stand up to. ●**-ant, -ante** *a* tough; **r. à la chaleur** heat-resistant; **r. au choc** shockproof ▮*nmf Mil Hist* Resistance fighter.

résolu [rezɔly] *pp de* **résoudre** ▮*a* determined, resolute; **r. à faire** determined to do. ●**résolution** *nf* (*décision*) decision; (*fermeté*) determination.

résonner [rezɔne] *vi* (*cris etc*) to ring out; (*salle*) to echo (**de** with).

résorber [rezɔrbe] *vt* (*chômage*) to reduce; (*excédent*) to absorb.

résoudre [rezudr] *vt* (*problème*) to solve; (*difficulté*) to clear up, resolve; **se r. à faire** (*se résigner*) to bring oneself to do.

respect [rɛspɛ] *nm* respect (**pour, de** for); **mes respects à** my regards *ou* respects to. ●**respecter** *vt* to respect; **qui se** respecte self-respecting. ●**respectueux, -euse** *a* respectful (**envers** to, **de** of).

respectif, -ive [rɛspɛktif, -iv] *a* respective.

respirer [rɛspire] *vi* to breathe; (*reprendre haleine*) to get one's breath back; (*être soulagé*) to breathe again ▮*vt* to breathe (in); (*exprimer*) *Fig* to exude, radiate. ●**respiration** *nf* breathing; (*haleine*) breath; **r. artificielle** *Méd* artificial respiration.

resplendissant [rɛsplɑ̃disɑ̃] *a* (*visage*) glowing (**de** with).

responsable [rɛspɔ̃sabl] *a* responsible (**de qch** for sth, **devant qn** to s.o.) ▮*nmf* (*chef*) person in charge; (*dans une organisation*) official; (*coupable*) person responsible (**de** for). ●**responsabilité** *nf* responsibility; (*légale*) liability.

resquiller [rɛskije] *vi* (*au cinéma, dans le métro etc*) to avoid paying; (*sans attendre*) to jump the queue, *Am* cut in (line).

ressaisir (se) [sər(ə)sezir] *vpr* to pull oneself together.

ressasser [r(ə)sase] *vt* (*ruminer*) to keep going over; (*répéter*) to keep trotting out.

ressemblance [r(ə)sɑ̃blɑ̃s] *nf* likeness, resemblance (**avec** to). ●**ressembler** *vi* **r. à** to look *ou* be like, resemble; **cela ne lui ressemble pas** that's not like him *ou* her ▮**se r.** *vpr* to look *ou* be alike.

ressentir* [r(ə)sɑ̃tir] *vt* to feel.

resserrer [r(ə)sere] *vt* (*nœud, boulon etc*) to tighten; (*liens*) *Fig* to strengthen ▮**se r.** *vpr* to tighten; (*route etc*) to narrow.

resservir [r(ə)servir] *vi* (*outil etc*) to come in useful (again). **2 se resservir** *vpr* **se r. de** (*plat etc*) to have another helping of.

ressort [r(ə)sɔr] *nm* **1** (*objet*) spring. **2 du r. de** within the competence of; **en dernier r.** (*décider etc*) as a last resort.

ressortir* [r(ə)sɔrtir] *vi* (*aux être*) **1** to go *ou* come back out. **2** (*se voir*) to stand out; **faire r.** to bring out.

ressortissant, -ante [r(ə)sɔrtisɑ̃, -ɑ̃t] *nmf (citoyen)* national.

ressource [r(ə)surs] *nfpl (moyens)* resources; *(argent)* means, resources.

ressusciter [resysite] *vi* to rise from the dead; *(malade, pays)* to recover, revive.

restant [restɑ̃] *a* remaining; **poste restante** poste restante, *Am* general delivery.

restaurant [restɔrɑ̃] *nm* restaurant.

restaurer [restɔre] **1** *vt (réparer, rétablir)* to restore. **2 se restaurer** *vpr* to (have something to) eat. ● **restaurateur, -trice** *nmf (hôtelier, hôtelière)* restaurant owner. ● **restauration** *nf* **1** restoration. **2** *(hôtellerie)* catering.

reste [rest] *nm* rest, remainder (**de** of); *Math* remainder; *pl (de repas)* leftovers; **un r. de fromage/***etc* some left-over cheese/*etc*; **au r., du r.** moreover, besides.

rester [reste] *vi (aux être)* to stay, remain; *(calme, jeune etc)* to keep, stay, remain; *(subsister)* to stay, remain; **il reste du pain/***etc* there's some bread/*etc* left (over); **il me reste une minute/***etc* I have one minute/*etc* left; **l'argent qui lui reste** the money he ou she has left; **reste à savoir** it remains to be seen; **en r. à** to stop at; **restons-en là** let's leave it at that.

restituer [restitɥe] *vt (rendre)* to return, restore (**à** to).

restreindre* [restrɛ̃dr] *vt* to limit, restrict (**à** to) ▌ **se r.** *vpr (faire des économies)* to cut back ou down. ● **restriction** *nf* restriction; **sans r.** unreservedly.

résultat [rezylta] *nm (score, d'examen etc)* result; *(conséquence)* outcome, result.

résumer [rezyme] *vt* to summarize; *(situation)* to sum up ▌ **se r.** *vpr (orateur etc)* to sum up; **se r. à** *(se réduire à)* to boil down to. ● **résumé** *nm* summary; **en r.** in short; *(en récapitulant)* to sum up.

rétablir [retablir] *vt* to restore; *(vérité)* to re-establish ▌ **se r.** *vpr* to be restored;

(malade) to recover. ● **rétablissement** *nm Méd* recovery.

retaper [r(ə)tape] *vt (maison, voiture etc)* to do up.

retard [r(ə)tar] *nm* lateness; *(sur un programme etc)* delay; **en r.** late; *(retardé)* backward; **en r. dans qch** behind in sth; **en r. sur qn/qch** behind s.o./sth; **rattraper son r.** to catch up; **avoir du r.** to be late; *(sur un programme)* to be behind (schedule); *(montre)* to be slow; **avoir une heure de r.** to be an hour late; **prendre du r.** *(montre)* to lose (time). ● **retardataire** *nmf* latecomer. ● **retardement** *nm* **bombe à r.** time bomb.

retard/er [r(ə)tarde] *vt* to delay; *(date, montre, départ)* to put back; **r. qn** *(dans une activité)* to put s.o. behind ▌ *vi (montre)* to be slow; **r. de cinq minutes** to be five minutes slow. ● **—é, -ée** *a (enfant)* backward.

retenir* [rətnir] *vt (empêcher d'agir, contenir)* to hold back; *(souffle)* to hold; *(réserver)* to book; *(se souvenir de)* to remember; *(fixer)* to hold (in place); *(chiffre) Math* to carry; *(chaleur, odeur)* to retain; *(candidature, proposition)* to accept; **r. qn prisonnier** to keep s.o. prisoner.

▌ **se retenir** *vpr (se contenir)* to restrain oneself; **se r. de faire** to stop oneself (from) doing; **se r. à** to cling to.

retent/ir [r(ə)tɑ̃tir] *vi* to ring (out) (**de** with). ● **—issant** *a* resounding; *(scandale)* major.

retenue [rətny] *nf* **1** *(modération)* restraint. **2** *(de salaire)* deduction; *(chiffre) Math* figure carried over. **3** *(punition) Scol* detention; **en r. in** detention.

réticent [retisɑ̃] *a (réservé)* reticent; *(hésitant)* reluctant.

retirer [r(ə)tire] *vt (sortir)* to take out; *(ôter)* to take off; *(éloigner)* to take away; *(plainte, candidature, argent)* withdraw; **r. qch à qn** *(permis etc)* to take sth away from s.o.; **r. qch de**

(*gagner*) to derive sth from ‖ **se r.** *vpr* to withdraw, retire (**de** from); (*mer*) to ebb.

retomber [r(ə)tɔ̃be] *vi* to fall (again); (*pendre*) to hang (down); (*après un saut*) to land; (*intérêt*) to slacken; **r. dans l'erreur** to be wrong again; **r. sur qn** (*responsabilité*) to fall on s.o. ● **retombées** *nfpl* (*radioactive*) fallout.

rétorsion [retɔrsjɔ̃] *nf Pol* retaliation; **mesure de r.** reprisal.

retouche [r(ə)tuʃ] *nf* alteration; touching up. ● **retoucher** *vt* (*vêtement*) to alter; (*photo, tableau*) to touch up.

retour [r(ə)tur] *nm* return; (*de fortune*) reversal; **être de r.** to be back (**de** from); **en r.** (*en échange*) in return; **par r.** (*du courrier*) by return (*of post*), *Am* by return mail; **à mon retour** when I get *ou* got back (**de** from); **r. en arrière** flashback; **match r.** return match *ou Am* game.

retourner [r(ə)turne] *vt* (*aux avoir*) (*matelas, steak etc*) to turn over; (*terre*) to turn; (*vêtement, sac etc*) to turn inside out; (*tableau etc*) to turn round; (*compliment, lettre*) to return; **r. contre qn** (*argument*) to turn against s.o.; (*arme*) to turn on s.o. ‖ *vi* (*aux être*) to go back, return. ‖ **se retourner** *vpr* (*pour regarder*) to turn round, look round; (*sur le dos*) to turn over *ou* round; (*dans son lit*) to toss and turn; (*voiture*) to overturn; **se r. contre** *Fig* to turn against.

rétracter [retrakte] *vt*, **se r.** *vpr* to retract.

retrait [r(ə)trɛ] *nm* withdrawal; (*de bagages*) collection; **en r.** (*maison etc*) set back.

retraite [r(ə)trɛt] *nf* **1** (*d'employé*) retirement; (*pension*) (retirement) pension; (*refuge*) retreat; **r. anticipée** early retirement; **prendre sa r.** to retire; **à la r.** retired; **mettre à la r.** to pension off. **2** *Mil* retreat; **r. aux flambeaux** torchlight tattoo. ● **retraité, -ée** *a* retired ‖ *nmf* senior citizen, pensioner.

retrancher [r(ə)trɑ̃ʃe] *vt* **1** (*passage etc*)

to cut (**de** from); (*argent, quantité*) to deduct (**de** from). **2 se retrancher** *vpr* **se r. dans/derrière** *Fig* to take refuge in/behind.

retransmettre [r(ə)trɑ̃smɛtr] *vt* to broadcast. ● **retransmission** *nf* broadcast.

rétrécir [retresir] *vt* to narrow; (*vêtement*) to take in ‖ *vi* (*au lavage*) to shrink ‖ **se r.** *vpr* (*rue etc*) to narrow.

rétribuer [retribɥe] *vt* to pay, remunerate; (*travail*) to pay for.

rétro [retro] *a inv* (*personne, idée etc*) old-fashioned.

rétroactif, -ive [retroaktif, -iv] *a* (*mesure etc*) retrospective; **augmentation avec effet r.** retroactive (pay) increase.

rétrograde [retrograd] *a* retrograde. ● **rétrograder** *vi* (*reculer*) to move back; *Aut* to change down ‖ *vt* (*fonctionnaire, officier*) to demote.

rétrospectif, -ive [retrospektif, -iv] *a* retrospective ‖ *nf* (*de films*) retrospective. ● **rétrospectivement** *adv* in retrospect.

retrouss/er [r(ə)truse] *vt* (*manches*) to roll up ● **—é** *a* (*nez*) turned-up.

retrouver [r(ə)truve] *vt* to find (again); (*rejoindre*) to meet (again); (*forces, santé*) to get back, regain; (*se rappeler*) to recall ‖ **se r.** *vpr* (*se trouver*) to find oneself (back); (*se rencontrer*) to meet (again), **s'y r.** (*s'orienter*) to find one's way *ou* bearings.

rétroviseur [retrovizœr] *nm Aut* (rearview) mirror.

réunion [reynjɔ̃] *nf* (*séance*) meeting; (*jonction*) joining. ● **réunir** *vt* (*objets*) to collect, gather; (*convoquer*) to call together, assemble; (*relier*) to join; (*rapprocher*) to bring together; (*qualités etc*) to combine.

réuss/ir [reysir] *vi* to succeed, be successful (**à faire** in doing); **r. à** (*examen*) to pass; **r. à qn** to work (out) well for s.o.; (*aliment, climat*) to agree with s.o. ‖ *vt* to make a success of. ● **—i** *a* successful. ● **réussite** *nf* **1** success. **2 faire des réussites** *Cartes* to play patience.

revaloir [r(ə)valwar] *vt* **je vous le revaudrai** (*en bien ou en mal*) I'll pay you back.

revaloriser [r(ə)valɔrize] *vt* to revalue; (*salaires etc*) to raise.

revanche [rəvɑ̃ʃ] *nf* revenge; *Sp* return game; **en r.** on the other hand.

rêve [rɛv] *nm* dream; **faire un r.** to have a dream; **maison de r.** dream house.

revêche [rəvɛʃ] *a* bad-tempered, surly.

réveil [revɛj] *nm* waking (up); *Fig* awakening; (*pendule*) alarm (clock); **à son r.** when he wakes (up) *ou* woke (up).

réveiller [reveje] *vt* (*personne*) to wake (up); (*sentiment, souvenir*) *Fig* to revive, awaken ▮ **se r.** *vpr* to wake (up); *Fig* to revive, awaken. ●**réveillé** *a* awake. ●**réveille-matin** *nm inv* alarm (clock).

réveillon [revɛjɔ̃] *nm* (*repas*) midnight supper (*on Christmas Eve or New Year's Eve*). ●**réveillonner** *vi* to take part in a *réveillon*.

révéler [revele] *vt* to reveal (**que that**) ▮ **se r.** to be revealed; **se r. facile**/*etc* to turn out to be easy/*etc*. ●**révélation** *nf* revelation.

revenant [rəvnɑ̃] *nm* ghost.

revendiquer [r(ə)vɑ̃dike] *vt* to claim; (*exiger*) to demand. ●**revendication** *nf* claim; demand.

revendre [r(ə)vɑ̃dr] *vt* to resell. ●**revendeur, -euse** *nmf* retailer; (*d'occasion*) secondhand dealer; **r. (de drogue)** drug pusher; **r. de billets** ticket tout.

revenir* [rəvnir] *vi* (*aux être*) to come back, return; (*mot*) to come *ou* crop up; (*coûter*) to cost (**à qn** s.o.); **r. à** (*activité, sujet*) to go back to, return to; (*se résumer à*) to boil down to; **r. à qn** (*forces, mémoire*) to come back to s.o., return to s.o.; **r. à soi** to come round *ou* to; **r. de** (*surprise*) to get over; **r. sur** (*décision, promesse*) to go back on; (*passé, question*) to go back over; **r. sur ses pas** to retrace one's steps; **faire r.** (*aliment*) to brown.

revenu [rəvny] *nm* income (**de** from); (*d'un État*) revenue (**de** from); **déclaration de revenus** tax return.

rêv/er [reve] *vi* to dream (**de** of, **de faire** of doing) ▮ *vt* to dream (**que** that). ●**-é** *a* ideal.

réverbération [reverberasjɔ̃] *nf* (*de lumière*) reflection.

réverbère [reverber] *nm* street lamp.

révérence [reverɑ̃s] *nf* reverence; (*salut d'homme*) bow; (*salut de femme*) curts(e)y; **faire une r.** to bow; to curts(e)y.

rêverie [revri] *nf* daydream; (*activité*) daydreaming.

revers [r(ə)ver] *nm* (*de veste*) lapel; (*de pantalon*) turn-up, *Am* cuff; (*d'étoffe*) wrong side; *Tennis* backhand; (*coup du sort*) setback; **le r. de la médaille** *Fig* the other side of the coin.

réversible [reversibl] *a* reversible.

revêtir* [r(ə)vetir] *vt* to cover (**de** with); (*habit*) to put on; (*route*) to surface. ●**revêtement** *nm* (*surface*) covering; (*de route*) surface.

rêveur, -euse [revœr, -øz] *nmf* dreamer.

revient [rəvjɛ̃] *nm* **prix de r.** cost price.

revirement [r(ə)virmɑ̃] *nm* (*changement*) about-turn, *Am* about-face; (*de situation, d'opinion, de politique*) reversal.

réviser [revize] *vt* (*leçon*) to revise; (*machine, voiture*) to service, overhaul; (*jugement*) to review. ●**révision** *nf* revision; service, overhaul; review.

revivre* [r(ə)vivr] *vi* to live again; **faire r.** to revive ▮ *vt* (*incident etc*) to relive.

révocation [revɔkasjɔ̃] *nf* (*de fonctionnaire*) dismissal.

revoir* [r(ə)vwar] *vt* to see (again); (*texte, leçon*) to revise; **au r.** goodbye.

révolte [revɔlt] *nf* rebellion, revolt. ●**révolter 1** *vt* to sicken. **2 se révolter** *vpr* to rebel, revolt (**contre** against). ●**révoltant** *a* (*honteux*) revolting. ●**révolté, -ée** *nmf* rebel.

révolu [revɔly] *a* (*époque*) past; **avoir trente ans révolus** to be over thirty (years of age).

révolution [revɔlysjɔ̃] *nf* (*changement,*

rotation) revolution. ● **révolutionnaire** *a* & *nmf* revolutionary.

revolver [revɔlvɛr] *nm* gun, revolver.

révoquer [revɔke] *vt* (*fonctionnaire*) to dismiss.

revue [r(ə)vy] *nf* **1** (*magazine*) magazine; (*spécialisée*) journal. **2** (*de music-hall*) variety show. **3** *Mil* review; **passer en r.** to review.

rez-de-chaussée [redʃose] *nm inv* ground floor, *Am* first floor.

rhabiller (se) [sərabije] *vpr* to get dressed again.

Rhin [rɛ̃] *nm* **le R.** the Rhine.

rhinocéros [rinɔserɔs] *nm* rhinoceros.

rhubarbe [rybarb] *nf* rhubarb.

rhum [rɔm] *nm* rum.

rhumatisme [rymatism] *nm Méd* rheumatism; **avoir des rhumatismes** to have rheumatism.

rhume [rym] *nm* cold; **r. de cerveau** head cold; **r. des foins** hay fever.

ri [ri] *pp de* **rire**.

riant [rjɑ̃] *p prés de* **rire** ‖ *a* cheerful, smiling.

ricaner [rikane] *vi* (*sarcastiquement*) to snigger, *Am* snicker; (*bêtement*) to giggle.

riche [riʃ] *a* rich; (*personne, pays*) rich, wealthy; **r. en** (*vitamines etc*) rich in ‖ *nmf* rich *ou* wealthy person; **les riches** the rich. ● **richesse** *nf* wealth; (*de sol, vocabulaire*) richness; *pl* (*trésor*) riches; (*ressources*) wealth.

ricocher [rikɔʃe] *vi* to rebound, ricochet. ● **ricochet** *nm* rebound, ricochet.

rictus [riktys] *nm* grin, grimace.

ride [rid] *nf* wrinkle; ripple. ● **rider** *vt* (*visage*) to wrinkle; (*eau*) to ripple ‖ **se r.** *vpr* to wrinkle. ● **ridé** *a* wrinkled.

rideau, -x [rido] *nm* curtain; (*de magasin*) shutter; (*écran*) *Fig* screen (**de** of).

ridicule [ridikyl] *a* ridiculous ‖ *nm* (*moquerie*) ridicule; (*de situation etc*) ridiculousness; **tourner en r.** to ridicule. ● **se ridiculiser** *vpr* to make a fool of oneself.

rien [rjɛ̃] *pron* nothing; **il ne sait r.** he

knows nothing, he doesn't know anything; **r. du tout** nothing at all; **r. d'autre/de bon/***etc* nothing else/good/*etc*; **r. de tel** nothing like it; **de r.!** (*je vous en prie*) don't mention it!; **ça ne fait r.** it doesn't matter; **pour r.** (*à bas prix*) for next to nothing; **r. que** just, only ‖ *nm* (*mere*) nothing, trifle; **un r.** de a hint *ou* touch of; **en un r. de temps** (*vite*) in no time.

rieur, -euse [rijœr, -øz] *a* cheerful.

rigide [riʒid] *a* rigid; (*carton, muscle*) stiff; (*personne*) *Fig* inflexible; (*éducation*) strict.

rigole [rigɔl] *nf* (*conduit*) channel; (*filet d'eau*) rivulet.

rigoler [rigɔle] *vi Fam* to laugh; (*s'amuser*) to have fun; (*plaisanter*) to joke (**avec** about). ● **rigolade** *nf Fam* fun; (*chose ridicule*) joke, farce. ● **rigolo, -ote** *a Fam* funny.

rigueur [rigœr] *nf* rigour; harshness; strictness; (*précision*) precision; **être de r.** to be the rule; **à la r.** if absolutely necessary. ● **rigoureux, -euse** *a* rigorous; (*climat, punition*) harsh; (*personne, morale, sens*) strict.

rillettes [rijet] *nfpl* potted minced pork.

rime [rim] *nf* rhyme. ● **rimer** *vi* to rhyme (**avec** with); **ça ne rime à rien** it makes no sense.

rincer [rɛ̃se] *vt* to rinse; (*verre*) to rinse (out). ● **rinçage** *nm* rinsing; (*opération*) rinse.

ring [riŋ] *nm* (*boxing*) ring.

ringard [rɛ̃gar] *a* (*démodé*) *Fam* old-fashioned, unfashionable.

riposte [ripost] *nf* (*réponse*) retort; (*attaque*) counter(attack).

rire* [rir] *vi* to laugh (**de** at); (*s'amuser*) to have a good time; (*plaisanter*) to joke; **faire qch pour r.** to do sth for a joke *ou* a laugh ‖ *nm* laugh; *pl* laughter; **le r.** (*activité*) laughter; **le fou r.** the giggles.

ris [ri] *nm* **r. de veau** *Culin* (calf) sweetbread.

risque [risk] *nm* risk; **au r. de faire qch** at

the risk of doing sth; **les risques du métier** occupational hazards; **à vos risques et périls** at your own risk; **assurance tous risques** comprehensive insurance. ●**risquer** *vt* to risk; *(question, regard)* to venture, hazard; **r. de faire** to stand a good chance of doing. ●**risqué** *a* risky.

ristourne [risturn] *nf* discount.

rite [rit] *nm* rite; *(habitude) Fig* ritual.

rivage [rivaʒ] *nm* shore.

rival, -ale, -aux [rival, -o] *a* & *nmf* rival. ●**rivaliser** *vi* to compete (**avec** with, **de** in). ●**rivalité** *nf* rivalry.

rive [riv] *nf* *(de fleuve)* bank; *(de lac)* shore.

riverain, -aine [rivrɛ̃, -ɛn] *nmf* riverside resident; *(de lac)* lakeside resident; *(de rue)* resident.

rivière [rivjɛr] *nf* river.

riz [ri] *nm* rice; **r. au lait** rice pudding. ●**rizière** *nf* paddy (field), ricefield.

RMI [ɛrɛmi] *nm abrév (Revenu minimum d'insertion)* = income support, *Am* = welfare.

RN *abrév* = route nationale.

robe [rɔb] *nf* *(de femme)* dress; *(d'ecclésiastique, de juge)* robe; **r. du soir** evening dress *ou* gown; **r. de grossesse/ de mariée** maternity/wedding dress; **r. de chambre** dressing gown, *Am* bathrobe.

robinet [rɔbinɛ] *nm* tap, *Am* faucet; **eau du r.** tap water.

robot [rɔbo] *nm* robot; **r. ménager** food processor, liquidizer.

robuste [rɔbyst] *a* sturdy, robust.

roc [rɔk] *nm* rock.

rocaille [rɔkaj] *nf* *(terrain)* rocky ground. ●**rocailleux, -euse** *a* rocky, stony.

roche [rɔʃ] *nf* *(substance)* rock. ●**rocher** *nm* *(bloc)* rock. ●**rocheux, -euse** *a* rocky.

rock [rɔk] *nm* *(musique)* rock ‖ *a inv* **chanteur/opéra r.** rock singer/opera.

rod/er [rɔde] *vt (moteur, voiture)* to run in, *Am* break in. ●**-age** *nm* running in,

Am breaking in.

rôd/er [rode] *vi* to roam (about); *(suspect)* to prowl (about). ●**-eur, -euse** *nmf* prowler.

rogner [rɔɲe] *vt* to trim, clip ‖ *vi* **r. sur** *(réduire)* to cut down on.

rognon [rɔɲɔ̃] *nm Culin* kidney.

roi [rwa] *nm* king; **fête** *ou* **jour des rois** Twelfth Night.

rôle [rol] *nm* role, part; *(d'un père etc)* job; **à tour de r.** in turn.

romain, -aine [rɔmɛ̃, -ɛn] **1** *a* & *nmf* Roman. **2** *nf* *(laitue)* cos (lettuce), *Am* romaine.

roman [rɔmɑ̃] **1** *nm* novel; **r. d'aventures** adventure story; **r.-fleuve** saga. **2** *a (langue)* Romance; *Archit* Romanesque. ●**romancier** *nm* novelist.

romanichel, -elle [rɔmaniʃɛl] *nmf* gipsy.

romantique [rɔmɑ̃tik] *a* romantic.

romarin [rɔmarɛ̃] *nm Bot Culin* rosemary.

rompre* [rɔ̃pr] *vt* to break; *(pourparlers, relations)* to break off ‖ *vi* to break *(Fig* **avec** with); *(fiancés)* to break it off ‖ **se r.** *vpr (corde etc)* to break; *(digue)* to burst. ●**rompu** *a* **1** *(fatigué)* exhausted. **2** **r. à** *(expérimenté)* experienced in.

romsteck [rɔmstɛk] *nm* rump steak.

ronces [rɔ̃s] *nfpl (branches)* brambles.

rond [rɔ̃] *a* round; *(gras)* plump; *(ivre) Fam* tight ‖ *adv* **tourner r.** *(machine etc)* to run smoothly; **dix francs tout r.** ten francs exactly ‖ *nm (cercle)* circle, ring; **en r.** *(s'asseoir etc)* in a ring *ou* circle; **tourner en r.** *(toupie etc)* & *Fig* to go round and round. ●**r.-point** *nm* *(pl* **ronds-points)** *Aut* roundabout, *Am* traffic circle. ●**ronde** *nf (de soldat)* round; *(de policier)* beat, round; *(danse)* round (dance); **à la r.** around. ●**rondelle** *nf (tranche)* slice. ●**rondement** *adv (efficacement)* briskly. ●**rondin** *nm* log.

ronfler [rɔ̃fle] *vi* to snore; *(moteur)* to hum. ●**ronflement** *nm* snore; hum; *pl* snoring; humming.

rong/er [rɔ̃ʒe] *vt* to gnaw (at); *(ver, mer,*

rouille) to eat into (*sth*); **r. qn** (*maladie*) to consume s.o.; **se r. les ongles** to bite one's nails. ●—**eur** *nm* (*animal*) rodent.

ronronnement [rɔ̃rɔnmɑ̃] *nm* purr(ing). ●**ronronner** *vi* to purr.

roquefort [rɔkfɔr] *nm* Roquefort (cheese).

roquette [rɔkɛt] *nf* Mil rocket.

rosbif [rɔsbif] *nm* **du r.** (*rôti*) roast beef; (*à rôtir*) roasting beef; **un r.** a joint of roast *ou* roasting beef.

rose [roz] **1** *nf* (*fleur*) rose. **2** *a* (*couleur*) pink; (*situation, teint*) rosy ‖ *nm* pink. ●**rosé** *a* pinkish ‖ *a* & *nm* (*vin*) rosé. ●**rosier** *nm* rose bush.

roseau, -x [rozo] *nm* (*plante*) reed.

rosée [roze] *nf* dew.

rosser [rɔse] *vt* to thrash.

rossignol [rɔsiɲɔl] *nm* (*oiseau*) nightingale.

rot [ro] *nm* Fam burp. ●**roter** *vi* Fam to burp.

rotation [rɔtasjɔ̃] *nf* rotation.

rotin [rɔtɛ̃] *nm* cane, rattan.

rôtir [rotir] *vti*, **se r.** *vpr* to roast; **faire r.** to roast. ●**rôti** *nm* **du r.** roasting meat; (*cuit*) roast meat; **un r.** a joint; **r. de porc** (*joint of*) roast pork. ●**rôtissoire** *nf* (*roasting*) spit.

rotule [rɔtyl] *nf* kneecap.

rouage [rwaʒ] *nm* (*de montre etc*) (working) part; (*d'organisation etc*) Fig cog.

roucouler [rukule] *vi* to coo.

roue [ru] *nf* wheel.

rouer [rwe] *vt* **r. qn de coups** to beat s.o. black and blue.

rouet [rwɛ] *nm* spinning wheel.

rouge [ruʒ] *a* red; (*fer*) red-hot ‖ *nm* (*couleur*) red; (*vin*) Fam red wine; (*à lèvres*) lipstick; **r. (à joues)** rouge; **le feu est au r.** Aut the (traffic) lights are red. ●**r.-gorge** *nm* (*pl* **rouges-gorges**) robin. ●**rougeur** *nf* redness; (*due à la gêne ou à la honte*) blush(ing); *pl* Méd rash, red spots. ●**rougir** *vi* (*de honte*) to blush (**de** with), go red; (*de colère, de joie*) to flush (**de** with), go red.

rougeole [ruʒɔl] *nf* measles.

rouget [ruʒɛ] *nm* (*poisson*) mullet.

rouille [ruj] *nf* rust ‖ *a inv* (*couleur*) rust(-coloured). ●**rouiller** *vi* to rust ‖ **se r.** *vpr* to rust; (*esprit, sportif etc*) Fig to get rusty. ●**rouillé** *a* rusty.

rouleau, -x [rulo] *nm* (*outil, vague*) roller; (*de papier, pellicule etc*) roll; **r. à pâtisserie** rolling pin; **r. compresseur** steamroller.

roulement [rulmɑ̃] *nm* (*bruit*) rumbling, rumble; (*de tambour, de tonnerre*) roll; (*ordre*) rotation; **par r.** in rotation.

rouler [rule] *vt* to roll; (*brouette*) to push, wheel; (*crêpe, ficelle, manches etc*) to roll up; **r. qn** (*duper*) Fam to cheat s.o. ‖ *vi* to roll; (*train, voiture*) to go, travel; (*conducteur*) to drive ‖ **se r.** *vpr* to roll; **se r. dans** (*couverture etc*) to roll oneself (up) in. ●**roulant** *a* (*escalier*) moving; (*meuble*) on wheels; **chaise roulante** wheelchair.

roulette [rulɛt] *nf* (*de meuble*) castor; (*de dentiste*) drill; (*jeu*) roulette.

roulis [ruli] *nm* (*de navire*) roll(ing).

roulotte [rulɔt] *nf* (*de gitan*) caravan.

Roumanie [rumani] *nf* Romania. ●**roumain, -aine** *a* & *nmf* Romanian ‖ *nm* (*langue*) Romanian.

round [rawnd, rund] *nm* Boxe round.

rouspéter [ruspete] *vi* Fam to complain, grumble.

rousse [rus] *voir* **roux.**

rousseur [rusœr] *nf* **tache de r.** freckle. ●**roussir** *vt* (*brûler*) to scorch, singe ‖ *vi* (*feuilles*) to turn brown.

route [rut] *nf* road (**de** to); (*itinéraire*) way, route; (*chemin*) Fig path, way; **r. nationale/départementale** main/secondary road; **grand-r.** main road; **en r.** on the way, en route; **en r.!** let's go!; **par la r.** by road; **sur la bonne r.** Fig on the right track; **mettre en r.** (*voiture etc*) to start (up); **se mettre en r.** to set out (**pour** for); **une heure de r.** an hour's drive; **bonne r.!** Aut have a good trip!

routier, -ière [rutje, -jɛr] *a* **carte/sécurité routière** road map/safety ‖ *nm* (*ca-*

mionneur) (long distance) lorry *ou Am* truck driver.

routine [rutin] *nf* routine; **contrôle de r.** routine check.

rouvrir* [ruvrir] *vti*, **se r.** *vpr* to reopen.

roux, rousse [ru, rus] *a* (*cheveux*) red, ginger; (*personne*) red-haired ‖ *nmf* redhead.

royal, -aux [rwajal, -o] *a* (*famille, palais etc*) royal; (*cadeau, festin etc*) fit for a king. ● **royaume** *nm* kingdom. ● **Royaume-Uni** *nm* United Kingdom. ● **royauté** *nf* monarchy.

ruban [rybã] *nm* ribbon; (*de chapeau*) band; **r. adhésif** sticky *ou* adhesive tape.

rubéole [rybeɔl] *nf* German measles, rubella.

rubis [rybi] *nm* (*pierre*) ruby; (*de montre*) jewel.

rubrique [rybrik] *nf* (*article de journal*) column; (*catégorie, titre*) heading.

ruche [ryʃ] *nf* (bee)hive.

rude [ryd] *a* (*pénible*) tough; (*hiver, voix*) harsh; (*grossier*) crude; (*rêche*) rough. ●**—ment** *adv* (*parler, traiter*) harshly; (*très*) *Fam* awfully.

rudiments [rydimã] *nmpl* rudiments.

rue [ry] *nf* street; **être à la r.** (*sans domicile*) to be on the streets. ● **ruelle** *nf* alley(way).

ruer [rɥe] **1** *vi* (*cheval*) to kick (out). **2 se ruer** *vpr* (*foncer*) to rush, fling oneself (**sur** at). ● **ruée** *nf* rush.

rugby [rygbi] *nm* rugby. ● **rugbyman,** *pl* **-men** [rygbiman, -men] *nm* rugby player.

rug/ir [ryʒir] *vi* to roar. ●**—issement** *nm* roar.

rugueux, -euse [rygø, -øz] *a* rough.

ruine [rɥin] *nf* (*décombres*) & *Fig* ruin; **en r.** (*édifice*) in ruins; **tomber en r.** (*bâtiment*) to become a ruin, crumble; (*mur*) to crumble. ● **ruiner** *vt* (*personne, santé etc*) to ruin ‖ **se r.** *vpr* (*en dépensant*) to be(come) ruined, ruin oneself. ● **ruineux, -euse** *a* ruinous.

ruisseau, -x [rɥiso] *nm* stream; (*caniveau*) gutter. ● **ruisseler** *vi* to stream (**de** with).

rumeur [rymœr] *nf* (*protestation*) clamour; (*murmure*) murmur; (*nouvelle*) rumour.

ruminer [rymine] *vi* (*vache*) to chew the cud.

rupture [ryptyr] *nf* break(ing); (*de fiançailles, relations*) breaking off; (*de pourparlers*) breakdown (**de** in); (*brouille*) break (up), split; (*de contrat*) breach; (*d'organe*) *Méd* rupture.

rural, -aux [ryral, -o] *a* rural; **vie/école/** *etc* **rurale** country life/school/*etc*.

ruse [ryz] *nf* (*subterfuge*) trick; **la r.** (*habileté*) cunning; (*fourberie*) trickery. ● **rusé, -ée** *a* & *nmf* cunning *ou* crafty (person).

Russie [rysi] *nf* Russia. ● **russe** *a* & *nmf* Russian ‖ *nm* (*langue*) Russian.

rustique [rystik] *a* (*meuble*) rustic.

rythme [ritm] *nm* rhythm; (*de travail*) rate; (*de la vie*) pace; **au r. de trois par jour** at a rate of three a day. ● **rythmé** *a* rhythmic(al). ● **rythmique** *a* rhythmic(al).

S

S, s [ɛs] nm S, s.

s' [s] voir **se, si.**

sa [sa] voir **son²**.

SA abrév (société anonyme) Com plc, Am Inc.

sabbat [saba] nm (Jewish) Sabbath.

sable [sabl] nm sand. ● **sabler** vt (route) to sand; **s. le champagne** to celebrate with champagne.

sablé [sable] nm shortbread biscuit ou Am cookie.

sablier [sablije] nm hourglass; Culin egg timer.

sablonneux, -euse [sablɔnø, -øz] a (terrain) sandy.

saborder [sabɔrde] vt (navire) to scuttle.

sabot [sabo] nm 1 (de cheval etc) hoof. 2 (chaussure) clog. 3 (de frein) Aut shoe; **s. (de Denver)** Aut (wheel) clamp.

sabot/er [sabɔte] vt to sabotage; (bâcler) to botch. ● **—age** nm sabotage.

sabre [sabr] nm sabre, sword.

sac [sak] nm 1 bag; (grand et en toile) sack; **s. (à main)** handbag; **s. à dos** rucksack; **s. de voyage** travelling bag. **2 mettre à s.** (ville) Mil to sack.

saccade [sakad] nf jerk, jolt; **par saccades** in fits and starts. ● **saccadé** a (geste, style) jerky.

saccager [sakaʒe] vt (détruire) to wreck.

saccharine [sakarin] nf saccharin.

sacerdoce [saserdɔs] nm (fonction) Rel priesthood; Fig vocation.

sachant, sache(s), sachent etc [saʃɑ̃, saʃ] voir **savoir**.

sachet [saʃɛ] nm (small) bag; **s. de thé** teabag.

sacoche [sakɔʃ] nf bag; (de vélo, moto) saddlebag.

sacre [sakr] nm (de roi) coronation; (d'évêque) consecration. ● **sacrer** vt (roi) to crown; (évêque) to consecrate.

sacré [sakre] a (saint) sacred; **un s. menteur/etc** Fam a damned liar/etc.

sacrifice [sakris] nm sacrifice. ● **sacrifier** vt to sacrifice (à to, pour for) ▌ **se s.** vpr to sacrifice oneself (à to, pour for).

sadisme [sadism] nm sadism. ● **sadique** a sadistic ▌ nmf sadist.

safari [safari] nm safari; **faire un s.** to be ou go on safari.

sage [saʒ] a wise; (enfant) good, well-behaved ▌ nm wise man, sage. ● **sagement** adv wisely; (avec calme) quietly. ● **sagesse** nf wisdom; good behaviour.

sage-femme [saʒfam] nf (pl sages-femmes) midwife.

Sagittaire [saʒiter] nm le S. (signe) Sagittarius.

Sahara [saara] nm le S. the Sahara (desert).

saign/er [seɲe] vti to bleed. ● **—ant** [seɲɑ̃] a (viande) Culin rare. ● **saignement** nm bleeding; **s. de nez** nosebleed.

saillant [sajɑ̃] a projecting, jutting out.

sain [sɛ] a healthy; (moralement) sane; (jugement) sound; (nourriture) wholesome; **s. et sauf** safe and sound, unhurt.

saindoux [sɛdu] nm lard.

saint, sainte [sɛ, sɛt] a holy; (personne) saintly; **s. Jean** Saint John; **la Sainte Vierge** the Blessed Virgin ▌ nmf saint. ● **s.-bernard** nm (chien) St Bernard. ● **S.-Esprit** nm Holy Spirit. ● **S.-Siège** nm Holy See. ● **S.-Sylvestre** nf New Year's Eve.

sais [sɛ] voir **savoir**.

saisie [sezi] nf Jur seizure; **s. de données** Ordinat data capture; **opérateur de s.** keyboard operator.

saisir [sezir] vt 1 to grab (hold of), seize; (occasion) to jump at; (comprendre) to understand; Jur to seize; (frapper) Fig to strike; **se s. de** to grab (hold of), seize. **2** (*viande*) Culin to fry briskly.

saison [sɛzɔ̃] *nf* season; **en/hors s.** in/out of season; **en pleine** *ou* **haute s.** in (the) high season; **en basse s.** in the low season. ● **saisonnier, -ière** *a* seasonal.

salt [se] *voir* **savoir.**

salade [salad] **1** *nf* (*laitue*) lettuce; **s. (verte)** (green) salad; **s. de fruits/etc** fruit/etc salad. **2** *nfpl* (*mensonges*) Fam stories, nonsense. ● **saladier** *nm* salad bowl.

salaire [salɛr] *nm* wage(s), salary.

salaison [salɛzɔ̃] *nf* Culin salting; *pl* (*denrées*) salt(ed) meat *ou* fish.

salarial, -aux [salarjal, -o] *a* **accord/etc s.** wage agreement/etc. ● **salarié, -ée** *a* wage-earning ‖ *nmf* wage earner.

salaud [salo] *nm* Fam Péj bastard, swine.

sale [sal] *a* dirty; (*dégoûtant*) filthy; (*mauvais*) nasty. ● **saleté** *nf* dirtiness; filthiness; (*crasse*) dirt, filth; (*action*) dirty trick; *pl* (*détritus*) rubbish, Am garbage.

sal/er [sale] *vt* Culin to salt. ● **—é** *a* (*goût, plat*) salty; (*aliment*) salted; **eau salée** salt water. ● **salière** *nf* saltcellar, Am saltshaker.

salir [salir] *vt* to (make) dirty; (*réputation*) Fig to tarnish ‖ **se s.** *vpr* to get dirty. ● **salissant** *a* (*métier*) dirty, messy; (*étoffe*) that shows the dirt.

salive [saliv] *nf* saliva.

salle [sal] *nf* room; (*très grande, publique*) hall; Th theatre, auditorium; (*de cinéma*) cinema, Am movie theater; (*d'hôpital*) ward; (*public*) Th audience; **s. à manger** dining room; **s. de bain(s)** bathroom; **s. de classe** classroom; **s. d'embarquement** Av departure lounge; **s. d'exposition** Com showroom; **s. de jeux** (*pour enfants*) games room; (*avec machines à sous*) amusement arcade; **s. d'opération** Méd operating theatre.

salon [salɔ̃] *nm* sitting room, lounge; (*exposition*) show; **s. de beauté/de coiffure** beauty/hairdressing salon; **s. de thé** tearoom(s).

salope [salɔp] *nf* (*femme*) Fam Vulg bitch. ● **saloperie** *nf* Fam (*action*) dirty trick; (*camelote*) junk.

salopette [salɔpɛt] *nf* (*d'enfant, d'ouvrier*) dungarees, Am overalls.

salubre [salybr] *a* healthy. ● **salubrité** *nf* healthiness; **s. publique** public health.

saluer [salɥe] *vt* to greet; (*en partant*) to take one's leave of; (*de la main*) to wave to; (*de la tête*) to nod to; Mil to salute.

salut [saly] **1** *nm* greeting; wave; nod; Mil salute ‖ *int* Fam hello!, hi!; (*au revoir*) bye! **2** *nm* (*de peuple etc*) salvation; (*sauvegarde*) safety. ● **salutation** *nf* greeting; **je vous prie d'accepter mes salutations distinguées** (*dans une lettre*) yours faithfully, Am sincerely.

samedi [samdi] *nm* Saturday.

SAMU [samy] *nm abrév* (*service d'assistance médicale d'urgence*) emergency medical service.

sanction [sɑ̃ksjɔ̃] *nf* (*approbation, peine*) sanction. ● **sanctionner** *vt* (*confirmer, approuver*) to sanction; (*punir*) to punish.

sandale [sɑ̃dal] *nf* sandal.

sandwich [sɑ̃dwitʃ] *nm* sandwich; **s. au fromage/etc** cheese/etc sandwich.

sang [sɑ̃] *nm* blood. ● **sanglant** *a* bloody. ● **sanguin, -ine 1** *a* **vaisseau/groupe s.** blood vessel/group. **2** *nf* (*fruit*) blood orange, ruby-red orange.

sang-froid [sɑ̃frwa] *nm* self-control, calm; **garder son s.-froid** to keep calm; **avec s.-froid** calmly; **de s.-froid** (*tuer*) in cold blood.

sangle [sɑ̃gl] *nf* (*de selle, parachute*) strap.

sanglier [sɑ̃glije] *nm* wild boar.

sanglot [sɑ̃glo] *nm* sob. ● **sangloter** *vi* to sob.

sanitaire [saniter] *a* (*conditions*) sanitary; (*personnel*) medical; **installation s.** bathroom fittings.

sans [sɑ̃] ([sɑ̃z] *before vowel and mute h*) *prép* without; **s. faire** without doing; **s. qu'il le sache** without him *ou* his knowing; **s. cela, s. quoi** otherwise; **s. plus** (but) no more than that; **s. faute** without fail; **s. importance** unimportant; **s. argent** penniless; **ça va s. dire** that goes without saying. ● **s.-abri** nmf inv homeless person; **les s.-abri** the homeless. ● **s.-gêne** a inv inconsiderate ‖ nm inv lack of consideration.

santé [sɑ̃te] nf health; **en bonne/mauvaise s.** in good/bad health; **(à votre) s.!** (en trinquant) (your good) health!, cheers!; **maison de s.** nursing home.

saoul [su] = **soûl.**

saper [sape] vt to undermine.

sapeur-pompier [sapœrpɔ̃pje] nm (pl **sapeurs-pompiers**) fireman.

saphir [safir] nm (pierre) sapphire.

sapin [sapɛ̃] nm (arbre, bois) fir; **s. de Noël** Christmas tree.

sarbacane [sarbakan] nf peashooter.

sarcasme [sarkasm] nm sarcasm; **un s.** a piece of sarcasm.

Sardaigne [sardɛɲ] nf Sardinia.

sardine [sardin] nf sardine.

SARL abrév (société à responsabilité limitée) Ltd, Am Inc.

sarrasin [sarazɛ̃] nm buckwheat.

sas [sɑs] nm Nau Av airlock.

Satan [satɑ̃] nm Satan.

satellite [satelit] nm satellite; **télévision par s.** satellite TV; **antenne s.** satellite dish; **pays s.** satellite (country).

satiété [sasjete] nf **manger/boire à s.** to eat/drink one's fill.

satin [satɛ̃] nm satin.

satire [satir] nf satire (contre on). ● **satirique** a satiric(al).

satisfaction [satisfaksjɔ̃] nf satisfaction. ● **satisfaire*** vt to satisfy (s.o.) ‖ vi **s. à** (conditions etc) to fulfil. ● **satisfaisant** a (acceptable) satisfactory. ● **satisfait** a satisfied, content (de with).

saturer [satyre] vt to saturate (de with).

satyre [satir] nm Fam sex fiend.

sauce [sos] nf sauce; (jus de viande) gravy; **s. tomate** tomato sauce.

saucisse [sosis] nf sausage. ● **saucisson** nm (cold) sausage.

sauf[1] [sof] prép except (que that); **s. avis contraire** unless you hear otherwise; **s. erreur** barring error.

sauf[2], **sauve** [sof, sov] a (honneur) intact; **avoir la vie sauve** to be unharmed.

sauge [soʒ] nf Bot Culin sage.

saule [sol] nm willow; **s. pleureur** weeping willow.

saumon [somɔ̃] nm salmon ‖ a inv (couleur) salmon (pink).

sauna [sona] nm sauna.

saupoudrer [sopudre] vt to sprinkle (de with).

saur [sɔr] am **hareng s.** smoked herring, kipper.

saura, saural etc [sora, sore] voir **savoir.**

saut [so] nm jump, leap; **faire un s.** to jump, leap; **faire un s. chez qn** to drop in on s.o., pop round to s.o.

sauté [sote] a & nm Culin sauté.

sauter [sote] vi to jump, leap; (bombe) to go off, explode; (fusible) to blow; (se détacher) to come off; **faire s.** (détruire) to blow up; (arracher) to tear off; (casser) to break; Culin to sauté; **s. à la corde** to skip, Am jump rope; **ça saute aux yeux** it's obvious ‖ vt (franchir) to jump (over); (mot, repas, classe) to skip. ● **saute-mouton** nm (jeu) leapfrog.

sauterelle [sotrel] nf grasshopper.

sautiller [sotije] vi to hop.

sauvage [sovaʒ] a (animal, plante) wild; (tribu, homme) primitive; (cruel) savage; (farouche) unsociable; (illégal) unauthorized ‖ nmf unsociable person; (brute) savage.

sauve [sov] a voir **sauf**[2].

sauvegarder [sovgarde] vt to safeguard; Ordinat to save.

sauver [sove] **1** vt to save; (d'un danger) to rescue (de from); (matériel) to salvage; **s. la vie à qn** to save s.o.'s life. **2 se sauver** vpr (s'enfuir) to run away ou off; (partir) Fam to get off, go. ● **sauvetage** nm rescue; **canot de s.** lifeboat; **ceinture de s.** life belt. ● **sauveteur** nm rescuer.

● **sauveur** nm saviour.

sauvette (à la) [alasovet] adv **vendre à la s.** to peddle on the streets (illegally).

savant [savɑ̃] a learned, scholarly; (manœuvre etc) masterly ▮ nm scientist.

saveur [savœr] nf (goût) flavour.

savoir* [savwar] vt to know; (nouvelle) to know, have heard; **s. lire/nager/etc** to know how to read/swim/etc; **faire s. à qn que** to inform ou tell s.o. that; **à s.** (c'est-à-dire) that is, namely; **(pas) que je sache** (not) as far as I know; **je n'en sais rien** I have no idea; **un je ne sais quoi** something or other ▮ nm (culture) learning, knowledge. ● **s.-faire** nm inv know-how, ability. ● **s.-vivre** nm inv good manners.

savon [savɔ̃] nm **1** soap; (morceau) (bar of) soap. **2 passer un s. à qn** (gronder) Fam to give s.o. a dressing-down ou a talking-to. ● **savonner** vt to wash with soap. ● **savonnette** nf bar of soap. ● **savonneux, -euse** a soapy.

savourer [savure] vt to enjoy, savour, relish. ● **savoureux, -euse** a tasty.

saxophone [saksɔfɔn] nm saxophone.

scalpel [skalpɛl] nm scalpel.

scandale [skɑ̃dal] nm scandal; **faire s.** (livre etc) to scandalize people; **faire un s.** to make a scene. ● **scandaleux, -euse** a shocking, outrageous. ● **scandaliser** vt to shock, scandalize.

Scandinavie [skɑ̃dinavi] nf Scandinavia. ● **scandinave** a & nmf Scandinavian.

scanner [skaner] nm Méd Ordinat scanner.

scaphandre [skafɑ̃dr] nm (de plongeur) diving suit; (de cosmonaute) spacesuit; **s. autonome** aqualung.

scarabée [skarabe] nm beetle.

scarlatine [skarlatin] nf scarlet fever.

scarole [skarɔl] nf endive.

sceau, -x [so] nm (cachet, cire) seal. ● **sceller** vt **1** (document etc) to seal. **2** (fixer) Tech to cement. ● **scellés** nmpl (cachets de cire) seals.

scénario [senarjo] nm (dialogues etc) film script, screenplay; (déroulement)

Fig scenario. ● **scénariste** nmf Cin scriptwriter.

scène [sɛn] nf **1** Th (plateau) stage; (décors, partie de pièce) scene; (action) action; **mettre en s.** (pièce, film) to direct. **2** (dispute) scene; **faire une s. (à qn)** to make a scene; **s. de ménage** domestic quarrel.

sceptique [sɛptik] a sceptical, Am skeptical ▮ nmf sceptic, Am skeptic.

schéma [ʃema] nm diagram. ● **schématique** a diagrammatic; (succinct) Péj sketchy.

scie [si] nf (outil) saw. ● **scier** vt to saw.

sciemment [sjamɑ̃] adv knowingly.

science [sjɑ̃s] nf science; (savoir) knowledge; **sciences humaines** social science(s); **étudier les sciences** to study science. ● **s.-fiction** nf science fiction. ● **scientifique** a scientific ▮ nmf scientist.

scinder [sɛ̃de] vt, **se s.** vpr to divide, split.

scintiller [sɛ̃tije] vi to sparkle, glitter; (étoiles) to twinkle.

scission [sisjɔ̃] nf (de parti etc) split (in).

sciure [sjyr] nf sawdust.

sclérose [skleroz] nf **s. en plaques** multiple sclerosis.

scolaire [skɔler] a **année/etc s.** school year/etc. ● **scolariser** vt (enfant) to send to school. ● **scolarité** nf schooling.

scooter [skuter] nm (motor) scooter.

score [skɔr] nm Sp score.

scorpion [skɔrpjɔ̃] nm scorpion; **le S.** (signe) Scorpio.

scotch [skɔtʃ] nm **1** (boisson) Scotch, whisky. **2**® (ruban adhésif) sellotape®, Am scotch® tape. ● **scotcher** vt to sellotape, Am to tape.

scout [skut] a & nm scout.

script [skript] nm (écriture) printing.

scrupule [skrypyl] nm scruple; **sans scrupules** unscrupulous; (agir) unscrupulously. ● **scrupuleux, -euse** a scrupulous.

scruter [skryte] vt to examine, scrutinize.

scrutin [skrytɛ̃] nm (vote) voting, ballot; (opérations électorales) poll(ing).

sculpter [skylte] vt to carve, sculpture. ● **sculpteur** nm sculptor. ● **sculpture** nf (art, œuvre) sculpture; s. sur bois woodcarving.

SDF [esdeef] nm abrév (sans domicile fixe) person of no fixed abode.

se [s(ə)] (s' before vowel or mute h) pron 1 (complément direct) himself; (féminin) herself; (non humain) itself; (indéfini) oneself; pl themselves; il se lave he washes himself.
2 (indirect) to himself; to herself; to itself; to oneself; se dire to say to oneself.
3 (réciproque) each other, one another; (indirect) to each other, to one another; ils s'aiment they love each other ou one another; ils ou elles se parlent they speak to each other ou one another.
4 (possessif) il se lave les mains he washes his hands.
5 (passif) ça se fait that is done; ça se vend bien it sells well.

séance [seɑ̃s] nf 1 Cin show(ing), performance. 2 (d'assemblée) session, sitting. 3 s. tenante at once.

seau, -x [so] nm bucket, pail.

sec, sèche [sek, sɛʃ] a dry; (fruits, légumes) dried; (ton) curt, harsh; **frapper un coup s.** to knock (sharply), bang; **bruit s.** (rupture) snap ‖ adv (boire) neat, Am straight ‖ nm à s. dried up, dry; (sans argent) Fam broke; au s. in a dry place.

sécateur [sekatœr] nm pruning shears, secateurs.

sèche [sɛʃ] voir sec. ● **sèche-cheveux** nm inv hair drier. ● **sèche-linge** nm inv tumble dryer, Am (clothes) dryer.

sécher [seʃe] 1 vti to dry ‖ se s. vpr to dry oneself. 2 vt (cours) Scol Fam to skip ‖ vi (ignorer) Scol Fam to be stumped. ● **séchage** nm drying.

sécheresse [seʃrɛs] nf dryness; (de ton) curtness; Mét drought.

séchoir [seʃwar] nm s. à linge drying

rack, clothes horse.

second, -onde¹ [sgɔ̃, -ɔ̃d] a & nmf second ‖ nm (adjoint) second in command; (étage) second floor, Am third floor ‖ nf Rail second class; Scol = fifth form, Am = eleventh grade; (vitesse) Aut second (gear). ● **secondaire** a secondary.

seconde² [sgɔ̃d] nf (instant) second.

secouer [s(ə)kwe] vt to shake; (paresse, poussière) to shake off; s. qch de qch (enlever) to shake sth out of sth.

secourir [skurir] vt to assist, help. ● **secourisme** nm first aid. ● **secouriste** nmf first-aid worker.

secours [s(ə)kur] nm assistance, help; pl (aux victimes) aid, relief; (premiers) s. Méd first aid; au s.! help!; porter s. à qn to give s.o. assistance; sortie de s. emergency exit; roue de s. spare wheel.

secousse [s(ə)kus] nf jolt, jerk; Géol tremor.

secret, -ète [səkrɛ, -ɛt] a secret; (cachottier) secretive ‖ nm secret; en s. in secret, secretly.

secrétaire [səkreter] 1 nmf secretary; s. médicale (doctor's) receptionist; s. d'État Secretary of State. 2 nm (meuble) writing desk. ● **secrétariat** nm (bureau) secretary's office; (métier) secretarial work; de s. (école, travail) secretarial.

secte [sekt] nf sect.

secteur [sektœr] nm Mil Com sector; (de ville) district; (domaine) Fig area; Él mains.

section [seksjɔ̃] nf section; (de ligne d'autobus) fare stage; Mil platoon.

séculaire [sekyler] a (tradition etc) ageold.

sécurité [sekyrite] nf (matérielle) safety; (tranquillité) security; s. routière road safety; S. sociale = social services, Social Security; ceinture de s. seat belt; en s. safe; secure.

sédatif [sedatif] nm sedative.

sédentaire [sedɑ̃ter] a sedentary.

sédiment [sedimɑ̃] nm sediment.

séduire* [sedɥir] *vt* to charm, attract; (*abuser de*) to seduce. ● **séduisant** *a* attractive. ● **séducteur, -trice** *nmf* seducer. ● **séduction** *nf* attraction.

segment [sɛgmã] *nm* segment.

ségrégation [segregasjõ] *nf* segregation.

seigle [sɛgl] *nm* rye; **pain de s.** rye bread.

seigneur [sɛɲœr] *nm Hist* lord; **S. Rel** Lord.

sein [sɛ̃] *nm* breast; *Fig* bosom; **donner le s. à** to breastfeed; **au s. de** (*parti etc*) within; (*bonheur etc*) in the midst of.

Seine [sɛn] *nf* **la S.** the Seine.

séisme [seism] *nm* earthquake.

seize [sɛz] *a* & *nm* sixteen. ● **seizième** *a* & *nmf* sixteenth.

séjour [seʒur] *nm* stay; (**salle de**) **s.** living room. ● **séjourner** *vi* to stay.

sel [sɛl] *nm* salt; **s. de mer** sea salt; **sels de bain** bath salts.

sélection [selɛksjõ] *nf* selection. ● **sélectionner** *vt* to select.

self(-service) [self(sɛrvis)] *nm* self-service restaurant *ou* shop.

selle [sɛl] *nf* (*de cheval*) saddle. ● **seller** *vt* (*cheval*) to saddle.

sellette [sɛlɛt] *nf* **sur la s.** (*personne*) under examination, in the hot seat.

selon [s(ə)lõ] *prép* according to (**que** whether); **c'est s.** *Fam* it (all) depends.

semaine [s(ə)mɛn] *nf* week; **en s.** (*opposé à week-end*) in the week.

semblable [sãblabl] *a* similar (**à** to); **être semblables** to be alike *ou* similar ‖ *nm* fellow (creature).

semblant [sãblã] *nm* **faire s.** to pretend (**de faire** to do); **un s. de** a semblance of.

sembler [sãble] *vi* to seem (**à** to); **il (me) semble vieux** he seems *ou* looks old (to me) ‖ *v imp* **il semble que** (+ *sub ou indic*) it seems that, it looks as if; **il me semble que** (+ *indic*) I think that, it seems to me that.

semelle [s(ə)mɛl] *nf* (*de chaussure*) sole; (*intérieure*) insole.

semer [s(ə)me] *vt* **1** (*graines*) to sow; **semé de** *Fig* strewn with, dotted with. **2** (*concurrent, poursuivant*) to shake off.

● **semence** *nf* seed.

semestre [s(ə)mɛstr] *nm* half-year; *Univ* semester. ● **semestriel, -ielle** *a* half-yearly.

semi- [səmi] *préf* semi-.

séminaire [seminɛr] *nm* **1** *Univ* seminar. **2** *Rel* seminary.

semi-remorque [səmirəmɔrk] *nm* (*camion*) articulated lorry, *Am* semi (trailer).

semoule [s(ə)mul] *nf* semolina.

sénat [sena] *nm Pol* senate. ● **sénateur** *nm Pol* senator.

sénile [senil] *a* senile. ● **sénilité** *nf* senility.

sens [sãs] *nm* **1** (*faculté*) sense.
2 (*signification*) meaning, sense; **avoir du bon s.** to have sense, be sensible; **ça n'a pas de s.** that doesn't make sense.
3 (*direction*) direction; **s. giratoire** *Aut* roundabout, *Am* traffic circle; **s. interdit** *ou* **unique** (*rue*) one-way street; **'s. interdit'** 'no entry'; **s. dessus dessous** [sãdsydsu] upside down; **dans le s./le s. inverse des aiguilles d'une montre** clockwise/anticlockwise, *Am* counterclockwise.

sensation [sãsasjõ] *nf* feeling, sensation; **faire s.** to cause a sensation; **à s.** (*film etc*) *Péj* sensational. ● **sensationnel, -elle** *a* sensational.

sensé [sãse] *a* sensible.

sensible [sãsibl] *a* sensitive (**à** to); (*douloureux*) tender, sore; (*progrès etc*) noticeable. ● **sensibilité** *nf* sensitivity.

sensuel, -elle [sãsɥɛl] *a* (*sexuel*) sensual; (*musique, couleur etc*) sensuous. ● **sensualité** *nf* sensuality; sensuousness.

sentence [sãtãs] *nf Jur* sentence.

senteur [sãtœr] *nf* (*odeur*) scent.

sentier [sãtje] *nm* path.

sentiment [sãtimã] *nm* feeling; **avoir le s. que** to have a feeling that; **meilleurs sentiments** (*sur une carte de visite etc*) best wishes. ● **sentimental, -aux** *a* sentimental.

sentinelle [sātinɛl] *nf* sentry.

sentir* [sātir] *vt* to feel; (*odeur*) to smell; (*goût*) to taste; **s. bon** to smell good; **s. le parfum**/*etc* to smell of perfume/*etc*; **s. le poisson**/*etc* (*avoir le goût de*) to taste of fish/*etc*; **je ne peux pas le s.** (*supporter*) *Fam* I can't stand *ou* bear him; **se s. fatigué**/*etc* to feel tired/*etc*; **se faire s.** (*effet etc*) to make itself felt ▮ *vi* to smell.

séparation [separɑsjɔ̃] *nf* separation; (*en deux*) division, split; (*départ*) parting.

séparer [separe] *vt* to separate (**de** from); (*diviser en deux*) to divide, split (up); **plus rien ne nous sépare de la victoire** nothing else stands between us and victory ▮ **se s.** *vpr* (*se quitter*) to part; (*couple*) to separate; **se s. de** (*objet aimé, chien etc*) to part with. ● **séparément** *adv* separately.

sept [sɛt] *a & nm* seven. ● **septième** *a & nmf* seventh; **un s.** a seventh.

septante [sɛptɑ̃t] *a & nm* (*en Belgique, Suisse*) seventy.

septembre [sɛptɑ̃br] *nm* September.

septennat [sɛptena] *nm Pol* seven-year term (of office).

sépulture [sepyltyr] *nf* burial; (*lieu*) burial place.

séquelles [sekɛl] *nfpl* (*de maladie etc*) aftereffects; (*de guerre*) aftermath.

séquence [sekɑ̃s] *nf* (*de film*) sequence.

sera, serai [s(ə)ra, s(ə)rɛ] *voir* être.

Serbie [sɛrbi] *nf* Serbia.

serein [sərɛ̃] *a* serene.

sergent [sɛrʒɑ̃] *nm Mil* sergeant.

série [seri] *nf* series; (*ensemble*) set; **s. noire** *Fig* series of disasters; **de s.** (*article etc*) standard; **fabrication en s.** mass production; **fins de s.** *Com* oddments.

sérieux, -euse [serjø, -øz] *a* (*personne, doute etc*) serious; (*fiable*) reliable; (*bénéfices*) substantial; **de sérieuses chances de...** a good chance of... ▮ *nm* seriousness; (*fiabilité*) reliability; **prendre au s.** to take seriously; **garder son s.** to keep a straight face; **manquer**

de s. (*travailleur*) to lack application. ● **sérieusement** *adv* seriously; (*travailler*) conscientiously.

seringue [s(ə)rɛ̃g] *nf* syringe.

serment [sɛrmɑ̃] *nm* (*affirmation*) oath; (*promesse*) pledge; **prêter s.** to take an oath; **faire le s. de faire** to swear to do.

sermon [sɛrmɔ̃] *nm Rel* sermon; (*discours*) *Péj* lecture.

séropositif, -ive [seropozitif, -iv] *a Méd* HIV positive. ● **séronégatif, -ive** *a Méd* HIV negative.

serpent [sɛrpɑ̃] *nm* snake; **s. à sonnette** rattlesnake.

serpenter [sɛrpɑ̃te] *vi* to meander.

serpentin [sɛrpɑ̃tɛ̃] *nm* (*ruban*) streamer.

serpillière [sɛrpijɛr] *nf* floor cloth.

serre [sɛr] **1** *nf* greenhouse. **2** *nfpl* (*d'oiseau*) claws, talons.

serrer [sɛre] *vt* (*tenir*) to grip; (*presser*) to squeeze, press; (*nœud, vis*) to tighten; (*poing*) to clench; (*taille*) to hug; (*frein*) to apply; (*rapprocher*) to close up; **s. la main à qn** to shake hands with s.o.; **s. les dents** *Fig* to grit one's teeth; **s. qn** (*embrasser*) to hug s.o.; (*vêtement*) to be too tight for s.o.; **s. qn de près** (*talonner*) to be close behind s.o. ▮ *vi* **s. à droite** *Aut* to keep (to the) right. ▮ **se serrer** *vpr* (*se rapprocher*) to squeeze up *ou* together; **se s. contre** to squeeze up against. ● **serré** *a* (*nœud, budget etc*) tight; (*gens*) packed (together); (*lutte*) close; (*cœur*) *Fig* heavy.

serre-tête [sɛrtɛt] *nm inv* headband.

serrure [sɛryr] *nf* lock. ● **serrurier** *nm* locksmith.

servante [sɛrvɑ̃t] *nf* (maid)servant.

serveur, -euse [sɛrvœr, -øz] *nmf* waiter, waitress; (*au bar*) barman, barmaid.

serviable [sɛrvjabl] *a* helpful, obliging.

service [sɛrvis] *nm* service; (*travail*) duty; (*pourboire*) service (charge); (*dans une entreprise*) department; *Tennis* serve, service; **un s.** (*aide*) a favour; **rendre s.** to be of service (**à qn** to s.o.), help (**à qn** s.o.); **s. (non) compris** service (not) included; **s. après-vente** *Com* aftersales service; **s. d'ordre** (*policiers*) police; **être de s.** to be on duty; **s. à café** coffee service *ou* set.

serviette [sɛrvjɛt] *nf* **1** towel; **s. de bain/ de toilette** bath/hand towel; **s. hygiénique** sanitary towel *ou* Am napkin; **s. (de table)** napkin, serviette. **2** (*sac*) briefcase.

servile [sɛrvil] *a* servile.

servir* [sɛrvir] **1** *vt* to serve (**qch à qn** s.o. with sth, s.o. to s.o.); (*convive*) to wait on ▮ *vi* to serve ▮ **se s.** *vpr* (*à table*) to help oneself (**de** to).
2 *vi* (*être utile*) to be useful, serve; **s. à qch/à faire** (*objet*) to be used for sth/to do *ou* for doing; **ça ne sert à rien** it's useless, it's no good *ou* use (**de faire** doing); **à quoi ça sert de protester/***etc* what's the use *ou* good of protesting/*etc*; **ça me sert à faire/de qch** I use it to do/as sth; **s. à qn de guide/***etc* to act as a guide/*etc* to s.o.
3 se servir *vpr* **se s. de** (*utiliser*) to use.

serviteur [sɛrvitœr] *nm* servant.

ses [se] *voir* **son²**.

session [sesjɔ̃] *nf* session.

set [sɛt] *nm* **1** Tennis set. **2 s. (de table)** (*napperon*) place mat.

seuil [sœj] *nm* doorstep; (*entrée*) doorway; (*limite*) Fig threshold.

seul, seule [sœl] **1** *a* (*sans compagnie*) alone; **tout s.** by oneself, on one's own, all alone; **se sentir s.** to feel lonely *ou* alone ▮ *adv* (**tout) s.** (*rentrer, vivre etc*) by oneself, on one's own, alone; (*parler*) to oneself; **s. à s.** (*parler*) in private.
2 *a* (*unique*) only; **la seule femme/***etc* the only woman/*etc*; **un s. chat/***etc* only one cat/*etc*; **une seule fois** only once; **pas un s. livre/***etc* not a single book/*etc* ▮ *nmf* **le s., la seule** the only one; **un s., une seule** only one, one only; **pas un s.** not (a single) one.

seulement [sœlmɑ̃] *adv* only; **non s.... mais encore...** not only... but (also)....

sève [sɛv] *nf* Bot sap.

sévère [sever] *a* severe; (*parents etc*)

strict. ● **sévérité** *nf* severity; strictness.

sévices [sevis] *nmpl* brutality.

sevrer [səvre] *vt* (*enfant*) to wean.

sexe [sɛks] *nm* sex; (*organes*) genitals. ● **sexualité** *nf* sexuality. ● **sexuel, -elle** *a* sexual; **éducation/vie sexuelle** sex education/life.

sextuor [sɛkstyɔr] *nm* sextet.

shampooing [ʃɑ̃pwɛ̃] *nm* shampoo; **s. colorant** rinse; **faire un s. à qn** to shampoo s.o.'s hair.

shooter [ʃute] **1** *vti* Fb to shoot. **2 se shooter** *vpr* (*avec une drogue*) Fam to inject oneself (**à** with).

short [ʃɔrt] *nm* (pair of) shorts.

si¹ [si] **1** (= **s'** [s] *before* **il, ils**) *conj* if; **si je pouvais** if I could; **s'il vient** if he comes; **je me demande si** I wonder whether *ou* if; **si on restait?** (*suggestion*) what if we stayed?
2 *adv* (*tellement*) so; **pas si riche que toi** not as rich as you; **un si bon dîner** such a good dinner; **si bien que** with the result that.
3 *adv* (*après négative*) yes; **tu ne viens pas? – si!** you're not coming? – yes (I am)!

si² [si] *nm* (*note de musique*) B.

Sicile [sisil] *nf* Sicily.

SIDA [sida] *nm* Méd AIDS. ● **sidéen, -enne** *nmf* AIDS sufferer *ou* victim.

sidérurgie [sideryrʒi] *nf* iron and steel industry.

siècle [sjɛkl] *nm* century; (*époque*) age.

siège [sjɛʒ] *nm* **1** (*meuble, centre*) & Pol seat; (*de parti etc*) headquarters; **s. (social)** (*d'entreprise*) head office. **2** Mil siege. ● **siéger** *vi* (*assemblée etc*) to sit.

sien, sienne [sjɛ̃, sjɛn] *pron poss* **le s., la sienne, les sien(ne)s** his; (*de femme*) hers; (*de chose*) its; **les deux siens** his *ou* her two ▮ *nmpl* **les siens** (*sa famille*) one's (own) people.

sieste [sjɛst] *nf* siesta; **faire la s.** to take *ou* have a nap.

siffler [sifle] *vi* to whistle; (*avec un sifflet*) to blow one's whistle; (*gaz, serpent*) to hiss **∥** vt (chanson) to whistle; (chien) to whistle to; (faute, fin de match) Sp to blow one's whistle for; (acteur) to boo. ● **sifflement** nm whistling, whistle; hiss(ing).

sifflet [sifle] nm (instrument) whistle; pl (des spectateurs) Th boos; **(coup de) s.** (son) whistle.

sigle [sigl] nm (initiales) abbreviation; (prononcé comme un mot) acronym.

signal, -aux [siɲal, -o] nm signal; **s. d'alarme** Rail alarm, communication cord.

signalement [siɲalmɑ̃] nm (de personne) description, particulars.

signaler [siɲale] **1** vt (faire remarquer) to point out (**à qn** to s.o., **que** that); (indiquer) to indicate, signal; (dénoncer à la police etc) to report (**à** to). **2 se signaler** vpr **se s. par** to distinguish oneself by.

signalisation [siɲalizasjɔ̃] nf signalling; Aut signposting; **s. (routière)** (signaux) road signs.

signature [siɲatyr] nf signature; (action) signing. ● **signer 1** vt to sign. **2 se signer** vpr Rel to cross oneself.

signe [siɲ] nm (indice) sign, indication; **s. particulier/de ponctuation** distinguishing/punctuation mark; **faire s. à qn** (geste) to motion (to) s.o. (**de faire** to do).

signet [siɲɛ] nm bookmark.

signification [siɲifikasjɔ̃] nf meaning. ● **signifier** vt to mean, signify (**que** that).

silence [silɑ̃s] nm silence; Mus rest; **en s.** in silence; **garder le s.** to keep quiet ou silent (sur about). ● **silencieux, -euse 1** a silent. **2** nm (d'arme) silencer. ● **silencieusement** adv silently.

silex [sileks] nm (roche) flint.

silhouette [silwet] nf outline; (en noir) silhouette; (ligne du corps) figure.

silicium [silisjɔm] nm silicon.

sillage [sijaʒ] nm (de bateau) wake.

sillon [sijɔ̃] nm furrow; (de disque) groove.

sillonner [sijone] vt (traverser) to cross;

(en tous sens) to criss-cross.

similaire [similer] a similar.

similicuir [similikɥir] nm imitation leather.

simple [sɛ̃pl] a simple; (non multiple) single; (employé) ordinary **∥** nmf **s. d'esprit** simpleton **∥** nm Tennis singles. ● **simplement** adv simply. ● **simplicité** nf simplicity. ● **simplification** nf simplification. ● **simplifier** vt to simplify.

simulacre [simylakr] nm un **s. de** Péj a pretence ou Am pretense of.

simuler [simyle] vt to simulate; (feindre) to feign.

simultané [simyltane] a simultaneous. ● **—ment** adv simultaneously.

sincère [sɛ̃ser] a sincere. ● **sincèrement** adv sincerely. ● **sincérité** nf sincerity.

singe [sɛ̃ʒ] nm monkey, ape. ● **singeries** nfpl antics.

singulariser (se) [səsɛ̃gylarize] vpr to draw attention to oneself.

singulier, -ière [sɛ̃gylje, -jer] **1** a (peu ordinaire) peculiar, odd. **2** a & nm Gram singular; **au s.** in the singular.

sinistre [sinistr] **1** a (effrayant) sinister. **2** nm disaster; (incendie) fire. ● **sinistré, -ée** a (population, région) disaster-stricken **∥** nmf disaster victim.

sinon [sinɔ̃] conj (autrement) otherwise, or else; (sauf) except (**que** that); (si ce n'est) if not.

sinueux, -euse [sinɥø, -øz] a winding.

sinus [sinys] nm inv Anat sinus. ● **sinusite** nf sinusitis.

siphon [sifɔ̃] nm siphon; (d'évier) trap, U-bend.

sirène [siren] nf **1** (d'usine etc) siren. **2** (femme) mermaid.

sirop [siro] nm syrup; (à diluer) (fruit) cordial, fruit drink; **s. contre la toux** cough medicine ou mixture.

site [sit] nm (endroit) site; (environnement) setting; **s. (touristique)** (monument etc) place of interest.

sitôt [sito] adv **s. levée, elle partit** as soon as she was up, she left; **pas de s.** not for some time.

situation [situɑsjɔ̃] *nf* situation, position; (*emploi*) position; **s. de famille** marital status. ● **situer** *vt* to situate, locate ‖ **se s.** *vpr* (*se trouver*) to be situated. ● **situé** *a* (*maison etc*) situated (à in).

six [sis] ([si] *before consonant*, [siz] *before vowel*) *a & nm* six. ● **sixième** *a & nmf* sixth ‖ *nf Scol* = first form; *Am* = sixth grade.

sketch [skɛtʃ] *nm* (*pl* **sketches**) *Th* sketch.

ski [ski] *nm* (*objet*) ski; (*sport*) skiing; **faire du s.** to ski; **s. de fond** cross-country skiing; **s. nautique** water skiing. ● **skier** *vi* to ski. ● **skieur, -euse** *nmf* skier.

slalom [slalɔm] *nm Sp* slalom.

slip [slip] *nm* (*d'homme*) briefs, (under)pants; (*de femme*) panties, knickers; **s. de bain** (swimming) trunks.

slogan [slɔgɑ̃] *nm* slogan.

SMIC [smik] *nm abrév* (*salaire minimum interprofessionnel de croissance*) guaranteed minimum wage.

smoking [smɔkiŋ] *nm* (*costume*) dinner jacket, *Am* tuxedo.

SNCF [esenseef] *nf abrév* (*Société nationale des chemins de fer français*) French railways, *Am* French railroad system.

sniffer [snife] *vt* **s. de la colle** *Arg* to sniff glue.

snob [snɔb] *nmf* snob ‖ *a* snobbish.

sobre [sɔbr] *a* sober.

sociable [sɔsjabl] *a* sociable.

social, -aux [sɔsjal, -o] *a* social. ● **socialiste** *a & nmf* socialist.

société [sɔsjete] *nf* society; (*compagnie*) company; **s. anonyme** *Com* (public) limited company, *Am* incorporated company.

sociologie [sɔsjɔlɔʒi] *nf* sociology. ● **sociologue** *nmf* sociologist.

socle [sɔkl] *nm* (*de statue, colonne*) plinth, pedestal; (*de lampe*) base.

socquette [sɔkɛt] *nf* ankle sock.

sœur [sœr] *nf* sister; *Rel* nun, sister.

sofa [sɔfa] *nm* sofa, settee.

soi [swa] *pron* oneself; **chacun pour s.** every man for himself; **en s.** in itself; **cela va de soi** it's self-evident (**que** that). ● **s.-même** *pron* oneself.

soi-disant [swadizɑ̃] *a inv* so-called ‖ *adv* supposedly.

soie [swa] *nf* **1** silk. **2** (*de porc etc*) bristle.

soient [swa] *voir* **être**.

soif [swaf] *nf* thirst (*Fig* de for); **avoir s.** to be thirsty; **donner s. à qn** to make s.o. thirsty.

soigner [swaɲe] *vt* to look after, take care of; (*maladie*) to treat; (*présentation*) to take care over; **se faire s.** to have (medical) treatment.

‖ **se soigner** *vpr* to take care of oneself, look after oneself. ● **soigné** *a* (*vêtement*) neat, tidy; (*travail*) careful; (*personne*) well-groomed. ● **soigneux, -euse** *a* careful (**de** with); (*propre*) neat, tidy. ● **soigneusement** *adv* carefully.

soin [swɛ̃] *nm* care; (*ordre*) tidiness, neatness; *pl Méd* treatment, care; **avec s.** carefully, with care; **avoir** *ou* **prendre s. de qch/de faire** to take care of sth/to do; **les premiers soins** first aid.

soir [swar] *nm* evening; **le s.** (*chaque soir*) in the evening(s); **à neuf heures du s.** at nine in the evening; **repas du s.** evening meal. ● **soirée** *nf* evening; (*réunion*) party.

sois, soit [swa] *voir* **être**.

soit 1 [swa] *conj* (*à savoir*) that is (to say); **s. ... s. ...** either ... or .... **2** [swat] *adv* (*oui*) very well.

soixante [swasɑ̃t] *a & nm* sixty. ● **soixantaine** *nf* **une s. (de)** (*nombre*) (about) sixty. ● **soixantième** *a & nmf* sixtieth.

soixante-dix [swasɑ̃tdis] *a & nm* seventy. ● **s.-dixième** *a & nmf* seventieth.

soja [sɔʒa] *nm* (*plante*) soya; **germes de s.** beansprouts.

sol¹ [sɔl] *nm* ground; (*plancher*) floor; (*territoire*) soil.

sol² [sɔl] *nm* (*note de musique*) G.

solaire [sɔler] *a* solar; (*rayons, chaleur*) sun's; **crème/huile s.** sun(tan) lotion/oil.

soldat [sɔlda] *nm* soldier; **simple s.** private.

solde [sɔld] **1** *nm* (*de compte*) balance. **2** *nm* **en s.** (*acheter*) at sale price, *Am* on sale; *pl* (*marchandises*) sale goods; (*vente*) (clearance) sale(s). **3** *nf Mil* pay.

solder [sɔlde] **1** *vt* (*articles*) to clear, sell off. **2** *vt* (*compte*) to pay the balance of. **3 se solder** *vpr* **se s. par un échec**/*etc* to end in failure/*etc*. ● **soldé** *a* (*article etc*) reduced.

sole [sɔl] *nf* (*poisson*) sole.

soleil [sɔlɛj] *nm* sun; (*chaleur, lumière*) sunshine; **au s.** in the sun; **il fait (du) s.** it's sunny, the sun's shining; **coup de s.** *Méd* sunburn; **prendre un bain de s.** to sunbathe.

solennel, -elle [sɔlanɛl] *a* solemn.

solex® [sɔlɛks] *nm* moped.

solfège [sɔlfɛʒ] *nm* rudiments of music.

solidaire [sɔlidɛr] *a* **être s.** (*ouvriers etc*) to show solidarity (**de** with); (*pièce de machine*) to be interdependent (**de** with). ● **solidarité** *nf* solidarity; (*d'éléments*) interdependence.

solide [sɔlid] *a* solid; (*argument*) sound; (*vigoureux*) robust ▮ *nm Ch* solid. ● **solidement** *adv* solidly. ● **solidité** *nf* solidity; (*d'argument etc*) soundness.

soliste [sɔlist] *nmf Mus* soloist.

solitaire [sɔlitɛr] *a* (*vie, passant etc*) solitary; (*tout seul*) all alone ▮ *nmf* loner; **en s.** on one's own. ● **solitude** *nf* solitude; **aimer la s.** to like being alone.

solliciter [sɔlisite] *vt* (*audience, emploi etc*) to seek; **s. qn** (*faire appel à*) to appeal to s.o.

solo [sɔlo] *a inv* & *nm Mus* solo.

soluble [sɔlybl] *a* (*substance, problème*) soluble; **café s.** instant coffee.

solution [sɔlysjɔ̃] *nf* (*d'un problème etc*) & *Ch* solution (**de** to).

solvable [sɔlvabl] *a Fin* solvent.

sombre [sɔ̃br] *a* dark; (*triste*) sombre, gloomy; **il fait s.** it's dark.

sombrer [sɔ̃bre] *vi* (*bateau*) to sink; **s. dans** (*folie, sommeil etc*) to sink into.

sommaire [sɔmɛr] *a* summary; (*repas, tenue*) scant ▮ *nm* summary, synopsis.

somme [sɔm] **1** *nf* sum; **faire la s. de** to add up; **en s.**, **s. toute** in short. **2** *nm* (*sommeil*) nap; **faire un s.** to take *ou* have a nap.

sommeil [sɔmɛj] *nm* sleep; **avoir s.** to be *ou* feel sleepy.

sommelier [sɔməlje] *nm* wine waiter.

sommer [sɔme] *vt* **s. qn de faire qch** (*enjoindre*) & *Jur* to summon s.o. to do sth.

sommes [sɔm] *voir* **être**.

sommet [sɔmɛ] *nm* top; (*de la gloire etc*) *Fig* height; **conférence au s.** summit (conference).

sommier [sɔmje] *nm* (*de lit*) base.

sommité [sɔmite] *nf* leading light, top person (**de** in).

somnambule [sɔmnɑ̃byl] *nmf* sleepwalker; **être s.** to sleepwalk.

somnifère [sɔmnifɛr] *nm* sleeping pill.

somnoler [sɔmnɔle] *vi* to doze, drowse.

somptueux, -euse [sɔ̃ptɥø, -øz] *a* sumptuous.

son¹ [sɔ̃] *nm* **1** (*bruit*) sound. **2** (*de grains*) bran.

son², **sa**, *pl* **ses** [sɔ̃, sa, se] (**sa** *becomes* **son** [sɔ̃n] *before a vowel or mute h*) *a poss* his; (*de femme*) her; (*de chose*) its; (*indéfini*) one's; **son père/sa mère** his *ou* her *ou* one's father/mother; **son ami(e)** his *ou* her *ou* one's friend; **sa durée** its duration.

sondage [sɔ̃daʒ] *nm* **s. (d'opinion)** opinion poll.

sonde [sɔ̃d] *nf Géol* drill; *Nau* sounding line; *Méd* probe; **s. spatiale** space probe.

songe [sɔ̃ʒ] *nm* dream.

song/er [sɔ̃ʒe] *vi* **s. à qch/à faire qch** to think of sth/of doing sth. ● **—eur, -euse** *a* thoughtful.

sonner [sɔne] *vi* to ring; (*cor, cloches etc*) to sound; **on a sonné** (*à la porte*) someone has rung the (door)bell ▮ *vt* (*cloche*) to ring; (*domestique*) to ring for; (*cor etc*) to sound; (*l'heure*) to strike.

sonnerie [sɔnri] nf (son) ring(ing); (appareil) bell; (au bout du fil) ringing tone, Am ring; **s. occupée** engaged tone, Am busy signal.

sonnette [sɔnɛt] nf bell; **coup de s.** ring; **s. d'alarme** alarm (bell).

sonore [sɔnɔr] a (rire) loud; (salle, voix) resonant; (salle, voix) Fam to throw out; **s'en s., se d'affaire** to pull ou come through.

— **sonorité** nf (de salle) acoustics; (de violon etc) tone.

sonorisation [sɔnɔrizasjɔ̃] nf (Fam sono) (matériel) sound equipment ou system. — **sonoriser** vt (salle) to wire for sound.

sont [sɔ̃] voir **être**.

sophistiqué [sɔfistike] a sophisticated.

soprano [sɔprano] nmf (personne) Mus soprano.

sorbet [sɔrbɛ] nm Culin water ice, sorbet.

sorcellerie [sɔrsɛlri] nf witchcraft. — **sorcier** nm sorcerer. — **sorcière** nf witch; **chasse aux sorcières** Pol witchhunt.

sordide [sɔrdid] a (affaire etc) sordid; (maison etc) squalid.

sort [sɔr] nm **1** (destin, hasard) fate; (condition) lot. **2** (maléfice) spell.

sorte [sɔrt] nf sort, kind (de of); **toutes sortes de** all sorts ou kinds of; **en quelque s.** in a way; **de (telle) s. que** (+ sub) so that, in such a way that; **faire en s. que** (+ sub) to see to it that.

sortie [sɔrti] nf **1** (porte) exit, way out; (promenade à pied) walk; (en voiture) drive; (excursion) outing; (de film, disque) release; (de livre, modèle) appearance; Ordinat output; pl (argent) outgoings; **à la s. de l'école** when the children come out of school. **2 s. de bain** (peignoir) bathrobe.

sortir* [sɔrtir] vi (aux être) to go out, leave; (venir) to come out; (pour s'amuser, danser etc) to go out; (film etc) to come out; (numéro gagnant) to come up; **s. de** (endroit) to leave; (université) to be a graduate of; (famille, milieu) to come from; (légalité, limites) to go

beyond; **s. de table** to leave the table; **s. de terre** (plante, fondations) to come up; **s. de l'ordinaire** to be out of the ordinary; **s. indemne** to escape unhurt (de from).

▮ vt (aux avoir) to take out (de of); (film, modèle, livre etc) to bring out; (expulser) Fam to throw out; **s'en s., se s. d'affaire** to pull ou come through.

SOS [ɛsoɛs] nm SOS; **SOS médecins** emergency medical services.

sosie [sɔzi] nm (de personne) double.

sot, sotte [so, sɔt] a foolish ▮ nmf fool. — **sottise** nf foolishness; (action, parole) foolish thing; **faire des sottises** (enfant) to be naughty.

sou [su] nm **sous** (argent) money; **elle n'a pas un ou le s.** she doesn't have a penny; **machine à sous** fruit machine, Am slot machine.

soubresaut [subrəso] nm (sudden) start.

souche [suʃ] nf (d'arbre) stump; (de carnet) stub, counterfoil; (de vigne) stock.

souci [susi] nm (inquiétude) worry; (préoccupation) concern (de for); **se faire du s.** to worry, be worried; **ça lui donne du s.** it worries him ou her. — **se soucier** vpr **se s. de** to be worried ou concerned about. — **soucieux, -euse** a worried, concerned (de qch about sth).

soucoupe [sukup] nf saucer; **s. volante** flying saucer.

soudain [sudɛ̃] a sudden ▮ adv suddenly. — **soudainement** adv suddenly.

Soudan [sudã] nm Sudan.

soude [sud] nf Ch soda.

souder [sude] vt (avec de la soudure) to solder; (par soudure autogène) to weld; (groupes etc) Fig to unite (closely). — **soudure** nf (substance) solder.

souffle [sufl] nm puff, blow; (haleine) breath; (respiration) breathing; (de bombe etc) blast; **s. (d'air)** breath of air. — **souffler** vi to blow; (haleter) to puff ▮ vt (bougie) to blow out; (par une explosion) to blow down, blast; (chuchoter) to whisper; **s. son rôle à qn** Th to prompt s.o.; **ne pas s. mot** not to breathe a word. ● **soufflet** nm (instrument) bellows. ● **souffleur, -euse** nmf Th prompter.

soufflé [sufle] nm Culin soufflé.

souffrance [sufrãs] nf **1** souffrance(s) suffering. **2 en s.** (colis etc) unclaimed.

souffr/ir* [sufrir] **1** vi to suffer; **s. de** to suffer from; (gorge, pieds etc) to have trouble with; **faire s. qn** to hurt s.o. **2** vt (endurer) to suffer; **je ne peux pas le s.** I can't bear him. ● **souffrant** a unwell.

soufre [sufr] nm sulphur, Am sulfur.

souhait [swɛ] nm wish; **à vos souhaits!** (après un éternuement) bless you! ● **souhaiter** vt (bonheur etc) to wish for; **s. qch à qn** to wish s.o. sth; **s. faire** to hope to do; **s. que** (+ sub) to hope that. ● **souhaitable** a desirable.

soûl [su] a drunk. ● **soûler** vt to make drunk ∥ **se s.** vpr to get drunk.

soulager [sulaʒe] vt to relieve (**de** of). ● **soulagement** nm relief.

soulever [sulve] vt to lift (up), raise; (poussière, question) to raise; (le peuple) to stir up; (sentiment) to arouse; **cela me soulève le cœur** it makes me feel sick ∥ **se s.** vpr (malade etc) to lift oneself (up); (se révolter) to rise (up). ● **soulèvement** nm (révolte) uprising.

soulier [sulje] nm shoe.

souligner [suliɲe] vt (d'un trait) to underline; (faire remarquer) to emphasize (**que** that).

soumettre* [sumɛtr] **1** vt (pays, rebelles) to subdue; **s. à** (assujettir) to subject to ∥ **se s.** vpr to submit (**à** to). **2** vt (présenter) to submit (**à** to). ● **soumis** a (docile) submissive; **s. à** subject to. ● **soumission** nf submission.

soupape [supap] nf valve.

soupçon [supsɔ̃] nm suspicion. ● **soupçonner** vt to suspect (**de** of, **d'avoir fait** of doing, **que** that). ● **soupçonneux, -euse** a suspicious.

soupe [sup] nf soup. ● **soupière** nf (soup) tureen.

soupente [supãt] nf (sous le toit) loft.

souper [supe] nm supper ∥ vi to have supper.

soupeser [supəze] vt (objet dans la main) to feel the weight of.

soupir [supir] nm sigh. ● **soupirer** vi to sigh.

soupirail, -aux [supiraj, -o] nm basement window.

souple [supl] a supple; (tolérant) flexible. ● **souplesse** nf suppleness; flexibility.

source [surs] nf **1** (point d'eau) spring; **eau de s.** spring water; **prendre sa s.** (rivière) to rise (**à** at, **dans** in). **2** (origine) source; **de s. sûre** on good authority.

sourcil [sursi] nm eyebrow.

sourd, sourde [sur, surd] **1** a deaf (Fig **à** to) ∥ nmf deaf person. **2** a (douleur) dull; **bruit s.** thump. ● **s.-muet** (pl sourds-muets), **sourde-muette** (pl sourdes-muettes) a & nmf deaf and dumb (person).

souricière [surisjɛr] nf mousetrap; Fig trap.

sourire* [surir] vi to smile (**à** at); **s. à qn** (fortune) to smile on s.o. ∥ nm smile; **faire un s. à qn** to give s.o. a smile.

souris [suri] nf (animal) & Ordinat mouse (pl mice).

sournois [surnwa] a sly, underhand.

sous [su] prép (position) under(neath), beneath; **s. la pluie** in the rain; **s. le nom de** under the name of; **s. Charles X** under Charles X; **s. peu** (bientôt) shortly.

sous- [su] préf (subordination, subdivision) sub-; (insuffisance) under-.

sous-alimenté [suzalimãte] a underfed.

sous-bois [subwa] nm undergrowth.

sous-chef [suʃef] nmf second-in-command.

souscrire* [suskrir] vi **s. à** (payer, approuver) to subscribe to. ● **souscription** nf subscription.

sous-développé [sudevlɔpe] a (pays) underdeveloped.

sous-directeur, -trice [sudirɛktœr, -tris] nmf assistant manager ou manageress.

sous-emploi [suzãplwa] nm underemployment.

sous-entendre [suzɑ̃tɑ̃dr] vt to imply.

sous-estimer [suzɛstime] vt to under-estimate.

sous-louer [sulwe] vt to sublet.

sous-marin [sumarɛ̃] a underwater; **plongée sous-marine** skin diving ‖ nm submarine.

sous-officier [suzɔfisje] nm noncommissioned officer.

soussigné, -ée [susiɲe] nmf **je s.** I the undersigned.

sous-sol [susɔl] nm (d'immeuble) basement.

sous-titre [sutitr] nm subtitle.

soustraire* [sustrɛr] vt Math to take away, subtract (**de** from); **s. qn à** (danger etc) to shield s.o. from. ● **soustraction** nf Math subtraction.

sous-verre [suvɛr] nm inv (encadrement) (frameless) glass mount.

sous-vêtements [suvetmɑ̃] nmpl underwear.

soutane [sutan] nf (de prêtre) cassock.

soute [sut] nf (magasin) Nau hold.

soutenir* [sutnir] vt to support, hold up; (opinion) to uphold, maintain; (candidat etc) to back, support; (effort, intérêt) to sustain, keep up; (thèse) to defend; **s. que** to maintain that ‖ **se s.** vpr (blessé etc) to hold oneself up (straight); (se maintenir, durer) to be sustained.

souterrain [sutɛrɛ̃] a underground ‖ nm underground passage.

soutien [sutjɛ̃] nm support; (personne) supporter; **s. de famille** breadwinner. ● **s.-gorge** nm (pl **soutiens-gorge**) bra.

souvenir [suvnir] nm memory; (objet) memento; (cadeau) keepsake; (pour touristes) souvenir; **en s. de** in memory of. ● **se souvenir*** vpr **se s. de** to remember, recall; **se s. que** to remember ou recall that.

souvent [suvɑ̃] adv often; **peu s.** seldom; **le plus s.** usually, more often than not.

souverain, -aine [suvrɛ̃, -ɛn] a sovereign ‖ nmf sovereign. ● **souveraineté** nf sovereignty.

soyeux, -euse [swajø, -øz] a silky.

soyons, soyez [swajɔ̃, swaje] voir **être**.

spacieux, -euse [spasjø, -øz] a spacious, roomy.

spaghetti(s) [spageti] nmpl spaghetti.

sparadrap [sparadra] nm Méd sticking plaster, Am adhesive tape.

spasme [spasm] nm spasm.

spatial, -aux [spasjal, -o] a **station/etc spatiale** space station/etc; **engin s.** spaceship, spacecraft.

speaker [spikœr] nm, **speakerine** [spikrin] nf Rad TV announcer.

spécial, -aux [spesjal, -o] a special; (bizarre) peculiar. ● **spécialement** adv (exprès) specially.

spécialiser (se) [səspesjalize] vpr to specialize (**dans** in). ● **spécialiste** nmf specialist. ● **spécialité** nf speciality, Am specialty.

spécifier [spesifje] vt to specify (**que** that).

spécimen [spesimɛn] nm specimen; (livre etc) specimen copy.

spectacle [spɛktakl] nm **1** (vue) sight, spectacle. **2** (représentation) show; **le s.** (industrie) show business. ● **spectateur, -trice** nmf Sp spectator; Th Cin member of the audience; pl Th Cin audience.

spectaculaire [spɛktakylɛr] a spectacular.

spéculer [spekyle] vi Fin Phil to speculate; **s. sur** (tabler sur) to bank ou rely on.

spéléologie [speleɔlɔʒi] nf (activité) potholing, Am spelunking.

sperme [spɛrm] nm sperm, semen.

sphère [sfɛr] nf (boule, domaine) sphere.

sphinx [sfɛ̃ks] nm sphinx.

spirale [spiral] nf spiral.

spirituel, -elle [spiritɥɛl] a **1** (amusant) witty. **2** (pouvoir, vie etc) spiritual.

spiritueux [spiritɥø] nmpl (boissons) spirits.

splendide [splɑ̃did] a (merveilleux, riche, beau etc) splendid. ● **splendeur** nf splendour.

spontané [spɔ̃tane] a spontaneous.

● **spontanéité** *nf* spontaneity.

● **ort** [spɔr] *nm* sport; **faire du s.** to play sport *ou Am* sports; **(de) s.** (*chaussures, vêtements*) casual, sports; **voiture/veste/terrain de s.** sports car/jacket/ground.

● **sportif, -ive** *a* (*personne*) fond of sport *ou Am* sports; (*association, journal*) sports; (*allure*) athletic ▮ *nmf* sportsman, sportswoman.

● **ot** [spɔt] *nm* **1** (*lampe*) spotlight. **2 s.** (*publicitaire*) *Rad TV* commercial.

● **print** [sprint] *nm* Sp sprint.

● **quare** [skwar] *nm* public garden.

● **quash** [skwaʃ] *nm* (*jeu*) squash.

● **quelette** [skɔlɛt] *nm* skeleton.

● **table** [stabl] *a* stable. ● **stabiliser** *vt* to stabilize ▮ **se s.** *vpr* to stabilize.

● **tade** [stad] *nm* **1** Sp stadium. **2** (*phase*) stage.

● **tage** [staʒ] *nm* training period; (*cours*) (*training*) course. ● **stagiaire** *a* & *nmf* trainee.

● **tagner** [staɲe] *vi* to stagnate.

● **talle** [stal] *nf* (*box*) & Rel stall.

● **tand** [stãd] *nm* (*d'exposition etc*) stand, stall; **s. de ravitaillement** *Sp* pit; **s. de tir** (*de foire*) shooting range.

● **tandard** [stãdar] *nm* Tél switchboard. **2** *a inv* (*modèle etc*) standard. ● **stan-dardiste** *nmf* (*switchboard*) operator.

● **tarter** [starter] *nm* **1** Aut choke. **2** Sp starter.

● **tation** [stasjɔ̃] *nf* (*de métro, d'observa-tion etc*) & Rad station; (*de ski etc*) resort; **s. de taxis** taxi rank, Am taxi stand; **s. (thermale)** spa. ● **s.-service** *nf* (*pl* stations-service) Aut service station, petrol *ou Am* gas station.

● **stationnaire** [stasjɔnɛr] *a* stationary.

● **stationn/er** [stasjɔne] *vi* (*être garé*) to be parked. ● **—ement** *nm* parking.

● **tatique** [statik] *a* static.

● **tatistique** [statistik] *nf* (*donnée*) statis-tic; **la s.** (*techniques*) statistics ▮ *a* sta-tistical.

● **tatue** [staty] *nf* statue.

● **tatuer** [statɥe] *vi* **s. sur** Jur to rule on.

● **tature** [statyr] *nf* stature.

● **statut** [staty] *nm* **1** (*position*) status. **2 statuts** (*règles*) statutes.

● **steak** [stɛk] *nm* steak.

● **sténo** [steno] *nf* (*personne*) stenogra-pher; (*sténographie*) shorthand, steno-graphy; **prendre en s.** to take down in shorthand. ● **sténodactylo** *nf* shorthand typist, Am stenographer. ● **sténogra-phie** *nf* shorthand, stenography.

● **stéréo** [stereo] *nf* stereo; **en s.** in stereo ▮ *a inv* (*disque etc*) stereo.

● **stérile** [steril] *a* sterile; (*terre*) barren. ● **stériliser** *vt* to sterilize. ● **stérilité** *nf* sterility; (*de terre*) barrenness.

● **stérilet** [sterilɛ] *nm* IUD, coil.

● **stéroïde** [steroid] *nm* steroid.

● **stéthoscope** [stetɔskɔp] *nm* stethoscope.

● **stigmatiser** [stigmatize] *vt* (*dénoncer*) to stigmatize.

● **stimul/er** [stimyle] *vt* to stimulate. ● **—ant** *nm* Fig stimulus; Méd stimu-lant. ● **stimulateur** *nm* **s. cardiaque** pace-maker.

● **stipuler** [stipyle] *vt* to stipulate (**que** that).

● **stock** [stɔk] *nm* Com & Fig stock (**de** of); **en s.** in stock. ● **stocker** *vt* (*provisions*) to store, stock.

● **stop** [stɔp] **1** *int* stop ▮ *nm* (*panneau*) Aut stop sign; (*feu arrière*) Aut brake light, stoplight. **2** *nm* **faire du s.** Fam to hitchhike. ● **stopper 1** *vti* to stop. **2** *vt* (*vêtement*) to mend (invisibly).

● **store** [stɔr] *nm* blind, Am (window) shade; (*de magasin*) awning.

● **strabisme** [strabism] *nm* squint.

● **strapontin** [strapɔ̃tɛ̃] *nm* tip-up *ou* fold-ing seat.

● **stratégie** [strateʒi] *nf* strategy. ● **stra-tégique** *a* strategic.

● **stress** [strɛs] *nm* Psy stress. ● **stressant** *a* stressful. ● **stressé** *a* under stress.

● **strict** [strikt] *a* strict; (*tenue, vérité*) plain; (*droit*) basic; **le s. minimum** the bare minimum. ● **strictement** *adv* strictly; (*vêtu*) plainly.

● **strident** [stridã] *a* shrill, strident.

● **strophe** [strɔf] *nf* verse, stanza.

structure [stryktyr] *nf* structure.
studieux, -euse [stydjø, -øz] *a* studious; *(vacances etc)* devoted to study.
studio [stydjo] *nm* Cin TV studio; *(logement)* studio flat *ou* Am apartment.
stupéfait [stypefε] *a* amazed (**de** at, by).
• **stupéfaction** *nf* amazement.
stupéfier [stypefje] *vt* to amaze. • **stupéfiant 1** *a* amazing. **2** *nm* drug, narcotic.
stupeur [stypœr] *nf* **1** *(étonnement)* amazement. **2** *(inertie)* stupor.
stupide [stypid] *a* stupid. • **stupidité** *nf* stupidity; *(action, parole)* stupid thing.
style [stil] *nm* style; **meubles de s.** period furniture. • **styliste** *nmf* *(de mode etc)* designer.
stylé [stile] *a* well-trained.
stylo [stilo] *nm* pen; **s. à bille** ballpoint (pen), biro®; **s. à encre, s.-plume** fountain pen.
su [sy] *pp de* **savoir**.
suave [sɥav] *a* *(odeur, voix)* sweet.
subalterne [sybaltεrn] *a* & *nmf* subordinate.
subconscient [sypkɔsjɑ̃] *a* & *nm* subconscious.
subir [sybir] *vt* to undergo; *(conséquences, défaite, perte)* to suffer; *(influence)* to be under; **s. qn** *(supporter)* Fam to put up with s.o.
subit [sybi] *a* sudden. • **subitement** *adv* suddenly.
subjectif, -ive [sybʒεktif, -iv] *a* subjective.
subjonctif [sybʒɔ̃ktif] *nm* Gram subjunctive.
subjuguer [sybʒyge] *vt* to subjugate, subdue; *(envoûter)* to captivate.
sublime [syblim] *a* & *nm* sublime.
submerger [sybmεrʒe] *vt* to submerge; **plaine/etc submergée** flooded plain/etc; **submergé de travail** Fig overwhelmed with work.
subordonn/er [sybɔrdɔne] *vt* to subordinate (**à** to). • **-é, -ée** *a* subordinate (**à** to); **être s. à** *(dépendre de)* to depend on

‖ *nmf* subordinate.
subsidiaire [sybsidjεr] *a* subsidiar
question s. *(de concours)* deciding que tion.
subsister [sybziste] *vi* *(rester)* to remai
(vivre) to get by, subsist.
substance [sypstɑ̃s] *nf* substance; **en** Fig in essence. • **substantiel, -ielle** substantial.
substituer [sypstitɥe] *vt* to substitute (
for); **se s. à qn** to take the place of s.c
subterfuge [sypterfyʒ] *nm* subterfuge.
subtil [syptil] *a* subtle.
subtiliser [syptilize] *vt* *(dérober)* Fam t
make off with.
subvenir* [sybvənir] *vi* **s. à** *(besoins*
frais) to meet.
subvention [sybvɑ̃sjɔ̃] *nf* subsidy. • **sub**
ventionner *vt* to subsidize.
subversif, -ive [sybvεrsif, -iv] *a* subver
sive.
suc [syk] *nm* *(gastrique, de fruit)* juice
(de plante) sap.
succéder [syksede] *vi* **s. à qn** to succee
s.o.; **s. à qch** to follow sth, come afte
sth. ‖ **se s.** *vpr* to follow one another.
succès [syksε] *nm* success; **s. de librai**
rie *(livre)* best-seller; **avoir du s.** to b
successful, be a success; **à s.** *(auteur*
film etc) successful; **avec s.** success
fully.
successeur [syksεsœr] *nm* successor
• **successif, -ive** *a* successive. • **suc**
cession *nf* succession; *(série)* sequence
(de of); *(patrimoine)* Jur inheritance
estate; **prendre la s. de qn** to succeed
s.o.
succomber [sykɔ̃be] *vi* *(mourir)* to die; **s.**
à ses blessures to die of one's wounds.
succulent [sykylɑ̃] *a* succulent.
succursale [sykyrsal] *nf* Com branch.
sucer [syse] *vt* to suck. • **sucette** *nf*
lollipop; *(tétine)* dummy, comforter,
Am pacifier.
sucre [sykr] *nm* sugar; *(morceau)* sugar
lump; **s. cristallisé** granulated sugar; **s.**
en morceaux lump sugar; **s. en poudre,**
s. semoule caster sugar, Am finely

ground sugar; **s. d'orge** barley sugar.

ucr/er [sykre] *vt* to sugar, sweeten.
●**—é** *a* sweet, sugary.

ucreries [sykrəri] *nfpl* (*bonbons*)
weets, *Am* candy.

ucrier [sykrije] *nm* (*récipient*) sugar
owl.

ud [syd] *nm* south; **au s.** in the south;
(*direction*) (to the) south (**de** of); **du s.**
(*vent*, *direction*) southerly; (*ville*) southern; (*gens*) from *ou* in the south;
Amérique/Afrique du S. South Amer-
ica/Africa; **l'Europe du S.** Southern
Europe.
a inv (*côte*) south(ern). ●**s.-africain,**
-aine *a & nmf* South African. ●**s.-**
américain, -aine *a & nmf* South American. ●**s.-est** *nm & a inv* south-east. ●**s.-**
ouest *nm & a inv* south-west.

uède [sɥɛd] *nf* Sweden. ● **suédois, -oise**
a Swedish ∥*nmf* Swede ∥*nm* (*langue*)
Swedish.

uer [sɥe] *vi* (*personne, mur etc*) to
sweat; **faire s. qn** *Fam* to get on s.o.'s
nerves. ● **sueur** *nf* sweat; **(tout) en s.**
sweating.

uffire* [syfir] *vi* to be enough *ou*
sufficient (**à** for); **ça suffit!** that's enough!; **il suffit de faire** one only has to
do; **il suffit d'une goutte/etc pour faire a**
drop/*etc* is enough to do∥ **se s.** *vpr* **se s.**
(à soi-même) to be self-sufficient.
● **suffisant** *a* 1 sufficient, adequate. 2
(*vaniteux*) conceited. ● **suffisamment**
adv sufficiently; **s. de** enough, sufficient.

suffixe [syfiks] *nm Gram* suffix.

suffoquer [syfɔke] *vti* to choke, suffocate. ● **suffocant** *a* stifling, suffocating.

suffrage [syfraʒ] *nm Pol* (*voix*) vote; **s.**
universel universal suffrage.

suggérer [sygʒere] *vt* (*proposer*) to
suggest (**à** to, **de faire** doing, **que** (+
sub) that). ● **suggestion** *nf* suggestion.

suicide [sɥisid] *nm* suicide. ● **suicidaire** *a*
suicidal. ● **se suicider** *vpr* to commit
suicide.

suie [sɥi] *nf* soot.

suinter [sɥɛ̃te] *vi* to ooze, seep.

suis [sɥi] *voir* **être, suivre.**

Suisse [sɥis] *nf* Switzerland; **S. alle-**
mande/romande German-speaking/
French-speaking Switzerland. ● **suisse**
a & nmf Swiss; **les Suisses** the Swiss.
● **Suissesse** *nf* Swiss woman *ou* girl,
Swiss *inv*.

suite [sɥit] *nf* (*reste*) rest; (*continuation*)
continuation; (*de film, roman*) sequel;
(*série*) series, sequence; (*appartement,*
escorte) & *Mus* suite; *pl* (*séquelles*)
effects; **faire s. (à)** to follow; **donner s.**
à (*demande etc*) to follow up; **par la s.**
afterwards; **par s. de** as a result of; **à la**
s. one after another; **à la s. de** (*derrière*)
behind; (*événement etc*) as a result of;
de s. (*deux jours etc*) in a row.

suivre* [sɥivr] *vt* to follow; (*accom-*
pagner) to go with, accompany;
(*cours*) *Scol* to attend; (*malade*) to
treat; **s. (des yeux** *ou* **du regard)** to
watch; **se s.** to follow each other.
∥ *vi* to follow; **faire s.** (*courrier*) to
forward; **'à s.'** 'to be continued';
comme suit as follows. ● **suivant¹,**
-ante *a* next, following ∥*nmf* next
(one); **au s.!** next!, next person! ● **sui-**
vant² *prép* (*selon*) according to.

sujet¹, -ette [syʒɛ, -ɛt] *a* **s. à** (*maladie etc*)
subject *ou* liable to ∥ *nmf* (*personne*) *Pol*
subject.

sujet² [syʒɛ] *nm* 1 (*question*) & *Gram*
subject; (*d'examen*) question; **au s. de**
about; **à quel s.?** about what? 2 (*raison*)
cause.

sultan [syltã] *nm* sultan.

super [syper] 1 *a inv* (*bon*) *Fam* great,
super. 2 *nm* (*supercarburant*) four-star
(petrol), *Am* premium gas.

superbe [syperb] *a* superb.

supercherie [syperʃəri] *nf* deception.

superficie [syperfisi] *nf* surface; (*di-*
mensions) area. ● **superficiel, -ielle** *a*
superficial.

superflu [syperfly] *a* superfluous.

supérieur, -eure [syperjœr] *a* (*étages,*
partie etc) upper; (*qualité, air, ton*)
superior; (*études*) higher; **à l'étage s.**

on the floor above; **s. à** (*meilleur que*) superior to ▌ *nmf* superior. ● **supériorité** *nf* superiority.

superlatif, -ive [syperlatif, -iv] *a & nm Gram* superlative.

supermarché [sypermarʃe] *nm* supermarket.

superposer [syperpoze] *vt* (*objets*) to put on top of each other.

superproduction [syperprodyksjɔ̃] *nf* (*film*) blockbuster.

superpuissance [syperpɥisɑ̃s] *nf Pol* superpower.

supersonique [sypersonik] *a* supersonic.

superstar [syperstar] *nf* superstar.

superstitieux, -euse [syperstisjø, -øz] *a* superstitious. ● **superstition** *nf* superstition.

superviser [sypervize] *vt* to supervise.

supplanter [syplɑ̃te] *vt* to take the place of.

supplé/er [syplee] *vt*, *vi* **s. à** (*compenser*) to make up for. ● **—ant, -ante** *a & nmf* (*personne*) substitute, replacement.

supplément [syplemɑ̃] *nm* (*argent*) extra charge, supplement; (*revue*) supplement; **en s.** extra; **un s. de** (*information etc*) extra, additional. ● **supplémentaire** *a* extra, additional.

supplice [syplis] *nm* torture.

supplier [syplije] *vt* **s. qn de faire** to beg *ou* implore s.o. to do; **je vous en supplie!** I beg *ou* implore you!

support [sypor] *nm* **1** support; (*d'instrument etc*) stand. **2** (*moyen*) *Fig* medium; **s. audio-visuel** audio-visual aid.

support/er¹ [syporte] *vt* (*malheur, conséquences etc*) to bear, endure; (*résister à*) to withstand (*heat etc*); (*soutenir*) to support (*arch etc*); (*frais*) to bear; **je ne peux pas la s.** I can't bear her. ● **—able** *a* bearable.

supporter² [syporter] *nm Sp* supporter.

supposer [sypoze] *vt* to suppose, assume (**que** that); (*impliquer*) to imply (**que** that); **à s. *ou* en supposant que** (+ *sub*) supposing (that). ● **supposition** *nf* assumption, supposition.

suppositoire [sypozitwar] *nm Méd* suppository.

supprimer [syprime] *vt* to get rid of, remove; (*mot*) to cut out, delete; (*tra etc*) to cancel; (*tuer*) to do away with; **des emplois** to axe jobs; **s. qch à qn** to take sth away from s.o. ● **suppressio** *nf* removal; deletion; cancellation; a: ing.

suprématie [sypremasi] *nf* supremacy.

suprême [syprem] *a* supreme.

sur [syr] *prép* on, upon; (*par-dessu* over; (*au sujet de*) on, about; **six** dix six out of ten; **un jour s. deux** ever other day; **six mètres s. dix** six metr by ten; **coup s. coup** blow after blow; ce (*often which*, and then; (*maintenan* and now; **s. votre gauche** to your lef

sur- [syr] *préf* over-.

sûr [syr] *a* sure, certain (**de of**, **que** that (*digne de confiance*) reliable; (*lieu*) safe (*goût*) discerning; (*jugement*) sound **c'est s. que** (+ *indic*) it's certain tha **s. de soi** self-assured; **bien s.!** of course

surboum [syrbum] *nf Fam* party.

surcharge [syrʃarʒ] *nf* **1** overloading (*poids*) extra load; **s. de travail** extra work. **2** (*correction de texte etc*) altera tion. ● **surcharger** *vt* (*voiture etc*) to overload (**de** with).

surchauffer [syrʃofe] *vt* to overheat.

surclasser [syrklase] *vt* to outclass.

surcroît [syrkrwa] *nm* increase (**de** in); **s., par s.** in addition.

surdité [syrdite] *nf* deafness.

surélever [syrelve] *vt* to raise (the heigh of).

sûrement [syrmɑ̃] *adv* certainly.

surenchère [syrɑ̃ʃer] *nf Com* higher bid ● **surenchérir** *vi* to bid higher.

surestimer [syrestime] *vt* to overestimate.

sûreté [syrte] *nf* safety; (*de l'État*) security; (*garantie*) surety; **être en s** to be safe; **mettre en s.** to put in a safe place; **épingle/***etc* **de s.** safety pin/*etc* **pour plus de s.** to be on the safe side.

surexcité [syreksite] *a* overexcited.

surf [sœrf] *nm Sp* surfing; **faire du s.** to go surfing, surf.

surface [syrfas] *nf* surface; (*dimensions*) (surface) area; **faire s.** (*sous-marin etc*) to surface; (**magasin à**) **grande s.** hypermarket.

surgelé [syrʒəle] *a* (*viande etc*) (deep-)frozen ▮ *nmpl* (deep-)frozen foods.

surgir [syrʒir] *vi* to appear suddenly (**de** from); (*problème*) to arise.

surhomme [syrɔm] *nm* superman. ● **surhumain** *a* superhuman.

sur-le-champ [syrləʃɑ̃] *adv* immediately.

surlendemain [syrlɑ̃dmɛ̃] *nm* **le s.** two days later; **le s. de** two days after.

surligner [syrliɲe] *vt* to highlight. ● **surligneur** *nm* highlighter (pen).

surmener [syrmøne] *vt*, **se s.** *vpr* to overwork. ● **surmenage** *nm* overwork.

surmonter [syrmɔ̃te] *vt* **1** (*obstacle, peur etc*) to get over, overcome. **2** (*être placé sur*) to be on top of.

surnaturel, -elle [syrnatyrel] *a* & *nm* supernatural.

surnom [syrnɔ̃] *nm* nickname. ● **surnommer** *vt* to nickname.

surnombre [syrnɔ̃br] *nm* **en s.** too many.

surpasser [syrpase] *vt* to surpass (**en** in) ▮ **se s.** *vpr* to excel *ou* surpass oneself.

surpeuplé [syrpœple] *a* overpopulated.

surplace [syrplas] *nm* **faire du s.** (*dans un embouteillage*) to be unable to move, be hardly moving.

surplomber [syrplɔ̃be] *vti* to overhang.

surplus [syrply] *nm* surplus; *pl Com* surplus (stock).

surprendre [syrprɑ̃dr] *vt* (*étonner*) to surprise; (*prendre sur le fait*) to catch; (*conversation*) to overhear. ● **surprenant** *a* surprising. ● **surpris** *a* surprised (**de** at, **que** (+ *sub*) that); **je suis s. de te voir** I'm surprised to see you. ● **surprise** *nf* surprise.

surréservation [syrrezervasjɔ̃] *nf* overbooking.

sursaut [syrso] *nm* (sudden) start *ou* jump; **s. de** (*énergie etc*) burst of.

● **sursauter** *vi* to jump, start.

sursis [syrsi] *nm Mil* deferment; (*répit*) *Fig* reprieve; **un an (de prison) avec s.** a one-year suspended sentence.

surtout [syrtu] *adv* especially; (*avant tout*) above all; **s. pas** certainly not; **s. que** especially since *ou* as.

surveiller [syrveje] *vt* (*garder*) to watch, keep an eye on; (*contrôler*) to supervise; (*épier*) to watch; **s. son langage/sa santé** *Fig* to watch one's language/health. ▮ **se surveiller** *vpr* to watch oneself.

● **surveillant, -ante** *nmf* (*de lycée*) supervisor (in charge of discipline); (*de prison*) (prison) guard, warder; (*de chantier*) supervisor. ● **surveillance** *nf* watch (**sur** over); (*de travaux, d'ouvriers*) supervision; (*de la police*) surveillance, observation.

survenir [syrvønir] *vi* to occur.

survêtement [syrvetmɑ̃] *nm Sp* tracksuit.

survie [syrvi] *nf* survival. ● **survivre** *vi* to survive (**à qch** sth); **s. à qn** to outlive s.o., survive s.o. ● **survivant, -ante** *nmf* survivor.

survoler [syrvɔle] *vt* to fly over; (*question*) *Fig* to go over (quickly).

susceptible [syseptibl] *a* **1** (*ombrageux*) touchy, sensitive. **2 s. de faire** likely *ou* liable to do; (*capable*) able to do.

susciter [sysite] *vt* (*sentiment*) to arouse; (*ennuis, obstacles etc*) to create.

suspect, -ecte [syspe(kt), -ekt] *a* suspicious, suspect; **s. de** suspected of ▮ *nmf* suspect.

suspend/re [syspɑ̃dr] *vt* **1** (*accrocher*) to hang (up) (**à** on). **2 s. à** to hang from. **2** (*destituer, interrompre*) to suspend. ● **—u** *a* **s. à** hanging from; **pont s.** suspension bridge. ● **suspension** *nf* (*d'hostilités, d'employé etc*) & *Aut* suspension.

suspens (en) [ɑ̃syspɑ̃] *adv* **1** (*affaire*) in abeyance. **2** (*dans l'incertitude*) in suspense.

suspense [syspens] *nm* suspense; **film à s.** thriller, suspense film.

suspicion [syspisjɔ̃] *nf* suspicion.

suture [sytyr] *nf Méd* stitching; **point de s.** stitch (*in wound*). ● **suturer** *vt* to stitch up.

svelte [svɛlt] *a* slender.

SVP [ɛsvepe] *abrév* (*s'il vous plaît*) please.

syllabe [silab] *nf* syllable.

symbole [sɛ̃bɔl] *nm* symbol. ● **symbolique** *a* symbolic. ● **symboliser** *vt* to symbolize.

symétrie [simetri] *nf* symmetry.

sympa [sɛ̃pa] *a inv Fam* = **sympathique.**

sympathie [sɛ̃pati] *nf* liking, affection; (*affinité*) affinity; (*condoléances*) sympathy; **avoir de la s. pour qn** to be fond of s.o. ● **sympathique** *a* nice, pleasant; (*accueil, geste*) friendly.

symphonie [sɛ̃fɔni] *nf* symphony. ● **symphonique** *a* **orchestre s.** symphony orchestra.

symptôme [sɛ̃ptom] *nm* symptom.

synagogue [sinagɔg] *nf* synagogue.

synchroniser [sɛ̃krɔnize] *vt* to synchronize.

syncope [sɛ̃kɔp] *nf Méd* blackout; **tomber en s.** to black out.

syndicat [sɛ̃dika] *nm* **1** (*d'ouvriers*) (trade) union, *Am* (labor) union; (*de patrons etc*) association. **2 s. d'initiative** tourist (information) office. ● **syndiquer** *vt* to unionize ▮ **se s.** *vpr* (*adhérer*) to join a (trade *ou Am* labor) union. ● **syndiqué, -ée** *nmf* (trade *ou Am* labor) union member.

syndrome [sɛ̃drom] *nm Méd & Fig* syndrome.

synonyme [sinɔnim] *a* synonymous (**de** with) ▮ *nm* synonym.

synthèse [sɛ̃tɛz] *nf* synthesis. ● **synthétique** *a* synthetic.

synthétiseur [sɛ̃tetizœr] *nm* synthesizer.

Syrie [siri] *nf* Syria. ● **syrien, -ienne** *a & nmf* Syrian.

système [sistɛm] *nm* (*structure, réseau etc*) & *Anat* system; **le s. immunitaire** the immune system; **le s. D** *Fam* resourcefulness; **s. d'exploitation** *Ordinat* operating system. ● **systématique** *a* systematic; (*soutien*) unconditional.

T

T, t [te] *nm* T, t.

t' [t] *voir* **te.**

ta [ta] *voir* **ton**[1].

tabac [taba] **1** *nm* tobacco; *(magasin)* tobacconist's (shop), *Am* tobacco store. **2** *nm* **passer qn à t.** *Fam* to beat s.o. up. **3** *a inv (couleur)* buff.

table [tabl] *nf* **1** *(meuble)* table; *(d'école)* desk; *(nourriture)* fare; **t. de nuit/ d'opération** bedside/operating table; **t. basse** coffee table; **t. à repasser** ironing board; **t. roulante** (tea) trolley, *Am* (serving) cart; **mettre/débarrasser la t.** to set *ou* lay/clear the table; **être à t.** to be sitting at the table; **à t.!** (food's) ready!; **mettre sur t. d'écoute** *(téléphone)* to tap. **2** *(liste)* table; **t. des matières** table of contents.

tableau, -x [tablo] *nm* **1** *(peinture)* picture, painting; *(image)* picture; **t. de maître** *(peinture)* old master. **2** *(panneau)* board; *(liste)* list; *(graphique)* chart; *(noir)* (black)board; **t. d'affichage** notice board, *Am* bulletin board; **t. de bord** *Aut* dashboard.

tabler [table] *vi* **t. sur** to count on *ou* rely on.

tablette [tablɛt] *nf (de chocolat)* bar, slab; *(de lavabo etc)* shelf; *(de cheminée)* mantelpiece.

tableur [tablœr] *nm Ordinat* spreadsheet.

tablier [tablije] *nm (vêtement)* apron; *(d'écolier)* smock.

tabou [tabu] *a & nm* taboo.

tabouret [taburɛ] *nm* stool.

tac [tak] *nm* **répondre du t. au t.** to give tit for tat.

tache [taʃ] *nf* spot, mark; *(salissure)* stain; **faire t. d'huile** *Fig* to spread. **● tacher** *vt*, **se t.** *vpr (tissu etc)* to stain **||** *vi (vin etc)* to stain.

tâche [tɑʃ] *nf* task, job.

tâcher [tɑʃe] *vi* **t. de faire** to try *ou*

---

tacheté [taʃte] *a* speckled, spotted.

tacite [tasit] *a* tacit.

tact [takt] *nm* tact; **avoir du t.** to be tactful.

tactique [taktik] *a* tactical **||** *nf* **la t.** tactics; **une t.** a tactic.

tag [tag] *nm* tag *(spray-painted graffiti)*. **● tagueur, -euse** *nmf* graffiti artist, tagger.

Tahiti! [taiti] *nm* Tahiti. **● tahitien, -ienne** [taisjɛ̃, -jɛn] *a & nmf* Tahitian.

taie [tɛ] *nf* **t. d'oreiller** pillowcase.

taillader [tɑjade] *vt* to gash, slash.

taille [tɑj] *nf* **1** *(hauteur)* height; *(dimension, mesure)* size; **de haute t.** *(personne)* tall; **de petite t.** short; **de t. moyenne** *(objet, personne)* medium-sized; **être de t. à faire** *Fig* to be capable of doing; **de t.** *(erreur)* *Fam* enormous. **2** *Anat* waist; **tour de t.** waist measurement.

taille-crayon(s) [tɑjkrɛjɔ̃] *nm inv* pencil sharpener.

tailler [tɑje] *vt* to cut; *(haie, barbe)* to trim; *(arbre)* to prune; *(crayon)* to sharpen; *(vêtement)* to cut out.

tailleur [tɑjœr] *nm* **1** *(personne)* tailor. **2** *(costume féminin)* suit.

taillis [tɑji] *nm* copse, coppice.

tain [tɛ̃] *nm* **glace sans t.** two-way mirror.

taire* [tɛr] *vt* to say nothing about **||** *vi* **faire t. qn** to silence s.o. **|| se t.** *vpr (ne rien dire)* to keep quiet **(sur qch** about sth); *(cesser de parler)* to stop talking, fall silent; **tais-toi!** be *ou* keep quiet!

talc [talk] *nm* talcum powder.

talent [talɑ̃] *nm* talent; **avoir du t. pour** to have a talent for.

talkie-walkie [talkiwalki] *nm (poste)* walkie-talkie.

talon [talɔ̃] *nm* **1** heel; **(chaussures à)**

talons hauts high heels; **talons aiguilles** stiletto heels. **2** (*de chèque, carnet*) stub, counterfoil.

talus [taly] *nm* slope, embankment.

tambour [tãbur] *nm* **1** (*de machine etc*) & *Mus* drum; (*personne*) drummer. **2** (*porte*) revolving door. ●**tambourin** *nm* tambourine. ●**tambouriner** *vi* (*avec les doigts etc*) to drum (**sur** on).

tamis [tami] *nm* sieve. ●**tamiser** *vt* (*farine etc*) to sift; (*lumière*) to filter.

Tamise [tamiz] *nf* **la T.** the Thames.

tampon [tãpɔ̃] *nm* **1** (*marque, instrument*) stamp. **2** (*bouchon*) plug, stopper; (*de coton etc*) wad; *Méd* swab; **t. hygiénique** *ou* **périodique** tampon; **t. à récurer** scrubbing *ou* scouring pad. **3** (*de train etc*) & *Fig* buffer; **état t.** buffer state.

tamponner [tãpɔne] *vt* **1** (*lettre etc*) to stamp. **3** (*visage etc*) to dab; (*plaie*) to swab. **3** (*train, voiture*) to crash into. ●**tamponneuses** *afpl* **autos t.** bumper cars, dodgems.

tandem [tãdɛm] *nm* **1** (*bicyclette*) tandem. **2** (*duo*) *Fig* pair; **en t.** (*travailler etc*) in tandem.

tandis que [tãdik(ə)] *conj* (*pendant que*) while; (*contraste*) whereas, while.

tanguer [tãge] *vi* (*bateau, avion*) to pitch.

tanière [tanjɛr] *nf* den, lair.

tank [tãk] *nm* *Mil* tank.

tanker [tãkɛr] *nm* (*navire*) tanker.

tann/er [tane] *vt* (*cuir*) to tan. ●**—é** *a* (*visage*) weather-beaten, tanned.

tant [tã] *adv* (*travailler etc*) so much (that); **t. de** (*pain, temps etc*) so much (que that); (*gens, choses etc*) so many (que that); **t. de fois** so often, so many times; **t. que** (*autant que*) as much as; (*aussi longtemps que*) as long as; **en t. que** (*considéré comme*) as; **t. bien que mal** more or less, so-so; **t. mieux!** good!, I'm glad!; **t. pis!** too bad!, pity!

tante [tãt] *nf* aunt.

tantôt [tãto] *adv* **1 t. . . . t.** sometimes . . . sometimes, now . . . now. **2** (*cet après-midi*) this afternoon.

taon [tã] *nm* horsefly, gadfly.

tapage [tapaʒ] *nm* din, uproar.

tape [tap] *nf* slap.

tape-à-l'œil [tapalœj] *a inv* flashy, gaudy.

taper [tape] **1** *vt* (*enfant, cuisse*) to slap; (*table*) to bang ∥ *vi* (*soleil*) to beat down; **t. sur qch** to bang on sth; **t. du pied** to stamp one's foot; **t. sur les nerfs de qn** *Fam* to get on s.o.'s nerves; **t. dans l'œil à qn** *Fam* to take s.o.'s fancy ∥ **se taper** *vpr* (*travail*) *Fam* to do, take on; (*repas, vin*) *Fam* to put away. **2** *vti* **t.** (**à la machine**) to type. ●**tapant** *a* **à midi t.** at twelve sharp; **à huit heures tapant(es)** at eight sharp.

tapir (se) [sətapir] *vpr* to crouch (down).

tapis [tapi] *nm* carpet; **t. de bain** bathmat; **t. roulant** (*pour marchandises*) conveyor belt; (*pour personnes*) moving walkway; (*pour voyageurs*) (*abattre*) to floor s.o.; **mettre sur le t.** (*sujet*) to bring up for discussion. ●**t.-brosse** *nm* doormat.

tapisser [tapise] *vt* (*mur*) to (wall)paper; to hang with tapestry. ●**tapisserie** *nf* (*papier peint*) wallpaper; (*broderie*) tapestry. ●**tapissier, -ière** *nmf* (*qui pose des tissus etc*) upholsterer; **t.(-décorateur)** interior decorator.

tapoter [tapɔte] *vt* to tap; (*joue*) to pat ∥ *vi* **t. sur** to tap (on).

taquin, -ine [takɛ̃, -in] *a* (*fond of*) teasing. ●**taquiner** *vt* to tease.

tard [tar] *adv* late; **plus t.** later (on); **au plus t.** at the latest; **sur le t.** late in life.

tarder [tarde] *vi* (*lettre, saison*) to be a long time coming; **t. à faire** to take one's time doing; **ne tardez pas** (*agissez tout de suite*) don't delay; **elle ne va pas t.** she won't be long; **sans t.** without delay; **il me tarde de faire** I long to do.

tardif, -ive [tardif, -iv] *a* late; (*regrets*) belated. ●**tardivement** *adv* late.

tarif [tarif] *nm* (*prix*) rate; *Aut Rail* fare; (*tableau*) price list, tariff; **plein t.** full price; *Aut Rail* full fare. ●**tarification** *nf* (*price*) fixing.

tarir [tarir] *vti,* **se t.** *vpr (fleuve etc)* & *Fig* to dry up.

tartare [tartar] *a* sauce t. tartar sauce.

tarte [tart] **1** *nf* (open) pie, tart. **2** *a inv Fam* (*sot*) silly. ● **tartelette** *nf* (small) tart.

tartine [tartin] *nf* slice of bread; **t.** (de beurre/de confiture) slice of bread and butter/jam. ● **tartiner** *vt* (beurre etc) to spread; **fromage à t.** cheese spread.

tartre [tartr] *nm* (de bouilloire) scale, fur; (de dents) plaque, tartar.

tas [tɑ] *nm* pile, heap; **un** *ou* **des t. de** (*beaucoup*) *Fam* lots of; **mettre en t.** to pile *ou* heap up; **former qn sur le t.** (*au travail*) *Fam* to train s.o. on the job.

tasse [tas] *nf* cup; **t. à café** coffee cup; **t. à thé** teacup; **boire la t.** *Fam* to swallow a mouthful (*when swimming*).

tasser [tase] *vt* to pack, squeeze (sth, s.o.) (dans into); (terre) to pack down ∎ **se t.** *vpr* (*se serrer*) to squeeze up; (sol) to sink, collapse; (*se voûter*) to become bowed; **ça va se t.** (*s'arranger*) *Fam* things will pan out.

tâter [tate] *vt* to feel; (sonder) *Fig* to sound out ∎ *vi* **t. de** (prison) to have a taste of, experience ∎ **se t.** *vpr* (hésiter) to be in *ou* of two minds. ● **tâtonner** *vi* to grope about. ● **tâtons (à)** *adv* **avancer à t.** to feel one's way (along); **chercher à t.** to grope for.

tatou/er [tatwe] *vt* (corps, dessin) to tattoo. ● **—age** *nm* (dessin) tattoo.

taudis [todi] *nm* slum, hovel.

taupe [top] *nf* (animal, espion) mole.

taureau, -x [tɔro] *nm* bull; **le T.** (signe) Taurus. ● **tauromachie** *nf* bull-fighting.

taux [to] *nm* rate; **t. d'alcool/de cholestérol/etc** alcohol/cholesterol/etc level; **t. d'intérêt** interest rate.

taxe [taks] *nf* (impôt) tax; (de douane) duty; **t. à la valeur ajoutée** value-added tax; **t. de séjour** tourist tax. ● **taxer** *vt* **1** (objet de luxe etc) to tax. **2 t. qn de** to accuse s.o. of. **3** (prendre, voler) *Fam* to swipe (**qch à qn** sth from s.o.). ● **taxé** *a* taxed.

taxi [taksi] *nm* taxi.

taxiphone [taksifɔn] *nm* pay phone.

Tchécoslovaquie [tʃekɔslɔvaki] *nf* Czechoslovakia. ● **tchèque** *a* & *nmf* Czech ∎ *nm* (langue) Czech.

te [t(ə)] (**t'** before vowel or mute h) *pron* **1** (complément direct) you; **je te vois** I see you. **2** (indirect) (to) you; **il te parle** he speaks to you; **elle te l'a dit** she told you. **3** (réfléchi) yourself; **tu te laves** you wash yourself.

technicien, -ienne [tɛknisjɛ̃, -jɛn] *nmf* technician. ● **technique** *a* technical ∎ *nf* technique. ● **technocrate** *nm* technocrat. ● **technologie** *nf* technology. ● **technologique** *a* technological.

teckel [tekel] *nm* (chien) dachshund.

tee-shirt [tiʃœrt] *nm* tee-shirt.

teindre* [tɛ̃dr] *vt* to dye; **t. en rouge/etc** to dye red/etc ∎ **se t.** *vpr* **se t. (les cheveux)** to dye one's hair. ● **teinture** *nf* dyeing; (produit) dye. ● **teinturerie** *nf* (boutique) (dry) cleaner's. ● **teinturier, -ière** *nmf* dry cleaner.

teint [tɛ̃] *nm* **1** (de visage) complexion. **2 bon** *ou* **grand t.** (tissu) colourfast.

teinte [tɛ̃t] *nf* shade, tint. ● **teinter** *vt* to tint; (bois) to stain.

tel, telle [tel] *a* such; **un t. homme/livre/ etc** such a man/book/etc; **un t. intérêt/ etc** such interest/etc; **de tels mots/etc** such words/etc ∎ **que** such as, like; **que je l'ai laissé** just as I left it; **comme t.** as such; **t. ou t.** such and such; **rien de t. que...** (there's) nothing like...; **Monsieur Un t.** Mr So-and-so; **t. père t. fils** like father like son.

télé [tele] *nf* (téléviseur) *Fam* TV; **à la t.** on TV; **regarder la t.** to watch TV.

télé- [tele] *préf* tele-.

télécarte® [telekart] *nf* phonecard.

télécommande [telekɔmɑ̃d] *nf* remote control. ● **télécommander** *vt* to operate by remote control.

télécommunications [telekɔmynikasjɔ̃] *nfpl* telecommunications.

télécopie [telekɔpi] *nf* fax. ● **télécopieur** *nm* fax (machine).

téléfilm [telefilm] *nm* TV film.

télégramme [telegram] *nm* telegram.

télégraphier [telegrafje] *vt (message)* to wire, cable. ● **télégraphique** *a* **poteau/fil t.** telegraph pole/wire.

téléguider [telegide] *vt* to operate by remote control.

télématique [telematik] *nf* telematics, computer communications.

téléobjectif [teleɔbʒektif] *nm* telephoto lens.

téléphérique [teleferik] *nm* cable car.

téléphone [telefɔn] *nm* (tele)phone; **coup de t.** (phone) call; **passer un coup de t. à qn** to give s.o. a ring *ou* a call; **au t.** on the (tele)phone; **avoir le t.** to be on the (tele)phone; **t. portatif** mobile phone. ● **téléphoner** *vt (nouvelle etc)* to (tele)phone (à to) **‖** *vi* to (tele)phone; **t. à qn** to (tele)phone s.o., call s.o. (up). ● **téléphonique** *a* **appel/etc t.** phone *ou* telephone call/etc.

télescope [teleskɔp] *nm* telescope.

télescoper [teleskɔpe] *vt Aut Rail* to smash into; **se t.** to smash into each other.

téléscripteur [teleskriptœr] *nm (appareil)* teleprinter.

télésiège [telesjeʒ] *nm* chair lift.

téléski [teleski] *nm* ski tow.

téléspectateur, -trice [telespektatœr, -tris] *nmf* (television) viewer.

téléviser [televize] *vt* to televise; **journal télévisé** television news. ● **téléviseur** *nm* television (set). ● **télévision** *nf* television; **à la t.** on (the) television; **regarder la t.** to watch (the) television; **programme/etc de t.** television programme/etc.

télex [teleks] *nm (service, message)* telex.

telle [tel] *voir* **tel**.

tellement [telmã] *adv (si)* so; *(tant)* so much; **t. grand/etc** que so big/etc that; **crier/etc t. que** so shout/etc so much that; **t. de** *(travail etc)* so much; *(soucis etc)* so many; **pas t.!** *(pas beaucoup)* not much!

téméraire [temerer] *a* rash, reckless.

témoigner [temwaɲe] **1** *vi Jur* to give evidence, testify *(contre* against); **t. de qch** *(personne, attitude etc)* to testify to sth **‖** *vt* **t. que** *Jur* to testify that. **2** *vt (gratitude etc)* to show (à **qn** (to) s.o.) ● **témoignage** *nm* **1** evidence, testimony; *(récit)* account; **faux t.** *(délit)* perjury. **2** *(d'affection etc) Fig* token (**de** of); **en t. de** as a token of.

témoin [temwɛ̃] **1** *nm* witness; **t. oculaire** eyewitness; **être t. de** *(accident etc)* to witness **‖** *a* **appartement t.** show flat *ou Am* apartment. **2** *nm Sp* baton.

tempérament [tãperamã] *nm (caractère)* temperament.

température [tãperatyr] *nf* temperature; **avoir de la t.** *Méd* to have a temperature.

tempéré [tãpere] *a (climat, zone)* temperate.

tempête [tãpet] *nf* storm; **t. de neige** snowstorm, blizzard.

temple [tãpl] *nm (romain, grec)* temple; *(protestant)* church.

temporaire [tãporer] *a* temporary.

temporel, -elle [tãporel] *a (terrestre)* worldly.

temporiser [tãporize] *vi* to procrastinate.

temps¹ [tã] *nm (durée, période, moment)* time; *Gram* tense; **t. d'arrêt** pause, break; **en t. de guerre** in wartime; **avoir/trouver le t.** to have/find (the) time *(de faire* to do); **il est t.** it is time *(de faire* to do); **il était t.!** it was about time!; **ces derniers t.** lately; **de t. en t.** [dətãzãtã] from time to time; **en t. utile** [ãtãzytil] in good *ou* due time; **en même t.** at the same time *(que* as); **à t.** *(arriver)* in time; **à plein t.** *(travailler etc)* full-time; **à t. partiel** *(travailler etc)* part-time; **dans le t.** *(autrefois)* once; **avec le t.** *(à la longue)* in time; **tout le t.** all the time; **de mon t.** in my time.

temps² [tã] *nm (climat)* weather; **il fait beau/mauvais t.** the weather's fine/bad; **quel t. fait-il?** what's the weather like?

tenable [tənabl] *a* bearable.

tenace [tənas] *a* stubborn, tenacious.

tenailles [tənaj] *nfpl* (*outil*) pincers.

tenant, -ante [tənā, -āt] *nmf* **le t. du titre** *Sp* the title holder.

tendance [tādās] *nf* (*penchant*) tendency; (*évolution*) trend (**à** towards); **avoir t. à faire** to tend to do, have a tendency to do.

tendancieux, -euse [tādāsjø, -øz] *a Péj* tendentious.

tendeur [tādœr] *nm* (*à bagages*) elastic strap, *Am* bungee.

tendre[1] [tādr] **1** *vt* to stretch; (*main*) to hold out (**à qn** to s.o.); (*bras, jambe*) to stretch out; (*muscle*) to tense, flex; (*arc*) to bend; (*piège*) to set, lay; (*filet*) to spread; (*tapisserie*) to hang; **t. qch à qn** to hold out sth to s.o.; **t. l'oreille** *Fig* to prick up one's ears ∥ **se tendre** *vpr* (*rapports*) to become strained.
2 **vt. à qch/à faire** to tend towards sth/to do. ● **tendu** *a* (*corde*) tight; (*personne, situation, muscle*) tense; (*main*) held out; (*rapports*) strained.

tendre[2] [tādr] *a* **1** (*viande*) tender; (*bois, couleur*) soft. **2** (*personne*) affectionate (**avec** to). ●**—ment** [-əmā] *adv* tenderly. ● **tendresse** *nf* affection, tenderness.

ténèbres [tenɛbr] *nfpl* darkness.

teneur [tənœr] *nf* (*de lettre*) content; **t. en alcool/**etc alcohol/etc content (**de** of).

tenir* [tənir] *vt* (*à la main etc*) to hold; (*promesse, comptes, hôtel*) to keep; (*rôle*) to play; (*propos*) to utter; **t. sa droite** (*conducteur*) to keep to the right; **t. la route** (*véhicule*) to hold the road; **t. pour** to regard as; **je le tiens!** (*je l'ai attrapé*) I've got him!
∥ *vi* (*nœud etc*) to hold; (*neige*) to last; (*résister*) to hold out; (*offre*) to stand; **t. à qn/qch** to be attached to *ou* fond of s.o./sth; **t. à la vie** to value life; **t. à faire** to be anxious to do; **t. dans qch** (*être contenu*) to fit into sth; **t. de qn** to take after s.o.; **tenez!** (*prenez*) here (you are)!; **tiens!** (*surprise*) well!, hey!
∥ *v imp* **il ne tient qu'à vous** it's up to you

(**de faire** to do)
∥ **se tenir** *vpr* (*avoir lieu*) to be held; (*rester*) to remain, stay; **se t. debout** to stand (up); **se t. droit** to stand up *ou* sit up straight; **se t. par la main** to hold hands; **se t. bien** to behave oneself; **se t. à** to hold on to; **s'en t. à** (*se limiter à*) to stick to.

tennis [tenis] *nm* tennis; (*terrain*) (tennis) court; **t. de table** table tennis ∥ *nmpl* (*chaussures*) plimsolls, *Am* sneakers.

ténor [tenɔr] *nm Mus* tenor.

tension [tāsjɔ̃] *nf* tension; **t. (artérielle)** blood pressure; **avoir de la t.** *Méd* to have high blood pressure.

tentacule [tātakyl] *nm* tentacle.

tente [tāt] *nf* tent.

tenter[1] [tāte] *vt* (*essayer*) to try; **t. de faire** to try *ou* attempt to do. ● **tentative** *nf* attempt; **t. de suicide** suicide attempt.

tent/er[2] [tāte] *vt* (*faire envie etc*) to tempt; **tenté de faire** tempted to do. ●**—ant** *a* tempting. ● **tentation** *nf* temptation.

tenture [tātyr] *nf* (*wall*) hanging; (*de porte*) drape, curtain.

tenu [təny] *pp de* tenir ∥ *a* **t. de faire** obliged to do; **bien/mal t.** (*maison etc*) well/badly kept.

tenue [təny] *nf* **1** (*vêtements*) clothes, outfit; **t. de combat** *Mil* combat dress; **t. de soirée** evening dress. **2** (*conduite*) (good) behaviour; (*maintien*) posture; **manquer de t.** to lack (good) manners. **3** (*de maison, hôtel*) running; (*de comptes*) keeping. **4** **t. de route** *Aut* road-holding.

ter [ter] *a* **4 t.** (*numéro*) 4B.

térébenthine [terebātin] *nf* turpentine.

tergal® [tergal] *nm* Terylene®, *Am* Dacron®.

terme [term] *nm* **1** (*mot*) term. **2** (*fin*) end; **mettre un t. à** to put an end to; **à court/long t.** (*conséquences etc*) short-/long-term. **3** **moyen t.** (*solution*) middle course. **4** **en bons/mauvais termes** on good/bad terms (**avec qn** with s.o.).

terminal, -aux [terminal, -o] **1** *a* final; (*phase*) *Méd* terminal ∥ *a* **& nf** (**classe**)

terminale *Scol* = sixth form, *Am* = twelfth grade. **2** *nm* (*d'ordinateur, pétrolier*) terminal.

terminer [tɛrmine] *vt* to end; (*achever*) to finish, complete. ● **se t.** *vpr* to end (*par with, en in*). ● **terminaison** *nf* (*de mot*) ending.

terminus [tɛrminys] *nm* terminus.

termite [tɛrmit] *nm* (*insecte*) termite.

terne [tɛrn] *a* (*couleur etc*) dull, drab; (*personne*) dull. ● **ternir** *vt* (*métal, réputation*) to tarnish; (*meuble*) to dull.

terrain [tɛrɛ̃] *nm* (*sol*) & *Fig* ground; (*étendue*) land; (*à bâtir*) plot, site; **un t. a piece of land; t. de camping** campsite; **t. de football/rugby** football/rugby pitch; **t. de jeux** (*pour enfants*) playground; (*stade*) playing field; **t. de sport** sports ground, playing field; **t. d'aviation** airfield; **t. vague** waste ground, *Am* vacant lot; **céder/gagner/perdre du t.** *Mil* & *Fig* to give/gain/lose ground; **véhicule tout t.** *ou* **tous terrains** off-road *ou* all-terrain vehicle.

terrasse [tɛras] *nf* **1** (*balcon, plateforme*) terrace. **2** (*de café*) pavement *ou Am* sidewalk area; **à la t.** outside.

terrasser [tɛrase] *vt* (*adversaire*) to floor, knock down; (*accabler*) *Fig* to overcome.

terre [tɛr] *nf* (*matière, monde*) earth; (*sol*) ground; (*opposé à mer*) land; *pl* (*domaine*) land, estate; *Él* earth, *Am* ground; **la T.** (*planète*) Earth; **à** *ou* **par t.** (*poser, tomber*) to the ground; **par t.** (*assis, couché*) on the ground; **sous t.** underground; **t. cuite** (baked) clay, earthenware. ● **t.-à-terre** *a inv* down-to-earth. ● **t.-plein** *nm* (earth) platform; (*au milieu de la route*) central reservation, *Am* median strip.

terreau [tɛro] *nm* compost.

terrer (se) [sɛtɛre] *vpr* (*fugitif, animal*) to hide, go to ground.

terrestre [tɛrɛstr] *a* (*vie, joies*) earthly; **la surface t.** the earth's surface; **globe t.** globe (*model*).

terreur [tɛrœr] *nf* terror. ● **terrible** *a*

awful, terrible; (*formidable*) *Fam* terrific. ● **terrifier** *vt* to terrify. ● **terrifiant** *a* terrifying; (*extraordinaire*) incredible.

terrien, -ienne [tɛrjɛ̃, -jɛn] *a* land owning; **propriétaire t.** landowner. ▌*nmf* (*habitant de la terre*) earth dweller, earthling.

terrier [tɛrje] *nm* **1** (*de lapin etc*) burrow. **2** (*chien*) terrier.

terrine [tɛrin] *nf* (*récipient*) *Culin* terrine; (*pâté*) pâté.

territoire [tɛritwar] *nm* territory.

terroir [tɛrwar] *nm* (*sol*) soil; (*région*) region; **du t.** (*accent etc*) rural.

terroriser [tɛrɔrize] *vt* to terrorize. ● **terrorisme** *nm* terrorism. ● **terroriste** *a* & *nmf* terrorist.

tertiaire [tɛrsjɛr] *a* **secteur t.** service *ou* tertiary sector.

tes [te] *voir* **ton**[1].

test [tɛst] *nm* test. ● **tester** *vt* (*élève, produit*) to test.

testament [tɛstamɑ̃] *nm* **1** *Jur* will. **2** **Ancien/Nouveau T.** *Rel* Old/New Testament.

testicule [tɛstikyl] *nm* *Anat* testicle.

tétanos [tetanos] *nm* *Méd* tetanus.

têtard [tɛtar] *nm* tadpole.

tête [tɛt] *nf* head; (*visage*) face; (*d'arbre*) top; (*de lit*) head; (*de page, liste*) head, (*coup*) *Fb* header; **t. nucléaire** nuclear warhead; **tenir t. à qn** (*s'opposer à*) to stand up to s.o.; **faire la t.** (*bouder*) to sulk; **faire une drôle de t.** to give a funny look; **tomber la t. la première** to fall headlong; **calculer qch de t.** to work sth out in one's head; **se mettre dans la t. de faire qch** to get it into one's head to do sth; **à la t. de** (*entreprise, parti*) at the head of; (*classe*) at the top of; **de la t. aux pieds** from head to toe; **en t.** *Sp* in the lead; **se payer la t. de qn** *Fam* to make fun of s.o.; **j'en ai par-dessus la t.** *Fam* I've had enough of it; **ça me prend la t.** *Fam* it gets on my nerves *ou* under my skin.

tête-à-queue [tɛtakø] *nm inv* **faire un t.-à-queue** *Aut* to spin right round.

tête-à-tête [tetatɛt] adv (seul) in private, alone together ▌nm inv tête-à-tête.

téter [tete] vt to suck; **t. sa mère** (bébé) to feed (at one's mother's breast); **le bébé tète** the baby is being fed (at the breast); **donner à t. à** to feed. ● **tétée** nf (de bébé) feed. ● **tétine** nf (de biberon) teat, Am nipple; (sucette) dummy, Am pacifier.

têtu [tety] a stubborn, obstinate.

texte [tɛkst] nm text; Th lines.

textile [tɛkstil] a & nm textile.

texture [tɛkstyr] nf texture.

TGV [teʒeve] abrév = **train à grande vitesse.**

Thaïlande [tailɑ̃d] nf Thailand. ● **thaïlandais, -aise** a & nmf Thai.

thé [te] nm (boisson, réunion) tea. ● **théière** nf teapot.

théâtre [teatr] nm (art, lieu) theatre; (œuvres) drama; (d'un crime) Fig scene; (des opérations) Mil theatre; **faire du t.** to act. ● **théâtral, -aux** a theatrical.

thème [tɛm] nm theme; (traduction) Scol translation, prose.

théologie [teɔlɔʒi] nf theology.

théorie [teɔri] nf theory; **en t.** in theory. ● **théorique** a theoretical.

thérapeutique [terapøtik] a therapeutic ▌nf (traitement) therapy. ● **thérapie** nf Psy therapy.

thermal, -aux [tɛrmal, -o] a **station thermale** spa; **eaux thermales** hot springs.

thermomètre [tɛrmɔmɛtr] nm thermometer.

thermos® [tɛrmɔs] nm ou f inv Thermos® (flask ou Am bottle), vacuum flask.

thermostat [tɛrmɔsta] nm thermostat.

thèse [tɛz] nf (proposition, ouvrage) thesis.

thon [tɔ̃] nm tuna (fish).

thym [tɛ̃] nm Bot Culin thyme.

tibia [tibja] nm shin bone.

tic [tik] nm (contraction) twitch, tic; (manie) Fig mannerism.

ticket [tikɛ] nm ticket; **t. de quai** Rail platform ticket.

tiède [tjɛd] a (luke)warm, tepid; (vent) mild; (accueil, partisan) half-hearted. ● **tiédir** vi to cool (down); (devenir plus chaud) to warm up.

tien, tienne [tjɛ̃, tjɛn] pron poss **le t., la tienne**, **les tien(ne)s** yours; **les deux tiens** ▌nmpl **les tiens** (ta famille) your (own) people.

tiens, tient [tjɛ̃] voir **tenir.**

tiercé [tjɛrse] nm (pari) place betting (on the horses); **jouer/gagner au t.** = to bet/win on the horses.

tiers, tierce [tjɛr, tjɛrs] a third ▌nm (fraction) third; (personne) third party; **assurance au t.** third-party insurance. ● **T.-Monde** nm Third World.

tige [tiʒ] nf (de plante) stem, stalk; (barre) rod.

tigre [tigr] nm tiger. ● **tigresse** nf tigress.

tigré [tigre] a (rayé) striped.

tilleul [tijœl] nm lime (tree); (infusion) lime tea.

timbale [tɛ̃bal] nf **1** (gobelet) (metal) tumbler. **2** Mus kettledrum.

timbre [tɛ̃br] nm **1** (tampon, vignette) stamp; (cachet de la poste) postmark. **2** (sonnette) bell. **3** (d'instrument, de voix) tone (quality). ● **t.-poste** nm (pl **timbres-poste**) (postage) stamp. ● **timbrer** vt (affranchir) to stamp (lettre).

timide [timid] a (gêné) shy, timid; (timoré) timid. ● **—ment** adv shyly; timidly. ● **timidité** nf shyness.

tinter [tɛ̃te] vi (cloche) to ring; (clefs, monnaie) to jingle; (verres) to chink.

tique [tik] nf (insecte) tick.

tiquer [tike] vi (personne) to wince.

tir [tir] nm (sport) shooting; (action) firing, shooting; Fb shot; **(stand de) t.** shooting ou rifle range; **t. à l'arc** archery; **ligne de t.** line of fire.

tirage [tiraʒ] nm **1** (de journal) circulation; (édition) edition; (quantité) (print) run; Typ Phot printing. **2** (de loterie) draw; **t. au sort** drawing of lots. **3** (de

cheminée) draught.
tirailler [tiraje] **1** *vt* to pull (away) at; **tirailler entre** (*possibilités etc*) torn between. **2** *vi* (*au fusil*) to shoot wildly.
tire [tir] *nf* **vol à la t.** *Fam* pickpocketing.
tire-au-flanc [tiroflɑ̃] *nm inv* (*paresseux*) shirker.
tire-bouchon [tirbuʃɔ̃] *nm* corkscrew.
tirelire [tirlir] *nf* moneybox, *Am* coin bank.
tirer [tire] *vt* to pull; (*langue*) to stick out; (*trait, rideaux, conclusion*) to draw; (*balle, canon*) to shoot, fire; *Typ Phot* to print; **t. de** (*sortir*) to pull *ou* draw *ou* take out of; (*obtenir*) to get from; (*nom, origine*) to derive from; (*produit*) to extract from; **t. qn de** (*danger, lit*) to get s.o. out of.
‖ *vi* to pull (*sur* on, at); (*faire feu*) to shoot, fire (*sur* at); *Fb* to shoot; **t. au sort** to draw lots; **t. à sa fin** to draw to a close.
‖ se tirer *vpr* (*partir*) *Fam* to beat it; **se t. de** (*travail, problème*) to cope with; (*danger, situation*) to get out of; **se t. d'affaire** to get out of trouble. ● **tiré** *a* (*traits, visage*) drawn; **t. par les cheveux** *Fig* far-fetched.
tiret [tire] *nm* (*trait*) dash.
tireur [tirœr] *nm* gunman; **t. d'élite** marksman; **t. isolé** sniper; **un bon/ mauvais t.** a good/bad shot.
tiroir [tirwar] *nm* (*de commode etc*) drawer.
tisane [tizan] *nf* herb(al) tea.
tison [tizɔ̃] *nm* (fire)brand, ember. ● **tisonnier** *nm* poker.
tiss/er [tise] *vt* to weave. ● **—age** *nm* (*action*) weaving.
tissu [tisy] *nm* material, cloth, fabric; *Biol* tissue; **du t.-éponge** (terry) towelling, *Am* toweling.
titre [titr] *nm* (*nom, qualité*) title; *Com* bond; (*diplôme*) qualification; (*gros*) **t.** (*de journal*) headline; **t. de propriété** title deed; **t. de transport** ticket; **à quel t.?** (*pour quelle raison*) on what grounds?; **à ce t.** (*en cette qualité*) as

such; (*pour cette raison*) therefore; **au même t.** in the same way (**que** as); **à t. d'exemple** as an example; **à t. exceptionnel** exceptionally; **à t. privé** in a private capacity; **à juste t.** rightly.
tituber [titybe] *vi* to reel, stagger.
titulaire [tityler] *a* **être t. de** (*permis etc*) to be the holder of; (*poste*) to hold **‖** *nmf* (*de permis, poste*) holder (**de** of).
toast [tost] *nm* **1** (*pain grillé*) piece *ou* slice of toast. **2** (*allocution*) toast; **porter un t. à** to drink (a toast) to.
toboggan [tɔbɔgɑ̃] *nm* **1** (*de terrain de jeux etc*) slide. **2** *Aut* flyover, *Am* overpass.
toc [tɔk] **1** *int* **t. t.!** knock knock! **2** *nm* **du t.** (*camelote*) trash; **bijou en t.** imitation jewel.
toi [twa] *pron* **1** (*après une préposition*) you; **avec t.** with you. **2** (*sujet*) you; **t., tu peux** you may; **c'est t. qui ...** it's you who .... **3** (*réfléchi*) **assieds-t.** sit (yourself) down; **dépêche-t.** hurry up. ● **t.-même** *pron* yourself.
toile [twal] *nf* **1** cloth; (*à voile, sac etc*) canvas; **une t.** a piece of cloth *ou* canvas. **2** (*tableau*) painting, canvas. **3** **t. d'araignée** (spider's) web.
toilette [twalet] *nf* (*action*) wash(ing); (*vêtements*) clothes, outfit; **articles de t.** toiletries; **cabinet de t.** washroom; **eau/trousse de t.** toilet water/bag; **faire sa t.** to wash (and dress); **les toilettes** (*W-C*) the toilet(s), *Am* the men's *ou* ladies' room; **aller aux toilettes** to go to the toilet *ou Am* to the men's *ou* ladies' room.
toit [twa] *nm* roof; **t. ouvrant** *Aut* sunroof. ● **toiture** *nf* roof(ing).
tôle [tol] *nf* **la t.** sheet metal; **une t.** a metal *ou* steel sheet; **t. ondulée** corrugated iron.
tolér/er [tɔlere] *vt* (*permettre*) to tolerate, allow; (*supporter*) to tolerate, bear. ● **—ant** *a* tolerant (**à l'égard de** of).
tollé [tɔle] *nm* outcry.
tomate [tɔmat] *nf* tomato; **sauce t.** tomato sauce.

tombe [tɔ̃b] *nf* grave; *(avec monument)* tomb. ● **tombale** *af* pierre t. gravestone, tombstone. ● **tombeau, -x** *nm* tomb.

tomber [tɔ̃be] *vi (aux être)* to fall; *(température)* to drop, fall; *(vent)* to drop (off); **t. malade** to fall ill; **t. (par terre)** to fall (down); **faire t.** *(personne)* to knock over; *(gouvernement)* to bring down; **laisser t.** *(objet)* to drop; *(projet etc) Fig* to drop, give up; **tu tombes bien/mal** *Fig* you've come at the right/ wrong time; **t. de sommeil** to be ready to drop; **t. un lundi** to fall on a Monday; **t. sur** *(trouver)* to come across. ● **tombée** *nf* **t. de la nuit** nightfall.

tombola [tɔ̃bɔla] *nf* raffle.

tome [tɔm] *nm (livre)* volume.

ton¹, ta, *pl* **tes** [tɔ̃, ta, te] *(ta becomes* **ton** [tɔ̃n] *before a vowel or mute h) a poss* your; **ton père** your father; **ta mère** your mother; **ton ami(e)** your friend.

ton² [tɔ̃] *nm (de voix etc)* tone; *(de couleur)* shade, tone; **de bon t.** *(goût)* in good taste. ● **tonalité** *nf Tél* dialling tone, *Am* dial tone.

tond/re [tɔ̃dr] *vt (mouton)* to shear; *(gazon)* to mow. ● **—euse** *nf* shears; *(à cheveux)* clippers; **t. (à gazon)** (lawn)mower.

tonifier [tɔnifje] *vt (muscles, peau)* to tone up; *(personne)* to invigorate.

tonique [tɔnik] **1** *a (accent) Ling* tonic. **2** *a (froid, effet)* tonic, invigorating ‖ *nm Méd* tonic; *(cosmétique)* tonic lotion.

tonne [tɔn] *nf (poids)* metric ton, tonne; **des tonnes de** *(beaucoup) Fam* tons of.

tonneau, -x [tɔno] *nm* **1** *(récipient)* barrel, cask. **2** *(manœuvre) Av* roll; **faire un t.** *Aut* to roll over. **3** *(poids) Nau* ton.

tonnelle [tɔnɛl] *nf* arbour, bower.

tonner [tɔne] *vi (canons)* to thunder ‖ *v imp* **il tonne** it's thundering. ● **tonnerre** *nm* thunder; **coup de t.** burst *ou* crash of thunder, thunderclap; **du t.** *(excellent) Fam* terrific.

tonton [tɔ̃tɔ̃] *nm Fam* uncle.

tonus [tɔnys] *nm* energy, vitality.

top [tɔp] *nm (signal sonore) Rad* stroke.

toque [tɔk] *nf (de fourrure)* fur hat; *(de jockey)* cap; *(de cuisinier)* hat.

toqué [tɔke] *a (fou) Fam* crazy. ● **toquade** *nf Fam (pour qch)* craze *(pour* for); *(pour qn)* infatuation *(pour* with).

torche [tɔrʃ] *nf (flamme)* torch; **t. électrique** torch, *Am* flashlight.

torchon [tɔrʃɔ̃] *nm (à vaisselle)* tea towel, *Am* dish towel; *(de ménage)* duster, cloth.

tordre [tɔrdr] *vt* to twist; *(linge, cou)* to wring; *(barre)* to bend; **se t. la cheville/ le pied** to twist *ou* sprain one's ankle/ foot ‖ **se t.** *vpr* to twist; *(barre)* to bend; **se t. de douleur** to be doubled up with pain; **se t. (de rire)** to split one's sides (laughing). ● **tordant** *a (drôle) Fam* hilarious. ● **tordu** *a* twisted; *(esprit)* warped.

tornade [tɔrnad] *nf* tornado.

torpille [tɔrpij] *nf* torpedo. ● **torpiller** *vt Mil & Fig* to torpedo.

torréfier [tɔrefje] *vt (café)* to roast.

torrent [tɔrɑ̃] *nm (mountain)* stream, torrent; **un t. de** *(injures, larmes)* a flood of; **il pleut à torrents** it's pouring (down). ● **torrentiel, -ielle** *a (pluie)* torrential.

torsade [tɔrsad] *nf (de cheveux)* twist, coil.

torse [tɔrs] *nm Anat* chest; *(statue)* torso; **t. nu** stripped to the waist.

torsion [tɔrsjɔ̃] *nf* twisting; *Phys Tech* torsion.

tort [tɔr] *nm* **avoir t.** to be wrong *(de faire* to do, in doing); **tu as t. de fumer!** you shouldn't smoke!; **être dans son t.** *ou* **en t.** to be in the wrong; **donner t. à qn** *(accuser)* to blame s.o.; *(faits etc)* to prove s.o. wrong; **faire du t. à qn** to harm *ou* wrong s.o.; **à t.** wrongly; **parler à t. et à travers** to talk nonsense; **à t. ou à raison** rightly or wrongly.

torticolis [tɔrtikɔli] *nm* **avoir le t.** to have a stiff neck.

tortiller [tɔrtije] *vt* to twist, twirl ‖ **se t.** *vpr (ver, personne)* to wriggle; *(en* *dansant, des hanches*) to wiggle.

tortue [tɔrty] *nf* tortoise; *Am* turtle; (*de mer*) turtle.

torture [tɔrtyr] *nf* torture. ●**torturer** *vt* to torture; **se t. les méninges** *Fam* to rack one's brains.

tôt [to] *adv* early; **au plus t.** at the earliest; **le plus t. possible** as soon as possible; **t. ou tard** sooner or later; **je n'étais pas plus t. sorti que...** no sooner had I gone out than ....

total, -aux [tɔtal, -o] *a & nm* total; **au t.** all in all, in total. ●**totalement** *adv* totally. ●**totaliser** *vt* to total. ●**totalité** *nf* entirety; **la t. de** all of; **en t.** (*détruit etc*) entirely; (*payé*) fully.

toubib [tubib] *nm* (*médecin*) *Fam* doctor.

touche [tuʃ] *nf* (*de clavier*) key; (*de téléphone*) (push-)button; **téléphone à touches** push-button phone; **une t.** de (*un peu de*) a touch of; (*ligne de*) **t.** *Fb Rugby* touchline.

toucher [tuʃe] *vt* to touch; (*paie*) to draw; (*chèque*) to cash; (*cible*) to hit; (*émouvoir*) to touch, move; (*concerner*) to affect ▌*vi* **t. à** to touch; (*sujet*) to touch on; (*but, fin*) to approach ▌**se t.** *vpr* (*lignes, mains etc*) to touch ▌*nm* (*sens*) touch; **au t.** to the touch. ●**touchant** *a* (*émouvant*) moving, touching.

touffe [tuf] *nf* (*de cheveux, d'herbe*) tuft; (*de plantes*) cluster. ●**touffu** *a* (*barbe, haie*) thick, bushy.

toujours [tuʒur] *adv* always; (*encore*) still; **pour t.** for ever; **essaie t.!** (*quand même*) try anyhow!; **t. est-il que...** the fact remains that ....

touple [tupi] *nf* (*spinning*) top.

tour[1] [tur] *nf* **1** (*bâtiment*) tower; (*immeuble*) tower block, high-rise. **2** *Échecs* castle, rook.

tour[2] [tur] *nm* **1** (*mouvement etc*) turn; (*de magie etc*) trick; (*excursion*) trip, outing; (*à pied*) stroll, walk; (*en voiture*) drive; **t. de cartes** card trick; **t. de poitrine**/*etc* chest/*etc* measurement *ou* size; **faire le t. de** to go round; (*question, situation*) to review; **faire un t.** (*à pied*)

to go for a stroll *ou* walk; (*en voiture*) to go for a drive; (*court voyage*) to go on a trip; **jouer un t. à qn** to play a trick on s.o.; **c'est mon t.** it's my turn; **à qui le t.?** whose turn (is it)?; **à son t.** in (one's) turn; **à t. de rôle** in turn; **à t.** in turn, by turns.

2 *Tech* lathe; (*de potier*) wheel.

tourbillon [turbijɔ̃] *nm* (*de vent*) whirlwind; (*d'eau*) whirlpool; (*de neige, sable*) swirl. ●**tourbillonner** *vi* to whirl, swirl.

tourelle [turɛl] *nf* turret.

tourisme [turism] *nm* tourism; **faire du t.** to go sightseeing *ou* touring; **agence/office de t.** tourist agency/office. ●**touriste** *nmf* tourist. ●**touristique** *a* **guide/***etc* **t.** tourist guide/*etc*; **route t., circuit t.** scenic route.

tourmenter [turmɑ̃te] *vt* to torment ▌**se t.** *vpr* to worry (oneself). ●**tourmenté** *a* (*mer, vie*) turbulent, stormy; (*expression, visage*) anguished.

tourne-disque [turnədisk] *nm* record player.

tournée [turne] *nf* **1** (*de livreur etc*) round; (*de spectacle*) tour. **2** (*de boissons*) round.

tourner [turne] *vt* to turn; (*film*) to shoot; (*difficulté*) to get round; **t. en ridicule** to ridicule; **t. le dos à qn** to turn one's back on s.o. ▌*vi* to turn; (*tête, toupie*) to spin; (*moteur*) to run, go; (*usine*) to run; (*lait*) to go off; (*Terre*) to revolve, turn; **t. autour de** (*objet*) to go round; (*maison, personne*) to hang around; **t. bien/mal** (*évoluer*) to turn out well/badly.

▌**se tourner** *vpr* to turn (vers to, towards). ●**tournant 1** *a* **pont t.** swing bridge. **2** *nm* (*de route*) bend, turning; (*moment*) *Fig* turning point. ●**tournage** *nm* *Cin* shooting, filming.

tournesol [turnəsɔl] *nm* sunflower.

tournevis [turnəvis] *nm* screwdriver.

tourniquet [turnikɛ] *nm* **1** (*barrière*) turnstile. **2** (*pour arroser*) sprinkler.

tournoi [turnwa] *nm* *Sp & Hist* tournament.

tournoyer [turnwaje] *vi* to spin (round), whirl.

tourterelle [turtərɛl] *nf* turtledove.

Toussaint [tusɛ̃] *nf* All Saints' Day.

tousser [tuse] *vi* to cough.

tout, toute, *pl* **tous, toutes** [tu, tut, tu, tut] **1** *a* all; **tous les livres**/*etc* all the books/*etc*; **t. l'argent/le temps/le village**/*etc* all the money/time/village/*etc*, the whole of the money/time/village/*etc*; **toute la nuit** all night, the whole (of the) night; **tous (les) deux** both; **tous (les) trois** all three; **t. un problème** quite a problem.

2 *a* (*chaque*) every, each; (*n'importe quel*) any; **tous les ans/jours**/*etc* every *ou* each year/day/*etc*; **tous les cinq mois/mètres** every five months/metres; **à toute heure** at any time.

3 *pron pl* (**tous** [tus]) all; **ils sont tous là, tous sont là** they're all there.

4 *pron m sing* **tout** everything; **elle dépense t.** she spends everything, she spends it all; **t. ce que je sais** everything that *ou* all that I know; **t. ce qui est là** everything that *ou* all that is there; **en t.** (*au total*) in all.

5 *adv* (*tout à fait*) quite; (*très*) very; **t. simplement** quite simply; **t. petit** very small; **t. neuf** brand new; **t. seul** all alone; **t. droit** straight ahead; **t. autour** all around; **t. au début** right at the beginning; **le t. premier** the very first; **t. au plus** at the very most; **t. en chantant**/*etc* while singing/*etc*; **t. rusé qu'il est** however sly he may be; **t. à coup** suddenly, all of a sudden; **t. à fait** completely; **t. de même** all the same; (*indignation*) really!; **t. de suite** at once.

6 *nm* **le t.** everything, the lot; **un t.** a whole; **pas du t.** not at all; **rien du t.** nothing at all.

toutefois [tutfwa] *adv* nevertheless.

toux [tu] *nf* cough.

toxicomane [tɔksikɔman] *nmf* drug addict. ● **toxicomanie** *nf* drug addiction.

toxique [tɔksik] *a* poisonous, toxic.

trac [trak] *nm* **le t.** (*peur*) the jitters; (*de candidat*) exam nerves; *Th* stage fright; avoir **le t.** to be *ou* become nervous, have *ou* get nerves.

tracas [traka] *nm* worry. ● **tracasser** *vt*, **se t.** *vpr* to worry.

trace [tras] *nf* (*quantité, tache, vestige*) trace; (*marque*) mark; *pl* (*de bête, pneus*) tracks; **traces de pas** footprints; **suivre les traces de qn** *Fig* to follow in s.o.'s footsteps.

trac/er [trase] *vt* (*dessiner*) to draw; (*écrire*) to trace; **t. une route** to mark out a route. ● **-é** *nm* (*plan*) layout; (*ligne*) line.

tract [trakt] *nm* leaflet.

tracter [trakte] *vt* (*caravane etc*) to tow. ● **tracteur** *nm* tractor.

traction [traksjɔ̃] *nf* **t. arrière/avant** *Aut* rear-/front-wheel drive.

tradition [tradisjɔ̃] *nf* tradition. ● **traditionnel, -elle** *a* traditional.

traduire* [traduir] *vt* **1** to translate (*de* from, *en* into); (*exprimer*) *Fig* to express. **2 t. qn en justice** to bring s.o. before the courts. ● **traducteur, -trice** *nmf* translator. ● **traduction** *nf* translation.

trafic [trafik] *nm* **1** *Aut Rail etc* traffic. **2** *Com Péj* traffic, trade; **faire le t. de** to traffic in, trade in. ● **trafiquer 1** *vi* to traffic, trade. **2** *vt Fam* to tamper with. ● **trafiquant, -ante** *nmf* trafficker, dealer; **t. d'armes/de drogue** arms/drug trafficker *ou* dealer.

tragédie [traʒedi] *nf Th & Fig* tragedy. ● **tragique** *a* tragic.

trahir [trair] *vt* to betray; (*secret*) to give away, betray ▮ **se t.** *vpr* to give oneself away, betray oneself. ● **trahison** *nf* betrayal; (*crime*) treason.

train [trɛ̃] *nm* **1** train; **t. à grande vitesse** high-speed train; **t. couchettes** sleeper; **t. auto-couchettes** (car) sleeper. **2 en t.** (*forme*) on form; **se mettre en t.** to get (oneself) into shape. **3 être en t. de faire** to be (busy) doing; **mettre qch en t.** to get sth going. **4** (*allure*) pace; **t. de vie** life style. **5** (*de pneus*) set; (*de péniches, véhicules*) string. **6 t. d'atterrissage** *Av* undercarriage.

traîne [tren] nf 1 (de robe) train. 2 à la t. (en arrière) lagging behind.

traîneau, -x [treno] nm sledge, sleigh, Am sled.

traînée [trene] nf (de peinture etc) streak.

traîner [trene] vt to drag; **faire t. en longueur** (faire durer) to drag out ▮ vi (jouets, papiers etc) to lie around; (s'attarder) to lag behind, dawdle; (errer) to hang around; **t. (par terre)** (robe etc) to trail (on the ground) ▮ **se t.** vpr (avancer) to drag oneself (along); (par terre) to crawl; (durer) to drag on.

train-train [trɛ̃trɛ̃] nm routine.

traire* [trer] vt (vache) to milk.

trait [tre] nm 1 line; (en dessinant) stroke; (caractéristique) feature, trait; pl (du visage) features; **t. d'union** hyphen; **d'un t.** (boire) in one gulp; **avoir t. à** (se rapporter à) to relate to. 2 **cheval de t.** draught ou Am draft horse.

traite [tret] nf 1 (de vache) milking. 2 Com bill, draft. 3 **d'une (seule) t.** (sans interruption) in one go.

traité [trete] nm Pol treaty.

traiter [trete] vt (se comporter envers) & Méd to treat; (problème, sujet) to deal with; (marché) Com to negotiate; (matériau, produit) to treat, process; **t. qn de lâche/etc** to call s.o. a coward/etc.
▮ vi to negotiate, deal (avec with); **t. de** (sujet) to deal with. ● **traitant** a **médecin t.** regular doctor. ● **traitement** nm 1 treatment; **t. de données/de texte** data/word processing; **machine à ou de t. de texte** word processor. 2 (gains) salary.

traiteur [tretœr] nm (fournisseur) caterer; **chez le t.** (magasin) at the delicatessen.

traître [tretr] nm traitor. ● **traîtrise** nf treachery.

trajectoire [traʒektwar] nf (de fusée, missile etc) path.

trajet [traʒe] nm trip, journey; (distance) distance; (itinéraire) route.

trampoline [trãpolin] nm trampoline.

tram(way) [tram(wɛ)] nm tram, Am streetcar.

tranche [trãʃ] nf (morceau) slice; (bord) edge; (partie) portion; (de salaire, impôts) bracket; **t. d'âge** age bracket.

tranchée [trãʃe] nf trench.

tranch/er [trãʃe] vt 1 to cut. 2 vt (difficulté, question) to settle ▮ vi (décider) to decide. 3 vi (contraster) to contrast (avec, sur with). ● **—ant** a (couteau, voix) sharp ▮ nm (cutting) edge; **à double t.** Fig double-edged.

tranquille [trãkil] a quiet; (mer) calm; (conscience) clear; (esprit) easy; **laisser t.** to leave alone; **soyez t.** don't worry. ● **tranquillement** adv calmly. ● **tranquillité** nf (peace and) quiet; (d'esprit) peace of mind.

tranquillis/er [trãkilize] vt to reassure; **tranquillisez-vous** set your mind at rest. ● **—ant** nm Méd tranquillizer.

trans- [trãz, trãs] préf trans-.

transaction [trãzaksjɔ̃] nf Com transaction.

transatlantique [trãzatlãtik] a transatlantic ▮ nm (paquebot) transatlantic liner; (chaise) deckchair.

transe [trãs] nf **en t.** in a trance.

transférer [trãsfere] vt to transfer (à to). ● **transfert** nm transfer.

transformer [trãsfɔrme] vt to change, transform; (maison) to carry out alterations to; (essai) Rugby to convert; **t. en** to turn into ▮ **se t.** vpr to change, be transformed (en into). ● **transformateur** nm Él transformer. ● **transformation** nf change, transformation; alteration.

transfuge [trãsfyʒ] nm Mil renegade ▮ nmf Pol renegade.

transfusion [trãsfyzjɔ̃] nf **t. (sanguine)** (blood) transfusion.

transgresser [trãsgrese] vt (loi, ordre) to disobey.

transi [trãzi] a (personne) numb with cold.

transistor [trãzistɔr] nm transistor (radio).

transit [trãzit] nm transit; **en t.** in transit;

salle de t. *Av* transit lounge. ● **transiter**
vt **(faire) t.** to send in transit ‖ *vi* to be in
transit.

transitif, -ive [trãzitif, -iv] *a Gram* transitive.

transition [trãzisjɔ̃] *nf* transition.
● **transitoire** *a* (*qui passe*) transient;
(*provisoire*) transitional.

transmettre* [trãsmetr] *vt* (*message etc*)
to pass on (à to); *Phys Tech* to transmit; *Rad TV* to broadcast.

transparent [trãsparã] *a* clear, transparent. ● **transparence** *nf* transparency.

transpercer [trãsperse] *vt* to pierce, go
through.

transpirer [trãspire] *vi* (*suer*) to sweat,
perspire. ● **transpiration** *nf* perspiration.

transplanter [trãsplãte] *vt* (*organe*,
plante etc) to transplant.

transport [trãspor] *nm* (*action*) transport, transportation (**de** of); *pl*
(*moyens*) transport; **moyen de t.** means
of transport; **transports en commun**
public transport; **frais de t.** transport
costs.

transporter [trãsporte] *vt* to transport,
convey; (*à la main*) to carry, take; **t.**
d'urgence à l'hôpital to rush to hospital
ou Am to the hospital. ● **transporteur**
nm **t. (routier)** haulier, *Am* trucker.

transversal, -aux [trãsversal, -o] *a* **rue/**
etc **transversale** cross street/*etc*.

trapèze [trapez] *nm* (*au cirque*) trapeze.
● **trapéziste** *nmf* trapeze artist.

trappe [trap] *nf* (*dans le plancher*) trap
door.

trapu [trapy] *a* (*personne*) stocky, thickset.

traquer [trake] *vt* to track *ou* hunt
(down).

traumatiser [tromatize] *vt* to traumatize.
● **traumatisme** *nm* (*choc*) trauma.

travail, -aux [travaj, -o] *nm* (*activité, lieu*)
work; (*à effectuer*) job, task; (*emploi*)
job; (*façonnage*) working (**de** of); *Écon*
Méd labour; *pl* work; (*dans la rue*)
roadworks, *Am* roadwork; (*aménage-*
ment) alterations; **travaux pratiques**

Scol Univ practical work; **travaux**
manuels *Scol* handicrafts; **travaux for-**
cés hard labour; **travaux ménagers**
housework; **t. au noir** moonlighting.

travaill/er [travaje] *vi* to work (à **qch** at
ou on sth) ‖ *vt* (*discipline, rôle, style*) to
work on; (*façonner*) to work. **2** *vi* (*bois*)
to warp. ● **—eur, -euse** *a* hard-working
‖ *nmf* worker.

travailliste [travajist] *a Pol* Labour ‖ *nmf*
Pol member of the Labour party.

travers [traver] **1** *prép & adv* à **t.**
through; **en t. (de)** across. **2** *adv* **de t.**
(*chapeau, nez etc*) crooked; (*com-*
prendre) badly; (*regarder*) askance;
aller de t. *Fig* to go wrong; **j'ai avalé**
de t. it went down the wrong way. **3** *nm*
(*défaut*) failing.

traverse [travers] *nf* **1** *Rail* sleeper, *Am*
tie. **2** **chemin de t.** short cut.

travers/er [traverse] *vt* to cross, go
across; (*foule, période, mur*) to go
through. ● **—ée** *nf* (*voyage*) crossing.

traversin [traversɛ̃] *nm* bolster.

travesti [travesti] *nm Th* female impersonator; (*homosexuel*) transvestite.

trébucher [trebyʃe] *vi* to stumble (**sur**
over); **faire t. qn** to trip s.o. (up).

trèfle [trefl] *nm* **1** (*plante*) clover. **2**
(*couleur*) *Cartes* clubs.

treillis [treji] *nm* **1** latticework); (*en*
métal) wire mesh. **2** (*tenue militaire*)
combat uniform.

treize [trez] *a & nm inv* thirteen. ● **trei-**
zième *a & nmf* thirteenth.

tréma [trema] *nm Gram* di(a)eresis.

trembl/er [trãble] *vi* to shake, tremble;
(*de froid, peur*) to tremble (**de** with);
(*flamme, lumière*) to flicker; (*voix*) to
tremble. ● **—ement** *nm* (*action, frisson*)
shaking, trembling; **t. de terre** earthquake.

trémousser (se) [sətremuse] *vpr* to
wriggle (about).

tremper [trãpe] **1** *vt* to soak, drench;
(*plonger*) to dip (**dans** in) ‖ *vi* to soak;
faire t. qch to soak sth ‖ **se t.** *vpr* (*se*
baigner) to take a dip. **2** *vt* (*acier*) to

temper.

tremplin [trɑ̃plɛ̃] *nm Natation & Fig* springboard.

trente [trɑ̃t] *a & nm* thirty; **un t.-trois tours** (*disque*) an LP. ● **trentaine** *nf* une **t. (de)** (*nombre*) (about) thirty. ● **trentième** *a & nmf* thirtieth.

trépied [trepje] *nm* tripod.

trépigner [trepiɲe] *vi* to stamp (one's feet).

très [trɛ] *adv* ([trɛz] *before vowel or mute h*) very; **t. aimé/critiqué/**etc (*with past participle*) much *ou* greatly liked/criticized/*etc*.

trésor [trezɔr] *nm* treasure; **le T. (public)** (*service*) public revenue (department). ● **trésorerie** *nf* (*bureaux d'un club etc*) accounts department; (*gestion*) accounting. ● **trésorier, -ière** *nmf* treasurer.

tressaillir* [tresajir] *vi* (*frémir*) to shake, quiver; (*de joie, peur*) to tremble (de with).

tresse [trɛs] *nf* (*cordon*) braid; (*cheveux*) plait, *Am* braid. ● **tresser** *vt* to braid; (*cheveux*) to plait, *Am* braid.

tréteau, -x [treto] *nm* trestle.

treuil [trœj] *nm* winch, windlass.

trêve [trɛv] *nf Mil* truce; (*répit*) *Fig* respite.

tri [tri] *nm* sorting (out); **faire le t. de** to sort (out).

triangle [trijɑ̃gl] *nm* triangle. ● **triangulaire** *a* triangular.

tribord [tribɔr] *nm Nau Av* starboard.

tribu [triby] *nf* tribe. ● **tribal, -aux** *a* tribal.

tribunal, -aux [tribynal, -o] *nm Jur* court; (*militaire*) tribunal.

tribune [tribyn] *nf* **1** (*de salle publique etc*) gallery; (*de stade*) (grand)stand; (*d'orateur*) rostrum. **2 t. libre** (*dans un journal*) open forum.

tricher [triʃe] *vi* to cheat. ● **tricherie** *nf* cheating, trickery; **une t.** a piece of trickery. ● **tricheur, -euse** *nmf* cheat, *Am* cheater.

tricolore [trikɔlɔr] *a* **1** (*cocarde etc*) red, white and blue; **le drapeau t.** the French

flag. **2 feu t.** traffic lights.

tricot [triko] *nm* (*activité, ouvrage*) knitting; (*chandail*) sweater, jumper; **un t.** (*ouvrage*) a piece of knitting; **en t.** knitted. ● **tricoter** *vti* to knit.

tricycle [trisikl] *nm* tricycle.

trier [trije] *vt* (*séparer*) to sort (out); (*choisir*) to pick *ou* sort out.

trimbal(l)er [trɛ̃bale] *vt Fam* to cart about, drag around.

trimestre [trimɛstr] *nm* (*période*) *Com* quarter; *Scol* term. ● **trimestriel, -ielle** *a* (*revue*) quarterly; **bulletin t.** end-of-term report *ou Am* report card.

tringle [trɛ̃gl] *nf* rail, rod; **t. à rideaux** curtain rail *ou* rod.

trinquer [trɛ̃ke] *vi* to chink glasses; **t. à la santé/**etc **de qn** to drink to s.o.'s health/*etc*.

trio [trijo] *nm* (*groupe*) & *Mus* trio.

triomphe [trijɔ̃f] *nm* triumph (**sur** over). ● **triompher** *vi* to triumph (**de** over); (*jubiler*) to be jubilant. ● **triomphant** *a* triumphant.

tripes [trip] *nfpl Culin* tripe; *Fam* guts.

triple [tripl] *a* treble, triple ▮ *nm* **le t.** three times as much (**de** as). ● **tripler** *vti* to treble, triple. ● **triplés, -ées** *nmfpl* (*enfants*) triplets.

tripoter [tripote] *vt* to fiddle about *ou* around with.

triste [trist] *a* sad; (*couleur, temps, rue*) gloomy, dreary; (*lamentable*) unfortunate, sorry. ● **tristement** [-əmɑ̃] *adv* sadly. ● **tristesse** *nf* sadness; (*du temps etc*) gloom(iness), dreariness.

trivial, -aux [trivjal, -o] *a* coarse, vulgar.

troc [trɔk] *nm* exchange, barter.

troène [trɔɛn] *nm* (*arbuste*) privet.

trognon [trɔɲɔ̃] *nm* (*de fruit*) core; (*de chou*) stump.

trois [trwa] *a & nm* three. ● **troisième** *a & nmf* third. ● **troisièmement** *adv* thirdly.

trolley(bus) [trɔle(bys)] *nm* trolleybus.

trombe [trɔ̃b] *nf* **trombe(s) d'eau** (*pluie*) rainstorm, downpour; **en t.** (*entrer etc*) *Fig* like a whirlwind.

trombone [trɔ̃bɔn] *nm* **1** *Mus* trombone.

2 (*agrafe*) paper clip.

trompe [trɔ̃p] *nf* (*d'éléphant*) trunk.

tromper [trɔ̃pe] *vt* to deceive, mislead; (*être infidèle à*) to be unfaithful to; (*échapper à*) to elude ∎ **se t.** *vpr* to be mistaken, make a mistake; **se t. de route**/*etc* to take the wrong road/*etc*; **se t. de date**/*etc* to get the date/*etc* wrong.

trompette [trɔ̃pɛt] *nf* trumpet. ● **trompettiste** *nmf* trumpet player.

tronc [trɔ̃] *nm* 1 (*d'arbre*) & *Anat* trunk. 2 *Rel* collection box.

tronçon [trɔ̃sɔ̃] *nm* section. ● **tronçonner** *vt* to cut (into sections). ● **tronçonneuse** *nf* chain saw.

trône [tron] *nm* throne.

trop [tro] *adv* too; too much; **t. dur**/*etc* too hard/*etc*; **t. fatigué pour jouer** too tired to play; **boire**/*etc* **t.** to drink/*etc* too much; **t. de sel**/*etc* (*quantité*) too much salt/*etc*; **t. de gens**/*etc* (*nombre*) too many people/*etc*; **un franc**/*etc* **de t.** *ou* **en t.** one franc/*etc* too many; **t. souvent** too often; **t. peu** not enough; **se sentir de t.** *Fig* to feel in the way.

trophée [trɔfe] *nm* trophy.

tropiques [trɔpik] *nmpl* **les t.** the tropics. ● **tropical, -aux** *a* tropical.

trop-plein [trɔplɛ̃] *nm* (*dispositif, liquide*) overflow; (*surabondance*) *Fig* excess.

troquer [trɔke] *vt* to exchange (**contre** for).

trot [tro] *nm* trot; **aller au t.** to trot. ● **trotter** [trɔte] *vi* (*cheval*) to trot.

trotteuse [trɔtøz] *nf* (*de montre*) second hand.

trottiner [trɔtine] *vi* (*personne*) to patter *ou* trot along.

trottinette [trɔtinɛt] *nf* (*jouet*) scooter.

trottoir [trɔtwar] *nm* pavement, *Am* sidewalk; **t. roulant** moving walkway.

trou [tru] *nm* hole; (*d'aiguille*) eye; (*village*) *Péj* dump; **t. de (la) serrure** keyhole; **t. (de mémoire)** *Fig* lapse (of memory).

trouble [trubl] 1 *a* (*liquide*) cloudy; (*image*) blurred; (*affaire*) shady; **voir**

t. to see things blurred. 2 *nmpl* (*de santé*) trouble; (*révolte*) disturbances, troubles.

troubler [truble] *vt* to disturb; (*vue*) to blur; (*liquide*) to make cloudy; (*esprit*) to unsettle; (*inquiéter*) to trouble ∎ **se t.** *vpr* (*liquide*) to become cloudy; (*candidat etc*) to become flustered. ● **trouble-fête** *nmf inv* killjoy, spoilsport.

trouer [true] *vt* to make a hole *ou* holes in; (*silence, ténèbres*) to cut through.

trouille [truj] *nf* **avoir la t.** *Fam* to have the jitters. ● **trouillard** *a* (*poltron*) *Fam* chicken.

troupe [trup] *nf* (*groupe*) group; *Th* company; **les troupes** (*armée*) the troops.

troupeau, -x [trupo] *nm* (*de vaches*) & *Fig Péj* herd; (*de moutons, d'oies*) flock.

trousse [trus] *nf* 1 (*étui*) case, kit; (*d'écolier*) pencil case; **t. à outils** toolkit; **t. à pharmacie** first-aid kit; **t. de toilette** sponge *ou* toilet bag, dressing case. 2 *nfpl* **aux trousses de qn** *Fig* on s.o.'s heels.

trousseau, -x [truso] *nm* 1 **t. de clefs** bunch of keys. 2 (*de mariée*) trousseau.

trouver [truve] *vt* to find; **aller/venir t. qn** to go/come and see s.o.; **je trouve que** (*je pense que*) I think that; **comment la trouvez-vous?** what do you think of her? ∎ **se t.** *vpr* to be; (*être situé*) to be situated; (*dans une situation*) to find oneself; **se t. mal** (*s'évanouir*) to faint; **il se trouve que** it happens that. ● **trouvaille** *nf* (lucky) find.

truander [tryɑ̃de] *vi* (*tricher*) *Fam* to cheat.

truc [tryk] *nm* 1 (*astuce*) trick; (*moyen*) way; **trouver le t.** to get the knack (**pour faire** of doing). 2 (*chose*) *Fam* thing.

truffe [tryf] *nf* 1 (*champignon*) truffle. 2 (*de chien*) nose.

truffer [tryfe] *vt* (*remplir*) to stuff (**de** with).

truie [trɥi] *nf* (*animal*) sow.

truite [trɥit] *nf* trout.

truqu/er [tryke] *vt* (*photo etc*) to fake;

(*élections, match*) to rig, fix. ●—**age** *nm*
Cin (special) effect; (*action*) faking;
rigging.

trust [trœst] *nm Com* (*cartel*) trust;
(*entreprise*) corporation.

tsigane [tsigan] *a* & *nmf* (Hungarian)
gipsy.

TSVP [teesvepe] *abrév* (*tournez s'il vous
plaît*) PTO.

TTC [tetese] *abrév* (*toutes taxes com-
prises*) inclusive of tax.

tu¹ [ty] *pron* you (*familiar form of
address*).

tu² [ty] *pp de* **taire**.

tuba [tyba] *nm* **1** *Mus* tuba. **2** *Sp Nau*
snorkel.

tube [tyb] *nm* **1** tube. **2** (*chanson, disque*)
Fam hit.

tuberculose [tyberkyloz] *nf* TB, tuberculosis.

tuer [tɥe] *vt* to kill; (*d'un coup de feu*) to
shoot (dead), kill; (*épuiser*) *Fig* to wear
out ▮ **se t.** *vpr* to kill oneself; to shoot
oneself; (*dans un accident*) to be killed;
se t. à faire *Fig* to wear oneself out
doing. ●**tuant** *a* (*fatigant*) exhausting.
●**tueur, -euse** *nmf* killer.

tue-tête (à) [atytet] *adv* at the top of
one's voice.

tuile [tɥil] *nf* **1** tile. **2** (*malchance*) *Fam*
(stroke of) bad luck.

tulipe [tylip] *nf* tulip.

tumeur [tymœr] *nf* tumour, growth.

tumulte [tymylt] *nm* (*désordre*) turmoil.

tunique [tynik] *nf* tunic.

Tunisie [tynizi] *nf* Tunisia. ●**tunisien,
-ienne** *a* & *nmf* Tunisian.

tunnel [tynel] *nm* tunnel; **le t. sous la
Manche** the Channel Tunnel.

turban [tyrbã] *nm* turban.

turbine [tyrbin] *nf* turbine.

turbulences [tyrbylãs] *nfpl Av etc* turbulence.

turbulent [tyrbylã] *a* (*enfant*) disruptive,
boisterous.

turfiste [tyrfist] *nmf* racegoer.

Turquie [tyrki] *nf* Turkey. ●**turc, turque**
a Turkish ▮ *nmf* Turk ▮ *nm* (*langue*)
Turkish.

turquoise [tyrkwaz] *a inv* turquoise.

tuteur, -trice [tytœr, -tris] *nmf Jur*
guardian. **2** *nm* (*bâton*) stake, prop.
●**tutelle** *nf Jur* guardianship; *Fig* protection.

tutoyer [tytwaje] *vt* **t. qn** to use the
familiar *tu* form to s.o.

tutu [tyty] *nm* ballet skirt, tutu.

tuyau, -x [tɥijo] *nm* **1** pipe; **t. d'arrosage**
hose(pipe); **t. de cheminée** flue; **t.
d'échappement** *Aut* exhaust (pipe). **2**
(*renseignement*) *Fam* tip. ●**tuyauterie**
nf (*tuyaux*) piping.

TVA [tevea] *nf abrév* (*taxe à la valeur
ajoutée*) VAT.

type [tip] *nm* (*modèle*) type; (*individu*)
Fam fellow, guy; **le t. même de** *Fig* the
very model of ▮ *a inv* (*professeur etc*)
typical. ●**typique** *a* typical (**de** of).

typé [tipe] *a* **être très t.** to have all the
usual distinctive features.

typhoïde [tifɔid] *nf Méd* typhoid.

typhon [tifɔ̃] *nm Mét* typhoon.

typographie [tipɔgrafi] *nf* typography,
printing.

tyran [tirã] *nm* tyrant. ●**tyrannie** *nf*
tyranny.

tzigane [dzigan] *a* & *nmf* (Hungarian)
gipsy.

U

U, u [y] *nm* U, u.

Ukraine [ykrɛn] *nf* Ukraine.

ulcère [ylsɛr] *nm* ulcer, sore.

ULM [yelɛm] *nm abrév* (*Ultra-Léger Motorisé*) *Av* microlight.

ultérieur [ylterjœr] *a* later. ●**—ement** *adv* later.

ultimatum [yltimatɔm] *nm* ultimatum.

ultime [yltim] *a* final, last.

ultramoderne [yltramɔdɛrn] *a* ultramodern.

ultra-secret, -ète [yltrasəkrɛ, -ɛt] *a* top-secret.

ultraviolet, -ette [yltravjɔlɛ, -ɛt] *a* ultraviolet.

un, une [œ̃, yn] **1** *art indéf* a, (*devant voyelle*) an; **une page** a page; **un ange** [œ̃nɑ̃ʒ] an angel. **2** *a* one; **la page un** page one; **un kilo** one kilo; **un type** (*un quelconque*) some *ou* a fellow; **un jour** one day. **3** *pron & nmf* one; **l'un** one; **les uns** some; **le numéro un** number one; **j'en ai un** I have one; **l'un d'eux/l'une d'elles** one of them; **la une** (*de journal*) page one.

unanime [ynanim] *a* unanimous. ●**unanimité** *nf* à **l'u.** unanimously.

uni [yni] *a* united; (*famille etc*) close; (*surface*) smooth; (*couleur, étoffe*) plain.

unième [ynjɛm] *a* (*after a number*) (-)first; **trente et u.** thirty-first; **cent u.** hundred and first.

unifier [ynifje] *vt* to unify.

uniforme [yniform] **1** *nm* (*vêtement*) uniform. **2** *a* (*régulier*) uniform.

union [ynjɔ̃] *nf* union; (*association*) association; (*entente*) unity.

unique [ynik] *a* **1** (*fille, espoir etc*) only; (*prix, marché*) single, one; **son seul et u. souci** his *ou* her one and only worry. **2** (*exceptionnel*) unique. ●**uniquement**

adv only.

unir [ynir] *vt* (*deux pays etc*) to unite, join (together); (*efforts*) to combine; **u. la force au courage** to combine strength with courage; **u. deux personnes** (*amitié*) to unite two people **s'u.** *vpr* (*étudiants etc*) to unite; (*se marier*) to be joined together.

unisexe [ynisɛks] *a* (*vêtements etc*) unisex.

unisson (à l') [alynisɔ̃] *adv* in unison (de with).

unité [ynite] *nf* (*de mesure, élément*) & *Mil* unit; (*cohésion, harmonie*) unity. ●**unitaire** *a* (*prix*) per unit.

univers [yniver] *nm* universe.

universel, -elle [yniversɛl] *a* universal.

université [yniversite] *nf* university; à **l'u.** at university, *Am* at college. ●**universitaire** *a* **ville/etc u.** university town/*etc*.

urbain [yrbɛ̃] *a* **population/etc urbaine** urban *ou* city population/*etc*. ●**urbanisme** *nm* town planning, *Am* city planning.

urgent [yrʒɑ̃] *a* urgent. ●**urgence** *nf* (*cas*) emergency; (*de décision, tâche etc*) urgency; **mesures/etc d'u.** emergency measures/*etc*; **état d'u.** *Pol* state of emergency; (**service des**) **urgences** (*d'hôpital*) casualty (department), *Am* emergency room; **faire qch d'u.** to do sth urgently.

urine [yrin] *nf* urine. ●**uriner** *vi* to urinate.

urne [yrn] *nf* **1** (*électorale*) ballot box; **aller aux urnes** to go to the polls, vote. **2** (*vase*) urn.

usage [yzaʒ] *nm* use; (*habitude*) custom; *Ling* usage; **faire u. de** to make use of; **d'u.** (*habituel*) customary; **à l'u. de** for the use of; **hors d'u.** broken, not in use.

●**usagé** a worn. ●**usager** nm user.
user [yze] vt (vêtement, personne) to
wear out; (consommer) to use (up)
‖ vi **u. de** to use ‖ **s'u.** vpr (tissu, machine) to wear out. ●**usé** a (tissu etc)
worn (out); (personne) worn out.
usine [yzin] nf factory; **u. à gaz** gasworks; **u. métallurgique** ironworks;
ouvrier d'u. factory worker.
usité [yzite] a in common use.
ustensile [ystãsil] nm utensil.
usuel, -elle [yzɥɛl] a everyday, ordinary.

usure [yzyr] nf (détérioration) wear (and
tear); **avoir qn à l'u.** Fig to wear s.o.
down.
usurper [yzyrpe] vt to usurp.
utérus [yterys] nm Anat womb.
utile [ytil] a useful (à to).
utiliser [ytilize] vt to use, utilize. ●**utilisateur, -trice** nmf user. ●**utilisation** nf
use. ●**utilité** nf use(fulness); **d'une
grande u.** very useful.
utilitaire [ytiliter] a utilitarian; **véhicule
u.** commercial vehicle.
UV [yve] nmpl abrév (ultraviolets) UV.

V

V, v [ve] *nm* V, v.

a [va] *voir* aller[1].

vacances [vakɑ̃s] *nfpl* holiday(s), *Am* vacation; **en v.** on holiday, *Am* on vacation; **prendre ses v.** to take one's holiday(s) *ou Am* vacation; **les grandes v.** the summer holidays *ou Am* vacation. ● **vacancier, -ière** *nmf* holiday-maker, *Am* vacationer.

vacant [vakɑ̃] *a* vacant.

vacarme [vakarm] *nm* din, uproar.

vaccin [vaksɛ̃] *nm* vaccine; **faire un v. à** to vaccinate. ● **vaccination** *nf* vaccination. ● **vacciner** *vt* to vaccinate.

vache [vaʃ] **1** *nf* cow; **v. laitière** dairy cow. **2** *nf* (*peau de*) **v.** (*personne*) *Fam* swine **ǁ** *a* (*méchant*) *Fam* nasty. ● **vachement** *adv Fam* (*très*) damned; (*beaucoup*) a hell of a lot.

vaciller [vasije] *vi* to sway, wobble; (*flamme, lumière*) to flicker.

vadrouille [vadruj] *nf* **en v.** *Fam* roaming *ou* wandering about.

va-et-vient [vaevjɛ̃] *nm inv* (*mouvement*) movement to and fro, (*de personnes*) comings and goings.

vagabond, -onde [vagabɔ̃, -ɔ̃d] *nmf* (*clochard*) tramp, *Am* hobo. ● **vagabonder** *vi* to roam *ou* wander about; (*pensée*) to wander.

vagin [vaʒɛ̃] *nm* vagina.

vague [vag] **1** *a* vague; (*regard*) vacant; (*souvenir*) dim, vague **ǁ** *nm* **regarder dans le v.** to gaze into space; **rester dans le v.** (*être évasif*) to keep it vague. **2** *nf* (*de mer*) & *Fig* wave; **v. de chaleur** heat wave; **v. de froid** cold spell *ou* snap. ● **vaguement** *adv* vaguely.

vain [vɛ̃] *a* (*futile*) vain, futile; (*mots, promesse*) empty; **en v.** in vain, vainly. ● **vainc/re*** [vɛ̃kr] *vt* to beat, defeat; (*surmonter*) to overcome. ● **—u, -ue**

nmf defeated man *ou* woman; *Sp* loser. ● **vainqueur** *nm* victor; *Sp* winner.

vais [ve] *voir* aller[1].

vaisseau, -x [veso] *nm* **1** *Anat Bot* vessel. **2** (*bateau*) ship, vessel; **v. spatial** spaceship.

vaisselle [vesel] *nf* crockery; (*à laver*) washing up, dirty dishes; **faire la v.** to do the washing up, wash *ou* do the dishes.

valable [valabl] *a* (*billet, motif etc*) valid.

valet [vale] *nm Cartes* jack.

valeur [valœr] *nf* value; (*mérite*) worth; *pl* (*titres*) *Com* stocks and shares; **avoir de la v.** to be valuable; **mettre en v.** (*faire ressortir*) to highlight; **objets de v.** valuables.

valide [valid] *a* **1** (*personne*) fit, able-bodied. **2** (*billet etc*) valid. ● **valider** *vt* to validate. ● **validité** *nf* validity.

valise [valiz] *nf* (*suit*)case; **v. diplomatique** diplomatic bag *ou Am* pouch; **faire ses valises** to pack (one's bags).

vallée [vale] *nf* valley.

valoir* [valwar] *vi* to be worth; (*s'appliquer*) to apply (**pour** to); **v. mille francs/cher/etc** to be worth a thousand francs/a lot/etc; **un vélo vaut bien une auto** a bicycle is just as good as a car; **il vaut mieux rester** it's better to stay; **il vaut mieux que j'attende** I'd better wait; **ça ne vaut rien** it's no good, it's worthless; **ça vaut la peine** *ou Fam* **le coup** it's worth while (**de faire** doing); **faire v.** (*faire ressortir*) to highlight; (*argument*) to put forward; (*droit*) to assert.

ǁ *vt* **v. qch à qn** (*causer*) to bring *ou* get s.o. sth.

ǁ se valoir *vpr* (*objets, personnes*) to be as good as each other; **ça se vaut** *Fam* it's all the same.

valse [vals] *nf* waltz. ● **valser** *vi* to waltz.

valve [valv] *nf* (*clapet*) valve.

vampire [vɑ̃pir] *nm* vampire.

vandale [vɑ̃dal] *nmf* vandal. ●**vandalisme** *nm* vandalism.

vanille [vanij] *nf* vanilla; **glace**/*etc* **à la v.** vanilla ice cream/*etc*.

vanité [vanite] *nf* vanity. ●**vaniteux, -euse** *a* vain, conceited.

vanne [van] *nf* **1** (*d'écluse*) sluice (gate), floodgate. **2** (*remarque*) *Fam* dig, jibe.

vanter [vɑ̃te] *vt* to praise **‖ se v.** *vpr* to boast, brag (**de** about, of). ●**vantard, -arde** *nmf* bighead, boaster.

vapeur [vapœr] *nf* (*brume, émanation*) vapour; **v.** (**d'eau**) steam; **cuire à la v.** to steam; **bateau à v.** steamship.

vaporiser [vaporize] *vt* to spray. ●**vaporisateur** *nm* (*appareil*) spray.

varappe [varap] *nf* rock-climbing.

variable [varjabl] *a* variable; (*humeur, temps*) changeable. ●**variation** *nf* variation.

varicelle [varisel] *nf* chicken pox.

varices [varis] *nfpl* varicose veins.

vari/er [varje] *vti* to vary (**de** from). ●**-é** *a* (*diversifié*) varied; (*divers*) various.

variété [varjete] *nf* variety; **spectacle de variétés** *Th* variety show.

variole [varjɔl] *nf* smallpox.

vas [va] *voir* **aller¹**.

vase [vaz] **1** *nm* vase. **2** *nf* (*boue*) mud, silt.

vaseline [vazlin] *nf* Vaseline®.

vaseux, -euse [vazø, -øz] *a* **1** (*boueux*) muddy, silty. **2** (*faible, fatigué*) off colour. **3** (*idées etc*) woolly, hazy.

vaste [vast] *a* vast, huge.

Vatican [vatikɑ̃] *nm* **le V.** the Vatican.

va-tout [vatu] *nm inv* **jouer son v.-tout** to stake one's all.

vaudeville [vodvil] *nm Th* light comedy.

vaurien, -ienne [vorjɛ̃, -jen] *nmf* good-for-nothing.

vaut [vo] *voir* **valoir.**

vautour [votur] *nm* vulture.

vautrer (se) [səvotre] *vpr* to sprawl; **se v. dans** (*boue, vice*) to wallow in.

va-vite (à la) [alavavit] *adv Fam* in a hurry.

veau, -x [vo] *nm* (*animal*) calf; (*viand*) veal; (*cuir*) calfskin, (calf) leather.

vécu [veky] *pp de* **vivre ‖** *a* (*histoire et* true, real-life).

vedette [vədet] *nf* **1** *Cin Th* star; **en** (*personne*) in the limelight. **2** (*cano* motor boat, launch.

végétal, -aux [veʒetal, -o] *a* **huile**/*e* **végétale** vegetable oil/*etc* **‖** *nm* plan ●**végétarien, -ienne** *a & nmf* vegeta ian. ●**végétation 1** *nf* vegetation. **2** *nf* *Méd* adenoids.

véhicule [veikyl] *nm* vehicle; **v. tou** **terrain** off-road *ou* all-terrain vehicle

veille [vej] *nf* **1 la v.** (**de**) the day befor à **la v. de** (*événement*) on the eve of; **la v** **de Noël** Christmas Eve. **2** (*état*) wake fulness.

veillée [veje] *nf* (*soirée*) evening; (*réu* nion) evening get-together; (*mortuaire* vigil.

veiller [veje] *vi* to stay up *ou* awake (*sentinelle etc*) to keep watch; **v. à** qc to see to sth, attend to sth; **v. à ce qu** (+ *sub*) to make sure that; **v. sur qn** to watch over s.o. **‖** *vt* (*malade*) to sit with watch over. ●**veilleur** *nm* **v. de nui** night watchman. ●**veilleuse** *nf* (*de voiture*) sidelight, *Am* parking light; (*de cuisinière*) pilot light; (*lampe allu mée la nuit*) night light.

veine [ven] *nf* **1** *Anat Bot Géol* vein. **2** (*chance*) *Fam* luck; **avoir de la v.** to be lucky. ●**veinard, -arde** *nmf Fam* lucky devil.

véliplanchiste [veliplɑ̃ʃist] *nmf* windsur fer.

vélo [velo] *nm* bike, bicycle; (*activité*) cycling; **faire du v.** to cycle, go cycling; **v. tout terrain** mountain bike. ●**vélo drome** *nm Sp* velodrome, cycle track. ●**vélomoteur** *nm* (lightweight) motor cycle.

velours [v(ə)lur] *nm* velvet; **v. côtelé** corduroy. ●**velouté** *a* soft, velvety; (*au goût*) mellow, smooth **‖** *nm* smooth ness; **v. d'asperges**/*etc* (*potage*) cream of asparagus/*etc* soup.

elu [vəly] *a* hairy.

enaison [vənɛzɔ̃] *nf* venison.

endange(s) [vɑ̃dɑ̃ʒ] *nf(pl)* grape harvest.

endre [vɑ̃dr] *vt* to sell; **v. qch à qn** to sell s.o. sth, sell sth to s.o.; **à v.** (*maison etc*) for sale ∎ **se v.** *vpr* to be sold; **ça se vend bien** it sells well. ●**vendeur, -euse** *nmf* (*de magasin*) sales *ou* shop assistant, *Am* sales clerk; (*de voitures etc*) salesman, saleswoman.

vendredi [vɑ̃drədi] *nm* Friday; **V. saint** Good Friday.

vénéneux, -euse [venenø, -øz] *a* poisonous.

vénérable [venerabl] *a* venerable.

venger [vɑ̃ʒe] *vt* to avenge ∎ **se v.** *vpr* to get one's revenge, get one's own back (**de qn** on s.o., **de qch** for sth). ●**vengeance** *nf* revenge, vengeance.

venin [vənɛ̃] *nm* poison, venom; *Fig* venom. ●**venimeux, -euse** *a* poisonous, venomous; (*haineux*) *Fig* venomous.

venir* [v(ə)nir] *vi* (*aux être*) to come (**de** from); **v. faire** to come to do; **viens me voir** come and see me; **je viens/venais d'arriver** I've/I'd just arrived; **en v.** (*conclusion etc*) to come to; **où veux tu en v.?** what are you getting *ou* driving at?; **les jours/etc qui viennent** the coming days/etc; **faire v.** to send for, get.

vent [vɑ̃] *nm* wind; **il y a ou il fait du v.** it's windy; **coup de v.** gust of wind.

vente [vɑ̃t] *nf* sale; **v.** (**aux enchères**) auction (sale); **en v.** (*disponible*) on sale; **point de v.** sales outlet, point of sale; **prix de v.** selling price; **salle des ventes** auction room.

ventilateur [vɑ̃tilatœr] *nm* (*électrique*) & *Aut* fan; (*dans un mur*) ventilator.

ventouse [vɑ̃tuz] *nf* (*pour fixer*) suction grip; **cendrier/etc à v.** suction-grip ashtray/etc.

ventre [vɑ̃tr] *nm* stomach, belly; (*utérus*) womb; **avoir/prendre du v.** to have/get a paunch; **avoir mal au v.** to have a

stomach-ache; **à plat v.** flat on one's face.

ventriloque [vɑ̃trilɔk] *nmf* ventriloquist.

venu, -ue¹ [v(ə)ny] *pp de* venir ∎ *nmf* **nouveau v., nouvelle venue** newcomer; **le premier v.** anyone ∎ *a* **bien v.** (*à propos*) timely; **mal v.** untimely.

venue² [v(ə)ny] *nf* (*arrivée*) coming.

ver [vɛr] *nm* worm; (*larve*) grub; (*de fruits, fromage etc*) maggot; **v. de terre** (earth)worm; **v. à soie** silkworm.

véranda [verɑ̃da] *nf* veranda(h); (*en verre*) conservatory (*room attached to house*).

verbe [vɛrb] *nm Gram* verb.

verdict [vɛrdikt] *nm* verdict.

verdir [vɛrdir] *vti* to turn green. ●**verdoyant** *a* green. ●**verdure** *nf* (*arbres etc*) greenery.

véreux, -euse [verø, -øz] *a* (*fruit etc*) wormy; (*malhonnête*) *Fig* dubious, shady.

verger [vɛrʒe] *nm* orchard.

verglas [vɛrgla] *nm* (black) ice, *Am* sleet. ●**verglacé** *a* (*route*) icy.

vergogne (sans) [sɑ̃vɛrgɔɲ] *a* shameless ∎ *adv* shamelessly.

véridique [veridik] *a* truthful.

vérifier [verifje] *vt* to check, verify; (*comptes*) to audit. ●**vérification** *nf* checking, verification; audit(ing).

vérité [verite] *nf* truth, (*de personnage, tableau etc*) trueness to life; **en v.** in fact, **dire la v.** to tell the truth. ●**véritable** *a* true, real; (*non imité*) real, genuine. ●**véritablement** *adv* really.

vermeil, -eille [vɛrmɛj] *a* bright red ∎ *nm* **carte vermeil** senior citizen's rail pass.

vermine [vɛrmin] *nf* (*insectes, racaille*) vermine.

vermoulu [vɛrmuly] *a* worm-eaten.

verni [vɛrni] *a* (*chanceux*) *Fam* lucky.

vernir [vɛrnir] *vt* to varnish; (*poterie*) to glaze. ●**vernis** *nm* varnish; glaze; **v. à ongles** nail polish *ou* varnish. ●**vernissage** *nm* (*d'exposition de peinture*) first day.

verra, verrai *etc* [vera, verɛ] *voir* **voir**.

verre [ver] *nm* glass; **boire** *ou* **prendre un v.** to have a drink; **v. de bière**/*etc* glass of beer/*etc*; **v. à bière**/*etc* beer/*etc* glass; **v. de contact** contact lens. ● **verrière** *nf* (*toit*) glass roof.

verrou [veru] *nm* bolt; **fermer au v.** to bolt; **sous les verrous** behind bars. ● **verrouiller** *vt* to bolt.

verrue [very] *nf* wart.

vers[1] [ver] *prép* (*direction*) towards, toward; (*approximation*) around, about.

vers[2] [ver] *nm* (*de poème*) line; *pl* (*poésie*) verse.

versant [versã] *nm* slope, side.

verse (à) [avers] *adv* in torrents; **pleuvoir à v.** to pour (down).

Verseau [verso] *nm* **le V.** (*signe*) Aquarius.

vers/er [verse] *vt* **1** to pour; (*larmes, sang*) to shed. **2** (*argent*) to pay. ● **—ement** *nm* payment. ● **—eur** *a* **bec v.** spout.

verset [verse] *nm* *Rel* verse.

version [versjɔ̃] *nf* (*de film, d'incident etc*) version; (*traduction*) *Scol* translation, unseen.

verso [verso] *nm* back (of the page); **'voir au v.'** 'see overleaf.'

vert [ver] *a* green; (*pas mûr*) unripe ∎ *nm* green.

vertical, -ale, -aux [vertikal, -o] *a & nf* vertical; **à la verticale** vertically.

vertige [vertiʒ] *nm* (*feeling of*) dizziness; (*peur de tomber dans le vide*) vertigo; *pl* dizzy spells; **avoir le v.** to be *ou* feel dizzy; **donner le v. à qn** to make s.o. (feel) dizzy. ● **vertigineux, -euse** *a* (*hauteur*) dizzy.

vertu [verty] *nf* virtue; **en v. de** in accordance with. ● **vertueux, -euse** *a* virtuous.

verveine [verven] *nf* (*plante*) verbena.

vésicule [vezikyl] *nf* **v. biliaire** gall bladder.

vessie [vesi] *nf* bladder.

veste [vest] *nf* jacket, coat.

vestiaire [vestjer] *nm* cloakroom, *Am* locker room; (*casier*) locker.

vestibule [vestibyl] *nm* (entrance) hall.

vestiges [vestiʒ] *nmpl* (*restes, ruines*) remains; (*traces*) traces, vestiges.

veston [vestɔ̃] *nm* (suit) jacket.

vêtement [vetmã] *nm* garment, article of clothing; *pl* clothes; **vêtements de sport** sportswear; **industrie**/*etc* **du v.** clothing industry/*etc*.

vétéran [veterã] *nm* veteran.

vétérinaire [veteriner] *a* veterinary ∎ *nmf* vet, veterinary surgeon, *Am* veterinarian.

vêtir* [vetir] *vt*, **se v.** *vpr* to dress. ● **vêtu** *a* dressed (**de** in).

veto [veto] *nm inv* veto; **mettre son v. à** to veto.

vétuste [vetyst] *a* dilapidated.

veuf, veuve [vœf, vœv] *a* widowed ∎ *nm* widower ∎ *nf* widow.

veuille(s), veuillent *etc* [vœj] *voir* **vouloir.**

veut, veux [vø] *voir* **vouloir.**

vexer [vekse] *vt* to upset, hurt ∎ **se v.** *vpr* to be *ou* get upset (**de** at). ● **vexant** *a* upsetting.

VF [veef] *nf abrév* (*version française*) **film en VF** film dubbed into French.

viable [vjabl] *a* (*entreprise etc*) viable.

viaduc [vjadyk] *nm* viaduct.

viager, -ère [vjaʒe, -er] *a* **rente viagère** life annuity ∎ *nm* life annuity.

viande [vjãd] *nf* meat.

vibrer [vibre] *vi* to vibrate; (*être ému*) to thrill (**de** with); **faire v.** (*auditoire etc*) to thrill. ● **vibration** *nf* vibration.

vice [vis] *nm* vice; (*défectuosité*) defect.

vice- [vis] *préf* vice-.

vice versa [vis(e)versa] *adv* vice versa.

vicieux, -euse [visjø, -øz] **1** *a* depraved ∎ *nmf* pervert. **2** *a* **cercle v.** vicious circle.

vicinal, -aux [visinal, -o] *a* **chemin v.** byroad, minor road.

vicomte [vikɔ̃t] *nm* viscount. ● **vicomtesse** *nf* viscountess.

victime [viktim] *nf* victim; (*d'un accident*) casualty; **être v. de** to be the victim of.

victoire [viktwar] *nf* victory; *Sp* win.
●**victorieux, -euse** *a* victorious; *(équipe)* winning.

victuailles [viktɥɑj] *nfpl* provisions.

vidange [vidɑ̃ʒ] *nf Aut* oil change.
●**vidanger** *vt* to empty, drain.

vide [vid] *a* empty ▮ *nm* emptiness, void; *(absence d'air)* vacuum; *(trou, manque, espace)* gap; **emballé sous v.** vacuum-packed; **à v.** empty.

vidéo [video] *a inv & nf* video; **jeu v.** video game. ●**vidéocassette** *nf* video (cassette). ●**vidéoclip** *nm* video *(of rock group etc)*.

vide-ordures [vidɔrdyr] *nm inv* (rubbish *ou Am* garbage) chute. ●**vide-poches** *nm inv Aut* glove compartment.

vider [vide] *vt* to empty; *(lieu)* to vacate; *(poisson, volaille) Culin* to gut; **v. qn** *Fam (chasser)* to throw s.o. out; *(épuiser)* to tire s.o. out ▮ **se v.** *vpr* to empty. ●**videur** *nm (de boîte de nuit)* bouncer.

vie [vi] *nf* life; *(durée)* lifetime; **le coût de la v.** the cost of living; **gagner sa v.** to earn one's living; **en v.** living; **à v., pour la v.** for life; **donner la v. à** to give birth to.

vieil, vieille [vjɛj] *voir* **vieux**.

vieillard [vjejar] *nm* old man, *pl* old people. ●**vieillesse** *nf* old age.

vieillir [vjejir] *vi* to grow old; *(changer)* to age ▮ *vt* **v. qn** *(vêtement etc)* to age s.o. ●—**i** *a (démodé)* old-fashioned.

Vienne [vjɛn] *nm ou f* Vienna.

viens, vient [vjɛ̃] *voir* **venir**.

vierge [vjɛrʒ] *nf* virgin; **la V.** *(signe)* Virgo ▮ *a (femme, neige etc)* virgin; *(feuille de papier, film)* blank; **être v.** *(femme, homme)* to be a virgin.

Viêt Nam [vjetnam] *nm* Vietnam. ●**vietnamien, -ienne** *a & nmf* Vietnamese.

vieux (*or* **vieil** *before vowel or mute h*), **vieille**, *pl* **vieux, vieilles** [vjø, vjɛj] *a* old; **être v. jeu** *(a inv)* to be old-fashioned; **v. garçon** bachelor; **vieille fille** *Péj* old maid ▮ *nm* old man; *pl* old people; **mon v.!** *(mon ami) Fam* mate!, pal! ▮ *nf* old

woman; **ma vieille!** *(ma chère) Fam* dear!

vif, vive [vif, viv] *a (enfant, mouvement)* lively; *(alerte)* quick, sharp; *(intelligence, vent)* keen; *(couleur, lumière)* bright; *(froid)* biting; *(pas)* quick, brisk; *(imagination)* vivid; **brûler qn v.** to burn s.o. alive ▮ *nm* **le v. du sujet** the heart of the matter; **à v.** *(plaie)* open.

vigilant [viʒilɑ̃] *a* vigilant.

vigile [viʒil] *nm (gardien)* watchman; *(de nuit)* night watchman.

vigne [viɲ] *nf (plante)* vine; *(plantation)* vineyard. ●**vigneron, -onne** *nmf* wine grower. ●**vignoble** *nm* vineyard; *(région)* vineyards.

vignette [viɲɛt] *nf Aut* = road tax disc; *(de médicament)* price label *(for reimbursement by Social Security)*.

vigueur [vigœr] *nf* vigour; **entrer en v.** *(loi)* to come into force. ●**vigoureux, -euse** *a (personne etc)* vigorous.

vilain [vilɛ̃] *a (laid)* ugly; *(enfant)* naughty; *(impoli)* rude.

villa [villa] *nf* (detached) house.

village [vilaʒ] *nm* village. ●**villageois, -oise** *nmf* villager.

ville [vil] *nf* town; *(grande)* city; **aller/ être en v.** to go (in)to/be in town; **v. d'eaux** spa town.

vin [vɛ̃] *nm* wine, **v. ordinaire** *ou* **de table** table wine.

vinaigre [vinɛgr] *nm* vinegar. ●**vinaigrette** *nf* French dressing, *Am* Italian dressing.

vingt [vɛ̃] *([vɛ̃t] before vowel or mute h and in numbers 22–29)* *a & nm* twenty; **v. et un** twenty-one. ●**vingtaine** *nf* **une v. (de)** *(nombre)* about twenty. ●**vingtième** *a & nmf* twentieth.

viol [vjɔl] *nm* rape. ●**violation** *nf* violation. ●**violer** *vt (femme)* to rape; *(loi, lieu)* to violate. ●**violeur** *nm* rapist.

violent [vjɔlɑ̃] *a* violent; *(remède)* drastic. ●**violemment** [-amɑ̃] *adv* violently. ●**violence** *nf* violence; **acte de v.** act of violence.

violet, -ette [vjɔlɛ, -ɛt] **1** *a & nm (couleur)*

purple, violet. **2** *nf* (*fleur*) violet.

violon [vjɔlɔ̃] *nm* violin. ● **violoncelle** *nm* cello. ● **violoncelliste** *nmf* cellist. ● **violoniste** *nmf* violinist.

vipère [viper] *nf* adder, viper.

virage [viraʒ] *nm* (*de route*) bend; (*de véhicule*) turn; (*revirement*) *Fig* change of course.

virer [vire] **1** *vi* to turn, veer; **v. au bleu/etc** to turn blue/*etc*. **2** *vt* (*expulser*) *Fam* to throw out. **3** *vt* (*somme*) *Fin* to transfer (**à** to). ● **virement** *nm Fin* (*bank ou credit*) transfer.

virevolter [virvɔlte] *vi* to spin round.

virgule [virgyl] *nf Gram* comma; *Math* (decimal) point; **2 v. 5** 2 point 5.

viril [viril] *a* virile, manly; (*force*) male.

virtuel, -elle [virtɥɛl] *a* potential; *Phys Ordinat* virtual.

virtuose [virtɥoz] *nmf* virtuoso.

virulent [virylɑ̃] *a* virulent.

virus [virys] *nm Méd Ordinat* virus.

vis¹ [vi] *voir* **vivre, voir.**

vis² [vis] *nf* screw.

visa [viza] *nm* (*de passeport*) visa; (*timbre*) stamp, stamped signature; **v. de censure** (*d'un film*) certificate.

visage [vizaʒ] *nm* face.

vis-à-vis [vizavi] *prép* **v.-à-vis de** opposite; (*à l'égard de*) with respect to; (*envers*) towards ‖ *nm inv* (*personne*) person opposite; (*bois, maison etc*) opposite view.

viser [vize] **1** *vi* to aim (**à** at); **v. à faire** to aim to do ‖ *vt* (*cible*) to aim at; (*concerner*) to be aimed at. **2** *vt* (*document*) to stamp. ● **visées** *nfpl* (*desseins*) *Fig* aims; **avoir des v. sur** to have designs on. ● **viseur** *nm Phot* viewfinder; (*d'arme*) sight.

visible [vizibl] *a* visible. ● **visibilité** *nf* visibility.

visière [vizjer] *nf* (*de casquette*) peak; (*en plastique etc*) eyeshade; (*de casque*) visor.

vision [vizjɔ̃] *nf* (*conception, image*) vision; (*sens*) (eye)sight, vision. ● **visionneuse** *nf* (*pour diapositives*) viewer.

visite [vizit] *nf* visit; (*personne*) visitor; (*examen*) inspection; **rendre v. à, faire une v. à** to visit; **v. (à domicile)** *Méd* (house) call *ou* visit; **v. (médicale)** medical examination; **v. guidée** guided tour; **heures/etc de v.** visiting hours/*etc*. ● **visiter** *vt* to visit. ● **visiteur, -euse** *nmf* visitor.

vison [vizɔ̃] *nm* mink.

visser [vise] *vt* to screw on.

visuel, -elle [vizɥɛl] *a* visual. ● **visualiser** *vt* (*afficher*) *Ordinat* to display.

vit [vi] *voir* **vivre, voir.**

vital, -aux [vital, -o] *a* vital. ● **vitalité** *nf* vitality.

vitamine [vitamin] *nf* vitamin.

vite [vit] *adv* quickly, fast; (*tôt*) soon; **v.!** quick(ly)! ● **vitesse** *nf* speed; *Aut* gear; **boîte de vitesses** gearbox; **à toute v.** at top *ou* full speed; **v. de pointe** top speed; **en v.** *Fam* quickly.

viticole [vitikɔl] *a* (*région*) wine-growing; **industrie v.** wine industry. ● **viticulteur** *nm* wine grower. ● **viticulture** *nf* wine growing.

vitre [vitr] *nf* (window)pane; (*de véhicule, train*) window. ● **vitrail, -aux** *nm* stained-glass window. ● **vitrier** *nm* glazier.

vitrine [vitrin] *nf* (*de magasin*) (shop) window; (*meuble*) display cabinet, showcase.

vivable [vivabl] *a Fam* (*personne*) easy to live with; (*endroit*) fit to live in.

vivacité [vivasite] *nf* liveliness; (*d'émotion*) keenness; (*agilité*) briskness; **v. d'esprit** quick-wittedness.

vivant [vivɑ̃] *a* (*en vie*) alive, living; (*récit, rue*) lively ‖ *nm* **de son v.** in one's lifetime; **bon v.** jovial fellow.

vive¹ [viv] *voir* **vif.**

vive² [viv] *int* **v. le roi/etc!** long live the king/*etc*!; **v. les vacances!** hurray for the holidays *ou Am* the vacation!

vivement [vivmɑ̃] *adv* quickly, briskly; (*répliquer*) sharply; (*regretter*) deeply; **v. demain!** I can hardly wait for tomorrow!; **v. que** (+ *sub*) I'll be glad when.

vivier [vivje] *nm* fish pond.

vivifier [vivifje] *vt* to invigorate.

vivre* [vivr] **1** *vi* to live; **elle vit encore** she's still alive; **faire v.** (*famille etc*) to support; **le v. vieux** to be old; **facile à v.** easy to get along with; **v. de** (*fruits etc*) to live on; (*travail etc*) to live by; **avoir de quoi v.** to have enough to live on **I** *vt* (*vie*) to live; (*aventure, époque*) to live through; (*éprouver*) to experience. **2** *nmpl* food, supplies.

VO [veo] *nf abrév* (*version originale*) film **en VO** film in the original version.

vocabulaire [vɔkabylɛr] *nm* vocabulary.

vocal, -aux [vɔkal, -o] *a* (*cordes, musique*) vocal.

vocation [vɔkasjɔ̃] *nf* vocation, calling.

vociférer [vɔsifere] *vti* to shout angrily.

vodka [vɔdka] *nf* vodka.

vœu, -x [vø] (*souhait*) wish; (*promesse*) vow; **faire le v. de faire** to (make a) vow to do; **tous mes vœux!** (my) best wishes!

vogue [vɔg] *nf* fashion, vogue; **en v.** in fashion, in vogue.

voici [vwasi] *prép* here is, this is; *pl* here are, these are; **me v.** here I am; **v. dix ans/etc** ten years/etc ago; **v. dix ans que** it's ten years since.

voie [vwa] *nf* (*route*) road, (*rails*) track, line; (*partie de route*) lane; (*chemin*) way; (*de gare*) platform; (*de communication*) line; **pays en v. de développement** developing country; **v. publique** public highway; **v. navigable** waterway; **v. sans issue** dead end; **sur la bonne v.** on the right track.

voilà [vwala] *prép* there is, that is; *pl* there are, those are; **les v.** there they are; **v., j'arrive!** all right, I'm coming!; **v. dix ans/etc** ten years/etc ago; **v. dix ans que** it's ten years since.

voile¹ [vwal] *nm* (*étoffe qui cache, coiffure etc*) **& Fig** veil. ● **voiler¹** *vt* (*visage etc*) to veil; **se v.** *vpr* (*personne*) to wear a veil; (*ciel, regard*) to cloud over.

voile² [vwal] *nf* (*de bateau*) sail; *Sp* sailing; **bateau à voiles** sailing boat,

Am sailboat; **faire de la v.** to sail, go sailing. ● **voilier** *nm* sailing ship; (*de plaisance*) sailing boat, *Am* sailboat. ● **voilure** *nf Nau* sails.

voiler² [vwale] *vt*, **se v.** *vpr* (*roue*) to buckle.

voir* [vwar] *vti* to see; **faire** *ou* **laisser v. qch** to show sth; **fais v.** let me see, show me; **v. qn faire** to see s.o. do *ou* doing; **voyons!** (*sois raisonnable*) come on!; **y v. clair** (*comprendre*) to see clearly; **je ne peux pas la v.** (*supporter*) *Fam* I can't stand (the sight of) her; **on verra bien** we'll see; **ça n'a rien à v. avec** that's nothing to do with.

I se voir *vpr* to see oneself; (*se fréquenter*) to see each other; **ça se voit** that's obvious.

voirie [vwari] *nf* (*enlèvement des ordures*) refuse collection; (*routes*) public highways.

voisin, -ine [vwazɛ̃, -in] *a* (*pays, village etc*) neighbouring; (*maison, pièce*) next (**de** to); (*idée, état etc*) similar (**de** to) **I** *nmf* neighbour. ● **voisinage** *nm* (*quartier, voisins*) neighbourhood; (*proximité*) closeness.

voiture [vwatyr] *nf* car; (*de train*) carriage, coach, *Am* car; **v. de course/de tourisme** racing/private car; **v. d'enfant** pram, *Am* baby carriage; **en v.!** *Rail* all aboard!

voix [vwa] *nf* voice; (*d'électeur*) vote; **à v. basse** in a whisper; **à haute v.** aloud; **à portée de v.** within earshot.

vol [vɔl] *nm* **1** (*d'avion, d'oiseau*) flight; (*groupe d'oiseaux*) flock, flight; **v. libre** hang gliding; **v. à voile** gliding. **2** (*délit*) theft; **v. à main armée** armed robbery; **v. à l'étalage** shoplifting; **c'est du v.!** (*trop cher*) it's daylight robbery!

volaille [vɔlaj] *nf* **la v.** (*oiseaux*) poultry; **une v.** (*oiseau*) a fowl.

volatiliser (se) [səvɔlatilize] *vpr* (*disparaître*) to vanish (into thin air).

volcan [vɔlkɑ̃] *nm* volcano.

voler [vɔle] **1** *vi* (*oiseau, avion etc*) to fly. **2** *vt* (*prendre*) to steal (**à** from); **v. qn to**

rob s.o. ‖ *vi* to steal. ● **volant 1** *a* (*tapis etc*) flying. **2** *nm Aut* (steering) wheel; (*objet*) *Sp* shuttlecock; (*de jupe*) flounce. ● **volée** *nf* flight; (*groupe d'oiseaux*) flock, flight; (*suite de coups*) thrashing; *Tennis* volley; **sonner à toute v.** to peal *ou* ring out. ● **voleur, -euse** *nmf* thief; **au v.!** stop thief!

volet [vɔlɛ] *nm* **1** (*de fenêtre*) shutter. **2** (*de programme, reportage etc*) section, part.

volière [vɔljɛr] *nf* aviary.

volley(-ball) [vɔlɛ(bɔl)] *nm Sp* volleyball.

volontaire [vɔlɔ̃tɛr] *a* (*voulu*) (*geste etc*) deliberate, voluntary; (*opiniâtre*) wilful, *Am* wilful ‖ *nmf* volunteer. ●—**ment** *adv* voluntarily; (*exprès*) deliberately.

volonté [vɔlɔ̃te] *nf* (*faculté, intention*) will; (*désir*) wish; **il a de la v.** he has willpower; **bonne v.** goodwill; **mauvaise v.** ill will; **à v.** (*quantité*) as much as desired.

volontiers [vɔlɔ̃tje] *adv* gladly, willingly; **v.!** (*oui*) I'd love to!

volt [vɔlt] *nm Él* volt. ● **voltage** *nm* voltage.

volte-face [vɔltəfas] *nf inv* about turn, *Am* about face; **faire v.-face** to turn round.

voltiger [vɔltiʒe] *vi* to flutter.

volume [vɔlym] *nm* (*de boîte, de son, livre*) volume. ● **volumineux, -euse** *a* bulky, voluminous.

volupté [vɔlypte] *nf* sensual pleasure.

vom/ir [vɔmir] *vt* to bring up, vomit ‖ *vi* to vomit, be sick. ●—**issement** *nm* vomiting.

vont [vɔ̃] *voir* **aller**[1].

vorace [vɔras] *a* (*appétit, lecteur etc*) voracious.

vos [vo] *voir* **votre**.

vote [vɔt] *nm* (*action*) vote, voting; (*suffrage*) vote; (*de loi*) passing; **bureau de v.** polling station, *Am* polling place. ● **voter** *vi* to vote ‖ *vt* (*loi*) to pass; (*crédits*) to vote.

votre, *pl* **vos** [vɔtr, vo] *a poss* your. ● **vôtre** *pron poss* **le** *ou* **la v.**, **les vôtres** yours; **à la v.!** (*toast*) (your) good health!, cheers! ‖ *nmpl* **les vôtres** (*votre famille*) your (own) people.

voudra, voudrai *etc* [vudra, vudre] *voir* **vouloir**.

vouer [vwe] *vt* (*promettre*) to vow (à to); (*consacrer*) to dedicate (à to).

vouloir[*] [vulwar] *vt* to want (**faire** to do); **je veux qu'il parte** I want him to go; **v. dire** to mean (**que** that); **je voudrais rester** I'd like to stay; **je voudrais un pain** I'd like a loaf of bread; **voulez-vous me suivre** will you follow me; **si tu veux** if you like *ou* wish; **en v. à qn d'avoir fait qch** to be angry with s.o. for doing sth; **v. du bien à qn** to wish s.o. well; **je veux bien (attendre)** I don't mind (waiting); **que voulez-vous!** (*résignation*) what can you expect!; **sans le v.** unintentionally; **ne pas v. de qch/de qn** not to want sth/ s.o.; **veuillez attendre** kindly wait. ● **voulu** *a* (*requis*) required; (*délibéré*) deliberate.

vous [vu] *pron* **1** (*sujet, complément direct*) you; **v. êtes** you are; **il v. connaît** he knows you. **2** (*complément indirect*) (to) you; **il v. l'a donné** he gave it to you. **3** (*réfléchi*) yourself, *pl* yourselves; **v. v. lavez** you wash yourself; you wash yourselves. **4** (*réciproque*) each other; **v. v. aimez** you love each other. ● **vous-même** *pron* yourself. ● **vous-mêmes** *pron pl* yourselves.

voûte [vut] *nf* (*plafond*) vault; (*porche*) arch(way). ● **voûté** *a* (*personne*) bent, stooped.

vouvoyer [vuvwaje] *vt* **v. qn** to use the formal *vous* form to s.o.

voyage [vwajaʒ] *nm* trip, journey; (*par mer*) voyage; **aimer les voyages** to like travelling; **faire un v., partir en v.** to go on a trip; **être en v.** to be (away) travelling; **bon v.!** have a pleasant trip!; **v. de noces** honeymoon; **v. organisé** (*package*) tour; **agent/agence de voyages** travel agent/agency. ● **voyager**

vi to travel. ● **voyageur, -euse** *nmf*
traveller; (*passager*) passenger; **v. de**
commerce commercial traveller.

voyant¹ [vwajɑ̃] **1** *a* (*couleur*) gaudy. **2**
nm (*signal*) (warning) light; (*d'appareil*
électrique) pilot light.

voyant², -ante [vwajɑ̃, -ɑ̃t] *nmf* clairvoyant; **les non-voyants** the blind, the
visually handicapped.

voyelle [vwajɛl] *nf* vowel.

voyou [vwaju] *nm* hooligan.

vrac (en) [ɑ̃vrak] *adv* (*en désordre*) in a
muddle, haphazardly; (*au poids*) loose.

vrai [vrɛ] *a* true; (*réel*) real; (*authentique*)
genuine **‖** *adv* **dire v.** to be right (in what
one says). ●—**ment** *adv* really.

vraisemblable [vrɛsɑ̃blabl] *a* (*probable*)
likely, probable; (*plausible*) plausible.
●—**ment** [-əmɑ̃] *adv* probably.

vrombir [vrɔ̃bir] *vi* to hum.

VRP [veerpe] *nm abrév* (*voyageur repré-*
sentant placier) sales rep.

VTT [vetete] *nm abrév* (*vélo tout terrain*)
mountain bike.

vu [vy] **1** *pp de* **voir ‖** *a* **bien vu** well
thought of; **mal vu** frowned upon. **2**
prép in view of; **vu que** seeing that.

vue [vy] *nf* (*spectacle*) sight; (*sens*)
(eye)sight; (*panorama, photo, idée*)
view; **en v.** (*proche*) in sight; (*en évi-*
dence) on view; (*personne*) *Fig* in the
public eye; **à v.** (*tirer*) on sight; **à**
première v. at first sight; **à v. d'œil**
(*grandir etc*) rapidly, for all to see; **de**
v. (*connaître*) by sight.

vulgaire [vylgɛr] *a* (*grossier*) vulgar,
coarse; (*ordinaire*) common.

vulnérable [vylnerabl] *a* vulnerable.

W

W, w [dubləve] *nm* W, w.
wagon [vagɔ̃] *nm Rail* (*de voyageurs*) carriage, coach, *Am* car; (*de marchandises*) wag(g)on, truck, *Am* freight car. ● **w.-lit** *nm* (*pl* **wagons-lits**) sleeping car, sleeper. ● **w.-restaurant** *nm* (*pl* **wagons-restaurants**) dining car, diner.
walkman® [wɔkman] *nm voir* **baladeur**.
wallon, -onne [walɔ̃, -ɔn] *a & nmf* Walloon.
watt [wat] *nm Él* watt.
w-c [(dublə)vese] *nmpl* toilet, *Am* men's *ou* ladies' room.
week-end [wikɛnd] *nm* weekend; **partir en w.-end** to go away for the weekend
western [wɛstɛrn] *nm* (*film*) western.
whisky, *pl* **-ies** [wiski] *nm* whisky, *Am* whiskey.

X

X, x [iks] *nm* X, x; **rayon X** X-ray; **film classé X** adults-only film, '18' film, *Am* X-rated film.
xénophobe [ksenɔfɔb] *a* xenophobic ▮ *nmf* xenophobe. ● **xénophobie** *nf* xenophobia.
xérès [gzeres] *nm* sherry.
xylophone [ksilɔfɔn] *nm* xylophone.

Y

Y, y[1] [igrɛk] *nm* Y, y.
y[2] [i] **1** *adv* there; (*dedans*) in it; *pl* in them; (*dessus*) on it; *pl* on them; **elle y vivra** she'll live there; **j'y entrai** I entered (it); **allons-y** let's go; **j'y suis!** (*je comprends*) now I get it!; **je n'y suis pour rien** I have nothing to do with it, that's nothing to do with me.
2 *pron* (= *à cela*) **j'y pense** I think of it; **je m'y attendais** I was expecting it; **ça y est!** that's it!
yacht [jɔt] *nm* yacht.
yaourt [jaur(t)] *nm* yog(h)urt.
yeux [jø] *voir* **œil**.
yoga [jɔga] *nm* yoga.
yo-yo [jojo] *nm inv* yoyo.

Z

Z, z [zɛd] *nm* Z, z.
zapper [zape] *vi* (*téléspectateur*) to flick channels, channel-hop.
zèbre [zebr] *nm* zebra. ● **zébré** *a* striped (**de** with).
zèle [zɛl] *nm* zeal; **faire du z.** to overdo it.

ro [zero] *nm* (*chiffre*) zero, nought;
ans un numéro) 0 [əʊ]; (*température*)
ro; (*rien*) nothing; **deux buts à z.** *Fb*
o nil, *Am* two zero; **partir de z.** to
art from scratch.

ste [zest] *nm* **un z. de citron** a piece of
mon peel.

gzag [zigzag] *nm* zigzag; **en z.** (*route*
c) zigzag(ging). ●**zigzaguer** *vi* to
gzag.

nc [zɛg] *nm* (*métal*) zinc.

zodiaque [zɔdjak] *nm* zodiac.

zona [zona] *nm* *Méd* shingles.

zone [zon] *nf* zone, area; (*domaine*) *Fig*
sphere; (*faubourgs misérables*) shanty
town; **z. bleue** restricted parking zone;
z. industrielle industrial estate *ou*
park.

zoo [zo(o)] *nm* zoo. ●**zoologique** *a*
zoological; **jardin** *ou* **parc z.** zoo.

zoom [zum] *nm* (*objectif*) zoom lens.

zut! [zyt] *int* *Fam* oh dear!, heck!